The Cambridge Grammar of the English Language

The Cambridge Grammar *of the* English Language

RODNEY HUDDLESTON
GEOFFREY K. PULLUM

in collaboration with LAURIE BAUER
BETTY BIRNER
TED BRISCOE
PETER COLLINS
DAVID DENISON
DAVID LEE
ANITA MITTWOCH
GEOFFREY NUNBERG
FRANK PALMER
JOHN PAYNE
PETER PETERSON
LESLEY STIRLING
GREGORY WARD

PUBLISHED BY THE PRESS SYNDICATE OF THE UNIVERSITY OF CAMBRIDGE
The Pitt Building, Trumpington Street, Cambridge, United Kingdom

CAMBRIDGE UNIVERSITY PRESS
The Edinburgh Building, Cambridge CB2 2RU, UK
40 West 20th Street, New York, NY 10011-4211, USA
477 Williamstown Road, Port Melbourne, VIC 3207, Australia
Ruiz de Alarcón 13, 28014 Madrid, Spain
Dock House, The Waterfront, Cape Town, 8001, South Africa

http://www.cambridge.org

First published 2002
Third printing 2005

Printed in the United Kingdom at the University Press, Cambridge

Typefaces Adobe Minion 10/13 pt & FFTheSans *System* LaTeX 2ε [TB]

A catalogue record for this book is available from the British Library.

Library of Congress cataloguing in publication data

Huddleston, Rodney D.
The Cambridge grammar of the English language /
Rodney Huddleston, Geoffrey K. Pullum
p. cm.
Includes bibliographical references and index.
ISBN 0 521 43146 8 (hardback)
1. English language – Grammar. I. Pullum, Geoffrey K. II. Title.
PE1106.H74 2002 425–dc21 2001025630

ISBN 0 521 43146 8 (hardback)

Contents

Contributors

RODNEY HUDDLESTON held lectureships at the University of Edinburgh, University College London, and the University of Reading before moving to the Department of English at the University of Queensland, where he won an 'Excellence in Teaching' award; he is a Fellow of the Australian Academy of the Humanities, and in 1990 was awarded a Personal Chair. He has written numerous articles and books on English grammar, including *The Sentence in Written English* (1971), *An Introduction to English Transformational Syntax* (1976), *Introduction to the Grammar of English* (1984) and *English Grammar: An Outline* (1988). He was the founding editor of the *Australian Journal of Linguistics* (1980–85).

GEOFFREY K. PULLUM taught at University College London for seven years before moving to the University of California, Santa Cruz, where he served as Dean of Graduate Studies and Research and is currently Professor of Linguistics. He was a Fellow at the Center for Advanced Studies in the Behavioral Sciences in 1990–91. His many publications cover not only English grammar and the theory of syntax but also a large number of other topics in linguistics. His scholarly books include *Rule Interaction and the Organization of a Grammar* (1979), *Generalized Phrase Structure Grammar* (1985, with Gerald Gazdar, Ewan Klein, and Ivan A. Sag), and *Phonetic Symbol Guide* (1986, 2nd edn 1996, with William A. Ladusaw). He has also published a collection of satirical essays on linguistics, *The Great Eskimo Vocabulary Hoax* (1991), and given many popular lectures and radio talks on language.

LAURIE BAUER holds a Personal Chair in Linguistics in the School of Linguistics and Applied Language Studies, Victoria University of Wellington, New Zealand. He has published widely on English word-formation and New Zealand English, and is a member of the editorial boards of the *Yearbook of Morphology* and *English World-Wide*. His major publications include *English Word-formation* (1983), *Introducing Linguistic Morphology* (1988), *Watching English Change* (1994), and *Morphological Productivity* (2001), and he is the joint editor, with Peter Trudgill, of *Language Myths* (1998).

Betty J. Birner is an Assistant Professor in the Department of English at Northern Illinois University. She is the author of *The Discourse Function of Inversion in English* (1996), as well as co-author, with Gregory Ward, of *Information Status and Noncanonical Word Order in English* (1998). She held a postdoctoral fellowship at the University of Pennsylvania's Institute for Research in Cognitive Science from 1993 to 1995, and has served as an expert witness in the area of text interpretation.

Ted Briscoe is a member of staff at the Computer Laboratory, University of Cambridge. His broad research interests are computational and theoretical linguistics, and automated speech and language processing. He teaches an advanced course on Natural Language Processing and is heavily involved in the teaching of the Laboratory's contribution to the M.Phil. in Computer Speech, Text, and Internet Technology, run jointly with the Engineering Department. From 1990 until 1996 he was an EPSRC Advanced Research Fellow undertaking research at Macquarie University in Sydney, University of Pennsylvania in Philadelphia, and Xerox European Research Centre in Grenoble, as well as at the Computer Laboratory. He has published around fifty research articles.

Peter Collins is Associate Professor of Linguistics and Head of the Linguistics Department at the University of New South Wales. He has also taught linguistics at Sydney University and Macquarie University, and is currently the Editor of the *Australian Journal of Linguistics*. Recently published books include *Australian English: The Language of a New Society* (1989, with David Blair), *Cleft and Pseudo-cleft Constructions in English* (1991), *English Grammar* (1998), *The Clause in English* (1999, edited with David Lee), *English Grammar: An Introduction* (2000, with Carmella Hollo), and *English in Australia* (2001, with David Blair).

Anita Mittwoch is Associate Professor Emeritus in the Department of English, The Hebrew University of Jerusalem. Her main work has been in the area of aspect, adjuncts, and events in grammar, and she is the author of numerous articles in books and journals, including *Linguistics and Philosophy*, *Journal of Linguistics*, *Natural Language Semantics*, and *Linguistic Inquiry*. She was President of the Israel Association for Theoretical Linguistics in 1991–95 and 1997–99.

Geoffrey Nunberg is a Principal Scientist at the Xerox Palo Alto Research Center and a Consulting Professor of Linguistics at Stanford University. Before going to PARC in 1986, he taught at UCLA, Stanford, and the University of Rome. He has written on a range of topics, including semantics and pragmatics, information access, written language structure, multilingualism and language policy, and the cultural implications of digital technologies. He is usage editor and chair of the usage panel of the *American Heritage Dictionary* and has also written on language and other topics for general magazines. His many publications include *The Linguistics of Punctuation* (1990).

JOHN PAYNE currently holds the post of Senior Lecturer in the Department of Linguistics at the University of Manchester. He has been Head of the Department, and also Head of the School of English and Linguistics. He has held appointments as visiting scholar or lecturer at, among others, the University of California at Los Angeles, the Australian National University (Canberra), and LaTrobe University (Melbourne), and he has been an exchange visitor with the Freie Üniversität Berlin and the USSR Academy of Sciences. He has published widely on typology and syntactic theory, and was a member of the EUROTYP group on noun phrase structure.

FRANK PALMER was Professor of Linguistic Science at the University of Reading from 1965 until his retirement in 1987, and is a Fellow of the British Academy. He is the author of journal articles on linguistic theory, English, and Ethopian languages, and of many books, including *Grammar* (1971, 2nd edn 1984), *The English Verb* (1974, 2nd edn 1987), *Mood and Modality* (1986, 2nd edn 2001), and *Grammatical Roles and Relations* (1994). His professional engagements have involved extensive travel in North and South America, Asia, North Africa, and Europe, and in 1981 he was Distinguished Visiting Professor at the Foreign Languages Institute, Beijing.

PETER PETERSON is a Senior Lecturer in the Department of Linguistics at the University of Newcastle, Australia. He is Reviews Editor and Associate Editor of the *Australian Journal of Linguistics.* His principal areas of current research are English syntax, particularly coordination and apposition-like structures, Lexical-Functional Grammar, and the acquisition of English as a Second Language. He is a contributing author in a forthcoming textbook for TESL, and has helped to establish the Newcastle ESL Corpus, a large database of unscripted conversations with French and Polish learners of English.

LESLEY STIRLING is a Senior Lecturer in the Department of Linguistics and Applied Linguistics at the University of Melbourne. Prior to taking up her appointment there she spent seven years at the Centre for Cognitive Science and the Department of Linguistics at the University of Edinburgh, and has also held a visiting appointment at the Institute of Cognitive Science, University of Colorado at Boulder. Her research has been mainly in the areas of anaphora, discourse analysis, speech processing, and Australian English. Her publications include *Switch-reference and Discourse Representation* (1993), *Anaphora* (2001, special issue of the *Australian Journal of Linguistics*, edited with Peter K. Austin), and papers in the *Belgian Journal of Linguistics*, *Language and Cognitive Processes*, and *Speech Communication.* In 1996 she was awarded the Crawford Medal for her research by the Australian Academy of the Humanities.

Gregory Ward is Professor and Chair of the Department of Linguistics at Northwestern University (Illinois). He has also taught at the Université Charles de Gaulle – Lille 3 (1996) and at the 1993 and 1997 LSA Linguistic Institutes. His main research area is discourse, with specific interests in pragmatic theory, information structure, and reference/anaphora. His 1998 book with Betty Birner – *Information Status and Noncanonical Word Order in English* – explores the discourse functions of a broad range of non-canonical syntactic constructions in English and other languages. With Laurence R. Horn, he is currently co-editor of the *Handbook of Pragmatics* (2002) and, also with Horn, co-author of the pragmatics entry in the *MIT Encyclopedia of the Cognitive Sciences* (1999). From 1986 to 1998, Ward was a consultant at AT&T Bell Laboratories (Murray Hill, NJ), working on speech synthesis and intonational meaning. In 2003, he will be a Fellow at the Center for Advanced Study in the Behavioral Studies in Palo Alto.

Notational conventions

Abbreviations of grammatical terms and special symbols

Where appropriate, page references are given to the initial explanation. For the symbols used in phonological representations, see p. 13.

A	adjunct
Adj	adjective
AdjP	adjective phrase
Adv	adverb
AdvP	adverb phrase
AmE	American English
AusE	Australian English
BrE	British English
C, Comp	complement
Coord	coordinate
d	dependent
D	determinative
declar	declarative
Det	determiner
DP	determinative phrase
exclam	exclamative
FCF	final combining form (p. 1661)
GEN	genitive
h	head
IC	immediate constituent
ICF	initial combining form (p. 1661)
impve	imperative
interrog	interrogative
LOC	locative
Mkr	marker
Mod	modifier
N	noun
N/A	not applicable
N/D	non-distinctive
Nec	necessity (p. 176)
Nom	nominal
NP	noun phrase
NPI	negatively-oriented polarity-sensitive item (p. 822)
NZE	New Zealand English

o	oblique
O	object
O^d	direct object
O^i	indirect object
$O_{ditrans}$	object of ditransitive (pp. 296–7)
O_{mono}	object of monotransitive (pp. 296–7)
O_{trans}	object of transitive (pp. 296–7)
P	predicator
PC, PredComp	predicative complement
pl	plural
Poss	possibility (p. 176)
PP	preposition phrase
Prep	preposition
PPI	positively-oriented polarity-sensitive item (p. 822)
Q–A	question–answer (p. 897)
REL	relative
S	subject
S_{intr}	subject of intransitive (pp. 296–7)
S_{trans}	subject of transitive (pp. 296–7)
sg	singular
Subj-det	subject-determiner
T_d	deictic time (p. 125)
T_m	matrix time (p. 160)
T_o	time of orientation (p. 125)
T_r	time referred to (p. 125)
T_{sit}	time of situation (p. 125)
univ	universal
V	verb
VGp	verb group (p. 1213)
VP	verb phrase
&	conjunction (logical) (p. 1294)
$\vee$	inclusive disjunction (p. 1294)
$\veebar$	exclusive disjunction (p. 1294)
$<$	is anterior to (p. 125)
$>$	(i) is greater/stronger than; (ii) is posterior to (p. 125); (iii) precedes (labile ordering constraint) (p. 452)
$\gg$	precedes (rigid ordering constraint) (p. 452)
~	(i) grammatical correspondence; (ii) the meaning of the morphological base (p. 1631)
$X \rightarrow Y$; $Y \leftarrow X$	*X* is morphological source of *Y* (p. 1633)

Presentation of examples

Italics are used for all expressions cited in orthography.

Bold italics are used to emphasise that we are citing a lexeme in abstraction from any of its inflectional forms, as in 'the verb ***go***' (p. 27).

"Double quotation marks" enclose meanings, or propositions.

Underlining (single or double) and square brackets serve to highlight part of an example.

SMALL CAPITALS are used, where appropriate, to indicate focal stress: *I* DID *tell you.*

Arrows mark intonation, with ↗ representing a rising pitch, ↘ a falling pitch, as in *Is it a boy* ↗ *or a girl* ↘*?*

The symbol '—', as in '*what Kim bought* —', represents a gap (p. 49).

The symbol '·' marks a morphological division within a word or a component part of a word, as in '*work·er·s*' or 'the suffix *·s*'.

Subscript indices, such as '*i*' or '*j*', mark pairs of items related as antecedent and anaphor (p. 48); thus in '$Jill_i$ *said* she_i *would help*', the pronoun *she* is to be interpreted as anaphoric to the antecedent *Jill*.

The following symbols indicate the status of examples (in the interpretation under consideration):

*	ungrammatical	**This books is mine.*
#	semantically or pragmatically anomalous	*#We frightened the cheese.*
%	grammatical in some dialect(s) only	*%He hadn't many friends.*
?	of questionable grammaticality	*?Sue he gave the key.*
!	non-standard	*!I can't hardly hear.*

The slash symbol '/' separates alternatives: *The picture seemed excellent/distorted* represents an abbreviation of the two examples *The picture seemed excellent* and *The picture seemed distorted.* Similarly, *I asked you not to leave / *to don't leave until tomorrow* is an abbreviation of *I asked you not to leave until tomorrow* and **I asked you to don't leave until tomorrow.* The slash is flanked by spaces unless both alternatives consist of a single word.

Parentheses enclose optional elements: *The error was overlooked (by Pat)* is an abbreviation of *The error was overlooked by Pat* and *The error was overlooked.*

The letters 'A' and 'B' represent different speakers in an interchange, as in A: *Where's the key?* B: *It's in the top drawer.*

Specialist passages

Certain passages are set off from the main text by being printed in smaller type against a shaded background, as illustrated here. They are designed mainly for the specialist grammarian rather than the more general reader, being mostly concerned with linguistic argumentation in favour of the analysis presented in the main text. Such passages can be omitted without loss of continuity.

Tree diagrams

Tree diagrams for the expressions listed in [1–40] below are given on the pages indicated. The conventions used in the diagrams are explained in the commentaries on [1] (the major concepts), [3] (for the 'gap' notation), and [8] (for the abbreviatory triangle).

Preface

This book aims to bridge the large gap that exists between traditional grammar and the partial descriptions of English grammar proposed by those working in the field of linguistics. We do not assume any familiarity with theoretical linguistics on the part of the reader and aim for as comprehensive a coverage as space allows, but we have made significant changes to the traditional analysis to take account of the progress that has been made by linguists in our understanding of English grammar.

The task of producing a new grammar of English that incorporates as many as possible of the insights achieved in modern linguistics is too great for two people, and we are fortunate to have been able to enlist the help of a team of distinguished linguists. A grammar, however, requires a very high degree of integration between the parts, so that it would not have been possible simply to put together a collection of papers by different scholars writing within their area of specialisation. Instead, one or both of us have worked closely with the other contributors in co-authoring the chapters concerned: we are grateful to them for their willingness to engage in this somewhat unusual kind of collaboration. They are not of course to be held responsible for any shortcomings in the description relating to topics whose primary coverage is in other chapters than those that bear their names.

The lengthy business of producing this grammar has occupied one of us (RDH) for over a decade, most of it full-time, and the other (GKP) part-time for over six years. Naturally, many intellectual and personal debts have piled up during the lengthy process of research, consultation, collaboration, writing, revising, and editing. We cannot hope to convey the full extent of these debts, but we will attempt to sketch the outlines of those that are the most central.

The project has benefited from the support and advice provided by a group of eminent linguists who served as a Board of Consultants: Barry Blake, Bernard Comrie, Greville Corbett, Edward Finegan, John Lyons, Peter Matthews, Keith Mitchell, Frank Palmer, John Payne, Neil Smith, Roland Sussex, and the late James D. McCawley.

During the first six years of the project, workshops were held regularly in Brisbane and Sydney to develop ideas for the framework and content of the grammar: we are grateful for the contributions to these workshops provided by Ray Cattell, Peter Collins, Peter Fries, David Lee, Pam Peters, and Peter Peterson. Pam Peters and staff at Macquarie University helped us with gathering data by providing online access to the Brown, ACE, and LOB corpora.

A number of scholars were good enough to let us have comments on one or more whole draft chapters: Barry Blake (a stalwart, who studied eight chapters with care), Bas Aarts, Francis Bond, Jill Bowie, Bernard Comrie, Greville Corbett, Annabel Cormack, David Denison, Edward Finegan, David Lee, James D. McCawley, Peter Matthews,

Keith Mitchell, Frank Palmer, Mário Perini, Peter Peterson, Aimo Seppänen, Neil Smith, and Mariangela Spinillo. Others commented on specific topics: Vic Dudman (tense, modality, conditionals), Peter Fries (verb inflection and auxiliaries); Janet Holmes and Anne Pauwels (gender); Henk Kylstra (numerals); John Lyons (clause type); Gregory Ward and Arnold Zwicky (unbounded dependencies). Edmund Weiner of Oxford University Press made available to us lexicographical data on *themself.* Aimo Seppänen provided us with comments, draft material, and corpus examples on a wide range of topics, including extraposition, relative clauses and verb complementation. John Payne also contributed ideas on a considerable number of issues that lie outside the two chapters bearing his name. Frank Palmer and Roland Sussex gave invaluable advice on matters of presentation.

Some scholars who did not end up being full collaborators in the drafting of any particular chapter nonetheless provided crucial draft material for particular sections or for notes at various points in the book: Ray Cattell (on light verbs), David Denison (on issues in the history of English), and David Lee (on the meanings of prepositions). Jill Bowie and Tom Mylne worked for the project in a research support role, and did enormously useful work; we thank them warmly. Tom also played a major part in compiling the index, while James Huddleston provided valuable additional help with this massive task.

Our more general intellectual debts will, we hope, be obvious, though not as obvious as they would have been if we had been writing a linguistics monograph with literature citations rather than a descriptive grammar with none. It should be kept in mind that we have maintained strictly a policy of not interrupting our exposition at all with references to the grammatical literature or source citations for examples, even in the footnotes. Those who wish to see a brief summary listing of some of the literature that influenced us most and a few works that we would recommend for additional information should turn to our 'Further Reading' section at the end of the book.

Special mention should be made here, however, of the work of Randolph Quirk and his colleagues, whose Survey of English Usage and the series of grammars resulting from it culminated in the publication of *A Comprehensive Grammar of the English Language* in 1985. Although the present work often pursues a very different theoretical approach and analysis from that of Quirk *et al.*, their grammar proved an indispensable source of data and ideas. We might never have attempted this grammar if Quirk, Greenbaum, Leech and Svartvik had not pointed the way.

The University of Queensland provided a special projects grant to launch our work in 1989, while the Australian Research Council provided the major financial support in the form of two Large Grants covering the period 1990–1996 and a Senior Research Fellowship funding RDH's full-time involvement from 1994 to 1998. GKP's work involved five visits to the project's Australian headquarters totalling over a year, together with two sabbatical quarters in California. These were made financially possible by the Gladys Krieble Delmas Foundation (New York), various grants programmes at the University of Queensland, Cambridge University Press, and the Division of Humanities and Department of Linguistics at the University of California, Santa Cruz.

We are also grateful to staff at Cambridge University Press, notably to Judith Ayling in the early part of the project and then to Kate Brett, who has provided invaluable support over the last few years. Thanks are due too to Leigh Mueller for her very thorough work as copy-editor.

Last of all, though only to ensure the pragmatic prominence associated with final constituents, we note that each of us is in the position of having married just a couple of years before starting work on this enormous task, and with some surprise we note that both our marriages have survived it. This is mainly because of great forbearance, resilience, unselfishness, supportiveness, and love supplied by our spouses.

Barbara Scholz faced five consecutive years of summertime choices between dislocation and desertion as her partner (GKP) decamped to Australia to work full-time on the grammar through the Australian winter. But through the years, whether she stayed behind or moved to Australia, she was unfailingly supportive and even enthusiastic about the project. Her generosity and fortitude is deeply appreciated.

Vivienne Huddleston provided an immense amount of warm hospitality to members of the project – in early years at the annual Brisbane workshops, and later to overseas contributors staying in her home for lengthy periods of collaboration with RDH. And she accepted with extraordinary patience and good humour prolonged and ever-increasing neglect during a writing process that went on three or four years longer than it was ever supposed to. And in the final stages of the work she provided more direct help with the proof-reading and indexing.

Both Vivienne and Barbara took a positive interest in the grammar itself, and we often derived benefit from examples they spotted or observations they made. We owe them more than could be expressed by the words of an acknowledgement note.

RDH · GKP

1

Preliminaries

Geoffrey K. Pullum
Rodney Huddleston

1 The aim of this book

This book is a description of the grammar of modern Standard English, providing a detailed account of the principles governing the construction of English words, phrases, clauses, and sentences. To be more specific, we give a synchronic, descriptive grammar of general-purpose, present-day, international Standard English.

Synchronic versus diachronic description

A **synchronic** description of a language is a snapshot of it at one point in time, the opposite of a **diachronic** or historical account. English has a rich history going back over a millennium, but it is not the aim of this book to detail it. We include only a few notes on historical points of interest that will assist the reader to understand the present state of the language.

Of course, at any given moment English speakers with birthdates spread over about a century are alive, so the idea of English as it is on one particular day is a fiction: the English used today was learned by some speakers at the end of the twentieth century and by others near the beginning. But our practice will be to illustrate relevant points mainly with examples of use of the language taken from prose produced since the mid twentieth century. Examples from earlier periods are used only when particularly apposite quotations are available for a point on which the language has not subsequently changed. Wherever grammatical change has clearly occurred, our aim will be not to describe the evolutionary process but rather to describe the current state of the language.

Description versus prescription

Our aim is to **describe** and not **prescribe**: we outline and illustrate the principles that govern the construction of words and sentences in the present-day language without recommending or condemning particular usage choices. Although this book may be (and we certainly hope it will be) of use in helping the user decide how to phrase things, it is not designed as a style guide or a usage manual. We report that sentences of some types are now widely found and used, but we will not advise you to use them. We state that sentences of some types are seldom encountered, or that usage manuals or language columnists or language teachers recommend against them, or that some form of words is normally found only in informal style or, conversely, is limited to rather formal style, but we will not tell you that you should avoid them or otherwise make recommendations about how you should speak or write. Rather, this book offers a description of the context common to all such decisions: the linguistic system itself.

General-purpose versus special-purpose

We exclude from consideration what we refer to as **special-purpose** varieties of the language. Newspaper headlines, road signs, notices, and the like have their own special styles of abbreviation (*Man bites dog, arrested*; *EXIT ONLY THIS LANE*), and we do not provide a full treatment of the possibilities. Likewise, we do not provide a description of any special notations (chemical formulae, telephone numbers, email addresses) or of the special language found in poetry, heraldic descriptions, scientific works, chemical compound naming, computer jargon, mathematical proofs, etc. To some small extent there may be idiosyncratic grammatical patterns found in such areas, but we generally set them aside, avoiding complicated digressions about usages found within only a very narrow range of discourse.

Present-day English versus earlier stages

Modern English is generally defined by historians of English to be the English used from 1776 onwards. The recent part of the latter period (say, since the Second World War) can be called Present-day English. Linguistic changes have occurred in the grammar of English during the Modern English period, and even during the last half-century. Our central aim is to describe Present-day English in its standard form. This means, for example, that we treat the pronoun system as not containing a contrast between familiar and respectful 2nd person pronouns: the contrast between *thou* and *you* has been lost, and we do not mention *thou* in this grammar. Of course, this does not mean that people who use *thou* (actors in period plays, people addressing God in prayers, or Quakers who have retained the older usage) are making a mistake; but they are not using the general-purpose standard Present-day English described in this book.

Grammar versus other components

A **grammar** of a language describes the principles or rules governing the form and meaning of words, phrases, clauses, and sentences. As such, it interacts with other components of a complete description: the **phonology** (covering the sound system), the **graphology** (the writing system: spelling and punctuation), the dictionary or **lexicon**, and the **semantics**.

Phonology and graphology do not receive attention in their own right here, but both have to be treated explicitly in the course of our description of inflection in Ch. 18 (we introduce the concepts that we will draw on in §3 of this chapter), and Ch. 20 deals with one aspect of the writing system in providing an outline account of the important system of punctuation.

A lexicon for a language deals with the vocabulary: it brings together information about the pronunciation, spelling, meaning, and grammatical properties of the **lexical items** – the words, and the items with special meanings that consist of more than one word, the idioms.

The study of conventional linguistic meaning is known as **semantics**. We take this to cut across the division between grammar and lexicon. That is, we distinguish between **lexical semantics**, which dictionaries cover, and **grammatical semantics**. Our account of grammatical meaning will be quite informal, but will distinguish between semantics (dealing with the meaning of sentences or words as determined by the language system itself) and **pragmatics** (which has to do with the use and interpretation of sentences as used in particular contexts); an introduction to these and other concepts used in describing meaning is given in §5 of this chapter.

A grammar itself is divisible into two components, **syntax** and **morphology**. Syntax is concerned with the way words combine to form phrases, clauses, and sentences, while morphology deals with the formation of words. This division gives special prominence to the **word**, a unit which is also of major importance in the lexicon, the phonology and the graphology.

Standard versus non-standard

Perhaps the most subtle concept we have to rely on is the one that picks out the particular variety of Present-day English we describe, which we call Standard English. Briefly (for we will return to the topic below), we are describing the kind of English that is widely accepted in the countries of the world where English is the language of government, education, broadcasting, news publishing, entertainment, and other public discourse.

In a large number of countries (now running into scores), including some where most of the people have other languages as their first language, English is used for most printed books, magazines, newspapers, and public notices; for most radio and television broadcasting; for many or most film scripts, plays, poetry, and other literary art; for speeches, lectures, political addresses, proclamations, official ceremonies, advertisements, and other general announcements. In these countries there is a high degree of consensus about the appropriate variety of English to use. The consensus is confirmed by the decisions of broadcasting authorities about the kind of English that will be used for public information announcements, newscasts, commentaries to broadcasts of national events such as state funerals, and so on. It is confirmed by the writing found in magazines, newspapers, novels, and non-fiction books; by the editing and correcting that is done by the publishers of these; and by the way writers for the most part accept such editing and correcting of their work.

This is not to say that controversy cannot arise about points of grammar or usage. There is much dispute, and that is precisely the subject matter for prescriptive usage manuals. Nonetheless, the controversy about particular points stands out against a backdrop of remarkably widespread agreement about how sentences should be constructed for such purposes as publication, political communication, or government broadcasting. This widespread agreement defines what we are calling Standard English.

National versus international

Finally, we note that this book is not intended to promote any particular country's variety of Standard English as a norm; it is to apply internationally. English is the single most important language in the world, being the official or de facto language of the United Kingdom, the United States of America, Canada, Australia, New Zealand, South Africa, and dozens of others, and being the lingua franca of the Internet. Many varieties of English are spoken around the world – from lectures in graduate schools in Holland to parliamentary proceedings in Papua New Guinea – but interestingly the vast majority of the variation lies in pronunciation and vocabulary. The number of differences in grammar between different varieties of Standard English is very small indeed relative to the full range of syntactic constructions and morphological word-forms.

Nevertheless, there undoubtedly are differences of this kind that need to be noted. For example, the use of the verb *do* following an auxiliary verb, as in %*I'm not sure that I'll go, but I may do* is not found in American English, and conversely the past participle verb-form *gotten*, as in %*I've just gotten a new car*, is distinctively American. We use the symbol '%' to mark constructions or forms that are restricted to some dialect or dialects in this way.

The regional dialects of Standard English in the world today can be divided into two large families with regional and historical affinities. One contains standard educated Southern British English, henceforth abbreviated **BrE**, together with a variety of related dialects, including most of the varieties of English in Great Britain, Australia, New Zealand, South Africa, and most other places in the British Commonwealth. The second dialect family we will refer to as American English, henceforth **AmE** – it contains the dialects of the United States, Canada, and associated territories, from Hawaii and Alaska to eastern Canada.

2 Prescriptivism, tradition, and the justification of grammars

The topic of prescriptivism and its relation to the long tradition of English grammatical scholarship needs some further discussion if the basis of our work, and its relation to other contributions to the field, is to be properly understood. It relates to the issue of how the statements of a grammar are justified: what the support for a claimed grammatical statement might be.

2.1 Prescriptive and descriptive approaches: goals and coverage

The distinction between the prescriptive and descriptive approaches to grammar is often explained by saying that prescriptivists want to tell you how you **ought** to speak and write, while descriptivists want to tell you how people actually **do** speak and write. This does bring out the major difference between the two approaches: it is a difference in goals. However, it is something of an oversimplification, because writing a descriptive grammar in practice involves a fair amount of idealisation: we need to abstract away from the errors that people make, especially in speech (this point is taken up again in §3 below). In addition, it glosses over some significant differences between the kinds of works prescriptivists and descriptivists characteristically produce.

Differences in content

The basic difference in goals between prescriptive and descriptive works goes hand in hand with a striking difference in topics treated. The subject matters overlap, but many topics dealt with by prescriptive works find no place in a descriptive grammar, and some topics that must be treated in a descriptive grammar are universally ignored by prescriptive works.

The advice of prescriptivists is supplied in works of a type we will refer to as **usage manuals.** They are almost invariably arranged in the style of a dictionary, containing an alphabetically arranged series of entries on topics where the issue of what is correct or acceptable is not altogether straightforward. In the first few pages of one usage manual we find entries on *abacus* (should the plural be *abaci*?), abbreviations (which ones are acceptable in formal writing?), *abdomen* (is the stress on the second syllable or the first?), *abduction* (how does it differ in meaning from *kidnapping*?), and so on. These points concern inflection, formal writing, pronunciation, and meaning, respectively, and on all of them a degree of variation and occasional uncertainty is encountered even among expert users of English. Not all of them would belong in a grammatical description. For example, our grammar does cover the plural of *abacus* (Ch. 18, §4.1.6), but it does not list abbreviations, or phonological topics like the placement of stress in English words, or lexical semantic topics like the distinction between *abduction* and *kidnapping*. These we take to be in the province of lexicon – matters for a dictionary rather than a grammar.

Usage manuals also give a great deal of attention to matters of style and effective expression that lie beyond the range of grammar as we understand it. Thus one prescriptive usage dictionary warns that *explore every avenue* is a tired cliché (and adds that it makes little sense, since exploration suggests a more challenging environment than an avenue); that the phrase *in this day and age* 'should be avoided at all costs'; that *circling round* is tautologous (one can only circle by going round) and thus should not be used; and so on. Whether or not one thinks these are good pieces of advice, we do not take them to fall within the realm of grammar. A sentence like *In this day and age one must circle round and explore every avenue* may be loaded with careworn verbiage, or it may even be arrant nonsense, but there is absolutely nothing **grammatically** wrong with it.

There are also topics in a descriptive grammar that are uniformly ignored by prescriptivists. These include the most salient and well-known principles of syntax. Prescriptive works tend to be highly selective, dealing only with points on which people make mistakes (or what are commonly thought to be mistakes). They would never supply, for example, the grammatically important information that determinatives like *the* and *a* precede the noun they are associated with (*the house*, not **house the*),[1] or that modal auxiliaries like *can* and *must* are disallowed in infinitival clauses (**I'd like to can swim* is ungrammatical), or that in subordinate interrogative clauses the interrogative element comes at the front (so we get *She asked <u>what</u> we needed*, not **She asked we needed <u>what</u>*). Native speakers never get these things wrong, so no advice is needed.

2.2 Disagreement between descriptivist and prescriptivist work

Although descriptive grammars and prescriptive usage manuals differ in the range of topics they treat, there is no reason in principle why they should not agree on what they say about the topics they both treat. The fact they do not is interesting. There are several reasons for the lack of agreement. We deal with three of them here: (a) the basis in personal taste of some prescriptivist writers' judgements; (b) the confusion of informality with ungrammaticality; and (c) certain invalid arguments sometimes appealed to by prescriptivists. These are extraneous features of prescriptive writing about language rather than inherent ones, and all three of them are less prevalent now than they were

[1]Throughout this book we use an asterisk to indicate that what follows is ungrammatical.

in the past. But older prescriptive works have exemplified them, and a few still do; their influence lingers on in the English-speaking educational world.

(a) Taste tyranny

Some prescriptivist works present rules that have no basis in the way the language is actually used by the majority of its native speakers, and are not even claimed to have any such basis – as though the manual-writer's own judgements of taste took precedence over those of any other speaker of the language. They expect all speakers to agree with their judgements, no matter what the facts of language use might show.

For example, one usage manual, discussing why it is (supposedly) incorrect to say *You need a driving instructor who you have confidence in,* states that 'The accusative *whom* is necessary with the preposition *in,* though *whom* is a word strangely shunned by most English people.' We take the implication to be that English people should not shun this word, since the writer (who is English) does not. But we are inclined to ask what grounds there could be for saying that *whom* is 'necessary' if most English people (or speakers of the English language) would avoid it.

The same book objects to *centre (a)round,* calling it incorrect, although 'probably more frequently used than the correct *centre on*'. Again, we wonder how *centre (a)round* can be determined to be incorrect in English if it is indeed more commonly used by English speakers than what is allegedly correct. The boundary would appear to have been drawn in the wrong place.

Prescriptive works instantiating this kind of aesthetic authoritarianism provide no answer to such obvious questions. They simply assert that grammar dictates things, without supporting their claim from evidence. The basis for the recommendations offered appears to lie in the writer's taste: the writer quoted above simply does not like to see *who* used where it is understood as the object of a preposition, and personally hates the expression *centre around.* What is going on here is a universalising of one person's taste, a demand that everyone should agree with it and conform to it.

The descriptivist view would be that when most speakers use a form that our grammar says is incorrect, there is at least a prima facie case that it is the grammar that is wrong, not the speakers. And indeed, even in the work just quoted we find the remark that '*Alright* is common, and may in time become normal', an acknowledgement that the language may change over time, and what begins as an isolated variant on a pattern may eventually become the new pattern. The descriptive grammarian will always adopt a stance of something more like this sort, thus making evidence relevant to the matter at hand. If what is involved were a matter of taste, all evidence would be beside the point. But under the descriptive viewpoint, grammar is not a matter of taste, nor of aesthetics.

This is not to say that the expression of personal aesthetic judgements is without utility. The writer of a book on usage might be someone famous for brilliant use of the language, someone eminently worthy of being followed in matters of taste and literary style. It might be very useful to have a compendium of such a person's preferences and recommendations, and very sensible for a less expert writer to follow the recommendations of an acknowledged master of the writer's craft (assuming such recommendations do reliably accord with the master's practice). All we are pointing out is that where the author of an authoritarian usage manual departs from recommendations that agree with the way most people use the language, prescriptivist and descriptivist accounts will necessarily disagree. The authoritarian prescriptivist whose recommendations are out of step with the usage of others is at liberty to declare that they are in error and should change their ways; the descriptivist under the same circumstances will assume that it is precisely the constant features in the usage of the overwhelming majority that define what is grammatical in the contemporary language, and will judge the prescriptivist to be expressing an idiosyncratic opinion concerning how the language ought to be.

(b) Confusing informal style with ungrammaticality

It has been a common assumption of prescriptivists that only formal style is grammatically correct. The quotation about *whom* given above is representative of this view, for *whom* can be a marker of relatively formal style, being commonly replaced by *who* in informal style (see Ch. 5, §16.2.3, for a detailed account of the use of these two forms). There are two related points to be made here. The first is that it is important to distinguish between the two contrasts illustrated in the following pairs:

[1]	i	a. *It is clear whom they had in mind.*	b. *It's clear who they had in mind.*
	ii	a. *Kim and I saw the accident.*	b. [!]*Kim and me saw the accident.*

In [i], both versions belong to Standard English, with [a] somewhat formal, and [b] neutral or slightly informal. There is no difference in grammaticality. But in [ii], the [a] version is standard, the [b] version non-standard; we use the '!' symbol to mark a construction or form as ungrammatical in Standard English but grammatical in a non-standard dialect. Construction [iib] will be heard in the speech of speakers of dialects that have a different rule for case inflection of pronouns: they use the accusative forms (*me, him, her, us, them*) whenever the pronoun is coordinated. Standard English does not.

A common view in the prescriptivist tradition is that uses of *who* like [1ib] are not grammatically correct but are nevertheless 'sanctioned by usage'. For example, Fowler, one of the most influential prescriptivists of the twentieth century, wrote: 'The interrogative *who* is often used in talk where grammar demands *whom*, as in *Who did you hear that from?* No further defence than "colloquial" is needed for this.' This implies a dichotomy between 'talk' and 'grammar' that we reject. The standard language embraces a range of styles, from formal through neutral to informal. A satisfactory grammar must describe them all. It is not that formal style keeps to the rules and informal style departs from them; rather, formal and informal styles have partially different rules.

(c) Spurious external justifications

Prescriptive grammarians have frequently backed up their pronouncements with appeals to entirely extraneous considerations. Some older prescriptive grammars, for example, give evidence of relying on rules that would be better suited to the description of classical languages like Latin than to Present-day English. Consider, for example, the difference between the uses of accusative and nominative forms of the personal pronouns seen in:

[2]	a. *It is I.*	b. *It's me.*

With *who* and *whom* in [1i] we saw a construction where an accusative form was associated with relatively formal style. In [2], however, it is the sentence with the nominative form *I* that belongs to (very) formal style, while accusative *me* is neutral or informal (again, see Ch. 5, §16.2.1 for a fuller description of the facts). Confusing informality with ungrammaticality again, a strong prescriptivist tradition says that only [2a] is grammatical. The accusative *me* is claimed to be the case of the direct object, as in *It hurt me*, but in [2] the noun phrase after the verb is a predicative complement. In Latin, predicative complements take nominative, the same case as the subject. An assumption is being made that English grammar too requires nominative case for predicative complements. Use of the accusative *me* is regarded as a departure from the rules of grammar.

The mistake here, of course, is to assume that what holds in Latin grammar has to hold for English. English grammar differs on innumerable points from Latin grammar; there is no reason in principle why the assignment of case to predicative complements should not be one of them. After all, English is very different from Latin with respect to case: the nominative–accusative contrast applies to only a handful of pronouns (rather than to the full class of nouns, as in Latin). The right way to describe the present situation in Standard English (unlike Latin) is that with the pronouns that have a nominative–accusative case distinction, the choice between the cases for a predicative complement noun phrase varies according to the style level: the nominative is noticeably formal, the accusative is more or less neutral and always used in informal contexts.

Another kind of illegitimate argument is based on analogy between one area of grammar and another. Consider yet another construction where there is variation between nominative and accusative forms of pronouns:

[3] a. *They invited me to lunch.* b. %*They invited my partner and I to lunch.*

The '%' symbol is again used to mark the [b] example as typically used by some speakers of Standard English but not others, though this time it is not a matter of regional variation. The status of the construction in [b] differs from that of *It's me*, which is undisputedly normal in informal use, and from that of !*Me and Kim saw her leave*, which is unquestionably non-standard. What is different is that examples like [b] are regularly used by a significant proportion of speakers of Standard English, and not generally thought by ordinary speakers to be non-standard; they pass unnoticed in broadcast speech all the time.

Prescriptivists, however, condemn the use illustrated by [3b], insisting that the 'correct' form is *They invited my partner and me to lunch.* And here again they seek to justify their claim that [3b] is ungrammatical by an implicit analogy, this time with other situations found in English, such as the example seen in [a]. In [a] the pronoun functions by itself as direct object of the verb and invariably appears in accusative case. What is different in [b] is that the direct object of the verb has the form of a coordination, not a single pronoun. Prescriptivists commonly take it for granted that this difference is irrelevant to case assignment. They argue that because we have an accusative in [a] we should also have an accusative in [b], so the nominative *I* is ungrammatical.

But why should we simply assume that the grammatical rules for case assignment cannot differentiate between a coordinated and a non-coordinated pronoun? As it happens, there is another place in English grammar where the rules are sensitive to this distinction – for virtually all speakers, not just some of them:

[4] a. *I don't know if you're eligible.* b. **I don't know if she and you're eligible.*

The sequence *you are* can be reduced to *you're* in [a], where *you* is subject, but not in [b], where the subject has the form of a coordination of pronouns. This shows us not only that a rule of English could apply differently to pronouns and coordinated pronouns, but that one rule actually does. If that is so, then a rule could likewise distinguish between [3a] and [3b]. The argument from analogy is illegitimate. Whether [3b] is treated as correct Standard English or not (a matter that we take up in Ch. 5, §16.2.2), it cannot be successfully argued to be incorrect simply by virtue of the analogy with [3a].

The claim that [1ib] (*It's clear who they had in mind*) is ungrammatical is supported by the same kind of analogical reasoning. In *They had me in mind*, we have accusative *me*, so it is assumed that the grammar likewise requires accusative *whom*. The assumption here is that the rules of case assignment are not sensitive to the difference in the position of the pronoun (after the verb for *me*, at the beginning of the clause for *who*), or to the difference between interrogative and personal pronouns. There is, however, no basis for assuming that the rules of grammar cannot make reference to such differences: the grammar of English could assign case to clause-initial and non-clause-initial pronouns, or to interrogative and non-interrogative pronouns, in slightly different ways.[2]

We should stress that not all prescriptive grammarians exhibit the shortcomings we have just catalogued – universalising taste judgements, confusing informality with ungrammaticality, citing spurious external justifications, and arguing from spurious analogies. There are usage manuals that are accurate in their understanding of the facts, clear-sighted in their attitudes towards usage trends, and useful in their recommendations; such books can be an enormous help to a writer. But the good prescriptive manuals respect a crucial tenet: that their criterion should always be the use of the standard language by its native speakers.

As we have said, to some extent good usage manuals go far beyond grammar into style, rhetoric, and communication, giving advice about which expressions are overused clichés, or fail to make their intended point, or are unintentionally ambiguous, or perpetuate an unfortunate malapropism, or any of a large number of other matters that lie beyond the scope of this book. But when it comes to points of grammar, the only legitimate basis for an absolute judgement of incorrectness in a usage manual is that what is being rejected is **not in the standard language**.

The aspects of some prescriptivist works that we have discussed illustrate ways in which those works let their users down. Where being ungrammatical is confused with merely being informal, there is a danger that the student of English will not be taught how to speak in a normal informal way, but will sound stilted and unnatural, like an inexpert reader reading something out from a book. And where analogies are used uncritically to predict grammatical properties, or Latin principles are taken to guarantee correct use of English, the user is simply being misled.

[2] A further type of invalid argument that falls under the present heading confuses grammar with logic. This is illustrated in the remarkably widespread but completely fallacious claim that non-standard [!]*I didn't see nobody* is intrinsically inferior to standard *I didn't see anybody* because the two negatives cancel each other out. We discuss this issue in Ch. 9, §6.2.

The stipulations of incorrectness that will be genuinely useful to the student are those about what is actually not found in the standard language, particularly with respect to features widely recognised as characteristic of some definitely non-standard dialect. And in that case evidence from use of Standard English by the people who speak it and write it every day will show that it is not regularly used, which means prescriptive and descriptive accounts will not be in conflict, for evidence from use of the language is exactly what is relied upon by descriptive grammars such as we present here.

The evidence we use comes from several sources: our own intuitions as native speakers of the language; the reactions of other native speakers we consult when we are in doubt; data from computer corpora (machine-readable bodies of naturally occurring text),[3] and data presented in dictionaries and other scholarly work on grammar. We alternate between the different sources and cross-check them against each other, since intuitions can be misleading and texts can contain errors. Issues of interpretation often arise. But always, under the descriptive approach, claims about grammar will depend upon evidence.

3 Speech and writing

There are significant and interesting differences between spoken and written language, but we do not regard written English as a different language from spoken English. In general, we aim to describe both the written standard variety that is encountered in contemporary newspapers, magazines, and books and the spoken standard variety that is heard on radio and television programmes in English-speaking countries.

'Speaker' and 'utterance' as medium-neutral terms

Most of what we say will apply equally to the spoken and written varieties of the language. As there is no non-technical term covering both one who utters a sentence in speech and one who writes a sentence, we will follow the widespread practice in linguistics of extending the ordinary sense of 'speaker' so as to subsume 'writer' – a practice that reflects the fact that speech is in important respects more basic than writing.[4] We likewise take 'utterance' to be neutral between the mediums, so that we will refer to both spoken and written utterances.

Practical bias towards written English

Despite our neutrality between speech and writing in principle, there are at least three reasons why the reader may perceive something of a bias in this work towards data from

[3] The computer corpora that we have made use of are the Brown corpus of a million words of American English; the London/Oslo/Bergen (LOB) corpus of British English; the Australian Corpus of English (ACE); and the *Wall Street Journal* corpus distributed by the Association for Computational Linguistics. The British National Corpus (BNC) was only released to scholars working outside the UK after the book was in final draft. We have also drawn on a variety of other sources, including collections of our own from sources such as magazines, newspapers, plays, books, and film scripts.

[4] Since our discussion of sentences will very often make reference to the way they are used we will have very frequent occasion to talk of speakers, and in order to avoid repeatedly using the term 'speaker' we will often simply use the 1st person pronoun *I*. Given that the book has joint authorship this pronoun could not be used in reference to any specific person, and hence is available as a convenient variant of 'the speaker'.

written English. To the extent that it is present, it stems from practical considerations rather than matters of principle. We will discuss here the three factors motivating the choices we have made.

Citation of forms and examples

First, we normally follow the usual practice in grammars of citing words or sentences in their written form. This is mainly a matter of practical convenience: it is much more straightforward typographically, and more widely accessible to readers, to supply examples in this form. In certain cases – as, for example, in describing the inflectional forms of verbs and nouns in Ch. 18 – it is necessary to indicate the pronunciation, and for this purpose we use the system of transcription described in §3.1.2 below. Representations in written form are given in italics, while phonological representations are enclosed in obliques.

Accessibility of print sources

Second, we make frequent use of genuinely attested examples (often shortened or otherwise modified in ways not relevant to the point at issue), and it is significantly easier to obtain access to suitable large collections, or corpora, of written data in a conveniently archived and readily searchable form than it is for speech.

Error rates in speech

Third, and most importantly, it must be acknowledged that the error content of spoken material is higher than that of written material. Those who have listened to tape recordings of spontaneous conversation are likely to have been struck by the high incidence of hesitation noises, false starts, self-corrections, repetitions, and other dysfluencies found in the speech of many people. It is not hard to see why speech contains a higher number of errors than writing. The rapid production of speech (quite often several words per second) leaves little time for reflection on construction choices or planning of sentence structure, so that at normal conversational pace slip-ups of the kind mentioned are very common. As a result, what speakers actually come out with reflects only imperfectly the system that defines the spoken version of the language. Hardly noticed by the listener, and often compensated for by virtually unconscious repair strategies on the part of the speaker, these sporadic interruptions and imperfections in speech production are inherently outside the purview of the grammarian (the discipline of psycholinguistics studies them in order to learn about the planning, production, and perception of speech). They therefore have to be screened out through judicious decision-making by a skilled native speaker of the language before grammatical description is attempted. The original speaker is not always available for the tedious editing task, and so someone else has to interpret the transcript and remove the apparent errors, which means that misunderstandings can result (word sequences that were actually due to slips might be wrongly taken to represent grammatical facts).

Written English has the advantage that its slow rate of composition has generally allowed time and opportunity for nearly all these slips and failures of execution to be screened out by the actual author of the sentence. This provides a practical reason for us to show a preference for it when selecting illustrative examples: we have very good reason to believe that what ultimately gets printed corresponds fairly closely to what the writer intended to say.

The nature of the written medium and the slower sentence-planning environment permits the construction of longer sentences than typically occur in speech, but we take this to be a matter of degree, not a matter of written English instantiating new possibilities that are completely absent from the spoken language. The basic point of most written material is that people who are ordinary native speakers of the language should read it and understand it, so the pressure will always be in the direction of keeping it fairly close to the language in which (ignoring the speech errors referred to above) ordinary people talk to each other.

Thus while we acknowledge a tendency for the exemplification in this grammar to be biased towards written English, we assume that the goal of providing a description that is neutral between spoken and written English is not an unreasonable one. Sharp divergences between the syntax of speech and the syntax of writing, as opposed to differences that exist between styles within either the spoken or the written language, are rare to the point of non-existence.

3.1 The representation of English pronunciation

This section provides an introduction to the system of representation we use in this book in those cases where it is necessary to indicate the pronunciation of words or word sequences. Developing a system that will be readily usable by non-specialists is by no means a trivial enterprise; English has a remarkably complex vowel system compared to most other languages, and one of the most complex patterns of fit between sound and spelling found in any language. Taken together, these facts raise some significant and unavoidable difficulties even if only one variety of English is under consideration. But an additional problem is that English is a global language with something like 400 million native speakers pronouncing the language in many different ways: pronunciation differs across the world more than any other aspect of the language.

3.1.1 Rhotic and non-rhotic accents

We will use the term **accent** for varieties of a language distinguished by pronunciation, opposing it to **dialect**, which applies to varieties distinguished by grammar or vocabulary. The most important accent distinction in English concerns the sound we represent as /r/. Most speakers in the BrE family of dialects have a **non-rhotic accent**: here /r/ occurs in **pre-vocalic** position, i.e. when immediately preceding a vowel, as in *run* or *area*, but not in **post-vocalic** position, after the vowel of a syllable. For example, in a non-rhotic accent there is no /r/ in any of the words in [1] (as pronounced in isolation):

[1]	i a. *mar, bear, floor, stir, actor*	b. *care, hire, bore, sure, cure*
	ii a. *hard, torque, term, burn*	b. *hammered*

The words in [i] all end in a vowel sound, while those in [ii] end in a vowel followed by just one consonant sound; note that the letter *e* at the end of the words in [ib] and of *torque* in [iia], and also that before the *d* in [iib] are 'silent' – i.e. there is no vowel in this position in the spoken form. In many of the non-rhotic accents such pairs of words as *mar* and *ma*, *floor* and *flaw*, or *torque* and *talk* are pronounced the same. A non-rhotic accent is thus one which lacks post-vocalic /r/.

Most speakers in the AmE family of dialects, by contrast, have a **rhotic accent**, where there is no such restriction on the distribution of /r/: all the words in [1] are pronounced with an /r/ sound after the (final) vowel, or (in the case of *stir* and *term*) with a rhotacised ('*r*-coloured') vowel sound, a coalescence of /r/ with the vowel.[5]

The English spelling system reflects the pronunciation of rhotic accents: in non-rhotic accents post-vocalic /r/ has been lost as a result of a historical change that took place after the writing system became standardised.

Linking and intrusive /r/

A further difference between non-rhotic and rhotic accents is seen in the pronunciation of such words and word sequences as those given in [2], where we use the symbol '·' to mark grammatical boundaries within a word (in these examples, between base and suffix):

[2]	i	a. *marr·ing, sur·est, soar·ing*	b. *the fear of death*
	ii	a. *saw·ing, thaw·ing*	b. *the idea of death*

In non-rhotic accents the words in [ia] are all pronounced with /r/: the dropping of post-vocalic /r/ in the words *mar, sure, soar* does not apply here because the addition of a suffix beginning with a vowel makes the /r/ at the end of the base pre-vocalic. Similarly the word sequence [ib] is usually pronounced with an /r/ at the end of *fear* because the initial vowel of the next word makes it pre-vocalic.

The /r/ in pronunciations of [2i] in non-rhotic accents is called a **linking** /r/. Within a word, as in [ia], linking /r/ is obligatory; in word boundary position, as in [ib], the /r/ is optional though strongly preferred in most styles of speech. In [ii], where there is no *r* in the spelling, an /r/ pronounced at the end of the bases *saw·* and *thaw·* or of the word *idea* is called an **intrusive** /r/. Word-boundary intrusive /r/ in the pronunciation of sequences like [iib] is very common; word-internal intrusive /r/ in words like those in [iia] is much less common and quite widely disapproved of.

Rhotic accents do not have intrusive /r/ at all: they maintain a sharp distinction between [2i] and [ii], with /r/ appearing only in the former. And although they pronounce /r/ in the forms in [i], this is not linking /r/, since the bases *mar, sure, soar,* and *fear* have /r/ in these accents even when not followed by a vowel.

3.1.2 An accent-neutral phonological representation

Where we need to give pronunciations of words or larger expressions, it would be inconsistent with our goals to confine ourselves to one accent, but to attempt a complete listing of the pronunciations in each significant regional or other variety would be tedious. We therefore present here a unitary way of representing pronunciations for major BrE and AmE accents, whether rhotic or non-rhotic. For this purpose it is necessary to indicate more distinctions than would be needed in a system constructed for any one accent. In

[5] The correlation between the rhotic vs non-rhotic accent distinction and that between the BrE and AmE family of dialects is not perfect. Ireland, Scotland, the west of England, and some English-speaking Caribbean countries have rhotic accents and yet belong to the BrE family, and, conversely, there are various non-rhotic accents within the United States, including some working-class northeastern varieties and some upper-class southeastern varieties. The term 'rhotic' derives from the Greek name of the letter *r*.

particular, since it cannot be determined from the pronunciation in a non-rhotic accent where post-vocalic /r/ would occur in a rhotic one (for example, southern British English has /tɔːk/ for both *torque* and *talk*), post-vocalic /r/ will have to be shown in some way even though it is not pronounced in the non-rhotic accents. Other differences have to be dealt with similarly.

The system we adopt is set out in [3], with illustrative examples in which the letter or letter sequence that symbolises the sound in question is underlined. Some notes on the system follow below.

[3]

SHORT VOWELS

ɒ	*odd, lot, lost*	e	*get, fell, friend, endeavour*
æ	*gas, fat, pan*	i	*happy, pennies, maybe*
ʌ	*gut, much, done*	ɪ	*kit, build, women*
ə	*alone, potato, stringent, sofa*	ɪ	*wanted, luggage, buses*
ə^{r}	*lunar, driver, actor*	ʊ	*look, good, put*

LONG VOWELS

ɑː	*spa, calm, father*	ɔː	*awe, dawn, caught, fall*
ɑː^{r}	*are, arm, spar*	ɔː^{r}	*or, corn, warn*
ɜː^{r}	*err, bird, work, fur*	uː	*ooze, blue, prune, brew, through*
iː	*eel, sea, fiend, dream, machine*		

DIPHTHONGS

aʊ	*owl, mouth, plough*	eə^{r}	*air, bare, pear*
eɪ	*aim, day, eight, grey*	oʊ	*owe, go, dough, toe, goat*
aɪ	*I, right, fly, guy*	ɔɪ	*oil, boy*
ɪə	*idea*	ʊə^{r}	*poor, sure, dour*
ɪə^{r}	*ear, fear, pier, mere*		

TRIPHTHONGS

aɪə^{r}	*ire, pyre, choir*	aʊə^{r}	*our*

CONSONANTS

b	*boy, sobbing*	ŋ	*sing, drink, dinghy*
d	*day, address*	θ	*thigh*
dʒ	*judge, giant, germ*	p	*pie*
ð	*this, although, bathe*	r	*rye, wrist*
f	*food, phonetics, if, off, rough*	s	*see, kiss, city, psychology*
g	*good, ghost, guide*	ʃ	*show, sure, charade, schmuck*
h	*hood*	t	*tall, pterodactyl*
j	*yes, fjord*	tʃ	*chin, watch*
k	*cat, chorus, kiss, brick, Iraqi*	v	*view, love, of*
l	*lie, all*	w	*wet*
m	*me, thumb, damn*	z	*zeal, peas*
n	*nigh, knife, gnaw, pneumatic*	ʒ	*measure, evasion, beige, rouge*

DIACRITICS

n̩	syllabic /n/ (likewise for /l̩/, etc.)	ˈ	stressed syllable (*aˈloof, ˈsofa*)

Notes on the transcription system

Post-vocalic /r/

This is represented by a superscript /ʳ/. In rhotic AmE, it is pronounced as a separate /r/ consonant or coalesces with the preceding sound to give a rhotacised vowel. In non-rhotic BrE it is not pronounced at all – though, as we noted above, a word-final /ʳ/ will typically be pronounced in connected speech as a pre-vocalic linking /r/ when followed by a word beginning with a vowel. Pre-vocalic /r/ corresponds to an *r* in the spelling. We do not include intrusive /r/ in our representations, since it is predictably present (between a low vowel or /ə/ and a following vowel) in those accents that have it.

/ɪ/, /ə/, and /ɨ/

The unstressed vowel in the second syllable of *orange, wanted, wishes, lozenge,* etc., is a significant difficulty for an accent-neutral transcription. In BrE it is typically identical with the vowel of *kit,* which we represent as /ɪ/; in most AmE and some Australian varieties it is usually identical with the second vowel of *sofa,* /ə/. Many of its occurrences are in the inflectional endings; but there is one inflectional suffix in English that contains /ɪ/ in virtually all accents, namely ·*ing,* and there are suffixes containing a vowel that is /ə/ in all accents (e.g. ·*en* in *written*). Hence we need a third symbol for the vowel that varies between accents. We use /ɨ/. This has been used by American phonologists as a phonetic symbol for a vowel slightly less front than /ɪ/ and slightly higher than /ə/, so it is a good phonetic compromise, and visually suggests the /ɪ/ of those BrE accents that have a minimal contrast between *counted* /ˈkaʊntɪd/ and *countered* /ˈkaʊntəd/. It should be kept in mind, however, that it is used here not with an exact phonetic value but rather as a cover symbol for either /ɪ/ or /ə/ according to accent.

/ɒ/ versus /ɑ/

For the vowel of *pot, rock, not,* etc., we use /ɒ/. Most varieties of AmE never have /ɒ/ phonetically in any context, so the American pronunciation can be derived simply by replacing our /ɒ/ by /ɑ/ everywhere. Hence there is no possibility of ambiguity.

/oʊ/ versus /əʊ/

For the vowel of *grow, go, dough,* etc., we write /oʊ/, in which the 'o' makes the phonological representation closer to the spelling; for most BrE speakers /əʊ/ would be a phonetically more appropriate representation.

/ɔː/ versus /ɑː/

BrE has distinct vowels in *caught* and *calm*: we represent them as /ɔː/ and /ɑː/ respectively. AmE standardly has the same vowel here, so for AmE the transcription /ɔː/ should be read as /ɑː/.

/æ/ versus /ɑː/

Both BrE and AmE have distinct vowels in *fat,* /fæt/, and *calm,* /kɑːm/, but there are a considerable number of words where most BrE accents have /ɑː/ while AmE (but also some accents within the BrE family) has /æ/. Very few of these arise in our examples, however, so instead of introducing a third symbol we give separate BrE and AmE representations when necessary.

/ʌ/ versus /ə/

The opposition between /ʌ/ and /ə/ is a weak one in that there are very few word-pairs kept distinct solely by this vowel quality difference. It is absent in many AmE accents – those in which *butt* and *but* are pronounced alike in all contexts, in which *just* has the same pronunciation whether it means "merely" or "righteous", and in which *lust* always rhymes with *must* regardless of stress. We show the distinction between these vowels here (it is generally clear in BrE), but for many Americans both vowels could be written as /ə/.

/juː/ versus /uː/

In many words that have /juː/ following an alveolar consonant in BrE, AmE has /uː/. Thus *new*, *tune*, *due* are /njuː/, /tjuːn/, /djuː/ in BrE but usually /nuː/, /tuːn/, /duː/ in AmE. We write /juː/ in these cases; for AmE, ignore the /j/.

Intervocalic /t/

We ignore the AmE voicing of intervocalic /t/, contrasting *latter* as /lætəʳ/ and *ladder* as /lædəʳ/ with the medial consonants distinguished as in BrE accents.

3.2 Pronunciation and spelling

The relation between the sounds shown by our transcription and the ordinary English spelling of words is a complex one, and certain analytical concepts will help in keeping clear about the difference.

Symbols and letters

When we match up written and spoken forms we find that in the simplest cases one letter corresponds to one sound, or **phoneme:** *in* /ɪn/, *cat* /kæt/, *help* /help/, *stand* /stænd/, and so on. But very often the match is more complex. For example, in *teeth* the two-letter sequence *ee* corresponds to the single phoneme /iː/ and *th* to /θ/; in *plateau* the three-letter sequence *eau* corresponds to /oʊ/ (a diphthong, analysed phonologically as a single phoneme); in *through* the last four letters correspond to the phoneme /uː/.

We will use **symbol** as a technical term for a unit of writing that corresponds to a phoneme, and we will refer to those symbols consisting of more than one letter as **composite symbols.**[6] The letter *e* can form **discontinuous composite vowel symbols** with any of the letters *a*, *e*, *i*, *o*, *u*: *a . . . e* as in *pane*, *e . . . e* as in *dene*, *i . . . e* as in *bite*, *o . . . e* as in *rode*, and *u . . . e* as in *cute*.

Vowels and consonants

The categories **vowel** and **consonant** are defined in terms of speech. Vowels have unimpeded airflow through the throat and mouth, while consonants employ a significant constriction of the airflow somewhere in the oral tract (between the vocal cords and the lips). The terms can be applied to writing derivatively: a **vowel symbol** is a symbol representing a vowel sound, and a **consonant symbol** is a symbol representing a consonant sound. We will speak of a **vowel letter** or a **consonant letter** only in the case

[6] 'Digraph' is widely used for a two-letter symbol and 'trigraph' is also found (though much less frequently) for a three-letter symbol, but there is no established term for a four-letter symbol, and no cover term for composite symbol.

of non-composite symbols: a single letter constituting a whole symbol may be called a vowel letter if it is a vowel symbol or a consonant letter if it is a consonant symbol. Thus *y* is a vowel letter in *fully* (representing /i/); it is a consonant letter in *yes* (it represents /j/); and in *boy* it is just part of a complex vowel symbol (representing /ɔɪ/). Similarly, *u* is a vowel letter in *fun* (/ʌ/), a consonant letter in *quick* (/w/), and part of a composite symbol in *mouth* (/aʊ/).[7]

It should be noted, however, that *r* counts as a consonant letter even in non-rhotic accents, as shown by the rule of final consonant letter doubling in inflected forms discussed in Ch. 18, §2.2.1: *map/mapping, bat/batting, trek/trekking, pin/pinning*, etc., are parallelled by *mar/ marring*, with *r* doubling like other consonant letters. Similarly, the *e* of the suffix ·*ed* counts as a vowel symbol even when no vowel is pronounced (e.g. it determines consonant doubling in forms like *sipped* /sɪpt/ and *banned* /bænd/). In both cases, of course, the spelling corresponds more closely to an earlier stage of the language than to the contemporary language.

4 Theoretical framework

The primary goal of this grammar is to describe the grammatical principles of Present-day English rather than to defend or illustrate a theory of grammar. But the languages human beings use are too complex to be described except by means of a theory. In this section we clarify the relation between description and theory in this book, and outline some of our most important theoretical distinctions.

4.1 Description and theory

The problem with attempting to describe English without having a theory of grammar is that the language is too big to be described without bringing things together under generalisations, and without a theory there are no generalisations.

It does not take much reflection to see that there is no definite length limit to sentences in English. Sentences 100 words long, or longer, are commonly encountered (especially in writing, for written sentences are on average longer than spoken ones). And, given any sentence, it is always easy to see how it could have been made even longer: an adjective like *good* could be replaced by *very good*, or a verb like *exceed* could be supplied with a preceding adverb to make something like *dramatically exceed*, or a noun like *tree* could be replaced by *tall tree*, or the words *I think* could be added at the beginning of a whole declarative clause, or the words *and that's what I told the police* could be added at the end, and so on through an endless series of different ways in which almost any grammatical sentence of English could be lengthened without the result being something that is recognisably not English.

The importance of the fact that English sentences can be constructed to be as long as might be necessary to express some meaning is that it makes the sentences of English impossible to encapsulate in a list. The number of sentences that have been spoken or

[7] It will be clear, then, that we do not follow the traditional practice of simply dividing the alphabet into five vowels (*a, e, i, o, u*) and twenty-one consonants: we will see that the traditional classification does not provide a satisfactory basis for describing the spelling alternations in English morphology.

written so far is already astronomically vast, new ones are being produced every second around the world by hundreds of millions of people, and no matter what the information storage resources available, the problem is that there would be no way to decide where to end the list.

An alternative to listing sentences is therefore needed. To describe the sentences that belong to English we have to provide a general account of their structure that makes their form follow from **general** statements, not about particular sentences but about sentences of English quite generally. We need to bring together the principles that sentences all conform to, so that we can use those principles to appreciate the structure of new sentences as they are encountered, and see how new ones can be constructed. This means developing a **theory** of the ways in which sentences can be put together by combining words. This book is an attempt to summarise and illustrate as much as possible of what has so far been determined about the ways in which sentences can be constructed in English, and it presupposes a theory that classifies the words of the dictionary and specifies ways in which they are combined to form sentences.

We emphasise, however, that it is not the aim of this book to convince the reader of the merits of the theory for general linguistic description. Quite the reverse, in a sense: wherever it is possible to make a factual point overshadow a general theoretical point, we attempt to do that; whenever a theoretical digression would fail to illuminate further facts about English, we curtail the digression; if ever the facts at hand can be presented in a way that is neutral between competing theoretical frameworks, we try to present them that way.

However, a significant amount of space is devoted here to arguing carefully that the particular analysis we have decided to adopt, within the framework of theory we assume, is the right **analysis**. What we mean by that is that even someone with a different idea about how to design a theory of syntax would have to come to a conclusion tantamount to ours if they considered all the facts. It is necessary for us to provide arguments concerning specific grammatical analyses in this book because, although this grammar is descriptive like the great traditional grammars that have been published in the past, it is not traditional in accepting past claims and analyses.

We depart from the tradition of English grammar at many points, sometimes quite sharply. For example, in this book the reader will find nothing of 'noun clauses', 'adjective clauses', or 'adverb clauses', because that traditional distinction in subordinate clause classification does not divide things satisfactorily and we have abandoned it. The reader will likewise find nothing of the traditional distinction between *since* as a preposition (*I haven't seen them since Easter*), *since* as an adverb (*I haven't seen them since*), and *since* as a subordinating conjunction (*I haven't seen them since they went overseas*), because we have concluded that this multiplication of categories for a single word with a single meaning makes no sense; we claim that *since* belongs to the same category (preposition) in all of its occurrences. On these and many other aspects of syntactic analysis we depart from traditional analyses (we draw attention to the major cases of this kind in Ch. 2). At such points we provide detailed arguments to convince the reader that we have broken with a mistaken tradition, and – we hope – made the correct decision about how to replace it.

The reader will therefore find much more discussion of grammatical concepts and much more syntactic argumentation than is usually found in grammars of English. It is supplied, however, not to establish some wider theoretical point applying to other languages, but simply to persuade the reader that our description is sound. While the application of grammatical theories to the full range of human languages is an important matter within linguistics, it is not the purpose of this book to develop that point. Detailed technical or descriptive discussions that can be skipped by non-specialists without loss of continuity have been set off in smaller type with a shaded background.

4.2 Basic concepts in syntax

Three essential concepts figure in the theory we use to describe English syntax in this grammar. Each is very simple to grasp, but together they permit extremely broad and powerful theories to be constructed for indefinitely large collections of sentences. We express them tersely in [1].

[1] i Sentences have parts, which may themselves have parts.
ii The parts of sentences belong to a limited range of types.
iii The parts have specific roles or functions within the larger parts they belong to.

The idea that sentences have parts which themselves may have parts, i.e. that larger stretches of material in a sentence are made up by putting together smaller stretches, is the basis of 'constituent structure' analysis. The idea that the parts fall into a limited range of types that we can name and refer to when giving a grammatical description is the root of the concept of 'syntactic categories'. And the idea that the parts also have specific roles or functions, or special slots that they fill in the larger parts they belong to, is the idea of 'grammatical functions'. The next three subsections are devoted to explaining these three fundamental ideas.

4.2.1 Constituent structure

Sentences contain parts called **constituents.** Those constituents often have constituents themselves, and those are made up from still shorter constituents, and so on. This hierarchical composition of wholes from parts is called **constituent structure**.

Consider a simple one-clause sentence like *A bird hit the car.* It is divisible in the first instance into two parts, *a bird* (the subject) and *hit the car* (the predicate). The phrase *a bird* is itself made up of smaller parts, *a* and *bird*; so is *hit the car*, which we divide into *hit* and *the car*; and finally *the car* also has two parts, *the* and *car.* This structure can be represented as in [2].

[2]

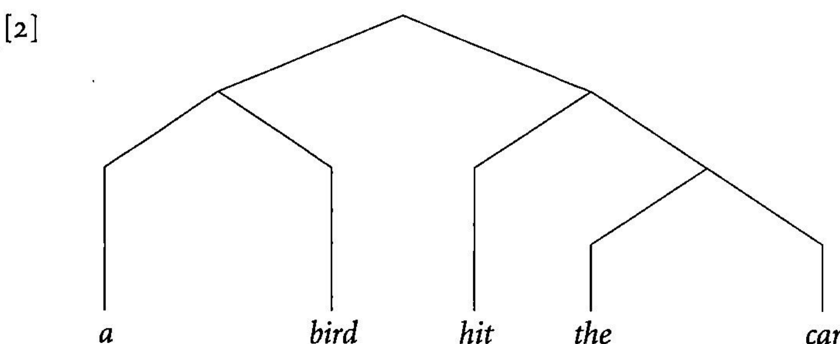

Such representations of the constituent structure are called **trees** or tree-diagrams (though the trees are upside down, with the root at the top and the ends of the smallest branches at the bottom). The words are the smallest constituents, and the points closer to the root where branches join identify the larger constituents. *A bird*, for example, is identified as a constituent because this word sequence can be traced via the branches to a single point in the tree; similarly with *the car* and *hit the car*. The sequence *bird hit*, on the other hand, is not a constituent, as there is no point in the tree that leads down branches to just these two words and no others.

The parts of the sentence shown at the first level down, *a bird* and *hit the car* are said to be the **immediate constituents** of the sentence; similarly, *hit* and *the car* are the immediate constituents of *hit the car*. The words are the **ultimate constituents** of the sentence.

The evidence that this is the correct analysis of the sentence comes from the whole of the rest of the grammar, all of which provides, by virtue of the coherence of the description it gives, the evidence that the lines of separation have been drawn in the right place. We can give an illustrative example of how other parts of the grammar can provide supportive evidence by considering where we can insert an adverb such as *apparently* (indicating that what the rest of the sentence asserts appears to be true). A rough account of where English grammar permits it to be positioned (at least in clauses as simple as our example) is that it can be anywhere in the clause it modifies, provided it does not interrupt a constituent. This is illustrated in [3], where the grammatical [a] examples conform to this rule, and the ungrammatical [b] ones do not:

[3]	i	a. *Apparently a bird hit the car.*	b. **An apparently bird hit the car.*
	ii	a. *A bird apparently hit the car.*	b. **A bird hit apparently the car.*
	iii	a. *A bird hit the car, apparently.*	b. **A bird hit the apparently car.*

The five words of our example sentence permit six different logically possible placements for *apparently* that are between words (before any of the five words, or after the last one), but only three are permissible. Breaking the sentence into constituents in exactly the way we have done, we are able to make a general statement about where an adverb like *apparently* (a 'modal' adverb) can be positioned in it: such an adverb must not interrupt a constituent of the clause. Hence [ib] above is disallowed because it would interrupt the constituent *a bird*; [iib] is disallowed because it would interrupt *hit the car*; and [iiib] is disallowed because it would interrupt *the car*. Inspecting the diagram in [2], we see that each of these uninterruptible sequences is a constituent smaller than the whole sentence.

The full support for a decision in grammatical description consists of confirmation from hundreds of mutually supportive pieces of evidence of many kinds, this being only one very simple example.

4.2.2 Syntactic categories

Diagram [2] shows just the hierarchical part–whole relationships in the sentence. This is only the starting-point for a description, identifying the constituents that have to be described. The next step is to classify these constituents, to say what **syntactic category** they belong to. For words, these syntactic categories correspond to what are traditionally called the 'parts of speech', and most of the categories for larger constituents are based on the ones for words. Where we need to refer to just the categories that have words as members, we will call them **lexical categories.**

Lexical categories

Any theory of syntax of the general sort we provide, and most types of dictionary, must include a list of the lexical categories or parts of speech assumed. For nearly all theories and nearly all dictionaries, **noun**, **verb**, **adjective**, and **adverb** will be among them, these being terms that have a history going back to the grammar of Classical Latin and Classical Greek some 2,000 years ago, but they are apparently applicable to almost all human languages. Our complete list is given, with some illustrations of membership, in [4]:

[4]	CATEGORY	LABEL	EXAMPLES
i	noun	N	*tree, pig, sugar, hatred, union, Picasso, London*
ii	verb	V	*do, fly, melt, think, damage, give, have, be, must*
iii	adjective	Adj	*good, nice, big, easy, ugly, helpful, reddish, fond*
iv	adverb	Adv	*obviously, easily, helpfully, frankly, soon, so, too*
v	preposition	Prep	*of, to, by, into, between, over, since, toward(s)*
vi	determinative	D	*the, this, that, a(n), some, all, every, each*
vii	subordinator		*that, for, to, whether, if*
viii	coordinator		*and, or, but, nor*
ix	interjection		*ah, damn, gosh, hey, oh, ooh, ouch, whoa, wow*

This scheme differs in several respects from the classification familiar from traditional grammar. Our determinatives are traditionally subsumed under the adjective category: they are said to be 'limiting adjectives' as distinct from the 'descriptive adjectives' illustrated in [4iii] – though some traditional grammars do recognise the articles *the* and *a(n)* as a distinct part of speech. We also take subordinators and coordinators to be distinct categories, not subclasses of the traditional conjunction category. Conversely, we regard pronouns as a subclass of nouns, not a distinct primary category. Our reasons for departing from the traditional analysis are given in the relevant chapters.

Phrasal categories

Constituents containing more than one word (more specifically, containing a central and most important word augmented by appropriate accompanying words that elaborate its contribution to the sentence) are called **phrases**, and are assigned to **phrasal categories.**[8] The lexical categories have corresponding phrase types that are in a sense expansions of them. A phrase consisting of a noun and the constituents that go with it most closely is a **nominal**; a nominal plus a determinative makes a **noun phrase**; a verb and its various complements makes up a **verb phrase**; a noun phrase and a verb phrase make up a **clause**; and so on. The full list of phrasal categories we employ in this book, together with our abbreviatory labels for them and an example phrase of each type, is given in [5].[9]

[8] There are circumstances in which phrases may consist of a single word: see the discussion of 'singulary branching' in §4.2.3.

[9] The term 'sentence' does not figure here. As will be explained more fully in Ch. 2, §1, a sentence in our terms is typically either a main clause or a coordination of main clauses.

[5]

	CATEGORY	LABEL	EXAMPLE
i	clause	Clause	*she saw something in there*
ii	verb phrase	VP	*saw something in there*
iii	noun phrase	NP	*this clear case of dedication to duty*
iv	nominal	Nom	*clear case of dedication to duty*
v	adjective phrase	AdjP	*very eager for further news*
vi	adverb phrase	AdvP	*quite separately from this issue*
vii	preposition phrase	PP	*right out of the area*
viii	determinative phrase	DP	*almost every*

We can represent the structure of sentences in more detail than is done in a diagram like [2] if we show the category to which each constituent belongs, as in [6].

[6]

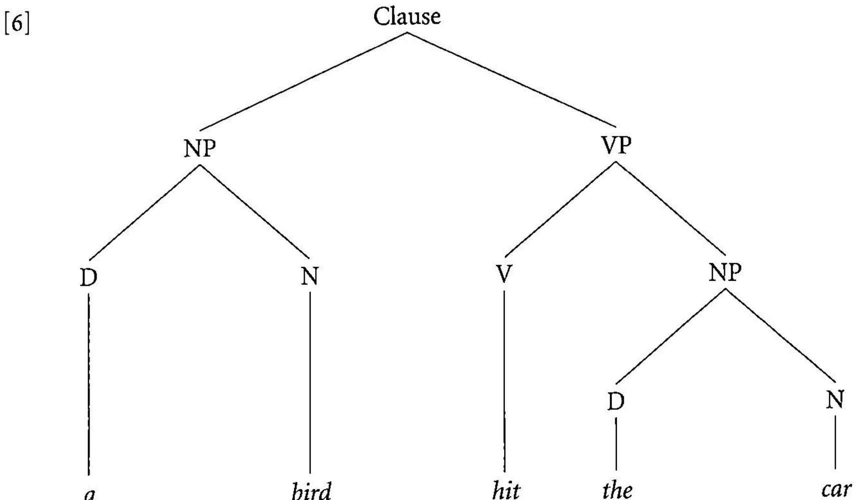

4.2.3 Grammatical constructions and functions

The third central theoretical idea we must introduce is that constituents always have particular roles to play in the **constructions**, the larger units, that they belong to. We call these roles **grammatical functions.** In our example sentence the phrases *a bird* and *the car* belong to the same category, NP, but they have different functions, subject and object respectively. They belong to the same category because they are alike in their internal structure (both have a noun as the major element), but they have different functions because they stand in different relations to the verb. The opposite type of situation is illustrated in such a pair as:

[7] a. *<u>His guilt</u> was obvious.* b. *<u>That he was guilty</u> was obvious.*

Here the underlined constituents have the same function (subject) but belong to different categories (NP and clause respectively). They have the same function because they stand in the same relation to the predicate, and they belong to different categories because the first is centred on a noun (*guilt*) while the second is centred, ultimately, on a verb (*was*). We say that the subject is **realised** by an NP in [a], by a clause in [b].

Heads and dependents

There is a set of functions that to a large extent apply in the same way within all phrasal categories. The first division we make is that between the **head** and the various **dependents** that can combine with it.

The head, normally obligatory, plays the primary role in determining the **distribution** of the phrase, i.e. whereabouts in sentence structure it can occur. Note, then, that while *his guilt* and *that he was guilty* can both function as subject they differ in other aspects of their distribution – we can have, for example, *The news that he was guilty was devastating*, but not **The news his guilt was devastating* (we need a preposition: *The news of his guilt was devastating*), and this difference is attributable to the fact that the head of the former is a noun while the (ultimate) head of the latter is a verb.

Dependents, often optional, are syntactically subordinate elements. The term 'dependent' reflects the fact that in any given construction what kinds of dependent are permitted depends on the head. For example, *too* (with the sense "excessively") can function as dependent to an adjective or adverb (*too careful, too carefully*), but not to a noun or verb (**their too extravagance, *You shouldn't too worry*). Similarly *sufficiently* can function as dependent to an adjective, adverb, or verb, but not to a noun (*sufficiently good, sufficiently often, practised sufficiently, *sufficiently reason*).

Predicate and predicator as special cases of the head function

Within this framework, what is traditionally called the **predicate** is a special case of the head function: the predicate is the head of a clause. Similarly, the term **predicator** is commonly used for the function of the verb itself, i.e. for the head of a verb phrase. We will retain the traditional terms, which indicate the characteristic semantic role of the element concerned, but it should be kept in mind that they are particular kinds of head.

Subtypes of dependent

Dependent is a very general function, and for many purposes we need to distinguish different subtypes of dependent according to their more specific relation to the head. At the first level of subdivision we distinguish **complements**, **modifiers**, and **determiners**, illustrated here in NP structure:

[8]	i	*the photographs <u>of their dog</u> that they had brought with them*	[complement]
	ii	*the photographs of their dog <u>that they had brought with them</u>*	[modifier]
	iii	*<u>the</u> photographs of their dog that they had brought with them*	[determiner]

In these examples, *of their dog* **complements** the head noun *photographs*; *that they had brought with them* **modifies** the head nominal *photographs of their dog*; and *the* **determines** the head nominal *photographs of their dog that they had brought with them*. At the next level we distinguish different kinds of complement, such as subject (*<u>the photographs</u> are excellent*), object (*He destroyed <u>the photographs</u>*), predicative (*these are <u>excellent photographs</u>*), and so on. A head element is said to **govern** its complements.

The determiner function is found only in the structure of the NP, whereas complements and modifiers occur quite generally. Note that the function 'determiner' is distinct from the lexical category 'determinative' (D). These need to be distinguished for the same reason as we distinguish subject and NP. Thus although *this* functions as determiner in *this height*, it functions as modifier in the structure of an AdjP in examples like *She is about this tall.* Conversely, while the determiner function is realised by a determinative in *a doctor*, it is realised by a genitive NP in *my neighbour's doctor.*[10]

Non-headed constructions

Although the functions of head and dependent apply to a very wide range of constructions, we must also allow for non-headed constructions, as in:

[9] i *She bought [a hamburger, some chips and a glass of milk].* [coordination]
ii *A storm damaged – or so I'm told – the roof of their house.* [supplementation]

The underlined NPs in [i] are of equal syntactic status: we cannot say that one is head and the others dependents. Each of them has the same function within the bracketed construction, that of **coordinate.** In [ii] the underlined constituent is what we call a **supplement:** instead of being integrated into the constituent structure of the sentence as a dependent or coordinate, it is loosely attached, set off from the rest in speech by separate intonational phrasing and in writing by punctuation. Note that it interrupts the sentence at a point where a dependent could not occur, between the predicator and the object: compare [3iib] above.[11] These two types of non-headed construction are described in Ch. 15.

Diagrammatic representation of functions

Functions, we have said, are essentially relational concepts: to specify the function of a constituent is to say what its relation is to the construction containing it.[12] One way to capture this would be to write the name of the function on the line (branch) of the diagram joining the constituent to the construction. The first level in the structure of our model sentence might then look as in [10].

[10]

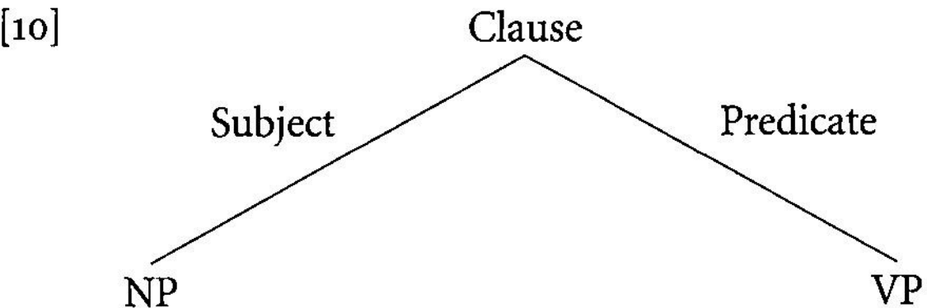

In more complex cases, though, diagram design becomes a problem, and we have found it preferable to present the functional labels separated from the category labels by a colon, and written above them in diagrams. In this format the analysis of our earlier example sentence looks as in [11].

[10] In other works 'determiner' is often used as a category term. The corresponding function is then sometimes called 'specifier', sometimes called 'determinative', and sometimes not clearly distinguished from the category term.

[11] It must be emphasised, therefore, that [3iib] was marked as ungrammatical with the understanding that *apparently* is integrated into the structure (as indicated by the absence of any punctuation). If *apparently* were set apart as a supplement, the sentence would not be ungrammatical – but it would be a different sentence from [3iib].

[12] 'Grammatical relation' is indeed commonly used as an alternative term to 'grammatical function'.

[11]

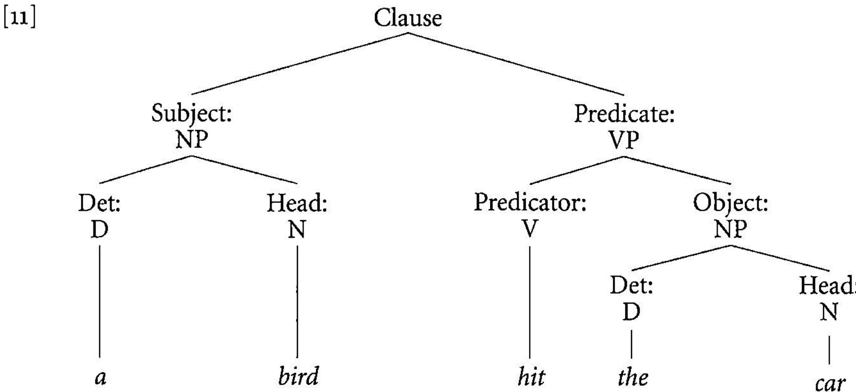

(Note that we use 'Det' as the abbreviation for the function 'determiner', and 'D' for the category 'determinative'.)

Singulary branching

We have said that dependents are often optional, and this implies that we can have a head on its own, without any dependents. Compare, for example:

[12] i *Some children were playing in the park.*
ii *Children were playing in the park.*

The underlined expressions are NPs functioning as subject of the clause: *children* is the head, determined by *some* in [i], but standing alone in [ii]. The relevant parts of the structure are thus as in [13].

[13]

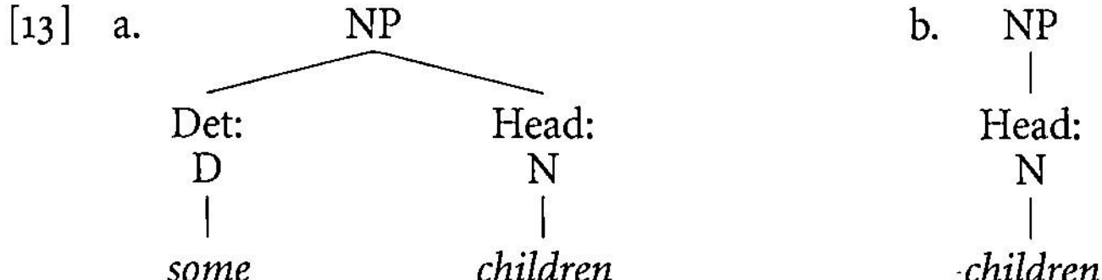

In [b] there is a single branch descending from the category label NP, and this part of the tree-diagram is said to exhibit **singulary branching**, in contrast to the **binary branching** of [a].

4.3 Morphology, inflectional and lexical

A grammar, we have said, is divided into two major components, syntax and morphology. This division follows from the special status of the word as a basic linguistic unit, with syntax dealing with the combination of words to make sentences, and morphology with the form of words themselves. In some respects the formation of words is comparable to the formation of larger units, but in others it is significantly different, and it is these differences that motivate dividing the grammar into two separate components.

Words, lexemes, and inflection

The term 'word', as used in traditional grammar, has two rather different senses. We can approach the difference by asking how many distinct words there are in, for example:

[14] *You are working hard, but your sister is working even harder.*

It is clear that the third and ninth words are not distinct: they are tokens (instances) of the same word. But what about *hard* and *harder*: are these the same word or different words? The answer depends on what you mean by 'word'. In one sense they are obviously different: *harder* has a suffix that is missing from *hard*. This enables it to occur in constructions like that of *Your sister works harder than you*, where it could not be replaced by *hard*; and conversely *hard* could not be replaced by *harder* in *Your sister works very hard*. So from a syntactic point of view they are different words. But there's another sense in which they are traditionally said to be 'different forms of the same word'. The perspective this time is that of the dictionary, which would have just one entry, labelled *hard*. The same applies to *are* and *is* in [14]: syntactically these are different words, but lexically (i.e. as far as the dictionary is concerned) they are the same. In order to avoid possible misunderstanding we will restrict the term **word** to the syntactically-oriented sense, so that *hard* and *harder* are different words, and likewise *are* and *is*. For the more abstract, lexically-oriented sense we will use the term **lexeme**. *Hard* and *harder* are then forms of the same lexeme, as are *are* and *is*.

In many cases it makes no difference whether we take a syntactic or a lexical perspective. Lexemes such as *the* and *and* are **invariable**, i.e. there is only one word corresponding to each. Also invariable are lexemes like *efficiently*: although *more efficiently* is in some respects like *harder*, it is not a single word, but a sequence of two, and hence *efficiently* and *more efficiently* are not forms of a single lexeme. **Variable** lexemes, by contrast, are those which have two or more forms. Where we need to make clear that we are considering an item as a lexeme, not a word, we will represent it in bold italics. ***Hard***, for example, represents the lexeme which has *hard* and *harder* – and also *hardest* – as its forms.[13] Similarly *are* and *is*, along with *be*, *been*, *being*, etc., are forms of the lexeme ***be***. In example [14], then, we have two occurrences of the lexeme ***hard***, but only one of the word *hard*, and of course just one of the word *harder*. A variable lexeme is thus a word-sized lexical item considered in abstraction from grammatical properties that vary depending on the syntactic construction in which it appears.

The variation found in variable lexemes is known, more specifically, as **inflection**, and the various forms are called **inflectional forms** of the lexeme. For the most part, inflectional categories apply to large sets of lexemes. Almost all verb lexemes, for example, inflect for tense (e.g. preterite *took* vs present tense *take*), most nouns inflect for number (e.g. singular *dog* vs plural *dogs*), many adjectives one or two syllables in length inflect for grade (e.g. plain *old* vs comparative *older* vs superlative *oldest*). The inflectional contrast of nominative case vs accusative case (e.g. *we* vs *us*), however, applies to just a handful of pronoun lexemes.

[13] We minimise the use of bold type for lexemes, because in many cases it would simply distract. If we are simply listing adjective lexemes that can occur in the construction *They are difficult to please*, for example, we will generally list them as '*difficult, easy, hard, impossible, tough*', etc., rather than '*difficult*, ***easy***, ***hard***, *impossible*, ***tough***', etc.; the fact that ***easy*** is inflectionally variable and *difficult* invariable has no relevance in that context.

Inflectional morphology and lexical word-formation

The distinction between words and lexemes provides the basis for the division of morphology into two branches: **inflectional morphology** and **lexical word-formation.**

Inflectional morphology deals with the inflectional forms of variable lexemes. It has something of the character of an appendix to the syntax, the major component of the grammar. Syntax tells us when a lexeme may or must carry a certain inflectional property, while inflectional morphology tells us what form it takes when it carries that inflectional property. For example, a rule of syntax stipulates that a verb in construction with the perfect auxilary ***have*** must carry the past participle inflection (as in *They have killed it, She had rung the bell*), while inflectional morphology describes how the past participles of verbs are formed from the **lexical base**: *killed* is formed from the base *kill* by adding the suffix *·ed*, *rung* from *ring* by changing the vowel, and so on.

Lexical word-formation, by contrast, is related to the dictionary. It describes the processes by which new lexical bases are formed and the structure of complex lexical bases, those composed of more than one morphological element. The traditional term is simply 'word-formation': we add 'lexical' to exclude the formation of words by inflectional processes.

The three major processes involved in lexical word-formation are the following:

[15] i COMPOUNDING: forming a new base by combining two bases
ii DERIVATION: forming a new base by adding an affix to an existing base
iii CONVERSION: forming a new base using the pronunciation/spelling of a base of related meaning in some other category

An example like *blackbird* illustrates compounding: it is formed by combining two smaller bases, *black* and *bird*. *Efficiently* illustrates derivation: an affix (the suffix *·ly*) is added to an adjective base (*efficient*) to form an adverb. Another example, this time not involving a change from one category to another, is the derivation of *inefficient* by adding the prefix *in·* to the same base. And conversion is illustrated by the underlined verb in *I managed to elbow my way to the front.* The base *elbow* is primarily a noun (having the singular form *elbow* and the plural form *elbows*) denoting a part of the body. The verb base *elbow* (the base of the lexeme whose forms are *elbow, elbows, elbowed, elbowing*) is formed from the noun by conversion – the shape of the noun is simply borrowed to make a verb of related meaning.

4.4 Defining grammatical concepts

A grammatical description of a language inevitably draws on a large repertoire of grammatical terms and concepts – **noun, verb, preterite, imperative, subject, object**, and countless more. A question arises concerning how these concepts are to be explained and defined.

Traditional grammar's notional definitions

It is useful to begin by considering the kind of definition familiar from dictionaries and traditional school grammars, which are known as **notional definitions**, i.e. they are based on the meaning of the expressions being classified, not on their grammatical properties. These are typical examples:

[16]			
i	NOUN:	the name of a person, place, or thing	[notional definitions]
ii	PRETERITE:	a tense expressing past action or state	
iii	IMPERATIVE:	a clause expressing a command	

To determine whether a word is a noun, for example, one asks what it means or denotes; to determine the tense of a verb one asks in what time period it locates the action or state expressed by the verb; and so on.

Such definitions have long been criticised by linguists. Indeed, it takes only a moment or two's reflection to see that they do not provide satisfactory criteria for determining the correct classification of words or verb-forms or clauses. Take first the definition of preterite, and consider such examples as the following:

[17] i a. *The finals started yesterday.* b. *You said the finals started tomorrow.*
ii a. *I gave them his address.* b. *I regret giving them his address.*

In [i] we find *started* associated with past time in [a] but with future time in [b], as indicated by the temporal modifiers *yesterday* and *tomorrow* respectively. The *started* of [ia] thus satisfies the definition for preterite tense, while that of [ib] clearly does not. Nevertheless, everyone agrees that *started* in [ib] is a preterite form: this represents a different use of the same form as we have in [ia], not a different form, for the phenomenon is quite general, applying to all verbs, not just ***start***. The opposite kind of problem arises in [ii]. Here the [a] and [b] versions are alike not in the form of the verb, but in the time of the associated event, which is located in the past. Both verbs therefore satisfy the definition of preterite tense, but while *gave* is certainly a preterite form, *giving* is not.

The notional definition thus gives the wrong results in both the [b] examples, excluding the *started* of [17ib], and including the *giving* of [iib]. If definitions are supposed to give necessary and sufficient conditions for belonging to some category, this one fails completely, for it gives neither: [ib] shows that past time reference is not necessary for a word to be a preterite verb form, and [iib] shows that it is not sufficient either. The problem is that the relation between the grammatical category of tense (form) and the semantic category of time (meaning) is highly complex, whereas the notional definition assumes the former can be defined directly in terms of the latter.

The same kind of problem arises with imperative clauses.[14] Compare:

[18] i a. *Go to bed.* b. *Sleep well.*
ii a. *Please close the door.* b. *Would you mind closing the door.*

'Command', in the everyday sense of the term, is too narrow and specific for the meaning typically conveyed by imperatives: we will use the term 'directive' to cover commands, orders, requests, and other acts whose aim is to get the addressee to do something. With this modification, [ia] and [iia] both clearly satisfy the definition. But [ib] does not:

[14] Strictly speaking, the traditional category of imperative applies in the first instance to verb-forms rather than clauses. We take the view, however, that there are no imperative verb-forms in English, and hence consider the concept of imperative as it applies to clauses; the argument is in no way affected by this modification.

if I say this I am not telling you, or asking you, to sleep well, but expressing the hope or wish that you will. Yet grammatically it belongs with [ia] and [iia]: it is clearly an imperative clause. Conversely, [iib] conveys the same kind of meaning as [iia], but has a quite different grammatical structure: it is not imperative but interrogative. Again, then, satisfying the terms of the definition is not necessary for a clause to be imperative (as [ib] shows), nor is it sufficient (as [iib] shows). The relation between form and meaning here is too complex for one to be able to determine whether a clause is imperative or not simply on the basis of its meaning.

The traditional definition of noun is unsatisfactory for a somewhat different reason. The problem here is that the concept of 'thing' (or perhaps 'name') is too vague to provide a workable criterion. There are countless abstract nouns such as *absence, fact, flaw, idea, indeterminacy, lack, necessity*, etc., so 'thing' cannot be intended as equivalent to 'physical object'; but we have no way of telling whether a word denotes (or is the name of) a thing unless we already know on independent, grammatical, grounds whether it is a noun. Take, for example:

[19]	i	*I was annoyed at their <u>rejection</u> of my proposals.*	[noun]
	ii	*I was annoyed that they <u>rejected</u> my proposals.*	[verb]

These have essentially the same meaning, but *rejection* is a noun and *rejected* a verb. What enables us to tell that *rejection* but not *rejected* belongs to the category of noun is not that *rejection* denotes a thing while *rejected* does not, but that they figure in quite different grammatical constructions. Thus *rejection* contrasts with *rejections* as singular vs plural, whereas *rejected* contrasts with *reject* as preterite vs present tense. The transitive verb *rejected* takes a direct object (*my proposals*), but nouns do not take direct objects, so we need a prepositional complement in [i] (*of my proposals*). Similarly, *rejected* takes a nominative subject (*they*), whereas *rejection* takes a genitive like *their* or a determinative like *the*. And if we wanted to add some modification we would need an adjective in [i] (e.g. *their <u>immediate</u> rejection of my proposals*), but an adverb in [ii] (*that they <u>immediately</u> rejected my proposals*).

The problem with notional definitions is that they do not refer to the kinds of property that motivate the use in the grammar of the theoretical concepts being defined. The reason we need such concepts as noun, preterite, imperative clause in writing a grammar of English is that they enable us to make general statements about words, about the inflection of verbs, about the structure of clauses. Lexemes fall into a number of major categories on the basis of their inflection, the kinds of dependent they take and the function in larger constructions of the phrases they head: noun belongs in this system of lexeme categories. Verbs have a variety of inflectional forms, and the preterite is one of these. Clauses show structural contrasts on one dimension according to the presence or absence of a subject, its position relative to the verb, and the inflectional form of the verb, so that we have contrasts between such sets as (a) *You are punctual*, (b) *Are you punctual?*, (c) *Be punctual*: 'imperative clause' is one of the terms in this system of clausal constructions.

A satisfactory definition or explanation of concepts like noun, preterite, and imperative clause must therefore identify the grammatical properties that distinguish them from the concepts with which they contrast. The discussion of *rejection* and *rejected* in [19] illustrated some of the major ways in which nouns differ from verbs. As for the preterite, it is distinguished in part by its form (in regular verbs it is marked by the suffix ·*ed*, though this also marks the past participle), in part by its distribution (like the present tense, but unlike other forms, a preterite form can occur as the verb of a declarative main clause: *Kim gave it away*, but not, for example, **Kim given it away*), in part by its lack of agreement with the subject (with the single exception of the verb ***be***), and so on. Imperative clauses differ from declaratives and interrogatives in the form of the verb ***be*** (*Be punctual* vs *You are punctual*), the optionality of a 2nd person subject (*you* is omissible in *You be punctual*, but not in *You are punctual*), the formation of the negative (compare *Don't be punctual*, formed with auxiliary ***do***, and *You aren't punctual*, with no ***do***), and so on.

In this grammar we will be at pains, therefore, to specify the distinctive grammatical properties of the concepts we introduce. This is not to suggest that we are not interested in the meaning, but rather to say that we need to distinguish between grammatical concepts and semantic ones; indeed, making such a distinction is a prerequisite for describing the relation between them.

General and language-particular definitions

In criticising the traditional notional definitions, we assumed that they were intended to enable us to determine what expressions in English belong to the categories concerned. It must be emphasised, however, that most of the terms that figure in a grammatical description of English are not unique to English but appear in the grammars of other languages too – in some cases, in the grammars of all languages. There are therefore two issues to be considered in defining or explaining such terms. At one level there is the issue of what grammatical properties distinguish one category from another in English. We call this the **language-particular** level. This is the level we have been concerned with so far. A language-particular definition will enable us to decide which expressions in the language concerned belong to the category. At another level there is the issue of what principled basis we have for using the same grammatical terms in the grammars of different languages, given that the language-particular distinctive properties will vary from language to language. We call this the **general** level. The fact, for example, that the negative imperative *Don't be punctual* requires auxiliary ***do*** while the negative declarative *You aren't punctual* does not is clearly a specific fact about English: it belongs in the language-particular definition of imperative clause for English, but not in a general definition.

It might then be suggested that the traditional notional definitions should be construed as applying at the general rather than the language-particular level. Certainly they are not intended to apply uniquely to English. But at the same time there can be no doubt that as they are presented in school textbooks, for example, they purport to be language-particular definitions: the student is meant to be able to apply them to decide whether a given word in English is a noun, whether a verb is in the preterite, whether a clause is imperative. In effect, the traditional definitions aim to work at both levels simultaneously, and our objection is that the levels need to be distinguished, and approached differently. At the language-particular level, as we have argued, it is necessary to focus on form: to specify the grammatical features that distinguish expressions which belong to the category from those that do not. At the general level it is quite legitimate to invoke meaning: languages serve to express meaning, and it is rare to find grammatical distinctions that have no correlation at all with semantic distinctions.

We need to make it clear when giving a general definition that it is to apply at the general level, not the language-particular. And we need to acknowledge that the correlation between grammatical form and meaning is typically complex rather than one-to-one. The general definitions we propose for the categories discussed above are as follows:

[20] i NOUN: a grammatically distinct category of lexemes of which the morphologically most elementary members characteristically denote types of physical objects (such as human beings, other biological organisms, and natural or artificial inanimate objects)

ii PRETERITE: a grammatically distinct inflectional form of the verb whose primary use is to locate the situation in past time (relative to the time of utterance)

iii IMPERATIVE: a grammatically distinct clause construction whose members are characteristically used to issue directives

The move to an avowedly general definition, together with the reference to characteristic use of the most elementary members, enables us to avoid the vagueness of the term 'thing' (or 'name') in [16i]. The fact that such lexemes as ***rejection***, ***arrival***, ***idea*** do not denote physical objects is not a problem for a definition at this level. By virtue of the distinctive grammatical properties specified in the language-particular definition, these lexemes belong to the same category as ***girl***, ***boy***, ***daffodil***, ***window***, etc., and this category as a whole satisfies the general definition of noun because it contains lexemes like these last examples that do denote physical objects. Note that the abstract nouns ***rejection*** and ***arrival*** are morphologically derived from lexemes of another category (verb); morphologically elementary nouns, such as ***girl***, ***boy***, etc., characteristically denote kinds of physical object.

Definition [20ii] allows for the fact that verb inflections often have more than one use. In [17ia] (*The finals started yesterday*), we have the past time use. In [17ib] (*You said the finals started tomorrow*) the preterite form *started* is within a subordinate clause functioning as complement to *said*: this is a case of what is traditionally called indirect reported speech. Your actual words will have been, say, *The finals start tomorrow*, but present tense *start* is shifted into the preterite *started* in my report. Another use of the preterite is seen in *I wish the finals started tomorrow*, where it indicates counterfactuality: we understand that the finals do not start tomorrow. Of these three uses, it is the one that indicates past time that is primary. The others are found only in special contexts, such as the complement of a preterite verb of reporting or the complement of ***wish***. This verb-form therefore qualifies for the label **preterite**.

Definition [20iii] likewise overcomes the problems we noted in [16iii]. The language-particular criteria assign *Sleep well* to the same category as *Go to bed* and *Please open the door*, and since most clauses with this form are normally used as directives we call the category imperative clause. *Would you mind closing the door* is excluded from the category at the language-particular level: it does not have the distinctive grammatical form of imperative clauses in English.

The grammatical distinctiveness requirement in general definitions

It will be noted that the general definitions in [20] all impose a condition of grammatical distinctiveness. This requirement means that the general term being defined will be applicable in the grammar of a given language only if it can be given a distinct language-particular definition in that language.

A significant weakness of traditional grammars of English is that they incorporate a number of categories that in fact have no place in a grammar of Present-day English, although they are perfectly valid for Latin (and in some cases older stages of English). A simple example is provided by the dative case inflection. A traditional dictionary or schoolbook definition is given in [21i], while our proposed revision is given in [ii]:

[21]	i	DATIVE:	the case of nouns, etc., expressing the indirect object or recipient
	ii	DATIVE:	a grammatically distinct case characteristically used to mark the indirect object

Definition [i] suggests that in *He gave Caesar a sword*, for example, *Caesar* is in the dative case, as it is in indirect object function and expresses the semantic role of recipient. And that indeed is the analysis found in many traditional grammars and school textbooks (especially older ones). But Present-day English has no dative case. In the Latin counterpart of the above sentence ***Caesar*** has a different form (*Caesarī*) from the one it has when functioning as subject (*Caesar*) or direct object (*Caesarem*), so the distinctiveness condition of definition [ii] is satisfied for Latin. In English it is not satisfied: the form is simply *Caesar* whether the function is subject, direct object, or indirect object. There is no noun, not even a pronoun, with a distinct inflectional form for the indirect object, and hence no basis at all for including dative among the inflectional categories of the English noun.[15]

5 Semantics, pragmatics, and meaning relations

Few grammars even attempt to describe the ways in which sentences are formed without making reference along the way to meaning and how sentences express it. After all, few would take it to be controversial that a human language such as English is in some sense a system for framing thoughts and making meaningful messages expressible, and this would make it a natural supposition that meaning and grammar would be to some extent intertwined. This grammar, while not attempting a full and detailed semantic description of the language (which would be an unrealistically large and difficult enterprise), touches on the topic of meaning frequently. But as we will explain, we do not treat meaning as a unitary phenomenon.

The semantics/pragmatics distinction

We treat the analysis of meaning as divisible in the first instance into two major domains. The first deals with the sense conventionally assigned to sentences independently of the contexts in which they might be uttered. This is the domain called **semantics**. The second

[15] Our definition omits the reference to recipients in the traditional definition because this will appear in the definition of indirect object – a grammatically distinct subtype of object characteristically expressing the recipient.

deals with the way in which utterances are interpreted in context, and the ways in which the utterance of a particular sentence in a certain context may convey a message that is not actually expressed in the sentence and in other contexts might not have been conveyed. This is the domain called **pragmatics**.

Truth-conditional and non-truth-conditional aspects of semantics
Within semantics we then make a further division between those aspects of the meaning of sentences that have to do with truth and those that do not. Consider the sentence:

[1] *I have just had a letter from the tax inspector.*

The most important thing that speakers of English know about the meaning of this sentence is the conditions under which it could be used to make a true statement. But there is certainly more to meaning than that. For one thing, the meaning of *Have you just had a letter from the tax inspector?* is such that it cannot be conventionally used to make a statement at all, so we cannot describe its meaning by specifying the conditions under which it would be used to make a true statement. Truth conditions are nonetheless important to specifying meaning exactly. In the brief survey that follows, we begin with truth-conditional meaning, then consider other aspects of sentence meaning, and finally turn to pragmatics, to the interpretation of sentences in context.

5.1 Truth conditions and entailment

Sentences vs propositions

Sentences as such are not true or false: they do not themselves have **truth values**. It makes no sense to ask whether [1], considered as a sentence of English, is true or false. The question of true or false arises only with respect to its use on particular occasions, for this question depends crucially on who utters the sentence, and when. This is why we said above that knowing the meaning of this sentence involves knowing the conditions under which it could be used to make a true statement – more succinctly, it involves knowing its **truth conditions**. The speaker, whoever it might be, must have received a letter from the tax inspector a short time before uttering the sentence.

The abstract entities that do have truth values we call **propositions**. We say, then, that declarative sentences can be used in particular contexts to **assert** propositions. And it is clear from what has been said that sentence [1] can be used to assert indefinitely many different propositions, depending on who says it and when. To describe the truth conditions of [1] is to say what conditions would have to be satisfied in order for the proposition it was used to assert in particular contexts to be true. Having made this general point, however, we will follow the widespread practice of talking of a sentence as being true under such-and-such conditions as a shorthand way of saying that the proposition asserted by the sentence under those conditions would be true.

If two sentences have different truth conditions they necessarily have different meanings. Consider the two pairs in:

[2]		a.		b.	
	i	a.	*The UK is a monarchy.*	b.	*The UK has a queen as sovereign.*
	ii	a.	*The committee approved of my plan.*	b.	*The committee approved my plan.*

At the turn of the twenty-first century the propositions asserted by saying [ia] and [ib] were both true. But clearly that could change: the succession of a male sovereign to the throne would allow [ia] to continue to assert a true proposition, but [ib] would assert a false proposition under those circumstances. The sentences accordingly have different truth **conditions**: circumstances could obtain under which one would express a truth and the other a falsehood. Similarly, though perhaps less obviously, in [ii]. For [iia] to be true, it is sufficient for the committee to feel broadly favourable to my plan, but for [iib] to be true it is necessary that they actually took some action to give my plan the go-ahead signal. The conditions under which the first would be true are not quite the same as those under which the second would be true, so the meanings differ.

Entailments

One way of describing truth conditions is in terms of **entailments**. An entailment is defined as follows (the definitions in this chapter use '≡' to symbolise the relation 'is by definition equivalent to'):

[3] *X* entails *Y* ≡ If *X* is true, then it follows necessarily that *Y* is true too.

In the first instance, entailment is a relation between propositions, since it is propositions, strictly speaking, that have truth values. But we can apply the concept derivatively to sentences, as illustrated in:

[4]	i *Kim broke the vase.*	[entails [ii]]
	ii *The vase broke.*	[entailed by [i]]
	iii *Kim moved the vase.*	[does not entail [ii]]

If the proposition asserted by [i] in any context is true, then the proposition asserted by [ii] in that same context must also be true. The first proposition entails the second, and sentence [i] entails sentence [ii]. If *X* entails *Y*, then it is inconsistent to assert *X* and deny *Y*. It is inconsistent, for example, to say *#Kim broke the vase but the vase didn't break* (the '#' symbol indicates that what follows is grammatical but semantically or pragmatically anomalous). In the case of [iii] and [ii] there is no such inconsistency: *Kim moved the vase but the vase didn't break.* And [iii] of course does not entail [ii]: it is perfectly possible for [iii] to be true and [ii] false.

We can state entailments in a variety of equivalent ways: we can say that *Kim broke the vase* entails that the vase broke, or that it entails "The vase broke", or that it entails *The vase broke.* Whichever mode of presentation we adopt, it follows from the definition given in [3] that if *X* entails *Y* then *X* cannot be true unless *Y* is true. And that is to say that *Y* is a condition for the truth of *X*. So to give the entailments of a sentence is to give its truth conditions.

Closed and open propositions

A refinement of our notion of proposition is called for in discussing certain constructions. What we have described so far as propositions could be described more precisely as **closed propositions**. They are closed in the sense of not leaving anything available to be filled in: a proposition like "Sandy showed me that at the office last week" identifies what was done, who did the showing, what was shown, where it happened, and when this occurred. There are also **open propositions**, which have a place left open. Consider the meaning of *What did Sandy show you at the office last week?*: it could be represented informally as "Sandy showed you *x* at the office last week", where *x* is a placeholder, or **variable**, for a piece of information not supplied. The point of open interrogative sentences like *What* *did Sandy show you at the office last week?* is typically to present an open proposition to the addressee in the guise of a request that the missing piece of information be supplied in response. An open proposition yields a closed proposition when the necessary extra piece of information is provided to fill the position of the variable.

5.2 Non-truth-conditional aspects of sentence meaning

Illocutionary meaning and propositional content

In making the point that there is more to sentence meaning than truth conditions we invoked the distinction between declaratives and interrogatives. Compare, then, such a pair as:

[5] a. *Kim broke the vase.* b. *Did Kim break the vase?*

We do not use [b] to make a statement. It therefore does not have truth conditions or entailments. Nevertheless, it is intuitively obvious that [a] and [b] are partially alike and partially different in both form and meaning. As far as the form is concerned, they differ in what we call **clause type**, with [a] declarative, [b] interrogative, but in other respects they are the same: [b] is the interrogative **counterpart** of [a]. The semantic correlate of clause type is called **illocutionary meaning**. The illocutionary meaning of [a] is such that it would characteristically be used to make a statement, while [b] has the illocutionary meaning of a question.

What [a] and [b] have in common is that they express the same proposition. We use 'express' here in a way which is neutral between statements and questions: [a] can be used to assert the proposition that Kim broke the vase, and [b] to question it, but in both cases the proposition is expressed. A distinctive property of questions is that they have answers, and the answers to the kind of question we are concerned with here are derivable from the proposition expressed, "Kim broke the vase", and its negation, "Kim didn't break the vase." While they differ in illocutionary meaning, we will say that [a] and [b] are alike in their **propositional meaning**, that they have the same **propositional content.**

Conventional implicature

Sentences with the same illocutionary meaning may have the same truth conditions and yet still differ in meaning. Consider the following pairs:

[6]	i	a. *She is flying up there <u>and</u> taking the train back.*	b. *She is flying up there <u>but</u> taking the train back.*
	ii	a. *<u>Max</u> agreed that his behaviour had been outrageous.*	b. *<u>Even Max</u> agreed that his behaviour had been outrageous.*
	iii	a. *I've just realised I've got to work out <u>my sales tax.</u>*	b. *I've just realised I've got to work out <u>my bloody sales tax</u>.*

Take first the pair in [i]. Both [ia] and [ib] are true provided that she is flying up there and coming back on a train. They have the same truth conditions, the same entailments. There is, in other words, no context in which the statement made by one would be true, while that made by the other would be false. They therefore have the same propositional meaning. Yet we do not perceive them as entirely **synonymous**, as having entirely the same meaning. We would use [ia] in neutral cases and reserve [ib] for cases where there is some relevant contrast related to the second coordinate – perhaps one would have expected her to use a return flight and she is acting counter to that expectation, or it might be that although she will be going up there at air travel speed she will have much more time for reading on the slow return trip, and so on. The precise nature of the contrast is not made explicit, but the use of *but* rather than the neutral coordinator *and* indicates that the two parts are being presented as involving some sort of contrast. As we have said, this extra meaning contributed by the choice of *but* rather than *and* is not part of the propositional meaning: it would not be legitimate for you to respond to [ib] by saying, *That's false, though I concede that she is flying up there and taking the train back.*

Similarly with [6ii], except that here the two sentences differ not in the choice of one word rather than another, but in the presence or absence of a word, namely *even. Even* conveys that it is somehow noteworthy that the property of having agreed that his behaviour was outrageous applies to Max: it is less expected that Max should have agreed than that the others who agreed should have done so. Again, this is not part of the propositional meaning. The truth conditions of [iia–iib] are the same: there is no context where one could be true and the other false. But it is intuitively clear that the sentences do not have exactly the same meaning.

The same applies in [6iii]. *Bloody* serves in some rather vague way to express anger or ill will towards sales tax reporting regulations, or towards the idea of having to work out sales taxes, or something of the sort. But the anger or ill will is not expressed as part of the propositional meaning: the truth conditions for [iiib] are exactly the same as those for [iiia].

We will handle the non-propositional meaning conveyed by items such as *but, even,* and *bloody* in these examples in terms of the concept of **conventional implicature**. In uttering [6ib], I indicate, or **implicate**, that there is some kind of contrast between her taking the train back and flying up there, but I do not actually state that there is. And analogously for the others. Unlike entailments, conventional implicatures are not restricted to sentences that are characteristically used to make statements. *Is she flying up there but taking the train back?, Did even Max agree that his behaviour had been outrageous?* and *Have you ever had to do a bloody sales tax report?* carry the above implicatures even though they do not themselves have truth conditions.

5.3 Pragmatics and conversational implicatures

Pragmatics is concerned not with the meaning of sentences as units of the language system but with the interpretation of utterances in context. Utterances in context are often interpreted in ways that cannot be accounted for simply in terms of the meaning of the sentence uttered.

Let us again illustrate the point by means of a few representative examples:

[7] i *Do you think I could borrow five dollars from you?*
ii *If you agree to look after my horses after I die, I'll leave you my whole estate.*
iii *Some of the audience left the room before the first speaker had finished.*

Imagine that Sue and Jill are at the cash register in a cafeteria buying sandwiches. Jill has $20 in her hand. Sue finds she only has a few cents in her purse, and utters [i]. As far as the literal meaning of the sentence is concerned, this is a question as to whether or not

Jill thinks Sue could borrow five dollars from her. It has two possible answers: "Yes" (i.e. "I do think you could") and "No" (i.e. "I don't think you could"). But for Jill to respond *Yes, I do* would seem strange and uncooperative in this context. It would force Sue to be more direct: *Well, lend it to me then, right now, because I can't afford to pay for this sandwich.*

What would normally be expected of Jill would be to act on the basis of the following reasoning. We both have to pay for our sandwiches. Sue has reached the cash register and, after finding her purse almost empty, is asking whether in my opinion it would be possible for me to extend a $5 loan. Sue can see that I have $20, and sandwiches only cost about $5, so I could obviously afford it. Sue must see that the answer to the question is "yes". Why am I being asked for my opinion about my financial status? What is the point of this question? The only reasonable conclusion is that Sue actually wants me to advance such a loan, right now.

The message "Please lend me $5" is thus indirectly conveyed by a question that does not itself actually express it. A cooperative addressee will understand the speaker's intention immediately, without consciously going through the process of reasoning just sketched. But for the student of language it is important to see: (a) that "Please lend me $5" is not the semantic meaning of sentence [7i], but the pragmatic meaning of an utterance of [i] in a certain range of contexts; (b) that the pragmatic interpretation can be derived in a systematic way from the interaction between the sentence meaning and the context.

Semantics is thus concerned with the meaning that is directly expressed, or encoded, in sentences, while pragmatics deals with the principles that account for the way utterances are actually interpreted in context. A central principle in pragmatics, which drives a great deal of the utterance interpretation process, is that the addressee of an utterance will expect it to be **relevant**, and will normally interpret it on that basis.

This principle of relevance was very evident in our first example: the relevance of Sue's question was that she needed Jill to lend her the money. It is equally important in deriving the pragmatic interpretation of [7ii]. This sentence does not actually make the statement that you won't get the estate if you don't agree to look after my horses: that is not part of the sentence meaning. A proposition of the type "if P then Q" does not require "P" to be true in order for "Q" to be true.[16] We therefore need an explanation for this fact: anyone who is told *If you agree to look after my horses after I die then I'll leave you my whole estate* will always assume that the bequest will not be forthcoming without the agreement to look after the horses. Why? Because otherwise it would not have been relevant to mention the horses. If that part of the sentence had some relevance, it must be as a necessary condition for getting the bequest, and we normally try to find an interpretation for an utterance that makes everything in it relevant. The semantics of the sentence does not tell us that the horse care will be a precondition for the bequest, but the pragmatics of interpreting the utterance certainly does.

[16] If this is not obvious, consider the sentence *If a house collapses directly on me I will die.* This does not entail that provided no house falls on me I will be immortal. Eventually I will die anyway. Or consider *If you need some more milk there's plenty in the fridge.* This does not state that there is plenty of milk in the fridge only if you need some. If there is milk in there, it will be there whether you need it or not. A sentence meaning "if P then Q" will often strongly suggest "if not P then not Q", but that is not part of the semantic meaning.

Consider, finally, example [7iii], as uttered, say, in the context of my giving you an account of a weekend seminar I recently attended. You will infer that not all of the audience left the room before the first speaker had finished. But again that is not part of the meaning of the sentence. *Some* does not **mean** "not all". The "not all" interpretation can be accounted for by pragmatic principles. I am describing an event at which I was present, so I presumably know whether or not all of the audience left before the first speaker had finished. Suppose I know that all of them left. Then I would surely be expected to say so: such a mass walkout would be much more worth mentioning than one where only part of the audience left. So the natural assumption is that I said *some* rather than *all* because it would not have been true to say *all*: what other reason could I have for making the weaker statement?

Compare this with the case where you ask *Have all the questionnaires been returned?* and I reply *I don't know: some have, but I can't say whether they all have.* If *some* meant "not all" this would be incoherent, but clearly it is not. This time my reason for saying *some* rather than *all* is not that it would be false to say *all*, but merely that I do not have enough knowledge or evidence to justify saying *all.*

We will again invoke the concept of implicature in describing the above interpretations of utterances of [7i–iii], but we will classify them more specifically as **conversational implicatures**. We will say, for example, that an utterance of [7iii] in the context described conversationally implicates "Not all of the audience left before the first speaker had finished".

Relation between entailment and the two kinds of implicature

The differences between entailment, conventional implicature, and conversational implicature are summarised in [8].

[8]			
	ENTAILMENT	semantic	truth-conditional
	CONVENTIONAL IMPLICATURE	semantic	non-truth-conditional
	CONVERSATIONAL IMPLICATURE	pragmatic	non-truth-conditional

Implicatures are distinguished from entailments in that they are not truth conditions; hence they are not restricted to sentences that can be used to make statements. The two types of implicature are distinguished according to whether they are part of the conventional meaning of sentences or derive from the interaction between the sentence meaning and the context of utterance by means of general principles of conversational cooperation. In this book we will be much more concerned with conversational implicatures than with conventional ones, as they play a larger part in the interpretation of discourse; we will take them to represent the default case, therefore, and when the term implicature is used without qualification it is intended to be understood in the conversational sense in the absence of indications to the contrary. The verb corresponding to 'implicature' is **implicate**; in addition, we will use the term **convey** in a way which is neutral between entail and (conventionally or conversationally) implicate.

Conversational implicatures are not part of sentence meaning at all. They are suggested to the hearer by the combination of the sentence meaning and the context, but they are not part of what is **said**. Nevertheless, many of them are of very general application, so that we can say that such-and-such an implicature will normally accompany the utterance of a given sentence unless special factors exclude that possibility. In such cases it is convenient to talk about the sentence normally implicating something – e.g. that [7iii] normally implicates that not all of the audience left before the first speaker had finished. This is to be understood as a shorthand way of saying that an utterance of the sentence in a normal context would carry that implicature in the absence of factors which exclude it. We will therefore apply the term to sentences in the following sense:

[9] *X* normally **conversationally implicates** $Y \equiv X$ does not entail *Y* but in saying *X* the speaker makes an implicit commitment to the truth of *Y* in the absence of indications to the contrary.

When such 'indications to the contrary' are present, we will say that the implicature is **cancelled**. Take, for example:

[10] *Some <u>if not all</u> of the delegates had been questioned by the police.*

Without the underlined sequence, *some* would again trigger a "not all" implicature – that not all of the delegates had been questioned by the police. This implicature, however, is inconsistent with *if not all*, which explicitly allows for the possibility that all of the delegates had been questioned. The implicature is therefore cancelled, i.e. is here not part of the interpretation. A context where the request-to-borrow implicature of [7i] could be cancelled might be one where I'm concerned with the legality of borrowing: perhaps I'm the treasurer of some institution and am uncertain whether I am permitted to go into debt.

The possibility of cancellation is an essential feature of conversational implicatures. If something conveyed by an utterance were an invariable component of the interpretation of the sentence, whatever the context, it would be part of the sentence meaning, either a conventional implicature or an entailment. Some conversational implicatures, however, are very **strong** in the sense that it is not easy to imagine them being cancelled – and these run the risk of being mistaken for components of sentence meaning. But it is important to make the distinction. It would be impossible, for example, to give a satisfactory account of quantification in the noun phrase if the "not all" component in the interpretation of *some* were not recognised as merely a conversational implicature.

5.4 Pragmatic presupposition

Finally, we consider the relation of **presupposition**, exemplified in:

[11] i *She has stopped trying to secure her son's release.*
ii *She hasn't stopped trying to secure her son's release.* [all presuppose [iv]]
iii *Has she stopped trying to secure her son's release?*
iv *She formerly tried to secure her son's release.*

Presupposition has to do with informational status. The information contained in a presupposition is backgrounded, taken for granted, presented as something that is not currently at issue. In [11] all of [i–iii] presuppose that she formerly tried to secure her son's release: what is at issue is not whether she tried to secure his release in the past but whether she is doing so now.

This example brings out an important property of presupposition, namely that it is generally unaffected by negation or questioning. When a sentence is negated, the negation characteristically applies to that part of the content that is presented as being at issue. If she in fact never tried to secure her son's release, [ii] is strictly speaking true, but it would normally be a very inefficient or misleading way of conveying that information. A simpler, more direct and more explicit way of doing so would be to say *She never tried to secure her son's release.* The fact that I didn't say this but said [ii] instead will lead you to infer that the negation applies to the stopping, so that [ii] implicates that she is still trying. Similarly with questioning. If I didn't know, and wanted to find out, whether she formerly tried to secure her son's release, I would be expected to ask *Did she try to secure her son's release?* If I ask [iii] instead, the natural inference will be that I am trying to find out about the present state of affairs.

The kind of reasoning just described is similar in kind to that invoked in discussing conversational implicatures, reflecting the fact that both phenomena are pragmatic.[17] Like conversational implicature, presupposition applies in the first instance to utterances, but we can apply it derivatively to sentences with the same 'normally' qualification as before:

[12] *X* normally presupposes *Y* ≡ in saying *X* the speaker, in the absence of indications to the contrary, takes the truth of *Y* for granted, i.e. presents it as something that is not at issue.

Again, then, we allow that in special circumstances a presupposition may be cancelled. Consider, for example, the following exchange:

[13] A: *Have you stopped using bold face for emphasis?*
B: *No I haven't (stopped using bold face for emphasis); I've always used small caps.*

A's question presupposes that B formerly used bold face for emphasis. But suppose it turns out that A was mistaken in believing this. B answers the question with a negative, and since this reflects the form of the question it too would normally presuppose that B formerly used bold face for emphasis. But in the context given here that presupposition is cancelled.

The presupposition associated with the verb ***stop*** coincides with an entailment when *X* is positive and declarative, as in [11i], but with a conversational implicature when *X* is negative or interrogative, as in [11ii–iii]. You cannot stop doing something that you have never done before, so [11i] cannot be true unless [11iv] is true. This gives the latter the status of an entailment. But it is not an entailment of the negative [11ii], as evident from the example in [13]. Nevertheless, if I say [11ii] I will normally be taken to have implicitly committed myself to [11iv], and the latter therefore counts as a conversational implicature. Likewise with the interrogative [11iii], which does not have entailments.

This represents the most usual pattern for presuppositions. For the most part they are entailed if *X* is positive and asserted to be true, and otherwise they are conversationally implicated. But this is not a necessary feature of presuppositions: we will see that they do not always follow this pattern.

[17] An alternative view is that presupposition is a logical or semantic concept. On one version of this account, a presupposition is a proposition that must be true if the presupposing proposition (or the sentence expressing it) is to be either true or false. In the case of [11], for example, in a context where [iv] was false, where she had never tried to secure her son's release, [i–ii] would be neither true nor false: they would simply lack a truth value (or would take a third truth value distinct from both truth and falsity). We do not adopt that concept of presupposition here, and take the view that if a proposition is not true, then it is false.

2

Syntactic overview

Rodney Huddleston

Given the length and nature of this book, there will be relatively few readers who begin at the beginning and work their way through the chapters in order to the end. We envisage, rather, that readers will typically be reading individual chapters, or parts thereof, without having read all that precedes, and the main purpose of this syntactic overview is to enable the separate chapters to be read in the context of the grammar as a whole.

We begin by clarifying the relation between sentence and clause, and then introduce the distinction between canonical and non-canonical clauses, which plays an important role in the organisation of the grammar. The following sections then survey very briefly the fifteen chapters that deal with syntax (as opposed to morphology or punctuation), noting especially features of our analysis that depart from traditional grammar.

1 Sentence and clause

Syntax is concerned with the way words combine to form sentences. The sentence is the largest unit of syntax, while the word is the smallest. The structure of composite words is also a matter of grammar (of morphology rather than syntax), but the study of the relations between sentences within a larger text or discourse falls outside the domain of grammar. Such relations are different in kind from those that obtain within a sentence, and are outside the scope of this book.

We take sentences, like words, to be units which occur sequentially in texts, but are not in general contained one within another. Compare:

[1] i *Jill seems quite friendly.*
ii *I think Jill seems quite friendly.*
iii *Jill seems quite friendly, but her husband is extremely shy.*

Jill seems quite friendly is a sentence in [i], but not in [ii–iii], where it is merely part of a sentence – just as in all three examples *friend* is part of a word, but not itself a word.

In all three examples *Jill seems quite friendly* is a clause. This is the term we apply to a syntactic construction consisting (in the central cases) of a subject and a predicate. In [1ii] one clause is contained, or embedded, within a larger one, for we likewise have a subject–predicate relation between *I* and *think Jill seems quite friendly.* In [iii] we have one clause coordinated with another rather than embedded within it: *her husband* is subject, *is extremely shy* predicate and *but* is the marker of the coordination relation. We will say, then, that in [i–ii] the sentence has the form of a clause, while in [iii] it has the form of a coordination of clauses (or a 'clause-coordination').[1] Within this framework, the clause is a more basic unit than the sentence.

To say that sentence [1ii] **has the form of** a clause is not to say that it consists of a clause, as the term 'consists of' is used in constituent structure analysis of the type introduced in Ch. 1, §4.2. There is no basis for postulating any singulary branching here, with the clause functioning as head of the sentence. This is why our tree diagram for the example *A bird hit the car* had the topmost unit labelled 'clause', not 'sentence'. 'Sentence' is not a syntactic category term comparable to 'clause', 'noun phrase', 'verb phrase', etc., and does not figure in our constituent structure representations.

Most work in formal grammar makes the opposite choice and uses sentence (abbreviated S) rather than clause in constituent structure representations. There are two reasons why we do not follow this practice. In the first place, it creates problems for the treatment of coordination. In [1iii], for example, not only the whole coordination but also the two clauses (*Jill seems quite friendly* and *but her husband is extremely shy*) would be assigned to the category sentence. The coordination, however, is quite different in its structure from that of the clauses: the latter are subject–predicate constructions, while the coordination clearly is not. Most importantly, assigning the whole coordination to the same category as its coordinate parts does not work in those cases where there is coordination of different categories, as in:

[2] *You must find out [<u>the cost</u> and <u>whether you can pay by credit card</u>].*

Here the first coordinate, *the cost*, is an NP while the second is, on the analysis under consideration, a sentence, but the whole cannot belong to either of these categories. We argue, therefore, that coordinative constructions need to be assigned to different categories than their coordinate parts. Thus we will say, for example, that *Jill seems quite friendly* is a clause, while [1iii] is a clause-coordination, *Jill and her husband* an NP-coordination, and the bracketed part of [2] an NP/clause-coordination (a coordination of an NP and a clause).

The second reason why we prefer not to use 'sentence' as the term for the syntactic category that appears in constituent structure representations is that it involves an unnecessary conflict with the ordinary, non-technical sense of the term (as reflected, for example, in dictionary definitions). Consider:

[3] a. *The knife <u>I used</u> was extremely sharp.* b. *I'm keen <u>for it to be sold</u>.*

The underlined sequences are not sentences in the familiar sense of the term that we adopted above, according to which sentences are units of a certain kind which occur in succession in a text. The underlined expressions nevertheless contain a subject (*I*, *it*) and a predicate (*used* and *to be sold*), and hence belong in the same syntactic category as expressions like *Jill seems quite friendly*. If we call this category 'sentence' rather than 'clause', the term 'sentence' will have two quite different senses.

[1] Traditional grammar classifies the sentences in [1] as respectively simple, complex, and compound, but this scheme conflates two separate dimensions: the presence or absence of embedding, and the presence or absence of coordination. Note that in *I think Jill seems quite friendly, but her husband is extremely shy* there is both embedding and coordination. We can distinguish [i–ii] from [iii] as non-compound (or clausal) vs compound; [i–ii] could then be distinguished as simple vs complex clauses but no great significance attaches to this latter distinction, and we shall not make further use of these terms.

2 Canonical and non-canonical clauses

There is a vast range of possible clause constructions, and if we tried to make descriptive statements covering them all at once, just about everything we said would have to be heavily qualified to allow for numerous exceptions. We can provide a simpler, more orderly description if in the first instance we confine our attention to a set of basic, or **canonical**, constructions, and then describe the rest derivatively, i.e. in terms of how they differ from the canonical constructions.

The contrast between canonical and non-canonical clauses is illustrated in the following examples:

[1]	CANONICAL	NON-CANONICAL
i	a. *Kim referred to the report.*	b. *Kim did not refer to the report.*
ii	a. *She was still working.*	b. *Was she still working?*
iii	a. *Pat solved the problem.*	b. *The problem was solved by Pat.*
iv	a. *Liz was ill.*	b. *He said that Liz was ill.*
v	a. *He has forgotten the appointment.*	b. *Either he has overslept or he has forgotten the appointment.*

Dimensions of contrast between canonical and non-canonical constructions

The examples in [1] illustrate five major dimensions of contrast between canonical and non-canonical clauses. In each case the canonical clause is syntactically more basic or elementary than the non-canonical one.

The examples in [1i] differ in polarity, with [a] positive and [b] negative. In this example, the negative differs from the positive not just by virtue of the negative marker *not* but also by the addition of the semantically empty auxiliary ***do***.

The contrast in [1ii] is one of clause type, with [a] declarative and [b] interrogative. The syntactic difference in this particular pair concerns the relative order of subject and predicator: in [a] the subject occupies its basic or default position before the predicator, while in [b] the order is inverted. In the pair *She finished the work* and *Did she finish the work?* the interrogative differs from the declarative both in the order of elements and in the addition of the auxiliary ***do***. All canonical clauses are declarative; non-canonical clauses on this dimension also include exclamatives (*What a shambles it was!*) and imperatives (*Sit down*).

In [1iii], canonical [a] is active while [b] is passive. These clauses differ strikingly in their syntactic form, but their meanings are very similar: there is a sense in which they represent different ways of saying the same thing. More precisely, they have the same propositional content, but differ in the way the information is presented – or 'packaged'. The passive is one of a number of non-canonical constructions on this dimension. Others include preposing (e.g. *Most of them we rejected*, contrasting with canonical *We rejected most of them*), the existential construction (e.g. *There were several doctors on board*, contrasting with *Several doctors were on board*), and the *it*-cleft (e.g. *It was Pat who spoke first*, contrasting with *Pat spoke first*).

The underlined clause in [1ivb] is subordinate, whereas [a] is a main clause. In this example, the non-canonical clause is distinguished simply by the presence of the subordinator *that*, but many kinds of subordinate clause differ from main clauses more radically, as for example in *This tool is very easy to use*, where the subordinate clause consists of just the VP subordinator *to* together with the predicator, with both subject and object left unexpressed. The clause in which a subordinate clause is embedded is called the **matrix** clause – in [ivb], for example, subordinate *that Liz was ill* is embedded within the matrix clause *He said that Liz was ill.* Subordination is recursive, i.e. repeatable, so that one matrix clause may be embedded within a larger one, as in *I think he said that Liz was ill.*

Finally, the underlined clause in [1vb] is coordinate, in contrast to non-coordinate [a]; it is marked as such by the coordinator *or.* A greater departure from canonical structure is seen in *Jill works in Paris, and her husband in Bonn*, where the predicator *works* is missing.

It is of course possible for non-canonical constructions to combine, as in:

[2] *I can't understand why I have not been questioned by the police.*

The underlined clause here is negative, interrogative, passive, and subordinate. But these are independent properties, and we can describe the structure in terms of its difference from canonical clause structure on four separate dimensions.

Counterparts

In the examples of [1] we presented the non-canonical clauses side by side with their canonical **counterparts**, i.e. canonical clauses differing from them simply as positive rather than negative, declarative rather than interrogative, and so on. Where a clause combines two non-canonical features, its counterpart with respect to each feature will be non-canonical by virtue of retaining the other. Thus *It wasn't written by Sue* has as its active counterpart *Sue didn't write it* (non-canonical by virtue of being negative) and as its positive counterpart *It was written by Sue* (non-canonical by virtue of being passive).

It must be emphasised, however, that not all non-canonical clauses have grammatically well-formed counterparts. Compare, for example:

[3]		a.	b.
	i	a. *I can't stay any longer.*	b. **I can stay any longer.*
	ii	a. *Have they finished yet?*	b. **They have finished yet.*
	iii	a. *Kim was said to be the culprit.*	b. **Said Kim to be the culprit.*
	iv	a. *There was an accident.*	b. **An accident was.*
	v	a. *If it hadn't been for you, I couldn't have managed.*	b. **It had been for you.*

Example [ia] has no counterpart differing from it as positive vs negative, and similarly there is no declarative counterpart to interrogative [iia]. There is no active counterpart to the passive [iiib], partly because ***say*** + infinitival (with this sense) is restricted to the passive construction, partly – and more generally – because there is no element corresponding to the subject of an active clause. Existential [iva] differs from the one cited above (*There were several doctors on board*) in that again there is no non-existential counterpart. And finally [va] contains a subordinate clause with no main clause counterpart. *It had been for you* is of course grammatical in the interpretation where *it* refers to something identifiable in the context (cf. *The parcel had been for you*), but that is not how *it* is interpreted in [va].

Syntactic processes

We follow the practice of much traditional and modern grammar in commonly describing non-canonical structures in terms of syntactic processes. We talk, for example, of subject–auxiliary inversion, of passivisation and relativisation, or preposing and postposing, and so on. It should be made clear, however, that such process terminology is merely a convenient descriptive device. When we say, for example, that *Is she still working?* involves subject–auxiliary inversion, we are not suggesting that a speaker actually starts with the declarative *She is still working* and then reverses the order of the first two elements. Apart from the inherent implausibility of such an interpretation of process terminology, it cannot be reconciled with the point illustrated in [3], namely that in many cases a non-canonical clause has no grammatically well-formed canonical counterpart.[2] It is always possible to translate the process description into an equivalent one couched in purely static terms. In the present example, we are merely saying that the order of the auxiliary and the subject is the opposite of that found in canonical clauses.

Extension of the apparatus for the representation of syntactic structure

The kind of syntactic analysis and representation we introduced in Ch. 1, §4.2, works well for canonical constructions, but needs some extension to cater for certain kinds of non-canonical construction. Compare, for example:

[4] a. *Liz bought a watch.* b. *I wonder <u>what Liz bought</u>.*

While [a] is a canonical clause, the underlined clause in [b] is non-canonical in two respects: it is interrogative and subordinate. It is the interrogative feature that distinguishes it from the canonical [a], inasmuch as *what* is understood as object of *bought* although its position relative to the verb differs from that of the object *a watch* in canonical [a]. (Clause [a] is not the declarative counterpart of *what Liz bought* because it contains the NP *a watch*, but it illustrates a comparable declarative structure.) The representations we propose are as in [5].

[5]

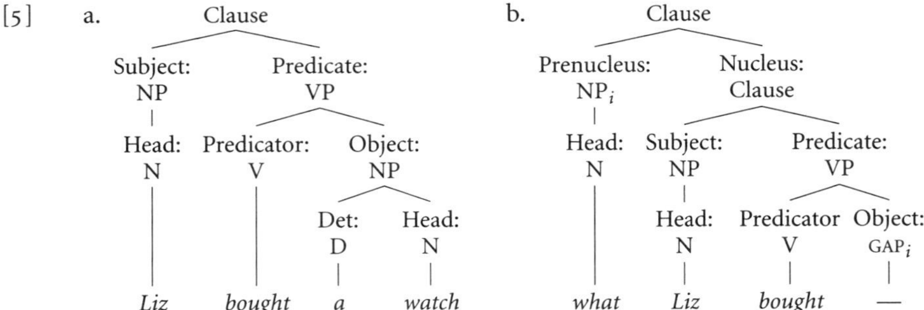

Structure [a] needs no commentary at this stage: it is of the type introduced in Ch. 1. In [b] *what* precedes the subject in what we call the **prenucleus** position: it is followed by

[2] Note also that what we present in this book is an informal descriptive grammar, not a formal generative one: we are not deriving the 'surface structure' of sentences from abstract 'underlying structures'. Thus our process terminology is not to be interpreted as referring to operations performed as part of any such derivation.

the **nucleus**, which is realised by a clause with the familiar subject–predicate structure. Within this nuclear clause there is no overt object present. But the prenuclear *what* is understood as object, and this excludes the possibility of inserting a (direct) object after *bought*: **I wonder what Liz bought a watch.* We represent this by having the object realised by a **gap**, an abstract element that is **co-indexed** with *what* (i.e. annotated with the same subscript index, here '*i*'): this device indicates that while *what* is in prenuclear position, it also functions in a secondary or derivative sense as object of *bought*.

Note that it would not be satisfactory to replace the 'prenucleus' label by 'object', and then simply dispense with the object element on the right of *bought*. Functions, we have said, are relational concepts and 'object' is a relation between an NP and a VP construction. Directly labelling *what* as object would not show that it is object of the VP headed by *bought*. This can be seen more easily by considering such an example as [6], where the bracketed clause has the structure shown in [7]:

[6] *I can't remember [what Max said Liz bought __].*

[7]

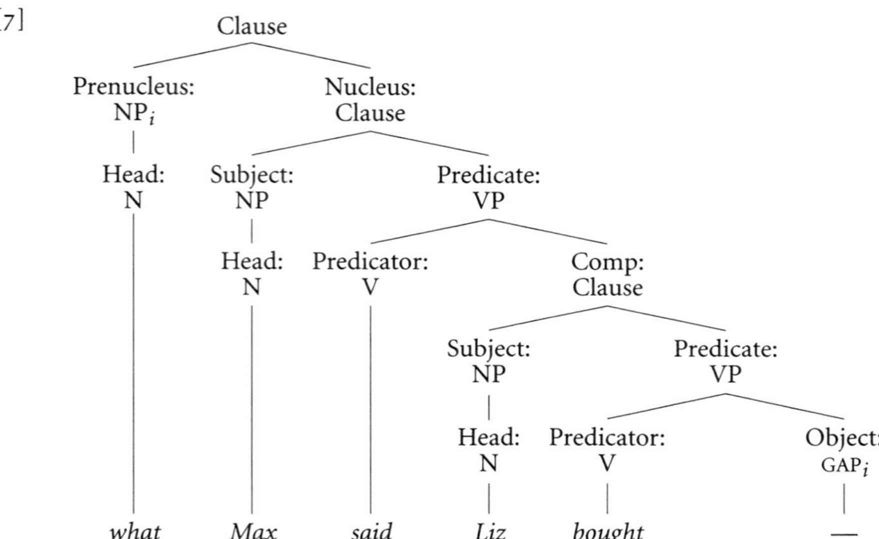

What is in prenuclear position in the clause whose ultimate head is the verb *said*, but it is understood as object of *bought*, not *said*. Simply labelling *what* as object would not bring this out, whereas the co-indexed gap device does serve to relate *what* to the *bought* VP whose object it is.

We make use of the same device to handle subject–auxiliary inversion. Compare the structures in [8] for canonical *He is ill* and interrogative *Is he ill?* The nucleus in [b] is identical to structure [a] except for the gap, and this accounts for the fact that the functional relations between *he*, *is*, and *ill* are the same in the two clauses: *he* is subject, *ill* is predicative complement, and *is* in [b] is shown to be predicator by virtue of its link to the gap element that fills the predicator position directly. Main clause interrogatives like *What had Liz bought?* will thus have one prenucleus + nucleus construction (*had* + *Liz bought*) functioning as nucleus within another (*what* + *had Liz bought*).

[8]

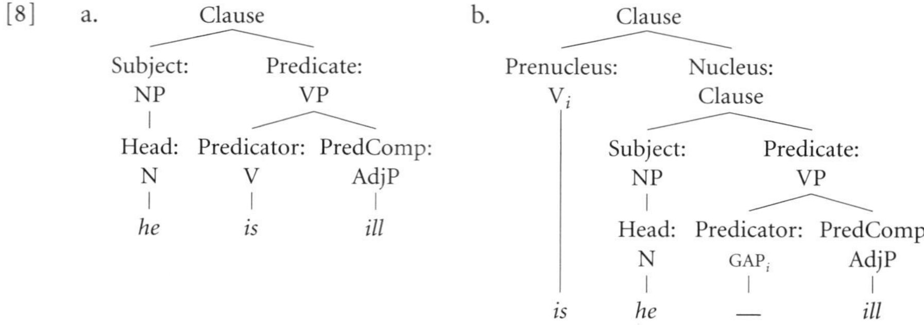

Organisation of the grammar

The distinction between canonical and non-canonical clauses plays a major role in the organisation of the present grammar. The early chapters deal predominantly with the structure of canonical clauses, and with units smaller than the clause: phrases headed by nouns, adjectives, adverbs, and prepositions. Chs. 9–16 then focus on non-canonical constructions; subordination requires more extensive treatment than the other dimensions mentioned above, and is covered in Chs. 11–14. The final chapter devoted to syntax (Ch. 17) deals with deixis and anaphora, phenomena which cut across the primary part-of-speech distinction between nouns, verbs, etc. There follow two chapters dealing with the major branches of morphology, and we end with a short account of punctuation.

3 The verb

The head of a clause (the predicate) is realised by a VP, and the head of a VP (the predicator) is realised by a verb. The verb thus functions as the ultimate head of a clause, and is the syntactically most important element within it: properties of the verb determine what other kinds of element are required or permitted.[3]

Inflection

Most verbs have six inflectional forms, illustrated here for the lexeme ***take***:

[1]

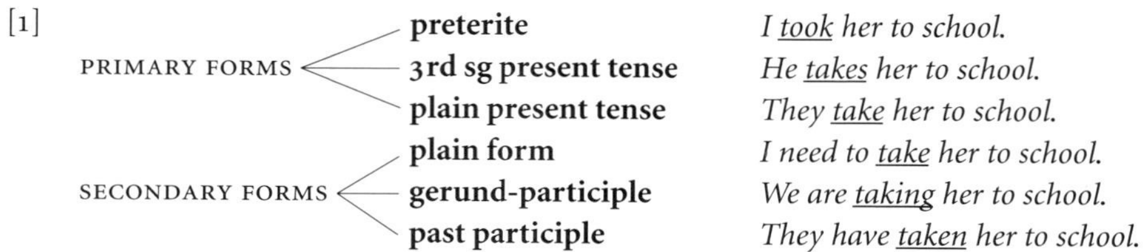

Auxiliary verbs also have negative forms (*She isn't here, I can't help it*, etc.), while the verb ***be*** has two preterite forms (*was* and *were*) and three present tense forms (*am, is, are*). The *were* of *I wish she were here* we take to be an irrealis mood form, a relic of an older system now found only with the verb ***be*** with a 1st or 3rd person singular subject.

[3] Since the verb is the ultimate head, we can identify clauses by the verb. In [6] of §2, for example, we can refer to the most deeply embedded clause as the *buy* clause.

The plain form occurs in three main constructions, one of which has two subtypes:

[2]			
i		IMPERATIVE	*Take great care!*
ii		SUBJUNCTIVE	*It is essential [that he take great care].*
iii	a.	*TO*-INFINITIVAL	*I advise you [to take great care].*
	b.	BARE INFINITIVAL	*You must [take great care].*

Note, then, that on our account imperative, subjunctive, and infinitival are clause constructions, not inflectional forms of the verb. *To* in [iiia] is a VP subordinator, not part of the verb.

Finite and non-finite

These terms likewise apply to clauses (and by extension VPs), not to verb inflection. Finite clauses have as head a primary form of a verb or else a plain form used in either the imperative or the subjunctive constructions. Non-finite clauses have as head a gerund-participle or past participle form of a verb, or else a plain form used in the infinitival construction.

Auxiliary verbs

Auxiliary verbs are distinguished syntactically from other verbs (i.e. from lexical verbs) by their behaviour in a number of constructions, including those illustrated in:

[3]	AUXILIARY VERB	LEXICAL VERB
i	a. *I have not seen them.*	b. **I saw not them.*
ii	a. *Will you go with them?*	b. **Want you to go with them?*

Thus auxiliary verbs can be negated by a following *not* and can invert with the subject to form interrogatives, but lexical verbs cannot. To correct [ib/iib] we need to insert the dummy (semantically empty) auxiliary ***do***: *I did not see them* and *Do you want to go with them?* It follows from our syntactic definition that ***be*** is an auxiliary verb not only in examples like *She is working* or *He was killed* but also in its copula use, as in *They are cheap* (cf. *They are not cheap* and *Are they cheap?*).

Our analysis of auxiliary verbs departs radically from traditional grammar in that we take them to be heads, not dependents. Thus in *She is writing a novel*, for example, *is* is a head with *writing a novel* as its complement; the constituent structure is like that of *She began writing a novel.* Note, then, that *is writing* here is not a constituent: *is* is head of one clause and *writing* is head of a non-finite subordinate clause.

Tense and time

There are two tense systems in English. The primary one is marked by verb inflection and contrasts preterite (*She was ill*) and present (*She is ill*). The secondary one is marked by the presence or absence of auxiliary ***have*** and contrasts perfect (*She is believed to have been ill*) and non-perfect (*She is believed to be ill*). The perfect can combine with primary tense to yield compound tenses, preterite perfect (*She had been ill*) and present perfect (*She has been ill*).

We distinguish sharply between the grammatical category of tense and the semantic category of time. In *It started yesterday, You said it started tomorrow*, and *I wish it started tomorrow*, for example, *started* is a preterite verb-form in all three cases, but only in the first does it locate the starting in past time. Once this distinction is clearly drawn, it is easy to see that English has no future tense: ***will*** and ***shall*** belong grammatically with ***must***, ***may***, and ***can***, and are modal auxiliaries, not tense auxiliaries.

Aspect and aspectuality

We make a corresponding distinction between grammatical aspect and semantic aspectuality. English has an aspect system marked by the presence or absence of the auxiliary ***be*** contrasting progressive (*She was writing a novel*) and non-progressive (*She wrote a novel*). The major aspectuality contrast is between perfective and imperfective. With perfective aspectuality the situation described in a clause is presented in its totality, as a whole, viewed, as it were, from the outside. With imperfective aspectuality the situation is not presented in its totality, but viewed from within, with focus on the internal temporal structure or on some subinterval of time within the whole. The main use of progressive VPs is to express a particular subtype of imperfective aspectuality.

Mood and modality

Again, mood is a matter of grammatical form, modality a matter of meaning. Irrealis *were*, mentioned above, is a residual mood-form, but the main markers of mood in English are the modal auxiliaries ***can***, ***may***, ***must***, ***will***, ***shall***, together with a few less central ones.

Three main kinds of modal meaning are distinguished:

[4]	i DEONTIC	*You must come in immediately.*	*You can have one more turn.*
	ii EPISTEMIC	*It must have been a mistake.*	*You may be right.*
	iii DYNAMIC	*Liz can drive better than you.*	*I asked Ed to go but he won't.*

Deontic modality typically has to do with such notions as obligation and permission, or – in combination with negation – prohibition (cf. *You can't have any more*). In the central cases, epistemic modality qualifies the speaker's commitment to the truth of the modalised proposition. While *It was a mistake* represents an unqualified assertion, *It must have been a mistake* suggests that I am drawing a conclusion from evidence rather than asserting something of whose truth I have direct knowledge. And *You may be right* merely acknowledges the possibility that "You are right" is true. Dynamic modality generally concerns the properties and dispositions of persons, etc., referred to in the clause, especially by the subject. Thus in [iii] we are concerned with Liz's driving ability and Ed's willingness to go.

All three kinds of modality are commonly expressed by other means than by modal auxiliaries: lexical verbs (*You don't need to tell me*), adjectives (*You are likely to be fined*), adverbs (*Perhaps you are right*), nouns (*You have my permission to leave early*).

4 The clause: complements

Dependents of the verb in clause structure are either complements or modifiers. Complements are related more closely to the verb than modifiers. The presence or absence of particular kinds of complement depends on the subclass of verb that heads the clause: the verb *use*, for example, requires an object (in canonical clauses), while *arrive* excludes one.

Moreover, the semantic role associated with an NP in complement function depends on the meaning of the verb: in *He murdered his son-in-law*, for example, the object has the role of patient (or undergoer of the action), while in *He heard her voice* it has the role of stimulus (for some sensation). Ch. 4 is mainly concerned with complements in clause structure.

Subject and object

One type of complement that is clearly distinguished, syntactically, from others is the subject: this is an external complement in that it is located outside the VP. It is an obligatory element in all canonical clauses. The object, by contrast, is an internal complement and, as just noted, is permitted – or **licensed** – by some verbs but not by others. Some verbs license two objects, indirect and direct. This gives the three major clause constructions:

[1]	INTRANSITIVE		MONOTRANSITIVE			DITRANSITIVE			
	a. *She*	*smiled*	b. *He*	*washed*	*the car*	c. *They*	*gave*	*me*	*the key*
	S	P	S	P	O^d	S	P	O^i	O^d

The terms intransitive, monotransitive, and ditransitive can be applied either to the clause or to the head verb. Most verbs, however, can occur with more than one 'complementation'. *Read*, for example, is intransitive in *She read for a while*, monotransitive in *She read the newspaper*, and ditransitive in *She read us a story*.

Example [1c] has the same propositional meaning as *They gave the key to me*, but *to me* is not an indirect object, not an object at all: it is syntactically quite different from *me* in [1c]. Objects normally have the form of NPs; *to me* here is a complement with the form of a PP.

Predicative complements

A different kind of internal complement is the predicative (PC):

[2]	COMPLEX-INTRANSITIVE			COMPLEX-TRANSITIVE			
	a. *This*	*seems*	*a good idea / fair.*	b. *I*	*consider*	*this*	*a good idea / fair.*
	S	P	PC	S	P	O^d	PC

We use the term **complex-intransitive** for a clause containing a predicative complement but no object, and **complex-transitive** for one containing both types of complement.

The major syntactic difference between a predicative complement and an object is that the former can be realised by an adjective, such as *fair* in these examples. Semantically, an object characteristically refers to some participant in the situation but with a different semantic role from the subject, whereas a predicative complement characteristically denotes a property that is ascribed to the referent of the subject (in a complex-intransitive) or object (in a complex-transitive).

Ascriptive and specifying uses of the verb *be*

Much the most common verb in complex-intransitive clauses is *be*, but here we need to distinguish two subtypes of the construction:

[3]	ASCRIPTIVE	SPECIFYING
	a. *This is a good idea / fair.*	b. *The only problem is the cost.*

The ascriptive subtype is like the construction with *seem*: the PC *a good idea* or *fair* gives a property ascribed to "this". Example [b], however, is understood quite differently: it serves to identify the only problem. It specifies the value of the variable *x* in "the *x* such that *x* was the only problem". Syntactically, the specifying construction normally allows the subject and predicative to be reversed. This gives *The cost is the only problem*, where the subject is now *the cost* and the predicative is *the only problem*.

Complements with the form of PPs

The complements in [1–3] are all NPs or AdjPs. Complements can also have the form of subordinate clauses (*I know you are right, I want to help*), but these are dealt with in Ch. 11 (finite clauses) and Ch. 14 (non-finites). In Ch. 4 we survey a range of constructions containing prepositional complements. They include those illustrated in:

		a.	b.
[4]	i	a. *He referred to her article.*	b. *He blamed the accident on me.*
	ii	a. *This counts as a failure.*	b. *He regards me as a liability.*
	iii	a. *She jumped off the wall.*	b. *She took off the label.*

The verbs *refer* and *blame* in [i] are prepositional verbs. These are verbs which take a PP complement headed by a specified preposition: *refer* selects *to* and *blame* selects *on*. (*Blame* also occurs in a construction in which the specified preposition is *for*: *He blamed me for the accident.*) Although the *to* in [ia] is selected by the verb, it belongs in constituent structure with *her article* (just as *on* in [ib] belongs with *me*): the immediate constituents of the VP are *referred* + *to her article*. *Count* and *regard* in [ii] are likewise prepositional verbs; these constructions differ from those in [i] in that the complements of *as* are predicatives, not objects.

The clauses in [4iii] look alike but are structurally different: the VP in [iiia] contains a single complement, the PP *off the wall*, while that in [iiib] contains two, *off* and the NP *the label*. *Off* is a PP consisting of a preposition alone (see §7 below). It can either precede the direct object, as here, or follow, as in *She took the label off*. Complements which can precede a direct object in this way are called particles.

5 Nouns and noun phrases

Prototypical NPs – i.e. the most central type, those that are most clearly and distinctively NPs – are phrases headed by nouns and able to function as complement in clause structure: *The dog barked* (subject), *I found the dog* (object), *This is a dog* (predicative). The three main subcategories of noun are common noun (e.g. *dog* in these examples), proper nouns (*Emma has arrived*), and pronouns (*They liked it*). As noted in Ch. 1, §4.2.2, we take pronoun to be a subcategory of noun, not a distinct primary category (part of speech).

Determiners and determinatives

One important kind of dependent found only in the structure of NPs is the determiner: *the book, that car, my friend*. The determiner serves to mark the NP as definite or indefinite. It is usually realised by a determinative or determinative phrase (*the, a, too many, almost all*) or a genitive NP (*the minister's speech, one member's behaviour*). Note then the distinction between **determiner**, a function in NP structure, and **determinative**, a lexical category. In traditional grammar, determinatives form a subclass of adjectives: we follow the usual practice in modern linguistics of treating them as a distinct primary category.

Just as the determiner function is not always realised by determinatives (as illustrated by the genitive NP determiners above), so many of the determinatives can have other functions than that of determiner. Thus the determinative *three* is determiner in *three books*, but modifier in *these three books*. Similarly, determinative *much* is determiner in *much happiness* but a modifier in AdjP structure in *much happier*.

Modifiers, complements, and the category of nominal

Other dependents in NP structure are modifiers or complements:

[1]	i a. *a young woman*	b. *the guy with black hair*	[modifiers]
	ii a. *his fear of the dark*	b. *the claim that it was a hoax*	[complements]

In these examples, the first constituent structure division is between the determiner and the rest of the NP, namely a head with the form of a **nominal**. *Young woman* in [ia], for example, is head of the whole NP and has the form of a nominal with *woman* as head and *young* as modifier. The nominal is a unit intermediate between an NP and a noun. The three-level hierarchy of noun phrase, nominal, and noun is thus comparable to that between clause, verb phrase, and verb.

In an NP such as *a woman*, with no modifier or complement, *woman* is both a nominal and a noun – so that, in the terminology of Ch. 1, §4.2.1, we have singulary branching in the tree structure. For the most part, however, nothing is lost if we simplify in such cases by omitting the nominal level and talk of the noun *woman* as head of the NP.

The underlined elements in [1], we have said, function in the structure of a nominal; as such, they are, from the point of view of NP structure, **internal dependents**, as opposed to the **external dependents** in:

[2] a. *quite the worst solution* b. *all these people*

The underlined elements here modify not nominals but NPs, so that one NP functions as head of a larger one. *Quite* is, more specifically, an NP-peripheral modifier, while *all* in [b] is a predeterminer. There are also post-head peripheral modifiers, as in [*The director alone*] *was responsible.*

The internal pre-head dependent *young* in [1ia] is called, more specifically, an attributive modifier. The most common type of attributive modifier is adjectival, like this one, but other categories too can occur in this function: e.g. nominals (*a federal government inquiry*), determinatives (*her many virtues*), verbs or VPs (in gerund-participle or past participle form: *a sleeping child, a frequently overlooked problem*). With only very restricted exceptions, attributive modifiers cannot themselves contain post-head dependents: compare, for example, **a younger than me woman* or **a sleeping soundly child.*

Indirect complements

The complements in [1ii] are licensed by the heads of the nominals, *fear* and *claim*: we call these **direct** complements, as opposed to **indirect** complements, which are licensed by a dependent (or part of one) of the head. Compare:

[3] a. *a better result than we'd expected* b. *enough time to complete the work*

The underlined complements here are licensed not by the heads *result* and *time*, but by the dependents *better* (more specifically by the comparative inflection) and *enough*. Indirect complements are not restricted to NP structure, but are found with most kinds of phrase.

Fused heads

In all the NP examples so far, the ultimate head is realised by a noun. There are also NPs where the head is **fused** with a dependent:

[4] i a. *I need some screws but can't find* [*any*]. b. [*Several of the boys*] *were ill.*
ii a. [*Only the rich*] *will benefit.* b. *I chose* [*the cheaper of the two*].

The brackets here enclose NPs while the underlining marks the word that functions simultaneously as head and dependent – determiner in [i], modifier in [ii]. Traditional grammar takes *any* and *several* in [i] to be pronouns: on our analysis, they belong to the same category, determinative, as they do in *any screws* and *several boys*, the difference being that in the latter they function solely as determiner, the head function being realised by a separate word (a noun).

Case

A few pronouns have four distinct case forms, illustrated for ***we*** in:

[5]	NOMINATIVE	ACCUSATIVE	DEPENDENT GENITIVE	INDEPENDENT GENITIVE
	we	*us*	*our*	*ours*

Most nouns, however, have a binary contrast between genitive and non-genitive or plain case (e.g. genitive *dog's* vs plain *dog* – or, in the plural, *dogs'* vs *dogs*).

Case is determined by the function of the NP in the larger construction. Genitive case is inflectionally marked on the last word; this is usually the head noun (giving a head genitive, as in *the child's work*) but can also be the last word of a post-head dependent (giving a phrasal genitive, as in *someone else's work*).

Genitive NPs characteristically function as subject-determiner in a larger NP. That is, they combine the function of determiner, marking the NP as definite, with that of complement (more specifically subject). Compare, then, *the minister's behaviour* with *the behaviour of the minister*, where the determiner and complement functions are realised separately by *the* and *of the minister* (an internal complement and hence not a subject). The genitive subject-determiner can also fuse with the head, as in *Your behaviour was appalling, but* [*the minister's*] *was even worse.*

Number and countability

The category of number, contrasting singular and plural, applies both to nouns and to NPs. In the default case, the number of an NP is determined by the inflectional form of the head noun, as in singular *the book* vs plural *the books*. The demonstratives ***this*** and ***that*** agree with the head, while various other determinatives select either a singular (*a book*, *each book*) or a plural (*two books*, *several books*).

Number (or rather number and person combined) applies also to verbs in the present tense and, with ***be***, in the preterite. For the most part, the verb agrees with a subject NP whose person–number classification derives from its head noun: [*The nurse*] *has arrived* ~ [*The nurses*] *have arrived.* There are, however, a good few departures from this pattern, two of which are illustrated in:

[6] a. [*A number of boys*] *were absent* b. [*Three eggs*] *is plenty.*

The head of the subject NP in [a] is singular *number*, but the subject counts as plural; conversely, in [b] the head noun is plural, but the subject NP is conceived of as expressing a single quantity.

Nouns – or, more precisely, senses of nouns – are classified as count (e.g. *a dog*) or non-count (*some equipment*). Count nouns denote entities that can be counted, and can combine with the cardinal numerals *one, two, three*, etc. Certain determiners occur only, or almost only, with count nouns (*a, each, every, either, several, many*, etc.), certain others with non-count nouns (*much, little, a little*, and, in the singular, *enough, sufficient*). Singular count nouns cannot in general head an NP without a determiner: *Your taxi is here*, but not **Taxi is here.*

6 Adjectives and adverbs

The two major uses of adjectives are as attributive modifier in NP structure and as predicative complement in clause structure:

[1]	ATTRIBUTIVE MODIFIER	PREDICATIVE COMPLEMENT
	a. *an excellent result*	b. *The result was excellent.*

Most adjectives can occur in both functions; nevertheless, there are a good number which, either absolutely or in a given sense, are restricted to attributive function (e.g. *a sole parent*, but not **The parent was sole*), and a few which cannot be used attributively (*The child was asleep*, but not **an asleep child*).

Adjectives may also function postpositively, i.e. as post-head modifier in NP structure: *something unusual, the money available.*

The structure of AdjPs

The distinction between modifiers and complements applies to the dependents of adjectives too: compare *It was* [*very good*] or *He seems* [*a bit grumpy*] (modifiers) and *She is* [*ashamed of him*] or *I'm* [*glad you could come*] (complements). Complements always follow the head and hence are hardly permitted in attributive AdjPs – though they commonly occur in postpositives (*the minister* [*responsible for the decision*]). Complements generally have the form of PPs or subordinate clauses: with minor exceptions, adjectives do not take NPs as complement.

The structure of AdjPs is considerably simpler than that of clauses or NPs, and we need only two category levels, AdjP and adjective. In examples like those in [1], *excellent* is both an AdjP (consisting of just a head) and an adjective, but as with nominal we will simplify when convenient and omit the AdjP level.

Adverbs and AdvPs

Adverbs generally function as modifiers – or as supplements, elements prosodically detached from the clause to which they relate, as in *Unhappily, the letter arrived too late.* Unlike adjectives, they do not occur in predicative complement function: *Kim was unhappy* but not **Kim was unhappily.*

As modifiers, adverbs differ from adjectives with respect to the categories of head they combine with: adjectives modify nominals, while adverbs modify other categories (including NPs). Thus the adverb *almost* can modify verbs (*She* [*almost died*]), adjectives (*an* [*almost inaudible*] *response*), adverbs (*He spoke* [*almost inaudibly*]), or NPs (*They ate* [*almost the whole pie*]).

Not all adverbs can modify heads of all these categories, however, and differences on this dimension make the adverb the least homogeneous of the traditional parts of speech. Some unity is accorded to it, however, by the fact that a high proportion of adverbs are morphologically derived from adjectives by suffixation of ·*ly*, as in pairs like *excellent* ~ *excellently*. In this grammar, moreover, we have significantly reduced the syntactic heterogeneity of the adverb category by redrawing the boundary between adverbs and prepositions: see §7 below.

Adverbs can themselves be modified in a similar way to adjectives: compare *quite excellent* and *quite excellently*. However, only a very small number of adverbs license complements, as in *independently of such considerations*. As with adjectives, we need only two category levels, AdvP and adverb, and again we will often simplify by omitting the AdvP level in examples like *a [remarkably good] performance*.

7 Prepositions and preposition phrases

One of the main respects in which the present grammar departs from traditional grammar is in its conception of prepositions. Following much work in modern linguistics, we take them to be heads of phrases – preposition phrases – which are comparable in their structure to phrases headed by verbs, nouns, adjectives, and adverbs. The NPs in *to you*, *of the house*, *in this way*, etc., are thus complements of the preposition, and the underlined expressions in *a few minutes before lunch* or *straight after lunch* are modifiers.

Complements of a preposition, like those of a verb, may be objects, as in the examples just cited, or predicatives, as in *They regard him [as a liability]* or *It strikes me [as quite reasonable]*. Some prepositions, moreover, can take AdvPs or clauses as complement: *I didn't meet him [until recently]* and *It depends [on how much they cost]*. Within this framework, it is natural to analyse words such as *before* as a preposition in *I saw him [before he left]* (with a clause as complement) as well as in *I saw him [before lunch]* (with an NP as complement). And just as phrases of other kinds do not necessarily contain a complement, so we allow PPs with no complement. Thus in *I hadn't seen him [before]*, for example, *before* is again a preposition. And in *I saw him [afterwards]* we have a preposition *afterwards* that never takes a complement. Many of traditional grammar's adverbs and most of its subordinating conjunctions, therefore, are here analysed as prepositions.

Preposition stranding

An important syntactic property of the most central prepositions is that they can be **stranded**, i.e. occur with a gap in post-head complement position. Compare:

		a.	b.
[1]	i	a. *She was talking [to a man].*	b. *I cut it [with a razor-blade].*
	ii	a. *[To whom] was she talking?*	b. *the razor-blade$_i$ [with which$_i$] I cut it*
	iii	a. *Who$_i$ was she talking [to __$_i$]?*	b. *the razor-blade$_i$ that I cut it [with __$_i$]*

In [i] we have the ordinary construction where *to* and *with* have an NP complement, with the whole PP occupying its basic position in the clause. In [ii] the PP is in prenuclear position, in an interrogative clause in [iia], a relative clause in [iib]. In [iii], however, the preposition is stranded, with the complement realised by a gap. In [iiia] the gap is co-indexed with the interrogative phrase *who* in prenuclear position, while in [iiib] it is co-indexed with *razor-blade*, the head of the nominal containing the relative clause as modifier.

8 The clause: adjuncts

We use the term 'adjunct' to cover modifiers in clause (or VP) structure together with related supplements, such as the above *Unhappily, the letter arrived too late* (see §15).

Ch. 8 is complementary to Ch. 4. The latter focuses on core complements (subjects, objects, predicatives) and complements realised by PPs where the preposition is specified by the verb; Ch. 8 is mainly concerned with adjuncts, but also covers certain types of complement that are semantically related to them. Manner expressions, for example, are mostly adjuncts, but there are a few verbs that take manner complements: in *They treated us badly*, the dependent *badly* counts as a complement by virtue of being obligatory (for *They treated us* involves a different sense of *treat*). Similarly, while locative expressions are generally adjuncts in clauses describing static situations, as in *I spoke to her in the garden*, those occurring with verbs of motion are generally complements, licensed by the verb of motion. We distinguish here between source and goal, as in *Kim drove from Berlin to Bonn*, where the source *from Berlin* indicates the starting-point, and the goal *to Bonn* the endpoint.

The adjuncts considered are distinguished, and named, on a semantic basis. They include such traditional categories as time (or temporal location, as we call it, in order to bring out certain similarities between the spatial and temporal domains), duration, frequency, degree, purpose, reason, result, concession, and condition, as well as a number of less familiar concepts.

9 Negation

Negative and positive clauses differ in several respects in their syntactic distribution, i.e. in the way they combine with other elements in larger constructions. Three such differences are illustrated in:

[1]		NEGATIVE CLAUSE	POSITIVE CLAUSE
	i	a. *He didn't read the report, not even the summary.*	b. **He read the report, not even the summary.*
	ii	a. *He didn't read the report, and nor did his son.*	b. *He read the report, and so did his son.*
	iii	a. *He didn't read it, did he?*	b. *He read it, didn't he?*

Negative clauses allow a continuation with *not even*, but positive clauses do not. The connective adjunct *nor* (or *neither*) follows a negative clause, whereas the corresponding adjunct following a positive clause is *so*. The third difference concerns the the form of the confirmation 'tag' that can be appended, with [iiia] taking a positive tag (*did he?*), and [iiib] taking a negative one (*didn't he?*).

Clauses which count as positive by the above criteria may nevertheless contain negative elements within them, and we accordingly distinguish between **clausal negation**, as in [1ii], and **subclausal negation**, as in:

[2] i *Not for the first time, she found his behaviour offensive.*
ii *We'll do it in no time.*
iii *They were rather unfriendly.*

These do not allow *not even* (e.g. **They were rather unfriendly, not even towards me*), take *so* rather than *nor* (e.g. *Not for the first time, she found his behaviour offensive, and so indeed did I*), and take negative confirmation tags (*We'll do it in no time, won't we?*).

Polarity-sensitive items

A number of words or larger expressions are sensitive to polarity in that they favour negative over positive contexts or vice versa. Compare:

[3] i a. *She doesn't live here any longer.* b. **She lives here any longer.*
ii a. *He was feeling somewhat sad.* b. **He wasn't feeling somewhat sad.*

(We set aside the special case where [iib] is used to deny or contradict a prior assertion that he was feeling somewhat sad.) We say, then, that *any longer* is negatively oriented, and likewise (in certain senses at least) *any, anyone, ever*, determinative *either, yet, at all*, etc. Similarly *somewhat* is positively oriented, and also *some, someone, pretty* (in the degree sense), *already, still*, and others.

It is not, however, simply a matter of negative vs positive contexts: *any longer*, for example, is found in interrogatives (*Will you be needing me any longer?*) and the complement of conditional *if* (*If you stay any longer you will miss your bus*). These clauses have it in common with negatives that they are not being used to make a positive assertion: we use the term **non-affirmative** to cover these (and certain other) clauses. *Any longer* thus occurs in non-affirmative contexts, and we can also say that *any longer* is a non-affirmative item, using this as an alternative to negatively-oriented polarity-sensitive item.

The scope of negation

One important issue in the interpretation of negatives concerns the scope of negation: what part of the sentence the negation applies to. Compare, for example, the interpretation of:

[4] i *Not many members answered the question.* [*many* inside scope of *not*]
ii *Many members did not answer the question.* [*many* outside scope of *not*]

These sentences clearly differ in truth conditions. Let us assume that there are a fairly large number of members – 1,000, say. Then consider the scenario in which 600 answered, and 400 didn't answer. In this case, [ii] can reasonably be considered true, but [i] is manifestly false.

The difference has to do with the relative scope of the negative and the quantification. In [4i] *many* is part of what is negated (a central part, in fact): "The number of members who answered was not large". In [ii] *many* is not part of what is negated: "The number of members who didn't answer was large". We say, then, that in [i] *many* is inside the scope of *not*, or the negation, or alternatively that the negative has scope over *many*. Conversely, in [ii] *many* is outside the scope of the negation or, alternatively, *many* has scope over the negation, since it applies to a set of people with a negative property.

In [4] the relative scope of *not* and *many* is determined by the linear order. But things are not always as simple as this. Compare:

[5] i *You need not answer the questionnaire.* [*need* inside scope of *not*]
ii *You must not answer the questionnaire.* [*must* outside scope of *not*]
iii *I didn't go to the party because I wanted to see Kim.* [ambiguous]

In [i] the negative has scope over *need* even though *need* comes first: "There isn't any need for you to answer"; in [ii], by contrast, *must* has scope over the negative: "It is necessary that you not answer". In abstraction from the intonation, [iii] is ambiguous as to scope. If the *because* adjunct is outside the scope of the negation, it gives the reason for my not going to the party: "The reason I didn't go to the party was that I wanted to see Kim (who wasn't going to be there)". If the *because* adjunct is inside the scope of negation, the sentence says that it is not the case that I went to the party because I wanted to see Kim (who was going to be there): here there is an implicature that I went for some other reason.

10 Clause type and illocutionary force

As a technical term, 'clause type' applies to that dimension of clause structure contrasting declaratives, interrogatives, imperatives, etc. The major categories are illustrated in:

[1] i DECLARATIVE *She is a good player.*
ii CLOSED INTERROGATIVE *Is she a good player?*
iii OPEN INTERROGATIVE *How good a player is she?*
iv EXCLAMATIVE *What a good player she is!*
v IMPERATIVE *Play well!*

We distinguish systematically between categories of syntactic form and categories of meaning or use. For example, *You're leaving?* (spoken with rising intonation) is syntactically a declarative but would be used to ask a question.

A question defines a set of possible answers. On one dimension we distinguish between polar questions (*Is this yours?* – with answers *Yes* and *No*), alternative questions (*Is this Kim's or Pat's?* – in the interpretation where the answers are *Kim's* and *Pat's*), and variable questions (*Whose is this?* – where the answers specify a value for the variable in the open proposition "This is *x*'s").

Making a statement, asking a question, issuing an order, etc., are different kinds of speech act. More specifically, when I make a statement by saying *This is Kim's*, say, my utterance has the **illocutionary force** of a statement. The illocutionary force typically associated with imperative clauses is called directive, a term which covers request, order, command, entreaty, instruction, and so on. There are, however, many different kinds of illocutionary force beyond those associated with the syntactic categories shown in [1]. For example, the declarative *I promise to be home by six* would generally be used with the force of a promise, *We apologise for the delay* with the force of an apology, and so on.

Indirect speech acts

Illocutionary meaning is often conveyed indirectly, by means of an utterance which if taken at face value would have a different force. Consider, for example, *Would you like to close the window*. Syntactically, this is a closed interrogative, and in its literal interpretation it has the force of an inquiry (with *Yes* and *No* as answers). In practice, however, it is most likely to be used as a directive, a request to close the door. Indirect speech acts are particularly common in the case of directives: in many circumstances it is considered more polite to issue indirect directives than direct ones (such as imperative *Close the window*).

11 Content clauses and reported speech

Ch. 11 is the first of four chapters devoted wholly or in part to subordinate clauses. Subordinate clauses may be classified in the first instance as finite vs non-finite, with the finites then subclassified as follows:

[1] i	RELATIVE	*The one <u>who laughed</u> was Jill.*	*This is the book <u>I asked for</u>.*
ii	COMPARATIVE	*It cost more than <u>we expected</u>.*	*He isn't as old as <u>I am</u>.*
iii	CONTENT	*You said <u>that you liked her</u>.*	*I wonder <u>what he wants</u>.*

Of these, content clauses represent the default category, lacking the special syntactic features of relatives and comparatives.

We do not make use of the traditional categories of noun clause, adjective clause, and adverb clause. In the first place, functional analogies between subordinate clauses and word categories do not provide a satisfactory basis for classification. And secondly, a high proportion of traditional adverb (or adverbial) clauses are on our analysis PPs consisting of a preposition as head and a content clause as complement: *before <u>you mentioned it</u>, if <u>it rains</u>, because <u>they were tired</u>*, and so on.

Clause type

The system of clause type applies to content clauses as well as to main clauses. The subordinate counterparts of [1i–iv] in §10 are as follows:

[2] i	DECLARATIVE	*They say <u>that she is a good player</u>.*
ii	CLOSED INTERROGATIVE	*They didn't say <u>whether she is a good player</u>.*
iii	OPEN INTERROGATIVE	*I wonder <u>how good a player she is</u>.*
iv	EXCLAMATIVE	*I'll tell them <u>what a good player she is</u>.*

(There is, however, no subordinate imperative construction.) One special case of the declarative is the mandative construction, as in *It is important <u>that she be told</u>*. In this version, the content clause is subjunctive, but there are alternants with modal *should* (*It is important <u>that she should be told</u>*) or a non-modal tensed verb (*It is important <u>that she is told</u>*).

Content clauses usually function as complement within a larger construction, as in [2]. They are, however, also found in adjunct function, as in *What is the matter, <u>that you are looking so worried</u>?* or *He won't be satisfied <u>whatever you give him</u>*. The content clause in this last example is a distinct kind of interrogative functioning as a conditional adjunct – more specifically, as what we call an exhaustive conditional adjunct.

Reported speech

One important use of content clauses is in indirect reported speech, as opposed to direct reported speech. Compare:

[3] i *Ed said, 'I shall do it in my own time.'* [direct report]
ii *Ed said that he would do it in his own time.* [indirect report]

The underlined clause in [i] is a main clause, and the whole sentence purports to give Ed's actual words. The underlined clause in [ii] is a subordinate clause and this time the sentence reports only the content of what Ed said.

12 Relative constructions and unbounded dependencies

The most central kind of relative clause functions as modifier within a nominal head in NP structure, as in:

[1] a. *Here's [the note which she wrote].* b. *Here's [the note that she wrote].*

The relative clause in [a] is a *wh* relative: it contains one of the relative words *who, whom, whose, which, when,* etc. These represent a distinct type of 'pro-form' that relates the subordinate clause to the antecedent that it modifies. The *that* in [b] we take to be not a pro-form (i.e. not a relative pronoun, as in traditional grammar) but the subordinator which occurs also in declarative content clauses like [2i] in §11. We call this clause a *that* relative; often, as here, *that* can be omitted, giving a 'bare relative': *Here's [the note she wrote].* In all three cases the object of *wrote* is realised by a gap (cf. §2 above): in [a] the gap is co-indexed with *which* in prenuclear position, and this is co-indexed with the antecedent *note*; in [b] and the version with *that* omitted the gap is simply co-indexed with the antecedent *note*.

The relative clauses in [1] are **integrated**: they function as a dependent within a larger construction. They are to be distinguished from **supplementary** relative clauses, which are prosodically detached from the rest of the sentence, as in *We invited Jill, who had just returned from Spain.* The two kinds of relative clause are traditionally distinguished as restrictive vs non-restrictive, but these are misleading terms since relative clauses that are syntactically and phonologically integrated into the sentence are by no means always semantically restrictive.

Consider finally the construction illustrated in:

[2] *I've already spent what you gave me yesterday.* [fused relative construction]

The underlined sequence here is an NP, not a clause; it is distributionally and semantically comparable to expressions that are more transparently NPs, such as *the money which you gave me yesterday* or the very formal *that which you gave me yesterday.* The underlined NP in [2] belongs to the **fused relative construction**, a term reflecting the fact that *what* here combines the functions of head of the NP and prenuclear element in a modifying relative clause.

Unbounded dependency constructions

Relative clauses belong to the class of **unbounded dependency constructions**, along with open interrogatives, exclamatives, and a number of others. The distinctive property of these constructions is illustrated for *wh* relatives in:

[3] i *Here's the note$_i$ [which$_i$ she wrote __$_i$].*
ii *Here's the note$_i$ [which$_i$ he said she wrote __$_i$].*
iii *Here's the note$_i$ [which$_i$ I think he said she wrote __$_i$].*

In each of these *which* is understood as object of *wrote*: we are representing this by co-indexing it with a gap in the position of object in the *write* clause. In [ii] the *write* clause is embedded as complement in the *say* clause, and in [iii] the *say* clause is in turn embedded as complement within the *think* clause. And clearly there is no grammatical limit to how much embedding of this kind is permitted. There is a dependency relation between the gap and *which*, and this relation is unbounded in the sense that there is no upper bound, no limit, on how deeply embedded the gap may be in the relative clause.

13 Comparative constructions

Comparative clauses function as complement to *than*, *as*, or *like*. They differ syntactically from main clauses by virtue of being structurally reduced in certain specific ways. Consider:

[1] a. *She wrote more plays than [he wrote __ novels].* b. *He's as old as [I am __].*

In [a] we have a comparison between the number of plays she wrote and the number of novels he wrote: we understand "she wrote *x* many plays; he wrote *y* many novels; *x* exceeds *y*". The determiner position corresponding to "*y* many" must be left empty, as evident from the ungrammaticality of **She wrote more plays than he wrote five novels.* In [b] we understand "He is *x* old; I am *y* old; *x* is at least equal to *y*", and not only the modifier corresponding to *y* but also *old* itself is inadmissible in the comparative clause: **He's as old as I am old.*

The *more* of [1a] is an inflectional form of the determinative ***many***, syntactically distinct from the adverb *more* in phrases like *more expensive.* The latter is an analytic comparative, i.e. one marked by a separate word (*more*) rather than inflectionally, as in *cheaper.* Similarly, *less* is the comparative form of determinative **little** in *I have less patience than you* and an adverb in *It was less painful than I'd expected.*

Example [1a] is a comparison of inequality, [b] one of equality – where being equal is to be understood as being at least equal. Comparisons of equality are also found following *same* (*She went to the same school as I did*), *such* (*Such roads as they had were in appalling condition*), and with *as* on its own (*As you know, we can't accept your offer*).

14 Non-finite and verbless clauses

Non-finite clauses may be classified according to the inflectional form of the verb. Those with a plain form verb are infinitival, and are subdivided into *to*-infinitivals and bare infinitivals depending on the presence or absence of the VP subordinator *to.* Including verbless clauses, we have, then, the following classes:

[1] i	TO-INFINITIVAL	*It was Kim's idea to invite them all.*
ii	BARE INFINITIVAL	*She helped them prepare their defence.*
iii	GERUND-PARTICIPIAL	*Calling in the police was a serious mistake.*
iv	PAST-PARTICIPIAL	*This is the proposal recommended by the manager.*
v	VERBLESS	*He was standing with his back to the wall.*

The suffix 'al' in 'infinitival', etc., distinguishes the terms in [i–iv], which apply to clauses (and, by extension, to VPs), from those used in this grammar or elsewhere for inflectional forms of the verb.

Most non-finite clauses have no overt subject, but the interpretation of the clause requires that an understood subject be retrieved from the linguistic or non-linguistic context. There are also non-finite clauses in which a non-subject NP is missing: *John*$_i$ *is easy* [*to please* __$_i$] (where the missing object of *please* is understood as *John*) or *This idea*$_i$ *is worth* [*giving some thought to* __$_i$] (where the complement of the preposition *to* is understood as *this idea*). Clauses of this kind we call **hollow** clauses.

To-infinitivals containing an overt subject are introduced by *for*, as in [*For them to take the children*] *could endanger the mission.* We take this *for* to be a clause subordinator, comparable to the *that* of finite declaratives.

The catenative construction

Non-finite clauses occur in a wide range of functions, as complements, modifiers, and supplements. One function that is worth drawing attention to here is that of **catenative** complement in clause structure:

[2] i	a. *Max seemed to like them.*	b. *Jill intended to join the army.*
ii	a. *Everyone believed Kim to be guilty.*	b. *She asked me to second her motion.*

The term 'catenative' reflects the fact that this construction is recursive (repeatable), so that we can have a chain, or concatenation, of verbs followed by non-finite complements, as in *She intends to try to persuade him to help her redecorate her flat.* The term 'catenative' is applied to the non-finite complement, and also to the verb that licenses it (*seem, intend, believe,* and *ask* in [2]) and the construction containing the verb + its complement. We take the view that these non-finite clauses represent a distinct type of complement: they cannot be subsumed under the functions of object or predicative complement that apply to complements in VP structure with the form of NPs. Auxiliary verbs that take non-finite complements are special cases of catenative verbs: in *You may be right, She is writing a novel,* and *They have left the country,* for example, the underlined clauses are catenative complements.

In [2i] the non-finite complement immediately follows the catenative verbs, whereas in [ii] there is an intervening NP: we refer to [i] and [ii] as respectively the simple and complex catenative constructions. In [ii] (but not in all cases of the complex construction) the intervening NP (*Kim* in [iia], *me* in [iib]) is object of the matrix clause. Cutting across this distinction is an important semantic one, such that *Max* in [ia] and *Kim* in [iia] are **raised** complements, whereas the corresponding elements in the [b] examples (*Jill* in [ib], *me* in [iib]) are not. A raised complement is one which belongs semantically in a lower clause than that in which it functions syntactically. Thus in [ia] *Max* is syntactically subject of *seem*, but there is no direct semantic relation between *Max* and *seem*: note, for example, that [ia] can be paraphrased as *It seemed that Max liked them*, where *Max* belongs both syntactically and semantically in the subordinate clause. Similarly, in [iia] *Kim* is syntactically object of *believe*, but there is no direct semantic relation between *believe* and *Kim*. Again, this is evident when we compare [iia] with the paraphrase *Everyone believed that Kim was guilty*, where *Kim* is located syntactically as well as semantically in the *be* clause.

15 Coordination and supplementation

Ch. 15 deals with two kinds of construction that differ from those covered above in that they do not involve a relation between a head and one or more dependents.

Coordination

Coordination is a relation between two or more elements of syntactically equal status. These are called the coordinates, and are usually linked by a coordinator, such as *and*, *or* or *but*:

[1]	i	[*She wants to go with them*, *but she can't afford it*.]	[clause-coordination]
	ii	*I've invited* [*the manager and her husband*].	[NP-coordination]
	iii	*She'll be arriving* [*tomorrow or on Friday*].	[NP/PP-coordination]

We take the bracketed sequences in [i–ii] as respectively a clause-coordination (not a clause) and an NP-coordination (not an NP). Coordinates must be syntactically alike, but the syntactic likeness that is required is in general a matter of function rather than of category. Thus in the clauses *She'll be arriving tomorrow* and *She'll be arriving on Friday*, the underlined phrases have the same function (adjunct of temporal location), and this makes it possible to coordinate them, as in [iii], even though the first is an NP and the second a PP. This adjunct clearly cannot be either an NP or a PP: we analyse it as an NP/PP-coordination.

Coordinations can occur at practically any place in structure. In *Kim bought two houses*, for example, we can replace each of the constituents by a coordination: *Kim and Pat bought two houses*, *Kim bought and sold two houses*, and so on. This means that when we are describing constructions we do not need to say for each function that if it can be filled by an *X* it can also be filled by an *X*-coordination: this can be taken for granted, with exceptions dealt with specifically in Ch. 15.

One important distinctive property of coordination is that there is no grammatical limit to the number of coordinates that may combine in a single construction. Instead of the two coordinates in [1ii], for example, we could have *the manager, her husband, the secretary, your uncle Tom, and Alice* or a coordination with any other number of coordinates.

Supplementation

We use the term supplementation for a construction containing an **anchor** and a **supplement**, an element related semantically to the anchor but not integrated into the syntactic structure as a dependent. Supplements are detached prosodically from the anchor, typically having the character of an interpolation or an appendage (an element added loosely at the beginning or end of a clause). Examples are the underlined expressions in:

[2] i *Her father – he's the guy talking to the Mayor – has agreed to finance the deal.*
ii *I finally volunteered to go first, a decision I quickly came to regret.*

As mentioned in §12, we include under this heading what are traditionally called non-restrictive relative clauses.

16 Information packaging

We noted in §2 above that there are a number of non-canonical constructions which characteristically differ from their more basic counterparts not in truth conditions or illocutionary meaning but in the way the informational content is presented: we call these **information-packaging** constructions. Some examples are given in [1], with their more basic counterparts listed in the right-hand column:

[1] i	PREPOSING	*This one I'm giving to Jill.*	*I'm giving this one to Jill.*
ii	POSTPOSING	*He gave to charity all the money she had left him.*	*He gave all the money she had left him to charity.*
iii	INVERSION	*In the bag were two knives.*	*Two knives were in the bag.*
iv	EXISTENTIAL	*There is one guard outside.*	*One guard is outside.*
v	EXTRAPOSITION	*It's clear that it's a forgery.*	*That it's a forgery is clear.*
vi	CLEFT	*It was a bee that stung me.*	*A bee stung me.*
vii	PASSIVE	*I was attacked by their dog.*	*Their dog attacked me.*

'Inversion' in [iii] is short for 'subject–dependent inversion', as opposed to subject–auxiliary inversion. In the particular example given here, there is inversion of the subject *two knives* and the locative complement *in the bag*. In *Soon afterwards came the second package* we have inversion of the subject and a temporal adjunct.

In [1i–iii] the only syntactic difference between the two versions is in the linear order of the elements, whereas in [iv–vii] there are differences in syntactic function. In the existential example, the dummy (semantically empty) pronoun *there* is subject, while *one guard* is **displaced subject**, and similarly in the extraposition example the dummy pronoun *it* is subject and *that it's a forgery* is **extraposed subject**. The terms 'displaced subject' and 'extraposed subject' denote elements which are not themselves subject but which are interpreted semantically as though they were, and characteristically correspond to the subject of the more basic construction. Extrapositional *it* can also appear in object function, as in *I find it strange that no one noticed the error*; in this case the embedded content clause functions as extraposed object.

A cleft clause contains the elements of the more basic counterpart divided into two: one (here *a bee*) is foregrounded and functions as complement of the verb *be*; the other (*stung me*) is backgrounded and placed in a subordinate (relative) clause. The example in [1vi] is, more specifically, an *it*-cleft (having the dummy pronoun *it* as subject of *be*), contrasting with the 'pseudo-cleft' *What stung me was a bee*, where the backgrounded component is located in a fused relative construction.

A passive clause like that in [1vii] differs from its active counterpart in the way the semantic roles are aligned with syntactic functions. The object of the active appears as subject of the passive, and the subject of the active appears as the complement of the preposition *by*; in addition, the passive contains the auxiliary verb *be*, taking a past-participial complement. We refer to the *by* phrase as the internalised complement: it is an internal complement of the passive VP, whereas the element in the active to which it corresponds, namely the subject, is an external complement. The internalised complement is generally optional: clauses in which it is present we call long passives, as opposed to short passives like *I was attacked.*

Pragmatic constraints

Use of the information-packaging constructions in discourse tends to be more constrained than that of the syntactically more basic constructions. Two important factors involved in these constraints are the familiarity status of the information expressed and the weight of syntactic constituents.

Information that is familiar, or **old**, is information that the speaker assumes to be shared by speaker and addressee. If it is derivable from the preceding discourse, it is discourse-old information; addressee-old information covers this together with other information that the addressee is assumed to be familiar with. Information that is not old is **new**.

Weight has to do with the length or complexity of constituents. Thus *the book she was reading* is heavier than *the book*, but the latter is heavier than *it.* Postposing, as in [1ii], generally depends on the constituent concerned being relatively heavy: replacement of *all the money she had left him* by, say, *ten dollars*, would very strongly favour the version where the object occupies its default position immediately after the verb.

17 Deixis and anaphora

The last of the chapters on syntax deals with deixis and anaphora, phenomena which cut across the division between the parts of speech and which are found in both canonical and non-canonical clause constructions.

Deictic expressions include temporal *now*, *yesterday*, *today*, *tomorrow*, locative *here* and *there*, demonstrative ***this*** and ***that***, the personal pronouns ***I***, ***we***, and ***you***, and primary tense. The property common to such expressions is that their reference is determined in relation to certain features of the utterance-act: essentially, when and where it takes place, who is speaking to whom, the relative proximity of entities to the speaker.

Anaphora is the relation between an anaphor and an antecedent, as in *Jill has left her car in the road*, in the interpretation where the reference is to Jill's car. *Jill* is here the antecedent and *her* the anaphor: the interpretation of the anaphor derives from that of the antecedent. We will often represent the anaphoric relation by co-indexing antecedent and anaphor: *Jill*$_i$ *has left her*$_i$ *car in the road.* In this example, the anaphor is a personal pronoun; we call such anaphors 'pro-forms', a term which also covers various forms which are not pronouns, such as *so* (*Grapes are expensive*$_i$ *and likely to remain* <u>*so*</u>$_i$ *for some time*), *do so* (*I haven't told them*$_i$ *yet, but I'll do so*$_i$ *tomorrow*), and ***one*** (*This banana*$_i$ *is green: have you got a riper one*$_i$*?*). Anaphors may also be gaps, as in the elliptical *I'd like to help you*$_i$ *but I can't* __$_i$.

An anaphor generally follows its antecedent, but under restricted conditions it may precede, as in *If you can* __$_i$, *please come a little earlier next week*$_i$.

3

The verb

RODNEY HUDDLESTON

1 Inflectional categories of the verb

This section is concerned with the question of what inflectional distinctions apply in the English verbal system: how many different forms of a lexeme need to be recognised, and how are they to be named? The question of how the forms of a lexeme are derived from its lexical base is a morphological one, and is dealt with in Ch. 18.

1.1 Summary presentation of the categories

We begin with a brief listing of the inflectional categories of verbs. Each inflectional category will be taken up in turn in §§1.3–9, after an explanation of the concept of syncretism.

Lexical vs auxiliary verbs

The two main types of verbs in English are the **auxiliary** verbs, comprising a small list of verbs with very specific syntactic properties, and the non-auxiliary verbs, i.e. all the rest of the verbs in the dictionary, which we will call the **lexical** verbs. The two types of verb differ in inflectional morphology as well as syntax.

Lexical verbs: the six-term paradigm

The set of inflectional forms of a variable lexeme is called a **paradigm**, and virtually all lexical verbs have a paradigm with six forms, as illustrated in [1].

[1]

			take	***want***	***hit***
Primary	preterite		*took*	*wanted*	*hit*
	present tense	3rd sg	*takes*	*wants*	*hits*
		plain	*take*	*want*	*hit*
Secondary	plain form		*take*	*want*	*hit*
	gerund-participle		*taking*	*wanting*	*hitting*
	past participle		*taken*	*wanted*	*hit*

Auxiliary verbs

The auxiliary verbs depart from the above system in three main ways.

(a) Negative forms

Auxiliaries, unlike lexical verbs, have an extra set of primary forms: the **negative** forms. Thus ***can*** has the preterite form *couldn't*, and the auxiliary verb ***have*** has the 3rd person singular present tense form *hasn't*, but we do not have **tookn't* in the paradigm of ***take***, or **wantsn't* for ***want***.

(b) Modal auxiliaries

The **modal** auxiliaries, ***can***, ***may***, ***must***, etc., are **defective**, i.e. they lack certain inflectional forms and hence cannot occur in constructions requiring these forms. All of them lack all of the secondary forms and hence are excluded from such constructions as **I'd like to <u>can</u> swim* (no plain form), **I regret not <u>canning</u> swim* (no gerund-participle), **I have could swim since I was three* (no past participle). In addition, ***must*** and one or two others lack preterite forms (**I must see the Dean yesterday*). A further special property of the modal auxiliaries is that they have a single present tense form that occurs with all subjects (there is no 3rd person singular present tense form with a suffixed ·*s*).

(c) Additional forms for ***be***

Be shows more person–number agreement than other verbs, and also has an irrealis mood form *were*.

In [2] we show the paradigms for ***have*** and ***can***, the latter having only primary forms. Notice the complete lack of secondary forms with the latter.

[2]

			have		***can***	
			neutral	negative	neutral	negative
Primary	preterite		*had*	*hadn't*	*could*	*couldn't*
	present tense	3rd sg	*has*	*hasn't*	*can*	*can't*
		plain	*have*	*haven't*		
Secondary	plain form		*have*	–	–	–
	gerund-participle		*having*	–	–	–
	past participle		*had*	–	–	–

In [3] we give the paradigm of the primary forms of ***be***; the secondary forms are *be* (plain form), *being* (gerund-participle), and *been* (past participle).

[3]

		Neutral			Negative		
		1st sg	3rd sg	Other	1st sg	3rd sg	Other
Primary	Present tense	*am*	*is*	*are*	*aren't*	*isn't*	*aren't*
	Preterite	*was*		*were*	*wasn't*		*weren't*
	Irrealis	*were*		–	*weren't*		–

1.2 Syncretism

When two or more forms of a lexeme are identical we say that there is **syncretism** between them, or that they are **syncretised.** For example, there is syncretism between the preterite and past participle of ***want***: both are **realised** as *wanted.*

The justification for recognising syncretism

We recognise two forms with the spelling *wanted* (the preterite and the past participle), instead of just one (labelled '*ed*-form', perhaps), because allowing syncretism permits the grammar to be stated in more general terms than if we dealt directly with the realisations. Consider, for example:

		a.		b.	
[4]	i	a.	*She wanted the car.*	b. *She took/*taken the car.*	[preterite]
	ii	a.	*She had wanted the car.*	b. *She had taken/*took the car.*	[past participle]

Take has *took* and *taken* as overtly distinct forms, with preterite *took* occurring, for example, in construction [i], as the first (or only) verb of a canonical clause, and past participle *taken* in [ii], the perfect construction. If we extend the distinction from ***take*** to ***want*** (and other such verbs) the *wanted* of [ia] will be analysed as a preterite form and that of [ib] as a past participle, and this enables us to say that the first (or only) verb of a canonical clause can appear in the preterite form but not the past participle, and conversely that a verb in construction with the perfect auxiliary ***have*** must be in the past participle form.

Principles for deciding how much syncretism to allow

Traditional grammar postulates a great deal more syncretism than we have in [1]: instead of the six forms we propose there are no less than thirty in the traditional analysis.[1] This gives a very misleading account of the contemporary language, one that fails to recognise that during the course of its historical development English has lost much of its earlier inflectional system. We have based the analysis of [1–3] on the following principles:

[5] i An inflectional distinction is accepted between two forms only if there is at least one lexeme with a stable contrast in realisation between those two forms.

ii Inflectional distinctions involving agreement properties are not generalised from one lexeme to another.

Principle [i] requires that a proposed inflectional distinction be morphologically marked – signalled by some actual prefix or suffix or some other overt distinction – in at least one lexeme. Inflection is **morphosyntactic**: an inflectional difference is a difference in morphological form that reflects a difference in syntactic properties. For example,

[1] Leaving aside the forms consisting of more than one word (*will take, has taken*, etc.), the traditional paradigm is as follows:

FINITE	Indicative		Subjunctive		Imperative	NON-FINITE	
	Past	Pres	Past	Pres	Pres		
1st sg	*took*	*take*	*took*	*take*		Infinitive	*take*
2nd sg	*took*	*take*	*took*	*take*	*take*	Gerund	*taking*
3rd sg	*took*	*takes*	*took*	*take*		Present participle	*taking*
1st pl	*took*	*take*	*took*	*take*		Past participle	*taken*
2nd pl	*took*	*take*	*took*	*take*	*take*		
3rd pl	*took*	*take*	*took*	*take*			

the difference in form between *took* and *taken* reflects the syntactic difference between preterite and past participle, so this difference is not just syntactic but morphosyntactic. But if a syntactic distinction is never marked by a difference in morphological form there is no reason for saying that it is morphosyntactic, hence no reason for saying that it is inflectional. Consider, for example:

[6] i *I'm warning you, [take careful note of what they say].* [imperative]
ii *It is essential [that he take careful note of what they say].* [subjunctive]

The bracketed clauses represent two syntactically distinct constructions: imperative and subjunctive. But no matter what lexeme we might select in such clauses, the form of the verb is always the same. This is true even with the verb ***be***, which has more distinctions of form than any other verb: compare *Be patient* and *It is essential [that he be patient]*. It follows that we have no reason to say that the constructions contain different inflectional forms of the verb: imperative and subjunctive are different syntactic types of clause, but those terms do not pick out different inflectional forms of the verb.

Principle [5ii] distinguishes agreement features from others involved in inflection. To say that *X* agrees with *Y* is to say that if *Y* changes then *X* must change too. In the preterite such agreement is found between the verb and the subject with ***be*** but not with other verbs:

[7] i a. *She was ill.* b. *They were ill.* [verb agrees with subject]
ii a. *She looked ill.* b. *They looked ill.* [no agreement]

When we change the subject from *she* to *they* in [i] we must change the preterite from *was* to *were*: there are two preterite forms whose person–number properties match those of the subject. But in [ii] *looked* remains constant, so that there is no basis for saying that the preterite of ***look*** agrees with the subject. Here, then, there is just one preterite form and it has no person–number properties at all. And the same of course applies to all verbs other than ***be***.

We will now return to the analysis presented in §1.1, comparing it with traditional grammar in the light of these principles, and explaining the terminology adopted.

1.3 The past participle

Perfect and passive

The past participle is used in two constructions, the perfect and the passive, where it prototypically follows the auxiliaries ***have*** and ***be*** respectively:

[8] i *I have written him a long letter.* [perfect]
ii *The letter was written by her secretary.* [passive]

Virtually all verbs appear in the perfect construction, whereas the passive is largely restricted to transitive verbs like ***write*** in [ii] or 'prepositional' verbs such as ***refer*** or ***rely*** (i.e. verbs which take a complement with a specified preposition: ***refer*** + *to*. . . , ***rely*** + *on* . . .), as in *This matter was referred to in my earlier letter*. The verbs ***be***, ***die***, ***seem***, for example, do not occur in the passive. But there are no verbs where the form used in the passive is different from that used in the perfect. For this reason we take the perfect and passive constructions to involve different uses of the same inflectional form, not different forms.

Clause-head and attributive uses

The past participle is also found without the perfect and passive auxiliaries, as in:

[9] i *I came across a letter written ten years ago.* [head of clause]
ii *He showed me a hurriedly written first draft.* [attributive]

Such constructions almost always involve the passive use of the past participle: [i] and [ii], for example, are comparable to *The letter was written ten years ago* and *The first draft was written hurriedly*, which contain the passive auxiliary ***be***. Construction [9i] allows the past participle to be followed by the same range of dependents as it can have in [8ii]: compare *I came across a letter written by her secretary.* For this reason we analyse *written ten years ago* as a clause with the verb *written* as its head. But *written* in [9ii] cannot be followed by dependents in this way (**a hurriedly written by her secretary first draft*), and *hurriedly written* does not have the structure of a clause: we will refer to it as an attributive VP.

The concept of participle

The central idea in the traditional concept of participle is that it is a word formed from a verb base which functions as or like an adjective. A second general property of participles is that these words are also used in combination with an auxiliary to form a compound tense, aspect, mood, or voice.

The adjective-like character of *written* is seen in [9]. The most elementary type of noun-modifier is an adjective (as in *a long letter, a careless draft*), so *written* is like an adjective in that it heads an expression with the same noun-modifying function as an adjective. The secondary feature of forming compound tenses is illustrated in [8] – note that here, certainly in the perfect use in *have written*, there is nothing adjective-like about the form. It is its use in the perfect construction that provides the basis for the 'past' component of the name, for the perfect is a kind of past tense. No element of pastness applies to the passive use, but it is predominantly the passive that is involved in noun-modifying constructions like [9], which fit the central part of the definition of participle. 'Past participle' is therefore a reasonably good name for a form with the above spread of uses. It should be emphasised, however, that the inclusion of 'past' in the name does not imply that the past participle is itself a tensed form: it is a participle which occurs in construction with the past tense auxiliary ***have***.

Participle as verb-form vs participial adjective

The formulation we used above – 'a word formed from a verb base which functions as or like an adjective' – is non-committal as to whether the word is in fact a verb or an adjective. Dictionary definitions commonly use the expression 'verbal adjective', implying a subtype of adjective. That certainly won't do for the examples above, where the words concerned are verbs, but there are other constructions where words of this kind are indeed to be classified as adjectives. In such cases we talk of a **participial adjective**, reserving 'participle' itself for verbs. Compare:

[10] i *It was broken deliberately, out of spite.* [past participle form of verb]
ii *It didn't look broken to me.* [past-participial adjective]
iii *It was broken.* [ambiguous]

The verb *broken* in [i] denotes an event, while the adjective *broken* in [ii] denotes a state – and the ambiguity of [iii] lies precisely in the fact that it can be interpreted in either of these ways. We take the verb to be more basic, with the adjective formed from it (cf. Ch. 19, §3.4).

We will look more fully at this distinction in Ch. 16, §10.1.3; here we draw attention to certain grammatical differences which justify drawing a distinction between verbs and adjectives with words of this kind.

(a) Complementation

Certain types of complement are found with verbs but not with adjectives – notably objects and predicative complements. The following are therefore unambiguously verbs:

[11] i *He quickly spent the money given him by his uncle.* [verb + indirect object]
ii *They sacked those considered guilty of bias.* [verb + predicative comp]

(b) Occurrence with *seem*

Verbs such as *seem, appear, look, remain* take AdjPs as complement, but not participial clauses. This is why *broken* in [10ii] is unambiguously an adjective, and why the ambiguity of [10iii] is resolved in favour of the adjective (state) reading if we replace *be* by *seem*: *It seemed broken.* Compare, similarly:

[12] i *The picture seemed excellent/distorted.* [*seem* + adjective]
ii **The boss seemed considered guilty of bias.* [*seem* + verb]

(c) Modification by *very* or *too*

The degree adverbs *very* and *too* can modify adjectives but not verbs: *It was very/too dangerous* (adjective), not **It very/too frightened me* (verb).

[13] i *He was [very frightened] / [too frightened to move].* [adjective]
ii **The plants were [very/too watered] by the gardener.* [verb]

Note, however, that not all adjectives take this modification – we can hardly have *?It didn't look very/too broken to me*, for example. Criterion (c) therefore works in only one direction: if the word in question can be modified by *very* or *too* it must be an adjective, not a verb, but if it can't be so modified it could be either.

In the light of this distinction between participial adjectives and participle forms of verbs we can clarify the nature of the functional resemblance between participle and adjective that forms the basis for the general definition. In examples like [9] it is not a matter of the word *written* itself having a function like that of an adjective, but of *written* being head of an expression whose function is like that of an expression headed by an adjective, i.e. of an AdjP. The functional resemblance is at the level not of words but of larger constituents, such as those underlined in *a letter written ten years ago* and *a very old letter*. At the level of words, verbs and adjectives differ significantly with respect to the dependents they take.

1.4 The gerund-participle

This form covers the gerund and present participle of traditional grammar, which are always identical in form.

The traditional present participle

This has uses comparable to those of the past participle:

[14] i *The train to Bath is now approaching Platform 3.* [with progressive auxiliary]
ii *The train approaching Platform 3 is the 11.10 to Bath.* [head of clause]
iii *He threw it in the path of an approaching train.* [attributive]

Constructions [ii–iii] are those where the present participle is functionally comparable to an adjective in that it is head of an expression modifying a noun, and in [i] it combines with an auxiliary to form the progressive aspect. It is called the 'present' participle because the time associated with it is characteristically the same as that expressed or implied in the larger construction containing it (but see also §7). In [i] and [ii] the time of approaching is simultaneous with the time of speaking, but that is because the larger construction has present tense *is*. There would be no change in the form or meaning of *approaching* if we changed *is* to *was* to give *The train to Bath was approaching Platform 3*. 'Present', therefore, is to be understood in a relative rather than absolute sense: the approaching is present relative to the time given in the larger construction. Again, however, it must be emphasised that the traditional present participle is not a tensed form of the verb.

Verb-form vs participial adjective

As with the past participle, we need to distinguish cases where the word in question is a verb from those where it is an adjective. Compare:

[15] i *They are entertaining the prime minister and her husband.* [form of verb]
ii *The show was entertaining.* [participial adjective]
iii *Her parents are entertaining.* [ambiguous]

The verbal interpretation of [iii] is "Her parents are entertaining some guests", the adjectival one roughly "Her parents have entertaining qualities". The constructions can be distinguished grammatically by the same criteria as we used for past participles in §1.3.

(a) Complementation

Verbs can take NP objects, whereas adjectives normally do not. Compare, for example, *Kim loves Pat* with the ungrammatical **Kim is fond Pat.* The ungrammaticality of the latter results from a requirement of the adjective *fond*: it requires a PP complement with *of* (*Kim is fond of Pat*). Consider, then:

[16] i *You're frightening me.* [form of verb]
ii *Such a prospect is frightening indeed.* [participial adjective]

The object *me* in [i] is a clear indication that *frightening* must here be a verb, and since the verb ***frighten*** (in the relevant sense of "cause fright") is more or less impossible without an object, *frightening* in [ii] will be interpreted as an adjective. Note that ***frighten*** differs in this respect from ***entertain***, which does occur quite readily without an object (cf. *They like to entertain*): this is why [15iii] can have a verbal as well as an adjectival interpretation.

(b) Occurrence with *seem*

We have noted that verbs like *seem* take AdjPs as complement, but not participial clauses. They can therefore substitute for *be* in [15ii] but not in [i]:[2]

[17] i *They are/*seem entertaining the prime minister and her husband.* [verb]
ii *The show was/seemed entertaining.* [adjective]

(c) Modification by *very* or *too*

As these degree adverbs can modify adjectives but not verbs they can be inserted in [15ii] but not [15i]:

[18] i **They are very entertaining the prime minister and her husband.*
ii *The show was very entertaining.*

Ambiguities between verb and adjective, as in [15iii] (*Her parents are entertaining*) are possible, but they are not common.

The traditional gerund

A gerund is traditionally understood as a word derived from a verb base which functions as or like a noun, as in:

[19] i *Destroying the files was a serious mistake.*
ii *I regret destroying the files.*

Destroying the files could be replaced by *the destruction of the files*, where *destruction* is clearly a noun. The primary difference between a gerund and a participle, therefore, is that while a participle is functionally comparable to an adjective, a gerund is functionally comparable to a noun. There is also a secondary difference: that gerunds do not combine with auxiliaries in the way that participles do.

Verb vs noun

As with the participle, we have used the formulation 'as or like' in talking of the functional resemblance between a gerund and a noun, leaving open the issue of whether the word is verb or noun. Dictionaries tend to define the gerund as a verbal noun, but there are strong grounds for analysing *destroying* in [19] as a verb, and for drawing a distinction between such words and others ending in ·*ing* which genuinely are nouns and which we refer to therefore as **gerundial nouns**:

[20] i *He was expelled for killing the birds.* [form of verb]
ii *She had witnessed the killing of the birds.* [gerundial noun]

The main grammatical differences are as follows:

(a) Complementation

Verbs and nouns differ in the kinds of complement they take. Most notably, transitive verbs can take NP objects whereas the corresponding nouns take an *of* PP: compare *the*

[2] Participial clauses were found with *seem* in the nineteenth century (and even occasionally in the twentieth), as in *The storms seemed clearing away from his path*: the loss of this construction has strengthened the category distinction between verb and adjective.

birds in [20i] with *of the birds* in [ii]. Note also that we find predicative complements with verbs but not with nouns: *He has a fear of seeming unintelligent*, but not **He has a fear of the seeming unintelligent*.

(b) Modification by adjective or adverb

Nouns are characteristically modified by adjectives, but the corresponding modifiers of verbs are adverbs:

[21] i *He was expelled for wantonly killing the birds.* [adverb + verb]
ii *She had witnessed the wanton killing of the birds.* [adjective + noun]

(c) Determiners

The and comparable determiners combine with nouns, not verbs. Thus we cannot have **the killing the birds* – only the NP *the killing of the birds* or the VP *killing the birds*.

(d) Plural inflection

Gerundial nouns can very often inflect for plural, as in *These killings must stop*. This is never possible with the verbs: **Killings the birds must stop*.

Note again, then, that the functional resemblance between *destroying* in [19] and the noun *destruction* is not at the level of words but at the level of the larger constituents that they head – between the clause *destroying the files* and the NP *the destruction of the files* rather than between the verb *destroying* and the noun *destruction*. At the level of the word, verb and noun are quite sharply distinct by virtue of the different dependents they take. Where no such dependents are present, ambiguities can arise:

[22] i *Kim hates writing thank-you letters.* [verb]
ii *Kim hadn't been involved in the writing of the letter.* [noun]
iii *Kim had been talking about writing.* [ambiguous]

In [i] the presence of a following object shows *writing* to be a verb; in [ii] *the* and the *of* phrase show it to be a noun; and in [iii], where it occurs alone, it could be either. In the verb interpretation of [iii] *writing* will have an understood object (very likely a letter) and also an understood subject (very likely it is a matter of Kim writing); in the noun interpetation *writing* denotes the phenomenon and is comparable to *speech*, which is unambiguously a noun.[3]

A distinction between gerund and present participle can't be sustained

Historically the gerund and present participle of traditional grammar have different sources, but in Modern English the forms are identical. No verb shows any difference in form in the constructions of [14] and [19], not even ***be***. The historical difference is of no relevance to the analysis of the current inflectional system, and in accordance with principle [5i] we reject an analysis that has gerund and present participle as different forms syncretised throughout the class of verbs. We have therefore just one inflectional form of the verb marked by the ·*ing* suffix; we label it with the compound term 'gerund-participle' for the verb-form, as there is no reason to give priority to one or other of

[3] Both noun and verb can take genitives as dependent, as in *I can't read his writing* (noun) and *There would be no point in his writing another letter at this stage* (verb); we discuss this issue in Ch. 14, §1.6.

the traditional terms. The compound term serves also to bring out the relationship between this form and the past participle: the gerund-participle has a considerably wider distribution than the past participle (which doesn't, for example, occur in constructions like [19i]), and yet the two forms have it in common that they head expressions modifying nouns, as in [9] and [14ii–iii].[4] This grammar also takes the view that even from the point of view of syntax (as opposed to inflection) the distinction between gerund and present participle is not viable, and we will therefore also not talk of gerund and present participle constructions: we argue the case for this position in Ch. 14, §4.3.

In summary, words with a verb base and the ·*ing* suffix fall into the following three classes:

[23]	i	*She had witnessed the* <u>*killing*</u> *of the birds.*	[gerundial noun]
	ii	a. *He was expelled for* <u>*killing*</u> *the birds.*	[gerund-participle form of verb]
		b. *They are* <u>*entertaining*</u> *the prime minister.*	
	iii	*The show was* <u>*entertaining*</u>.	[participial adjective]

1.5 The plain form

The last of the secondary forms, the plain form, is used in the following three constructions:

[24]	i	<u>*Be*</u> *on your guard.*	[imperative]
	ii	*It is essential* [*that she* <u>*be*</u> *on her guard*].	[subjunctive]
	iii	*It is important* [*to* <u>*be*</u> *always on your guard*].	[infinitival]

We pointed out in §1.2 that there is never any morphological difference between the form a verb has in the imperative construction and the form it has in the subjunctive construction, and we can now add that the form concerned is also identical with that used in the infinitival construction.

Given that the three constructions in [24] always select identical verb-forms, it is inappropriate to take imperative, subjunctive, and infinitival as inflectional categories. That, however, is what traditional grammar does, again retaining distinctions that were valid at an earlier stage of the language but have since been lost: they have no place in the inflectional system of Present-day English.

As far as terminology is concerned, there is no reason to pick out one of the three constructions as more basic than the others. This time, however, a compound term, 'imperative-subjunctive-infinitive', would be far too unwieldy, and we have therefore chosen the term 'plain form', which is oriented towards morphology rather than meaning or syntax. The form consists simply of the lexical base, the plain base without any suffix or other modification.

Precisely because it is the morphologically most elementary form, this is the one we use as the **citation form** for verbs, i.e. the one we put in bold face to represent the lexeme as a whole.

[4] Some modern grammars use '-*ing* form' for gerund-participle and '-*en* form' for past participle (the ·*en* suffix of *taken*, *eaten*, etc., being one that is never used to form preterites). These labels have mnemonic value but are unsuitable as general terms: they do not relate the categories concerned to comparable ones in other languages.

Infinitival *to* is not part of the verb

The traditional practice for citation of verbs is to cite them with the infinitival marker *to*, as in '*to be*', '*to take*', and so on. That is an unsatisfactory convention, because the *to* is not part of the verb itself. It is not a (morphological) prefix but a quite separate (syntactic) word. This is evident from the fact that it can stand on its own in elliptical constructions as in [25i], need not be repeated in coordination as seen in [25ii], and can be separated from the verb by an adverb as seen in [25iii] (the so-called 'split infinitive construction', discussed in Ch. 6, §7.1):

[25] i *I haven't read it yet but I hope <u>to</u> shortly.*
ii *I want <u>to</u> [<u>go out</u> and <u>get some exercise</u>].*
iii *I'm trying <u>to</u> gradually <u>improve</u> my game.*

1.6 The present tense forms

Most verbs have two present tense forms, with the choice between them normally determined by agreement with the subject. The 3rd person singular form *takes* is so called, therefore, because it occurs with 3rd person singular subjects. The other form, *take*, occurs with 1st and 2nd person singular and all plural subjects. It might be called the 'non-3rd-person-singular present tense'; we have preferred 'plain present tense' partly because it is simpler, partly to draw attention to the fact that with verbs other than ***be*** this form is syncretised with the plain form.

Syncretism between the plain present tense and the plain form

This syncretism is the most problematic feature of our analysis. An alternative would be to say that lexical verbs have only five inflectional forms, that the *take* of *They take no notice of her* is not a different inflectional form from the plain form but merely a further use of it, beyond the three illustrated in [24]. There are nevertheless several points that can be made in support of an analysis where the plain present tense is recognised as a distinct inflectional form.

(a) Overt morphological contrast with *be*

The main point is that with the verb ***be*** we do not have syncretism between the plain form and a present tense form. The examples in [24] contrast with:

[26] *You <u>are</u> on your guard.* [present tense]

This is a very sharp distinction. The imperative, subjunctive, and infinitival in [24] are morphologically identical, but the present tense is morphologically distinct from them. This is sufficient to establish an inflectional contrast, in accordance with principle [5i]. There are other respects in which the plain present tense differs from the plain form.

(b) Tense contrast

The two forms occupy very different positions within the verbal system: the present contrasts in tense with the preterite, while the plain form is tenseless. The difference is brought out by such examples as these:

[27] i a. *I think they <u>take</u> their son to school by car.* [present tense]
b. *I thought they <u>took</u> their son to school by car.* [preterite]
ii a. *We demand that they <u>be</u> reinstated.* } [plain form]
b. *We demanded that they <u>be</u> reinstated.* }

The tense contrast in [i] is not matched in [ii]; traditional grammar takes the *be* of [ii] to be a present subjunctive, but there is no justification for assigning tense to it (or for regarding *I be* and *I were* as contrasting in tense: see §1.7 below).

(c) Person–number contrast

The plain present contrasts with the 3rd person singular present: it is normally restricted to plural or 1st/2nd person subjects, whereas in the imperative, subjunctive, and infinitival constructions the form of the verb is unaffected by the subject. If we replace *they* by *she* in [27ia], *take* changes to *takes*, but the same replacement in [iia] has no effect on the verb.

(d) Defective morphology of the modal auxiliaries

The modals have only tensed forms. They lack a plain form, just as they lack a past participle and gerund-participle. Compare:

[28] i *They can recite it by heart.* [present tense]
ii **Can recite it by heart by the end of the week.* [imperative]
iii **It is important for them to can recite it by heart.* [infinitival]

Instead of [ii] and [iii] we would have to use *be able*: *Be able to recite it by heart by the end of the week*, *It is important for them to be able to recite it by heart.* Similarly in the subjunctive: *It is essential that they be able to recite it by heart*; *can* is not impossible here, but that is because the subjunctive alternates with a tensed construction: *It is essential that they are able to / can recite it by heart* (cf. Ch. 11, §7.1.1).

1.7 The preterite and irrealis *were*

Three uses of the preterite

The preterite has three distinct uses illustrated in [29]:

[29] i *She always took her dog with her.* [past time]
ii *If he took the later plane tonight he wouldn't have to rush.* [modal remoteness]
iii *Kim said I took things too seriously.* [backshift]

The difference between these is most easily seen by comparing them with the corresponding present tense forms:

[30] i *She always takes her dog with her.*
ii *If he takes the later plane tonight he won't have to rush.*
iii *Kim said I take things too seriously.*

With [29i] and [30i] the difference is straightforwardly a matter of time: *took* indicates that I am talking about a time in the past. The difference between [29ii] and [30ii], however, is not one of time: in both cases I'm talking about future time. They belong to two different kinds of conditional construction which we call **remote** and **open**: [30ii] presents his taking the later plane tonight as an open possibility, whereas [29ii] presents it as a more remote one. Such a difference belongs to the area of meaning called modality, so that we speak of the preterite here as expressing modal remoteness (as explained in §6.1). The modal remoteness use is also found in the complement of the verb *wish*, as in *I wish I had my umbrella with me.* The time here is present, but the clause has a counterfactual interpretation, i.e. you understand that I don't have my umbrella with me. Finally, [29iii] and [30iii] could both be used to report Kim's saying to me: *You take things too seriously.* The present tense of the original utterance is retained in [30iii] but replaced in [29iii] with a preterite; we will keep the traditional term **backshift** here, saying that preterite *took* is a backshifted counterpart of present *take.*

Of the three uses illustrated in [29] the past time one is clearly the most basic. The modal remoteness use is found (with lexical verbs) only in a few subordinate constructions, and backshift is restricted to cases of explicit or implicit reported speech, or comparable kinds of subordination. By virtue of its past time use, therefore, we say that *took* is a past tense, and since we also regard the perfect as a past tense we refer to *took* more specifically as the preterite.[5] This term is applicable to past tenses that are expressed inflectionally, rather than by means of an auxiliary, like the perfect.

The mood contrast between *was* and *were*

With 2nd person and plural subjects, *were* is the form of ***be*** used for past time, modal remoteness, and backshift, but with 1st and 3rd person singular subjects, there are two forms to account for, *was* and *were*:

[31]	i	*I was very busy.*	[preterite]
	ii	*If I were less busy I would go with you.*	[irrealis]

There are three issues to consider here. First, we take up the descriptive issue of where the two forms are found, i.e. of their 'distribution'. The main use of irrealis *were* is to express modal remoteness, but for some speakers it extends to certain related constructions, where it has something of the character of a hypercorrection. The second issue concerns the relation between what we are calling 'irrealis' *were* and the subjunctive construction of *It is essential* [*that she be on her guard*] ([24ii]), since traditional grammar analyses both as subjunctive. Third, we explain why we do not extend the irrealis category beyond the 1st and 3rd person singular of ***be***.

The modal remoteness use of irrealis *were* and preterite *was*

The main use of irrealis *were* is in subordinate constructions where the preterite of other verbs has the modal remoteness meaning – remote conditionals (with *if, as if, as though,* etc.), and the complement of *wish, would rather,* etc.:[6]

[32]	i	*He talks to me as if I were a child.*	[modal remoteness]
	ii	*I wish I were going with you.*	

Preterite *was*, however, is very widely used instead of irrealis *were* in these constructions, especially in informal style: *He talks to me as if I was a child, I wish I was going with you.*[7]

[5] An alternative, AmE, spelling is 'preterit'.

[6] Occasional examples are found of irrealis *were* in main clauses: %*Such a move were ill-advised* ("would be"). This is archaic, reflecting a stage of the language before a modal auxiliary was required in the main clause of an explicit or implicit remote conditional.

[7] *Was* has been in competition with *were* for 300–400 years, and in general the usage manuals regard it as acceptable, though less formal than *were*. Two places where *were* cannot be replaced by *was* are inverted conditionals (*I would certainly join them, were I not working on a project of my own*) and the fixed phrase *as it were*; *if I were you* bears some resemblance to a fixed phrase and *was* is less usual here than in conditionals generally.

Extended uses of irrealis *were*

For some speakers, irrealis *were* is not restricted to the modal remoteness constructions, but is found also in certain backshift and past time uses that bear some resemblance to them:

[33] i	%*She phoned to ascertain whether he were dining at the Club.*	[backshift]
ii	%*He looked at me as if he suspected I were cheating on him.*	
iii	%*If he were surprised, he didn't show it.*	[past time]

In [i] we have backshift in a closed interrogative (the 'original question' was "Is he dining at the Club?"). This construction allows *if* in place of *whether* (*to ascertain if he were dining*. . .), and this can be seen as providing a link to the central uses of irrealis *were*. In [ii] the backshift is in the complement of *suspect*, which in turn is within a conditional construction (though not, in this case, a modally remote one). Example [iii] is a conditional, but of the open type, not the remote (for a past time remote conditional requires a preterite perfect: *If he had been surprised, he would have shown it*). *Was* is much more usual than *were* in the constructions of [33], and for most speakers probably the only possibility. *Were* here clearly has something of the character of a 'hypercorrection': prescriptive grammar used to insist on *were* rather than *was* in modal remoteness constructions, and this may have led to the avoidance of *was* in certain neighbouring constructions.[8]

Irrealis and subjunctive

One striking weakness of the traditional analysis is that it treats the verbs of *I be* and *I were* as present and past tenses of a single mood, the subjunctive: this is quite unjustified in terms of the contemporary language. In general they appear in different constructions and are not in direct contrast, but in the one place where it is marginally possible to have a contrast the meaning difference is clearly not one of time but of modality:

[34] i	*If that be so, the plan will have to be revised.*	[subjunctive use of plain form]
ii	*If that were so, the plan would have to be revised.*	[irrealis]

Both are concerned with present time, but [ii] suggests much more than [i] that 'that' is not so. In its normal use, i.e. in modal remoteness constructions, irrealis *were* does not refer to past time, and there is no synchronic reason to analyse it as a past tense form. Similarly, *be* is not a present tense form because it has no tense at all, as we argued above on the basis of its failure to undergo backshift in constructions like [27iib] (*We demanded that they be reinstated*). Moreover, we have seen that there is no inflectional distinction between this *be* and the ones that occur in the imperative and infinitival constructions. The plain form *be*, therefore, has no inflectional property of either tense or mood; 1st/3rd person singular *were* is likewise a non-tensed form, but it does have mood.

[8] Examples like [i] and [iii] are mentioned in some usage manuals, and generally treated as incorrect; but they are found in the writings of highly prestigious authors. Another type of example we have encountered is: *The two theoretical extremes of such a scale of formal explicitness would be (a) the case where no information at all were expressed formally, and (b) the case where no information were expressed pragmatically.* *Were* is here in a relative construction embedded within a main clause containing a modal remoteness use of *would.*

The general term **subjunctive** is primarily used for a verbal mood that is characteristically associated with subordinate clauses with a non-factual interpretation. We are extending the term so that it applies to a syntactic construction rather than a verb-form, but our subjunctive clauses are still characteristically subordinate and non-factual. We need a different term for 1st/3rd person singular *were*: we call it **irrealis**, a general term applying to verb moods associated with unreality (i.e. where the proposition expressed is, or may well be, false).

Irrealis category applies only to ***be*** with a 1st/3rd person singular subject

The distinction between *was* and *were* in [31] is not sufficient to justify generalising a mood system to all verbs. As we have noted, *was* is a variant of *were* in the modal remoteness constructions, so that if we said that *took*, for example, could be the realisation of either a preterite or an irrealis, there would be no way of telling in cases like [29ii] (*If he took the later plane tonight he wouldn't have to rush*) whether it corresponded to *was* or to *were*, and hence no way of deciding whether it was preterite or irrealis. The encroachment of *were* into territory normally occupied by *was* exemplified in [33] is further evidence that we are not dealing here with a clear case of semantic or syntactic contrast. If we were to say that all verbs had a preterite–irrealis distinction we would be claiming that the massive coalescence of realisational forms that has taken place in the development of English has not produced a change in the system of verb inflection itself, but merely large-scale syncretism. It is much more plausible to say that irrealis *were* is an unstable remnant of an earlier system – a system which has otherwise been replaced by one in which the preterite has expanded its use in such a way that it now serves to express modal remoteness as well as past time.

1.8 Primary and secondary forms and the category of finiteness

Primary forms: forms with tense or mood inflection

The first division we have made within the verbal paradigm is between the primary and secondary forms: leaving aside the verb ***be***, the primary forms are the tensed ones, i.e. the preterite and present tense forms. These can be regarded as primary in that they are the ones that are found in canonical clauses: the secondary forms appear in various kinds of non-canonical clause, especially subordinate ones. Irrealis *were* is not used in canonical clauses, but is best classified with the tensed forms as it is normally in alternation with preterite *was* and occurs in constructions (such as those in [32–33]) which select tensed forms of other verbs. The primary forms can therefore be defined as the ones that are inflected for tense or mood, and the secondary forms as the remainder.

1.8.1 Finiteness as a syntactic rather than inflectional category in English

In the traditional analysis of English verb inflection the first division is between the finite and non-finite forms, but the revision we have made means that the finite/non-finite distinction is no longer definable simply in terms of inflection. We will see that there are grounds for not discarding it altogether, however, and we therefore reinterpret it as a syntactic category of the clause, rather than as an inflectional category of the verb. Clauses whose verb is a primary form are finite, those whose verb is a past participle or gerund-participle are non-finite, but those with a plain form verb can be either, depending on the construction:

[35]
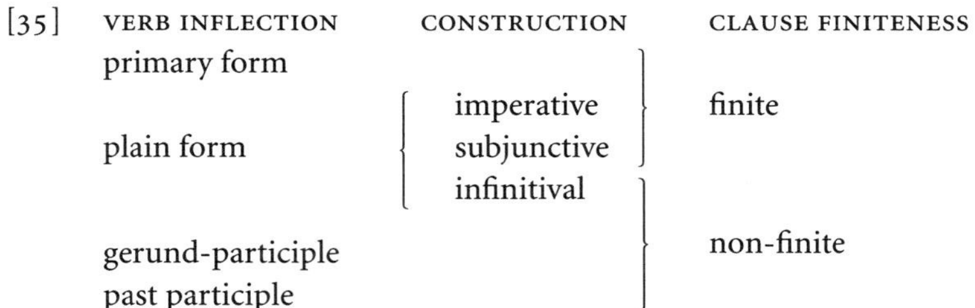

VERB INFLECTION
CONSTRUCTION
CLAUSE FINITENESS
primary form
plain form
imperative
subjunctive
infinitival
finite
gerund-participle
past participle
non-finite

Finite and non-finite as general categories

Non-finite clauses are characteristically subordinate, and non-finiteness can be seen as an instance of the phenomenon known as 'desententialisation', the loss of properties that are associated with a clause standing alone as a full sentence. The general term 'finite' is related to its everyday sense of "limited". More specifically, a finite verb is characteristically limited with respect to person and number. In its traditional application to English, for example, *takes* is finite in that it is limited to occurrence with a 3rd person singular subject. Being limited is thus a matter of being marked for the relevant categories. Generalising beyond person–number, we can think of finite verbs or clauses as marked for more categories than non-finite ones. This accounts for the connection between non-finiteness and subordination: a subordinate clause occurs within the structure of some larger clause and is commonly less explicit than a main clause because information which in a main clause has to be encoded in the grammatical structure can be simply inferred from the larger context.

Compare, for example:

[36]	i	*The boy was seen by the guard.*	[finite, main]
	ii	*The boy who was seen by the guard was her son.*	[finite, subordinate]
	iii	*The boy seen by the guard was her son.*	[non-finite, subordinate]

The underlined clause in [ii] differs from [i] by virtue of having as subject not *the boy* but the relative pronoun *who*, whose interpretation is derivable from the main clause, but in other respects it is just the same. In [iii], however, the structural accompaniment of subordination is much greater: the subject is missing altogether and so is the passive auxiliary ***be*** and the preterite inflection.

1.8.2 Constructions with a plain form verb: imperative, subjunctive, and infinitival

The prototypical finite clause contains a tensed verb (or irrealis *were*), but there are grounds for extending the boundaries of the category to include the imperative and subjunctive constructions too. These differ from infinitivals in significant ways, being much closer to the prototypical finite construction.

(a) Imperatives

These differ from non-finites in that they are virtually always main clauses.[9] They are like finite clauses, moreover, in that they take auxiliary ***do*** in the negative – compare:

[9] Note that although *You told me to be on my guard* can be used to report your saying *Be on your guard*, the subordinate clause *to be on my guard* is infinitival, not imperative (cf. Ch. 10, §9.8).

[37] i *They* <u>*don't*</u> *leave until tomorrow.* [tensed]
ii <u>*Don't*</u> *leave until tomorrow.* [imperative]
iii *I advise you* <u>*not*</u> *to leave* / **to* <u>*don't*</u> *leave until tomorrow.* [non-finite]

The subject can even occur in post-auxiliary position (*Don't you talk to me like that!*), a position which is otherwise quite impossible in clauses with secondary verbs. It is true that they usually have no subject, but the understood subject is recovered from the nature of the construction itself (as *you*) rather than from an element in the larger construction, as it most often is with non-finites.

(b) Subjunctives

These exclude auxiliary ***do***, and are usually subordinate: subjunctive main clauses are restricted to fixed phrases (*So be it!*, *Be that as it may*, etc.) or frames (*Long live. . . !*, *Far be it from me to. . . , etc.*). In other respects, however, they are more like tensed clauses than non-finites. In the first place the subject is an obligatory element. Secondly, the most productive use of the subjunctive construction takes the same subordinator as is found with tensed declaratives, *that*, as in the earlier *We demand that he be reinstated*, etc. And, thirdly, except in more or less fixed expressions, the subjunctive alternates with a tensed construction:

[38] i *It is important* [*that she* <u>*be*</u> *reinstated immediately*]. [subjunctive]
ii *It is important* [*that she* <u>*is*</u> / <u>*should be*</u> *reinstated immediately*]. [tensed]

(c) Infinitivals

These are almost invariably subordinate, and the range of functions is closely comparable to that of gerund-participials and past-participials, which are clear cases of the non-finite construction. Like gerund-participials and past-participials, infinitivals usually have no overt subject. Those that do contain a subject are introduced by a different subordinator from that used in tensed declaratives, *for* rather than *that*, and personal pronouns appear in accusative case, not nominative as in tensed clauses. Compare:

[39] i *It is unusual* [<u>*for*</u> <u>*him*</u> *to be so late*]. [infinitival]
ii *It is annoying* [<u>*that*</u> <u>*he*</u> *is so late*]. [finite]

It is clear, then, that although infinitivals have the same verb-form as imperatives and subjunctives, they belong more closely with gerund-participials and past-participials in terms of their distribution and structure. Infinitivals, gerund-participials, and past-participials constitute the non-finites of traditional grammar: we have retained the membership of the class while changing the interpretation and definition.

1.9 Negative forms

The primary forms of auxiliaries can normally be either **neutral** or **negative**. The neutral ones are so called because they can occur in both positive and negative clauses:

[40] i *She* <u>*will*</u> *read it.* } [neutral form]
ii *She* <u>*will*</u> *not read it.* }
iii *She* <u>*won't*</u> *read it.* [negative form]

The clause is positive in [i], negative in [ii–iii], but only in [iii] is the negation marked inflectionally on the verb. In [ii] the negation is **analytic**, marked by a separate word (*not*), with the form of the verb, *will*, being the same as in the positive clause. The full set of negative forms is given in Ch. 18, §5.5.

Negative inflection vs contraction

Forms like *won't* are commonly regarded as 'contractions' of *will* + *not*, and so on, but there are compelling reasons for analysing them differently from cases like *she'll* (from *she* + *will*), *they've* (*they* + *have*), etc. *Won't* is, by every criterion, a single grammatical word, an inflectional form of ***will***. *She'll* is not a single grammatical word, hence not an inflectional form. Rather, *'ll* (pronounced /l/) is a **clitic** form of *will*, i.e. a reduced form that is joined phonologically (and orthographically) to an independent word called its **host**. The host in the case of *she'll* is the pronoun *she*. The written forms *she'll*, *they've*, etc., are pronounced as single monosyllabic words phonologically but correspond to two-word sequences syntactically.

Evidence for this analysis is seen in:

[41]	i	*Won't* / **Will not she be glad?*	[not replaceable by *will not*]
	ii	*He says she'll read it, but she* WON'T / *will* NOT.	[contrastive negation]

Example [i] shows that *won't* is not always replaceable by *will not* (as *she'll* always is by *she will*), and in such cases a contraction analysis is not viable. In [ii] the small capitals indicate contrastive negation marked by stress. A clitic cannot bear stress (cliticisation is an extreme case of the phonological reduction that is available only for words that are unstressed). Note, for example, that in *He says she won't read it, but she* WILL, the stress prevents the reduction of *she* WILL to SHE'LL: if *won't* involved cliticisation like *she'll*, therefore, it would not occur with emphatic negation.

A further point is that the phonological form of *won't* is not predictable by general rule from *will* + *not* (as the form of *she'll* is a predictable reduction of *she* + *will*). The irregularity of the negative form *won't* is comparable to that of the preterite form *would*: such irregularity is a common phenomenon in inflectional morphology, but is not explicable in terms of cliticisation. Not all the negative auxiliary forms are irregular, of course, but the fact that some are is an indication that we are dealing with inflection.

The historical **origin** of the negative forms as contractions of the word *not* in casual styles of speech is nonetheless transparent. In writing this is reflected in the use of the apostrophe, which once indicated a vowel omitted. And in consequence the negative forms are therefore like genuine synchronic contractions (e.g. clitic *'ll*) in one respect: they are felt to be informal, and are generally avoided in the most formal styles, especially in writing (see Ch. 9, §2.1).

Notice that this book is **not** written in strictly formal style, and we make considerable use of negative auxiliaries.

Negative of plain form

Do is exceptional in that it has a negative of the plain form, used solely in the imperative: *Don't eat it. Don't* can of course also be a plain present tense form, as in *They don't eat it*: we have syncretism, just as we do with neutral *do*.

The plain form *don't* differs from the present tense in that it doesn't agree with the subject, and hence can combine with a 3rd person singular, such as *anybody*.

[42]	i	*Don't anybody eat it!*	[imperative: no agreement – plain form]
	ii	*Doesn't anybody eat it?*	[interrogative: agreement – present tense]

2 Auxiliary verbs

The auxiliary verbs of English are the following:

[1]	i	***can, may, will, shall, must, ought, need, dare***	[modals]
	ii	***be, have, do,*** %***use***	[non-modals]

Some of them appear in idioms – ***be*** *going,* ***have*** *got, had better/best, would rather/sooner* (as in *It is going to rain, I've got a headache,* etc.) – and in such cases it is just the first verb (***be***, ***have***, *had*, *would*) that is an auxiliary, not the whole idiom.

Need, ***dare***, ***have***, ***do***, and ***use*** are dually categorised: they belong to both auxiliary and lexical verb classes. Compare:

[2]		AUXILIARIES	LEXICAL VERBS
i	a.	*Need I bother?*	b. *Do I need to bother?*
ii	a.	*I daren't tell you any more.*	b. *No one had dared to contradict him.*
iii	a.	*They had finished.*	b. *They had a fight.*
iv	a.	*She doesn't agree with you.*	b. *She does her best.*
v	a.	%*You usedn't to worry about it.*	b. *You didn't use to worry about it.*

These matters are taken up in the discussion of the individual auxiliary verbs in §2.5; ***use*** differs from the others in that [va] and [vb] belong to different varieties, and for many speakers only [vb] is possible, with ***use*** for them belonging exclusively to the class of lexical verbs.

The syntactic properties which distinguish auxiliaries from the open class of lexical verbs are discussed in §2.1, while §2.4 presents the further properties which distinguish, within the auxiliaries, between the modals and the rest. We have listed the auxiliaries in [1] as lexemes, subsuming *could, would, should, might,* as preterite forms, under ***can***, ***will***, ***shall***, ***may***, respectively. For the last two, however, this raises certain problems that we take up in §9.8.4.

2.1 Distinctive syntactic properties of auxiliary verbs

The NICE constructions: Negation, Inversion, Code, and Emphasis

Auxiliaries differ very strikingly from lexical verbs in their syntactic behaviour. In the first place, there are four non-canonical constructions that are found with auxiliary verbs, but not with lexical verbs. This is illustrated by the contrast between auxiliary ***have*** and lexical ***see*** in [3], where [i] represents the canonical structure in which both are allowed, and [ii–v] the special constructions that are restricted to auxiliaries:

[3]	AUXILIARY VERB	LEXICAL VERB	
i	a. *He has seen it.*	b. *He saw it.*	
ii	a. *He has not seen it.*	b. **He saw not it.*	[Negation]
iii	a. *Has he seen it?*	b. **Saw he it?*	[Inversion]
iv	a. *He has seen it and I have too.*	b. **He saw it and I saw too.*	[Code]
v	a. *They don't think he's seen it but he HAS seen it.*	b. **They don't think he saw it but he SAW it.*	[Emphasis]

The acronym 'NICE'

The short labels for the constructions illustrated here are 'Negation', 'Inversion', 'Code', and 'Emphasis', and the initial letters of these give rise to the acronym 'NICE'. We will need to refer to them frequently in what follows, so it will be convenient to call them the **NICE constructions.**

'Negation' is clear; 'Inversion' means subject–auxiliary inversion; 'Emphasis' means emphasis on an auxiliary realised by heavy stress. 'Code' is the least transparent of the four terms. The idea is that when someone says *He has seen it* and I reply by saying *I have too*, I am speaking in a kind of code: such clauses can't be understood without a key. The key is provided by the preceding context, which in this example enables us to interpret *I have too* as "I have seen it too".

The ungrammatical examples [3iib–vb] can be corrected by inserting the verb ***do*** (and changing *saw* to the plain form *see*), but performing this operation on [iia–va] leads to ungrammaticality:

[4]	AUXILIARY VERB	LEXICAL VERB	
i	a. **He does not have seen it.*	b. *He did not see it.*	[Negation]
ii	a. **Does he have seen it?*	b. *Did he see it?*	[Inversion]
iii	a. **He has seen it and I do too.*	b. *He saw it and I did too.*	[Code]
iv	a. **They don't think he's seen it but he DOES have seen it.*	b. *They don't think he saw it but he DID see it.*	[Emphasis]

The ***do*** in [ib/iib/ivb] is a semantically empty, or **dummy** auxiliary verb introduced to permit the formation of negative, inverted, and emphatic constructions whose canonical counterpart contains no semantically contentful auxiliary verb. These constructions are commonly called ***do*-support** constructions: in the absence of an ordinary auxiliary they require the support of dummy ***do***. We will refer to this ***do***, therefore, as **supportive *do*.** The status of ***do*** in the code construction [iiib] is more problematic and subject to dialect variation; this issue will be taken up in §2.1.4 after an outline account of the three central ***do***-support constructions in §§2.1.1–2.1.3.

Other distinctive properties of auxiliary verbs

There are other differences between auxiliary verbs and lexical verbs besides those where we have the interaction with ***do*** illustrated in [3–4]. Auxiliary verbs characteristically occupy a different position from lexical verbs relative to various adjuncts, and it is only auxiliary verbs that inflect for negation and have reduced forms. We deal with these matters in §2.1.5.

2.1.1 Primary verb negation

The first ***do***-support construction we will call, more precisely, **primary verb negation**:

[5]		POSITIVE	PRIMARY VERB NEGATION
	i	a. *That is reasonable.*	b. *That isn't / is not reasonable.*
	ii	a. *That seems reasonable.*	b. *That doesn't / does not seem reasonable.*

The [b] examples illustrate the most elementary kind of negative clause, that where the negative marker is associated with a primary verb-form – preterite or present tense (or irrealis *were*). The negation can be marked inflectionally, by means of a negative form of the verb such as *isn't* or *doesn't*, or analytically, by means of *not* modifying the verb. In either case, the verb must be an auxiliary. Where the corresponding positive contains no auxiliary, ***do*** must therefore be added, as in [ii].

Primary verb negation compared with other kinds of negation

Primary verb negation is to be distinguished from non-verbal negation and non-imperative secondary negation, which do not take supportive ***do***:

[6]			
	i	a. *They didn't go to Paris.*	[primary verb negation]
		b. *No one went to Paris.*	[non-verbal negation]
		c. *They went not to Paris but to Berlin.*	[non-verbal negation]
	ii	a. *He didn't promise to help them.*	[primary verb negation]
		b. *He promised not to help them.*	[non-imperative secondary negation]

Non-verbal negation commonly involves some negative word other than *not*, as in [ib], and when it is marked by *not* the *not* belongs within some larger constituent, such as the PP-coordination *not to Paris but to Berlin* in [ic] (cf. Ch. 9, §3.1). In [ii] we have a clear syntactic and semantic distinction between [a] and [b]. In [iia] it is the finite matrix clause that is negated – it is the negation of *He promised to help them*, and says that no promise was made. In [iib], by contrast, *not* belongs in the non-finite subordinate clause, which has the secondary verb-form *help* as its head: this time he did make a promise, but it was a promise to refrain from doing something.

We have labelled [6iib] 'non-imperative secondary negation' because imperatives take ***do***-support even though the verb is in a secondary form, the plain form. But imperatives also differ from clauses with a primary verb-form in that verbal negation always requires ***do***, even when there is another auxiliary, such as ***be***; compare, then:

[7]			
	i	*You aren't put off by his manner.*	[primary verb negation]
	ii	*Don't be put off by his manner.*	[imperative negation]

It is therefore only primary verb negation that follows the general rules for ***do***-support constructions: the imperative represents an exceptional extension of the use of supportive ***do***.

2.1.2 Subject–auxiliary inversion

The second ***do***-support construction is subject–auxiliary inversion, where the subject occurs after an auxiliary verb instead of in its default pre-verbal position:

[8]		DEFAULT ORDER	SUBJECT–AUXILIARY INVERSION
	i	a. *She can speak French.*	b. *Can she speak French?*
	ii	a. *She speaks French.*	b. *Does she speak French?*

In this type of inversion the verb preceding the subject is always a primary form (again, preterite or present tense, or irrealis *were*); the verb in question must be an auxiliary, with ***do*** added if this requirement would not otherwise be met, as in [ii].

Constructions involving subject–auxiliary inversion

(a) Closed interrogatives

This is the construction illustrated in [8]. Inversion is generally restricted to main clauses – compare the subordinate interrogative [*I wonder*] *whether he has got it* (but see Ch. 11, §5.3.1).

(b) Open interrogatives

Here inversion accompanies the placement in prenuclear position of a non-subject interrogative phrase. As with closed interrogatives, inversion is normally limited to main clauses:

[9]	SUBJECT + VERB ORDER	SUBJECT–AUXILIARY INVERSION
i	a. *Who told you that?*	b. *What did she tell you?*
ii	a. *And after that you went where?*	b. *And where did you go after that?*
iii	a. *I wonder what she is doing.*	b. *What is she doing?*

In [ia] the interrogative phrase is itself subject: inversion occurs only after non-subjects, as in [ib]. In [ii] the inverted construction with the interrogative phrase in prenuclear position contrasts with the uninverted one where it appears in the same position as in corresponding non-interrogatives (cf. *I went to the station*). In [iii] the uninverted [a] is subordinate, while [b] is a main clause.

(c) Exclamatives

Here inversion is optional after a non-subject exclamative phrase in prenuclear position:

[10]		
i	a. *What a fool I have been!*	b. *What a fool have I been!*
ii	a. *How hard she tried!*	b. *How hard did she try!*

The uninverted construction is much the more common (see Ch. 10, §8.1.3).

(d) Initial negative constituents

Inversion occurs with a negative non-subject element in prenuclear position:

[11]		
i	a. *He found not one of them useful.*	b. *Not one of them did he find useful.*
ii	a. *Somewhere he mentions my book.*	b. *Nowhere does he mention my book.*

In [ia] we have the default subject + verb order when the negative is within the VP; inversion applies when it precedes the subject, as in [ib]. In [ii] we see the contrast between having the positive *somewhere* and the negative counterpart *nowhere* at the beginning of the clause: only *nowhere* demands inversion.

Inversion with negatives is not limited to main clauses: we get *He pointed out that not once had she complained*. But it only applies with clausal negation – compare uninverted *Not long afterwards, he moved to Bonn*, which has subclausal negation (*not* applies only to modify *long* within the temporal adjunct *not long afterwards*), the clause itself being positive (see Ch. 9, §1.2).

(e) Initial *only*

Only is not a marker of negation: *He has only seen her once* (unlike *He hasn't seen her once*) is a positive clause. But it has a close connection with negation, for such an example entails that he has not seen her more than once. And this connection with negation is reflected in the fact that as far as inversion is concerned it behaves just like a negative:

[12] i a. *He found only two of them useful.* b. *Only two of them did he find useful.*
ii a. *She had complained only once.* b. *Only once had she complained.*

As with negatives, inversion does not apply unless *only* has scope over the clause: compare *Only a few days later, he moved to Bonn,* where *only* applies just to *a few days* within the initial AdvP.

(f) Initial *so/such*

These behave like *only*, though they do not have any similar connection with negation:

[13] i a. *We had so little time that we had to cut corners.* b. *So little time did we have that we had to cut corners.*
ii a. *He would make such a fuss that we'd all agree.* b. *Such a fuss would he make that we'd all agree.*

We also have inversion after initial *so* when it is functioning as a connective adjunct, as in *You got it wrong and so did I* (see Ch. 17, §7.7.3).

(g) Other fronted elements

In relatively formal style inversion may occur following the preposing of a wide variety of elements. A few attested examples are as follows:

[14] i *Thus had they parted the previous evening.*
ii *They were bound by time... yet were they simultaneously timeless.*
iii *Tourism will continue to grow... Particularly is this the case in Queensland,...*
iv *Many another poem could I speak of which sang itself into my heart.*
v *The more wives he had, the more children could he beget.*
vi *Well did I remember the crisis of emotion into which he was plunged that night.*

(h) Conditional inversion

In conditional constructions an inverted subordinate clause may be used instead of *if* + clause with default order (see Ch. 8, §14.2, and Ch. 11, §4.7):

[15] a. *If he had seen the incident he'd have reported it to the police.* b. *Had he seen the incident he'd have reported it to the police.*

(i) Optative *may*

[16] *May you both enjoy the long and happy retirement that you so richly deserve.*

Optative clauses express hopes and wishes (Ch. 10, §10). This inverted construction with *may* generally belongs to formal style, though it is also found in various fixed phrases such as *May the best man win!* or *May you be forgiven!*

Classification of subject–auxiliary inversion constructions

The above constructions fall into two main classes: those where inversion is 'triggered' by the presence of some special kind of non-subject phrase in initial position, and those without any such triggering phrase. The triggered inversion constructions may be subclassified as optional or obligatory according as there is or is not alternation with subject + verb order:

[17]

UNTRIGGERED	TRIGGERED	
	obligatory	**optional**
Closed interrogatives	Open interrogatives	Exclamatives
Conditional inversion	Initial negative	Other fronted elements
Optative *may*	Initial *only*	
	Initial *so*/*such*	

Subject–auxiliary inversion vs subject postposing

Subject–auxiliary inversion is to be distinguished from subject postposing, as in *In the bottom right-hand corner could be seen a small arrow* or *Good morning, said Kim.* Auxiliaries are not significantly involved in this construction, as is evident from these examples, where the subject appears after the lexical verbs *seen* and *said.* The structures resulting from subject–auxiliary inversion and subject postposing may, however, sometimes appear superficially the same:

[18] i *Where <u>is</u> <u>the auditor's report</u>?* [subject–auxiliary inversion]
ii *More damaging <u>is</u> <u>the auditor's report</u>.* [subject postposing]

The difference can be brought out by noting that a postposed subject can be moved over a sequence of verbs, freely including secondary forms: *More damaging <u>had been</u> the auditor's report.* Subject–auxiliary inversion, by contrast, places the subject after a single auxiliary, so we have, say, *Where <u>had</u> the auditor's report <u>been</u>?*, not **Where <u>had been</u> the auditor's report?*

Exclamative and *so*/*such* phrases, however, can trigger either subject–auxiliary inversion or subject postposing:

[19] i a. *How often had he regretted his impetuosity!*
b. *So cold had it been that they had called off the match.* } [subject–auxiliary inversion]
ii a. *How ungracious had been their response!*
b. *So wet had been the pitch that they'd abandoned play.* } [subject postposing]

Structure

We suggested in Ch. 2, §2, that clauses with subject–auxiliary inversion have the auxiliary verb in prenuclear position, with a gap occupying the basic position of the predicator in the nucleus – see the tree diagram given there for interrogative *Is he ill?* According to this analysis the part of the clause following the auxiliary forms a constituent (a clause realising the nucleus function), and some support for this analysis is provided by the possibility of having a coordination after the auxiliary (cf. Ch. 15, §4.6):

[20] i *Is [<u>he the president</u> and <u>his daughter the secretary</u>]?*
ii *Have [<u>you loved me</u> and <u>I been so inconsiderate as to make myself unworthy of your love</u>]?*

2.1.3 Emphatic polarity

In the third ***do***-support construction, stress is placed on the primary verb to emphasise the positive or negative polarity of the clause. Again, the verb must be an auxiliary, so that ***do*** must be added if the unemphatic counterpart doesn't contain one:

[21]	UNEMPHATIC POLARITY	EMPHATIC POLARITY
i	a. *I will / I'll be there.*	b. *That's not true: I WILL be there.*
ii	a. *She moved the picture.*	b. *She DID move the picture: I saw her.*

Emphatic polarity to be distinguished from emphatic lexical content

The construction illustrated in [21ib/iib] is to be distinguished from that where stress is used to emphasise the lexical content of the verb, not its polarity: *He* WROTE *it, though he wouldn't* RECITE *it.* Compare:

[22] i *You* DID *promise – I heard you.* [emphasis on positive polarity]
ii *You* PROMISED *– I heard you.* [emphasis on lexical content]

A likely context for [i] is where you have denied promising: the issue is whether or not you promised. A context for [ii] is where you have indicated that you won't do something I want you to do: I'm reminding you that you promised in order to get you to do it after all, the important thing being that you committed yourself to doing it by making a promise. It is only when the stress emphasises the polarity that an auxiliary verb is required.

Emphatic positives

Very often an emphatic positive serves to contrast the positive with a corresponding negative proposition that has been expressed or implicated in the preceding discourse, and in this case it will often involve ellipsis: *You don't think I'm serious, but I* AM*!* Other uses of the emphatic positive are illustrated in:

[23] i *Kim's the one who* DID *make a donation.*
ii *He didn't win, but he* DID *come in the first half dozen.*
iii *I* DO *think you could be more tolerant.* *I* AM *pleased you can join us.*

In [i] there is a contrast with an implicit negative, but not the negative of this clause itself: the contrast is with the people who didn't make a donation. In [ii] the contrast is not with the negative of the proposition being asserted but with something stronger – winning. In other cases an emphatic positive may be used just to indicate the strength of one's beliefs or feelings, as in [iii].

Emphatic polarity in negatives

Emphatic negatives are seen in:

[24] i *He thinks they are cheating, but they are* NOT / AREN'T.
ii *You're wrong: I did* NOT / DIDN'T *move it.*
iii *He never* DID *understand how she felt.*

Examples [i–ii] have primary verb negation, and hence require an auxiliary verb for this reason as well as because of the emphatic polarity. The stress falls on the negative element: the verb itself if it is a negative form or else the *not*. The negation in [iii] is non-verbal (marked by *never*): the unemphatic version is *He never understood how she felt.* Supportive ***do*** is therefore added to [iii] just to carry the stress that marks emphatic polarity.[10]

[10] Auxiliary ***do*** was used more widely in earlier stages of the language, and in certain genres one comes across archaic uses that go beyond our ***do***-support constructions – e.g. in legal language (*The person before the court is charged that at Newborough, on or about the 14th day of June, 1997, he did murder one James Robinson*).

2.1.4 Code: elliptical stranding and the pro-verb *do*

In the code construction the VP of a clause is reduced, with the remainder of its semantic content being recoverable from the context. In the simplest case we have ellipsis of the complement of an auxiliary verb:

[25]	FULL VERSION	REDUCED VERSION
i	a. *Pat [can help him too].*	b. *I can help him and Pat [can __ too].*
ii	a. *Pat [is in debt as well].*	b. *I'm in debt and Pat [is __ as well].*

In [ib] we understand "Pat can help him too" but the "help him" is left unexpressed, recoverable from the preceding clause. Similarly in [iib] there is ellipsis of *in debt.* The **site** of the ellipsis is shown by the gap symbol '__', and we say that the verbs *can* and *is* are **stranded,** i.e. left on their own before the site of ellipsis. While auxiliary verbs can be stranded in this way, lexical verbs cannot: ***want***, for example cannot be stranded to give **I want to go and Pat wants __ as well.*

Old-verb stranding vs new-verb stranding

The stranded auxiliary verb may have the informational status of **discourse-old** or **discourse-new** (cf. Ch. 16, §2):

[26]		
i	*Kim has seen the report and I think Pat has __ too.*	[old-verb stranding]
ii	*I'll help you if I can __.*	[new-verb stranding]

In [i] the stranded *has* is discourse-old in the sense that it, as well as the missing material (*seen the report*), occurs in the preceding context. But in [ii] stranded *can* is new to the discourse. The distinction is of significance because new-verb stranding allows a slightly narrower range of possibilities – compare:

[27]		
i	*He is to present a paper in the morning session and I am __ too.*	[old]
ii	**I didn't bother to phone the results to her because I knew Kim was __.*	[new]

In [i] ***be*** can be stranded because it, along with its understood infinitival complement *to present a paper in the morning session,* occurs in the first clause. In [ii], however, *Kim was to phone the results to her* can't be reduced to *Kim was* because this time the ***be*** is not found in the preceding context (we need *Kim was to __* or else *Kim was to do so*).

Stranding with idioms

With the idioms beginning with an auxiliary we find the following contrasts:

[28]			
i	a. A: *Would you rather stay at home?*	B: *Yes, I would __.*	[old]
	b. A: *Do you want to stay at home?*	B: *Yes, I'd rather __.*	[new]
ii	a. A: *Have you got a pen?*	B: *Yes, I have __.*	[old]
	b. A: *Do you need a pen?*	B: **No, I've got __.*	[new]

In [ia] *would rather* in B's response is discourse-old and hence only the auxiliary need be retained (though it is still possible to repeat *rather*); in [ib] it is discourse-new, so *rather* can't be left out. *Have got* is different, however, because *got* is a verb, and more specifically a lexical one, and hence can't be stranded. In [ii], therefore, only [a], with stranding of auxiliary *have,* is possible (instead of **I've got* in [ib] we need *I've got one*).

Differences between stranding and the central *do*-support constructions

(a) Stranding not restricted to primary forms

One difference between stranding and the ***do***-support constructions covered in §§2.1.1–3 is that while the auxiliaries in the latter are always primary forms, this is not so with stranding:

[29] i *I don't think she has seen it, but she may have __.* [plain form]
ii *This one needs to be repaired; the other already has been __.* [past participle]
iii %*He said I was being unfair, but I don't think I was being __.* [gerund-participle]

This construction is subject to some regional variation: AmE doesn't allow [iii], but it does have [i–ii], even if they are less usual than versions in which the second auxiliary is omitted.

(b) The infinitival marker *to* may be stranded under restricted conditions

A second important difference between stranding and the ***do***-support constructions is that stranding is not completely restricted to auxiliary verbs. It is also found with the infinitival subordinator *to* under certain conditions (see Ch. 17, §7.3):[11]

[30] i *I want to go and Pat wants to __ as well.*
ii **I advise you not to go; to __ would be very dangerous.*

The use of the verb *do* in code

We have noted that auxiliary verbs can be stranded but lexical verbs cannot. If the full version contains a lexical verb the reduced version is formed by means of ***do***; but if the full version contains an auxiliary verb (other than supportive ***do***), then a primary form of ***do*** is excluded:

[31]	VERSION WITHOUT *DO*	VERSION WITH *DO*
i	a. **I hated it and Pat hated too.*	b. *I hated it and Pat did too.*
ii	a. *I am well and Pat is too.*	b. **I am well and Pat does too.*

This is the same pattern as applies with primary verb negation, inversion, and emphasis. There is, however, an important difference – in code ***do*** is not limited to primary forms, and where secondary forms are involved versions with and without ***do*** are in alternation, not mutually exclusive:

[32]	VERSION WITHOUT *DO*	VERSION WITH *DO*
i	a. *I've seen it; Pat may have too.*	b. %*I've seen it; Pat may have done too.*
ii	a. *I haven't read it but I will soon.*	b. %*I haven't read it but I will do soon.*

As indicated by the % annotation, the [b] versions are not admissible to all speakers: BrE speakers accept such forms while AmE speakers mainly reject them. It is plausible to suggest that correlating with the difference in admissibility of these [b] versions is a difference in the grammatical status of ***do*** in code. In BrE the ***do*** of code constructions is a pro-form: in [31ib] and [32ib/iib] reduction is achieved not by ellipsis but by the substitution of a verb that stands for the whole antecedent VP. The verbal pro-form ***do*** bears some resemblance to the nominal pro-form ***one***, so that the alternation between

[11] We also find a few lexical verbs appearing with ellipsis in constructions like *I tried to help him and Pat tried __ as well.* We take the view, however, that this is not the same elliptical construction as is found with auxiliaries, and hence is not a case of a NICE construction: we take up this issue too in Ch. 17, §7.4.

the different kinds of reduction seen in [32] is similar to that found in NP reduction in pairs like:

[33] i *The second version was no better than [the first].* [no pro-form]
ii *The second version was no better than [the first one].* [*one* as pro-form]

In both of these we understand "the first version": in [ii] but not [i] there is a head noun *one* that substitutes for the antecedent *version*, just as in [32] the [b] versions but not the [a] ones have a head verb ***do*** that substitutes for the antecedents *seen it* and *read it*.[12]

In the dialect where examples like [32] are inadmissible, the ***do*** used in code is restricted to primary forms and can therefore be assimilated to the supportive ***do*** used in primary verbal negation, inversion, and emphasis. Here, then, [31ib] will be elliptical, like [31iia]. It differs in that reinstatement of the ellipted material requires that ***do*** be dropped: the full form is *I hated it and Pat hated it too*, not **I hated it and Pat did hate it too*. But this is a general property of the ***do***-support constructions: if we change interrogative *Did he hate it?* into its declarative counterpart we likewise drop ***do*** (*He hated it*). For this dialect, then, the code construction always involves ellipsis. Leaving aside the case where we have stranding of the infinitival marker *to*, it is a matter of ellipting the complement of an auxiliary verb, and if the full form contains no auxiliary then ***do*** must be inserted to permit complement ellipsis to apply.

Code in combination with negation, inversion, and emphasis

The code construction can combine with any of the other NICE constructions:

[34] i a. A: *Was he ill?* B: *No, he was not / wasn't __.* [primary verb negation]
b. A: *Did he go?* B: *No, he did not / didn't __.*
ii a. *Kim can't help her; neither can I __.* [subject–auxiliary inversion]
b. *No one else complained, so why did you __?*
iii a. *They say I can't read it, but I* CAN *__.* [emphatic polarity]
b. *He won't believe I wrote it, but I* DID *__*
c. *%He won't believe I wrote it, but I* DID *do.*

Note that in [ii] and the versions of [i] with analytic negation the auxiliary is not situated immediately before the site of ellipsis because the subject or *not* intervenes (as *rather* likewise intervenes in [28ib]): stranding is not to be understood as implying adjacency to the site of the missing dependents.

The ***do*** in the [b] examples of [34] is required quite independently of code: this is therefore the supportive ***do*** in BrE as well as in AmE. In [iiic] *did* is a form of supportive ***do*** combining with the pro-form ***do*** in BrE: this pro-form ***do*** is thus a lexical verb, not an auxiliary.

2.1.5 Position and form

The four NICE constructions have all involved some kind of interaction between auxiliaries and ***do***; in this section we turn to some further properties distinguishing auxiliaries from lexical verbs, but here there is no special relationship with ***do***.

[12] For reasons given in Ch. 5, §9.5, however, we analyse examples like [33i] in terms of a fusion of modifier and head rather than ellipsis of the head.

Position of adverbs

Auxiliaries differ from lexical verbs in their position relative to various adverbs, notably frequency adverbs (such as *always*, *usually*, *often*, *sometimes*, *never*) and modal adverbs (such as *possibly*, *probably*, *certainly*). Such adverbs tend to precede lexical verbs but to follow auxiliaries:

[35]	LEXICAL VERB	AUXILIARY VERB
i	a. *He always looks miserable.*	b. *He is always miserable.*
ii	a. *They probably go by bus.*	b. *They have probably gone by bus.*

With lexical verbs the opposite ordering (with the adverb following the verb and preceding its complement) is excluded: **He looks always miserable*; **They go probably by bus.*[13] With auxiliaries the verb + adverb order shown above is the usual one, but the reverse order of adverb + verb is also possible: compare *He always is miserable*; *They probably have gone by bus*. One special case where the latter order might be found is with emphatic polarity, with stress on the auxiliary.

Quantificational adjuncts

A comparable difference in position between auxiliaries and lexical verbs is found with certain determinatives, such as *all*, *both*, *each* (Ch. 5, §9.2), that are semantically associated with the subject:

[36]	LEXICAL VERB	AUXILIARY VERB
i	a. *All the players took a card.*	b. *All the players had taken a card.*
ii	a. *The players all took a card.*	b. *The players all had taken a card.*
iii	a. **The players took all a card.*	b. *The players had all taken a card.*

In the [i] versions *all* belongs syntactically and semantically in the subject: it functions within the NP *all the players* and it quantifies over players. Such items can be positioned outside the NP, and the [ii] versions show *all* in pre-verbal position. If the verb is an auxiliary, it can follow the verb, as in [iiib] – which is preferred over [iib]. But it cannot follow a lexical verb, as is evident from the ungrammaticality of [iiia].

Negative inflection and reduced forms

Auxiliaries differ from lexical verbs in that they have an inflectional contrast between negative and neutral forms: see §1.9. And finally, most of them have phonologically reduced forms when unstressed – weak forms such as /həv/ or /əv/ for *have*, or clitics such as /v/ (as in *I've seen it*): see Ch. 18, §§6.1–2.

2.2 Issues of definition and analysis

Auxiliary verb as a general term

A general definition of auxiliary verb is that it denotes a closed class of verbs that are characteristically used as markers of tense, aspect, mood, and voice. These categories are also commonly expressed by verb inflections (as primary tense is in English, for

[13] These examples must be distinguished from examples like *He looks, always, quite miserable* and *They go – probably – by bus*, where the adverb is set off by commas or dashes in writing and by intonation and phrasing in speech. These involve what we call supplements, which interrupt the clause rather than forming an integrated part of its structure (see Ch. 15, §5).

example): auxiliaries tend to express the same kinds of meaning as inflections, but are syntactically separate words.

In English, auxiliary verbs are defined at the language-particular level by the NICE properties – their ability to appear in the constructions described above involving negation, inversion, code, and emphasis. The class of verbs with these properties clearly satisfies the above general definition. The modals express mood, perfect ***have*** we analyse as a marker of tense, progressive ***be*** and ***use*** are aspect markers, and passive ***be*** marks voice. ***Do*** has no independent meaning, appearing as the default auxiliary in the ***do***-support constructions, but these constructions themselves have a significant association with modality, the area of meaning expressed by the category of mood.

Core and non-core uses of auxiliaries

All the auxiliaries are used in construction with a verb bearing one of the secondary inflections: the modals and ***use*** with a plain form, progressive ***be*** with a gerund-participle, ***have*** and passive ***be*** with a past participle. We refer to this as the **core** use of the auxiliaries: it is by virtue of this use that these verbs in English satisfy the general definition of auxiliary verb, as explained above. ***Be*** and ***have***, and the *would* of the idiom *would rather*, however, also occur without a following verb of this kind: we refer to this, by contrast, as the **non-core** use. The distinction between these two uses is illustrated in:

[37]	CORE USES	NON-CORE USES
i	a. *He isn't telling the truth.*	b. *He isn't honest.*
ii	a. *I haven't bought it.*	b. %*I haven't any money.*
iii	a. *Would you rather go alone?*	b. *Would you rather I didn't tell her?*
iv	a. *They can't resist it.*	b. [no non-core use]

In [ia] we have the progressive ***be***, in construction with the gerund-participle *telling*, while [ib] illustrates the copula ***be*** with the AdjP *honest* as predicative complement, a non-core use of ***be***. In [iia], perfect ***have*** is in construction with the past participle *bought*, but in [iib] ***have*** has the "possess" sense and takes the NP *any money* as object. This construction is subject to variation: many speakers would say *I don't have any money*, with ***have*** here a lexical verb: see §2.5.6. In [iiia] we have a core use of *would*: the idiom *would rather* is here in construction with the plain form *go*, whereas in the non-core use shown in [iiib] it has a finite clause as complement.

These three are the only auxiliaries with non-core uses in modern English.[14] All the other auxiliaries are like ***can***, which has only the core use, as shown in [iv]. Examples like *They can't resist it and I can't either* illustrate code, and are covered by the core category.

It is in their core uses that the auxiliaries are markers of tense, aspect, mood, and voice. As observed above, this is what makes the general term 'auxiliary verb' applicable to this class. But the non-core uses are consistent with our applying the term 'auxiliary' to the non-core cases too, given the distinction we have drawn between general and language-particular definitions (Ch. 1, §4.4). The non-core ***be*** of [ib], ***have*** in [iib] (subject to the variation noted), and *would* as used in [iiib] belong to the same subclass of English verbs as those in the [a] examples because they too have the NICE properties. The subclass defined by the NICE properties

[14] Here we are setting aside certain thoroughly archaic uses involving the omission of understood verbs of motion after modals, e.g. *I must away* "I must go away".

satisfies the general definition of auxiliary verb because its members are characteristically used as markers of tense, aspect, mood, and voice.[15]

Analysis

The main analytic issue concerns the status of the core auxiliaries. A widely adopted view is that they are dependents of the following lexical verb. We call this the **dependent-auxiliary analysis**. The view adopted in this book, however, is that they are verbs taking non-finite complements. For reasons explained below, we refer to this as the **catenative-auxiliary analysis**. We will illustrate the two contrasting analyses by reference to example [38]:

[38] *She is writing a novel.*

(a) The dependent-auxiliary analysis

Under the dependent-auxiliary analysis, [38] is a simple clause. Core auxiliaries are contrasted with **main verbs**, so that *is writing* forms a syntactic unit in which the main verb *writing* is head and the core auxiliary *is* is a dependent. As indicated by the term, core auxiliaries are never heads in the dependent-auxiliary analysis.

(b) The catenative-auxiliary analysis

The catenative-auxiliary analysis says that *writing a novel* in [38] is a non-finite complement of *is*. The tree-structure of [38] is therefore the same as that of, say, *She began writing a novel*, where *begin* is a lexical verb, not an auxiliary. On this view, there is no contrast between auxiliary verbs and main verbs. *Is* in [38] is just as much a main verb as *writing*: both are heads of their respective clauses. We call this the catenative-auxiliary analysis because it treats the core auxiliaries as belonging to the larger class of **catenative** verbs. These are verbs which take non-finite complements:

[39] *She promised [not to forget [to arrange [to collect the key]]].*

To collect the key is complement of the catenative verb *arrange*, *to arrange to collect the key* is complement of *forget*, and *not to forget to arrange to collect the key* is complement of *promise*. As the example shows, the construction is recursive: it can be repeated, yielding a chain or 'concatenation' of such verbs. Hence the name 'catenative'.

The syntactic evidence strongly favours the catenative analysis of the English core auxiliaries. We will not give the supporting arguments here, but will postpone further discussion to Ch. 14, §4.2, so that the arguments can be presented in the context of a detailed study of the catenative construction in which lexical verbs like *begin*, *promise*, *forget*, *arrange*, and all of the auxiliaries participate.

2.3 Combinations of auxiliary verbs

Combinatorial restrictions

Like the lexical catenative verbs seen in [39], the core auxiliaries can be chained together in sequence. The restrictions on their combination are as follows:

[15] Many grammars restrict the term 'auxiliary' to the core uses; 'operator' is then sometimes used for the larger class containing the NICE verbs in all their uses. The view taken here, however, is that it is this larger class that is of importance in the syntax of English (by virtue of their role in the NICE constructions), and this therefore is the one to which we apply the familiar term 'auxiliary'.

[40] i Auxiliary ***do*** cannot combine with any other auxiliary (including the non-core ones): **He doesn't have read it*, **Did she be working?* The only exception is the imperative, as in *Don't be making so much noise when your father comes home.*
ii The modals are mutually exclusive. Except in coordination, they cannot combine: **He will can swim soon*, **She may will help you.*
iii Aspectual ***use*** is likewise mutually exclusive with the modals: **He wouldn't use to go by bus*, **He used to can speak French.*

Order restrictions

In addition to the above restrictions about which auxiliaries may be co-members of a sequence of auxiliaries, there are also rigid restrictions on the order in which auxiliaries can appear in any such sequence; for example:

[41] i a. *She <u>could</u> <u>have</u> won first prize.* b. **She <u>had</u> <u>could</u> win first prize.*
ii a. *He <u>has</u> <u>been</u> reading my mail.* b. **He <u>is</u> <u>having</u> read my mail.*

We need to allow for combinations of up to four auxiliaries,[16] appearing in the order shown in the following display:

[42]	I	II	III	IV
	modal ***can/will/...*** aspectual ***use***	perfect ***have***	progressive ***be***	passive ***be***

Given that the auxiliaries are optional but have a fixed position in the sequence, there are sixteen possibilities provided for in [42], ignoring the choice between different items from column I, but including the case where no auxiliary at all is selected. They are illustrated in [43], where *will* is used as a representative choice from column I and ***take*** is used as the lexical verb heading the complement to the last auxiliary.

[43]	MODAL	PERFECT	PROGRESSIVE	PASSIVE	LEXICAL VERB
i					*takes*
ii				*is*	*taken*
iii			*is*		*taking*
iv			*is*	*being*	*taken*
v		*has*			*taken*
vi		*has*		*been*	*taken*
vii		*has*	*been*		*taking*
viii		*has*	*been*	*being*	*taken*
ix	*will*				*take*
x	*will*			*be*	*taken*
xi	*will*		*be*		*taking*
xii	*will*		*be*	*being*	*taken*
xiii	*will*	*have*			*taken*
xiv	*will*	*have*		*been*	*taken*
xv	*will*	*have*	*been*		*taking*
xvi	*will*	*have*	*been*	*being*	*taken*

[16] We ignore here the verb ***have*** in its obligation or necessity sense (*I <u>have</u> to leave now*), which is an auxiliary for some speakers but not others: see §2.5.6 below.

Structures containing two secondary forms of ***be*** (progressive and passive), such as *They may be being overlooked* or *They may have been being overlooked*, are avoided by some speakers, but they do occasionally occur.[17]

Determination of inflectional form

Each core auxiliary fully determines the inflectional form of the next verb in the sequence, whether it be a lexical verb or another auxiliary of one kind or another. The forms required are as shown in [44], where double underlining in the examples marks the auxiliary in question, single underlining the verb whose form it determines:

[44]	AUXILIARY	NEXT VERB	EXAMPLES		
i	modal	plain form	*will sing*	*may be seen*	*must have eaten*
ii	perfect	past participle	*has sung*	*had been seen*	*must have eaten*
iii	progressive	gerund-participle	*is singing*	*was being seen*	*has been eating*
iv	passive	past participle	*was sung*	*was being seen*	*has been eaten*

It is on this basis that we distinguish instances of auxiliary ***be*** as progressive or passive: the ***be*** of *was eating* is recognisable as the progressive auxiliary because it is followed by a gerund-participle, and that of *was eaten* as the passive auxiliary because it is followed by a past participle. And similarly these rules show why the progressive and passive auxiliaries are placed in that order in [42]: in *was being seen* it is the first ***be*** that is followed by a gerund-participle, the second by a past participle (contrast **was been eating*).

2.4 Distinctive properties of modal auxiliaries

The central modal auxiliaries have five distinctive properties: they have only primary forms, they don't show any agreement with the subject, they take bare infinitival complements, they are required in remote conditionals, and the use of their preterites with the modal remoteness meaning is much less restricted than is the case with other verbs.

(a) Only primary forms

The modal auxiliaries have no secondary inflectional forms and hence cannot occur in constructions which require one. Compare, then, the following examples with ***can*** and the semantically similar ***be*** *able*, where the differences in grammaticality show that ***can*** is a modal while ***be*** is not:

[45]		a.	b.
	i	a. **I'd like to can swim.*	b. *I'd like to be able to swim.*
	ii	a. **I will can swim soon.*	b. *I will be able to swim soon.*
	iii	a. **Can swim by June!*	b. *Be able to swim by June!*
	iv	a. **I regret not canning swim.*	b. *I regret not being able to swim.*
	v	a. **I have could swim for six years.*	b. *I have been able to swim for six years.*

Constructions [i–iii] require the plain form (the *to*-infinitival, bare infinitival, and imperative constructions respectively), [iv] the gerund-participle, [v] the past participle. As evident from the acceptability of the [b] examples, this is a grammatical restriction, not a restriction attributable to the meaning. We noted above that, leaving aside coordination,

[17] These constructions did not enter the language until the twentieth century – and even simpler progressives like *is/was being taken* were not fully established until the second half of the nineteenth century.

the modals cannot combine (**He may must work tomorrow*; **They must will help you*).[18] This can now be seen to be a consequence of their morphological defectiveness: the verb following a modal must be in the plain form, and modals do not have plain forms, so the verb following a modal can never be another modal.

(b) No agreement

The modal auxiliaries do not display the usual person–number agreement with the subject in the present tense: *can, may, must*, etc., occur with any kind of subject. The normal distinction between a 3rd person singular and a plain present tense is therefore missing. Again, this is a morphological oddity.

(c) Bare infinitival complement

The central modal auxiliaries take bare infinitival complements – and no other kind of complement. Most verbs with infinitival complements take *to*; the few others that take bare infinitivals generally differ from the modals in their complementation by taking an NP before the plain form verb: compare non-modal *They <u>make</u> us work* with modal *They <u>must</u> work.*

(d) Remote conditionals

The first verb of the apodosis of a remote conditional must be a modal auxiliary:

[46] i *If you came tomorrow,* [*you <u>could</u> help with the flowers*].
ii **If you came tomorrow,* [*you <u>were</u> able to help with the flowers*].

The apodosis is the part enclosed in brackets: the matrix clause minus the conditional adjunct. We can correct [ii] by changing *were* to *would be*, but this change involves adding modal *would.*

(e) Modally remote preterite

The preterites of the modal auxiliaries – *could, might, would, should* – can be used with the modal remoteness meaning without the grammatical restrictions that apply in the case of other verbs, where it is found only in a small set of subordinate constructions. Compare:

		a.	b.
[47]	i	*I wish* [*you <u>could</u> move it*].	*I wish* [*you <u>were</u> able to move it*].
	ii	*<u>Could</u> you move it?*	*<u>Were</u> you able to move it?*

In [i] the preterites are in the complement of *wish*, where all verbs have the modal remoteness meaning. But [ii] is a main clause: the preterite *were* of [b] can therefore only indicate past time, whereas *could* in [a] is ambiguous between a past time meaning ("were able") and a modally remote non-past time meaning ("would be able").[19] The modal remoteness meaning of the preterite is much more common with the modal auxiliaries than the past time meaning: *should*, indeed, is no longer used with the past time meaning, and for many speakers the same applies to *might.*

[18] Some non-standard dialects allow combinations of modals, but even here they are restricted to a few specific sequences. For example, there are dialects with %*It might could break* but none with **It could might break.*

[19] This point is related to (d) in that the preterite *could* of [46i] is a special case of the use we are concerned with here. We have given them as separate properties, however, because the use in (d) is not restricted to preterite forms: see §§2.5.2–5.

2.5 The auxiliaries considered in turn

In this section we look at the individual auxiliaries with respect to the properties of §2.1 and §2.4; they are listed here with short labels, and exemplified with ***will***:

[48] AUXILIARY PROPERTIES

[A]	Primary verb negation	*It will not work.*
[B]	Subject–auxiliary inversion	*Will it rain?*
[C]	Emphatic polarity	*I WILL help you.*
[D]	Stranding	*He won't attend, but I will __.*
[E]	Exclusion of ***do*** in code	**Ed will go and I do too.* ("I will go")
[F]	Precede adverb/quantifier	*They will probably/all accept.*
[G]	Negative forms	*It won't help.*
[H]	Reduced forms	*She'll be here soon.*

[49] MODAL AUXILIARY PROPERTIES

[I]	Only primary forms	**It's expected to will finish soon.*
[J]	No agreement	*She will/*wills win.*
[K]	Only bare infinitival complement	*It will be / *to be over.*
[L]	Can occur in remote apodosis	*If it weren't for her I would give up.*
[M]	Modally remote preterite in main clause	*I would ask you to treat it seriously.*

2.5.1 Can and will; *would rather*

Can and ***will*** are the most straightforward of the modal auxiliaries: they have all the above properties.

A special use of *would* is in the idioms *would rather, would sooner, would as soon.* These expressions take not only bare infinitivals but also finite clause complements, as in *I would rather she did it alone.* In this use, therefore, *would* differs from normal modals in property [K]. With a bare infinitival it has the negation property [A] only under restricted conditions. Compare:

[50] i *She would rather [not go first].*
ii *She would* NOT / WOULDN'T *rather [go first].*
iii *Wouldn't she / Would she not rather [go first]?*

In [i] the *not* belongs in the non-finite complement: it negates secondary *go*, not primary *would.* It is [ii–iii] therefore which illustrate primary verb negation, but this construction is possible only under the conditions shown here. In [ii] it serves as the denial of the corresponding positive: it implies a context where someone has said or suggested that she would rather go first. In [iii] it appears in a negative question with positive bias.

Would in these idioms clearly exhibits property [M], the ability of the preterite to occur in main clauses with the modal remoteness meaning: *I'd rather do it myself* indicates a present time preference, but is weaker, more tentative, than *I will do it myself.* For past time we need *have*, as in *I would rather have done it myself.*

2.5.2 *Must*

Must is a very clear member of the modal auxiliary class, with properties [A–K] applying unproblematically. It differs from ***can*** and ***will***, however, in that it has no preterite, and therefore property [M] is not applicable. For some speakers it still has property [L], occurring in a remote apodosis, as in %*If he had stayed in the army he must surely have become a colonel.* However, such examples are rare and of marginal status; the remote conditional normally requires a preterite modal.

2.5.3 *Shall* and *may*

These are the last two central members of the modal auxiliary class. ***Shall*** has all of properties [A–M]. ***May*** has all except [H] and, for many speakers, [G]: it has no reduced forms and the negative form %*mayn't* is rare – the normal or only present tense negation is the analytic *may not.*

With both verbs, however, the relation between the preterite and present tense forms raises certain problems. In the case of ***shall***, some major uses of the preterite *should* – as in *You should be more careful* – have no close analogues in the present tense: the meaning is thus not systematically derivable from the meanings of ***shall*** and the preterite, so that in these uses *should* is idiomatic, requiring independent description.

The case of ***may*** is somewhat different: here there is evidence that for some speakers *may* and *might* have diverged to the extent that they are no longer inflectional forms of a single lexeme, but belong to distinct lexemes, ***may*** and ***might***, each of which – like ***must*** – lacks a preterite; we take up this point in §9.8.4.

2.5.4 *Ought*

Ought behaves very largely like a modal auxiliary. It differs most notably in respect of property [K]: it takes a *to*-infinitival complement, *He ought to take more care.* There is a growing tendency, however, for it to be constructed with a bare infinitival in non-affirmative contexts (particularly negatives), bringing it closer to the central modals: %*You ought not/oughtn't take any notice,* %*Ought we invite them both?* and the like are found, especially in AmE, as well as the more usual forms with *to.* The negative form *oughtn't* has declined in frequency over the last century, and is now somewhat marginal for some speakers.

In stranding constructions, it occurs much more readily when old than when new:

[51] i A. *Ought we to invite them both?* B. *Yes, I think we* <u>*ought*</u> __. [old]
ii ?*He's considering telling the police, but I don't think he* <u>*ought*</u> __. [new]

It would be normal in [ii] to use the *to* stranding construction instead: *I don't think he ought to. Ought* has no reduced forms [H], and it also lacks a preterite counterpart, so that property [M] is again not applicable.[20] The absence of a preterite makes it ill-adapted to the remote apodosis construction: examples like ?*If he had stayed in the army he ought to have become a colonel* are of very questionable acceptability.

2.5.5 *Need* and *dare*

Both modal auxiliaries and lexical verbs

We have noted that these verbs can behave as modal auxiliaries or as lexical verbs, though the auxiliary use is rare in AmE:

[20] *Ought* derives historically (as indeed does *must*) from a preterite – and this is synchronically reflected in certain non-standard dialects where it behaves as a lexical verb taking ***do*** in the ***do***-support constructions, for it is the preterite of ***do*** that appears: !*You didn't ought to speak like that.*

[52] MODAL AUXILIARY | LEXICAL VERB

i a. *He needn't/daren't tell her.* b. *He doesn't need/dare to tell her.*
ii a. *Need/Dare he tell her?* b. *Does he need/dare to tell her?*
iii a. *No one need/dare go out alone.* b. *No one needs/dares to go out alone.*

As lexical verbs they take ***do***-support in primary verb negation and subject–auxiliary inversion, and have a distinct 3rd person singular present tense form. Because of this difference in inflectional form shown in [iii], we will distinguish separate lexemes for auxiliary and lexical ***need*** and ***dare***. As lexical verbs they take a wider range of complementation than the auxiliaries (e.g. an NP as object: *He needs a haircut* or *I dare you to say that to his face*), but in this section we will confine our attention to the simple catenative construction of [52], where they have just an infinitival complement, like the auxiliaries.

Need and *dare* as modal auxiliaries

The auxiliaries, unlike the lexical verbs, are restricted to non-affirmative contexts (negatives, interrogatives, and related constructions):

[53] i **I regret that the Senate need/dare take such action.* [modal auxiliary]
ii *I regret that the Senate needs/dares to take such action.* [lexical verb]

Within these limitations, modal auxiliary ***need*** and ***dare*** have virtually all the auxiliary and modal properties. The main exception is [H]: they have no reduced forms. In addition ***need*** has no preterite form, so that [M] (modal remoteness use of the preterite) is not applicable. As for [L], occurrence in a remote apodosis, they are quite acceptable in a past time conditional marked by *have*: *If you'd told me they were going to be late, I needn't have cancelled my violin class*; *Even if my life had depended on it, I daren't have jumped*. Otherwise they are somewhat marginal: *If you were more efficient you needn't work such long hours*; *?Even if my life depended on it, I daren't jump*.

Blurring of auxiliary–lexical distinction with *dare*

The auxiliary and lexical constructions are not always as sharply distinct as they are in [52]. In the first place, lexical ***dare*** commonly occurs in non-affirmative contexts without *to*: *She wouldn't dare ask her father*. Secondly, it – like modal ***dare*** – can be stranded: *The sensible thing would be to ask my father, but I wouldn't dare*. And thirdly, while other modals have highly irregular preterites, the regular form *dared* is found in both constructions:

[54] i *With a bold arm he dared once more to obstruct them.* [lexical]
ii *He dared not obstruct them.* [auxiliary]

In [i] *dared* can be seen to be lexical from the *to* and the fact that the clause is affirmative; [ii], however, has primary verb negation, so lexical ***dare*** would require ***do***-support: *He didn't dare obstruct them*. As a result of these factors there are places where it is impossible to determine whether ***dare*** is modal or lexical: there is nothing in *Few of them dare/dared stand up to him*, for example, to force one analysis over the other.[21]

[21] It is typical in text for about half the occurrences of lexical ***dare*** in non-affirmative contexts to be without *to*, but for almost all affirmative tokens to have *to*. A much rarer type of blend is seen in *The professor in turn dares not tolerate the influence in his classes of such an organisation*, with a 3rd person singular present form taking primary negation. *Dared* has replaced the now archaic *durst* as preterite of the modal, but the forms *dare* and

The auxiliary–lexical distinction is maintained with *need*

The blurring of the distinction noted for ***dare*** is not found with ***need***: lexical ***need*** can't be stranded, *needed* is invariably lexical (it is not used in the NICE constructions), and *to* is only exceptionally omitted with lexical ***need***. One difference between ***dare*** and ***need*** is that with ***dare*** even the lexical verb occurs predominantly in non-affirmative contexts (as the modal obligatorily does), whereas lexical ***need*** very commonly occurs in affirmative contexts (*We need to consider both options*), reinforcing the contrast with the modal verb.

2.5.6 *Have, have got, had better*

We need to consider three uses of ***have*** on its own, and two uses where it is part of an idiom.

(a) Perfect *have*

This is a clear auxiliary, with all of properties [A–H]. The canonical, primary verb negation and subject–auxiliary constructions are seen in:

[55] *She has eaten it.* *She hasn't eaten it.* *Has she eaten it?*

As well as the primary forms shown here, it has a plain form (*She may have eaten it*) and a gerund-participle (*She regrets having eaten it*), but not a past participle.

(b) Dynamic *have*

This is a lexical verb in all varieties of English:

[56] i	*He had a swim.*	*He didn't have a swim.*	*Did he have a swim?*
ii	*He had it painted.*	*He didn't have it painted.*	*Did he have it painted?*

It has none of the auxiliary properties [A–H] – cf. **He hadn't a swim*, **Had he a swim?*, etc. As the label 'dynamic' indicates, it expresses an event rather than a state. In [i] it is used as a 'light verb' (Ch. 4, §7): the main semantic content is in the following noun. Similar is its use with the meaning "experience": *I didn't have any difficulty in persuading her.* In [ii] it is a catenative verb taking an object and a past-participial complement; it can also take a bare infinitival: *Did she have you retype it?*

(c) Stative *have* and the idiom *have got*

Where ***have*** expresses a state rather than an event it is replaceable by the idiom ***have** got* (subject to conditions outlined below):

[57] i	a. *She has a swim every day.*	b. **She has got a swim every day.*	[dynamic]
ii	a. *She has a swimming-pool.*	b. *She has got a swimming-pool.*	[stative]
iii	a. *She has to swim each day.*	b. *She has got to swim each day.*	[stative]

Stative ***have*** occurs either with an NP object, as in [ii], expressing possession and similar relations (cf. *She has many virtues / two sons*), or as a catenative verb with a *to*-infinitival complement, as in [iii], where the meaning is of obligation or necessity, much like that of ***must*** (see §9.11). Note that in spite of its semantic similarity

daren't are commonly used where normally a backshifted preterite would be found (*He knew she dare not tell her father*), and even occasionally in ordinary past time contexts (*Kim daren't tell them so I had to do it myself*).

to ***must*** this ***have*** has none of the modal properties [I–M]. For example, it has secondary forms and hence can appear in the progressive (*I'm having to work late tonight*), the perfect (*I've had to do it all myself*), and with a modal (*We may have to cancel it*). There is therefore no case at all for including it in the syntactic class of modal auxiliaries.

The idiom ***have*** *got* derives historically from a perfect construction. This is transparent in BrE, where *got* is the past participle of ***get***, so that there is homophony between the idiom of [iib]/[iiib] and the perfect with ***get***, as in *She has got arrested, She has got him a tie for Christmas.* In AmE the past participle of ***get*** is generally *gotten*, making the constructions overtly distinct. In both varieties, however, the perfect origin of ***have*** *got* is reflected in the fact that the ***have*** component of it is an auxiliary, absolutely incompatible with ***do*** (* *We don't have got enough tea*).

While dynamic ***have*** is invariably a lexical verb, stative ***have*** can behave as either a lexical verb or, in some varieties, an auxiliary. This means that for the negative we have either *don't have* or *haven't* (or the analytic forms with *not*), and analogously with inversion. If we include ***have*** *got* too, we find therefore the following possibilities:

[58] i	a. *I have enough tea.*	*I don't have enough tea.* %*I haven't enough tea.*	*Do I have enough tea?* %*Have I enough tea?*
	b. *I have got enough tea.*	*I haven't got enough tea.*	*Have I got enough tea?*
ii	a. *I have to read it all.*	*I don't have to read it all.* %*I haven't to read it all.*	*Do I have to read it all?* %*Have I to read it all?*
	b. *I have got to read it all.*	*I haven't got to read it all.*	*Have I got to read it all?*

Have *got vs* ***have***

There are several respects in which ***have*** *got* is more restricted in its use than ***have***:

[59]	***have*** *got*	***have***
i	Informal	Stylistically neutral
ii	Characteristically BrE	
iii	Usually present tense of ***have***	All inflectional forms of ***have***
iv	Excludes habitual reading	Non-habitual or habitual

Have *got* is restricted to informal style, but is otherwise very common, especially in BrE. The ***have*** of ***have*** *got* has no past participle form (**She had had got a Ph.D.*): in this respect it is like the ordinary perfect auxiliary. Unlike the perfect ***have***, however, the idiomatic ***have*** also has no gerund-participle: %*She almost regrets having got a Ph.D.* has only the non-idiomatic meaning "having obtained", and hence requires *gotten* in AmE. The plain form is very marginal: ?*She may have got plenty of money but that doesn't mean she can push us around.* The preterite is certainly possible (*She had got too much work to do*), but it is fairly uncommon: ***have*** *got* occurs predominantly in the present tense. To the extent that the plain form is excluded, the ***have*** here has property [I] (only primary forms), but it has none of the other modal properties and cannot be regarded as a member of the modal auxiliary class.

The meaning difference [59iv] is seen most clearly in the catenative construction:

[60] i	*I've got to mow the lawn.*	[single obligation]
ii	*I have to mow the lawn.*	[single or habitual obligation]

While [ii] can have a habitual interpretation ("It is my regular job to mow the lawn") or a non-habitual one (a matter of some single future act of mowing), [i] has only the latter.

Stative ***have***: lexical or auxiliary (*doesn't have* vs *hasn't*)

In AmE stative ***have*** always behaves as a lexical verb (and is preferred over ***have*** *got*). In BrE the lexical use has become common too, and the auxiliary use is tending to sound relatively formal or old-fashioned (with ***have*** *got* or lexical ***have*** preferred). The auxiliary use is hardly possible with a habitual interpretation: *Have you to mow the lawn?*, for example, shows the same restriction as ***have*** *got* in [60i].

(d) *Had better/best*

These are idioms containing auxiliary *had*:

[61] *I had better tell them.* *I hadn't better tell them.* *Had I better tell them?*

Had has the reduced form *'d*, but the reduction can here go one stage further, with *had* dropping altogether, and only the *better* remaining: *You better go now.*[22] The *had* does not have a past time meaning: in [61], for example, we are concerned with what is the best course of action now, not at some time in the past. This weakens the relationship of the *had* to non-idiomatic ***have***, and it is questionable whether it should be regarded synchronically as a form of ***have*** or as a distinct lexeme.

If we take *had* as a form of ***have***, it will have property [M], preterite with modal remoteness rather than past time meaning. If we take it as a distinct lexeme, we will say that it has been reanalysed as a present tense form (like *must* and *ought*), and it will have property [J], no agreement. In either case, it has only primary forms, [I], and takes only a bare infinitival complement, [K]. On these grounds it undoubtedly should be included among the non-central members of the modal auxiliary class. Like *must* and *ought*, it is questionable in a remote apodosis, [L]: ?*If tomorrow's vote went against the proposal, you'd better let me know at once.*[23]

2.5.7 *Be*

We distinguish the following uses of ***be***:

[62] i	*She was a lawyer.*	[copula ***be***]
ii	*She was sleeping peacefully.*	[progressive ***be***]
iii	*They were seen by the security guard.*	[passive ***be***]
iv	*You are not to tell anyone.*	[quasi-modal ***be***]
v	*She has been to Paris twice already.*	[motional ***be***]
vi	*Why don't you be more tolerant?*	[lexical ***be***]

The ***be*** of [i–iii] has all of properties [A–H], and needs no further commentary.

Quasi-modal *be*

This has clear semantic affinities with the central modal auxiliaries, and syntactically it resembles them in having property [I] (as well as [A–H]). That is, it can't appear in a

[22] This is so common that in non-standard speech (especially that of children) one sometimes hears examples like !*We better go in, bettern't we?*, with *better* reanalysed as itself an auxiliary verb.

[23] *Had* also occurs in the idiom *had rather*, a variant of the *would rather* dealt with in §2.5.1; in BrE the *had rather* variant is somewhat archaic.

secondary form: **I resent being not to tell anyone*, **The meeting had been to be chaired by the premier.*[24] It lacks all the other modal auxiliary properties, however: it has agreement forms, it takes an infinitival with *to*, it can't occur in a remote apodosis, and its preterites do not occur with the modal remoteness meaning. The label 'quasi-modal' indicates that in spite of its one modal property (and its modal meaning) this ***be*** doesn't in fact qualify grammatically for inclusion in that class.

Motional *be*

This occurs only in the past participle form after perfect ***have***, and hence most of the auxiliary properties don't apply. It does, however, exhibit auxiliary property [D], stranding: *She's not coming to the Exhibition tonight because she has been __ already.*

Lexical *be*

This is found with *why* + **do** and with *if*:

[63] i	a. *Why don't you be more tolerant?*	b. *Why doesn't he be more tolerant?*
ii	a. *If you don't be quick you'll lose.*	b. *If he doesn't be quick he'll lose.*
iii	a. %*If you be quick you'll win.*	b. **If he be/bes quick he'll win.*

The *why* construction [i] is virtually restricted to the negative: ?*Why do you be so intolerant?* is at best very marginal. Pragmatically [i] conveys "You/He should be more tolerant" and thus bears some resemblance to the imperative, but syntactically it is quite distinct from the imperative construction by virtue of having a present tense form, not a plain form. This is evident from the person–number contrast between *don't* in [ia] and *doesn't* in [ib], for imperatives with a 3rd person singular subject do not differ in verb-form from those with a 2nd person subject (cf. *Somebody open the door, please*). The same person–number contrast is seen in the conditional construction [ii/iii], which again conveys that you/he should be quick (in order to win / avoid losing). This time, however, some speakers allow *be* in the positive, but with no corresponding 3rd person singular form.

Two points about ***be*** follow from the data of [63]. The first is that in these constructions it behaves as a lexical verb, taking ***do***-support in present tense negatives. The second is that for speakers who use construction [iiia] the lexical and auxiliary uses correspond to different lexemes, for the inflectional forms are different. Lexical ***be*** has only the one realisational form *be*, but it realises either the plain form (when taking ***do***-support) or (in positive conditionals) a present tense form, distinct from the *are* that we have with auxiliary ***be***.

2.5.8 *Do*

Like several of the items considered above, **do** belongs to both the auxiliary and lexical verb classes:

[64] i	*Do you like it?*	*I don't understand.*	*She* DOES *love him.*	[auxiliary **do**]
ii	*I did my best.*	*He's doing the washing.*	*What can we do?*	[lexical **do**]

Auxiliary ***do*** is virtually restricted to the ***do***-support constructions discussed in §§2.1.1–4 (where it is mutually exclusive with other auxiliaries), and to negative and emphatic imperatives. Elsewhere it is archaic, as in *I do hereby bequeath...*, and the like. Lexical

[24] This represents a historical change: constructions of this kind were used until the early nineteenth century, as in *You will be to visit me in prison with a basket of provisions.*

do of course combines with auxiliary ***do*** when the latter is required: *I didn't do very well.*

2.5.9 *Use*

This is the most marginal of the auxiliaries. For many speakers, especially younger ones, it does not belong in the class at all; many others have it as both auxiliary and lexical verb (with the former belonging to somewhat more formal style). We therefore find both:

[65] i	a. %*He usedn't to like it.*	b. %*Used he to live alone?*	[auxiliary]
ii	a. *He didn't use to like it.*	b. *Did he use to live alone?*	[lexical verb]

Choice between the negative variants is sometimes avoided in informal style by using *never*: *He never used to like it.* The version with analytic negation, *He used not to like it,* could be construed either as an auxiliary with primary verb negation, or else as a lexical verb with negation of the non-finite complement. *Usedn't* is pronounced without an internal /t/ and sometimes written *usen't*; similarly *used to* is pronounced with a single /t/ and hence is homophonous with the *use to* of [ii], and the spelling *used* is sometimes found instead of *use* in these negative and inverted constructions.

Use does not normally appear as an auxiliary in the emphatic polarity or stranding constructions:

[66] i	**He claims neither of us used to reply but we* USED *to.*	[emphatic polarity]
ii	**Kim used to like it and I used __ as well.*	[verb stranding]

Contrastive stress on ***use*** can only emphasise the past aspectual meaning, not the polarity, so the only possibility in [i] is *but we* DID. In [ii] the only possibilities are *to*-stranding (*and I used to as well*) or ***do*** (*and I did, as well*).

Morphologically, ***use*** is highly defective: it has no present tense, no gerund-participle, and no past participle.[25] The plain form is found only in construction with auxiliary ***do***, as in [65ii]. We have seen that it is mutually exclusive with the modal auxiliaries, but it is clearly not itself a member of the modal auxiliary class. It lacks properties [I] and [K–M], while [J] is irrelevant because *used* is a preterite form so the issue of agreement doesn't arise. It is also semantically quite distinct from the modal auxiliaries: the meaning it expresses is aspectual, not modal.

3 Tense, aspect, and mood: preliminaries

3.1 Categories of form and categories of meaning

The remainder of this chapter is concerned with the verbal systems of tense, aspect, and mood, which are marked inflectionally on the verb in just one case (the distinction between present and preterite tense) and otherwise analytically by auxiliaries. We will not, however, be dealing with the voice system in this chapter: although the passive is characteristically marked by auxiliary ***be***, the voice system involves contrasts in the structure of the clause as a whole and a somewhat different kind of meaning contrast, so that it is more appropriately dealt with in Ch. 16. Some attention will be given also

[25] Except that the preterite perfect *had used* is occasionally found: *When Arthur had been a boy at school, he had used to play football.*

to various semantically related expressions which are not members of the syntactic class of auxiliary verbs, but the main focus will be on the auxiliaries themselves. Items such as ***begin*** or ***finish***, for example, are lexical verbs expressing aspectual meaning, whereas progressive ***be*** is an aspectual auxiliary requiring fuller discussion.

The four systems and their marking

There are four systems to be considered, two of tense, and one each of aspect and mood:

[1]	System	Terms	Marking	Example
i	Primary tense	Preterite	preterite inflection	*went*
		Present	present tense inflection	*goes*
ii	Secondary tense	Perfect	***have*** (+ past participle)	*has gone*
		Non-perfect	[unmarked]	*goes*
iii	Aspect	Progressive	***be*** (+ gerund-participle)	*is going*
		Non-progressive	[unmarked]	*goes*
iv	Mood	Modal	modal aux (+ plain form)	*can go*
		Non-modal	[unmarked]	*goes*

We will also use the terms **simple preterite** and **simple present** for examples like *went* and *goes* which are unmarked in respect of all three analytic systems. In discussing the meanings we will use the term **situation** to cover actions, processes, events, states, relations, etc. – i.e. for whatever is expressed by a clause.

Tense

The general term **tense** applies to a system where the basic or characteristic meaning of the terms is to locate the situation, or part of it, at some point or period of time. English has two tense systems, illustrated in:

[2]				
i	a. *She went to school.*	b. *She goes to school.*	[preterite vs present]
ii	a. *He may have known her.*	b. *He may know her.*	[perfect vs non-perfect]

In [i] the verb-forms refer respectively to past and present time, so that this is a very obvious example of a contrast of tense. We saw in §1.7 that the same inflectional contrast can convey other meanings too. In *If she went with us tomorrow she'd have plenty of time* vs *If she goes with us tomorrow she'll have plenty of time*, for example, the time is the same (future) in both, the difference being that the first presents her going with us as a more remote possibility than the second. But this meaning difference is found only in a restricted range of constructions, such as conditionals: it is examples like [i] that illustrate the basic meanings of the forms.

In [2ii] the perfect auxiliary ***have*** (in combination with the following past participle) serves to locate the knowing in past time and given that this can again be regarded as the basic meaning we analyse ***have*** as a tense auxiliary. We shall see that the inflectional preterite and the analytic perfect have a great deal in common, and we shall use the term **past tense** to cover them both: for reasons explained in §6.3, we take the inflectional preterite to be the primary past tense and the perfect the secondary past tense.[26]

[26] The perfect is often regarded as an aspect rather than a tense; the term 'phase' (distinct from both tense and aspect) is also used.

Aspect

The term **aspect** applies to a system where the basic meanings have to do with the internal temporal constituency of the situation. Compare:

[3]

	PRESENT	PRETERITE
NON-PROGRESSIVE	*She goes to school.*	*She went to school.*
PROGRESSIVE	*She is going to school.*	*She was going to school.*

If we change present tense *She goes to school* to preterite *She went to school* we change from present to past time, but if we change it to *She is going to school* the time (and the tense) remains the same. The difference is a matter of how the speaker views the situation. The progressive takes an internal view, looking at it from the inside, as it were, as something ongoing, in progress. The unmarked, non-progressive, version takes an external view: there is no explicit reference to any internal phase or to any feature of the temporal flow (such as whether the situation is conceived of as instantaneous or having duration through time).

There are a considerable number of verbs which express aspectual meaning. ***Begin*** and ***finish***, for example, are semantically similar to progressive ***be*** in that they too take an internal view, focusing on the initial or final phase of the situation. They do not belong to the grammatical class of auxiliary verbs, however, and we will refer to them therefore as lexical aspectual verbs.

Mood

It is not so easy to give a succinct account of the kind of meaning characteristically associated with **mood**. The unmarked mood is associated with factual assertions, whereas the marked terms involve various kinds of non-factuality or non-actuality, indicating that the situation is merely possible, is predicted or inferred rather than known, and so on. Compare:

[4] i *She goes to school.* [non-modal (unmarked)]
ii *She may/must go to school.* [modal]

As a main clause, [i] is characteristically used as an unqualified assertion. *She may go*, by contrast, indicates that the situation possibly obtains or is permitted, while *She must go to school* typically conveys that I deduce from evidence that she goes to school or that I am imposing a requirement that she go to school.

The mood system differs from the aspect and analytic tense system in that there are a handful of modal auxiliaries, not just one. Note in particular that we depart from traditional grammar in analysing ***will*** and ***shall*** as modal auxiliaries, not future tense markers: this issue is taken up in §10.1. And again the same kind of meaning as is expressed by the auxiliaries of mood can also be conveyed by other means, e.g. adverbs like *perhaps*, adjectives like *possible*, the imperative construction (*Go to school*), and so on.

Distinct terms for form and meaning

It will be clear from the above preliminary survey that a single form does not always convey the same meaning (the preterite being a striking example) and that the same kind of meaning can be expressed by very different formal means. This makes it important to distinguish carefully between categories of form and categories of meaning, so that the complex relation between them can be described. To facilitate this we will use different terms for the formal systems and the associated areas of meaning:

[5]

FORM	CHARACTERISTIC MEANING
Tense	Time
Aspect	Aspectuality
Mood	Modality

The adjectives 'aspectual' and 'modal' can apply to form or meaning depending on the noun they modify.

3.2 Kinds of situation and aspectuality

3.2.1 A broad classification of situations

States, activities, accomplishments, and achievements

The interpretation and use of tense, aspect, and (to a lesser extent) mood depends on the kind of situation expressed in the clause. A broad classification is given in [6], with examples in [7]:

[6]

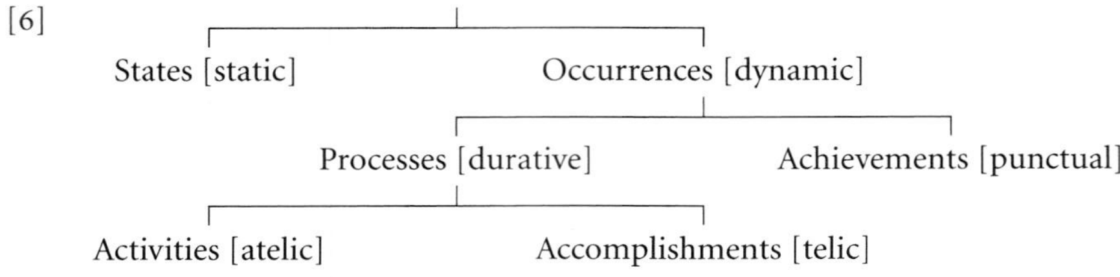

[7] i *The flag is red. He likes her. They believed in God.* [states]
ii *He's playing golf. He read to them. I had walked in the park.* [activities]
iii *He's writing a note. He read the note. I had walked home.* [accomplishments]
iv *I declare the meeting closed. I found the key. He had died.* [achievements]

The categories apply in the first instance to meanings and then derivatively to the forms that express them – but it must be emphasised that a single expression can often be interpreted as applying to situations of different types. Except where otherwise noted, we will be concerned with situations in abstraction from the features contributed by tense, aspect, and mood, so that, for example, *He is playing tennis, He was playing tennis, He played tennis* all involve the same situation of his playing tennis.

Singulary vs multiple situations

Before outlining the differences between these various kinds of situation, we need to introduce a further distinction, between **singulary** and **multiple** situations:

[8] i *I was born on Good Friday. The President has resigned.* [singulary]
ii *He went with her a few times. She usually cycles to work.*
iii *She cycles to work. He was winking at me.* } [multiple]

A multiple situation comprises more than one instance of the same subsituation, as in [ii–iii], where we have multiple occurrences of his going with her, her cycling to work, and his winking at me. In [ii] the multiplicity is overtly expressed by adjuncts, but it does not have to be, as is evident from [iii]. Often the same form can be used for a singulary or a multiple situation: *She cycled to work* allows both single occasion and habitual interpretations, *She immediately knocked at the door* may involve a single knock or repeated knocks, and so on.[27]

We will consider multiple situations in §3.2.4; in the meantime we will confine our attention to singulary ones.

3.2.2 States vs occurrences

The first contrast is between static and dynamic situations – between states and occurrences. States exist or obtain, while occurrences happen, take place. Occurrences involve change, while states do not. States have no internal temporal structure: they are the same throughout their duration, having no distinguishable phases.

State-occurrences

The transitions into and out of a state are therefore not part of the state itself; where we are concerned with a state together with these transitions we will speak of a 'state-occurrence'. Thus *She reigned for thirty years*, for example, is dynamic by virtue of covering the transitions: it denotes a situation that happened.

Linguistic differences between states and occurrences

The distinction between the two main types of situation is reflected linguistically in a number of ways; the major ones are listed here summarily.

(a) Progressive aspect

This does not normally occur with expressions denoting states:

[9]	i	**The flag is being red.*	[state]
	ii	*He is playing tennis.*	[occurrence]

(b) Simple present

This combines freely with states but not with occurrences.

[10]	i	a. *The flag was red.*	b. *The flag is red.*	[state]
	ii	a. *She married Tom.*	b. *She marries Tom.*	[occurrence]

While [ib] is the present time counterpart of [ia], [iib] resists a comparable interpretation – it can hardly be used for an event actually taking place at the time of speaking.

(c) Adjuncts of temporal location

These can refer to a point within the duration of a state but not, in the non-progressive, of an occurrence:

[11]	i	*At midnight / When he left she was still at her desk.*	[state]
	ii	*At midnight / When he left she made herself an omelette.*	[occurrence]
	iii	*At midnight / When he left she was making herself an omelette.*	

In [i] midnight or the time of his leaving are internal to the static situation of her being at her desk, whereas in [ii] they are presented as giving the time of occurrence of her making herself an omelette: the progressive is needed if they are to be interpreted as internal to the situation, as in [iii].

[27] A singulary situation interpretation of the examples in [8iii] is in fact also possible, though it is much less salient than the multiple.

(d) Pseudo-clefts with *do*

Various constructions such as the pseudo-cleft can relate to occurrences but not to states:

[12] i **What she did next was know German.* [state]
ii *What she did next was learn German.* [occurrence]

3.2.3 Achievements, accomplishments, and activities

The labels for the three kinds of occurrences initially suggest situations with human agents, but they are to be understood as applying quite generally. *The fire destroyed the building*, for example, is just as much an accomplishment as *Tom destroyed the building*.

Achievements and processes distinguished as punctual vs durative

Achievements are conceived of as **punctual**, i.e. as being instantaneous, as occurring at a point in time, whereas processes – like states – are conceived of as **durative**, as having duration.

Accomplishments and activities distinguished as telic vs atelic

The two kinds of process, accomplishments and activities, are distinguished by the fact that the former are **telic**: they have an inherent terminal point beyond which they cannot continue. Activities (and states) are **atelic**. Writing or reading some particular letter or note, walking some specific distance (*We walked six kilometres*) or to some specific destination (*We walked to the post office*) are accomplishments. Once we have covered six kilometres, the situation of our walking six kilometres is necessarily terminated: we can carry on walking (for that is an activity), but not walking six kilometres. Accomplishment expressions are often essentially composite, as in this example. The verb *walk* on its own is an activity verb in that it does not itself imply any necessary conclusion: the telic property comes from adding a complement of distance or destination, which converts an atelic expression into a telic one. Similarly *read* and *write* are atelic, but adding an object that is 'bounded' yields a telic expression. Compare here:

[13] i *She's writing a note.* [telic: accomplishment]
ii *She's writing notes.* [atelic: activity]

Here [i] is telic because the object is bounded: the situation must necessarily come to an end when that particular note is written. But in [ii] no bounds, limits, are set and the situation can go on indefinitely. There are some verbs, however, which incorporate the telic property within their own meaning. *Melt* and *evaporate*, for example, are telic in themselves: they denote a change from one state to another, and the occurrence is necessarily complete when the second state is reached.

Complex structure of accomplishments

Accomplishments have a complex structure involving two conceptually distinguishable phases: a pre-terminal phase, which has duration, and a terminal phase, which is punctual. Activities and achievements have a simple structure. By virtue of its pre-terminal phase an accomplishment is like an activity in that both are durative, both are processes. By virtue of its punctual terminal phase an accomplishment is like an achievement; some grammars apply the term telic to both, but since the question of whether the situation can in principle **continue** indefinitely doesn't arise with achievements, we will regard them rather as 'quasi-telic'.

Linguistic differences

The distinction between accomplishments, activities, and achievements is reflected in the following ways:

(a) Lexical aspectual verbs

Achievement expressions do not normally occur as complement to the lexical aspectual verbs, whereas process expressions do:

[14] i *He began to work / write a letter. He stopped snoring / reading it.* [processes]
ii **He began to reach the summit. *He stopped finding the key.* [achievements]

(Recall that we are concerned at this stage only with singulary situations: *He kept reaching the summit before me* is quite normal but involves repeated achievements.) There are also more specific differences, the most important of which concerns the contrast between *finish* and *stop*; compare:

[15] i *He stopped/finished painting the house.* [accomplishment]
ii *He stopped/finished talking.* [activity]

With accomplishments, *finish* necessarily encompasses the terminal phase, whereas *stop* does not: thus *He finished painting the house* entails that he had painted it, whereas *He stopped painting the house* does not – it strongly implicates that he had not. (That this is only an implicature follows from the possibility of saying *I won't stop until I've finished*, which shows that stopping can coincide with finishing.) With activities, the difference is less sharp, for both versions of [ii] entail that he had talked. *Finish*, however, lends a quasi-telic quality to the situation expressed in its complement (his talking): it suggests reaching some independently established endpoint. *He finished talking* conveys that he said all he had or wanted to say, whereas *He stopped talking* does not.

(b) Occurrence with progressive aspect

Similarly, processes occur freely with progressive aspect, whereas achievements tend to resist it:

[16] i *I was working.* [activity]
ii *I was writing a novel.* [accomplishment]
iii *?I was recognising her.* [achievement]

A complication arises, however, with verbs like *die*. In the non-progressive these behave clearly as achievement expressions: they have a punctual interpretation and do not occur with the lexical aspectual verbs. Compare *He finished painting the house last week* (accomplishment) and *#He finished dying last week* (achievement). Nevertheless, such verbs occur quite freely in the progressive: *He was dying*. This of course has a durative rather than a punctual interpretation, and we will therefore refer to situations expressed by *die* and the like as 'extendable achievements', in contrast to 'strict achievements' like [iii].

(c) Entailments and implicatures from the progressive

[17] i *I was working* entails that I worked. [activity]

ii *I was writing a novel* does not entail that I wrote a novel, but strongly implicates that I had not (yet) written the novel. [accomplishment]

iii *He was dying* implicates that he would subsequently die and entails that he had not (yet) died. [extendable achievement]

Accomplishments have separable pre-terminal and terminal phases, such that occurrence of the former does not guarantee occurrence of the latter. In [ii] the progressive normally picks out a segment from the pre-terminal phase, and hence *I was writing a novel* does not say whether or not I subsequently completed it – but it does implicate that at the time in question I had not done so. (Note that the negative implicature must be formulated in terms of 'the', i.e. 'the same', novel: [ii] does not of course convey that I had not written some other novel at some previous time.) Activities do not have separable phases, and hence the fact that an activity was in progress at some time is sufficient to ensure that it took place, happened: hence the entailment in [i]. The issue of such entailments does not generally arise with strict achievements because of their resistance to the progressive; extendable achievements, however, are in this respect rather similar to accomplishments. The negative implicature "he had not (yet) died" in [iii] is like that of the accomplishment in [ii] (but stronger: see §8.1): there is a necessary terminal point not yet reached at the time referred to in the progressive. An extendable achievement differs from an accomplishment, however, by virtue of the strong implicature that the terminal point was or will be reached. Thus whereas *He is writing a novel but I suspect he'll soon give up* is perfectly natural, *He is dying but I suspect he'll recover soon* is not. We have spoken here of an implicature because of the possibility of cancellation, as in *When I last saw him he was dying, but now you would hardly know he had been ill*; such examples are quite acceptable to many speakers at least: others might insist on *he seemed to be dying* or the like, and for them subsequent reaching of the terminal point has the strength of an entailment.

(d) Expressions of duration

The admissibility and interpretation of such expressions also differentiates between the three kinds of dynamic situation:

[18] i a. **He reached the summit for an hour.* [achievement]

b. **He was dying for an hour.* [extendable achievement]

c. *He played tennis for an hour* / **in an hour.* [activity]

d. *He walked a mile in an hour* / **for an hour.* [accomplishment]

ii a. *It took him an hour to reach the summit / die.* [achievements]

b. **It took him an hour to play tennis.* [activity]

c. *It took him an hour to walk a mile.* [accomplishment]

iii a. *He reached the summit in an hour.* [duration of preceding activity]

b. *He arrived home / went to Ed's for two days.* [duration of ensuing state]

Duration adjuncts like *for an hour*, interpreted as giving the duration of the situation, are inadmissible with expressions denoting achievements (usually including extendable ones, but see §8.1(d)) and accomplishments, as shown in [i]. Activities freely allow such adjuncts, but not those like *in an hour*. These latter give the time taken to reach the intrinsic terminal point, and hence occur readily with accomplishments. *For* phrases are often possible with expressions that **can** denote accomplishments, but they induce an activity interpretation. Compare:

[19] i *He read the book in an hour.* [accomplishment]
ii *He read the book for an hour.* [activity]

Example [ii] strongly implicates that he didn't finish the book (on the occasion in question).

Constructions involving *take* + duration complement measure the time of the situation through to the terminal point, and hence do not occur with activities (or states). Since the terminal phase is a point, the duration complement gives the time spent on the pre-terminal phase in the case of accomplishments. With achievements, which don't have a pre-terminal phase, it gives the time of some preliminary activity not explicitly expressed (e.g. moving towards the summit in [18iia] or looking for the key in *It took him an hour to find the key*).

Similarly an *in* phrase with an achievement is interpreted as giving the duration of such a preceding activity situation, as in [18iiia]. The mirror image of this is where a *for* phrase gives the duration not of the situation (achievement or accomplishment) actually expressed but of the implied resultant state, as in [iiib].

3.2.4 Multiple situations

Iterative, repeated, and serial multiplicity

There are three main ways in which a situation can be multiple rather than singulary:

[20] i *She knocked at the door* [sc. more than once]. [iterative]
ii *She saw him twice / several times last week.* [repeated]
iii *She usually mows the lawn herself.* [serial]

Verbs like *knock*, *nod*, *wink*, etc., can denote a singulary punctual situation (an achievement) or a multiplicity of such subsituations: *She knocked at the door* can involve a single knock or more than one. We will use the term **iterative** for this kind of multiplicity, which is a matter of the inherent meaning of the verbs. **Repeated** is used for the case illustrated in [ii], where there is an indication of how many subsituations are involved; nothing further need be said about this type. **Serial** multiplicity is that where the recurrence of the subsituations is unbounded; there may be an indication of frequency, such as *usually* in [iii], but this is not necessary. Thus in its salient interpretation *She mows the lawn herself* is no less serial than [iii]: we take it to describe her habitual behaviour.

Classification of subsituations and of overall situation

The analysis of multiple situations is more complex than that of singulary ones, since we need to distinguish between the classification of the subsituations and that of the overall situation.

(a) Iterative multiplicity

With iterative multiplicity, the subsituations (as noted above) are achievements, but the overall situation is an activity. Hence the possibility of the progressive, or a *for* phrase: *She was knocking at the door*; *She knocked at the door for a moment or two.*

(b) Serial multiplicity

Here the individual subsituations can belong to any of the categories:

[21] i *She usually knows the answer to his questions.* [states]
ii *She usually gets up at six.* [achievements]
iii *She usually mows the lawn herself.* [accomplishments]
iv *She usually plays tennis at the week-end.* [activities]

But the overall situation itself is best regarded as a state. Although the subsituations may be dynamic, the overall situation is not: it is a state of affairs characterised by the serial occurrence of the subsituations. Serial situations do not have all the properties of states given in §3.2.2 (and hence are not prototypical states), but they are state-like with respect to properties (b) and (c). That is, they occur freely in the simple present, as in the examples just given, and a time adjunct can refer to an interval within the duration of the overall situation: *At the time I went to stay with them she usually mowed the lawn herself.* Moreover, as we shall note in the next subsection, serial states, like ordinary ones, have imperfective interpretations.

3.2.5 Perfective and imperfective aspectuality

The two most general categories of aspectuality are illustrated in:

[22] i *He died last week. I'll write again soon. He reigned for a year.* [perfective]
ii *He lives in Bonn. He often cycles to work. He is working.* [imperfective]

With perfective aspectuality, the situation is presented in its totality, as a complete whole; it is viewed, as it were, from the outside, without reference to any internal temporal structure or segmentation. The concept of complete whole is independent of time, so that perfective aspectuality is compatible with any time-sphere: past in *He declared it a fake*, present in *I declare this meeting open*, future in *It is essential* [*that he declare everything he's bought*]. With imperfective aspectuality, the situation is not presented in its totality; it is viewed from within, with focus on some feature of the internal temporal structure or on some subinterval of time within the whole.

In languages such as Russian there are distinct verb-forms whose basic meanings correspond closely to these two aspectualities, and these languages are therefore said to have perfective and imperfective aspect. English, of course, is not such a language: the simple present and preterite can both be used either perfectively or imperfectively. With reference to English, therefore, the terms will be used wholly for categories of meaning and interpretation.[28] A special case of imperfectivity, however, is that where a dynamic situation is presented as ongoing, in progress: this we refer to as **progressive** aspectuality, and since it is the basic function of the ***be*** + gerund-participle construction to express it, this construction is called progressive aspect.

The interpretation of the non-progressive depends on the kind of situation involved. Normally (but see also §5.2) it is perfective with occurrences, i.e. dynamic situations, but imperfective with states, whether ordinary or serial. Compare:

[23] i *He played golf on Wednesday.* [perfective]
ii *Even in those days he played golf every Wednesday.* [imperfective]

[28] It will be clear, then, that 'perfective' has a quite different sense from 'perfect'; in some works on English, however, 'perfective' is used with the meaning that (following the most usual practice) we give to 'perfect'.

Example [i] expresses a single activity; it is considered as a whole and located as a whole (by the preterite) in past time. By contrast, [ii] expresses a serial state; it is not considered as a whole, as is evident from the fact that in spite of the preterite the situation may still obtain at the time of speaking (the *even* is likely to suggest that it does). That is, the preterite locates in past time not the situation as a whole, but that part of it that I am talking about (the part that coincides with 'those days') – this makes clear that I am taking an internal view. Further evidence for this internal orientation comes from the fact that a time adjunct can refer to an interval of time within the duration of a state, just as it can with progressive aspect for an occurrence: see [11] above, where the adjunct has an internal interpretation in imperfective [i] and [iii], but not in perfective [ii].

4 Primary tense

English has two primary tense categories, preterite and present, marked by verb inflection. We examine them in this section, for the most part, with reference to the simple preterite and present, i.e. to examples without any auxiliaries of mood, secondary tense, or aspect – *She worked/works hard*; *It started/starts on Tuesday*; *He expected/expects to lose.*

4.1 Past, present, and future as relational categories

Relation between time referred to and time of orientation

The semantic categories past, present, and future are inherently relational: one time is defined by its relation to another. Consider such examples as:

[1]	i	*He died of lung cancer.*	[past time]
	ii	*I promise to let you have it back tomorrow.*	[present time]
	iii	*If you see her tomorrow give her my best regards.*	[future time]

When we say of [i], for example, that the time of dying is past, this is understood as a time earlier than now, than the time at which I utter the sentence. We will speak of the two terms in the relation as **the time referred to**, symbolised T_r, and **the time of orientation**, symbolised T_o. In [i], T_r is the time of dying, T_o is the time of utterance, and the relation is "earlier than", or to use a more technical term "anterior to". In [ii], T_r is the time of promising, T_o again the time of utterance, and the relation is "simultaneous with". In [iii], T_r is the time of your seeing her, T_o the time of utterance, and the relation is "later than", or "posterior to". These three relations may be symbolised as shown in:

[2]	i	Past time	T_r anterior to T_o	$T_r < T_o$
	ii	Present time	T_r simultaneous with T_o	$T_r = T_o$
	iii	Future time	T_r posterior to T_o	$T_r > T_o$

In addition to T_r and T_o we need two other temporal concepts: T_{sit}, **the time of the situation**, and T_d, **deictic time**.

Time referred to and time of situation

Where the aspectuality is perfective, the T_r for the primary tenses is simply the time of the whole situation, T_{sit} – this is so in all the examples in [1]. Where the aspectuality is imperfective, however, T_r will normally be just some point or interval within T_{sit}.

Compare:

[3] i *He <u>died</u> of lung cancer.* (=[1i]) [T_r coextensive with T_{sit}]
ii *I already <u>knew</u> how to do it.* [T_r included within T_{sit}]

In [ii] the preterite in *knew* refers to some contextually given time included within the situation of my knowing how to do it, a situation which may well still obtain in the present (cf. also the above comments on *Even in those days he played golf every Wednesday* ([23ii] of §3)): this is why we need to distinguish between T_r and T_{sit} – and why our general definition of a tense system stipulated that the basic meaning of the terms was to locate in time the situation **or some part of it**.

Time of orientation and deictic time

For primary tense T_o is normally the time of speaking or writing. We use the term **deictic time** to allow for the fact that in special circumstances it can be the time of **decoding** rather than that of **encoding**. Compare:

[4] i *I am writing this letter while the boys are at school.* [T_o is time of encoding]
ii *You are now leaving West Berlin.* [a written notice] [T_o is time of decoding]

In ordinary speech the time of encoding and the time of decoding are identical, but in writing they can be different. Where this is so, the default identification of T_o, as in [i], is with the time of encoding, the writer's time, but in notices like [ii] it is identified as the time of decoding, the addressee's time.[29] The difference between these is not marked linguistically in any way and the term deictic time covers both cases: it is defined by the linguistic event itself.

T_o, we have said, is normally identified as T_d; in this case, illustrated in [1], we say that the tense is **interpreted deictically**. But it is not invariably interpreted in this way. Consider:

[5] i *If she beats him he'll claim she <u>cheated</u>.* [non-deictic past]
ii *If you eat any more you'll say you <u>don't</u> want any tea.* [non-deictic present]

The preterite and present tense inflections on ***cheat*** and ***do*** indicate that T_r is respectively anterior to and simultaneous with T_o, but here T_o is clearly not T_d. The time of the (possible) cheating is not anterior to the time of my uttering [5i], but to the time of his (possibly) making a claim of cheating. Similarly in [5ii] the time of your not wanting any tea is not simultaneous with my utterance but with your future utterance. This is why we need to distinguish the concepts of T_o and T_d: they do not necessarily coincide, even though they usually do.

The four temporal categories: summary

The four times we have distinguished are repeated for convenience in:

[6]			
i	T_{sit}	time of situation	
ii	T_r	time referred to	identified with T_{sit} when aspectuality is perfective
iii	T_d	deictic time	normally the time of utterance
iv	T_o	time of orientation	identified as T_d in the default case

[29] The same applies to recorded speech, as for example in radio broadcasts – *You have been listening to 'The Goon Show'.*

Using '/' to indicate the identification of one time with another, we can represent the temporal interpretation of [1i], *He died of lung cancer*, as $T_r/T_{sit} < T_o/T_d$.

The main use of the tenses is to express the relation between T_r and T_o. Whether T_r is identified with T_{sit} or just part of it is a matter of aspectuality and is not encoded by tense. As far as the identification of T_o is concerned, tense does not distinguish between a deictic T_o and a future T_o; the former is the default identification but it can be overridden to yield a non-deictic interpretation in cases like [5]. However, the distinction between a past and a non-past T_o is relevant to the meaning of the tenses: we will take this up in §5.2, confining our attention in this section to cases involving a non-past T_o.[30]

4.2 The present tense

4.2.1 Present time reference

Contrast between occurrences and states in basic use

The basic use of the present tense, we have said, is to indicate that $T_r = T_o$, where T_o is non-past; in the absence of indications to the contrary, T_o is identified more specifically as T_d. To see more clearly what this involves, we need to invoke the distinction between occurrences and states:

[7] i *I promise to let you have it back tomorrow.* (=[1ii]) [occurrence]
ii *I live in Berlin.* [state]

Occurrences are interpreted perfectively, so that T_r is identified as T_{sit}. For [i], therefore, we have $T_r/T_{sit} = T_o/T_d$: the time of promising coincides with the time of speaking. The verb *promise* is here being used 'performatively' (Ch. 10, §3.1). I perform the act of promising by virtue of saying *I promise*, and hence the time taken to promise is precisely the same as the time taken to utter the sentence. States, by contrast, are interpreted imperfectively, with T_r included within T_{sit}. In [ii] $T_r = T_o/T_d$, but clearly T_{sit} is not coextensive with T_r: it extends without specified limits on either side. I am simply referring to the present time and saying that the situation of my living in Berlin obtains at that time. I say nothing about when it began or how long it will continue.

There is therefore a major difference between occurrences and states with respect to the interpretation of the simple present: dynamic situations are **coextensive with** T_r, whereas static situations **include** T_r.

States: no distinction between limited and unlimited situations

In English, the same grammatical construction is used for states applying over an (implicitly) limited period, as in [8i], and those which hold for all time or are outside time altogether, as in [ii]:

[8] i *She has a headache. She is Austrian. France is a republic.* [limited]
ii *The sun rises in the east. Two plus two is four. God is omnipotent.* [unlimited]

[30] Some writers use 'zero-point' for our T_d, while others talk of the time of utterance/speech. Alternative terms for deictic and non-deictic uses of the tenses are 'absolute' and 'relative' respectively – unfortunate terms given that in either case T_r is located relative to T_o.

Occurrences: constraints on basic use of simple present

The requirement that a dynamic situation be temporally coextensive with the utterance imposes severe constraints on what dynamic situations can be expressed in the simple present. Consider:

[9] *I do 'The Times' crossword.*

This cannot naturally be interpreted as describing a single situation because it takes longer to do 'The Times' crossword than it does to utter [9]. Only some small internal phase of the accomplishment of doing the crossword could be coextensive with the utterance, and hence if I were concerned with a single such phase I would need to use the progressive aspect: *I am doing 'The Times' crossword.* As it stands, however, [9] receives a serial state interpretation: "I habitually do 'The Times' crossword". This state interpretation is imperfective, so that T_{sit} simply includes T_r: the period of time over which my habitually doing the crossword obtains includes T_r and extends without specified limits on either side.

The use of the simple present for dynamic situations is thus very restricted. The main cases (leaving aside fiction) are the following:

(a) The performative use of verbs

[10] *I beg you not to tell anyone.* *I advise you to accept.* *I object strongly to that proposal.* *Passengers on Flight QF312 are requested to proceed to Gate 4.*

(b) Running commentaries and demonstrations

[11] i *Adams steps forward, tries to drive, he's bowled!*
ii *I add two cups of flour and fold in gently.*
iii *We begin by calculating the correction factor, CF:* [calculation given] *and continue by calculating the various sums of squares:* [calculations given]...

The coextensiveness between T_{sit} and T_d is subjective rather than objective: I present the happenings as simultaneous with my utterance even if strictly speaking they are not. Commentaries are generally restricted to a range of conventional contexts where the speaker is specifically assigned the role of commentator, as in the radio cricket commentary example [i]. A demonstration, as in [ii], can be thought of as a commentary on one's own actions. Example [iii], from a statistics textbook, illustrates the written analogue of a demonstration (with *we* involving the addressee in the calculations).

(c) Informal commentaries with preposed locatives

[12] *There it goes.* *Here comes the bus.* *Up he goes.* *Down she falls.*

These are semi-formulaic, with a limited range of locatives and verbs. Non-pronominal subjects are normally postposed, as in the bus example. This case might be extended to cover such examples as *Pop goes the weasel*, found in children's rhymes and stories.

Further restrictions with non-assertives

Cases (b) and (c) are restricted to declaratives – or, more generally, to assertive utterances. There is, for example, no question corresponding to *Here comes the bus: *Does here come the bus?* is ungrammatical and *Does the bus come here?* corresponds to *The bus comes here*, whose natural interpretation is as a serial state. It is possible, however, to have questions corresponding to the performative category: *Do you promise not to tell anyone?*; *Do you, John,* *take Mary to be your lawful wedded wife?* The tense here anticipates, as it were, the answer: the time of your promising (or declining to promise) is that of your answer, not my question. In speech the answer is expected to be given immediately, so there is effectively no difference in the time; in writing, of course, there is likely to be a significant time difference between question and answer, and it is clearly the time of answering that is relevant (cf. *Do you consent to the terms and conditions outlined above?*).

4.2.2 The 'timeless' use of the present tense

The present tense can be regarded as the default term in the primary tense system: in some cases it is used without any specific reference to present time, or to any time at all, but simply because the conditions for the preterite do not obtain.

(a) Synopses and stage directions

One such case is in synopses of TV programmes, films, novels, operas, etc., as in [13i], and in stage directions, as in the bracketed part of [13ii]:

[13] i *Hugo walks out on Darcy, Harry defies government orders and operates on Jenny Pope, and Tom goes on a wild goose chase to rescue Valmai Winters.*

ii DOOLITTLE. *Afternoon, gentlemen. Afternoon, maam.* [*He touches his hat to Mrs Pearce, who disdains the salutation and goes out. He winks at Higgins, thinking him probably a fellow sufferer from Mrs Pearce's difficult disposition, and follows her.*]

This use of the present tense differs from that considered above in that dynamic situations do not have to be short enough to be coextensive with the utterance. *Harry operates on Jenny Pope*, for example, cannot be used for a single present time accomplishment because an operation cannot be performed in the time taken to utter a sentence and hence cannot be viewed perfectively as occurring at T_d. But [i] is not concerned with a real situation occurring at T_d, and hence there is no obstacle to presenting the situation perfectively. If I had seen the TV programme or whatever, I would report its content using the preterite (unless making use of the 'historic present', §4.2.3). The perspective for a synopsis, however, is not that of a past performance (so that the preterite would be inappropriate) but of a work that can be performed (or read) at any time, and is in that sense timeless.

(b) Focus on present existence of works created in the past

A similar use of the 'timeless' present tense is seen in:

[14] i *Describing individuals coping with ordinary life and social pressures, she* [Jane Austen] *uses a sharp satiric wit to expose follies, hypocrisies and false truths.*

ii *That's not exactly what the Bible says.*

iii *Rubens is a master of those parts of his art which act immediately on the senses, especially in the portrayal of the tumult and energy of human action in full power and emotion.*

Writing has a permanence lacking in speech, and where past writings have been preserved they can be read now, and we can talk about them from the perspective of their present and potentially permanent existence rather than that of their past creation. And what holds of writing applies of course to other kinds of creation, as illustrated in [iii].[31]

By contrast, when the concern is with the act of creation itself, then a preterite is required: *Jane Austen wrote 'Emma' in 1815*.

(c) Captions

Similarly, photographs and drawings can give a permanence to what would otherwise be a transient historical occurrence, and captions then use the present tense, as in the following newspaper examples:

[15] i *David Boon (above) is startled into belated action after Indian wicket-keeper Chandra Pandit threw down his stumps at the non-striker's end.*

ii *Aboriginal protesters occupy part of the old Parliament House in Canberra yesterday.*

Note the contrast between the tense and the time adjunct in [ii]. The tense reflects the permanence of the photographic record while the adjunct *yesterday* (like the dates in [16]) gives the time when the occupation actually took place.[32]

(d) Chronicles of history

Past events can also be expressed in this timeless present tense when they are seen as part of a chronicle forming a permanent record of history:

[16] *1434 Cosimo dei Medici begins his family's control of Florence.*

1435 Congress of Arras: Burgundians withdraw support from England, in favour of France.

1438 Albert I becomes Emperor – the first Habsburg Emperor.

4.2.3 Extension of the present tense into past time territory

In [14–15] the present tense is used to give a timeless, permanent perspective to what could also have been conceptualised as past occurrences. There are a number of other places, too, where the present tense encroaches into past time territory:

(a) The historic present in narrative

The present tense is used for past time situations in informal conversational narration or in fiction:

[17] *There was I playing so well even I couldn't believe it and along comes this kid and keeps me off the table for three frames!*

This can be regarded as a metaphorical use of the present tense, a device conventionally used (in English and a very wide range of languages) to make the narrative appear more vivid by assimilating it to the here-and-now of the speech act. Note that in the example cited the speaker switches from preterite in the first two verbs to the present in the last two.

[31] Present tense cross-references to other parts of a single work may perhaps be regarded as a special case of this category: *This matter is discussed in Chapter 2*; *The results of the experiment are shown in Figure 3*. It is also possible to write *was discussed* or *will be discussed*, taking the perspective of the writer or reader progressing through time from beginning to end of the work. Forward references like *We take this matter up in the final chapter* can be construed indifferently as comparable to [14] or as 'futurates' like [20ii] below.

[32] Captions to illustrations in books often use the timeless present tense too (*Dick Purfoy seeks his fortune*; *Mr Meekin administers consolation*), but a preterite is equally possible, to match the narrative text (*D'Artagnan began to renew the acquaintance with Groslow*).

(b) 'Hot news'

The present tense is widely used in news headlines (spoken, as in [18i], or written, as in [ii]) for dynamic situations in the recent past:

[18] i *UN aid reaches the stricken Bosnian town of Srebrenica.*
ii *Probe clears Speaker over bike payout.* *Ailing pensioner gets Govt death notice.*

The texts beneath the headlines in [ii] use past tenses, preterite (*An independent inquiry yesterday cleared former Speaker Leo McLeay of any favourable treatment in his $65,000 bicycle accident compensation claim*) or present perfect (*An 84-year-old Bathurst man recovering from a stroke has received a letter...*), but in headlines the simple present is shorter and more vivid. This might be regarded as a metaphorical extension of the use of the present tense in commentaries.

(c) The past evidential use with verbs of communication

[19] i *Your mother tells me you're off to Paris tomorrow.*
ii *I hear we're getting some new neighbours.*

Your mother's telling me about your departure and my hearing about our neighbours are past time occurrences, and yet the present tense is used. It serves to background the communication occurrences themselves and to foreground their content, expressed in the subordinate clause. The main clause provides, as it were, the evidence for believing or entertaining this content. The primary purpose is therefore normally to impart this content – or to seek confirmation of it. The verbs most commonly used in this way are: *say, tell, inform* (these latter two typically with a 1st person indirect object, or else in the passive with a 1st person subject, as in *I'm told you're off to Paris tomorrow*), and *hear, gather, understand* (these typically have a 1st person subject, with the communicator optionally expressed in a *from* phrase: *I gather from Angela that you're short of money again*). Because the main clause is backgrounded, it generally does not contain elaboration by adjuncts, and in particular will not include temporal specification. In [19i], for example, it would be unacceptable to add *just before she left this morning* or the like. And similarly it would be inconsistent with the backgrounding of the main clause to add that the original communicator no longer believed what they had said – e.g. to add to [19i] *but she now realises you're not going till next week.*

4.2.4 Future time reference in main clauses: the present futurate

The simple present tense can also be used for future time situations: we look first at main clauses and turn to subordinate clauses in the following two subsections. The main clause case we refer to as the **futurate**:

[20] i *The next high tide is around 4 this afternoon.* *There is a solar eclipse on Tuesday.* *When is the next full moon?*
ii *The new Kevin Costner film opens at the Eldorado on Saturday.* *When do lectures end this year?* *She is president until next May.*
iii *If he doesn't help me, I 'm finished.* *If you don't do better next month you are fired.* *Either he plays according to the rules or he doesn't play at all.* *If I get it for less, do I keep the change?*

As evident from the last example in [ii], the time can be a period extending from the present into the future.

Main uses of the futurate

The futurate construction is subject to severe pragmatic constraints: the clause must involve something that can be assumed to be known already in the present. The three most common uses involve cyclic events in nature, scheduled events, and conditionals.

(a) Cyclic events in nature

The present tense is used for recurrent events whose time of occurrence can be scientifically calculated, as in [20i]. Here the scientific evidence for the future occurrence of the situation is clearly such as to warrant including it under what is currently known. We do not, by contrast, use the simple present for future weather. We say *It's going to rain soon* or *It will rain soon*, not *It rains soon*: such events are not conceived of as being within the domain of what is known.

(b) Scheduled events

The examples in [20ii] express future situations that have already been arranged, scheduled by human agency. The evidence for treating these as falling within the domain of what is known might not satisfy the demands of a philosopher concerned with the theory of knowledge, but it is sufficient in the ordinary use of language. The element of current schedule/arrangement is seen in such a contrast as we find in

[21] i *Australia <u>meets</u> Sweden in the Davis Cup final in December.*
ii *Australia <u>beats</u> Sweden in the Davis Cup final in December.*

The present tense is quite natural in [i] (in a context where Australia and Sweden have already qualified for the final), but not in [ii], since this conveys that not only the finalists but also the result has already been arranged. Note that subjective certainty is not enough: I might feel quite certain, on the basis of the skills, experience, and past performance of the teams, that Australia will win, but that does not sanction the simple present *beats*.

(c) Conditionals

We can have a futurate to indicate that the consequence of the condition being fulfilled is inevitable or already decided, as in [20iii]. The first example conveys that if he doesn't help me nothing can prevent my being finished. The second would normally be said by someone with the power to fire you and hence would serve as a threat. The third is only indirectly a conditional (Ch. 15, §2.2.4) but, as spoken by one with the authority to stop him playing, its natural interpretation is "If he doesn't play according to the rules, he doesn't play at all". With a question, as in the fourth example, control switches to the addressee: it is (prototypically) you who decide whether I keep the change. Not all future conditionals with simple present main clauses belong in this category. *What happens if there is a power failure?*, for example, belongs under (b): it is asking what arrangements have been made to deal with this contingency.[33]

Reinforcement by temporal expressions

The cyclic and scheduled event cases are characteristically accompanied by a temporal expression specifying (or questioning) the future time, as in [20i–ii]. Very often, the significant information to be conveyed (or obtained) is precisely the time of the future situation.

[33] It can also have a serial state interpretation, with *if* equivalent to *when* or *whenever*; in this case, the time reference is present.

Progressive futurate

The present progressive is also used in main clauses with a futurate interpretation. It is found in case (b), scheduled events, and to a limited extent case (c), conditionals:

[22] i *The new Kevin Costner film <u>is opening</u> at the Eldorado on Saturday.*
ii *Either he plays according to the rules or he <u>is not playing</u> at all.*

Futurate vs modal *will*

In all the above examples modal *will* could be used instead of the futurate construction. In [20i–ii] substituting *will* wouldn't make much difference: *will* does not indicate that the situations are conceived of as falling within the domain of what is known, but the scientific calculability of the first set and current scheduling of the second could be inferred from the nature of the situations involved. But the contrast is clear in [21]: adding *will* makes [ii] no less acceptable than [i]. Compare also such a pair as *When do we meet again?* and *When will we meet again?* The first is asking about current arrangements, the second is not. In [20iii] the simple present is more forceful, more dramatic than *will*, emphasising the inevitability of the consequence. We will take up the relation between these structures when considering the semantic/pragmatic status of ***will*** in §9.5.

Present futurate involves a present time component

Although the futurate locates the situation in future time, there are grounds for saying that it involves a component of present time as well: the future situation is determinable from the state of the world now. The present time element is reflected linguistically in two related ways.

(a) Contrast between present and preterite futurate

[23] i *My mother <u>is</u> arriving tomorrow / the following day.*
ii *My mother <u>was</u> arriving tomorrow / the following day.*

The future time of arriving is the same in both: what differs is the time of the scheduling, present in [i], past in [ii]. Such contrasts are more readily found in the progressive, but they are not entirely excluded from the simple forms, as seen in [24] below.

(b) Possibility of separate time specification

[24] i *The match <u>now</u> starts <u>next Monday</u>, not Tuesday, as I said in my last letter.*
ii *<u>At that stage</u> the match didn't start <u>till next Tuesday</u>.*

Here the adjuncts *next Monday* and *till next Tuesday* specify the time of the future situation, whereas *now* and *at that stage* give the time of the arrangement or schedule. The temporal interpretation is therefore complex – we understand [i] not as simply "future" but as "future in present", contrasting with the "future in past" of [ii].

Examples [23–24] involve the scheduled event use of the futurate, but it is arguable that such an analysis applies to the futurate construction generally: that it involves a future component associated with the situation itself and a present (or past) component associated with the state of affairs in which the occurrence of the future situation is determined. Performative *I object* and futurate *I leave tomorrow* contrast not as "present" vs "future", but as "simple present" vs "future in present".

Is the tense contrasting with the preterite a present tense or a non-past?

Given that English has no future tense, some modern grammars contrast the two primary tenses as past (preterite) vs non-past. The view taken here, however, is that 'present' is a more appropriate term than 'non-past'. It is true that in subordinate clauses this tense is readily used for both present and future situations, but this is certainly not so in main clauses – and it is fitting to select the general term for the category on the basis of main clause usage. The discussion of the futurate has shown that in main clauses the use of the present tense for future situations is extremely restricted and, moreover, involves an element of present time too.

4.2.5 **Deictic future time in subordinate clauses**

Contrast in temporal interpretation of subordinate and main clauses

In certain kinds of subordinate clause the present tense can be used for future situations without the pragmatic constraints that we have observed for main clauses, i.e. for the futurate. Consider first such pairs of subordinate and main clause as:

[25]	SUBORDINATE	MAIN
i	a. *Don't go until I am feeling better.*	b. *I am feeling better.*
ii	a. *I'll be disappointed if we have wet weather.*	b. *We have wet weather.*
iii	a. *Keep a record of how much you spend.*	b. *How much do you spend?*

In each pair the interpretation of the subordinate clause is quite different from that of the corresponding main clause. The subordinate clauses all have a future interpretation. They do not belong to the futurate construction, however: there is no present time element in their meaning and they are not subject to the pragmatic conditions applying to the futurate – we will refer to them as **pragmatically unrestricted futures**. The main clauses [ib] and [iib] have present time state interpretations: the pragmatic conditions for a natural futurate interpretation are not met in these examples. The salient interpretation of [iiib] is likewise a present time state (a serial state, concerned with recurrent spending); it also allows a futurate interpretation implying a current arrangement for future spending (cf. "How much has been allotted to you to spend?"), but there is no such meaning in subordinate [iiia].

The three subordinate examples differ slightly from one another, but they have it in common that the simple present is not used to make a future time **assertion**. Take [25i] first. In a normal utterance of main clause [ib] I assert the proposition that it expresses (essentially, "I am feeling better now") – and thus commit myself to its being true. But in subordinate [ia] I am not asserting that I am / shall be feeling better at some future time: there is no reference to any specific time. In [iia] there may be reference to a specific time, that of a forthcoming holiday perhaps, but clearly the proposition that we have wet weather at this future time is not asserted to be true: it is merely entertained as a possibility. Since there is no assertion in [ia] and [iia], they are not subject to the pragmatic conditions which apply to the future time use of the simple present tense in main clauses, clauses which **are** characteristically used for assertions.

In [25iii] we have interrogative clauses expressing questions, and hence an extra step is needed in the explanation, for the main clause [iiib] will not itself be used to make an assertion. The prototypical use of a main clause interrogative is to ask the addressee to answer the question it expresses. And the answer will prototypically be given as an assertion (e.g. *I spend $200 per week*). But in the subordinate [iiia] you are not being asked to answer the question now, hence not to make an assertion – so again the pragmatic conditions applying to the assertive use of the simple present do not apply.

Subordinate constructions allowing pragmatically unrestricted futures

The major kinds of subordinate clause where a simple present can be used for a pragmatically unrestricted future are found in the following constructions:

(a) Temporal constructions

The present tense may be used in a clausal complement of *after, before, as soon as, once,* etc., or in a fused relative with *when*:

[26] *I'm drinking it now, before it goes off. We'll leave as soon as it stops raining. Clean up before you leave. Will you be seeing Kim when you are in Bonn?*

(b) Conditional constructions

A future interpretation of the present tense is found in the complement of *if, unless, provided, supposing, on condition,* the verbs *assume* and *suppose*, and in the exhaustive conditional construction:

[27] *She's mad if she goes tomorrow. We'll be staying until Friday unless the weather changes. It should last till next pay-day provided you're careful. Let's assume we are returned with a good majority. Suppose he lets you in. I'm leaving next week whether the job is finished or not.*

(c) Integrated relative clauses

[28] *Anyone who misses tomorrow's meeting is irresponsible. A prize will be given to everyone who gets the right answer. Keep any letters he sends you.*

(d) Embedded interrogative clauses

[29] *I don't mind what you do. Let me know who wins.*

The context has to be such that the answer only becomes available in the future. This is not the case in a context such as *I know / Do you know ...*, and hence only a futurate interpretation is possible in *I know / Do you know when they arrive* and the like.

(e) Comparative clauses

[30] *I'll be able to do it in less time than it takes them. Next time do as he says.*

These in fact are temporally ambiguous between present time ("than it takes them now", "as he says now") and future time.

(f) Complement of *bet, wager,* and *hope*

[31] *I bet it rains again tomorrow. He's hoping she doesn't find out.*

Will is equally possible here. The construction generalises to the deverbal nouns *bet, wager, hope* (*My hope is that she changes her mind*), but not to the adjective *hopeful*.

(g) The covert mandative construction

[32] *It is essential that he finishes the job tomorrow. I insist that she goes too.*

The covert mandative alternates with the more common subjunctive mandative (*that he finish*) and *should*-mandative (*that he should finish*): cf. Ch. 11, §7.1.1.

4.2.6 Future interpretation of a non-deictic present tense

A third construction where a present tense is used with a future time situation was illustrated earlier:

[33] *If you eat any more you'll say you don't want any tea.* (=[5ii])

We interpret the time referred to by present tense *don't* as future, not present. This construction differs from those dealt with in the last subsection, in that here the present tense does express simultaneity. The simultaneity, however, is not with T_d, but with the time referred to in the matrix *say* clause. The temporal relation is $T_r = T_o$, but T_o is identified non-deictically, as future.

Two sources for a future interpretation of a subordinate clause

It follows from what we have said that a future interpretation of a subordinate clause may arise in one or other of the following ways:

[34]	i	$T_r > T_o/T_d$	as in [26–32]	[posterior to present T_o]
	ii	$T_r =$ future T_o	as in [33]	[simultaneous with future T_o]

We need to allow for these two ways of arriving at the same end result because neither on its own will cover all the data. Case [i] will not account for [33], because it doesn't cater for the contrast in this environment between a present tense and a preterite – recall [5i] above, *If she beats him he'll claim she cheated.* Here the cheating is clearly interpreted as anterior to the claim, so that we have "$T_r <$ future T_o", i.e. the preterite counterpart of [34ii]. But nor can [34ii] be generalised to cover [26–32]. Although most of the latter have a matrix clause with a future time, not all of them do: there can be no question of the matrix clause providing a future T_o in [31–32] or the first example in each of [26–29] (*I'm drinking it now, before it goes off; She's mad if she goes tomorrow*, etc.).

No less important is the fact that where the matrix clause does have future time reference it often need not be simultaneous with the future time of the subordinate clause:

[35] i *I'll finish it before you return.*
ii *If you miss her tomorrow, you'll have another chance of seeing her next week.*
iii *Those who pass the test tomorrow will be notified in writing next week.*
iv *I'm quitting at the end of the year whether I pass tomorrow's test or not.*
v *My time for the marathon next year will certainly be worse than it is tomorrow.*

Since the subordinate T_r here cannot be simultaneous with a T_o identified with the matrix T_r, the interpretation again cannot be given by [34ii]. All of the constructions in §4.2.5 allow for a future in the subordinate clause that is not simultaneous with a future referred to elsewhere in the sentence and hence require analysis [34i]. We will therefore restrict [34ii] to constructions where there is a potential tense contrast, with the preterite interpreted as "$T_r <$ future T_o" and the present tense as "$T_r =$ future T_o". The clearest cases involve content clause complements of verbs of saying, thinking, feeling, etc., as in [33].

4.3 The preterite, as used to express anteriority

In this section we examine the use of the preterite to indicate that T_r is earlier than T_o; its use for modal remoteness and in backshift will be taken up in §6, after consideration of the secondary past tense, the perfect.

4.3.1 Past time reference

The basic use of the preterite is to locate T_r as anterior to T_o, where T_o is identified as T_d:

[36] i *I promised to let you have it back tomorrow.* [occurrence]
ii *I lived in Berlin.* [state]

Occurrences

Here, as in the present tense, the aspectuality is perfective. With a past time occurrence, therefore, T_r coincides with T_{sit}, and since T_r is in the past, T_{sit} must be wholly in the past. However, there is no requirement that it be of short duration, as a dynamic present time situation must normally be: in the present, $T_r = T_o/T_d$ and hence has to be of the same duration as T_d, whereas in the past, $T_r < T_o/T_d$ and hence is not subject to any such constraint. In [36i] T_r/T_{sit} is short, but in *The glacier moved only about 50 metres during the next century* it is 100 years long.

No analogue of pragmatic constraints on dynamic use of present tense

It follows that the severe constraints on the use of the simple present for occurrences (noted in §4.2.1) do not apply in the preterite. Compare, for example:

[37] i *I do 'The Times' crossword.* (=[9]) [present: serial state]
ii *I did 'The Times' crossword.* [past: occurrence or serial state]

We have seen that an interpretation of [i] as a singulary dynamic situation is generally ruled out, but such an interpretation is perfectly natural for [ii], which can refer to a single doing of the crossword as readily as to habitual doing of the crossword. With the preterite, therefore, greater importance attaches to adjuncts and context in selecting between occurrences and serial states: compare the effect of adding on the one hand *yesterday* (inducing a dynamic interpretation), and on the other *regularly* or *whenever I could find the time* (which yield interpretations as serial states).

States

Here the aspectuality is imperfective, so that T_r does not coincide with T_{sit}: with the preterite, therefore, the state does not have to be wholly in past time (cf. [3ii], *I already knew how to do it*). Very often there will be an implicature that the state no longer obtains, but it is not an entailment. If we add *in those days* to [36ii] this encourages an interpretation where I no longer live in Berlin, but if we expand it instead to *I already lived here in Berlin at that time* we get an interpretation where I still live in Berlin. Compare also such examples as *I liked her as soon as I met her and we've been good friends ever since.* If the state still obtains in the present the question arises: Why is a preterite used, rather than a present tense? And the answer of course is that we use a preterite because we are **talking about** some time in the past – T_r is in the past. The state obtained at T_r but (unlike an occurrence) is not co-extensive with it. In this respect, the preterite is precisely parallel to the present tense.

We noted in connection with [37] that the distinction between occurrences and serial states is less clearly drawn in the preterite than in the present tense, and the same applies with ordinary (non-serial) states. Thus whereas present tense *I live in Berlin* is quite obviously a state, preterite *I lived in Berlin* can be construed in either way:

[38] i *At that time I lived in Berlin.*
ii *After the War I moved to Germany; I lived in Berlin for three years and then spent a few months in Cologne.*

In [i] it is a state, but in [ii] it is presented as one of a sequence of occurrences. In [i] it is seen as obtaining at T_r but extending without specified limits before and after T_r; in [ii] it is viewed in its totality, and its time simply is T_r. The perfective aspectuality in [ii] embraces the transition into and out of the state, resulting in what we have called a state-occurrence.

4.3.2 Past time reference in combination with politeness/diffidence

The preterite is commonly used in preference to the present in examples like the following, where it is considered somewhat more polite:

[39] i *I wanted to ask your advice.*
ii *I wondered whether I could see you for a few minutes.*

The politeness/diffidence feature is also found with the past progressive: *I was hoping to see the Manager.* The prototypical case (for either aspect) is that illustrated in [39], a declarative with 1st person subject, but 3rd person subjects can be used when I am talking on someone else's behalf: *My daughter was hoping to speak to the Manager.* And the same usage carries over into interrogatives, with a switch to 2nd person subject: *Did you want to see me?*

Politeness/diffidence feature as an implicature

This conventional use of the preterite is quite consistent with its basic past time meaning. It would not be correct to say that [39i], for example, is an ambiguous sentence, interpretable in one sense as describing my wants at some time in the past and in another as a more polite, more diffident version of *I want to ask your advice.* Rather, the first of these interpretations corresponds to what the sentence means, and the second is a context-dependent implicature deriving from that basic, literal meaning. In the absence of any contextual indication that I am referring to some definite time in the non-immediate past, T_r will here be interpreted as immediate past time. As the situations are states, not occurrences, use of the preterite does not entail that the state no longer obtains. And since there is nothing to suggest that the state has ended, the interpretation will be that the state also obtains at T_d, so that [39] conveys "I want to ask your advice", "I wonder whether I can see you for a few minutes". The added politeness associated with the preterite comes from avoiding explicit reference to the immediate present: I distance myself slightly and thus avoid the risk of appearing too direct, possibly brusque.

4.3.3 The past futurate

The preterite can be used for arranged or scheduled situations located posterior to some time in the past, in what we are calling the futurate construction (§4.2.4):

[40] i *Originally entries closed tomorrow, but they've decided to allow another week.*
ii *I was leaving for Sydney the next day so couldn't spend much time with them.*

The progressive, [ii], is used for the futurate as readily as in the present tense but the simple preterite is very rare and generally of somewhat marginal acceptability: normally one would use a more explicit formulation such as *Originally, entries were due/scheduled/going to close tomorrow.*

A major reason why the simple preterite is so much less readily used in the futurate than the simple present is that the pragmatic constraints on the basic use of the simple present with dynamic situations do not apply with the simple preterite, as noted above. *The match starts on Tuesday*, for example, can't be used for a present time occurrence: it can only be a futurate (leaving aside the barely possible serial state interpretation). With *The match started on Tuesday*, however, there is nothing to block the basic meaning of the preterite, with the match starting in past time: if the past time applies to the arrangement rather than the starting, therefore, one will not normally associate the preterite with the verb *start* itself.[34] The past progressive futurate *The match was starting on Tuesday* does dissociate the preterite from *start* (so that the structure is more like that of *The match was due to start on Tuesday*, etc.), and the futurate interpretation is further facilitated by the fact that the basic meaning of progressive aspect is pragmatically very unlikely here.

4.3.4 Non-deictic anteriority

The preterite expresses the relation $T_r < T_o$, with T_o non-past; normally T_o is identified as T_d, but it can also be some future time identified in a matrix clause. This has already been illustrated in [5i]; further examples are:

[41] i *If you don't buy it you will soon regret that you missed such a bargain.*
ii *If you don't buy it you will soon envy the one who did.*

The missing in [i] and the buying in [ii] are here anterior to the (potential) future regret and envy, not to T_d. This is similar to the non-deictic use of the present tense to express simultaneity with a future T_o, as discussed in §4.2.6. The two cases are not completely parallel, however, in that the preterite is used in this way in a somewhat wider range of constructions than the present tense – notably in relative clauses, as in [41ii].

Note that we can replace *did* in [41ii] by *does*, but this does not change the temporal location of the situation. While preterite *did* indicates that the buying is anterior to the future envying, present tense *does* does not indicate that the buying is simultaneous with it; the present tense here conveys posteriority of T_r relative to T_o/T_d, so that the interpretation is to be accounted for by [34i] rather than [34ii].

5 Perfect tense

The secondary tense system contrasts the perfect, marked by ***have*** + past participle, and the non-perfect, which is unmarked. The perfect, marked analytically, and the preterite, marked inflectionally, constitute the two past tenses: they have it in common that in their basic meanings they both express the temporal relation of anteriority. This is seen most clearly in such examples as:

[1]	i *He wrote it last week.*	[preterite]
	ii *He is believed [to have written it last week].*	[perfect tense]

[34] It nevertheless is quite possible if the context does exclude the basic past time meaning, as in *We had to get up very early because the train left at six*: what necessitated our getting up early can't have been the subsequent event itself but the fact that it was scheduled.

5.1 The perfect as a non-deictic past tense

In its basic use the preterite is usually interpreted deictically, locating T_r as anterior to T_o/T_d, i.e. as anterior to now. The perfect tense, by contrast, is normally non-deictic. Consider:

[2]	i	*He was believed [to* *have written* *it the previous week].*	[$T_r <$ past T_o]
	ii	*He is believed [to* *have written* *it last week].* (=[42ii])	[$T_r <$ present T_o]
	iii	*He hopes [to* *have written* *it by next week].*	[$T_r <$ future T_o]

Here the past T_o in [i] is established by the preterite in the matrix clause, the present T_o in [ii] by the present tense in the matrix clause, and the future T_o in [iii] by the lexical properties of the verb *hope* (in combination with the adjunct *by next week*). The perfect tense itself expresses "$T_r < T_o$", and the temporal identification of T_o is given by the larger context; this latter aspect of the interpretation is discussed further in §7.

Compound tenses

In order to bring out the contrast between preterite and perfect tenses most clearly, examples have been chosen where the perfect occurs in a clause lacking primary tense. When we combine the perfect with a primary tense, marked by the inflection on ***have***, we have a compound tense expressing two temporal relations. We will use superscripts to distinguish the T_r–T_o pairs related by primary and secondary tense:

[3]	i	*At that time I* *had written* *two chapters.*	[preterite: $T^1_r < T^1_o$; perfect: $T^2_r < T^2_o$]
	ii	*Now I* *have written* *four chapters.*	[present: $T^1_r = T^1_o$; perfect: $T^2_r < T^2_o$]

The preterite perfect [i] locates the writing anterior to an intermediate time which is anterior to the time of speaking – it is doubly anterior. This interpretation derives from the combination of the meanings of the two past tenses as follows. The preterite (the primary past tense) indicates that T^1_r, the time specified more precisely by the adjunct *at that time*, is anterior to T^1_o, which is identified deictically as the moment of speaking. And the perfect (the secondary past tense) indicates that T^2_1, the time of writing, is anterior to T^2_o, which is identified non-deictically as T^1_r. (T^2_r is interpreted as the time of writing as a whole because the situation is dynamic, hence perfective.) Notice that there is no essential difference between this and an example like [2i], which is likewise doubly anterior. In both, the perfect locates the writing as anterior to some T_o which is identified via other features of the sentence as anterior to T_d; the difference is that in [2i] the relevant other feature is the preterite marked on *was believed*, whereas in [3i] it is the preterite carried by ***have*** itself.

The present perfect [3ii] locates the writing anterior to the time of speaking – there is only one past tense here. But it is still non-deictic. The perfect again locates T^2_r, the time of writing, anterior to T^2_o; this is not identified deictically as the time of speaking, but rather non-deictically as T^1_r, which the present tense locates as simultaneous with T^1_o/T_d. This is the major difference between the present perfect and the simple preterite, as in *I wrote four chapters*, which locates the writing anterior to T_o/T_d in a single step. The different temporal relations expressed in the preterite perfect, present perfect and simple preterite (assuming deictic primary tense in all cases) are shown schematically in [4]; the implications of the difference between present perfect and simple preterite are taken up in §5.3 below.

[4] i preterite perfect: *had written*

$T_r^2 \quad < \quad T_o^2/T_r^1 \quad < \quad T_o^1/T_d$

writing — intermediate time — now

ii present perfect: *has written*

$T_r^2 \quad < \quad T_o^2/T_r^1 = T_o^1/T_d$

writing — now

iii simple preterite: *wrote*

$T_r \quad < \quad T_o/T_d$

writing — now

5.2 Complex anteriority: continuative and non-continuative perfects

An important difference between the two past tenses is that the perfect can locate T_r either wholly before T_o or as beginning before but extending forward to include T_o. Only the former possibility is available with the preterite. Compare:

[5]	NON-CONTINUATIVE (T_r wholly before T_o)	CONTINUATIVE (T_r before and up to T_o)
i	a. *He may have told her last week.*	b. *He may have been here ever since.*
ii	a. *He told her last week.*	b. **He was here ever since.*

The case where T_r begins before but extends forward to T_o is called the **continuative** reading: the situation continues throughout that period. This is illustrated in [ib], where his being here covers a period beginning in the past and extending up to now. The deviance of [iib] shows that the preterite cannot be used for this meaning – only for the **non-continuative** reading where T_r is wholly before T_o, as in the [a] examples.

The temporal relation "T_r wholly before or before and up to T_o" we will call **complex anteriority**; **simple anteriority** is the relation "T_r wholly before T_o". We can then say that the basic use of the perfect is to express complex anteriority with non-deictic T_o, while that of the preterite is to express simple anteriority with deictic T_o.

Non-continuative as default reading

The non-continuative reading of the perfect is much the more frequent, and can be regarded as the default one. The continuative reading virtually requires reinforcement by time adjuncts, such as *since* or *for* phrases (cf. *He has been ill for the last four days*):[35]

[6]		
i	*She has lived in Berlin ever since she married.*	[continuative]
ii	*She has lived in Berlin.*	[non-continuative]

In [i] the situation lasts from her marriage up to now (and in the absence of contrary indications will presumably continue into the future). In [ii] the absence of the duration adjunct (unless it is clearly recoverable from the context, as in response to the question *Where has she lived since she married?*) forces the non-continuative reading: her living in Berlin is said to have taken place at some indefinite time in the past. Notice, then, that

[35] The requirement is not absolute: *It's been very hot, hasn't it?* could be used in a context where it is still very hot, emphasising the duration of the heat. In many languages the perfect has only a non-continuative reading and translations of examples like [6i] will have simple present tenses.

a continuative reading has imperfective aspectuality, while a non-continuative one has perfective aspectuality.

Continuative restricted to atelic situations

A further restriction on the continuative perfect is that in the non-progressive it allows only atelic situations (ones without an inherent terminal point: §3.2.3):

[7] i *He has lived here / visited her regularly ever since they met.*
ii **He has written another poem / found his keys again ever since he came home.*

In [i] we have two states, ordinary (living here) and serial (visiting her regularly); in [ii] an accomplishment (writing another poem) and an achievement (finding his keys again). Activities are possible (*He has talked non-stop ever since he arrived*), though the progressive would be somewhat more likely (especially without the *non-stop*: *He has been talking ever since he arrived*). Dropping the *ever* makes [ii] grammatical: an ordinary *since* phrase is compatible with a non-continuative reading, giving the period within which the occurrence is located. Examples like *She has lived in Berlin since then* are therefore ambiguous; the continuative reading is more salient, but the other is possible too (cf. *Since then she has lived in Berlin and Paris, as well as London*).

5.3 Present perfect vs the simple preterite

5.3.1 Present perfect as a compound tense

When primary tense combines with the perfect it gives the temporal location not of the situation itself but of the T_o that the situation (or the part of it referred to) is anterior to. With the preterite, this yields double anteriority, as noted above. Compare:

[8]	i *She went to work.*	[preterite non-perfect]
	ii *When he got up she had gone to work.*	[preterite perfect]

In [i] her going to work is anterior to now, while in [ii] it is anterior to a time (the time when he got up) that is itself anterior to now. The motivation for the compound tense here is to relate the time of one situation to that of another. Consider now the present tense:

[9]	i *I promise to do it tomorrow.*	[present non-perfect]
	ii *I have promised to do it tomorrow.*	[present perfect]
	iii *I promised to do it tomorrow.*	[preterite non-perfect]

Example [i] locates my promise as simultaneous with now, while [ii] locates it as anterior to now. But [iii] too locates it as anterior to now. The difference is that [iii] does so directly, whereas [ii] does so indirectly: the promise is anterior to a time which is simultaneous with now. Nevertheless, the end result, in terms of the temporal location of the promise, is the same (cf. diagram [4]). So what is the point of using a compound tense rather than the simple preterite?

The difference in meaning and use between the present perfect and the simple preterite reflects the fact that the former is a compound tense combining past and present, whereas the latter is a simple tense, just past. In the simple preterite T_d is involved only **passively**, as T_o in the anteriority relation $T_r < T_o$: here T_d is not here referred to, talked about. In the present perfect, however, T_d is **actively** involved: the primary tense is present, expressing the relation $T^1_r = T^1_o$, so that T_d doesn't just identify T_o but is equated with

T_r, and hence T_d is referred to, talked about, just as in the basic use of the simple present. With the simple preterite the focus is on the past situation (or, in the case of states, the past segment of it being talked about); with the present perfect the primary focus is on the present.

Past time adjuncts normally excluded from present perfect

The present perfect involves reference to both past and present time: it is concerned with a time-span beginning in the past and extending up to now. It is not used in contexts where the 'now' component of this is explicitly or implicitly excluded:

[10] i	*I saw her last week / two minutes ago.*	[explicit exclusion of now]
ii	*Who wrote 'Moby Dick'?*	[implicit exclusion of now]

Except under conditions outlined below, time adjuncts like *last week, two minutes ago,* etc., which refer to times wholly before now, are incompatible with the present perfect: we cannot replace *saw* by *have seen* in [i]. Example [ii] illustrates the case of past situation focus: the existence of 'Moby Dick', and hence the writing of it, is taken for granted, and the issue concerns a particular feature of the past situation, the identity of the writer. Compare *Who has written this note?*, which might be said in a context where the note has just been discovered, with the focus on its present existence.[36]

5.3.2 The experiential perfect

Grammars commonly distinguish four major uses of the present perfect: the **continuative**, the **experiential** (or 'existential') perfect, the **resultative** perfect, and the perfect of **recent past**. These can be thought of as a classification of the main ways in which the concept of a time-span up to now can be involved in the use and interpretation of the present perfect – or as different ways in which the past situation may have 'current relevance'. The continuative has been dealt with already, and can be distinguished reasonably sharply from the non-continuative: compatibility with such expressions as *ever since* provides a criterion. The three categories within the non-continuative are not mutually exclusive, but they are useful nevertheless.

The experiential/existential perfect is seen in:

[11] i *I've finally finished.* *We've now walked ten miles.*
ii *This is / That was the best meal I've had all week.*
iii *His sister has been up Mont Blanc twice.*

This use of the present perfect is concerned with the occurrence of situations within the time-span up to now. The connection with now is clearest and most direct when the completion of an accomplishment takes place at (or virtually at) T_d, as in [i]. The possibility of having present time adjuncts like *now* or *at present* shows clearly that we have present time meaning as well as present tense form. These bear some resemblance to continuatives – the walking ten miles, for example, has occupied a period up to now. However, they cannot take continuative adjuncts like *ever since* (**We've*

[36] A special case of implicit exclusion is found in the use of the simple preterite for politeness/diffidence, as in *I wondered if I could see you for a moment* (§4.3.2). *Have wondered* could not be substituted here because it conveys (by virtue of the perfective aspectuality) that the wondering situation is over, which is the reverse of what I want to convey. (Progressive *have been wondering* is possible, however, because it has imperfective meaning.)

now walked ten miles ever since we started), and they are interpreted perfectively, not imperfectively.

The connection with now is also apparent in [11ii], illustrative of a common type involving superlatives or ordinal numerals (cf. *It's the first/third time you've said that today*). There is an actual or potential series of occurrences within the time-span up to now (with *first* only one is actualised, but there could have been more). In the *this is* version of [ii] the meal is presumably still taking place, but it is nevertheless presented perfectively (progressive *I've been having* would be out of place), for the issue is its ranking in a series, which applies to it as a whole.

The connection with now is less direct in [11iii]: the ascents could be quite a long time in the past. The focus, however, is not on their occurrence at some particular time in the past but on the existence of the situation within the time-span. The connection with now is the potential for occurrence, or recurrence, of the situation at any time within the time-span up to now. Thus [iii] implicates that his sister is still alive, while *I haven't been to the market yet* implicates that the possibility of my going to the market still exists (it hasn't closed down).[37]

Experiential perfects vs simple preterites

Compare now the following pairs:

[12] i a. *It is better than it <u>has ever been</u>.* b. *It's better than it <u>was</u>.*
ii a. *<u>Have</u> you <u>seen</u> Jim?* b. *<u>Did</u> you <u>see</u> Jim?*

In [ia] the comparison is between its quality now and its quality at any time within the time-span – clearly the potential for it to be of such and such a quality still exists. In [ib] the comparison is between now and then; the past is contrasted with the present, the 'then' situation is over and excludes now.

Example [12iia] brings out the point that there may be limits to the time-span beyond those inherent in the situation itself. The inherent limit is that Jim (and you) must be alive, but in the salient interpretation I will have in mind a much shorter span than this: the time of his current visit to our vicinity, today, the period since we were last together, or whatever it might be. It would not be acceptable for you to answer *yes* on the strength of having seen him before this time-span. Whatever the limits on its beginning, however, the time-span stretches up to now. But [iib] is very different. Assuming again that you know Jim and have seen him perhaps many times, you need to determine more specifically what I am asking. This time, however, it is not a matter of placing limits on the start of the time-span up to now, but of finding which particular, definite past time I am asking about – your visit to Jim's sister last month, or whatever it might be, but a time that is over, exclusive of now.

Past time adjuncts in experiential perfects

This use of the present perfect allows for the inclusion, under restrictive conditions, of a past time adjunct:

[13] i a. *He <u>has got</u> up at five o'clock.* b. *He <u>got</u> up at five o'clock.*
ii a. *We <u>'ve</u> already <u>discussed</u> it yesterday.* b. *We <u>discussed</u> it yesterday.*

[37] The implicature may be weaker: that the same **kind** of situation is still possible. *Nixon has been impeached*, for example, can still be acceptable even though Nixon has since died, given a context where the issue is the occurrence within the time-span of situations of the kind 'impeachment of a president'.

In [ia] "at five o'clock" is a crucial part of the potentially recurrent situation: the issue is that of his getting up at this early hour; there is no reference to any specific occasion, as there is in the simple preterite [ib]. In [iia] the *already* indicates that I'm concerned with the occurrence of the situation of our discussing it within a time-span up to now and cancels the normally excluding effect of *yesterday* evident in [iib].

5.3.3 The resultative perfect

[14] i *She has broken her leg.* *He has closed the door.* *They've gone away.*
ii *She's been to the bank.* *She has run ten kilometres.*
iii *I've tried to phone her, but she's not answering.*

The clearest cases of the resultative perfect are illustrated in [i], where the situation is one that inherently involves a specific change of state: breaking a leg yields a resultant state where the leg is broken, closing the door leads to the door's being closed, going away (from place *x*) results in a state where one is no longer at place *x*, and so on. The connection with the present in this resultative use is that the resultant state still obtains now. *She has broken her leg* does not **mean** "Her leg is broken", but this is the likely implicature unless the context selects an experiential interpretation. Cases like [i] are known more specifically as the perfect of **continuing result**: the resultant state begins at the time of occurrence of the past situation itself and continues through into the present.

Examples like [14ii] may be interpreted resultatively in a much vaguer sense. *Be*, as used here, means "go and return" and hence does not yield a resultant state "not at place *x*" as *go* does. A resultative interpretation of *She's been to the bank* is thus not derivable directly from the meaning but is heavily dependent on pragmatics – it might be, for example, "She has some money", but it could equally be "The cheques are deposited", or whatever. Similarly there is no state resulting inherently from running ten kilometres, so an implicature like "She is tired" or "She is hot" is heavily dependent on context.

Example [14iii] illustrates the phenomenon of 'nil results', the failure to obtain the expected or intended result – in this example, that of making contact with her. In the broader sense that goes beyond case [i], the resultative is clearly not mutually exclusive with the experiential: [ii] and [iii] have both components in their interpretation – and similarly [13iia] is likely to have the resultative implicature "We don't need to discuss it again".

5.3.4 The perfect of recent past

[15] i *It has been a bad start to the year, with two fatal road accidents overnight.*
ii *I've discovered how to mend the fuse.*
iii *She has recently/just been to Paris.*

One respect in which a past situation may be connected with now is that it is close in time to now. It is clear from examples like [11iii] (*His sister has been up Mont Blanc twice*) that it does not have to be recent, but there is nevertheless a significant correlation between the present perfect and recency, whereas the simple preterite is quite indifferent as to the distance between T_r and T_o. The present perfect is therefore the one most frequently used in news announcements, as in the radio bulletin example [15i]. It is arguable that the experiential and resultative categories are broad enough to cover all non-continuative uses, but recency adds an important component to the account. For example, [15ii] has a continuing result interpretation: the discovery resulted in my knowing how to mend the fuse and this knowledge persists. Such knowledge can persist for a long time, so there is nothing in the idea of continuing result itself to exclude my having made the discovery years ago. But in fact the normal interpretation involves a recent discovery. We have noted that experiential perfects like [12iia] (*Have you seen Jim?*) impose limitations on the time-span up to now beyond those inherent to the situation, and these additional limitations also involve recency.

Adjuncts of recency

As illustrated in [15iii], the present perfect admits the adjuncts *recently* and *just*, which of course signal a perfect of recent past (when they are used deictically, in contrast to the non-deictic use in *She had recently/just been to Paris*). But recency as such is not sufficient to sanction a time adjunct: **I have seen him a minute ago* is no better than **I have seen him a year ago*. *Recently* and *just* do not refer to definite times in the past, but indicate an indefinite time within a short interval stretching back from their T_o (which in their deictic use is identified as T_d). They are comparable, therefore, to expressions like *within the last few years*, where recency is not an issue, but which combine quite freely with the present perfect.[38]

5.4 Non-present perfects

The distinction between the present perfect and the simple preterite is neutralised elsewhere in the verbal system, so that when ***have*** carries any other inflection than the present tense the perfect may correspond to either a present perfect or a simple preterite. Compare, for example:

[16]	i	a.	*He <u>has lost</u> his key so he can't get in his room.*	[present perfect]
		b.	*He <u>had lost</u> his key so he couldn't get in his room.*	[preterite perfect]
		c.	*He seems to <u>have lost</u> his key so he can't get in his room.*	[non-finite perfect]
	ii	a.	*He <u>lost</u> his key while he was running home.*	[simple preterite]
		b.	*He <u>had lost</u> his key while he was running home.*	[preterite perfect]
		c.	*He seems to <u>have lost</u> his key while he was running home.*	[non-finite perfect]

In [i] the non-present perfects *had lost* and *have lost* correspond to present perfect *has lost*, while in [ii] they correspond to the simple preterite *lost*. It does not follow, however, that the non-present perfects are ambiguous: it is rather that they are not subject to the restrictions and specialisation that apply to the present perfect (and which are attributable to the fact that it is in contrast with the simple preterite). In the case of the preterite perfect, for example, we have the temporal relations $T_r^2 < T_o^2$/ $T_r^1 < T_o^1$; in [ib] the context suggests that the focus is on T_r^1, the intermediate point (when he was unable to get in his room because of the earlier loss of his key), whereas in [iib] the focus is on T_r^2, the time of losing the key, but both are special cases of a single more general meaning which is neutral as to focus on T_r^1 or T_r^2.

[38] There are some relatively small-scale differences between AmE and BrE with respect to the choice between the present perfect and the simple preterite – cases where AmE may prefer a simple preterite where BrE prefers or requires a present perfect. One case concerns situations in the recent past, where *I just saw them*, for example, might be preferred in AmE, *I've just seen them* in BrE. Another case concerns the aspectual adjuncts *already* and *yet*: for discussion, see Ch. 8, §8.

5.5 Omissibility of the perfect

Under certain conditions the perfect may be omitted with little or no effect on the temporal interpretation. The construction to be considered here has the perfect in a subordinate clause following such prepositions as *after*, *as soon as*, or *before*:

[17] i *She left after / as soon as / before he had spoken to her.* [perfect]
ii *She left after / as soon as / before he spoke to her.* [non-perfect]

The temporal relation between her leaving and his speaking to her is effectively the same in [ii] as in [i], being indicated by the preposition. In [ii] we have a single T_r in the subordinate clause, identified perfectively as the time of his speaking. In [i] there is reference to two times, with T_r^2 the time of his speaking and T_r^1 an intermediate point to which T_r^2 is anterior. But there is no significant gap between T_r^2 and T_r^1, so that it doesn't make any appreciable temporal difference whether the time of her leaving is specified in relation to one or the other.

The contrast between the perfect and non-perfect takes on more significance when T_{sit} is of relatively long duration, especially with *as soon as* and (to a lesser extent) *before.* Thus while the perfect is omissible in *She left the country as soon as she had completed her thesis* (with punctual T_{sit}), it is not omissible in *She left the country as soon as she had written her thesis* (where the thesis-writing situation is too long to be compared with the country-leaving one). Similarly *She left the country before she had written her thesis* allows (and indeed suggests) that she had started writing when she left and is thus not equivalent to *She left the country before she wrote her thesis*, which indicates that the leaving preceded the whole of the thesis writing.

The perfect is also omissible in the gerund-participial complement of certain catenative verbs such as *regret*: see §7 below.

5.6 Scope of the perfect

There are three issues relating to the semantic scope of the anteriority expressed by the perfect that merit brief mention; two are discussed here, one in §9.8.

(a) Multiple situations

[18] i *Every time I've seen them, they've been drinking.* [ambiguous]
ii *Every time I see them, they've been drinking.* [unambiguous]

Example [i] has two interpretations: one where I've always seen them **after** they've been drinking, and one where I've always seen them **as** they were drinking. Example [ii] has only the first type of reading: I always see them after they've been drinking.

The ambiguity of [18i] can be seen as a matter of the scope of the anteriority relation expressed by the main clause perfect. In the first interpretation each drinking subsituation is anterior to the corresponding subsituation of my seeing them: we refer to this as a narrow scope reading since the anteriority applies just to the simple subsituation of their drinking. In the second, wide scope, reading, the anteriority applies to the complex subsituation of my seeing them as they are drinking. The wide scope reading is excluded in [ii] because the *see* clause is in the simple present tense.

(b) *Should/would like* + perfect

[19] i *I should/would have liked to meet her.* [default version]
ii *I should/would like to have met her.* [lowered *have*]
iii *I should/would have liked to have met her.* [pleonastic *have*]

Constructions [ii] and [iii] are often used to convey the same meaning as [i]. We refer to [i] as the default version in that there is a single anteriority relation applying to the liking situation: ***have*** has scope over the following past participle, as usual. In [ii] ***have*** is syntactically in construction with ***meet*** while related semantically to ***like***: ***meet*** is lower in the constituent structure than ***like***, so we can think of ***have*** as having been 'lowered' into the complement of ***like***. In [iii] the second ***have*** is pleonastic in that it does not express a second anteriority relation. Strictly speaking, [ii] and [iii] are ambiguous: they also have interpretations in which anteriority applies to the meeting. These interpretations are pragmatically somewhat unlikely in the examples chosen, but become more salient if we change *met her* to *finished it*: *I should like to have finished it* can mean "I should like to be in the situation of having finished it" (and such a normal scope interpretation is the only one available in *I should like to have finished it by the end of the week*).

6 Further uses of the past tenses

6.1 Modal remoteness

Modal contrasts between preterite and present tense

In some constructions the preterite expresses modal rather than temporal meaning. Compare the preterite and present tenses in the following pairs of subordinate clauses:

[1]	PRETERITE: PRESENT TIME	PRESENT TENSE: PRESENT TIME
i	a. *I wish he was here.*	b. *I'm glad he is here.*
ii	a. *If he was here, he'd be upstairs.*	b. *If he is here, he'll be upstairs.*

[2]	PRETERITE: FUTURE TIME	PRESENT TENSE: FUTURE TIME
i	a. *I'd rather you went tomorrow.*	b. *I bet you go tomorrow.*
ii	a. *If you went tomorrow, you'd see Ed.*	b. *If you go tomorrow, you'll see Ed.*

In each pair the time of the situation expressed in the subordinate clause is the same: present in [1], future in [2]. The difference is a matter of modality, of how the subordinate clause is presented with respect to its factuality, likelihood, and so on. We refer to clauses with a preterite tense expressing such modal meaning as **modal preterite clauses**. Normally, as in [1ia/iia], preterite tense *was* is replaceable by irrealis mood *were*.

The interpretation of modal preterite clauses depends on the type of matrix construction containing them. The subordinate clause in [1ia] has a counterfactual interpretation: because of the meaning of *wish* we understand that he is not here. Example [ib], with matrix *glad*, conveys that he is here, but *I think/hope he is here* leaves it open: the present tense is the default one, and covers both factual and various kinds of non-factual cases. In the conditionals in [1ii] we have a more direct contrast, since *if* can be used with either preterite or present tense. The difference is that [iib] presents his being here as an open possibility, whereas [iia] presents it as a remote possibility. Very often the preterite is used when the subordinate proposition is known to be false, but it is not restricted to such cases. It is perfectly possible to say, for example, *I don't know whether he's here, but I doubt it: if he was here, he'd be upstairs.*

Where the time of the situation is future, as in [2], the difference between preterite and present tense is not quite so sharp. In [ia] the preterite can be seen as acknowledging the possibility that you won't go tomorrow: I'm expressing a mere preference, not an expectation, demand, or the like. In the conditional [2ii], the preterite version again presents the possibility of the condition being satisfied, of your going tomorrow, as more remote than the present tense version.

Remote and open conditional constructions

The most common use of modal preterite clauses is in conditional constructions. We refer to examples like [1iia] and [2iia] as **remote conditionals** and [1iib] or [2iib] as **open conditionals** – and we use **modal remoteness** as a label for the meaning of the preterite in all the above examples, a label general enough to cover all the more specific interpretations that we have illustrated. See Ch. 8, §14.2, for a fuller discussion of the difference in meaning between the two types of conditional construction.

The open conditional is the default type, while remote conditionals have the following properties:

[3] i Subordinate clause: must contain a preterite (or irrealis *were*) expressing modal remoteness.
ii Matrix clause: must contain a modal auxiliary, in the preterite if possible.[39]

Open conditionals of course do not require a modal auxiliary in the matrix, but only those that do contain one have a remote counterpart. Consider, for example:

[4] i *If you see Jill, tell her I'm waiting to hear from her.*
ii *If it rains, we're going to take a taxi.*
iii *If they are here, they're in the kitchen.*

In [i] the matrix clause is imperative, hence tenseless: very obviously, then, there is no possibility of changing to preterite tense to mark remoteness. In [ii–iii] the matrix clause has present tense, but does not contain a modal auxiliary: it is possible to switch tenses (*If it rained we were going to take a taxi*; *If they were here, they were in the kitchen*), but the result is not a remote conditional but an open one with changed time reference. We will develop this point further when we examine the meaning and use of ***will***.

Modal remoteness in combination with past time reference

In the modal preterite clauses considered so far, the time of the situation has been present or future; when it is past, we need a preterite perfect:

[5]	PRETERITE PERFECT: PAST TIME	SIMPLE PRETERITE: PAST TIME
i	a. *I wish <u>I had accepted her offer</u>.*	b. *I'm glad <u>I accepted her offer</u>.*
ii	a. *If <u>it had come yesterday</u> he would surely have told her.*	b. *If <u>it came yesterday</u> he will surely have told her.*

[39]'If possible' in [ii] allows for the occurrence in the present tense of those modals like ***must*** which have no preterite form (cf. §6.2.1).

Again *wish* yields a counterfactual interpretation: I didn't accept the offer. Usually, past-time remote conditionals are also interpreted counterfactually: you are likely to infer from [iia] that it didn't come yesterday. But that cannot be part of the meaning actually expressed since, as in the present time case, it would be perfectly possible to say: *I don't know whether it came yesterday, but I doubt it: if it had come yesterday he would surely have told her.*

In the [b] examples in [5] the primary past tense, the preterite, has its basic use of expressing past time, but in [ia/iia] it serves to express modal remoteness and is therefore not available to locate the situation in past time. As a result, the secondary past tense, the perfect, has to be brought into service to fulfil this latter function. This is the one place where the perfect is interpreted deictically: it locates the accepting her offer and the coming as anterior to T_o, and T_o can only be identified as T_d.

Preterite perfects with a doubly remote interpretation

In [5ia/iia], we have noted, the preterite expresses modal remoteness and the perfect expresses temporal anteriority. With present and future time, it is possible for both past tenses to function modally yielding a (fairly rare) **doubly remote** construction. For conditionals we therefore have the following three-way contrasts:

[6]	i	a.	*If they <u>are</u> still alive they will be horrified.*	[open: present time]
		b.	*If they <u>were</u> alive now they would be horrified.*	[remote]
		c.	*If they <u>had been</u> alive now they would have been horrified.*	[doubly remote]
	ii	a.	*If they <u>go</u> tomorrow they will meet her son.*	[open: future time]
		b.	*If they <u>went</u> tomorrow they would meet her son.*	[remote]
		c.	*If they <u>had gone</u> tomorrow they would have met her son.*	[doubly remote]

In [i] the difference between [b] and [c] is not very tangible: [ic] adds an extra dose of modal remoteness, as it were, but it still does not encode counterfactuality (cf. again, *I don't know whether they are still alive, but I doubt it: certainly, if they had been . . .*). In [ii] there is a sharper difference. Here [iic] **is** presented as counterfactual, in the sense that it conveys that they will not be going tomorrow. It suggests that the issue of their going tomorrow has already been decided negatively – for example, by virtue of their having gone already or of it having been arranged that they will go at some other time.[40]

The doubly remote preterite perfect is also found with other cases of the modal preterite:

[7]	i	a.	*I wish they <u>were</u> here now.*	[remote: present time]
		b.	*I wish they <u>had been</u> here now.*	[doubly remote]
	ii	a.	*I'd rather you <u>went</u> tomorrow.*	[remote: future time]
		b.	*I'd rather you <u>had gone</u> tomorrow.*	[doubly remote]

[40]The doubly remote construction is not available for past time because the perfect construction is not recursive. The formal resources don't allow for more than two past tenses, and in [5ia/iia] the perfect is serving its basic function of expressing anteriority and hence cannot contribute to the expression of modal remoteness. Analogously, it is not possible to express double anteriority in the remote construction. The remote counterpart of open *If it had already died when she phoned, he will have told her* is *If it had already died when she phoned he would have told her*, where there is no difference in the form of the subordinate clause: since the preterite is being used modally we have only one anteriority relation expressed, the other being inferred from the *already*. Without the *already*, the example does not specify whether the death preceded or coincided with the phoning.

As with the conditionals, there is little discernible difference in the present time case, but a clear one with future time. Thus [iib] again conveys that it has already been settled that you won't be going tomorrow.

Formal marking of modal remoteness

We have been concerned so far with cases where modal remoteness is expressed by the same formal means, preterite tense, as the temporal relation of anteriority. There are three ways, however, in which the meanings may be differentiated.

(a) Irrealis *were*

With a 1st or 3rd person singular subject, irrealis *were* is often used instead of preterite *was*, especially in more formal style: *If he were/was less dogmatic we could solve the problem in no time.* This issue has been discussed in §1.7.

(b) ***Be*** + infinitival

There is one use of quasi-modal ***be*** that serves as a marker of the remote conditional construction, with ***be*** appearing in either preterite or irrealis form:

[8] *If she was/were to return now, we would be in real trouble.*

This is equivalent to *If she returned now,...*; quasi-modal ***be*** cannot occur in the open construction except with a quite different sense, so the only open conditional corresponding to [8] is *If she returns now, we will be in real trouble.*

(c) *Had + have*

Instead of an ordinary preterite perfect, a non-standard 'double perfect' is often found:

[9] i !*If it had've come yesterday he would surely have told her.*
ii !*I wish he hadn't've left.*

This is largely restricted to speech (or the written representation of speech). It appears to be increasing in frequency, and though it is not as yet established as a standard form, it is used by many who in general speak standard English. From a grammatical point of view it is a curious construction in that *had* is followed by a plain form, not a past participle; it is normally reduced to /əv/, and in writing is sometimes spelled *of*, indicating that it is not perceived as a form of ***have***.[41]

6.2 The backshifted preterite

6.2.1 Backshifted preterite vs ordinary preterite

The third major use of the preterite is in backshifting:

[10] i	*I have too many commitments.*	[original utterance: present tense]
ii	*Jill said she had too many commitments.*	[backshifted report: preterite]

We are concerned with [ii] in the interpretation where it reports Jill's prior utterance of [i] – or of any other sentence expressing that proposition, for this kind of report purports to give the content of what was said, not the actual wording used. In [i] ***have*** is in the present tense, whereas in [ii] it is in the preterite: the term **backshifted**

[41] A further non-standard variant has *would have*: !*If it would have come yesterday he would surely have told her.* Very often, however, the first verb is reduced to *'d* and it is then unclear whether this is to be taken as a reduced form of *would* or of *had*: *if she'd have done it* is ambiguous.

preterite is intended to suggest this change from an original present to a preterite. We retain the traditional terminology for its mnemonic value, but emphasise that back-shift is not conceived of here as a syntactic process: we are not proposing that *had* is syntactically derived by changing the present tense of an underlying *have* into a preterite. The issue to be considered is simply what the preterite means in this construction.

Why backshift involves a special use of the preterite

The first question we need to ask is why backshift cannot be subsumed under the basic use of the preterite. After all, no one says that *she* has some special use or meaning in [10ii]: it is used in the same way as in the main clause *She had too many commitments*, namely in definite reference to some contextually identifiable female. Why can't we say, similarly, that the preterite in *had* is used in its ordinary way, again as in *She had too many commitments*, to locate T_r as anterior to T_o/T_d? Given its context, this T_r would be identifiable, more specifically, as the time when Jill said [i].

There are two reasons why such an account would not work, why we need to recognise a backshifted preterite as distinct from an ordinary one.

(a) Backshifting within the scope of a modally remote preterite

[11] i *If he knew she <u>had</u> too many commitments, he would do something about it.*
ii *I wish he <u>realised</u> that she <u>had</u> too many commitments.*

Example [i] is a remote conditional, with the preterite in *knew* expressing modal remoteness, not past time: the time of knowing is present. So too (certainly in the salient interpretation, the one we are concerned with here) is the time of her having too many commitments: it is a matter of knowing in the present about a situation obtaining in the present. And the same applies to the *wish* construction [ii]. In both, therefore, we have the preterite form *had* even though there is no reference at all to past time: this cannot represent the ordinary use of the preterite. Nor would it be valid to subsume the preterite in *had* in these examples under the modal remoteness use which applies to the matrix clause preterite verbs *knew* and *realised*. For clearly the unlikelihood in [i] and the counterfactuality in [ii] apply to his knowing/realising but not to her having too many commitments. There is no modal remoteness meaning attaching to *had*, for, certainly in [ii], you will in fact infer that she does have too many commitments. From a semantic point of view, therefore, the preterite carried by ***have*** must be distinguished from that carried by ***know*** or ***realise***, and this distinction is reflected in the grammar in that irrealis *were* is not substitutable for *was* in this construction: *If he knew she was/*were too busy, he would do something about it*; *I wish he realised that she was/*were too busy.*

(b) Acceptability of present tense forms of modal auxiliaries

[12] i *We knew we <u>must</u> leave by noon yesterday to have any chance of catching her.*
ii *She said I <u>ought</u> to invite them both, but I didn't take her advice.*

The modals ***must*** and ***ought*** have no preterite forms, and hence cannot occur with the past time meaning associated with the preterite: examples like #*We must leave by noon yesterday, so we did* and #*I ought to invite them both but I didn't* are nonsensical. They can appear in the present tense in examples like [12], however, which would require a preterite if one were available: compare *We knew we had/#have to leave by noon yesterday*;

She said I was/#am morally obliged to invite them both, but I didn't. We can account for the acceptability of [12] by allowing that with verbs having only present tense forms these forms can occur where otherwise a backshifted preterite would be needed. But this of course requires that we draw a distinction between a backshifted preterite and an ordinary one.

Conditions for backshift

A backshifted preterite can occur when either of the following conditions obtains:

[13] i The **tense** of the matrix clause is past.
ii The **time** of the matrix clause situation is past.

The reference to past tense in [i] allows for backshifting after a perfect as well as after a preterite:

[14] *I have never said she had too many commitments.*

In the great majority of cases, the two conditions in [13] are satisfied jointly, as in [10ii], but either alone is sufficient:

[15] i *I wish he realised that she had too many commitments.* [satisfies [13i]]
ii *I remember telling him that she had too many commitments.* [satisfies [13ii]]

In [15i] (repeated from [11]) the matrix clause has a past tense (*realised*), but the time is present; in [15ii] the matrix clause, with *telling* as its verb, has no tense (it is non-finite) but the time of the telling is understood as past by virtue of properties of *remember*, and this is sufficient to sanction backshift in the *have* clause.[42]

Backshifting of an 'original' preterite

In the examples so far, the 'original utterance' has been in the present tense; when it is in the preterite, the backshifted construction has a preterite perfect:

[16] i *I had too many commitments.* [original utterance: simple preterite]
ii *Jill said she had had too many commitments.* [backshifted: preterite perfect]

Meaning of the backshifted preterite

The backshifted preterite represents a distinct use of the preterite that differs in meaning from a preterite in its primary use. Compare, for example:

[17] i *She had too many commitments.* [ordinary preterite]
ii *Jill said she had too many commitments.* (=[10ii]) [backshifted preterite]

Ordinary preterites are normally deictic: [i] locates T_r as anterior to a T_o that is identified with T_d, here the time of speaking. But a backshifted preterite is non-deictic: it indicates that T_o is identified by the matrix clause. In [ii], therefore, the T_r for the *have* clause is simultaneous with a T_o identified as the time of Jill's utterance. Given that the latter is in the past, we end up with the same result as for [i], namely that T_r is anterior to the time of my utterance. However, we end up with this result via a different and more complex route than in [i]. And examples like [15i] show that the end result is not always the same

[42] Again, the possibility of having *must* here shows that the *had* of [15ii] is a backshifted preterite, not an ordinary one: *I remember telling him that we must leave by noon yesterday.*

as with an ordinary preterite, because in [15i] the time referred to in the matrix clause is present, not past.

Let us examine the difference more precisely. We have seen that two factors are involved in locating T_r: (I) the relation between T_r and T_o; (II) the identification of T_o. The values of these variables are different for the two kinds of preterite in [17]:

[18] i Ordinary preterite ([17i]) (I) $T_r < T_o$ (II) T_o is non-past
ii Backshifted preterite ([17ii]) (I) $T_r = T_o$ (II) T_o is past

In the ordinary use, the anteriority expressed by the preterite is a matter of relation (I); there is no anteriority in (II), where the more specific interpretation, applying in [17i], identifies T_o with T_d. In a backshifted case like [17ii], by contrast, the anteriority expressed by the preterite is a matter of (II), with the past T_o identified by the past T_r of the matrix *say* clause. In the backshifted use the relation between the subordinate T_r and its T_o is not directly expressed by the preterite. Thus (I) in [18ii], $T_r = T_o$, is not part of the meaning of the preterite here: it is a default value arising from the **absence** of any expression of anteriority.[43] When anteriority **is** expressed, by the perfect, as in [16ii], we have:

[19] Backshifted preterite + perfect ([16ii]) (I) $T_r < T_o$ (II) T_o is past

The perfect is required here for the same reason as in past time remote conditionals (§6.1): the primary past tense is not being used to express the anteriority relation $T_r < T_o$, and hence the secondary past tense has to be introduced for that purpose. And for [15i] we have:

[20] Backshifted preterite ([15i]) (I) $T_r = T_o$ (II) T_o is present

(I) again has the default value $T_r = T_o$, and T_o is again identified by the T_r of the matrix *realise* clause, but since the latter is present, the combination of factors (I) and (II) here yields a present time situation. The fact that backshift applies even when the matrix clause identifying the T_o has preterite form without past time reference shows that backshift is a grammatical phenomenon, akin to agreement: the *had* here agrees in tense with the verb of the matrix clause without there being any strictly semantic motivation for its preterite form.

Backshift not confined to indirect reported speech

We introduced the concept of a backshifted preterite with an example involving indirect reported speech, [10]. It is important to emphasise, however, that the backshifted preterite is used much more generally than in reported speech. Compare:

[21] i *This meant that Jill had too many commitments.*
ii *That Jill had too many commitments was undeniable.*

Conversion to indirect reported speech not a matter of grammatical rule

There is a second respect in which we must beware of being misled by the traditional account associating backshift with indirect reported speech. The term 'backshift' may suggest an operation performed on the 'original' utterance to convert it into indirect reported speech – with, for example, Jill's original *have* becoming *had* when I report her utterance. Converting into indirect reported speech, however, is not a matter of applying

43 The relation can equally be that of posteriority when the corresponding present tense of the 'original utterance' has a future interpretation: compare *I'll stay until you are better* with *I said I'd stay until you were better*, where *were* is interpreted as posterior to the past T_o defined by the T_r of *said*.

rules of grammar that are specific to this purpose. When I make an indirect report of Jill's speech, I purport to give the content of what she said – as opposed to quoting the actual wording, which is direct reported speech. In [10], the content of Jill's utterance [i] is the proposition "I [sc. Jill] have too many commitments", and hence my report must also express this proposition. But leaving aside the issue of the tense, the way I express this proposition is just the same as if I were expressing it quite independently of her utterance. The subject could be *Jill*, *she*, *you* (if I am talking to Jill), *I* (if it is Jill who is talking), and so on: as remarked above, there is nothing special about the use of *she* in [10i]. What is special about the tense is that it is non-deictic: T_o is identified not with the reporter's T_d but with the original speaker's, and the preterite encodes this anteriority of T_o.[44] We have seen that backshift extends far beyond reported speech, as illustrated in [21], where there is no 'original speech' to convert. What [21i–ii] have in common with our initial example [10ii] (*Jill said that she had too many commitments*) is that the preterite tense of the content clause is non-deictic, taking its T_o from the matrix clause rather than immediately from T_d. This is how backshift is to be interpreted, not as converting one tense into another.

Non-subordinate backshift

Backshift normally occurs in subordinate clauses under the conditions given in [13], but it can also be found in main clauses as a literary device for representing thoughts or interior monologue:

[22] i *Would she be home before he left, she wondered.*
ii *Max was getting more and more anxious. What could have happened to her? Would she be home before he left? Ought he to contact her mother?*

Example [i] illustrates the case where the reporting verb is parenthetical: *would she be home before he left* is therefore syntactically a main clause, not a complement of *wonder*. Example [ii] illustrates what is often called 'free indirect speech', an essentially literary device for representing thoughts or interior monologue without any overt reporting verb at all (cf. Ch. 17, §10.2). The backshift itself (alone or in combination with other features) signals the adoption of a non-deictic T_o; note that the appearance of present tense *ought* in [ii] shows this to be just like the ordinary, subordinate, type of backshift construction.

6.2.2 Obligatory vs optional backshifting

A backshifted preterite may be pragmatically equivalent to a present tense

Very often, the use of a backshifted preterite is optional. Jill's *I have too many commitments* may be given in indirect reported speech in two ways:

[23] i *Jill said she had too many commitments.* [backshifted: preterite]
ii *Jill said she has too many commitments.* [non-backshifted: present tense]

Corresponding to the original present tense we have a preterite in [i] but a present tense in [ii]. The two reports do not have the same meaning, but in many contexts the difference

[44] With the modals *must*, *ought*, etc., in examples like [12], the anteriority of T_o cannot be formally expressed, but is pragmatically inferred.

between them will be of no pragmatic significance. The difference is that in [i] the T_r for the *have* clause is simultaneous with the T_o identified as the time of Jill's utterance, whereas in [ii] it is simultaneous with a T_o identified as the time of my utterance. But suppose Jill's utterance took place quite recently and there has been no change in her circumstances between then and now: in this context, if she had too many commitments then, she will still have too many commitments now, and the change in T_o will not affect the validity of the report in any way.

Four types of 'original utterance'

The options for reporting the two simple primary tenses and the two compound tenses are as follows:

[24]	ORIGINAL	BACKSHIFTED	NON-BACKSHIFTED
i	*I <u>am</u> ill.*	*She said that she <u>was</u> ill.*	*She said that she <u>is</u> ill.*
ii	*I <u>broke</u> it.*	*She said that she <u>had broken</u> it.*	*She said that she <u>broke</u> it.*
iii	*I <u>have seen</u> it.*	*She said that she <u>had seen</u> it.*	*She said that she <u>has seen</u> it.*
iv	*I <u>had left</u>.*		*She said that she <u>had left</u>.*

With an original preterite perfect (case [iv]), there is no possibility of a backshifted version: it would require a combination of three past tenses, which is beyond the formal resources available. In the other three cases, however, backshifting is always possible, and constitutes the default option; it provides, strictly speaking, a more faithful report in that it uses the same T_o as the original speaker.

Backshift with a complex original utterance

When the original utterance is complex, with a primary subordinate clause embedded in a main clause, the options are as shown in:

[25]		
i	*I <u>am</u> leaving before he <u>returns</u>.*	[original utterance]
ii	*She said she <u>was</u> leaving before he <u>returned</u>.*	[backshifted + backshifted]
iii	*She said she <u>was</u> leaving before he <u>returns</u>.*	[backshifted + non-backshifted]
iv	*She said she <u>is</u> leaving before he <u>returns</u>.*	[non-backshifted + non-backshifted]

It is not possible, however, to have non-backshifted + backshifted (**She said she <u>is</u> leaving before he <u>returned</u>*): once one has exercised the option of selecting a deictic tense, the option of selecting a non-deictic, backshifted, one is no longer available. Thus if there is more than one level of embedding, as when the original utterance is *I'm sorry I'm leaving before he returns*, we can have a backshifted preterite corresponding to all three present tenses, the first two or just the first one, but these are the only possibilities.

Condition on use of deictic rather than backshifted tense

In the non-backshifted type of report, I use a deictic tense, taking T_o from my own utterance rather than the original one. This is subject to the following pragmatic condition:

[26] It must be reasonable to assume that the temporal relation between the situation and the reporter's T_d is the same as that between the situation and the original T_d.

A deictic, non-backshifted, report indicates that the original utterance (or belief, etc.) is still applicable and relevant.

Consider the following examples with respect to condition [26]:

[27] i a. *Jill said she had/has a weak heart.*
b. *Jill said she had/has a headache.*
ii a. *Jill said the payment was / is due next week.*
b. *Jill said the payment was / is due on Tuesday.*

Deictic *has* will be much more widely appropriate in [ia] than in [ib] because having a weak heart can be assumed to last much longer than having a headache. Jill's utterance needs to have been quite recent for *has* to be appropriate in [ib], whereas it could be quite distant in [ia] – provided she hasn't died. The 'original' present tense in [ii] had future time reference. In [iia] the condition for the use of deictic *is* is satisfied because the (alleged) payment date is future relative to my utterance as well as to Jill's. Whether *is* is appropriate in [iib] depends on the time reference of *Tuesday*: *is* is appropriate if the reference is to the Tuesday following my report, but not if it is to a Tuesday falling between Jill's utterance and mine – compare *Jill said the payment was due yesterday*, where a backshifted preterite is obligatory.

Factors affecting choice between backshifted and non-backshifted versions

Where condition [26] is satisfied, both backshifted and non-backshifted versions are in principle possible. A number of factors are relevant to the choice between them:

(a) Reporter's attitude to the content

If I endorse or accept the original, this will somewhat favour the deictic present version, and conversely if I reject it this will favour backshift:

[28] i *She said she doesn't need it, so I'll let Bill have it.* [accepted: non-backshifted]
ii *She said there was plenty left, but there's hardly any.* [rejected: backshifted]

But the opposite combinations certainly cannot be excluded: *She said it's illegal, but I'm sure it's not* (rejected, but non-backshifted), *She said it was excellent, so why don't we go?* (accepted, but backshifted).

(b) Indication of deictic future

Consider the following reports of *I'm leaving at the weekend*, where the situation is in future time:

[29] i *She said she was leaving at the weekend.* [backshifted]
ii *She said she's leaving at the weekend.* [deictic]

If there has been a week-end between the original utterance and the report, [ii] is excluded because it does not satisfy condition [26]: the week-end referred to is posterior to the original but anterior to the report. But if no week-end has intervened, [ii] will be more informative than [i] precisely because it indicates that the time of leaving is still in the future. If this information is not readily retrievable from elsewhere, [ii] is likely to be favoured.

(c) Focus on original

If the focus is on the original utterance or belief, with a contrast between 'then' and 'now', this will favour the backshifted version:

[30] *I thought it was mine.* [backshifted]

One context for this is where it has just been established that it **is** mine: *thought* would here be strongly stressed, indicating a contrast between past thinking and present knowing (of the same proposition). Another context is where it has just been established (or claimed) that it is not mine: here the contrast is between what I thought in the past and what is known/claimed in the present. In either case the past time location of the thinking is foregrounded, focused, and this favours the backshifted version, preserving the original T_o: deictic *is* would hardly be possible here.

(d) Present perfect reporting clause

The present perfect focuses on the present rather than the past (§4.3), and tends therefore to favour the non-backshifted version, using a present T_o. Compare the following reports of *I can't afford it*:

[31] i *She said she couldn't afford it.* [simple preterite report: backshifted]
ii *She has said she can't afford it.* [present perfect report: non-backshifted]

The reverse pairings are of course possible, but those shown in [31] are the most frequent.

(e) Simplification

Where the original utterance or belief is in the present tense, the backshifted and non-backshifted versions differ merely in primary tense, preterite vs present. But where the original is in the simple preterite they differ as preterite perfect vs simple preterite, i.e. as compound vs simple tense. In this case the non-backshifted version may be preferred precisely for its greater simplicity. Note that condition [26] will always be satisfied with an original simple preterite: if the situation was anterior to the original utterance, it will also be anterior to the report. Both backshifted and non-backshifted versions will therefore always be available. It is doubtful whether either of them can in general be regarded as the default version: it depends on the nature of the situation. Consider:

[32] i *She asked me where I was / had been born.*
ii *She said she wrote / had written it herself.*
iii *She said she loved / had loved him when she was at college.*
iv *She said she loved / had loved him.*

In [i] *was* cannot be interpreted as a backshifted preterite: it can be assumed that she did not ask, #*Where are you born?* In [ii], assuming that the *write* situation is a single occurrence, not a serial state, *wrote* will again not be interpretable as backshifted: non-serial (perfective) *I write it myself* is too unlikely. Similarly in [iii], assuming that the *when* adjunct modifies **love**, not ***say***: *I loved him when I was at college* is very much more likely as the original than is *I love him when I am at college* (with the implicature of "then, but not at other times"). In none of these cases, then, is the preterite perfect necessary in order to ensure the intended temporal interpretation – and the principle of simplification is likely to favour the non-backshifted version with the simple preterite. In [iv], however, the subordinate situation is a state, and there is no temporal adjunct: in the absence of any counter-indications from the context the version with *loved* will be interpreted as a report of *I love him.* If it is intended to report *I loved him,* it will therefore be necessary to use the backshifted preterite perfect *had loved.*

6.3 Primary vs secondary past tense

We have been referring to the preterite and the perfect as respectively primary and secondary past tenses; there are three reasons for distinguishing them in this way.

(a) Relation to T_d

In languages in general, tense systems prototypically locate T_r relative to T_o/T_d, i.e. they are deictic, and we have seen that the English preterite is most often interpreted in this way, whereas the perfect is generally non-deictic. The preterite is thus a clearer instance of a tense than is the perfect. Moreover, when they combine in the preterite perfect to express double anteriority, it is the preterite that encodes the first move back from T_d, while the perfect encodes a further move back beyond that: the primary/secondary contrast has been shown in our notation by the superscript numerals, as in [44–45] of §5.

(b) Degree of grammaticalisation

The primary tense system is more highly grammaticalised than the secondary one. One obvious reflection of this is that it is marked inflectionally rather than analytically. The perfect marker ***have*** is a member of the small closed class of auxiliary verbs, so that the perfect can properly be regarded as a grammatical category, but analytic marking of this kind represents a lesser degree of grammaticalisation than inflection. No less important, however, is the fact that the preterite is in contrast with another tense, the present, whereas the perfect merely contrasts with its absence. The present perfect and the preterite perfect are compound tenses (involving two T_r–T_o relations), whereas the present non-perfect and the preterite non-perfect are simple tenses (involving a single T_r–T_o relation): non-perfect is not a tense. The present tense is distinct from the absence of primary tense (*She is / They are ill* vs *She is / They are believed to be ill*), but there is no such distinction with secondary tense. A third factor commonly involved in grammaticalisation is discrepancy between form and meaning: highly grammaticalised elements tend to develop uses which depart from their core meaning. The preterite is used for modal remoteness and to indicate backshift as well as with its core meaning of locating T_r anterior to T_o, whereas the perfect is almost restricted to this latter use.

(c) Anteriority expressed by the perfect when the preterite not available

We have noted that when the preterite is used for modal remoteness or in backshift (to locate T_o), the perfect takes over the role of expressing the anteriority of T_r relative to T_o: see [16]. It similarly has this role in non-finite clauses, which lack primary tense altogether: compare finite *He died in 1806* with non-finite *He is believed to have died in 1806*.

7 Temporal interpretation of constructions without primary tense

In general, the concept of T_r is relevant to the interpretation of tenseless constructions as well as tensed ones. Suppose I say *Please open the window*, for example. This is an imperative clause with *open* a tenseless form of the verb – a plain form. The (potential) opening of the window, however, is not timeless: you will understand, in the absence of indications to the contrary, that my intention is for you to open the window in the immediate future, i.e. the time just following my utterance. In this case, the interpretation is linked to the imperative form of the clause.

It is not necessary to survey all kinds of constructions containing non-tensed verbs: the main issues can be seen by considering briefly just two, non-finite clauses functioning as complement to catenative verbs or as modifier in NP structure.

The catenative construction

[1]	i	*I remembered [going to Sydney at Christmas].*	$[T_r < T_m]$
	ii	*I enjoyed [going to Sydney at Christmas].*	$[T_r = T_m]$
	iii	*I intended [going to Sydney at Christmas].*	$[T_r > T_m]$

The bracketed gerund-participial is complement of the preceding verb, which belongs to the class we have called catenatives (cf. §2.2 above). In [i] we understand the time of my going to Sydney to be anterior to the time of remembering. The time of remembering is the time referred to in the matrix clause, the one in which the non-finite clause is embedded. We call this **matrix time**, symbolised T_m, while T_r is the time referred to in the clause under consideration, the gerund-participial. The annotation on the right thus says that the T_r for the *go* clause is anterior to the matrix time. In [ii], the time of going and the time of enjoying are simultaneous, while in [iii] the time of going is posterior to T_m, the time referred to in the *intend* clause.

Because the *go* clause is tenseless it does not itself express any relation between its T_r and some T_o. Rather, the T_r is related directly to the matrix time, and the different interpretations of [33i–iii] are attributable to the semantic properties of the matrix verbs *remember, enjoy,* and *intend.* Catenative verbs may thus be classified according to the temporal interpretation that they permit for their complement. A sample of such a classification is given in [2], with examples in [3]:

[2]	i	Class 1:	anterior	*forget*$_1$	*recall*	*recollect*	*remember*$_1$
	ii	Class 2:	anterior or simultaneous	*admit*	*deny*	*regret*	*resent*
	iii	Class 3:	simultaneous	*begin*	*believe*	*like*	*seem*
	iv	Class 4:	simultaneous or posterior	*may*	*must*	*need*	*will*
	v	Class 5:	posterior	*aim*	*intend*	*propose*	*want*

[3]	i	Class 1		*I remember telling you about it.*	$[T_r < T_m]$
	ii	Class 2	a.	*He resents her taking the car while he was out.*	
			b.	*He resents not having access to his own file.*	$[T_r = T_m]$
	iii	Class 3		*She is believed to be in hiding.*	
	iv	Class 4	a.	*She may be his sister.*	
			b.	*She may abdicate.*	$[T_r > T_m]$
	v	Class 5		*She wants to finish it when you return.*	

Forget$_1$ and *remember*$_1$ take gerund-participial complements, and are to be distinguished from *forget*$_2$ and *remember*$_2$, which take infinitivals and belong to Class 3 (*I forgot to turn off the oven*). With Class 2 verbs, the choice between anterior and simultaneous interpretations depends on the aspectuality of the complement clause. In [3ii], for example, the *take* clause in [a] is perfective, while the *have* clause in [b] is imperfective.

If the matrix time is present, a complement interpreted as simultaneous is generally subject to the pragmatic constraints on perfective situations that apply to the present tense:

[4] i *I do 'The Times' crossword.* (=[9] of §4) [present habitual]
ii *He seems to do 'The Times' crossword.* [present habitual]
iii *He may do 'The Times' crossword.* [present habitual or future]

We noted in §4.2.1 that [i] normally requires a serial state (habitual) imperfective reading, resisting a singulary (dynamic) perfective one, and the same applies to the infinitival clause of [ii]. *Seem* belongs to Class 3, with $T_r = T_m$, and since *seem* is here in the present tense the tenseless *do* of its complement is interpreted like a present tense. *May* belongs to Class 4, and in the interpretation where the complement time is simultaneous with the matrix time, the *do* will again be interpreted as habitual: "It may be that he does 'The Times' crossword". In the interpretation where the complement time is posterior to the matrix time the constraint does not of course apply, and [iii] can be interpreted with a singulary doing of the crossword in future time.

There is a slight blurring of the distinction between simultaneous and posterior interpretations in two cases, illustrated in:

[5] i *I can't understand them leaving tomorrow.*
ii *I desperately want this card to be an ace.*

Understand belongs to Class 2, but what is simultaneous with the matrix time in [i] is not the leaving itself but the schedule or arrangement for them to leave: [i] is comparable to *I can't understand why they leave tomorrow*, where *leave* is a present tense with a futurate interpretation. (Alternatively, the finite construction could have a progressive: *why they are leaving.*) *Want* in [ii] we have assigned to Class 5, but one might argue that the time of the card being (potentially) an ace is now; what lies in the future is of course the revelation as to whether it is an ace or not.

The perfect auxiliary *have*

Most but not all catenative verbs allow their non-finite complement to be headed by the perfect auxiliary ***have***. Thus we can have *He seemed to have offended them* but not **He began to have offended them*, or again *I expected him to have finished by six*, but not **I made him have finished by six*. With *begin* and *make* the matrix and subordinate situations are not temporally separable, so that the latter cannot be marked as anterior to the former by means of the perfect construction.

Where the non-finite complement does have perfect *have* as its verb, the semantic properties of the catenative verb again play a role in determining the temporal interpretation. Compare:

[6] i *He resents [her having taken the car while he was out].* } [$T_r < T_o$; $T_o = T_m$]
ii *She is believed [to have been in hiding].* }
iii *She wants [to have finished it when you return].* [$T_r < T_o$; $T_o > T_m$]

T_r in the annotations is the time referred to in the underlined past-participial clause; the perfect, as we have seen, locates this T_r as anterior to some T_o. The properties of the catenative verb then locate this T_o with respect to the matrix time. Here there are only two possibilities, not the three of [1] or [3]: the T_o is simultaneous with T_m in [6i–ii], posterior to it in [6iii]. Note, then, that there is no temporal difference between [6i] and [3iia]: in both, the time of her taking the car is anterior to the time of the *resent* clause (which is simultaneous with T_d, the time of utterance). Catenative verbs of Class 4 or 5, however, allow the perfect to locate the past-participial time as posterior to the matrix time, as in [6iii]. Here, in contrast to [3v], the finishing (if her want is fulfilled) will be anterior to your return.

Non-finite clauses functioning as modifier in NP structure

In the following gerund-participials the time associated with the underlined verb is interpreted relative to T_d, the time of utterance:

[7] i *Just about anyone living in the area at that time is at risk.* [$T_r < T_d$]
ii *The guy sitting next to your wife was on television last night.* [$T_r = T_d$]
iii *Anyone misbehaving at tonight's meeting won't be invited next week.* [$T_r > T_d$]

In [i] the adjunct *at that time* will be understood in context as referring to some time in the past, and that is the time of the living: "anyone who lived in the area at that time". The salient interpretation of [ii] is that the guy is sitting next to your wife now, at the time of speaking. And in [iii] it is a matter of misbehaving on some future occasion, the meeting to be held tonight. Such examples bring out clearly the tenseless nature of the gerund-participial: the verb itself gives no indication of the location of T_r, which is determined by other elements in the sentence or by the context. Very often the participial T_r is simultaneous with T_m (as in *The guy sitting next to you at lunch looked very frail*; *Some of those waiting outside are showing signs of impatience*; etc.), but this is not so in any of the examples in [7]. Given that the verb leaves quite open the location of T_r, one needs to be able to retrieve it from elsewhere, and T_m is then one particularly accessible source, but this is not to say that simultaneity with T_m is a meaning expressed by the construction.

The same applies with passive past-participials. Those in [8] match [7] above:

[8] i *Those arrested yesterday will appear in court this afternoon.* [$T_r < T_d$]
ii *The allegations contained in this report will be strenuously denied.* [$T_r = T_d$]
iii *Proposals submitted after today won't be considered till next month.* [$T_r > T_d$]

Infinitival modifiers in NP structure

The infinitival construction allows a narrower range of temporal interpretations than the participial, being in general restricted to simultaneity or posteriority to T_m, as in [9i–ii] respectively:

[9] i *She was the only one to talk to him.* [$T_r = T_m$]
ii *She was looking for someone to talk to.* [$T_r > T_m$]

Temporal location is closely bound up with modality: the infinitival commonly conveys non-actuality, which tends to be associated with posteriority. The temporal difference between [i] and [ii] thus correlates with the difference in modality: in [i] the talking is actual, whereas in [ii] it is potential.

8 Progressive aspect

8.1 Progressive aspectuality

The progressive, marked by the auxiliary ***be*** + a following gerund-participle, has as its basic use the expression of progressive aspectuality: hence, of course, the name. There are also some specialised uses (§8.3) which cannot be subsumed under this meaning, and this is why we are distinguishing between progressive aspect, a category of syntactic form, and progressive aspectuality, a category of meaning.[45]

Progressive aspectuality involves the following features, two of which are strong implicatures rather than part of the meaning proper:

[1] i The situation is presented as in progress, ongoing, at or throughout T_r.
ii The situation is viewed imperfectively.
iii T_r is a mid-interval within T_{sit}. [implicature]
iv The situation is presented as durative.
v The situation is presented as dynamic.
vi The situation is presented as having limited duration. [implicature]

(a) Situation in progress at/throughout T_r

[2] i *He was reading the letter when the phone rang.*
ii *They were talking about it over lunch.*
iii *I am reading 'Middlemarch' at the moment.*

In [i] the T_r is specified by the adjunct *when the phone rang*, and at this point the reading was in progress, ongoing. The formulation 'at/throughout' allows for T_r to be a point, as in this example, or a period, as in [ii]. Some situations are not strictly continuous but allow for gaps, and the concept of 'in progress at T_r' is perfectly consistent with T_r actually coinciding with such a gap, as in [iii]. One is unlikely to read 'Middlemarch' at a single sitting: there will be reading interspersed with periods when one is doing other things (such as sleeping). But this is of no linguistic significance, for the gaps are treated as part of the situation – note for example that *It took me six months to read 'Middlemarch'* gives the time between start and finish, including all these gaps. Thus in [iii] it is the situation with gaps included that is presented as ongoing, so that I needn't be engaged in actual reading at T_d. The remaining features clarify what is meant by 'in progress'.

(b) Imperfectivity

Progressive aspectuality is a special case of imperfectivity (§3.2.5): in presenting a situation as in progress I am necessarily taking an internal view. Compare:

[3] i *When he arrived she phoned the police.* [perfective]
ii *When he arrived she was phoning the police.* [imperfective]

Assuming the phoning is a single occurrence, not a serial state, the non-progressive is interpreted perfectively: the phoning is viewed as a whole, without internal temporal structure, and therefore the *when* adjunct gives the time of the phoning as a whole. (Semantically, his arrival and her phoning are said to be simultaneous, but pragmatically we interpret it as 'loose simultaneity', with the phoning immediately following his arrival.) In [ii] the progressive gives an imperfective interpretation, so the *when* adjunct specifies the time at which the phoning was in progress, with the implicature that it had started before his arrival and continued after it: see (c) below.

[45] The progressive may be blocked or inhibited by certain formal factors: sequences of the form *be/been* + *being* tend to be avoided (cf. §2.3) and progressive ***be*** can hardly appear in the gerund-participial form by virtue of the 'doubl-*ing*' constraint (Ch. 14, §5.6.1).

The perfective/imperfective contrast is particularly important in the present tense because of the constraint that a present time perfective interpretation is normally possible only when the situation is of short enough duration to be co-extensive with the utterance:

[4] i *His daughter mows the lawn.* [salient reading: serial state]
ii *His daughter is mowing the lawn.* [salient reading: single occurrence]

Mowing the lawn does not satisfy that condition, so that a single occurrence reading is not normally available for [i], which we interpret as a serial state, with habitual lawn-mowing. The imperfective meaning in [ii], by contrast, allows for T_d to be **included** within T_{sit}, giving the interpretation where a single occurrence of mowing is now in progress. In the present tense, therefore, the progressive is much the more frequent aspect for dynamic situations. It would, however, be a mistake to see "habitual" vs "non-habitual" as the difference in **meaning** between [i] and [ii] (or, worse, between the present non-progressive and the present progressive generally). A single occurrence interpretation of [i] is not semantically excluded, but merely pragmatically unlikely: it could occur as a timeless or historic present or as a futurate – and if embedded, for example in a conditional construction, it could easily take a single future occurrence interpretation. Nor does [ii] exclude a serial state interpretation: compare *His daughter is mowing the lawn until he is well again.* The "habitual' vs "non-habitual" contrast is thus a difference in salient interpretations arising from the interaction between the meaning of the aspects and the pragmatic constraints on present perfectivity. Note that in the preterite the non-progressive *His daughter mowed the lawn* allows a single occurrence reading as readily as the progressive *His daughter was mowing the lawn.*

Measure phrases

With past time, inclusion of a measure indicator tends to favour a perfective reading and hence to make the progressive less likely:

[5] i a. *She walked five miles.* b. *She was walking five miles.*
ii a. *She wrote two novels.* b. *She was writing two novels.*

Progressive [ib] suggests that the distance had been determined in advance – she was on a five-mile walk; [iib] suggests that she was writing the novels simultaneously. And in a pair like *She hit him twice* vs *She was hitting him twice* it is difficult to contextualise the progressive at all.

(c) The mid-interval implicature

The T_r of a progressive is normally interpreted as a **mid-interval** of T_{sit} – i.e. as a point or period that excludes the beginning and the end. This is very evident in [3–5]. In [4ii], for example, the mowing started in the past and will continue for at least some time into the future; in [5iib] the writing started before T_r and presumably continued afterwards; and so on. The mid-interval feature is of greatest significance with accomplishments, where the progressive implicates incompleteness:

[6] i a. *She wrote a novel.* b. *She was writing a novel.*
ii a. *He has learnt to swim.* b. *He has been learning to swim.*

In [ia] the novel was finished, for T_r coincides with T_{sit} and hence includes the terminal phase. But in [ib] it was not finished at T_r, because this is interpreted as a mid-interval of T_{sit}, one which therefore excludes the punctual terminal phase (whether or not the terminal phase was reached after T_r is not said). Similarly, on the resultative interpretation of the perfect examples with *learn*, [iia] indicates that he now knows how to swim, whereas [iib] implicates that he doesn't.

The mid-interval feature is an implicature, not part of the meaning proper

This is evident from the fact that we can specify the time of the beginning or end or both:

[7] i *From the moment I arrived he was trying to provoke me.*
ii *He was watching TV until the power went off.*
iii *Between 10 and 11 I was working in the library.*
iv *From after dinner until nearly midnight I was filling in my tax return.*

In [iii] *between 10 and 11* may or may not specify the boundaries of my working in the library. Suppose that in response to the question *What did you do yesterday?*, I say, *From 9 to 10 I was at the phonology lecture, between 10 and 11 I was working in the library, and then I had a game of squash*: here the adjunct will be taken to delimit T_{sit}. But if [6iii] is said in response to *Where were you between 10 and 11?*, it will be taken to delimit only T_r: it could be that I worked there all morning. The same applies to [iv], where filling in my tax return is an accomplishment. Possible continuations are *It took me all that time to do it* (indicating that the terminal phase is included in the T_r of [iv], thus cancelling the implicature of incompleteness) and *I'll have to finish it tonight* (preserving the incompleteness implicature).

The interpretive/explanatory use of the progressive

The mid-interval implicature is also cancelled in what is sometimes called the 'interpretive' or 'explanatory' use of the progressive:

[8] *When I said 'the boss' I was referring to you.*

Here the saying and referring are strictly simultaneous, coextensive, so that the T_r for *was referring* is the whole T_{sit}. The progressive is not required here but is more usual than the non-progressive; the internal (imperfective) view is appropriate to the explanatory function of the clause – in emphasising duration, the progressive metaphorically slows down or extends the situation in order to be able to focus on clarifying its nature.

Cancellation consistent with imperfectivity

The fact that the mid-interval factor is a cancellable implicature is quite consistent with the imperfective meaning of the progressive. Imperfective meaning involves taking an internal view of the situation (which obviously applies in all the above examples) and not presenting it in its totality – but this is not the same as presenting it as incomplete. The progressive does not itself identify T_r with T_{sit}, but is not inconsistent with other features of the sentence or context making that identification. In the absence of such features, or of features including just the beginning point ([7i]) or just the endpoint ([7ii]), it will strongly implicate that T_r is a mid-interval of T_{sit}.

(d) Duration

For a situation to be in progress, it must have duration: there can be no progress within a punctual situation. A conflict is thus liable to arise between an achievement type situation and progressive aspectuality: examples like *I've just found my key* resist conversion to the progressive. There are, however, ways of resolving the conflict:

[9] i a. *She nodded.* b. *She was nodding.*
ii a. *The train arrived.* b. *The train was arriving.*

Here [ia] can be interpreted punctually as an achievement involving a single nod or as an activity involving a sequence of nods, whereas [ib] selects the latter reading.[46] Compare similarly: *She was knocking on the door.* In [iib] the effect of the progressive is precisely to change a punctual situation into a durative one, giving an extendable achievement (§3.2.3). The mid-interval factor is also important here: the train had not yet arrived at T_r (though there is a strong implicature that subsequently it would). *Die* is similar, but allows a much greater extension in time and (in the perfect) for modification by a duration adjunct: *He has been dying for several weeks now*, but not **The train has been arriving for two minutes now. They were kissing* can be interpreted in either way: as an ongoing activity of repeated kisses, or as a single extended kiss.

The feature of duration is, however, of much more general relevance. Perfective aspectuality does not exclude duration (perfectivity is not limited to achievements), but it does not express duration, hence does not focus it. The progressive, by contrast, does highlight the duration. This is so even where the clause contains a duration adjunct: *They were arguing all through the meal* emphasises the duration more than *They argued all through the meal*: it takes an internal view, with the activity ongoing throughout the period. Similarly in accomplishments where the mid-interval implicature is cancelled, as in the relevant contextualisation of [7iii–iv], highlighting of duration is effectively the only difference between progressive and non-progressive – compare *Between 10 and 11 I worked in the library* and *From after dinner until nearly midnight I filled in my tax return.*

Duration is also the major relevant factor in the frequent use of the progressive for a situation presented as a frame or background for a perfective situation:

[10] i *The accident occurred as she was cleaning the windows.*
ii *I was doing some work in the garden when the police arrived.*

Where two situations are of the same duration and simultaneous, it is possible to use the progressive for either, both, or neither:

[11] i *She was reading while he watched TV.* [progressive + non-progressive]
ii *She read while he was watching TV.* [non-progressive + progressive]
iii *She was reading while he was watching TV.* [progressive + progressive]
iv *She read while he watched TV.* [non-progressive + non-progressive]

Serial states

With situations of this kind the feature of duration tends to be accompanied by an emotive overtone, usually of disapproval, when emphasised by such adjuncts as *always, continually, constantly, everlastingly, forever, perpetually.* Compare:

[12] i a. *He always loses his temper.* b. *He's always losing his temper.*
ii a. *They always meet at the market.* b. *They're always meeting at the market.*

[46] A single nod interpretation is possible for [9ib] in the special context where the situation is 'frozen' in a photograph or slowed down (and thus given duration) in a slow motion film.

Notice first that *always* is interpreted differently in the two aspects: in the progressive we understand "constantly", whereas in the non-progressive it has its basic meaning, "on all occasions" – e.g., for [ia], on all occasions of his playing table tennis, losing at cards, or whatever, for [iia] on all occasions of their meeting or going to the market. The progressive indicates continual unpredictable recurrence of the subsituation – typically, though not necessarily, an undesirable one.

(e) Dynamicity

The major difference between progressive aspectuality and imperfectivity in general is that the former is inconsistent with a purely static situation: it conveys some measure of dynamicity. Compare the contrasting aspects in

[13] *When I left, Jill had her head buried in a book but Ed was watching TV.*

Having one's head buried in a book is a state whereas watching TV is an occurrence (an activity), and this is why the *have* clause has non-progressive aspect, the *watch* clause progressive. T_r (specified by the *when* adjunct) is the same for both, and in both it is included in T_{sit}: the only difference is in the static vs dynamic character of the situations. Notice, moreover, that if Kim's situation had been conceptualised, with little objective difference, as reading, the progressive aspect would have been used, since reading, like watching TV, is an activity.

Expressions denoting purely static situations do not combine felicitously with progressive aspect: *The Earth is round/flat*; *The solution consists of salt and vinegar*; *This contains lots of calcium*; *He has a mole on his shoulder*; *She is tall for her age* – and not #*The Earth is being round/flat*; #*The solution is consisting of salt and vinegar*, etc. There are, however, several ways in which the progressive can combine with a basically stative expression to yield a dynamic interpretation:

[14]	i	*He is being tactful.*	[agentive activity]
	ii	*He's making more and more / fewer and fewer mistakes.*	[waxing/waning]
	iii	*She is cycling to work this week.*	[temporary state]

Agentive activity

Non-progressive *He is tactful* is static: we interpret *tactful* as denoting a personal quality. Progressive *He is being tactful* ([14i]), by contrast, is dynamic: we interpret it as involving agentive activity, as describing his present behaviour, "He is behaving tactfully". (There may also be a suggestion that he is putting on an act.)

Waxing and waning situations

Non-progressive *He makes mistakes* expresses a serial state. The dynamicity in progressive [14ii] comes from the element of change: the subsituations are not constant, but are waxing or waning. The state in the non-progressive need not be a serial one: compare *He looks very much like his father* and *He is looking more like his father every day.*

Temporary state

She cycles to work again typically has a serial state interpretation, and this time the dynamicity in the progressive version [14iii] comes from the feature of temporariness – see (f) below. We interpret non-progressive *She cycles to work* as giving her regular mode of travel to work, whereas in the progressive it is temporary (perhaps she normally goes by car, but this week it is off the road, so she is going by bicycle). The link between temporariness and dynamicity is that a temporary state can be thought of as moving – 'progressing' – towards its endpoint. Again, the examples given are of serial states, but the phenomenon applies to ordinary states too: compare *She lives with her parents* vs *She is living with her parents.* The first suggests that it is a permanent arrangement (relatively speaking, of course), the second that it is only a temporary one. It must be emphasised, however, that temporariness is not sufficient to sanction the use of the progressive. There are 'strongly stative' verbs, such as *belong, contain, matter, own,* which remain in the non-progressive even when the state is temporary: *It doesn't matter at this stage; At the moment she owns both blocks, but she's selling one next week.* The waxing/waning type of dynamicity sanctions the progressive significantly more generally: *It is mattering more and more which university you get your degree at; Each year more and more people are owning their own home.*

(f) The limited duration implicature

The progressive often implicates that the situation is of limited duration, temporary. The clearest case is the one just illustrated in [14iii], where temporariness provides the essential feature of dynamicity. It is also evident in cases like [14i], as an accompaniment to the agentive activity feature. *He is being tactful* focuses on current behaviour and hence is likely to be interpreted as applying to a situation of shorter duration than *He is tactful,* which generally suggests a personality trait and hence a relatively permanent situation. (Notice, however, that this latter suggestion can be cancelled: *He is very tactful this morning.*) We have also seen that in pairs like [4] (*His daughter mows the lawn* vs *His daughter is mowing the lawn*) the salient interpretations differ sharply with respect to the duration of the situations, again a relatively permanent (serial) state vs temporary current activity.

Attention is often drawn to the paradox that in some cases (such as these) the progressive conveys limited duration, whereas in others it conveys extended duration, most obviously in cases like [9iib] (*The train was arriving*), where it gives duration to a situation that would otherwise be punctual. The paradox arises because neither limited duration nor extended duration is a feature of the meaning of the progressive. Both are implicatures deriving from the interaction between the meaning of the progressive and other factors, which are different in the two cases. For example, limited duration can arise when dynamicity is imposed on a situation which is basically a state, and extended duration arises when the feature of duration (which **is** part of the meaning) is imposed on a situation which is basically punctual. That limited duration is not part of the meaning of the progressive is evident from the complete acceptability of examples like *This must have been going on ever since the beginning of time* – or those like [12] above.

8.2 Some verb classes

The distinction between states and occurrences is not sharply drawn in objective reality: there is scope for differences in the way a situation is conceptualised and in the properties lexicalised in particular verbs. The above difference between *have one's head buried in a book* (static) and *read a book* (dynamic) illustrates the relevance of conceptualisation. The relevance of particular lexical properties is seen in the following contrasts:

[15] i a. *He wears a wig.* b. *He is wearing a wig.*
ii a. *He has a wig on.* b. **He is having a wig on.*

[16] i a. *He suffers from bronchitis.* b. *He is suffering from bronchitis.*
ii a. *He is ill with bronchitis.* b. **He is being ill with bronchitis.*

The contrast in [15i] is essentially like that in [4] (*His daughter mows / is mowing the lawn*): the salient interpretation of [15ia] is as a serial state with regular, habitual wearing of the wig, while that of [15ib] is for a single occurrence, present activity. In addition, [15ib] can be used for a temporary serial state (*He is wearing a wig these days*). A single occurrence reading of the non-progressive is readily available with past or future time (*That day he wore a wig; He'll wear a wig for the wedding*), but hardly in the present. The salient interpretation of [15iia] is that of a single situation – a multiple reading requires an adjunct (*He always has a wig on*) or indication from context. The progressive is then not used either for a temporary serial state or for an ongoing single situation. The same contrasts are found in [16]. We will therefore look briefly at four verb classes falling around the boundary between states and occurrences.

Verbs of perception and sensation (*see, hear, feel, smell, taste,* etc.)

The sense verbs *feel, smell,* and *taste* are used in three quite clearly distinguishable ways, indicating: (a) evocation or production of the sensation by the stimulus for the experience, as in *The plum feels hard* (intransitive); (b) experience or detection of the sensation by the experiencer, as in *I can feel something hard* (normally transitive); (c) deliberate action on the part of the experiencer to acquire or obtain the sensation, as in *I felt it to make sure it wasn't too hard* (normally transitive). With the senses of sight and hearing we have different verbs:

[17]	PRODUCTION	EXPERIENCE	ACQUISITION
i	*It looked square.*	*I could see it.*	*I looked at it.*
ii	*It sounded shrill.*	*I could hear it.*	*I listened to it.*
iii	*It felt hard.*	*I could feel it.*	*I felt it.*
iv	*It smelt horrible.*	*I could smell it.*	*I smelt it.*
v	*It tasted sweet.*	*I could taste it.*	*I tasted it.*

The **acquisition** situations are unproblematically dynamic and readily occur with progressive aspect: this is the default aspect in the present tense for singulary situations (*Carry on – I'm listening,* not ?*Carry on, I listen*).

The **production** situations are states, so that the aspect is generally non-progressive. The progressive is found with waxing/waning situations (*It's tasting sweeter every day*) or, mainly with *look* and to a lesser extent with *sound,* for temporary situations (*You're looking gorgeous; It's sounding ominous*).

The **experience** situations are less straightforward. With a state interpretation, the default construction is that with modal ***can***, as in [17]: ***can*** + progressive is not possible at all here. The non-modal construction is at the boundary between stative and dynamic: *I heard a plane pass overhead* contrasts clearly with *I could hear planes passing overhead* as dynamic (an achievement) vs stative, but we can also have *I heard the tap dripping,* which is also state-like, differing little from *I could hear the tap dripping.* In the present tense the simple form tends to sound somewhat more dramatic, suggesting a quasi-dynamic interpretation: *Yes, I see it now; I smell something burning.* The progressive is possible, especially when the focus is on the quality of the sense organs or the channel (*She's not hearing very well these days*; *I'm hearing you loud and clear*), or when the sensation is understood to be hallucinatory (*I must be seeing things*; *She is hearing voices*).

Verbs of hurting

There is a small set of verbs associated mainly with various kinds of pain which again fall at the boundary between stative and dynamic: *ache, hurt, itch, feel sick/well*, etc. These occur equally readily in either aspect – compare *My neck aches* (where the non-progressive indicates a state) and *My neck is aching* (where the progressive suggests an activity).

Verbs of cognition, emotion, and attitude (*believe, fear, regret*, etc.)

These constitute a large and important class of stative verbs: *agree, believe, fear, forget, hope, intend, know, like, love, realise, regret, remember, suppose, think, understand, want, wish, wonder*, etc. As such, they occur in the simple present with imperfective meaning:

[18] *I believe it's illegal.* *I fear you've made a mistake.* *She knows where they are.*
He loves you. *I suppose it's too late.*

(*See, hear*, and *feel* also belong here when used, for example, with a finite content clause as complement: *I see/hear/feel that it's not working properly.*)

None of these verbs completely excludes the progressive, however, though they differ with respect to how easily they take it. In the case of *know*, for example, it is just about restricted to the waxing/waning case (*He claims that fewer and fewer students are knowing how to write English when they come up to university*). The following illustrate ways in which a dynamic factor can be added to the basic stative meaning:

[19] i *I'm thinking we ought to accept.* *She's regretting she stayed behind.*
ii *Don't interrupt me when I'm thinking.* *They're loving every minute of it.*
iii *You're forgetting you said you'd help.* *He's not realising what he's saying.*
iv *I'm hoping you can help me.* *He was wondering if he could ask your advice.*

In [i] the progressive suggests limited duration; the focus is on the present moment, suggesting that the states have not obtained for a long time (e.g. I've just come round to thinking this). In [ii] the progressive yields an activity reading: we interpret *think* and *love* here as equivalent to dynamic *cogitate* and *enjoy*. In [iii] I am concerned with explaining, interpreting, commenting on something you or he has just said: the progressive adds the feature of duration to enable us to focus on what is (or was) going on (cf. [8]). Finally in [iv] the progressive adds an element of tentativeness: the first example avoids any danger of apparent brusqueness that might attach to *I hope you can help me*. The effect is similar to that of the preterite for diffidence/politeness (§4.3.2), and in the *wonder* example the preterite and progressive features combine to produce this effect. It is not so clear how the politeness derives from the progressive. One factor is no doubt length/complexity: polite formulations are often more complex than ordinary ones (compare *I wonder whether you'd mind opening the door* with *Open the door*). Another may be the restricted duration feature: the temporariness of the hoping acknowledges that you may not want to help me.

Stance verbs (*stand, lie, sit*)

The class of 'stance' or 'position' verbs, the most frequently occurring members of which are *stand, lie*, and *sit*, falls at the boundary between states and activities. When they are used of fixed or (relatively) permanent positions, these verbs are construed as denoting states and normally occur in the non-progressive; when they apply to temporary positions, for example with human or animate subjects, they tend to be construed rather as activities and to favour the progressive:

[20] i *The church stands at the top of the hill.* *The village lay beside the gorge.*
ii *He is standing near the entrance.* *They were lying on the beach.*

Particularly in narrative, however, the progressive is found for permanent positions, as in *We reached the knoll and the peak was standing majestically above the glacier*: the limited duration feature reflects the narrator's experience of the situation, rather than the objective state itself. With temporary positions, the non-progressive is possible: *They lay on the beach, sunning themselves*; *We'll sit here and watch you playing.* But the non-progressive is not normally used for a present time situation (leaving aside serial states): in response to *Have you seen Kim?*, I might say *She's in the garden* or *She's sitting in the garden*, but not *She sits in the garden.*

8.3 Non-aspectual uses of the progressive

There are two uses of progressive aspect where the meaning cannot be accounted for in terms of progressive aspectuality. In both cases there is future time reference, one involving the futurate, the other modal *will.*

(a) The progressive futurate

[21]	i a. *The sun sets at five tomorrow.*	b. #*The sun is setting at five tomorrow.*
	ii a. *I phone her tonight.*	b. *I'm phoning her tonight.*
	iii a. *She has her operation tomorrow.*	b. *She's having her operation tomorrow.*
	iv a. *It expires tomorrow / in five years*	b. *It's expiring tomorrow / in five years.*

The progressive is restricted to cases where human agency or intention is involved – hence the anomaly of examples like [ib]. The difference between non-progressive and progressive is fairly clear in pairs like [ii]. The non-progressive suggests a schedule or plan: perhaps I regularly phone her on the first Sunday in the month, or perhaps the call is part of some larger plan or arrangement – it's hardly possible if I'd simply said, casually, *I'll phone you tonight.* The progressive [iib] could be used in these schedule/plan scenarios, but it is not limited to them: it could be that I have simply formed the intention to phone her (without consulting her or anyone else about the matter) and am waiting till I think she'll be in. In [iii] there is little difference – because the greater range of the progressive just illustrated is here restricted by the fact that operations normally involve formal scheduling. A further point is that the progressive tends to be used for the relatively near future. In [ivb], for example, *tomorrow* is appreciably more natural than *in five years*, whereas there is no such difference in [iva].

(b) *Will* + progressive

[22]	i *When we get there, they'll probably still be having lunch.*	[aspectual meaning]
	ii *Will you be going to the shops this afternoon?*	[special meaning]
	iii *When the meeting ends we'll be flying to Bonn.*	[ambiguous]

In [i] we simply have the ordinary use of the progressive to express progressive aspectuality: the lunch will be still in progress at the time of our arrival. This is not how we interpret [ii], however. The meaning can best be seen by comparing it with the non-progressive counterpart, *Will you go to the shops this afternoon?* The salient interpretation of the latter is as a request to you to go to the shops, and the role of the progressive in [ii] is to avoid such an interpretation. The progressive indicates that the matter has already been settled rather than being subject to decision now. Compare, similarly, *We won't buy any more* (interpretable as a refusal, made here and now) vs *We won't be buying any more* (following prior decision), or *Will he help us?* ("Is he willing?", decision still to be made) vs *Will he be helping us?* ("Has it been decided that he will?").

The distinctness between the two meanings is seen clearly in the ambiguity of [22iii]. On the progressive aspectuality reading, we will already be flying to Bonn when the meeting ends; on the 'already decided future' interpretation, the *when* adjunct says when we will leave. The first is imperfective, with reference to a mid-interval; the second is perfective, just as in the non-progressive *we'll fly*, which, however, suggests that the decision is being made now. This use is particularly common with *will*, but it is also found with, for example, the idiom *be going*, as in *Are you going to be helping them again this year?* (where the non-progressive might again be construed as a request).

9 Mood and modality

The distinction between mood and modality is like that between tense and time, or aspect and aspectuality: mood is a category of grammar, modality a category of meaning. Mood is the grammaticalisation of modality within the verbal system. The term 'mood' is most usually applied to inflectional systems of the verb, as in the contrast between indicative, subjunctive, and imperative in such languages as Latin, French, and German. As far as English is concerned, historical change has more or less eliminated mood from the inflectional system, with irrealis mood confined to 1st/3rd person singular *were*, which is moreover usually replaceable by the ordinary preterite form *was* (§1.7). The main mood system, therefore, is analytic rather than inflectional, marked by the presence or absence of special words, the modal auxiliaries.[47]

9.1 Modality and its expression

The domain of modality

The area of meaning referred to as modality is rather broad and finds expression in many areas of the language besides mood; it is, moreover, not sharply delimited or subdivided, so that we shall need to make frequent reference to the concept of prototypical features and to allow for indeterminacy at the boundaries of the categories. We begin this section, therefore, with a brief account of the central area covered by modality and of its linguistic manifestations.

[47] This use of 'mood' is not widely adopted in works on English grammar; we take the extension of the term to analytic systems to be parallel to the use of tense and aspect for analytic systems as well as inflectional ones.

Speaker's attitude to factuality or actualisation

Modality is centrally concerned with the speaker's attitude towards the factuality or actualisation of the situation expressed by the rest of the clause.

A declarative main clause like *He wrote it himself* we will regard as **unmodalised**: in normal use the speaker is committed, without qualification or special emphasis, to the factuality of the proposition expressed. *He must have written it himself*, by contrast, is **modalised**: although I still commit myself to the factuality of his having written it himself, my commitment is qualified in the sense that the truth of the proposition is not presented as something that is directly known but as something that is inferred. A somewhat different kind of modality is found in (the most salient interpretation of) *You must help him*, which is concerned not so much with factuality as with the actualisation of a future situation, your helping him: I impose on you the obligation to bring this situation about.

Necessity and possibility

Although the two examples just given involve different kinds of modality, they are united by the fact that they both express the concept of necessity. This and the related concept of possibility are core concepts in modality (and it is primarily these that the branch of logic known as modal logic is concerned to explicate and formalise). Modal possibility is illustrated in examples corresponding to the above with *may* substituted for *must*. *He may have written it himself* expresses the possibility of his having written it himself: it indicates an open attitude to the truth of the proposition. Similarly *You may help her* expresses the possibility of your helping her: I give permission and thus remove a potential barrier to the actualisation of that situation.

Extension beyond speaker's subjective attitude

Modality is in the first instance a matter of the speaker's attitude, but it applies by extension to the attitude of persons referred to in the sentence. In *Kim thinks he must have written it himself*, for example, *must* indicates Kim's attitude, not mine, but we shall of course still regard it as expressing modal necessity. Furthermore, the concept of modality also extends to cases where it is not a matter of subjective attitude on the part of the speaker (or others), but of something more objective. *If x is a prime number between 90 and 100 it must be 97*, for example, is likely to be interpreted as expressing not the speaker's subjective attitude to the truth of "*x* is 97" but objective, mathematical necessity.

The linguistic expression of modality

Major areas of the language, other than the analytic mood system, where modality may be expressed include:

(a) Lexical modals

We use this term for items expressing the same kind of meaning as the modal auxiliaries, but which do not belong to the syntactic class of auxiliary verbs. It covers adjectives like *possible*, *necessary*, *likely*, *probable*, *bound*, *supposed*, adverbs like *perhaps*, *possibly*, *necessarily*, *probably*, *certainly*, *surely*, verbs like *insist*, *permit*, *require*, and nouns like *possibility*, *necessity*, *permission*, and similar derivatives.

(b) Past tense

The preterite is commonly used to express what we have called modal remoteness, and the perfect is occasionally used in this way too (§6.1). The difference in modal meaning between present tense *If you do that again you will be fired* and preterite *If you did that again you would be fired* (open possibility vs remote possibility) is in many languages expressed by means of an inflectional mood system.

(c) Other verb inflection

The residual irrealis *were* has only the modal remoteness meaning just illustrated for the preterite; it represents the remnant of an inflectional mood system in English. In addition, the plain form of the verb is commonly used with a modal sense. In finite clauses, it is used mainly in the imperative and mandative constructions, which are covered respectively in (d) and (e) below. In non-finite clauses, the plain form is used in the infinitival construction, where it is often associated with non-actuality in contrast with the gerund-participial construction. Compare:

[1]	i	a. *He's the one to do the job.*	b. *He's the one doing the job.*
	ii	a. *I want to talk to her.*	b. *I enjoy talking to her.*

In [ib] the doing is actual, whereas in [ia] it is not: the meaning is comparable to that of *the one who should do the job* or *the one whom we should get to do the job*, with modal *should*. Similarly [iib] conveys that I actually do talk to her, whereas the talking in [iia] is non-actualised, merely potential. It is not fortuitous that the modal auxiliaries themselves take infinitival complements, not gerund-participials.

(d) Clause type

The default clause type, the declarative, is associated with factual statements and, as suggested above, can (in the absence of any other relevant marking) be regarded as unmodalised. The other major types, however, are closely associated with modality. Imperatives are characteristically used as directives, with the speaker typically wanting the actualisation of some future situation. The interrogative types are characteristically used to express questions to which the speaker doesn't know the answer – and in the case of a polar question the speaker will usually regard both positive and negative answers as possibly true.

(e) Subordination

While the use of a declarative main clause typically conveys the speaker's commitment to the truth of the proposition expressed, such a commitment is often lost under subordination – compare main *He is ill* with subordinate *I/They think he is ill.* This is not to say that subordination necessarily involves modalisation: this will depend on the properties of the construction, for in *I/They know he is ill*, for example, my commitment to the truth of "He is ill" remains. Nevertheless, there is a significant association between subordination and markers of modality. In languages with an inflectional subjunctive, for example, this mood characteristically indicates non-factuality in subordinate clauses. In English the modal remoteness use of the preterite is in general restricted to subordinate clauses, and certain uses of some of the modal auxiliaries are characteristic of subordinate clauses too (e.g. the 'emotive' use of *should* in examples like *It's strange that he should be so quiet*). The mandative construction is a subordinate one, and the modal meaning (involving the necessity or desirability of actualisation) is often marked by a plain form or by *should*, as in *It's essential that he be / should be told.* One construction involving subordination that is particularly important in connection with the modal auxiliaries is the conditional: the remote conditional construction requires a modal auxiliary in the matrix clause and has a modal use of the preterite in both subordinate and matrix clauses, and even the open conditional very often has a modalised matrix clause too.

(f) Parentheticals

These contain lexical modals such as *think*, *seem*, etc.: *He is, I think / it seems, almost bankrupt*. They are also relatable to subordinate constructions (*I think / It seems he is almost bankrupt*); see Ch. 10, §5.3.

In this section we focus on the modal auxiliaries – we shall not, for example, be dealing systematically with the lexical modals, though we shall refer to a number of them for purposes of contrast and clarification. The modal auxiliaries have a considerable range of uses: in the next subsection we consider three major dimensions along which these uses may be compared. We then deal with the individual auxiliaries, focusing first on the present tense forms (and the idiomatic uses of *should*) before taking up the preterite forms. The remaining subsections examine the relation between the modals and perfect tense, negation, and interrogative clause type.

9.2 Dimensions of modality

In describing the meanings and use of the modal auxiliaries we will make distinctions on three major dimensions, which we refer to as **strength**, **kind**, and **degree**.

9.2.1 Strength of modality

Necessity vs possibility: strong vs weak modality

The first dimension concerns the **strength** of commitment (prototypically the speaker's commitment) to the factuality or actualisation of the situation. This is where we distinguish the core modal concepts of necessity and possibility: necessity involves a strong commitment, possibility a weak one.

Internal negation vs external negation

In order to describe the logical relation between necessity and possibility we need to consider their interaction with negation, and here we must distinguish between **internal negation** and **external negation**:

[2]	i	*He may not have read it.*	[internal negation]
	ii	*He can't have read it.*	[external negation]
	iii	*He can't not have read it.*	[external + internal negation]

In [i] the negation applies semantically to the complement of *may*: "It is possible that he didn't read it". We say in such cases that the modal **has scope over** the negative, or that the negation falls within the scope of the modal: it is in this sense that the negation is 'internal'. In [ii], by contrast, the negative applies to the modal itself: "It is not possible that he read it". Here then the negative **has scope over** the modal auxiliary rather than falling within its scope, i.e. the negation is external to the scope of the modal (see Ch. 9, §1.3.1, for the concept 'scope of negation'). The two kinds of negation can combine, as in [iii]: "It is not possible that he didn't read it".

A second example (omitting the combination of negatives, which would be much less natural than it is in [2]) is seen in:

[3]	i *You mustn't eat it all.*	[internal negation]
	ii *You needn't eat it all.*	[external negation]

In [i] the negative applies to the eating, not the modal obligation: "It is necessary that you not eat it all"; it is thus internal, within the scope of the modal. In [ii] the negative applies to the obligation: "It isn't necessary for you to eat it all"; here then it is external, outside the scope of the modal.[48]

The scope of the negation is generally transparent when the modality is expressed by lexical modals in constructions where there is a clear syntactic distinction between a matrix clause containing the lexical modal and a subordinate clause, as in the glosses given for [2–3]. In such cases a *not* in the subordinate clause marks internal negation, while a *not* in the matrix clause marks external negation. When we have negation with a modal auxiliary we can therefore test whether it is internal or external negation by finding a paraphrase with a lexical modal, and seeing whether the negative is in the subordinate clause (as in *It is necessary that you not eat it all*) or the matrix one (as in *It isn't necessary for you to eat it all*). It should be borne in mind, however, that such paraphrases will often be much less idiomatic than the versions with modal auxiliaries.

Logical relation between necessity and possibility

The following examples illustrate the equivalence between pairs of clauses expressing modal necessity and possibility:

[4]		NECESSITY	POSSIBILITY	
	i	*He must be guilty.*	*He can't be not guilty.*	[Nec *P*] = [not-Poss not-*P*]
	ii	*He must be not guilty.*	*He can't be guilty.*	[Nec not-*P*] = [not-Poss *P*]
	iii	*He isn't necessarily guilty.*	*He may be not guilty.*	[not-Nec *P*] = [Poss not-*P*]
	iv	*He isn't necessarily not guilty.*	*He may be guilty.*	[not-Nec not-*P*] = [Poss *P*]

In the annotations on the right we use 'Nec' for necessity and 'Poss' for possibility, independently of how they are expressed: *must, need, necessary, necessarily*, and so on, all express modal necessity, while *can, may, possible, possibly, perhaps* all express possibility. '*P*' stands for the propositional content that is modalised or negated: in this case, "He is guilty". 'Not-*P*' indicates internal negation, while 'not-Nec' and 'not-Poss' indicate external negation, with the negative having scope over the modal necessity or possibility.

Semantic strength vs pragmatic strength

When considering the strength of the modality expressed in a clause it important to bear in mind the distinction between semantics and pragmatics. Compare, for example:

[5]	i	a. *You must come in immediately.*	b. *You must have one of these cakes.*
	ii	a. *You may take your ties off.*	b. *You may leave now.*

Example [ia] is likely to be used as an instruction to come in: it is strong in that it doesn't countenance your not doing so. Example [ib] contains the same modal *must*, but, as used

[48] Alternative terms that will be found in the literature are 'propositional negation' for 'internal negation', and 'modal negation' for 'external negation'.

at an afternoon tea-party or the like, the modality would be considerably less strong – it will be taken as an offer rather than an order. We will talk of this as **pragmatic weakening**: *must* is a semantically strong modal, but in this context its strength is reduced. The opposite case is illustrated in [ii]. Here [iia] has weak modality: the salient interpretation is as giving permission, allowing you a choice as to whether or not to take your tie off. But [iib], as used in the context of a boss talking to a secretary, will be construed as an instruction, not mere permission: here we have **pragmatic strengthening**.

Medium modality

There is a third category on the scale of strength which we call **medium modality**, though intuitively it is closer to the strong end than to the weak. It is expressed by *should*, *ought*, and comparable lexical modals such as *probable*, *likely*, *appear*, *seem*:

[6]	i	*The meeting must be over by now.*	[strong]
	ii	*The meeting should be over by now.*	[medium]
	iii	*The meeting may be over by now.*	[weak]

With [ii] we confine our attention at this stage to the interpretation "The meeting is probably over by now" (ignoring, for example, its use in a context where I know the meeting is still going on and am saying that this state of affairs is not right). In the "probably" interpretation, [ii] is weaker than [i] in that it allows for the possibility that the meeting is not over: with [ii], unlike [i], I could add *but it may not be.* At the same time, [ii] is stronger than [iii] in that it presents the likelihood of the meeting being over as greater. Thus [iii] is consistent with such continuations as *but it's unlikely to be*, whereas [ii], in its "probably" interpretation, is not. Note, moreover, that the common formula *may or may not* (e.g. *You may or may not believe this*) presents "*P*" and "not-*P*" as equally likely, but we do not similarly say *should or should not.*

Medium modality and negation

A significant feature of medium strength modality is that there is little difference, pragmatically, between external and internal negation:

[7]	i	*He isn't likely to be ready.*	[external negation]
	ii	*He is likely not to be ready.*	[internal negation]

Construction [i] is the more frequent but it tends to be interpreted pragmatically as [ii] (for further discussion, see Ch. 9, §5). Semantically [i] allows that the likelihood of his being ready may be around 50% as well as low, but in the 50% case one would generally say, more simply and clearly, *He may be ready*, so that [i] tends to be used only in the low probability case, "He is unlikely to be ready", and this is equivalent to [ii]. Note that in a simple clause construction with *probably* the negation is normally semantically as well as pragmatically internal. For example, *He is probably not ready*, with *not* following *probably* and inside its scope, is normal while ?*He isn't probably ready* is very marginal. Similarly, it is internal negation that we have with *should* and *ought* (see §9.4).

9.2.2 Kind of modality

It is a difficult matter to decide how many different senses should be recognised for a given modal auxiliary, but certain broad categories can be motivated by clear cases of ambiguity and by differences with respect to such matters as the scope of negation. We begin here with the distinction between **epistemic** and **deontic** modality, and then introduce a third category of **dynamic** modality; these distinctions cut across those of strength, and we will restrict the term **kind** of modality to this dimension of differentiation.

Epistemic vs deontic modality

The contrast between the two major categories is seen in the sharply different interpretations of *must* and *may* in [8i–ii] and the ambiguity of [8iii]:

[8]		STRONG	WEAK	
	i	a. *He must have been delayed.*	b. *He may have been delayed.*	[epistemic]
	ii	a. *You must pull your socks up.*	b. *You may stay if you wish.*	[deontic]
	iii	a. *You must be very tactful.*	b. *He may sleep downstairs.*	[ambiguous]

The ambiguity in [iii] is very clear, with [iiia] interpretable as either "I am forced to conclude (from the evidence) that you are very tactful" (epistemic) or "Be very tactful" (deontic), and [iiib] as either "Perhaps he sleeps downstairs" (epistemic) or "He can sleep downstairs" (deontic). (Strictly speaking, [i–ii] are ambiguous too, but the interpretations that we have ignored here are unlikely and need fairly elaborate contextualisation.)

Prototypically, epistemic modality concerns the speaker's attitude to the factuality of past or present time situations while deontic modality concerns the speaker's attitude to the actualisation of future situations.

'Epistemic' is derived from the Greek for "knowledge": this kind of modality involves qualifications concerning the speaker's knowledge. The unmodalised *He has been delayed* presents the truth of the proposition as something I know, whereas [8ia] presents it as something I arrive at by inference and in [ib] I merely put it forward as a possibility. 'Deontic' is derived from the Greek for "binding", so that here it is a matter of imposing obligation or prohibition, granting permission, and the like. In [iia], for example, I am telling you to pull your socks up and in [iib] I give you permission to stay. The person, authority, convention, or whatever from whom the obligation, etc., is understood to emanate we refer to as the **deontic source**.

There are numerous expressions that are used both deontically and epistemically, and the same phenomenon is found in many other languages too. In general it is plausible to regard the deontic uses as more basic, with the epistemic ones arising by extension to the domain of reasoning of concepts primarily applicable in the domain of human interaction, such as compelling and permitting.

Dynamic modality

The clearest cases of dynamic modality are concerned with properties and dispositions of persons, etc., referred to in the clause, especially by the subject NP. Again, the category can be justified by the existence of very clear cases of ambiguity:

[9]			
	i	*She can stay as long as she likes.*	[deontic]
	ii	*She can easily beat everyone else in the club.*	[dynamic]
	iii	*She can speak French.*	[ambiguous]

Example [i] gives (or reports) permission, while [ii] is concerned with her ability, and [iii] can be interpreted in either way, deontically as authorising her to speak French or dynamically as reporting her ability to do so.

The boundary between dynamic and deontic modality is, however, somewhat fuzzy. Examples like *The most we can expect is a slight cut in the sales-tax* ([21i] below) do not belong clearly with either [i] or [ii] in [9]. We put them in the dynamic category on the grounds that no person or institution is identifiable as a deontic source – they might be glossed with "permissible", but not with "permission" (e.g. "the most it is permissible to expect", but not "the most we have permission to expect").

Dynamic ability is less central to modality than deontic permission in that it does not involve the speaker's attitude to the factuality or actualisation of the situation. It does not apply as generally to the modal auxiliaries as do deontic and epistemic modality, and the clear ambiguities illustrated above for *can* are not found with the other auxiliaries.[49]

9.2.3 Degree of modality and modal harmony

Degree of modality has to do with the extent to which there is a clearly identifiable and separable element of modal meaning.

Contrast between unmodalised and modalised clauses

The difference between high and low degree modality is most easily seen by comparing pairs of clauses where one member is unmodalised, the other modalised:

[10]		UNMODALISED		HIGH DEGREE MODALITY
i	a.	*They <u>know</u> her.*	b.	*They <u>may know</u> her.*
ii	a.	*Your passport <u>is</u> in the drawer.*	b.	*Your passport <u>should be</u> in the drawer.*
iii	a.	*The letter <u>arrived</u> yesterday.*	b.	*The letter <u>will have arrived</u> yesterday.*

[11]		UNMODALISED		LOW DEGREE MODALITY
i	a.	*Strange as it <u>seems</u>, I believe you.*	b.	*Strange as it <u>may seem</u>, I believe you.*
ii	a.	*It's odd that he <u>is</u> so late.*	b.	*It's odd that he <u>should be</u> so late.*
iii	a.	*She <u>is</u> one year old tomorrow.*	b.	*She <u>will be</u> one year old tomorrow.*

In [10] the [b] examples differ very sharply and obviously in meaning from their unmodalised counterparts: the introduction of a modal auxiliary into the structure therefore adds a high degree of modal meaning. In [11], on the other hand, it is difficult to detect any meaning difference at all between the [a] and [b] examples: here, then, we have a low degree of modality. Degree, in this sense, is quite a different matter from strength. Our examples cover the scale of strength from weak *may* through medium *should* to strong *will* – but low degree modality is most often found at the upper end of the scale of strength, especially with *will* and, in the 1st person, *shall.*

Modal harmony

The low degree of modality in [11ib] can be attributed to the fact that it repeats, or is in **harmony** with, the modality expressed in the larger construction. *Strange as it seems / may seem* functions as a concessive adjunct: the meaning of *strange as it seems* is "although it seems strange". *May* can be used concessively on its own (as in *It may be expensive, but it's worth every penny* – [16] below), but in [11ib] it is reinforcing, not adding, concessive meaning. Compare, similarly, the optional use of *may* in the exhaustive conditional construction, *I'm going to appoint her <u>whatever you say / may say</u>.* Something comparable to modal harmony can be seen in [11iib] where the optional use of *should* is dependent on the presence of an emotive word such as *odd, surprising, remarkable* in the matrix clause.

[49] Some scholars operate with just a two-way distinction between epistemic and 'root' modality.

The most common and central cases of modal harmony are found with verb–adverb combinations, as in:

[12] i *The meeting must surely be over by now.* [strong]
ii *The meeting should probably be over by now.* [medium]
iii *The meeting may possibly be over by now.* [weak]

The verb and adverb are of the same strength and combine to express a single feature of modal meaning rather than two independent ones. They are very different from examples like *It may surely have been an accident*, where *may* (weak) and *surely* (strong) express independent modal meanings. The meaning of this non-harmonic combination is "Surely it is possible that it was an accident", with *possible* inside the scope of *surely*.

Will, a special case of low degree modality

The low degree of modality in the *will* of [11iiib], *She will be one year old tomorrow*, is not attributable to modal harmony. There is, rather, a strong association between *will* and the temporal concept of futurity, and the degree of modal meaning is in general significantly less with future time situations than with past and present time ones. We have noted that there are severe pragmatic constraints on the use of a main clause simple present for future time, so that with examples like *It will be dark soon* the unmodalised counterpart is not normally acceptable. *Will* can therefore be regarded as the default means of indicating future time; we take up this issue in §9.5.1.

9.3 Necessity and possibility: *must*, *need*, *may*, and *can*

Two modal auxiliaries, *must* and *need*, express modal necessity, and two, *may* and *can*, express possibility. *Need*, however, is restricted to non-affirmative contexts, and both *must* and *need* lack preterite counterparts; they are, moreover, jointly much less frequent than the possibility ones, and they cover a narrower range of distinguishable uses than *may* and *can*.[50]

9.3.1 Epistemic necessity and possibility

The main auxiliaries of epistemic necessity and possibility are respectively *must* and *may*, as in *He must/may have done it deliberately*. In its epistemic use *can*, like auxiliary *need* in all its uses, is restricted to non-affirmative contexts.

Scope of negation

Epistemic *must* and *may* normally take internal negation, with *need* and *can* being used for external negation. We therefore have the following semantic equivalences corresponding to [4ii–iii]:

[13] i a. *He mustn't have done it deliberately.* [internal negation: Nec not-*P*]
b. *He can't have done it deliberately.* [external negation: not-Poss *P*]
ii a. *He needn't have done it deliberately.* [external negation: not-Nec *P*]
b. *He may not have done it deliberately.* [internal negation: Poss not-*P*]

[50] We use ordinary italics in this section rather than bold because we are concerned only with the present tense forms; preterite *could* and *might* are taken up in §9.8.

In each pair, however, type [a] is quite rare and restricted (indeed unacceptable for many speakers):[51] in negative contexts, *must* and *need* are usually interpreted deontically. In the mood system, therefore, epistemic possibility can be regarded as more basic, less restricted, than epistemic necessity.

Subjective and objective uses

Must and *may* are most often used subjectively, to express the speaker's judgement, but objective uses are also found. Let us take them in turn.

Must

With epistemic modality, subjective *must* characteristically involves what we have described as pragmatic weakening. This accounts for the clear difference in strength in:

[14]	i	A: *What has happened to Ed?* B: *He <u>must</u> have overslept.*	[subjective]
	ii	*If I'm older than Ed and Ed is older than Jo, I <u>must</u> be older than Jo.*	[objective]

Objective [ii] involves strict semantic necessity, but subjective [i] will be interpreted as confident inference. And [ii] doesn't differ significantly from the unmodalised version with *am*, whereas [i] is much weaker than *He has overslept.* An appropriate pragmatic gloss is "This is the only explanation I can think of", rather than "This is the only possibility there is", which holds for [ii]. It must be emphasised, however, that semantically *He must have overslept* entails that he has overslept (as "Nec-*P*" entails "*P*"), and this is why it would be anomalous, inconsistent, to say – in the context, for example, of his having failed to turn up for an early rendez-vous – *#He must have overslept, though it might alternatively be that he has had problems with his car.*

Because of the pragmatic weakening found with subjective *must*, [13ia] is not pragmatically equivalent to [ib], which is stronger, more categorical. *Can't* would be preferred when the matter is regarded as obvious and particularly in denying something that has been asserted (*He says it was Jill but it can't have been*), with *mustn't* used – by those for whom it is not restricted to deontic modality – when it's a question of arriving at a negative conclusion (*He mustn't have told her after all*).

May

This is likewise most often used subjectively: I don't know that the proposition is false and put it forward as a possibility. But it can also be used objectively, where it is a matter of public knowledge, as it were, rather than the speaker's knowledge:

[15]	i	*He <u>may</u> have left it downstairs: I'll just go and see.*	[subjective]
	ii	*He <u>may</u> have misled Parliament: there's going to be an inquiry.*	[objective]

The distinction here, however, is less significant (and less easy to draw) than with *must*, as it does not correlate with any appreciable difference in strength. In either case the strength can be increased by adding adverbial *well*: *He may well have left it downstairs*, "It is quite likely".

[51] This is why we used *necessarily* rather than *need* in presenting the logical relations between necessity and possibility in [4iii–iv]: *He needn't be guilty* is less likely than *He isn't necessarily guilty.*

The 'don't know' implicature and concessive *may*

Epistemic *may* usually triggers a strong implicature that I don't know that the proposition is true. If I knew that it was true, I would normally be expected to use the unmodalised form – *He's ill*, say, rather than the much weaker *He may be ill.*

This implicature can be cancelled, however, yielding a rather special case of pragmatic strengthening:

[16] *It may be expensive, but it's worth every penny.* [concessive *may*]

Here *may* is interpreted concessively, "I concede that it is expensive"; in this use it is typically followed by *but* or the like.

Harmonic combinations

Must and *may* commonly occur in harmonic combination with an adverb of comparable meaning, with the modal elements simply reinforcing each other:

[17] i *It must surely be valid. It must necessarily have involved deception.*
ii *He may perhaps have left already. She may possibly be ill.*

They also appear harmonically in the complements of verbs, etc., of the same strength: *He insisted that there must have been a mistake*; *I suggest that he may be lying. May* is also used harmonically in concessive adjuncts like *strange as it may seem* ([11ib]).

Time of the situation

With *must* and *need* the time is generally present or past, as with prototypical epistemic modality. If the time is future, they are most likely to be interpreted deontically – compare *He must have told her yesterday* (past and epistemic) with *He must tell her tomorrow* (future and deontic). The future + epistemic combination is not impossible, and is somewhat more likely in conjunction with harmonic *surely* (which is not used deontically): *It must surely rain soon.* Epistemic *may*, on the other hand, occurs freely with future situations – where its deontic use is much less frequent than that of *must.* Compare:

[18] i a. *He may come back tomorrow.* b. *You may do better next time.*
ii a. *He must come back tomorrow.* b. *You must do better next time.*

The salient interpretations here are epistemic for *may*, and deontic for *must.* Epistemic *can* is barely possible with a future: compare *They may not finish until tomorrow* (where the salient reading is epistemic) and *They can't finish until tomorrow* (where it is a question of factors preventing actualisation, hence deontic or dynamic modality).

9.3.2 Deontic necessity and possibility

Deontic necessity, i.e. strong obligation, is expressed (in affirmative contexts) by *must*: *You must attend the lectures.* Deontic possibility, i.e. permission, is expressed by *may*, in formal style, or *can*, informal: *You may/can attend the lectures.*

Scope of negation

Deontic *must* behaves like epistemic *must* in that it normally takes internal negation. Deontic *may*, however, behaves differently from epistemic *may*: like *can*, it usually takes external negation. The semantic equivalences corresponding to [13] are as follows:

[19]	i	a. *You mustn't attend the lectures.*	[internal negation: Nec not-*P*]
		b. *You may not / can't attend the lectures.*	[external negation: not-Poss *P*]
	ii	a. *You needn't attend the lectures.*	[external negation: not-Nec *P*]
		b. ?*You may/can not attend the lectures.*	[internal negation: Poss not-*P*]

We saw in §9.3.1 that with epistemic modality possibility is less restricted than necessity, but the reverse is the case with deontic modality. This is particularly clear in [ii]: [iia] is perfectly acceptable for all speakers, whereas [iib] is at best very marginal, with a sharp prosodic boundary being required after the auxiliary to keep it out of the scope of *not*. But even in a pair like [i], assuming a subjective interpretation with the speaker imposing obligation or giving permission, deontic possibility is more restricted than necessity. Giving permission implies the power to withhold permission and hence to impose a barrier to actualisation: subjective *may/can* tacitly invokes this power. This is why, for example, it would be quite inappropriate to replace *must* by *may* in [5ib] (*You must have one of these cakes*): *You may have one of these cakes* conflicts with the social equality of host and guest. *Must*, by contrast, is commonly used when there is no question of the speaker having the power, or the wish, to require actualisation: it is often pragmatically weakened, to be interpreted in terms of advice or exhortation rather than requirement. *You mustn't take any notice of him* is thus not pragmatically equivalent to *You may not / can't take any notice of him*: the latter is inappropriate because the situation is not of the kind that needs authorisation.

Subjective and objective

Prototypical deontic modality is subjective, with the speaker as the deontic source, the one who imposes the obligation or grants permission.[52] But it can also be objective, most obviously in reports of rules and regulations – compare:

[20]	i	a. *You* <u>*must*</u> *clean up this mess at once.*	[subjective]
		b. *You* <u>*may/can*</u> *have one more turn.*	
	ii	a. *We* <u>*must*</u> *make an appointment if we want to see the Dean.*	[objective]
		b. *We* <u>*may/can*</u> *borrow up to six books at a time.*	

However, with objective necessity there is a tendency to use *have*, *have got*, or *need* rather than *must*: *We have (got) / need to make an appointment.* With possibility some speakers use *may* for speaker's permission, *can* for objective permission, but the choice between these verbs is more often a matter of style, with *may* more formal than *can*. The subjectivity is particularly clear in an example like *You may join us with pleasure*, where the pleasure is mine, not yours, and only in the subjective use do we find the pragmatic weakening of obligation to an offer and strengthening of permission to obligation illustrated in [5ib/iib] (*You must have one of these cakes, You may leave now*).

The objective examples [20ii] have 1st person subjects, but this of course is not necessary (with a subject such as *you*, however, they could be interpreted subjectively or objectively according as the speaker was laying down a rule or merely reporting one). Conversely, a 1st person subject is quite consistent with subjective modality, as in *I must do something about this leak*, where I impose on myself, or voluntarily accept, an

[52] In questions, subjectivity involves the addressee as deontic source, as in *May/Can I attend the lectures?*, asking for your permission. The same may apply in conditionals, as in *I'll have this one,* <u>*if I may*</u>, "if you will allow me" (a fixed expression, where *may* is not replaceable by *can*).

obligation to do something (again, more likely than an objective reading reporting an obligation imposed by someone else). This is found quite commonly with illocutionary verbs, as in *I must admit it's better than I expected* – a rather special case, for the utterance itself normally effects actualisation, i.e. I make the admission by saying *I must admit*. . .[53]

Time of situation

Deontic modality generally applies to future situations: I can oblige or permit you to do something in the future, but I can't oblige or permit you to have done something in the past. Deontic modality can combine with past or present situations only with general requirements, conditions, options, etc., as in [20ii] (present) or *Candidates must have completed at least two years of undergraduate study* (past).

9.3.3 Dynamic necessity and possibility

Dynamic possibility

This covers a considerable range of uses, including the following:

(a) What is reasonable or acceptable

[21] i *The most we can expect is a slight cut in the sales-tax.*
ii *You can always say you're too busy.*

May could appear as a very formal alternative to *can* in [i], but not in the intrinsically informal [ii]. The *always* in [ii] facilitates internal negation: *You can always not answer the phone.* As noted in §9.2.2, this use falls at the periphery of the dynamic category.

(b) What is circumstantially possible

[22] i *It can easily be shown that the argument is fallacious.*
ii *Water can still get in.*

In this case, actualisation is possible because it is not prevented by factual or physical circumstances. *May* is again found in formal style, such as scientific writing, especially in combination with a passive (it is virtually excluded in [ii], partly by informal *get*, partly by the likelihood of it being interpreted epistemically rather than dynamically).

(c) What is sometimes the case: the 'existential' use

[23] i *These animals can be dangerous.*
ii *Poinsettias can be red or yellow.*

We can gloss [i] as "These animals are sometimes dangerous" or "Some of these animals are dangerous" – by virtue of this relationship with the existential quantifier *some*, the modality here is sometimes called 'existential'. The modal and the quantifier often combine harmonically, as in *These animals can sometimes be dangerous. He can be very tactless/helpful* shows this use with a singular subject, expressing characteristic behaviour. Example [ii] shows the existential use combined with *or*, with the interpretation "Some poinsettias are red, others yellow" (generally with the implicature that these are the only alternatives). This combination of *can* + *or* can also be regarded as harmonic, and as in the other such combinations the auxiliary could be omitted without significant

[53] There are two special uses of *may* that fall at the periphery of deontic modality. One is in the idiom *may as well* (e.g. *We/You/They may as well accept*), used to suggest a course of action in default of any better. The other is the optative *may* of *May you be forgiven!*, etc., mentioned in §2.1.2.

loss: *Poinsettias are red or yellow. May* is again possible in formal style, but it differs from *can* in that it readily allows internal negation (like epistemic *may*): *The hairs are there all the time, although they may not grow noticeably before puberty* ("sometimes they don't").

(d) Ability

[24] i *She can run the marathon in under three hours.* [potential]
ii *I can hear something rattling.* [currently actualised]

Ability is a matter of internal properties on the part of the subject-referent; it represents a grammatically distinct use in that *may* is excluded even in the most formal style. Two subcases can be distinguished: potential and currently actualised. The latter is found with sense verbs and various verbs of cognition, and here there is low-degree modality: [ii] differs little from *I hear something rattling.* By contrast, [i] differs very sharply from the unmodalised *She runs the marathon in under three hours.* The latter is interpreted as a serial state, with multiple runnings, whereas [i] could be said on the basis of a single marathon under three hours – indeed she may not have run a marathon at all but merely displayed potential in training. In this potential ability case, the degree of difference from the unmodalised version will depend very much on the pragmatics of the situation concerned. There is, for example, little effective difference between *She can speak fluent French* and *She speaks fluent French*, because it is not easy to see how one could justifiably assert the former without repeated actualisations of the ability.

Dynamic necessity

Dynamic *must* is seen in:

[25] i *Ed's a guy who must always be poking his nose into other people's business.*
ii *Now that she has lost her job she must live extremely frugally.*

Example [i] represents prototypical dynamic modality in that it is a matter of someone's properties/disposition: the necessity arises from some internal need, rather than being imposed by some deontic source. An approximate equivalent in terms of negated possibility is *who can't help poking his nose into other people's business.* This use is thus comparable to the ability use of *can* – but whereas ability is a very frequent use of *can*, internal need is a fairly rare use of *must.* No equivalence is to be found here matching that shown in [19i] and [13i]: *He mustn't swim* cannot be interpreted as equivalent to *He can't swim* in the dynamic sense. The boundary between deontic and dynamic is somewhat blurred in explicit or implicit conditional constructions like *These plants must have plenty of water if they are to survive*: the plants need the water, but there may be an implicit obligation on relevant persons to ensure they have it.

Example [25ii] is more peripheral to the dynamic category, involving circumstantial necessity, comparable to the circumstantial possibility of [22] above. It is not a matter of obligation imposed by a deontic source, but simply force of circumstance. But *must* is less likely than *have* or *need* in such cases.[54]

[54] Dynamic *must* is sometimes found in the harmonic idiom *must needs*: *Apart from the radio and a small decca set, there are none of the modern aids to navigation on board so the skipper and his mate must needs be master of their craft.*

9.4 Idiomatic *should*, and *ought*

Should is the preterite form of ***shall*** but, as noted in §2.5.3, in some uses (the more frequent ones) the meaning is not derivable from that of ***shall*** + preterite inflection. We deal with these idiomatic uses in this section and take up the non-idiomatic ones in §9.8.

9.4.1 Medium strength modality

In its most frequent use, *should* expresses medium strength deontic or epistemic modality and is generally interchangeable with *ought* (+ *to*):

[26] i	*You should / ought to tell your mother.*	[deontic]
ii	*The next road on the left should / ought to be King Street.*	[epistemic]
iii	*He should / ought to do better this time.*	[ambiguous]

In the deontic interpretation of [iii] it is a matter of what is expected **of** him, whereas in the epistemic interpretation it is a matter of what I expect will happen. In the former case I could add *but I don't suppose he will*, while a possible continuation for the latter is *judging by the amount of training he's done.*

The deontic use

Deontic *should/ought* is usually subjective, indicating what the speaker considers 'right' – whether morally (*One should always tell the truth*) or as a matter of expediency (*We should buy now while the market is depressed*). They are weaker than *must* in that they allow for non-actualisation: *I should stop now but I'm not going to.* With past or present time they are commonly used when it is known that the situation was/is not actualised, in which case they convey criticism: *He shouldn't have gone to bed so late*; *You should be doing your homework instead of watching television.* One difference between *should* and *ought* is that only the former is normally used in issuing indirect directives (Ch. 10, §9.6), such as instructions: *The right-hand column should be left blank*, "Leave the right-hand column blank".

The epistemic use

Epistemic *should/ought*, again usually subjective, has a strength comparable with *probable*, but differs from it in that it involves inference (compare the difference between epistemic *must* and *certainly*). This means that the concept of 'right' is also relevant here: in [26ii], if the next road is not King Street, then I shall have failed to make the right inference.

Primacy of the deontic use

The deontic use of *should/ought* is more basic than the epistemic use. An epistemic reading is hardly possible with past time situations. Note, for example, the contrast between *must/may* and *should/ought* in:

[27] i	*She must/may have left yesterday.*	[epistemic]
ii	*She should / ought to have left yesterday.*	[deontic[55]]

[55] In this deontic reading the past time applies to the modality: it is a matter of what was (or would have been) right, not of what is right now. Deontic *must* and *may* cannot be used in this way with *have* for past obligation or permission: see §9.8.

More generally, there are many cases where the interpretation is purely deontic, but few where it is purely epistemic. If you ask where the key is and I reply, *It should be in the desk drawer*, there is an epistemic component in the meaning ("You'll probably find it there"), but there is likely to be a deontic component too ("If it isn't there, it's not in its right place"). If you are sending a manuscript to a publisher and I say, *They should accept it*, this can have a purely deontic reading ("It would be wrong of them not to accept it", with no epistemic judgement as to whether they will) or it can have an epistemic reading ("I'm fairly confident that they will"), but this is again not wholly free of deontic meaning: my expectation that they will accept is inseparable from the judgement that that is the right thing for them to do.

The primacy of deontic *should/ought* is also reflected in the fact that an epistemic reading is much less likely with unfavourable situations than with favourable ones. Thus if we replace *accept* by *reject* in this last example the epistemic reading becomes very unlikely. The primacy of the deontic use (where the situation is characteristically in the future) may also explain why *should/ought* are used epistemically in inferring consequences from causes but not the other way round, so that they could substitute for *must* in *He's better now: he must be able to return to work*, but not in *He's back at work now: he must be better.*

Negation

Should/ought normally take internal negation: *You shouldn't eat so much* exhorts you to refrain from eating so much. There are no equivalent items taking external negation, i.e. no items related to them as *need* is to *must* or *can* to epistemic *may*, but this is to be attributed to the fact that with medium strength modality there tends to be no pragmatic difference between external and internal negation (§9.2.1).[56]

9.4.2 Low-degree modality

There are several constructions, predominantly subordinate ones, where *should* (but not *ought*) appears with low-degree modality, i.e. with little discernible modal meaning of its own:

[28]	i	*It is essential/desirable that he should be told.*	[mandative]
	ii	*We invited her husband too, lest he should feel left out.*	[adversative]
	iii	*We invited her husband too, in order that he should not feel left out.*	[purposive]
	iv	*It's surprising that he should have been so late.*	[emotive]
	v	*If you should experience any difficulty, please let me know.*	[conditional]

In the first two, *should* is a somewhat less formal alternative to a plain form verb (*that he be told, lest he feel*).

Mandative *should*

In the mandative construction we have something similar to a harmonic combination of modal auxiliary + matrix predicative element, for the predicative items concerned have deontic meaning. The use of *should* here, however, is grammaticalised in that

[56] *Should* is often used with *why* with an implicature that there is no (deontic or epistemic) reason for actualisation: *Why should we let him get away with it?*; *Why should it have been Max who told her?* ("I don't think it was"). A further special use of *should* is in certain Yiddishisms that have gained wide currency, e.g. *I should be so lucky*, where it conveys non-actualisation ("I am not / won't be so lucky").

it combines as readily with items of strong modality (*necessary, essential, imperative,* etc.) as with those of medium strength (*desirable, advisable, right,* etc.) – see Ch. 11, §7.1.1.

Emotive *should*

This occurs primarily with predicative lexemes indicating surprise or evaluation: *odd, remarkable, surprising, good, bad, a pity,* etc. The *should* clause can generally be replaced by an unmodalised one: compare [28iv] with *It's surprising that he was so late.*[57] This emotive *should* is also found in main-clause interrogatives used with the force of rhetorical questions: *I was walking in the park and who should I meet but Angela Cooke!* ("to my surprise I met...").

Conditional *should*

This expresses slightly greater doubt than the non-modal counterpart: compare [28v] with *If you experience any difficulty,...* This is why it cannot be used when there is no element of doubt at all, as in *If you're my father, why don't you help me?* and the like. It is usually found in open conditionals, but the remote construction is also possible: compare *If there should be any opposition, they will/would not go ahead with the plan* (where *will* indicates open, *would* remote).

9.5 *Will*

In general *will* conveys a lower degree of modal meaning than the auxiliaries considered so far; nevertheless, it has much in common with them semantically and pragmatically as well as syntactically.

9.5.1 Epistemic modality, including futurity

There are three uses of *will* that fall within the general area of epistemic modality:

[29]	i	*They <u>will</u> have made the decision last week.*	[central-epistemic]
	ii	*She <u>will</u> beat him easily.*	[futurity]
	iii	*If they are here, they'<u>ll</u> be upstairs.*	[conditional consequence]

The central-epistemic use is found with past and present time situations and the futurity use, of course, with future time. The conditional consequence use, on the other hand, applies with any of the three time spheres, and for that reason provides a bridge or link between the first two uses.

The central-epistemic use

The past time case, marked by perfect *have*, is illustrated in [29i], the present in:

[30] [Knock on door] *That <u>will</u> be the plumber.*

This use is normally restricted to 2nd or 3rd person subjects: we will not say, for example, #*I will/shall have offended him by what I said at yesterday's meeting* (where epistemic *may*

[57] Actualisation is not always conveyed: *It is unthinkable that she should give up without a fight,* for example, involves a potential future situation whose actualisation is unthinkable. An unmodalised form is not possible here, but an infinitival construction is, especially with a modalised main clause: *It would be unthinkable for her to give up without a fight.*

or *must* could occur quite readily). It therefore excludes *shall*, which always has deontic meaning with 2nd/3rd person subjects.

Strength and degree of modality

Semantically *will* is strong, entailing the factuality of the situation. This is why we can't say #*They will have made the decision last week though it's just possible that they have postponed it until the next meeting*: it is self-contradictory. Usually, however, there is a considerable amount of pragmatic weakening. For example, [29i] is epistemically much weaker than *They made the decision last week*: the latter presents it as something I know, whereas the former presents it as a confident prediction. In such cases, therefore, we have a sharp difference between modalised and unmodalised versions, with a high degree of modality attaching to *will*. The difference from the unmodalised version is of the same general kind as we find with epistemic *must* and *may*, and it is for this reason that we refer to this as the 'central-epistemic' use: it falls very centrally within the area of epistemic modality.

The examples given have involved subjective modality, but *will* can also be used objectively. In this case, as with *must*, there is less pragmatic weakening, and hence a lower degree of modality:

[31] *Ed is Tom's father and Tom is Bill's father, so Ed <u>will</u> be Bill's grandfather.*

Here the evidence for the factuality of Ed's being Bill's grandfather is so strong that I could equally well have used unmodalised *is*: the effect of *will* is just to present Ed's being Bill's grandfather as something that follows from what has just been said, rather than as a matter of direct knowledge.

Will vs *must*

Will has the same semantic strength as *must*, and in its central-epistemic use it can generally be replaced by *must* with relatively little change of meaning. *Must* conveys the idea of conclusion, and is often used in explanations: *Ed's late – he must have overslept.* With central-epistemic *will* it is more a matter of assumption or expectation, very often with a suggestion of future confirmation, as in: *I can't tell you what the word means but it will be in the dictionary.* Compare futurity *You will find it in the dictionary. Will* would therefore hardly substitute for *must* in *You were mad to tell her: you must have known how upset she would be*, for it is hardly a case where the issue of future confirmation would arise. *Will* seems, moreover, to allow somewhat more pragmatic weakening than *must*, which also makes it less appropriate in this context. The idea of future confirmation is similarly unlikely to be relevant in *This must be the best restaurant in town*, though *will* would also be avoided for this present time meaning because it would most likely be misinterpreted as indicating futurity.

Futurity

We have emphasised that in main clauses a simple present tense can be used for future time only under strict pragmatic conditions: *We leave for Sydney tomorrow* but not, normally, #*You understand when you receive Kim's letter tomorrow.* The default way of locating the situation in future time is by means of *will*: *You will understand when you receive Kim's letter tomorrow.*

Varying degree of modality

In such cases the temporal component of meaning appears pre-eminent, but futurity is accompanied by varying degrees of modal meaning. This can be seen by comparing the following contrasts between past and future:

[32]	PAST TIME	FUTURE TIME
i	a. *He was two yesterday.*	b. *He will be two tomorrow.*
ii	a. *She beat him in under an hour.*	b. *She will beat him in under an hour.*

In [i] there is little perceptible difference between [a] and [b] other than the temporal one: *will* here comes close to being simply a marker of futurity, with the modal component reduced to a minimum. It is not quite zero, however, for the truth of [b] is contingent on his surviving until tomorrow. In this example *will be* is interchangeable with futurate *is*, but the existence of a present futurate is not a necessary condition for *will* to be perceived as having a minimal degree of modality. Compare, for example, *It was soon too dark to play any more* and *It will soon be too dark to play any more*, where *will be* is not replaceable by *is*. If the *will* sentence is uttered on the playing field as the light fades, the modal component will again be minimal. In [ii], however, the temporal difference between [a] and [b] is accompanied by a significantly greater modal difference: [iia] reports a past event while [iib] is clearly perceived as a prediction, not a factual statement about the future. However confident I may be about the match, innumerable factors could intervene to prevent the prediction coming true. The epistemic status of [iib] is thus quite sharply different from that of [iia]. Similar are examples like *It will be a long time before we have another summer like this*, *You won't recognise him*, and so on.

Variation in the degree of modal qualification associated with *will* can also be seen by comparing the *will* construction with the present futurate in cases where the latter is acceptable:

[33]	PRESENT FUTURATE	FUTURITY *WILL*
i	a. *He is two tomorrow.*	b. *He will be two tomorrow.*
ii	a. *Australia meets Sweden in the Davis Cup final in December.*	b. *Australia will meet Sweden in the Davis Cup final in December.*

In [i] there is no effective difference between the two constructions, whereas in [ii] the difference is quite sharp. As we noted in §4.2.4, [iia], with unmodalised *meets*, is appropriate only in a context where the semi-finals have been played, so that the finalists have already been determined, whereas [iib], with modal *will meet*, could be used earlier in the competition, predicting the outcome of the intermediate matches. *Will meet* is thus pragmatically considerably weaker than *meets*: it requires less supporting evidence, less 'epistemic warrant'.

It is evident, therefore, that futurity *will* potentially carries a significant amount of modal meaning. The modality concerned is of the epistemic kind, since it is generally a matter of limitations to the speaker's knowledge. There is a close intrinsic connection between futurity and modality: our knowledge about the future is inevitably much more limited than our knowledge about the past and the present, and what we say about the future will typically be perceived as having the character of a prediction rather than an unqualified factual assertion.

Non-occurrence of futurity *will* in temporal clauses

When adjuncts and the complements of temporal prepositions such as *after, before, as soon as,* etc., take the simple present, not the *will* construction, when the reference is to future time:

[34] i *I'll buy one when the price comes / *will come down.*
ii *We'll go for a walk as soon as it stops / *will stop raining.*

Here I do not **assert** that the price will come down or that it will stop raining, but simply take the occurrence of these events for granted. The modal qualification which *will* conveys (in varying degrees) would therefore be out of place: the grammar requires the unmodalised forms.

Futurity *will* in conditional protases

With future time conditionals the protasis (the subordinate clause) may or may not contain *will*:

[35] i *If [the price comes down in a few months], I'll buy one* [sc. then].
ii *If [the price will come down in a few months], I'm not going to buy one now.*

Version [i] illustrates the usual construction: [ii] is quite rare. In [i] I again do not assert that the price will come down (but merely entertain it as a possibility) and therefore the modal qualification associated with *will* is here too out of place. In [ii], however, *will* does appear in the protasis because the modal meaning it expresses is part of the proposition that is conditionally entertained. In [i] the condition is a matter of the future occurrence of an event, whereas in [ii] it is a matter of the present predictability of an event (it might be glossed as "If it is the case that the price will come down in a few months", a type of gloss quite inappropriate for [i]). Note that the behaviour of *will* here matches that of the other epistemic modals – compare, for example, *If the price may come down in a few months, I'm not going to buy one now.*[58]

Conditional consequence

Will is very often used in the apodosis of conditional constructions, whether the time is past, present, or future:

[36] i a. *If it rained last night [the match will have been cancelled].* [past time]
b. *If it rains tonight [the match will be cancelled].* [future time]
ii a. *If he's still in Bath, [he'll be at his mother's].* [sc. now] [present time]
b. *If he's still in Bath when you arrive, [he'll be at his mother's].* [future time]

In none of the three time spheres is *will* required. We therefore have such contrasts as the following:

[37] i *If Ed signed the petition [he was / will have been the only one of us who did].*
ii *If he's still in Bath [he is / will be at his mother's].*
iii *If you're late again tomorrow, [you are / will be fired].*

Again, the version with *will* is pragmatically somewhat weaker than the one with the simple preterite or present. This is perhaps clearest with past time. If I'm uncertain

[58] The epistemic modality expressed by *will* or *may* in these conditional protases is of the objective type: it is not a matter of the speaker's subjective judgement.

whether Ed signed but know that no one else among us did, then I will use the simple preterite *was*: *will have been* conveys a lesser degree of confidence in the conclusion. Compare, similarly, *If he said that, he was mistaken*: in a context where I have no doubt that "that" is false, *will have been* would be out of place. With future time, the simple present tense (the futurate construction) is rare; in [iii] it strengthens the threat by emphasising the ineluctability of the consequence.

As suggested above, the use of *will* for conditional consequence can be seen as providing a link between the central-epistemic and futurity uses. Examples [36–37] are alike in that *will* indicates the predictability of the consequence, yet the past/present time cases have clear affinities with the central-epistemic *will*, and the future cases with the *will* of futurity. Note that in all three time spheres, strong *will* contrasts with weak epistemic *may*.

Differences from the modals of necessity and possibility

Modal adverbs

Will does not combine harmonically with modal adverbs as *must* does with *surely/necessarily* or *may* with *perhaps/possibly*. Adverbs of any strength, *possibly*, *probably*, *certainly*, etc., can all be added to epistemic *will* (just as they can to corresponding clauses without a modal auxiliary): *They will surely/probably/perhaps have made the decision last week*; *She will certainly/very likely/possibly beat him easily*. The adverbs are of high-degree modality, quite different in meaning from *will*, so that when they are added they bring a distinct modal meaning rather than harmonically reinforcing that of *will*.

Negation

A second important difference between *will* and the modals of necessity and possibility is that it does not enter into any contrast between external and internal negation such as we find between *needn't* and *mustn't* or *can't* and *may not*. *She won't have read it yet* (central epistemic) and *She won't win as easily next time* (futurity) have internal negation and there are no comparable forms in which the negation applies to the modality.

Both these differences between *will* and the modals of necessity and possibility can be related to the degree of modality involved: in contrast to *must*, *may*, etc., *will* is a low-degree modal.

9.5.2 **Dynamic modality**

Under this heading we consider those uses of *will* where dispositions or properties of the subject-referent are involved.

(a) Volition

[38] i *Jill won't sign the form.*
ii *They have found someone [who will stand in for you while you're away].*
iii *I will be back before six.*

Example [i] implies unwillingness or refusal on Jill's part; in [ii] *will* might be glossed as "is prepared/willing to"; and in [iii] the auxiliary conveys the idea of intention.

Difference between *will* and *want*, *be willing*, etc.

It must be emphasised, however, that *will* does not have the same meaning as *want*, *be willing*, *be prepared*, *intend*, and the like. In the first place *will* expresses strong modality (as noted above for the epistemic uses), whereas *intend* and *want* are of medium strength, with *willing* and *prepared* still weaker. For example, [38iii] entails actualisation, so that it would be inconsistent to add *but I may not be able to manage it* (whereas *I intend/ want to be back before six but may not be able to manage it* is perfectly acceptable). Secondly, with *will* there is normally no contrast between external and internal negation such as we find between, say, *She isn't willing to receive any payment* and *She is willing not to receive any payment.* Example [38i] entails her future non-signing of the form, and hence is best regarded as having internal negation (like *mustn't*), but there is no way of negating just the volitional component, leaving open the issue of future actualisation – nothing comparable to *She doesn't mind whether she signs the form or not* (hence nothing comparable to *needn't*).

These points indicate that even in the volitional use *will* has a low degree of modality: the modal meaning is not sharply separable from the non-modal component. Volition and futurity are not contrasting meanings of *will*, so that one has no feeling of ambiguity between volitional and non-volitional future in examples like [38iii] (any more than one has a feeling of ambiguity between volitional and non-volitional past in the unmodalised *I was back before six*). Volition is better regarded as an implicature overlaid upon futurity – an implicature deriving from the assumption that the subject-referent is in control, e.g. in [38iii] that I have control over the time of return. With a 1st person subject, moreover, volition tends to trigger a further implicature of commitment – and you might ask *Is that a promise?* in order to get me to make the commitment explicit.

Heightening of volitional meaning

The separateness of the volitional component is heightened in an example like [38i] uttered in a context where she has already expressed her intentions – *I've told her how urgent it is but she won't sign the form.* This interpretation differs from that where I am simply predicting her future non-signing. But the difference is not so much between volition and mere futurity as between current, present volition and volitional future, for the presumption must be in any case that non-signing is subject to her control and hence volitional. It is the combination of volition with present time (time distinct from that of the actualisation) that makes the modal component more separable. Such heightened modality is more likely in the negative than the positive: I am more likely to report refusal by *she won't* than agreement by *she will* (in the positive the present orientation would favour *she's going to*). Other factors which similarly tend to heighten the volitional component are illustrated in:

[39]	i	*I* <u>*WILL*</u> *solve this problem.*	[strongly stressed modal]
	ii	<u>*Will*</u> *you lend me your pen?*	[closed interrogative]
	iii	*I'll wash if [you* <u>*will*</u> *dry].*	[conditional protasis]

A strongly stressed *will*, especially with a 1st person subject, tends to convey determination. A closed interrogative, especially with a 2nd person subject, characteristically questions willingness and indirectly conveys a request (Ch. 10, §9.6.1). Futurity *will* rarely occurs in a conditional protasis, as noted above, but volitional *will* is quite unexceptionable, as in [iii], where your willingness is clearly part of the proposition that is conditionally entertained.[59]

[59] One special case of volitional heightening is in subordinate elliptical constructions with comparative *as* (*He receives a large allowance to spend as he will*) or relative *what* (*Do what you will*).

Extension to inanimates

Volition implies a human or animate agent, but something akin to a metaphorical extension of volitional *will* is found with inanimates when it is a matter of satisfying human wants, as in *The lawnmower won't start* (someone is trying to start it) or *The books won't fit on one shelf.* These again appear freely in conditionals: *Give me a call if the engine won't start.*

(b) Propensity

[40] i *He will lie in bed all day, reading trashy novels.*
ii *Oil will float on water.*

Here we are concerned with characteristic or habitual behaviour of animates or general properties of inanimates. A simple present could be substituted with little effect: this use is therefore fairly sharply distinct from futurity, though in many cases there is a connection through conditional consequence – compare [ii] with *If you pour oil on water it will float.* Strong stress on the auxiliary conveys the speaker's emotive response to the situation – usually exasperation, disapproval, resignation, or the like: *He* WILL *pour the tea-leaves down the sink.*

9.5.3 Deontic modality

[41] *You will report back for duty on Friday morning.* [speaker's requirement]

The deontic use of *will* is a matter of implicature: if I predict your agentive actions (or someone else's) in a context where I have the authority to require them, I will be understood as tacitly invoking that authority. The evidence for the prediction is that I am telling you to do something and you are required to do as I say. The same implicature is found with *be going* (in informal speech), as in the sports coach's *You're going to go out there and give them all you've got.*

9.6 *Shall*

9.6.1 Deontic modality

Three deontic uses of *shall* are seen in:

[42] i *The committee shall meet at least four times per year.* [constitutive/regulative]
ii *You shall have your money back tomorrow.* [speaker's guarantee]
iii *Shall I close the window?* [direction-seeking]

(a) The constitutive/regulative use

This is used in constitutions, regulations, and similar legal or quasi-legal documents. The subject is normally 3rd person.

(b) Speaker's guarantee

In [42ii] I give an undertaking that you will get your money back: I put myself under an obligation to ensure that the situation is actualised. This use is relatively uncommon and differs from the central cases of deontic modality in that the obligation is placed on the speaker. It is found with 2nd and 3rd person subjects.

(c) *Shall* in direction questions

Example [42iii] is what we call a direction question (Ch. 10, §4.6): I'm asking you to tell me whether to close the window or not. The prototypical answer is an imperative (e.g. *Yes, please do*), not a declarative with *shall*. This use occurs mainly with 1st person subjects, and for many varieties *will* would be quite impossible here with this meaning.

9.6.2 **Non-deontic uses and the choice between *shall* and *will***

With a 1st person subject, *shall* occurs as a variant of *will* as follows:

[43]	i	*I shall never understand why she left.*	[futurity]
	ii	*If the rules have changed as much as you suggest we shall have done most of this work for nothing.*	[consequence]
	iii	*I shall do as she says.*	[volition]

We have noted that conditional consequence very often involves future time (cf. *If we don't leave now we shall miss the bus*), but [ii] shows again that it does not have to. The other epistemic use of *will*, the central-epistemic one of *That will be the plumber*, is not found with a 1st person subject, and there is accordingly no corresponding use of *shall*. The *shall* of [43i–ii] occurs also in the interrogative – e.g. for futurity, *When shall I be well enough to leave hospital?* The interrogative counterpart of [iii], however, *Shall I do as she says?*, has a deontic meaning, like [42iii] above.[60]

There is a well-known prescriptive rule that treats *shall* and *will* as complementary:

[44]		Traditional prescriptive rule	1ST PERSON	2ND/3RD PERSON
	i	Futurity (so-called future tense)	*shall*	*will*
	ii	Volition/determination	*will*	*shall*

The classic illustration contrasts the drowning man's *I shall drown and no one will save me* (expressing futurity) and *I will drown and no one shall save me* (expressing a determination to drown). It is quite clear, however, that this rule is not valid.

As for [44i], we must allow *will* as well as *shall* for the 1st person – and modern usage manuals recognise this. *Will* (including the contracted variant *'ll*) is in fact very much more common, and indeed in AmE *shall* is quite rare. There is also a style difference, with *shall* tending to be somewhat more formal. Part [ii] of rule [44] is unsatisfactory for two reasons. Firstly, with a 1st person subject there is again variation between *will* and *shall*: *We will/shall never surrender. Will* is here more frequent than *shall* – even more so than is the case with futurity. Secondly, with a 2nd/3rd person subject both *will* and *shall* are possible but they have different meanings. For subject-referent's volition, *will* occurs with all three persons – e.g. *I've said I won't sign, You've said you won't sign, She's said she won't sign.* The 2nd/3rd person *shall* of *You/They shall have my answer tomorrow* we have labelled 'speaker's guarantee': it indicates the speaker's

[60] Non-deontic *shall* is not wholly restricted to 1st person subjects. Some speakers allow it in 2nd person interrogatives like *Shall you take a taxi?*, where *Will you take a taxi?* is likely to be taken as a request rather than a question about your intentions. This use is uncommon and for many speakers sounds old-fashioned and formal; the more usual way of avoiding the request interpretation is by use of the progressive *Will you be taking a taxi?* There is also an archaic use of *shall* in an open protasis, still found in some legal language: *If the tenant shall at any time fail to keep the demised premises as aforesaid the landlord may do all things necessary to effect or maintain such insurance. Shall fail* here is semantically indistinguishable from *fails*; this use of *shall* is comparable to that of *should* in [28iv].

determination or promise that the situation will be actualised. With a 1st person subject the distinction between volition and speaker's guarantee is not so sharp since the subject-referent is (or includes) the speaker. Nevertheless, there is good reason to treat *I shall let you have my answer tomorrow* as volition, since this *shall* can be replaced without change of meaning by the ordinary volitional *will*: *I will let you have my answer tomorrow.*

9.7 *Had better* and auxiliary *dare*

The idiom *had better* and the modal auxiliary *dare* have a much narrower range of use than the items discussed above, both being restricted to just one of the three kinds of modality:

[45] i *You/I had better telephone her.* [deontic]
ii *I daren't tell her.* [dynamic]

Deontic *had better*

This is generally subjective, giving the speaker's judgement as to the best course of action. Unlike *should* but like *must*, it doesn't countenance non-actualisation: *He should / #must / #had better tell her but I don't suppose he will.* This makes it semantically strong, but it is normally pragmatically weaker than *must*, less a matter of the speaker's will. The modality is always in present time: compare again *He should / *must / *had better have done it himself.* Negation is normally internal, whether marked after or before *better*: *He had better not tell her*; *He hadn't better tell her.*

Dynamic *dare*

This means essentially "have the courage" – a matter of the subject-referent's disposition. In declarative main clauses auxiliary *dare* is normally negative, and the negation is external: *I daren't open the door*, "I don't have the courage to". This entails that I won't open the door, which puts *dare* with the weak modals (cf. *I can't open the door*).

9.8 The preterite forms *could, might, would, should*

We have distinguished three uses of the preterite: past time, backshift, and modal remoteness. It is a distinctive property of the modal auxiliaries that the modal remoteness use is much more frequent and less restricted than the past time use – the complete reverse of what holds for other verbs.

9.8.1 Past time

Could and *would* are quite commonly used with past time meaning but, significantly, the majority of examples involve dynamic modality, the kind that is least different from the type of meaning expressed by lexical verbs. Past time *might* is seen in such attested examples as:

[46] i *When my father was attached to a cavalry regiment at Brighton before we moved to Stonehurst, my parents might attend an occasional concert at the Pavillion.*
ii *The completion of the canal increased the ease with which the Mons coal might be sent to Nord.*

This use is, however, very rare, and somewhat formal or literary in style: for many speakers *might* is restricted to the backshifted and modal remoteness senses. And *should* is not used at all with past time meaning.

Past time *could*

Present tense *can* is matched by *could* in all the deontic and dynamic uses given in §9.3:

[47]	i	*In those days we could borrow as many books as we wished.*	[permission]
	ii	*The most we could expect was a slight cut in sales-tax.*	[reasonable/acceptable]
	iii	*Water could still get in.*	[circumstantial possibility]
	iv	*He could be very tactless at times.*	[existential]
	v	*She could run the marathon in under three hours.*	[potential ability]
	vi	*I could hear something rattling.*	[actualised ability]

Restriction on use of *could* in affirmative contexts

An important restriction is that *could* does not normally appear in affirmative contexts when it is a matter of actualisation of a single situation viewed perfectively. Compare:

[48]	i	*I left early but still couldn't get a seat.*	[non-affirmative]
	ii	**I left early and could get a good seat.*	[affirmative]

In [ii] we need *was able.* Similarly imperfective *rattling* in [47vi] is not replaceable by perfective *rattle* – cf. *Last night I heard / *could hear the clock strike two.* The restriction applies also to *can*, but is less obvious because of the general restriction on the perfective present. Thus in a timeless synopsis (§4.2.2) where this general restriction doesn't apply, we find the same contrast between *able* and *can*: *She starts early and is able to / *can finish on time.*

Past time *would*

This is used with dynamic modality (volition or propensity) and with futurity:

[49]	i	*I had no money on me but he wouldn't lend me any.*	[volition]
	ii	*Whenever he heard her coming he would quickly put out his pipe.*	[propensity]
	iii	*Only a few months later their love would change to hate.*	[futurity]

Volition

The restriction just noted for *could* applies also with volitional *would.* It is normally excluded from affirmative contexts with singulary dynamic situations, so that we couldn't replace *wouldn't* in [49i] by *would* – we would use unmodalised *lent me some* (or *was willing to lend me some*, etc.). This time the restriction doesn't apply to *will* (cf. *I haven't any money on me but fortunately Ed will lend me some*).[61]

Propensity

This normally involves a serial state, as in [49ii], but there is a use of *would* which can be regarded as a special case of the propensity use and where we do find singulary actualisation in an affirmative context: *He* WOULD *call round just when I wanted an early*

[61] The contexts allowing *would* are a little broader than the ordinary non-affirmative ones: for example, *just* permits *would* but not *any*: *The text would just fit on one page*, but not **I just had any money.*

night. The modal is always stressed – with an emotive effect like that of stressed propensity *will*. But *will* differs from *would* in not allowing reference to a single actualisation – if, in response to a jocular remark, I say *He* WILL *have his little joke*, I am describing his typical or habitual behaviour, not a particular instance of it, as in the *would* example. The connection with the ordinary case of propensity is that the event is presented as typical. What it is typical of is not expressed, but we infer something like "typical of the inconvenient/annoying things that he does or that happen (to me)".

Futurity

Would is also used to indicate futurity in the past, futurity relative to the time referred to by the preterite, as in [49iii]. As with *will*, actualisation is entailed – and the actualisation is virtually required to have already taken place, so that a simple preterite could have been used instead: *A few months later their love changed to hate*. The difference is in the choice of T_o: *changed* is a deictic past, while *would* has a past T_o, and [49iii] therefore has some affinity to non-subordinate backshift (§6.2.1). This use of *would* is restricted to narrative and similar genres.

9.8.2 Backshift

Could, *would*, *should*, and *might* occur as backshifted preterites. Compare:

[50] i *I can/may/will/shall see her shortly.* [original utterance: present tense]
ii *I knew I could/might/would/should see her shortly.* [backshifted: preterite]

In this construction the distinction between a present tense and a modally remote preterite is lost:

[51] i a. *I can win if I really try.* b. *I could win if I really tried.*
ii a. *He said I could win if I really tried.* b. *He said I could win if I really tried.*

The backshifted reports of [ia], an open conditional, and [ib], a remote conditional, are identical. In open [iia] the preterite in *could* (and *tried*) indicates that T_o is in the past, whereas in remote [iib] it indicates modal remoteness and the location of T_o is not expressed. The open conditional interpretation is the more likely because the open conditional construction is the default one. It is clear, however, that the remote interpretation is grammatically possible, for we have examples like *He knew he would be in trouble if they were to check his alibi*, where this use of ***be*** is found only in the remote construction (cf. §6.1).

9.8.3 Modal remoteness

Three broad subcases of the modal remoteness use can be distinguished: in remote conditionals and the complement of *wish*, to indicate tentativeness, and a special use applying just to *could* and *might*.

(a) Remote conditionals and the complement of *wish*

We have seen that the distinction between open and remote conditional constructions is marked syntactically by tense. One major use of the preterite modals, therefore, is in the apodosis of a remote conditional, where they contrast with the present tense forms of an open conditional:

[52] i *If he pays the fare [I can/may/will/shall take a taxi].* [open: present]
ii *If he paid the fare [I could/might/would/should take a taxi].* [remote: preterite]

We also include here cases where the condition is implicit – most obviously those where a condition is inferrable from the context, as when *I wouldn't sign* is interpreted as "I wouldn't sign if I were you".

The relation between *would* and *should* matches that between *will* and *shall* described in §9.6.2. *Might* in this construction is generally epistemic: it could not, for example, substitute for the *could* of deontic permission in *If he hadn't misbehaved he could have come with us.*

Remote apodosis requires a modal auxiliary

In Present-day English the apodosis of a remote conditional must contain a modal auxiliary:

[53]		−MODAL AUXILIARY	+MODAL AUXILIARY	
i	a.	*If he's here, he's upstairs.*	b. *If he's here he'll be upstairs.*	[open]
ii	a.	**If he were here, he were upstairs.*	b. *If he were here he'd be upstairs.*	[remote]

The difference between [53ia] and [ib] is quite slight, and many grammars implicitly or explicitly treat the *would* construction [iib] as the remote counterpart of [ia] (as well as of [ib]): in such an analysis *would* is regarded as simply a marker of the remote conditional construction. The view taken in this grammar, however, is the one reflected in the display [53], namely that remote *would* is to be paired with open *will* – that [iib] differs semantically from [ia] not just as remote vs open but by virtue of containing modal "will". Evidence for this view comes from considering examples where the presence or absence of *will* in the open construction is of greater significance:

[54] i *If Oswald didn't shoot Kennedy someone else did.* [open; − ***will***]
ii *If Oswald didn't shoot Kennedy someone else will have.* [open; + ***will***]
iii *If Oswald hadn't shot Kennedy someone else would have.* [remote; + ***will***]

It is common knowledge that President Kennedy was shot, and with this background knowledge one would naturally use [i] rather than [ii]. Given that someone shot Kennedy, then if Oswald didn't, necessarily someone else did: the conclusion that someone else shot him is so certain and obvious that the epistemic qualification expressed by *will* in [ii] would be out of place. *Will* is used when the conclusion is somewhat less secure, as in our earlier example [36], *If it rained last night the match will have been cancelled*: here it is (we may assume) very reasonable to draw the conclusion, but it certainly doesn't follow necessarily from the premise since it's not impossible for a match to be played in the rain. Now consider the remote conditional [54iii]. What is striking here is that although (in view of the common knowledge mentioned) we accept [i] as true, we do not have any similar reason to accept [iii] as true. Example [iii] implicates that Oswald did shoot Kennedy but envisages a different world from our own in which he didn't, and there is no common knowledge that establishes that Kennedy would have been shot in such a world – that establishes that his shooting (by Oswald or someone else) was inevitable. The conclusion in [iii] therefore does not have the absolutely secure status that it does in [i], and that is why we perceive a difference between them with respect to truth. This is important because, in general, open–remote pairs do not differ in this way: compare *If he pays the fare I can take a taxi* with *If he paid the fare I could take a taxi* – or *If it rained last night the match will have been cancelled* with *If it had rained last night the match would have been cancelled.* An analysis which takes [iii] as the remote counterpart of [i] must therefore treat the meaning difference between them as exceptional.

No such problem arises in our analysis because for us [iii] is not the remote counterpart of [i]. It is the counterpart of [ii], which would be appropriate in a context where it was not known that Kennedy was shot, and where the conclusion was therefore again less secure than it is in [i]. (For further discussion of these issues, see Ch. 8, §14.2.2.)

Wish (together with certain similar expressions: Ch. 11, §7.2) requires a preterite in a finite complement, so that we have such contrasts as:

[55] i *I'm glad you can/will join us.* [*be glad* + present]
ii *I wish you could/would join us.* [*wish* + preterite]

We group the remote conditional and *wish* constructions together because in both the preterite is here obligatory, and the contrast illustrated in [52] and [55] reinforces the inflectional relationship between *can* and *could*, *will* and *would*, etc.: they are different forms of a common lexeme required in different grammatical constructions.[62]

(b) The tentative use

[56] i a. *He'll be about sixty.* b. *He'd be about sixty.*
ii a. *Can you pass the salt, please.* b. *Could you pass the salt, please.*
iii a. *You may be right.* b. *You might be right.*

The difference between present tense and preterite is much less tangible here than in (a) above: the preterite introduces a rather vague element of tentativeness, diffidence, extra politeness, or the like. The intended context for [i] is that of answering such a question as *How old is he?* (we are not concerned here with the interpretation of [ib] as an implicit conditional, "He'd be about sixty now if he were still alive"). In such a context the unmodalised *He is sixty* makes an unqualified assertion. Example [ia] is less assured: it involves what we have called the central-epistemic use of *will.* And [ib] is then marginally weaker still, less confident. In [ii] we have indirect speech acts: questions about your ability are conventionally used as requests. In such cases the preterite is generally regarded as slightly more diffident, more polite. Finally, in [iii] we have epistemic possibility; for some speakers at least the preterite version [iiib] suggests a slightly lower degree of possibility than [iiia] – they would find *may* a little more encouraging than *might.* Note that with epistemic ***can*** only the preterite version with *could* is used.

Further cases of tentative preterites are seen in:

[57] i *It might/could be described as an act of provocation.* [dynamic]
ii *Might/Could I have a little more sugar?* [deontic]
iii *Would you tell them we're here.* [polite request]
iv *... and, I would suggest, it's too expensive anyway.* [indirect performative]
v *I would/should like to see him tomorrow.* [tentative version of *want*]
vi *They would appear to have gone without us.* [redoubled qualification]

[62] The contrast illustrated in [55] for *can/could* and *will/would* is not found with *shall/should* because *wish* is oriented to present (or past) time: we cannot therefore have **I wish I should/would be able to attend* matching *I'm glad I shall/will be able to attend.* The contrast is also rather marginal for the *may/might* pair: we have *I'm glad the Grade 12 boys may attend* but *I wish the Grade 12 boys might attend* is very unlikely: it would be very much more natural here to have *could.*

Example [i] corresponds to the use of *may/can* glossed in §9.3.3 as "what is reasonable or acceptable". Example [ii] is a request for permission, slightly more diffident than the version with *may/can* – still further politeness can be achieved by extra length, as in the harmonic combination *May/Might I be permitted to have a little more sugar?* The *would* of [iii] is volitional, again more diffident/polite than *will. Would* is also volitional in [iv] but actualisation is immediate, so that I make the suggestion ('perform' the act of suggesting: see Ch. 10, §3.1) in uttering the sentence, just as I do in the non-modal *I suggest. I would suggest* is less direct than *I suggest*, hence again more diffident.

Would/should like in [57v] is more or less a fixed phrase, contrasting as a whole with *want.* While *want* assigns a future interpretation to its complement (§7), *like* assigns a present interpretation (as in *I like to see him*); if the seeing is to be future, therefore, the liking must be too, hence the need for ***will***. The preterite supplies the tentative feature, accepting that I may not be able to see him. However, a present tense conveys that the situation is a serial state (*I like to see him* conveys that I periodically do) and so does *will* (cf. *When you're older you will probably like to see him*), whereas *would/should like* + infinitival allows a singulary situation, as in [v], and is to this extent idiomatic. The expression can also be used in indirect requests as a more elaborate alternative to the *would* of [iii]: *Would you like to tell them we're here.* Compare also [iv] with *I should like to thank you for your kind hospitality*, which is an indirect expression of thanks, with *thank* another illocutionary verb.

In [57vi] *appear* is a lexical modal of medium strength, qualifying my commitment to the truth of the modalised proposition: compare unmodalised *They have gone without us* with modalised *They appear to have gone without us. Would* then adds further modal qualification, so that [vi] provides a double hedge against being wrong. There is no intermediate term with *will*, for *They will appear to have gone without us* has futurity, not central-epistemic *will.* The same effect is found in *would seem, I would think*, etc.[63]

(c) Special use of *might* and *could*

[58] i *You were mad to drive so fast: you <u>might</u>/<u>could</u> have been killed.*
ii *We <u>could</u>/<u>might</u> be in Africa.* [knowingly uttered in France]
iii *You <u>might</u>/<u>could</u> have cleaned up instead of leaving it to me to do.*

These do not fall into either of the above major categories: there is no implicit condition, but the preterite conveys much more than a slight element of tentativeness. In [i] the (circumstantial) possibility existed but was not actualised: you weren't killed. Example [ii] can also be regarded as unactualised circumstantial possibility, but differs from [i] in that there is no element of cause and effect (as your being killed was a possible result of your driving so fast); it can be glossed as "It is as though we were in Africa – we're not, but judging from appearances there's no reason why we should not be". Example [iii] is a conventional informal expression of reproach: "You didn't clean up but should

[63] Remote *would* can occur in the protasis of an open conditional: *Come on Friday if that would be more convenient* or *If you would just move your bag I'll open the window.* In *If only 400 weapons would destroy the Soviets, what would 17,000 weapons do to the world?* we have an open conditional with *would* in both protasis and apodosis: we understand "If it is the case that 400 weapons would destroy the Soviets . . . ", not "If it were the case that . . . ".

have done"; the possibility here is probably best regarded as deontic (like *should* in this gloss), with pragmatic strengthening. A present time example (hardly permitting *could*) is *You might take your feet off the sofa*; the implicature is that your feet shouldn't be on the sofa.

9.8.4 The status of *should* and *might* as preterites

It is clear from the data presented in §§9.8.1–3 that the relation between *should* and *shall* and between *might* and *may* is significantly less systematic than that between *could* and *can* or *would* and *will.* While *could* and *would* are unquestionably the preterite counterparts of present tense *can* and *will* respectively, the status of *should* and *might* as preterite forms is far less clear-cut.

We take the view that the analysis of *should* as the preterite counterpart of *shall* is justified by the relationship between them in backshift and conditionals. Compare:

[59]	i	a.	*I shall easily finish before she returns.*	[original utterance]
		b.	*I knew [I should/*shall easily finish before she returned].*	[backshifted report]
	ii	a.	*If they offer me the job I shall certainly accept.*	[open conditional]
		b.	*If they offered me the job I should/*shall certainly accept.*	[remote conditional]

Shall is inadmissible in the [b] constructions: it is replaced by *should* just as other present tense forms are replaced by uncontroversial preterites. Thus no general account of these constructions can be given unless *should* is analysed as a preterite form.

The uses of *should* described in §9.4 can then be said to be idiomatic, since the meaning is not derivable from the meanings of ***shall*** and the preterite combined. It is exceptional for inflectional forms to be idiomatic in this way: in general, inflection differs from lexical word-formation in that the meanings of inflected forms are predictable from the components whereas this is very often not so with lexical word-formation. But exceptions to this generalisation are not restricted to the preterite forms of the modals: the comparative forms *earlier* and *later* have idiomatic senses, and there are also numerous plural nouns that are idiomatic (cf. Ch. 5, §3.2.1).

With *might* matters are complicated by the existence of significant dialect variation:

[60]	i	a.	*It may rain before we get home.*	[original utterance]
		b.	*I thought [it might/%may rain before we got home].*	[report]
	ii	a.	*If you come back tomorrow, you may find him in.*	[open conditional]
		b.	*If you came back tomorrow, you might/%may find him in.*	[remote conditional]

In Dialect A, *may* is inadmissible in [ib/iib], and for this dialect, therefore, the argument presented for *should* applies to *might* too: it has to be analysed as the preterite form of ***may***. But in Dialect B *may* is found in these constructions – and also in perfect constructions that are ungrammatical in Dialect A, such as %*The whole thing may never have happened if it hadn't been for a chance meeting.*

There can be no doubt that in Dialect B *may* has been reanalysed as lexically distinct from *might*: they are forms of different lexemes, both present tense forms. If they were different tenses of the same lexeme, only the preterite form would be able to occur in [60ib/iib]. Such a reanalysis will no doubt have been facilitated by two factors. One is the existence in the modal system of ***must*** and ***ought***, which likewise do not have preterite forms – note that both of them occur readily in construction [60ib], if only marginally in [iib]. The other factor is that in other constructions the meaning difference between *may* and *might* is not like that characteristically associated with tense; in particular, *might* is hardly used to indicate past time.

Conservative usage manuals tend to disapprove of the Dialect B usage, but it is becoming increasingly common, and should probably be recognised as a variant within Standard English.[64]

9.9 Modal auxiliaries and the scope of the perfect

Perfect *have*, when following a modal auxiliary, may belong semantically in the complement of the modal or may have scope over the modal:

[61]	i	*She must <u>have</u> saved him.*	[internal perfect]
	ii	*She could <u>have</u> saved him if she'd tried.*	[external perfect]

In [i] the modality is present, with the past time expressed by the perfect applying to the saving: "I am forced to conclude that she saved him". In [ii], by contrast, the past time applies to the modality, to the non-actualised ability: "It would have been possible for her to save him". The scope difference is just like that found with negation, and we use parallel terminology, contrasting internal and external perfect. In [i] the syntax matches the semantics: the modal precedes *have* and is outside its scope. In [ii] the perfect has extended scope, attributable to the fact that ***can*** lacks the past participle form that would be needed if it were to follow *have*.

External perfects are found as follows:

[62]	i	*He needn't / ought to / should / might / could <u>have</u> told her.*	[deontic]
	ii	*We might/could <u>have</u> been in Africa.*	[circumstantial possibility]
	iii	*If he hadn't lied she would/might <u>have</u> forgiven him*	[remote apodosis]
	iv	*I wish I could <u>have</u> persuaded her.*	[non-epistemic *could*]

The deontic case [i] allows *need* but not *must*; *might* and *could* here have the pragmatically strengthened interpretation of reproach (cf. [58iii]). Example [62ii] is the past time counterpart of [58ii], and [62iii] involves explicit or implicit remote conditionals, which differ in the present regard from open conditionals:

[63]	i	*If he <u>had stayed</u> in the army he <u>would have become</u> a colonel.*	[remote]
	ii	*If he <u>stayed</u> in the army he <u>will have become</u> a colonel.*	[open]

In [ii] the possible staying in the army and the consequential becoming a colonel are in past time, whereas in [i] only the former necessarily is: the becoming a colonel is simply subsequent to staying in the army and this includes the case where it is still in the future. The difference becomes clearer if we add a time adjunct such as *before the*

[64] As a present-tense form the *may* of Dialect B is exceptional in that it occurs in some constructions, such as [60ib/iib], which do not normally admit present-tense forms. We would handle this in terms of an extension in the use of the present-tense form (associated with the lack of a preterite counterpart). Its distribution is very different from that of a preterite form in that it doesn't occur with past time meaning: we would not therefore want to analyse it as a preterite form, or as a tensed form which neutralises the preterite–present distinction.

end of the decade: in [i] but not [ii], this could refer to the current decade, hence to a time in the future. This indicates that ***will*** is inside the scope of the perfect in [i] but not [ii]: [i] can be thought of as a consequential future in the past, [ii] as consequential predictability about the past. Other modal auxiliaries in remote conditionals likewise fall within the scope of *have*, as in [61ii], etc. Certain cases of non-epistemic *could* are covered by [62i–ii], but it is also found in wishes, as in [62iv], or in remote protases (*It would have been better if you could have done it yourself*).

Ambiguity concerning the kind of modality may thus be accompanied by ambiguity in the scope of the perfect:

[64]	i	*He <u>needn't</u> <u>have</u> told her.*	[epistemic or deontic]
	ii	*He <u>might</u> <u>have</u> killed her.*	[epistemic or dynamic]

In [i] the perfect is internal in the epistemic reading ("It isn't necessarily the case that he told her"), external in the deontic ("He didn't have to tell her"). Similarly with [ii]: "It might be that he killed her" (epistemic), "His killing her was a possible but unactualised consequence of what he did" (dynamic).

External perfects convey propositions of opposite polarity: positive *You should have told her* implicates that you didn't, while negative *You shouldn't have told her* implicates that you did. A positive implicature arises whether the negation is internal, as in this *shouldn't* example, or external, as in *You needn't have told her*, which also implicates that you did. Thus we can't say #*I did what I should have done* (instead we need *I did what I had to do*). Nevertheless, we can say *I don't know whether he told her, but he certainly should have done*. With *should have*, therefore, there may be some doubt as to whether the proposition of opposite polarity is true. That is not so, however, with *might/could* in [62i]: here there is no doubt that we were not in fact in Africa. And similarly for the *wish* construction in [62iv]: the complement of *wish* is counterfactual, so it follows from [62iv] that I couldn't persuade her, and hence that I didn't.

9.10 Modal auxiliaries in negative and interrogative clauses

Negation

There is a general tendency for strong or medium modals to take internal negation, and for weak modals to take external negation:

[65]	i	*He <u>mustn't</u>/<u>shouldn't</u> go with them.*	[strong/medium: internal negation]
	ii	*He <u>can't</u> go with them.*	[weak: external negation]

Negation of a weak modal entails non-actualisation, so that even in [ii] there is negation associated with the going, but indirectly rather than directly, as in [i]. Exceptions to the above pattern are of two kinds.

(a) Exceptions involving specific items

Strong *need* (which in declarative main clauses is always negative) takes external negation. Weak ***may*** takes internal negation when epistemic or existential: *He may not have seen it* contrasts with *He can't have seen it*, which follows the basic pattern. Otherwise weak ***may*** and ***can*** take internal negation only when separated from *not* by other words or a clear prosodic juncture (§9.3.2).

(b) Exceptions involving specific constructions

Negative interrogatives, used as questions biased towards a positive answer, have external negation irrespective of the strength of the modality: *Mustn't it be wonderful to have so many admirers?* ("Is it not the case that it must be wonderful?", not "Is it the case that it must not be wonderful?"), *Shouldn't you tell them we'll be late?* A special case of this is in tags: *We must stop soon, mustn't we?*

Interrogatives

The use of modal auxiliaries in interrogatives is in general predictable from their use in declaratives: only a few further points need be made, several of which relate to the common use of modalised questions as indirect speech acts (Ch. 10, §9.6.1). For *shall*, see §9.6.

Must and *need*

In declaratives these differ essentially as semantically positive (*must*) vs negative (*needn't*), but in interrogatives both can appear in the positive: *Must/Need we stay to the end?* For either version the positive answer is *Yes we must* and the negative is *No we needn't.* However, a lexical modal is more likely in such questions: *Do we have to stay to the end? Must* readily occurs in such indirect speech acts as *MUST you interrupt when I'm speaking?* This conveys that there is no necessity and that therefore you shouldn't interrupt.

Can, ***may***, and ***will***

For epistemic possibility ***can*** is much preferred over ***may***, and in either case the tentative preterite forms *could* and *might* are more likely: *Could/Might it be a forgery?* Questions about deontic possibility are commonly used as indirect requests, for permission (*May/Can I go with him?*) or other things (*May/Can I have some sugar?*). Tentative *could* and *might* express diffidence, and would not appear in the answer (A: *Could/Might I have a try?* – B: *Yes you can/may*). Dynamic ***can*** (ability) and ***will*** (volition) similarly appear frequently in indirect requests, prototypically with a 2nd person subject: *Can/Could/Will/Would you help me.*

Should

This generally has a deontic interpretation in interrogatives: *Should he go by bus?* Because *should* takes internal negation, the modality is effectively outside the scope of the question, which presupposes that he should do one of two things, go by bus or not go by bus. There is a special epistemic use in open interrogatives, normally with *why*, as in *Why should he have resigned?* This is ambiguous between a deontic reading "Why was the right thing for him to do to resign?" and an epistemic one not predictable from the use of *should* in declaratives, "Why do you assume/think he resigned?"

9.11 Lexical modals, *have* (*got*), and quasi-modal *be*

(a) Strong modality

Have and *have got*

[66] i *You <u>have (got)</u> to come in now.* [deontic]

ii *Now that she has lost her job she <u>has (got)</u> to live extremely frugally.* [dynamic]

iii *This <u>has (got)</u> to be the worst restaurant in town.* [epistemic]

Have and *have got* are most commonly used for deontic necessity, as in [i]. Here they characteristically differ from *must* in being objective rather than subjective: with [i] I'm likely to be relaying someone else's instruction but with *You must come in* it's more likely that I am myself telling you to. With dynamic necessity, as in [ii], they are more likely than *must*. The epistemic use of [iii] is widely found in AmE, but is still fairly rare in BrE. The differences between *have* and *have got* are dealt with in §2.5.6.[65]

Quasi-modal *be*

[67] i *You are to come in at once.* [deontic necessity]
ii *He is to be left alone.* [passive: strong deontic]
iii *These ideas are to be found throughout his later work.* [passive: weak dynamic]

Be is commonly used for deontic necessity, as in [i], where it is comparable to subjective *must* or (more closely) objective *have*. With a passive the interpretation can be strong deontic, "must" ([ii]), or weak dynamic, "can" ([iii]); there is no active counterpart to the latter. Negation here follows the generalisation of §9.10: internal in the strong case (*He is not to be left alone*, "must not"), external in the weak case (*They are not to be found in his later work*, "cannot").

Be is also used for future situations:

[68] i *There's to be one more meeting.* [present schedule]
ii *The lecture was to be followed by a buffet lunch.* [past schedule]
iii *Only two weeks later he was to have a severe heart attack.* [future in the past]

Examples [i–ii] involve arrangements or schedules; [ii] doesn't indicate whether the situation was actualised, but an implicature of non-actualisation can be expressed by using perfect tense: *The lecture was to have been followed by a buffet lunch.*[66] Example [iii], which belongs to fairly formal style, does entail that the event took place; *was to* could here be replaced by *would*.

There are special uses of *be* in conditionals:

[69] i *If we are to get there on time we must leave immediately.* [open protasis]
ii *If she was/were to come home now, we'd be in real trouble.* [remote protasis]

Example [i] suggests purpose: "in order to get there on time". In remote conditionals *be* generally serves merely to reinforce the remote modality (combining harmonically with the preterite tense or irrealis mood): [ii] is interpreted as "If she came home now, we'd be in real trouble".

Lexical *need*

This is very similar in meaning to auxiliary *need*, but there are some differences:

[70] i a. *You don't need to cut the grass.* b. *You needn't cut the grass.*
ii a. *He didn't need to tell her.* b. *He needn't have told her.* (=[62i])

There is some tendency for lexical *need* to favour a dynamic interpretation more than auxiliary *need* or *must*. In [i], for example, I'm likely to prefer [a] if it's a matter of the grass not having grown enough to need cutting (dynamic), but [b] if I'm simply

[65] The deontic meaning is attenuated in examples like *A satisfactory solution to this problem has yet to emerge* (where *got* could not be added). What is primarily conveyed is that the solution has not yet emerged.

[66] This is an external perfect in the sense of §9.9. We have noted that quasi-modal *be* resembles the modal auxiliaries in that it has only primary forms. It cannot therefore occur after perfect *have* and takes an external perfect instead.

exempting you, perhaps because someone else will be doing it (deontic). With past time necessity there is a sharp contrast illustrated in [ii]. In its salient deontic interpretation, [iib] conveys that he did tell her, [iia] does not: we could add *so he didn't* to [a] but not [b].

Necessary, *necessarily*, *surely*, etc.

[71] i *It is necessary* [*that they be told*] / [*for them to be told*]. [deontic]
ii *It doesn't necessarily follow that he's lying.* [epistemic]

Necessary is used for objective deontic but not epistemic necessity; it takes a mandative or infinitival complement. *Necessarily*, by contrast, is used for epistemic necessity, especially in non-affirmative contexts like [ii]. It is normally objective and does not allow the pragmatic weakening found with *must*. It can also be used dynamically: *The democratic process is necessarily vicious in its campaign characteristics*, "by its nature".

Consider next *surely* and *certainly*:

[72] i *You're surely not going to accept his offer.* } [epistemic]
ii *I certainly enjoyed it.* *It certainly does belong to her.* }

Surely is used only epistemically, and characteristically with persuasive intent, inviting agreement. It is subjective and does not fall within the scope of a negative. Thus *It surely needn't have been an accident* (unlike *surely must* or *needn't necessarily*) is non-harmonic, with negated *need* inside the scope of positive *surely*: "It is surely the case that it needn't have been an accident". Epistemic *certainly* belongs with the strong modals but does not suggest any reasoning from evidence. The examples in [ii] emphasise my commitment to the modalised propositions (perhaps in response to a challenge), implying direct knowledge, so that they are pragmatically stronger than counterparts that have *must* or are unmodalised.

Bound, *sure*, and *certain* + infinitival are used epistemically, often (unlike *must*) with a future situation: *He's bound to be here soon.* All allow internal negation (*He's bound not to like it*) whereas external negation tends to be restricted to contexts of denial or contrast (*It's not* CERTAIN *to be over, but it's* LIKELY *to be*). More rarely, *bound* is used deontically, and here external negation is quite readily permitted: *You're not bound to answer* ("needn't"). Deontic necessity is commonly glossed as "obligation", but the noun *obligation* covers the range of *should* as well as *must* (cf. *He had a clear obligation to return it, but refused*). *Obliged* is somewhat stronger: *I was obliged to return it* entails that I did.

(b) Medium modality

Epistemic

Here we have such items as *probably*, *probable*, *likely*, and the verbs *appear*, *seem*, *expect*:

[73] i *It is probably in the desk drawer.* *It should probably be in the desk drawer.*
ii *The wet weather is expected to last several days.*

Probably combines harmonically with *should*, so that there is little difference between the examples in [i]. With *expect* there can also be a deontic component overlaid upon the basic meaning, as in *Everyone was expected to bring their own food*, "it was assumed they would because there was an obligation to do so".

The participial adjectives *supposed* and *meant* have developed specialised meanings expressing medium deontic modality: *You're supposed/meant to do it this way.* They differ from *should/ought* in being objective. The normal position for *not* is in the matrix, but (except in contrastive contexts) it is interpreted as marking internal negation: *We're not supposed to tell anyone. Supposed* is occasionally found in an epistemic sense: *It is supposed to have been posted yesterday,* "it's alleged to have been"; compare deontic *It was supposed to be posted yesterday,* "should have been".

Dynamic

This is expressed by such verbs as *intend, want,* etc. As noted earlier, negation of medium modality tends to be interpreted more specifically as internal negation, e.g. *I don't want her to go* as "I want her not to go".

(c) Weak modality

Possible, possibly, perhaps, maybe

These express epistemic possibility: *It is possible that I misled you*; *They have possibly/perhaps/maybe misunderstood. Possible* and *possibly* are objective, *perhaps* and *maybe* usually subjective. The subjectivity of *perhaps* is reflected in its occurrence in interrogatives outside the scope of the question: *Has he perhaps missed his train?,* where the question is "Has he missed his train?" and *perhaps* indicates that I think he may have.

Able

This is similar to ***can***, but has a somewhat narrower range of meaning: it is used for objective but not subjective permission (*Undergraduates are able to borrow up to six books*) and it can't replace *can* in the 'existential' use (*These animals can be dangerous,* [23i]) or for present actualised ability (*I can hear something rattling,* [24ii]) – *She is able to hear extremely high notes* is a matter of potential ability.

Dynamic *willing*

This is weaker than medium strength *want,* so that *He was not willing to do it* is not pragmatically equivalent to *He was willing not to do it.* It differs from prototypical weak modals in that *He was not willing to do it* does not entail (though it strongly implicates) that he did not do it, for one could add *but he was forced to.*

Allow, permit, and *let*

These can express deontic possibility, permission, but (unlike the expression *give permission*) they are also used more generally in a causative sense similar to *enable,* as in *The good weather allowed us to finish the job a day early.* Because of this causative meaning the time of the complement situation is simultaneous with that of the modality – i.e. they belong to Class 3 of §7 (like *believe*), not Class 4 (like *may*). This is why they cannot normally be used performatively: we say *I will allow him to stay until tonight,* not *I allow . . .* External negation, *He didn't allow/permit/let her take it,* strongly implicates non-actualisation of the complement situation, i.e. that she didn't take it, but this can be cancelled by contrastive stress, as in HE *didn't allow her to take it: it was her* MOTHER *who did.*

10 Future time

10.1 The lack of a future tense in English

One of the most obvious respects in which we have departed from traditional grammar in this book is that we do not recognise a future tense for English. Traditional grammar treats *will* (and, in the 1st person, *shall*) as a future tense auxiliary, proposing a tense system with three terms:

[1]	PAST	PRESENT	FUTURE	
	took	*takes*	*will take*	[traditional tense system]

The view taken here, by contrast, is that while there are numerous ways of indicating future **time**, there is no grammatical category that can properly be analysed as a future **tense**. More particularly we argue that *will* (and likewise *shall*) is an auxiliary of mood, not tense.

The case against the traditional analysis

(a) The three-term system does not cater for the relation between *will* and *would*

One major argument against [1] is that *would* is the preterite counterpart of *will*. The relation between *would* and *will* is just like that between *could* and *can*. We have distinguished three uses for the preterite (past time, backshift, and modal remoteness), and *would* is found in all three, as seen in §9.8. *Will take*, therefore, does not belong in a one-dimensional system with *took* and *takes* any more than *has taken* does: the contrast between preterite and present is independent of the presence or absence of ***will***, just as it is independent of the presence or absence of ***have***. Even if we provisionally accept that ***will*** is a future tense auxiliary, [1] must be modified so as to allow for two dimensions of contrast:

[2]		PAST	PRESENT
	NON-FUTURE	*took*	*takes*
	FUTURE	*would take*	*will take*

(b) ***Will*** belongs grammatically with ***can***, ***may***, ***must***, etc.

We have seen (§2.4) that a whole cluster of grammatical properties distinguish ***can***, ***may***, ***must***, and a few more from the other verbs of English. They constitute a syntactic class whose central members are strongly differentiated from ordinary verbs – and ***will*** belongs very clearly among these central members. This argument is not itself decisive: it would in principle be possible to say that the verbs in question formed a class of tense/mood auxiliaries. But it does place the onus of proof on defenders of the future tense analysis to demonstrate why ***will*** (and ***shall***) should be differentiated from the others as tense auxiliaries vs mood auxiliaries.

(c) ***Will*** belongs semantically with ***can***, ***may***, ***must***, etc.

The survey in §9 shows that ***will*** belongs in the same semantic area as the uncontroversial modal auxiliaries, and the same applies to ***shall***. The difference in interpretation between a simple present tense and its counterpart with *will* is to a very large extent a matter of modality. Compare, for example:

[3]		PRESENT TIME	FUTURE TIME
	SIMPLE PRESENT	*That <u>is</u> the doctor.*	*They <u>meet</u> in the final in May.*
	WILL + PLAIN FORM	*That <u>will be</u> the doctor.*	*They <u>will meet</u> in the final in May.*

In each pair the time is the same, but the version with *will* is epistemically weaker than the simple present. Note also that all of the auxiliaries in question can be used with situations that are in past, present, or future time. Compare, then *will* and *may* in:

[4]	PAST TIME	PRESENT TIME	FUTURE TIME
i	*He will have left already.*	*He will be in Paris now.*	*He will see her tomorrow.*
ii	*He may have left already.*	*He may be in Paris now.*	*He may see her tomorrow.*

For [ii] the past time interpretation is attributable to perfect *have*, while the present and future time interpretations can be accounted for in terms of the mechanism discussed in §7: *may* allows either a present or future interpretation to be assigned to its complement. Under the analysis proposed for *will*, [i] will be handled in exactly the same way.

Notice, moreover, that *may* and *will* are themselves present tense forms. In examples like [4] this present tense encodes the time of the modal judgement, and it is possible for the present tense modal to be modified by the time adjunct *now*: *Now we will/may not be in time to see the start.* And in dynamic uses of *will* this present time meaning tends to be more salient. In *I've asked him to help us but he won't*, for example, *won't* indicates his present disposition (compare *but he can't*, indicating present inability), and in *This door won't lock* I am talking about the present properties of the door (compare *You can't lock this door*).

Data like that shown in [3] does not by itself refute a future tense analysis: there are languages (such as French) where the translation equivalents do contrast as present vs future tense. What is decisive is the combination of arguments (a)–(c), and the extent of the grammatical and semantic likeness involved in (b) and (c). If one looks at the verbal system of English without any preconception that the tripartite division between past, present, and future time will inevitably be reflected in a system of three corresponding tenses, then the evidence is overwhelming for grouping ***will, shall, may, can, must***, etc., together as auxiliaries of the same kind.

Clausal constructions with a future time interpretation

Although English has no future tense it has a range of constructions which select or permit a future time interpretation. They are illustrated in:

[5]			
	i	*Give her my regards.*	[imperative]
	ii	*It is essential [that she tell the truth].*	[mandative]
	iii	*The match starts tomorrow.*	[main clause present futurate]
	iv	*If [she goes], I'll go too.*	[subordinate present]
	v	*I may/will [see her tomorrow].*	[bare infinitival]
	vi	*I intend/want [to see her tomorrow].*	[*to*-infinitival]
	vii	*I intend/am [seeing her tomorrow].*	[gerund-participial]

In [i–ii] the modality is deontic, which characteristically involves futurity of the situation. In [iii–iv] we have present tense verbs: these allow future interpretations under the conditions described in §§4.2.4–5. Constructions [v–vii] are non-finite: the temporal interpretation depends on properties of the matrix clause, as discussed in §7.

10.2 Idiomatic *be going*

One case of a future-time *to*-infinitival that merits attention is that found in the complement of the idiom ***be** going*, as in *He's going to be too hot.* Historically the idiom clearly derives from the progressive auxiliary ***be*** + the lexical verb ***go*** (compare the literal ***be*** *going* of *Now he's going through the second tunnel*), but in construction with a *to*-infinitival complement the meaning of motion and progressivity has been lost. The idiom differs from ordinary ***be*** *going* in that *going* is virtually inseparable from the following *to*; in some varieties the *to* may be incorporated into a compound verb [gənə], as discussed in Ch. 18, §6.3.

Differences between *be going* and *will*

The most salient feature of the meaning of idiomatic ***be*** *going* is that it locates the complement situation in future time: we need therefore to examine how it differs from the much more frequent ***will*** (beyond the obvious syntactic fact that it takes a *to*-infinitival complement rather than a bare one).

(a) Style

Be *going* is characteristic of relatively informal style, whereas ***will*** is entirely neutral.

(b) Inflection

The ***be*** component of the idiom has the full set of inflectional forms except for the gerund-participle (**being going* is excluded in the same way as literal progressives like **being taking*). As a result, it occurs in a wider range of environments than ***will***, as in *She had been going to tell me, He may be going to resign*, etc.

(c) ***Be*** *going* has greater focus on matrix time

We turn now to differences in interpretation. Both the ***be*** *going* and ***will*** constructions involve two times, one associated with the infinitival complement, the other with the matrix, i.e. ***be*** *going* and ***will*** themselves. The subordinate time is always future with ***be*** *going*; we have seen that ***will*** allows other possibilities but we confine our attention here to future cases. The matrix time depends on the matrix tense, e.g. usually present with *is going*, past with *was going*. The first meaning difference, then, is that with ***be*** *going* there is significantly greater focus on the matrix time than is normally the case with ***will***. Compare:

[6] i *The dog's going to / will take the roast.*
ii *The secretary is going to / will give you a timetable.*
iii *If you're going to / ?will lose your temper, I'm not going to / won't play.*

The difference is very clear in an example like [i]: in a context where there is immediate danger of the dog taking the roast one would use *is going*, which focuses on the present danger – ***will*** lacks the implicature of immediacy commonly found with ***be*** *going*. In [ii] *will* invites a conditional interpretation ("if you ask") whereas *is going* suggests that instructions have already been given to the secretary. (Conditionality is implied with *is going* in [i], but it is of a negative kind: "if nothing is done to stop it".) In [iii] the present focus of *is going* is evident from the fact that the most salient contextualisation is one where you have already shown signs of, or started, losing your temper.[67] *Will* would be very unnatural in this example; we have noted that it occurs in conditional protases only under restrictive conditions, and these are not satisfied in [iii] since it does not lend itself to an interpretation in terms of objective predictability ("if it is predictable that you will lose your temper").

[67] ***Be*** *going* also occurs as an alternative to quasi-modal ***be*** in goal/purpose-oriented conditionals (cf. [69i] §9.1): *If we are going to get there on time we must leave immediately*; ***will*** is quite impossible in this sense.

The futures in [6] are all relatively close ones, but this is not a necessary feature of ***be** going*, merely one factor that makes current focus appropriate. The future situation is clearly not close in *I'm going to retire in ten years' time*, but instead we have present intention or arrangement.[68] We invoked the concept of current (present) focus in contrasting the present perfect with the simple preterite (§5.3), but the difference between ***be** going* and ***will*** is only loosely comparable. There is no present focus at all in the simple preterite, while in the present perfect it is very strong (as reflected in the impossibility, generally, of having past time adjuncts like *yesterday*); with ***will*** and ***be** going* the contrast is much less extreme, for some present focus is possible with *will* (*Now we will have to wait until Friday*; *I won't put up with it*; etc.) and the present focus in *is going* does not exclude future time adjuncts (*I'm going to read it tomorrow*).

(d) Preterite: ***be** going* doesn't entail that the complement situation was actualised

[7] *He was going to / would marry his tutor at the end of the year.*

Here we have a future in the past (with *would* restricted to formal narrative style). ***Will***, we have seen, is semantically strong, so that the *would* version entails that he did marry her. *Was going* does not have this entailment and quite often there will be an implicature of non-actualisation.[69] This ties in with the current focus mentioned above: *was going* focuses on the intention/arrangement obtaining at the past time referred to, rather than the marrying situation itself.

(e) Intention vs willingness or volition

[8] *I have asked her to join us but she's not going to / won't.*

Won't here conveys dynamic volition; ***be** going* can also carry a dynamic overtone, but it tends to be a matter of intention rather than willingness. *Won't* suggests explicit refusal more than *isn't going*. The contrast is sharper in the preterite, where one would expect *wouldn't*, not *wasn't going*; the latter would be appropriate, however, if she later changed her mind and did join us.

[68] Extreme closeness, immediate futurity, is explicitly encoded in *about* or the less frequent *on the point of*. ***Be** going* and these expressions can be modified by *already* or *just* (in its temporal sense), whereas futurity *will* cannot: *She was already going/about to tell us* (where *going* allows for a greater temporal gap than *about*); *He was just going/about to eat it.*

[69] Such an implicature is more pronounced in the preterite perfect: *He had been going to marry his tutor* implicates, though of course does not entail, that he didn't do so.

4

The clause: complements

Rodney Huddleston

This is the first of two chapters on the structure of the clause. The focus of this chapter is on complements of the verb, while Ch. 8 is mainly concerned with adjuncts. We exclude from consideration here complements with the form of subordinate clauses: these are dealt with in Ch. 11 (finite clauses) and Ch. 14 (non-finites).

1 Elements of clause structure: an overview

The major functions in the structure of the clause are the **predicator** (**P**), **complements** of the predicator (**C**), and **adjuncts** (**A**), as illustrated in:

[1]	*He*	|	*always*	|	*reads*	|	*the paper*	|	*before breakfast.*
	C		A		P		C		A

The predicator is a special case of the head function. Complements are more central to the grammar than adjuncts: they are more closely related to the verb and more clearly differentiated by their syntactic properties. Those in this example are, more specifically, subject and object respectively, two sharply distinct syntactic functions. Adjuncts, on the other hand, tend to be differentiated primarily by their semantic properties – *always* is an adjunct of frequency, *before breakfast* an adjunct of temporal location, and so on. Complements are dependents of the verb (or VP), while adjuncts may be dependents (modifiers), as in this example, or supplements, elements that are more loosely attached to the clause (see Ch. 15, §5).

Many grammars restrict the term 'complement' to non-subject elements. The view taken here is that although subjects do have special properties, they also have important affinities with the object and other complements.

It is a common practice to use V rather than P in representing clause structure, with V therefore used for both a function and a category. Such a dual use of V is unlikely to create problems, but we nevertheless prefer to maintain here the distinction between function names and category names that we systematically draw elsewhere, and hence we follow the also quite widespread practice of using P for the function and restricting V to the category.

In clauses containing an auxiliary verb, such as *She may like it*, some grammars analyse auxiliary + lexical verb as forming a 'verb group' unit realising (in our terms) a single P function. Under the analysis presented in this book, *may* is the predicator of the main clause, and *like* that of a subordinate clause functioning as complement of *may*. The contrast between these two analyses is discussed in Ch. 14, §4.2. In this chapter we will for the most part avoid the issue by concentrating on examples without auxiliary verbs.

1.1 Types of complement and canonical clause structures

Core complements and obliques

We distinguish between **core** and **non-core** complements. Prototypically core complements have the form of NPs, non-core complements that of PPs. The core complements in [2] are underlined.

[2]					
	i	*Kim*	*gave*	*Pat*	*the key.*
	ii	*Kim*	*gave*	*the key*	*to Pat.*
		C	P	C	C

All three complements are core in [i], but only the first two are in [ii].

NPs functioning as core complements are related directly to the verb, while those functioning within PPs are related to the verb only indirectly, via the preposition. An NP related to the verb by a preposition in this way is referred to as an **oblique**. In [2ii], the phrase *to Pat* is a complement of *give*, but the NP *Pat* is an oblique.

The preposition characteristically makes a contribution to identifying the semantic role of the NP. In this example Pat is recipient, and although a recipient is inherently involved in the semantics of *give*, the preposition *to* can be regarded as identifying the NP that has this role.

External and internal complements

Among the core complements one has special status: the subject (S). The first constituent structure division in canonical clauses is between the subject and the predicate, the function realised by the VP. In such cases, therefore, S is **external** to the VP, not a constituent of it.

English is what is known typologically as a subject-prominent language, inasmuch as the subject is very sharply set apart syntactically from other clause elements: we find a whole cluster of distinctive properties associated with it. In [2] *Kim* is S, while *the key*, *Pat*, and *to Pat* are non-subject complements, **internal** to the VP.[1]

Transitivity

The default type of internal core complement is an object (O). Whereas all canonical clauses contain an S, they may or may not contain an O, depending on the nature of the verb. This yields the important contrast referred to as **transitivity** – a **transitive** clause contains an O, an **intransitive** one does not:

[3] i *I fainted.* [intransitive: S–P]
ii *They destroyed all the evidence.* [transitive: S–P–O]

The category of transitivity applies to both clauses and verbs: *I fainted* is an intransitive clause because it contains no object, and *faint* is an intransitive verb because it has no object as dependent. More precisely, transitivity applies to **uses** of verbs, for although *faint* is always intransitive many verbs can occur either with or without an object. For example, *read* is intransitive in *She read* and transitive in *She read the letter*; likewise *open*

[1] The terms 'internal' and 'external' are more often applied to semantic elements ('arguments') than to syntactic complements, but in a comparable way, so that in *Pat took the key* the subject *Pat* expresses an external argument and the object *the key* an internal one.

is intransitive in *The door opened* and transitive in *She opened the door.* We refer to such verbs as **dual-transitivity** verbs.

The transitive class of verbs and clauses can be divided into **monotransitive** and **ditransitive** subclasses according as there is just one object (a **direct** object, O^d) or two (**indirect**, O^i, + direct):

[4] i *She wrote a novel.* [monotransitive: S–P–O^d]
ii *She told him the truth.* [ditransitive: S–P–O^i–O^d]

Complex-intransitives and complex-transitives

One further subtype of (internal) complement is the **predicative complement** (PC), illustrated by *quite competent* in:

[5] i *Ed seemed quite competent.* [complex-intransitive: S–P–PC^s]
ii *She considered Ed quite competent.* [complex-transitive: S–P–O–PC^o]

From a semantic point of view a PC tends to be more like a predicator than an ordinary complement such as a subject or object. In [5], for example, *Ed* and *she* serve to refer to or pick out particular persons, but the PC does not: rather, it denotes a property that is predicated of the person referred to by *Ed.* This is the basis for the term 'predicative complement': syntactically a PC is a complement, but semantically it characteristically has a predicative function.[2] In these examples the PC has the form of an AdjP; it can also be realised as an NP, as in *Ed seemed a decent guy*, but even here it expresses a property rather than referring to a person.

We refer to the constructions in [5i] and [ii] (and these uses of *seem* and *consider*) as respectively **complex-intransitive** and **complex-transitive**: on the transitivity dimension [i] is intransitive and [ii] is transitive, but each contains a further predication expressed in the PC, so that the structures are more complex than the ordinary intransitives and transitives in [3]. The PC is related in both examples to *Ed*, which, however, is S in [i] and O in [ii]. The labels PC^s and PC^o thus indicate whether the PC is **subject-oriented** (subjective) or **object-oriented** (objective).

However, the orientation is normally predictable from the transitivity, with the PC oriented towards O in transitive clauses, and towards S in intransitives. Thus if we put *think* in a passive clause the PC is automatically re-oriented to S: *Ed was considered quite competent.*

Notice that in the latter example the PC *quite competent* is semantically predicated of Ed, but *Ed* is not syntactically the subject of *quite competent.* In [i], *Ed* is subject of *seemed* (or the VP *seemed quite competent*). In [ii], *Ed* is not subject at all, but object (of *considered*). We will therefore speak of *Ed* not as the subject of the PC but as its **predicand.**

The predicative elements in [5] are core complements (extending this category now to cover AdjPs as well as NPs); they are also found as obliques in non-core complements, as in *She regarded him as quite competent / a decent guy*, where the AdjP/NP is complement of the preposition *as*, not of the verb *regarded.*[3]

[2] There is a minor clause construction in which such expressions combine directly with the subject in a verbless clause: *Ed quite competent?* (see Ch. 10, §4.8.3).

[3] Predicative elements can also be adjuncts, as in *He wrote most of his poetry drunk*: the contrast between predicative and ordinary (non-predicative) thus cuts across that between complements and adjuncts, though it has less grammatical significance in the case of adjuncts.

Comparison with constructions containing finite clause complements

The verbs *seem* and *consider* in [5] allow a paraphrase involving a finite subordinate clause, as in:

[6] i *It seemed that Ed was quite competent.*
ii *She considered that Ed was quite competent.*

Such paraphrases highlight the fact that two predications are expressed in [5], for now they are located in separate clauses.[4] Syntactically, however, the constructions are very different, precisely because [6i–ii] contain subordinate clauses while [5i–ii] do not: in [5] *Ed* and *quite competent* are complements of *seem* and *think*, whereas in [6] they are not.[5] The overlap between the verbs entering into the two constructions is relatively small: there are many like *stay* and *make* appearing in [5] but not [6], or like *happen* and *know*, with the opposite distribution.

[7]		a.	b.
	i	*Ed stayed silent.*	**It stayed that Ed was silent.*
	ii	*She made Ed angry.*	**She made that Ed was angry.*
	iii	**Ed happened diabetic.*	*It happened that Ed was diabetic.*
	iv	**I knew Ed diabetic.*	*I knew that Ed was diabetic.*

Copular clauses

The commonest complex-intransitive construction has *be* as predicator:

[8] *Ed was quite competent.*

It is useful to have a separate term for such clauses because there are a number of distinguishable semantic and syntactic relations involved: we will therefore refer to them as **copular clauses**. This is based on the traditional idea of *be* as a copula, a syntactic link relating PC to S; in some cases (though certainly not all) *be* has little semantic content but primarily serves the syntactic function of filling the verbal predicator position, and thus carrying the tense inflection.[6]

Five canonical constructions

In summary, the core complements yield two dimensions of structural contrast, a ternary one involving O and a binary one involving PC:

[9]	ORDINARY	COMPLEX
INTRANSITIVE	*I left.* (S–P)	*I got better.* (S–P–PC)
MONOTRANSITIVE	*I took the car.* (S–P–O)	*I kept it hot.* (S–P–O–PC)
DITRANSITIVE	*I gave Jo a key.* (S–P–O–O)	

Valency

The categories presented in [9] are defined in terms of particular kinds of complement (O and PC), but it is also useful to have a more general classification based simply on

[4] Notice that even with clausal subordination *quite competent* is still a predicative complement, not a predicator: the subordinate predicator is the verb *was*.

[5] Some modern grammars have an analysis of [5ii] in which *Ed quite competent* is a verbless clause (technically, a 'small clause').

[6] The term 'copular' is widely used for [5i] and the like as well as [8]; we prefer to restrict it to the latter, using 'complex-intransitive' for the more general construction, partly to bring out the parallel between [5i] and [5ii], partly because complex-intransitive verbs other than *be* are not mere syntactic copulas but do express semantic predication.

the number of complements, and for this we will use the term **valency**. A monovalent verb is thus a verb which combines with just one complement, like the *die* of [9], and so on. Classifications in terms of transitivity and valency are compared in [10], where the complements are underlined:

[10]		TRANSITIVITY	VALENCY
i	*He died.*	intransitive	monovalent
ii	*This depends on the price.*	intransitive	bivalent
iii	*Ed became angry.*	intransitive (complex)	bivalent
iv	*He read the paper.*	monotransitive	bivalent
v	*He blamed me for the delay.*	monotransitive	trivalent
vi	*This made Ed angry.*	monotransitive (complex)	trivalent
vii	*She gave him some food.*	ditransitive	trivalent

Note that examples like [ii], where *on the price* is a non-core complement, and [iii], where *angry* is a predicative complement, are grouped with [i] in terms of transitivity, but with [iv] in terms of valency.[7] There are also quadrivalent verbs, as in *I bet you $10 that it rains* or *I'll trade you this bicycle for your binoculars*.

1.2 Complements vs adjuncts

Complements, we have said, are more closely related to the verb than adjuncts. Core complements are generally more sharply differentiated from adjuncts than are non-core complements, and there is some uncertainty, and disagreement among grammarians, as to how much should be subsumed under the function complement.[8] We review here the major factors involved in the distinction; (a)–(e) have to do with syntactic differences, while (f)–(h) deal with semantic issues.

(a) Licensing

The most important property of complements in clause structure is that they require the presence of an appropriate verb that **licenses** them. Compare:

[11] i a. *She mentioned the letter.* b. **She alluded the letter.*
ii a. *She thought him unreliable.* b. **She said him unreliable.*

In [i], the verb *mention* licenses an O (*the letter*), but *allude* does not. Similarly in [ii] *think* licenses O + PC°, but *say* does not. By contrast an adjunct such as *for this reason, at that time, however*, etc., is not restricted to occurrence with a particular kind of verb.

This type of dependence between complements and their head verbs is commonly referred to as **subcategorisation**: verbs are subcategorised according to the **complementation** they take, i.e. the different kinds and combinations of complement they

[7] We follow the most usual terminology here in spite of the mixture of Greek- and Latin-based prefixes. The term 'valency' is used in several different ways. For some, valency covers not just the number but also the kind of complements: in this sense (for which we will use the term 'complementation'), all the verbs in [10] have different valencies. For others, valency is based on the number of semantic 'arguments' rather than syntactic complements (see §1.2 for the relation between these); an alternative term for this sense is 'adicity', with [i] and [ii] being respectively 'monadic' and 'dyadic'.

[8] Some restrict it to core complements, taking the presence of the preposition in, say, *He alluded to her letter* as sufficient to make the post-verbal element an adjunct; this makes the boundary between complement and adjunct easier to draw, but in our view it does not draw it in a satisfactory place, as will be apparent from the following discussion.

license. Different patterns of complementation are found with different subcategories (classes) of verb: 'intransitive', 'monotransitive', etc., are names of verb subcategories in this sense: *allude* can't occur in [i] because it doesn't belong to the class of verbs that license O, namely monotransitive verbs; and *say* can't occur in [ii] because it does not belong to the class of verbs that license O + PC° complementation, namely complex-transitive verbs.

We emphasise two points about names like 'intransitive' and 'monotransitive'. First, the different patterns of complementation define a large number of different verb subcategories, but only a few very general ones have established names. For example, there is no name for the class of verbs like *inquire, wonder*, etc., which take interrogative clauses as complement (*He inquired/*believed/*wanted whether it was ready*). Second, most verbs allow more than one pattern of complementation. For example, *think* is not restricted to complex-transitive clauses, but is found in intransitives (in *Let me think for a moment* the PP is an adjunct), in ordinary monotransitives (*She was obviously thinking uncharitable thoughts*), with a PP headed by *of* (*I was thinking of someone else*), with a declarative clause as complement (*She thought that he was unreliable*), and so on.

Licensing of complements often involves syntactic determination of the type of complement phrase or clause that is licensed. The issues of the choice of preposition and the choice of subordinate clause construction each deserve separate discussion.

Choice of preposition

PPs functioning as non-core complement often have the preposition specified by the verb:

[12] i *It consists of egg and milk.* *He didn't look at her.* *It depends on the cost.*
ii *He gave it to Pat.* *He supplied them with sufficient food.* *I blame it on Kim.*

The prepositions here are not replaceable without loss of grammaticality (**It consists with sugar and water*) or an unsystematic change in the meaning (the difference in meaning between *He didn't look at them* and *He didn't look for them* is not fully derivable from the difference between *at* and *for*).

In [12i] the preposition immediately follows the verb, whereas in [ii] it is separated from the verb by another complement (O), but in either case the occurrence of the PP is dependent on the occurrence of the right kind of verb (cf. **It contains of egg and milk*; **He bought it to Pat*, etc.). These PPs thus very clearly qualify as complements by our licensing criterion. The first two examples in [ii] may be contrasted with *He threw it to/towards/past Pat* and *He set out with/without sufficient food*, where we have a choice of preposition; here *with/without sufficient food* is an adjunct while *to/towards/past Pat* is still a complement as it is licensed by *throw*, but it is less clearly a complement (less distinct from an adjunct) than those in [12].

Choice of subordinate clause construction

When a clause functions as complement in the structure of a larger clause, the verb of the latter determines what kind of subordinate clause is permitted – whether declarative, interrogative, or exclamative, whether finite, infinitival, gerund–participial, and so on:

[13] i *Whether we go abroad / *That we go abroad depends on the cost.*
ii *He tends to be lazy / *being lazy / *that he is lazy.*

Example [i] shows that *depend* licenses an interrogative clause, but not a declarative, as its external complement, [ii] that *tend* licenses an infinitival, not a gerund–participial or a finite clause, as its internal complement. As before, the complements require an appropriate verb: we can't, for example, have *Whether he wins counts on the weather, *He enjoys to be lazy.[9]

Clauses, like PPs, can be either complements or adjuncts:

[14] i *He doesn't know whether or not she likes him.* [complement]
ii *I'm inviting him, whether or not she likes him.* [adjunct]

The subordinate clause is a complement in [i], for it requires a verb like *know* as opposed, say, to *intend*; but it is an adjunct in [ii], where there is no such restriction. The meaning is clearly different in the two cases: "He doesn't know the answer to the question 'Does she like him or not?'" and "It doesn't matter whether she likes him or not: I'm still inviting him".

(b) Obligatoriness

A second important property of complements is that they are sometimes obligatory, whereas adjuncts are always optional. Compare:

[15] i a. *She perused the report.* b. **She perused.* [obligatory complement]
ii a. *She read the report.* b. *She read.* [optional complement]
iii a. *She left because she was ill.* b. *She left.* [optional adjunct]

We understand obligatoriness in a similar way to determination of a preposition by the verb: an element is obligatory if it can't be omitted without loss of grammaticality or an unsystematic change of meaning. Loss of grammaticality is illustrated in [ib], an unsystematic change in meaning in *She ran the business* vs *She ran*, where we have different senses of *run*. Obligatory complements with the form of PPs or subordinate clauses are illustrated in *It consists of egg and milk, He blamed the accident on me, This proves that it's possible, He tends to be lazy.*

This criterion is stronger than that of licensing. Licensing is a matter of a verb **allowing** a certain pattern of complementation, whereas here we are talking about the verb **requiring** it.

Obligatory complements are more distinct from adjuncts than are optional ones: they are complements in the most literal sense, in that they are needed to complete the structure headed by the verb. Both allowing and requiring complements are covered by the concept of subcategorisation mentioned above: *peruse* and *read*, for example, are differentiated in that *peruse* belongs only to the monotransitive class while *read* is a dual-transitivity verb, belonging to both monotransitive and intransitive classes.

The [a] examples in [15i–ii] are both monotransitive clauses: although the complement is obligatory in one and optional in the other this is not sufficient reason for saying that we have different constructions, for in other respects they are alike. For example, both have passive counterparts, as in *The report was perused/read by her*, and the complement can be questioned in the same way, as in *What did she peruse/read?*; and so on. If an element is obligatory, and hence a complement, with some verbs, then in the absence of counter-evidence we will take it to be a complement rather than an adjunct when it is optional too.

[9] Where the superordinate clause is complex-intransitive it is the PC that licenses the external complement: cf. *Whether we go abroad/*That we go abroad is dependent on many factors.* This is one of the factors that makes a PC more like a predicator than is an ordinary complement.

Examples involving non-core complements are given in:

[16] i *She put/deposited the money in her bank account.*
ii *Lunch was followed/spoilt by the President's annual speech.*

In her bank account and *by the President's annual speech* are obligatory with *put* and *follow*, and hence complements. With *deposit* and *spoil* they are optional, but we again want to say that the constructions with *put* and *deposit* are the same, and likewise for those with *follow* and *spoil*. In [i] *in her bank account* can in both cases be replaced by *into her bank account*, which qualifies as a complement by the licensing criterion, since it requires the presence of a verb of the appropriate kind (compare *She deposited/*found the money into her bank account*). The *by* phrase in [ii] is more problematic. Here the primary requirement is that the clause be passive, which is not a matter of licensing by the verb. Nevertheless, the factor of licensing does arise in cases like *How successful we are will be determined by how hard we all work*. The subordinate interrogative clause within the *by* phrase here is licensed by *determine*, just as it is in subject function in the corresponding active *How hard we all work will determine how successful we are*. We will therefore take the final elements in [16] as complements, whether they are obligatory or optional, though in the latter case they are somewhat peripheral instances of that function.

There are other cases, however, where we shall not want to generalise a complement analysis from obligatory to optional occurrences. Most obviously, the verb *be* almost always requires an internal complement, but allows a great range of different kinds of expression to fill that position and many of these are certainly not always complements:

[17] i a. *Jill is in her study.* b. *The meeting was on Monday.* [complement]
ii a. *Jill signed it in her study.* b. *We signed it on Monday.* [adjunct]

The place and time expressions in [i] are obligatory and hence complements, but in [ii], where they are optional, they are prototypical adjuncts. Another example is that of manner dependents: with one or two verbs such as *treat* these are obligatory, but (for reasons we will take up in (c) below) we shall not want to take them as complements in the usual case where they are optional:

[18] i *She treated us remarkably well.* [obligatory: complement]
ii *She carried out all the duties remarkably well.* [optional: adjunct]

Nevertheless, obligatoriness is an important factor in the distinction between complements and adjuncts. If a dependent is obligatory, that is sufficient to make it a complement, and the clearest types of complement (such as O, PC, etc.) are obligatory with some verbs besides *be*.

(c) Anaphora

The fact that complements are more closely related to the verb than adjuncts is reflected in the scope of certain **anaphoric expressions**, notably *do so*. Anaphoric expressions are those which derive their interpretation from an **antecedent**. Compare, for example, *Jill signed the petition and Pam did so too* with *Jill visited my mother and Pam did so too*, where the first instance of *did so* is interpreted as "signed the petition" and the second as "visited my mother". The relevance of *do so* to the distinction between complements and adjuncts is seen in the following examples:

[19] i a. **Jill keeps her car in the garage but Pam does so in the road.*
b. *Jill washes her car in the garage but Pam does so in the road.*
ii a. **I didn't read all the reports but I did so most of them.*
b. *I didn't cover this topic last time but I shall do so on Tuesday.*
iii a. **She rode her bicycle and she did so to school.*
b. *She performed all the tasks and she did so remarkably well.*

The antecedent for *do so* must embrace all internal complements of the verb: it therefore cannot itself combine with such a complement. In [ia] *in the garage* is a complement of *keep* (it is obligatory when *keep* has the sense it has here), and therefore must be included in the antecedent for *do so*. This means that *Pam does so* has to be interpreted as "Pam keeps her car in the garage", yet the inclusion of *in the road* to contrast with *in the garage* in the first clause requires the interpretation "Pam keeps her car": the ungrammaticality results from this conflict. But in [ib] *in the garage* is an adjunct in the *wash* clause, and hence need not be included in the antecedent of *does so*:[10] we interpret it as "Pam washes her car", with *in the road* added as an adjunct contrasting with *in the garage* in the first clause. In [iia] *all the reports* is likewise a complement of *read* (optional this time, however): *did so* must therefore be interpreted as "read all the reports", so that we can't add *most of them* as another O. In [iib], by contrast, *do so* is interpreted as "cover this topic", showing that *last time* is an adjunct. In [iii] the final phrase does not contrast with anything in the first clause, but the rule excluding the addition of a complement to *do so* is still operative: *to school* is complement in *She rode her bicycle to school*, whereas *remarkably well* is adjunct in *She performed all the tasks remarkably well.* Note that the data in [19] lend support to the position adopted in (b) above, namely that certain kinds of element can be either complements or adjuncts: locative *in the road*, for example, is a complement in [ia] and an adjunct in [ib].

Do so provides a useful diagnostic: if a dependent (other than the subject) can combine with *do so* this is sufficient to show that it is an adjunct. But inability to combine is not sufficient to show that a phrase is not an adjunct: there are semantic restrictions on the kind of VP that can serve as antecedent (see Ch. 17, §7.5). For example, we cannot say **Kim died in 1995 and Pat did so last year*, but this doesn't indicate that *in 1995* and *last year* are here complements: the deviance doesn't result from combining a complement with *do so* but from using *do so* with the wrong kind of antecedent. This is evident from the fact that the deviance remains if we drop the time expressions altogether: **Kim died and Pat did so too.*

(d) Category

In the simplest cases, complements have the form of NPs, adjuncts that of adverbs (Adv) or adverb phrases (AdvP):

[20]	*Unfortunately,*	*Kim*	*often*	*reads*	*things*	*too quickly.*
	A:Adv	C:NP	A:Adv	P:V	C:NP	A:AdvP

[10] We say 'need not' because adjuncts can be included within the antecedent, as in *Jill washes her car in the garage and Pat does so too.*

We review summarily the major categories, confining our attention to cases where they function within the structure of the clause.

NPs

Complements are most often NPs, and conversely NPs are usually complements. Some NPs can occur with adjunct function, but they tend to belong to very restricted semantic types, mainly time or manner:

[21] i *They saw her this morning / last week.* [time adjunct]
ii *You should hold them this way.* [manner adjunct]

A distinctive property of such NPs is that they cannot be replaced by personal pronouns: *They saw her then/*it, You should hold them so/*it.* Similarly there are no corresponding interrogatives with the pronoun *what* or relatives with *which*: *When/*What did they see her?, How/*What should you hold them?; the time when/*which they saw her, the way that/*which you should hold them.*

AdvPs

The characteristic function of AdvPs is to modify the verb. In general they are adjuncts, but we have noted that they qualify as complements with the few verbs like *treat* where they are obligatory. AdvPs also occur as complement to the verb *be* in its specifying sense (§5.5.1):

[22] i *She writes exceptionally clearly.* [adjunct]
ii *They treat us quite abominably.* [complement of *treat*]
iii *The only way to do it is very, very slowly.* [complement of specifying *be*]

PPs

Phrases headed by a preposition prototypically have an NP as complement; PPs of this kind occur readily either as adjunct or complement:

[23] i a. *She did it [without difficulty].* b. *I slept [on the floor].* [adjunct]
ii a. *He relied [on his mother].* b. *I put it [underneath the mat].* [complement]

The most obvious complements are those where the preposition is specified by the verb, as in the *rely* + *on* example (and those in [12] above), but there are also cases where the preposition has its full lexical content, as in [23iib]. For reasons explained in Ch. 7, we interpret the category of preposition more broadly than in traditional grammar, allowing for example that a PP may consist of just a preposition. PPs of this kind are likewise found as adjunct (*We slept downstairs*) or complement (*We took the bed downstairs*). Those consisting of preposition + declarative clause, however, are predominantly adjuncts, with complement function largely limited to copular clauses of various kinds:

[24] i *You'll catch him [if you run].* *They left [because the baby was sick].* [adjunct]
ii *It's [because you eat so fast] that you get indigestion.* [complement]
iii *That was [long before we were married].* [complement]

Subordinate clauses

Finite subordinate clauses – content clauses, as we call them – are generally complements, but are occasionally found as adjuncts too:

[25] i *I hadn't noticed that she was looking so worried.* } [complement]
ii *Whether or not I give my approval depends on many factors.*
iii *What had happened, that she was looking so worried?* } [adjunct]
iv *He'll do it, whether or not I give my approval.*

The complements in [i–ii] meet the licensing criterion, the first requiring a verb like *notice*, the second, one like *depend*.

Non-finite clauses are distributed more evenly between the two functions:

[26] i *He tried to please his mother.* } [complement]
ii *I regret having lived here so long.*
iii *He did it to please his mother.* } [adjunct]
iv *I understand the problem, having lived here so long.*

AdjPs

The characteristic function of AdjPs is predicative – but both complements and adjuncts can be predicative:

[27] i *She was disgusted at his betrayal.* [predicative complement]
ii *Disgusted at his betrayal, she went back to Paris.* [predicative adjunct]

(e) Position

Complements are more restricted than most adjuncts as to what positions they can occupy in the clause. In general, there is a basic or default position for a given kind of complement, with its occurrence in other positions being permitted only under a limited set of conditions. Consider, for example, the position of the underlined complements in the following:

[28]	BASIC (DEFAULT) POSITION	NON-BASIC POSITION
i	a. *She will accept the proposal.*	b. *Will she accept the proposal?*
ii	a. *An old badger lived in the garden.*	b. *In the garden lived an old badger.*
iii	a. *He gave the beer to Kim.*	b. *To Kim he gave the beer.*

The basic position of the subject is before the predicator, as in [ia/iia], and no other complement can come between them. In [ib] the subject follows the auxiliary verb, a construction limited largely to main clause interrogatives and to declaratives containing a restricted range of elements in initial position (*Only then* / **Because she is desperate will she accept the proposal*). Example [iiia] shows the basic position for the PP complement *to Kim*; it can occur initially, as in the preposing construction [iiib], but this is relatively unusual and restricted in discourse distribution – for example, it would not be an appropriate response to such questions as *What happened next?*, *What did Ed do with that beer?*, and so on. Adjuncts, on the other hand, generally have considerably greater mobility. With some, such as *however*, *fortunately*, and the like, the distinction between basic and non-basic positions is not applicable, and with those where it does apply, occurrence in a non-basic position tends to be less restricted than with complements.

In the afternoon we played tennis, for example, is a more usual kind of construction than *To Kim he gave the beer.*

(f) Argumenthood

In the simplest cases the propositional meaning of a clause (ignoring the component contributed by the tense) can be described in terms of a **semantic predicate** together with one or more **arguments**. The semantic predicate represents some property, relation, process, action, etc., and the arguments represent the entities involved – the bearer of the property, the terms in the relation, etc. Prototypically, the semantic predicate corresponds to the syntactic predicator, and the arguments correspond to complements.[11] In our initial example, *He always reads the paper before breakfast*, the complements *he* and *the paper* are arguments of *read*, but the adjuncts *always* and *before breakfast* are not: semantically, they are concerned with circumstances of the situation (frequency and temporal location respectively) rather than entities involved in the reading.

The correlation between semantic arguments and complements is complicated by two factors:

Dummies

Although complements usually correspond to arguments, there are some that do not. The clearest case is that of **dummies**, semantically empty NPs consisting of a pronoun and having a purely syntactic function:

[29] a. *It upset me that she didn't write.* b. *She finally made it to the shore.*

In [a] *me* and *that she didn't write* are arguments of *upset*, but *it* is not: it is a dummy pronoun filling the subject position. It makes no independent contribution to the meaning of the clause, which is the same as that of *That she didn't write upset me*. In [b] the object *it* is part of an idiom, again without independent meaning of its own; the clause means roughly "She finally (after some effort) reached the shore".

Raised complements

In some constructions a complement expresses an argument not of the semantic predicate expressed by its syntactic head, but of one in some subordinate position:

[30] a. *Pat seems to have misled them.* b. *They intended Kim to see it.*

In [a] *Pat* is a syntactic complement (subject) of *seem* but not an argument of it. The meaning is the same as in *It seems that Pat misled them*, where it is clear that *Pat* is related both syntactically and semantically to *mislead*, not *seem*. Similarly [b] has *Kim* as complement (object) of *intend* but it is an argument of *see*, not of *intend* (compare again *They intended that Kim should see it*). We will refer to complements of this kind as **raised**: syntactically they are complements of an element which is superordinate to (higher in the constituent structure than) the one they are construed with semantically.[12]

[11] In syntax we have a distinction between **predicator** (the function of the verb) and **predicate** (the function of the VP); the analogous distinction in semantics is between **simple predicate** and **complex predicate**. In *Kim loves Pat*, we have a simple predicate *love* relating *Kim* and *Pat*, but we can also think of *love Pat* as a complex predicate denoting a property attributed to Kim: a complex predicate can thus be formed by incorporating an argument. For present purposes, however, we will understand a semantic predicate to be of the simple kind: it is in this sense that it corresponds to a syntactic predicator.

[12] The term 'raised' was originally used in an approach where there is an abstract level of analysis in which the complement is located in a subordinate clause and then raised by a syntactic transformation into the higher clause; our definition of the term carries no such implication and covers a somewhat wider range of cases, including for example *He drank himself to death*, where *himself* relates semantically to *death*, not directly to *drink*.

(g) Selection

Semantic predicates commonly impose **selection restrictions** on their arguments. For example, the first argument of *enjoy*, and the second of *frighten*, are normally required to represent animate beings:

[31]		RESTRICTIONS ADHERED TO	RESTRICTIONS VIOLATED
	i	a. *Kim enjoyed the concert.*	b. #*The cheese enjoyed the cool breeze.*
	ii	a. *They frightened the cat.*	b. #*They frightened the ironing-board.*

Examples like [ia] and [iia] are perfectly normal, whereas [ib] and [iib], which violate selection restrictions, are anomalous.

Since these restrictions involve arguments of the semantic predicate, then it follows from what was said about arguments in (f) above that they apply to complements: *enjoy* selects an animate subject, *frighten* an animate object.[13]

(h) Role

The arguments of a semantic predicate bear various **roles** in the situation, such as agent (roughly, performer of an action) and patient (undergoer of an action). Traditional school grammar defines subject and direct object in terms of these roles: the subject is said to be the performer of the action and the direct object the undergoer. But this is a massive oversimplification, implying that there is an invariant role associated with each of these complement types. There is in fact no such invariance: the roles depend on the semantic properties of the verb. Compare, for example:

[32]			
	i	*Kim shot the intruder.*	[S: agent; O: patient]
	ii	*Kim wrote the letter.*	[S: agent; O: factitive]
	iii	*Kim heard an explosion.*	[S: experiencer; O: stimulus]

Example [i] describes a situation in which Kim did something to the intruder, and here the traditional roles do apply. But in [ii] it is not a matter of Kim doing something to the letter, for the letter did not exist prior to the writing – note that *I wrote it* would not be a coherent response to the question *What did you do to the letter?* There is thus no patient in the situation described in [ii]. We will refer to the role of the object here as 'factitive', indicating something that comes into existence by virtue of the process expressed in the verb. It is even clearer that [iii] does not describe an agent–patient situation: Kim did not do something to an explosion. The clause here describes not an action performed by Kim but an event of sensory perception, and the roles we will use for this type of situation are 'experiencer', for the one who has the perception, and 'stimulus', for what is perceived. We take up the issue of describing and classifying roles in §2: the point being made here is just that there is no single semantic role that is associated with a given type of complement such as subject and object. The role depends on the meaning of the verb rather than being simply determined by the meaning of the complement expression itself. This contrasts sharply with what we find with prototypical adjuncts. If, for example, we add *at that time* or *certainly* to the examples in [32] these adjuncts will have the same interpretation in each case, determined by their own content.

[13] We use the standard term 'selection restriction' here, but it should not be interpreted in too negative a way, as ruling out examples like [31ib/iib] as anomalous. A selection restriction implies that the argument is of a particular type, and this often serves to further specify the interpretation of an NP; in *He ate everything we had in the house*, for example, the selection restriction imposed by *eat* on its second argument will normally lead us to interpret *everything* as "all the food".

Where the complement has the form of a PP we again need to distinguish those where the preposition potentially has contrastive content (e.g. *They pushed it to/towards/past their house*) and those where it is specified by the verb (e.g. *This gave a big advantage to their house*). With *push* the preposition is crucial for determining the role – compare *They pushed it from their house*, where we have a 'source' rather than a 'goal'. But with *give* it is the verb that plays the major part in assigning the role. This use of *to* is clearly related to that of *They pushed it to their house*, but the role is not identical: it is by virtue of the *give* that we interpret their house specifically as 'recipient'. The choice of preposition is not arbitrary, but nor is its content sufficient to identify the role by itself.

Semantic roles need some further discussion, and the next section is devoted to that topic.

2 Semantic roles

We suggested in §1.2 that the arguments of a semantic predicate play various roles in the situation represented by the clause: we turn now to the issue of describing these semantic roles. In the first instance they apply to the entities involved in the situation, but we will follow the widespread practice of applying them, derivatively, to syntactic constituents of the clause. In *Pat objected*, for example, we will say that *Pat* has the semantic role of agent.

2.1 Some preliminary issues

Generality

In an example like *Kim loves Pat* we can begin by distinguishing the roles of *Kim* and *Pat* as respectively 'lover' and 'loved', roles specific to this particular verb. But there is an obvious likeness between these roles and those found with other verbs of emotion, such as *adore, fear, hate, like, respect,* so that we might describe the role of *Kim* as 'experiencer of emotion' and that of *Pat* as 'stimulus of emotion'. At a higher level of generality we can group together verbs of emotion and verbs of perception, such as *feel, hear, see, smell, taste,* with the roles now simply 'experiencer' and 'stimulus'.

There are, however, limits to this process of generalisation. Most obviously, we cannot generalise across **all** verbs and find one semantic role invariably filled by the subject argument of canonical clauses and another by the direct object argument. This is the point made in §1.2 in criticising the traditional schoolbook definitions of subject and direct object as respectively performer and undergoer of the action expressed by the verb. These roles apply to examples like *Kim shot the intruder*, but certainly not to all, e.g. not to *Kim heard an explosion*. We will see below that there is an important insight underlying the traditional definitions, but it is not a matter of finding a constant role associated with the subject and direct object.

It is by no means clear that (as assumed in some modern work) a small number of general roles can be established (perhaps in the order of a dozen or so) such that all arguments can be assigned to one or other of these roles, with no two arguments in the same clause having the same role.

We will not therefore attempt a systematic and comprehensive description of clause structure in terms of semantic roles. But we will frequently invoke them in a less ambitious way in describing the arguments corresponding to complements of various sorts – subjects, direct or indirect objects, or obliques governed by different prepositions. The level of generality of the roles invoked will then vary according to the needs of the case in question. In *Kim gave the key to Pat*, for example, the role of *Pat* may be described as goal or, more specifically, as recipient: the more general role is relevant to the selection of the preposition *to*, while the more specific one is needed in relating this structure to the alternant with an indirect object, *Kim gave Pat the key*, since other subtypes of goal are not permitted here (cf. *He sent the culprit to the back of the room*, but not **He sent the back of the room the culprit*).

Semantic role vs presentational status

Although semantic role is a major determinant of syntactic function, it is not the only one. This is evident from such pairs as:

		a.	b.
[1]	i	a. *Kim shot Pat.*	b. *Pat was shot by Kim.*
	ii	a. *Kim married Pat.*	b. *Pat married Kim.*
	iii	a. *Kim's writing resembles Pat's.*	b. *Pat's writing resembles Kim's.*
	iv	a. *Kim's promotion preceded Pat's.*	b. *Pat's promotion followed Kim's.*
	v	a. *Kim bought the car from Pat.*	b. *Pat sold the car to Kim.*

In [i] the [a] version is active and [b] is its passive counterpart. Both describe the same situation, so that each of *Kim* and *Pat* has a constant role, agent and patient respectively. The difference, then, is not a matter of the roles that the arguments have in the situation but of what we will call their **presentational status**. Other things being equal, [a] will be interpreted as being primarily about Kim, [b] as being primarily about Pat. The active is syntactically more elementary than the passive. We can therefore say that the default alignment of argument and syntactic function associates agent with subject and patient with object, while the passive departs from this default, aligning patient with subject and agent with the complement of the preposition *by*.

However, presentational status is not relevant only to choice between constructions of different complexity. It may also be the chief determinant of the alignment of arguments with syntactic functions in cases like [1ii–v], with no syntactic complexity differences. The [a] and [b] cases again describe the same situation, and neither is more complex than the other. In [ii] *marry* (in the sense it has here) is semantically **symmetric**: *X married Y* and *Y married X* entail each other. It follows that there is no linguistically significant difference between the semantic roles of the two arguments: both are agents. Either can be aligned with the subject without any difference in syntactic construction. The choice between them depends on whether the event is presented from Kim's perspective or Pat's. In [iii] *resemble* is likewise symmetric,[14] so that again the choice between [a] and [b] depends on perspective, not role. The only difference is that this time the common role is not agent, but rather one that we will subsume under 'theme'.

Example [1iv] differs from [ii–iii] in that [a] and [b] contain different lexical verbs, *precede* and *follow*. These verbs (as used here) are **converses** in that each of *X precedes Y* and *Y follows X* entails the other. Again the difference is not in the situation itself, but in

[14] The difference in perspective here is very much the same as that found in *Kim's handwriting is as bad as Pat's is* and *Pat's handwriting is as bad as Kim's is*, where the syntactic difference, however, is not a matter of which argument is realised as subject and which as object, but rather of which is realised as subject of the superordinate clause and which as subject of the subordinate one.

the way it is presented, [a] giving greater prominence to Kim's promotion, [b] to Pat's.[15] Differences in presentational status thus determine not simply which argument is aligned with subject and which with object, but also which lexical verb is selected. Different verbs are needed because neither *precede* nor *follow* is symmetric, like *marry*, and this implies that the arguments do not have identical roles – they might be distinguished at a very specific level as 'prior' and 'subsequent'. But the difference between these is of no significance for more general roles, and these too we will include under the concept of theme.

In [1v], *buy* and *sell* are likewise converses: [a] and [b] entail each other. Both describe the same situation, but again from different perspectives. It is worth emphasising in this connection that *buy* and *sell* do not differ according to whether it is the buyer or the seller who initiates the deal: [a] and [b] are both consistent with either party making the first move. We very often take the perspective of the one who initiates the deal, but there may be other factors which override this. In one respect, then, *Kim* and *Pat* are both agents, just as they are in the *marry* example [ii]. In another respect, however, they are obviously different since the car goes **to** Kim **from** Pat – and this time, in contrast to [iv], the difference is of significance at higher levels of generality, where we will analyse *Kim* as goal and *Pat* as source. But either goal or source can be aligned with subject in a syntactically elementary construction, depending on the lexical properties of the particular verb selected.

2.2 Some major semantic roles

We present here briefly the major roles that we shall have occasion to invoke. We focus on prototypical instances with no attempt to provide rigorous criteria to determine precisely when an argument bears a given role. As made clear in the discussion of [1], we allow that in certain circumstances two arguments of a single verb may have the same role (as in *Kim married Pat*, where both *Kim* and *Pat* are agents). We also allow that a single argument may have more than one role (as in *Kim bought the car from Pat*, where *Kim* is both agent and goal, *Pat* both agent and source).

(a) Causer

The **causer** role involves direct or immediate causation of an action or event – the role of the subject argument in *Kim signed the letter*, *The dog snarled*, *The rain ruined the crop*, etc. The qualification 'direct or immediate' is introduced to clarify the analysis in cases where we have a chain of causation, as in *Pat made Kim sign the letter*, where Kim is the direct/immediate causer in the signing situation, and Pat can be regarded as indirectly causing the signing. Here *Pat* is not an argument of *sign*, and hence has no role relative to it: the causer role for *sign* is assigned to *Kim*, just as in the canonical clause *Kim signed the letter.*

(b) Agent

This is a subtype of causer, the type found in *<u>Kim</u> signed the letter* and *<u>The dog</u> snarled* but not *<u>The rain</u> ruined the crop*. The prototypical agent is animate and acts consciously,

[15] Each of [1iva–b] has a passive counterpart (*Pat's promotion was preceded by Kim's* and *Kim's promotion was followed by Pat's*) so that the presentational difference between [a] and [b] is not identical to that in [1i]; the point being made here, however, is that it is the same kind of difference, namely one relating to presentation rather than inherent properties of the situation being described.

volitionally. Whether or not a causer is an agent depends in part on the verb, in part on other factors. Thus *murder* takes an agent, but with many verbs the subject argument may or may not be agentive. Compare, then:

[2]	i	a. *My uncle returned.*	b. *I coughed to remind them I was waiting.*	[agent]
	ii	a. *My headache returned.*	b. *I coughed.* [involuntarily]	[non-agent]

As just noted, an agent is normally animate, or at least conceived of as like an animate being, so that while the subject argument will be interpreted as agent in [ia] it does not have this role in [iia] (where it is not even causer, merely theme). And it is not just the inherent properties of the subject argument that affect the issue. For example, [iib] readily allows a non-agentive interpretation (an involuntary cough), but the purpose adjunct in [ib] excludes this (requiring a deliberate, purposeful cough). Compare, similarly, *You've broken the window* with *I suggest you break the window* and imperative *Break the window*: the role of *you* (the overt or understood subject) with respect to the breaking may be that of a non-agentive causer in the first, but must be that of agent in the second and third.[16]

(c) Instrument

This is the role of an entity prototypically used by an agent in performing an action:

[3]	*I cut the lace with the knife.*	[instrument]

There is a close relation between an instrument and a causer, and some entities can fill either role. Thus in *The knife cut the lace* the subject *the knife* bears the causer role. Note that this does not entail that anyone used the knife (perhaps it was accidentally knocked off the table and fell onto the lace, cutting it as it did so): we will therefore invoke the instrument role only where there is an explicit or implicit agent using the instrument.

(d) Patient

A prototypical patient is affected by an action performed by some causer, especially an agent – the agent (or causer) does something to the patient. Compare:

[4]	i	*They hit me.*	*They kissed us.*	*They did cruel things to him.*	[patient]
	ii	*They like me.*	*They remember us.*	*They listened to him.*	[non-patient]

(e) Experiencer and stimulus

These roles are associated with subject and internal complement respectively in:

[5]	i	*He hates me.*	*We heard a bang.*	*The thought of being alone scares me.*
	ii	*They believe me.*	*We know the reason.*	*She realises that it's impossible.*

Experiencer and stimulus prototypically appear in situations of emotional feeling or sensory perception, as in [i]. The experiencer is the one who feels or perceives, while

[16] In an example like *They advised the twins not to be photographed together* the agentivity conferred on *the twins* by the verb *advise* is indirect, involving an implicit chain of causation in the sense explained in (a) above: the (direct) agent of *photograph* is not expressed. The indirectness of the agentivity is more apparent in examples with an explicit chain of causation, as in *The twins wouldn't let themselves be photographed together* or *The twins had him photograph them separately.*

the stimulus is the second argument, what arouses the feeling or is perceived. We will also extend these roles to the field of cognition, as in [ii] (where the last example has the stimulus expressed by a subordinate clause). The labels are not as intuitively appropriate in the case of cognition, for while it is normal to talk of 'experiencing' emotion and sensory perceptions, it is much less so for cognitive states. Nevertheless, in all three fields – emotion, perception, and cognition – we are concerned with the internal state of some animate or animate-like being which is characteristically not under its immediate control. (The experiencer may exercise control, in which case the argument will also have the agent role, as with the understood subject of *hear* in *Hear what I have to say before making up your mind.*)

(f) Theme

This role has a rather wide application, illustrated in:

[6] i *She fell off the balcony.* *She's on the balcony.* *She ran home.*
ii *He gave me the key.* *The key is mine.*
iii *She went mad.* *It made her angry.* *She was in a happy frame of mind.*

The most central case concerns movement and location in space, as in [i]: the theme is the entity that moves or is located. In *She ran home* the role of theme combines with that of agent. Many expressions, such as the *precede* and *follow* of [1iv], have senses in the field of time as well as space, and we will thus allow for temporal as well as spatial themes. Also analogous to movement and location in space are transfer and possession, and we assign the theme role to *the key* in both examples in [ii]. By further extension it applies to entities that change or have properties, as in [iii] and, we have suggested, the arguments of *resemble* in [1iii].[17]

(g) Primary and secondary theme

In a situation of transfer there may be two themes, moving in opposite directions as it were:

[7] i *I swapped two of my records for one of Ed's compact discs.* } [theme + theme]
ii *Ed swapped one of his compact discs for two of my records.* }
iii *I bought the car from Ed for $1,000.* [primary + secondary theme]

In [i–ii] there is no basis for differentiating between the two themes as semantic roles: the difference between them is essentially one of perspective. But in a case like [iii] there is a situational difference between the themes. *The car* is the **primary theme** and *$1,000* is the **secondary theme**. The secondary theme (characteristically a sum of money, the price) presupposes a primary one, but not conversely: in *I obtained the car from Ed (for $1,000)* the version without the *for* phrase does not entail that any price was paid, whereas the interpretation of, say, *He charged me $1,000* requires that we supply a primary theme.

[17] The use of 'theme' for a semantic role has little connection with the everyday sense of the term but is now well established; an older use of the term which still has a wide currency (and is more directly related to the everyday sense) corresponds closely to what we here call 'topic', a concept having to do with presentational status, not a semantic role.

(h) Factitive theme

A further special case of theme is illustrated by the role of *a hole* in:

[8] *They made a hole in the roof.* *A hole appeared in the roof.*

A **factitive** theme comes into existence by virtue of the process expressed, and cannot be simultaneously agent or patient.

(i) Path, source, goal, and location

These occur in situations involving the theme role:

[9] i *She ran from the post office via the railway station to the bus-stop.*
ii a. *Kim gave the key to Pat.* b. *The light went from red to green.*
iii a. *She is on the balcony.* b. *The meeting is at noon.*

In the central case where the theme moves, as in [i], the starting-point is the **source** (*the post office*), the endpoint is the **goal** (*the bus-stop*), and the intermediate point is the **path** (*the railway station*). We will then extend these roles, as we did with theme, from the central field of space to the fields of possession and the ascription of properties/states. Thus in [ii] (where the themes are *the key* and *the light*) the sources are *Kim* (also agent) and *red*, while the goals are *Pat* and *green*. The clauses in [i] and [ii] are dynamic, whereas [iii] is static, so here there is no going from source to goal, but simply location, either spatial (*on the balcony*) or temporal *at noon*.

(j) Recipient

This is the subtype of goal applying in the field of possession. Thus in the above *Kim gave the key to Pat* the goal *Pat* is, more specifically, **recipient**.

(k) Beneficiary

The **beneficiary** is the role of the argument, usually animate, that something is obtained for or done for, e.g. the role of *you* in *I've bought you a present* or *I'll open the door for you*. In the central case on which the term is based, the beneficiary is intended to benefit but it also covers situations where the reverse intention holds, as in *You poured me a drink laced with arsenic*, or *I'll break your neck for you*.

2.3 Subject and direct object selection in canonical transitive clauses

The major factor determining the alignment of arguments with syntactic functions in canonical clauses is semantic role. Here we focus on transitive clauses, asking which argument is expressed as subject, and which as direct object. The key principle is given in [10i] and illustrated in [10ii]:

[10] i In canonical clauses with one agent and one patient, the agent is aligned with S, the patient with O^d.
ii *Kim shot Pat.* [S (*Kim*) = agent, O^d (*Pat*) = patient]

There are no exceptions to this principle, which underlies the schoolbook tradition mentioned above where subject and object are defined as respectively performer and undergoer of the action. We noted that these definitions are unsatisfactory because their formulation implies that all clauses are of the agent–patient type (and because they do not cater for non-canonical clauses like passives). Nevertheless, the alignment in other canonical clauses can be seen, to a very significant extent, as derivative, as reflecting the relative likeness of the arguments to agent and patient. We consider briefly three cases.

(a) Potential agentivity

Many verbs allow a given position to be filled by an agent or a non-agent, with other features of the role remaining constant; this argument will then be aligned with S in either case:

[11]	S AS AGENT	S AS NON-AGENT
i	a. *Kim destroyed the flowers.*	b. *The rain destroyed the flowers.*
ii	a. *Kim overtook me.*	b. *The rock overtook me.*

In [ia/iia] the salient interpretations have *Kim* as agent; in [ib] and [iib] *the rain* and *the rock* are not agents but their roles are like that of *Kim* in other respects, *the rain* being causer in [ib], and *the rock* theme in [iib] (describing a situation, let us say, in which a dislodged rock rolls past me down a hillside).

(b) Experiencer + stimulus clauses

Verbs of emotion or psychological state fall into two main classes according to the way these roles align with S and O:

[12]	EXPERIENCER:S, STIMULUS:O	STIMULUS:S, EXPERIENCER:O
i	a. *We enjoyed the show.*	b. *The show delighted us.*
ii	a. *We deplored their decision.*	b. *Their decision appalled us.*

The existence of these two patterns of alignment reflects the fact that both experiencer and stimulus bear some resemblance to a prototypical agent. On the one hand, the experiencer is an animate, sentient being, like an agent; on the other, the stimulus has something of the character of a causer. Most of the *enjoy* class verbs can occur fairly readily in constructions that assign agentivity to the experiencer, constructions such as the imperative (especially when negative) or the complement of verbs like *try*: *Don't despise/hate/pity me*; *I'm trying to like / to enjoy / not to resent it.* Similarly, verbs of the *delight* class generally allow agentivity to be assigned to the stimulus, indeed in a somewhat wider range of constructions: *Don't annoy/humiliate/intimidate him*; *I'm trying to amuse/encourage/shock them*; *He deliberately frightened/offended/unnerved them.*[18] The *delight* verbs also tend to occur more readily than *enjoy* verbs in dynamic situations, where the similarity between stimulus and causer is closer than in states. Finally, a number of the *delight* class verbs also have senses involving physical activity with the subject expressing a causer: *agitate, crush, depress, disarm, floor, move, repel, wound,* etc.

In the field of emotion many more verbs pattern like *delight* than like *enjoy*. In the field of perception, by contrast, the predominant pattern has the experiencer expressed as S: *I saw/heard/felt/smelled/tasted them.* The other alignment is seen in *It dazzled/deafened me*, where the experiencer is much like a patient (and the literal sense of *deafen* is straightforwardly causative). In the field of cognition it is again predominantly the

[18] Verbs which accommodate agentivity less readily include *abhor, deplore* from the *enjoy* class, *appal, concern* ("worry") from the *delight* class. Some of the latter class also tolerate the assignment of 'indirect' agentivity to the experiencer, as in *Don't be intimidated/offended/unnerved by his behaviour.*

experiencer that is aligned with S: *I know/forget/remember the answer*; as noted above, it is questionable whether the other role is appropriately categorised as a stimulus, and certainly it tends to be very different from a causer, so that it has very little claim, as it were, to be aligned with S. The opposite alignment, of stimulus with S and experiencer with O, does occur, but with extended senses of verbs whose primary sense is physical: *The answer eludes/escapes me*; *A worrying thought struck me.*

(c) Presentational status as deciding factor

To conclude this discussion, we return to the examples introduced in [1ii–v]. Here we find two arguments with equal claims to subject alignment in terms of [10] and its analogical extension: in [1ii] with *marry* and [iv] with *buy/sell* the two parties are equally agentive; in [iii] with *resemble* and [iv] with *precede/follow* the two arguments are themes and equally non-agentive. It is in this case, then, that the alignment is determined not by role but by what we are calling presentational status, with the subject expressing the argument from whose perspective the situation is viewed.

3 The subject

At the general level the subject may be defined as that functional element in the structure of the clause that prototypically expresses: (i) the semantic role of agent, and (ii) the presentational status of topic. In canonical clauses in English where there is a single agent, this is always aligned with the subject, and there is a significant tendency for the subject to refer to the topic, to what the utterance is primarily about.

Corresponding canonical and non-canonical clauses may differ with respect to the choice of subject:

[1]	CANONICAL	NON-CANONICAL
i	a. *Kim opened the parcel.*	b. *The parcel was opened by Kim.*
ii	a. *One nurse is here.*	b. *There is one nurse here.*

The existence of such pairs can be seen as reflecting the fact that there are two components of meaning involved in the above definition of subject, one having to do with semantic role, the other with presentational status. The two factors may conflict rather than combine in determining the choice of subject. In [1i] the agent is *Kim*, but I might wish to present the situation as primarily about Kim or about the parcel: in the former case agent role and topic status combine and I would select alternant [a], while in the latter they conflict and I would select [b], giving precedence to presentational status over semantic role. In [ii] there is no agent, but of the two roles that are involved, the theme *one nurse* rates as more like an agent than the location *here* and is aligned with S in the canonical alternant [a] (note that *be* allows for agentivity to be conferred on the theme by other factors, as in imperative *Be here if you possibly can*: see §2 above). The situation, however, is one that does not lend itself to a topic–comment presentation, and alternant [b] allows *one nurse* to be expressed in non-subject position with non-topic status. In general, semantic role is the determining factor in the choice of subject in canonical clauses, while presentational status determines the choice between canonical and non-canonical constructions.

All canonical clauses contain a subject, and the interpretation of subjectless non-canonical clauses always involves an 'understood subject' in some sense – for example, imperative *Speak up* and infinitival *Kim was ordered* to leave are interpreted with *you* and *Kim* as unexpressed subjects. This cannot be said of any other complement, so that we can think of the subject as the 'primary' complement. On this basis we will use the metaphor of 'promotion' and 'demotion' in describing the relation of construction [b] to [a] in [1] and the like: in [i] the switch from [a] to [b] involves demoting *Kim* to non-subject and promoting *the parcel* in its place, whereas in [ii] we have demotion of *one nurse* with insertion in its place of the semantically empty element *there*, another dummy pronoun.

As mentioned in §1.1, the subject is sharply distinguished from other clause elements in English by a number of grammatical properties: it is the aim of this section to examine these insofar as they involve intra-clausal syntax. We list these properties in §3.1 and then consider the analysis of certain non-canonical constructions in the light of this list.

3.1 Distinctive grammatical properties of the subject

(a) Category

The prototypical subject has the form of an NP. In [2], for example, identification of the subject is completely straightforward on this basis:

[2] i *The moral objections are more important.*
ii *An upturned seat lay across the path.*

In [i] there is only one NP; in [ii] there are two, but the second, *the path*, is complement within the PP *across the path* and hence does not function directly in the structure of the clause. These examples were chosen as ones where the order can be reversed (*More important are the moral objections*; *Across the path lay an upturned seat*) without changing the subject.

Subordinate clauses can also function as subject, as in *That he was guilty was obvious to everyone*; such subjects are, however, non-prototypical, as is reflected in the existence of a more frequent (non-canonical) alternant in which the subject function is assumed by the dummy NP *it* and the subordinate clause is extraposed: *It was obvious to everyone that he was guilty*. Other categories appear as subject only under very restrictive conditions. The major issue, therefore, is what distinguishes a subject NP from NPs in other clause functions, especially object.

(b) Position

The default position of the subject is before the predicator, external to the VP constituent. In transitive clauses, linear order is the most important factor distinguishing the subject from the object, whose basic position is after the predicator, internal to the VP.

Compare, for example, the following, with *you* as S, *their arguments* as O:

[3]	S BEFORE P	O BEFORE P [ungrammatical]
i	a. *You heard their arguments.*	b. **You their arguments heard.*
ii	a. *Their arguments you heard.*	b. **Their arguments heard you.*

Version [ia] illustrates the basic order S–P–O. In [iia] the object is preposed, but the subject remains in the position before the predicator. The [b] examples have the object before the predicator, and both are completely ungrammatical. S can be separated from P by an adjunct (*You never heard their arguments*), but not by a complement. Non-canonical constructions where S follows P involve subject–auxiliary inversion or subject postposing: see (e)–(f) below and §3.2.3.

(c) Case

In finite clauses a personal pronoun with distinct nominative and accusative forms appears in the nominative when subject, and in the accusative when object: compare *I know them* (with nominative *I* as S, accusative *them* as O) and *They know me* (nominative *they* as S, accusative *me* as O).

In many languages case plays the major role in distinguishing subject and object, and in such languages the order of elements is characteristically very free. In English, however, the loss of any inflectional distinction between nominative and accusative except in a handful of pronouns has resulted in order becoming the primary marker of clause functions, and this limits the scope for varying the order, as illustrated above. Note that O–P–S is excluded even where the NPs are pronouns with a nominative–accusative contrast: *Them know I. This underlines the slender role of case in English syntax: typically in a language with case-marked subject and object, such positional reversals are permitted.

(d) Agreement

Person–number inflection in the verb is determined by agreement with the subject:

[4]	i *The minister knows the candidates.*	[*knows* agrees with *the minister*]
	ii *The candidates know the minister.*	[*know* agrees with *the candidates*]

As with case, verb agreement plays a lesser role in marking the subject in Present-day English than in many languages, and again this is due to the large-scale loss of inflectional contrasts: leaving aside the verb *be*, there is no person–number inflection in the preterite, and in the present tense we have only a two-way contrast between 3rd person singular and any other person–number combination (as in the above *knows* vs *know*). Thus in *You know the candidates* the verb-form *know* provides no indication that the subject is *you*. It is worth observing, however, that although more often than not the subject is not directly identifiable by pronominal case and verbal person–number, inflection still has a significant indirect role: the subject status of *you* in *You know the candidates* is indicated by the fact that if we replace ***you*** by ***she*** the form required will be nominative *she* and *know* will have to be replaced by 3rd person singular *knows*.

(e) Subject–auxiliary inversion

In closed interrogative main clauses and various other constructions, the subject follows the predicator instead of preceding it, as in canonical clauses: compare canonical *She can swim* and *She likes it* with closed interrogative *Can she swim?* and *Does she like it?* The predicator has to be an auxiliary verb, and these constructions are accordingly said to involve subject–auxiliary inversion.

This property provides an indirect way of identifying the subject in structures not illustrating inversion: *you* can be confirmed as subject of *You know the candidates* because it is *you* that comes to occupy the post-auxiliary position when we convert this declarative to the corresponding closed interrogative *Do you know the candidates?*

(f) Open interrogatives

The rules forming open interrogatives likewise distinguish sharply between subject and non-subject elements:

[5] i *Who bought it?* [interrogative element as subject: basic order]
ii *What did you buy?* [interrogative element as non-subject: inverted order]

If the interrogative element is subject, the order is the same as in the declarative (cf. *Someone bought it*), but if it is non-subject, then the interrogative element is usually placed in front position, triggering subject–auxiliary inversion.

(g) Tags

Interrogative tags attached to a declarative clause contain a subject pronoun that agrees with the subject of that clause:

[6] i *You know the others, don't you?*
ii *The candidates know the minister, don't they?*

The tag has the form of an elliptical closed interrogative consisting of auxiliary + personal pronoun, the choice of pronoun being determined by the subject of the declarative: *you* agrees with *you* in [i], *they* with *the candidates* in [ii] (see Ch. 10, §5.1). Note that this holds even when the declarative clause does not have the elements in the basic order, as in *The others you know, don't you?*; *Even clearer is the second point, isn't it?*

(h) Coordination

Since its default position is external to the VP, the subject can enter straightforwardly into construction with a VP-coordination:

[7] *Sue typed the letter and posted it herself.*

This illustrates what we call 'basic coordination', where the coordinates *typed the letter* and *posted it herself* both have the status of constituents in the clauses *Sue typed the letter* and *Sue posted it herself.* It is to be distinguished from the much less frequent non-basic coordination *Sue typed, and her father posted, the letter*: here the coordinates *Sue typed* and *her father posted* are not normal constituents in that they don't have constituent status in the clauses *Sue typed the letter* and *Her father posted the letter.* (This is reflected by the commas and the corresponding sharp prosodic breaks when spoken.) A prototypical subject has, therefore, the distinctive property that it can combine with a basic coordination where the coordinate parts consist of the verb together with other dependents.

(i) Obligatoriness

In general, the subject is an obligatory element: subjectless clauses are found only in certain specific non-canonical constructions such as non-finites and imperatives.[19] Whether a clause has an object or not depends on the lexical properties of the verb (e.g. *appear* excludes one, while *use* normally requires one), but a subject is required in all canonical clauses.

One corollary of this is that English has dummy subjects, as in *It is raining* or *It is time to go home*, where *it* satisfies the syntactic need for a subject but has no identifiable

[19] Or in casual style, where certain pronoun subjects may be ellipted at the beginning of a main clause, as in *Had a marvellous time at the beach yesterday*, with "I" understood (see Ch. 17, §7.8.1).

meaning. The fact that the subject is obligatory is reflected in the possibilities for reducing clauses when material is recoverable from the context. *Sue has eaten them already*, say, can be reduced to *She has* (e.g. in answer to the question *Has Sue eaten them already?*), but not to **Has* or **Has eaten*. *She has* is what we will refer to as a **maximal finite reduction**, i.e. a finite clause that can't be reduced any further, and this construction must contain a subject together with an auxiliary or the pro-form *do*.

(j) Uniqueness

There can be no more than one subject per clause. By contrast it is possible for a clause to contain two objects (though of different subtypes), as in *She gave me the key*.

Notice that in examples like *Jane and her husband are right* we have a coordination of NPs, not of subjects: *Jane and her husband* constitutes a single subject. For example, agreement and tags treat the coordination as a whole as subject, not the separate parts: the verb required with *Jane and her husband* is *are*, and the tag would be *aren't they?*

3.2 Subject in non-canonical clauses

In the light of the above properties we consider here whether various non-canonical constructions differ from their basic counterparts in the choice of subject or merely in its position.

3.2.1 The passive and preposing constructions

Passive clauses and clauses with preposing differ from canonical clauses in radically different ways. Compare:

[8] i *She took the others.* [canonical]
ii *The others were taken by her.* [passive]
iii *The others she took.* [preposing]

We use examples with minimal lexical content in order to facilitate the manipulation needed in applying the various tests. *The others* might be interpreted in context as "the other photographs", "the other lectures", "the other books", and so on. In [ii] the subject function has clearly been reassigned from *she* to *the others*, whereas in [iii] *she* remains subject and we simply have a special position for O – we may think of it as having been preposed from its basic position. The difference is shown in the following table, which indicates for each of the two NPs whether or not it has the subject properties (b)–(i) of § 3.1.

[9]

	[8i]		[8ii]		[8iii]	
	she	*the others*	*her*	*the others*	*she*	*the others*
(b) POSITION	✓	×	×	✓	✓	×
(c) CASE	✓	×	×	✓	✓	×
(d) AGREEMENT	✓	×	×	✓	✓	×
(e) INVERSION	✓	×	×	✓	✓	×
(f) OPEN INTERROGATIVES	✓	×	×	✓	N/A	
(g) TAGS	✓	×	×	✓	✓	×
(h) COORDINATION	✓	×	×	✓	N/D	
(i) OBLIGATORINESS	✓	×	×	✓	N/A	

(b) Position

In [8ii] *the others* is in subject position; in [iii] *the others* is in front position but it is still *she* that occupies the basic S position, just preceding P.

(c) Case

In [8ii] *the others* can be replaced by nominative *they*; in [iii] a personal pronoun replacing *the others* would have to be accusative: *Them, she took.*

(d) Agreement

In [8ii] *were* agrees with *the others*; in [iii] if we replace the preterite by the present we get *The others, she takes*; replacing *she* by *you* would yield *The others, you take.* The verb agrees with *she* or *you.*

(e) Subject–auxiliary inversion

For [8ii] the form is *Were the others taken by her?* Preposing of a complement is extremely rare in closed interrogatives (but not ungrammatical: we cannot exclude examples like *I did the first half; the second half should we leave for Pat to finish?*). However, we can apply the inversion test more clearly by taking another construction involving subject–auxiliary inversion, namely one where the preposed element is negative, as in *None of the others did she take seriously.* Again, it is *she*, not the preposed element, that behaves like a subject.

(f) Open interrogatives

For [8ii] we have *Which ones were taken by her?* For [iii], the criterion is not applicable ('N/A'), since this kind of preposing is incompatible with the open interrogative construction.

(g) Tags

The evidence from tags is straightforward. For [8ii], we get *weren't they?*, where *they* has *the others* as its antecedent. For [iii], we get *didn't she?*

(h) Coordination

For [8ii] we can have the basic coordination *The others were taken by her and gave us great pleasure.* In [iii] both S and O are external to the VP, and for this reason coordination no longer distinguishes clearly between them – hence the entry 'N/D' (non-distinctive) in the table. It is possible to have a coordination of VPs, as in *The others she took and published in a magazine*, but the coordinates *took* and *published in a magazine* are not ordinary VPs, as they do not contain the object; moreover it is also possible for O to combine with a coordination, as in *The others, she took but the editor rejected.*

(i) Obligatoriness

The maximal finite reduction for [8ii] is *They were*; but this parameter is not applicable to [iii], since if we reduce it to *She did* we no longer have a preposing construction.

The syntactic effect of preposing is thus merely to change the order of elements: it does not affect the alignment of semantic roles with grammatical functions. Non-canonical clauses of this kind, however, do not allow the full range of manipulation available in canonical clauses. Passivisation, by contrast, does affect the role–function alignment: to use the metaphor introduced above, it 'promotes' the element that is object in the active to subject in the passive, and assigns the active subject the status of oblique within a PP headed by *by*. This PP is a non-core complement we refer to as an **internalised complement**, since it is internal to the VP but corresponds to the external complement of the active; it is almost invariably omissible (compare [8ii] with *The others were taken afterwards*).

3.2.2 The extraposition and existential constructions

Consider now the extraposition and existential constructions in the light of the uniqueness property (j), which says that there can be no more than one subject per clause:

[10] i a. *That he loved her was obvious to everyone.* [canonical]
b. *It was obvious to everyone that he loved her.* [extraposition construction]
ii a. *Several options are open to us.* [canonical]
b. *There are several options open to us.* [existential construction]

Evidence that subject function is uniquely filled by dummy *it* and *there*

The underlined expressions in [10ib/iib] have the same semantic role as the identical items in [ia/iia], which clearly are subjects. Syntactically, however, they are very different. By the criteria for subjecthood that we have presented, the subjects of [ib/iib] are uniquely the dummy NPs *it* and *there*. This is evident from the following table showing the value of *it*, *that he loved her*, *there*, and *several options* with respect to the subject properties (b)–(i) listed in §3.1:

[11]	*it*	*that he loved her*	*there*	*several options*
(b) POSITION	✓	×	✓	×
(c) CASE	N/A	N/A	N/A	×
(d) AGREEMENT	✓	×	✓	×
(e) INVERSION	✓	×	✓	×
(f) OPEN INTERROGATIVES	N/A	N/A	N/A	×
(g) TAGS	✓	×	✓	×
(h) COORDINATION	✓	×	✓	×
(i) OBLIGATORINESS	✓	×	✓	×

(b) Position

It and *there* have the property of occupying the default subject position.

(c) Case

For the most part the case criterion is not applicable to these constructions: pronouns with a nominative–accusative contrast cannot substitute for dummy *it* and *there*, nor for the extraposed clause. As for the post-verbal NP in the existential construction, pronouns with a nominative–accusative contrast are rare, but where they occur they are accusative. In answer to the question *Who is there who could help her?*, one could respond with *Well, there's always me.* Nominative *I* does not occur, indicating that the post-verbal NP has lost the subject case property.[20]

[20] Matters are not so clear with NP-coordinations; some speakers might say ?*He realised that there were now only his father and he remaining*, or perhaps ?*He realised that there were now only his father and he himself remaining*; but this seems to be more a fact about the uncertainty of pronoun case in coordination than about subjecthood in existentials – see Ch. 5, §16.2.2.

(d) Agreement

In extraposition the verb agrees with *it*. Clauses generally have the default 3rd person singular feature, but a clause-coordination can have a plural interpretation, as reflected in the *are* of *To promise you'll do something and to actually do it are two quite different things.* There can be no extraposition counterpart of this precisely because *are* does not agree with *it*. Compare also (with different positions for *both*) *To work hard and to play hard are both important* and *It is important both to work hard and to play hard.*

With the existential construction, however, matters are more complicated. In the first place, we find variation according to style-level in the present tense. When the copula is cliticised to the subject in informal style, many speakers use the 3rd person singular form irrespective of the number of the post-verbal NP: %*There's only two problems remaining.* This pattern suggests the verb agreement is simply with *there*, treated as a 3rd person singular pronoun like *it*.

When the copula is pronounced as a full independent word, the person–number properties of the verb match those of the post-verbal NP – compare *There is only one problem remaining* and *There are only two problems remaining.* Contrasts of this kind appear at first to indicate that the post-verbal NP is subject, but consideration of a wider range of data shows that this is not so. Compare:

[12] i *There tends to be a single pre-eminent factor in the breakup of a marriage.*
ii *There tend to be several contributing factors in the breakup of a marriage.*

Ultimately, the choice between the verb-forms *tends* and *tend* is determined by the person–number of the underlined NP, but that NP cannot be the subject of ***tend***, for it is not located in the ***tend*** clause, but in the ***be*** clause. The situation here is comparable to that found in relative clauses, such as those enclosed in brackets in *the copy [which was ready]* and *the copies [which were ready]*. The choice between *was* and *were* in the relative clauses depends ultimately on the number of the underlined nominal, which is the antecedent for the relative pronoun *which*. Nevertheless it is *which*, not the antecedent nominal, that is subject of the relative clause. Relative *which* has no inherent person–number properties, but 'inherits' them from its antecedent. Similarly, the dummy pronoun *there* does not have inherent person–number properties but inherits them from the NP that it 'displaces' as subject. In [10ii], *several options* is subject in the canonical version [a], and *there* displaces it as subject in the existential version [b], taking on its 3rd person plural features. In [12] *there* is subject of the ***tend*** clause, but it is a raised subject, and is understood as subject of the ***be*** clause, and it is by virtue of its understood function in that clause that it inherits the person–number features of the underlined NPs. As far as the subject–verb agreement rule is concerned, therefore, it is *there* which counts as subject: the complication is that it inherits its agreement features from the NP it displaces as subject.[21]

(e) Subject–auxiliary inversion

It is the dummy pronouns *it* and *there* that appear in post-auxiliary position: *Was it (really) obvious to everyone that he loved her?*; *Are there (really) several options open to us?*

[21] A further complication arises in existentials when the verb is followed by an NP-coordination, as in *There was/?were a bottle of wine and several glasses on the table. Were* tends to be unidiomatic with an NP-coordination when the coordinate that is adjacent to it is singular, even though the coordination as a whole (*a bottle of wine and several glasses*) is plural. Plural agreement, however, occurs readily in lists: *There are still Brown, Jones, Mason and Smith to interview.*

(f) Open interrogatives

In extraposition neither *it* nor the extraposed clause can be questioned, so this test is not applicable. In the existential construction the post-verbal NP can be questioned and then clearly behaves like a non-subject: *How many options are there available to us?*

(g) Tags

It and *there* are repeated in interrogative tags: compare *It is important both to work hard and to play hard, isn't it / *aren't they?* and *There are several options open to us, aren't there/*they?*

(h) Coordination

Neither *it* nor *there* commonly enter into construction with a coordination of VPs, but examples like *It was obvious to everyone that he loved her and had been from the very beginning* and *There are several options open to us and have been since the start* are acceptable, indicating that the dummy pronouns behave like subjects here too.

(i) Obligatoriness

The minimal finite reductions of our extraposition and existential examples are *It was* and *There are*, with *it* and *there* satisfying the subject requirement.

Conclusion

It is clear that the subjects of the extraposition and existential constructions are *it* and *there* respectively. Both are dummy elements, without any inherent semantic content. The elements that correspond to the subjects of the more basic constructions, i.e. *that he loved her* in [10ib] (*It was obvious to everyone that he loved her*) and *several options* in [10iib] (*There are several options open to us*), we call respectively the **extraposed subject** and the **displaced subject**. These terms are intended to capture the fact that they are semantically like the subject of their basic counterpart, but they are not to be interpreted as kinds of subject. The subject is a syntactic function, and these elements are no more subjects than a former president is a president or than an imitation diamond is a diamond. The label 'extraposed subject' also serves to distinguish the element concerned from an extraposed object, as in *She made it clear <u>that she disapproved of our plan</u>*, where *it* is object.

3.2.3 Subject–auxiliary inversion and subject postposing

Three positions for the subject

[13] i	*<u>The financial arguments</u> had been equally flawed.*	[basic position]
ii	*Had <u>the financial arguments</u> been equally flawed?*	[post-auxiliary position]
iii	*Equally flawed had been <u>the financial arguments</u>.*	[postposed position]

There are three main positions for the subject, as illustrated here. The **basic position**, we have noted, is before the predicator; certain adjuncts can intervene, as in *The financial arguments clearly had been equally flawed*, but complements cannot. The subject occurs in **post-auxiliary position** in the various constructions involving subject–auxiliary inversion; except in negative imperatives (e.g. *Don't <u>anyone</u> touch it*, where *don't* is a plain form), the auxiliary must have a primary inflection (preterite or present tense or else irrealis *were*). Finally a subject in **postposed position** follows the predicator in final position in the clause; usually there is also a preposed complement or adjunct in front position, as in [iii].

Distinguishing the two non-basic positions

In clauses containing an auxiliary verb but no lexical verb, the two non-basic positions look superficially the same:

[14] i *Where were the children's toys?* [post-auxiliary]
ii *Under the bed were the children's toys.* [postposed]

They can be easily distinguished, however, by adding a non-auxiliary verb: *Where were the children's toys hidden?* reveals that [i] has the subject in post-auxiliary position, and *Under the bed were hidden the children's toys* shows that [ii] has a subject in postposed position.

Subject postposing affects order, not function

We have assumed that *the financial arguments* is subject in all three of the examples in [13], and hence that they differ only in the order of elements, not in the assignment of functions to *equally flawed* and *the financial arguments.* This is very obvious in the case of [ii], but is worth demonstrating for [iii], since this construction is sometimes found as an alternant of the existential: compare *Over her desk was a photograph of her grandparents* and *Over her desk there was a photograph of her grandparents.* Evidence that *the financial arguments* is subject of [13iii] is provided by agreement (cf. *Equally flawed is the financial objection*), the interrogative tag (*Equally flawed had been the financial arguments, hadn't they?*) and, very marginally, case (*?Equally flawed are they*).

The order X–P–S

In spite of the importance of position in marking the subject, it interacts with other factors. The order X–P–S is excluded where X is O, but not for other values of X. A non-object X can even occasionally take the form of an NP:

[15] i *A thorough rogue was James Bacharach.* [PC–P–S]
ii *The following morning came news of her father's arrest.* [A–P–S]
iii **A loud explosion heard the children.* [O–P–S]

The ban on O–P–S reflects the fact that NPs in S and O function can be of the same semantic type, so that the meaning of the NPs themselves may give no indication as to which is S and which O. In *Kim admires Pat,* for example, there is nothing but the order to tell us who is the admirer and who the admired. In [ii], by contrast, the initial NP is a time expression and can thus be interpreted as adjunct while the final NP can only be S, given that *come* is intransitive. In [i] the NPs differ in definiteness, and while the second is clearly referential the first can be interpreted as an ascriptive property term.

4 Direct and indirect objects

The object is a core complement contrasting with subject and predicative complement; the contrast between O (internal) and S (external) is very sharp, that between O and PC (both internal) rather less so, though the area of uncertainty is quite small. Of the two types of object, the direct object (O^d) occurs in both monotransitive and ditransitive clauses, whereas the indirect object (O^i) occurs in canonical clauses only in ditransitives.

At the general level, the direct object may be defined as a grammatically distinct element of clause structure which in canonical agent–patient clauses expresses the patient role. Direct object arguments are associated with a wide range of semantic roles, but in other canonical clauses than those expressing agent–patient situations, the direct object has the same grammatical properties as the NP expressing the patient in agent–patient clauses.

The general definition of indirect object is that it is a distinct element of clause structure characteristically associated with the semantic role of recipient. Again this is not the only role we find (though the range is much narrower than with the direct object), but indirect objects behave grammatically like the NP expressing the recipient with verbs like *give, lend, offer, sell.*

The terms **direct** and **indirect** are based on the idea that in ditransitive clauses the O^d argument is more directly affected or involved in the process than the O^i argument. In *I gave Kim the key*, for example, it is the key that is actually transferred, while Kim is involved only as an endpoint in the transfer. Characteristically the O^d in ditransitives is obligatory while the O^i is omissible, as in *He lent (them) his car, She offered (us) $400 for it*, and it is plausible to see this as reflecting a more direct involvement, a greater centrality on the part of the O^d argument.

In languages with richer case systems than English, direct and indirect objects are characteristically marked by accusative and dative case respectively. English has lost its earlier dative case, so that the two types of object are somewhat more alike than in such languages. One manifestation of this is seen in the relation between active and passive clauses. In English the subject of a passive can correspond either to active O^d (*<u>Kim</u> was seen by Pat* ~ *Pat saw <u>Kim</u>*) or to active O^i (*<u>Kim</u> was given the key by Pat* ~ *Pat gave <u>Kim</u> the key*), but in languages with dative O^i a passive subject normally corresponds only to active O^d.

In the following subsections we consider the grammatical properties of objects in English, looking first at monotransitive clauses, and then at ditransitives.

4.1 The object in canonical monotransitive clauses

The object has fewer distinctive properties than the other core complements: it is characterised as much by the absence of S and PC properties as by the presence of clear positive properties of its own.

(a) Category: normally NP

The prototypical object has the form of an NP. Thus *He entered the lounge* has *the lounge* as O, but there is no object in *He went into the lounge*, where the internal complement *into the lounge* has the form of a PP. Similarly, the Os are as underlined in the following pairs:

[1]	i	a. *He climbed <u>the mountain</u>.*	b. *He climbed up the mountain.*
	ii	a. *He supplied <u>eggs</u> to them.*	b. *He supplied <u>them</u> with eggs.*

Again, the PPs *up the mountain, to them, with eggs* are non-core complements, not objects. NPs readily occur as S or PC, so this property serves to differentiate objects from non-core complements and adjuncts. It is not fully decisive, however, since a limited range of NPs are found in these latter functions, as in *They went* <u>*that way*</u>, *She arrived* <u>*this morning*</u>.[22] Subordinate clauses show varying degrees of similarity to NP objects, but (with minor exceptions) we prefer to use the more general term complement for them in view of the absence of well-motivated criteria to determine which are objects and which are not (see Ch. 11, §8.3).

(b) Selective obligatoriness

Although there is a great deal of overlap between the classes of transitive and intransitive verbs, we nevertheless find some which require an O, at least for a given sense of the verb (and excluding highly restricted contexts). Thus the O is non-omissible in such examples as: *He accosted* <u>*her*</u>; *We kept* <u>*the old battery*</u>; *He delineated* <u>*the problem*</u>; *This entailed* <u>*a considerable delay*</u>; *We forced* <u>*a showdown*</u>; *I used* <u>*a knife*</u>; and so on.

(c) Correspondence to passive subject

The object of an active clause prototypically corresponds to the subject of a related passive:

[2] a. *Pat overlooked* <u>*the error*</u>. [O] b. <u>*The error*</u> [S] *was overlooked (by Pat).*

The term 'related passive' applies to the actual passive counterpart (*The error was overlooked by Pat*) or one differing from the latter by the absence of the *by* phrase, the internalised complement (*The error was overlooked*).

It must be emphasised, however, that such a correspondence does not hold for all objects, and that the subject of a passive does not always correspond to the object of the verb in the active:

		a.	b.
[3]	i	*His uncle owned* <u>*two yachts*</u>.	<u>*Two yachts*</u> *were owned by his uncle.*
	ii	*His uncle had* <u>*two yachts*</u>.	**Two yachts* *were had by his uncle.*
	iii	*He has drunk out of* <u>*this glass*</u>.	<u>*This glass*</u> *has been drunk out of.*

We see from [i–ii] that there is a related passive when the verb is *own* but not when it is *have*, and yet there is no independent syntactic evidence for assigning different functions to *two yachts*. Whether or not there is an acceptable related passive for a given active clause depends on the interaction of pragmatic, semantic, syntactic, and lexical factors: it cannot satisfactorily be reduced to a simple matter of the presence or absence of O in the active. Example [iii] illustrates the second point, that it is not only transitive clauses that have related passives. *This glass* in [a] corresponds to the subject of the passive [b], but it is functioning as complement of a preposition, not as object of *drink*.

Nevertheless, correspondence with a passive subject is an important property of objects and provides a valuable diagnostic which we will call the **passive test:** if a core complement NP of an active clause can be converted into the subject of a related passive, then it is an object. This formulation excludes *this glass* in [iii] since it is not a core complement. And it provides a sufficient but not a necessary condition: *two yachts* passes the test in

[22] In special cases, moreover, it is possible for an object to have the form of a PP, as in *He considered* <u>*under the mat*</u> *an unsafe place for the key*: note that *under* here does not serve to relate *the mat* to *consider* or *he*.

[i] and hence qualifies as an object, but the fact that it fails the test in [ii] does not mean that *two yachts* is not here an object.

(d) Position

The prototypical position for O is immediately after P. Non-parenthetical adjuncts cannot normally intervene between P and O: *She saw Tom often* or *She often saw Tom*, but not **She saw often Tom.*

The main departures from this order are illustrated in the [b] members of the following pairs, where underlining marks P and O:

[4]	i	a. *He brought the clothes in.*	b. *He brought in the clothes.*
	ii	a. *I returned the books to Jo.*	b. *I returned to Jo all the books I'd borrowed.*
	iii	a. *She rejected the others.*	b. *The others she rejected.*

In [ib] O is separated from P by *in*, which we refer to as a 'particle' (cf. §6.2); this order is not permitted when O is an unstressed personal pronoun (**He brought in it*). In [iib] an O that is heavy is placed in end position (see Ch. 16, §4 for details) – in [iia], by contrast, the O is not heavy enough and must precede the PP (**I returned to her the books*). In [iii], the default order is as in [a], while [b] is an instance of the preposing construction, with *the others* occupying the prenuclear position; O can also occur in this position in open interrogatives (*Which ones did she reject?*) and various other unbounded dependency constructions (cf. Ch. 12, §7).

4.2 Object and extraposed object

Comparable to the distinction between subject and extraposed subject is that between object and extraposed object:

[5]	i	*It was necessary to postpone the meeting.*	[subject + extraposed subject]
	ii	*We thought it necessary to postpone the meeting.*	[object + extraposed object]

We have seen that in examples like [i] it is the NP *it*, not the subordinate clause *to postpone the meeting*, that has the distinctive subject properties, and in [ii] it is again *it*, not the subordinate clause, that functions as object. *It* in [ii] occupies the post-verbal object position, and corresponds to the subject of a related passive: *It was thought necessary to postpone the meeting*, not **To postpone the meeting was thought it necessary*. We therefore refer to the subordinate clause *to postpone the meeting* in [ii] as an extraposed object, again with the understanding that this is not a kind of object. It is semantically like an object, but does not fill that position syntactically. Note that while [i] has an alternant in which the subordinate clause does function as subject (*To postpone the meeting was necessary*) the extraposed clause in [ii] cannot replace the *it* (**We thought to postpone the meeting necessary*).

Extraposed objects usually occur in complex-transitive clauses, as in [5ii], where *it* is object and *necessary* predicative complement. But it is not limited to this construction, as is evident from such examples as [6] (see Ch. 11, §4.3).

[6] *I put it to you that you knew what the consequences would be.*

4.3 Ditransitive clauses

Alternation with prepositional construction

Most ditransitive clauses have alternants with a single object and a PP complement with *to* or *for* as head:

[7] DITRANSITIVE: S–P–O^i–O^d MONOTRANSITIVE: S–P–O^d–C

i a. *I sent Sue a copy.* b. *I sent a copy to Sue.*

ii a. *I ordered Sue a copy.* b. *I ordered a copy for Sue.*

As the above formulation makes clear, it is only the [a] examples that we analyse as ditransitive, as double-object constructions. In [b] the PP *to/for Sue* is not an indirect object, not an object at all, having none of the properties outlined in §4.1 above, and the NP *Sue* is of course an oblique, hence not a possible object of the verb.

This departs from the traditional analysis where the PPs *to Sue* and *for Sue* (or just the NP within them) are taken to be indirect objects. The traditional account appears to be based solely on the fact that the semantic role (recipient or beneficiary) of *Sue* is the same in [b] as in [a]. But *Sue* also has that role in the passives *Sue was sent a copy* and %*Sue was ordered a copy*, yet no one would want to say it was indirect object here: it is clearly subject. We have seen that the grammar allows for varying alignments of semantic role and syntactic function: syntactic functions must be assigned on the basis of syntactic properties, not semantic ones.

O^i and O^d distinguished by order

When both objects follow P (as in all canonical clauses) their relative order is fixed, with O^i preceding O^d.[23] If we switch the order of the two NPs we change their functions, yielding a clause with a quite different meaning or else an anomaly:

[8] i a. *They offered all the overseas students one of the experienced tutors.* [O^i–O^d]

b. *They offered one of the experienced tutors all the overseas students.* [O^i–O^d]

ii a. *He gave Sue the key.* [O^i–O^d]

b. #*He gave the key Sue.* [anomalous]

The effect of the switch is comparable to that of switching S and O NPs in a monotransitive: *Ed saw Kim* vs *Kim saw Ed* or *Kim enjoyed the concert* vs #*The concert enjoyed Kim.* In the ditransitive case, however, the switch almost always results in anomaly, because in the great majority of such clauses O^i is human (or at least animate) and O^d inanimate, as in [iia].

In constructions where an object occupies prenuclear position, O^d–S–P–O^i (with the first post-verbal element being O^i, as in the canonical construction) is strongly preferred to O^i–S–P–O^d:

[9] O^d–S–P–O^i O^i–S–P–O^d

i a. *The key he gave Sue.* b. ?*Sue he gave the key.*

ii a. *The key which he lent me didn't fit the lock.* b. ?*The one who(m) I lent the key didn't return it.*

iii a. *He asked what I bought her.* b. **He asked who(m) I bought presents.*

iv a. *What a lot of hardship he caused them!* b. **What a lot of them he caused great hardship!*

[23] Some varieties of English, particularly BrE varieties, allow the order O^d–O^i when both Os are personal pronouns, as in %*He gave it her* rather than the more widespread *He gave her it.*

Speakers vary considerably in their judgements of the [b] examples, particularly of those where the corresponding prepositional construction has *to*, as in [ib/iib], rather than *for*, as in [iiib/ivb]. Nevertheless, there is very widespread agreement that the [b] examples are significantly **less** acceptable than the [a] ones.

Ditransitives and their related passives

Two passive constructions need to be distinguished according to which object the passive subject corresponds to:

[10] i	a. *I sent Sue a copy.*	b. *I ordered Sue a copy.*	
ii	a. *Sue was sent a copy.*	b. ?*Sue was ordered a copy.*	[first passive]
iii	a. ?*A copy was sent Sue.*	b. **A copy was ordered Sue.*	[second passive]

We use the term **first passive** for the one where the subject corresponds to the first object, O^i, and **second passive** for [iii], where it corresponds to the second object, O^d. These terms also reflect the order of preference: the first passive tends to be quite strongly favoured over the second. Ditransitive verbs vary considerably in how readily they occur in passive clauses. In general, where O^i corresponds to the complement of *to* in the prepositional alternant [7i], characteristically having the semantic role of recipient, the first passive is fully acceptable, as in [10iia]; judgements vary as to the acceptability of second passives like [10iiia]: many find them unacceptable,[24] and they are textually quite rare. Where O^i corresponds to the complement of *for* in [7ii], with the semantic role of beneficiary, neither passive is completely acceptable, but many speakers find the first marginally possible.

Ditransitive O^i and O^d compared with monotransitive O^d

We have been assuming that the second object of a canonical ditransitive can be identified with the single object of a monotransitive (as O^d) while the first is a distinct type of object (O^i). This is not entirely unproblematic, however, as is evident from the following examination of the properties of O^i and what for convenience we will refer to as 'monotransitive O^d' and 'ditransitive O^d'.

(a) Passives

We have noted that the first passive (with the subject corresponding to O^i) is preferred over the second (where the subject corresponds to ditransitive O^d). This makes O^i somewhat more like monotransitive O^d than is ditransitive O^d. However, the marginality of [10iib] shows that it by no means behaves like a prototypical monotransitive O^d.

(b) Post-verbal position

It is of course O^i rather than ditransitive O^d that characteristically occupies the position immediately following P, as in [10i]. It is, however, significantly more resistant to departures from this position than is monotransitive O^d, as we see from the next two points.[25]

[24] Acceptability is greater when we have a personal pronoun + *by* phrase: *This copy was given me by my grandfather.*

[25] Note also that O^i does not readily allow a particle to intervene between it and P: examples like *I gave John back his sunglasses* are more acceptable than ?*I gave back John his sunglasses*, an order that many speakers find unacceptable. The issue is complicated by the fact that the presence of a particle will often favour a PP complement over an O^i. Thus while *He sent his students out a questionnaire* may be more acceptable than ?*He sent out his students a questionnaire*, it is appreciably less so than *He sent out a questionnaire to his students* or *He sent a questionnaire out to his students.*

(c) Object postposing

Unlike monotransitive O^d and ditransitive O^d, O^i cannot be postposed when heavy:

[11]	i	*He gave to charity everything he earned from the concert.*	[monotransitive O^d]
	ii	*He gave Sue immediately all the spare keys he had had cut.*	[ditransitive O^d]
	iii	**He gave a second chance all those who had scored 40% or more.*	[O^i]

The ban on S–P–O^d–O^i is comparable to that on O–P–S. Order is the primary factor distinguishing O^i from O^d as well as S from O, and the grammar excludes structures which reverse the normal O^i–O^d and S–P–O orders.

(d) Prenuclear position

As we have seen in [9], clauses with prenuclear O^i are of low acceptability, whereas ditransitive O^d occurs as readily in this position as monotransitive O^d – compare the [a] examples with *The key he lost, The key which he tried didn't fit, He asked who(m) I had invited, What a lot of them he had offended!*

(e) Predicand

Unlike monotransitive O^d and ditransitive O^d, O^i cannot be the predicand for a predicative adjunct:

[12]	i	*She ate the steak almost raw.*	[monotransitive O^d as predicand]
	ii	*He served her her steak almost raw.*	[ditransitive O^d as predicand]
	iii	**He offered her the steak fiendishly hungry.*	[O^i as predicand]

In [i–ii] the property expressed by the adjunct *almost raw* is predicated of the steak, expressed as O^d, but [iii] illustrates the impossibility of having O^i as predicand: it can't mean that she was in a state of fiendish hunger as he offered her the steak (the asterisk applies to this interpretation: it is grammatical with the subject *he* as predicand).

(f) Control

In infinitival purpose clauses an O can be left unexpressed if it is recoverable from the superordinate clause O – which is said to 'control' the gap, or missing element. The controlling element can be monotransitive O^d or ditransitive O^d, but not O^i:

[13]	i	*He wanted it to spend __ on his children.*	[monotransitive O^d as controller]
	ii	*She gave him it to spend __ on his children.*	[ditransitive O^d as controller]
	iii	**She sent him it to prove __ wrong.*	[O^i as controller]

In [i–ii] we understand *to spend on his children* as "to spend it on his children": there is a missing O (a gap marked by '__') recoverable from the O^d *it* of *want* or *give.* But [iii], where the intended interpretation is "She sent him it to prove him wrong", thus with O^i as controller, is ungrammatical. (The infinitivals here are 'hollow clauses': see Ch. 14, §6, for further discussion.)

Conclusion

On balance, ditransitive O^d has greater syntactic affinity with monotransitive O^d than does O^i, justifying our analysis of the canonical double-object construction as containing O^i + O^d.[26] The most important distinctive property of O^i is (d), its resistance to front

[26] Some modern grammars take the opposite view, regarding the first internal complement as O^d and the second as not an O at all. Languages with a ditransitive construction fall broadly into two types, one where the O which characteristically has a recipient role behaves syntactically like a monotransitive O, and one where it

position, for (e)–(f) involve fairly infrequent constructions and certainly don't apply to all O^ds.

O^i not found in canonical clauses without O^d

In canonical clauses containing just one object, that object is always a direct object, even if it corresponds semantically to the indirect object of a ditransitive clause:

[14] i	*She teaches the first-year students introductory logic.*	[$O^i + O^d$]
ii	*She teaches introductory logic.*	[O^d, with semantic role of ditransitive O^d]
iii	*She teaches the first-year students.*	[O^d, with semantic role of ditransitive O^i]

Although the semantic roles of *introductory logic* in [ii] and *the first-year students* in [iii] are different, there is no syntactic basis for assigning different structures to these clauses. Except in certain non-canonical constructions (such as the passive), therefore, O^i is found only in combination with O^d.

Note, in support of this analysis, that the internal complement in [14iii] does not have the major O^i property of resisting prenuclear position: *These students she has never taught, the students whom she taught, Who does she teach?, What a lot of first-class students she taught!* are completely acceptable, just like the equivalent constructions based on [ii], *Logic she has never taught, the subject which she taught*, and so on. The case is comparable to that involving different kinds of relation between monotransitive and intransitive constructions:

[15] i	*She rang the bell twice.*	[S + O^d]
ii	*She rang twice.*	[S, with semantic role of monotransitive S]
iii	*The bell rang twice.*	[S, with semantic role of monotransitive O^d]

It is uncontroversial that *she* in [ii] and *the bell* in [iii] have the same syntactic function, subject, even though the semantic roles are different, and we are saying that *introductory logic* in [14ii] and *the first-year students* in [14iii] likewise have the same syntactic function, this time direct object, in spite of the semantic difference.

5 Predicatives and related elements

A predicative complement is oriented towards a predicand, normally S in intransitives, O in transitives. In both cases it may be classified as either **depictive** or **resultative** as in [1], where double underlining marks the predicand, single underlining the predicative.

[1]	INTRANSITIVE	TRANSITIVE
DEPICTIVE	*Kim seemed uneasy.*	*He found Kim intolerant.*
RESULTATIVE	*Kim became angry.*	*He made Kim happy.*

The resultative PC typically occurs with verbs that denote a change of state. The PC denotes the state of the predicand argument at the end of the process. A depictive PC gives a property of the predicand argument at the time of the situation under consideration, without any such factor of change.

is the other O that does; the terms O^i and O^d are appropriate for the second type, with 'primary object' and 'secondary object' for the first type (the primary object covering the monotransitive O and the ditransitive O with recipient role). We are treating English as belonging to the second type, but it is not a clear-cut member; in general, the clear members are those where O^i is marked by a distinct case, the dative, contrasting with accusative for O^d, as in such languages as German and Latin (or Old English).

The central type of predicative complement has the form of an AdjP, as in [1] above, or else of an NP used non-referentially, as in [2]:

[2] i *Kim remained a keen supporter of the proposal.*
ii *The publicity made Kim a liability.*

The underlined NPs are not here used to refer to some person, as the complement NP *Kim* is, but rather denote characteristics ascribed to Kim, as the AdjPs in [1] do. The likeness between AdjP and NP in such constructions is seen in pairs like *This idea sounds promising* and *This idea sounds a promising one.*

The underlined complements in [1–2] express semantic predicates – hence the term predicative complement. At the general level, we thus define a predicative complement as a grammatically distinct complement of the verb characteristically expressing a semantic predicate. This semantic predicate applies to the predicand, generally subject or object. Syntactically predicatives are complements, but semantically they are comparable to verbs in predicator function.

The semantic similarity between predicative complements and predicators is particularly evident in pairs like:

[3]	PREDICATIVE COMPLEMENT	PREDICATOR
	a. *Kim is fond of animals.*	b. *Kim loves animals.*

The meanings of the clauses here are more or less the same, while the syntactic structures are very different. *Love* is a verb, and its two arguments *Kim* (experiencer) and *animals* (stimulus) are aligned with S and O, external and internal core complements. *Fond*, by contrast is an adjective, and has the experiencer aligned with S, a complement of the verb *be*, rather than of *fond* itself, and the stimulus aligned with the complement of *of*, thus with an oblique element within the AdjP.[27] The relation between semantic and syntactic structure is thus less straightforward in [a] than in [b]. This provides one reason for applying the term 'complex' to clauses containing PC, with [2i], for example, a complex-intransitive clause and [2ii] a complex-transitive one.

A second, related, reason is that while the PCs in [1–2] express semantic predicates, the predications concerned are themselves arguments of a superordinate semantic predicate, *seem*, *find*, etc.[28] We thus have two semantic predications encoded within a single syntactic subject–predicate construction. It may be that the *be* of [3i] should be regarded as semantically empty, serving the purely syntactic function of carrying the tense inflection, which has to be associated with a verb: note in this connection that translation equivalents in a good number of languages contain no verb. However, there are undoubtedly constructions where *be* does express a semantic predicate (e.g. in *The chief culprit was Kim*: see §5.5), and we will simplify by assuming that it does in all cases.

Clauses with extraposed subject or object

[4] i *It is unfortunate that it rained.* [intransitive: extraposed subject as predicand]
ii *I find it easier to go by bus.* [transitive: extraposed object as predicand]

In clauses of this kind it is the extraposed element that serves as predicand for *unfortunate*

[27] Since *Kim* is a complement of *love* but not of *fond*, it follows that while *love* is bivalent (has two complements), *fond* is monovalent (has only one). However, as semantic predicates *love* and *fond* are both dyadic (have two arguments).

[28] Alternatively we might say that the predicate itself, conceptualised as a state, constitutes the argument.

and *easier*. This reflects the fact that these elements behave semantically like the subject or object even though they do not have that syntactic function.

In the following sections we begin by presenting the syntactic properties that distinguish the central type of predicative complement from an object. We turn next to the relation between predicatives and the semantic roles of location, goal, and source. §5.3 introduces a distinction (cutting across those made above) between obligatory and optional predicatives (e.g. *He looked young* vs *He died young*), and in so doing recognises that some predicatives are adjuncts rather than complements. The final section examines various semantic and syntactic distinctions within copular clauses.

5.1 Distinctive syntactic properties of PCs

Three syntactic differences between PCs and objects

(a) Category: PC function can be filled by AdjP or bare role NP

The crucial syntactic property of PC is that it can have the form either of an AdjP or of a bare role NP (a count singular with no determiner, such as *President of the Republic*, *treasurer*, etc.). Usually it can have the form of an ordinary NP too, but what distinguishes PC from O is the admissibility of an AdjP or bare role NP.

[5]	PREDICATIVE COMPLEMENT	OBJECT
i	a. *He seemed a nice guy / nice.*	b. *He met a nice guy / *nice.*
ii	a. *I consider it bad advice / bad.*	b. *I gave her bad advice / *bad.*
iii	a. *She remained treasurer.*	b. **She questioned treasurer.*
iv	a. *They appointed him secretary.*	b. **They promised him secretary.*

Examples [i–ii] illustrate the possibility of replacing an ordinary NP by an AdjP in the case of PC, and the impossibility of doing so with O. Examples [iii–iv] show bare role NPs functioning as PC and the ungrammaticality that results from putting them in O function: the NPs in [iiib/ivb] need determiners (e.g. *She questioned the treasurer*; *They promised him a secretary*).

The ability of AdjPs to function as PC but not O reflects the fact that a PC characteristically expresses a property, while O (like S) characteristically refers to someone or something: AdjPs denote properties but are not used referentially. Similarly, the restriction on bare role NPs reflects the fact that they too cannot be used referentially; note in this connection that they are equally excluded from subject function: **Treasurer has resigned.*

(b) Passives: no correspondence with a passive subject

A negative property is that PC – unlike a prototypical O – never corresponds to the subject of a related passive clause: it always very clearly fails the passive test.

[6]	PREDICATIVE COMPLEMENT	OBJECT
i	a. *Ed became a minister.*	b. *Ed attacked a minister.*
ii	a. **A minister was become by Ed.*	b. *A minister was attacked by Ed.*

Again, this reflects the important semantic distinction that underlies the syntactic contrast of PC and O mentioned in (a). O is semantically the same kind of element as the S of a canonical clause in that both are characteristically used referentially and express arguments, not semantic predicates: the voice system allows for different alignments of arguments with syntactic functions. The prototypical PC, on the other hand, is non-referential and expresses a semantic predicate, so that it is quite unlike a canonical S and remains unaffected by the voice system.

We have noted that some objects fail the passive test (e.g. *His uncle had two yachts*, but not **Two yachts were had by his uncle*; *This colour doesn't suit me*, but not **I am not suited by this colour*; and so on). This is therefore a less decisive criterion than the first: if an NP complement of a verb can be converted into the subject of a related passive this establishes that it is an object, not a PC, but failure to pass this test is not sufficient to establish that it is a PC.

(c) Case: nominative possible for a PC

In languages with richer case systems, PC commonly agrees in case with its predicand: PC^s and O^d then tend to contrast in case as nominative vs accusative. In English, however, case is of only the most marginal relevance for PC. The nominative–accusative contrast is found only among the personal pronouns and with interrogative/relative ***who***, but both kinds of pronoun occur as PC only under quite restricted conditions.

The personal pronouns are mainly used referentially and, as we have noted, PC is characteristically non-referential. Their appearance in PC function is virtually limited to specifying uses of the verb *be*, where the PC differs quite significantly from the central type of PC with respect to both form and meaning. Nevertheless, formal style does here have nominative case, so that we may contrast *It was he who wrote it* (nominative: PC) and *They saw him* (accusative: O). The distinction is lost in informal style, which has accusative for both PC and O, but the possibility of a nominative personal pronoun in formal style does differentiate PC from O, at least in certain constructions.[29]

Who likewise rarely occurs as PC except with the verb *be*. Formal style distinguishes between nominative *who*, as in *I wonder who she is* (PC: *whom* impossible), and accusative *whom*, as in *I wonder whom she invited* (O). Again the distinction is lost in informal style, which in this case has the nominative *who* for both (*who she is / who she invited*) rather than the accusative.

The question of number in NPs

Because an NP functioning as PC is characteristically non-referential, it tends not to select independently and contrastively for number. Very often, the number matches that of the predicand:

		a.	b.
[7]	i	a. *She seems a reliable witness.*	b. *They seem reliable witnesses.*
	ii	a. *She considered him a fool.*	b. *She considered them fools.*

Note that we cannot replace the singular PCs in [a] by the plural ones of [b], or vice versa.

This is not, however, a matter of syntactic agreement. There are innumerable examples where a PC differs in number from its predicand:

[8] i *They were a nuisance / a problem / a huge success / an example to us all.*
ii *That so-called work of art is simply four pieces of driftwood glued together.*

[29] Nominative PCs are found predominantly in the *it*-cleft construction and in more or less fixed expressions like *Those are they*; see Ch. 5, §16.2.1, for details.

What is required is semantic compatibility, not syntactic agreement (for fuller discussion of this issue, see Ch. 5, §19).

Predicative obliques

Predicative elements may occur as complement of a preposition instead of being related directly to the verb. Much the most common preposition is *as*:

[9]		INTRANSITIVE	TRANSITIVE	
	i	a. *That counts as excellent.*	b. *I regard her as indispensable.*	[AdjP]
	ii	a. *She served as treasurer.*	b. *They chose her as secretary.*	[bare role NP]

Again the predicand is S in the intransitive, and normally O in the transitive.[30] The complements of *as* we analyse as **predicative obliques**, and the *as* phrases themselves (*as excellent*, etc.) as **marked predicative complements**.

Imperfect match between syntax and semantics

A handful of verbs such as *constitute, provide, represent* include within their range of uses one where the semantic relation between subject and internal complement is similar to that found with the verb *be*. This use is illustrated in [10i], which may be contrasted with [10ii]:

[10] i a. *Changes in the basic wage-rate constitute an argument for raising prices.*
b. *Sue Brown provides an excellent example of a woman who has achieved outstanding success in the world of business while bringing up a large family.*
c. *This proposal represents a serious threat to our standard of living.*
ii a. *We must constitute a new and more democratic committee of management.*
b. *The government provides the necessary funds.*
c. *Jill represents her school at tennis.*

In [i], but not in [ii], the verbs could be replaced with virtually no perceptible change of meaning by *be* (or by *count* + *as*, where the complement of *as* is a predicative oblique). It would be a mistake, however, to suggest that this indicates that the internal complements are predicatives in [i], but objects in [ii]. There are no syntactic grounds for assigning different structures to the two sets of examples, and we will analyse the internal complement as an object in both: what [i] shows is that with these verbs an object can be semantically similar to a predicative complement.

The first syntactic argument that the internal complements in [10i] are objects is that we cannot replace them by AdjPs or bare role NPs – cf. **This proposal represents intimidatory*; **She constituted/provided treasurer.* Secondly, the *provide* example in [10i] has a straightforward passive counterpart: *An excellent example of a woman who has achieved outstanding success in*

[30] The verb *strike* is exceptional in having S as predicand in a transitive construction: compare *I regard him as a liability* (normal, O as predicand) and *He strikes me as a liability* (exceptional, S as predicand). The behaviour of *strike* here correlates with its exceptional alignment of semantic roles and syntactic functions. Like *regard* it belongs to the field of cognition, yet it aligns experiencer and stimulus with O and S respectively, instead of the usual S and O (cf. §2.3), and this exceptional alignment in turn reflects the fact that the sense involved here is a secondary one relative to that of *He struck me on the chin.*

the world of business while bringing up a large family is provided by Sue Brown. The relevant uses of *constitute* and *represent* do not so readily occur in the passive, but the underlined part of the following attested example shows that passives are not excluded with these verbs, merely less frequent:

[11] *It would be possible to take sport in general, or indeed one particular sport such as cricket, and explain the material and ideological conditions surrounding its production in a specific socio-cultural order such as that constituted by Australia.*

Note, moreover, that the range of complementation patterns for *provide* is the same as in other uses, so that the above bivalent constructions can be matched with trivalent *Sue Brown provides us with an excellent example*... and *The government provides us with the necessary funds.*

The semantic similarity between the objects in [10i] and predicative complements is reflected in the fact that the former tend to match the subject in number. Compare [ib], for example, with *Sue Brown and her sister provide excellent examples*... or [ic] with *These proposals both represent serious threats to our standard of living.* The fact that such number matching is found with objects that are semantically similar to predicatives provides further support for the view advanced above that it is a matter of semantic compatibility, not grammatical agreement.

On the construction *She made him a good wife*

Another verb that can take an object semantically resembling a predicative complement is *make*, but here matters are complicated by the fact that *make* also appears in the complex-transitive construction, where it does take a predicative complement:

[12]	i	*She made him a good husband.*	[PC°: complex-transitive construction]
	ii	*She made (him) a good wife.*	[O: ordinary transitive construction]
	iii	*She made (him) a teddy-bear.*	

In [i] *a good husband* is a straightforward example of a predicative complement: it can be replaced by an AdjP or bare role NP (*She made him happy/treasurer*). In [iii] *a teddy-bear* is equally clearly a direct object: it occurs either alone or with an indirect object, and in the former case corresponds to a passive subject (*A teddy-bear was made by her*).

What then of [12ii]? From a semantic point of view *a good wife* is like *a good husband* except that it applies to the subject *she* rather than the object *him*. And indeed *a good wife* here is commonly analysed as a predicative complement. We would again argue, however, that from a syntactic point of view [ii] belongs with [iii], not with [i] – that *a good wife* is an object, comparable to those in [10i].

As before, the first and crucial point is that *a good wife* cannot be replaced by an AdjP or bare role NP: **She made exemplary/treasurer* (and *She made him grateful/secretary* can only have *him* as predicand and hence must belong with [12i], not [ii]). The second point is that the range of complementation patterns is again the same as in [iii], with the direct object optionally preceded by an indirect object. And both ditransitive versions alternate with a prepositional construction: *She made a teddy-bear for him* and *She made a good* *wife for him* (or, if the latter sounds slightly unnatural, compare *She'll make an excellent stepmother for his children*). If *a good wife* were predicative complement, *She made him a good wife* would belong to a construction type unique to *make*. It differs from [iii] in that there is no related passive, but many other objects fail the passive test too, and given that there is no automatic correspondence between object and passive subject it is not surprising that an object semantically resembling a predicative should fail.[31]

5.2 Location, goal, and source

Relation between locative complements and predicative complements

One common type of complement to the verb *be* is a locative expression, as in *The letter is on the table*. The structural similarity between this and, say, *The letter is highly offensive* suggests that assigning a location to something is comparable to assigning it a property. One respect in which locative complements resemble predicatives is that they too are oriented towards a particular element, subject in intransitives, object in transitives:

[13]	INTRANSITIVE: S-ORIENTATION	TRANSITIVE: O-ORIENTATION	
i	a. *Sue remained calm.*	b. *I kept it handy*	[PC]
ii	a. *Sue remained outside.*	b. *I kept it in the drawer*	[locative]

Moreover, there is a significant degree of overlap between the verbs which take the two kinds of complement. Further examples of verbs which license both include the following (those in [i] being intransitive, those in [ii] transitive):

[14]		PREDICATIVE COMPLEMENT	LOCATIVE COMPLEMENT
i	*get*	*They got angry.*	*They got into the car.*
	go	*He went mad.*	*He went to hospital.*
	stay	*She stayed calm.*	*She stayed inside.*
ii	*drive*	*He drove them mad.*	*He drove them to the bank.*
	get	*They got me angry.*	*They got me to the shore.*
	leave	*They left me unmoved.*	*They left me in the waiting-room.*

However, there are also numerous verbs which take only one or the other, and for this reason we will not assimilate the locatives to the predicatives, but will regard them as syntactically distinct kinds of complement that exhibit certain semantic resemblances.[32]

[31] A semantic relation similar to that holding between *She made a teddy-bear* and *She made a good wife* is found between *She made a table out of the remaining timber* and *She made a man (out) of him* and again we will want to say that the underlined NP is object in both. *A table* clearly qualifies as object by the passive test: *A table was made out of the remaining timber*. The corresponding example with *a man* as subject is not acceptable: **A man was made out of him*; however, similar examples such as *I'm sure a world-class tennis player could be made out of him* are reasonably acceptable, certainly much better than the results of trying to convert a PC into a passive subject. Note, moreover, that both examples have a counterpart with *into*, which supports their analysis as belonging to the same construction: *She made the remaining timber into a table* and *She made him into a man.*

[32] Note, moreover, that some of the verbs that occur with both kinds of complement, such as *drive* and *turn*, have a different sense and a very restricted range of permitted complements in the PC construction.

A few examples of verbs that take predicatives but not locatives are given in:

[15]		PREDICATIVE COMPLEMENT	LOCATIVE COMPLEMENT
i	*become*	*He became anxious.*	**He became in the city centre.*
	seem	*Kim seemed angry.*	**Kim seemed at the back of the queue.*
	sound	*They sounded strange.*	**They sounded in a cave.*
ii	*call*	*They called him stupid.*	**They called him in the wrong team.*
	make	*She made him happy.*	**She made him onto the platform.*
	render	*This rendered it useless.*	**This rendered it in the wastebin.*

Nevertheless, the semantic similarities observed above make it fruitful to generalise the semantic roles of location, source, and goal beyond the field of space. We will thus look first at spatial location and then extend the application of these roles to states and possession (for further discussion of spatial location and extension of the roles to the dimension of time, see Ch. 8, §§5–6).

Location and change of location in space

Locative complements cover expressions associated with the roles of source, goal, and location. Source and goal apply in situations involving movement, source representing the initial location, goal the final one; where there is no movement the role is simply that of location. Compare:

[16] *Angela went [from Berlin] [to Bonn] but Henry remained [in Berlin].*
Theme Source Goal Theme Location

The prepositions *from* and *to* serve as markers of source and goal. They indicate that their complement NPs express the initial and final locations respectively: Angela started off in Berlin and ended in Bonn. *In* by contrast is part of the expression of the location itself, and as such contrasts with other prepositions – for example, *near* or *outside.*

With goal, however, a preposition may also be part of the location expression:

[17] i a. *Ed fell [in the pool].* b. *She put Ed [on the bus].*
ii a. *Ed slipped [under the car].* b. *She pushed Ed [behind the curtain].*

The prepositions here are not markers of goal: they do not indicate that the NP expresses the final location. They serve, rather, to describe the final location. The goal marker *to* cannot be added before the PPs in [17] (cf. **Ed fell to in the pool,* **Ed slipped to under the car,* etc.), but with *in* and *on* it can form a compound preposition:

[18] a. *Ed fell [into the pool].* b. *She put Ed [onto the bus].*

The meaning is the same as in [17i], the difference being simply a matter of whether the goal role is morphologically marked or not. Note that the grammatical order of components in the compounds *into* and *onto* does not match the semantic order: we understand "to [in the pool]", "to [on the bus]", the final locations being "in the pool" and "on the bus", as in [17i].

Sources behave rather differently. Compare:

[19] i a. *Ed ran [from the scene].* b. *He pulled Ed [from the wreckage].*
ii a. *Ed emerged [from under the car].* b. *He pulled Ed [from behind the curtain].*

From marks the source in all of these. In [i] the source location is expressed simply by an NP (we understand "at the scene", "in the wreckage"), whereas in [ii] it is expressed by a PP headed by a locative preposition: the marker of source, unlike that of goal, is not omissible in such cases. Source can also be expressed by *out*, as in *Ed ran out of the house.*

States

The extension of the locational roles from the field of space to that of states (properties) is most clearly motivated by the use of the same markers for source and goal. Compare:

[20]		SPATIAL SOURCE + GOAL	STATE SOURCE + GOAL
	i	a. *He went [from Berlin] [to Bonn].*	b. *It went [from bad] [to worse].*
	ii	a. *I sent it [from Berlin] [to Bonn].*	b. *I changed it [from green] [to red].*

In [a] *from* marks the initial location in space, *to* the final one; in [b] *from* marks the initial state, *to* the final one. The AdjPs *bad, worse, green, red* are predicative obliques and the PPs containing them marked predicative complements.

We have seen that a spatial goal often remains unmarked, and thus we can regard the PCs in *His condition got worse* and *I made it red* as similarly unmarked state goals. There is no marker of spatial location, so that the prototypical state equivalent will likewise be an unmarked PC: *It seemed satisfactory, He considers it worthless.* We have noted that the source marker *from* is not omissible like the goal marker *to* and this correlates with the absence of unmarked PCs associated with the source role: thus we have *It became red* (goal), but not **It ceased green* (source). Compare also *It turned [from green] [to red]* (two prepositions) and *It turned red* (no preposition, with PC interpreted as goal, not source).

The parallel between spatial and state location is also seen in the fact that states are often expressed by PPs headed by prepositions whose primary meaning is spatial: *in a terrible state, in good condition, in good spirits, in a bad temper, out of sorts, on top of the world.* Such expressions can occur with verbs like *seem* which, as noted above (cf. [15]), do not take spatial location complements: *She seemed miserable / in a terrible state / *in the lounge.*[33] In addition, *to* can mark state goals with a small range of abstract NPs such as *sleep, death, distraction* – compare:

[21]				
	i	*He went to sleep.*	*We stabbed it to death.*	*The noise drove us to distraction.*
	ii	*He fell asleep.*	*We shot it dead.*	*The noise drove us mad.*[34]

Semantically, the underlined expressions here are state goals (marked in [i], unmarked in [ii]). Syntactically, they are locative complements in [i], predicative complements in [ii] – note that the NPs in [i] cannot be replaced by AdjPs (or bare role NPs), and that these *to* phrases do not occur with any of the verbs that license PCs but not locative complements.

[33] This does not apply with *become* and *make*: see Ch. 6, §2.1.

[34] In the depictive construction the AdjP version is required (*He remained asleep / * in sleep*) unless appropriate dependents are added (*He remained in a deep sleep*).

Into with state goals

With some verbs a state goal is expressed as complement to *into*:

[22] i *Enrico turned [from a frog] [into a handsome prince].*
ii *Enrico / The frog turned [into a handsome prince].*

Here we take the whole compound preposition as marker of the goal role, with the NP *a handsome prince* expressing the final state. Such NPs tend to have the same number as that of the NP expressing the theme: cf. *Enrico and his brother turned into handsome princes* – or, with a different verb, *He developed into a fine young man* ~ *They developed into fine young men.* We have argued that this does not mean that these NPs are syntactically predicatives, and given that neither an AdjP nor a bare role NP can occur as complement to *into* we will take *into a handsome prince* as a locative complement. Note that *turn* does also occur with a predicative (*He turned nasty*), whereas *develop* does not.

In [22i] theme, source, and goal are all expressed separately. Construction [ii], however, which contains no *from* phrase, allows two interpretations, according as the subject expresses theme alone (*Enrico*) or theme and source combined (*the frog*): *Enrico* simply picks out the one undergoing the change, while *the frog* does this but at the same time defines the source state – the prince was (presumably) still Enrico but not still a frog.

Possession

Another field where we can invoke the roles of location, source, and goal is that of possession:

[23] i *These houses are Kim's.*
ii a. *These houses belong to Kim.* b. *Kim owns these houses.*
iii *The estate passed from Kim to Pat.*
iv a. *Kim sold the house to Pat.* b. *Pat bought the house from Kim.*

Example [iii] illustrates straightforward change of possessor, with *from* marking initial possessor, *to* the final one: *Kim* and *Pat* can be regarded as possessional source and goal. In [i–ii], where there is no change of ownership, we can, by extension of the analogy, take *Kim* as possessional location, with the *to* in [iia] and the genitive case in [i] as markers.[35] Genitive NPs of this kind are best analysed as predicative complements, as they are found only with a subset of verbs that take such complements: e.g. intransitive *be, become, remain, stay,* transitive *call, consider, declare, make.* The non-genitives, however, are very sharply different from predicative complements. In particular, possessional location, source, and goal can all be aligned with the subject, as in [iib], [iva], and [ivb] respectively. Similarly, O^{d} expresses source in *They robbed her of all her jewellery* and goal in *They presented her with a certificate of merit,* while O^{i} expresses source in *They fined her $100* and goal in *They gave her $100.*

[35] The preposition *to* in [iia] does not fit in with the usual pattern since it is normally associated with goal rather than location; note that *belong* is also used in the field of space but here does not take *to*: *The shirts belong in the top drawer.*

5.3 Obligatory and optional predicatives

Predicatives may be either **obligatory** or **optional**.

[24]

	OBLIGATORY	OPTIONAL
INTRANSITIVE	*Kim became ill.*	*They departed content.*
TRANSITIVE	*He made Kim angry.*	*He washed it clean.*

Obligatory *ill* and *angry* here cannot be omitted without loss of grammaticality (**Kim became*) or an unsystematic change of meaning (the sense of *make* in *He made them angry* is not the same as in *He made them*). Optional *content* and *clean*, by contrast, can be omitted without any change to the rest: *They departed content* entails *They departed*, and *He washed it clean* entails *He washed it.*

Intransitives

Little further need be added here concerning complex-intransitives, where we have the four combinations shown in:

[25]

	OBLIGATORY	OPTIONAL
DEPICTIVE	*They look fantastic.*	*He died young.*
RESULTATIVE	*The boss got angry.*	*The pond froze solid.*

Note that although *die* in *He died young* entails a change of state, the change does not involve his age, so that *young* has a depictive, not a resultative, interpretation – this is why we use the terms depictive and resultative for the predicative, rather than static vs dynamic, which apply to the situation as a whole. *The parcel came open* is then ambiguous between obligatory resultative ("Its state changed from closed to open") and optional depictive ("It was already open when it arrived" – cf. the unambiguous *It arrived open*).

Transitives

Corresponding examples of complex-transitives are as follows:

[26]

	OBLIGATORY	OPTIONAL
DEPICTIVE	*He kept Kim warm.*	*He ate the steak almost raw.*
RESULTATIVE	*This got me furious.*	*He painted the fence blue.*

An ambiguity matching that of *The parcel came open* might be *You've made the tea too weak.* The obligatory resultative reading would be appropriate in a scenario where after the tea has been made you found it too strong and added water, but too much: you have produced a change of state such that it is now too weak. No such change is involved in the optional depictive reading: you merely failed to use enough tea-leaves when making the tea, so that its initial state is too weak.

Transitives with obligatory resultatives

Within the category of transitives with obligatory resultatives there is a further distinction to be drawn:

[27] i *He made himself unpopular.* [internal complementation obligatory]
ii *He talked himself hoarse.* [internal complementation optional]

In neither case can we drop the PC leaving the rest unchanged: *He made himself* is somewhat unidiomatic, but in any case has a different sense of *make* and in *He talked himself* the reflexive is adjunct, not object. The resultative PC is thus in both cases obligatory. But in [ii] we can drop the PC and its predicand together, giving *He talked*, whereas [i] cannot similarly be reduced to **He made*. *Make* requires internal complementation, but *talk* does not. Example [i] represents the default case, while [ii] illustrates a quite unusual and restricted type of construction. The meaning is "He became hoarse as a result of talking". It is not possible to replace the reflexive by any other kind of NP – cf. **He talked his audience bored*, "His audience became bored as a result of his talking". The obligatory presence of a reflexive in [ii] would seem to be related to the fact that intransitive verbs with agentive subjects do not allow optional resultative predicatives. For example, non-agentive *The water ran hot* allows a resultative interpretation (it became hot as the water from the hot tank reached the tap), but we cannot have *Kim ran hot* with the meaning "Kim became hot as a result of running." ?*He talked hoarse* is perhaps marginally acceptable in a depictive sense, but it cannot have a resultative meaning: addition of the reflexive makes *talk* an agentive transitive in which the O can serve as a predicand for the resultative predicative. It is also possible to have a PP expressing a state goal: *He cried himself to sleep*; *He drank himself into a stupor*.

Transitives with optional depictives: O vs S as predicand

Predicatives in transitive clauses normally have O as predicand, but optional depictives can also have S:

[28] i *They served <u>the coffee</u> <u>black</u>.* [O as predicand]
ii *<u>They</u> served the coffee <u>blindfolded</u>.* [S as predicand]

This second construction is not possible with resultatives: *She chopped the wood tired*, for example, cannot mean that she became tired through cutting the wood, only that she was (already) tired when she cut it.

Optional depictive predicatives as adjuncts

Obligatory predicatives are clearly complements, dependent on the occurrence of an appropriate verb. With optional ones, however, there are grounds for saying that while the resultatives are complements, the depictives are adjuncts. Resultatives are either obligatory (as in the *He talked himself hoarse* construction) or else need to be licensed by the verb. Optional depictives, however, are less restricted in their occurrence. One manifestation of this has just been noted: they can occur in transitive clauses with either S or O as predicand. Another is that they can occur in combination with an obligatory predicative or in the ditransitive construction:

[29] i *They look <u>even more fantastic</u> <u>naked</u>.*
ii *They served <u>us</u> our coffee <u>black</u>.*

We will therefore regard such predicatives as adjuncts, so that the predicative/non-predicative contrast cuts across that between complements and adjuncts.

Like numerous other kinds of adjunct, predicatives may be integrated into the structure as modifiers, or detached, as supplements:

[30] i *They left <u>empty-handed</u>.* [modifier]
ii *<u>Angry at this deception</u>, Kim stormed out of the room.* [supplement]

The supplements are positionally mobile and are set apart prosodically. The modifiers are of course more like the complements, especially in cases where they occur very frequently with a particular verb, as with *leave* in [i], *die* in *He died young*, *bear* in the passive *He was born rich*, and so on.

As phrases as predicative adjuncts

Predicatives marked by *as*, like unmarked ones, can function as complement or adjunct. The complement use was illustrated in [9] above (*That counts as excellent*, etc.), while the adjunct use is seen in:

[31] i *He was happy [as a junior assistant].*
ii *[As a former member] we can offer you the following terms.*
iii *[As a former member] I offer you both the following advice.*

The adjuncts can take any pragmatically appropriate NP as predicand: for example, *a former member* has *you* (O^i) as predicand in [ii], but *I* (S) in [iii] – and reducing *you both* to *you* in [iii] results in ambiguity, with either S or O^i interpretable as predicand. The adjuncts also differ from complements in that the NP cannot be replaced by an AdjP, but it can still have the form of a bare role NP: *[As treasurer] I recommend that we seek approval for a modest increase in the subscription rate.*

5.4 Classification of verbs taking predicative complements

Class 1 verbs: complex-intransitives with depictive PCs

[32] *Kim felt lonely / an intruder. Her son remained ill / a danger. That seems plausible / a good idea. Pat proved reliable / a great asset.*

Aside from *be* (discussed in §5.5) the main members of this class are given in [33]:

[33]					
i	*feel*	*look* INF	*smell* ADJ	*sound* INF	*taste* ADJ
ii	*continue* ADJ INF	*keep* ADJ	*remain*	*stay*	
iii	*appear* INF	*seem* INF		*prove* INF	

Those marked 'INF' also take infinitival complements, so that there is alternation between, for example, *She appeared anxious* and *She appeared to be anxious.* (With *look* and *sound* the constructions are not wholly equivalent. In *She looked happy* the signs of happiness are presented as more immediately or directly visible than in *She looked to be happy.*) The annotation 'ADJ' indicates that the PC is restricted, or virtually restricted, to AdjPs to the exclusion of NPs. Compare *She kept calm* but not (as a complex-intransitive) **She kept the calmest person in the group.* The verbs in [i] are sense verbs (at least in their primary meaning), those in [ii] indicate continuation of the state, while set [iii] contains the two verbs of seeming and the odd one out, *prove.* Within set [ii] *continue* is quite rare in comparison with the others. It is used quite readily in talking of the weather, as in *It continues cold* or *The weather continued sultry.* For the rest, examples like %*Finding suitable accommodation for students continued difficult* are attested, but infinitival *continued to be difficult* would be preferred by most speakers.

The sense verbs and the verbs of seeming license a *to* phrase where the oblique NP expresses the experiencer: *The proposal looks very promising to me.* These same verbs also commonly occur with a *like* phrase instead of an NP: *Kim felt like an intruder; It seemed like a good idea.*

There are, in addition to the verbs in [33], a number that appear with such a limited range of PCs that the combinations are more or less fixed phrases or idioms:

[34] *go hungry/naked, hold true, lie flat, loom large, pass unnoticed, play rough / the fool, plead guilty/innocent, rest assured, run wild, stand corrected/firm*

Class 2 verbs: complex-intransitives with resultative PCs

[35] *He became ill / our main ally.* *The work got too difficult for them.*

[36]

become	*come* ADJ	*fall*	*get* ADJ INF	*go* ADJ
grow ADJ	*turn* ADJ			

These are all verbs of becoming. *Get* differs from *become* in three respects: it belongs to relatively informal style; it is for most speakers restricted to adjectival PCs; and it more readily accommodates an agentive subject, as in *The dog tried to get free.* In particular we find *get* rather than *become* with *ready*: *Get ready.*

The other verbs in [36] take only a very limited range of PCs. The main items permitted by each as the head of the PC are listed in [37].

[37]	i	*fall*	*asleep, ill, pregnant, prey* (*to* NP), *sick, silent, victim*
	ii	*come*	*loose, open, right, true*; ordinal adjectives (*I came third*)[36]
	iii	*go*	*bad, mad, wrong,* colour adjectives
	iv	*turn*	*bad, nasty, sour,* colour adjectives
	v	*grow*	*long, old, tall,* adjectives denoting psychological states (*bored, impatient, tired*), comparative AdjPs (*You grow more beautiful each day*)

Although we have marked *go* and *turn* as taking adjectival complements, they can also take an NP denoting a colour: *It went/turned a strange colour.*

There are other verbs that are found only with one or two items, in what are basically just fixed phrases:

[38] *blush scarlet, break loose, burst open, drop dead, freeze solid, run hot/cold, slide open/shut, spring open, walk free, wax eloquent, wear thin, work loose*

Class 3 verbs: complex-transitives with depictive PCs

[39] *She believed it prudent / an advantage to be out of town.* *We proved it genuine / a fake.* *They kept their marriage secret / a secret.*

There are considerably more verbs in this class, and we therefore list separately those with the 'INF' annotation indicating the possibility of an infinitival complement instead of the PC: compare the *believe* and *prove* examples in [39] with *She believed it to be prudent to stay out of town* and *We proved it to be genuine.*

[36] There is a different sense of *come* (roughly "act as though one were") where it does take an NP complement, as in *Don't come the concerned father with me.* Likewise *come* licenses an infinitival complement, but with a somewhat different meaning, so that *Her wish came true*, for example, is not equivalent to #*Her wish came to be true.*

[40]						
	i	*believe* INF	*certify* INF	*consider* INF	*declare* INF	*deem* INF
		feel INF	*find* INF	*hold*$_1$ ADJ INF	*judge* INF	*like* INF
		prefer INF	*presume* INF	*profess* INF	*pronounce* INF	*prove* INF
		reckon INF	*report* INF	*rule* INF	*think* INF	*want* INF
	ii	*account*	*brand*	*call*	*designate*$_1$	*esteem*
		have ADJ	*hold*$_2$	*imagine*	*keep*	*label*
		leave	*rate*	*term*	*wish* ADJ	

Hold$_1$ means roughly "consider", as in *I hold you responsible for her safety*, while *hold*$_2$ is close to "keep", as in *She held the door open for us*; *They held us hostage* (in both cases the range of PCs is quite limited). Some verbs in [ii] do enter into the infinitival complement construction but without the semantic equivalence that obtains in [i]. For example, *He wished himself different from the sort of person he thought he was* is closer to *He wished that he were different* than to *He wished himself to be different* (which indicates wanting to change). *He imagined himself unmarried* does have an interpretation equivalent to *He imagined himself to be unmarried* (i.e. "He thought he was unmarried" – cf. *He imagined himself indispensable*) but it also has another interpretation, probably more salient, in which he knew he wasn't unmarried but imagined what it would be like if he were.

A few verbs not included above, such as *acknowledge*, *confess*, *suppose*, appear in the complex-transitive construction, but normally only with a reflexive object: *He confessed himself puzzled by her response*, but not **He confessed the decision indefensible.*

Class 4 verbs: complex-transitives with obligatory resultative PCs

[41]		
	They appointed her ambassador to Canada.	*You drive me mad.*
	They made him anxious/treasurer.	*They created her a life peer.*

Some of these verbs take only NPs as PC: they are listed separately in [42] with the annotation 'NP'.

[42]						
	i	*drive* ADJ	*get*	*make*	*put* ADJ	*render*
		send ADJ	*set* ADJ	*turn* ADJ		
	ii	*appoint* NP INF	*baptise* NP	*christen* NP	*create* NP	*crown* NP
		designate$_2$ NP INF	*elect* NP INF	*name* NP	*proclaim* NP INF	*vote* NP

The verbs in [i] are the transitive analogues of the intransitive verbs of becoming. *Make*, informal *get*, and relatively formal *render* are the main ones, with the others restricted to a narrow range of adjectival complements. *Turn* takes the same type as intransitive *turn* (e.g. colour terms); *drive* and *send* occur with such items as *crazy*, *mad*, *insane*; *set* generally with *alight*, *free*, *right*, *straight*; and *put* also with *right* and *straight*.

The NP complement of the verbs in [42ii] can normally be a bare role NP: *They crowned him King*; *They elected her president*. *Baptise* and *christen* (at least in its literal sense) are exceptions, but we take this to be a semantic rather than a grammatical restriction, and not a sufficient reason for excluding them from the class of complex-transitive verbs. Some allow optional *as*: *They elected her (as) president* (see §6.1.2).

The primarily semantic distinction between depictive and resultative PCs is not always easy to draw. We have distinguished two senses of *designate* with one taking a depictive ("officially classify", as in *They have designated*$_1$ *it a disaster area*), and the other a resultative ("choose, appoint", as in *They have designated$_2$ Kim the next Attorney-General*), and it may be that some others should likewise be dually classified. Compare, for example, *We had half the children sick* (depictive) vs *We had the meal ready in half an hour* (resultative).

Class 5 verbs: complex-transitives with optional resultatives

[43] *We hammered it flat.* *Kim knocked him senseless.* *You should paint the house green.* *She rubbed herself dry.* *He pushed the door open.* *I'll wipe it clean.*

There are many verbs of this type, usually taking a small range of AdjPs (though again such NPs as *an unusual colour* are possible instead of colour adjectives). A small sample, with typical adjectives, is given in [44]:

[44]	*boil* (*hard*)	*bore* (*stiff*)	*brush* (*flat*)	*drain* (*dry*)	*fill* (*full of* NP)
	frighten (*silly*)	*jerk* (*open*)	*plane* (*smooth*)	*shoot* (*dead*)	*wash* (*clean*)

5.5 Copular clauses

5.5.1 Ascriptive and specifying uses of *be*

Two of the most important kinds of copular clause are illustrated in:

[45] i *His daughter is very bright / a highly intelligent woman.* [ascriptive]
ii *The chief culprit was Kim.* [specifying]

In the ascriptive use, PC denotes a property and characteristically has the form of an AdjP or a non-referential NP; the subject is most often referential and the clause ascribes the property to the subject-referent. Thus [i], for example, ascribes to his daughter the property of being very bright or being a highly intelligent woman. The specifying use defines a variable and specifies its value. We might represent [ii] therefore as "The *x* such that *x* was the chief culprit was: Kim"; it serves to specify, or identify, who the chief culprit was. We will refer to the semantic roles joined by *be* as **theme** and **property** in the ascriptive case, and as **variable** and **value** in the specifying case.

Many copular clauses can be interpreted in either way.

[46] i *His first proposal was a joke.*
ii *The victim was his sister.* } [ambiguous: ascriptive or specifying]

The ascriptive interpretation of [i] is "His first proposal was laughable": *a joke* gives an evaluation of his proposal. A context for the specifying interpretation might be one, say, where the question has been raised as to what would be the best way of opening a speech: his proposal was then to open it with a joke. Here the two interpretations are sharply different, and the specifying one is highly context-dependent. In [ii], which is much more typical, this is not so. The specifying reading identifies who the victim was; the ascriptive reading doesn't do this but merely says that she was related to him as sister. In the ascriptive use he may have several sisters, while the specifying one implicates that he has only one – and in the negative *The victim was not his sister* the ascriptive reading is perfectly consistent with his not having a sister, while the specifying one strongly implicates that he does.

Cleft clauses

There is one special copular construction, the *it*-cleft, that is restricted to the specifying use. Thus *It was Kim who was the chief culprit* conveys essentially the same as [45ii] – and *It was his sister who was the victim* corresponds unambiguously to the specifying reading of [46ii]. (Compare also for [46i]: *It was a joke that he proposed first.*) Fused relative constructions can occur in either type. The matrix *be* clause is known as a pseudo-cleft in the case where the copula has the specifying sense.

[47]	i	*It was peace and quiet that he wanted most.*	[specifying: *it*-cleft]
	ii	*What he wanted most was peace and quiet.*	[specifying: pseudo-cleft]
	iii	*What he wanted most was unobtainable.*	[ascriptive]
	iv	*What he gave her was a worthless piece of jewellery.*	[ambiguous]

In [i–ii] we have a variable defined as "the *x* such that he wanted *x* most" and its value is specified as "peace and quiet". In the *it*-cleft, the subject *it* corresponds just to the bare "*x*", and the definition of the variable is given in the relative clause at the end; in the pseudo-cleft [ii] the syntax matches the semantics more directly, with the "*x*" and its definition given in the fused relative construction functioning as S. In [iii] we have the same fused relative with the meaning "the *x* such that he wanted *x* most", but this time *be* + PC does not specify the value of *x*; the fused relative is here quite strongly referential, and the clause is used to say something about the referent, ascribing the property "unobtainable" to it. Example [iv] can be taken in either way: the specifying use identifies what he gave her as a worthless piece of jewellery, while the ascriptive use describes it as such. A context for the former is where you don't know what he gave her and my purpose is to inform you, whereas a likely purpose in the ascriptive reading is to express a judgement about the thing that he gave her. This is not to say that an evaluative term like *worthless* is needed for the ascriptive use: the ambiguity remains if we drop it, being still a matter of identification vs description, but the difference is then less salient. Precisely because the fused relative can occur in both types, it can be combined with the *it*-cleft to make the specifying sense explicit: *What it was that he wanted most was peace and quiet*; *What it was that he gave her was a worthless piece of jewellery.* (For further discussion of cleft clauses, see Ch. 16, §9.)

The contrast in meaning between the two kinds of copular clause is particularly clear when the PC has the form of an AdjP:

[48]	i	*The man they've appointed is too big for his boots.*	[ascriptive]
	ii	*What you are, my boy, is too big for your boots.*	[specifying]

Example [i] is a straightforward ascriptive clause with *too big for his boots* denoting a property ascribed to the subject-referent. *Too big for your boots* in [ii] clearly also denotes a property, but it is not a property ascribed to the subject-referent, for the subject does not refer to a person. Here, then, *too big for your boots* specifies the value of the variable "the *x* such that you are *x*". If we substitute this value for *x* in "you are *x*" we obtain "you are too big for your boots", which is an entailment of [ii]. (For further discussion of the interpretation of *be* clauses, see Ch. 5, §8.3.)

5.5.2 Formal differences between ascriptive and specifying copular clauses

(a) Reversibility

The specifying construction normally allows the alignment of semantic roles with syntactic functions to be reversed, so that we can have either variable as S and value as PC or value as S and variable as PC:

[49]	VARIABLE AS S – VALUE AS PC	VALUE AS S – VARIABLE AS PC
i	a. *What he wants is peace and* QUIET.	b. *Peace and* QUIET *is what he wants.*
ii	a. *Is what he wants peace and* QUIET?	b. *Is peace and* QUIET *what he wants?*

In order to help exclude irrelevant interpretations we have marked the focal stress (by small capitals), which in the default case falls within the element with the role of value. We give both declarative and interrogative versions to demonstrate that the first NP in both [a] and [b] is indeed the subject. No such realignment of roles and functions is possible in the ascriptive construction: the property role is always aligned with PC.

[50]	THEME AS S – PROPERTY AS PC	*PROPERTY AS S – THEME AS PC
	a. *What he wants is unobtainable.*	b. **Unobtainable is what he wants.*

Under certain conditions the ascriptive construction allows the order of S and PC to be switched:

[51]	S – P – PC	PC – P – S
	a. *Her third novel was even better.*	b. *Even better was her third novel.*

That the subject of [b] is *her third novel*, not *even better*, is evident from agreement (cf. *Even better* <u>*were*</u> <u>*her next two novels*</u>), the impossibility of forming a closed interrogative by inverting the first two elements (**Was* <u>*even better*</u> <u>*her third novel*</u>?), and so on.

The difference may therefore be summarised as follows. Given a clause 'X – *be* – Y', then if *be* is specifying, we can normally switch to 'Y – *be* – X', retaining the structure 'S – P – PC' (as in [49]), but changing the alignment between syntactic functions and semantic roles. But if *be* is ascriptive the switch to 'Y – *be* – X' will result either in ungrammaticality (as in [50b]) or in a change in syntactic structure (as in [51b], a special case of subject–dependent inversion: see Ch. 16, §5).

Reversibility as a source of ambiguity

The reversibility of the specifying construction is a further potential source of ambiguity, for it means that either S or PC may encode the variable. In abstraction from intonation such examples as the following can be taken with either S or PC as variable:

[52]		
i	*What he wanted to know was what I told her.*	[variable as S, value as PC OR
ii	*What I told her was what he wanted to know.*	value as S, variable as PC]

One interpretation has the variable expressed by *what he wanted to know* ("the *x* such that he wanted to know *x*") and the value by *what I told her*: "It was the answer to the question 'What did I tell her?' that he wanted to know". The other interpretation has the variable expressed by *what I told her* ("the *x* such that I told her *x*") and the value by *what he wanted to know*: "It was the answer to the question 'What did he want to know?' that I told her". The default position for the main stress is on *told* for the first interpretation and on *know* for the second.[37]

[37] We have cited examples where the meaning difference between the S-as-variable and S-as-value readings is very clear because in one case *what he wanted to know* is a fused relative and *what I told her* a subordinate interrogative whereas in the other case it is the other way round. It should be emphasised, however, that the

Restrictions on reversibility

We will assume that the variable-as-S version represents the canonical alignment and that the value-as-S version is the 'reversed' one. The variable-as-S version is in general significantly more frequent and it is the only one allowed in the *it*-cleft construction (compare [47i] with **Peace and quiet was it that he wanted most*). Moreover, the variable-as-S version characteristically has the main stress at the end, which represents the default place for it in general – compare [49i–ii].

Nevertheless, there are certain conditions under which the reversed version is required:

[53] i *Look over there!* [*THAT'S the guy you should ask.*]
ii *She took down some books but* [*THOSE weren't the ones I needed*].
iii *THAT* / *?His FATHER is who you should ask.*
iv *THAT* / *?Ill HEALTH was why he resigned.*

In [i] the value is expressed by demonstrative *that* used deictically and with human reference: it can only occur as S (**The guy you should ask is THAT*). Example [ii] illustrates the case where the value is a demonstrative used anaphorically with a preceding antecedent (here *some books*). Examples [iii–iv] represent a somewhat problematic case of the specifying construction, with the variable expressed by an open interrogative clause (cf. Ch. 12, §5.4).

(b) Connectedness of value and variable

[54] i *What I asked you was whether she had seen him* / **that she had seen him.*
ii *What I regretted was that she had seen him* / **whether she had seen him.*

In [i] the value can be a closed interrogative but not a declarative clause, but in [ii] it is the other way round. This is because of the way the variables are defined. In [i] we have "the *x* such that I asked you *x*", and *ask* (in the relevant sense) can take a closed interrogative but not a declarative clause as complement – *I asked you whether she had seen it* / **that she had seen it*. Conversely for the variable "the *x* such that I regretted *x*" in [ii]. Similarly in [48ii] above the value can take the form of an AdjP (*too big for your boots*) because the definition of the variable ("the *x* such that you are *x*") allows a property term.

The form and interpretation of the value element are thus closely connected with the way the variable is defined. Some of the manifestations of this connectedness are as follows.

Reflexives and reciprocals

[55] i *My long-term goal is to get myself* / **me elected to Council.* } [specifying]
ii *All we did was give each other* / **us a little encouragement.*
iii *My long-term goal is of great importance to me* / *?myself.* } [ascriptive]
iv *All we did was of great importance to us* / **each other.*

We have a reflexive pronoun in [i] because the understood subject of *get* is *I*. Although unexpressed, it can be recovered on the basis that if I have a goal that constitutes an action then, other things being equal, I can be assumed to have the agent role. Similarly in [ii] the subject of *give* is recoverable from within the variable as *we*, which sanctions reciprocal *each other* and excludes *us*. Such reflexives and reciprocals are not

difference is not dependent on the presence of an extra factor like this. Thus *The one who got the job was the one who won the prize* and *The one who won the prize was the one who got the job* are likewise ambiguous according to which NP encodes the variable. They can be used, normally with stress on *prize*, to specify, identify who got the job ("It was the one who won the prize who got the job") or, with stress on *job*, to specify who won the prize ("It was the one who got the job who won the prize").

confined to clauses where the value has the form of a non-finite clause: the same principle applies to examples like *What you are, my boy, is rather too sure of yourself* (cf. [48ii]), which entails *You are rather too sure of yourself.* In the ascriptive construction, by contrast, there is no such connectedness between PC and S, so the accusative forms are now permitted. The reciprocal is straightforwardly excluded, as shown in [iv], whereas in [iii] a reflexive is marginally acceptable as an alternant to the more usual accusative – it is an example of what we call an 'override reflexive' (see Ch. 17, §3.1.4).

Aspectual agreement

[56] i *What she did next was correct/*correcting the proofs.*
ii *What she was doing was correcting/*correct the proofs.*

When the clause specifies a value for a variable involving "do *x*" there must be agreement in the aspectual system progressive vs non-progressive. Thus non-progressive *did* in [i] requires non-progressive *correct*, while progressive *was doing* in [ii] selects *correcting.*

Non-affirmative items

[57] i *What he never did was show some/any sign of remorse.* [specifying]
ii *The part he didn't read had been interesting to some/*any of us.* [ascriptive]

A non-affirmative item in the value element may be sanctioned by a negative within the variable. Example [i] entails *He never showed any sign of remorse*, where *any* is straightforwardly within the scope of *never*, and this then allows non-affirmative *any* in the specifying construction. In ascriptive [ii], however, the negative embedded within the subject does not have scope over the PC.

(c) Category

In the specifying construction the variable element normally has the form of an NP,[38] whereas the value can be expressed by a phrase of any category or a subordinate clause. Thus the value has the form of an AdvP in *It was only very reluctantly that she agreed*, an AdjP in [48ii], a PP in *The best place for it is under the bed*, and so on. In the ascriptive construction a subordinate clause can function as S but not in general as PC: it expresses not a property but the bearer of a property.[39] Compare, then, the role of the *whether* clause in:

[58] i *Whether he'll survive is uncertain.* [ascriptive: S only]
ii *The question occupying us all is whether he'll survive.* [specifying: PC as value]
iii *Whether he'll survive is the question occupying us all.* [specifying: S as value]

(d) Interrogative and relative *who*

Who cannot be used to question properties, hence can't be an ascriptive PC. *Who is he?*, for example, can only be specifying. To question properties we need *what... like*,

[38] The one exception is an open interrogative, as illustrated in [53iii–iv].

[39] Infinitival clauses can function as PC under certain conditions. The most productive case involves purpose infinitivals, as in *This is to clean the lens with*: the property is that of serving a particular purpose. Other cases like *He is to blame, The house is to let*, are lexically very restricted.

what, or *how* (Ch. 10, §7.7). Similarly for the relative: *He's not the man who I thought he was* is concerned with identity. And where the issue concerns properties, not identity, we have *He's not the man that he used to be,* where *that* cannot be replaced by *who.*

(e) Referentiality and definiteness

NPs in ascriptive PC function are non-referential and cannot have the form of a personal pronoun; they are characteristically indefinite, as in *Kim is a successful lawyer.* Such examples illustrate the common use of ascriptive copular clauses to indicate class membership: *This is a weed,* "This belongs to the class of weeds". Very often they involve gradable terms: *What a hopeless cook he is!*; *He's such a bore.* Definite NPs are not excluded; among the clearest examples we find superlatives, kin or similar relations, offices or roles and the like: *She's the nicest person you could hope to meet / the headmistress's daughter / the secretary of the bushwalking club.* These could also be specifying, but if we drop *the* from the last the ambiguity dissolves: *She is secretary of the bushwalking club* can only be ascriptive, for bare role NPs are always non-referential. In the specifying construction the variable NP is characteristically definite, as in *The ones he invited were Kim and Max* (where the value is definite too) or *What he wanted was an umbrella* (where the value is indefinite). Such cases carry an implicature of exhaustiveness and contrast: he didn't invite anyone besides Kim and Max, and there are others whom he might have invited but didn't. It is possible for the variable NP to be indefinite, in which case there is no such implicature: *An example of what I mean was his behaviour at dinner last night.*[40] The variable NP is always interpreted descriptively, never purely referentially (in the sense of Ch. 5, §8). Compare:

[59] i *The man next to Tom / That guy with the beard is a scoundrel.* [ascriptive]
ii *The one who got the job / The one who set up the deal was Max.* [specifying]

In [i] it may be that I am simply wanting to tell you that a certain person is a scoundrel and indifferently choose either *the man next to Tom* or *that guy with the beard* as a means of getting you to see who I am talking about: in this case the NPs are used referentially. But the subject NPs in [ii] can't be freely interchanged in this way: their content is essential to what I am saying, for in the one case I am telling you who got the job and in the other I am telling you who set up the deal, so that the two versions cannot be different ways of making the same point. In some cases the variable NP has a form which doesn't permit a purely referential use: e.g. NPs with a fused or restrictive relative containing an *about* phrase, as in *What / The thing I like about Ed is his hair* (hence the deviance of ascriptive **What / *The thing I like about Ed is black*).

(f) Predicative complements with verbs other than *be*

Ascriptive PCs occur freely with other verbs, whereas the specifying construction is almost wholly restricted to *be* clauses:

[60] i *It was/*seemed/*became John who took responsibility for the accounts.*
ii **He considered what she needed a complete rest.*

[40] The implicature of exhaustiveness is also lost if we add such adverbs as *primarily, chiefly, mainly*: *It was primarily the cost that put me off.*

These can be remedied by replacing *seemed* by *seemed to be* and *became* by *came to be* in [i] and adding *to be* before *a complete rest* in [ii]. Note that in [ii] it is the relationship between the complements that is inadmissible, not their form: compare *He considered what she had done a complete disaster*, with ascriptive PC. Because the PCs governed by these other verbs are ascriptive, the constructions are not reversible: *Pat became Kim's lover* is not equivalent to ?*Kim's lover became Pat* (which suggests a fantasy world where the lover turned into Pat).[41]

6 Special verb + preposition combinations and related types of complementation

Our major focus in this section is on prepositional complements of verbs where the combination of verb and preposition is distinctive in one or more of the following ways:

[1] i The preposition is specifically selected by the verb rather than being in potential contrast with other prepositions – e.g. *Kim referred to your book.*

ii The preposition can be positioned between the verb and a simple NP object – e.g. *She put in her application.*

iii The verb + preposition combination forms an idiom, or is part of one – e.g. *I gave up the struggle* ("abandoned"), *This gave the lie to her critics* ("showed to be wrong").

Transitive and intransitive prepositions

We include in the category of prepositions not only words like *to* in [1i/iii], but also *in* in [1ii] and *up* in [1iii]. As used here, *in* and *up* are traditionally analysed as adverbs: explanation and justification for their treatment as prepositions is given in Ch. 7, §2.4. Prepositions, like verbs, head a range of different construction types, and one major distinction is between transitive and intransitive constructions. In *He put it [in the box]*, the NP *the box* is object of *in*, and we apply the term transitive to the PP or to *in* itself (as used here), just as in *He [opened the door]*, where *the door* is object of *opened*, we say that *opened the door* is a transitive VP and that *open* (as used here) is a transitive verb. Similarly, in *He brought the chairs in* the preposition has no object and we apply the term intransitive to the PP consisting of *in* alone or to the preposition *in* itself (as used here). On this basis we take the *to* of [i/iii] as a transitive preposition (with *your book* and *her critics* as object), and the *in* of [ii] and the *up* of [1iii] as intransitive prepositions. Strictly speaking, an intransitive preposition may have a complement other than an object NP – e.g. *owing* in *owing to the rain* has a PP complement. In this section, however, we will be concerned only with intransitive prepositions that have either no complement at all or else a predicative, as in *That counts [as satisfactory]*.

[41] A specifying use of *become* cannot be excluded altogether, however, as can be seen from such an example as *The genuinely interesting question, then, becomes:what factors determine the degree of realism or distortion in conventional images of Jews.* The PC here identifies the genuinely interesting question, and subject and predicative complement could be switched. *Remain* allows a specifying PC somewhat more readily, as in *His weight remained 60 kgs* (contrast **His weight became 60 kgs*), with the marginal possibility of reversal to *60 kgs remained his weight*; cf. also *What I like best about Bill remains his sense of humour*, where the S can't be purely referential.

Selection of preposition by the verb

The preposition *to* of *Kim referred to your book* in [1i] is to be distinguished from that of *Kim flew to Boston* in that the latter may contrast systematically with such other prepositions as *towards, round, from, over,* and so on, whereas the former permits no such replacement. The dictionary entry for *refer* must specifically mention *to*, whereas that for *fly* need say only that the verb takes complements of goal, source, and path. For purposes of comparison we will refer to the *to* of *Kim referred to your book* as a **specified** preposition, and that of *Kim flew to Boston* as an **unspecified** preposition.

Prepositional verbs

Verbs like *refer* which select a specified preposition we call **prepositional verbs**. This category covers not only verbs where the PP is the sole complement but also those where it combines with one or more other complements, like *congratulate* in *He congratulated her on her promotion.* It also covers those where the specified preposition takes a predicative complement, like *count* in the above *That counts [as satisfactory]*. We examine constructions containing prepositional verbs in §6.1.

Positioning between verb and object: particles

The usual position for an object is immediately after the verb unless it is internally complex or heavy, in which case it may occur in postposed position, as in *She found in the woods a large number of exotic toadstools.* Clauses like *She put in her application* in [1ii] depart from the usual pattern by virtue of having a complement positioned between the verb and a simple object, i.e. one that is not heavy. Words which can occur as complement in this position we call **particles**; they are mainly intransitive prepositions like the *in* of this example, but there are also a few other types, such as the adjective *short* in *We cut short the debate.* The particle + object construction is dealt with in §6.2.

Idioms and verbal idioms

An idiom is an expression larger than a word whose meaning cannot be systematically derived from meanings that the parts have when used independently of each other. We apply the term **verbal idiom** to idioms whose major element is a verb.

A large number of verbal idioms contain intransitive prepositions, as in the *give up* of [1iii]: we survey the various constructions containing idioms of this kind in §6.3. In §6.4 we look at verbal idioms consisting of verb + NP object + transitive preposition, such as *give the lie to* in [1iii]; and in §6.5 we introduce briefly various other types of verbal idiom.

The following further examples of verbal idioms illustrate two general points that should be borne in mind:

		a.	b.
[2]	i	a. *He took me to task for wearing jeans.*	b. *She made up her mind to resign.*
	ii	a. *You're pulling my leg.* ("teasing me")	b. *He had no idea how ill I was.*

(a) Idioms need not be syntactic constituents

An idiom is a lexical unit, and there is no requirement that lexical units coincide with syntactic ones. In [2i], for example, the PP *to task* is part of the idiom, but is separated from the verb by the object and hence doesn't form a syntactic constituent with the verb. In [ib/iia] the genitive inflection in *her* and *my* is part of the idiom, while the lexeme component (***she***, ***I***) is not, though in [ib] the pronoun must be anaphorically linked to the subject (cf. **We made up Jill's mind to resign*). In [iia], moreover, there is compelling evidence that the syntactic structure is the same in the idiomatic interpretation as in the literal one, for in either case we can have a related passive, as in *I don't like having my leg pulled.* It is clear, then, that *my leg* in [iia] is syntactically the object of *pull.* Similarly in [ib] *her mind* is object – cf. the adjectival passive *Her mind is made up.* In [iib] *idea* is head of the NP object: the determiner *no* isn't strictly part of the idiom for we can have other dependents here (*He hadn't the faintest idea . . . / Did he have any idea . . .*), though there are severe restrictions on what they can be (cf. **He had a rather novel idea how ill I was*).

(b) Idioms can license complements

Make up one's mind has essentially the same meaning as *decide*, and like the latter it licenses an infinitival complement, such as *to resign* in [2ib]. Similarly in [iib], *have . . . idea* is comparable to *know* and takes the same range of clausal complements, in this example the exclamative *how ill I was.* Note that the complement here is not licensed by the noun *idea* alone, for we cannot have, say, **The idea how ill I was hadn't entered his mind.*

It follows that when we list items taking a particular type of complement, we need to allow for the inclusion of verbal idioms.

The term 'phrasal verb'

Sequences like those underlined in the [a] examples of [3] are commonly classified as 'phrasal verbs':

[3]		a.		b.
	i	a.	*Kim referred to your book.*	b. *He flew to the capital.*
	ii	a.	*He put in his application.*	b. *He carried in the chairs.*
	iii	a.	*I look forward to seeing you.*	b. *I ran forward to the desk.*
	iv	a.	*He paid tribute to his parents.*	b. *He sent money to his parents.*

The term 'phrasal verb' implies that the combinations concerned form syntactic constituents belonging to the category verb. The view taken here, however, is that the underlined expressions in the [a] examples in [3], despite their idiomatic interpretations, do not form syntactic constituents, any more than the underlined word sequences in the [b] examples form constituents. It is for this reason that we do not use the term 'phrasal verb' in this grammar.[42]

6.1 Prepositional verbs

Prepositional verbs, we have said, are those which select a PP complement containing a specified preposition together with its own complement.[43] In §6.1.1 we compare the syntax of clauses containing prepositional verbs with that of clauses containing verbs taking transitive PP complements headed by unspecified prepositions; then in §6.1.2 we survey the major clause constructions containing prepositional verbs.

[42] For some writers the phrasal verb category is defined more narrowly to include only combinations of verb + intransitive preposition, as in [3iia], and perhaps also the non-idiomatic type of [iib].

[43] As usually employed, the term 'prepositional verb' applies to the sequence of verb + preposition, thus to *refer to* in [3ia]: since we don't analyse that as a single constituent, we apply the term just to the verb, i.e. in this case to *refer* itself.

6.1.1 Comparison between constructions with specified and unspecified prepositions

The comparison we are concerned with here is between clauses like those in the [a] and [b] members of such pairs as:

[4]

		SPECIFIED PREPOSITION	UNSPECIFIED PREPOSITION
i	a.	*I referred to her book.*	b. *I flew to Boston.*
ii	a.	*I came across some old letters.*	b. *I swam across the river.*
iii	a.	*I skated over the problem.*	b. *I skated over the frozen pond.*
iv	a.	*I waded through my ironing.*	b. *I waded through the mud.*

The [a] examples, in contrast to the [b] ones, contain prepositional verbs. As illustrated in [iii–iv] there are numerous verb + preposition combinations where the preposition can be either specified or unspecified: in the specified case the combination forms a verbal idiom.

We will compare the two types with respect to four parameters: fronting of the preposition along with its complement, coordination of PPs, positioning of adjuncts before the preposition, formation of prepositional passives. The comparison shows that it is necessary to distinguish two types of specified preposition, **mobile** ones like the *to* of [4ia], and **fixed** ones like the *across* of [iia]. The mobile ones behave in essentially the same way as unspecified prepositions, while the fixed ones do not permit variation in their position relative to the verb.

(a) Fronting of the preposition + NP

The main constructions at issue here are relatives and open interrogatives. Also relevant are *it*-clefts where the foregrounded element (the complement of *be*) is a PP. We illustrate first with cases that have an unspecified preposition:

[5]

i	*the city to which I flew*	[relative]
ii	*To which city did you fly?*	[open interrogative]
iii	*It was to Boston that I flew.*	[*it*-cleft]

There are alternants with a stranded preposition (*the city which I flew to*, etc.), but it is the version cited in [5] that is of interest for present purposes, for it shows that *to* and the following NP form a constituent.

Consider now the behaviour of specified prepositions in these constructions, the mobile *to* selected by *refer* and the fixed *across* selected by *come*:

[6]

		MOBILE PREPOSITION	FIXED PREPOSITION
i	a.	*the book to which I referred*	b. **the letters across which I came*
ii	a.	*To which book did you refer?*	b. **Across which letters did you come?*
iii	a.	*It was to her book that I referred.*	b. **It was across these letters that I came.*

The mobile preposition behaves just like the unspecified one in [5], whereas the fixed one does not. *Across* cannot be moved to the left of *come*, so only the versions with stranded prepositions are admissible: *the letters which I came across*; *Which letters did you come across?*; *It was these letters that I came across.*

(b) Coordination of PPs

Unspecified prepositions can be readily repeated in coordination:

[7] *I flew to Boston and to New York.*

With specified prepositions we again find the mobile and fixed types behaving differently:

[8] a. *I referred to her book and to several others.* b. **I came across these letters and across some family photographs.*

(c) Position of adjuncts

An adjunct can be readily inserted between the verb and an unspecified preposition:

[9] *I flew regularly to Boston.*

The same applies to mobile specified prepositions, but not to fixed ones:

[10] a. *I referred repeatedly to her book.* b. **I came eventually across these letters.*

(d) Prepositional passives

In the prepositional passive construction the preposition remains next to the verb, and this time we don't have a systematic difference in behaviour between mobile and fixed specified prepositions. With unspecified prepositions the prepositional passive is not generally admissible, but it is not wholly excluded. Passives are much more widely available with specified prepositions, but they are not admissible in all cases. Compare, for example:

[11] i a. **Boston was flown to next.* b. *This bed has been slept in.*
ii a. **Such principles were stood for.* b. *Her book was referred to.*
iii a. **Some old letters were come across.* b. *These matters must be seen to.*

In [i] we have unspecified prepositions, in [ii] mobile specified ones (cf. *the principles for which we stand*), and in [iii] fixed specified ones (cf. **the matters to which we must see*).

Distinction between mobile and fixed specified prepositions applies in transitive clauses

The mobile vs fixed distinction applies also to prepositions following an object NP:

[12]

	MOBILE PREPOSITION	FIXED PREPOSITION
i	a. *He referred me to a specialist.*	b. *He got me through the biology test.*
ii	a. *the specialist to whom he referred me*	b. **the test through which he got me*
iii	a. *To whom did he refer you?*	b. **Through which test did he get you?*
iv	a. *It was to an ophthamologist that he referred me.*	b. **It wasn't through the biology test that he got me.*
v	a. *He referred me to an optometrist, but not to an ophthalmologist.*	b. **He got me through the biology test, but not through the anatomy one.*

In the [a] examples we have the transitive use of *refer*, and as with the intransitive use considered above the specified preposition *to* can be fronted along with its complement in relatives and open interrogatives, extracted with its complement in the *it*-cleft, and repeated in coordination. The [b] examples contain the transitive idiom *get through*, "help pass", and here the specified preposition *through* cannot be moved or repeated.

Constituent structure

The constituent structure of clauses containing specified prepositions is best regarded as identical to that of matching clauses with unspecified prepositions. This means that in all the above examples where the preposition immediately precedes an NP it combines with the latter to form a transitive PP. The bracketing for our model examples with *refer to* and *come across* is thus as follows:

[13] a. *I [referred] [to her book].* b. *I [came] [across some old letters].*

Where the position of the preposition is fixed we take the verb + preposition combination to be **fossilised**, i.e. it blocks the application of the syntactic processes that can normally apply to such combinations.

There is no support for the common view according to which specified prepositions form a constituent with the verb, giving bracketings like those in [14].

[14] a. *I [referred to] [her book].* b. *I [came across] [some old letters].*

These structures imply that there has been a reanalysis such that the preposition has come to be incorporated into the verb instead of heading a PP. Structure [14a], however, is inconsistent with the data presented in [6], [8], and [10], which show that syntactically the preposition belongs with the NP, its complement, not with its governing verb. If the structure were as shown in [14a], we have no account of why the preposition can be fronted along with the NP, of why the preposition can be repeated in coordination, of why an adjunct can be inserted before *to*.

The analysis of clauses with fixed specified prepositions is less clear. The data of [6], [8], and [10] are this time not inconsistent with the bracketing shown in [14b]. But nor are they inconsistent with that shown in [13b]: we can simply say that the sequence is fixed rather than variable. This indeed is the only plausible solution in the case of fixed prepositions in transitive clauses like *He got me through the biology test*, [12ib]: here the preposition is separated from *get* by the object, and hence cannot form a syntactic constituent with it.

The reanalysis account [14b] would be required if there were positive evidence that the VP behaved like a verb + object construction – for example, if an adjunct could occur immediately before a heavy NP. We have no attested examples of this type, however, and constructed ones appear to be unacceptable:

[15] i **He came across later that morning a letter she wrote just before her marriage.*
ii **We must see to immediately the various matters that your father raised.*

The fossilisation account avoids the need to assign different structures to the *refer to* and *come across* examples, and is in any case needed for the transitive case illustrated with *get* NP *through.*

6.1.2 Constructions containing prepositional verbs

In this section we survey the patterns of complementation found with prepositional verbs. We distinguish the following six structures:

[16] I	verb – [prep + O]	*I <u>referred</u> [<u>to</u> her book].*
II	verb – O – [prep + O]	*I <u>intended</u> it [<u>for</u> Kim].*
III	verb – [prep + O] – [prep + O]	*He <u>looked</u> [<u>to</u> her] [<u>for</u> guidance].*
IV	verb – [prep + PC]	*It <u>counts</u> [<u>as</u> too short].*
V	verb – O – [prep + PC]	*They <u>regard</u> it [<u>as</u> successful].*
VI	verb – [prep + O] – [prep + PC]	*I <u>think</u> [<u>of</u> it] [<u>as</u> indispensable].*

In I–III the final NP is object of its governing preposition, while in IV–VI it is a predicative complement. The distinction we have drawn among complements of the verb between objects and predicatives applies also to the complements of prepositions, though the preposition governing a PC is almost always *as* – in the lists below we will include the preposition taking a PC only when it is not *as*.

Structure I: verb – [prep + O], as in *refer* [*to her book*]

This is the type focused on in §6.1.1, where the preposition + NP forms the only complement of the verb. There are a great many prepositional verbs of this kind; a small sample are given in [17], where '–P' indicates that prepositional passives like [11] are unacceptable, and 'F' that the combination is fossilised, with the preposition more or less fixed in position, as illustrated for *come across* in [6], [8], and [10].[44]

[17]				
	abide by	*account for*	*ask after* F	*ask for*
	bank on	*believe in*	*break into*	*break with* –P F
	call for	*call on*	*come across* –P F	*come between* –P F
	come by F	*come into* –P F	*come under* –P	*consist of* –P
	count on	*dawn on* –P	*decide on*	*dispose of*
	draw on	*dwell on*	*fall for* –P	*feel for* –P
	fuss over F	*get at* F	*get over* –P F	*get round* F
	go off –P F	*grow on* –P F	*hit on* F	*hold with* –P
	hope for	*keep to*	*lay into* F	*look after* F
	look for	*make for* –P F	*part with*	*pick on*
	pore over F	*run into* F	*see about* F	*see to* F
	stand by –P F	*stand for* –P	*stem from* –P	*take after* –P F
	tamper with	*tell on* F	*testify to*	*wait on*

We also include under the present heading such combinations as *blossom into* and *turn into*, where the complement of the preposition is semantically like a predicative but doesn't qualify syntactically as a predicative complement as it cannot have the form of an AdjP or bare role NP (see §5.2).

Structure II: verb – O – [prep + O], as in *intend it* [*for Kim*]

In this construction the verb has two complements, an object and a PP. The subject of related passives always corresponds to the object of the verb, not that of the preposition: *It was intended for Kim*, not **Kim was intended it for*. The preposition can almost always be fronted or extracted along with its complement and repeated in coordination, as illustrated for *refer... to* in [12], but there are a few informal expressions like the *get... through* of [12] where this is not possible; such fossilised combinations are again

[44] In fact the three constructions in [6] differ somewhat in this regard: *the goods of which he had disposed*, for example, is much more acceptable than *?Of which items did he dispose first?* or *?It was of his own car that he disposed first.* We have marked with 'F' only those which resist occurrence in all three. Note also that a verb + preposition combination may be more fossilised in one meaning than in another: the position of *at*, for example, is fixed in *I must get a plumber to look at this tap* ("examine with a view to repairing"), but not in *Everyone was looking at the organist.*

marked 'F' below:

[18]	*accuse . . . of*	*address . . . to*	*assure . . . of*	*charge . . . with*
	confine . . . to	*convince . . . of*	*deprive . . . of*	*draw . . . into*
	entitle . . . to	*explain . . . to*	*get . . . through* F	*help . . . with*
	hold . . . against	*incite . . . to*	*interest . . . in*	*introduce . . . to*
	let . . . into F	*let . . . off* F	*persuade . . . of*	*protect . . . from*
	read . . . into	*refer . . . to*	*rob . . . of*	*see . . . through* F
	subject . . . to	*suspect . . . of*	*treat . . . to*	*warn . . . of/about*

Two special cases of Structure II are shown in:

[19] i a. *He supplied weapons to them.* b. *He supplied them with weapons.*
ii a. *She gave the key to Pat.* b. *She gave Pat the key.*

In both there is alternation between [a] and [b]. With *supply* both alternants belong to the prepositional construction, selecting different NPs as object and different prepositions. With *give* the prepositional construction [a] alternates with the ditransitive (double-object) construction [b]. These alternations are dealt with in §8.

- Structure III: verb – [prep + O] – [prep + O], as in *look* [*to her*] [*for guidance*]

Here the verb selects two prepositions:

[20]	*agree with . . . about*	*appeal to . . . for*	*argue with . . . about/over*
	arrange with . . . for	*boast to . . . about*	*complain to . . . about*

- Structure IV: verb – [prep + PC], as in *count* [*as too short*]

[21]	*act*	*count*	*do* "serve"	*double*	*emerge*
	function	*masquerade*	*pass as/for*	*pose*	*rate*
	resign	*retire*	*serve*	*stand*	

This is the prepositional equivalent of the complex-intransitive construction. *Pass* allows *for* as the preposition, as in *He had passed for dead.*

- Structure V: verb – O – [prep + PC], as in *regard it* [*as successful*]

[22]	i	*accept*	*acknowledge*	*adopt*	*bill*	*brand*
		cast	*categorise*	*characterise*	*choose*	*class(ify)*
		condemn	*confirm*	*construe*	*count*	*define*
		denounce	*depict*	*describe*	*diagnose*	*disguise*
		dismiss	*enlist*	*establish*	*give*	*hail*
		have	*identify*	*instal*	*intend*	*interpret*
		know	*mean*	*perceive*	*portray*	*present*
		recognise	*regard*	*represent*	*scorn*	*see*
		suggest	*take as/for*	*treat*	*use*	*view*
	ii	*appoint*	*consider*	*designate*	*elect*	*imagine*
		nominate	*ordain*	*proclaim*	*rate*	*report*

This is the prepositional equivalent of the complex-transitive construction. Again we have an exceptional case where *for* is allowed as well as *as*: *He took it as obvious* and *He took them for dead.* With the verbs in [ii] the *as* is optional: *They appointed Kim (as) treasurer*; the version without *as* belongs to the complex-transitive construction discussed in §5.4.

- Structure VI: verb – [prep + O] – [prep + PC], as in *think* [*of it*] [*as indispensable*]

[23] *agree on* *conceive of* *look (up)on* *refer to* *think of*

In this relatively unusual construction the predicand for the predicative is complement of the first preposition – i.e. the predicative *indispensable* applies to *it.* Note that there is no construction where the predicand is complement of a preposition but the predicative is not.[45]

6.2 The 'verb – particle – object' construction

Particle exemplified and defined

We use the term **particle** for words like *down* in [24i], as opposed to *downstairs* in [ii]:

[24] i a. *She brought down the bed.* b. *She brought the bed down.*
ii a. **She brought downstairs the bed.* b. *She brought the bed downstairs.*

Down is a one-word phrase functioning as complement of the verb, and the term 'particle' can be applied to the word or the phrase it constitutes. The distinctive property of particles is that they can be positioned between the verb and an NP object with the form of a proper noun or determiner + common noun. This is what distinguishes *down* from *downstairs* in [24]: both can follow the object, but only *down* can precede it. In general, object NPs of the above form follow the verb immediately, without intervening adjuncts or complements, and particles constitute the major exception to this ordering. It is necessary to refer to the internal structure of the object NP because there are no relevant restrictions on what can come between the verb and an NP that is heavy: *She brought downstairs the bed that she had recently inherited from her grandmother.* Since particles are here defined by reference to structure [ia], we will not invoke the category in intransitive clauses: there is no equivalent difference between *down* and *downstairs* in *She came down* and *She came downstairs.*

The most central particles are prepositions – intransitive prepositions, of course, since they are one-word phrases.[46] The class of particles also contains some adjectives and verbs, but these are restricted to a fairly small number of verbal idioms (*He made clear his intentions*; *They cut short their holiday*; *She let go his hand*), whereas prepositional particles are found readily in both idioms like *She brought down the price* and in non-idiomatic, or **free**, combinations like [24i]. A sample of these prepositional particles is

[45] The construction 'verb – [preposition + NP] – PC (unmarked)' is possible only where the predicand is subject, as in *He looks to me somewhat insecure*, with *somewhat insecure* applying to *he*, not *me.*

[46] The term particle is used in a variety of ways, but normally for a class of uninflected words. Our use of the term reflects the way it is most commonly applied in English.

given in [25]:[47]

[25]	*aboard* T	*about* T	*across* T	*ahead*	*along* T
	apart	*around* T	*aside*	*away*	*back*
	by T	*down* T	*forth*	*forward*	*home*
	in T	*off* T	*on* T	*out* %T	*over* T
	round T	*through* T	*together*	*under* T	*up* T

The annotation 'T' indicates that the preposition can also be transitive, i.e. can take an object NP, as in *She brought me down the mountain* (*out* is marked '%T' because the transitive use seen in *He jumped out the window* is normal in AmE, but not in BrE).

Contrast between the constructions 'V – particle – NP' and 'V – [preposition + NP]'

In view of the large overlap between the particle and transitive preposition categories, we will examine the difference between them in such constructions as:

[26] V – PARTICLE – NP V – [PREPOSITION + NP]
a. *She took off the label.* b. *She jumped [off the wall].*

In [a] *off* is a particle, an intransitive preposition functioning as complement of the verb, with *the label* a separate complement of the verb – more specifically, *the label* is object. In [b], by contrast, *off* is a transitive preposition with *the wall* as its object, so that *off the wall* is a PP forming a single complement of the verb. The constructions differ syntactically in the following ways:

(a) The 'particle + NP' order can usually be reversed, 'preposition + NP' cannot

[27] i a. *She took off the label.* b. *She jumped off the wall.*
ii a. *She took the label off.* b. **She jumped the wall off.*

The distinctive property of particles is that they **can** precede the object, but in general they don't have to, so that we have alternation between the two clause structures illustrated in [ia] and [iia]. In [ib], however, *off the wall* forms a single clause element, and the order within this phrase is fixed.

Important though it is, this test is not as straightforward as (b) below: there are a small number of alternations between transitive PPs and sequences of NP + intransitive preposition (illustrated in [33] below), and also cases where a particle cannot be shifted around the object (§6.3.1).

(b) Only a transitive preposition can be followed by an unstressed personal pronoun

The NP following a transitive preposition (its object) can have the form of an unstressed personal pronoun, but the NP following a particle can't: objects of this kind must immediately follow the governing verb.

[28] a. **She took off it.* b. *She jumped off it.*

This provides the simplest test for determining which structure we have in a given instance: if the NP can be replaced by an unstressed personal pronoun, it must be the transitive prepositional construction.[48]

[47] The list could be expanded by adding various nautical terms such as *aft, aloft, ashore, astern.* There are others largely restricted to one or two verbs: *leave behind.*

[48] The qualification 'unstressed' allows for a particle to precede a pronoun bearing contrastive stress. In the context of removing people from a list, for example, with Jill mentioned as a possibility for removal, I might conceivably say: *I'm certainly not going to take off* HER.

(c) Transitive PPs can normally be fronted/foregrounded, particle + NP sequences cannot

In fairly formal style a transitive preposition can be fronted along with its complement in such constructions as relatives and open interrogatives, and similarly transitive preposition + NP can be the foregrounded element in the *it*-cleft construction; a particle + NP sequence, by contrast, does not form a constituent and cannot be fronted or foregrounded in this way:

[29] i	a. **the label* [*off which she took*]	b. *the wall* [*off which she jumped*]
ii	a. **Off which label did she take?*	b. *Off which wall did she jump?*
iii	a. **It was off this label that she took.*	b. *It was off this wall that she jumped.*

This test provides a sufficient but not a necessary condition for the transitive PP construction: we noted in §6.1.1 that some prepositional verbs select transitive prepositions that are fixed in position (see [12] above).

(d) A transitive preposition can normally be repeated in coordination of phrases

[30]	a. **Did she take <u>off the red label</u> or <u>off the yellow one</u>?*	b. *Did she jump <u>off the wall</u> or <u>off the balcony</u>?*

Example [b] is well formed because the underlined sequences in *Did she jump <u>off the wall</u>?* and *Did she jump <u>off the balcony</u>?* are constituents. Conversely, [a] is deviant because in *Did she take <u>off</u> <u>the red label</u>?* and *Did she take <u>off</u> <u>the yellow one</u>?* the sequences *off* + NP are not constituents.

(e) A manner adverb can generally be inserted between verb and transitive preposition

[31]	a. **She took carefully off the label.*	b. *She jumped fearlessly off the wall.*

In [b] the complement of the verb is a PP and complements of this kind can be separated from the verb by such adjuncts as manner adverbs (except with the fixed specified prepositions). In [a], however, *the label* is object of the verb and cannot be separated from the verb in this way: [a] is comparable to **She removed carefully the label.*

Homonymous sequences

Given the large degree of overlap between particles and transitive prepositions, it is not surprising that the same item can often be found with the same verb, interpreted now as particle, now as transitive preposition:

[32]	PARTICLE	TRANSITIVE PREPOSITION
i	a. *He shouted <u>down</u> his opponent.*	b. *He shouted* [*<u>down</u> the phone*].
ii	a. *They turned <u>in</u> the fugitives.*	b. *They turned* [*<u>in</u> the wrong direction*].
iii	a. *She ran <u>off</u> another copy.*	b. *She ran* [*<u>off</u> the road*].
iv	a. *He got <u>over</u> his message clearly.*	b. *He got* [*<u>over</u> his disappointment*] *quickly.*

These are easily differentiated by the criteria given above (the only complication being that the *get* + *over* in [ivb] is fossilised). The structural difference between the [a] and [b] members correlates with a very sharp difference in meaning, with all four of the particle examples and the last of the transitive preposition ones involving a rather high degree of idiomatisation.

Alternation between transitive PPs and sequences of NP + intransitive preposition

The distinction between transitive prepositions and particles is slightly complicated by the existence of a few pairs like:

[33]	TRANSITIVE PP	NP + INTRANSITIVE PREPOSITION
i	a. *She read [through the prospectus].*	b. *She read [the prospectus] through.*
ii	a. *She looked [over the letters].*	b. *She looked [the letters] over.*

Initially these pairs look like [27ia/iia] (*She took off the label* ~ *She took the label off*), but on closer examination we can see that they are not, that *through* and *over* are not particles here, but transitive prepositions in [a] and (non-particle) intransitive prepositions in [b]. This is evident from the fact that in [a] we can substitute unstressed personal pronouns: *She read through it, She looked over them.* We can also have an intervening adverb, as in *She read carefully through the prospectus.* There is a fair amount of fossilisation in the prepositional construction, so that ?*the prospectus through which she was reading*, for example, is somewhat awkward and unlikely, but its status is nevertheless clearly different from the sharply ungrammatical **the label off which she took.* The alternation shown in [33] is restricted to certain combinations involving *through* and *over. Over* occurs readily as a particle elsewhere: *He knocked over the vase / *it* ~ *He knocked the vase / it over. Through*, however, is a somewhat marginal member of the particle class: as an intransitive preposition it generally follows the object, but it is found as a particle in *She was determined to see through the project* ("see it through to completion"), which contrasts with the transitive preposition use in *She quickly saw through his little game* ("perceived the true nature of it").

6.3 Verbal idioms containing intransitive prepositions

6.3.1 Lexicalisation and fossilisation

The intransitive prepositions that are found in verbal idioms are ones which in free combinations have locative meanings: *in, out, up, down*, etc. In free combinations it is usually possible to add further locative specification:

[34]			
i	*I jumped off (the wall).*	*I fell in (the dam).*	*I climbed down (the tree).*
ii	*I ran ahead (of him).*	*I got out (of the box).*	*I jumped down (from the wall).*

In [i] the optional elements are NPs (so that *off, in*, and *down* will be transitive prepositions when the NPs are present). In [ii] they are PPs.

Such specification may be omitted because it is recoverable anaphorically, from previous mention: *She climbed onto the wall and immediately jumped off* (understood as "jumped off the wall"); *She walked with us most of the way, and then suddenly ran ahead* (understood as "ran ahead of us"). Often, however, it is simply implicit in the context. The examples in [35] will be understood in suitable contexts as if they included the parenthesised words:

[35] i a. *I didn't put sugar in (your tea).* b. *I'll take the tablecloth off (the table).*
ii a. *Don't go away (from me/here).* b. *I must put the cat out (of the house).*
iii a. *Come back (to me / this place).* b. *He put his coat on (himself / his body).*

There is considerable variation in the naturalness or likelihood of including such contextually derivable specification. In [35], for example, the filled out versions in the [b] cases are less likely than those in [a]. Including the parenthesised parts of the [b] examples, especially [iiib], would normally be regarded as involving an unnecessary specification of the obvious.

We find a great range of meanings with prepositional verbs, from those where there is still a transparently clear connection with the literal locative relation to others which are much more opaque. Consider, for example, the seven different senses of *take in* illustrated in [36], where [i] is clear from the sense of *take* and the contextual interpretation of *in*, while [vii] is idiomatic and completely unpredictable from the meanings of *take* and *in*.

[36] i *We'd better take in the children's toys.* ["move into the house"]
ii *They supplement their income by taking in students.* ["renting to"]
iii *I've taken in your trousers, because they were too loose.* ["tighten"]
iv *Grammar takes in syntax and morphology but not phonology.* ["includes"]
v *I thought we might take in a show after dinner.* ["see"]
vi *I was too tired to take in what she was saying.* ["grasp"]
vii *I'm not surprised he was taken in: he's as gullible as a child.* ["deceived"]

One type of extended meaning commonly found involves what we have called aspectuality (Ch. 3, §3.2), especially that of completion or perfectivity. This is illustrated in [37i], while the examples in [ii] have such other aspectual meanings as repetition and duration:

[37] i *break up, catch up, come up (to someone), cut down, drink up/down, eat up, fill up, fizzle out, give up, lace up, round up, sell out, shrivel up, wear out, write up*
ii *beaver away, fire away, work away; carry on, go on, keep on, push on*

Verb + intransitive preposition idioms are an important feature of the English vocabulary; there are great numbers of them, and they are very frequent indeed, especially in informal speech. They tend to involve simple everyday verbs rather than more learned ones, and common verbs like *bring, come, give, go, have, let, make, put, take*, etc., are found in large numbers of such idioms, often with a considerable range of meanings, as illustrated above for *take in*.

Lexicalisation may be accompanied in varying degrees by what we are calling **fossilisation**, the loss of the ability to undergo the range of manipulation found with comparable free combinations. Three areas where such loss is found are:

(a) Preposing (*Down it went* ~ **Down it broke*)

In free combinations, intransitive locative prepositions can generally appear in front position, with postposing of the subject if it is not a personal pronoun: *Up went the balloon*; *Down they glided*; *In came Kim*; *Away we ran.* A relatively small number of verbal idioms are found in this construction, as in [38i], where the concept of movement in a given direction, physical or metaphorical, remains fairly strong, but with the majority such preposing is excluded, as illustrated in [ii]:

[38] i *Down it went.* *Off came his shirt.* *Up go the ratings.* *In went the sun.*
ii **Down it broke.* **Off went the milk.* **Up pay the patrons.* **In gave the bandit.*

(b) Insertion of adjunct (*climbed slowly up* ~ **gave slowly up*)

In free combinations, adjuncts (e.g. of manner) can be inserted before an intransitive preposition in complement function, but this possibility is greatly reduced in idioms, as seen in:

[39] i a. *She climbed slowly up.* b. *She led him triumphantly out.*
ii a. **She gave slowly up.* b. **She knocked him triumphantly out.*

Adjuncts before intransitive prepositions are not excluded altogether: we can have *They pressed resolutely on* or *It faded gradually away*, contrasting with **They carried resolutely on* or **He passed gradually away* ("died"), and so on. But in general the close association between the verb + preposition sequence inhibits this kind of separation, and the further the meaning is from that of a literal combination the less likely it is that such insertion will be acceptable.

(c) Order alternation (*took off the label* ~ *took the label off*)

As we noted in §6.2, intransitive prepositions can generally either precede or follow the object of the verb: compare [27ia/iia], *She took <u>off</u> <u>the label</u>* ~ *She took <u>the label</u> <u>off</u>.* There are some cases, however, where the intransitive preposition can only precede the object (unless the latter can have the form of an unstressed personal pronoun), and this restriction can be seen as a clear case of fossilisation: the lexical unity bars the usual syntactic separability. In the following examples the order alternation is permitted in one sense of the verb + prepositional particle combination but not, or at best only very marginally, in another – and the fossilised one is clearly further removed from the literal meaning of the components:

[40] i a. *He carried out the chairs.* b. *He carried the chairs out.*
ii a. *He carried out his threat.* b. ?*He carried his threat out.*
iii a. *He put on his hat.* b. *He put his hat on.*
iv a. *He put on an act.* b. ?*He put an act on.*

Other examples of idioms where the particle normally precedes the object are given in:

[41]

buy in [food]	*drum up* [support]	*find out* ["discover"]
fork out [money]	*give forth* [sound]	*give off* [sound]
hold out [prospects]	*knock up* [score in sport]	*lay out* [requirements]
let out [cry]	*pass out* [samples]	*pour out* [feelings]
put down [plane: "land"]	*put out* [leaf, of plant]	*put up* [resistance]
ride out [recession]	*start up* [conversation]	

There are also cases where the intransitive preposition must follow the object (unless the latter is heavy) – and where the preposition is therefore by definition not a particle. Most of these involve free combinations as in our earlier *She brought the bed downstairs* ([24iib]). But the restriction does apply to some idioms, and again we can find combinations where alternation is possible in one sense but not another:

[42] i a. *I turned off the tap.* b. *I turned the tap off.*
ii a. **His arrogance turned off people.* b. *His arrogance turned people off.*

Examples of idioms virtually requiring the order verb – object – preposition are:[49]

[43]	*answer back*	*ask round/over*	*boss about/around*
	draw out [person]	*get up* [out of bed]	*have down* [as guest]
	have on ["tease"]	*have out*	*leave alone*
	order about	*take aback*	*work over* ["beat up"]

6.3.2 Constructions containing verb + intransitive preposition idioms

Verbal idioms of this kind are found in the following structures (again leaving aside those containing subordinate clauses as complement):

[44]	I	verb – prep	*He gave in.*
	II	verb – prep – O	*She mixed up [the tickets].*
	III	verb – O^i – prep – O^d	*I ran [him] off [another copy].*
	IV	verb – prep – transitive PP	*We look forward [to your visit].*
	V	verb – O – prep – transitive PP	*I let [her] in [on a little secret].*
	VI	verb – prep – (*as*) PC	*She ended up [(as) captain].*
	VII	verb – O – prep – [*as* + PC]	*This showed [him] up [as spineless].*

'Prep' here stands for the intransitive preposition functioning as a complement of the verb.

Structure I: verb – prep, as in *give in*

This is an extremely common pattern; we give only a small sample of such idioms:

[45]	*back down*	*bear up*	*branch out*	*butt in*	*catch on*
	climb down	*close in*	*come apart*	*come on*	*come to*
	crop up	*die down*	*die out*	*drag on*	*fall out*
	get by	*grow up*	*move on*	*own up*	*pass away*
	pay up	*settle down*	*sit down*	*sit up*	*take off*

Structure II: verb – prep – O, as in *mix up [the tickets]*

The examples given here all allow the PP to precede the object (*mix up the tickets*) or follow it (*mix the tickets up*); for examples restricted to one or other order, see [40–43] above:

[46]	*beat up*	*bring about*	*bring up*	*call off*	*cast aside*
	cross off	*cut back*	*dig up*	*dream up*	*explain away*
	fight off	*fill out*	*give back*	*have back*	*head off*
	hold up	*lay on*	*let off*	*live down*	*make up*
	pay back	*put down*	*read out*	*seal off*	*set back*

[49] One tendency worth noting is for intransitive prepositions with locative meaning to be able to precede the object with verbs involving motion rather than state: *She put/kept her hat on* but *She put/*kept on her hat*; *I took/left the curtains down* but *I took/*left down the curtains.*

Just as numerous ordinary verbs have dual transitivity, so there are verb + intransitive preposition idioms that occur with or without an object: *I gave up the attempt* or *I gave up.*

Structure III: verb – O^i – prep – O^d, as in *run* [*him*] *off* [*another copy*]

[47]	*bring up*	*get in*	*give back*	*order in*	*pack up*
	pass down	*pay back*	*send over*	*serve out*	*write out*

The meanings of such combinations are at the more transparent end of the spectrum, and indeed *bring up* and *pass down* can be regarded as free combinations. In all of them there is alternation with a prepositional construction with *to* or *for*: *I'll give you back your money* ~ *I'll give your money back to you*; *I'll get you in some food* ~ *I'll get some food in for you.* With two objects, there are in principle three positions for the intransitive PP:

[48] i *I still have to pay back* [*my father*] [*that loan*]. [PP – O^i – O^d]
ii *I still have to pay* [*my father*] *back* [*that loan*]. [O^i – PP – O^d]
iii *I still have to pay* [*my father*] [*that loan*] *back.* [O^i – O^d – PP]

But [ii], with the PP between the two objects, is much the most usual; [i] is not possible if the indirect object is an unstressed personal pronoun (as it is very likely to be in this relatively complex structure), and [iii] requires that both objects be quite short.

Structure IV: verb – prep – transitive PP, as in *look forward* [*to your visit*]

The idiom here contains verb + intransitive preposition + transitive preposition. As with prepositional verbs, we take the transitive preposition to belong syntactically with the following NP, so that *look* has two PP complements, one consisting of the intransitive preposition alone, the other of the transitive preposition together with its object. In this example, the second PP can be separated from the first by an adjunct (*I was looking forward eagerly to her return*) or by fronting in a relative clause (*It's not the sort of event to which you'd expect him to be looking forward so eagerly*). Others show varying degrees of fossilisation: those marked 'F' in the list below are unlikely to be found with fronting of the transitive preposition (compare *the difficulty which we had run up against*, where the preposition is stranded, with the barely possible fronted version ?*the difficulty against which we had run up*). Again as with prepositional verbs, there is often a related passive whose subject corresponds to the object of the preposition: *Her return had been eagerly looked forward to*; '–P' indicates that such passives are of low acceptability.

[49]	*cash in on*	*come down on* F	*come up with* –P F	*cry out for* –P
	cut down on F	*face up to*	*fall back on* –P	*fit in with* –P
	get along with –P	*get by on* –P	*get on without* –P F	*go off with* –P
	hold out for –P	*keep up with* –P F	*lash out at*	*lead up to* F
	look out for F	*make up for* F	*own up to*	*put up with* F
	run up against F	*settle up with*	*stand up to*	*tie in with* –P

Structure V: verb – O – prep – transitive PP, as in *let* [*her*] *in* [*on a little secret*]

This is the transitive counterpart of Structure IV. For the most part the object precedes the PPs: *She put* [*his bad temper*] *down* [*to stress*], not **She put down* [*his bad temper*] [*to stress*], but there are a few items which allow the object to follow the intransitive PP: *He played off* [*one*] [*against the other*]. Passive subjects always correspond to the object of the verb, never that of the preposition: *His bad temper was put down to stress*, not **Stress was put his bad temper down to*. 'F' again indicates that the transitive preposition resists movement to front position or foregrounding: **the shock for which he intended to let me in*.

[50]	*bring in on* F	*fob off on(to)*	*fob off with*	*give up to*
	help on with F	*let in for* F	*let in on* F	*play off against*
	put down to F	*put up to* F	*take out on*	*take up on* F

Structure VI: verb – prep – (as) PC, as in *end up* [(*as*) *captain*]

There are relatively few idioms of this kind, and we therefore group together those where the final element is an ordinary PC (*It turned out* [*better than we had expected*]) and those where it is marked by *as* (*He came across/over* [*as rather indecisive*]).

[51]	*come across as*	*come over as*	*end up (as)*	*finish up (as)*
	step down as	*take over as*	*turn out*	*wind up (as)*

The annotation '(*as*)' here indicates *as* may occur when the predicative is an NP, but not when it is an AdjP: *She ended up broken-hearted / captain / as captain.*

Structure VII: verb – O – prep – [*as* + PC], as in *show* [*him*] *up* [*as spineless*]

This is the transitive counterpart of Structure VI, with the object now the predicand of the predicative. Again, there are few idioms of this kind and with the somewhat marginal exception of *make out* (*?They made it out worse than it was*) the predicative is oblique, complement to *as* or *for*:

[52]	*give up for*	*lay down as*	*pass off as*	*put down as*
	rule out as	*set up as*	*write off as*	

6.4 Verbal idioms containing NP + transitive preposition

We are concerned here with idioms like the underlined sequences in:

[53] i *She lost patience* [*with the secretary*].
ii *They cast doubt* [*on his motives*].
iii *We lost sight* [*of our goal*].
iv *They made good use* [*of the extra time*].

The main point of syntactic interest in idioms of this form concerns the passive. The four idioms cited are all different in that [i] takes no passive, [ii] an ordinary passive, [iii] a prepositional passive, and [iv] a passive of either kind:

[54]	ORDINARY PASSIVE	PREPOSITIONAL PASSIVE
i	**Patience was lost with the secretary.*	**The secretary was lost patience with.*
ii	*Doubt was cast on his motives.*	**His motives were cast doubt on.*
iii	**Sight was lost of our goal.*	*Our goal was lost sight of.*
iv	*Good use was made of the extra time.*	*The extra time was made good use of.*

The following idioms are classified according to which of these four types they belong to:

[55]

NO PASSIVE	ORDINARY	PREPOSITIONAL	EITHER TYPE
cross swords with	*cast doubt on*	*catch sight of* F	*make a fuss of*
curry favour with	*do justice to*	*give the lie to*	*make an example of*
find favour with	*give credence to*	*give way to*	*make use of*
get the better of F	*keep tabs on*	*lay claim to*	*pay attention to*
give birth to	*make an attempt on*	*lay hold of* F	*pay tribute to*
give the lie to	*make mention of*	*lose sight of*	*put a stop to*
lose patience with	*raise an objection to*	*lose touch with* F	*see much/little of*
make friends with	*shed tears over* F	*make fun of* F	*take advantage of*
		make love to	*take exception to*
		pay court to	*take note of*
		set eyes on	

As before, 'F' indicates that the idiom is fossilised to the extent that the preposition resists fronting or foregrounding: *those with whom he had crossed swords*, but hardly $^{?}$*those of whom he had got the better*. The prepositional passive here is exceptional, for elsewhere it is found only when the preposition immediately follows the verb: compare *Her article was referred to*, but not **Her article was referred the students to* (matching active *They referred the students to her article*).

On a separate dimension we find differences in the extent to which it is possible to add dependents to the post-verbal noun. Some virtually exclude all additions: *cross swords with, give birth to, catch sight of, set eyes on, put a stop to*. Others allow limited adjectival modification: *cast serious doubt on, keep close tabs on, make passionate love to, take careful note of*. Others again allow determiners and post-head dependents: *lose all patience with, pay more attention than ever to*. Note that while the prepositional passive disfavours modification of the noun, it certainly does not exclude it:

[56] *The report highlighted the poor underground conditions and warned they had to be taken particular note of during the tunnel's design phase.*

6.5 Other types of verbal idiom

Verb + adjective

Idioms including adjectives are illustrated in:

[57] i *break even, come true, hold good/true, lie low, stand tall, work loose*
ii *He cut short the debate.* ~ *He cut the debate short.*
iii *She didn't see/think fit to respond.* *I'll make sure it's ready.*

The items in [i] belong in the complex-intransitive construction: *We broke even* has the structure S–P–PC^{s}. There are also, as noted in §5.4, numerous combinations like *blush scarlet, lie flat* which are not strictly idioms in that the meanings are derivable from the parts, but which allow very little choice in the adjective position. *Short* in [ii] is a particle; a few other adjectival particles are found in non-idiomatic *cut open, make clear, put right/straight*. The items in [iii] are syntactically exceptional, for normally extrapositional *it* would be required (cf. *She didn't think it necessary to respond; I'll make it obvious that I'm dissatisfied*); with *make clear*, the *it* is optional: *He made (it) clear that he meant business.*

- Verb + verb

[58] i *give* NP *to understand*; *let* NP *be*, *make* NP *do*; *knock/send* NP *flying*
ii *make do with*; *have done with*, *put paid to*

The idioms in [i] fit into what we call the complex catenative construction (Ch. 14, §3): the verb has two complements, an object and a non-finite clause. The idioms in [ii] cannot be matched with free combinations of words of the same kind, and it is best to treat the two verbs as forming a verb complex functioning as a single predicator. Similarly with *He let slip that he hadn't read it*; *I let go of the rope.* Some speakers have the alternations *He let slip the opportunity* ~ *He let the opportunity slip* and *He let go the rope* ~ *He let the rope go*; here *slip* and *go* are particles.

- Verb + noun, verb + PP

Innumerable idioms contain nouns (or NPs) or PPs: *He bought a pup*; *I'll put it on the back burner*; and so on. Some of these license complements that the verb on its own can't take, such as the subordinate clauses in: *I've half a mind to accept your offer*; *He had in mind to change his will*; *It brought to light how devious he had been.*[50]

7 Light verbs

7.1 General issues

Light verbs – or, more properly, light uses of verbs – are illustrated in the right-hand column of:

[1]	ASSOCIATED VERB ALTERNANT	LIGHT VERB ALTERNANT
i	a. *She kissed him.*	b. *She gave him a kiss.*
ii	a. *I calculated the costs.*	b. *I made a calculation of the costs.*
iii	a. *He looked at my draft.*	b. *He had a look at my draft.*
iv	a. *We rested.*	b. *We took a rest.*
v	a. *She danced.*	b. *She did a dance.*

As used here, the underlined verbs are semantically 'light' in the sense that their contribution to the meaning of the predication is relatively small in comparison with that of their complements. This is evident from the fact that the [b] examples have syntactically simpler alternants, [a], which do not contain the light verbs. The main semantic content is located not in the light verb, but in the noun functioning as head of the direct object. In the central cases, this noun is related to a verb: the lexical bases are often identical, as with *kiss*, *look*, and *rest*, or the noun may be derived from the verb by affixation, as with *calculation*. Generally, the verb is morphologically more basic than the noun, but it is not invariably so: in the pair *I showered* and *I had a shower*, for example, it would be implausible to take *shower* as primarily a verb. For this reason we refer to the verbs in

[50] There are also a large number of idioms containing non-referential *it* as object of a verb or preposition, as in *They don't hit it off* or *We'll have to make the best of it*: see Ch. 17, §2.5.

the [a] examples as the **associated verb**, a term which leaves open the issue of whether the verb or noun is more basic.

The light use of the above verbs contrasts with their ordinary use, where they have their full semantic content, as in *She gave him an orange*; *I made a paper-hat*; *He had a Rolls-Royce*; *We took all we could find*. In some cases there is ambiguity between the two uses. An obvious example is *I had a bath*: the light verb interpretation is "I bathed (in a bath)", while the ordinary verb interpretation is "I owned a bath". Less obvious is *I had a shave*: the light interpretation is "I shaved (myself)", the ordinary one "I had someone shave me". Or again, for *He gave me a lick* the light interpretation is "He (a dog, perhaps) licked me", the ordinary one: "He allowed me to have a lick (of his ice-cream, perhaps)". Some of the verb + NP + preposition sequences covered in §6.4 involve light verbs: *make mention of* (compare *She made mention of an earlier draft* ~ *She mentioned an earlier draft*), *raise an objection to*, *make use of*, *pay attention to*, *take note of*. But the combination of light verb and noun is fairly productive, and by no means all such combinations can be regarded as lexical units.

Syntactic and semantic differences between the constructions

The use of a light verb and noun tends to yield a significant increase in syntactic versatility over that of the associated verb construction. Most importantly, it generally allows for dependents to be added to the noun, allowing a considerably greater range of elaboration by modifiers and determiners. Consider, for example:

[2] i *She gave him an unusually passionate kiss.*
ii *We took a well-earned rest.* *She had an enduring influence on him.*

Example [i] is less awkward than *She kissed him unusually passionately*, while *well-earned* and *enduring* in [ii] have no close adverbial counterparts that could be used with the associated verbs. A special case of such dependents involves quantification:

[3] i *I've already had two showers today.*
ii *She made three very astute comments on his suggestion.*
iii *He gave a scream.*

Here [i] is equivalent to *I've already showered twice today*, but [ii] is not equivalent to *She commented three times very astutely on his suggestion*: the latter quantifies the event (three acts of commenting), whereas [3ii] quantifies the product of the event – light *make* here is like the ordinary *make* of *She made a model car* in that the object has a factitive role, with the comments, like the car, being produced by the action.[51] The most usual determiner with light verbs is the indefinite article, and this too introduces quantification, which may make the meaning somewhat different from that of the associated verb construction. Thus [3iii], for example, is not fully equivalent to *He screamed*, for it involves a necessarily quite short and continuous event, while *He screamed* is not so restricted, covering also cases where the screaming is prolonged and intermittent. Similarly, [1ib] specifies a single kiss whereas [ia] does not, and hence could apply to a situation where she covered him with kisses.

[51] Note that the light verb could appear in a relative clause modifying the noun: *The comments which she made on his plan infuriated him.*

Semantic differences are particularly common with *have*, as illustrated in such examples as:

[4] i a. *He drank my milk.* b. *He had a drink of my milk.*
ii a. *He walked in/to the park.* b. *He had a walk in/*to the park.*
iii a. *He lay down.* b. *He had a lie down.*
iv a. *He pitied them.* b. *He had/took pity on them.*

In [i] the [a] version conveys that he drank it all, whereas in [b] he drank only part of it. In [ii] both allow *in the park* as a location adjunct, but only [a] allows *to the park* as goal: [b] presents the situation as an activity, more specifically a recreational one, whereas verbal *walk* is more general, covering cases of accomplishments. In [iii] the light verb version is again more specific: it is used when the purpose of lying down is to rest – not, for example, to undergo a medical examination. The difference is greater in [iv], where [a] describes a state, whereas [b] is dynamic: he felt pity and did something for them.

Complementation

Where there are elements following the noun, as in [1iib/iiib], there is some indeterminacy as to whether they are complements of the noun itself or of the light verb. Consider, for example:

[5] i *He gave a demonstration of this technique to the postgraduates.*
ii *He gave the postgraduates a demonstration of this technique.*

Are the underlined PPs in [i] complements of *demonstration* or of *give*? Semantically it makes no difference, precisely because light *give* contributes so little meaning; and syntactically there is little evidence to resolve the issue. The noun can certainly take these complements in other constructions (cf. *His demonstration of this technique to the postgraduates was impressive*), but the alternation between [i] and [ii], which unquestionably has *the postgraduates* as a complement of *give*, argues that *to the postgraduates* in [i] can likewise be interpreted as one. The data from relativisation suggests that both PPs can be taken as complements of either the noun or the verb:

[6] i *the demonstration which he gave of this technique to the postgraduates*
ii *the demonstration of this technique to the postgraduates which he gave last week*
iii *the demonstration of this technique which he gave to the postgraduates last week*

In [i] both PPs are complements of *give*, in [ii] they are both complements of *demonstration*, and in [iii] the first is a complement of *demonstration*, the second of *give*. We will assume, therefore, that for the most part both analyses are valid, and focus here on the one where such post-nominal elements are complements of the light verb.

In general, the complements are the same as those of the noun when it is used independently of the light verb. These may of course be the same as those for the associated verb, as in [7i–ii], but they may be different, as in [7iii–vi]:

[7] i a. *His appeal for clemency failed.* b. *He made an appeal for clemency.*
ii *He appealed for clemency.*
iii a. *It was my third try at opening it.* b. *I had a try at opening it.*
iv *I tried to open it.*
v a. *I enjoyed my tour of the factory.* b. *I made a tour of the factory.*
vi *I toured the factory.*

There is, however, a little more to it than this. In the first place, properties of the light verb in its ordinary use may affect the complementation. In particular, *give*, *make*, and *do* are ditransitive verbs, and under certain conditions take an indirect object in their light use too, whereas nouns of course do not take any objects as complement: *He gave me a description of the thief*; *He made the staff a new offer*; *He did us a report on the accident.*

Secondly we sometimes find PPs which could not occur with the noun independently of the light verb:

[8]	i	a. **His blame for it on Kim is unfair.*	b. *He put/laid the blame for it on Kim.*
	ii	*He blamed it on Kim.*	
	iii	a. **I enjoy a good read of his books.*	b. *I had a read of his book.*
	iv	*I read his book.*	

In [ib] *on Kim* can only be a complement of *put/lay*, not of *blame*, and the preposition *on* reflects that of the associated verb, as seen in [ii]. With *read*, the *of* in [iiib] is the default preposition found when its complement corresponds to the direct object of an associated verb, matching that in [7v] above, but elsewhere the noun *read* does not normally take a complement corresponding to the object of the verb, as we see from [8iiia].

7.2 Survey of the main light verbs

Give

Some examples of light *give* are:

[9]	i	a. *She sighed.*	b. *She gave a sigh.*
	ii	a. *She kissed him.*	b. *She gave him a kiss.*
	iii	a. *She advised him.*	b. *She gave him advice.*
	iv	a. *She described him (to me).*	b. *She gave (me) a description of him.*

She gave a sigh

In [9ib] light *give* has just one complement other than the subject, and it is normally impossible to add a second as indirect object: **She gave me a sigh.* The complementation here is therefore quite different from that of ordinary *give*, and reflects the properties of the associated verb *sigh*, and the noun derived from it, which do not license an additional complement. In [10] we give a sample of items that behave in essentially the same way; they denote bodily actions, and many – like *sigh* – involve the ingress or egress of air:[52]

[10]	*cough*	*fart*	*gasp*	*grunt*	*hiss*	*laugh*
	lurch	*moan*	*scowl*	*shrug*	*shudder*	*squeak*

She gave him a kiss

In [9iib] the direct object of the associated verb appears as indirect object of *give*. The latter still differs from ordinary *give*, however, in that there is no alternation with a *to* phrase: **She gave a kiss to him.* Some further items like *kiss* are:

[11]	*bath*	*clout*	*cuddle*	*hit*	*hug*	*kick*
	punch	*push*	*shower*	*squeeze*	*wash*	*wipe*

[52] *Scowl* differs from the others in that the associated verb optionally takes *at* + NP, and this NP appears as indirect object of the light verb: *He gave me a scowl.*

This is a homogeneous set: semantically, they involve physical action in which the direct object of the associated verb has a patient role; syntactically, the nouns do not normally take PP complements (**Her kiss of him was passionate*).

She gave him advice

Example [9iiib] also has an indirect object corresponding to the direct object of [a], but this time there is alternation with a *to* phrase: *She gave advice to him.* A few items following this pattern are given in [12]:

[12]	*answer*	*consideration*	*encouragement*	*help*	*reply*

Except for the first and last these are non-count nouns (like *advice*). Some take PP complements in other constructions: *consideration* and *encouragement* indeed allow *of* (*Further consideration of the matter is clearly called for*), but *of* is not possible here with light *give.*

She gave (me) a description of him

Finally, in [9ivb] the direct object of the associated verb appears as complement to *of,* not as indirect object – because that function is reserved for the NP which in the associated verb construction appears in the optional *to* phrase, *She described him (to me)*. We also have the prepositional alternant *She gave a description of him to me.* Other nouns following this pattern include:

[13]	*definition*	*demonstration*	*explanation*	*illustration*	*imitation*
	impersonation	*indication*	*performance*	*portrayal*	*presentation*

Make

Ordinary *make* takes a subject, direct object, and optionally either an indirect object or a *for* phrase. Light *make* is seen in:

[14]			
i	a. *He leapt from the balcony.*	b. *He made a leap from the balcony.*
ii	a. *He inspected the wreckage.*	b. *He made an inspection of the wreckage.*
iii	a. *He offered us $100.*	b. *He made us an offer of $100.*
iv	a. **He donated them $100.*	b. *He made them a donation of $100.*

He made a leap from the balcony

Example [14i] illustrates the case where the complementation matches that of the noun and of the associated verb. There are many examples of this kind; in the following sample the parentheses show the kind of complements found, with 'inf' indicating a *to*-infinitival clause, as in *He made a promise to donate $100*, and '*that*' a declarative content clause, as in *He made a recommendation that the offer be rejected*:

[15]	*appeal* (*to*)	*attempt* (inf)	*boast* (*that*)	*call* (*on*)
	comment (*about*/*on*)	*dash* (*for*)	*decision* (*that*/inf)	*discovery* (*that*)
	escape (*from*)	*fuss* (*about*)	*grab* (*at*)	*guess* (*at*)
	improvement (*on*)	*inquiry* (*about*/*into*)	*objection* (*to*)	*observation* (*that*)
	reference (*to*)	*remark* (*about*)	*retreat* (*from . . . to*)	*start* (*on*)

He made an inspection of the wreckage

In [14iib] the NP corresponding to the direct object of the associated verb is governed by a preposition, the one that the noun takes when it appears without *make.*[53] With the following nouns the preposition is *of* unless otherwise indicated:

[16]	*analysis*	*attack (on)*	*calculation*	*choice*	*contribution*
	copy	*disclosure*	*investment*	*note*	*payment*
	reduction (in)	*request (for)*	*search*	*study*	*survey*

He made us an offer of $100

Example [14iiib] has an indirect object – but its semantic role is that of recipient, like that of the indirect object of the verb *offer* in [14iiia], not beneficiary, the role found with ordinary *make* (as in *He made me a cake*). This construction is then generalised to certain cases where the associated verb does not take an indirect object, as in [14iv], where *donate* takes a *to* phrase (*He donated $100 to them*). Example [14ivb] is perhaps slightly marginal in acceptability (*He made a donation to them of $100* is more likely), but it is much more acceptable than [14iva]. Similar items are marked with '?' in the following list:

[17]	?*confession*	?*consignment*	*gift*	*payment*
	proposal (that/inf)	?*protest (about)*	?*suggestion (that)*	

Have and *take*

We consider these two verbs together as there is a considerable overlap in the nouns they take. Sample sets of nouns are as follows:

[18]	*HAVE* OR *TAKE*				
	bath	*break*[54]	*drink*	*guess*	*lick (of)*
	look (at)	*pity (on)*	*rest*	*shave*	*shower*
	sip	*sleep*	*swim*	*walk*	*wash*

[19]	*HAVE* ONLY				
	chat (with)	*cry*	*dream (about)*	*fight (with)*	*grumble*
	influence (on)	*kiss*	*laugh*	*look (for)*	*meeting (with)*
	need (inf/*for*)	*quarrel (with)*	*talk (with)*	*think (about)*	*try (at)*

[20]	*TAKE* ONLY				
	decision (inf)	*dive*	*leap*	*photograph (of)*	*step*

Light *take* is dynamic and normally agentive, whereas *have* has a somewhat wider range of use: compare, for example, *He took a decision to assert himself* (dynamic) and *He has a need to assert himself* (stative). Where both verbs are possible, there is a tendency for *take* to be favoured in AmE, *have* in BrE and AusE.

A number of the nouns combining with *have* are also found with (ordinary) *give* with a causative sense, "cause to have, let have": *He gave me a shave / a read of his newspaper.*

[53] The expression *make an impression on* is exceptional in that the *on* (and indeed the noun *impression* with this sense) is restricted to the *make* construction: *He made a favourable impression on them*, but not **His impression (on them) was favourable.*

[54] Here the associated verb requires complementation: *Let's have/take a break*, but *Let's break (off) for lunch.*

Some of them hardly appear elsewhere (as nouns) and are found in very informal style, especially in AusE: *Can I have a borrow/lend of your pen / a carry of the baby?* or *He gave me a borrow/lend of his pen / a carry of the baby*, but not **I was grateful for the borrow/lend of his pen*, etc.[55]

Do

Light *do* is seen in *She did a somersault / an imitation of her teacher*. Some other nouns:

[21]

cleaning N	*dance*	*dive*	*drawing*	*knitting* N
report (on)	*sewing* N	*sketch (of)*	*sprint*	*tango*
thinking N	*translation (of)*	*turn*	*work* N	*writing* N

Those marked 'N' are non-count nouns, and often occur with *some*: *She did some work.*

Other light verbs

There are various other verbs appearing with a much narrower range of nouns: *offer an apology / a suggestion*; *pay attention (to) / a call (on) / a visit (to)*; *put the blame on / an end/stop to*; *raise an objection (to)*.

8 Verbs with multiple patterns of complementation

Most verbs allow more than one complementation, i.e. they occur in two or more constructions differing in respect of the complements. For example, *make* occurs with just a direct object in *They made some cakes*, with indirect and direct object in *They made me a filing-cabinet*, with object + predicative in *They made me impatient*, and so on. This section examines a selection of such cases of multiple complementation where the verb meaning remains constant or exhibits a systematic change, and where the same contrast applies to a number of verbs. We exclude from consideration at this point alternations between canonical clause constructions and various non-canonical ones such as the passive and the existential, as these are dealt with in Ch. 16; we also continue to exclude cases involving complements with the form of finite or non-finite clauses.

The majority of these patterns of contrasting complementation will be dealt with under three headings: transitive vs intransitive (§8.1), ditransitive vs monotransitive (§8.2), and further core vs non-core contrasts (§8.3). Each covers four main types, as illustrated summarily below.

Transitive/intransitive contrasts

[1]

	$S_{intr} = S_{trans}$		$S_{intr} = O_{trans}$	
I	*They shot him.* *They shot at him.*	II	*The sun radiates heat.* *Heat radiates from the sun.*	[O vs PP comp]
III	*She drank some water.* *She drank.*	IV	*He broke the vase.* *The vase broke.*	[+O vs –O]

The four transitive/intransitive pairs here differ on two cross-cutting dimensions. In I–II the contrast is between an object (*him*, *heat*) and a non-core complement with the

[55] *Think* appears only with *have*: *I had a think about it*, but not **He gave me a think about it* or **That was a good think* (cf. *That's good thinking*; *That's an interesting thought*).

form of a PP, while in III–IV it is simply between the presence and the absence of an object (*some water, the vase*). On another dimension, I and III have it in common that the subject is unaffected, i.e. the intransitive subject (*they, she*) is the same, and has the same semantic role, as the transitive subject: $S_{intr} = S_{trans}$. In II and IV, however, the intransitive subject (*heat, the vase*) corresponds to the object of the transitive: $S_{intr} = O_{trans}$.

Ditransitive/monotransitive contrasts

[2]	$O^d_{mono} = O^d_{ditrans}$		$O^d_{mono} = O^i_{ditrans}$	
I	*I gave her the key.*	II	*I envied him his freedom.*	[O vs PP comp]
	I gave the key to her.		*I envied him for his freedom.*	
III	*They offered us $100.*	IV	*They fined us $100.*	[+O^i vs –O^i]
	They offered $100.		*They fined us.*	

The four types here differ on two cross-cutting dimensions that are similar to those in [1]. In I–II the contrast is between a ditransitive construction containing two internal core complements, $O^i + O^d$, and a monotransitive one containing O^d + a non-core complement with the form of a PP, while in III–IV it is between a ditransitive construction and a monotransitive containing just one internal complement (O^d). And in I and III the single object, O^d, of the monotransitive construction (*the key, $100*) corresponds to the direct object of the ditransitive, whereas in II and IV the single object of the monotransitive (*him, us*) corresponds to the indirect object of the ditransitive. Only a small number of verbs are found in constructions II and IV.

Further core/non-core contrasts

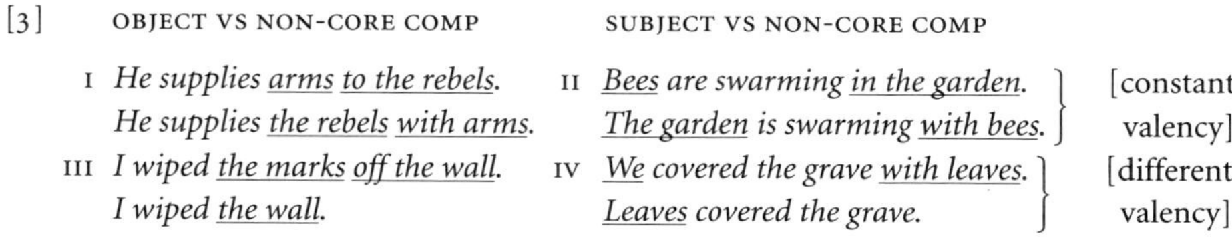

[3]	OBJECT VS NON-CORE COMP		SUBJECT VS NON-CORE COMP	
I	*He supplies arms to the rebels.*	II	*Bees are swarming in the garden.*	[constant valency]
	He supplies the rebels with arms.		*The garden is swarming with bees.*	
III	*I wiped the marks off the wall.*	IV	*We covered the grave with leaves.*	[different valency]
	I wiped the wall.		*Leaves covered the grave.*	

Again the pairs of clauses fit into a two-dimensional pattern. In I–II the matched clauses have the same valency, the same number of complements, but differ in the way they are aligned with the semantic roles, whereas in III–IV one member has one more complement (non-core) than the other. On the other dimension, I and III are alike in that the core complement whose content and semantic role varies is object (*arms* vs *the rebels, the marks* vs *the wall*), whereas in II and IV it is subject (*bees* vs *the garden, we* vs *leaves*).

Separate complements vs combined complement

In addition to the major kind of contrast seen in [1–3] we need to recognise the following relatively minor type:

[4]	i	*She kissed him on the cheek.*	[separate complements]
	ii	*She kissed his cheek.*	[combined complement]

In [i] *him* and *on the cheek* are separate complements of *kiss*, while [ii] has just a single internal complement – but the content of the single complement incorporates that of both internal complements of [i]. Contrasts of this kind are discussed in §8.4.

In many cases a verb will enter into more than one of the above contrasts:

		a.	b.
[5]	i	a. *They sold us the house.*	b. *He was dripping blood.*
	ii	a. *They sold the house.*	b. *He was dripping with blood.*
	iii	a. *The house sold.*	b. *Blood was dripping from him.*

With *sell* [ia] and [iia] show contrast III of [2], while [iia] and [iiia] show contrast IV of [1]. With *drip*, the contrast between [ib] and [iib] belongs under I of [1], while that between [iib] and [iiib] belongs under II of [3]. In the interests of simplicity of presentation we will focus in what follows on the contrasting pairs rather than attempt to bring together for particular verbs the full range of constructions in which they appear.

8.1 Transitive/intransitive contrasts

There are a great number of dual-transitivity verbs in English, verbs which occur in both transitive and intransitive constructions – such verbs greatly outnumber those that are restricted to just one or other of the two constructions. We look in turn at the four types of contrast distinguished in [1] above.

8.1.1 Type I: *They shot him* vs *They shot at him*

In contrasts of this type an NP appears either as direct object of the verb, yielding a transitive construction, or as complement of a preposition, yielding an intransitive, while the subject remains constant. There are several different cases of this contrast.

(a) Conative intransitives

		a.	b.
[6]	i	a. *The horse kicked me.*	b. *The horse kicked at me.*
	ii	a. *He cut the meat.*	b. *He cut at the meat.*

The intransitives here are known as **conatives** in that they imply endeavour in contrast to the success expressed in the transitives. Example [ib] says that the horse kicked in my direction, as though trying to kick me, whereas [ia] says that it did make contact. In [ib] he performed a cutting action on the meat, but it doesn't say that he succeeded in cutting through it, as in [iia]. Similarly for the *shoot* pair: in *They shot him* he was hit, whereas in *They shot at him* they may have missed – and use of the prepositional construction rather than the simpler transitive will often implicate that they did miss. Other verbs found in such contrasts include:

[7]	*claw*	*hit*	*nibble*	*poke*	*push*
	smell	*sniff*	*spray*	*squirt*	*strike*

The preposition is generally *at*, but *on* is sometimes also possible: *He nibbled his biscuit* vs *He nibbled at/on his biscuit.* The meaning difference between transitive and intransitive is perhaps not so clear here, but it can be brought out by noting that we can say *He nibbled his biscuit away* but not **He nibbled at/on his biscuit away.* Compare similarly *She sipped her wine* vs *She sipped at her wine*: even the transitive involves little intake of wine, but it is still potentially greater than with the preposition.

(b) Directional movement

[8] i a. *She climbed the tree.* b. *She climbed up the tree.*
ii a. *We swam the river.* b. *We swam across the river.*
iii a. *They fled the building.* b. *They fled from the building.*

There is generally less objective difference between transitive and prepositional constructions here. In some cases the transitive conveys a completeness lacking in the prepositional version: [ia], for example, entails that she reached the top of the tree, whereas [ib] does not. Similarly, *They roamed the woods* suggests a fuller coverage of the area than *They roamed in the woods.* The transitive may also suggest a somewhat more significant achievement: if, for example, I use a small stepladder to reach something from a high shelf, I'm more likely to use the prepositional construction *I climbed up the stepladder* than transitive *I climbed the stepladder.* Again, compare *She jumped over the fence/pebble*: with *fence* the transitive version (*She jumped the fence*) is equally natural, but with *pebble* it is not.

In general, the prepositional construction allows a range of prepositions in addition to those where the meaning is close to that of the transitive construction: *She climbed down the tree*; *We swam along the river*; *They fled towards the building.*

(c) Consultation and contest

[9] i a. *Kim met the Dean.* b. *Kim met with the Dean.*
ii a. *Kim will be playing Pat.* b. *Kim will be playing against Pat.*

This pattern is found with a fairly small number of verbs including:

[10] *battle* *box* *consult* *fight* *visit*

Version [9ia] applies to a wider range of situations than [ib]: the latter suggests a meeting arranged for purposes of consultation, whereas the former could also be used of a chance and inconsequential meeting on a bus. In general, such clauses are semantically symmetrical: [ia/ib] entail that the Dean met (with) Pat, and [iia/iib] that Pat will be playing (against) Kim. But there are also some metaphorical uses where the NPs could not be felicitously reversed: *He was battling (with/against) cancer.*

(d) Emission

[11] i a. *He was dripping blood.* b. *He was dripping with blood.*
ii a. *Her voice oozed charm.* b. *Her voice oozed with charm.*

The verbs here denote the emission of a physical substance or, by figurative extension, of an abstract quality. They are a relatively small subset of those found in the Type II contrast dealt with in §8.1.2 below. The transitive construction, unlike the intransitive, allows the addition of a goal, at least with physical emission: *He was dripping blood all over the carpet.*

(e) Others

[12] i a. *They were speaking French.* b. *They were speaking in French.*
ii a. *He always talks politics.* b. *He always talks about politics.*
iii a. *We're flying Qantas.* b. *We're flying by/with Qantas.*

In [i–ii] we have the verbs *speak* and *talk* in construction with NPs denoting languages or subject matter. In [iii] the NP denotes an airline. The final NPs in [iia/iiia] are somewhat marginal instances of the object function, failing the passive test fairly clearly (**Politics must not be spoken over dinner*; **Qantas is flown by nearly half the passengers on this route*), and not allowing replacement by a personal pronoun (**He always talks it* and **We're flying it* are unacceptable with *it* referring to subject matter and an airline).

8.1.2 Type II: *The sun radiates heat* vs *Heat radiates from the sun*

This differs from Type I in that the subject of the intransitive corresponds not to the subject of the transitive but to its object. Further examples are seen in [13]:

[13]	i	a. *His wound was oozing blood.*	b. *Blood was oozing from his wound.*
	ii	a. *The bush sprouted new shoots.*	b. *New shoots sprouted from the bush.*
	iii	a. *The reforms will benefit women.*	b. *Women will benefit from the reforms.*

Most verbs showing this contrast denote the emission of some substance – or some quality, in the case of metaphorical uses, as in *He oozes charm.* The two arguments can be subsumed under the semantic roles of source and theme. In the transitive version, the source is expressed as subject, the theme as object, while in the intransitive the source is expressed as the complement of *from* and the theme as subject. Other verbs belonging in this semantic group include:

[14]	*bleed*	*dribble*	*drip*	*emanate*	*exude*
	leak	*seep*	*spew*	*spurt*	*squirt*

8.1.3 Type III: *He drank some water* vs *He drank*

Type III contrasts are those where the transitive contains an object that is lacking in the intransitive, and the subject remains constant ($S_{intrans} = S_{trans}$). In most pairs of this type, the transitive construction is semantically more basic in that the intransitive is interpreted as having an unexpressed object. For example, *He read* entails that there was something that he read, a book perhaps or some other written text; similarly *He married* entails that he married **someone**. *Read* and *marry* thus inherently involve two arguments though only one need be expressed. The interpretation of the intransitives in such cases therefore requires the recovery of the unexpressed object. In addition, some verbs enter into transitive–intransitive pairs where it is the intransitive that can be regarded as more basic. This is seen in *She smiled* vs *She smiled a wistful smile*, where the latter differs little in meaning from *She smiled wistfully.*

The examples in [15i] illustrate various cases where a basically transitive verb appears in an intransitive construction, while those in [ii] show transitive constructions containing basically intransitive verbs. We do not claim that the categories are exhaustive or that the boundaries between them are always clear.

[15]	i	a. *Apply liberally.* (e.g. "this lotion")	[omission of object in instructions]
		b. *They won.* (e.g. "the match")	[unexpressed definite object]
		c. *I must shave.* ("myself")	[unexpressed reflexive object]
		d. *We had met before.* ("one another")	[unexpressed reciprocal object]
		e. *They clapped.* ("their hands")	[unexpressed body-part object]
		f. *That dog bites.* ("people")	[unexpressed human object]

g. *She doesn't drink.* ("alcohol") [specific category indefinites]
h. *He read for a while.* ("some reading matter") [normal category indefinites]

ii a. *They were talking nonsense.* [extension of intransitive]
b. *He died a long and agonising death.* [extension by cognate object]
c. *She smiled her assent.* [object of conveyed reaction]

The first case is different in kind from the others in that it is a matter of a particular register (a variety of language associated with a limited range of social situations or functions – such as the register of newspaper editorials, sermons, parliamentary debates, etc.). The others all involve lexical properties of particular verbs, and for these we list a sample of verbs that are found in the pattern concerned and, for contrastive purposes, a few that aren't (marked with an asterisk).

(a) Omission of object in instructional register: *Apply liberally*

Intransitives of this kind are characteristic of the register of giving instructions, as in directions for use, recipes, etc. The understood object is identifiable from the context. Very often a written instruction physically accompanies the item in question: [15ia], for example, is taken from the label on a bottle of sunscreen lotion. Alternatively, there may be prior mention of the item: *Trace design on to tracing paper, then transfer __ on to table mat with dressmakers' carbon paper* ("transfer the design").[56] Such intransitives usually occur in imperative clauses, but are also found in non-finite subordinate clauses: *Cook for 15–20 minutes, turning __ once during cooking*; *To open __, pull lever.* As noted above, occurrence in these intransitives need not be specified lexically for individual verbs: it is, rather, a property of this particular register.

(b) Unexpressed definite object: *They won*

The unexpressed object is here recoverable from the context and has a definite interpretation, as in (a); the difference is that this time the omission of the object is not restricted to a given register, but is instead restricted to particular verbs. Intransitive *win* is interpreted as "win a contest", and which contest it was can be determined from the context. In *They played the club champions and won*, for example, it is identifiable as the match they played against the club champions, but equally *They won* could be used in a situation where a match has just been played and it could then be interpreted as implicitly referring to this match even if there had been no overt reference to the match. But the verb *enjoy* cannot similarly be used intransitively, with the object of enjoyment identified in these ways. Thus we cannot have **They played the club champions and enjoyed* ("enjoyed the match"), and if I meet you as you come out of the movies I cannot say **Did you enjoy?* ("enjoy the movie"). Further verbs and examples:

[16]					
i	*answer*	*ask*	*attend*	*drive*	*fail* (test)
	fit	*follow*	*interrupt*	*lead*	*lose* (contest)
	obey	*prosecute*	*pull*	*telephone*	*watch*
ii	Excluded:	**punish*	**teach*	**write*	

[56] As can be seen from this example the instructional register often uses other reduction strategies besides the omission of the object – notably the omission of determiners. Indeed we also find omission of the subject: *Must be diluted before use.* The phenomenon here bears some similarity to the omission of subject + *be* in notices, e.g. *Not for drinking* placed beside a tap.

[17] i *I asked her where it was but she didn't answer. There's a meeting tonight but I can't attend. They've charged him but I don't who's going to prosecute.*
ii **He wants to learn but I shan't teach.*

In [17i] we understand "answer me / my question", "attend the meeting", "prosecute him"; [ii] is ungrammatical in the interpretation "teach him". Some verbs appear in such intransitives only under restricted conditions. For example, I might throw you a ball and say *Catch!* but we don't have prior mention cases like **I threw him the ball but he failed to catch.* Similarly, *Shall I dry?* ("the dishes") is quite acceptable in, say, a context of washing-up, but we would not say **The dishes were still wet so I dried* ("them").

(c) Unexpressed reflexive object: *I must shave*

[18] i	*bathe*	*shave*	*shower*	*wash*	
ii	*disrobe*	*dress*	?*strip*	*undress*	
iii	*cram*	*launch*	*load*	*pack*	[+ goal]
iv	*jerk*	*pull*	*yank*		[+ *free*]
v	*behave*[57]	*hide*	*identify* (*with*)	*prepare*	*worry*
vi	Excluded:	**clothe*	**perjure*		

[19] i a. *We crammed* (*ourselves*) *into the back seat.* b. *He pulled* (*himself*) *free.*
ii a. *They clothed themselves in black.* b. **They clothed in black.*

The salient interpretation of *I must shave* is "I must shave myself". The verbs in [18iii] take a complement with the role of goal (like *into the back seat*) and those in [18iv] take *free* as resultative predicative complement. The intransitive versions are in most cases much more frequent than the overt reflexives; although one can shave or wash others, and so on, the default object is reflexive and there is a strong tendency to leave it unexpressed. This makes it difficult to identify the verbs concerned very precisely. Thus we can have *I must go and wash/bathe/shower*, but a reflexive object is unlikely with *bathe* or *shower* (a possible context might be one where a nurse asks: *Are you able to shower yourself?*); similarly in [ii] an overt reflexive is somewhat marginal with *strip*. We do not include here cases where the presence or absence of a reflexive affects the agentivity of the clause, as in *He got himself arrested* vs *He got arrested*, or *She proved herself reliable* ("showed herself to be") vs *She proved reliable* ("turned out to be").

(d) Unexpressed reciprocal object: *We had met before*

[20] i	*court*	*divorce*	*embrace*	*kiss*	*marry*
ii	*cross*	*hit*	*miss*	*touch*	
iii	*consult*	*fight*	*meet*		
iv	Excluded:	**help*	**love*	**resemble*	

[21] i a. *They kissed* (*each other*) *passionately.* b. *The lines cross* (*each other*) *here.*
ii b. *They resemble each other closely.* b. **They resemble closely.*

[57] With *behave* the overt reflexive is normally restricted to cases of good behaviour: it could be inserted into *They behaved well*, but not *They behaved appallingly*; "well" or the like is understood in examples like *Behave!*, where no manner adjunct is expressed.

One or two of the verbs are semantically symmetrical: *Kim married Pat*, for example, entails *Pat married Kim* (for the primary sense of *marry*). But generally reciprocity is merely common rather than necessary. For example, *Kim kissed Pat* very clearly does not entail *Pat kissed Kim*, as the one kissed can be entirely passive (and can indeed be inanimate: *Kim kissed the cross*). Nor does *Kim divorced Pat* entail *Pat divorced Kim*, since it involves Kim initiating the proceedings, and so on. Again, the intransitive versions tend to be commoner than the reciprocal transitives.

(e) Unexpressed body-part object: *They clapped*

[22] i *blink* (eyes) *clap* (hands) *nod* (head) *shrug* (shoulders)
ii Excluded: **bat* (an eyelid) **crane* (neck) **gnash* (teeth) **stub* (toe)

[23] i a. *I nodded* (*my head*). b. *He shrugged* (*his shoulders*).
ii a. *She craned her neck to see.* b. **She craned to see.*

These verbs denote gestures involving a particular part of the body. The intransitive version is in most cases more common – and it is questionable with such verbs as *squint* and *wink* whether a transitive use with *eye* as object is acceptable at all. One or two cases of the omission of a reflexive object are very similar to the present type (though the verbs denote bodily care rather than gestures): *I shaved* = *I shaved myself*, but both versions will normally be understood as "I shaved my face" (rather than my legs, say); *I washed* = *I washed myself* with both suggesting (though not as strongly) hands, or hands and face.[58]

(f) Unexpressed human object: *That dog bites*

[24] i *admonish* *advise* *caution* *warn*
ii *amaze* *amuse* *disturb* *offend* *please*
iii *bite* *kick* *prick* *sting*
iv Excluded: **alert* **injure* **like*

[25] i a. *I'd advise you against buying it.* b. *I advise against buying it.*
ii a. *I must alert you to a new danger.* b. **I must alert to a new danger.*

We interpret the intransitives as having a human object, but it may be either general (arbitrary people), as in *That dog bites*, or specific, e.g. *you* in particular, as in a salient interpretation of *Take care: it may bite.* The verbs in [24ii–iii] appear more readily in intransitives when the situation is habitual or unactualised – e.g. *He never fails to please*, *I'll aim to please*, but hardly ?*His behaviour at lunch pleased.*

(g) Specific category indefinites: *She doesn't drink*

[26] *bake* *drink* *eat* *expect* *wash*

[27] *Have you eaten yet?* *We're eating at six.* *She's expecting again.*

[58] The relatively recent bodily-care verb *floss* allows omission of a body-part object but doesn't take a reflexive: *I flossed* (*my teeth*)/**myself.* Somewhat similar is *change*, which has an intransitive use with "one's clothes" understood: *I must go and change for dinner. Point* and *wave* characteristically involve a particular body-part (finger and hand respectively), but allow other kinds of objects too, as in *I pointed the ruler at it, She waved a flag to signal that the path was clear*; we will not therefore want to say that intransitive clauses containing these verbs have "finger" and "hand" as part of their meaning.

Intransitive *drink* is ambiguous according as the unexpressed object is understood specifically as alcoholic drink or more generally, as in case (h) below. *Expect* has a special sense (found only in the progressive) where *baby* can be either present or left understood: "She's pregnant again". *Eat* in [27] is likely to be interpreted with some contextually determined meal as implicit argument, though in cases like *He was eating* the interpretation is more general. There are innumerable things one can wash but *I was washing* (ignoring the reflexive interpretation) will generally be interpreted as involving clothes/sheets/towels, items covered by the noun *washing* (as in *I must hang out the washing*). Likewise with *bake*, where the intransitive use applies to cakes, pies, and the like, as opposed, say, to various other kinds of food that can be baked, such as potatoes or apples.

(h) Normal category indefinites: *He read for a while*

[28]	i	*cook*	*darn*	*draw*	*drink*	*drive*	*dust*
		eat	*fly*	*hunt*	*iron*	*knit*	*marry*
		paint	*read*	*sew*	*study*	*teach*	*type*
	ii	Excluded:	**devour*	**fix*	**peruse*		

[29] *They were eating/drinking/*devouring.* *I want to read/*peruse.*

The unexpressed object here is interpreted as an indefinite member of the typical, unexceptional category for the verb in question – reading matter for *read*, food for *eat*, and so on. Thus *He read for a while* wouldn't normally be used of a situation where he was reading short-answer examination questions: this is not the usual kind of reading. Nor would I say *I had been eating* if it had been grass, say: that is too exceptional to be subsumed under the ordinary activity of eating. Similarly, *She spent the afternoon writing* suggests some kind of composition: one would hardly use this if she had been writing labels or addressing envelopes. Because of this kind of restriction, no sharp line can be drawn between the present case and (g) above.

A great many verbs enter into this contrast: the lexical process of extending the use of a basically transitive verb by omission of an indefinite object is very productive. There are differences, however, in how readily a verb occurs in the intransitive construction. As with case (f) above – which is indeed very similar to the present one – the most accommodating contexts tend to be those involving generalisations rather than particular events. Thus *It is better to love than to hate* and *He loves/hates with great passion* are more acceptable than *He's going to love/hate* or *At that time he loved/hated.* Compare similarly *He likes to organise* with *?This morning he organised* or *He would never steal* with *?He had lunch at the castle yesterday and stole when he was left alone.*

With a considerable number of verbs the intransitive construction is characteristically used for an activity and the transitive one for an accomplishment. This is so, for example, with *I ironed* vs *I ironed your shirt*, *We read* vs *We read the report*, and so on. This is one reason why adding *something* often fails to provide a satisfactory paraphrase of the intransitive: *We read* (activity) does not mean quite the same as *We read something* (accomplishment).[59] Notice in this connection the contrast between *eat/drink* and *eat/drink up*: the preposition *up* gives an accomplishment meaning and is

[59] Note that while *We were reading* entails *We read*, *We were reading something* does not entail *We read something* (assuming that *something* has constant reference).

inconsistent with the intransitive use being considered here – **When I left they were still eating up.*[60]

(i) Extension of intransitive: *They were talking nonsense*

Intransitive *talk* denotes an activity which does not inherently involve an object-argument, but it is possible to include one, such as *nonsense* (with the semantic role of factitive). Other examples:

[30] *hum* *run* *sing* *speak* *walk* *weep*

[31] *She hummed a familiar tune.* *She ran a marathon.* *I sang the wrong words.* *He speaks Greek.* *I walked the last two miles.* *She wept tears of joy.*

The objects tend to be selected from a quite narrow range of types – in the case of *weep* the head can only be *tear*. We might also include here *push*, *shove*, etc., which allow a *way* object before a goal complement: *They pushed (their way) to the front* (cf. Ch. 8, §4.4). Two special cases are given in (j)–(k) below.

(j) Extension by cognate object: *He died a long and agonising death*

A cognate object is one where the head noun is a nominalisation of the verb, as *death* is of *die*, and so on. In some cases the selection of a cognate object is of no syntactic significance: *They built a hideous building* and *I can smell an appalling smell* belong to the same construction as *They built a mansion* and *I can smell rotting meat. Sing* is arguably basically intransitive, but it allows many objects besides the cognate *song* and hence was included under (i) above. But there are also verbs where the cognate object is not freely replaceable by a non-cognate one:

[32] i *cough* *grin* *laugh* *sigh* *snore* *yawn*
ii *die* *dream* *live* *sleep* *think*

[33] *He grinned a wicked grin.* *She always dreams the same dream.* *He lives a life of drudgery.* *She slept the sleep of the just.* *He was thinking lewd thoughts.*

The semantic role might again be said to be factitive. Modification of the noun is just about obligatory:[61] *?He died a death*; *?He grinned a grin.* It is semantically comparable to modification of the verb (cf. *He died slowly and agonisingly*; *He grinned wickedly*).

(k) Object of conveyed reaction: *She smiled her assent*

[34] i *grin* *laugh* *nod* *sigh* *smile* *wave*
ii *mumble* *roar* *scream* *whisper*

[35] *He grinned his appreciation.* *I nodded my agreement.* *He roared his thanks.*

The verbs in [34i] involve non-verbal communication; the meaning of *She smiled her assent* is approximately "She signalled her assent by smiling": the object thus hardly expresses an argument of *smile* – and cannot be made into a passive subject: **Her assent was smiled.* The verbs in [34ii] are manner-of-speaking verbs and allow a wider range of objects (e.g. *He roared the command*) and passives are not in principle excluded (*On the parade ground commands must be roared, not whispered*).

[60] *Eat/drink up* have intransitive uses of type (b), as in *You haven't finished your milk: drink up*, but these have accomplishment interpretations.

[61] In canonical clauses, that is: a construction without modification is found in relative clauses, as in [*the dream*] *I dreamt last night*, [*the life*] *she led then*, etc.

8.1.4 Type IV: *He broke the vase* vs *The vase broke*

Pairs of this type differ from those considered above in that the subject of the intransitive corresponds not to the subject of the transitive but to its object: $S_{intrans} = O_{trans}$, i.e. the semantic role of the intransitive subject is the same as that of the transitive object. In the *break* pair, for example, *the vase* is subject of the intransitive and object of the transitive, having the same semantic role in both cases, that of theme, the entity that undergoes the change of state. A great many dual-transitivity verbs enter into this type of contrast. We will consider here four cases of it, classified by properties of the intransitive.

[36]	i	*The vase broke.*	[non-agentive dynamic intransitive]
	ii	*The ladder leant against the wall.*	[non-agentive static intransitive]
	iii	*The dog walked round the block.*	[agentive intransitive]
	iv	*She doesn't frighten easily.*	['middle' intransitive]

(a) Non-agentive dynamic intransitives: *The vase broke*

This is much the most usual case: the subject, *the vase*, is non-agentive, and the clause expresses a dynamic situation, as does the transitive *He broke the vase.* The transitive differs from the intransitive in including an extra argument with the role of causer, potentially agent, which is expressed as subject in accordance with the general rule that a single actual or potential agent is aligned with the subject in canonical clauses (§2.3).

Very often there is also a copular counterpart containing an adjective morphologically related to the verb:

[37]		TRANSITIVE	INTRANSITIVE	COPULAR
	i	*I opened the door.*	*The door opened.*	*The door was open.*
	ii	*I widened the gap.*	*The gap widened.*	*The gap was wide(r).*
	iii	*I tore my shirt.*	*My shirt tore.*	*My shirt was torn.*

The copular version describes the state resulting from the dynamic situation expressed in the transitive–intransitive pair. (In [ii] the verb is derived from the adjective, and conversely in [iii], which is also interpretable as a passive clause – see Ch. 16, §10.1.3.)

A sample of verbs found in contrasts of the type *He broke the vase* ~ *The vase broke* is given in [38], together with a few which are excluded (those lacking the intransitive use marked '*I', and those lacking the transitive use marked '*T'):

[38]						
	i *bend*	*blacken*	*bounce*	*change*	*collapse*	*crack*
	crease	*divide*	*drop*	*drown*	*explode*	*float*
	freeze	*grow*	*improve*	*melt*	*move*	*roll*
	sink	*slow*	*smash*	*turn*	*vary*	*wake*
	ii Excluded:	*construct* *I	*destroy* *I	*endanger* *I	*hit* *I	*touch* *I
		die *T	*emerge* *T	*fall* *T	*occur* *T	*perish* *T

[39]	i	a. <u>*This*</u> *changed* <u>*the situation*</u>.	b. <u>*The situation*</u> *changed.*
	ii	a. <u>*They*</u> *destroyed* <u>*the farm*</u>.	b. *<u>*The farm*</u> *destroyed.*
	iii	a. *<u>*The frost*</u> *perished* <u>*the fruit*</u>.	b. <u>*The fruit*</u> *perished.*

It must be emphasised that we are concerned here with a lexical relationship which is subject to a fair amount of idiosyncratic variation for particular items. Thus *break* occurs only transitively in the context of records or laws/rules (*He broke the 100m record*, but not **The 100m record broke*), and with a body-part object a matching subject will generally be interpreted as experiencer rather than causer (*I've broken my arm*). *Grow* appears in both constructions when applied to plants but is used only intransitively of people or animals (*They grew lots of tomatoes/*children*). Intransitive *move* with animates (*He moved*) has a sense involving movement of part of the body which doesn't apply in the transitive (*They moved him*), and conversely the transitive has a sense in *It moved me to tears* that is not found in the intransitive (**I moved to tears*). With *change*, the transitive use (*I changed my views*) and the intransitive use (*My views changed*) have virtually the same meaning. With *bounce, drop, roll* we hardly have an adjectival copular counterpart: *The ball was bounced* is a passive clause.

(b) Non-agentive static intransitive: *The ladder leant against the wall*

With a relatively small number of verbs the intransitive denotes a state and the transitive the bringing about of that state: *I leant the ladder against the wall.* This is found with verbs of position, such as *hang, rest, sit, stand*, and a few others such as *hurt* (*My arm is hurting* ~ *You are hurting my arm*).

(c) Agentive intransitives: *The dog walked round the block*

With a few primarily intransitive verbs the intransitive subject has an agent role (combined with that of theme), and the transitive then involves getting the person or whatever to act in the given way: *We walked the dog round the block.*[62] Compare similarly: *The prisoners marched to the guardroom* ~ *He marched the prisoners to the guardroom.* In the transitive, the agentivity of the dog/prisoners is much reduced: the primary agent is the one expressed as subject. The clear cases of pairs of this kind involve movement in some direction (in *She jumped the horse* it cannot be a matter of jumping on the spot). Other verbs include *canter, gallop, run, walk* – but hardly *jog, meander, saunter*, and the like.

(d) 'Middle' intransitives: *She doesn't frighten easily*

In this case the transitive use is primary and the intransitive is interpreted as having an unexpressed causer. Cross-linguistically, the primary use of the general term **middle** is for a term in a system of voice – it applies to a voice that is in some sense intermediate between active and passive. The term is certainly not applicable to English in this sense: there are just two categories in the syntactic system of voice in English, active and passive. *She doesn't frighten easily* is active in form, but it has some semantic affinity with the passive, and it is in this semantic sense that it can be thought of as intermediate between ordinary actives and passives: we put scare quotes around the term to signal that it is being used in an extended sense and is not to be interpreted as denoting a formal category in the voice system.

Intransitives like *She doesn't frighten easily* characteristically have the following properties:

[40] i A causer (normally human) is implied but can't be expressed in a *by* phrase.

[62] The meaning of transitive *walk* in *I'll walk you home* is more specialised: "escort on foot".

ii The clause is concerned with whether and how (especially how readily) the subject-referent undergoes the process expressed in the verb.

iii The clause is negative, or is headed by a modal auxiliary (especially *will*), or contains an adjunct of manner (such as *well* or *easily*).

iv The clause expresses a general state, not a particular event.

The implication of a causer ([40i]) is what makes such clauses semantically similar to passives: compare *She isn't easily frightened.* But the causer cannot be expressed: **She doesn't frighten easily by noises in the dark.*[63] Property [ii] shows that these intransitive actives are by no means identical in meaning to passives. Compare *The shirt irons well*, which says something about the quality of the shirt, with *The shirt was ironed well*, which tells of the skill of the ironer. Properties [iii] and [iv] exclude such examples as **She frightens* and **There was a sudden noise outside and she frightened immediately.*

A sample of verbs occurring in 'middle' intransitives is given in:

[41]	i	*alarm*	*amuse*	*demoralise*	*embarrass*	*flatter*	*frighten*
		intimidate	*offend*	*pacify*	*please*	*shock*	*unnerve*
	ii	*clean*	*cut*	*hammer*	*iron*	*read*	*wash*

The restrictions given in [40] normally apply in full to the verbs in [41i], but those in [ii] allow single event interpretations, contrary to [40iv]: *The meat cut surprisingly easily*; *The milk kept for ten days*; *The tin hammered flat*; *The shirt washed cleaner than I'd expected.*[64] *Sell* is less restricted again, allowing unmodified structures like *The house sold.*

In addition, numerous verbs subsumed under case (a) above can appear in clauses with an interpretation like those we have been considering: *The door won't open*; *These rods bend quite easily*; *The handle doesn't turn.* These could be used of situations where someone is trying to open the door, bend the rods, or turn the handle. However, these are not the only possible contextualisations, and there is no justification for analysing them as structurally ambiguous. As observed above, the 'middle' intransitive is not a syntactically distinct construction in English, and there is also no sharp semantic distinction between such clauses and the intransitives covered under (a); it is sufficient to note that the central instances are those involving verbs like *frighten*, *read*, *cut*, etc., which are subject (in varying degrees) to the restrictions outlined in [40].

8.2 Ditransitive/monotransitive contrasts

8.2.1 Type I: *I gave her the key* vs *I gave the key to her*

The indirect object generally expresses arguments with the semantic role of recipient or beneficiary, and these arguments are also commonly expressed by PPs headed by *to*

[63] A further structural difference from the passive is that the subject always corresponds to an object in a transitive construction. There are therefore no analogues of prepositional passives like *The house can be easily broken into*: **The house breaks into easily.*

[64] The last three examples illustrate alternatives to the more usual manner adjunct mentioned in [40iii]: an adjunct of duration and a resultative PC. Note that **The tin won't/doesn't hammer* is not acceptable: there is no issue of whether the tin can undergo the process of hammering, only of whether it has a certain result. Similarly *read* has to do with readability, not legibility, so that **Your paper won't/doesn't read* is not acceptable: there can't be an issue as to whether it can be read, only as to how it sounds or is evaluated when read (*It reads well / like a confession*).

and *for* respectively. We distinguish five verb classes according to which of the following constructions they license: ditransitive, monotransitive with *to* phrase, monotransitive with *for* phrase.

[42]	$O^i + O^d$	O^d + NON-CORE COMP	
i	a. *I gave her the key.*	b. *I gave the key to her.*	[O^i or *to*]
ii	a. **I explained her the problem.*	b. *I explained the problem to her.*	[*to* only]
iii	a. *I bought her a hat.*	b. *I bought a hat for her.*	[O^i or *for*]
iv	a. **I borrowed her the money.*	b. *I borrowed the money for her.*	[*for* only]
v	a. *I spared her the trouble.*	b. **I spared the trouble to/for her.*	[O^i only]

The [a] examples are ditransitive, whereas the [b] ones are monotransitives containing a non-core complement after the direct object. Examples of verbs belonging to the five classes are given in:

[43]					
i O^i OR *TO*	*award*	*bequeath*	*bring*	*cable*	*deny*
	feed	*give*	*hand*	*kick*	*leave*$_1$
	lend	*offer*	*owe*	*pass*	*post*
	promise	*read*	*sell*	*send*	*show*
	take	*teach*	*tell*	*throw*	*write*
ii *TO* ONLY	*announce*	*confess*	*contribute*	*convey*	*declare*
	deliver	*donate*	*exhibit*	*explain*	*mention*
	narrate	*refer*	*return*	*reveal*	*say*
	submit	*transfer*			
iii O^i OR *FOR*	*bake*	*build*	*buy*	*cook*	*design*
	fetch	*find*	*get*	*hire*	*leave*$_2$
	make	*order*	*reach*	*rent*	*reserve*
	save$_1$	*sing*	*spare*$_1$	*write*	
iv *FOR* ONLY	*acquire*	*borrow*	*collect*	*compose*	*fabricate*
	obtain	*recover*	*retrieve*	*withdraw*	
v O^i ONLY	*allow*	*begrudge*	*bet*	*charge*	*cost*
	envy	*excuse*	*fine*	*forgive*	*permit*
	refuse	*save*$_2$	*spare*$_2$	*strike*	*tax*
	tip	*wish*			

The subscripts indicate different senses. For *leave* we have *He left*$_1$ *everything to his wife* ("bequeathed"), Class [i], and *I've left*$_2$ *some spaghetti for you*, Class [iii]. For *save* and *spare* we have *I'll save*$_1$ *you some porridge* ("keep"), *I can't spare*$_1$ *you any more* ("let you have"), Class [iii], and *This will save*$_2$*/spare*$_2$ *you the bother*, Class [v]. The *for* construction is possible only with the first sense: *I'll save some porridge for you* and *I can't spare any more for you* but not **This will save/spare the bother for you.*

It will be noted that items of very similar meaning may belong to different classes, especially [i] and [ii]. Compare, for example, *She gave/*donated her old school $500; He gave me back / *returned me the books I'd lent him; They showed/*revealed/*exhibited us the jewellery recovered from the wreckage.* In such cases there is a tendency for it to be the Latinate and/or more formal words that exclude O^i.

With verbs allowing an alternation between ditransitive and prepositional constructions, the difference between them is very largely a matter of information packaging. Thus in accordance with the general tendencies described in Ch. 16, §2, *He gave his son a couple of CDs* is likely to be preferred over the prepositional counterpart *He gave a couple of CDs to his son*, and conversely *He gave the spare copy to one of his colleagues* is likely to be preferred over the ditransitive counterpart *He gave one of his colleagues the spare copy*. If O^d is a personal pronoun, the prepositional construction is favoured, especially if the other NP is not a pronoun – examples like %*I gave Kim it* are inadmissible for most speakers, especially in AmE.

In addition, however, there are certain points to be made concerning the semantic role of O^i and the oblique NP.

Recipients

In the most central ditransitive construction O^i has the semantic role of recipient. With such verbs as *give, hand, throw* there is actual transfer of the theme (expressed as O^d) to the recipient; with *bequeath, offer, owe, promise* there is an arrangement or commitment for the recipient to receive the theme later.[65] With such verbs as *tell, read, show, teach,* O^i and O^d are aligned with less central cases of recipient and theme: the O^i-referent comes to hear, see, or learn what is expressed by O^d, rather than to have it. Verbs of verbal communication, of saying, characteristically belong to the *to*-only class: *He said something offensive to us*, not **He said us something offensive. Tell* is the main exception, but there is also a productive set expressing the means of communication (*cable, fax, phone*, etc.: *I'll fax you a copy*).

Recipient vs locative goal

The preposition *to* can mark a recipient or a locative goal – compare: *She offered the manuscript to the university library* (recipient) and *She took her son to the university library* (locative goal). It is only in the recipient case, however, that there is alternation with a ditransitive:[66]

[44] i	a. *I gave/sent some cash to him.*	b. *I gave/sent him some cash*	[recipient]
ii	a. *I moved/sent Kim to the back.*	b. **I moved/sent the back Kim*	[locative]

Beneficiaries – of goods or services

For marks the oblique as having a beneficiary role, and we can then distinguish (not always sharply) between beneficiaries of goods and beneficiaries of services. In *I'll get another glass for you* we have a beneficiary of goods (the glass is for you), in *Let me open the door for you* we have a beneficiary of services (it is the deed that is for you, not the door). The O^i alternant tends to be restricted to cases where it is a matter of goods rather than services:

[45] i	a. *I'll do a quiche for you.*	b. *I'll do you a quiche.*	[goods]
ii	a. *I'll do the washing-up for you.*	b. **I'll do you the washing-up.*	[service]

[65] In the extended sense of *owe* seen in *She owes her immense success to sheer hard work* the oblique NP does not have a recipient role, and here the O^i alternant is not possible: **She owes sheer hard work her immense success.*

[66] For some speakers there may be a further difference in some cases between the ditransitive and prepositional alternants, with the latter more consistent with a failure of the transfer, thus more likely than the O^i-alternant in examples like *He teaches logic to Grade 10 students, but they don't seem to learn anything* or *I sent my report to the boss but she never received it.*

The goods-beneficiary characteristically occurs with verbs of obtaining or creating – and in [45] *do* has the latter meaning ("make") in [i] but not in [ii]. Compare similarly *I fixed a drink for her* ~ *I fixed her a drink*, where *fix* means "make/prepare", with *I fixed the tap for her* ~ **I fixed her the tap*, where it means "repair".[67] Notice, moreover, that even with verbs of obtaining or creating a *for* phrase may have a wider range of interpretation than O^i: in *I made some cakes for her* it may have been my intention that she should have the cakes but it could also be that I did the job for her (perhaps she had been told to make some cakes for her employer and I was helping her out) but *I made her some cakes* has only the interpretation where the cakes are for her.

It is plausible to relate this restriction on an O^i-beneficiary to the fact that a goods-beneficiary is much closer than is a services-beneficiary to a recipient, the most central semantic role for O^i. In *He made her some cakes* we understand that he intended that the cakes be transferred to her; this is comparable to *He offered her some cakes* (where O^i has a recipient role) since in neither case is there an entailment of actual transfer.

A few verbs can take either a recipient or a goods-beneficiary; in the oblique alternant the roles are distinguished by the preposition, but in the ditransitive alternant the distinction is not encoded. Compare *Could you rent me your cottage for the week-end* ("to me": recipient) and *Could you rent me a car for the week-end*, as said by boss to secretary, say ("for me": beneficiary). Or again, *He wrote her a letter* (on the salient reading, the letter is a communication to her: recipient) and *He wrote her a cheque* (the cheque is for her: beneficiary).[68]

O^i-only verbs

These include verbs of permission or its opposite (*allow*, *refuse*), where O^i has a recipient role. But there are also verbs here where the role of O^i is source rather than goal (recipient), most clearly *charge*, *cost*, and *fine*: in *They charged Ed $10* the money is transferred away from Ed, not to him.[69]

Other prepositions

Isolated cases are found where the non-core complement corresponding to the indirect object of the ditransitive has some other preposition than *to* or *for*:

[46]	i	a. *Can I ask you a favour?*	b. *Can I ask a favour of you?*
	ii	a. *I played him a game of chess.*	b. *I played a game of chess with/against him.*
	iii	a. *They bear you no ill will.*	b. *They bear no ill will towards you.*

With *ask* the *of* version is somewhat formal, and unlikely where the direct object expresses a 'concealed question' (Ch. 11, §5.3): *He asked me my name / the time* ~ ?*He asked my name / the time of me.* Conversely, with a direct object like *a great deal* the ditransitive is hardly possible: *That's asking a great deal of her* ~ ?*That's asking her a great deal.*

[67] A service-beneficiary is more acceptable when the O^i is a personal pronoun (especially 1st or 2nd person), and when the utterance has directive force: *Could you iron me my white shirt* is more acceptable than ?*I ironed my brother his white shirt.* Speakers vary considerably in their judgements on such examples.

[68] *Send* takes either *to* or *for*, but it seems that O^i always has a recipient interpretation: *He sent Kim a cheque* means that he sent it to her, not for her. *Send* thus belongs in [44ii] and [43i].

[69] The inclusion of *wish* in this class is problematic. A *to* phrase is possible in initial position, as in *To all who have retired we wish happiness and long life*, but not normally within the VP, especially when the complements are relatively short: *I wish you good luck*, but not **I wish good luck to you.*

8.2.2 Type II: *I envied him his freedom* vs *I envied him for his freedom*

Type II differs from Type I in that the single object of the monotransitive corresponds to the indirect object of the ditransitive rather than its direct object. The prepositions found here are *for* and *with*:

[47]		$O^i + O^d$	O^d +NON-CORE COMP
	i	a. *I can't forgive him his lies.*	b. *I can't forgive him for his lies.*
	ii	a. *He served us a sumptuous meal.*	b. *He served us with a sumptuous meal.*

In the [b] construction there is only one object, so that it is syntactically a direct object even though it corresponds semantically to the indirect object in [a].

Only a handful of verbs belong here:

[48]					
i	O^i OR *FOR*:	*envy*	*excuse*	*forgive*	
ii	O^i OR *WITH*:	*issue* BrE	*leave*	?*provide*	*serve*

Those in [ii] occur freely with *with* but in the ditransitive construction *issue* is found in BrE but not AmE (%*They issued us a ticket*) and *provide* is at best very marginal in the ditransitive construction. The sense of *leave* involved here is that seen in *This left us (with) no alternative but to cancel the show. Issue, provide,* and *serve* also occur in the *to* construction discussed in §8.2.1, so that for *serve*, for example, we have the following three possibilities:

[49]			RECIPIENT	THEME
	i	*They served the guests minestrone soup.*	O^i	O^d
	ii	*They served the guests with minestrone soup.*	O^d	Comp of *with*
	iii	*They served minestrone soup to the guests.*	Comp of *to*	O^d

8.2.3 Type III: *They offered us $100* vs *They offered $100*

In general, the indirect object (or the corresponding PP complement) can be omitted without loss of grammaticality or change in the meaning of the verb. The most clearcut exception is *wish*: *They wished us a safe journey* but not *They wished a safe journey.* With one or two others a single internal complement is possible only under restricted conditions: with *deny*, for example, O^i is omissible in *They denied (him) his request to take the computer home* but not in *They denied him promotion*; with *give* it is omissible in *They gave us $100*, but not in *They gave us a beating* (the 'light' use of *give*).

Where only one internal complement is present, an O^i may or may not be understood:

[50]			
	i	*She gave $100.*	[O^i understood]
	ii	*She fetched a glass.*	[no O^i understood]

Give (in the sense it has here) inherently involves three arguments, and though no recipient is expressed in [i] one is understood. But the interpretation of [ii] does not require that we supply a beneficiary. In [i] the understood recipient is definite: I assume it will be clear from the context who she gave the money to. In other cases it is indefinite, typically a general human recipient: *This kind of work can give immense satisfaction.*

Understood indirect objects a subset of those with recipient role

Cases where an O^i (or corresponding PP complement) is absent but understood always involve the semantic role of recipient rather than beneficiary. Compare, for example, *He offered them some cakes* with *He made them some cakes*: if we drop *them* from the former there will still be a recipient understood (recoverable from the context), but if we drop *them* from the *make* clause to give *He made some cakes* there is no understood beneficiary, no suggestion that the cakes were for some third party. Similarly if we drop the O^i from *I bought her a hat* to give *I bought a hat* there is again no implicit beneficiary: *buy* inherently involves transfer to the buyer (expressed as the subject) but not to a beneficiary.

With verbs whose O^i is associated with the recipient role, omission of the O^i usually leaves the recipient understood but there are a few where this is not so, where the recipient is not an inherent part of the meaning. Compare:

		a.	b.
[51]	i	a. *We haven't awarded anyone a prize.*	b. *We haven't awarded a prize.*
	ii	a. *He read them a story.*	b. *He read a story.*

There is an implicit recipient in [ib], but not in [iib].

8.2.4 Type IV: *They fined us $100* vs *They fined us*

Considerably less usual is the case where the single object of the monotransitive corresponds to the indirect object of the ditransitive: the role of *us* in *They fined us $100* is the same as in *They fined us*.

With *fine*, this is the only possibility, but there are other verbs such as *charge* that allow both types of omission:

		a.	b.
[52]	i	a. *They fined us $100.*	b. *They charged us $100.*
	ii	a. **They fined $100.*	b. *They charged $100.*
	iii	a. *They fined us.*	b. *They charged us.*

Tip follows the pattern of *fine* while the verbs in [53] follow that of *charge*:

[53]	*bet*	*cost*	*envy*	*excuse*	*forgive*
	refuse	*show*	*teach*	*tell*	

Again there is a distinction to be drawn between understood elements that are definite and those that are indefinite. Compare, for example, *I asked him the price but he wouldn't tell me* (sc. "the price": definite) and *He tells lies / dirty jokes* (addressee indefinite). *Cost* appears in examples like [52iii] only in informal style (*That'll cost you*, with "a lot" understood) or in the idiom *It cost us dear* (where the syntactic analysis of *dear* is unclear).

8.3 Further core/non-core contrasts

8.3.1 Type I: *He supplies arms to the rebels* vs *He supplies the rebels with arms*

In this type we have two internal complements, with the object of one corresponding to the oblique of the other. Several different cases can be distinguished.

(a) *Present/blame*

		a.	b.
[54]	i	a. *He presented a prize to Kim.*	b. *He presented Kim with a prize.*
	ii	a. *He blamed the accident on Kim.*	b. *He blamed Kim for the accident.*

With *present* the roles are theme (*a prize*) and recipient (*Kim*), and when they are not aligned with the object they take the prepositions *with* and *to* respectively. There are a number of verbs that follow this pattern, and some that occur only with *with* (*They* *armed us with knives*, but not **They armed knives to us*):

[55]						
i	*TO* OR *WITH*	*credit*	*entrust*	*furnish*	*issue*	*present*
		provide	*serve*	*supply*	*trust*	
ii	*WITH* ONLY	*arm*	*equip*	*regale*	*reward*	*saddle*

This contrast is similar to that between *He gave the prize to Kim* and *He gave Kim the prize*, except that in the second construction the NP expressing the theme is oblique (complement of *with*) instead of being a core complement (direct object). A few verbs, as noted in §8.2.2 above, are found in all three constructions. In addition, *supply* allows a beneficiary with *for* instead of a recipient with *to*: *He supplies arms for the rebels.*

In some cases the range of NPs found as oblique is somewhat greater than that allowed as object. For example, if we replace *a prize* in [54i] by *a dilemma* only [b] is acceptable. Conversely with *entrust*: we have *He entrusted his children to her* and *He entrusted her with his children*, but if we replace *her* by *her care* only the *to* construction is permitted. There are also differences among the verbs as to whether the non-core complement can be omitted: *serve* allows omission of either (*They served the guests*; *They served the wine*), *present* allows omission of the recipient (*He presented the prizes*), *entrust* requires two internal complements (**He entrusted me / his savings*).

The contrast with *on* and *for* seen in [54ii] is unique to *blame*. We can omit the *for* phrase (*He blamed Kim*) but not the *on* phrase (**He blamed the accident*).

(b) *Spray/load*

[56]	THEME AS OBJECT	LOCATIVE AS OBJECT
i	a. *She sprayed <u>paint</u> <u>onto the wall</u>.*	b. *She sprayed <u>the wall</u> <u>with paint</u>.*
ii	a. *She loaded <u>hay</u> <u>onto the cart</u>.*	b. *She loaded <u>the cart</u> <u>with hay</u>.*

Here one argument has the role of theme, the other that of locative. In [a] the object is aligned with the theme and in [b] with the locative. When the theme is expressed as oblique the preposition is always *with*, whereas in the [a] version a range of locative prepositions is found – e.g. *over* in [ia] or *into* in [iia]. If only one internal complement is included it will normally be the object, and while both kinds of object are possible in this case the locative is somewhat more likely (*She loaded the cart*).

The meanings of the [a] and [b] versions in [56] are not quite the same. Where the locative is expressed as object, it characteristically has what has been called a **holistic** interpretation. The [a] examples could be used of a situation in which only a small portion of the wall had paint sprayed on it or where the hay occupied only a small part of the cart, whereas the [b] versions indicate a fuller coverage of the wall, a fuller loading of the cart. It is, however, difficult to capture the difference precisely. *She sprayed me with water*, for example, certainly does not require that she sprayed me all over. And in *She sprayed the wall with paint all over* the *all over* undoubtedly adds new meaning instead of merely reinforcing what is already expressed in [ib]. The best way to get at the difference in meaning is to take NPs of the same kind (more precisely, both definite) and introduce an explicit indication of completeness, such as the verb *finish*:

[57] i *She finished spraying <u>the paint</u> <u>on the wall</u>.*
ii *She finished spraying <u>the wall</u> <u>with the paint</u>.*

What emerges from such a comparison is that it is the object-argument that determines when the situation is complete/finished. In [i] the spraying was finished when the paint was used up, regardless of how much of the wall was covered; conversely, in [ii] it was finished when the wall was covered.

While *spray* and *load* appear in both constructions there are other verbs limited to one or the other:

[58] i a. *She put the tea in the cupboard.* b. **She put the cupboard with the tea.*
ii a. **She filled cordial into the glass.* b. *She filled the glass with cordial.*

The asterisk in [ib] applies to the interpretation where *the tea* expresses the theme, here the entity moved: the sentence is perfectly acceptable with *the cupboard* expressing the theme and *with* a locative preposition, i.e. when the structure is the same as in [ia]. In [59] we give a sample of verbs from the three classes: those in [i] follow the pattern of *spray* and *load* in allowing either theme or locative as object, those in [ii] are like *put* in licensing only the theme-as-object construction, and those in [iii] are like *fill* in that they appear only in the locative-as-object version.

[59]						
i	THEME OR LOC	*brush*	*cram*	*hang*	*inject*	*pack*
		plant	*shower*	*smear*	*spread*	*sprinkle*
ii	THEME ONLY	*immerse*	*lean*	*place*	*push*	*stand*
iii	LOC ONLY	*cover*	*decorate*	*drench*	*litter*	*surround*

(c) *Drain*

[60] THEME AS OBJECT — LOCATIVE AS OBJECT
i a. *I drained water from the pool.* b. *I drained the pool of water.*
ii a. *I removed leaves from the pool.* b. **I removed the pool of leaves.*
iii a. **He deprived food from us.* b. *He deprived us of food.*

This case is like that found with the *spray/load* verbs, except that this time the locative is source rather than goal and the preposition used with the theme NP in [b] is *of* rather than *with*. In the [a] version other prepositions than *from* are often available, such as *off* or *out* + *of*. Sample verbs following the complementation patterns of *drain*, *remove*, and *deprive* respectively are shown in:

[61]						
i	THEME OR LOC	*bleed*	*clean*	*clear*	*empty*	*strip*
ii	THEME ONLY	*eject*	*eradicate*	*extract*	*omit*	*withdraw*
iii	LOC ONLY	*acquit*	*cheat*	*divest*	*purge*	*rob*

There are few clear members of class [i]; for some speakers, verbs such as *cleanse*, *cull*, *leech*, *plunder* belong in the class too, while for others they belong in [ii] or [iii].

(d) *Engrave*

[62] THEME AS OBJECT — LOCATIVE AS OBJECT
i a. *I engraved my initials on the ring.* b. *I engraved the ring with my initials.*
ii a. *I scratched my initials on the ring.* b. **I scratched the ring with my initials.*
iii a. **I labelled my initials on the ring.* b. *I labelled the ring with my initials.*

This again is very much the same contrast as we have with *spray* and *load*. This time the theme is a factitive theme: the (representation of) my initials is created by the act of engraving. There is no difference here comparable to that illustrated in [57]. Sample verbs:

[63]						
i	THEME OR LOC	*embroider*	*inscribe*	*mark*	*stamp*	*tattoo*
ii	THEME ONLY	*carve*	*copy*	*draw*	*print*	*write*
iii	LOC ONLY	*adorn*	*brand*	*decorate*	*illustrate*	*tag*

(e) *Hunt*

[64]	QUEST AS OBJECT	LOCATIVE AS OBJECT
i	a. *They hunted deer in the woods.*	b. *They hunted the woods for deer.*
ii	a. **She searched her key in her bag.*	b. *She searched her bag for her key.*

The verbs we are concerned with here take as internal arguments a locative and what may be called a quest – the entity being looked for or sought. Quest is a quite specific semantic role, and it remains unclear whether it could be satisfactorily subsumed under one of the more general roles we have postulated. The object expresses the quest in [a] and the location in [b], where the quest is aligned with the complement of *for*. The verbs below are classified according as they allow both kinds of object in this way, or only a locative, as in [64ii]:

[65]						
i	QUEST OR LOC	*fish* I	*hunt* I	*mine* I	*poach* I	*stalk*
ii	LOC ONLY	*check* I	*dredge* I	*examine*	*inspect*	*investigate*
		ransack	*scour*	*search* I	*survey*	*watch* I

The annotation 'I' indicates that the verb also appears in an intransitive construction with two PPs, *for* again marking the quest: *They hunted for deer in the woods*; *She searched for her key in her bag.* We haven't given any verbs appearing in construction [64ia], but not [64ib]; *They discovered deer in the woods* has the syntactic structure of [ia] but the object is not associated with the quest role, and hence the inadmissibility of **They discovered the woods for deer* needs no special noting.[70]

(f) *Hit*

[66]		
i	a. *He hit the stick against the fence.*	b. *He hit the fence with the stick.*
ii	a. *He stabbed his knife into me.*	b. *He stabbed me with his knife.*
iii	a. *He pierced the pin through my hat.*	b. *He pierced my hat with the pin.*

Here the [a] and [b] examples are equivalent. In [b] the *with* phrase is instrument and the object has the role of patient. In [a] the PP is a locative, and an important feature of this construction is that the locative is obligatory: it cannot be omitted without changing the way in which the object is interpreted. The [a] examples, that is, do not entail that he hit the stick, that he stabbed his knife, that he pierced the pin – but they do entail that he hit the fence, stabbed me, and pierced my hat. In the construction with a locative PP, [a], the object has the role of theme, which it does not otherwise have with these verbs (and given the equivalence with [b] it might be said to combine this with the instrument role).

[70] A candidate for a verb taking only the structure with quest as object is *ferret*: *She ferreted the secret out of him* but not **She ferreted him for the secret.* However, the locative here is source, not location, as in [64].

Such examples are to be distinguished from the following, where [a] and [b] are not equivalent, and where the semantic role associated with the object is the same in both:

[67] i a. *He threw his racquet against the net.* b. *He threw the net with his racquet.*
ii a. *He broke his stick on the fence.* b. *He broke the fence with his stick.*

Here the [a] examples do entail that he threw his racquet and broke his stick – and they do not entail that he threw the net and broke the fence. In these cases there is no significant relation between the [a] and [b] structures, and the locative and instrument can usually combine, as in *He threw his racquet against the net with a makeshift catapult.*

Verbs found in the contrast shown in [66] include:

[68] *bang* *bash* *beat* *hammer* *jab* *knock*
pound *strike* *tap* *thump*

The locative preposition with these is generally *against*, except for *jab*, which takes *in* or *into*. There are some verbs where the [a] and [b] structures are not equivalent but where the semantic role associated with the object is still different in the two cases. *He poked his pencil through the paper* is not equivalent to *He poked the paper with his pencil*, but nevertheless has an obligatory locative and a theme role associated with the object. *Smash* can behave in a similar way: *He smashed his crow-bar against the gate* allows an interpretation where the crow-bar is not broken, but there is also no entailment that the gate was broken, as there is in *He smashed the gate with his crow-bar. Smash* can also simply follow the pattern of [67]: the salient interpretation of *He smashed the vase against the wall* has him smashing (breaking) the vase.

(g) *Build*

[69] GOAL AS OBJECT — SOURCE AS OBJECT

i a. *She built a shelter out of the stones.* b. *She built the stones into a shelter.*
ii a. *They produce fuel from sugar.* b. **They produce sugar into fuel.*
iii a. **I changed a bedroom from the attic.* b. *I changed the attic into a bedroom.*

These all involve a change of state. We have extended the concepts of source and goal from the domain of spatial location to that of state (§5.2), taking the initial state to be source and the resultant state to be goal, so we can say that *build* allows either goal or source to be aligned with the object. The preposition for a non-core goal, as in [b], is *into*, while a non-core source has *out* + *of*, *from*, or *with* (*I made a stew with the leftovers*). As illustrated in [69], some verbs allow only one of the two alignments. Sample verbs, classified according to the role expressed by the object, are:

[70]						
i	GOAL/SOURCE	*assemble*	*bake*	*carve*	*cut*	*develop*
		form	*grow*	*make*	*mould*	*sculpt*
ii	GOAL ONLY	*compose*	*construct*	*derive*	*design*	*manufacture*
iii	SOURCE ONLY	*alter*	*change*	*fold*	*turn*	*work*

A number of verbs allowing only the source as object – *alter*, *change* and *turn* from the ones cited in [iii] – also figure in a construction where both source and goal are expressed as non-core complements, with the object expressing the theme, the entity whose state changes: *She wants to change the room from an attic into a bedroom.*

8.3.2 Type II: *Bees are swarming in the garden* vs *The garden is swarming with bees*

This contrast is like the last except that the core complement involved is subject rather than object. Again we distinguish various cases, but as they are effectively intransitive analogues of some of the transitive cases covered under Type I, we can deal with them quite briefly.

(a) *Swarm/abound*

[71]	THEME AS SUBJECT	LOCATIVE AS SUBJECT
i	a. *Fish abound in the lake.*	b. *The lake abounds with fish.*
ii	a. *Vermin were crawling over him.*	b. *He was crawling with vermin.*
iii	a. *Sweat dripped down his face.*	b. *His face dripped with sweat.*
iv	a. *Wild music resounded in the hall.*	b. *The hall resounded with wild music.*

This is analogous to the *spray/load* contrast. Again we have a theme and a locative, such that either can be aligned with a core complement (here subject) and the other with a non-core element. The locative subject version characteristically has *with* in the non-core complement, but some verbs allow other prepositions, as in *The lake abounds in fish. In* is the most usual preposition in the version with the theme as subject, but others occur here more readily, as seen in the above examples – and in case [iiia] we could have a whole range: *from*, *off*, *over*, and so on.

A considerable number of verbs exhibit this contrast; further examples are given in [72], grouped into broad semantic classes:

[72]						
i	*blaze*	*flicker*	*glimmer*	*glitter*	*shimmer*	*shine*
ii	*buzz*	*clatter*	*echo*	*resonate*	*ring*	*whir*
iii	*abound*	*bloom*	*blossom*	*bristle*	*crawl*	*creep*
	quiver	*sprout*	*swarm*	*teem*	*throng*	*writhe*

The verbs in [i] have to do with light, those in [ii] with sound, and those in [iii] with concrete objects, generally in large numbers. Abstract qualities are also found in figurative language: *Anger blazed in his eyes* ~ *His eyes blazed with anger.*

In some cases there is a difference in meaning between the two versions of a kind analogous to that discussed for *spray/load*. The locative subject version, *The garden was swarming with bees*, has a holistic interpretation: we understand that more or less the whole garden was occupied by the swarming bees. But there is no such implicature in the theme subject version *Bees were swarming in the garden*: here they could all have been in just one corner of the garden. It must be emphasised, however, that this semantic difference is found only under quite limited conditions: even with verbs like *swarm* it can be lost with a change in the location (*The night air swarmed with midges* ~ *Midges swarmed in the night air*) or a change in the preposition (*The bush was swarming with bees* ~ *Bees were swarming over the bush*).[71]

[71] Since *swarm* doesn't lend itself to the expression of an achievement, as opposed to an activity, we cannot here bring out the difference in meaning between the two constructions by using examples with *finish*, analogous to [57] above.

(b) *Develop*

[73] GOAL AS SUBJECT
a. *A major international crisis developed out of the incident.*

SOURCE AS SUBJECT
b. *The incident developed into a major international crisis.*

This is the intransitive analogue of the *build* contrast shown in [69]. But only a few verbs are involved, mainly *develop, evolve, grow*. Such verbs as *alter, change, turn* again allow only the source as the core complement: *The incident turned into a major crisis*, not **A major crisis turned out of / from the incident.*

8.3.3 Type III: *I wiped the marks off the wall* vs *I wiped the wall*

Here the contrast is between a trivalent construction with object + non-core complement and a bivalent one with just an object as internal complement. We leave aside cases where the non-core complement is simply omissible (*He removed the key from the table* vs *He removed the key*) and focus on the case where the object of the bivalent construction corresponds to the oblique of the trivalent construction.

[74] a. *Kim washed the stain out of the towel.* b. *Kim washed the towel.*

In [a] the roles of the internal arguments *the stain* and (*out of*) *the towel* are theme and source; but the absence of an expressed or understood theme in [b] means that there is no basis for interpreting *the towel* as source: it can more appropriately be regarded as patient. The object of *wash* can express a theme only if the source is also expressed: **Kim washed the stain.* Nor can the theme be expressed as an oblique (**Kim washed the towel of the stain*): this is what distinguishes *wash, wipe*, etc., from verbs like *drain* and *empty* discussed in case (c) in §8.3.1. There are a fair number of verbs behaving like *wash* and *wipe*; further examples are given in:

[75]	*brush*	*dust*	*filter*	*hose*	*lick*	*prune*
	purge	*rinse*	*rub*	*scrape*	*soak*	*sweep*

8.3.4 Type IV: *We filled the bucket with water* vs *Water filled the bucket*

As in Type III we have here a distinction between a trivalent and a bivalent construction, the former having object + non-core complement within the VP, the latter just object. This time, however, the oblique of the trivalent corresponds to the subject of the bivalent.

[76]
- i a. *We opened the door with the master-key.* b. *The master-key opened the door.*
- ii a. *We offended her with our complaints.* b. *Our complaints offended her.*
- iii a. *We covered the grave with leaves.* b. *Leaves covered the grave.*
- iv a. *We dried the clothes in the sun.* b. *The sun dried the clothes.*
- v a. *We slept three in the tent.* b. *The tent slept three.*
- vi a. *We included your father in the list.* b. *The list included your father.*
- vii a. *We made a stew from the leftovers.* b. *The leftovers made a stew.*
- viii a. *We saw a big change in that week.* b. *That week saw a big change.*
- ix a. *We could buy a house for that amount.* b. *That amount could buy a house.*

The interesting point to note about these examples is that when we drop the subject NP from the trivalent construction the obligatory subject function is taken over not by the object, but by the complement of the preposition. Only [i] and [iv] allow a third construction where the subject of the bivalent corresponds to the object of the trivalent (*The door opened with the master-key*; *The clothes dried in the sun*) – the contrast between the [a] examples and these is a transitive/intransitive contrast of the kind covered in §8.1.4.

The non-core complements in the [a] examples of [76] have a range of roles. *With the master-key* in [ia] is an instrument. The bivalent version [ib] is available only with a limited range of instruments: compare, for example, *We ate it with a spoon* vs #*A spoon ate it.* The *with* phrases in [iia] and [iiia] have some similarity to an instrument, but are nevertheless distinct. The salient interpretation of [iia], in contrast to [ia], is non-agentive: we didn't use our complaints to offend her, as we used the master-key to open the door in [i]. And in [iiia] the distinction between the *with* phrase and an instrument is evident from the possibility of combining them: *We covered the grave with leaves with a garden-fork.* The PP in [iiia] can be identified with the non-core complement used in the *spray/load* construction of §8.3.1, and the NP *leaves* can be regarded as having the theme role. The [a] and [b] versions of [iii] differ in terms of the kind of situation involved: [iiia] is dynamic, expressing an occurrence, while [iiib] has not only a dynamic interpretation but also (and more saliently) one where it describes a state. A considerable number of verbs enter into the contrasts illustrated here for *offend* and *cover*; further examples are given in:

[77]	i LIKE *OFFEND*	*affect*	*amuse*	*appall*	*bewilder*	*depress*
		discourage	*enthrall*	*humiliate*	*hurt*	*worry*
	ii LIKE *COVER*	*adorn*	*bathe*	*clutter*	*fill*	*flood*
		line	*litter*	*stain*	*surround*	*wreathe*

The PPs in [76iv–vii] are various kinds of locatives. Only a few verbs, closely related semantically to those used in [76], enter into these contrasts: for example, *heat* and *scorch* are found in [iv], *feed* and *house* in [v], *incorporate* and *omit* in [vi], *bake* and *weave* (both rather unlikely in the bivalent version, however) in [vii]. In [viii] (where it is hard to find a convincing replacement for *see*) the PP is a temporal. Finally, the *for* phrase in [ix] expresses the price role and the trivalent–bivalent contrast is found with a few related verbs such as *obtain, reserve*, etc.[72]

8.4 Contrasts between separate complements and a single combined complement

(a) Oblique of trivalent incorporated into object of bivalent

[78] i	a. *She kissed him on the cheek.*	b. *She kissed his cheek.*
ii	a. *She praised him for his sincerity.*	b. *She praised his sincerity.*

Here [a] has two internal complements while [b] has only one, but the content of that one complement covers that of the two complements of [a]. The object of [a], *him*,

[72] Note that *sell* differs from *buy* in entering into the transitive–intransitive contrast instead: *We sold the house for $200,000* or *The house sold for $200,000* but not **$200,000 sold the house.*

corresponds to the genitive *his* functioning as subject-determiner within the object NP of [b]. An alternative pattern is for it to correspond to the complement in an *of* phrase (*She praised the auditors for their diligence* ~ *She praised the diligence of the auditors*). In [ia] the PP expresses a body-part location (and allows a variety of locative prepositions), while in [iia] the oblique expresses a property and the normal preposition is *for*. Verbs following the patterns of *kiss* and *praise* are illustrated in [79i–ii] respectively:

[79]	i	*bang*	*bump*	*hammer*	*hit*	*kick*	*poke*
		prick	*punch*	*scrap*	*smack*	*tap*	*touch*
	ii	*admire*	*appreciate*	*censure*	*commend*	*denounce*	*despise*
		envy	*fear*	*like*	*need*	*respect*	*value*

These may be contrasted with such verbs as *break* and *discern*, which allow only the bivalent construction: *She broke his arm* (not **She broke him in/on the arm*); *She discerned his anxiety* (not **She discerned him for his anxiety*).

(b) Oblique of bivalent incorporated into subject of monovalent

[80] a. *<u>The shares</u> increased <u>in value</u>.* b. *<u>The value of the shares</u> increased.*

This contrast is like those considered in (a) except that the core complement involved is subject rather than object. Again we can have either a genitive, as in *The shares' value increased* or an *of* phrase, as in the example cited. This intransitive contrast is found in clauses expressing a change of state involving the increase or decrease of some measurable property such as price, length, weight, etc. Other verbs found here include:

[81] *appreciate* *decline* *decrease* *drop* *fluctuate* *soar*

5

Nouns and noun phrases

John Payne
Rodney Huddleston

This chapter is concerned with the structure of noun phrases (NPs) and with the syntax of two lexical categories that function primarily within that structure: **nouns** and **determinatives**.

1 Distinctive properties of nouns and NPs

Summary of defining properties of NPs

[1] i	NP FUNCTION	NPs are prototypically capable, when placed in an appropriate case-form, of functioning as a complement in clause structure, i.e. as subject (*The doctor arrived*), object (*We need a doctor*), or predicative complement (*Kim is a doctor*).
ii	NP STRUCTURE	Except in what we refer to as the fused-head construction (*Two of them were broken*; *Many would disagree*; *It benefits the rich*), NPs consist of a noun as head, alone or accompanied by one or more dependents.

Summary of defining properties of nouns

[2] i	INFLECTION	Nouns prototypically inflect for number (singular vs plural) and for case (plain vs genitive).
ii	FUNCTION	Nouns characteristically function as head in NP structure.
iii	DEPENDENTS	Various dependents occur exclusively or almost exclusively with nouns as head: certain determinatives (*a book*, *every day*), pre-head AdjPs (*good news*), relative clauses (*people who work*). Conversely, nouns differ from verbs and prepositions in that they do not take objects: *I dislike it* but not **my dislike it*.

Inflection of nouns

The four inflectional forms of prototypical nouns are illustrated in [3] for regular ***dog*** and irregular ***child***:

[3]	PLAIN	GENITIVE	PLAIN	GENITIVE
SINGULAR	*dog*	*dog's*	*child*	*child's*
PLURAL	*dogs*	*dogs'*	*children*	*children's*

Not all nouns have contrasting singular and plural forms: *equipment*, for example, has no plural counterpart, and *outskirts* no singular; we take up these matters in §3.2.

Personal pronouns have a different set of inflectional forms, as illustrated in:

[4]

NOMINATIVE	ACCUSATIVE	DEPENDENT GENITIVE	INDEPENDENT GENITIVE	REFLEXIVE
I	*me*	*my*	*mine*	*myself*
he	*him*	*his*	*his*	*himself*
she	*her*	*her*	*hers*	*herself*

Pronouns included in the category of nouns

Traditionally pronouns are regarded as a separate part of speech, but there are strong grounds for treating them as a subcategory of noun. They differ inflectionally from prototypical nouns and permit a narrower range of dependents, but they qualify as nouns by virtue of heading phrases which occur in the same functions as phrases headed by nouns in the traditional sense, i.e. common and proper nouns. This functional likeness between common nouns, proper nouns, and pronouns is illustrated for the three main clause-structure complement functions in:

[5]

	COMMON/PROPER NOUN	PRONOUN	
i	a. *[The boss] / [Liz] was late.*	b. *[She] was late.*	[subject]
ii	a. *I'll tell [the boss] / [Liz].*	b. *I'll tell [her].*	[object]
iii	a. *It was [the boss] / [Liz] who left.*	b. *It was [she/her] who left.*	[predicative]

Other functions of NPs

In addition to their prototypical function as complements in clause structure, NPs may appear with a number of other functions, including the following:

[6]

i	*I was talking [to the doctor].*	[complement in PP]
ii	*I like [Sue's analysis of the passive construction].*	[subject-determiner in NP]
iii	*Fred arrived the day before yesterday.*	[adjunct in clause]
iv	*The nail was [three inches long].*	[modifier in AdjP]
v	*Fred arrived [a whole day late].*	[modifier in AdvP]
vi	*The wreck was discovered [a mile under the sea].*	[modifier in PP]
vii	*She was writing a treatise on [the opera 'Carmen'].*	[modifier in NP]
viii	*I finally met his wife, a distinguished anthropologist.*	[supplement]
ix	*Elizabeth, your taxi is here.*	[vocative]

In [ii] the relation of the NP *Sue's* to the larger (bracketed) NP bears significant resemblance to that between a subject NP and the verb in clause structure, and for this reason we analyse *Sue's* as **subject-determiner**, i.e. as combining the functions of subject and determiner. The functions in [iii–ix] allow only a quite restricted range of NPs.[1]

Inclusion of dummies in the category of NP

We naturally include in the category of NP any noun-headed unit which, while not functioning in all of the clausal complement positions (subject, object, predicative complement), nevertheless occurs in at least one. This covers the dummy *there* of:

[7] *There are several options open to us.* [subject]

[1] There are one or two NPs that are specialised to the modifying functions [iv–vi]: *It's [a damn sight better than last time]*; *It's [a tad small]*. These NPs do not occur as complement in clause structure.

We argued in Ch. 4, §3.2.2, that the subject here is *there*, not *several options*, and this is sufficient to establish that this semantically empty *there* qualifies as an NP, even though it occurs only as a subject in clauses like [7] or, derivatively, as object in the related raised object construction *I believe there to be several options open to us.*

Inclusion of bare role NPs in the category of NP

Also included in the category of NP are **bare role NPs** such as *president, deputy leader of the party* – bare in the sense that they do not contain a determiner. These qualify as NPs by virtue of occurring as the predicative complements of verbs like *be, become, appoint, elect*, but singular NPs of this kind are exceptional in that they cannot occur as subjects or objects, where a determiner such as the definite article *the* is required:

[8]	i	*I'd like to be president.*	[predicative complement]
	ii	*I'd like to meet *president / the president.*	[object]

2 Overview of noun classes and NP structure

Common nouns, proper nouns, and pronouns

Nouns can be divided in the first instance into three major classes: common nouns, proper nouns, and pronouns.

[1]	i	*The manager has just arrived.*	[common noun]
	ii	*Sue has just arrived.*	[proper noun]
	iii	*She has just arrived.*	[pronoun]

The main use of proper nouns is as head of an NP that serves as a **proper name**. They also have various other uses: in *He thinks he's [another Einstein]*, for example, the bracketed NP has a proper noun as head, but is not itself a proper name. It should also be borne in mind that not all proper names have proper nouns as head: the heads (underlined) of such names as *The Open University* and *Rhode Island*, for example, are common nouns. Pronouns fall into various more specific classes such as personal pronouns, interrogative pronouns, relative pronouns, etc.: they differ from ordinary nouns in that they allow a much narrower range of dependents, and in particular they do not combine with determiners. Pronouns and proper nouns are discussed in §§10 and 20 respectively; no separate section is needed for common nouns, which constitute the default category, lacking the special properties of the others.

Count and non-count nouns

A second important distinction is between count and non-count nouns:

[2]	i	a. *She was reading [a book].*	b. *May I have [another cake]?*	[count]
	ii	a. *She was reading [poetry].*	b. *May I have [some more cake]?*	[non-count]

Count nouns can combine with low numerals: *three books, ten cakes.* Many nouns allow both count and non-count interpretations, as illustrated here for *cake*. As a count noun *cake* denotes an individuated, separate entity, while as a non-count noun it denotes a substance.

Nominals

Intermediate between the noun and the NP we recognise a category of **nominals**:

[3] a. *the old man* b. *that book you were talking about*

In [a] the definite article *the* serves as determiner with respect to *old man*, while demonstrative *that* in [b] determines *book you were talking about.* The underlined expressions are not single words, hence not nouns, but nor are they themselves NPs – they cannot function as subject, object, etc., in clause structure (cf. *_Old man_ *gave it to me*; **Where can I find book you were talking about?*).

In these examples, the nominals are head of the NPs, but they can also function as pre-head dependent in NP structure, a function which cannot be realised by an NP:

[4] i a. *another United States warship* b. *those Ministry of Defence officials*
ii a. **another The United States warship* b. **those the Ministry of Defence officials*

In [i] *United States* and *Ministry of Defence* modify *warship* and *officials* respectively. They are larger than single words but again do not qualify as NPs (cf. **United States is sending a warship*, **She has joined Ministry of Defence*). To realise a function in clause structure we need to add a determiner to form an NP from the nominal: *The United States is sending a warship*; *She has joined the Ministry of Defence.* But the resultant NPs can't replace the nominals in pre-head dependent position, as shown in [ii].

Structures for the NPs in [3a] and [4ib] are shown in:

[5]

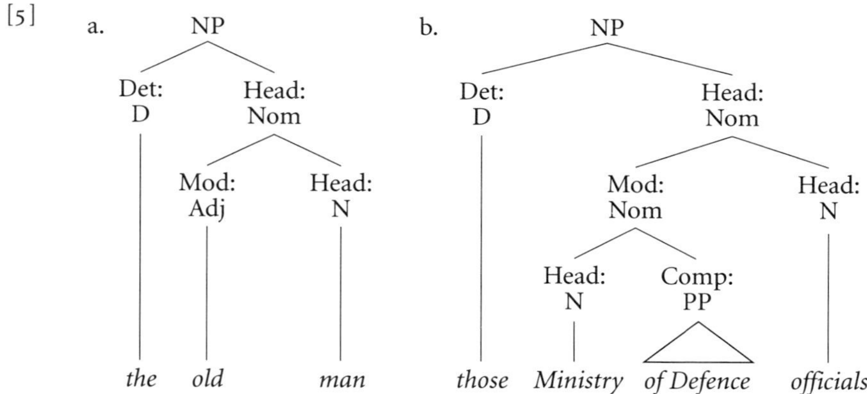

As explained in Ch. 2, §5, we generalise the concept of nominal to cover the case where the head of an NP is a single noun. Just as *old* in *the old man* is both an AdjP and an adjective, so *man* in *the man* is both a nominal and a noun; similarly in *those Ministry officials*, the modifier is realised by a nominal consisting of the noun *Ministry*. We simplify the tree diagrams by omitting the higher-level constituents if they consist of just a head element.

Functions in the structure of the NP

An NP consists of a head element, alone or accompanied by one or more dependents. Some kinds of dependent precede the head, others follow: we speak of **pre-head** and **post-head** dependents.

Head and ultimate head

We have seen that the head position can be filled by a noun, as in *the <u>man</u>*, or a nominal, as in *the <u>old man</u>*. In the latter example, the nominal itself has the noun *man* as head, and we will refer to this as the **ultimate head** of the NP, i.e. the final head element in a line running from the NP through any intermediate heads until we reach the level of the word. Except in most cases of the fused-head construction, therefore, the ultimate head in NP structure is a noun.

Determiner

From a grammatical point of view, the most important dependent is the determiner: in many cases this element is obligatory. The determiner position can be filled by a determinative (or a phrase headed by a determinative, i.e. a DP) or else by an NP, almost always in genitive case:

[6]	i	*He broke [<u>the</u> glass].*	[determinative]
	ii	*He broke [<u>the teacher's</u> glass].*	[genitive NP]

Note then that we distinguish between **determiner**, a function in the structure of the NP, and **determinative**, a word-category. As the examples show, the determiner position is not always filled by a determinative (or DP): *the teacher's* in [ii] has the same relation to the head *glass* as *the* in [i], but it has itself a structure where *the* is determiner and ***teacher*** is head, and hence is an NP. Conversely, while determinatives function most distinctively as determiner in NP structure, most of them are not restricted to that function. For example, determinative *all* is determiner in *all children* but modifier in *all the children* (an NP, with *the* as determiner) or *I was <u>all confused</u>* (an AdjP).

Internal dependents: modifiers and complements

Dependents which are immediate constituents of a nominal rather than of an NP we refer to as **internal dependents**. The determiner by contrast is an **external dependent**: see the structures represented in [5].

Further examples of internal dependents in pre-head position are given in:

[7]	i	*the <u>two</u> mistakes I made*	[determinative]
	ii	*an <u>extremely old</u> manuscript*	[AdjP]
	iii	*<u>Ministry of Defence</u> officials*	[nominal]
	iv	*some <u>wonderfully warm</u> <u>woollen</u> blankets*	[AdjP + adj]

Determinatives like *two* function as internal dependent when they follow a determiner, as in [i], but otherwise function as determiner, as in *I found [<u>two</u> mistakes]*. Other types of pre-head internal dependent do not presuppose the presence of a determiner, as is evident from [iii]. The construction is recursive, so that in [iv], for example, *woollen* modifies *blankets* to form the nominal *woollen blankets*, and then *wonderfully warm* modifies this to form the larger nominal *wonderfully warm woollen blankets*, which enters into construction with the determiner *some* to form the whole NP.

Internal dependents in post-head position are illustrated in:

[8]	i	*a house <u>as big as I have ever seen</u>*	[AdjP]
	ii	*the nightlife <u>in Paris</u>*	[PP]
	iii	*the proposal <u>which she made</u>*	[relative clause]
	iv	*the photographs <u>of Paris</u> <u>which her father had taken</u>*	[PP + relative clause]

Like those in pre-head position, these dependents form a nominal with the head, and again the construction is recursive. In [iv], for example, the PP *of Paris* combines with the noun *photographs* to form the nominal *photographs of Paris*, and this in turn is postmodified by the relative clause yielding a larger nominal which is determined by *the*. *Photographs of Paris which her father had taken* is thus the immediate head of the NP, while the noun *photographs* is the ultimate head.

Within the category of internal dependents we will draw a distinction between modifiers and complements. The pre-head dependents in [7] are modifiers, while complements are seen in *the finance minister*, *our legal advisor*, and the like. Of the post-head dependents in [8], *of Paris* is a complement and the rest modifiers.

External modifier: predeterminer and peripheral

External dependents are immediate constituents of an NP, not a nominal. The determiner, which we have already covered, is external in this sense. In addition there are external modifiers, which modify an NP. These are of two kinds, **predeterminer modifiers** (or simply **predeterminers**) and **peripheral modifiers**.

[9]	i	a. *He destroyed [both those copies].*	[predeterminer (modifier)]
		b. *It's [two thirds the price of the other one].*	
		c. *She had [such a brilliant idea].*	
	ii	a. *[Even this house] is too expensive.*	[peripheral modifier]
		b. *We couldn't manage with [the car alone].*	
		c. *He took [by far the most difficult path].*	

Predeterminer modifiers have a variety of forms, including the determinatives *all* and *both*, fractions, multipliers (*twice*, *three times*, etc.), and a small range of adjectives (e.g. *such* in [ic]) or AdjPs (*[How large a piece] do you need?*). A predeterminer modifier normally precedes a determiner: in *both copies*, for example, *both* is determiner, not predeterminer as in [ia], and in *such brilliant ideas* the *such* is an internal modifier.

Peripheral modifiers have the form of adverbs, PPs, or reflexive pronouns (*Jill herself*). They occur either initially or finally, and in the former case precede any predeterminer: *[Even such a pessimist as your father] admits the prospects are improving.*

Tree structures for [9ia/iib] are as in [10].

[10]

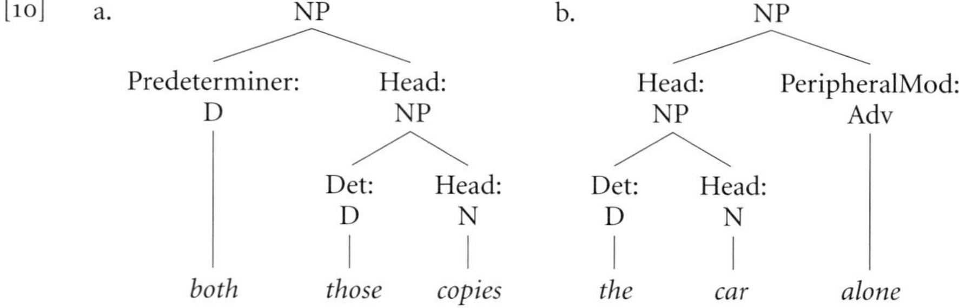

Sample structure for NP containing multiple dependents

To conclude this overview of the structure of NPs (with non-fused heads), we give the structure for an example containing multiple dependents in [11], where the triangle notation is used for elements whose internal structure is not analysed.

[11]

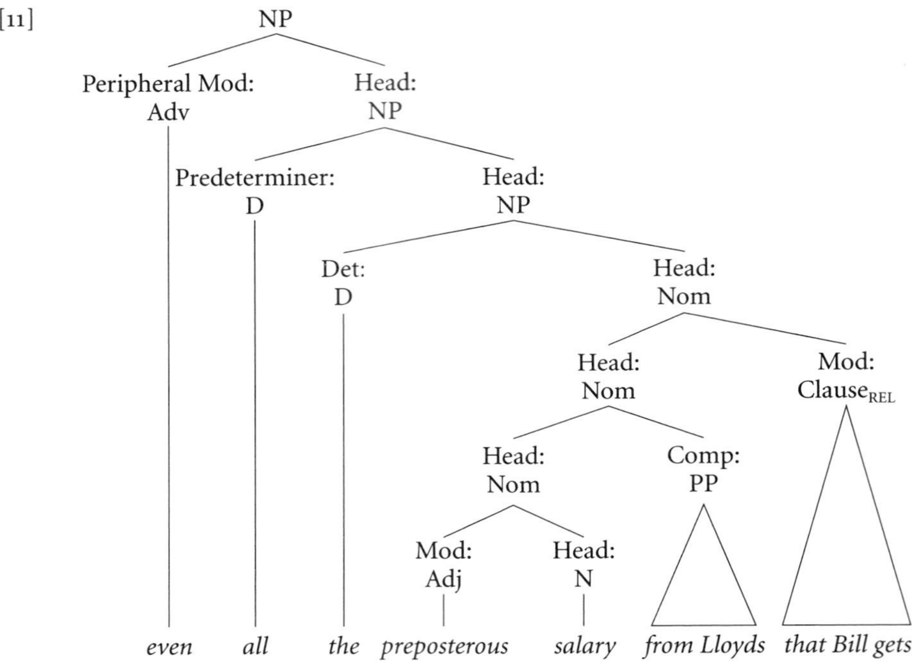

Fused-head constructions

Fused-head NPs are those where the head is realised jointly with a dependent function. The major case is where the head is fused with a dependent in NP structure – an internal modifier, a determiner, or (occasionally) a predeterminer:[2]

[12]	i	a. *He ignored [the most important of her criticisms].*	[modifier-head]
		b. *This proposal would benefit [the rich].*	
	ii	a. *Four boys played croquet and [two] played tennis.*	[determiner-head]
		b. *[Many] would agree with you on that point.*	
	iii	*Jo earns three times that amount, and I earn [double].*	[predeterminer-head]

The bracketed expressions here are NPs, and the underlined expressions combine the function of head with that of a dependent. In [i] *most important* is understood in part in the same way as in the non-fused construction *the most important criticisms*, but in [i] it is also occupying the head position, with *of her criticisms* as complement. In some cases it would be possible to simply add a separate head without changing the meaning: for example, we could replace *many* in [iib] by *many people* and *double* in [iii] by *double that amount*. This is not possible in cases like [i], however, and it is for this reason that we analyse the construction in terms of fusion of the head with a dependent function rather than in terms of ellipsis of the head.[3] Tree-diagrams for NPs with fused heads are given in §9 (p. 412).

[2] A more complex case of fusion is between the head and the initial element of a relative clause, as in *He quickly devoured [what was left of the shepherd's pie]*. This fused relative construction is discussed in Ch. 12, §6.3.

[3] There is one other construction, a minor one, where we recognise an NP that does not have a noun as head. This is what we call a hybrid NP, with a gerund-participial VP as head: *There was [no stopping her]*. For discussion, see Ch. 14, §1.6.

On one dimension, we can distinguish different types of fused-head according to the syntactic category of the head. On another, we can distinguish among them on the basis of their structure and interpretation. Here we have the following three types.

(a) Simple fused-head NPs

This type is illustrated in the *two* of [12iia] and *double* of [iii]. Here a head can be added that is recoverable from an antecedent: *two boys* and *double that amount.*

(b) Partitive fused-head NPs

The most important of her criticisms ([12ia]) is a **partitive NP**; other examples are *most of the boys, two of these chairs*, and so on. The NP contains an *of* PP and denotes a subset of the set denoted by the complement of *of*, i.e. by the **partitive oblique**. The examples given are explicitly partitive, but we also have implicit partitives, where the *of* phrase is missing but recoverable, as in *He made ten mistakes but most were fairly trivial*: we understand "most of them".

(c) Special fused-head NPs

The remaining two examples in [12], *the rich* and *many*, fall into neither of the above relatively straightforward categories and have what we call special interpretations. *The rich* is here understood as "rich people", and *many* as "many people", but special interpretations do not always incorporate "people". In *They are striving for* [*the unobtainable*], for example, we understand "that which is unobtainable".

Subordinate clauses excluded from the NP category

Certain kinds of subordinate clause – those commonly called 'noun clauses' in traditional grammar – bear some resemblance to NPs, but do not qualify for inclusion in that category. Compare:

[13]	i	*That he was guilty was obvious to everyone.*	[declarative content clause]
	ii	*Whether it will work remains unclear.*	[interrogative content clause]
	iii	*For her to be so late is most unusual.*	[infinitival clause]
	iv	*Finding suitable lodgings proved to be difficult.*	[gerund-participial clause]

Such clauses are like NPs in that they function as subject or internal complement of a verb. But their distribution is by no means the same as that of NPs. For example, such clauses occur as extraposed subject, as in *It was obvious to everyone that he was guilty*, etc., whereas all but a very narrow range of NPs are excluded from this position. Most importantly, subordinate clauses differ markedly from NPs in their internal structure. In [i–iii] we have a subordinator and a clearly verbal head. The gerund-participial construction in [iv] does not allow a subordinator and has a closer relation to an NP than the other types of subordinate clause, but here too there are good reasons for treating it as a clause rather than an NP, as argued in Ch. 14, §1.6.

3 Number and countability

The grammatical term **number** is the name of the system contrasting singular and plural. Some languages have more than two terms in the number system: it is not uncommon, for example, for there to be a dual category, indicating "two" (with plural then characteristically expressing the meaning "more than two"). There are a few places in English where a feature dual is relevant (e.g. in *both* and *either*), but the number system itself simply contrasts singular and plural ("more than one").

The number system applies primarily to nouns and NPs – with the number of an NP generally but not invariably matching that of its head noun. The system is relevant in four main areas of the grammar:

[1] i Noun inflection: characteristically, plural nouns are morphologically marked (*dog·s*) while singular nouns are unmarked, identical with the lexical base (*dog*).
ii Agreement and selection within the NP: *this dog* vs *these dogs* (agreement), *a dog* but *several dogs* (selection).
iii Pronoun–antecedent agreement: *My dog hid its bone* vs *My dogs hid their bones.*
iv Subject–verb agreement: *The dog likes her* vs *The dogs like her.*

We deal with these issues in §§3.2, 3.4, 17, and 18, but first we need to examine the distinction between count and non-count nouns, since this interacts in important ways with the number system.

3.1 Count and non-count nouns

As the terms indicate, **count** nouns denote entities that can be counted, while **non-count** nouns denote entities that cannot be counted:

[2] i *We need another plate.* [count]
ii *We need some more crockery.* [non-count]

Test for countability: occurrence with cardinal numerals

A simple test for count nouns is the ability to combine with the cardinal numerals *one, two, three*, etc.:

[3] i *one plate ~ two plates ~ three plates* [count]
ii **one crockery ~ *two crockeries ~ *three crockeries* [non-count]

The count vs non-count distinction applies to senses or uses of nouns

Many nouns can be used with either a count or a non-count interpretation:

[4] i *Would you like [another chocolate]?* [count]
ii *Would you like [some more chocolate]?* [non-count]

Chocolate in [ii] denotes a food substance, whereas in [i] it denotes an individual unit consisting of that substance (in either case there may be additional matter beside the pure chocolate substance: filling, nuts, etc.). We regard this as a case of **polysemy**, not **homonymy**. Homonymy is the phenomenon where distinct lexical items happen to be pronounced and spelled alike. A standard example is *bank*, where we distinguish two homonymous lexical items, one denoting a financial institution, the other the sloping margin of a river. These happen to derive ultimately from the same etymological source, but they have come into English via different routes and, more importantly, they are not perceived as being semantically related. But in the case of [4] there is a clear relation between the two meanings, and we therefore take them to be senses of a single lexical item. *Chocolate* accordingly exhibits polysemy: it has more than one sense.

It follows that when we speak of count nouns and non-count nouns it is to be understood that we are concerned with nouns as used with a count and non-count interpretation respectively. There are, certainly, some nouns, such as *piece*, which have no established non-count use, and others, such as *crockery* above, which have no established count use. These are simply the limiting cases; the dual use of *chocolate* is not remotely exceptional but is representative of an extremely widespread phenomenon. The following sample should give some idea of how pervasive it is:

[5]	COUNT	NON-COUNT
i	a. *This proposal has three advantages.*	b. *They took advantage of us.*
ii	a. *He's promoting a new slimming aid.*	b. *Foreign aid has been reduced again.*
iii	a. *I quoted two authorities in support.*	b. *They don't have much authority.*
iv	a. *It is certainly a fine building.*	b. *There's plenty of building going on.*
v	a. *Both covers were torn.*	b. *The trees provided useful cover.*
vi	a. *There are three details I would add.*	b. *They didn't go into much detail.*
vii	a. *Change over to another discipline.*	b. *We need rather more discipline.*
viii	a. *My three main duties are as follows.*	b. *She has a strong sense of duty.*
ix	a. *She wants a football for Christmas.*	b. *Let's play football.*
x	a. *Australia won more golds than ever.*	b. *It isn't really made of gold.*
xi	a. *That's one of my two pet hates.*	b. *He still seems full of hate.*
xii	a. *I can't see a single white hair.*	b. *He has blond hair.*
xiii	a. *Several improvements were made.*	b. *There's been little improvement.*
xiv	a. *These are our two major necessities.*	b. *I see little necessity for change.*
xv	a. *She's written five papers already.*	b. *We haven't got much paper left.*
xvi	a. *I have several reasons for concern.*	b. *He's little reason to doubt her word.*
xvii	a. *We've three sausages left.*	b. *I don't like sausage.*
xviii	a. *I've just had another good sleep.*	b. *I've not had much sleep.*
xix	a. *The word has two different spellings.*	b. *They should be taught spelling.*
xx	a. *These animals have two stomachs.*	b. *I haven't much stomach for it.*
xxi	a. *All previous studies are flawed.*	b. *The question needs more study.*
xxii	a. *Bear these truths constantly in mind.*	b. *There's some truth in what he says.*
xxiii	a. *The gadget has several uses.*	b. *It's not much use complaining now.*
xxiv	a. *I've read her most important works.*	b. *They haven't put in enough work.*
xxv	a. *These are my two main worries.*	b. *It's a source of great worry to me.*

Count and non-count conceptualisations

A count noun denotes a class of individuated entities of the same kind. *Boy*, for example, denotes the class of boys. The individual entities are atomic in the sense that they cannot be divided into smaller parts of the same kind as the whole. A boy consists of parts – head, arms, legs, etc. – but these parts are not themselves boys. The entities denoted by non-count nouns may be uncountable for a variety of reasons, of which we will consider just two at this point. One very salient case is that of nouns denoting physical substances: *water, milk, soil, silver, hydrogen*, and so on. The substances denoted by such words are not inherently bounded: particular amounts can be separated out and put in individual containers, but (in their primary senses) such nouns do not apply to separate amounts. Water, milk, soil, silver, and hydrogen are not atomic. An amount of water can be divided arbitrarily into parts which are themselves (amounts of) water. There is no individuation by non-count nouns of this type, hence no basis for counting.

A second type of non-count noun is illustrated by our original example, *crockery*. This covers a variety of objects – plates, dishes, cups, saucers, etc. – united by their shared function with respect to food and drink. The subdivisibility feature applies here only to a limited extent. Given a reasonably large amount of crockery, it could be divided into two parts each of which would itself constitute crockery, but such subdivision cannot be carried out arbitrarily, as it can with substances. Thus the handle of a cup, or indeed a whole cup, does not constitute crockery. What distinguishes crockery from water is that it is heterogeneous while water is homogeneous. Any subamount of water is still water, but crockery is made up of entities of different kinds. *Crockery* denotes a heterogeneous **aggregate** of parts. Nevertheless, that aggregate, like a substance, is not inherently bounded, so that we can add or subtract pieces, and still be left with crockery. This is what makes it uncountable. We can count the individual plates, dishes, cups, saucers, etc., that make up crockery, but not the aggregate itself. A sample of other non-count nouns denoting heterogeneous aggregates of this type is given in:

[6]	*baggage*	*bedlinen*	*clothing*	*cutlery*	*equipment*	*footwear*
	furniture	*jewellery*	*luggage*	*machinery*	*tableware*	*underwear*

Count/non-count polysemy

In some cases, the existence of paired count and non-count senses is entirely predictable, so that it is not necessary for a dictionary to list both: one can be inferred from the other. But very often we find pairings that are restricted to particular items, so that both senses have to be specified for the lexical items concerned. Consider the following pairs.

(a) Drink/food substances and servings

[7] i *I don't like beer.* [non-count]
ii *She offered me another beer.* [count]

Names of drinks are primarily non-count, but systematically allow count interpretations where the noun denotes a serving of the drink – a glass, bottle, cup, or whatever. The paired senses illustrated in [7] are found also with *coffee, tea, lemonade, orange-juice, brandy*, and so on – including drinks known by proprietary names, such as *Ovaltine, Milo*, and the like. This is one of the regular cases where the secondary sense, here "serving of...", is predictable and need not be listed. With foods we have a contextually much more restricted count sense applicable to ordering in restaurants, cafés, etc.:

[8] i *I'm going to have pork.* [non-count]
ii *That makes five porks and two turkeys, please.* [count]

(b) Foods and varieties

[9] i *We're having cheese for lunch.* [non-count]
ii *These are two of my favourite cheeses.* [count]

Example [i] represents the primary sense, while [ii] has the secondary sense "kind/variety of cheese". This too is a case where the count sense is predictable and does not need individual listing: compare *an excellent brandy, a slightly bitter coffee, a very popular bread, a mild mustard*, and so on.

(c) Animals and food

[10] i *I was lucky enough to catch a salmon today.* [count]
ii *We're having salmon for dinner.* [non-count]

The primary sense here is the count one, with *salmon* denoting a fish of a particular species; in the secondary non-count sense it denotes a food substance. This extension of meaning applies very generally with fish. It is also found with poultry: *chicken, turkey,* etc. Similarly with *lamb,* but for *cow, pig, sheep, deer* there are separate terms for the meat: *beef, pork, mutton, venison.* Note also that the food sense can be further reinterpreted as count with the restaurant order sense mentioned in (a) above: *One roast beef and two lambs, please.*

(d) Abstracts and event instantiations

[11] i a. *Considerable injustice was revealed during the enquiry.*
b. *Serious harm was done to the project's prospects.* } [abstract, non-count]
ii a. *Two fundamental injustices were revealed during the enquiry.*
b. **Two serious harms were done to the project's prospects.* } [event, count]

There are a large number of nouns denoting abstract concepts which are non-count in their primary sense. With some there is a secondary count sense denoting an event which constitutes an instance of the abstract concept, as with *injustice* in [ii]. But this extension is not regular and predictable. Although events in which injustice is instantiated are countable, events in which harm is instantiated are not. The same variability is found with abstract nouns derived from verbs. Compare, for example, *discussion* and *permission,* abstract nouns derived from *discuss* and *permit* respectively:

[12] i a. *Full discussion of the land question is vital.*
b. *Permission is required.* } [abstract, non-count]
ii a. *Two discussions of the land question took place.*
b. ?*Two separate permissions are required.* } [event, count]

Events which instantiate discussion are clearly countable, but those which instantiate permission are at best only marginally countable.

(e) Abstracts and results

[13] i *Necessity is the mother of invention.* [abstract, non-count]
ii ?*There were two separate inventions of the light-bulb.* [event, count]
iii *Edison was honoured for three separate inventions.* [result, count]

Nouns which denote results, however, are more generally countable than those denoting events: the count result sense of *invention* in [iii], for example, is fully acceptable, whereas the event sense in [ii] is again at best very marginal.

(f) Nonce substance interpretations of primarily count nouns

Concrete nouns whose primary sense is count may be 'coerced' into a non-count use, where the entities are reinterpreted as substance rather than individuals:

[14] i *The termite was living on a diet of book.*
ii *There was cat all over the driveway.*

These involve a somewhat contrived extension of the sense of *book* and *cat* – one that is in principle applicable quite generally, and that clearly does not need to be listed in dictionary entries.

The count vs non-count contrast and the system of number

Count nouns can be either singular or plural, whereas non-count nouns are generally singular. The singular non-count nouns in [6], for example, have no plural counterparts: **bedlinens*, **clothings*, **cutleries*, and so on. And where a noun has distinct count and non-count senses, occurrence of the plural form will normally force the count interpretation, as in *a box of chocolates*, *its advantages*, *these aids*, etc. We do, nevertheless, find some non-count plurals, so that the two systems of count vs non-count and singular vs plural cut across each other:

[15]		COUNT	NON-COUNT
	SINGULAR	*I'd like <u>an apple</u>.*	*I'd like <u>some cheese</u>.*
	PLURAL	*I'd like <u>some biscuits</u>.*	*I'd like <u>some oats</u>.*

Oats, unlike the ordinary plural *biscuits*, has no established singular counterpart and does not take numeral dependents: **an oat*, **two oats*.

Cross-linguistic differences in lexicalisation and conceptualisation

Whereas the count/non-count distinction appears to play a role in most if not all languages, the ways in which particular entities are conceptualised and lexicalised may vary considerably. One area in which there is variability is the treatment of more-or-less identical small entities (particles) which can be gathered together into a substance: if the particles are very small and non-significant, then the conceptualisation is likely to focus on the substance. Languages may differ, however, in how small an entity has to be to be treated as insignificant. In English for instance, the basic noun for "dust", "sand", "wheat", and "grass" is a non-count noun denoting the substance, just like *water*: cf. **one dust*, **one sand*, etc. If we want to talk about the individual particles, we have to use a syntactic construction headed by a separate particle-denoting count noun: *<u>particle</u> of dust*, *<u>grain</u> of sand*, *<u>ear</u> of wheat*, *<u>blade</u> of grass*. On the other hand, larger entities such as peas, strawberries, and potatoes are individuated in English and lexicalised as count nouns: *one pea*, *one strawberry*, *one potato* (we can also have *some mashed potato*, but this is a homogeneous substance prepared from potatoes). When peas, strawberries, and potatoes are gathered together, we simply pluralise the count noun: *peas*, *strawberries*, or *potatoes*. In Russian, by contrast, peas, strawberries, and potatoes are basically conceptualised as gathered, like grass, into substances denoted by non-count nouns, e.g. *trava* "quantity of grass", *gorox* "quantity of peas", *klubnika* "quantity of strawberries", *kartoška* "quantity of potatoes". Non-basic count forms, often referred to as 'singulative', are then required to denote individual units: blades of grass, separate peas, etc.

Similar, but less systematic, differences in lexicalisation can also be found with concrete nouns denoting aggregates, and with abstract nouns. In English, for example, *furniture* is a non-count singular noun and *contents* is a non-count plural. In French, the treatment is the reverse: *meubles* "furniture" is plural and *contenu* "contents" is singular. In English, information is conceptualised as a substance (*plenty of information* / **one information*) and for individual 'particles' we use a composite nominal *item/piece of information*; in French, on the other hand, the basic term is count (*une information* "an item of information").

Determiners in combination with count and non-count singular nouns

Some determiners combine with both count and non-count singular nouns:

[16]					
i	COUNT	*<u>the</u> house*	*<u>this</u> piece*	*<u>my</u> father*	*<u>no</u> pianist*
ii	NON-COUNT	*<u>the</u> equipment*	*<u>this</u> crockery*	*<u>my</u> clothing*	*<u>no</u> milk*

Similarly for *that*, other genitives, *some* and *any*, *which* and *what*. There are others, however, that are wholly or predominantly restricted to one or other class of noun.

(a) Incompatible with count singular nouns

[17] *a little* *enough* *little* *much* *sufficient*

[18]

		COUNT		NON-COUNT
i	a.	*Why has he so much/little priest?	b.	Why was there so much/little damage?
ii	a.	*He damaged a little knee.	b.	She drank a little water.
iii	a.	*He has got enough/sufficient son.	b.	He has got enough/sufficient strength.

Example [iia] is of course grammatical with *little* an adjective and *a* the indefinite article ("He damaged a small knee"): we are concerned here with *a little* as determinative. With nouns having both count and non-count senses, the occurrence of one of these items selects a non-count interpretation: *There isn't much chocolate left*; *We need a little discipline*; *Does it provide enough cover?*

(b) Incompatible with non-count singular nouns

[19] *another* *each* *either* *every* *neither* *one*

[20]

		COUNT		NON-COUNT
i	a.	Each/Every boy won a prize.	b.	*He broke each/every crockery.
ii	a.	I'll accept either/neither proposal.	b.	*I can repair either/neither damage.
iii	a.	Choose one/another leader.	b.	*Choose one/another clothing.

Occurrence of such a determiner with a noun that has both count and non-count senses selects the former: *He examined every chocolate in the box*; *Neither discipline appeals to her very much*; *One cover was torn.*

(c) The indefinite article *a*

In general, *a* selects a count singular noun: *a cup*, but not **a crockery*. *Would you like a chocolate?* therefore yields a count interpretation of *chocolate*. Under restricted conditions, however, *a* can combine with a non-count singular:

[21]

i	a.	A number of problems remain.	b.	He wastes a great deal of time.
ii	a.	I have a high regard for them.	b.	Jill has a good knowledge of Greek.

Number and *deal* in [i] are quantificational nouns: they serve here to quantify (imprecisely) problems and time. *Deal* is restricted to the singular; ***number*** can inflect for plural (*Huge numbers of bees were swarming in the garden*), but in this imprecise quantificational sense it doesn't allow cardinal numerals (**Two numbers of problems remain*). *Regard* in the sense it has in [iia] has no plural (**We both have high regards for them*). *Knowledge* in [iib] is a clear case of a non-count noun: it has no established plural and combines with the determinatives *much*, *little*, *enough* (*They have little knowledge of the matter*). The effect of the *a* is to individuate a subamount of knowledge, her knowledge of Greek, but this individuation does not yield an entity conceptualised as belonging to a class of entities of the same kind: **Jill has an excellent knowledge of Greek and Liz has another*; **They both have excellent knowledges of Greek.*

(d) *All* as determiner

As determiner (as opposed to predeterminer), *all* in a singular NP is normally restricted to non-count nouns:

[22] a. **All cup had been broken.* b. *All fear had evaporated.*

It can, however, combine with count singulars denoting periods of time: *She spent all week marking exam papers*; *We were at home all morning.*

(e) Absence of determiner

Singular NPs with no determiner cannot normally have a count common noun as head:

[23]	i	a. **She married Englishman.*	b. *She always drinks water.*
	ii	a. **There had been a lot of vandal.*	b. *There had been a lot of vandalism.*

Chocolate is bad for your teeth or *I bought a bar of chocolate* therefore involve the non-count sense of *chocolate.*[4]

3.2 Singular and plural nouns

Most nouns have both singular and plural forms:

[24]	i	SINGULAR	*dog*	*fox*	*child*	*mouse*	*sheep*
	ii	PLURAL	*dogs*	*foxes*	*children*	*mice*	*sheep*

The singular is identical with the lexical base and the plural is formed from the base by suffixation or some other morphological process: this is a matter of inflection, and the formation of plural nouns is described in detail in Ch. 18, §4.1. The only point we need to make here is that with a small number of irregular nouns the plural form is identical with the singular, as with *sheep* in [24]; we refer to plurals that are identical with the lexical base as **base plurals**. This case is clearly distinct from that where a noun has a singular form but no plural, for base plurals can occur in the same positions as ordinary plurals. Compare, then:

[25]		NO PLURAL FORM	BASE PLURAL
	i	a. **these equipment*	b. *these sheep*
	ii	a. **The equipment are ready.*	b. *The sheep are ready.*

In examples like those in [24] the plural form applies to a set containing two or more of the entities to which the singular applies; nothing further need be said about such cases in this section. Our main focus will be on **plural-only nouns**, nouns which have either no singular form at all (as with *cattle* or *clothes*) or no singular form with a matching meaning (as with *glasses* in the sense "spectacles" or *greens* "green vegetables").[5] We will also consider, by way of contrast, singular nouns whose form resembles that of a plural noun (e.g. *mumps*, *mathematics*, and the like).

3.2.1 Plural-only nouns with the ·*s* ending

Bipartites

One quite large class of plural-only nouns consists of words denoting objects made up of two like parts: we refer to these as **bipartites.**[6] They include names of articles of clothing, tools, and optical aids, as in [26i–iii] respectively.

[4]Non-count nouns are often called 'mass' nouns. We have preferred 'non-count,' in part because it reflects clearly the test we use for determining whether a noun is count or non-count, in part because 'mass' is not suitable for the full range of non-count nouns. The term 'mass' is readily applicable with nouns like *water* or *coal* that denote substances but it is less evident that it applies transparently to abstract non-count nouns such as *knowledge, spelling, work.*

[5]Plural-only nouns are often referred to by the equivalent Latin term, 'pluralia tantum.' Some grammars, however, use this term for only a subset of plural-only nouns.

[6]They are sometimes called 'summation plurals,' though some writers use this term for other kinds of plural-only nouns too.

[26] i	*bloomers*	*breeches*	*briefs*	*britches* AmE	*corduroys*
	drawers	*flannels*	*jeans*	*knickerbockers*	*knickers*
	overalls BrE	*pajamas* AmE	*panties*	*pants*	*pyjamas* BrE
	shorts	*slacks*	*tights*	*trousers*	*trunks*
ii	*bellows*	*clippers*	*cutters*	*forceps*	*nutcrackers*
	pincers	*pliers*	*scales*	*scissors*	*secateurs*
	shears	*snippers*	*tongs*	*tweezers*	
iii	*binoculars*	*clip-ons*	*glasses*	*goggles*	*spectacles*

The bipartite nature of the objects is reflected in the common occurrence of these nouns in construction with *pair*: *a pair of trousers/shears/spectacles.*

The garment terms in [26i] denote clothes that are worn over the lower part of the body and cover the legs to varying degrees (or at least provide holes for them to pass through): it is of course the duality of the legs that is the source of the bipartite form of the garments. There are many words of this kind, some of them (such as *drawers*) now somewhat dated, others (such as *bloomers*) denoting garments worn in earlier times. Clothes for the upper body are not treated as bipartite even where they cover the arms; note in connection with this contrast between the upper and lower parts of the body that English has the word *sleeve* for the part of a garment covering an arm, but no comparable word for the part covering a leg. BrE *overalls*, however, denotes a garment covering both parts of the body; AmE here has singular *overall*, a term which in BrE denotes only a non-bipartite garment shaped like a coat. Several of the words in [i] have singular forms denoting a type of cloth, with the bipartite plural having a sense incorporating the meaning "trousers": corduroys, for example, are trousers made of corduroy. Two other words that might be included as peripheral members of this group denote straps for holding up trousers: *braces* in BrE and *suspenders* in AmE.

Bipartite tools typically have two mobile parts which come together and move apart. In the original type of scales, the two parts were trays at the end of a pivoted bar; changes in design have resulted in an object that is no longer physically bipartite, and while the plural form *scales* is applied to such objects in BrE, AmE has a singular: cf. (*a pair of*) *kitchen scales* vs *a kitchen scale.* There is similarly variation (though not regional) between (*a pair of*) *nutcrackers* and *a nutcracker.*

The bipartite nature of the optical words in [26iii] comes from their containing two pieces of glass (or glass substitute) for the eyes. *Glasses* itself is also found in various compounds: *field-glasses*, *sunglasses*, etc.

The bipartite structure of the three kinds of object motivates the construction with *pair*, and the plural form of the noun. But the two parts are essentially joined and do not have independent functions, and there is no singular form denoting just one of them: *He had *torn his left slack / *damaged the lower shear / *cracked the right spectacle.*[7] Thus while *He has a pair of shoes* entails *He has two shoes*, no such relation holds between *He has a pair of slacks/scissors/glasses* and *He has *two slacks / ?two scissors / two glasses.*

Outside the *pair* construction, bipartite plurals characteristically apply to single garments, tools, or optical devices: *I've torn my trousers*; *These scissors need sharpening*; *Where are the binoculars?* There is some uncertainty and variation among speakers as to

[7] Singular *trouser* is occasionally found (%*He had snagged his left trouser on the wire*), but for most speakers such examples are quite unacceptable.

how readily they can also be applied to a plurality of such objects. Compare:

[27] i a. *Corduroys are still fashionable.* b. %*I'll get both these trousers cleaned.*
ii a. *All the scissors need sharpening.* b. ?*Have you got two tweezers I can borrow?*

Example [ia] illustrates the generic use and is completely acceptable: it would be quite inappropriate to say *Pairs of corduroys are no longer fashionable* because the *pair* construction focuses on the individual objects. In [iia] we have reference to all members of some definite set of bipartite objects; this too has a high degree of acceptability, but this time the version with *pairs of scissors* would be acceptable too, though probably somewhat disfavoured relative to [iia] itself. Example [ib] is subject to variation between speakers: some find it acceptable, while others would require *both (these) pairs of trousers.* Example [iib] is significantly worse: there can be few speakers who find this as acceptable as *Have you got two pairs of tweezers I can borrow?* There may also be differences between the various bipartite nouns, with ?*I've only got two jeans* being perhaps worse than [iib]. Overall, however, bipartite plurals cannot be said to satisfy the test for count nouns.

It should be noted, finally, that there is a restricted use of bipartite nouns as singulars:

[28] i *This scissor reportedly never needs sharpening.*
ii *Ever wondered why someone can't design a flannel-lined jean?*
iii *Venetians were a wide-topped breeches narrowing to button or tie below the knee.*

Note that in [iii] (where *Venetians* denotes a garment) *breeches* retains the ·*s* ending: we take it to have been reanalysed as a non-inflectional suffix, like that in *mumps*, etc. discussed in §3.2.3 below. Examples like [28] are most likely to be encountered in the language of commerce or in non-fictional writing such as a historical survey of clothing, tools, and so on. The crucial feature of this usage is that the reference is to types, not individual specimens. For the latter the plural form is required (*These scissors* / **This scissor will have to be sharpened*), and it is for this reason that bipartites fall within our definition of plural-only nouns.[8]

Plurals denoting substances consisting of particles

[29] *dregs* *Epsom salts* *grits* AmE *oats*

The plurality of the particles accounts for the plural form of the nouns, but the individual particles are themselves of no significance, and this correlates with the lack of a singular form and the non-occurrence with cardinal numerals and comparable quantifiers: **one oat*, **two oats*, **several oats*, **how many oats*. (?*How much oats* is better, but of marginal status because of the conflict between *much* and plurality.) *Chives* might be included here, though the components would be described as blades, rather than particles. There are of course non-count singulars denoting substances consisting of particles: *sand*, *gravel*, *rice*, *sugar*, *salt* (as for use in cooking, for example, in contrast to *Epsom salts*), but the particles tend to be relatively larger in the case of the plural nouns (i.e. relative to the total amount of substance under consideration). In the case of such foods as peas and noodles the particles are large enough to be counted, so that ***pea*** and ***noodle*** are count nouns, even though they most often occur in the plural in contexts where one would be unlikely to be concerned with the number.

[8] The uninflected base is also found in compounds or as an attributive modifier: *a trouser-press*, *changes in forcep design*.

Plurals denoting aggregates of entities

[30]	*arms*	*clothes*	*contents*	*covers*	*dishes*
	goods	*groceries*	*leftovers*	*munitions*	*odds-and-ends*
	refreshments	*remains*	*spoils*	*supplies*	*valuables*

These are cover-terms for sets of entities of unlike kind: the plurality of the entities again matches the plural form, while their heterogeneity prevents counting. The aggregate nature of the denotation is comparable to that of the non-count singulars given in [6] above, and the difference in number between the singular and plural forms is difficult to explain in general terms. One grammatical difference is that the singulars but not the plurals occur in *of* complements to nouns like *item* and *piece*:

[31] i a. *an item of clothing* b. **an item of clothes*
ii a. *a piece of jewellery* b. **a piece of valuables*

Contents (as in *the contents of the drawer*) contrasts with singular *content* (*the content of the essay*); the latter is virtually restricted to the singular. Non-count *covers* denotes bedcovers, subsuming sheets, blankets, quilt, or whatever, and contrasts with count ***cover*** as used, for example, for a bookcover. Non-count *dishes*, as in *I must do/wash the dishes*, subsumes plates, cups, saucers, etc., in contrast to count ***dish***, denoting a shallow bowl.

Plurals denoting areas containing a plurality of entities without clear boundaries

[32] *bushes* *mountains* *plains* *steppes* *woods*

These can be ordinary count plurals (*We should plant a few bushes*; *She climbed two mountains in one day*), but they have non-count interpretations in examples like [33]:

[33] a. *He threw it in the bushes.* b. *She lives in the mountains.*

Here we understand an area containing bushes or mountains that are not perceived as discrete enough to be countable. Note the sharp contrast between [a] and *He threw it in two bushes* and the absurdity of asking, in connection with [b], *How many mountains does she live in? Catacombs* and *ruins* have affinities with this type of plural.

Other plural-only nouns

[34]						
	i	*beginnings*	*belongings*	*furnishings*	*goings-on*	*lodgings*
		makings	*proceedings*	*savings*	*surroundings*	*writings*
	ii	*amends*	*damages*	*deserts*	*dues*	*earnings*
		proceeds	*reparations*	*reprisals*	*returns*	*wages*
	iii	*apologies*	*compliments*	*condolences*	*regards*	*remembrances*
	iv	*alms*	*arrears*	*ashes*	*auspices*	*brains*
		credentials	*customs*	*elders*	*eye-drops*	*folks*
		genitals	*grassroots*	*greens*	*grounds*	*guts*
		heads	*heavens*	*holidays*	*humanities*	*letters*
		looks	*mains*	*minutes*	*odds*	*particulars*
		reams	*spirits*	*tails*	*troops*	*wits*

The nouns in [34i] contain the suffix ·*ing* attached to a verb base. For most there is also a singular form, but the meaning relation is not that of a normal singular–plural pair. For example, *The movement had its beginnings in the seventeenth century* does not imply that it had more than one beginning. *Lodgings* can denote a single rented place of accommodation (*My lodgings are next to the post office*) or a plurality of such places (*Their lodgings are several miles apart*). *Makings* means roughly "potential": *Kim has the makings of a fine writer.* Plural-only *savings* denotes money that one has saved out of income or whatever (*We may have to draw on our savings*), whereas ***saving***, with both singular and plural forms, denotes a reduction in time or money (*You can make a big saving / big savings by buying at the hypermarket*). Singular *writing* has a variety of senses, but none quite matches that of plural *writings*, which applies to literary output. *Belongings* and *furnishings* denote aggregates, like those in [30].

The nouns in [34ii] have to do with compensation and reward for what has been done; *earnings* could also have been included in [i]. For most, the singular form exists, but not with the standard sense relation to the plural. *Wages* simply means "pay"; compare *I haven't received this week's wages yet* and *There has been little increase in the average weekly wage this year. Returns* differs little from one sense of *return*: *I'm not satisfied with the return/returns on my investment.*

The nouns in [34iii] are used in relatively formal expressions of feelings: *Please accept my condolences*; *My father sends his regards. Thanks* and *congratulations* might be added here or in [ii].

Finally, [34iv] contains a set of miscellaneous plural-only nouns. *Heads* and *tails* apply in the tossing of coins. *Elders* means "those who are older": *Show more respect for your elders. Eye-drops* can be a straightforward plural of *eye-drop* (*He put two eye-drops in each eye*), but in *a bottle of eye-drops* it denotes a quantity of liquid. Plural-only non-count *brains* is seen in examples like *Use your brains* or *She has brains* (which is close in meaning to *She has a good brain*); contrast the ordinary count *brains* of *She examined the brains of the victims.* Others that can also be ordinary plurals with a count sense are: *customs* (as in *customs and excise*); *grounds* (*the palace grounds*); *looks* (*Kim has good looks*); *spirits* (*They are in good spirits*). *Folks* is used with genitive determiners in the same meaning as *family*, and is informal in style: *My folks are pretty dumb.* It can also be used as a form of address, and is not restricted in this case to family members: *goodbye, folks!* (For *folk* as a plural form, see §3.2.2 below.)

Most of the nouns in [34] not only lack a singular form but also exclude cardinal numerals with the plural: **seven amends*; **three folks of mine.* However, *minutes* "written record of a meeting" is marginally countable: *Three separate minutes were kept of the meeting.* Similarly with *arrears*: *There are three separate arrears on this account.*

Functionally restricted plural-only nouns

[35]	i	*at loggerheads with*	*at odds with*	*for keeps*
		in cahoots with	*in the doldrums*	*on friendly terms with*
	ii	*I'm no longer friends with him.*		

There are a good number of more or less fixed phrases containing non-count plurals, as in [i]. In [ii] the plurality of *friends* derives from the fact that two people are involved in the relation (cf. *We are no longer friends*), but the plural appears in predicative complement function with a singular subject. This plural-only non-count use is to be distinguished from the ordinary use seen in *They are friends of mine* (cf. *He's a friend of mine*; *They are two old friends of mine*); the *friends with* construction focuses on the relationship, while the ***friend** of* construction gives a descriptive property of the predicand.

3.2.2 Other plural-only nouns

(a) Foreign plurals with no singular counterpart

[36] *genitalia* *minutiae* *regalia*

See also §3.2.4 for some foreign plurals that have been partially reanalysed as singular.

(b) Uninflected plural-only nouns

There are a few plural-only nouns that are not morphologically marked as plural:

[37] i *cattle* *livestock* *police* *poultry*$_1$ *vermin*
ii *folk* *people*$_1$

The lack of a singular–plural contrast is seen in such pairs as:

[38] a. *These cattle belong to my uncle.* b. **This cattle belongs to my uncle.*

The items in [37i] cannot be used with low numerals, but are found with high round numerals (and hence might be classified as 'quasi-count nouns'). Their denotation is thought of en masse, with none of the individuation into atomic entities that the use of a low numeral implies. Genuine count nouns (usually of somewhat more specific meaning) must be substituted in order for this individuation to take place. Compare:

[39] i *a thousand <u>cattle</u>* **seven <u>cattle</u>* *seven <u>cows</u>*
ii *two hundred <u>police</u>* **four <u>police</u>* *four <u>policemen</u> / <u>police officers</u>*

An alternative, in the case of *cattle*, is to use a quantificational noun construction: *seven head of cattle. Poultry*$_1$ denotes hens and other fowl; it is distinguished from the non-count singular-only *poultry*$_2$, which denotes the meat of these birds (*Poultry is cheaper than beef*).

Folk and *people*$_1$, by contrast, do occur with low numerals: *these three city folk, two people*;[9] they can therefore be regarded as exceptional count nouns, differing from normal ones only in the absence of a singular. *People*$_1$ is distinguished from ***people***$_2$, a noun with regular singular and plural forms: compare *They are a very family-oriented people*$_2$ and *Similar customs are found among many peoples*$_2$ *of the world.* Instead of **one people*$_1$ we have *one person*, ***person*** being an ordinary noun with singular and plural forms. *Persons* is then in competition with *people*$_1$; the latter is considerably more common, *persons* often (though not invariably) being associated with legal or quasi-legal contexts (cf. *Persons using the footbridge do so at their own risk*). *Folk* has a similar meaning to *people*$_1$, but its use is mostly restricted to a few standard collocations: *country folk, city folk, island folk, the folk around here.* It can also be used with proper name modifiers, with the same connotations of group identity: *Virginia folk, East Anglia folk.* (For plural-only *folks*, containing the regular plural suffix, see [34iv] above.)

3.2.3 Singular nouns with the ·*s* ending

There are a number of nouns in English which appear to have the same ending as plural nouns but which are in fact singular. One clear example is the disease name *shingles.* There is a singular noun *shingle* but it is not related semantically (or etymologically) to

[9] There is, however, a slightly old-fashioned use with the sense "family" which is non-count: *My people have lived in these parts for several generations.*

shingles. The existence of the singular form *shingle* helps give *shingles* the appearance of a plural form, but this appearance is misleading: it is singular. Evidence for saying that it is grammatically singular is provided by examples like:

[40] *Shingles is/*are often excruciatingly painful; I hope I never get it/*them.*

This case is to be distinguished from that illustrated in:

[41] i *<u>A very pleasant three days</u> was spent with Kim's aunt in Brighton.*
ii *<u>Three ounces of sugar</u> is rather too much.*

Here *days* and *ounces* are plural nouns even though the NPs containing them are construed as singular, as shown by the 3rd person singular verb-forms *was* and *is*. These involve semantically motivated recategorisation: in [i] the nominal *three days* is recategorised as singular by virtue of denoting a continuous stretch of time, while in [ii] the NP *three ounces of sugar* is recategorised as singular by virtue of denoting a quantity. There is a clear distinction between these constructions (discussed in §3.4 below) and the *shingles* case, but we will see that there are some examples whose assignment to one or other type is more problematic.

An isolated example of the *shingles* type is the non-count noun *news*, as in *This news is encouraging. News* is morphologically analysable into *new* + *s*, but *new* is not a noun, nor ·*s* here an inflectional suffix. Other cases we discuss in groups.

(a) Diseases and ailments

[42]	i	*bends*	*hives*	*mumps*	*rabies*	*rickets*	*shingles*
	ii	*haemorrhoids*	*hiccups*	*measles*			

The terms in [i] are singular nouns, behaving like our model example *shingles*. Some, such as *bends* (which occurs with the article *the*), are etymologically plurals, but as disease names they are not systematically related to the forms without ·*s*. The words in [ii] are different. *Hiccup* is a singular noun denoting an involuntary spasm of the respiratory organs producing a characteristic sound, and *hiccups* can be a straightforward plural counterpart: *I heard two further hiccups and then there was silence. Hiccups* can also denote the condition where one is producing such spasms, and in this case it can be construed as singular or plural for purposes of subject–verb agreement: *Hiccups is/are unpleasant, I concede, but it/they are hardly life-threatening. Hiccups* is thus best treated as a plural noun, with the NP it heads optionally recategorised as singular by virtue of being interpreted as denoting a condition rather than the spasms themselves: this is to handle it like [41]. The same applies to *haemorrhoids*. And probably also to *measles*, except that here the use of *measle* and *measles* for the spots that characterise the disease is relatively uncommon; many speakers will have only the form *measles* denoting the disease and for them it is likely to belong with the singular nouns in [42i].

(b) Nouns with the ·*s* ending in both singular and plural

[43]	*barracks*	*crossroads*	*gallows*	*headquarters*	*innings*	*kennels*
	links	*means*	*mews*	*rapids*	*waterworks*	

Waterworks is illustrative of a handful of compounds in ·*works*: *gasworks*, *ironworks*, etc. *Innings* is used in connection with such games as cricket: for baseball the term is *inning*, with *innings* a regular plural. *Kennels* here denotes an establishment where dogs are bred or looked after while their owners are away; *kennels* can also be the ordinary plural of *kennel*, "small hut for a dog". *Links* denotes a golf-course (and is often compounded with *golf*).

The words in [43] are count nouns with identical singular and plural forms:

[44] i *This barracks is in urgent need of repair.*
ii *These two barracks have been used to accommodate refugees.*

In several cases at least, the ·*s* transparently has its source in the ordinary plural suffix, but it is not serving to mark these words themselves as plural. *Crossroads* applies to a place where roads cross but it denotes the intersection, a singular concept, not the roads as such. The ·*s* is part of the lexical base of these words, not an inflectional suffix added to it. BrE *licensed premises* ("pub") belongs here too, and so for many people does *splits* as used in gymnastics, etc.: *a licensed premises, a finely executed splits. Series* and *species* might also be included, though it is doubtful if these are perceived as containing a morphological ending ·*s* at all.

(c) Nouns in ·*ics*

[45]	i	*acoustics*	*classics*	*economics*	*ethics*	*linguistics*	*mathematics*
		mechanics	*phonetics*	*physics*	*politics*	*semantics*	*statistics*
	ii	*athletics*	*gymnastics*				

The nouns in [i] denote fields of study (with some having other meanings too); those in [ii] various sporting activities. For some of them there is a related singular noun without the ·*s* (*acoustic, classic, ethic, statistic*), and these have regular count plurals:

[46] i *The new concert hall has two distinct acoustics.*
ii *Two distinct ethics are in conflict in this school.*
iii *Two newly published statistics reveal that alcohol is good for you.*

Where there is no form without ·*s* we still find plural agreement for some uses:

[47] i *His politics are somewhat to the left of my own.*
ii *I recall the mental gymnastics that were required to keep up with him.*
iii *I'm afraid the mechanics of the market are beyond me.*

There can be no doubt that the ·*ics* words in [46–47] are plurals. But in the case of *phonetics*, for example, there is no noun *phonetic*, and *phonetics* itself behaves as a non-count singular, as evident from the *much* and *it* in:

[48] *There is unfortunately not much phonetics in the course: it's my best subject.*

It would be quite implausible to analyse *phonetics* as a plural noun that is merely recategorised as singular: it is simply a singular noun. Historically, ·*ics* consists of ·*ic* + the plural suffix, but it is arguable that they have undergone reanalysis, combining into a single suffix indicating a field of study. But as is often the case with reanalysis, there is variation in the present-day system – between singular and plural agreement with such words as *athletics* and *mathematics*, for example. With such words, and those that have both a field of study sense and some other sense, it is difficult to decide whether singular behaviour in the field of study sense should be handled by saying that the form is morphologically singular (like *shingles*) or in terms of recategorisation of a plural NP (like our *two ounces of sugar* example).

(d) Games

[49] i *billiards* *checkers* AmE *draughts* BrE *fives* *ninepins*
ii *cards* *darts* *dominoes* *skittles*

As names of games these normally take singular agreement, but those in [ii] can also be ordinary plurals applied to the entities used in the game:

[50] i *Billiards/Dominoes is one of my favourite games.*
ii *I've only three dominoes left.*

The natural solution for [49ii] is to say that these are plural nouns, with the NP they head being recategorised as singular when interpreted as denoting the game (a singular concept) rather than the pieces. But the nouns in [49i] apply only to the game (ignoring irrelevant senses), and are therefore better treated as simply singular nouns, with the ·*s* part of the lexical base.[10]

3.2.4 Variation between singular and plural construals

There are a number of nouns with Latin plural endings where English usage is divided as to whether they are construed as singular or plural:

[51] i *algae* *bacteria* *criteria* *data* *insignia*
media *phenomena*
ii *ephemera* *erotica* *exotica* *paraphernalia* *trivia*

We thus find %*this algae* and %*these algae*, %*the data that is relevant* and %*the data that are relevant*, %*too much trivia* and %*too many trivia*, and so on. Those in [i] are historically plurals of the unequivocally singular forms:

[52] *alga* *bacterium* *criterion* *datum* *insigne*
medium *phenomenon*

These singulars, however, are – in varying degrees – uncommon in comparison with their plural counterparts, and this has led to some speakers reanalysing the forms in [51i] as singulars, inflectionally unrelated to the forms in [52]. *Alga*, *bacterium*, and *insigne* are particularly rare outside specialised registers, and many speakers will be familiar only with their counterparts in [51]. Some of the items in [51i] are treated as count singulars with regular plural counterparts: !*bacterias*, !*criterias*, %*insignias*, !*medias*, !*phenomenas*. Of these, however, only *insignias* has gained any significant degree of acceptance, and that in AmE rather than BrE: the others are still regarded as clearly non-standard, as indicated by the annotation. It should be noted, however, that this reanalysis has taken place in the history of *agenda* and *candelabra*, former plurals which are now uncontroversial singulars with the regular plurals *agendas* and *candelabras*.[11]

As for the singular use of the forms in [51], all except *criteria* and *phenomena* are well enough established to be regarded as standard. With *data* the singular construal is particularly common in the field of computing and data-processing, where *datum* is hardly applicable. The most frequent use of *media* is in the phrase *the media*, applied to

[10] For some speakers *draughts* belongs in [ii], being applicable to the pieces as well as the game. The coordination *cowboys and indians* also belongs in [ii], but with the singular forms denoting participants.
[11] *Candelabra*, however, is still encountered as a plural of a rare *candelabrum*.

the means of mass communication, the press, radio, and television, where both singular agreement and plural agreement are well established.

3.3 Non-count quantificational nouns

The most straightforward type of quantification involves a quantifier in determiner or modifier function: *many books*, *these three houses*. But quantification can also be expressed by means of a noun as head with an *of* PP as complement. We are concerned in this section with the case where the quantificational noun is non-count, as in *a lot of people*.

There are three versions of this non-count quantificational noun construction to be considered, as illustrated in [53], where double underlining marks the quantificational noun and single underlining marks what we shall call the **oblique**, the NP complement of *of*:

[51]	SINGULAR	PLURAL
i	a. [*A lot of work*] *was done.*	b. [*A lot of errors*] *were made.*
ii	a. [*A great deal of work*] *was done.*	b. *[*A great deal of errors*] *were/was made.*
iii	a. *[*Dozens of work*] *was/were done.*	b. [*Dozens of errors*] *were made.*

In [i] the number of the whole NP depends on the oblique: we will say that *lot* is **number-transparent** in that it allows the number of the oblique to percolate up to determine the number of the whole NP. In [ii], singular *deal* selects a singular oblique, while in [iii] plural *dozens* selects a plural oblique. (We include both *was* and *were* in [iib] and [iiia] to show that the ungrammaticality is not a matter of subject–verb agreement but lies within the NP.)

The obliques may be either **partitive** or **non-partitive**:

[54] i [*A lot of the delegates*] *complained.* [partitive]
ii [*A lot of people*] *complained.* [non-partitive]

In [i] the whole NP picks out a subset of the set referred to by *the delegates*, whereas there is no such subset relation involved in [ii]. The partitive obliques are normally definite and are distinguished from the non-partitives in that they occur in the fused-head construction:

[55] i [*Many of the delegates*] *complained.* [partitive]
ii *[*Many of delegates*] *complained.* [non-partitive]

Instead of [55ii] we have simply [*Many delegates*] *complained*, where there is no embedding of one NP within another.

(a) Number-transparent quantificational nouns

The *lot* in [53i] is to be distinguished from that of *We have two lots of visitors coming this afternoon, one at 2.30 and the other at 4*, where *lot* is a count noun meaning "group". In the use illustrated in [53i] it has been bleached of its original meaning and is a non-count noun, with the bracketed NPs meaning respectively "much work" and "many errors". The *of* complement can be omitted in ellipsis, but it remains understood and continues to determine the number of the NP headed by *lot*, as is evident from the verb-forms in:

[56] i A: *Where did all the money go?* B: *A lot was spent on travel.*
ii A: *What happened to the protesters?* B: *A lot were arrested.*

In [i] *a lot* is understood as "a lot of the money" and hence is singular, in [ii] as "a lot of the protesters", and hence plural.

The main number-transparent nouns are as follows:

[57]						
i	*lot*	*plenty*				
ii	*lots*	*bags*	*heaps*	*loads*	*oodles*	*stacks*
iii	*remainder*	*rest*				
iv	*number*	*couple*				

Singular *lot* takes *a* as determiner, and allows a very limited amount of premodification, as in *A whole/huge lot of time has been wasted.*[12] *Plenty* is singular in form but does not permit any determiner or modifier: *plenty of butter/friends*, not **a remarkable plenty of butter/friends*. The plural forms in [ii] occur without determiners; *lots* is informal and the others very colloquial. These latter hardly allow partitive obliques: compare, for example, *They have oodles of money* but hardly *?Oodles of the money had already been spent. Remainder* and *rest* take the definite article *the* and allow only a partitive oblique: *the remainder/rest of the time/errors*, not **the remainder/rest of time/errors.*

Number and *couple* permit only plural obliques, partitive or non-partitive: *a number of the protesters/*money, a couple of days/*hope.* Both occur in singular form with an obligatory determiner (usually *a*, but others are possible as shown in [58]), and in addition ***number*** can occur in the plural, and take a limited range of adjectival modifiers:

[58] i *We found [huge numbers of ants] swarming all over the place.*
ii *If [this number of people] come next time we'll bring in professional caterers.*
iii *[Any number of people] could have done a better job than that.*
iv *[The couple of mistakes she had made] were easily corrected.*
v *[An unusually large number of people] have applied this year.*
vi *[How large a number of students] have enrolled, did you say?*

The definite article *the* does not occur with *number* in the sense we are concerned with here. In the number-transparent sense it indicates an imprecise number, but elsewhere it indicates a precise number, and in that case it can take *the*, as in *The number of protesters arrested has not been revealed*, where the subject NP is singular by virtue of having singular non-transparent *number* as head.

(b) Non-count quantificational nouns selecting a singular oblique

One clear case here is *deal*, as in [53ii] (*a great deal of work*, but not **a great deal of errors*). Non-partitive obliques are construed as non-count. In Standard English *deal* requires an adjectival modifier, normally *great* or *good*, as well as the indefinite article. Informal *smidgen* and *bit* are also of this type: *a smidgen/bit of improvement*, but not **a smidgen/bit of improvements*. The sense of *bit* here is different from that of non-quantificational *bit*, "piece", as in *two bits of cheese. Amount* and *quantity* are for many speakers likewise restricted to singular obliques, but here we find divided usage with respect to examples like *%a large amount/quantity of stamps.* Conservative usage manuals tend to condemn such examples, while more liberal ones recognise that they are quite common – especially when there would be no question of specifying a precise number, as in *a large amount of pebbles.* Compare also the non-count plural oblique in *a huge amount/quantity of stolen goods.* But in any case *amount* and *quantity* differ from *deal* in that they are count nouns: *Two small quantities of silver had been discovered.*

[12] *Lot* can occur in the complement of *hell/heck*, and in *A hell of a lot of people are going to be disappointed* the plural feature percolates up from *people* to the topmost NP. See §14.1 for more on this construction.

(c) Non-count quantificational nouns selecting a plural oblique

Dozens in [53iii] (*dozens of errors*, but not **dozens of work*) is representative of the following class:

[59] *dozens* *scores* *tens* *hundreds* *thousands* *millions* *billions* *zillions*

We distinguish these plural nouns from the singular forms that appear in cardinal numerals and comparable quantifiers:

[60] i	a. *dozens of spiders*	b. *hundreds of voters*	[head noun + complement]
ii	a. *a dozen spiders*	b. *three hundred voters*	[determiner + head noun]

The head in [i] is *dozens/hundreds*, whereas in [ii] it is *spiders/voters*. The crucial difference is that the plural nouns in [i] cannot be related directly to the noun whose denotation is quantified: they require *of* (cf. **dozens spiders*, **hundreds voters*). The quantifiers can occur with a definite *of* phrase in the partitive fused-head construction (*a dozen of the spiders, three hundred of these voters*), but in the simplest construction they occur as dependents of a following head, as in [ii].

The plural nouns in [59] are non-count in that they cannot take numerals as dependent; instead we have iteration of the head noun + complement construction:

[61] i	a. **ten thousands of stars*	b. *tens of thousands of stars*
ii	a. **seven thousand millions of stars*	b. *thousands of millions of stars*

Tens is largely restricted to this iterated construction: *?tens of mistakes*. The construction does, however, allow *many* or certain definite determiners (*many thousands of stars, the thousands of stars you can see, those millions of people living in poverty*).

Syntactic structure of NPs like *a number of protesters*

The analysis we have assumed for *a number of protesters* takes *number* as head and *of protesters* as complement – and analogously for the other quantificational noun constructions covered above. An alternative analysis found in many works takes *protesters* as head and *a number of* as a complex quantifier. Simplified tree structures will be as follows:

[62]

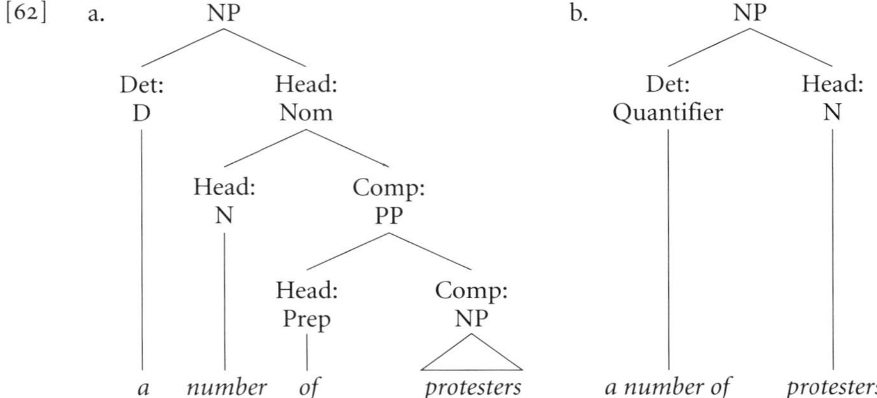

The main motivation for analysis [b] is that the grammatical number of the whole NP is plural. In [b] this follows from the general rule that the number of an NP derives from its head, whereas in [a] special provision has to be made, with the grammatical number percolating upwards from the oblique rather than being determined by the head.

We believe, however, that there are compelling arguments in favour of analysis [a] which far outweigh this point.

(a) Evidence that *of* forms a constituent with the oblique, not with (*a*) *number*

[63] i *Most students like continuous assessment but [a number _ prefer the old examination system].*

ii *We called a meeting of the first-year students, [of whom a number _ had complained about the assessment system].*

Example [i] shows that if the oblique is omitted in ellipsis the *of* drops too, as is the case with PPs generally. In [ii] the oblique is not dropped but relativised, and *of whom* is clearly a PP occupying prenuclear position in the relative clause. There is no plausible way of reconciling these constructions with analysis [b].

(b) Pre-head dependents of *number*

Analysis [62b] effectively treats *a number of* as a fixed phrase: it doesn't provide a structure with potential for replacements and expansion. But we have seen that *a* is replaceable by certain other determiners (e.g. *this* or *any*, as in [58ii–iii]); that ***number***, although non-count, has both singular and plural forms; and that *number* can take adjectival modifiers (as in [58v–vi]) – note in particular the position of the interrogative phrase in *how large a number of students*. To cater for these constructions analysis [62b] would need to assign to complex quantifiers a structure that duplicates in many respects what we already have for the NP.

3.4 Number agreement and selection within the NP

Restrictions on the combination of elements within an NP that have to do with number are of two kinds, **agreement** and **selection**:

[64] i a. *this book* / **this books* b. *these books* / **these book* [agreement]

ii a. *one doctor* / **one doctors* b. *two doctors* / **two doctor* [selection]

We say there is agreement in [i] because *this* and *these* are inflectional forms of a single lexeme ***this***: the agreement rule requires the singular form *this* when the head itself is singular, and the plural form *these* when the head is plural. But in [ii], *two* is not the plural counterpart of *one* any more than *three* is: *one* and *two* are not forms of a single lexeme differing simply with respect to an inflectional property. We talk here, then, of selection: *one* selects a singular head, *two* a plural one.

Agreement

There are just two dependents that agree in number with the head, the demonstratives ***this*** and ***that***:

[65] a. *this girl* ~ *these girls* b. *that boy* ~ *those boys*

The *these kind of dogs* construction

Exceptionally, the nouns ***kind***, ***sort***, and ***type*** can occur in the singular with a plural demonstrative. Compare:

[66] i a. *[This kind of dog] is dangerous.* b. *[These kinds of dogs] are dangerous.*

ii *[These kind of dogs] are dangerous.*

The examples in [i] follow the normal agreement rule, but [ii] does not. The meaning of the bracketed NP in [ii] is like that of the one in [ia] in that we have a single kind of dog, not a plurality, as in [ib]; cf. also *dogs of this kind.* Construction [ii] involves number-transparency as in the *a number of protesters* construction discussed in §3.3 above, for the plural number of the whole NP is determined by that of the oblique *dogs*, but this time the plural number carries over to the demonstrative determiner too. The construction is very well established, and can certainly be regarded as acceptable in informal style.

Selection

Determiners such as *the, which, no* are indifferent as to the number of the head, whereas others are selective.

(a) Dependents that select a singular head

[67]	i *a*	*one*	*each*	*every*	*either*	*neither*
	ii *much*	*little*	*a little*			

As noted earlier, those in [i] combine with count singulars, those in [ii] with non-count singulars.[13] *A* belongs in set (c) below when compounded with *other* or combined with *further* or *additional.* The quantifiers in [ii] marginally permit certain non-count plurals such as *oats*: ?*We haven't got much oats left* (§3.2.1).

(b) Dependents that select a plural head

[68]	i *two*	*three*	*one and a half*	2.3 (/tuː pɔɪnt θriː/)	
	ii *both*	*several*	*many*	*few*	*a few*
	iii *numerous*	*countless*			
	iv *we*	*you*			

Those in [i] are illustrative of numerals greater than one, whether integral or not: compare *half an apple* and *one and a half apples.* The items in [iii] are adjectives: *numerous objections, countless mistakes.* The 1st and 2nd person determinatives *we* and *you* are seen in *we veterans, you youngsters.*[14]

(c) Dependents that select a singular or quantified plural head

[69] *another* *an additional* *a further* *a good*

[70] i [*Another body/*bodies*] *had been discovered.*
ii [*Another three bodies*] *have been discovered.*
iii [*A further few/*many volunteers*] *were needed.*
iv *He ate* [*a good three hefty steaks*] *before leaving the table.*

A plural head is permitted only if it is quantified by a numeral or by *few.* With singular heads, *a good* is restricted to occurrence with abstract nouns like *time, period, distance, way, stretch, weight,* and measure nouns like *day, hour, week*: *We have a good stretch still to cover* or *It took me a good day to finish the assignment.*

[13] *One* selects a singular head even when it occurs in DPs headed by *more* like *more than one* or *one more*: see [6] of §11. However, it selects a plural in examples like [*one in ten*] *students,* where *one in ten* is a DP indicating proportion ("10% of"). The head is also plural when determined by the coordinations *one or two* and *one or more.*

[14] The requirement for a plural head with *you* does not apply in vocative NPs: *Why did you miss the train, you fool?* – nor in the exclamatory construction *You bastard!* Such NPs can never occupy a complement position in ordinary clause structure: **You fool are late!*

Respecification of plural measure phrase nominals as singular

Certain kinds of plural nominal can be respecified as singular:

[71] i [*That ten days we spent in Florida*] *was fantastic.* [period of time]
ii [*This twenty dollars*] *isn't going to get us very far.* [sum of money]
iii [*This next two miles*] *isn't going to be difficult.* [distance]
iv [*This last fifty bars*] *clearly isn't Beethoven.* [stretch of music]
v [*That two pounds of sugar you bought*] *isn't going to be enough.* [quantity]

The underlined nominals here are plural with respect to their internal form (they have plural nouns as head) but they are conceptualised as denoting single entities: a period of time, a sum of money, a distance, a stretch of music, a quantity. This singular conceptualisation overrides the plurality of form, so that they are treated as singular heads – just like *that period of ten days*, *this sum of twenty dollars*, and so on.[15]

Such respecification is in general optional. Besides [71], for example, we find:

[72] i [*Those ten days we spent in Florida*] *were fantastic.*
ii [*These twenty dollars*] *aren't going to get us very far.*
iii [*These next two miles*] *aren't going to be difficult.*
iv [*These last fifty bars*] *clearly aren't Beethoven.*
v [*Those two pounds of sugar you bought*] *aren't going to be enough.*

However, with quantifiers that select singular heads, respecification is the only option:

[73] i [*Every ten days we've spent on the project*] *has/*have cost a fortune.*
ii [*Each fifty bars*] *was/*were a new challenge.*

The respecification of plural nominals as singular is clearly similar to the occurrence of quantified plurals with *another* and the other items in [69]. In particular the nominal must again be quantified by a numeral or by *few*: *That few/*many days we spent in Florida was fantastic.* Moreover, respecification of plural measure nominals as singular is found with *another*, etc., as well as with the items shown in [71] and [73]. But *another*, etc., also occur with plural nominals that are not measure phrases and that do not permit respecification. Compare:

[74] i [*Another three days*] *are/is going to be needed.* [respecification permitted]
ii [*Another three bodies*] *have/*has been discovered.* [respecification disallowed]

Three days in [i] is a measure phrase that can be conceptualised as denoting a single period of time, in which case we have respecification as a singular, just as we do with *this*, *every*, etc. But *three bodies* in [ii] is not a measure phrase and cannot undergo respecification, as shown by the verb-form, or by the impossibility of replacing *another* by *this* or the like: *Where did they find these/*this three bodies? Another* and *a(n) additional further/good* can thus combine with nominal heads that are both conceptually and formally plural.

4 The determiner function

The determiner is a key function in the structure of the NP. When a determiner is added to a nominal, a construction at the NP level is formed. In the case of nominals headed

[15] The respecification of a plural head as singular is also found in fused-head NPs where the head is a numeral: *Then it would be reasonable to suppose that he showed the diamonds to you, his customer. Or showed you twenty-five of them perhaps. Then he sent that twenty-five back to Antwerp by the Euro-Securo couriers.* We interpret *that twenty-five* anaphorically as "that batch of twenty-five diamonds".

by singular count nouns, addition of a determiner is generally obligatory:

[1] i *[*New car*] *was stolen.* [bare count singular nominal]
ii [*The*/*One*/*Ally's new car*] *was stolen.* [determiner + nominal]

In [i], the nominal *new car*, headed by the singular count noun *car*, cannot by itself constitute an NP which is capable of acting as the subject of the clause. In [ii], the addition of the determiners *the*, *one*, and *Ally's* to this same nominal forms the NPs *the new car*, *one new car*, and *Ally's new car*. Each determiner has its own specialised meaning. However, one general function of all determiners is to add a specification of definiteness (as with *the* or *Ally's*) or indefiniteness (*one*). In their primary use, proper names are inherently definite: we defer consideration of them until §20.

Determined and bare NPs

NPs containing a determiner we call **determined NPs**. Under certain circumstances, nominals can themselves form NPs in the absence of a determiner, and we speak here of **bare NPs**. Nominals headed by plural count nouns or by non-count nouns can freely be admitted as indefinite by default, forming bare indefinite NPs such as *new cars* in *We used to buy new cars*, or *Danish cheese* in *We used to prefer Danish cheese*. Compare then [1] with the plural [2]:

[2] i [*New cars*] *were stolen.* [bare NP]
ii [*The*/*Two*/*Ally's new cars*] *were stolen.* [determined NP]

In [i] the nominal *new cars* forms a bare indefinite NP, while in [ii] the addition of determiners forms NPs in the same way as in [1], with *the new cars* and *Ally's new cars* definite, *two new cars* indefinite. There are, however, various exceptional cases where bare count singular nominals are admitted as NPs – compare *Henry became treasurer*; *Ed went to school*; *What time did you have breakfast?*; *We are monitoring the situation day by day*: these constructions are discussed in §8.5.

Types of determiner

We distinguish the following types of determiner:

[3]				
i	BASIC DETERMINERS	determinatives	*the tie*	*those shoes*
		DPs	*almost every tie*	*at least two shoes*
ii	SUBJECT-DETERMINERS	genitive NPs	*my tie*	*the boy's shoes*
iii	MINOR DETERMINERS	plain NPs	*what colour tie*	*this size shoes*
		PPs	*over thirty ties*	*up to thirty shoes*

Distinction between determiner and determinative

We distinguish, then, between the concepts of determiner, a **function** in the structure of the NP, and determinative, a **category** of words (and certain larger expressions) whose distinctive syntactic property concerns their association with the determiner function. Determinatives (or phrases headed by them) constitute the most basic kind of determiner, but not all determiners have this form, as seen in [3ii–iii]. Conversely, most determinatives can occur in one or more functions besides that of determiner, as in [4i–v], or combine the function of determiner with that of head in the fused-head construction, as in [4vi–viii]:

[4]	i	[*All* the vases] are broken.	[predeterminer]
	ii	[*The three rings*] were stolen.	[modifier in nominal]
	iii	*The problem isn't* [*that serious*].	[modifier in other phrase]
	iv	*We are* [*three in number*].	[predicative complement]
	v	*The remark was* [*both offensive*] *and irrelevant.*	[marker of coordination]
	vi	*He gave ten copies to me and* [*six*] *to the others.*	[simple fused head]
	vii	*I had taken lots of books but all (of them) were novels.*	[partitive fused head]
	viii	*They couldn't find much to criticise.*	[special fused head]

Traditionally, different uses of the determinatives are largely handled in terms of differences in part-of-speech classification. For example, *both* is traditionally an adjective in *both sides*, a pronoun in *both of them*, an adverb in *both Jill and her husband*. Within the framework adopted in this book it is generally more appropriate to handle these differences in terms of function rather than category: we deal with this issue in some detail in our discussion of the fused-head construction in §9. The syntactic distinction between determinatives and adjectives is discussed in Ch. 6, §2.4.2.

Basic determiners

These generally have the form of determinatives alone or with a limited range of modifiers (such as *almost* and *at least* in [3i]). We include in the category of determinatives certain complex expressions (such as *a few*, *many a*, cardinal numerals expressing numbers greater than 100) whose internal structure is not describable in terms of general rules of syntax applying elsewhere. The main members of the determinative category are as follows:

[5]	i	*the, a*	articles
	ii	***this, that***	demonstrative determinatives
	iii	***we**, you*	personal determinatives
	iv	*all, both*	universal determinatives
	v	*each, every*	distributive determinatives
	vi	*some, any*	existential determinatives
	vii	*one, two, three, . . .*	cardinal numerals
	viii	*either, neither*	disjunctive determinatives
	ix	***no***	negative determinative
	x	*another*	alternative–additive determinative
	xi	*a few, a little, several, . . .*	positive paucal determinatives
	xii	***many, much, few, little**, . . .*	degree determinatives
	xiii	*enough, sufficient*	sufficiency determinatives
	xiv	*which, what, whichever, whatever*	interrogative and relative determinatives[16]

Those in bold face exhibit inflectional variation: ***this*** and ***that*** inflect for number; ***we*** inflects for case (nominative *we*, accusative *us*); ***no*** has distinct dependent and independent forms (*no* and *none*); and the degree determinatives inflect for grade (*much, more, most*, etc.).

[16]The relative series also contains the archaic forms *whichsoever* and *whatsoever*. There is also a minor use of *such* that belongs with the determinatives: see §12. We might also include *last* and *next* as used in temporal deictic expressions such as *last week, next year*, etc., where they contrast with the central determinative *this*.

As determiners, the definite article *the* and those in [5ii–iv] mark the NP as definite, while the indefinite article and [v–xiii] mark it as indefinite; the items in [xiv] are indefinite as interrogatives, definite as relatives. Basic determiners are dealt with in §§6–7.

Subject-determiners

Genitive NPs like those in [3ii] combine the function of determiner with that of subject of the NP: hence the term **subject-determiner**. As determiners, they specify an NP as definite: *Ally's new cars* is in this respect like *the new cars belonging to Ally*, where definiteness is instead specified by the basic determiner *the*. Genitive NPs function not only as determiner but also as fused determiner-head (*This car isn't as big as Ally's*), predicative complement (*Everything here is Ally's*), oblique genitive (*a friend of Ally's*), and as subject of a gerund-participial clause (*I object to [Ally's being given extra privileges]*). Most personal pronouns have two genitive forms, dependent (*my*) and independent (*mine*). The syntax and semantics of genitive NPs are described in §§16.3–6.

Minor determiners

The determiner function can also be filled by a narrow range of plain-case NPs and PPs. The NPs are of two kinds. Firstly, there are those headed by nouns denoting elementary properties, such as *size*, *shape*, and *colour*. These occur most readily in interrogatives: [*What size hat*] *do you take?* They are also possible with a demonstrative, as in *They don't stock* [*that size shoes*], but here there is a strongly preferred alternant in which the embedded NP functions as post-head modifier rather than determiner: *They don't stock* [*shoes that size*].

The second kind of plain NP found in determiner function is a weekday name, or one of the temporal pronouns *yesterday* and *tomorrow*, as in *Sunday morning*, *tomorrow evening*, etc. We take the second noun as head since this is the one which marks the number of the whole NP: compare *Sunday morning* and *Sunday mornings*. Note also the contrast with *this morning*, where *this* is a basic determiner.

PP determiners normally have a cardinal numeral as complement of the preposition:

[6] *around ten thousand copies, between fifty and sixty tanks, close to a hundred tickets, from ten to fifteen judges, in excess of ninety delegates, over a million people, under ten new drugs, up to twenty minutes*

These PPs are semantically comparable to DPs like *more than ten thousand*, etc., and we will return to them briefly in our discussion of the latter (§11).

Determiner as a dependent function, not a type of head

The analysis presented in this chapter differs from that adopted in much work in recent formal grammar in that we take elementary NPs like *the book* to be headed by the noun *book*, not the determinative *the*. This is of course implied by our retention of the term 'noun phrase'.

There are two main reasons for our decision to retain the traditional conception of such expressions as headed by the noun. Firstly, it is the noun (or nominal) which defines the selectional properties of the phrase. For example, a verb like *assassinate* selects a human NP as object (one can assassinate a president, but not a dog), whereas there is no verb in English which selects an object phrase determined by *the* as opposed to *no*. This is because the basic semantic function of the determiner is to indicate whether the phrase is definite or indefinite (whether it denotes something assumed to be identifiable), and this is independent of the role the phrase otherwise plays in the larger construction in which it occurs. The second reason for taking the noun as head is that while there is a wide range of ordinary NPs that contain no determiner (NPs like *Kim, money, women,* ***they***), NPs that do not have a noun as ultimate head (NPs like *both, several, the largest*) are highly restricted in their form and use.

The determiner, then, is a kind of dependent – contrasting with complements and modifiers. As we have seen, moreover, it need not be realised by a determinative, but can itself have the form of an embedded NP, in either genitive or plain case.

5 Quantification

The determiners, we have seen, serve to mark the NP as definite or indefinite, but at the same time the basic ones characteristically express quantification. (In this they contrast with the genitive NP determiners, which combine the marking of definiteness with the expression of the subject-argument.) We use quantification and quantifier as semantic terms, noting that there is no one-to-one relation between them and the syntactic category of determinatives. For example, various kinds of quantification are expressed by words of other categories, adverbs such as *very, always, sometimes, rarely,* adjectives such as *numerous, whole, complete,* nouns such as *lot, number,* and so on. And certain determinatives – for example, demonstrative ***this*** and ***that*** – do not express quantification. Nevertheless, there is an important correlation between determinatives and quantification, so that it will be helpful to deal with certain general issues relating to quantification before we examine the determinatives in turn in §§6–7.

Predication property

In discussing the meaning of quantifiers we will make use of the concept of **predication property**, which may be explained by reference to such examples as the following:

[1] i a. [*Three students*] *coughed.* b. *They arrested* [*three students*].
ii a. [*Enough money*] *is available.* b. *Kim gave them* [*enough money*].

The predication property is given by the clause in abstraction from the quantified NP itself: in [i] we therefore have the predication properties of being an *x* such that *x* coughed, or such that they arrested *x*, and in [ii] those of being *x* such that *x* is available or such that Kim gave them *x*. The examples in [i] then say that the number of members of the set denoted by the head *students* that have the predication property is three. Those in [ii] likewise indicate that the size of the subquantity of money that has the predication property meets some criterion of sufficiency.

5.1 Existential quantification, universal quantification, and negation

Two important types of quantification are illustrated in:

[2] EXISTENTIAL QUANTIFICATION UNIVERSAL QUANTIFICATION
a. [*Some of the meat*] *was fresh.* b. [*All of the meat*] *was fresh.*

Existential quantification indicates a quantity or number greater than zero, and has *some* as its most straightforward expression. The term 'existential' reflects the fact that elementary examples like [a] assert the existence of a quantity of meat that was fresh, i.e. a quantity having the predication property. **Universal quantification** is expressed by a number of quantifiers of which *all* is the most prototypical. Universal quantification can be defined in terms of existential quantification and negation. The meaning of [b], for example, is "It is not the case that some of the meat wasn't fresh" – which can be expressed as *None of the meat wasn't fresh.* We thus have the following equivalences:

[3] i a. [*All of the meat*] *was fresh.* ≡ b. [*None of the meat*] *wasn't fresh.*
ii a. [*Some of the meat*] *was fresh.* ≡ b. [*Not all of the meat*] *wasn't fresh.*

In each pair, the truth conditions for [a] and [b] are identical.

The following pairs involving a single negation are also equivalent, with the doubly underlined word having scope over the one with single underlining (see Ch. 9, §1.3.1 for explanation of the concept 'having scope over'):

[4] UNIVERSAL — EXISTENTIAL
i a. [*Not all of the meat*] *was fresh.* ≡ b. [*Some of the meat*] *wasn't fresh.*
ii a. [*All of the meat*] *wasn't fresh.* ≡ b. [*None of the meat*] *was fresh.*

In [ia] *all* is within the scope of the negation ("It is not the case that all of the meat was fresh"), while in [ib] *some* has scope over the negative ("Some of the meat had the property that it wasn't fresh"). In abstraction from prosody, the clause *All of the meat wasn't fresh* is ambiguous with respect to scope. In one interpretation the negative has scope over the quantifier ([*All of the meat*] *wasn't fresh*), making it simply an alternant of [ia]; this is the kind of interpretation we have in the proverb *All that glitters is not gold.* In a second interpretation, the one indicated by the notation in [iia], *all* has scope over the negative ("All of the meat had the property of not being fresh"); this is equivalent to [iib]. Examples like *All of the meat wasn't fresh* are relatively infrequent: it is much more common to use one or other of the unambiguous equivalents, [ia] or [iib].

Now in [4ia/b] and [iia] the quantifier and the negative are grammatically distinct, as reflected in the underlining of two elements. In [iib], however, quantification and negation are simultaneously expressed in *none.* The grammar doesn't allow *[*not some of the meat*] (matching universal [*not all of the meat*]), but the meaning "not some" is expressed as *none. None* is thus to be analysed as a negative existential quantifier, i.e. a quantifier combining negation and existential quantification, with the negation having scope over the quantification.

Non-affirmative *any*

The examples so far have had the quantified NP located before the verb, in subject function. When we turn to postverbal NPs we find a third possible expression of existential quantification, *any.* Compare [4] above with the following:

[5] i a. *He hadn't eaten* [*all of the meat*]. ≡ b. *He hadn't eaten* [*some of the meat*].
ii a. *He hadn't eaten* [*all of the meat*]. ≡ b. *He had eaten* [*none of the meat*].
b′. *He hadn't eaten* [*any of the meat*].

In [ia] the negative has scope over *all* ("It is not the case that he had eaten all of the meat"). This is equivalent to [ib], where *some* has scope over the negation: "There was some of the meat that he hadn't eaten". Version [ib] is much less likely than [ia], though the construction is certainly admissible (cf. *I didn't agree with some of the things he said*). Construction [iia], with the meaning "all of the meat had the property that he hadn't eaten it", is somewhat marginal and contrived: *He hadn't eaten all of the meat* would generally be interpreted with the negative having wide scope, as in [ia]. Much more likely than [iia], then, is a version where negation has scope over existential quantification. And this can take either of two forms, one with the negative existential quantifier *none*, and one with a negative having scope over *any*. In the context of a wide scope negative, *any* is normally used instead of *some* to express existential quantification; we will use the asterisk notation for **He hadn't eaten* [*some of the meat*], with the proviso that it could be used in the special context of denying a previous utterance of *He had eaten some of the meat* or the like.

Any can also be used in interrogative contexts, as in *Had he eaten any of the meat?* Here *Had he eaten some of the meat?* is also possible, but it suggests the questioner is disposed to think the answer may well be positive, whereas *any* is neutral, giving no indication of the speaker's attitude to the possible answers (see Ch. 10, §4.7.4). However, *any* cannot substitute for *some* in *He had eaten some of the meat*: in the sense we are concerned with here, *any* is restricted to **non-affirmative** contexts (negatives, interrogatives, and various others, as described in Ch. 9, §4.4). This gives us three expressions of existential quantification: basic *some*, non-affirmative *any*, and negative ***no***.

Count NPs

So far we have used non-count NPs; count examples are as follows:

[6] a. *He had eaten* [*all of the pies*]. b. *He had eaten* [*some of the pies*].

Example [a] entails that there were none of the pies that he hadn't eaten, while existential [b] entails that not all the pies had the property that he hadn't eaten them. There is a complication in the existential case, however, in that *some* in [b] indicates not just a number greater than zero but a number no less than two. This complication does not apply to *none* and *any*. Compare, then:

[7] i a. *He hadn't eaten* [*all of the pies*]. b. *He hadn't eaten* [*some of the pies*].
ii a. *He hadn't eaten* [*all of the pies*]. ≡ b. *He had eaten* [*none of the pies*].
b′. *He hadn't eaten* [*any of the pies*].

In [i], [b] entails [a] but is not equivalent to it since [a] but not [b] would be true if he had eaten all but one. The examples in [ii] are equivalent in the same way as their counterparts in [5]. And the versions with existential quantification, [7iib/b′], are very strongly preferred over the one with universal quantification, [7iia], just as [5iib/b′] are preferred over [5iia].

Duality

The examples in [7] convey that there were at least three pies. Suppose we take a scenario in which I know that there are just two. I would then use *both* rather than *all*: *He had eaten both of the pies.* There is no distinct simple determinative that would replace *some* in this scenario: we would have to say *He had eaten one or other of the pies* or *He had eaten one of the two pies.* We do, however, have *either* and *neither* as replacements for *any* and *none* respectively. This gives the following pattern corresponding to [7]:

[8] i a. *He hadn't eaten* [*both of the pies*].
ii a. *He hadn't eaten* [*both of the pies*]. b. *He had eaten* [*neither of the pies*].
b′. *He hadn't eaten* [*either of the pies*].

As before, [iib/b′] are strongly preferred over [iia].

The following table shows the classification of the simple quantifiers introduced so far:

[9]

	UNIVERSAL	EXISTENTIAL		
		basic	**non-affirmative**	**negative**
NEUTRAL	*all*	*some*	*any*	***no***
DUAL	*both*		*either*	*neither*

All, we have noted, is not normally used in a context where it is known that the set has just two members: compare *Cars were parked on both/#all sides of the road.* However, the "more than two" component in examples like *He had eaten all of the pies* is an implicature not an entailment. The right answer to the question *Have all (the) mistakes been corrected?* in a situation where there were exactly two mistakes and both have been corrected is "Yes", not "No". And of course no such "more than two" implicature can arise in non-count cases like *all of the meat.* It is for these reasons that we have labelled *all* 'neutral': there is no explicit indication of the size of the set or quantity.

In the dual series the "two" meaning is more prominent in universal *both* than in existential *either* and *neither.* Compare, for example, the interrogatives:

[10] a. *Did he eat both of the pies?* b. *Did he eat either of the pies?*

A "yes" answer to [a] entails that he ate two pies, while a "yes" answer to [b] does not: it is merely that there are two pies under consideration. The greater prominence of "two" in *both* is reflected in the syntax of coordination. *Both, either*, and *neither* are the three words that can function to mark the first member of a coordination construction, and while *both* is limited to binary coordinations, *either* and *neither* are not. Thus we have *both Kim and Pat* but not **both Kim, Pat, and Alex*, whereas *either Kim, Pat, or Alex* and *neither Kim, Pat, nor Alex* are admissible.

Free choice *any* and *either*

Besides their use as an existential quantifier in non-affirmative contexts, *any* and *either* can be used with what is called a **free choice** sense:

[11] a. *Any of these computers will do.* b. *Either of these computers will do.*

Again, *any* here implicates a set of three or more computers while *either* presupposes a set of just two. The interpretation is that if you choose arbitrarily from among the set of computers – i.e. make a free choice – the one you choose will have the predication property, i.e. in this case it will do ("satisfy the requirements"). In the free choice case, the quantifier is always stressed. Where relevant, we will distinguish the two senses with subscripts: any_n and $either_n$ represent occurrence of these items with the non-affirmative existential sense, while any_f and $either_f$ represent occurrences of them with the free choice sense.

Any_f and $either_f$ are not excluded from non-affirmative contexts, so that there may be ambiguity between the two senses, as in:

[12] *Were [<u>any</u>/<u>either</u> of the students] allowed to take part?*

In the non-affirmative existential sense, this asks if there was at least one of the students who was allowed to take part. In the free choice sense (with stressed quantifier) it asks whether permission to take part was available generally, i.e. whether a student chosen arbitrarily from the set could take part. What is at issue in this second interpretation is whether or not restrictions applied as to which or how many students were allowed to take part.

Free choice *any* and *either* often implicate universal quantification. This is so in the examples cited: [11] implicates that all or both of the computers will do and a "yes" answer to the free choice reading of [12] implicates that all or both students had permission to take part. This component of the meaning is not an entailment. Imperative *Take any*$_f$/*either*$_f$ *of the computers*, for example, is not an instruction to take all or both of them; indeed in such contexts there will tend to be an implicature limiting the number to one: "Take any/either one of the computers".

The free choice quantifiers are admissible only in a certain range of contexts. *We haven't had any rain for two months*, for example, admits only the non-affirmative reading, while **I had been for a long walk and was feeling hungry, so I ate any/either of the pies* excludes not only the non-affirmative reading (by virtue of being a positive declarative main clause) but also the free choice one.

Distributivity and the universal quantifiers *each* and *every*

The concept of **distributive** quantification can best be explained by means of the contrast illustrated in:

[13] i *Five students voted against the proposal.* [distributive]
ii *Five students lifted the piano onto the stage.* [non-distributive: joint]

In [i] the predication property ("*x* voted against the proposal") applies to the five students individually: there were five votes against the proposal. We say in such cases that the predication is interpreted distributively. The salient interpretation of [ii] by contrast is that the predication property ("*x* lifted the piano onto the stage") applies to the five students jointly, collectively: they lifted it together. Here then the predication is interpreted non-distributively.

In this example there is no syntactic marking of the difference between the two interpretations. Thus [ii] could in principle be interpreted distributively, with the students individually lifting the piano onto the stage in turn: this is merely pragmatically unlikely. There are, however, two universal quantifiers, *each* and *every*, which explicitly indicate that the predication property applies distributively. Compare:

[14] i *Every student voted against the proposal.*
ii *Each student lifted the piano onto the stage.* } [distributive]

Here [ii] has the pragmatically unlikely interpretation where the students individually lifted the piano, so that there were as many acts of lifting the piano onto the stage as there were students: perhaps it was a toy or miniature piano, perhaps they had some mechanical aid.

Existential presupposition of universal quantification

It is normally presupposed, taken for granted, that a universally quantified set is not empty. *All left-handed philosophers* presupposes that there exist left-handed philosophers, *all/both Kim's children* presupposes that Kim has children, *each/every pie* and *all the pies* presuppose the existence of pies belonging to a set that will be identifiable in the context, and so on. There are certainly cases where such existence is not entailed, but we still find a distinction between universal *all* and free choice *any*:

[15] *All/Any candidates who score 100% on the test will receive a $100 prize.*

This does not entail that there will actually be candidates who score 100%. The use of *all* nevertheless suggests a disposition to believe that some candidates will do so, whereas free choice *any* is more neutral. The distributive universal quantifiers *each* and *every* behave like *all* in such cases.

5.2 Scalar entailments and implicatures

Cardinal numerals

Numeral determinatives are generally interpreted as giving the exact **cardinality** of a set, i.e. the exact number of members that it contains. An elementary example like [16i] will then be understood as conveying the propositions [ii–iii]:

[16] i *Max has [<u>four</u> children].*
ii "Max has no less than four children" [lower bound]
iii "Max has no more than four children" [upper bound]

Proposition [ii] gives the **lower bound** to the cardinality of the set, the minimum number: "at least four"; [iii] gives the **upper bound**, the maximum number: "not exceeding four". If, for example, I say [i] in response to the question *How many children has Max got?*, you would clearly infer that Max has exactly four children. But the two components [ii–iii] differ in status. Proposition [ii] is an entailment: if it is false, then necessarily [i] itself is false. But [iii] is only an implicature, albeit a strong one: it is possible for [i] to be true while [iii] is false. Suppose, for example, that in order to qualify for extra child benefit one has to have at least four children: in the context of talking to the benefits clerk I could truthfully say that I have four children even if I have five, because the only thing that is relevant here is whether the lower bound condition is satisfied. Or take the case where we are expecting an unusually large number of guests to dinner, say fourteen. I could then ask *Have we got fourteen dining chairs?* and the answer *Yes* would again convey only that the lower bound condition was satisfied – you could add, without contradiction, *in fact we've got sixteen.*

The relation between a pair of numerals such as *five* and *four* is thus as illustrated in:

[17] i *Max has five children* **entails** *Max has four children*
ii *Max has four children* **implicates** *Max doesn't have five children*

Adding *at least* cancels the implicature: *Max has at least four children* allows that there may well be more than four. Adding *at most* converts the upper bound implicature into an entailment: *Max has at most four children* entails *Max doesn't have five children.* But at the same time it removes the lower bound entailment: *Max has at most four children* does not entail that he has (no less than) four children, or indeed that he has three.

The implicature [17ii] is standardly called a **scalar implicature.** It is an obvious property of the cardinal numerals (and of the numbers that they express) that they are ordered: *five* comes between *six* and *four*, and so on. We talk of this ordered arrangement as a **scale**. Other things being equal, the expectation is that a speaker will make the strongest statement that is consistent with what they know to be true. If I know that Max has five children, I will normally be expected to say so, rather than making the weaker statement that he has four. The most obvious reason for saying *four* rather than *five* is that it would not be true to say *five*, so [16i] will generally convey [16iii]. But since there could be other reasons for choosing the weaker statement, [16iii] is an implicature, not an entailment. More generally, the selection of a particular term on some scale implicates the negation of stronger ones.

All and *some*

There is likewise a scalar relation between *all* and *some*: *all* is stronger than *some*. This gives rise to essentially the same pattern of entailments and implicatures:

[18] a. *All of her children have emigrated.* b. *Some of her children have emigrated.*

Here [a] entails [b], and [b] implicates the negation of [a], i.e. *Not all her children have emigrated.*[17] Again the implicature is a strong one, but it is easy to demonstrate that it is not an entailment. Suppose she has five children. One plausible context for [b] is where I know that three of them have emigrated and simply don't know about the other two; here I choose [b] over [a] not because [a] is false but because I don't know whether it is true or false. (Notice that replacing *her* in [b] by *my* strengthens the implicature: I would normally be expected to know whether all my own children have emigrated.) A second point is that if [b] entailed the negation of [a] it would be logically impossible for [a] to entail [b]. But clearly [a] does entail [b]: if all of them have emigrated, then necessarily some of them have.

Proportional and non-proportional quantification

The "not all" implicature is not found with all uses of *some*:

[19] i *There were some children in the park.*
ii *I saw some children climb over the fence.* } [non-proportional use of *some*]

In construction [i], with dummy *there* as subject, substitution of *not all* for *some* is not permitted: *#There were not all children in the park.* The latter is not pragmatically intelligible, and cannot express an implicature of [i]. As for [ii], we are concerned with the reading where *some* is unstressed, reduced to /səm/ (or /sm/). In this case there is no particular larger set of children that I have in mind of whom it would not be true that I saw them all climb over the fence. Again, then, I'm not implicating that I didn't see all of a certain set of children climb over the fence. *Some* conveys "not all" only when it is interpreted **proportionally**, i.e. when there is a certain set involved such that the issue arises as to whether all members of that set have the predication property. The partitive construction is one which forces such a proportional interpretation, for the set concerned is expressed in the partitive oblique. In [18b], we are concerned with the set of her children, and *some* is interpreted relative to this set: by virtue of this it contrasts with *all* and implicates "not all". But it isn't only in partitives that *some* has a proportional interpretation. Consider:

[20] i *Some people misunderstood the question.*
ii *Some people don't know how to say 'No'.* } [proportional use of *some*]

[17] Strictly speaking, the entailment relation holds only if the universally quantified set is not empty: see the discussion of [15] above. *All candidates who score 100% will win a prize* does not itself entail *Some candidates who score 100% will win a prize* – but it and *Some candidates will score 100%* taken together do have this entailment.

In [i] there is an implicit set of people who were asked the question (perhaps the candidates in an examination, perhaps the voters in a referendum, and so on), so *some* is interpreted proportionally: it contrasts with *all* and implicates "not all". In [ii] I am talking about people in general, but people in general constitute a set, so again we have the "not all" implicature.

Proportional *most*

Most likewise has proportional and non-proportional uses, though in this case they are somewhat more clearly distinguished, with the non-proportional use being the superlative of ***many*** and ***much***. We distinguish the uses by means of subscripts, with $most_p$ representing the proportional sense, $most_s$ the non-proportional, superlative sense:

[21] i *$Most_p$ students would regard that as unreasonable.* [proportional]
ii *It's the Pyschology Department that attracts (the) $most_s$ students.* [superlative]

In [i] the predication property applies to a high proportion of students, while in [ii] it is a matter of the Psychology Department attracting the largest number of students, i.e. a larger number than the other departments. Again, proportional *most* is weaker than *all* and hence triggers a "not all" implicature: "Not all students would regard that as unreasonable".

Scalar relation between *all*, $most_p$, and *some*

$Most_p$ is weaker than *all* but stronger than proportional *some*, so that they can be arranged on a scale as shown in [22], where '>' means "is stronger than":

[22] *all* > $most_p$ > *some*

Each of these quantifiers entails any to its right and implicates the negation of any to its left:

[23] i *I knew all of the delegates.* [entails [ii–iii]]
ii *I knew most of the delegates.* [entails [iii], implicates negation of [i]]
iii *I knew some of the delegates.* [implicates negation of [i–ii]]

Multal quantification

Multal quantification is the name given to the quantification expressed by such items as *many, much, a lot, a great deal*, and so on. In most (but not all) of its uses *some* enters into a scalar relationship with the multal quantifiers as illustrated in:

[24]	PROPORTIONAL	NON-PROPORTIONAL
i	a. *Many people think it's a conspiracy.*	b. *We're having a lot of friends round.*
ii	a. *Some people think it's a conspiracy.*	b. *We're having some friends round.*

In both the proportional and non-proportional cases [i] entails [ii], while [ii] has a "not multal" implicature, i.e. [iia] implicates that the proportion of people who think this is less than high, and [iib] implicates that the number of friends we're having round is less than large. We specify the implicature here as "not multal", rather than as "not many" because *not many* is interpreted not as "less than many" but as "few" (cf. Ch. 9, §5 and footnote 18 below.).

The proportional uses of the multal quantifiers cannot, however, be simply added to the scale in [22] because *all, most*, and *some* do not presuppose that the set in question is large. Suppose, for example, that Ed makes six mistakes. If four were trivial,

I could say *Most of them were trivial*, but *Many of them were trivial* would not be appropriate. *All* and *most*$_p$ do not therefore entail *many/much*. *Many* and *much* implicate "not all", but whether they implicate "not most$_p$" will be very much context-dependent.

Paucal quantification

Paucal quantification is expressed by such quantifiers as *a few*, *a little*, *several*, *a bit*, etc. These enter into a scalar relation with the multal quantifiers. Compare:

[25] i a. *I disagreed with many of his points.* b. *I made a lot of mistakes.*
ii a. *I disagreed with a few of his points.* b. *I made a few mistakes.*

The examples in [i] entail those in [ii] and the latter have a strong "not multal" implicature.

There is no such relation between *some* and the paucal quantifiers. The paucal quantifiers entail *some* (for example, [25iib] entails *I made some mistakes*), but *some* clearly does not implicate "less than paucal". *Some* is applicable to an area of the quantificational scale that includes the paucal area. The lower bound for *a few* is three, but two qualifies as 'some', and *some* can readily be used without any suggestion that the upper bound is low.

Negative quantifiers

The scale in [22] cannot be expanded by adding anything to the right of *some*. In particular, we cannot continue with ***no***. Compare the following pair with [18] above:

[26] a. *Some of her friends voted for him.* b. *None of her friends voted for him.*

Example [b] doesn't implicate the negation of [a] (*It is not the case that some of her friends voted for him*): it entails it. ***No*** is thus not a weaker quantifier than existential *some*: it combines negation with existential quantification, and for this reason it does not belong on the scale of positive quantifiers given in [22].

Few is likewise to be excluded by virtue of being negative. The relation between *many* and *few* is comparable to that between *some* and ***no***:

[27] a. *Many of her friends voted for him.* b. *Few of her friends voted for him.*

Again, [b] entails the falsity of [a] rather than merely implicating it. Note, then, the difference in the following:

[28] i *Some <u>if not all</u> / <u>indeed all</u> of her friends voted for him.*
ii **Few <u>if not many</u> / <u>indeed many</u> of her friends voted for him.*

If not all in [i] cancels the "not all" **implicature** of *some* by admitting the possibility that all voted for him, while *indeed all* cancels it by asserting that all did. But these devices cannot cancel the "not multal" **entailment** of *few*.

Few, however, does not mean "less than many": it means "the opposite of many". *Many* and *few* are antonyms, like *good* and *bad*, *big* and *small*, *old* and *young*, etc. We noted above that negating *many* tends to yield a paucal interpretation. Compare, then:

[29] a. *He didn't obtain many votes.* b. *He obtained few votes.*

Example [a] conveys that he obtained a small number of votes. But this is an implicature: it could be that he received a fair number of votes but nevertheless somewhat fewer than would merit the description *many*. *Few*, however, could not be used in this latter scenario: [b] entails, rather than merely implicating, that he obtained no more than a small number of votes. Thus [a] and [b] are not equivalent: [b] entails [a], while [a] implicates [b].[18]

As a negative, *few* enters into a scalar relation with ***no***, and if we consider just proportional uses we can also include *not all* on the negative scale even though it is not a single word:

[30] ***no*** > *few* > *not all*

We put ***no*** on the left because it is the strongest of the three, in the sense of being most restrictive. Compare:

[31] i	*None of her friends voted for him.*	[entails [ii–iii]]
ii	*Few of her friends voted for him.*	[entails [iii], implicates negation of [i]]
iii	*Not all of her friends voted for him.*	[implicates negation of [i–ii]]

The truth conditions for [i] are narrower, more restrictive, than those for [ii], and the latter are in turn more restrictive than those for [iii].

The entailments and implicatures deriving from [30] follow the same principles as with the positive scale [22]. The stronger terms entail the weaker, while the weaker implicate the negation of the stronger, as indicated in the annotations given on the right in [31]. The implicature from *few* to "not none" is often very strong, like that from *some* to "not all", and this is likely to be the case in the particular example we have here. But in other cases it is clearer that we are dealing with an implicature, not an entailment. Suppose, for example, we are about to mark a set of exam papers. I might say *Few will do as well as Kim Jones in last year's exam: of that we can be quite sure.* This expresses confidence that at most a small number will equal Kim's (outstanding) performance last year, but it doesn't say that at least some will do so. The "not none" implicature can be cancelled in the same way as was illustrated for the "not all" implicature of *some* in [28i]:

[32] *Few <u>if any</u> / <u>indeed none</u> of them did as well as Kim.*

A few and *few*

These are both paucal quantifiers in that they involve a low upper bound. But they contrast as positive vs negative (cf. Ch. 9, §3.3). This results in the differences summarised in:

[33]	*a few*	*few*
i Upper bound is low	implicated	entailed
ii Lower bound is greater than zero	entailed	implicated

(*A few* entails, in fact, that the lower bound is greater than two.) Notice, then, that *a few* works in just the opposite way from *few* with respect to the cancellation of implicatures. Compare [28ii] and [32] with:

[34] i *A few <u>if not many</u> / <u>indeed many</u> of her friends voted for him.*
ii **A few <u>if any</u> / <u>indeed none</u> of them did as well as Kim.*

[18] When *not* modifies *many* within a DP, however, we have a paucal entailment: *Not many of her friends voted for him* does not allow an interpretation where a good number voted but not enough to qualify as many.

6 The articles and the category of definiteness

The term **article** is used for the special subcategory of determinatives that provide the most basic expression of definiteness and indefiniteness. In this section we examine in turn the two articles *the* and *a*, explaining what is meant by the contrast between definite and indefinite NPs.

6.1 The definite article *the*

The definite article *the* is the most basic indicator of definiteness. It is illustrated in [1], which shows that it is compatible with all types of common noun: count singular, count plural, and non-count.

[1] *Bring me [the ladder/ladders/cement]!*

Use of the definite article here indicates that I expect you to be able to identify the referent – the individual ladder, the set of ladders, the quantity of cement that I am referring to.

Identifiability

The concept of identifiability expressed by the definite article is best understood in terms of pre-empting a question with *which?* Compare, for example:

[2] i *Where did you park the car?*
ii *The father of one of my students rang me up last night.*
iii *The first person to run the mile in under four minutes was Roger Bannister.*

Example [i] illustrates the frequent case where the addressee can be assumed to be familiar with the referent of the definite NP: you have been driving the car and presumably know a good deal more about it than that it is a car – what colour and make of car it is, and so on. You thus don't need to ask *Which car?*: you know which one I'm referring to.[19]

Familiarity of this kind is not, however, a necessary condition for the felicitous use of *the*. In [2ii], for example, I don't say who the student is and so can't expect you to know who the father is. Nevertheless, I have a particular student in mind and the property of being father of that student provides distinctive, hence identifying, information about the referent. It wouldn't make sense, therefore, to ask #*Which father of one of your students?* (*Which one of your students?* would of course make sense, but the *which* question here relates to the embedded NP *one of my students*, which is indefinite.)

The kind of identifiability signalled by *the* is thus of a relatively weak kind. This is further illustrated in [2iii], where the predicate provides stronger identifying information. The head nominal of the definite NP in subject function defines a unique individual, so again the question #*Which first person to run the mile in under four minutes?* would be incoherent. But you can recognise that the description can only be met by a unique individual without knowing who the individual is: it is the predicate in [iii] that says who he is. *The* indicates, therefore, that the head gives identifying information that pre-empts

[19] If you did respond to my utterance of [2i] by asking *Which one?*, this would indicate that there had been a breakdown in communication, that I had been mistaken in assuming that you would be able to identify which car I was referring to.

a *which* question, but the information expressed in the head certainly need not pre-empt a *who* question.

Count singular NPs: identifiability and uniqueness

In the case of definite count singular NPs, identifiability is normally due to the recognition that there is only one relevant entity satisfying the description expressed in the head. In [2iii] there is necessarily only one person who was the first to perform the feat in question. In [2ii] there can likewise be only one person who is father of the student I have in mind. And in [2i] there is a unique car in the context that is relevant: the context will be one where we are aware that you had been driving a particular car, and this is the one I'm referring to.

Under certain circumstances, however, the definite article can be appropriate with a count singular even when the context does not strictly limit the number of entities satisfying the description given in the nominal to just one:

[3] i *Put your cup down on <u>the arm of your chair</u>.*
ii *He married <u>the daughter of his bank manager</u>.*

An (arm-)chair has two arms, but the definite article in [i] is in order on the assumption that it doesn't matter which one you choose. Again, then, the definite article signals my expectation that you don't need to ask *Which arm of my chair?* In [ii] it could be that the bank manager has in fact two daughters, but *the* is again appropriate on the assumption that you don't need to ask *Which one?*: perhaps the other is already married, or too young to marry, perhaps you don't know that there are two, and perhaps it simply doesn't matter, the important point being only that his bank manager was the father of the woman he married.

Existential presupposition

In general, use of the definite article presupposes the existence of the entity, set, or quantity that the addressee is expected to be able to identify. For example, [3ii] presupposes that his bank manager has a daughter. In the example as given, the existence of the daughter is entailed, but the presupposition typically carries over to contexts in which there is no such entailment, as in *He thinks it would be to his advantage to marry the daughter of his bank manager*. This includes negative contexts, such as *He didn't, after all, marry the daughter of his bank manager*: this still takes it for granted that the bank manager has a daughter. It is possible to cancel the existential presupposition, but this would normally only be done in a context where one is denying what has been said or suggested by someone else. In such a context one could say, for example, *He can't have married the daughter of his bank manager: his bank manager doesn't have a daughter.*

Plural and non-count NPs: totality

The account of identifiability by virtue of uniqueness can be extended to plural and non-count definite NPs:

[4] i *Where did you put <u>the keys</u> / <u>the milk</u>?*
ii *<u>The parents of one of my students</u> came round to see me last night.*

These are like the count singulars in [2i–ii], except that the uniqueness applies now to a set or quantity rather than to an individual. It is to be understood, however, that the set or quantity is maximal: we are concerned with the totality of the keys, milk, and parents.

If you had five keys, say, there will be a number of subsets containing four, three, or two keys, but these are irrelevant: it is the set as a whole that is presented as identifiable by virtue of there being in the context a unique maximal set of keys (the keys that you were recently using to open a door or safe, perhaps).

It is important to note, however, that the concept of totality implied by the definite article is somewhat weaker than that expressed by universal quantification: if the set consists of a number of essentially similar entities, then the use of the definite article does not entail that every individual entity has the predication property. Compare:

[5] a. *The bathroom tiles are cracked.* b. *All the bathroom tiles are cracked.*

In [a] it is not necessarily the case that every individual tile is cracked: rather, the totality of the tiles gives the impression of being cracked. If I wish to indicate that every individual tile is cracked, I must make that explicit, for example by adding the universal quantifier *all* as a predeterminer, as in [b].

Types of context in which the identifiability requirement is satisfied

The following examples illustrate a range of contexts in which the use of the definite article is appropriate:

[6] i *Could you do something about the hum?*
ii *The president has been assassinated.*
iii *They have a cat and two dogs. The cat is over fifteen years old.*
iv *My car won't start; I think the battery is flat.*
v *She grabbed me by the arm.*
vi *Everybody wants to be a member of the most popular team.*
vii *They are interviewing the man who mows her lawn.*
viii *The racquet dropped from Andre Agassi's hand as if his fingers had grown numb.*

In [i] the hum is identifiable from sensory features of the situation: I assume you can hear it. Similarly, I might say *Pass me the hammer* in a context where you can see it, or *Does the draught worry you?* in a context where you can feel it. Example [ii] illustrates the case where identifiability derives from non-linguistic knowledge shared by speaker and addressee. If [ii] is uttered as 'hot news', the most likely interpretation is that the definite NP refers to the person they know as the president of their country. But of course, in another exchange, for example between two journalists who report on a particular country, the reference may well be to the president of that country, identifiable through shared knowledge of the country.

In [6iii] the first sentence introduces a particular cat into the discourse, so the referent of *the cat* in the second is identifiable by virtue of this prior mention. In [iv] the battery is identifiable through its association with the car that has just been introduced into the discourse: it is interpreted as the battery of that car. Example [v] is similar, with the arm in question identified by association with the object-referent: it was my arm. An alternative formulation in this case would use the genitive pronoun: *She grabbed me by my arm*. There are, however, severe restrictions on the construction with *the*. In the first place the referent of the determined NP is prototypically a body-part (cf. ?*She grabbed me by the tie*). Secondly, the body-part NP and the NP with which it is associated are respectively oblique and direct complements of a single verb (this kind of interpretation is not available with *I used the arm to help me get over the fence*).

In [6vi] it is the modifier *most popular* that enables the team to be identified: it is singled out by its position at the top of the scale of popularity. The modifier can thus be said to **establish** identifiability. The same applies to the relative clause in [vii]. The definite article is not of course required, but its use indicates that *man who mows her lawn* is being presented as a description of a unique person.

A less usual case is illustrated in [6viii], the first sentence in a newspaper sports article. The sentence forces you to recognise a unique racquet even though the NP itself contains no other information about it than that it is a racquet. It is thus only from the predication property that you obtain the information necessary to understand what racquet it is, and we can say then that it is the predication that establishes identifiability. Similarly with a notice such as *Beware of the dog!* This serves to inform readers that there is a (single) dog in the vicinity, and warns them to beware of that dog.

Stress

The definite article is generally unstressed in connected speech. Stressed use of the definite article, in the form /ðiː/, is highly unusual, but is found with proper names in examples like *Was it* THE *Bill Gates that he was talking about?* (discussed in §20.4), or with common nouns, as in *Is that* THE *book you're looking for?* (where I am seeking confirmation that the entity concerned is indeed the unique book that you're looking for).

Functions beside determiner

[7] i *She ran* [*the fastest she had ever run*]. } [modifier]
ii *The longer we stay,* [*the more*] *chance there is we'll be caught.* }

The occurs as modifier in construction with superlatives and comparatives: see Ch. 13, §§4.4.2, 6.3.4. The bracketed phrases here belong respectively to the categories AdvP and DP. Note that in [ii] *the more chance* is an NP, but *the* here modifies *more*: it is not determiner with *more chance* as head.

Unlike most determinatives, *the* is completely excluded from fused-head function:

[8] i **There's a spider in the bath. Get rid of* [*the*] *immediately!* [*it*]
ii **Do you prefer this version or* [*the Kim did*]*?* [*the one*]
iii **Wine from Australia is now more popular than* [*the from France*]. [*that*]

Instead of *the* we need the forms shown on the right. *It* and *the one Kim did* are not fused-head NPs, while *that from France* is (see [9] of §9).

6.2 The indefinite article *a*

The indefinite article *a* is the most basic indicator of indefiniteness for singular count nouns. Its incompatibility with plurals is due to its historical origin as an unstressed form of the numeral *one*. The indefinite article is then unstressed in connected speech, but has a liaison form *an* (see Ch. 18, §6.4).

With indefinite NPs the addressee is not being expected to be able to identify anything. NPs headed by singular count nouns permit a direct contrast between indefinite *a* and definite *the*:

[9] a. *Bring me a ladder!* b. *Bring me the ladder!*

One possible scenario for the use of *a* is that there are two or more ladders in your field of vision, especially ones differing in significant ways, such as size. In this case *the* would be inappropriate since you would not be able to identify a unique ladder (so that the question *Which ladder?* would not be pre-empted). Another possible scenario is one in which there are no ladders at all in the field of vision, and therefore no clues to help identify a unique ladder.

Quantitative and non-quantitative indefiniteness.

A can express two kinds of indefiniteness, quantitative and non-quantitative:

[10]	QUANTITATIVE	NON-QUANTITATIVE
i	a. *She has just bought [a new car].*	b. *Jill is [a doctor].*
ii	a. *[A student] has complained about it.*	b. *As [a doctor], Jill should know better.*
iii	a. *Jill found [a book on Greek syntax].*	b. *Jill has [a good knowledge of Greek].*

Quantitative *a* expresses existential quantification. By virtue of selecting a singular head it indicates "one", and we have the usual scalar implicature in the [a] examples that she bought no more than one car, and so on. But the issue of how many is backgrounded with *a*: where the distinction between one and more than one is important we use cardinal *one* rather than *a*. The quantification is generally non-proportional, as in [ia/iiia], but [iia] shows that a proportional use is possible: I could be talking here about a student belonging to a definite set of students. We then have the "not all" implicature, but again the contrast with *all* is much less salient with *a* than with *one*. *A* is found only in determiner function. It is thus not used in partitives or other fused-head NPs: this gap is filled by *one*.

The non-quantitative use of *a* is found in ascriptive predicative complements indicating simple set membership, as in [10ib/iib]. Here, what is being said is that Jill belongs to the set denoted by the noun *doctor*, i.e. that she belongs to the set of doctors. The singular NP in the predicative complement position matches the singularity of the predicand *Jill*, but is not in itself quantitative, and could not in this use be replaced by *one*. *A* is also used non-quantitatively in combination with non-count nouns, as in [10iiib]: see the discussion of [21] in §3. Generic *a*, as in *A lion is a ferocious beast* ([14iia] of §8), is likewise non-quantitative.

Constraint on occurrence of *a* in attributive modifiers

Being essentially a marker of indefiniteness, *a* occurs in determiner function and, unlike cardinal numerals, cannot itself function as modifier: compare *its one redeeming feature* and **its a redeeming feature*. However, *a* can occur in certain kinds of expression which can in general function as either determiner or modifier, notably cardinal numerals and genitives. We illustrate first with cardinal numerals and genitives containing *one*:

[11]	DETERMINER	MODIFIER
i	a. *[one hundred] charges*	b. *these [one hundred] charges*
ii	a. *[one colleague's] house*	b. *the [one dollar's] worth of coins*

(We have varied the nouns in [ii] because only a narrow range of measure phrases can occur as attributive genitive NPs – see §16.3.) Now *a* can replace *one* when the numeral or genitive NP is in determiner function, but not when it is modifier: we can't have **these [a hundred] charges* or **the [a dollar's] worth of coins*. Instead, *a* is simply dropped when the numeral or genitive is in modifier function following a determiner:

[12]		
i	a. *[a hundred] charges*	b. *these [hundred] charges*
ii	a. *[a colleague's] house*	b. *the [dollar's] worth of coins*

This rule applies only when *a* would be in initial position in the modifier. *A* is thus retained in such examples as the following:

[13] i *the [more than a hundred] charges that had been laid against them*
ii *the [almost a dollar's] worth of coins that he had in his pocket*

7 Other determinatives

In this section we examine in turn the groups of determinatives given in [5] of §4 other than the two articles. Our major focus will be on their use in determiner function, with other uses being dealt with more summarily.

7.1 The demonstrative determinatives *this* and *that*

There are two demonstrative determinatives, proximal ***this*** and distal ***that***. Both inflect for number, and when in determiner function agree with the head: compare singular *this book* with plural *these books*, or singular *that book* with plural *those books*.

Demonstratives, like the definite article, mark the NP as definite. In saying *this book* or *that book*, for example, I assume you are able to identify which book I am referring to. In the plural the demonstratives indicate in the same way as *the* that the totality of the set has the predication property. Compare, then, the following with [5] of §6:

[1] a. *Those bathroom tiles are cracked.* b. *All those bathroom tiles are cracked.*

What the demonstratives add to basic definiteness is, in the central cases, the notion of spatial deixis:

[2] a. *Read me this book!* b. *Fetch me that book!*

Proximal *this* indicates that the book is relatively close to the speaker, distal *that* that it is less close – though the notion of closeness is partially subjective.

The demonstratives are also used anaphorically:

[3] i *Jones was playing chess. This new hobby that he had just discovered was taking up all of his time.*
ii *I suggested we call the police, but he didn't like that idea.*

Here the interpretation of the underlined NPs derives in part from their antecedents: in [i] the new hobby is understood to be chess, and in [ii] the idea he didn't like is that of calling the police. In both cases we could have *the* instead of the demonstrative, but *this* and *that* mark the anaphoric relationship more clearly or explicitly. The deictic and anaphoric uses of demonstratives are discussed in detail in Ch. 17, §5.

Functions besides determiner

[4] i *Those cards are Kim's; [these] are yours.* [simple fused-head]
ii *[All those of them that were contaminated] we destroyed.* [partitive fused-head]
iii *It's a little late, but [that] doesn't matter.* [special fused-head]
iv *We don't need [this much] sugar.* [modifier]

The fused-head constructions are discussed in §9.2. The modifier use is found with the singular forms in construction with gradable adjectives (*The food wasn't [that bad]*), adverbs (*I hadn't expected to finish* [*this quickly*]), and the core degree determinatives, as in [iv].

7.2 The personal determinatives *we*$_{d}$ and *you*$_{d}$

[5] i [*We*$_{d}$ *supporters of a federal Europe*] *will eventually win the argument.*
ii [*You*$_{d}$ *students*] *should form a society.*

We$_{d}$ and *you*$_{d}$ here are the determinative counterparts of the 1st and 2nd person plural pronouns ***we***$_{p}$ and ***you***$_{p}$ that we have in *We*$_{p}$ *will eventually win the argument* and *You*$_{p}$ *should form a society.* Like the demonstratives, ***we***$_{d}$ and *you*$_{d}$ mark the NP as definite, but this time what is expressed in addition to definiteness is person deixis: ***we*** denotes a set containing the speaker, *you* a set containing at least one addressee but not the speaker. ***We***$_{d}$, like the pronoun, inflects for case, with nominative *we* contrasting with accusative *us*; the distribution of these case-forms is described in §16.2.

It should be noted that the personal determinatives are exactly parallel to other definite determiners such as the demonstratives and the definite article in, for example, permitting the universal quantifier as a predeterminer. Compare:

[6] i a. *all we*$_{d}$ *supporters of a federal Europe* b. *all you students*
ii a. *all those supporters of a federal Europe* b. *all the students*

This property distinguishes them from the personal pronouns, which permit *all* only when postmodified: *All we/you who support a federal Europe will win the argument*, but not **All we/you will win the argument.*

In [7], however, *we* and *you* are pronouns:

[7] i *We*$_{p}$, *the supporters of a federal Europe, will eventually win the argument.*
ii *You*$_{p}$, *the students, should form a society.*

Here, the determiner of *supporters* and *students* is clearly the definite article, and the NPs formed with the definite article are full NPs in their own right which stand in supplementary apposition to the personal pronouns *we* and *you* (see Ch. 15, §5, for discussion of this construction). One reflection of this difference is that the personal determiners can only be the 1st person plural ***we*** and the 2nd person plural *you* (with the exception noted in footnote 14), while all the personal pronouns regardless of person and number occur in the appositional construction. We illustrate this with the 1st person singular *I*, the 2nd person singular *you*, and the 3rd person plural *they*:

[8]	DETERMINER + HEAD	APPOSITIONAL CONSTRUCTION
i	a. **I president declare the meeting open.*	b. *I, the president, declare the meeting open.*
ii	a. **You proponent of a federal Europe should support this proposal.*	b. *You, the proponent of a federal Europe, should support this proposal.*
iii	a. **They poets are our guides.*	b. *They, the poets, are our guides.*

7.3 The universal determinatives *all* and *both*

All and *both* express universal quantification, with *both* applied only to sets with exactly two members. As noted in §5.1, *all* is neutral with respect to the size of the set but by virtue of the contrast with *both* it generally strongly implicates "more than two" when used in count plural NPs. Compare, for example:

[9] a. [*Both parents*] *were interviewed.* b. [*All parents*] *were interviewed.*

In [a] there are two parents involved, and it is very likely, though not of course necessary, that they were parents of the same person. But [b] would not be used for the parents of one person: we would be talking about the parents of a group of people, for example pupils at a school.

Countability and number

The duality meaning restricts *both* to count plural heads; *all* also occurs readily with non-count heads and, much less generally, with count singulars:

[10] i *They used up* [*all the sugar*]. [non-count]
ii *She had spent* [*all* (*the*) *morning*] *in the library.* [count singular]

Universal quantification with count singulars involves quantification over parts, just as in the non-count case. The morning is a period of time that can be subdivided into smaller periods, just as the sugar can be subdivided into smaller quantities of sugar. The count singular use is therefore restricted to cases where there is some relevant subdivision: we say *She read all the book*, but not *#She went out with all her brother.*

All vs *whole*

When used with singular heads, *all* is in competition with the adjectival modifier *whole*:

[11] i a. *I drank* [*all the whisky*]. b. *?I drank* [*the whole whisky*].
ii a. *You will need* [*all your patience*]. b. *#You will need* [*your whole patience*].
iii a. *?Tell me* [*all the truth*]. b. *Tell me* [*the whole truth*].
iv a. *I haven't read* [*all the book*]. b. *I haven't read* [*the whole book*].
v a. *I spent* [*all the day*] *cooking.* b. *I spent* [*the whole day*] *cooking.*
vi a. *?I broke* [*all the plate*]. b. *?I broke* [*the whole plate*].
vii a. **I spent* [*all a day*] *cooking.* b. *I spent* [*a whole day*] *cooking.*
viii a. [*All the committee*] *have voted.* b. [*The whole committee*] *has voted.*

In [i] we have a non-count concrete noun. It denotes a substance subdivisible into quantities of the same kind, and *all* is perfectly natural, but *whole* is not. In [ii] we have the abstract non-count *patience*, and here the preference for *all* is greater. With *truth* the preference is for *whole*, but *the whole truth* has something of the character of a fixed phrase. In [iv–vi] we have singular count nouns, and there is here no preference for one over the other. Both versions of [vi] are questionable because plates, unlike books and days, are not so readily thought of as subdivisible – or at least not with respect to breaking, for the examples would be acceptable with such a verb as *painted.* In [vii] we have a sharp difference in grammaticality: *all* is incompatible with an indefinite determiner while *whole* is not. In [viii] the head noun is a collective; *all* foregrounds the individual members and virtually requires *have* rather than singular *has*, while *whole* has more of a unifying effect and favours *has* over *have.*

Modification

All permits modification while the "exactly two" meaning of *both* excludes it: *Almost all* / **Almost both the candidates were interviewed.* Similarly with *not*: *Not all* / **Not both students take that view. Not all* conveys "less than all", which potentially covers a considerable range; "less than both", by contrast, could only be "just one" or "neither".

Relation between determiner and predeterminer constructions

All and *both* are unique among the determinatives in that they function as either determiner or predeterminer:

[12] i [*All*/*Both* *students*] *failed the philosophy exam.* [determiner]
ii [*All*/*Both* *the students*] *failed the philosophy exam.* [predeterminer]

With *both* such pairs are equivalent. *Both students* (in contrast to *two students*) is definite: it denotes the totality of an identifiable set. *The* expresses nothing more than definiteness, so adding it to the already definite *both students* has no effect on the meaning.

All, however, has a somewhat restricted use as a determiner. The universality of *all* naturally gives rise to generic interpretations, as in *All philosophers live long*; but elsewhere *all* occurs more naturally as a predeterminer than as a determiner, with the *all* version of [12i] thus considerably less likely than that of [12ii] (or the partitive fused-head construction *All of the students failed the philosophy exam*). The determiner construction, however, is certainly not excluded:

[13] i *We will be informing the market that the business is continuing to run as a separate entity, with all key staff remaining in place.*
ii *All students who have failed must see their tutors tomorrow.*
iii *All three visitors left early.*
iv *We spent all day at the beach.*

In [i] the primacy adjective *key* lexico-morphologically indicates a unique set, making it unnecessary to indicate definiteness by means of *the.* Example [ii] illustrates the use of determiner *all* in signs, notices, and injunctions, [iii] before a numeral internal modifier, and [iv] with a time-period noun. Again, *all* could be replaced by weaker *the* in all these examples.[20] Since a unique set is indicated and *all* indeed makes a stronger statement of totality than required for definiteness, *all* must be considered as a definite determiner. Note in this connection that it is possible, though unusual, for it to appear in the oblique NP in the partitive, as in [*Over 40% of all first-year logic students*] *go on to do a major in that field.*

Fused-heads

[14] i *Her friends have got their results:* [*all*/*both* (*of them*)] *have passed.* [partitive]
ii [*All here*] *admire her.* } [special]
iii [*All I want*] *is peace and quiet.* }

All and *both* commonly occur in explicitly or implicitly partitive fused-head NPs; a special case of this is the adjunct use in *They had both/all (of them) passed.* In addition *all* occurs in special fused-head NPs, with a human interpretation ("all people") in [ii], a non-human one in [iii]. *All* in [ii] is more formal and less common than *everyone.* But we could not substitute *everything* in [iii] because of the distributive meaning of *every.* In this inanimate use, *all* is generally followed by a dependent, such as the relative clause modifier in [iii]. *All* on its own tends to be restricted to more or less fixed phrases such as *above all, All is well, All is not lost.*

[20] Such a replacement of *all* by *the* is not possible in NPs with adjunct function: *He worked at home all day / *the day.*

The both of us

Fused-head NPs of this kind are used by some speakers in informal style: %*They had invited the both of us.* More widely accepted would be *the two of us* or *both of us.* Syntactically *the both of us* is exceptional in that *both* cannot follow *the* (i.e. cannot occur in internal modifier function) in NPs with a noun head: **the both students.* The partitive oblique is restricted to personal pronouns: **the both of the students.*

Other functions

[15] i *She did it [all by herself].* *I'm [all wet].* *The coat is [all wool].* [modifier]
ii *They invited [both Kim] and Pat.* [marker of coordination]

All can modify PPs, AdjPs, AdvPs, and NPs. *All wool* in [i] has *all* as a peripheral modifier in the NP, not a determiner, as it is in *[All wool] is tax-free* (see [6ii] of §13). *All* is also used as an intensifying modifier of AdjPs, AdvPs, or DPs that have *the* or *that* as modifier: *I feel [all the better for it]*; *The exam wasn't [all that difficult]*. The plural meaning of *both* excludes it from such modifying constructions, but it is used (in correlation with *and*) as a marker of coordination. There is no corresponding use of *all* for multiple coordination: **They invited all Kim, Pat, and Alex.*

Distributivity

All and *both* usually yield a distributive interpretation, i.e. one where the predication property applies individually to the members of the set:

[16] i *All members of the committee voted in favour of the resolution.*
ii *Both students bought a present for the teacher.*

In [i] the vote was unanimous: the members voted individually in favour of the resolution. If it was a majority vote rather than unanimous we wouldn't use *all*, but would simply say *the members of the committee* (or, in this particular case, *the committee*). Similarly, we understand from [ii] that two presents were bought for the teacher.

All and *both* do not explicitly exclude a non-distributive interpretation (as *each* and *every* do), but the preference for a distributive reading is somewhat stronger with *both* than with *all*. Compare:

[17] i *All/Both the students together had managed to lift the piano onto the stage.*
ii *All/Both the students had handed in only five essays.*

In [i] *together* forces a non-distributive, joint, reading, and some speakers feel that *both* is not completely felicitous here. If we drop *together*, the *all* version continues to allow the joint interpretation, whereas the acceptability of *both* becomes problematic: inherently it strongly favours a distributive interpretation, but this clashes with the usual expectation that more than one person is needed to lift a piano. The preferred interpretation of [ii] is distributive, with five essays handed in per student. The non-distributive interpretation has a total of five essays handed in, and while *all* allows this interpretation it is hardly possible with *both*. The non-distributive reading can be forced by adding *between them*, and again some speakers will find *both* somewhat less fully acceptable than *all*.

Reciprocal properties

[18] i *All/Both of them had been to the same school.*
ii *All/Both copies were identical/alike.*

In the absence of further context we will interpret [i] reciprocally, i.e. as "the same school as each other" (rather than "the same school as the person just mentioned"), and we likewise have a reciprocal interpretation in [ii]: "identical to / like each other". Such properties are compatible with *each*, which indicates that they can be construed as distributable: *Each of them had been to the same school*; *Each copy was identical/alike.* Nevertheless, they are less straightforwardly distributable than others, and there are again speakers who find *both* less than fully acceptable here.[21]

7.4 The distributive determinatives *each* and *every*

Each and *every* explicitly indicate a distributive interpretation of the predication property, and this is reflected in the selection of a singular head. Compare, then, [17ii] above with:

[19] *Each / Every student handed in only five essays.*

If there were ten students, fifty essays were handed in: it can't be that the students as a group handed in only five. This is the normal interpretation for *both* too, but it selects a plural head. Plural *both students* is definite in that it refers to an identifiable set of two; singular *each/every student*, however, is indefinite: our concern here is with the individual students, and they do not individually satisfy the criterion of being identifiable.

Differences between *each* and *every*

(a) *Each*, unlike *every*, normally involves an identifiable set

Although an NP like *each student* is itself indefinite, we understand that there is some definite set of students to which the quantification applies. This, however, is not necessarily so with NPs determined by *every*. Compare:

		a.		b.
[20]	i	a.	*Last year <u>each student</u> passed.*	b. *Last year <u>every student</u> passed.*
	ii	a.	*<u>Each philosopher</u> admires Aristotle.*	b. *<u>Every philosopher</u> admires Aristotle.*
	iii	a.	**We lunch together <u>each other day</u>.*	b. *We lunch together <u>every other day</u>.*

In [i] I'm talking specifically about last year's course, so there must be an identifiable set of students involved, the ones who took that course. In contexts like this, *each* and *every* are equally appropriate. But the difference is clear in [ii]. Here [iib] is interpreted generically (like *all philosophers*, except for the explicit marking of distributivity); [iia], however, doesn't have this generic interpretation: rather, we recognise some contextually identified set of philosophers, each of whom admires Aristotle. With time (and other measure) expressions, the identifiable set requirement with *each* is not so evident, for we can have *We lunch together each day*; nevertheless, *every* occurs more freely in this kind of context, as is evident from the contrast in [iii]. Compare similarly *I see her every two or three days*, but not **I see her each two or three days.*

(b) The distributive meaning is stronger with *each* than with *every*

We have said that both items indicate distributivity, reflected syntactically in the singular head. With *each*, however, this feature is stronger in that the predication property is generally construed as applying **separately** to the individual members of the set. Compare

[21] There is a prescriptive tradition of condemning this use of *both*, though the more empirically based usage manuals recognise that it is well established. Curiously, manuals which condemn it invoke the concept of tautology or redundancy, but there is no more reason to say that *both* is redundant in *Both copies were alike* than there is in *Both copies were defective.*

such examples as the following, where *every* is considerably more likely or natural than *each*:

[21] i *Each/Every city in the region was destroyed by the earthquake.*
ii *I enjoyed each/every minute of it.*

In [i] it is likely that the earthquake destroyed the cities more or less simultaneously, which is more consistent with *every* than with *each*: the latter suggests they were destroyed separately. In [ii] *enjoy every minute of* is a common expression: you understand that it was enjoyable throughout, from beginning to end. The version with *each*, however, focuses more literally on the sequence of individual minutes.[22]

(c) *Every* but not *each* implicates a set with more than two members

Like *all*, *every* is not normally used when it is known that the set has just two members. Only *each* is appropriate in examples like *Cars were parked on each side of the road.*

(d) *Every* can be used with abstract nouns with multal rather than universal meaning

[22] i *There is every possibility that she will make a complete recovery.*
ii *I have every reason to believe that they were conspiring against us.*

This represents a secondary use of *every*, where the primary universal distributive meaning is lost: in [i] you understand that there is a very good chance of her recovery, and in [ii] that I have strong reasons for my belief (cf. Ch. 16, n. 16). The loss of the primary meaning is such that it is not clear that the NPs in [22] are construed as count rather than non-count; certainly, *every* in this sense can combine with non-count nouns, as in *He gave them every encouragement.*

(e) *Each* but not *every* can be used as a fused determiner-head

		a.	b.
[23]	i	*Each (of them) was cut in two.*	**Every (of them) was cut in two.*
	ii	*They sold for two dollars each.*	**They sold for two dollars every.*

Every has only a dependent use, requiring a following head. We can correct [ib] by inserting *one* to satisfy this requirement: *Every one (of them) was cut in two*, but this is hardly possible in [iib]. Fused-head NPs with *each* are normally explicitly or implicitly partitive; *Each to* %*his/their own* and its variant *To each* %*his/their own* are fixed phrases with the form of special fused-head NPs where *each* means "everyone".

(f) *Every*, but not *each*, permits modification

[24] a. *[Almost every student] passed.* b. **[Almost each student] passed.*

(g) *Every*, but not *each*, can occur as modifier following a genitive determiner

[25] a. *They scrutinised [her every move].* b. **They scrutinised [her each move].*

The NP in [a] means "every move she made". The construction is possible with only a narrow range of nouns as head, probably all abstract.

Each and *every* also differ (reflecting certain of the above contrasts) in the compounds into which they enter: *each* compounds with *other* in the reciprocal *each other*, *every* with ·*body*, etc., in *everybody, everyone, everything, everywhere.* They can also coordinate for emphatic effect: *Each and every contestant will win a prize.*

[22] Compare also the idiomatic expressions *every inch* and *every bit* as used in examples like *She was every inch a philosopher* or *It was every bit as good as I'd hoped.*

7.5 The existential determinatives *some* and *any*

Some and *any* express existential quantification, as explained in §5.1. They occur primarily in determiner function, where they mark the NP as indefinite. Leaving aside the free choice sense of *any* (*any*$_f$), they are polarity-sensitive items, with *some* having a positive orientation, *any* a negative orientation. Compare:

[26] i a. *We've got some milk.* b. **We've got any milk.*
ii a. **We haven't got some milk.* b. *We haven't got any milk.*

This relationship between *some* and *any* is discussed in Ch. 9, §4.3 (where we note that there are some special contexts in which examples like [iia] are acceptable).

Some in determiner function

Existential *some* is found with the following range of uses:

(a) Basic non-proportional use, selecting plural and non-count heads

[27] i *There are some letters for you.* [plural]
ii *We need some sugar.* [non-count]

Some is here a prototypical existential quantifier, indicating a quantity greater than zero; by virtue of the plural head in [i] there must be at least two. In this use *some* is non-proportional: we are not concerned with a subset of letters belonging to a certain larger set. There is accordingly no "not all" implicature, but often there will be a "not multal" implicature – that the number of letters or amount of sugar is not particularly large. This *some* is normally unstressed and pronounced /səm/. In negative declaratives, we typically have *any* in place of *some.*

(b) "Considerable quantity" use, selecting plural and non-count heads

[28] i *It was some years before she saw him again.* [plural]
ii *We discussed the problem at some length.* [non-count]

Here *some* cannot be phonologically reduced to /səm/, and there is no replacement by *any* in negative contexts. *Some* is here again non-proportional, but it indicates a quantity significantly above zero, so this time there is no evident "not multal" implicature. *Quite* is often found as peripheral modifier, increasing the quantity indicated: *We discussed the problem at quite some length.* It is normally restricted to heads denoting some kind of measure – cf. **There were quite some people at the demonstration.*

(c) Vague count singular use

[29] i *When I arrived, some student was waiting outside the door.*
ii *Some idiot must have left the oven on!*
iii *Some day I will win the lottery.*

With count singular heads, *some* is in competition with the indefinite article *a*, which is much more common and represents the default choice. *Some* conveys that the identity is of little importance: you are not expected to pursue the question of who the student was in [i], and so on. In this interpretation, *some* commonly occurs with *or other* following the head, as in *Some student or other was waiting outside the door*; in this construction *or other* is arguably a modifier rather than a coordinate. In examples like [ii], the head noun *idiot* is what is known as an **epithet**, an emotive expression which serves to indicate annoyance with the individual concerned rather than to give an objective description. *Some* is more natural than *a* with epithets: *An idiot has left the oven on* suggests that *idiot* is being used as an ordinary descriptive noun. Finally, in [iii], the indefinite article would not be possible, though *some* could here be replaced without detectable change of meaning by *one*. This case is restricted to a handful of nouns such as *day*, *time*, and *place*. NPs of this kind bear some resemblance to compounds (such as *somewhere*) but differ in that they are syntactically composite. It is possible, for instance, to insert the adjective *other* between the determiner and the noun: *some other day*.

(d) Exclamatory use with stressed SOME

[30] a. *Those are SOME elephants!* b. *SOME hotel that was! An utter disgrace!*

With strong (but not contrastive) stress, *some* has a special interpretation indicating an emotive response to something exceptional. The speaker's attitude may be favourable, as is quite likely in [a] ("remarkable elephants"), or unfavourable, as in [b]. The examples given have plural and count singular heads; non-counts are less usual but certainly not excluded (*That was SOME crockery they were using!*).

(e) Basic proportional use

[31] i	*Some people left early.*	[plural]
ii	*I think some candidate expressed a view on this issue*	[count singular]
iii	*Some cheese is made from goat's milk.*	[non-count]

Here, in contrast most directly to use (a), we are concerned with quantity relative to some larger set, so that there is a clear "not all" (and indeed "not most") implicature: "Not everyone left early, most people didn't leave early", and so on. As with use (a), *any* would generally be used in negative declarative contexts: *I don't think any people left early*. In this use, however, *some* is stressed, and not reducible to /səm/. It can be modified by such expressions as *at least* or (less likely) *at most*: *At least some people thought it was worthwhile*. It can be the focus of *only*: *Only SOME people read the whole report*. It is mainly found with plural and non-count heads. But count singulars are also possible, as in [ii]: we don't here have the special indeterminate interpretation given under (c) above for non-proportional *some*.

Any in determiner function

For *any* we have a major distinction between two uses that we call non-affirmative (*any*$_n$) and free choice (*any*$_f$).

(a) Non-affirmative *any*$_n$

Any$_n$ has essentially the same sense as *some* in its basic non-proportional and proportional uses, but is restricted to non-affirmative contexts – prototypically either negative declaratives or else interrogatives.

The non-proportional use is seen in:

[32] i	*There aren't any letters for you.*	[plural]
ii	*We don't need any sugar.*	[non-count]
iii	*I haven't got any job lined up for you today, I'm afraid.*	[count singular]

The count singular case is relatively uncommon. We noted above that the indefinite article *a* is generally preferred over *some* for count singulars, and since *a* – unlike *some* – is not polarity-sensitive, that preference carries over to non-affirmative contexts. Thus I would normally say, for example, *I haven't got a car* rather than *I haven't got any car*. The latter cannot be ruled out, but it needs some special context, as when I make an emphatic riposte to someone who thinks I do have a car. *Any*$_n$ is found with various singular abstract nouns where the distinction between count and non-count is somewhat blurred: *They didn't make any attempt to justify their decision* (cf. *They didn't make an attempt / much attempt to justify their decision*, with count and non-count interpretations respectively). In general, the choice between singular and plural with count nouns is determined by the same factors as apply with *no*: see §7.8. Note, for example, that one would normally say *They haven't got any children* rather than *They haven't got any child*.

The proportional use of *any*$_n$ is illustrated in:

[33] i *I don't think any people left early.* [plural]
ii *I don't think any candidate expressed a view on this issue.* [count singular]
iii *I don't think any cheese is made from goat's milk.* [non-count]

The count singular case is less restricted here than in the non-proportional use, reflecting the fact that proportional *some* is also found with count singulars.

Any$_n$ is usually but by no means always unstressed. It can be stressed, for example, when it is the focus of negation: *I don't think* ANY *people left early*. The negative orientation of *any*$_n$ can be reinforced by the polarity-sensitive *at all* or *whatever*: *We hadn't made any progress at all / whatever.*

(b) Free choice *any*$_f$

[34] i *Any computers with defective keyboards should be returned.* [plural]
ii *Any policeman will be able to tell you.* [count singular]
iii *Any remaining dirt will have to be removed.* [non-count]

Any$_f$ occurs with all three of the main kinds of head: plural, count singular, and non-count. It indicates that there is a free choice: an arbitary member (or subquantity) can be selected from the set (or quantity) denoted by the head and the predication property will apply to it. In [ii], for example, there is a free choice as to which policeman can be selected, but no matter which policeman it is, that policeman will be able to tell you. *Any*$_f$ implicates that the free choice will only have to be made once, but this implicature can be cancelled. In [ii], since the first policeman selected will normally provide the required information, it will not be necessary to ask another one. However, in [i] the modal *should* imposes an obligation to apply the free choice until all defective computers are selected. Note that this obligation to return all defective computers is not related to the plurality of the nominal: *Any computer with a defective keyboard should be returned* implicates the same obligation.

For these reasons *any*$_f$ bears some resemblance to the universal quantifier *all*: compare *All computers with defective keyboards should be returned.*[23] It is clear, however, that *any*$_f$ does not **mean** "all". There is, for example, a clear difference between *Come on, anyone, join me up here on the stage*, which asks for one volunteer to come up on stage, and *Come on, everyone, join me up here on the stage*, which asks less prudently for everyone in the audience to come up on stage.

[23] *Any* is sometimes found coordinated with *all*: *He hadn't seen the indictment but asserted that he was totally innocent of any and all charges.*

Free choice *any*$_f$ is best treated as having the same sense as *some* in its basic proportional use, with a special added implicature: when I say *Any*$_f$ *first-year student could solve this puzzle* I assert that some first-year student could solve this puzzle and also implicate that I have no particular first-year student in mind, but rather am prepared to allow the claim to be applied to whatever arbitrary first-year student you might pick. I do not **state** that every first-year student could solve the puzzle, but very strongly implicate a belief in that proposition, because my claim risks being shown to be false unless it is in fact true that every first-year student could solve the puzzle.

Differences between *any*$_f$ and *any*$_n$

There are several differences between the two *any*'s. We noted that *any*$_n$ is usually unstressed: *any*$_f$, by contrast, is always stressed. Secondly, while *any*$_n$ is restricted to non-affirmative contexts, *any*$_f$ is not polarity-sensitive. The *any*$_f$ examples given above are all in affirmative contexts, but in a negative context we can have a contrast between the two senses:

[35] i [*We don't publish any*$_n$ *letters*:] *we only accept commissioned articles.*
ii [*We don't publish just any*$_f$ *letters*:] *we reject more than half of those submitted.*

Example [i] is equivalent to *We publish no letters.* In [ii] the free choice is negated: we ourselves are making a selection, accepting some letters, rejecting others. Thirdly, *any*$_f$, unlike *any*$_n$, permits modification, for example by the adverb *almost.* Compare:

[36] i *Jan will read* [*almost any*$_f$ *computer magazines*].
ii *Jan couldn't find* [*almost any*$_n$ *computer magazines*] *in the shop.*

Restriction of *some* and *any*$_n$ to quantitative indefinites

Unlike the indefinite article and bare NPs, *some* and *any*$_n$ are excluded from non-quantitative indefinites.

(a) Ascriptive predicative complements

Some and *any*$_n$ are not used in ascriptive predicative complements indicating simple set membership. Instead we find the indefinite article for count singulars (as in [10ib/iib] above) and bare NPs for plural and non-count heads. Compare:

	a.	b.
[37] i	*Jill is a doctor.*	**Jill is some doctor.*
ii	*Jill and Ed are doctors.*	**Jill and Ed are some doctors.*
iii	*As doctors, they should know that.*	**As any doctors, they should know that.*
iv	*This liquid is sulphuric acid.*	**This liquid is some sulphuric acid.*
v	*Jill wasn't a student.*	**Jill wasn't any*$_n$ *student.*

This is not to say that *some* and *any*$_n$ are wholly excluded from predicative complements:

[38] i *Mary and Frieda are* [*some friends of ours that we met on holiday in Ibiza*].
ii *This is* [*some sulphuric acid we have left over from the last experiment*].
iii *Jill wasn't* [*any*$_n$ *student of mine*].

These, however, do not belong to the ascriptive *be* construction: the predicative does not indicate membership of a set or type, but identity. Thus [37vb] is inadmissible with the sense "It is not the case that Jill was a member of the set of students", but [38iii] can be treated as equivalent to "It is not the case that Jill was one of my students", with the second *be* used in its specifying sense.

(b) Generics

Some is likewise excluded from generic NPs. Only the [a] examples in [39] allow generic interpretations:

		a.	b.
[39]	i	a. [<u>A</u> *lion*] *is a ferocious beast.*	b. [<u>*Some*</u> *lion*] *is a ferocious beast.*
	ii	a. [*Lions*] *are ferocious beasts.*	b. [<u>*Some*</u> *lions*] *are ferocious beasts.*
	iii	a. [*Sulphuric acid*] *is a dangerous substance.*	b. *[<u>*Some*</u> *sulphuric acid*] *is a dangerous substance.*

(c) Individuated non-count NPs

Some and *any*$_n$ cannot replace *a* in examples like *Jill has a good knowledge of Greek* (=[21iib] of §3): **Jill doesn't have any good knowledge of Greek.*

(d) Further contrasts with bare plural NPs

In other constructions, NPs with *some* contrast with bare plural NPs as quantitative versus non-quantitative indefinites:

[40] i [<u>*Some*</u> *seats*] / [*Seats*] *are available at fifty dollars.*
ii *Everybody went to the post office to buy* [<u>*some*</u> *stamps*] / [*stamps*].

The version of [i] with *some* could be used by a box-office clerk at the theatre indicating that more than one seat is available at fifty dollars. The version with bare *seats*, by contrast, might well be a sign outside the theatre and could reasonably be left on display as long as not every seat had been sold – it does not exclude the case where only one seat is left. In [ii], where the subject is the distributive *everybody*, the use of *some* conveys that more than one stamp was bought by each person, whereas bare *stamps* simply indicates that each person was engaged in stamp-buying, regardless of the number of stamps actually bought.

Relation between *some* and *any*$_n$ and the indefinite article

Consider a set of examples such as the following:

		a.	b.
[41]	i	a. *We need a chair.*	b. *We don't need a chair.*
	ii	a. *We need some chairs.*	b. *We don't need any*$_n$ *chairs.*
	iii	a. *We need some furniture.*	b. *We don't need any*$_n$ *furniture.*

The indefinite article allows only count singular heads, and hence is excluded from [ii–iii]. The occurrence of *some* and *any*$_n$ in [ii–iii] with essentially the same role as that of *a* in [i] makes it tempting to see *some* and *any*$_n$ as indefinite articles too, ones selecting plural or non-count heads. There are indeed works that adopt such an analysis, but we will not follow that approach here, for two reasons, involving data already presented. In the first place, *some* and *any*$_n$ are not restricted to plural and non-count heads, but are also found, albeit less frequently, with count singular heads, as in [30], for example. They may therefore contrast with the indefinite article rather than being in complementary distribution with it. Secondly, as illustrated in [37–40], there are also respects in which *some* and *any*$_n$ are distributionally more restricted than the indefinite article, inasmuch as they are restricted to quantitative uses.

Other functions of *some* and *any*$_n$

(a) Fused determiner-head

[42] i a. *I need some dollar coins; have you got* <u>*some*</u> *I could borrow?* } [simple]
b. *I wanted to borrow some dollar coins but she didn't have* <u>*any*</u>.
ii a. *Can I have* <u>*some*</u> *of this custard?* } [partitive]
b. *There are a lot of applicants but I don't think* <u>*any*</u> *are suitable.*

iii *The film is disappointing – <u>some</u> might put it more strongly than that.* [special]

Any$_n$ has no special fused-head use corresponding to the *some* of [iii], "some people".

(b) Modifier

[43] i *Have you got [<u>some</u>/<u>any</u> more] milk?*
ii *Are you feeling [<u>any</u> better] / [<u>any</u> more relaxed]?*

In [i] *some* and *any* modify *more* in a DP (see §11). In [ii] *any*$_n$ functions as degree modifier of comparatives; *some* is found in this construction in AmE, but is regarded as either very colloquial or non-standard: %*I'm feeling some better.* The standard form with positive orientation is *somewhat*: *I'm feeling somewhat better. Some* and *any*$_n$ are also used as degree modifiers in clause structure, but primarily in informal AmE: %*She may be oversimplifying some*; %*That wouldn't help us any.*

Some with the sense "approximately", as in *We had some thirty applications for the position*, we take to be a different word, belonging to the adverb category.

7.6 Cardinal numerals

The cardinal numerals are primarily determinatives but they have a secondary use in which they inflect for number and hence belong in the noun category: *They set off in <u>threes</u> / enrolled in their <u>hundreds</u>.* In practice, only low or round numerals are used in this way.[24]

The form of cardinal numerals

The cardinal numerals can express any number, and therefore themselves form an infinite subset of the determinative category. Numerals expressing whole numbers from "0" to "99" are single words (*zero*/*nought, three, thirteen, thirty, thirty-three*, etc.); those expressing higher numbers are syntactically complex (*three hundred, three hundred and thirty-three*, etc.), as are those involving fractions (*one and a half*).[25]

The rules which govern the internal structure of the syntactically complex numerals are sui generis, and, with one minor exception, this internal structure is unaffected by the wider syntactic context. We will therefore treat all numerals as belonging to the lexical category determinative, on a par with other unmodified determinatives, and for this reason we describe their form in Ch. 19, §5.10.1.

The one place where the form of the numeral is affected by the syntactic structure of the NP involves numerals which begin with the multiplier "1": *one hundred, one thousand, one million*, etc. The form *one* here can be freely replaced by the indefinite article to give *a hundred, a thousand, a million*, etc. Note that this article must be considered as an integral part of the numeral, and not as an independent determiner. *A hundred days*, for example, has the structure determiner + head, not determiner + modifier + head: the whole NP is clearly plural, not singular, as it would be if *a* were the determiner.[26]

[24] Numerals are often used metalinguistically, as the names of symbols: *They added a '3' before all the Brisbane telephone numbers.*

[25] Fractional numbers smaller than one, however, are expressed by nouns or NPs in predeterminer modifier function: see §12.

[26] Contrast *a marvellous hundred days*, where *a* is determiner and quite independent of *hundred*: see §3.4 for discussion of this construction.

However, when the numeral is in modifier function, initial *a* is dropped in accordance with the rule given in §6.2, so corresponding to, say, *every one hundred days* we have not **every a hundred days*, but *every hundred days*.

Interpretation and modification

As noted in §5.2, the numerals are usually interpreted as giving the exact cardinality of a set, but the "not more than" component has the status of an implicature. *Five people complained* implicates but does not entail that no more than five complained. They allow a significant range of modifiers such as *at least* or *at most*, and various expressions of approximation: *some fifteen mistakes*, etc.

Numerical vs singulative *one*

At the first level we distinguish three items *one*: a personal pronoun (*One should keep oneself informed of these matters*), a common noun that is generally used anaphorically and has a plural form *ones* (*a red car and three black ones*), and the determinative that is our concern in the present section.

Determinative *one* belongs in the set of cardinal numerals, but it has some uses that are not matched by the higher numerals. We therefore distinguish two uses, which we will call **numerical** (*one*$_n$) and **singulative** (*one*$_s$):

[44]	NUMERICAL *ONE*	SINGULATIVE *ONE*
i	a. *We have one*$_n$ *son and two daughters.*	b. *She arrived one*$_s$ *rainy morning.*
ii	a. *Only / At least one*$_n$ *student failed.*	b. *Not one*$_s$ *student failed.*
iii	a. *I need one*$_n$ *or more volunteers.*	b. *For one*$_s$ *reason or another they didn't charge us.*
iv	a. *That one*$_n$ *mistake cost him his job.*	b. [no use of *one*$_s$ as modifier]
v	a. [no emotive use of *one*$_n$]	b. *That's* ONE$_s$ *big elephant.*

One$_n$ contrasts with the higher cardinal numerals: [ia] contrasts with *We have two sons*, and so on. *One*$_s$ does not enter into such contrasts: compare [ib] with **She arrived two rainy mornings*. We observed that the indefinite article *a* arose historically by weakening of *one*: *one*$_s$ behaves in many respects like a stressed counterpart of *a*. In [ii] we see that *one*$_n$ takes modifiers in the same way as other cardinals: *at least*, *at most*, *more than*, etc., and can be the focus of such NP-level modifiers as *only* (§13). These constructions are incompatible with *one*$_s$, but the latter permits *not*. This *not* is not generally found with higher cardinals (**Not five students failed the exam*),[27] but it is commonly found with *a*: compare *Not one*$_s$*/a day passed without Fred losing his glasses*. The numerical nature of *one*$_n$ is seen in the coordination with *or more* in [iiia] (cf. *three or more*); the corresponding coordination for *one*$_s$ is with *another*, as in [iiib]: it's a matter of what reason, not how many reasons.[28] This association with *another* is seen also in examples like *One*$_s$ *problem followed another*. *One*$_n$ can function as modifier following a determiner, as in [iva]; again, other cardinals appear here too: *Those two mistakes cost him his job*. *One*$_s$, however, is restricted to determiner function – like the indefinite article. Finally, [vb] shows *one*$_s$ carrying heavy stress for emotive effect: it conveys that the elephant is exceptionally big. The construction is similar to that illustrated in [30] for *some*. Note

[27] Such combinations are permitted with expressions of measure, as in *I saw her not five minutes ago*.

[28] Here *one*$_s$ is replaceable by *some* (in what we called the vague count singular use): *for some reason or another*. We find a similar interchangeability in *One*$_s$*/Some day soon I'll make amends*.

that highlighting *one* here has nothing to do with a contrast between one and more than one. Somewhat similar is the use of *one*$_s$ in combination with the head noun *hell* in *We had one*$_s$ *hell of a week-end*; in this case, however, *one*$_s$ is not stressed and can be replaced by *a*.

Fused-head NPs

Cardinal numerals occur commonly in simple and partitive fused-head NPs, and *one*$_n$ follows this pattern. *One*$_s$ is found in the simple type, where it fills the gap resulting from the inability of *a* to function as fused-head, and in the special type with the interpretation "a person":

[45]	i	a. *Kim has written four novels, and Pat has written two/one*$_n$.	[simple]
		b. *Mary bought a book, and I bought *a/one*$_s$ *as well.*	[simple]
	ii	*They gave us four copies but two/one*$_n$ *of them seemed defective.*	[partitive]
	iii	*He behaved like one*$_s$ *who considers himself born to rule.*	[special]

Zero and *nought*

Zero and BrE *nought* are marginal members of the set of cardinal numerals. They act like cardinals in arithmetic operations (*zero/nought times ten*), in percentages (*zero percent*), in decimals (*zero/nought point two*), and temperature measures (*zero/nought degrees Celsius*). *Zero*, but not *nought*, also functions as a determiner comparable to *no* (which is not a cardinal numeral, and does not take part in any of the rules for numeral formation):

[46] a. *They made zero/no errors.* b. *They have zero/no chance of winning.*

Zero is quite rare in comparison with *no*; its origin as a mathematical term for the number "0" tends to give utterances with *zero* a pseudo-scientific character. *Zero* differs from *no* in that it is not a marker of negation. The difference is brought out, for example, by the reversed polarity tag test for clause polarity (Ch. 9, §1.1): contrast *They made zero errors, didn't they?* and *They made no errors, did they?*[29]

7.7 The disjunctive determinatives *either* and *neither*

Either as determiner: non-affirmative and free choice uses

Either selects a count singular head: *either parent*, but not **either children* or **either information*. Like *any*, it has a non-affirmative use (*either*$_n$) and a free choice use (*either*$_f$):

[47]	i	a. *He didn't like either*$_n$ *teacher.*	b. **He liked either teacher.*
	ii	a. *Did either*$_n$ *boy have a key?*	b. **Either boy had a key.*
	iii	a. *You can take either*$_f$ *computer.*	b. **She had taken either computer.*

The inadmissible [b] examples are affirmative and also exclude a free choice interpretation.

Duality: *either* in relation to *any* and *both*

Either differs from *any* in that it presupposes a selection from a set of two that is assumed to be identifiable by the addressee. *Either teacher* in [47ia] is thus equivalent to *either*

[29] There are a number of other words expressing "0" found in specialised registers, such as giving scores in various sports – e.g. *nil* (soccer, etc.) or *love* (racquet sports).

of the two teachers. Its association with duality makes *either* like *both*. The difference is most straightforwardly seen in pairs like:

[48] i a. *Did either boy have a key?* (=[47iia]) b. *Did both boys have a key?*
ii a. *If either parent dies, Jill will inherit the business.* b. *If both parents die, Jill will inherit the business.*

In [i] the conditions under which the answer to the question is "yes" are clearly different: in [b] each of the two boys must have had a key, but in [a] only one need have had one. Similarly in [ii] the condition under which Jill will inherit the business is different: in [b] she'll inherit if each of the parents dies, but in [a] it is sufficient that one parent dies. *Both* thus indicates the totality of the set: it is a universal quantifier. *Either*$_n$ is an existential quantifier: it indicates at least one member. This is reflected in the fact that *both* selects a plural, while *either* selects a singular. And it follows that while *both boys* is definite, *either boy* is indefinite.

The presupposition of a definite set of two distinguishes dual *either* from neutral *any*. *Either* could be replaced by *any* in [47], preserving the contrast between the admissible [a] and inadmissible [b] examples, but with the implicature now that we are concerned with more than two teachers, boys, or computers. *Any*, however, does not presuppose a definite set at all, so a closer *any* counterpart of [47ia] would have an explicit partitive phrase: *He didn't like any of the teachers*, etc. As with *both*, restriction to a set of exactly two rules out modification: compare *He liked hardly any/*either of the teachers* or *Almost any/*either of the computers would do the job.*

Either as a marker of coordination

Like *both*, *either* functions not only as determiner in NP structure but also as the marker of the first term in a coordinative construction:

[49] i a. *either parent* b. *both parents*
ii a. *either her father or her mother* b. *both her father and her mother*

While *both* is paired with the coordinator *and*, *either* is paired with *or*; the relation between [a] and [b] in the coordinations [ii] thus matches that between the NPs [i]. *Or*-coordinations (discussed in Ch. 15, §2.2) express the semantic relation known as **disjunction**: hence our classification of *either* as a disjunctive determinative. The relation between the uses as NP-determiner and coordination-marker is not quite as close with *either* as with *both*. In the first place, the distributional restrictions on *either* in NPs illustrated in [47] do not hold for *either* in coordinations: compare [47iib], for example, with *Either her father or her mother had a key.* Secondly (as we noted in §5.1), the duality feature is weakened: while *either*-coordinations are characteristically binary, multiple ones like *either Kim, Pat, or Alex* are also possible.

Special use: *on either side*

[50] *They planted roses on either side of the driveway.*

Here *either* is equivalent to *each*, and since a set of two is still presupposed *either side* is equivalent to *both sides*. This use of *either* is found with a very small set of nouns, such as *side, end, extreme*, and is not subject to the syntactic restrictions illustrated in [47].

Neither

Neither functions likewise as determiner (*neither parent*) or marker of an initial coordinate (*neither her father nor her mother*), and represents the lexicalisation of "not + either". Example [47ia] is thus equivalent to *He liked neither teacher*. Similarly *Neither boy had a key* means "It is not the case that either boy had a key" and is equivalent to *Both boys didn't have a key*. This equivalence is the same as that between *Neither Max nor Ed had a key* and *Both Max and Ed didn't have a key*, and is discussed more fully in our account of coordination (Ch. 15, §2.4).

Fused-head NPs

Either and *neither* commonly occur as head in explicitly or implicitly partitive fused-head NPs:

[51] i *Let me know if [either/neither of the students] turns up.* [explicitly partitive]
ii *There were two flats available, but [neither] was suitable.* [implicitly partitive]

7.8 The negative determinatives *no* and *none*

No as determiner with count and non-count heads

[52] i a. *No juvenile was admitted.* b. *No juveniles were admitted.* [count]
ii *No bread was baked that day.* [non-count]

With count heads *no* indicates that not one member of the set under consideration has the predication property, and with non-count heads it indicates that there isn't any subquantity of the quantity under consideration that has the predication property. The set/quantity under consideration is that denoted by the head subject to any implied contextual restrictions. If I say, for example, *No student had read Bloomfield's 'Language'*, I will normally be understood as talking not about students in general but about the students in a particular course.

Neutralisation of the singular–plural distinction

Examples [52ia–b] are semantically equivalent: the distinction between singular and plural is here neutralised. In this example there is little pragmatic difference between the two versions, but in some cases one or other may be preferred or required:

[53] i a. *He has no father.* b. #*He has no fathers.*
ii a. *He has no child.* b. *He has no children.*

In [i] the singular is required because one doesn't have more than one (biological) father. The singular is also more natural in *He has no job/jobs*: it is of course possible to have two or more jobs, but the normal expectation is that people have just one. In [ii], by contrast, we would normally use the plural version: it is more usual to have two or more children than just one. It is arguable, indeed, that the plural in general represents the default choice.

Relationship with *not* + *a/one/any*$_n$ and *neither*

In general, *no* is equivalent to *not* (or a negative verb inflection) + *a*, *one*$_s$, or *any*$_n$.

[54] i a. *No boy(s) in the class passed.* b. *I know no boy(s) in the class.*
ii a. *Not a/one*$_s$ *boy in the class passed.* b. *I don't know a/one*$_s$ *boy in the class.*
iii a. ?*Not any*$_n$ *boy(s) in the class passed.* b. *I don't know any*$_n$ *boy(s) in the class.*

Construction [ii], especially the version with *one*$_s$, is somewhat more emphatic than the others, but is of course restricted to singular heads. *Not* cannot normally modify *any*, so that while [iiib] is admissible, [iiia] is at best very marginal (see §11).

When the conditions for the use of *neither* are satisfied, it will normally pre-empt the use of *no*, just as *either* and *both* pre-empt *any* and *all*: *Parking was permitted on neither/#no side of the road.*

He's no doctor

One place where the *no* version is semantically distinct is in ascriptive predicative complements. Compare:

[55] a. *He isn't a doctor.* b. *He's no doctor.*

Version [a] simply says that he isn't a member of the class of doctors, while [b] says that he doesn't have the properties of a doctor. Similarly, *He's no friend of mine* implies that I know him and that his behaviour to me is not what one would expect of a friend, while *He's not a friend of mine* says only that he doesn't belong to the class of friends of mine – it could be that I hardly know him, or indeed that I don't know him at all. This usage is also found with proper names: *She's no Florence Nightingale* says that she doesn't have the qualities she would need to qualify as 'another Florence Nightingale' (cf. Ch. 9, §3.2.1).

no mean achievement

A further special use of *no* is in examples like *That was no mean achievement* or *She made no small contribution to our project.* These convey that it was in fact a major achievement or contribution.

Fused-head NPs: use of the independent form *none*

No is always dependent, requiring a following head; the corresponding independent form is *none.* Compare:

[56] i a. *No student was present.* b. *None (of the students) was present.*
ii a. *No students were present.* b. *None (of the students) were present.*

The relation between *no* and *none* is closely comparable to that between *my* and *mine* (and other genitive pronoun pairs), and we will likewise regard them as inflectional forms of a single determinative, with the [b] examples thus fused-head NPs. As shown in [56], both forms occur in either singular or plural NPs. Both can also take such modifiers as *almost*: *almost no students, almost none.*

All three types of fused-head are found with *none*:

[57] i *Kim had lots of money left, but Pat had [none].* [simple]
ii *There were few jobs available, and [none (of them)] seemed suitable.* [partitive]
iii *The prizes were presented by [none other than the President herself].* [special]

Example [iii] emphasises that it was the President herself who presented the prizes, not any lesser person. The special type is quite rare; it is characteristically found with *other*, as here, or *but* (*None but a lawyer would respond in such a way*).

No and *none* as modifiers outside NP structure

No often modifies comparatives: *no bigger, no more interesting, no different, no longer. None* occurs as an alternant of *not* modifying *too* (*The structure looked none too sound*), and with *the* + comparative (*I felt none the worse for my ordeal*).

7.9 The alternative-additive determinative *another*

The alternative-additive determinative *another*

Determinative *another* derives historically from the compounding of the indefinite article and the adjective *other*; the consequence of this for the modern language is that the existence of the determinative *another* blocks the co-occurrence of the indefinite article and *other* as separate syntactic constituents: **an other book.* Determinatives other than the indefinite article precede *other* without such compounding, as is evident from the variable position of the numeral in [58ii]:

		a.	b.
[58]	i	a. *another three examples*	b. **a three other examples*
	ii	a. *the other three examples*	b. *the three other examples*

Alternative and additive senses

[59] i *I would like [another banana].*
ii *Harriet supports [one$_s$ team], and I support [another].*
iii *I'll make [one$_n$ dish], and you can make [another].*
iv *Masha consumed [yet another banana].*

Another has alternative and additive senses. Example [i] can be interpreted in either way. In the alternative interpretation I would like a **different** banana: the implicature is that I want a banana to replace the one I already have (perhaps it is too green). In the additive interpretation I would like an **additional** banana (perhaps I've already eaten the one or ones I had). In the additive sense, therefore, *another banana* is equivalent to *one more banana.* However, it must be noted that the alternative and additive senses are not mutually exclusive: maybe I'm still hungry, and so want an additional one, but at the same time want a riper one than the last.

In some contexts, one or the other sense is highlighted. The contrast in [59ii], for example, is with singulative *one* and this highlights the alternative sense. Singulative *one* is the *one* that cannot be replaced by a numeral: *#Harriet supports two teams, and I support another* (cf. [44]). In [59iii], however, we have numerical *one*, which is naturally followed by the additive sense of *another*; this *one* can be replaced by any other numeral: *I'll make [two dishes], and you can make [another]* (= an additional one). The modifier *yet* in [59iv] is only compatible with the additive sense.

As would be expected from its historical origins, *another* selects singular count nouns, as in *another day* (**another days*). It can, however, also select quantified nominals, as in *another three days, another few days*: see §3.4 for discussion of this construction.

Fused-head NPs

Another readily functions as fused determiner-head, as in [59ii–iii]. These are of the simple type, while a partitive fused-head is seen in *Kim found two of the missing reports and then Pat found another (of them).*

7.10 The positive paucal determinatives *a little, a few, several,* etc.

The paucal determinatives indicate an imprecise small quantity or number. *A little* selects non-count heads, *a few* and *several* select plural count heads:

[60] i *I only have [a little money].* [non-count]
ii *I found [a few / several mistakes].* [plural count]

In the case of the plurals, the lower bound is three: two doesn't qualify as a few or several.

The complex forms *a few* and *a little*

These have internal structure in that they contain the indefinite article *a*. *A few mistakes* with *a few* as determiner is structurally quite different from *the few mistakes*, where *the* is determiner and the degree determinative *few* is modifier – and of course *a little money* is structurally distinct from *a little boy*, where *little* is an adjective in modifier function. The only internal expansion permitted for *a little* is the addition of *very* (*a very little money*), while *a few* admits *very*, *good*, and *fair*; the internal structure of these forms is thus sui generis, and as with the cardinal numerals we include them among the lexical determinatives. They can also combine with the peripheral modifier *quite*. Compare then:

[61] a. [*a very few*] *mistakes* b. *quite* [*a few*] *mistakes*

Very in [a] serves to lower the upper bound: the number is not much greater than the minimum of three. *Quite* in [b] by contrast raises the upper bound, as do the adjectival modifiers in *a good/fair few*: the number is appreciably greater than three.

A few vs *several*

One clear syntactic difference between these is that *several* can function as modifier (following a definite determiner) or as predicative complement: *its several advantages*; *Its advantages are several. A few*, but not *several*, can combine with *quite*, as in [61b], and also with *not*: *not a few* implies a relatively large number. *Only* occurs readily with *a few*, but is hardly idiomatic with *several. At least* can occur with either, but also more readily with *a few*.

Some speakers feel that the upper bound can be somewhat greater with *several*, but that is difficult to establish. *A few* contrasts with *many* more directly than does *several* (though not so directly as does *few*), and for this reason the "not multal" implicature conveyed by *a few* seems somewhat stronger than that conveyed by *several*. Thus a salesperson would be more likely to say that their product had several advantages over a competitor than that it had a few.

Fused-head NPs

All three forms are used as head in simple or partitive fused-head NPs: *Kim made about ten mistakes and Pat made a few too* (simple); *She took about twenty photographs and a few* (*of them*) *were very good indeed.*

Various and *certain*

These are somewhat marginal members of the determinative category, less clearly distinct from adjectives than most. Both occur with plural heads:

[62] a. [<u>*Various*</u> *items*] *are missing.* b. [<u>*Certain*</u> *problems*] *remain.*

In [a] *various* acts as a determiner rather similar to *several*: a relatively small number of items are missing. It differs from *several* in indicating more explicitly that the items are different; note, however, that this component of variety can also sometimes be found in the modifier use of *several* following a subject-determiner, as in *their several opinions. Certain* in [b] implies that the problems could be specified. In this example, *certain* is non-proportional, while in other cases it can be proportional, with a strong "not all" implicature: *Such action might be justifiable in certain circumstances.*

Certain occurs (in relatively formal style) as head in a partitive fused-head: *Certain of the delegates had expressed strong opposition to the proposal.* The same applies, for some speakers, primarily AmE, to *various*: %*He summoned a number of men (those who had been professional entertainers in civilian life) from various of his units.* This makes *certain* and *various* more like the clear determinatives, distinct, for example, from the adjective *numerous.* They also differ from adjectives in not allowing a generic interpretation. *Various tiger populations are dangerous,* for example, means that a small set of tiger populations are dangerous, not that any tiger populations which show variety are dangerous. *Numerous tiger populations are dangerous,* by contrast, can be given a generic interpretation: populations which consist of large numbers of tigers are dangerous.

Certain is also used in singular NPs in combination with *a*:

[63] i *This gave her a certain authority.*
ii *To a certain extent I agree with you.*
iii *It's a certain bet that the price will rise again before the end of the year.*

The *certain* of [iii] is semantically distinct from that of [i–ii]; it is replaceable by *sure* and is clearly an adjective in modifier function. In [i–ii], unlike [iii], there is a strong association with *a*, and it may be best to treat *a certain* as a complex determinative. In cases like [i], indeed, we could not omit *certain* and retain *a*: #*This gave her an authority. A certain* here serves to individuate a kind of authority. In [ii] *a certain* is equivalent to *some* with a paucal implicature: "to a limited extent".

7.11 The degree determinatives *many, much, few, little*

These form a distinct group of determinatives in that they inflect for grade. ***Many*** and ***few*** select count plural heads, ***much*** and ***little*** non-count singulars:

[64]	COUNT PLURAL	NON-COUNT
i	a. *He made [many mistakes].*	b. *Has he got [much money]?*
ii	a. *He made [more mistakes than you].*	b. *Has he got [more money than you]?*
iii	a. *He made [(the) most mistakes].*	b. *Has he got [(the) most money]?*
iv	a. *He made [few mistakes].*	b. *He has got [little money].*
v	a. *He made [fewer mistakes than you].*	b. *He has got [less money than you].*
vi	a. *He made [(the) fewest mistakes].*	b. *He has got [(the) least money].*

We have used interrogative examples for ***much*** because the plain form *much* is largely restricted to non-affirmative contexts (see Ch. 9, §4.1.2). The grammar of comparison is described in Ch. 13, and our discussion of the comparative and superlative forms in this section can be brief, focusing on certain issues concerning the structure of NPs.

The plain forms

The plain forms express imprecise quantification. *Many* and *much* are multal quantifiers, meaning approximately "a large number/quantity of"; their antonyms *few* and *little,* meaning "a small number/quantity of", are paucal quantifiers. *Few* and *little* differ from *a few* and *a little* as negative vs positive; the difference in meaning was presented summarily in §5.2 above, and is treated in detail in Ch. 9, §3.3. All four plain forms accept a wide range of modifiers: *unusually many, amazingly few, this much, very little,* and so on. As determiners they mark the NP as indefinite.

Use as modifiers in NP structure

Except for *much*, the plain forms can also occur as modifier following a definite determiner: *her many virtues, those few outstanding mistakes, the little money that remains.*[30] *A few* and *a little* cannot occur as modifiers, but the rather sharp contrast that we find in determiner function between negative *few* or *little* and positive *a few* or *a little* is largely neutralised with *few* and *little* as modifiers. In the first place, determiner *few* implicates but does not entail a number above zero, but by virtue of the existential presuppositions associated with definite NPs modifier *few* has to be interpreted as greater than zero: *The few mistakes they made were relatively trivial* entails that they made at least some mistakes. Secondly, while a determiner can mark a clause as negative, an internal modifier never can. Compare, for example, *She hadn't offered a very convincing excuse, had she?* (positive tag attached to a negative clause) and *She had offered a not very convincing excuse, hadn't she?* (negative tag attached to positive clause). Similarly with *few*:

[65]	i *Few people came to the meeting, did they?*	[determiner; negative clause]
	ii *The few people who came to the meeting all supported the proposal, didn't they?*	[modifier; positive clause]

Many in combination with *a*

Many combines with *a* to form two kinds of complex determinative:

[66] i *[Many a man] has been moved to tears by this sight.*
ii *[A great many complaints] had been received.*

Many a is syntactically inert: nothing can intervene between *many* and *a*, and *many* cannot even be replaced in this position by its antonym *few*. Like *a*, *many a* always functions as determiner. It is found in proverbs such as *There's many a slip twixt cup and lip*, and in the frequency adjunct *many a time*, but is elsewhere somewhat formal or archaic. The *many* component indicates a large number, but the *a* has an individuating and distributive effect requiring a count singular head.

Great in *a great many* can be replaced by *good*, but one or other of these adjectives is required; for the rest, these expressions are syntactically comparable to *a few*. They function as determiner or fused determiner-head (simple or partitive).

The superlative forms and proportional *most*

We have distinguished two senses of *most* (§5.2), one proportional (*most*$_p$) and one the superlative of ***many*** or ***much*** (*most*$_s$). Both select plural or non-count heads:

[67] i	a. *[Most$_p$ people] enjoyed it.*	b. *[Most$_p$ cheese] is made from cow's milk.*
ii	a. *Kim had scored [(the) most$_s$ runs].*	b. *Kim had made [(the) most$_s$ progress].*

There is no analogous distinction for *fewest* or *least*: these cannot indicate a small proportion, but have only the superlative sense.

Proportional *most*$_p$

Most$_p$ indicates a number or subquantity that is at least greater than half of the set or quantity concerned, but in many contexts it will be interpreted as a considerably higher proportion. It marks the NP as indefinite, and can never occur as modifier.

[30] *Much* is marginally possible in this function if it is itself modified: ?*all the not very much money that he earns.*

The and the superlatives

As illustrated in [67ii], superlative *most*$_s$ and also *fewest* and *least* occur with or without *the*; the version with *the* is considerably more frequent. We analyse this *the* as modifying the comparative quantifier, rather than as determiner in NP structure: the whole NP is indefinite, just as it is when *the* is omitted. *The* is here functioning in the same way as in *It was Jill who had spoken* [*the most eloquently*]. Note, then, the contrast between [67ii] and, say, *Jill had put forward* [*the most promising proposals*]. In the latter *the* is determiner in NP structure, marking the NP as definite; if we drop *the* here we get an indefinite NP, and *most promising* can only be interpreted as "highly promising", rather than as a strict superlative.

The comparative forms

The determinatives *more*, *fewer*, and *less* likewise occur in determiner function, marking the NP as indefinite:

[68] i *She drinks* [*more*/ *less milk than you*].
ii *There's* [*more milk*] *in the fridge if you need some.*

In [i] we have a straightforward comparative, while in [ii] *more* is interpreted as "additional, further". The comparative forms cannot occur as modifier: **I can't find* [*the more milk that you said was in the fridge*]. There is, however, a construction comparable to the superlative one in [67ii], where *the* modifies the comparative form:

[69] i *That's* [*all the more reason why we should take professional advice*].
ii [*The more alternative occupations*] *there are available,* [*the fewer women*] *you will find who take in lodgers.*

The bracketed NPs here are indefinite, and the underlined sequences are DPs; again this *the* is found outside NP structure, as in *He had found that* [*the more afraid*] *a man was, the easier it was to kill him.*

Fused-head NPs

All the forms in [64] are found as fused heads. A few examples are given in:

[70]	i	*He expected to get a lot of votes but ended up with* [*relatively few*].	[simple]
	ii a.	[*Much of the book*] *was incomprehensible.*	[partitive]
	b.	*I found about twenty mistakes, but* [*most*$_p$] *were relatively minor.*	
	iii a.	*They had found* [*much*/ *little to criticise*] *in his thesis.*	[special]
	b.	[*Many*/ *Few*] *would disagree with you on that point.*	
	c.	*Kim isn't* [*much of an actor*] / [*any more of an actor than Pat*].	

Other functions

Much and ***little*** (all forms) occur as degree adjunct in clause structure: *Jill little realised what they were planning*; *It didn't hurt as much as last time.* The plain forms *much* and *little* modify comparative expressions: *much better, little different, much more cheese, little less intrusive. Very much* modifies a wider range of expressions: *very much in control, very much an intellectual.* (*More* and *less* modify adjectives, adverbs, etc., but we take these to be degree adverbs, rather than comparative forms of ***much*** and ***little***: see Ch. 13, §4.1.1.) The degree determiners can also function directly as predicative complement: *Their enemies were many.* This, however, is a relatively uncommon and formal construction: a formulation in which they appear as determiner to a noun would usually be preferred, as in *They had many enemies.*[31]

7.12 The sufficiency determinatives *enough*, *sufficient*

As determiners, *enough* and *sufficient* select count plural or non-count heads:

[71] i [*Enough*/*sufficient* *people*] *attended the meeting to form a quorum.*
ii *I haven't got* [*enough*/*sufficient* *money*].

They express imprecise quantification, being concerned with the lower bound required to satisfy some explicit or implicit need or purpose. In [i] it is a question of how many people were needed to form a quorum; suppose that in a particular case twenty was the minimum (maybe there were thirty members and the rules stipulated a quorum of two thirds), then [i] indicates that at least twenty people attended. In [ii] no indication is given of the need or purpose, but one must be recoverable from the context – it could be quite specific (e.g. to come to the movies with you) or quite general (e.g. to satisfy my needs). *Enough* and *sufficient* do not say anything about the upper bound; in cases like [i], however, where we are concerned with a proportion of some set, we have the familiar "not all" implicature: I convey that not all members attended.

Expression of need/purpose, or result

Enough and *sufficient* license purpose expressions with the form of PPs with *for* (*enough money for a taxi*), or infinitival clauses (such as *to form a quorum* in [71i]). AmE allows an alternative construction in which they take a resultative content clause: %*There was enough hot water that we could all have baths.*

Sufficient as determinative or adjective

Unlike *enough*, *sufficient* belongs to the category of adjectives as well as being a determinative:

[72] i *This isn't* [*a sufficient reason for dismissing them*]. [adjective]
ii *Those aren't* [*sufficient reasons for dismissing them*]. [adjective or determinative]

In [i] *sufficient* differs from the sufficiency determinatives in two respects: it is in modifier function and the head is count singular. The meaning is approximately "sufficiently good/strong": it is quantifying not the reason itself, but a property of it. Example [ii] is then ambiguous: in the adjectival reading it is simply a plural counterpart of [i] ("Those aren't sufficiently good reasons"); in the determinative reading, *sufficient* is replaceable by *enough*, so that we are here quantifying reasons.

Fused-head NPs

The sufficiency determinatives function as head in all three types of fused-head NP, with the special ones having non-count interpretations:

[73] i *I had some money on me, but not enough*/*sufficient to get a taxi.* [simple]
ii *I don't think enough*/*sufficient of us are here to form a quorum.* [partitive]
iii *You've already said enough*/*sufficient to convince me.* [special]

[31] A special and idiomatic case has predicative *many* in front position with a singular temporal expression as subject: *Many's the time I've found them playing computer games well after midnight.*

Modifier uses

The sufficiency determinatives are not permitted in pre-head modifier position. *Enough*, however, has the syntactic peculiarity of being able to appear as post-head modifier and it can also occur in this function with verbs, adjectives, and adverbs:

[74] i *We have time enough to complete the task.* [noun]
ii *I don't like it enough to buy it at that price.* [verb]
iii *The furniture isn't robust enough for that kind of treatment.* [adjective]
iv *They don't speak clearly enough for me to be able to hear.* [adverb]

Note, however, that it doesn't modify the core degree determinatives. It contrasts rather than combines with them, so that we have *enough money* (or *money enough*), not **much enough money*. To a limited extent *enough* can also modify PPs, and here – as in NPs – it precedes the head (*I wasn't enough in control for that*) or follows it (*I wasn't in control enough for that*).

The determinative *sufficient* is much more limited in its distribution, occurring only as determiner in NP structure (or fused determiner-head). The gap is filled by the adverb *sufficiently*: compare *like it sufficiently, sufficiently robust, sufficiently clearly, sufficiently in control*. The fact that *sufficient* is paired with a ·*ly* adverb in this way makes it the most adjective-like of the determinatives.

7.13 The interrogative determinatives *which, what, whichever, whatever*

The interrogative determinatives belong to the larger set of interrogative words that includes also *who, when, where, why*, etc. – and *what* as a pronoun. The determinatives in ·*ever* are found only in the exhaustive conditional construction: [*Whichever*/*Whatever present you buy for him,*] *he won't be satisfied*; this construction is discussed in detail in Ch. 11, §5.3.6, and the forms will not be considered further here.

Which vs *what*

The interrogative words, by their very nature, mark the NP as indefinite, but *which* shares with *either* and *each* the property of involving a set that is identifiable by the addressee: answers to a *which* question make a selection from this set. Compare:

[75] *Which / What videos have been released this week?*

Suppose I go into the video store and use the *which* version of question [75]: *which* indicates that I expect you to be able to identify a unique set of videos, perhaps those on display in the store; I will be understood as requesting the kind of answer that selects from this set in the most relevant way to me the ones released this week. *Which* can be used in a directive way to force the addressee to recognise a unique set in the absence of any contextual clues. Consider, for example, the question *Which video shall we watch tonight?* This might be used in a context, say, where we have hired seven videos from the video store to last the week, and you will then be already aware of the unique set from which the answer is to be selected. But it is also possible that there is no such previously established set (perhaps we are merely planning a trip to the video store), and *which* then serves itself to establish one in a way that is comparable to the establishing use of the definite article (as in [6viii] of §6.1). You are forced, as it were, to recognise a set consisting of the videos that we might choose.

Fused-head NPs

Which occurs freely in explicitly or implicitly partitive fused-head NPs: [*Which of the candidates*] *shall we interview first?*; *They had hired several videos and were arguing about* [*which*] *to watch.* Determinative *what*, however, does not function as a fused-head – cf. *[*What of these videos*] *have you already seen?* The *what* that occurs as head in NP structure is a pronoun, differing sharply in meaning from the determinative. The pronoun *what* is non-personal (contrasting with personal ***who***: *What/Who did you see?*), whereas the determinative is indifferent as to the gender of the head noun.

7.14 The relative determinatives *which, what, whichever, whatever*

Fused relatives

The relative determinatives occur in the fused relative construction (Ch. 12, §6). *Which* is restricted to the free choice subtype:

[76] i *We bought* [*what/whatever/*which/whichever tickets were available*]. [ordinary]
ii *We can use* [*what/whatever/which/whichever edition you want*]. [free choice]

Like interrogative *which*, fused relative *which* and *whichever* are selective. It follows that, unlike *what* and *whatever*, they select count nouns as head. Compare:

[77] i *We'll use* [*whatever/whichever edition is available*]. [count singular]
ii *I gave them* [*whatever/*whichever help I could*]. [non-count]

Whichever in [i] signals that I expect you to be able to identify a set of editions from which one will be selected. *What* (but not *whatever*) in the ordinary fused relative has a paucal interpretation: *We bought what tickets were available* conveys that few tickets were available.

The relative NPs in the fused construction can plausibly be regarded as definite: the examples in [76], for example, are comparable to *We bought the tickets that were available* and *We can use the edition you want to use* (not *some tickets* or *an edition*). The ·*ever* compounds – and *what* or *which* in the free choice construction – are indeterminate (see §8.3 below). For example, [77i] can be glossed as "We'll use the edition that is available, no matter which it is".[32] For the rest NPs determined by *what* can be referential or indeterminate. *We bought what tickets were available* can be interpreted either referentially (e.g. the two tickets in the front stalls) or indeterminately (the tickets that were available, no matter which they were).

Fused-head NPs

Which and *whichever* occur as fused heads: *There are several editions of the play – you can use* [*which you like*]; *We'll borrow* [*whichever of the computers is available*]. But as with interrogatives, *what* and *whatever* in head function are pronouns, contrasting with personal ***who*** and ***whoever***.

[32] There is a subtle distinction between *whichever* and the free choice quantifier any_f. A child who is told *You can have whichever present you like for Christmas* would have to choose a unique present, for *whichever*, though indeterminate, is definite. On the other hand, a child who is told *You can have* any_f *present you like for Christmas* might claim to be allowed to choose a multiplicity of presents: with indefinite any_f the parent only **implicates** that no more than one present is to be chosen (see §7.5 above).

Supplementary relatives

The only relative determinative found outside the fused construction is *which*. It occurs in supplementary but not integrated relatives:

[78] *The meeting lasted until midnight, at [which stage] everyone was exhausted.*

Again the relative NP is definite – comparable, for example, to demonstrative *that stage*. Determinative *which* does not occur in fused-head NPs: in *He works at the post-office, [which is just down the road]* the head *which* is a pronoun. The pronoun is non-personal, contrasting with ***who***, while the determinative occurs with personal and non-personal heads.

8 Referential and non-referential uses of NPs

8.1 Reference and denotation

In this grammar, we make a distinction between the semantic properties **reference** and **denotation**. We will say that a linguistic expression has reference if, by using it on a given occasion, a speaker intends it to pick out some **independently distinguishable** entity, or set of entities, in the real world (or in some fictional world). By 'independently distinguishable', we mean distinguishable by properties other than those inherent in the meaning of the expression itself. We will say that an expression used in this way is **referential**, that it is used to **refer to** the entity in question, and we call this entity the **referent** of the expression.

Consider the following elementary example:

[1] *Mary washed her car.*

The subject NP *Mary* is a proper name and as such is the most basic kind of referential expression. In an ordinary utterance of sentence [1],[33] the NP serves to pick out a certain individual named *Mary*, an entity distinguishable by properties other than her name (for example, her appearance, where she lives, etc.). We say, then, that the speaker refers to this entity by means of the NP or, by extension and more simply, that the NP itself refers to it. Reference is clearly **context-dependent**: the NP *Mary* can be used on different occasions to refer to indefinitely many distinct individuals, so what its referent is on any particular occasion will depend on the context. The pronoun *her* in [1] is also referential; in a salient interpretation it too refers to Mary, this time by virtue of the anaphoric relation between the pronoun and its antecedent, the NP *Mary*. Finally, the object *her car* is referential: it picks out a particular car, distinguishable by properties not expressed in the NP, such as colour, make, registration number, and so on.

Not all of the linguistic expressions in [1] are referential, however. The verb *washed* is not referential: rather than picking out a particular entity, it indicates the relation that obtained between Mary and the car. This we speak of as denotation: the verb ***wash*** denotes a relation between two arguments *x* and *y* such that *x* cleans *y* using some liquid (typically water). Similarly, in *Mary is very talkative* the adjective *talkative* is

[33] The qualification 'ordinary' excludes special cases where a sentence is simply used as an example, as in a linguistic discussion, a language-teaching class, or whatever. In what follows we will take it for granted that we are concerned only with ordinary uses.

non-referential and denotes a property of an argument *x* such that *x* talks a lot. Denotation is not context-dependent in the way that reference is: while [1] can be used on different occasions to refer to different people and different cars, the relation between the subject-referent and the object-referent is the same. Denotation is thus a matter of the meaning of expressions in the language system, while reference is not. An ordinary monolingual dictionary is largely concerned with describing the denotation of lexemes and idioms, but it does not and could not give the referents of referential expressions.

Referential expressions are generally NPs.[34] Nouns (or nominals), by contrast, are not themselves referential. Thus while the NP *her car* in [1] is referential, the noun *car* is not. Rather, it denotes the set of entities of a certain kind (prototypically four-wheeled road vehicles powered by an engine); the particular car referred to by the NP *her car* in a given utterance of [1] will then be a member of the set denoted by the noun **car**. This set is said to be the **denotation** of ***car*** (with the same term thus used for the semantic relation and for the set denoted). *Mary* is an NP that happens to consist of just a noun, but it is by virtue of being an NP in [1] that it is referential, not by virtue of being a noun. Considered as a noun, *Mary* is non-referential, and denotes the set of individuals named *Mary*: this is reflected in uses like *There are two Marys in my class.*

8.2 The contrast between referential and non-referential NPs

Referential expressions, we have said, are generally NPs – but NPs aren't always referential. Compare:

[2] i *Did Mary telephone while I was out?* [referential]
ii *Did anyone telephone while I was out?* [non-referential]

In [i] I refer to a certain person and ask whether this person telephoned. In [ii], by contrast, *anyone* is not used referentially: I am not asking whether a certain person phoned.

Coreferential pronouns as test for referentiality

In straightforward cases like [2], the difference can be brought out by testing whether a coreferential personal pronoun can be added in a separate main clause:

[3] i *Did Mary$_i$ telephone while I was out? She$_i$ promised to call today.*
ii *Did anyone$_i$ call while I was out? *She$_i$/*He$_i$/*They$_i$ promised to call today.*

In [i] *she* derives its interpretation from its anaphoric link with *Mary*: the two NPs refer to the same person, and hence are **coreferential**. In [ii], however, *anyone* is non-referential and, unlike *Mary*, cannot stand as antecedent for a personal pronoun in this context. Referential 3rd person NPs can always serve as antecedent for an anaphoric personal pronoun in a following main clause, while the clearest cases of non-referential NPs cannot.

Consider some further examples:

[4] i a. *One car in the race broke down and it had to be repaired.* [coreferential]
b. **No car in the race broke down and it had to be repaired.*
ii a. *Three students arrived early; they had taken a taxi.* [coreferential]
b. *No students arrived on time; they had all overslept.* [not coreferential]

[34] Under restricted conditions, PPs can also be referential. In *Under the table is the best place to hide*, for example, the PP *under the table* refers to a particular place. Titles of books, films, etc., can also be used referentially and need not have the form of NPs: *They saw 'What's up, Doc?' three times.*

Examples [ia–b] exhibit the same clear distinction as we had in [3]: *one car in the race* is referential and serves as antecedent for the pronoun *it*, while *no car in the race* is non-referential and cannot serve as antecedent for a pronoun in a separate main clause. *Three students* in [iia] is again unproblematically antecedent for the coreferential *they*. Example [iib] shows that the test must be applied with care: although *they* is perfectly acceptable here, *no students* is not its antecedent and there is no relation of coreference between the two NPs. *No students* is non-referential, but is understood here as "none of the students", i.e. as involving a set of students of whom none arrived on time, and it is this set that *they* refers to. The difference between [iia] and [iib] is evident from the fact that [iia] entails that three students had taken a taxi, whereas [iib] does not entail that no students had overslept.

NPs that can only be used non-referentially

Negative NPs like those in [4ib/iib] are always non-referential. Other kinds of inherently non-referential NPs are illustrated in [5]:

[5]	i	*[<u>Either</u> city] might win the Olympics.*	[determinative *either*]
	ii	*The matron interviewed [<u>each</u> boy] in turn.*	[determinative *each*]
	iii	*I wonder [<u>who</u>] told her.*	[interrogative]
	iv	*I was elected <u>treasurer</u> two years ago.*	[bare role NP]

Certain determinatives, such as *either* and *each* in [i–ii], mark an NP as non-referential. The pronoun test works clearly in [i]: we could not continue with *It has excellent facilities*, with *it* anaphoric to *either city*. We could have *They have excellent facilities*, but this is like [4iib]: *either city* involves a set of two cities, and *they* refers to this set. Similarly, we could not continue [5ii] with *he* used as an anaphor to *each boy*, but could use *they* to refer to the implicit set of boys. Other items of this kind include *any*, *every* – and the negative *no* and *neither*. *Who* in [5iii] is representative of the class of interrogative NPs, which are all clearly non-referential; *who told her* expresses an (embedded) question, and it is the corresponding NP in the answer (such as *<u>Tim</u> told her*) that is referential. *Treasurer* in [iv] is a bare role NP restricted to the function of predicative complement: by virtue of having no determiner such NPs cannot occupy characteristically referential positions such as subject (for other kinds of bare NP that are always non-referential, see §8.5 below).

NPs which can be used referentially or non-referentially

Most types of NP can be used either referentially or non-referentially. The proper name *Mary*, for example, can be used non-referentially even when it constitutes a full NP, as in *<u>Mary</u> is still one of the most popular girl's names.* This represents a **metalinguistic** use of *Mary*: the case where we cite a linguistic expression in order to say something about it qua linguistic expression. It is obvious that *Mary* does not here refer to a person, but it would also be a mistake to say that it refers to a name: it **is** a name. In the following section we consider various non-referential uses of NPs besides this metalinguistic case. These uses exploit the fact that even potentially referential NPs also have a denotation of the type "*x* such that . . ."; for example, even a proper name like *Mary*, which is prototypically referential, has a denotation "the individual *x* such that *x* is named Mary".

8.3 Some special cases of non-referential NPs

(a) Ascriptive interpretations

[6] i *Mary is a Manchester United supporter.*
ii *Kim became Pat's lover / the heir to a large fortune.*

Ascriptive NPs are those that function as predicative complements in the ascriptive as opposed to specifying construction (see Ch. 4, §5.5.1). In [i] I am not telling you that Mary is the same as some individual that I know as a Manchester United supporter: I'm simply saying that Mary is a member of the set of Manchester United supporters – I'm not specifying who she is, but ascribing a property to her. Similarly in [ii], where the ascriptive NP is definite rather than indefinite: the clause doesn't describe a change of identity, but Kim's coming to be in the lover relation to Pat, or the heir to a large fortune.

(b) Descriptive interpretations

Descriptive interpretations arise in constructions which contain *be* in its reference-specifying rather than ascriptive use. In these cases, we have a definite NP as predicand and another definite NP as predicative complement. We made the point in §6 that a definite NP is assumed to contain enough information to identify some entity or set of entities in the relatively weak sense of pre-empting a *which* question. However, the fact that an NP identifies some entity or set of entities in this sense does not mean that it is being used referentially. Consider, then:

[7] i *The Vice-Chancellor is that guy over there by the piano.*
ii *Paul is that guy over there by the piano.*
iii *I'm Kim Lane.*
iv [*Cassius Clay*] *is* [*Mohammed Ali*].

In [i] *that guy over there by the piano* is referential, but *the Vice-Chancellor* is not: I'm not making two references to a certain person and saying that this person is identical to himself.[35] Rather, I assume you know there is some contextually relevant person who satisfies the description *the Vice-Chancellor* and am telling you who this person is: the individual referred to by the NP *that guy over there by the piano.* The same applies in [ii]: a proper name can be descriptive, just as an NP with a common noun as head can be. Thus *Paul* is here non-referential but acts as a description of some individual by virtue of his name ("the individual *x* such that *x* is named Paul"), and the referential NP *that guy over there by the piano* specifies the value of the variable *x*. In [iii] it is the subject *I* that is referential, while the predicative complement *Kim Lane* is descriptive: I'm not saying that I'm identical to myself, but giving my name. Example [iv] is naturally interpreted like [i–ii], saying that the individual named Cassius Clay is the person you already know as Mohammed Ali, but it can also be interpreted like [iii], saying that the person you already know as Cassius Clay also has the name Mohammed Ali. This interpretation emerges strongly if we add *now*: *Cassius Clay is Mohammed Ali now.* These examples are

[35] One place where the subject and predicative complement of *be* can both be referential is in examples like *Max was Macbeth*, "Max played the part of Macbeth". This represents a special use of *be* that cannot be subsumed under either the specifying or ascriptive use.

reference-specifying in the sense that, following their utterance, the descriptive NP can be used referentially.[36]

(c) Definiendum and definiens interpretations

A further use of specifying *be* is in definitions. In this case, both predicand and predicative complement are indefinite NPs (either a singular NP determined by the indefinite article, or a bare plural). Consider, then:

[8] i *A pentagon is a regular figure with five sides.*
ii *Pentagons are regular figures with five sides.*

Here I am not telling you that a particular pentagon (or a particular set of pentagons) has the property of being a regular figure with five sides, nor indeed that a typical pentagon has this property (this would be a generic interpretation, see (i) below). Rather, I am specifying what the definition of the expression *pentagon* is. Both NPs are then non-referential: the predicand represents the definiendum (the entity whose definition is to be specified), and the predicative complement represents the definiens (the entity providing the definition). These examples are similar to the reference-specifying examples in (b), since I am telling you how a term can appropriately be used, but reference is not involved.

(d) Indeterminate interpretations

[9] i *The boy who wrote this email must be expelled.* } [referential or
ii *I think Ed's CD player was stolen by a friend of his.* } indeterminate]

These examples are ambiguous, with the underlined NPs having either a referential or a non-referential interpretation. Take first the underlined NP in [i]. This could be used as a way of picking out a particular individual (Smith Junior, say); in this referential interpretation, then, I'm saying that Smith Junior must be expelled. A context for this interpretation might be one where an investigation has already taken place into who wrote the offending email, and the culprit has been apprehended.[37] Alternatively, however, it could be that no investigation has yet taken place, so that the culprit is not yet known. In this case, the underlined NP can be used non-referentially to say that the individual denoted ("the *x* such that *x* is a boy who wrote this email") must be expelled, whoever this individual might turn out to be. We term this the **indeterminate** use of the NP. The indeterminate interpretation can be expressed unequivocally by *Whichever boy wrote this email must be expelled* (fused relative), or *The boy who wrote this email must be expelled, whoever it is* (NP + exhaustive conditional adjunct). Note, then, that the indeterminate use is akin to the descriptive use outlined in (b) above, but it is not identical: following the utterance of the sentence, the indeterminate NP does not automatically have a referential use.

[36] Example [7iv] also has another and less likely interpretation where neither NP is referential: here I am merely saying that *Cassius Clay* and *Mohammed Ali* are names of the same person, though I don't know who it is that bears these names. The only use of such a sentence would be in a context where we are discussing examples of things which have two different names. The classic philosophers' example *The morning star is the evening star* is of the same kind: it has two reference-specifying interpretations in which either I specify the morning star as the entity you know as the evening star, or vice versa. But it can also be used to assert that there is a single celestial body which has these two names.

[37] It should be noted that in the referential use, the property given in the NP does not in fact have to apply to the referent. It could be that speaker and addressee are both convinced that Smith Junior is the culprit, even though he is not; in that case *the boy who wrote this email* would still successfully pick out Smith Junior and I would still be saying that Smith Junior must be expelled.

Indeterminate NPs can serve as antecedent for personal pronouns (we could continue [i], for example, with *He has brought the school into disrepute*): as is evident from the formulation in §8.2, inability to be antecedent for an anaphoric pronoun in an independent clause is a sufficient but not a necessary condition for the non-referential use of a 3rd person NP.

The referential versus indeterminate distinction also applies in the case of indefinite NPs, as in [9ii]. In the referential use I am picking out an individual whom I could distinguish by independent properties – compare *a friend of his named Jones.* On the other hand, I might have no idea who the thief is, but deduce from the fact that there has been no break-in that only a friend, someone who had access to the house, could have done it. In that case, *a friend of his* is being used indeterminately, to indicate what property the thief must have (whoever it actually is). Of course you, the addressee, cannot judge from the utterance of [9ii] alone whether I was using the NP referentially or indeterminately; a response such as *So you know who did it then?* would serve to seek confirmation that a referential use had been intended.[38]

(e) Non-specific interpretations

[10]	i	*I want to meet* <u>*the genius who can solve this equation*</u>.	[referential or non-specific]
	ii	*I'm going to marry* <u>*the man of my dreams*</u>.	
	iii	*I intend to date* <u>*a Norwegian*</u>.	

These examples too are ambiguous according as the underlined NP is interpreted referentially or non-referentially. In [i], for example, the NP can be used referentially to pick out the person who I know (or believe) to be the genius who can solve this equation; this is the specific interpretation and the referent will again be independently distinguishable – perhaps I know his or her name, perhaps I have merely seen the solution scribbled on the blackboard and am referring to the unknown person who wrote it. But there is also an interpretation where I don't know that there is in fact anyone who can solve the equation, and hence am not referring to anyone. This type of non-referential NP is called **non-specific**. Such interpretations arise in the scope of verbs like *want* which create hypothetical worlds: what is wanted may involve entities that do not necessarily exist.

Other verbs (or verbal idioms) that create such hypothetical contexts include *be going* and *intend*, and also *desire, ask for, look for, seek, dream.* In the referential (specific) interpretation of [10ii] there exists an actual person who satisfies the description *man of my dreams*; in the non-specific, non-referential, interpretation such a person exists so far only in my dreams, and hence is not independently distinguishable.

Non-specific interpretations are classically illustrated by indefinite examples such as [10iii]. The interpretation in question is that I haven't found anyone to date yet, but want to find someone to date who is a Norwegian: for some reason, being Norwegian is an essential property I'm looking for in my date. This contrasts with the referential specific

[38] The term 'attributive' is often used for what we have here called the 'indeterminate' use of NPs. We prefer the latter term in order to avoid conflict with the syntactic use of 'attributive' as applied to adjectives functioning as pre-head modifier to a noun (contrasting with their 'predicative' function). The concept of indeterminate use of an NP can be extended to pronouns, as in *I wonder which of the boys told her:* <u>*he*</u> *must have wanted to embarrass me.* The pronoun is equivalent to the indeterminate NP *the boy who told her.*

interpretation where there is a particular person I have in mind – compare *I intend to date a Norwegian my brother introduced me to last night.* The bare plural NP *Norwegians* could similarly be interpreted in either way.

(f) Negative-bound interpretations

[11] i *My sister now has a car_i. She bought it_i with the royalties from her novel.*

ii *My sister doesn't have a car_i. *She bought it_i with the royalties from her novel.*

In [i] *a car* is referential, and can be antecedent for the following pronoun *it.* But in [ii] *a car* is within the scope of the negative and non-referential. I do not pick out some particular car and say that my sister doesn't have it: she simply has no car. Such **negative-bound** interpretations typically emerge with indefinite NPs: if I say *My sister doesn't now have the car,* I am referring to a particular car and saying that she does not now have it. However, definite negative-bound NPs are found, as in *I don't have the slightest idea,* "I have no idea, not even a minimal one".

(g) NP-bound interpretations

[12] i *Every first-year student has to learn two languages.*

ii *Some students have a boyfriend.*

iii *Most people got the salary they deserved.*

iv *Each of them wants to marry a film-star.*

NP-bound interpretations of NPs arise in the scope of other NPs that are quantified, such as the subjects in these examples. In [i] the quantified NP *every first-year student* is naturally interpreted as having *two languages* within its scope. This means that each student has an individual set of two languages to learn. For pragmatic reasons, there is likely to be a great deal of overlap between these sets: if there are forty students, for example, it is highly unlikely that any college would have the resources to offer eighty languages, as would be needed if there were no overlap. But this is irrelevant: what is crucial for the NP-bound interpretation is that there be three or more languages from which each student selects (or is assigned) a set of two. This contrasts with the referential interpretation where two particular languages, German and Chinese, say, have to be learnt by each student, i.e. all students learn the same two languages. In this referential interpretation *two languages* is outside the scope of the quantified NP. Note that the passive counterpart *Two languages have to be learnt by every first-year student* allows the same two interpretations but with the referential one somewhat more salient than in the active. But the construction with existential *there* – *There are two languages that every first-year student has to learn* – does not permit the NP-bound interpretation as *two languages* is in a higher clause than the quantified NP.

In [12ii] the NP-bound interpretation is the only natural one: each student has their own boyfriend (with the possibility of incidental overlap). The situation where they all had the same boyfriend would normally be considered so unusual that it would need to be expressed more explicitly, so a referential interpretation of *a boyfriend* is hardly possible. A bare plural *boyfriends* would require the NP-bound interpretation; it differs from the singular in that while *a boyfriend* implicates just one boyfriend per student, *boyfriends* leaves it quite open as to whether the students concerned have one or more boyfriends.

In [12iii] we have the less usual case where a definite NP is NP-bound: "for most people x, x got the salary x deserved". Here "the salary x deserved" applies separately to each person x, but in each case x's deserts define a unique salary, so that the definite article is in order. A referential interpretation would be possible but unlikely: I would be saying that most people got a particular salary ($40,000, say), which is what they all deserved.

Finally, [12iv] shows that NP-bound and non-specific interpretations of the same NP are not mutually exclusive. The sentence therefore has three interpretations. Firstly, *a film-star* may be referential, referring to a particular individual. Secondly, it may be NP-bound but specific: each of them has a particular film-star in mind, but not the same one in each case. Thirdly, there is the NP-bound non-specific interpretation where they don't have any particular film-star in mind.

(h) Multiple-situation-bound interpretations

[13]	i	*<u>The president</u> has been assassinated three times.*	[repeated multiple situation]
	ii	*<u>The police</u> are getting younger.*	[serial multiple situation]
	iii	*I usually have lunch with <u>a colleague</u>.*	[ambiguous]

Multiple-situation-bound interpretations arise when the NP is in the scope of an expression denoting a multiple situation, in the sense of Ch. 3, §3.2.4. They are very much akin to the NP-bound interpretations just discussed in that both involve quantification, but this time the quantification is over situations rather than entities. Example [i] involves a repeated multiple situation – i.e. one where a specific indication is given of the number of occurrences, in this case three. Only the non-referential interpretation makes sense in this example: there were three assassinations, each of a different president. If *the president* were referential and hence outside the scope of the multiple situation it would be a matter of a single president being assassinated three times, a physical impossibility. In [ii] the multiple situation is of the serial type, with the number of occurrences in principle unlimited. I am comparing the age of the police at different times, and at each time it is a matter of the age of those who are in the police force at that time. A non-bound, referential, interpretation would be saying that those who now make up the police force are getting younger – again a physical impossibility. Example [iii] is then ambiguous according as *a colleague* is likewise within the scope of a serial multiple situation or is referential: in the latter case it is always the same colleague I lunch with, while in the non-referential case there is variation between one occasion and another.

(i) Generic interpretations

Generic interpretations arise with NPs that are within the scope of expressions denoting the situation type we call **unlimited states.**[39] Unlimited states potentially hold for all time (or at least for as long as the entities which take part in them exist). Examples of clauses with referential subjects expressing unlimited states are *Leo is a lion* and *I like Hilda.* Unlimited states can be contrasted with limited states, as in *Leo is angry* or *I am in Paris,* which are understood to hold for a limited period of time unless an explicit indication is given to the contrary.

[39] Some works use the term 'generic' more broadly covering also such multiple-situation-bound interpretations as *I smoke <u>a cigar</u> / <u>cigars</u> after dinner.* We believe, however, that there is no difference in principle between this and the examples in [13], and wish to reserve the term 'generic' for the interpretation of NPs in the scope of unlimited states. Multiple situations are similar to unlimited states, but distinct.

Generic interpretations are illustrated in [14]:

[14] i a. *Lions are ferocious beasts.* b. *Italians like pasta.*
ii a. *A lion is a ferocious beast.* b. *An Italian likes pasta.*
iii a. *The lion is a ferocious beast.* b. *The Italians like pasta.*

The denotation of bare indefinite NPs is itself unlimited in the scope of unlimited states, and so examples like [ia] are naturally interpreted generically, with *lions* understood as "any lion or set of lions that exists". The interpretation of singular indefinites in the same context, like *a lion* in [iia], is correspondingly "any lion that exists". The generic use of a singular definite like *the lion* is also possible in the context given in [iiia], but is an example of the restricted 'class' use of the definite article (see §8.4 below). If instead of lions, we were talking about doctors, the definite singular would not generally be possible: compare the generic *Doctors are kind people* with *The doctor is a kind person* (which only has a non-generic, referential interpretation). In *The lions are ferocious beasts*, the plural definite *the lions* would also obligatorily be interpreted non-generically. The [b] examples illustrate the generic use of nationality nouns like *Italian* (as well as the generic use of non-count nouns like *pasta*). This time the restricted class use of the definite article has a plural rather than a singular NP. The definites in [iii] could both also have a non-generic interpretation where they refer to a particular lion and a particular set of Italians.

With predicates that can only be applied to a set, a singular indefinite generic such as *a lion* is inadmissible:

[15] *Lions* / **A lion* / *The lion will soon be extinct in this part of Africa.*

8.4 Restricted non-referential uses of the articles

In this section, we cover non-referential uses of NPs determined by the definite and indefinite articles that are permitted only with a restricted set of head nouns.

(a) Class uses of the definite article

NPs determined by the definite article can denote the entire class denoted by the head noun, rather than individual members or subsets within that class.

[16] i a. *The African elephant will soon be extinct.* [singular]
b. *The invention of the hydrogen bomb was the next step.*
c. *This chapter describes the English noun phrase.*
d. *The human brain has fascinated me ever since I was a child.*
ii a. *We studied the Hittites in the final year.* [plural]
b. *The Greeks defeated the Persians at Issus.*

The boundaries of this usage with singular nouns are somewhat indeterminate, but it is clearly facilitated in the context of species ([ia]), inventions ([ib]), and areas of study, interest, or expertise ([ic–d]). Compare, for example, **The hospital doctor is overworked* with *The hospital doctor is an endangered species round here*, or **The tabloid newspaper is a disgrace* with *Hugo has turned the tabloid newspaper into a research industry*. With plurals, the class use is restricted to nouns that denote nations. The interpretation of [iia] is that we studied the Hittites qua nation, rather than any particular Hittites, and similarly for [iib].

(b) Fixed expressions containing the definite article

A number of fixed expressions require the definite article. In such cases, it is largely arbitrary that the definite article is required rather than a bare noun (and often both are possible).

[17]	i	*Wolfgang can play the piano / the violin / the drums.*	[musical instruments]
	ii	*Hilda can dance the waltz / the rumba.*	[dances]
	iii	*I have (the) flu / (the) measles / (the) mumps / (the) chicken pox.*	[illnesses]
	iv	*I listened to the radio / spoke to her on the telephone.*	[transfer of information]
	v	*We took/caught the bus / the train / the boat.*	[transport]
	vi	*I take my nap in the morning.*	[times]

Nouns denoting musical instruments take the definite article in the context of the verb *play*, when it is clear that what is important is the activity rather than the particular instrument that is played on a given occasion. When the interpretation is that of an academic subject, however, in the context of the verb *study*, either a bare NP or one with the definite article NP is possible: *Wolfgang is studying (the) piano at the Royal College.* Nouns denoting dances in the activity sense also take the definite article, as in [ii]. However, if an individual performance is indicated, the normal range of determiners is possible: *Hilda danced a frenzied rumba, followed by a sedate waltz.* Some common infectious diseases optionally take the definite article, as in [iii]; cf. also *(the) hiccups.* With *the plague*, the article is obligatory. Most diseases are non-count: *He has rubella / AIDS / Alzheimer's disease* – but note *He has a cold/headache.* In [iv] we have the definite article used in expressions concerned with devices and institutions for the transfer of information, even though it is the activity or action that is relevant rather than the device used on a particular occasion. Compare, however, *watch something on (the) television* with the article optional, and *watch (some) television*, where *television* is non-count. No article is used in *watch something on tape/video*, and the like, where the recording medium rather than the recording device is intended. For postal and similar institutions, we also have the article: *put something in the post/mail.* However, no article is used after *by*: *by post, by telephone*, etc. With transport terms, the article is used in examples like [v], where there is no reference to any particular vehicle, but again, there is no article after *by*: *by bus.* Example [vi] illustrates the article with temporal nouns following the preposition *in*: no particular morning is being singled out. With seasons the article is optional: *Hedgehogs hibernate in (the) winter.* In addition, a number of idiomatic expressions require the definite article, presumably for historical reasons. Examples include: *pass something on the nod* ("without discussion"); *be on the blink* ("out of order"); *be left in the lurch* ("in severe difficulty").

(c) The indefinite article in expressions of price, rate, etc.

[18]	*She has a salary of [$80,000 a year].*	*[How many hours a day] do you work?*
	He was going at [50 miles an hour].	*It costs [$20 a yard/person].*

The underlined NP is interpreted distributively, like one with *each* (which in some contexts can be used instead of *a*: compare *How many hours do you work each day?*). A somewhat more formal alternant is a PP with *per* + bare NP, as in *$80,000 per year* (though in cases like *The output per worker has increased dramatically* or *The cost is $200 per person per week* only the *per* construction is acceptable).

8.5 Restricted non-referential interpretations of bare NPs

Here we cover cases similar to those dealt with in §8.4, i.e. cases where only a restricted range of head nouns is found. This time, however, our concern is with bare NPs. We confine our attention to singular count nouns, which normally require a determiner.

(a) Bare role NPs

[19] i *Henry became treasurer.*
ii *As treasurer, I strongly support this proposal.*
iii *The role of treasurer will fall to Henry.*

NPs such as *treasurer, deputy leader of the party,* occur as the predicative complements of verbs like *be, become, appoint, elect,* as oblique predicative governed by *as,* and as complement of the preposition *of* following nouns like *role, part,* or *position.* They cannot occur as subjects (**I'm told treasurer strongly supports this proposal*) or objects (**We dismissed treasurer*): in these positions they require a determiner. The interpretation of bare role NPs is invariably definite: in [19], for example, we are concerned with the office of treasurer in some particular organisation. They are therefore invariably replaceable by their counterparts with determiner *the,* as in *Henry became the treasurer,* and so on.

It is important to note that only NPs which genuinely allow role interpretations can function in this manner. The verb *become,* for example, also allows non-role nouns such as *miser* as head of the predicative complement, but such nouns require determiners: *Fred became *miser / a miser when he lost his job.*

(b) Fixed expressions or frames

[20] i *Ed is in hospital / went to school / went off stage.* [activities linked to locations]
ii *They are out of place / off target / on call.* [indications of status]
iii *We went by bicycle / communicate by email.* [transport and media]
iv *We had lunch on the terrace.* [meals]
v *at dawn, by daybreak, before sunrise* [times]
vi *arm in arm, back to back, day after day, mouthful by mouthful, side by side, mile upon mile* [repeated nouns]
vii *from father to son, from beginning to end, between husband and wife, mother and child* [matched nouns]

The examples in [i] are illustrative of a number of restricted expressions connected with common activities of everyday life where no determiner is permitted, even when the noun involved is in other uses a singular count noun denoting a location which would require a determiner. In these cases, the noun acts as an indication of the associated activity, and does not have its standard denotation. Contrast, for example, *Ed is in bed* (resting/asleep) with referential *There are fleas in the bed*; or *Ed is in prison* (serving time) with *There was a riot in the prison*; or again *Ed is in church* (at a service) with *There is a new pulpit in the church.* The nouns which permit this use are severely restricted. We do not have for example **Ed is at desk* (studying), **Ed is at computer* (working), **Ed is in kitchen* (cooking). Nevertheless there are a fair number of them: others include the underlined nouns in such expressions as *on campus, in class, at college, settle out of court, at sea* (as a sailor), *at table* (for a meal), *leave town, start university.*

The examples in [20ii] relate to what we may call 'status': whether or not something is in its proper place, whether or not someone is available or engaged in their proper activity. These fixed expressions are comparable to those with non-count nouns such as *at work*, *at play*. The bare NPs in [iii] occur after the preposition *by*: compare the definite NPs in [17iv]. Meals are generally expressed by bare NPs, except when a particular occasion is singled out: compare [20iv] with *We had a nice lunch at the Savoy*. Note also *at/by dinner*, where the meal indicates a time of day. Bare NPs are used for times of day following the prepositions *at*, *by*, *before*, *until*, *after*, as in [20v]; note, however, that *morning*, *daytime*, *evening*, and *dark* take *in* + *the* instead of *at*: *in the* / **at morning*. The examples in [vi–vii] are illustrative of a number of expressions involving repetition of the same noun or contrasting nouns; for the category status of the expressions in [vi], see Ch. 7, §4.3. Similarly, in coordinate structures, bare NPs can optionally be used in repetition: *We searched endlessly for a spring or a cave to spend the night, but neither spring nor cave could be found.*

9 Fused-head and elliptical NPs

9.1 Overview of the fused-head construction

Fused-head NPs are those where the head is combined with a dependent function that in ordinary NPs is adjacent to the head, usually determiner or internal modifier:

[1]	i	*Where are the sausages? Did you buy [some] yesterday?*	[determiner-head]
	ii	*The first candidate performed well, but [the second] did not.*	[modifier-head]

Form of the fused head

In general, the expression in fused-head position can occur in the dependent position in NPs where it is not fused with the head. Thus *some* occurs with just the determiner function in *some sausages* and *second* with just the internal modifier function in *the second candidate*. These latter examples involve the **dependent** use of *some* and *second*, while [1] illustrates the **independent** use:

[2]	i	*Did you buy [some sausages] yesterday?*	[dependent use]
	ii	*Did you buy [some] yesterday?* (from [1i])	[independent use]

There are two small-scale departures from this pattern.

Contrasting dependent and independent forms

A handful of items have distinct inflectional forms for dependent and independent uses:

[3]	i	DEPENDENT	*my*	*your*	*her*	*our*	*their*	*no*
	ii	INDEPENDENT	*mine*	*yours*	*hers*	*ours*	*theirs*	*none*

The dependent forms are used in (pure) determiner function, the independent ones in head function. The independent genitive pronouns occur in fused heads and also pure heads, whereas the independent negative determinative *none* appears (in NP structure) only as a fused head:

[4]	i	*Kim's car had broken down and [mine] had too.*	[determiner-head]
	ii	*Don't touch that: it's [mine].*	[(pure) head]
	iii	*They made several mistakes, but [none] were serious.*	[determiner-head]

Compound determinatives

In some cases the syntactic fusion of determiner and head is reflected in the morphological compounding of a determinative base and a noun base, as in *something, nobody,* etc. These compound forms are discussed in §9.6 below.

Types of fused-head construction

There are three main types of fused-head construction: simple, partitive, and special. The partitive may be explicit, with an *of* phrase in post-head modifier position, or implicit, with ellipsis of the *of* phrase. Compare, then:

[5]	i	*While Kim had lots of books, Pat had [very few].*	[simple]
	ii	*[Few of her friends] knew she was ill.*	[explicitly partitive]
	iii	*We made numerous suggestions but [few] were taken up.*	[implicitly partitive]
	iv	*[Few] would have expected it to turn out so well.*	[special]

Simple and implicitly partitive constructions

These are usually interpreted anaphorically, i.e. via an antecedent. We understand [5i], for example, as "very few books" and [5iii] as "few of the suggestions". It is also possible for the interpretation to derive from something in the situation of utterance. Perhaps, for example, there is a packet of biscuits on the table: you take a biscuit from the packet and I say *Can I have one too?* The fused-head NP *one* is here interpreted as "a biscuit" – or "one of those biscuits", for the distinction between the simple and implicitly partitive cases may in certain cases be neutralised. We look further into the interpretation of these two types in Ch. 17, §6.1.

Explicitly partitive constructions

Here the head is followed by a complement consisting of *of* + a partitive oblique, an NP which can be plural, non-count, or, under restricted conditions, count singular:

[6]	i	a. *some of the books*	b. *all of them*	[plural]
	ii	a. *some of the meat*	b. *all of it*	[non-count singular]
	iii	a. *some of the morning*	b. *all of it*	[count singular]

In [i], the partitive oblique denotes a set and the matrix NP (the one with the fused head) denotes a subset of that set; similarly in [ii] the partitive oblique denotes a quantity and the matrix NP denotes a subquantity of that quantity. We use 'subset' here in the technical sense which does not require that a subset be smaller than the set concerned: this allows for [ib] as well as [ia].[40] Count singulars are admissible as partitive obliques only if they can be interpreted as divisible into parts in some relevant way. The clearest cases are those involving time periods, as in [iii]. We can also have, for example, *Some of the loaf had mould on it,* but not *#Some of the car was muddy*: we need a noun head, as in *Parts of the car were muddy.*

Partitive obliques are normally definite: we would not have #[*Two of some windows*] *were broken.* Indefinites cannot be wholly excluded, however: acceptability improves if the indefinite NP contains an information-rich internal modifier of the type that would in principle justify use of the definite article (cf. the discussion of definiteness-establishing

[40] A subset which is smaller than the set is known technically as a 'proper subset'. In non-technical usage *subset* is interpreted as "proper subset": this is a case therefore where an implicature of the familiar "not all" type is taken to be actually part of the meaning of the form.

modification in [6vi–vii] of §6). Such a modifier would be the relative clause in [*One of some windows which we were fitting at the Sears Tower*] *was broken, and that's why I'm late.*

Partitive NPs do not invariably have fused heads: there are various quantificational nouns that can occur as head, either with a separate determiner (*the majority of the books, a lot of the meat*) or in bare NPs (*lots/dozens of the books*).

Representation of NPs with fused heads

Simplified tree-diagrams are given in [7] for three NPs with fused heads: *few of her friends, someone I know* and *the second* (as used in [1ii]).

[7]

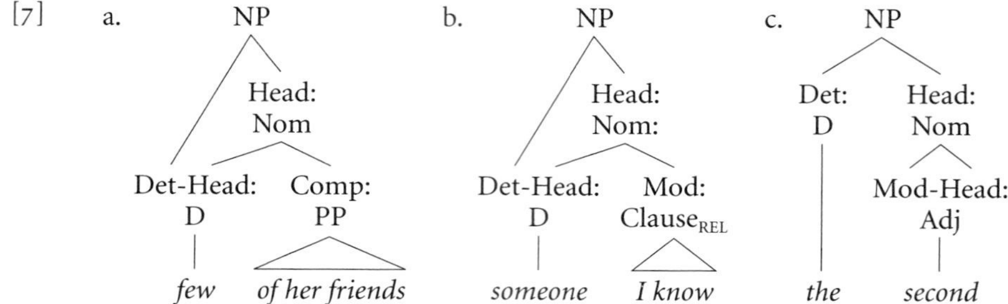

9.2 Fusion of determiner and head

Exclusions

The great majority of determiners can fuse with the head, but there are a small number of exceptions, which fall into two groups.

(a) *What, **we**, you*

These items belong to both determinative and pronoun categories: in determiner function they are determinatives, in head function they are pronouns (see §9.5 below). Note that *what, **we**,* and *you* do not occur in constructions comparable to those involving simple or partitive fused-head constructions:

[8] i a. *What books did he give Kim, and what did he give Pat?*
b. *We students will leave first, you follow as soon as you can.*
ii a. *[*What of these books*] have you read?*
b. *[*You of the team*] have let the rest of us down.*

The underlined NPs in [i] are not interpreted anaphorically as "what books" and "you students", and the partitives in [ii] are ungrammatical.

(b) *The, a, every*

The two articles and *every* do not occur in head function at all: they require the presence of a separate head. In the case of the articles, the gap created by their inability to fuse with the head is filled by demonstrative ***that*** and singulative *one* respectively.

[9]	i a.	*Alice's performances were better than [those/*the of Helen].*	[count plural]
	b.	*Alice's performance was better than [that/*the of Helen].*	[count singular]
	c.	*Alice's cooking was better than [that/*the of Helen].*	[non-count]
	ii	*I haven't got a pen: can you lend me [one/*a]?*	[count singular]

In the case of *every*, what we have in place of a determiner-head fusion is a construction with *every* as determiner and pro-nominal *one* as head:

[10] i *He received over a hundred letters and replied to [every one / *every (of them)].*
ii *[Every one / *Every of the apples] was rotten.*

Partitives

(a) Determinatives restricted to the partitive subtype

A number of determinatives function as fused head only in partitives:

[11] i *I found some old letters in the attic; [certain of them] dealt with political issues.*
ii *They had borrowed two videos but there wasn't time to watch [either (of them)].*
iii *We used to have two spare keys, but [both (of them)] have disappeared.*

With *certain* the *of* phrase is hardly omissible, and the same applies to *various*. Like *either* in [ii] are *neither* and *which*: all involve choosing from some set. *Each* would also belong here, were it not for the minor special use mentioned below. *Both* indicates the whole of some definite set; as a determiner-head it is always partitive, but it can also occur as fused predeterminer-head (see §9.4 below).

(b) Definites

Of the definite determiners only the universal quantifiers *all* and *both* occur freely as fused head in partitives. Genitives are completely excluded: **Kim's of the shares had already been sold.* (The meaning here could be expressed as *Those of the shares that were Kim's had already been sold.*) Of the demonstratives, only *those* appears in partitives, and then only under restricted conditions:

[12] i **[Those of the accidents] are discussed in greater detail in Chapter 7.*
ii *[Those of the above accidents which involve special circumstances or matters of particular medical interest] are discussed in greater detail in Chapter 7.*
iii *[Those of you with a train to catch] had better leave now.*

Those is admissible in this construction only if the partitive PP is followed by a modifier – a relative clause in [ii], a PP in [iii]. It is this modifier which serves to establish the definiteness of the set expressed by the matrix NP.

(c) Quantificational adjuncts

One use of fused-head partitives that merits separate mention here is that where they function as quantificational adjunct in clause structure:

[13] i *Her parents both felt she had been exploited.*
ii *They had none of them intended to cause so much ill will.*

The quantificational adjuncts serve to quantify the subject. Example [i] is thus equivalent to *Both her parents felt she had been exploited* and [ii] to *None of them had intended to cause so much ill will.* Universal *all*, *both*, and *each* can occur as implicit partitives, while the set of determinatives found in explicit partitives is considerably larger: these three together with existential *some*, *any*, *none*, cardinal numerals, multal *many* and *much*, paucal *few*, *a few*, and *several*. The implicit partitives can occur in preverbal position, as in [i]; explicit partitives are somewhat questionable in this position, strongly preferring post-auxiliary position. Compare *?Her parents both of them felt she had been exploited* and *Her parents had both of them felt she had been exploited.*

Fused determiner-heads with special interpretations

We consider five cases of this construction:

(a) Personal: "people"

[14] i [Those who break the rules] must expect to be punished.
ii [Few] would quarrel with that assessment.

Example [i] can be glossed as "(Those) people who break the rules . . ."; the construction requires a clausal modifier and the plural form *those*. There is no contrast with proximal *these*, and the deictic, demonstrative meaning of ***that*** is bleached away.

In [14ii], we likewise understand "few people"; postmodification is not required (but nor is it excluded). This pattern, relatively uncommon, is found with paucal *few*, multal *many*, universal *all*, and existential *some*. *All* is here equivalent to the compound determinative *everybody*, which is much more usual; *each* is found but only in more or less fixed expressions like *Each to* %*his/their own*. *Some* differs from *somebody* by virtue of being plural. Non-affirmative *any* is not used in this way, and negative *none* is largely restricted to constructions with *but* or *other*, as noted in §7.8. *None but a lawyer* is equivalent to *nobody but a lawyer*, but *none other than the President herself* is idiomatic and doesn't allow replacement of *none* by *nobody*.

(b) Non-personal

[15] i [Not much / Little] has happened while you've been away.
ii You said [enough to convince me I was wrong].

This pattern is found mainly with quantifiers that do not form compounds with ·*thing*: multal *much*, paucal *little*, and the sufficiency quantifiers *enough* and *sufficient*. For universal quantification we generally have *everything*, but *all* is used in a very restricted range of cases, usually with a following modifier, as in [*All I did*] *was express an opinion*.[41]

(c) Singular demonstratives

[16] i [This] doesn't look like Jill's writing.
ii The rules allow 16-year-olds to buy alcohol, but [that] is going to change.
iii What's [all this I hear about a move to sack the chief executive]?
iv The banquet costs $50, but you could get a decent meal for [half that].

The singular forms of the demonstratives behave somewhat differently from the plurals. Proximal *these* is used in the simple fused-head construction, interpreted anaphorically (*Those questions are too advanced: I recommend you focus on* [*these*]) or directly from the context (*Can I have one of these?* – "one of these biscuits", perhaps). *Those* is used in the same way, but also (with neutralisation of the distal vs proximal distinction) in examples like [12ii–iii] and [14i]. The singular forms can be used with a separate head recoverable anaphorically, as in:

[17] i That sausage has only 25 % meat, but [this] has 90%.
ii This model is more suitable than [that].

or – in the case of *that* only – in examples like [9ib–c]. The construction of [17], however, is somewhat less likely than one with pro-nominal *one* (*this one*, *that one*), and

[41] There are places where *all* neutralises the personal vs non-personal distinction, as in partitive obliques: *best of all*. The same applies with certain fixed phrases with *none*: *second to none*.

is not normally used with human antecedents (**I prefer the previous candidate to this*). The singular demonstratives in head position thus fall predominantly in the special interpretation category.

(d) Quantification of predicatives: *much of a . . .*

[18] i *Ed isn't [much of a husband].*

ii *It turned out to be [more/less of a problem than we'd expected].*

Plain *much*, comparative *more* and *less*, and sufficiency *enough* are used as degree quantifiers for properties expressed in predicative NPs. *Husband* doesn't usually denote a gradable property, but in this construction we understand the quantification to apply to the degree to which Ed has the properties that are taken to characterise a good husband. Syntactically, *much* is a determiner-head taking a PP complement in which *of* is followed by an NP with the form *a* + nominal. *Much* here is strongly non-affirmative: compare **Ed is much of a husband.* This construction is to be distinguished from that where *very much* appears as peripheral modifier. Compare, for example, *He's [very much an actor]* and *He isn't [very much of an actor]*, where the first has *actor* as head, the second, *much*. The first is concerned with the degree to which he can be said to be an actor, the second with how good an actor he is.

(e) Genitives with a locative interpretation: *Kim's, the doctor's*

[19] i *There's a party at [Kim's] tonight.*

ii *I'd better take you to [the doctor's].*

Kim's in [i] is understood as "Kim's place, the place where Kim lives". Note that, except in the informal speech of young people, personal pronouns cannot be used in this way: *%There's a party at mine tonight.* The genitive in [ii] has a more specific interpretation, "the doctor's surgery" – similarly with *the hairdresser's, the grocer's*, etc., "the hairdresser's/grocer's shop", or with proper names referring to stores: *Sainsbury's.* In this second type there is often a strong implicature of purpose. In [19ii], for example, it will normally be a matter of taking you there to consult the doctor: I wouldn't use this construction if it were a matter of your going there to play chess with the doctor's daughter.

9.3 Fusion of internal modifier and head

The head does not fuse so readily with an internal modifier as with a determiner, as evident from the ungrammaticality of such examples as:

[20] i **Because the existing bridge is too narrow, we will have to build [a new].*

ii **The retreating troops were captured, but [the advancing] managed to escape.*

iii **Bill likes the linguistics lecturer, but I prefer [the sociology].*

The adjective *new*, the verb *advancing*, and the noun *sociology* require a following head, such as ***one***. The cases where fusion is possible are as follows.

(a) Determinatives

Those determinatives which can function as internal modifier as well as determiner can in general occur as fused modifier-head as well as determiner-head:

[21] i *This copy is defective but [the other two] are fine.*
ii *I've corrected most of the mistakes but [these few here] are still to be done.*
iii *I didn't like it myself, but I respect the views of [the many who did].*

Much the most common case has a cardinal numeral as head, as in [i]. *Every* is again excluded, and so too this time is *various*, while the others are hardly admissible unless accompanied by a following modifier, as in [ii–iii].

(b) Superlatives and definite comparatives

[22] i *I went up that skyscraper in Boston, but [the tallest] is in Chicago.*
ii *There are two sisters, but [the elder] is already married.*
iii **Hugo has a big house, but Karl has [a bigger].*

The fact that acceptability deteriorates with indefinitely determined comparatives suggests an explanation based on definiteness. Superlatives are **ranking expressions**: they inherently pick out a unique entity as of higher rank than the rest, as do comparatives when comparison is made between two entities. They are therefore more like definite determiners than are ordinary adjectives, which serve only to constrain the denotation of the nouns they modify. This is reflected in the position of superlatives and comparative adjectives: they are typically closer to the determiner than other adjectives (§15). However, the possibility of fusion with the head must in the last resort be stated in syntactic terms, for other adjectives which have a similar ranking function, for example *main*, cannot be used in the same way: **There's obviously some kind of switch at the front, but [the main] is at the back.*[42]

Superlatives occur in the special interpretation type in a construction with a genitive personal pronoun as determiner, and special interpretations are also found with *former*, *latter*, and *same*:

[23] i *George was at [his most obstructive].*
ii *They invited Watson and Gates, but as usual [the latter] was unable to come.*

Example [i] illustrates the common type where the NP is complement to *at*; it says that George was particularly obstructive, locating his obstructiveness at the maximum level. *Best* and *damnedest* also occur as complement to **do**: *He did his best/damnedest to frustrate our plan. The former/latter/same* are used as anaphors (see Ch. 17, §9.4); in [ii], for example, *the latter* is understood as "Gates".

(c) Ordinal adjectives

[24] i *The first student wanted to take linguistics, but [the second] did not.*
ii *I wanted to catch the next train, because [the last] will be too late.*
iii *After having a first child, I didn't want [a second].*

The fact that ordinal adjectives are also ranking expressions links this phenomenon to (b) above. However, as is demonstrated by [iii], there appears to be no constraint against the NP being indefinitely determined. Ordinal fused heads occur with special interpretations in dates (*the second of June*, "second day") and in proper names (*George II*, spoken as *George the Second*).

[42] As well as taking a partitive complement (e.g. *the biggest of them*), superlatives can, when in predicative function, take a bare plural as oblique: *He isn't the most reliable of colleagues.*

(d) Modifiers denoting colour, provenance, and composition

[25] i *Henrietta likes red shirts, and I like [blue].*
ii *Knut wanted the purple wallpaper, but I wanted [the mauve].*
iii *Henrietta likes Russian vodka, and I like [Polish].*
iv *Knut wanted the French caterers, but I wanted [the Italian].*
v *I prefer cotton shirts to [nylon].*
vi *Knut likes malt whisky, but I prefer [blended].*

The NPs here are either bare or have a definite determiner; there is significant loss of acceptability when the determiner is indefinite:

[26] i ?*Harvey bought a red shirt and I bought [a blue].*
ii ?*I bought some Chinese food rather than [some Indian].*
iii ?*I bought a cotton shirt rather than [a nylon].*

(e) Adjectives denoting basic physical properties such as age and size

[27] i *Lucie likes young dogs, but I prefer [old].*
ii *Lucie likes big dogs, but I prefer [small].*

The boundaries to what is admissible are hard to define, but there appears to be considerable degradation with adjectives denoting more complex physical properties or with evaluative adjectives, for example those denoting character:

[28] i ?*Lucie likes smooth-coated dogs, but I prefer [shaggy].*
ii **Lucie likes friendly dogs, but I prefer [aggressive].*

As with type (d) above, acceptability is reduced, indeed here lost altogether, when the NP is indefinitely determined: **Lucie bought a young dog, but I bought [an old].*

(f) Modifier-heads with special interpretations

[29] i *[The French] do these differently from [the Dutch].*
ii *[The rich] cannot enter the kingdom of Heaven.*
iii *How will the new system affect [the very poor]?*
iv *We are going to attempt [the utterly impossible].*
v *This is verging on [the immoral].*
vi *They like to swim in [the nude].*

A rather restricted range of adjectives – beyond those covered in (b) and (c) – occur in fused-head constructions with special interpretations. The NPs are determined by the definite article – we couldn't even substitute a demonstrative: **these very poor.* Examples [i–iii] illustrate a subtype denoting categories of human being; these NPs are characteristically used generically, as here. *The French* and *the Dutch* denote the inhabitants of France and Holland; for other nationality adjectives of this kind, see Ch. 19, §5.6.2. NPs like those in [ii–iii] can be paraphrased by means of *those* + relative clause: *those who are rich / very poor.* This subtype includes adjectives based on past participle forms or similar denominal derivatives in *·ed*: *the disadvantaged, the intellectually gifted, the unemployed, the hard-hearted,* and so on. Two non-generic cases are *the deceased* and *the accused,* which can be used in singular or plural reference. Note also the fused-head restrictive modifier in proper names like *Ivan [the Terrible].*

Examples [29iv–v] illustrate a second subtype, with an abstract rather than concrete interpretation. Paraphrases here may have the form *that* + relative clause or fused relative: *that which is utterly impossible, what is immoral.* Neither type of paraphrase applies in [vi], where *in the nude* is an idiom meaning "naked". See also §16.7 for the use of *own* in special fused-head constructions.

It is possible, though very rare, for the AdjP functioning as fused head to contain a post-head modifier: *the pure in heart.* In a dependent use AdjPs of this kind can only follow the head noun: *people pure in heart,* not **pure in heart people.* We must allow, therefore, for a head to fuse with a post-head modifier, as well as for the usual case where the fusion is with a pre-head modifier.

Fused modifier-heads contrasted with non-fused heads realised by de-adjectival nouns

The construction we have been concerned with in this section is to be distinguished from that where the head position is filled by a noun morphologically derived by conversion from an adjective:

[30] *Kim is* [*an* <u>*intellectual*</u>]. [determiner + head]

Intellectual here is simply a noun that happens to be derived from an adjective, whereas *French, Dutch, rich, poor, impossible,* and *immoral* in [29] are themselves adjectives.

The difference is clearest with the *rich* and *poor* type, which differ from *intellectual* in two respects. In the first place, *intellectual* inflects for number (cf. *Kim and Pat are intellectuals*), whereas *the rich* and *the very poor* are plural NPs with no inflectional plural marking on the head. Secondly, while the adjective *intellectual* takes adverbs as modifier, as in *Kim is* [<u>*remarkably*</u> *intellectual*], the noun *intellectual* does not. Instead of **Kim is* [*a* <u>*remarkably*</u> *intellectual*], we have *Kim is* [*a* <u>*remarkable*</u> *intellectual*], with the noun modified by the adjective *remarkable. Rich* and *poor,* by contrast, take adverbs as modifier, as in *the extremely rich* and *the very poor*: this is clear evidence that they retain their category status as adjectives.

The nationality adjectives *French* and *Dutch* are non-gradable, and with these only the first difference applies: the lack of plural inflection. Conversely, *impossible* and *immoral* in [29iv–v] are obligatorily singular, so here only the second difference applies: the adverbial modification. In both cases, however, the one difference is sufficient to establish that the head word has not been converted into a noun, especially in view of the fact that *the French* and *the immoral* clearly belong with *the rich* by virtue of the obligatory definite article.

9.4 Fusion of predeterminer and head

To a very limited extent the head may also fuse with a predeterminer modifier. There are two cases to consider:

(a) Fractions and multipliers

[31] i *I earn half the amount Bill does, and Mary earns* [<u>*two thirds*</u>].

ii *I earn three times the amount Bill does, and Mary earns* [<u>*double*</u>/<u>*half*</u>].

iii ?*I earn three times the amount Bill does, and Mary earns* [<u>*twice*</u>].

These belong to the simple fused-head construction, interpreted anaphorically as "two thirds the amount Bill does", and so on. In [i–ii] the predeterminer is respectively a nominal and a noun, while in [iii] *twice* is an adverb, which is appreciably less acceptable. (Fractions can also occur as non-fused heads in a partitive construction: *Mary had already spent [two thirds of her allowance].*)

(b) Universal quantifiers

[32] i *Both/All these issues were ignored in the first draft, but [both/all] are now adequately covered.*
ii *Two judges had given both/all the competitors a grade of B+, but one had given [both/?all] an A.*

The analysis here is rather problematic since *both* and *all* can function as determiner, and examples of this kind could be construed as implicitly partitive determiner-heads, "both/all of them". Be that as it may, *all* occurs here less readily than *both*, the *all* version of [ii] (where the fused-head NP is non-subject) being of very questionable acceptability. Preference would generally be given, even with *both*, to one or other of two equivalent formulations: *both/all of them* or *them both/all.*

9.5 The fused-head analysis compared with alternatives

The constructions we have been concerned with in this section are not analysed in terms of functional fusion in traditional grammar, or indeed in modern treatments either. Traditional grammars tend not to provide wholly explicit accounts, but in general offer a combination of two kinds of analysis, one involving pronouns, the other ellipsis:

[33] i *There are a dozen applications and [several] look quite promising.* [pronoun]
ii *There were two pieces left and Kim, as always, chose [the larger].* [ellipsis]

Several is traditionally analysed as an adjective in examples like *several applications*, but as a pronoun in examples like [i]. *Larger*, however, is treated as an adjective not only in *the larger piece*, but also in [ii]: the latter is said to be elliptical, with *piece* understood.

We believe it is fair to say that traditional grammar provides no justification for handling the examples in [33] in different ways, and this itself must count against the analysis: a unitary treatment is to be preferred on grounds of simplicity and generality.

Problems with the traditional pronoun analysis

(a) Lack of generality

The first point to note about the pronoun analysis is, indeed, that it clearly cannot be generalised to cover all cases. This approach says that a word belongs to different part-of-speech categories according to whether or not it is (in our terms) head of the NP, and there are several reasons why this won't do as a general solution. In the first place, fusion of dependent and head is possible with comparative and superlative adjectival expressions: to include inflected forms like *larger* and *largest* and the plain-form heads of analytic comparatives and superlatives such as *more/most important* would make the pronoun category open-ended and completely change its character. Secondly, in the construction where a genitive determiner is fused with the head, as in *Jill's proposal was an improvement on her husband's*, the head word is a noun; to treat *husband's* and the like as pronouns would lose the distinction between pronouns and common or proper nouns. The pronoun analysis is traditionally invoked only for our determinatives (other than cardinal numerals) and it cannot be extended beyond those.

(b) Differences from genuine pronouns with respect to dependents

A second point is that the words concerned take different dependents from pronouns – but the same ones as they take when functioning as non-fused determiner. Compare:

[34]	DEPENDENT USE	INDEPENDENT USE
i	a. *not much cheese*	b. *not much of the cheese*
ii	a. *very little cheese*	b. *very little of the cheese*
iii	a. *almost enough cheese*	b. *almost enough of the cheese*

This argues against any part-of-speech distinction between the two uses – contrast again the case of *intellectual* in [30], which takes different dependents in the independent (noun) use from those it takes in the dependent (adjective) use.

(c) Genitive case

The forms we analyse as fused heads either cannot occur in the genitive at all or do so only very rarely. **All's*, **many's*, **few's*, **some's*, for example, are completely excluded, while *each's* is occasionally attested but of somewhat questionable status. A pronoun analysis provides no account of why this should be so, while the fused analysis does suggest a reason: the form is simultaneously determiner and head, and for full acceptability its case should match both functions. The genitive marking in *many people's expenses* goes on the head, not the determiner, and hence there is a conflict between case and determiner function in **many's expenses.* (See also the discussion of case in fused relatives, Ch. 12, §5.3.)

Ellipsis

Ellipsis does not provide a general solution either. There are several cases where it is not possible to reinstate a separate head element, the two most important of which are seen in:

[35]				
i	*many of us*	*two of the windows*	*much of it*	*all of the meat*
ii	*the rich*	*the very poor*	*the immoral*	*the utterly impossible*

In [i] we have partitives, and we cannot in examples like these add a noun before *of* – cf. **many ones of us*, **much quantity of it*, etc. The NPs in [ii] belong to the special type of fused modifier-head construction: see [29] above. Although the first two denote sets of people, we cannot insert the noun *people* here without changing the meaning, for *the rich* and *the very poor* are interpreted generically, while *the rich people* and *the very poor people* are not. It is likewise impossible to add a separate head noun in examples like those in [23].

A less obvious problem with an ellipsis analysis arises when we consider the relationship between the present NP construction and clauses with missing heads. Compare:

[36] i *Alice performed the Schubert and [Helen _ the Rachmaninov].* [clause]

ii *Alice's performance of the Schubert and [Helen's of the Rachmaninov]* [NP]

In [i] the head of the clause, the predicator, is missing, but recoverable from the underlined antecedent in the preceding clause: this is the construction known as gapping (Ch. 15, §4.2). It is tempting to say, by analogy, that in [ii] the head of the NP is missing but recoverable as *performance* from the preceding NP. The two constructions are not, however, as similar as this pair of examples at first suggests. Two significant differences are illustrated in:

[37] i a. *Alice performed the Schubert immediately after [Helen _ the Rachmaninov].
b. Alice's performance of the Schubert took place immediately after [Helen's of the Rachmaninov].
ii a. Alice attempted to play the Schubert and [Helen _ the Rachmaninov].
b. *Alice's attempt to play the Schubert and [Helen's the Rachmaninov]

In the first place, gapping is in general restricted to coordinative constructions, hence the ungrammaticality of [ia]. There is, however, no such restriction on the fused-head NP construction, and [ib] is perfectly well formed. Secondly, gapping can involve the omission of a sequence of elements which do not together form a constituent: this is illustrated in [iia], where there is ellipsis of *attempted* + *to play*. There is nothing comparable in the NP, however, with [iib] completely ungrammatical. No viable fusion analysis could be devised to handle gapping: we have to describe this construction in terms of the omission of elements recoverable from an antecedent. But there is nothing in the NPs that requires this approach, and since it cannot be sustained for the constructions shown in [35], it cannot be accepted as providing a satisfactory alternative to the fused-head analysis.

A third approach: change of function without change of category

A third solution that is compatible in principle with our framework is to handle such pairs as the following in the same kind of way:

[38] i a. *The shirt is made of [nylon].* [noun as head]
b. *He was wearing [a nylon shirt].* [noun as modifier]
ii a. *[Many people] would agree with you.* [determinative as determiner]
b. *[Many] would agree with you.* [determinative as head]

In [i] we simply have a single category appearing in two different functions: *nylon* is head in [ia], internal modifier in [ib]. This is the kind of analysis we have adopted in numerous places in the present grammar, so the question naturally arises as to whether a solution of this kind could handle the constructions under consideration in this section. It would involve saying that in [ii] *many* belongs to the same category, determinative, in both cases, but functions as determiner in [iia], head in [iib].

The reason we have not adopted this solution is that it does not handle cases like:

[39] i *I prefer cotton shirts to [nylon].* (=[25v])
ii *I earn three times the amount Bill does, and Mary earns [double].* (=[31ii])

To say that *nylon* in [i] was a noun in head position would not distinguish this construction from *I prefer cotton to nylon.* The crucial difference is that in [i] but not this latter example *nylon* is understood as having modifier function. The fused-head analysis enables us to make this distinction: *nylon* combines the functions of modifier and head in [39i], but functions simply as head in *I prefer cotton to nylon*, just as it does in [38i]. Similarly in [39] *double* is a noun, but it would not be satisfactory to say that it was functioning simply as head of the NP object of *earns*: it is understood as having a predeterminer modifier function matching that of *three times* in the object of the first clause.

Overlap between determinative and pronoun categories

The fused-head analysis avoids the need to recognise a large amount of overlap between the pronoun and determinative categories. In the present grammar there are just four items that belong in both categories: *what*, *which*, ***we***, and ***you***.

[40]	DETERMINATIVE	PRONOUN
i	a. [*What* boy] *could resist such an offer?*	b. [*What*] *happened?*
ii	a. *It may be free, in* [*which* case] *I'll go.*	b. *I need a job* [*which*] *pays well.*
iii	a. [*We*/*You* Irish] *will have his support.*	b. [*We*/*You*] *will have his support.*

(a) *What* and *which*

With these items there is a difference of meaning between determinative and pronoun, so their assignment to separate categories is unproblematic. The interrogative and relative pronouns *what* (and *whatever*) and the relative pronoun *which* are non-personal, contrasting with personal ***who***, while the determinatives are neutral as to the personal vs non-personal contrast. Note that there is no interrogative pronoun *which*: the *which* of [*Which* (*of them*)] *do you want?* is likewise neutral in gender and functions as a fused determiner-head.

(b) ***We*** and ***you***

Here there is no comparable difference in meaning, but there are other grounds for recognising a category distinction. We take ***we*** and ***you*** to be primarily pronouns because they enter into systematic contrast with the 3rd person and 1st person singular personal pronouns, and have inflectional forms – genitive and reflexives – which are quite inapplicable to determinatives. There could be no question of analysing these items as uniquely determinatives, with independent occurrences, i.e. those without a following noun (which of course constitute the overwhelming majority), belonging to the fused-head construction. We regard the *we*/*you students* construction, therefore, as involving an extended, secondary use in which they have been reanalysed as determinatives.

(c) Borderline case: singular demonstratives

It is less clear how the demonstratives *this* and *that* should be treated. A case could be made for treating them too as belonging to both determinative and pronoun categories. In head function, we have seen, they cannot occur in partitives, and they do not commonly occur in simple fused-head constructions like [17]: they belong predominantly to the special subtype of fused-head construction, with little semantic motivation for saying that they have determiner as well as head function. Moreover, while they freely occur with a following personal head (*this girl*, *that boy*), a personal interpretation of them in head function is permitted only under restricted conditions: *This is my husband*, but not – with a personal interpretation – **This said he would help me*. We have nevertheless found it preferable to assign demonstratives uniquely to the determinative category, functioning in NP structure as determiner or fused determiner-head. One reason is that there is no well-motivated place to draw a boundary between determinative and pronoun uses. The plural forms fall in naturally with the fused-head analysis, and singular examples like [17] and [9ii–iii] match corresponding plural forms. A second point is that the demonstratives differ quite sharply from prototypical pronouns in the way they combine with other elements in the structure of NPs. Pronouns do not in general take quantifiers as pre-head dependents: of the personal pronouns only ***we*** and plural ***you*** allow *all*, and then only in the presence of a post-head modifier such as a relative clause. The demonstratives, however, allow *all* quite freely, and in addition take other predeterminers: *half this*, *double* / *three times that*, and so on. There is no difference with regard to such quantification between demonstratives in (determiner-)head position and those in pure determiner position. And again, post-head relative clauses and PPs are commonly found in NPs headed by demonstratives (see [16iii] for a relative clause example), but are very rare with pronouns.

9.6 Compound determinatives

Compound determinatives such as *somebody* occur as determiner-head with the syntactic fusion of the two functions marked by the morphological compounding of a determinative base with a nominal one. The central members are:

[41]	i	*everybody*	*somebody*	*anybody*	*nobody*
	ii	*everyone*	*someone*	*anyone*	*no one*
	iii	*everything*	*something*	*anything*	*nothing*
	iv	*everywhere*	*somewhere*	*anywhere*	*nowhere*

The determinative bases are universal distributive *every* and three existential quantifiers: positively-oriented *some*, non-affirmative or free choice *any*, and negative *no*. The nominal bases are personal ·*body* and ·*one* (which are wholly equivalent), non-personal ·*thing*, and locative ·*where*. An informal variant of ·*where* in AmE is ·*place*. The analysis of the locatives as heads of NPs is motivated by their use as object in constructions like *Have you got anywhere to spend the night?*[43]

Special post-head dependents

Because determiner and head are fused it is not possible for these forms to take internal pre-head dependents. The counterparts of such dependents in non-fused NPs are located after the head:

[42] i *[No <u>sensible</u> ideas] / [Nothing <u>sensible</u>] will emerge from the meeting.*

ii *I don't want [a <u>gold</u> watch] / [anything <u>gold</u>] for my anniversary.*

We refer to such post-head dependents as **restrictors**. There can be no more than one of this kind per NP:

[43] i *[No <u>sensible</u> <u>new</u> ideas] / *[Nothing <u>sensible</u> <u>new</u>] will emerge from the meeting.*

ii *I don't want [an <u>expensive</u> <u>gold</u> watch] / *[anything <u>expensive</u> <u>gold</u>] for my anniversary.*

Else and *more*

The compound determinatives share with the determiner-heads *all*, *much*, and *little* the property of taking *else* or (in the case of those expressing existential quantification) *more* as immediate post-head dependent: *everything else*, *nothing else than a few scraps of bread*, *something more*, *anything more than that. Else* can precede a restrictor like those in [42]: *nothing else sensible*, *anything else gold.* This is not possible, however, if there is a *than* complement, in which case *other* is required instead of *else* and follows the restrictor: compare **nothing else sensible than this* and *nothing sensible other than this.*

Post-head modifiers

The compound determinatives take the same range of post-head modifiers as common nouns, for example PPs and relative clauses: *everything in the collection*, *something (that) you need to know*, and so on. These ordinary modifiers must follow any restrictor: *everything fashionable in the collection*, not **everything in the collection fashionable*, and so on. This ordering restriction departs from the general rule that from a syntactic point of view the ordering of post-head internal dependents is completely free (see §15).

[43] There are one or two nouns formed by conversion from compound determinatives: *He's [a <u>nobody</u>]*, *Would you care for [a little <u>something</u>]?*

Something of...

Something can indicate degree in combination with an *of* phrase complement:

[44] i *It was something of a surprise that he wasn't sacked on the spot.*
ii *She's something of an actor.*

The meaning is "It was to some extent a surprise", "She can to some extent be described as an actor".[44] This construction bears some resemblance to that found with *much* (cf. [18] above), but is not restricted to predicative complements: *Something of a problem has arisen.* Nor is it restricted to obliques determined by *a*: *She has something of her mother's charm and tenacity.*

Pre-head dependents

The compound determinatives take the same pre-head modifiers as the determinative bases they contain (see §11):

[45] i a. *[Not every] supervisor would agree.* b. *[Not everyone] would agree.*
ii a. *They did [hardly any] work.* b. *They did [hardly anything].*

Analysis as compound determinatives

These words are traditionally analysed as pronouns but are here assigned to the determinative category. They have it in common with pronouns that they always function as head in NP structure. The reason for nevertheless regarding them as determinatives at the primary level is that they take the same pre-head modifiers as ordinary determinatives, as illustrated in [45]. In the [a] examples, *not every* and *hardly any* are DPs functioning as determiner in NP structure; in the [b] examples *not everyone* and *hardly anything* are DPs functioning as determiner-head in NP structure. On this analysis *not everyone* and *hardly anything* can be handled in terms of constructions that are needed anyway for the DP rather than by setting up special NP constructions. Note also that while they share with pronouns, as we have noted, the property that they always function as head in NP structure, they differ from pronouns in that they freely take post-head modifiers, as illustrated above. Moreover, they differ semantically from the core pronouns in that they are not interpreted deictically or anaphorically.

9.7 Ellipsis of postmodifiers

The fused-head analysis makes it unnecessary to posit ellipsis of heads or pre-head dependents; the only cases of ellipsis in NP structure thus involve internal post-head dependents:

[46] i *You say she's [a friend of Bill's], but I think she's [a relation _].*
ii *[An article on this topic] is more likely to be accepted than [a book _].*

We understand "a relation of Bill's", "a book on this topic": the post-head dependents are ellipted to avoid repetition. The ellipsis involved here is of a quite general kind applicable to post-head constituents: compare *I sent my daughter to Paris, and Mary sent her son _.*

[44] A variant of *something* in this construction is *somewhat*: *It was somewhat of a problem. Somewhat* must therefore be admitted as a marginal member of the category of compound determinatives, but elsewhere it is a degree adverb, as in *It was somewhat difficult to understand.* In non-standard English *something* extends into this degree adverb territory: [!]*I loved her something rotten*, "terribly, greatly".

In *I use* [*a teaspoon* *of garlic powder*] *in this recipe, and Mary uses* [*a tablespoon* _] _, we have ellipsis of *of garlic powder* in NP structure, and of *in this recipe* in clause structure.

A special case of post-head ellipsis in the NP occurs in what we have been calling implicit partitives:

[47] i *I didn't see any of the movies, but Lucille saw* [*some* _].
ii *A great many people saw the play and* [*the majority* / *almost all* _] *enjoyed it.*

Here we have ellipsis of *of them*, with the antecedent for the partitive oblique being the underlined NP. In [i] there is a partitive PP in the preceding clause, but in [ii] there is not: the *of* is inherent in the partitive construction, and does not have to be recoverable from an antecedent. *Some* and *almost all* in these examples are fused determiner-heads, but *majority* is not: ellipsis of the *of* phrase is possible in either case.

10 Pronouns

Pronouns constitute a closed category of words whose most central members are characteristically used deictically or anaphorically.

[1] i *I love you.* [deictic pronouns]
ii *Tell Mary$_i$ I want to see her$_i$.* [anaphoric pronoun]

In [i] *I* and *you* are deictic in that they are interpreted in relation to certain features of the utterance-act: they refer to persons with the roles of speaker and addressee respectively. In the salient reading of [ii] *her* is anaphoric in that it derives its interpretation from the expression *Mary*, its antecedent: in this simple example the pronoun is coreferential with its antecedent. Syntactically, pronouns function as head in NP structure, and for that reason belong to the larger category of nouns. What distinguishes them from other nouns (common nouns and proper nouns) is that they permit a much narrower range of dependents. Usually they form full NPs by themselves, as in [1]. Most distinctively, they do not take determiners.

Precisely because of their close association with deixis and anaphora, detailed discussion of the meaning and use of pronouns is largely deferred until Ch. 17. Here we review fairly summarily the various subcategories of pronoun, and then take up the question of the syntactic difference between pronouns and other nouns.

10.1 Subcategories of pronoun

The category of pronouns recognised in this book is somewhat smaller than in traditional grammar since a number of our determinatives are traditionally analysed as pronouns when they occur in what we are calling the fused-head NP construction: this issue has been discussed in §9.5. On the other hand, we include in the pronoun category certain words such as *today* which are traditionally analysed as common nouns or adverbs. This gives, then, five main categories: personal, reciprocal, interrogative, relative, and temporal.

10.1.1 Personal pronouns

This is the largest category, and can usefully be subdivided into core and more peripheral members.

Core members

Personal pronouns are so called because they are the ones that are classified according to the deictic category of person. More specifically, this is the category that contains the 1st and 2nd person pronouns, associated with the speaker and addressee roles in the utterance-act. There are eight core members of the category, classified also for number and (in the 3rd person singular) gender. Each has up to five inflectional forms, as shown in [2]:

[2]

<table>
<tr><th rowspan="3">PERSON</th><th rowspan="3">NUMBER</th><th rowspan="3">GENDER</th><th colspan="4">Non-reflexive</th><th>Reflexive</th></tr>
<tr><th>nominative</th><th>accusative</th><th colspan="2">genitive</th><th>plain</th></tr>
<tr><th colspan="2">plain</th><th>dependent</th><th>independent</th><th></th></tr>
<tr><td>1st</td><td>sg</td><td></td><td>I</td><td>me</td><td>my</td><td>mine</td><td>myself</td></tr>
<tr><td>2nd</td><td>sg</td><td></td><td colspan="2">you</td><td>your</td><td>yours</td><td>yourself</td></tr>
<tr><td rowspan="3">3rd</td><td rowspan="3">sg</td><td>masculine</td><td>he</td><td>him</td><td colspan="2">his</td><td>himself</td></tr>
<tr><td>feminine</td><td>she</td><td>her</td><td>her</td><td>hers</td><td>herself</td></tr>
<tr><td>neuter</td><td colspan="2">it</td><td colspan="2">its</td><td>itself</td></tr>
<tr><td>1st</td><td>pl</td><td></td><td>we</td><td>us</td><td>our</td><td>ours</td><td>ourselves</td></tr>
<tr><td>2nd</td><td>pl</td><td></td><td colspan="2">you</td><td>your</td><td>yours</td><td>yourselves</td></tr>
<tr><td>3rd</td><td>pl</td><td></td><td>they</td><td>them</td><td>their</td><td>theirs</td><td>themselves</td></tr>
</table>

The inflectional forms divide first into reflexive and non-reflexive categories. Reflexives are primarily used when there is a close structural relation between the pronoun and an overt or covert antecedent: typically, the antecedent is subject of the clause containing the pronoun. Compare, then, *Ed hurt himself* (antecedent as subject) and *She had pushed Ed away but hadn't intended to hurt him* (antecedent in different clause). Reflexives have only a plain case-form. There are thus no genitive reflexives: *Ed has left his/*himself's umbrella behind.* The non-reflexives do have a genitive vs non-genitive case distinction. In the non-genitive most distinguish nominative vs accusative (a contrast otherwise found only in interrogative/relative ***who***); ***you*** (singular and plural) and ***it***, however, have only a plain form. In the genitive all except ***he*** and ***it*** exhibit a distinction between dependent and independent forms that is found only in personal pronouns and the determinative ***no***. The system of case is described in §16.

Singular *they*

They is commonly used with a singular antecedent, as in *Someone has left their umbrella behind.* As such, it fills a gap in the gender system of the core personal pronouns by virtue of being neutral as to sex. For some speakers singular ***they*** has a distinct reflexive form *themself*: %*Someone has locked themself in the attic.*[45] For discussion of singular ***they***, see the section on gender, §17.2.4.

Pronoun *one*

The pronoun ***one*** belongs with the personal pronouns on two counts, as illustrated in:

[3]	i	*One shouldn't take oneself too seriously.*	[reflexive form]
	ii	*One can't be too careful in these matters, can one?*	[subject of tag]

In the first place it has (in addition to plain *one* and genitive *one's*) a reflexive form *oneself*: reflexive forms are not found outside the personal pronoun system. In the second place,

[45] There is also a singular ***we*** with *ourself* as reflexive form. This is an honorific pronoun used by monarchs, popes, and the like: it is hardly current in Present-day English.

it can function as subject of interrogative tags, again a distinctive property of personal pronouns (see Ch. 10, §5.1).

One differs from the core 3rd person personal pronouns in that it cannot be used as an anaphor to another NP: **A politician shouldn't take oneself too seriously.* Indeed, for some speakers (primarily AmE) *one* can itself be the antecedent for a personal pronoun anaphor:

[4] i *%What is one to do when he is treated like this?*
 ii *%One should do their best to ensure that such disputes are resolved amicably.*

Examples like [i] are now less common than they used to be, in line with the general decline in the use of the purportedly sex-neutral ***he***. Type [ii] is quite rare: singular ***they*** is not well established as anaphor to *one*.

As evident from these examples, ***one*** is neutral as to sex, but that is not the most significant respect in which it differs from the 3rd person singular pronouns in [2] (and hence it could not be fitted into that system as a fourth gender). For most speakers ***one*** is used only non-referentially – in talking about people generally rather than in reference to a particular individual. It is in competition with the non-referential use of ***you***, as in *What are you to do when you are treated like this?*, and so on. ***One*** belongs to a more formal style than ***you***, and of course makes clear that there is no reference to the addressee in particular (as there could be in *You shouldn't take yourself too seriously*). There are speakers, however, who in certain contexts use ***one*** instead of ***I*** to refer to themselves: *%One suddenly realised that one was being followed.* This usage is associated with upper-class BrE – and is regarded by many other speakers as pretentious.

Dummy *there*

[5] i *There is an obvious solution to this problem, isn't there?*
 ii *I believe there to be no obvious solution to this problem.*

Historically *there* is a locative preposition (an adverb in traditional accounts), but it came to be used in various constructions where it is bleached of all locative meaning and has been reanalysed as a pronoun. These constructions fall in the information-packaging area, and are described in Ch. 16, §6. It occurs only in subject function except in the complex catenative construction shown in [ii], where it is a raised object. It has only a plain case-form.

As a pronoun *there* can best be regarded as a peripheral member of the personal pronoun category. It has the distinctive personal pronoun property of being able to occur as subject in an interrogative tag, as in [5i]. And it is comparable with the other dummy pronoun, ***it***, a core member of the category.

Universal personal pronouns of the type *us all*

		a.	b.
[6]	i	a. *They've invited us all.*	b. *It's an insult to us both.*
	ii	a. *She likes you all.*	b. *I'm counting on you both to help.*
	iii	a. *This applies to them all.*	b. *I expect them both to take part.*

Here we take *all* and *both* to be incorporated into a compound pronoun. These forms are to be distinguished from the sequences found in the much more general construction seen in:

[7] i a. *We all/both enjoyed it.* b. *We had all/both enjoyed it.*
ii a. *You each qualify for a prize.* b. *You will each qualify for a prize.*
iii a. *They all five of them complained.* b. *They are all five of them complaining.*

In this construction the underlined expressions are quantificational adjuncts functioning in clause structure. This is evident from the fact that when the verb is an auxiliary they preferentially follow rather than precede it, as in the [b] examples. Note also the possibility of inserting an adjunct after the pronoun and before the quantificational adjunct in [a]: *We certainly all/both enjoyed it.* No such insertions are permitted in [6]: **She likes you certainly all.* A further important difference is that in the adjunct construction the pronoun can be replaced by NPs with common noun heads: *The girls all/both enjoyed it.* Again, such replacements are quite impossible in [6]: **They've invited the girls all.*

The adjuncts in [7] have the form of fused-head NPs. As the examples show, the pattern extends beyond *all* and *both*, covering *each* and partitives that are excluded from [6]: **It's an insult to us each*, **This applies to them all five of them.* The combinations in [6] are thus not predictable by any general rule, and are best regarded as compound forms; they are limited to the six accusative forms cited.

10.1.2 Reciprocal pronouns

There are two reciprocal pronouns, *each other* and *one another*, with no semantic contrast between them:

[8] i *The children gave each other / one another a present.*
ii *Kim and Pat met each other's / one another's parents only four years later.*

Like the universal personal pronouns, the reciprocals are written as two orthographic words but are single grammatical words. They bear some resemblance to the reflexive forms of personal pronouns in that they are anaphorically linked to an overt or covert antecedent that must be relatively close. Compare, for example, [8], where the antecedent is subject of the clause containing the reciprocal, with the ungrammatical **The children thought that I should give each other a present*, where the antecedent is separated from the anaphor by the subject of the lower clause. The reciprocals differ from the reflexives in that they have genitive forms, as in [8ii]. And of course they do not exhibit contrast of person (*We/You/They underestimated each other*): it is for this reason that they fall outside the system of personal pronouns. The reciprocals are discussed in detail in Ch. 17, §4.

10.1.3 Interrogative and relative pronouns

Interrogative and relative constructions make a gender distinction within the pronouns between personal (***who***) and non-personal (*what* or ***which***). Leaving aside the compounds in ·*ever*, the forms are as follows:

[9]

	NON-PERSONAL		PERSONAL		
	Plain	Genitive	Nominative	Accusative	Genitive
INTERROGATIVE / FUSED RELATIVE	*what*	–	*who*	*whom*	*whose*
OTHER RELATIVE	*which*	*whose*	*who*	*whom*	*whose*

Note that interrogative and fused relative *which* is a determinative, not a pronoun (and hence is not included in [9]). Personal ***who*** is usually human, but can also be non-human animate: see §17.3. Examples illustrating the non-personal vs personal distinction are given in:

[10]		NON-PERSONAL	PERSONAL
i	INTERROGATIVE	*What did he want?*	*Who did you see?*
ii	FUSED RELATIVE	*Take [what you want].*	*Marry [who you want].*
iii	OTHER RELATIVE	*the car [which came first]*	*the boy [who came first]*

Fused relative ***who*** is virtually restricted to the free-choice construction illustrated here: compare *[*Who said that*] *was wrong.*

In addition to the above forms, there are compounds in *·ever*, which are found only in fused relatives ([*Whoever said that*] *was wrong*) and in the exceptional interrogative construction that functions as exhaustive conditional adjunct (*I shan't be attending the meeting,* [*whoever takes over as chair*]). These interrogative and relative pronouns are discussed more fully in the chapters that deal with the interrogative and relative constructions in general: see Ch. 10, §7, and Ch. 12, §§3.5.1–2, 6.4.

10.1.4 Deictic temporal pronouns

Yesterday, *today*, *tonight*, and *tomorrow* are not traditionally analysed as pronouns, but belong in this subclass of nouns by virtue of their inability to take determiners. Compare, for example, *Today* / **The today is my birthday.* They are also semantically like the central pronouns ***I*** and ***you*** in that they are characteristically used deictically. Unlike the temporal prepositions *now* and *then*, the pronouns have genitive forms: *today's*, etc. For further discussion of their syntactic analysis, see Ch. 6, §5.1.

10.2 The structure of NPs with pronouns as head

Pronouns usually constitute whole NPs by themselves, but some allow a very limited range of modifiers, such as the integrated relative clause in *you who worked on both the projects*.

Pronouns do not permit determiners

A defining property of pronouns in English is that they do not permit determiners: **the they*, **some you*, **our each other*.[46] Items traditionally analysed as pronouns but excluded from the pronoun category because they can take determiners include echo ***what*** and the pro-nominals ***one*** and ***other***:

[11]			[common nouns, not pronouns]
i	A: *I bought a new car.*	B: *You bought a what?*	
ii	A: *Which operas do you like?*	B: *The ones by Mozart.*	
iii	A: *Which books do I need?*	B: *The three others.*	

Echo ***what*** is syntactically very different from the interrogative pronoun *what*. It can replace words of more or less any category, and can take on the inflectional properties of that category – cf. *You bought three whats?* or even *They had whatted the car?* Pro-nominal ***one*** and ***other*** are likewise very different from such pronouns as ***it*** and ***they***. As

[46] In examples like *Is it a he or a she?* the forms *he* and *she* are common nouns, not pronouns. The meaning and the syntax are clearly different from those of the pronouns.

the examples show, they inflect for number, and in the structure of the NP they take the same range of dependents as ordinary common nouns.

Pre-head internal dependents normally excluded too

Pronouns do not normally allow internal pre-head dependents: **Extravagant he bought a new car*; **I met interesting them all*. The qualification 'normally' caters for one minor exception, the use of a few adjectives such as *lucky, poor, silly* with the core personal pronouns:

[12] i *Lucky you! No one noticed you had gone home early.*
ii *They decided it would have to be done by poor old me.*

The adjective is semantically non-restrictive, and the NP characteristically stands alone as an exclamation, as in [i]. It can be integrated into clause structure, as in [ii], but not as subject (**Poor you have got the night shift again*). The pronoun must be in accusative or plain case (compare *Silly me!* and **Silly I!*).

Post-head dependents

A very limited range of post-head modifiers are found.

(a) Interrogative and fused relative pronouns

Interrogatives take *else* and emotive modifiers such as *on earth, the hell*: *What else do you need?*; *Who on earth could have done this?* Interrogative and fused relative pronouns allow PPs: *Who in Paris would wear a hat like that?*; *Whatever in the report was written by Harry was simply ignored.* They can also serve as antecedent for integrated relative clauses, but these occur in delayed position and hence do not form part of the NP itself:

[13] i *Who do you know who would wear a hat like that?*
ii *Whatever they have that has a Paris label is bound to fetch a higher price.*

(b) Personal pronouns

Personal pronouns with human denotation may be modified by integrated relative clauses:

[14] i *I/We who have read the report know that the allegations are quite unfounded.*
ii *He who controls testosterone controls the sexual universe.*

The 3rd person use is archaic, characteristic of proverbs (*He who laughs last laughs longest*) or new forms modelled on the proverbial use, as in [ii]: the pronoun is used non-referentially. In Present-day English this type of meaning would usually be expressed in a construction with *those* as fused determiner-head: *Those who control testosterone control the sexual universe.*

External modifiers

Peripheral modifiers combine with NPs, and a number are largely indifferent as to the internal structure of the NP. In particular, certain focusing modifiers combine readily with personal pronouns and to a lesser extent with reciprocals: *I love* [*only you*]; *Let's invite* [*just them*]; *They criticise* [*even each other*].

Predeterminer modifiers are more sensitive to the structure of the head NP, and are virtually incompatible with pronouns. The one exception is that *all* combines with the 1st and 2nd person plural pronouns provided they are modified by a relative clause or PP, *all we who have signed up for the course*; *all you in the front*.

11 Determinative Phrases

Most of the determinatives that are semantically quantifiers optionally take dependents, thus forming phrase-level constituents, DPs. Some of the expressions that function as dependents in DP structure can also be peripheral modifiers in NP structure (see §13):

[1]	MODIFIER IN DP	MODIFIER IN NP
i	a. [*Not many*] *people saw her leave.*	b. [*Not a single person*] *saw her leave.*
ii	a. [*Almost all*] *copies were lost.*	b. [*Almost the whole batch*] *was lost.*
iii	a. [*At least ten*] *people were killed.*	b. [*At least an hour*] *was wasted.*

In the [a] examples the underlined expression modifies the immediately following word, forming a phrase which is a dependent of the head noun, whereas in the [b] examples it modifies the following phrase, an NP. It is not always as easy as in these examples, however, to determine which is the appropriate structure to assign.

We review in this section the various syntactic and semantic types of dependent found in DP structure. The DPs are enclosed in brackets with the heads underlined.

(a) The absolute negation marker *not*

Not occurs most readily with *many* (as in [1ia]), *much*, *all*, *every*, and *enough*. It is also permitted with *sufficient*, *a few*, and *a little*, but not (as a DP-level modifier) with *both*, *each*, *few*, *little*, *some*, and at best only marginally with *any* (cf. Ch. 9, §3.1). *Not* can occur before singulative *one* (*Not one computer was working*) and, under quite restrictive conditions, with cardinal numerals in general (*Not three miles from where they live is a most beautiful lake*), but these are cases where it may be better to treat *not* as a peripheral modifier in NP structure, as in [1ib].

(b) Approximation and precision

[2] i *The platoon contained* [*approximately twenty*] *soldiers.*
ii [*Almost no*] *seats were taken.*
iii *We have* [*exactly/hardly enough*] *fuel to get us home.*

Such adverbs as *approximately*, *roughly*, *about*, *almost*, *nearly*, *practically*, *exactly*, *just*, *precisely*, and the idioms *nigh on* ("almost"), *spot on* ("exactly") occur with numerals, and some of them with *all*, *every*, *any*$_{\text{f}}$, *no*, *enough*, *sufficient*. *All of* probably belongs here too, as used in examples like *They had recruited* [*all of fifty*] *volunteers*. The approximate negators *hardly*, *barely*, *scarcely* can modify *any*$_{\text{n}}$, *enough*, *sufficient*, and numerals ([*Barely twenty*] *people attended the meeting*). The adverb *some* expresses approximation only with numerals, as in [*some thirty*] *students*.[47]

(c) Degree

The degree determinatives ***many***, ***much***, ***few***, and ***little*** are the ones that are most like adjectives, and in particular they take a very similar range of degree modifiers to gradable adjectives, including *very*, *so*, *too*, *how*, *this*, *that*, *amazingly*, *distressingly*, and the like (but not *slightly*, and others of this kind):

[3] i *He hasn't* [*very much*] *patience.*
ii *They gave us* [*too little*] *time for discussion.*

[47] Approximation is also expressed by certain grammatically distinct constructions, as in [*thirty or so*] *students* (coordination) or [*thirty-odd*] *students* (affixation).

Adverbs denoting degrees of completeness such as *fully, totally, completely, marginally,* and *partially* can modify the sufficiency quantifiers *enough* and *sufficient. Fully* can also modify numerals, while *absolutely* occurs with universal *all* and *every* and negative *no*:

[4] i *We have [marginally enough] material to finish the job.*
ii *There are [fully twenty] unanswered letters in your in-tray.*
iii *[Absolutely all] his friends had deserted him.*

(d) Comparison

The comparative forms of the degree determinatives, *more, less,* and *fewer* take PP complements with the form *than* + quantifier (usually a numeral), and pre-head modifiers realised by a quantificational determinative (numeral, *many, much, some, a few, no,* etc.), adverb (*considerably*), or NP (*a lot,* etc.):

[5] i *[More / Less / Fewer than twenty] people came to the meeting.*[48]
ii *[Considerably / A lot more than fifty] protesters were arrested.*
iii *You can have [no / a little more] money.*

The *than* phrase can occur later (so that it is no longer part of the DP): *more people than twenty.* Where the complement of *than* is non-quantificational this is the only option: *more people than expected,* but not **more than expected people.* In [iii] the salient interpretation of *more* is "further, additional", but a *than* phrase (explicit or implicit) generally requires the strict comparative interpretation of "greater amount". Complications arise where *one* occurs as complement of *than* or as pre-head modifier:

[6] i *[More than one] glass was broken.*
ii *[One more] application has been received (than we had expected).*

The presence of *one* selects a singular head noun (*glass, application*), even though *one* is not head of the DP. In [i] this results in a clear discrepancy between form and meaning: *more than one glass* is syntactically singular but denotes a plurality of glasses. In [ii] we have the same discrepancy in the version with the *than* phrase: leaving aside the unlikely scenario where we had expected zero applications, the interpretation is that a plurality of applications have been received. However, without the *than* phrase and with *more* interpreted as "additional" the clause reports the receipt of a single application, but with the implicature that at least one other had been received earlier.[49]

(e) Upper and lower bound

[7] i *We have [at least enough] fuel to get to Woking.*
ii *[At the very most twenty] people will agree to help.*

The PPs *at most* and *at least* (together with the fuller forms with *the very*) mark the upper and lower bounds ("no more than", "no less than"). They occur mainly with numerals, *some, a few, a little, enough,* and *sufficient. Several* accepts *at least* but hardly *at most.*

[48] A variant of *more than* that is sometimes found is *greater than,* as in *It reserves the right to treat any Application in the Public Offer for greater than 20,000 Sale Shares as an Application in the Institutional Offer.* Since *greater* is an adjective, however, we need to treat *20,000* as head of the DP: this is another case where a comparative expression (*greater than*) has been reanalysed to function as an adverbial modifier (cf. Ch. 13, §4.5).

[49] Note that a singular is not permitted with *no*: *no more applications,* not (as a count singular) **no more application,* even though we can have singular *no application.* This, together with the fact that in the fused-head construction we have the dependent form *no,* not independent *none* (*No/*None more have been received*) argues that *more* is head of the construction.

(f) PPs: condition, exception, proportion, and addition/subtraction

[8] i [*Few*, *if any*,] *guests will arrive on time.*
ii [*All but/except a few*] *helicopters have crashed.*
iii [*One in ten*] *students take drugs.*
iv *There's room for* [*ninety thousand minus a few hundred*] *spectators.*

Here we have PPs in post-head modifier function. There are alternants in which the PP is delayed, so that it is not a constituent of the DP: *Few guests, if any, will arrive on time*; *All helicopters but/except a few have crashed*; *One student in ten takes drugs*; *There's room for ninety thousand spectators minus a few hundred.* With numerals there is also a PP expressing totality, as in [*Thirty-five in all*] *supporters were arrested after the game*, but this is strongly disfavoured relative to the version with delayed PP (*Thirty-five supporters in all were arrested after the game*).

The conditional type serves to cancel implicatures, as described in §5.2. The exception construction is found only with *all*: with *every*, *no*, *any* the PP can only occur after the head noun, as in *Every helicopter but one has crashed.*

PPs in lieu of DPs

The same kind of meaning as we find in a number of the above DP constructions can also be expressed by the PPs given in [6] of §4, such as [*around ten thousand*] *copies*, [*between fifty and sixty*] *tanks*, [*from ten to fifteen*] *judges*, etc. It is clear that in the last two there can be no question of treating the numerals as head: *between* takes a coordination as complement, while *from* takes two complements, a numeral and a *to* PP. We need therefore to recognise that a restricted range of PPs can function as determiner – just as a restricted range can function as subject in clause structure, as in *From London to Manchester is 180 miles* or *Under the mat is a silly place to hide a key.*

12 **Predeterminer modifiers**

Predeterminer modifiers, or predeterminers, are one type of external modifier, i.e. they enter into construction with an NP, not a nominal, as explained in §2. There are four subtypes, illustrated in:

[1] i *She had lost* [*all her money*]. [universal quantifier]
ii *He had eaten* [*half a bar of chocolate*]. [fraction]
iii *They wanted to charge us* [*twice the amount they had quoted*]. [multiplier]
iv [*How serious a problem*] *is it?* [adjectival]

The first three express various kinds of quantification, while the adjectival type is restricted to occurrence before the indefinite article *a*. As implied by their name, the NP they modify generally contains a determiner. There are two very restricted cases, however, where the NP has a pronoun as head: *all* can occur as external modifier to an NP headed by ***we*** or *you* provided there is a following modifier (*all you who were present at the meeting*), and fractions and multipliers can combine with a fused relative construction (*I sold it for half/twice what I had paid*).

(a) Universal quantifiers

[2] i *all the books/sugar/morning*, *all these books*, *all that work*, *all Kim's friends*
ii *both the houses*, *both these animals*, *both those cups*, *both my parents*

All and *both* occur before the definite determiners: the definite article, the demonstratives, and genitives.[50] For further discussion of these constructions, see §7.3.

When *all* occurs immediately before a cardinal numeral, as in *all three proposals*, we take *all* to be the determiner and the cardinal numeral an internal modifier. *All three proposals*, unlike *three proposals*, is definite (I assume you can identify them), so it is *all* that is the marker of definiteness, and we have seen that the definiteness of an NP depends on the determiner. Note, moreover, that the relation of *all three proposals* to *all the three proposals* is the same as that of *all proposals* to *all the proposals*: in each pair *all* is determiner in the version without *the* and predeterminer in the one with *the*.

(b) Fractions

[3] i *John had already wasted [half his share of the legacy].*
ii *He had to sell his shares for [exactly one half the amount he paid for them].*
iii *It only took [a quarter / one third / two fifths the time I thought it would].*

Predeterminers expressing fractions have the form of NPs. *Half, quarter, third*, etc., are nouns, as is evident from the fact that they take determiners (cardinal numerals or the indefinite article *a*) and inflect for number (as in *fifths* in [iii] – cf. also *three quarters, two thirds*). There is an alternative construction in which the fractional noun functions as head of the topmost NP, with a following partitive complement: *half of his share . . .*, *exactly one half of the amount . . .*, *a quarter of the time . . .*, etc.

Half behaves somewhat differently from the other fractional nouns. In the first place, it can occur without a determiner, as in [i]. Secondly, it cannot take the plural form in the predeterminer construction, though the anomaly of #*two/both halves the amount* is paralleled by that of # *three thirds the amount*.[51] Thirdly, it occurs with a much wider range of NP heads than the others. All can occur with abstract nouns such as *amount, time, size, height* with a definite determiner, but in the predeterminer construction concrete nouns accept only *half*, and then without any determiner before it: *half the cake* but not **a half/third the cake* (instead we have partitive *a half/third of the cake*). Similarly, only undetermined *half* can occur before indefinite *a*: *half a day*, but not **one half/third a day*.

(c) Multipliers

[4] i *She earns [two/three/four times the salary I earn].*
ii *Kim won $10,000, but Pat won [twice/thrice that].*
iii *We've had [double/triple/quadruple the number of applications I had expected].*

Forms consisting of cardinal numeral + *times*, as in [i], are clearly NPs. *Twice* and the archaic *thrice* in [ii] are adverbs, occurring elsewhere as frequency adjuncts, like the *times* NPs: *I saw her twice / three times*. The category status of *double, triple*, and the quite rare *quadruple* is somewhat unclear: we take them to be nouns on the basis of their occurrence in the expressions *in doubles/triples*; they also occur as internal modifier, where they are probably to be analysed as adjectives (*double/triple glazing*). Multipliers occur only with definite NPs, and there is no corresponding partitive construction (**double of my salary*).

[50] One further, somewhat marginal, possibility is for *all* to occur before interrogative *which* in a certain very restricted type of context. Suppose I say *I've read all the books*, assuming you can identify the set concerned (all the books on some reading list, perhaps), when in fact you can't (there may be two reading lists): you could then ask *All which books?*, with the aim of eliciting identifying information about the set.

[51] The plural is possible, however, in the partitive construction: *both halves of the apple*. This indicates that the two constructions are not absolutely equivalent: the partitive allows ***half*** to be interpreted in a more physical sense as "half-portion".

(d) Adjectival predeterminers

A very limited range of adjectives and AdjPs occur before the indefinite article. Three types can be distinguished.

Such and exclamative *what*

[5] EXTERNAL MODIFIER / INTERNAL MODIFIER

i a. *It was [such a disaster].* b. *She had shown [such promise].*

ii a. *[What a disaster] it was!* b. *[What promise] she had shown!*

The adjectives *such* and exclamative *what* occur as external rather than internal modifier in construction with *a*: compare **a such/what disaster*. In non-count or plural NPs, as in the [b] examples, they are in internal position: there is no determiner here and no reason to say that the adjective is in predeterminer position. *Such* differs from *what* in that it can follow certain determiners other than *a*: *one such device, all/several/many such problems* (and indeed it can follow *a* if there is another adjective intervening, as in *a further such error*). In this latter construction, however, it has only the "kind" sense ("one device of this kind", etc.), whereas in initial position it can be a matter of either kind (*such a person, such letters*) or degree (as in the examples of [i]).[52]

AdjPs introduced by the degree modifiers *as, so, how, too, this,* and *that*

[6] i a. *It's [as fine a show as I've seen].* b. **They're [as fine shows as I've seen].*

ii a. *It's [so good a bargain I can't resist buying it].* b. **They're [so good bargains I can't resist buying them].*

iii a. *[How serious a problem] is it?* b. **[How serious problems] are they?*

AdjPs of this form can function as pre-head modifier only in external position, before *a*. Their distribution is thus more restricted than that of *such* and *what* above. Note, for example, that while *such a good bargain* is equivalent to *so good a bargain*, the plural *such good bargains* has no counterpart **so good bargains*, as seen in [iib]. For further discussion, see Ch. 6, §3.3.

The degree adverb or determinative need not be modifying the adjective itself: it may be part of an AdvP modifying the adjective, as in *It was so blatantly biased a report that no one took any notice of it.* The restriction to NPs determined by *a* does not apply to AdjPs in post-head internal modifier function: *He had a nose so long he reminded me of Pinocchio*; *He had hair so long that it reached down to his knees.*

AdjPs introduced by the degree adverbs *more* and *less*

[7] a. *This is [more serious a problem than the other].* b. *This is [a more serious problem than the other].*

With AdjPs of this form, there is alternation between the external position [a] and the internal [b]. Again, the external position is available only in combination with *a* – compare the bare NP *These are [more serious problems than the others]*. Note also that inflectional comparatives are restricted to internal position: *Kim is a better player than Pat*, not **Kim is better a player than Pat.*

[52] There is a minor use of *such* found primarily in legal register where it is a determinative rather than an adjective: *Completion of the transactions will take place on 21 December 1999 or [such other date as the parties may agree].* The NP here is count singular, so *such* (meaning roughly "any") must be in determiner function.

Combinations of predeterminers

It is possible, though rare, for a predeterminer to modify an NP which itself contains a predeterminer of a different kind:

[8] i *Even if I had [double all the money he has], I wouldn't be able to afford that house.* [multiplier + univ quantifier]
ii *Give me [even three times one thousandth the amount you win on the lottery], and I will be very happy.* [multiplier + fraction]
iii *If I had [even half such a brain as you do], I'd be prime minister by now.* [fraction + adjective]

13 Peripheral modifiers

This section is concerned with those external modifiers occurring at the periphery of the NP, mainly in initial position (before any predeterminer) but in a few cases in final position.

Almost all the semantic types involved are found with the same kind of meaning in other constructions, especially clauses and AdjPs or AdvPs. Indeed, it is not always evident from the linear position of an adverb whether it is functioning in the structure of a clause or of an NP. Consider, for example:

[1] *Possibly (,) the best actress in the world will take the role of Emma.*

Here the modal adverb *possibly* can have scope over the clause or over the subject NP. In the former case (where the adverb would most likely be followed by a comma) the interpretation is "It is possibly the case that the best actress in the world will take the role of Emma"; in the latter case (which does not admit a comma) we understand "The person who is possibly the best actress in the world will take the role of Emma". The difference can be brought out syntactically by passivisation:

[2] i *Possibly, the role of Emma will be taken by [the best actress in the world].*
ii *The role of Emma will be taken by [possibly the best actress in the world].*

The position of the clause-level adjunct remains constant when we passivise, but that of the NP-level peripheral modifier does not, for it is a constituent of the NP whose function changes from subject to complement of *by*. These examples are structurally unambiguous: in [i] *possibly* can only belong in the clause, while in [ii] it immediately follows a preposition and hence must belong in the NP.

We review briefly in turn six semantic categories of peripheral modifier.

(a) Focusing modifiers

[3] i *[Only the corner of the painting] had been damaged.*
ii *[Jill alone] has the authority to sign cheques.*
iii *He wasn't familiar with [even the broad outlines of the proposal].*
iv *We specialise in [principally the following three areas].*
v *[The bottom drawer too] needs some attention.*

Focusing modifiers attach to phrases of almost all categories, and are discussed further in Ch. 6, §7.3.

(b) Scaling modifiers

[4] i *We were faced by* [*easily the worst situation we had ever seen*].
ii *Kim had come to* [*almost the same conclusion as us*].
iii *After* [*hardly a moment's hesitation*] *he agreed to all their demands.*
iv [*Not the least of my worries*] *is that my hearing is deteriorating.*
v *I'd asked him not to make a fuss, but he was doing* [*exactly that*].

These have it in common that they are permitted with only a restricted range of NPs – compare, for example, **We were faced by easily a disaster* or **Not the problem is that my hearing is deteriorating.* The sanctioning element typically has to do with some scalar property. All of them have analogues in the structure of DPs, as described in §11 above; they have some affinity with the category of degree adjuncts in clause structure (Ch. 8, §11), but cover a rather broader range of semantic territory. Various subtypes can be recognised, as illustrated in [i–v] respectively.

Reinforcement: *absolutely, altogether, entirely, fully, quite, much, by far, easily*
All of these items can modify superlatives, as in [4i], but the last two are restricted to this construction, whereas the others are found also with such adjectives as *same* and *wrong*: *quite* / **by far the wrong job, entirely*/**easily the same conclusion.*

Approximation: *almost, nearly, practically, virtually, essentially, quite, much, rather*
These modify superlatives, like the reinforcement modifiers, but in addition occur more readily than the latter with indefinite NPs: *rather*/ **absolutely a good idea. Quite* and *much* have both reinforcement and approximation uses: compare *quite the worst response* (reinforcement: "absolutely") and *quite a good idea* (approximation: "fairly good"); *much the best solution* (reinforcement: "by far") and *much the same size* (approximation: "virtually"). *Nearly* and *much* can themselves be modified by *very*: *They had chosen very nearly*/*much the same material.* This type also includes a number of idioms or fixed phrases: *all but, more or less, to all intents and purposes,* informal *as good as.*

Negative approximation: *hardly, barely, scarcely*
These indicate approximation to the negative end of the scale; see Ch. 9, §3.3.

Absolute negation: *not*
As a peripheral modifier in NP structure, *not* is found with superlatives, as in [4iv], and in various forms of quantification: *Not a single complaint had been received*; *Not a soul had noticed her plight.* It also occurs in coordinative constructions: *They had chosen* [*not Paris*] *but Rheims as the venue for the conference* (Ch. 15, §2.6).

Precision: *exactly, precisely*
These are found with such adjectives as *right* and *wrong* (*exactly the right answer*); with abstract nouns like *way, height* (*He responded in* [*precisely the way I expected*]); with demonstratives, as in [4v]; interrogative and relative *what*, etc. (*I did* [*exactly what you asked me to*]). In certain cases they can occur in post-head position: *It lasts* [*ten minutes exactly*]; [*What precisely*] *do you want?*

(c) Frequency, domain, modal, and evaluative modifiers

Modifiers of these types characteristically function in clause structure (see Ch. 8, §§9, 15–17), but they are also found in NP structure, as in:

[5] i *With [invariably the most unconvincing explanations], he would attempt to excuse his erratic behaviour.*
ii *I'd rate this as [architecturally the most impressive building in the city].*
iii *After [possibly the worst performance of his career], he was booed off the stage.*
iv *With [unfortunately very limited qualifications], he has little prospect of getting a job.*

Such adverbs as *invariably* in [i], and also *always, consistently, repeatedly, usually,* occur with heads denoting events or results. Domain modifiers are realised by adverbs such as *architecturally, politically, economically, socially,* or corresponding PPs of the form *from a political point of view,* etc. Modal modifiers (*possibly, probably, surely, definitely,* etc.) and evaluative modifiers (*unfortunately, happily, sadly, regrettably,* etc.) comment on properties expressed in the NP: "It is possible that this was the worst performance of his career", "It is unfortunate that his qualifications are very limited".

(d) Quantifying modifiers in predicatives

[6] i *She is [every inch a philosopher].*
ii *The sweater is [all wool].*

These modifiers occur in NPs functioning as predicative complement: we can't say **The proposal was made by every inch a philosopher,* and the *all wool* of [ii] is understood quite differently from that in *All wool is imported,* where *all* is determiner. Other such modifiers include *wholly, exclusively, half.*

(e) Reflexive pronouns

[7] *[The manager herself] had approved the proposal.*

In this construction an NP with the form of a reflexive pronoun functions as post-head modifier within a larger NP; it is an external rather than internal modifier in that the immediate constituents of the matrix NP are *the manager + herself* (not *the + manager herself*). Where, as in this example, the matrix NP is subject, there is an alternative construction with the reflexive as a clause-level adjunct: *The manager had approved the proposal herself.* See Ch. 17, §3.2, for further discussion.

(f) Combinations

An NP may contain more than one peripheral modifier, with multiple layers of embedding:

[8] i *Make sure you invite [Jill herself too].*
ii *[Even merely a formal apology] would be acceptable.*
iii *After [financially certainly the worst crisis this decade], the emerging economies will take some time to recover.*

The bracketed NP in [i] has the NP *Jill herself* as head and the adverb *too* as peripheral modifier; at the next level, the NP *Jill* is head and the NP *herself* is peripheral modifier. A peripheral modifier is thus in peripheral position (initial or final) in the NP of which it is an immediate constituent, but need not be in peripheral position in a larger NP containing it.

14 Internal dependents

Internal dependents of the head noun are dependents contained within the nominal constituent. They therefore follow the determiner (if there is one) and any other pre-head external dependents. Internal dependents can be distinguished in terms of position as **pre-head** or **post-head**. In terms of function we distinguish **complements** and **modifiers**.

[1]	PRE-HEAD	POST-HEAD	
i	a. *a* [*linguistics student*]	b. *a* [*report on the crash*]	[complement]
ii	a. *a* [*first-year student*]	b. *a* [*report in the paper*]	[modifier]

Adjectives in pre-head position, as in *a brilliant student*, are traditionally called **attributive**, and we will generalise this term to all pre-head internal dependents. One special case of the post-head modifier is the integrated appositive, as in *the poet Wordsworth*; we will deal with appositives separately, in §14.3.

14.1 Complements

Categories of complement

Pre-head complements are usually realised by nominals, but a small number of adjectives can also function as complements:

[2]			
i	a. *a flower seller*	b. *an income tax adviser*	[nominal]
ii	a. *a legal adviser*	b. *an ecological expert*	[adjective]

Post-head complements have the form of PPs or clauses:

[3]		
i	*the journey to Rome / back*	[PP]
ii	*the rumour that the city had been captured*	[declarative content clause]
iii	*the question whether they were guilty*	[interrogative content clause]
iv	*the question 'Is God dead?'*	[main clause]
v	*the decision to abandon the project*	[*to*-infinitival clause]

Clauses in complement function are usually subordinate, but main clauses are found in direct reported speech or citation, as in [iv]. Nouns, unlike verbs, do not permit objects and hence do not normally take NPs as complement – NPs occur as oblique complements, related to the head by a preposition; compare, for example, the clause *They destroyed the city* with the NP *their destruction of the city*.[53]

Complements vs modifiers

The distinction between these two kinds of dependent is essentially the same as in clause structure, but in the NP they are not as clearly differentiated syntactically. Note in particular that while complements of a verb are not infrequently recognisable as such by

[53] A minor exception is found in examples like [*The journey this way*] *is less hazardous*. A comparable clause construction is *Let's go this way*, where the NP is a locative complement, not an object.

virtue of being obligatory, the contrast between obligatory and optional elements is of virtually no relevance to distinguishing complements from modifiers in NP structure. Compare, for example the verb *peruse* and the noun *perusal*. The former requires an object (*Jill perused the documents*, but not **Jill perused*), but the noun can be found quite naturally without a complement: *After a quick perusal, Jill pushed the documents to one side*. The one exception is the noun *denizen*, which requires a complement: *They are denizens of the forest* but not **They are denizens*.[54]

We consider in turn the other syntactic and semantic criteria presented in Ch. 4, §1.2.

(a) Complements must be licensed by the head noun

The licensing criterion is the most basic criterion for complement status of post-head dependents. In the case of subordinate clauses the choice between the types illustrated in [3] depends on the noun: compare *the fact that he was ill* with **the fact whether he was ill* and **the fact for him to be ill*, and so on. With PP complements the head noun determines the choice of preposition or the range of permitted choices. The default preposition is *of*, and this is often the only possibility, as in *the King of France*. Nouns like *report* and *injury* permit either default *of* or a more specific preposition (*a report on/of the crash, an injury to/of the wrist*), but subtle differences in meaning are involved. A report **on** the crash is likely to be the result of a detailed investigation into its causes, whereas a report **of** the crash can be simply an announcement that a crash has taken place. Similarly, an injury **to** the wrist is likely to be caused by an external force, whereas with an injury **of** the wrist the cause is not emphasised. *Journey* licenses prepositions denoting motion (*the journey <u>to</u> Rome / <u>from</u> here / <u>back</u>*) but not *of* (**the journey of the continent*).

With deverbal nouns we find the following relations between clause and NP:

[4]		CLAUSE	NP
	i	a. *Muriel rejected <u>the plan</u>.*	b. *Muriel's rejection <u>of the plan</u>*
	ii	a. *The school banned <u>alcohol</u>.*	b. *the school's ban <u>on alcohol</u>*
	iii	a. *Fiona relies <u>on public support</u>.*	b. *Fiona's reliance <u>on public support</u>*

In [i] we have the common case where the verb takes an object while the noun takes default *of*. Example [ii], however, shows that not all nouns corresponding to transitive verbs take *of*: *ban* takes *on*, *address* takes *to*, *entry* takes *into*, and so on. Where, as in [iii], a verb takes a PP complement rather than an object, the noun takes the same preposition.

This kind of licensing does not apply directly with pre-head complements. However, such complements typically have close paraphrases involving post-head complements where a forced choice of preposition is observable. Compare, for example, *an <u>alcohol</u> ban* and *a ban <u>on alcohol</u>*, *a <u>wrist</u> injury* and *an injury <u>to the wrist</u>*. Similarly, corresponding to *a <u>legal</u> adviser* ([2ii]) we have *an adviser <u>on legal matters</u>*.

(b) Scope of anaphora

In clause structure any internal dependent that can combine with anaphoric *do so* must be an adjunct because it takes as antecedent a verb together with all its internal complements.

[54]The complement is usually an *of* PP, but occasional examples are found with a genitive subject-determiner: *The Dock Leaf had shed one generation of low-life drinkers, and discovered another. <u>Its denizens</u> now were young, unemployed and living six to a three-bedroom rented flat along Shore Road.* For the alternation between *of* PPs and genitives, see §16.5.3.

To a limited extent the pro-nominal ***one*** behaves in the same way in NP structure:

[5] i a. ?*I prefer the poems of Goethe to the ones of Schiller.* [complements]
b. ?*I have the key to the basement but not the one to the attic.*
c. ?*I've told my history tutor, but I can't find my French one.*
ii a. *I prefer the poems in Part I to the ones in Part II.* [modifiers]
b. *This key is identical to the one in the door.*
c. *I don't want a British nanny: I want a French one.*

The examples in [i], where ***one*** is in construction with an internal complement, show varying degrees of infelicity, but those in [ii], where it is in construction with a modifier, are impeccable. *French* in [ic] is a noun (denoting an academic subject), whereas in [iic] it is an adjective. This test distinguishes between the two senses of the ambiguous nominal *criminal lawyer* (with *criminal* an adjective in both). In the sense "lawyer who works in the field of criminal law", *criminal* is a complement and resists combination with ***one***: ?*I needed a civil lawyer, but he had found me a criminal one.* But in the sense "lawyer who is criminal", *criminal* is a modifier and combines readily with ***one***: *It turned out that he was an honest lawyer, not a criminal one, as I'd been led to expect.*

This test does not work, however, with nouns derived from verbs. The following, for example, are fully acceptable although the PPs are complements licensed by the head nouns *ban* and *proof*:[55]

[6] i a. *I support the ban on smoking, but not the one on alcohol.*
ii a. *The proof of Pythagoras' theorem is more clearly formulated than the one of Parseval's equality.*

(c) Correlation with syntactic category

Within NP structure we do not observe the clause-level correlation between complement and NP: as we have noted, nouns do not (with minor exceptions) take NPs as complement. Nevertheless, just as adverbs typically correspond to adjuncts in the clause, so adjectives are typically modifiers in the NP: adjectival complements like that in *legal adviser* are exceptional.

(d) Positional mobility

Complements are generally more restricted than modifiers. With respect to the internal dependents of the NP, this is most clearly observable with pre-head complements, which must be positioned adjacent to the head noun, following any modifiers. We have for example *a brilliant legal adviser* (modifier + complement), but not **a legal brilliant adviser*. Post-head complements by contrast only have a tendency to follow the head noun directly: see §15 below.

(e) Complements express semantic arguments of the head noun

This criterion holds for the NP in much the same way as for the clause. Its application is particularly straightforward when the noun is a semantic predicate denoting some property, relation, process, or action (whether a nominalisation or not), and the

[55] The deviance of examples like **Your reliance on me is just as bad as Kim's one on Pat* is due to the fact that pro-nominal ***one*** is a count noun and hence cannot have non-count *reliance* as antecedent: it has nothing to do with the complement status of the PPs.

complement represents an involved entity: the bearer of the property, a term in the relation, etc. However, we also take as complement those *of* PPs that are semantically related to the head in such ways as:

[7]	i	*the dirtiness <u>of the water</u>*	[o has non-human property h]
	ii	*the younger sister <u>of Mary</u>*	[o has kin relation h]
	iii	*the anger <u>of the older staff</u>*	[o has feeling h]
	iv	*the writing <u>of the book</u>*	[o is result of h]
	v	*the rays <u>of the sun</u>*	[o is natural source of h]
	vi	*the spire <u>of the cathedral</u>*	[o has inherent part h]
	vii	*the most expensive car <u>of the man who lives next door</u>*	[o is owner of h]
	viii	*her stupid nitwit <u>of a husband</u>*	[o is predicand of h]

In the annotations on the right, o = oblique (the NP within the underlined PP: *the water*, etc.), and h = head (the head of the matrix NP: *dirtiness*, etc.). Many NPs with *of* complements alternate with the subject-determiner construction: compare [ii], for example, with *Mary's younger sister*. We compare the two constructions in §16.5.3.

Examples [7i–iv] illustrate the straightforward cases: *dirtiness* denotes a property and the water bears that property; *sister* denotes a relationship in which Mary is one term; *anger* denotes an emotional process in which the older staff are experiencers; *writing* is an action of which the book is a result. The complement status of the PPs in [v–vii] is also relatively obvious, even though the head in each case denotes a physical object rather than a property, relation, process, or action. Rays do not exist without a source, so the sun is plausibly taken as an involved entity. Similarly, spires do not exist in isolation of the buildings of which they are a part. Most controversial is perhaps the complement status of the *of* phrase in examples like [vii], where the oblique represents the owner. However, owners are from a semantic point of view plausibly taken as entities involved in the things they possess. The grammatical evidence also points towards complement status: owners are typically expressed by the subject-determiner function, whose complement status in other cases is relatively uncontroversial; pro-nominal *one* is also infelicitous: #*my car and the one of the man who lives next door.*

Example [7viii] belongs to a distinctive syntactic construction where the oblique is constrained to be determined by the indefinite article *a*. The relation between the oblique and the head is like that between the predicand and the predicative complement in the clausal construction *Her husband is a stupid nitwit.* We can also relate [i] to *The water is dirty*, but this involves a change in the category and form of the noun *dirtiness* to the adjective *dirty*, whereas in [viii] the noun *nitwit* remains constant.[56]

One significant difference between clauses and NPs is the lack of any counterpart in NPs to dummy and raised complements. There are thus no NP counterparts to clauses like *It is noisy in the hall* or *Kim is certain to win* – compare **the noisiness of it in the hall*

[56]The singular nouns *hell* and *heck* occur in a frozen version of this construction: *It created a hell/heck of a problem.* The popular spelling *a helluva problem* might appear to suggest a reanalysis, making *problem* the head, but the possibility of intensificatory modification, as in *an absolute hell of a problem*, argues that *hell* remains syntactic head of the construction.

and *the certainty of Kim to win (or, with subject-determiners, *its noisiness in the hall and *Kim's certainty to win).

(f) Semantic roles of complements depend on the head noun

This property of complements is a natural consequence of their being semantic arguments, and is no less applicable to the NP than to the clause. In clause structure the roles associated with the subject and object depend on the meaning of the verb (e.g. Kim and Pat are respectively agent and patient in *Kim shot Pat*, but experiencer and stimulus in *Kim saw Pat*); in NP structure the same applies with the subject-determiner (as described in §16.5) and PP complements, especially those headed by *of*. Compare, for example, *the resignation of the secretary*, where the secretary is agent, and *the assassination of the secretary*, where the secretary is patient – and the examples in [7] provide further illustration of this point.

(g) Semantic selection restrictions in NPs involve complements

This property too is a natural consequence of the semantic argument status of complements. A spire is an inherent part of a building, and this imposes a semantic selection restriction on the denotation of the complement. While we can have *the spire of the cathedral*, we cannot have #*the spire of the rocket* or #*the spire of Mary*. Similarly, a speech can only be made by a person, so we have *the speech by the mayor*, but not #*the speech by coffee*.

Indirect complements

The complements considered so far have all been **direct**, in that they are licensed by the head noun itself. **Indirect** complements are those where the licensor is another dependent of the head (or part of one). In the following examples single underlining marks the indirect complement, brackets enclose the other dependent and double underlining marks the element within it that licenses the complement.

[8] i *a [larger] galaxy than initial measurements suggested* [*than* PP]
ii *[so great] a loss that we're likely to go bankrupt* [declarative content clause]
iii *[too dangerous] a proposal for parliament to accept* [infinitival]

Indirect complements are licensed by: comparative expressions (see Ch. 13, §1.3); the degree adverbs *so* and *too* (Ch. 11, §4.6); the sufficiency determinatives *enough* and *sufficient*, and the adverb *sufficiently* (see §7.12 above); and a number of attributive adjectives, such as *easy*, in *some [very easy] people to get on with* (Ch. 14, §6.3).

The post-head position of these complements correlates with the fact that PPs and clauses are not permitted within pre-head dependents except under very restricted conditions: [8i], for example, may be contrasted with **a larger than initial measurements suggested galaxy*, and so on. In most cases there is an alternative construction in which the licensor too occurs after the head of the NP: *a galaxy larger than initial measurements suggested*. One exception involves comparative *same*: *the same problem as you had*, but not **the problem same as you had*. It is also usually possible for the complement to be further delayed so that it occurs later in the clause rather than within the NP: *We have suffered so great a loss this year that we're likely to go bankrupt*. The exception this time is the adjective + hollow clause construction: **We've got some very easy people at the office to get on with*.

14.2 Modifiers

Attributive modifiers

Internal modifiers in pre-head position are realised by DPs, AdjPs, VPs with past participle or gerund-participle heads, and nominals in plain or genitive case:

		a.	b.	
[9]	i	a. *another three days*	b. *the barely forty students present*	[DP]
	ii	a. *his wry attitude*	b. *many very angry farmers*	[AdjP]
	iii	a. *the defeated army*	b. *her recently published article*	[VP]
	iv	a. *the gleaming showroom*	b. *three steadily melting marshmallows*	[VP]
	v	a. *its entertainment value*	b. *those Egyptian cotton shirts*	[nominal]
	vi	a. *a dogs' home*	b. *a young children's edition*	[nominal]

A few prepositions are also found, as in *the downstairs toilet.* For determinatives and adjectives we recognise a single higher-level category, DP and AdjP, whereas for verb and noun we recognise two, VP and clause for the verb, nominal and NP for the noun, and in the latter two cases the attributive modifier position admits expressions belonging to the intermediate but not to the highest category (with the small-scale exception of measure genitives, which we take up in §16.3). The attributes in [iii–iv] are thus VPs, not clauses, and those in [v–vi] are nominals, not NPs.

The internal structure of attributive modifiers is subject to severe constraints. They can contain their own pre-head dependents, as in the [b] examples in [9], but for the most part attributive modifiers cannot contain post-head dependents: compare **many [very angry at this betrayal] farmers*, **her [recently published in 'Nature'] article*, **those [Egyptian cotton of the highest quality] shirts*, and so on. VPs do not allow any relaxation of this constraint. With plain-case nominals, post-head dependents are found with institutional proper names, as in *a [Ministry of Defence] official.* AdjPs allow a narrow range of short post-head dependents, as in *[better than expected] results* – see Ch. 6, §3.3. DPs take few post-head dependents even in determiner function (see §11), but in general those that are permitted within determiners are admissible in attributes too, as in *the [more than twenty] complaints they received.*

There are numerous adjectives which, either absolutely or in a given sense, occur only in attributive modifier function (e.g. *a mere child*, but not **The child is mere*), and others that are excluded from this function (*Corruption was rife*, but not **rife corruption*); we deal with these issues in Ch. 6, §4.

Nonce-formations

In addition to regular formations like those in [9], we also find **nonce-formations**:

[10] i *my do-it-yourself skills, the buy-me glitter of the duty-free shop*
ii *a no-frills airline, a no-fuzzy-edge guarantee, an all-or-nothing approach*
iii *huge floor-to-ceiling windows, the custard-pie-in-your-face front cover*

The examples in [i] are constructed from VPs headed by plain-form verbs; those in [ii] contain determiners; those in [iii] are nominals with post-head dependents in the form of PPs. These attributes are nonce-formations in that forms of these types are not systematically admissible in this construction. Some of them have the status of well-established forms (e.g. *do-it-yourself, floor-to-ceiling*), but many – such as *custard-pie-in-your face* in [iii] – are simply concocted on-the-hoof. One even finds word-sequences that elsewhere do not form constituents, as in the attested example *his 'best-of' retrospective album*. (See also Ch. 19, §4.3.3.)

Post-head modifiers

The general constraints on attributive modifiers do not apply to those in post-head position: they readily take their own post-head dependents, and for expressions based on verbs and nouns we have expressions of the highest-level category, clause and NP. NPs, however, are rare because with modifiers, as with complements, dependent NPs are usually related to the head by means of a preposition, rather than directly. Modifiers with the form of PPs are extremely common in post-head position, but those containing complements do not occur attributively (leaving aside nonce-formations).

(a) Determinatives and DPs

The default position for these modifiers is before the head, but certain types can follow:

[11] *a/one day more* *two days [less than we had expected]* *money enough*

The comparative determinatives *more, less, fewer* can occur after the head provided there is a determiner. Thus we have a post-head alternant for *one more day* but not for *more days*: compare *One day more* / **Days more will be needed.* In NP structure determinative *enough* usually functions as determiner, but it is permitted as post-head modifier provided it is not modified: *I have money enough*, but not **I have money almost enough.*

(b) Adjectives and AdjPs

The basic rule for the placement of adjectives and AdjPs is that single adjectives and phrases without their own post-head dependents occur in attributive position, while others occur **postpositively**, i.e. after the head of the NP, as in *members [dissatisfied with the board's decision]*. Special rules apply with compound determinatives like *somebody, anything*, etc.: see §9.6. For the rest, there are certain specific adjectives that can or must occur postpositively. Representative examples are given in [12] (see also Ch. 6, §4.2):

[12] i *the only day suitable, years past, proof positive, matters financial, all things Irish*
ii *the people present, the cars involved, the students concerned, the city proper*
iii *the heir apparent, the body politic, the president elect, the devil incarnate, the poet laureate, a notary public*
iv *the house [currently ablaze], all people [now alive], the ones asleep*

The examples in [12i] alternate with the attributive construction: compare *the only suitable day*, etc. The postpositive use of these adjectives is subject to severe restrictions. Adjectives in ·*able* or ·*ible*, like *suitable* and *possible*, require an attributive superlative or *only*: compare *the best result possible* and **the result possible.* Postpositive *past* occurs with temporal nouns (cf. **approaches past*), and *positive* only with *proof.* The last two examples have general nouns as head and denote domains; the adjectives *financial* and *Irish* are like restrictors (§9.6) in that they must immediately follow the head.

The adjectives in [12ii] occur both attributively and postpositively, but with a difference in sense. Postpositive *present* (or *absent*) denotes a temporary state of affairs: compare *the present government.* The same applies to *involved* and *concerned*, though here the attributive sense differs more (cf. *deeply involved activists, concerned parents*). Postpositive *proper* means "in the strict/proper sense of the term". With *net* and *gross* the choice of position depends not on the meaning but on the head: they follow specific sums (*fifty dollars net*) but otherwise precede (*my net income*).

The examples in [12iii] are fixed phrases, with no attributive alternant. The adjectives in [iv] are ones which are altogether excluded from attributive position.

(c) NPs

[13] i *a man my age, shoes this size, the results last year, houses this side of the lake*
ii *fifty miles an hours, a salary of [$20,000 a year], ten dollars a head*

Leaving aside the appositives to be discussed in §14.3, modifiers with NP form are limited to those denoting age, size, and similar properties, or non-referential distributive indefinities like those in [ii] (discussed in §8.4 above).

(d) PPs

[14] i *a woman [of great wisdom], a school [of this type], the man [with black hair], the church [near the river], friends [from Boston], Jill's career [as a journalist]*
ii *the temperature [outside], the floor [below], the year [before]*
iii *his behaviour [after his wife left him], the car [as we know it today]*

A very great range of PPs can function as post-head modifier. Those in [i] illustrate the most frequent pattern, with the preposition having an NP as complement. In the last example, with *as*, the oblique NP is interpreted predicatively: Jill was a journalist. We also find prepositions without complements, generally locative or temporal, as in [ii]; and in [iii] the prepositions have clauses as complement.

(e) Clauses

[15] i *Where's [the book I lent you]?* [relative]
ii *Kim is [the person to do the job].* [infinitival]
iii *[People living near the site] will be seriously disavantaged.* [gerund-participial]
iv *She came across [some letters written by her grandmother].* [past-participial]

Finite clauses in modifier function are all relatives: post-head content clauses are complements. For the three types of non-finite clause in [ii–iv], see Ch. 14, §8.2.

Multiple dependents

Nominals commonly contain more than one internal modifier:

[16] i *some [blue cotton blankets]*
ii *the [star on the horizon with the reddish tint]*
iii *the [gleaming star on the horizon]*

We take the modifiers to modify the head successively rather than simultaneously: i.e. we recognise a layered structure with one nominal inside another. In [i], for example, the ultimate head *blankets* is modified by the noun *cotton* to give the nominal *cotton blankets*, and this in turn is modified by *blue* to give *blue cotton blankets*. This construction is known as **stacked modification**, or **stacking**; see also Ch. 6, §3.2.

Syntactic evidence for such a layered structure comes from coordination and anaphora. We can have coordination at any of the three levels: *blue cotton blankets and sheets*; *blue cotton blankets and silk sheets*; *blue cotton blankets and white silk sheets*. And any of the three heads can be the antecedent for various kinds of anaphoric expression (see Ch. 17, §6.1). In *I prefer those blue cotton blankets to these*, for example, *these* can be interpreted as "these blankets", "these cotton blankets," or "these blue cotton blankets". Examples like [iii], with a pre-head and a post-head modifier are structurally ambiguous according to which modifier is applied to the head noun first: the immediate constituents can thus be either *gleaming star + on the horizon* or *gleaming + star on the horizon*. Usually, as in this example, it will make no practical difference whether it is taken in one way or the other.

The constructions in [16] are to be distinguished from such as the following:

[17] i *some [Egyptian cotton shirts]*
ii *an [interesting and very promising proposal]*
iii *the [award of the contract to the other firm]*

In [i] *Egyptian* modifies *cotton*, and the nominal *Egyptian cotton* in turn modifies *shirts*. This is **submodification**, modification of a modifier; again see Ch. 6, §3.2. In [ii] there is just one modifier, realised by an AdjP-coordination. And in [iii] the two underlined PPs are complements of *award*, and as such are related to the head at the same structural level: *award of the contract* does not here form a nominal.

14.3 Appositive modifiers

Appositive dependents are ones which when substituted for the matrix NP in a declarative clause systematically yield a clause which is an entailment of the original:

[18] i	a. *She sang in [the opera 'Carmen'].*	b. *She sang in 'Carmen'.*
ii	a. *It was founded in [the year 1850].*	b. *It was founded in 1850.*
iii	a. *[The verb 'use'] is transitive.*	b. *'Use' is transitive.*

In each of these pairs, [a] entails [b]. The appositive thus provides a formulation that can stand instead of the NP containing it.

We are concerned here with appositives as integrated dependents in NP structure, as distinct from supplementary appositives like that in *The information was given me by Kim Jones, the President of the Students' Union*: see Ch. 15, §5, for this latter construction. Integrated appositives are usually semantically restrictive, as in [18]. Thus *'Carmen'* in [i] restricts the denotation of the nominal headed by *opera*: the opera 'Carmen' contrasts with other operas. Analogously in [ii–iii], where *1850* and *'use'* restrict the denotation of the nominals headed by *year* and *verb*. Typically, integrated appositives provide identifying information, so that the matrix NP is definite. However, they do not have to be semantically restrictive, as is evident from examples like:

[19] *This is [my husband George].* [non-restrictive integrated appositive]

As an integrated appositive *George* belongs in the same intonation unit as the head, instead of being pronounced as a separate intonation unit, as in supplementary apposition. But there is no entailment or implicature that I have more than one husband: the integrated construction simply provides a succinct way of saying that the person concerned is my husband and is named George.

Appositive modifiers are very often proper names, but there are other possibilities too, as illustrated in [18]. It is also possible for a proper name to occur as head with a definite NP as appositive: *['Carmen' the opera] is performed more often than ['Carmen' the ballet]*.

Appositives vs complements

We have said that substitution of an appositive for the matrix NP **systematically** yields entailments. This distinguishes appositives from complements realised by content clauses:

[20] i [*The suggestion that they cheated*] *was quite outrageous.*
ii *They omitted to mention* [*the fact that he is insolvent*]. [complement]

Example [i] clearly does not entail *That they cheated was quite outrageous*: the latter presupposes that they cheated and says that the cheating was quite outrageous, while in [i] it is the suggestion that was outrageous, probably because they didn't in fact cheat. The content clause thus does not qualify as an appositive; it is a complement licensed by the head noun *suggestion*, just as in the clausal construction *He suggested that they cheated* it is a complement licensed by the verb *suggested*. Example [ii], however, does entail *They omitted to mention that he is insolvent*. But this is attributable to the semantic properties of the noun *fact*: it is not a systematic feature of the noun + content clause construction. We accordingly don't regard this example either as satisfying the condition for analysis as an appositional construction: syntactically, it is just like [i].

Appositive obliques

Appositives with the form of proper names may be related to the head via the preposition *of*, rather than being directly related to it, as in the above examples.

[21] i a. *She was born in* [*the month of May*]. b. *She was born in May.*
ii a. *It took place in* [*the city of Berlin*]. b. *It took place in Berlin.*

Again, [a] entails [b] in each pair, and just as in the [a] examples of [18] we understand that 'Carmen' is an opera, 1850 a year, and *use* a verb, so [21ia/iia] categorise May as a month and Berlin as a city. Following the terminology used for predicatives in Ch. 4, §5.1, we call the PPs *of Berlin* and *of May* **marked appositives**, and the NPs *Berlin* and *May* **appositive obliques**. The oblique is a proper name, and the head is *month* or a term denoting some politico-geographical entity such as *city, town, suburb, village, settlement, state, county, canton, province.* The construction is characteristically definite, since the oblique is a proper name, but it is possible for the matrix NP to be indefinite, as in *There's a city of Manchester in England, and one in New Hampshire too*, reflecting the secondary use of proper names to denote a set of bearers of the name (§20.4).

14.4 Composite nominals vs compound nouns

The syntactic construction consisting of an attributive dependent + head, forming a composite nominal, is to be distinguished from a morphological compound noun:

[22] i a. *some new cars* b. *two London colleges* [composite nominals]
ii a. *some shortbread* b. *two ice-creams* [compound nouns]

New and *London* are separate words, adjective and noun respectively, functioning as attributive modifiers, while *short* and *ice* do not themselves have the status of words: they are bases, again adjective and noun respectively, forming part of a compound word.

What distinguishes the syntactic construction from the compound noun is that the component parts can enter separately into relations of coordination and modification, as seen in:

		a.	b.
[23]	i	a. *[new and used] cars*	b. *various [London and Oxford] colleges*
	ii	a. *new [buses and cars]*	b. *various London [schools and colleges]*
	iii	a. *[four new and two used] cars*	b. *[two London and four Oxford] colleges*
	iv	a. *two [reasonably new] cars*	b. *two [south London] colleges*
	v	a. *two new [diesel-driven cars]*	b. *two London [theological colleges]*

Coordination is illustrated in [i–iii]: in [i] we have coordination in the modifier, in [ii] coordination in the head, and in [iii] delayed right constituent coordination (see Ch. 15, §4.4). The other examples involve modification – within the modifier in [iv] (hence submodification), and within the head in [v] (hence stacking).

Compound nouns, by contrast, do not submit to this kind of manipulation. Take *ice-cream*, for example:

		a.	b.
[24]	i	a. *[*ice- and custard-*]*creams*	b. *ice-creams and custard-creams*
	ii	a. **ice-*[*lollies and creams*]	b. *ice-lollies and ice-creams*
	iii	a. *[*two ice- and ten custard-*]*creams*	b. *two ice-creams and ten custard-creams*
	iv	a. *[*crushed ice-*]*cream*	b. *cream made of crushed ice*
	v	a. **ice-*[*Italian cream*]	b. *Italian ice-cream*

The [a] examples here match the coordination and modification constructions in [23], but because *ice* and *cream* are bases, not words, the results are inadmissible. For coordination, we need the [b] versions of [24i–iii], where *ice-creams* remains intact. And similarly, *ice-cream* can only be modified as a whole, as in [vb]. *Crushed ice-creams* is possible with the structure *crushed [ice-creams]* ("ice-creams that are crushed"), but not with the structure of [iva] and the meaning expressed by [ivb].

The five constructions thus provide diagnostic tests for distinguishing between syntactic constructions and compounds.[57] In principle, satisfaction of any of the tests is sufficient to demonstrate that a sequence of elements forms a syntactic construction. Consider the examples in [25], which illustrate various functions and semantic roles of noun pre-head dependents; they all straightforwardly pass the first test (coordination of the first element), as shown in [26], and hence qualify as syntactic constructions:

[25] i a. *blackcurrant sorbet* (composition: "made of blackcurrants")
b. *cooking apple* (purpose: "for cooking")
c. *gas cooker* (instrument: "using gas") } [modifier]

ii a. *television screen* (inherent part: "screen of a television")
b. *microfilm reader* (theme: "device for reading microfilms") } [complement]

[26] i a. *I'd like [a blackcurrant and passion-fruit sorbet], please.*
b. *We sell [both cooking and eating apples].*
c. *You can use [a gas or electric cooker], it doesn't matter.*

ii a. *[Television and computer screens] have different resolutions.*
b. *[Microfilm and microfiche readers] are not the same.*

[57] The last test, separate modification of the head, is less useful than the others, because such modification will often be blocked by the ordering constraints discussed in §15. In *linguistics student*, for example, *linguistics* is a complement and must immediately precede the head, so no independent modification of *student* is permitted.

It might be claimed that the reason why examples like *ice-cream* fail the tests is purely semantic: an ice-cream is not transparently a cream made of ice. Since there is an element of unpredictability in the way the denotation of *ice-cream* is related to the denotation of its parts, we should not then expect either *ice* or *cream* to be independently modifiable. Likewise, only elements which are semantically comparable can be coordinated: since the role of ice in making ice-creams is not the same as that of custard in making custard-creams, and since an ice-lolly is a lolly made of ice in a sense that an ice-cream is not, we could expect *ice-cream* to fail the coordination tests. There are, however, pairs of N + N combinations in which the semantic relations involved seem both transparent and equivalent, but which nevertheless fail the coordination tests:

[27]	i	*sunrise* ~ *sunset*	*[*The sunrise and set*] *were both magnificent.*
	ii	*backache* ~ *toothache*	**I'm suffering from* [*back and toothache*].
	iii	*teardrop* ~ *raindrop*	**Her face was a sea of* [*tear and raindrops*].
	iv	*swimwear* ~ *sportswear*	**This is* [*a swim and sportswear shop*].
	v	*blackbird* ~ *bluebird*	**There are* [*both black and bluebirds*] *in the area.*

If, as we believe to be the case, these examples cannot be explained on semantic grounds, a syntactic difference must exist between the examples in [25] and those in [27]: the former are syntactic constructions and the latter are compounds.

The semantic relations involved in composite nominals and compound nouns may be exactly the same: for example, *cutlery box* denotes a box for cutlery, and *matchbox* denotes a box for matches. *Cutlery box* seems to pass the coordination test, e.g. *I collect antique* [*cutlery and wine-glass boxes*], but *matchbox* does not: **I collect antique* [*match and dinky-car boxes*]. As the orthography suggests, *cutlery box* is then a syntactic construction, and *matchbox* is basically a compound. Nevertheless, the fact that two superficially identical structures coexist as competing realisations of the same semantic relationship means that it is often possible to reanalyse the component elements of a compound as independent constituents. For example, *washing-machine* is basically a compound: it denotes a machine for washing, but specifically a machine for washing clothes. It must fail the first coordination test because the other devices for handling clothes are not of the same form: we have a *tumble-dryer* rather than a *drying-machine*, and a *press* rather than a *pressing-machine*. Nevertheless, *washing-machine* can be coerced into passing the coordination test in the situation where we have a new invention which carries out all three processes: this might be called a combined *washing-, drying-, and pressing-machine.*

It is commonly pointed out that tests such as those illustrated in [23] do not yield a sharp division between composite nominals and compound nouns. A good deal of the apparent blurring of the distinction, however, is attributable to reanalysis of the type just illustrated. For the rest, we take the view, here as in so many other areas of grammar, that the existence of borderline cases does not provide a reason for abandoning a distinction that can be recognised in a great range of clear cases. To abandon the distinction requires that we treat all N + N combinations as composite nominals or else treat them all as compounds. Each of these approaches raises more problems than it solves. The all-composite-nominals approach provides no explanation for data like [27], and it leaves a major and arbitrary gap in the rules for forming compound nouns: given the wide range of compound types described in Ch. 19, §4.2, why should there be none formed from N + N combinations?

The all-compounds approach, on the other hand, requires that we allow for open-ended recursive formations within morphology, resulting in a serious weakening of the distinction between syntax and morphology: we will have to allow for compounds to contain coordinations of arbitrary length (*the* [*United States, New Zealand, . . . , and Soviet Union representatives*]), PPs (*a* [*Ministry of Agriculture and Food proposal*]), and even interpolations (*They are cancelling all* [*history, philosophy and even, I believe, linguistics classes*]).

Both approaches, moreover, raise the problem of the relation between N + N combinations and Adj + N combinations: the coordination and modification tests of [24] apply to both. The problems just mentioned become even more serious if the unitary approach is extended to these – as would seem necessary given that we can have N + Adj + N combinations like *London theological college* or coordinations of N + Adj combined with N, as in *brick or wooden houses.* But if, nevertheless, the unitary approach is not extended, so that a distinction between composite nominals and compounds is recognised for Adj + N combinations on the basis of the coordination and modification tests, the question arises as to why these same tests are deemed irrelevant for N + N combinations.

Various non-syntactic criteria have been proposed as differentiating between composite nominals and compound nouns, as in such pairs as composite *black bird* ("bird which is black") and *blackbird* ("species of bird"):

[28] i STRESS: the composite nominal has primary stress on the second element (*black-ˈbird*), while the compound has it on the first (*ˈblackbird*).

ii ORTHOGRAPHY: the composite nominal is written as two orthographic words, the compound as one.

iii MEANING: while the meaning of the composite nominal is straightforwardly predictable from the component parts, that of the compound is not – it is specialised, denoting a particular species.

iv PRODUCTIVITY: in the composite nominal the dependent can be replaced by any other adjective that is semantically compatible with the head, whereas there is a quite limited number of compounds with the form Adj + *bird.*

The correlation between these criteria and the syntactic tests of coordination and modification is, however, very imperfect, and since we are concerned with the delimitation of a syntactic construction we will naturally give precedence to the syntactic tests in the many cases of divergent results.

In the first place, there are many combinations that clearly pass the tests for composite nominals that have primary stress on the first element – forms like *biology teacher, cooking apple, television screen, income tax.* Conversely, there are some compounds, such as *full stop* ("period") or, for many speakers, *hotdog,* that have stress on the second element.

Orthography does not provide a decisive criterion because in many cases there are alternant forms: *daisy wheel, daisy-wheel,* or *daisywheel,* for example. And there are compounds, such as the above *full stop,* that are written as two orthographic words.

Thirdly, semantic specialisation may be found in composite nominals as well as compounds. The coordination *desktop and internet publishing,* for example, shows *desktop publishing* to be a composite nominal, but the meaning is specialised, since it denotes publishing by use of computer programs accessible to a desktop computer, rather than publishing using the top of a desk. Conversely, the meaning of such compounds as *backache* or *raindrop* is as transparent as that of numerous composite nominals.

Finally productivity is a gradient matter, and cannot provide a criterion for a binary distinction. Syntactic processes are overall more productive than morphological ones within the lexicon, but this is a tendency, not a matter of productive vs non-productive.

15 Order of elements in NP structure

The preceding sections have introduced the main kinds of dependents that we distinguish in describing NP structure, and we must now say something further about the order in which they occur. The ordering constraints are of two kinds, which we call **rigid** and **labile** ordering constraints. Violation of a rigid ordering contraint results in clear ungrammaticality, as when the determiner is placed after the head instead of before it – compare *the unicorn* and **unicorn the*. A labile ordering constraint, on the other hand, gives the preferred order in the default case: departures from this order will often be of questionable acceptability but they may also be justified by considerations of scope and information packaging. Compare:

[1] i *I want to buy* [*a large black sofa*] / ?[*a black large sofa*].
ii *I want to buy a* [*black large sofa*], *not those other colours of large sofa you insist on showing me.*

In the absence of special factors, a modifier of size precedes one of colour: *a large black sofa* represents the preferred order while *a black large sofa* is very unnatural. But this constraint can be overridden, as in [ii]: the context here is one where it has already been established that I want a large sofa, so that now only the colour is at issue. *Black* is thus interpreted restrictively, picking out a subset of the set of large sofas, and in this context it can precede *large*.

We will represent rigid and labile constraints by means of the symbols '⋙' and '>' respectively: 'Determiner ⋙ Head' indicates that the determiner obligatorily precedes the head, while 'General property > Colour' gives the default order of modifiers of these two semantic types.

Main rigid ordering constraints

The basic order of elements can be expressed in terms of the template shown in [2]:

[2] Pre-head external modifiers ⋙ Determiner ⋙ Pre-head internal modifiers ⋙ Pre-head complement ⋙ Head ⋙ Post-head internal dependents ⋙ Post-head external modifiers

The following NP contains one each of the above seven functions, in the order shown:

[3] *all those grossly over-rewarded financial advisers in the city too*

Pre-head external modifiers

For these modifiers we have rigid ordering:

[4] Peripheral external modifiers ⋙ Predeterminer external modifiers

[5] i *even all the shareholders* [peripheral (focusing) + predeterminer]
ii *financially such a mess* [peripheral (domain) + predeterminer]

Pre-head internal modifiers

For these we need to distinguish two sets, **early** and **residual**:

[6] Early pre-head modifiers > Residual pre-head modifiers

The early modifiers are realised by determinatives and superlative, ordinal, and primacy adjectives; their default position is before any other modifier:

[7] i *the two vital reports* [determinative + residual]
ii *the largest unsupported structure* [superlative + residual]
iii *the second unsuccessful attempt* [ordinal + residual]
iv *the key new proposal* [primacy + residual]

When compatible early modifiers combine, they may generally do so in any order (with possible scope differences):

[8] i a. *the two largest buildings* b. *the largest two buildings*
ii a. *the second brightest child* b. *the brightest second child*
iii a. *the key second proposal* b. *the second key proposal*

Whereas the [a] and [b] examples are more or less equivalent in [i], those in [ii] are not. In its salient interpretation [iia] denotes the runner-up to the brightest child, or there may have been two groups of children ranked for brightness, giving two children who are brightest in their group, and this is the second of these two. The meaning of [iib] is quite different: it picks out the brightest from the set of second children (most plausibly, second in order of birth). The examples in [iii] can be interpreted as equivalent, with the proposal concerned being simultaneously the key proposal and the second proposal. But they are more likely to be interpreted differently, with [iiib] denoting the second in the set of key proposals, and [iiia] the key one among the second proposals.

Evidence that the ordering in [6] is labile is provided by such examples as:

[9] i *a seemingly interminable two hours* [residual + determinative]
ii *their woefully spoilt youngest child* [residual + superlative]
iii *an unsuccessful second attempt* [residual + ordinal]
iv *her highly influential key address* [residual + primacy]

Residual pre-head modifiers

Here we have the labile ordering stated in [10] and illustrated in [11]:

[10] Evaluative > General property > Age > Colour > Provenance > Manufacture > Type

[11] *an [attractive tight-fitting brand-new pink Italian lycra women's] swimsuit*

Evaluative modifiers represent the speaker's evaluation, rather than an objectively definable general property. The central examples are *good* and *bad*; others include *annoying, attractive, boring, despicable, excellent, ghastly, mind-numbing, oppressive, perfect, revolting, tasty, valuable*, and so on.

General property modifiers include those denoting properties that can be objectively distinguished using the senses: size (*big, small*), dimension (*long, tall, short, wide, narrow, fat, thin*), sound (*loud, faint*), touch (*rough, smooth*), taste (*sweet, sour*). Less central examples include: *ear-splitting, enormous, foul-smelling, inaudible, minuscule, obese, tight-fitting, vast.* Also belonging under the same heading are modifiers denoting human properties, such as *cruel, intelligent, irascible, jealous, kind, pompous, rude, snooty, wise.* We note that, when a sense modifier and a human property modifier apply non-restrictively, there is no real preferred order: *her fat cruel husband* and *her cruel fat husband* are indistinguishable.

Age modifiers include *old, new*, and *young*, along with *ancient, brand-new, modern, up-to-date*, etc. Colour modifiers include the basic colour terms *black, white, red*, *yellow, green, brown, blue, pink, orange, grey, purple*, together with a host of non-basic ones, e.g. *crimson, vermilion, carmine, blue-green, powder-blue*. Provenance modifiers are typically nationality adjectives, such as *French, Italian, Chinese, Venezuelan*, or other geographical and politico-geographical proper names, for example *Queensland* in *an old Queensland sofa*.

Manufacture modifiers either denote the material out of which something is composed, or the mode of its manufacture. Composition modifiers can be adjectival, for example *wooden* and *woollen*, but are typically nouns: *cotton, iron, jade, nylon, polyester, satin, wood, wool*. Mode modifiers are typically participles, e.g. *carved, enamelled*. We also include under this heading genitive proper name nominals, as in *a delicious Sainsbury's pie*. Modifiers indicating type are mainly nominals but also include a number of adjectives: *fancy-dress costume, photograph album, dessert spoon, lap-top computer, passenger aircraft, winter overcoat, digestive biscuit*. Into this class naturally fit genitive nominals such as *men's department, women's clothes, children's diseases, old people's home, summer's day, winter's day*.

The labile nature of constraint [10] can be seen in the fact that while *a new cotton shirt*, say, is normally preferred over *a cotton new shirt*, the latter is not ungrammatical. It is admissible, for example, in a context where there has been talk of new shirts, and the concern is with different kinds of new shirt.

Post-head internal dependents

General labile constraints

Post-head internal dependents are subject to the two labile constraints [12], as illustrated in [13], where double underlining is used for complements, single underlining for modifiers:

[12] i Light post-head complements > Post-head modifiers
ii Light dependents > Heavy dependents

[13] i a. *the attack on the prime minister in the tabloid press*
b. ?*the attack in the tabloid press on the prime minister*
ii a. *the rumour in the tabloid press that income tax would be cut*
b. ?*the rumour that income tax would be cut in the tabloid press*
iii a. *the rumour that income tax would be cut which was published in 'The Times'*
b. *the rumour which was published in 'The Times' that income tax would be cut*

In [13i] we have a light complement and in accordance with [12i] it will normally precede the modifier: [13ia] is preferred over [13ib]. In [13iia–b] the complement is heavy, so [12i] is irrelevant. Since the modifier is light, it will normally precede the complement in accordance with constraint [12ii]: [13iia] is the preferred member of the pair. Finally, in [13iii] both dependents are heavy, so neither of the constraints is applicable, and both versions are perfectly acceptable.

Specific rigid constraints

Although the order of post-head internal dependents is essentially labile, certain specialised types are subject to rigid ordering constraints:

[14] i Immediate post-head dependents ≫ Residual post-head dependents
ii *else* ≫ Restrictors ≫ Residual post-head dependents

Constraint [14i] is illustrated in:

[15] i a. *a trip abroad to Paris* b. **a trip to Paris abroad*
ii a. *the opera 'Carmen' by Bizet* b. **the opera by Bizet 'Carmen'*
iii a. *the body politic of France* b. **the body of France politic*

Dependents which immediately follow the head are appositives (*the opera 'Carmen'*), prepositions without complements (*a trip abroad*), single adjectives in fixed phrases (*the body politic*): in each case, the attempt to insert a light complement between them and the head results in ungrammaticality.

Constraint [14ii] concerns the position of the modifiers we call restrictors. These are AdjPs or nominals without any post-head dependents of their own which modify the compound determinatives: *something very nice*, *everything gold* (see §9.6). These restrictors cannot occur in pre-head position because of the fused nature of the construction, and are forced into post-head position, with only *else* allowed between them and the head:

[16] i a. *something highly original by Bach* b. **something by Bach highly original*
ii a. *nothing else significant by Schubert* b. **nothing significant else by Schubert*

Post-head external modifiers and postposing

There is rigid ordering between the two types of post-head modifier:

[17] Emphatic reflexives ⩾ Focusing modifiers
[18] a. *the author herself too* b. **the author too herself*

Clausal post-head internal dependents are often **postposed** to a position following the short post-head focusing modifiers, as in:

[19] i *the one man alone who can help you on this*
ii *the possibility too that the prisoners would be released*

The postposed dependent occupies a special position within the NP, but outside the structure imposed by the basic order constraint in [2].

16 Case

16.1 Preliminaries

Case as a general term

The term case applies in the first instance to a system of inflectional forms of a noun that serve to mark the function of an NP relative to the construction containing it. Compare, for example:

[1]		FUNCTION OF NP	CASE OF PRONOUN
i	*I slept soundly.*	subject of clause	nominative
ii	*Please help me.*	object of clause	accusative
iii	*Where is my bag?*	subj-det of NP	genitive

The pronouns in [i–ii] are heads of NPs functioning in clause structure: the nominative *I* marks that NP as subject, while accusative *me* marks it as object. At the general level, the nominative is a case whose primary function is to mark the subject of both intransitive and transitive clauses, while the accusative is a case whose primary function is to mark the direct object of a transitive clause. The genitive is somewhat different in that its primary function is to mark one NP as a dependent in the structure of a larger NP. In [iii] *my* is a dependent in the structure of the NP *my bag*. More specifically, we analyse the dependent NP as subject-determiner within the matrix NP.

Plain case: neutralisation of the nominative–accusative contrast

In Present-day English the contrast between nominative and accusative is found with only a handful of pronouns. At earlier stages of the language the contrast applied to the whole class of nouns but the inflectional distinction has been lost except for these few pronouns. We will use the term **plain case** for the form that neutralises the distinction between nominative and accusative, contrasting simply with the genitive:

[2]		FUNCTION OF NP	CASE OF NOUN
i	*[The doctor] slept soundly.*	subject of clause	plain
ii	*Please help [the doctor].*	object of clause	plain
iii	*[the doctor's] bag*	subj-det of NP	genitive

Distinction between case and syntactic function

While case characteristically serves as a marker of syntactic function, it is important not to lose sight of the distinction between the inflectional category of case and the functions that it may mark. It is a common practice in much traditional grammar, especially traditional school grammar, to say that nouns functioning as (head of the) subject are in nominative case, while those functioning as (head of the) object are in accusative case, but this is to confuse the two sets of concepts. According to this traditional account, *doctor* is nominative in [2i] and accusative in [ii], but in fact there is no inflectional distinction between these two occurrences of the noun *doctor*. *The doctor* is subject in [i], object in [ii], but the difference in function is not marked by any difference in the internal form of the NP: there is therefore no contrast of case here, and as indicated in [2] we assign both instances of *doctor* to the same case, the plain case. Case, then, is only one among a variety of possible markers of syntactic function, and as far as Present-day English is concerned the linear position of an NP relative to the verb plays a larger role in the marking of syntactic function than does inflectional case.[58]

Terminology: 'nominative' vs 'accusative' or 'subjective' vs 'objective'

The classical terms 'nominative' and 'accusative' are quite opaque, and some modern grammars have replaced them by the more transparent 'subjective' and 'objective' respectively. The view taken here, however, is that the correlation between case and syntactic function is so complex that these new terms run the risk of creating confusion, and we have therefore preferred to retain the traditional terms – which also have the advantage that they are much more widely used in the grammars of other languages. As we will note in detail below, the nominative is not restricted to subject function (cf. *It was I who found it*, %*They've invited Kim and I to lunch*) and the accusative is likewise not restricted to object function, and indeed not excluded from subject function (*Kim objected to him being given such preferential treatment*; *For him to go alone would be very dangerous*).

[58] Case as an inflectional category is quite distinct from the 'abstract case' invoked in some modern theories of formal grammar: all overt NPs have case in this abstract sense, regardless of their surface form.

No dative case in English

The earlier case system of English distinguished not only nominative, accusative, and genitive, but also dative (a case which characteristically serves to mark indirect object function). The loss of inflectional endings has resulted in this case dropping out of the system altogether, for it is not even retained in the personal pronouns. Compare, then:

[3]	i	*We took him to the zoo.*	[direct object; accusative case]
	ii	*We showed him the animals.*	[indirect object; accusative case]

No pronoun has different forms in these constructions, and there is thus no basis for distinguishing two inflectional cases here. Again, traditional school grammars often analyse *him* as a dative case in examples like [ii], but this is one of those places where an analysis that is valid for Latin (or Old English) has been inappropriately carried over to Present-day English.[59]

Inflectional and analytic case

Although case is prototypically marked inflectionally, there are languages where it is marked analytically, by special grammaticised words. Japanese is a language of this type, with subject, direct object, and indirect object marked by distinct postpositions. Some grammars of English also postulate a certain amount of analytic case: *to*, for example, has been regarded as a marker of dative case in clauses like [4a] and *of* as a marker of genitive case in NPs like [4b]:

[4]	a. *I gave the money to Kim.*	b. *the father of the bride*

The view taken here, however, is that English has only inflectional case, that prepositions are not case markers. The rationale for taking *to* as a dative marker is that *to Kim* is allegedly an indirect object, but we have argued in fact that it is not – that although it has the same semantic role as the NP *Kim* of *I gave Kim the money* it does not have the same syntactic function (cf. Ch. 4, §4.3). Leaving aside the nominative–accusative contrast in pronouns, the core syntactic functions in clause structure are not marked by inflectional case, and there is no justification for treating *to* as an analytic case marker here but as an ordinary preposition in *I explained the matter to Kim*, *I spoke to Kim*, *He referred to Kim*, and so on. Similarly for *of*. Semantically, the relation of *the bride* to *father* is the same in [4b] as in *the bride's father*, but syntactically there is a major difference: in the latter *the bride's* is determiner (or subject-determiner), whereas in [4b] *of the bride* is simply a complement, and as such it is similar to the post-head PPs in *a view of the river*, *a number of animals*, *his marriage to Jennifer*, *her insistence on a recount*. There are a large number of prepositions in English and overall their role is very different from that of inflectional case markers; some of them have relatively grammaticised uses, but we do not believe it would be possible to make a principled and rigorous syntactic distinction between case-marker and other uses.

Variants of the genitive: dependent and independent

Most of the personal pronouns have two genitive forms, which we refer to as **dependent** and **independent**:

[5]	i	*Where shall I park my car?*	[dependent]
	ii	*Jill's car is in the carport: where shall I park mine?*	[independent]

[59] A considerable amount of modern work applies the term 'dative' to a semantic role (essentially, the recipient role) or the corresponding syntactic function. Given that 'dative' is applicable to an inflectional case in many languages, this seems to us an unfortunate extension of the term.

My is required in [i], where the genitive is a dependent of the head noun *car*, but in [ii], where the genitive itself is head of the object NP, we have the independent form *mine*. We take this to be a relatively minor matter, and regard *my* and *mine* as variants of the genitive case. The distinction is not comparable to that between *I* and *me*: these are distinct primary cases, not variants of the plain case.

We have, then, three major cases: nominative, accusative, genitive. The plain case represents a neutralisation of the nominative–accusative opposition, and independent and dependent genitives are contextual variants of the genitive.

Pronouns with more than two case-forms

Most nouns, we have noted, have just two cases, plain and genitive. The following table lists those pronouns which distinguish nominative and accusative, and/or independent and dependent genitives. They constitute most of the personal pronouns together with the interrogative and relative pronoun ***who***:

[6]

<table>
<tr><th></th><th>NOMINATIVE</th><th>ACCUSATIVE</th><th colspan="2">GENITIVE</th></tr>
<tr><th></th><th colspan="2">PLAIN</th><th>Dependent</th><th>Independent</th></tr>
<tr><td>PERSONAL</td><td></td><td></td><td></td><td></td></tr>
<tr><td></td><td>I</td><td>me</td><td>my</td><td>mine</td></tr>
<tr><td></td><td>we</td><td>us</td><td>our</td><td>ours</td></tr>
<tr><td></td><td colspan="2">you</td><td>your</td><td>yours</td></tr>
<tr><td></td><td>he</td><td>him</td><td colspan="2">his</td></tr>
<tr><td></td><td>she</td><td>her</td><td>her</td><td>hers</td></tr>
<tr><td></td><td>they</td><td>them</td><td>their</td><td>theirs</td></tr>
<tr><td>INTERROGATIVE/RELATIVE</td><td></td><td></td><td></td><td></td></tr>
<tr><td></td><td>who</td><td>whom</td><td colspan="2">whose</td></tr>
</table>

16.2 Nominative and accusative

We look first at the contrast between nominative and accusative case, where we find a considerable amount of variation and instability in the system. There are a number of constructions where the nominative is associated with formal style, the accusative being strongly preferred in informal speech and writing. Because of the tendency of older prescriptive grammar to accept only formal style as 'grammatically correct', there has been a tradition of criticising the accusative alternants, and the stigmatism attaching to such accusatives has given rise to a certain amount of hypercorrection, with nominatives being used in constructions where the traditional rules call for an accusative. Or at least this is the situation with the personal pronouns and determinatives: with interrogative and relative ***who*** the reverse situation obtains, the accusative *whom* being the case associated with formal style. We will therefore consider the personal pronouns and ***who*** separately, and for the former we begin with non-coordinate constructions, leaving the special problems found with coordination to §16.2.2.

16.2.1 Non-coordinate personal pronouns/determinatives

Constructions where nominative case is obligatory

There is just one function where pronouns appear in the nominative case to the exclusion of the accusative, irrespective of style level: subject of a finite clause. Compare:

[7] NOMINATIVE / ACCUSATIVE

	NOMINATIVE	ACCUSATIVE
i	a. *I made up some new curtains.*	b. **Me made up some new curtains.*
ii	a. *Did we see that movie or not?*	b. **Did us see that movie or not?*
iii	a. *We saw that movie, didn't we?*	b. **We saw that movie, didn't us?*
iv	a. *I think he is mad.*	b. **I think him is mad.*

These examples illustrate a variety of finite-clause subjects: non-inverted subject in [i], inverted subject in [ii], inverted subject in an interrogative tag in [iii], and subject of a finite subordinate clause in [iv]. In all these environments, an accusative subject is completely ungrammatical, as seen in the [b] versions.

Even in this construction, however, we find variation with the personal determinative ***we***, with nominative *we* being the norm but very colloquial and dialectal varieties having accusative *us*:

[8] i *We anarchists almost toppled the militarist-industrial-financial Establishment.*
ii *Perhaps this is why we all taunted and teased him, because he was different and us kids don't like anything different.*

Constructions where nominative and accusative are in alternation

There are a number of constructions where both cases are found. In most, the nominative is restricted to formal (or very formal) style, with the accusative appearing elsewhere.

(a) Subjective predicative complement

[9]		
i	a. *It is I who love you.*	b. *It's me who loves you.*
ii	a. *It is I she loves.*	b. *It's me she loves.*
iii	a. *Yes, it is she!*	b. *Yes, it's her!*
iv	a. *This is he / These are they.*	b. *This is him / These are them.*
v	a. ?*The only one who objected was I.*	b. *The only one who objected was me.*
vi	a. **This one here is I at the age of 12.*	b. *This one here is me at the age of 12.*

Probably the most frequent use of a nominative case predicative is in the *it*-cleft construction, as in [i–ii]. And here we can make a distinction according to whether the pronoun would be in nominative or accusative case in the non-cleft counterpart: compare [i] with *I love you* and [ii] with *She loves me*. In the former, the accusative version [ib] certainly has an informal flavour, whereas in the latter the nominative version [iia] seems very formal and the accusative [iib] relatively neutral in style. Nominatives are also found with *it* + *be* without a following relative clause, as in [iiia]. This is considered very formal – and in response to the question *Who's there?* the nominative version *It is I* would be widely perceived as pedantic. The other main construction where a nominative is quite commonly found, again in formal style, is with a demonstrative as subject, as in [iv]. It might also be used in *if I were he* (but hardly ?*if you were I*). Elsewhere, it is again likely to be perceived as somewhat pedantic. Most speakers would avoid examples like [va] – which is easily done by reversing the order (*I was the only one who objected*). The context for [vi] is one where we are looking at an old photograph; it is difficult to imagine that anyone would use a nominative in construction with the following PP that we have here.

Languages with fuller case systems than Present-day English often have case agreement between a predicative complement and its predicand; this indeed was the situation in older stages of English. With only a handful of pronouns showing a nominative–accusative contrast, however, it would be inappropriate to talk of case agreement in English. In [9], for example, all the subjects are in plain case, so it is not a matter of whether the predicative matches the subject in case. Notice, moreover, that the issue of a contrast in case between subjective and objective predicatives doesn't arise for it is impossible to have a personal pronoun in objective predicative complement function. This is because an objective predicative can only be ascriptive, and personal pronoun predicatives can only be of the specifying type: see Ch. 4, §5.4.2.

(b) Subject of a gerund-participial in adjunct function

[10] i *We were in Greville's office, I sitting in his swivel chair behind the vast expanse of desk, Annette sorting yesterday's roughly heaped higgledy-piggledy papers back into the drawers and files that had earlier contained them.*

ii *He could think of a few himself, I expect, him being so much in the business already.*

Here the difference is straightforwardly one of style level, nominative being the formal variant, accusative the informal.

(c) Complement of comparative *than* and *as*

	a.	b.
[11] i	*She is older than he.*	*She is older than him.*
ii	*She went to the same school as I.*	*She went to the same school as me.*
iii	*I've not met a nicer man than he*	*I've not met a nicer man than him.*
iv	**It affected the others more than I.*	*It affected the others more than me.*
v	**She is older than we both/all.*	*She is older than us both/all.*

If the complement of *than* or *as* can be expanded by the addition of a verb to which the pronoun is subject, then formal style has a nominative, informal style an accusative. In [i–iii], for example, we can expand the [a] versions to *older than he is, the same school as I went to, a nicer man than he is.* According to the traditional account, the pronouns in [i–iii] are subjects of elliptical clauses and therefore 'should' appear in the same case as when the verb is present. Whether the pronouns in [i–iii] are properly analysed as reduced clauses is a difficult question that we discuss (without in fact resolving) in Ch. 13, §2.2, but whatever the answer the accusatives are clearly fully acceptable in informal style. Some speakers may find the nominative less likely in [iii] than in [i–ii]: in [i–ii] the pronoun is matched against the subject of the matrix clause, but this is not so in [iii]. In [iv] expansion of the complement of *than* would put the pronoun in object position (*It affected the others more than it affected me*), and in comparative constructions of this kind the pronoun is invariably accusative. Note finally that if the pronoun is followed by *both* or *all*, as in [v], accusative case is the only possibility (see §10.1.1).

(d) Subject of (other) verbless clauses

	a.	b.
[12] i	*He was morose, she full of life.*	*He was morose, her full of life.*
ii	*What, he a republican?*	*What, him a republican?*

Example [i] belongs to the gapping construction (Ch. 15, §4.2); the nominative is readily used in formal style, while the accusative seems very informal or colloquial. Example [ii] belongs to the bare predication polar echo construction (Ch. 10, §4.8.3), which is itself generally a somewhat informal construction, so the accusative pronoun is more likely; nevertheless, a nominative, as in [iia], is certainly possible. There is also the verbless counterpart of the gerund-participial adjunct discussed in (b) above:

[13] *I knew people thought ours an unlikely alliance, I neat and quiet, he restless and flamboyant.*

Again accusative *me* and *him* could be used as subject in a more informal style. In [12–13] the clauses, though verbless, nevertheless contain a predicative element. In constructions without such an element following the subject, nominative case is less likely:

		a.	b.
[14]	i	a. *Gary took the call, not I.*	b. *Gary took the call, not me.*
	ii	a. A: *Who ordered a taxi?* B: ?*I.*	b. A: *Who ordered a taxi?* B: *Me.*
	iii	a. A: *I'm going home.* B: *I too.	b. A: *I'm going home.* B: *Me too.*

Few people would use a nominative in [i], fewer still in [ii], where it would sound excessively pedantic (even more so, probably, with a negative: ?*Not I*), and in [iii] it can be regarded as completely unacceptable. If the accusative is felt to be too informal for the context, the construction can easily be avoided altogether: *I didn't take the call, Gary did; I did; So am I.*[60]

(e) Following exclusive *but*

		a.	b.
[15]	i	a. *Nobody but she can do it.*	b. *Nobody but her can do it.*
	ii	a. *I trust nobody but she.	b. *I trust nobody but her.*
	iii	a. *Nobody can do it but she.	b. *Nobody can do it but her.*

Again, [ia] is the formal variant, [ib] the informal. The nominative is normally restricted to the construction where *but* + pronoun immediately follows (or is part of) the subject: compare [ia] and [iia/iiia]. The alternation between nominative and accusative reflects the fact that the category status of *but* in this construction – as coordinator or preposition – is somewhat problematic: see Ch. 15, §2.5.

(f) Subject of clausal complement of *with/without*

Pronouns in this position normally appear in accusative case:

[16] i *We set off again, the Rover going precariously slowly in very low gear up hills, with me staying on its tail in case it petered out altogether.*

ii *With me out of the way, there would be no one to curb his excesses.*

Note that this is one place where a gerund-participial in complement function cannot take a genitive subject, but unlike the construction dealt with in (b) above the accusative is not here an informal alternant to a nominative.[61]

Constructions where accusative case is obligatory

Finally there are a number of constructions where only an accusative case is permitted: direct and indirect object, object of a preposition (other than *than* and *as*, covered above), and subject of an infinitival clause introduced by the subordinator *for*:

		a.	b.
[17]	i	a. *The police arrested him on Friday.*	b. *The police arrested he on Friday.
	ii	a. *She handed me the tapes.*	b. *She handed I the tapes.
	iii	a. *Pamela was standing near me.*	b. *Pamela was standing near I.
	iv	a. *For him to go alone would be risky.*	b. *For he to go alone would be risky.

[60] Whatever the case, the deictic pronoun ***I*** is much more likely in constructions like [14ii–iii] than the usually anaphoric **he** or **she**.

[61] Nominatives are occasionally attested (e.g. *If I kept it secret, I could not use it without he in time asking awkward questions as to where I had obtained all the money), but they are rare enough to be set aside as errors.

Accusatives are also the only option for the left- and right-dislocation constructions (which are themselves characteristic of informal style):

[18] i *Me, I wouldn't trust him further than I could throw him.*
ii *I don't much care for it, me.*

The non-clausal construction where a pronoun is modified by an adjective is likewise restricted to accusatives: *Silly me!* And we can almost certainly include here too the displaced subject in the existential construction (see Ch. 4, §3.2.2):

[19] i A: *Who is there who could help?* B: *Well, there's always me/*I, I suppose.*
ii A: *Don't forget Liz.* B: *Yes, there's certainly her/*she to consider.*

As we saw with the subject of a finite clause, the case-assignment rule does not apply so absolutely with determinative ***we*** as it does with pronouns:

[20] i *Nobody asked us workers how we felt about it.*
ii %*The real work of universities . . . is now being made increasingly difficult for we workers.*
iii %*What a delightful invitation, for we workers to submit something to your splendid publication.*

The nominatives in [ii–iii] (both taken from a university staff newsletter) are further examples of what can be regarded as hypercorrections.

16.2.2 Coordinative constructions

For one variety of English, coordination has no bearing on case: the case of a coordinate pronoun is the same as that of a pronoun that could substitute for the whole coordination. Some examples conforming to this rule are as follows:

[21] i *At 4 pm this afternoon my ministers and I formally took office.*
ii *He and Luckman were sentenced to life imprisonment.*
iii *He and I have some of our biggest arguments over Conservative social issues.*
iv *You know you can trust Andrea and me.*
v *I saw them and their children in the park.*
vi *There has always been pretty intense rivalry between him and me.*

Compare [i–iii] with the non-coordinate nominatives *I took office*, *They were sentenced . . .*, *We have . . .*, and [iv–vi] with the accusatives . . . *you can trust us*, *I saw them*, . . . *between us*. This is the pattern advocated by the usage manuals, but for many speakers the case-assignment rules are sensitive to the syntactic distinction between coordinate and non-coordinate pronouns.

Coordinate accusatives corresponding to non-coordinate nominatives

[22] i a. !*Tina and me sat by the window looking down on all the twinkling lights.*
b. !*She and us are going to be good friends.*
ii a. !*Me and Larry are going to the movies.*
b. !*Him and me fixed up the wagon while the others went to town.*

In the variety illustrated in [i] the accusative is used only for a coordinate following the coordinator: coordinators are treated in the same way as prepositions for case-assignment purposes. In [ii] the accusative is used irrespective of the position of the pronoun within the coordination.

The accusatives in [22] are non-standard and strongly stigmatised, especially the pattern in [ii]. They show, however, that the only completely secure territory of the nominative in Present-day English is with pronouns functioning as the whole subject in a finite clause.

Coordinate nominatives corresponding to non-coordinate accusatives

[23] i a. %*The present was supposed to represent Helen and I, that was the problem.*
b. %*Any postgrad who has any concerns about working conditions or security in shared offices is welcome to approach either Ann Brown or I with them.*
c. %*It would be an opportunity for you and I to spend some time together.*
d. %*He had intended to leave at dawn, without you or I knowing anything about it.*
ii a. %*They've awarded he and his brother certificates of merit.*
b. %*There's a tendency for he and I to clash.*

Single pronouns replacing the coordinations would have to be in accusative case: *us* in [i] and [iib], *them* in [iia]. One particularly common use of this construction is in the expression *between you and I*, and indeed usage manuals often discuss it under that heading. It must be emphasised, however, that these nominatives are found quite generally in coordinations functioning in positions where single accusative pronouns are used. The pattern shown in [i], with the nominative as final coordinate, is much more common than the one in [ii], where the nominative occurs as first (or both first and final) coordinate.

There can be little doubt that the quite common use of this construction is related to the stigmatism attaching to accusatives in subject coordinations like those in [22]: people are taught that *Me and Kim will do it* and *Kim and me will do it* are incorrect, and many generalise their avoidance of such coordinate accusatives to other functional positions. The schoolteacher's strictures focus primarily on the 1st person singular pronoun (since this is where children most commonly depart from the standard variety), and in construction [23], with final-only nominative, *I* is overwhelmingly the most frequent form that is found. Compare [23] with the much less widely used:

[24] i %*They've invited the Smiths and we to lunch.*
ii %*Liz will be back next week, so I've asked Ed to return the key to you or she.*

Because these coordinate nominatives are perceived to be associated with avoidance of stigmatised accusatives in subject coordinations they are often described as hypercorrections. This is to imply that they are 'incorrect', not established forms in the standard language. Construction [23i] with *I* as final coordinate is, however, so common in speech and used by so broad a range of speakers that it has to be recognised as a variety of Standard English, and we will reserve the term hypercorrection for examples like [23ii] and [24].

Note that the distinction between 1st person singular and other personal pronouns is also evident in such constructions as:

[25] i *They like the same kind of music as you and we.*
ii *They like the same kind of music as you and I.*

Example [i] belongs to the same style level as *They like the same kind of music as we* – i.e. it is very formal. But [ii] is not felt to be stylistically restricted in the same way; many speakers who do not themselves use examples like [23i] would nevertheless feel much more comfortable with [25ii] than with [25i].

16.2.3 *Who* and *whom*

The situation with the interrogative or relative pronoun ***who*** is significantly different from that obtaining with the personal pronouns. Style differences in the personal pronouns have nominative as formal, accusative as informal, but with ***who*** the alternations are typically between accusative *whom* as formal and nominative *who* as informal or relatively neutral.

[26]	ACCUSATIVE	NOMINATIVE
i	a. *Whom did you meet?*	b. *Who did you meet?*
ii	a. *He didn't say whom he had invited.*	b. *He didn't say who he had invited.*
iii	a. *those whom we consulted*	b. *those who we consulted*

Whom and style level

In short simple constructions like those in [26] there is a rather sharp style contrast between *whom* and *who*: *whom* is strikingly more formal than *who*. It would be a mistake to say, however, that *whom* is confined, or even largely confined, to formal style. In more complex constructions than the above, *whom* is not infrequently found in combination with lexical or syntactic features which are characteristic of relatively informal style. A few attested examples are given in:

[27] i *A pretty young co-ed named Junko gets into the game and thus meets a youngster with whom she has an affair.*

ii *The next musician whom I got to know well was a much younger man whom I have already mentioned, Sidney Lewis.*

iii *He double-crosses the five pals with whom he lives, cheats a waitress (Juliet Prowse) and cynically uses a magazine editress (Martha Hyer) to get ahead.*

iv *Jeffrey had grown a beard and was associating with a scruffy crowd of radicals, many of whom were not even British.*

v *Hugh wasn't impressed with this ingratiating barman whom Roddy had raked up.*

vi *These include the deros of the inner urban areas and most of the abos, most of whom haven't got a skerrick, and spend most of what little they have on the terps getting rotten.*

None of these could be described as formal in style; the last in particular, an Australian example, is strikingly informal, containing as it does the clippings *deros* ("derelicts"), *abos* ("Aborigines"), *terps* ("turpentine"), and such other features as *haven't got a skerrick* and *getting rotten*.

Survey of functions

(a) Subject and predicative complement

Nominative is required in both these functions:

[28]		
i	a. **Whom wrote the editorial?*	b. *Who wrote the editorial?*
ii	a. **the man whom came to dinner*	b. *the man who came to dinner*
iii	a. **Whom could it be?*	b. *Who could it be?*

We are concerned here with the subject of the interrogative or relative clause itself: for the construction where ***who*** is subject of a clause embedded within the interrogative or relative, see (e) below. A predicative complement realised by ***who*** is always subjective:

the objective predicative in clauses like *He considered her the victim* cannot be questioned or relativised by ***who***.

(b) Object of verb

Here *whom* and *who* are in alternation, as illustrated in [26]. The alternation is also found in post-verbal interrogative objects:

[29] a. *Who is going to marry whom?* b. *Who is going to marry who?*

The formal feel of *whom* is most apparent in main clause interrogatives: examples like [26ia] are widely perceived to be very formal indeed (verging on the pedantic), with nominative *who* considered preferable in almost all contexts. *Whom* is just about impossible as a single-word question: in response to *I met a friend of yours on the bus this morning* one would say *Oh, who?*, not *Oh, whom?* With relatives the nominative is felt to be more informal than with the interrogatives, probably because it can easily be avoided in integrated relatives by means of a non-*wh* construction: *those we consulted* or *those that we consulted* (but note the accusative object in [27v] above). Supplementary relatives are normally of the *wh* type, and here *whom* is not uncommon, and not strongly formal in tone; the following, for example, appeared in a video chainstore's magazine giving synopses of new releases:

[30] *Award-winning journalist Nelson Keece (Gary Busey) is coldly detached from his chosen subject, serial killer Stefan (Arnold Vosloo), whom he catches in the act of murder.*

(c) Fronted object of a stranded preposition

[31] i a. *Whom are you referring to?* b. *Who are you referring to?*
ii a. *someone whom we can rely on* b. *someone who we can rely on*

The versions with *who* have a slightly informal flavour, and again relative *who* will often be avoided in favour of the non-*wh* construction *someone (that) we can rely on*. The construction with accusative *whom* is fairly rare in comparison with *who* + stranded preposition or fronted preposition + *whom* (as in [33] below). Nevertheless, examples of *whom* + stranded preposition are certainly attested, providing further evidence that *whom* is not restricted to markedly formal style.

[32] i *Nobody cares to guess how many votes he may get, nor whom he is most likely to take them from.*
ii *The first royalty whom mama ever waited on in the White House was Queen Marie of Rumania, . . .*
iii *And that's the man whom you've been eating your heart out over?*

(d) Object of a preceding preposition

[33] i a. *To whom are you referring?* b. **To who are you referring?*
ii a. *someone on whom we can rely* b. **someone on who we can rely*

This is the one place where the accusative is normally the only option: the nominative [b] versions are clearly ungrammatical. One qualification concerns constructions in which the PP stands alone or in post-verbal position:

[34] i A: *You should give them away.* B: *To who?*
ii *Who said what to who?*

Who here is acceptable in informal style: in terms of their grammaticality status these examples are closer to [31ib/iib] than to [33ib/iib].

The particular accusative examples cited as [33ia/iia] are very formal in tone, and in most contexts would be avoided in favour of the stranded preposition construction shown in [31] above. But there are many places where the stranded construction is impossible or would be extremely awkward:

[35] i *Her whole life centred around her six surviving daughters, one son, and nine grand-children, of whom I was the youngest.*
ii *There were many in the colony for whom a resumption of the transport system meant a supply of cheap labour.*

It is where there is no stranding alternant that the accusative *whom* is most likely to be perceived as more or less neutral in style rather than as a distinctively formal marker. The most common construction where stranding is not an available alternant is with partitives, as in: *some of whom, all/both/many/few/none/two of whom*, etc.

The preposition + *whom* construction is much more common in relatives than in interrogatives. It is certainly not excluded from the latter, however; one type worth illustrating is that where we have a coordination of interrogative clauses or phrases:

[36] *Since the earliest days of Australian sports coverage the issues have been, more subconsciously than consciously, what should be reported, by whom, for whom, to what purpose and in what form.*

(e) Subject of an embedded content clause

[37] a. %*those whom he thought were guilty* b. *those who he thought were guilty*

Here **who** is subject of the content clause functioning as complement of *thought*: it is not subject of the relative clause itself but of a finite clause embedded within the relative clause. In this construction there is variation between accusative *whom* and nominative *who*. The accusative construction is very largely restricted to relative clauses; it does not appear to occur in main clause interrogatives, and is rare and of doubtful acceptability in subordinate ones:

[38] i a. **Whom do you think will win?* b. *Who do you think will win?*
ii a. ?*I told her whom you think took it.* b. *I told her who you think took it.*

Attested examples of relative *whom* are given in [39], where [i] represents the usual type with a tensed verb (*thought*), while [ii] has a plain-form verb in the mandative construction:

[39] i *A man with a large waxed moustache and a mop of curly damp hair, whom Hal thought might be his uncle Fred, said, 'That's a fine bird you're carving, Bert.'*
ii *It turns out that the woman, whom the police have asked not be identified, was a talented pianist and an unpublished writer.*

Prescriptive grammarians commonly treat this *whom* as a hypercorrection: since the pronoun is in subject function, the argument goes, it should be nominative and the accusative is therefore incorrect, attributable to a concern to avoid the common 'error' of using nominative *who* in place of accusative *whom*. This is another place, however, where we believe it is invalid to talk in terms of hypercorrection. The accusative variant has a long history and is used by a wide range of speakers; examples are quite often encountered in quality newspapers and works by respected authors. It has to be accepted as an established variant of the standard language.[62] Thus there are in effect two dialects with respect to the case of embedded subjects, though they are not distinguished on any regional basis. Dialect A, which selects nominative, has more speakers and is the one recommended by the manuals, but there is no reason to say that it is inherently better or more grammatically correct than Dialect B, which selects accusative: the dialects just have different rules.

The alternation between *who* and *whom* can be attributed to the tension between the function of ***who*** with respect to the embedded content clause and its position in the relative clause. The two relevant factors are:

[40] i ***Who*** is subject of a finite content clause.
   ii ***Who*** is in prenuclear position preceding the subject of the relative clause.

In Dialect A it is factor [i] that determines the case, as nominative, while in Dialect B [ii] is the determining factor, at least in formal style (and excluding the rather rare construction where ***who*** is in predicative complement function). In Dialect B the crucial distinction is therefore between relative clause subject and non-subject. And it is worth noting that this distinction is of importance elsewhere in relative clauses: bare relatives are normally not admissible when it is the relative clause subject that is relativised, but allow relativisation of other elements, including the subject of an embedded clause. Compare, for example, **She's the <u>student</u>$_i$ [__$_i$ had made the complaint]* (where the gap is relative clause subject) with *She's the <u>student</u>$_i$ [he accused__$_i$]* (object) and *She's the <u>student</u>$_i$ [he said [__$_i$ had made the complaint]]* (embedded subject).

16.3 Six types of genitive construction

We turn now to the genitive case, where we distinguish six constructions, as follows:

[41]	i	*[<u>Kim's</u> father] has arrived.*	[I: subject-determiner]
	ii	*No one objected to [<u>Kim's</u> joining the party].*	[II: subject of gerund-participial]
	iii	*Max's attempt wasn't as good as [<u>Kim's</u>].*	[III: fused subject-determiner-head]
	iv	*She's [a friend of <u>Kim's</u>].*	[IV: oblique genitive]
	v	*All this is <u>Kim's</u>.*	[V: predicative genitive]
	vi	*He lives in [an <u>old people's</u> home].*	[VI: attributive genitive]

The genitives in Types I–V are full NPs, while that in Type VI can be just a nominal.

In this section we present a short overview of all six constructions; in §16.5 we look more fully at Type I, and the ways Type VI differs from it.

Type I: subject-determiner

In [41i] *Kim's* is a genitive NP functioning as subject-determiner within the matrix NP *Kim's father*; genitive case marks *Kim* as standing in a relation of dependence within this matrix NP. *Kim's father* itself has plain case and can occur in the full range of NP positions; it is interpreted as definite ("the father of Kim", not "a father of Kim").

[62] *Whom* is occasionally found as subject not of an embedded clause but of the relative clause itself, with a parenthetical expression after the subject: **Mr Dawkins lashed out at the Senators, including those of his own party <u>whom</u>, he believed, should have shown more loyalty.* Unlike the examples in [37a] and [39], however, this does not represent an established usage, and we believe it is properly regarded as ungrammatical, a genuine hypercorrection.

As noted above, the genitive subject-determiner is itself a full NP. In *this company's computers*, for example, it is clear from the singular form that *this* is a dependent of *company*, not *computers*; we accordingly have the NP *this company's* functioning as subject-determiner within a larger NP. Where the genitive NP contains a post-head dependent, as in *the people next door's behaviour*, the case marker attaches at the end rather than on the head (*people*): we take up this issue in §16.6.

The construction is recursive, i.e. we can have one such construction within another, as in *Kim's father's business*, where the first *'s* suffix marks ***Kim*** as subject-determiner of *Kim's* ***father***, and the second marks the latter as subject-determiner within the topmost NP *Kim's father's business*.

Type II: subject of gerund-participial

In [41ii] the genitive marks the subject of a gerund-participial clause in complement function – in this example, the clause is object of the preposition *to*. Historically, this construction is an offshoot from Type I: what was originally a noun came to be reanalysed as a verb and to behave as the head of a clause rather than an NP (see further discussion in Ch. 14, §1.5). This genitive marks the relation of *Kim* not to a matrix NP but to a clause; in this construction, then, the subject function does not combine with that of determiner. One major difference between Types I and II in Present-day English is that the genitive marking the subject of a gerund-participial alternates with plain (or accusative) case: *No one objected to Kim joining the party.*

Type III: fused subject-determiner-head

Kim's in [41iii] is an instance of the fused-head construction discussed in §9.2. As in the Type I construction, the genitive marks the relation between a dependent element and a matrix NP containing it. Usually, as in this example, the two NPs are co-extensive, but they do not have to be – the matrix NP may also contain a predeterminer or a post-head dependent:

[42] i *Only one of Ed's attempts was successful, but [both Kim's] were.*
ii *Ed's production of 'Hamlet' was more successful than [Kim's of 'Macbeth'].*

Thus in [41iii], no less than in [41i], we need to recognise a plain-case NP as well as the genitive one. The structures for the two examples are as follows:

[43]
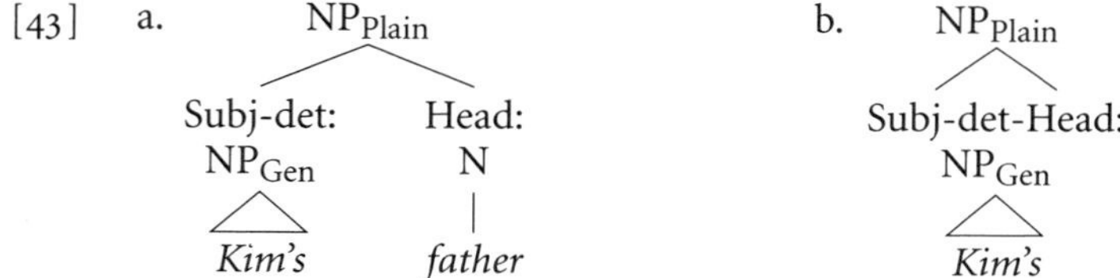

Type IV: oblique genitive

We refer to the genitive in [41iv] as oblique because it is related to the head noun *friend* obliquely, via the preposition *of*, rather than immediately, as in *Kim's friend*.[63] The PP *of Kim's* is post-head dependent within the matrix NP. Type I genitives fill

[63] The oblique genitive construction is commonly referred to as the 'double genitive'. For the reasons given in §16.1, however, we do not regard *of* as a genitive case marker, and hence there is only one genitive here, not two.

the determiner position, where they mark the NP as definite, while the oblique allows the relation between subordinate and matrix NPs to be expressed while leaving the determiner position free to be filled by other kinds of determiner.[64] Compare, then:

[44]	PRE-HEAD	POST-HEAD: OBLIQUE
i	a. *a _Kim's_ *friend*	b. *a friend of* _Kim's_
ii	a. **those* _Kim's_ *friends*	b. *those friends of* _Kim's_
iii	a. _Kim's_ *friend*	b. **the friend of* _Kim's_
iv	a. ?_Kim's_ *friend that I met in Paris*	b. *the friend of* _Kim's_ *that I met in Paris*
v	a. *all/both* _Kim's_ *friends*	b. *all/both friends of* _Kim's_
vi	a. _Kim's_ *every move*	b. *every move of* _Kim's_

Examples [ib/iib] show the oblique in combination with an indefinite or demonstrative determiner; the [a] versions are inadmissible because the determiner position is doubly filled – by *a*/*those* and by the Type I genitive *Kim's*. In [iiia] *Kim's* marks the matrix NP as definite, and the [b] version is excluded: the meaning would not be distinct from that of [iiia], and the simpler Type I construction is required. Where there is a post-head dependent, such as the relative clause in [iv], *the* is permitted in the oblique construction, while the pre-head version tends to be somewhat marginal. In [v] *all* and *both* can be predeterminers as well as determiners, and hence both constructions are possible, though the simpler [a] version is quite strongly preferred. Both versions are possible in [vi] too, because *every* can function as modifier as well as determiner; the [a] version, however, is limited to a quite narrow range of heads, so we can have *every friend of Kim's*, but not **Kim's every friend.*

Type V: predicative genitive

In [41v] the genitive marks the relation between *Kim* and the predicand *all this*, a relation like that expressible by *belong* + *to*. *Kim's* here is thus not part of some matrix NP, as it is in Types I and III–IV: here, then, the predicative complement function is realised directly by a genitive NP. Genitive predicative complements are usually subjective, as in this example, but they can also be objective: *Let's call it* _Kim's_; *I regard it as* _Kim's_.

As there is no reason to exclude the fused-head construction from predicative complement position, there may be structural ambiguity between Types III and V. Consider the case where A says, *I've got my towel but I can't find Kim's*, and B replies, *This is Kim's.* The first *Kim's* is Type III and one will tend to take the second in the same way, but outside such contexts *This is Kim's* will be Type V. The two readings here amount to the same thing, but we could not dispense with Type V, treating all such cases as fused heads: there is, for example, no basis for a fused-head analysis in examples like *Everything that is mine is yours.*

Type VI: attributive genitives

In [41vi], *an* _old people's_ *home*, the genitive is an attributive modifier within a nominal. At the top level of structure we have *an* as determiner and *old people's home* as head: it is clear that *an* cannot belong within the genitive expression, which is here plural. These genitives, moreover, can be preceded by other attributes, as in *a luxurious old people's home*, where *luxurious* modifies *old people's home.*

We distinguish two subtypes of attributive genitive:

[64]The range of semantic relations between subordinate and matrix NPs is, however, considerably narrower in the oblique construction: see §16.5.3.

(a) Descriptive genitives

[45] *a glorious [summer's day], a [Sainsbury's catalogue], two [bachelor's degrees], a [women's college], these very expensive [ladies' gloves], an [all girls' school]*

The square brackets enclose the nominal containing the genitive attribute. Descriptive genitives are themselves generally nominals, not NPs, as in all these examples except the last. Here, *all girls'* has NP status by virtue of having *all* as a peripheral modifier, giving the meaning "school exclusively for girls".

Descriptive genitives are unusual in that they are a somewhat unproductive category. For example, while it is possible to have *a summer's day* and *a winter's day*, corresponding forms for the other seasons are quite marginal: ?*a spring's day*; ?*an autumn's day*. Similarly, we have *a ship's doctor*, but not #*a school's doctor* – instead a plain-case nominal is used, *a school doctor*. The great majority of descriptive genitives denote humans (or animals); compare, for example, *fisherman's cottages* (cottages typical of those lived in by a fisherman) and **country's cottages* – instead of the latter we again have plain-case *country cottages*.

(b) Measure genitives

[46] *[an hour's delay], [one week's holiday], this [hour's delay], a second [one hour's delay], the [one dollar's worth of chocolates] he bought*

Genitives of this kind measure just temporal length or value: we do not have, for example, **They had [a mile's walk]* (spatial distance) or **We bought [a pound's carrots]* (weight). Value measures take the noun *worth* as head, while the temporal ones allow any semantically appropriate noun as head. An alternative means of expressing measure is to use a compound adjective, as in *a [two-hour delay], a [five-mile walk], an [eight-pound baby]*, etc.; this is less restricted than the genitive, though it is not admissible with *worth*.

Measure genitives commonly occupy initial position in the NP, as in the first two examples in [46], in which case they resemble subject-determiners (Type I genitives). That they are attributive modifiers, not determiners, however, is evident from the last three examples, where they follow a determiner (immediately or with an intervening adjectival attribute). When they occur in this position, i.e. after a determiner, they are subject to the constraint described in §6.2, so that the indefinite article is dropped: instead of **this [an hour's delay]* we have *this [hour's delay]*. In this case the measure genitive (*hour's*) has the status of a nominal, but otherwise measure genitives are full NPs.

Because they are modifiers not determiners, measure genitives do not confer definiteness on the NP. While *a friend's dog*, with Type I genitive, is definite ("the dog of a friend"), *an hour's delay* is indefinite ("delay of an hour"). Nor can they occur initially with nouns that require a count interpretation: **We played [an hour's game of squash]*; instead we need the compound adjective construction *We played a [one-hour game of squash]*.

16.4 Genitive pronouns

Dependent and independent forms

Five personal pronouns have two distinct contextual variants of the genitive case, dependent and independent: *my* ~ *mine, our* ~ *ours, your* ~ *yours, her* ~ *hers, their* ~ *theirs*. The dependent forms are used in constructions of Types I–II, the independent ones in

Types III–V (while Type VI excludes personal pronouns altogether):

[47] i [*My father*] *has arrived.* [I: subject-determiner]
ii *No one objected to* [*my joining the party*]. [II: subject of gerund-participial]
iii *Max's attempt wasn't as good as* [*mine*]. [III: fused subject-determiner-head]
iv *She's* [*a friend of mine*]. [IV: oblique genitive]
v *All this is mine.* [V: predicative genitive]

Independent genitives can stand alone as NPs functioning in the structure of main clauses. The dependent ones can function as subject in one type of subordinate clause, the gerund-participial, but in main clauses they require the support of a following head element, as in Type I. The head can be fused with a modifier (*My second attempt was even worse than* [*my first*]), but not with the dependent genitive itself (**Max's attempt wasn't as good as* [*my*]): fusion with the subject-determiner is structure III and requires the independent form, as in [47iii].

Traditional grammar's contrast between 'possessive adjectives' and 'possessive pronouns'

The dependent and independent genitives are often analysed in traditional grammar as 'possessive adjectives' and 'possessive pronouns' respectively, but we find this an unsatisfactory way of handling the difference between the two sets of forms. Both are genitive forms of the personal pronouns, and *my* and *mine* are both pronouns, just as *I* and *me* are. As pronouns, they are heads of NPs: *my* and *mine* are genitive NPs, like such expressions as *Kim's* or *the doctor's*, which can replace them. It is important to note that *my* is replaceable by expressions of this kind just as much as *mine* is. Moreover, *my* can be coordinated with such NPs, as in *He did it without my or the doctor's approval.* And in constructions of Type II an adjective analysis makes no sense at all: *my* is functioning as subject of a clause, not a modifier in NP structure.

Distributional restrictions on certain genitive pronouns

For the most part, any genitive can occur in all of constructions I–V, assuming that the correct choice is made between the dependent and independent forms, where relevant. There are, however, a number of restrictions applying to a few pronouns.

Its

This form is largely restricted to the constructions where dependent forms are used, i.e. I–II. Examples are very occasionally found in III and V, but we have no attested instances of IV and constructed examples seem clearly unacceptable:

[48] i *The Guardian seems to respect its readers more than the Sun respects its.* [III]
ii **The Bank is being sued by a rich client of its.* [IV]
iii *The council appears to be guilty of the illegal sale of houses that were not its to sell in the first place.* [V]

Instead of [ii] we would have *one of its rich clients* – or else we could have ***they*** rather than ***it***: *a rich client of theirs.* (See footnote 68 for another Type III example.)

Interrogative *whose*

This occurs in all constructions except the gerund-participial subject (II) and the oblique (IV), though its use in the fused-head construction (III) is rare:

[49] i *Whose book is that?* [I]
ii **I wonder whose being short-listed for the job he resented most.* [II]
iii A: *My suggestion was ignored again.* B: *Whose wasn't?* [III]
iv **I wonder a friend of whose he was.* [IV]
v *Whose could it be?* [V]

Relative whose

This occurs mainly in Type I, though it is just possible in Type IV in supplementary relatives:

[50] i *She wrote personally to those [whose proposals had been accepted].* [I]
ii **He felt deeply hostile to Georgina, [whose informing the College of his escapade had caused so much trouble].* [II]
iii **Students whose papers were marked by Jones were at a significant disadvantage relative to those [whose were marked by Smith].* [III]
iv *I was going to visit Lucy, [a friend of whose had told us of the accident].* [IV]
v **The police are trying to contact the person [whose it was].* [V]

16.5 Subject-determiner genitives

16.5.1 Combination of determiner and subject functions

Type I genitives combine the syntactic functions of determiner and subject. They are mutually exclusive with the basic determiners and for this reason their analysis as a special type of determiner is unproblematic, whereas the idea that they are also subject of the NP is more controversial. We believe, however, that this treatment is justified by significant structural resemblances between these genitives and the subject in clause structure; we will also see, when we turn to consider (in §16.5.2) the semantic relations between Type I genitives and the head of the NP that there are likewise important semantic resemblances between them and subjects of clauses.

Genitives as complements

In the first place we have seen that a genitive can occur separately from the determiner in the oblique genitive construction. Compare again, then:

[51] a. *Kim's cousin* b. *a cousin of Kim's*

On one dimension these differ as definite vs indefinite. In [a] the genitive is itself determiner, and as such it marks the matrix NP as definite, as we have noted. In [b] the genitive is located within a post-head dependent and the determiner position is filled by the indefinite article. On another dimension, however, *Kim's* stands in the same relation to *cousin* in both constructions: it expresses an argument of the head *cousin*. In [b] *of Kim's* is a complement, and in view of the likeness just observed we take *Kim's* to be a complement in [a] too. It then differs from other complements in NP structure in ways that resemble those in which the subject differs from other complements in clause structure.

Structural position

The subject in both NP and clause structure precedes the head and constitutes an external rather than internal complement. This parallelism is most obvious in nominalisations, where the NP is headed by a noun morphologically derived from a verb. It is then possible to make a direct comparison between NP and clausal structures, as in:

[52] a. b.

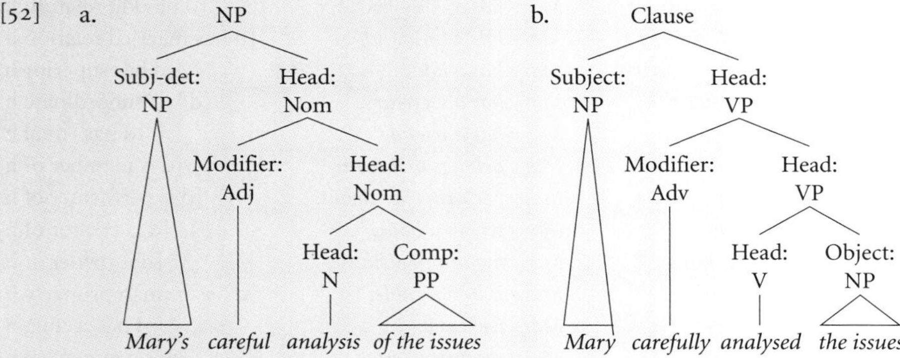

To bring out the parallelism, we use the label 'head' in [b] rather than the more specific 'predicate' or 'predicator'. Just as the verb *analysed* is the ultimate head of the clause, so the noun *analysis* is the ultimate head of the NP. Nouns take oblique complements as opposed to objects, so the internal complement of *analysis* is the PP *of the issues* rather than directly *the issues*. The nominal *analysis of the issues* is directly parallel to the VP *analysed the issues*: both can be modified by a pre-head modifier, the adjective *careful* in the case of the nominal and the adverb *carefully* in the case of the VP. The subject-determiner then completes the NP as the subject completes the clause.

Reflexives and their antecedents

The subject of a clause is the prototypical antecedent for any reflexive anaphor in the same clause, blocking any higher subject from acting as antecedent. The subject-determiner has an analogous role in NP structure. Compare:

[53]	i a. *<u>Sue</u> analysed <u>herself</u>.*	b. *Jill said [that <u>Sue</u> analysed <u>herself</u>].*	[clause]
	ii a. *<u>Sue's</u> analysis of <u>herself</u>*	b. *Jill's note on [<u>Sue's</u> analysis of <u>herself</u>]*	[NP]

In clause [ia] *herself* has the subject *Sue* as antecedent, and in [ib] it is still anaphorically linked to *Sue*, the subject of its own clause: it cannot be linked to *Jill*, the subject of the higher clause. And the same applies in the NPs in [ii]: in [iib] it is linked to the subject of the NP in which it appears as oblique, not the subject of the higher NP. (See Ch. 17, §3.1, for fuller discussion.)

16.5.2 Semantic comparison with the subject in clause structure

Range of semantic relations

The range of semantic relations between the genitive NP and the head is vast, and largely parallel to that found between subject and predicate in clause structure. Some of this variety is illustrated in [54]: the semantic distinctions made are typical of those known cross-linguistically to have different structural realisations even though they are similarly expressed in English. NPs are given in the left-hand column, and can be compared to clauses in the middle column, where the semantic relation between the subject and the NP within the predicate is parallel to that between the genitive and the head nominal. The right-hand column contains a generalised schema of each semantic relation:

[54]			
i	*Mary's green eyes*	*Mary has green eyes.*	[d has body part h]
ii	*Mary's younger sister*	*Mary has a younger sister.*	[d has kin relation h]
iii	*Mary's husband*	*Mary has a husband.*	[d has married relation h]
iv	*Mary's boss*	*Mary has a boss.*	[d has superior h]
v	*Mary's secretary*	*Mary has a secretary.*	[d has subordinate h]
vi	*Mary's friend*	*Mary has a friend.*	[d has equal h]
vii	*Mary's team*	*Mary belongs to a team.*	[d is member of h]
viii	*Mary's debut*	*Mary performs her debut.*	[d is performer of h]
ix	*Mary's book*	*Mary writes a book.*	[d is creator of h]
x	*Mary's new house*	*Mary owns a new house.*	[d is owner of h]
xi	*Mary's honour*	*Mary is honourable.*	[d has human property h]
xii	*Mary's anger*	*Mary feels angry.*	[d has feeling h]
xiii	*Mary's letter*	*Mary receives a letter.*	[d is recipient of h]
xiv	*Mary's obituary*	*Mary is the topic of an obituary.*	[d is human topic of h]
xv	*Mary's surgery*	*Mary undergoes surgery.*	[d is undergoer of h]
xvi	*the room's Persian carpet*	*The room contains a Persian carpet.*	[d is location of h]
xvii	*this year's new fashions*	*This year is a time of new fashions.*	[d is time of h]
xviii	*the sun's rays*	*The sun emits rays.*	[d is natural source of h]
xix	*the cathedral's spire*	*The cathedral has a spire.*	[d has inherent part h]
xx	*the war's ancient origins*	*The war has ancient origins.*	[d has cause h]
xxi	*the flood's consequences*	*The flood has consequences.*	[d has result h]
xxii	*the lock's key*	*The lock has a key.*	[d has associated part h]
xxiii	*the summer's heat*	*The summer is hot.*	[d has non-human property h]

In the annotations on the right 'd' stands for dependent (i.e. the subject-determiner NP) and 'h' for head (i.e. the nominal which the genitive determines); thus in [i], for example, 'd' represents Mary and 'h' represents green eyes.

The semantic analysis given here is considerably more specific than that which underlies the semantic roles presented in Ch. 4, §2.2, with the roles listed here being special cases of those more general roles. For example, performer ([viii]) and creator ([ix]) are central types of agent, and undergoer ([xv]) is a clear case of patient. The list given in [54] is not intended to be exhaustive, and indeed could not be, since ultimately the semantic relation that holds between subject-determiner and head nominal is not predetermined. Rather the interpretation is dependent on what semantic relation the context allows.

For example, *Mary's green eyes* in [i] is in isolation most likely to be interpreted as "the eyes which Mary sees with" (i.e. "Mary has green eyes as body part"), but other contextualisations are possible. Mary might be a university ophthalmologist who is conducting research into the optical properties of differently coloured eyes ("Mary is researcher into green eyes"). Or Mary might have a phobia about green eyes ("Mary is fearer of green eyes"). Or Mary might be an avant-garde sculptor who makes sculptures of green eyes ("Mary is creator of green eyes").

Similarly, *Mary's letter* in [iii] could be interpreted as "the letter Mary received" ("Mary is recipient of the letter"); or as "the letter Mary wrote" ("Mary is creator of the letter"); or as "the letter Mary posted" ("Mary is poster of the letter"); or it might have been written by Shakespeare, and Mary does research into it ("Mary is researcher into the letter"). The possibilities are endless, but they are all ones which can be parallelled by a clause which contains the subject-determiner as subject.

Nominalisations

In [54] we chose NPs that do not involve nominalisations, which to some extent need separate treatment. Or rather, this is so for **event nominalisations**, where the head noun is morphologically derived from a verb and denotes an event. Compare:

[55]	i a.	*Jill's departure*	*Jill departed.*	[event nominalisations]
	b.	*Ed's destruction of the file*	*Ed destroyed the file.*	
	ii a.	*Max's invention*	*Max invented something.*	[other nominalisations]
	b.	*Edith's proposal*	*Edith proposed something.*	
	c.	*Nigeria's population*	*Nigeria is populated.*	

The nominalisations in [ii] are essentially like the examples of [54] in allowing a range of interpretations for the subject NP. The most salient ones are those that match the corresponding clause, with Max the inventor in [iia], Edith the proposer, i.e. the creator of the proposal, in [iib], and Nigeria the location in [iic] (for *population* denotes the people who populate a given place). But other construals are possible. For example, if a class of science students is asked to write essays on different nineteenth-century inventions, Max might be allocated an essay on the light bulb, and is therefore researcher. Similarly in [iib], Edith could be a recipient of the proposal. And for [iic] imagine that the United Nations passes a resolution requiring population growth in each country to be monitored by a neighbouring country: then *Nigeria's population* might be interpreted as "the population Nigeria monitors" (the generalised researcher relation again).

With event nominalisations such as we have in [55i], however, it is hardly possible to assign a semantic role to the subject-determiner different from that of the subject of the corresponding clause. This is particularly so in examples like [ib] which contain another complement besides the subject. Here Ed can only be the destroyer, the agent, and the file that which is destroyed, the patient. In event nominalisations, therefore, the role of the subject-determiner is determined by the predicate expressed in the noun head to the same extent as the role of the subject of the clause is determined by the predicate expressed in the verb head.

16.5.3 Alternating patterns of complementation

In the structure of NPs, as in the structure of clauses, we often find that an element with a given semantic role may be aligned with complements of different kinds:

[56]	i a.	*Van Dyck's portrait of Charles I*	[creator as subject-determiner]
	b.	*the portrait of Charles I by Van Dyck*	[creator as *by* oblique]
	ii a.	*the flood's consequences*	[cause as subject-determiner]
	b.	*the consequences of the flood*	[cause as *of* oblique]

We have seen that the subject-determiner characteristically allows a range of roles, so that [ia] could be construed with Van Dyck having some other role than that of creator, such as owner; the oblique construction, however, is more specific, so that [ib] allows only the creator construal.

In [56i] the NPs are bivalent, i.e. contain two complements, while in [ii] they are monovalent, i.e. have just one complement (see Ch. 4, §1.1, for the concept of valency).

We will examine the two cases in turn, confining our attention to alternations involving the subject-determiner.

Bivalent constructions

In event nominalisations corresponding to transitive clauses, we typically have three possible alignments:

[57] i *Alexander the Great's conquest of Persia* [subject-determiner + *of* oblique]
ii *Persia's conquest by Alexander the Great* [subject-determiner + *by* oblique]
iii *the conquest of Persia by Alexander the Great* [*of* oblique + *by* oblique]

Version [iii] has two obliques, the others a subject-determiner + one oblique. In obliques it is the complement associated with the role of agent that takes *by*, while other roles take the default preposition *of*. In the mixed constructions, pattern [i] is more usual than [ii]: there is a preference for the more active role to be aligned with the subject-determiner, and for the other to be aligned with an oblique, which will therefore take the preposition *of*.

No system of voice in the NP

The relation between [57i] and [ii] bears some resemblance to that between active and passive clauses:

[58] i *Alexander the Great conquered Persia.* [active]
ii *Persia was conquered by Alexander the Great.* [passive]

Alexander the Great is subject in [57i/58i] and *by* oblique in [57ii/58ii], while *Persia* is subject in [57ii/58ii], and *of* oblique in [57i], object in [58i] – nouns don't take objects, *of* obliques being the default counterpart to the object of a verb. The parallel, however, is by no means sufficient to justify analysing the NPs [57i–ii] as differing in voice: there is no system of voice in the NP. The reasons for not generalising the system of voice from the clause to the NP are as follows:

(a) The system of voice in the clause involves just one of a number of contrasts in the alignment of complement types with semantic roles (see Ch. 4, §8). It differs from others (such as that illustrated in *Kim gave the book to Pat* vs *Kim gave Pat the book*) in that the terms are marked by formal differences that concern the verb, not just the NP complements: in this example, *conquered* vs *was conquered.* There is no difference of this kind in NP structure.

(b) For the NP, we have three contrasting structures, as shown in [57], not just the two that we find for the clause, illustrated in [58]. There would be no way of determining the voice of the double-oblique construction: it is like the putative active in having the patient role aligned with the *of* oblique, but like the putative passive in having the agent role aligned with the *by* oblique.

(c) The *by* oblique in NPs is associated with a narrower range of semantic roles than the *by* oblique in clauses. In NPs it always has an agentive role, whereas in clauses it can express, for example, the experiencer. Compare, then, *These facts were known by his father* and **the knowledge of these facts by his father.*

Monovalent constructions: subject-determiners compared with *of* phrases

In bivalent constructions a subject-determiner can combine with an *of* phrase, but in monovalent ones the two kinds of complement tend to be in competition with each other:

[59]	GENITIVE SUBJECT-DETERMINER	*OF* + NON-GENITIVE
i	a. *Mary's sister*	b. *the sister of Mary*
ii	a. *the accident's result*	b. *the result of the accident*

In [i] one would generally prefer the [a] version, but in [ii] the [b] version. We review here a number of factors favouring one or the other; the first involves a structure that excludes the genitive as ungrammatical, while with the others it is a matter of preferences, as in [59].

(a) Semantic relation between the NP and the head noun

Certain semantic relations are excluded from the subject-determiner construction but permitted in the *of* phrase one. These are illustrated in:

[60] i	**Roman coins' collection*	*the collection of Roman coins*	[h is collection of d]
ii	**shrub's two kinds*	*the two kinds of shrub*	[h is type of d]
iii	**red wine's glass*	*the glass of red wine*	[h is quantity of d]
iv	**gold's colour*	*the colour of gold*	[h is colour of d]
v	**honour's men*	*the men of honour*	[h has human property d]
vi	**despair's cry*	*the cry of despair*	[h has source d]
vii	**unemployment's problem*	*the problem of unemployment*	[h has content d]
viii	**washed silk's dress*	*the dress of washed silk*	[h has composition d]
ix	**twelve years' girl*	*the girl of twelve years*	[h has age d]
x	**purple's veil*	*the veil of purple*	[h has colour d]
xi	**2%'s rise*	*the rise of 2%*	[h has size d]
xii	**the cross's sign*	*the sign of the cross*	[h has form d]
xiii	**the hay stack's painting*	*the painting of the hay stack*	[h is depiction of d]
xiv	**all battles' battle*	*the battle of all battles*	[h is supreme example of d]

There is also no genitive counterpart of the predicative construction *the stupid nitwit of a husband* discussed in §14.1 (cf. **a husband's stupid nitwit*), or of partitives like *the youngest of the boys* (**the boys' youngest*).

(b) Semantic character of the NP

NPs denoting humans and (to a lesser extent) animals occur with much greater frequency as subject-determiners, e.g. *Mary's green eyes* and *the cat's paw* are much preferred to *the green eyes of Mary* and *the paw of the cat* (cf. also [59i]). However, there is also a (less strong) preference for NPs denoting times and geographical entities to be subject-determiners, e.g. *October's weather* is preferred to *the weather of October*, and *London's pubs* is preferred to *the pubs of London*. Least preferred as subject-determiners are NPs denoting other inanimates, e.g. *the roof of the house* is preferred to *the house's roof* (cf. [59ii]).

(c) Syntactic character of the NP

Most strikingly, pronouns are very strongly preferred as subject-determiners, and rarely found as the complement of *of*: compare *her money* and *your nose* with the very unnatural *the money of her* and *the nose of you*. However, pronouns are not totally excluded from the *of* construction. We have examples like *The only portrait of her can be found in the National Gallery*, where *her* as human topic is intended as relatively lower on the semantic hierarchy: *her only portrait* could also be interpreted as creator or owner. There are also almost idiomatic phrases like *That will be the death/undoing/making of him*, where again a low role (undergoer) seems to be intended.

Secondly, other things being equal, relatively short, head-final NPs will generally prefer subject-determiner position while relatively long NPs with post-head dependents will generally prefer the oblique position:

[61] i a. *the city's usual rush-hour traffic* b. *the usual rush-hour traffic of the city*
ii a. *a relatively young designer from Italy's creations* b. *the creations of a relatively young designer from Italy*

Version [a] is preferred in [i], [b] in [ii]. This reflects the general linguistic tendency for heavy dependents to be positioned to the right of the head.

(d) Morphological character of the NP

A small tendency has been noted for the regular plural ending to be avoided in subject-determiners: in speech, *the king's horses* and *the kings' horses* are not distinguishable, whereas *the horses of the king* and *the horses of the kings* are.

Comparison with oblique genitives

The oblique genitive construction is semantically less general than the subject-determiner construction. The semantic roles available to the oblique genitive NP are those in the top half of the hierarchy given in [54], while the construction is either questionable or clearly unacceptable with those in the lower half. Compare:

[62] i *those green eyes of Mary's* *that younger sister of Mary's*
that husband of Mary's *that boss of Mary's*
that secretary of Mary's *that friend of Mary's*
that team of Mary's *that debut of Mary's*
that book of Mary's *that new house of Mary's*
ii ?*that honour of Mary's* ?*that anger of Mary's*
?*that letter of Mary's* **that obituary of Mary's*
**that spire of the cathedral's* **that heat of the summer's*

The oblique genitive therefore does not generally contrast with the non-genitive *of* phrase construction, since this is disfavoured by animate dependents and virtually excluded in the case of personal pronouns. There is no possibility, for example, of **those green eyes of her* competing with *those green eyes of hers.* Nevertheless, we note two cases where there is competition. Firstly, it has been established that relatively long and heavy post-head dependents can favour the *of* phrase construction over the subject-determiner construction; this carries over to a competition between the oblique genitive and simple *of* phrases. We are more likely to have *those green eyes of Mary's* than *those green eyes of Mary*; equally, however, *those green eyes of the girl who lives next door* is considerably favoured over *those green eyes of the girl who lives next door's.* Secondly, in the special case of the equal relationship the difference between the two constructions can indicate different perspectives. We gloss *Mary's friends* (the plural of [54vi]) as "d has equal h", indicating that the relationship is viewed from Mary's perspective, and *those friends of Mary's* is understood in the same way. In *those friends of Mary,* however, the perspective is that of the friends, so that an appropriate gloss would have the terms reversed, giving "h has equal d".

16.6 Head and phrasal genitives

Genitive NPs are usually marked as such by the inflection of the head noun: we refer to these as **head genitives**. It is also possible for the marking to be located on the last word of a (final) post-head dependent, and these we call **phrasal genitives**. Compare, then, the following, where underlining marks the head and the genitive suffix:

[63]	HEAD GENITIVE	PHRASAL GENITIVE
i	a. [*Edward's*] *daughter*	b. [*the King of England's*] *daughter*
ii	a. [*everyone's*] *responsibility*	b. [*everyone else's*] *responsibility*
iii	a. [*somebody's*] *initiative*	b. [*somebody local's*] *initiative*
iv	a. [*the doctor's*] *house*	b. [*a guy I know's*] *house*

In [ib], for example, the head of the genitive NP is *King* but the suffix's attaches to *England*, the last word of the phrase *the King of England*. The range of phrasal genitive constructions is greater in informal, especially spoken, styles than in formal and written ones. In the latter it is normally restricted to post-head dependents with the form of a PP, including *else*, as in [ib/iib]. In informal speech it is also found with relative clauses ([ivb]), and the occasional postpositive AdjP ([iiib]). Acceptability decreases as the weight or complexity of the post-head dependent increases, as illustrated in the following examples:

[64] i a. [*the Head of Department's*] *speech*
b. ?[*the Head of the newly formed Asian Studies Department's*] *speech*
ii a. [*the man she was speaking to's*] *reaction*
b. ?[*the man she and her friend had been complaining to's*] *reaction*
c. #[*the man she and her friend had been complaining to so angrily's*] reaction

Example [ia] is acceptable in any style, and [iia] is fully acceptable in informal speech, but the rest are marginal and would generally be avoided in favour of other constructions, notably *the* + N + PP (*the speech by the Head of the newly formed Asian Studies Department*). And in [ii] version [c] can be regarded as significantly worse than [b]: examples of this degree of complexity are certainly unacceptable.

Why we need to distinguish the head and phrasal genitive constructions

In both head and phrasal genitives the genitive marking is on the last word. It is not possible to have genitive marking on the head if there is a post-head dependent: we cannot have *[*the Head's of Department*] *speech* or *[*the man's she was speaking to*] *reaction*.[65] Why then, it might be asked, do we need to distinguish between head and phrasal genitives – can't we treat all genitives as phrasal genitives (i.e. marked on the final word), with examples like *Edward's daughter, the manager's departure*, etc., simply having the head as the final word? The reason why this would not do, why we need to distinguish head and phrasal genitives, is that the morphological realisation of genitive case is sensitive to the distinction. This can be seen in such pairs as:

[65]		
i	a. [*my*] *facial expression*	b. [*the man opposite me's*] *facial expression*
ii	a. [*my friend's*] *father*	b. [*a friend of mine's*] *father*

[65] Exceptions to this rule are occasionally found in the Type III construction (i.e. with a fused determiner-head): *I could feel the hair stand up on the back of my neck like* [*a dog's that is going to get into a fight*]. The relative clause is too long to accept the *'s* marker at the end, but one would have expected this to lead to the avoidance of the genitive: *like that of a dog that is going to get into a fight*. Examples of the kind cited are not acceptable and frequent enough to qualify as grammatical.

In [i] the genitive is marked on the pronoun ***I***: in the head genitive construction [a] the pronoun is realised as *my* but in the phrasal genitive as *me's*. In [ii] we have two genitives: in [iia] one is again realised as *my* and the other as *friend's*, whereas in [iib] they combine in the single word *mine's*. Both *me's* and *mine's* thus have double case-marking, an inner case and an outer case. In *me's* the inner case is accusative, required because the pronoun is object of the preposition *opposite*, while in [iib] the inner case is genitive because the pronoun is functioning in the oblique genitive construction. The phrasal genitive is the outer case, morphologically added to the form that realises the inner case. In examples like [*the King of England's*] *daughter* the inner case of *England's* is the plain case, which has no morphological marking, but the principle is the same: the outer genitive is added to the form required by ***England*** within the inner NP *the King of England*. In *the man she was speaking to's* we only have an outer layer of case because the last word of the inner NP, *to*, is a preposition, not a noun, and hence does not have any inner case.

Genitive as an inflectional case, not a construction marked by a cliticised word

We have been assuming that all the examples in [63–65] have genitive **case-inflection**, but we need to show that this analysis is to be preferred over one in which the genitive marker is a **clitic**, a separate syntactic word that merges phonologically with the preceding word – as *'m* is a clitic that merges with *I* in *I'm ill* (see Ch. 18, §6.2).

An obvious difference between *'m* and the genitive marker is that the latter can never stand alone as a phonologically independent word, whereas clitic *'m* alternates with the non-clitic *am*. This is not a conclusive argument for rejecting a clitic analysis of the genitive, however. Although cliticisation happens to be always optional in English, there are languages where it is not; for example, the French subject personal pronouns *je*, *tu*, etc., are obligatorily cliticised onto the verb. The English genitive marker could in principle be a clitic of this kind.

Argument for inflectional status of head genitives

The status of the genitive as an inflectional case is most evident in head genitives. With the personal pronouns, no other analysis is possible. *My*, *our*, *your*, *his*, *her*, and *their* are completely irregular forms and could not be divided into two consecutive syntactic words: their relationship to ***I***, ***we***, ***you***, ***he***, ***she***, and ***they*** is a matter of inflectional morphology. In nouns such as *cats*, *dogs*, *horses*, the genitive is marked by a suffix whose form varies according to the phonological properties of the base to which it attaches. As described in detail in Ch. 18, §2.1.1, we have /ɪz/ after sibilants (/hɔː^{r}s·ɪz/ *horse's*), /s/ after voiceless non-sibilants (/kæt·s/ *cat's*), and /z/ after voiced non-sibilants (/dɒg·z/ *dog's*). Such alternation is not inconsistent with the second element being a clitic, but what does provide further evidence for an inflectional analysis is that genitive formation is sensitive to the internal **morphological** structure of the noun. Compare, for example:

[66] SINGULAR | PLURAL

i a. [*the duck's*] *plumage* /dʌk·s/   b. [*the ducks'*] *plumage* /dʌks/ */dʌks·ɪz/

ii a. [*the goose's*] *plumage* /guːs·ɪz/   b. [*the geese's*] *plumage* */giːs/ /giːs·ɪz/

In [ia] and [iia] the genitive NPs are singular, and the forms follow the regular rule just given, with /s/ after the /k/ of *duck* and /ɪz/ after the sibilant /s/ of *goose*. The plural form *ducks*, however, also ends in sibilant /s/, but we do not form the genitive by adding the /ɪz/ ending:

instead of */dʌks·ɪz/ we have the 'bare genitive' /dʌks/, bare in the sense that it is simply the same, phonologically, as the non-genitive (plain) plural form *ducks*. It might be claimed that the form of the genitive just depends on whether the noun is singular or plural, without reference to the internal structure of the word. This possibility is ruled out, though, by nouns with irregular plurals like *goose*. The form *geese* is also plural, but this time the bare genitive is impossible, and the regular /ɪz/ affix must be used. The generalisation which can be made is that the bare genitive is obligatory when the plural of the noun is formed regularly with ·*s*, but the regular 's genitive form is required when the plural is not formed with ·*s*. The realisation of the genitive is crucially bound up, therefore, with the inflectional formation of the noun, and this – like the suppletive genitives of the personal pronouns – rules out an analysis where the genitive is formed by the addition of a separate word cliticised to the noun.

The status of the phrasal genitive

The argument from suppletion applies only to head genitives: *my*, *our*, etc. (and the independent counterparts *mine*, *ours*, etc.), are always head of the genitive NP. The argument from the contrast between regular and bare genitives, however, does have some application to phrasal genitives. Compare, for example:

[67] i	[<u>*one*</u> *of my students'*] *assignment*	%/stjuːdənts/	%/stjuːdənts·ɪz/
ii	[<u>*one*</u> *of my mice'<u>s</u>*] *tail*	*/maɪs/	/maɪs·ɪz/

In [i] ("the assignment of one of my students") the genitive is associated with the regular plural noun *students*: here we find some variation among speakers, with some having a bare genitive, others the regular /ɪz/ attachment. In [ii] ("the tail of one of my mice") the plural noun is irregular and the genitive must be marked by the /ɪz/ attachment. Again, then, the rule for forming the phrasal genitive is sensitive to the internal morphological structure of the noun with which it is associated, indicating that the marker /ɪz/ is a morphological affix, not a syntactic clitic.

We conclude that both head and phrasal genitives involve case inflection. With head genitives it is always a noun that inflects, while the phrasal genitive can apply to words of most classes.

Genitives and non-headed constructions

So far we have been concerned with genitive case-marking on an NP, i.e. on a headed construction. It can also appear on non-headed constructions, an NP-coordination or a supplementation.

(a) Coordination

When a subject-determiner is realised by an NP-coordination, genitive case may be marked on each coordinate or just on the final one:

[68] i	[<u>*Kim's*</u> *and* <u>*Pat's*</u>] *views*	[multiple marking]
ii	[<u>*Kim*</u> *and* <u>*Pat's*</u>] *views*	[single marking]

The distinction in [68] cuts across that between head and phrasal genitives. In terms of the latter distinction *Pat's* is a head genitive in both, and similarly both constructions allow a phrasal genitive, as in:

[69] i	[<u>*Kim's*</u> *and* <u>*the guy next door's*</u>] *views*	[multiple marking]
ii	[<u>*Kim*</u> *and* <u>*the guy next door's*</u>] *views*	[single marking]

In both versions of [68] and of [69] the whole coordination is genitive, and the difference is a matter of how the genitive case is realised – on each coordinate or only the last. Each coordinate is an NP, and hence for each NP there is in principle the possibility of having either a head or a phrasal genitive.

When one or more of the coordinates is a personal pronoun, the construction with marking on the final coordinate is of at best marginal acceptability:

[70] i a. [*his and her*] *views* b. [*my and her*] *views* [multiple marking]
ii a. ?[*you and Kim's*] *views* b. *[*Kim and your*] *views* [single marking]

Even the one with marking on all coordinates may sound somewhat awkward with some of the pronouns, such as *my* in [ib]. We review more comprehensively the range of possible structures in Ch. 15, §3.4, but one further point to be made here is that the single marking construction with a pronoun as the final coordinate will never have the *'s* suffix. Thus ?*These are Kim and yours* is the only possible form: **These are Kim and you's* is excluded because ***you*** is head of the final coordinate, and hence what is needed is a head genitive, not a phrasal one.

(b) Supplementation

A supplementation consisting of one NP as anchor and another as supplement may likewise have either multiple or single marking:

[71] i [*the Prime Minister's, Mr Howard's,*] *tax package* [multiple marking]
ii [*the Prime Minister, Mr Howard's*] *tax package* [single marking]

The multiple-marking version is preferred in writing, no doubt because it allows the supplement to be set off by paired commas. In speech, however, it is the single-marking version that is usually heard.

16.7 The adjective *own* in construction with genitives

The adjective *own* is unique in that it is virtually restricted to occurring after a genitive subject-determiner.[66] It occurs with a following head or as fused modifier-head.

(a) *Own* in pre-head position

[72] i a. *The children had to make* [*their own beds*]. } [restricted uses]
b. *Sue set up* [*her own marketing business*]. }
ii a. *Jill prefers* [*her own car*]. } [general use]
b. [*Jill's own car*] *is out of service.* }

Restricted uses are those where the genitive subject-determiner must be a personal pronoun, while the general use allows other types of genitive NP too, such as *Jill's* in [iib]. The interpretation of [ia] is that the children had to make their beds themselves – no one else would do it for them. In this use the genitive pronoun must be anaphorically linked to the subject. *The children had to make my own bed*, for example, does not have this interpretation and belongs to the general construction. The restricted use illustrated in

[66] The only exceptions are set phrases, as in *They won by an own goal* or *Own brands are often the best value* ("Supermarkets' own brands of goods"). *Own* naturally can't occur following the subject of a gerund-participial: **No one would object to your own giving yourself a modest pay-rise*. The underlined sequence is a VP, not a nominal, and hence cannot take an adjectival modifier.

[ib] is found with verbs of possession, acquisition, or causing to possess; *own* emphasises that the business was hers. The antecedent in this example is the subject, but there are other possibilities, as in *They gave Sue her own business.*

The adjective likewise has an emphatic role in the general construction: in [72ii] it emphasises that the reference is to Jill's car as opposed to someone else's. A natural context for [iib], for example, is one where Jill has had to go in some other car because hers is unavailable. A 3rd person pronoun in this construction will often be anaphorically linked to the subject, as in [iia], but again it is not required to be. Compare, for example:

[73] i *Bill advised Fred to take his own car.*
ii *Bill offered to let Fred take his own car.*

The most likely interpretation of *his* is "Fred's" in [i] and "Bill's" in [ii], and while in [i] the antecedent is the understood subject of the *take* clause, in [ii] it is not.

(b) *Own* as fused modifier-head

[74]	i	*Your proposal is no better than my own.*	[simple]
	ii	a. A: *Is this your father's?* B: *No, it's my own.*	[special]
		b. *I've got a car of my own.*	
		c. *She is living on her own.*	

Here, no less than in (a) above, a genitive personal pronoun appears in the dependent form: the independent form occurs only when the pronoun itself is in head function. Thus *my own*, not **mine own.*

Own occurs in two of the three types of fused-head construction we have distinguished. As it is an adjective (in plain grade) it cannot occur in the partitive type: compare *three of the books* and **my own of the books.* Example [74i] is of the simple type, with *my own* interpreted anaphorically as "my own proposal"; it is an emphatic version of *mine.* The others illustrate various special uses. *My own* in [iia] is predicative complement, equivalent to the predicative genitive in *It's mine.* In [iib] *a car of my own* means "a car which belongs to me", while in [iic] *on her own* means "by herself" (cf., similarly, *She did it on her own*). In these examples [iib–c] the genitive subject-determiner must be a personal pronoun linked to an antecedent (cf. **I've got a car of their own*). And here there is no possibility of dropping *own* and having the genitive as fused head: [iib] is not equivalent to the unlikely *I've got a car of mine.* The same restrictions apply to various idiomatic expressions that belong to the special fused-head construction: *I want to get my own back* ("get revenge"); *It's at times like this that she really comes into her own* ("shows her real value"); *We have to look after our own* ("look after those related to or otherwise associated with us").

Modification

In some of its uses *own* can be modified by the adverb *very*: *This is my very own work.* This gives extra emphasis to the point that the work is mine, not someone else's. The complement *of one's own* can be modified by *all*: *a room all of my own* ("a room which is entirely mine").

17 Gender and pronoun–antecedent agreement

17.1 Gender as a grammatical category

The grammatical category of gender applies in the first instance to a system of noun classes differentiated by the agreement patterns they enter into with associated words. In languages where gender plays a greater role in the syntax than it does in English these agreement patterns characteristically hold between a head noun and various dependents within the NP, such as articles and attributive adjectives.

Elementary examples from French and German are given in [1]:

[1]	i	a. *un grand château*	"a big castle"	[masculine]
		b. *une grande maison*	"a big house"	[feminine]
	ii	a. *der Garten*	"the garden"	[masculine]
		b. *die Wand*	"the wall"	[feminine]
		c. *das Haus*	"the house"	[neuter]

French has just two genders, and [i] illustrates the inflectional agreement of the indefinite article and the adjective ***grand*** ("big") with head nouns of masculine and feminine gender. The term gender is then applied, secondarily, to these dependents: *un* and *une* are the masculine and feminine forms of the indefinite article, *grand* and *grande* masculine and feminine (singular) forms of the adjective. German has three genders; the examples in [ii] ignore adjective agreement, but show agreement between the article and the head noun, with *der*, *die*, *das* respectively (nominative singular) masculine, feminine, and neuter forms of the definite article.

In this example, the head noun is what we call the **source** of agreement, while the dependent article or adjective is the **target**.[67] The head noun is source in the sense that the target derives its gender from this noun. It is for this reason that we said that gender applies in the first instance to a system of noun classes: the source in gender agreement is a noun (or NP). The names for gender categories are then based on semantic characteristics of these noun classes. The masculine and feminine gender classes are so called because these are the classes to which nouns denoting respectively males and females characteristically belong. In both French and German these classes also contain many words that denote inanimates (necessarily so in French, of course, since there is no other gender class), and for this reason it is important to distinguish carefully between the grammatical terms **masculine** and **feminine** and the semantic or extralinguistic terms **male** and **female**.

Until relatively recently it was usual to make a parallel distinction between **gender** (grammatical) and **sex** (extralinguistic) – comparable, for example, to that between tense and time. In the social sciences, however, 'sex' came to be used to refer to biological attributes and 'gender' to the social construction of sex, and this usage has been incorporated into linguistics. A book on 'language and gender' will therefore not be primarily concerned with gender as a grammatical category, but will cover such matters as differences between the speech of men and women. Our concern in this section, however, is

[67] A more usual term than 'source' is 'controller'; we have preferred the former, however, because we use 'controller' for the element which determines the interpretation of certain ellipted elements, such as the missing subject in *Kim wants __ to leave*: see Ch. 14, §11.

with gender in the old, strictly grammatical sense, as defined above, and because in this area, as indicated above, the relation between form and meaning is by no means one-to-one, we will not risk possible confusion by using 'gender' for the semantic categories as well: we will speak therefore of masculine and feminine gender, male and female sex. It is important, moreover, to bear in mind that while noun gender systems often have a significant correlation with the categories of male and female they do not necessarily do so. Etymologically, 'gender' derives ultimately from Latin *genus* ("kind, sort"), and the basis for differentiating between various kinds of noun is not necessarily the sex of their denotation. Some languages have gender systems based on such contrasts as animate vs inanimate, human vs non-human, strong vs weak, large vs small, and some have more specific categories correlating with insects, liquids, edibles, and so on. And indeed, in English, gender differences are reflected not only in the contrast between the personal pronouns *he*, *she*, and *it* but also in that between the relative pronouns *who* and *which*, where the difference is not based on sex.

English differs from languages like French and German in two important respects. In the first place, there is no gender agreement between dependents and head noun within NP structure, matching that seen in [1]. Gender is not an inflectional category in English. Gender classes can be differentiated only on the basis of relations with pronouns, as illustrated in [2], where the identical indices mark the anaphoric relation between the pronoun and the (head of the) antecedent:

[2]	i	*The King$_i$ declared himself$_i$ satisfied.*	[masculine]
	ii	*The Queen$_i$ declared herself$_i$ satisfied.*	[feminine]
	iii	*The machine$_i$ had switched itself$_i$ off.*	[neuter]

Secondly, the choice of pronoun is determined by denotation or reference, not by purely syntactic properties of the antecedent. We have observed that in French and German, nouns denoting males and females are generally masculine and feminine respectively, but for the rest the gender of a noun is not predictable from its meaning. The dictionary entries for French *château* and *maison*, German *Garten*, *Wand*, and *Haus* must explicitly record their gender, but no lexical specification of this kind is needed in English.

Because of these differences some linguists argue that English simply has no gender system, that the category of gender is irrelevant to English. That is not the view we take here: we regard the differences between English and French or German as a difference in the degree to which gender is grammaticalised in these languages, not in whether or not they have a category of gender. In French and German, agreement between pronoun and antecedent works in a very similar way to agreement between dependent article or adjective and head noun, but not identically: it is somewhat more semantically oriented. And restrictions on pronoun–antecedent pairing in English have sufficient in common with those obtaining in French and German to justify treating them as involving agreement of gender. Note in this connection that while pronoun choice in English depends on the meaning or reference of the antecedent there are places where the linguistic form of the antecedent restricts the choice of pronoun. Compare, for example:

[3] a. *The dog$_i$ has lost his$_i$/its$_i$ bone.* b. *Fido$_i$ has lost his$_i$/*its$_i$ bone.*

The dog and *Fido* could be used to refer to the same male animal, but the fact that the latter has a proper noun as head excludes the use of the neuter pronoun ***it*** that is found as an alternative to ***he*** in [a]. Similarly with human babies:

[4] a. *Her baby*$_i$ *had lost its*$_i$ *rattle.* b. **Her son*$_i$ / **Max*$_i$ *had lost its*$_i$ *rattle.*

Again, *her baby, her son,* and *Max* could all be used to refer to the same person, but only the first permits neuter *it* as pronoun.

We will say, therefore, that English does have gender, although it is only weakly grammaticalised, being based purely on pronoun agreement. There are two systems of pronoun–antecedent agreement to consider, one involving the personal pronouns (which agree with their antecedent in person and number as well as gender), the other the relative pronouns *who* and *which.* We will examine these in turn.

17.2 Agreement between personal pronouns and their antecedents

17.2.1 Nature of the agreement relation

Personal pronouns agree with their antecedent in person and number; in the 3rd person singular they also agree in gender. We illustrate here with reflexive forms of the pronouns as target:

[5]

		GENDER	PERSON	NUMBER
i	*I*$_i$ *may hurt myself*$_i$.		1st	
ii	*You*$_i$ *may hurt yourself*$_i$.		2nd	
iii	*The King*$_i$ *may hurt himself*$_i$.	masculine		singular
iv	*The Queen*$_i$ *may hurt herself*$_i$.	feminine	3rd	
v	*The dog*$_i$ *may hurt itself*$_i$.	neuter		
vi	*We*$_i$ *may hurt ourselves*$_i$.		1st	
vii	*You*$_i$ *may hurt yourselves*$_i$.		2nd	plural
viii	*The children*$_i$ *may hurt themselves*$_i$.		3rd	

We assume that there are two pronouns ***you***, a singular one with *yourself* as its reflexive form and a plural one with *yourselves* as reflexive form. As the distinction is marked only in the reflexive, examples like *You may have missed your chance* are ambiguous between singular and plural interpretations.

We have suggested that restrictions on the pairings of pronouns with antecedents have sufficient in common with those on pairings of articles or attributive adjectives and head noun in [1] for us to treat them as a matter of agreement. Nevertheless, there are significant differences between the two types of agreement.

(a) No fixed structural relation between antecedent and personal pronoun

The antecedent source and personal pronoun target do not occupy fixed positions in a syntactic construction like the noun as head and article as determiner or adjective as modifier in the French and German examples. Compare, then:

[6] i *The King*$_i$ *says he*$_i$ *will see you tomorrow.*

ii *The King*$_i$ *wants you to help him*$_i$.

iii *We found the King*$_i$ *examining one of the recommendations of his*$_i$ *advisors.*

iv *I'm looking for the King*$_i$. *He*$_i$ *sent for me this morning.*

Subject to various restrictions described in Ch. 17, §2.3, the antecedent NP and the pronoun can occupy the full range of NP functions. Note in particular that they do not need to be in the same sentence, as seen in [iv]. The functions of pronoun and antecedent are here quite independent: in [i] they are both subjects, in [ii] the antecedent is subject, the pronoun object (of a different clause), in [iii] the antecedent is object, the pronoun subject-determiner in NP structure, and so on. The inflectional case of the pronoun depends entirely on the function of the pronoun itself: the function of the antecedent is irrelevant.

Replacement of the masculine pronouns by feminine or neuter ones in such examples does not lead to ungrammaticality – it merely excludes *the King* as a possible antecedent for the pronoun. And similarly, a masculine pronoun does not have to have *the King* as antecedent:

[7] i *The King*$_i$ *says she*$_j$ *will see you tomorrow.*
ii *The King*$_i$ *says he*$_j$ *will see you tomorrow.*

The reflexive forms are more constrained in their distribution, and in examples like [5] or the earlier [2] replacement of one reflexive by another does lead to ungrammaticality:

[8] i **The King*$_i$ *declared herself*$_i$ *satisfied.*
ii **The Queen*$_i$ *declared itself*$_i$ *satisfied.*
iii **The machine*$_i$ *had switched himself*$_i$ *off.*

But even reflexive forms are not restricted to a particular functional relation – the antecedent, for example, is not invariably subject: *She was telling Max*$_i$ *some home-truths about himself*$_i$.

(b) The pronouns can be used non-anaphorically – without an antecedent

Except for the 3rd person reflexive forms, the personal pronouns do not require an antecedent for their interpretation: they can refer directly to entities that have not been mentioned (and are not subsequently mentioned). This represents much the most frequent use of the 1st and 2nd person pronouns, and is illustrated in the subject pronouns in [5i–ii] and [vi–vii]. However, the 3rd person pronouns can also be used non-anaphorically. In such cases the referent is usually present in the situation, but even that is not necessary: see Ch. 17, §2.3.1. In addition *it* has non-anaphoric uses with no referent at all – dummy uses as in *It is raining*, *We finally made it to the shore*, etc.

(c) Gender agreement requires consistency rather than complete identity of relevant features

Consider such a set of examples as:

[9] i *My tutor wants to see me.*
ii *My tutor*$_i$ *wants me to go and see her*$_i$.
iii *My tutor*$_i$ *wants me to go and see him*$_i$.

The noun *tutor* does not encode any information about the sex of the person. Example [i] is not ambiguous as to whether the tutor is male or female: it is simply non-specific, just as it is non-specific as to whether the tutor is married or single, well-qualified or under-qualified, and so on. In [ii–iii] *tutor* is head of the NP that is the antecedent of feminine *her* and masculine *him* respectively, but because *tutor* is itself non-specific we cannot say that both antecedent and pronoun are feminine in [ii], masculine in [iii]. The pronoun encodes a property of the person that is not encoded in the antecedent. What is required for an NP to qualify as a possible antecedent for a pronoun is that it be consistent or compatible with the meaning of the pronoun. Agreement in gender between personal pronoun and antecedent, therefore, is agreement of a somewhat looser kind than agreement in person and number (or than agreement in gender between article/adjective and head noun in French or German).

17.2.2 Masculine, feminine, and neuter

Core uses of *he*, *she*, and *it*

In the most straightforward cases, ***he*** is used for males, ***she*** for females, and ***it*** for entities which are neither male nor female:

[10] i *My father*$_i$ *has lost his*$_i$ *watch.*
ii *One woman*$_i$ *said she*$_i$ *would make a formal complaint.*
iii *Have you seen my diary*$_i$*? I had it*$_i$ *a few minutes ago.*

We include here cases where *it* has a clause as antecedent or is used as a dummy element:

[11] i *I'd like to help*$_i$ *but I'm afraid it*$_i$ *is just not possible.*
ii *It looks as though we're going to be late.*

She with non-females

There are two cases where ***she*** can be used as an alternant of ***it*** for entities that are neither female nor male.

(a) Countries considered as political entities

[12] i *This country*$_i$ */ England*$_i$ *has no sense of her*$_i$*/its*$_i$ *place in the world.*
ii *From this map of England*$_i$ *you can see that it*$_i$*/*she*$_i$ *lies north of the 50th parallel.*
iii *England*$_i$ *has won its*$_i$*/their*$_i$*/*$^?$*her*$_i$ *first victory over Australia for five years.*

She is not used when the country is considered as a geographical entity, as in [ii], and it is very marginal when the country name is used for a sporting team, as in [iii].

(b) Ships and the like

[13] i *The Titanic*$_i$ *sank on her*$_i$*/its*$_i$ *maiden voyage.*
ii *It*$_i$*/She*$_i$ *is a beauty, this Ferrari*$_i$*.*

Ships represent the classic case of this extended use of *she*, but it is found with other kinds of inanimates, such as cars. There is considerable variation among speakers as to how widely they make use of this kind of personification. It is often found with non-anaphoric uses of ***she***: *Here she is at last* (referring to a ship or bus, perhaps), *Down she comes* (with *she* referring, say, to a tree that is being felled).

It with animates

It is by no means restricted to entities that are neither male nor female: it is often in competition with ***he*** and ***she*** rather than mutually exclusive with them. We distinguish two cases:

(a) Non-humans

[14] i *The bull*$_i$ *turned his*$_i$*/its*$_i$ *head.*
ii *The cow*$_i$ *was lying on her*$_i$*/its*$_i$ *back.*
iii *The dog*$_i$ *looked as if he*$_i$*/she*$_i$*/it*$_i$ *needed a good brush.*

In cases like this, the difference between ***it*** on the one hand and ***he*** or ***she*** on the other does not lie in the referent itself: it is a matter of whether the speaker chooses to encode the sex of the referent. As is evident from [i–ii], encoding of sex in the antecedent does not require that it also be encoded in the pronoun. Again, what is required is simply consistency: an NP headed by *dog* is consistent with all three pronouns, one headed by *bull* or *cow* with only two, as shown. There is nothing in the meaning of ***it*** that would make it inapplicable here: it does not mean "neither male nor female". In many cases the neuter pronoun is used because the speaker doesn't know what the sex is, though we may also use ***he*** or ***she*** in such contexts, making an arbitrary assumption about the sex. Use of a masculine or feminine pronoun is generally more likely with pets, domestic animals, and creatures ranked high in the kingdom of wild animals (such as lions, tigers, elephants, etc.). It indicates a somewhat greater degree of interest in or empathy with the referent than does ***it***. As remarked above, ***he*** or ***she*** is obligatory if the animal is referred to by a proper name.

(b) Humans

[15] *The baby$_i$ lost his$_i$/her$_i$/its$_i$ rattle.*

With human antecedents ***it*** can be used for babies. Because the normal pronouns for humans are ***he*** and ***she***, the use of ***it*** tends to have a dehumanising effect, and it is more likely in the context of a maternity hospital with lots of potentially undifferentiated babies than in that of a private home with just one or two: ***it*** in this latter context would tend to suggest resentment or antipathy. As noted above, ***it*** is not used when the antecedent head noun is *son* or *daughter*: there is here no motivation for failing to encode the sex of the baby.[68]

17.2.3 Common noun gender classes

It follows from the above discussion that we need to classify common nouns according to their compatibility with the 3rd person singular pronouns. In the first place, we classify them as **single-gender**, **dual-gender**, and **triple-gender** common nouns according as they are compatible with just one, with two, or with all three of the core singular pronouns ***he***, ***she***, and ***it***.

As will be clear from the discussion above, a dual-gender noun is not to be interpreted as a noun which has two genders: it is a noun which can head the antecedent to a pronoun of either of two genders. *Tutor*, for example, is a dual-gender noun in that it can serve as antecedent to either ***he*** or ***she***, but we are not saying that *tutor* itself can be either a masculine or a feminine noun. This would incorrectly imply that *My tutor wants to see me* ([9i]) was ambiguous according as it contained an instance of masculine or feminine *tutor* – and it would raise pointless problems with examples like *No tutor should be expected to put up with that kind of treatment*, where there is no reference to any particular tutor. Likewise *parent* is not ambiguous, synonymous in one sense with *mother* and in

[68] An exceptional attested example where ***it*** is used non-referentially in talking of humans as a whole is: *Darwin felt that a so-called lower form of life, like an amoeba, could be as adapted to its environment as a human is to its – humans in other words, are not necessarily closer to some evolutionary ideal than other animals.* What makes ***it*** appropriate here is that humans are being likened to other animals rather than differentiated from them: the likeness is reflected in the use of the same pronoun. In this example, moreover, the use of ***it*** solves the problem of finding a pronoun subsuming males and females: see §17.2.4.

another with *father*: it is a more general noun, distinct in meaning from both these more specific terms. This type of case is to be distinguished from that illustrated by *diner*, for example. *Diner* does have two meanings: in one sense, "railway restaurant carriage", it is a single-gender noun taking ***it*** as pronoun, while in another, "person dining", it is a dual-gender noun taking ***he*** or ***she***. Similarly *fellow* as a colloquial term for "man" is a single-gender noun taking ***he***, but with the meaning "member of a learned society" it is a dual-gender noun taking ***he*** or ***she***.

Single- and dual-gender nouns are subclassified according to the particular pronoun or pronouns permitted. This gives seven classes in all:

[16]			
	SINGLE-GENDER	masculine	***he*** only
		feminine	***she*** only
		neuter	***it*** only
	DUAL-GENDER	masculine/feminine	***he*** or ***she***
		masculine/neuter	***he*** or ***it***
		feminine/neuter	***she*** or ***it***
	TRIPLE-GENDER		***he***, ***she***, or ***it***

(a) Single-gender masculine nouns

[17]						
	bachelor	*boy*	*bridegroom*	*chap*	*husband*	*king*
	man	*monk*	*policeman*	*son-in-law*	*stepson*	*widower*

This class contains *man* and a number of more or less colloquial synonyms; various kinship or similar terms involving marriage relations; a good number of occupational terms compounded from *man*; and names of various social ranks such as *duke*, *count*, *squire*.

(b) Single-gender feminine nouns

[18]						
	actress	*bride*	*girl*	*heroine*	*nun*	*policewoman*
	princess	*queen*	*spinster*	*widow*	*wife*	*woman*

This class is significantly larger than the last: its members include not only feminine counterparts to the masculines in (a) above, but also a fair number derived by suffixation from dual-gender nouns, such as *actress* and *heroine* in this list. The morphological marking of gender is discussed in Ch. 19, §5.3.

(c) Single-gender neuter nouns

[19]						
	arrival	*beer*	*fact*	*finger*	*garage*	*glove*
	idea	*piece*	*sincerity*	*thing*	*title*	*window*

This is the largest class, containing abstract nouns and concrete inanimates.

(d) Dual-gender masculine/feminine nouns

[20]						
	actor	*atheist*	*dwarf*	*friend*	*hero*	*manager*
	narrator	*nurse*	*parent*	*person*	*poet*	*writer*

This class is far larger than the single-gender masculine and feminine classes put together. It contains words denoting humans without specification of sex; many of them are derived morphologically by various processes, as described in Ch. 19, §5.7.1. There are also a few words denoting non-humans, such as *god* and *angel*.

(e) Dual-gender masculine/neuter nouns

[21]	*brother*	*buck*	*bull*	*cock*	*drake*	*father*
	gander	*gelding*	*he-goat*	*ram*	*stallion*	*tom-cat*

This is a quite small class. It contains the names for males of various animal species (particularly farm animals), together with male kinship terms applicable to animals as well as to humans. With the kinship terms, the masculine pronoun is more likely than the neuter.

(f) Dual-gender feminine/neuter nouns

[22]	*boat*	*car*	*country*	*cow*	*earth*	*hen*
	lioness	*mare*	*mother*	*she-goat*	*ship*	*sister*

This class contains names for the female of various animals, female kinship terms matching the male ones in (e), and terms denoting boats and the like. There is no clear boundary between nouns which allow this extended use of ***she*** and those which do not, and hence belong in Class (c); as remarked above, there is considerable variation among speakers as to how widely they use ***she*** for inanimates.

(g) Triple-gender nouns

[23]	*baby*	*blackbird*	*child*	*dog*	*elephant*	*frog*
	goat	*horse*	*infant*	*lion*	*octopus*	*snake*

This class contains a few words for young humans and terms denoting animals without specification of sex. As mentioned above, ***he*** and ***she*** are less likely to be used for lower animals (other than pets) than for higher ones, but it would not be feasible to assign some animal terms to Class (g) and others to Class (c).

17.2.4 Singular pronouns denoting humans without specification of sex

Many singular NPs with human reference or denotation include no specification of sex:

[24] i *<u>My tutor</u> wants to see me.* (=[9i])
ii *I'm having lunch with <u>a friend from College</u>.*
iii *<u>Someone</u> has borrowed my stapler.*
iv *<u>The successful candidate</u> will be required to take up duties in January.*
v *<u>No one in the class</u> had noticed the mistake.*

Cases like [i] present no problem for the selection of an anaphoric personal pronoun. *My tutor* refers to a specific person, and I can use ***he*** or ***she***, as appropriate: *<u>My tutor</u>$_i$ wants me to go and see <u>her</u>$_i$* or *<u>My tutor</u>$_i$ wants me to go and see <u>him</u>$_i$*. Similarly in [ii], though it might be that I don't wish to reveal the sex of the person concerned (this could of course also be the case in [i], though it is very much less likely). In [iii] there is again a particular person involved, but since I presumably do not know who this person is I cannot select an anaphoric pronoun in the same way as in [i–ii]. In [iv] there is no reference to any particular person: the intended context is one where a number of people including at least one man and one woman have applied for a job and no one has yet been selected. Finally in [v] we are not concerned with any single individual: assuming again that the class is of mixed sex, this example illustrates the frequent case where a nominal represents a variable ranging over a set containing both males and females.

What is needed, therefore, is a pronoun that simply expresses the meaning "human", without specification of sex.[69] And English, of course, does not have a personal pronoun with this as its primary meaning.[70]

Various strategies for dealing with this problem are illustrated in:

[25] i *Everyone had cast* {%*his* / %*her* / *his or her* / *his/her* / *their*} *vote.*

[25] i	*Everyone had cast* %*his* *vote.*	[purportedly sex-neutral ***he***]
ii	*Everyone had cast* %*her* *vote.*	[purportedly sex-neutral ***she***]
iii	*Everyone had cast* *his or her* *vote.*	[disjunctive coordination]
iv	*Everyone had cast* *his/her* *vote.*	[composite]
v	*Everyone had cast* *their* *vote.*	[singular ***they***]
vi	*All had cast their votes.*	[avoidance]

Versions [iii–iv] have variants with the component pronouns in the reverse order: *her or his, her/his.*

(a) Purportedly sex-neutral *he*

He has traditionally been regarded as the grammatically 'correct' choice in opposition to singular ***they***; it is characteristic of relatively formal style. The issue of the choice between ***he*** and ***they*** has concerned writers on usage for some 200 years, but since this use of ***he*** represents one of the most obvious and central cases of sexism in language, the matter has received much more widespread attention since the early 1980s in the context of social changes in the status of women.

The fact that the primary meaning of ***he*** contains the component "male" makes it an unsatisfactory pronoun for use in a secondary sense that covers females as well as males. Use of the male term to subsume females is a form of linguistic inequality that can be seen as related to and tending to reinforce social inequality. The strong and persuasive criticisms that have been made of sex-neutral ***he*** by supporters of the feminist movement have led to a marked reduction in its use. Many people now systematically avoid it, and we have accordingly annotated it with the percentage sign in [25i].

The objection to the use of ***he*** as a sex-neutral pronoun is particularly compelling where the antecedent has to do with some kind of employment. Consider, for example:

[26] i %*A Member of Parliament should always live in his constituency.*
ii %*The successful candidate will be required to take up his duties in January.*
iii A: *They're going to appoint a new manager.*
B: %*Well, I hope he does a better job than the present one has.*

Examples [i–ii] can easily be read as conveying that the speaker or writer regards it as the default case for a Member of Parliament or the successful candidate to be male. And in [iii] it is questionable whether B intends the ***he*** to be sex-neutral at all: it is most likely to be interpreted as reflecting an assumption on B's part that the new manager will be male. It is for this reason that we have labelled ***he*** as **purportedly** sex-neutral: it is

[69] Strictly speaking the relevant concept is "animate", for the issue arises with animals as well as with humans. ***It*** is of course more generally available with animals, but it could not be used anaphorically to such an antecedent as *which of Fido, Rex, and Lassie* (names of dogs). We will simplify, however, by ignoring such cases, focusing on the issue raised with human antecedents.

[70] Attempts have been made, beginning in the nineteenth century, to create new pronouns to fill this gap: these neologisms include *thon, unus, co,* and a good few others. Such forms have failed to gain acceptance in the past, and there is no reason to expect that they will be any more successful in the future.

not a genuinely sex-neutral form, for the primary, male, meaning will often colour the interpretation in varying degrees.

There are some places where the distinction between basic ***he*** and sex-neutral ***he*** can be somewhat blurred, as in the following attested example:

[27] *An independent counsel cannot let himself get caught up in a political process.*

This is formulated as a judgement about limitations on the legitimate behaviour of independent counsels in general: *an independent counsel* is here non-referential, and ***he*** therefore has a purportedly sex-neutral interpretation. But the statement was made as an indirect criticism of a particular male independent counsel, suggesting that he had let himself get caught up in a political process. In this kind of context ***he*** is less likely than it is in [26] to give offence or to be systematically avoided.

(b) Purportedly sex-neutral *she*

This represents a new and very much minority usage that can be thought of as the linguistic equivalent of affirmative action, consciously introducing linguistic discrimination in favour of females to counterbalance the effects of the long tradition of linguistic discrimination in favour of males implicit in purportedly sex-neutral ***he***. Some writers alternate between ***he*** and ***she***: in a book on language, for example, one might use one pronoun as anaphoric to *the speaker* and the other as anaphoric to *the addressee*. ***She*** could also be used by a wider range of speakers in non-referential examples like [27] in a context where the relevance of the general statement is its applicability to some particular female.

(c) Disjunctive coordination

He *or* ***she*** has long been used as a means of avoiding the sexist bias of ***he*** without resorting to singular ***they***. It is more common in relatively formal style, but it is by no means rare in, for example, informal conversation. It is likely to be regarded as somewhat 'clumsy' if repeated frequently, especially where reflexive forms are involved:

[28] ?*Everyone agreed that he or she should apply him- or herself without delay to the task which he or she had been assigned.*

(d) Composite forms

Use of such forms is a relatively recent strategy, a simplification of the coordination approach; it is normally restricted to written texts. For the nominative, *(s)he* and *s/he* are alternants of *he/she*.

(e) Singular *they*

The use of ***they*** with a singular antecedent goes back to Middle English, and in spite of criticism since the earliest prescriptive grammars it has continued to be very common in informal style. In recent years it has gained greater acceptance in other styles as the use of purportedly sex-neutral ***he*** has declined. It is particularly common with such antecedents as *everyone, someone, no one*; indeed its use in examples like *No one$_i$ felt that they$_i$ had been misled* is so widespread that it can probably be regarded as stylistically neutral. Somewhat more restricted is its use with antecedents containing common nouns as head:

[29] i *The patient$_i$ should be told at the outset how much they$_i$ will be required to pay.*
ii *But a journalist$_i$ should not be forced to reveal their$_i$ sources.*
iii *A friend of mine$_i$ has asked me to go over and help them$_i$ with an assignment.*

The antecedents in [i–ii] are non-referential; they have multiple-situation-bound interpretations of the type discussed in §8.3: it's a matter of the patient being told at the outset of each treatment, of the journalist not being forced to reveal sources for any of their reports. Examples of this kind are common in conversation (including relatively formal radio or television interviews), but in formal writing ***they*** will often be avoided in this type of context in favour of one of the other strategies illustrated in [25]. Example [iii] is a rare case where the antecedent is referential: the speaker knows the sex of the referent but uses ***they*** to avoid indicating whether the friend is male or female. ***He*** and ***she*** could not be used in a sex-neutral sense in such a context, while *he or she* and *he/she* would generally be avoided as too formal in style and as making the intention to conceal the sex too obvious.

The prescriptive objection to examples like [25v] and [29] is that ***they*** is a plural pronoun, and that such examples therefore violate the rule of agreement between antecedent and pronoun. The view taken here is that ***they***, like ***you***, can be either plural or singular. Plural is of course the primary sense, but the use we are concerned with here involves a secondary, extended sense, just as purportedly sex-neutral ***he*** involves a secondary, extended sense of ***he***. The extension to a singular sense has not been reflected in subject–verb agreement, just as the historical extension of ***you*** from plural to singular (replacing ***thou***) did not have any effect on the form of the verb. With ***they*** we therefore have a conflict between the number it has as an agreement target (plural or singular) and the number it has as source for subject–verb agreement (plural only): the former is more semantically oriented.

Singular ***they*** has two reflexive forms, *themselves* and *themself*:

[30] i *Everyone promised to behave themselves.*
  ii %*Someone had apparently locked themself in the attic.*

Themselves is morphologically marked as plural, and hence creates a number conflict with the singular antecedent. Such a conflict is of little consequence with *everyone* as antecedent since this implies a plural set, but is potentially more problematic with an antecedent like *someone*. Examples of the morphologically singular *themself* are attested in the standard dialect from the 1970s onwards, but they are very rare and acceptable only to a minority of speakers; the use of this form is, however, likely to increase with the growing acceptance of ***they*** as a singular pronoun.

The use of ***they*** with a singular antecedent is comparable with that where the antecedent is a disjunctive coordination of singular NPs:

[31] i *Let me know if your father or your brother changes their mind.*
  ii *Let me know if your father or your mother changes their mind.*

His could substitute for *their* in [i], but few if any speakers would find ***he*** acceptable in [ii] (which is a further indication that it is not a genuinely sex-neutral pronoun). In this kind of context, the morphologically plural reflexive *themselves* is also of very doubtful acceptability, with *themself* clearly preferable for those who have adopted this form:

[32] *Either the husband or the wife has perjured *himself/?themselves/%themself.*

(f) Avoidance

The avoidance strategy chooses a formulation that does not require a pronoun with an antecedent of the relevant kind. In the case of [32], for example, we could simply say

Either the husband or the wife has committed perjury. The most general avoidance strategy is to use a plural antecedent. This is particularly useful in cases like [29i–ii], where *they* is still not regarded as completely acceptable in formal writing:

[33] i *Patients should be told at the outset how much they will be required to pay.*
ii *But journalists should not be forced to reveal their sources.*

In this book we ourselves commonly employ a much more specific avoidance strategy, using ***I*** and ***you*** instead of *the speaker* and *the addressee* respectively so that we do not need to select a pronoun anaphoric to these latter NPs; since the book has joint authorship, ***I*** could not be interpreted as referring to any particular individual and is therefore free to be used non-referentially.

17.2.5 Person and number

Person–number agreement between a personal pronoun and its antecedent works in very much the same way as person–number agreement between a verb and its subject, as described in §18: an NP which, as subject, determines a 3rd person singular verb will, as antecedent, determine a 3rd person singular pronoun, and so on. For this reason, we can deal with pronouns relatively briefly, though we will see that there are some differences between the two agreement systems.

(a) Collectives and partitives

Singular NPs headed by a collective noun such as *committee* may be interpreted as either singular or plural for the purposes of subject–verb agreement, and the same holds for antecedent–pronoun agreement:

[34] i *The committee$_i$ hasn't yet made up its$_i$ mind.*
ii *The committee$_i$ haven't yet made up their$_i$ mind/minds.*

Here the pronoun matches the verb-form, singular in [i], plural in [ii]. It is possible, however, to switch from singular verb to plural pronoun – but one would not normally switch from a plural verb to a singular pronoun in close proximity:

[35] i *The committee$_i$ hasn't yet made up their$_i$ mind.*
ii **The committee$_i$ haven't yet made up its$_i$ mind.*

A plural pronoun is particularly likely where there is an overt plural oblique:

[36] i *A group of bystanders were having their names and addresses taken down.*
ii *A group of bystanders was having their names and addresses taken down.*
iii #*A group of bystanders was having its names and addresses taken down.*

Version [i] is unproblematic, and [ii] is possible though the singular verb has no evident semantic motivation: it is likely to be due just to the application of what we call the simple (subject–verb) agreement rule. But there is no comparable reason for having a singular pronoun, as in [iii]. There is, moreover, a strong pragmatic reason in this example for having a plural pronoun: the names and addresses belong to the members of the group as individuals, i.e. distributively, not to the group as a unit (note that replacing plural *names and addresses* by singular *name and address* in [iii] would make it pragmatically worse).

Note, however, that a plural reflexive pronoun could not occur as complement with a singular verb:

[37] i *A group of bystanders were behaving themselves rather badly.*
ii *A group of bystanders was behaving itself/*themselves rather badly.*

Partitives with *one* as head (e.g. *one of the boys*) take singular pronouns:

[38] i *[One of the boys]$_i$ was behaving himself$_i$ rather badly.*
ii *[One of the boys]$_i$ had forgotten his$_i$ lunch.*

And this type of construction often gives rise to the problem discussed in §17.2.4 above of selecting a singular pronoun that does not specify sex: *[One of the children]$_i$ had forgotten their$_i$ lunch.*

1st and 2nd person partitive obliques

If the partitive oblique is 1st or 2nd person plural, we find the following pattern, very much along the lines sketched above for 3rd person obliques:

[39] i a. *[A group of us]$_i$ are in the process of getting ourselves$_i$ ready for the election.*
b. *[A group of you]$_i$ are behaving yourselves$_i$ rather badly.*
ii a. *[A group of us]$_i$ has spent all morning filling in our$_i$ application forms.*
b. *[A group of you]$_i$ is going to have your$_i$ results sent to you$_i$ by email.*
iii a. *[A group of us]$_i$ is in the process of getting itself$_i$ ready for the election.*
b. *[A group of you]$_i$ is behaving itself$_i$ rather badly.*

In [i] the antecedent is construed as plural with respect to subject–verb agreement. Here the pronoun takes its person and number from the partitive oblique: *themselves* would be very marginal here. In [ii] the antecedent takes a 3rd person singular verb but a 1st or 2nd person plural pronoun; many will feel that this difference makes the construction less than fully felicitous (and would feel more comfortable with a plural verb), but for others it is acceptable and explicable in terms of the potentially more mechanical nature of subject–verb agreement. Agreement with the oblique is again hardly possible with reflexives, *ourselves, yourselves* being excluded from [iii], *themselves* from [37ii].

In the *one of*... construction, there is a slight difference between 1st and 2nd person:

[40] i a. *[One of us]$_i$ will have to move his$_i$/her$_i$/their$_i$/our$_i$ car.*
b. *[One of you]$_i$ will have to move his$_i$/her$_i$/their$_i$/your$_i$ car.*
ii a. *[One of us]$_i$ is going to hurt himself$_i$/herself$_i$/%themself$_i$/themselves$_i$/*ourselves$_i$.*
b. *[One of you]$_i$ is going to hurt himself$_i$/herself$_i$/%themself$_i$/themselves$_i$/yourself$_i$.*

In [i], where we have a genitive pronoun, the 1st and 2nd person behave alike. All four pronouns are possible. *His* and *her* are applicable if the whole set consists of males or females respectively (cf. also the sex-neutral issue discussed in §17.2.4 above). With *one of us* as antecedent *our car* has a distributive interpretation: we each have a car, and for one person *x* among us, *x* will have to move *x*'s car. (*Our* could also be co-indexed with *us* rather than *one of us*; in this case there is only one car, belonging to us as a group.) The same applies with *your car* in [ib]. The difference between 1st and 2nd person is seen in [ii], where we have reflexive forms of the pronoun. Since ***we*** can only be plural, the reflexive form is *ourselves*, which clashes with the singular *one* in the subject/antecedent. But ***you*** can be singular or plural and hence we can avoid such a clash with singular *yourself*. Even here, however, acceptability diminishes the closer the reflexive is to a 3rd person singular verb: ?*[One of you]$_i$ always behaves yourself$_i$ badly when we have guests.*

(b) Coordination

Where the antecedent is an *and*-coordination, the choice of pronoun is quite straightforward:

[41] i [*Kim and I*]$_i$ *have had* <u>*our*</u>$_i$ *applications turned down.*
ii [*You and Kim*]$_i$ *need to get* <u>*your*</u>$_i$ *passports renewed.*

Kim and I refers to a group containing the speaker and hence takes ***we*** as pronoun in accordance with the ordinary meaning of ***we*** – note that ***we*** is the pronoun that would be used to refer to a group consisting of Kim + the speaker when there was no antecedent expression. Analogously for ***you*** in [ii].

With *or*-coordinations of singulars we can also get 1st and 2nd person plural pronouns:

[42] i [*Either Kim or I*]$_i$ *will have to move* <u>*our*</u>$_i$ *car.*
ii [*You or Kim*]$_i$ *will need to take* <u>*your*</u>$_i$ *secretary to the meeting to take minutes.*

The coordinations here are likely to be interpreted exclusively, making them like *one of us/you. His, her,* and *their* would then just be possible here, as in [40i], but *our* and *your* are the preferred forms. But problems can arise with non-genitives, as with the following reflexives:

[43] i ?[*Either Kim or I*]$_i$ *may find* <u>*ourselves*</u>$_i$ *having to chair the meeting.*
ii ?[*You or Kim*]$_i$ *may find* <u>*yourself*</u>$_i$/<u>*yourselves*</u>$_i$ *having to chair the meeting.*

The plurality of *ourselves* and *yourselves* clashes with the singular meaning, and singular *yourself* appears to relate exclusively to *you* rather than the whole coordination. The rules for coordination provide no fully satisfactory solution in such cases, and in monitored speech or writing one would normally avoid the construction.

Note that while in subject–verb agreement some usage manuals say that the final element of an *or*-coordination should determine the form of the verb, such a rule could not apply with pronoun agreement:

[44] i #<u>*Kim or I*</u> *may have* <u>*my*</u> *application knocked back.*
ii <u>*Kim or I*</u> *will have to move* <u>*my*</u> *car.*

The antecedent for *my* has to be *I*, not *Kim or I*. Example [i] is therefore anomalous, and in [ii] there is only one car involved, mine.

17.3 Agreement between relative pronouns and their antecedents

We are concerned here with the contrast between the relative pronouns ***who*** and ***which***, which contrast in gender as personal vs non-personal. This second gender system differs from the one that figures in personal pronoun agreement in two main respects: (a) it applies with plurals no less than with singulars; and (b) no distinction is made according to whether the antecedent denotes a male or a female. Compare then:

[45]	SINGULAR	PLURAL
i	a. *the* <u>*man*</u> <u>*who*</u> *lost* <u>*his*</u> *head*	b. *the* <u>*men*</u> <u>*who*</u> *lost* <u>*their*</u> *heads*
ii	a. *the* <u>*woman*</u> <u>*who*</u> *lost* <u>*her*</u> *head*	b. *the* <u>*women*</u> <u>*who*</u> *lost* <u>*their*</u> *heads*
iii	a. *the* <u>*house*</u> <u>*which*</u> *lost* <u>*its*</u> *roof*	b. *the* <u>*houses*</u> <u>*which*</u> *lost* <u>*their*</u> *roofs*

For the relatives there is no difference between masculine singular *man* and feminine singular *woman*, as there is for the personal pronouns in [ia] and [iia]; but the contrast between *who* with the lexemes **man** and **woman**, and *which* with **roof** applies in the plural [b] examples as well as in the singular [a].

Likeness between the contrasts *which* vs *who* and *it* vs *he* or *she*

With singular antecedents, **which** is for the most part found with nouns that take **it**, and **who** with those that take **he** or **she**. With human nouns, **which** is possible only with nouns denoting infants without specification of sex:

[46] i a. *The baby had lost his/her/its rattle.* b. *the baby who/which took the rattle*
ii a. *The boy had lost his/*its rattle.* b. *the boy who/*which took the rattle*

Nouns denoting animals can thus take **which** or **who**, just as they can take **it** or else **he** or **she**. And if an animal is referred to by means of a proper noun then **which** is excluded, just as **it** is:

[47] i a. *The dog had lost his/her/its bone.* b. *the dog who/which took the bone*
ii a. *Fido was wagging his/*its tail.* b. *Fido, who/*which was barking again*

The use of **who** rather than **which** with animals, like that of **he** or **she** rather than **it**, indicates a greater amount of interest or empathy. The primary, obligatory use of **who** is with persons, and its extension to animals suggests that they are being treated as relatively like persons: hence the label 'personal' for this pronoun.

Imperfect match between *which* vs *who* and *it* vs *he* or *she*

In spite of the similarities illustrated in [46–47], the relative and personal pronoun contrasts are not quite the same. It is for this reason that we use separate labels, **non-personal** for ***which***, **neuter** for ***it***. The differences are as follows:

(a) ***Who***, unlike ***she***, is not used with nouns denoting ships, etc.

[48] *The ship, which/*who was on its/her maiden voyage, was way behind schedule.*

Inanimates always take **which**.

(b) Human collectives can take **who**, but not **he** or **she**

[49] i *The committee, who haven't yet completed their report, must be in disarray.*
ii **The committee, who haven't yet completed his report, must be in disarray.*
iii *The committee, which hasn't yet completed its report, must be in disarray.*

A singular collective noun like *committee* can be given either a unitary or a set interpretation (§18.2). In the set interpretation the focus is on the individual members of the committee, and this overrides the morphosyntactic singular feature, so that in subject–verb agreement it behaves like a plural, and takes plural **they** as anaphoric personal pronoun. Since the individual members of the committee are humans, this interpretation takes personal **who** as relative pronoun. Hence the combination of *who*, *have*, and *their* in version [i]. In the unitary interpretation, the focus is on the committee as a single entity, so that it behaves as a singular for subject–verb agreement. But this single entity itself is not a human being, so that **who** and **he** or **she** are not permitted – this gives the combination *which*, *has*, and *its* in version [iii], while excluding [ii]. Some speakers also allow %*which hasn't yet completed their report*: this involves a shift of focus from unitary to set, but it doesn't affect the point at issue in this section. The set interpretation sanctions **who**, but neither interpretation can sanction **he** or **she** because in neither case is *committee* understood as denoting a single male or female person.

(c) ***Which*** can itself serve as antecedent to ***he*** or ***she***

[50] i That's the dog { *who attacked his owner.*
ii That's the dog *which attacked its owner.*
iii That's the dog *which attacked his owner.* }

In addition to the congruent combinations of ***who*** with ***he*** or ***she*** and ***which*** with ***it***, the non-congruent combination of ***which*** with ***he*** or ***she*** is also possible, though less likely. The other mismatch, of ***who*** and ***it***, is of very questionable acceptability: ?*That's the dog who attacked its owner.*

18 Subject–verb agreement

18.1 Simple agreement

Agreement between the subject, as source, and the verb, as target, is limited to clauses where the verb is of one of the following kinds:

[1] i a present tense form of a verb other than a modal auxiliary
ii a preterite form of the verb ***be***

Compare, then:

[2] VERB AGREES WITH SUBJECT

i a. *The nurse wants to see him.* b. *The nurses want to see him.*
ii a. *The dog was sleeping.* b. *The dogs were sleeping.*

[3] NO VARIATION IN THE VERB

i a. *The nurse will see you now.* b. *The nurses will see you now.*
ii a. *The dog slept all day.* b. *The dogs slept all day.*

In [2] the choice between the inflectional forms *wants* and *want*, *was* and *were* is determined by the subject, whereas in [3] the modal auxiliary *will* and the preterite *slept* remain constant even though the subject changes.

The agreement involves number and person together: *wants* is a 3rd person singular present tense form, while *want* is the plain present tense form, occurring with any other kind of subject – 3rd person plural or else 1st or 2nd person singular or plural (cf. *They/I/You/We want to see him*). Similarly, *was* is the 1st/3rd singular preterite form of ***be***, while *were* is the form occurring with any other subject – 1st/3rd plural or 2nd person. And in the present tense of ***be*** there is a three-way distinction between *am* (1st person singular), *is* (3rd person singular), and *are* (2nd person and plural).

Relatively little needs to be said about 1st and 2nd person subjects: most of the complexity in this area has to do with the contrast between singular and plural in 3rd person subjects. For this reason we will for the most part speak, for convenience, of 'singular verbs' and 'plural verbs'.

The examples in [2] illustrate what we will call **simple agreement**, which may be defined initially as follows:

[4] In simple agreement, the verb agrees with a subject with the form of an NP whose person–number classification derives from its head noun.

Thus *wants* and *was* agree respectively with *the nurse* and *the dog*, which are 3rd person singular NPs by virtue of having *nurse* and *dog* as their head; *want* and *were* agree with *the nurses* and *the dogs*, which are 3rd person plural NPs by virtue of having *nurses* and *dogs* as head noun.

Extensions of simple agreement

(a) Relative clauses

[5] i a. *the nurse [who wants to see him]* b. *the nurses [who want to see him]*
ii a. *the dog [that __ was sleeping]* b. *the dogs [that __ were sleeping]*

The default pattern in relative clauses is that the subject takes its person–number properties from its antecedent. In [i] *who* is construed as 3rd person singular in [a] and 3rd person plural in [b] by virtue of its anaphoric relation to the antecedent *nurse* and *nurses* respectively. In [ii] the subject is realised by a gap rather than an overt NP (see Ch. 12, §3.5.6), but this gap likewise inherits the person–number properties of the antecedent.[71]

(b) Subjects with the form of clauses or phrases of other categories than NP

We can extend the concept of simple agreement to cover constructions where the subject is a clause or some other kind of phrase than an NP. These are treated as 3rd person singular:

[6] i *That he is trying to hide something is all too plain.* [declarative clause]
ii *Why he resigned remains a mystery.* [interrogative clause]
iii *Not informing the neighbours was a serious mistake.* [gerund-participial clause]
iv *From here to London is over fifty miles.* [PP]
v *Rather too big for your boots is what you are, my boy.* [AdjP]

The default category in the system of person is 3rd and, certainly for the purposes of agreement, singular is the default number, so in the absence of any motivation for 1st or 2nd person or for plural, subjects like those in [6] take 3rd person singular verbs.

Departures from simple agreement

There are many places where the rule of simple agreement is not followed. A sample of attested written examples is given in:

[7] i **The Directors believe that [the effect of the above resolutions] are in the best interests of the Company and strongly recommend you to vote in favour of them.*
ii **But at this stage, [the accuracy of the quotes] have not been disputed.*
iii **Cognitive scientists seek . . . to model the ways in which [the ability to perform such tasks] are acquired, changed or impaired.*
iv **In this case a woman may continue to use both names provided [the use of both commonly known names] are disclosed.*
v *?It is part of one's linguistic competence to be able to control and interpret variations of word-order and grammatical structure of the kind that are exemplified in the sentences cited above.*
vi *[A number of special units] are available for patients requiring hospitalisation.*
vii *[The committee] were informed that the proposal to close the canal had been made by the British Transport Commission . . .*

[71] In a similar way, the dummy pronoun *there* takes on the agreement properties of the displaced subject: see Ch. 4, §3.2.2.

Examples [i–iv] – from a letter to shareholders from the chairperson of a major British company, a newspaper, government instructions relating to academic grant applications, a formal notice in a credit union office – are unquestionably ungrammatical, but examples of this kind are not uncommon, even in written texts. They clearly involve processing errors: the subjects are relatively complex, and the verb has been made to agree with a plural NP within the subject rather than with the singular subject NP itself. The position of the plural NP immediately before the verb has presumably given it greater salience for the writer at the time of choosing the verb than the singular NP containing it. In the case of [i] and [iv], and perhaps [ii] also, the selection of the plural NP as agreement source is facilitated by the fact that it could substitute for the larger subject NP with little change to the meaning: *The Directors believe that the above resolutions are in the best interests of the Company*, and so on.

This phenomenon is often described in terms of the concept of 'proximity': the verb agrees with the proximate preceding NP. The proximate preceding NP is the one whose head is closest to the verb: in [7i] the NPs *the effect of the above resolutions* and *the above resolutions* both immediately precede the verb, but the second is the proximate one since its head *resolutions* is closer to the verb than *effect*, the head of the first. English clearly has no general rule saying that the verb agrees with the proximate preceding NP (which is why we have starred these examples), but we will see that there are places where proximity is a relevant factor in more acceptable departures from simple agreement – and indeed one such case is seen in [vi].

Example [7v], from a textbook by an eminent linguist, is more acceptable than [i–iv], but still cannot be covered by any established rule of grammar. The underlined verb is in a relative clause whose subject has singular *kind* as antecedent, so the simple agreement rule would predict *is* rather than *are*. The latter form matches the plurality of the sequence *variations of word-order and grammatical structure*, and again the sentence could be reformulated with this as antecedent for the relative clause: *to control and interpret the kind of <u>variations of word-order and grammatical structure</u> that <u>are</u> exemplified in the sentences cited above.*

Examples [7vi–vii] are fully acceptable and grammatical: they illustrate cases where more specific rules require or permit the general rule of simple agreement to be overridden. We will survey a variety of such override constructions in §§18.2–3, and in §18.4 we look at the interaction between coordination and agreement.[72]

18.2 Semantically motivated overrides with collective and number-transparent nouns

Two of the most common overrides of the simple agreement rule are found with singular collective nouns and with the number-transparent quantificational noun construction introduced in §3.3 above:

[8] SINGULAR COLLECTIVE AS HEAD OF SUBJECT NP

i	*<u>The committee</u> <u>has</u> not yet come to a decision.*	[simple agreement]
ii	*<u>The committee</u> <u>have</u> not yet come to a decision.*	[plural override]

[72] Examples like *More than one glass was broken* and *One more application has been received than we had expected* ([6] of §11) follow the simple agreement rule and hence do not need to be dealt with here: what is noteworthy about such examples is the mismatch between the syntactic number of the subject NP and its meaning.

[9] NUMBER-TRANSPARENT NOUN AS HEAD OF SUBJECT NP

i *A number of spots have/*has appeared.* [plural override]

ii *Heaps of money has/*have been spent.* [singular override]

With collectives the override applies only in the case where the subject has a singular noun as head: with a plural head we have a plural verb in accordance with the simple agreement rule (*The committees have not yet completed their reports*). The number-transparent construction has overrides of both types: in [9i] we have a singular head (*number*) but a plural verb, while in [9ii] we have a plural head (*heaps*) but a singular verb. We consider the collective and number-transparent constructions together in this section because the plural override in [9i] is similar to that in [8ii] – and the division between collective and number-transparent nouns is by no means sharply drawn.

Optional vs obligatory override

The essential difference between the two constructions is that with collectives the override is optional, whereas in the number-transparent construction it is obligatory. As the examples show, *this committee* can take either a singular or a plural verb, whereas *a number of spots* requires a plural verb.[73]

The optionality of the override with collectives reflects the fact that there is potentially a difference of meaning between the versions with singular and plural verbs. From one perspective a committee is a single entity, but since a committee (normally) consists of a plurality of members it can be conceptualised as denoting this plural set. The construction with a plural verb focuses on the members of the committee rather than on the committee as a unit. The plural override is therefore not permitted with predicates that are applicable to the whole but not to the individual members; it is, moreover, of questionable acceptability if the collective has *one* (or *a/another*) as determiner:

[10] i *The committee consists/*consist of two academic staff and three students.*

ii *This committee, at least, is/*are not chaired by one of the premier's cronies.*

iii *One committee, appointed last year, has/?have not yet met.*

The version with singular agreement may reflect a focus on the collection as a whole, or may just result from application of the simple agreement rule. The plural version is more common in BrE than in AmE – and in informal style than in formal written style, where some writers may have the feeling that the singular is grammatically more correct. It must be emphasised, however, that the plural construction is unquestionably fully grammatical in Standard English, and this is generally recognised by the usage manuals. The plural override is particularly likely with predicates that necessarily apply to individuals rather than collective wholes, and it is virtually required if a quantifying adjunct such as *all* is included in the clause:

[11] i *The other crew were not even born at the time I won my first championship.*

ii *The class have/?has now all received certificates of merit.*

[73] Examples of a singular verb with *a number* are occasionally attested, as in this one from an editorial in an Australian national newspaper: *In the past year a number of illegal drug operations has been uncovered in relatively close proximity.* They are too rare, however, to qualify as an established variant in Standard English: they can be regarded as hypercorrections attributable to an overzealous application of the simple agreement rule. And one case where no one would consciously apply the simple agreement rule is with *lot* as head: *A lot of people like/*likes it.*

In the case of the number-transparent *a number of spots*, by contrast, there is no potential meaning difference, just as there is none with the semantically similar *some spots*.

Complementation

A second difference between *committee* and number-transparent *number* is that the latter occurs predominantly with an *of* complement, and if there is no such complement expressed one must be recoverable anaphorically from the context. *A number have accepted the offer*, for example, is elliptical: it can only be properly interpreted if an oblique can be reconstructed (e.g. partitive *of the shareholders* or non-partitive *of shareholders*). This is not so with *committee*. *The committee has/have finally reached a decision* is interpretable as it stands: it does not require contextual information about the members of the committee.

Consider now the nouns in:

[12] i	*administration*	*army*	*band*$_1$	*board*	*class*$_1$
	clergy	*couple*$_1$	*crew*	*enemy*	*family*
	government	*intelligentsia*	*jury*	*party*$_1$	*public*
	staff	*team*	*union*	*university*	*woodwind*
ii	*band*$_2$	*batch*	*bunch*	*class*$_2$	*couple*$_2$
	flock	*group*	*herd*	*host*	*majority*
	minority	*number*	*party*$_2$	*rash*	*set*

The nouns in [i] occur freely, usually, or invariably without an *of* complement, while those in [ii] are found predominantly or invariably with an overt or understood *of* complement. (*Band*$_1$ denotes a musical band, while *band*$_2$ means "group", as in *a band of ruffians*. *Class*$_1$ applies to a class at school or university, while *class*$_2$ denotes a class derived by classification, as in *a class of words*. *Couple*$_1$ denotes a man and woman who are married or in a comparable relationship, while *couple*$_2$ means "a set of (approximately) two", as in *a couple of days*. *Party*$_1$ denotes a political party, while *party*$_2$ again means "group", as in *a party of hitchhikers*. *Clergy* and *intelligentsia* are, for pragmatic reasons, normally restricted to the singular, with *the* as determiner.)

The nouns in [12i] behave straightforwardly like our model collective *committee*: the plural override is optional and there is a potentially clear difference between singular and plural conceptualisations. Those in [ii] are less homogeneous. *Bunch*, for example, can apply to a set of things fastened or closely grouped together or simply to a group of people; the unitary conceptualisation is strongly favoured in the former sense while override is likely in the second: *A bunch of flowers was presented to the teacher* vs *A bunch of hooligans were seen leaving the premises*. The plural override is most likely where the construction simply provides a quantification, as in this latter example with *bunch* or *A group of onlookers were injured*. For many speakers, especially of BrE, simple agreement in such cases sounds unacceptably pedantic: %*A bunch of hooligans was seen leaving the premises*.

The clear cases of number-transparent singular nouns are *lot*, *number*, and *couple*$_2$. *Majority* and *minority* are borderline cases; plural override is surely obligatory in such examples as [13i], but one does encounter examples with singular verbs, as in [13ii]:[74]

[74] There can be no override in examples like *The government's majority is likely to be reduced*, which is parallel to the use of *number* in *The number of fatalities has risen*. With the expression *the silent majority* plural override is optional: *The silent majority takes/take a different view*.

[13] i *The majority of her friends are/*is Irish.*
ii %*The fact the overwhelming majority of Americans doesn't want the President impeached does not necessarily mean that that would be the right decision.*

One final point to make is that the collective plural override never applies with non-count nouns like *crockery, luggage,* etc., that denote aggregates of heterogeneous entities (§3.1): *Her crockery was/*were very ornate; The luggage has/*have been lost.*

18.3 Further overrides and alternations

(a) Measure phrases

We have already noted that plural measure nominals can be respecified as singular for the purposes of agreement and selection within the NP. This carries over to subject–verb agreement, whether or not there is any marker of singular number within the NP:

[14] i *<u>That ten days we spent in Florida</u> <u>was</u> fantastic.* (=[71i] of §3)
ii *<u>Twenty dollars</u> <u>seems</u> a ridiculous amount to pay to go to the movies.*
iii *<u>Five miles</u> <u>is</u> rather more than I want to walk this afternoon.*
iv *<u>Three eggs</u> <u>is</u> plenty.*

This is the opposite of the collective override: here an NP that is formally plural is conceptualised as referring to a single measure (of time, money, distance, or whatever) and accordingly takes a singular verb. The measure override is characteristically found with *be* or other complex-intransitive verbs (such as *seem* in [ii]). In [ii], where the predicative complement is a singular NP, the override is obligatory (**Twenty dollars seem a ridiculous amount to pay*); in [iii–iv] it is optional but quite strongly preferred.

(b) Proportional constructions

There are a variety of constructions expressing proportion. Consider first:

[15] i *[One <u>student</u> in a hundred] takes/*take drugs.* } [simple agreement]
ii *In a hundred students, [only <u>one</u>] takes/*take drugs.* }
iii *[One in a hundred <u>students</u>] takes/take drugs.* [optional singular override]

In all cases *out of* could replace *in*. Examples [i–ii] follow the simple agreement rule: the subject has a singular head (underlined), and the verb must be singular too. In [iii], however, the head is plural, but the verb can be singular as well as plural. The optional singular override is clearly motivated by the presence of *one*, and the synonymy with [i–ii]. (For the structure of the subject NP in [iii], see §11.)

Proportional constructions with *per cent* (BrE) and *percent* (AmE)

[16] i *One percent of students *takes/take drugs.*
ii *One percent of the electorate takes/take drugs.*
iii *One percent of the cheese was/*were contaminated.*

Percent is best analysed here as a noun taking an *of* complement (and for that reason we have used here the single-word AmE spelling). It belongs with the number-transparent nouns, with plural *students* in [i] requiring a plural verb and singular *cheese* in [iii] a singular verb: compare *a lot of students* and *a lot of the cheese.* In [ii] the head of the oblique is *electorate,* and since this is a collective noun, singular agreement can be overridden, just as in *The electorate aren't going to like this.*

(c) Fused relatives

The following examples illustrate simple agreement:

[17] i [*What money remains*] *is in the bank.*
ii [*What errors were made*] *were relatively minor.*
iii [*What amuses you*] *doesn't necessarily amuse everybody else.*

The bracketed expressions are fused relative constructions belonging to the category of NP. In these examples the relativised phrase is subject in the subordinate clause and the whole fused relative construction is subject of the matrix clause, so the issue of number agreement arises in both clauses: in [i], for example, there are two singular verbs, *remains* in the subordinate clause, *is* in the matrix. In *I have already committed what money remains* (where the fused relative is object) it arises only in the subordinate clause, and in *What she says amuses me* (where the relativised element is object) it arises only in the matrix.

In [17i–ii] *what* is a determinative functioning as determiner to a head noun, *money* and *errors* respectively. This head noun determines the number in both clauses, hence the two singular verbs in [i] and the two plural verbs in [ii]. Nothing further need be said about this construction: complexities arise only where *what* is a pronoun, as in [iii].

In general, the pronoun *what* has the default value singular. This accounts for the singular verbs *amuses*, and *doesn't* in [17iii] – and for the deviance of examples like **What he bought have all been broken* even in a context in which he bought a plurality of things, such as half a dozen plates. There may, however, be a plural override when the relativised phrase or the whole fused relative construction is predicand to a plural NP in predicative complement function:

[18] i a. *He withdrew his motion for* [*what were obviously very sound reasons*].
b. *He has given me* [*what appear to be forged banknotes*].
c. [*What appeared to be forged banknotes*] *were lying all over his desk.*
ii a. [*What we need*] *are managers with new ideas and the will to apply them.*
b. [*What is needed*] *are managers with new ideas and the will to apply them.*
c. [*What are needed*] *are managers with new ideas and the will to apply them.*

In [i] the plural predicative is within the subordinate clause, whereas in [ii] it is in the matrix clause. In [ic] the subordinate verb *appeared*, being a preterite, doesn't show agreement, but the plural construal of *what* is manifest in the plural verb of the matrix. Where, as here, we have a plural construal in the subordinate clause, the whole fused relative is construed as plural: we could not replace *were* by *was*. Where a plural predicative in the matrix results in a plural override in that clause, there may or may not be a matching override in the subordinate clause: in [iic] there is, but in [iib] the default singular *is* is retained.

Where the plural predicative that motivates the plural verb is in the matrix, the override is optional: *are* could be replaced by *is* in [18iia–c]. Where the plural predicative is in the subordinate clause matters are not so clear-cut: a singular verb would be possible in [ib] (*appears*), but not in [ia] or [ic] (**was*).

(d) Interrogatives

In general, the interrogative pronouns *who* and *what* take the default value of singular. Compare:

[19] i a. *Who wants some more ice-cream?* b. *What remains to be done?*
ii *Which (of these) is/are yours?*

There is no presupposition in [i] that only one person wants some more ice-cream or that only one thing remains to be done: the default singular allows for either singular or plural answers. In [ii], with determinative *which* as fused determiner-head, we have a singular or plural verb according to whether the answer is presupposed to be singular or plural.

The default singular values for *who* and *what* can, however, be overridden when there is a presupposition that the answer is plural:

[20] i *What are going to be the deciding factors?*
ii *Who haven't yet handed in their assignments?*
iii *Who have excelled themselves in this year's coxed pairs?*
iv *What have pointed ears and long tails?*

In [i] the override is obligatory: this case is similar to those discussed for fused relatives such as [18i], with the plural PC *the deciding factors* forcing a plural construal of *what*. A likely context for [20ii] is one where I'm addressing a group of students and assuming that a plurality of them haven't handed in their assignments; singular *hasn't* would be possible (but without indicating any expectation of a plural answer and favouring singular *assignment* if there is only one each). In [20iii], coxed pairs involve three people (two rowers and the cox), so the presupposition is again that the answer is plural. The reflexive has to be plural, and this favours a plural verb. Finally, [iv] presupposes a generic bare plural as answer, e.g. *foxes*, but the motivation for a plural override is relatively small since the answer could be given in the form of a generic singular, e.g. *a fox*.

(e) Singular override with *one of X who* . . .

NPs of the form '*one of* Det N relative-clause' may have one or other of two structures, depending on whether the relative clause belongs in the embedded NP (with N as head) or the upper one (with *one* as fused determiner-head). Compare, for example:

[21] i *Max is [one of the people the previous head had appointed].* [Type I]
ii *[One of her colleagues whom she deeply admired] had betrayed her.* [Type II]

In [i] the relative clause modifies *people*: there is a set of people whom the previous head had appointed, and Max is a member of this set. But this is not how we interpret [ii] (or at least it is not the natural interpretation of [ii]). The relative clause belongs in the topmost NP, not the one with *colleagues* as head: it is not a matter of there being a set of colleagues whom she admired, but of there being one colleague whom she admired.

The relativised element in these examples is object. Where it is the subject that is relativised, the expectation would be that the number of the verb would be determined by the antecedent, giving a plural verb in Type I, and a singular in Type II. In practice, however, singular verbs are often found as alternants of plurals in Type I:

[22] i *He's [one of those people who always want to have the last word].* } [Type I]
ii *He's [one of those people who always wants to have the last word].* }
iii *He's [one of her colleagues who is always ready to criticise her].* [Type II]

Examples [i] and [iii] follow the ordinary rules, but [ii] involves a singular override. It can presumably be attributed to the salience within the whole structure of *one* and to the influence of the Type II structure (it is in effect a blend between Types I and II). But it cannot be regarded as a semantically motivated override: semantically the relative clause modifies *people*. This singular override is most common when the relative clause follows *those* or *those* + noun.

(f) *Any* and *none, either* and *neither* as fused determiner-heads

Any and *none* naturally take singular verbs when they are construed as non-count singular – for example, when they have a singular NP as oblique partitive, as in *Has any of the money been recovered?* or *None of the food was contaminated.* When they quantify over a plural set, they take either plural or singular verbs:

[23] i *Please let me know immediately if [any of the set texts] are/is unavailable.*
ii *He made quite a few mistakes but [none (of them)] were/was very serious.*

The alternation correlates with the fact that as pure determiners *any* and *no* can combine with plural or singular heads.

Either and *neither* quantify over sets of two and as pure determiners take only singular heads. In the fused determiner-head construction the default verb-form is singular; plurals are also found, but they are likely to be avoided in formal style:

[24] i *Has/Have [either of the candidates] arrived yet?*
ii *He made two mistakes but [neither (of them)] was/were very serious.*

(g) 3rd person override in cleft relatives

[25] i *It is I [who am at fault].* [simple agreement]
ii *It is me [who is at fault].* [3rd person override]

Example [i] follows the general rules for relative clauses, with the relative pronoun *who* being construed as 1st person singular by virtue of its anaphoric relation to *I*. In the less formal [ii], however, the antecedent is in accusative case, and here the 1st person property is not carried over to *who*; the latter therefore takes on the default 3rd person feature.

18.4 **Coordination within the subject**

Rules which determine the agreement feature values of coordinate structures as a whole on the basis of the values of each of the coordinates are generally known as **resolution rules**.

(a) Coordination with *and*

In general a subject with the form of a coordination of NPs linked by *and* takes a plural verb, as in *Mary and John are here*, etc. It doesn't matter whether the individual coordinates are singular or plural: the coordination as a whole here denotes a set containing at least two members, and hence takes a plural verb.

And-coordinations with a singular verb

There are several constructions, however, where the verb is singular. One case is seen in:

[26] i *[Eggs and bacon] is/*are my favourite breakfast.*
ii *[The hammer and sickle] was/*were flying over the Kremlin.*
iii *[Your laziness and your ineptitude] amazes/amaze me.*

Such examples can be regarded as involving a singular override similar to that found with measure phrases: the subject is conceptualised as a single unit and this determines the singular verb. In [i] the predicative *my favourite breakfast* can only apply to eggs and bacon as a unit, and hence a plural verb is impossible. If we change the predicative to, say, *good for you*, both singular and plural verbs are possible, but with a difference of meaning. In *Eggs and bacon is good for you* the subject is again conceptualised as a single unit (a meal consisting of eggs and bacon), whereas in *Eggs and bacon are good for you* the two foods are separately good for you. In [ii] the coordination is between two nouns rather than two NPs, but again we have a unitary conceptualisation: the subject refers to a flag. In [iii] both singular and plural verbs are possible, the singular conveying that the laziness and ineptitude form a single cause of amazement, the plural conveying that each of them is a cause of amazement. The choice between singular and plural conceptualisations is more readily available with abstract NPs, as here, than with concrete NPs: compare, for example, **John and his father amazes me.*

A second case where an *and*-coordination takes singular agreement is illustrated in:

[27] i [*The chair of the finance subcommittee, and the source of all our problems,*] *has* *voted in favour of cuts for the twenty-first time.*
 ii [*Our chef and chauffeur*] *has decided to emigrate.*

The singular verbs reflect the fact that the subject as a whole refers to a single person. The chair of the finance subcommittee and the source of all our problems are one and the same person, and likewise our chef and our chauffeur. In [ii] we could have *Our chef and chauffeur have decided to emigrate*, but this would entail that two separate people are involved; the same applies in principle to [i], but in practice the second coordinate would be very unlikely to be used to refer to a distinct person.

Finally, coordinations of NPs containing distributive *each* or *every* take singular verbs:

[28] i [*Each dog and each cat*] *has/*have to be registered.*
 ii [*Every complaint and every suggestion*] *was/*were thoroughly investigated.*

And-coordinations of clauses

Subjects with the form of an *and*-coordination of clauses generally take singular verbs:

[29] i [*That the form was submitted on the very last day and that the project had not been properly costed*] *suggests that the application was prepared in a rush.*
 ii [*How the dog escaped and where it went*] *remains a mystery.*

It is nevertheless possible to have a plural verb when the predicate treats the coordinates as expressing separate facts, questions, or the like:

[30] i [*That the form was submitted on the very last day and that the project had not been properly costed*] *are two very strong indications that the application was prepared in a rush.*
 ii [*How the dog escaped and where it went*] *are questions we may never be able to answer.*

(b) Coordination with *or*

The use of *or* indicates that the coordinates are to be considered separately. In the case of *or*, therefore, a coordination of two singulars does not yield a plural, as it generally does with *and*. With symmetric uses of *or* – those where the coordinates are of fully equal status and could be reversed – the resolution rules give fully acceptable results only where the coordinates have the same number, i.e. all are singular or all are plural:

[31] i	[(*Either*) *Mary or John*] *is/*are sure to go.*	[sg *or* sg = sg]
ii	[(*Either*) *Mary or the twins*] *?is/?are sure to go.*	[sg *or* pl = ?sg/?pl]
iii	[(*Either*) *the twins or Mary*] *?is/?are sure to go.*	[pl *or* sg = ?sg/?pl]
iv	[(*Either*) *the twins or their parents*] *are/*is sure to go.*	[pl *or* pl = pl]

In [i] and [iv] the whole coordination has the same number as each coordinate, singular in [i], plural in [iv]. But where the coordinates are of different number, neither singular nor plural agreement feels right: whichever we choose, there will be conflict between the number of the verb and the number of one of the coordinates. Usage manuals generally invoke the principle of proximity, saying that the verb should agree with the nearest coordinate. This rule would select *are* in [ii] and *is* in [iii]. In practice, however, many speakers tend to feel uncomfortable with both forms and will typically find ways of avoiding the conflict, e.g. by using a modal auxiliary, which has no agreement properties: *(Either) Mary or the twins will be sure to go.*

The acceptability of a plural verb with coordinates of mixed number, or indeed with coordinates that are all singular, is increased in such contexts as the following:

[32] i *I don't think [(either) Mary or the twins] are/?is going to help you.*
  ii *I don't think [(either) Mary or John] is/are going to help you.*

Here the coordination is within the scope of a negative and a negated *or* entails that all coordinates fail to have the property in question. Example [i] thus conveys that both Mary and the twins are not going to help you, and analogously for [ii]. This makes the plural *are* sound better, though it would still generally be avoided in [ii] in formal style.

One also occasionally finds plural verbs with singular coordinates when *X or Y* is thought of inclusively rather than exclusively, i.e. as "X or Y or both":

[33] *?Problems arise when emotional involvement or lack of experience prevent an objective appraisal of the situation.*

Or in supplements

In the following, *or* introduces a supplement rather than an element which is strictly coordinate with the preceding NP:

[34] i *His proposal, or rather the ramifications of it, are/*is going to have a serious effect on our plans.*
  ii *Her eyes, or rather the visible one, was/*were pale blue.*
  iii *Arhythmia, or irregular contractions of the ventricles, is/*are a serious heart condition.*

In [i–ii] the underlined NP represents a correction of the preceding one. It therefore supersedes the first NP and determines the number of the verb, plural in [i], singular in [ii]. In [iii] the supplement is merely an explanatory and parenthetical reformulation of the first NP, and it is therefore the latter that determines the number of the verb.

Person

Where one of the coordinates is 1st or 2nd person singular there tends to be a preference for agreement with the final coordinate, except that the 1st person singular form *am* is felt to be awkward and the construction is likely to be avoided in monitored style:

[35] i *You mustn't go unless [either I or your father] comes/?come with you.*
  ii *I don't think [either your father or I] have/?has had much say in the matter.*
  iii *[Either your father or I] ?am/?is going to have to come with you.*

(c) Coordination with *neither . . . nor*

A clause with a *neither . . . nor* coordination as subject can be thought of semantically in either of two ways (see Ch. 15, §2.4):

[36] i *Neither Mary nor John will help.*
ii "It isn't the case that either Mary or John will help"
iii "Both Mary and John will not help"

The conceptualisation given in [ii] incorporates an *or*-coordination, while that given in [iii] shows *neither... nor* to be like (*both...*) *and*. This then yields the following agreement patterns:

[37] i	[*Neither Mary nor John*] *is/are here yet.*	[*neither* sg *nor* sg = sg/pl]
ii	[*Neither Mary nor the twins*] *are/?is here yet.*	[*neither* sg *nor* pl = pl/?sg]
iii	[*Neither the twins nor Mary*] *are/?is here yet.*	[*neither* pl *nor* sg = pl/?sg]
iv	[*Neither the twins nor their parents*] *are/*is here yet.*	[*neither* pl *nor* pl = pl]

In [i] the singular verb matches the singular that is found with an *or*-coordination of two singulars, while the plural verb matches the conceptualisation "Both Mary and John are not here yet". We have seen that *or*-coordinations of coordinates with unlike number are problematic, so the singular verb in [ii–iii] is of questionable acceptability (especially in [ii], where the nearest coordinate is plural). The "both . . . and + not" conceptualisation, however, sanctions the plural verb: this can certainly be regarded as fully acceptable and is strongly preferred over the singular.

(d) *Not only . . . but also*

In constructions of this kind, number is determined by the second coordinate:

[38] i *Not only Mary / her parents but also Helen has been questioned.*
ii *Not only Mary / her parents but also the twins have been questioned.*

(e) Coordination with *and not* or *but not*

Coordinations with *and not* and *but not* follow a simple rule. Since only the first coordinate has the property ascribed to it by the predicate, it is the first coordinate that determines the form of the verb:

[39] i a. *Ed, and not the twins, is/*are here.* b. *The twins, and not Ed, are/*is here.*

19 Number in predicatives and their predicands

19.1 The semantic nature of matching number

Very often the number of an NP functioning as predicative matches that of its predicand:

[1]	SINGULAR PREDICAND	PLURAL PREDICAND
i	a. *My daughter is a doctor.*	b. *My daughters are doctors.*
ii	a. *#My daughter is doctors.*	b. *#My daughters are a doctor.*

Here the predicand is subject and the predicative NP must have the same number as the subject, singular in [a], plural in [b]. Similarly where the predicand is object in the complex-transitive construction:

[2] i *He considers his colleague a complete idiot / #complete idiots.*
ii *He considers his colleagues complete idiots / #a complete idiot.*

In these examples the predicative is a complement of the verb, but we find the same matching of number when it is within an *as* phrase adjunct:

[3] i *As a doctor* / #*doctors, my daughter makes vital decisions.*
ii *As doctors* / #*a doctor, my daughters make vital decisions.*

This phenomenon bears an obvious resemblance to agreement, and indeed it is commonly said that a predicative agrees with its predicand. We have noted, however, that it is not a straightforward matter to distinguish between grammatical agreement and mere semantic congruence, and in this instance we believe that an account in terms of semantics is more appropriate than one in terms of grammatical agreement. It is for this reason that we have marked the unacceptable examples above with the symbol '#' rather than '*'. We will see that the requirement for matching number applies only in a semantically restricted range of cases: it does not have the generality that would justify the postulation of a grammatical rule of agreement.

No agreement of person

One initial point to make is that there is certainly no agreement between predicative and predicand with respect to the category of person: the relationship between predicative and predicand is therefore clearly different from that holding between subject and verb (predicator). Compare, for example:

[4] i *I am [a doctor who believes/*believe in euthanasia].*
ii *It is I who am master now.*
iii *You are obviously [someone who has/*have thought carefully about this issue].*
iv *[The one who is causing all the trouble] is you.*

In [i] the matrix subject *I* is 1st person, while the predicative – the NP headed by *doctor* – is 3rd person. The difference in person is reflected in the contrast between the verb-forms *am* and *believes*. *Am* is 1st person singular agreeing with *I*, while *believes* is 3rd person singular agreeing with *who*, which takes its person–number properties from its antecedent *doctor*. Conversely in the matrix clause of [ii] the subject is 3rd person while the predicative is 1st. Example [iii] has a 2nd person subject with 3rd person predicative, while [iv] has the opposite arrangement.

No agreement of gender

Similarly we do not have gender agreement between predicative and predicand, as we do between a pronoun and its antecedent. Predicatives are headed by nouns with their own inherent content which can independently determine the gender features involved:

[5] i *[Your brother] is clearly [a problem which/*who we will have to resolve].*
ii *[The dean] is [an obstacle which/*who I didn't foresee].*

In these examples, the relative clause is semantically applicable only to the head noun of the predicative complement (e.g. it is possible to resolve a problem, but not a brother), and the relative pronoun has to be the non-personal *which*.

In examples like the following the gender of the predicative does seem to vary so as to match that of the predicand:

[6] i *[This house] is [a shambles which is going to take days to sort out].*
ii *[The government] are [a shambles who don't deserve to be in power].*

The switch from *which* to *who* here, however, is due to the fact that *shambles* can be interpreted as a human collective noun; this sanctions the *who* (together with the plural verb) in [ii]. But it is simply a semantic fact that *shambles* can be predicated of both human and non-human entities.

Similarly, the match between personal pronoun and the matrix subject in the following can be accounted for semantically:

[7] [*The younger daughter*] *is* [*a doctor*$_i$ *who*$_i$ *is dedicated to her*$_i$/$^{\#}$*his*$_i$ *patients*].

Doctor is a dual-gender noun that does not itself encode information about sex, but the anaphoric link between the genitive personal pronoun, relative *who*, and *doctor* gives the predicative a female or male interpretation. The anomaly of *his* here simply reflects the semantic fact that the property of being a doctor who is dedicated to his patients is an inappropriate one to ascribe to a female.

No agreement of number

As for number, we find numerous cases where predicative and predicand differ in grammatical number. We will illustrate in turn from the specifying and ascriptive uses of the copula distinguished in Ch. 4, §5.5.

Specifying *be*

[8] i [*The only thing we need now*] *is* [*some new curtains*].
ii [*The major asset of the team*] *is* [*its world-class opening bowlers*].

Here the subject (predicand) is singular, the predicative complement plural: clauses of this kind are commonplace. Since this construction is generally reversible we likewise find plural subject with singular predicative complement: *Its world-class opening bowlers are the major asset of the team.* Compare also *The Morning Star and the Evening Star are both Venus.*

Number mismatches that result in unacceptability are due to semantic incompatibility between the terms:

[9] i $^{\#}$[*The person who complained most*] *was* [*my parents*].
ii $^{\#}$[*The two people who complained most*] *were* [*my parents and my uncle*].

The incompatibility results from identifying a single person with a set of two in [i], and identifying a set of two with a set of three in [ii]. Example [ii] could not be handled in terms of agreement of grammatical number, since both elements are plural, and it would therefore be inappropriate to invoke violation of grammatical agreement in [i], for the nature of the anomaly is the same in both cases.

Ascriptive *be*

With this use of *be* number mismatches most often have a plural subject in construction with a singular predicative, but the opposite pairing is also found:

[10] i a. [*Our neighbours*] *are* [*a nuisance*].
b. [*The people who live out there*] *are* [*a minority cult group*].
c. [*The accidents*] *were* [*the result of a power failure*].
d. [*These results*] *were really* [*something to be proud of*].
ii a. [*His Ph.D. thesis*] *was* [*simply four unrelated articles collected together*].
b. [*This gadget*] *is* [*five different tools in one*].

Overall, the cases of mismatches are too prevalent for them to be treated as exceptions to a grammatical rule of agreement holding generally between predicate and predicand – as involving overrides comparable to those suggested in our discussion of subject–verb agreement. A more satisfactory approach is to provide a semantic account of the restricted range of cases where mismatches result in unacceptability of the kind illustrated in [1ii] (#*My daughter is doctors*; #*My daughters are a doctor*).

19.2 Distributive and non-distributive predicatives in non-quantificational constructions

In this section we leave aside clauses involving explicit quantification in the subject (as in *All my daughters are doctors*) or the predicate (*My daughters are all doctors*): such quantification creates complications that we will take up in §19.3 below. Our account will be concerned exclusively with ascriptive predicative constructions.

Within this domain we distinguish between predicatives which have a **distributive** and those which have a **non-distributive** interpretation.

[11] i	*My daughters are doctors.* (=[1ib])	[distributive]
ii	*Ed's daughters are a pest.*	[non-distributive]

Distributive predicatives combine with plural predicands and the property they express is ascribed to the individual members of the set referred to by the predicand (or to various subsets of that set). In [i], for example, the property of being a doctor is ascribed distributively to each of my individual daughters. In [ii], by contrast, the property of being a pest is ascribed non-distributively to the set of Ed's daughters as a whole.

The distributive interpretation is subject to the following rule:

[12] With semantically plural predicands, pluralised forms of predicatives are ascribed distributively, singular forms non-distributively.

This accounts for the interpretations in [11], where the predicative is pluralised in [i] but singular in [ii]. The latter contrasts with the distributive interpretation obtained by pluralising the predicative: *Ed's daughters are pests.* This is like [11i]: it ascribes the property of being a pest not to the daughters as a combined set but to each of them individually. The formulation of [12] in terms of semantically plural predicands caters for examples like *This group are doctors*, where *this group* is grammatically singular but refers to a plural set of individuals (this group of delegates, perhaps), and the property of being a doctor is ascribed distributively to these individuals.

It is then necessary to distinguish between different types of property, **non-collective**, **neutral**, and **collective**.

Non-collective properties

These properties are ascribable only to individual entities. ***Doctor*** expresses a property of this kind. Example [1ia], *My daughter is a doctor*, thus illustrates the ascription of the property of being a doctor to an individual person. Thus [1iib], #*My daughters are a doctor*, is semantically anomalous because the predicative is not in its pluralised form, and hence the property of being a doctor must be ascribed non-distributively to the set consisting of my daughters as a whole, which is of course incoherent. In [1ib], *My* *daughters are doctors*, the pluralised form indicates that the property of being a doctor is ascribed distributively to the individual daughters.

Neutral properties

These can be ascribed to individual entities but they can also be ascribed collectively to a set. Compare, then:

[13]	i	*Our neighbour is a nuisance.*	
	ii	*Our neighbours are a nuisance.* (=[10ia])	[non-distributive]
	iii	*Our neighbours are nuisances.*	[distributive]

Here, [i] has a singular subject and the predicative ascribes a property to the individual it refers to. Example [ii] has a plural subject and the predicative ascribes the property of being a nuisance to the set it refers to as a whole: they are collectively a nuisance. And in [iii] the subject is again plural and the predicative ascribes the property of being a nuisance to each member of the set it refers to: each of them is individually a nuisance. A sample of other nouns denoting neutral properties is as follows:

[14]	*delight*	*disgrace*	*embarrassment*	*godsend*	*mess*
	obstacle	*pest*	*pigsty*	*problem*	*tip*

Shambles has no plural form, and hence cannot be used distributively: *This room is a shambles*, *These rooms are a shambles*, but not **These rooms are shambles.*

Collective properties

These properties are ascribed to sets, even when used in the plural with a distributive interpretation:

[15]	i	#*This stamp is a superb collection of rare issues.*	
	ii	*Bill's stamps are a superb collection of rare issues.*	[non-distributive]
	iii	*Bill's stamps are superb collections of rare issues.*	[distributive]

Example [i] is excluded because *this stamp* refers to an individual entity which cannot have a collective property ascribed to it. A grammatically singular subject is permitted if it refers to a set: *This is a superb collection of rare issues.* In [ii] the property expressed in the predicative is ascribed to the set of Bill's stamps as a whole. Example [iii] is less likely, but possible with a distributive interpretation which assigns the collective property not to the individual stamps but to subsets of them.

Nouns like ***twin*** can express either a non-collective or a collective property, the latter interpretation being possible only if the noun is plural. Compare:

[16] i *Bill is a twin.*
ii *Bill and Fred are twins.*
iii *Bill, Fred, and Mary are twins.*
iv *Bill and Fred, and Mary and Jane are twins.*

Example [i] ascribes the non-collective property of being a twin (of someone) to the individual Bill. In the salient interpretation of [ii] the collective property of being twins of each other is ascribed non-distributively to the set consisting of Bill and Fred. Since the set concerned must have just two members, [iii] can only have an interpretation where the non-collective property of being a twin of someone is ascribed distributively to Bill, Fred, and Mary. And the most likely interpretation of [iv] has the collective property of being twins of each other ascribed distributively to two subsets of the set referred to by the subject, one consisting of Bill and Fred, the other of Mary and Jane.

19.3 Distributive interpretations in quantified constructions

Distributivity of the kind considered above does not mean that the property expressed in the predicative necessarily applies to every individual in the set referred to by the subject. Consider, for example:

[17] *The office buildings downtown are skyscrapers.* [distributive]

This does not explicitly say (and thus does not have as a truth condition) that every individual office building downtown is a skyscraper (the old courthouse, for example, might be a single-storey edifice). To ensure an interpretation in which every atom either individually (in the case of distributive predicatives) or collectively (in the case of non-distributive ones) possesses the predicative complement property, explicit quantification is required. This is illustrated in the examples in [18], which have distributive interpretations, still in accordance with rule [12]:

[18] i *<u>All</u>/<u>Both</u> the office buildings downtown are skyscrapers.*
ii *The office buildings downtown are <u>all</u>/<u>both</u> skyscrapers.*

We find, however, that rule [12] does not apply in all cases of explicit quantification in that distributive interpretations can be obtained without pluralisation:

[19] i *Ed's daughters are a nuisance.* [non-distributive]
ii *Both Ed's daughters are nuisances / a nuisance.* [distributive]

In [i], only the collective interpretation of *a nuisance* is possible, since the only interpretation which can apply in the absence of pluralisation or quantification is the non-distributive one. With the presence of the quantifier *both* in [ii], however, the versions with *nuisances* and *a nuisance* are equivalent, having distributive interpretations in which each daughter individually is a nuisance. The semantic basis for the effect of the quantifier here is clear. *Both* itself yields a distributive interpretation (see §7.3), so that it is not essential for distributivity to be marked by pluralisation of the predicative, which can therefore maintain its basic singular form.[75] The plural, however, remains the default option, with the singular available only with a restricted range of predicatives. We could not, for example, have a singular in the *both* version of [18]: *#Both the office buildings downtown are a skyscraper.*

20 Proper names, proper nouns, and vocatives

20.1 The distinction between proper names and proper nouns

The central cases of **proper names** are expressions which have been conventionally adopted as the name of a particular entity – or, in the case of plurals like *the Hebrides*, a collection of entities. They include the names of particular persons or animals (*Mary*, *Smith*, *Fido*), places of many kinds (*Melbourne*, *Lake Michigan*, *the United States of*

[75] The quantifiers *each* and *every* are themselves explicitly distributive and as quantifiers in subject NPs enforce singularity on the whole clause, including the predicative complement: *Each/Every office building downtown is a skyscraper*. This can be seen as a fully grammaticalised version of the principle that distributive quantification removes the need for plural forms.

America), institutions (*Harvard University, the Knesset*), historical events (*the Second World War, the Plague*). The category also covers the names of days of the week, months of the year, and recurrent festivals, public holidays, etc. (*Easter, Passover, Ramadan*). In many cases there are different versions of a proper name, typically with one more formal than the other(s): *the United States of America* vs *the United States, the US, the States*, or *Elizabeth* vs *Liz* and *Lizzie*.

In their primary use proper names normally refer to the particular entities that they name: in this use they have the syntactic status of NPs.[76] For the most part, however, they can also be nominals that are parts of larger NPs: such nominals may be attributive modifiers or heads that are accompanied by dependents that are not part of the proper name itself. Compare:

		a.	b.	
[1]	i	a. *She lives in New Zealand.*	b. *Clinton was re-elected.*	[full NP]
	ii	a. *the New Zealand government*	b. *the Clinton administration*	[modifier]
	iii	a. *the New Zealand of my youth*	b. *the new Clinton*	[head]

Proper nouns, by contrast, are word-level units belonging to the category noun. *Clinton* and *Zealand* are proper nouns, but *New Zealand* is not. *America* is a proper noun, but *The United States of America* is not – and nor are *The United States* or *United* and *States* on their own. Proper nouns function as heads of proper names, but not all proper names have proper nouns as their head: the heads of such proper names as *The United States of America, the Leeward Islands, the University of Manchester*, for example, are common nouns. Proper names with common nouns as head often contain a smaller proper name as or within a dependent, but they do not need to: compare *Madison Avenue* and *Central Avenue*, or *Harvard University* and *The Open University*. We noted above that many proper names have alternant versions, and one type of alternation is between a formal name with a common noun as head and a less formal version with the common noun omitted: *The Tate Gallery* vs *The Tate*.

Proper nouns are nouns which are specialised to the function of heading proper names. There may be homonymy between a proper noun and a common noun, often resulting from historical reanalysis in one or other direction. For example, the underlined word in *the Earl of Sandwich* is a proper noun, while that in *a ham sandwich* is a common noun. Similarly proper *Rosemary* (a female name) is homonymous with common *rosemary* (denoting a type of shrub). As this formulation indicates, we take such cases to involve pairs of different words, so that we can still say that proper *Sandwich* and *Rosemary* are specialised to the proper name use. Note by contrast that we don't have homonymy in pairs like *the University of Manchester* and *I haven't yet decided which university to apply to*: there is a single word *university*, functioning as the head of a proper name NP in the first case and of an ordinary NP in the second. The difference, of course, is that while the University of Manchester is a university, Sandwich is not a sandwich, and so on.

20.2 The form of proper names

Most proper names, in their primary use, are NPs. The names of various kinds of artefact – the **titles** of written works, movies, TV programmes, etc. – allow a wider range

[76] Also included under the primary use is the non-referential use of proper names in identification statements: see §8.3 above.

of forms, including main clauses (e.g. declarative *White Men Can't Jump*, interrogative *Who's Afraid of Virginia Woolf?*, imperative *Kiss Me Kate*) and subordinate interrogatives (*How the West was Won*; *How to Marry a Millionaire*). Even when they have the form of NPs, titles are much less constrained than other kinds of proper name and are excluded from the following account.

To a large extent the syntactic structure of proper names conforms to the rules for the structure of ordinary NPs, but there are a number of respects in which they depart from the general pattern. We consider first the question of determiners, and then look at the structure of proper names with composite heads.

20.2.1 Strong and weak proper names

By virtue of its use to refer to a particular entity or collection of entities that bears the name, a proper name is inherently definite. This excludes the inclusion of an indefinite determiner, and makes the marking of definiteness unnecessary. We distinguish, then, between **strong** proper names like *Kim* or *New York*, where there is no determiner, and **weak** proper names like *the Thames* or *the Bronx*, where definiteness is redundantly marked by the definite article *the*. In some names *the* is optional, so that we have both strong and weak versions: e.g. *Gambia* or *the Gambia*.[77]

Weak proper names normally lose the definite article when they don't constitute a full NP – when they are modifying the head of an NP or are themselves modified:

[2] i *a Thames cruise, two United States warships, both Republic of Chad delegates*
 ii *It was [a very different Thames from the one I remembered from my youth].*

These are positions where the grammar allows nominals, not NPs, so the dropping of the article reduces the proper name to nominal form.[78] There are, however, differences among weak proper names as to how readily they enter into these constructions. It is virtually impossible, for example, to drop the article from *the Hague*: **two Hague councillors, *an impressively modernised Hague.*

Plural proper names are always weak. Plural names apply to mountain ranges (*the Alps, the Himalyas, the Urals*); island groups (*the Bahamas, the Hebrides, the Maldives*); occasional other geographical entities (*the Netherlands, the Balkans, the Dardanelles*). Groups of performers may have weak plural names (*the Beatles*) or strong collective singulars (*Abba*).

Among weak singular names with proper nouns as head we find the following types:

[3]	i	*the Argentine, the Ukraine, (the) Sudan, (the) Yemen*	[countries]
	ii	*the Crimea, the Caucasus, the Ruhr*	[geographically defined regions]
	iii	*the Colisseum, the Pantheon, the Parthenon*	[famous buildings]
	iv	*the (River) Thames, the Potomac, the Bosphorous*	[rivers, straits]

[77] Whether proper names are strong or weak is, from a cross-linguistic perspective, a rather arbitrary matter. Personal names like *Mary* are weak in modern Greek, but strong in English. Similarly, river names are invariably weak in English, but in Bulgarian some are strong and some weak. Nevertheless, as we shall see, there are some generalisations that can be made about the strong/weak distinction **within** English.

[78] There are some cases where the article is exceptionally retained in attributive modifier function, as in *The Gap State High School.* This refers to a state high school in a suburb of Brisbane called *The Gap*; such schools in suburbs with strong names have no article (cf. *Kenmore State High School*), so we can infer that *the* forms a constituent with *Gap* rather than being an immediate constituent of the matrix NP. Note, however, that the matrix NP in this case is itself a proper name: in ordinary NPs the article drops in the usual way: *Gap residents are protesting against this decision.*

v *the Adriatic, the Atlantic, the Mediterranean* [seas, oceans]
vi *the Gobi, the Sahara, the Negev* [deserts]
vii *the Eiger, the Jungfrau, the Matterhorn* [Swiss Alpine peaks]
viii *the Knesset, the Kremlin, the Pentagon* [political/military authorities]
ix *the Bodleian, the Guggenheim, the Tate* [libraries, galleries, etc.]
x *the Bible, the Koran, the Talmud* [religious tracts]
xi *The Economist, The Guardian, The Times* [newspapers, periodicals]

There are in addition isolated weak names in other categories: e.g. *the Hague* as a city name, *the Bronx* naming a district in Manhattan. The names in [i] are relatively exceptional: countries usually have strong names (and note *Argentina* as a strong version of *the Argentine*). Names of the categories illustrated in [ii–vi] are normally weak, but region names formed from Latinate proper nouns in ·*ia* are strong: *Scandinavia, Siberia, Transylvania.* Names of individual mountains (as opposed to ranges) are generally strong, but those in the Swiss Alps may have weak names, as in [vii]. The categories in [viii–x] are normally weak, as are the names of newspapers (with capitalised *The*). Periodicals often have strong names as their official titles: *New Scientist, Journal of Linguistics*; in most contexts, however, a weak alternant is used: *I doubt whether the New Scientist would publish a paper like that.*

20.2.2 Proper names with simple and composite heads

The head of a proper name is the name less the article in the case of weak names. This may be **simple**, i.e. a single noun (including compounds of various kinds: *Fortescue-Smythe, Alsace-Lorraine*), or **composite**, i.e. a nominal with internal syntactic structure.

Simple heads

In strong proper names, simple heads are normally proper nouns: *Kim, Jones, Boston, Italy*, etc. Within a family, however, there are constraints on the use of given names, so that kin terms are commonly used instead when a child is referring to an adult, or when one is talking to a child: *Mum/Mom/Mummy/Mother wants you*; *Have you seen Grandma/Granny/Nana?* In such cases the terms have the status of proper names, though they belong syntactically to the category of common nouns. One or two other common nouns can similarly be used with the status of proper names in restricted contexts: *Have you seen Nurse?*

Composite heads

The main kinds of composite head structures are illustrated in [4]:

[4] i *Kim Jones, Emma Ann Barton, J. C. Smith, John C. Smith, J. Edgar Hoover*
ii *Queen Mary, Pope John Paul, Major White, Nurse Fox, Dr Brown, Mr Black*
iii *British Columbia, Upper Saxony, North America, the Northern Territory, New York, Long Island, Good Friday, the Iron Duke, the National Gallery*
iv *Oxford Road, Harvard University, the Ford Foundation, Christ's College*
v *Lake Michigan, Mount/Mt Everest, the River Thames, Ward 17*
vi *The Isle of Skye, the Bay of Biscay, the University of Sydney, John of Gaunt, Massachusetts Institute of Technology, the Institute of Modern Art*
vii *Henry Cotton Senior, Peter the Great, (King) George the Fifth / V*

Combinations of given and family names

Personal names typically consist of a combination of one or more given (first, Christian) names and a family name (surname), as in [4i]; given names may be reduced to an initial letter. This construction is unique to personal names, and there is no convincing evidence for treating one element as head.

Appellations

The underlined elements in [4ii] are appellations, pre-head modifiers of personal names, expressing the status of the individual concerned.[79] The kinds of status they indicate include: royal/aristocratic office or rank (*King, Queen, Prince, Earl, Lord, Emperor, Count,* etc.); clerical office (*Pope, Archbishop, Sister*); military and police rank (*Private, Captain, Squadron Leader, Admiral, Inspector*); political office (*President, Senator, Governor, Councillor*); judicial office (*Judge*); academic status (*Dr, Professor*). The default set of appellations – *Mr, Ms, Mrs, Miss, Master* – indicate sex and in some cases also marital or maturity status. It is arguable whether appellations form part of the proper name or are an embellishment of it; the case for including them within the name would seem to be stronger in cases like *King George* or *Pope John* (where a particular personal name is chosen for use with the appellation on accession to the office) than with others. Some combinations of appellations are permitted: *<u>Professor</u> <u>Sir</u> Ernest Rutherford, <u>Her Majesty Queen</u> Elizabeth.*

Other pre-head dependents

Pre-head dependents may, as in ordinary NPs, have the form of adjectives ([4iii]) or nouns – generally nouns that are themselves proper names ([iv]), or **descriptors** indicating what kind of entity the name applies to ([v]). The descriptors are generally omissible: compare *Everest, the Thames,* and so on. The others tend to be an essential part of the name, but in a few cases are omissible too, as when *the States* is used as an informal variant of *the United States.* As elsewhere, the construction is recursive: compare [*New* [*South Wales*]] or [[*Cambridge University*] *Press*].

Genitives, such as *Christ's* in [4iv], we take to be modifiers not determiners. They occur readily in names that are themselves functioning as modifier within a larger construction, as in *a <u>Christ's College</u> don*: this is a construction which accepts nominals but not full NPs in modifier position. Such genitives cannot normally contain a determiner – compare *King's College, Women's College,* etc.

Post-head dependents

These most often have the form of PPs, generally headed by *of,* as in [4vi]. The oblique NP in this construction is commonly another proper name. A different kind of post-head dependent is seen in [4vii]: *Junior* is an adjective while the other two have the form of fused modifier-head NPs. Such post-head dependents as *the Great* occur only in proper names.

20.3 **Embellishments**

Proper names may occur, with the status of nominals, as head of a larger NP that refers to the bearer of the name:

[79] The term 'title' is more commonly used than 'appellation', but we have used 'title' for the proper name of a literary work or comparable artefact, and from a grammatical point of view appellations and titles are quite different.

[5] i *architect Norman Foster, mother of two Eileen Jones, special agent Cully, well-born Hampshire gentleman John Grant, nuclear physicist Lord Rutherford*
ii *beautiful Italy, dear old Mr Smithers, poor Henry, sunny Italy, historic Virginia; the inimitable Oscar Wilde, the distraught Empress Alexandra*
iii *Who's [this Penelope who's been sending you emails]?, [That Senator Fox] should be locked up, [Your Mr Jenkins] has been arrested again!*

The underlined elements are semantically non-restrictive dependents that we refer to as **embellishments** of the proper name. The examples in [5] illustrate three main kinds of embellishment: nominal and adjectival attributive modifiers, and determiners.

Nominal modifiers generally occur with personal names and serve to categorise the person concerned. The construction is to be distinguished from the one where the proper name is an appositive: in *architect Norman Foster* the proper name is head and *architect* an omissible embellishment, whereas in *the architect Norman Foster* the head is *architect* and the proper name is an omissible appositive dependent.[80] We noted above that it is arguable whether appellations should be regarded as part of the proper name or as embellishments; certainly expressions like *Secretary of State Colin Powell* or *Prime Minister Tony Blair*, used more extensively in AmE than in BrE, bear a significant resemblance to those in [5i].

Adjectives occur as embellishments of proper names in two constructions: in bare NPs or in ones determined (redundantly) by *the*, as in the last two examples of [5ii]. The bare NP construction is restricted to a fairly small set of adjectives with emotive colouring: *beautiful* and *ugly*, *young* and *old*, and so on. The determined NP construction allows a somewhat larger range including *beautiful, dazzling, incomparable, inimitable, irrepressible, unfortunate, wretched*, and adjectives denoting emotional states such as *distraught, furious, jealous*. Such adjectives can in general modify the head of weak proper names: *the ill-fated Titanic.*

The main determiners that are used as embellishments are the demonstratives and genitive personal pronouns, as in [5iii]. The genitive indicates a close relationship: *your Mr Jenkins* suggests that you are a close acquaintance of Mr Jenkins. Often it is a parental relationship: *[My Jennifer] has won the school prize again.*

20.4 Secondary uses of proper names

In their primary use proper names are inherently definite, and for this reason their heads do not select from the determiner system in the same way as ordinary heads in NP structure. Proper names also have various secondary uses where this inherent definiteness is lost, and where determiners are thus selected in the ordinary way.[81] Five such uses may be distinguished:

[80] The presence or absence of *the* does not serve to distinguish apposition from non-apposition in the case of such titles as *Emperor, Empress, Archduke*, which occur in both strong and weak proper names: *Emperor Haile Selassie* or *the Emperor Haile Selassie. The emperor Haile Selassie*, however, is possible though unlikely as an appositive construction.

[81] Note, then, that in its primary use a noun such as *Kim* is non-count: it is only in certain of the secondary uses that it can combine with numerals and hence qualify as a count noun.

(a) To denote a set of bearers of the name

[6] i [*The Mary that you met yesterday*] *is my fiancée.*
ii *I've never met* [*an Ophelia*] *before.*
iii *There are* [*two Showcase Cinemas*] *in Manchester.*
iv *Shall we invite* [*the Smiths*]*?*
v *Was it* [THE *Bill Gates*] *he was talking about?*

This use exploits the fact that names are quite typically not uniquely assigned. Although there is only one country named *Zaire*, there are thousands of people named *Mary*. The name *Mary* can then denote the set of people bearing this name, rather than some specific individual, as in the primary use. As a set-denoting noun, the name *Mary* then takes a full range of dependents, including determiners and restrictive modifiers, comparable to those permitted by common nouns. In [i], for example, I select from amongst the set of people named *Mary* the particular one that you met yesterday, and in [ii] I say that I have never met a person named *Ophelia*. Example [iii] illustrates the use of a proper name with a common noun head: it says there are two cinemas with that name in Manchester. A more specific use is seen in [iv]: *the Smiths* refers to an identifiable group of people with the surname *Smith*; here it will be a married couple or a family, but in other contexts it might be a dynasty. In [v] the stressed article indicates reference to the famous bearer of the name, as opposed to other people with that name.

(b) To denote a set of entities having relevant properties of the bearer of the name

[7] i *We need* [*another Roosevelt*].
ii *She's* [*no Florence Nightingale*].

In [i] we understand "another person with the properties associated with Roosevelt", while [ii] says that she doesn't have the properties needed to qualify as another Florence Nightingale.

(c) To denote a set of manifestations of the bearer of the name

[8] i *This is not* [*the Paris I used to know*].
ii *This is* [*a United States I prefer to forget*].
iii [*The young Isaac Newton*] *showed no signs of genius.*

In [i] I distinguish between a previous manifestation of Paris (which may have been a pleasant one), and a current manifestation. Example [ii] shows that, in this use, a normally plural name can head a singular NP – when we are concerned with a single manifestation. In [iii] the adjective *young* is used restrictively: what is referred to is the manifestation of Isaac Newton in his youth, rather than as an established scientist; such a use should be contrasted with the non-restrictive embellishment use of the adjective in *Young Isaac Newton went off to Cambridge.*

(d) To denote a set of products created by the bearer of the name

[9] i *The gallery has acquired* [*a new Rembrandt*].
ii *Let's listen to* [*some Beethoven*] *tonight.*

In [i] the gallery has acquired a new picture by Rembrandt, and in [ii] I want us to listen to some music by Beethoven. As this latter example demonstrates, this use allows non-count as well as count interpretations.

This use covers various commercial products: in *She was driving* [*a Ford*], for example, we understand "a car manufactured by Ford (i.e. the Ford Motor Company)". This case is to be distinguished, however, from *She was driving* [*a Cortina*], where *Cortina* is a tradename but not a proper name. It is not a name assigned to an **individual**: rather, it is a term coined to denote a **kind**. The same applies to a great number of commercial names. In *I bought* [*some Maltesers*], for example, ***Malteser*** is simply a common noun denoting a kind of chocolate confection.

(e) To denote a set of copies/editions, etc., of the entity bearing the name

[10] i *Can I borrow* [*your Guardian*] *for a few minutes?*
ii *The film was reviewed in* [*yesterday's Herald-Tribune*].

This use is largely restricted to proper names belonging to the category of titles. These examples involve newspaper titles: we understand "your copy of 'The Guardian' ", "yesterday's edition of the '(New York) Herald-Tribune' ". The particular interpretation will depend on the kind of work bearing the title: compare *last night's 'Carmen'* ("performance"), *Peter Hall's 'Hamlet'* ("production").

20.5 NPs in vocative function

NPs serving as terms of address are said to be in **vocative** function:[82]

[11] *What do you think, Senator Fox?*

The main kinds of NP that can realise the vocative function are illustrated in:

[12] i	*Mary, Smith, Mary Smith, Mr/Dr Smith, Sir John*	[personal names]
ii	*Mum/Mom/Mummy; son, daughter, aunt, uncle, cousin*	[kin terms]
iii	*Your Majesty, Your* (*Royal*) *Highness, Ma'am, sir, madam*	[status terms]
iv	*driver, officer* ("member of police force"), *waiter, vicar*	[occupational terms]
v	*buddy* (AmE), *mate* (BrE/AusE), *gentlemen, ladies, guys*	[general terms]
vi	*darling, dear, honey, love, sweetheart, gorgeous, handsome*	[terms of endearment]
vii	*fatty, idiot, imbecile, nitwit, slowcoach, swine*	[derogatory terms]
viii	*you, you-all* (Southern US), *you with the glasses*	[2nd person pronoun]
ix	*somebody, anybody, everybody, someone*	[compound determinatives]

Personal nouns are used alone or with certain appellations. The use of a surname alone, once quite prevalent in Victorian Britain, is now restricted to a very few contexts, such as certain British public schools and the armed forces (addressing those of low rank). Forms like *Mary Smith* are also contextually restricted, but may be used in the classroom, especially if there is more than one Mary in the class. The kin terms include those that can be used with the status of proper names, but also others, such as *son* or *cousin*, that are hardly possible as proper names. (As a vocative, *son* can be applied to any young male, and in this sense it belongs with the general terms in [v].) The status terms include a good number of appellations. There are also special vocative terms for aristocrats and others of especially high status: *Your Majesty, Ma'am* (for the Queen), *My Lord, Your*

[82] The term 'vocative' is standardly used for both a function, as here, and, where relevant, a case (contrasting with nominative, accusative, etc.) used in vocative function. English of course has no vocative case, and hence 'vocative' is used in this grammar exclusively for the function.

Honour (for a judge), and so on. Some appellations and other terms have *Mr* or *Madam* added for the vocative: *Mr President, Madam Chair/%Chairman. Sir* and *Madam* are the polite terms for strangers (or in certain contexts for those of higher social rank); *Mr* and *Mrs* would generally be considered non-standard or impolite as vocatives, though *Miss* is used for girls or young women (and schoolteachers). The occupational terms in [iv] are not used as appellations, and as vocatives are normally used only when the person addressed is engaged in the relevant occupation.

General human nouns are often accompanied by such dependents as *my, old, young*: *my boy/girl, old chap* (BrE), *young man.* Genitive *my* is also often used with the terms of endearment: *my darling*; some of these terms are used as attributes to personal names or general nouns, as in *darling Anna, my dear friends.* Vocative *gorgeous, handsome*, and the like are syntactically NPs with fusion of modifier and head of a type permitted only in vocative function. Derogatory terms are commonly accompanied by determinative *you*, as in *you stupid bastard*, etc. The pronoun *you* (or *you-all*) in [12viii], by contrast, is head of the vocative NP. Among the compound determinatives ([ix]) the *some·* and *any·* forms are used when no specific person is addressed: *Fetch me a chair, somebody!* One further vocative type is the fused relative in, say, *Come out, whoever you are!*, characteristically used when I can't see you or otherwise don't know who you are.

Vocatives can be used to call someone (*Kim, dinner's ready!*), to attract their attention, to single out one person among a group as the addressee, and so on. It will be clear from the above survey, however, that vocative terms generally convey a considerable amount about the speaker's social relations or emotive attitude towards the addressee, and their primary or sole purpose is often to give expression to this kind of meaning, as in *Yes, sir!* or *I agree, my dear, that it's quite a bargain.*

A vocative can stand alone without any sense of ellipsis, and for this reason cannot be regarded as a dependent of the verb. It is best regarded as a kind of interpolation – one that can appear, like certain adjuncts, in front, central, or end position (cf. Ch. 8, §20).

6

Adjectives and adverbs

Geoffrey K. Pullum
Rodney Huddleston

1 **Preliminaries**

The last three chapters have dealt with the two most fundamental lexical categories (parts of speech) in English, verbs and nouns. Nouns are the commonest words in text, the most abundant in the dictionary, and the most productively added to the language by word-formation processes and borrowing. Verbs are fundamental in the sense that they function as head in clause structure, and they are second only to nouns in text and dictionary frequency. All canonical clauses contain at least a noun and a verb, and the simplest ones contain just one of each: *Rain fell*; *People change*; *Kim disappeared.*

But there are not enough nouns and verbs to express every shade of meaning needed. There is a noun to denote water, but not different nouns for water at various temperatures. There is a verb to denote falling (indeed, several: *fall, drop, sink, plummet, . . .*), but not enough different verbs to denote falling at all the different speeds we might want to distinguish, or in all the different ways things might fall.

In English the necessary finer gradations of meaning are expressed by means of words (and phrases) that alter, clarify, or adjust the meaning contributions of nouns and verbs. The words used to modify nouns are typically **adjectives**, and the words that similarly modify verbs are **adverbs**:

[1]	i a. [*<u>Heavy</u> rain*] *fell.*	b. [*<u>Young</u> people*] *change.*	[adjective]
	ii a. *Rain* [*fell <u>heavily</u>*].	b. *People* [*change <u>slowly</u>*].	[adverb]

Many of the adverbs that modify verbs can also modify adjectives and other adverbs. The primary syntactic distinction, therefore, is between adjectives, which modify only nouns, and adverbs, which modify all the other categories – verbs, adjectives, prepositions, determinatives, and other adverbs. Compare, for example:

[2]	i	*They made a lot of* [*unnecessary <u>changes</u>*].	[noun]
	ii	*They had* [*<u>worried</u> unnecessarily*].	[verb]
	iii	*Their response was* [*unnecessarily <u>long</u>*].	[adjective]
	iv	*They had treated him* [*unnecessarily <u>harshly</u>*].	[adverb]

Here the noun *changes* is modified by the adjective *unnecessary*, while the verb *worried*, the adjective *long*, and the adverb *harshly* are all modified by the adverb *unnecessarily.*

In addition to modifying nouns, adjectives may have a predicative function: *The rain was <u>heavy</u>*; *They are <u>young</u>.* In these examples the adjectives are syntactically complements of the verb *be*, but semantically they constitute the main part of the predicate. As a lexeme, *be* makes little if any contribution to the meaning, but serves the syntactic function of carrying the tense inflection (and showing agreement with the subject). The combination of *be* + adjective is then comparable to a verb with its own lexical content. The similarity is seen in such pairs as:

[3]	i	a. *She* [*was awake*].	b. *She* [*awoke*].
	ii	a. *She* [*was dead*].	b. *She* [*died*].

Adjectives almost always denote states, with verbs used for dynamic situations, as in these examples – though there are also many verbs that denote states, such as *know* and *resemble*. Whereas many verbs take objects, there are only one or two adjectives that are transitive (e.g. *worth* and *like*), so NPs within the predicate are normally related to an adjective by means of a preposition: compare verbal *She likes animals* with adjectival *She is fond of animals*.

For verb and noun we have recognised two levels of syntactic unit based on them: for the verb these are the verb phrase and the clause, and for the noun they are the nominal and the noun phrase. For adjective and adverb we need only a single higher-level unit: the adjective phrase and the adverb phrase. The structure of expressions headed by adjectives and adverbs is less complex than that of those headed by verbs and nouns – in particular, they have no analogue of the subject and determiner functions which motivate the distinction between the two higher-level units for verbs and nouns.

Adjectives and adverbs are numerous in English; there are many thousands of each, and they are very frequent in use: almost every sentence of more than but trivial length contains adjectives and/or adverbs.

The adjective and the adverb are more alike than any other pair of part-of-speech categories, and it is for this reason that we deal with them together in this chapter. There are a great many adverbs that are morphologically derived from adjectives by suffixation of *·ly*. And the possible ways of expanding adverbs into AdvPs are, broadly speaking, a subset of those available for expanding adjectives into AdjPs. We have noted that adjectives can have a predicative as well as a modifying function, and the reduced possibility for expansion of the adverb can be attributed at least in part to the fact that adverbs have no predicative function.

2 Criterial properties of adjectives

At the general level, adjectives may be defined as a syntactically distinct class of words whose most characteristic function is to modify nouns. They typically denote properties – most centrally in the domains of size, shape, colour, worth, and age. If a language has adjectives,[1] it will always have one that means "good" (an adjective denoting the property of having positive worth or value), and nearly always another meaning "bad"; virtually always it will have a size adjective meaning "large", and probably also one meaning "small", and some others; it is extremely likely to have an adjective with the meaning "old", may well have another meaning "young" or "new", and it is very likely to have some colour adjectives meaning "black", "white", "red", "green", etc. The core semantic

[1] There are some languages that have either no adjective lexemes at all or only a tiny handful.

function of adjectives seems to be to provide terms for individual properties of the kinds just listed, and usually other properties as well: physical properties like hardness and heaviness, human tendencies like kindness and cruelty, properties like speed of movement, and so on.

As a general definition, the above provides a basis for deciding which lexical category in a language (if any) we should call 'adjective', but it does not enable us to decide whether some particular lexeme in English is an adjective or not. For this purpose we need to consider the distinctive syntactic properties.

Central members of the adjective category have the cluster of syntactic properties given in [1], where the adjectives in the examples are all underlined:

[1]	i	FUNCTION	They can appear in three main functions: attributive (*happy people*), predicative (*They are happy*), postpositive (*someone happy*).
	ii	GRADABILITY	They are gradable, and hence accept such degree modifiers as *very, too, enough*, and have inflectional or analytic comparatives and superlatives (*happier, happiest, more useful, most useful*).
	iii	DEPENDENTS	They characteristically take adverbs as modifiers (*remarkably happy, surprisingly good*).

No one of these properties is unique to adjectives, and many adjectives do not have the full set of properties. However, words that do have this combination of properties are clearly distinct from words of other categories. And of course adjectives also have negative properties that distinguish them from other categories: for example, they don't inflect for number or tense, they cannot be modified by (other) adjectives and, with a very small number of exceptions, they do not take NPs as complement.

We will take in turn the three groups of properties given in [1], and then examine the criteria for distinguishing adjectives from nouns and determinatives.

2.1 Function

The three main functions: attributive, predicative complement, and postpositive

[2]	i	*my new job*	*all other possibilities*	*good work*	[attributive]
	ii	*This is new.*	*They seem suitable.*	*We found it easy.*	[predicative comp]
	iii	*something important*	*a man full of his own importance*		[postpositive]

Attributive adjectives are those functioning as pre-head internal dependent in the structure of the NP. Internal dependents are those which are part of a nominal, and hence in NPs containing a determiner they are located between the determiner and the head noun, as in the first two examples in [2i]. Attributive AdjPs are almost always modifiers rather than complements (cf. Ch. 5, §14).

Predicative complements are dependents in clause structure, licensed by particular verbs, such as intransitive *be* and *seem* or transitive *find* in [2ii].

Postpositive adjectives function as post-head internal modifier in NP structure. They commonly occur after the compound determinatives *something, anyone, nobody*, etc., but under restricted conditions they occur in NPs with nouns as head. Postpositive adjectives are much less frequent than attributive and predicative ones: adjectives are admissible in this position only under severe syntactic constraints.

Strictly speaking it is AdjPs that occur in these functions, but we can talk of attributive, predicative, and postpositive uses of an adjective with the understanding that the adjective is head of an AdjP in the function in question. The AdjP will consist of the head adjective alone or accompanied by its dependents.

The majority of adjectives can occur in all of these three main functions, as illustrated for *happy* in [1i]. Nevertheless there are a significant number of adjectives which, either absolutely or with a certain meaning, are restricted to attributive function (e.g. *mere, former, main*) or excluded from it (e.g. *alone, asleep, glad* "happy/pleased"). Adjectives that can function predicatively can also occur in postpositive function (subject to the syntactic constraints alluded to above), but there are a handful of adjectives that qualify as such solely by the ability to occur in postpositive function: *the president elect, gifts galore*.

Further adjectival functions

[3]	i	*such a nuisance* *so serious a problem*	[predeterminer]
	ii	*the rich* *the bigger of the two* *the most useful of them*	[fused modifier-head]
	iii	*He died young.* *They served the coffee blindfolded.*	[predicative adjunct]
	iv	*Furious, he stormed out of the room.*	

Predeterminer AdjPs occur as external modifier in NP structure, preceding the definite article *a*. This construction is subject to highly restrictive structural conditions described in §3.3. All adjectives that can head a predeterminer AdjP can also be used attributively – cf. *such tools, a serious problem.*

The **fused modifier-head** AdjPs in [3ii] combine the functions of internal modifier and head in NP structure; this construction is described in Ch. 5, §9.3. An adjectives that can function in this construction can also be used attributively.

Finally, the AdjPs in [3iii–iv] function as **predicative adjunct**. Those in [3iii] are integrated into clause structure and hence modifiers, while that in [iv] is detached and hence a supplement. All adjectives that can function as predicative adjunct can also function as predicative complement.

Functional potential as the feature distinguishing adjectives from adverbs

It is function that provides the primary basis for the distinction between adjectives and adverbs. Consider such adjective–adverb pairs as those in:

[4]		ADJECTIVE	ADVERB
	i	a. *a rapid improvement*	b. *It rapidly improved.*
	ii	a. *a surprising depth*	b. *surprisingly deep/deeply*
	iii	a. *Progress was rapid.*	b. *We progressed rapidly.*

In [i–ii] the underlined word is in modifier function, and the adjective member of the pair occurs when the modifier is modifying a noun (*improvement* in [ia], *depth* in [iia]), and the adverb occurs when it is modifying a verb (*improved* in [ib]) or else an adjective or another adverb (*deep* and *deeply* respectively in [iib]). While *rapid* in [ia] is attributive, in [iiia] it is predicative complement, and adverbs cannot function as predicatives: in

[iiib] *rapidly* is modifying the verb, just as in [ib], differing only in its position relative to the head.

For the most part, the forms that occur in attributive and predicative function are distinct from those modifying verbs, adjectives, or adverbs: in a great number of cases, as in [4], the adverb is morphologically derived from the adjective by suffixation of ·*ly*. Where there is overlap, as with such lexemes as ***fast***, ***hard***, ***early***, or such inflected forms as *better* or *worse*, we treat the item concerned as belonging to both categories. Whether any given instance is an adjective or adverb can be determined indirectly by seeing which member of pairs like *rapid/rapidly* or *surprising/surprisingly* could replace it, or directly, on the basis of the function:

[5] ADJECTIVE — ADVERB

i a. *an early departure* — b. *They departed early.*

ii a. *Kim's performance was better.* — b. *Kim performed better.*

Predicative complements of *become*, *make*, *seem*

Predicative adjectives most often occur as complement to the verb *be*, but *be* allows such a wide range of complements that its value as a diagnostic is quite limited. Much more useful from this point of view are the verbs *become* and *make*, and to a lesser extent *seem*, *appear*, *feel*, *look*, *sound*, which take a more restricted range of complements. In particular, they wholly or largely exclude PP complements. Compare [6], where the complements are adjectives, with [7], where they are PPs:

[6] i a. *The car is rusty.* — b. *The car became rusty.*

ii a. *They are impatient.* — b. *This made them impatient.*

iii a. *They are all content.* — b. *They all seem content.*

[7] i a. *The car is in the garage.* — b. **The car became in/into the garage.*

ii a. *They are behind schedule.* — b. **This made them behind schedule.*

iii a. *They are all outside.* — b. **They all seem outside.*

We are of course concerned here with *make* as a complex-transitive verb ("cause to be"): other uses of *make* allow PPs, but not as predicative complement.

Seem, *appear*, etc., allow predicative PPs with idiomatic meanings, such as *in a bad temper*, *in good working order*, *in good shape*, *out of control*, *under the weather.* But even these are normally excluded by *become* and *make*: compare *He seems in a bad temper*; **He became in a bad temper*; **This made him in a bad temper.*

Predicative adjuncts in front position: the predicand requirement

Predicatives require an overt or understood predicand. In *Kim seemed sad*, the predicand is the subject *Kim*; in *I consider his behaviour outrageous*, it is the object *his behaviour*; and in *Be careful*, it is the understood 2nd person subject.

This requirement provides the basis for distinguishing between adjectives and prepositions functioning as head of a phrase in front position in the clause. Compare:

[8] i *Upset, the children had daubed paint on the walls.* [AdjP]

ii *Upstairs, the children had daubed paint on the walls.* [PP]

In [i] *upset* is in predicative function, with the subject *the children* as predicand: the sentence entails that the children had been upset. In [ii] *upstairs* is an adjunct of location and has no predicand: its role is to indicate where the event took place, not to give the location of the children. Of course, if the event took place upstairs it is a reasonable inference that the children were upstairs, but this is incidental, and not in fact an entailment. One could imagine a scenario, for example, where the children were standing on ladders outside the house and had a paintbrush attached to a long pole which they put through the window. The point can, however, be made more simply by contrasting such a pair as:

[9] i **Upset, there was nothing going on.*
ii *Upstairs, there was nothing going on.*

Upset is unacceptable here because it has no predicand, whereas the location adjunct *upstairs*, having no such requirement, is fine. The same distinction is found with the adjective *alone* and the preposition *ashore*: *Ashore/*Alone, there was much drunkenness.*

This is not to say that PPs in front position cannot be predicative. Idiomatic PPs like those mentioned above as admissible complements to *seem* – i.e. *in a bad temper, under the weather*, etc. – function predicatively, and in front position require a predicand: *In a bad temper, Max seemed intent on ruining everybody's fun*, but not **In a bad temper, there was nothing to do.* But *in a bad temper* is a phrase with *in* as its head, and phrases headed by *in* can in general freely occur non-predicatively: *In winter there isn't much to do.* The predicand requirement thus provides a test that applies to head words:

[10] Adjectives cannot head clause-initial phrases unless they are related to a predicand, whereas prepositions can.

2.2 Grading

Gradable and non-gradable adjectives

The prototypical adjective is **gradable**: it denotes a property that can be possessed in varying degrees. The degree can be questioned or indicated by means of a degree adverb: *[How good] is it?*; *She seems [very young]*; *Things are getting [rather serious]*.

There are, however, a great many adjectives that are non-gradable. The following small sample will give an idea of how extensive the class of non-gradable adjectives is:

[11]						
	alphabetical	*ancillary*	*chief*	*equine*	*federal*	*glandular*
	latter	*left*	*marine*	*medical*	*obtainable*	*orthogonal*
	phonological	*pubic*	*residual*	*syllabic*	*tenth*	*utter*

It should be emphasised, however, that the distinction between gradable and non-gradable – like that between count and non-count in nouns – applies to uses or senses of adjectives rather than to adjectives as lexemes. Many items can be used with either a gradable or a non-gradable sense (often with the latter representing the primary meaning of the adjective). Compare:

[12]	NON-GRADABLE SENSE	GRADABLE SENSE
i	a. *the public highway*	b. *a very public quarrel*
ii	a. *Christian martyrs*	b. *not very Christian behaviour*
iii	a. *a British passport*	b. *He sounds very British.*
iv	a. *The door was open.*	b. *You haven't been very open with us.*

On so-called 'absolute' adjectives

Adjectives such as the following are traditionally classified as 'absolutes':

[13]						
	absolute	*complete*	*correct*	*equal*	*essential*	*eternal*
	ideal	*impossible*	*perfect*	*supreme*	*total*	*unique*

There has been a prescriptive tradition of saying that such adjectives are non-gradable, and hence should not be used in comparative constructions or with degree modifiers such as *very*, *somewhat*, etc. *Unique* is especially picked on: students are vilified for writing *highly unique* or *one of the more unique features* or *the most unique person*. The meaning of *unique*, it is claimed, guarantees that it is absolutely non-gradable: a thing is unique if and only if it is the sole thing that has the property under consideration. Hence, the reasoning goes, I cannot speak of a piece of jewellery as 'very unique': if its uniqueness is not absolute then it is not unique at all. Likewise, some hold, an object cannot be more unique than another, since an absolute degree of uniqueness is the only degree of uniqueness there is.

Only the most conservative of manuals still present this rule without qualification. Others recognise that it conflicts with established usage, as illustrated in such examples as:

[14] i *His technical ignorance had proved* [*even more complete than he had thought*].
ii *A* [*more perfect*] *rake has seldom existed.*
iii *The* [*most essential*] *characteristic of mind is memory.*

As for *unique*, we find *more unique* meaning "more nearly unique", but the adjective has also acquired the sense "exceptional, unusual", which quite readily accepts degree modification: *this rather unique situation*, *the most unique person I've ever met*, and so on.

Gradability itself is not an all-or-nothing matter. Even conservative manuals accept that adjectives such as *complete*, *perfect*, *total*, *unique* admit the degree adverbs *almost* and *nearly*, but these are incompatible with most of the adjectives in [11]. And there are differences among the adjectives in [13]: *essential* accepts interrogative *how* more readily than most of the others, *unique* (in the "exceptional" sense) accepts *rather* more readily than most of the others, and so on. But these are matters of semantic compatibility, not of grammaticality.

Gradability not restricted to adjectives

The gradable vs non-gradable contrast applies with adverbs in the same way as with adjectives: *soon* and *quickly* are gradable, *alphabetically* and *phonologically* are not. It is function, not grading, that distinguishes adverbs from adjectives.

More important for present purposes is that nouns and verbs can be gradable (though the proportion of gradable words in these categories is much smaller). The noun *success*, for example, is gradable: one can have varying degrees of success. Similarly with *problem*: something can be a problem in varying degrees. The same applies to such verbs as *love*, *like*, *enjoy*: these are just as gradable as the adjectives *fond*, *likeable*, *enjoyable*.

What distinguishes adjectives and adverbs from nouns and verbs, therefore, is not that the former may take degree dependents while the latter may not. It is a matter of the syntactic constructions used to express grading.

Modification by the degree adverbs *very* and *too*

The degree adverbs *very* and *too* modify adjectives and adverbs, but not nouns and verbs:

		a.	b.	
[15]	i	a. *She was* [*very helpful*].	b. *His delivery was* [*too hurried*].	[Adj]
	ii	a. *She acted* [*very helpfully*].	b. *He spoke* [*too hurriedly*].	[Adv]
	iii	a. **It wasn't of* [*very help*].	b. **He is in a* [*too hurry*].	[N]
	iv	a. **You haven't* [*very helped*] *us.*	b. **He had* [*too hurried*].	[V]

The adverb *very* ("to a high degree") is to be distinguished from the adjective *very* ("exact, true"). The latter does not express degree and can of course modify nouns, as in *That's the very thing we're looking for* or *The child was the very picture of innocence.* Similarly the degree adverb *too* ("excessively") is to be distinguished from the focusing adverb *too* ("in addition"), which can occur in post-head position in phrases of any of the major categories – cf. [*Kim too*] *was present*; *They play the piano and* [*sing too*].

With nouns and verbs the closest counterparts to the constructions in [15i–ii] contain the determinative *much*: (*very*) *much* and *too much*. *Much* is a polarity-sensitive item and hence distributionally more restricted than *very* (see Ch. 9, §4.1.2): it is for this reason we are using negatives for the [a] examples. Compare, then:

[16]			
i	a. *You haven't* [*helped us* (*very*) *much*].	b. *He* [*worries too much*].	[V]
ii	a. *It wasn't* [(*very*) *much help*].	b. *It was* [*too much trouble*].	[N]
iii	a. *It wasn't* [(*very*) *much of a success*].	b. *He's in* [*too much of a hurry*].	[N]

With verbs, *much* functions as head of a degree modifier in the VP. With nouns there are two constructions to consider. In [ii], *much*, together with its dependents, functions as determiner with the noun as head of the NP; *much* here is restricted to occurrence with non-count singular nouns. In construction [iii], *much* is fused determiner-head with an *of* phrase complement; the noun in that PP must be a count singular determined by *a*.

Under restricted conditions, adjectives and adverbs can also take *much* as degree modifier, but for present purposes the major point is that they are distinguished from nouns and verbs by their ability to take *very* and *too* in central constructions like [15i–ii].

In general, PPs don't take *very* and *too* as degree modifiers. Some of the idiomatic PPs mentioned above as admissible complements of *seem*, etc., do allow them, but with *much* as an alternative construction:

[17]		
i	a. **It was* [*very before lunch*].	b. **We placed it* [*too above the floor*].
ii	a. *He's* [*very* (*much*) *in the know*].	b. *He was* [*too* (*much*) *out of sorts to join in*].

Inflectional and analytic grade

The second respect in which grading in adjectives and adverbs is syntactically distinctive concerns comparison. Gradable adjectives and adverbs enter into a system of grade, marked inflectionally or analytically.

The inflectional system

A large number of adjectives and a few adverbs inflect for grade, but verbs and nouns do not:

[18]	PLAIN	COMPARATIVE	SUPERLATIVE	
i	*flat*	*flatter*	*flattest*	[Adj]
ii	*soon*	*sooner*	*soonest*	[Adv]
iii	*enjoy*	**enjoyer*	**enjoyest*	[V]
iv	*success*	**successer*	**successest*	[N]

For the most part determinatives and prepositions do not inflect for grade either, but there are a handful of exceptions, the determinatives ***much***, ***many***, ***little***, and ***few*** (e.g. *few, fewer, fewest*) and the prepositions ***near***, ***close***, and ***far***. Such forms as *inner*, *outer*, and *upper* are morphologically related to the prepositions *in*, *out*, and *up*, but it is a derivational relationship, not an inflectional one. *Inner* is not the comparative form of a lexeme ***in***, but a distinct lexeme which belongs to the category of adjectives. It differs from the preposition in that it cannot take an NP complement (*in*/**inner the woods*), and it differs from inflectional comparatives in that it cannot take a *than* complement (**This is inner than that*). The same applies to *outer* and *upper*, and such forms as *innermost* are likewise adjectives formed by derivation, not inflectional superlatives.

Analytic comparatives and superlatives

With adjectives and adverbs, analytic comparatives and superlatives are formed by means of the degree adverbs *more* and *most* in pre-head position:[2]

[19] i *useful* — *more useful* — *most useful* — [Adj]
ii *seriously* — *more seriously* — *most seriously* — [Adv]

Verbs and nouns can combine with *more* in the constructions illustrated in [16]:

[20] i *He [worries more than I do].* [V]
ii *It was [more trouble than it was worth].* [N]
iii *It was [more of a success than I'd expected].* [N]

The *more* in [20] is the inflectional comparative form of the determinative ***much*** of [16], rather than an adverb serving as an analytic marker of the comparative: see Ch. 13, §4.1.1, for this distinction. In the verbal construction, *more* follows the head rather than preceding it, as with adjectives and adverbs. Compare, then: *It was more enjoyable than usual* and *I enjoyed it more than usual.* In [20ii], *more* is in determiner function and again excludes count singular heads. Unlike *much*, however, it accepts count plurals (*It caused more problems than usual*): *more* is the inflectional comparative of ***many*** as well as of ***much***. With count singular nouns, we again have the distinctive *of* + *a* construction, as in [20iii].

In general, PPs don't allow analytic comparatives: compare, for example, prepositional **They arrived more before lunch than I did* with adverbial *They arrived earlier than I did.* However, the idiomatic PPs that allow *very* and *too*, as in [17ii], also accept *more*: *They now seem more in control than they were last week.*

Placement of *enough*

The third place where we find differences in the expression of grading depending on the category of the head concerns the determinative *enough*. Compare first:

[21] i a. *He wasn't [old enough].* — b. **He wasn't [enough old].* — [Adj]
ii a. *He can't speak [clearly enough].* — b. **He can't speak [enough clearly].* — [Adv]
iii a. *He doesn't [care enough].* — b. **He doesn't [enough care].* — [V]
iv a. *There isn't [enough time].* — b. *There isn't [time enough].* — [N]
v a. *He isn't [enough of a scholar].* — b. **He isn't [of a scholar enough].* — [N]

When the head is an adjective, adverb, or verb, *enough* follows, as in [i–iii]. With nouns there are again two constructions. In [iv], which admits plural and non-count singular nouns, *enough* can occur in either pre-head or post-head position. The pre-head version [iva] is, however, much the more usual; as it stands, [ivb] is perhaps only

[2] On the question of which adjectives and adverbs take inflectional comparatives and superlatives, and which take analytic ones, see Ch. 18, §3.2.

marginally acceptable, but it improves considerably if we add a complement licensed by *enough*: *There isn't time enough for that.* In construction [v], *scholar* is not head of the whole NP but part of the *of* phrase complement, and for this reason it must follow *enough.*

In [21i–iv] the head word has no dependent other than *enough*; consider next some cases where it also has a complement:

[22] i	a. *He isn't [keen enough on the idea].*	b. ?*He isn't [keen on the idea enough].*
ii	a. *He didn't [care enough about me].*	b. *He didn't [care about me enough].*
iii	a. **He doesn't [like enough the idea].*	b. *He doesn't [like the idea enough].*

In [i–ii] the complement has the form of a PP; with adjectives the preferred position for *enough* is between the head and the complement, as in [ia], whereas with verbs there is no clear preference for this position over one where it follows the complement, as in [iib]. One completely general rule, however, is that *enough* cannot intervene between the head and an NP complement (leaving aside the case where a heavy NP is postposed – see Ch. 16, §4). This applies whatever the category of the head. As far as the verb is concerned, the deviance of [iiia] is the same as that of **He didn't read carefully the report*: modifiers cannot in general intervene between a verb and its object.

Like *much*, *enough* does not generally occur with PPs: **We left enough before the end of the meeting to catch our train.* It is found with the idiomatic PPs that allow the other kinds of grading. The positional possibilities are illustrated in:

[23] i *I'm not [enough in control of things to go away for a week].*
ii **I'm not [in enough control of things to go away for a week].*
iii ?*I'm not [in control enough of things to go away for a week].*
iv ?*I'm not [in control of things enough to go away for a week].*

The normal position for *enough* is before the head, as in [i]. In accordance with the general rule given in the last paragraph, it cannot come between a preposition and an NP complement. This is illustrated in [ii] – which is to be understood with *enough* a modifier to *in*, not determiner to *control* (compare *We're in enough trouble as it is*, where *enough trouble* is an NP, so that the construction belongs with [21iva]). The positions shown in [23iii–iv] are marginally possible; there is some variation in judgements on these constructions, and also with respect to different prepositional idioms: *He wasn't in love with her enough to give up his career*, for example, seems fine.

2.3 Adverbs as dependents

Pre-head modifiers of adjectives characteristically belong to the adverb category, as in attributive *a [highly controversial] proposal* or predicative *The proposal is [highly controversial]*. This feature is related to the last in that adverbial modifiers commonly indicate degree. But this is by no means their only semantic function: compare *her [often irate] father-in-law*, where *often* is a frequency modifier, or *an [obviously phonological] issue*, where *obviously* is a modal modifier – and *phonological* is non-gradable.

This property distinguishes adjectives from nouns. We have noted that characteristically single-word modifiers of nouns are adjectives, while those modifying verbs are adverbs, and – leaving aside *very* and *too* – modifiers of adjectives and adverbs are, broadly speaking, a subset of those that modify verbs. This is illustrated in [24], where double underlining marks the head, and single underlining the modifier:

[24]		HEAD	MODIFIER
i	*They were subjected to [excessive force].*	noun	adjective
ii	*She [worries excessively].*	verb	adverb
iii	*He was [excessively persistent].*	adjective	adverb
iv	*They had been driving [excessively fast].*	adverb	adverb

The form of the dependent thus provides a test for distinguishing between predicative complements with the form of an AdjP and those with the form of a bare NP. Compare *That's stupid* and *That's nonsense*, for example. *Stupid* is an adjective taking adverbs as modifier (*That's utterly stupid*), while *nonsense* is a noun taking adjectives as modifier (*That's utter nonsense*).

2.4 Adjectives in comparison with words of other categories

In the last three sections we have presented the positive features of adjectives, and seen how they distinguish adjectives from other words. In this section we aim to develop our account of adjectives a little further by comparing them in turn with nouns, determinatives, and verbs. The distinction between adjectives and prepositions is discussed in Ch. 7, §2.2.

2.4.1 Adjectives vs nouns

The properties of nouns have been described in detail in Ch. 5, but the ones most relevant to distinguishing nouns from adjectives are repeated summarily in:

[25] i Phrases with a noun as non-fused head can occur as subject, object, or predicative complement in clause structure.
ii Count nouns inflect for number.
iii Nouns characteristically take adjectives as pre-head modifiers.
iv Nouns take determiner dependents.

In *They had left [some rotten apples] on the table*, for example, *apples* qualifies as a noun by all four criteria: it is head of the phrase in object function, it is in plural form, contrasting with singular *apple*, it is modified by the adjective *rotten*, and determined by the determinative *some*. As far as property [i] is concerned, we should exclude, for diagnostic purposes, clauses headed by *be* in its specifying sense, since phrases of any major category can occur as subject or predicative complement in clauses of this type. In *Rather more humble is how I'd like him to be*, for example, the subject is an AdjP.

The adjective and noun properties in [1] and [25] for the most part distinguish clearly between the two categories. Where the criteria give conflicting results we have homonymy:

[26] i *It was a very professional performance.* [Adj]
ii *She did better than all the professionals.* [N]

Attributive *professional* in [i] is modified by *very*, indicating that it is an adjective, while the plural form in [ii] must be a noun: the singular form *professional* is thus a noun homonymous with the adjective. Similarly, for speakers who accept such examples as %*It's a very fun thing to do*, etc., *fun* is an adjective homonymous with the noun *fun* of *We had some great fun*. Such cases of homonymy, where the adjective and noun are closely related in meaning, result from the lexical word-formation process of conversion: see Ch. 19, §3.[3]

Though the distinction between adjectives and nouns is generally quite clear, there are two places where further commentary is merited.

(a) Nouns as attributive modifiers

It is important to emphasise that it is not only adjectives that can function as pre-head modifier in the structure of a nominal. A variety of other categories are found in this function (as described in Ch. 5, §14.2), in particular nouns (or nominals):

[27] *a government inquiry* *student performance* *a London park* *the Clinton administration* *the Caroline factor* *the biology syllabus* *a computer error*

Traditional school grammar (though not scholarly traditional grammar) tends to analyse the underlined nouns here as adjectives – or to say that they are 'nouns used as adjectives'. From our perspective, this latter formulation represents a confusion between categories and functions: they are not nouns used as adjectives, but nouns used as attributive modifiers. Apart from pronouns, just about any noun can appear in this function – including proper nouns, as in the *London*, *Clinton*, and *Caroline* examples. These words can all appear as head of an NP in subject or object function, where they are uncontroversially nouns; to analyse them as adjectives when they are functioning attributively would make the adjective category far too heterogeneous, and require an unwarranted and massive overlap between the adjective and noun categories.[4]

Attributive nouns fail to qualify as adjectives by virtue of the grading and adverbial dependents criteria. They don't take *very* or *too* or the analytic comparative marker *more* as modifier. More generally, they don't take adverbs as modifier: to the extent that they accept pre-head modifiers, the modifiers are of the same kind as are found modifying nouns functioning as head in NP structure. Compare, for example:

[28] i	a. *the federal government*		b. *a federal government inquiry*
ii	a. *mature students*		b. *mature student performance*

Here *government* and *student* take the adjectives *federal* and *mature* as modifiers, not adverbs: cf. **a federally government inquiry* and **maturely student performance*. Often the modifier is another noun, as in *psychology student performance* ("the performance of students of psychology"). This difference in the category of modifiers applies equally in cases where there is homonymy between adjective and noun. Thus *a characteristically French response* has *French* as an adjective modified by an adverb, while *an Old French dictionary* has *French* as a noun modified by an adjective.

[3] One also comes across nonce-conversions, new uses that have not been established in the language, as in this attested example of *cutting-edge* as an adjective: *It's very innovative – it's very cutting-edge for Australia.*

[4] We will not take an attributive modifier to be a noun unless it occurs with the same meaning as head of an NP. In a *maiden voyage*, for example, *maiden* does not have the same meaning as in *a young maiden from Perth*, and will thus be analysed as an adjective even though it has no adjective properties other than that of occurring in attributive function: it cannot be used predicatively or postpositively, and it doesn't admit any dependents.

The examples in [27] differ from the simplest type of attributive adjective construction in that there is no matching predicative construction. Compare:

[29] i a. *a red jacket* b. *The jacket is red.*
ii a. *a government inquiry* b. **The inquiry is government.*

However, nouns denoting the material of which something is composed do show this kind of relationship: compare a *cotton sheet* and *The sheet is cotton.* This may appear to make these nouns more adjective-like, but again the modifier test shows that they belong to the noun category, for they are modified by adjectives, not adverbs: *a pure cotton sheet* and *This sheet is pure cotton.*

(b) Adjectives as fused modifier-heads in NP structure

Certain kinds of adjective can function as head of a subject or object NP when the head is fused with a modifier – this is why criterion [25i] is formulated in terms of a non-fused head. Some examples of NPs with adjectives as fused modifier-head are given in:

[30] i *They will be playing modern music, but I prefer [classical].*
ii *She has answered [the most important of your criticisms].*
iii *They claim the changes will benefit [only the very poor].*

This case is very different from that of homonymy between adjective and noun illustrated in [26]. Although the underlined words bear some functional resemblance to nouns, they do not have enough in common with nouns to justify their assignment to the noun category. Example [i] belongs to the type of fused-head construction that is interpreted anaphorically: we understand "classical music" by virtue of the antecedent *music.* In the absence of such an antecedent we would normally have to supply a noun as head. In [ii–iii] *important* and *poor* are like adjectives in other functions with respect to grading: *most important* is an analytic superlative and *poor* has *very* as modifier. For detailed description of the fused-head construction, and a fuller discussion of this issue, see Ch. 5, §9.

2.4.2 **Adjectives vs determinatives**

This book follows the practice of most work in modern linguistics in recognising a primary part-of-speech distinction between adjectives and determinatives. In traditional grammar, by contrast, determinatives are wholly or almost wholly subsumed under the adjective category – they are said to be 'limiting adjectives', as opposed to 'descriptive adjectives'. There is some variation in the treatment of the definite and indefinite articles: while these are usually classified as adjectives in twentieth-century traditional grammar, along with other determinatives, some works recognise the article as a distinct part of speech.

The articles

The articles *the* and *a* are unquestionably very different, both syntactically and semantically, from prototypical adjectives such as *good* or *bad* or *happy.* They serve to mark the NP as definite or indefinite, not to express properties attributed to the denotation of the head. They are non-gradable, and they cannot be used predicatively. And in most circumstances they cannot be omitted from an NP with a count singular common noun as head: we have *I bought the book* or *I bought a book*, but not **I bought book.* There are thus strong grounds for distinguishing *the* and *a* from adjectives at the primary level of classification.

Criteria for determinatives

Words like *this* and *that* or *some* and *any* can be seen to have more in common with the articles than with *good* and *bad* and *happy.*

(a) Mutual exclusiveness with the articles

The clearest members of the determinative category cannot combine with the articles. Thus we have *a good book*, but not **a this book*, and so on. This criterion admits the following items as determinatives:

[31]	*another*	*any*	*each*	*either*	*enough*	*every*
	much	*neither*	***no***	*some*	*that*	*this*
	we$_{d}$	*what*$_{int/rel}$	*whatever*	*which*	*whichever*	*you*$_{d}$

Also admitted by this criterion are the complex forms *a few* and *a little.* The items ***we***$_{d}$ and you$_{d}$ (as in *we/you students*) are distinguished from the pronouns **we** and ***you***, and the *what* in [31] is the interrogative or relative determinative; exclamative *what* can combine with *a*, as in *What a disaster it was!*, and is best included in the adjective category (see below).

(b) Admissibility of count singular NPs

Cardinal *one* does not qualify by criterion (a) since it can follow *the* – though it is mutually exclusive with *a* (*the one problem that remains*, but not **a one problem that remains*). *One* is nevertheless like the articles and those determinatives in [31] that do not require plural or non-count heads in that it allows count singular nouns to occur as head of an NP. Compare again, then, *I bought one/neither book* (with *one* and *neither* determinatives) and **I bought good book* (with *good* an adjective).

(c) The partitive construction

The other cardinal numerals are semantically like *one* and a number of the determinatives in [31] in that they have to do with quantification, and syntactically this similarity is brought out by their ability to occur as fused determiner-head in a partitive construction. Adjectives cannot occur in this construction unless in comparative or superlative grade. Compare:

[32] a. *one/three/which/neither of them* b. **(the) good of them*

Instead of [b] we need *the good ones among them* or the like. Words not included in [31] that are admitted to the determinative category on the basis of this criterion are:

[33]	*all*	*both*	*certain*	*few*	*little*	*many*
	several	*sufficient*	*various*		cardinal numerals	

Consideration of selected items

Many, few, much, little

These items are admitted to the determinative category by criterion (c): cf. *many of them*, *much of it*, etc.; *much* also satisfies criterion (a). They nevertheless bear a considerable resemblance to adjectives. ***Many*** and ***few*** can occur as predicative complement: *Her virtues are many.* More importantly, all four are gradable, and have inflectional comparative and superlative forms. Even with grading, however, there is one syntactic feature which differentiates them from adjectives. Compare:

[34] i a. *He made [so many mistakes].* b. **He made [so numerous mistakes].*
ii a. *He gave me [so much sugar].* b. **He gave me [so hard work].*
iii a. [no count singular] b. *He made [so big a fuss].*

Adjectives modified by *so* cannot function as pre-head dependent in NP structure except as a predeterminer before the indefinite article, but the determinatives *many, much,* etc., can. Thus *so numerous* cannot function as an internal modifier, but *so many* can function as determiner. This difference applies not just to *so* but to all the items that can modify adjectives in construction [iiib] (see §3.3 below). Compare, for example, *How many mistakes did they make?* and **How numerous mistakes did they make?*

Sufficient

We have classified *sufficient* as both a determinative and an adjective. It is a determinative when it is replaceable by *enough,* as in *sufficient helpers* or *sufficient help,* and it is an adjective in *a sufficient reason,* where it means "satisfactory, good enough". The determinative *sufficient* meets criteria (a) and (c), and since it doesn't occur with count singular heads (b) is inapplicable. It is, however, more limited in its distribution than *enough,* for it cannot occur in post-head position. Thus we have *time enough* but not **time sufficient,* and *good enough* but not **good sufficient.* Instead of the latter we have *sufficiently good,* and this relationship with a ·*ly* adverb differentiates *sufficient* from central members of the determinative category.

Exclamative *what*

We take this – unlike interrogative and relative *what* – to be an adjective. It fails all of the determinative criteria (a)–(c). Compare, for example, the count singular exclamative *What a great book that is!* with interrogative *What book is that?*, where *a* is required in the former but inadmissible in the latter. The distribution of exclamative *what* is comparable to that of the adjective *such,* and in *what a great book* it is functioning as predeterminer like the AdjP *so big* in [34iiib] above.

2.4.3 Adjectives vs verbs

Primary forms of verbs, and also the plain form, are clearly distinct from adjectives: it is only with the gerund-participle and past participle forms that problems arise, for there are many adjectives that are homophonous with these forms of verbs. We need to consider two cases, one where the verb or adjective follows the verb *be,* and one where it modifies a noun.

Following the verb *be*

Gerund-participle and past participle forms of verbs follow *be* as a marker of progressive aspect and passive voice respectively, whereas adjectives follow *be* as a copula. Compare:

[35]	VERB		ADJECTIVE
i	a. *She was sleeping.*	[progressive]	b. *This was disturbing.*
ii	a. *He was killed.*	[passive]	b. *He was very distressed.*
iii	a. *They were seen.*		b. *He was drunk.*

This distinction is discussed for gerund-participles in Ch. 3, §1.4, and for past participles in Ch. 3, §1.3, and Ch. 16, §10.3, and hence can be dealt with here quite summarily. One test for adjectival status is the possiblity of replacing *be* by other complex-intransitive verbs such as *seem* and *become*. Thus we have *This seemed disturbing, He became very distressed, He appeared drunk*, but not **She seemed sleeping, *He became killed, *They appeared seen*. A second test is modification by *very* and *too*, as discussed in §2.2 above: *very* is present in [iib] and can be added to [ib/iiib], but not to any of the [a] examples. A third, much less general, factor is meaning: the adjective *drunk* is semantically distinct from the past participle verb-form of *The milk had already been drunk*.

The two constructions are also often distinguished by the different patterns of complementation of verbs and adjectives. Most obviously, gerund-participles of transitive verbs take objects, whereas no participial adjective does: in *She was mowing the lawn*, therefore, *mowing* is very clearly a verb. Conversely, a verbal reading of *disturbing* in [35ib] can be excluded because there is no object: contrast verbal *This was disturbing me*. (The verb *disturb* can occur without an object, but [35ib] cannot plausibly be construed as an intransitive use.)

Past participles following *be* have a passive rather than perfect interpretation and (leaving aside cases of semantic specialisation as in the *drunk* example) the same normally applies to corresponding adjectives. Thus *distressed* in [35] denotes a state resulting from being distressed in the passive verbal sense. There are, however, a few exceptions. *Kim is retired*, for example, means that Kim is in the state resulting from having retired. Similarly, *They are gone* means that they are in the state resulting from having gone or departed.[5]

Modifying a noun

[36]		VERB	ADJECTIVE
	i	a. *a <u>sleeping</u> child*	b. *some <u>disturbing</u> news*
	ii	a. *a rarely <u>heard</u> work by Purcell*	b. *her very <u>worried</u> parents*

Two of the criteria we used in the construction with *be* are inapplicable in this modifying construction, and the distinction between verbs and adjectives is here not so sharply drawn, certainly in the past participle case. Since there is no verb *be* in [36], the issue of replacing it by *seem, become*, etc., does not arise. And complements are virtually excluded with attributive modifiers, so we do not have clearly verbal constructions like **a mowing the lawn gardener*.

Very again provides a sufficient but not a necessary condition for adjective status; it is present in [36iib], and can be added in [ib], but not in [ia/iia]. Similarly, semantic divergence from the verb is sufficient to establish adjective status, as in *a <u>winning</u> smile* or, less obviously, *the <u>winning</u> team*, which means not "the team that is/was winning" but "the team that wins/won".

In general, we will take the form as a verb if it cannot function as a predicative adjective. We have already seen that *sleeping* has no predicative adjective use; cf. also *a <u>smiling</u> face, the <u>sinking</u> ship, a <u>dying</u> man*, etc. Similarly with the past participle *heard* in [36iia] – or *this frequently <u>visited</u> shrine, the <u>murdered</u> man*, etc.

Again, past participles and corresponding adjectives in attributive position are usually interpreted passively: a rarely heard work is a work which one rarely hears. But here too

[5] The adjective *gone* also has various specialised meanings in informal style, including "pregnant" (cf. *She's five months gone*) and "infatuated" (cf. *He's quite gone on her*).

there are a fairly small number of exceptions: *fallen rocks, a failed businessman, the escaped prisoner, a grown man, the recently departed guests.* The category status of these items is rather problematic, but since they cannot occur as predicative adjectives, they are perhaps best regarded as verbs.

3 The structure of AdjPs

AdjPs, like other major phrasal categories, may be of considerable internal complexity: they may contain complements following the head, and modifiers in either pre-head or post-head position.

3.1 Complementation

Many adjectives license complements in post-head position. Like the post-head complements in NP structure, those in AdjPs almost invariably have the form of PPs or clauses.

Optional and obligatory complementation

For the most part, complements in AdjP structure are optional elements: they qualify as complements by virtue of being licensed by the head rather than being obligatory. Compare:

[1] i a. *He was [afraid of dogs].* b. *He was [afraid].*
ii a. *Kim was [very keen to take part].* b. *Kim was [very keen].*
iii a. *He's [happy to leave it to you].* b. *He's [happy].*

In some such cases, however, the interpretation depends on recovering an understood complement from the context. This is so in [iib], for example, which contrasts in this regard with [iiib].

There are some adjectives that take a complement that is syntactically obligatory when the AdjP is in non-attributive function:

[2] i a. *They are [mindful of the danger].* b. **They are [mindful].*
ii a. *We were [loath to accept their help].* b. **We were [loath].*
iii a. *They were [fraught with danger].* b. *They were [fraught].*

As usual, we take a complement to be obligatory if its omission results in an unsystematic change in the meaning of the head. This is the case with [iii]: *fraught* in [a] means roughly "full (of), charged, accompanied (by)", while in [b] it means "anxious, distressed, causing anxiety/distress". A high proportion of adjectives that require a complement when used predicatively or postpositively cannot occur at all in attributive function, but there are others that can, in which case there is no complement. Compare:

[3] i a. *This is [tantamount to a confession].* b. **their tantamount confession*
ii a. *They were [heedless of the danger].* b. *this heedless destruction of the forests*

The underlined complements in the [a] examples are obligatory, but *heedless* – unlike *tantamount* – can be used in attributive function, where complements are hardly possible.

Adjectives that do not license complements

A large number of adjectives do not license complements of any kind. It is hard or impossible to find or envisage complements occurring with such adjectives as:

[4]	*ambulatory*	*bald*	*concise*	*dead*	*enormous*	*farcical*
	gigantic	*hasty*	*immediate*	*jaunty*	*lovely*	*main*
	nefarious	*ostentatious*	*purple*	*quiet*	*red*	*regular*
	salty	*tentative*	*urban*	*vivid*	*wild*	*young*

PP complements

We review here a range of constructions with PP complements. For each of the prepositions concerned we give a few examples of AdjPs containing a complement, followed by a sample of adjectives that license complements headed by this preposition. In the lists of adjectives we underline those where (for a given sense of the adjective) the complement is wholly or virtually obligatory in non-attributive constructions.[6]

Adjective + *about*

[5] *annoyed <u>about the delay</u>* *concerned <u>about the cost</u>* *mad <u>about you</u>*

[6]	*aggrieved*	*angry*	*annoyed*	*concerned*	*cross*	*delighted*
	glad	*happy*	*knowledgeable*	*mad*	*pleased*	*reasonable*

In many cases, *about* alternates with *at* (*annoyed <u>at the delay</u>*). With *mad* in the sense "angry", *at* and *about* are possible, but when it indicates enthusiasm or love only *about* is used, and here the complement is obligatory; both senses belong to informal style.

Adjective + *at*

[7] *aghast <u>at the news</u>* *indignant <u>at the allegations</u>* *pleased <u>at being invited</u>*
adept <u>at making people feel at home</u> *good <u>at chess</u>* *hopeless <u>at arithmetic</u>*

[8]	*adept*	*aghast*	*alarmed*	*amazed*	*amused*	*angry*
	astonished	*bad*	*brilliant*	*clever*	*delighted*	*disgusted*
	gifted	*good*	*hopeless*	*indignant*	*mad*	*marvellous*
	pleased	*puzzled*	*skilled*	*superb*	*talented*	*terrible*

Semantically these adjectives fall into two groups. In one (*aghast, indignant*, etc.) the adjective denotes a psychological reaction to the phenomenon expressed in the complement of *at*: here *at* is generally replaceable by *about*. In the other (*adept, good*, etc.) the adjective denotes a property, capacity, or failing and the *at* phrase indicates its domain.

Adjective + *by*

[9] *very distressed <u>by these insinuations</u>* *completely unaffected <u>by the changes</u>*

[10] *amused* *distressed* *hurt* *unaffected* *unperturbed* *worried*

This construction is confined to adjectives deriving from past participles in their passive use; it is discussed in Ch. 16, §10.1.3.

[6] We do not provide a list for *against*, but there is one adjective that selects complements headed by this preposition: *No security system is <u>proof</u> against the truly professional burglar.*

Adjective + *for*

[11] *responsible for the poor performance* *bad for you* *greedy for power*

[12]	*answerable*	*anxious*	*bad*	*difficult*	*eager*	*easy*
	good	*grateful*	*greedy*	*necessary*	*responsible*	*sorry*

Adjective + *from*

[13] *divorced from reality* *remote from everyday life* *distinct from each other*

[14]	*alienated*	*averse*	*different*	*differentiated*	*distant*	*distinct*
	divorced	*free*	*immune*	*remote*	*removed*	*separated*

Averse, *different*, and *immune* also take *to* (which is strongly favoured in the case of *averse*). With *free*, *from* alternates with *of*.

Adjective + *in*

[15] *bathed in sunlight* *fortunate in our choice* *confident in my ability* *covered in dust* *dressed in military uniform* *engaged in a court battle* *steeped in history*

[16]	*bathed*	*clothed*	*confident*	*covered*	*decisive*	*domiciled*
	dressed	*embroiled*	*engaged*	*fortunate*	*inherent*	*interested*
	lacking	*lucky*	*rooted*	*secure*	*steeped*	*swathed*

Covered also takes *with*, which is preferred over *in* in examples like *covered with a blanket.*

Adjective + *of*

[17] *afraid of dogs* *capable of murder* *fond of children* *sure of his facts* *indicative of its importance* *supportive of her husband* *very kind of you*

[18]	i	*afraid*	*ashamed*	*aware*	*beloved*	*bereft*	*capable*
		certain	*characteristic*	*cognisant*	*conscious*	*constitutive*	*convinced*
		desirous	*destructive*	*devoid*	*distrustful*	*fond*	*full*
		heedless	*ignorant*	*illustrative*	*indicative*	*mindful*	*productive*
		proud	*reminiscent*	*representative*	*respectful*	*scared*	*short*
		suggestive	*supportive*	*sure*	*tired*	*wary*	*worthy*
	ii	*careless*	*considerate*	*generous*	*good*	*honest*	*idiotic*
		kind	*naive*	*noble*	*pleasant*	*silly*	*stupid*

Beloved incorporates a past participle, which accounts for the fact that the semantic roles are ordered as in a passive clause: compare *This tactic is much beloved of administrators* and *This tactic is loved by administrators.* The adjectives in [18ii] commonly occur in combination with *it* + extraposed subject, as in *It was very kind of you to wash the dishes*, alternating with a construction with a personal subject: *You were very kind to wash the dishes.*

Adjective + *on/upon*

[19] *based on/upon firm evidence* *bent on/upon vengeance* *incumbent on/upon us* *set on/upon regaining power* *a bit tough on the audience* *sweet on her*

[20]	i	*based*	*bent*	*contingent*	*dependent*	*incumbent*	*intent*	*reliant* *set*
	ii	*big*	*easy*	*hard*	*keen*	*severe*	*sweet*	

Upon occurs as a somewhat more formal alternant to *on* with the adjectives in [20i], but not those in [ii] – where *big* and *sweet* are markedly informal.

Adjective + *to*

[21] *accustomed to getting his own way* *allergic to morphine* *beholden to no one*
good to me *responsible to the president* *similar to mine* *subject to revision*

[22]

accustomed	*allergic*	*allied*	*answerable*	*attributable*	*attuned*
averse	*beholden*	*comparable*	*conducive*	*congruent*	*connected*
devoted	*different*	*distasteful*	*due*	*equal*	*equivalent*
generous	*good*	*hospitable*	*hostile*	*impervious*	*inclined*
inferior	*injurious*	*integral*	*kind*	*liable*	*mean*
nice	*opposed*	*parallel*	*prone*	*proportional*	*receptive*
reconciled	*related*	*resigned*	*resistant*	*responsible*	*similar*
subject	*subordinate*	*subservient*	*superior*	*susceptible*	*tantamount*

Adjective + *toward(s)*

[23] *very friendly towards us* *strongly inclined towards the other candidate*
respectful towards authority *not very sympathetic towards new ideas*

[24] *antagonistic* *friendly* *hostile* *inclined* *respectful* *sympathetic*

Except perhaps with *inclined*, *to* occurs as an alternant of *towards*.

Adjective + *with*

[25] *careful with money* *conversant with the rules* *fed up with the noise*
good with her hands *happy with the result* *obsessed with sex* *tinged with gold*

[26]

angry	*annoyed*	*bored*	*browned off*	*busy*	*careful*
cautious	*comfortable*	*compatible*	*concerned*	*connected*	*consonant*
content	*conversant*	*covered*	*cross*	*delighted*	*depressed*
disappointed	*disgusted*	*distressed*	*effective*	*enchanted*	*familiar*
fed up	*firm*	*fraught*	*friendly*	*furious*	*gentle*
good	*happy*	*harsh*	*impatient*	*obsessed*	*occupied*
parallel	*pleased*	*reckless*	*riddled*	*rife*	*satisfied*
sick	*skilful*	*stricken*	*strict*	*taken*	*tinged*

Adjective + comparative *as* or *than*

[27] a. %*different than it used to be* b. *the same as last time*

[28] a. %*different* *other* b. *same* ?*similar* *such*

The adjectives in [28a] express comparison of inequality and take *than*; those in [b] express comparison of equality and take *as*: for detailed description, see Ch. 13. *Different* also takes comparative complements headed by *from* or *to*, with *than* of questionable acceptability in BrE, while *similar* normally takes *to*, with *as* marginal in all varieties.

Clausal complements

The range of clausal complements found in AdjP structure is illustrated in:

[29] i *I'm [glad that you were able to come].* [declarative content clause]
ii *She was [insistent that the charge be dropped].* [mandative]
iii *I'm not [sure whether that will be possible].* [interrogative]
iv *I was [amazed what a fuss he made].* [exclamative]

v *She is [willing <u>to renegotiate the deal</u>].* [*to*-infinitival]
vi *Kim is [hard <u>to please</u>].* [hollow infinitival]
vii *She was [busy <u>marking assignments</u>].* [gerund-participial]
viii *The offer is certainly [worth <u>considering</u>].* [hollow gerund-participial]

Interrogatives and exclamatives, however, may also be related to the adjective via a preposition, rather than directly, as in the above examples: compare *They weren't interested <u>in</u> why we were protesting* or *They seemed surprised <u>at</u> how strongly we felt about the issue.* All these constructions are dealt with in the chapters on subordinate clauses: see Ch. 11 for the ones involving finite clauses, and Ch. 14 for those involving non-finites.

NP complements

In the structure of phrases headed by adjectives, as in those headed by nouns, NPs are usually related to the head via a preposition, rather than immediately. There are, however, four adjectives that license NP complements: *due*, *like*, *unlike*, and *worth*. Compare:

[30] i *The book turned out to be [worth <u>seventy dollars</u>].*
ii *Jill is [<u>very like her brother</u>].*

The NP complement of *worth* expresses the value of the predicand. It may denote a sum of money, as in [30i], or a more abstract value, as in *I'm sure you'll find this [worth <u>the effort</u> / <u>your time</u>]*. *Like* and *unlike* are used to express comparison of equality and inequality respectively: they are dealt with along with other comparative expressions in Ch. 13, §5.6. *Like* and *unlike*, moreover, belong to the category of prepositions as well as that of adjectives: we discuss in Ch. 7, §2.2, the issue of distinguishing between adjectival and prepositional constructions consisting of head + NP complement.

Due

In the sense in which it can take an NP complement, *due* is semantically and syntactically similar to the past participle of the verb *owe*, as used in passive constructions. Compare:

[31]	VERBAL *OWE*	ADJECTIVAL *DUE*
i	a. *The bank now owes you $750.*	b. ___
ii	a. *You are now owed $750.*	b. *You are now due $750.*
iii	a. *$750 is now owed you.*	b. *$750 is now due you.*
iv	a. *The bank now owes $750 to you.*	b. ___
v	a. *$750 is now owed to you.*	b. *$750 is now due to you.*

Examples [ia/iva] are active, and have no counterpart with *due*, but in the three passive examples with *owed*, there is an equivalent construction with *due*. Semantically, there are three entities involved: the creditor ("you"), the debt ("$750"), and the debtor ("the bank"). In [ii], the creditor is expressed as subject and the debt as object – reflecting the fact that in active [ia] *you* is indirect object and *$750* direct object. In [iii/v] the debt is expressed as subject, and the creditor as either object or complement of the preposition *to* – reflecting the alternation between the two active constructions [ia/iva]; [iiib] is predominantly AmE, with BrE favouring [vb]. With the verb *owe*, the debtor is expressed as subject in the active and (optionally) as complement of *by* in the passive:

You are now owed $750 by the bank, etc. In general, the debtor is not expressed in the *due* construction, but some speakers accept *by* or *from* phrases: [%] *$750 is due (to) you by/from the people you worked for last month.* This results in a highly exceptional AdjP containing two complements.

Indirect complements

We have been concerned so far with complements that are licensed by the adjective lexeme in head position. AdjPs may also contain indirect complements, complements licensed by a modifier of the head, or by the comparative inflection:

[32] i *The bill wasn't [as large as we'd expected].*
ii *I'm [fonder of them than you].*
iii *They were [so small you could hardly see them].*
iv *This is still [too hot to drink].*

Here single underlining indicates the indirect complement (a PP in [i–ii], a clause in [iii–iv]), while double underlining indicates the modifier or inflectional suffix that licenses it. As illustrated in [ii], an indirect complement can combine with a direct one.

3.2 Modification

Modifiers in the structure of AdjPs may have the form of AdvPs, determinatives, NPs, PPs, and, under very restricted conditions, relative clauses:

[33] i *She is [quite incredibly generous].* [AdvP]
ii *It surely isn't [that important].* [determinative]
iii *The nail was [two inches long].* [NP]
iv *The view was [beautiful beyond description].* [PP]
v *He is now [the fattest he's ever been].* [relative clause]

Relative clauses occur only with superlatives; the construction is discussed in Ch. 12, §4.1, and need not be considered further here. The other types of modifier we will review in turn, but first we should make two general points.

Stacked modification vs submodification

AdjPs may contain more than one layer of modification, and in such cases we need to distinguish between the structures illustrated in [34], where underlining indicates the lower-level construction:

[34] i *his [occasionally very offensive] behaviour* [stacked modification]
ii *his [quite unbelievably offensive] behaviour* [submodification]

In [i] *very* modifies *offensive*, and then at a higher level *occasionally* modifies *very offensive*: we understand that occasionally his behaviour was very offensive. Here both cases of modification have an adjectival head (*offensive* being an adjective and *very offensive* an AdjP), and in such constructions we say there is **stacked** modification. In [ii], by contrast, *quite* modifies the adverb *unbelievably*, and it is the resultant AdvP *quite unbelievably* that modifies the adjective *offensive*: here the lower level of modification is within the modifier, not the head, and we refer to this as **submodification**. Tree structures for the bracketed phrases are as follows:

[35] a. STACKED MODIFICATION b. SUBMODIFICATION

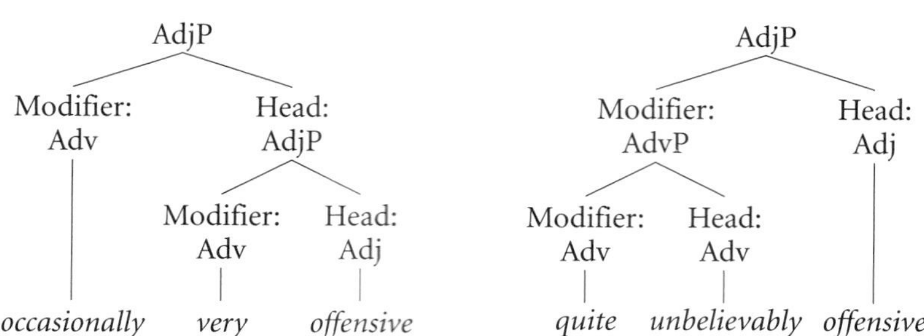

Distinction between comparative and non-comparative forms affects modification

A considerable proportion of modification in AdjP structure has to do with the expression of degree with gradable adjectives, as in <u>*very*</u> *good* and <u>*extremely*</u> *old*, etc. What kind of degree modifiers are permitted depends in part on whether the phrase is comparative or not. Compare:

[36]

	NON-COMPARATIVE	COMPARATIVE
i	a. <u>*very*</u>/*<u>*much*</u> *young*	b. <u>*much*</u>/*<u>*very*</u> *younger*
ii	a. <u>*this*</u> / *<u>*this much*</u> *expensive*	b. <u>*this much*</u> / *<u>*this*</u> *more expensive*
iii	a. *<u>*far*</u> *excellent*	b. <u>*far*</u> *superior*

Non-comparatives like *young* allow *very*, while comparative *younger* does not: it takes *much*, or (with submodification) *very much*, modifiers which are for the most part inadmissible with non-comparatives. Similarly, determinative *this* is found with non-comparative *expensive*, but not with comparative *more expensive*, which again requires *much*: *this much more expensive*. Again, *far* occurs with comparatives, but not with non-comparatives.

The comparatives in [36ib–iiib] are respectively inflectional, analytic, and lexical. Modification of an analytic comparative yields a submodification structure along the lines of [35b]: in *far more expensive*, for example, *far more* is an AdvP modifying *expensive*. The lexical forms (mainly *different*, *superior*, *inferior*, *preferable*) can in some respects also behave like non-comparatives. We can have, for example, either *very different* or (*very*) *much different*. The comparatives considered here are comparatives of inequality: for comparatives of equality, see Ch. 13, §4.4.1.

AdvPs

The most common type of modifier is an AdvP, consisting of an adverb alone (*unbelievably offensive*), or an adverb together with its own modifier (<u>*quite unbelievably*</u> *offensive*). In the former case we will often say simply that the modifier is an adverb (rather than an AdvP), and – in keeping with our general practice – we have omitted the AdvP constituent in the tree diagram [35a]. The use of adverbs as modifiers in AdjP structure is described in §7.2 below.

Determinatives

The determinatives that function as degree modifiers are illustrated in [37]:

[37]	i	[The bigger] it is, [the more likely] it is to break down.	[the]
	ii	They are [this tall].	[this]
	iii	The meals aren't [that expensive].	[that]
	iv	It's [no better than it was before].	[no]
	v	We're not getting [any younger].	[any]
	vi	It's [much smaller than I expected].	[much]
	vii	They spent a lot of money, but it's [little better than it was before].	[little]
	viii	I'm feeling [a little disappointed].	[a little]
	ix	I thought you were [old enough to know better].	[enough]
	x	He seemed [all confused].	[all]

The occurs with inflectional and analytic comparatives (see Ch. 13, §4.4.2), and with *same*: *Everything seems [the same as it was before]*.

The demonstratives *this* and *that* are discussed in Ch. 17, §5.4. Both are used deictically, with some accompanying gesture indicating the degree intended. *That* is also used anaphorically (*Max is in his eighties and Kim is about that old too*) or, in informal style, with the sense "particularly", as in [37iii]. In this latter use, *that* is restricted to non-affirmative contexts. The demonstratives also occur with *much* in a submodification construction, as in *She's about [this much taller than me]*, where *this much* is a DP modifying *taller*.

No, *any*, *much*, and *little* occur in comparisons of inequality. *Much* and *little* are also found with various adjectives formed from past participles: *They don't seem much inclined to leave / much impressed by his argument*. Somewhat different is the use of *very much* in examples like *He seemed very much separate from the rest of the group*. This doesn't indicate a high point on a gradable scale of separateness: rather, it emphasises that he was indeed separate from the rest of the group. ***Good*** is exceptional in that it accepts *no*, *any*, and (in non-affirmative contexts) *much* in the plain form as well as in the comparative: *This car is no good*; *The radio reception wasn't any/much good*.

Enough is positioned after the head. If the AdjP also contains a complement, there is a strong preference for *enough* to precede it: *careful enough with money* rather than *?careful with money enough*, and so on. It licenses a *for* phrase (*good enough for most purposes*) or a clause (such as *to know better* in [37ix]) which functions as indirect complement in the AdjP. Note, then, that we take the immediate constituents in [37ix] to be *old enough* + *to know better*, not *old* + *enough to know better*: this is because a complement will be placed between *enough* and the indirect complement licensed by *enough*, as in *fond enough of them to make this sacrifice*.

All, as in [37x], *all confused*, means "completely". In addition, it occurs, as in NP structure, before *the* and *that*: *I feel all the better for it* (suggesting a somewhat higher degree than *the better for it*) and *It wasn't all that good* (hardly distinguishable from *that good*).

NPs

Only a narrow range of NPs are used to modify adjectives:

[38]	i	*three years old*	*five centimetres thick*	*a foot wide*	*two hours long*	
	ii	*a great deal smaller*	*a (whole) lot different*	*lots better*	*heaps worse*	
	iii	*a bit lax*	*a smidgin overripe*	*a tad greasy*	*a trifle shy*	*plenty big enough*

The NPs in [i] are measure phrases, while the others are quantificational NPs (see Ch. 5, §3.3). Those in [ii] occur only with comparatives. *A tad* and *a trifle* differ from the others in that they do not occur in NP structure with an *of* complement: *a bit of trouble*, but not **a trifle of trouble. Plenty* occurs (in informal style) in combination with *enough*, indicating a degree clearly above that which qualifies as enough. The construction without *enough*, as in *%plenty hot*, is informal AmE. Expressions like *stone cold* or *time-poor* are best regarded as compound adjectives: see Ch. 19, §4.3.1.

PPs

Modifiers with the form of PPs are found in both post-head and pre-head position:

[39] i *cautious to excess*   *clear in his mind*   *dangerous in the extreme*   *deaf in both ears*   *very good for a beginner*   *happy beyond belief*   *polite in her manner*   *young at heart*   *too long by a mile*   *not very good at all*

ii *these [in some respects highly controversial] ideas*   *his [at times very offensive] behaviour*   *this [in my view quite outrageous] suggestion*   *an [on the whole persuasive] argument*   *their [to some extent perfectly valid] objections*

The default position in predicative AdjPs is after the head, as in [i], but the construction with pre-head PP modifiers in attributive AdjPs, as in [ii], is certainly possible, though very restricted with respect to the kinds of PPs permitted.[7]

3.3 Structural differences correlating with the function of the AdjP

Not all AdjPs can occur in all four of the functions that can be realised by AdjPs: attributive, predicative, postpositive, and predeterminer. Some of the restrictions concern the adjective lexeme itself: *mere*, for example, is always attributive, while *tantamount* is never attributive. Restrictions of this kind are dealt with in §4. There are also restrictions relating to the syntactic structure of the AdjP. For example, *keen on golf* is excluded from attributive position not because of any restriction on the head *keen*, but because it contains the complement *on golf*. It is syntactic restrictions of this kind that we are concerned with here.

(a) Predeterminer AdjPs

AdjPs occurring in predeterminer position in NP structure, before the article *a*, must meet one or other of the following conditions:

[40] i The AdjP begins with one of the modifiers *how, as, so, too, this, that.*

ii The AdjP has *such* or exclamative *what* as head.

[7] In addition to the four categories of modifier considered above, one finds a few adjectives (including one or two participial ones): *icy cold, freezing cold, red-hot, boiling hot, scalding hot.* These expressions have the character of fixed phrases, however: this is not a productive construction. One also occasionally finds more complex modifying expressions comparable to the nonce-formations that occur much more readily as attributive modifiers in NP structure (cf. Ch. 5, §14.1): *He usually looks happy not just [things-are-OK happy], but [things-are-so-exciting-and-wonderful happy]*.

In the following examples underlining marks the AdjP, and brackets enclose the NP:

[41] i *[How big a company] is it? It was [so serious a matter that we called the police]. Don't make [too big a fuss]. I've never seen [that big a spider] before. *They have [quite big a house]. *It's [excessively big a risk].*

ii *It's [such a pity] you can't come. [What a waste of time] it was! *She's [excellent a pianist].*

The modifiers listed in [40i] need not modify the adjective head: the AdjP may involve submodification, with *how*, etc., modifying an adverb, as in *[How ridiculously trivial a complaint] it had turned out to be!*

(b) Attributive AdjPs

AdjPs functioning as internal pre-head modifier in an NP are subject to three constraints on their structure.

Virtual exclusion of post-head dependents

Attributive AdjPs, like other attributive modifiers, hardly permit post-head complements or modifiers. Compare:

[42]	PREDICATIVE	ATTRIBUTIVE
i	a. *She's [very good at chess].*	b. **a [very good at chess] friend*
ii	a. *She's [generous to a fault].*	b. **a [generous to a fault] sister*
iii	a. *It's [easy to find].*	b. **an [easy to find] place*

The ungrammatical examples in [b] can be corrected by putting the AdjPs after the head: *a friend very good at chess* (or of course by using a relative clause: *a friend who is very good at chess*). In cases like [iii], where the complement is a hollow infinitival, it is also possible to place just the clause after the head noun, giving *an easy place to find.* Similarly with comparatives: **a younger than you leader* can be corrected to either *a leader younger than you* or *a younger leader than you.*

The ban on post-head dependents is not absolute, as is evident from such examples as:

[43] *a [big enough] room a [better than average] result the [larger than expected] profit his [hard as nails] attitude to the workers a [ready-to-eat] TV meal*

The postmodifier *enough* occurs quite readily. Comparative complements are permitted provided they are very short, usually *than* or *as* + a single word, which cannot be a referential NP. Compare the examples in [43] with, say, **a better than ours result, *the larger than we expected profit*, etc. The last example in [43], *ready-to-eat*, has a hollow infinitival clause, but it has something of the character of a fixed phrase. We might also find *some easy-to-read children's books* or *hard-to-beat prices*, but not **the ready-to-paint surface* or **a hard-to-clean oven*, etc.

Pre-head NP modifiers not permitted

[44]		
i	a. *They are [a great deal better].*	b. **some [a great deal better] proposals*
ii	a. *She is [three years old].*	b. **a [three years old] child*

Example [ib] may be contrasted with the well-formed *some much better proposals*: the inadmissible *a great deal* is an NP, whereas *much* is a determinative.[8] Similarly, the NP *three years* is permitted in the predicative AdjP, but not in the attributive. Instead we have *a three-year-old child*, with no plural marking on *year*: *three-year-old* is a compound adjective (see Ch. 19, §4.3.3).

Initial *how, as, so, too, this, that* not permitted

[45] i a. *How safe are these cars?* b. **How safe cars are these?*
ii a. *This coffee is too sweet.* b. **I don't like too sweet coffee.*

In NPs determined by the indefinite article, AdjPs of this kind appear in predeterminer position, as in *How safe a car is it?*, but in other kinds of NP this alternative is not available. Note the contrast between [iib] and the well-formed *I don't like excessively sweet coffee.* Instead of **a this long letter* we can have either predeterminer *this long a letter* or postpositive *a letter this long.*[9]

(c) Postpositive AdjPs

AdjPs follow the head in two kinds of NP construction:

[46] i *They want [someone young].* [compound determinative as fused head]
ii *They want [a leader younger than you].* [ordinary noun as head]

In [i] the AdjP follows *someone*, which functions as fused determiner-head (cf. Ch. 5, §9.6); here there is no possibility of the AdjP occurring in attributive modifier position, and there are accordingly no structural constraints on postpositive AdjPs. In [ii] the head is an ordinary noun, so that attributive AdjPs are permitted provided they satisfy the conditions given under (b) above. For NPs that do satisfy those conditions, moreover, the attributive position is generally the default, and in many cases the only possibility:

[47] i a. *They chose [a young leader].* b. **They chose [a leader young].*
ii a. *We saw [a black swan].* b. **We saw [a swan black].*

Postpositive AdjPs without a post-head dependent of their own are generally restricted to the fused-head construction of [46i] or to a restricted set of adjectives, as described in Ch. 5, §14.2.

(d) Predicative AdjPs

With AdjPs in predicative position it is not a matter of certain kinds of dependents being excluded but of their being construed as clause-level modifiers. Compare:

[48] i a. *his often irrational behaviour* b. *His behaviour was often irrational.*
ii a. *a probably futile attempt* b. *The attempt will be probably futile.*

In the [a] examples the underlined adverb is clearly a modifer within the attributive AdjP, whereas in [b] it is more natural to take it as a modifier in clause structure. It does not make any semantic difference, however, and there may well be indeterminacy

[8] An exceptional case where an NP modifier is permitted is seen in *She's a lot better player than me*; here the indefinite article of *a lot* is lost following an indefinite article determining the matrix NP (compare *a player who is a lot better than me*).

[9] Examples are found where *too* + adjective occurs attributively in NPs containing a determiner: *She slid her feet round [the too-warm sheets] in search of a cool place* or *They sat in [the too-perfect living-room created by their mother]*, but such examples are somewhat marginal and are punctuated as compound adjectives.

as to whether a modifier belongs in the structure of the clause or of the AdjP. Since *very* cannot modify verbs, examples like *It is very late* can only have the adverb in the AdjP, and other cases of degree modification can be assumed to have the same analysis.

4 Restricted function for adjectives

The default is for an adjective to be able to function in any of the attributive, postpositive, and predicative functions: *any intelligent person* (attributive), *anyone intelligent* (postpositive), *anyone who is intelligent* (predicative). But there are a number of items that are restricted in function, and many adjectival constructions and meanings of adjectives that are associated with restrictions on function. The major distinction we need to make is between adjectives which – either absolutely or in a given sense – are restricted to attributive function and those which are excluded from it. We refer to these as, respectively, **attributive-only** adjectives and **never-attributive** adjectives. A small subset of the latter occur only postpositively: these are **postpositive-only** adjectives.

4.1 Attributive-only adjectives

Adjectives wholly restricted to attributive function

Adjectives that do not normally occur except as (heads of) attributive modifiers include:[10]

[1]	*damn*	*drunken*	*ersatz*	*erstwhile*	*eventual*	*former*
	frigging	*future*	*latter*	*lone*	*maiden*	*main*
	marine	*mere*	*mock*	*only*	*own*	*premier*
	principal	*putative*	*self-confessed*	*self-same*	*self-styled*	*soi-disant*
	sole	*umpteenth*	*utter*	*veritable*	*very*	*would-be*

Thus we have *that damn noise*, but not **That noise is damn*; *a drunken sailor* but not **a sailor who was drunken*; and so on. Three of these items, *former*, *latter*, and *own* are exceptional among attributive-only adjectives in that they can occur in the fused modifier-head construction: *She chose the former/latter*; *I prefer my own.*

There are also numerous compound adjectives that are attributive-only – adjectives based on gerund-participles or past participles, as in *a fund-raising dinner* or *a Sydney-based engineering company*. Again we do not find **The dinner was fund-raising* (cf. *The dinner was to raise funds for*...) or **The company is Sydney-based* (cf. *The company is based in Sydney*).

Meaning differences between attributive and non-attributive uses

There are numerous cases where an attributive adjective has a meaning that it cannot have in predicative function, or where the semantic relation between the adjective and the head nominal is different from that which it bears to its predicand when it is used predicatively. Compare, for example:

[10] The qualification 'normally' means that they have no established non-attributive use. It excludes nonce-uses, as when one says, in jocular vein, *His ignorance could only be described as utter.*

[2]	ATTRIBUTIVE-ONLY USE	PREDICATIVE USE
i	a. *the late queen* ("recently deceased")	b. *She is late.* ("behind schedule")
ii	a. *my old school* ("former")	b. *He is old.* ("has lived a long time")
iii	a. *a hard worker* ("one who works hard")	b. *The work is hard.* ("difficult")
iv	a. *complete nonsense* ("absolute")	b. *The work is complete.* ("finished")
v	a. *the lawful heir* ("lawfully determined")	b. *It is quite lawful.* ("legal")

Thus *She is late* cannot mean "She recently died", *This school is old* cannot mean "This is the school I (or someone else) formerly attended", and so on.

Potential differences between attributive-only and ordinary attributive adjectives

Ordinary attributive adjectives can be used predicatively with the same sense: we can call these **ascriptive** adjectives since they can occur as complement to the verb *be* in its ascriptive sense (Ch. 4, §5.5.1). Ascriptive attributive adjectives characteristically have the four properties illustrated summarily for *shy* in [3], whereas most attributive-only adjectives lack one or more of them.

[3]		
i	ENTAILMENT	*X is a shy N* entails *X is an N* (e.g. *Tom is a shy man* entails *Tom is a man*).
ii	SUBSET	*A shy N* gives an answer to the question *What kind of an N is X?* (e.g. *A shy man* is an answer to the question *What kind of a man is Tom?*)
iii	MODIFIABILITY	*Shy* can itself be modified (e.g. *a very shy man*).
iv	PRO-FORM	*Shy* can modify the pro-form ***one*** (e.g. *Tom is the shy one*).

(a) The entailment property

If some entity falls within the denotation of a nominal containing an ascriptive adjective, it also falls within the denotation of the nominal formed by omitting that adjective. Most attributive-only adjectives also have this property, but some do not. Compare:

[4] i *Tom is a lone parent* entails *Tom is a parent.*
ii *Tom is the putative father* does not entail *Tom is the father.*

(b) The subset property

The nominal *man* denotes the set of all men, and *shy man* denotes a smaller set included within it. The adjective here is thus semantically restrictive. Ascriptive adjectives are not always used restrictively. For example, *the industrious Chinese* can be interpreted restrictively or non-restrictively. In the former case it denotes just a subset of the Chinese, whereas in the latter it denotes the full set of Chinese, who are said to have the property of being industrious. All ascriptive adjectives have the potential to be used restrictively, however. As for attributive-only adjectives, many also have this property, but there are a good number that do not. Compare:

[5] i *A marine biologist* is an answer to the question *What kind of a biologist is she?*
ii *A mere child* is not an answer to the question *What kind of a child is she?*

We must of course distinguish between a genuine answer and a jocular response. One might say *A mere child* in response to the question in [ii], but it doesn't answer the question. *Mere child* does not denote one subset of children.

(c) Modifiability

Shy accepts modifiers by virtue of being gradable, but non-gradable ascriptive adjectives generally accept modifiers of some kind, as in *strictly alphabetical order* or *a wholly European initiative*, and so on. Some attributive-only adjectives are gradable or otherwise modifiable, but a significant number are not. Compare:

[6]	i	a. *a hard worker*	b. *a very hard worker*
	ii	a. *the late queen*	b. **the very/apparently late queen*

(d) Pro-form

One is a count noun, so this property is relevant only in the case of count NPs. With that limitation, it normally applies with ascriptive adjectives, whereas attributive-only adjectives again give mixed results. Compare:

[7]	i	a. *the main objections*	b. *the main ones*
	ii	a. *an utter disgrace*	b. **an utter one*

Some types of attributive-only adjectives

Attributive-only adjectives are too numerous and semantically heterogeneous to permit a simple and exhaustive classification. Instead we will here illustrate and comment on some of the most important semantic types.

(a) Degree and quantifying attributives

One group has to do with the degree to which the property expressed in the head nominal applies in a given case. *Kim is an absolute genius*, for example, is comparable to *Kim is absolutely brilliant*, where *absolutely* is an adverbial degree modifier of the adjective *brilliant*. In this sense *absolute* cannot be used predicatively: **The genius is absolute*. NPs containing adjectives of this kind are given in:

[8]	i	*a complete fool*	*a definite advantage*	*the extreme end*
		an outright lie	*a perfect stranger*	*a positive joy*
		a pretty mess	*pure nonsense*	*a real help*
		a right idiot	*sheer arrogance*	*total disarray*
		a true heroine	*an utter disgrace*	*the very edge*
	ii	*a blithering idiot*	*a crashing bore*	*a thumping majority*

Those in [i] for the most part indicate maximum degree, and thus have an emphatic effect; *pretty*, however, indicates moderate degree, like the adverb in *pretty messy*. Those in [ii] express high degree, and are again emphatic. They are representative of a set of attributive-only adjectives ending in the suffix ·*ing* belonging to informal style; they tend to combine with only one or two nouns as head (cf. also *raving lunatic*, *gibbering idiot*), though *thumping* and *whopping* have a wider distribution.

The degree adjectives in [8] have the entailment property (an absolute genius is a genius), but mostly lack the other properties in [3]. Thus *absolute genius* is not understood as defining a particular kind of genius; we don't find **a very absolute genius* (though *a very definite advantage* is quite normal); and we can't substitute *one* for the head (**Kim is a genius, in fact an absolute one*). *Precise* (as in *the precise moment*) and *proper (I want a proper job)* bear some resemblance to this group.

In the following, the adjective expresses various other kinds of quantification:

[9]	*her complete works*	*the entire class*	*full agreement*
	further instalments	*a lone parent*	*an occasional truck*
	the odd lizard	*the only escape*	*scant attention*
	a single objection	*the usual place*	*the whole book*

The quantification applies to frequency with *occasional*, *odd*, and *usual* (e.g. *You might see the odd lizard*, "You might see a lizard from time to time", etc.). These quantifying adjectives all have the entailment property but mostly lack the subset property – though *lone parent* can be said to denote a kind of parent (analogously for *only* in the collocation *an only child*). They are heterogeneous with respect to the other properties – compare *a very occasional truck* but not (in the relevant sense) **a very odd lizard*; and *the only ones* but not **her complete ones.*

(b) Temporal and locational attributives

Our next group have to do with the relative time at which the description expressed in the head applies, or with location in space:

[10]	i	*his current girlfriend*	*an erstwhile gangster*	*the eventual outcome*
		his former wife	*future progress*	*a new friend*
		my old school	*the original plan*	*past students*
		the present manager	*the previous attempt*	*its ultimate demise*
	ii	*the lower lip*	*her right eye*	*the southern states*

We can also include in this group the adjectives *former* and *latter* that are used to indicate relative location within the text (e.g. *the former/latter observation*).

Some of these items lack the entailment property: *She's his former wife*, for example, doesn't entail *She's his wife*. They fail the subset test, and again show variation with respect to the other properties. Note, for example, that *old* doesn't accept modification in *my old school* but we can have *a very old friend* ("one who has been a friend for a very long time").[11] For the pro-form test, compare *his current one* and **an erstwhile one.*

(c) Associative attributives

In a large class of attributive adjective constructions, the property expressed by the adjective does not apply literally to the denotation of the head nominal, but rather to some entity associated with it. Some examples are given in [11]:

[11]	*clerical duties*	*criminal law*	*foreign affairs*
	a historical novelist	*a lunar landing*	*a marine biologist*
	a mathematical genius	*a medical journal*	*a medieval scholar*
	a military expert	*a moral dilemma*	*musical analysis*
	a nuclear physicist	*Platonic realism*	*urban policy*

Literally, duties are not clerical, but clerical duties are associated with being a clerk. Criminal law is not itself criminal but is the branch of the law that concerns crime. Similarly, foreign affairs aren't themselves foreign, but concern relations with foreign countries; and so on. Adjectives of this kind have a classifying function similar to that

[11] *New* is attributive-only in certain collocations but not others. *She is new* might be used to say that someone has recently become a student or employee, for example, but not that she has recently become a friend or wife.

commonly realised by nominals: compare *clerical duties* with *office duties*, *a lunar landing* with *a moon landing*, *a mathematical genius* with *a computer genius*, *a military expert* with *a safety expert*.

A good number of the adjectives of this kind are derived from nouns by means of suffixes like ·*al* and ·*ar*. In some cases the head noun may also be morphologically derivative in such a way that two associative links are involved in the interpretation. A nuclear physicist, for example, works in the field of nuclear physics, and nuclear physics is concerned with the nuclei of atoms.

Many of these adjectives can also be used ascriptively, with a different sense or semantic function. Compare, for example, *criminal behaviour* or *a highly moral person*. There may even be ambiguities between the associative and ascriptive uses, as in the case of *a criminal lawyer* (discussed in Ch. 5, §14.1).

Associative attributives all have the entailment property, and also the subset property: their function is to classify, so naturally they define a subset. They mostly lack the other two properties, though some accept such modifiers as *purely* (e.g. *purely clerical duties*).

(d) Process-oriented attributives

[12]	*a big eater*	*a fast worker*	*a firm believer*
	a hard worker	*a heavy smoker*	*a rapid reader*
	a slow learner	*a sound sleeper*	*a strong advocate*

These bear some resemblance to the associative type, since *a big eater*, for example, denotes not someone who is big, but someone who eats a lot. The property expressed by the adjective thus applies not to the denotation of the nominal but to an associated process. It describes the degree or manner of this process, and in most cases there is a paraphrase in which the corresponding adverb modifies the verb: *one who works fast / believes firmly*, etc. These adjectives differ from the associatives, however, in that they are gradable (cf. *a very big eater*), and they do not all naturally pass the subset test. *A big eater* would hardly make a natural answer to the itself unlikely question *What kind of an eater is he?*

(e) Modal attributives

[13]				
	i	*the actual cause*	*an apparent discrepancy*	*a certain winner*
		the likely benefits	*a possible explanation*	*a potential customer*
		the probable result	*the putative father*	*the true course of events*
	ii	*a self-confessed thief*	*the self-styled prince*	*the soi-disant emperor*
	iii	*ersatz champagne*	*a mock trial*	*a would-be novelist*

The adjectives in [i] are clearly modal in meaning and have corresponding adverbs which function as adjunct in related clausal constructions: *that which is actually the cause*, *something which is apparently a discrepancy*, *one who will certainly be a winner*. They thus express a modal qualification to the applicability of the nominal. For this reason, those expressing medium or weak modality (cf. Ch. 3, §9.2.1) fail the entailment test: *He's a potential customer*, for example, does not entail *He's a customer*. The items in [ii–iii] likewise fail this test: a self-styled prince isn't necessarily a prince (in fact there's a strong implicature that he isn't), and even a self-confessed thief may have made a false confession.

They mostly fail the other tests, though a few allow modification (*an absolutely certain winner*) or accept *one* as head (*not a possible flaw but an actual one*).

(f) Particularising attributives

[14] i	*a certain house*	*a particular area*	
ii	*the chief reason*	*the main objection*	*our premier scientists*
	the prime suspect	*the principal factor*	*the ultimate perk*

These adjectives serve to pick out a specific member or group of members of the set denoted by the head. Those in [ii] all indicate a high ranking in importance, and have some affinity with superlatives: we refer to them as **primacy** adjectives.[12]

Particularising attributives pass the entailment test but not the subset one: a certain house is not a kind of house, and so on. They allow the pro-form *one* (cf. *the main one*), but do not normally accept modification.

(g) Expressive attributives

[15] i	*my dear mother*	*her poor father*	*the wretched car*
ii	*a bleeding nitwit*	*the bloody tax inspector*	*a fucking investigation*

These items are all semantically non-restrictive. They pass the entailment test, but fail the other three. Those in [ii] are illustrative of a quite large number of attributive-only **expletives**, items that make no contribution to the propositional meaning of the clause but express the speaker's ill-will, irritation, anger, agitation, or in some cases enthusiastic approval (*You're a bloody genius!*). These expletives vary considerably in expressive strength, with *damn(ed)* at the low end of the scale and regarded as quite mild, *fucking* at the high end, and widely regarded as coarse and offensive.

(h) Hypallage: transferred attributives

[16]	*smoked [a discreet cigarette]*	*a drunken brawl*	*their insane cackle*
	a nude photo of the mayor	*a quiet cup of tea*	*your own stupid fault*

This is another case where the adjective does not apply literally to the head nominal. It wasn't the cigarette that was discreet, but the way it was smoked. Similarly it was the participants in the brawl that were drunk, the people cackling who were (apparently) insane, the mayor who was nude, the tea-drinking event that was quiet, the person at fault who was stupid.

Traditional rhetorical analysis uses the term **transferred epithet** or the word **hypallage** (from the Greek for "exchange") for such cases. There is considerable variation with respect to how well established adjectives are in this usage. *Drunken* is very often used in this way, with a fair range of nouns (*drunken speech/walk/behaviour*, etc.). There are numerous expressions like *insane cackle* (*casual glance, hasty browse, hostile gaze, cold stare, impudent grin*, etc.), but with some at least of these there is no restriction to the attributive construction: *His gaze was openly hostile*; *That grin was impudent*. Nouns denoting representations, such as *photo, picture, statue*, readily take *nude* as a transferred attributive, but few other adjectives are used in this way. (In *a beautiful photo of their baby*, for example, the adjective is interpreted ascriptively – cf. *This photo is beautiful*.)

[12] For many speakers *key* also belongs here, but in AmE it is coming to be used predicatively, as in % *This point is absolutely key*. *Chief* has a minor predicative use in front position in the clause and with an *among(st)* phrase complement: *Chief among them is the issue of cost*.

The expressions *a quiet cup of tea* and *your own stupid fault* are likely to be recognised as familiar or unexceptional, but *a discreet cigarette* is not: it represents a nonce-use, an extension of the established pattern.[13]

Transferred attributives pass the entailment test. Results on the other tests are largely negative, except for the *nude photo* type, though some accept modification (*an outrageously drunken brawl, a very quiet cup of tea*).

4.2 Never-attributive adjectives

We turn now to adjectives which cannot occur in attributive position – again, either absolutely or in a given sense.

Adjectives which can occur predicatively or postpositively, but not attributively

These fall into three groups:

(a) Adjectives formed with the *a·* prefix

One group of very clearly non-attributive adjectives comprises those formed with the prefix *a·* that originates in the Middle English preposition *an* "in, on". We list them (excluding some like *abed* and *afire* that are rather archaic) in [17]:

[17]	*ablaze*	*afloat*	*afoot*	*afraid*	*aghast*	*agleam*
	aglimmer	*aglitter*	*aglow*	*agog*	*ajar*	*akin*
	alight	*alike*	*alive*	*alone*	*amiss*	*askew*
	asleep	*averse*	*awake*	*aware*	*awash*	*awry*

Phrases like *a child who was asleep* do not have attributive paraphrases: **an asleep child* is strongly ungrammatical. Note, however, that expansion by modification or coordination can greatly improve the acceptability of the attributive use: compare **their awake children* and *their still awake children* or **She flashed me an aware glance* with the attested *She flashed me an aware, amused glance. Alert* and (somewhat marginally) *aloof* are permitted in attributive function, though they occur much more readily as predicatives.

(b) Adjectives with complements

Because adjectives with complements cannot in general have attributive function, those adjectives with obligatory complements are normally excluded from this position. A sample of these are given in [18] with an indication of the type of complement they take (a PP headed by the preposition given, or an infinitival clause):

[18]	*able* (INF)	*accustomed* (*to*)	*apt* (INF)	*conscious* (*of*)	*desirous* (*of*)
	devoid (*of*)	*fond* (*of*)	*fraught* (*with*)	*intent* (*on*)	*liable* (INF)

Some license more than one type of complement: *accustomed*, for example, licenses an infinitival as well as a *to* PP; for fuller lists, see §3.1 above and Ch. 14, §8.1. Compare, then, predicative *The minister is desirous of meeting with them* and attributive **the desirous minister*. Again, expansion may improve acceptability, as seen is this attested example of attributive *fond: Gina Verity, . . . , would be seen by any court in the way that I had seen*

[13] The extended use of hypallage for humorous effect is a notable stylistic device of the British author P. G. Wodehouse. Examples from his writings include: *He uncovered the fragrant eggs and I pronged a moody forkful; I balanced a thoughtful lump of sugar on the teaspoon; I fumbled with a fevered foot at the self-starter of the car.*

her at first, as a relaxed, tolerant and fond mother doing her best in difficult circumstances. A number of the items in [18] can occur attributively with a different sense:

		a.	b.
[19]	i	a. *They are able to talk.*	b. *an able worker*
	ii	a. *We are accustomed to hard work.*	b. *his accustomed manner*
	iii	a. *I was conscious of the danger.*	b. *a conscious effort*
	iv	a. *I'm very fond of them.*	b. *fond memories*
	v	a. *It is fraught with danger.*	b. *a rather fraught evening*

Note that [iib] and [ivb] illustrate attributive-only uses of the adjectives.

There are also a number of adjectives such as *embroiled, involved, short* whose complements are optional, but which still cannot occur attributively with the same meaning. Thus there are no attributive counterparts of *I don't want to get embroiled* (sc. in a certain situation), *How many students were involved?, We are still short* (e.g. of chairs).

(c) A small set of other adjectives

[20]	i	*faint*	*ill*	*poorly*	*sick*$_{\text{d}}$ BrE	*unwell*	*well*	
	ii	*bereft*	*content*	*drunk*	*glad*	*present*	*rife*	*sorry*

Those in [20] have to do with medical health or condition. The relevant sense of *faint* is thus that seen in *I feel faint* ("as if I'm about to lose consciousness"). The restriction does not apply to *ill* when it is modified: *They were charged with neglecting their mentally ill daughter.*[14] The subscript on *sick* is mnemonic for 'dynamic': the use of *sick* in *be sick* with the sense "vomit". This is a semantically exceptional adjective in that it is inherently dynamic in meaning. It is distinct from *sick* in its stative sense ("unwell"), which can be used attributively, as in *his very sick mother. Well* is used attributively in the construction *He's not a well man*, but in general it is excluded from attributive use: compare **his well mother.*

Bereft and *rife* have senses in which they take obligatory complements and hence belong under (b) above: *bereft of ideas* and *rife with rumours.* The senses we are concerned with here are illustrated in *She felt bereft and friendless* (e.g. following the loss of a friend) and *Corruption was rife.* Never-attributive *content* is to be distinguished from the ordinary adjective *contented*, and *drunk* from attributive-only *drunken.* The *glad* and *sorry* of *I'm glad/sorry* are to be distinguished from the attributive-only uses in the idioms *glad tidings* and *glad rags*, and such expressions as *a sorry state of affairs.* The relevant sense of *present* is seen in *Only fifteen members were present.* It can in fact be used attributively, but only in the phrase *present company*; in *the present members*, for example, it has the attributive-only sense "current".

Postpositive-only adjectives

A handful of adjectives are restricted to postpositive function:

[21]	i	*restaurants aplenty*	*flowers galore*	*the city proper*
	ii	*Attorney General designate*	*the President elect*	*a Nobel laureate*

Aplenty and *galore* are somewhat dated. *Proper* here means "in the strict sense of the term", and is distinct from the attributive-only sense of *a proper job* and the ascriptive

[14] A distinct (and attributive-only) sense of *ill* is found in the proverb *It's an ill wind that blows nobody any good.*

sense of *His behaviour was not considered proper.* The adjectives in [ii] occur with a very narrow range of heads: *designate* and *elect* with nominals denoting various kinds of roles to which one may be appointed or elected, *laureate* mainly with *Poet* or *Nobel* (*prize*).

4.3 Two intensificatory attributive constructions

We conclude this section by drawing attention to two intensificatory constructions containing adjectives in attributive function:

[22] i *It was a* [*long, long way*]. [intensificatory repetition]
ii *A* [*tiny little bird*] *flew in.* [intensificatory tautology]

We take these to involved stacked modification (Ch. 5, §14.2), so that the immediate constituents of the bracketed nominals are *long* + *long way* and *tiny* + *little bird.*

Intensificatory repetition

The effect of the repetition in [22] is like that of modifying the adjective by *very*: "It was a very long way". It is thus restricted to gradable adjectives: we will not find **I hurt my left, left hand*, and the like. There are usually just two occurrences of the adjective, but there is no grammatical limitation to two, and three or even more may be found, especially in informal style or in expressive telling of anecdotes, as in the attested example *That's become a big, big, big issue at our school.*

By no means every gradable adjective is found in this construction, but many are, frequent and basic adjectives in the language more so than rare or erudite ones. The construction is used more frequently in children's stories and other language addressed to children (*a big, big elephant*; *a naughty, naughty boy*), and thus may have a patronising or jocular tone if over-used, but it is unquestionably established and quite common in serious prose usage addressed to adults, both spoken and written. Among the adjectives that are common in the intensificatory repetition construction are the following:

[23]							
bad	*big*	*bright*	*cold*	*cool*	*cruel*	*deep*	*fine*
good	*great*	*hard*	*heavy*	*high*	*hot*	*huge*	*large*
long	*low*	*nasty*	*real*	*sad*	*short*	*sick*	*small*
smart	*soft*	*tight*	*tiny*	*tough*	*vast*	*wide*	*wild*

However, plenty of other adjectives are also found in the construction, including not only other relatively short high-frequency words (*awful, close, dark, lovely, nice, picky, pretty, strong, stupid, touchy, ugly, weak*) but also longer and less frequent ones, as in these attested examples:

[24] i *In numerous, numerous instances, what he told us has turned out to be true.*
ii *This has become a powerful, powerful weapon for the government.*
iii *The company has faced a series of major, major setbacks.*

The construction should be distinguished from that where a repetition arises in hesitant speech, or as recapitulation: *We have a unique,* [pause] *unique opportunity here.* The recapitulatory nature of the repetition can be rendered explicit by an adverb: *We have a unique, simply unique, opportunity here.* This latter type of repetition is found also with predicative adjectives: *It was gorgeous,* (*absolutely*) *gorgeous.*

Intensificatory repetition is also distinct from the ironic use of repetition, as in *Is this the final final draft?*, which asks whether this is really the last in a series of drafts each of which was supposed to be the last.

Intensificatory tautology

In [22ii], *a tiny little bird*, there is a sequence of two adjectives with identical or nearly identical meanings, interpreted as "a very little bird": we accordingly call this **intensificatory tautology**. It belongs to informal style, and is found with a very narrow range of adjective meanings – normally "very small" or "very big" (e.g. *a huge big box*).

The adjective *great* is not much used for expressing largeness in contemporary English: *It was great*, for example, means "It was extremely good", and likewise *They have a great house* means "They have a wonderful house", not "They have a big house". One of the places where *great* retains its "large" sense, however, is in this intensificatory tautology construction, as in *an enormous great house, a great big hole*, and so on. Some of the attributive-only degree adjectives with the ·*ing* suffix are also found here: *a whopping great hole, a thumping big majority*, and so on.

5 Adverbs: delimitation of the category

5.1 Adverbs as modifiers of heads that are not nouns

We noted at the beginning of this chapter that the words that modify verbs are in general distinct from the words that modify nouns. Compare:

[1]		MODIFIER OF NOUN		MODIFIER OF VERB
	i	a. *old houses*		b. **They endured old.*
	ii	a. **her quite enjoyment of it*		b. *She quite enjoyed it.*
	iii	a. *a remarkable/*remarkably change*		b. *It changed remarkably/*remarkable.*

Old and *remarkable* are adjectives, modifying nouns but not verbs, while *quite* and *remarkably* are adverbs, modifying verbs (or VPs) but not nouns. In a great number of cases, there are morphologically related pairs of adjective and adverb, with the latter derived from the former by suffixation of ·*ly*, as with *remarkable* and *remarkably* in [iii].

This provides the starting point for a definition of adverb: a grammatically distinct category of words whose members are characteristically used to modify verbs but not nouns. Broadly speaking, however, the words that can modify verbs can also modify adjectives and other adverbs – and many can also modify expressions of additional categories other than nouns (or nominals). Compare, for example:

[2]			
	i	a. *They [almost suffocated].*	[verb]
		b. *The article was [almost incomprehensible].*	[adjective]
		c. *She [almost always] gets it right.*	[adverb]
		d. *[Almost all] the candidates failed.*	[determinative]
		e. *They are [almost without equal].*	[PP]
		f. *She read [almost the whole book] in one day.*	[NP]
	ii	a. *He [behaved annoyingly].*	[verb]
		b. *We'd had enough of his [annoyingly unpredictable] behaviour.*	[adjective]
		c. *They are late [annoyingly often].*	[adverb]
		d. *Annoyingly, they hadn't left us any milk.*	[clause]

Almost is amongst the most versatile, occurring not just with verbs, adjectives, and adverbs, as in [ia–c], but also with determinatives, PPs, and NPs. Note that it is necessary to distinguish between nouns and NPs. Adverbs do not occur as attributive modifiers within a nominal, but many can occur as external modifier with an NP as head. *Almost the whole book*, for example, has the NP *the whole book* as head, and may be contrasted with **She congratulated him on his* [*almost* <u>*success*</u>], where it is inadmissibly functioning as modifier of the noun *success*. In [ii] we see *annoyingly* in construction with not only a verb, adjective, and adverb, but also a whole clause.[15]

The most important defining property of adverbs thus needs to be given in the form:

[3] Adverbs characteristically modify verbs and other categories except nouns, especially adjectives and adverbs.

Heterogeneity of the adverb category

The fact that adverbs can modify such a wide range of expressions makes the category somewhat heterogeneous, for by no means all adverbs occur with all of the heads illustrated in [2]. For example, *very* "to a high degree" and *too* in the sense "excessively" modify adjectives and adverbs (and a few PPs), but not verbs or NPs or clauses. Their inability to modify verbs makes them sharply different from prototypical adverbs: compare *I enjoyed it considerably* and **I enjoyed it very*, or *He worries excessively* and **He worries too* (possible only with a quite different sense of *too*). Such adverbs as *moreover* and *nevertheless* modify clauses, but not verbs or predicative adjectives. Adverbs such as *only* and *even* differ from most adverbs by virtue of their ability to occur with a particularly wide range of heads, e.g. a content clause in *I regret* [*only* <u>*that I couldn't do more to help*</u>], a non-idiomatic PP in *They open* [*even* <u>*on Christmas Day*</u>]. To say that a word is an adverb thus gives only a very rough indication of its syntactic distribution. A fuller description needs to include a statement of which categories it can modify.

It is worth emphasising, however, that some degree of unity is brought to the category of adverbs by the fact that all the types of expression that accept adverbs as modifier take some that are derived from adjectives by means of the ·*ly* suffix. For example, the class of connective adverbs containing *moreover* and *nevertheless* also includes de-adjectival *consequently*. Similarly, the class of adverbs which, like *almost* in [2if], modify NPs includes *absolutely*, *possibly*, and numerous other ·*ly* adverbs – cf. *absolutely the best way of handling the situation*.

It is also the case that no ·*ly* adverb modifies nouns. This is the hallmark modifying function from which adverbs are absolutely excluded. (There are words ending in ·*ly* that can modify nouns, as in *a likely story*, *the ugly building*, *my only daughter*, *this lovely party*; but these are adjectives, not adverbs: see Ch. 19, §5.8.)

Reducing the extension of the adverb category

In the practice of traditional grammar (as reflected, for example, in the classification of words in dictionaries), the adverb is a miscellaneous or residual category – the category to which words are assigned if they do not satisfy the more specific criteria for nouns, verbs, adjectives, prepositions, and conjunctions. Nouns function as (head of

[15] *Annoyingly* in [2iid] is prosodically detached from the rest, and hence is a supplement rather than a modifier, but the relations are similar in the case of adverbs. Examples with an adverb integrated into the structure as a modifier of a clause are <u>*Suddenly*</u> *there was a tremendous crash* or <u>*Perhaps*</u> *you made a mistake*.

the) subject or object in clause structure, and (mostly) inflect for number and combine with determiners. Verbs function as head in clause structure and inflect for tense. Adjectives can normally function as attributive modifier in the structure of a nominal, and/or as predicative complement. Traditional prepositions take NP complements. Traditional conjunctions introduce subordinate clauses or coordinates. With fairly small-scale exceptions (including interjections), all other words are assigned to the adverb category.

In the present grammar we have endeavoured to make the adverb a more coherent category. To this end we have significantly reduced its membership in the following ways.

Major change: adverbs and prepositions

The main difference between our analysis and traditional grammar with respect to the adverb category concerns the boundary between adverbs and prepositions. We count as prepositions words that take other kinds of complement than NPs, and we also include in the preposition category some words that occur without any complement. In our analysis, then, the underlined words in [4] are prepositions, not adverbs:

[4] i [<u>According</u> *to Mary,*] *we have no chance of winning.*
ii *The basket is <u>outside</u>.*

We discuss this issue in detail in Ch. 7, §2.4, and here will make only two brief points.

(a) PPs, no less than AdvPs, can function as adjunct in clause structure; the difference is then primarily a matter of their internal structure, and there are no good reasons for restricting PPs to phrases with an NP complement. From this point of view, there is a strong case for taking the head + complement phrase *according to Mary* in [4i] as a PP rather than an AdvP.

(b) *Outside* in [4ii] is complement of the verb *be*, a function that does not admit ·*ly* adverbs; note that in cases where we have an adjective–adverb pair with the latter derived from the former by ·*ly* suffixation, it is the adjective, not the adverb, that appears in this position. *Outside* cannot plausibly be said to be modifying the verb, and there are thus good grounds for removing it and similar words from the adverb category.

Minor changes: pronouns and determinatives

We also exclude the following from the adverb category:

[5] i *yesterday, today, tomorrow, tonight* [pronouns]
ii *the, this, that, all, any, a little,* ***much***, ***little***, *enough* [determinatives]

Traditional grammar takes the items in [5i] to be nouns in examples like [6i] and adverbs in [6ii–iii]:

[6] i *<u>Yesterday</u> was the first day for weeks that it hasn't rained.*
ii *They arrived <u>yesterday</u>.*
iii [*Their behaviour <u>yesterday</u>*] *was quite embarrassing.*

There is, however, no need to distinguish the *yesterday* of [i] and [ii] in terms of category as well as function. There are a considerable number of NPs that can function as adjunct in clause structure – adjunct of temporal location (*They arrived <u>last week</u>*), duration (*They stayed <u>a long time</u>*), frequency (*They tried <u>many times</u>*), manner (*They did it <u>this way</u>*), and so on. *Yesterday* in [ii] thus fits in with this pattern: an adjunct of temporal location realised by an NP with a deictic pronoun as head. As for [iii], *yesterday* is here modifying the noun *behaviour*, which makes it unlike an adverb. Compare, for example, **Their behaviour so badly was quite embarrassing.* To correct this we must replace the noun *behaviour* by a verb (*Their behaving so badly was quite embarrassing*) or the adverb *badly* by an adjective (*Their bad behaviour was quite embarrassing*).

The same general point applies to the items in [5ii], which are traditionally analysed as adjectives in examples like [7i] and adverbs in [7ii]:

[7] i a. *We haven't got [much time].* b. *She wrote [this book].*
ii a. *We didn't [like it much].* b. *She is [this tall].*

Again, we do not need to distinguish in terms of category as well as function, for the dual use applies to a significant proportion of the words that function as basic determiners. Determinatives which in NP structure select plural heads (such as *these, those, we, you, both, several, many, few, a few*) naturally do not occur as modifiers to verbs, adjectives, and adverbs. The same applies to those that select count singulars (*a, each, every, either, neither, another*). But apart from the interrogatives and relatives, virtually all determinatives that can occur in NP structure with a non-count singular head can also function as modifier to verbs and/or adjectives and adverbs: see the account of individual items given in Ch. 5, §7.

5.2 The morphological form of adverbs

Adverbs differ from nouns, verbs, and adjectives in that the great majority of them are morphologically complex: there are relatively few adverbs with simple bases like *as, quite, soon*. For this reason, we survey the morphological form of adverb lexemes in this section, rather than in Ch. 19.

(a) De-adjectival adverbs in ·*ly*

A very high proportion of adverbs are formed from adjectives by suffixation of ·*ly*. Many Adj + ·*ly* forms can be paraphrased as "in an Adj manner/way" (e.g. *careful·ly, hasti·ly*, etc.), or "to an Adj degree" (*extremely, surprisingly*, etc.), but numerous ·*ly* adverbs do not have this kind of meaning, and those that do can generally be used in other senses too, as described in Ch. 8. It must be emphasised, therefore, that there is no simple and regular semantic relation between adjectives and their ·*ly* adverb counterparts. Thus in such pairs as the following the adverb cannot be paraphrased in any uniform way on the basis of the adjective:

[8] i a. *their final performance* b. *They finally left.*
ii a. *the individual members* b. *We must examine them individually.*
iii a. *a real disappointment* b. *I really enjoyed it.*
iv a. *a total failure* b. *She's totally absorbed in her work.*

There are also pairs where the meaning of the adverb is related much less directly to that of the adjective than in [8]: compare *bare* ~ *barely, hard* ~ *hardly, scarce* ~ *scarcely, late* ~ *lately, present* ~ *presently, short* ~ *shortly.*

Adjectives that do not form ·*ly* adverbs

Although a great many adjectives form the base for ·*ly* adverbs, there are also many that do not. Adjectives that do not accept the ·*ly* suffix include the following:

[9]	i	*afraid*	*aghast*	*alive*	*asleep*	*awake*	*awash*
	ii	*inferior*	*junior*	%*major*	*minor*	*senior*	*superior*
	iii	*friendly*	*leisurely*	*lonely*	*poorly*	*silly*	*ugly*
	iv	*hurt*	*improved*	*surrounded*	*unexplained*	*written*	*Paris-based*
	v	*American*	*British*	*Chinese*	*European*	*Iraqi*	*Parisian*
	vi	*blue*	*brown*	*orange*	*purple*	*scarlet*	*yellow*
	vii	*big*	*content*	*drunk*	*fake*	*fat*	*female*
		foreign	*good*	*key*	*little*	*long*	*macho*
		male	*modern*	*nuclear*	*old*	*prime*	*sick*
		small	*sorry*	*tall*	*urban*	*woollen*	*young*

We ignore at this point cases of homonymy between adverb and adjective: see (c) below.

The adjectives in [9i–iv] illustrate morphological constraints: ·*ly* does not attach to adjectives beginning with the prefix *a*· or, in general, ending with the Latin comparative suffix ·*or*, or to adjectives that themselves end in *ly* (whether or not this represents the adjective-forming suffix ·*ly*). Thus there are no adverbs **afraidly*, **inferiorly*, **friendlily*, etc. The '%' annotation on *major* reflects the fact that %*majorly*, "in a major way, to a considerable degree", has recently come to be used by some, predominantly younger, speakers. Likewise most adjectives based on past participles do not form adverbs, though there are some exceptions, such as *tiredly* or *determinedly*.

Semantic constraints are illustrated in [9v–vi]. The ·*ly* suffix does not attach to adjectives derived from place-names, nor in general to those denoting colours. There are, however, a few colour terms that are occasionally found: *blackly*, *whitely*, *greenly*, *redly* (e.g. *The Huntleys' farmhouse rose redly out of the red Herefordshire earth, as if it had, over the centuries, just slowly emerged from it*).

Finally, [9vii] gives a miscellaneous set of other adjectives without adverbial counterparts in ·*ly*. Note that the set includes a number of very common short adjectives denoting size or age. *Good* has a morphologically unrelated adverbial counterpart, *well*. *Content* and *drunk* are to be distinguished from *contented* and *drunken*, which do form ·*ly* adverbs.

Adverbs in ·*ly* derived from non-adjectival bases

[10]	i	*bodily*	*namely*	*partly*	*purposely*	*matter-of-factly*
	ii	*accordingly*	*exceedingly*	*jokingly*	*longingly*	

In [i], ·*ly* attaches to a noun or, in *matter-of-factly*, to a phrase; for *daily*, *hourly*, etc., see (c) below. The bases in ·*ing* in [ii] exist as verbs, but not (or hardly) as adjectives.

(b) Other morphologically complex adverb lexemes

[11]	i	*afresh*	*again*	*aloud*	*anew*	*apace*	
	ii	*almost*	*already*	*also*	*altogether*	*always*	*anyhow*
		anyway	*somehow*	*sometimes*	*somewhat*		

iii	*edgeways*	*lengthways*	*sideways*	*clockwise*	*crabwise*	*crosswise*
	likewise	*otherwise*	*moneywise*	*healthwise*	*plotwise*	*weatherwise*
iv	*forthwith*	*furthermore*	*indeed*	*maybe*	*meantime*	*meanwhile*
	moreover	*nevertheless*	*nonetheless*	*nowadays*	*oftentimes*	*doubtless*
v	*never*	*neither*	*nor*	*once*	*thrice*	*twice*

The prefix *a·* forms adjectives (such as *afraid*), prepositions (*along*), and also adverbs, as in [i]. The adverbs in [ii] are compounds beginning with a determinative base: in none of them is the meaning predictable from the parts. The examples in [iii] end in *·wise* or *·ways*, which sometimes yield alternants, as in *lengthwise* ~ *lengthways*. The last four illustrate a more recent use of *·wise*, with the sense "as regards", which yields numerous nonce-forms, largely restricted to informal style, and more common in AmE than in BrE. There are also nonce-forms compounded with *fashion*, as in *doggy-fashion*. Set [iv] contains a miscellaneous group of compounds, together with the derivative *doubtless*. The first three items in [v] are negative forms, while the last three are morphologically irregular forms based on numerals. We might also include in the present category the underlined expressions in such examples as *It <u>sort of</u> collapsed*, *It looks <u>kind of</u> dangerous*, *He <u>as good as</u> admitted it*. These are best regarded as having been reanalysed as adverbs modifying the following verb or adjective. Note, for example, that *sort of collapsed* is a finite VP in predicate function: the verb *collapsed* must be head of this VP, not complement of *of*. For further examples of reanalysed comparative expressions like *as good as*, see Ch. 13, §4.5.

(c) Adverbs that are homonymous with adjectives

There are a good number of adverbs that are identical in form with adjectives. The overlap is greater in non-standard speech, and within the standard variety there are some adverbs of this kind that are restricted to informal style. Compare:

[12]	ADJECTIVE	ADVERB
i	a. *She's a <u>hard</u> worker.*	b. *She works <u>hard</u>.*
ii	a. *It's a <u>real</u> gem.*	b. *That's <u>real</u> nice of you.*
iii	a. *They make <u>regular</u> payments.*	b. !*They pay the rent <u>regular</u>.*

Hard is one that is stylistically neutral; there is an adverb *hardly*, but its meaning is quite different, and there is no alternation between *hard* and *hardly* in [ib]. The use of *real* in [iib] is very informal: other styles would have *really*. And [iiib] is clearly non-standard, the standard variety requiring the *·ly* form *regularly*. Many examples of this last kind are familiar to speakers of Standard English through popular culture, e.g. song lyrics, as in !*Love me tender*, !*Treat me nice*. It should be noted that this non-standard usage is restricted to cases where the adverb follows the head: we do not find **She tender loved him* and the like.

One further general point to be made is that the distinction between adjective and adverb is not always entirely obvious. Adjectives can occur in predicative function with verbs other than *be*, as in *They sat <u>still</u>* or *We laid them <u>flat</u>*. Thus although we can have both *The moon shone brightly* and *The moon shone bright* these clauses do not have to be assigned the same structure: *bright* in the second is best taken as a predicative adjective (cf. *The moon was bright*), not an adverb.

Pairs where the adverb differs significantly in meaning from the adjective

In a number of cases the adverb differs in meaning from the adjective in varying degrees:

[13]							
	about	*dead*	*even*	*far*	*ill*	*jolly*	*just*
	only	*pretty*	*sometime*	*still*	*straight*	*very*	*well*

The adverb uses are illustrated in:

[14] *About five people were present.* *You're dead right.* *He won't even talk to me.*
This one is far better. *He won't speak ill of her.* *We had a jolly good time.*
It was just big enough. *I've only got two dollars.* *It's pretty dangerous.*
We must get together sometime. *I still love you.* *He went straight to bed.*
You are very kind. *She speaks French well.*

The meaning of *very* in *very kind* is clearly different from that of the adjective in *this very room* or *the very edge of the cliff*, but there is a further adverbial use of *very* whose meaning is quite close to that of the adjective – namely the use where *very* modifies superlatives or comparative *same*, as in *the very best hotel* or *the very same point.*

Pairs where there is little if any difference in meaning

A sample of adjective–adverb pairs of this kind is given in:

[15]						
i	*daily*	*hourly*	*weekly*	*deadly*	*kindly*	*likely*
ii	*downright*	*freelance*	*full-time*	*non-stop*	*off-hand*	*outright*
	overall	*part-time*	*three-fold*	*wholesale*	*worldwide*	
iii	*bleeding*	*bloody*	*damn(ed)*	*fucking*		
iv	*clean*	*clear*	*dear*	*deep*	*direct*	*fine*
	first	*flat*	*free*	*full*	*high*	*last*
	light	*loud*	*low*	*mighty*	*plain*	*right*
	scarce	*sharp*	*slow*	*sure*	*tight*	*wrong*
v	*alike*	*alone*	*early*	*extra*	*fast*	*hard*
	how(ever)	*late*	*long*	*next*	*okay*	*solo*

Those in [15i] contain the suffix ·*ly*, but since it appears on the adjective too it cannot be identified with the suffix that derives adverbs from adjectives. This set includes words whose base denotes a period of time (*a monthly magazine* vs *It is published monthly*). The others are illustrated in *deadly poison* vs *deadly poisonous* and *the likely result* vs *He'll very likely die.*

The items in [15ii] are compounds: *It's a downright lie* vs *It's downright false.* Those in [iii] are representative of expletives which occur as attributive-only adjectives and systematically exclude the ·*ly* suffix, giving *a bloody disgrace* vs *bloody disgraceful.*

The items in [15iv] all have adverb counterparts in ·*ly*, so there are three constructions to consider:

[16]	a.	b.	
i	a. *a deep wound*	b. *the wrong decision*	[adjective]
ii	a. *It cut deep into his flesh.*	b. *He guessed wrong.*	[adverb]
iii	a. *They were deeply distressed.*	b. *He acted wrongly.*	[adverb]

The adverbs with and without the ·*ly* suffix are not freely interchangeable, but differ in a variety of ways, only some of which can be mentioned here. *Firstly* and *lastly* alternate with *first* and *last* as connective adjuncts used in enumeration (*First/Firstly I would like to thank my parents, . . .*), but not normally elsewhere (*It was first / *firstly noticed last week*). Adverbial *scarce* is archaic or literary relative to *scarcely*: *She could scarce/scarcely remember what she'd said.* Adverbial *dear* is largely restricted to modifying such verbs as *cost* and *pay*: compare *It cost us dearly/dear* but *They loved her dearly/ *dear.* Adverbial *direct* is restricted to post-head position and situations of movement or transfer: compare *We went directly/direct to New York*, but *It won't affect us directly/ *direct* and *We live* [*directly/ *direct opposite the park*]. By contrast, *mighty* (more common in AmE than in BrE) occurs as a pre-head modifier of adjectives and adverbs: *mighty impressive*; *mightily* mainly occurs as postmodifier to a verb (*He laboured mightily against the elements*). *Slow* occurs only with verbs of motion, especially *go* and *drive*, and cannot occur in preverbal position: *Don't go so slowly/slow*, but *It improved slowly/*slow* and *They slowly/ *slow moved away.*

There are no forms in ·*ly* for the items in [15v] (leaving aside *nextly*, which has virtually disappeared from use, and the semantically quite distinct *hardly* and *lately*). *How* is not traditionally analysed as an adjective, but that is the appropriate category to assign it to in examples like *How are you?* and *How was the concert?*, where it is in predicative complement function – compare the adjectives in answers to these questions, such as *I am <u>well</u>* and *It was <u>excellent</u>.* Likewise *however*, though as an adverb this also has a distinct use as a connective adjunct.

Adverbial *long*, as in *It won't last long*, has a temporal meaning: "a long time". Its distribution is quite exceptional for an adverb, in that it can head phrases functioning as internal complement to a few verbs such as *take*, *have*, *need*, *spend*, *give*, and *be*:

[17] i a. *Take <u>as long as you like</u>.*
b. *You won't have <u>very long</u> to wait.*
ii a. *<u>How long</u> can you give me?*
b. *I won't be <u>long</u>.*

The underlined phrases are functionally comparable to NPs: compare *Take <u>as much time as you like</u>*; *You won't have <u>more than ten minutes to wait</u>*; *<u>How much time</u> can you give me?*; *I won't be <u>more than ten minutes</u>.* It is nevertheless clear from the dependents of *long* in [17] (*as*, *very*, *how*) that it is an adverb, not a noun. Notice, moreover, that such AdvPs cannot replace temporal NPs in subject function: *<u>A long time</u> / *<u>Long</u> had passed since their last meeting* (except, somewhat marginally, in passives – *How long was spent on the job?*). In post-verbal position, *long* tends to prefer non-affirmative contexts: *She didn't stay long*, but not **She stayed long* – compare pre-verbal (and somewhat formal) *I had long realised that it was dangerous.*

Inflected forms

The overlap between adjective and adverb is somewhat greater with comparatives and superlatives than with the plain form. Compare:

[18] i a. **They are singing loud.* b. *They are singing louder than usual.*
ii a. **Kim was moving slow.* b. *Kim was moving the slowest of them all.*

Note in this connection that the irregular *better* and *best* are forms of both the adjective

good and the adverb ***well***, and *worse* and *worst* of both the adjective ***bad*** and the adverb ***badly***.

Other lexically simple adverb lexemes

Finally, there are a number of adverb lexemes that are morphologically simple but not homonymous with adjectives, though some of them are homonymous with words of other categories. They include the following:

[19]						
	as	*but*	*either*	*else*	*ever*	*least*
	less	*more*	*most*	*no*	*not*	*often*
	perhaps	*please*	*quite*	*rather*	*seldom*	*so*
	some	*soon*	*though*	*thus*	*too*	*way*
	why	*yes*	*yet*			

In examples like *as big as usual* the first *as* is an adverb, while the second (which requires a complement) is a preposition. *But* is an adverb in the construction *We can but hope* ("only"), but more often is a coordinator (*old but alert*) or preposition (*nothing but trouble). Either* is an adverb when functioning as a connective adjunct (*Kim didn't like it either*); elsewhere it is a determinative. For the analysis of *else*, see footnote 5 of Ch. 7. *Least, less, more,* and *most* are adverbs when functioning as markers of analytic comparative constructions but determinatives when they are inflectional forms of ***little*** and ***much*** or ***many*** (see Ch. 13, §4.1.1). *No* is an adverb when it is in construction with a clause, as in *No he isn't* (contrasting with *Yes he is*), but a determinative in *no money*. The determinative analysis carries over to cases like *It's no better than it was* in accordance with the treatment proposed for the items in [5ii] above. *Please* is of course a verb in *This won't please them*, but it has been reanalysed as an adverb in *Please don't tell anyone* or *Wait here a moment, please*, where it is functioning as adjunct. *Some* is an adverb in *They had invited some thirty guests* ("approximately"), but a determinative in *They had invited some friends over*, and again the determinative analysis extends to %*She may be oversimplifying some*, where the meaning is broadly the same. *Though* is an adverb when used in the sense "however" (*It wasn't very successful, though*); elsewhere it is a preposition, usually taking a clausal complement and alternating with *although (He couldn't help us, though he certainly tried*). Finally, *way* is an adverb in *It was way too big*, but a noun, of course, in *Do it this way*.

6 The structure of AdvPs

Adverbs head full phrases (AdvPs) that may, like AdjPs, contain modifiers and/or complements. Overall, however, adverbs occur with dependents less often than adjectives. Only a few license complements, and even modifiers are excluded by a number of those that are not formed by ·*ly* suffixation, such as:

[1]						
	about	*also*	*but*	*either*	*however*	*moreover*
	neither	*nor*	*perhaps*	*please*	*therefore*	*though*

6.1 Complementation

Only adverbs with the ·*ly* suffix license direct complements. Elsewhere, we take the ability to take a complement as an indication that a word belongs to some other category, such as preposition: see Ch. 7, §2.4.

PPs

Direct complements in AdvP structure almost always have the form of PPs. In the following examples, the AdvP is enclosed in brackets, with double underlining marking the head and single underlining the preposition which it licenses:

[2] i *The subsidiary is today operating [almost entirely separately from the rest of the company].*
ii *The duel solves disputes [independently of abstract principles of justice].*
iii *We should make our decision [independently of whether we plan to take immediate action to implement it].*
iv *Purchase of State vehicles is handled [similarly to all State purchases].*
v *Foreign firms in US markets are treated [equally with their US counterparts].*
vi %*There were some people who reacted [differently than you did].*

The complement of the preposition is usually an NP, but it can also be an interrogative content clause in the case of *independently of* and a comparative clause with *differently than*. Other prepositions occurring with *differently* are *from* and *to* (see Ch. 13, §5.4), while *independently* can also take *from*.

This construction is to be distinguished from that where a PP following an adverb is a separate dependent of the verb, as in:

[3] *The two plaintiffs' lawyers also dissented [separately] from most of the major recommendations in the report.*

Here the *from* phrase is a complement of *dissent*, whereas in [2i] it is a complement of *separately* – note that the verb *operate* in [2i] does not license a *from* complement.

The complementation in [2] matches that of the adjectives from which the adverbs are derived. Compare *The subsidiary is [separate from the rest of the company]*; *Neither part is [independent of the other]*; *This condition is [independent of how much experience the candidate has had]*; and so on.

It is only with a few adverbs, however, that the complementation carries over from the adjective in this way. Adverbs licensing the prepositions in [2] are virtually limited to those mentioned, together with the following:

[4] i	*to*:	*analogously*	*comparably*	*identically*	*similarly*
ii	*with*:	*concomitantly*	*concurrently*	*consistently*	*simultaneously*

For PPs

There is, however, one kind of PP complement that is less restricted in its occurrence, namely the *for* PP that occurs in evaluative adjuncts like those in:

[5] i *[Fortunately for me,] my mother was unusually liberal-minded.*
ii *[Luckily for them,] Mr Keswick decided not to call their bluff.*
iii *[Happily for the middle class,] the workers hate pointy-headed intellectuals.*

Note that while the adjectives *fortunate* and *lucky* license PP complements of this kind, *happy* does not. Thus *Happily for him, it failed* is not paralleled by **Its failure was happy for him*; here the adverb takes a complement appropriate to the sense (roughly, "luckily"), and that sense is not really found in the adjective (except in a few odd phrases like *a happy coincidence*). Other adverbs that take complements of this kind include the negative counterparts *unfortunately*, *unluckily*, *unhappily*, and the following:

[6]	*annoyingly*	*comfortingly*	*encouragingly*	*gratifyingly*	*humiliatingly*
	pleasantly	*pleasingly*	*rewardingly*	*satisfyingly*	*thankfully*

The adjective bases denote psychological reactions, judgements, or attitudes of sentient beings to events that concern them, while the *for* phrase complement denotes the experiencer of the emotion or attitude.

Clauses

Although numerous adjectives license clausal complements, there are no cases where this carries over to the adverb. Compare, for example, adjectival *eager to please* and *furious that he had lost* with adverbial **eagerly to please* and **furiously that he had lost.* There are, however, two adverbs, *directly* and *immediately*, that take declarative content clause complements even though the adjectives *direct* and *immediate* do not:

[7] i *He came to see me [directly he got the letter].*
ii *You can watch the programme, but [immediately it's over] you're to go to bed.*

Indirect complements

AdvPs may contain indirect complements: clauses or PPs licensed not by the lexical head of the AdvP, but by a modifier, or by the comparative inflection. The indirect licensing of the complements in the following examples is like that in the AdjPs given in [32] of §3:

[8] i *He didn't read it [as carefully as he should have done].*
ii *She works [harder than he does].*
iii *She spoke [so softly that I couldn't make out what she said].*
iv *He had read the paper [too hurriedly to be able to see its shortcomings].*

As before, single underlining marks the complement, double underlining the licensor.

6.2 **Modification**

Modification within the AdvP is very similar to modification within the AdjP, as described in §3.2, and need be dealt with here only summarily.

Stacked modification vs submodification

This distinction applies to AdvPs in the same way as to AdjPs. Compare:

[9] i *She loses her temper [only very rarely].* [stacked modification]
ii *They had sung [quite remarkably well].* [submodification]

In [i], *very* modifies *rarely* and *only* modifies *very rarely*, whereas in [ii] *quite* modifies *remarkably* and *quite remarkably* modifies *well.* Note, then, that in both examples the underlined expression is an AdvP contained within the larger AdvP that is enclosed in brackets; it functions as head in [i], and modifier in [ii].

Both constructions are be distinguished, of course, from stacked modification within an AdjP. In *This is a [generally highly competitive] market*, for example, *highly* modifies the adjective *competitive*, and *generally* modifies the AdjP *highly competitive*. We have here a sequence of two adverbs, *generally* and *highly*, but they do not form an AdvP (like *quite remarkably* in [9ii]), and are not even contained within a larger AdvP (like *only very* in [9i]).

Categories of modifier

The modifier function is realised by the same range of categories as in AdjPs. Relative clauses occur only with superlatives, as in *She ran [the fastest she had ever run]*. The other categories we review briefly in turn.

AdvPs

Adverbs commonly modify other adverbs, as in [9]. It is possible for an adverb in ·*ly* to modify another adverb of that same form:

[10] i *They are fairly evenly matched.*
ii *He reads surprisingly slowly.*
iii *They had done the job really incredibly meticulously.*

Sequences of ·*ly* adverbs, however, run the risk of sounding stylistically clumsy, and certainly those with more than two will tend to be avoided in monitored prose. Thus an AdvP like *practically totally incomprehensibly*, while perfectly grammatical, is unlikely to occur in edited text.

An adverb modifying another adverb normally indicates degree or is of the focusing type, like *only* in [9i]. Such adverbs thus have a narrower range of semantic functions than those occurring in the structure of AdjPs, especially attributive AdjPs. For example, while we can have *his [occasionally intemperate] remarks*, with the frequency adverb *occasionally* modifying the adjective *intemperate*, there is no AdvP *occasionally intemperately*. If these adverbs occurred in succession (*He spoke occasionally intemperately*) they would be separate modifiers of the verb – and it would be much more natural to put the first before the verb (*He occasionally spoke intemperately*).

Determinatives

The same items occur as in AdjP structure:

[11] i *The bigger it is, [the sooner] it disintegrates.* [*the*]
ii *I hadn't expected to be able to do it [this easily].* [*this*]
iii *I'm afraid we didn't do [all that well].* [*that*]
iv *She can run [much faster than me].* [*much*]
v *They had performed [little better than the previous time].* [*little*]
vi *I had [no sooner] got into bed than the phone rang.* [*no*]
vii *She doesn't seem to have grown [any less] extravagant.* [*any*]
viii *He had answered [a little indiscreetly].* [*a little*]
ix *You didn't express yourself [clearly enough].* [*enough*]
x *They had begun [all enthusiastically].* [*all*]

Note that when modifying *too* the determinative ***no*** appears in the independent form: *It was [none too] successful.*

NPs

[12] i *We arrived [three hours late].*
ii *He works [a great deal harder than he used to].*
iii *Things are moving [a bit slowly].*
iv *She died [later that morning].*

There are far fewer adverbs than adjectives that accept measure phrase modifiers: such modifiers occur with ***early*** and ***late***, and also in phrases headed by ***soon*** (*two hours sooner, a day too soon,* though not **a week soon*). The post-head NP in [iv] has no analogue in AdjP structure; similarly with that in *twice a week* (cf. Ch. 5, §8.4).

PPs

[13] i *They had behaved [badly in the extreme].*
ii *[Later in the day] the situation had improved slightly.*
iii *[Increasingly of late,] one of the latter varieties may dominate, particularly merlot.*

PPs occur less readily as postmodifier in AdvPs than in AdjPs, but they are certainly possible. In [ii] we take *later* as head on the grounds that the phrase can be reduced more readily to *later* than to *in the day* (*?In the day the situation had improved slightly*); this analysis is extended to [12iv], though here *that morning* could stand on its own. The position of the idiomatic PP *of late* in [13iii] – as part of a sequence that would be prosodically detached – suggests that it is construed syntactically as a modifier of *increasingly* rather than as a separate modifier of the verb.

7 The external syntax of AdvPs

AdvPs function almost exclusively as modifiers, or supplements. They occur as complement only to a small handful of verbs and prepositions, as in:

[1] i *You'll have [to word your reply very carefully].*
ii *It is now only occasionally that they travel interstate.*
iii *I didn't hear about it [until recently].*
iv *There's no way they can treat us [except leniently].*

A few verbs such as *word, phrase, treat,* and *behave* take manner phrases that qualify as complements by virtue of being obligatory. AdvPs are also occasionally found as complement of *be* in its specifying sense, as in the cleft clause [ii]. A few AdvPs can also function as complement of a preposition, as in [iii–iv], the latter being a case of 'matrix licensing' (Ch. 7, §5.1). Note also the complement use of phrases headed by *long* illustrated in [17] of §5.

The use of AdvPs as adjuncts (modifiers in clause structure or supplements to a clause) is mainly dealt with in Ch. 8, since the various semantic categories of adjunct we need to distinguish – manner, means, frequency, purpose, condition, etc. – can also be realised by expressions of other categories, primarily PPs. We do take up in the present chapter, however, the issue of the linear position of AdvPs in clause structure, since PPs do not in general show the same range: this is the topic of §7.1. In §7.2 we survey the use of AdvPs as modifiers of adjectives and adverbs. And finally, in §7.3, we examine the use of adverbs as focusing modifiers. For adverbial modifiers in NP structure, see Ch. 5, §§12–13.

7.1 Linear position of AdvPs in clause structure

Front, end, and central positions

We distinguish three main positions for adjuncts, as described in Ch. 8, §20.1. **Front** position is before the subject. **End** position is after the verb, and perhaps some or all of its dependents. **Central** position in clauses headed by a lexical verb is between the subject and the verb; for clauses headed by an auxiliary verb it can again be between subject and verb, but is more often just after the verb (and hence not always clearly distinct from end position). We illustrate in [2], where the adjunct *happily* can be either an evaluation or a manner adjunct:

[2]		SEMANTIC TYPE	POSITION
i	*Happily, they watched TV until dinner.*	evaluation	front
ii	*They happily watched TV until dinner.*	manner	central
iii	*They watched TV happily until dinner.*	manner	end
iv	*They watched TV until dinner happily.*	manner	end

Placement in end position immediately after a lexical verb is possible when no object is present (*They watched happily until dinner*) but impossible in [2]: **They watched happily TV until dinner.* The latter is excluded by the general prohibition against separating a head from an NP functioning as its object (except where heavy complements are postposed) – recall the discussion of **He doesn't like enough the idea* in §2.2).

As noted in Ch. 8, §20.2, an adjunct immediately following a catenative auxiliary verb may belong either in the clause headed by the auxiliary or in the non-finite clause functioning as its complement. Compare:

[3] i *I would frankly [want a lot more money than that for it].* [speech act-related]
ii *I would [frankly explain to him what the position was].* [manner]

Note then the different possibilities in [4] for placement of the modality adjunct *probably*, which belongs in the upper clause, and the manner adjunct *contentedly*, whose basic position is in the *watch* clause:

[4]			
i	a. *Probably they would watch TV for hours.*	modality	front
	b. *They probably would watch TV for hours.*	modality	pre-auxiliary
	c. *They would probably watch TV for hours.*	modality	post-auxiliary
ii	a. ?*Contentedly they would watch TV for hours.*	manner	front
	b. ?*They contentedly would watch TV for hours.*	manner	pre-auxiliary
	c. *They would contentedly watch TV for hours.*	manner	post-auxiliary
	d. *They would watch TV contentedly for hours.*	manner	end
	e. *They would watch TV for hours contentedly.*	manner	end

VP-oriented and clause-oriented AdvP adjuncts

Modality *probably* is oriented towards the clause as a whole rather than more specifically to the VP, whereas it is the other way round with manner *contentedly*. This distinction can be generalised to the other semantic types discussed in Ch. 8, so that we will distinguish, for purposes of setting out the relevant generalisations about AdvP positioning, two significantly different groups of adjunct types:

[5]	VP-ORIENTED ADJUNCTS	
i	MANNER	*She walked unsteadily to the door.*
ii	MEANS OF INSTRUMENT	*Planets can be detected radio-telescopically.*
iii	ACT-RELATED	*They deliberately kept us waiting.*
iv	DEGREE	*The share price has increased enormously.*
v	TEMPORAL LOCATION	*She subsequently left town.*
vi	DURATION	*We were staying in a motel temporarily.*
vii	ASPECTUALITY	*Some of the guests are already here.*
viii	FREQUENCY	*Do you come here often?*
ix	SERIAL ORDER	*The play was next performed in 1901.*
[6]	CLAUSE-ORIENTED ADJUNCTS	
i	DOMAIN	*Politically, the country is always turbulent.*
ii	MODALITY	*This is necessarily rather rare.*
iii	EVALUATION	*Fortunately this did not happen.*
iv	SPEECH ACT-RELATED	*Frankly, I'm just not interested.*
v	CONNECTIVE	*Moreover, he didn't even apologise.*

Only rather broad and approximate flexible generalisations about adjunct placement and sequence can be made. There is a great deal of variation in use, and features of context, style, prosody, and euphony play a role in some decisions. However, a useful rule of thumb can be framed in terms of the distinction between the adjunct types in [5] and those in [6]. The generalisation, in two parts, can be stated thus:

[7] i AdvPs realising VP-oriented adjuncts are more closely associated with the VP constituents, and more likely to be positioned in the VP or adjacent to the VP.

ii AdvPs realising clause-oriented adjuncts are less closely associated with the VP constituents and less likely to be positioned in the VP or adjacent to the VP.

The statement about positioning in [7i] correlates with a semantic observation, namely that VP-oriented adjuncts denote modifications of the details of the predicate of a clause: if the predication corresponds semantically to a type of action, adjuncts of these types tend to specify aspects such as the way in which the action was carried out, the time it took, the degree to which it was carried out, or the order in which it was done relative to other actions.

There is also a semantic observation relevant to [7ii]. Clause-oriented adjuncts represent modifications of the applicability of the clause content. That is, their semantic effect is to characterise how the propositional content of the clause relates to the world or the context: the sphere of discourse within which it holds (domain), the array of possible situations within which it is true (modality), the extent to which its obtaining is a good or a bad thing (evaluation), or the attitude the speaker has towards its obtaining (speech act-related). Clause-oriented adjuncts have meaning contributions that are much more external to the content of the proposition.

Putting the syntactic and semantic observations together, we see that the closeness of the adjuncts in linear proximity to the predicator at the heart of a clause tends to correlate with the closeness of what the adjuncts express to the content of the predication.

Adjunct orientation and linear position

The rough generalisation in [7] can be adapted to yield a more detailed guide to AdvP positioning if we note that front position is furthest from the VP, central position is closer, and end position means being in or adjacent to the VP. Clause-oriented adjuncts often favour front position; VP-oriented adjuncts favour end position. Central position before an auxiliary is a less common alternative to front position; and central position after an auxiliary may be found with either, since it is ambiguous with respect to clause or VP orientation.

It follows from this that if a clause-oriented AdvP and a VP-oriented AdvP are both in central position, they will be in that order, or will acquire a different and perhaps unusual meaning if not in that order:

[8] i a. *They had luckily already left.* b. ?*They had already luckily left.*
ii a. *It probably sometimes fails.* b. ?*It sometimes probably fails.*

The [b] examples are not fully acceptable: [ib] has an aspectuality adjunct before an evaluation adjunct, and [iib] has a frequency adjunct before a modality adjunct; both illustrate clause-oriented adjuncts closer to the verb than VP-oriented ones.

Prosodic detachment and AdvP positioning

Adjuncts in any of the three basic positions may be **prosodically detached**, i.e. set off from the rest of the clause by intonational phrase boundaries. In this case they have the status of supplements, elements that occupy a linear position but are not integrated into the structure of the clause, as modifiers are (see Ch. 15, §5). In writing, supplementary adjuncts are often set off by punctuation, most often commas, but it is important to note that there is a great deal of variation in usage on this point, some authors putting in such commas far more often than others. In the examples below, however, we systematically indicate prosodic detachment and integration respectively by the presence and absence of a comma.

Prosodic detachment is more likely and more appropriate for adjuncts that are out of the positions their semantic type would normally determine for them. Thus, for example, if a means adjunct were ever to be in front position, or if a speech act-related adjunct were placed in end position, prosodic detachment would be demanded:

[9] i a. ?*Statistically, we analysed it.* b. **Statistically we analysed it.*
ii a. ?*Are you a spy, honestly?* b. **Are you a spy honestly?*

The [a] examples in [9], with an intonation break separating the adverb from the rest of the clause, are not fully acceptable; but they are better than the [b] examples, in which they are prosodically integrated into the clause.

It is particularly natural for front position adjuncts to be prosodically detached. With central position adjuncts, prosodic detachment marks the adjuncts as interpolations, and thus indicates that front or end would be their more normal position.

There is a difference between clause-oriented and VP-oriented adjuncts regarding detachment, though in illustrating it we shall mark disfavoured examples with '?' rather than '*' in recognition of the considerable variability found, in both intonation in speech and the use of commas in writing. The relevant generalisations are set out in [10], with examples following.

[10] i VP-ORIENTED ADJUNCTS

a. VP-oriented adjuncts often prefer end position, where prosodic detachment is not normal except to separate the indication of manner from the rest of the clause, perhaps as a kind of afterthought.

b. Central position (after the tensed auxiliary if there is one) is an alternative, especially if this means the adjunct is adjacent to the lexical verb of the VP it is semantically associated with, rather than being separated from it by secondary forms of auxiliaries. Prosodic detachment in this case is not normal, but would signal that the adjunct was an interpolation.

c. Front position is highly unusual for VP-oriented adjuncts, and if used will normally require prosodic detachment.

ii CLAUSE-ORIENTED ADJUNCTS

a. Clause-oriented adjuncts tend to prefer front position, where prosodic detachment is normal.

b. Central position (preferably after the auxiliary if there is one) is an alternative, with prosodic detachment often preferred.

c. End position is strongly disfavoured unless there is prosodic detachment.

[11] VP-ORIENTED ADJUNCT (MANNER)

i	a. ?*Expertly, Chris had repaired it.*	b. ?*Expertly Chris had repaired it.*
ii	a. *Chris, expertly, had repaired it.*	b. ?*Chris expertly had repaired it.*
iii	a. *Chris had, expertly, repaired it.*	b. *Chris had expertly repaired it.*
iv	a. *Chris had repaired it, expertly.*	b. *Chris had repaired it expertly.*

[12] CLAUSE-ORIENTED ADJUNCT (EVALUATION)

i	a. *Luckily, Chris had forgotten it.*	b. *Luckily Chris had forgotten it.*
ii	a. *Chris, luckily, had forgotten it.*	b. ?*Chris luckily had forgotten it.*
iii	a. *Chris had, luckily, forgotten it.*	b. *Chris had luckily forgotten it.*
iv	a. *Chris had forgotten it, luckily.*	b. **Chris had forgotten it luckily.*

Manner adjuncts are generally not placed in front position, as the marks on both examples in [11i] indicate, but, again, in some contexts such sentences will be encountered; in particular, where the manner in which some action is taken is crucial to the context of the action, a manner adjunct might perhaps be found in front position (*Smoothly the boat slid down the ramp into the water*). Similarly, although [11iib] is not a normal positioning of an integrated manner adjunct, it should not be assumed that such sentences will never be encountered. Similar remarks hold for [12iib] (consider *We fortunately hadn't gone very far*, which has the same structure), though [12ivb] seems implausible enough to be marked as ungrammatical.

Survey of semantic types

To indicate in summary form where AdvPs can be positioned with full or partial acceptability, we will exhibit a sequence of words with indicators of acceptability for each of the potentially available positions in which a given adjunct might occur. We will put '✓' where it would be acceptable, '?' where it might occur but would be disfavoured (not fully acceptable), and '*' where it is outright ungrammatical, or else so implausible (because some other reading would be assumed) that we can treat it as ungrammatical. These marks apply to readings in which the adjunct is prosodically integrated, not detached. Thus for *frankly* as a manner adverb combining with *Chris won't talk about it*, we would write [13], which is interpreted as in [14]:

[13] *frankly* MANNER *Chris * won't √ talk √ about it √*

[14] i *Frankly Chris won't talk about it* and *Chris frankly won't talk about it* have no chance of being interpreted with *frankly* as a manner adjunct (both would be interpreted with *frankly* as speech act-related).

ii Any of *Chris won't frankly talk about it*, *Chris won't talk frankly about it*, and *Chris won't talk about it frankly* are fully acceptable with the manner adjunct reading.

We do not put any mark between *about* and *it* since these are not separate dependents in clause structure, and no integrated adjunct could occur here.

We now summarise how the classes of adjuncts listed in [5–6] are typically positioned in clauses.

Manner, means, and instrument

[15] i *erratically* MANNER * *Bill* * *would* √ *stagger* √ *around* √

ii *arithmetically* MEANS * *it* * *was* √ *established* √ *today* √

Adjuncts of manner, means, and instrument must normally be within the VP whose head they modify, in either end position (which is preferred) or central position. Manner adjuncts may sometimes be found preposed (*Erratically he staggered across the room*), but this is not at all common.[16]

Act-related

[16] ACT-RELATED

foolishly (subjective) √ *she* √ *has* √ *gone* * *to the police* *

deliberately (volitional) ? *they* ? *were* √ *delaying* √

Act-related adjuncts of the subjective subtype (*carefully*, *foolishly*, *rudely*, *wisely*, etc.) occur in front or central position: end position is possible only with prosodic detachment. For the volitional subcategory (*deliberately*, *intentionally*, and so on) the preference is for central position, following the auxiliary if there is one; end position is an available alternative.

Degree

[17] i *almost* DEGREE * *I* √ *died* *

ii *thoroughly* DEGREE * *I* √ *agree* * *with you* √

There are significant differences among degree adverbs. Some, such as *almost*, *nearly*, *quite*, normally occur only in central position. Others, such as *thoroughly*, *enormously*, *greatly*, occur in either central or final position. With this second set, end position is the default, and acceptability in central position depends on the verb. Thus *He enormously admires them* is fine, but we cannot have **The price has enormously gone up*.

[16] In earlier centuries manner adjuncts could be preposed with subject–auxiliary inversion: *Gladly would I accept your invitation if I could*; but this is seldom found in Present-day English.

Temporal location, duration, aspectuality, and frequency

[18] i	*earlier*	TEMPORAL LOCATION	√ *she* ? *had* √ *left* ? *for Chicago* √
ii	*temporarily*	DURATION	? *we* ? *are* √ *staying* √ *with mother* √
iii	*already*	ASPECTUALITY	? *our guests* ? *are* √ *here* √
iv	*often*	FREQUENCY	? *he* ? *would* √ *visit her* √

AdvPs expressing temporal location prefer central position; they are also acceptable in front position, and mostly in end position too (though a longer one, such as *subsequently*, would be questionable in end position in [i]). Duration, aspectuality, and frequency adjuncts are similar except that they are less likely to be in front position (but for a use of *already* in front position see example [10ii] in Ch. 8, §8).

Serial order

[19] i	*last*	SERIAL ORDER	* *I* ? *had* √ *eaten* √ *the previous day* *
ii	*next*	SERIAL ORDER	* *'Salome'* ? *was* √ *performed* √ *in 1926* ?

The serial order adverbs *again*, *first*, *last*, and *next* generally resist front position quite strongly, and must precede the temporal adjuncts with which they frequently occur. Front position is not impossible for the word *next* in [ii], but the sentence *Next 'Salome' was performed in 1926* would be interpreted with *next* as a simple temporal location adjunct ("What happened after that was that *'Salome'* was performed in 1926"), not with the reading where *next* has the serial order sense ("The next time *'Salome'* was performed was in 1926").

Domain and modality

[20] i	*politically*	DOMAIN	√ *this* ? *will* ? *become* ? *very unpleasant* √
ii	*probably*	MODALITY	√ *she* √ *will* √ *go* √ *with them* √

Domain adjuncts prefer front position and also accept end position, but in central position normally require prosodic detachment. For modality adjuncts the preferred position is central; they occur readily in front position, and are also found in end position (but often with prosodic detachment).

Evaluation and speech act-related

[21] i	*unfortunately*	EVALUATION	√ *they* ? *had* ? *set out* ? *too late* ?
ii	*frankly*	SPEECH ACT-RELATED	√ *this* ? *is* ? *becoming* ? *a joke* ?

Both of these types of adjunct are most often prosodically detached. When prosodically integrated both can occur in front position, and the evaluation type also centrally.

Connective

In general, connective adjuncts most often occur with prosodic detachment. In this case front position is preferred, but with numerous alternatives. In writing, it is common to find them in immediate post-subject position (as in *The plan, however, had one serious flaw*), but this is markedly more formal, and less common in speech. There are nevertheless some connectives that can be prosodically integrated – like the centrally positioned *nevertheless* in this sentence. *So* is exceptional in being more or less invariably integrated and in front position.

The so-called 'split infinitive'

In infinitival clauses containing the marker *to*, there are two variants of the pre-verbal central position, one in which the adjunct precedes *to*, and one in which it follows:

[22] i *We ask you [not to leave your seats].* [pre-marker]
ii *We ask you [to please remain seated].* [post-marker]

The construction with an adjunct in post-marker position is traditionally called a 'split infinitive'. There has been prescriptive pressure against it for more than a century; in fact it is probably the best-known topic in the whole of the English pedagogical grammatical tradition. Disapproval of the construction leads many writers (and subeditors) to avoid it in favour of pre-marker placement of the adjunct. That is, in written English, sentences like those in [23i] will be found as alternatives to sentences like those in [23ii].

[23] i a. *I want really to humiliate him.* b. *We aim utterly to ignore it.* [pre-marker]
ii a. *I want to really humiliate him.* b. *We aim to utterly ignore it.* [post-marker]

No rational basis for the prescriptive rule

Prescriptive condemnation of the 'split infinitive' did not arise until the second half of the nineteenth century. The construction can be found in the literature of the preceding several hundred years, but it became more popular in English writing as the nineteenth century went on, and the adoption of the rule in prescriptive grammar reflected disapproval of this change. No reason was ever given as to why the construction was supposedly objectionable, however.

It should be noted that the term 'split infinitive' is a misnomer: nothing is being split. In Latin there is an infinitive form of the verb, which is traditionally translated into English by means of *to* + the plain form. Latin *amare*, for example, is translated as *to love*. But while *amare* is a single word, *to love* is not: it is a sequence of two words. Thus the fact that no adjunct can be positioned within *amare* provides no basis for expecting that it should be contrary to grammatical principles to position one between *to* and *love*. Moreover, we will argue in Ch. 14, §1.4.2, that in such a VP as *to love her* the immediate constituents are *to* and *love her*, so that *to love* does not form a syntactic constituent, let alone a word. From a grammatical point of view, therefore, the adjunct in *to genuinely love her* does not split anything.

Avoiding ambiguity

Prescriptive rules and recommendations are often motivated by the wish to achieve clarity of expression, in particular to avoid ambiguity – cf., for example, the discussion of the traditional rule concerning the placement of *only* in §7.3 below. A curious feature of the 'split infinitive' rule, however, is that following it has the potential to reduce clarity, to create ambiguity.

A modifier placed between *to* and a following verb will always be interpreted as modifying that verb, but one located before the *to* can in principle be interpreted as modifying either the following verb or a preceding verb in a matrix clause. Compare first the following unambiguous examples:

[24] i *I urge you [to really immerse yourself in the topic].*
ii *I hope [eventually to have my own business].*
iii *I want desperately [to see him again].*

In [i] *really* belongs in the infinitival clause: it is a matter of your really immersing yourself, not of my really urging you. In [ii] *eventually* will also be interpreted as modifying the infinitival: it is my having my own business that is in the future, for my hoping is in the present. In [iii], by contrast, *desperately* is interpreted as modifying *want*, not *see*: the adjunct here belongs in the matrix clause (where it is in end position, after the lexical verb). Modifiers with the same linear position between a matrix verb and infinitival *to* can thus occupy different positions as far as the constituent structure is concerned.

Compare now:

[25] i *The board voted [to immediately approve building it].*
ii *The board voted immediately to approve building it.*

In [i] *immediately* unambiguously modifies *approve*: the board decided (perhaps after months of debate with opponents) that they would give immediate approval for some building project. This violates the prescriptive rule, however, so one might seek to remedy that by placing the adverb to the left of *to*, as in [ii]. But this is ambiguous, and indeed much the more salient and natural interpretation is the one where *immediately* modifies *voted*: they voted immediately that the proposal should be approved. Note, moreover, that we do not fare any better if we move the adverb to the right instead of to the left:

[26] i *The board voted to approve immediately building it.*
ii *The board voted to approve building it immediately.*

The salient interpretation of [i] has *immediately* modifying *building*. In [ii] the adverb can be interpreted as modifying any of the three verbs, but the one where it modifies *approve* is the least likely of the three. It is clear, then, that for the intended meaning, version [25i] is far superior to any of the others.

Current usage

Placement of a modifier after infinitival *to* is not uncommon in either speech or writing (including works of many of the most prestigious authors). Among the adverbs that particularly lend themselves to placement in this position are those marking degree (such as *really* and *utterly* in [23ii]), *actually*, *even*, *further*, and so on:

[27] i *I hadn't expected her to almost break the record.*
ii *Following this rule has the potential to actually create ambiguities.*
iii *I wouldn't advise you to even consider accepting their offer.*
iv *It's important not to further complicate an already very tense situation.*

Such examples are unquestionably fully acceptable. Note, moreover, that it is not just adverbs that can appear in post-marker position: we also find PPs (e.g. *at least*, *in effect*, *in some measure*) and NPs (e.g. *one day*).

Modern usage manuals are generally aware of the points made above, and present the rule only with the qualification that a 'split infinitive' is acceptable if it improves clarity or avoids awkwardness. Nevertheless, there can be no doubt that in careful or edited writing adjuncts are often consciously placed in pre-marker (or end) position in order to avoid infringing the traditional rule.

7.2 Adverbial modifiers of adjectives and adverbs

In the structure of attributive AdjPs, adverbs (or AdvPs) can be used with virtually any of the semantic functions that they have in clause structure. In the following examples, the labels on the right match the ones used in the account of adjuncts presented in Ch. 8.

[28] i *his [quietly confident] demeanour* [manner]
ii *their [unintentionally humorous] remarks* [act-related]
iii *his [internationally famous] daughter-in-law* [spatial location]
iv *his [recently very aggressive] behaviour* [temporal location]
v *his [permanently sullen] expression* [duration]
vi *an [already quite difficult] situation* [aspectuality]
vii *her [sometimes very harsh] criticisms* [frequency]
viii *his [again totally uncomprehending] response* [serial order]
ix *an [extremely valuable] contribution* [degree]
x *the [consequently inevitable] decline* [reason]
xi *their [nevertheless very valid] objection* [concession]
xii *the [otherwise preferable] course of action* [condition]
xiii *a [philosophically very naive] argument* [domain]
xiv *a [probably unintentional] slight* [modality]
xv *their [fortunately quite rare] misunderstandings* [evaluation]
xvi *this [frankly rather unsavoury] character* [speech act-related]

The degree function, however, is by far the most common, and in AdvPs and predicative AdjPs it is virtually the only possibility apart from that of the focusing adverbs *only*, *even*, etc. Moreover, degree modifiers are found in AdjP and AdvP structure much more frequently than in clause structure, because verbs are less readily gradable than adjectives and adverbs. For these reasons we will focus in the remainder of this section on degree modification, though we will not repeat the semantic classification of degree modifiers presented in Ch. 8, §11.

Degree adverbs in ·*ly*

A great many adverbs function as degree modifiers. The following is a sample of ·*ly* adverbs that can be used in this way:

[29]

absolutely	*amazingly*	*awfully*	*barely*	*completely*	*considerably*
dreadfully	*easily*	*enormously*	*entirely*	*exceedingly*	*excessively*
extensively	*extremely*	*fairly*	*fantastically*	*fully*	*greatly*
hardly	*highly*	*hugely*	*immensely*	*incredibly*	*infinitely*
intensely	*largely*	*moderately*	*nearly*	*noticeably*	*partly*
perfectly	*positively*	*practically*	*profoundly*	*purely*	*really*
reasonably	*relatively*	*remarkably*	*simply*	*slightly*	*strikingly*
strongly	*sufficiently*	*supremely*	*suspiciously*	*terribly*	*totally*
tremendously	*truly*	*unbelievably*	*utterly*	*virtually*	*wonderfully*

For some of these the primary meaning has to do with manner, with the degree meaning secondary. Compare:

[30]	MANNER	DEGREE
i	a. *They behaved dreadfully.*	b. *I'm dreadfully sorry.*
ii	a. *He was acting suspiciously.*	b. *The kids are suspiciously quiet.*
iii	a. *She solved the problem easily.*	b. *She speaks easily the most fluently.*

In [ia] *dreadfully* means "very badly" ("in a dreadful manner"), whereas in [ib] it simply indicates a very high degree ("extremely"). In [iia] *suspiciously* likewise indicates manner ("in a manner that gave rise to suspicion"), while in [iib] it is a matter of the kids being quiet to a degree that caused suspicion. *Suspiciously* does not occur with this extended sense as a modifier of verbs.

As a manner adverb, *easily* means "with ease"; as a degree adverb it occurs mainly with superlatives or expressions indicating sufficiency (*easily loud enough, easily sufficient*). The interpretation is that the degree expressed in the head is achieved by a considerable margin; in [30iiib] she excelled the others in fluency by such a margin, and in *She's easily good enough* she is considerably higher on the relevant scale than the minimum necessary to count as good enough.

Fairly indicates a moderately high degree: *The weather has been fairly good* ("quite, reasonably"). This is very different from the manner sense of *They played fairly*, etc. *Fairly* does not occur in clause structure with the same sense as in AdjPs or AdvPs: it cannot, for example, replace *quite* in *I quite liked it.* It is found in clause structure, however, as a synonym of *positively*, as in *They fairly jumped at the idea.*

Degree adverbs without the ·*ly* suffix

Other adverbs that function as degree modifier include the following:

[31]						
	about	*almost*	*altogether*	*as* –v	*bloody*	*damn* –v
	dead –v	*downright*	*even* –v c	*extra* –v	*far* c	*how*
	however	*indeed*	*jolly* –v	*just*	*least*	*less*
	mighty –v	*more*	*most*	*not*	*outright*	*plain* –v
	pretty –v	*quite*	*rather*	*real* –v	*so*	*somewhat*
	still c	*too* –v	*very* –v	*way* c	*well*	*yet* c

The 'c' subset

The items marked 'c' occur with comparisons of inequality or (in most cases) *too*:

[32] i	*far less useful*	*far too old*	**far old*
ii	*still better*	**still too expensive*	**still expensive*
iii	*way better*	*way too dangerous*	**way dangerous*

The relevant sense of *still* is seen in:

[33] i *I enjoyed the evening but it would have been still better if you had been there.*

ii *Tuesday is possible, but Friday would be better, and Sunday better still.*

In this sense *still, even, yet,* and *again* are equivalent: these are the ones that do not combine with *too. Still too expensive* and *still expensive* are possible as attributive AdjPs with *still* having its aspectual sense.

The '–v' subset

The items in [31] marked '–v' do not occur with the same sense as modifiers of verbs.[17] Their use as modifiers of adjectives is illustrated in:

[34]						
	as tall as Kim	*damn rude*	*dead right*	*even better*	*extra careful*	*jolly good*
	mighty generous	*plain wrong*	*pretty stupid*	*real kind*	*too big*	*very old*

[17] Strictly speaking we should also have marked *more, most, less, least* as –v, since in clause structure they are forms of the determinatives **much** and **little** rather than adverbs. Moreover, *not* (expressing "zero degree") does not belong syntactically with the degree modifiers in clause structure.

But we do not find *I as enjoyed it as Kim, *I damn hated it, *They dead hit the target, etc. In clause structure *as*, *too*, and *very* modify *much* rather than modifying the verb directly: *I enjoyed it as much as Kim*; *You indulge yourself too much*; *I regret it very much*. *Pretty* also combines with *much*, but with the meaning "just about, more or less": *I've pretty much ruined my chances*. In addition, *still* and its synonyms occur in clause structure in combination with *more*, the comparative form of **much**. Compare [33i], for example, with *I enjoyed the party, but I would have enjoyed it still more if you had been there*. *Damn* and *jolly* combine with *well* to form clause-level modifiers with emphatic meaning: *I damn/jolly well hope you're right*.

We have noted that informal *real* alternates with *really*, and it is only the latter form that occurs in clause structure: *I really/*real like him*. *Dead* and *plain* combine with a quite narrow range of adjectives. Compare, for example, *dead bored* and **dead interested* or *plain silly* with **plain bright*. There are others that are even more restricted in their occurrence, largely confined to one or two fixed phrases: *fast asleep*, *wide open*, *wide awake*.[18]

The primary sense of *too* is to indicate a higher degree than the maximum that is consistent with meeting some condition, achieving some purpose, actualising some situation:

[35] i *She was too tired to continue.*
ii *We didn't go out: it was too wet.*

In [i] the degree of tiredness was greater than the maximum consistent with her continuing: the sentence thus entails that she didn't continue. In this sense, *too* licenses an indirect complement with the form of an infinitival clause or a *for* phrase (*too valuable for this kind of use*). This indirect complement indicates the condition, purpose, or potential situation, but does not have to be overtly expressed. In [ii], for example, there is no complement in the *wet* phrase, but we understand "too wet to go out". In informal style, *too* can be used with more or less the sense of *very*, as in *You are too kind* or *That's too bad* ("very unfortunate"). In negative contexts it can be glossed as "particularly": *I wasn't too impressed*; *It wasn't too bad* ("It was tolerable").

Submodification and iteration

It is possible to have non-coordinate sequences of degree adverbs, involving either submodification of one by another or iteration of the same word:

[36]	i	*way more useful*	*almost unbelievably greedy*	*quite amazingly irresponsible*
		just barely alive	*not entirely too eager*	*bloody nearly completely useless*
	ii	*very, very good*	*much, much better*	*far, far more interesting*

The examples in [ii] illustrate the adverbs that iterate most readily, but the construction is not limited to these – cf. *It's quite, quite beautiful* or *You're too, too kind*.

[18] Because there are degree modifiers that combine with adjectives and adverbs but not verbs, some modern grammars assign the items in [29] and [31] to a distinct lexical category called 'intensifier'. This cannot be regarded as an improvement on the traditional analysis, however, for the number of –v items is very small in comparison with the total number of items that can function as degree modifier in the structure of AdjPs and AdvPs: there is no basis for making a primary category distinction here. The term 'intensifier' is also used as a functional term, but again this is no improvement on the traditional 'degree modifier'. A large proportion of degree adverbs indicate a relatively high degree, but there are a good number that do not, and it is semantically inappropriate to apply the term 'intensifier' to the modifiers in phrases like *moderately cool*, *slightly unusual*, *barely noticeable*, etc.: in this book 'intensifier' is used only for those indicating a high degree.

Linear position

Degree modifiers generally precede the head. *Still* and its synomyms, however, optionally follow, as in [33ii]. In addition, the preferred position for *indeed* is after the head (reflecting its transparent resemblance to a PP):

[37] *We are fortunate indeed to live in such a wonderful country.*

This example belongs to quite formal style; elsewhere *indeed* normally modifies a head that contains its own degree modifier, typically *very*, as in *very good indeed.* Post-head position is not possible in an attributive AdjP. Instead, *indeed* is delayed and appears after the head of the NP: *a very good book indeed.*

7.3 Focusing modifiers

We conclude this section with a survey of the kind of modifying function realised by such adverbs as *only* and *also* in:

[38] i *You can [only <u>exit from this lane</u>].*
ii *Jill had [also <u>attended the history seminar</u>].*

In writing, both of these examples are ambiguous, with the interpretations given in:

[39] i a. "The only thing you can do from this lane is exit"
b. "This is the only lane from which you can exit"
ii a. "Those attending the history seminar included Jill as well as others"
b. "The seminars Jill attended included the one on history as well as others"
c. "The things Jill attended included the history seminar as well as others"
d. "The things Jill did included attending the history seminar as well as others"

Thus if the lane is on a motorway, then in [ia] you are prohibited from continuing along the motorway, and in [ib] you are prohibited from exiting from other lanes. A context for [iia] is one where Kim and Pat attended the history seminar: Jill did too. For [iib] it might be that she attended the history seminar as well as the philosophy seminar. For [iic] she may have attended the history seminar as well as some committee meeting. And in [iid] it might be that Jill attended the history seminar as well as giving a lecture on semantics.

The square brackets in [38] enclose the constituents in which *only* and *also* are modifiers, with underlining marking the head. But it follows from the ambiguities that in order to understand the meaning contribution of *only* and *also* it is not sufficient to identify the syntactic head that they modify: one must know which element they apply to semantically. This element is called the **focus** – hence the term **focusing modifier** for this type of modifier. In [38i] the focus is *exit* in the case of interpretation [39ia], and *this lane* (or just *this*) for interpretation [39ib]. Similarly, the focus of [38ii] for the four interpretations given is respectively *Jill, history, the history seminar, attended the history seminar.* Note that the first of these, *Jill,* is not part of the head constituent that *also* syntactically modifies.

Focusing modifiers occur in a wide range of constituent types: all the major phrasal categories, and in some cases whole clauses. They are, moreover, predominantly realised by adverbs. It is for these reasons that we deal with them in the present chapter.

Only has a restrictive meaning, *also* an additive one. These represent the two main kinds of focusing modifier, and we will consider them in turn. But we should first note that neither of them can be made complement of *be* in a cleft clause:

[40] i **It is only that you can exit from this lane.*
ii *It is also that Jill had attended the history seminar.*

Example [i] is ungrammatical, while [ii] is not a cleft clause. It is not a cleft counterpart of *Also, Jill had attended the history seminar.* Thus the complement of *be* here is not *also* but the content clause: compare *It* ("the problem", perhaps) *is that Jill had attended the history seminar.*

7.3.1 Restrictive focusing modifiers

Adverbs that function as focusing modifiers of the restrictive type include the following:

[41]	*alone*	*but*	*exactly*	*exclusively*	*just*	*merely*
	only	*precisely*	*purely*	*simply*	*solely*	

Range of constructions accepting restrictive focusing modifers

It is a characteristic of focusing adverbs that they modify a wide range of constructions:

[42] i	*He loves* [*only* <u>*his work*</u>].	[NP]
ii	*It's the sort of thing that could happen* [*only* <u>*in America*</u>].	[PP]
iii	*The problem is* [*only* <u>*temporary*</u>].	[AdjP]
iv	*He agreed* [*only* <u>*somewhat reluctantly*</u>] *to help us.*	[AdvP]
v	*He apparently* [*only* <u>*works two days a week*</u>].	[VP]
vi	*I regret* [*only* <u>*that I couldn't be there to see it*</u>].	[declarative content clause]
vii	*I need to know* [*only* <u>*how much it will cost*</u>].	[interrogative]
viii	*I remembered* [*only* <u>*what a close shave we'd had*</u>].	[exclamative]
ix	*She forbade* [*only* <u>*his living there*</u>], *not just visiting.*	[gerund-participial]
x	[*Only* <u>*to help you*</u>] *would I have anything to do with him.*	[*to*-infinitival clause]
xi	*Things will* [*only* <u>*get worse*</u>].	[bare infinitival]
xii	*We had it* [*only* <u>*checked once*</u>].	[past-participial]
xiii	*Only* <u>*disturb me if there's a genuine emergency.*</u>	[imperative clause]

They cannot, however, modify any other kind of main clause than an imperative. Compare [42iv], for example, with [43i]:

[43] i A: *What's the matter?* B: **Just there's nothing to do.*
ii A: *What's the matter?* B: *There's just nothing to do.*

B cannot reply to A's question by *just* (or *simply*, *only*, etc.) + main clause. Instead we can place *just* in the VP, as in [ii], or use a construction with *it is* (*It's just that there's nothing to do*). Nor do focusing adverbs modify nouns or nominals (as opposed to NPs): in *my only reservation*, for example, *only* is an adjective, and as such it is not replaceable by the other items in [41].[19]

[19] There are other limitations which apply to the additive type too. For example, they cannot modify a vocative element (**Hey, only* <u>*Pat*</u>*, would you like one of these biscuits*), coordinators (**You can have cheese and biscuits only* <u>*or*</u> *dessert* – i.e. you can't have both), or parts of idioms (**My opponent gave only* <u>*in*</u>).

Interpretation of *only*

The meaning of an elementary and unambiguous example like [44i] can be broken down into the two propositions given as [iia–b]:

[44] i *Only Kim resigned.*
ii a. "Kim resigned"
b. "Nobody except Kim resigned"

Proposition [iia] is a presupposition: it is [iib] that constitutes the foregrounded part of the information, the main assertion. The "except" component of the main proposition is based on the focus – *Kim.*

In some cases the relevant concept is not "except", but "more than". Compare:

[45] i *Sue is only a tutor.*
ii *I saw them only yesterday.*

The natural interpretation of [i] is that Sue is located on the hierarchy of academic positions no higher than the rank of tutor. And for [ii] we understand "as recently as yesterday". There can be ambiguity between the two kinds of interpretation. *I've only got a Mini,* for example, might be understood in context as "I've only got one car, a Mini" or "The car I've got is no grander than a Mini". Example [45ii] is in fact ambiguous in this way, for it could also be interpreted in the "except" sense: "Yesterday was the only time I saw them". And indeed the same applies with [45i]: it could be saying that Sue has only one job.[20]

Negation

We observed that proposition [44iia] is presupposed, and this is reflected in the fact that it is normally preserved under negation, as in:

[46] *Not only Kim resigned.*

This conveys that Kim resigned and that someone else did too. Matters are more complex when *only* has the "not more than" sense. *Sue isn't only a tutor* (ignoring the case where it is denying that she has only one job) would require a context where it has been claimed that Sue was only a tutor, and in this case it would be saying that she isn't a tutor but holds some higher position. *Only yesterday* in the sense "as recently as yesterday" cannot occur within the scope of negation (see Ch. 9, §1.3, for this concept): the natural interpretation of *I didn't see them only yesterday* has the "except" sense of *only,* "Yesterday was not the only time I saw them".

It will be apparent from what was said about [46] that negation relates restrictive *only* and additive *also.* It follows from [46] that there was **also** someone else who resigned. This relationship is reflected in the fact that *also* is often used correlatively with *not only*:

[47] i *He <u>not only</u> apologised, he <u>also</u> sent flowers.*
ii *She'll be working late <u>not only</u> today but <u>also</u> every other day this week.*

Similarly with synonyms of *only* and *also*: primarily *simply, merely, just* on the one hand, *too* on the other (see also Ch. 15, §2.7).

[20] For the interpretation of *only* + *if,* see Ch. 8, §14.2.1.

Scopal focus and informational focus

In speech, the focus of a focusing modifier is commonly marked by stress. But the main stress in a clause certainly does not have to fall at this point. Compare:

[48] i *They only gave me a* SANDWICH *for lunch.*
ii *Only Kim preferred the* ORIGINAL *version.*

In [i] the main stress is on *sandwich*, and this will be interpreted as the focus of *only*: "They didn't give me anything except a sandwich for lunch". In [ii], however, the focus of *only* is *Kim*, but for reasons of contrast the main stress falls on *original*: we understand "No one except Kim preferred the original version – everyone else preferred some later version".

It is a common practice to use the term 'focus' for the constituent carrying the main stress as well as for the constituent that a focusing modifier applies to. This of course stems from the fact that they coincide in the default case. It will be clear from what has just been said, however, that they are distinct concepts, and it is potentially confusing to use the same term for both. We will therefore distinguish them as **scopal focus** and **informational focus** respectively. The latter denotes the constituent carrying the main stress, and represents the principal new information in the clause, or intonation group: see Ch. 16, §2.

Scopal focus is the type we are concerned with in this section. Focusing modifiers are scope-bearing items, and the scopal focus is the contrastive element in their scope. In [48ii], for example, the scope of *only* is the whole clause, since the meaning of the whole clause is affected by it. That is, the restriction to Kim applies to the variable *x* in the open proposition "*x* preferred the original version". The scope is thus the whole clause and the scopal focus is *Kim*.

The scope does not always embrace everything in the sentence. Compare:

[49] *Pat said that only Kim preferred the* ORIGINAL *version.*

Here *Pat said that* is outside the scope of *only*, and this means that neither *Pat* nor *said* could possibly be the scopal focus of *only*. For example, [49] cannot mean that nobody except Pat said that Kim preferred the original version. (For further discussion of the concept of scope, which applies to many elements besides focusing modifiers, see Ch. 8, §1, and Ch. 9, §1.3.) In the rest of this chapter, the term 'focus' when used without modification is to be understood as 'scopal focus'.

Linear position of focusing modifier relative to focus

There are two questions to consider concerning the order of focusing modifier and focus: does the modifier precede the focus, and is it adjacent to the focus? These two parameters yield the following combinations of values, where double underlining marks the modifier and single underlining the focus:

[50]		PRECEDES?	ADJACENT?
i	*We found only one mistake.*	yes	yes
ii	*We only found one mistake.*	yes	no
iii	*Technology alone cannot solve these problems.*	no	yes
iv	*Technology cannot alone solve these problems.*	no	no

Which of these four possibilities are admissible in a given instance depends on the particular focusing adverb concerned. The modifier is also occasionally found following part of the focus and preceding the rest. This is what we have in [43ii], where the focus is the rest of the clause, *There's nothing to do.*

Position of *only*

Only usually precedes its focus. Unlike *just, purely,* and *simply,* however, it can also follow, as in *This is for your eyes only* or *I'm giving these to special friends only.* Such examples seem slightly formal in style, and *only* is relatively unlikely to occur in post-head position within a subject NP: *Kim only went to the movies,* for example, will normally be construed with *only* modifying *went to the movies,* not *Kim.*

When *only* precedes the focus and the latter is contained within the VP, *only* is commonly non-adjacent, functioning syntactically as modifier to the whole VP, as in [50ii]. There is a long-standing prescriptive tradition of condemning this construction and saying that in writing *only* should be placed immediately before its focus. It is recognised that one needs to distinguish here between speech and writing, because in speech the focus will usually be prosodically marked (as noted above, the scopal focus usually coincides with the informational focus). In writing, however, there is generally no analogue of stress, and hence no comparable way of marking the intended focus. For this reason, the prescriptive argument goes, the focus should be marked by placing *only* immediately before it.

This is another of those well-known prescriptive rules that are massively at variance with actual usage, including the usage of the best writers. The more empirically based manuals recognise this, and cite numerous literary examples that violate the rule, such as those in [51], where the focus is marked by underlining:

[51] i *I [only saw Granny <u>at carefully spaced intervals</u>].*
ii *Boris doesn't eat shanks so, of course, I [only cook them <u>when he's away</u>].*

Examples of this kind are clearly impeccable. There is no grammatical rule requiring that *only* be adjacent to its focus. And all that can validly be said from the perspective of style is that the general injunction to avoid potential confusion or misinterpretation should be respected as usual. In the absence of contextual indications to the contrary, *saw* and *Granny* in [i] are not plausible candidates for the status of focus: it is not necessary therefore to place *only* adjacent to the PP to indicate that it is the intended focus. Similarly, in [ii], the context provided by the first clause together with the connective *so* makes it obvious that *when he's away* is the intended focus, and it is therefore quite mistaken to insist that *only* must be placed after *cook them.* Such examples may be contrasted with those in [52], where there is significantly greater potential for misinterpretation, and hence a stronger case for recommending that *only* be placed next to the intended focus:

[52] i *You can only access the web at this workstation.*
ii *Last Christmas he only gave money to his children.*

In [i] either *the web* or *this* might reasonably be taken as focus, yielding an ambiguity between the readings "At this workstation accessing the web is all you can do" and "This is the only workstation at which you can access the web". And in [ii] both *money* and *children* might be plausible candidates for focus: "He didn't give his children anything except or more than money" or "His children were the only ones to whom he gave money". But of course, the issue of whether there is any real danger of misinterpretation will depend on the context in which the sentences are used.

Alone

Association with NPs

The syntax of *alone* is strikingly different from that of other restrictive focusing adverbs. Leaving aside cases where it is non-adjacent to its focus, it occurs only in post-head position in NP structure, with the head of the NP as its focus. Compare:

[53]	i	a. [*Only <u>the president</u>*] *has the key.*	b. [*<u>The president</u> alone*] *has the key.*	[NP]
	ii	a. [*Only <u>reluctantly</u>*] *did he relent.*	b. *[*<u>Reluctantly</u> alone*] *did he relent.*	[AdvP]
	iii	a. *Things can* [*only <u>improve</u>*].	b. **Things can* [*<u>improve</u> alone*].	[VP]

Notice, moreover, that while the default place for the main stress in [ia] is *president*, in [ib] it is *alone*.

Two senses of *alone*: upper bound and lower bound

As a focusing modifer, *alone* has two senses, as illustrated in:

[54] i *Los Angeles alone made a profit on the Olympic Games.*
"Only Los Angeles made a profit on the Olympic Games" [upper bound sense]
ii *Los Angeles alone has more murders than Britain.*
"Los Angeles by itself has more murders than Britain" [lower bound sense]

In [i] *alone* is equivalent to *only*: Los Angeles made a profit, but no other city did. We call this the 'upper bound' sense, since it places an upper bound or limit on the set of cities that made a profit on the Olympic Games – in this case, a limit of one. *Only* cannot substitute for *alone* in the natural interpretation of [ii]: it is not saying that nowhere but Los Angeles has more murders than Britain, but that if you count only those murders that take place in Los Angeles the number will exceed the number of murders committed in Britain. This is the 'lower bound' sense: it's not that you can't go beyond Los Angeles, but that you don't need to, for this city is sufficient to satisfy the condition of having more murders than Britain.

There may be ambiguity between the two senses:

[55] *Musical excellence alone makes the drama memorable.*

In the upper bound sense nothing but musical excellence makes the drama memorable – other features, such as the plot and the dialogue, do not. In the lower bound sense the music is so excellent that it suffices to make the drama memorable irrespective of other features. We have noted that *only* cannot have the lower bound sense, but *just* can, provided it is adjacent to the focus. Compare:

[56] i *They paid her $50,000 for just that one performance.*
ii *They just paid her $50,000 for that one performance.*

Here [i] is ambiguous between upper and lower bound interpretations: "There was only one performance that they paid her $50,000 for" vs "That one performance on its own earned her $50,000". Example [ii] does not permit the latter interpretation, though it does allow for something other than *that one performance* to be focus (e.g. "They paid her only $50,000 for that one performance").

Alone non-adjacent to its focus

When it has the lower bound sense and the subject as its focus, *alone* is sometimes found in post-auxiliary position:

[57] i *This surplus is alone larger than the total sales listed for aircraft.*
ii *New interactive technologies cannot alone solve the problems of education.*

Multiple occurrences of restrictive focusing modifiers

Multiple occurrences are permitted under the conditions illustrated in [58]:

[58] i *Only Kim has only one job.*
ii *And just exactly who do you think you are?*
iii *He sacked her purely and simply because he felt threatened by her.*

In [i] the two occurrences of *only* have different foci; the meaning is "Everyone (in some contextually determined set) except Kim has more than one job". In [ii] *just* modifies *exactly*, but the two adverbs mean effectively the same, so this is a case of intensificatory tautology. This construction is limited to *just* + *exactly* or *precisely*. In [iii] *purely* and *simply* likewise have the same meaning, so here we have coordinative tautology – restricted, among focusing adverbs, to this one fixed phrase.

Partial restrictive focusing modifiers

The restriction expressed by the items listed in [41] is total; it may also be partial, as in:

[59] i *I was concerned mainly about the cost.*
ii *I was mainly concerned about the cost.*

The focus here is *the cost*, or (equivalently) *about the cost*. The sentences do not say (as they would with *only*) that I wasn't concerned with anything except the cost, but rather that I wasn't concerned with anything else to the same extent: any other concerns were relatively minor. Other items of this kind are as follows (the set includes some PPs):

[60]	*chiefly*	*especially*	*mainly*	*mostly*	*notably*
	particularly	*primarily*	*at least*	*for the most part*	*in particular*

7.3.2 Additive focusing modifiers

Focusing modifiers of the additive type include the PP *in addition* and the following:

[61]	*also*	*as well*	*too*	*even*

There are other items that bear some semantic similarity to these but do not have the same syntactic versatility in that they do not occur as modifiers in a wide range of construction types. They include *nor*, *neither*, *either* (discussed in Ch. 9, §1.1, and Ch. 15, §2.4), and various comparative expressions, such as *similarly*, *likewise*, *equally*.

Interpretation of additive *too* compared with restrictive *only*

The contrast between the meaning contributed by additive modifiers and that contributed by restrictive ones may be seen by comparing *too* with *only*, as analysed in [44] above:

		a.	b.
[62]	i	a. *Kim too resigned.*	b. *Only Kim resigned.*
	ii	a. "Kim resigned"	b. "Kim resigned"
	iii	a. "Someone besides Kim resigned"	b. "No one except Kim resigned"

Both [ia] and [ib] entail that Kim resigned: the obvious difference between additive *too* and restrictive *only* is shown in [iii]. But there is also a difference with respect to the status of the component propositions given in [ii–iii]. We saw that with *only* the main assertion is [iiib], with [iib] being backgrounded. With *too*, however, it is [iia] that is the main assertion, and [iiia] that is backgrounded. And in fact [iiia] (unlike [iib]) is not an entailment, not a truth condition, but merely a conventional implicature. The only scenario in which [ia] can be false is one where Kim didn't resign. To see more easily that this is so, consider a situation in the future. You say *Pat will sign the cheque* and I respond *Kim too will sign it.* And suppose that in fact Pat does not sign, and only Kim does so: it is clear that the prediction I made will be judged to have turned out to be true, not false.

Correlating with this is a difference with respect to negation. We have seen that negating [62ib] affects [iiib]: *Not only Kim resigned* says that there was someone else besides Kim who resigned. But we can't negate [ia] so as to cancel [iiia], while leaving [iia] intact. **Not Kim too resigned* is ungrammatical, and *Kim too didn't resign* has *too* outside the scope of negation, so that the two components are "Kim didn't resign" and "Someone besides Kim didn't resign".

Position of *also*, *too*, and *as well*

[63]	i	a. *Sue <u>also</u> bought a CD.*	b. *Sue bought a CD <u>too</u>.*
	ii	a. *We plan to visit Paris <u>also</u>.*	b. *I <u>too</u> think the proposal has merit.*
	iii	a. *<u>Also</u>, it was pouring with rain.*	b. *I realised <u>too</u> that he was in great pain.*

The preferred position for *also* is central, as in [63ia]; auxiliaries tend to precede *also*, as in *Sue had also bought a CD.* End position is certainly possible, as in [iia]. In both [ia] and [iia] *also* can have a variety of foci – e.g. *Sue* or *a CD* or *bought a CD* in [ia], *We* or *Paris* or *to visit Paris* or *plan to visit Paris* in [iia]. In informal style *also* can occur in front position, with the whole clause as focus, as in [iiia].

Too most often occurs at the end of the VP, as in [63ib]. Here it can have the same range of foci as *also* in [ia]; and indeed it can have the whole clause as focus, so that an alternant of [iiia] is *It was pouring with rain too.* A second possibility is for *too* to occur as postmodifier in a non-final NP, as in [iib]. Note, then, that [iib] is structurally different from [ia]: in [ia] *also* is premodifier in the VP, while the *too* of [iib] is part of the subject, and can have only *I* as its focus. Example [iiib] illustrates the fairly rare case where *too* precedes a post-verbal focus. There is no reason here, however, to analyse *too* as a premodifier of the following content clause: it is a modifier of *realised*, the structure being like that of *I realised suddenly that he was in great pain.*

The distribution of the idiomatic AdvP *as well* is similar to that of *too*, the preferred position being at the end of a VP. It can replace *too* in [63iiib], but not so readily in [iib]. In addition, it can, in informal style, occur in front position with the clause as focus, e.g. in the position of *also* in [iiia].

The relation of addition is closely associated with coordination, and *also*, *too*, and *as well* commonly occur in coordinates marked by *and* or *but*: *We saw Kim [and <u>also</u> Pat] at the wedding* or *She was bright [and energetic <u>too</u> / <u>as well</u>].*

Even

Even differs from the other items in [61] in that it contributes an extra component of meaning, and can be negated. Let us consider the positive and negative together:

[64] i a. *Even Kim resigned.* b. *Not even Kim resigned.*
ii a. "Kim resigned" b. "Kim didn't resign"
iii a. "Someone besides Kim resigned" b. "Someone besides Kim didn't resign"
iv a. "Kim was the one least likely or least expected to resign" b. "Kim was the one least likely or least expected not to resign"

Propositions [iia/iiia] are the same as with *too* in [62]: it is for this reason that *even* belongs with the additive modifiers. Moreover, the status of these propositions is the same: [iia] is the main assertion, while [iiia] is a backgrounded conventional implicature. With *too* the information that someone other than Kim resigned will be retrievable from the prior discourse, but this need not be so with *even.*

Because [64iia] is the main assertion it is affected by negation, so in [iib] we have its negative counterpart. And [iiib] is likewise negative: Kim is added to the set of those who didn't resign.

The component of the meaning distinctively associated with *even* is [64iv]. *Even* indicates that the proposition expressed is being compared with one or more related propositions and judged stronger or more surprising. In the case of [64ia] there is implicit reference to a set of people who might have resigned – the members of some committee or society, perhaps – and Kim is judged to be the member of that set who was least likely to resign (or to be among a subset who were least likely to do so).

Consider some other examples:

[65] i *Your task will be difficult, maybe even impossible.*
ii *She can't have voted against the proposal: she didn't even attend the meeting.*
iii *We can't even afford to go to the movies, let alone the theatre.*
iv *He smiled, yet even so I sensed a deep terror within him.*

In [i–iii] both terms in the comparison are overtly expressed. In [i] to say that your task will be impossible is to make a stronger claim than that made by saying that it will be difficult. Example [ii] illustrates a common form of argument, where one negative proposition is presented as following from a second stronger one: the claim that she didn't attend the meeting is stronger than the claim that she didn't vote against the proposal. In [iii] the stronger term in the comparison is presented before the weaker, with the latter introduced by the idiom *let alone* – expressions such as *never mind, not to mention, still less* are used in the same way. In [iv] *even* modifies the pro-form *so*: we understand "even though he smiled". It is more surprising that I should have sensed a deep terror within him when he smiled than if he hadn't done so. (For discussion of *even though* and *even if,* see Ch. 8, §14.1.3.)

Position

Even is typical of focusing adverbs in being able to occur in a wide range of positions:

[66] i *<u>Even</u> you would have enjoyed dancing tonight.*
ii *You would <u>even</u> have enjoyed dancing tonight.*
iii *You would have enjoyed <u>even</u> dancing tonight.*

iv *You would have enjoyed dancing even tonight.*
v *You would have enjoyed dancing tonight, even.*

It usually precedes the head it modifies, but in informal speech it occasionally follows, as in [v]. Where it modifies a VP there will typically be a number of possible foci, with the intended one being marked prosodically in speech. Thus the focus of *even* in [ii] could be *dancing*, *tonight*, or *you* – which are the only possible foci in [iii], [iv], and [i] respectively.

Multiple occurrences

It is possible, though rare, for a clause to contain two instances of *even*:

[67] *Not even digital tape recorders, which everyone is ballyhooing, can even approach the new adapter format.*

7

Prepositions and preposition phrases

GEOFFREY K. PULLUM
RODNEY HUDDLESTON

1 The category of prepositions

This book employs a definition of the category of prepositions that is considerably broader than those used in traditional grammars of English. The purpose of this section is to give an overview of the items that are assigned to the category of prepositions under our analysis.

Traditional definition

The general definition of a preposition in traditional grammar is that it is a word that governs, and normally precedes, a noun or pronoun and which expresses the latter's relation to another word. 'Govern' here indicates that the preposition determines the case of the noun or pronoun (in some languages, certain prepositions govern an accusative, others a dative, and so on). In English, those pronouns that have different (non-genitive) case forms almost invariably appear in the accusative after prepositions, so the issue of case government is of less importance, and many definitions omit it.

In our framework we substitute 'noun phrase' for the traditional 'noun or pronoun'. With that modification, the traditional definition can be illustrated by such examples as the following, where the preposition is underlined.

[1] i *Max sent a photograph <u>of</u> his new house <u>to</u> his parents.*
ii *They are both very keen <u>on</u> golf.*

In [i] the preposition *of* relates the NP *his new house* to the noun *photograph* (we understand that the new house is depicted in the photograph), while *to* relates the NP *his parents* to the verb *send* (we understand his parents to have been the recipients of the photograph). Similarly, in [ii] *on* relates the NP *golf* to the adjective *keen* (the semantic relation is like that between direct object and verb in *They both very much like golf*: the semantic role associated with *golf* is that of stimulus for the emotional feeling).

Prepositions as heads

In this book, in keeping with much work in modern linguistics, we adopt a significantly different conception of prepositions. We take them to be heads of phrases – phrases comparable to those headed by verbs, nouns, adjectives, and adverbs, and containing dependents of many different sorts. This change in conception leads to a considerable increase in the set of words that are assigned to the category of prepositions. Before turning to a description of the full membership of the category, we will explain, by reference to words that are uncontroversially prepositions, why they should be regarded as heads of phrases taking various kinds of dependent.

Modifiers

Note first that some prepositions can take modifiers like those found in other phrases:

[2] i *She died [two years after their divorce].*
ii *She seems [very much in control of things].*
iii *It happened [just inside the penalty area].*

These modifiers, marked with single underlining, are found also in AdjPs (*two years old*), NPs (*very much a leader*), and VPs (*She [just managed to escape]*).

Prepositions followed by constituents that are not NPs

Secondly, it is not only 'nouns or pronouns' (NPs in our terms) that occur after prepositions:

[3]	i	*The magician emerged [from behind the curtain].*	[PP]
	ii	*I didn't know about it [until recently].*	[AdvP]
	iii	*We can't agree [on whether we should call in the police].*	[interrogative clause]
	iv	*They took me [for dead].*	[AdjP]

In [i], one PP (underlined) is embedded inside a larger one (enclosed in brackets). This parallels the way one NP is embedded inside a larger NP in *a house that size*, or one clause is embedded inside another in *That she survived is a miracle.* In [ii], *until* has an AdvP as complement, instead of the NP that it has in examples like *until last week.* In [iii], *on* takes an interrogative clause complement rather than an NP, as in *We can't agree [on a course of action]*. And in [iv], *dead* is an AdjP, which has a predicative function, with *me* as predicand.

It is important to note that different prepositions license different types of complement. *Until* can take an AdvP but not an interrogative clause, while *on* can take an interrogative clause but not an AdvP, and so on. This is entirely parallel to the way verbs, nouns, and adjectives select particular types of complement. And the fact that the AdjP in [3iv] is predicative means that in the structure of the PP, as in that of the VP (or clause), we must make a distinction between objects and predicative complements. Compare:

[4]		OBJECT	PREDICATIVE COMPLEMENT	
	i	a. *She consulted a friend.*	b. *She considered him a friend.*	[clause]
	ii	a. *She bought it [for a friend].*	b. *She took him [for a friend].*	[PP]

Extending the membership of the preposition category

Once it is recognised that prepositions head phrases comparable in structure to those headed by verbs, nouns, adjectives, and adverbs, we need to take a fresh look at what words belong in the category. When we do this, we find there are strong grounds for including a good number of words beyond those that are traditionally recognised as prepositions.

Traditional grammar's subordinating conjunctions

We have noted that prepositions take complements that are not NPs, such as the PP, AdvP, interrogative clause, and AdjP in [3]. This conflicts with the general definition for 'preposition' given in most traditional grammars and dictionaries, though in practice traditional grammarians would have no hesitation in classifying *from, until, on,* and *for* in [3] as prepositions. Traditional grammarians thus tacitly accept that there can be PP, AdvP, or AdjP complements of prepositions. They do not, however, allow declarative content clauses. A word otherwise similar to a preposition but taking a declarative content clause complement is traditionally analysed as a 'subordinating conjunction'. This is not a policy that can be justified. Consider the analogy with verbs that take both NP and declarative content clause complements:

[5]	NP COMPLEMENT	DECLARATIVE COMPLEMENT
i	a. *I remember the accident.*	b. *I remember you promised to help.*
ii	a. *He left [after the accident].*	b. *He left [after you promised to help].*

No one suggests that the difference in the category of the complement between the [a] and [b] examples requires us to assign *remember* to different parts of speech in [i]. It would traditionally be treated as a verb in both cases. There is no reason to handle *after* in [ii] any differently: it can be analysed as a preposition in both cases. Or take the following pairs, where the complement clause is declarative in [a], and interrogative in [b]:

[6]	DECLARATIVE COMPLEMENT	INTERROGATIVE COMPLEMENT
i	a. *I assume he saw her.*	b. *I wonder whether he saw her.*
ii	a. *the fact that he saw her*	b. *the question whether he saw her*
iii	a. *glad that he saw her*	b. *unsure whether he saw her*
iv	a. *He left [after he saw her].*	b. *It depends [on whether he saw her].*

The head words in [i–iii], those with double underlining, belong uncontroversially to the same category in [a] as in [b] (verb, noun, and adjective respectively). We are proposing that the same applies in [iv]. The difference in the type of complement between [a] and [b] in [iv] no more justifies a part-of-speech distinction in the head than the similar difference in [i–iii]. *After* in [iva] and *on* in [ivb] are both appropriately analysed as prepositions.

We therefore include in the preposition category all of the subordinating conjunctions of traditional grammar, with three exceptions. The exceptions are, first, *whether*; second, those occurrences of *if* that are equivalent to *whether* (as in *Ask him if he minds*); and, third, *that* when it introduces a subordinate clause. These items we take to be markers of subordination, not heads of the constructions in which they figure: see Ch. 11, §8.1, for detailed discussion of this issue.

A subset of traditional adverbs

The traditional account does not allow for a preposition without a complement, but within a framework where prepositions function as heads of phrases, like verbs, nouns, adjectives, and adverbs, there is again no principled basis for imposing such a condition. Compare:

[7]	WITH COMPLEMENT	WITHOUT COMPLEMENT
i	a. *She was eating an apple.*	b. *She was eating.*
ii	a. *She's [the director of the company].*	b. *She's [the director].*
iii	a. *I'm [certain it's genuine].*	b. *I'm [certain].*
iv	a. *I haven't seen her [since the war].*	b. *I haven't seen her [since].*

The presence or absence of a complement has no bearing on the classification of the head in [i–iii], where in both the [a] and [b] members of the pair *eating* is a verb, *director* a noun, and *certain* an adjective. There is no reason to treat [iv] any differently, and we accordingly take *since* as a preposition not only in [a], but also in [b], where traditional grammar analyses it as an adverb.

We also include in the preposition category certain words like *downstairs*, which never take complements. We look further at the relation between prepositions and adverbs in §2.4, where we note that moving a subset of traditional adverbs into the preposition category reduces the heterogeneity of the adverb category.

Grammaticised uses of prepositions

A number of the most frequent and central prepositions have what we call **grammaticised** uses:

[8] i *He was interviewed by the police.*
ii *They were mourning the death of their king.*
iii *You look very pleased with yourself.*

Here the preposition has no identifiable meaning independent of the grammatical construction in which it occurs. Example [i] is a passive clause, and *by* marks the element that is subject of the corresponding active, *The police interviewed him. Of their king* in [ii] is complement of the noun *death*, and corresponds to the subject of the clausal construction *Their king died.*

With very minor exceptions, nouns do not take NP as internal complement: instead, the NP is related to the head noun by a preposition. Compare, for example, the clause *They destroyed the city* with the NP *their destruction of the city*, where the NP *the city* is related to the noun *destruction* by means of the grammaticised preposition *of*. Other prepositions than the default *of* are seen in *Kim's marriage to Pat* and *the ban on smoking.* Adjectives behave in very much the same way: compare *proud of her achievements*, *keen on opera* and *very pleased with yourself* (from [8iii]). Many verbs, of course, do take NPs as internal complement, but there are others that take a PP complement introduced by a certain grammaticised preposition: *It depends on the weather*; *I owe everything to her*; and so on.

In their grammaticised uses, prepositions often serve the same kind of functions as inflectional cases. Compare, for example, *the death of their king* and *their king's death*, with *their king* related to the head noun by the preposition *of* and genitive case respectively. Similarly *to* in *I gave it to Kim* marks a role that in many languages is marked by the dative case (cf. Ch. 5, §16.1).

In such uses, prepositions cannot take modifiers like those in [2], and they are virtually restricted to occurrence with NP complements. The traditional definition thus covers these grammaticised uses quite adequately. However, there are a good number of uncontroversial prepositions that have no grammaticised uses: *behind*, *below*, *since*, *underneath*, etc. And the ones that do have such uses have non-grammaticised ones too. The grammaticised uses of *by*, *of*, and *with* in [8], for example, may be contrasted with the non-grammaticised uses seen in *I left the parcel by the back-door*, *That is of little importance*, and *He's with Angela*. An adequate account of prepositions must thus cover much more than the grammaticised uses. The traditional definition is too restrictive to allow this to be done.

Position of the preposition relative to its complement

The traditional definition specifies that prepositions usually precede the NP they govern. Simplified versions often omit the qualification 'usually', but it is indispensable for two reasons. In the first place, a very small number of English prepositions can follow the complement: compare *notwithstanding the weather* (head + complement) and *the weather notwithstanding* (complement + head) – we deal with these items in §4.2. Secondly, we have to allow for cases like *What are you looking at?*, where the complement appears in prenuclear position in the clause and the preposition is said to be **stranded** – this matter is discussed in §4.1. Preposition stranding is restricted to various kinds of non-canonical construction such as open interrogatives, relatives, etc.: in canonical constructions traditional prepositions (with the minor exception of the *notwithstanding* type) always do precede their complements. But so do verbs, adjectives, and adverbs. The location of prepositions before their complements is thus not a distinguishing feature of the category. Moreover, we have argued that not all prepositions have complements, and where they don't the issue of relative position obviously doesn't arise.

It should be clear that the term 'preposition' is by no means ideal for our purposes, for it is etymologically divisible into a base *position* and a prefix *pre·* meaning "before". However, the term is so thoroughly established that we have found it best to retain it despite the shift in sense, and the application to a category of words not defined by linear order at all.

It is helpful that the first syllable of 'preposition' is pronounced /pre/, as in *prep* ("homework"), not /pri/, as in *pre-war*, where the "before" meaning is transparent. *Preposition* thus falls together with such words as *supposition* or *proposition*, in which there is no longer a prefix that makes an independent contribution to the meaning.

There are languages where words of the category in question characteristically follow the NP complement, as in Japanese, and in grammars of such languages they are generally called 'postpositions'. However, in most such languages transitive verbs follow their objects, so again order is not distinctive. Rather, there is a general typological distinction between head + complement and complement + head languages. The term 'postposition' is transparently analysable into a meaningful prefix and a base, and when it is contrasted with 'preposition' the etymological meaning of 'pre·' is revived.

Because position relative to the complement reflects general typological features, one wouldn't want to regard Japanese postpositions as representing a different primary category from English prepositions. For example, the phrase *Tōkyō ni* clearly has a structure parallel to that of its English translation *to Tokyo*. The term 'adposition' is accordingly used by some linguists as a more general term covering both 'postposition' and 'preposition'. This term is not used, however, to form a term for the phrases headed by adpositions. There is no established term 'adposition phrase'.

It has to be recognised, therefore, that the term 'preposition' is ambiguous. In one sense it is neutral as to linear position, and in the other it is restricted to words which precede their complements. In this book we are using it in the former sense, but since we are describing a language where these words do characteristically precede their complements the dual usage should not create any problems. All that is necessary here is that the reader should see that in our sense of the term there is no contradiction in saying that *the weather notwithstanding* is a preposition phrase headed by the preposition *notwithstanding*.

General definition

The number of prepositions is far smaller than the number of nouns, verbs, adjectives, or adverbs, and though new prepositions are added to the language from time to time there is no freely productive morphological process for forming them. We have pointed out that the removal of the traditional requirement that all prepositions take NP complements means that the class is somewhat larger than is often suggested, but in comparison with the others it remains a relatively closed class (i.e. one that does not readily accept the addition of new members).

The most central members have meanings which, at least in origin, have to do with relations in space. The situation may be either static (*Kim is in Boston*) or dynamic (*Kim went to Boston*). The most frequent preposition, *of*, derives from a word meaning "away from". This feature of prepositions, together with their grammaticised uses, provides the basis for a general definition of the category along the following lines:

[9] PREPOSITION: a relatively closed grammatically distinct class of words whose most central members characteristically express spatial relations or serve to mark various syntactic functions and semantic roles.

2 Distinctive properties of prepositions in English

2.1 Overview

The most important properties that distinguish prepositions from lexemes of other categories are as follows:

[9] i COMPLEMENTS The most central prepositions can take NP complements; in addition, non-expandable content clauses are almost wholly restricted to occurrence as complement to a subset of prepositions. More generally, most prepositions license a complement of one kind or another.

ii FUNCTIONS All prepositions can head PPs functioning as non-predicative adjunct; many can also head PPs in complement function.

iii MODIFIERS A subset of prepositions are distinguished by their acceptance of such adverbs as *right* and *straight* as modifiers.

In addition, of course, there are negative properties: prepositions are distinguished from verbs and nouns, for example, in that they don't inflect for tense or number and don't take determiners as dependents.

Complements

(a) NPs

We have seen that traditional grammar in effect defines prepositions as words taking NP complements, and though we have rejected that definition it remains the case that the prototypical PP has the form of a preposition as head and an NP as complement. No adverb takes an NP complement, and only four adjectives do, namely *worth*, *due*, *like*, and *unlike.* With very few exceptions, therefore, the only words that take NP complements are verbs and prepositions, and prepositions are generally easily distinguished from verbs in terms of function and inflection (see §2.3 below). Occurrence with NP complements is thus an important distinguishing property of prepositions, and in general those that take complements of this type are the clearest members of the class: prepositions that do not take NP complements are admitted into the class by virtue of being similar in other respects to these central members.

(b) Non-expandable content clauses

Declarative content clauses are non-expandable if they do not permit the subordinator *that.* Almost all words that license complements of this kind are prepositions, though there are also prepositions that take expandable content clauses, like heads of other categories:

[2] i *We left* [*before the meeting ended*]. [non-expandable]
ii *I'll come with you* [*provided (that) it doesn't rain*]. } [expandable]
iii *I* [*know (that) you've done your best*].

In [i] it is not possible to insert *that* (**We left before that the meeting ended*), and this is sufficient to establish that *before* is a preposition. With *provided,* however, *that* is permitted, as it is with the verb *know* in [iii], and here we therefore need further evidence that it is a preposition. There are also two adverbs, *directly* and *immediately,* that take non-expandable content clause complements: see Ch. 6, §6.1.

(c) Complementation in general

Prepositions allow a wide range of complement types, a rather large subset of those licensed by verbs. Most prepositions license an obligatory or optional complement; those that do not are almost wholly restricted to the spatial domain. As we shall see in §2.4, it is the pattern of complementation that provides the most general criterion for distinguishing prepositions from adverbs.

Functions

(a) Non-predicative adjunct

The ability of PPs to function as an adjunct in clause structure that is not in a predicative relation to the subject is one of the main respects in which prepositions differ from adjectives, as explained in Ch. 6, §2.1. Compare, for example:

[3] i a. *Tired of the ship, the captain saw an island on which to land.* } [AdjP]
b. **Tired of the ship, there was a small island.*
ii a. *Ahead of the ship, the captain saw an island on which to land.* } [PP]
b. *Ahead of the ship, there was a small island.*

In [ia] *tired of the ship* is an AdjP predicated of the subject: it entails that the captain was tired of the ship. The deviance of [ib] is then attributable to the fact that there is no appropriate subject for the AdjP to be predicated of. No such constraint applies to the PP *ahead of the ship* in [ii]: [iia] does not entail that the captain was ahead of the ship, and [iib] is perfectly well-formed.

A number of prepositions have arisen by conversion from adjectives, and it is the ability to occur as head of non-predicative adjuncts that shows such conversion to have taken place:

[4] i [Opposite the church] *there is a path leading down to the lake.*
ii [Contrary to popular belief,] *Eskimos don't have huge numbers of 'snow' words.*

Occurrence as a non-predicative adjunct also distinguishes, for the most part, prepositions from gerund-participle and past participle forms of verbs. Compare:

[5] i [*Owing to my stupid bank,*] *there's no money for the rent.* [preposition]
ii [*Owing money to my stupid bank,*] *I have to live very frugally.* } [verb]
iii *[*Owing money to my stupid bank,*] *there's no money for the rent.* }

Owing can be either a preposition or the gerund-participle of ***owe***. As a preposition it takes a *to* phrase complement and is non-predicative; as a verb, it can take a direct object + *to* complement, but it then needs a predicand, an understood subject, such as *I* in [ii]: "as I owe money to my stupid bank, I must live very frugally". The lack of any such predicand in [iii] makes the example ungrammatical. Example [i], however, is fine: the predicand requirement applies to *owing* as a verb but not as a preposition.

(b) Complement

The ability of many prepositions to head phrases in complement function is an important property distinguishing them from adverbs, which can appear as complements only under extremely restricted conditions. Particularly useful from a diagnostic point of view are cases where the complement is obligatory.

One such case is the goal complement of certain transitive verbs such as *put* or *place* and a few intransitives such as *dart* and *slither*:

[6] i a. *I put it in the drawer.* b. **I put it.*
ii a. *He darted behind the curtain.* b. **He darted.*

The [a] examples here have prototypical PPs consisting of preposition + NP complement. But other forms can be assigned to the PP category on the basis of their ability to occur in this position. Compare:

[7] PREPOSITION ADVERB
i a. *I put it in/downstairs/away.* b. **I put it adjacently.*
ii a. *He darted off/indoors.* b. **He darted immediately.*

Phrases consisting of such words as *in, downstairs, away, off, indoors* by themselves are distributionally like uncontroversial PPs such as *in the drawer* or *behind the curtain*, and are accordingly assigned to the same category. Prototypical adverbs, those formed from adjectives by suffixation of ·*ly*, do not occur in these positions.

A second case of an obligatory complement is in clauses with the verb *be* as head:

[8] i a. *Jill is in the office.* b. **Jill is.*
ii a. *The proposal is without merit.* b. **The proposal is.*

The [b] examples are admissible if elliptical, with a complement recoverable from the preceding text (*Max isn't in the office, but Jill is* __), but otherwise *be* normally requires an internal complement. Leaving aside the specifying use of *be*, which allows complements of just about any category (cf. Ch. 4, §5.5), adverbs cannot in general function as complement to *be*. Where we have morphologically related adjective–adverb pairs it is the adjective that is required in this function: *Jill is sad*, not **Jill is sadly*. The fact that the underlined words in [7ia/iia] can occur as complement to *be* is thus further support for their classification as prepositions: compare *Jill is in/downstairs/*locally.*

Modifiers

There are a small number of adverbs such as *right* and *straight* which occur with a certain sense as modifiers of prepositions but not (in Standard English) of verbs, adjectives or adverbs:

[9]	i	*They pushed it [right under the bed].*	[preposition]
	ii	**They were [right enjoying themselves].*	[verb]
	iii	**I believe the employees to be [right trustworthy].*	[adjective]
	iv	**The project was carried through [right successfully].*	[adverb]

Not all prepositions accept these modifiers – they occur primarily with prepositions indicating spatial or temporal relations. But they are not restricted to phrases containing preposition + NP:

[10] i *They pushed it [right in/inside].*
ii *She ran [straight upstairs].*

The occurrence of such highly restricted modifiers with words like *in*, *inside*, and *upstairs* as well as in uncontroversial PPs thus provides further evidence for recognising PPs without complements.

2.2 Prepositions vs adjectives

Central members of the preposition category such as *of*, *to*, *in* differ syntactically in numerous ways from central members of the adjective category such as *good*, *big*, *new*. At the periphery, however, we have to recognise some items which belong to both categories, and some cases of adjectives and prepositions that are exceptional by virtue of having properties that are normally restricted to the other category.

The properties most relevant to distinguishing between prepositions and adjectives are as follows:

[11] i Prepositions but not adjectives can occur as head of a non-predicative adjunct in clause structure.
ii AdjPs, other than those restricted to attributive or postpositive function, can mostly occur as complement to *become*; in general, PPs cannot.
iii Central adjectives accept *very* and *too* as degree modifiers, and have inflectional or analytic comparatives and superlatives; in general, prepositions do not.
iv Central prepositions license NP complements; in general, adjectives do not.
v Central prepositions accept *right* and *straight* as modifiers; adjectives do not.
vi Prepositions taking NP complements can normally be fronted along with their complement in relative and interrogative constructions, as in *the knife [with which she cut it]* or *I don't know [to whom you are referring]*; in general, adjectives cannot.

Property [i] was presented in §2.1 above and provides the most decisive criterion for distinguishing between prepositions and adjectives.

In this section we consider the analysis of a number of problem items, and some cases of overlap between the categories.

Worth

Worth belongs to the categories of noun and adjective. The noun use (as in *You should make an estimate of your net worth*) is unproblematic and need not be considered further. As an adjective, however, *worth* is highly exceptional. Most importantly for present purposes, it licenses an NP complement, as in *The paintings are* [*worth thousands of dollars*]. In this respect, it is like a preposition, but overall the case for analysing it as an adjective is strong.

Functional properties

It is the more specific properties associated with predicative function that establish that *worth* belongs to the adjective category. It readily occurs as complement to *become*, and when functioning as adjunct it must have a predicand:

[12] i *What might have been a $200 first edition suddenly became* [*worth perhaps 10 times that amount*].

ii [*Worth over a million dollars,*] *the jewels were kept under surveillance by a veritable army of security guards.*

iii *[*Worth over a million dollars,*] *there'll be ample opportunity for a lavish lifestyle.*

In [ii] the predicand of the *worth* AdjP is the subject *the jewels*, whereas in [iii] there is no such predicand and the result is inadmissible.

Grading and modification

Worth is hardly gradable, so there is little evidence in this area to count for or against its classification as an adjective. An analytic comparative seems just possible: *It was more worth the effort than I'd expected it to be.* This construction is not incompatible with a preposition analysis, though it occurs with prepositions in idiomatic or secondary senses rather than in their primary sense, and this is clearly not an idiomatic or secondary sense of *worth. Very* is excluded: **It was very worth the effort.* Instead we can have *very much*: *It was very much worth the effort.* But the sense here is "decidedly" rather than "to a high degree", and in this sense *very much* is quite admissible with adjectives – cf. *The ship was very much unique in its class.*

Enough provides no useful diagnostic evidence in favour of either analysis, for it cannot normally combine with *worth* in any position: **The proposal didn't seem enough worth the sacrifices it would require for us to accept it* or **It didn't seem worth the sacrifices enough for us to go through with it.* Nor do the adverbs *straight* and *right* provide evidence in favour of one analysis over the other. They do not occur with *worth*, but since they are incompatible with many prepositions as well as with adjectives no weight can be attached to this. Overall, then, there is nothing in the area of grading and modification that is inconsistent with the analysis of *worth* as an adjective or that would favour its analysis as a preposition.

Fronting with complement in relatives, etc.

Worth differs from prepositions with respect to property [11vi]. Compare:

[13] i *This was far less than the amount* [*which she thought the land was now worth*].

ii **This was far less than the amount* [*worth which she thought the land was now*].

Here the complement of *worth* is relativised as *which*: in [i] *which* alone is fronted, whereas in [ii] *worth* is fronted with it, resulting in sharp ungrammaticality.

We conclude that although *worth* differs markedly from central members of the adjective category, the evidence shows that that is the category to which it belongs.

Like and *unlike*

These items belong to both adjective and preposition categories. One quite restricted use of the adjectives is as attributive modifier, as in *Like poles repel, unlike poles attract,* "poles which are like/unlike each other". For the rest, the adjective and preposition uses are as illustrated in:

[14] i *John is* [(*very*) <u>*like*</u> *his father*]. } [adjective]
ii *John is becoming* [*more* <u>*like*</u> *his father*] *every day.* }
iii [<u>*Like*</u> *his father,*] *John had been called to give evidence.* } [preposition]
iv [*Just* <u>*like*</u> *in the summer,*] *there is dust all over the house.* }

The adjective occurs in predicative complement function, with *be like* meaning "resemble". It accepts modification by *very* and analytic comparison, though it is also possible to have *John is very much like his father.* The preposition *like* occurs as head of an adjunct. While the adjective is related to a predicand, the preposition is not. This is evident in [iv], but even in [iii] the adjunct is not interpreted predicatively: we understand the clause as saying that John had been called to give evidence, just as his father had, rather than as saying that John was like his father. The fact that both had been called to give evidence doesn't establish that they were alike: [iii] does not entail *John was like his father.* Moreover, in its prepositional use, *like* is not gradable: we could not insert *very* in [iii].

There are thus good grounds for distinguishing between an adjective and a preposition *like* – but the adjective, no less than the preposition, can take an NP complement. And the same applies to *unlike.*[1]

Due

Due also belongs to both adjective and preposition categories. It is straightforwardly an adjective when used as an attributive modifier (*the due sum, with due diligence, pay them due respect*), and when used predicatively with either no complement (*The rent is now due*) or an infinitival complement (*We are due to arrive in less than an hour*). The adjective also licenses an NP or *to* phrase complement, while *due* as a preposition takes an obligatory *to* phrase:

[15] i *We are* [*due* <u>*a refund of about fifty dollars*</u>]. [adj + NP comp]
ii *Sincere thanks are* [*due* <u>*to all those who gave so generously*</u>]. [adj + PP comp]
iii [*Due* <u>*to the rain,*</u>] *the match was cancelled.* [prep + PP comp]

Due does not take any relevant kind of modification, and the classification of these examples is based on the predicand test: *due* requires a predicand when it has the senses illustrated in [i–ii], but not when understood as in [iii]. The status of *due* as an adjective

[1] *Like* can also take a clause as complement. In the case of the adjective, this is a comparative clause: *He was like* <u>*he always is*</u> *– sullen and unco-operative.* In the case of the preposition, it is a non-expandable content clause: *It looks like* <u>*we're going to have some rain*</u>.

in [i–ii] seems clear, and example [i] thus confirms that there are exceptional adjectives taking an NP as complement: note in fact that it is the adjective, not the preposition, that licenses this form of complement.

The construction illustrated in [15iii] has been subject to a great deal of prescriptive criticism: it is commonly claimed that this usage is incorrect, that *due to* in such cases should be replaced by *owing to* or *because of*. The prepositional usage is, however, unquestionably well established, and this is recognised by the more empirically-based manuals. The sense of *due* in [15iii] is the same as that in:

[16] *The delay was due to a signal failure.*

Historically, this *due* is an adjective – and the prescriptive objection to [15iii] is in effect that *due* there is not admissible because, being an adjective, it requires a predicand. Given, however, that *due* is now established as a preposition, there is no reason why that analysis should not apply to [16] as well as to [15iii], i.e. to all occurrences of *due* in this causal sense, for PPs are not in general excluded from functioning as complement to *be*.

Near, close, far

These lexemes too belong to both categories, though the prepositional uses are much more common than the adjectival. All three occur as attributive adjectives, in examples like *a near relative, close friends, the far side of the building*. The comparative form *further* also belongs to the adjective category when it has the sense "additional": *There are some further issues to be discussed*. The adjective *close* is used predicatively in examples like *The election result is going to be very close* (cf. *a closely fought election*) or *Kim and Pat are getting very close* (in the sense of *close friends*). But for the most part, non-attributive uses involve the prepositions.

Consider first ***near***:

[17] i *We should put it* [*near*/*nearer the pool*].
ii *This place is a dead end, but* [*near*/*nearer the city*] *there's plenty going on.*

Near has a locative meaning and the phrases it heads are distributionally like uncontroversial locative PPs such as *in the pool* or *beyond the city*. Most importantly, examples like [ii] show that ***near*** fails the predicand test for adjectives. ***Near*** can also be fronted along with its complement, as in *the tree near which we had parked*. It accepts *right* as modifier: *We found it right near the house*. In general, it does not occur as complement to *become*: **The water had become near the house*; acceptability is greater, however, when ***near*** has no complement: ?*The storm was becoming nearer*. With respect to grading, on the other hand, ***near*** behaves like an adjective. It inflects for grade (hence our use here of the bold face representation), and it accepts modification by *very* and *too*: *You have put it very*/*too near the pool*. It is thus highly exceptional in its syntax, combining a number of adjectival properties with those of the preposition.

The same applies with ***close*** and ***far***, except that they do not license an NP complement. Thus while ***near*** takes as complement either an NP, as above, or a *to* phrase (*near*/*nearer to the pool*), ***close*** takes only a *to* phrase and ***far*** only a *from* phrase.[2]

[2] The complement of *from* can be a gerund-participial: *Far from advancing our cause, this made things much more difficult for us*. Unlike the others, *far* can also be a degree adverb, as in *It was far better than last year*.

The following examples show that ***close*** and ***far*** fail the adjective test of requiring a predicand:

[18] i *[Closer to election day,] the audience is much larger.*
ii *[Not very far from their house] the road deteriorates into a dirt track.*

Further cases of overlap or conversion

[19]	*absent*	*adjacent*	*consequent*	*contrary*	*effective*
	exclusive	*irrespective*	*opposite*	*preliminary*	*preparatory*
	previous	*prior*	*pursuant*	*regardless*	*subsequent*

These items all qualify as prepositions by virtue of being able to occur as head of an adjunct with no predicand, as in such examples as:

[20] i *[Absent such a direct threat,] Mr Carter professes to feel no pressure.*
ii *[Right adjacent to the church] there is a liquor store.*
iii *[Consequent on this discovery,] there will doubtless be some disciplinary action.*
iv *He had not been seen in the area [prior to this].*
v *The plan will go ahead [regardless of any objections we might make].*

Irrespective and *regardless*, although historically adjectives (as reflected in their morphological form), are now virtually restricted to the preposition category. The other items in [19] occur in addition as adjectives in attributive function – compare *absent friends, the adjacent building, the consequent loss of income*, etc. In the case of *absent, effective, exclusive, opposite, preliminary*, and *preparatory*, there are also complement uses which are clearly adjectival: *Five of them were absent*; *The film was very effective*; *This club seems very exclusive*; and so on. With the others, however, there is little reason to distinguish the complement use from the clearly prepositional adjunct: compare, for example, *This was prior to the election* and *This happened prior to the election*. NP complements are licensed only by a few of the prepositions: *opposite* (*opposite the church*) and, in specialised registers, *absent* (as in [20i], "in the absence of") and *effective* (*Effective 1 July the fee will be increased to $20*).

2.3 Prepositions vs verbs

For the most part, verbs are clearly distinguishable from prepositions by their ability to occur as head of a main clause and to inflect for tense. There are, however, a number of prepositions that have arisen through the conversion of secondary, non-tensed, forms of verbs:

[21] i *[Barring accidents,] they should be back today.*
ii *There are five of them [counting/including the driver].*
iii *[Pertaining to the contract negotiations,] there is nothing to report.*
iv *[Given his age,] a shorter prison sentence is appropriate.*

The basis for analysing the underlined words here as prepositions is that there is no understood subject. This is effectively the same criterion as we have used in distinguishing prepositions from adjectives: prepositions can be used in adjunct function without a predicand, i.e. an element of which they are understood to be predicated. The preposition *counting* in [ii], for example, is to be distinguished from the gerund-participial verb-form in:

[22] [*Counting his money before going to bed last night,*] *Max discovered that two $100 notes were missing.*

The boundary between the prepositional construction [21] and the verbal [22] is slightly blurred by the usage illustrated in:

[23] i [*Turning now to sales,*] *there are very optimistic signs.*
ii [*Bearing in mind the competitive environment,*] *this is a creditable result.*
iii [*Having said that,*] *it must be admitted that the new plan also has advantages.*

These differ from [22] in that no subject for the underlined verb is recoverable from the matrix clause. They are similar to what prescriptivists call the 'dangling participle' construction illustrated in examples such as **Walking down the street, his hat fell off,* ungrammatical in the sense where it was he, not his hat, that was walking down the street. Unlike the latter, however, the examples in [23] are generally regarded as acceptable. They differ from the prepositional construction in that there is still an understood subject roughly recoverable from the context as the speaker or the speaker and addressees together. Syntactically, they differ from the prepositions with respect to the dependents permitted: the verbs in [23i–ii], for example, accept the same dependents as in tensed constructions. In [i] we have the adjunct *now* as well as the complement *to sales*, and we could add other adjuncts such as *briefly* or *if I may.* Similarly, in [ii] the PP complement *in mind* is part of the idiom *bear in mind*, and again we could add adjuncts (e.g. *bearing in mind, as we must, the competitive environment*). In [iii] *having* is a form of the perfect auxiliary, and – unlike any preposition – takes an obligatory past-participial complement; little expansion is possible this time, but that is because *having said that* is a more or less fixed phrase in this use.

The main prepositions that are homonymous with the gerund-participle or past participle forms of verbs are as follows:

[24]					
	according † T	*allowing* F	*barring* †	*concerning*	*counting*
	excepting	*excluding*	*failing* †	*following*	*including*
	owing † T	*pertaining* T	*regarding*	*respecting*	*saving* †
	touching †	*wanting* †	*given*	*gone* † BrE	*granted*

The symbol '†' indicates that the preposition differs in complementation and/or meaning from current usage of the verb: we have prepositional *according to Kim* but not verbal **They accorded to Kim*, and so on. *Gone* differs from *given* and *granted* in that the corresponding verb is not understood passively; it is used, in informal style, with expressions of time or age as complement: *We stayed until gone midnight* ("after"); *He's gone 60* ("over").

As prepositions, the items in [24] take an obligatory complement – an NP, except for those marked T or F, which take a *to* or *for* phrase respectively. The prepositions *during, notwithstanding,* and *pending* contain the ·*ing* suffix, but are not homonymous with a verb.

There are also a few deverbal prepositions that take content clause complements: *given, granted, provided, providing, seeing* (see Ch. 11, §4.8).

2.4 Prepositions vs adverbs

Adverbs are traditionally defined as words that modify verbs, adjectives, and other adverbs. Elements traditionally regarded as modifying the verb are, in our framework, adjuncts, but prepositions also occur as heads of phrases with this function. Almost every semantic type of adjunct can be realised by a phrase with either an adverb or a preposition as head. In the following, for example, the first underlined word in each clause is an adverb, the second a preposition:

[25]	i	*She did it carefully / with great care.*	[manner]
	ii	*They communicate electronically / by email.*	[means]
	iii	*They live locally / in the vicinity.*	[spatial location]
	iv	*The prices went up astronomically / by a huge amount.*	[extent]
	v	*I haven't seen her recently / since August.*	[temporal location]
	vi	*She's working with us temporarily / for a short time.*	[duration]
	vii	*They check regularly / at regular intervals.*	[frequency]
	viii	*I loved her immensely / with all my heart.*	[degree]
	ix	*It failed consequently / for this reason.*	[reason]

Thus in [i] we can have either *She did it carefully* (where *carefully* is an adverb) or *She did it with great care* (where *with* is a preposition), and similarly with the others. The labels on the right give the semantic type of adjunct, matching those used in the description of adjuncts given in Ch. 8, §1.[3] It is clear then that the property of being able to head a phrase in adjunct function does not itself help distinguish prepositions from adverbs.

The traditional definition of preposition says that they have (in our terms) an NP complement, but we have shown that stipulation to be unwarranted (and it is not in fact observed in practice). However, we will not depart further from the traditional account than is justified. Prototypical prepositions have NP complements, and other items will be admitted into the preposition category only if there is positive evidence to support such an extension beyond the core members.

Words without dependents

Consider first words without dependents – words which by themselves constitute a full phrase. Several types can be distinguished.

(a) Prepositions that optionally take NP complements

The case for allowing prepositions with no complements is most compelling where the same word occurs either with or without an NP complement, as in *The owner is not in the house* ~ *The owner is not in.* There are several reasons for saying that these two instances of *in* belong to the same category.

Firstly, as illustrated in [7] of §1, the relation between the constructions with and without the NP complement is the same as is found with verbs, nouns, and adjectives: there is no more reason for saying that *in* here belongs to two different categories than

[3] It is because of this functional similarity that the PPs here are traditionally called 'adverbial phrases'. From our perspective, that term represents a confusion of functions and categories: we say that the two sets of expressions in [25] have the same function but belong to different categories, and in terms with the form 'X phrase' the 'X' indicates the category of the head word.

for saying that *eating* does in *She was eating an apple* and *She was eating*, and so on. In particular, there is no functional difference between *in the house* and *in*, just as there is none between *eating an apple* and *eating*.

Secondly, the same modifiers are permitted whether the NP complement is present or not. Compare:

		a.	b.
[26]	i	*He'd left [two hours before the end].*	*He'd left [two hours before].*
	ii	*She went [straight inside the house].*	*She went [straight inside].*

Thirdly, a considerable proportion of prepositions show a similar alternation between occurrence with NP and occurrence without. A sample of them is shown in [27].

[27]				
aboard	*about*	*above*	*across*	*after*
against	*along*	*alongside*	*apropos*	*around*
before	*behind*	*below*	*beneath*	*besides*
between	*beyond*	*by*	*down*	*for*
in	*inside*	***near***	*notwithstanding*	*off*
on	*opposite*	*outside*	*over*	*past*
round	*since*	*through*	*throughout*	*to*
under	*underneath*	*up*	*within*	*without*

Most of these belong to the domains of space and time, predominantly the former, but there are a few with other meanings: *apropos, besides, nothwithstanding, without.*[4] There is a good deal of variation with respect to how readily they occur without a complement. *In, on, over, under, up,* for example, are very common in this use, whereas *to* is restricted to secondary senses (*He pulled the door to,* "just not completely closed"; *He came to,* "recovered consciousness"; etc.), and the use of *against* and *for* without a complement is mainly restricted to contexts involving voting: *We had a huge majority, with only two people voting against.*

Occurring with no NP complement is not a property found just occasionally with one or two prepositions, or only with marginal items. It is a property found systematically throughout a wide range of the most central and typical prepositions in the language.

(b) Compounds with *here, there,* and *where*

[28]								
i	*hereat*	*hereby*	*herefrom*	*herein*	*hereof*	*hereon*	*hereto*	*herewith*
ii	*thereat*	*thereby*	*therefrom*	*therein*	*thereof*	*thereon*	*thereto*	*therewith*
iii	*whereat*	*whereby*	*wherefrom*	*wherein*	*whereof*	*whereon*	*whereto*	*wherewith*

Half a dozen or so preposition bases form compounds with *here, there,* and *where.* Most are archaic, though some – particularly the ·*by* series – are merely rather formal. The *where* forms are relatives. There is also a series in ·*abouts*: *hereabouts* (with *hereabout* a variant in AmE), *thereabouts* (most often used in the expression *or thereabouts,* "or roughly that"), and interrogative *whereabouts.*

(c) Spatial terms

Among the words that do not license NP complements there are a fair number belonging to the spatial domain that occur as goal complement with such verbs as *come* and *go,*

[4] Prepositional *apropos* on its own means roughly "talking of that" (e.g. *I went to a College reunion on Friday; apropos, did you ever hear what happened to Webster?*) In addition, *apropos* can be an adjective meaning "appropriate, suitable": *His behaviour was not exactly apropos.*

and also, in most cases, as locative complement to *be*:

[29] i a. *They went ashore.* b. *They are ashore.*
ii a. *I'll take them downstairs.* b. *They are downstairs.*
iii a. *Kim is coming home.* b. *Kim is home.*
iv a. *Let's put everything indoors.* b. *Everything is indoors.*

There are good grounds for putting words of this kind in the preposition category.

In the clause, prototypical adverbs generally occur in adjunct rather than complement function. They are not entirely excluded from functioning as complement (cf. *They treat us appallingly*, etc.: see Ch. 8, §2.1), but this usage is relatively exceptional. No adverb in ·*ly* could substitute as goal complement for the underlined words in the [a] examples in [29]. Leaving aside its specifying use, *be* does not license adverbs in ·*ly* as complement, so none could substitute for the underlined words in the [b] examples either. Notice, moreover, that *ashore*, *downstairs*, etc., in these [b] examples cannot reasonably be said to 'modify' the verb. They no more modify the verb than does *young* in *They are young.* Thus although they are traditionally analysed as adverbs, it is arguable that they do not in fact satisfy the traditional definition.

These words are syntactically very like the prepositions in [27] except that they cannot take NP complements. Compare, for example, *They went/are aboard* and *They went/are ashore.* Some of them can be modified by *right* and *straight*, as in *They are right downstairs* or *We went straight indoors.* We accordingly include these too in the preposition class. They may be contrasted with the adverb *locally*, which belongs semantically in the spatial domain but is syntactically quite different from these prepositions.

The main prepositions of this kind are as follows:

[30]					
i	*abroad*	*abreast*	*adrift*	*aground*	*ahead*
	aloft	*apart*	*ashore*	*aside*	*away*
ii	*here*	*there*	*where*		
	hence	*thence*	*whence*		
iii	*east*	*north*	*south*	*west*	
iv	*aft*	*back*	*forth*	*home*	*together*
v	*downhill*	*downstage*	*downstairs*	*downstream*	*downwind*
	uphill	*upstage*	*upstairs*	*upstream*	*upwind*
vi	*indoors*	*outdoors*	*overboard*	*overhead*	*overland*
	overseas	*underfoot*	*underground*		
vii	*backward(s)*	*downward(s)*	*eastward(s)*	*forward(s)*	*heavenward(s)*
	homeward(s)	*inward(s)*	*leftward(s)*	*northward(s)*	*onward(s)*
	outward(s)	*rightward(s)*	*seaward(s)*	*skyward(s)*	*southward(s)*
	upward(s)	*westward(s)*			

The words in [30i] contain the prefix *a*·, which originates historically in a form of the preposition *on.* They are the result of fusion of the preposition with its complement. The same prefix is found in some of the prepositions that optionally take NP complements, such as *aboard.* Except for *aside*, the words in [30i] occur both as goal (*They went abroad*) and as complement of *be* (*They are abroad*). In its spatial sense *aside* occurs only in dynamic contexts: *He pushed them aside*, but not **They are aside. Apart* and *aside* also have a secondary sense "not including/considering": *Apart/Aside from this, I have no complaints*; in this sense, they can in fact take an NP complement, but one which precedes rather than follows the head (see §4 .2).

Here and *there* ([30ii]) are deictic expressions, discussed in detail in Ch. 17, §9.1; *where* is the corresponding interrogative and relative form. All three have both dynamic and static uses: e.g. *Where did she go?* and *Where is she?* The forms *hence, thence*, and *whence* incorporate the meaning "from". As spatial terms, they are restricted to dynamic contexts and are somewhat archaic: *They travelled to Calais and thence to Paris.* They also have secondary senses in the realm of reasoning (*Hence it follows that*...). There is, in addition, an archaic triple incorporating the meaning "to": *hither, thither, whither.* Note also the archaic or dialectal *yonder*, meaning something like "there" but typically locating at some distance from the speaker; it has a marginal determinative use (*yonder hills* "those hills over there") but is a preposition in *He was headed over yonder.*

The compass terms in [30iii] are primarily nouns (often spelled with an initial capital): *She comes from the North of England.* As prepositions, they are used dynamically in examples like *We were travelling east*; in their static use they require an *of* phrase complement, as in *It is 50 miles north of Paris.* The prepositions are often modified by the adverb *due* "exactly": this occurs only with compass terms and belongs in a class with *straight* and *right* as adverbs modifying only prepositions. In addition to the simple forms cited, there are compounds such as *north-east, south-west*, etc.

The words in [30iv] form a miscellaneous group, all morphologically simple, apart from *together.* They all occur as complement of *be*, as in *We'll be home soon*, with the exception of *forth*, which has directional meaning and occurs with verbs of going (*go forth, venture forth, sally forth*, etc.). Another directional item that might be added here is AusE *bush* "off into the forest or countryside", as in *Once hatched, the chicks immediately head bush on their own.*

The remaining items in [30] are compounds. *Overland* and *underfoot* are marginal members, morphologically like the others but syntactically different in that they do not occur as goal or complement of *be. Overland* functions as path (Ch. 8, §4.3), as in *They travelled overland from Paris to Athens.* The items in [30vii] have variants with and without ·*s*: *homeward* or *homewards*, etc. Only the forms without ·*s* are used attributively (*the homeward journey, a backward move*). Elsewhere, AmE also normally uses the forms without ·*s*, while BrE allows both forms, generally preferring the ·*s* variant (though *forwards* is more restricted in use than *forward*).

(d) Non-spatial terms

Outside the spatial domain there are only a handful of prepositions beyond those given in [27] that occur without a complement. Almost all belong to the temporal domain:[5]

[31]	i	*now*	*then*	*when*	
	ii	*afterward(s)*	*beforehand*	*henceforth*	*thenceforth*

Now, then, and *when* are the temporal counterparts of spatial *here, there*, and *where. Afterward* (AmE) and *afterwards* (most other varieties) have essentially the same meaning

[5] *Why* has certain affinities with prepositions in that it can occur as complement to *be*, as when you say, for example, *I won't be seeing them again*, and I ask: *Why is that?* This is a somewhat unusual construction, however: semantically it is quite different from *Where is Kim?* or *Kim is out.* The *why* is not interpreted predicatively, the meaning being essentially the same as that of *Why is that so?*; for this reason, we do not regard this use as incompatible with the analysis of *why* as an adverb. One borderline case is *else*. This is an adverb when following *or*, as in *Hurry up or else you'll miss the bus*, but arguably a preposition when it postmodifies interrogative heads and compound determinatives: *who else, why else, something else than this.* The function of internal postmodifier in NP structure is characteristic of PPs rather than AdvPs, and note also that since the head can be the adverb *why* it would be implausible to take *else* as an adjective here.

as the simple form *after*, and similarly *beforehand* means much the same as *before*; *henceforth* and *thenceforth* are compounds of the prepositions *hence/thence* and *forth*. The case for analysing single-word temporal terms as prepositions is weaker than with spatial ones, since they occur predominantly as adjunct rather than complement. Those in [31] are closely related to forms whose assignment to the preposition class is strongly motivated, and *now*, *then*, and *afterward(s)* accept modification by *right* and/or *straight*. Most single-word forms in the domain of time location, duration, and frequency, however, are adverbs: *previously, subsequently, immediately, shortly, soon, long, always, often, frequently*, etc.

Words with PP complements

Consider next words taking PP complements, as in:

[32] i *Everything has been badly delayed* [<u>*owing*</u> *to a computer failure*].
ii [<u>*According*</u> *to Kim,*] *most of the signatures were forged.*
iii *We had to cancel the match* [<u>*because*</u> *of the weather*].
iv *She suddenly jumped* [<u>*out*</u> *of the window*].
v *They gave me a knife* [<u>*instead*</u> *of a fork*].

The traditional definition of preposition excludes the underlined words, precisely because they are not followed by NPs. For the most part, these and other words of the same kind are therefore analysed as adverbs in traditional grammar.[6] In some cases, however, the similarity between the whole bracketed expression and a PP is recognised, and catered for by analysing the first two words as a single unit. This unit does have an NP as complement, and hence is traditionally analysed as a preposition – what is often called a 'complex preposition'. We discuss the concept of complex preposition in detail in §3, but three points can be made briefly here with respect to the particular kind of 'complex preposition' found in these examples.

In the first place, there is a good deal of inconsistency in the traditional account, as reflected in the practice of dictionaries, as to which combinations are analysed as complex prepositions and which as sequences of adverb + preposition. For example, *owing to* and *out of* are listed as prepositions, but *according to, because of*, and *instead of* are treated as adverb + preposition. Modern descriptive grammars have tended to extend the category of complex prepositions, and there is accordingly some variation in dictionary practice, depending on how far they are influenced by such work.

Secondly, the complex preposition analysis fails to provide a satisfactory account of the optionality of the complement in cases like [32iv–v]. If the NP is omitted, the *of* drops too. Compare, then:

[33]		
i	a. *I ran* [<u>*through*</u> *the tunnel*].	b. *I ran* [<u>*out*</u> *of the house*].
ii	a. *I ran* [<u>*through*</u>].	b. *I ran* [<u>*out*</u>].

The complex preposition analysis is saying that *out of* is the same kind of unit as *through*, but the data in [33] shows that this is clearly not so. If *out of* were like *through*, the form

[6] Our primary concern in this discussion will be with the internal structure of the bracketed phrases, but there is one point that should be made about syntactic function. Some of these phrases can appear as complement to *be*: *This voucher is* [<u>*instead*</u> *of the watch I intended to get for you*]. As we observed earlier, an analysis as an adverb is hardly consistent with the traditional definition: the *instead* phrase is not modifying the verb but is in a predicative relation to the subject.

we would have in [iib] would be **I ran out of.* It is *out*, not *out of*, that is syntactically similar to *through*: for example, both head phrases that can function as complement to motion verbs like *run*. The difference between *out* and *through* is a matter of their complementation: *through* takes an NP, while *out* takes a PP with *of*.[7]

The third point concerns the motivation for the complex preposition analysis. It seems clear that the recognition of units like *out of* as a complex preposition is intimately related to the restrictive definition of prepositions, which requires them to have an NP complement. *Out* does not have an NP complement in *out of the house*, but if the *of* is grouped with *out* then we can say that there is an NP complement and hence treat the whole sequence like *through the window*. But as we have noted, there is no justification for restricting prepositions to words that take NP complements, and in practice traditional grammar does not exclude the occurrence of prepositions with certain other types of complement: examples like *The magician emerged [<u>from</u> behind the curtain]* ([31i] of §1) show that a preposition can take a PP complement.

In the present grammar we are taking prepositions to function as heads of phrases that allow a rich range of complementation. We have seen that there are functional differences between PPs and AdvPs, but these do not by any means apply in all cases. The most general syntactic difference between prepositions and adverbs, therefore, concerns their complementation.

Most prepositions license an obligatory or optional complement; as described above, those that do not, with only a handful of exceptions, belong in the spatial domain, which is where the sharp functional differences apply.

Adverbs, by contrast, usually occur without a complement: none of them take obligatory complements, and most of them do not even license optional ones. The adverbs that license complements all contain the ·*ly* suffix, as in *The lawsuit was filed [<u>simultaneously</u> with the consent decree]*, and words of this kind can be readily assigned to the adverb category on independent grounds.

This provides, then, a reasonably clear basis for distinguishing between prepositions and adverbs. If a word not ending in the ·*ly* suffix licenses a complement, it is not an adverb; if a word other than those of the type covered in [30–31] fails to license a complement, it is not a preposition.

3 Idiomatic and fossilised expressions headed by a preposition

One of the hallmarks of English is the remarkable profusion of idiomatic and semi-idiomatic constructions into which prepositions enter. These extend the inventory of expressions in English in a way that is equivalent to adding hundreds of new words to the dictionary. In this section we illustrate and review a range of expressions of this kind in which the first word belongs to the traditional category of preposition.

Many consist simply of preposition + noun, or preposition + determinative + noun:

[1] i *for example, in abeyance, in person, in sum, on purpose, under protest*
ii *after a fashion, in a word, on the spot, under the weather, with one voice*

[7] In some varieties of English *out* also allows an NP complement: see §5.1 below.

These are simply PPs with a preposition as head and an NP as complement: syntactically, there is nothing further to be said. Less straightforward are those where the noun is followed by a second preposition, as in *in accordance with* + NP. We consider these in §3.1, and then cover other structural types more briefly in §3.2.

3.1 Expressions of the type *for the sake of X, at odds with X*

Our concern in this section is with expressions consisting of a preposition followed by a noun (sometimes preceded by *the* or *a*), followed in turn by a second preposition and an NP (or gerund-participial), as in:

[2] i *He did it [for the sake of his son].*
ii *I'm [at odds with my boss].*

We will represent such expressions schematically as:

[3] Prep_1 (Article) N_1 Prep_2 *X*

The article, in those containing one, is usually *the*, but *a* is also found, as in *with a view to finishing the report.* In some cases even the *X* element is specified as part of the idiom, as in *in point of fact, in the nick of time, in the twinkling of an eye*, and so on. Usually, however, this part is independently variable: countless NPs could replace *his son* and *my boss* in [2]. A sample of such expressions, omitting the *X* element, is given in [4], where they are arranged alphabetically on the basis of N_1:

[4]			
	in accordance with	*on account of*	*in addition to*
	under the aegis of	*in aid of*	*under the auspices of*
	in back of	*in/on behalf of*	*at the behest of*
	in case of	*in charge of*	*in comparison with*
	in compliance with	*in conformity with*	*in consequence of*
	in contact with	*by dint of*	*with effect from*
	with the exception of	*in exchange for*	*at the expense of*
	in (the) face of	*in favour of*	*by (the) force of*
	in front of	*on (the) ground(s) of*	*at the hands of*
	in league with	*in lieu of*	*in (the) light of*
	in line with	*at loggerheads with*	*by means of*
	in the name of	*at odds with*	*on pain of*
	on the part of	*in place of*	*in (the) process of*
	in quest of	*in/with reference to*	*in/with regard to*
	in relation to	*in/with respect to*	*in return for*
	at (the) risk of	*for (the) sake of*	*in search of*
	in spite of	*in step with*	*on the strength of*
	in terms of	*on top of*	*in touch with*
	at variance with	*in view of*	*with a view to*
	by virtue of	*for/from want of*	*by way of*

These differ in two respects from **free expressions** such as:

[5] *She put it [on the photo of her son].* [free expression]

In the first place, they are in varying degrees idiomatic, so that the meaning of the whole is not derivable in a fully systematic way from the meanings of the components.

Secondly, they do not permit the full range of syntactic manipulation that applies with free expressions – manipulations involving additions, omissions, and replacements. Those where no manipulation at all of the pre-*X* sequence is permitted are said to be fully fossilised.

A number of such manipulations of the free expression – including, for comparative purposes, one inadmissible one – are shown in [6]:

[6]	i	*She has lost [the photo of her son].*	[occurrence without $Prep_1$]
	ii	*She put it [on the photo].*	[omission of Prep2 + *X*]
	iii	*She put it [on the crumpled photo of her son].*	[modification of N_1]
	iv	*She put them [on the photos of her son].*	[number change in N_1]
	v	*She put it [on this photo of her son].*	[determiner change]
	vi	*She put it [on her son's photo].*	[genitive alternation]
	vii	*She put it [on the photos and drawings of her son].*	[coordination of N_1]
	viii	*She put it [on the photos of her son and of Kim].*	[coordination of $Prep_2$ + *X*]
	ix	**the son <u>of whom</u> she put it [on the photo]*	[fronting of $Prep_2$ + *X*]

In [i] the sequence following $Prep_1$ occurs on its own as an NP in object function. In [ii] the sequence following N_1, i.e. *of X*, has been dropped. In [iii] an attributive adjective has been added, modifying N_1. Example [iv] contrasts with the original with respect to the number of N_1, plural instead of singular. In [v] there has been a change in the determiner, from *the* to *this.* In [vi] we have a genitive subject-determiner in place of the original *the* as determiner + *of her son* as complement. The next two examples involve coordination: of N_1 in [vii], and of the sequence $Prep_2$ + *X* in [viii]. Finally, in [ix] *X* has been relativised and placed in prenuclear position in the clause, along with $Prep_2$, and in this case the result is ungrammatical.

The most fossilised of the expressions in [4], such as *in case of, by dint of, in lieu of, by means of, on pain of, in quest of, in search of, in spite of, in view of, by virtue of, by way of,* disallow all of these manipulations. Compare *She achieved this [by dint of hard work]*, for example, with:

[7]	i	**[Dint of hard work] achieves wonders.*	[occurrence without $Prep_1$]
	ii	**She achieved this [by dint].*	[omission of $Prep_2$ + *X*]
	iii	**She achieved this [by pure dint of hard work].*	[modification of N_1]
	iv	**She achieved this [by dints of hard work].*	[number change in N_1]
	v	**She achieved this [by the dint of hard work].*	[determiner change]
	vi	**She achieved this [by hard work's dint].*	[genitive alternation]
	vii	**She achieved this [by dint and way of hard work].*	[coordination of N_1]
	viii	**She achieved this [by dint of hard work and of sheer persistence].*	[coordination of $Prep_2$ + *X*]
	ix	**the hard work <u>of which</u> she achieved this [by dint]*	[fronting of $Prep_2$ + *X*]

The only place where there may be some doubt is [viii]; some speakers may find this marginally acceptable, but there is at least a very strong preference for the version with only one *of* (i.e. with the coordination simply within *X*: *by dint of hard work and sheer persistence*).

The less fossilised expressions in [4] allow one or a few changes, but none of them allow all. Moreover, the manipulations cannot be ordered in a strict hierarchy such that if a given manipulation is permitted then all others below it in the hierarchy will be permitted too. For example, *in/on behalf of* allows genitive alternation but not omission of $Prep_2$ + X, but it is the other way round with *in front*:

[8] i a. *I'm writing [in/on behalf of my son].*
b. *I'm writing [in/on my son's behalf].* [genitive alternation]
c. **I'm writing [in/on behalf].* [omission of $Prep_2$ + *X*]
ii a. *She was sitting [in front of the car].*
b. **She was sitting [in the car's front].* [genitive alternation]
c. *She was sitting [in front].* [omission of $Prep_2$ + *X*]

In testing for the various properties, one must ensure that relevant aspects of meaning remain constant. Compare [iia], for example, with *She was sitting [in the front of the car]*. This is well-formed, but the sense of *front* is quite different: it means "She was sitting in the front portion of the car, the driver's seat or the adjacent one", while [iia] means that she was sitting outside the car, near the front end, or between the car and the observer.

Syntactic structure

There are at least three different syntactic structures that might be assigned to expressions like those in [4]. They are illustrated here (with simplification of the X component) for the expression *in front of the car*:

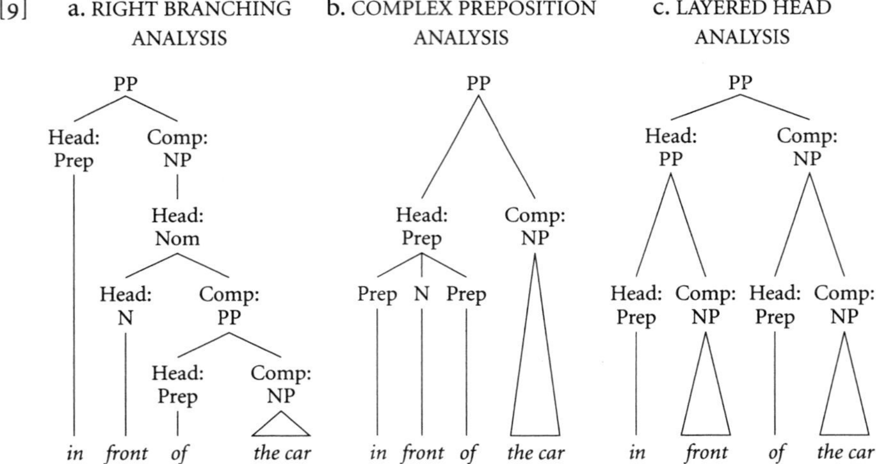

Arguments against the complex preposition analysis

Structure [9a] is essentially the same as that which we assign to the free expression *on the photo of her son*: the sequence N_1 $Prep_2$ *X* is an NP functioning as complement to *in*. This is called a right branching analysis since the embedded *X* element is located in the tree at the end of a series of steps down to the right. Structure [b] treats *in front of* as a complex preposition, but we have not attempted to assign functions to the component parts of it. Structure [c] divides the whole expression first into *in front* as head and *of the car* as complement: the *of* phrase is licensed by *in front* as a unit. We call this the 'layered head analysis' since it has one PP functioning as head within another.

Much modern work in descriptive grammar adopts the complex preposition analysis, thus treating *in front of* as similar to the simple preposition *behind*. The close semantic relation between *in front of* and *behind* (and similarly *on top of* and *underneath* or *in spite of* and *despite*) gives the complex preposition concept some initial intuitive appeal, but semantic relations of this kind do not provide a reliable guide to syntactic analysis. There are innumerable examples of idioms that cannot be analysed by treating specific strings of words as complex syntactic units: cases in which the parts to which the idiomatic interpretation is assigned do not occur contiguously. Consider:

[10] i *That salesman really took us both for a ride.* (*take X for a ride* = "deceive X")
ii *I've kept these problematic data on the back burner for a while now.* (*keep X on the back burner* = "postpone dealing with X")
iii *She took the students to task for their tardiness.* (*take X to task* = "upbraid X")

The underlined parts constitute idioms that cannot be analysed by positing complex syntactic units, because the special meanings here are not associated with a string of contiguous words.

Nor does the relative resistance of the expressions in [4] to the manipulations illustrated in [6] provide convincing evidence in favour of the complex preposition analysis. Most of them allow at least one manipulation that is inconsistent with this analysis. We have observed, for example, that *in/on behalf of X* alternates with *in/on X's behalf*, as in [8i]. This shows that *behalf of X* must be an NP, for the alternation is essentially the same as that in non-idiomatic NPs: compare *the behaviour of the president* ~ *the president's behaviour*. The fact that *in/on behalf of* doesn't allow other manipulations must therefore be handled in terms of the fossilisation that very often accompanies idioms: idioms are lexical units whose syntactic components very often cannot be independently varied. Or take the case of *in front of*. The same argument applies here as with *out of* (see [33] of §2): if *in front of* really were syntactically like *behind*, it would be possible to omit just the X component. Compare, however:

[11] i a. *It is behind the car.* b. *It is behind.*
ii a. *It is in front of the car.* b. **It is in front of.*

Instead of [iib] we have *It is in front*: syntactically, the *of* forms a constituent with *X*, and it is this constituent (a PP), not *X*, that is optional. *In front of* cannot, therefore, be a complex preposition, but it resists other manipulations, and thus exhibits a high degree of fossilisation.

Expressions like *by dint of*, which effectively disallow all manipulation, differ from *in/on behalf of* and *in front of* simply in the degree of fossilisation involved. There is no reason to say that they differ in kind, that in these cases there has been a reanalysis yielding a complex preposition.

The arguments we have used here are of the same general kind as those invoked in rejecting complex (multiword) verbs such as *refer to* (Ch. 4, §6) or complex determinatives such as *a number of* (Ch. 5, §3.3). There is a clear family resemblance between these concepts; in all of them the motivation for grouping together two or more words into a complex unit is essentially semantic, and the analysis is unable to provide a satisfactory account of the syntactic data.

It is worth noting that there is one place where we can argue that a reanalysis has taken place, with the result that *of* has been incorporated into a unit with a preceding noun. This is with *kind* and *sort*, as in He *kind of lost control.* Here *kind of* is omissible (*He lost control*) and is a modifier in VP structure: the head of the construction must be *lose*, the verb. *Kind* has clearly not assumed verbal properties, for it doesn't inflect as a verb. But there is no comparable evidence for reanalysis in such cases as *refer to*, *a number of*, *in front of*, etc.

The right branching analysis

We have seen that an analysis along the lines of [9a] is required in those cases where there is alternation with a genitive construction, as in the *in/on behalf of* type. Other expressions in [4] which permit this alternation are: *under the aegis of, under the auspices of, at the behest of, at the expense of, in favour of, at the hands of, in the name of, on the part of, in place of, for (the) sake of.*

Less direct evidence for a right branching structure applies in such cases as:

[12] A: *The murder charge was dropped on the grounds of diminished responsibility.*
B: *I don't think it should have been dropped on those grounds.*

The use of the anaphoric demonstrative *those* indicates that *the grounds of diminished responsibility* is construed as an NP.

The layered head analysis

Strong evidence for an analysis like [9c] is provided by fronting of $Prep_2$ + relativised *X*:

[13] i *He was [in league with the guys from down the road].*
ii *the guys from down the road, <u>with whom</u> he was [in league]*

If the *with* phrase were a dependent in the NP headed by *league* it would not normally behave in this way: compare the deviance of [6ix] (**the son of whom she put it on the photo*). The layered head analysis treats the *with* phrase as a dependent of the PP *in league*, not of the noun *league*. The expressions in [4] where such fronting is permitted are a subset of those with *with* as $Prep_2$: *in compliance with, in conformity with, in contact with, in line with, at loggerheads with, at odds with, in touch with, at variance with.*

Where we do not have positive evidence of the kinds given above for the right branching and layered head analyses, it is difficult to choose between them. It is reasonable, however, to prefer the layered head analysis in those cases where N_1 cannot occur elsewhere (with the same meaning) with $Prep_2$ + *X* as dependent. Compare, for example:

[14] i a. *[Comparison with earlier results] supports such a hypothesis.*
b. *You could have predicted the [consequence of your action].*
ii a. **The [front of the car] was strewn with daffodils.*
b. **The [view of his remorse] led them to be lenient.*

Comparison and *consequence* can take PP complements with *with* and *of* respectively, and this lends some plausibility to a right branching structure for *in comparison with* and *in consequence of.* Conversely, the absence of such complementation for *front* and *view* in relevant senses provides some support for a layered head analysis of *in front of* and *in view of.*[8] But the effect of fossilisation is to reduce the amount of positive evidence available, and as a result there may be some indeterminacy as to the correct syntactic analysis in some cases.

Compound prepositions

In a small number of cases there has been coalescence of $Prep_1$ + N_1 into a single compound preposition. One very clear case is *because*, as in *<u>because</u> of the weather*: historically, *because* derives from *by cause*, but the connection with *by* is no longer apparent. Another compound is *instead*, as in *He gave me a knife [<u>instead</u> of a fork]*. There is still a noun *stead*, but it is of very limited distribution, occurring in such expressions as *This will stand you in good stead for future dealings with him* or *I attended the meeting in her stead.* The latter construction might suggest that *stead* allows genitive alternation, but in fact there is no systematic alternation

[8] Example [14iia] is fine for describing a scene where the daffodils are on the front part of the car itself but, as noted in connection with [8ii], that is not the sense of *front* that we have in *in front of the car.*

between *instead of X* and in *X's stead*: compare, for example, *They gave it to me instead of her* ~ **They gave it to me in her stead.*

The layered head analysis is clearly very similar to one involving a compound preposition: [9c] takes *in front* as a constituent just as *instead* is a constituent in *instead of a fork*. The difference is that the former is syntactically composite while the latter is not, but there is no sharp difference between the two cases.

3.2 Other types of expression: *on the grounds that ..., up against, in brief*

There are three other kinds of expression to be considered.

(a) Expressions licensing content clauses or infinitivals

[15] i	a.	*in the event*	*on the basis*	*on the grounds*	*to the effect*
	b.	*for all*	*for fear*	*on condition*	
ii		*in case*	*in order*	*in two minds*	

The expressions in [ia] are followed by declarative content clauses although the nouns *basis*, *event*, and *grounds* do not normally take such complements elsewhere. Compare:

[16] i a. [*In the event that something happens to me*] *give them this letter.*
b. *[*The event that something happens to me*] *would shock my family.*
ii a. *She declined,* [*on the basis that she was too tired*].
b. *[*The basis that she was too tired*] *was unsatisfactory.*
iii a. *He defends guns* [*on the grounds that they enhance public safety*].
b. *[*The grounds that handguns enhance public safety*] *are implausible.*

Nevertheless, there is some evidence that the content clause is syntactically a dependent of the preceding noun:

[17] i *Something may happen to me, and* [*in that event*] *please give them this letter.*
ii *I can't believe she declined* [*on that basis*].
iii *His wife doesn't think they can be defended* [*on such grounds*].

In that event in the context of [i] is equivalent to *in the event that something happens to me*, and it is plausible to see the content clause in the latter as serving, like demonstrative *that* in the former, to define some unique event. Similarly, [17ii/iii] could be used following [16iia/iiia] respectively: *that basis* and *such grounds* are interpreted anaphorically with *the basis that she was too tired* and *the grounds that they enhance public safety* as their antecedents, suggesting that these latter expressions are NPs.

We therefore analyse *in the event that something happens to me* as a PP consisting of the preposition *in* and an NP containing a content clause complement. In terms of constituent structure it is thus like the bracketed PP in *This follows* [*from the fact that they contested the will*]. It differs from the latter in that the content clause complement is not licensed by the head noun itself but by the sequence *in the event*, as illustrated in [16i]: it is in this sense that *in the event* is idiomatic. Analogously for *on the basis*, *on the grounds*, and *to the effect*.

In the event that something happens to me means essentially the same as *if anything happens to me*, and for this reason some works analyse *in the event that* as a 'complex conjunction'. In our framework, where most subordinating conjunctions are included in the preposition category, this is to assign an analysis very like that of [9b] (but with *that* a subordinator rather than a preposition, and *something happens to me* a clause, not an NP). Again, however, there is no syntactic justification for making the first division between *in the event that* and the clause: *that* belongs with *something happens to me* just as *of* belongs with *the car* in *in front of the car* (see Ch. 11, §8.1).

The expressions in [15ib] also take content clauses:

[18] i [*For all that I'm not guilty,*] *I'll still be a suspect in the eyes of history.*
ii *She didn't reply,* [*for fear she might offend him*].
iii *They donated a print of the film* [*on condition it was not shown commercially*].

In [i] the content clause is clearly licensed by *for all* ("although"), not by *all* alone. And while the nouns *fear* and *condition* do license content clause complements, in the construction shown in [ii–iii] it may be best to analyse *for fear* and *on condition* too as heads, like *for all* in [i]. *For fear* differs from the expressions of [15ia] in that we couldn't have a demonstrative instead of the content clause: **I didn't reply for that fear either.* And the absence of a determiner in [18iii] supports an analysis with *on condition* as the head. The bracketed PPs thus have structures along the lines of [9c] or else have compound prepositions as head.

Consider, finally, the expressions in [15ii], illustrated in:

[19] i *You'd better take an umbrella* [<u>*in case*</u> *it rains*].
ii *We set out early* [<u>*in order*</u> *to avoid the rush-hour traffic*].
iii *I'm* [<u>*in two minds*</u> *whether to accept their offer*].

When the nouns *case, order,* and *minds* occur without the preceding *in* they do not have the same meaning and do not accept clausal complements (cf. **Consider the case it rains,* etc.). We therefore take the first constituent division to be between the underlined expression and the following clause. This gives a layered head structure like [9c], with *in case, in order,* and *in two minds* PPs taking clausal complements – except that again the first two might alternatively be considered compound prepositions.

In case takes a non-expandable declarative clause (*that* is not permitted: **in case that it rains*), and also allows a PP (*in case of rain*). *In order* takes a *to*-infinitival or a declarative clause in which *that* is more or less obligatory (*in order that we might get some peace and quiet*). *In two minds* – meaning "undecided", a more obvious case of an idiom – licenses an interrogative clause, infinitival or finite (*I was in two minds whether I should accept their offer*); it also takes a PP complement, *about* + NP (*about their offer*) or *as to* + interrogative clause (*as to whether to accept their offer*).

(b) Sequences of preposition + preposition

In examples like *He emerged* [<u>*from behind*</u> *the curtain*] or *She went* [<u>*down to*</u> *the post office*] we have 'free' sequences of prepositions: there is nothing idiomatic or fossilised about such cases. Our concern here is not with these but with such combinations as:

[20]				
i	*out of*	*because of*		
ii	*up to*	*up against*	*upon*	
iii	*in between*	*into*	*onto / on to*	
iv	*as to*	*as for*	*as from*	*as per*

Out of in [i] shows a high degree of fossilisation. It is virtually impossible to separate the two components or to repeat *of* in coordination: cf. **the door of which she had come out* or **All the furniture will have to be taken out of the dining-room and of the lounge.* We have seen, however, that there is good syntactic evidence against treating *out of* as a composite preposition, namely that if the following NP is omitted the *of* must drop too: *They came out of the building* or *They came out. Because of* is similar, except that instead of omitting *of* + NP we can replace it by a content clause: *because of the rain* or *because it was raining.*

Metaphorical or idiomatic uses of *up to* are illustrated in:

[21]	i	*Up to page 400, the book does not mention transformations.*	["prior to"]
	ii	*I've asked Jake to help, but I'm not sure he's up to it.*	["fit or competent for"]
	iii	*It's up to you to set the guidelines.*	["a responsibility for"]
	iv	*That child is up to something.*	["doing (illicitly and/or furtively)"]

In [i] the meaning can be related via metaphorical extension to the free combination sense seen in *They had climbed up to the summit by lunchtime*: the direction referred to in [i] is not towards a more elevated point in space but towards a higher point on the scale determined by treating the reading of a book as like a climb with the beginning of the book at the bottom and the end at the top. *Up to page 400* refers to the portion of the book that extends from the lowest point of this scale 'upward' until page 400 is reached. The senses in [ii–iv] are clearly idiomatic. A person is described as being up to some activity if they are fit, capable, or competent enough for it (the sense in [ii]). A task is described as being up to a person who has responsibility and discretion for it (the sense in [iii]). And a person is described as being up to something in a different sense from [ii] if they are involved in nefarious and probably reprehensible activity (the sense in [iv]).

There is no good reason, however, for saying that idiomatisation is accompanied here by syntactic reanalysis. In [21iii] and probably also [21ii] it is possible to repeat *to* in coordination: cf. *It's up to you, or to your staff, to set the guidelines* or *I'm not sure that Jake is up to this, or to anything else that needs stamina.* We thus analyse *up to you* as *up* + *to you,* and similarly for the others. This is probably the appropriate way to handle *up against* too. This is found as a free combination in *The balloon is up against the ceiling* and as an idiom in *We're up against a criminal mastermind* – or *We're up against it* ("facing very adverse circumstances"), where the idiom includes the pronoun *it.*

The case of *upon,* however, is different: as reflected in the orthography, this is a compound preposition which occurs as a slightly formal alternant of *on* in some but not all uses of the latter. Compare: *We placed it on/upon the roof*; *On/Upon hearing the news, she phoned her sister*; *She's writing a thesis on/*upon the poetry of Judith Wright.*

The free combination of *in* and *between* is seen in *He placed his fingers in between his toes.* In *I managed to mow the lawn in between the showers* we understand "in the intervals between the showers"; though this sense tends to be noted separately in dictionaries, it is perfectly consistent with an analysis which matches that of the free combination, i.e. *in* + *between the showers. Into,* however, is a compound, as again reflected in the orthography. *Onto* is likewise a compound, whereas *on to* can be either a free combination or a variant spelling of the compound. The free combination is seen in *We travelled on to Manchester* ("onward as far as Manchester"), the compound in %*The ball dropped on to the carpet* ("to a position on the carpet"). In AmE the compound is spelled *onto,* while both *onto* and *on to* are found in BrE.[9]

[9] One place where the distinction between compound and non-compound uses is somewhat blurred is in complements to the verb *hold,* as in *Hold on to / onto the railing.* The spelling *onto* is certainly found here, but the meaning is not that of the compound in its ordinary use.

The expressions in [20iv] beginning with *as* are illustrated in:

[22] i *There's no doubt* [*as to her suitability*] / [*as to whether she's suitable*].
ii [*As for your other objections,*] *I'll return to them next week.*
iii [*As from tomorrow*] *the library will close at 9 p.m.*
iv *We'll be meeting at six,* [*as per usual*].

The underlined expressions bear no clear relation to free expressions, and are probably best analysed as compound prepositions. *As to* licenses an NP or interrogative clause complement, *as for* an NP or gerund-participial, *as from* an NP. In [iv] *as per* takes an adjectival complement in an idiom of the type we now turn to.

(c) Preposition + adjective combinations: *in brief*

[23]	*at first*	*at last*	*for certain*	*for free*	*for sure*	*in brief*
	in full	*in private*	*in short*	*in vain*	*of late*	*of old*

PPs of this kind consist of a preposition as head and an adjective as complement. In the case of the informal expression *for free*, the adjective is related to a predicand: in *You can have the other book for free*, for example, we understand that the other book is free. The other adjectives do not stand in any such relation to a predicand: in *I tried in vain to persuade her*, for example, *in vain* simply means "vainly". This use of adjectives has some affinity with that seen in *out of the ordinary* or *verging* [*on the impossible*], where *ordinary* and *impossible* function as fused modifier-heads in NP structure, but the absence of *the* in [23] means that we have no syntactic justification for extending the fused-head analysis to these expressions: we treat them simply as preposition + adjective idioms.

One such expression, *in common*, licenses a *with* phrase complement: *Jill has a lot in common with her brothers.*[10]

4 The position of a complement relative to the head preposition

In the default case, a preposition precedes its complement, as in *with pride, to the car,* etc. In this section we review three constructions that depart in various ways from this pattern.

4.1 Preposition stranding: *What was she referring to?*

In constructions like the following the preposition is said to be **stranded**:

[1] a. *What was she referring to?* b. *This is the book she was referring to.*

Here *to* is stranded in that its complement is missing from the normal post-head position – missing, but recoverable from elsewhere in the construction. In [i] the

[10] One idiom that does not belong with any of the structural types considered above is *what with*, used to introduce a reason adjunct, as in [*What with all the overtime at the office and having to look after his mother at home,*] *he'd had no time to himself for weeks.* This idiom has developed out of an otherwise almost obsolete use of *what* to introduce lists or coordinations, especially of PPs – and indeed *what with* is characteristically followed by a coordination, as in the example given. A rare example of this *what* with a preposition other than *with* is: *What between the duties expected of one during one's lifetime, and the duties exacted from one after one's death, land has ceased to be either a profit or a pleasure.*

understood complement is the interrogative phrase *what* in prenuclear position, while in [ii] *she was referring to* is a relative clause with the complement of *to* recoverable from the nominal *book* that the clause modifies: we understand that she was referring to some book.

Stranding can be represented by means of the gap symbol, co-indexed with the element which supplies the interpretation, the antecedent (see Ch. 2, §2):

[2] a. *What*$_i$ *was she referring to* __$_i$? b. *This is the book*$_i$ *she was referring to* __$_i$.

The traditional prescriptive rule against preposition stranding

There has been a long prescriptive tradition of condemning preposition stranding as grammatically incorrect. Stranded prepositions often, but by no means always, occur at the end of a sentence, and the prescriptive rule is best known in the formulation: 'It is incorrect to end a sentence with a preposition.' The rule is so familiar as to be the butt of jokes, and is widely recognised as completely at variance with actual usage.[11] The construction has been used for centuries by the finest writers. It would be almost impossible to find a writer who does not use it. Everyone who listens to Standard English hears examples of it every day.

Instead of being dismissed as unsupported foolishness, the unwarranted rule against stranding was repeated in prestigious grammars towards the end of the eighteenth century, and from the nineteenth century on it was widely taught in schools. The result is that older people with traditional educations and outlooks still tend to believe that stranding is always some kind of mistake. It is not. All modern usage manuals, even the sternest and stuffiest, agree with descriptive and theoretical linguists on this: it would be an absurdity to hold that someone who says *What are you looking at?* or *What are you talking about?* or *Put this back where you got it from* is not using English in a correct and normal way.

Syntactic constructions where preposition stranding is found

Stranded prepositions occur in the constructions illustrated in [3]:

[3]	i	*Your father*$_i$ *I'm even more deeply indebted to* __$_i$.	[preposing]
	ii	*Who*$_i$ *are they doing it for* __$_i$?	[open interrogative]
	iii	*What a magnificent table*$_i$ *the vase was standing on* __$_i$!	[exclamative]
	iv	*He's the one* [*who*$_i$ *I bought it from* __$_i$].	[*wh* relative]
	v	*He's the one*$_i$ [(*that*) *I bought it from* __$_i$].	[non-*wh* relative]
	vi	*Kim went to the same school*$_i$ *as* [*I went to* __$_i$].	[comparative]
	vii	*His performance*$_i$ *was easy* [*to find fault with* __$_i$].	[hollow clause]
	viii	*The bed looks as if* [*it*$_i$ *has been slept in* __$_i$].	[passive]

In constructions [3i–iv] the antecedent for the gap occupies prenuclear position within the clause, and here it is in principle possible to avoid the stranding construction

[11] The 'rule' was apparently created ex nihilo in 1672 by the essayist John Dryden, who took exception to Ben Jonson's phrase *the bodies that those souls were frighted from* (1611). Dryden was in effect suggesting that Jonson should have written *the bodies from which those souls were frighted*, but he offers no reason for preferring this to the original.

by placing the preposition before its complement in what we call the **PP fronting** construction:

[4] i *To your father I'm even more deeply indebted.* [preposing]
ii *For whom are they doing it?* [open interrogative]
iii *On what a magnificent table the vase was standing!* [exclamative]
iv *He's the one [from whom I bought it].* [*wh* relative]

In [3v–viii] the antecedent is not in prenuclear position, and stranding cannot be avoided by placing the preposition in front of its complement. In the case of non-*wh* relatives, however, we can avoid stranding simply by switching to a *wh* relative construction and using PP fronting, as in [4iv]. Stranding in comparative clauses can often be avoided by using a more reduced form: compare [3vi] with *Kim went to the same school as I did.* With hollow clauses it will be necessary to change to a different construction; in the case of [3vii] we could use extraposition to give *It was easy to find fault with his performance*, but other kinds of hollow clauses would require different strategies. Finally, for passives like [3viii] stranding of the preposition can be avoided by switching to an active construction: *The bed looks as if [someone has slept in it].*

Examples like *We played squash together last Tuesday, but I haven't seen her since* are not relevant here. Although *since* is interpreted as *since last Tuesday*, the omission of the complement is restricted to certain prepositions: compare **She's coming back next Tuesday and I intend to stay here until.* Thus *since* is not stranded, but merely allows – unlike *until* – a choice between uses with and without a complement.

Style level

There is a tendency for preposition stranding to be avoided in the most formal style. Hence, if what is desired is a public speaking manner that sounds lofty, solemn, or remote, *To whom may we appeal?*, for example, will be preferred over *Who can we appeal to?* And for a deeply serious funeral oration a phrase like *a colleague to whom we are so much indebted* will be preferred over *a colleague we're so indebted to.* But in most contexts stranding will often be considered more appropriate than the fronting construction. Stranded prepositions are not even markers of distinctively informal style. They are found in nearly all styles. We will see below that there are conditions under which stranding is preferred over PP fronting, and the use of PP fronting in such cases runs the risk of creating an impression of pedantry or stuffiness.

In the remainder of this section we will be concerned with the choice between preposition stranding and PP fronting, and hence will confine our attention to the constructions where PP fronting is in principle available – i.e. preposing, open interrogatives, exclamatives, and relatives. The examples above were chosen as ones where both versions are acceptable, stranding in [3i–v], PP fronting in [4i–iv]. Very often, however, only one version is admissible or else one is strongly preferred over the other. We group such cases into two sets: those where PP fronting is inadmissible or disfavoured relative to stranding, and those where stranding is inadmissible or disfavoured relative to PP fronting.

Constructions in which PP fronting is inadmissible or disfavoured

(a) The fused relative construction

[5] i *Somebody has to clean [what$_i$ grafitti artists write on __$_i$].* [stranding]
ii **Somebody has to clean [on what grafitti artists write].* [PP fronting]

The fused relative construction is discussed in Ch. 12, §6, and it will be clear from the analysis presented there why PP fronting is not possible. Briefly, *what graffiti artists write on* in [i] is an NP in which the head element is fused with the relative phrase in the subordinate clause: *what* is here equivalent to *that + which*. PP fronting places the PP in prenuclear position in the clause – compare *that on which graffiti artists write*. Because *what* represents a fusion of the head and the relative pronoun, the *on* in [ii] has been placed before the head of the NP: the resulting ungrammaticality is comparable to that of **Somebody has to clean [on that which graffiti artists write]*.

(b) Subordinate interrogative clauses functioning as complement of a preposition

[6] i *We can't agree on [which grant$_i$ we should apply for __$_i$].* [stranding]
ii **We can't agree on [for which grant we should apply].* [PP fronting]

In [i] the bracketed interrogative clause is complement of *on*; putting *for* at the front results in a sequence of two prepositions, and although there is no general ban on such sequences they are not permitted when the second involves PP fronting.

(c) Complement of prepositional verb or verbal idiom

In many cases the stranding construction is preferred or required when the preposition is specified by the verb or a verbal idiom, as in *account for, ask for, come across, consist of, face up to, look out for, tie in with*, etc. (see Ch. 4, §6). Compare:

[7] i a. *What$_i$ are you asking for __$_i$?*
b. *?For what are you asking?*
ii a. *My brother$_i$ you can certainly rely __ on$_i$.*
b. *?On my brother you can certainly rely.*
iii a. *That wasn't the one [which$_i$ we were looking out for __$_i$].*
b. *?That wasn't the one [for which we were looking out].*
iv a. *This is the sort of English [which$_i$ I will not put up with __$_i$].*
b. *?This is the sort of English [with which I will not put up].*[12]

It is not possible, however, to give any simple, general rules. Much depends on individual verb + preposition combinations. Some are fossilised, so that the preposition must be adjacent to the verb: compare *the documents which he had come across* and **the documents across which he had come*. Many such combinations belong to informal style and will thus resist occurrence with the noticeably formal PP fronting construction. Compare, for example, informal *pick on* and neutral *dispose of*, as in *?the people on whom he was always picking* and *the goods of which he had disposed*.

The acceptability of PP fronting may be affected by other factors. While the preposing in [7iib] is questionable, for example, a *wh* relative with the same verb and preposition is undoubtedly acceptable: *He's certainly someone on whom you can rely*. Or compare:

[8] i **I wonder for what he was hoping.*
ii *I am not able to say for what kind of outcome he was hoping.*

[12] This example is based on a much-quoted joke attributed to Sir Winston Churchill, who is said to have annotated some clumsy evasion of stranding in a document with the remark: *This is the sort of English up with which I will not put.* Unfortunately, the joke fails because it depends on a mistaken grammatical analysis: in *I will not put up with this sort of English* the sequence *up with this sort of English* is not a constituent, *up* being a separate complement of the verb (in the traditional analysis it is an adverb). Churchill's example thus does not demonstrate the absurdity of using PP fronting instead of stranding: it merely illustrates the ungrammaticality resulting from fronting something which is not a constituent.

Subordinate interrogatives tend to disfavour PP fronting, as illustrated in [i], which seems clearly inadmissible; in [ii], however, the relative formality of *I am not able to say* and *what kind of outcome* matches that of PP fronting, and the result is acceptable, though very markedly formal.

Constructions in which stranding is inadmissible or disfavoured

(a) The gap precedes a content clause

[9] i **Who$_i$ did she declare to __$_i$ that she was not going to take any more abuse?*
ii *To whom did she declare that she was not going to take any more abuse?*

Construction [i] is ungrammatical because the gap following *to* is located before a content clause (functioning as second complement of the verb *declare*).

(b) The PP is itself complement of a larger PP

[10] i **Which couch$_i$ did you rescue the pen from under __$_i$?*
ii *From under which couch did you rescue the pen?*

In *I rescued this pen from under your couch* the PP *under your couch* is complement of the preposition *from*, and *under* cannot be stranded in this context. To remove the ungrammaticality we must front the matrix PP, as in [ii]. Fronting just the smaller PP leaves *from* stranded, and the result is again unacceptable: **Under which couch$_i$ did you rescue the pen from __$_i$?*

This case is to be distinguished from the following, where stranding is permitted (and in fact preferred):

[11] i *Which account$_i$ did you take the money out of __$_i$?*
ii *Out of which account did you take the money?*

The difference here is that *of* is specifically selected by the head *out*, whereas in [10] *under* is potentially in contrast with other prepositions (such as *behind*).

(c) Elliptical interrogatives where the NP consists of more than one word

[12] i a. A: *I've got an interview at 2.* B: *Who$_i$ with __$_i$?*
b. A: *I've got an interview at 2.* B: *With whom$_i$?*
ii a. A: *I've got an interview at 2.* B: **Which tutor$_i$ with __$_i$?*
b. A: *I've got an interview at 2.* B: *With which tutor$_i$?*

Here B's response has the form of an interrogative clause consisting of just a preposition and its NP complement. In [i] the NP complement is the single word *who(m)*, and both stranding and PP fronting constructions are permitted. In [ii], however, the NP complement contains more than the interrogative word itself, and in such cases stranding is prohibited.

(d) The gap occurs at the end of the subject NP

[13] i **To the left is a door [which$_i$ the key to __$_i$ has been lost].*
ii *To the left is a door [to which the key has been lost].*

In *The key to this door has been lost* the PP *to this door* is the final element in the subject NP, and a preposition heading a PP in this position cannot normally be stranded, as illustrated in [i]. But such a PP can be fronted, as in [ii]. For further discussion of this kind of constraint, see Ch. 12, §7.3.

(e) The PP is in adjunct function

Stranding occurs most readily when the PP is functioning as complement; with adjunct PPs stranding is often prohibited or of doubtful acceptability, though there are certainly some cases where it is permitted. Compare:

[14] i a. **What circumstances*$_i$ *would you do a thing like that under* _$_i$?
b. *Under what circumstances would you do a thing like that?*
ii a. ?*That was the party [which*$_i$ *we met Angela at* _$_i$].
b. *That was the party [at which we met Angela].*
iii a. *What year*$_i$ *were you born in* _$_i$?
b. *In what year were you born?*

Wholly or marginally acceptable cases of stranding in adjuncts, such as [iiia] and [iia], tend to involve short and frequent prepositions in adjunct types that go naturally enough with the VP to be almost like complements.

(f) The preposition *than*

[15] i **They appointed Jones, [who*$_i$ *no one could have been less suitable than* _$_i$].
ii *They appointed Jones, [than whom no one could have been less suitable].*

Fronting of *than* + NP is rare and confined to very formal style. Stranding is inadmissible in the somewhat formal style of [i], where it is in a supplementary relative clause. The integrated relative ?*He's the only one*$_i$ *I was taller than* _$_i$ is better, but still very marginal. For the most part, both constructions are avoided (cf. *He's the only one who is shorter than me*). In comparisons of equality, which take *as* instead of *than*, both stranding and PP fronting are unacceptable: **They appointed Jones, who*$_i$ *no one was as suitable as* _$_i$ and **They appointed Jones, as whom no one was as suitable.*

4.2 Prepositions following their complement in PP structure

Notwithstanding, apart, aside

These items either precede or, less often, follow their complement. *Apart* and *aside* take a *from* phrase complement when they precede, but an NP when they follow:

[16] i a. *[Notwithstanding these objections,] they pressed ahead with their proposal.*
b. *[These objections notwithstanding,] they pressed ahead with their proposal.*
ii a. *[Apart/Aside from this,] he performed very creditably.*
b. *[This apart/aside,] he performed very creditably.*

The construction with the complement before the preposition bears some resemblance to an absolute construction with a subject–predicate structure. Compare:

[17] i *No one – [including missionaries] – had any right to intrude on their territory.*
ii *No one – [missionaries included] – had any right to intrude on their territory.*

In [i] *including* is a preposition derived by conversion from the gerund-participle form of a verb, and taking a following complement. In [ii] *included* is the past participle form of the verb, and there is no basis for saying that it has been converted into a preposition: *missionaries* is interpreted as the subject of a passive clause. *Notwithstanding, apart,* and *aside,* however, are not used predicatively (cf. **These objections are notwithstanding* or **This is apart/aside*), and hence a subject–predicate analysis of [16ib/iib] would not be valid: instead we treat them as exceptional PP constructions in which the complement precedes the head.

Ago and *on* following expressions denoting periods of time

More problematic is the analysis of the bracketed phrases in:

[18] a. *She died [ten years ago].* b. *[Ten years on] nothing had changed.*

Etymologically, *ago* derives from a past participle form *agone* (the prefix *a·* + the past participle of *go*), so that *ten years ago* has its origin in a subject–predicate construction comparable to that in [17ii] except that the past participle is active rather than passive. *Ago* is of course no longer construed as a past participle, but how the construction should now be analysed is unclear: it is syntactically highly exceptional. Expressions like *ten years* occur as optional modifiers modifying prepositions (*ten years before her death*) and adverbs (*ten years earlier*), but with *ago* such an expression is obligatory, which indicates that it has the status of a complement. Traditional grammar classifies *ago* as an adverb, but on the basis that it takes a complement we analyse it as a preposition, in accordance with the criteria given in §2.4. It is even more exceptional than *notwithstanding*, etc., in that it always follows its complement.

On, in the sense it has in [18b], namely "later", likewise cannot occur without the accompanying phrase: **On, nothing had changed.* We again take the dependent to be a complement, therefore, and treat *on* in this sense like *ago*, as a preposition that follows its complement.[13]

4.3 PPs of the form *spoonful by spoonful*

Expressions like *spoonful by spoonful, step by step, day by day, one by one* begin with a noun or cardinal numeral but do not have the distribution of NPs, being normally restricted to adjunct function. Compare:

[19] i a. **I used spoonful by spoonful.* b. **One by one exited.*
ii a. *I drank my milk spoonful by spoonful.* b. *They exited one by one.*

For this reason we take the head to be the preposition *by*, with the phrase as a whole, therefore, an exceptional PP construction. The constituent structure (ignoring the internal structure of the NPs) will be as follows:

[20]

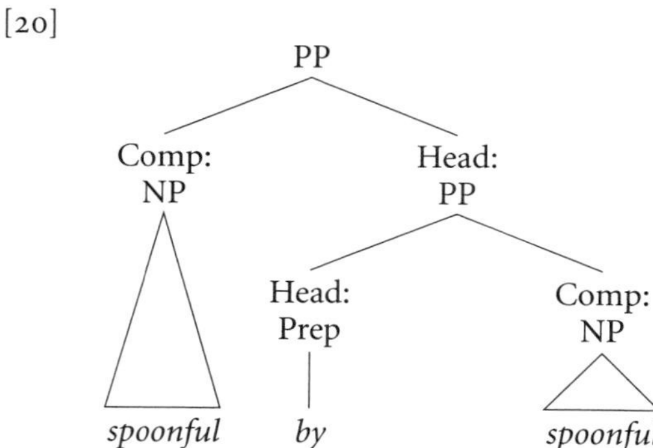

[13] One further case where a preposition follows its complement is in the idiom *(all) the world over*, which is essentially equivalent to the syntactically regular construction *all over the world*.

The distinction between internal and external complements applies to this minor type of PP as well as to clauses and NPs. The second NP is an internal complement in that it forms a PP with the head *by*, and the first NP is then an external complement.[14]

In the examples given, the two complements are identical single-word NPs. A minor variant has modification in one or both: (*dogged*) *step by dogged step*. The same kind of structure also seems applicable to such adjunct expressions as *one at a time*, as in *She marked them one at a time*.[15]

It is arguable that a PP analysis along these lines is also appropriate for a number of lexicalised phrases like *arm in arm*, *face down*, *side by side*, *back to back*, *inside out* which function either as adjuncts or as predicatives: *They were walking arm in arm* or simply *They were arm in arm*. In the case of *face down* and *inside out*, however, the inner PP is intransitive, consisting of a head preposition alone. These expressions have their origin as verbless clauses, and we discuss them further in Ch. 14, §10.

4.4 Preposing in PP structure

The domain for preposing is usually the clause, but it can also be a PP. Compare the examples in [21], where the structure of [iib] is as shown in [22]:

[21]	i	a. *I gave some of them to Angela.*	[basic]
		b. *Some of them$_i$ I gave __$_i$ to Angela.*	[preposing]
	ii	a. [*Though it seems incredible,*] *sales of these cars are falling.*	[basic]
		b. [*Incredible$_i$ though it seems __$_i$,*] *sales of these cars are falling.*	[preposing]

[22]

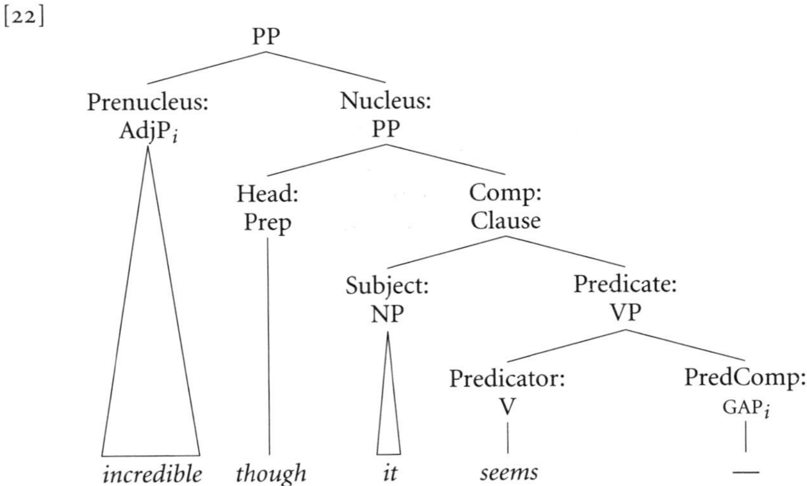

[14] We do not, however, need to recognise a category intermediate between PP and preposition, comparable to VP and nominal. There are major distributional differences between a VP and a clause and between a nominal and an NP, but there are no comparable grounds for having an intermediate category in the structure of PPs.

[15] But not in *She marked one at a time*, where *one at a time* does not form a constituent: *one* is object, and *at a time* is an ordinary PP adjunct. We do not include in the PP construction expressions like *day after day* or *quarrel after quarrel*. These are NPs, with the first noun as head and the PP as dependent. This is evident from the fact that their distribution depends on the first noun. *Day after day*, for example, can function as subject,

In [21ib] the preposed *some of them* occupies prenuclear position in the clause; the notation '__' marks the corresponding gap in the nucleus. In [iib], however, the preposed *incredible* appears in prenuclear position within the PP, while the gap is located within the clause functioning as complement of the preposition.[16] In this construction, then, the preposition follows part, but not all, of its complement.

Restriction to *though* and *as*

Preposing in PP structure applies only with *though* or *as* as head. Note, for example, that while *though* is elsewhere interchangeable with *although*, the latter cannot replace it in [21iib]. *Though* always has concessive meaning; *as* is most often used with that meaning too, but it can also be used with the sense "since, given that". Compare:

[23] i *This brouhaha, [colourful$_i$ as it is __$_i$,] would have little significance outside of Idaho if it did not reflect some of the larger problems facing the NRA.*

ii *This exhibition, [composed as it is __$_i$ of a large number of small works,] cannot have been an easy one to select.*

In [i] we understand that the brouhaha would have had little significance in spite of being colourful, but in [ii] the exhibition can't have been easy to select because it is composed of a large number of small works. *Though* could thus replace *as* in [i], but not in [ii]. In the concessive sense *as* occurs only in the preposing construction: *as it is colourful* cannot be substituted for the bracketed PP in [i] without changing the meaning from concessive to causal.

Form and function of the preposed element

In the examples given above, the gap is in predicative complement function. Other examples of this kind are as follows:

[24] i *The house, [close to the highway$_i$ though it is __$_i$,] seems quiet and secluded.*

ii *The house, [close$_i$ though it is __$_i$ to the highway,] seems quiet and secluded.*

iii %*[As bad$_i$ as last week was __$_i$,] this week promises little respite for the premier.*

iv *[Gifted exponent of the classical guitar$_i$ though he is __$_i$,] his excursions into jazz have on the whole been considerably less convincing.*

v %*[As big a hit as it is __$_i$ in Europe,] Timotei never made it out of the test market in the US.*

As illustrated in [i–ii], the preposing may affect the whole of the predicative element or just the first part of it: in [ii] the complement of *close* remains within the nucleus. With concessive *as* some speakers have a preposed predicative adjective modified by the adverb *as*: see example [iii]. *As bad as* here looks like a comparison of equality (such as we have in, for example, *It was as bad as expected*), but that is not how it is interpreted: the meaning of the PP is simply "though last week was bad".

When the preposed predicative complement is an NP, it normally has no determiner, even when it is count singular, as in [24iv]. In the more basic construction, without preposing, the NP here would require the indefinite article: *though he is a gifted exponent of the classical guitar*. In the variety that allows the adverb *as* as modifier, however, the

object, or adjunct (*Day after day was wasted*; *They wasted day after day*; *She worked on it day after day*), while *quarrel after quarrel* does not allow the adjunct function. Note, moreover, that the PP can be followed by another PP within the same NP: *They climbed [flight after flight of stairs]*.

[16] Preposing within a PP, like preposing in general, is an unbounded dependency construction: see Ch. 12, §7.

article can appear in a preposed NP, but not in initial position: see [24v], where *a* follows the AdjP.[17] The version without adverbial *as* would again have a bare NP (*big hit*ᵢ *as it is* _ᵢ *in Europe*), while the basic version would have just the article (*though it is a big hit in Europe*). Note that with NPs it is again possible for a post-head dependent to be positioned in the nucleus: compare the initial PP in [24iv] with *Gifted exponent*ᵢ *though he is* _ᵢ *of the classical guitar.*

It is also possible to prepose other elements, such as a degree modifier or the complement of an auxiliary verb:

[25] i *I can't come, I'm afraid,* [*much*ᵢ *as I would like* _ᵢ *to*].
ii [*Try*ᵢ *as I might* _ᵢ,] *I couldn't improve my time.*
iii [*Apologise*ᵢ *though he did* _ᵢ,] *Jill declared she would never forgive him.*

5 The structure and functions of PPs

5.1 Complementation

In this section we review fairly summarily the kinds of complement found in PPs.

(a) Object NPs

The prototypical preposition takes an NP as complement: *in the garden*, *to Paris*, etc. As we will see under (b) below, the distinction drawn in clause structure between an object and a predicative complement applies to PP structure too. The NPs *the garden* and *Paris* in the above examples are thus objects, and the contrast of transitive vs intransitive can be applied to prepositions as well as to verbs. *In*, for example, is transitive in *She stayed in the house*, and intransitive in *She stayed in.*

A number of prepositions that take objects have been identified in §2: [24] lists those that are derived by conversion from verbs, while [27] lists those with either an object or no complement at all. The following take an obligatory complement (though some of them accept other types than an object NP):

[1]						
	i	*amid(st)*	*among(st)*	*as*	*at*	*bar*
		beside	*come*	*despite*	*during*	*ere*
		from	*into*	*less*	*like*	*minus*
		of	*onto*	*per*	*plus*	*save*
		than	*till*	*times*	*unlike*	*until*
		upon	*versus*	*via*	*with*	
	ii	*à la*	*chez*	*circa*	*contra*	*modulo*
		pace	*re*	*sans*	*vis-à-vis*	

The items in [ii] are borrowings from French or Latin (*sans* being archaic or jocular, as in *sans teeth*, "without teeth"). The *as* in [i] is the comparative *as* of *She had saved as much* [*as twenty dollars*]: for *He struck me* [*as an impostor*] see (b) below. *Beside* usually means "close to" (*Come and sit beside me*) or "wide of", but it is also used with the same meaning

[17] An exception to the rule that a preposed NP cannot begin with a determiner is seen in the following example from journalistic prose: *No intellectual though he is on many issues, Mr Bush can out-wonk most people when it comes to public education.* It is questionable whether this construction is well enough established to be considered grammatical.

as *besides*, "in addition to"; the object is obligatory in either case, whereas with *besides* it is optional. *Come* takes a future time expression as complement: *Come the end of the year, we should be free of all these debts.* Historically, this is a subjunctive clausal construction, with *come* a plain form verb and *the end of the year* its subject; synchronically, however, its function and internal structure are like those of a PP (compare *by the end of the year*), and it is plausible to suggest that *come* has been reanalysed as a preposition.

Between vs among

The complement of *between* and *among* is required to be semantically plural. Syntactically, it generally has the form of a plural NP (*between/among the trees*) or an *and*-coordination of NPs (*I found it hard to choose between/among cornflakes, bran flakes, oat flakes, and muesli*). In addition, *among* readily accepts a collective singular (*among the crowd*), and *between* accepts a singular determined by distributive *each* or *every* (*There will be a five-minute interval between each lecture* – we understand "between each lecture and the next").[18]

There is a well-known prescriptive rule saying that *between* is required when the complement denotes a set of two, and *among* when it denotes a larger set. This rule is based on the etymology of *between*, and is empirically quite unjustified, as is now recognised by most usage manuals. The restriction to a set of two does not apply to the *between* examples given in the last paragraph, nor to the following, where *among* is not acceptable:

[2] i *I have sand between/#among my toes.*
ii *I never eat between/#among meals.*
iii *He hid it somewhere between/#among the back door, the shed, and the oaktree.*

The difference between the prepositions is thus not a matter of the size of the set denoted by their complement. It is, rather, that with *between* the members of the set are considered individually, whereas with *among* they are considered collectively. In [2i], for example, the sand is located between one toe and the one(s) adjacent to it, and similarly in [ii] we are concerned with the time between one meal and the next. In [iii] the back door, the shed, and the oaktree define the boundary points of a triangular area.

Such examples may be contrasted with the following, where only *among* is acceptable:

[3] i *Among/#Between the meals that we had, several stand out as exceptional.*
ii *Police paced among/#between the crowd.*

Here the members of the set are taken all together. Such verbs as *choose, divide, share* can accept both prepositions, though the collective interpretation of *among* will normally require a set of more than two: *I can't choose between/#among the two of them.*

(b) Predicative complements

The main preposition taking a predicative complement is *as*: this is the prepositional analogue of the verb *be*. The whole *as* phrase may function as complement or adjunct in the larger construction containing it:

[4] i *I regard their behaviour [as outrageous].* [complement]
ii *[As treasurer] I recommend we increase the fees by 10%.* [adjunct]

[18] *Between* is sometimes found with *or* or *to* instead of *and*: *This forces many to choose between work or having a family* and *Lambs are usually marked at between 1 to 6 weeks.* These are blends between the regular constructions *choose between X and Y* and *choose X or Y*, and *between 1 and 6 weeks* and *from 1 to 6 weeks.* It is doubtful if they are well enough established to be considered grammatical.

The complement is predicative in that it is related to a predicand: the object *their behaviour* in [i], the subject *I* in [ii]. In the complement use, the *as* is selected by the verb – in this example, by the prepositional verb *regard* (see Ch. 4, §6.1.2).

Syntactic differences between predicatives and objects

In the discussion of clause structure we noted three syntactic differences between predicative complements and objects: a predicative can be realised by an AdjP or bare role NP; it can never correspond to the subject of an equivalent passive clause; and it can under certain conditions be realised by a nominative case pronoun (cf. Ch. 4, §5.1). Compare:

		a.	b.
[5]	i	a. *Kim was ill/treasurer.*	b. **Kim attacked ill/treasurer.*
	ii	a. **The treasurer was been by Kim.*	b. *The treasurer was attacked by Kim.*
	iii	a. *It was I who told them.*	b. **Kim attacked I.*

In [i/iii] the underlined complement is predicative in [a], object in [b], while in [ii] it is a subject corresponding in [a] to the predicative complement of the active (*Kim was the treasurer*) and in [b] to the object of the active (*Kim attacked the treasurer*). The nominative case factor is irrelevant with *as* since (in the sense we are concerned with here) it does not license personal pronouns as complement. The other two differences are illustrated in the contrast between *as* and *into* in:

		a.	b.
[6]	i	a. *He regards your answer as correct.*	b. **This turned your answer into correct.*
	ii	a. **My guide was acted as by Kim.*	b. *The matter will be looked into by Kim.*

The AdjP *correct* is acceptable with *as* but not with *into*, which takes an object. And the deviance of [iia] is attributable to the fact that in the active *Kim acted as my guide* the complement of *as* is predicative. The passive voice factor, however, is of less significance for the complements of prepositions than for the complements of verbs, for there are many transitive prepositions which also cannot be stranded in the passive construction – cf. **This setback was continued despite by Kim* (corresponding to *Kim continued despite this setback*).

The important factor is thus the form of the complement: *as*, like the verb *be*, allows AdjPs and bare role NPs. AdjPs are of course the more sharply distinct from object NPs, but they are not permitted in all cases. For example, *as* phrases in adjunct function permit bare role NPs, as in [4ii], but not AdjPs. Compare:

[7]	i	**As ill, Kim withdrew from the competition.*	[complement of preposition]
	ii	*Being ill, Kim withdrew from the competition.*	[complement of verb]

The category of number in predicative NPs

The predicative complement of *as*, like that of a verb, characteristically matches its predicand in number when it has the form of an NP. Compare *as* and *from*:

		a.	b.
[8]	i	a. *I regard her as a friend / #friends.*	b. *I bought it from a friend / friends.*
	ii	a. *I regard them as friends / #a friend.*	b. *I bought them from friends / a friend.*

We have noted, however, that this is a matter of semantic compatibility rather than grammatical agreement (compare, for example, the plural + singular combination in *I regard them as a nuisance*): see Ch. 4, §§5.1–2, Ch. 5, §19.

Predicative complements with prepositions other than *as*

[9] i *I took him for harmless.*
ii *The situation went from bad to worse.*
iii *I don't want to make an announcement qua head of department.*

For takes a predicative complement after two verbs, *take* and *pass* (as in *He passed for dead*). *From* and *to* take predicatives in clauses expressing a change of state: see Ch. 4, §5.2. *Qua* is another preposition borrowed from Latin, very similar in meaning to *as*, which could substitute for it in [iii]. It belongs to formal style, and perhaps its most characteristic use is between two instances of the same noun: *It wasn't a very good novel qua novel* ("considered as a novel"). It differs from *as* in that the complement must be a bare NP, whether it denotes a role or not.[19]

Adjectives occur as complement in a few expressions like *in brief*, *of old*, but these are idioms, and as there is no predicand we have no reason to analyse the complement as predicative (see §3.2 above).

Prepositions taking reducible clauses as complement

[10] i [*Although she was moderately rich,*] *she lived very frugally.*
ii [*Although moderately rich,*] *she lived very frugally.*

In [i] *although* has a content clause as complement, but the subject and predicator can be omitted, leaving just the predicative complement, as in [ii]. This latter construction differs from the one with *as* precisely by virtue of its relation with the full content clause. The *as* phrases in [4] cannot be expanded in this way: **I regard their behaviour as it is outrageous* is ungrammatical, while *As I am treasurer, I recommend we increase the fees by 10%* has a quite different meaning from [4ii], with *as* now having a causal sense. For this reason we take *moderately rich* in [10ii] to be a reduced clause, and classify *although* as taking a reducible clause as complement.

(c) Complements with the form of a PP

The complement of a preposition may itself have a preposition as its head. There are two cases to distinguish:

[11] i *We didn't see anyone* [*apart from Jill*]. [specified by matrix prep]
ii *They have lived here* [*since before the war*]. [not specified]

In [i] the head of the larger PP, *apart*, takes a PP complement headed by *from*: the *from* is thus specified by the head of the matrix construction. In [ii], however, *before* is not specified by *since* but makes an independent contribution to the meaning, and potentially contrasts with other prepositions – compare, for example, *They have lived here* [*since just after the war*]. The distinction is comparable to that found in clause structure between *They referred to her article* (where *to* is specified by the verb *refer*) and *They went to Paris* (where *to* is not specified by *go* and potentially contrasts with other prepositions, such as *towards*, *over*, etc.).

[19] Dictionaries differ in their grammatical classification of *qua* (which derives from the ablative form of the relative pronoun "who"): while some treat it as a preposition, others call it a conjunction or an adverb. It is clearly not a coordinating conjunction, but it doesn't fit the traditional definition of a subordinating conjunction either, for it cannot introduce a subordinate clause. It is like a preposition, and unlike an adverb, in that it obligatorily occurs with a following NP.

Complements headed by specified prepositions

Prepositions specified by the preceding head are *of*, *to*, *from*, *for*, *on*, and *with*:

[12] i *She took it [out of the box].*
 ii *She was sitting [next to her sister].*
 iii *They were running [away from us].*
 iv *She would have broken the record [but for the appalling weather conditions].*
 v *[Consequent on the fire,] the shop closed.*
 vi *[Together with Jim,] I moved the piano.*

Prepositions which select *of* as head of their complement include the following:

[13] i	*because*	*exclusive*	*irrespective*		
ii	*abreast*	*ahead*	*instead*	*regardless*	*upward(s)*
	east	*north*	*south*	*west*	
iii	*alongside*	*inside*	%*off*	*out*	*outside*

Those in [i] do not occur without a complement, though the adjective *exclusive* can, and *because* also takes a clausal complement. With the prepositions in [ii–iii] the complement is optional, those in [iii] also allowing an NP complement.

Off licenses an *of* phrase only in AmE (%*He fell off of the wall*). Conversely, *out* usually takes an *of* PP: an NP complement is primarily AmE (or informal), and generally restricted to NPs determined by *the* in combination with such verbs as *look*, *jump*, *go*, etc. Compare %*He jumped/looked out the window* and **He jumped out bed* or **I took it out my pocket*, etc.

Inside of commonly occurs with time periods (*She'd finished inside of a week*), but is otherwise restricted to AmE. *Outside* takes *of* rather than an NP when the meaning is "except" (*Outside of us two, no one knew what was going on*), but with the locative sense *of* is again restricted to AmE (%*outside of Boston*).

Prepositions selecting *to* as head of their complement include the items in [14] (where boldfacing, in accord with our usual conventions, identifies the two lexemes that – exceptionally for prepositions – have inflected comparative and superlative forms):

[14]	*according*	***close***	*contrary*	*counter*	*due*	*further*
	near	*next*	*owing*	*pertaining*	*preliminary*	*preparatory*
	previous	*prior*	*pursuant*	*subsequent*	*thanks*	*unbeknown(st)*

For the most part the *to* phrase complement is obligatory when these items are prepositions. The exceptions are ***close*** and ***near***, as in *Bring it a little closer/nearer*; ***near*** also takes an object. *Further to*, as in *Further to our correspondence, I am happy to enclose details of the property*, is an idiom: in other senses *further* (the comparative form of ***far***) can occur without a complement. Many of the items in [14] are converted from adjectives, as discussed in §2.2; *thanks*, however, is an isolated case of a preposition converted from a noun. The meaning of *thanks to X* is something like "because of X". When X is human (or animate) we find an extra dimension of personal responsibility deserving of recognition; there may be an implicit element of gratitude, either sincere (*Thanks to Jim, we're safe and well*) or ironical (*Thanks to you, all my clothes are soaking wet*).

Only a few items select the other grammaticised prepositions. *On* is selected only by *consequent*, and *with* only by *together*, as in [12v–vi]. The others are selected as follows:

[15]	i	*allowing*	*but*	*except*		[select *for*]
	ii	*apart*	*aside*	*away*	***far***	[select *from*]
		downstage	*upstage*	*downstream*	*upstream*	

But selects *for* only in the conditional sense illustrated in [12iv] ("if it hadn't been for the appalling weather conditions"); elsewhere it takes an object (*Anyone but you would have jumped at the opportunity*). *Except* requires *for* in the conditional interpretation (it can substitute for *but* in [12iv]), and elsewhere takes either a *for* complement or an object: *Everyone liked it except Kim / except for Kim*. With *away* and ***far*** the complement is optional; *apart* and *aside* with the sense "except" require a complement – a *for* phrase if it follows, an NP if it precedes (see §4.2).

Complements headed by non-specified prepositions

The prepositions that most readily take PP complements of the potentially contrastive type are *from*, *since*, and *till* or *until*. *From* is used in the spatial or temporal domains, the others just in the temporal one. *Since* is illustrated in [11ii], the others in:

[16] i *He emerged [from under the bed].*
ii *The meeting lasted [from just before twelve] [until/till after six].*

To is generally not used in this way: we say *He crawled under the bed* rather than ?*He crawled to under the bed* (see Ch. 8, §4.3). It is certainly not wholly excluded, however: we can have *They have moved to across the river* ("They have relocated to a place across the river").

The PPs *here*, *there*, *now*, *then* occur as complement to a wider range of prepositions than do such PPs as *under the bed* or *after six*. We find, for example, *They live near here*; *Put it on there*; *I found it behind here*; *You should have told me before now*; *He certainly stayed past then*.

(d) Complements with the form of an AdvP

This construction is very restricted, the most clearly acceptable combinations being those marked by the plus signs in [17], where the top row gives the heads, the left column the complements:

[17]		*before/ere*	*for*	*till/until*
i	*later*		+	+
ii	*lately, recently*			+
iii	*ever, once*		+	
iv	*long*	+	+	

In [18] we give one example of each combination, with the PP bracketed and the complement underlined.

[18] i *Why don't you save it [for later]?*
ii *I didn't hear about it [until later].*
iii *[Until recently] there wasn't even a road.*
iv *Why don't you listen [for once]?*
v *You'll be feeling better [before long].*
vi *He won't have that car [for long].*

(e) Complements with the form of clauses

[19] i *This happened [after Stacy left].* [non-expandable declarative]
ii *I'll do it [provided that you help me].* [expandable declarative]
iii *[Although (we were) nearly exhausted,] we pressed on.* [reducible declarative]
iv *Let me repeat, [lest there be any doubt about the terms].* [subjunctive]
v *They ignored the question [of whether it was ethical].* [interrogative]
vi *We can't agree [on how much to charge].* [infinitival interrogative]
vii *They're talking [about moving to New York].* [gerund-participial]
viii *He's not as enthusiastic [as he used to be].* [comparative]

Non-interrogative infinitivals are found with the expressions *in order* and *so as*: *He only mentioned it [in order to embarrass his wife]* or *We left at dawn [so as to miss the rush-hour traffic]*. Constructions with clausal complements are dealt with in the context of our discussion of subordinate clauses in Chs. 11, 13, and 14. Note that in *They kept blaming him [for what he had done]* the underlined constituent is not a clause but an NP (a fused relative), and hence does not belong under the present heading.

(f) Double complementation

We suggested in §3.1 that in examples like *in league with the guys from down the road* the *with* phrase is complement of *in league*, while *league* is complement of *in*: we have a layered structure of the kind shown in diagram [9c] of §3. There are also non-idiomatic examples that have such a layered structure:

[20] i *[From Boston to Providence] is not far.*
ii *[To Los Angeles from Chicago] is the path of the fabled Route 66.*
iii *[Across the road from the post office] there is a children's playground.*

In [i] *Boston* is complement of *from*, and *to Providence* is complement of *from Boston*: thus at the top level the head of the whole PP is the smaller PP *from Boston*, and at the next level *from* is head of this latter PP. In support of this analysis, note that *to Providence* is clearly a complement because it cannot be omitted, and it is also clear that it is not a dependent of *Boston*, for it depends crucially on the presence of *from*. The bracketed PP in [ii] is similar, but has *to* rather than *from* as the ultimate head. Example [iii] is not so clear because *from the post office* is omissible. Nevertheless, it qualifies as a complement because it is licensed by *across the road*: note the contrast, for example, between this construction and *on the road from the post office*, where *from the post office* is a dependent of *road*, so that the structure is simply *on* as head + *the road from the post office* as object. (*Downstream from where we were camped* is somewhat similar, but here *down* and *stream* are compounded, so syntactically there is only one layer of complementation, and the construction is covered under [15ii].)

(g) Matrix-licensed complements

Some prepositions appear with a wide range of complements that are licensed not by the preposition itself but by an element in the matrix clause to which the PP in question bears a modifier relation. One clear case of a preposition of this kind is *except*, as illustrated in the following examples:

[21] i *There's nobody here* [*except the cleaners*]. [NP]
ii *I've been everything* [*except president*]. [bare role NP]
iii *I don't know where to look* [*except in the garden*]. [PP]
iv *I have felt every imaginable way* [*except proud of myself*]. [AdjP]
v *This thesis treats the topic in every way* [*except competently*]. [AdvP]
vi *There is nothing any of us can do* [*except be cautious*]. [bare infinitival]
vii *I don't intend to do anything* [*except to wait for news*]. [*to*-infinitival]
viii *I can't think what to advise* [*except staying home*]. [gerund-participial]
ix *He said not a thing* [*except that he was sorry*]. [declarative content clause]
x *They told me everything* [*except whether I'd passed*]. [closed interrogative]
xi *I asked little* [*except what they had been doing*]. [open interrogative]
xii *She asked nothing* [*except that they be reprimanded*]. [subjunctive clause]

What this indicates is not that *except* licenses complements of all the different phrasal categories in the grammar, but rather that it takes as its complement something licensed by features of the clause containing it. That is, the internal syntax of a PP with a head like *except* is, unusually, not independent of the syntax of the matrix clause in which it appears: we accordingly speak of the underlined expressions as **matrix-licensed complements** of *except*.

That it is the matrix clause, not *except* itself, that licenses the complements in [21] is evident from the fact that if we shift *except* PPs from one example to another at random we will get some starkly ungrammatical results. Compare, for example, **There's nobody left here except be cautious*; **I've been everything except that they be reprimanded*; **I can't think what to advise except proud of myself*; and so on.

What makes the examples in [21] admissible is that they entail or implicate [22i–xi] respectively:

[22] i *The cleaners are here.*
ii *I have not been president.*
iii *I know to look in the garden.*
iv *I have not felt proud of myself.*
v *This thesis does not treat the topic competently.*
vi *We can be cautious.*
vii *I intend to wait for news.*
viii *I advise staying home.*
ix *He said (that) he was sorry.*
x *They didn't tell me whether I'd passed.*
xi *I asked what they had been doing.*
xii *She asked that they be reprimanded.*

The underlined expressions are directly admissible in these contexts, and this is sufficient to sanction their occurrence as complement to *except* in the corresponding member of set [21].

The grammatical relationship between the corresponding clauses in [21] and [22] is, however, in some cases quite loose. Although we can say that the polarity is changed (positive to negative and negative to positive), and that such features as tense, aspect, and mood are left unchanged, there is no simple syntactic manipulation of the clauses in [21] that systematically yields the clauses in [22]. For example, if we change [21viii] in the same way as [21iii], we get the anomalous *#I can think to advise staying home.*

Except is representative of a wider class of prepositions with matrix-licensed complements. Other members are *bar, but, excepting, excluding, save,* and *including.*[20] The first five of these are semantically close to *except*, but *including* has the opposite meaning, so that the corresponding clause that licenses the complement directly does not differ in polarity:

[23] i a. *I have felt every imaginable way [including proud of myself].*
b. *I have felt proud of myself.*
ii a. *I have looked everywhere, [including in the garden].*
b. *I have looked in the garden.*
iii a. *He said quite a lot, [including that he was sorry].*
b. *He said that he was sorry.*

Comparative *as* and *than* can be followed by a similarly wide range of expressions provided they are licensed by the matrix construction. Compare:

[24] i a. *He should have said more [than that he was sorry].*
b. *He said that he was sorry.*
ii a. *She asked nothing more [than that they be reprimanded].*
b. *She asked that they be reprimanded.*

As and *than*, however, also take comparative clauses as complement, and in cases like *He has more enemies [than friends]* it is arguable that *friends* should be analysed as a reduced clause: see Ch. 13, §2.2, for discussion of this issue.

5.2 Modification

In this section we survey the kinds of modifier found in the structure of PPs.

(a) Idiomatic PPs with gradable meanings

We have seen that there are a number of idiomatic PPs that are gradable, and as far as their external syntax is concerned they bear significant resemblances to adjectives – PPs such as *in a bad temper, in control, out of sorts, out of order, on top of the world.* These take degree expressions as modifier:

[25] i *She seemed [completely in control of the situation].*
ii *That remark was [wholly out of order].*
iii *I was feeling [very much out of sorts].*

For the choice between *very much* and *very* or *too much* and *too*, see Ch. 6, §2.2.

[20] To a certain extent, *beyond* behaves in a similar way, as in this AusE example: *He is understood to have been given no assurances [beyond that the Coalition did not believe Labor's cross-media regulations were effective]* (corresponding to *He was given the assurance that the Coalition did not believe Labor's cross-media regulations were effective*).

(b) NPs indicating spatial and temporal extent

[26] i *We live [two miles / a few minutes' walk beyond the post office].*
ii *It happened [ten minutes / a long time after the accident].*

This is a common type of modification of PPs headed by spatial and temporal prepositions.

(c) PP-specialised pre-head modifiers (*right*, *straight*, etc.)

As mentioned in §2.1, there are a few adverbs which occur as modifiers in PPs but not in phrases of other categories. These PP-specialised modifiers include *clear*, *right*, *smack*, and *straight*:[21]

[27] i *The bank robber was [clear across the state] before the police were alerted.*
ii *The ball went [right out of the park].*
iii *Torbin drove his car [smack into the rear end of a truck] this morning.*
iv *When he saw me, he walked [straight into the other room].*

Clear conveys movement to a distant point that breaks free and clear of restraints: *flew clear out of sight, went clear over the house, drove clear across town.*

Right denotes exactitude or immediacy of location or direction, either literally or metaphorically, the connection to the adjective *right* "correct" being that the prepositional description is fully and literally correctly satisfied: *ran right up a tree, collapsed right in front of me, went right back to her mother, fell right into my hand, heading right for the shore. Right* may also emphasise completion, as in *ate it right up, came right up to me, fell right over on its side.*

Informal *smack* indicates complete exactitude of location, often but not always combined with a suggestion (perhaps metaphorical) of impact: *dropped smack on top of the other one, walked smack into the door, lay smack in the centre.*

Straight describes the accuracy and directness of a path either in space (*climbed straight up the tree, sailed straight between the goalposts*) or time (*met straight after lunch*) or both (*went straight to the police*), and thus connects to the sense of the adjective *straight* "not bent".

(d) Other adverbial modifiers

[28] i *The ball had landed [very clearly beyond the base-line].*
ii *You will find it [immediately on the left of the post office].*
iii *They had arrived [shortly after midnight].*
iv *That all happened [way before Kim's appointment].*
v *I regard it as [quite obviously and uncontroversially within the dean's powers].*

Like VPs, AdjPs, and AdvPs, PPs may be modified by any of an open class of AdvPs expressing extent, precision, epistemic status, etc., preceding the head. The range of AdvPs permitted is determined not by grammatical rule but by the kind of modification that is appropriate to the meaning of the phrase. Thus *shortly* "a short time", for example, modifies temporal prepositions such as *before* and *after*, but not spatial ones like *from* or *to*.

[21] The word *spot* also occurs in this function in a very restricted way, in the idiom *spot on*, where it connotes exactness of position on some point: *We were spot on with our estimate of the cost.*

(e) *All*

[29] i *There were troops [all round the building].*
ii *He had blood [all over his shirt].*

All indicates completeness: in [i] the building was completely surrounded. *All over* is partly idiomatic, for if we omit *all* the natural preposition to use would be *on* rather than *over* – and *on* does not accept *all* as modifier (**He had blood all on his shirt*). *All* also occurs with some of the idiomatic PPs that are used predicatively: *I was all of a dither*; *It's all up in the air now.*

(f) Directional preposition modifiers (*over in the corner*)

Certain directional prepositions are frequently found functioning as pre-head modifiers in PPs. The clearest cases are *down, out, over, round,* and *up.*

[30] i *[Down under the house] it was cool.*
ii *I saw you last night [out on the edge of town].*
iii *My ball went right [over into the neighbours' garden].*
iv *I think dad may be [round at the pub].*
v *You'll find it [up on top of the filing cabinet].*

To a limited extent these modifiers can be iterated: *right up over the house, up round the corner.* They modify the sense of the head preposition by indicating the path that should be envisaged: there are several ways one might go into the neighbours' garden, but *over into the neighbours' garden* suggests a path going over the fence. They are particularly common with *here* and *there*: *over here, out there, up in here, down over there,* etc.

We can see that it is the last preposition in the relevant preposition sequences that is the head, because the last preposition is the one that determines whether the whole phrase is admissible in a given context:

	a.	b.
[31] i	*I placed it [up on the shelf].*	*I placed it [on the shelf].*
ii	**I placed it [up to the attic].*	**I placed it [to the attic].*
iii	*He headed [over into the next valley].*	*He headed [into the next valley].*
iv	**He headed [over on that hill].*	**He headed [on that hill].*

The [a] examples, with the modifier, are admissible only if the [b] ones, without the modifier, are admissible. The verb *place*, for example, licenses a PP with *on* as head, but not *to*, so both examples in [i] are admissible and both in [ii] are not. Analogously for the verb *head* in [iii–iv].

(g) Post-head modifiers

[32] i *[Downstairs in the kitchen] were several other guests.*
ii *[Underneath on a low shelf] stood the dishwasher detergent.*
iii *You'll find it [outside the back door by the garbage bin].*
iv *We're having a great time [over here in Guernsey].*
v *[Astern of us on the horizon] we saw the sails of a galleon.*

These examples illustrate PPs functioning as post-head modifiers within a PP. Semantically, *in the kitchen* in [i] modifies *downstairs* just as it modifies *sat* in a VP like *sat in the kitchen.* Syntactically, the fact that the underlined PPs are within the bracketed PPs is shown by such tests as constituent order; in [ii] and [v], for example, the containing PP has been preposed as a unit.

5.3 Functions of PPs

We have already seen from the account of the internal structure of PPs that one PP can function within a larger one, as head, complement, or modifier:

[33] i *Sue was still [at odds with her parents] on this issue.* [head in PP]
ii *She lives [just down the street from Kim's].* [complement in PP]
iii *I'm [down here by the back door].* [modifier in PP]

For the most part, however, PPs function in other constructions, as in:

[34] i *I gave the key to Sue.* [complement in clause]
ii *She put the key in her bag.* [complement in clause]
iii *They are under the table.* [complement in clause]
iv *She had slept in the attic.* [adjunct in clause]
v *Where's [the key to the safe]?* [complement in NP]
vi *They bought [a house with a flat roof].* [modifier in NP]
vii *There are now [fewer than a hundred] seats left.* [complement in DP]
viii *[Only one in twenty] candidates were shortlisted.* [modifier in DP]
ix *They are still [very keen on surfing].* [complement in AdjP]
x *He was [tired to the point of exhaustion].* [modifier in AdjP]
xi *He likes to do things [differently from everyone else].* [complement in AdvP]
xii *I'll be seeing her [later in the week].* [modifier in AdvP]

In [i], *to Sue* is a PP complement whose head preposition is specified by the verb: this type is discussed in Ch. 4, §8.2.1. *In her bag* in [ii] is a goal complement, and *under the table* in [iii] a locative complement, while in [iv] *in the attic* is an adjunct in the clause: complements and modifiers where the head preposition is not specified by the verb are dealt with in Ch. 8. The remaining examples show PPs functioning as complement or modifier in the structure of NPs and DPs (see Ch. 5, §§11, 14), AdjPs and AdvPs (Ch. 6, §§3, 6).

PPs with quantificational complements

Certain types of PP containing a numeral or measure phrase have a distribution like that of a DP or NP rather than of an ordinary PP. Compare:

[35] i a. *She wrote [over fifty novels].* b. *She wrote [between forty and fifty novels].*
ii a. *I spent over a year here.* b. *I spent between ten months and a year here.*

In [i] the underlined PPs function as determiner in the bracketed NPs. *Over fifty* denotes a number larger than fifty, and as such is a suitable realisation of the determiner function; similarly, *between forty and fifty* denotes a number within the specified range. In [ii] the complements are an NP and an NP-coordination, and the PPs function as object of *spend*. See Ch. 5, §§4, 11, for further examples.

The prepositions or prepositional idioms used in this way include the following:

[36] i *around* *over* *under*
ii *close to* *up to* *in excess of*
iii *from . . . to* *between* (+ *and*-coordination)

PPs as subject and object in clause structure.

PPs of the type shown in [35ii] have a distribution like that of an NP, and hence can function as object (as in the examples given) or subject (cf. *Over a year was spent on this problem*). It is also possible, though unusual, for PPs denoting places or times to fill the subject and object functions:

[37] i a. *Under the mat is the place where we used to leave the key for the boys.*
b. *Under the mat isn't a very sensible place to leave the key.*
c. *Before the end of the week would suit me better.*
d. *Will at the week-end suffice, or do you need it sooner than that?*
ii a. *We must prevent under the desk from getting too untidy.*
b. *We asked where to put it, and the man recommended just above the front door.*
c. *They won't consider after Christmas, of course, to be soon enough.*

In the case of the subject, the verb is usually *be*, in either its specifying or its ascriptive sense, as in [ia–ib] respectively, but a restricted range of other verbs are also possible, as illustrated in [ic–id]. The underlined phrases in [ii] are interpreted in the same way as *the area under the desk, the area just above the front door, some time after Christmas*, and syntactically they behave in the same way as these NPs. In particular, they correspond to the subject of related passive clauses: compare *Under the desk must be prevented from getting too untidy* or *After Christmas won't of course be considered to be soon enough.*

6 Grammaticised prepositions

Some prepositions have become **grammaticised** in the sense of having specific syntactic roles in the language that are not determined by their meanings. A preposition like *under* is an example of a preposition that is clearly not grammaticised. It is an ordinary lexical item with a meaning, and it is used where a preposition is permitted and the meaning that it has is the appropriate one. No rule of sentence formation or condition on complement licensing needs to single it out in any way. Indeed, any syntax for English that did make specific mention of it would be insufficiently general. In all contexts where it can appear, other prepositions can appear too: beside *Put it under the table* we have *Put it above the table, Put it near the table*, and so on.

The grammaticised prepositions are not like *under*. Each of them is specifically mentioned in the definition of at least one grammatical construction or the statement of some grammatical condition on the distribution of some class of lexical items. For example, the verb *dispose* (meaning "get rid", etc.) cannot be used correctly without *of* being present as the preposition marking its complement: *They disposed of the box* is grammatical but **They disposed the box* is not. And other prepositions are not permitted where the *of* appears: **They disposed at/below/on/through/under the box.*

This section surveys the semantic and syntactic properties of those prepositions that are grammaticised in this sense. To set these facts in context it will be useful to begin with some general remarks about the meanings associated with the most basic prepositions of English.

6.1 Meanings of prototypical prepositions

Basicness of location

Most of the central prepositions in English (or any language) have meanings that are quite clearly locational in origin. More specifically, they concern either spatial location or change of location, or extensions of those notions into the dimension of time, or notions derived more broadly from them through other metaphors.

Landmark and trajector

In formulating expressions about spatial relationships, typically one entity is taken as a reference point (or area) with respect to which another is located. Let us call the reference point or area the **landmark** and the item whose location or movement is specified the **trajector**. For example, in *The pen is on the table*, the pen is the trajector and the table is the landmark. In *He collapsed in the bedroom*, the trajector is the event of him collapsing and the landmark is the bedroom. Trajectors can be physical objects, abstract objects, or situations such as events and states; landmarks are typically physical objects or places (points or regions) in space, or else something metaphorically represented in those terms.

Location and change of location

While *Kim is at the supermarket* simply gives Kim's location, *Kim walked from the post-office to the supermarket* indicates a change of location. A change of location involves (explicitly or implicitly) an initial location and a final location: we refer to these as **source** and **goal** respectively. In this example, then, *from* marks the source and *to* the goal. There are two other prepositions besides *at* that have distinct source and goal counterparts, as shown in:

[1]	LOCATION	GOAL	SOURCE
i	*at*	*to*	*from*
ii	*on*	*on/onto*	*off*
iii	*in*	*in/into*	*out*

Double underlining indicates that the preposition can occur without a complement, giving the following range of possibilities:[22]

[2]	LOCATION	GOAL	SOURCE
i	*I'm at Heathrow.*	*I went to Heathrow.*	*I departed from Heathrow.*
ii a.	*It is on the floor.*	*It fell on/onto the floor.*	*I lifted it off the floor.*
b.	*The roof is still on.*	*She jumped on.*	*I fell off.*
iii a.	*It is in the box.*	*It fell in/into the box.*	*I took it out of the box.*
b.	*The doctor is in.*	*She jumped in.*	*They won't come out.*

The source prepositions *off* and *out* can also be used for static location, contrasting with *on* and *in* respectively. Compare *The car is on/off the road* and *The boss is in her office / out of her office.* Since in a source use such as *He fell off the ledge* he was on the ledge to start with, but not on it at the end, we can regard static *off* and *out* as the semantically negative counterparts of *on* and *in*.

One other source preposition is *away*, which occurs with a *from* complement or on its own: *I walked away* (*from them*). Like *off* and *out*, it is also used for static location, where it contrasts with *at*: compare *She is at home / away from home*. In its source use, it often alternates with *from*: *He moved away from the window / from the window*. It could not, however, be used with *departed* in [2i], and *from* is normally used when the source is paired with a goal, as in *She flew from London to Glasgow*.

[22] We noted in §2.4 that *to* can also occur without a complement, but only in secondary senses, which are not relevant to the present discussion.

Adding *away* and the static uses of *off* and *on* to [1] gives:[23]

[3]

	LOCATION		CHANGE OF LOCATION	
	Positive	**Negative**	**Goal**	**Source**
i	*at*	*away*	*to*	*away/from*
ii	*on*	*off*	*on/onto*	*off*
iii	*in*	*out*	*in/into*	*out*

There are no other source prepositions beside the four given here. Many of the other spatial prepositions, however, can be used both for location and for goal. Thus for *under*, for example, we have *The key is under the mat* (location) and *I put the key under the mat* (goal).

Ordinary location and endpoint location

Two cases of static location are to be distinguished, as illustrated in:

[4]

	ORDINARY LOCATION	ENDPOINT LOCATION
i	a. *There is a light over the table.*	b. *The cottage is over the hill.*
ii	a. *A large snake lay across our path.*	b. *They live across the river.*

In the [a] examples the preposition simply indicates the position of the trajector relative to the landmark. In the [b] examples, however, there is an implicit path from some point of orientation (in the default case the current position of the speaker) to the trajector. Thus the location of the cottage in [ib] is at the end of an implicit path or journey: to get to where the cottage is, you go over the hill. Similarly, in [iib]: to get to where they live, you go across the river, i.e. they live on the other side of the river from the point of orientation. For further discussion of the concepts of location, goal, and source, see Ch. 4, §5.2, Ch. 8, §4.3.

Plasticity of meaning

All prepositions demonstrate a considerable degree of flexibility in the way that they apply to locative situations. There are systematic ways in which such flexibility is shown, across differing prepositional meanings.

Containment and *in*

Whereas *in* prototypically denotes a relation in which the trajector is a physical object completely contained within a clearly bounded landmark (*the man in the study*), there are many cases in which the notion of containment applies only loosely. For example, in *the flowers in the vase* only a part of the trajector is contained within the confines of the landmark (cf. also *the woman in the white blouse*). And in *the bird in the tree* the boundaries of the landmark do not manifest themselves in the kind of concrete physical form characteristic of a prototypical container such as a building. Similarly a corner is a landmark with relatively ill-defined boundaries. Thus the trajector in *the chair in the corner* is not totally enclosed by the corner, but is contained in a vaguely delimited area of space that is nearer the corner than the middle of the room.

[23] *Into* has a very restricted locational use indicating distance travelled: *They camped five miles into the forest.* In addition it is used in static situations outside the spatial domain in examples like *He's into basket-weaving now*, an informal way of saying that he has gone into, or embarked upon, basket-weaving – metaphorically a journey into a new region of activity. *To* is used for static location with a narrow range of NP complements, such as those headed by *left* or *right* or compass terms: *It is situated a little to the north of the cathedral.* *From* can be used in static situations to indicate origin, as in *She is from London.*

Different aspects of a landmark may be prominent in different examples. In *the water in the vase*, for example, it is the sides that define the contained region, whereas in *the cracks in the vase* the surface of the object defines it.

Functional considerations may also come into play. A foot is described as being in a stirrup (in spite of being only partially contained by the landmark) but a finger is not described as being in a ring, even though the topographical relationships are similar. The difference is that the function of a stirrup is to hold a foot in a particular position, so it is naturally seen as a landmark, but there is no such function for a ring (being small and mobile, the ring is easily seen as a trajector). The same point applies to the contrast between *the bulb in the socket and #the jar in the lid*. The function of a socket is to hold a bulb, so the description is in terms of containment, but holding a jar in place is not the function of a lid.

Support and *on*

Similar points can be made about examples containing *on*. The prototypical situation for *on* is one in which trajector and landmark are in physical contact with each other, with the landmark located below the trajector and supporting it (as with *the pen on the desk*). However, an example like *the poster on the wall* diverges somewhat from this scenario: the physical contact and support apply in the horizontal rather than the vertical plane.

In *the wrinkles on his face* the vertical separation between landmark and trajector is notional rather than actual, as we see from the fact that a similar situation can be construed in terms of embedding rather than separation (*the wrinkles in his skin*). Similarly, the objective nature of the relationships in cases such as *the writing on the paper, the writing in the margin* is less important than the way in which these relationships are construed. We use *on the paper* because the paper serves as a background against which the writing is displayed, but we say *in the margin* because the landmark is a restricted area, and that motivates a construal in terms of containment.

Vehicles such as buses, trucks, trains, and large boats can be construed as containers (*She's in that bus over there*), but if the context is such that the role of the vehicle as transporter is salient, then the relationship between trajector and landmark is more likely to be construed in terms of support (*She'll be on the next bus*). Small boats and cars are normally conceptualised as containers rather than supporting surfaces (*I was sitting in a tiny little boat*), perhaps because of the close proximity of the external boundary of the trajector and the internal boundary of the landmark.

Point location and *at*

The preposition *at* provides a particularly clear example of the processes of abstraction involved in the expression of spatial relationships. The function of *at* is to describe two entities as having precisely the same spatial location, each entity being construed as a point. This means that some degree of idealisation is inevitably inherent in its use.

Consider, for example, the contrast between *John is in the supermarket* and *John is at the supermarket*. If one were standing outside the supermarket, it would be more natural to use *in* than *at*, since the discrepancy between the physical size of the person and the building makes a containment construal appropriate. But *at* becomes progressively more natural as the viewpoint shifts further away from the situation. Speaking from home, one says *John is at the supermarket*. This is because distance facilitates abstraction – naturally enough, for as we move away from objects in our visual field, their image on the retina grows smaller, approximating gradually to a point.

A consequence of the abstraction associated with *at* is that, if I arrange a meeting with someone and use the phrase *at the library*, there may be difficulties when the time of meeting arrives, since it does not specify whether the rendezvous is inside or outside the building. This distinction is lost when the building is conceptualised as a point.

An example like *The cafe is at the highway* seems at first sight a counterexample to this account of the meaning of *at*, since an entity like a highway surely cannot be construed as a point. In fact, however, the typical context of use for such an example is a situation in which we are referring to travel along a road that intersects with the highway at some point ahead and the cafe is located at precisely this point. The following examples constitute similar cases: *The bomb exploded at 1,000 feet* (intersection of downward path of the bomb with the plane of 1,000 feet); *We'll hold a lifeboat drill at the equator* (intersection of ship's course with equator line); *The horse fell at the water jump* (intersection of steeplechase route with obstacle line). In all of these there is an implicit notion of path and a point where the path crosses some non-parallel line.

Implicit paths are also present in abstract form in the following examples: *The bird has a white band at its neck* (the visual scan route along the bird intersects the white band line); *The bird is at the top of the tree* (the upward scan of the tree intersects with the plane of the bird's height); *There are bubbles at the surface* (the upward scan through the liquid intersects with the plane of the surface). Notice that this notion of a mental path has no role in comparable examples with *on*, such as *The bird has a white band on its neck* or *There are bubbles on the surface.*

There is further evidence for saying that *at* involves the notion of path. A sentence like *The cyclists are at Dijon* would only be natural if Dijon were one of a series of points on a journey (such as the Tour de France cycle race). Otherwise, the size of a city like Dijon in relation to a group of cyclists would make it much more natural to conceive of the city as a container rather than as a point (hence *They took this photo when they were in Dijon*).

Metaphorical extensions from the locative domain

The locative domain is the source for a large variety of semantic extensions to non-locative domains through metonymy and metaphor. Such processes help to explain numerous facts that might seem puzzling at first sight – for example, the fact that *out* means "active in the visual field" in *The sun is out*, but "inactive in the visual field" in *The light is out.*

There is certainly some degree of arbitrariness in the use of prepositions to express non-locative meanings. For example, although certain emotional states are metaphorically construed as containers of the experiencer (*in love, in pain, in ecstasy, in despair, in anger*), this is by no means always the case (**He's in hate*; **She's in happiness*). Similarly, there is no obvious reason why *on* rather than *in* is used in such expressions as *The building is on fire.* However, the degree of arbitrariness is lower than might at first be thought if the role of metonymy and metaphor were not appreciated. We will illustrate first with *out*, and then with the pair *up* and *down.*

Out

One important factor in some of these extended prepositional meanings has to do with perspective, and this is particularly relevant to those associated with *out.* Take, for example, the contrast mentioned above: *The sun is out* means that the sun is visible, whereas *The light is out* means that the light is invisible. The difference here is attributable to contrasting perspectives. In both cases there is an implicit opposition between an inner and an outer area. The difference is that in the *sun* example the observer-conceptualiser is located in the outer area, so that any other entity in that area (in this case the sun) is within the observer's visual field. By contrast, in the *light* example the perceiver is conceptualised as located in the inner area so that *out* indicates that the trajector (the light) is outside that field. There is independent support for this claim: the coming about of the first kind of situation is construed in terms of movement towards the observer, using the verb *come* (*The sun came out*), whereas the coming about of the second situation is construed as movement away from the observer, using the verb *go* (*The light went out*).

Both these situations connect to other extended uses. The notion of movement into the observer's visual field is associated with movement into the observer's domain of awareness or understanding (*work out the answer, figure out, find out, sound someone out*). Also related are expressions like *everything turned out all right* or *I've sorted it out* where the result (or outcome) of a process comes to be known or available, and becoming available in this way is conceptualised as emerging from an inner space where the trajector was previously hidden.

Conversely, the notion of exit from the observer's visual field extends not only to processes involving exit from other perceptual areas (*The noise drowned out the music*) but also movement into domains outside the observer's consciousness (*He tried to blot out the memory*). This notion further modulates into the process of unavailability of a particular phenomenon or resource (*The supplies ran out*; *The bulb burned out*), and there are various idioms that express such ideas with the human experiencer expressed as clause subject (*We're out of gas*; *I'm tired out*).

There is also a conceptual link between the notion of exit from a landmark and that of change from a normal to an abnormal state, such as from consciousness into unconsciousness, or from self-control into lack of control. Hence the use of *out* in an extensive and growing set of verb + preposition idioms, including *black out, bomb out, fade out, flip out, freak out, knock out, lash out, pass out, pig out, psych out, space out, tune out, wig out, zone out.*

Up and *down*

Some of the metaphors associated with the up–down axis play an important role in the extension of meaning generally, not just in the domain of prepositions. They include:

(a) Status. We talk of 'high' and 'low' status, and to achieve higher status is to go 'up' in the world, while to lose status is to go 'down' in the world; compare also *look up to someone* and *look down on someone*, or *put someone down* ("make someone feel inadequate/unimportant").

(b) Size. *Up* and *down* are used in various expressions indicating respectively increase and decrease in size: *blow up a balloon, fatten up cattle, scale up a map, let down a tyre, scale down a map.* Compare again *high* and *low* in *high/low prices, high/low achievement.*

(c) Degree of activity or intensity. Again *up* correlates with 'high' degree and *down* with 'low' degree: compare *wake up, liven up, brighten up, cheer up, speed up, start up, pep up, perk up, wind up, keyed up, tense up, psych up* with *calm down, slow down, shut down, settle down, quieten down, get someone down.*

Increasing size is also perceptually associated with the notion of approach, as might be expected from the fact that the retinal image expands as an entity approaches an observer, so that it is no accident that *up* expresses this meaning in such collocations as *go up to someone, walk up, come up, creep up, loom up, sidle up*, and so on. The association between *up* and the notion of approach probably also helps to explain why *up* is used in various expressions having to do with coming or bringing into existence, such as *conjure up an image, dream up an excuse, make up a story, whip up a dessert.*

The notion of approach is in turn related to that of completion of a process on a more abstract level, given that both notions involve movement towards a goal. Hence such expressions as *cut up, settle up* (a bill), *even up, balance up, square up, use up, sum up, carve up.*

When *up* and *down* are used geographically, the choice between them is sometimes arbitrary. Movement along such linear spaces as streets or railway tracks on level ground is sometimes expressed with *up* and sometimes with *down.* Naturally, if there is a slope the direction of increasing elevation is much more likely to be called *up the street,* but in many circumstances what one person refers to as a short distance up the street might be referred to by another as a short distance down the street.

Where the choice is not arbitrary, there are various different geographical metaphors motivating uses of *up* and *down* in connection with travel to towns, cities, etc., and they sometimes conflict.

Up is almost always used for travel that goes perceptibly up a hill, so that people use the phrase *up to Kuranda* when speaking about travel from the coastal city of Cairns in Queensland to the town of Kuranda in the nearby hills. But the ascent must be perceptible: although the ground between Illinois and Colorado steadily increases in elevation for 1,000 miles, so that Denver is actually a mile higher than Chicago, no Chicagoan says *going up to Denver.*

Up and *down* are also commonly used in association with north and south respectively: cf. *They live up north* or *We travelled down from France into Spain.* This of course correlates with the convention in maps of putting northern areas above southern ones.

A less common and more localised use of *up* in England is for travel from less prestigious to more prestigious cities – this is a special case of the metaphor relating to status mentioned above. People in England often use the phrase *going up to London* or *going up to town,* even though this may involve travel south. In addition, universities, in particular the long-established universities of Oxford and Cambridge, are conceptualised as if they towered above the surrounding area: attending Oxford or Cambridge is generally called 'going up to university', and being expelled from those universities is called 'being sent down'.

6.2 **Syntactic uses of grammaticised prepositions**

We now summarise the syntactic uses of the main grammaticised prepositions in English, indicating the semantic roots of those syntactic uses where this is possible. We consider *as* and *than, at, by, for, from, in, of, on, to,* and *with.*[24]

[24]Note that all of these are monosyllabic. The majority of them (*as, at, by, for, from, of, than,* and *to* but not *in, on,* or *with*) have strong and weak pronunciations, the weak ones (with the vowel [ə]) being used when the preposition is completely unstressed. We omit *against* and *toward(s)*, which are specified in the complementation of very few items: the former occurs with *proof* and the latter with a few adjectives and associated nouns such as *friendly* and *friendliness* (see Ch. 6, §3.1).

As and *than*

These occur in comparisons of equality and inequality respectively:

[5] i *Kim is as tall [as Pat].*
ii *Kim is taller [than Pat].*
iii *[As you may have noticed,] several members are absent.*

In [i–ii] the bracketed PP is a complement, licensed by the degree adverb *as* and the comparative inflection. *Than* is restricted to PPs in complement function, while *as* can head comparative adjuncts, as in [iii]. These constructions are described in detail in Ch. 13.

In addition, *as* has the uses illustrated in:

[6] i *[As they were checking the proofs,] they came across a serious error.*
ii *[As it was raining] we had to take a taxi.*
iii *I regard her [as my best friend].*

The *as* PPs in [i–ii] are adjuncts of temporal location and reason respectively, the former being clearly related to the comparative use. In [iii] *as* takes a predicative complement, as described in §5.1 above: here it plays a role among prepositions analogous to the role that *be* plays among verbs.

At

As discussed in §6.1, the core lexical meaning of *at* expresses location in a specific geographical position conceived as a point in the plane. Thus *at the North Pole* is a typical literal use. The static meaning can be extended to cover movement of a trajector headed for such a spot (*The truck was coming right at me*) or the point where a path intersects with a non-parallel line (*We were stopped at the Albanian border*). It extends metaphorically into temporal meaning, with the progress of time conceptualised as a one-dimensional line, allowing it to be used for exact times corresponding to points at certain distances along the line (*at three o'clock*).

At is only marginally a grammaticised preposition, but it is grammatically selected in the complements of certain verbs, nouns, and adjectives, as in:

[7]	COMP OF VERB	COMP OF NOUN	COMP OF ADJECTIVE
i	*She laughed at me.*	*her attempt at a compromise*	*agog at this*
ii	*We rejoiced at the news.*	*our joy at the news*	*delighted at the news*
iii	*She excels at chess.*	*her skill at chess*	*good at chess*

The examples in [i] represent the clearest case, with other prepositions being completely excluded: cf. **laughed on me*, **attempt to a compromise*, etc.

There is also a semi-productive semantic contrast between constructions with direct objects and constructions with *at* PPs, as described in Ch. 4, §8.1.1. The semantic difference is that in the transitive case the action is direct and has its effect, while in the version with the *at* PP the action is aimed or attempted but not successful:

[8] i a. *Jerry shot a rabbit so let's have it for dinner.*
b. *Jerry shot at a rabbit but it got away.*
ii a. *The creature clawed my face and now I look terrible.*
b. *The creature clawed at my face so I dropped it before I got hurt.*

By

By has a locative meaning expressing proximity (*by the wall*), an intransitive version of that meaning, "near the contextually retrievable location" (*They stood by and watched*), a dynamic variant of that signifying motion past a point (*Many people passed by*), and temporal analogues of the latter (*Time was passing by*), in addition to idioms like *by myself* (not "near myself" but "alone"), *side by side* ("adjacent"), *day by day* ("continuously through a sequence of days"), *by night* ("during the night").

The fact that in simple and stereotypical cases causes, agents, instrumentalities, methods, and routes are close at hand has permitted various extended meanings to evolve, including instrument or technique used (*by unscrewing it, by hand*), cause (*do something by mistake*), mode of transport (*by boat, by car*), or route of access (*They came in by the window*).

By has also assumed an array of other meanings: marking the extent of differences in comparisons (*We won the game by two points*), time deadlines (*Be here by ten o'clock*), products in multiplication and area measurement (*The problems had been multiplied by two*; *Our room is twenty feet by thirty feet*), units used in selling a commodity (*sold by the pound*), identification marks (*I recognised him by his hair*), and many others (books listing phrasal verbs and other idioms list more than fifty distinguishable uses of *by* in particular expressions).

Most importantly among this large array of lexical and idiomatic meanings, for our present purposes, the preposition *by* is used to head complements in passive clauses and in NPs:

[9] i	a. *The plan was approved by the boss.*	b. *the approval of the plan by the boss*
ii	a. *The boss was hated by everyone.*	b. *a new book by Italo Calvino*

In spite of the similarity suggested by pairs like those in [i], there are significant differences between the constructions, and we do not analyse [ib] as a passive NP (cf. Ch. 5, §16.5.3). In the clausal construction, *by* marks the internalised complement of the passive, corresponding to the subject of the active counterpart (*The boss approved the plan*; *Everyone hated the boss*). In the NP construction, *by* marks a complement with the semantic role of agent. Note, then, that as hating is non-agentive there is no NP corresponding to [iib]: **the hatred of the boss by everyone.* A special case of the agent NP is seen in [iib], where it identifies the creator of an object such as a work of art. This construction allows such paraphrases as *a new book from Italo Calvino, a new book from the hand of Italo Calvino*, etc., but these are not possible in passive clauses: **It was written from Italo Calvino*; **It was written from the hand of Italo Calvino.*

For

For is perhaps the most polysemous of the prepositions of English, with a plethora of subtly distinct meanings and a small set of grammaticised uses in addition.

Among the most basic meanings of *for* are "in favour of" (*My position on the tax cut is that I'm for it*); "as a favour to" (*I took the garbage out for you*); intended recipient (*I have a package for Mr Markby*); beneficiary (*Say a prayer for me*) and "on behalf of" (*I am appearing for the defence in this case*); duration (*We stayed for a week*); distance (*We walked for five miles*). In a variety of idiomatic combinations it can convey something more like "as a result of" (*It was somewhat the worse for wear*); reason or purpose

(*He wouldn't help for some reason*; *He kept quiet for fear of making a fool of himself*; *We were only doing it for fun*); suitability (*time for reading*); destination (*heading for the city*); consideration in relation to (*lovely weather for the time of year*); and numerous other senses in idiomatic combinations with various verbs, adjectives, and nouns. There may be some common core of positive or favourable orientation towards a goal here, but at best it is very general and vague.

Complementation of verbs

A fair number of verbs select *for* PPs as complement, as in:

[10] *I can't account for these results. We didn't allow for human error. He asked for help. I begged for mercy. He blamed me for the delay. Good intentions alone count for nothing. We exchanged it for a new model. I'm hoping for some respite. I paid $5 for it. We must provide for the children. Why do you stand for such nonsense? Why not try for promotion? Wait for me.*

With *pass* and *take*, *for* is used instead of the usual *as* with a predicative complement: *I took him for a friend of mine.* At the boundary between complement and modifier status is the beneficiary element in clauses like *They bought a tie for me*; with many verbs this alternates with a ditransitive construction (*They bought me a tie*), as discussed in Ch. 4, §8.2.1.

Complementation of nouns, adjectives, and prepositions

[11] i *the blame for our failure   cause for complaint   consideration for others*
a desire for revenge   lust for power   a request for help   a reward for bravery
ii *Jogging can be [bad for you]. The task was [easy for most of them].*
iii *I would have failed [but for you]. I enjoyed it all [except for the ending].*

With some of the nouns the construction matches that of the corresponding verb, but with others the verb takes a direct object. Compare *They lust for power* vs *They desire revenge.*

From

In its most basic meaning *from* marks the source location, contrasting with *to*, marking goal, as discussed in §6.1: *She drove from London to Carlisle.* Like *to*, it extends to duration in time (*It lasted from Sunday to Friday*), and change of state (*It went from bad to worse*). Other metaphorical extensions include that where *from* marks cause, as in *They died from malnutrition.* This use is highly restricted, however, for causes are not in general expressed by a *from* PP: if a tornado is the cause of the destruction of a house, we cannot therefore use *from* in a passive clause (**The house was destroyed from a tornado*). *From* has not been grammaticised in this role.

Complementation of verbs

Bivalent and trivalent verbs selecting *from* are illustrated in [12i–ii] respectively:

[12] i *My copy differs from yours. Have you heard from Sue? I couldn't keep from laughing. Please refrain from smoking. Kim suffers from asthma.*
ii *The rules bar employees from entering the competition. He hid it from me. Keep everyone from talking. I learnt it from Ed. She saved him from death.*

With such verbs as *hear* and *learn*, *from* marks the source in the sense of the one from whom the message/information comes. There are a considerable number of verbs of prevention and abstention (to characterise the range of meanings very roughly), where the use of *from* derives via the fairly transparent metaphor of intended actions as spatial goals. To hold someone back from an object or location is to physically hold them in a place that is back away from that object or location, and to hold someone back from doing something is to hold them back so that they will not perform the action. Verbs (and verbal idioms) expressing prevention are listed in [13i]. Similar remarks hold for abstention, which is holding oneself back from some action. Verbs (and verbal idioms) expressing abstention are listed in [13ii].

[13]	i	*ban*	*bar*	*block*	*delay*	*discourage*	*disqualify*
		dissuade	*distract*	*divert*	*enjoin*	*exclude*	*exempt*
		forbid	*hinder*	*hold back*	*inhibit*	*keep*	*preclude*
		prevent	*prohibit*	*protect*	*restrain*	*restrict*	*stop*
	ii	*abstain*	*back away*	*back off*	*cease*	*desist*	*draw back*
		hang back	*hold back*	*hold off*	*keep*	*recoil*	*refrain*
		shrink	*shy away*	*step back*	*withdraw*		

Many of the prevention verbs permit not only a direct object denoting the preventee (*prevent him from seeing it*) but also, alternatively, a direct object denoting the action prevented (*prevent it*). However, not all do: *They dissuaded him from doing it*, but not **They dissuaded his action.* Some of the prevention verbs allow a gerund-participial clausal complement without the *from*: *prevent the boy leaving, stop them doing it. Keep* differs from the others in that without a *from* complement it has a continuative sense: compare [12], for example, with *Keep everyone talking* and *I kept crying.*

Complementation of other categories

[14] i *<u>abstention from</u> sex*   *<u>freedom from</u> harassment*   *<u>protection from</u> the sun's rays*
ii *<u>different from</u> other people*   *<u>free from</u> intimidation*   *<u>immune from</u> prosecution*
iii *<u>apart from</u> anything else*   *<u>aside from</u> these advantages*   *<u>far from</u> being contrite*

In some cases *from* alternates with other prepositions – e.g. *protection* (and the base verb *protect*) takes *against*, *different* takes *to* or *than*, and so on. Complements with adverbs are rare, but a very few adverbs, e.g. *separately*, take *from* PPs (*separately from the rest*; see Ch. 6, §6.1).

In

In is the basic preposition for expressing interior location (*in the box*). It extends through the usual temporal metaphor to mark a time period conceived as a container within which an event is located (*That happened in the winter*, "at a time included in the winter") or to mark a time period used to provide an upper bound on a delay, a period during which, hence by the end of which, an event will occur (*I'll be ready in a few minutes*, "by the end of a period consisting of a few minutes").

Complementation

In plays a relatively small role in complementation, but there are a number of verbs, nouns, and adjectives which select PPs with *in* as head. Examples include:

[15] i *Do you believe in God? He won't confide in me. He deals in used cars. Don't engage in politics. I can't interest them in the scheme. It's bound to result in a lot of ill will. She succeeded in changing their views.*
ii *his confidence in her a dealer in illegal drugs an interest in religion*
iii *dangers [inherent in the system] interested in reptiles*

A number of the governing items have to do with the concepts of trust and confidence, and the need for the dictionary to specify that they take *in* is evident from the fact that a range of other prepositions are found in this semantic domain. Thus *about* is selected by *certain, confident, secure, sure*; *by* by *swear*; *for* by *speak, vouch*; *of* by *certain, confident, sure* (as an alternant of *about*); *on* by *bank, bet, count, depend, gamble, rely*; and *to* by *commit, entrust, swear.* Note similarly the range of prepositions found with such adjectives of intellectual attitude as *interested in, attentive to, fascinated by, mindful of,* and *obsessed with.*

Of

Of is the most highly grammaticised of all prepositions. Its original basic locative meaning was like that of *away/from,* indicating source, but this disappeared early on, and a complex historical development led to its expressing a large number of meanings, as "movement away" gave way to concepts like geographic origin, belonging, selection from a set, and many others. It is used predominantly, but not exclusively, in PPs with complement function.

Complement in the structure of NPs

With minor exceptions, nouns do not license non-genitive NPs as complement. Subordinate NPs are related to the head noun by genitive case or by prepositions, and *of* is the default preposition used for this function. The contrast between verbs and nouns in this respect is illustrated in:

[16]			
i	a. *The emperor died.*	b. *They assassinated the emperor.*	[clauses]
ii	a. *the emperor's death*	b. *the emperor's assassination*	[NPs]
iii	a. *the death of the emperor*	b. *the assassination of the emperor*	

In [i] *the emperor* is related directly to the verb (as subject in [a] and direct object in [b]). In [ii] the subordinate NP is marked by genitive case, functioning as subject-determiner, and in [iii] it is complement of *of.*

The NPs in [16ii–iii] are nominalisations: the head noun is morphologically derived from a verb. The alternation between the genitive and *of* constructions is found with other head nouns too, but the *of* construction allows a much wider range of semantic relations between the subordinate NP and the head, as illustrated in [17] and discussed in detail in Ch. 5, §16.5.3:

[17]		
i	a. *her former husband's house*	b. *the house of her former husband*
ii	a. *Dick Brown's son-in-law*	b. *the son-in-law of Dick Brown*
iii	a. **the students' majority*	b. *the majority of the students*
iv	a. **water's glass*	b. *a glass of water*

Complement in the structure of AdjPs and AdvPs

Like nouns, adjectives do not (with very few exceptions) take NPs as post-head complement. Subordinate NPs are related to the head adjective by means of a preposition, and again *of* can be regarded as the default preposition in this construction. A list of adjectives selecting *of* is given in Ch. 6, §3.1; further examples are as follows:

[18] *I feel ashamed of myself.* *They seem bereft of ideas.* *She is convinced of his guilt.*
It is full of water. *It is good of you to help.* *We're short of money.*

Adverbs seldom take complements, but at least one – *independently* – inherits from its adjectival base the property of selecting an *of* complement (see Ch. 6, §6.1).

Complement in the structure of VPs and PPs

Verbs and prepositions, by contrast, do take NP complements, so prepositions in general, and *of* in particular, play a smaller role in their complementation. Nevertheless, there are a number of verbs and prepositions which do select *of* complements; they are illustrated in [19], the verbs in [i] being bivalent, those in [ii] trivalent:

[19] i *She approves of the plan.* *Beware of the dog.* *He disposed of the old bulb.*
We partook of a simple meal. *The book treats of the fauna of New Zealand.*
ii *We apprised* her *of the facts.* *I convinced* her *of his guilt.* *They deprived* him *of his liberty.* *You expect too much of them.* *He robbed me of my wallet.*
iii *ahead of* her *rivals* *because of the danger* *instead of tea* *out of the box*

Of indicating cause may be included here as it is virtually restricted to occurrence with *die*: *He died of a broken heart.* With *expect* (and likewise *demand*) *of* alternates with *from*. There are also cases where it alternates with *about*, which has its ordinary lexical meaning: *They had spoken of/about their wartime experiences*; *He's thinking of/about moving to Sydney.*

Other functions of *of* PPs

There are a few cases where *of* is not selected by the head and thus makes an independent contribution to the meaning. In [20i–iii] the *of* phrase is respectively modifier in NP structure, predicative complement, and adjunct in clause structure:

[20] i *a matter of no importance* *a frame of steel* *a girl of a sunny disposition*
a man of honour *a boy of sixteen* *the best novelist of her time*
ii *It is of no importance.* *The frame is of steel.* *She is of a sunny disposition.*
iii *We like to go to the beach of a week-end.* *He did it of his own accord.*

The predicative complements in [ii] match the modifiers in [i], but the predicative construction allows a narrower range of semantic types. Compare, for example, **The man is of honour* or **The boy is of sixteen.* Leaving aside idioms and fixed phrases such as *of course, of late, of necessity*, etc., *of* PPs are rarely found as clause adjuncts. The only productive case is for indicating time in multiple situations, as in the *of a week-end* example in [iii]: the NP denotes a time period and must begin with the indefinite article.

On

The spatial use of *on* was discussed in §6.1. The temporal use is seen in such phrases as *on Tuesday, on the first of June, on hearing this news.* It is found with a limited range of NPs indicating ongoing actions or states (*on fire, on the march, on your guard*), or reason (*on her advice*).

On PPs in complement function

On is selected in the complementation of various verbs, nouns, and adjectives, as illustrated in [21i–iii] respectively:

[21] i *We can't decide on a colour. It depends on the cost. We feed them on raw meat. I can't improve on that. Look on her as a friend. Don't rely on him. He spent it on drink. The stress will tell on her. They're waging war on us.*
ii *an attack on my honour a ban on gambling their expenditure on drink an improvement on his first attempt reliance on his parents war on want*
iii *dependent on his parents hard on the poor intent on revenge keen on golf*

Adjunct of disadvantage

[22] *I was looking after the neighbours' dog for the week-end, and it died on me.*

One special use of *on* is to indicate that the referent of its complement is adversely affected by the event expressed in the clause: in this example, I'm going to have to give bad news to the neighbours (and might even be thought to be responsible).[25]

To

To is the basic English preposition for indicating the goal in physical movement: *She went to Paris.* Secondary senses include the endpoint in a change of state: *I came to my senses*; *He went to sleep*; *They beat him to death*; *The snow turned to water*; *The lights turned from red to green.* In the temporal domain it can be used for the endpoint in a period of duration (*I'll be available from two to three*), and in clock times (*ten to six* – AmE also has *ten of/before six*). Other kinds of endpoint or limit are seen in such expressions as *wet to the skin, generous to a fault, notes to the value of $100.*

Complementation of verbs

A large number of verbs and verbal idioms select complements with *to*, with varying degrees of similarity to the basic goal meaning. Examples are as follows:

[23] i *It doesn't matter to me what you do. Does that seem reasonable to you?*
ii *He apologised to us. They lied to me. I'm speaking to you. Talk to me.*
iii *Give it to me. I lent it to your wife. He transferred his assets to his children.*
iv *Does this apply to them all? This belongs to me. I can't compare it to yours. She devotes herself to her work. It'll expose you to ridicule. Listen to me. They lost to United. It reduced him to a wreck. Please see to the guests.*

The *to* phrase is associated in [i] with the role of experiencer (in the sense of Ch. 4, §2.2), in [ii] with the addressee in an act of communication, and in [iii] with the recipient in situations of giving, transfer, and the like. Many trivalent verbs in the fields of communication and giving/transfer show alternation between a construction with object + *to* PP and one with two objects: *She showed the new draft to her tutor* ~ *She showed her tutor the new draft*; see Ch. 4, §8.2.1 for discussion.

Other *to* complements

To is selected by a good number of nouns and adjectives and a few prepositions:

[25] It is common for languages to express this meaning by a dative case rather than a prepositional construction; this is the basis for the terms 'ethic dative' and 'dative of disadvantage' that are used for such expressions. We do not apply these terms to English in accordance with our policy of distinguishing between case and function: English has no dative case.

[24] i *an answer to the question* *a burden to us all* *cruelty to animals* *the entrance to the cave* *a hindrance to progress* *the key to the safe* *his marriage to Sue*
ii *answerable to no one* *kind to us* *similar to yours* *susceptible to flooding*
iii *according to you* *owing to the rain* *prior to the exam* *thanks to this delay*

Note that some of the *to* complements of nouns correspond to direct objects of verbs: compare *She answered the question*; *They entered the cave.* One or two ·*ly* adverbs, such as *similarly*, inherit the *to* complementation from the base adjective.

With

With has as its most basic meaning the notion of accompaniment, as expressed by **comitative** adjuncts – e.g. *Christopher Robin went down with Alice*, meaning roughly "Christopher Robin and Alice went down together". From this root meaning, via associations between copresence and various kinds of involvement, metaphorical extensions spread out into notions like location (*I left the keys with my neighbour*); properties (*a boy with black hair, someone with intelligence, a car with a powerful engine*); means or instrument (*undo it with a pin, achieve it with military force*); manner (*skated with skill, writes with passion, spent money with gay abandon*); agreement (*I'm with you on this matter*). The distinction between modifiers and complements is not easy to draw in the case of *with* phrases, and some of the complements illustrated below certainly have strong affinities with these meanings.

Complementation of verbs

[25] i *I agree with you.* *They charged him with perjury.* *I'll deal with it myself.* *Let's dispense with the formalities.* *Will you help me with my homework?* *Please don't mess with my stuff.* *I wouldn't trust them with my car.*
ii *We covered the floor with sawdust.* *They supplied the terrorists with guns.* *The garden was swarming with bees.*

The NP complement of *with* in [ii] can occur as a direct complement of the verb in related constructions: *Sawdust covered the floor*; *They supplied guns to the terrorists*; *Bees were swarming in the garden* (see Ch. 4, §8.3).

Other *with* complements

[26] i *comparison with the first version* *contact with outer space* *help with my taxes*
ii *angry with you* *familiar with the rules* *riddled with corruption*

8

The clause: adjuncts

Anita Mittwoch
Rodney Huddleston
Peter Collins

1 Preliminaries

This chapter continues the description of clause structure begun in Ch. 4. The latter introduced the primary functions of predicator, complement, and adjunct. The predicator is the head of the clause, the function realised by the verb. Within the category of complement we distinguished between core and non-core complements: characteristically core complements have the form of NPs while non-core ones are realised by PPs. The major focus of Ch. 4 was on the core complements, subjects, objects, and predicatives; predicatives are semantically comparable to predicators, while subject and object are associated with a fairly wide range of semantic roles such that the interpretation in particular cases is largely dependent on the semantic properties of the predicator. In this chapter, by contrast, our focus is on those elements (primarily adjuncts but also certain less central kinds of complement) that express relatively constant kinds of meaning, such as manner, spatial or temporal location, duration, condition, and so on. As explained in Ch. 15, §5, the term 'adjunct' covers modifiers in the VP or clause together with related supplements.

Semantic categories

The elements concerned express a very wide range of semantic categories, and we cannot hope to provide a fully comprehensive coverage. The following examples illustrate the main categories that will be dealt with in this chapter, with the annotation on the right giving the name and the section or subsection in which it is discussed:

[1]	i	*She presented her case very eloquently.*	[manner: §2.1]
	ii	*They opened it with a tin-opener.*	[instrument: §2.2]
	iii	*We solved the problem by omitting the section altogether.*	[means: §2.2]
	iv	*I foolishly omitted to lock the back-door.*	[act-related: §3]
	v	*He slept in the TV room.*	[spatial location: §§4–5]
	vi	*He hurried from the scene.*	[source: §4–5]
	vii	*She went to New York for Christmas.*	[goal: §4–5]
	viii	*We made the mistake of travelling via Heathrow.*	[path: §4–5]
	ix	*I crawled towards the door.*	[direction: §4.4]
	x	*They walked five miles.*	[extent: §5]
	xi	*I woke up at five.*	[temporal location: §6]
	xii	*Ken slept for ten hours.*	[duration: §7]

xiii	*It was already light.*	[aspectuality: §8]
xiv	*I often read in bed.*	[frequency: §9]
xv	*She read the book for the third time.*	[serial order: §10]
xvi	*We enjoyed it very much.*	[degree: §11]
xvii	*He left the door open in order to allow late-comers to enter.*	[purpose: §12.2]
xviii	*They had to walk because of the bus-strike.*	[reason: §12.3]
xix	*As the sun sank, the light intensified so that the hills glowed.*	[result: §12.4]
xx	*I'll come along, though I can't stay very long.*	[concession: §13]
xxi	*We'll get there before dinner if the train is on time.*	[condition: §14]
xxii	*Technically, he did not commit an offence.*	[domain: §15]
xxiii	*The accident was probably due to a short-circuit.*	[modality: §16]
xxiv	*Fortunately, we got there on time.*	[evaluation: §17]
xxv	*Frankly, I'm disappointed.*	[speech act-related: §18]
xxvi	*There is, moreover, no justification for making an exception.*	[connective: §19]

Organising principles

Broadly speaking, elements belonging to the later categories in this list are less tightly integrated into the structure of the containing clause than the earlier ones. Thus elements which qualify as complements by the criteria of Ch. 4 are found only among those in the top part of the list, while those in the bottom part often have the status of supplements, prosodically detached from the rest of the sentence.

Partial overlap of categories

For the most part the categories in [1] are mutually exclusive: a given complement or adjunct in an unambiguous clause will not generally belong to more than one category. There are, however, a small number of exceptions, as illustrated in:

[2]	i	a. *He's going to buy the house if he can afford it.*	[basic conditional]
		b. *He's going to buy the house if I'm not mistaken.*	[modal conditional]
		c. *He's going to buy the house, if you must know.*	[speech act-related conditional]
	ii	a. *She has gone home because she was feeling ill.*	[basic reason]
		b. *She has gone home, because her light is off.*	[speech act-related reason]

In [ia] the *if* phrase is a basic, or ordinary, conditional adjunct, giving a condition on his buying the house. In [ib] it expresses a modal qualification to the proposition that he is going to buy the house. And in [ic] it relates to my act of assertion: "If you must know, I'll tell you". Similarly, in [iia] the *because* phrase is a basic, or ordinary, reason adjunct, saying why she has gone home, while in [iib] it relates to my speech act in that it gives the reason why I am able to assert that she has gone home.

Descriptive parameters

Among the issues we will consider in looking at the various types of complement and adjunct are the following.

(a) Focus potential

Most, but by no means all, of the elements to be considered can be the informational focus (marked by the main stress) in such constructions as interrogatives expressing alternative questions, contrastive negation, and *it*-clefts. Compare:

[3] i a. *He returned yesterday.* [temporal location]
b. *Did he return yesterday or on Tuesday?* [alternative question]
c. *He didn't return yesterday but on Tuesday.* [contrastive negation]
d. *It was yesterday that he returned.* [cleft]
ii a. *He returned, fortunately.* [evaluation]
b. **Did he return fortunately or surprisingly.* [alternative question]
c. **He didn't return fortunately but surprisingly.* [contrastive negation]
d. **It was fortunately that he returned.* [cleft]

The cleft construction allows a narrower range of elements to be focused than alternative questions and contrastive negation. For example, adverbs in ·*ly* are less readily focused in a cleft: compare *Did they grow quickly or reasonably fast?* and ?*Was it quickly that they grew?*[1] Elements that cannot be focused in any of these constructions are adjuncts rather than complements, and in many cases are supplements rather than modifiers. Thus while *yesterday* in [ia] is a modifier within the VP, *fortunately* in [iia] is not: it is a supplement with the clause *he returned* as its 'anchor'.

(b) Restrictiveness

A further, and related, difference between *yesterday* in [3ia] and *fortunately* in [iia] is that the latter has no bearing on the truth of the utterance. Example [ia] is true only if he returned yesterday: if he returned not yesterday but the day before, it is false. We will say, then, that *yesterday* is **restrictive**. But [iia] is true if he returned: if you respond *That's not true* you are denying that he returned, not disputing my evaluation of the event as fortunate. *Fortunately* is therefore said to be **non-restrictive.** Elements that are inherently non-restrictive in this way are again always adjuncts, but they do not wholly coincide with those that lack focus potential. A modal adjunct like *probably*, for example, cannot be focused (**Did he return probably or possibly?*), but it is clearly relevant to the truth of the proposition expressed: while [iia] entails that he returned, *He probably returned* obviously does not.

(c) Questioning

Most types of adjunct can be questioned. For example, an interrogative phrase can function as adjunct of temporal location, as in *When did he return?* But again, the evaluation adjunct of [3iia] behaves differently: interrogative phrases cannot have this function. Where questioning is possible, it is relevant to ask further what form the interrogative phrase takes. Use of the same interrogative word indicates a degree of likeness between categories that in other respects may be different. For example, we will see that there are grounds for distinguishing purpose and reason, but they nevertheless have it in common that both can be questioned by *why*: compare [1xvii–xviii] with *Why did he leave the door open?* ("for what purpose?") and *Why did they have to walk?* ("for what reason?").

[1] The complement of *be* in the cleft construction – what we call the 'foregrounded element' – need not carry the focal stress, as explained in Ch. 16, §9.4.1, but for the purposes of the present chapter we can simplify by considering only the prototypical case where it does. The unmodified term 'focus' in this chapter is to be understood as informational focus, as distinct from the scopal focus of adverbs such as *only* and *even*: see Ch. 6, §7.3, for this distinction.

(d) Relative scope

In many cases it is important to determine the scope of a dependent relative to other elements in the clause. One important issue concerns the scope of an element relative to a negative. Compare, for example:

[4] i *I didn't buy it because it was too expensive.* [adjunct has wider scope]
ii *I didn't appoint him just because he was my son.* [negative has wider scope]

Scope is the semantic analogue of constituent structure in syntax: it has to do with the way the meaning of the whole sentence is built up from the meanings of its parts. In [i] the negation applies to my buying it, and then the adjunct applies to my not buying it. We say, therefore, that the adjunct here has scope over the negation (or has wider scope than the negation). This can be brought out by such a gloss as "The fact that it was too expensive is the reason why I didn't buy it", where the negative is in a subordinate clause and "reason" is in the matrix. In [ii] the negation doesn't apply to my appointing him but to my doing so just because he was my son: the sentence implicates that I did appoint him, but for some other reason.[2] Here then the negation has scope over the reason adjunct, and we can gloss as "It is not the case that I appointed him just because he was my son", with the negative in the matrix and the reason in the subordinate clause. In abstraction from prosody, a clause may be ambiguous as to the relative scope of adjunct and negative. *I didn't appoint him because he was my son*, for example, can be interpreted like [i] ("That's the reason why I didn't appoint him"), or like [ii] without the *just*.

There are also places where we need to consider the scope of one adjunct relative to another:

[5] i *He usually doesn't attend departmental meetings, fortunately.*
ii *He probably sees them regularly.*

In [i] *fortunately* has scope over *usually* ("It is fortunate that he usually doesn't attend departmental meetings", not "It is usually fortunate that he doesn't attend departmental meetings"). In [ii] *probably* has scope over *regularly* ("It is probable that he sees them regularly", not "It is regularly probable that he sees them"). In both these examples, the element with narrow scope is a frequency adjunct, while the one with wide scope belongs to one of the categories towards the end of our list in [1]: evaluation and modality respectively.

(e) Bounding potential

Some types of dependent are closely related to the aspectuality of the clause, and our discussion will draw on the aspectual categories of perfective vs imperfective and the situation types states, activities, accomplishments, and achievements presented in Ch. 3, §3.2. In particular, some elements have a bounding effect. Compare, for example:

[6] i *She ran.* [unbounded: activity]
ii *She ran to the station / two miles.* [bounded: accomplishment]

Example [i] is unbounded and can take a duration adjunct with *for* but not *in*: *She ran for ten minutes / *in ten minutes*. But adding a goal such as *to the station* or an extent adjunct such as *two miles* makes the clause bounded, and this is reflected in the fact

[2] That this is an implicature, not an entailment, is evident from the acceptability of examples like *I don't know whether I will appoint him at all, but I certainly won't appoint him just because he's my son.*

that we can now have *in* but not *for* in the duration adjunct: *She ran to the station in twenty minutes* / **for twenty minutes*.

(f) Syntactic realisation

We are concerned under this heading with the internal form of the complement or adjunct. The main categories are as follows:

[7]	i	*She folded the napkins carefully.*	[AdvP]
	ii	*She cut it with a razor-blade.*	[PP]
	iii	*I was annoyed because they had overcharged me.*	[PP]
	iv	*She didn't consult us before signing the contract.*	[PP]
	v	*I hadn't seen them before.*	[PP]
	vi	*They arrived last week.*	[NP]
	vii	*Had I known this at the time, I wouldn't have bought it.*	[finite clause]
	viii	*We were saving up to buy a new car.*	[non-finite clause]
	ix	*Realising he couldn't win, Tom began to lose heart.*	[non-finite clause]
	x	*His assignment completed, Ed went down to the pub.*	[non-finite clause]
	xi	*Hands on their heads, the prisoners filed from the room.*	[verbless clause]

Example [i] illustrates the common case of an adjunct realised by an AdvP. Prototypically, the adverb is derived from an adjective by suffixation of ·*ly*, and the relation between such adverbs and their head or anchor is comparable to that between a predicative adjective and its predicand. Thus here the folding is careful, and in *Fortunately, no one was injured* the fact that no one was injured is fortunate. In [ii–v] the adjuncts are realised by PPs of various kinds: the complement of the preposition is an NP in [ii], a content clause in [iii], a gerund-participial in [iv], while in [v] there is no complement at all. It will be recalled that the category of prepositions we are working with includes many items that are traditionally analysed as subordinating conjunctions or adverbs.

While AdvPs and PPs constitute the bulk of adjuncts, there are other possibilities. A small number of categories allow NPs, as in [7vi] (temporal location). Finite (content) clauses are even more restricted in their range; [vii] illustrates the case of a clause with subject–auxiliary inversion functioning as conditional adjunct, alternating with the *if* PP *if I had known this at the time*. The remaining examples in [7] involve non-finite clauses (infinitival, gerund-participial, and past-participial) and verbless clauses. Infinitivals can function as purpose adjuncts, as in [viii] (where the clause alternates with the PP *in order to buy a new car*), but for the rest non-finite and verbless clauses generally have a less specific semantic function in the clause. The examples in [ix–x] can be construed as indicating temporal location and/or reason, that in [xi] as manner perhaps, but this is a matter of pragmatic inference: the semantic category is not explicitly marked either grammatically or lexically. For this reason, relatively little attention will be given to adjuncts of this kind in the present chapter.

(g) Linear position

We discuss the linear position of adjuncts in the final section of the chapter. The primary distinction we draw is between **front**, **central**, and **end** position:

[8]	i	*Fortunately there was plenty of time.*	[front]
	ii	*There was fortunately plenty of time.*	[central]
	iii	*There was plenty of time, fortunately.*	[end]

Further distinctions will be drawn within the central position, based on the contrast between auxiliary and lexical verbs. We use the terms 'front' and 'end' in preference to 'initial' and 'final' as the former pair more readily accommodate the fact that more than one adjunct can occur in these positions:

[9] i *Yesterday just outside the back door I found a large grass snake.*
ii *We slept in the garage for three weeks while the house was being repaired.*

2 Manner, means, and instrument

Elements belonging to the manner, means, and instrument categories characteristically describe how, in what way, the process expressed in the VP is performed:

[1] i *She walked slowly away.* [manner]
ii *He got in by breaking the door down.* [means]
iii *I broke the nut with a hammer.* [instrument]

Examples like these can be differentiated quite clearly as manner, means, and instrument respectively, but the boundaries between the three categories are far from sharp, in terms of either meaning or grammatical form.

Questioning

All three elements can in principle be questioned by *how*:

[2] i A: *How did they perform?* B: *Extremely well.* [manner]
ii A: *How did you manage to get in?* B: *By breaking the door open.* [means]
iii A: *How are you supposed to eat it?* B: *With chopsticks.* [instrument]

In practice, though, *how* is not often used to question manner. Other question forms involve PPs like *in what manner/way, by what means* or (for instruments) *what... with* but again these are not commonly used for questioning manner.

2.1 Manner

Prototypically a manner element is an adjunct with the form of an AdvP, where the head is a gradable adverb formed from an adjective by suffixation of ·*ly*; the AdvP modifies the verb (or residual VP) as an AdjP modifies a nominal. Compare, for example:

[3]	MANNER ADJUNCT	ATTRIBUTIVE ADJP
i	a. *She departed very hastily.*	b. *a very hasty departure*
ii	a. *He laughed raucously.*	b. *raucous laughter*
iii	a. *We examined the damage carefully.*	b. *a careful examination of the damage*

Non-gradables are found, but much less commonly: *The volumes are sold separately*; *We own the property jointly*. Manner adjuncts usually occur in clauses expressing dynamic situations, but they are also found with states, as in this last example with *own* or *I know them personally*, *He lay snugly in bed*, and so on. Many manner adjuncts combine only with verbs expressing actions performed by animate agents: *nonchalantly, sadly, skilfully, sloppily*, etc.

Manner complements

With some verbs a manner dependent has the syntactic status of a complement:

[4] a. *She behaved outrageously.* b. *They treated her pretty shabbily.*

In the senses they have here, these verbs require a manner dependent, for *She behaved* on its own means approximately "She behaved well", while the sense of *treat* in *They treated her* is quite different from that of [b] (involving medical treatment or paying for her). Other verbs where a manner complement is more or less obligatory for the sense in question are *word* (*We worded the motion carefully*) and *dress* (*He dresses very shabbily*; *dress* on its own generally means "get dressed"). With *live* a manner phrase is one of a range of permitted complement types (*live frugally, live in Durham, live in the fifteenth century*). And with *give* the manner complement *generously* can occur instead of the usual object.

NPs and PPs

Manner elements may also have the form of NPs (*Do it this way*) or, more often, PPs. Prepositions heading manner phrases include *with* and *without*:

[5] i *She handled it with great care.*
ii *They treated us without much consideration.*

Manner PPs and AdvPs readily coordinate: *She handled the situation skilfully and with great tact.* PPs like those in [5] occur predominantly in clauses expressing human actions. When they have concrete NPs as complement, *with* and *without* often have instrumental function (as in [1iii]) – and indeed the use of these prepositions in both functions is a reflection of the similarity between manner and instrument. A further reflection of the similarity is that clauses with a manner *with* phrase, like those with an instrumental *with* phrase, may have a close paraphrase with the verb *use*: compare *She handled the situation with great skill* (manner) ~ *She used great skill in handling the situation* and *She cut it with a scalpel* (instrument) ~ *She used a scalpel to cut it.*

One major class of manner PPs have *in* with an NP complement headed by such nouns as *manner, way, style, fashion*:

[6] i *He had responded in a studiously nonchalant manner.*
ii *They had been behaving in the usual way.*
iii *We're furnishing the house in a modern style / the Italian fashion.*

There is partial overlap between this kind of phrase and the ·*ly* AdvP. We find numerous equivalent pairs like *intelligently* ~ *in an intelligent way* or *spontaneously* ~ *in a spontaneous manner*, and so on. But *I found it easily, He speaks too quickly, Drive slowly*, and the like do not have natural counterparts with *manner* or *way*, whereas the PPs in [6] do not have natural counterparts with the form of AdvPs. For [i] *studiously nonchalantly* is possible but likely to be avoided because of the sequence of two quite long ·*ly* adverbs. *Usually* is not available as a replacement in [ii] because it has a frequency rather than a manner meaning, and [iii] illustrates the case where there is no adverb at all derived from the adjective (**modernly, *Italianly*). *Way* NPs can occur as manner dependents on their own, without the governing preposition *in*: *Do it this way*; *I cooked it (in) the Italian way.*

Another common type of manner PP (discussed in more detail in Ch. 13, §§5–6) has comparative *as* or *like* as head: *I did it exactly as you told me to*; *He talks just like his father.*

In addition we need to recognise a miscellaneous group of manner PPs, such as *in a loud voice*, *at maximum volume*, *under his breath*.

Implications for resultant state

Manner adjuncts typically give information about how a process is carried out, but in some cases this will have implications for the state resulting from the process. Compare:

[7] a. *He shut the door noisily.* b. *He sealed the window hermetically.*

In [a] *noisily* describes the manner of shutting the door, but has no bearing on the resultant state: the door is simply shut. But in [b] the window ended up not just sealed, but hermetically sealed. Similarly *They painted the house badly* (resulting in a badly painted house), *I tied the knot loosely* (yielding a loose knot), *You've mended the dress perfectly*, and so on. The entity that ends up in the relevant state is not always overtly expressed, as in *He wrote illegibly* (resulting in illegible writing).

Adverbs having both manner and other uses

Most ·*ly* adverbs that occur as manner dependents can also occur with one or more other meanings, as illustrated in:

[8]	MANNER	OTHER USE
i	a. *He sang badly.*	b. *They wounded him badly.*
ii	a. *He behaved rudely.*	b. *Rudely, he turned his back on them.*
iii	a. *He'll behave typically.*	b. *This typically happens after a long drought.*
iv	a. *I can't think politically.*	b. *Politically, it was a disaster.*
v	a. *She explained it clearly.*	b. *She is clearly a great asset.*
vi	a. *She smiled happily.*	b. *Happily, I was able to get my money back.*
vii	a. *They discussed it frankly.*	b. *Frankly, it's a disgrace.*

In the [b] examples, the AdvP belongs to one of the semantic categories discussed elsewhere in this chapter: *badly* here indicates degree, *rudely* belongs to the act-related category, *typically* indicates frequency, *politically* is a domain adjunct, *clearly* is modal, *happily* is evaluative, and *frankly* speech act-related. In the manner use, the adverb modifies just the verb together with any internal complements, while in most of the other uses it has a broader application. In [iib], for example, *rudely* applies to the act wherein he turned his back on them. Similarly *politically* specifies the domain within which *it was a disaster* is true, while in [viib] *frankly* relates to the illocutionary act of saying *it's a disgrace.*

Secondary manner adjuncts

There is a class of adverbs derived from adjectives denoting feelings or moods that have a double use comparable to that exemplified in [8], except that the 'other use' still has very much to do with manner. We therefore call this other semantic category **secondary manner**, with **primary manner** the term now used for the manner adverbs of the [a] examples. Adverbs belonging to this type include *angrily*, *bitterly*, *gloomily*, *moodily*, *serenely*:

[9]	PRIMARY MANNER	SECONDARY MANNER
i	a. *He shouted angrily at them.*	b. *Angrily, he stormed out of the room.*
ii	a. *He peered gloomily at her.*	b. *Gloomily they packed their bags.*
iii	a. *She smiled serenely.*	b. *Serenely she led the premier onto the stage.*

Like the [b] examples in [8ii–vii], the secondary manner adjuncts can have scope over a primary manner adjunct:

[10] i *Angrily, Ed grasped her tightly by the wrist.*
ii *Cleverly, Ed spoke loudly enough for the neighbours to hear.*

Cleverly belongs to the act-related category, and the secondary manner adjuncts are undoubtedly very similar to these. Note, however, that *cleverly* applies to the act of speaking but not to the manner of doing so: Ed didn't speak in a clever way, he simply spoke loudly, and that was a clever thing to do (presumably because it enabled the neighbours to hear). *Angrily* gives information about Ed's mood, but it seems that this will be reflected in some way in the manner in which the act is performed.

Secondary manner dependents differ from primary ones in that they cannot be complements (**Angrily he worded the letter*) and cannot be focused. They normally occupy front position, a position where primary manner adjuncts are rarely found. Such adverbs as *happily* and *sadly* can indicate either secondary manner or evaluation. *Sadly Kim left the room*, for example, is ambiguous according as it is Kim or me, the speaker, who is sad.

Implied manner: the cognate object construction

[11] a. *She fought a heroic fight.* b. *He died a long and agonising death.*

A cognate object is one where the head noun is a nominalisation of the verb: *fight* and *death* are nominalisations of the verbs *fight* and *die*. As the head noun itself is already implied by the verb it does not normally occur on its own: *#He died a death.* Rather, the noun is modified in some way, as by the adjectives in these examples. And these adjectives typically describe the process expressed in the clause and thus have the same kind of function as a manner adverb. Thus [i] means essentially the same as *She fought heroically*; [ii] likewise describes the manner of his dying but in this case there is no adverb *longly* available to express the same meaning in a manner adjunct.

2.2 Means and instrument

By and *with* phrases

Means and instrument adjuncts are characteristically realised by PPs headed by *by* (or *by means*) and *with* (or *without*) respectively:

[12] i a. *She travels to work by bus.*
b. *Sometimes you have to translate a noun in one language by a verb in another.*
c. *He had gained access to the board by highly dubious means.*
d. *They communicate by means of sign language.*
e. *Ed annoyed them by constantly interrupting.*
ii a. *She opened my door with the master-key.*
b. *She managed to gain entry without a key.*
c. *They ate with chopsticks / with their fingers.*
d. *I translated the passage with the help of a dictionary.*
e. *You can see the star with the naked eye.*

The instrumental NP is normally concrete, those denoting body-parts being a special case. (In [iid] the *help* NP is abstract, but it contains the concrete NP *a dictionary* within it.) Instruments normally occur in clauses where the subject (in the case of active clauses) has an agent role, as in [ia–d]. *See* doesn't require an agent role for its subject, but it is consistent with one, and the instrumental in [iie] makes an agent interpretation more likely. There are also constructions (besides the obvious short passives), however, where the agent is implicit rather than overtly expressed:

[13] a. *The master-key opened the door.* b. *The door opened with the master-key.*

Both of these convey that someone used the master-key to open the door; for further discussion of these constructions see Ch. 4, §8.3.3.

Means adjuncts likewise occur most often with an agentive subject (where the clause is active), but there is no semantic requirement for an explicit or implicit agent. A non-agent subject is readily permitted when *by* has a gerund-participial as complement, as in [12ie]; note that this could apply equally to situations where Ed deliberately or unintentionally annoyed them. Note also that the verb in the gerund-participial complement of *by* can be *use*, which can give rise to a means adjunct effectively equivalent to an instrument: *They got in by using the master-key / with the master-key.*

Other forms

Other prepositions are sometimes found, but with a restricted range of complements. In *he wrote it by hand* the *by* has an instrumental function. In *She went there on foot* and *She worked it all out on the computer*, the *on* phrases are interpreted respectively as means and instrument. In a few cases we find NPs rather than PPs:

[14] a. *I'll send it (by) airmail.* b. *Next time we're going to fly Qantas.*

In addition means and instrument can be realised by adverbs in such expressions as *lift mechanically*, *analyse statistically*, *examine spectroscopically*. This, however, is extremely limited; note, for example, that while *treat surgically* and *communicate electronically* are perfectly possible, we could not replace the adverbs here with *pharmaceutically* or *postally*, even though in both cases there are adjectives from which the adverbs could be derived.

The internalised complement in passive clauses

We use the term **internalised complement** for the element in a passive clause that corresponds to the subject (the external complement) of the active counterpart. Its semantic role is the same as that of the active subject, and varies according to the meaning of the verb, as explained in Ch. 4, §2: agent in *They were questioned by the police*, experiencer in *They were despised by the police*, and so on. In general, therefore, it falls outside the scope of the present chapter, but there are two brief points to be made about it here.

Marking of the internalised complement

The prepositional marker of the internalised complement, *by*, is the same as the marker of means. Compare, then:

[15] i *The information was obtained by their competitors.* [internalised complement]
ii *The information was obtained by subterfuge.* [means]

The *by* phrase in [i] is an internalised complement, that in [ii] a means adjunct. *By subterfuge*, but not *by their competitors*, could answer a *how* question. The two *by* phrases can easily combine: *A great deal of information was obtained by their competitors by subterfuge.* The distinction is less straightforward when *by* has a subjectless gerund-participial complement:

[16] i *The plan had been sabotaged by leaking the report to the media.*
ii *He had sabotaged the plan by leaking the report to the media.*
iii *Leaking the report to the media had sabotaged the plan.*

Example [i] has an analysis in which the *by* phrase is a means adjunct, matching that in the active clause [ii]; here the understood subject of the gerund-participial is the same as the understood internalised complement. Yet the gerund-participial can itself function as the subject of an active clause, as in [iii]. This suggests that the *by* phrase in [i] could be an internalised complement. We do not perceive [i] to be ambiguous, however, because [iii] itself is understood with the subject indicating means: whoever leaked the report had sabotaged the plan by doing so.

AdvP in lieu of internalised complement

A number of verbs allow an AdvP instead of a quantified complement:

[17] i *It was widely believed that the proposal had been leaked by the minister herself.*
ii *It is popularly known as 'Singapore daisy'.*

Widely is understood as "by many people", and *popularly* as "by most ordinary/lay people". Similarly: *She was universally admired*, "by everyone". The verbs concerned are generally stative, with the understood complement having the semantic role of experiencer (but note also *The land is publicly owned / owned by the public*).

3 Act-related adjuncts

Contrast between manner adjuncts and act-related adjuncts

We noted in §2.1 that most adverbs that can function as manner adjunct can also appear in some other semantic category. In particular, there are some – such as *carefully, carelessly, discreetly, ostentatiously, stupidly*, etc. – that function as manner adjuncts to verbs denoting actions of animate beings (mainly humans) and which also belong to what we refer to as the act-related category. The distinction between the manner and act-related categories is illustrated in the following pairs:

[1]	MANNER ADJUNCT	ACT-RELATED ADJUNCT
i	a. *He spoke to them quite rudely.*	b. *Rudely, he spoke only to her husband.*
ii	a. *He answered the question foolishly.*	b. *Foolishly, he answered two questions.*
iii	a. *He closed the door carefully and then answered my question.*	b. *Carefully, he closed the door before answering my question.*

In [ia] it was the **way** he spoke to them that was rude, whereas in [ib] it was the **act** of speaking only to her husband that was rude – it may be that he spoke to her husband quite politely, while rudely ignoring her. Similarly, in [iia] *foolishly* describes the way he answered the question (he gave a foolish answer), whereas in [iib] it evaluates the act of answering two questions. In this latter case the answers may have been clever, but perhaps he was only asked to answer one question. In [iiia] he closed the door in a careful way – taking care to make the minimum noise perhaps, or in such a way as to ensure that the door wouldn't spring open again. In [iiib] it was the very act of closing the door that was careful: he may well have been taking care to ensure that no one would overhear his answer. The act-related adjuncts are thus concerned with the act in abstraction from its manner. Another way of bringing out the difference is to consider the comparison classes: in [iiia], for example, closing the door carefully may be compared with closing it noisily, slamming it, and so on, whereas in [iiib] the act of closing the door may be compared with other possible acts in the context, such as opening the door or leaving it open, closing the window, and the like.

In these examples, the semantic difference is reflected in the different syntactic positions. Front position normally allows only the act-related interpretation; end position usually indicates the manner interpretation, but could generally allow the act-related reading if set apart from the residue prosodically or by punctuation (as in *He answered two questions, foolishly*). That position would hardly be possible for *carefully*, which is probably due to the fact that *carefully* is much more oriented towards manner than *foolishly* or *rudely*: one would be unlikely to use [iiib] if he had slammed the door, whereas [ib] and [iib], as noted, are quite compatible with his having spoken politely and answered cleverly (*carefully* is thus not so clearly distinguished as the others from the secondary manner adjuncts of §2.1). With adverbs like *rudely* and *foolishly* central position gives the act-related reading, while with *carefully*, for the reasons just suggested, the distinction is somewhat blurred:

[2] a. *He <u>foolishly</u> answered two questions.* b. *He <u>carefully</u> closed the door.*

The two kinds of adjunct can combine in a single clause, with the act-related one having scope over the manner:

[3] i *He <u>foolishly</u> spoke <u>rather impolitely</u> to the boss's husband.*
ii *She <u>carefully</u> dresses <u>sloppily</u>.*

The fact that *careful* and *sloppy* are more or less opposites brings out sharply the difference between the two kinds of adjunct, for there is no contradiction in [ii]: we understand that she takes care to give the appearance of being sloppily dressed.

Subjective and volitional subtypes of act-related adjuncts

The act-related adjuncts cited in [1] are **subjective** in that they involve an evaluation of the act by the speaker. It's my judgement that his speaking only to her husband was rude, that it was foolish to answer two questions, that closing the door before answering my question was a careful thing to do. Note, however, that in making an evaluation of the act, I am also making one of the actor: he was rude to speak only to her husband and foolish to answer two questions, and he was being careful in closing the door. This distinguishes the act-related adjuncts from evaluative proposition-related ones like *Unfortunately he answered two questions* (see §17).

There is a second type of act-related adjunct that does not involve this kind of subjective evaluation. We refer to these as **volitional**:

[4] i *The clerk <u>deliberately</u> gave her the wrong change.*
ii *<u>Reluctantly</u> the clerk later gave her another five pounds.*

The adverbs here belong in the act-related category since we are not concerned with the manner in which the act was performed; they do not, however, reflect a subjective evaluation of the act but relate to the intentions or willingness of the agent, the clerk.

Realisation

Act-related adjuncts most often have the form of adverbs, such as:

[5] SUBJECTIVE

carefully	*carelessly*	*cleverly*	*considerately*	*delicately*
discreetly	*foolishly*	*immaturely*	*lavishly*	*manfully*
nonchalantly	*ostentatiously*	*prudently*	*studiously*	*stupidly*
surreptitiously	*tactfully*	*tactlessly*	*unceremoniously*	*wisely*

[6] VOLITIONAL

accidentally	*deliberately*	*freely*	*inadvertently*	*knowingly*
purposely	*reluctantly*	*unwittingly*	*voluntarily*	*willingly*

PPs are also found: *with his usual tact, without any consideration for the rest of us* (subjective), *by accident, on purpose, under duress, with reluctance* (volitional).

The adverbs in [5] occur also as manner adjuncts, as illustrated in [1], while those in [6] are very largely specialised to the act-related category. *Deliberately* indicates manner with such verbs as *speak*, but with a somewhat different sense ("carefully and slowly"), while *reluctantly* and several others have a manner interpretation in construction with such verbs as *act*.

A good number of the subjective adverbs allow paraphrases where the adjective from which they are derived is used predicatively: *It was foolish of him to answer two questions; He was foolish to answer two questions.* Such paraphrases are not available with the volitional adverbs. Compare, for example, **It was deliberate of the clerk to give her the wrong change.* We do have *He was reluctant/willing to answer the question* but since this does not entail that he answered the question the meaning is quite different from that of *He reluctantly/willingly answered the question.*

Restrictiveness and focus

The main difference between the two subtypes is that the subjective ones are always non-restrictive, while the volitional ones can be restrictive. Only the latter, therefore, can be focus of an interrogative or of contrastive negation:

[7]	i	a. *Did he close the door* CAREFULLY?	[manner reading only]
		b. *Did he go* WILLINGLY?	[act-related: volitional]
	ii	a. **He didn't answer two questions foolishly but wisely.*	[subjective]
		b. *He didn't mislead us inadvertently but quite deliberately.*	[volitional]

Instead of [iia] we need one of the adjectival versions, such as *It wasn't foolish but wise of him to answer two questions.*

The subjective ones, indeed, do not readily occur in closed interrogatives even in non-focus position. Compare:

[8]	i	*?Did he rudely speak only to her husband?*	[subjective]
	ii	*Did you deliberately leave me the smallest piece?*	[volitional]

The open interrogative *Who so rudely interrupted the speaker?* is perfectly acceptable, because here there is a presupposition that someone interrupted the speaker, and this act can therefore be evaluated as rude.

Imperative clauses do not accommodate subjective act-related adjuncts. Volitional ones are very rare, but not wholly excluded, particularly in negatives: *Don't deliberately offend any of them.*

Both types can have scope over a negative: *I foolishly didn't pay enough attention to what she said*; *The director deliberately didn't mention any names.* But with some of the subjective ones (e.g. *carefully*), it would be more usual to select a verb such as *refrain, omit, avoid* that incorporates the negative meaning within it than to use a syntactically negative clause. Thus *The director carefully refrained from mentioning any names* is somewhat more natural than *The director carefully didn't mention any names.*

The agent

An act implies an agent, and the adjuncts discussed in this section are related to the agent via the act. We have seen that clauses containing an adjunct of the subjective subtype can generally be quite closely paraphrased with a clause containing a predicative adjective whose predicand refers to the agent: *Ed rudely interrupted* ~ *Ed was rude to interrupt* or *It was rude of Ed to interrupt.* Even though such paraphrases are not available with the volitional ones, the latter are still concerned with attitudes, intentions, etc., on the part of the agent: *Ed deliberately misled us*, for example, ascribes intention to Ed.

We have so far confined our attention to active-voice clauses describing actions. We must now turn to some less straightforward cases.

States

[9] i *Jill rightly / mistakenly/ foolishly believes/ thinks that Nigel had told the police.*
ii *Jill wisely / foolishly/ deliberately lives a long way from her place of work.*

Here the clauses describe states, not acts, but a restricted subset of the adjuncts listed above can occur in clauses of this kind. What sanctions them is that the subject-referent is assumed to be responsible for the state. This is reflected in the fact that we again have approximate paraphrases with a predicative adjective: *Jill is right/mistaken/foolish to believe . . .*; *It is wise/foolish of Jill to live (such) a long way from her place of work.*

Long passive clauses (passive clauses containing an internalised complement)

[10] i *The gate was carelessly left open by the hikers.*
ii *The lecturer was rudely interrupted by several members of the audience.*
iii *Dick was wisely taught the tricks of the trade by Donald.*
iv *Ed was reluctantly sent to boarding-school by his stepfather.*

In passive clauses the complement of *by* corresponds to the subject of the active, and in the default case it is therefore this NP that refers to the agent to which the adjunct relates. In [i], for example, carelessness is attributed to the hikers. In this example, the subject is inanimate and hence could not be associated with the agent role. In [ii] the subject is human, but again the rudeness is attributed to several members of the audience, not the lecturer: being interrupted is not (normally) something over which one has control and hence the subject of the passive is not associated with an agent role. Examples [iii–iv] also have a default reading in which the wisdom and reluctance are attributed to the agent expressed by the complement of *by*, i.e. to Donald and Ed's stepfather. But they also have a less salient reading in which the default is overridden, with the wisdom and reluctance being attributed to Dick and Ed, the referents of the passive subject.[3] Here we

[3] For some speakers this second reading is more readily available if the adjunct is positioned before the passive auxiliary: *Dick wisely was taught the tricks of the trade by Donald.*

understand that Dick had an agent role in initiating Donald's teaching him the tricks of the trade, that Ed likewise had an agent role in agreeing to go to boarding-school (or at least accepting the decision). From the point of view of meaning, therefore, we effectively have two acts, and two agents, in such cases – and the act-related adjunct applies to the one that is implicit rather than the one that is explicitly expressed. The two acts are both explicitly expressed in structures like *Dick wisely got himself taught the tricks of the trade by David* or *Ed reluctantly allowed his stepfather to send him to boarding-school.* In this second interpretation [iii–iv] are comparable to the embedded passive of examples like *They advised the twins* *not to be photographed together*, discussed in Ch. 4, fn. 16, where the understood subject is assigned an agent role by virtue of being embedded as complement to the verb *advise.*

Short passives (those without an internalised complement)

[11] i *The letter was inadvertently posted without a stamp.*
ii *The lecturer was rudely interrupted several times.*
iii *Dick was wisely taught the tricks of the trade.*

In examples like these the internalised complement is implicit rather than overtly expressed, and the default interpretation relates the adjunct to the understood agent – to the person who posted the letter, the people who interrupted, the one who taught Dick the tricks of the trade. But the default reading can be overridden in examples like [iii] in the same way as in [10iii].

Other cases of an implicit act

We suggested that in the non-default reading of [10iii–iv] and [11iii] there is an implicit act (and hence agent) in addition to the one overtly expressed in the passive clause. There are also active voice clauses in which an adjunct relates to an implicit act and agent:

[12] i *The document may have unintentionally got into Soviet hands.*
ii *The four brands found unwittingly to contain 'Enterococcus faicium' were supplied by a different laboratory.*

In [i] we understand *unintentionally* to apply to the act of allowing the document to get into Soviet hands, and in [ii] *unwittingly* in the *contain* clause likewise applies to the implicit act of manufacturing the brands. Examples of this kind will tend to be avoided in carefully monitored text, but they certainly occur in less formal styles.

4 Location and change of location in space

The term 'location' applies primarily to the domain of space, but it is common practice, both in linguistics and in the ordinary use of language, to extend the concept to other domains, especially time. This extension is motivated by the clear parallels in the use of prepositions in the two domains (see Ch. 19, §5.4, where we examine the role of prepositional elements in lexical morphology). In this section we look at spatial location and change of location, but precisely because this is the primary domain for the application of the concept of location, we will largely omit the specification 'spatial'.

4.1 Overview of categories

Adjuncts and complements expressing location and change of location in space are very frequent and quite varied in form and meaning. The most elementary case is that of spatial location itself, without any motion from one place to another:

[1] i *We met under the station clock.* [(spatial) location]
ii *George remained at home.*

We analyse the underlined elements as adjuncts or complements of **spatial location**, or simply **location**.

More complex is the case where we have a change of location, or motion.

[2] i *John ran from the attic to the kitchen.* [source + goal]
ii *She took her passport out of the drawer.* [source]
iii *Kim put the key under the mat.* [goal]

Example [i] specifies two locations: John began in the attic and ended in the kitchen. *From the attic* indicates the **starting-point**, *to the kitchen* the **endpoint**; we will refer to them in the domain of space as respectively **source** and **goal**. In [ii] only the source is specified (her passport was initially in the drawer), and in [iii] only the goal (the key was finally under the mat).

It is also possible to specify an intermediate location (or indeed more than one), which we call **path**:

[3] i *Don't travel via London if you can avoid it.* [path]
ii *I drove from school through the tunnel to the station.* [source + path + goal]
iii *John ran down the stairs into the kitchen.* [path + goal]
iv *She has come from London via Singapore.* [source + path]

In addition, one can indicate the **direction** of motion:

[4] i *We are travelling north.* [direction]
ii *She ran from the car towards the house.* [source + direction]
iii *They turned left onto the main highway.* [direction + goal]

4.2 Location

Location elements can be complements or adjuncts:

[5]	COMPLEMENT	ADJUNCT
i	a. *The stew is in the oven.*	b. *We had breakfast in the kitchen.*
ii	a. *The books are stored next door.*	b. *Next door they sell jewellery.*
iii	a. *The accident occurred at the corner.*	b. *I read the report at home.*

The underlined elements in the [a] examples are part of the complementation of the verb. In some cases they are obligatory, not omissible without loss of grammaticality (though they might be replaceable by complements of a different kind). In [ia], for example, **The stew is* is not an admissible clause on its own (leaving aside the case of ellipsis: *The vegetables aren't in the oven, but the stew is _*). Elsewhere, as in [iia/iiia], the complement is not strictly obligatory, but nevertheless has a strong link with the verb: it represents an integral feature of the situation expressed in the clause. The adjuncts in the [b] examples are all optional and do not depend for their admissibility on the presence of a particular class of verb. Note also the difference with respect to the *do so* test (Ch. 4, §1.2):

[6] i *I read the report at home and Henry did so at the office.*
ii **The first accident occurred at the corner and the second did so at the roundabout.*

Location of situation or location of theme

[7] i *I saw your father in London.* [location of situation]
ii *I saw your father at the window.* [location of theme]
iii *I saw your father on the bus.* [ambiguous]

In the natural interpretation of [i] the adjunct *in London* indicates where the event as a whole took place. In [ii], however, *at the window* is likely to be construed as saying where your father was when I saw him: I myself was elsewhere – in the road, perhaps. Example [iii] can then be interpreted in either way, as saying where the event took place or where your father was. The element whose location is described in cases like [ii] has the semantic role of theme (cf. Ch. 4, §2.2).

The theme may be aligned with the subject or object of the clause, and the locative can then be said to have either subject or object orientation:

[8] SUBJECT ORIENTATION / OBJECT ORIENTATION
i a. *The key remained in my pocket.* b. *I found the key in my pocket.*
ii a. *The child was on her shoulders.* b. *She carried the child on her shoulders.*

It is also possible for the theme to be the object of a preposition, as in *I caught a glimpse of her at the window.*

Some special cases of location elements

Contact with body-part

[9] i a. *She poked him in the ribs.* b. *She poked his ribs.*
ii a. *He patted her on the shoulder.* b. *He patted her shoulder.*
iii a. *He was wounded in the foot.* b. *His foot was wounded.*

The locatives in the [a] examples do not specify the location of either participant (or of the event as a whole), but indicate which part of the patient's body was affected. These examples with two complements in the VP are approximately equivalent to their counterparts in [b], which have just one, with the body-part noun heading the object NP.[4] Note that where the location is questioned, as in *Where did he hit you?*, there is no corresponding [b] version: we need something like *What part of your body did he hit?* (see Ch. 4, §7.4, for further discussion of the alternation in [9]).

Temporal interpretation of locatives

[10] i *She wrote the book in Cape Town.*
ii *I was ill in Calcutta.*
iii *In the zoo he wanted an ice-cream.*

Location adjuncts can often be used to give, by implication, the time of an event. A purely spatial interpretation might apply in [i] if, for example, Cape Town is connected with the content of the book. But it can also be taken as a shorthand way of saying *She*

[4] The qualification 'approximately' is needed because in certain cases the two constructions are not interchangeable. A doctor, for example, might poke your ribs as part of a medical examination, but we would not describe this situation as 'poking you in the ribs'.

wrote the book when she was in Cape Town. Such a temporal interpretation is especially common for locatives in construction with stative verbs, as in [ii–iii].

Metonymic locatives

[11] i *I met her at Jill's 21st birthday party.*
ii *There may well be some unpleasantness at the meeting.*

The NP complements of *at* here refer to events, but the association between such events and their venue yields a spatial location interpretation of the whole PP. (There is, however, some blurring of the distinction between space and time here: these examples can also be taken as giving the time of the event – cf. the discussion of [10] above.)

Metaphorical locatives

[12] i *Nobody would dare talk in Smith's class.*
ii *I read this in a book on wild flowers.*
iii *In our family birthdays are not celebrated.*
iv *In medicine you can't afford to make mistakes.*

Locative phrases with *in* often denote some metaphorical space. In [i] Smith's class is not a physical location, but a social location. In [ii] it is the book as an abstract rather than a physical location that provided the information I obtained. And so on. Physical and metaphorical locations can combine: *In my dream, I was walking with Paula in Hyde Park.*

Iteration of location adjuncts and complements

[13] i a. *I heard him at the Albert Hall, in London.*
b. *I heard him in London, at the Albert Hall.*
c. *In London I heard him at the Albert Hall.*
d. #*At the Albert Hall I heard him in London.*
ii *He is staying in the annexe, on the top floor, in Room 201.*

Location may be given by a series of phrases differing in their degree of specificity: *at the Albert Hall* is more specific than *in London*, and *in Room 201* is more specific than *on the top floor*, which is in turn more specific than *in the annexe*. The examples in [i] illustrate the relative positions of the phrases: note that preposing applies to the less specific, as shown by the contrast between [ic] and [id].

Combination of location adjunct with locative complements

[14] i *In Brisbane we keep our cats indoors at night.*
ii *Here lots of people go to the beach every week-end.*

These examples have a location adjunct combining with a location complement in [i], and a goal in [ii]. The adjunct is less specific than the complement.

Questioning

Location dependents can generally be questioned by *where*:

[15] i *Where did you have lunch today?* [adjunct]
ii *Where are you living these days?* [complement with subject orientation]
iii *Where do you keep the stickytape?* [complement with object orientation]

Realisation

Most location dependents have the form of a PP. A sample of prepositions (and prepositional idioms) heading such phrases is given in:

[16] i	*abroad*	*downhill*	*downstairs*	*here*	*hereabouts*	*home*
	indoors	*nearby*	*overseas*	*there*	*where*	
ii	*above*	*across*	*against*	*around*	*at*	*away*
	before	*behind*	*below*	*between*	*beyond*	*by*
	down	*east*	*in*	*in front*	*inside*	*near*
	next	*off*	*on*	*on top*	*opposite*	*out*
	outside	*over*	*past*	*through*	*throughout*	*under*
iii	*back*	*into*	*to*	*towards*		

The items in [i] occur without complements in the PP: *He lives abroad*; *Nearby, some children were playing cricket.* For *here* and *there* see Ch. 17, §9.1. *Home* marks location only as a subject-oriented complement: *Are you home?*, *We stayed home*, but not **I keep my computer home* or **Home, the children were playing cricket.* Besides *where* we have the compound determinatives *anywhere, everywhere, nowhere, somewhere. Where* commonly introduces PPs with the form of fused relatives: *The keys aren't where they should be.* Similarly *wherever*: *You can sleep wherever you like.*

The prepositions in [16ii] take complements (NPs or further PPs), though most can also occur without: *They were playing outside* (*the caravan*); *She is out* (*of the country*). For a number of them, however, the construction without a complement is largely excluded from location function. Compare:

[17]		LOCATION	GOAL
i	a.	*She was working across the road.*	b. *She swam across the river.*
ii	a.	**She was working across.*	b. *She swam across.*
iii	a.	*She was across.*	b. *She got across.*

Intransitive *across* can express location only in examples like [17iiia], where it indicates the location resulting from movement. *Before* is much more commonly used in the temporal domain than in the spatial, where *in front* is more usual (*before the altar, in front of her brother*).

The prepositions in [16iii], *back, into, to, towards*, occur predominantly with change of location, but they are not completely excluded from simple location:

[18] i *They camped five miles into the forest.*
ii *Liz is back from London already.*
iii *The entrance is to the right of the letter-box.*
iv *The school is situated towards the end of the highway.*

Example [18i] is similar to [17iiia] in that the location is understood as the endpoint of motion not expressed in the clause itself: they had been travelling into the forest and stopped to camp after covering five miles. Example [18ii] likewise implies prior motion: Liz went to London and has now returned. In [18iii–iv] the implied movement is conceptual or potential rather than actual. Locate the letter-box and then move to the right: that is where the entrance is. Imagine yourself travelling along the highway: some place near the end of it is where the school is situated. *Onto* is not used in this way, though it has a metaphorical locative sense in *The police are onto him already.*

Location is also expressed by a handful of adverbs, such as *locally, internationally, nationally, regionally, worldwide*: *They work locally.*

4.3 Change of location: goal, source, path, and direction

The dependents having to do with change of location are normally complements, requiring the presence of some verb expressing motion, or the causation of motion. Note again that these elements have to be included in the scope of *do so*: **Kim went to London and Pat did so to New York.*

The central cases of complements of source and goal are found in clauses expressing the change of location of a theme element. The source gives the initial location of the theme, and the goal the final location:

[19] i *Angela drove from Berlin to Bonn.* [subject orientation]
ii *Angela took the TV from the lounge into her bedroom.* [object orientation]

The theme role is aligned with the subject in [i], and the object in [ii], so we may again distinguish between subject and object orientation (cf. [8] above).

In [19i] Angela was originally in Berlin and finally in Bonn. Similarly in [ii] the TV started off in the lounge and ended up in Angela's bedroom. Note, then, that *from* and *to* are not part of the description of the initial and final locations. The initial locations are Berlin and the lounge (or 'in Berlin' and 'in the lounge'): *from* serves, rather, as a marker of the source category, indicating that its complement represents the initial location. Similarly, the final locations are (in) Bonn and in her bedroom, with *to* being a marker of the goal category.

Omission of contextually understood source and goal

With some verbs of directed motion, especially but by no means only the deictic verbs *come* and *go*, a source and/or goal may be left unexpressed but contextually implied:

[20] i a. *He has gone.* b. *Are you going?*
ii a. *I'm coming.* b. *Are you coming?*
iii a. *Have they arrived yet?* b. *We'll be arriving at seven.*

Example [ia] will often be interpreted in a face-to-face conversation as "He has gone from here" (understood source), and in a context mentioning a party, for example, [ib] is likely to imply "Are you going to the party?" (understood goal). Example [iia] will often imply movement from where I currently am to where you are; [iib] might involve your coming to where I am or our both going to a party or whatever. In a face-to-face conversation [iiia] will most likely be understood as "Have they arrived here yet?", while in [iiib] the goal will probably be some other place, but it will have to be recoverable from the context. (See also Ch. 17, §9.2.)

Bounding potential of goal

With most verbs of motion, including all verbs expressing manner of motion (*walk, drive, swim, fly*, etc.) the presence of a goal has the effect of making the clause bounded; the other change of location elements do not have this effect. Compare:

[21] i *She drove to Berlin in/*for eight hours.* [goal]
ii *She drove from Bonn in/for eight hours.* [source]
iii *She walked through the forest for/in eight hours.* [path (*for*) or *goal* (*in*)]

In [i] the source, although not expressed, is contextually implied. This means that the length of the trip is delimited, and driving this distance must be an accomplishment, must be bounded. We can therefore have a duration adjunct with *in* but not with *for* (see §1 above). In [ii] we have a source but no overt goal. A goal can be implied by the context yielding a bounded process, which sanctions the duration adjunct with *in*; but there need not be a contextually derivable goal, and in the absence of an implied goal the clause expresses an unbounded situation, an activity, which sanctions the adjunct with *for*. In [iii] *through the forest* can express path or goal. In the former case there is no implication that she reached the end of the forest; here walking along this path is an unbounded activity, which sanctions *for*. In the goal interpretation the end of the forest is reached; the journey was from one end of the forest to the other, which means that it was bounded, so that *in* is sanctioned.

Licensing of change of location complements

Goal, source, path, and direction complements are generally licensed by verbs expressing motion, including causative verbs of movement such as *put* or *send*. Three further special cases merit brief mention.

Verbs of sound emission

The primary meaning of such verbs as *roar* and *whistle* has to do with the emission of various kinds of sound rather than with motion, but they can be used in a secondary sense to indicate motion accompanying or causing such sounds:

[22] i a. *A bullet <u>whistled</u> <u>past my head</u>.* b. *The motor bikes <u>roared</u> <u>up the hill</u>.*
ii a. *She <u>rustled</u> <u>out of the room</u>.* b. *The train <u>chugged</u> <u>into the station</u>.*

The *way* construction

[23] a. *We <u>made our way</u> <u>to the station</u>.* b. *Jill had to <u>elbow her way</u> <u>to the exit</u>.*

The verb *make* on its own does not license change of location complements, but it forms an idiom with an object NP of the form *x's way*, meaning approximately "progress", and this does license them, as in [a]. This provides the basis for a fairly productive construction in which *make* is replaced by verbs giving information about the manner of progress. In [b] Jill's progress to the exit was achieved by using her elbows (cf. also *She elbowed me out of her way*). The movement denoted by the *way* construction has to be one that consists of a series of stops and starts, rather than being continuous movement.

Be + goal

The verb *be* can have a motional sense in construction with the perfect. Compare:

[24] i a. *Jill has been to Moscow.* b. *Jill has gone to Moscow.*
ii a. **Jill was to Moscow twice.* b. *Jill went to Moscow twice.*

The difference between *be* and *go* (apart from the restriction of *be* to the perfect, as shown in [iia]) is that *be* entails subsequent departure from the goal location. In [ib] Jill could still be in Moscow (indeed the most likely scenario is that she is), but in [ia] she can't. Typically she will have returned to the original source location, but it is possible for her to have moved to some third location.

Omission of goal marker

Goal is much the most frequent of the change of location elements, and the specific goal marker *to* is often omissible. Compare, for example, source and goal in the following pairs:

[25]	SOURCE	GOAL
i	a. *Where did she come from?*	b. *Where did she go (to)?*
ii	a. *She's travelling from here by car.*	b. *She's travelling here by car.*
iii	a. *He emerged from under the bridge.*	b. *He swam under the bridge.*
iv	a. *He came out of the room.*	b. *He went in(to) the room.*

The source in all these examples is marked – by *from* or *out* + *of*. As for the goal, the marker *to* is optional with *where*: in *Where did she go?* the *where* questions the final location, just as it does in *Where did she go to?* The *to* is generally impossible with *here* and *there*: ?*She's travelling to here by car.*[5] In [iiib] the preposition *under* is part of the description of the location, not a marker of its status as goal. *Under the bridge* can express location without motion or change, as in *He was camping under the bridge.* And indeed precisely because there is no goal marker in [iiib] itself, the example is ambiguous between the goal reading (He wasn't under the bridge to start with but was at the end of the event described) and a location reading (roughly, "He was swimming around under the bridge").[6] In [iv] the goal marker *to* is again optional, though this time it is not a separate word but part of a compound. As we remarked in Ch. 4, §5.2, the position of *to* in the compound doesn't match the interpretation of the phrase: the final location is "in the room", so conceptually we have "to + in the room". *To* is likewise an optional component of the compound *onto*: *She jumped on(to) the platform.*

Whence and *whither* are relative and interrogative words for source and goal respectively; *whither* is archaic, *whence* somewhat less so in relative constructions. Even here the source as often as not is marked by *from*: *the place from whence he came.*

Realisation of goal

The prototypical goal is marked by the preposition *to*, as a word on its own or compounded with *in* or *on*. In either case the preposition requires an overt complement; if the final location is omissible by virtue of being contextually recoverable, as discussed in connection with [20], then the marker *to* is omitted as well as the complement expressing the final location. Compare then:

[26] i *Kim went to the meeting, and Pat went as well.*
ii *Kim went into the church but Pat wouldn't go in with her.*

Because the goal marker *to* is omissible, most of the expressions that can function as location can also function as goal:

[27]		
i	a. *I found it next to the garage.*	b. *I put it next to the garage.*
ii	a. *It was lying between the posts.*	b. *It fell between the posts.*

[5] This might be acceptable if *here*, accompanied by a gesture, refers to a location on a map. For some speakers, *to* can also occur after *back*: %*She's coming back to here.*

[6] There is also a salient reading of [25iiib] in which *under the bridge* indicates the path: he was swimming along a river and passed under the bridge. In languages where prepositions govern a range of cases, the goal and location interpretations of the preposition are often distinguished by the case of the complement NP. For example, Latin and German have accusative case for the goal and path readings, and respectively ablative and dative case for the location reading.

One important exception is *at*. Instead of **He went to at school*, we have an NP complement: *He went to school*. A different kind of exception is *out*, which with verbs of motion is restricted to source: *She stayed out of the room* (location); *She went out of the room* (source, not goal). (*From* is also excluded from goals, but doesn't occur in location either.) Some prepositions which occur predominantly in source or direction expressions are found as goal under restricted conditions: *It landed just off the highway*; *Place it well away from the fire*; *The bomb dropped towards the end of the highway*; *They moved south*. The latter (certainly in its salient interpretation) says that they moved to a new location, in the south; it may be contrasted with *They walked south*, where *south* indicates direction (cf. *They walked south for two hours*).

A few verbs are exceptional in that they do not take *to* as a marker of goal. *Arrive* takes *at* instead of *to*: *They'll be arriving at Heathrow from Paris shortly after noon*. It does, however, allow *into* (as well as *in* and *on*): *They arrived into Heathrow in the middle of the night*. *Put* (and similar verbs such as *place*) take *in(to)* and *on(to)*, but normally not *to* alone: *He put it in(to) the cupboard* / *on(to) the top shelf* / **to the cupboard*.

Fused relatives with *where* or *wherever* occur as goal, alone or with a governing preposition: *Put it back where you found it*; *She swam to where the river divides*. The verb *reach* assigns a goal interpretation to its object, which is obligatory: *She reached Bonn at six*; **She reached at six*.

Realisation of source

Source complements generally have the form of PPs headed by *from*, *away*, *off*, *out*. *From* takes as complement an NP or a PP headed by a locative preposition: *She emerged from the garden* / *from behind the wall* / *from under the bridge*. But again *at* is dropped: *He came home from school*, not **from at school*. Like the goal marker *to*, *from* requires an overt complement. *Away* occurs alone (*She walked away*) or with a *from* phrase as complement (*She walked away from him*). *Off* and *out* occur alone or with complements, NP and *of* PP respectively: *Kim jumped off (the pier)*; *He came out (of the room)*. *Out* can combine with a *from* phrase: *She came out from behind the bush*.

Realisation of path

Via is the prototypical preposition marking path: in the domain of space it occurs uniquely with paths. It takes an NP as complement, not a locative PP: *She came via the bridge* / **via over the bridge*. *Along* is usually associated with path too: *They strolled along the castle wall* (which doesn't specify where the stroll started or finished); it can, however, also be used for location, as in *He lives just along the corridor*. NPs headed by *way* also commonly occur in path function: *Don't go that way to the beach, go this way*.

In addition, many PPs that can express simple location or initial and final locations can also express intermediate location, and hence path. Compare, for example:

[28]	i	a.	*I ran across the bridge.*	[goal]
		b.	*I ran across the bridge to the old church.*	[path]
	ii	a.	*The noise came from up the hill.*	[source]
		b.	*They walked from the station up the hill to the new Civic Centre.*	[path]

In [ia] *across the bridge* gives the final location whereas in [ib] it gives an intermediate location.[7] In [iia] *up the hill* gives the initial location (*from* being the source marker), while in [iib] it is an intermediate location within the journey from station to Civic Centre.

Realisation of direction

Direction elements can be prospective or retrospective in orientation, with the former very much the more common. The prospective type are oriented towards a later location, the retrospective type towards an earlier location.

The morphological base *·wards* is a distinctive component of a number of prospective direction phrases: *eastwards, northwards, forwards, backwards, inwards, outwards,* etc., and *towards*, where *·wards* is compounded with the goal marker *to*.[8] While *to* alone marks goal, *towards* marks direction: the complement of the preposition is only a potential final location. The compass terms are also used without *·wards*: *They went south/southwards.* Other prospective direction phrases include *left* and *right* (or *to the left/right*). The preposition *at* occurs with a good number of verbs (*He shot an arrow at the rabbit*) and *for* with a few (*The ship made for the harbour*). These are closely related to goals: the intention was that the arrow hit the target, that the ship reach the harbour.

NPs with *way* as head can function as direction as well as path – compare:

[29] i *Which way did you come?* [path]
ii *Which way did he go?* [direction (or path)]

Example [i] has an implied goal ("here") and *which way* asks about the route taken to get here. Example [ii] can be interpreted likewise with an implied goal (though not "here", of course), but a very salient interpretation has the goal unspecified, and the question asking about direction, equivalent to *In which direction did he go?*

Retrospective direction elements are not distinct in form from source. Compare:

[30] i *Get away from it.*
ii A: *Can you tell me the way to the station?* B: *You are walking away from it.*

In [i] *away from it* expresses source: the initial location is where 'it' is. In [ii], however, *away from it* expresses direction: the station doesn't give your initial location. Rather, your unspecified initial location was closer to the station than your current one.

Constituency of source + goal constructions

Source and goal can certainly be treated syntactically as separate elements of clause structure, as is evident from examples like:

[31] i *From London she went to New York.*
ii *It was to New York that she went next from London.*

But there is a close relationship between them, and they can also be construed as forming a unit together:

[32] i *We walked from Sunshine Beach to Noosa, which is a beautiful stretch of coast.*
ii *We drove from Manchester to London, a distance of 180 miles.*

[7] There is a sense in which the goal in [28i] incorporates a path: the final location is on the other side of the bridge, but *across the bridge* also indicates the path taken to get there. Prepositions like *across, through, up, down* differ from *at, in, on* in combining path with goal in this way.

[8] An alternant of *·wards* is *·ward*, found primarily in AmE.

The antecedent for the relative pronoun *which* in [i] is *from Sunshine Beach to Noosa*, and expressions of this kind can function as subject: *From Sunshine Beach to Noosa is a beautiful stretch of coast.* Similarly, [ii] may be compared to *From Manchester to London is a distance of 180 miles.*

4.4 Metaphorical extension of the locative categories to other domains

We observed at the beginning of this section that there are conceptual and linguistic similarities between the domain of space and various other domains, such as time. For this reason, the categories introduced above have a broader application than has been described so far. Source and goal especially, representing primarily the terminal points in spatial movement, can be applied to many other processes conceived of as involving progression. Compare, for example:

[33] i *I read the article from page 15 to page 60.*
ii *The dressmaker took in the skirt from the waist down.*
iii *We drank our way through a magnum bottle of whisky.*
iv *We came to a decision / arrived at a decision / reached a decision.*
v *We managed to get through that meeting without any mishap.*
vi *The tradition is transmitted from father to son and from teacher to pupil.*
vii *I couldn't get the message across.*

In [i] the process is one of reading rather than movement of a theme element, but the relationship with the central case of movement is very close. The article has physical form, and *page 15* and *page 60* refer to places within it. In [ii] the process of taking the skirt in applies to an area of the skirt and the waist is a place in that area where the process began. Example [iii], involving the *way* construction of [23] above, expresses a process of drinking a bottle of whisky, with completion of that process treated like reaching a spatial goal. And in [iv] the process of deciding is conceptualised like movement to a goal. Analogously with [v–vii].

The concepts of location, source, and goal can be applied to states:

[34]	SPACE	STATES
i	a. *Liz is in London.*	b. *The situation is bad.*
ii	a. *Liz went from London to New York.*	b. *The situation went from bad to worse.*

In [ib] we have location in a state, and in [iib] change from one state to another. On the basis of such parallels between space and states we can talk of state location, state source, and state goal, as discussed in Ch. 4, §5.2.

Orientation and topography

We also find, within the general domain of space, that the categories associated primarily with change of location can apply without there being any movement:

[35] i *The house faces towards the forest.* [direction]
ii *The arrow points north / to the exit.* [direction/goal]
iii *The road runs from the village to the castle.* [source + goal]
iv *The valley broadens out into a fertile plain.* [goal]
v *The track winds its way along the banks of the river.* [path]

These do not involve any change of location, but express static situations. The adjuncts are therefore not bounding. There is, however, a very clear connection between these static situations and dynamic ones involving motion. In [iii] and [v], for example, the road and the track do not themselves move, but one can move from one location to another by travelling along them. And similarly in [iv] one could walk along the valley, coming to the fertile plain as goal. In [i], if I start walking in a straight line from the front of the house I will be walking towards the forest. In [ii] we can envisage an extension of the arrow, and if we go along this imaginary line, starting at the arrow-head, we will go north or to the exit. The terms 'source' and 'goal' have their primary application in the field of motion, but given this conceptual similarity and the similarity of form (reflected in the prepositions used) we can generalise the categories so that they apply in both the dynamic and static cases.

One difference between the static and dynamic types is that [iii] is equivalent to *The road runs from the castle to the village*, whereas *Kim ran from the village to the castle* is not equivalent to *Kim ran from the castle to the village.* These latter examples describe movement in opposite directions, whereas the road examples describe the same situation from different perspectives. As a consequence of this feature of [35iii], it is also equivalent to *The road runs* <u>*between the village and the castle*</u>. Here *the village* and *the castle* are coordinated, indicating that the locations expressed have equal status. They are not differentiated as source and goal, and can be thought of as terminal points or locations that define an extent of space.[9] Expressions of extent are the topic of our next section.

5 Spatial extent and scalar change

5.1 Overall extent and terminal-point extent

Consider the following set of examples:

[1] i *She walked to Hyde Park Corner.*
ii *She walked from her hotel to Hyde Park Corner.*
iii *She walked three miles.*

We have discussed clauses like [i–ii] as involving change of location, with *from her hotel* as source and *to Hyde Park Corner* as goal. From that point of view, they answer *where* questions: *Where did she walk to?*; *Where did she walk to Hyde Park Corner from?* But (assuming that in [i] the source is contextually implied) they can also be thought of as answering *how far* questions: *How far did she walk?* From this point of view they indicate spatial extent. A measure phrase like *three miles* in [iii] will normally unequivocally indicate extent. We will say that phrases like *three miles* express **overall extent**, while those in [i–ii] can express **terminal-point extent**, i.e. extent defined by specification of one or both of the terminal points, source and goal.

Overall extent is commonly expressed by measure phrases, as in [1iii], but measure phrases can also appear in the specification of the terminal points:

[2] i *She dived* <u>*from a height of 30 feet above the pool*</u>. [source]
ii *The plane soared* <u>*to a height of 35,000 feet*</u>. [goal]

[9] A *between* phrase is not incompatible with the dynamic sense of *run*. The most obvious use is in what we are calling multiple situations, as in *The tram runs between the village and the castle.* Here the tram makes multiple journeys, some starting at the village, others at the castle. Again, then, we have terminal locations without differentiation as source and goal.

From and *to* here mark source and goal, as usual, with the complement of the preposition specifying an initial location 30 feet above the pool and a final location 35,000 feet above sea-level.

5.2 Extent in various domains

Like location, extent can apply in the domain of time as well as space:

[3] i *The kite rose several hundred metres.* [spatial extent]
ii *The meeting lasted three hours.* [temporal extent: duration]

The standard term for temporal extent is 'duration', and these elements will be discussed under that heading in §7, after a consideration of temporal location: in this section, therefore, we confine our attention to non-temporal extent.

Dynamic and static spatial extent

As with spatial location, we find expressions of spatial extent in both dynamic and static situations. The above examples are all dynamic, while [4i–ii] are static:

[4] i *The tower rises to a height of 200 metres.*
ii *The road runs along the river for 20 miles / as far as the eye can see.*

Spatial dimensions

[5] i *He fell several metres, landing in a bed of nettles.* } [vertical]
ii *The tree has grown to its maximum height.* }
iii *The children cycled another three miles.* } [horizontal]
iv *They had to push their bicycles (for) half a mile up the hill.* }
v *The oil slick expanded to an area of thousands of square miles.* } [area]
vi *They extended the grounds by 5 acres / to a total of 55 acres.* }

These examples illustrate various dimensions of spatial extent. The differences are purely lexical, the range of grammatical constructions being the same throughout. The term 'distance' is commonly used for the category of spatial extent elements in the one-dimensional, especially horizontal, sphere.

Extension of spatial extent to scalar change

The same kinds of construction are found in such examples as:

[6] i *The price / A jar of coffee has gone up another two dollars.*
ii *The Dow Jones industrial average rose from 9892 through the psychological barrier of 10000 to a record level of 10073.*
iii *The temperature dropped to 5°.*
iv *She increased her philosophy mark from 70% to 85%.*

These do not involve movement in physical space, but change in value along some scale – increase or decrease. We refer to this therefore as the domain of **scalar change**. Although there is no change of physical location, the verbs used include many whose primary meaning has to do with spatial movement, as in [i–iii], and the extent of change is expressed in the same way as spatial extent. In [i], then, we have *another two dollars* expressing overall extent, while [ii–iv] have expressions of terminal-point extent, and again we can talk of *to* as marking the goal of scalar change, *from* the source. Example

[iii] even has a path, marked by *through*. The semantic role of theme likewise generalises to the element that moves along the scale in this figurative way: the price or a jar of coffee, the Dow Jones industrial average, and so on.

Overall extent in scalar change

One respect in which the scalar change constructions differ from those considered earlier concerns the expression of overall extent:

[7]		SCALAR CHANGE	SPATIAL MOVEMENT
	i	a. *The temperature fell 10°.*	b. *She cycled ten miles.*
	ii	a. *The temperature fell by 10°.*	b. *She cycled for ten miles.*

In [i] overall extent is expressed by NPs, and in [ii] by PPs, but the preposition for scalar change is *by*, while that for spatial movement is *for*. Note that the scale may incidentally have to do with spatial measurement (*They have widened the road by two metres*) or indeed with measurement of temporal duration (*They have shortened the semester by a week*): in terms of meaning and form, these clearly belong in the scalar change construction.

5.3 Non-temporal extent: further syntactic and semantic issues

Complement status of non-temporal extent elements

While elements expressing extent in the temporal domain (duration) are generally adjuncts, those in the spatial and scalar change domains have the properties of complements.

(a) Licensing by verb

The presence of these extent elements is strongly dependent on the presence of an appropriate verb. To take just a few examples, replacement of *fall, grow, cycle* in [5i–iii] by such verbs as *sit, die, think* would clearly lead to ungrammaticality.

(b) *Do so* anaphora

In general, extent elements cannot fall outside the scope of anaphoric *do so*:

[8] i **Jill pushed her bicycle half a mile and Liz did so even further.*
ii **Last week the Dow Jones share index fell 3%; this week it did so another 2%.*
iii **Coles have raised the price by $5, while the corner shop has done so by $8.50.*

Bounding potential

Adding an extent element to a clause expressing a process has the effect of making it bounded (and this too, indeed, is a property more characteristic of complements than of adjuncts). Note, then, the change from *for* to *in*:

[9]			
	i	a. *The temperature rose for four days.*	b. *The temperature rose 20° in four days.*
	ii	a. *The share price went up for weeks.*	b. *It went up from £3 to £5 in a week.*
	iii	a. *The shrub grew for years.*	b. *The shrub grew a whole foot in a year.*

Extent complements do not have this effect with stative clauses: examples like [4] are unbounded.

Realisation

(a) PPs

Extent complements commonly have the form of PPs. As we have noted, terminal-point extent has source marked by *from* and goal by *to*, and in overall extent *for* is used in the spatial domain, *by* in scalar change – see [7].

(b) AdvPs

A small number of adverbs (including *extensively*) serve to express extent, primarily in scalar change, as in *The price went up <u>astronomically</u>.*

(c) NPs

[10] i *The price went up <u>£2</u>.*
ii *They lowered the net <u>three metres</u> into the water.*
iii *I hadn't expected them to walk <u>that distance</u>.*
iv *Ed walked <u>the last few miles</u>; Bill rode <u>them</u> on a donkey.*

Extent NPs are usually indefinite and non-referential, as in [i–ii] and all the earlier examples. But definites are possible, as illustrated in [iii–iv]: note especially the accusative case pronoun in [iv].

The syntactic status of extent NPs is somewhat problematic. In general, they differ quite sharply from objects. Usually we can add the preposition *by* or *for*: *The price went up (by) £2*; *The path continues (for) another three miles.* This is not possible, however, in the second clause of [10iv] (cf. **Bill rode for them on a donkey*). They are questioned by *how far/much* rather than *what*: *How far / *What does the path continue?*; *How much / *What has the Dow Jones fallen this week?* Clauses where an extent NP follows an object, as in [10ii], are very different from ditransitive clauses: we shall certainly not want to analyse *the net* here as an indirect object, and *three metres* as direct object. Making such phrases subject of a passive clause usually results in ungrammaticality: **£2 was gone up by the price*; **Another three miles was/were continued by the path.* Nevertheless, there are some cases where such passivisation is possible, primarily when the NP is definite: *The last few miles will have to be walked*; *It is now nearly fifty years since the/a mile was first run in under four minutes.* We argued in Ch. 4, §4.1, that passivisation does not provide a necessary and sufficient condition for object status, but it may nevertheless be best, in the present case, to admit extent NPs as object only in those constructions where they can be made subject of a passive.

5.4 Scalar location

To conclude this section we should consider briefly the locational counterpart of scalar change. Simple location on a scale is commonly expressed by *be* with an NP as predicative complement, but we also find *at* PPs with *be* or a comparable verb such as *stand*. Compare the following, for example, with [6] above:

[11] i *The price / A jar of coffee is $12.*
ii *The Dow Jones industrial average currently stands at 9437.*
iii *The temperature is 10°.*
iv *Her philosophy mark was 70%.*

With some scales, however, there is a special verb taking a measure complement. Compare:

	a.	b.
[12] i	a. *A jar of coffee <u>is</u> $12.*	b. *A jar of coffee <u>costs</u> $12.*
ii	a. *This case <u>is</u> over 20 kilos.*	b. *This case <u>weighs</u> over 20 kilos.*
iii	a. *My other table <u>is</u> six foot by four.*	b. *My other table <u>measures</u> six foot by four.*

These verbs differ syntactically in various ways. *Measure* allows an AdjP as complement: *The table measures just over three foot wide. Cost* permits an object expressing the person, etc., that has to pay the cost: *That jar of coffee cost me $12.* We have questions with *what* or *how much*: *What / How much does it cost?* (except that *how long*, etc., would be more likely than *how much* with *measure*).

6 Temporal location

6.1 Adjuncts and complements

We turn now to the domain of time, where we find many similarities with the domain of space. There are also important differences, the most important of which is that time is indicated not only by phrasal elements, but also by the verbal category of tense.

Temporal location is the analogue of spatial location, and like their spatial counterparts elements of temporal location are predominantly adjuncts, but with a few verbs they have the status of complements, with either subject or object orientation:

[1]	i	*I read your thesis <u>last week</u>.*	[adjunct]
	ii	*The staff meeting is <u>tomorrow</u>.*	[complement: subject orientation]
	iii	*I've arranged a meeting <u>for Tuesday at ten</u>.*	[complement: object orientation]

Adjuncts normally locate in time the situation expressed by the verb together with its complements, e.g. the situation of my reading your thesis in [i]. Complements give the temporal location of the theme element, as expressed by the subject in [ii] and the object in [iii]. Such themes are normally events: we can have *The staff meeting is tomorrow* or *The accident occurred around lunch-time*, but not *#Jill is tomorrow* or *#My car occurred around lunch-time.*[10] The exception is with the verb *live*, as in *Voltaire lived in the eighteenth century*. (One might prefer to say that this gives the temporal location of Voltaire's life rather than Voltaire himself, but *live* is still exceptional in taking a human theme in combination with a temporal complement.)

Only a small number of verbs (or verbal idioms) take complements of temporal location; clear examples include:

[2]	i	*be*	*happen*	*live*	*occur*	*take place*	[S orientation]
	ii	*arrange*	*fix*	*keep*	*put*	*schedule*	[O orientation]

An adjunct of temporal location can co-occur with a complement:

[3]	i	*Christmas falls <u>on a Tuesday</u> <u>this year</u>.*
	ii	*He <u>later</u> scheduled yet another meeting <u>for the following Tuesday</u>.*

Change of temporal location

While many verbs express change of spatial location, very few express change of temporal location:

[4]	i	*The meeting has (been) moved <u>from Tuesday morning to Thursday afternoon</u>.*
	ii	*We have postponed our holiday <u>until the end of September</u>.*
	iii	*They adjourned the meeting <u>until next week</u>.*

Cases of this kind are restricted to situations involving the scheduling of events. While spatial expressions of the kind *from X to Y* are readily used to indicate either change of location or extent, temporal expressions of this kind are almost always used for extent,

[10] Examples like *Jill is tomorrow* might in fact occur in casual speech as a shorthand way of giving the temporal location of some event involving Jill; for example, at a conference it might be used to convey "Jill's paper is (scheduled for) tomorrow".

i.e. for duration (see §7). Nothing further need be said about the change of temporal location construction [4], and hence this section is called simply 'temporal location'.

6.2 Semantic types

Situations (or themes) are located in time in three different ways.

(a) Deictically – in relation to the time of utterance

[5] i *I saw her yesterday.*
ii *It'll be all over a year from now.*

Yesterday refers to the day preceding the one when I utter [i], and *a year from now* identifies a period a year later than the time I utter [ii] (see Ch. 17, §10, for a fuller account of temporal deixis). The range of temporal deictic expressions is illustrated in:

[6]	*now*	*yesterday*	*today*	*tomorrow*	*this morning*
	tonight	*last night*	*tomorrow night*	*last week*	*next week*
	two days ago	*in two weeks*	*in a week's time*	*these days*	*in earlier times*

The temporal counterparts of spatial *here* and *there* are *now* and *then*, but while *there* is readily used both deictically and anaphorically, *then* is almost always anaphoric. Such expressions as *in two weeks, in a week's time, in earlier times* can be used anaphorically as well as deictically. The deictic use is seen in *She's arriving in two weeks* ("in two weeks from now"), the non-deictic in *She was due to arrive in two weeks* ("in two weeks from some contextually given point of orientation"). This kind of expression can also have a durational rather than locational meaning: *She wrote the report in two weeks.*

(b) In relation to calendar and clock times and comparable points of orientation

[7] i a. *He lived in the third century BC.*
b. *The Company was founded on 1 January 1978.*
ii a. *Sarah is arriving at three o'clock / on 3 May / on Monday.*
b. *We finished the job at noon / at the end of May / at the week-end.*

The examples in [i] provide an absolute, or context-independent, specification of temporal location. The year of the birth of Christ was adopted by convention precisely as a point of orientation that would permit such context-independent time specification. The expressions in [ii] are context-dependent: the times concerned, 3 o'clock, 3 May, Monday, etc., recur cyclically and to understand their reference we need to know which cycle is intended. In the default case this is determined deictically, by means of the tense and the time of utterance in combination. In [iia] the tense is present and the adjunct is interpreted as referring to the next cyclic occurrence of the point or period in question following the time of utterance. In [iib] the tense is past, and the reference is to the last cyclic occurrence preceding the time of utterance.

Expressions like those in [7ii] thus have a default use in which they are interpreted deictically. But they are also commonly used non-deictically, especially in combination with preterite tense. Here the relevant cycle is determined by other features of the context. Elementary examples are:

[8] i *Mary arrived yesterday at three o'clock.*
ii *We all met in Paris last Monday. I got there at 3 o'clock, the others at four.*

In [i] there are two time expressions in the one clause – *yesterday* is deictic, but *at three o'clock* is not: its reference is determined relative to yesterday, not to the day of speaking.

In [ii] *last Monday* in the first sentence is deictic, the other adjuncts non-deictic: again we interpret them as referring to Monday's cycle, not today's.

Other expressions referring to cyclic or otherwise recurrent times or events work in the same way: festivals (*at Christmas/Easter, for Ramadan*), seasons (*in the spring*), meals (*after lunch*), regular sporting events (*during the Olympic Games*), political events (*before the Federal election*), and so on. The default interpretations of *I'll see you at the Olympics* and *I met her at the Olympics* have reference to the next and last Olympic Games relative to the time of utterance. But again the default deictic interpretation can easily be overridden: *I came back to England in 1948 and got a job in London shortly before the Olympic Games.* The periods or events may be familiar only locally: *on sports day* for a school, perhaps, *during Orientation Week* for a university.

(c) In relation to other times or situations

[9] i *The company collapsed <u>during the Second World War</u>.*
ii *She became a recluse <u>after the death of her husband</u>.*
iii *He retired to his study <u>when the guests arrived</u>.*
iv *They arrived <u>earlier than we had expected</u>.*
v *She made a complaint about his behaviour and <u>soon afterwards</u> she was sacked.*
vi *By a strange coincidence Kim and I got engaged <u>on the same day</u>.*

In [i] the company's collapse is related temporally to the Second World War, and so on. Example [iv] illustrates the quite common case when the time of an event is related to a time at which it might have taken place. In [v] *soon afterwards* is interpreted anaphorically: the first clause, the antecedent, describes an event and the following adjunct locates the time of the sacking by reference to that event, "soon after she made her complaint".[11] Example [vi] can also have an anaphoric interpretation ("the same day as the event described in the previous sentence"), but in the more salient interpretation *on the same day* relates the times of Kim's getting engaged and my getting engaged to each other.

6.3 The form of temporal location expressions

PPs

The most common form is that of a PP; further distinctions can be made according to the complementation of the PP. In the following survey we first list head prepositions, and then give examples containing full PPs.

(a) With NP complement

[10]	*after*	*ago*	*at*	*before*	*between*	*by*
	during	*in*	*into*	*on*	*since*	*toward(s)*

[11] i *I spoke to her <u>before the meeting</u> / <u>during the interval</u>.*
ii *They must have escaped <u>between 9 a.m. and noon</u>.*
iii *We're leaving <u>in three weeks</u> / <u>in three weeks' time</u>.*
iv *The accident happened <u>three weeks into the vacation</u>.*

[11] The antecedent for an anaphoric expression can also be a temporal location dependent of the kinds mentioned in (a) and (b). In *I met Jill yesterday; she had spent the previous day in court,* deictic *yesterday* provides the antecedent for anaphoric *the previous day* ("the day before yesterday"). And similarly in *They married in 1980 and the following year they moved to Rome* the context-independent *in 1980* is the antecedent for anaphoric *the following year* ("the year following 1980"). See Ch. 17, §10, for a detailed discussion of temporal anaphora.

Into requires a measure phrase modifier, such as *three weeks* in [iv]. *After* and *before* take a semantically wider range of complements than the others, including NPs denoting human beings: *Sarah arrived before me.* This is equivalent to *Sarah arrived before I did,* with a clause as complement. *The Examiners' Meeting finished before the Selection Committee Meeting* is ambiguous between this kind of clausal interpretation ("before the Selection Committee Meeting finished") and one like [11i] (where one meeting finished before the other began). *Ago* follows its complement (*a year ago*): see Ch. 7, §4.2.

(b) With declarative content clause complement

[12] *after* *as* *as soon as* *before* *once* *since*

[13] i *Jill has sold over 200 policies since she joined the company.*
ii *I want to leave before it gets dark.*
iii *We'll invite you over once we are settled in.*
iv *She phoned just as I was leaving.*

Since, irrespective of the type of complement, is largely restricted in BrE to occurrence with the perfect, as in [13i]; it can, however, be used with simple tenses in the construction *It is now nearly a year since he died.* AmE allows preterites rather more widely: %*Since you went home we redecorated our bedroom.*

The content of the subordinate clause is usually presupposed, taken for granted: [i] presupposes that she joined the company, [ii] that it will get dark, and so on; see Ch. 11, §7.4. *Before* is sometimes used, especially in directives, to indicate purpose and avoidance: *Come away from there before you get hurt* conveys that you are in danger of getting hurt and directs you to come away so as to avoid that happening. This of course is one case where the presupposition relation does not hold: it doesn't presuppose that you will get hurt, for you won't if you come away. When the subordinate clause refers to future time, as in [ii–iii], we usually have a non-modal present tense (compare #*I want to leave before it will get dark*).

The construction illustrated in [13] has no analogue in the spatial domain. Spatial prepositions do not take content clause complements – compare, for example, **He found it near she was sitting* (we need a fused relative: *near where she was sitting*). The event described in a clause can implicitly define a time, but it cannot define a place.

(c) With non-finite or verbless complement

[14] *after* *before* *between* *on* *once* *since*

These take gerund-participials, and in addition *once* licenses past-participial or verbless clauses:

[15] i *I must have lost it between getting on the train and going to the buffet-car.*
ii *On hearing them return, he hid under the bed.*
iii *Once in bed they usually fall asleep pretty soon.*

(d) With no complement

[16] *after* *afterward(s)* *before* *beforehand* *now*
since *then* *throughout* *when*

[17] a. *I had seen her several times since.* b. *When are they coming?*

Afterward is generally restricted to AmE; *afterwards* is also found in AmE as an alternant and is the only form used elsewhere. *After,* as an alternant of *afterwards,* occurs with premodifiers such as *shortly* (*Kim came at 6 and Pat arrived shortly after*); on its own it is somewhat non-standard ([!]*I never saw her after*).

(e) PPs introduced by *when, whenever, while*

[18] a. *His heart sank when he heard the news.* b. *You can leave whenever you like.*

The internal structure of the underlined PPs is not entirely clear. For the most part they can be regarded as fused relatives (comparable to the fused relative NP in *What he had bought was worthless*), but in some respects the initial words are like prepositions governing content clauses. We discuss this issue in Ch. 12, §6.4; here we will simply refer to them as *when* PPs, etc.

When PPs are among the most common and central temporal location expressions. *Whenever*, on the other hand, is quite restricted in this function: it mostly occurs in phrases expressing frequency. In addition to the finite constructions shown in [18] we find the following:

[19]	i	*While waiting for the bus I read the paper.*	[gerund-participial]
	ii	*When asked to step forward, he blushed.*	[past-participial]
	iii	*I can't read when/while on duty.*	[verbless]

NPs

The following nouns are illustrative of those that head temporal location NPs:

[20]	i	*yesterday*	*today*	*tomorrow*	*tonight*	*Sunday*	*Monday*
	ii	*morning*	*afternoon*	*evening*	*day*	*night*	*week*
		month	*year*	*instant*	*moment*	*second*	*minute*

Those in [i] can stand alone without dependents: *I saw her yesterday.* The use of the names of days of the week in this way (*They arrive Sunday*) is commoner in AmE than in BrE. The nouns in [ii] require dependents, such as the demonstratives *this* and *that*. *Next* and *last* occur widely, but with restrictions. *Last* is always deictic and doesn't occur with *morning* and *afternoon* (instead we have *yesterday morning/afternoon*). *Next week* is deictic, while *next day* is non-deictic (instead of the deictic version we have *tomorrow*) and [?]*next night* is hardly possible at all (cf. again deictic *tomorrow night*). *The* occurs only in combination with another dependent: *the following year, the night we first met, the day before yesterday*,[12] but not **She resigned the day.* Most temporal location NPs are definite, but indefinites are possible, e.g. with *some, one*, or *another* as determiner: *Some days she felt quite elated*; *One day I'll get my revenge*; *We can do that another day.*

Some NP structures are specialised to time location: *tomorrow week* "(in) a week from tomorrow", *three weeks next Tuesday* "(in) three weeks from next Tuesday", *a week on Monday* "(in) a week from next Monday", and so on.

AdvPs

Heads of temporal location AdvPs include the following:

[21]	*currently*	*earlier*	*early*	*formerly*	*immediately*	*late*
	lately	*later*	*nowadays*	*recently*	*soon*	*subsequently*

We list *earlier* and *later* separately from *early* and *late* because, in addition to their ordinary comparative uses (*Kim arrived earlier/later than Pat*), they have lexicalised uses meaning "before" and "afterwards" (*She had resigned three days earlier/later*).

[12] Note the structural contrast between this latter NP (with *day* as head) and the PP *two days before yesterday* (with *before* as head).

Gerund-participial and past-participial clauses

We observed in §1 that with clauses of this form in adjunct function the nature of the relation of the subordinate clause to the matrix is not explicitly marked but has to be pragmatically inferred. In examples like the following, it is plausible to infer a temporal relation:

[22] i *Driving along the highway, we passed a long line of lorries.* ["as we drove . . . "]
ii *This done, he walked off without another word.* ["when this was done"]

6.4 **Further issues**

Referential vs non-referential

Most temporal location expressions are referential, but some are not:

[23] i *I'd rather have had the party last Sunday.* [referential]
ii *I'd rather have had the party on a Sunday.* [non-referential]

In [i] *last Sunday* is deictic and refers to one particular Sunday, the last one before today, the day of speaking. In [ii], by contrast, I am not referring to a certain Sunday – other things being equal, any Sunday would do or would have done.

In these examples, the distinction is marked in the form of the adjunct itself. Many expressions are like *last Sunday* in that they always refer to a particular time (e.g. *yesterday, tomorrow, a week ago, during the Second World War*, etc.). Some, however, can be interpreted in either way:

[24] i *I'm going to Paris in (the) spring if I can finish this report in time.* [referential]
ii *Have you ever been to Paris in (the) spring?* [non-referential]
iii *I'd like to go to Paris in (the) spring.* [ambiguous]

In [i] I'm referring to the spring following the time of utterance, and in [ii] to springtime in general, while [iii] allows both interpretations.

The distinction between referential and non-referential is relevant to constraints on the use of the present perfect. This compound tense is incompatible with referential temporal location in the past (see Ch. 3, §5.3): **I haven't been to a party last Sunday.* The non-referential *I haven't been to a party on a Sunday*, however, is admissible.

Temporal location and causation

Temporal location adjuncts are often accompanied by an implicature of causation:

[25] i *When John attacked Bill the police arrested him.*
ii *On hearing this news, he phoned his solicitor.*

The natural interpretation is that the police arrested John because he attacked Bill, and that he phoned his solicitor as a result of hearing the news.

Intervals of time vs points of time

An expression of temporal location can denote either an interval or a point of time:

[26] i *Mary arrived yesterday.* [interval]
ii *Mary arrived at four o'clock.* [point]

An interval (period, stretch) of time has duration, while a point of time is not conceived of as having duration. *Yesterday* in [i] denotes a 24-hour interval of time, and Mary's arrival took place some time during that interval. *At four o'clock* in [ii], by contrast, gives the point of time at which Mary arrived, not an interval during which she did.

Most temporal location expressions denote intervals: *on Monday, while I was in*

America, *after dinner*, *before John arrived.* Temporal location expressions denoting points of time, moments, commonly have the form of PPs with *at* as head: *at midnight*, *at that very moment. At* tends not to occur with nouns denoting periods such as *day*, *week*, etc.: we have *on that day*, not *#at that day.* It is not, however, restricted to point expressions: *at lunch-time*, *at the end of her life. At that time* is anaphoric, and could be interpreted in either way, depending on the antecedent. Nor is *on* restricted to intervals: *on the stroke of midnight*, *on the hour.*

Temporal location adjuncts and aspectuality

The temporal relation between the adjunct and the situation denoted by the rest of the clause depends on: (a) the nature of the adjunct, whether it denotes an interval or a point of time; and (b) the aspectuality of the situation. Compare:

[27]		ADJUNCT	SITUATION
i	*I lived in New York last year.*	interval	imperfective
ii	*I arrived on Monday.*	interval	perfective
iii	*I was still awake at midnight.*	point	imperfective
iv	*I arrived at midnight.*	point	perfective

Example [i] is readily understood as indicating that my living in New York filled the whole of last year, and is compatible with my living there earlier and/or later.[13] In [ii] my arrival occupies only a small part of Monday: the time occupied by the situation is included in that denoted by the adjunct. In [iii] we have the opposite effect: the time of the adjunct is included in that of the situation. Finally, in [iv] the times of the adjunct and of the situation are simultaneous.

The same kind of interaction applies when the adjunct has the form of a *when* PP:

[28]			
i	*When I was at school I was friends with Kim.*	interval	imperfective
ii	*When we were on holiday Kim came to see us.*	interval	perfective
iii	*When Kim arrived, we were having lunch.*	point	imperfective
iv	*When the clock struck twelve, the bomb exploded.*	point	perfective

The aspectuality labels apply to the matrix clause, but the subordinate clause is imperfective in [i–ii], perfective in [iii–iv]: hence the interpretation of the adjunct as denoting an interval in [i–ii] and a point in [iii–iv]. Again, then, in [i] we interpret the subordinate and matrix situations as largely coinciding. In [ii] the time of the matrix situation (Kim's coming to see us) is included in the time of the subordinate situation (our being on holiday). Conversely, in [iii] the time of the subordinate situation (Kim's arriving) is included in that of the matrix situation (our having lunch). Finally, [iv] is interpreted with the two situations simultaneous.

The simultaneity in the case where both clauses are perfective does not have to be interpreted too strictly, however. Consider such examples as the following:

[29] i *When he caught Atherton he broke the record for the highest number of catches in test cricket.*
ii *When I read her thesis I realised why you think so highly of her.*
iii *When the principal came in, everybody stood up.*
iv *#When she wrote her thesis she applied for a job at Harvard.*

[13] Interval adjuncts may, however, be contextually restricted. In *Were you at the University on Monday?*, the question may relate to only part of Monday – for example, the hours when you are usually there.

In [i] matrix and subordinate situations are different facets of a single instantaneous event: he broke the record in catching Atherton. Here then we necessarily have strict simultaneity. In [ii] my reading her thesis will have taken a significant amount of time, but we can conceptualise my coming to the realisation that she merits your high regard as occupying the same time. But in [iii] the most likely scenario is that the standing up was in response to the principal's arrival. This belongs with the examples in [25]: everybody stood up because the principal came in. In this case the events can't be strictly simultaneous: the standing up must be fractionally later. It does not follow, however, that *when* means "immediately after": it expresses simultaneity, but a certain amount of leeway is allowed as to what constitutes simultaneity. This is why [iv] is anomalous even if she applied for the job immediately after writing the thesis. The two situations cannot be conceptualised as simultaneous, and hence we need either to replace *when* by *after*, or else to use a preterite perfect: *When she had finished her thesis she applied for a job at Harvard.*

Deictic location expressions and deictic tense

We have seen that temporal location is often achieved by means of deictic expressions. At the same time, primary tense is usually interpreted deictically (Ch. 3, §4.1). There is then normally a requirement that a deictic tense not conflict with a deictic adjunct: **Her uncle died tomorrow.* Some constructions that merit brief comment in the light of this constraint are illustrated in:

[30] i *John was coming tomorrow but he has now postponed his visit.*
ii *They fixed the interview for tomorrow.*
iii *They wanted the flat tomorrow.*
iv *I thought the match started tomorrow.*
v *. . . it was getting late; they must waste no more time; Cassandra arrived tonight for dinner . . .*

The first clause of [i] contains a futurate progressive: at some time in the past there was a plan for John to come tomorrow (but that plan has subsequently been changed). There is no semantic conflict here because the preterite relates to the past time at which the schedule obtained and *tomorrow* relates to the time of coming. Example [ii] belongs to the construction discussed in §6.1 above (see [1iii]): the verb tense gives the time of the fixing, but *tomorrow* is a complement with object orientation, giving the temporal location of the theme, the interview. Example [30iii] looks as though it might likewise belong to this construction, but in fact it does not. There is no sense in which it locates the flat in time: *#The flat is tomorrow* (unlike *The interview is tomorrow*) is incoherent. We have to recognise here a clash between syntactic form and meaning: *want* here means "want to have", and while there is only one clause, the preterite relates to the wanting and *tomorrow* to the implicit having. In [iv] the preterite in *started* is not deictic: the tense here is backshifted, matching the ordinary deictic tense of *thought.* In [v] we have a shift of the deictic centre in free indirect style: see Ch. 17, §10.2

Negation

In general, subordinate clauses contained within temporal location expressions are positive. Compare, for example:

[31] i *I left home before my parents divorced*
ii *#I left home before my parents didn't divorce.*

My parents getting divorced defines a time relative to which I can locate my leaving home, but their not getting divorced does not, hence the anomaly of [ii]. Negatives are not wholly inadmissible, however, and [ii] certainly does not violate any rule of grammar. Consider:

[32] i *I'll be pleased when I no longer have to get up at this ungodly hour.*
ii *When/After Liz didn't come home, we alerted the police.*

In [i] the negative subordinate clause represents a change of state, and such a change can readily define a time. Example [ii] suggests that Liz had been expected to come home within some time interval; there is therefore a time at which she failed to come home – or a time at which her absence was conceptualised as a failure to come home. This type of example is another case where temporal location has a causal implicature: we alerted the police because she didn't come home.

7 Temporal extent: duration

7.1 Similarities and differences between the temporal and spatial domains

Parallels

When we turn to extent in time, duration, we again find striking similarities in conceptualisation and expression between the temporal and spatial domains. In particular, such concepts as starting-point and endpoint, terminal-point extent and overall extent, are applicable to duration as well as to spatial extent. Compare, for example:

[1]	SPATIAL EXTENT	TEMPORAL EXTENT
i	a. *The path goes <u>from the village</u> <u>past the castle</u> <u>to the lake</u>.*	b. *The session ran <u>from 10 a.m.</u> <u>through lunch</u> <u>to 5 p.m.</u>*
ii	a. *The path runs <u>from under the bridge</u> <u>to just beyond the castle</u>.*	b. *The meeting lasted <u>from just after lunch</u> <u>to shortly before dinner</u>.*
iii	a. *The path goes (<u>for</u>) <u>another mile</u>.*	b. *We are staying (<u>for</u>) <u>another week</u>.*

In [i–ii] we have a starting-point marked by *from* and an endpoint marked by *to*, and in [i] there is also an intermediate point. The complement of *from* and *to* is in [i] an NP, in [ii] a PP of the type that could be used for spatial or temporal location. In both domains, locational *at* is dropped in starting-point and endpoint locations: *from the village*, *from 10 a.m.*, not **from at the village*, **from at 10 a.m.* In [i–ii] the extent is specified by reference to terminal points, while in [iii] it is specified by an overall measure, expressed in both domains by an NP or a PP headed by *for*. Notice, moreover, that some verbs whose primary meaning involves spatial movement can be used for duration – see *run* in [ib] or *go* itself, as in *The teaching semester goes from the end of February to the beginning of June.*

Differences between the domains

The syntax and semantics of duration is, however, far from identical to that of spatial extent, and for this reason we are not generalising the categories of source, goal, and path to duration, but will use the more general categories of starting-point, endpoint, and intermediate point.

Starting-point and endpoint prepositions

One of the most obvious differences concerns the prepositions. *Since* is commonly used (in clauses in the perfect) to mark the durational starting-point, while *until/till* is the most usual preposition for the endpoint, with *to* largely restricted to constructions containing a *from* phrase as well: compare *She was in hospital from Monday until/to Thursday* and *She was in hospital until/*to Thursday.*[14]

Complements and adjuncts

A second important difference is that duration expressions most often function as adjuncts rather than complements. The contrasting adjuncts and complements in the following examples match those given for temporal location in [1] of §6:

[2] i *I was in Hong Kong all week.* [adjunct]
ii *The staff meeting lasted (for) five hours.* [complement: S orientation]
iii *I've scheduled the course from 1 May to 15 June.* [complement: O orientation]

The adjunct gives the duration of the situation as a whole, while the complements give the duration of the theme, expressed by the subject in [ii] and the object in [iii]. As with temporal location, such themes are normally events, but some verbs allow physical object themes: *He lived from 1848 to 1912*; *That cheese won't last long.*

Intermediate point

Time is envisaged as a straight line, so that for duration we cannot have alternative routes between the terminal points, as we can in the domain of space. When an intermediate point is expressed, therefore, it does not specify the path taken but indicates continuity, the absence of intermission. This is seen in the *through lunch* adjunct in [1ib]: the session continued right through from 10 a.m. to 5 p.m. without any break for lunch.

7.2 The contrast between bounding and non-bounding duration elements

An important distinction is to be drawn between **bounding** and **non-bounding** duration elements:

[3]	BOUNDING	NON-BOUNDING
i	a. *I studied law for six years.*	b. *I reached the summit in two hours.*
ii	a. *I lived in College all year.*	b. *I wrote the report in two days.*

The situations in [ia/iia], considered in abstraction from the duration adjunct, are imperfective: studying law is an activity, and living in College is a state. Adding the adjunct has the effect of bounding the situation, making it perfective. Precisely because the temporal extent is specified, the situation is presented in its totality. In [ib/iib], by contrast, the situations considered in abstraction from the adjunct are perfective: reaching the summit is an achievement, and writing the report is an accomplishment. Since the situations are already bounded, therefore, adding a duration adjunct cannot have the bounding effect that it has in the [a] cases.

There are in many cases approximate paraphrases in which duration is expressed by an NP in object function:

[4]		
i	a. *I spent six years studying law.*	b. *It took me an hour to reach the summit.*
ii	a. *#I spent all year living in College.*	b. *It took me two days to write the report.*

[14] It is worth noting, however, that the *until* is not incompatible with complements expressing spatial location, as in *I had a good flight: I was able to sleep from Berlin until Bahrein.* This is shorthand for *I was able to sleep from when we left Berlin until we arrived in Bahrein*; it is analogous to the use of spatial location to indicate temporal location illustrated in [10] of §4.

The *spend* construction implies activity by an agent, and hence doesn't provide a paraphrase for the *living in College* example. *Spend* can also be used with expressions like *write the report*, but in that case the expression does not count as bounded. Example [3iib] entails that I completed the work, but *I spent two days writing the report* does not (though there will often be an implicature that I did). We could say, for example, *I spent the next two days writing the report but had to break off before I had finished because my mother was taken ill.* For variants of the *take* construction, see Ch. 14, §6.3.[15]

Some combinations of verb + complements are compatible with either type of duration adjunct:

[5]	BOUNDING	NON-BOUNDING
i	a. *The fruit ripened for four weeks.*	b. *The fruit ripened in four weeks.*
ii	a. *He cleaned the house for two hours.*	b. *He cleaned the house in two hours.*

This is because the ripening of the fruit and his cleaning the house can be viewed either perfectively or imperfectively. In the perfective case the fruit got to the stage of being ripe, he completed the job of cleaning the house. Here a non-bounding adjunct is allowed, giving the time taken to reach these final states: "It took the fruit four weeks to ripen"; "It took him two hours to clean the house". In the imperfective the inherent endpoint is not necessarily reached: the process could have continued beyond the period given in the duration adjunct.

7.3 Bounding duration elements

Overall vs terminal-point extent

Like spatial and scalar change extent, duration may be specified overall or by means of endpoints:

[6]	OVERALL SPECIFICATION	TERMINAL POINT SPECIFICATION
i	a. *He did housework all morning.*	b. *He did housework from 9 until 12.*
ii	a. *I have been here (for) a week.*	b. *I have been here since Monday.*
iii	a. *Mary wrote letters for half an hour.*	b. *Mary read in bed until she fell asleep.*

In [ib] both terminal points are specified. In [iib] *since Monday* specifies the starting-point; no endpoint can be expressed and the present perfect indicates that the situation continues to obtain at the time of utterance. And in [iib] *until she fell asleep* specifies the endpoint, with the starting-point being left implicit (a plausible inference is that she read from the time she went to bed).

Questioning

The usual way of questioning bounding duration is with *how long*: *How long did she live in College?*; *How long did she study medicine?* We also find *for how long*, but it is much less usual. It is in principle possible to question the complement in a terminal-point expression: *From when will the price be increasing?*; *Until when can I keep it?* But such forms are not common; in many cases it would be more natural to use questions with *start* and *stop*: *When did he start/stop doing housework? Since when* is mainly confined to indirect speech acts, as in *Since when have you been in charge here?* This conveys that you are behaving as though you were in charge when in fact you are not.

[15] There is a construction comparable to [4i] involving a special use of the verb *be*: *She was two weeks finishing the report.*

Restrictions on dependents of the verb

With clauses containing process verbs, the status as perfective or imperfective is usually determined by dependents of the verb. In [6iii], for example, Mary's writing letters is imperfective because the number of letters isn't specified. If we add a determiner expressing or implying a specified quantity, the result is ill-formed: **Mary wrote a letter / the letters for an hour.* Compare, similarly:

[7] i *Mary drove along country lanes for half an hour.*
ii **Mary drove ten miles along country lanes for half an hour.*
iii **Mary drove along country lanes to the village for half an hour.*

Mary's driving along country lanes is an imperfective situation, but specifying the spatial extent (distance) in [ii] or the goal in [iii] makes it perfective and hence incompatible with the bounding duration adjunct.

Duration of resultant state

Achievements are punctual, i.e. have no duration; except in special circumstances, therefore, they are incompatible with bounding duration adjuncts:

[8] a. **She noticed my error all morning.* b. **I spotted a hawk for five minutes.*

One case in which such adjuncts are permitted with punctual verbs is when the adjunct can be understood as measuring the state resulting from the achievement, if this state can be taken as planned or intended by the agent of the achievement:

[9] a. *I borrowed the book for a week.* b. *I sent him out for half an hour.*

The result of borrowing the book was that I had it, and this state lasted for a week.[16] The result of sending him out was that he was out (of the room, let us assume), and again the adjunct gives the duration of this state. The examples in [8] do not lend themselves to this kind of interpretation, since noticing and spotting are not subject to control.

Bounding duration adjuncts with multiple situations

So far we have only considered singulary situations; multiple situations involve what we have called serial states (Ch. 3, §3.2.4), and like singulary states they are imperfective and therefore allow bounding adjuncts. Note then that while a single occurrence of my cycling to school is an accomplishment, incompatible with a bounding adjunct, the multiple situation of my repeatedly cycling to school permits an adjunct of this kind:

[10] i **I cycled to school this morning for half an hour.*
ii *I cycled to school for the next three years.*

The adjunct in [ii] gives the duration of the state of affairs in which I went to school by bicycle.

Punctual verbs can likewise occur with bounding duration adjuncts if the clause expresses a multiple situation:

[11] i *I spotted a hawk every morning for a month.*
ii *I woke up with a headache all last week.*

Here we have repeated, multiple, hawk-spotting and waking up, not singulary situations. Spotting a hawk every morning and waking up of a morning are imperfective, and hence

[16] There is also an interpretation where it is a matter of permission or an arrangement to have the book for a week (a library book, say): here, it could be that I returned it early, or that the week has not yet elapsed.

permit bounding by a duration adjunct. In [i] the multiple nature of the situation is indicated by the frequency adjunct *every morning*; without it, it would be very difficult to get a multiple situation interpretation, and hence ?*I spotted a hawk for a week* will generally be considered anomalous, like [8b]. In [11ii] the duration adjunct itself is sufficient to supply the multiple situation interpretation: a single waking up with a headache can't last all week.

Two sources for bounding duration adjuncts

There are thus two factors that can make a bounding adjunct admissible: it can serve to bound a singulary situation that would otherwise be imperfective, and it can bound a multiple situation. It is therefore possible for a clause to contain two bounding duration adjuncts, one of each kind:

[12] *She broadcast <u>for half an hour</u> every Sunday <u>for forty years</u>.*

For half an hour gives the duration of the individual broadcasts, while *for forty years* gives the duration of the multiple situation.

Bounding duration elements and scope in negative clauses

In negative clauses a bounding duration element may fall within the scope of the negative or may itself have scope over the negation. Compare:

[13] i a. *The strike lasted <u>two days</u>.*
b. *The strike didn't last <u>two days</u>.* [negative has scope over adjunct]
ii a. **I noticed my error <u>until later</u>.*
b. *I didn't notice my error <u>until later</u>.* [adjunct has scope over negative]

In [i] *two days* is part of the complementation of *last*, and [ib] is straightforwardly the negation of [ia]: "It is not the case that the strike lasted two days". Here, then, the duration dependent is within the scope of the negative: it is part of what is negated. Example [iia] is anomalous for reasons given above: my noticing my error is punctual and doesn't permit an interpretation where the duration adjunct applies to a resultant state. By contrast, [iib] is perfectly well-formed, and cannot therefore be the direct negation of [iia]: it does not have the anomalous meaning "It is not the case that I noticed my error until later". Rather, *until later* gives the duration of my not noticing my error. Unlike its positive counterpart, the negative *I didn't notice my error* can be construed as imperfective, and hence permits a bounding duration adjunct, saying how long this negative state of affairs lasted.

Ambiguities can then arise according to whether it is the duration adjunct or the negative that has the wider scope:

[14] i a. *The family lived in the house <u>for a year</u> / <u>until 1990</u>.*
b. *The family didn't live in the house <u>for a year</u> / <u>until 1990</u>.* [ambiguous]
ii a. *He went to New York <u>for two weeks</u>.*
b. *He didn't go to New York <u>for two weeks</u>.* [ambiguous]

If we interpret [ib] with the negative having the wider scope, it says that [ia] is not true: it might be, for example, that they stayed only six months, or moved out before 1990. If the adjunct has wider scope it means that the situation of their not living in the house lasted for a year or until 1990; here there is an implicature that they started living in the house at the end of the year, or in 1990. Example [iia] has a resultant state interpretation, and the wide scope negative interpretation of [iib] denies that he went to New York for a stay of two weeks (perhaps he went for only one). When the adjunct has scope over the negation it applies to the state of his not going: it may be, for example, that he had to postpone his departure, and went only at the end of the two weeks.

The scope of the adjunct can interact in this way with a negative that is implied rather than overtly expressed:

[15] i *I doubt whether the family have lived in the house all year.*
ii *I don't think the family have lived in the house all year.*

There is no negative marker in [i], but it means the same as [ii], and displays the same scope ambiguity.

Realisation of overall extent duration elements

(a) PPs

PPs in this function usually consist of *for* plus an NP denoting an interval of time: *for three weeks, for a long time, for the rest of his life, for the duration of the festival. For* can also take certain adverbs as complement: *for ever, for long. In* can occur in place of *for* in negative perfect clauses, especially in AmE: *I haven't been to Scotland in ten years.* Other prepositions found here are *over, through,* and *throughout*: *She worked on her thesis over/through/throughout the Christmas break.*

(b) NPs

NPs have as head a noun denoting a time interval, such as *hour, day, week,* etc.:

[16] i	*two days*	*a week*	*three months*	*the whole year*
ii	*all day*	*all year round*	*this week*	*next month*

Expressions like those in [i] can also occur as complement to *for*, while those in [ii], certainly the ones with initial *all*, cannot. Moreover, NPs like the first three of [i] cannot be too far separated from the verb. Compare:

[17] i	a. *He stayed (here) a month.*	b. *He stayed (here) for a month.*
ii	a. **I studied the report two days.*	b. *I studied the report for two days.*
iii	a. *We argued about it all weekend.*	b. **We argued about it for all weekend.*

Duration NPs can be found in constructions like *What was the total number of hours slept?*; *The long hours worked by the miners had clearly exacerbated the problem* (or abbreviated versions in a statistical table, for example: *Number of hours slept,* etc.). *Slept* and *worked* here are past-participial passive clauses, with a duration phrase as understood subject. The comparable main clause construction, however, is not possible: **Over ten hours was slept by one of the patients.*

(c) AdvPs

Duration is also expressed by a number of adverbs, most of them with the ·*ly* suffix:

[18]	*always*	*briefly*	*indefinitely*	*long*	*momentarily*
	permanently	*provisionally*	*temporarily*		

[19] i *I have always known that things would turn out OK in the end.*
ii *She has been working here longer than the others.*

Always is more often used for frequency, but in examples like [i] it indicates how long, not how often. In its plain form *long* is generally a non-affirmative item: *They didn't stay long*, but not **They stayed long.*

Realisation of terminal-point duration elements

As noted in §7.1, the prepositions *from* and *to* used for the starting-point and endpoint in spatial extent are used for duration too (*They are open from 9 to 5*), though *to* is hardly used except in combination with *from*. In addition there are three prepositions specialised to the temporal domain. *Since* is used with the perfect to mark the starting-point, with the endpoint obligatorily left implicit. *Until* and its somewhat more informal variant *till* mark the endpoint, with the starting-point either implicit or marked by *from*:

		a.	b.
[20]	i	*He'd been in Paris <u>since 1962</u>.*	**He'd been in Paris <u>since 1962</u> <u>till 1970</u>.*
	ii	*He'll be here <u>until/till 10</u>.*	*He'll be here <u>from 3</u> <u>until/till 10</u>.*

The complements of the prepositions can be PPs instead of NPs: *from shortly before lunch until a little after dinner.* The complement of *from* often contains *on* or *onwards* (*from that time on/onwards*) – and an alternant of *from now on* is the intransitive preposition *henceforth. Since* and *until/till*, unlike *from* and *to*, take content clause complements: *since I last saw her*, *until it stops raining. Since* can occur without a complement with the interpretation "since then": *We met in 1990 and have been friends ever since. Since* can take a gerund-participial (*I haven't spoken to him since leaving home*), while *until/till* can take a past-participial (*Stay until ordered to leave*) or a verbless clause (*It should not be touched until dry* "until it is dry"). In AmE *through* is often used for the endpoint in preference to *until/till.* It has the advantage of being more explicit: *We'll be in Paris from May through July* makes clear that the endpoint is the end of July, whereas *We'll be in Paris from May until July* does not say whether the endpoint is the beginning or end of July (or some time in the middle).

Duration vs location

Location with a durational implicature

PPs headed by *during* and *between* and with a temporal NP as complement express location in time, but may imply duration. Compare, for example:

		a.	b.
[21]	i	*My son was born <u>during the recess</u>.*	*He died <u>between 8 a.m. and 1 p.m.</u>*
	ii	*I worked at home <u>during the recess</u>.*	*He rested <u>between 8 a.m. and 1 p.m.</u>*

In [i] the PP expresses a time interval within which the birth/death occurred: clearly the latter did not occupy the whole of the interval. In [ii], however, there is an implicature that the situation did last for the whole of the interval. This durational implicature can, however, be cancelled: *I worked at home several times during the recess* and *He rested between 8 a.m. and 1 p.m. for two periods of about thirty minutes each. During* phrases do not normally provide answers to *how long* questions (e.g. *During the recess* is not an answer to *How long were you in Paris?*); for many speakers the same applies with *between*, while for others the implicature can be strong enough to allow it to answer such a question (A: *How long were you in the library?* B: *%Between three and about half past four*).

Since phrases can express location or duration

With *since*, however, there is a clear contrast between the two categories of adjunct:

[22] i *I've moved house since you left.* [temporal location]
ii *I've been here since four o'clock.* [duration]
iii *He's been ill again since then.* [ambiguous]

Example [iii] can be interpreted as locating his illness at some time between then and now or as saying that he has been ill throughout this period. Durational *since* allows *ever* (*I've been lonely ever since you left*) and provides answers to *how long* questions (A: *How long have you been here?* B: *Since four o'clock*).

7.4 Non-bounding duration adjuncts

These adjuncts have the form of PPs with *in* or *within* as head and a temporal NP as complement. They are found in clauses expressing singulary achievements or accomplishments:

[23] i *The doctor arrived in/within half an hour.* [achievement]
ii *They built the house in/within a year.* [accomplishment]

An achievement itself has no duration: the adjunct therefore measures a period that ends at the time of the achievement and begins at the time when it was in some sense set in train or at a time that is a relevant point of orientation in some other way. In [i] the starting-point is likely to be the time the doctor was called. In *She reached the summit in two hours* the default interpretation is that the starting-point was when she set out on the climb. But it doesn't have to be: compare *We should reach the summit in another two hours.* Here we may well have already done part of the climb and I am taking the moment of utterance as the starting-point of the two-hour period.

Accomplishments do have duration, and the adjunct measures that. In a context where the builders have already been working on a house for some months, we would normally use an achievement expression, *They will finish building the house in another year*, rather than the accomplishment *build the house* itself. But there may be indeterminacy over the location of the starting-point: the interval could begin with a subinterval that was merely preparatory, rather than strictly part of the building as such.

Just as bounding duration adjuncts are incompatible with clauses denoting singulary perfective situations (accomplishments and achievements), so non-bounding duration adjuncts cannot appear with clauses denoting imperfective situations (activities and states): #*I wrote letters in an hour.*

Non-bounding duration adjuncts can hardly be questioned directly: ?*Within how long a period did they build the house?* Instead we use the *take* construction: *How long did it take them to build the house?*

Shortness implicature

The construction with *in/within* suggests that the duration was somewhat short relative to some norm or expectation. This is reflected in the fact that it is infelicitous to modify with *at least*: *They will build the house in at most a year / *at least a year*; *The doctor will arrive in at most an hour / *at least an hour.* No such implicature is associated with the *take* construction: *It will take at least a year to build the house.*

Durational and locational *in*

There is a clear semantic affinity between the *in* considered here and the one used for temporal location, as in *They'll be arriving in ten days.* In the latter *ten days* gives the length of the period between now and their arrival, but the clause isn't interpreted as saying how long they will take to arrive. The distinction between the durational and locational senses is seen in the ambiguity of:

[24] *I'll write the report in two weeks.* [ambiguous: duration or location]

The durational sense tells how long I'll take, the locational sense tells when I'll write it – at the end of the two weeks. The locational sense usually involves future time: *I wrote the report in two weeks*, for example, will normally have a durational interpretation. *Write the report* is an accomplishment expression; if we replace it by an achievement expression, as in *I'll complete the report in two weeks*, there is little effective difference between the two readings. A clear contrast is found with the expression *in time*: compare *We managed to finish in time* ("within the time allotted") and *In time he will realise how much he owes you* ("eventually").

8 **Polarity-sensitive aspectual adjuncts**

We are concerned in this section with a small class of adverbs or AdvPs consisting of *still* and *already*, *yet* and *any longer/more*. These are polarity-sensitive items of the kind discussed in detail in Ch. 9, §4; *still* and *already* characteristically occur in positive clauses, *yet* (in its main use) and *any longer/more* in negatives.

Primary use of *still* and *already*: continuation and inception

Non-perfect affirmative constructions

[1] i a. *Liz is/was still here.* b. *Liz is/was already here.*
ii a. *Liz still goes/went to school.* b. *Liz already goes/went to school.*
iii a. *Liz is/was still cooking dinner.* b. *Liz is/was already cooking dinner.*

The situations here are all imperfective: in [i] we have a singulary state, in [ii] a serial state (a multiple situation, with the going to school repeated habitually), while [iii] is progressive. *Still* and *already* are not adjuncts of temporal location: the time referred to in the clause is precisely the same as it would be if the adjuncts were omitted. Very often, the clause contains another adjunct which does serve to locate the situation in time: *Liz was still/already here at eight o'clock*. The meaning of *still* and *already* is aspectual rather than simply temporal: it has to do with what we have referred to as the 'internal temporal constituency of the situation' (Ch. 3, §3.1). With *still* it is a matter of the situation continuing to obtain, while with *already* we are concerned with the time of the situation's inception, beginning.

Still emphasises that the situation obtains/obtained at the time referred to, and involves an implicit or explicit contrast – generally with what might have been expected or with some comparable situation:

[2] i *Liz was still here at eight o'clock – she usually goes home around seven.*
ii *Liz has sold her flat in London but she still has a house in the country.*

The situation in the *still* clause lasted till later than might have been expected or than the contrasted situation. Like the aspectual verb *continue*, *still* carries a presupposition that the situation also obtained prior to the time referred to: *I continue to think / still think it was a mistake* asserts that I think this now and presupposes that I did so earlier, too.

Already also emphasises that the situation obtains at the time referred to, and again there is an implicit or explicit contrast, but this time it is a matter of the *already* situation beginning earlier. *Liz is already here* suggests that I (or you, or someone else) might have expected her not to be here until later. Compare, then:

[3] i *Liz was already here at eight o'clock; she usually gets here around nine.*
ii *Liz has bought a flat in Paris though she already has a house in the country.*
iii *Jill still goes to school, whereas Liz is already at university.*

Example [iii] shows *still* and *already* in successive clauses contrasting the stage in life that Jill and Liz have reached. The school stage has lasted later for Jill, and the university stage has begun earlier for Liz.

Negation

[4] i a. *She still isn't here.* b. #*She already isn't here.*
ii a. ?*She isn't still here.* b. ?*She isn't already here.*
iii a. *She isn't here any more.* b. *She isn't here yet.*

Still readily has scope over a negative, as in [ia]: we simply have continuation of a negative state of affairs. In the primary sense we are concerned with here, *already* can't have scope over a negative, as seen in [ib]. In [ii] the negative has scope over the aspectual adjunct. These examples are of doubtful acceptability: they could hardly be used except to contradict a prior assertion of the corresponding positives. It is on this basis that *still* and *already* are included in the class of positively-oriented polarity-sensitive items. Normally, one would use the corresponding negatively-oriented items *any more/longer* and *yet*, as in [iii]. Here [iiia] presupposes that she formerly was here and carries the implicit suggestion that this situation might have been thought to still obtain. And [iiib] suggests that she will be here in the (not very distant) future.

Still and *already* are certainly not wholly excluded from falling within the scope of a negative, but they do so only under restricted conditions, as illustrated in:

[5] i a. *You don't still believe it, do you?* b. *You're not already a member, are you?*
ii a. *I hope you don't still read comics.* b. *I hope you don't already subscribe.*
iii a. *If you're not still a member, now's the time to rejoin.* b. *If you're not already a member, do consider joining.*

In [i–ii] the positive situation seems likely to obtain or at least to be a real possibility. In [ia] it looks as though you still believe it (though you shouldn't), and in [ib] it looks as though you might already be a member (a pity, because I was thinking of offering you a subscription). In [iia] I have some reason to think you may still read comics (but I hope that isn't so, given your age), while in [iib] it could be that you already subscribe (but I hope not). The examples in [iii] are conditional, with [iiia] hardly possible unless the issue of your being still a member has already been raised; compare also relative clauses in construction with *anyone*, etc.: *Anyone who isn't still/already a member should consider taking advantage of this offer.*

Interrogatives

[6] i a. *Is Jill still at school?* b. *Is Jill already at school?*
ii a. %*Is Jill at school any more?* b. *Is Jill at school yet?*

For inception, both *already* and *yet* are found. *Yet* is the neutral choice, while *already* suggests an inclination to think that the answer may well be positive: the relationship matches that between *some* and the more neutral *any* (cf. Ch. 9, §4.3). For continuation, the form normally used in interrogatives is *still*, as in [ia], but some speakers have *any more* as an alternant. *Any longer/more* can, however, be used with a somewhat different sense:

[7] i *Do we still have to put up with these conditions?*
ii *Do we have to put up with these conditions any longer?*

Example [i] asks whether the situation continues to obtain now, whereas [ii] asks whether it will continue to obtain beyond now, in the future.

Still and *already* with the perfect

[8] i a. **He has still read the report.* b. *He has already read the report.*
ii a. *He has still not read the report.* b. **He has already not read the report.*

Already very often occurs with a positive perfect, as in [ib]: he is in the state resulting from earlier reading the report. We can't have *still* here: the state wherein he has read the report necessarily continues indefinitely, so it doesn't make sense to assert that it still obtains at the present moment. The negative [iia], however, makes perfect sense: the state wherein he hasn't read the report continues until he does read it.[17] But [iib] is again excluded: as noted above, *already* in its primary sense does not take scope over a negative.

Use of *still* and *already* in cases of progression

[9] a. *He has still read only twenty pages.* b. *He has already read twenty pages.*

Still and *already* are often used of situations where it is a matter of progressing along some scale. *Already* suggests a relatively high degree of progression; *still* typically combines with *only* to suggest a relatively low degree. *So far* or *up to now* could be substituted for *still* and *already* giving *He has read twenty pages so far*; this says how many pages he has read during the period with now as terminal point, but without any indication as to whether this is relatively many or few. *Already* is often used with temporal expressions: *It is already five o'clock, so he must be home by now.* The low degree counterpart would usually have *only* by itself rather than *still only*, as in *It's only five o'clock, so he won't be home yet.*

Already for 'mounting process'

In the *already* example in [9], the suggestion of a relatively high degree of progression can be regarded as a special case of the implicature that the situation obtains at an earlier time than might have been expected: there has been greater progression than might have been expected. In other cases, however, it is not a matter of the situation obtaining at an earlier time than expected, but of it being a stage in a potentially mounting process:

[17] *Still* also appears with the perfect in the 'progression' use discussed below: see [9a].

[10] i *He already owns two newspapers and a TV station: this takeover must be stopped.*
ii *There is now at least an even chance that this nation of almost 200 million people will shortly erupt in murderous violence. Already, protests of various sorts have taken place, mostly in provincial cities.*
iii *It isn't clear whether Brazil, which already wasn't making payments on the principal of its foreign debt, will come out of the moratorium in a better state to service its debt.*

An undesirable situation obtains at the time in question, and it is envisaged that things may get worse. In this use *already* can be placed in front position, as in [ii], or have scope over a negative, as in [iii].

Already and *yet* with a perfective

In BrE, and some varieties of AmE, the aspectual adjuncts are restricted to imperfective situations, as illustrated above. Other varieties of AmE, however, allow *already* and *yet* to occur in perfective examples, as in:

[11] i A: *Can I speak to Ed, please?* B: %*He already left yesterday.*
ii %*Did he leave yet?*

Already may also follow the verb: %*He left already* (with main stress on *left*). This use of *yet* (criticised in some usage manuals) is restricted to informal style.

Yet in affirmative contexts

[12] i *I have yet to see a better account than the one you proposed ten years ago.*
ii *There may yet be an election before Christmas.*

Yet can occur with essentially the meaning of *still* in a quite restricted range of affirmative contexts. Example [i] illustrates its use with *have* + infinitival; it entails that I haven't yet seen a better account. The significant feature of [ii] is the modal *may*: the construction indicates that a possibility still exists. Another case is seen in *There's hope for me / you / . . . yet*, but this is a more or less fixed formula. Some varieties of English, however, allow *yet* with the sense "still" in a wider range of structures, such as %*Her father is here yet.*

9 Adjuncts of frequency

Adjuncts of frequency express quantification in the clause in a way which is comparable to that of quantifiers in the structure of NPs:

[1]

	FREQUENCY ADJUNCT IN CLAUSE	QUANTIFIER IN NP
i	a. *She lectured twice.*	b. *She gave two lectures.*
ii	a. *She always wins.*	b. *She wins every match.*
iii	a. *People sometimes misunderstand this question.*[18]	b. *Some people misunderstand this question.*
iv	a. *Students usually prefer assignments.*	b. *Most students prefer assignments.*

[18] *Sometimes* can also convey much the same meaning as modal *may*: compare *These animals sometimes bite* and *These animals may bite.*

Frequency modification generally indicates a multiple situation

Frequency adjuncts quantify situations, and except in the special case of one or zero quantity, therefore, they serve to mark that the clause expresses a multiple situation. Compare:

[2] i *She cycled to work.* [singulary or multiple]
ii *She cycled to work three times / every day / quite often.* [multiple]
iii *She cycled to work just once.* [singulary]

Clauses that express permanent states or non-repeatable occurrences such as *Barbara is from Cardiff* or *Fred was born on New Year's Day 1965* do not therefore permit the addition of frequency adjuncts.

Bounding vs non-bounding frequency adjuncts

Frequency adjuncts can be subdivided into two main types:

[3] i *She lectured ten times.* [bounding]
ii *She lectured regularly / quite frequently / every day.* [non-bounding]

Multiple situations are inherently imperfective, regardless of whether the subsituation is imperfective or perfective. A **bounding frequency adjunct** in its turn makes the imperfective multiple situation perfective, whereas a non-bounding adjunct leaves it imperfective. The bounding type cannot therefore be in the scope of bounding duration adjuncts:

[4] i **She lectured ten times for one semester.*
ii *She lectured regularly / quite frequently / every day for one semester.*

With bounding adjuncts it is a matter of how many times, while with non-bounding ones it is characteristically a matter of how often. Note, however, that an expression like *three times a week* is non-bounding: it specifies how many times per week, but not how many times in an absolute sense. Compare:

[5] i A: *How many times did you meet?* B: *We met twice.* [bounding]
ii A: *How often / How many times a week did you meet?* B: *We met twice a week.* [non-bounding]

A non-bounding frequency adjunct can have scope over a bounding one:

[6] *I always proofread an article three times.* [non-bounding + bounding]

Here the subsituations of the multiple situation modified by *always* are themselves multiple situations as they involve three occurrences of the singulary subsituation of reading an article.

Iterative verbs

Verbs such as *cough, hit, kick, kiss, knock, nod, pat, wink* are potentially iterative. *She knocked at the door* can apply to a situation where she gave a single knock or to one where she gave several knocks (see Ch. 3, §3.2.4). When a bounding frequency adjunct combines with such a verb it can be interpreted in either of two ways, as in:

[7] *Ben kicked Beth twice.* [ambiguous]

In one interpretation, he gave her two kicks (in more or less immediate succession); in the other, there were two occasions on which he gave her an unspecified number of kicks.

The form of bounding frequency adjuncts

The class of bounding frequency expressions contains the adverbs *once* and *twice* (and archaic *thrice*), NPs with *times* as head, PPs consisting of *on* + NP with ***occasion*** as head.[19] *Once* and *on one occasion* can indicate either frequency or temporal location:

[8] FREQUENCY / TEMPORAL LOCATION

	FREQUENCY	TEMPORAL LOCATION
i	a. *We only met once.*	b. *I once liked this kind of music.*
ii	a. *We met on just one occasion.*	b. *On one occasion it caught fire.*

In [a] we are concerned with how many times, while in [b] the adjunct locates the situation at some indefinite time in the past. The idiom *once upon a time* has only the temporal location use.

The form of non-bounding frequency adjuncts

These display a much wider and more varied range of forms, illustrated in:

[9] i *always, constantly, continually, ever, frequently, intermittently, invariably, never, normally, occasionally, often, periodically, rarely, regularly, repeatedly, seldom, sometimes, sporadically, usually*

ii *each/every day, every two weeks, every other/second week, every time; whenever . . .*

iii *once a day, once every half-hour, twice a year, three times each month, four times per year, on three occasions each year, on several occasions per year*

iv *now and again, again and again, off and on, on and off, from time to time, as a rule, for the most part*

Those in [i] are adverbs. The universally quantified *always* can indicate frequency (*She always won*) or duration (*I've always liked her*). *Never* usually indicates frequency (*He never answers my letters*, "always doesn't"), but can also be used for temporal location (*He never answered my last letter*, "at no time"). *Ever* is polarity-sensitive, as discussed in Ch. 9, §4.3; like *never* it can be used for frequency (*Do you ever go to the movies?*) or temporal location (*Did you ever see 'Gone with the Wind'?*).

In [9ii] we have NPs with a time-interval noun as head and *each* or *every* as quantifier; there may be a postmodifier (*every day when it isn't raining, every time I see her*). There are also expressions where such NPs are embedded within larger phrases, as in *on the first Sunday of every month*. We also include *whenever* in this group, since in its main use it is interpreted as *every time*: *He blushes whenever / every time she speaks to him.* It can also be used under restricted conditions for non-referential temporal location with the sense "at any time": *You can let me have it back whenever you like.*

The expressions in [9iii] consist of those that function as bounding frequency adjuncts (other than *never*) together with a postmodifier that cancels the bounding effect – compare *We met twice* (bounding) and *We met twice a week* (non-bounding) in [5] above. In the *on three occasions each year* type, *each year* is probably a separate adjunct rather than a postmodifier (as suggested by its position in *Each year we had lunch together on about three occasions*), but it still serves to cancel the bounding effect: *For the next several years we had lunch together on about three occasions every month.* The clear postmodifiers are NPs introduced by *a* or else PPs with *per* as head (cf. Ch. 5, §8.4). Example [9iv]

[19] Instead of being head of their respective NPs, *times* and *occasion* may occur in the complement of quantificational nouns.

contains a variety of frequency idioms. In addition NPs like *a great deal*, *a lot*, etc., may blend frequency with duration and degree: see §11.

Frequency and time

The subsituations of a multiple situation are typically located at different times. In the salient, serial-state interpretation of *She cycles to work*, for example, the individual events of her cycling to work will necessarily take place at different times – very likely, different days. Particularly when the subsituations take place at regular intervals, there is then a close relation between the expression of frequency and the expression of temporal location. Compare then:

[10]	i	*He visits his parents every Christmas.*	[frequency]
	ii	*He visits his parents at Christmas.*	[temporal location]
	iii	*He always visits his parents at Christmas.*	[frequency + temporal location]

Every Christmas in [i] is a frequency adjunct, indicating how often. But at the same time, it gives the temporal location of the subsituations: it could therefore be used in answer to the question *When does he visit his parents?* In [ii] *at Christmas* is an adjunct of temporal location, giving the time of the subsituations. The meaning of [ii] is not the same as that of [i], since [ii] does not explicitly say that the visiting takes place every year; this is made explicit in [iii], which combines a frequency adjunct with one of temporal location. Nevertheless, clauses like [ii] that contain just an adjunct of temporal location will often be interpreted as conveying regularity and hence frequency (the implicature being strengthened if *at Christmas* is placed at the front of the clause: *At Christmas he visits his parents*). Compare, similarly, the minimal difference between *George phones my mother on the first Sunday of every month / every other Sunday* (frequency) and *George phones my mother on the first Sunday of the month / on alternate Sundays* (temporal location). Both versions could answer either a frequency question (*how often?*) or a temporal location question (*when?*).

This kind of relation between frequency and temporal location is not confined to cases of repetition at regular intervals. The same pattern is found with *whenever* or *every time* and *when*:

[11]	i	*He blushes whenever / every time she speaks to him.*	[frequency]
	ii	*He blushes when she speaks to him.*	[temporal location]
	iii	*He always blushes when she speaks to him.*	[frequency + temporal location]

No doubt as a result of such close relationships, many grammars treat frequency adjuncts as a subtype of time adjunct. Conceptualisation of frequency as being a matter of time is encouraged by the fact that the word 'time' iself is used in frequency expressions such as *three times* or *every time it rains*. Nevertheless, there are compelling grounds for treating frequency as conceptually distinct from time. Frequency adjuncts quantify (sub)situations, and that is not the same as quantifying times. Consider first the following examples with bounding frequency adjuncts:

[12] i *This quartet has only been performed twice, once in Bath and once in Glasgow.*
ii *This question, which the examiners include in the paper every year, has been answered correctly just three times.*
iii *The victim was stabbed three times.*

The most likely scenario for [i] is that the performances took place at different times, but this is not a necessity: it is perfectly possible that both were held on the same evening. Similarly in [ii]: it could be that the three correct answers were all given at the same time – in last year's exam, held on 1 November, let us say. And in [iii] it is possible, certainly for some speakers, that the three stabbings were carried out simultaneously by three different assailants.

The same applies with the non-bounding type:

[13] i *Parents usually love their children.*
ii *A quadratic equation usually has two different solutions.*

In its most likely interpretation [i] is saying something about most parents, not most times. And since [ii] expresses a timeless truth, the quantification can only be over situations, not times.

Scope in negative clauses

In general, frequency adjuncts can have scope over a negative or fall within its scope, but there are restrictions concerning linear position and particular items. Some examples are given in:

[14]	ADJUNCT HAS WIDER SCOPE	NEGATIVE HAS WIDER SCOPE
i	a. *I always didn't answer the phone.*	b. *I didn't always answer the phone.*
ii	a. *I sometimes didn't answer the phone.*	b. *I didn't ever answer the phone.*
iii	a. *I usually didn't worry about it.*	b. *I didn't usually worry about it.*
iv	a. *Every Sunday he didn't shave.*	b. *He didn't see her every week-end.*

In [i–iii], the scope depends on linear order: the first of the underlined items has scope over the second. Thus [ia] is logically equivalent to *I never answered the phone* and [ib] is equivalent to [iia]. *Sometimes* is strongly polarity-sensitive, and can hardly fall within the scope of negation: instead we have *ever*, as in [iib]. With *usually* the two constructions are pragmatically equivalent (in the absence of contrastive stress), as in [iii]. In [iva] it's a matter of how often he omitted to shave; the adjunct could occur at the end, but front position makes the scope clearer. In [ivb] he saw her less frequently than every week-end; here the adjunct could not be fronted.

Bounding adjuncts like *four times* can have wide or narrow scope:

[15] *He didn't vote four times.* [ambiguous as to scope]

It can be interpreted as "Four times he failed to vote", with the adjunct having wider scope; or it can be read as "It's not the case that he voted four times" (he only voted twice, let us say), and here the negation has wider scope.

Scope relations with quantified NPs

Frequency adjuncts quantify situations and if the clause also contains a quantified NP the issue arises as to which quantifier has the wider scope. Consider the following pairs:

[16] QUANTIFIED NP HAS SCOPE OVER FREQUENCY ADJUNCT
i *One of my friends has been sacked two or three times in the last few months.*
ii *Some people were late much more often than me.*

[17] FREQUENCY ADJUNCT HAS SCOPE OVER QUANTIFIED NP
i *If you sack someone two or three times a year the public will lose confidence.*
ii *People in ex-communist countries kill themselves more often than others in Europe.*

In [16i] it is the same person who was sacked on two or three different occasions, and in [16ii] there is a group of people each of whom was late much more often than me. In these examples, then, the quantified NP has scope over the adjunct: we ascribe a property involving a frequency quantification to the referent(s) of the NP. By contrast, in [17i–ii] (both attested examples) it is not the same person who is sacked, we may assume, and it is not particular individuals within the set of people in ex-communist countries who commit suicide more often than other people. Here we start with the quantification of situations: each subsituation may involve a different person being sacked or committing suicide.

Contextual restrictions on the domain of non-bounding frequency quantification

Compare the interpretation of *always* in:

[18] i *There is always somewhere where it is raining.*
ii *I always handwash this blouse.*

Example [i] illustrates the relatively rare case where the frequency adjunct is interpreted without restriction: at every moment of every day of every year there is somewhere where it is raining. By contrast, [ii] does not entail that I spend my life handwashing the blouse: *always* here is interpreted with an unexpressed restriction, "on all occasions when I wash this blouse I do so by hand". Again, this is comparable to quantification in NPs. In *All students take Introduction to Phonology*, for example, we interpret the subject NP as containing some pragmatically recoverable restriction on the domain – typically, all students in a particular department of a particular institution.

The restriction is often stated explicitly, usually by an adjunct of temporal location or condition applying to the subsituations:

[19] i *The teacher sometimes gives us a hint when /if he sets a difficult problem.*
ii *Pamela usually sets the alarm clock before she goes to sleep.*

Association with focus

The effect of the hidden restriction may be to cause differences in truth value between clauses with contrastive stress associated with different elements. Compare:

	a.	b.
[20] i	*FIDO barked at the postman today.*	*Fido barked at the POSTMAN today.*
ii	*FIDO usually barked at the postman.*	*Fido usually barked at the POSTMAN.*

In [i], where there is no frequency quantification, the [a] and [b] versions have the same truth value. But the addition of *usually* in [ii] destroys the equivalence between the two versions. Suppose, for example, that the postman came 120 times, and that Fido barked at him 50 times, while our other dog, Whisky, barked at him 110 times: in this scenario, [iia] (with focus on *Fido*) will be false, but [iib] (with focus on *postman*) can still be true if most of Fido's barking was provoked by the arrival of the postman in contrast with other visitors. In [iia], therefore, the hidden restriction is "when the postman came", whereas in [iib] it is "when people came", or perhaps just "when he barked".

Frequency adjuncts with the progressive

Except where there are explicit or implicit indications to the contrary, clauses with progressive aspect characteristically denote singulary rather than multiple situations and hence resist modification by frequency adjuncts. Compare:

[21] i a. *She cycles to work.* b. *She is cycling to work.*
ii a. *She usually cycles to work.* b. ?*She is usually cycling to work.*

The salient interpretation of [ia] involves a multiple situation (repeated cycling to work), and hence it readily accommodates the addition of *usually* in [iia]. The salient interpretation of [ib], by contrast, is singulary, so that it resists the addition of *usually*. A multiple reading of [ib] can be obtained by adding an adjunct of temporal location such as *this week*, but the short time span involved leaves *usually* infelicitous. However, [iib] is acceptable with an overt or covert adjunct giving the temporal location of the subsituations: *She is usually cycling to work at this time of the morning.*

The combination of the progressive with such adjuncts as *always* generally has an idiomatic interpretation, as in *She is always/constantly filing her fingernails.* In the absence of any evident restriction, this conveys a subjective judgement, usually negative, suggesting excessive frequency.

10 Adjuncts of serial order

These characteristically pick out one of a series of repeated events, indicating its temporal order relative to others in the series:

[1] i *I went to New York <u>for the second time</u> in 1976.*
ii *The oratorio was <u>first</u> performed in 1856.*
iii *The oratorio was performed <u>again</u> the following year.*
iv *The oratorio was performed <u>yet again</u> yesterday.*

These examples all express singulary situations, but these singulary situations are related to an implied multiple situation. In general the existence of such a multiple situation is entailed: [i], for example, entails that I went to New York at least twice. In the case of *first*, however, its existence is merely implicated: [ii] implicates, but does not entail, that there were further performances after the first.

Again, as in [1iii], places the repeated event anywhere after its first occurrence. *Yet again* places it anywhere after its second occurrence, with the suggestion that this degree of repetition is in some way surprising or notable.

Adjuncts of serial order cannot be directly questioned. They have the form of PPs or AdvPs. The PPs prototypically consist of *for + the X time*, where *X* is an ordinal numeral or *last*. The adverbs are *first*, *next*, *last*, and *again*.

Scope

Adjuncts of this type may or may not have scope over the subject of the clause. Compare:

[2] i *Mary Smith performed the sonata <u>for the third time</u> last year.*
ii *A woman has been elected president <u>for the second time</u>.*
iii *People are dying of TB <u>again</u>.*

In the reading of [i] where the subject is inside the scope of *for the third time* it was Mary Smith herself who performed on all three occasions, whereas when the subject is outside the scope of the adjunct there is no indication of who performed before. The ambiguity is thus a matter of whether what was repeated was Mary's performing the sonata, or *x*'s performing it. Similarly in [ii]: it may or (much more likely) may not have been the same woman. In the only pragmatically plausible interpretation of [iii] the adjunct has wider scope than the subject: we can assume that people do not die twice.

Again can also be used to indicate restoration of a previous state:

[3] i *Ann opened the window, and then a few minutes later she closed it again.*
ii *The lawnmower broke down, and I couldn't get it going again.*

What is repeated here is not the events (Ann's closing the window, my getting the lawnmower going) but earlier states (the window being closed, the lawnmower operating).

11 Degree

Degree as a kind of quantification

Among the categories considered so far, a number inherently involve quantification:

[1] i *She walked a long way.* [spatial extent (distance)]
ii *The price has gone up a lot.* [scalar change extent]
iii *The strike lasted a long time.* [temporal extent: duration]
iv *They go out very often.* [frequency]

In this section we take up other kinds of quantification, such as are illustrated in:

[2] i *She likes it a lot.*
ii *I've completely finished marking these assignments.*
iii *He almost forgot the doctor's appointment.*

We will use the traditional term **degree** as a cover term for all of these, though its intuitive applicability is greater for some than for others. *A lot* in [2i] represents the prototypical case: *like* denotes a gradable property that can apply with varying levels of intensity, and the degree adjunct indicates the level that applies in the situation in question. *Finish marking these assignments* in [ii] denotes an accomplishment, and *completely* emphasises that the terminal point was reached. In [iii] we are concerned with the conditions that must be satisfied in order for "He forgot the doctor's appointment" to be true: *almost* indicates the extent to which these conditions were satisfied. Example [i] differs from [ii–iii] in that it can be seen as an answer to a *how much* question, and hence is a more central member of the degree category. We can say *How much does she like it?* but not **How much have you finished marking these assignments?* or **How much did he forget the doctor's appointment?*

In some cases we find a blending of degree with frequency and duration. *Ed talks a great deal*, for example, could answer a *how much* question and the NP *a great deal* occurs as a prototypical degree adjunct in such clauses as *I like it a great deal.* At the same time, however, there is a clear affinity with duration (*You've talked a great deal already* implies that you've talked for a long time) and frequency (*Ed talks a great deal* denotes a multiple situation and strongly suggests that Ed talks often as well as long).

Subgroups of degree adjuncts

We will divide degree adjuncts into seven subgroups, illustrated as follows:

[3] i *I absolutely reject that suggestion.* [maximal]
ii *I much regret confiding in her.* [multal]
iii *I rather like that idea.* [moderate]
iv *I had modified it slightly.* [paucal]
v *I doubt whether he understood it at all.* [minimal]
vi *I nearly made a serious mistake.* [approximating]
vii *I trusted her enough to let her borrow the file.* [relative]

We will examine the subgroups in turn, providing further examples without attempting to be exhaustive. But first, two general points should be made. As with many other categories, we find adverbs that can appear now with manner function, now with degree function:

[4]

	MANNER	DEGREE
i	a. *He sang rather badly.*	b. *He badly misrepresented my position.*
ii	a. *She answered the question perfectly.*	b. *I perfectly understand your reasoning.*

Secondly, some members of the class of degree adverbs are often quite restricted with respect to the type of verb or VP they can modify. We have, for example, *I completely forgot, I badly needed it, I greatly admire her, I deeply dislike them,* but not **I thoroughly forgot, *I utterly needed it, *I perfectly admire her, *I deeply like it.* Some items are found only in one or two idiomatic combinations: *roundly condemn/defeat, clean forget,* and so on.

(a) The maximal subgroup

[5] *altogether absolutely completely entirely fully perfectly quite thoroughly totally utterly wholly*

[6] i *She finally eliminated the problem altogether/completely/entirely.*
ii *I absolutely/fully/quite/thoroughly agree with you.*

These items indicate a degree at the top end of the scale. For the most part they do not permit further intensification by a degree adverb (**very absolutely/utterly*), but we can have *very fully, more completely than ever before,* etc. *Thoroughly* readily takes intensification in *They examined it very thoroughly,* but here it is probably best regarded as a manner adjunct (and certainly does not itself indicate maximal degree). Most can indicate either completion of an accomplishment, as in [6i], or extremely high degree of a gradable property, as in [ii]. Again, however, there are idiosyncratic restrictions applying: compare *She utterly eliminated the problem* and **She utterly finished the work.* In such pairs as *calculate ~ miscalculate, estimate ~ overestimate, behave ~ misbehave,* the second member differs from the first in having a gradable sense that permits this kind of degree modification:

[7]

	a.	b.
i	**He utterly calculated her response.*	*He utterly miscalculated her response.*
ii	**I completely estimated his strength.*	*I completely overestimated his strength.*

Quite belongs in this group when modifying an accomplishment (*Have you quite finished?*) or – more often – a gradable property that inherently involves high degree. But with gradable properties such as are expressed by *like*, it marks moderate degree:

[8] i *She quite adores them.* [maximal]
ii *She quite likes them.* [moderate]

Note also the maximal interpretation in *I quite understand.*

The maximal items can generally be positioned centrally or at the end of the clause (though *quite* is limited to central position). In end position they will typically carry the stress, reinforcing their height on the scale of degree; the contrast is particularly noticeable in such pairs as *I absolutely agree with you* and *I agree with you absolutely* or *This totally ruined the evening* and *This ruined the evening totally.*

(b) The multal subgroup

[9]	*badly*	*bitterly*	*deeply*	*far*	*greatly*	*immensely*
	largely	*much*	*particularly*	*profoundly*	*so*	*strongly*
	tremendously	*vastly*	*well*	*a great deal*	*a lot*	*for the most part*

[10] i *He badly needs a haircut.*
ii *She bitterly/deeply/strongly resents the way she has been treated.*
iii *I would far/much prefer to do it myself.*
iv *He had for the most part understood what they said.*
v *I do so hope everything works out as you would wish.*

This subgroup covers a range on the scale from above the midpoint to near the top end. Items such as *immensely* and *tremendously* belong in the upper region and resemble the maximal ones in that they hardly admit further intensification themselves (**very immensely*). *Far* generally indicates distance, but is used by extension for degree when it is a matter of scalar difference, as in comparison (*far prefer* – note that it also occurs as a modifier of adjectives and adverbs in comparatives like *far better, far more consistently*) or with such verbs as *exceed* (*It far exceeded her expectations*). In some cases, manner and degree seem to merge: *laugh heartily, squeeze tightly, work hard. So* may license a result clause: *He grieved so, (that) we thought he would never recover* (some speakers would find *so much* more natural). Without such a result clause, *so* tends to be found primarily in informal style: *Do you have to stare so?*

One item that is noticeably absent from the list in [9] is *very*, which modifies adjectives and adverbs but not verbs. Instead we have *much*, but this is subject to considerable restrictions. In end position it normally behaves as a non-affirmative item unless it is itself modified by a degree adverb: *I don't like it much, I like it very much*, but not **I like it much.* It can occur in central position in affirmative contexts with a limited range of verbs such as *appreciate, enjoy, outrank, prefer, surpass, underestimate*: *I much appreciate your concern.* In some cases, we find that unmodified affirmative *much* is permitted in passives but not in the corresponding active:

[11] i *She had been much abused by her stepfather.*
ii **Her stepfather had much abused her.*

(c) The moderate subgroup

[12]	*moderately*	*partially*	*partly*	*quite*	*rather*	*somewhat*

[13] i *Things have changed somewhat.*
ii *I rather think you're right.*

This subgroup, like the following, has significantly fewer members than (a)–(b): there is greater lexical variation at the upper end of the scale (the list given in [9], in particular, could easily be extended).

(d) The paucal subgroup

[14] *a bit* *a little* *little* *slightly*

[15] i *I slightly regret not accepting their offer.*
ii *We discussed it a little.*
iii *He little realised what he was letting himself in for.*

Little represents a lower degree than *a little*, and is the antonym of *much* (as it is in NP quantification). It generally behaves as a negative, as explained in Ch. 9, §3.3. In end position it tends to require its own modifier: *She likes him very little*, but not **She likes him little*; note, however, that we can have *It matters little* (*what you say now*). Paucal adjuncts tend not to occur with verbs which inherently involve a high degree: *He liked/*[?]*adored her a little*; *It had slightly damaged/*[#]*ruined her prospects.*

(e) The minimal subgroup

[16] i *at all* *in the least* *in the slightest* *so much as*
ii *barely* *hardly* *scarcely*

[17] i *If it rains at all, we'll move to the church hall.*
ii *He hardly understood what she was saying.*

The items in [16i] are non-affirmative: *I didn't like it in the least*, but not **I liked it in the least.* Those in [16ii], by contrast, are negative: [17ii], for example, could be continued: *and nor indeed did I.* It does not entail that he didn't understand, but the degree to which he did understand was so small that it is treated syntactically as negative. These negative items readily occur with non-affirmative *at all*: *We hardly enjoyed it at all.* The non-affirmative set include some items restricted to idiomatic combinations, as in *I don't care a damn/fig.* A variant of this is *I don't give a damn/fig*, where the final NP is syntactically object rather than adjunct, and indeed there are other cases of non-affirmative objects that are pragmatically equivalent to *at all* – compare *I didn't understand a word.*

(f) The approximating subgroup

[18] *all but* *almost* *as good as* *kind of* *more or less* *nearly*
practically *sort of* *virtually*

[19] i *He almost lost his balance.*
ii *Ed as good as / more or less admitted it was his fault.*
iii *She had sort of promised to help him.*

Almost, *nearly*, and *practically* trigger a strong negative implicature: [19i], for example, conveys that he didn't in fact lose his balance, but came very close to doing so.[20] The complex expressions *more or less*, *as good as*, *kind of*, *sort of* (belonging to informal style, especially the last three) indicate that the conditions for application of the verbal expression are approximately satisfied: what is conveyed here is not so much that an

[20] The implicature is of the scalar type discussed in Ch. 5, §5.2. If I bet that Sue will have almost finished her thesis by the end of the year and in fact she has completely finished it by then, I will be deemed to have won my bet, just as if I bet that she will have written most of her thesis by the end of the year.

admission and promise were not in fact made, as that the acts did not qualify as an admission and promise in the strictest sense.

(g) The relative subgroup

[20] *enough* *less/least* *more/most* *sufficiently* *too much*

[21] i *He had studied enough to scrape a pass.*
ii *I understood it more than I'd expected, but that isn't saying very much.*
iii *He needed the money too much to be able to turn down such an offer.*

We call these the 'relative' subgroup because they do not identify some constant area of the scale but quantify the degree relative to some other situation. *Enough* and *sufficiently* indicate a lower bound: in [21i] the degree or extent to which he had studied was not lower than that required to scrape a pass. *More/most* and *less/least* are inflectional forms of ***much*** and ***little*** (discussed in detail in Ch. 13, §4.1.1); in [ii] the degree of understanding is compared to that of the expected understanding, which could in principle be almost anywhere on the scale, though the following clause happens to suggest it was quite low. *Too much* indicates an upper bound: the degree of need was above the highest level at which he would be able to turn down the offer, so that [iii] entails that he wasn't able to turn it down. Again, however, we don't know whereabouts on the scale this upper bound lies.

Too, like *very*, can't modify verbs: *much* is therefore required in [21iii]. *Too*, and the other items in [20], can modify adverbs, so AdvPs consisting of one of the earlier adverbs as head and one of these as modifier will to some extent belong in the relative subgroup. The qualification 'to some extent' is needed because most of the adverbs in subgroups (a)–(b) that permit modification by these items are not neutral, but will still mark a high position on the scale. *Ed resented it more bitterly than I did*, for example, does indicate that Ed resented it to quite a high degree.

Negation

To the extent that degree adjuncts can combine with clausal negation, they normally fall within its scope:

[22] *I don't fully understand what you mean.* [adjunct in scope of negation]

The meaning here is "It is not the case that I fully understand what you mean", not "I fully fail to understand what you mean". Where there is a need to quantify the degree of a negative situation it is usually expressed lexically rather than by clausal negation:

[23] i a. *He very much dislikes them.* b. ?*He very much doesn't like them.*
ii a. *I absolutely reject the idea.* b. ?*I absolutely don't accept the idea.*

Nevertheless, narrow scope negation is not entirely excluded:

[24] *I very much don't want you to go with them.* [negation in scope of adjunct]

Where the adjunct is within the scope of the negative, we need to distinguish between ordinary and metalinguistic negation (see Ch. 9, §1.2):

[25] i *I don't like her much.* [ordinary negation]
ii *I don't rather like her: I absolutely adore her.* [metalinguistic negation]

The first clause in [ii] could normally only be used in a context where it had been suggested that I rather like her: the negative rejects that proposition not because it is false but because it falls short of indicating the degree of my liking her. In what follows we ignore cases of this kind and consider below only narrow scope ordinary negation.

Maximal degree

One case is illustrated in [22]: the negative indicates "less than fully", with an implicature that the degree is still high (i.e. not very much less than fully). Negation of *quite* implicates "almost": *I don't quite agree* entails that I don't agree, but suggests that I'm not far from doing so. This is also the interpretation when it's a matter of reaching some endpoint, as in *I haven't completely finished.* Examples like *I absolutely adore her,* where the verb itself indicates high degree, do not permit ordinary negation.

Multal and moderate degree

The multal case is illustrated in [25i], and similarly *They don't meet a great deal* or *He wasn't badly wounded.* Negation indicates a lower degree than that expressed by the adjunct – and this will usually be interpreted as quite low, in the paucal range. Thus while [25i] is consistent with my liking her moderately, it generally implicates a lower degree than that. Many of the multal degree adverbs resist ordinary negation. Take *He bitterly regretted it,* for example: in the negative we would be much more likely to use *much* than *bitterly,* giving *He didn't regret it much.* The moderate degree items are also unlikely to occur with a negative; note here that *quite* has the maximal interpretation in negation, not the moderate one.

Paucal, minimal, and approximating degrees

A little and *slightly* likewise resist negation. *A bit,* by contrast, is commonly negated, and then behaves like the minimal items *at all,* etc. *They didn't enjoy it a bit / at all* indicates a zero degree of enjoyment, as does the less emphatic *They didn't enjoy it. Little, barely, hardly, scarcely,* being themselves negative, do not occur in the scope of another negative. Ordinary negation is also normally incompatible with the approximating items *almost,* etc.

The relative subgroup

These readily undergo negation. *He hadn't studied enough to scrape a pass,* the negative of [21i], indicates a lower degree than the lower bound defined by the positive and hence entails that he didn't scrape a pass. *He hadn't been worrying too much to be able to sleep* indicates a lower degree than the upper bound defined by the positive and hence entails that he could sleep. But *too much* can occur in the negative with a paucal meaning when there is no explicit or implicit infinitival complement: *I didn't enjoy it too much* is simply an informal alternant of *I didn't enjoy it very much.*

12 **Cause and result**

In this section we are concerned with adjuncts of the kinds illustrated in:

[1]	i	*We booked early* <u>*so that we could be sure of getting good seats*</u>.	[purpose]
	ii	*Two of us couldn't get on the plane* <u>*because the airline had overbooked*</u>.	[reason]
	iii	*The airline had overbooked,* <u>*so that two of us couldn't get on the plane*</u>.	[result]

We take purpose and reason to be subtypes of a more general category 'cause': they have it in common, for example, that they can be questioned by *why.* Thus [1ii] provides an answer to the question *Why did you book early?* and [ii] to *Why couldn't two of you get on the plane?*

The examples also illustrate connections between cause and result. *So* is used to indicate either purpose or result, as in [1i/iii]. And the semantic equivalence between [ii] and [iii] shows that cause of the reason subtype stands in a converse relationship with result: if *X* caused *Y*, then *Y* resulted from *X*, and vice versa. The difference is a matter of which of the situations is presented as superordinate and which as subordinate. In [ii] the airline's overbooking is treated as subordinate and expressed within an adjunct of cause (more specifically, of reason), whereas in [ii] it is the other situation, our not being able to get on the plane, that is expressed as a subordinate clause, this time within an adjunct of result.

It must be emphasised, however, that from a grammatical point of view adjuncts of cause are very much more important than those of result, in terms of both frequency and the range of constructions available for expressing them. One aspect of this is illustrated in the following examples, where both situations are expressed in main clauses:

[2] i *Two of us couldn't get on the plane: the airline had overbooked.*
ii *The airline had overbooked: two of us couldn't get on the plane.*
iii *The airline had overbooked; <u>for this reason</u> / <u>as a result</u> / <u>because of this</u> / <u>consequently</u> two of us couldn't get on the plane.*

In [i–ii] the cause–result relationship is not expressed, but left to be pragmatically inferred. In [iii] the second clause begins with an adjunct related anaphorically to the first clause, and in this construction the adjunct belongs to the cause (reason) category. Note that although *as a result* contains the noun *result* it is an adjunct of cause: we understand "as a result of the airline having overbooked"; the adjunct itself, therefore, gives the cause, and indicates that what follows is the result.

12.1 The two subtypes of adjuncts of cause

Cause can in general be questioned by *why* or *what...for*, but as noted above such questions can elicit two different kinds of answer, purpose or reason:

[3] i *Why did you get up so early?/What did you get up so early for?*
ii *(I got up early) in order to do some gardening while it was still cool.* [purpose]
iii *(I got up early) because I couldn't sleep.* [reason]

Differences between purpose and reason

The central cases of purpose imply intention and design – usually on the part of the agent of the matrix clause. As a result, purpose adjuncts differ from those of reason in the following respects.

Temporal relations

The time of the situation expressed or implied in a purpose adjunct is characteristically later than that of the matrix situation: purpose is generally future-oriented. It is also possible for the two situations to be simultaneous.

[4] i *He borrowed $50 from me <u>in order to pay his rent</u>.* [later]
ii *He walked home <u>in order to save the bus fare</u>.* [simultaneous]

With reason, by contrast, the subordinate situation is usually earlier or simultaneous with the matrix, though it is also possible for it to be later:

[5] i *He was angry because he couldn't find his keys.* [simultaneous]
ii *He was late because he had overslept.* [earlier]
iii *He didn't want to go with them because it would be dark soon.* [later]

Entailment

The proposition expressed in the subordinate clause is entailed in the case of reason adjuncts but not with purpose, when the situation time is later than that of the matrix. Example [3iii] entails that I couldn't sleep, while [5i–iii] entail respectively that he couldn't find his keys, that he had overslept, and that it would be dark soon. By contrast, [3ii] implicates that I did some gardening, but certainly does not entail it: maybe a sudden thunderstorm forced me to change my plans. Similarly [4i] does not entail that he paid his rent: maybe he was unable to resist the temptation to spend the money on drink. These future-oriented purpose adjuncts involve aims and intentions, and there is no guarantee that aims and intentions are realised.

Reason may implicate purpose

The close relation between purpose and reason is reflected in the fact that a clause with a reason adjunct very often implicates one with a purpose adjunct, and vice versa. For example, [3ii] implicates and is implicated by [6i], and there is a similar relation in [6ii]:

[6] i *I got up early because I wanted to do some gardening while it was still cool.*
ii a. *He got up at 4.30 because his plane left at six.* [reason]
b. *He got up at 4.30 in order to catch the six o'clock plane.* [purpose]

Note, however, that the differences mentioned above concerning entailments still apply: the complement of *because* expresses an entailment, but that of *in order* does not. Thus [6i] entails that I wanted to do some gardening while it was still cool (though not, of course, that I actually did do some). The subordinate clause in [6iia] is a preterite futurate, interpreted as "his plane was scheduled to leave at six", and again this is an entailment, whereas [iib] does not entail that he caught the plane.

12.2 **Purpose**

Realisation

(a) PPs with clausal complements – finite clauses or infinitivals

The prepositions found here are *in order* (finite or infinitival), *so* (finite), *so as* (infinitival):

[7] i *May I request a postponement in order that I might make adequate preparation?*
ii *He withdrew the remark in order to appease his colleagues.*
iii *Please phone everybody before the meeting so that we can be sure of a quorum.*
iv *He phoned everybody before the meeting so as to be sure of a quorum.*

In the finite construction, the subordinator *that* is readily omissible after *so*, but hardly after *in order*, which is somewhat more formal and considerably less frequent. The finite construction usually contains a modal auxiliary, such as *might* in [i], *can* in [iii]; clauses without modals are certainly possible, however, especially in the negative, and we also find examples of the subjunctive construction with *in order*:

[8] i *We think we have to fight in order that Cuba is integrated into the Latin American system.*
ii *I'll try and get home a little earlier than usual so we don't have to rush.*
iii *The administration had to show resolve in order that he not be considered a lame-duck president.*

(b) Ungoverned clauses: infinitivals or finites with *may/might*

[9] i *We left early to miss the rush-hour.*
ii *He requested an adjournment that he might have adequate time to study the documents.*

Here the subordinate clause functions as purpose adjunct itself, rather than being governed by a preposition. Example [i] illustrates the most frequent type of purpose adjunct, while [ii] by contrast is very rare and formal: instead of the content clause that we have here, we would usually have a PP headed by *in order* or *so*.[21] Ungoverned infinitivals are always positive: a negative requires a governing preposition. In *He modified the story somewhat in order not to offend his parents*, for example, we cannot omit *in order*.

(c) PPs with NP complements

[10] i *I did it for fun / for your sake / for her benefit.*
ii *He called in Kim [with a view to / with the intention of obtaining some professional advice].*

Example [i] illustrates the purposive use of *for*, while the construction in [ii] depends for its purposive meaning on the lexical content of the head noun, and the noun *purpose* itself could of course substitute for *intention*.

Syntactic function

Purpose elements are usually adjuncts, but they are also found as predicative complements: *This is in order that the local delegates can be officially informed.*

Further remarks on infinitival clauses

(a) Infinitivals with an overt subject

Infinitivals governed by *so* + *as* cannot contain a subject: if a subject has to be expressed after *so*, the finite construction is required. Both infinitivals that are governed by *in order* and those that are ungoverned may have a subject preceded by the subordinator *for*, though this construction is much less common than the subjectless one:

[11] *(In order) for the flavours to mingle properly, the dish should be cooked very slowly in a low oven.*

(b) Governed infinitivals with no subject

In subjectless clauses governed by *in order* or *so as*, the antecedent for the missing subject is the subject of the matrix clause:

[12] *He resigned in order / so as to avoid any conflict of interest.*

[21] In traditional grammar the term 'final clause' is used for the type of subordinate clause illustrated in [7–9]. *In order*, *so* (*that*), and *so as* are treated as subordinating conjunctions constituting part of the subordinate clause.

(c) Ungoverned subjectless infinitivals with no other missing element

[13] i *He resigned to avoid any conflict of interest.*
ii *They sent Sue to New York to manage the photography department.*
iii *The meeting was adjourned by the Head of Department to provide time for consultation with course committees.*
iv *The goods were sold at a loss to make room for new stock.*
v *The new prison has no outside windows to make it more secure.*

The default case is illustrated in [i], where the matrix subject provides the antecedent for the missing subordinate subject. But in ungoverned clauses there are other possibilities. In [ii] the antecedent is matrix object: it is Sue who is to manage the photography department. The matrix clause in [iii] is passive; it can be interpreted with the complement of *by*, *the Head of Department*, as antecedent, but we can also take the whole matrix situation as providing the interpretation. This reflects the fact that *The Head of Department provided time for consultation by adjourning the meeting* entails *Adjourning the meeting provided time for consultation.* There is no *by* phrase in [iv], but we can still interpret it with either the seller of the goods or the selling of the goods as making room for new stock. In [v] the matrix is active: it's the design or building of the prison with no outside walls that was intended to make it more secure. These examples indicate that the missing subject in a purpose infinitival does not have to be syntactically controlled.

(d) Ungoverned infinitivals with a missing non-subject

[14] i *I bought them$_i$ for the children to play with __$_i$.*
ii *I bought them$_i$ to read __$_i$ on the train.*
iii *She gave me this box$_i$ to put the loose change in __$_i$.*
iv *They gave the flowers$_i$ to Linda to present __$_i$ to the soloist.*
v *The flat$_i$ was bought (by Ralph) to use __$_i$ as a pied à terre in London.*

The subordinate clauses here are 'hollow' non-finites in the sense of Ch. 14, §6: the '__$_i$' marks the position of a missing object, of the verb or of a preposition, that is linked to the element in the matrix bearing the same index. This element is object of the matrix in [i–iv], subject in [v]. In [i] the infinitival has its own subject, but in the others the subject is missing too. The antecedent for the missing subordinate subject is marked by double underlining. This construction is found only with ungoverned infinitivals: we cannot insert *in order* or *so as* in these examples.

Purpose infinitivals and unbounded dependency constructions

[15] i *Who have they gone to Paris to see __ this time?*
ii *These are the kinds of student [that this school exists to cater for __].*

Non-subject elements in infinitival purpose adjuncts can be questioned or relativised, as in these examples, where it is the matrix clause, not the infinitival, that is interrogative or relative. This construction occurs most readily, but by no means exclusively, when the matrix clause expresses motion, as in [i].

Infinitivals in clause and NP structure

[16] i *Two other books to read on holiday were lent to me by Fay.* [NP modifier]
ii *She lent me them to read on holiday.* [clause adjunct]
iii *She lent me two books to read on holiday.* [ambiguous]

Infinitival clauses similar to the ones we have been considering are also found as modifier in the structure of NPs, as in [i]. The position of the clause here rules out an analysis as an adjunct in clause structure: it can only be part of the subject NP. In [ii] the infinitival must be an adjunct in clause structure because the pronoun *them* cannot take such dependents. Examples like [iii] can then be analysed in either way, but with little effective difference in meaning. As a clause adjunct it specifies her purpose in lending me two books, as an NP modifier it gives descriptive information about the books – "books which were for reading on holiday".

Implicit purpose

We noted above that reason adjuncts often implicate purpose: for example, [6iia], *He got up at 4.30 because his plane left at six*, implicates that he got up then in order to catch the six o'clock plane. The same kind of implicature may be triggered by a conditional:

[17] i *If you want to catch the six o'clock plane, you will have to get up at 4.30.*
ii *In order to catch the six o'clock plane, you will have to get up at 4.30.*

A purpose implicature is particularly common where it is a matter of avoiding some undesirable situation:

[18] i *Come in before you get wet.*
ii *The children had to be watched carefully lest they stray with their new rubber surf-floats beyond the orange and yellow flags.*
iii *Keep well away in case you get hurt.*
iv *He delayed his departure for fear of missing something.*

The underlined adjuncts might be interpreted as "so that you don't get wet", "so that they wouldn't stray . . . beyond the orange and yellow flags", "so that you don't get hurt", "so that he wouldn't miss anything". But the prepositions that introduce them do not themselves mean "so that . . . not": the purpose interpretation arises only if the content of the subordinate and matrix clauses is conducive to it. Compare the above with, for example:

[19] i *Come in before your father gets home.*
ii *He trembled lest they should see through his disguise.*
iii *Take your umbrella in case it rains.*
iv *She was never game to join in for fear of being ridiculed.*

These clearly cannot be glossed in terms of "so that . . . not", but there is no reason to say that the prepositions have a different meaning here than in [18]. Notice, moreover, that [19iii] still implicates purpose, but a purpose whose content is not so simply derivable from what is expressed: we understand something like "Take your umbrella in order to avoid getting wet if it rains". Depending on the context, there could likewise be a purpose implicature in [19i]: "Come in before your father comes home in order to avoid possible unpleasant consequences if he comes home and finds that you are not yet in".

Purpose and deontic necessity

Purpose adjuncts are commonly found with matrix clauses expressing deontic necessity, one special case being that where it is a matter of satisfying rules and regulations:

[20] i *Significantly more permanent positions will have to be created to fulfill the requirements of the day-to-day running of the museum from 1988.*
ii *How many credit points are needed to obtain a degree?*

Scope and focus

In negative clauses purpose adjuncts may have wider or narrower scope than the negative; in the latter case they can be the focus, as they can also be in alternative questions:

[21] i *He doesn't eat much, to keep his weight down.* [adjunct has wider scope]
ii *I didn't come here to have a quarrel.* [negative has wider scope]
iii *Did you say that to please her or to annoy her?*

12.3 **Reason**

Realisation

Adjuncts that explicitly express reason mostly have the form of PPs, though there are also a few adverbs, such as *consequently, therefore, thus,* that express reason as well as having a connective function.

(a) Preposition + declarative content clause

The following prepositions take finite clauses as complement:

[22] *as* *because* *for* *inasmuch as* *seeing* *since*

All except *seeing* take a non-expandable content clause, i.e. one not permitting the subordinator *that*. The relatively formal *for* has certain syntactic properties in common with coordinators, including the impossibility of fronting the phrase it introduces (see Ch. 15, §2.11). *Because* has been illustrated above, the others are seen in:

[23] i *As I still have work to do, I can't come to the film tonight.*
ii *He avoided answering, for he was afraid of implicating his wife.*
iii *Inasmuch as they have apologised, I consider the matter closed.*
iv *Seeing (that) you have come, you might as well stay.*
v *Since Mars has an elliptical orbit its distance from the sun varies considerably.*

Because is the most central and versatile of the reason prepositions. A PP with *because* as head can occur in subject or predicative complement function as well as adjunct:

[24] i *Because some body parts have already been turned into commodities does not mean that an increasing trade in kidneys is desirable.*
ii *The reason I didn't call you was because the phone was out of order.*

Because could be replaced by *the fact that* in [i], *that* in [ii], and these latter versions would be widely preferred in formal style. In the subject structure [i], *because* is often modified by *just*, and the matrix VP is more or less restricted to *doesn't mean*: *Just because you're older than me doesn't mean you can order me around.*

(b) Preposition + PP or NP

[25] *because [of]* *due [to]* *for* *from* *in view [of]*
on account [of] *out [of]* *owing [to]* *through*

[26] i *The lecture was cancelled [due to / owing to / on account of her indisposition].*
ii *[Because of / In view of her political activities,] they treated her with suspicion.*
iii *He said it out of sheer spite.*
iv *They were unable to concentrate [for/through lack of sleep]*

Of is also found, as in *He died of a heart attack*, but the PP here is a complement of *die* and would not generally be thought of as answering a *why* question.

(c) Implicated reason

There are also, as so often, various constructions which have a more general circumstantial meaning, but which may be interpreted in appropriate contexts as giving a reason for the matrix situation:

[27] i *Having known the candidate for ten years, I can vouch for his reliability.*
ii *With six people away sick, we can't meet the deadline.*

Scope and focus

Reason adjuncts may fall within the scope of a negative or have scope over it. Compare:

[28] i *I'm not going just because Sue will be there.* [negative has scope over adjunct]
ii *I'm not going because I can't afford to.* [adjunct has scope over negative]
iii *I'm not going because Sue will be there.* [ambiguous]

In [i] the negative has wide scope: the fact that Sue will be there is not the reason why I'm going. In [ii] the adjunct has wide scope: the fact that I can't afford it is the reason why I'm not going. And [iii] can be interpreted in either way. The scope will normally be indicated prosodically – see Ch. 9, §1.3.2.

This does not apply to all the reason prepositions, however. Of those taking clausal complements, only *because* can fall within the scope of a negative: *I'm not going since Kim suggested it*, for example, is unambiguously interpreted like [28ii]. Those taking phrasal complements mostly behave like *because*, but the *of* complement of *die* cannot have scope over a negative: *He didn't die of a broken heart*, but not **He didn't die, of a new wonder drug.*

The PPs that cannot fall within the scope of a negative cannot be focused either, and nor can they be used in answer to a *why* question. Compare:

[29] i *It was [because/*since/*as he lied] that he was sacked.*
ii *Are you going [because/*since/*as Sue will be there]?*
iii A: *Why aren't you coming with us?* B: *[Because/*Since /*As I'm not well.]*

These restrictions indicate that the PPs headed by *since*, *as*, etc. are not as integrated into the structure of the clause as *because* PPs: they are not constituents of the VP, but are attached at a higher position in the constituent structure, or else have the status of supplements.

Why can have scope over a negative, which is relatively unusual for interrogative adjuncts; *what . . . for*, however, cannot occur in the negative construction:

[30] i a. *Why did you miss the lecture?* b. *Why didn't you go to the lecture?*
ii a. *What did you miss the lecture for?* b. **What didn't you go to the lecture for?*

12.4 Result

Adjuncts of result are characteristically expressed either by a PP with *so* as head and a content clause as complement, or by a PP with *with* as head and an NP complement with the form *the result* + content clause:

[31] *They had gambled away all their money, [so / with the result that they didn't even have the fare to get home].*

Nothing further need be said about the *with the result* type, where the result meaning is indicated lexically by the head noun within the complement of the PP. The resultative *so* construction merits examination, however, because this preposition is also used to express purpose. We thus have a contrast between:

[32] i *He left early so that he could have some time with his son.* [purpose]
ii *He had to work late so that he couldn't have any time with his son.* [result]

In [i] the *so* PP says why he left early, what his purpose was in doing so, whereas in [ii] it gives the result or consequence of his having to work late.[22]

Semantic differences between the result and purpose constructions

[33] i The subordinate clause is entailed with result but generally not with purpose.
ii Result does not imply intentionality or agentivity.

We noted in §12.1 that with prototypical purpose adjuncts there is no entailment that the purpose was achieved. For example, [32i] does not entail that he was able to have time with his son: we could without inconsistency add *but when he got home he found that his son had gone to visit some friends.* By contrast, [32ii] does entail that he couldn't have any time with his son, and such an entailment relation always holds in the case of result adjuncts. Purpose, we have seen, implies intention (though this is not always overtly expressed in the matrix clause), but result does not, as evident from examples like:

[34] *We'd had 6 inches of rain overnight, so that the track was completely flooded.*

Syntactic differences between result and purpose

[35] i Resultative *so* is not replaceable by *in order.*
ii Result adjuncts cannot be fronted: they occur in end position.
iii Modality: result adjuncts do not permit the subjunctive construction, and they occur freely without modal auxiliaries.
iv Result adjuncts are characteristically prosodically detached, with the status of supplements.
v Omission of the subordinator *that* from the resultative construction affects the syntactic status of *so*: see Ch. 15, §§10–11.

Unlike *so, in order* is restricted to purpose: it can substitute for *so* in [32i], but not in [ii]. We have noted that purpose *so* PPs are occasionally fronted, but this is not possible with result. Point [35iii] reflects the semantic fact that the content of a result adjunct is entailed: there is therefore no need for any modal qualification, as illustrated in [34]. Point [35iv] is reflected in the inability of result adjuncts to fall within the scope of negation or to be focused:

[36] i *He has never spent much, so that he now has a tidy sum saved up.*
ii **It's so that the track was completely flooded that we'd had six inches of rain overnight.*

In [i] the adjunct has to have scope over the negative: it gives the result of his not spending much.

[22] The term 'consecutive clause' is thus traditionally applied to adjuncts like that in [32ii] (where *so that* is again treated as a subordinating conjunction).

Ambiguity and blurring of the distinction between result and purpose

The syntactic differences given in [35] are not sufficient to indicate in all cases whether a *so* PP is an adjunct of purpose or result. Compare:

[37] i *He's come home early so we can all go to the movies together.*
ii *A relatively simple switching mechanism reverses the cycle so that the machine literally runs backward, and the heat is extracted from outdoor air and turned indoors.*

In abstraction from prosody, [i] is ambiguous, with a sharp difference between the result and purpose interpretations. But in [ii] the difference is somewhat blurred. We understand this to entail the subordinate clause governed by *so*, which makes it like a result construction, but at the same time the subordinate situation came about by design: the purpose or intention was realised.

- *So* as a marker of result and as a degree adverb

There is also a close semantic relationship between the constructions shown in:

[38] i *He loves her passionately, so that he is even willing to give up his job for her.*
ii *He loves her so passionately that he is even willing to give up his job for her.*

In [i] *so* is head of a PP functioning as adjunct of result: this is the construction we have been discussing. In [ii] *so* is an adverb of degree modifying *passionately*; it licenses the content clause following *passionately*, which expresses the result of his loving her to the degree he does. The net effect is thus essentially the same.

- Implicit result with *until*

A content clause complement of *until* often implicates result:

[39] *He drank until he couldn't walk in a straight line any more.*

The *until* PP is a duration adjunct, indicating the endpoint of the period during which he drank. At the same time, there is an implicature that his being unable to walk in a straight line was the result of his drinking.

13 Adjuncts of concession

13.1 Concessive meaning

An elementary example of a clause containing a concessive adjunct is:

[1] *Sonia doesn't speak French although she grew up in Paris.*

The concessive preposition *although* expresses a contrast between the subordinate clause *she grew up in Paris* and the superordinate clause *she doesn't speak French*. The meaning involves the following three features:

[2] i The subordinate clause is entailed.
ii The truth of the subordinate clause might lead one to expect that the superordinate clause would be false.
iii In fact, the truth of the subordinate clause does not detract from the truth of the superordinate clause.

This gives the following three components in the meaning of [1]: she grew up in Paris; the fact that she grew up in Paris might very well lead you to expect that she would (have learnt to) speak French (the language spoken by native inhabitants of Paris); in fact, she doesn't speak French.

Since it follows from [1] both that Sonia grew up in Paris and that she doesn't speak French, it is possible to switch the two clauses:

[3] *Sonia grew up in Paris, although she doesn't speak French.*

What was originally the subordinate clause is now the head one, and vice versa: the difference between the versions is primarily a matter of information packaging, of which piece of information is given greater prominence by virtue of being made the head. The implicature of course changes: for [3] we have "the fact that she doesn't speak French might lead one to expect that she did not grow up in Paris".

It is also possible to have a juxtaposition of two main clauses, with the semantic relationship between them expressed by a concessive adverb in the second:

[4] i *Sonia doesn't speak French; <u>nevertheless</u>, she grew up in Paris.*
ii *Sonia grew up in Paris; <u>nonetheless</u>, she doesn't speak French.*

The internal form of these adverbs reflects fairly transparently the concessive meaning given above as [2iii].

Variation in the strength of the contrary-to-expectation implicature

In the example we began with there was a very sharp conflict between the subordinate and superordinate clauses, in that Sonia's having grown up in Paris provides strong grounds for expecting that she would speak French. But the implicature that one might expect the superordinate clause to be false need not be as strong as this. Compare (this time with the concessive adjunct in front position):

[5] i *<u>Although Sam was extremely rude to her</u>, Beth defended him.*
ii *<u>Although many Gurkhas speak English</u>, almost none speak Cantonese.*
iii *<u>Although carrots are good for you</u>, eating too many can actually be harmful.*

In [i] the fact that Sam was extremely rude to Beth provides reasonable grounds for thinking she might not defend him. In [ii] (taken from an article dealing with the employment of Gurkhas as private bodyguards in Hong Kong) the fact that many Gurkhas speak English doesn't provide very strong grounds for expecting that some Gurkhas (more precisely, a number greater than almost none) would speak Cantonese: what is important here is the contrast between English and Cantonese. In [iii] the fact that carrots are good for you is obviously a good reason for thinking that eating them won't be harmful, but the superordinate clause here contains the *too* of excess: eating too much of anything is likely to be harmful. Again, then, it's primarily a matter of contrasting the beneficial effects of carrots in general with the harmful effects of carrots in excess.

13.2 Syntactic issues

Realisation

Concessive adjuncts have the form of PPs, mainly headed by the items in [6i], or adverbs, as in [6ii]:

[6] i *although* *though* *despite* *in spite* *notwithstanding* *albeit*
ii *nevertheless* *nonetheless* *still* *yet*

The adverbs behave as connective adjuncts: they are considered further in §19.

Although and *though*

Although and *though* are alternants, the latter slightly more informal. Their complement may be a full content clause (as in [1] and [5]) or it may be reduced to a participial and verbless clause:

[7] i *Though living in Holland he works in Germany.*
ii *Although elected to the Council he can't take up his seat.*
iii *Though an American citizen, he has never lived in the States.*

Though commonly occurs with *even*, which serves to reinforce the concessive meaning:

[8] *He knew they were there even though he couldn't see them.*

Despite, in spite, notwithstanding, for, albeit

[9] i *[In spite of / Despite the recession,] travel agents seem to be doing well.*
ii *[In spite of / Despite having grown up in Paris,] Sonia doesn't speak French.*
iii *[Notwithstanding Ed's reservations,] the agreement is the best I could hope for.*
iv *[For all our good intentions,] the meeting soon broke up in acrimony.*
v *The book covers the whole field, [albeit somewhat superficially].*

Despite takes an NP complement, *in spite* a PP with *of* + NP, and in either case a gerund-participial can replace the NP. *Notwithstanding* usually takes an NP complement (which can precede the head: see Ch. 7, §4.2). In its concessive use, *for* takes an NP complement beginning with *all*. *Albeit* is restricted to formal style, and takes only a verbless clause as complement.

Scope, focus, and questioning

Concessive adjuncts cannot be directly questioned: there is, for example, no (ordinary) question to which *although she was ill* is an answer. For the most part, they cannot fall within the scope of an element in the matrix, but there are two constructions where they can:

[10] i *She didn't reject his offer in spite of his wealth but because of it.*
ii *Shall we go for a walk even though it does look like rain?*

In [i] we have a contrast between concession and reason: his wealth wasn't something that detracted from, or stopped, her rejecting his offer but the reason why she did. Such a contrast reflects the fact that a concessive construction can be roughly paraphrased in terms of reason in combination with two negatives: *She rejected his offer in spite of his wealth* conveys "His wealth was not (as you might have expected) a reason for not rejecting his offer". This construction is possible only with *in spite* or *despite*, and is generally restricted to cases where the speaker is contradicting another remark or being jocular.

In [10ii] the matrix has question force and the adjunct falls within the scope of the question. Such questions, however, are biased (in the sense discussed in Ch. 10, §4.7): I'm suggesting that we go for a walk. This construction also allows *in spite / despite*, but hardly *though* without the *even*, or *although*.

13.3 Semantically related constructions

(a) *Whereas*, *while/whilst*, *when*

[11] i *Whereas many Gurkhas speak English, almost none speak Cantonese.*
ii *While/Whilst the first act was excellent, the second seemed rather dull.*
iii *He gave me a beer when what I'd asked for was a shandy.*

Whereas can substitute for *although* in most cases, but not felicitously in ones like our original example: #*Sonia doesn't speak French, whereas she grew up in Paris.* It expresses contrast, but hardly conveys the suggestion that the superordinate clause might be expected to be false; it might be regarded as a peripheral member of the class of concessive prepositions. The primary meaning of *while* and *whilst* is durational, but they have a secondary sense equivalent to *whereas*, as in [ii]: the meaning expressed here is contrast, not co-duration. *When* normally has a temporal meaning, but it too conveys contrast in cases like [iii]. This use is quite restricted; the *when* PP must come at the end and it could not be used in examples like [i–ii]. It seems to require a context that is consistent with the primary temporal meaning, so that the contrastive, concessive meaning is probably best handled as an implicature, rather than a distinct sense of *when*.

(b) Coordination with *but*

The contrast expressed in clauses containing concessional adjuncts can also be expressed in a coordinative construction with *but*:

[12] i *Sonia doesn't speak French although she grew up in Paris.* } [subordination]
ii *Although she grew up in Paris, Sonia doesn't speak French.* }
iii *Sonia grew up in Paris but she doesn't speak French.* [coordination]

While the *although* PP can occur in either of the positions shown, the corresponding main clause always occupies first position in the coordination. For the syntactic differences between *although*, a preposition, and *but*, a coordinator, see Ch. 15, §2.1. *But* has a somewhat wider range of use than *although*; most notably, *but*-coordinations involving contrastive negation (with *but* expandable as *but rather*) do not have counterparts with *although*:

[14] i *She doesn't sit and mope but (rather) makes the best of the situation.*
ii #*Although she doesn't sit and mope, she makes the best of the situation.*

(c) Conditionals

There is quite a close relation between *though*, which is primarily concessive, and *if*, which is primarily conditional. In combination with *even* they typically contrast as in:

[14] i *I'm going out, even if it rains.* [conditional]
ii *I'm going out, even though it's going to rain.* [concessive]

Example [ii] says that it is going to rain (but I'm going out nevertheless), while [i] leaves it open as to whether it will rain (but I'm going out whether it does or not). *Even if* may be used, however, in a context where the complement of *if* is known to be true, and *even though* is occasionally found where the complement is not presented as true:

[15] i *You don't have to defend everything Ed does, even if he is your brother.*
ii *Will mere debate on that proposition, even though it be free and untrammelled, remove the dross and leave a residue of refined gold?*

In [i] there will normally be no doubt that Ed is your brother, so that the conditional is pragmatically equivalent to a concessive. In [ii] the non-factual status of the subordinate clause is reflected in its subjunctive form.

If is also interpreted concessively in the following construction:

[16] i *The respect he inspires demonstrates the moral authority of his heroic, if contradictory, personality.*
ii *It's funny, it's good, and it's a parody, if a little blunt.*

If is here equivalent to concessive *though* (or *albeit*): [i] entails that his personality is contradictory, [ii] that 'it' is a little blunt. This concessive meaning arises when *if* links attributive modifiers or predicative complements. Note finally that *if* and *though* are interchangeable in idiomatic combination with *as*: *He behaves as if/though he owned the place.*

14 Conditional adjuncts and conditional constructions

Protasis and apodosis

The prototypical conditional adjunct consists of a PP with *if* as head and a content clause as complement:

[1] i [*If you touch that wire,*] *you will get an electric shock.*
ii [*If she earns $1,000 a week,*] *she is better off than me.*
iii [*If she bought it at that price,*] *she got a bargain.*
[*if* + protasis + apodosis]

The subordinate clause functioning as complement of *if* (marked here by single underlining) we call the **protasis**, and the matrix clause minus the adjunct (marked by double underlining) is the **apodosis**. We use the term **conditional construction** for the matrix including the adjunct.[23]

Application of the concepts of true and false to protasis and apodosis

As is evident from the examples in [1] protasis and apodosis can refer to future, present, or past time. The time sphere does have some limited bearing on the interpretation, but the basic meaning is the same in all three cases, and we want to be able to make general statements that apply irrespective of the time sphere. The terms true and false can be applied straightforwardly to examples like [1ii–iii], and it will be convenient to extend them to [1i] as well. A context in which the protasis of [1ii] or [1iii] is true is one in which she does in fact earn $1,000 a week or did in fact buy it at that price, and a context in which the protasis of [1i] is true is a future context in which you do in fact touch that wire – one in which the condition comes to be **satisfied**. Analogously for the apodoses.

[23] Traditional grammar takes *if* to be a subordinating conjunction, not a preposition, and many modern works follow this analysis; *if* is therefore commonly regarded as forming part of the protasis. We are using 'conditional adjunct' for the constituent including *if*, and protasis just for the subordinate clause. Protasis and apodosis derive from Greek; it may be helpful to note that the *pro·* prefix means "before" (as also in *prologue*, etc.): the protasis is logically prior to the apodosis. In logic the terms 'antecedent' and 'consequent' generally correspond to protasis and apodosis respectively, but we will see that the correspondence is not complete. (This sense of 'antecedent' is quite different from the grammatical one, but the prefix *ante·*, this time Latin, again means "before".) Note also that we use 'conditional construction' rather than 'conditional clause', because the latter could be understood as applying to either the subordinate clause or the superordinate one.

The distinction between open and remote conditional constructions

One important distinction within the rather wide variety of conditional constructions is that between **open** and **remote** versions. This is illustrated in [2i–ii], interpreted with the time of the protasis respectively future and present:

[2]		OPEN	REMOTE
	i	a. *If you get it right, you'll win $100.*	b. *If you got it right, you'd win $100.*
	ii	a. *If Ed is here he can come too.*	b. *If Ed was/were here he could come too.*

A remote conditional must have a modal auxiliary as the apodosis verb (usually *would, should, could,* or *might*) and a modal preterite or irrealis *were* in the protasis.

The open conditional can be regarded as the default conditional construction: we will examine it first, returning to remote conditionals in §14.2.

14.1 Open conditional constructions

14.1.1 Meaning and implicatures of open *if* conditionals

Let us, for convenience, represent the *if* conditional construction schematically as '*If P* (*then*) *Q*', with the understanding that this covers not only cases where the adjunct is at the front (*If it rains we'll cancel the match*) but also those where it is at the end (*We'll cancel the match if it rains*). The interpretation of open conditional constructions then involves the following components:

[3] i Invariant meaning: the truth values of *P* and *Q* are related in such a way as to exclude the combination where *P* is true and *Q* false.
ii Consequence implicature: *Q* is a consequence of *P*.
iii Only-if implicature: if not-*P*, then not-*Q*.
iv Don't-know implicature: the speaker doesn't know whether *P* and *Q* are true or false.

Invariant meaning: excludes the combination of a true *P* and a false *Q*

What is common to all constructions fitting the *If P* (*then*) *Q* schema is that they exclude the case where *P* is true and *Q* false. Take the examples in [1]. Suppose you touch the wire and don't get a shock, or she earns $1,000 a week and is not better off than me, or she bought it at that price and didn't get a bargain: in such cases [1i–iii] are unquestionably false.

Consequence implicature: *Q* is a consequence of *P*

In most cases it is not simply a matter of *Q* being true when *P* is true: the conditional construction generally conveys that *Q* is a consequence of *P*, that *Q* follows from *P*. Very often, the relationship is one of cause and effect. An obvious example is [1i]: touching the wire will cause you to get an electric shock. Similarly in [2ia]: getting it right (correctly answering a question, let us assume) will earn you $100. In these examples the time is future, but the cause–effect relationship can of course apply in other time spheres: *If they touched the wire they* (*invariably*) *got an electric shock.*

A second common type of consequence is inference. Here the truth of *Q* is seen as following from that of *P*:

[4] i *If Ed is your brother and Max is Ed's son, then Max is your nephew.*
ii *If the key is not in my pocket, I have left it in the door.*
iii *If Jill was at the meeting she probably told / may have told him the news.*

In [i] the inference is a necessary one, given the meanings of *brother, son,* and *nephew,* but typically the grounds for inferring *Q* from *P* are not as strong as this. In [ii], for example, there could in principle be many other places where the key might be, but I tacitly exclude all possibilities other than the two expressed in *P* and *Q*. Example [iii] illustrates the frequent case where the apodosis contains an expression of epistemic modality (cf. §14.1.2).

The consequence relation has to be treated as an implicature rather than an entailment because there are certain special uses of *if* where it does not apply:

[5] i *If he won the coveted prize, it was because of his divine playing of the rondo.*
ii *If our house was spacious, the place next door was immense.*

In the intended context for [i] it has been established that he won the prize: the apodosis here gives the reason for his having done so, not a consequence. In [ii] we understand that both *P* and *Q* are true, but the immensity of the place next door is not a consequence of the spaciousness of our house. It differs from *Our house was spacious and/but the place next door was immense* in that the first clause is syntactically and informationally subordinate: the context is likely to be one where I have been talking about our house and am now turning to the size of the house next door. A characteristic feature of this construction is that the clause ascribes a scalar property to two entities, such that the second outdoes the first.

The consequence implicature differs from those considered below in that it doesn't normally allow explicit cancellation: there are here no close analogues of the cancellation of the only-if implicature seen in [8] or that of the don't-know implicature seen in [11].

Relevance protases

One further special case where *Q* is not a consequence of *P* involves 'relevance protases':

[6] i *If you need some help, Helen is willing to lend a hand.*
ii *If you're interested, Dick's coming to the party too.*

Here *Q* is true independently of whether *P* is true. Nevertheless, such examples are consistent with the invariant meaning of *if*, which excludes only the case where *Q* is false and *P* true. In uttering [6] I'm asserting *Q*, with *P* expressing a condition on the **relevance** of *Q*. Such examples might be regarded as a shorthand way of saying something like *If you need some help you will be interested to know that Helen is willing to lend a hand* or *If you're interested it is worth telling you that Dick is coming to the party.* There is thus some implicit predication in which the actually expressed *Q* is an argument.

The only-if implicature: if not-*P*, then not-*Q*

A conditional construction generally implicates that if the condition is not satisfied the matrix situation does not or will not obtain either – that if *P* is not true, then *Q* is not true either. This implicature is related to the last. If there is a cause and effect relation between *P* and *Q* then in the absence of the cause there will be no effect. If you don't touch the wire you won't get an electric shock, if you don't get the answer right you won't win $100. The inferential consequence case commonly involves two mutually exclusive possibilities. So if the key is in my pocket I haven't left it in the door. More generally, this implicature derives from the fact that *If P (then) Q* is a weaker statement than *Q* on its own. Compare:

[7] i *I'm going to the beach this week-end if it's fine.*
ii *I'm going to the beach this week-end.*

Clause [i] is weaker, more restrictive, than [ii], so if I'm going to the beach whether it's fine or not I would be expected to say [ii], not [i]. So [i] implicates that I'm going only if it's fine.

This, however, is a matter of conversational informativeness, not of truth conditions. *If P (then) Q* does not entail *If not-P (then) not-Q*. There is no inconsistency in:

[8] i *If it's fine this week-end I'm going to the beach, and in fact I'll probably go even if it's wet.*
ii *If you invite the Smiths as well, there won't be enough room for everybody – indeed I think you've already invited too many as it is.*

And clearly the relevance protasis construction seen in [6] likewise does not have the truth of *Q* dependent on that of *P*.

The only-if implicature brings *if* PPs within the domain of what we would think of as conditions in the ordinary sense of that word. For example, [7i] will generally be interpreted as "I'm going to the beach this week-end on condition that it's fine". But this kind of gloss is inapplicable in cases like [8], [6], [5]; as usual, then, it must be borne in mind that the general term 'conditional' is assigned to the *if* construction on the basis of its characteristic use and that there are some less central uses of *if* that do not impose conditions in the everyday sense of that term.

The don't-know implicature: the speaker doesn't know whether *P* and *Q* are true or false

Many conditionals relate to future time and here it will normally be the case that at the time of utterance I can't know whether or not the condition will be satisfied. For example, in [2ia], I don't know whether you will get it right, but I do know that if you do you will win $100. The same implicature is found in other time spheres:

[9] i *If Jill is still here, she <u>is</u> / <u>will be</u> in her office.*
ii *If she bought it, she got a bargain.*

Example [i] implicates that I don't know whether Jill is still here, whether she is in her office, and analogously for [ii]. Again, this implicature relates to the issue of informational strength: *If P (then) Q* is weaker than *P and Q*, so if I choose the weaker version this is likely to be because I haven't the knowledge to justify the stronger. Compare, for example, *Jill is still here: she's in her office* or *She bought it and got a bargain.* These are much more informative than the conditional versions, and something along these lines is therefore what I could be expected to say if I knew that *P* was true.

As before, my not knowing whether *P* is true or false is an implicature, not an entailment, and in the present and past time spheres it is significantly weaker than the consequence and only-if implicatures. Indeed we have already encountered examples where it does not apply – the examples given in [5]. One common case where there is no such implicature is where *P* has just been asserted or established, and I use a conditional construction to make a comment on it or draw an inference from it. For example, [1iii] (*If she bought it at that price, she got a bargain*) might well be said on learning that she bought it at such-and-such a price. There is also a special use of the conditional construction where *P* is self-evidently true:

[10] *She's eighty if she's a day.*

This is an emphatic way of asserting that she's eighty: since she is obviously a day old it follows from [10] that she's eighty. Note that this is another case where the consequence implicature doesn't apply: her being eighty is not a result of her being a day old, nor a reasonable inference from it. The 'don't know' implicature can also be explicitly cancelled:

[11] *If he proposes – and he will – she'll probably turn him down.*

In demonstrating that the 'don't know' component is an implicature, not an entailment, we have so far been concentrating on the case where I know that *P* is true. If I know that *P* is false I would normally use a remote rather than an open conditional. Compare:

[11] i a. #*If I am you I will accept the offer.* b. *If I were you I would accept the offer.*
ii a. *If Ed broke it he will have told her.* b. *If Ed had broken it he'd have told her.*

Example [ia] is pragmatically anomalous. It can be assumed that I know that I am not you, and there is no apparent reason for not using the remote version [ib]. Example [iia] is perfectly acceptable – but it will normally carry the don't-know implicature: it suggests that I don't know whether or not he told her he had broken it. If I know, or am confident, that he didn't break it, I would normally use the remote [iib].

The open construction, however, is not inconsistent with a context in which I know that *P* is false. There is in fact one use of an *if* construction that has the falsity of *P* as an implicature:

[13] *If that is Princess Anne, I'm a Dutchman.*

This is a conventional emphatic way of saying that that is not Princess Anne. Since I'm obviously not a Dutchman (if I were I'd have to use some other patently absurd apodosis such as *pigs can fly*), *P* must be false too. We will take up in §14.2.1 the question of why a remote conditional would be inappropriate here.

Logical equivalences

With respect to the invariant meaning stated in [3i], *If P (then) Q* is equivalent to *If not-Q (then) not-P* and also to *Q or not-P*. Compare, for example:

[14] i *If Jill is here she is in her office.* [*If P (then) Q*]
ii *If Jill is not in her office then she is not here.* [*If not-Q (then) not-P*]
iii *Jill is in her office, or she is not here.* [*Q or not-P*]

These all exclude the scenario where Jill is here but not in her office. But because of the implicatures typically associated with *if* conditionals, switching from one of these constructions to another will often have a major effect on the interpretation. Compare this time:

[15] i *If she leaves, I leave.* [*If P (then) Q*]
ii *If I don't leave, she doesn't leave.* [*If not-Q (then) not-P*]
iii *I leave or she doesn't leave.* [*Q or not-P*]

These are pragmatically very different. In the singulary future interpretation we understand from [i] that my leaving will be a consequence of her leaving. One scenario, for example, is where I'm making a threat: if you sack her, you'll lose me too. But in [ii] (and [iii]) the consequence relation is quite different: her not leaving will be a consequence of my not leaving.

Multiple situations

All but one of the examples considered so far have expressed singulary situations. With multiple situations the conditional adjunct generally has narrow scope relative to the multiple quantification:

[16] *She cycled to work if she got up early enough.*

In the salient interpretation we are concerned here with habitual cycling to work, and the condition applies to the individual events. We thus have multiple instances of cycling-to-work-if-she-got-up-early-enough. In cases like this, *if* implies *when*, and as with adjuncts of temporal location like *when* phrases there will often be an accompanying frequency adjunct (making the multiple quantification explicit rather than implicit, as in [16]): *She always/often/sometimes cycled to work if she got up early enough.* Example [16] conveys that there were at least some occasions when she got up early enough and cycled to work, but the construction doesn't actually entail that the condition is sometimes satisfied. You will infer from [16] that she sometimes got up early enough because if she hadn't done so I wouldn't have enough evidence for my assertion. But it would be possible to say, for example, *These machines switch themselves off if the temperature rises above 40° Celsius* in a context where they had been designed to do that but hadn't actually been tested.[24]

14.1.2 Issues of time, modality, and polarity

Time of apodosis situation independent of that of protasis situation

In most of the examples considered so far the protasis and apodosis situations have been in the same time-sphere, both future, both present, or both past. But they do not need to be: all combinations are possible, though some are much more frequent than others. Compare, then:

[17]

		PROTASIS	APODOSIS
i	*If she leaves, I leave too.*		future
ii	*If they don't come, we're wasting our time.*	future	present
iii	*If it doesn't rise, you didn't put enough bicarb in.*		past
iv	*If that's Jill over there, I'll ask her to join us.*		future
v	*If she's here, she's in her office.*	present	present
vi	*If he knows the answer, he got it from you.*		past
vii	*If they batted first they will probably win.*		future
viii	*If Kim said that, you are entitled to compensation.*	past	present
ix	*If Kim didn't do it, Pat did.*		past

(We ignore the time of the modality in [vii]: it is the winning that is in the future.)

[24] It is possible for a conditional adjunct to have scope over a multiple situation, as in *She cycled to work if I remember correctly*. The adjunct here, however, belongs to the modal category discussed in §18.

Non-modal present tense in future time protases

A future time protasis usually has a non-modal present tense:

[18] i *If you see Ed at tomorrow's meeting, tell him I'll phone him at the week-end.*
ii *If it rains tomorrow, we'll postpone the match until next week-end.*

There are no main clauses that have precisely the same interpretation as the underlined subordinate clauses. Compare:

[19] i a. *You see Ed at tomorrow's meeting.* b. *You will see Ed at tomorrow's meeting.*
ii a. *#It rains tomorrow.* b. *It will rain tomorrow.*

The interpretation of [19ia] is present futurate – roughly "The arrangement is that you see him then". Example [19iia] is pragmatically anomalous, because the situation concerned isn't one that is arranged or scheduled in advance. The [b] versions differ from the subordinate clauses in [18] by virtue of containing a modal auxiliary that serves to qualify the assertion being made. (See Ch. 3, §10.1, for arguments that *will* expresses modal rather than temporal meaning.)

In general, epistemic modals are not used in conditional protases, but they are certainly not excluded:

[20] *If we will have an unusually wet winter (as the meteorological office predicts), the threat of a serious water shortage will recede, for the time being at least.*

The bracketed phrase suggests the kind of context in which this might be used. The proposition that we will have an unusually wet winter has been put forward by the meteorological office, and I am entertaining it conditionally and drawing a conclusion from it. The modality is here part of the proposition expressed by *P*: we could paraphrase as *If it is true that we will have an unusually wet winter, . . .* This type of construction is discussed in more detail in Ch. 3, §9.5.1.

Modal qualification in the apodosis

We have observed that in remote conditionals the apodosis verb must be a modal auxiliary. No such requirement applies with open conditionals, but modals are nevertheless very common in open apodoses: the conditional construction is conducive to the expression of modality. Examples are given in:

[21] i *If it rains tomorrow it will/may make things very difficult for us.* [future]
ii *If he is not at work he will/may be watching the cricket.* [present]
iii *If the meeting finished on time, he will/may have caught the 3.15 train.* [past]

Other modals are of course used too; *must*, for example, is often used when *Q* is a conclusion deduced or inferred from *P*. In [i], a modal is required, in accordance with general constraints applying to future time situations in main clauses. We could have *If the report isn't ready by tomorrow, you lose your job*, but *lose* here is a present futurate: the decision about your losing your job in the circumstances described has already been made, so that the contingent future situation is arranged at present time. This may be felt to make the threat marginally stronger than in the version with *will*. A non-modal version of [ii] would be very natural: it would indicate a slightly higher degree of confidence in the conclusion than with *will* (and much higher than with *may*) – a higher degree of confidence that the only possible scenarios are that he is at work and that he is watching the cricket. Non-modal preterites are also unproblematic in principle. An example was given in [1iii]: *If she bought it at that price, she got a bargain.* My judgement here is that at the price in question it was undoubtedly a bargain. *Caught* could substitute for *will / may have caught* in [21iii], but seems less likely than a modalised version; it indicates complete confidence that nothing could have interfered with his presumed intention of catching the 3.15 train provided the meeting finished on time.

Subjunctive construction in the protasis

Consistently with its non-factual status, the protasis verb may be in the plain form, marking the subjunctive construction:

[22] *If such a demonstration <u>be</u> made, it will not find support or countenance from any of the men whose names are recognised as having a right to speak for Providence.*

In Present-day English, however, this construction is very rare and formal (not comparable to the use of irrealis *were* in remote conditionals). It is virtually restricted to the verb *be*.

Polarity-sensitive items

If adjuncts have much in common, semantically and syntactically, with interrogatives. *If Jill is here, she's in her office*, for example, implicitly raises the question of whether Jill is here, but leaves the question unanswered. And *if* sanctions polarity-sensitive items in very much the same way as interrogatives.

[23] i a. *It will give us an advantage if they are <u>already</u> here.*
b. *I'll be surprised if they are here <u>yet</u>.*
ii a. *If <u>anyone</u> has a solution to this problem, please let me know.*
b. *If <u>someone</u> has a solution to this problem, please let me know.*

Already is positively-oriented, *yet* negatively-oriented and both can occur in interrogatives: *Are they already here?*, *Are they here yet?* Example [ia] is oriented towards a positive answer (it's their being here already that will give us the advantage), while [ib] is oriented towards the negative: *I'll be surprised* suggests an expectation that they are not here yet. The difference between [iia] with non-affirmative *anyone* and [iib] with affirmative *someone* matches that between *Has anyone a solution to this problem?* and *Has someone a solution to this problem?*, where the latter suggests a slightly greater inclination to think that the answer could be positive.

Factors of this kind account for the differences in:

[24] i *If you are <u>at all</u> worried about the project, don't get involved.*
ii ?*If you were <u>at all</u> worried about the project, why didn't you let me know?*
iii ?*If you improve your performance <u>at all</u>, we give you a bonus.*

Example [i] readily accepts non-affirmative *at all*: you may well not be worried at all. But the reproachful *why didn't you* in [ii] conveys that I think you were worried (and should have let me know), and so *at all* is here infelicitous. Similarly in [iii] we're making a conditional offer, and this suggests a positive orientation to the satisfaction of the condition.

14.1.3 *If* in combination with *only* and *even*

Only if

[25] i *I'll cook only if you clean up.*
ii *Students are admitted into the second year only if they achieve a grade of 5 or higher in the first year.*
iii *She cycled to work only if it was fine.*

An *if* phrase is often the scopal focus of *only*, which as usual may immediately precede (as in these examples) or be separated (*I'll only cook if you clean up*, etc.). In the former case, the whole *only if* phrase may precede the apodosis (*Only if you clean up will I cook*), but the order shown in [25] is much more usual, and we will therefore describe the meaning with reference to the schematic representation *Q only if P*.

[26] i Invariant meaning: The truth values of *P* and *Q* are related in such a way as to exclude the combination where *P* is false and *Q* is true.
ii Sufficient condition implicature: *Q* if *P*.

Invariant meaning: excludes combination of false *P* and true *Q*

The *Q only if P* construction rules out the case where *P* is false and *Q* true. Thus [25i] rules out the case where I cook and you don't clean up; [ii] rules out that where students are admitted into second year without achieving a grade of 5 or higher in the first year; [iii] rules out that where she cycled to work in bad weather. *P* thus expresses a **necessary condition**, a condition that must be satisfied if *Q* is to be true.

Sufficient condition implicature: *Q* if *P*

Besides expressing a necessary condition, *P* is characteristically taken to express a sufficient condition, one whose satisfaction is all that is required for *Q* to be true. The natural interpretation of [25i] is that I'm offering to cook provided you agree to clean up. Similarly we will assume from [ii] that any student obtaining a first-year grade of 5 will be admitted into second year. And [iii] conveys that she did cycle to work when it was fine. But it is clear that *Q only if P* does not actually **entail** *Q if P*. Consider, for example:

[27] i *A will is valid only if it has been signed in the presence of two witnesses.*
ii *You are entitled to a pension only if you are a permanent resident.*
iii *The red light goes on only if the blue light is on, but it doesn't go on if the green light is also on.*

It is common knowledge that there are other conditions on the validity of a will than the one expressed in [i] – for example, the testator must be of sound mind and not acting under duress. Example [ii] omits the obvious condition on pensions concerning age (or health): we don't assume that all permanent residents are currently entitled to a pension. And in [iii] the second coordinate adds a second condition but is not judged to be inconsistent with the first. To make explicit that *P* expresses a condition that is both necessary and sufficient we need to combine *if* and *only if* (or use some equivalent formulation): *I will accept your proposal if and only if my lawyer assures me that it is legal.*

Logical equivalences

By virtue of the invariant meaning [26i], *Q only if P* is equivalent to *If not-P (then) not-Q* and *If Q (then) P*. Compare:

[28] i *You qualify for a rebate only if your annual income is less than $70,000.*
ii *If your annual income is not less than $70,000 you don't qualify for a rebate.*
iii *If you qualify for a rebate your annual income is less than $70,000.*

The third version, however, will again often be pragmatically very different from the others. Compare the following examples with modal *will*:

[29] a. *I'll do it only if you pay me.* b. *You'll pay me if I do it.*

Version [a] will tend to be construed as giving you a choice as to whether you pay me or not (though if you don't I won't do it). Version [b], by contrast, would then sound very peremptory: I'm not giving you a choice, but telling you.

We have seen that adding *only* to *Q if P* is logically equivalent to switching the protasis and apodosis: *Q only if P* is logically equivalent to *P if Q*. This may at first appear puzzling, but it is in fact predictable from the meanings of *if* and *only*: there is no need to regard *only if* as an idiom. Consider the meaning contribution of *only* in the non-conditional *Only permanent residents qualify for a rebate.* This entails that people other than permanent residents do not qualify for a rebate (cf. Ch. 6, §7.3). Similarly, [28i] entails that you don't qualify for a rebate in other situations than that in which your annual income is less than $70,000. In other words, it excludes the scenario in which "You qualify for a rebate" is true, and "Your annual income is less than $70,000" is false. But we have seen that the invariant meaning of *if* is that it excludes the combination of a true protasis and a false apodosis, so we arrive at *If you qualify for a rebate, your annual income is less than $70,000*, i.e. [28iii].

Even if

[30] i *I'm going to the party even if Kim is going too.*
ii *I'm going to the party if Kim is going too.* [entailment of [i]]
iii *I'm going to the party.* [implicature of [i]]

Q even if P entails *Q if P*: [i] entails [ii]. In addition it implicates *Q* by itself: [i] conveys that I'm going to the party. *Even* has as scopal focus the whole content clause *Kim is going too*; it indicates that my going to the party is less expected if Kim is going too than if Kim is not going (cf. Ch. 6, §7.3). But if I'm going in the less expected case, it can be inferred that I'm also going in the more expected one – so I'm going in either case.

This implicature does not go through if the scopal focus of *even* is not the content clause as a whole, but a scalar element within it:

[31] i *You'll have to repeat the whole year even if you fail (just)* ONE *exam.*
ii *You'll have to repeat the whole year.* [not an implicature of [i]]

Here we understand having to repeat if you fail (just) one exam to be less expected than having to repeat if you fail more than one – but not than having to repeat if you don't fail any. In [30] the comparison is between positive and negative (Kim is going vs Kim is not going), but in [31] it is between points on a scale (one vs more than one). This gives the following interpretations:

[32] i "I'm going whether Kim is going or not."
ii "You'll have to repeat the year whether you fail one exam or more."

The scale may be an implicit one. *You'll have to repeat the whole year even if you fail PE* does not imply that you'll have to repeat the whole year whether you fail PE or not, but that you have to repeat it whether you fail PE or some more important part of the course.

As noted in §14.1.1, *even if P* may be used in a context where the truth of *P* is not in question: *Even if you are my elder brother, you haven't the right to tell me what to do.* In such cases the conditional implies a concessive: *Although you are my elder brother you haven't the right to tell me what to do.*

14.2 Remote conditional constructions

14.2.1 Meaning and implicatures

Let us consider now the difference in interpretation between remote and open conditionals. Further examples illustrating the contrast are given in:

[33]		OPEN	REMOTE
	i	a. *If he tells her she will be furious.*	b. *If he told her she would be furious.*
	ii	a. *If you are under 18 you need parental approval.*	b. *If you were under 18 you would need parental approval.*
	iii	a. *If he bought it at that price, he got a bargain.*	b. *If he had bought it at that price, he would have got a bargain.*

In [3] we presented four components involved in the interpretation of open conditionals, and the first three of these apply equally to the remote construction. In the first place, the remote conditional, like the open, excludes the case where *P* is true and *Q* false. Thus [ib] no less than [ia] excludes the case where he tells her and she is not furious; similarly, both versions of [ii] and [iii] exclude the case where you are under 18 and don't need parental approval, where he bought it at that price and didn't get a bargain. Secondly, the remote construction implicates that *Q* is a consequence of *P*. Thirdly, it again has the only-if implicature: if you weren't under 18 you wouldn't need parental approval, and so on.

The remote construction differs from the open in that it entertains the condition as being satisfied in a world which is potentially different from the actual world.

Present and past time protases

Let us consider first cases where the time of the protasis situation is present or past, as in [33ii–iii]. Remote conditionals of this type generally implicate that *P* is false, or at least likely to be. And by the only-if implicature *Q* will likewise be false, or probably false. A salient context for [iiib], for example, is one where I know that he missed the opportunity of buying it at the price in question: *P* is false, the condition is not satisfied in the world as it actually is. I thus imagine a world differing from the actual one by virtue of *P* being true in that world, and draw conclusions about other features of this imaginary world – namely that *Q* is also true, that he got a bargain. Very often, we reason about the properties of worlds potentially different from the actual world in order to make inferences about the latter:

[34] *If Ed had been here at ten o'clock, it wouldn't have been possible for him to attend the departmental staff meeting at 10.30, as he did. So it wasn't Ed who committed the crime.*

I imagine a world in which Ed was here at ten o'clock: in this world (which I assume to be like the actual world in other respects as far as is consistent with Ed's being here at ten o'clock) he can't have been at the staff meeting. In the actual world he was, so the actual world must differ from the imaginary world with respect to the truth of *P*: in the actual world *P* must be false. And since (let us assume this to have been established) the crime was committed here at ten o'clock, it can't have been Ed who committed it.

It is important to emphasise, however, that a present or past time remote conditional does not entail that *P* is false (in the actual world): this is why we spoke above of the condition being satisfied in a world which is **potentially** different from the actual world. In the first place, it may well be that I don't know whether *P* is true or false:

[35] *I don't know whether he broke it or not, but I doubt it; if he had done he would probably have told her about it.*

Secondly, there is one use of the remote construction, not common but nevertheless clearly established, where I know or am confident that *P* is in fact true:

[36] *If he had escaped by jumping out of the window he would have left footprints in the flower-bed beneath. And that is precisely what we found.*

I begin by presenting the world in which he jumped out of the window as potentially different from the actual world. But it turns out that the consequential property *Q* obtains in the real world as well as the imaginary one – and the natural explanation for *Q* is *P*, so the inference is that *P* does in fact hold of the actual world. The strategy here, then, is to reconstruct what happened by working back from consequences to their causes.[25]

Note also that there are occasions where a remote conditional would be inappropriate even though I know that *P* is actually false:

[37] a. *If Grannie is here she is invisible.* b. *If Grannie were here she'd be invisible.*

The context here is one where someone has suggested that Grannie is here and I wish to pour scorn on the idea. This is achieved by the open conditional [a], where I show that that suggestion has an absurd consequence: since *Q* ("Grannie is invisible") is patently false, *P* ("She is here") must be false too. The rhetorical effect is drastically diminished in the remote version. Here I imagine a world differing from the actual one in that *P* is true. But once we envisage a world that differs in this respect from the actual one, the possibility arises that it could differ in other respects too: perhaps in this imaginary world people can be invisible. One can still argue from [b] that Grannie is not actually here (in the same way as one argues from [34] that Ed wasn't here at ten o'clock), but the demonstration is less immediate, less direct than in the open version. Similarly with [13] above: *If that's Princess Anne, I'm a Dutchman* is a conventional way of ridiculing the idea that that is Princess Anne, but we do not say #*If that were Princess Anne I would be a Dutchman.*

The remote construction is of course also inappropriate in those cases considered in §14.1.1 where the truth of *P* is contextually given, or self-evident:

[25] For this reason the commonly used term 'counterfactual conditional' is not an appropriate one for the grammatical class of remote conditionals (even if restricted to those with a past or present time protasis): it is best applied to **uses** of remote conditionals when the protasis situation is false.

[38] i a. *If our house was spacious, the place next door was immense.* b. *If our house had been spacious, the place next door would have been immense.*
ii a. *Even if you are my elder brother you haven't the right to tell me what to do.* b. *Even if you were my elder brother you wouldn't have the right to tell me what to do.*
iii a. *She's eighty if she's a day.* b. #*She'd be eighty if she were a day.*

Examples [ib] and [iib] are possible, but would not be used in a context where it is taken for granted that our house is spacious, or where I'm talking to my elder brother.

Future time protases

Where the time of the protasis is future, the remote conditional generally conveys that satisfaction of the condition in the actual world is relatively unlikely. In [33i], for example, the remote version suggests a lesser likelihood of his telling her than does the open one. And it is the remote construction that would normally be used following an assertion that the condition will not be satisfied:

[39] *He won't resign. If he did he would lose most of his superannuation entitlement.*

Again, however, unlikelihood is an implicature, and provides neither a necessary nor a sufficient condition for selecting the remote construction in preference to the open. Compare:

[40] i *I would be most grateful if you would/could give me the benefit of your advice.*
ii *If we offered you the post, when could you start?*
iii *If you die in a few minutes that was an overdose you just took.*

Example [i] does not convey that I regard it as unlikely that you will – much less that you can – give me the benefit of your advice. The reason for choosing the remote construction in such cases will generally be that it is considered more polite than the open version, *I will be most grateful if you will/can give me the benefit of your advice.* It is more polite in that it more clearly allows for your not wanting to give the advice. Similarly, [ii] does not convey that we are unlikely to offer you the post, though it remains somewhat less encouraging than its open counterpart with *offer* and *can.* On the other hand, the open conditional [iii] is perfectly consistent with a context in which I think it unlikely that you will die: the reason for preferring the open construction here is essentially the same as with [37] above. The remote *If you died in a few minutes that would have been an overdose you just took* conjures up a world potentially different from the actual one, but we don't want the issue to be confused by other possible differences between this imaginary world and the actual one. The issue is simply whether what you took was an overdose, and that can be settled by waiting to see whether you die in a few minutes in the actual world.

Only if and *even if*

The remote vs open contrast is the same in combination with *only* and *if* as in the examples given in [33]. Compare, then:

[41] i a. *I'll cook only if you clean up.* b. *I'd cook only if you cleaned up.*
ii a. *I'm going to the party even if Kim is going too.* b. *I'd be going to the party even if Kim was going too.*
iii a. *You'll have to repeat the whole year even if you fail just* ONE *exam.* b. *You'd have to repeat the whole year even if you failed just* ONE *exam.*

The open versions were discussed as [25i], [30i], and [31i] above. The remote [41ib] makes greater allowance for your not cleaning up than [ia], perhaps out of politeness/diffidence, perhaps because it seems unlikely that you will agree. But there's still an implicature that satisfaction of the condition will be sufficient to ensure that I cook. *Even* likewise has the same interpretation in the remote versions as in the open ones. Thus [iib] implicates that Kim is not going to the party, whereas [iia] leaves it open, but both versions convey that I am in fact going to the party. Example [iiib] suggests that your failing one exam is relatively unlikely, while [iiia] again leaves it open; both indicate that repetition will be required in the event of failure in one or more exams but not otherwise.

If only

Quite distinct from *only if* is the construction where *only* occurs in the protasis indicating something like a wish for the satisfaction of the condition:

[12] i *He would get a distinction if only he would buckle down to some hard work.*
ii *I could have solved the problem myself if only I'd had a little more time.*

The wish meaning is particularly evident when the apodosis is omitted: *If only I'd had a little more time!* In this idiomatic sense *if only* occurs predominantly in remote conditionals, but it is found also in the open type: *He'll get a distinction if he will only buckle down to some hard work.*

14.2.2 The form of remote conditionals

Tense and mood restrictions

The verb of the protasis must be the irrealis form *were* or a preterite with the modal remoteness meaning. The verb of the apodosis must be a modal auxiliary; this too must be a modally remote preterite, except where the modal has only a present tense form.

With 1st/3rd person singular subjects preterite *was* is somewhat informal in comparison with irrealis *were.* The most common modal auxiliaries occurring in the apodosis are *would, should, could,* and *might*; for other modal forms, see Ch. 3, §§5, 9.8.4.[26]

Protasis and apodosis times

As with open conditionals, all combinations of protasis and apodosis times are possible.

[43]		PROTASIS	APODOSIS
i	*If I went tomorrow, I would have more time in Paris.*	future	future
ii	*If they didn't carry out tomorrow's inspection after all we would be wasting our time cleaning up like this.*	future	present
iii	*If tomorrow's experiment didn't work, the Russians' original prediction would have been wholly accurate.*	future	past

[26] Philosophers sometimes use the terms 'indicative conditional' and 'subjunctive conditionals' for open and remote conditionals respectively. These terms reflect the way in which the distinction is characteristically marked in Latin, but in English it is marked quite differently. Given that the grammatical marking of the distinction varies considerably across languages, appropriate general terms should be based on the common meaning difference.

iv	*If you loved me you would come with me.*	present	future
v	*If she were here she would be in her office.*		present
vi	*If I were ill I would have stayed at home.*		past
vii	*If I had won the lottery I would buy a sports car.*	past	future
viii	*If I had followed your advice, I would be rich now.*		present
ix	*If Kim hadn't told her, I would have done so.*		past

The combination of a present or past apodosis with a future protasis, as in [ii–iii], is very rare. In [iii], for example, it would be more natural to say something like *would have been vindicated*: the vindication is future, simultaneous with the imagined failure of the experiment.

The preterite verb forms express modal remoteness, not past time; past time therefore has to be marked by the secondary past tense, the perfect, as shown by the underlining of ***have*** in [43]. In a past time apodosis, perfect ***have*** appears in the plain form following *would* (or other modal); in a past time protasis, perfect ***have*** itself carries the modal preterite inflection. A variant form for the protasis has *had've*: *If I had've followed your advice, I would be rich now*; we also find *I'd've*, etc., where it is debatable whether the *'d* might also be construed as a cliticised form of *would*. These variants are increasingly common in informal speech, but are still generally regarded as non-standard. The preterite perfect can also occur with future time reference: this is the doubly remote construction which we take up below.

The modal apodosis requirement

The fact that the apodosis must contain a modal auxiliary means that a high proportion of open conditionals do not have remote counterparts. Note, for example, that imperatives have the verb in the plain form, which excludes the possibility of a modal:

[44] a. *If it rains, bring the washing in.* b. [no remote counterpart]

Consider also the case of declaratives, as illustrated in:

[45]	i	a. *If Ed's still here, he'll be in his office.*	b. *If Ed were still here, he'd be in his office.*
	ii	a. *If Ed's still here, he's in his office.*	b. [no remote counterpart]
	iii	a. *If Jill didn't sign the cheque, her husband will have.*	b. *If Jill hadn't signed the cheque, her husband would have.*
	iv	a. *If Jill didn't sign the cheque, her husband did.*	b. [no remote counterpart]

In [i–ii] the time of the protasis is present. Version [ib] is the remote counterpart of [ia], with both apodoses containing modal ***will***; compare similarly *If Ed's still here he may be in his office* and *If Ed were still here he might be in his office*. In [iia] there is no modal in the apodosis and therefore no remote counterpart. In this case, there is relatively little difference between [ia] and [iia], and [ib] is commonly regarded as the remote version of [iia] (or of both [ia] and [iia]: grammars tend not to be very explicit on this point).

In [45iii–iv] the time of the protasis is past. The grammatical differences between the four versions are the same as in [i–ii], but this time there is a potentially greater pragmatic difference between [iiia] and [iva]. Suppose Jill and her husband have a bank account in their joint names with either of them able to sign cheques. Then if I know the cheque was signed (and have no reason to suspect forgery), I can say [iva]: there is no need for any modal qualification. The *will* in [iiia] suggests, therefore, that I don't actually know whether the cheque was signed. In [iiia], then, her husband's having signed the cheque doesn't follow so securely from Jill's not having done so as it does in [iva]. Now in [iiib] the salient interpretation is that Jill did in fact sign the cheque (i.e. that *P* is false). But I'm imagining a world in which she didn't, and in this imaginary world, I don't have the same grounds for concluding that her husband did sign it as I do in [iva], because it isn't necessarily a property of this world that the cheque was signed. In terms of the basis for concluding *Q* from *P*, therefore, [iiib] is closer to [iiia] than to [iva], and this correlates with the fact that it differs from [iiia] in only one respect (remote vs open), whereas it differs from [iva] in two (remote vs open, and presence vs absence of ***will*** in the apodosis). Note that it would be quite reasonable in the context proposed to take the view that [iva] was true while [iiib] was false.[27]

The open construction with ***will***, [45iiia], is not a common one: there are various other ways of expressing roughly the same meaning, e.g. by means of modal adjuncts such as *probably*, *surely*, etc. But these alternatives are not available in the remote construction because of the modal auxiliary requirement, so that the *would* construction is, by contrast, of very high frequency. The view taken here, however, is that this difference in frequency does not invalidate an analysis in which [iiib] is formally and semantically more closely or directly related to [iiia] than to [iva].

Protases with *be* + *to* and *should*

[46]	i	a. #*If it is to rain, I'll cancel the show.*	b. *If it were to rain, I'd cancel the show.*
	ii	a. *If Kim should die, Ed will take over.*	b. *If Kim should die, Ed would take over.*

There is an idiomatic use of what we call 'quasi-modal ***be***' that occurs only in remote conditionals like [ib]. In the open conditional *If we are to survive we'll have to drastically reduce expenditure* the protasis suggests purpose ("In order to survive, we'll have to drastically reduce expenditure"), which is why [ia] is pragmatically anomalous. In the remote conditional, this quasi-modal ***be*** serves merely to reinforce the remote meaning: the protasis of [ib] means "if it rained" but with a slightly stronger implicature of unlikelihood. It occurs predominantly in future time protases.[28] The examples in [ii] illustrate the special conditional use of *should*, which is found without any difference in the form of the protasis itself in both open and remote conditionals.

Omission of *if* and subject–auxiliary inversion

In the examples above, the protasis has the form of a PP with *if* as head and a content clause as complement; under certain conditions it can instead take the form of an ungoverned content clause with subject–auxiliary inversion:

[47] i <u>*Had I had any inkling of this,*</u> *I would have acted differently.*
ii <u>*Were that to happen*</u> *we would be in a very difficult situation.*

These are equivalent to *If I had had any inkling of this, . . .* and *If that were to happen, . . .* This construction is found mainly with *had* and *were*, though a few other auxiliaries are also possible (cf. Ch. 11, §4.7). It excludes negative verb-forms: *had Jill not signed the cheque*, but not **hadn't Jill signed the cheque.* It is restricted to remote conditionals

[27] This point reinforces what was said above in connection with [37], *If Grannie is here she's invisible* and *If Grannie were here she'd be invisible.* See also the discussion in Ch. 3, §9.8.3, of the contrast between *If Oswald didn't shoot Kennedy someone else did* and *If Oswald hadn't shot Kennedy someone else would have.*

[28] Another use of ***be*** that is restricted to remote conditionals is seen in *If it hadn't* <u>*been*</u> *for you, I would have missed the train*: "but for you".

except that the special conditional *should* allows inversion in both open and remote constructions. *If Kim should die*, for example, is replaceable by *should Kim die* in [46iia] as well as [iib].

The doubly remote conditional construction

[48] i *If you had told me you were busy I would have come tomorrow.*
ii *If you had come tomorrow you would have seen the carnival.*
iii *If your father had been alive today he would have been distraught to see his business disintegrating like this.*

Ordinary remote conditionals have preterite tenses (or irrealis mood) expressing modal remoteness, not past time. In [48] the underlined perfect auxiliaries ***have*** also express modal rather than temporal meaning. In [i] the apodosis situation is future; in [ii] both protasis and apodosis situations are future; and in [iii] both situations are located in present time. We refer to this, therefore, as the **doubly remote conditional**: the remoteness is signalled twice, once by the preterite inflection, once by perfect ***have***.

Where the time is future the doubly remote construction indicates not only that *P* and *Q* are false, but also that the possibility of the future situation being actualised has already been foreclosed by a past event. In [i–ii], for example, it might be that I or you have come today, with the assumption that that precludes our coming again tomorrow.

Modal preterites vs other preterites

There may be ambiguity between a remote conditional and an open one with preterites expressing past time rather than modal remoteness:

[49] *If we weren't home by ten o'clock the landlady would lock us out.*

This can be a remote conditional corresponding to the open *If we aren't home by ten o'clock the landlady will lock us out.* In this case the salient interpretation refers to a singulary situation in the future (cf. *If we weren't home by ten o'clock tonight, . . .*). But [49] can also be an open conditional expressing a multiple situation in the past: "Whenever we weren't home by ten o'clock, . . . ". With a non-modal apodosis such as *the landlady locked us out* only the open reading is possible – and an irrealis protasis such as *if I weren't home by ten o'clock* permits only the remote reading. The meaning contrast is very sharp: it is a clear case of ambiguity.

Less straightforward is the distinction between a preterite marking a remote conditional and one that arises through backshift. Compare:

[50] i *He said that if they were convicted they would be liable to a life sentence.*
ii *He said that if Sue hadn't signed the cheque her husband would have.*

Here [i] could be a backshifted report of the open conditional *If they are convicted they will be liable to a life sentence* or a report (necessarily without backshift) of remote *If they were convicted they would be liable to a life sentence.* Example [ii] could likewise be a backshifted report of open *If Sue didn't sign / hasn't signed the cheque her husband will have* or a non-backshifted report of remote *If Sue hadn't signed the cheque her husband would have.* But it can also be a backshifted report of remote *If Sue didn't sign the cheque her husband would.* In cases like [50] the meaning differences are much more subtle than in [49], a matter of the modality of the conditional rather than of time; it is likely that speakers will in many cases be unaware of the fact that the grammar makes available these different interpretations.

Mixed constructions

In some cases we find a modal preterite in the protasis but not in the apodosis:

[51] i *If you needed some help, Helen is willing to lend a hand.*
ii *I'll come on Tuesday if that would suit you better.*

Example [i] has what we have called a relevance protasis: it is the remote counterpart of [6i] above (*If you need some help, Helen is willing to lend a hand*). It doesn't look like a remote conditional because the apodosis doesn't have a preterite verb, but if we fill in the unexpressed superordinate structure we get the usual form for a remote apodosis: *If you needed some help, you would be interested to know that Helen is willing to lend a hand.* The remote version would be pragmatically more likely with past time reference: *If you'd needed some help, Helen was willing to lend a hand.* In [ii] we have an implicit remote conditional embedded within an open one: "I will come on Tuesday if it would suit you better if I came on Tuesday". The overt protasis in [ii] contains a modal auxiliary and hence belongs with the type illustrated in [20].

14.3 *Unless*

Unless occurs in open conditionals and, less freely, remote ones:

[52]	i	*The report will be ready soon* <u>*unless*</u> *the printer breaks down again.*	[open]
	ii	*He will be in London now,* <u>*unless*</u> *the plane was delayed.*	
	iii	*She always cycled to work* <u>*unless*</u> *it was raining.*	
	iv	*I wouldn't suggest such a plan* <u>*unless*</u> *I thought it was feasible.*	[remote]

Unless means "except if" or, more explicitly, "in all circumstances except if". *Q unless P* thus has the following entailments:

[53] a. If not-*P*, then *Q*. b. If *P*, then not-*Q*.

In other words, not-*P* is a sufficient and necessary condition for *Q*. For example, [52i] entails that if the printer doesn't break down again the report will be ready soon and that if the printer does break down again the report won't be ready soon. The implicature of the remote version, as in [iv], is that not-*P* is false or probably false: [iv] conveys that I do think it is feasible.

An *unless* conditional is often pragmatically equivalent to an *if* conditional with a negative protasis. Compare [52i], for example, with:

[54] *The report will be ready soon if the printer doesn't break down again.*

If we take *P* and *Q* to have the same values as in [52i] (i.e. *P* = "the printer breaks down again", *Q* = "the report will be ready soon"), then [54] clearly expresses component [a] of [53]: if not-*P*, then *Q*. The [b] component – If *P*, then not-*Q* – comes from what we have called the only-if implicature – hence the pragmatic equivalence between *Q unless P* and *Q if not P*. But there are numerous differences between the two constructions, many places where *unless* cannot replace *if not* and a few where *if not* can't replace *unless*.

Where *if not* cannot be replaced by *unless*

[55] i *We're going to the beach this week-end <u>if it doesn't rain</u> – and indeed we may still go even if it does.*
ii *<u>If it wasn't exactly a bargain</u>, it wasn't unreasonably expensive either.*
iii *I'm cancelling the order <u>if the goods aren't ready yet</u>.*
iv *Will you be going to the beach <u>if it isn't fine</u> / <u>if it isn't raining</u>?*
v *It'll be better <u>if you don't say where you're going</u>.*
vi *<u>If Philip doesn't find a better job and if Paula doesn't get a substantial pay-rise</u>, they won't be able to pay the mortgage.*
vii *I'll invite Jill <u>only/even if Kim isn't coming</u>.*

Examples [i–ii] are cases where the only-if implicature doesn't apply: they are therefore inconsistent with the meaning of *unless*. The inadmissibility of *unless* in [iii] is due to *yet*, a non-affirmative item. While *yet* is permitted in the "If not-*P*, then *Q*" part of the meaning of *unless* conditionals (the part expressed in [55iii]), it is not compatible with the other component, "If *P*, then not-*Q*": **If the goods are ready yet I'm not cancelling the order*. In [iv] the conditional adjunct falls within the scope of a question – but the question relates only to the "If not-*P*, then *Q*" component, not to "If *P*, then not-*Q*". *Unless* is not wholly excluded from questions, but it occurs only in biased ones, such as *How can you ever face them again unless you apologise?*, which conveys that I think you won't be able to face them again unless you apologise. Example [v] involves a comparison between the current state of affairs and one in which the condition is satisfied: again, then, it is only the "If not-*P*, then *Q*" component that is of concern. The inability of *unless* to substitute for *if not* in [vi–vii] matches the general behaviour of *except*. For [vi] compare **Unless Philip finds a better job and unless Paula gets a substantial pay-rise, they won't be able to pay the mortgage* and **They've questioned everybody except Kim and except Pat*. Instead the coordination has to be within the complement of the preposition: *unless Philip finds a better job and Paula gets a substantial pay-rise* and *except Kim and Pat*. Similarly, [vii] may be compared with **They are inviting only / even everybody except Jill*.

Where *unless* can't be replaced by *if not*

[56] i *I'm going climbing tomorrow <u>unless it's wet</u>, in which case I'll do my tax-return.*
ii *We can go now <u>unless you would rather wait till it stops raining</u>.*

In [i] *in which case* is a relative phrase with the positive clause *it's wet* as its antecedent: the relative clause is interpreted as "If it is wet I'll do my tax-return". The version with *if it's not wet* as adjunct has a negative subordinate clause and hence would not provide the appropriate antecedent. In [ii] *would rather* is a positively oriented polarity-sensitive item: it is not normally possible with negatives, and hence not with *if not*.

14.4 Other explicitly or implicitly conditional constructions

(a) Reduction of the complement of the conditional preposition

We have been concerned so far with constructions where *if* (or *unless*) has a full content clause as complement. Other possibilities are illustrated in:

[57] i *This product will/would stay fresh for two weeks, <u>if kept refrigerated</u>.*
ii *There'll probably be a vacancy in June; <u>if so</u>, we'll let you know.*
iii *We may be able to finish tomorrow; <u>if not</u> it will certainly be done by Friday.*

iv *You won't get your money till next month, if then.*
v *Some, if not all, of your colleagues will disagree with that view.*
vi *We'll get it finished by tomorrow if necessary/possible.*

In [i] the protasis has the form of a past-participial. This is found in both open and remote constructions: the full versions would be *if it is kept refrigerated* and *if it were kept refrigerated.* Past-participials are found also with *unless*: *Do not take any further action unless requested to do so.* In [ii–iii] the protasis is a pro-form standing for a clause (cf. Ch. 17, §7.7.2) with *so* positive and *not* its negative counterpart. *If so* is interpreted as "if there is a vacancy in June", *if not* as "if we aren't able to finish tomorrow". Examples [iv–v] illustrate the construction where an *if* phrase serves to cancel an implicature of the apodosis. On its own, *you won't get your money till next month,* for example, implicates that you will get your money next month: *if then* indicates that you may not get it even then. In [vi] the protasis is an AdjP headed by one or other of the modal adjectives *necessary* and *possible.* They can be modified (*if absolutely necessary*, *if at all possible*), but not replaced by other adjectives (**if useful*). The understood clausal subject can be reconstructed from the apodosis: "if getting it finished by tomorrow is necessary/possible".

Condition and concession

With other predicative elements than *necessary* and *possible*, the adjunct may have a concessive interpretation. Compare:

[58] i *The house is sumptuous, if slightly smaller than we'd have liked.*
ii *She is bright, if not a genius.*

Example [i] has only a concessive reading, with *if* equivalent to *though.* In [ii], where both apodosis and protasis contain related scalar predicatives and the protasis is negative, two clearly distinct interpretations are available. One is concessive, matching that of [i]: "She is bright, though she is not a genius". The other is conditional: it can be glossed as "She is bright, perhaps even a genius" or "If she is not a genius, she is at least bright". In the concessive reading *P* is assumed to be true, while the conditional reading leaves it open whether *P* is true or false.

If only

[59] i *I'll go with them, if only to get some exercise.*
ii *It was hard work, if only because of the searing heat.*

There is a use of *if only* distinct from that considered in §14.1.3 above, one where the scopal focus of *only* is a single element of clause structure – a purpose adjunct in [i], a reason adjunct in [ii]. Example [i] says that I will go with them, but concedes that my only purpose might be to get some exercise. Similarly [ii] says it was hard work, though maybe the only reason was that it was so hot. The same meaning can be expressed by the form *if for no other reason than . . .*

(b) *If . . . then*

When placed at the front of the matrix an *if* adjunct is often followed by a correlative *then*, especially in cases where the connection is inferential:

[60] *If it wasn't Jill who left the gate open then it must have been Nat.*

This *then* occurs predominantly in main clauses; in embedded contexts it is often of questionable acceptability: ?*Since if it wasn't Jill who left the gate open, then it must have been Nat, we'd better call him in for questioning.*

(c) Other items governing content clause protases

A handful of words or expressions can be used instead of *if* in conditional adjuncts:

[61] i *provided* *as/so long as* –T *on condition*
ii *assuming* *supposing* *in the event* *in case* –T

[62] i *The meeting will start at 5.30, provided (that) there is a quorum.*
ii *You can go wherever you like, as long as you are back by 7.*
iii *You may borrow the book on condition (that) you return it tonight.*
iv *Assuming (that) everybody agrees, the project will get under way next month.*
v *The announcement would look well in 'The Times', supposing (that) one were to waste money in that way.*
vi *In the event (that) they are again indicted their case will be randomly assigned to a federal judge.*
vii *You can call this toll-free number in case you need emergency service.*

Items in [61] marked '–T' exclude the subordinator *that* in the content clause; with the others it is optional. The underlined expressions in [i–iii] express necessary and sufficient conditions: they are equivalent to *if and only if. Assuming* and *supposing* are verbs heading gerund-participial clauses. The conditional use of *in case* is rare (especially in BrE) in comparison with its use as head of a reason adjunct (with an implicature of purpose): *Many shoppers are starting to hold back on spending in case the economy falters*, "because of / to guard against the possibility that the economy might falter". The close relation between the two uses is seen in an example like:

[63] *All major airlines that travel between Canada and Britain have contingency plans to reroute airplanes in case negotiations fail.*

The *in case* phrase can be construed as a reason adjunct in the *have* clause (saying why they have contingency plans), or a conditional adjunct in the *reroute* clause (giving the condition under which the planes would be rerouted).

(d) Constructions with phrases rather than clauses

The expressions *in the event* and *in case* from [61] can license PP complements as well as content clauses (*In the event of a tie, the chair shall have a casting vote*) – and the verb *assuming* can take an NP (*assuming favourable weather*, "if the weather is favourable"). Other conditional expressions taking phrasal complements include *barring* and *but* + *for* (this latter occurring in the remote construction), and there are also PPs whose conditional role derives from the meaning of a noun contained within them, such as *case* or *condition*:

[64] i *Barring any further delays, the project should be completed on time.*
ii *But for this hitch, the project would have been completed on time.*
iii *In that case / On that condition I will / would accept your offer.*

(e) Relative constructions with conditional interpretations

[65] i *Anyone who thinks they can take advantage of us will be disappointed.*
ii *Anyone who thought they could take advantage of us would be disappointed.*

Constructions where a relative clause is embedded within an NP with *any* as determiner can be paraphrased by conditional constructions: *If anyone thinks they can take advantage of us, they will be disappointed.* It is just possible to have modal preterites in the relative and matrix clauses, as in [ii], which corresponds to the remote conditional *If anyone thought they could take advantage of us they would be mistaken.*

(f) Coordinate and juxtaposed constructions with conditional interpretations

[66] i *Say that again and you're fired.*
ii *Ask them to stay after five, they'll demand 50% overtime.*
iii *One more remark like that and you're fired.*
iv *Hurry up or we'll miss the train.*
v *Either you agree to my terms or the deal is off.*
vi *Suppose I had the same number of peas as there are atoms in my body, how large an area would they cover?*

Constructions such as these do not have the form or literal meaning of conditionals, but they serve indirectly to convey conditional meaning. In [i] we have an *and*-coordination where the first coordinate is an imperative; it is not taken as a directive to say that again, however, but as a conditional threat: "If you say that again you're fired". Example [ii] is similar except that the clauses are merely juxtaposed rather than coordinated: "If you ask them to stay after five they'll demand 50% overtime". In [iii] the first coordinate is simply an NP, but we understand "If you make one more remark like that, you're fired". In [iv] the coordinator is *or*, and this time the implicated conditional is arrived at by negating the first coordinate: "If you don't hurry up, we'll miss the train". Similarly in [v], where the first coordinate is declarative: "If you don't agree to my terms the deal is off". (See Ch. 10, §9.5, and Ch. 15, §§2.2.3–4, for further analysis of such indirect speech acts.)

Example [66vi] illustrates a special use of the verb *suppose*. The first clause is again syntactically imperative, but it is pragmatically equivalent to an *if* phrase: "If I had the same number of peas as there are atoms in my body, how large an area would they cover?" The clause following the imperative *suppose* clause is characteristically interrogative. Indeed, the *suppose* clause often stands on its own with question force: *Suppose I hadn't brought along enough money?*, "What would we do if I hadn't brought along enough money?" *Supposing* is often used in this way too: *Supposing he was seen?*, "What would happen if he was seen?"

(g) NPs

[67] i *The appointment of his nephew as finance minister will/would be a mistake.*
ii *A ban on federal funding for stem cell research will/would be very damaging.*
iii *Any contribution towards defraying our costs will/would be most appreciated.*
iv *With another $100,000 he will/would be able to buy that luxurious town-house.*

The NPs functioning as subject in [i–iii] and complement of *with* in [iv] do not refer to any actual appointment, ban, contribution, or sum of money, and the clauses are again interpreted as conditionals – open or remote according to the form of the verb. Example [i], for instance, can be glossed as "If his nephew is appointed finance minister, this will be a mistake" (open) or "If his nephew were appointed finance minister, this would be a mistake" (remote). Compare [iv] with non-conditional *With the $500,000 inherited from his father he bought a luxurious town-house*, where the underlined NP is referential.

14.5 Scope, focus, and stacking

A conditional adjunct generally has scope over a negative in the matrix, but there are also cases where the negative has scope over the adjunct. Compare, then:

[68] i *We won't go bankrupt if we budget carefully.* [wide scope adjunct]
ii *We won't go bankrupt if we get the carpets cleaned.* [wide scope negative]

We understand from [i] that our not going bankrupt will be a consequence of our budgeting carefully; the negative is entirely within the apodosis, and we could substitute a pragmatically equivalent positive: *We will overcome our financial problems if we budget carefully.* But the interpretation of [ii] is that going bankrupt will not be a consequence of getting the carpets cleaned. Example [i] can be analysed as "If *P*, then *Q*", where *Q* happens to be negative, but [ii] has the meaning "not [If *P*, then *Q*]".[29] In [ii] *if* could be replaced by *because.* Wide scope negation is not possible with *only/even if*, *unless*, or *provided.*

Because conditional adjuncts generally have wide scope, they do not readily occur as focus in alternative questions, contrastive negation, or clefts:

[69] i *Do you fill in this form if you're a citizen or if you're an alien?*
ii *Here you don't get promoted if you show initiative but if you put in long hours.*
iii *It's if Herbert is appointed that I foresee trouble.*

Such constructions tend to be avoided in favour of non-conditionals – e.g. *Is this form for citizens or for aliens?*; *Here you don't get promoted for showing initiative but for putting in long hours*; etc. The cleft type is greatly improved by the addition of *only*: *It's only if Herbert is appointed that I foresee trouble. Unless* is impossible in all three constructions.

There is no interrogative word with conditional meaning: questioning requires a PP containing a noun with the appropriate meaning: *Under what conditions / On what terms would you agree to sell?*

Stacking

The conditional construction is recursive in that an *if* phrase can occur at successive layers in the constituent hierarchy:

[70] *If the proposal is adopted prisoners will be entitled to a personal TV set if they enrol for a course at the Open University.*

If the proposal is adopted functions at the first layer, having scope over the rest of the sentence, while *if they enrol for a course at the Open University* functions at the second layer, modifying *prisoners will be entitled to a personal TV.* Recursion of this kind is known as **stacking**. Stacking of conditional adjuncts is comparatively rare: the resultant construction tends to be somewhat hard to process, especially if the conditional adjuncts are adjacent.

[29] This then is one of the cases alluded to in footnote 20, where the grammatical apodosis doesn't match the logical consequent: *we won't go bankrupt* is the apodosis but it doesn't express the consequent. Another case is that where the conditional adjunct is within the scope of the quantification implied in a multiple situation as in [16], *She cycled to work if she got up early enough.*

14.6 Exhaustive conditionals

The exhaustive conditional construction is illustrated in:

[71]	GOVERNED	UNGOVERNED
i	a. *I'm buying it* [*regardless of whether we can really afford it (or not)*].	b. *I'm buying it* [*whether we can really afford it or not*].
ii	a. *The business will fail* [*no matter who takes over as manager*].	b. *The business will fail* [*whoever takes over as manager*].

Both versions of [i] are equivalent to *I'm buying it if we can really afford it and I'm buying it if we can't really afford it*: I'm buying it under either of these two conditions. These two conditions constitute an exhaustive set: one of them must be satisfied. This is the motivation for applying the term **exhaustive conditional** to this construction. This type of adjunct is semantically non-restrictive (i.e. it can be dropped without affecting the truth of the proposition expressed): [ia/b] both entail that I'm buying it.

All four of the examples in [71] contain a subordinate clause, but in [ia/iia] the subordinate clause is complement of a preposition while in [ib/iib] it functions immediately, directly, as an adjunct in clause structure. We will therefore distinguish these two subtypes of exhaustive conditional as respectively **governed** and **ungoverned**. We will look first at the syntactically more straightforward governed construction, and then return to the ungoverned one in §14.6.2.

14.6.1 The governed construction

Here the adjunct has as head one of the items in [72]:

[72] *independently* *irrespective* *regardless* *no matter*

Independently is an adverb, *irrespective* and *regardless* (as used here) prepositions, while *no matter* is an idiom with the form of an NP which might be regarded as having been reanalysed as a preposition. *No matter* takes a subordinate clause as complement, as in [71iia], while the others normally take *of* + subordinate clause, as in [ia].

The subordinate clauses are uncontroversially interrogative. They can be either closed, marked by *whether*, or open, marked by one of the interrogative words *who*, *what*, *which*, *when*, *where*, etc. By virtue of the meaning of the items in [72] the adjunct indicates that the answer to the question corresponding to the subordinate interrogative has no bearing on the matrix. Thus [71ia], with a closed interrogative, allows for two possibilities, one where we can afford it, one where we can't, but in either case I'm buying it. The open interrogative in [iia] allows for an open-ended set of possibilities, one for each possible new manager, but in any of these cases the business will fail.

The exhaustiveness presupposition

The answers to the question corresponding to the interrogative clause define an exhaustive set of cases in the sense that one of them must apply. For example, [71iia] presupposes that someone will take over as manager, just like the corresponding question "Who will take over as manager?" Or consider such an example as *I'll be attending the meeting regardless of whether it is held on Thursday or Friday.* In one salient interpretation the interrogative corresponds to the alternative question "Will the meeting be held on Thursday or Friday?", where the answers are "Thursday" and "Friday". Although there are in principle other possible days, the presupposition here is that the meeting will in fact be held on one or other of these two days, so again all real possibilities are provided for, and it follows that I will be attending the meeting.

Definite NP complement in lieu of open interrogative clause

[73] *I'm buying it [regardless of what the price is] / [regardless of the price].*

We also find definite NPs in the governed construction. The alternation seen in [73] is the same as we have in other environments permitting subordinate interrogatives: *I don't know what the price is / the price.* The NP is interpreted in the same way as the interrogative, and for this reason it is sometimes referred to as a 'concealed question' (cf. Ch. 11, §5.3).

14.6.2 The ungoverned construction

Here the adjunct has the form of a subordinate clause (or clause-coordination). The syntactic analysis of these clauses is discussed in Ch. 11, §5.3.6, where it is argued that they are best treated as interrogative, with the open type, however, displaying significant formal resemblances to fused relatives, giving them something of the character of a relative–interrogative blend. The exhaustive conditional is the only place where interrogative clauses function as adjunct rather than complement.

The closed type

Closed interrogatives in the ungoverned construction are a subset of those found in the governed one: they must contain an *or*-coordination. Compare:

[74]	GOVERNED	UNGOVERNED
i	a. *I'm buying it [regardless of whether we can afford it].*	b. **I'm buying it [whether we can afford it].*
ii	a. *I'm buying it [regardless of whether we can afford it or not].*	b. *I'm buying it [whether we can afford it or not].*
iii	a. *He'll resign [regardless of whether he is found guilty or innocent].*	b. *He'll resign [whether he is found guilty or innocent].*

Closed interrogatives characteristically express questions that can be distinguished as polar or alternative on the basis of how they define the set of answers (cf. Ch. 10, §§4.3–5). Compare the main clauses:

[75] i *Can we afford it?* [polar]
ii *Can we afford it or not?* } [alternative]
iii *Will he be found guilty or innocent?* }

The answers to a polar question consist of the proposition expressed in the question itself together with its polar opposite. The answers to the question in [i], for example, are "We can afford it" and "We can't afford it". The answers to an alternative question are all expressed in the question itself: it contains an *or*-coordination where each coordinate represents one answer. In the case of [iii], for example, the answers are "He will be found guilty" and "He will be found innocent". Example [ii] belongs with [iii] rather than [i] in that the answers are given by the coordinates linked by *or*, just as they are in [iii].

The constraint that excludes [74ib] while allowing [74iib/iiib] can therefore be stated as follows:

[76] The closed interrogative in the ungoverned construction must correspond to an alternative question.

The presence of an *or*-coordination is not itself sufficient. *Will one or other of your colleagues be elected?*, for example, can only express a polar question: the answers are "Yes, one or other of them will be elected" and "No, one or other of them won't be elected", not "One of them will be elected" and "*Other of them will be elected". The corresponding ungoverned exhaustive conditional is therefore excluded: **I'll be happy whether one or other of your colleagues is elected.*

It should also be noted that in the alternative question type, the interrogative subordinator can only be *whether*, not *if*. In conditionals, *if* can only have its primary, conditional meaning, so that *I won't serve on the committee if you're on it or if I'd be expected to chair it* does not belong to the exhaustive conditional construction. *If* is excluded from the governed construction too, but that follows from the general rule that *whether* is normally required in closed interrogatives functioning as complement of a preposition.

The open type

In the open construction there is a major difference in form between the governed and ungoverned subordinate clauses: the interrogative word in the latter is compounded with ·*ever*. Elsewhere *ever* is associated with interrogative words only in an emotive sense (and is usually though not always written as a separate word), but in the exhaustive conditional it has a 'free choice' sense. Compare:

[77]	i	*What ever did she give him?*	[emotive *ever*]
	ii	*Whatever she gave him, he grumbled.*	[free choice *ever*]

In [i] *ever* is comparable to *on earth* and suchlike expressions, whereas in [ii] the meaning is comparable to that of *any* in its free choice sense: for any value of *x* in "she gave him *x*", he grumbled.[30] In the governed construction this free choice meaning is expressed by the governing item, *regardless, irrespective, no matter, independently*; in the ungoverned construction it is expressed within the interrogative word. The meaning of [ii] is thus the same as that of *No matter what she gave him, he grumbled.*

Relationship with fused relatives

Free choice ·*ever*, we have noted, does not appear elsewhere in interrogative clauses, but it is found in fused relatives. In terms of its form the ungoverned open exhaustive conditional resembles a fused relative, but it differs sharply in its external syntax and meaning. Compare:

[78]	i	a.	*The business will fail whoever takes over as manager.*	[conditional]
		b.	*Whoever takes over as manager will have a hard job ahead.*	[fused relative]
	ii	a.	*Whatever she gave him, he grumbled.*	[conditional]
		b.	*Whatever she gave him he devoured voraciously.*	[fused relative]

In [i], the conditional is a clause functioning as adjunct while the fused relative is an NP functioning as subject. Unlike the conditional, the fused relative here denotes a person: it

[30] The matrix may restrict the range to which the free choice applies, as in *Whatever (else) that bird is, it isn't a kookaburra.* The implicature here is that I don't know what the bird is, but I do know it isn't a kookaburra.

might be roughly analysed as "the/any person *x* such that *x* takes over as manager". Unlike the fused relative, the conditional contrasts on one dimension with a closed interrogative (cf. *The business will fail whether Smith or Jones takes over as manager*) and on another with a governed construction containing an open interrogative (cf. *The business will fail irrespective of who takes over as manager*). Similarly in [ii]; here the fused relative is interpreted (by virtue of its relation to the matrix verb *devour*) as denoting food. We noted in §14.4 a close relationship between (non-fused) relative constructions containing free choice *any* and ordinary conditionals, and there is likewise a close relationship between fused relatives with free choice ·*ever* and exhaustive conditionals. Thus [ib] is equivalent to *The person, whoever it is, who takes over as manager will have a hard job ahead*, where the underlined sequence is an interrogative in exhaustive conditional function.

With *wherever* and *whenever* the difference in meaning between the exhaustive conditional and fused relative constructions is less obvious but nonetheless real:

[79] i a. *You must get this message to him, wherever he is.* [conditional]
b. *Put it back wherever you found it.* [fused relative]
ii a. *I'm determined to go to the wedding, whenever it is.* [conditional]
b. *He blushes whenever he sees her.* [fused relative]

Example [ia] means "Irrespective of where he is, you must get this message to him", while [ib] means "Put it back in the place where you found it". Similarly [iia] means "I'm determined to go to the wedding, no matter when it is held", and [iib] means "He blushes on any occasion when he sees her".

Restricted range of interrogative words

[80] i **Whyever he behaved as he did, he owes us an apology.*
ii *Regardless of why he behaved as he did, he owes us an apology.*

Free choice ·*ever* cannot combine with *why* in ungoverned exhaustive conditionals any more than it can in fused relatives; in [80], therefore, only the governed version is available. The ungoverned conditional further resembles the fused relative in that it allows only one ·*ever* compound (except in coordination).

14.6.3 Further issues

Reduction of the subordinate clause

[81] i a. *However arbitrary the decision, you can't change it.*
b. *Such proposals, however promising, must be uncompromisingly rejected.*
ii a. *Whether eaten raw or cooked, fennel is good for you.*
b. *Whether intentionally or not, she had deeply offended him.*

The subordinate clause may be reduced to a non-finite or verbless construction. Example [ia] is reduced by the omission of the verb *be* to a structure consisting of predicative + subject, while the subordinate clause in [ib] consists just of the predicative element: we understand "however promising they might be". The adjunct in [iia] is a past-participial, while that in [iib] is verbless. These examples are of the ungoverned construction; to a lesser extent reduction is found also in the governed construction, especially with *no matter* (cf. *Such proposals, no matter how promising, must be uncompromisingly rejected*).[31]

[31] *No matter* also allows the interrogative to be reduced idiomatically to *what*: *He wouldn't go back, no matter what*, "no matter what might happen".

Subjunctive form and modal *may*

The subordinate clause in an exhaustive conditional may have subjunctive form:

[82] i *Whenever and wherever a number of human beings are gathered for a common purpose – whether it be a sporting club or a multinational corporation, a Kindergarten committee or a state – there will inevitably be a struggle for power.*
ii *Whatever republican model be proposed, it is unlikely to be approved at the referendum.*
iii *There isn't a single state-subsidised company, be it drama or opera or dance, that is not in a state of crisis.*

This construction belongs to relatively formal style and is virtually restricted to the verb *be*, but within those limitations it is by no means uncommon, especially in the ungoverned construction, as in these examples. As illustrated in [iii], an alternant of the *whether* construction with *be* has inversion instead of a subordinator.[32] The structural relation between *whether it be good or bad* and *be it good or bad* is comparable to that between *if it were possible* and *were it possible.*

The variable question construction very often contains the epistemic modal ***may***:

[83] *Whatever people may say, my mind is made up.*

The possibility meaning of ***may*** ties in with the fact that all possible answers to the question "What will/do people say?" are allowed for.

Remote exhaustive conditionals

All our examples so far have been of open conditionals; the remote construction is also possible, though quite rare:

[84] *[Whatever / Irrespective of what we had decided,] someone would have objected.*

Analogous constructions

[85] i *It doesn't matter what we say: he's going to give up the course anyway.*
ii *Believe it or not, Eric has been short-listed for a managerial position.*
iii *Say what you like: it's a big improvement on his last effort.*

Example [i] is equivalent to *No matter what we say / Whatever we say, he's going to give up the course (anyway)*, but *it doesn't matter what we say* is a main clause, not an adjunct embedded within a matrix clause. Similarly in [ii–iii], where the underlined element is an imperative; they can be glossed as "whether you believe it or not" and "whatever you say".

15 **Domain adjuncts**

Adjuncts of this kind restrict the domain to which the rest of the clause applies:

[1] i *Economically, the country is in sharp decline.*
ii *Officially, we shouldn't really be discussing the matter.*
iii *As far as the law is concerned, what he did is not a crime.*
iv *From a linguistic point of view, there are no primitive languages.*

[32] Compare also the idiomatic historical relic *come what may* (with a fused relative as subject of *come*), "whatever happens".

Example [i] does not entail that the country is in sharp decline: it might be, for example, that the country's cultural life is flourishing. The property of being in sharp decline is thus ascribed to the country only with respect to the economic domain. The clause usually expresses a state, but occurrences are not excluded, as in *From an economic perspective, we acted foolishly.*

Realisation

Domain adjuncts generally have the form of AdvPs or PPs of the following kinds:

[2] i AdvP *morally, weatherwise*
ii PP *from a moral point of view / perspective, as far as the weather (is concerned), as regards the weather, regarding the weather, with respect to the weather*

Adverbs are mostly derived from adjectives by suffixation of ·*ly* (or ·*ally*), but there are also (especially in AmE) those formed from nouns by suffixation of ·*wise*. Domain adverbs are not gradable and cannot be lexically negated: *very morally* and *immorally*, for example, do not function as domain adjuncts. Clauses with a de-adjectival adverb as domain adjunct cannot be paraphrased by clauses with a predicative adjective applying to a clausal subject: compare [1i] with **It is economic that the country is in sharp decline.* Omission of *be concerned* from the PP frame *as far as... be concerned* is increasingly common in speech: *We're a lot better off than we were, as far as conditions of work*; *As far as dealing with teenagers, he doesn't have a clue.* This construction is still widely condemned by prescriptivists, and generally avoided in formal style.

In addition to AdvPs and PPs of the above kinds, we also find gerund-participials and past-participials with appropriate verbs: *economically speaking, speaking economically, considering the matter from an economic point of view, considered / looked at from an economic perspective*, and so on. There are also adjuncts belonging to other semantic categories which simultaneously serve to restrict the domain, notably adjuncts of spatial location and a narrow range of conditional constructions:

[3] i *In this country giving bribes to secure foreign contracts is permitted.*
ii *If we consider the matter from an economic point of view, the country is in sharp decline.*

Omitting *in this country* from [i] would result in a statement understood to apply universally: it is for this reason that the adjunct can be regarded as defining the domain to which the residue applies rather than merely adding a specification of location.

Focus and questioning

Domain adjuncts can be the focus of a question, of negation, and in a cleft construction, and the PP type allows for occasional questioning:

[4] i *Can the country stand on its own feet economically?*
ii *Linguistically but not ethnically the inhabitants have much in common with their northern neighbours.*
iii *It is only from an economic-rationalist viewpoint that the policy is defensible.*
iv *From what point of view, then, do you think the country is in decline?*

16 **Modal adjuncts**

Kinds of modality

Adverbs such as *necessarily*, *probably*, *possibly*, *surely* belong among the quite diverse set of forms expressing modal meaning (see Ch. 3, §9.1). Other items in the set include verbs, especially the modal auxiliaries, and adjectives, such as *necessary*, *probable*, etc. Verbs function as predicator, and in complement position adjectives too are predicative, so in these two cases the modality is expressed by means of predication, whereas the adverbs typically involve modification. Compare:

[1]		MODAL PREDICATION	MODAL MODIFICATION
	i	a. *He must have made a mistake.*	b. *He has surely made a mistake.*
	ii	a. *They should be in Berlin by now.*	b. *They are probably in Berlin by now.*
	iii	a. *It is possible that they are related.*	b. *They are possibly related.*

The adjunct may indeed combine with a verb in what we have called modal harmony, i.e. with dual or reinforced expression of a single modal meaning: *He must surely have made a mistake*; *They should probably be in Berlin by now.*

We saw in Ch. 3, §9, that modal auxiliaries can be used to express a range of different kinds of modality, epistemic, deontic, or dynamic. Modal adjuncts, however, are predominantly used for epistemic modality, where it is a matter of the speaker's assessment of the truth of the proposition expressed in the residue or the nature of the speaker's commitment to its truth. Modal adjuncts are not used to express deontic modality (obligation, permission, etc.). Compare, for example:

[2]			
	i	a. *You must return it to her tomorrow.*	b. *You surely return it to her tomorrow.*
	ii	a. *He can/may stay until six.*	b. *Possibly he stays until six.*

In the salient interpretation of [ia] I impose on you the obligation to return it to her tomorrow, but [ib] cannot have this deontic meaning: *surely* has an epistemic meaning and the present tense is interpreted as a futurate: "Surely the arrangement is that you return it to her tomorrow". The intended interpretation of [iia] is that he has permission to stay until six, but again [iib] can't have that deontic meaning: it has an epistemic reading combining with either a multiple situation ("Perhaps he habitually stays until six") or a futurate ("Perhaps the arrangement is that he stays until six").

Modal adjuncts are, indeed, often referred to as 'epistemic adjuncts'. We prefer the more general term because in spite of the above restrictions there are some uses that fall outside the epistemic category. Compare, for example, the two uses of *necessarily* in:

[3] i *You're his uncle, so necessarily he's your nephew.*
ii *Twice as many people turned up as we had been told to expect, so necessarily things were a little chaotic for a while.*

In [i] *necessarily* has an epistemic interpretation: given that the proposition "You're his uncle" is true, the proposition "He's your nephew" is necessarily true: its truth is absolutely guaranteed. In [ii], by contrast, it's not a matter of the truth of one proposition following from that of another, but of one situation being the result of another: the unexpectedly large number of people caused the chaos. *Unavoidably* could substitute for *necessarily* in [ii], but hardly in [i]. Examples like [ii] can be included in the category we have called dynamic modality, here a matter of the interaction between one situation and another.

Note also that while modal adjuncts are not used deontically on their own, *possibly* can be used in modal harmony with deontic ***can*** in requests for permission or action:

[4] i *Could I possibly borrow your bicycle for half an hour?*
ii *Could you possibly come a little earlier next week?*

Consider, finally, the adverb *hopefully*, as used in:

[5] *The good weather will hopefully last for another week.*

Here we are concerned not with knowledge and probability but with desire. This is a type of modality not expressed by the modal auxiliaries, though it has some connection with deontic modality: if I say *You must come in now* this is likely to imply that I want you to come in now.[33]

Strength of modality

In discussing the meanings of the modal auxiliaries we distinguished three levels of strength, according to the speaker's commitment to the truth of the proposition, or to the actualisation of the situation, expressed by their complement. *Must, need, will,* and *shall* are strong, *should* and *ought* are medium, *can* and *may* are weak. *Necessarily, probably, possibly* are then examples of adverbs belonging respectively to the three categories.

Modal adverbs, however, are considerably more numerous than the auxiliaries, and are not so easily classified on this dimension. In the following list, we distinguish four levels, adding a 'quasi-strong' category between the strong of *necessarily* and the medium of *probably*:

[6]						
	i	*assuredly*	*certainly*	*clearly*	*definitely*	*incontestably*
		indubitably	*ineluctably*	*inescapably*	*manifestly*	*necessarily*
		obviously	*patently*	*plainly*	*surely*	*truly*
		unarguably	*unavoidably*	*undeniably*	*undoubtedly*	*unquestionably*
	ii	*apparently*	*doubtless*	*evidently*	*presumably*	*seemingly*
	iii	*arguably*	*likely*	*probably*		
	iv	*conceivably*	*maybe*	*perhaps*	*possibly*	

Some of these show the familiar contrast between manner and non-manner uses:

[7]		MANNER ADJUNCT	MODAL ADJUNCT
	i	a. *I could see her clearly.*	b. *He had clearly been irresponsible.*
	ii	a. *He was flirting too obviously.*	b. *He was obviously flirting.*

But such items are in the minority: most of the adverbs in [6] do not occur with a matching manner use.

The strong items (of which [6i] gives only a sample) commit the speaker to the truth of the modalised proposition. An unmodalised assertion such as *Kim chaired the meeting* or *Pat is in love* also commits me to the truth of the propositions expressed: addition of a strong modal adjunct emphasises that commitment or makes it more explicit. *Kim*

[33] The modal use of *hopefully* (as distinct from the manner use of *He was looking hopefully around*) was quite rare until around the 1960s, when it acquired considerable popularity, but also aroused strong (in some cases quite intemperate) opposition from conservative speakers. It has become thoroughly established, and the opposition has abated somewhat in the last few years.

definitely chaired the meeting suggests a context in which the truth of the proposition had been questioned; *Pat is obviously in love* presents the truth as easily perceived. *Surely* is a borderline member of this category: it may suggest less than complete certainty, and is often used with an implicit request for confirmation by the addressee. *Unavoidably* and *ineluctably* are concerned with the actualisation of situations rather than the truth of propositions.

Turning now to the weak category, [6iv], the main members, *maybe, perhaps, possibly*, indicate that the proposition is not known to be false, with the chances of its being true falling in the range from slight to more or less fifty-fifty. They thus readily occur in combination with a proposition and its negation: *Maybe he told her, maybe he didn't.* The form of the informal idiom *as like as not* would lead one to expect that it too belonged in this category, but in fact the meaning is close to "probably". *Conceivably* puts the chances at the low end of the scale.

Probably explicitly allows for the possibility that the proposition is not true, but rates the chances of its being true as greater than even. It can occur in contexts like:

[8] i *He may be still in his office, but he's probably gone home by now.*
ii *He's probably gone home by now, though he could be still in his office.*

In abstraction from the modality, the propositions are inconsistent, but the weak modal in one and the medium modal in the other allow them to be combined without contradiction. *Likely* has the same meaning but differs syntactically in BrE in that it more or less requires a modifier, as in: *He has quite likely gone home by now. Arguably* indicates that an argument can be mounted for accepting the proposition as true, and implies that I find such an argument plausible or persuasive.

Apparently, seemingly, and *presumably* in [6ii] indicate that I don't know, cannot be certain, that the proposition is true: I'm merely judging by appearances or making a presumption. We put these at a higher level on the scale of strength than *probably*, because they do not so directly allow for the possibility that the proposition is false: they suggest a qualified acceptance of the proposition. Note the quite sharp contrast between the first two and the corresponding verbs. We can say, for example, *He appeared to like them but in fact couldn't stand the sight of them*, but not #*He apparently liked them but in fact couldn't stand the sight of them. Evidently* can likewise be used to indicate lack of direct knowledge: *They said they would come, but have evidently changed their minds.* But it can also behave like a class [i] item, meaning much the same as *clearly*, and like it and a number of other class [i] items allows further strengthening by *quite*: *Quite evidently, the man's a fraud.* In spite of its form, *doubtless* belongs at level [ii], not [i]: it is noticeably weaker than *without doubt.*

One adverb not included in the above classification is *allegedly*, as in:

[9] *Max had allegedly falsified the accounts.*

Allegedly absolves me from responsibility for the residual proposition: the latter has the status of an allegation, and I can't say whether it is true. As with *apparently* and *seemingly*, the fact that the qualification is expressed adverbially rather than by a predicative element serves to background it, and make it less accessible to denial. The verbal version *It was alleged that Max had falsified the accounts* readily allows the expression of a contrary view (*but I'm sure he hadn't*), but [9] does not accommodate that kind of continuation.

Forms with negative affixes

A few modal adverbs contain one of the negative prefixes *in·* and *un·*, but the set of modal adverbs does not contain any pair of opposites. We have *possibly*, but not *impossibly*, *indubitably* and *unquestionably* but not *dubitably* or *questionably*. *Arguably* and *unarguably* are both found but are not opposites, for the former indicates that an argument can be given for the proposition being true, the latter that no argument can be given against it. All the ones with negative prefixes belong in the strong category. Note that *improbably* is not an exception: it does not function as a modal adjunct in examples like *Improbably, he had accepted our proposal without hesitation.* The meaning here is "Improbable as it may seem, he had accepted our proposal without hesitation": *improbably* is an evaluative adjunct of the type discussed in §17 below.

Negation

In general, modal adjuncts have scope over a negative:

[10] i a. *She obviously didn't enjoy it.* b. *She didn't enjoy it, obviously.*
ii a. *He probably hasn't told her.* b. *He hasn't told her, probably.*

The meaning in [i] (both versions) is "It is obvious that she didn't enjoy it" and in [ii] "It is probable that he hasn't told her". To bring the modality within the scope of the negation we need to express it predicatively, e.g. *It isn't obvious that she enjoyed it*; *It isn't likely that he has told her.*

Most modal adjuncts behave in the same way, but there is not complete uniformity. Cases where a negative has scope over the adjunct are seen in:

[11] i *Those who do best at school aren't necessarily the cleverest.*
ii *It wasn't definitely sabotage but that is the most likely explanation.*
iii *He couldn't possibly have done it by himself.*

Epistemic *necessarily* occurs much more often within the scope of a negative than otherwise: examples like [3i] above are quite rare in ordinary speech. *Not necessarily* is logically equivalent to *possibly not*, but much more frequent. *Not definitely* is possible, as in [11ii], but it would be more usual to use a predicative construction such as *It is not certain that*... The occurrence of *possibly* within the scope of negation is virtually limited to the case where it is in modal harmony with ***can***, as in [iii]; *perhaps* could not replace *possibly* here.

Questioning of modality

In general, modality is more readily questioned by a predication than a modification construction. Compare:

[12] i a. *Are they likely to be offended?* b. #*Will they probably be offended?*
ii a. *Is it possible that he was poisoned?* b. *Was he perhaps poisoned?*

In [i] the [a] version is very strongly preferred over [b], which is very unnatural in most contexts. And in [ii], while [a] clearly questions the modality, the *perhaps* in [b] is likely to be construed as outside the scope of the question: I'm asking if he was poisoned, with *perhaps* indicating that I think that his having been poisoned is a possibility to be considered.

Nevertheless, there are certainly cases where a modal adjunct is in the scope of a question. *Will he probably die?* seems quite reasonable, and *Won't he probably die?* is fully acceptable; the negative question here is biased towards the positive answer *He will probably die.* Similarly, examples like [11], or their positive counterparts, can readily be questioned. Because epistemic *necessarily* predominantly occurs in the scope of a negative, a question like *Are those who do best at school necessarily the cleverest?* is typically biased towards a negative answer.

Double modality

It is perfectly possible to have more than one modal qualification, but no more than one can normally be expressed by means of an adverb. Compare, for example:

[13] i *It is certainly possible that he told her. / Certainly he may have told her.*
ii **Certainly he possibly/perhaps told her.*

Other forms

A few PPs have meanings very similar to those of adverbs listed above: *without doubt/question, in all probability/likelihood.* There are others with no close adverbial equivalent, such as *in my opinion/judgement*, and the like. *According to Kim* belongs in a group with *allegedly* in absolving me from personal responsibility for the assertion, but specifies who is responsible for it. Parentheticals also very often serve to indicate epistemic status, and conditional adjuncts too can function in this way:

[14] i a. *You didn't do it on purpose, I'm sure.*
b. *One of you, she suggests, should write a report for the local paper.*
ii a. *If I'm not mistaken, that's a kookaburra over there.*
b. *We're in for a wet week-end if the weather forecast is anything to go by.*

17 Evaluative adjuncts

[1] i *Fortunately the commandos got away before their presence was discovered.*
ii *Ironically he did best in the subject he liked least.*
iii *Ominously, these two economic trends are connected.*

With adjuncts of this kind the residual proposition is presented as a fact, and the adjunct expresses the speaker's evaluation of it. They are therefore subjective, and in this respect (as in others too) resemble the subjective type of act-related adjunct discussed in §3. There are quite a large number of evaluative adverbs, a sample of which is given in:

[2]	*absurdly*	*amazingly*	*annoyingly*	*appropriately*	*bewilderingly*
	curiously	*disappointingly*	*fortunately*	*funnily*	*happily*
	importantly	*improbably*	*inexplicably*	*ironically*	*luckily*
	mercifully	*miraculously*	*oddly*	*ominously*	*paradoxically*
	predictably	*regrettably*	*sadly*	*shamefully*	*strangely*
	surprisingly	*thankfully*	*unaccountably*	*understandably*	*unfortunately*

There are also PPs of similar meaning: *to my amazement*, *by good fortune*, *contrary to what we'd been led to expect*, and so on.

For the adverbs in [2] (with the exception of *improbably*, *thankfully*, and *unaccountably*) there are two corresponding adjectival constructions:

[3] i *Amazingly he escaped with only a scratch.* [evaluative adjunct]
ii *He escaped with only a scratch, which was amazing.* [supplementary relative]
iii *It was amazing that he escaped with only a scratch.* [superordinate adjective]

In [ii] the adjective is predicative in a supplementary relative clause whose subject has the residue as antecedent. In [iii] the residue is embedded as extraposed subject of a clause containing the adjective as predicative complement (there is also a less common variant without extraposition: *That he escaped with only a scratch was amazing*). Construction [ii] is much closer in meaning to [i] than is [iii]. In [iii] the "amazing" feature is foregrounded, with the residue backgrounded, presupposed, whereas in [i] it is the residue that constitutes the main new information. In [ii] the "amazing" feature is backgrounded relative to the residue, as it is in [i], though it still differs by virtue of being expressed predicatively rather than adverbially. Note, for example, that the relative clause can take an interrogative tag: *He escaped with only a scratch, which was amazing, wasn't it?* The adjunct construction doesn't readily take a tag at all because the truth of the residue is not in doubt, but when a tag is used it questions the residue, not the adjunct: *Fortunately, he'll be away for at least three weeks, won't he?*

Negation

Evaluative adjuncts always take scope over clausal negation, though a few adverbs can take a subclausal negative as part of the adjunct itself:

[4] i *Surprisingly, he hadn't been detected.* [adjunct has scope over negative]
ii **He hadn't been surprisingly detected.* [negative has scope over adjunct]
iii *Not surprisingly, he had been detected.* [subclausal negation]

In [i] it is the fact that he hadn't been detected that is surprising. In [ii] the negation applies to "Surprisingly he had been detected", but the result is ungrammatical; [ii] becomes grammatical if *surprisingly* is set apart prosodically from the residue, in which case the meaning is as in [i]. In [iii] *not* has scope only over *surprisingly*: the clause as a whole is positive.

Residue as asserted information

The residue in the adjunct construction is presented as new, factual information. Such adjuncts do not, therefore, occur in interrogatives, imperatives, or pragmatically presupposed subordinate clauses:

[5] i **Did the soldiers fortunately get away?*
ii **Fortunately catch the last bus.*
iii **Since Deidre fortunately recovered from her illness, she has lived in California.*

The *since* of [iii] is intended in its temporal sense. Causal *since* can introduce new information, and hence permits an evaluative adjunct in its complement: *Since she is unfortunately too ill to travel, she can't attend the wedding.*

Reported speech

[6] *Jill told me she had unfortunately been too ill to attend the wedding.*

Here *unfortunately* expresses Jill's evaluation of the situation, not mine. But it is relatively uncommon for evaluative adjuncts to be retained in reported speech in this way: they are not a central part of what was said and thus liable to be omitted when it is reported.

18 Speech act-related adjuncts

The adjuncts considered in this section are more peripheral than any treated so far, inasmuch as they relate not to the situation or proposition expressed in the clause but to the speech act performed in uttering the clause (or to the speech act that is expected as a response). For this reason, they do not have any bearing on the truth value of the statement expressed in the residue.

Manner adjuncts

Compare first the following examples of manner adjuncts:

[1]	SITUATIONAL ADJUNCT	SPEECH ACT-RELATED ADJUNCT
i	a. *Ed spoke frankly about his feelings.*	b. *Frankly, it was a waste of time.*
ii	a. *His daughter spoke briefly about her ordeal.*	b. *Briefly, your expenditure must not exceed your income.*
iii	a. *Ruth told me confidentially that she is thinking of resigning.*	b. *Confidentially, Ruth is thinking of resigning.*

In the [a] examples, the adverb relates to the situation described in the clause containing it: hence the label 'situational adjunct'. Thus *frankly* and *briefly* describe the way in which Ed and his daughter spoke, and *confidentially* specifies the way Ruth told me her news (or the terms under which she told me). In the [b] examples, by contrast, the adverb describes my speech act: [ib] can be glossed approximately as "I tell you frankly that it was a waste of time", and analogously for [iib/iiib]. But the adjunct in [b] is not part of the expression of a proposition and hence doesn't introduce a truth condition: if I'm not in fact speaking frankly, [ib] would be infelicitous, but not actually false.

In questions, the speech act-related adjunct may relate to the question itself or the response it aims to elicit:

[2] i *Confidentially / Frankly, what do you think of the plan?* [addressee-oriented]
ii *Frankly, who gives a damn anyway?* [speaker-oriented]
iii *Briefly, what are the chances of success?* [ambiguous]

In [i] *confidentially* or *frankly* relates to your response: I'm inviting you to reply in confidence or with frankness. In [ii] *who gives a damn anyway?* is an indirect speech act, a rhetorical question that conveys an assertion ("Nobody gives a damn anyway"), and it's me who is speaking frankly. Non-rhetorical questions are usually addressee-oriented like [i], but as evident from [iii] they also allow a speaker-oriented adjunct: it can be a matter of your giving a brief answer or of my asking a brief or succinct question (here I might be following up on a relatively lengthy utterance of mine or yours).

Form

Speech act-related manner adjuncts have the form of AdvPs, as in [1–2], or PPs, such as *in brief, in all honesty*, etc. We also find gerund-participials in which the verb *speak* is modified by an adverb: *Candidly speaking, they both drink far too much.* Here *candidly* is a situational manner adjunct within the subordinate clause, and the subordinate clause as a whole is a speech act-related adjunct within the matrix clause.

Purpose, reason, concession, and condition

There are various other kinds of adjunct that can relate to the speech act as well as functioning ordinarily to give information about the situation described in the clause.

[3] i *To cut a long story short, Ed accepted their offer and left the country.*
ii *Well, since you ask, I shan't be seeing her again.*
iii *Dick's coming to the party, in case you're interested.*
iv *Jill's on the verge of a breakdown, though I don't suppose you could care less.*
v *If you must know, I wasn't even short-listed.*

In [i] the infinitival is a purpose adjunct – but it is my purpose, not Ed's. My purpose in saying what I do is to cut the story short. Such purpose clauses tend to suggest manner – compare *to put it bluntly*. The *since* phrase in [ii] is a reason adjunct, giving the reason not for my not seeing her again, but for telling you that I shan't be. Similarly in [iii] I'm telling you that Dick's coming to the party because of the possibility that you may be interested. In [iv] the *though* phrase is a concessive adjunct understood as relating not to Jill's being on the verge of a nervous break-down but again to my telling you that she is. Finally in [v] we have a conditional adjunct: "If you must know, I'll tell you that . . . ". A rather curious conditional adjunct is *if you remember/recall*, as in *You promised to do the cooking today, if you remember.* This gives the utterance the force of a reminder, but is idiomatic in that there is no evident expanded version in which it serves as a situational conditional adjunct.

Such adjuncts can be found with questions:

[4] i *Are you nearly ready, because the bus leaves in ten minutes?*
ii *What time will you be back, in case anyone calls?*
iii *Where are you going, if I may ask?*

Why? can also be used as a response to a question: you ask *Have you ever been to Pontefract?* and I respond *Why?*, asking why you asked or want to know.

Adjuncts relating to felicity conditions for the speech act

[5] i *It's going to be a hard winter, because the storks are migrating early.*
ii *Is Irene still in Rome, because I've not heard from her since August?*
iii *Since you're so clever, what's the square root of 58,564?*

In [i] the adjunct indicates that one of the conditions for the felicitous performance of the illocutionary act of assertion is satisfied, namely that I have evidence for the truth of what I'm asserting. This case has much in common with the modal adjuncts discussed in §16 since it bears on the epistemic status of the superordinate proposition; we include it here as it clearly has the form of a reason adjunct, so that it can be construed as giving a reason for making the speech act, like the *since* phrase in [3ii] or the *because* phrase in [4i]. Moreover, adjuncts relating to felicity conditions occur readily in questions, which modal adjuncts do not. For example, [5ii–iii] would normally be used as inquiries, and the adjuncts indicate that two of the felicity conditions for an inquiry are satisfied – that I don't myself know the answer, and that you may well know it.

Metalinguistic adjuncts

One special case of the speech act-related adjunct is concerned with the selection of particular words used in the residue:

[6] i *Metaphorically (speaking), French is descended from Latin.*
ii *They literally live in glass-houses.*
iii *To use a fashionable term, their decor looks postmodern.*
iv *The place stinks, if you will pardon the expression.*
v *You may take the 'elevator', as you are American.*

Metaphorically and *literally* (two of the adverbs most commonly used in this function) clarify how *descended* and *glass-houses* are to be understood; the other examples similarly relate to the selection of the words *postmodern, stinks, elevator.* Because they relate to the actual language used in the clause, we refer to these adjuncts as **metalinguistic**.

19 Connective adjuncts

The final category of adjunct we shall consider serves to relate the clause to the neighbouring text or, in the limiting case, to the context:

[1] i *Jill was the only one with a Ph.D. Moreover, she had considerable teaching experience.*
ii *There's a good movie on at the Regal. Alternatively we could have a quiet evening at home.*
iii *Right, last week we were examining the Bloomfieldian concept of the morpheme.*

Moreover and *alternatively* here express the relation between the clause they introduce and what precedes. *Moreover* indicates a relation of addition; in this example the clause containing it presents a further positive property concerning Jill. *Alternatively* indicates a relation of choice; the issue in this example is to decide on what to do for the evening, with the first sentence presenting (somewhat indirectly) one possibility, and the second another. *Right* in [iii] (in the context we intend for it) is the first word of the discourse, but it can be subsumed under the category of connective if that term is understood in a suitably broad sense. It relates the residue to the context, seeking the attention of the audience for the commencement of some activity, in this example a lecture or seminar.

Connective elements often link units smaller than the clause. In *An unexpected and, moreover, very significant piece of information has just come to hand*, for example, *moreover* indicates the relation between the AdjP *very significant* and the preceding *unexpected*. We take up such cases in Ch. 15, §4.1, confining our attention here to connectives functioning as adjunct to a clause. The link may be with a preceding sentence, as in [1i–ii], or with a preceding stretch of text of indefinite length. It can equally be between a clause and a preceding clause in the same sentence, or between a clausal residue and a preceding element in the same clause. The following examples show *nevertheless* relating its clause to a variety of preceding elements in the same sentence:

[2] i *He has never had the disease himself but he can nevertheless identify it.*

ii *The shoes are expressly designed for those of us whose feet are no longer youthful, but who nevertheless like to be fashionably shod.*

iii *Although he affects a gruff exterior in many instances, nevertheless he is fundamentally a man of warm heart and gentle disposition.*

iv *Challenged by the passiveness of the music-hall and, later, by the twanging whines of American country and western music, it has nevertheless survived and is now undergoing a revival.*

v *This almost trivial example is nevertheless suggestive, for there are some elements in common between the antique fear that the days would get shorter and shorter and our present fear of war.*

Example [i] illustrates the common case where *nevertheless* relates a main clause to a preceding coordinate. Coordination is likewise involved in [ii], but this time the clauses are subordinate – integrated relative clauses. Another very common case is represented in [iii], where the connective adjunct has a **reduplicative** role: the relation between the main and subordinate clauses is already marked by *although*, so that *nevertheless* simply marks this relationship a second time. In [iv] *nevertheless* links its clause to the initial non-finite subordinate clause; precisely because this initial adjunct has the form of a non-finite clause, its relationship to the matrix is not explicitly marked within the adjunct itself. This time, therefore, *nevertheless* does not reduplicate what is already marked, but serves to indicate that the *challenge* clause is construed as "although it was challenged . . . ". Finally, in [v] *nevertheless* indicates a relationship between the clause and an element within the subject: the contrast is between the suggestiveness of the example and its near triviality.

Most connective adjuncts link their clause to preceding material, as is the case with the above *moreover*, *alternatively*, and *nevertheless*. There are, however, some correlative pairs (or larger sets) of connectives where the first member relates its clause to what follows and the second (or last) relates its to what precedes:

[3] *On the one hand, normal daily life is largely concerned with the problems of the present or those of the quite near future; on the other hand, the universities live in a world with a quite different time-scale, and the problems which exercise the academic mind belong to that world.*

The clear and central cases of connective adjuncts have the following properties:

[4] i They do not impose additional truth conditions on their clause.

ii They cannot fall within the scope of negation, be questioned, or be focused.

In [1i] (*Moreover, she had considerable teaching experience*), for example, the truth of the clause depends simply on whether she did in fact have considerable teaching experience. There is no way in which this condition could be satisfied and yet the whole clause be considered false on the grounds that the proposition expressed didn't stand in a "moreover" relation to what precedes. Consider, then:

[5] i *Jill was the only one without a Ph.D. She did not, moreover, have any teaching experience.*

ii **Jill had just finished her Ph.D. She didn't have considerable teaching experience moreover but nevertheless.*

In [i] *moreover* follows *not* but nevertheless has scope over it: it relates a negative property to what precedes. Example [ii] attempts to say that the relation between the proposition "She had considerable teaching experience" and that expressed in the preceding sentence is not of the "moreover" kind but of the "nevertheless" kind. The very clear ungrammaticality of the example shows that it is quite impossible to express that meaning by contrasting *moreover* and *nevertheless* by means of such a construction as *not... but.*

It will be evident from earlier sections of this chapter that the properties in [4] are not unique to connective adjuncts (they apply equally, for example, to the speech act-related adjuncts discussed in §18): these properties have to be taken in conjunction with their crucial role of serving to relate the clause to surrounding text or context. It should also be borne in mind that there are many ways of relating one clause to another besides the use of a connective adjunct. Coordinators are one such device; syntactically, these have distinctive properties that lead us to analyse them differently from connective adjuncts. Nevertheless, the division between coordinators and connective adjuncts is not entirely clear-cut, and items such as *yet* and *so* have some uses where they are clearly connective adjuncts, others where they are very similar to coordinators (see Ch. 15, §2.10).

Pure and impure connectives

A distinction can be drawn, though again not sharply, between **pure** and **impure** connective adjuncts. Pure connectives like *moreover* and *also* have no other function than that of connecting their clause to the surrounding text (or context), while the impure ones combine that function with one of those discussed in earlier sections. This impure type may be illustrated by *therefore.* Compare such a set of examples as the following:

[6] i *<u>Because his son had been charged with importing illegal drugs</u>, Ed had decided to resign from the School Board.*
ii *His son had been charged with importing illegal drugs, and <u>for this reason</u> Ed had decided to resign from the School Board.*
iii *His son had been charged with importing illegal drugs, and Ed had decided to resign from the School Board.*
iv *His son had been charged with importing illegal drugs; Ed had <u>therefore</u> decided to resign from the School Board.*

Sentence [i] has the form of a single clause (with subordinate clauses embedded within it); the underlined sequence is a PP functioning as adjunct of reason within this larger clause. In [ii] we have a coordination of clauses, with the information about the son's being charged expressed in a main clause. *For this reason* is interpreted anaphorically, with the first main clause as its antecedent, so that it is understood like the *because* PP in [i], and like the latter it functions as reason adjunct within the clause containing it. In [iii] the reason adjunct is omitted; the clauses are linked only by the coordinator *and*, and the cause–effect relation between the clauses is merely implicit, one of the range of implicatures associated with *and*, inferrable from the specific content of the clauses (cf. Ch. 15, §2.2.3). In [iv] there is no coordinator (though *and* could of course be inserted), and *therefore* serves both to connect the second clause to the first and to indicate the reason for the decision. The meaning of [iv] is very similar to that of [ii], but the reason relation is expressed less directly, less explicitly. Note, for example, that *for this reason* can be the focus of a cleft clause or fall within the scope of negation, whereas *therefore* cannot:

[7] i *It was for this reason / *therefore that Ed had decided to resign.*
ii *However, Ed hadn't decided to resign for this reason / *therefore but because of his disagreement with the school's policy on corporal punishment.*

It is also arguable that *therefore* does not contribute to the truth conditions of its clause in the way that *for this reason* does. Imagine a context where the son was charged and Ed decided to resign, but exclusively because of the disagreement described in [7ii]. In this scenario [6i–ii] will certainly be judged false, and [iii] true but misleading, while the status of [iv] is less clear, but seems to lie somewhere between the two.

Types of pure connectives

We suggest here a few broad subcategories of pure connectives, though we would not want to claim that they are either sharply distinct or exhaustive.

(a) Ordering

[8] *I have two objections to your proposal. In the first place, it hasn't been adequately costed. Secondly, it violates the spirit of our agreement with Father.*

Connective adjuncts are often used to signal the structure of a piece of discourse by identifying separate points, as *in the first place* and *secondly* mark the two objections in [8]. Examples of adjuncts of this type are:

[9] i *first, firstly, in the first place, first of all, for a start, for one thing, on the one hand*
ii *second, secondly, in the second place, second of all* (AmE), *on the other hand, third, . . . , for another (thing), next, then*
iii *finally, last, lastly, last of all, in conclusion*

Those in [i] mark the first point, and thus relate their clause to what follows rather than (or as well as) to what precedes. Some speakers have a preference for *first* over *firstly* that doesn't carry over to other forms of ordinal numerals. Those in [ii] mark a second or subsequent point, while those in [iii] mark the last in the series; *in sum* might be added here, though it indicates more than just the order of the point. Besides such forms as those in [9], we also find numerical figures and letters: *[1], A, (a)*, etc.

(b) Addition and comparison (likeness and contrast)

[10]	*alternatively*	*by contrast*	*also*	*besides*	*conversely*
	either	*equally*	*further(more)*	*however*	*in addition*
	in comparison	*instead*	*likewise*	*moreover*	*neither*
	nor	*on the contrary*	*rather*	*similarly*	*too*

This list includes a number of focusing adverbs, discussed further in Ch. 6, §7.3. *Neither* and *nor* belong to both the class of coordinators and that of connective adverbs (again, see Ch. 15, §2.4, for discussion). *Either* and *too* are polarity-sensitive, with *either* occurring in negative contexts, *too* preferring positives:

[11] i *Kim didn't like it, and Pat wasn't greatly impressed either.*
ii *Kim thought it was wonderful, and Pat enjoyed it too.*

The felicitous use of these connectives requires that the similarity be between propositions that are informationally in the foreground, not presupposed. Compare, for example:

[12] i *Kim has stopped smoking and Pat has given it up too.*
ii #*Kim has stopped smoking and Pat used to smoke too.*

In [i] the likeness is between "Pat has given up smoking" and "Kim has stopped smoking", which are both asserted. In [ii], however, it is between "Pat used to smoke", which is asserted, and "Kim used to smoke", which is not asserted in the first clause but merely presupposed as a precondition for stopping.

To the list given in [10] we can add such expressions as *again* or *at the same time*:

[13] i *If you have 12 hours to spare, put your feet up and over-indulge. 'War and Peace' it is not but then again, in these grim times, maybe that's a blessing.*
ii *He did not want to appear to be running hat in hand to Premier Krushchev's doorstep. At the same time he took pains not to rule out an eventual meeting with the Soviet leader.*

These have primary meanings in which they indicate serial order and temporal location respectively, but in examples like [13] these meanings have been bleached away, leaving only a comparative connective meaning. The same applies with *in the same way*. *By the same token* is an idiom specialised to the connective function. Comparative expressions like *better* or *what is more important* lie at the boundary between connective adjuncts and the evaluative type discussed in §17 above. There are also comparatives in the next category.

(c) Elaboration and exemplification

[14] *for example* *for instance* *in other words* *more precisely* *that is (to say)*

[15] *The proposal has a lot to commend it. It would, for example, considerably reduce the amount of time spent travelling from one centre to another.*

(d) Markers of informational status

Such items as *by the way*, *incidentally*, *parenthetically* signal the informational status of their clause. They indicate a change of topic or digression, generally suggesting that the new information is less important. They have much in common with the speech act-related adjuncts of §18.

Impure connectives

Adjuncts combining the connective function with some other are illustrated in:

[16] i CONCESSION *nevertheless, nonetheless, still, though, yet*
ii CONDITION *anyway, in that case, otherwise, then*
iii REASON/RESULT *accordingly, as a result, consequently, hence, in consequence, so, therefore, thus*

20 Linear position of adjuncts

20.1 Front, central, and end positions

We distinguish three main positions for adjuncts, illustrated in:

[1] i *The next day she sold her car.* [front]
ii *They probably saw her.* [central]
iii *She spoke very confidently.* [end]

In clauses containing a subject and a lexical verb, front position is before the subject, central position is before the verb, and end position is after the verb.

The choice of position for an adjunct is strongly influenced by (a) its internal form; and (b) its semantic category. Central position disfavours long or heavy adjuncts. Thus (leaving aside the case of prosodically detached interpolations) adjuncts consisting of or containing subordinate clauses do not occur in central position, and PPs or NPs are for the most part less likely in this position than AdvPs. All three positions readily accept adverbial adjuncts, and in Ch. 6, §7.1, we examine the role of semantic category in determining or restricting the position of adjuncts.

Multiple occurrences

In all three positions, it is possible to have more than one adjunct (and in such cases it might be more appropriate to talk of 'zones' rather than 'positions'):

[2] i *For this reason, as soon as the meeting was over, he called his solicitor.*
ii *He probably deeply regretted having agreed to take part.*
iii *She left immediately in order to catch the early train.*

Such multiple occurrences, however, occur much more readily in end zone than in front or central zone.

Lexical verbs vs auxiliaries

One of the syntactic properties distinguishing auxiliary verbs from lexical verbs concerns the position of certain types of adjunct. Compare, then, the following, where the [a] examples have lexical *see* as verb, and the [b] ones the perfect auxiliary *have*:

[3]	LEXICAL VERB	AUXILIARY VERB
i	a. *They probably saw her.* (=[1ii])	b. *They probably had seen her.*
ii	a. **They saw probably her.*	b. *They had probably seen her.*

With the lexical verb the modal adjunct *probably* can precede but it cannot occur between the verb and its complement, as seen in [iia]. With auxiliary *have*, by contrast, the order shown in [iib] is not only possible but quite strongly preferred over that shown in [ib]. For this reason we will take the central position to cover not only the pre-verbal position illustrated in [ia–b], but also the post-auxiliary position of *probably* in [iib]. And the property distinguishing the two classes of verb is that with lexical verbs central adjuncts precede the verb while with auxiliaries they preferentially follow. In clauses with subject–auxiliary inversion, a post-auxiliary adjunct follows the subject as well as the auxiliary: *Have they really gone to Montreal?*

Central position in *to*-infinitivals

A centrally positioned adjunct may precede or follow the marker *to*:

[4] i [*For him never to play again*] *would be a great pity.* [pre-marker]
ii [*For him to never play again*] *would be a great pity.* [post-marker]

The construction where the adjunct occurs between *to* and the following verb, as in [ii], is traditionally said to contain a 'split infinitive'; it is discussed in Ch. 6, §7.1.

Clauses without a subject

If a clause has no subject the overt distinction between front and central (pre-verbal) position is lost. To a large extent, however, it remains possible to assign an initial adjunct to one or other of the two positions:

[5] i *If it rains, bring the washing in.* [front]
ii *He complained about [never receiving any support from the boss].* [central]

The position of the conditional adjunct in [i] can be equated with the one it occupies in *If it rains, you bring the washing in* (rather than the somewhat unlikely *You, if it rains, bring the washing in*, where the adjunct has the status of an interpolation). In [ii], by contrast, we can confidently treat *never* as central within the *receive* clause because it cannot precede the subject in a gerund-participial: compare *He complained about [the staff never receiving any support from the boss]* and **He complained about [never the staff receiving any support from the boss]*.

Some constituent structure contrasts in complex clauses

Where one clause is embedded within another, we may need to consider whether an adjunct belongs in the subordinate clause or the matrix:

[6] i *He says [he saw her yesterday].* [subordinate clause adjunct]
ii *He told me [you're getting married] yesterday.* [matrix clause adjunct]
iii *He told me you wanted it yesterday.* [ambiguous]

The subordinate clause is bracketed in [i–ii], with *yesterday* inside it in [i], giving the time of the seeing, but outside it, in the matrix clause, in [ii], giving the time of the telling. Example [iii] can be interpreted with *yesterday* either inside the subordinate clause, giving the time of your wanting, or else in the matrix clause, giving the time of his telling. In [ii] *yesterday* can precede the subordinate clause – and changing the order in [iii] in this way makes *yesterday* unambiguously a matrix clause adjunct (*He told me yesterday you wanted it*).

With a non-finite subordinate clause we have a comparable distinction in the case of an adjunct located between matrix and subordinate verbs:

[7] i *I regret [impetuously volunteering to take part].* [subordinate clause adjunct]
ii *I regret deeply [volunteering to take part].* [matrix clause adjunct]

In [i] *impetuously* modifies *volunteering*, while in [ii] *deeply* modifies *regret*. In the former case the adjunct is in central (pre-verbal) position in the subordinate clause, while in [ii] it is in end zone in the matrix (following the verb, but preceding the non-finite complement). The difference is reflected in the different alternative positions available for the adjuncts. In [i] we can move *impetuously* from central position in the subordinate clause to end zone (with naturalness increased by adding a modifier such as *so*): *I regret [volunteering so impetuously to take part]*. In [ii], by contrast, *deeply* can be moved from end zone to central position in the matrix clause: *I deeply regret volunteering to take part.*

20.2 Central position in auxiliary constructions

Preference for post-auxiliary over pre-verbal position

We have said that where the verb is an auxiliary rather than a lexical verb, central adjuncts characteristically occur after the verb (post-auxiliary position) rather than before it (pre-verbal position). Consider first the case where the auxiliary is copular *be*:[34]

[8]	POST-AUXILIARY (PREFERRED)	PRE-VERBAL (LESS FAVOURED)
i	a. *It was certainly very good.*	b. *It certainly was very good.*
ii	a. *They are always cheerful.*	b. *They always are cheerful.*
iii	a. *He is already in hospital.*	b. *He already is in hospital.*

The degree of preference for the post-auxiliary position is variable. It is less, for example, with modal adjuncts (as in [i]) than with frequency ones ([ii]), while in [iii], with the aspectual adjunct *already*, the [b] version is less disfavoured in AmE than in BrE. In general, the pre-verbal version is considerably improved by placement of stress on the verb, and even more when such stress is accompanied by ellipsis of post-verbal elements:

[9]		
i	A: *They seem very cheerful today.*	B: *They always* ARE__.
ii	A: *He should be in hospital.*	B: *He already* IS__.

The special case of negation

When the auxiliary verb is negated, the choice between the two orders is determined by relative scope rather than by any general preference for post-auxiliary position:

[10]	POST-AUXILIARY: NARROW SCOPE	PRE-VERBAL: WIDE SCOPE
i	a. *It wasn't regularly available.*	b. *It regularly wasn't available.*
ii	a. *They aren't always co-operative.*	b. *They sometimes aren't co-operative.*
iii	a. *It wasn't necessarily his fault.*	b. *It probably wasn't his fault.*

The post-auxiliary adjunct falls within the scope of the negative, while the pre-verbal one has scope over the negative. Thus in [i], version [a] can be glossed as "It isn't the case that it was regularly available" and [b] as "It was regularly the case that it wasn't available". A good number of items have preferences (of varying strengths) for one or other scope relation: *always* and *necessarily*, for example, prefer narrow scope, while *sometimes* and *probably* prefer (quite strongly) wide scope.

Auxiliaries with non-finite complements

We turn now to the less straightforward case where the auxiliary verb has a non-finite complement. Here the issue arises as to whether an adjunct located between the auxiliary and the following verb is in post-auxiliary position in the matrix clause (the clause with the auxiliary as predicator) or pre-verbal position in the non-finite subordinate clause:

[11]		
i	a. *He had [deeply offended her].*	[subordinate clause adjunct]
	b. *He had probably [offended her].*	[matrix clause adjunct]
ii	a. *He may [regularly write his own speeches].*	[subordinate clause adjunct]
	b. *He may obviously [write his own speeches].*	[matrix clause adjunct]

[34] Recall that in this book auxiliary verbs are distinguished from lexical verbs by their behaviour in negative, interrogative, and similar constructions. Auxiliaries in construction with a secondary form of a verb, such as *will* in *They will buy it* or *have* in *I have seen it*, are analysed as catenative verbs taking non-finite complements: see Ch. 3, §2.2, and Ch. 14, §4.2.

The distinction thus matches that illustrated in [7] with the lexical catenative verb *regret*. The difference is reflected in the fact that the adjunct can be moved to the left of the auxiliary if it belongs in the matrix, but not if it belongs in the subordinate clause:

[12] i a. **He deeply had offended her.* b. **He regularly may write his own speeches.*
ii a. *He probably had offended her.* b. *He obviously may write his own speeches.*

The asterisk in [12ib] applies to the reading where *may* has the epistemic meaning that it has in [11ii] ("It may be that he regularly writes his own speeches"): it is admissible with deontic *may* ("He is regularly allowed to write his own speeches"), but the adjunct then does belong in the matrix, and we no longer have an alternant of [11iia].

The syntactic constituent structure in these examples matches the semantic scope of the adjunct, just as it does in the *regret* examples in [7]. But the semantic content of the auxiliaries, especially *have*, *be*, and *will*, is such that we do not always have the sharp semantic contrasts that are seen in [7] and [11]. One consequence is that it is not always clear whether an adjunct located between an auxiliary and the following verb belongs in the matrix or in the subordinate clause. Consider such examples as:

[13] a. *She is still working.* b. *Do you often have lunch together?*

The place of *still* and *often* in the constituent structure is a good deal less obvious than that of the adjuncts in the earlier examples. The best test is to see whether the adjunct can be moved to the left of the auxiliary: if so, this is strong evidence that it belongs in the matrix. We have illustrated this test in [12]; applying it to [13] indicates that *still* and *often* are matrix adjuncts, for we can have *She still* IS *working* or (with ellipsis) *She still* IS__, while a possible response to [13b] is *Yes, we often* DO__.

Incongruent positioning

A more significant consequence of the relatively weak scope contrasts found with auxiliaries is that central adjuncts may be positioned 'incongruently', i.e. located syntactically in a way that does not match their semantic scope. Compare, for example:

[14] i a. *He undoubtedly must have misinterpreted her letter.* [pre-verbal]
b. *He must undoubtedly have misinterpreted her letter.* [post-aux]
c. *He must have undoubtedly misinterpreted her letter.* [incongruent]
ii a. *The party will be long remembered.* [pre-verbal]
b. *The party will long be remembered.* [incongruent]

In [i] *undoubtedly* has wide scope semantically: "It is undoubtedly the case that he must have misinterpreted her letter". The preferred position is after *must*, i.e. post-auxiliary position in the topmost clause. The position before *must* is also completely acceptable. In version [ic], however, *undoubtedly* cannot be in the topmost clause, the one to which it belongs semantically, and hence can be regarded as incongruently positioned. Such clauses are encountered, but they are considerably less likely than the ones where there is congruence between the syntactic position and the semantic scope. In [ii] *long* belongs semantically with *remember*; in version [iia] it belongs in the *remember* clause, while in [iib] it is located syntactically in the *be* clause. Examples of this kind, where the adjunct occurs to the left of its expected position (rather than to the right, as in [ic]), are found with a very restricted range of adjuncts: compare, for example, *The supply will be drastically reduced* with **The supply will drastically be reduced.*

9

Negation

Geoffrey K. Pullum
Rodney Huddleston

1 **Introduction**

A pair of clauses such as *It is raining* and *It isn't raining* are said to differ in **polarity**. The first is a **positive clause** or a clause with **positive polarity**, while the second is a **negative clause** or a clause with **negative polarity**. For the most part positive represents the default polarity, in the sense that positive constructions are structurally and semantically simpler than negative ones. To a very large extent, therefore, a description of polarity is a matter of describing the special properties of negatives – and it is for this reason that we have called this chapter 'Negation' rather than 'Polarity'.

1.1 **Tests for clause polarity**

Negation is marked by words (*not, no, never*, etc.) or by affixes (e.g. *·n't, un·*), but very often the effect of adding a negative word or the suffix *·n't* is to make the whole clause negative. Hence the distinction drawn above between *It is raining* and *It isn't raining* as positive and negative clauses. We will therefore begin by surveying four useful diagnostic tests for determining the syntactic polarity of a clause. They are illustrated in [1]:

[1]	NEGATIVE CLAUSE	POSITIVE CLAUSE
i	a. *He didn't read it, not even the abstract.*	b. **He read it, not even the abstract.*
ii	a. *He didn't read it; neither/nor did I.*	b. *Ed read it; so did I.*
iii	a. *Ed didn't read it, did he?*	b. *Ed read it, didn't he?*
iv	a. *Not once did Ed read it.*	b. *After lunch Ed read it.*

Single underlining marks the clauses whose polarity is indicated in the headings, while the double underlining in [i–iii] marks the crucial feature of the diagnostic.

Clause continuations with *not even*

Negative clauses allow a continuation with *not even* + complement or adjunct, as in [1ia]. This is comparable to *Ed didn't even read the abstract*, but instead of *the abstract* being integrated into the structure of the clause, it is added on, as a prosodically detached supplement. When the clause is negative, the following *even* is commonly preceded by *not*, as here, but *not* is inadmissible after a positive clause. (For the meaning of *even*, see Ch. 6, §7.3.)

Connective adjuncts

In [1ii] the underlined clause is followed by an anaphorically reduced clause introduced by a connective adjunct. Following a negative clause we find *neither* or *nor*, whereas a positive clause is followed by *so*. Note that switching the connective adjuncts leads to ungrammaticality: compare **Ed didn't read it; so did I* and **Ed read it; neither/nor did I.* A contrast of the same kind applies when the connective adjunct is located at the end of the following clause:

[2] a. *Ed didn't read it, and I didn't either.* b. *Ed read it, and I did too.*

Again we may contrast **Ed didn't read it and I didn't too* and **Ed read it and I did either.* (The connective adjuncts *neither, nor, either* and *so, too* are not restricted to occurrence in reduced clauses, but the reduced construction provides the simplest test for our purposes.)

Reversed polarity tags

Did he? and *didn't he?* in [1iii] are reduced interrogative clauses, known as **tags**. They represent the most common type of interrogative tag, being used to seek confirmation of what has been said in the clause to which they are attached. This type of tag reverses the polarity of the preceding clause, so we have negative clause + positive tag in [iiia], positive clause + negative tag in [iiib].

These are not the only type of clause + tag construction: it is possible to have positive clause + positive tag, as in *Ed read it, did he?* and some speakers allow negative clause + negative tag, as in %*Ed didn't read it, didn't he?* But these are clearly different intonationally and in their pragmatic effect from those in [1iii], as described in Ch. 10, §5: our diagnostic is based on the most neutral type of confirmation tag.

Subject–auxiliary inversion with prenuclear constituents

The test illustrated in [1iv] involves the form of the clause itself rather than constraints on what may follow it. Negative clauses in which the negation is marked on a constituent in prenuclear position have obligatory subject–auxiliary inversion. Compare [iva], for example, with **Not once Ed read it.* There is, by contrast, no inversion in the positive [ivb]. Nor do we have inversion in negative *After lunch Ed didn't feel well* since the negation is marked on the verb, not on the PP *after lunch.*

Obligatory subject–auxiliary inversion is not limited to negative clauses: inversion is obligatory following connective *so* in [1iib] and following a prenuclear phrase introduced by *only* (*Only occasionally did Ed read these reports*) – see Ch. 3, §2.1.2. This test thus needs to be used in combination with the others, but we will see that it nevertheless proves useful in drawing the distinction between a negative clause and a positive clause containing subclausal negation. This is one of the distinctions to which we now turn.

1.2 An overview of negation types

The framework in terms of which we shall describe negation involves four major contrasts: **verbal** vs **non-verbal**, **analytic** vs **synthetic**, **clausal** vs **subclausal**, and **ordinary** vs **metalinguistic**. We illustrate in examples [3–6], and then discuss each distinction in turn.

[3]

	VERBAL	NON-VERBAL
i	a. *He doesn't dine out.*	b. *He never dines out.*
ii	a. *I did not see anything at all.*	b. *I saw nothing at all.*

[4] ANALYTIC / SYNTHETIC

i a. *The report is not complete.* b. *The report isn't complete.*

ii a. *Not many people liked it.* b. *Nobody liked it.*

[5] CLAUSAL / SUBCLAUSAL

i a. *She didn't have a large income.* b. *She had a not inconsiderable income.*

ii a. *We were friends at no time.* b. *We were friends in no time.*

[6] ORDINARY / METALINGUISTIC

i a. *She didn't have lunch with my old man: he couldn't make it.* b. *She didn't have lunch with your 'old man': she had lunch with your father.*

ii a. *Max hasn't got four children: he's got three.* b. *Max hasn't got four children: he's got five.*

The first two contrasts have to do with the expression of negation, i.e. with matters of form, while the second two have to do with meaning, i.e. with the interpretation of negation.

(a) Verbal vs non-verbal negation

In verbal negation the marker of negation is grammatically associated with the verb, the head of the clause, whereas in non-verbal negation it is associated with a dependent of the verb: an adjunct in [3ib], object in [3iib]. This distinction is needed to account for the occurrence of the auxiliary *do*, which is required in the [a] examples of [3], but not the [b] ones. Within verbal negation we then distinguish three subcategories:

[7] i a. *You didn't hurt him.* b. *You aren't tactless.* [primary]

ii a. *Don't hurt him.* b. *Don't be tactless.* [imperative]

iii a. *It's important not to bend it.* b. *It's important not to be seen.* [secondary]

In **primary** verbal negation the negative marker is associated with a primary verb-form: here *do* is required if there is no other auxiliary verb. In **imperative** verbal negation *do* is required even if the corresponding positive does contain an auxiliary verb, as in [iib]. The third category comprises all constructions other than imperatives containing a secondary verb-form: infinitivals, subjunctives, gerund–participials, and so on. Auxiliary *do* does not occur in these constructions. We label this category **secondary** with the understanding that this is a shorthand for 'non-imperative secondary'.

(b) Analytic vs synthetic negation

Analytic negation is marked by words whose sole syntactic function is to mark negation, i.e. *not* and also *no* in the use in which it contrasts with *yes*, as in answering a question, for example. Synthetic negation is marked by words which have some other function as well. Synthetic verbal negation is marked inflectionally, by negative verb-forms. Synthetic non-verbal negation is marked by elements of three kinds:

[8] i ABSOLUTE NEGATORS — *no* (including compounds *nobody*, *nothing*, etc., and the independent form *none*), *neither*, *nor*, *never*

ii APPROXIMATE NEGATORS — *few*, *little*; *barely*, *hardly*, *scarcely*; *rarely*, *seldom*

iii AFFIXAL NEGATORS — *un·*, *in·*, *non·*, *·less*, etc.

We treat examples like *He had no money* as cases of synthetic negation because *no* combines the function of marking negation with that of determiner in NP structure. As a determiner, it expresses quantification. These two functions are separated in the analytic negative *He did not have any money.*

The distinction between the absolute and approximate negators is illustrated in:

[9] a. *None of them supported her.* b. *Few of them supported her.*

In [a] the number of them who supported her is zero, whereas in [b] it merely approximates to zero – it is located towards the bottom of the scale, in the area that contains zero. Example [b] in fact has a positive implicature – that some of them supported her. It nevertheless has important features in common with [a] that motivate its analysis as negative – note, for example, that the reversed polarity tag for both examples is *did they?*

The affixal negators are prefixes (*un·happy*) or suffixes (*care·less*). The main discussion of these is in Ch. 19, §5.5, but we look briefly in §3.4 below at the relation between verbal and affixal negation – at the contrast, for example, between *They are not common* and *They are uncommon.*

(c) Clausal vs subclausal negation

This distinction relates to the tests for polarity given in §1.1: as made clear there, these are tests that differentiate between negative and positive clauses. Clausal negation is therefore negation that yields a negative clause, whereas subclausal negation does not make the whole clause negative. The distinction is seen very clearly when we apply the tests to such a pair of examples as those in [5ii]:

[10] i	a. *We were friends at no time, not even when we were at school.*	b. **We were friends in no time, not even within a few days.*
ii	a. *We were friends at no time, and neither were our brothers.*	b. *We were friends in no time, and so were our brothers.*
iii	a. *We were friends at no time, were we?*	b. *We were friends in no time, weren't we?*
iv	a. *At no time were we friends.*	b. **In no time were we friends.*

The tests show clearly that *We were friends at no time* has clausal negation while *We were friends in no time* has subclausal negation. The former allows a *not even* continuation, takes *neither* as a following connective adjunct, takes a positive tag, and requires inversion when *at no time* is placed in prenuclear position. Conversely, *We were friends in no time* does not permit *not even,* takes *so* as connective adjunct, takes a negative tag, and does not have inversion when *in no time* is preposed (the form required is *In no time we were friends*).

One further difference is that the example with *at no time* has an equivalent with verbal negation whereas the one with *in no time* does not:

[11] a. *We weren't friends at any time.* b. **We weren't friends in any time.*

The negation in *in no time* thus relates only to the phrase, which means "in a very short period of time": it doesn't negate the clause as a whole.

Affixal negation is always subclausal. Compare, for example:

[12] i	*These terms aren't negotiable, are they?*	[verbal negation: clausal]
ii	*These terms are non-negotiable, aren't they?*	[affixal negation: subclausal]

Clausal negation is a matter of syntax, while affixal negation is purely morphological. For the rest we take clausal negation as the default case, and survey in §3.2.2 the main places where negative markers other than affixes yield subclausal negation.

(d) Ordinary vs metalinguistic negation.

Consider finally the contrast between the examples in [6]. In [ia] (*She didn't have lunch with my old man: he couldn't make it*) the negative indicates that it is not the case, not **true**, that she had lunch with my old man. But that is not how the negative is understood in (the intended interpretation of) [ib]: *She didn't have lunch with your 'old man': she had lunch with your father.* The latter would normally be used in a context where you had said *She had lunch with my old man.* In uttering [ib] I am not disputing the truth of what you said but rejecting the formulation you used: I'm objecting to your referring to your father as your 'old man'. Similarly, *She doesn't live in a* /kæsl̩/, *she lives in a* /kɑsl̩/ might be used to reject your pronunciation of *castle.*

An important case of metalinguistic negation is illustrated in [6iib], *Max hasn't got four children, he's got five*: here it is used to deny an implicature. We argued in Ch. 5, §5.2, that *Max has four children* **entails** that he has no less than four and **implicates** that he has no more than four. *Max hasn't got four children: he's got three* ([6iia]) is thus ordinary negation. It denies the entailment of the positive, i.e. it indicates that *Max has got four children* is false. *Max hasn't got four children, he's got five* ([iib]) denies the implicature. It is not saying that *Max has got four children* is false, and hence is not ordinary negation. Again I would typically use the metalinguistic negative in a context where you had just said that Max has four children: I am correcting what you said not because it is false but because it doesn't go far enough. It is metalinguistic in the sense that it is saying that *four* was the wrong word to use (among those yielding a true statement).

1.3 Scope and focus of negation

The notions **scope of negation** and **focus of negation** will be introduced together in this section because they are tightly interlinked. The **scope** of negation is the part of the meaning that is negated. The **focus** is that part of the scope that is most prominently or explicitly negated. We will explain these concepts by reference to the most elementary type of negation, verbal negation of declaratives.

1.3.1 The concept 'having scope over'

The scope of a negative is most easily seen by considering the semantic effect of removing the negative element. We will illustrate by first exhibiting in [13] a case where the negative element ·*n't* has scope over everything in a sentence, and then in [15] adding to it some material over which the negative element does not have scope, pointing out the semantic difference that results.

In the following pair, [a] is negative, and [b] is its positive counterpart:

[13] a. *Liz didn't delete the backup file.* b. *Liz deleted the backup file.*

Each of the clause constituents *Liz, deleted,* and *the backup file* in [b] makes a contribution to the meaning; we can therefore give the truth conditions of [b] as a list of statements:

[14] i "A deletion operation took place"
ii "The deletion operation was performed by Liz"
iii "The deletion operation was performed on the backup file"

Each of these has to be true in order for [13b] to be true. And the falsity of any one of them is sufficient to make [13a] true. That is, the negated sentence [13a] is true if either there was no act of deletion, or if any deletion operation that occurred was performed by someone other than Liz, or if any deletion operation that occurred was performed on something other than the backup file. The status of the propositions in [14] thus changes as we switch from [a] to [b]: the falsity of any one of them establishes the truth of [a], but also the falsity of [b]. All three components are therefore said to be **inside the scope** of the negation – or, to put it another way, the negative **has scope over** all three of them.

The negative can therefore be said to have scope over the whole clause, i.e. over everything in the clause (except itself): we can say that **the scope of the negation** here is "Liz deleted the backup file".

Now compare the following examples, in which an extra clause has been added to each of the sentences:

[15] a. *Liz didn't delete the backup file and Sue wrote the report.* b. *Liz deleted the backup file and Sue wrote the report.*

The truth conditions for [15b] consist of those given in [14] together with

[16] "Sue wrote the report"

But this is also a truth condition for [15a]: if Sue didn't write her report then both examples in [15] are false. The status of [16] is thus not affected by the negation: it is **outside the scope** of the negative. So the scope of the negative is the same in [15a] as in [13a], namely "Liz deleted the backup file".

Notice that [15a] has the form of a coordination of clauses, and it is quite generally the case that a negative in one clause does not have scope over another clause that is coordinate with it. There is, though, an exception to this: a negative can have scope over a clause-coordination that involves gapping (Ch. 15, §4.2). Compare the following:

[17] a. *Kim wasn't at work on Monday or Pat on Tuesday.* b. *Kim was at work on Monday or Pat on Tuesday.*

These involve the following components of meaning:

[18] i "Kim was at work on Monday"
ii "Pat was at work on Tuesday"

Because of the meaning of *or* the truth of either one of these is sufficient to establish the truth of [17b]. But for [17a] to be true, both of [18i–ii] must be false. The negation thus affects the status of both: both fall within its scope. In this construction, therefore, the negative has scope over the whole coordination.

Elements whose meaning is not truth-conditional

Not all elements in a sentence contribute to its truth conditions. Consider the connective adjunct *however* in:

[19] a. *Ed noticed a problem; Liz, however, did<u>n't</u> delete the backup file.* b. *Ed noticed a problem; Liz, however, deleted the backup file.*

Here [b] can be analysed into three components of meaning:

[20] i "Ed noticed a problem"
ii "Liz deleted the backup file"
iii "There is some relation of apparent contrast between [i] and [ii]"

The nature of the contrast is not made explicit; one plausible possibility is that the problem concerns the backup file and the speaker considers Ed's noticing the problem as a reason for not deleting the backup file (so that the problem could be investigated). Now [20iii] does not constitute a truth condition for [19b]: you cannot argue that the latter was false simply because there is in fact no relation of contrast between the components. And because it does not affect the truth of the sentence it cannot fall within the scope of the negative in [19a]: the scope of the negative here is "Liz deleted the problem", just as it is in [13a] and [15a].

Semantic and syntactic identification of scope

Scope is in the first instance a semantic concept, and we have been identifying the scope of negation in semantic terms – saying, for example, that the scope of the negative in [19a] is "Liz deleted the backup file". Where a relevant component of meaning is expressed by a separate syntactic constituent, however, we can equally well refer to it in terms of its form. In a case like [19a], then, we can say that the clause *Ed noticed a problem* and the adjunct *however* are outside the scope of the negative.

1.3.2 Relative scope: wide scope negation and narrow scope negation

Scope is the semantic analogue of syntactic constituent structure, and in many cases the syntactic structure reflects the scope of negation in an obvious and elementary way. Compare:

[21] i a. *She didn't say that she knew him.* b. *She said that she didn't know him.*
ii a. *She didn't promise to help him.* b. *She promised not to help him.*

In [i] the scope of the negative in [a] is "she said that she knew him", while in [b] it is "she knew him". Thus the negative has scope over *say* in [ia] but not in [ib], and this correlates with the fact that in [ia] *say* is located within the subordinate clause functioning as complement of the negated verb *do*, whereas in [ib] the negative is located within the clause functioning as complement to *say*. Similarly, the negative has scope over *promise* in [iia], but not in [iib], and again the negative is in the matrix clause in [iia] but the subordinate clause in [iib].

The concept of scope applies to numerous other kinds of element besides negation markers, including verbs. Compare, for example:

[22] a. *She tried to stop offending them.* b. *She stopped trying to offend them.*

In [a] *stop* is syntactically within the complement of *try* and semantically within its scope, and conversely in [b]: here *try* is within the syntactic complement and semantic scope of *stop*. In [21iib], then, it is not simply that *promise* is outside the scope of the negative: the negative is inside the scope of *promise*. We are concerned here, then, with **relative scope**: we have two scope-bearing elements and the issue is which has scope over the other.

As far as negation is concerned, the clearest cases are those like [21] where relative scope is reflected in the contrast between matrix and subordinate clauses.[1] Less obvious

[1] Even here, however, matters are not entirely straightforward. With auxiliary verbs the issue arises as to whether a following *not* belongs in the matrix or the subordinate clause (see §2.3.2), and we will also find

are cases where relative scope is not marked by clause subordination in this way. We will consider two such cases here, involving the scope of negation relative to adjuncts in clause structure and relative to quantifiers; the issue also arises with respect to coordinators (see Ch. 15, §2.2.2) and modal auxiliaries (Ch. 3, §9.3.1).

(a) Relative scope of negation and adjuncts in clause structure

Consider first the relative scope of negation and an adjunct such as *intentionally.*

[23] i *Liz intentionally deleted the backup file.*
ii *Liz intentionally didn't delete the backup file.* [adjunct has scope over negative]
iii *Liz didn't intentionally delete the backup file.* [negative has scope over adjunct]

The truth conditions for positive [23i] can be given as follows:

[24] i "Liz deleted the backup file"
ii "Liz did what she did intentionally"

Now [23ii] cannot be true by virtue of [24ii] being false: it can only be true if [24i] is false. Thus [24ii] is a condition for the truth of both [23i] and [ii] and hence outside the scope of negation in [23ii]. And since [24ii] is the meaning contributed by *intentionally*, we can say that *intentionally* in [23ii] is outside the scope of negation. In [23i] what was intentional was Liz's deleting the backup file, whereas in [23ii] what was intentional was Liz's not deleting the backup file, so the negative is inside the scope of *intentionally*: it contributes to specifying what it was that was done intentionally.

The interpretation of [23iii] is quite different. This can be true by virtue of it being false that Liz acted intentionally. So this time *intentionally* is inside the scope of negation, rather than the other way round. An equivalent way of expressing the difference is to say that in [23ii] the negative has **narrow** scope relative to the adjunct, whereas in [23iii] it has **wide** scope.

We noted that in the most elementary cases relative scope is reflected in a contrast between matrix and subordinate clauses, as in [21], and in cases like [23ii–iii] the difference in meaning can be brought out by means of glosses involving clause subordination:

[25] i "Liz acted intentionally in not deleting the backup file" [meaning of [23ii]]
ii "Liz didn't act intentionally in deleting the backup file" [meaning of [23iii]]

When the negative has narrow scope, it appears in the subordinate clause of the gloss; when it has wide scope, it appears in the matrix clause of the gloss.

Contraries and contradictories

The contrast between [23ii] and [23iii] can also be brought out by noting that they stand in different semantic relations to the positive [23i]:

[26] i *Liz intentionally didn't delete the backup file* and *Liz intentionally deleted the backup file* are **contraries**: they cannot be both true, but they can be both false.
ii *Liz didn't intentionally delete the backup file* and *Liz intentionally deleted the backup file* are **contradictories**: they cannot be both true, but they cannot be both false either.

that in certain circumstances non-verbal negation within a subordinate clause can have scope over the matrix (see §3.2.1).

Both [23i] and [23ii] are false if Liz deleted the backup file unintentionally, but there is no context in which both [23i] and [23iii] are false.

Relative scope and the contrast between clausal and subclausal negation

The difference in scope of the negatives in [23ii–iii] is reflected in the fact that while the latter behaves straightforwardly as a negative clause, the former does not:

[27]	NARROW SCOPE: SUBCLAUSAL	WIDE SCOPE: CLAUSAL
i	a. *<u>*Liz intentionally didn't delete the backup file*</u>*, and neither did Sue.*	b. <u>*Liz didn't intentionally delete the backup file*</u>*, and neither did Sue.*
ii	a. *<u>*Liz intentionally didn't delete the backup file*</u>*, did she?*	b. <u>*Liz didn't intentionally delete the backup file*</u>*, did she?*

The *neither* continuation is permitted in [b] but not [a] (*and so* . . . would be somewhat awkward in [a], but the inadmissibility of *neither* is sufficient to establish a clear difference). Similarly *did she?* as a reversed polarity tag seeking confirmation of what is said in the preceding clause can be added in [b] but not in [a]. Thus [23iii] is a negative clause, but [23ii] is not.

It should not be assumed, however, that in negative clauses the negative necessarily has scope over every element in the clause. One case where this is not so is [19a]. Here the negative does not have scope over *however*, but that does not prevent the clause being negative: compare *Liz, however, didn't delete the backup file and neither did Sue* (where the *neither* continuation shows that the clause is negative), or *Liz, however, didn't delete the backup file, did she?* (where the tag shows the clause is negative). We will see, moreover, that the exceptions are not confined to cases like this where the element outside the scope of negation is non-truth-conditional.

Relative scope and linear order

An obvious syntactic difference between [23ii] and [23iii] is that *intentionally* precedes *didn't* in the former while *didn't* precedes *intentionally* in the latter. The semantic difference in scope is marked syntactically by a difference in linear order. In both examples, then, the element with wider scope precedes the one with narrower scope. This represents the default case:

[28] Given a construction containing two scope-bearing elements, the one which comes first will generally have scope over the one which comes later.

As implied by the 'generally', relative scope does not always correlate directly with relative order in this way. One factor that may override it is intonation. Compare:

[29]		
i	*Liz didn't delete the backup file intentionally.*	[negative has scope over adjunct]
ii	*Liz didn't delete the backup file – intentionally.*	[adjunct has scope over negative]

In the intended pronunciations of these, *intentionally* falls in the same intonational phrase as *didn't* in [i], whereas in [ii] it is prosodically detached. In [i], the default pattern is observed: the negative has scope over the following adjunct. But in [ii] the prosodic offsetting of the adjunct allows it to take scope over the whole of what precedes.

A similar illustration is provided by reason adjuncts:

[30]		
i	*Because it cost $50 she didn't buy it.*	[adjunct has scope over negative]
ii	*She didn't buy it because it cost $50.*	[ambiguous]

In [i] we find the default pattern: the adjunct comes first and has scope over the negative. The narrow scope of the negative here can again be brought out by a roughly equivalent sentence in which it appears in a subordinate clause (underlined): *The $50 price caused her not to buy it.* Here we understand that $50 was too high a price. Example [ii], however, is ambiguous. It can have an interpretation following the default pattern, with the negative having scope over the adjunct; here the adjunct will be in the same intonational phrase as *didn't.* In this interpretation we understand that $50 was a good price, but that this price did not lead her to buy it – and there is an implicature that she did buy it, for some other reason. But [ii] can also have the same interpretation as [i]. This departs from the default pattern given in [28], and the adjunct would form a separate intonational phrase (and in writing it might well be preceded by a comma to remove the ambiguity).

(b) Relative scope of negation and quantifiers

The issue of relative scope also arises when negation combines with quantification:

[31] i	*He hasn't got many friends.*	[negative has scope over quantifier]
ii	*Many people didn't attend the meetings.*	[quantifier has scope over negative]

Here [i] is the contradictory of *He has many friends*: one will be true, the other false. But [ii] is not even the contrary of *Many people attended the meetings*: both could easily be true. Given a large enough set of people, it is perfectly possible for the subset attending and the subset not attending to both qualify as 'many'. Again the narrow scope of the negative in [ii] is brought out by a gloss with a negative in a subordinate clause: "There were many people who didn't attend the meetings". Note, however, that [ii] behaves as a negative clause: cf. *Many people didn't attend the meetings, not even the first one* or *Many people didn't attend the meetings, did they?* This confirms the point made above that in negative clauses the negative does not necessarily have scope over all other elements in the clause.

Linear order

The examples in [31] follow the default pattern where relative scope matches relative linear order. Again, however, the default may be overridden under certain circumstances:

[32] i	*I didn't agree with many of the points he made.*	[scope ambiguous]
ii	*Everybody didn't support the proposal, but most did.*	[wide scope negation]

Example [i] can be interpreted with either the negative or the quantifier having scope over the other. With wide scope negation it is like [31i], the contradictory of *I agreed with many of the points he made.* In this reading there weren't many points that I agreed with. The wide scope quantification reading can be expressed unambiguously by fronting the quantified NP: *Many of the points he made I didn't agree with.* In this second reading there were many points that I disagreed with; it is a less likely reading of [32i] than the one with wide scope negation, but certainly possible, especially with a clear change of intonation contour on *many.* Without the *but* clause, [32ii] would be ambiguous in the same way: *most did*, however, forces the interpretation where the negative has scope over the quantifier, as it unambiguously does in *Not everybody supported the proposal.* Again the intonation can assist in making the meaning clear: the reading with wide scope negation reading will typically be encouraged by high pitch on *EVerybody.*

Because the preferred (most likely) interpretation matches scope with order of appearance in the sentence, if we change the order – for example, by switching from active to passive – we will change the preferred interpretation:

[33] i *Many members didn't back the proposal.* [narrow scope negative]
ii *The proposal wasn't backed by many members.* [wide scope negative preferred]

A prosodic override is virtually impossible in [i]: *many* has scope over the negative. In [ii] the preferred reading has *many* within the scope of the negative ("there weren't many who supported the proposal"), though it is just possible for this to be overridden, making it equivalent to [i].

Equivalence between wide scope universal and narrow scope existential quantification

[34] i *All of them didn't have a clue what he meant.* [wide scope universal]
ii *None of them had a clue what he meant.* [narrow scope existential]

These are semantically equivalent (cf. Ch. 5, §5.1). In [i] the universal quantifier *all* has scope over the negative: all of them had a negative property. In [ii] *none* expresses the negation of existential quantification: "it is not the case that any of them had a clue what he meant". (A more emphatic version is *Not one of them had a clue what he meant*, with negative and quantifier expressed separately, and the one with wider scope coming first.) Although [34i–ii] are equivalent, version [ii] is quite strongly preferred. This preference for a formulation with existential quantification within the scope of the negative over universal quantification with scope over the negative is reflected in the possibilities for overriding order in clauses combining negation with universal quantification:

[35] i *All of the members didn't support the proposal.*
ii *The proposal wasn't supported by all of the members.*

Here [i] can be interpreted with wide scope negation ("Not all of the members supported the proposal"): it allows a prosodic override of the narrow scope negation reading much more readily than [33i] because *None of the members supported the proposal* would be preferred over the narrow scope negation reading of [35i]. Conversely, override is hardly possible in [ii]. The normal reading here has wide scope negation ("not all"): instead of overriding the order to put *all* outside the scope of negation one would normally use *any* instead of *all* (*The proposal wasn't supported by any of the members*), with the negative having scope over an existential quantifier.

1.3.3 Focus

In all but the most trivial negative clauses there are several different conditions whose failure to hold would cause the clause to be strictly true. Which condition is intended can be indicated by a speaker through the device of stressing the most closely associated word. A constituent marked by stress as being crucial to the way in which an instance of negation should be understood is called the **focus** of that negation.[2]

Negation focus, falsity conditions, and prosody

Let us again compare a negative clause and its positive counterpart:

[36] a. *Your children don't hate school.* b. *Your children hate school.*

[2] Throughout this chapter 'focus' is to be understood in the sense of 'informational focus': see Ch. 6, §7.3, for the distinction between two concepts of focus.

One way of giving the truth conditions for the positive [b], one which highlights the contribution of the separate words, is as follows:

[37] i a. "Somebody's children hate school" b. "You are that person"
ii a. "Some relatives of yours hate school" b. "They are your children"
iii a. "There is some attitude your children harbour towards school" b. "That attitude is hatred"
iv a. "There is something your children hate" b. "That thing is school"

In order for [36b] to be true, each of these conditions must be true; but for [36a] to be true it is sufficient that any one of the conditions be false. From this point of view, negative statements run the risk of being relatively uninformative. It could be that somebody's children hate school, but not yours – or indeed that no one's children hate school; it could be that some relatives of yours hate school, but not your children – or indeed that none of your relatives hate school. And so on.

English provides ways of making negatives more informative by giving some indication as to which condition fails to hold. The way we are concerned with here involves the use of stress and intonation to highlight the part of the clause that is associated with that condition. Consider, for example, the four ways of saying [36a] shown in [38], where the small capitals indicate heavy stress and raised or changing pitch:

[38] i *YOUR children don't hate school.*
"If there are children who hate school, they are not yours"
ii *Your CHILDREN don't hate school.*
"If any of your relatives hate school, it is not your children"
iii *Your children don't HATE school.*
"If your children harbour an attitude towards school, it is not hatred"
iv *Your children don't hate SCHOOL.*
"If your children do hate something, it's not school"

The part of the clause that is prosodically highlighted is the focus. In [38i] the focus is *your*, and this indicates that what makes the positive *Your children hate school* false is the non-satisfaction of the condition associated with *your*. Hence the gloss we have provided for this reading, "If there are children who hate school, they are not yours", which locates the failure to satisfy the set of conditions given in [37] specifically in [ib]. Similarly, the glosses given for [38ii–iv] reflect the choice of *children*, *hate*, and *school* respectively as focus.

Narrower and broader negation focus

In this very simple example we have taken the focus to be simply the stressed word itself. But it does not have to be just that word: it can be a constituent that includes the stressed word. The focus in *Your CHILDREN don't hate school*, for example, could be the whole NP *your children*, and the interpretation in this case would be "If there are some people who hate school, they are not your children". Here, then, the focus is broader than we took it to be in our interpretation of [38ii]. Similarly, the focus in *Your children don't hate SCHOOL* need not be as narrow as *school*: it can also be the VP *hate school*, and here the interpretation would be along the lines of "If your children have some property, it's not that of hating school".

To illustrate this variation in how broad a focus is selected, consider the following more complex example:

[39] i *At least Max didn't wear a green mohair* SUIT *to the wedding.*

ii a. "At least the green mohair garment Max wore to the wedding wasn't a suit"

b. "At least the green garment Max wore to the wedding wasn't a mohair suit"

c. "At least the garment Max wore to the wedding wasn't a green mohair suit"

d. "At least what Max did wasn't to wear a green mohair suit to the wedding"

e. "At least Max wearing a green mohair suit to the wedding didn't happen"

We confine our attention to the case where the stress is placed on *suit*. This allows five different choices of focus, each a constituent containing the word *suit*. The glosses given in [ii] correspond to progressively broader foci. In [iia] the focus is taken to be *suit*; [iib] makes *mohair suit* the focus; [iic] makes it *green mohair suit*; [iid] makes it *wear a green mohair suit to the wedding*; and [iie] makes it the whole clause. The later paraphrases are probably more plausible in normal contexts than the first two, but all are possible.

There are default assumptions for both main stress and focus of negation. The neutral place in a clause to put the heaviest stress is on the last stressed syllable of the lexical head of the last phrasal constituent of the VP. When this is the stress pattern, the focus is quite likely to be taken by the hearer to be the whole clause that corresponds semantically to the scope of the negation. Consider a normal pronunciation of the sentence *I don't know why they appointed him to the job*. The heaviest stress is likely to be on *job*, and given that stress the focus of the negation will probably be taken to be the entire scope of *not*, i.e., the whole clause meaning "I know why they appointed him to the job".

Positive implicatures resulting from the choice of focus

The focus of negation serves to narrow down the condition whose non-satisfaction makes the negative true and the positive counterpart false. But in picking out one condition one often implicates that the other conditions for the truth of the positive are in fact satisfied. The glosses we gave in [38] did not incorporate these implicatures. We glossed *YOUR children don't hate school* as "If there are children who hate school, they are not yours". But very often it will be interpreted more strongly as "There are children who hate school, but they are not yours". Thus in addition to the negative component "they are not yours", we have the positive implicature "there are children who hate school". It is clear that this is an implicature, not an entailment: to select *your* as focus is not to actually **say** that somebody else's children hate school. It would be perfectly coherent, for example, to say *I don't know about other people, but I'll certainly concede that* YOUR *children don't hate school.*

Such positive implicatures tend to be stronger with narrow focus than with broad. Thus if *I haven't done my* TAX *return yet*, say, is interpreted with the whole clause as focus it will not convey any positive implicatures of this kind. Compare this with a narrow focus example discussed earlier, *She didn't buy it because it cost $50* ([30ii]). The reading where the negative has scope over the reason adjunct will normally have the stress on *$50*, and focus on *because it cost $50*. It will then have a very strong positive implicature that she did buy it, giving the interpretation that she bought it for some reason other than its price. (But again, this is not an entailment: it could be that I don't know whether she bought it or not but am merely quite confident that she would not have allowed the mere price to induce her to buy it.)

Focus of negation as a special case of informational focus

The concept of focus applies in all main clauses, not just negatives. Compare:

[40] i *Liz* INTENTIONALLY *deleted the backup file.*
ii *Liz* INTENTIONALLY *didn't delete the backup file.*
iii *Liz didn't* INTENTIONALLY *delete the backup file.* [focus of negation]

In all three cases the focus is *intentionally*, and in all three cases the effect of selecting this as focus is to give prominence to the associated piece of information – that Liz did what she did intentionally. Example [i] is positive and in [ii] the scope of the negation, "deleted the backup file" does not include the focus. Only in [iii] does the focus fall within the scope of a negative, but when it does, it serves as the focus of the negation. The effect of selecting as focus a constituent within the scope of negation is still to give prominence to the associated piece of information, but by virtue of giving it prominence I indicate that this is where you are to find the condition whose non-satisfaction makes the negative true.

2 Verbal negation

Negation of a clause is commonly marked on or adjacent to the verb of that clause, and we call that **verbal** negation. There are three types of clause that exemplify it, and the syntax is different in each case. We will deal first with clauses that have verbs inflected in a primary inflectional form, then with imperative clauses, and then with non-imperative clauses whose verbs are inflected in secondary forms.

2.1 Primary verbal negation

Positive clauses containing a primary form of an auxiliary verb may be negated by adding *not* after the verb, giving **analytic primary negation**, or by inflecting the verb in the negative, giving **synthetic primary negation**:

[1] i *Kim will be here later on.* [positive clause with auxiliary verb]
ii *Kim will not be here later on.* [analytic primary negation]
iii *Kim won't be here later on.* [synthetic primary negation]

In [i] we have the neutral present tense form *will* in a positive clause. In [ii] this neutral form *will* is modified by *not* in post-auxiliary position. In [iii] the negation is marked by the negative present tense form *won't.*

To negate a clause containing a primary form of a lexical verb it is necessary to add the semantically empty auxiliary that we have called supportive ***do***:

[2] i *Kim waved to us.* [positive clause with lexical verb]
ii *Kim did not wave to us.* [analytic primary negation]
iii *Kim didn't wave to us.* [synthetic primary negation]

Do takes on the inflectional properties (here preterite tense) that in the positive are carried by the lexical verb, and the latter now appears in the plain form. Again the negation may be marked analytically or synthetically by a negative form of ***do***.[3]

The choice between analytic and synthetic primary negation

Analytic and synthetic primary negation forms are not fully interchangeable. The main difference is one of style level.

The synthetic forms are a mark of informal style. While they are the default form in ordinary conversation and informal writing,[4] they are not used in very formal and solemn contexts or in some kinds of written (especially published) language. They are by no means absent from academic prose, but the author or speaker who uses them makes a definite style decision: the effect of using synthetic negative auxiliaries is to increase the sense of familiarity, intimacy, and accessibility. Compare the following pairs, where the [a] members belong to formal style, the [b] members to informal style:

[3] i a. *I do not accept, and will not condone or defend, this shameful policy.*
b. *I don't accept, and won't condone or defend, this shameful policy.*
ii a. *This is not to say that one could not conceive of a world in which aesthetic properties did not supervene on the physical; but the necessity of positing them does not seem to me an attractive prospect.*
b. *This doesn't mean that you couldn't imagine a world where aesthetic properties didn't supervene on physical ones; but having to assume them doesn't seem like an attractive prospect to me.*

While [ia] sounds grave and parliamentary, [ib] does not, and might be judged to sound too petulant in the context of a political speech. Likewise, [iia] has the tone of a published paper in analytic philosophy, while [iib] (in which various other changes are made in addition to the choice of synthetic negatives) has the flavour of a more informal explanation of the same ideas; it might be judged too patronising for appearance in some philosophy journals, but just right for a lecture. Naturally, there is much variation in style, and some academic writers choose to use a much more informal style than others.

The fact that synthetic negative auxiliaries are informal does not mean that analytic forms are neutral or preferable. Analytic forms sound unnatural in many conversational contexts unless there is some clear reason for their use, e.g., emphasis on the word *not* (*I did* NOT *sneak out by the back door when she arrived!*). Thus in an ordinary conversation, *I don't think so* or *Don't worry, I won't be long* are perfectly natural even in slow and careful speech, while *I do not think so* or *Do not worry, I will not be long* would be not just unusual but highly unnatural.[5]

[3] In earlier forms of English, non-auxiliary verbs in primary forms were also postmodified by *not*. Instances are preserved in various biblical and proverbial phrases (*I care not whether she lives or dies*; *He who knows not, and knows that he knows not, can be taught*), but the construction is no longer part of the productive syntax of the language.

[4] This applies to the synthetic forms that are fully acceptable; for the case of %*mayn't* and of *aren't* with a 1st person singular subject, see Ch. 18, §5.5.

[5] Such unnatural avoidance of negative auxiliaries is used in films to underscore the alienness of such characters as visitors from outer space.

Grammatical restriction on synthetic negatives: inadmissible in inverted conditionals
Although the difference is mainly stylistic, there is one construction that does not permit synthetic negatives, namely the inverted conditional (see Ch. 3, §2.1.2). Compare:

[4] i *Had it not been for the weather, the plan would have succeeded.*
ii **Hadn't it been for the weather, the plan would have succeeded.*

Synthetic verbal negation is a matter of inflection

The suffix ·*n't* is often mistaken for a reduced pronunciation of the word *not*. That is of course its etymology, but it is no longer an unstressed pronunciation of *not*; in the contemporary language it is a verbal suffix. There are syntactic, morphological, and phonological reasons for distinguishing between such pairs as *does not* and *doesn't*, as described in Ch. 3, §1.9.

Position of negator in clauses with subject–auxiliary inversion

Clauses with subject–auxiliary inversion normally have the subject immediately following the auxiliary verb. The negative marker will thus precede the subject in synthetic negation but follow the subject in analytic negation:

	a.	b.
[5] i	*She <u>doesn't</u> agree with me.*	*She <u>does</u> <u>not</u> agree with me.*
ii	*<u>Doesn't</u> she agree with me?*	**<u>Does</u> <u>not</u> she agree with me?*
iii	**<u>Does</u> she<u>n't</u> agree with me?*	*<u>Does</u> she <u>not</u> agree with me?*

Example [iiia] is ungrammatical for the reasons just given: ·*n't* is an inflectional suffix of the verb and hence can never be separated from the verb. In general the word *not* cannot come between the auxiliary and the subject, as shown in [iib]. The construction with *not* preceding the subject is not competely excluded, however: it is occasionally found as an alternant of the normal pattern where *not* follows the subject. Compare:

[6] i *Do most self-indulgent public officials not accept bribes?*
ii *Do not most self-indulgent public officials accept bribes?*

Construction [ii] is a survival of an older pattern where *not* was quite generally permitted in this position. In speech it would be highly unnatural except in extremely formal declamation. But in writing it will still be found in sources not permitting synthetically negated auxiliaries. It is normally restricted to cases where the subject is relatively long, where it serves to avoid the lengthy interruption between auxiliary verb and *not* which makes [i] too sound somewhat stilted.[6]

Subclausal primary negation

Primary negation is normally clausal. Subclausal cases are restricted to constructions where the negated verb falls within the scope of a preceding adjunct, as in *He often isn't there when you call him.* The reversed polarity tag would be *isn't he?*, and we could have continuations like *and so is his secretary.* What is negated here, then, is the predicate (that is, the VP), not the whole clause.

[6] We have noted, however, that synthetic negatives are not permitted in inverted conditionals, and this may facilitate the use of the construction with *not* preceding the subject: *She might have regretted her smallness <u>had</u> <u>not</u> all the parts been so well-proportioned.*

2.2 Imperative negation

Imperative clauses have a pattern of negation that cannot be reduced to the generalisations about the other types of negation, uniformly using the negative auxiliary *don't*. Positive and negative examples of the main types of imperative are shown in [7]:

[7]	POSITIVE IMPERATIVES	NEGATIVE IMPERATIVES
i	a. *Look at me.*	b. *Don't look at me.*
ii	a. *You look at me!*	b. *Don't you look at me!*
iii	a. *Everyone shout it out.*	b. *Don't everyone shout it out.*

Contrasts between imperatives and non-imperatives

Verbal negation in imperatives differs from that in other clauses in the following respects:

(a) Auxiliary ***do*** required even with auxiliaries

[8]	IMPERATIVE	DECLARATIVE
i	a. *Don't be afraid.*	b. *You aren't afraid.*
ii	a. *Don't have eaten all the pizza by the time I get back.*	b. *I hope [they haven't eaten all the pizza by the time I get back].*

Here auxiliary ***do*** appears in imperatives but not in comparable declaratives – because they contain auxiliary verbs, which permit primary verbal negation without the addition of supportive ***do***. The most usual case of this kind involves the verb ***be***, as in [i]. In [ii] we have the perfect auxiliary ***have***; this is quite rare in imperatives, so [iia] may seem somewhat contrived. Nevertheless, its grammatical status is sharply different from that of the clearly ungrammatical **Haven't eaten all the pizza by the time I get back!* The distinction between auxiliary verbs and lexical verbs is thus irrelevant to the formation of negative imperatives: ***do*** is required in all cases.[7]

(b) Order of subject and verb

The subject, in imperatives that have one, as in [7ii–iii], precedes the verb in the positive, but usually follows *don't* in the negative (but see also Ch. 10, §9.7.3). No such order change accompanies negation in other clause types.

(c) Synthetic negation is found even though imperatives have plain form verbs

The verb in imperative clauses is in the plain form: it is not a tensed form, as evident from the form of ***be*** in *Be careful* and the absence of the ·*s* suffix on *shout* in [7iii]. The negative imperative is the only construction containing an inflectional negative that is not a primary verb-form.

(d) Restrictions on analytic negation

In speech, verbal negation in imperatives is generally expressed synthetically, with *don't*. Analytic *do not* occurs mainly in writing and is a somewhat stronger marker of formal style than analytic negation is with primary verb-forms. It is particularly unlikely when the imperative has an overt subject, and in the case of *you* it can be regarded

[7] Verbally negated imperatives without ***do*** will occasionally be encountered, but they are conscious archaisms, surviving as relics, usually biblical, literary, or proverbial: *Fear not*; *Be not afraid*; *Waste not, want not*; *Judge not that ye be not judged*; etc. This construction is comparable to that illustrated in footnote 3.

as ungrammatical:

[9]	i	a. *Don't any of you think you have heard the last of this matter.*	b. *Do not any of you think you have heard the last of this matter.*
	ii	a. *Don't you renege on our deal.*	b. **Do not you renege on our deal.*

Note that there is no alternative version of the analytic construction where *not* follows the subject. This order is found only in interrogatives: *Do you not habitually renege on your promises?*

2.3 Secondary verbal negation

The final category of verbal negation covers clauses other than imperatives that contain a secondary verb-form: a plain form, past participle, or gerund-participle. Since imperatives have plain form verbs, this category might be called non-imperative secondary negation, but we will simplify by dropping the 'non-imperative' and speak of secondary negation. The category covers subjunctive and non-finite clauses with verbal negation.

2.3.1 Formal marking of secondary negation

Secondary verbal negation differs from the others in two respects. First, it never introduces the auxiliary verb ***do***. Second, it is always analytic: negative verb-forms are all primary except for the *don't* of imperatives. In all cases, then, secondary verbal negatives are formed by placing *not* as premodifier of the VP, as in the following subordinate clauses (enclosed in square brackets):

[10]		POSITIVE	NEGATIVE
	i	a. *It is vital [that he be told].*	b. *It is vital [that he not be told].*
	ii	a. *[Locking the doors] is unwise.*	b. *[Not locking the doors] is unwise.*
	iii	a. *[His accepting it] was a shock.*	b. *[His not accepting it] was a shock.*
	iv	a. *a plan [approved by the board]*	b. *a plan [not approved by the board]*
	v	a. *It looks bad [for them to smile].*	b. *It looks bad [for them not to smile].*
	vi	a. *They let me [wear high heels].*	b. *They let me [not wear high heels].*

Here [i] is subjunctive, [ii–iii] gerund-participial, [iv] past-participial, [v–vi] infinitival. The infinitival with *to* has an alternant where *not* follows *to*: *It looks bad [for them to not smile]*. Since *to* carries no identifiable contribution to meaning, there is no real possibility of any scope contrast between the two constructions: they are semantically equivalent. The one with *not* between *to* and the verb is a special case of the 'split infinitive' construction discussed in Ch. 6, §7.1.

Most clauses with secondary negation are subordinate clauses, but the minor clause types that have secondary verb-forms in main clauses with exclamatory or optative senses also show this pattern:

[11]	i	a. *A letter written on a computer!*	b. *A letter not written on a computer!*
	ii	a. *My only son getting into Harvard!*	b. *My only son not getting into Harvard!*
	iii	a. *Oh to have to visit England!*	b. *Oh to not have to visit England!*

2.3.2 Secondary negation with *not* following an auxiliary verb

When *not* comes between two verbs the issue arises as to which of them it negates. If the first verb is a lexical verb or a secondary form of an auxiliary, *not* belongs clearly with the following verb:

[12] i *She agreed [not to make a formal complaint].*
ii *Jill's instruction had been [not to take on any extra staff].*

These are straightforward cases of secondary negation, with *not* located syntactically in the infinitival clause. The matrix clauses with primary verb-forms are positive, as evident from the reversed polarity tags *didn't she?* and *hadn't it?*, and other tests. *Not* can modify a preceding verb only if it is a primary form of an auxiliary (or imperative *do*). This is the case we need to consider further.

(a) *Not* immediately following a primary form of an auxiliary

In this position *not* normally modifies the auxiliary verb and hence marks primary negation. This is so even when the auxiliary is not within the semantic scope of the negative:

[13] a. *They must not read it.* b. *They need not read it.*

In [a] *must* has scope over *not* ("it is required that they not read it"), whereas in [b] *not* has scope over *need* ("it is not necessary for them to read it") – cf. Ch. 3, §9.3.1. Nevertheless, *not* belongs syntactically in the matrix clause in both cases. Note, for example, that they take positive tags (*must they?*, *need they?*) – and that the analytic negation alternates with synthetic *mustn't* and *needn't.*

There are, however, three exceptions to the general rule, illustrated in:

[14] i *Jill's instruction was [not to take on any extra staff – in any circumstances].*
ii *You can [not answer their letters]: you're not legally required to respond.*
iii *You can't [not go with them].*

Not after ***be*** in its specifying sense

Example [14i] can be interpreted like [12ii] without the perfect tense feature: "Jill's instruction was that they not take on extra staff". The reversed polarity tag in this case would be *wasn't it?*, for the main clause is positive. The construction illustrates the specifying use of ***be*** with a clause in the complement position that happens to be subjectless and negative. In [14i] it is impossible to replace *was not* by *wasn't* and preserve the sense.

However, it is perfectly possible for the *not* to follow ***be*** in sentences of superficially similar form and belong to the copular clause (if the copula is in a primary form): compare the attested sentence *The sole purpose of the criminal law is not to amuse Mr Mortimer*, which we understand as denying that the purpose of the criminal law is to amuse Mr Mortimer, not as affirming the bizarre claim that its purpose is to avoid amusing him. The construction is therefore potentially ambiguous. We included the prosodically detached *in any circumstances* in [14i] because it strongly favours the secondary negation reading that we wish to illustrate.

Can not and possibility of abstention

The meaning of the first clause in [14ii] is "You are permitted not to answer their letters", with *can* thus having scope over *not.* In this use, the *not* will characteristically be stressed and prosodically associated with *answer* rather than *can* by means of a very slight break separating it from the unstressed *can.* The fact that the modal has scope over *not* makes this semantically comparable to [13a], but syntactically it differs in that it has secondary negation rather than the primary negation of [13a]. This is evident from the fact that the reversed polarity tag for the *can* clause is *can't you?* The meaning is quite different from that of *You can't/cannot answer their letters*, which has primary negation in the *can* clause, and where the negative has scope over the modal ("It is not possible or permitted for you to answer their letters").

In [14ii], therefore – unlike [13a] – the syntax matches the semantics, with the *not* located in the subordinate, non-finite, clause. But this construction is fairly rare, and sounds somewhat contrived. It would not normally occur with modals other than ***can*** and ***may***.

Can't not: secondary negation combined with primary negation

In [14iii] (*You can't not go with them*) the *not* follows a negative auxiliary: a verb cannot be negated twice, so the *not* can only belong in the non-finite clause. Note that the matrix clause is straightforwardly negative by virtue of the synthetic negation: the reversed polarity tag is *can you?*, just as it is for *You can't go with them*. Syntactically, two negatives do not cancel each other out to make a positive: there are two negative elements in [14iii] but the main clause remains syntactically negative.

In principle, this construction is possible with any auxiliary verb: *I won't not speak this time, I promise you.* It can even be used, and has been attested, when the auxiliary is supportive ***do***, to deny a negative assertion that has been made: *I DIDN'T not listen to you.* Compare also imperative *Don't not go just because of me.* These examples have one negative immediately within the scope of another, so that they cancel each other out semantically. *I won't not speak* is truth-conditionally (but not rhetorically) equivalent to *I will speak*; *I DIDN'T not listen* is similarly equivalent to *I DID listen*; *Don't not go* is equivalent to *Go.* In most circumstances the simpler positive would be preferred, but special circumstances can make the use of mutually cancelling negatives preferable.[8]

The *can* case in [14iii] differs from these in that the first negative has scope over *can*, so that *You can't not go with them* is not equivalent to *You can go with them*; it is equivalent to *You must go with them*, but there is sufficient pragmatic difference between *can't not* and *must* to motivate the use of both forms.

(b) *Not* syntactically separated from an auxiliary

Not can more readily mark secondary negation if it is adjacent to the secondary verb-form but not to the auxiliary. There are three distinct ways in which such a separation of the auxiliary from the negator can come about.

Infinitival *to* preceding *not*

The subordinator *to* can separate an auxiliary from *not.* One very clear case concerns infinitival *to* in the specifying ***be*** construction. Compare:

[15] a. *Their aim is not <u>to</u> change things.* b *Their aim is <u>to</u> not change things.*

[8] Three attested examples of mutually cancelling adjacent negative elements of this kind are found in the following interesting piece of dialogue from a film script. The situation is between a man, A, who has run into a woman, B, whom he had been dating but has not seen for a while.

A: *Don't think that I have [<u>not</u> called you]. I have<u>n't</u> [<u>not</u> called you]. I mean . . . , I don't mean that I have<u>n't</u> [<u>not</u> called you] because that's a double negative so as to say that I have called you. . .*
B: *When did you call?*
A: *I didn't. But I did<u>n't</u> [<u>not</u> call you] in the way that you might think that I didn't call you.* [i.e. as indicating that I didn't want to see you again]

Each occurrence of *not* is prosodically associated with ***call***, and marks secondary negation in the non-finite clause functioning as complement of the auxiliary.

In [a] we find the ambiguity between primary negation in the matrix clause and secondary negation in the infinitival clause that we mentioned in the discussion of [14i]; this ambiguity is resolved in favour of primary negation in the matrix if *is not* is replaced by synthetic *isn't*. In [b], by contrast, only the secondary negation reading is possible: the subordinator *to* marks the beginning of the infinitival VP of the subordinate clause, so *not* can only be in that subordinate clause.

Adjuncts between auxiliary and VP

A second case has an adjunct between the auxiliary and the *not*:

[16] i *You can simply not answer their letters, can't you?*
ii *They have always not enforced that regulation, haven't they?*

The intervening adjunct serves to dissociate the *not* from the auxiliary. Compare [16i] with [14ii] above: adding the *simply* facilitates the association of *not* with the non-finite clause. In [16ii] the universally quantified adverb *always* has scope over *not*, forcing the association of *not* with *enforce*, to give the meaning "waive".

Subject between auxiliary and *not*

A third possibility is for the subject to intervene between the auxiliary and its complement, when the matrix clause has subject–auxiliary inversion:

[17] i *Would you not put your feet on the sofa.*
ii *Can you not ask them to help you?*
iii *Did you not agree with her?*

The natural interpretation of [i] is as a request not to put your feet on the sofa: *not* belongs in the *put* clause, and there is no alternant with synthetic negation in the matrix clause (i.e. we can't replace *would you not* by *wouldn't you*). But [ii] is ambiguous. It can be interpreted like [i], i.e. as a request not to ask them (in which case a full stop might be preferred to the question mark); this reading would be forced if *please* were inserted before *not*. Or it can be interpreted with *not* having scope over the modal, equivalent to synthetic *Can't you ask them to help you?*; in this reading we have primary negation in the matrix clause.

Strictly speaking, [17iii] is likewise ambiguous between primary negation of the matrix and secondary negation of the complement. The latter reading would be assisted if there were a slight prosodic separation of *you* from *not*, as in [14ii], but this reading is strongly disfavoured as the relevant meaning could be expressed much more clearly by *Did you disagree with her?* Again we could insert an *always* to force the secondary negation construal: *Did you always not agree with her?*

3 Non-verbal negation

We turn now to constructions where the negator is not associated with the verb. We look first in §3.1 at analytic negation marked by *not*. Then in §§3.2–3 we consider synthetic negation marked by absolute and approximate negators respectively. Finally, in §3.4 we discuss the semantic difference between affixal negation and verbal negation. Analytic negation marked by *no* (as in answers to questions) is discussed in §7.

3.1 *Not* as a marker of non-verbal negation

The clearest cases where *not* marks non-verbal negation are illustrated in:

[1] i [*Not all of them*] *regarded it as a success.*
ii *He seemed* [*not entirely honest*].

These clauses contain primary forms of lexical verbs, which are not permitted with verbal negation: compare the verbal negation constructions *They did not all regard it as a success* and *He did not seem entirely honest* (which have synthetic alternants containing *didn't*).

When we turn to constructions with auxiliary verbs a contrast emerges because of the very strong tendency for *not* after an auxiliary to be interpreted as primary negation:

[2] i [*Not all of them*] *had regarded it as a success.*
ii *He was not entirely honest.*

The negation in [i] remains clearly non-verbal: *not* is part of the subject NP, and not in a position where there could be any doubt about that. In [ii], however, *not* follows the auxiliary, and the sentence is most likely to be interpreted as a case of primary verbal negation. Note that the reversed polarity tag for [1ii] would be *didn't he?*, whereas that for [2ii] would be *was he?*

As in the case of [17] in the previous section, our syntactic description does in fact entail that [2ii] is structurally ambiguous, with *not* marking either verbal or non-verbal negation, because we have said nothing to exclude the bracketed AdjP constituent in [1ii] from occurring as the complement of the copula. And indeed, the non-verbal negation reading can be forced if the copula is separated from the *not*; thus we might find *He was both not entirely honest and somewhat aggressive.*[9] Nonetheless, the likelihood that an example like [2ii] will be seen as ambiguous is very low in most contexts.

We now proceed to review a dozen constructions where things are not as subtle as this, and *not* can be shown to be quite clearly a marker of non-verbal negation. (An additional one where *not* functions as an anaphoric complement, as in *I think not*, is covered in §7.2.)

(a) The *not all* type

[3] i *Not all people have had the opportunities you have had.*
ii *Not often do we see her lose her cool like that.*
iii **I agree with not all your arguments.*
iv **He not often visits his parents.*

Not combines with a quantifier to form a negative phrase: *not all* is a negative DP, *not often* a negative AdvP. The *not* of course has scope over the quantifier. Such phrases can occur within the subject, as in [i], or before the subject, as in [ii]. The *not* here marks clausal negation, so *not often* in [ii] triggers subject–auxiliary inversion. These phrases are excluded from post-verbal position ([iii]) or central position ([iv]). Instead of [iii–iv] we need verbal negation: *I don't agree with all your arguments* and *He doesn't often visit his parents.*

[9] A further case is in predicative AdjPs modified by *so*, as in %*It was so not funny.* This is a relatively new construction, characteristic of the informal speech of younger speakers.

There are severe restrictions on what quantifiers take *not* as modifier in this construction (cf. Ch. 5, §11). Compare:

[4]	i	*not all*	*not every*	*not many*	*not much*	*not often*
	ii	**not both*	**not each*	**not most*	**not some*	?*not any*

In clauses with verbal negation *each, most,* and *some* do not readily occur within the scope of negation. The salient interpretation of *I hadn't read most of it,* for example, is "Most of it I hadn't read". There is therefore little need for a phrase that explicitly brings them within the scope of a negative.

Both can occur readily enough inside the scope of verbal negation: *I couldn't afford both of them.* But there is still little need for a phrase combining *not* with *both.* Suppose two swimmers have attempted to swim the Bering Straits but have not both succeeded. If we want to express the quantification in the subject we would very likely be in a position to say *Neither of them succeeded* or *Only one of them succeeded,* which are more informative, and hence generally preferable to the inadmissible **Not both of them succeeded.*

Not any is of doubtful acceptability. Normally one would instead use *no* or *none,* as in *None of her friends had supported her,* but *not any* is marginally acceptable as an emphatic alternant: ?*Not* ANY *of her friends had supported her.*

(b) *Not one*

[5] i *Not one person supported the proposal.*
ii *They had found not one mistake.*

Not one has a somewhat wider distribution than the items in [4i], in that it can occur post-verbally, as in [5ii]. We can also have *not* in combination with *a* or *a single*: *They had found not a single mistake.*

(c) *Not two,* etc.: "less than"

[6] i *Not two years ago this company was ranked in the top ten.*
ii *He was here not ten minutes ago.*

Not behaves differently in combination with numerals denoting numbers higher than one than in (b) above. In the first place, *not two,* etc., are largely confined to measure phrases, of time, distance, and the like. They could not replace *one* in such examples as [5ii]: **They found not two mistakes.* Secondly, *not* in [6] marks subclausal negation: the clauses are positive, as evident from the lack of inversion in [i], and the reversed polarity tags, which would be *wasn't it?* and *wasn't he?* The clauses in [5], by contrast are negative (though *not one* or *not a single*... can also occur in measure phrases with subclausal negation). The interpretation of *not* in [6] is "less than", and this sense is found also in such expressions as *not an hour ago, not long before his death, not far from the post office,* etc., which likewise do not mark clausal negation.

(d) *Not a little, not a few*

[7] *His speech had caused not a little confusion.*

Not can also combine with the determinatives *a little* and *a few.* These have paucal meaning, and the effect of the *not* is to negate the low upper bound on the quantification, giving "a fairly large amount/number" (compare the use of *no* in *no small achievement* in [29]). The negative thus has very narrow scope and the clause itself is positive – witness the tag *hadn't it?*

(e) *Not even, not only*

[8] i a. *Not even Ed approved of the plan.* b. *Not only Ed approved of the plan.*
ii a. *Not even then did he lose patience.* b. **Not only then did he lose patience.*

Not commonly combines with the focusing adverbs *even* and *only*. *Not even* generally marks clausal negation: the tag for [ia] would be *did he?* Clause [ib], by contrast, is positive. A tag would be rather unlikely here, but the construction readily allows a continuation with a positive connective adjunct: *Max approved of it too.* In [ii] we have inversion in [a], whereas the inversion in [iib] is ungrammatical.[10] The difference between *not even* and *not only* reflects the semantic difference: it follows from [ia] that Ed did not approve of the plan but from [ib] that he did approve of it. (In fact [ib] presupposes, takes for granted, that he approved of it: that is why it resists the addition of a confirmatory tag.)

Not only marks clause negation when it functions by itself as a clause adjunct: [<u>*Not only*</u> *was the acting appalling,*] *the movie was far too long.*

(f) *Not very, not quite*, etc.

[9] i *We had a*[<u>*not very*</u> *amicable*] *discussion.*
ii *It somehow sounded* [<u>*not quite*</u> *right*].
iii *I found his story* [<u>*not wholly*</u> *convincing*].
iv *He spoke* [<u>*not very*</u> *confidently*].
v [<u>*Not very*</u> *many of them*] *had been damaged.*

Not combines with various degree expressions that can modify adjectives, adverbs, or certain determinatives. In [i] it combines with an attributive AdjP, in [ii–iii] predicative AdjPs, in [iv] an AdvP, in [v] a DP. While [i–iv] illustrate subclausal negation, [v] is different: *not very many* behaves like *not many* in marking clausal negation and being limited to pre-verbal position.

(g) *Not unattractive*: *not* with affixally negated adjectives

[10] i *Morton was in his early fifties and* <u>*not unattractive to women*</u>.
ii *It was a* <u>*not undistinguished*</u> *private university with a large endowment.*
iii *They had fixed the walls, and purchased some* <u>*not inelegant*</u> *furniture.*

In general, attributive adjectives cannot be negated directly by *not*: cf. **a not large house* or **It looked not large.* The *not* + adjective construction illustrated in [10] is permitted only when the adjective consists of a base preceded by a productive and transparently negative prefix. Note then that we cannot have **a not anarchic society, *several not intrepid explorers*: *anarchic* and *intrepid* are etymologically divisible into negative prefix + base,

[10] *Not only then* would not be fronted even without inversion: to give it prominence we would use the cleft construction with verbal negation: *It wasn't only then that he lost patience. Not even* can occur with subclausal negation, and thus without inversion, when the focus is a measure phrase: *Not even two years ago this company was ranked in the top ten, wasn't it?*

but this analysis is not synchronically transparent.[11] A further condition is that the adjective must be gradable. This excludes examples like **a not immoral purpose*, **this not uncrystalline substance*, or **a not illegal act.* In these uses the adjectives are classificatory rather than gradable: purposes are either moral or not, substances either form crystals or they do not, acts are either legal or not.

There has been occasional prescriptive condemnation of the '*not un·*' construction, though most manuals are perfectly clear in their view that it is fully acceptable. It would certainly be mistaken to imagine that *attractive* should or could be substituted for *not unattractive* to express the same meaning. The two have different meanings. The adjective *attractive* denotes an appearance that ranks towards the positive end of a scale that has ugliness at the negative end, beauty at the positive end, and a range of indeterminate looks in the middle. The *un·* reverses the orientation of the scale to give an adjective denoting an appearance ranked towards the lower end of the scale. The *not* yields a negation of being towards the lower end of the scale, suggesting an appearance ranked towards the positive end, but only guardedly so, since the middle of the range is not excluded, and the phrase is too cautious to suggest that the user intended to indicate a high degree of beauty:

[11] Impressionistic graph of the meanings of *attractive* and *not unattractive*

attractive

not unattractive

UGLINESS INTERMEDIATE LOOKS BEAUTY

(h) *Not unnaturally*: negation of adverbs

[12] i *Not unexpectedly, Charles was late for the meeting.*
ii *Not unreasonably, he asked for payment in advance.*
iii *Not surprisingly, they didn't want any part of it.*

Again, adverbs cannot in general be negated directly by *not*: cf. **Not stupidly, he asked for payment in advance.* The exceptions illustrated in [12] are similar to those with adjectives in [10] – except that *surprisingly* (which is roughly synonymous with *unexpectedly*) accepts *not* even though it has no negative prefix. The *not* in [12] has scope over just the adverb: the clauses in [i–ii] are positive, while that in [iii] is negative by virtue of the verbal negation.

(i) *Not* with PPs

[13] i *Not at any stage of the proceedings did she contemplate giving up.*
ii *Not for the first time, she felt utterly betrayed.*

Not can modify a limited range of PPs, resulting either in clausal negation as in [i], or subclausal negation, as in [ii]. The difference here is again shown by the presence or absence of inversion. It correlates also with a difference in meaning: [i] entails that she did not contemplate giving up, while [ii] entails that she did feel utterly betrayed.

[11] A subtle point here derives from the fact there are adjectives treated as affixally negated by some speakers and not by others. For example, *impious* is pronounced /ɪm'paɪəs/ by some, making it clear that it is analysable into negative prefix + *pious*; but others pronounce it as /'ɪmpɪəs/, not related in pronunciation to *pious*. In general, *%a not impious man* is acceptable for the first group of speakers, but not for the second.

(j) *Not* in verbless clauses

[14] i *Not an accomplished dancer, he moved rather clumsily.*
ii *Not under any illusions about the matter, he continued to be cautious.*
iii *We need someone not afraid of taking risks.*

These are equivalent to the verbal constructions *not being an accomplished dancer, not being under any illusions about the matter, who is not afraid of taking risks.* As in these latter examples, the negative does not have scope beyond the subordinate clause: the matrix clauses in [14] are all positive.

(k) *Not* + *that* clause

[15] i *The film never quite generates his trademark level of icy paranoia. Not that it doesn't try.*
ii *I don't think they should be allowed to use our public health services – not that I have anything against immigrants, of course.*
iii *There are spare blankets in here, not that you'll have any need of them.*

This construction may be glossed as "This is not, however, to say/suggest that . . .". In each case, the *not* calls up a proposition that might be naturally assumed or expected in the context, and denies that it is in fact true. In [i] what is denied is that the film doesn't try to generate the icy paranoia usually found in the director's works; in [ii] that the speaker has xenophobic views; and in [iii] that there is reason to think that it will be useful to know where the spare blankets are kept because you might be cold enough to need them. None of these are linguistically explicit.

The syntactic analysis is somewhat problematic. In terms of function the construction occupies a non-embedded position, like a main clause. In terms of its structure, we might take *not* as modifying the content clause (as in *not all* it modifies *all*, and so on). If so, the whole construction will have the form of a subordinate clause even though it is not functionally subordinate; as with other cases of this kind (such as *That it should have come to this!*) there is implicit rather than explicit functional subordination.

(l) *Not* in coordination

[16] i *They are now leaving [not on Friday but on Saturday].*
ii *They are now leaving [on Saturday, not on Friday].*
iii *They've invited [you and your brother, but not me].*

Not is found in a variety of coordinative constructions (discussed further in Ch. 15, §2.6). In [i] *not* appears in the first coordinate, and there is an equivalent construction with verbal negation: *They aren't now leaving on Friday but on Saturday.* (The non-verbal version is admissible only by virtue of the coordination: compare **They are now leaving not on Friday.*) In [ii–iii] *not* belongs in the second coordinate – without a coordinator in [ii] (where the coordinates are conceived of as mutually exclusive), following coordinator *but* in [iii]. In all of these constructions the negation is subclausal, with *not* having scope over only one of the coordinates. Hence the tags or continuations seen in *They are now leaving not on Friday but on Saturday, aren't they?* and *They are now leaving on Saturday, not on Friday, and so are the Smiths.*[12]

[12] Where the *not* belongs in the second element, the negated phrase may be detached as a supplement, so that what precedes is a whole clause, which may take its own tag: *They are now leaving on Saturday, aren't they, not on Friday?*

The coordinates in construction [16ii] may be verbs, but the negation is still subclausal:

[17] *The night turned viciously cold under a sky crowded with stars that [shone, not twinkled,] in the diamond-clear air.*

The scope of the *not* is just the second coordinate, so this is not a case of verbal negation of the clause – which is why we do not have supportive do (cf. **shone, didn't twinkle).*

Unintegrated final *not*

[18] i %*I'm so glad those old people came to the party . . . not!*
ii %*Obviously the government is going to tell us the whole truth . . . not!*

This construction is found mainly in younger-generation speech (popularised and perhaps originated by characters in an American television comedy sketch) but is occasionally echoed in recent journalistic writing. As a humorous way to signal irony or insincerity, a final emphatic *not* is added following a clause, retracting the assertion made. A comparable effect can be achieved by attaching *I DON'T think* instead of *not.*

3.2 The synthetic absolute negators

The absolute negators are:

[19] i *no, none, nobody, no one, nothing, nowhere, no place* (informal AmE)
ii *neither, nor, never*

No and *none* are dependent and independent forms of the determinative ***no***, while the other items in [i] are compounds containing *no*: in spite of the orthography we take *no one* ("nobody") and *no place* ("nowhere") to be grammatically single words. The three words in [ii] are transparently related to *either, or,* and *ever.*[13]

3.2.1 Clausal negation

In the default case the negators in [19] mark clausal negation: we look at this construction first and then turn in §3.2.2 to the subclausal case. The examples in [20] illustrate the clausal negation behaviour of clauses containing these items:

[20]	i	*[Kim had done nothing about it,] and neither had Pat.*	[connective *neither*]
	ii	*[They never replied to your letter,] did they?*	[positive tag]
	iii	*In no city has she been entirely comfortable.*	[subject–auxiliary inversion]

Note that in [iii] we have subject–auxiliary inversion triggered by the preposing of the PP *in no city.* The negative property of *no* percolates upwards in a way that is similar to that in which the interrogative property percolates upwards in *In which city has she been entirely comfortable?* The negative or interrogative property percolates upwards from the determiner to the NP, and thence to the PP (see Ch. 10, §7.9).

[13] There is also an archaic alternant of *nothing,* namely *naught.* But as such it is now restricted to a handful of collocations, as in *It availed him naught, It will come to naught.* In AmE *naught* can also be a variant spelling of *nought* ("zero"), which is not syntactically a negation marker; it is discussed in Ch. 5, §7.6.

Alternation with verbal negation constructions

Clausal negation marked by the absolute negators is generally in alternation with verbal negation in which *no* is replaced by *any* in the case of [19i] and by *either*, *or*, and *ever* in the case of [19ii]. Compare:

[21]		NON-VERBAL NEGATION	VERBAL NEGATION
	i	a. *They showed no remorse.*	b. *They didn't show any remorse.*
	ii	a. *We liked none of them.*	b. *We didn't like any of them.*
	iii	a. *You did nothing about it.*	b. *You didn't do anything about it.*
	iv	a. *I knew neither of them.*	b. *I didn't know either of them.*
	v	a. *He neither knew nor cared where his children were.*	b. *He didn't either know or care where his children were.*
	vi	a. *She had never felt more alone.*	b. *She hadn't ever felt more alone.*

There are three restrictions that apply to the alternation between the non-verbal and verbal constructions.

(a) No verbal negation counterpart with negator in clause-initial constituent

Where the negator falls within the subject or an element preceding the subject, there is no direct verbal negation counterpart:

[22]			
	i	a. *Nobody knew where Kim was.*	b. **Anybody didn't know where Kim was.*
	ii	a. *At no stage did she complain.*	b. **At any stage she didn't complain.*
	iii	a. *I didn't go and neither did he.*	b. **I didn't go and either didn't he.*

In the case of [iib/iiib], the ungrammaticality of the verbal negation construction can be corrected by placing the element in post-verbal position: *She didn't complain at any stage* and *I didn't go and he didn't go either.*

(b) Verbal negation counterparts with *no* in predicative complements

Where *no* determines an NP in predicative complement function there may or may not be a verbal equivalent, depending on the interpretation of the negative NP. Compare:

[23]			
	i	a. *This is no place for a child.*	b. *This isn't any place for a child.*
	ii	a. *This is no time to give up.*	b. *This isn't any time to give up.*
	iii	a. *That is no way to behave.*	b. *That isn't any way to behave.*
	iv	a. *I'm no angel.*	b. ?*I'm not any angel.*
	v	a. *You are no electrician.*	b. ?*You're not any electrician.*
	vi	a. *He's no friend, is he?*	b. ?*He isn't any friend, is he?*

The examples in [i–iii] show the regular relationship between the two constructions, but in [iv–vi] the [b] versions are of questionable acceptability and in any case do not have the same meaning as the [a] versions. It is [iv–vi] that illustrate the usual pattern for predicative NPs with *no*: pairs like those in [i–iii] are largely limited to NPs with simple and basic head nouns like *place*, *time*, and *way*, and subjects like *this* or *that*. As discussed in Ch. 5, §7.8, the interpretations of the [a] examples in [iv–vi] involve the stereotypical qualities associated with the set that the head noun denotes: angels, electricians, and friends in this case. Thus to make [iva] true it is neither necessary nor sufficient that I should not be a member of the set of angels; the sentence claims that I do not have the stereotypical qualities of angels (perfect goodness, kindness, patience, or whatever). Analogously for [va/via]. For this sort of interpretation, the [b] versions are not appropriate paraphrases; they convey the literal meanings that the [a] meanings lack; for example, [ivb] means "I am not any specific member of the set of angels".

(c) Limitation on distance between verb and negator

In principle, non-verbal negators marking clausal negation can appear in any position in the clause. However, as the position gets further from the beginning of the clause and/or more deeply embedded, the acceptability of the construction decreases, simply because more and more of the clause is available to be misinterpreted as a positive before the negator is finally encountered at a late stage in the processing of the sentence:

[24] i a. *I am not satisfied with the proposal you have put to me in any way.*
b. ?*I am satisfied with the proposal you have put to me in no way.*
ii a. *As far as I can recall, I have not purchased food at the drive-through window of a fast-food restaurant on any street in this city.*
b. ?*As far as I can recall, I have purchased food at the drive-through window of a fast-food restaurant on no street in this city.*

When the negator is in a subordinate clause, particularly a finite one, and is significantly far away from the matrix clause verb, it will typically not be interpreted as negating the matrix clause, but rather will be heard as negating the subordinate clause in which it is located. Compare, for example:

[25] i *I was not trying to imply that Bob had offered bribes to any official.*
ii *I was trying to imply that Bob had offered bribes to no official.* [≠ [i]]
iii *I was trying to imply that Bob had not offered bribes to any official.* [= [ii]]

Example [ii] is not synonymous with [i]: it is, rather, an alternant of [iii]. Compare also:

[26] i *I cannot recall actually seeing a magpie attempting to steal anything.*
ii #*I can recall actually seeing a magpie attempting to steal nothing.* [≠ [i]]

In [26i] there is an occurrence of *anything* in a subordinate clause with primary verb negation in the matrix clause. If the primary verb negation is removed and the *anything* in the subordinate clause is replaced by *nothing*, we get [ii], but this is not equivalent to [i]. Example [ii] is understood with subordinate clause negation, either of the *steal* clause or the *attempt* clause; e.g., picking the *attempt* clause as the scope, the meaning is "I can recall actually seeing a magpie not attempting to steal anything". But seeing a bird not attempting to steal is hardly worth mentioning, so [ii] sounds bizarre.

It is not entirely impossible for a negator in a subordinate clause to negate the matrix one, merely unusual. Where it happens, the subordinate clause will virtually always be non-finite, usually infinitival:

[27] i *I don't know why they say they were forced to take their shoes off; [WE certainly forced them to do nothing of the kind].*
ii *[We are requiring people to pay nothing for the concert,] but nonetheless we are hoping for at least some donations at the door.*

Here the negator is located in the underlined infinitival clause but marks negation of the bracketed finite clause, as shown by the equivalence with the verbal negation versions *WE certainly didn't force them to do anything of the kind* and *We are not requiring people to pay anything for the concert.* In cases like this, then, the negative property percolates upwards from one clause into a higher one.

3.2.2 Subclausal negation

We review here three situations in which absolute negators mark subclausal negation.

(a) Negative NP as complement of preposition

[28] i *I could do a lot for this place* with no money at all.
ii *Kim regretted having married someone* with no ambition.
iii *It was a matter* of no consequence.
iv *They were arguing* about nothing.
v *She finished it* in no time.

The PPs in [i–iii] are semantically equivalent to clauses or PPs with clausal complements: compare *even if I had no money at all*, *who had no ambition*, *which had no importance*. And just as the negative in these latter constructions would not percolate upwards beyond the subordinate clause, so the scope of the negative in the PP examples does not percolate upwards into the containing clause. Example [iv] is, strictly speaking, ambiguous. It has an interpretation as clausal negation, equivalent to the verbal negative *They weren't arguing about anything*; much more likely, however, is the meaning "They were arguing about something completely trivial", and here the clause is positive (with *weren't they?* as tag). *In no time* in [v] is an idiom meaning "extremely quickly"; it is an instance of hyperbole: a desirably small amount of time implying a very high speed is overstated as being zero and thus implying infinite speed. Also idiomatic is the PP in *They were obviously* up to no good.[14]

(b) *No + mean, small*, etc.

[29] *Getting that degree was* no mean achievement, *wasn't it?*

Here, in contrast to [28v], we have understatement: we understand "quite an achievement", a positive meaning. Similarly: *His resignation was in no small measure involuntary, wasn't it?*

(c) Semantically clausal NP

[30] i *They predicted no rain.*
ii *They promised no increase in income tax.* } [ambiguously clausal or subclausal]

Example [i] has an ordinary clausal negation interpretation, equivalent to *They didn't predict any rain*. But it can also be interpreted as subclausal negation, with the NP serving as a compressed expression of a clause, "They predicted that there would be no rain". Similarly for [ii].[15]

3.3 The approximate negators

The class of approximate negators comprises the following seven words:

[31] i DETERMINATIVES: *few, little*
ii ADVERBS: *rarely, seldom; barely, hardly, scarcely*

[14] A non-prepositional idiom is *no end*, meaning "very much", as in *We enjoyed it no end and so did the others*, or *She had no end of a good time, didn't she?*

[15] This type is not mutually exclusive with (a) above, for such NPs can occur as complement to a preposition: *The weak US dollar is expected to weigh on equity and bond markets, despite no signs of inflation in Australia* ("despite there being no signs of inflation").

Few and *little* are determinatives. They function in NP structure as determiner (*Few people liked it*) or fused determiner-head (*Few of them liked it*). *Few* selects count plural heads, *little* non-count singulars. *Little* also functions as degree adjunct modifying verbs (*He little understood the implications of what he had done*) or comparatives (*He felt little better*). *Few* and *little* are the plain forms of the lexemes ***few*** and **little**, but the comparative and superlative forms (*fewer, fewest, less, least*) do not behave syntactically as negators.

The words in [31ii] are adverbs. *Rarely* and *seldom* are adverbs of frequency, while the other three are adverbs of degree, characteristically modifying verbs (*She hardly moved*), adjectives (*He was barely intelligible*), and a restricted range of determinatives (especially *any*: *There was scarcely any food left*).

We refer to these items as approximate negators on the basis of such contrasts as the following with absolute negators or verbal negation:

[32] i	a. *<u>Few</u> of them will survive.*	b. *<u>None</u> of them will survive.*
ii	a. *Ed <u>rarely</u> leaves the house.*	b. *Ed <u>never</u> leaves the house.*
iii	a. *She had <u>hardly</u> moved.*	b. *She had<u>n't</u> moved.*

While the [b] examples indicate absolute zero, those in [a] express an imprecise quantification which is close to or approximates zero. However, the fact that the approximate negators do not indicate absolute zero gives them a somewhat equivocal status with respect to the positive vs negative contrast. Take [iia], for example. This entails that Ed doesn't often leave the house, that he leaves the house no more often than occasionally, and in this respect has a negative meaning. On the other hand, it implicates that he sometimes does leave the house: in this respect it differs from [iib] and has to some extent a positive character. We will attempt to shed some light on the status of these forms by considering three issues: the nature of the "not zero" implicature, their likeness to prototypical negators with respect to what we will call the 'direction of entailment', and their behaviour in the constructions we have used to distinguish between negative and positive clauses. *Few* and *little* contrast with *a few* and *a little*, which are unequivocally positive, and it will help clarify the status of *few* and *little* to show how they differ from *a few* and *a little* in these three areas.

(a) Nature of the "not zero" implicature

As imprecise quantifiers, the approximate negators cover a range of the relevant scale of quantification. In general, they **entail** that the upper bound of that range is not high but only **implicate** that the lower bound is not zero. We can show the relations between *a few* and *few* in relation to multal *many* and the absolute negator ***no*** in a diagram. The arrows stand for two different relations according to the labels: 'E~' means 'entails the falsity of' and 'I~' means 'implicates the falsity of'.

[33]

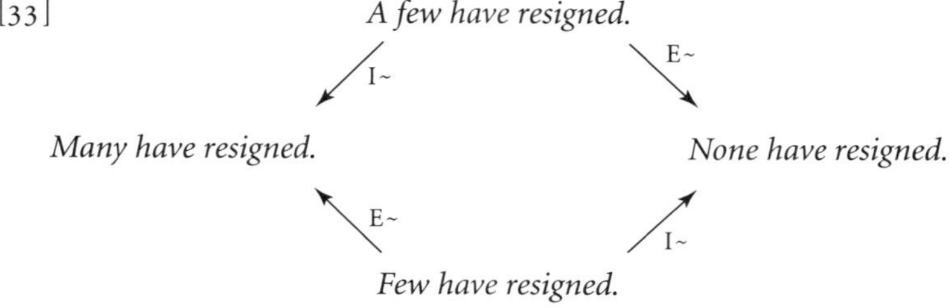

A few have resigned implicates that *Many have resigned* is false, and entails that *None have resigned* is false. The meaning of *a few* sets a lower bound of three, so if no one has resigned then *A few have resigned* is quite clearly false. If I know that many have resigned, then I would not normally use the sentence with *a few*, since to use *many* would be more informative. But the statement with *a few* would not be false in this context: if many have resigned, then it is necessarily true that a few have resigned. And it could be that I didn't yet know whether many had: I could still make the claim with *a few* without excluding the possibility that the stronger claim with *many* would also turn out to be true.

Now with *few* we have precisely the reverse situation: *Few have resigned* entails that *Many have resigned* is false, and implicates that *None have resigned* is false. The first of these is obvious, but it is not immediately obvious that the second is just an implicature, because it is a very strong implicature: I would be very unlikely to say *Few have resigned* unless I knew that at least some had resigned. But in other cases it can be less strong. Consider such an example as *Few of you will have experienced the kind of intimidation which our colleague Kim Jones has had to endure over the last several months.* Here it could well be that none of you have in fact experienced it: in this case I say *few* rather than *none* not because the latter would be false but because I do not have the knowledge to justify the stronger claim that it makes.

The difference between *a few* and *few* is reflected in constructions where the implicatures are cancelled (cf. Ch. 5, §5.2):

[34] i *A few of them, indeed quite a lot, had found the proposal offensive.*
ii *Few of them, if any, will find the proposal offensive.*

In [i] *indeed quite a lot* cancels the "not multal" implicature of *a few*: we could not substitute *few* for *a few* because entailments cannot be cancelled in this way. In [ii] *if any* cancels the "not zero" implicature of *few*, and again we could not substitute *a few*, which has "not zero" as an entailment.

There may of course be other features of the clause that strengthen such "not zero" implicatures into entailments. One such case is the common construction where *barely*, *hardly*, or *scarcely* is followed by *when*:

[35] *I had hardly arrived at the office when I was summoned to see the boss.*

The meaning is that I was summoned to see the boss virtually immediately after reaching the office. Here it is entailed, not merely implicated, that I did get to the office.

(b) Direction of entailment

The concept **direction of entailment** may be illustrated by comparing the entailments in two sets of sentences, the first unproblematically negative, the second equally clearly positive. The negative set is given in [36]:

[36] i *No one would deliberately injure <u>an animal</u>.*
ii *No one would deliberately injure <u>a mammal</u>.*
iii *No one would deliberately injure <u>a horse</u>.*
iv *No one would deliberately injure <u>a racehorse</u>.*
↓ direction of entailment

The VPs have meanings expressing successively harder conditions to satisfy: only certain animals are mammals; only some of those are horses; and only some horses are racehorses.

Yet if [i] makes a true statement then all the sentences below it do. Assuming an ordering where the most general is at the top and the most specific at the bottom, we can say that the quantified NP *no one* is **downward entailing**: each example entails any that are lower on the scale but does not entail any that are higher. If no one would deliberately injure a mammal then no one would deliberately injure a horse, but it does not follow from there being no one who would deliberately injure a horse that there is no one who would deliberately injure some other kind of mammal, such as a pig.

Consider now the positive set given in:

[37] i *Most people can afford to keep an animal.* ↑
ii *Most people can afford to keep a mammal.* | direction of entailment
iii *Most people can afford to keep a horse.* |
iv *Most people can afford to keep a racehorse.* |

Here the entailments work in the opposite direction. If most people can afford to keep a horse, then most people can afford to keep a mammal, but it doesn't follow from the fact that most people can afford to keep a mammal that they can afford to keep a horse: there could be lots of people who can afford to keep only a small mammal such as a cat. Here then we will say that the quantified NP is **upward entailing**.

Not all quantifying expressions induce one or other type of entailment. For example, *Exactly ten members of the class own a horse* neither entails nor is entailed by *Exactly ten members of the class own a mammal.* Where a quantifier does yield relevant entailments, however, we can ask whether they work in a downward direction, as with negative *no*, or in an upward direction, as with positive *most.* This test then shows *few* to pattern like *no*, while *a few* behaves like *most.* Compare, for example:

[38]	DOWNWARD ENTAILING	UPWARD ENTAILING
i	a. *Few good drivers ignore signs.*	b. *A few good drivers ignore signs.*
ii	a. *Few good drivers ignore big signs.*	b. *A few good drivers ignore big signs.*

The predicate *ignore big signs* defines a more restrictive condition than *ignore signs*, so from the fact that [ia] entails [iia] we know that *few good drivers* is a downward entailing quantified NP. But [ib] does not entail [iib]: there could be a few good drivers who ignore signs, though always small ones, but none who ignore big ones. It is [iib] that entails [ib]: if there are a few who ignore big signs there must be a few (at least these same ones) who ignore signs. So *a few good drivers* is an upward entailing quantified NP.

These results tie in with those obtained in considering the entailments and implicatures in (a) above. If *few* entailed "at least some" then we couldn't have the entailment that does in fact hold between [38ia] and [iia]: it certainly doesn't follow from the fact that at least some good drivers ignore signs that at least some ignore big signs. And similarly for the [b] examples. If *a few* entailed "not many", [iib] could not entail [ib], as in fact it does. It does not follow from the fact that not many drivers ignore big signs that the number who ignore signs of any size is also small.[16]

[16] Downward entailment does not provide a foolproof indication that the construction is negative. This is shown by the expression *at most. At most 25% of Australians own an animal* entails *At most 25% of Australians own a horse*, and so on, yet these clauses (unlike the equivalent ones with *no more than*) are positive – as is evident from the connective in such a continuation as *and at most 25% of New Zealanders do so too/*either*, or the tag in *At most 25% of Australians own an animal, don't they?*

The direction of entailment test gives the same results for the other approximate negators. It is illustrated for *seldom* in:

[39] i *I had seldom* *seen such birds.*
ii *I had seldom* *clearly seen such birds.*
iii *I had seldom* *clearly seen such birds through binoculars.*
iv *I had seldom* *clearly seen such birds through really powerful binoculars.*

The conditions imposed by the VPs of successive examples are, as before, increasingly hard to meet (more people will have seen such birds than will have clearly seen them; more will have clearly seen them than will have clearly seen them through binoculars; and so on). Again, then, we have downward entailment: if [i] is true then [ii] is true; if [i] and [ii] are true then [iii] is true; and so on downward into more and more specific claims. This downward entailment property is what the adverb *seldom* contributes, for notice that if *seldom* is removed the property disappears: it is not necessarily the case that if *I had seen such birds* is true then *I had clearly seen such birds* is true and that *I had clearly seen such birds through binoculars* is true, and so on.

Care should be taken when determining whether adverbs of this sort are downward entailing to make sure that the implicit context of comparison is not changed. For example, take the sentences in [40]:

[40] i *David rarely watches films.*
ii *David rarely watches violent films.*

It is natural to interpret [i] against a background consisting of all the days of David's life, so that if he watches only one film a year, [i] is true. And it is natural to interpret [ii] against a background of all of David's visits to the cinema, so that if 90% of the films he watches are violent ones, [ii] is false. Now, it is perfectly possible to envisage David watching just ten films in ten years, but with nine of the ten being violent films. In that case a natural interpretation of [i] is true (he watches very few films per year) and a natural interpretation of [ii] is false (in fact most of the films he sees are violent). But that is not grounds for doubting that *rarely* is downward entailing.

Selection of the reference class for assessing rarity is crucial to the interpretation of the word *rare*. The proper comparison is between the truth conditions of the two sentences given a constant choice of reference class. For example, if we fix the reference class as the set of days in David's life, then watching films on average ten times in ten years certainly counts as rarely watching films, so [i] is true; but by the same standard, watching violent films on average only nine times in ten years certainly counts as rarely watching violent films, so [ii] is true (as it would be even if **all** David's film choices were violent).

This is not to say that it is illegitimate to select the set of David's film viewing experiences as the reference class for evaluating the truth of [40ii]; but if we are concerned with whether [i] entails [ii], we should not shift reference class between sentences so that [i] is evaluated by reference to one class and [ii] is evaluated by reference to another. The claim of downward entailing is that if we select a reasonable reference class that makes [i] true, when we fix that class and use it to evaluate [ii], [ii] will also be true.

(c) The syntactic tests for negative polarity

Examples such as the following show that the approximate negators can mark clause negation:

[41] i a. *Little of the liquid spilled, not even when the flask fell over.* [*not even*]
b. *One seldom sees such birds, not even in Australia.*
ii a. *She hardly goes out these days, and neither does her son.* [connective]
b. *Little of the gas spilled, and little of the gas escaped, either.*
iii a. *Few good drivers ignore signs, do they?* [tag]
b. *Hardly any of them complained, did they?*
iv *Rarely does the possum emerge before dusk.* [inversion]

Matters here, however, are somewhat more complex than with the absolute negators: examples like those in [41] are not fully representative of the patterns found. There are four points that need to be noted.

Approximate negators mark clausal negation more readily when positioned early

The negators in [41] all precede the verb. In cases where they occur late in the clause the polarity tests often give much less clear-cut results. Compare, for example:

[42] i *Few of the boys had shown any interest in the proposal.*
ii *He had so far shown the visitors few of the sights of London.*

While '*had they?*' is perfectly acceptable as the tag for [i], '*had he?*' for [ii] is for many speakers at best marginal. And [i] allows the continuation *and nor indeed had many of the girls*, while *and nor indeed had his colleagues* is questionable as a continuation of [ii].

The strength of the "not zero" implicature may affect the syntactic polarity

[43] i *He's probably lying. It's barely conceivable that he could have done it himself.*
ii *She's barely alive.*

A positive tag is more acceptable for [i] than for [ii], and this would seem to correlate with the fact that [i] has a somewhat stronger negative flavour than [ii]: [i] suggests that I'm inclined to believe he couldn't have done it himself, while [ii] seems to be saying that she is alive, though only just.

The class of approximate negators is not entirely homogeneous

Rarely and *seldom* are somewhat weaker markers of clausal negation than the others. These two can be the focus for *only*, while the others cannot:

[44] i *She visits her parents only rarely.*
ii **She had read only few of the letters.*
iii **She had done only hardly anything about it.*

Note that [ii] can be corrected by replacing *few* by *a few*. The *only* strongly favours an interpretation where there are at least some occasions on which she visits her parents, and a *does she?* tag for [i] or a continuation like *and neither does her brother* would be quite unacceptable. It is also possible, for many speakers at least, for *rarely* to occur in front position without triggering subject–auxiliary inversion: *Rarely, the possum emerges before dusk.* Here we understand "very occasionally, on rare – but at least some – occasions", and the clause is syntactically positive.

The approximate negators can occur in subclausal negation like the absolute ones
Some of the constructions where the absolute negators mark subclausal negation, illustrated in §3.2.2, also permit approximate negators:

[45] i *I could do a lot for this place with <u>barely</u> any money at all.* (cf. [28i])
ii *Kim regretted having married someone with <u>little</u> ambition.* (cf. [28ii])
iii *They have predicted <u>little</u> rain for the next month.* (cf. [30])

3.4 Affixal negation in relation to verbal negation

We have noted that affixal negation is always syntactically subclausal, but from a semantic point of view it may or may not be equivalent to clausal negation. Compare:

	a.	b.
[46] i	*That model is <u>available</u>.*	*Such mistakes are <u>common</u>.*
ii	*That model is <u>not available</u>.*	*Such mistakes are <u>not common</u>.*
iii	*That model is <u>unavailable</u>.*	*Such mistakes are <u>uncommon</u>.*

Examples [iia] and [iiia] are equivalent, and both are contradictories of the positive [ia]. It is not possible for [ia] and [iia] to be both true, and it is also not possible for them to be both false, and the same holds for [ia] and [iiia]. In the [b] examples, however, the clausal and affixal negatives are not equivalent: while [iib] is again a contradictory of the positive [ib], the affixal negative [iiib] is not. It is not possible for [ib] and [iiib] to be both true, but it is possible for them to be both false – so [iiib] is the contrary of [ib]. This is evident from the fact that it makes perfect sense to say:

[47] *Such mistakes are not common, but they are not uncommon either.*

The difference between set [a] and set [b] in [46] is due to the fact that *common* denotes a gradable property whereas *available* does not (cf. Ch. 6, §2.2). *Common* and *uncommon* can be thought of as applying to non-adjacent areas on a single scale, as shown impressionistically in [48]:

[48]

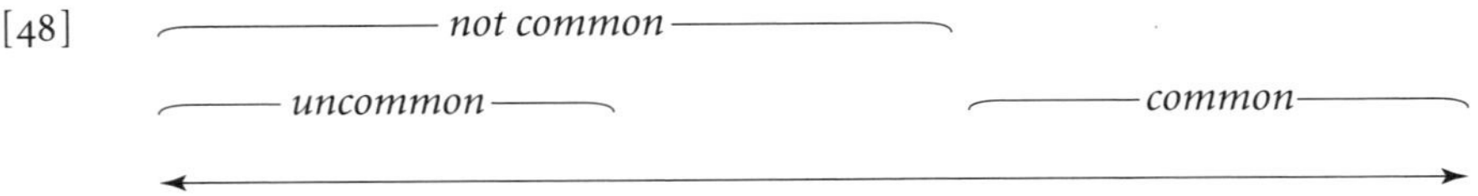

Frequencies in the middle area of the scale don't qualify as either common or uncommon, so *not common* covers a larger area of the scale than *uncommon*.

In practice, *Such mistakes are not common* will tend to be interpreted with the frequency falling towards the left part of the scale. But this is a matter of implicature, which we will take up in §5: for present purposes it is sufficient to note that examples like [47] demonstrate that *Such mistakes are not common* doesn't have the same meaning as *Such mistakes are uncommon.*

The difference is accentuated if we add the intensifier *very*:

[49] a. *Such mistakes are not very common.* b. *Such mistakes are very uncommon.*

Very common denotes a narrower area of the scale than *common*, located at the right of diagram [48], and similarly *very uncommon* a narrower area than *uncommon*, located at the left: the in-between area is therefore greater, and the difference in meaning more obvious.

4 Polarity-sensitive items

A significant number of items – specific words, fixed or variable phrases, and idiomatic expressions – are **polarity-sensitive**, i.e. sensitive to the polarity of the environment in which they occur. Some items are admissible in negative environments but not normally in positive ones, while others occur in positive environments but generally not in negative ones:

[1] i a. *She doesn't see him any longer.* b. *She knows him already.*
ii a. **She sees him any longer.* b. **She doesn't know him already.*

The aspectual adjunct *any longer*, for example, is acceptable in negative [ia] but not in positive [iia]. And conversely *already* is acceptable in positive [ib] but not in negative [iib] (ignoring the special case when it is used to contradict a previous utterance like [ib]). We need two pieces of new terminology for referring to these two kinds of item:

[2] i Items which prefer negative contexts over positive ones (such as *any longer*) are **negatively-oriented polarity-sensitive items**, or **NPIs**.
ii Items which prefer positive contexts over negative ones (such as *already*) are **positively-oriented polarity-sensitive items**, or **PPIs**.

Non-affirmative contexts

The reference to preferring negative contexts above is not incorrect, but it is only part of what needs to be said about the distribution of NPIs. The clauses in [1] are declarative main clauses. When we go beyond such data to consider interrogatives and certain types of subordinate clause we find that NPIs are not restricted to negatives:

[3] i *Do you need me any longer?* [interrogative]
ii *If [you play any longer], you'll get too tired.* [conditional]

In [i] *any longer* occurs in an interrogative clause, while in [ii] it occurs in a subordinate clause functioning as protasis in a conditional construction. Although these clauses are positive, they have it in common with [1ia] that they are not used to assert a positive proposition: the proposition is questioned or merely conditionally entertained. This larger class of contexts that admit NPIs we call **non-affirmative** contexts – and those that exclude them, by contrast, are **affirmative** contexts.

While NPIs are restricted to non-affirmative contexts, PPIs are not restricted to affirmative contexts. *Already*, for example, is just as acceptable as *any longer* in interrogative and conditional constructions:

[4] i *Have they already left?* [interrogative]
ii *If [he has already finished his work], we can leave immediately.* [conditional]

Thus NPIs and PPIs do not occur in mutually exclusive sets of environments. They are mutually exclusive in declarative main clauses, but not always elsewhere.[17]

[17] NPIs are often referred to as 'negative polarity items'. We avoid that term because it is open to misinterpretation. NPIs are not themselves negative items: the NPI *any*, for example, is to be distinguished from the negative word *no*. Nor, as we have just emphasised, are NPIs restricted to negative contexts. Alternative terms found in the literature for our 'affirmative' and 'non-affirmative' are 'assertive' and 'non-assertive'.

Varying strength of the restrictions

The NPI and PPI classes are by no means completely homogeneous: we find significant differences with respect to the distributional restrictions that apply. *Much*, for example, qualifies as an NPI by virtue of the unacceptability of clauses like **She loved him much*, but it is not wholly excluded from affirmative contexts, as is evident from examples like *She much regretted accepting their invitation.* By contrast, the NPI *at all* (*She did not love him at all*) is completely excluded from affirmative contexts. Similarly with PPIs. We have noted that *already* is quite acceptable in interrogatives, but *pretty* ("fairly") is not: examples like ?*Is she pretty happy?* are of doubtful acceptability.

It should also be borne in mind that in some cases the restrictions apply to one sense of an item but not to another. Thus *any* is non-affirmative in the sense it has in *She didn't make any changes* or *Did she make any changes?*, but it also has a 'free choice sense' which is not polarity-sensitive, as in *Take any card*, or *Any changes must be approved by the board* (cf. Ch. 5, §7.5). Where it will help exposition we will use subscripts to distinguish between different senses, referring to the NPI *any* as 'any_n'.

We will review the NPI and PPI classes in turn, and then examine correspondences between certain sets such as *any* (NPI), *some* (PPI), and *no* (negator). In the final subsection we take up in more detail the question of what constitutes a non-affirmative context.

4.1 Negatively-oriented polarity-sensitive items (NPIs)

The class of NPIs is quite large: it is not possible to give an exhaustive and definitive list. The most important ones, and a sample of the less important ones, are given in [5].

[5] i The *any* class of items: any_n, $anybody_n$, *any longer*, *any more* (AmE *anymore*), $anyone_n$, $anything_n$, $anywhere_n$

ii Miscellaneous grammatical items (mostly functioning as adjuncts): *at all*, $either_n$, $ever_n$, $long_n$, *much*, *till/until*, too_n, $what(so)ever_n$, yet_n

iii The modal auxiliaries *dare* and *need*

iv A few lexical verbs: *bother* (+ infinitival), *budge*, *faze*

v A large and probably open array of idioms, including: *can abide/bear/stand*, *can be bothered*, *could care less*,[18] *cost a bean*, *do a* (*single*) *thing* (*about*...), *drink/touch a drop*, *eat a bite/thing*, *give a damn/fig*, *have a clue*, *have a penny* (*to one's name*) (BrE), *have a red cent* (AmE), *hear/say a word/sound*, *hold a candle to*, *in ages*, *in donkey's years*, *lift a finger* (*to help*), *mind a bit*, *move a muscle*, *say a word*, *see a thing*, *see a* (*living*) *soul*, *so much as* (+ verb), *take a* (*blind*) *bit of notice*, *would hurt a fly*

We prefer 'affirmative' as it suggests the two most important features: positive in contrast to negative (an affirmative answer is a positive one) and declarative in contrast to interrogative (to affirm is to state, not to ask). 'Non-affirmative' can also be applied to items, providing an alternative term for NPIs, one which we have used in other chapters: in the present context we prefer NPI because we are dealing with the contrast between the two types of polarity-sensitive item.

[18] For many American speakers the expression *I couldn't care less* has lost its negation and the expression is now *I could care less*, still with the idiomatic meaning "I do not care at all". For these speakers, *care less* is no longer an NPI; *could care less* has become an idiom with a negative meaning (approximately the opposite of its literal meaning). This is not an uncommon development; it is seen again in the development from *I don't know beans about it* "I don't know anything about it" to *I know beans about it* with the same meaning.

The following examples provide matching negative and positive examples in declarative main clauses for a sample of these.

[6] i a. *Lee didn't budge an inch.* b. **Lee budged an inch.*
ii a. *They can't abide aniseed.* b. **They can abide aniseed.*
iii a. *You needn't come with us.* b. **You need come with us.*
iv a. *He didn't wait so much as a week.* b. **He waited so much as a week.*
v a. *She hasn't woken up yet.* b. **She has woken up yet.*
vi a. *I didn't see a living soul.* b. #*I saw a living soul.*
vii a. *Joe hasn't lifted a finger to help.* b. #*Joe has lifted a finger to help.*

The positive versions are either ungrammatical or have a quite different and often bizarre literal meaning. Thus while [via] means that I didn't see anyone, [vib] can only mean that in some way I actually saw a soul. Similarly, [viia] means that Joe did nothing to help, but [viib] can only mean that Joe's help consisted literally of raising a finger.

The subscripts attached to some of the items in [5] indicate that they have other senses in which they are not NPIs. Thus *any* and *either* have free choice senses (cf. Ch. 5, §§7.5, 7.7); *either* also has a non-NPI use as a marker of coordination (*She's arriving either on Monday or on Tuesday*); *ever* and *yet* are similarly not NPIs in *It will last for ever* and *He is yet to announce his decision*; nor is *long* an NPI as an adjective (*It lasted a long time*).

Too$_n$ means "very", as opposed to the ordinary *too* meaning "excessively": the difference is seen in the well-known ambiguity of the testimonial writer's *I can't recommend her too highly* ("it's impossible to overstate her good qualities" or, with *too*$_n$, "I can give only a lukewarm recommendation").

What(so)ever is an NPI, with the meaning "at all", only when functioning as an emphatic postmodifier in NP structure following *any* or ***no***: *There is no justification whatsoever for his behaviour*; *Have you any idea whatever of its value?*

The case with *till* and *until* is somewhat different. These are NPIs only when the clause has a punctual meaning (cf. Ch. 8, §7.3):

[7] i a. *We won't leave till six o'clock.* b. **We will leave till six o'clock.*
ii a. *We won't publish it until next year.* b. **We will publish it until next year.*
iii a. *We won't stay until the end.* b. *We will stay until the end.*

With verbs that are non-punctual and atelic, *till* and *until* are not polarity-sensitive, as shown in [iii]. But this is not a matter of a difference in the sense of *till/until*: it is simply that the polarity-sensitivity of these prepositions is limited to their occurrence with certain types of VP.

4.1.1 NPIs vs negative idioms

It will be noted that we have not included the word *not* or the inflectional suffix *·n't* in any of the NPIs. Thus we have listed *long* and *could care less* rather than *not long* or *couldn't care less*. The negative element is part of the context which admits the NPI, not part of the NPI itself. There are in fact a number of idioms which do include negators as subparts, and they behave quite differently from NPIs. Idioms of the type in question include the underlined phrases in [8]: *not half bad* "quite good", ***like*** *nothing better* "be pleased", and ***stop*** *at nothing* "use any means necessary".

[8] i *I tasted the caviar, and it was not half bad.*
ii *I would like nothing better than to attend the dinner.*
iii *George will stop at nothing to get that job.*

Notice that the positive counterparts are not available, or not available with related meanings: *half bad, like something better,* and *stop at something* are not positive counterparts to the expressions given in [8].

These idioms contain a negator, but do not negate the clause they belong to. NPIs, by contrast, do not contain a negator, but require that one of a certain range of properties be present in the context in which they appear in order that it be non-affirmative: negation is just one of the properties of this kind. The difference between the behaviour of negative-containing idioms and that of NPIs is seen when we contrast, say, the distribution of *not for long* with that of *not half bad.* At first they might seem parallel:

[9] i a. *They laughed, but not for long.* b. *It was salty, but not half bad.*
ii a. *It wasn't for long.* b. *It wasn't half bad.*

But the parallel rapidly breaks down:

[10] i a. *They didn't laugh loudly or for long.* b. #*It wasn't too salty or half bad.*
ii a. *No one laughs for long.* b. #*Nothing was half bad.*
iii a. *Few people laughed for long.* b. #*Few portions were half bad.*
iv a. *I doubt that he'll laugh for long.* b. #*I doubt that it was half bad.*
v a. *Did they laugh for long?* b. #*Was it half bad?*
vi a. *I'll leave if they laugh for long.* b. #*I'll leave if it's half bad.*

The '#' in the [b] cases indicates that the expected idiomatic meaning is not present (though some other meaning might be possible, e.g. with *half bad* meaning "50% putrescent"). As we see, *for long* does not have to be preceded by *not* or a negative auxiliary; it merely has to be in some sort of non-affirmative context. The situation with *not half bad* is quite different. Immediately before *half bad* must be either *not* or a negative auxiliary; merely having *half bad* in some non-affirmative context is not sufficient for it to count as an instance of the idiom *not half bad.*

The idiom *like nothing better* is likewise restricted to combinations involving those three words: [8ii] can be paraphrased by *There's nothing I'd like better than to attend the dinner,* but not by *I wouldn't like anything better than to attend the dinner.* The latter has only the literal meaning that nothing (not even winning a national lottery) tops dinner attendance on my preference list, whereas [8ii] is just a polite form of words carrying no such literal entailment.

Stop at nothing also exists only in negative form. ?*George will stop at something* would have to have a literal meaning and is hard to find any context for; [8iii] is not paraphrased by ?*George will not stop at anything to get that job.* It has a tighter structural restriction than *like nothing better* in that the word sequence *stop at nothing* (usually *will stop at nothing*) must be intact, so we do not find ?*There is nothing that George will stop at to get that job* with the NPI sense.

4.1.2 Variation in the strength of the negative orientation

We noted at the beginning of the discussion of polarity-sensitive items that there is variability with respect to the strength of their positive or negative orientation. As far as NPIs are concerned, there are two issues to be considered: (a) how strictly the restrictions apply in negative clauses, and (b) the occurrence of these items in other kinds of non-affirmative context, such as interrogatives.

The restriction to negative contexts in declarative main clauses

With some items things are fairly clear. Leaving aside certain special constructions dealt with in §4.4 below, the NPI *at all* is completely excluded from positive declaratives. *She didn't like it at all* is admissible, but **She liked it at all* is not, and so on. The same applies to the *any* series of words once we set aside the semantically distinct free choice uses. But for others we find that a word may be an NPI in some styles or registers and not in others. The item *much* is a particularly problematic case of this sort, and *long* and *many* have similar properties.

Contexts for *much*, *long*, and *many*

Much has a bewilderingly large set of distinct uses associated with different styles or registers. Compare:

[11] i a. *The new, more elaborated abstracts were <u>much</u> favoured among modernists.*
b. *Location theorists have given these matters <u>much</u> consideration.*
c. *This means <u>much</u> to the American tradition.*
d. *The design of an interlocking frame is <u>much</u> like a mechanical puzzle.*
e. *The president spent <u>much</u> of the weekend at his summer home on Cape Cod.*
ii a. *Thank you very <u>much</u> for the lovely flowers.*
b. *So <u>much</u> has happened that I'm not sure I can remember it all.*
c. *When I wear these I look too <u>much</u> like my dad.*
d. *This is <u>much</u> better than the other one.*
e. *I'll tell you this <u>much</u>: I didn't pay full price.*
iii a. *The lecture was very long but it didn't really cover <u>much</u>.*
b. *I went sailing once but I didn't enjoy it <u>much</u>.*
c. *He isn't <u>much</u> of a dancer.*

In general terms the examples in [i] can be said to be more characteristic of written English, literary contexts, formal style, and the usage of older speakers. The uses illustrated in [ii–iii] are more likely to be found in spoken English, conversational contexts, informal style, or the usage of younger speakers. But this is only a rough guide. It is extraordinarily difficult to separate the constructions out in a rigorous way, because certain phrases from the literary language have become familiar sayings in everyday speech almost as quotations.

We can be more specific about the examples in [11i], which will give a sense of what we mean. In [ia], *much* is a premodifier of a past participle (in its passive use), and has an intensificatory meaning like "greatly" or "to a high degree". This is quite literary, but even this turns up in casual conversation through a number of fixed or partially fixed phrases that are in a sense borrowings from an earlier stage of the language; for example, the phrase *Much appreciated* is often used with the sense "Thank you". In [ib], *much* is determiner in NP structure, and means "a lot of"; again, this is literary, but while *We have much sugar* is extremely unlikely to occur in casual conversation, one might easily hear something like *The living room is a scene of much confusion, I'm afraid* in a semi-jocular echo of the formal construction. Something similar is true for [ic], where *much* is used as fused determiner-head. The phrase *much like* in [id] is distinctly literary in that context, yet the phrase *one is much like the next* has been adopted as a common turn of phrase in conversation. And *much of the weekend* in [ie] is slightly literary (*a lot of the weekend* would be more conversational), but *much of the time* is familiar in conversation.

There is an important difference between the cases in [11i] and those in [ii]. No cautions about literariness or formality need apply to the latter: all of them are fully natural in casual conversation in the contemporary language. It should be noted that *much* with an adverbial modifier like *very*, *so*, or *too* as in [iia–c] has a far wider distribution than *much* on its own. *Much* as a modifier of comparatives, as in [d], is very common (*much longer* is analogous to *very long*); and so are the phrases *this much* and *that much*, as in [e]. None of these illustrate NPIs.

That leaves the kind of use seen in [11iii]. These are the constructions in which *much* is an NPI. This is particularly clear in contrasts like these:

[12]	i	a. *I don't enjoy sailing much.*	b. **I enjoy sailing much.*
	ii	a. *We don't have much time.*	b. **We have much time.*
	iii	a. *Kim isn't much of a dancer.*	b. **Kim is much of a dancer.*

Much is thus certainly an NPI (and it is therefore on the list in [5]), despite the fact that looking at a random selection of occurrences of *much* would make it easy to think that one had found counterevidence to that statement. Many occurrences of *much* are, indeed, in affirmative environments. But nonetheless, if we focus on (say) the use of *much* as a post-verbal adjunct when occurring without its own premodifying adverb, it is clearly an NPI, as the sharp contrast between [12ia] and [b] shows. Instead of [12ib] we would have, in informal style, *I enjoy sailing a lot* / *a great deal.* The informal way to express the positive counterpart of the claim in [12iia] would be not [12iib] but something like *We have plenty of time.* And to express the positive counterpart of [12iiia] one would use something like *Kim is quite a dancer.*

The durational adverb *long* – which, like *much*, expresses multal quantification – exhibits similar behaviour. We have *She hasn't known him long* but not **She has known him long* (cf. *She has known him a long time*); but *long* can occur pre-verbally in (somewhat formal) positive clauses: *I have long thought that this should be changed.*

Multal *many* also shows some signs of negative orientation, though to a lesser extent. The sentences *Many were lost* and *We saw many flowers*, with no negation, are very slightly literary, whereas *Not many were lost* and *We didn't see many flowers*, with negation, are as common in casual conversation as in writing. But again, an example like ?*I'm not hungry because I've eaten many biscuits* sounds completely unnatural, with *a lot of biscuits* very strongly preferred in informal style.

Occurrence in contexts that are non-affirmative but positive

Negatives constitute the most central type of non-affirmative context, but we have noted that NPIs can occur in certain types of positive clause, such as interrogatives – this is precisely why we talk in terms of non-affirmative contexts rather than simply negative ones. These positive non-affirmative contexts all have various semantic or pragmatic links to negatives. There are, however, differences among the NPIs with respect to how strong or close these links need to be. Such differences can be illustrated by considering the non-affirmative context provided by closed interrogatives.

NPIs in closed interrogatives

Other things being equal, questions expressed by positive closed interrogatives are neutral as opposed to biased (cf. Ch. 10, §4.7). That is, they do not indicate any predisposition on the part of the questioner to think that one answer is more likely than the other. Now the inclusion of certain NPIs in the question has no effect on this neutrality, but with others bias towards a negative answer is introduced. Compare:

		a.	b.
[13]	i	a. *Did they have a dog?*	b. *Did they have any money?*
	ii	a. *Has she been to Paris?*	b. *Has she ever been to Paris?*
	iii	a. *Did they help him?*	b. *Did they lift a finger to help him?*

The possible answers to [ia] may be expressed as *Yes they did have a dog* and *No they didn't have a dog*: as we have said, there is no indication that one or other of these is expected to be the right answer. The answers to [ib] (omitting henceforth the *yes* and *no*) are *They had some money* and *They didn't have any money*, and again the question is quite neutral. The inclusion of *any* in the question does not indicate that the answer containing *any* is expected. The absence of any indication that a positive answer is favoured is sufficient to license the NPI *any*: this is the default existential quantifier for polar questions. Similarly, both questions in [ii] are neutral as between the answers *She has been to Paris* (*at some time*) and *She hasn't* (*ever*) *been to Paris.* This is not so in [iii]. While [iiia] is of course neutral, [iiib] is not: it is oriented towards the negative answer *They didn't lift a finger to help him.* The form of the question is such that the positive answer would be #*They lifted a finger to help him*, but since this (in the sense "They helped him") is anomalous, the question doesn't cater directly for a positive answer and hence indicates bias towards a negative one. The same applies to most of the other items in [5iv–v].

Pragmatic nature of strength contrasts

It is important to emphasise that the difference between (say) *any* or *ever* on the one hand and *budge* or *lift a finger* or *in ages* on the other is not a syntactic one. We are not saying that the former can occur in positive interrogatives while the latter cannot. The difference, rather, is pragmatic, having to do with the conditions under which they can be used in the expression of questions and with the interpretation of the resulting questions.

Take, for example, the phrase *in ages*, as in *I haven't tasted truffles in ages.* This is not easily contextualised in an interrogative: ?*Have you tasted truffles in ages?* would not be a highly appropriate way of simply asking someone whether it had been a very long time since they last tasted truffles. However, it might well be found in a context that was strongly biased in a direction suggesting a negative answer, as in [14i]. Similarly, the occurrence of the verb *budge* is almost entirely limited to negative clauses but one might encounter it in a biased context like [14ii].

[14] i *I don't think you know anything about truffles or any other gourmet foods. Do you eat truffles regularly? Have you even so much as tasted truffles in ages?*

ii *Did you budge an inch to let anyone else sit down? Not you; you just sat there hogging the whole couch as usual.*

4.2 Positively-oriented polarity-sensitive items (PPIs)

The class of PPIs is somewhat smaller than that of NPIs. The main members are listed in [15], while [16] provides a sample of positive examples contrasted with their inadmissible negative counterparts:

[15] i *some, somebody, someone, something, somewhere, somehow, somewhat*
ii the paucal determinatives *a few, a little, several, various*
iii the degree adverbs *pretty, fairly, quite*$_{\mathrm{p}}$, *far*$_{\mathrm{p}}$
iv aspectual *already, still*
v connective *so, too, as well*
vi the modal idioms *would rather, would sooner, would as soon*
vii illocutionary *I guess*

[16] i a. *They made some mistakes* — b. *They didn't make some mistakes.*
ii a. *It's pretty big.* — b. **It isn't pretty big.*
iii a. *It is still a mystery why he ran off.* — b. **It isn't still a mystery why he ran off.*
iv a. *Kim saw it, and so did Pat.* — b. **Kim saw it, but not so did Pat.*
v a. *This one is far better.* — b. **This one isn't far better.*
vi a. *I would rather die.* — b. **I wouldn't rather die.*
vii a. *I guess I agree.* — b. **I don't guess I agree.*

As a PPI *quite* means "fairly": with the sense "completely" *quite* is not polarity-sensitive (cf. *That's quite right* ~ *That's not quite right*). The *far* that acts as a PPI modifies comparative expressions for the most part, and means roughly "considerably"; as a measure of distance it is not polarity sensitive (cf. *They live / don't live far away*). *I guess* qualifies as a PPI where it serves to indicate the illocutionary force of the utterance: it is not polarity-sensitive when *guess* has its literal meaning (as in *I don't guess what's in my presents, I wait to be surprised when I open them on Christmas Day*).

Scope of negation

The negatives in the [b] examples in [16] have scope over the PPI. In general, PPIs are admissible with negatives over which they themselves have scope: this does not count as a non-affirmative context for the item concerned. Compare, for example:

[17] i *I would rather not commit myself.*
ii *Far more of them didn't understand it than did.*
iii *We already can't afford any luxuries: how will we deal with this new expense?*
iv *I still don't know how she did it.*
v *I didn't understand some of the points she was trying to make.*
vi *I'm afraid I couldn't stand several of her friends.*

In [i] the *not* belongs in the subordinate clause: it modifies *commit*, not *would rather.* Example [ii] says that the number of those who didn't understand was far greater than the number of those who did. Example [iii] says that the state of affairs wherein we can't afford luxuries already obtains. In [iv] the state of my not knowing how she did it still obtains. And in [v] some of the points she was trying to make had the property that I didn't understand them. Similarly [vi] says there were several of her friends whom I couldn't stand, not that the number whom I could stand was less than several. In all of these, then, the PPI itself is not affected by the negation and hence perfectly admissible.

The connective adjuncts *so*, *too*, and *as well*, however, cannot even take scope over negation:

[18] i **Kim didn't see it, and so didn't Pat.*
ii **Kim didn't see it, and Pat didn't see it too / as well.*

This of course is why we were able to include these items in our tests for clause polarity. There is, however, an appreciable difference in the strength of the restriction: [i] is completely ungrammatical, whereas [ii] might be regarded as marginally acceptable by some speakers provided the final adjunct is prosodically set off to some extent.

Metalinguistic and other overrides

A number of the PPIs can occur within the scope of negation when used in a metalinguistic or quasi-metalinguistic way:

[19] i A: *It's a pretty big fish.* B: *It isn't pretty big, it's absolutely gigantic.*
ii A: *He's pretty stupid.* B: *He's not pretty stupid, he's actually quite bright.*

In [i] we have a case of metalinguistic negation. B is not saying that the proposition "It is pretty big" is false, but is rejecting it on the grounds that it doesn't go far enough. In [ii], B is rejecting A's statement as false, so this is not metalinguistic negation; nevertheless B is repeating A's expression. We refer to this latter case as a **denial,** a contradiction of something that has been said and explicit assertion of an alternative to it. In talking about the unacceptability of PPIs in negative contexts we are setting aside such special uses; and the asterisk attached to the [b] examples in [16] is to be understood as applying to the ordinary use of the clauses in question.

PPIs may also be found in negative clauses that are embedded beneath a superordinate negative in such a way that the positive counterpart is implicated:

[20] i *You can't tell me that it isn't far better for some couples to divorce than to stay together.*
ii *Never think that I wouldn't rather be with you than at the office.*

You can't tell me that it isn't in [i] strongly implicates "it is", which sanctions the positively-oriented *far*; and in [ii], *never think that I wouldn't* strongly implicates *I would*, which sanctions the PPI *would rather*.

Interrogatives

Most PPIs can occur in interrogative clauses:

[21]	NEGATIVE INTERROGATIVE	POSITIVE INTERROGATIVE
i	a. *Wouldn't you rather stay here?*	b. *Would you rather stay here?*
ii	a. *Didn't Kim see it too / as well?*	b. *Did Kim see it too / as well?*
iii	a. *Isn't he pretty stupid?*	b. ?*Is he pretty stupid?*
iv	a. *Aren't they still/already in London?*	b. *Are they still/already in London?*
v	a. *Isn't there something wrong with it?*	b. *Is there something wrong with it?*

Negative interrogatives are normally used to ask biased rather than neutral questions, and when there is bias towards a positive answer this is sufficient to admit the PPIs even though they are in the scope of the negative. Illocutionary *I guess* and connective *so*, however, are restricted to declaratives. For the rest, the degree adverbs *pretty*, *fairly*, $quite_p$ occur significantly less readily in positive interrogatives than the others.

4.3 Correspondences between PPIs, NPIs, and negators

There is an important relationship between *some*, *any*$_n$, and ***no*** illustrated in such sets as:

[22] i *Kim made <u>some</u> mistakes.* [positive]
ii *Kim didn't make <u>any</u> mistakes.* [negative with verbal negation]
iii *Kim made <u>no</u> mistakes.* [negative with non-verbal negation]

In [ii–iii] the existential quantification falls within the scope of the negation, and (with the provisos mentioned in §4.2 above) *some* cannot occur in this environment. Thus [ii–iii] are negations of [i], differing in that the negation is expressed separately from the quantification in [ii] but not in [iii].

Broadly similar relationships are found with a number of other items, so that we can set up the following correspondences:

[23]		PPIs	NPIs	ABSOLUTE NEGATORS
i	a.	*some*	*any*	*no*
	b.	*someone/somebody*	*anyone/anybody*	*no one / nobody*
	c.	*something*	*anything*	*nothing*
	d.	*somewhere/someplace*	*anywhere/anyplace*	*nowhere / no place*
	e.	*sometimes*	*ever*	*never*
	f.	*sometime, once*	*anytime, ever*	*never*
	g.	*somewhat*	*at all*	
ii	a.	*still*	*any more / any longer*	*no more / no longer*
	b.	*already*	*yet*	
iii	a.	*so*		*neither/nor*
	b.	*too / as well*	*either*	
	c.		*either*	*neither*
	d.		*either . . . or*	*neither . . . nor*

These three displays need to be interpreted with some caution. In the first place, the relation between paired PPIs and NPIs is not identical in all cases. For example, the connection between *somewhat* and *at all* is considerably weaker and less systematic than that between *some* and *any*. Secondly it should be borne in mind that a number of the forms have a range of senses or uses, with the correspondences applying only to some of them. Take *some*, for example. Of the several senses distinguished in Ch. 5, §7.5, the connection with *any* and ***no*** is clearest in the basic existential quantificational sense illustrated in [22i]. But for certain uses, most clearly that seen in *That was* SOME *journey* ("a remarkable journey") or SOME *friend he was!*, there are no close negative counterparts.

A good number of polarity-sensitive items involve quantification. Broadly speaking, we find that the following generalisations hold:

[24] i Universal quantifiers are not polarity-sensitive.
ii Some multal quantifiers exhibit some degree of negative orientation.
iii Paucal quantifiers tend to have positive orientation (like *a few*) or to be approximate negators (*few*).
iv The most central existential quantifiers enter into the pattern of correspondences illustrated in [23i].

Note in this connection that those uses of *some* that go beyond simple existential quantification to indicate a fairly considerable quantity do not enter into such correspondences. *It took some time to rectify the problem*, for example, does not have a straightforward negative with *any* or *no*: #*It didn't take any time to rectify the problem*; a pragmatically closer negation here would be *It didn't take much time to rectify the problem.*

A further general point to be made is that certain of the NPIs have free choice senses in addition to their NPI senses. This applies to *any* and its compounds and to *either* when it functions as determiner or fused determiner-head in NP structure: *Take any of the computers*; *Ask anyone*; *You can have either of the printers. Ever* has a free choice sense when compounded with relative and interrogative words (*Take whatever you like* or *He'll grumble whatever you do*). Elsewhere *ever* can express universal quantification: *She had been ill ever since she returned from Paris* ("all the time"); *Ever the optimist, she was undeterred by these warnings.* Free choice and universal quantification are often related by implicature: *Anyone can do that* implicates "Everyone can do that" (see Ch. 5, §7.5).

We will now provide some further brief comments on the sets given in [23]:

(a) The *some* ~ *any* series ([23i])

In positive interrogatives the *some* and *any* words generally contrast:

[25] i	a. *Did Kim make <u>some</u> mistakes?*	b. *Did you tell <u>someone</u>?*	[PPI]
ii	a. *Did Kim make <u>any</u> mistakes?*	b. *Did you tell <u>anyone</u>?*	[NPI]

The positive orientation of *some* is reflected in the fact that while the versions in [ii] are quite neutral, those in [i] suggest a somewhat greater inclination on the part of the speaker to think that the answer may well be positive.

The variants in [23id] containing *place* rather than *where* belong to AmE (informal style).

Ever and *never* can function as adjuncts of frequency or temporal location. In the frequency sense they correspond straightforwardly to *sometimes*: *He sometimes loses his patience* ~ *He doesn't ever lose his patience* ~ *He never loses his patience.*[19] For the temporal location sense with past time the closest PPI is *once*: *She once liked them* ~ *She didn't ever like them* ~ *She never liked them.* For future time the PPI *sometime* can be used: *I hope they will change these rules sometime* ~ *... won't ever / will never change these rules.* AmE *anytime* most often has a free choice sense (*Feel free to call me anytime*), but it is found as an NPI in combination with *soon* and suchlike expressions as counterpart to *sometime*: *I expect it to end sometime soon* ~ %*I don't expect it to end anytime soon.*

Correspondence between *somewhat* and *at all* is seen in pairs like *I somewhat regret agreeing to take part* ~ *I don't at all regret agreeing to take part. Somewhat* is slightly formal in style, and *at all* occurs in a much wider range of syntactic constructions. For example, there is no positive counterpart with *somewhat* for *He hasn't worked at all this week. At all* commonly occurs as a reinforcing postmodifier in the structure of NPs containing *any* or ***no***, as in *I hadn't had any food at all* or *I'd had no food at all*:

[19] *Never* is likely to be preferred over verbal negation when *ever* immediately follows *not* or the negative verb; a more natural use of frequency *ever* is seen in *I don't think he ever loses his patience. Ever* can be used in juxtaposition to *never* with emphatic effect; this device is associated primarily with informal conversation, but can be found in other styles too: *Any risk of a prime minister abusing this power is effectively eliminated because he can never, ever put a political crony into the job.*

here the positive is simply *I'd had some food.* As a modifier of comparatives, *somewhat* can also be paired with *any*: *It was somewhat better than last time* ~ *It wasn't at all / any better than last time.*

The PPI *somehow* generally indicates manner (*They had somehow lost their way*), but can also have a reason sense (in *I somehow couldn't understand what he was getting at* the word *somehow* means something like "for some unknown reason" or "in some way that I cannot quite specify"). *Anyhow* exists, but not as the NPI counterpart, so this pair is not included in [23i]. As a manner adverb, *anyhow* is based on free choice *any* but with specialisation of meaning (*They had stacked everything into the cupboard anyhow,* "without care, haphazardly"). More often it has a concessive or connective meaning, like *anyway.*

(b) The aspectuals ([23ii])

The correspondence between the aspectual PPIs and NPIs is illustrated in:

		a.	b.
[26]	i	a. *Ed <u>still</u> lives with us.*	b. *Ed doesn't live with us <u>any more</u>/<u>longer</u>.*
	ii	a. *Jill has <u>already</u> finished.*	b. *Jill hasn't finished <u>yet</u>.*

In the aspectual sense *any more* is generally written *anymore* in AmE, and that spelling is spreading to BrE.[20] In positive interrogatives, some speakers allow *still* but not *any more / longer* in such examples as *Does he still live with you?* ~ %*Does he live with you any more?* A further difference is that *any more / longer* can be used for projection into the future in a way that has no counterpart with *still. I'm not working here any more* is ambiguous between a present time sense ("I no longer work here") and a futurate reading ("I don't intend to continue working here"), but *I'm still working here* has only the present time interpretation.

(c) The *either* ~ *neither* series ([23iii])

One use of *either* and *neither* is as connective adjuncts in the constructions we have used as a test of negative polarity for clauses:

		a.	b.
[27]	i	a. *Kim enjoyed it and so did Pat.*	b. *Kim didn't enjoy it and neither did Pat.*
	ii	a. *Kim enjoyed it and Pat did too.*	b. *Kim didn't enjoy it and Pat didn't either.*

Here *neither* is always in front position in a declarative clause, which excludes the possibility of a direct counterpart with verbal negation + the NPI *either*; the matching PPI is *so. Either* occurs in post-verbal position, matching *too* or *as well.* In this connective use, *nor* is a variant of *neither*, but has a slightly wider distribution (cf. Ch. 15, §2.4).

The *either* and *neither* of [23iiic] are the ones that function as existential quantifiers in NP structure: *He hadn't read either of them* ~ *He had read neither of them.* There is here no simple PPI counterpart; we can relate these to positive *He had read one of them*, but this differs from *either/neither* in that it doesn't indicate selection from a set of two, and *one*, moreover, is not polarity-sensitive. A closer match is with *He had read one or other of them*, where the complex expression *one or other* is a PPI. The items in [23iiid] are markers of coordination: this is the one place where we have absolute negators with non-negative counterparts that are not polarity-sensitive.

[20] The single word spelling is occasionally found in non-aspectual uses but this is not accepted as standard: **We don't know anymore than the others.* Regional AmE has a non-NPI use of *anymore* meaning roughly "nowadays": %*They're working together anymore.*

4.4 Non-affirmative contexts

We review in this section the constructions or lexical items that create contexts within which NPIs can occur. Negation is the most central of them, while the others have various kinds of semantic or pragmatic connection with negation. In the examples that follow we use single underlining to pick out the NPI and double underlining for the item which sanctions it.

Negators

All negators, whether expressing clausal or subclausal negation, sanction NPIs:

[28] i a. *Kim didn't do anything wrong.*
b. *No one did anything wrong.* [clausal negation]
c. *Hardly anyone liked it at all.*
ii a. *He seems not very interested in any of these activities.*
b. *It was a matter of little consequence for any of us.* [subclausal negation]
c. *It is unlikely anyone has noticed it yet.*

Recall, however, that the negative context begins at the point where the negator is located. An NPI is not sanctioned by a following negator: cf. **Anyone did nothing wrong* or **We had given anyone nothing.*

Interrogative clauses

We have observed that NPIs are commonly found in closed interrogatives, and for these nothing need be added to what has been said above. Positive open interrogatives, however, require some further discussion.

Open interrogatives

The way NPIs interact with positive open interrogatives is slightly different from the way they work in the semantically simpler closed interrogatives. Compare the following:

[29] i a. *Who helped her?* b. *Who did anything to help her?*
ii a. *Why did you help someone like George?* b. *Why would you lift a finger to help someone like George?*
iii a. *How come you like her?* b. **How come you like her much?*

In general, questions expressed by means of positive open interrogatives have positive presuppositions. When I ask [ia] I normally take it for granted that someone helped her and aim to find out who it was. Similarly [iia] presupposes that you helped George and [iiia] that you like her.

Introduction of an NPI, even one like *any* or *ever*, changes matters in various ways. It is not presupposed by [29ib] that someone did something to help her. It may suggest that no one did, though it doesn't need to – cf. *Who has any suggestions to make?*, which leaves it entirely open whether anyone does in fact have any.

In [29iib], with the more strongly negatively-oriented *lift a finger*, there is a negative implicature – that George doesn't deserve help, so that a proper stance would be for you not to lift a finger to help him. In effect, the question asks for a reason for departing from that presumption.

Example [29iiib] is ungrammatical, like the positive declarative **You like her much.* (Note the contrast with the fully acceptable *How come you like her so much?*) But again, there is no question of *much* being syntactically excluded from positive open interrogatives: we merely need to find contexts with an appropriate negative flavour, as in *Who cares much about it, anyway?*

Bare infinitival *why* interrogatives

[30] a. *Why tell them anything about it?* b. **Why not tell them anything about it?*

It might initially seem surprising that the NPI is permitted in the positive question [a] but excluded from the negative [b]. But again the explanation has to do with the conveyed meaning of the construction.

Although positive, [30a] conveys the negative suggestion that there is no reason to tell them anything about it. The negative meaning of the clause that would express this negative implicature allows naturally for NPIs. With *why not* interrogatives, on the other hand, there is a positive implicature. The conventional meaning of *Why not tell them about it?* is to suggest via a rhetorical question that you should tell them about it. The positive sense of the latter makes the NPI in [b] unacceptable.

Covertly negative lexical items with clausal or clause-like complements

Many verbs and adjectives that take clauses as complements are covertly negative in that they trigger entailments or implicatures involving the negation of the subordinate clause, and this is sufficient to sanction NPIs in those clauses. Certain of these items allow the complement to take the form of an NP or PP with an interpretation like that of a clause with NPIs still being sanctioned. In some cases the subordinate clause (or its equivalent) may be subject: this is one case where an NPI can precede the item that sanctions it, as in [34ii] and [36ii] below.

We group these covertly negative items into six classes: (a) failure, avoidance, and omission; (b) prevention and prohibition; (c) denial; (d) doubt; (e) counter-expectation; and (f) unfavourable evaluation.

(a) Expressions of failure, avoidance, and omission

NPIs are sanctioned in the complements (usually infinitival or gerund-participial complements) of lexical items (mostly verbs) expressing failure to do something or similar acts of avoidance or omission. Relevant verbs include *avoid, decline, fail, forget, neglect, refrain*, and a few others, e.g. *omit* in BrE.

[31] i *The authorities failed to do a thing to ensure the child's safety.*
ii *Lee forgot to take a blind bit of notice when they were giving directions.*
iii *I want you to refrain from moving a muscle until you're completely recovered.*
iv *We managed to avoid any further delays.*

Example [i] entails that the authorities didn't do a thing to ensure the child's safety. In [iv] the verb *avoid* has an NP as complement, understood roughly as "having any further delays".

(b) Expressions of prevention and prohibition

Lexical items expressing prevention, prohibition, banning, excluding, or otherwise stopping actions generally take gerund-participle complements in PPs headed by *from*, and NPIs are sanctioned in those complements. The verbs include *ban, hinder, keep, prevent, prohibit, stop*.

[32] i *We kept him from telephoning anyone before the police arrived.*
ii *I am prohibited from so much as naming any of the principals in this case.*

Again we have negative entailments: it follows from [i], for example, that he didn't telephone anyone before the police arrived.

(c) Expressions of denial

The verb *deny* is the central item here, but a close paraphrase will work the same way regardless of lexical content or syntactic structure.

[33] i *My client denies that he ever said any such thing.*
ii *My client denies any involvement in the matter.*
iii *My client completely rejects the notion that he ever said any such thing.*

Here we can paraphrase [i] as *My client says that he never said any such thing.* Example [ii] illustrates the case where the complement has the form of an NP: we understand "that he was in any way involved in the matter".

(d) Expressions of doubt

The class of dubitative items includes verbs (*doubt* being the clearest case), adjectives (*doubtful, dubious, sceptical*), and nouns (*doubt, scepticism*):

[34] i *I doubt that Lee has been to the theatre in ages.*
ii *That they will ever have a better opportunity is very much to be doubted.*
iii *I'm doubtful about the value of pursuing the matter any further.*
iv *She expressed scepticism about there being any point in continuing.*

There is a clear relation between doubt and negation: to doubt is to entertain the possibility that some proposition is false. The verb *doubt* with a declarative clause complement suggests an inclination to believe that the proposition is false (see Ch. 11, §5.3.3).

(e) Expressions of counter-expectation

A statement like *I'm surprised the car started* asserts that I have experienced a reaction to the discovery that the car started because that is counter to expectation: it implicates that I had a prior expectation that could be expressed as *The car won't start.* Such implicatures are enough to sanction NPIs in complements of such verbs or verbal idioms as *amaze, astonish, astound, bowl over, flabbergast, shock, surprise, take aback*, and corresponding adjectives:

[35] i *It astounds me that they took any notice of him.*
ii *It's surprising he lifted a finger, considering that he's a total stranger.*
iii *We were all amazed that he had been able to write anything during that time.*

(f) Expressions of unfavourable evaluation

A large array of lexical items expressing unfavourable evaluations, e.g. *absurd, excessive, foolish, monstrous, ridiculous, silly, stupid, unacceptable, unwise*, and many others, are capable of providing contexts for NPIs:

[36] i *It would be foolish to take any unnecessary risks.*
ii *Any more pudding would be quite excessive.*
iii *It was stupid of Basil ever to have mentioned the war.*

The implicature in [i] here is that we (or whoever) should not take any more risks than the absolute minimum, and [ii] implicates that we (or whoever) should not have any more pudding. The situation concerned will generally be in the domain of the potential rather than the actual: we would not say ?*It was foolish to take any unnecessary risks* in speaking of a single event in the past.

Downward entailing quantified NPs

All quantified NPs that are downward entailing in the sense explained in §3.3 sanction following NPIs. Compare:

[37] i a. *Few of the bees stung anyone.* b. **A few of the bees stung anyone.*
ii a. *At most ten students did any work.* b. **At least ten students did any work.*

Most downward entailing quantified NPs are negative and hence are already covered under (a) above, but we noted in footnote 15 that *at most* triggers downward entailment although it is not negative. As seen in [iia], it nevertheless sanctions following NPIs. *A few* and *at least* are upward entailing, and do not create non-affirmative contexts.

Although [37iia] is not itself negative, it has clear links with negation. *At most ten of the thirty students worked* entails that the other twenty (the majority) did not work: compare the negative paraphrase *No more than ten of the students worked, did they?*

At least ten of the thirty students worked, on the other hand, has no such negative entailment: in fact it suggests that some of the other twenty may have worked. *At least* can be paraphrased by *no less than*, but this yields a positive clause: *No less than ten of the students worked, didn't they?*

The degree adverb *too*

[38] i *By that time I was just too tired to budge.*
ii *It was too difficult for anyone else.*

Too in the sense "excessively" licenses an indirect complement with the form of an infinitival clause or a *for* PP. The *too* + positive infinitival construction can be paraphrased by *so* + negative finite clause: *I was so tired that I couldn't budge.* Similarly [ii] conveys "It was so difficult that no one else could do it / that it was not appropriate for anyone else". Note that *He wasn't too tired to have a couple of games of tennis* implicates that he did play, and this positive implicature excludes an NPI (ignoring again the denial use): **I wasn't too tired to budge.*

Prepositions (*against, before, without*)

Certain prepositions define contexts for NPIs, as illustrated in the [a] examples of [39]:

[39] i a. *She did it without any difficulty.* b. **She did it with any difficulty.*
ii a. *He left before anyone noticed it.* b. **He left after anyone noticed it.*
iii a. *I argued against taking any more.* b. **I argued in favour of taking any more.*

Again the NPIs are admissible because the clauses convey negative propositions: that she had no difficulty in doing it, that no one had noticed it, that I argued we (or whoever) should not take any more. No such negative propositions are conveyed by the [b] examples, which contain prepositions of opposite meaning: the NPIs are therefore inadmissible. *Without* and *before* sanction NPIs quite generally, but *against* does so only in the rather special sense it has here.

Only

[40] i *Only then did she realise she had any chance of winning.*
ii *She remained the only one capable of making any sense of it.*

Again, there is a very clear connection between *only* and negation. Example [i] entails that until then she hadn't realised she had any chance of winning, while [ii] entails that no one else was capable of making any sense of it. For further discussion, see Ch. 6, §7.3.

Comparative and superlative constructions

NPIs are commonly found in the complement of comparative *than* or *as*, and in relative clauses and partitive PPs in construction with superlatives. As usual, this reflects the close association between these constructions and negatives:

[41] i *She ran faster than she had ever run before.*
ii *The performance was as good as any you could hope to see.*
iii *It was the biggest fish I had ever seen.*

Example [i] entails that she had never previously run as fast; [ii] entails that no performance you could hope to see would be better than this one; and [iii] entails that I had never before seen a bigger fish.

Overt and covert conditionals

A clause embedded as complement of *if* generally allows NPIs, and so do clauses in various other constructions that have conditional interpretations. Consider:

[42] i *If you want anything, just call.*
ii *If I'd ever seen anything like that, I'd have reported it.*
iii *I would read your review, if I gave a damn about your opinion.*
iv *Drink any more and you'll have to get a taxi home.*

Example [i] is an open conditional; it envisages that you may or may not want something, without bias in favour of one or other of those possibilities. The mere absence of positive affirmation is sufficient to allow an NPI such as *any*. The remote conditional construction illustrated in [ii–iii] is more closely related to negation: [ii] implicates that I hadn't ever seen anything like that, and [iii] that I don't give a damn about your opinion. *Give a damn* is one of the more strongly negatively-oriented items, and occurs much more naturally in a remote conditional like [iii] than an open one. In [iv] an NPI is sanctioned by the conditional meaning even when there is no syntactically conditional construction: we interpret the imperative as equivalent to *if you drink any more* (cf. Ch. 10, §9.5).

5 Increased specificity of negation (*I don't want to hear about it*)

In various ways, negative clauses are often interpreted with increased specificity: they are taken to be making a stronger claim than they actually entail. One common instance of this phenomenon was discussed in §1.3.3, where we were examining the effect of selecting as focus an element falling within the scope of the negation. Thus *YOUR children don't hate school* is interpreted as saying not just that the conditions for the truth of the proposition "Your children hate school" are not all satisfied, but as indicating, more specifically, that it is the condition associated with *your* that is not satisfied.

Another common case of this general phenomenon is illustrated in:

[1] i a. *Mary doesn't like you.* b. *Mary dislikes you.*
ii a. *He doesn't have many friends.* b. *He has few friends.*
iii a. *The weather wasn't very good.* b. *The weather was rather poor.*

In each pair, [a] implicates [b], which has a more specific meaning.

Consider [1ia]. This would presumably be true if Mary had never even heard of you, and in this case [ib] would be false. But it would normally be quite pointless to say [ia] if this were the case, so this scenario can be ignored in interpreting it. It would also be true if Mary did know you but hadn't formed a judgement about you or had no feelings about you, positive or negative: in this case she neither likes you nor dislikes you, so [ia] is true and [ib] is false. However, if this were so, I would normally be expected to say so explicitly: *Mary doesn't like you, but she doesn't dislike you either.* Much the most likely scenario for [ia] is one where Mary dislikes you, and in the absence of indications to the contrary that is how it will generally be interpreted. The interpretation is more specific than the actual meaning of [ia] in that it ignores the various other conditions under which [ia] could be true.

Many in [1iia] is an imprecise multal quantifier: there's no clear lower bound such that twenty, say, would count as 'many' but nineteen would not. The scenario in which I can be confident in saying [iia], therefore, is one in which the number of friends falls well below what would count as many – i.e. one in which he has few friends. So [iia] will generally be taken as conveying that he has few friends. But again that is not what it means: it makes perfect sense to say *He doesn't have* MANY *friends, but he has a reasonable number.*[21] The implicature [iib] is thus more specific than [iia], excluding the middle ground on the numerical scale that lies between few and many.

Very in [1iiia] likewise has an imprecise multal meaning, and again the middle ground on the good–bad scale is discarded, so that [iiia] implicates [iiib]. It is easy to see that the meanings are different, for *very good* denotes a relatively small part of the scale at the top end, so that [iiia] places the weather within the large area of the scale below that top segment, whereas [iiib] places it towards the bottom end. The implicature can be cancelled, typically by using contrastive stress on *very*: *It wasn't* VERY *good, but it was quite reasonable.* This kind of implicature is found quite generally with multal quantification. A third example is provided by *She doesn't often lose her temper*, which implicates, but does not entail, *She rarely loses her temper.*

Our major concern in this section is with a further special case of this tendency to move to a more specific interpretation of a negative clause: the case where a clause containing a clausal complement has negation in the matrix clause interpreted as applying to the subordinate clause, as in the [a] examples of:

[2] MATRIX NEGATION — SUBORDINATE NEGATION
i a. *I don't want to hear about it.* b. *I want to not hear about it.*
ii a. *Mary didn't want you to tell them.* b. *Mary wanted you not to tell them.*

[21] Where *not* combines with *many* to form a DP *not many*, the paucal interpretation is an entailment, not an implicature: *not many* means "few". Note then that we can't say #*Not many people came to the meeting but a reasonable number did.*

In both pairs the negative marker is located in the topmost clause in [a], but in the complement of *want* in [b]. And in both cases [b] is an implicature of [a] with a somewhat more specific meaning.

This case is very similar to [1ia] above. Example [2ia] is true if **either** I have no feelings about the matter one way or the other, **or** I want to not hear about it (to be spared from hearing about it). In practice, the first of these possibilities is normally discounted, giving the more specific interpretation where it is the second condition that obtains – i.e. the interpretation expressed by [ib]. If I had no feelings about the matter, I would typically be expected to say so: e.g. by saying *I don't mind whether I hear about it or not.* But the fact that the truth of the latter would be sufficient to make [ia] true shows that [ia] does not have the same meaning as [ib]. This is why [ib] is an implicature of [ia], not an entailment. And again the implicature can be cancelled: *I don't want to hear about it and I don't want to not hear about it – I'm completely indifferent.*

Matrix verbs and adjectives allowing the subordinate negation implicature

The phenomenon illustrated in [2] is quite widespread: there are a good number of lexemes which behave like *want* in constructions containing a non-finite or finite subordinate clause. In [3] we list a sample of the verbs and adjectives concerned, classified into broad semantic groups:

[3] i WANTING: *choose, intend, mean, plan, want*
ii ADVICE: *advisable, advise, had better, be meant, recommend, ?suggest, be supposed*
iii PROBABILITY: *likely, ?probable*
iv OPINION: *%anticipate, believe, expect, feel, %figure, guess, imagine, reckon, suppose, think*
v PERCEPTION: *appear, feel, look, sound, seem*

The common semantic factor: 'medium strength'

The items in [3] all have to do with various kinds of modality, and they have it in common that their value on the dimension or scale we have called 'strength' is medium, as opposed to weak or strong: see Ch. 3, §9.2.1. Consider again *want,* which contrasts with weak *willing* and strong *insist.* Compare:

[4] i a. *I'm not willing to be included.* b. *I'm willing to not be included.* [weak]
ii a. *I don't want to be included.* b. *I want to not be included.* [medium]
iii a. *I don't insist on being included.* b. *I insist on not being included.* [strong]

It is clear that [b] is an implicature of [a] only in case [ii]. In [i], [a] actually entails [b], but [a] is much more informative than [b] and would not be used to convey the latter. In both [ii] and [iii], [b] entails [a], but the difference in meaning between [iiia] and [iiib] is very much greater than that between [iia] and [iib]. As we have seen, the only difference between [iia] and [iib] is that [iia] allows for the scenario in which I am indifferent as to whether I'm included or not. But [iiia] allows for a much greater range of possibilities than [iiib]: it could be, for example, that I want to be included, but am just not insisting on it. It is only in the medium strength case – where there is relatively little difference in meaning between matrix and subordinate negation – that the implicature applies.

The same holds for advice. Compare:

[5] i	a. *He didn't allow me to go.*	b. *He allowed me not to go.*	[weak]
ii	a. *He didn't advise me to go.*	b. *He advised me not to go.*	[medium]
iii	a. *He didn't order me to go.*	b. *He ordered me not to go.*	[strong]

Advise has medium strength in contrast to weak *allow* and strong *order*, and the implicature is found only in case [ii]. Again, [ia] is much more informative than [ib] (which it entails), and [iiib] is much more informative than [iiia] and could not be conveyed by it. But the difference between [iia] and [iib] is much less. They don't have the same meaning, of course, since [iia] is consistent with his not having offered any advice at all. If we assume that he did give some advice as to whether I should go, however, then [iib] can be inferred from [iia]. Note that the implicature is more likely to be present when *advise* is used performatively (Ch. 10, §3.1), as in *I don't advise you to go.*

Likely expresses medium strength epistemic modality. Compare this time:

[6] i	a. *It isn't possible that he's alive.*	b. *It is possible that he isn't alive.*	[weak]
ii	a. *It isn't likely that he's alive.*	b. *It is likely that he isn't alive.*	[medium]
iii	a. *It isn't certain that he's alive.*	b. *It's certain that he isn't alive.*	[strong]

As before, the implicature is found in the medium strength case [ii], but not in [i/iii]. In [i], [a] entails [b] and is much more informative. In [iii], [b] is much more informative than [a] and cannot be pragmatically inferred from it. But in [ii] there is relatively little difference between [a] and [b]. Like *many* in [1iia], *likely* is an imprecise term: the lower bound for what probability qualifies as 'likely' is fuzzy, just as it is for what number counts as 'many'. Suppose for the sake of argument we take the lower bound to be 60%: if there's a 60% chance he's alive then we'll accept *It's likely that he's alive* as true. In this case, [iia] puts the probability of his being alive at less than 60%, while [iib] puts it at 40% or less. The interpretation of [iib] is then more specific by cutting out the middle ground in the range 40% to 60%. Again this is comparable with the interpretation of negated multal quantification as paucal.[22]

Such verbs as *think* and *believe* are also often used to express medium strength epistemic modality, but differ in taking two arguments, with the subject associated with the role of experiencer (the one making the epistemic judgement). They contrast with strong *know*, but there is no syntactically comparable verb or adjective expressing weak modality. Compare, then:

[7] i	a. *She doesn't think he's alive.*	b. *She thinks he isn't alive.*	[medium]
ii	a. *She doesn't know he's alive.*	b. *She knows he isn't alive.*	[strong]

As before, [b] is an implicature of [a] only in the medium strength case: the difference in meaning between [iia] and [iib] is too great to be pragmatically ignored. Note, moreover, that although we have not provided a contrast with weak modality here there is no doubt that *think* belongs in the medium strength category. The weak case can be expressed in other ways, such as *She is quite open-minded as to whether he is alive* or (more naturally, but with negation) *She has no idea whether or not he is alive.*

[22] There is one catenative that allows the implicature which is semantically closer to multal *often* than to the modal items in [3], namely *tend*: compare *They don't tend to read the fine print* and *They tend not to read the fine print.*

The items in the perception category [3v] are very similar, and although there are no simple contrasts with strong or weak modality, it is clear that they belong in the medium category. As before, [a] implicates [b] in the pair:

[8] a. *He doesn't seem to understand.* b. *He seems not to understand.*

Conventionalisation of specificity increase

Not every item expressing medium strength modality permits the increased specificity implicature that we have been illustrating. Lexemes meeting the general semantic condition become associated with it on a piecemeal basis.

For example, while the implicature is found with *likely*, as illustrated in [6ii], it is very questionable with *probable*: *It's not probable that he's alive* is not a natural way of conveying "It is probable that he's not alive". Similarly, *I don't recommend that you tell them* conveys "I recommend that you not tell them" much more readily than *I don't suggest you tell them* conveys "I suggest you don't tell them".[23] There are, moreover, dialect differences with respect to some items, as indicated by the % annotation. Thus for some speakers, but not others, *I don't guess there's anybody home* can convey "I guess there isn't anybody home". At the same time, there are differences with respect to how readily the construction with subordinate negation is used. Thus *He seems not to have understood* is perfectly natural, whereas *I want to not go* is highly unusual, and normally sharply disfavoured relative to *I don't want to go.*

A clear indication of the importance of conventionalisation in this area is provided by cross-linguistic differences in the items which allow the implicature. In English the verb *hope* clearly belongs in the medium strength category, like *want*, but its negation is not pragmatically interpreted as applying to the subordinate clause. Thus *I don't hope you're late* does not implicate *I hope you're not late.* In German, however, the corresponding verb, *hoffen*, does permit the implicature, behaving like the English verbs in [3].

No subordinate negation implicature with modal auxiliaries

It will be noted that (leaving aside the *had* of the idiom *had better*) there are no modal auxiliaries among the verbs in [3]. At first glance the following might appear to behave in the same way:

[9] i *You mustn't tell anyone.* [strong]
ii *You shouldn't take the job.* [medium]

In both of these the negation is located syntactically in the matrix clause but applies semantically to the subordinate clause: in this respect they are like the examples we have been considering. There is, however, an important difference. The semantic association of the negation with the subordinate clause is this time not a matter of implicature but of sentence meaning. We noted in Ch. 3, §9.10, that a syntactically negative modal may or

[23] Note also the difference between the epistemic and deontic senses of *expect.* In the epistemic sense (roughly "think likely") the implicature generally goes through, but in the deontic sense ("think *x* should") its application is more restricted. Consider, for example, *We don't expect them to pay more than $100.* In the epistemic sense this implicates "We expect that they won't pay more than $100". But in the deontic sense (roughly "We don't regard them as having an obligation to pay more than $100") there is no subordinate negation implicature: it doesn't convey "We regard them as having an obligation not to pay more than $100".

may not fall within the semantic scope of the negation. The examples in [9] have what we call 'internal negation': the negation applies semantically to the non-finite complement of the modal, not to the modal itself. Thus [i] imposes or reports an obligation not to tell anyone. To negate the modality we use *need*: *You needn't tell anyone.* Note, moreover, that *must* expresses strong modality, whereas we have seen that the implicature only applies in the case of medium strength modality.

Should, on the other hand, does belong in the medium strength category, but the subordinate negation interpretation, approximately "The right thing for you to do is to not take the job", is still the meaning proper, not an implicature. Example [9ii] differs from the examples with a subordinate negation implicature in that it does not allow the less specific interpretation in which the negation applies semantically to the matrix: it doesn't mean "The right thing for you to do isn't to take the job". This is evident from the fact that one can't say: #*You shouldn't take the job and you shouldn't not take it either: it doesn't matter whether you take it or not.* The implicature arises only in cases where there is a syntactic contrast between matrix and subordinate negation like that found between [8a] and [8b], and the other pairs discussed.

The *can't seem to* construction

[10] a. *I can't seem to get it right.* b. *I seem not to be able to get it right.*

The meaning of [a] is the same as that of [b] – or of *It seems that I can't get it right.* Syntactically, *seem* falls within the complement of the negated modal auxiliary, but semantically it is outside the scope of the negative. This example differs from those considered above, however, in that modal *can* also belongs semantically within the complement of *seem*, rather than the other way round, as one would expect from the syntax.

This is another case where the interpretation is a matter of meaning proper, not implicature: *can't seem* (as used here) is simply an idiom meaning "seem unable". The essential parts of the idiom are ***can***, negation, and *seem*; note, for example, that *seem* is not here replaceable by *appear*. The mismatch between syntax and semantics here is probably related to the fact that ***can*** has no plain form, so we don't have **I seem not to can get it right.*

6 Multiple negation

When a clause contains two or more negative elements we need to distinguish cases where they express separate semantic negations from those where only one semantic negation is involved:

[1] i *I <u>didn't</u> say I <u>didn't</u> want it.* [two semantic negations]
ii *He consulted <u>neither</u> his wife <u>nor</u> his parents.* [one semantic negation]

In [i] we clearly have two semantic negations, one of *want* and one of *say*. In [ii], however, there is just one semantic negation: it has scope over the coordination and is syntactically expressed twice, once in each coordinate. The negation in [ii] is non-verbal, and the fact that there is only one semantic negation is evident from the version with verbal negation, which is semantically equivalent: *He didn't consult either his wife or his parents. Neither* and *nor* in [ii] are markers of coordination, and exhibit what can be regarded as **negative concord**, or agreement.

Constructions with semantic negations in separate clauses, as in [1i] or *I didn't promise [not to tell them]* are unremarkable and do not need to be considered further (for the special case where the negation markers are adjacent, as in *You can't not go*, see §2.3.2 above). Nor do we need to say any more here about affixal negation. This is always subclausal, and it can combine unproblematically with clausal negation, as in *Their behaviour was certainly not immoral* or *None of the problems seemed unimportant.* In §6.1 we will look briefly at constructions with separate semantic negations in a single clause, each of which could by itself mark clausal negation. Then in §6.2 we turn to concordial and similar types of negation.

6.1 Multiple semantic negation within a single clause

(a) Constructions where the first negation has scope over existential quantification

[2] i *None of them had no redeeming features.*
ii *No one, surely, has never experienced such temptation.*
iii *Never before had no one nominated for the position.*
iv *Neither investigator had no financial interest in the company.*
v *No one didn't consider it a retrograde move.*

By virtue of the relation between existential and universal quantification (see Ch. 5, §5.1) these are all equivalent to positive clauses with universal quantification: *All of them had some redeeming features*; *Everyone, surely, has at some time experienced such temptation*; *Before, someone had always nominated for the position*; *Both investigators had some financial interest in the company*; *Everyone considered it a retrograde move.* Note that it is the first negative that is replaced by a universally quantified counterpart in the paraphrase. Thus in [ii] *no one* precedes *never*, so we have *everyone* and *at some time*, but in [iii] *never* precedes *no one*, so we have *always* and *someone* (even though in the positive they do not occur in that order).[24]

The positive versions are of course easier to process and represent the default way of expressing the meanings concerned. The more complex forms would thus typically need some special motivation, such as contrast. In [2iii], for example, we are concerned with an occasion on which no one had nominated for the position in question, and [iii] contrasts this occasion with all previous ones of the relevant kind. Such contexts of contrast will often lead to one or other of the negative markers being stressed.

As far as the syntax is concerned, only one of the negators can mark clausal negation. The clauses in [2] are all negative and behave with respect to the tests for polarity just like clauses with a single negative. Compare, for example, *None of them had any redeeming features, did they?* and *None of them had no redeeming features, did they?*

[24] The same kind of relationship holds between disjunctive and conjunctive coordination, so that *Neither Kim nor Pat had no financial interest in the company* is equivalent to *Both Kim and Pat had some financial interest in the company.*

(b) Other types

[3] i [*He didn't say nothing:*] *he said it didn't matter.*
ii *Not all of them made no mistakes.*
iii *Not many / Few people found nothing to criticise.*
iv [*We not only made no progress:*] *we actually moved backwards.*

In [i] *nothing* follows the verbal negation, and this time the meaning involves existential quantification: "He did say something"; examples of this kind are used to contradict a negative assertion, in this case *He said nothing.* Example [ii] has negation of the universal quantifier *all* and is accordingly equivalent to a positive with existential quantification: *Some of them made some mistakes.* Example [iii], with negation of the multal quantifier *many* or combination of negation with paucal quantification in *few,* has no positive semantic equivalent of a comparable kind. But given a reasonably large set of people under consideration it will tend to be pragmatically equivalent to *Most people found something to criticise.*

One of the commonest cases has *not only* with scope over a negative, as in [3iv]. This differs from the other types in that we can drop the *not only* without affecting the other negative, giving *We made no progress: we actually moved backwards.*

6.2 Negative concord and pleonastic negation

We turn now to constructions where a single semantic negative is expressed more than once.

(a) The standard variety

There are a number of constructions in Standard English in which the negation of a clause is expressed at more than one point morphologically:

[4]	i	*Their action was neither illegal nor immoral.*	[disjunctive coordination concord]
	ii	*They aren't here, I don't think.*	[parenthetical concord]
	iii	*Not in my car, you're not.*	[negative retort]
	iv	*I wouldn't be surprised if it didn't rain.*	[pleonastic subordinate negative]

Disjunctive coordination concord

When a negative has scope over disjunctive coordination, it may be expressed verbally, as in *Their action wasn't (either) illegal or immoral,* or non-verbally, in the coordination itself, as in [4i]. In the latter case it is generally incorporated into all markers of coordination, and we can therefore talk of concord or agreement in polarity. Occasionally, however, we find *or* instead of *nor*: *Their action was neither illegal or immoral* (see Ch. 15, §2.4).

Parenthetical concord

A further minor case is seen in [4ii], where semantically there is a single negation, just as there is in the non-parenthetical versions *I don't think they are here* or *I think they aren't here.* In the parenthetical version the negation is expressed both in the anchor *they aren't here* and in the parenthetical *I don't think.* The negation in the parenthetical, however, is optional, for we can also have *They aren't here, I think.* The matching negation in [4ii] is comparable to the matching interrogatives in *Are they here, do you know?* (cf. Ch. 10, §5.3).

Negative retort

Example [4iii] might be said by B in response to A's saying *I'm just driving into town.* B's response is thus a reduced version of *You're not driving into town in my car.* The negated initial constituent represents new information, while the rest is discourse-old, recoverable from A's utterance. The effect is to emphatically reject a proposition or proposal that is more specific than the one just uttered.

Pleonastic negation in subordinate clauses

Example [4iv] is ambiguous between a reading with two semantic negations ("It would not come as a surprise to me if I were to learn that it didn't rain") and the one we are concerned with here, where there is only one semantic negation ("I wouldn't be surprised if it rained"). In this second interpretation the negative in the subordinate clause is pleonastic, an extra mark of something that has already been marked – in this case, in the matrix clause. Other examples are:

[5] i *No one can say what might not happen if there were another earthquake.*
ii *He is unable to predict how much of it may not turn out to be pure fabrication.*

The range of constructions where this pleonastic *not* is found is very restricted. In [4iv] the pleonastic *not* is in the protasis of a remote conditional where the apodosis has a negated expression of surprise (cf. also *I wouldn't wonder if . . .*). In [5i–ii] it is in an interrogative clause headed by modal ***may***. In all three examples the subordinate clause containing pleonastic *not* is strongly non-factual.

Negative concord in non-standard dialects

The clearest case of negative concord in English is found in non-standard dialects. This book is of course a grammar of Standard English, but the negative concord phenomenon is so widespread and salient that it deserves some mention here.

In many dialects, ranging from Cockney (spoken in the East End of London, England) to African American Vernacular English (AAVE, formerly known as Black English Vernacular, spoken in segregated African American communities in the USA), the absolute negators *no, no one, nothing,* etc., are used in negative clauses where the standard dialect has the NPIs *any, anyone, anything,* etc.:

[6]	NON-STANDARD	STANDARD
i	a. !*He didn't say nothin'.*	b. *He didn't say anything.*
ii	a. !*You gonna spend your whole life [not trustin' nobody]?*	b. *Are you going to spend your whole life [not trusting anybody]?*
iii	a. !*Nobody here didn't point no gun at nobody.*	b. *Nobody here pointed any gun at anybody.*

Each clause contains just one semantic negation and in the standard versions it is marked by a single negator. In the non-standard versions, however, it is marked by verbal negation and also on all the existentially quantified elements in the clause. We accordingly have negative concord between the verb and these elements.

Non-standard clauses with negative concord are characteristically homonymous with standard dialect clauses containing multiple semantic negation, such as [2v] and [3i] above. Standard *He didn't say nothing* means "He did say something (it's not true that he said nothing"). The bracketed clause of [6iia] could likewise be used in the standard dialect with the meaning "not being in a state of refusing to trust anyone". In principle [6iiia] could be used in Standard English to express a meaning containing four semantic negations, though in practice of course it would be far too complex to process. There are, however, some constructions – such as imperative *Don't nobody move!* – that cannot be used in the standard dialect to express multiple semantic negation.[25]

There is an extremely widespread tendency among Standard English speakers to regard dialects with negative concord as 'illogical' and 'inferior'. It is argued that by a rule of logic two negatives cancel each other out to make a positive. Thus just as *It isn't the case that she didn't move* (or *She didn't not move*) is equivalent to *She moved*, it is argued that *He didn't say nothing* is a double negative that can only mean "He said something" and hence should not be used to express the opposite of that meaning. But such an argument is completely invalid. The rule of logic that two negatives are equivalent to a positive applies to logical forms, not to grammatical forms. It applies to semantic negation, not to the grammatical markers of negation. And as far as the [a] examples of [6] are concerned, there is only a single semantic negation, so the rule of logic doesn't apply: it is completely irrelevant.[26] The pattern in the non-standard dialect is similar to the one found in the standard dialect of Italian, French, Spanish, Polish, Russian, and many other languages. For example, Italian *non* means "not" and *nessuno* means "nobody", but the meaning of *Non ti credo nessuno* is "Nobody believes you", not "Nobody doesn't believe you". Here again, then, we have two negative words marking a single semantic negation, just as we do in the non-standard English dialects. There is no more reason to condemn the latter as illogical than there is to condemn Italian, French, and so on. The difference between the [a] and [b] versions of [6] is a matter of grammar, not logic, and neither set can be regarded as intrinsically superior to the other.

Despite its non-standard character every experienced user of English needs to be passively acquainted with the negative concord construction in order to be able to understand English in such ordinary contexts as film soundtracks, TV dramas, popular songs, and many everyday conversations. Those who claim that negative concord is evidence of ignorance and illiteracy are wrong; it is a regular and widespread feature of non-standard dialects of English across the world. Someone who thinks the song title *I can't get no satisfaction* means "It is impossible for me to lack satisfaction" does not know English.[27]

7 Positive and negative polarity in responses and anaphora

7.1 Answers to polar questions and comparable responses

Yes and *no* answers

Yes and *no* serve as markers of positive and negative polarity in answers to questions. They may stand alone, or combine with a clause that expresses the answer more

[25] The same applies to the construction *without* + *no* (corresponding to standard *without* + *any*), as in !*Give me a large cheeseburger without no onions.* And also to the construction with negative concord between the verb and an approximate negator of degree, as in !*I can't hardly see* (corresponding to standard *I can hardly see*).

[26] Given that the term 'double negative' is strongly associated with the semantic rule whereby two negatives do cancel each other out, it is an unsatisfactory term for the negative concord construction. It is in any case inappropriate because there is no limitation to two, as we have seen.

[27] Negative concord was common in Old English and became virtually obligatory in the Middle English period. Its decline in the standard written language in the early Modern period may have had much to do with a nascent prescriptive tradition and its conscious comparison of English with Latin. In the nineteenth century negative concord re-emerged as a literary mark of non-standard usage, the gap in the historical record almost certainly concealing a continuous but largely unrecorded tradition in many spoken dialects.

explicitly:

[7] i a. A: *Is this car yours?* B: } *Yes* (*it is*). *No* (*it isn't*).
b. A: *Isn't this car yours?* B:
ii a. A: *He has gone, hasn't he?* B: } *Yes* (*he has*). *No* (*he hasn't*).
b. A: *He hasn't gone, has he?* B:

The choice between *yes* and *no* depends simply on the polarity of the answer – not, for example, on agreement vs disagreement with what may be suggested by the question. Polar questions, especially negative ones, may be biased, indicating the questioner's predisposition to think that one or other answer is the right one, but that has no bearing on the choice between *yes* and *no*. In [ib], for example, the appropriate response is *yes* if the car is B's and *no* if it isn't, irrespective of what A appears to expect is the case. Similarly with answers to tag questions, as in [ii].

**Yes it isn't* and **No it is* are thus ungrammatical as single clauses. In *Yes it is* and *No it isn't*, the *yes* and *no* can be regarded as a special type of adjunct, a polarity adjunct, which agrees in polarity with the clause – a further case of polarity concord in English. The adjunct can also be placed at the end of the clause, with prosodic detachment: *It is, yes* and *It isn't, no*. A response to [7i] with the form *No, it's Kim's* would not of course violate the polarity concord rule, because here we have not a single clause but a sequence of two, just as we do in *No it's not mine, it's Kim's*.

One respect in which the agreement vs disagreement factor is relevant concerns the choice between single-word and expanded responses. Suppose you ask *Didn't you post the letter after all, then?*, indicating that you think I didn't. If in fact I did post it, I would normally say *Yes I did*, not just *Yes*.

Responses to other kinds of speech act

Yes and *no* are used in response to statements in a similar but not identical way:

[8] i A: *She did very well.* B: *Yes* (*she did*). *No she didn't.*
ii A: *She didn't do very well.* B: *Yes she did.* *No* (*she didn't*).

In [i] the disagreeing negative response would not normally be reduced to *No*, and in [ii] the disagreeing positive answer could not be reduced to *yes*. It is in fact here possible to say *yes* to express agreement with the negative statement: "Yes, you're right".

Following directives, *yes* and *no* can be used to express intention to comply with a positive and negative directive. *No* is also used to indicate refusal to comply with a positive one, but *yes* is not an idiomatic way of refusing to comply with a negative directive:

[9] i A: *Remember to lock up.* B: *Yes* (*I will*).
ii A: *Don't forget to lock up.* B: *No* (*I won't*).
iii A: *Tell me who did it.* B: *No* (*I won't*).
iv A: *Don't tell them I did it.* B: ?*Yes I will.*

In [iv] B would more likely say just *I will* (*tell them*), or words to that effect. With directives expressed by certain kinds of interrogative clause (a type of indirect speech act, in the sense of Ch. 10, §9.6.1), a response may reflect the literal question meaning or the indirect directive meaning. Thus in response to *Would you mind coming a little earlier next week*, I might respond *No of course not, I'll come around six* ("No of course I wouldn't mind"), or *Yes of course, I'll come around six* ("Yes of course I'll come a little earlier").

Idiomatic negative answers with *not* and *no*

There are a number of idiomatic phrases that express an emphatic negative response to a question or other speech act. Some have *not*, others the determinative *no*:

[10]	i	*Not for all the tea in China!*	*Not likely!*	*Not on a bet!* (AmE)
		Not in a million years!	*Not on your life!*	*Not on your nelly!* (BrE)
	ii	*No fear!*	*No chance!*	*No way!*[28]

7.2 Anaphoric *so* and *not*

With predicates that take *so* as the anaphoric pro-form for a positive clausal complement, *not* is used as a pro-form for a negative (cf. Ch. 17, §7.7.2). We illustrate with answers to questions, but they occur more widely than this.

[11]	QUESTION	POSITIVE ANSWER	NEGATIVE ANSWER
	Are they reliable?	*I believe/think so.*	*I believe/think not.*
		I was told so.	*I was told not.*
		It seems so.	*It seems not.*

Not (like *so*) is here functioning as complement and marks non-verbal negation: it is not modifying the verb.

What accompanies the pro-form need not be a full matrix clause; a preposed AdvP functioning as clause adjunct will serve as well:

[12]	*Is the city beautiful?*	*Apparently so.*	*Apparently not.*
		Most definitely so.	*Most definitely not.*

Other adjuncts such as PPs are permitted with *not* but not *so*:

[13]	*Does it rain much?*	**On the whole so.*	*On the whole not.*
		**So in the winter.*	*Not in the winter.*
		**Usually so this early.*	*Usually not this early.*

Not can also introduce anaphorically reduced clauses used in response to other types of speech act or following a negative clause:

[14] i A: *I think you should leave now.* B: *Not without my money.*
ii *I won't go, not even if they beg me.*
iii *There aren't many wild rhinoceroses left, not in Africa or in Asia.*

Not is here understood respectively as "I won't leave", "I won't go", and "there aren't many rhinoceroses left".

[28] *No way* can also be integrated into clause structure as an emphatic negator, as in *No way is that a diamond!* The original manner meaning has here been bleached away, so that we understand "That is emphatically not a diamond".

10

Clause type and illocutionary force

RODNEY HUDDLESTON

1 Type as a grammatical system of the clause

The five major categories

Clause type is the grammatical system whose five major terms are illustrated in:

[1]	i	*You are generous.*	[declarative]
	ii	*Are you generous?*	[closed interrogative]
	iii	*How generous are you?*	[open interrogative]
	iv	*How generous you are!*	[exclamative]
	v	*Be generous.*	[imperative]

Characteristic use and general definitions

Each of the categories is associated with a characteristic use as follows:

[2]		CLAUSE TYPE	CHARACTERISTIC USE
	i	declarative	statement
	ii	closed interrogative	closed question
	iii	open interrogative	open question
	iv	exclamative	exclamatory statement
	v	imperative	directive

A closed question is one with a closed set of answers: for example, the answers to [1ii] are just "Yes" and "No". By contrast, [1iii] has any number of possible answers, and is therefore an open question; similarly with *Who attended the meeting?*, and so on. In [2iv] we have used 'exclamatory statement' rather than the more familiar 'exclamation', because an exclamatory meaning can be added to any of the use categories, but the special syntactic construction shown in [1iv] is associated just with a particular kind of statement. For example, the exclamatory command *Get the hell out of here* or the exclamatory question *What on earth are you doing?* belong syntactically with [1v] and [1iii] respectively, not with [1iv]. 'Directive' in [2v] is a cover term for requests, commands, instructions, and the like; traditional grammars tend to use the term 'command', but this is far too narrow and specific for our purposes if understood in its everyday sense.

The correlation shown in [2] provides the basis for general definitions of the clause type categories:

[3] Imperative clause is a grammatically distinct class of clause whose members are characteristically used to issue directives.

And similarly for the others.

Complex relation between form and meaning

We have spoken of 'characteristic' use because, as is so often the case, the correlation between major categories of grammatical form and categories of meaning or use is by no means one-to-one. Compare, for example:

[4]		CLAUSE TYPE	USE
i	*Passengers are requested to remain seated.*	declarative	directive
ii	*Would you mind opening the door for me.*	closed interrogative	directive
iii	*Sleep well.*	imperative	wish

Examples [i] and [ii] illustrate conventional ways of expressing a polite request, a kind of directive, but syntactically they belong to the same structural class as *You are generous* and *Are you generous?* respectively. And though [iii] belongs syntactically with *Be generous* it is not used to tell or ask somebody to do something, but to express a wish. Numerous further examples of this and other kinds will emerge during the course of the chapter. It is essential therefore to maintain a sharp conceptual distinction between the grammatical clause types and the categories of meaning or use – between declarative and statement, imperative and directive, and so on. The situation is closely parallel to that which obtains in the area of tense (form) and time (meaning), but whereas it is standard practice for grammars to distinguish terminologically between tense and time, many use 'question' both for form (our 'interrogative') and for meaning. Again we emphasise, therefore, that interrogatives aren't always used as questions, and not all questions have the syntactic form of interrogatives.

Clause type in subordinate clauses

Four of the clause type categories apply to subordinate clauses as well as to main clauses:

[5]	MAIN	SUBORDINATE	
i	*It's a bargain.*	*She says* <u>*that it's a bargain*</u>*.*	[declarative]
ii	*Is it a bargain?*	*I wonder* <u>*if it's a bargain*</u>*.*	[closed interrogative]
iii	*Which one is a bargain?*	*I know* <u>*which one is a bargain*</u>	[open interrogative]
iv	*What a bargain it is!*	*I realise* <u>*what a bargain it is*</u>*.*	[exclamative]

Imperatives, however, are normally restricted to main clauses.[1] Our main focus in this chapter will be on main clauses, with most of the material on subordinate clause types deferred till Ch. 11.

The type system applies to the clause, not the sentence

What we refer to here as 'clause type' is more often called 'sentence type', but given the way in which we have defined sentence and clause in this grammar (Ch. 2, §1), it is evident that it is to the clause, not the sentence, that the system applies. In the first place, the subordinate clauses of [5] are not sentences but are nevertheless classified for type. And secondly, in sentences with the form of a clause-coordination the coordinated

[1] For arguments against treating infinitivals like *I told them* <u>*to be quiet*</u> as subordinate imperatives, see §9.8. Examples like *It's time we were going home, because* <u>*don't forget we have to be up early in the morning*</u> are of somewhat marginal grammaticality, and the internal structure here remains like that of a main clause.

clauses do not have to be of the same type:

[6] i	*Come around six, or is that too early for you?*	[imperative + closed interrog]
ii	*You can come too, but please bring your lunch.*	[declarative + imperative]
iii	*What a fine player she is, and she's still only ten!*	[exclamative + declarative]

In [i] the first clause is imperative and the second closed interrogative: the sentence as a whole cannot be assigned to any of the type categories. And similarly with [ii–iii].

Clause fragments

We include within the category of clause various kinds of verbless construction, such as open interrogative *What about the others?* or exclamative *What a disaster!*

The clause types are mutually exclusive

Clause type is a grammatical system in the sense that no clause can belong to more than one of the categories: they are mutually exclusive. There can be ambiguity: *How many problems remain* (considered in abstraction from punctuation and prosody) can be an open interrogative ("What is the number of problems that remain?") or an exclamative ("What a lot of problems remain!"), but any particular instance of it will be one or the other, not simultaneously both.

Echo question not a clause type

Echo questions are illustrated in:

[7]	STIMULUS	ECHO QUESTION
i	a. *Give it to Angela.*	b. *Give it to who?*
ii	a. *Did you use a macro?*	b. *Did I use a what?*

Suppose you say [ia] and I don't quite catch the name: I might respond with [ib] to ask you to repeat it, and similarly in [ii]. The [b] examples are known as **echo questions**: they echo **the stimulus**, what has just been said, with a view to questioning some aspect of it. We examine this construction in §4.8, but we mention it in the present context to develop what has just been said about the concept of system. It is evident from [7] that the echo construction is not mutually exclusive with the clause type categories. In [i] the echo feature is superimposed on an imperative and in [ii] on a closed interrogative: from a syntactic point of view, echo question is therefore a different kind of category from the clause types, not a sixth term on the same dimension. With respect to clause type, then, [ia] and [ib] are both imperatives, [iia] and [iib] both closed interrogatives; in each pair [b] differs from [a] by virtue of being an echo question. This reinforces the need to distinguish carefully between the clause types and the categories of meaning/use: [ib], for example, is a question, but it is not syntactically interrogative.

2 Distinctive grammatical properties of the major clause types

Declarative is the default clause type: a clause is declarative if it lacks the special properties that define the other types. In this section, therefore, we outline the distinctive properties of the other four major types with respect to main clauses.

Closed interrogatives

[1] Closed interrogatives have subject–auxiliary inversion triggered by the clause type, and hence are always tensed.

[2]

	DECLARATIVE	CLOSED INTERROGATIVE
i	a. *It is true.*	b. *Is it true?*
ii	a. *They saw her.*	b. *Did they see her?*

Subject–auxiliary inversion is a *do*-support construction (Ch. 3, §2.1), so empty *do* is required if there would not otherwise be an auxiliary verb, as in [ii]. Subject–auxiliary inversion is not limited to closed interrogatives but other main clauses in which it occurs, with one exception, all have the inversion triggered by the placement of a non-subject element in initial position. In declarative *None of them did he consider satisfactory*, for example, the inversion is triggered by the initial negative. The one exception (in main clauses) is the optative *may* construction of *May you be forgiven!*[2]

Open interrogatives

[3] i Open interrogatives contain an interrogative phrase based on one of the interrogative words *who, whom, whose, which, what, when, where, how*, etc.
ii A non-subject interrogative phrase is usually fronted, and this triggers subject–auxiliary inversion.
iii Open interrogatives are usually tensed, but can also be infinitival.
iv Open interrogatives can be reduced to just the interrogative phrase.

[4]

i	*<u>Who</u> broke the window?*	[interrogative phrase as subject]
ii	*<u>Which one</u> did he choose?*	[non-subject interrogative phrase with inversion]
iii	*So you told him <u>what</u>, exactly?*	[non-fronted interrogative phrase]
iv	*<u>Why</u> make such a fuss?*	[infinitival]
v	*<u>Which one</u>?*	[reduction to interrogative phrase]

In [4i] the interrogative phrase is subject and occupies the same position as the subject of a declarative (*Kim broke the window*). In [4ii] the interrogative phrase is a non-subject in prenuclear position: we say that the interrogative phrase has been **fronted**. As usual, the process terminology is not to be interpreted literally: it is merely a shorthand way of saying that the interrogative phrase occupies front position rather than the post-verbal position of the corresponding element in a syntactically more basic clause (cf. *He chose <u>this one</u>*). In main clauses fronting of the interrogative phrase always triggers inversion, whereas in subordinate clauses it normally doesn't. (The qualification 'normally' is needed because inversion is possible in subordinate clauses under restrictive conditions discusssed in Ch. 11, §5.3.2: %*She asked <u>how could she help us</u>*.) Example [iii] shows that fronting of a non-subject interrogative phrase is not obligatory: the interrogative phrase here remains **in situ**, i.e. it occupies the same place as the corresponding element in a declarative clause. Example [iv] is a bare infinitival; *to*-infinitivals are also possible, as in *How to explain his attitude?* Reduced clauses like [v] are naturally heavily dependent on context for their interpretation.

[2] Untriggered non-interrogative inversion occurs also in subordinate clauses functioning as conditional adjunct: *<u>Had I known earlier</u>, I'd have done something about it* (see Ch. 11, §4.7).

Exclamatives

[5] i Exclamatives contain an initial exclamative phrase, based on one or other of the two exclamative words *what* and *how*.
ii They may be reduced to just a predicative exclamative phrase; otherwise they are always tensed.
iii They usually have subject + predicator order, but subject postposing and subject–auxiliary inversion are also possible.

[6] i *What a disaster it was!*
ii *How great would be their embarrassment if the error were detected!*
iii *How happy would he be if he could see her once more!*
iv *What a disaster!*

Examples [6i–iii] have fronting of a non-subject exclamative phrase; in [ii] this is accompanied by postposing of the subject *their embarrassment* and in [iii] by subject–auxiliary inversion. In [iv] the clause is reduced to the exclamative phrase, understood predicatively ("What a disaster it was!").

Imperatives

[7] i Imperatives are normally restricted to main clauses.
ii A 2nd person subject is omissible.
iii The verb is in the plain form.
iv In verbal negation, emphatic polarity, and code, supportive *do* is required even in combination with *be*.
v Verbal negatives with *you* as subject usually have the order *don't* + *you*.

The examples in [8] show how these properties distinguish imperatives from declaratives:

[8]	DECLARATIVE	IMPERATIVE
i	a. *You look after yourself.*	b. (*You*) *look after yourself.*
ii	a. *You are very tactful.*	b. *Be very tactful.*
iii	a. *Everybody stands up.*	b. *Everybody stand up.*
iv	a. *You aren't late.*	b. *Don't be late.*
v	a. *You don't worry about it.*	b. *Don't you worry about it.*

You look after yourself is ambiguous between declarative and imperative (it could be used as a statement about your behaviour or as a directive), but *Look after yourself* is unambiguously imperative (having only the directive interpretation). Examples [8ii–iii] have a difference in verb-form. Present tense *are* in [iia] contrasts with plain form *be*: ***be*** is the only verb lexeme that does not have syncretism between the plain form and one of the present tense forms. The difference in [iii] is of greater generality: here the plain form of the imperative contrasts with the 3rd person singular present tense form of the declarative, whatever the lexeme involved. In [8iv] *do* isn't needed in the declarative because *be* is an auxiliary verb, but it is nevertheless required in the imperative (cf. **Be not late*). Finally, in [8v] we have a difference in the position of the subject. Example [va] has the default S–P order; it is a statement, one that might well be followed by the question tag *do you?* In imperative [vb], a directive, the subject follows *don't*.

Closed and open interrogatives: subclasses of a larger class or distinct primary classes?

The terms 'closed interrogative' and 'open interrogative' suggest that they are subclasses of 'interrogative'. Yet what they have in common is much more a matter of meaning than of syntax: they both characteristically express questions. From a syntactic point of view, they are in fact strikingly different. The most important property of open interrogatives is the presence of an interrogative phrase, based on the special set of interrogative words – they can in fact be reduced to just an interrogative phrase, as seen in [4v]. The distinctive property of closed interrogatives (in main clauses) is subject–auxiliary inversion. Inversion is found in the open interrogative as well as the closed, but only as a secondary feature, triggered by the fronting of a non-subject interrogative phrase. As a result, closed *Did she win the race?* and *Who won the race?* share no syntactic feature distinguishing them from declarative *She won the race.* Note, moreover, that inversion is also found as a secondary feature in a variety of other constructions too, such as negatives like *Not once did she smile.*

It is for these reasons that we have treated closed and open interrogatives as each on a par with declarative, exclamative, and imperative within the syntactic system of clause type. It would not be helpful, however, to coin new terms for them without a shared component – and we will make use of 'interrogative' as a cover term, generally when the focus is on the relation with question rather than on the syntactic structure.

3 Some semantic and pragmatic preliminaries

Before looking systematically at the relation between the clause types and their meaning or use, we need to clarify some of the concepts we will be using in talking of meaning in this area.

3.1 Illocutionary force

Statement and directive are in the first instance pragmatic categories: we are concerned with the way the speaker is using the clause when uttering it in a particular context. A more specific term for this aspect of pragmatic meaning is **illocutionary force**. If, for example, I utter the clause *Tom has arrived* with the intention of thereby committing myself to the truth of the proposition "Tom has arrived", I have uttered it with the illocutionary force of a statement – or, to put it slightly differently, I have performed the **illocutionary act** of making a statement. If I say *Sit down* with the intention of telling you to sit down, my utterance has the illocutionary force of a directive – or, again, I have performed the illocutionary act of issuing a directive. And so on. Question is commonly used in the same kind of way: asking a question is a kind of illocutionary act contrasting with making a statement or issuing a directive.

More specific kinds of illocutionary force

Statement, directive, and question are very general categories of illocutionary force, but there are in addition innumerable more specific illocutionary categories. Some of these can be regarded as simply special cases of the more general categories. For example, *Bring the water to the boil* might be said with the force of a command, a request, advice, an instruction (e.g. in a recipe), all of which can be subsumed under the broader category of directive, for they all count as attempts to get you to do something.

In other cases, the specific illocutionary force is different in kind from the three general ones:

[1] *I promise to return the key tomorrow.*

The natural use of this is to make a promise, and a promise is different in kind from a statement. In making a statement I commit myself to the truth of some proposition, whereas in making a promise I commit myself to doing something – in the case of [1], to returning the key tomorrow.

Primary and secondary force

Strictly speaking, a natural utterance of [1] would be both a statement and a promise, though the promise is of course more important, more salient than the statement. We will speak of the promise force as **primary** and the statement force as **secondary**. Making the statement can be regarded as simply the means of making the promise. I make a promise by stating that I do, and the statement is true simply by virtue of my uttering the clause with the intention of making a promise. The greater salience of the promise over the statement is reflected in the way the utterance of [1] would most naturally be reported, in comparison with the way in which an utterance with primary statement force would be:

[2]	i	a. *I returned the key yesterday.*	[statement]
		b. *You said you returned the key yesterday.*	[report of statement]
	ii	a. *I promise to return the key tomorrow.* (=[1])	[promise]
		b. *You promised to return the key tomorrow.*	[report of promise]

You said you promised to return the key tomorrow, although possible, is much less natural than [iib] precisely because it reports [iia] as a statement, whereas [iib] reports it as a promise.

Notice, then, that whereas the clause types are mutually exclusive, the illocutionary categories are not: it is possible for an utterance to belong simultaneously to more than one such category. This applies, indeed, also to the general categories: *I order you to leave* would naturally be both a directive (the primary force) and a statement (secondary).

The performative use of verbs

The two illocutionary forces of [1] are expressed by quite different linguistic devices. The statement force derives from the declarative clause type, whereas the promise force derives from the presence of the verb *promise* itself. *Promise* belongs to the class of **illocutionary verbs**, verbs that denote illocutionary acts, and in [1] it is used **performatively**, i.e. to effect the performance of the illocutionary act it denotes. The performative use of ***promise*** in [1] may be contrasted with its non-performative use in examples like [2iib]. The latter is not a promise but simply a report of a promise, hence just a statement. The first device, declarative clause type, is a matter of grammar, and there is accordingly only a very small number of possible contrasts; the second device, the performative use of *promise*, is primarily a lexical matter, which allows for a large number of contrasts. In [3] we give a small sample of verbs that can be used performatively:

[3]					
	admit	*advise*	*apologise*	*ask*	*beg*
	bet	*claim*	*command*	*commend*	*concede*
	congratulate	*entreat*	*estimate*	*name*	*order*
	postulate	*promise*	*repudiate*	*resign*	*suggest*
	swear	*thank*	*urge*	*warn*	*welcome*

There are also expressions consisting of verb + dependent: *declare . . . open* (*I declare the meeting open*), *give one's word*, and so on. For convenience we will refer to such utterances as [1]/[2iia] as **performatives**.[3]

Perlocutionary effect

Illocutionary force contrasts with **perlocutionary effect**, the effect the utterance has on you, the addressee. If I say *Tom has arrived* with the illocutionary force of a statement, the default perlocutionary effect is that you will accept it as true. But of course statements do not invariably have this effect: you may know or believe me to be mistaken. Similarly, if I say *Sit down* with the illocutionary force of a directive, the default perlocutionary effect will be that you comply by sitting down; but again this is not the only possible result. Typically, then, an illocutionary force is associated with a particular perlocutionary effect which the speaker is aiming to achieve, but failure to achieve this effect does not normally deprive the utterance of its illocutionary force: a statement is still a statement even if it is not accepted as true, a directive is still a directive even if it is not complied with, and so on.

Verbs which denote illocutionary acts can normally be used performatively, like *promise* in [1]. Those – such as *persuade, convince, annoy, intimidate, impress* – which denote perlocutionary acts cannot similarly be used to perform those acts. I can warn you (an illocutionary act) that the car is unroadworthy by saying [4i], but I cannot persuade you (a perlocutionary act) that it is unroadworthy by saying [4ii]:

[4] i *I warn you that the car is unroadworthy.* [performative]
ii *I persuade you that the car is unroadworthy.* [non-performative]

(The second is indeed pragmatically unlikely: it needs some such continuation as *and yet you buy it nevertheless!*) Similarly, there are differences in the way I might ask you to clarify your illocutionary and perlocutionary intentions. Compare

[5] i a. *Is that a threat or a promise?*
b. *Are you asking me or telling me?* } [illocutionary]
ii a. *Is that intended to intimidate me?*
b. *Are you trying to annoy me or to amuse me?* } [perlocutionary]

When questioning the perlocutionary intention, one typically needs to include some such verb as *intend* or *try*, but this is generally not necessary when questioning the illocutionary intention. Saying *I'll be back at six* with the intention of making a promise is sufficient for the utterance to be a promise, but telling a joke with the intention of amusing the addressee is not sufficient to achieve that goal.

[3] Clauses like *I promise to return the key* and *I order you to leave* are ambiguous, having also less salient interpretations in which they are statements about my habitual behaviour ("I habitually promise to return the key / order you to leave"): in this interpretation they are not performatives since they do not themselves constitute a promise or order. The *tomorrow* in [2iia] makes the habitual reading even less salient, but it is still possible in principle.

Propositional and non-propositional components of meaning

The **propositional content** of a sentence is that part of its meaning that determines what propositions it can be used to express; clause type, however, contributes to **non-propositional meaning** (see Ch. 1, §5.2). Consider the relation between a declarative and its closed interrogative counterpart, as in:

[6]	DECLARATIVE	CLOSED INTERROGATIVE
i	a. *Kim is in Paris.*	b. *Is Kim in Paris?*
ii	a. *Pat saw them.*	b. *Did Pat see them?*

In each pair, [a] and [b] are partly alike and partly different in both form and meaning. In form, the closed interrogative contains the same elements as the declarative (sometimes with the addition of *do*, as in [ii]) but with a different order of subject and verb. As for meaning, what they have in common is that they have the same propositional content: both express the proposition "Kim is in Paris" or "Pat saw them". They differ in the non-propositional component, more specifically, in their **illocutionary meaning**. In a normal use of [a] the proposition is asserted, whereas in [b] it is questioned. In both [i] and [ii] the illocutionary force is separate from the propositional content of the utterance: when I use [ia] to make a statement I do not express the proposition that I am making a statement – I simply make it by uttering a declarative with the appropriate intention. Similarly, when I ask a question by means of [ib] I do not **say that** I am asking a question. Note, then, that the term 'express' is neutral as to illocutionary force. And the terms 'true' and 'false' can be applied to propositions or to statements, but not of course to questions.

A unique feature of performatives like [1], *I promise to return the key tomorrow*, is that here the (primary) illocutionary force is identified in the propositional content of the utterance. Thus [1] itself, for example, expresses the proposition "I promise to return the key tomorrow". As a result of this feature of performatives, the primary illocutionary force of the utterance is more explicit and precisely specified in such utterances than it normally is elsewhere.

Other non-propositional markers of illocutionary force

Clause type and the performative use of illocutionary verbs are not the only linguistic devices for indicating illocutionary force. Intonation plays an important role too, as we shall see, and there are also particular words, such as *please*, which serve this purpose. But these further devices are like clause type in that they do not contribute to the propositional content of the utterance. When I say, for example, *I'd like a cup of tea, please*, the *please* serves to indicate that I am making a request, that I am **asking** for a cup of tea, but I do not express the proposition that I am doing so. *Please* is quite irrelevant to the truth or falsity of the utterance, and hence does not express any part of its propositional content.

3.2 Indirect speech acts

Illocutionary force is very often conveyed indirectly rather than directly. Consider:

[7] *Do you know what time it is?*

A likely context for this (not the only possible one of course) is where I don't know the time, want to know the time, and believe you may well be able to tell me. In this context it would indirectly convey "What time is it?" This is why it would be thoroughly unco-operative in such a context for you to respond merely with *Yes*. *Yes* would answer the question that is actually asked, but not the one that I in fact want to have answered. Another plausible context for [7] is where it is addressed to a child (by a parent, say) when it is known to be past the child's bedtime: here my intention may well be to convey a directive to go to bed.

In either contextualisation, I perform two illocutionary acts simultaneously, one directly (a question as to whether you know what time it is), and one indirectly (a question as to what time it is, or a directive to go to bed). We will follow the established practice of referring to indirect illocutionary acts as **indirect speech acts** (with the understanding that the term covers writing as well as speech). Commonly, the direct act is obviously less important than the indirect one – as when the interest of the question whether you know the time is simply that if you do you will be able to answer the question that I really do want an answer to. There is an analogy here with performatives, and we will again, where appropriate, apply the terms 'primary' and 'secondary' to the different acts or forces. Thus just as in the performative *I promise to return the key tomorrow* the promise is primary and the statement secondary, so in the first contextualisation of [7] the question about the time is primary and that about your knowledge secondary. The difference is that in the performative case the primary act is direct, whereas in such cases as [7] it is not.

Definition of indirect speech act

An indirect speech act is one where (a) the propositional content actually expressed differs from that which the speaker intends to convey with some illocutionary force, or (b) where the illocutionary force is different from that normally conveyed by the clause type concerned.

Most cases are covered by condition (a). The propositional content expressed in [7], for example, is "You know what time it is", whereas the propositional content that I intend to convey is "What time is it?" (with question force) or "You go to bed" (with directive force). Case (b) is illustrated by [4iii] of §1, *Sleep well*. At the direct level it is a directive (the force characteristically associated with imperative clause type), but since sleeping well is not something that we normally regard as being under our control it will generally have the indirect force of a wish.[4]

Degrees of indirectness

There are varying degrees of indirectness, depending on how different the two propositional contents are. The first suggested contextualisation of [7], for example, is less indirect than the second because the propositional content of the conveyed "What time

[4]The sense of 'indirect' introduced in this section is quite different from the one it has in traditional grammar in such expressions as 'indirect question.' A traditional indirect question, such as the underlined clause in *She asked <u>who had done it</u>*, is in our terminology a subordinate interrogative, whereas an indirect question in the speech-act sense might be *I'd be interested to hear your view*, when used to convey "What is your view?" As it happens, both senses are applicable in [7], but to different parts of it. The subordinate clause *what time it is* is an indirect question in the traditional sense (it is a subordinate interrogative clause), whereas the whole utterance is an indirect question in the speech act sense (in the use where it conveys "What time is it?"). We will use 'indirect' solely in the speech-act sense.

is it?" is included as part of that which is actually expressed, whereas "You go to bed" is not. Intuitively (for we are not suggesting that the degree of indirectness can be precisely calculated), the following are less indirect again, though they still qualify as indirect speech acts:

[8] i *I should like to order two copies of the Penguin edition of Plato's 'Republic'.*
ii *May I remind you that you agreed to pay for the drinks?*

In the context of a letter to a bookshop, the writer of [i] will be taken to have performed the illocutionary act of ordering the goods, but the act is performed indirectly because the propositional content expressed is "I should like to order . . .", not "I (hereby) order . . .". The inference from "I should like to order" to "I order" is a very easy one to make in this context, for the wish to order can be fulfilled instantaneously simply by writing the letter (and perhaps enclosing payment). Nevertheless, "I should like to order" and "I order" are obviously not propositionally equivalent, and it is easy to imagine other contexts where the inference would not go through – e.g. in a conversation where the speaker adds: *but in my present financial plight I can't afford to do so.* Example [ii] conveys "I remind you that you agreed to pay for the drinks", but again that is not the same as the propositional content actually expressed. The question concerning permission is here vacuous since merely mentioning that you agreed to pay for the drinks itself reminds you of that fact, but this does not alter the fact that there is a difference between the propositional content expressed and that which I wish to convey.

The pervasive nature of indirect speech acts

Indirect speech acts are an immensely pervasive phenomenon. Some kinds of illocutionary act are more often performed indirectly than directly, either in general or in a certain range of contexts.

Requests

Take first the case of requests, not in general but in a context where speaker and addressee are social equals yet not closely intimate. Here a request is much less likely to be made directly than indirectly. Instead of the direct *Please open the window*, for example, I am likely to use one of the indirect directives in [9] or something along similar lines:

[9] i *Can/Could you (please) open the window.*
ii *Will/Would you (please) open the window.*
iii *Would you be good enough to open the window (please).*
iv *Would you mind opening the window (please)?*
v *Would you like to open the window (please)?*
vi *I wonder if I might trouble you to open the window?*

(There is some variation in the punctuation of interrogatives such as [iv], with a full stop reflecting the primary directive force, a question mark the secondary question force.)

Job applications

As a second example, consider the more specialised illocutionary act of applying for a job, an act normally performed in writing. Some of the formulations used for this purpose are illustrated in [10], where those in [i] are direct, the others indirect:

[10] i a. *I hereby apply for the position of Lecturer in Philosophy advertised in 'The Australian' of 30 November.*
b. *I apply for the position . . .*
c. *This is an application for . . .*
ii a. *I would/should like to apply . . .*
b. *I wish to apply / make application . . .*
c. *I am writing to apply . . .*
d. *I would/should like to be considered for . . .*
e. *I would/should be grateful if you would consider me for . . .*
f. *Please consider this letter as my formal application for . . .*
g. *I beg/wish to offer myself as a candidate for . . .*
h. *The purpose of this letter is to express my interest in securing . . .*
i. *I am very glad to have this opportunity to apply . . .*

Again, only a small minority of applications are performed directly, and there are innumerable variations on the indirect formulations exemplified in [ii].

Non-propositional markers of indirect force

We have explained the concept of indirect speech act primarily by reference to propositional content; non-propositional components may, however, relate to the illocutionary act which is conveyed indirectly rather than the one which is directly expressed. This is illustrated by the *please* of [9], *Can you please open the window*, etc., or of the earlier, *I'd like a cup of tea, please.* The latter is an indirect speech act in that the propositional content expressed ("I'd like a cup of tea") differs from that conveyed with directive force ("you give me a cup of tea"), but the *please* serves to signal this indirect directive force (marking it, more specifically, as a request): it does not relate to the direct statement. Similarly in [9] *please* works at the indirect level of request, not the direct level of question. The distinction between direct and indirect is therefore not to be identified with that between explicit and inexplicit: the *please* explicitly marks the above examples as requests, but they are still indirect because of the discrepancy between the propositional content expressed and that implied.

Prosody and punctuation commonly serve as markers of indirect force:

[11] i *Could you turn your radio down a little.*
ii *Isn't she fantastic!*

At the direct level these are questions, but I am unlikely to use them with question as the primary force: I would generally be indirectly conveying "Turn your radio down a little" (directive) and "How fantastic she is!" (exclamatory statement). In this use they would typically have falling intonation, rather than the rising intonation that is the most characteristic prosodic accompaniment of closed questions, and they are very often not punctuated with a question mark.

Such markers of the indirect force have the effect of increasing the difference in salience between the indirect speech act and the direct one, pushing the latter further into the background. In such an example as *Boy, am I ever hungry!* the combination of falling intonation with the non-propositional elements *boy* and *ever* causes the direct question force to be completely overshadowed by the indirect exclamatory statement force.

Idiomatic forms of indirect speech acts

As will be evident from the examples given, certain forms of expression are idiomatically or conventionally used in the performance of indirect speech acts. A clear distinction can be seen in such a pair as:

[12] a. *Can you turn the light on.* b. *Are you able to turn the light on?*

The construction with *can* is a much more frequent and natural way of making an indirect request than that with *be able*. It is certainly possible to make indirect requests with *be able*, but the degree of backgrounding of the direct inquiry force is significantly less than it is with *can*. With *can*, the inquiry force is commonly vacuous, in that the answer is self-evidently *Yes*, but this is not normal for *be able*. Thus in a context where it is obvious that you can turn the light on, [12a] is appropriate, or idiomatic, whereas [b] is not. Version [b] needs a context where there is genuine doubt as to your ability to turn the light on (e.g. one where you are carrying some shopping). This difference is reflected in the fact that the request marker *please*, which backgrounds the question force, would be very much more naturally inserted before *turn* in [a] than in [b]: *Can you please turn the light on*, but hardly *Are you able to please turn the light on.*

A similar, probably sharper, distinction is seen in

[13] a. *Have a good match.* b. *Win the match.*

Like the earlier *Sleep well*, [a] is likely to be used as an indirect wish, whereas it is hardly possible to convey a wish by means of [b]. The range of imperatives conventionally used as wishes is very limited: *Sleep well*, *Get well soon*, *Have a good . . .*, *Enjoy . . .*, but not many more.

To say that [12a] is an idiomatic way of making a request is not to say that it, or just the initial part, *can you*, is an idiom. An idiom (such as *kick the bucket* with the sense "die") is an expression whose meaning is not systematically derivable from its parts, but the request meaning conveyed by [12a] is derivable from the meanings of *can*, *you*, and the remainder of the clause together with the inference from an inquiry about your ability to do something to a request that you do it.

4 Kinds of question

4.1 Question as a semantic and as a pragmatic category

Semantic questions and their answers

The term 'question' is commonly used at both the semantic and pragmatic levels. At the semantic level, a question is distinguished by the fact that it defines a set of logically possible answers:

[1]	QUESTION	ANSWERS
i	a. *Have you seen it?*	b. *I have seen it.* *I haven't seen it.*
ii	a. *Who broke it?*	b. *I broke it.* *Kim broke it.* *The priest broke it.* *One of her children broke it . . .*

Instead of saying *I have seen it* in answer to [ia], I might say *Yes* or *I have* or *Yes, I have* or *Yes, I've seen it*, and so on. Although these are different in form they are equivalent, and we will regard them as (expressing) the same answer. Similarly for the negatives: *I have not seen it*; *I have not*; *I haven't*; *No*; *No, I haven't.* These all count as the same answer. It is in this sense of the term that we can say that [ia] defines a closed set of just two possible answers. Questions like [iia], on the other hand, define in principle an open set of answers: there are indefinitely many others besides those given in [iib]. It was this distinction that provided the basis for general definitions of closed and open interrogatives.

The distinction between answer and response

Answer is to be distinguished from **response**, which is a purely pragmatic concept. If you ask question [1ia], *Have you seen it?*, I could give any of the following as response, or of course indefinitely many others:

[2] i *No.* *I have.*
ii *I'm not sure.* *I can't remember.* *Possibly.* *Does it matter?*
iii *I've already told you that I have.* *It's on your desk.* *I saw it yesterday.*

The responses in [i] are answers, but the others are not. In [ii] I avoid giving an answer – whether on the grounds of insufficient knowledge or for some other reason. The responses in [iii] implicate or entail the answer *Yes*, but they are not logically equivalent to *Yes*: they are not themselves answers. With *It's on your desk* I interpret your question as indirectly asking "Where is it?", and answer that – *Have you seen my pen?*, for example, is a conventional way of indirectly conveying "Where's my pen?" The final response in [iii], *I saw it yesterday*, is not an answer because it contains extra information not called for in the question.

It is clear, then, that for a wide range of reasons one very often responds to a question in some other way than by giving an answer. And such a response will sometimes contain less information than an answer would, and sometimes more.

'The answer' and 'the right answer'

A semantic question defines a **set** of answers, but commonly one speaks of **the** answer to a question. Unless there are special features of the context indicating otherwise, the expression *the answer* is understood to mean "the right answer". Usually the right answer is the one that is true, but we will see below (§4.6) that there is a kind of question where 'right' cannot have this interpretation.

Pragmatic questions

Inquiry

The pragmatic concept of question is an illocutionary category. Prototypically, a question in this sense is an **inquiry**. To make a (genuine) inquiry is to ask a question to which one does not know the answer with the aim of obtaining the answer from the addressee. An inquiry can be thought of as effectively a kind of a directive – a directive (usually a request) to the addressee to supply the answer. The directive force is indirect, however, since the propositional content of the implied directive ("Tell me the answer to the question ...") is not the same as that which is actually expressed. As with the indirect directives discussed in §3.2, the request force can be signalled explicitly in the non-propositional component by the marker *please*, as in *What time is it, please?*

Not all questions are inquiries

The category of question is much broader than that of inquiry. Consider, for example:

[3] i A: *Ed's coming round tonight.* B: *Is he? I didn't know he was still in London.*
ii *What will become of her, I wonder?*
iii *What were the names of Henry VIII's six wives?*
iv *How can this problem be overcome? I suggest that the first step is . . .*

Example [i] illustrates the case where a question is used to indicate surprised or interested acknowledgement of new information. B's *Is he?* is not an inquiry: it doesn't seek to find out the answer, for A has just provided it, and B is not challenging what A has said. In [ii] I am wondering, not inquiring – probably not asking for an answer (much less 'the' answer). Question [iii] might be used in a quiz or exam: in this case it's not an inquiry since presumably I already know the answer, my aim being to test whether you do. And [iv] is intended as an expository question. Instead of asking you for the answer, I am directing your attention to a question whose answer I'm about to give you. Other cases of questions that are not inquiries include indirect speech acts like *Could you turn your radio down a little* or *Isn't she fantastic!* ([11] of §3), where the question force is secondary and very much backgrounded.

In comparison with a statement, a question on its own is informationally incomplete: it needs the answer to complete it. In an utterance with question as its primary force, I draw attention to this need for a completing answer. What we are calling an inquiry is then the special, but most common, case where I ask you to provide this answer.

4.2 Summary classification of questions

Questions can be classified in numerous different ways. In the following sections we will examine distinctions on the four dimensions shown in [4] where the first distinguishes three kinds of question, the others two each:

[4]	i	POLAR *Is it breathing?*	ALTERNATIVE *Is it alive or dead?*	VARIABLE *Why isn't it moving?*
	ii	INFORMATION *What time is it?*	DIRECTION *Shall I put some music on?*	
	iii	NEUTRAL *Have you read it?*	BIASED *Haven't you read it yet?*	
	iv	ORDINARY (NON-ECHO) *What's he going to do?*	ECHO *He's going to what?*	

Dimension [i] is based on the way the question defines the set of answers. Polar and alternative make up the class we have called closed question, and both are characteristically expressed by closed interrogatives. Variable questions are open questions, and are expressed by open interrogatives. We examine polar, alternative, and variable questions in turn in the next three sections.

For the other three dimensions the category in the left column of [4] can be regarded as the default, and §§4.6–8 will therefore focus respectively on direction questions (where the answers have the force of directives, not statements), biased questions (where the speaker is biased in favour of one answer over another) and echo questions (which seek repetition or clarification of what has just been said).

In addition, we take the view that while intonation may mark a question it does not mark interrogative clause type, and hence with respect to the syntactic form of (non-echo) polar questions we distinguish:

[5]	INTERROGATIVE QUESTION	DECLARATIVE QUESTION
	Are you ready?	*You're ready?*

4.3 Polar questions

Answers to polar questions

A polar question has as answers a pair of polar opposites, positive and negative. The answers to *Is it ready?* are *It is ready* and *It is not ready* (or equivalently *Yes* and *No*, or *Yes, it is* and *No, it's not*, and so on). The propositional content of one answer is expressed in the question itself, and that of the other is obtained by reversing the polarity.[5]

Usually it is the positive that is expressed in the question, but it can also be the negative, as in the biased question *Isn't it ready?*

Choice between *Yes* and *No* determined by answer

Yes and *no* are used in positive and negative answers respectively: the choice between them is determined by the polarity of the **answer**, with the polarity of the **question** being irrelevant. Thus *Yes, it is* and *No, it's not* are answers to both *Is it ready?* and *Isn't it ready? Yes* on its own, however, is relatively unlikely to be used as a response to a negative question.

The form of polar questions

Polar questions prototypically have the form of a closed interrogative clause, as in *Is it breathing?* in [4i]. They do not always have this form, however; other possibilities are shown in:

[6] i *Your aim that evening, then, was to go to the discotheque?*
ii *So you went to the party but your brother stayed at home?*
iii *Another cup of tea?*

Example [i] is what we are calling a declarative question: it has declarative not interrogative syntax, with the question meaning normally signalled by rising intonation or the punctuation; see §4.7.2 for further discussion. Example [ii] has the form of a coordination of declarative clauses: there are two clauses, but it is a single question. Finally, [iii] is a clause fragment.

4.4 Alternative questions

Answers to alternative questions

Alternative questions have as answers a set of alternatives given in the question itself. For example, the answers to *Is it right or wrong?* are *It's right* and *It's wrong*, which are derivable directly from the question. This example contains two alternatives, but there may be more: e.g. three in *Would you like to meet in the morning, the afternoon, or the evening?*

[5] Other terms for polar question include '*yes/no* question', 'general question', 'total question', 'nexus-question'.

The propositional content of an alternative question is, or is logically equivalent to, a disjunction of propositions, disjunction being the relation expressed by *or* (see Ch. 15, §2.2.1). Each of these propositions gives the content of one of the answers. The propositional content of *Is it alive or dead?*, for example, is "It is alive or dead", which is logically equivalent to "It is alive or it is dead".

The form of alternative questions

The essential feature of alternative questions is the coordinator *or* which relates the alternatives. The *or*-coordination is normally prosodically marked by a rise on the first coordinate and a fall on the final one, as indicated in [7], where we put ↗ after a word or phrase that is uttered with rising pitch and ↘ after a word or phrase that is uttered with falling pitch:

[7]	i	*Is it a boy↗ or a girl↘?*	[closed interrogative]
	ii	*Is it genuine↗ or is it a hoax↘?*	[coordination of closed interrogatives]
	iii	*You're staying here↗, or coming with us↘?*	[declarative]
	iv	*Tea↗ or coffee↘?*	[clause fragment]

With multiple coordination the intermediate coordinates take rising intonation, like the first: *Would you like orange juice↗, lemonade ↗, or coke↘?*

Alternative questions usually have closed interrogative syntax. In [7i] the *or*-coordination is within the clause, whereas in [ii] it is between clauses. In the latter case, then, we have two interrogative clauses but a single question. It is also possible for an alternative question to have the form of a declarative, as in [iii], or of a clause fragment, as in [iv]. Prosodically marked declaratives, however, are much less readily used for alternative questions than for polar ones; this is no doubt because questions with declarative form are biased, and alternative questions tend to be neutral.[6]

Or in alternative and polar questions

The coordinator *or* is an essential component of an alternative question, but it may also occur incidentally in a polar question: *Will I be able to get some tea or coffee at the bus station?* Here the answers are *Yes, you will* and *No, you won't*: I'm not asking which drink is available but whether or not I'll be able to get one or other of the drinks.

In writing there will often be ambiguity between an alternative question and a polar question that happens to contain an *or*-coordination, but the two cases are distinguished in speech by the intonation. An alternative question, we have noted, has a rise on the first coordinate and a fall on the last: a polar question will not distinguish the coordinates in this way but will normally have a rising pitch on the last:

[8]	i	*Are you free on Tuesday↗ or Wednesday↘?*	[alternative]
	ii	*Are you free on Tuesday or Wednesday↗?*	[polar]

The answers to the alternative question [i] are *I am free on Tuesday* and *I am free on Wednesday*. The polar question [ii] is equivalent to *Are you free on Tuesday or Wednesday, or not?*, its answers being *Yes, I am free on Tuesday or Wednesday* and *No, I'm not free on Tuesday or Wednesday*. It should again be borne in mind, however, that while the **answers** to the alternative and polar questions are sharply distinct, the **responses** may

[6] A special case is where the alternatives are identical: *Is it hot, or is it hot?* This serves as an indirect emphatic statement, "It is remarkably hot".

be less so. A co-operative addressee might respond to the polar question with *Yes, I'm free on Tuesday*, giving more specific information than is actually asked for.

The ambiguity which is found in the written form *Are you free on Tuesday or Wednesday?* is seen also when the coordination is between clauses:

[9] *Have you moved or are you about to move?*

The answers to the alternative question are *I have moved* and *I am about to move*, and those to the polar question are *Yes, I have moved or I am about to move* (unlikely as a response: you would generally give more specific information) and *No, I have not moved nor am I about to move*. The example is taken from a bank statement, where the continuation – *If so, please call us on the number below* – makes clear that the polar interpretation is intended, but it is equally easy to imagine contexts where the alternative one applies. Again, the ambiguity would be resolved in speech by the intonation.

One **grammatical** difference between the two kinds of question is that *or* cannot be paired with *either* when it is the marker of an alternative question. *Are you free on either Tuesday or Wednesday?*, for example, is unambiguously polar. This explains the anomaly of examples like *Would you prefer to watch with the light either on or off?* or (to an expectant mother) *Are you hoping for either a boy or a girl?* – the *either* forces a polar, yes/no, interpretation which conflicts with normal assumptions that there are no other possibilities than those expressed.

No alternative interrogative clause type corresponding to alternative question

Although [8i] and [ii] are, semantically, different kinds of question, they do not belong, grammatically, to different clause types. This is one reason why we have adopted different terminologies for subclassification at the two levels. Semantically we distinguish three kinds of question on the basis of the way they define the set of answers: polar, alternative, and variable. But grammatically there are just two subtypes of interrogative: closed and open.

The reason we do not treat the *or* of alternative questions as a clause type marker is that the coordination in which it figures may be between clauses, as in [7ii]. This is a clause-coordination, not a clause, so the issue of what clause type it belongs to doesn't arise. And as for the component clauses, *is it genuine* and *is it a hoax*, they have the same syntactic form as clauses expressing polar questions. Note that with embedded questions the clause subordinator *whether* can appear in both coordinates: *I don't know whether it's genuine or whether it's a hoax*. From a grammatical point of view, therefore, alternative questions are distinguished from polar questions not by the system of clause type but by a special use of coordination.

Polar-alternative questions

A special type of alternative question has the alternatives consisting of a positive and its negative counterpart. Questions of this kind are logically equivalent to polar questions, and we refer to them as **polar-alternative questions**:

[10] i a. *Are you ready or are you not ready?*
b. *Are you ready or aren't you ready?*
c. *Are you ready or aren't you?* [polar-alternative]
d. *Are you ready or not?*
e. *Are you, or are you not, ready?*
ii *Are you ready?* [polar]

As shown in [i], the second coordinate can be reduced by the omission of repeated material, and its position relative to the first can be varied, as in [ie]. With embedded polar-alternative questions there is also the possibility of having *or not* adjacent to the subordinator *whether*: *They want to know whether or not you're ready.*

The questions in [10] are logically equivalent in that they define the same set of answers. They do so, however, in different ways. Polar [ii] expresses a single proposition and the answers are provided by this and its polar opposite, whereas the polar-alternatives in [i] express two propositions, each of which provides an answer. The distinction between polar, alternative, and variable questions is based on the way they define the set of answers, and in accordance with the definitions given above, therefore, [i] and [ii] belong to different categories despite their logical equivalence. The term 'polar-alternative' is to be understood as denoting a subclass of alternative questions.

Apart from the issue of how the answers are derived, there are two other respects in which [10i] behave like alternative questions rather than polar ones. These involve the subordinate constructions illustrated in:

[11]	i	a. *I wonder/doubt whether it is alive.*	[polar]
		b. *I wonder/*doubt whether it is alive or dead.*	[alternative]
		c. *I wonder/*doubt whether it is alive or not.*	[polar-alternative]
	ii	a. **I'm marrying her whether you like her.*	[polar]
		b. *I'm marrying her whether you like her or hate her.*	[alternative]
		c. *I'm marrying her whether you like her or not.*	[polar-alternative]

While verbs like *wonder* license interrogative complements expressing all three kinds of question, *doubt* accepts only the polar type: the polar-alternative is excluded just as other alternative questions are (see Ch. 11, §5.3.3). Conversely, the ungoverned exhaustive conditional construction [ii] excludes the polar type, while allowing polar-alternatives as well as other alternative questions (see Ch. 11, §5.3.6).

Pragmatic differences between polar and polar-alternative questions

Although polar questions are logically equivalent to their polar-alternative counterparts, there are considerable pragmatic differences between them. The polar version is simpler and much more frequent: it can be regarded as the default version. We draw attention here to a selection of contexts favouring one rather than the other of the two.

(a) Polar-alternative emphasises choice

The explicit expression of the negative often has an emphatic effect. One reason for my emphasising the choice might be that you have failed to give a satisfactory response, i.e. an answer, to a previous polar question. In such a context, the polar-alternative question is likely to have an impatient, hectoring, or petulant tone, conveying "Make up your mind", "Give me an answer", or the like. The different versions of the polar-alternative, as illustrated in [10i], vary in the extent to which they convey such emotive meaning. In general, the less elliptical the form, the greater the emotive meaning is likely to be: compare *Are you going or not?* with the more insistent *Are you going or aren't you?* Typically, however, the version where the second coordinate is interpolated within the first, as in [10ie], is the most hectoring.

(b) Polar-alternative emphasises the exhaustiveness of the two alternatives

[12] a. *Was it good?* b. *Was it good or not?*

The answers to both polar [a] and polar-alternative [b] are simply *It was good* and *It wasn't good*, but (no doubt because of the tendency for the negative *It wasn't good* to be interpreted as "It was bad" – see Ch. 9, §5) [a] will often receive such non-answer responses as *It was okay*, *It wasn't too bad*, and the like. Such responses locate 'it' in the middle ground between good and bad. The polar-alternative can serve, then, to insist on a simple, unequivocal choice between 'good' and 'not good' – and again the emotive meaning of impatience or the like will be more evident in the less elliptical versions.

(c) Polar version preferred when answers are of unequal status for the speaker

[13] i *Have you any idea how much these things cost?*
ii *Will they agree to the proposal, do you think, or not?*
iii *Is it the sixteenth today?*

I might use [i] rhetorically, to convey that I believe that you haven't any idea of the cost: in this use (which is not the only one, of course) it would be a biased question, one where I am predisposed to one answer over another. In this case it would be very unnatural to add *or not*, for this would take away the rhetorical effect. Negative polar questions – e.g. *Don't you like it?* – are always biased, and will never be pragmatically equivalent to polar-alternatives. The polar-alternative, by expressing both positive and negative propositions, tends to assign them equal status.

In a case like [13ii] the effect is to give you full freedom to choose between them: it avoids any appearance of according greater likelihood to one answer. Especially in combination with the parenthetical *do you think*, the effect of the polar-alternative may then be to suggest a certain diffidence or deference to the addressee.

Bias is not the only factor that can make the answers of unequal status. Consider [13iii], for example. I might say this when my concern is to find out what date it is, and in that case a "yes" answer gives me the desired information but a "no" does not (so that a co-operative response would go further: *No, it's the fifteenth*, say). For this reason, the answers are of unequal value, and in such a context the polar-alternative version would be very unlikely. There are numerous other ways in which the answers might be of unequal status. To give just one, note that we say *Are you awake?*, not (normally) *Are you awake or not?* The latter suggests that positive and negative answers are on a par, but they are not. If you are awake you can answer *Yes*, but if you're not you can't answer *No*, so only one of the answers is a possible (true) response.

4.5 Variable questions

Answers to variable questions

Variable questions have a propositional content consisting of an open proposition, i.e. a proposition containing a variable (Ch. 1, §5.1). The answers express closed propositions derived by substituting a particular value for the variable. If we use the symbol 'x' for the variable, we can represent the propositional content of *What did they give her?* as "They gave her x", and the answers have different values for the variable x: *They gave her some books*; *They gave her the key*; *They gave her everything she asked for*; and so on.

Prototypically, there is no logical limit to the number of different possible values, so that the set of answers will be open-ended. It need not be so, however: a limit to the possible values may be incorporated into the question, as in *Which of the two proposals suits you better?*[7]

The form of variable questions

These questions have the form of an open interrogative clause. They are marked by a phrase containing an interrogative word – whose role is to express the variable. Details of the interrogative words and their properties are given in §7. The question may consist solely of the interrogative element, forming a clausal fragment: *Who?*; *What about the others?*; and so on.

Fronting of the interrogative phrase

When the interrogative phrase has a function other than that of subject of the interrogative clause, it is normally fronted to prenuclear position, and in main clauses this triggers subject–auxiliary inversion. Fronting of a non-subject interrogative phrase is not obligatory in main clauses: it can remain in situ, i.e. in the default position of corresponding non-interrogative phrases, following the verb. Open interrogatives with a post-verbal interrogative phrase generally occur, however, only in contexts of sustained questioning, such as quizzes and interrogations by legal counsel, police, and so on. Compare, then:

[14]		FRONTED: INVERSION	IN SITU: NO INVERSION
	i	a. *<u>Where</u> are those senses located?*	b. *And those senses are located <u>where?</u>*
	ii	a. *<u>What</u> were the results of that examination?*	b. *And the results of that examination were <u>what</u>?*

The [b] versions are attested examples used in court during the cross-examination of a medical witness. As such, they are quite distinct from echo questions: the aim was to elicit new information, not a repetition or clarification of what had just been said.

Infinitivals

Open interrogatives may have infinitival form, with or without *to*; in either case, no subject is permitted.

The *to*-infinitival construction

Two non-embedded cases of this are to be found:

[15]			
	i	*What to do in the event of fire*	[titular]
	ii	*How to persuade her to forgive him?*	[main clause]

Type [i] is a non-sentential construction: infinitivals of this kind are used as titles of books, articles, etc., or headings for lists, notices, and the like. They have the same function as an NP: compare *How to get rich quick* and *Five easy ways to get rich quick.* In [ii] the interrogative is a main clause, forming a sentence – note the difference in punctuation between [ii] and [i]. By virtue of forming a sentence, it will normally have illocutionary force: it's a matter of asking, or at least wondering. This type is somewhat rare and literary; one case of it is in interior monologue, where one is pondering over a question. The meaning here is essentially "How could he persuade her . . . ?"

[7] Other terms to be found in the literature as equivalent to our 'variable question' include '*x*-question', '*wh*-question', 'specific question', 'partial question', and 'information question'.

The bare infinitival construction

This is found only in main clauses, almost invariably with *why*:

[16] a. *Why be so soft with them?* b. *Why not accept his offer?*

These convey that I don't think there is any valid reason, and this leads to an interpretation as an indirect directive: "I suggest that you not be so soft with them / that you accept his offer". With negatives, a finite construction can be used in the same way: *Why don't you accept his offer?* A negative finite, however, does not have to be interpreted in this way. Thus *Why don't you let him drive your car?* can be interpreted literally as asking for your reasons or indirectly as suggesting you should let him, whereas *Why not let him drive your car?* has only the second interpretation.[8]

Single-variable vs multi-variable questions

All the variable questions given so far have contained a single variable, but it is possible for there to be more than one. Compare:

[17]	i *Who said that?*	[single-variable Q]
	ii *Who said what?*	[multi-variable Q]
	iii *Who said what to whom?*	

We are representing the propositional content of [i] as "*x* said that", with '*x*' as the variable; the content of [ii] can similarly be represented as "*x* said *y*", with two variables, and that of [iii] as "*x* said *y* to *z*", with three. We therefore distinguish [i] and [ii/iii] as respectively **single-variable** and **multi-variable** questions. As there is a straightforward match with the grammar, we can use the same terms to distinguish the corresponding grammatical categories: clause [i] is a single-variable open interrogative, while clauses [ii] and [iii] are multi-variable ones.

Coordination of interrogative phrases

It is possible for two or more interrogative phrases to be coordinated:

[18] i *How many sheets and how many towels do we need to take?*
ii *When and where did you see her?*

These two examples differ in that in [i] the two coordinate phrases are functionally alike (with the coordination as a whole understood as object of *take*), whereas in [ii] they are functionally distinct (*when* being an adjunct of temporal location, *where* one of spatial location). In answers to [i], phrases expressing the values of the variables will be coordinated, as in *We need to take six sheets and a dozen towels*, but in answers to [ii] they generally will not, as in *I saw her last Saturday at the Planetarium.*

Restriction on fronting of interrogative phrase

In multi-variable questions where the variables are not coordinate, no more than one interrogative phrase can be fronted:

[19] i *They did what to whom?*
ii *What did they do to whom?*
iii **What to whom did they do?*

[8] Bare infinitivals with *how* are occasionally attested, but they are of questionable acceptability: [?]*How leave the matter rest?* The interpretation is similar to those with *why*, suggesting that there is no way in which one could reasonably leave the matter rest.

Answers to multi-variable questions

Multi-variable questions may have either **singulary answers** or **multiple answers**:

[20] i *Who beat who?*
ii *Kim beat Max.* [singulary answer]
iii *Kim beat Max and Pat beat Bob.* [multiple answer]

A singulary answer simply provides a single value for each variable. A multiple answer provides sets of values – pairs if there are two variables, triples if there are three, and so on. Thus for "*x* beat *y*" in question [20i], the singulary answer [ii] provides the value "Kim" for "*x*" and "Max" for "*y*", whereas the multiple answer [iii] provides the pairs {"Kim", "Max"} and {"Pat", "Bob"} for the variable pair {"*x*", "*y*"}. For example, [ii] might be the answer when the question is used to inquire about the final match in some sporting competition, [iii] when it is used to inquire about the semi-finals.

A two-variable question with multiple answers can be used as an inquiry in a range of contexts differing with respect to what information I already have, as opposed to that which I am seeking to obtain:

[21] i I don't know the values of either variable.
ii I know the values of one variable but not the other.
iii I know the values for both variables, but not how they are paired.

Answer [20iii] would be used under condition [21i] when I simply know that two matches took place but don't know who the players were, or I know who played but not who won or lost. A context where [21ii] applies would be one where I know who has won through to the final but want to know who they beat in the semi-finals. Context [21iii] would obtain if I knew who was playing in the semi-finals and ask *Who beat who?* to find out the results. Or [21iii] might similarly apply to the answer to such a question as *Who's going to teach which courses this semester?* A likely context for this is the planning of a teaching-programme when we know who the teaching staff are and what the courses are: it is then just a matter of matching teachers with courses.

Multiple answer vs multiple response

Single-variable questions (and multi-variable ones where the variables are coordinate, as in [18]) have only singulary answers. Again, however, we need to invoke the distinction between answer and response, for sometimes a single-variable question can receive a multiple response:

[22] i *Where did she buy these books?* [single-variable Q]
ii *She bought them at Heffer's.* } [singulary answers]
iii *She bought them at Heffer's and Dillon's.* }
iv *She bought this one at Heffer's and that one at Dillon's.* [multiple response]

With [ii] we have a straightforward singulary answer: all the books were bought at one place. Answer [iii] is still singulary, but as the books were bought at more than one place a coordinate phrase is used to give the value of the variable. This situation then implicitly raises the multi-variable question of which books were bought at which shop, and [iv] gives the answer to this question, not to [i]: it gives more information than is needed to answer the question to which it was a response. As we have noted, a co-operative participant commonly provides more information than is directly asked for. The difference in directness can be brought out by contrasting the anomaly of [23i] with the naturalness of [ii]:

[23] i #*I know that she bought these books at Heffer's and Dillon's, but I don't know where she bought these books.*
ii *I know that she bought these books at Heffer's and Dillon's, but I don't know where she bought which.*

The single-variable *where she bought these books* in [i] is the embedded counterpart of [22i]. Example [23i] is anomalous because it is self-contradictory. Thus to know [22iii] is to know the answer to [22i], even in a context where [22iv] is true: information about the pairing of books with shops is not part of the answer. The multi-variable *where she bought which* in [23ii] is the embedded counterpart of *Where did she buy which?*, and the naturalness of the example shows that to know [22iii] is not sufficient to know the answer to this latter question: in the multi-variable case, information about the pairing is part of the answer.

Juxtaposition of variable and polar or alternative questions

It is not uncommon for a variable question to be followed by a polar or alternative question which pragmatically supersedes it:

[24] i *What's her name*↘*? Is it Anne*↗*?*
ii *What's her name*↘*? Is it Anne*↗ *or Anna*↘*?*

In [i] the polar question suggests an answer to the variable one. If the answer is positive, then answering the second also provides the answer to the first – though the typical form, *Yes*, shows that it is given in response to the polar question. If the answer is negative, then another answer to the variable question is needed – *No, it's Anna* (as we saw above, this kind of response is often given when the variable question is merely implicit). In [ii] the alternative question reformulates the variable one, narrowing down the range of possible answers; this time, whatever the answer to the second question is, it will simultaneously be an answer to the first. (To respond with *Neither: it's Amy* is not to answer the alternative question but to reject its presupposition: see §6.1 below.)

In either the polar or the alternative case, the second question will often be elliptically reduced:

[25] i *What's her name? Anne?*
ii *What's her name? Anne or Anna?*

Such reduction will be particularly likely when the full form would involve more lexical repetition than is the case with [24]: *Who do you think I am?* (*Do you think I am*) *Father Christmas?*; *What are you going to give him?* (*Are you going to give him*) *a book or just money?*

We have punctuated the questions in [24] and [25] as separate sentences, but they could also be integrated into a single written sentence: e.g., for [24], *What's her name – Anne?* With an alternative question, but not a polar, they can be separated simply by a comma: *What's her name, Anne or Anna?* Similarly, in speech there are different degrees of prosodic integration between the two questions. This is one of the places where it is difficult to draw a sharp distinction between a succession of two grammatical sentences on the one hand and a single sentence on the other.

4.6 **Direction questions**

Distinguished from information questions by the illocutionary force of the answers

The great majority of questions are **information questions**: when used as inquiries they seek to elicit information. The characteristic illocutionary force of their answers is that of a statement. There is also, however, a kind of question whose answers characteristically have the force of directives. They seek not information but direction, and we accordingly call them **direction questions**.[9] The distinction applies to all three of the polar, alternative, and variable categories of question. Compare:

[26]	INFORMATION QUESTION	DIRECTION QUESTION	
i	a. *Did he open the window?*	b. %*Shall I open the window?*	[polar]
ii	a. *Did he do it then or later?*	b. %*Shall I do it now or later?*	[alternative]
iii	a. *When did he come back?*	b. %*When shall we come back?*	[variable]

The answers to the information questions are *He opened the window / He didn't open the window*; *He did it then / He did it later*; *He came back at six* (or whenever): these would all have the force of statements. The answers to the direction questions are *Open the window / Don't open the window*; *Do it now / Do it later*; *Come back at six* (etc.): and these would have the force of directives. With the polar questions, *Yes* and *No* could of course be used in either case, but they would still have the statement force in response to [a] and directive force in response to [b]. We annotate the [b] examples with '%' because some varieties use *will* in place of *shall* here.

Distinction between direction and information questions only weakly grammaticalised

As far as unembedded questions are concerned, direction questions are not sharply distinguished in grammatical form from information questions. Matters are complicated by the fact that a response giving an answer to a question may, like utterances generally, have more than one illocutionary force. Consider, for example:

[27]		
i	a. *Do you promise not to tell him?*	b. *I promise not to tell him.*
ii	a. *Would you advise me to accept?*	b. *I would advise you to accept.*
iii	a. *Have I got to eat it all?*	b. *You have got to eat it all.*
iv	a. %*Shall I tell the police?*	b. *You shall tell the police.*

For convenience, we give the answers in unreduced form, rather than as *Yes, I do*, etc. Answer [ib] has the illocutionary verb *promise* used performatively, so that it is a promise as well as a statement. Similarly [iib] both makes a statement and gives advice: it differs from [ib] in that the advice force is indirect rather than direct, because we have *I would advise*, not *I advise*. Answer [iiib] is literally a statement but, in the context of answering question [iiia], stating that you have to eat it all amounts to telling you to do so. Here then we have an answer which is both statement and directive. However, from the point of view of its form, and more specifically of the relation between its form and that of its answer, there is nothing special about [iiia]. What makes [iva] different from the other questions is that *shall* here has a sense that is specialised to direction questions: [ivb] is not a possible answer precisely because the meaning of *shall* is not the same.

The semantic development of *shall* has led to a situation where it has a use in 1st person interrogatives that specifically marks direction questions. It can also be used with a futurity sense, as in the information question *Shall I ever need it again?* As a result, there is potential for ambiguity:

[28] *Shall I get my money back?* [direction or information question]

[9] Direction questions are also known as 'deliberative questions'.

As a direction question, this is concerned with the choice between future actions by the speaker: I'm asking you to tell me to retrieve it or not to do so. As an information question, it is concerned with predictions as to what will happen: will the money be returned or not?[10]

The case with *should* is less clear-cut. *Should I get my money back?* is ambiguous between a deontic reading ("Is getting my money back the right thing for me to do?") and an epistemic one ("Is it probable that I'll get it back?"). But the ambiguity is also found in *You should get your money back.* So the development of *should* has certainly not been entirely parallel to that of *shall.* Nevertheless, we do see something partly analogous. While *Yes, you should* is a perfectly natural (deontic) response to *Should I tell the police?*, it would be odd to respond in this way to *Should I open the window?*, said in a context where it is a matter of my possibly opening the window there and then. In this use *should* behaves like *shall* – and could not be replaced by *ought...to*, as it could in *Should I tell the police?*

Embedded direction questions have infinitival form

We have seen that with unembedded questions the distinction between direction and information questions is not matched by any sharp grammatical distinction; with embedded ones, however, the distinction is clearly marked. For here there is a construction, the infinitival interrogative, that is used exclusively for direction questions. Compare the following, as used, say, in the frame *I asked* __:

[29]	INFORMATION QUESTION	DIRECTION QUESTION	
i	a. *whether she told him*	b. *whether to tell him*	[polar]
ii	a. *whether he left then or later*	b. *whether to leave then or later*	[alternative]
iii	a. *how she got home*	b. *how to get home*	[variable]

Because they are embedded, these are questions only in the semantic sense, not in the pragmatic sense, as they do not themselves have illocutionary force. But we can relate them to unembedded questions by considering them in the suggested frame. *I asked whether she told him* reports my asking the information question "Did she tell him?", while *I asked whether to tell him* reports my asking the direction question "Shall I tell him?"[11] Note that subordinate interrogatives with *shall* do not express direction questions. *I must ask him whether I shall get my money back*, for example, lacks the ambiguity of [28], having only the information question interpretation.

Right answers to direction questions

It is because of the existence of direction questions that we cannot identify a 'right' answer with a true one (cf. §4.1). Right answers to information questions are true, but the categories true and false are not applicable to directives, and hence to the answers to direction questions.

[10] In neither interpretation is *You shall get your money back* an answer; with a 2nd or 3rd person subject *shall* indicates commitment on the part of the speaker, rather than obligation on the part of the subject-referent (cf. Ch. 3, §9.6.1). The positive answers to the two readings of [28] are therefore *Get your money back* and *You will get your money back.*

[11] We are concerned here with indirect reported speech, where one reports the content of what was said rather than the actual words, but for present purposes we can consider the idealised case where there is the closest possible match. The embedded infinitival construction does not always correspond to an unembedded *shall* question. *How shall I turn the machine on?* is hardly idiomatic whereas *I don't know how to turn the machine on* is; nevertheless, the answers to the infinitival question involve directions for turning the machine on.

If I use a direction question to ask you to tell me what to do, then the issue of whether the answer given is right or wrong is trivial. Consider, for example:

[30] A: *Shall I call a taxi for you?* B: *No, thanks. I'll enjoy the walk.*

A's question is an indirect offer, and it is up to B to accept or reject. The issue of whether the directive answer is right or wrong is comparable to that of whether a statement like *I promise to help you*, when used to make a promise, is true or false. This latter issue is trivial because the statement is made true simply by virtue of its being uttered with the relevant intention, and similarly B's directive answer to the direction question in [30] will be right simply by virtue of B's deciding to deliver that directive rather than another.

There are also cases, however, where the issue of what the right answer is to a direction question can arise in a non-trivial way. For example, such questions can be used to ask for advice:

[31] A: *Shall I take a taxi?* B: *No, you'd be better off walking.*

Here it is easy to imagine circumstances under which B could be said to have given bad advice, given the wrong answer – e.g., if the distance were too great for A to be able to walk it comfortably in the time available. Similarly when one puts a direction question to oneself, in wondering: what the right answer is in this case is of course a crucial issue. Determining what is the right answer to direction questions used to seek advice or in wondering involves a judgement as to what course of action is in the best interests of the one uttering the question (or, in *shall we* questions, of the group containing that person).

4.7 Biased questions

The distinction between neutral questions and biased questions

A biased question is one where the speaker is predisposed to accept one particular answer as the right one. A neutral question lacks such bias towards one answer rather than another: it is the default category on this dimension. The distinction between neutral and biased questions applies primarily to polar questions. Compare, for example:

[32] i *Did you get any annuity, superannuation, or other pension?* [neutral]
ii *Doesn't she like it?* [biased]

Example [i] is taken from an income tax form: it is addressed individually to all those filling in the form, and for any individual there is no expectation on the part of the 'speaker' (the Income Tax Commissioner) that the answer will be positive rather than negative, or vice versa. A plausible context for [ii], though not the only one, is that her behaviour or her remarks suggest that she doesn't like it: I ask the question to confirm whether this is so. In such a context the question is biased towards the negative answer *She doesn't like it.*[12]

[12] Alternative terms for 'neutral' and 'biased' are 'open' and 'conducive' respectively.

4.7.1 Kinds and degrees of bias

(a) Epistemic bias

There are different kinds of bias. It may be simply a matter of the speaker thinking, expecting, or knowing that one answer is the right one. We will refer to this kind of bias as **epistemic**, a term whose primary application is in the closely related field of modality. In the contextualisation of [32ii] suggested above, for example, the bias towards the negative answer will be an epistemic one.

(b) Deontic bias

Alternatively, it might be a matter of the speaker judging that one answer **ought** to be the right one. Again we will take over a term from the field of modality, and refer to this kind of bias as **deontic**. It is seen in the natural interpretations of:

[33] i *You're surely not going to let them get away with outrageous behaviour like that, are you?*
ii *Aren't you ashamed of yourselves?*

In [i] there is a deontic bias towards a negative answer: I convey a judgement that you ought not to let them get away with their outrageous behaviour. Example [ii] shows a deontic bias towards a positive answer: you ought to be ashamed of yourselves. But at the same time, [ii] has an epistemic bias towards a negative answer: it appears from your behaviour that you are not ashamed of yourselves.

(c) Desiderative bias

A third kind of bias, not greatly different from the deontic, is that where the speaker wants one answer to be the right one – **desiderative** bias, as we shall call it. For example, when I indirectly request something by means of such a question as

[34] *Can I have some more ice-cream?*

there will be a desiderative bias towards a positive answer: I want a *Yes* answer. The negative epistemic bias of [32ii] could also be accompanied by a positive desiderative bias. This could be the case in a context where *it* refers to something I am responsible for (a painting, say, that I have painted or chosen): I want her to like it but think she doesn't.

Different degrees of bias

We also find considerable differences in the degree or strength of the bias. Take, for example, the case illustrated in [13iii], where I ask, wanting to know the date:

[35] *Is it the sixteenth today?*

It is likely that there will be some positive bias here (primarily epistemic), for if I had no idea whether it was the sixteenth or not, it would generally be more natural to use the variable question *What date is it today?* But my confidence that I am right about the date can vary greatly. Similarly in [32ii] the negative bias could be a matter of a mere flimsy suspicion or a strongly supported conviction.

The limiting case is where the bias is complete: I am in no doubt at all as to what is the right answer.

[36] i A: *May I speak to Ms Jones?* B: *I'm afraid she's no longer here. Didn't you know that she went overseas yesterday?*
ii A: *I wasn't able to get a ticket.* B: *Weren't you? I'm sorry to hear that.*

In [i], assuming that B does not consider the possibility that A intended to deceive, B will be in no doubt that A didn't know that Ms Jones went overseas yesterday, i.e. that the answer to the question is negative. Nor is there any doubt in [ii]: A has just given the answer, and B accepts it. Where the bias is complete, as here, the question cannot have the force of an inquiry: the intention is not to elicit information. In [i] the question serves to inform A that Ms Jones went overseas yesterday: it is an indirect statement. In [ii] the question serves to acknowledge the information A has just supplied (cf. [3i] above).

Complete bias can also be found with variable questions, as in *Who's a clever girl?* In a context where the addressee or the speaker is a girl who has just done something clever, there will be no doubt as to what is the value for the variable in "*x* is a clever girl", and the question will therefore indirectly convey "What a clever girl you are!" or "What a clever girl I am!".

The encoding of bias

The inference that a question is biased towards a particular answer may be based simply on the context, together with assumptions about the speaker's intentions. This is likely to be the case in [35], for example. In other cases, bias may be reflected in the prosodic properties of the question. For example,

[37] *Have you any idea how much these knives cost?*

could be used as an indirect way of inquiring about the cost of the knives or as a rebuke to someone considered to be misusing a certain knife. In the first case there is some positive desiderative bias (I am no doubt hoping for a positive answer to the direct question, for otherwise you will not be able to answer the indirect question about the cost, the one I am primarily interested in), but it could be epistemically quite neutral (I have no reason to think that one answer rather than the other is actually the right one). In the rebuke use, on the other hand, there will be a strong negative epistemic bias: the suggestion is that the maltreatment of the knife indicates lack of awareness of its value.

Our focus in what follows will be on the grammatical marking of bias, on cases where the bias is reflected in the grammatical structure of the question. Declarative questions and negative interrogative questions are always quite strongly biased; note that neither of these would occur in the kind of context attested for the neutral question [32i]. In addition, a weaker bias can be conveyed by the use of positively- and negatively-oriented polarity-sensitive items, such as *some* and *any*. We take these three cases in turn; see also §5.2 for bias in tag questions.

4.7.2 Declarative questions

Positive declarative questions have an epistemic bias towards a positive answer, negative ones towards a negative answer:

[38] a. *They've finished?* b. *They haven't finished?*

The expected answer is here the statement with the same propositional content as the question – i.e. *They've finished* and *They haven't finished* respectively. In asking a declarative question I am typically seeking confirmation of a proposition that I am inclined, with varying degrees of strength, to believe. There may be deontic or desiderative bias as well as epistemic, but this is not inherent to the construction as such.

Lexical reinforcement of bias

The bias may be reinforced by lexical markers indicating confidence in the truth of the proposition expressed:

[39] i *They no doubt misunderstood her intentions?*
ii *You're surely not going to agree?*
iii *And the manager has been informed, of course?*
iv *There isn't any chance of her changing her mind, I take it?*

These confidence markers are outside the propositional content of the question, outside the scope of the question. The positive answer to [39i], for example, is not *They no doubt misunderstood her intentions*, but simply *They misunderstood her intentions.* Such markers would not naturally occur in interrogative questions, where comparable items are epistemically much weaker:

[40] i *Did they perhaps misunderstand her intentions?*
ii *Isn't there any chance of her changing her mind, I wonder?*

Responses to declarative questions

The bias of declarative questions is reflected in the fact that they can naturally receive confirmatory responses like *That's right, Exactly, Quite so*, which would be out of place with a neutral question. *Yes* can even occur here with a following negative, which is not normally possible: *Yes, there's no chance at all* is a plausible response to [39iv], but not to interrogative *Is there any chance of her changing her mind?* or even *Isn't there any chance of her changing her mind?*

Declarative questions as indirect speech acts

The illocutionary force of declarative questions is not that characteristically associated with the clause type, and hence they are indirect speech acts in the sense of §3.2. At the direct level they are statements, but the intonation overrides this to yield an indirect question. The indirectness is reflected in the fact that pragmatic inferences may be involved in determining the scope of the question, which need not be the whole of the propositional content. Consider, for example:

[41] i *I take it there isn't any chance of her changing her mind?*
ii *I hope you're not proposing to leave it like that?*
iii *I don't suppose I could borrow your car for a couple of hours?*

Example [41i] differs grammatically and semantically from [39iv], but pragmatically there is little difference. In [39iv] *I take it* is a parenthetical (§5.3), but in [41i] it occurs as part of a complex clause construction: *there isn't any chance of her changing her mind* is this time a subordinate clause, the grammatical complement of *take*, and its content is semantically integrated into that of the complex clause. Nevertheless, *I take it* is again outside the scope of the question: the expected answer is not *You take it there isn't any chance . . .* , but simply *There isn't any chance . . .* At the direct level, [41i] is a statement with the propositional content "I take it there isn't any chance of her changing her mind", but indirectly it is a question with the content "There isn't any chance of her changing her mind", or perhaps "It is true that there isn't any chance of her changing her mind". Example [ii] is just like [i], but [iii] involves two additional factors. One is that the negative is associated with the complement of *suppose* (cf. the discussion of increased specificity of negation in Ch. 9, §5), giving "Couldn't I borrow your car for a couple of hours?"; and the other factor is that the latter question in turn indirectly conveys a request to borrow the car.

4.7.3 Negative interrogative questions

Questions with negative interrogative form are always strongly biased. They typically allow a range of interpretations, and the epistemic bias can be towards either the negative or the positive answer. Consider:

[42] *Didn't I tell you Kim would be coming?*

One context for this is where it has become apparent that I have, or probably have, omitted to tell you that Kim would be coming. Here the bias is towards the negative answer (I didn't tell you). But I could equally use [42] in a context where I remember quite well having said that Kim would be coming: my prediction was not accepted at the time but has now been shown by Kim's presence to have been correct and I am asking you to admit that I was right. Here, then, the bias is towards the positive answer (that I did tell you).

Similarly with such examples as:

[43] i *Wasn't I right?*
ii *Isn't it all as simple as she predicted?*
iii *Aren't they spending Christmas with their uncle?*
iv *Isn't it raining?*

For [i] possible interpretations are: "It appears that I wasn't right – is that so?" (negative epistemic bias) and "It is now evident I was right – admit it" (positive). For [ii]: "It is looking as though it is not as simple as she predicted, isn't it?" (negative) and "It has turned out just as simple as she said it would, hasn't it?" (positive). For [iii]: "It seems I was wrong in thinking they are spending Christmas with their uncle" (negative) and "Remember they are spending Christmas with their uncle" (positive). A context for this latter, positively biased, interpretation could be one where you have suggested inviting them over for Christmas and I point out that they won't be able to come because they will be away at their uncle's – another case where a question is used not to obtain information but to indirectly impart it. For [iv], a negatively biased interpretation is "I thought it was raining but there is now evidence suggesting it is not" (for example, you may be showing signs of going out without protection against rain), and a positively biased one is "Let me remind you that it's raining" (e.g. in response to *Why aren't you going out?* – "Surely the fact that it is raining is reason enough!").

Negative interrogative questions typically suggest some element of contrast. We will consider this feature first in cases where the bias is negative, and then in those where it is positive.

Negative interrogative questions with negative bias

The negative epistemic bias commonly contrasts with a positive deontic bias. This was illustrated in [33ii] above, *Aren't you ashamed of yourselves?* The most salient interpretation here carries an implied contrast between the state of affairs which apparently obtains (negative) and my judgement of what should be the case (positive). When such a contrast reflects adversely on you, the question will be an indirect reproach or rebuke, as in [33ii]. This is also the natural interpretation of [44i], and a quite likely one for [44ii–iii]:

[44] i *Can't you think of a more positive response?*
ii *Didn't you turn the oven off?*
iii *Don't you know where it goes?*

In this interpretation [44i] conveys "It appears you can't think of a more positive response, but you ought to be able to". Similarly for [ii] we may have "You apparently didn't turn the oven off, but you ought to have done", and for [iii], "You have been told where it goes but have apparently forgotten". On the other hand, I may myself accept responsibility for the contrast between what is and what should be, and then the question may be accompanied by an apology. An alternative, apologetic, implicature of [iii], therefore, is "I should have told you where it goes but apparently didn't do so".

Such a contrast between what is and what should be (whether a matter for reproach or apology) is not, however, the only kind of contrast that may be suggested by the negative interrogative construction. The negative bias reading of [43iv], for example, is unlikely to suggest that it ought to be raining. There is still a contrast, however: between what now appears to be the case (negative: it's not raining) and what I previously thought to be the case (positive: it was raining).

Negative interrogative questions with positive bias

Where the epistemic bias is positive, there is commonly an implicit contrast between my belief in some proposition and previous unwillingness on the part of you or others to accept it. This is the context suggested for the positive bias interpretations of [42] and [43].

One case where such a contrast is not in evidence, or at least not obviously in evidence, is that where the question is used as indirectly equivalent to an exclamatory statement:

[45] *Aren't they lovely! Haven't they made a good job of it! Doesn't he talk fast!*
Haven't I been a fool! Didn't it rain!

The interpretations can be given in the form of exclamatives: "How lovely they are!"; "What a good job they made of it!"; "How fast he talks!"; "What a fool I have been"; "How it rained!" The indirect statement force is reflected in the falling intonation that marks this use. Such exclamatory questions typically involve gradable expressions – very often adjectives (predicative *lovely* or attributive *good*) or adverbs (*fast*), but also certain nouns (*fool*) or verbs (*rain*).

4.7.4 Positively- and negatively-oriented polarity-sensitive items (*some* vs *any*, etc.)

The distinction between contrasting pairs of items such as unstressed *some* vs *any*, or *already* vs *yet*, is discussed in detail in Ch. 9, §4.3; here we focus on the relation between this distinction and bias in questions.

Positive interrogative questions

Here, the selection of a positively-oriented item rather than its negatively-oriented counterpart confers some degree of positive bias. Compare:

[46] NEGATIVELY-ORIENTED ITEM — POSITIVELY-ORIENTED ITEM

i a. *Is anything wrong?* b. *Is something wrong?*

ii a. *Has anybody told Ed about it?* b. *Has somebody told Ed about it?*

iii a. *Have they gone yet?* b. *Have they gone already?*

In each pair [b] suggests that I am rather more inclined towards a positive answer than does [a]. The difference is particularly evident in [iii]: *already* is a stronger marker of positive bias than *some* and its compounds. The bias is potentially either epistemic or deontic/desiderative. The positively-oriented *somebody* in [iib], for example, could reflect some positive evidence that somebody has told him about it (e.g. he may have said something which suggests that he knows about it) or it could reflect the need for someone to tell him (e.g. it has been recognised that his behaviour is causing inconvenience and it is necessary that someone inform him of this).

Positively-oriented items with desiderative bias often appear in questions used as indirect speech acts of various kinds:

[47] i *Could you please do something about that noise.*

ii *Would you like some coffee?*

Example [i] is an indirect request, with the direct question force very much backgrounded. In the natural interpretation, I assume you can do something about the noise (so that there is complete positive bias) and ask you to do so. Negatively-oriented *anything* would be out of place here. Example [ii] would typically be used as an offer, a more hospitable one than the form with *any*: the positive bias signalled by *some* suggests that I am favourably inclined towards an acceptance of the offer, whereas *any* suggests indifference. In a more effusive offer such as *Would you care for some of this delicious coffee?* substitution of *any* for *some* would be unlikely, because of the inconsistency between the indifference of *any* and the enthusiasm of the rest.

Positive declarative questions

These always have a strong positive bias, as we observed in §4.7.2. For this reason they do not take negatively-oriented items:

[48] *There's something/*anything else you need?* **You have ever been to Paris?*

Negative interrogatives

Negatively-oriented items give these a negative bias:

[49] i *Haven't they seen anybody about it yet?*

ii *Wasn't I right about anything else?*

Question [i] expects the negative answer *They haven't seen anybody about it yet*, and analogously for [ii]. Example [ii] differs strikingly from [43i], *Wasn't I right?*: it allows only the negative bias interpretation, whereas [43i] allows both positive and negative.

Positively-oriented items occur in negative interrogatives with either bias, though the positive case will often be more salient:

[50] i *Didn't you like some of it?*

ii *Haven't you forgotten something?*

iii *Shouldn't someone do something about it?*

iv *Weren't some of them marvellous!*

Question [i] can be interpreted with positive bias, conveying "It wasn't all bad: there was some of it you liked, wasn't there?", or (less likely) with negative bias: "It apparently wasn't a complete success: there was some of it you didn't like, did you?" The others generally have positive bias. Example [ii] would typically convey "You have apparently forgotten something", and would often be used as a reminder (e.g. to a child to say *please* when asking for something). Similarly, [iii] is likely to be seeking agreement to the proposition that something should be done about it. Finally, [iv] illustrates the use of positively-oriented items in indirect exclamatory statements.

4.8 Echo questions

The prototypical use of the echo question is to question whether one has correctly heard what the previous speaker said – heard the **stimulus**, as we call it. My doubt as to whether I heard the stimulus correctly may arise because it was not perceptually clear (I may have had difficulty making it out above some background noise) or because its content is surprising or remarkable in such a way that I want to verify whether you did in fact say, or mean to say, what I apparently heard.

Polar, alternative, and variable echo questions

Echo questions are predominantly of either the polar or the variable kind, but alternative echoes are also possible:

[51]	STIMULUS	ECHO QUESTION	
i	A: *She's leaving on Saturday.*	B: *She's leaving on Saturday?*	[polar]
ii	A: *He gave it to Anne.*	B: *He gave it to Anne or Anna?*	[alternative]
iii	A: *He's proposing to resign.*	B: *He's proposing to what?*	[variable]

The polar echo question prototypically repeats the stimulus but with a rising intonation imposed on it; like ordinary polar questions, it has *Yes* and *No* as answers. The alternative echo question substitutes an *or*-coordination for part of the stimulus, and each answer will include just one of the coordinates; it generally has the rise + fall intonation pattern of ordinary alternative questions. The variable question, which – like the polar – prototypically also has rising intonation, substitutes an echo question word expressing a variable for part of the stimulus, and the answers involve replacing the variable by its possible values.

Modification of stimulus

The stimulus is often modified by reduction – by omitting parts or replacing them by shorter expressions such as pro-forms. An echo response to *Kim is going to try and persuade him to buy a microwave*, for example, could take one of many forms, including:

[52] i *To try and persuade him to buy a microwave / one / a what?*
ii *To buy a microwave / one / a what?*
iii *Kim/ Who is?*

And since the stimulus will normally be produced by a different speaker, there will be a change in deictic pronouns: *I like it* will be echoed as *You like it?*, and so on.

4.8.1 The contrast between echo and ordinary questions

Echo questions as indirect speech acts

The propositional content of echo questions is not the same as that which is actually expressed in the utterance, and such questions therefore belong to the class of indirect speech acts. The propositional content of the echo question in [51i] is not "She's leaving on Saturday", the content actually expressed, but something like "You said she's leaving on Saturday". (We say 'something like' for it could be "You're telling me . . .", "You're suggesting . . .", and so on: precisely because it is implicit rather than directly expressed there is some imprecision as to what it is.) And, correspondingly, the answer *Yes* is equivalent not to *She's leaving on Saturday*, but to *I said she's leaving on Saturday*. The difference between these two interpretations may not seem very important, but is of much greater significance in a case like:

[53] A: *Is he going to resign?* B: *Is he going to resign?*

The propositional content of B's echo question is clearly not "He's going to resign", but "You said he's going to resign", and a *Yes* answer in this context is equivalent to *I asked whether he is going to resign*, not to *He's going to resign*. The latter would be an answer to A's question, not B's – to an ordinary question, not an echo question. The same applies to the other kinds of question. For example, the propositional content of B's variable question in [51iii] is approximately "You said that he's going to *x*".

This indirectness is a crucial property distinguishing echo questions from ordinary questions. They are not distinguished simply by the fact that an echo question questions what has just been said, for it is perfectly possible to use an ordinary question to do that:

[54]	PREVIOUS UTTERANCE	ORDINARY QUESTION
i	A: *She's leaving on Saturday.*	B: *Did you say she's leaving on Saturday?*
ii	A: *He's proposing to resign.*	B: *What did you say he's proposing to do?*

Note that B's utterances here may be said with the same prosodic signals of incredulity or the like that commonly accompany echo questions: these prosodic features are likewise not what is crucial for the echo question. There is nothing special about B's questions in [54]: they are just ordinary questions whose subject matter happens to be the content of a previous utterance.

The following also belong to the category of ordinary questions, not echoes:

[55]		
i	A: *She's leaving on Saturday.*	B: *Is she?* [sc. *leaving on Saturday*]
ii	A: *He's proposing to resign.*	B: *What's he proposing to do?*

B's questions here are not echoes in the technical sense we are giving to that term in that they do have their face value. That is, they are genuinely questions as to whether she is leaving on Saturday and as to what he is proposing to do: assuming that what A said was true, the answers are *She's leaving on Saturday* and *He's proposing to resign*. Since A has already given the answers, B may be construed as challenging what A said or asking for repetition, but this is not a reason for identifying them with the echoes in [51]. (As we have seen, the polar question here could also be used simply to acknowledge, with surprise, what A has said.) The difference between these examples and the echoes is reflected in the difference in form: in [55] B's questions have the characteristic grammatical form of ordinary questions, but in [51] they do not.

4.8.2 The grammatical form of variable echo questions

We turn now to the form of echo questions, beginning with the variable kind. The variable echo question is grammatically marked by an echo-question word – *what* in the above examples. As there is here a fairly straightforward relation between grammar and meaning we can use the term 'variable echo' at both levels, speaking of a variable echo construction at the level of grammar and of a variable echo question at the level of meaning. And just as there is a difference in meaning between a variable echo question and a variable ordinary question, so there are differences in form.

Grammatical differences between variable echoes and open interrogatives

(a) Differences between *what/who* as echo-question words and as interrogative words

One difference between the two constructions is that these words, especially *what*, have a wider range of uses in variable echo clauses than in open interrogatives. For example, in [51iii], *He's proposing to what?*, the echo word *what* is a verb and combines with *to* to form a verb phrase, but interrogative *what* is not a verb and hence we need *do* in [55]. Note also:

[56]	i A: *He was enthusing about the film.*	B: *He was whatting about the film?*
	ii A: *They gave it to Angela Cooke.*	B: *They gave it to Angela who?*

Example [i] shows that echo *what*, unlike interrogative *what*, can inflect. And [ii] shows that echo *who* likewise differs from interrogative *who*: the latter must always be initial in the interrogative phrase.

(b) Position of echo-question and interrogative words, and subject–auxiliary inversion

In open interrogative clauses a non-subject interrogative element is normally fronted and triggers subject–auxiliary inversion; in variable echo clauses a non-subject question element always remains in situ and therefore never triggers inversion. Compare, for example, echo *He's proposing to what?* ([51iii]) with **What is he proposing to?*, or *They gave it to Angela who?* ([56ii]) with **Angela who did they give it to?* The absence of fronting and inversion serves of course to make the echo maximally like the stimulus that it echoes.

However, there are places where we find overlap between echoes and ordinary questions:

[57]	i *<u>Who</u> made a mistake?*	[subject]
	ii *And the purpose of that was <u>what</u>?*	[post-verbal non-subject]

Example [i] is the case where the interrogative or echo element is subject, and hence will be in pre-verbal position in either case. It could be either an ordinary question with answers like *The Secretary-General made a mistake* or an echo question with the latter as a possible stimulus and answers like *I said, 'The Secretary-General made a mistake'*. Question [ii] has non-subject *what* after the verb: this is a possible if rare position in open interrogatives, as well as the only possible one in echoes, so [ii] could be an ordinary question with such answers as *The purpose of that was to test the PH level* or an echo of a stimulus like the latter. The two interpretations would normally be distinguished prosodically: the echo construction will generally have a fall + sharp rise on the question word.

(c) Relation with clause type

The open interrogative is a clause type, and as such it is mutually exclusive with the other clause types. The variable echo construction, by contrast, is not a clause type. It is a construction on a quite independent dimension, and can combine with any of the clause types:

[58]	STIMULUS	VARIABLE ECHO QUESTION	
i	A: *She's a genius.*	B: *She's a what?*	[declarative]
ii	A: *Did Kim complain?*	B: *Did who complain?*	[closed interrogative]
iii	A: *What did he do last week?*	B: *What did he do when?*	[open interrogative]
iv	A: *What a fuss Ed made!*	B: *What a fuss who made?*	[exclamative]
v	A: *Give the key to Angela.*	B: *Give what to Angela?*	[imperative]

In each of these, B's echo question belongs to the same clause type as the corresponding stimulus, being derived from it by substituting a question element for some element of the stimulus.

The independence of the variable echo construction from clause type is explicable in terms of both form and meaning. As far as its form is concerned, it is marked simply by the presence of a question word, and there is no reason why this should not co-occur with any of the clause type markers. Notice in particular that the variable echo does not determine any features of order, which means that the order of elements in the clause is able to be determined by clause type (or other properties). As far as meaning is concerned, the variable echo question is indirect; at the direct level it is merely a partial repetition, citation, of the stimulus and hence there is no reason why the stimulus should not have an illocutionary force of the kind characteristically associated with any of the clause types.

Multi-variable echo questions

Like an ordinary question, an echo question can contain more than one variable. All the examples so far have been single variable echoes, but multi-variable echoes can be formed simply by substituting a question word for two or more elements in the stimulus:

[59]	STIMULUS	SINGLE VARIABLE ECHO	MULTI-VARIABLE ECHO
i	A: *Kim's a genius.*	B: *Kim's a what?*	B: *Who's a what?*
ii	A: *Give the key to Pat.*	B: *Give what to Pat?*	B: *Give what to who?*

Each question word will normally bear the main stress in its own intonation group.

Because the differences between interrogative words and echo-question words are relatively slight, there is scope for a great deal of potential ambiguity as to whether a word that does not trigger subject–auxiliary inversion is an interrogative word or an echo-question word. *Who's a what?*, for example, is given in [59i] as a two-variable echo of a declarative, but it could also be a single-variable echo of an open interrogative, used in response, say, to the stimulus *Who's a genius?* In the two-variable interpretation, *who* and *what* are both echo-question words, but in the single-variable reading only *what* is, *who* being an interrogative word. Similarly, *Who saw what?* can be a non-echo multi-variable open interrogative, a single-variable echo of a single-variable open interrogative (with a stimulus such as *Who saw the weasel?*) or a multi-variable echo of a declarative (with a stimulus like *The butler saw the weasel*).

4.8.3 The form of polar echo questions

Unlike the variable echo question, the polar echo is not, for the most part, expressed by any special grammatical construction: rather, the echo is signalled prosodically, by the rising intonation. A polar echo question can have the syntactic form belonging to any of the clause types. Polar counterparts of the variable echoes given in [58], for example, are as follows:

[60]	STIMULUS	POLAR ECHO QUESTION	
i	A: *She's a genius.*	B: *She's a genius?*	[declarative]
ii	A: *Did Kim complain?*	B: *Did Kim complain?*	[closed interrogative]
iii	A: *What did he tell her?*	B: *What did he tell her?*	[open interrogative]
iv	A: *What a fuss Ed made!*	B: *What a fuss Ed made?*	[exclamative]
v	A: *Give the key to Angela.*	B: *Give the key to Angela?*	[imperative]

The echo repeats the stimulus, with rising intonation signalling a request for repetition, or justification.

We have seen that rising intonation can also combine with declarative clause type to yield an ordinary polar (or alternative) question, and there is accordingly again potential ambiguity in examples like *She's a genius?* It can be an ordinary (direct) question whose answers are *She's a genius* and *She's not a genius*; or it can be, as in [60i], a polar echo (indirect) question whose answers are *I said she's a genius* and *I didn't say she's a genius.* In both cases the question is biased – towards an answer which expresses the same propositional content as is expressed in the direct question or implied in the indirect one. For example, in:

[61] a. *She gave it to him?* b. *She didn't give it to him?*

the expected answers for the ordinary question interpretations are, for [a], *She gave it to him* and, for [b], *She didn't give it to him*, whereas those for the echo question interpretations are respectively *I said, 'She gave it to him'* and *I said, 'She didn't give it to him'.*

The bare predication construction in polar echoes

[62]	STIMULUS	POLAR ECHO (BARE PREDICATION)
i	A: *Kim has resigned.*	B: *Kim resign?*
ii	A: *She's a genius.*	B: *Her a genius?*

One case where a polar echo does have a special syntactic form is the **bare predication** construction. The clause consists of a subject together with a non-finite VP (as in [i]), or simply a predicative complement (as in [ii]). The echo belongs to relatively informal style, and a personal pronoun subject will thus tend to take accusative case.

4.8.4 Repetition vs clarification echoes

The echoes considered so far have all been what we will call **repetition echo questions**, as their answers include a repetition of the stimulus. They are distinguishable from a more peripheral kind of echo used to seek clarification of some element in the stimulus – the **clarification echo question**. The distinction may be illustrated by means of a potentially ambiguous example, such as:

[63]			
i	A: *I've finally solved the problem of the missing cents.*	B: *You've finally solved what?*	[repetition]
ii	A: *I've finally solved it.*	B: *You've finally solved what?*	[clarification]

In [i] the echo *what* substitutes for *the problem of the missing cents*, which B has not properly perceived or understood. The answer would be *I said, 'I've finally solved the problem of the missing cents'*: this is the repetition echo interpretation. In [ii], by contrast,

B has heard perfectly well what A has said but does not know what A intended to refer to by the pronoun *it*. B seeks therefore not a repetition of the stimulus, but a reformulation that expresses A's intended meaning more successfully. Similarly, B's echo in [56ii], *They gave it to Angela who?*, was given above as a repetition echo, aiming to obtain repetition of *Cooke*, but it could also be used as a clarification echo to A's stimulus *They gave it to Angela*: A mistakenly assumes that the name *Angela* on its own is sufficient to pick out the intended referent, and B asks for a fuller referring expression.

One obvious use of the clarification echo is when the stimulus is an incomplete utterance like A's *I need to buy a new er, er, ...*; here B's echo response *You need to buy a new what?* aims to elicit the word or expression that A was trying to find.

Clarification echo questions can again be of the polar, alternative, or variable kind. In response to the stimulus *Give the key to Angela*, for example, we might have:

[64]	i	*Give her the front-door key?*	[polar echo]
	ii	*Give her the front-door key or the back-door one?*	[alternative echo]
	iii	*Give her which key?*	[variable echo]

There are intonational differences between clarification and repetition echoes, especially in the variable kind. For example, *You've finally solved what?* as a repetition echo (in [63i]) will have a fall followed by steep rise on *what*, but as a clarification echo (in [63ii]) it will have falling intonation.

The implicit propositional content for the repetition echo begins, roughly, "You said ...", whereas that for the clarification echo might be given as "You meant ...". And indeed the distinction between the two kinds of echo question can be made explicit by means of parentheticals using one or other of these verbs:

[65]	i	*Give the key to Angela, <u>did you say?</u>*	[repetition echo]
	ii	*Give her the front-door key, <u>do you mean?</u>*	[clarification echo]

In spite of these differences, the clarification echo belongs grammatically with the repetition echo in that it too exhibits the grammatical properties that distinguish the variable echo construction from the open interrogative. This is evident from the above examples. In *You need to buy a new what?*, the echo-question word *what* is a common noun with a determiner and adjectival modifier as dependents: interrogative *what*, by contrast, is a pronoun, unable to take such dependents. And in [64iii] the echo question element *which key* occurs in an imperative clause, whereas interrogative *which key* is a clause type marker, and can occur only in open interrogatives.

5 Interrogative tags and parentheticals

In this section we look at the form and interpretation of questions like:

[1]	i	*He's rather aggressive, <u>isn't he?</u>*	[interrogative tag]
	ii	*He's rather aggressive, <u>don't you think?</u>*	[interrogative parenthetical]

An interrogative clause is here added as a supplement to another clause, changing the illocutionary force of the utterance. The clause to which the interrogative is attached we refer to as the **anchor**, e.g. *he's rather aggressive* in [1]. In the default case the anchor is declarative, but it can belong to any of the five major clause types: closed interrogative in *Is it genuine, do you think?*, imperative in *Be quiet, will you!*, and so on (those with imperative anchors are discussed in §9.7).

No great significance attaches to the terminological distinction between tag and parenthetical, but it is useful to have a separate (and well-established) term for the construction shown in [1i], which we examine first.

5.1 The formation of interrogative tags

Reversed polarity and constant polarity tags

A tag is a short interrogative clause which may be negative or positive:

[2] i *Your friends made a good job of it, didn't they?* [negative tag]
ii *They haven't finished it, have they?* [positive tag]

In [i] a negative tag attaches to a positive anchor and in [ii] a positive tag attaches to a negative anchor: we refer to these as **reversed polarity tags**. It is also possible to have **constant polarity tags**, where the tag has the same polarity as the anchor. Thus in [i] we could have *did they?* instead of *didn't they?*, and in [ii] *haven't they?* instead of *have they?* The four possibilities are shown in:

[3]	POSITIVE ANCHOR	NEGATIVE ANCHOR	
i	a. *He is ill, isn't he?*	b. *He isn't ill, is he?*	[reversed polarity tag]
ii	a. *He is ill, is he?*	b. %*He isn't ill, isn't he?*	[constant polarity tag]

As far as the meaning is concerned, the important issue is not whether the tag is positive or negative, but whether it has reversed or constant polarity. Reversed polarity tags are much the more frequent, and constant polarity tags occur predominantly with positive anchors: many speakers reject examples like [iib]. A more formal variant of the inflectional negative *isn't he?* is the analytic negative *is he not?*

Formation of tags by reduction of full interrogatives

In the examples so far, the tag might be regarded as a reduced version of a full closed interrogative clause corresponding to the anchor. The tag in [2i], for example, might be derived from its anchor in three steps, as follows:

[4] i *your friends made a good job of it* [anchor]
ii *your friends didn't make a good job of it* [step I: reverse polarity]
iii *didn't your friends make a good job of it?* [step II: form interrogative]
iv *didn't they?* [step III: reduce]

For constant polarity tags, step I would of course be skipped. Although this procedure works in the great majority of cases, it runs into difficulties with anchors like those in:

[5] i *Few of them liked it, did they?*
ii *It's hardly fair, is it?*

The only way we could apply step I to the anchor *few of them liked it* would be to change this into *few of them didn't like it*, which would lead via steps II and III to the tag *didn't they?* But in fact the reversed polarity tag for this anchor is *did they?*, as in [5i]. The reason is that *few of them liked it* is in fact negative (see Ch. 9, §3.3), so the reversed polarity tag must be positive. It is a negative, however, with no positive counterpart, so step I can't be applied. The same applies with [ii].

Direct formation of the tag

It follows that we need rules to account for the tags directly, rather than by reduction of some full interrogative clause. The form of the tag is as in [6], and it can be derived by procedure [7]:

[6] Auxiliary as predicator + personal pronoun as subject (+ *not*)

[7] i Subject: if anchor subject is a personal pronoun, repeat it; otherwise take the anchor subject as antecedent and select the appropriate personal pronoun.

ii Auxiliary lexeme: if anchor predicator is an auxiliary, select the same lexeme, otherwise select *do*.

iii Auxiliary tense: same as anchor tense.

iv Auxiliary person–number properties (if any): determined by agreement with subject.

v Polarity: opposite to that of anchor for reversed polarity tags, the same for constant polarity tags.

vi Negation: if tag is negative, choose between the less formal synthetic negation (with negative form of auxiliary) and the more formal analytic negation (neutral auxiliary, with final *not*)

Step [i] will often require pragmatic information: the tag for the anchor *the boss has arrived* can be either *hasn't he?* or *hasn't she?*, depending on the sex of the boss. Step [ii] reflects the normal rules for closed interrogative formation: the closed interrogative is a *do*-support construction. Step [iv] selects person–number properties by reference to the tag subject rather than the anchor predicator to cater for cases like *Everybody has read it, haven't they?*, where the anaphoric personal pronoun for singular *everybody* is plural *they*. Steps [v] and [vi] handle the polarity of the tag and of the auxiliary in accordance with the account given above.

Tags based on subordinate clauses

Special provision must be made for the construction illustrated in:

[8] a. *I think it's legal, isn't it?* b. *I don't think it's legal, is it?*

In [a] the first constituent structure boundary is between *I think it's legal* and *isn't it?*: the tag is appended to the main clause *I think it's legal*, which is in this sense the anchor. But the form of the tag is based on the subordinate clause *it's legal*, so from this point of view it is the latter that is treated as anchor. This conflict reflects the mismatch between the grammatical structure of *I think it's legal* and its communicative meaning. Grammatically, *it's legal* is subordinate to the *think* clause, but communicatively it is the subordinate clause that is primary: *I think* simply expresses some modal qualification. The anchor is comparable to *It's probably legal*, where the modal qualification is expressed in a grammatically subordinate way, by an adverbial adjunct, or *It's legal, I think*, where the qualification is parenthetical: for both of these the procedure [7] would give *isn't it?* as tag quite straightforwardly.

Example [8b] is similar but has the added complication of negative polarity. *Is it?* is a reversed polarity tag, but the negative which it reverses is in the *think* clause. Again the form of the tag reflects the communicative meaning rather than the grammatical structure – by the process we call specificity increase (Ch. 9, §5) the negative is interpreted as applying to the complement of *think* ("I think it isn't legal"), so the tag is positive, just as it is in *It's probably not legal, is it?* or *It isn't legal, I think, is it?*

Other expressions allowing the tag to be based on a subordinate clause complement include: *I believe/suppose/guess/reckon*; *it seems/appears*; *it follows/this means*; and so on (cf. *It seems we made a mistake, didn't we?*; *It follows that we won't have to pay any more, will we?*).

Minor departures from the main pattern of tag formation

We find a number of departures from the forms predicted by [7] (but with a good deal of idiolectal and dialectal variation), all indicating that meaning rather than exact syntactic form is what is important in tag selection:

[9] i The non-prototypical auxiliary *ought* is sometimes replaced by the synonymous *should*: *You ought to have told them the whole truth, shouldn't you?*

ii The rules predict *mayn't it?* as the informal reversed polarity tag for *It may rain*, but most speakers do not have the form %*mayn't*; there is no clearly established way of filling the gap: possibilities include *mightn't it?*, *won't it?*, the more formal *may it not?*, or a structurally independent interrogative such as parenthetical *don't you think?*, *isn't that so?*, etc.

iii *Do* may be found as a variant of *have* in the tag to an anchor with *have got*: *He's got problems, doesn't he?* (which may be regarded as a blend of *He's got problems, hasn't he?* and *He has problems, doesn't he?*).

iv *Be* + 3rd person pronoun can occur as tag to a verbless anchor: *Lovely day, isn't it?*; *Beautiful ship, isn't she?*

5.2 The use and interpretation of tags

Reversed polarity tags

The illocutionary force of an utterance with the form anchor + tag depends on the prosody. The two principal patterns both have falling tone on the anchor; the tag itself is either rising or, more frequently, falling:

[10]	POSITIVE ANCHOR	NEGATIVE ANCHOR	
i	a. *He was here, wasn't he↗?*	b. *He wasn't here, was he↗?*	[rising tag]
ii	a. *He was here, wasn't he↘?*	b. *He wasn't here, was he↘?*	[falling tag]

(a) The rising tag

This expresses doubt or asks for verification: the question is biased towards an answer that confirms the anchor. A special case, involving a negative anchor, is prosodically distinguished by a somewhat wider pitch movement and the lack of any rhythmic break between anchor and tag. Here there is no such bias towards an answer with the same polarity as the anchor:

[11] *It isn't raining again, is it?* *It isn't my turn already, is it?*

If anything, there is a bias towards a positive answer, but in addition the construction has an emotive component of meaning – a suggestion of being afraid that the positive answer is the true one.

(b) The falling tag

The version with falling intonation on the tag does not express doubt: the question merely seeks acknowledgement that the anchor is true. Thus it can be used in a context where the anchor is obviously true: *Good gracious, you're up early this morning, aren't you?*, uttered at 4 a.m., say. There may be, as perhaps in this example, an implicit invitation to provide an explanation (*Yes, I've got a train to catch*). Or I may want you to admit something you didn't previously accept (*I was right all along, wasn't I?*). Or again I might be asking for your agreement to some minor uncontroversial proposition (*It's a lovely day again, isn't it?*). Thus an exclamative anchor will normally take a falling tag because I can hardly ask you to confirm my exclamation: *What a mess I've made of things, haven't I?* With an exclamative the truth of the proposition is not at issue (see §8.2), so that such an anchor is inconsistent with the expression of doubt. The falling tag may therefore have the character of a rhetorical question, where an answer-response is unnecessary.

Constant polarity tags

The characteristic intonation for constant polarity tags is slightly but not steeply rising. They do not, however, express doubt: the content of the anchor is typically something I am repeating or inferring from what you have just said or from what was said earlier. For many speakers they occur only in the positive. One use, commonly accompanied by *so* or a comparable item such as *oh, I see*, etc., carries an emotive meaning of disapproval, reproach, belligerence, or the like:

[12] i *So you have forgotten your homework again, have you?*
ii %*So you haven't done your homework, haven't you?*

These suggest a context where you have just revealed that you have forgotten your homework or failed to do it. Because the anchor proposition is implicitly attributed to you, this use lends itself to sarcasm, as when I say to someone who has performed badly: *So you're the one who was going to come back laden with prizes, are you?*

Such belligerence is not, however, a necessary feature of the constant polarity tag construction. A second use is where I accept what you say, indicating some surprise or at least acknowledging that the information is news to me:

[13] A: *Jones is coming over next semester.*
B: *Jones is coming, is he? In that case we can ask him to give some seminars.*

In both uses, the anchor proposition derives from the addressee, rather than representing a prior belief of the speaker. Exclamatives, which do not readily occur in such contexts, normally allow only reversed polarity tags.

5.3 Parentheticals

By **parentheticals** we mean expressions which can be appended parenthetically to an anchor clause but which also have a non-parenthetical use in which they take a declarative content clause as complement – expressions like *I think, don't you think?*, and so on. Compare:

[14]	NON-PARENTHETICAL USE	PARENTHETICAL USE
i	a. *<u>I think</u> it is quite safe.*	b. *It is quite safe, <u>I think</u>.*
ii	a. *<u>Don't you think</u> it is safe?*	b. *It is safe, <u>don't you think?</u>*
iii	a. *<u>Would you say</u> it is safe?*	b. *Is it safe, <u>would you say?</u>*
iv	a. *When <u>did she say</u> it'll be safe?*	b. *When will it be safe, <u>did she say?</u>*

In the parenthetical use they can, in general, interrupt the anchor instead of following it, as in, for example, *It is, I think, quite safe* or *Has there, would you say, been any serious attempt at compromise?*

In the parenthetical construction the anchor is syntactically a main clause, whereas the corresponding clause in the non-parenthetical construction is subordinate. And while the verbs *think* and *say* have complements in [a], in [b] they do not: in this construction verbs which (with the meanings they have here) normally require a complement occur without one. The syntactic structure signals that the anchor is the communicatively most important part of the message, with the parenthetical supplement correspondingly backgrounded.

Declarative anchor + declarative parenthetical: *It is quite safe, I think*

Many of the parentheticals here serve, like *I think*, to weaken the speaker's commitment to the truth of the anchor proposition: *I believe*, *I reckon*, *I guess*, *I suppose*, *I suggest*, *it seems*, *it appears*, etc. Others are somewhat stronger: *I'm sure, I have no doubt*. And some have concessive force: *it is true, I admit*.

In the non-parenthetical construction the matrix verb and its subject may also be backgrounded, but this is not signalled syntactically, being rather a matter of pragmatics, dependent on context and the content of the subordinate clause. *I believe that there is a God*, for example, will be taken as a statement about my beliefs, with the informational status of *believe* matching its syntactic status as verb of the main clause. This is not the natural way of taking *I believe that nominations close on Tuesday*, however. Here, the subordinate clause will generally be pragmatically foregrounded and the matrix *I believe* reduced in status to a modal qualifier, making it like the parenthetical in *Nominations close on Tuesday, I believe*. Note that while *Do you?* is a pragmatically perfectly natural response to the God example, it would be rather odd as a response to the nominations one, indicating that *I believe* had been taken as foreground material. With the parenthetical construction this response would be anomalous.

Declarative anchor + interrogative parenthetical: *It is quite safe, don't you think?*

The effect of the parenthetical is much like that of a tag (*isn't it?*): I seek your confirmation that the anchor proposition is true. Other such parentheticals include *wouldn't you say?*, *don't you reckon?*, and so on. One might also say *am I right?*, *don't you think so?*, and the like, but these would have the status of independent questions rather than parentheticals.

Interrogative anchor + interrogative parenthetical: *Is it safe, would you say?*

From a grammatical point of view we have here a sequence of two interrogative clauses, but in normal use I would be asking one question, not two. The parenthetical does not serve to ask a second question but to clarify the way the question expressed in the anchor clause is to be interpreted and answered: it is not part of the propositional content that is questioned. The parenthetical makes clear that I am asking for an expression of your opinion – and, indeed, a more formal variant might be *In your opinion, is it safe?*, where the adjunct *in your opinion* likewise does not contribute to the propositional content of the question.

The non-parenthetical *Would you say it is safe?* might well be interpreted in the same way, but again this is a pragmatic matter, not signalled in the syntactic structure. Note, for example, that *Did you say it's safe?* can be used as an indirect speech act to ask whether it is safe, i.e. essentially equivalent to *Is it safe, did you say?*, but it can also be used at face value as a question about what you said.

Other interrogative parentheticals that are appended to interrogative anchors include *would/do you reckon/guess/believe/argue?* We also find similar expressions with 3rd person subjects: *does she think?*, *did she say?*, etc. In general, the same items are used with closed and open interrogatives. An exception is *do you know?*, which appears as a parenthetical only with the closed type: *Are they valuable, do you know?*

Interrogative parentheticals with echo-question anchors

Parentheticals can also be appended to echo questions:

[15] i *He's going to what, did you say?*
ii *Did I help him, do you mean?*

Again the parenthetical does not express a second question, but clarifies the force of the whole – [i] is a repetition echo, [ii] a clarification echo.

Note that with these there is no comparable non-parenthetical construction. *Did you say that he's going to what?*, for example, is an (unlikely) echo of a question (with a stimulus like *Did I say that he's going to emigrate?*), whereas [15i] is an echo of a statement (with a stimulus like *He's going to emigrate*).

6 The presuppositions of information questions

Pragmatic Q–A presuppositions

In general, when I ask a question I presuppose that it has a right answer. We are concerned here with **pragmatic presupposition**: to presuppose something in this sense is to take it for granted, as not at issue, to present it as uncontroversial background. In the case of information questions, to presuppose that a question has a right answer is to presuppose that one of the possible answers is true.

There are several different kinds of pragmatic presupposition, and we will accordingly refer more specifically to the kind we are concerned with here as a **question–answer presupposition** ('Q–A presupposition'). The most straightforward case is perhaps that of the alternative question: we will look at this first, and then examine how the concept of Q–A presupposition applies to polar and variable questions.

6.1 Q–A presuppositions of alternative questions

The possible answers to [1i] are given in [ii], and its Q–A presupposition in [iii]:

[1] i *Is he leaving on Monday or Tuesday?* [alternative Q]
ii "He is leaving on Monday"; "He is leaving on Tuesday" [answers]
iii "He is leaving on Monday or Tuesday" [presupposition]

To presuppose that [i] has a right answer is to presuppose the **disjunction** (*or*-coordination) of the possible answers, i.e. "Either he is leaving on Monday or he is leaving on Tuesday", which is logically equivalent to [iii]. The presupposition of an alternative question can thus be derived simply by taking the corresponding statement.

The *or* in alternative questions and their presuppositions is interpreted exclusively – i.e. the question presents a set of alternatives with the presupposition that one, but only one, is true. Just as [1ii] does not countenance the possibility that he will not leave on Monday or Tuesday, so it does not countenance the possibility that he will leave on both days. This relation of mutual exclusiveness between the alternatives is perfectly consistent with the use of such expressions as *or both*:

[2]	i	*Would you like cheese, fruit, or both?*	[alternative question]
	ii	"You would like cheese"; "You would like fruit"; "You would like both fruit and cheese"	[answers]
	iii	"You would like cheese or fruit or both"	[presupposition]

The *or both* simply adds a third alternative, mutually exclusive with the first two, for "cheese" and "fruit" in the first two answers are interpreted as "just cheese" and "just fruit".

6.2 Q–A presuppositions of polar questions

The presuppositions of polar questions are arrived at in a similar way:

[3]	i	*Has the clock stopped?*	[polar question]
	ii	"The clock has stopped"; "The clock hasn't stopped"	[answers]
	iii	"(Either) the clock has stopped or it hasn't"	[presupposition]

To presuppose that [i] has a true answer is again to presuppose the disjunction of the answers listed in [ii], i.e. to presuppose [iii]. The Q–A presupposition of a polar question is therefore the disjunction of the corresponding statement and its polar opposite.

This applies equally when the question is negative:

[4]	i	*Didn't she see them?*	[polar question]
	ii	"She didn't see them"; "She did see them"	[answers]
	iii	"(Either) she didn't see them or she did"	[presupposition]

We have seen that negative questions are biased, but bias is perfectly consistent with presupposition. The presupposition is that one of the answers is true; the bias goes beyond this and favours one rather than the other as the true one.

The presuppositions in [3] and [4] are necessarily true: they are logical truths, tautologies. This will always be the case with polar questions: the disjunction of any proposition and its polar opposite is necessarily true. Polar questions clearly differ in this respect from alternative ones: [1], for example, is obviously not a logical truth. It should not be thought, however, that this property of polar presuppositions makes them vacuous: from a pragmatic point of view they can be of considerable significance. This may be illustrated by such an example as:

[5]	i	*Are you telling the truth?*	[polar question]
	ii	"(Either) you are telling the truth or you are not"	[presupposition]

The presupposition is what I take for granted, and the significance here is that the presupposition is so weak – it doesn't go beyond a mere tautology. In asking [5i] I take for granted the truth of [ii], but in so doing conspicuously fail to take for granted the truth of the proposition "You are telling the truth". The question entertains the possibility that you are not telling the truth, thereby casting doubt on your veracity. At the direct level [i] is clearly a question, not an accusation, but is not uncommon for such questions to be interpreted as indirect accusations.

6.3 Q–A presuppositions of variable questions

The presuppositions of variable questions cannot be derived in quite so simple a way as with alternative and polar questions. This is because the set of answers is prototypically open-ended: we shall not therefore derive the presupposition by taking the disjunction of the possible answers. Instead we derive it by substituting an appropriate indefinite phrase for the variable in the open proposition expressed in the question:

[6]	i	*Who wrote the editorial?*	[variable question]
	ii	"Person *x* wrote the editorial"	[open proposition]
	iii	"Someone wrote the editorial"	[presupposition]

We have seen that the answers to a variable question assign values to the variable(s) in the open proposition. To presuppose that [6i] has a right answer, therefore, is to presuppose that there is a true proposition in which a value is assigned to the variable in [ii] – and to presuppose this is to presuppose [iii]. Note that the latter does not constitute an **answer** to the question, and to give it as a response would be clearly unco-operative. This is precisely because it does not provide any information beyond that which the speaker presents as already established. Thus [iii] no more constitutes an answer to [i] in set [6] than it does in sets [2–4]. With alternative and polar questions an answer must be more specific than the presupposition by selecting one of the coordinates; with variable questions it must be more specific by genuinely providing a value for the variable.

It will be noted that in [6ii] the variable *x* is attached to 'person' instead of standing on its own, as in the formulations which, for simplicity of presentation, we have been using hitherto. 'Person' is needed to show that the variable ranges only over the set of persons: #*The lawnmower wrote the editorial*, for example, is not a possible answer to [6i]. 'Person', of course, is part of the meaning of *who*, and is encapsulated also in that of *someone*, which appears in the presupposition. For *when*, a comparable schema is given in:

[7]	i	*When did they move to Edinburgh?*	[variable question]
	ii	"They moved to Edinburgh at time *x*"	[open proposition]
	iii	"They moved to Edinburgh at some time"	[presupposition]

A detailed account of the presuppositions of variable questions must therefore draw on a description of the individual interrogative words: we take this up in §7 below.

Q–A presuppositions in relation to the set consisting of all the answers

Another, but equivalent, approach to an explanation of the Q–A presupposition of a variable question is to see it as following from every one of the answers. Thus instead of [6], for example, we might have:

[8]	i	*Who wrote the editorial?*	[variable question]
	ii	"Ian wrote the editorial"; "I wrote the editorial"; "One of the directors wrote the editorial"; . . .	[answers]
	iii	"Someone wrote the editorial"	[presupposition]

If Ian wrote the editorial, it follows that someone wrote it, and similarly for all other answers.

It is important to note, however, that the presupposition may follow not from the answer alone, but from the answer together with the premise that it **is** an answer. Consider [9i] and the sample of responses given in [ii]:

[9] i a. *What Soviet president won the Nobel Peace Prize?* [question]
b. "Some Soviet president won the Nobel Peace Prize" [presupposition]
ii a. *Mikhail Gorbachov won the Nobel Peace Prize.*
b. *Leonid Brezhnev won the Nobel Peace Prize.*
c. *Willy Brandt won the Nobel Peace Prize.*

The right answer is [iia], but this does not by itself entail [ib]: we need the additional premise "Mikhail Gorbachov is/was a Soviet president". Though false, [iib] is still an answer. By contrast, [iic] is true, but not a true answer, because the additional premise – "Willy Brandt is/was a Soviet president" – is false. Presuppositions thus play a significant role in the interpretation of responses to variable questions. If you interpret a response as an answer you add to its content whatever additional premise is needed for the presupposition to be entailed.

No such additional premises are needed with alternative and polar questions. Here the presupposition is a disjunction of the answers, and since any proposition "p" entails "p or q", any one answer will always entail the disjunction of the set of answers. In [1], for example, if "He is leaving on Monday" is true, then obviously "He is leaving on Monday or Tuesday" is also true.

6.4 Rejection of Q–A presuppositions

The Q–A presuppositions of alternative and variable questions are generally not logical truths, and they will not always be accepted by the addressee:

[10] i A: *Will Kim or Pat chair the meeting?* B: *Neither. I'm chairing it this time.*
ii A: *Who helped her?* B: *Nobody – she did it herself.*

B's responses here are not answers. They contradict the presuppositions of the questions: B rejects these presuppositions and hence cannot answer. Notice that although *nobody* has the grammatical form of an NP, it does not have reference and hence does not supply a value for the variable in the question. It indicates, rather, that there is no value of *x* such that "Person *x* helped her" is true.

6.5 Cancellation of Q–A presuppositions

We have said that Q–A presuppositions are pragmatic in nature: they are not invariant, immutable, as they would have to be to qualify as a semantic phenomenon. In particular, there are cases where I can use a variable question without taking it for granted that a value can be supplied for the variable. We will refer to this as **presupposition cancellation**: the question is used without the presupposition that characteristically accompanies a question.

Some examples are given in:

[11] i *Who cares?*
ii *What do I care? / What does it matter?*
iii *How do you know Jill didn't do it herself?*
iv *How should I know?*
v *Why should he do a thing like that?*

Question [i] is a conventional way of indirectly asserting "Nobody cares". Similarly [ii] typically conveys "I don't care at all / It doesn't matter at all". A difference between them is that in [i] there is nothing in the grammatical form of the sentence to indicate that the expected presupposition is cancelled, whereas in [ii] there is. It would be possible in principle to use [i] in a presupposition-preserving way, and this is reflected in the fact that it can be used as complement to *know*: *She knows who cares and who doesn't care.* This is not so with [ii] – cf. **She knows what I care / what it matters.* They involve semi-fixed expressions, with *what* here meaning "how much". Questions like [iii], beginning with *how do you know*, are often used to challenge what the addressee has just said. I am suggesting that you have not considered the possibility that Jill did it: I am therefore not taking it for granted that you know she didn't.

Question [11iv] is a conventional way of conveying "There's no reason why I should (be expected to) know". Modal *should* quite often occurs with presupposition cancellation, but is not an unequivocal marker of it. Question [11v], for example, could be used either with or without the Q–A presupposition. Suppose you say *I've just discovered that Max has been tampering with the computer*; I might then respond with [11v] in two different ways:

[12] i *Yes, I can't understand it. Why should he do a thing like that?*
ii *Oh, surely not! Why should he do a thing like that?*

The question in [i] presupposes that Max 'did a thing like that' (i.e. tampered with the computer), whereas in [ii] the presupposition is cancelled: it conveys that Max probably didn't do it. (Note that even in [i] *should* serves an emotive role, indicating puzzlement or surprise, rather than being part of the propositional content: the presupposition is "He did a thing like that for some reason", not "He should do a thing like that for some reason".) *Would* is possible instead of *should* in all these examples.

Negatively-oriented polarity-sensitive items generally serve to cancel the presuppositions of variable questions:

[13] i *When will you <u>ever</u> learn not to trust them?*
ii *Where could you find <u>anything</u> better?*

There is no presupposition here that you will at some time learn not to trust them or that you could find something better somewhere. On the contrary, these questions tend to convey the speaker's belief that you won't, that you couldn't.

The presupposition is also cancelled in the bare infinitival construction illustrated in [16] of §4. *Why invite them both?* suggests that there is in fact no reason to do so. Likewise in the negative finite *Why don't you invite them both?*, when it's a matter of some future situation – the presupposition is preserved in examples like *Why don't you like it?*

6.6 Secondary presuppositions

In addition to the Q–A presupposition that a question normally has simply by virtue of being a question, there may be further presuppositions that follow from it – we will refer to these as **secondary presuppositions**:

[14] i	*Has he stopped smoking?*	[polar question]
ii	"(Either) he has stopped smoking or he hasn't"	[Q–A presupposition]
iii	"He formerly smoked"	[secondary presupposition]

Here [ii] presupposes [iii]. If he has stopped smoking, then necessarily he formerly smoked and precisely because you can't stop doing something that you have never done I also wouldn't normally say *He hasn't stopped smoking* unless he had previously done so (cf. Ch. 1, §5.4). If [i] presupposes [ii] and [ii] presupposes [iii], it follows that [i] presupposes [iii]. When I ask [i], the issue is normally just whether he smokes now: I take it for granted that he formerly did. We call this a secondary presupposition because it doesn't derive directly from the question form itself, but depends crucially on the properties of the verb *stop*.

A second example is seen in:

[15]	i *Did he break it intentionally?*	[polar question]
	ii "(Either) he broke it intentionally or he didn't"	[Q–A presupposition]
	iii "He broke it"	[secondary presupposition]

If he didn't break it, the issue of whether he broke it intentionally doesn't arise, so in asking [i] I normally take [iii] for granted. But again [iii] is only a secondary presupposition of the question because it derives from properties of the verb + manner adverb construction.

7 Interrogative words and phrases

This section is concerned with the grammatical and semantic properties of the following interrogative words, and phrases based on them:

[1]	*how*	*what*	*when*	*where*	*which*
	who	*whom*	*whose*	*why*	

The interrogative subordinators *whether* and *if* are discussed in Ch. 11, §5.2: we confine our attention here, therefore, to the open interrogative words, which are used in both main and subordinate clauses. *Who* and *whom* are inflectional forms of the lexeme ***who***, and will here be treated together, the difference being a matter of case (Ch. 5, §16.2.3). The issue of the grammatical number of interrogative phrases, as reflected in subject–verb agreement, is discussed in Ch. 5, §18.

The dual role of interrogative words

Open interrogatives are marked as such by the presence of an open interrogative word, but these words all have some other role in the syntactic structure. Compare:

[2]	i a. *<u>Who</u> has taken my umbrella?*	b. *<u>What</u> mistakes did I make?*
	ii a. *<u>Someone</u> has taken my umbrella.*	b. *I made <u>some</u> mistakes.*

As well as marking the clause type, *who* in [ia] is head of the subject NP, like *someone* in [iia], and *what* in [ib] is determiner in the object NP, like *some* in [iib]. We refer to these two roles respectively as their **interrogative role** and their **core role**. In their interrogative role they serve as a variable that is replaced by a value in the set of answers; the core role differs from one to another, and hence has to be described individually.

7.1 *Which*

Which differs from all the other interrogative words in having a property we shall call 'selective'. It implies that the value which an answer substitutes for the question variable is to be selected from some definite set:

Which + partitive phrase

The set may be specified by a partitive phrase within the interrogative phrase itself:

[3] i *Which (one) of the chapters did you write?*
ii *Which of quiche, pizza, and lasagna would you prefer?*

A possible answer to [i] is *I wrote Ch. 3*, where *Ch. 3* refers to a member of the set referred to by *the chapters* in the question. The partitive phrase usually consists of *of* + definite NP, as in this example. An alternative to a definite NP is a coordination defining the set by listing its members, as in [ii]. Note, however, that we can't have an indefinite NP: *which of us / them / the boys / these books / your shares*, but not **which of boys / some books / any shares*. Instead of *of* we sometimes find *out of*: *Which out of the three cheapest ones do you think we should take?* A cardinal numeral commonly precedes the partitive: *which one/two of the chapters.*

Which without an overt partitive phrase

The set from which selection is made need not be specified in a partitive phrase, but may be given elsewhere or just be contextually implicit:

[4] i *Which would you prefer, quiche or pizza?*
ii *It comes in three colours, red, blue, and green. Which would you prefer?*
iii *Which chapter(s) did you write?*

In [i] the set is defined by the coordination which is added at the end, effectively converting the variable question into an alternative one. In [ii] the set is given in the preceding text, while in [iii] it is contextually given: we are talking about some book, and the chapters in that book constitute an identifiable set.

Which vs *what*

What cannot occur just before a partitive: **What of the chapters did you write?* It is also normally excluded before a cardinal numeral + partitive: *Which/*What one of them is defective?* Elsewhere, *what* is not grammatically excluded, though there will be a strong pragmatic preference for *which* in cases like [4ii], where the interrogative word constitutes the whole interrogative phrase and the set is given in the preceding text – *what* could substitute much more readily for *which* in [i], where the set is defined later.

When the interrogative word is determiner to a noun head, both *which* and *what* are possible:

[5] i *Which/What approach to the problem would you recommend?*
ii *Which/What king of England had six wives?*

In [i] the contrast is quite sharp. The set of approaches to a problem is not inherently clearly defined. Normally, therefore, one would present it as an identifiable set by using *which* only in a context where a number of possible approaches have been mentioned: the question implies a choice from such a contextually defined set. *What* does not have the selective feature and is the form one would use when there is no identified set to choose from. *What* is not inconsistent with there being a contextually defined set, as evident from the fact that it can be used in [ii], since the kings of England do form an identifiable set. In such cases the distinction between *which* and *what* is effectively neutralised: *which* encodes the fact that the choice is from an identifiable set while *what* doesn't, but as that is part of background knowledge it doesn't matter from a pragmatic point of view whether it is encoded or not. Compare, similarly, *Which/ What gear are we in?*, as said of a car with five gears.

7.2 *Whose*

Interrogative *whose* is genitive and (unlike relative *whose*) personal, so that presuppositions to *whose* questions contain *someone*:

[6]	QUESTION	PRESUPPOSITION
i	a. *Whose bicycle did she take?*	b. "She took someone's bicycle"
ii	a. *Whose is that?*	b. "That is someone's / belongs to someone"
iii	a. *Whose do you prefer?*	b. "You prefer someone's"

In [i] *whose* is determiner to a noun head, while [ii] is the predicative use, with answers like *It's mine.* In [iii] *whose* is a fused determiner-head, with the interpretation recoverable from the context – e.g. *Kim and Pat don't need their bicycles today: whose would you prefer to borrow?* This is a relatively infrequent construction: one would be more likely to use *which. Whose* can be used when the variable ranges over a contextually identifiable set, but it is hardly possible with a partitive *of* phrase: **Whose of the two of them would you prefer?*

7.3 *Who* and *whom*

Nominative *who* and accusative *whom* occur only in head function, contrasting with *whose* as non-genitive vs genitive, and with *what* as personal vs non-personal:

[7] i a. *Who is that?* [non-genitive]
b. *Whose is that?* (=[6ii]) [genitive]
ii a. *Who have you got as tutor this year?* [personal]
b. *What have you got as set text this year?* [non-personal]

Who vs *what* in predicative complement function

[8]	A:	B:	
i	A: *Who is Lesley?*	B: *She's their solicitor.*	[specifying *be*]
ii	A: *What is Lesley?*	B: *She's a solicitor.*	[ascriptive *be*]

In [i] we have the specifying *be* construction: the question asks about Lesley's identity, and the answer identifies her as their solicitor. Here *their solicitor* is used referentially. In [ii] *be* is ascriptive, and the NP *a solicitor* in the answer is non-referential (cf. Ch. 5, §8.3). The contextually most neutral interpretation of such *what* questions about people is that the variable ranges over occupations, as in this example. The context, however, may specify other kinds of property: the question *What are you?*, for example, could be a question about your political affiliation, your religion, or your martial art grade, when following such statements as *I'm Labour, I'm Catholic, I'm a Blue Belt* – and so on.

Who vs *which*

[9] i *There are two contestants left, Kim and Pat. Which/ Who do you think will win?*
ii *Who/ Which is Lesley?*

The contrast between **who** and *which* is similar to that between *what* and *which*. Unlike *which*, **who** does not encode that selection is to be made from an identifiable set, but it can substitute for *which* in cases where the set is defined in context, as in [i]. Again, we could add *of them* with *which* but not ***who***. (A partitive phrase with *of* or *out of* is not in general excluded with ***who***, however: *Who (out) of all the conductors you have worked with was the most inspiring?*) Both *who* and *which* are found in the specifying ***be*** construction, [ii]. With *who* the more likely interpretation is that *who* has the identifier role, *Lesley* the identified, as in [8i]: I don't know who Lesley is and am wanting to find out. With *which*, by contrast, the salient interpretation has *which* as identified and *Lesley* as identifier: I do know who Lesley is and am wanting to find out which of a certain set of persons (e.g. on a group photograph, or on a stage) is identifiable as her.

7.4 *When*

When is used to question time, and is used with a range of functions:

[10]	i	*When is she leaving?*	[adjunct (temporal location)]
	ii	*When is the concert?*	[complement]
	iii	*When would be a good time to meet?*	[subject of specifying *be*]
	iv	*When would the best time be for her lecture?*	[complement of specifying *be*]
	v	*Since when have you been in charge?*	[complement of preposition]

Question [i] presupposes "She is leaving at some time", but it is more general than *What time / At what time is she leaving?*, which normally refers to clock time, so that while *in August* is not an answer to the latter it is an answer to [i]. Similarly for [ii]. In the specifying *be* construction *when* could be replaced by *what* (or *what time*), and the answer would generally be given without *at*: *five o'clock* rather than *at five o'clock* (though *the afternoon* and *in the afternoon* are equally possible). One case of specifying *be* where *what* could not replace *when* is the *it*-cleft construction: *When/*What was it you saw her?*

Since when, as in [10v], is often used sarcastically, with cancellation of the presupposition. So as well as asking how long you have been in charge, it might be used to suggest that you are behaving as though you were in charge when in fact you are not.

7.5 *Where*

Where questions spatial location or goal and occurs in the same range of functions as *when*:

[11]	i	*Where are we going to have lunch?*	[adjunct (spatial location)]
	ii	*Where are you?* *Where are you going?*	[complement]
	iii	*Where would be a good place to meet?*	[subject of specifying *be*]
	iv	*Where would the best place be for her lecture?*	[complement of specifying *be*]
	v	*Where have you come from?*	[complement of preposition]

Example [i] presupposes "We are going to have lunch (at) some place". As complement, *where* can question location (*Where are you?*: "at what place?") or goal (*Where are you going?*: "to what place?"). In the latter case, *to* can be used, giving a structure like [v]: *Where are you going to?* In [iii–iv] we could again substitute *what*. In the prepositional construction [v] the preposition is normally *to* or *from* (though *at* is found in idiomatic

Where are we at?). The preposition is usually stranded, as in [v]: fronting of the preposition (*From where have you come?*) is confined to markedly formal style.[13]

7.6 *Why*

This has a narrower range of use than *when* and *where*, being restricted to adjunct function or the complement of the *it*-cleft construction; note, for example, that other specifying *be* constructions allow only *what*:

[12] i *Why is she going home?* [adjunct (cause)]
ii *Why is it that we keep getting the wrong results?* [*it*-cleft]
iii *What/*Why was the reason for her sudden departure?* [specifying *be*]

Why questions cause (reason or purpose): answers to [i] include *Because she's hungry*, *To get some food*, and so on. In adjunct function (but not in [ii]) *why* is replaceable by the idiomatic, and relatively informal, *what . . . for*: *Why did you do that?* or *What did you do that for?*

Presupposition cancellation

Question [12i] presupposes "She is going home for some reason", but *why* is often found with cancellation of the presupposition. Compare:

[13] i a. *Why is Max so naughty?* b. *Why am I naughty?*
ii a. *Why don't you go to the beach?* b. *Why not go to the beach?*
iii a. *Why don't you be more tolerant?* b. *Why not be more tolerant?*

In its salient interpretation [ia] presupposes that Max is naughty and asks for the cause, or explanation. Question [ib] can be used in a similar way, but I'm more likely to use it to ask for evidence or justification for the claim that I'm naughty: the presupposition is cancelled in this use, whether I'm naughty being the main issue, not something that is taken for granted. (A similar interpretation is possible for [ia], but the *so* makes it less likely.) *Why* questions with presupposition cancellation often contain modal *should*, as noted in §6.6. Example [iia] allows a face value interpretation where the presupposition is retained: "Why is it that you don't go to the beach?", but it can also be used when I don't think there is any valid reason and the cancellation of the presupposition results in an indirect directive: "You should go to the beach". The other three examples have only this directive interpretation: see §4.5.

Direction questions and *to*-infinitivals

Unlike the other interrogative words, *why* is not normally possible in direction questions. Thus %*Why shall I get my money back?* can only be an information question, with answers like *You will get your money back because the manufacturer has accepted responsibility for the defect.* In *to*-infinitivals, *why* is just possible in the titular use: *Why to vote yes in the referendum.*

[13] *Whereabouts* can be used instead of *where* to indicate that only an approximate answer is envisaged. However, the noun *whereabouts* (derived from the preposition by shift of stress from the last syllable to the first) is not an interrogative word: *His whereabouts aren't known* is declarative and has no embedded interrogative clause within it. Interrogative *whence* ("from where") and *whither* ("to where") are archaic. So too is *wherein*, which is the only one of the compounds of interrogative *where* + preposition that one is likely to encounter; its archaic status is seen in the fact that it does not require *do*-support but allows inversion of subject + lexical verb, as in *Wherein lies its appeal?*

Why in response to directives and questions

Why also differs from the other interrogative words in examples like:

[14] i A: *Get your money back.* B: *When?/ Why?*
ii A: *Did you see her?* B: *When?/ Why?*

B's *When?* in [i] asks for a more specific directive, whereas *Why?* asks for a reason for complying with the directive. Features such as time and place count as features of the action itself (getting your money back tomorrow is a different action from getting it back next week), but reason does not (getting your money back counts as the same action, whether you do it for this reason or for that). Similarly in [ii] *When?* asks for further specification of the propositional content of A's question: it is a clarificatory echo question, elliptical for *Did I see her when?* (cf. §4.8.4). *Why?*, by contrast, asks for A's reason for asking the question – and could accompany an answer to the question, as in *Yes, why?*

7.7 *How*

Interrogative *how* has a considerable range of uses which we will consider in turn.

(a) Adjectival predicative complement

[15] i a. *How are you (feeling)?* b. *How was the concert?* [PC^s]
ii a. *How did you find the seminar?* b. *How do you like your coffee?* [PC^o]

Adjectival *how* is used predicatively only, not attributively (we can't say **How films do you like?*, but need a periphrastic expression such as *what kind of*). In [i] the PC is subjective, and in [ii] objective. It is difficult to state the presuppositions precisely, because there is no word standing in the same relation to *how* as *someone* does to *who* or *somewhere* to *where*, for *somehow* can only be an adverb, not an adjective. Nor is there any comparable NP or PP standing in the same relation to *how* as *some time* does to *when* or *for some reason* to *why*.

The salient interpretation of [15ia] is as a question about your present state of health, with such answers as *I am well/ ill/ better, I have a headache*, and so on: the presupposition is thus roughly "You are in some state of health". Question [ib] would typically be used to ask for your subjective evaluation of the concert, with such answers as *It was good / fair / disappointing / a disaster.* An example like *How does the house look now?*, which has a more specific verb than *be*, seems to allow a wider range of values for the variable, though evaluative ones will still be the most likely; the presupposition is that the house has some property relating to its appearance.

Example [15iia] again asks for evaluation (*I found it enlightening / a waste of time*). The complex-transitive construction with *like* takes a very limited range of PC^{o}s – *black, white, sweet, hot, with cream*, etc., and the presupposition of [15iib] will be that you like your coffee with some property from this range.

Questioning of a predicative (like that of a predicator: see §7.10) is much more restricted than questioning an argument or circumstance. *How* occurs with relatively few copulative and complex-transitive verbs, so that [15] may be contrasted with examples like **How did she become?*, **How did you think the concert?*, etc. With *strike* it is only in the interrogative that the PC can have the form of an adjective rather than a PP: compare <u>*How*</u> *does it strike you?* and *It strikes me* <u>*as quite interesting*</u>.

(b) Adverbial degree modifier

[16] i [<u>How</u> *old*] *is your father?* [modifier of adjective]
ii [<u>How</u> *many*] *children have they got?* [modifier of degree determinative]
iii [<u>How</u> *seriously*] *are they taking his threat?* [modifier of adverb]
iv <u>How</u> *did you like the concert?* [modifier of verb]

How modifies adjectives, degree determinatives, adverbs, and verbs to question degree, extent, quantity. Only a very small number of verbs (*like, enjoy, please,* etc.) take *how* in its degree sense: with other verbs, degree is normally questioned with *how much*, as in *How much do you care about him?*

Whatever its category, the word modified by *how* is always gradable. The presupposition of the question then depends on the nature of the scale involved. Consider:

[17] a. *How deep is the water?* b. *How shallow is the water?*

While [b] presupposes that the water is shallow, [a] does not presuppose that it is deep – only that it has a value on the scale of depth, a value which may or may not fall within the range denoted by the unmodified adjective *deep.*

(c) Adjunct in clause structure, questioning means

[18] i A: *How did you get in?* B: *By climbing through the kitchen window.*
ii A: *How is she going to pay for it?* B: *By cheque.*
iii A: *How can I remove it?* B: *With a razor-blade.*

The presupposition is "You got in by some means / in some way", and so on. This represents the most usual sense of adverbial *how* when it modifies the verb.

(d) Adjunct in clause structure, questioning manner

[19] i A: *How did she speak?* B: *With a strong French accent.*
ii A: *How does he drive?* B: *Rather recklessly.*

The presupposition this time is "She spoke in some manner/way", etc. Very often such questions ask for evaluative judgements, as in [ii]. *How* can also occur as complement with those verbs requiring manner specification: *How do they treat you?* This again invites an evaluative answer, such as *Well* or *Badly.*

(e) Adjunct in clause structure, asking for evidence:

[20] i *How does he know she is going to resign?*
ii *How can you be so sure that it was an accident?*

This use is found with *know* and a few similar expressions, and serves to challenge what has been said or implied. There is no presupposition "He knows (in some way) that she is going to resign": I am calling into question the contention that she is going to resign.

(f) Questioning reason in the *it*-cleft construction, and in the idiom *how come*

[21] i *How is it you didn't tell me before?*
ii *How come the fridge is switched off?*

The use of *how* shown in [i] is restricted to the *it*-cleft construction: the closest non-cleft counterpart has *why* rather than *how*: *Why didn't you tell me before?* Like the latter, [i] presupposes "You didn't tell me before (for some reason)".

The idiom *how come*, a common alternant to *why* in informal speech, derives from a construction where *come* is a verb taking a clausal subject (cf. *How does it come to be that the fridge is switched off*). But it is best regarded as a compound interrogative word functioning as adjunct in a simple clause. Note, for example, that it is impossible to insert *that* after *come*, a strong indication that the following NP (*the fridge*) has been reanalysed as subject of a main clause. Moreover, the lack of any inflection on *come* works against its construal as a verb with a 3rd person singular subject. *How come* is nevertheless very exceptional as an interrogative expression in that it doesn't trigger subject–auxiliary inversion. It normally occurs in main clauses, but is not entirely excluded from subordinate interrogatives: *That's how come they stay No. 1.*

(g) In the idiom *how about*

[22] i *How about another drink?*
ii *How about helping me with the washing-up?*
iii *How about we leave the others until next week?*
iv *I think it's excellent; how about you?*

How about belongs to informal style – with *how's about* more informal still. The primary use is to put forward a suggestion. This may have the indirect force of an offer (as in a possible contextualisation of [i]), a directive (as in a likely interpretation of [ii]), and so on. The complement of *about* can be an NP, a gerund-participial clause, or a tensed declarative clause, as in [i–iii]. Besides its use in suggestions, the idiom can be used to introduce a change to a related topic – e.g. from the speaker's opinion to the addressee's in [iv]. *What about* is a possible variant except in [iii], where the complement is a tensed clause.

(h) In certain non-question idioms

[23] i *How do you do.*
ii *How dare you speak to me like that!*

The boundary between direct and indirect speech acts is by no means sharply drawn, but it is arguable that these are not questions indirectly conveying a greeting and a rebuke respectively, but simply a greeting and a rebuke at the direct level. *How do you do* may be contrasted with *How are you?*, which is used as a greeting, but is clearly also a question. *I'm very well* is an answer to the latter, but *I do very well* is archaic (in the sense "I am in good health"), so that [i] can no longer be regarded as defining a set of possible answers. Similarly it is difficult to accept that any declarative clause could properly be regarded as expressing an answer to [ii] or other rebukes beginning with *how dare.*

7.8 ***What***

What occurs as determinative or pronoun, with respectively *some* or *something* as the non-interrogative counterpart, and, in general, presuppositions of *what* questions can be derived by substituting these:

[24]	i a. *What class is she in?*	b. "She is in some class"
	ii a. *What did the doctor say?*	b. "The doctor said something"

Determinative *what* contrasts with *which* and *whose*, while pronoun *what* contrasts with these two and also with *who*/*whom*, *when*, and *where*: the meaning of *what* has been discussed above in relation to these contrasts.

What in verbless constructions

[25] i A: *Tom.* B: *What?* A: *Can you come here a moment?*
ii A: *I've just discovered something.* B: *What?*
iii A: *Kim's just got a new job:* B: *So what?*

In [i] *what?* serves to acknowledge a call; *yes?* would be a rather more polite alternative. In [ii] it is elliptical: we understand "What have you just discovered?"; this elliptical use is found with all the interrogative words. (*What?* can also be a repetition echo question, and [25ii] is thus ambiguous between the ordinary question interpretation just given and the echo question interpretation "What did you say?") The idiom *so what?* is a conventional way of expressing, none too politely, a lack of interest in what has just been said: the meaning is "What is the relevance/significance of that?".

What about? and *what if?*

[26] i A: *The car's in fine shape now.* B: *What about the tyres?*
ii A: *I've invited Peter.* B: *And what about Paul?*
iii A: *You know that knife I found?* B: *Yes, what about it?*
iv *What about a game of squash?*
v *What if we can't get back in time?*

What about is often used to introduce a new but related topic, as in [i–ii]; in [i] it serves to challenge what has been said, the implicature being that the judgement fails, or may have failed, to take account of the tyres. In [iii] the topic marked by *about* is not new, but old information: I'm asking you to say something about the topic that you introduced. *What about* can also be used to make suggestions, as in [iv]; *how about* could be substituted for it here, and also in [i–ii]. The interpretation of [v] is along the lines of "What will happen / will you do / shall I do if . . . ?"

7.9 Upward percolation of the interrogative feature: interrogative phrases

The markers of the open interrogative clause type are in the first instance words. We must also recognise a category of interrogative phrase, however, for it is whole phrases, not single words, that are affected by the fronting rule:

[27] a. *She took <u>which car</u>?* b. *<u>Which car</u> did she take?*

In [a] *which car* remains in situ, while in [b] it is fronted, but we can't have fronting of *which* alone: **Which did she take car?* We will say, therefore, that *which* is an interrogative word and *which car* an interrogative phrase. And since *which car* is an interrogative phrase by virtue of containing the interrogative word *which*, we can speak metaphorically of the interrogative feature as percolating upwards from the word *which* to the phrase *which car*.

This is a useful way of speaking because such upward percolation may involve more than one step, as we see from such examples as:

[28] a. *<u>What size shoes</u> do you take?* b. *<u>How big a hole</u> did it make?*

[29]

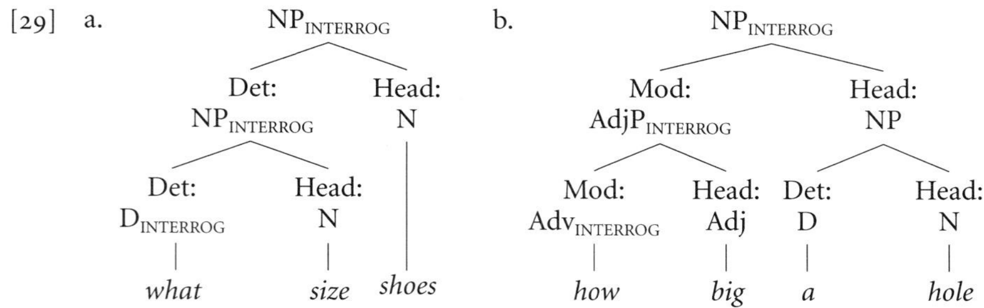

Both involve two steps. In [a] the interrogative feature first percolates up from the word *what* to the NP *what size*, and then from this to the higher NP *what size shoes*. Similarly in [b]: from *how* to the AdjP *how big*, and thence to the NP *how big a hole*. There may, therefore, be one interrogative phrase within another, and when fronting applies it is the topmost one that is fronted: compare **What size do you take shoes?*; **How big did it make a hole?*

The question then arises: what determines how far upwards the interrogative feature percolates? How far up the tree do we have to go before we come to the **maximal** interrogative phrase, i.e. the one that is fronted? The examples in [28] share two properties:

[30] i The maximal interrogative phrase is the highest phrase beginning with the interrogative word.
ii The maximal interrogative phrase is an element of clause structure.

In [28a], for example, *what size shoes* is higher in the tree than the other phrase beginning with *what*, namely *what size*; and *what size shoes* is a clause element, namely object, whereas *what size* is not (it is determiner in NP structure).

Usually, both these properties obtain – but not always:

[31] i	<u>*In which drawer*</u> *do you keep the bank statements?*	[fronted preposition]
ii	<u>*Which drawer*</u> *do you keep the bank statements* <u>*in*</u>*?*	[stranded preposition]

In [i] the fronted interrogative phrase is *in which drawer*; again the upward percolation involves two steps, from *which* to the NP *which drawer*, and then from this to the PP *in which drawer*. But although property [30ii] applies (*in which drawer* is a locative complement), property [30i] does not, for the maximal interrogative phrase begins with the preposition. In [31ii], by contrast, the upward percolation stops at the NP *which drawer*, which begins with the interrogative word but is not an element of clause structure, being complement of the preposition *in*. Here, then, the preposition is stranded in situ while its complement is fronted. In general, informal style conforms to [30i], formal style to [ii].

We should also note that a PP containing an interrogative phrase as complement will not always be an element of clause structure – it may be the complement in NP or AdjP structure, as in:

[32] i	a.	<u>*Which country*</u> *was she* <u>*the president of*</u>*?*	[informal]
	b.	<u>*Of which country*</u> *was she* <u>*the president*</u>*?*	[formal]
	c.	*<u>*The president of which country*</u> *was she?*	
ii	a.	<u>*What subjects*</u> *are you* <u>*interested in*</u>*?*	[informal]
	b.	<u>*In what subjects*</u> *are you* <u>*interested*</u>*?*	[formal]
	c.	*<u>*Interested in what subjects*</u> *are you?*	

Informal style continues to follow principle [30i], but the formal style conforms to neither [30i] nor [30ii]: it represents a compromise between the two principles. If the highest phrase beginning with the interrogative word is complement of a preposition, upwards percolation proceeds towards an element of clause structure as far as is consistent with the fronted interrogative phrase being a PP. This rather complex formulation is needed to exclude examples like [32ic/iic], where the inadmissibly fronted interrogative phrase is not a PP, while nevertheless allowing such structures as:

[33] *To the daughter of which famous statesman was he engaged?*

Here the fronted interrogative phrase is not the PP containing *which famous statesman* as complement, but the next higher PP. Upward percolation of the interrogative feature here involves four steps: from *which* to the NP *which famous statesman*, then to the *of* PP, then to the NP *the daughter of which famous statesman*, and finally to the fronted PP itself. The contrast between the fronted and stranded preposition constructions applies much more widely than in interrogatives, and is discussed in more detail in Ch. 7, §4.1.

7.10 Upward percolation of the question variable: the questioned element

The upward percolation of the grammatical feature interrogative has an analogue at the semantic/pragmatic level, as illustrated in:

[34] A: *Which team do you support?* B: *United.*

From a grammatical point of view, as we have seen, the fronting rule applies to the whole NP *which team*, not just to the interrogative word *which*. Similarly, from the point of view of the meaning, the answer substitutes *United* for the whole NP *which team*. We will therefore use the same metaphor, and speak of the question variable as percolating upwards from the interrogative word to the phrase containing it, and we will refer to *which team* as the **questioned element**, the one for which the answer provides a replacement, giving a value for the variable.

Although there is this similarity between form and meaning, quite extensive differences are to be found in the way the upward percolation works at the two levels. One small difference applies, in fact, to example [34], for a very limited subset of answers to A's question involve replacement of the interrogative determinative alone: *this team*, *your team*, etc. We will consider the major differences between syntactic and semantic upward percolation under three headings: determinative *whose*, PPs, and predications.

(a) Determinative *whose*

[35] A: *Whose father is on duty today?* B. *Kim's.*

The answer, without ellipsis, is *Kim's father is on duty today*, where it is just *whose* that is replaced. The syntactic interrogative phrase is *whose father*, but the semantic questioned element is just *whose*. Note that *Mr Roberts* is not a possible answer, even in a context where it is known that Mr Roberts is Kim's father. With determinative *whose*, upward percolation is obligatory at the syntactic level, but barred at the semantic level.

(b) PPs

[36] A: *To whom are you referring? / Who are you referring to?*
B: (*I'm referring to*) *your mother.*

The answer retains the preposition, making a substitution just for its NP complement. This is the usual case: in general there is no semantic percolation into a PP – and hence it is in the informal preposition stranding construction that we find the closer match between form and meaning.

There are nevertheless some exceptions, cases where the answer involves replacement of the whole PP:

[37] i a. A: *What are you closing the window for?*
B: (*I'm closing the window*) *because I'm cold* / *to cut out the noise.*
b. A: *What's the new boss like?*
B: (*The new boss is*) *quite pleasant.*
ii a. A: *Under what conditions would you take on the job?*
B: (*I'd take on the job*) *if they gave me adequate support staff.*
b. A: *In what way can I help you?*
B: (*You can help me*) *by minding the children for a couple of hours.*

In [i] we have the idioms *what...for* and *what... like*: the answers must provide a replacement for the whole PP. The same applies with certain very general PPs, such as *under what circumstances/conditions* and *in what way* in [ii], but this time the syntax matches, having obligatory percolation into the PP.

(c) Predication

[38] i A: *What did you do?* B: *I called the police.*
ii A: *What happened?* B: *The car rolled into the ditch.*

The syntactic interrogative phrase is *what*, but the semantic questioned element is in [i] the VP, the predicate, and in [ii] the whole clause. There is no verb among the interrogative words, and hence to question the predication it is necessary to use a very general verb together with the pronoun *what*; syntactically there is no percolation beyond the *what*, but semantically there is. *Do* is used to question the predicate, *happen* the whole clause. Just as the answer in [34] implicates "United is a team", so the answer in [38i] implicates "For me to call the police is for me to do something". This is why *I was older than my sister*, *I was seen by one of the guards*, etc., are not possible answers: the implicit propositions "For me to be older than my sister / seen by one of the guards is for me to do something" are not true. An answer to such a *do* question must denote a situation which is dynamic rather than static, and one in which the subject-referent has an agentive role (cf. Ch. 17, §7.6).[14] Similarly, the answer in [38ii] implicates "For the car to roll into the ditch is for something to happen". *Happen* also denotes a dynamic situation, but it need not be agentive; *I was older than my sister* is thus again not a possible answer to [38ii], but *I was seen by one of the guards* is.

Such predication questions may include specification of various circumstances of the situation denoted by the answer: *What did you do in the morning?*; *What happened to make you change your mind?* They may also include specification of an argument:

[39] i A: *What did you do to/with my hat?* B: *I dropped it in the mud / put it away.*
ii A: *What happened to your father?* B: *He was taken away for questioning.*

[14] An exception is the idiom '*What **be** X doing Y?*' (where *Y* is a locative or a gerund-participial): *What are your gloves doing on my desk?*; *What are you doing sleeping in my bed?* These convey "Why are your gloves on my desk?" and "How come you are sleeping in my bed?" – with the suggestion that the gloves shouldn't be there, that you shouldn't be sleeping in my bed.

With *do*, the preposition *to* indicates that the complement NP is associated with an affected, patient role, as in B's *I dropped it in the mud*. Another answer here might be *I sat on it*, where 'it' does not inherently have an affected, patient role, but is interpreted as having such a role because for *I sat on it* to be an answer to *What did you do to my hat?* implicates "To sit on your hat is to affect it". *With* involves disposing of something, putting it somewhere: *I put it away / gave it to Kim*. With *happen*, *to* indicates a less specific participant role: it will often be an affected patient, as in B's answer in [ii], but it can also be an agent (*He escaped through the bathroom window*). *Become* can be used with an *of* phrase in a related way (A: *What became of his sister?* B: *She went to China*).

7.11 Open interrogatives as an unbounded dependency construction

The open interrogative is what is known as an **unbounded dependency construction**, as illustrated in the following examples:

[40] i *What$_i$ did he [buy __$_i$]?*
ii *What$_i$ did she [say [he bought __$_i$]]?*
iii *What$_i$ do you [think [she said [he bought __$_i$]]]?*
iv *What$_i$ do you [think [she said [he wanted [to buy __$_i$]]]]?*

In all of these *what* occupies initial (prenuclear) position in the open interrogative clause but its core role is that of object of the verb *buy*. The *buy* clause is embedded within the interrogative clause and it will be evident from these examples that there is no limit as to how deeply embedded it may be. The paired brackets indicate clause boundaries, and by adding verbs that take clausal complements we can increase the number of clause boundaries between *what* and *buy*. The dependency relation between *what* and *buy* is thus unbounded: there is no grammatical limit on how many clause boundaries may separate them.

There are a number of constructions of this kind, including exclamatives and relatives. We discuss the general properties of this kind of construction in Ch. 12, §7, and here we will merely note that we show the relationship between *what* and *buy* by co-indexing *what* with a **gap** (__) located in the position of direct object to *buy* (cf. Ch. 2, §2). This gap pre-empts the filling of the direct object function by any other NP: **What did he buy some meat?*, etc.

7.12 Ambiguities concerning the role of an interrogative phrase in complex clauses

Two kinds of ambiguity can arise when an open interrogative clause has another clause embedded as complement within it. One concerns the core role of a fronted interrogative phrase, the other the interrogative role of an interrogative phrase that remains in situ.

Core role ambiguities resulting from fronting

Examples such as the following are ambiguous in that the interrogative phrase may have its core role in either of two clauses:

[41] i a. *When did they decide to leave?*
b. *When*$_i$ *did they* [*decide* [*to leave*] __$_i$]? [gap in *decide* clause]
c. *When*$_i$ *did they* [*decide* [*to leave* __$_i$]]? [gap in *leave* clause]
ii a. *Why do you think he lied?*
b. *Why*$_i$ *do you* [*think* [*he lied*] __$_i$]? [gap in *think* clause]
c. *Why*$_i$ *do you* [*think* [*he lied* __$_i$]]? [gap in *lie* clause]

In [ia] *when* may question the time of deciding ("When did they make the decision to leave?") or the time of leaving ("What was the time of leaving they decided on?"). Similarly in [iia] *why* can be reason adjunct in the *think* clause ("What makes you think he lied?") or in the *lie* clause ("In your opinion, why did he lie?").

Such ambiguities most often involve adjunct interrogative phrases, as in these examples. Under quite restricted conditions, however, ambiguity may arise involving a more central core function:

[42] i *Who do you expect to play?*
ii *Who*$_i$ *do you* [*expect* __$_i$ [*to play*]]? [gap as object of *expect*]
iii *Who*$_i$ *do you* [*expect* [*to play* __$_i$]]? [gap as object of *play*]

The question here is ambiguous according as it concerns your expectation as to who will play or who you will play: answers for the two interpretations might be respectively *I expect Jones to play* and *I expect to play Jones.* For reasons given in Ch. 14, §2, we analyse *I expect Jones to play* as having *Jones* as object of *expect*, whereas *I expect to play Jones* has *Jones* as object of *play*: on this account, therefore, the ambiguity in [i] results from the fact that *who* can be syntactically object of *expect* or of *play*.

The ambiguity in [42] is clearly dependent on the interrogative phrase being fronted, since the core positions are different. This is typically not so with the adjunct examples. The ambiguity of [41ia], for example, is found also in *They decided to leave when?*, just as it is in declarative *They decided to leave yesterday.*

Interrogative role ambiguities in multi-variable constructions

The ambiguities illustrated above have to do with the core role of an interrogative phrase but it is also possible for there to be ambiguity concerning its interrogative role. Such ambiguity can arise when one open interrogative clause is embedded within another and at least one of them is multi-variable:

[43] i *Who knows which universities offer the best courses in which subjects?*
ii *Kim knows which universities offer the best courses in medicine and Pat knows which universities offer the best courses in law.*
iii *Kim knows which universities offer the best courses in which subjects.*

The core functions of the three interrogative phrases in [i] are clear: *who* belongs in the *know* clause as subject, while *which universities* and *which subjects* belong in the *offer* clause as subject of the clause and complement of *in* respectively. The issue is: which of the two clauses is the multi-variable one?

Who clearly expresses a variable with respect to the *know* clause: we will say that *who* (or, more precisely, the interrogative component of *who*) has the *know* clause as its scope. Similarly for *which universities* in the *offer* clause: it has the *offer* clause as its scope. The issue can thus be put more specifically as: what is the scope of the interrogative component of *which subjects*? Is the variable it expresses associated with the *know* clause (making the main clause the multi-variable one) or with the *offer* clause (making the subordinate clause the multi-variable one)? The ambiguity can be brought out by using variables just for the propositional content of the *know* clause:

[44] i "*x* knows which universities offer the best courses in *y*"
ii "*x* knows which universities offer the best courses in which subjects"

Thus [i] corresponds to the reading where the *know* clause is multi-variable: this is the one for which [43ii] is an answer, since it supplies paired values {"Kim", "medicine"} and {"Pat", "law"} for the pair of variables {"*x*", "*y*"}. Different people are assumed to be informed about different fields, and the answer supplies a pairing of people with fields. By contrast, [44ii] matches the reading where the *know* question is a single-variable one: this is the one for which [43iii] is an answer, since it supplies a value for the variable "*x*". Here the presupposition is that someone is informed about the whole range of fields, and the answer identifies such a person.

From a formal point of view, the ambiguity is attributable to the fact that only one interrogative phrase can undergo fronting. In single-variable constructions the fronting of the interrogative phrase shows clearly which clause its interrogative role is associated with:

[45] i *She will say <u>what</u>$_i$ she saw _$_i$.* [*see* clause interrogative]
ii *<u>What</u>$_i$ will she say she saw _$_i$?* [*will* clause interrogative]

In both [i] and [ii] *what* is at the front of the clause over which it has scope. In multi-variable constructions only one phrase can have its scope marked in this way: the scope of the other(s) is not overtly signalled. Hence the scope ambiguity of [43i].

7.13 Modification of interrogative words

Interrogative phrases may contain a limited range of modifiers, as illustrated in:

[46] i a. [*What <u>ever</u>*] *did you do that for?* b. [*Why <u>ever</u>*] *would he do that?*
ii a. [*What <u>the hell</u>*] *is she trying to do?* b. [*Who <u>on earth</u>*] *can that be?*
iii a. [*Who <u>else</u>*] *will be there?* b. [*What <u>exactly</u>*] *do you mean?*

The items in [i–ii] express surprise or bafflement, and hence suggest that the speaker does not know the answer to the question. They tend to emphasise the open-endedness of the set of possible values for the questioned variable; as a result they are hardly compatible with *which*, for this involves selection from an identifiable set. They do not contribute to the propositional meaning, and we will refer to them as **emotive modifiers**. Variants of *hell* in [iia] are *heck, blazes, deuce, dickens, fuck*, etc.

These modifiers are constrained to occur immediately after an interrogative word in head, not dependent, function: *[*What <u>on earth</u> reason*] *could they have for rejecting it?*; *[*How <u>ever</u> much*] *did that cost?* The interrogative phrase must be in initial position: contrast **And after that you went* [*where <u>the hell</u>*]*?* Except in combination with *why*, *ever* is found written as part of the interrogative word: *Whatever did you do that for?*[15]

Interrogatives are among those words that accept *else* as postmodifier, as in [46iiia]. *Else* is semantically like *other* ("who other than those mentioned"); it licenses a *than* complement (*What else than this?*). The adverbs *exactly* and *precisely* may follow the head, as in [46iiib], or precede: *Just exactly who do you think you are?*

[15] The more conservative usage manuals say that *ever* should always be written separately in this interrogative construction, but that is in conflict with actual usage. This *ever* is semantically distinct from the *ever* that occurs – always as part of a compound – in fused relatives ([*<u>Whoever</u> said that*] *was mistaken*) and the exhaustive conditional construction (*I won't sell* [*<u>however</u> much you offer*]).

7.14 Complex-intransitive interrogatives: S–P–PC vs PC–P–S

A main clause of the form 'NP$_1$ *be* NP$_2$', where NP$_1$ is interrogative, may have one of two structures: S–P–PC or PC–P–S. Compare:

[47] S P PC / PC P S
a. *Who is editor of the magazine?* b. *What time is it?*

Example [a] represents the default order of clause elements, while [b] arises through fronting of the interrogative phrase and subject–auxiliary inversion. Answers might be, respectively, *Kim is* and *It's five o'clock*, with the interrogative phrase replaced by the subject *Kim* or predicative complement *five o'clock*. The structures can be distinguished by manipulating them in any of the three ways shown in:

[48] INTERROGATIVE S / INTERROGATIVE PC
i a. *Who will be editor of the magazine?* b. *What time will it be?*
ii a. *Who did he say was editor of the magazine?* b. *What time did he say it was?*
iii a. *Ask who is editor of the magazine.* b. *Ask what time it is.*

In [i] we have added modal *will*, so that the positions of *editor of the magazine* in [a] and *it* in [b] are now differentiated: *it* occurs after auxiliary *will*, indicating that it is subject, while *editor of the magazine* follows *be*, showing that subject–auxiliary inversion has not applied. In [ii] the interrogative phrase has its core role in a subordinate clause: in [a] it is linked to a gap in subject function (*Who$_i$ did he say* [__$_i$ *was editor of the magazine*]*?*), and in [b] to a gap in predicative complement function (*What time$_i$ did he say* [*it was* __$_i$]*?*). In [iii] the interrogative clauses are subordinate, so subject–auxiliary inversion is inapplicable: as a result it is clear that the subject of *is* is *who* in [a] but *it* in [b].

Example [47a] is itself unambiguous, as the post-verbal NP lacks the determiner that it would need if it were in subject function. Other features that may clearly signal the structure are verb agreement and case:

[49] INTERROGATIVE S / INTERROGATIVE PC
a. *Which is me?* b. *Which am I?*

Here *is* agrees with the subject *which* in [a], while *am* agrees with the subject *I* in [b]. Accusative *me* can only be PC; nominative *I* can occur as subject or (in formal style) as PC and hence does not serve to distinguish the structures. *Which is him?* is therefore S–P–PC, while *Which is he?* is ambiguous.

Ascriptive and specifying *be*

Where *be* is interpreted ascriptively, the PC–P–S structure is somewhat more likely, but it will be pragmatically clear from the content which NP is subject:

[50] i *Who is a friend of John's?* [interrogative S (S–P–PC)]
ii *What is your uncle?* [interrogative PC (PC–P–S)]

These may be glossed roughly as "Who belongs in John's circle of friends?" and "What does your uncle do?"

Where *be* is used in the specifying sense, either structure will generally be possible, and it will usually make no significant difference whether it is taken as one or the other:

[51] *What was the cause of the delay?* [PC–P–S or S–P–PC]

The tests of [48] allow either analysis: compare *What do you think was the cause of the delay?* or *What do you think the cause of the delay was?*; *We asked what was the cause of the delay* or *We asked what the cause of the delay was*; and so on.

8 Exclamatives and exclamations

8.1 The syntax of exclamatives

Exclamatives, we have said, are marked by one or other of the exclamative words *how* and *what*. These enter into the structure of an exclamative phrase, which is fronted when it is not subject:

[1]		EXCLAMATIVE SUBJECT	EXCLAMATIVE NON-SUBJECT
	i	a. *How much remains to be done!*	b. *How she hated it!*
	ii	a. *What strange people inhabit these parts!*	b. *What a disaster it was!*

Where the exclamative phrase is subject, the order is the same as in matching declaratives: compare *Much remains to be done* and *Strange people inhabit these parts.* Where the exclamative phrase is non-subject, the fronting is obligatory: there is no exclamative analogue of open interrogatives like *And the results of the examination were what?*

Like the open interrogative (cf. §7.11), the exclamative is an unbounded dependency construction, so that the initial exclamative phrase can be linked with a gap in a subordinate clause embedded within the exclamative clause, as in:

[2] i *How impossibly polite*$_i$ *she expected them [to be* $\_\__i$*]!*
ii *What a waste of time*$_i$ *they thought [it was likely [to be* $\_\__i$*]]!*

As evident from the above examples, the exclamative feature percolates upwards in the same way as the interrogative feature; in [1iia], for example, it goes from *what* to the NP *what strange people*, while in [2i] it goes from *how* to the AdvP *how impossibly*, and thence to the AdjP *how impossibly polite.* It may percolate up into a PP or stop at the NP complement, leaving the preposition stranded:

[3] i *With what unedifying haste he accepted the offer!* [fronting of preposition]
ii *What unsavoury people he associates with!* [stranding of preposition]

Ambiguity between exclamative and open interrogative

How and *what* can be either exclamative or interrogative, and in abstraction from the prosody/punctuation such examples as [1ia/iia] are ambiguous between an exclamative reading ("A remarkably large amount remains to be done"; "Remarkably strange people inhabit these parts") and an open interrogative reading ("What is the amount that remains to be done?"; "Who are the strange people that inhabit these parts?"). Where the clause is not ambiguous, as in the other examples given above, this is due to the distributional differences between exclamative and interrogative *how* and *what* or to differences in the order of elements in the clause. We will consider the exclamative words in the next two subsections, and then take up the issue of order.

Whereas there are a fair number of interrogative words, the exclamative class has only two members, *how* and *what*: clauses like *Who remains to be seen?* or *Which strange people inhabit these parts?* are unambiguously interrogative. Like interrogative words, exclamative *how* and *what* have a dual role: on one dimension they are markers of exclamative clause type, but they also have what we are calling a core role. And in their core role they show some differences from their interrogative counterparts in both grammar and meaning.

8.1.1 Exclamative *how*

We will consider two uses of *how*, both adverbial; the first is closely parallel to interrogative *how*, the second quite different.

(a) Modifying an adjective, degree determinative, or adverb

How commonly functions as a degree modifier. Compare the following exclamative and interrogative examples:

[4]	EXCLAMATIVE	OPEN INTERROGATIVE
i	a. *How tall they are!*	b. *How tall are they?*
ii	a. *How much time we wasted!*	b. *How much time did we waste?*
iii	a. *How quickly it grows!*	b. *How quickly does it grow?*
iv	a. *How very tactful he is!*	b. **How very tactful is he?*

In both constructions we are concerned with degree: with exclamative *how* the degree is remarkably great, with interrogative *how* it is to be indicated in the answer. Two differences are to be noted. In the first place, as illustrated in [iv], exclamative *how* can modify another degree modifier such as *very*, *absolutely*, *remarkably*, etc., whereas this is not possible with interrogative *how*. Secondly, while [ia] says that they are tall (remarkably tall), [ib] does not presuppose that they are tall, only that they have some degree, small or large, on the scale of tallness.

(b) Modifying a verb

[5]		
i	a. *How they deceived her!*	b. *How did they deceive her?*
ii	a. *How I hated it!*	b. #*How did I hate it?*

Here we find a sharp difference: exclamative *how* is again concerned with degree, whereas interrogative is rarely used in that way (cf. §7.7 above). Exclamative [ia] means "They deceived her greatly / to a remarkable degree or extent", while interrogative [ib] means "By what means / In what way did they deceive her?"

8.1.2 Exclamative *what*

What occurs in NPs with a following noun head: there is no exclamative counterpart to the interrogative *what* of *What did they bring with them?* In NPs with a noun head, we find the following patterns:

[6]	EXCLAMATIVE	OPEN INTERROGATIVE	
i	a. *What a game it was!*	b. *What game was it?*	[count singular]
ii	a. *What games he played!*	b. *What games did he play?*	[plural]
iii	a. *What music he played!*	b. *What music did he play?*	[non-count]

With count singulars, the NPs are overtly distinct, as shown in [i]: the exclamative has *what a*, the interrogative just *what*. In other cases, i.e. with plurals and non-count singulars, as in [ii–iii], there is no overt distinction in the form of the NP itself. We take interrogative *what* to be a determinative functioning as determiner; exclamative *what*, by contrast, is an adjective functioning as external or internal modifier (see Ch. 5, §§7.1.3, 12).

Interrogative *what* is concerned with identity: answers to questions [6iia/iiia] will identify the games/music (e.g. *He played cricket and tennis / Schubert's octet*). Exclamative *what*, by contrast, is concerned with quality and degree: [iia/iiia] indicate that the games/music he played were remarkable for their quality (though whether the speaker approves or disapproves is not indicated: the quality may be remarkably good or remarkably bad). However, if the head noun is gradable, the difference is like that described above for *how* in [4i–iii]: compare *What a size it was!* (its size was remarkable) and *What size was it?*

Differences between exclamative *what* and *how*

Style

How is associated with a somewhat formal style, especially in main clauses: *How well she plays!*, for example, is appreciably more formal than *What a fine player she is!*

Distribution

What occurs only as modifier in NP structure. *How* modifies adjectives, degree determinatives, adverbs, and verbs; it does not function immediately in NP structure, but phrases containing it can occur as external modifier in count singular NPs. (The distributional difference is similar to that between *such* and *so*: see §8.3.) Compare, then, the following exclamative phrases, which might occur in such a frame as '__ *we have on our hands!*'

		a.	b.	
[7]	i	*what a difficult problem*	*how difficult a problem*	[count singular]
	ii	*what difficult problems*	**how difficult problems*	[plural]
	iii	*what difficult work*	**how difficult work*	[non-count]

Although *what* is not directly in construction with the adjective *difficult*, it nevertheless indicates a remarkable degree of the property expressed by it, so that with count singulars the meaning of [a] is effectively the same as that of [b]. For plurals and non-count singulars, only the *what* construction is available.

8.1.3 Position of the subject

The normal position for the subject in exclamatives is before the predicator. A major grammatical difference between main clause exclamatives and open interrogatives is thus that whereas fronting of an interrogative phrase is obligatorily accompanied by subject–auxiliary inversion, fronting of an exclamative phrase is not:

[8] EXCLAMATIVE / OPEN INTERROGATIVE

a. *What a mistake they made!* b. *What mistake did they make?*

Subject–auxiliary inversion in exclamatives

However, subject–auxiliary inversion is available as an option in exclamatives, though it is relatively infrequent and characteristic of fairly literary style:

[9] i *How much clearer does it seem now that you have explained it yourself!*
ii *How rarely does one see such chivalry nowadays!*
iii *What a row would there have been if they had known you were here!*

The effect of course is to make the structure more like an interrogative, so that from a grammatical point of view there will often be ambiguity as to clause type. In abstraction from the prosody/punctuation, for example, [9i] can be either exclamative ("How much clearer it now seems") or interrogative ("To what extent does it now seem clearer?").

Example [iii] is unambiguously exclamative because *what* is here in a count singular NP, where the constructions are distinct. Inversion is not possible with *how* when it is modifying the verb, as in [5ia] (*How they deceived her!*): the inverted *How did they deceive her?* is unambiguously interrogative.

When the clause is grammatically ambiguous, it is not always as clear as one might expect which is the contextually appropriate reading. Consider, for example:

[10] *How often have I told you not to put your feet on the sofa!*

The most salient interpretation of this is as a rebuke and directive ("Don't put your feet on the sofa"), but in spite of the exclamatory prosody/punctuation this corresponds to the interrogative reading. In this interpretation the force at the direct level is that of question, but it is a rhetorical question which indirectly conveys "I have told you very many times not to put your feet on the sofa"; this is close to the meaning of an exclamative, but not quite the same. An unco-operative addressee could respond with, say, *forty-five times*, thereby answering the question at the direct level. Note, moreover, the clear style difference between [10] and [9ii]: the latter suggests the rather formal style that is characteristic of exclamative *how*, whereas [10] does not.

Subject postposing

It is also possible for the subject to be postposed when the exclamative phrase is an adjectival predicative:

[11] *How great would have been her disappointment if she had known what they had actually thought!*

8.1.4 Verbless exclamatives

An exclamative clause often consists of just the exclamative phrase (or of this plus a coordinator or the like), normally an NP or an AdjP:

[12] *What nonsense! What an insensitive way to behave! What a strange thing for him to say! How fantastic! How incredibly unlucky!*

The infinitival clauses here are relatives. The exclamative phrase is interpreted as a predicative complement, with *be* and the subject understood: "What nonsense that is!". It is also possible to omit just *be*, with an overt subject in final position: *What a terrible thing, that 'wailing wall' in Berlin!*

Another frequent verbless construction consists of an exclamative phrase followed by a declarative content clause, infinitival, or (less frequently) a gerund-participial:

[13] *How strange that nobody noticed the error! What a coincidence that they were on the same bus! How kind of you to let me know! What a nuisance having to do them all again!*

These can be regarded as involving the omission of *it* + *be*: compare *How strange it is/was that nobody noticed the error!* The subordinate clause thus functions as extraposed subject – and the infrequency of the gerund-participial reflects the fact that such clauses do not readily undergo extraposition.[16]

[16] An idiomatic verbless exclamative is *and how!*, added (in informal style) to what has just been said (by the same or another speaker) as an exclamatory intensifier: *She can certainly play the piano! – And how!*

8.2 Meaning and use of exclamative main clauses

Exclamative utterances normally have the force of exclamatory statements. Consider again our initial example:

[14] *How much remains to be done!* (=[1ia])

At the most general level of classification we include this in the statement family because of its resemblance to the straightforward statement *Much remains to be done.* The meaning of the latter is contained within that of the exclamative.

Nevertheless, exclamative utterances are by no means prototypical statements. The exclamatory component gives them a strongly subjective quality, so that they are not presented as statements of fact. Rather, they express the speaker's strong emotional reaction or attitude to some situation. The exclamative indicates that the situation obtains (e.g. [14] indicates that much remains to be done), and this is the statement component of the meaning – but this component is backgrounded relative to the emotive exclamatory component. Several more specific properties follow from this general account.

In the first place, because the statement component is backgrounded it is presented as uncontroversial, not at issue. Thus one normally doesn't envisage disagreement, dispute. This is reflected in the use of interrogative tags:

[15] i *What a disaster it was, wasn't it!* [reversed polarity tag]
ii ?*What a disaster it was, was it!* [constant polarity tag]

Example [i] (with falling intonation on the tag) is possible because such a tag can be used to seek agreement – but note that it is agreement with the subjective attitude (that the situation is remarkable), not just the statement component. However, [ii] would not normally be used because the constant polarity tag in this case would be seeking acknowledgement of the statement component, which is inconsistent with its background status.

Secondly, exclamatives do not give answers to (non-echo) questions: *How I enjoyed it!* is not an answer, and a very unlikely response, to *Did you enjoy it?* In part, this relates to what we have said about the backgrounded status of the statement component: information giving the answer to an explicit question will normally be foregrounded. But a more important reason is the semantic one that exclamative *how* and *what* express variables rather than constants. The construction indicates that the value of the variable is remarkable, but does not explicitly specify what it is. This is why exclamative utterances are not naturally assessed as true or false. Thus one would hardly express agreement by saying *Yes, that's true*: more normal would be something like *Yes, indeed*, or – where the exclamative phrase is non-subject – a reduced interrogative, such as *Yes, didn't she!* in response to *How she hated it!*

The resemblance between exclamatives and open interrogatives

The property of expressing a variable is of course common to both exclamative and interrogative uses of *how* and *what*, and it is a very widespread phenomenon in the world's languages that exclamative clauses bear strong formal resemblances to open interrogatives. (Because subject–auxiliary inversion generally does not apply in English exclamatives, their resemblance is greater to subordinate interrogatives, and this too is illustrative of the most common pattern.) We have seen that closed interrogatives like *Wasn't it a disaster!* or *Did she hate it!* are also commonly used as exclamatory statements, but with these the force is indirect: at the direct level, they are questions. In the exclamative construction, however, the exclamatory statement force has been grammaticalised: in spite of the resemblance, exclamatives are grammatically distinct from open interrogatives, as we have noted above, and they do not belong in the semantic category of question.

Exclamatives have a narrower range of uses than the other major clause types. And there are no cases where they are conventionally used with some indirect force, as various kinds of declarative and interrogative are used as indirect directives, or imperatives as components of conditional statements, and so on.

8.3 Non-exclamative exclamations

Not all exclamations take the form of exclamative clauses. The concept of exclamation is, moreover, a somewhat nebulous one, and it is not possible to present a well-defined set of grammatical constructions that express exclamatory meaning; very often, of course, it is signalled prosodically rather than, or as well as, by the lexicogrammatical form. We give here a sample of structures that are characteristically associated with such meaning.

(a) Closed interrogatives

As we have noted, closed interrogatives such as negative *Isn't it cold!* or positive *Is it cold!* can be used as rhetorical questions indirectly conveying exclamatory statements: the implicit meaning is close to that of the positive exclamative *How cold it is!*

(b) *So* and *such*

These words closely match *how* and *what* in their grammatical distribution, except that they are not exclamative and hence the phrase containing them is not obligatorily fronted. Compare, then, the following with [1] above:

[16]	i	a. *So much remains to be done!*	b. *She hated it so!*
	ii	a. *Such strange people inhabit these parts!*	b. *It was such a disaster!*

So resembles *how* in that it can modify an attributive adjective only in count singular NPs with following *a*, while *such* occurs in the three main kinds of NP, like *what*. The following therefore match [7] above, but would not be fronted, so that they might occur in the frame '*We have* __ *on our hands!*':

[17]	i	a. *such a difficult problem*	b. *so difficult a problem*
	ii	a. *such difficult problems*	b. **so difficult problems*
	iii	a. *such difficult work*	b. **so difficult work*

So and *such* are not markers of a distinct clause type since they can occur in any of the major clause types – closed interrogative (*Have you ever seen such chaos?*), open interrogative (*Why do you torment me so?*), imperative (*Don't be such a wet blanket!*), as well as the above declaratives. There is nevertheless a slight difference of meaning in that these non-declarative examples are implicitly comparative ("Have you ever seen such chaos as this?"; "Why do you torment me as you are doing?"; "Don't be such a wet blanket as you are being"), whereas the examples in [16] are not. The non-comparative use is more clearly exclamatory, and does not readily occur in non-declaratives. It is not altogether excluded, however: they can occur in interrogatives used with the indirect force of an exclamatory statement, as in *Haven't they such charming manners!*

(c) Extraposable NPs

NPs with the form *the* + . . . N + integrated relative clause / *of* phrase can stand on their own as exclamations:

[18] i *The money he spends on clothes!*
ii *The cost of these clothes!*
iii *The way he treats his wife!*

We call these 'extraposable NPs' because they can appear in extraposed subject position with predicates such as *amazing*: *It's amazing the money he spends on clothes* / *the cost of these clothes*; *It's a scandal the way he treats his wife*. The verbless examples in [18] are understood in much the same way as these with some generalised exclamatory predicate understood; the attitude implied is usually one of disapproval. An alternative to *the* + N + relative is the fused relative construction: *What some people will do to save a few dollars!* (compare: *The things some people will do . . . !*).

(d) Imprecative retorts

[19] A: *I'll invite them round for dinner.* B: *Like hell you will!*

The structure consists of an expletive + personal pronoun subject + auxiliary with anaphoric ellipsis of the complement.

9 Imperatives and directives

9.1 Subtypes of imperative clauses

The grammatical properties which together define the class of imperative clauses in English were summarised in §2. The most important points are:

[1] i The subject is an optional rather than obligatory element.
ii The verb is in the plain form.
iii Supportive *do* is used in relevant constructions with *be*, not just lexical verbs.

Ordinary imperatives vs *let*-imperatives

The main syntactic division within the class is between **ordinary imperatives** (the default subclass) and ***let*-imperatives**:

[2]	ORDINARY IMPERATIVE	*LET*-IMPERATIVE
i	a. *Open the window.*	b. *Let's open the window.*
ii	a. *Please let us borrow your car.*	b. *Let's borrow Kim's car.*

Let-imperatives are marked by a special use of *let* distinct from the normal use with the sense "allow". *Let* in the "allow" sense is found in all clause types (cf. declarative *He let us borrow his car*), including ordinary imperatives like [iia]. The *let* of [ib] and [iib] has been bleached of this meaning and serves as a marker of this special type of imperative construction.

Subtypes of *let*-imperative: 1st person inclusive vs open

The [b] examples in [2] are, more specifically, **1st person inclusive let-imperatives.** These contain an accusative form of ***we*** which can be, and usually is, contracted to *'s*, and whose reference normally includes the addressee(s) as well as the speaker. In [2ib/iib], for example, I'm proposing that you and I (or one of us) open the window and borrow Kim's car. (The *us* of [2iia], by contrast, is exclusive: it refers to me together with one or more other persons, excluding you.) The special use of *let* is also found in what we call **open *let*-imperatives:**

[3] i *If that is what the premier intends, let him say so.*
ii *Let that be a lesson to you.*
iii *Since I/we/you did most of the work, let me/us/you receive the credit.*

These usually have 3rd person reference, as with *him* and *that* in [i–ii], but in principle the full range of person–number combinations is permitted, as illustrated in [iii].

The 1st person inclusive *let*-imperative is certainly grammatically distinguishable from ordinary imperatives (by the potential contraction of *us* to *'s*), but the status of the open subtype is much more problematic: it could be argued that it simply involves a semantically special use of *let* and is not grammatically distinct from the ordinary imperative construction. It will nevertheless be convenient to treat them separately, after first examining clear cases of ordinary imperatives and then 1st person inclusive *let*-imperatives. (For simplicity we will generally, in discussing ordinary imperatives, leave the 'ordinary' understood.)

9.2 Ordinary imperatives

9.2.1 Omissibility of the subject

The prototypical imperative has no subject – and this of course immediately distinguishes it from most other main clause types. Normally, such clauses are interpreted as though they had *you* as subject: in *Tell her the truth*, for example, it is a matter of you, the addressee(s), telling her the truth. This is reflected in the use of reflexive pronouns in such examples as:

[4] a. *Get yourself/*you a new hat.* b. *Try to leave yourselves/*you plenty of time.*

The choice of the reflexive over the non-reflexive here matches that found in clauses with *you* as subject, such as *You never get yourself/*you a new hat, You always try to leave yourselves/*you plenty of time*, and so on.

Imperatives with overt subject

Imperatives do not always have the subject missing, however. *You* itself can appear as subject, or we may have a 3rd person NP:

[5] i *<u>You be wicket-keeper</u> and I'll bowl.* [2nd person subject]
ii *Somebody get me a screwdriver.* } [3rd person subject]
iii *All those in the front row take one step forward.* }

With a 2nd person subject, *be* is the only verb where the plain form and the present tense are not syncretised; with other verbs, therefore, there is potential ambiguity between imperative and declarative, as in *You give the first lecture.* As an imperative this would be some kind of directive for you to give the first lecture, and as a declarative it would be a statement about what you do (e.g. as part of some scheduled lecture programme). With a 3rd person subject, imperative and declarative will in the singular always have overtly distinct verb-forms, but in the plural again only with *be*. Thus [5ii] contrasts with declarative *Somebody gives me the screwdriver*, whereas [iii] is ambiguous between imperative (with directive force) and declarative (with statement force).[17]

3rd person subjects

The range of possible subjects is more limited in imperatives than in declaratives, though it is questionable how far this is a matter of grammatical rule. The subject must normally have personal denotation, and dummy or clausal subjects are thus categorically ruled out: **There be no more talking*; **That he's over 60 don't be forgotten.* The most likely 3rd person subjects are the compound determinatives (*someone, nobody, everybody*, etc., alone or with dependents – *Everybody over here stay still*; *Anybody with a faulty disk please let me know*), other fused determiner-head constructions with *of you* as complement (*Some/One of you give me a hand with this trunk*; *Those of you who've finished please put up your hands*), and bare plurals (*Passengers on flight QF2 please proceed to Gate 6*; *Gentlemen lift the seat*). Definite NPs with *the* are less likely, but possible (*The boy by the door please turn on the light*), and the same applies to proper names (*Kim move upstage a little*). These 3rd person definites occur somewhat more readily in coordinative constructions (*You and Kim play on the other court*; *You give the first four lectures and the others do the rest*). Personal pronouns other than *you* are very unlikely though they probably cannot be categorically ruled out, especially in the coordinative constructions just illustrated.

2nd person subjects

Given that *you* can be omitted, why is it sometimes retained? One factor is the need to mark contrast. In [5i], for example, *you* contrasts with *I*; compare, similarly, *You do the washing-up tonight please: Kim did it last night.* Where there is no such contrast, the addition of *you* has an emotive effect:

[6] i *(Just) you watch where you put your feet.*
ii *You mind your own business.*
iii *You sit down and have a nice cup of tea; everything is going to be all right.*
iv *You go back and tell him you need more time.*

Very often it contributes to a somewhat impatient, irritated, aggressive, or hectoring effect, as in a natural use of [i–ii]. But [iii–iv] show that it can also have very much the opposite effect of soothing reassurance, encouragement, support. Whether the effect is of the first or the second kind will of course depend on the tone of voice, the content, and the context. What the two cases have in common is perhaps that expression of *you* emphasises the speaker's authority. In the aggressive case, the *you* emphasises that I am telling you, not asking you, to do something. In the reassuring case, I assume the position of one who is assured, one who knows best what to do.

[17] It should be borne in mind that declaratives can be used as indirect directives: directive force is thus no guarantee that an ambiguous clause is construed as imperative. A common way of giving street directions, for example, is illustrated in *You take the first road on the right after the church*, which is normally intended (and pronounced) as a declarative, even though it is (indirectly) a directive. Note that the contextual conditions for an imperative with overt subject would not normally apply to such cases – see the final paragraph of this section.

9.2.2 Subject vs vocative in imperatives

In declarative clauses we find a very sharp grammatical distinction between the subject and a vocative (i.e. the underlined element in *We need to talk this over, my boy* or *Kim, I'm just slipping out to the shops*). One obvious factor is that the subject is obligatory whereas the vocative is optional. It follows that if only one of them is present it can only be the subject. In *Someone in the back row is not in tune*, for example, *someone in the back row* must be subject: there is no possibility of it being vocative.

In imperatives the two functions are less sharply distinct because they are both optional, so that it is possible to have either element without the other:

[7] i *Nobody move.* [subject]
ii *Kim, dear, just come and see what I've found.* [vocative]
iii *Someone in the back row(,) please turn on the fan.* [subject or vocative]

Nobody in [i] is unambiguously subject because a vocative can't be negative, and in [ii] *dear* marks the NP as unambiguously vocative, but in abstraction from punctuation and prosody *someone in the back row* in [iii] could be either.

Apart from the grammatical factor, there is a pragmatic reason why the distinction is less sharply drawn in imperatives than in declaratives. In declaratives subject and vocative are referentially quite independent. There is no intrinsic connection between the subject-referent and the addressee(s): the subject may of course refer to the addressee(s), but it then does so only coincidentally. But in imperatives the subject is always referentially tied to the addressee(s). This is perfectly consistent with the NP being grammatically 3rd person: *somebody* and *all those in the front row* in [5] are also interpreted as "somebody among you", "all those of you in the front row". It follows that with a few exceptions like those in [7i–ii], expressions which have the potential to function as imperative subject can also appear in vocative function, and vice versa.

Single NP in imperatives: subject or vocative?

NP in initial position

Where the NP is initial, vocative and subject will be distinguished prosodically: the vocative is set apart intonationally, whereas the subject is intonationally linked with the predicator; in writing, the vocative, but not the subject, is set off by a comma. The two functions can of course combine, with vocative + subject effectively the only possible order:

[8] i *You at the back(,) please make less noise.* [vocative or subject]
ii *Kim, you be umpire please.* [vocative + subject]

One grammatical difference is that a subject, but not a vocative, can serve as antecedent for a pronoun. Compare:

[9] i *Somebody at the front(,) write your name on the board.* [vocative or subject]
ii *Somebody at the front write their name on the board.* [subject only]

In [i] *your* is deictic, not anaphoric, and hence has no bearing on the status of the initial NP. In [ii], however, *their* is anaphoric to the initial NP, which requires that it be read as subject.

NP in final position

Here the distinction between subject and vocative is somewhat less determinate:

[10] i *Turn the fan on please, somebody.*
ii *Stand up all those who wish to leave.*

Final position is in other clause types a very common one for vocatives, and must surely be allowed in imperatives too. We will thus take *somebody* in [i] to be a vocative, just like that in interrogative *What time is it, somebody?* More problematic is [ii], where the final NP is prosodically integrated into the clause. With declaratives a final vocative need not be prosodically set apart as clearly as an initial one, but it still cannot carry the focal stress as the NP in [ii] can. Moreover it would be possible to have a clear vocative before the verb, as in *Now, children, stand up all those who wish to leave.* On the other hand, declarative subjects are allowed in final position only under very restrictive conditions, and there is certainly no declarative counterpart of [ii] with final subject: **Stood up all those who wished to leave.* The evidence from anaphora is not entirely conclusive. *Put their hands up all those who wish to leave* is less natural than the form with deictic *your*, but it is clearly more acceptable than, say, [9ii] would be if read with the initial NP in vocative function – and in any case its relative unnaturalness could be due to the fact that there are constraints on the use of anaphoric pro-forms when the antecedent follows rather than precedes. On balance, the evidence seems to favour the subject rather than the vocative analysis, but the matter is very far from clear-cut.

9.2.3 Imperatives with auxiliary *do*

Verbal negation

Like clauses of other types, negative imperatives may have the negation associated with the verb (verbal negation) or incorporated within some other element:

[11] i *Don't say anything that could compromise you.* [verbal negation]
ii *Say nothing that could compromise you.* [non-verbal negation]

In verbal negation, imperatives differ from other constructions in requiring the dummy auxiliary *do* unconditionally, not just when there is no other auxiliary present (see Ch. 9, §2.2). Compare, for example:

[12] i *You <u>weren't</u> sitting in that chair when your father returned.* [declarative]
ii *<u>Don't be</u> sitting in that chair when your father returns.* [imperative]

Do in combination with a subject

Imperatives with verbal negation may contain an overt subject; the subject then either precedes or (more often) follows *don't*:

[13]	SUBJECT + *DON'T*	*DON'T* + SUBJECT
i	a. *<u>You</u> <u>don't</u> be so cheeky.*	b. *<u>Don't</u> <u>you</u> be so cheeky.*
ii	a. *<u>Those with a bus to catch</u> <u>don't</u> hesitate to leave.*	b. ?*<u>Don't</u> <u>those with a bus to catch</u> hesitate to leave.*

With *you* the subject-first order is strongly disfavoured, whereas with other, especially longer, subjects, the subject-first order tends to be preferred and examples like [iib] are somewhat marginal. Contrastiveness will tend to favour the subject-second order: *The girls can board now, but don't the boys move until I say so.* The choice may also be determined by the scope of the negative:

[14] i *<u>One of you</u> <u>don't</u> forget to turn off the light.* [narrow scope negation]
ii *<u>Don't</u> <u>one of you</u> forget to sign the register.* [wide scope negation]

One is outside the scope of the negative in [i], inside in [ii]: the meanings can be contrasted as "One of you remember to turn off the light" and "All of you remember to sign the register".

Don't and *do not*

Analytic *do not* occurs as a somewhat more formal variant of inflectional *don't*, except that it is of somewhat doubtful acceptability in constructions like [13i] which have *you* as overt subject. The imperative differs from the interrogative in that the subject cannot come between *do* and *not*. Compare:

[15] i *Don't you tell her!/?* [imperative or interrogative]
ii *Do you not tell her?* [interrogative only]

Emphatic imperatives

Supportive *do* is also used in imperatives to emphasise the positive polarity and again it occurs unconditionally, not just in the absence of an auxiliary, as in non-imperatives:

[16] a. *Do hurry up.* b. *Do be careful.*

Here too it can either follow or precede an overt subject (though this is unlikely to be just *you*):

[17] i *Those with a bus to catch do please feel free to leave.*
ii *Do at least some of you make a commitment to contribute.*

9.2.4 Imperatives as directives

Whereas declarative clauses are prototypically concerned with the truth of propositions, imperatives are prototypically concerned with carrying out some future action. Imperatives are characteristically used as directives, and directives do not have truth values. The issue that arises with a directive is not whether it is true or false, but whether it is (subsequently) complied with. A directive expresses a proposition representing a potential situation: realising or actualising that situation constitutes compliance with the directive.

The terms 'directive' and 'compliance' are to be understood in a broader sense than they have as non-technical terms. There is no everyday word whose normal sense is general enough to embrace the quite wide range of (direct) uses of imperatives: we therefore extend the sense of 'directive' so that it covers not just orders, requests, instructions, and the like but also advice or merely giving permission. Similarly, 'compliance' covers obeying orders, acceding to requests, following advice, or simply doing what one is given permission to do. What is common to the various more specific kinds of directive is that they all 'promote' compliance – with varying degrees of strength, of course. At the stronger end of the spectrum, compliance is required, whereas at the weaker end it is merely accepted: the range of the imperative is therefore comparable to that of the deontic modals *must, should, may/can* together.

We list and illustrate below a sample of directive categories – with the proviso that since illocutionary force depends on the interplay of a whole variety of factors many of the examples could also be used in other ways than those suggested.

(a) Orders, commands, demands

[18] i a. *By the left, quick march!* b. *Get out of my way!*
ii a. *Release all detainees!* b. *Do as you're told!*
iii a. *Keep off the grass.* b. *Don't move!*

With orders, commands, and demands, compliance is required: failure to comply is not countenanced – or is liable to provoke sanctions. For a command, I generally need institutionalised authority to tell you to do something. A demand doesn't have this kind of backing, but I nevertheless forcefully insist on compliance. 'Order' is the most general term for a strong directive; it can cover commands, some demands, and directives issued by some legal authority to the public at large (... *By order of the Council*). A prohibition is an order not to do something.

(b) Requests, pleas, entreaties

[19] i a. *Please help me tidy up.* b. *Kindly lower your voices.*
ii a. *Open the door, will you?* b. *Give me one more chance, I beg you.*

Here I give you the option of not complying: I am asking, not telling – though very often it will be assumed that you will do as you are asked. It is of course possible for me to ask even when I have the authority to tell: I simply do not present myself as invoking the authority to require compliance. The examples in [19] illustrate various ways in which the 'asking' force is commonly signalled: by means of *please* or (less frequently) *kindly*, by an interrogative tag like *will you?*, or by a performative parenthetical like *I beg you.* There are other devices too, such as *just* in *Just hold the hammer for me a moment.*

The distinction between telling and asking is scalar rather than categorical, and many directives could be reported with either verb. For example, if I say to my spouse *Don't forget to buy some milk on the way home* this could lie somewhere in the middle ground, construable as indeterminate between telling and asking. Categories (a) and (b) together have been called 'wilful' directives: it is, with varying strength, my will that you comply.

(c) Advice, recommendations, warnings

[20] i a. *Keep your options open.* b. *Don't put all your eggs in one basket.*
ii a. *Wait until the price is right.* b. *Don't let yourself become too complacent.*
iii a. *Mind the step.* b. *Try your uncle, perhaps.*

These are a kind of non-wilful directive: compliance is not something I will, not for my benefit, but rather something I present as being in your interest. It is then up to you whether you comply or not. Suggestions belong in the same family, though here I am merely putting forward a possible course of action for you to consider: there is not the same accountability as there is with advice, in that I am not expected to be able to justify the action as being the best thing for you to do. Some kinds of warning (e.g. *Look out!*) may be very peripheral to this category in that immediate compliance can be more or less a reflex action.

(d) Instructions and expository directives

[21] i *Insert a cassette as illustrated with its labelled side facing you.*
ii *Dilute 1ml to 20ml with water, and gargle for 30 seconds.*
iii *Blend lemon juice, orange rind, and cornflour and add to the cottage cheese.*
iv *Take the first road on the right after the post office.*
v *Compare these figures with those shown in Table 1 above.*
vi *Take, for example, the case of my uncle.*

These too are non-wilful: compliance is primarily in your interest rather than mine, but is presented as necessary for the achievement of the relevant goal – using some appliance, cooking some dish, finding your way somewhere, etc.

Examples [21v–vi] are what we will call **expository directives**. Directives of this kind are used in various kinds of expository discourse, especially written, to engage the active participation of the addressee (there are many examples in the text of this book). They have it in common with instructions like [i–iv] that compliance will serve the purpose in hand: in this case, following the speaker's exposition.

(e) Invitations

[22] i a. *Come over and see my etchings.* b. *Bring your family too if you like.*
ii a. *Have some more soup.* b. *Feel free to call in at any time.*

These have some similarity with advice in that you can choose whether or not to comply (accept) and doing so is intended to be primarily for your benefit – but it is a matter of what you'd like rather than what is calculated to be in your best interest. Invitations may lie at the boundary between the wilful and non-wilful categories, since compliance may be something I'd like too. Where this is not so, they tend to merge with offers, where the speaker has an initiating and enabling role.

(f) Permission

[23] i a. *Yes, go ahead.* b. *Take as many as you'd like.*
ii a. [Knock at the door] *Come in.* b. *Yes, borrow it by all means.*

The action is something you want to do, but I have the authority to permit or prohibit it. Giving permission promotes compliance in the rather weak sense of not exercising power to stop it or, to put it more positively, removing a potential obstacle.

(g) Acceptance

[24] i *Well, tell her if you want to – it's all the same to me.*
ii *OK, buy it if you insist – it's your money, after all.*
iii *Take it or leave it – it's my final offer.*

This is the weakest kind of directive. Compliance is not something I positively want, but I haven't the authority or power to prevent it; I thus merely express acceptance, perhaps with defiance, perhaps with indifference. As [iii] shows, the acceptance use is not sharply distinct from that where the imperative is more or less equivalent to an exhaustive conditional. Compare, similarly:

[25] i *Say what you like, it won't make any difference.*
ii *Double your offer: I still won't sell.*

It is arguable that the imperatives here have lost all directive force, and that such examples are instances of indirect speech acts, with direct directive + statement indirectly conveying a concessive statement ("Whatever you say, it won't make any difference"; "Even if you double your offer, I still won't sell"). For other indirect uses of imperatives, see [29] and [39–41] below.

9.2.5 Agentivity in imperatives

Prototypically, compliance with a directive with the form of an ordinary imperative is a matter of future action by the addressee(s).

Preference for dynamic VPs

Compliance is a matter of **doing** something. This is why an imperative is likely to have a dynamic rather than a stative VP: *Apply for Australian citizenship* is more natural than *Be Australian* and *Help yourself to some more coffee* more so than *Want some more coffee*. Progressive *be* (like *be* generally) and perfect *have* are stative, and hence relatively infrequent in imperatives. This is especially so with the perfect, where essentially equivalent non-stative constructions of less or at least no greater structural complexity are available – compare:

[26] i *Have finished it before I return.* [perfect: stative *have*]
ii *Have it finished before I return.* [causative: dynamic *have*]
iii *Finish it before I return.* [dynamic *finish*]

Example [ii] uses the dynamic causative *have* rather than the perfect and is much more natural than [i]. This alternative will of course be available only in a limited set of cases (for example, the non-finite complement of *have* must be transitive), but simply dropping the perfect component, as in [iii], is a quite generally available option. The loss of perfect meaning will not normally be significant, because if you comply with [iii] you will necessarily comply with [i] as well.

Agentivity conferred by imperative construction itself

It must be emphasised, however, that there is no grammatical rule excluding inherently stative VPs from imperatives. The imperative construction can itself affect the interpretation of the VP, assigning an agentive role to the subject when it would not have (or not necessarily have) such a role in a corresponding declarative. Compare:

[27] i a. *Kim is patient.* b. *Be patient.*
ii a. *Kim saw what time it was.* b. *See what time it is.*

Declarative [ia] describes a state, and Kim has a non-agentive role, whereas in [ib] the imperative leads us to assign an agentive role to the understood subject-referent: we interpret it as a directive to exercise self-control, to refrain from acting impatiently. Similarly in [ii]: in declarative [a] the salient interpretation describes a happening, with Kim in the non-agentive role of perceiver, while [b] assigns an agentive role: "Find out / Go and look what time it is". Where the normal sense of a predicate is stative, acceptability of the imperative will thus depend on how readily it lends itself to such an agentive reinterpretation. For the earlier *Want some more coffee*, for example, we need the interpretation "Get yourself into the state where you want some more coffee", and this is a pragmatically rather unlikely directive.

Passive imperatives

Because the agentive role is associated with subject function, passive imperatives are relatively infrequent. This reflects the fact that in declaratives whose predicate assigns an agentive role to one of the arguments the argument concerned is aligned with the subject of the active, not the passive. Compare active *Kim attacked him* and passive *He was attacked by Kim*, where only the former has an agentive subject. Thus *Attack him* makes a perfectly natural imperative, but *Be attacked by Kim* does not. Passive imperatives are not ungrammatical, however, for the imperative construction can itself, as we have just seen, confer agentivity on a subject that is not assigned an agentive role by the predicate:

[28] i *Be warned!* ("Heed this warning")
ii *Don't be intimidated.* ("Don't allow yourself to be intimidated")
iii *Get checked out by your own doctor.* ("Get your own doctor to check you out")

Positive passives with *be* are not often found with directive force: [i] has something of the character of a fixed phrase. But negatives lend themselves more readily to such an agentive interpretation, as in [ii] or, say, *Don't be seen* ("Avoid being seen"). *Get* also facilitates an agentive interpretation, as in [iii], where *be* would be unidiomatic. It is more usual, however, to have a reflexive object here (*Get yourself checked out by your own doctor*), but this involves a different construction, one where it is not the imperative matrix clause itself that is passive.

Non-agentive imperatives and indirect speech acts

In certain cases the unnaturalness of an agentive interpretation is associated with the use of the imperative as an indirect speech act:

[29] i *Win $60,000 for an extra $1.10.*
ii *Sleep well. Get well soon. Have a good week-end. Enjoy your holiday.*

Example [i] illustrates a form commonly used in advertising. While it suggests that winning is subject to your control, that is not in fact so (we may assume): what is subject to your control is just paying the extra $1.10, but whether doing so results in your winning $60,000 is a matter of chance. Your role relative to the predicate actually expressed in the verb *win* is therefore non-agentive, and the imperative indirectly conveys another directive where the role is agentive – something like "Spend an extra $1.10 (on your Gold Lotto ticket or whatever) in order to give yourself a chance of winning $60,000".

Imperatives like [29ii] are normally interpreted as wishes. Sleeping well, recovering from an illness, and so on, are situations we do not normally think of as being under our control, and this inhibits a direct interpretation as directives. This use of imperatives as indirect wishes is highly conventionalised, but it is limited to a very narrow range of situations, hardly going beyond the types exemplified here. Note that these illustrate the way indirect speech acts may involve the backgrounding of the direct force without it being totally lost. Although enjoying oneself is generally not thought of as something you can choose to do, your role is not wholly passive, and *enjoy* can certainly be used in imperatives with full directive force (as in *Come on, join in and enjoy yourself*): there seems to be a residue of this directive force in the wishes.

Other non-agentive imperatives are found in constructions with a conditional interpretation: see §9.5.[18]

[18] Controlled compliance is incompatible with past time reference, and imperatives like *Please don't have eaten it* are highly exceptional and again not interpreted as genuine directives. This example might be used in addressing someone not actually present, expressing the hope that they have not eaten something (e.g. because I know it to have been contaminated and am concerned for their safety).

9.3 1st person inclusive *let*-imperatives

9.3.1 Grammatical properties

Dialect differences

This construction involves a specialised use of *let*, but there are dialect differences in the extent to which it has diverged from the ordinary verb *let* meaning "allow". We will therefore distinguish two varieties, Dialects A and B, on the basis of their rejection or acceptance of examples like [30ii]:

[30]		Dialect A	Dialect B
i	*Let's go for a walk.*	✓	✓
ii	%*Let's you and I/me make it ourselves.*	*	✓

Dialect A

This is the more conservative dialect, and here 1st person inclusive *let*-imperatives are analysable as containing the catenative verb *let* together with an NP object and (except in ellipsis) a bare infinitival clause as second complement. The object is *us*, actually or potentially contracted to *'s*, with an interpretation that includes the addressee(s) in the reference along with the speaker: *Let's go for a walk* proposes that you and I go for a walk, not that I go with some third person.[19]

The differences between this construction and an ordinary imperative may be illustrated with reference to the following pair:

[31]	1ST INCLUSIVE *LET*-IMPERATIVE	ORDINARY IMPERATIVE
	a. *Let us / Let's go with her.*	b. *Let her go with you.*

(a) Contraction of *us*

In 1st person inclusives *us* can be contracted to *'s*, whereas in ordinary imperatives, as indeed in all non-imperatives, it can't: *Don't make us/*'s look ridiculous*; *He won't let us/*'s join in.* As it stands, *Let us go with her* is ambiguous between a 1st person inclusive ("I propose that we go with her") and an ordinary imperative ("Allow us to go with her"), but if we reduce the *us* to *'s*, only the first possibility remains. Contraction reduces the pronoun to the status of a clitic (i.e. *let's* is phonologically like a single word); this is the usual form, with uncontracted *us* found only in relatively formal style (cf. *Let us pray*, as said in a church service).

(b) No subject allowed for *let*

The 1st person inclusive doesn't allow *let* to have a subject, whereas the ordinary imperative normally does. Compare **You let's go with her* with the ordinary imperative *You let her go with you.*

(c) Interrogative tags

Ordinary imperatives normally allow the addition of an interrogative tag with *you* as subject; comparable tags with 1st person inclusives have *we*. Compare:

[32] a. *Let's go with her, shall we?* b. *Let her go with you, will you?*

[19] As with the 1st person plural pronoun generally (see Ch. 17, §2.2.2), there are also peripheral uses where *us* refers just to the addressee(s), as when a parent says to a young child, *Now, let's just eat up these carrots*, or just to the speaker, as in the very informal *Let's have a look.*

(d) Scope of negation

Ordinary imperatives with catenative *let* as verb allow negation of either the imperative clause itself or of the infinitival complement, with a corresponding difference in the semantic scope of the negative. Both constructions are possible with 1st person inclusives, but without the semantic scope difference:

[33] i a. *Don't let's go with her.* b. *Don't let her go with you.*
ii a. *Let's not go with her.* b. *Let her not go with you.*

There is a very clear difference in meaning between [ib] and [iib]. In [ib] *let* is inside the scope of negation, so it is a matter of your not allowing something (her going with you); in [iib] the *let* is outside the scope of negation, so it is a matter of your allowing something (her not going with you). There is no comparable semantic difference between [ia] and [iia]. Both would normally be used to propose/suggest that we not go with her: the difference is simply stylistic, with [ia] a little more informal than [iia].

(e) *Let* not omissible in ellipsis

The verb *let* cannot be omitted in ellipsis in 1st person inclusives:

[34] i A: *Let her go with you.* B: *Yes, do. / No, don't.* [ordinary]
ii A: *Let's go with her.* B: **Yes, do.* / **No, don't.* [1st inclusive]

In [i] A addresses the ordinary imperative to some person C and another person B gives an elliptical response understood as "Yes, do let her go with you" or "No, don't let her go with you". But these are not coherent responses to a 1st person inclusive imperative; what we would get in [ii] (from the person to whom the directive was addressed) might be, for the positive, *Yes, let's*, with ellipsis only of *go with her.*

These properties of the 1st person inclusive indicate that *let* has here lost its propositional meaning. It does not contribute to the propositional content, does not help specify what action would constitute compliance with the directive. It serves, rather, as a marker of illocutionary meaning. In Dialect A, however, there is no compelling reason to suggest that there has been a reanalysis of the syntactic structure. The data are compatible with an analysis where *let* is still a catenative verb: it is semantically bleached and partly fossilised in its syntax.

Dialect B

This is the dialect that allows, in informal style, examples like [30ii], *Let's you and I/me make it ourselves.* This would appear to be widely enough used to qualify as acceptable informal style in Standard English.

Syntactically, this construction indicates that the specialisation of *let* has been taken a significant step further. The *'s* is not here replaceable by *us*; for this reason (and also because of the prosody) it is not plausible to treat the NP *you and I/me* as being in apposition to *'s*. It seems clear, rather, that *let* and *'s* have fused syntactically as well as phonologically, and are no longer analysable as verb + object: they form a single word which functions as marker of the 1st person inclusive imperative construction. The NP *you and I/me* will be interpreted not as object of *let* but as subject of the following verb.[20]

[20] Some speakers of Dialect B have a negative construction that provides even stronger evidence of reanalysis: %*Let's don't bother.* This is much less common than the construction with an NP after *let's*, and cannot be regarded as acceptable in Standard English. Its syntactic interest is that it shows conclusively that *let* is no longer construed as a verb: a subjectless *don't* could not appear in the complement of a catenative verb.

9.3.2 Use of 1st person inclusive imperatives

Like ordinary imperatives, 1st person inclusives are normally used as directives – but with a narrower range of subcategories than was illustrated for ordinary imperatives in §9.2.4. Compliance normally involves joint action by speaker and addressee(s), alone or with one or more others. I commit myself to the action and seek your agreement.[21] For this reason, a verbal response is normally expected, indicating agreement or refusal:

[35] A: *Let's go for a walk.*
B: *Okay, just let me put some shoes on. / Not just now: I must finish this letter.*

The force is thus of a proposal for joint action, which the addressee can accept or reject. The speaker's attitude towards compliance can range from strongly wanting it (*Come on, let's get going: the bus leaves in five minutes*) to merely accepting it (*Okay, let's invite Kim as well, if that's what you want*). With expository directives, the 1st person inclusive tends to suggest less inequality between speaker and addressee than the ordinary imperative, and where *us* is contracted it is less formal:

[36] i *Consider now the effect of increasing the velocity.* [ordinary imperative]
ii *Let's consider now the effect of increasing the velocity.* [1st incl *let*-imperative]

This is one use where no verbal response is expected: agreement is taken for granted.

9.4 Open *let*-imperatives

This construction – if it is indeed a syntactically distinct construction – is illustrated in:

[37] i *If he has any evidence to support his allegation, let him produce it.*
ii *Let anyone who thinks they can do better stand for office at the next election.*
iii *If this is what the premier really intends, let him not / don't let him pretend otherwise.*

These differ (in their salient interpretation) from prototypical ordinary imperatives with *let* in that they are not understood as directives to the addressee(s) to allow or permit something. They are roughly paraphrasable with deontic *should*: "he should produce it"; "anyone who thinks they can do better should stand for office"; "he shouldn't pretend otherwise". They can be used where the speaker has no specific addressee(s) in mind, e.g. in newspaper editorials, and the one(s) on whom the obligation is laid need not be among the audience. They are therefore somewhat peripheral members of the speech act category of directives. Nevertheless, they have it in common with more central directives that they define some future action and call for it to be carried out. As in 1st person inclusives, the *let* does not contribute to defining that future action, but serves as an illocutionary marker.

For this reason, it is again not possible to insert *you* as subject, or to have an interrogative tag such as *will you?* – indeed, no comparable tag at all is possible with these. And as with 1st person inclusives there is no semantic scope contrast with negatives. *Let ... not* is a great deal more likely than *don't let*, no doubt because such imperatives are characteristically used in relatively formal style, but *don't let* is not excluded, as in [37iii].

[21] A special case is where the action is in fact to be carried out by just one (typically the speaker). For example, I might say *Let's open the window* with the aim of securing your agreement to my opening it. But note that in this scenario I could still report the action subsequently by saying *We opened the window.*

There is, however, no positive grammatical property that sets such clauses apart as a distinct construction (as contraction of *us* does the 1st person inclusives). An alternative analysis, therefore, would be to group them grammatically with ordinary imperatives, treating the difference as a matter of meaning and use rather than form.

One advantage of this is that it avoids the problems raised by the very fuzzy boundary that would separate them. Consider the range illustrated in:

[38] i *Let the prisoners be brought in.*
ii *This proposal was first made, let it be noted, by the Liberal Party.*
iii *Let 'u', 'v', 'w' be the velocity components along the 'x', 'y', 'z' axes of a molecule moving with velocity 'q'.*
iv *Now, let me see, what's the best way of tackling the problem?*

Example [i] differs from *Bring the prisoners in* in that it is not so specifically addressed to those who are to bring the prisoners in. Nevertheless the audience is more directly involved than in cases like [37] – and of course a reformulation with *should* would here be much too weak to capture the meaning. *Let* clearly doesn't mean "allow", but it might be argued that it has a causative sense, and hence does contribute to the propositional content, with compliance being a matter of causing the prisoners to be brought in – compare the ordinary imperative *Have the prisoners brought in.*[22]

Let it be noted in [38ii] can be roughly glossed as "it should be noted", but it can be regarded as an expository directive to the addressee(s); it is comparable to an ordinary imperative with *note*: *Note that this proposal was first made...* Example [38iii] illustrates an expository device in scientific discourse, where the speaker assigns values to arbitrary symbols, by fiat, as it were, and invites the addressee to accept these decisions. Because the structure is conventionalised, it would not be possible to insert *you* as subject or add a *will you?* tag, but otherwise the meaning is consistent with *let* having its basic "allow" sense. Note, moreover, that such *let*-imperatives can be coordinated with ordinary ones in the expository use: *To keep things simple, let I be an open interval and assume that all functions mentioned have domain I.*

In [38iv] *let me see* is a conventional way of giving oneself time to think. As such, it doesn't permit manipulation of the usual kind (adding *you*, a tag, etc.), but this is no reason for denying that *let* here has the "allow" sense and contributes to the propositional content rather than being an illocutionary marker.

9.5 Imperatives interpreted as conditionals

When an imperative is the first element in a clause-coordination, it is commonly interpreted as a conditional:

[39] i *<u>Ask him about his business deals</u> and he quickly changes the subject.*
ii *<u>Do that again</u> and you'll regret it.*
iii *<u>Persuade her to agree</u> and I'll be forever in your debt.*
iv *<u>Don't make him the centre of attention</u> and he gets in a huff.*

Thus we understand "If you ask him about his business deals he quickly changes the subject", and so on. The examples illustrate the prototypical case, where the second clause is declarative and overtly linked to the imperative by *and*. The conditional interpretation

[22] *Let* has a causative sense not restricted to imperatives in the idiom *let ... know*: *I'll let you know* means "I'll tell you", i.e. "I'll cause you to know".

derives from the implicature of consequence that is commonly conveyed by *and* – compare *I'll offer him a 10% discount and he's bound to take it.* The first clause is usually positive, but it is just possible for it to be negative, as in [iv]; the form of the negative shows clearly that it is indeed the imperative construction that we are dealing with here.

Condition is not part of the meaning of the imperative, and the present examples can be regarded as involving indirect speech acts. The direct force of the imperative, that of directive, is lost or backgrounded in varying degrees.[23] In the salient interpretation of [39i] I am not directing you (even in the broad sense we have given to that term) to ask him about his business deals. No illocutionary force attaches to the imperative clause itself: the coordination has a force as a whole – that of a conditional statement. Example [ii] is similar except that a further step follows: the whole indirectly conveys "If you do that again you'll regret it", and this in turn conveys "Don't do that again", the opposite of what would be directly conveyed by the imperative clause standing on its own. The indirect negative directive results from the undesirability of the consequence expressed in *you'll regret it.* In [iii] the consequence is desirable, so that the conditional "If you persuade her to agree I'll be forever in your debt" conveys "Persuade her to agree", the meaning of the imperative itself. In such cases the distinction between direct and indirect is blurred: it is hardly possible to distinguish [iii] from, say, *Come over around seven and then we'll be able to avoid the rush hour traffic,* which surely directly conveys a directive to come around seven.

Relaxation of constraints applying to imperatives in their directive use

The use of imperatives to convey conditions is a highly conventionalised one, with the result that certain constraints on form and propositional meaning that normally apply to imperatives in their directive use are here relaxed:

[40]	i	*<u>Do that ever again</u> and I'll brain you.*	[negatively-oriented *ever*]
	ii	*<u>Feel slightly off-colour</u> and he thinks you're dying.*	[absence of agentivity]
	iii	*<u>Buy myself the slightest luxury</u> and I'm branded a spendthrift.*	[1st sg]
	iv	*<u>Express any misgivings</u> and he accused you of disloyalty.*	[past time reference]

Negatively-oriented items like *ever* are normally excluded from positive imperatives, but they occur readily in conditionals (cf. *if you ever do that again*), and the conditional meaning in [i] thus sanctions the *ever.* Imperatives used with directive force (other than those with open *let*) associate an agentive role with the subject, but conditionals of course do not, so that there is no suggestion in [ii] that feeling off-colour is under your control. The reflexive *myself* in [iii] shows that the understood subject is 1st person singular, a normal possibility for conditionals, but not imperatives with directive force. And in [iv] the tense of *accused* shows that we are concerned with past time ("if you expressed any misgivings"), whereas imperatives normally involve future situations. Note that *any* in [iv] is a further case of a negatively-oriented item like *ever* in [i]. Examples like [iii] and [iv] are comparatively rare, but they are possible; they provide further illustration of the way an indirect use can have repercussions on the formal and semantic properties of constructions.

[23] This distinguishes the *and* construction from the one with *or*: *Hurry up or we'll be late.* This conveys "If you don't hurry up we'll be late", but the full directive force of the imperative is retained. For further discussion of the *and* and *or* constructions, see Ch. 15, §2.2.3–4.

Clause type of second coordinate

The second clause can belong to other clause types than declarative; what is important is not the form but what the clause conveys:

[41] i *Invite one without the other and what a row there'll be.* [exclamative]
ii *Tell the truth and who'll believe you / what'll they do?* [open interrogative]
iii *Act in haste and repent at leisure.* [imperative]

Exclamatives, we have seen, have essentially the same force as declaratives and hence [i] needs no explanation. The interrogatives in [ii] would not be used as inquiries. The most likely interpretation of *who'll believe you?* is as a rhetorical question conveying "No one will believe you"; with *what'll they do?* the answer might again be contextually obvious or else be given immediately by the one who put the question (e.g. *They'll say you're being disloyal to your friends*). In [iii] the second imperative indirectly conveys approximately "You'll regret it (for a long time)".

Let-imperatives

Our conditional examples have all been of ordinary imperatives. Open *let*-imperatives are also possible: *Let anyone question what he says and he flies into a rage.* But 1st person inclusives are not used in this way: in normal use they always retain their directive force. For example, *Let's put up the price and they'll cancel the order* cannot be used like [39ii] to convey the opposite of what is expressed in the imperative ("If we put up the price they'll cancel the order, so let's not put up the price").

9.6 Non-imperative directives

9.6.1 Interrogatives as directives

Directives are very often conveyed indirectly by means of interrogatives. This is especially so with requests – particularly when speaker and addressee are not intimates. The imperative structure, we have noted, can be used for a wide range of directives, including orders: to make a request by means of an imperative may therefore run the risk of appearing too brusque or peremptory, even if illocutionary modifiers like *please* and *kindly* are added. In many circumstances indirect directives with interrogative form are considered more polite. This is not to suggest that there is any simple correlation between interrogative form and politeness with directives. In the first place, prosody plays an important and in part independent role: *Can you move your car?* will typically be more polite than *Move your car*, but this can be overridden by an impatient, emphatic tone of voice. Secondly it depends on the content of the interrogative: *Can you move your car* lends itself much more readily to use as a polite request than, say, *Must you park your car across my driveway?*

We find a great variety of interrogative directives, but four of the most important semantic categories concern: (a) your ability to do something; (b) your desire or willingness to do something; (c) the deontic necessity for you to do something; (d) the reason for you to do something:

[42] i *Can you open the door.* ("Open the door") [ability]
ii *Would you like to / Will you sign here?* ("Sign here") [desire/willingness]
iii *Must you talk so loud?* ("Don't talk so loud") [deontic necessity]
iv *Why don't you bring your radio?* ("Bring your radio") [reason]

(As noted in §3.2, there is some variation with respect to punctuation, with a full stop often preferred to a question mark in the ability or desire/willingness cases.)

(a) Ability questions

These lend themselves to indirect directive use since a likely reason for me to be interested in your ability to do something is that I want you to do it. Typical openers are:

[43] *can you, could you, is it possible (for you), will/would it be possible (for you), are you able, will/would you be able*

The versions with *can* are most frequent, and are especially likely in contexts where the answer is obviously "yes", so that the direct inquiry force is effectively lost; this will usually apply with such everyday examples as *Can you pass the salt*, etc. The forms with preterites (*could/would*, with the preterite indicating tentativeness) are regarded as more polite.

All the above could be negated: *can't you, couldn't you*, etc. Negative questions are always biased, and in the present case the negation adds some emotive component of meaning, perhaps impatience (*Can't you talk a little louder?*, suggesting you ought to be able to) or persuasiveness (*Couldn't you stay a little bit longer?*). Inflectional negatives always have the ability predicate within their scope; analytic ones with ***can*** are potentially ambiguous as to scope. *Can you not stand by the door*, for example, can have the *not* in the *can* clause or in the *stand* clause. In the first case it is a negative question conveying the positive directive "Stand by the door", and in the second it is a positive question conveying the negative directive "Don't stand by the door".

(b) Desire/willingness questions

These likewise have a natural connection with directives: if you want or are willing to do something you are likely to comply with a request to do it. Typical formulae are:

[44] i	*will/would you, would you like to / care to / be so kind as to*	[+ infinitival]
ii	*do/would you mind*	[+ gerund-participial]

Again the tentative preterite *would* adds to the effect of politeness. (Note that *want* occurs in this use with *do* but not *would*, and is appreciably less polite: *Do you want to clear the table so that we can have lunch?*) Inflectional negatives are possible for those taking infinitival complements, especially the first three (*won't/wouldn't you, wouldn't you like to*); they do not occur with *mind*, for the salient bias of the question would be positive, suggesting that you do/would mind. The analytic negatives *will/would you not* have the scope ambiguity illustrated above for *can*. Compare:

[45] i	*Will you not [take a seat]?*	[*not* in *will* clause]
ii	*Will you [not put your feet on the sofa].*	[*not* in *put* clause]

The pragmatically salient interpretations have primary verb negation in [i], "Take a seat", and secondary negation in [ii], "Don't put your feet on the sofa".

Closely related to desire/willingness is prospective intentional future, as in *Are/Aren't you going to tidy your room?* These express doubt as to whether you intend to do what you should do, and for this reason are quite well down the politeness scale.

(c) Deontic necessity questions

Deontic necessity is usually questioned by *must*, as in [42iii] or *have* (*Do you have to talk so loud?*), though *need, necessary*, etc., are also possible (cf. *Need you / Is it necessary to talk so loud?*). The situation denoted in the complement clause (your talking so loud) is one that I regard as undesirable, and the question has, in context, a clear negative bias: I don't think there is any necessity for you to talk so loud. Hence the implied directive – whose content is this time the opposite of that expressed in the complement clause. Suggesting that you are unnecessarily doing what I don't want does not of course make for a polite directive.

(d) Reason questions

These are usually expressed by means of *why* and have been discussed in §4.5. Here again the content of the implicit directive is the opposite of that expressed in the question, whether the latter is negative, as in [42iv], or positive, as in *Why accept less?* ("Don't accept less").

3rd person

The above examples all have *you* as subject, but just as imperatives can have 3rd person subjects, so can interrogatives with directive force: *Will everyone remember to sign the register.* It is also possible to have 3rd person subjects in examples like those given in [42]: *Can he come a little earlier tonight?*; *Would he like to return my wrench?*; *Must they talk so loud?*; *Why doesn't she bring her radio?* These aren't equivalent to imperatives because they are not addressed to the person(s) concerned, but can still have indirect directive force, suggesting that you should convey the directive to whoever is to comply.

1st person inclusive

Interrogatives used with essentially the same force as 1st person inclusive imperatives generally begin with *shall we* or *why*:

[46] i *Shall we go for a swim?*
ii *Why don't we eat out tonight?* *Why waste our time on it?*

At the direct level, [i] is a direction question whose answers are expressed by 1st person inclusive imperatives: in context the question is biased towards the positive answer, "Let's go for a swim", which it therefore indirectly conveys.

9.6.2 Declaratives as directives

Declaratives can be used with either direct or indirect directive force. The direct cases involve the performative construction (§3.1):

[47] i *I <u>order</u>/<u>beg</u> you to return her letters.*
ii *The riding of bicycles on the walkway is strictly <u>prohibited</u>.*

Among the many indirect cases, mention may be made of those involving (a) the speaker's wants or needs; (b) the addressee's future actions; (c) deontic necessity:

[48] i	*I <u>want</u> / <u>need</u> / <u>would like</u> someone to hold the ladder.*	[speaker's wants/needs]
ii	*You <u>are going to</u> / <u>will</u> apologise.*	[addressee's future actions]
iii	*You <u>must</u> / <u>have to</u> come in now.*	[deontic necessity]

The indirectness in these cases does not contribute to politeness. Case [48ii] in particular is strongly wilful and coercive: in telling you what you are going to do I conspicuously leave you no choice. Politeness can be achieved, however, by combining declarative and interrogative in a doubly indirect directive:

[49] *I wonder whether you would mind moving your car a little.*

The statement actually expressed conveys an indirect question ("Would you mind moving your car a little?"), and this in turn is interpreted as an indirect directive. This device generally involves the more polite of the interrogative constructions (note, for example, that *would* is not omissible from the *whether* clause), and the extra indirectness increases the impression of politeness.

9.6.3 Non-finite and verbless directives

Directives of this form are commonly used in written notices, where there is a need for brevity:

[50] i *Smoking prohibited.* *No visitors allowed beyond this point.* [non-finite]
ii *No smoking.* *No entry.* *Slow.* [verbless]

Non-finites are typically abbreviated passive performatives (cf. *Smoking is prohibited*). The verbless construction is commonly used in speech to indicate what one is ordering or asking for: *Two black coffees*; *The hammer, please*; *Two adults, please* ("I request admission for two adults"); *Single to Manchester* (as in booking transport); and so on.

9.7 Imperatives with interrogative tags

Ordinary and 1st person inclusive *let*-imperatives may be anchor to an interrogative tag:

[51] i *Help yourself, will you / won't you?* [positive ordinary imperative]
ii *Don't tell anyone, will you?* [negative ordinary imperative]
iii *Let's (not) go with them, shall we?* [1st person inclusive *let*-imperative]

The tags attached to imperatives cannot be derived by grammatical rules of the kind we suggested for tags attached to declaratives (§5.1). They can be regarded as elliptical versions of the full interrogatives *Will you help yourself?*, *Won't you help yourself?*, *Will you not tell anyone?*, *Shall we (not) go with them?*, but the reason truncated versions of these can be attached to the imperative anchors is that they are interrogatives of the types that are commonly used as indirect directives, as described in §9.6.1. The indirect force of the interrogative thus matches the direct force of the imperative anchor.

This is why we can have either a positive or a negative tag with the positive imperative in [51i], but only a positive tag with the negative imperative in [ii]. *Will you help yourself?* and *Won't you help yourself?* can both be used to convey "Help yourself", and hence both *will you?* and *won't you?* can be attached to *Help yourself.* "Don't tell anyone", however, can be indirectly conveyed by *Will you not tell anyone*, but not normally by ?*Won't you not tell anyone*, and hence only *will you?* is an appropriate tag for *Don't tell anyone.*

Nevertheless, the construction is conventionalised in that the tags correspond to only a subset of the interrogatives that can be used with indirect directive force. For example, *Can/Could/Will/Would you not touch it* could all convey "Don't touch it", but the tag for a negative ordinary imperative is virtually restricted to *will you?* With positives the range is considerably greater: the most frequent are the above *will you?*, *won't you?*, but *would you?*, *can you?*, *can't you?*, *could you?* and, especially in AmE, *why don't you?* are also common (and *wouldn't you?*, *couldn't you?* are possible):

[52] i *Just give me a hand with these boxes, would you?*
ii *Let me have your reply by the end of the week, can you / could you?*
iii *Watch where you're putting your feet, can't you?*

Can and *could* tend to retain some of their direct inquiry force. *Can't you?* typically conveys some impatience. *Won't you?* and *would you?* are generally the most polite. One context favouring *won't you?* is where the directive is a reminder or otherwise not unexpected: *Be there at six, as we agreed, won't you?* The normal tag for 1st person inclusives is *shall we?*, but *why don't we?* is also a possibility.

9.8 No subordinate imperative construction

Imperatives normally occur as main clauses: there is no grammatically distinct construction that can properly be regarded as the subordinate counterpart of a main clause imperative, as *whether she liked it* and *why she liked it* are the subordinate counterparts of the closed and open interrogative main clauses *Did she like it?* and *Why did she like it?* respectively.

Reporting of directives

Imperatives are generally used as directives, and directive speech acts can of course be reported. But they are reported by means of constructions where the subordinate clauses are syntactically and semantically very different from imperative clauses. Compare, for example:

[53] i *Leave her alone.* [imperative]
ii *Max ordered/ told/ asked/ advised me to leave her alone.* [infinitival]
iii *Max asked that I leave her alone.* [mandative subjunctive]

All three constructions contain the plain form of the verb, but the imperative differs from the other two in taking auxiliary *do* for verbal negation and emphatic polarity:

[54] i *Don't be late.* [imperative]
ii **He told me to do not be late.* [infinitival]
iii **He asked that I do not be late.* [mandative subjunctive]

In other clause types subordination does not exclude *do* in this way (compare main *Why didn't they like it?* and subordinate *He asked why they didn't like it*), so the data in [54] suggests we are dealing with different constructions, not main and subordinate versions of a single construction. Compelling evidence for this view comes from the fact that both infinitivals and mandatives allow a much wider range of subject–predicate combinations than we find with imperatives. There are, for example, no main clause imperatives matching the subordinate clauses in:

[55] i a. *The house was shown to be in need of repair.*
b. *She was the first one to realise its significance.*
c. *It's unusual for it to rain so much in August.*
d. *We can't afford for there to be more disruption.*
ii a. *He suggested that the meeting be postponed.*
b. *It is essential that there be no more disruption.*
c. *It's important that she get all necessary assistance.*

#Be in need of repair and *#Realise its significance* are pragmatically anomalous, while **It rain so much in August*, **There be more disruption*, and so on are ungrammatical.

The infinitival construction has a vastly greater range of use than the imperative, and examples like those in [55i] bear no significant relation to imperatives at all. The meaning is compatible with its use to report directives, but the interpretation of [53ii] as reports of directives depends crucially on the lexical verb in the matrix clause – *order*, *tell*, etc. The range of the mandative construction is more limited, but still considerably broader than that of the imperative, as evident from the lack of imperative counterparts to the subordinate clauses in [55ii]. The differences in form and meaning between either infinitivals or mandatives on the one hand and imperatives on the other cannot be explained in terms of subordination: we must recognise three syntactically quite distinct constructions.

10 Minor clause types

In this final section of the chapter we review summarily a number of main clause constructions that do not belong to any of the major clause types discussed so far. See also the elliptical constructions discussed in Ch. 17, §7.8.

Optatives

[1] i *Long live the Emperor.* *God save the Queen!* *God help you if you're not ready on time!* *Far be it from me to complain.* *So be it.*
ii *May all your troubles be quickly resolved!* *Long may she reign over us!*
iii *Would that he were still alive!* *Would to God I'd never set eyes on him!*

These three constructions express wishes. The examples in [i] are subjunctives. Though the subjunctive construction is fully productive in subordinate clauses, in main clauses it is found only in a narrow range of fixed expressions or formulaic frames. In some the subject occupies its basic position, while in others it is postposed to the end of the clause or to the right of *be*. Construction [ii], which belongs to somewhat formal style, has *may* in pre-subject position, meaning approximately "I hope/pray". There is some semantic resemblance between this specialised use of *may* and that of *let* in open *let*-imperatives, but syntactically the NP following *may* is clearly subject (witness the nominative form *she*). The construction has the same internal form as a closed interrogative, but has no uninverted counterpart. Construction [iii] is archaic; syntactically it consists of *would* as predicator with a finite clause complement (and optionally the PP *to God* as another complement), but is of course exceptional in that the understood subject (*I*) is not expressed. The subordinate clause is a modal preterite, with the same interpretation as in the regular construction with *I wish* (Ch. 11, §7.2).

Clauses with the subordinate form

[2] i *That it should have come to this!*
ii *To think that he was once the most powerful man in the land!*

The meaning is close to that of the exclamatives *How amazing it is that it should have come to this* / *to think that he was once the most powerful man in the land*, with subordinate clauses in extraposed subject function. The subordinate form of the clauses in [2] suggests that, when they stand on their own, as here, they are fragments, containing a subordinate clause but with the matrix frame omitted. Other infinitival constructions that are not overtly embedded include the *Oh to be in England* pattern (which also belongs in the optative category: "I wish I were in England") and the negative *Not to worry* ("Don't / Let's not worry"), which is rarely found with verbs other than *worry*.

Conditional fragments

[3] i *If only you'd told me earlier!*
ii *Well, if it isn't my old friend Malcolm Duce!*
iii *If you'd like to move your head a little.*
iv *Supposing something happens to part us, June?*

Various kinds of conditional adjunct can be used on their own, with the apodosis left unexpressed. Construction [i], with *if only* + modal preterite indicating counterfactuality, is used to express regret: "How unfortunate you didn't tell me earlier (because if you had done, things would have been better)" – see Ch. 8, §14.2.1. Construction [ii] involves a fixed frame of the form *if it/that isn't X*; it is used to express surprise at seeing *X* (so [ii] itself conveys "It is my old friend Malcolm Duce"). Construction [iii] is a further type of indirect directive: "Please move your head a little" (as said by doctor to patient, for example); the missing apodosis is understood along the lines of "that would be helpful". Example [iv] is understood as a question: "What if . . . ?"; the same construction can be used with directive force, as a suggestion or invitation: *Supposing we meet at six.* This fragment construction represents the most common use of conditional *supposing*; *suppose* can be used with the same meaning, but syntactically that gives an imperative clause rather than a fragment.

Verbless directives

[4] *Out of my way! On your feet! This way! Everybody outside! All aboard!*
Head up! Shoulders back! Careful! Off with his shoes! On with the show!

Fragmentary structures like these are commonly used for a peremptory type of directive, where immediate compliance is required. In many a verb could be supplied (*Get out of my way!*; *Come this way!*; *Everybody move outside*; *Put your shoulders back!*; *Be careful!*), but the *off/on* + *with* construction can't be expanded in this way. Military commands often take this form: *Eyes right!*; *At ease!*; etc. Other types of verbless directive have the form of NPs: *No talking!* or *Two coffees, please*, as used in restaurants, shops, etc.

Parallel structures

[5] *The sooner, the better. More haste, less speed. Out of sight, out of mind.*
No work, no pay. Once bitten, twice shy. Like father, like son.

There are numerous lexicalised expressions of this kind, fixed phrases, proverbs, and the like. They consist of a juxtaposition of two expressions of like form. The first two can be seen as elliptical versions of the correlative comparative construction (Ch. 13, §4.6) – cf. *The sooner you decide, the better it will be.* Some have a conditional interpretation (e.g. "If you do no work, you get no pay"). Some, such as the last, bear no clear resemblance to any productive syntactic construction. Similar parallelism is seen in pairs of imperative clauses like *Spare the rod, and spoil the child*, which also have conditional interpretations like those of the non-lexicalised examples discussed in §9.5.

11

Content clauses and reported speech

RODNEY HUDDLESTON

This chapter is concerned with one of the three major classes of finite subordinate clause; the other two classes, relative and comparative clauses, are covered in the next two chapters, while non-finite subordinate clauses are the topic of Ch. 14.

1 Subordinate clauses

A subordinate clause characteristically functions as dependent within some larger construction:

[1] i [*The book* *she recommended*] *is out of print.*
ii *He* [*knows* *that she is right*].
iii [*Although* *the paper is poorly written,*] *it contains some excellent ideas.*

The underlined clause is modifier of the noun *book* in [i], complement of *knows* in [ii], and complement of *although* in [iii]. Note that in [iii] *it contains some excellent ideas* is a clause contained within a larger construction (the clause that forms the whole sentence), but it has the function of head, and hence is a main clause, not a subordinate one.

Marking of subordination

Subordination is very often marked by some feature in the internal structure of the clause:

[2] i *It is clear* [*that he made a mistake*].
ii *They interviewed all those* [*she mentioned* __ *in her affidavit*].
iii *She's asking* [*how many copies we will want*].

One very simple case is illustrated in [i], where *that* serves directly to mark the clause as subordinate. In [ii] it is the absence of the understood object that distinguishes the subordinate clause from a main clause. And in [iii] what marks the clause as subordinate is the combination of a prenuclear interrogative phrase and the subject + predicator order, for the corresponding main clause has subject–auxiliary inversion (*How many copies will we want?*).

Not all subordinate clauses are structurally marked as such

English does not require that subordination be marked in the structure of the subordinate clause itself. In *He knows she is right*, for example, the underlined clause is subordinate by virtue of functioning as complement to *know* but it is structurally identical to the main clause *She is right.* We examine the conditions under which the marking is omissible in §3.1.

Marking may be sufficient to establish that a clause is subordinate

There are certain places where a clause can be marked as subordinate even though it is not functioning as dependent within some larger construction:

[3] i A: *What are they demanding?* B: [*That the sacked workers be reinstated.*]
ii *That it should have come to this!*
iii *He took advice from his daughter, who was manager of the local bank.*

The bracketed clause in [i] is the familiar case of an elliptical answer to a question, while [ii] illustrates a special, and rare, exclamatory construction consisting of a content clause without any governing predicate (cf. Ch. 10, §10). The underlined relative clause in [iii] functions as supplement rather than dependent, but it has subordinate clause form by virtue of containing the relative pronoun *who*.

This is why we began by saying that a subordinate clause **characteristically** functions as a dependent. It is also why we use the terms subordinate vs main rather than dependent vs independent. Notice, moreover, that a clause functioning as a dependent may have main clause rather than subordinate clause form, as in *The question they need to answer is why did no one check her references?* (see [21] of §5.3.1).

Finite and non-finite

A major division within subordinate clauses is between finite and non-finite clauses:

[4] i *He thinks that she is here.* } [finite]
ii *He insists that she be here.* }
iii *She wants to be here.* [non-finite]

Most finite clauses have primary forms of the verb – preterite or present tense forms or irrealis *were*. For reasons explained in Ch. 3, §1.8, we also include the subjunctive construction, as in [ii], in the finite class. Non-finite clauses have the verb in the gerund-participle or past participle form, or involve the infinitival use of the plain form, as in [iii]. They differ structurally from main clauses in much more radical ways than do finite subordinate clauses, and are dealt with separately in Ch. 14.

Relative, comparative, and content clauses

We distinguish three main classes of finite subordinate clause:

[5] i *I couldn't find the book that I wanted.* [relative]
ii *He gave me more copies than I wanted.* [comparative]
iii *You know that I wanted it.* [content]

Content clauses can be regarded as the default category on this dimension: they lack the special properties of relative and comparative clauses, and their structure is less different from that of main clauses. Notice, for example, that in [i] and [ii] *wanted* is understood as having an object that is not expressed, whereas in [iii] the object must be expressed, just as it must in main clauses. And those subordinate clauses that show no structural difference at all from main clauses belong in the content clause class, as in the above *I know she is right*.

The term **content clause** reflects this default status: it suggests that the clause is simply selected for its semantic content.

2 Clause type

The system of clause type applies to content clauses as well as to main clauses, except that we don't have imperative content clauses as argued in Ch. 10, §9.8. Compare, then, for the other types:

[1]	MAIN	SUBORDINATE (CONTENT)	
i	a. *They are in Paris.*	b. *He says* [(*that*) *they are in Paris*].	[declarative]
ii	a. *Is she ill?*	b. *He asked* [*whether/if she is ill*].	[closed interrogative]
iii	a. *What does he do?*	b. *I wonder* [*what he does*].	[open interrogative]
iv	a. *What a liar he is!*	b. *You know* [*what a liar he is*].	[exclamative]

We again take declarative to be the default category, and we defer discussion of the special properties of interrogative and exclamative content clauses until §§5–6.[1]

3 Subordinators in content clauses

Expanded (or *that*-) declaratives vs bare declaratives

Declarative content clauses are prototypically introduced by the subordinator *that*, but they are also found without any such marker of subordination:

[1]		
i	*He knows that you are here.*	[expanded declarative / *that*-declarative]
ii	*He knows you are here.*	[bare declarative]

Content clauses introduced by the subordinator *that* we call **expanded declaratives**, or simply *that*-declaratives; those without an introductory subordinator are **bare declaratives**.

Non-expandable vs expandable declaratives

Certain prepositions take declarative complements that are invariably bare. We call these **non-expandable**. The default class of **expandable declaratives** then comprises all others: they allow, in principle, for the subject–predicate construction to be expanded by a subordinator. This second classification is based, then, not on whether a subordinator is actually present or absent, but on whether or not the content clause is complement to an item which invariably excludes a subordinator, such as *if* and *before* in [2]:

[2]	NON-EXPANDABLE DECLARATIVE	EXPANDABLE DECLARATIVE
i	a. *I'll do it if* [*you pay me*].	b. *I'll do it provided* [(*that*) *you pay me*].
ii	a. *He left home before* [*she died*].	b. *You know* [(*that*) *he is guilty*].

[1] Blends between declarative and interrogative are occasionally attested: *There are, he thought, so few true means of forgetfulness in this life that why should he shun the medicine even when the medicine seemed, as it did, a little crude?* The *why should he . . .* interrogative (which has main clause syntactic form, evident in the subject–auxiliary inversion) is so strongly biased towards a negative answer that it indirectly conveys "he should not shun the medicine", and it is this interpretation that allows it to be subordinated by means of the declarative subordinator *that*.

3.1 Conditions under which *that* must or may appear

In expandable declaratives structural properties of the matrix may make the subordinator obligatory or, exceptionally, they may require that it be absent. We examine these cases first and then consider those where *that* is omissible.

Conditions under which *that* is obligatory

(a) When the content clause is subject or otherwise precedes the matrix predicator

[3] i *[That they were lying] is now quite obvious.*
ii *But [that he really intended to cheat us] I still can't believe.*

Compare these with *It is now quite obvious [(that) they were lying]*, where the content clause is in extraposed subject position, and *But I still can't believe [(that) he really intended to cheat us]*, where it is in post-verbal complement position. What distinguishes [3] from these is that in [3] *that* is needed to signal the start of a subordinate clause: if [i] began with *They were lying* this would be perceived initially as a main clause, whereas in the extraposed subject construction the matrix *It is now quite obvious* prepares the ground for a subordinate clause, and the marker of subordination does not therefore have the essential role that it does in [i]. The same applies in [ii], where we have a further contrast between [ii] itself and *He really intended to cheat us, I believe.* The absence of *that* in the latter indicates that *he really intended to cheat us* is indeed a main clause, and *I believe* is a parenthetical: we have here two main clauses in a supplementation relation, not one clause subordinated within another, as in [3].[2]

(b) The content clause is adjunct

[4] *He appealed to us to bring his case to the attention of the authorities that justice might be done.*

Content clauses usually function as complement, being licensed by some verb, noun, preposition, etc., in the matrix clause, but they are also occasionally found as adjuncts, as in [4]. Here *that* is needed to show the relation of *justice might be done* to the matrix structure.

(c) When the content clause is complement to comparative *than/as*

In comparative constructions *that* may distinguish a content clause from a comparative clause, as in:

[5]	i *He hired a taxi more often [than he drove my car].*	[comparative clause]
	ii *I'd rather (that) he hired a taxi [than that he drove my car].*	[content clause]

Example [i] illustrates the most usual case where *than* has a clause as complement: *he drove my car* is a comparative clause of the type described in Ch. 13, and it would be impossible to add *that.* In [ii], however, *than* has a content clause as complement: it contrasts with *(that) he hired a taxi*, which is licensed by the idiom *would rather.* Here the first *that* is optional, but the one in the complement of *than* is obligatory, serving to mark the clause as a content clause as opposed to a comparative.

[2] The difference between the subordination and supplementation constructions is perhaps even clearer in the case of interrogatives: compare *Whether it was deliberate I won't ask* (subordination) and *Was it deliberate, I ask myself?* (supplementation).

When *that* must be omitted

That is not permitted when the content clause is embedded within an unbounded dependency construction in such a way that its subject is realised by a gap:

[6] i *She thinks [(that) Max is the ringleader].* [*that* optional]
ii *Who does she think [__ is the ringleader]?* } [*that* excluded]
iii *Max is the one she thinks [__ is the ringleader].* }

That is allowed in [i] but not in [ii–iii] (these being unbounded dependency constructions in the sense of Ch. 12, §7): compare **Who does she think that is the ringleader?* and **Max is the one she thinks that is the ringleader.* In [ii] the subject of *is the ringleader* is realised by a gap linked to *who* in the superordinate interrogative clause. The content clause subject is likewise realised by a gap in [iii], where the content clause is embedded within a relative clause.[3]

The obligatory absence of *that* in such clauses is quite consistent with our saying that *think* selects an expandable declarative as complement. The inadmissibility of *that* in [6ii–iii] is not attributable to *think* but to non-lexical aspects of the structure: it is different in kind from the inadmissibility of *that* in the complement of prepositions like *if* and *before* in [2ia/iia].

Optional omission of *that*

The default case is the one where *that* is present as a marker of the subordinate status of the clause. Departures from this default case, declaratives without *that*, are more likely in informal than in formal style. For the rest, the relative likelihood of dropping the *that* depends largely on the structure of the matrix clause but also on that of the content clause itself. Factors which favour respectively the omission and the retention of *that* are illustrated in [7i–ii]:

[7] i a. *I think [it's a good idea].*
b. *She said [they'd had a wonderful holiday].*
c. *It's a good job [we left early].*
ii a. *One of them mentioned to me [<u>that</u> your secretary might be leaving].*
b. *It distresses me [<u>that</u> he is trying to lay the blame for the accident on us].*
c. *I didn't like his insinuation [<u>that</u> we had initiated the complaint].*
d. *She said [<u>that</u> because of the new regulations they had to lay off ten more staff].*
e. *It was possible [<u>that</u> she was ill and <u>that</u> her mother had gone to see her].*
f. *This motion, [<u>that</u> the subscription be increased by 50%,] was quickly defeated.*

In [ia–b] the content clause is complement to a common and quite general verb of cognition or communication, and in [ic] it is extraposed subject in a matrix clause containing *be* + a short predicative complement. In [ia], moreover, *I think* is likely to be backgrounded to the status of a modal qualification, informationally comparable to a parenthetical (cf. *It's a good idea, I think*); similarly with *it seems* in *It seems we made a mistake.*

Turning now to the examples with *that*, note that the verb in [7iia] is longer and less common than *say*, and also that the content clause is separated from the verb by another

[3] Acceptability is improved by adding between *that* and the gap an adjunct of the kind that could occur between *that* and an overt subject. Compare *She said that in her opinion Max was the ringleader* and ?*[the one] who she said that in her opinion was the ringleader.* We doubt whether such structures can be considered grammatical, however, and have not catered for them in formulating the constraint.

phrase. In [iib] the content clause is extraposed subject in a transitive matrix clause. In [iic] it is complement to a noun; omission is not impossible in this construction, but it is unlikely with a morphologically complex noun like *insinuation* (compare *The fact [it was illegal] didn't seem to worry him*, with the simple noun *fact* as head). In [iid] *that* is followed by a non-subject element (the PP *because of the new regulations*), and *that* signals that the phrase belongs in the subordinate clause, not the matrix. Omission of *that* is very unlikely in such cases, though probably not impossible in rather casual speech (*I think [often they don't realise how much it means to her]*). In [iie] the repetition of *that* makes clear that the coordination is between subordinate clauses: without the second *that* the second coordinate (*her mother had gone to see her*) could be construed as a main clause, and hence as being presented as a fact rather than a possibility. (In many cases, of course, it will be clear from the sense that the coordination is at the level of subordinate clauses, and the second *that* will then be readily omissible: *It is possible [that you are right and I am wrong]*.) Finally, in [iif] the content clause is a supplement to the NP *this motion* rather than being integrated into the structure of the NP as a complement of the head noun *motion*; the pressure to retain *that* is so great here that this construction might be included among those where the subordinator is strictly obligatory.[4]

How as subordinator

In very informal style *how* can be used without any trace of its usual manner (or degree) meaning, and in such cases it is arguable that it is no longer an interrogative word but has been reanalysed as a declarative subordinator, a variant of *that*:

[8] *He thought of the time he had ridden to Gavin and told him <u>how</u> his cattle were being rustled at the far end of the valley.*

In the salient interpretation *how* here is simply equivalent to *that*. The interrogative origin, however, is reflected in the fact that it is found only in the complement of items that allow interrogative as well as declarative complements: compare **I believed how his cattle were being rustled.*

3.2 The syntactic category of subordinator

The structure we propose for a *that* clause such as *that your secretary might be leaving* in [7iia] is as follows:

[9]

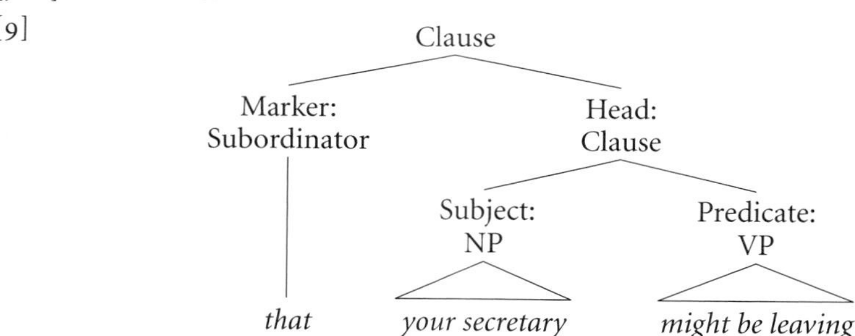

[4] A rather different kind of factor is involved in such an example as *I would ask that you keep me fully informed*, where *that* is hardly omissible. It serves here to distinguish the finite construction from the infinitival one of *I would ask you to keep me informed* (where *you* is object of *ask*).

There are two features of this analysis that require explanation: the initial constituent structure division into *that* + *your secretary might be leaving*, and the treatment of the second constituent (*your secretary might be leaving*) as the head. Note that it is because this element is head that we can apply the term 'clause' both to it and to the larger construction; more specifically, it is a bare clause while the larger one is an expanded clause.

The binary division into *that* + the rest

The main argument here comes from coordination: *that* may combine with a coordination of subject–predicate constructions.

[10] i *I told him* [*that the kitchen tap was dripping and the doorbell wasn't working*].
ii *I concluded* [*that I hadn't installed the program properly or else it was defective*].

Note that it would not be possible to argue that the coordination is simply between a *that* clause and a bare one (e.g. that the coordinates in [i] are *that the kitchen-tap was dripping* and *the doorbell wasn't working*). That would not account for the semantic difference between [ii] and the pragmatically less likely *I concluded that I hadn't installed the program properly or else that it was defective.* Example [ii] says that the conclusion I came to contained a disjunction, an *or*-coordination: I concluded that one or other of two possibilities obtained. The version with repeated *that*, by contrast, says that I came to one or other of two conclusions. The distinction is perhaps easier to see if we insert correlative *either*:

[11] i *I concluded* [*that either I hadn't installed the program properly or else it was defective*].
ii *I concluded* [*either that I hadn't installed the program properly or else that it was defective*].

Version [ii] is pragmatically rather unlikely because it suggests I can't now remember which of these conclusions I came to. What this contrast shows is that *that* in [10] serves to mark as subordinate the whole of the coordination that follows it. We need to say, therefore, that *that* enters into construction with either a clause or a coordination of clauses.

Why *that* is not the head

Omissibility

One obvious reason for treating *that* as a dependent element in the construction, rather than the head, is that it is frequently omissible: we have either *I know that it's wrong* or *I know it's wrong.* What we're suggesting is that *that* is simply a syntactic marker of subordination, and in contexts where the subordinate status of the clause is predictable from features of the matrix structure the marker may be omissible.

Licensing

A second argument is based on the contrast between such examples as:

[12] i *We insist* [*that the work be finished this week*].
ii **We hope* [*that the work be finished this week*].

Here we have subjunctive content clauses (as evident from the plain form *be*), and the contrast shows that such a clause can be licensed by *insist* but not by *hope.* If *that* were head with the bare clause as its complement we would have an exceptional situation where a verb determines the form not directly of its own complement but of the complement within the latter.

Position of preposed adjuncts

It is possible for a preposed adjunct that is part of the content clause to precede *that*:

[13] *The boat was such an attraction that I was afraid, [if he came near it again, that I should never see the last of him].*

The *if* phrase here is an adjunct not in the *be afraid* clause, but in the content clause that functions as complement of *afraid*. The most usual position for it would be after the *that*, but the fact that it can precede indicates that the *that* is construed as part of the subordinate clause itself, not as a head element taking the subordinate clause as its complement. The adjunct occupies initial position within the content clause, just as it does in the main clause counterpart *If he came near it again, I should never see the last of him.*

Whether

We treat *whether* in the same way: it (together with its variant *if*) is a marker of subordination in interrogatives, as *that* is in declaratives. *Whether* is not omissible in the same way as *that*: it is only the default clause type declarative that can dispense with a marker, *whether* being required to distinguish interrogative from declarative. However, it is restricted to closed interrogatives, with the open type being marked as interrogative by the initial interrogative phrase. Compare, then:

[14] i	*They didn't say [(that) they needed some help].*	[declarative]
ii	*They didn't say [whether they needed some help].*	[closed interrogative]
iii	*They didn't say [what help they needed].*	[open interrogative]

In all of these the bracketed expression is a clause; [i] has an omissible subordinator, [ii] a non-omissible one, while [iii] does not allow a subordinator at all, the initial prenuclear position being filled instead by the interrogative phrase *what help*. This phrase has the function of object within the content clause: it is not a head, with *they needed* as dependent. *Whether* differs from *what help* in that it has no role as complement or adjunct within the content clause, but the two expressions are alike in that they both mark the clause as interrogative. The similarity between *whether* and an interrogative phrase is reflected in the fact that certain limited patterns of coordination are permitted: *She didn't know whether or to what extent he was involved in the conspiracy.*

The similarity between *whether* and *that* is also seen in the following example, which is parallel to [13] above:

[15] *He wondered, [if the ceiling did drop, whether he and the other flights would be able to find their way back in this unfamiliar territory].*

The *if* phrase again belongs in the content clause: it relates not to his wondering but to their being able to find their way back. Nevertheless, it precedes *whether*. Note also that *whether* could here too be replaced by an interrogative phrase such as *how*.

4 Functions of declarative content clauses

In this section we review in turn the various functions in the structure of clauses and phrases that can be filled by declarative content clauses.

4.1 Subject

The prototypical subject is an NP; all verbs (and VPs) allow an NP as subject, but some license a content clause as well:

[1] i *Their failure to reply doesn't worry her.* [NP as subject]
ii *That they haven't replied doesn't worry her.* [content clause as subject]

Content clauses do not have the full set of subject properties listed in Ch. 4, §3.1. In particular, they cannot undergo subject–auxiliary inversion: **Doesn't that they haven't replied worry her?* Nevertheless, clauses have enough of the distinctive subject properties to make their analysis as subject unproblematic. They occupy the distinctive subject position before the verb, as seen in [1]. Note also such examples as:

[2] i *That the project has not been properly costed is a serious objection, isn't it?*
ii *That the project has not been properly costed and that the manager is quite inexperienced are just two of my objections to your proposal.*

Example [i] is the interrogative tag construction: the pronoun subject of the tag has as its antecedent the subject of the declarative clause, in this case *that the project has not been properly costed.* And the contrast between [i] and [ii] shows that subject–verb agreement holds between the verb and the initial element, a single clause in [i], a coordination of clauses in [ii].

Constructions containing a *that* clause as subject are illustrated in:

[3] i *That he tried to retract his statement is hardly surprising.* [complex-intransitive]
ii *That the work might be a forgery simply hadn't occurred to us.* [other active]
iii *That she did everything in her power to help cannot be doubted.* [passive]

We will give in turn a sample of governing expressions that license constructions [i] and [ii]; some of the verbs found in the passive [iii] are noted in §4.2 below, when we examine the corresponding active construction.

Subject of a complex-intransitive clause

The clausal subject of [3i] is licensed by *surprising*, the head of the predicative complement. Examples of predicatives allowing a declarative content clause as predicand are given in [4i] (adjectival) and [4ii] (with nouns as head):

[4]	i	*apparent*	*clear*	*critical*	*disconcerting*	*disgusting*
		distressing	*due* [*to*]	*evident*	*important*	*indisputable*
		inevitable	*obvious*	*remarkable*	*significant*	*striking*
		suggestive	*true*	*undeniable*	*vital*	*worrying*
	ii	*an accident*	*an asset*	*a consequence*	*a factor*	*an irony*
		a measure [*of*]	*a miracle*	*a reflection* [*of*]	*a source* [*of*]	*a tribute* [*to*]
		no consolation	*no reason* [*for*]	*testimony* [*to*]	*the fault* [*of*]	*the result* [*of*]

Subject of other active clause constructions

Declarative content clauses are also found as subject of such transitive and intransitive verbs as the following:

[5]	*amuse*	*bother*	*deter*	*disgust*	*enrich*	*help*
	illustrate	*indicate*	*influence*	*infuriate*	*matter*	*mean*
	offend	*reflect*	*reveal*	*show*	*suggest*	*surprise*

It should be borne in mind, however, that what licenses a subject of this kind is often not the verb alone, but the verb in combination with one or more complements – for example, such expressions as *bring home to* NP *that* . . ., *cloud the fact* (*that*) . . ., *leave* NP AdjP (e.g. *leave us confused*), *make sense*, *offer testimony to* . . ., *underline the point* (*that*) . . . .

Postposing of subject

It is possible for a content clause to occupy matrix final position as a postposed subject:

[6] *Even more disturbing is that the neighbours hadn't noticed his absence.*

This, however, is quite rare. It would be more usual to use one of the following constructions:

[7] i *Even more disturbing is the fact that the neighbours hadn't noticed his absence.*
ii *What is even more disturbing is that the neighbours hadn't noticed his absence.*
iii *It is even more disturbing that the neighbours hadn't noticed his absence.*

In [i] the content clause is complement to a noun (*fact*), in [ii] it is complement to *be* in a pseudo-cleft clause, and in [iii] it is extraposed subject.

4.2 Internal complement in clause structure

This section surveys constructions containing a declarative content clause within the matrix VP, as in:

[8] i *Everyone expected that he would resign.*
ii *They told us that the battery was flat.*

For reasons we will take up in §8.3, we do not analyse the content clauses in such constructions as objects: we take them simply as internal complements of the verb. We exclude from consideration at this stage those content clauses that are in construction with dummy *it* (as in *It seems that he was wrong*, for example): these are dealt with separately in §4.3.

In the default case, there is a related passive, with the content clause as subject ('Type I') or extraposed subject ('Type II'):

[9] i	*They cannot dispute that they misled us.*	[active]
ii	*That they misled us cannot be disputed.*	[passive, Type I]
iii	*It cannot be disputed that they misled us.*	[passive, Type II]

Type I passives are rare, and acceptable with only a fairly small number of verbs. Verbs in the following sample lists are marked '-P' only if they are excluded from Type II as well as Type I; '?P' indicates that the passive is questionable.

Content clause as the only internal complement: *She decided that it was a hoax*

[10]					
accept	*add*	*allege*	*care* –P	*claim*	*consider*
contend	*decide*	*dispute*	*fear*	*feel*	*find*
forget	*gather* –P	*guess*	*hope*	*imagine*	*maintain*
presume	*realise*	*reason*	*reflect*	*rejoice* –P	*suppose*
suspect	*think*	*threaten* ?P	*vote*	*wonder* –P	*worry* –P

Impossible and questionable passives may be illustrated by the contrast between *We gather that it was an accident*, *He threatened that the meeting would be disrupted*, and:[5]

[11] i **It is gathered that it was an accident.*
 ii ?*It was threatened that the meeting would be disrupted.*

With optional PP as first internal complement: *She suggested (to me) that he was ill*

[12]					
i	*admit*	*announce*	*assert*	*boast*	*brag* ?P
	complain	*confess*	*declare*	*disclose*	*explain*
	hint	*insist*	*let on* ?P	*mention*	*object*
	point out	*pray* ?P	*propose*	*protest*	*prove*
	remark	*reply*	*report*	*reveal*	*say*
	signal	*state*	*suggest*	*swear* ?P	*testify*
ii	*conclude*	*discover*	*elicit*	*gather* –P	*hear*
	infer	*learn*	*notice*	*observe*	*see*
iii	*agree*	*arrange*	*confirm*	*organise*	*plead*

With the verbs in [i] the optional PP is a *to* phrase whose NP indicates the recipient of some act of communication. In [ii] the preposition is *from*, indicating the source – either a speaker (*I gather from Kim that you are going to Paris*) or evidence (*I conclude from your silence that you have no objections*). In [iii] the preposition is *with*: *I had organised with the secretary that the meeting should be postponed.*

With NP as first internal complement: *You told me that you would help*

[13]					
i	*assure*	*convince*	*inform*	*notify*	*persuade*
	reassure	*remind*	*satisfy*	*tell*	*thank*
ii	*advise*	?*ask*	?*beg*	*caution*	?*command*
	forewarn	?*instruct*	?*order*	*promise*	*show*
	teach	*warn*			

With the verbs in [i] the NP is normally obligatory.[6] With the verbs in [ii] it is optional and those marked '?' (all of them mandative) occur much more readily without the NP object. It is the NP that corresponds to the subject of related passives, so that passives with the content clause as extraposed subject are restricted to constructions where the NP is omitted:

[14] i *We have been shown that the program is defective.*
 ii *It has been shown that the program is defective.*
 iii **It has been shown us that the program is defective.*

As complement to the verb *be*

[15] i *The reason he resigned was that he didn't get on with the boss.*
 ii *What she said was that she'd be contacting us later in the day.*
 iii *The fact/problem/rumour is he can't afford the rent.*

[5] *Wonder* allows passives in such modal contexts as *Can it be wondered that he feels insecure?*, but not normally in non-modal contexts like **It is wondered that he feels insecure.* For *worry* we have *I worry that he may have left it too late*, but not **It is worried that he may have left it too late*; *I'm worried that he may have left it too late* is perfectly acceptable, but this is not a passive clause since *worried* is here an adjective.

[6] The NP object is omissible when informal *how* is the subordinator: *He told how he'd had to sleep in the carport. Thank* appears in this construction with a limited range of objects, as in *I thank my good fortune I wasn't at home at the time* – with others the second complement is a *for* phrase (*I thank you for being so patient*).

Examples [i–ii] are straightforward instances of the specifying use of *be* described in Ch. 4, §5.5; the content clause identifies the value of the variable expressed in the subject.[7] Example [iii] can be spoken with two intonation groups, the first ending with stressed *is*, in which case it is hardly possible to have *that* in the content clause. Although the subject NP contains the definite article, there is no reference to any previously mentioned or independently definable fact, problem, or rumour. The effect here is to present the content clause as new information, rather than to specify the value of a variable – and in this interpretation it is certainly not possible to reverse the order of the elements related by *be*.

4.3 Content clauses in construction with *it*

4.3.1 *It* as subject

Extraposed subject

The clausal subject construction illustrated in [3] (*That he tried to retract his statement is hardly surprising*, etc.) is by no means rare, but it is nevertheless much more usual for the content clause to occur in extraposed subject function, at the end of the matrix clause:

[16] i *It is hardly surprising that he tried to retract his statement.*
ii *It simply hadn't occurred to us that the work might be a forgery.*
iii *It cannot be doubted that she did everything in her power to help.*

The relationship between the two constructions with and without extraposition is discussed in Ch. 16, §7.

The impersonal construction with *it* as subject

[17] i *It appeared/seemed that he was trying to hide his true identity.*
ii *It chanced / (so) happened / turned out that she had just been to the bank.*

In this construction the subject is semantically empty (as indicated by the term **impersonal**), so that the content clause represents the sole argument of the matrix clause. For [i] this can be brought out by a paraphrase containing an adverb instead of the matrix verb: *Apparently/Seemingly he was trying to hide his true identity.* Similarly the version of [ii] with *chance* as verb is approximately equivalent to *By chance, she had just been to the bank.* Some of the verbs concerned allow a further complement containing an NP with the semantic role of experiencer: *It seems to me she's probably right* or *It strikes me that we are losing control.* For other verbs in this impersonal construction, see [10i] of Ch. 16, §7.1.

We take the content clause in [17] to be an internal complement of the verb. The construction bears some resemblance to the one shown above in [16], where the content clause occurs in extraposed subject position, but differs from it in that the subordinate clause cannot occupy the actual subject position. Compare:

[18]	INTERNAL COMPLEMENT ONLY	EXTRAPOSED OR SUBJECT
i	a. *It seems that he was wrong.*	b. *It is obvious that he was wrong.*
ii	a. **That he was wrong seems.*	b. *That he was wrong is obvious.*

[7] We noted that *remain* is occasionally used with its complements interpreted as variable and value, and it too allows a content clause as value: *My main objection to your article remains that it is too speculative.*

In spite of this difference many grammars do in fact treat the content clauses in [17] as extraposed subjects: the ungrammaticality of [18iia] is accounted for by saying that with these verbs extraposition is obligatory. There are, however, a number of objections to this analysis.

No structural reason for extraposition to be obligatory

The contrast between [ia] and [iia] in [18] is quite different from that seen in:

[19] i *Isn't it obvious that he is wrong?* } [extraposition obligatory]
ii **Isn't that he is wrong obvious?*

Here it is reasonable to say that extraposition is obligatory, because [ii] is excluded by a general structural constraint preventing a finite clause occurring in the post-auxiliary position. But there's no such rule blocking [18iia]: finite clauses can occupy subject position if licensed by the verb or VP. Indeed, the inadmissibility of [18iia] is not attributable to the fact that the subject is a clause: no other kind of expression (besides impersonal *it*) would be acceptable here. Ordinary subjects are possible if we add an internal complement, but that changes the construction and makes it possible to have a content clause as well as an ordinary NP in subject position:

[20]	IMPERSONAL CONSTRUCTION	ORDINARY COMPLEX-INTRANSITIVE
i	a. *It seems that he was guilty.*	b. *It seems clear that he was guilty.*
ii	a. **That he was guilty seems.*	b. *That he was guilty seems clear.*
iii	a. **His guilt seems.*	b. *His guilt seems clear.*

In the [b] examples *seem* takes *clear* as predicative complement, and this licenses as subject either an NP (*his guilt* in [iiib]) or a content clause (*that he was guilty* in [iib]). Example [ib] is an alternant of [iib] and a straightforward case of the construction with extraposed subject. Similarly in the construction with an infinitival complement (the catenative construction):

[21] i *It seems to have surprised her that he was guilty.*
ii *That he was guilty seems to have surprised her.*
iii *His guilt seems to have surprised her.*

But examples [iia] and [iiia] in [20] show that *seem* can't occur in monovalent constructions. The deviance of [iia] has nothing to do with extraposition: it simply doesn't satisfy the complementation requirements of *seem.* The same applies with the other verbs illustrated in [17]: cf. **A meeting chanced*; **Their friendship happened* (not possible with the relevant sense of *happen* – compare *It so happened that they were friends*); **A disaster turned out.*

Coordination

Compare next:

[22] i *It seemed that he was trying to hide his true identity.*
ii *It was later confirmed that he was trying to hide his true identity.*
iii **It seemed and was later confirmed that he was trying to hide his true identity.*

Example [ii] is a clear case of the extraposition construction: if [i] also belonged to this construction it should be possible to coordinate the contrasting parts *seemed* and *was later confirmed.* However, [iii] shows that this can't be done, suggesting that the content clause does not have the same function in the two cases.

Complementation with *as if*

With *seem* and *appear* the content clause in what we are analysing as the impersonal construction can be replaced without any perceptible change of meaning by a phrase introduced by *as if* (or *as though* or *like*), a type of phrase also found with such verbs as *feel, look, smell, sound, taste* – and *be*:

[23] i *It seemed that / as if he was trying to hide his true identity.*
ii *It looked/was as if he was trying to hide his true identity.*

As if phrases cannot function as subject, so there is no question of an extraposed subject analysis for this construction: we must recognise an impersonal construction containing an internal complement with the form of an *as if* phrase. To cater for *It seems that*... we need only add that with *seem* and *appear* this internal complement can also have the form of a content clause.[8] The similarity between the content clause and the *as if* phrase is seen in examples like:

[24] *It seems to me as if / that they have a reasonable chance of winning; is that how it seems to you?*

The internal complement of *it seems* is here questioned by *how*, with either an *as if* phrase or a content clause providing an appropriate answer. Not only does this show the similiarity between the content clause and an *as if* phrase: it also shows the difference between both and an extraposed subject. Extraposed subjects can't be questioned: since the interrogative element would not itself be a clause, there would be no extraposition. With *It invariably annoys him that I work on Sundays*, for example, we can question the subject (*What invariably annoys him?*), but not the extraposed subject (**What does it invariably annoy him?*).

With *be*

There are several more or less idiomatic uses of *be* with *it* as subject and content clause as internal complement:

[25] i *It's not that I don't understand what you're trying to say.*
ii *It's just that there hasn't been time to consider the matter carefully.*
iii *It may be that we should have given him a second chance.*

In the salient interpretations (we ignore the unproblematic ones where *it* is simply anaphoric to some preceding NP such as *my objection* or *the best suggestion*) the *it* here has no clear reference and hence can hardly be regarded as defining a variable whose value is specified by the content clause. Example [i], with *not* and obligatory *that*, is an idiomatic way of denying the proposition expressed in the content clause. Positive [ii], again with *that* obligatory, is a way of presenting an explanation – I might have been showing reluctance to accept some proposal and say [ii] to explain why. Example [iii], with *may*, stressed *be*, and optional *that*, is equivalent to *Maybe/Perhaps we should have given him a second chance.* We noted above that *it* + *be* is like *it* + *seem* in allowing an *as if* phrase as complement (cf. [23]), and the examples in [25] should perhaps be analysed as belonging to the impersonal construction we have proposed for *seem*.

[8] *Feel, look,* and *sound* are very occasionally found with a content clause too: *It looks to me that a vendetta has struck up.* Content clauses differ from *as if* phrases in that they are restricted to the impersonal construction: compare *Ed seemed as if / *that he was trying to hide his true identity.*

4.3.2 The complex-transitive construction

[26] i *I find it hardly surprising that he tried to retract his statement.*
ii *They regard it as a discourtesy that you didn't notify them earlier.*

Example [i] may be compared with *I find his behaviour hardly surprising,* where the predicand of the predicative complement *hardly surprising* is an NP in object function. If the predicand is a content clause we normally need *it* as a dummy object, with the content clause in **extraposed object** position, as here. The content clause cannot itself occupy the position between verb and predicative complement, for a clausal complement cannot in general be followed within the VP by another complement; however, a version without the extrapositional *it* is possible if the content clause is preposed to prenuclear position:

[27] i **I find that he tried to retract his statement hardly surprising.*
ii *That he tried to retract his statement I find hardly surprising.*

A sample of complex-transitive verbs appearing in this construction is given in [28]; the notation '[*as*]' indicates that the predicative has the form of an *as* phrase, as in [26ii]:

[28]	*accept* [*as*]	*believe*	*call*	*confirm* [*as*]	*consider*
	declare	*deem*	*establish* [*as*]	*find*	*hold*
	judge	*make*	*present* [*as*]	*recognise* [*as*]	*see* [*as*]

4.3.3 Other constructions

[29] i *I take it you'll be accepting their offer.*
ii *He didn't like it that she had brought the children.*
iii *She resents it that they appointed someone less qualified than her.*
iv *You can depend on it that she'll find a solution.*
v *We owe it to you that we got off so lightly.*
vi *I put it to you that the man's a charlatan.*
vii *This brought it home to us that we were in great danger*

These are all different in various ways, but each type is restricted to a small number of governing expressions. *Take it* in [i] is a verbal idiom, which as a whole licenses the content clause; *have it* is another idiom of the same kind (cf. *Rumour has it that they're getting divorced*). *Like* has the same meaning in [ii] as elsewhere, but it doesn't license a content clause on its own (**He didn't like that she had brought the children*); *dislike* and *hate* probably behave in the same way. Example [iii] differs from [i–ii] in that the *it* here can be omitted without any apparent change in meaning; *resent* and *regret* are the main verbs that display this behaviour. In [iv] *it* is object of a preposition rather than of the verb; the preposition *on* cannot take declarative content clauses as complement, so again the *it* is obligatory. Verb + preposition combinations found in this construction, beside *depend on*, include *bank/rely on, get over, see to*, and there are also verbal idioms like *get wind of, take my word for*. Examples [v–vii] have one or more complements between *it* and the content clause. In [v], the content clause can be preposed, with omission of *it* (*That we got off so lightly we owe to you*); in [vii] the *it* can be dropped without change in the position of the content clause; and [vi] has neither type of alternant. The idiom *take for granted* belongs with [vii]: *He had taken (it) for granted that he would be given a second chance.*

4.4 Complement of an adjective

Adjectives in predicative function may take complements with the form of content clauses:

[30] i *He's [very conscious that they might not give him a second chance].*
ii *This made me [glad I'd stayed at home].*
iii *I'm [determined that he won't get the better of me].*

Adjectives that license declarative content clauses as complement include the following:

[31]						
i	*afraid*	*angry*	*aware*	*certain*	*confident*	*conscious*
	eager	*fearful*	*glad*	*grateful*	*happy*	*hopeful*
	positive	*proud*	*sad*	*sorry*	*sure*	*thankful*
ii	*amazed*	*amused*	*annoyed*	*determined*	*disgusted*	*distressed*
	disturbed	*irritated*	*pleased*	*surprised*	*upset*	*worried*

Those in [ii] are participial adjectives, and many others of this kind could be added. All the adjectives in [31] also take complements with the form preposition + NP, as in *He's afraid of snakes.* There is, however, a sense of *afraid* that is found only with a clausal complement – approximately "regret", as in *I'm afraid I can't help you.*

The present construction is to be distinguished from that dealt with in §4.3.1 above, where an adjective is followed by an extraposed subject. Compare:

[32] i *Max is certain that he is being victimised.* [complement in AdjP structure]
ii *It is certain that he is being victimised.* [extraposed subject in clause structure]

In [i] *certain* has two arguments, expressing Max's state of mind relative to the proposition that he is being victimised. In [ii] *it* is a dummy element, so that *certain* here has only one argument, just as in the non-extraposed counterpart *That he is being victimised is certain.* For the most part the adjectives licensing the two constructions are distinct, as is evident from a comparison of [31] with [4] above; note in particular that the participial adjectives taking a complement are based on past participles, while those taking a clause as (extraposed) subject are based on gerund-participles. *Certain* is the only item that occurs commonly in both constructions; in addition, *sure* occurs predominantly in construction [32i] but occasionally in [ii] (*It now seems sure there'll be an election before the end of the year*), and conversely *clear* usually appears in [ii] but is occasionally found in [i] (*I'm quite clear that he's not telling the truth*).

4.5 Complement of a noun or supplement

Content clauses commonly function as complement in NP structure:

[33] i *[The thought that we might need him] had simply never occurred to him.*
ii *He expressed [the opinion that we should advertise the position overseas].*
iii *We're looking for [evidence that the fire was deliberately lit].*

For the distinction between this construction and one with a relative clause modifier (e.g. *evidence that will convince them*), see Ch. 12, §3.1; and for argument that this construction involves complementation rather than apposition, see §8.2 below. A sample of nouns licensing declarative content clause complements is given in:

[34]					
i	*admission*	*agreement*	*argument*	*assertion*	*assumption*
	belief	*boast*	*claim*	*complaint*	*conclusion*
	discovery	*expectation*	*feeling*	*guess*	*hope*
	implication	*inference*	*knowledge*	*objection*	*promise*
	proof	*proposal*	*revelation*	*rumour*	*saying*
	statement	*suggestion*	*thought*	*warning*	*worry*
ii	*awareness*	*certainty*	*confidence*	*eagerness*	*inevitability*
	likelihood	*possibility*	*probability*	*sorrow*	*willingness*
iii	*chance*	*danger*	*evidence*	*fact*	*faith*
	idea	*impression*	*message*	*news*	*odds*
	opinion	*principle*	*proposition*	*prospect*	*sign*
	story	*tradition*	*view*		

Those in [i] and [ii] are derived from verbs and adjectives respectively; some of those in [iii] are also morphologically derivative but differ in meaning from the source.

With the deverbal nouns the element corresponding to the subject of the verb commonly appears as genitive subject-determiner; with agentive verbs it may also appear as complement in a *by* phrase and with non-agentives occasionally within an *of* phrase:

[35] i *our assumption that he was telling the truth*
ii *a proposal by one candidate that there should be a television debate*
iii *the earnest hope of all of us that she would quickly recover from her operation*

The adjectives from which the nouns in [34ii] are derived include some that take content clauses as complement (*aware*, *confident*, etc.) and others that license them as subject (*likely*, *probable*, etc.). Genitive determiners are then found in nouns deriving from the former, but not the latter:

[36] i *his confidence that he would get the job*
ii *the/*his probability that he would get the job*

the fact (*that*)

Among the nouns in [34iii] *fact* merits special mention as much the most frequent noun taking a content clause complement. It serves as a device for nominalising clauses by incorporating them into an NP that can occupy any ordinary NP position. Consider, for example:

[37] i *This theory is borne out by* [*the fact that children in co-educational schools often mature earlier than those who are segregated*].
ii *Are they indifferent to* [*the fact that the dog can easily pick up germs from the preceding patient*]*?*
iii *No amount of statistical explanation can disguise* [*the fact that, as a nation, we are still spending more than we are earning*].

Many prepositions like *by* in [i] allow NP complements but not declarative content clauses: use of *the fact* here is therefore necessary to accommodate the content clause within the *by* phrase. Similarly *indifferent* in [ii] and *disguise* in [iii] don't license content clauses: the former requires a *to* phrase, the latter an NP object. *The fact* is not limited, however, to cases where the content clause could not stand on its own. It commonly occurs, for example, in subject position, where it is in competition with two other constructions:

[38] i *The fact that it was illegal didn't worry him.* [NP as subject]
ii *That it was illegal didn't worry him.* [clause as subject]
iii *It didn't worry him that it was illegal.* [*it* + extraposed subject]

Construction [ii], with the content clause itself as subject, is much the least frequent of the three; use of *the fact* facilitates the incorporation of the content clause into the subject when there is a preference for positioning it early in the matrix clause, rather than later, as in the extraposition construction.

Like other cases of full nominalisation, *the fact* permits the introduction of adjuncts such as AdjPs that cannot modify clauses:

[39] *We should encourage the leaders of these societies to accept the unpleasant fact that they are responsible for their fates.*

NPs with *fact* as head and clause as complement are always definite: the clause identifies the fact. A coordination of clauses usually counts as a single fact, but can also be taken as a set of facts:

[40] i *It hides [the fact that the peace movement is still advancing and that clarification of the issues can bring a majority to secure the Scarborough decisions].*
ii *They are invited to consider [the facts that when a prisoner's letter home contained the word 'commies' it was suggested that 'People's Volunteers' should be substituted, and that the only address to which any prisoner's relatives could send letters was 'c/o the People's Committee for World Peace'].*

Postposed complements and supplements

In all the examples given so far the content clause has been integrated into the structure of the NP headed by the licensing noun. It is also possible for it to be postposed or detached as a supplement, as in [41i–ii] respectively:

[41] i a. *The possibility can't be ruled out that she will call an early election.*
b. *He presented evidence to the commission that the fire was deliberately lit.*
ii a. *I'm inclined to favour your first suggestion, that we shelve the proposal until after the election.*
b. *Avoiding one counsel of the Fabian tract, that a few of the larger school boards might well be saved for limited purposes because of their superior efficiency, the government came out for their abolition.*

The supplements have the whole of the preceding NP as anchor; they must be semantically compatible with it (identifying its content), but are not syntactically licensed by the head noun: *counsel*, for example, does not license content clause complements (cf. Ch. 15, §5.1).

Multi-word licensing

There are some instances of the sequence noun + content clause where the clause is not licensed by the noun alone. The clearest cases involve prepositional constructions like *to the effect*, *on the basis*, etc., discussed in Ch. 7, §3.2, but it is arguable that certain clausal constructions involving *have/give* or existential *there* + *be* are also of this kind:

[42] i *We had no idea it would be so difficult.*
ii *The present system has the disadvantage that it is inordinately complicated.*
iii *There's also the problem that two signatures are needed.*

Idea can certainly take a clausal complement (*The idea that he might be wrong had simply never occurred to him*), but hardly with *no*, and (as observed in Ch. 4, §6) the *have no/any idea* combination can license an interrogative complement, which is certainly not possible with *idea* on its own (*He had no idea what to do*, but not **A good idea what to do was suggested by Terry*). *Have no idea* is semantically like *not know*, and it appears to behave as an idiom with the same complementation as *know*. *Disadvantage* and *problem* are hardly able to take clausal complements on their own: *?The disadvantage that it is inordinately complicated had been overlooked*; *?The problem that two signatures are needed is quite serious.* Again, therefore, it is arguable that the content clause is a complement in the structure of the VP or clause rather than of the NPs headed by these nouns.

4.6 Content clauses licensed by *so*, *such*, and (in AmE) *enough*, *sufficient*(*ly*)

Delayed complements with *so* and *such*

In all varieties of English the adverb *so* and the adjective *such* license declarative content clauses occurring at the end of the matrix clause:

[43] i a. *The case was so heavy that I couldn't lift it.*
b. *So many people enrolled for the course that we had to move to a larger room.*
c. *It happened so quickly that we were taken completely offguard.*
d. *It was so at variance with his usual behaviour that we thought he was ill.*
e. *He'd so arranged the programme that we had lots of time to discuss the papers.*
ii a. *It was such a miserable day that we decided to stay at home.*
b. *He placed the boulder in such a way that the door couldn't swing shut.*
c. *Such strain is being placed on the marriage that it is likely to collapse.*

The content clause here is not adjacent to the *so* or *such* that licenses it, but is 'delayed' to the end of the matrix clause. This position is obligatory. In [ia], for example, we cannot have **It was so that I couldn't lift it heavy*; nor can [ib] have the content clause at the end of the subject phrase: **So many people that we had to move to a larger room enrolled for the course.* Note also that there may be multiple occurrences of *so* or *such* followed by a single content clause:

[44] i *So many defects had been found in so many of the components that the model had to be withdrawn from the market.*
ii *Some places are so lovely, so mystical, that they must be left intact for the sake of the human spirit.*

For these reasons we analyse the content clause as a complement in clause structure rather than as a complement of *so* and *such* themselves. This is a further case, therefore, of an indirect complement, one licensed not by the word which is the ultimate head of the construction containing it, but by an item embedded within some other dependent. In [43ib], for example, the immediate constituents are *so many people enrolled for the course* and *that we had to move to a larger room*. The ultimate head is *enrolled*, but it is the *so* within the subject that licenses the content clause.

So and *such* indicate degree/extent or manner and the content clause has a resultative meaning that can be brought out by such glosses as "The result of the case being as heavy as it was was that I couldn't lift it", "The result of his arranging the programme in the way he did was that we had plenty of time to discuss the papers", and so on. *So* occurs as modifier to a wide range of heads: adjective in [43ia], degree determinative in [ib], adverb in [ic], PP in [id], verb in [ie]; *such* in [ii] is a predeterminer modifier in NP structure, but it can also occur predicatively, as illustrated below.

The subordinator *that* is omissible, under the conditions that apply to content clauses generally (§3.1): *The case was so heavy I couldn't lift it*. One quite exceptional feature of this construction, however, is that *that* cannot be repeated in coordination:

[45] **The goods were so defective that they had to be recalled and that the manager was forced to resign.*

such that

When the adjective *such* is used predicatively the content clause generally follows immediately, but it does not have to:

[46] i *His circumstances were such that he could rarely afford a restaurant meal.*
ii *Such is the mystique of planning that people expect that fulfilment of the plan will follow automatically upon its announcement.*
iii *The angle of attack was such on take-off that several passengers reported hearing the fuselage scrape the runway.*

In [ii] the *such* is preposed and in [iii] it is followed by an adjunct. In all cases, however, the content clause is again located at the end of the matrix clause, just as in [43ii] above, and we will analyse it in the same way, as complement in the matrix clause. The only difference, a minor one, is that in this predicative construction the subordinator *that* is not omissible.

Such is also used postpositively, in which case the content clause is obligatory:

[47] *The approach aims to achieve a body of laws of empirical generalisations about human conduct such that one can both explain human behaviour and social change and gain the power to change society.*

so that

So occurs immediately before the content clause it licenses in three constructions, involving manner, result, and purpose adjuncts.

(a) Manner

[48] i *He'd arranged the programme so that we had lots of time to discuss the papers.*
ii *I apply the hay so that only the tops of the plants show above it.*

The *so* here can be glossed as "in such a way": it is a manner adjunct and licenses a resultative in the same way as the *so* of [43i] – note that [48i] is identical to [43ie] except for the position of the *so*. The construction with post-verbal manner *so* is, however, comparatively rare: *so* in this position is usually interpreted as in (b) or (c) below (and indeed the *so* phrase in [48i] is ambiguous between the manner reading considered here, and a "with the result that" reading like that of [49] below).

(b) Result

[49] *Most primary teachers are women so that suitable 'role models', to use the trendy phrase, are more abundant for girls than for boys.*

Here *so* is syntactically inseparable from the content clause which, moreover, cannot be omitted. In this construction, therefore, the content clause is best analysed as a complement of *so*, with the combination of *so* + content clause functioning as adjunct of result. Note then that here the resultative meaning is attributable not to the content clause itself, but to the phrase consisting of *so* as head and clause as complement; this phrase we take to be a PP, with *so* a preposition by virtue of taking a content clause as complement (see Ch. 15, §2.11).

(c) Purpose

[50] i *I disconnected the phone so that we could talk undisturbed.*
ii *So that his customers should not soil their hands, Brecht issued white gloves.*

Again the content clause is inseparable from *so*, and this time *so* + content clause can be preposed, as in [ii]: it is clear therefore that the content clause is a complement of *so* itself. The PP consisting of *so* + content clause functions as adjunct of purpose, with *so* equivalent to *in order.*

■ *enough, sufficient, sufficiently*

In AmE these degree modifiers license a complement with the form of a content clause or *so* + content clause:

[51] i %*The orchestra is far enough away from you that you miss the bow scrapes, valve clicks, and other noises incidental to playing.*
ii %*The calculation can usually be made with sufficient accuracy that it won't affect the final computation.*
iii %*The party is usually in a room small enough so that all guests are within sight and hearing of one another.*

(BrE would have to have an infinitival complement here: *far enough away from you for you to (be able to) miss the bow scrapes . . .*) The complement has to be final in the matrix clause like those in [43] and is again best analysed as belonging in the matrix clause.

4.7 Adjunct in clause structure

There are a handful of constructions where a declarative content clause functions as adjunct rather than complement.

(a) With subject + predicator order

[52] i *What has happened, that you are looking so worried?*
ii *'This is my party card', he said, holding it high, that all might see it.*
iii *The more we talked, the more I liked her.*

The type of content clause we have in [i] functions as adjunct to interrogative clauses. Semantically the adjunct can be regarded as resultative: the presupposition of the question can be glossed as "Something has happened with the result that you are looking worried". The content clause in [ii] is a purpose adjunct; the construction is rare and somewhat archaic, with Present-day English usually having *so that* rather than *that* alone. In [iii] *the more we talked* is the subordinate clause in the correlative comparative construction discussed in Ch. 13, §4.6; note that although it occurs in a comparative construction it does not have the distinctive properties of comparative clauses with respect to its internal form and hence belongs in the default category of content clauses. The initial element is always a comparative phrase modified by *the.*

(b) With subject–auxiliary inversion

[53] *Had they committed a similar crime here, they would have got a jail sentence.*

Here the content clause functions as a conditional adjunct, equivalent to the PP *if they had committed a similar crime here.* Only a subset of auxiliaries can occur in this construction: the great majority of cases involve *had, were,* or *should.*

By virtue of the subject–auxiliary inversion, the subordinate clause has the appearance of a main clause closed interrogative. This formal resemblance is one reflection of the significant semantic resemblances between conditions and questions. Compare:

[54] i *If you're free this afternoon, we can go and look at some houses.*
ii *Are you free this afternoon? If so, we can go and look at some houses.*

The conditional adjunct in [i] entertains two possibilities, one where you're free this afternoon and one where you're not, and these correspond to the two answers to the polar question in [ii]. The second sentence of [ii] begins with an *if* phrase where *so* is interpreted in terms of the positive answer to the preceding question; for the negative answer we have *not* (*If not, I'll look at the houses on my own*). Consider next the following set:

[55] i *Are you sitting comfortably? Then I'll begin.*
ii *He does little himself. He only plans. But his agents are numerous and splendidly organised. Is there a crime to be done, a paper to be abstracted, we will say, a house to be rifled, a man to be removed – the word is passed to the Professor, the matter is organised and carried out.*
iii *Dare a woman have a child, she's putting her job at risk.*
iv *Could he have cast himself in the part of Mr Copthorne, the villain and apostate, he would not have attempted to run away from his captors.*
v *Suddenly it seemed to him insane that they might hope to locate Gyp Carmer so casually, even were he to prove the thief.*

Here [i] (the first words of a radio programme for young children) is like [54ii] except that we have *then* instead of the *if* phrase in the second sentence: this time a positive answer is assumed. In [55ii] (from Conan Doyle's *The Adventures of Sherlock Holmes*, 1901–3) there is no question mark and no following adjunct; the underlined sequence is interpreted like a conditional adjunct ("If there is a crime to be done, ... "), but its syntactic status is somewhat obscure: it lies somewhere between [i], which is clearly an interrogative expressing a question, and [iii–v], which are conditional adjuncts. Example [iii] is unusual in that we have here an open conditional: these inverted conditional adjuncts normally occur in remote conditionals (except when introduced by modal *should*: see §7.1.2). For this reason, [iii] is not sharply different from [ii], though the latter does not represent an established construction in Present-day English, for *is* cannot introduce inverted conditionals. In [iv–v] we have remote conditionals, with [iv] a rare example of inversion with modal *could*. In [v] the irrealis form *were* and even more strikingly the focusing adverb *even* make the underlined clause clearly distinct from an interrogative. There is no doubt, then, that inversion can serve as a marker of a conditional, and that [iii–v] are not interrogative clauses but belong to the default declarative type of content clause.

4.8 Complement of a preposition or adverb

With prepositional governors we need to distinguish between non-expandable content clauses, which exclude *that*, and expandable ones, which allow it (§3):

[56] i a. *They left [before the meeting ended].* } [non-expandable]
b. *We'll invite them both [though I don't think he'll come]*
ii a. *I'll come along, [provided (that) I can leave early.* } [expandable]
b. *I was lucky [in that the other candidates withdrew].*

The non-expandable construction

The main items governing non-expandable content clauses are as follows:

[57]	*after*	*although*	*as*	*as if*	*as long as*	*as soon as*
	because	*before*	*for*	*for all*	*if*	*in case*
	lest	*like*	*once*	*since*	*though*	*till/until*
	unless	*when*	*where*	*whereas*	*directly*	*immediately*

The last two are adverbs, the others prepositions or prepositional idioms.

The expandable construction

Prepositions governing content clauses of this kind include those given in [58]; see also the discussion in Ch. 7, §3.2, of prepositional idioms that license content clauses: expressions such as *in order*, *on condition*, *for fear*, etc.

[58]	*but*	*considering*	*except*	*given*	*granted*
	in	*notwithstanding*	*now*	*provided*	*providing*
	save	*seeing*	*so*	*supposing*	

The subordinator *that* is obligatory with *in*, and effectively with *so* too, for *so* without *that* is construed as a connective adverb (cf. Ch. 15, §2.11). *But* occurs with a content clause complement in such constructions as:

[59] i *I don't doubt but that she meant it.*
ii *I wouldn't have taken any notice but that I feared they might upset Angela.*
iii *There wasn't a boy among them but would have gladly taken my place.*

Example [i] (conveying that I believe she meant it) illustrates the use with expressions of doubt in non-affirmative contexts; *but* is omissible, with the content clause then a complement of *doubt* (cf. §5.3.3 below). *That* is more or less obligatory in [ii], for without it *but* will generally be taken as a coordinator (but cf. the proverb *It never rains but it pours*, where *but* clearly has its prepositional meaning, "except"). In [iii] the subordinate clause has a gap in subject position (anaphorically linked to *a boy among them*), with *that* obligatorily omitted. This is a somewhat archaic construction, restricted to non-affirmative contexts; the "except" meaning of *but* gives an interpretation like that of a negative relative clause: "There wasn't a boy among them who would not gladly have taken my place".

5 Interrogative content clauses

Subordinate interrogatives, like main clause interrogatives, normally express questions, but because they are embedded there is no illocutionary force associated with them. A main clause interrogative such as *Where was she born?* is characteristically used to **ask** a question, i.e. as an inquiry, but the subordinate counterpart *where she was born* is not. It nevertheless **expresses** the same question as the main clause, with the same set of possible answers. As will be evident from this formulation, we continue to maintain a distinction between categories of grammatical form and categories of meaning: interrogative applies to the formal category, question to the semantic one.

Subordinate interrogatives are used in reporting inquiries, as in *They asked where she was born*, but have numerous other uses too, as in *They know where she was born* or *It depends where she was born.* We refer to the questions they express as **embedded questions**, avoiding the traditional term 'indirect question' for reasons given in Ch. 10, §3.2. In the default case, sentences whose meaning contains an embedded question can be glossed with the formula 'the answer to the question' – thus for the examples just given, "They know / It depends on the answer to the question 'Where was she born?' ".

5.1 Form

Absence of subject–auxiliary inversion

The main structural difference between subordinate and main clause interrogatives is that subject–auxiliary inversion does not generally apply in the subordinate construction:

[1]	MAIN	SUBORDINATE	
i	a. *Has he read it?*	b. *I wonder [whether/ if he has read it].*	[closed]
ii	a. *What did he do?*	b. *I know [what he did].*	[open]

Closed interrogative content clauses are generally marked by one or other of the subordinators *whether* and *if*, while open interrogatives are distinguished from declaratives by the presence of an interrogative phrase in initial position:

[2]	DECLARATIVE	INTERROGATIVE	
i	a. *I can't say [(that) it's his].*	b. *I can't say [whether/ if it's his].*	[closed]
ii	a. *I know [(that) he told Ed].*	b. *I know [who he told].*	[open]

Since main clause open interrogatives with the interrogative phrase as subject have no inversion, there is here no internal difference between the main and subordinate constructions:

[3]	MAIN	SUBORDINATE
	a. *What happened to Kim?*	b. *It's unclear [what happened to Kim].*

The absence of inversion results in a very considerable overlap between subordinate open interrogatives and relative constructions:

[4] OPEN INTERROGATIVE / RELATIVE

i a. *You know which I prefer.* b. *This is the version which I prefer.*

ii a. *I don't know what you want.* b. *I haven't got what you want.*

The distinction between these constructions is discussed in Ch. 12, §§3.1, 6.2.

Subject–auxiliary inversion is not wholly excluded from subordinate interrogatives, but it is largely restricted (in Standard English) to constructions where questions are cited, as in *Easily the most popular question put to the PM was: Why are we buying New Zealand carpets for the new Parliament House?*

We have noted that in main clause open interrogatives it is possible for the interrogative phrase to remain 'in situ' (*And after that you went where?*). In the subordinate construction, however, fronting is obligatory: *He wants to know* [*where you went after that*], not **He wants to know* [*after that you went where*]. But, as in main clauses, there can be more than one interrogative phrase, with just one of them occurring in initial position:

[5] i *They haven't told us* [*who is responsible for what*].

ii *I haven't found out yet* [*which projects they are assigning to whom*].

Infinitival interrogatives

A second difference between subordinate and main clause interrogatives is that with subordinates the distinction between information questions and direction questions is clearly marked grammatically, with direction questions having infinitival form (cf. Ch. 10, §4.6):

[6]	MAIN	SUBORDINATE	
i	a. *Where am I going?*	b. *I don't know* [*where I'm going*].	[information]
ii	a. *Where shall I go?*	b. *I don't know* [*where to go*].	[direction]

5.2 ***Whether* vs *if***

Closed interrogative subordinate clauses are marked as such by one or other of the interrogative subordinators *whether* and *if.* Typically these are interchangeable, as in [1ib] and [2ib] above, but this is not always so. We examine here constructions where *if* is excluded, and then consider factors favouring one or the other in constructions that permit both.

Constructions where only *whether* is permitted

(a) In the exhaustive conditional construction

[7] *I'm going to see her* [*whether*/**if you like it or not*].

(b) When the interrogative clause is infinitival

[8] *She can't make up her mind* [*whether*/**if to accept*].

(c) When the interrogative clause precedes the superordinate predicator

[9] i [*Whether*/**if this was the right decision remains unclear*]. [subject]

ii [*Whether*/**if it will work*] *we shall soon find out.* [preposed complement]

(d) When *or not* immediately follows the subordinator

[10] *I don't know [whether/*if or not she'll accept].*

When *or not* follows the first coordinate, either subordinator is permitted: *I don't know whether/if she'll accept or not.*

(e) As complement to *be* or as a supplement to an NP

[11] i *The question you have to decide is [whether/*if guilt has been established beyond reasonable doubt].*
ii *This question, [whether/*if the commissioner exceeded the terms of reference,] will need to be carefully investigated.*

Example [i] represents the specifying use of *be*: the interrogative specifies the value of the variable expressed in the subject, i.e. it identifies which question you have to decide. In [ii] the bracketed supplement specifies the content of 'this question' (cf. Ch. 15, §5.2).

(f) When the interrogative clause is complement of a preposition[9]

[12] *It depends on [whether/*if we have enough time left].*

Factors favouring one or other subordinator

In constructions where both *whether* and *if* are grammatically allowed, a preference for one over the other may arise from a variety of factors, including the following:

(a) Reports of questions used as indirect speech acts favour *if*

[13] i *I asked them if they'd like to stay to dinner.*
ii *He wants to know if you'd mind moving your car.*
iii *I suggested getting you to do it and he asked me if I'd taken leave of my senses.*

These examples would typically be used to report utterances of the unembedded questions *Would you like to stay to dinner?*; *Would you mind moving your car?*; *Have you taken leave of your senses?*; and the characteristic use of these would be as indirect speech acts (Ch. 10, §3.2) – the first as an offer/invitation, the second as a request, and the third as a statement ("You must have taken leave of your senses to make such a suggestion"). *If* tends to be preferred in cases of this kind. *Whether* would give more prominence to the question itself than to the indirect speech act: it focuses on the choice between possible answers. This preference for *if* generalises to cases like *I wonder if you could help me move these plants*: this is not a report of a question, but a statement used as an indirect question ("Could you help me move these plants?"), which in turn indirectly conveys a request.

(b) Style: *if* slightly more informal than *whether*

There is a small difference in style level: other things being equal, formal style will favour *whether*, informal style *if*.

[9] Occasional examples with *if* in this construction are attested, but they are at best of very marginal acceptability: *?I was excited for this new opportunity, and yet worried about if I would be able to find work.*

(c) Some matrix verbs favour *whether*

Such verbs include *explain*, *investigate*, *judge*, *ponder*, *study*, etc.:

[14] i *You should explain whether they are required to write detailed answers or only short ones.*

ii *They are investigating whether there is any way of closing the loophole.*

The verbs concerned tend to be ones which do not frequently take closed interrogative complements. There is some correlation here with factor (b), but it is clearly not simply a matter of style, for such verbs as *ascertain*, *inquire*, *recall*, etc., take *if* more readily than the above but do not differ from them in style level: *I'll inquire if we are required to write detailed answers or only short ones.*

Interrogative and conditional *if*

If is used as a marker of conditionality as well as of closed interrogative clause type – and there may be ambiguity between the two constructions:

[15] i *I won't tell her if you bring it back today.* } [conditional or interrogative]

ii *Let me know if you need any help.*

With conditional *if* the meaning of [i] is "If you bring it back today then I won't tell her (something contextually retrievable, e.g. that you borrowed her ring)". With interrogative *if* the meaning is "I won't tell her whether you bring it back today". *Whether* is interrogative, not conditional, and hence will disambiguate when substituted for *if*. In [ii] there is little pragmatic difference between the two interpretations. In the conditional interpretation I am asking you to tell me that you need help if you do, and in the interrogative interpretation to tell me whether or not you need help – but telling me you need help would be an appropriate response in either case, and failure to say anything could indicate non-fulfilment of the condition or a negative answer to the question.

The overlap between the conditional and closed interrogative markers is not surprising (and quite common cross-linguistically), for there is an evident semantic connection between conditions and questions, as discussed in §4.7 above.

5.3 Survey of constructions containing subordinate interrogatives

Classification of embedded questions

In Ch. 10 we distinguished numerous different kinds of question, but for present purposes it is sufficient to consider two dimensions of contrast. One is that between information questions and direction questions mentioned above, and the other is between polar, alternative, and variable questions. These dimensions cut across each other, yielding the following six categories:

[16]

	INFORMATION	DIRECTION
POLAR	*I don't know if it is possible.*	*I don't know whether to tell them.*
ALTERNATIVE	*I don't know if it's true or not.*	*I don't know whether to go or not.*
VARIABLE	*I don't know what he wants.*	*I don't know what to do.*

Variable questions are expressed by open interrogatives, polar and alternative questions by closed interrogatives, with alternative questions further marked by an *or*-coordination. As noted above, information questions are expressed by finite clauses, direction questions by infinitivals.

In the great majority of cases where subordinate interrogatives are found, all six categories are permitted. Cases where this is not so are discussed in §§5.3.2–4.

Licensing of subordinate interrogatives

Subordinate interrogatives mainly occur in complement function, where they have to be licensed by an appropriate head – for example, we can have *I forget whether Kim was present* but not **I regret whether Kim was present.* We will give sample lists of licensing heads as we look in turn at the various constructions involved, but it will be helpful to give at the outset a rough semantic classification of a sample of licensing expressions:

[17] i	ASKING:	*ask, inquire, wonder, investigate*	
ii	KNOWING:	*know, find out, remember, certain*	
iii	GUESSING:	*guess, estimate, predict, judge*	
iv	TELLING:	*tell, inform, point out, show*	
v	DECIDING:	*decide, determine, make up one's mind, agree*	
vi	DEPENDENCE:	*depend, have a bearing, influence, affect*	
vii	SIGNIFICANCE:	*significant, important, matter, care*	
viii	CONCERNING:	*concern, about, as to, regarding*	
ix	SURPRISE:	*amaze, amazed, amazing, surprise*	[open type only]
x	DISBELIEF:	*doubt*$_V$, *doubtful, question*$_V$, *questionable*	[closed type only]

Knowing covers coming to know, as with *find out, learn, discover.* The categories are to be interpreted as subsuming corresponding negatives, whether expressed analytically (*not know*), by a negative affix (*uncertain*), or lexically (*forget* in contrast to *remember*). We have given priority to verbs in selecting items to illustrate the classification but corresponding nouns generally belong in the same categories; for reasons explained in §5.3.3, however, it is only as verbs that *doubt* and *question* belong in category [x] (hence the subscripts): the homonymous nouns belong in [ii] and [i] respectively.

Concealed questions: embedded questions with the form of NPs

While embedded questions are generally expressed by means of interrogative clauses, they can also take the form of a definite NP, and are then known as **concealed questions**:

[18] i *I can't remember the kind of pizza she likes.*
ii *Can you tell me the time?*

The underlined NPs are equivalent to subordinate interrogatives: compare *I can't remember what kind of pizza she likes* and *Can you tell me what time it is?* NPs with this kind of interpretation are found only with items that license interrogative clauses. Thus we do not have a concealed question in *I don't like the kind of pizza she likes,* for *like* does not license interrogative complements (cf. **I don't like what kind of pizza she likes*). Not all items that do license interrogatives allow concealed question complements, however. We can have, for example, *I wonder what time it is,* but not **I wonder the time*: *wonder* does not license NP complements.[10]

[10] Except for certain types of anaphoric NP, as in *Surely John must have an inkling who's responsible? Gill Templar was wondering the same thing.*

5.3.1 As complement or supplement

We review here the various types of complement that can be realised by an interrogative clause; for each category we begin with examples and a sample of the governors that license the interrogative. We then turn briefly to interrogative clause supplements.

(a) Subject and extraposed subject

[19] i *Whether we do it now or later is immaterial.* [subject]
ii *It is immaterial whether we do it now or later.* [extraposed subject]

[20]	i	*bother*	*concern*$_1$	*interest*	*matter*	*worry*	
	ii	*arguable*	*certain*	*clear*	*crucial*	*debatable*	*immaterial*
		important	*interesting*	*obvious*	*predictable*	*relevant*	*significant*
	iii	*concern*	*issue*	*matter*	*problem*	*question*	*secret*
	iv	*affect*	*bear (on)*	*depend (on)*	*determine*	*influence*	

Those in [20i–iii] are respectively verbs, adjectives, and nouns. The items in [20iv] are verbs too; they are listed separately as they allow interrogatives both as subject and as internal complement: *Whether we win depends on how much effort we put in. Concern*$_1$ means roughly "be of relevance to or cause anxiety for", as in *Whether we accept or reject the offer doesn't concern you.* The noun *concern* in [iii] is related to this sense: *What I do is not your concern.* The noun *matter* requires some elaboration by means of a dependent, one with more content than just an article – *Whether these differences count or not is another matter / a matter of social convention / *a matter.*

In many cases the interrogative is not licensed directly by the verb or the head adjective/noun in the predicative complement, but indirectly via their dependents. In *How this problem can be resolved needs further study* and *Whether this is the best solution is open to debate*, for example, the crucial items are *study* and *debate*, which are not immediately in construction with the interrogative clause.

(b) Specifying predicative complement

Embedded interrogatives commonly occur with the role of value in the specifying construction discussed in Ch. 4, §§5.5.1–2. In this function, however, there is a choice between subordinate and main clause form:

[21] i *The main question is whether we have sufficient evidence to secure a conviction.*
ii *The main question is: Do we have sufficient evidence to secure a conviction?*

The interrogatives here serve to identify the main question, to specify the value of the variable expressed in the subject ("the *x* such that *x* is the main question"). The underlined content clause in [i] has the normal form for embedded interrogatives, while the complement in [ii] is realised by a main clause. What makes the main clause form possible here is that the question is identified by citing it – and it is cited in the form it has when it stands alone as a sentence. The subject NP generally has *question* as its head, or some semantically similar noun such as *problem*, *issue*, etc., or it can be a fused relative construction, such as *what we must ascertain*. Like most cases of the specifying construction, the examples in [21] are reversible: *Whether we have enough evidence to secure a conviction is the main question*, and similarly for [ii].

(c) The complex-transitive construction

[22] i *I consider how he cheated us less important than why he did.* [object]
ii *I consider it immaterial whether we do it now or later.* [extraposed object]

Interrogatives differ from declaratives in that they can intervene between the matrix verb and the predicative complement, as in [i] – but they also occur with extraposition, as in [ii]. We have not listed governors here since it is the PC of the matrix, rather than its verb, that licenses the interrogative in these constructions, and the items concerned (here *important* and *immaterial*) are among those that license interrogative subjects or extraposed subjects.

(d) Internal complement licensed by the matrix verb

[23] i *We'll* [*establish what caused the malfunction*].
ii *We* [*investigated whether the contract is valid*].

[24] i	*ascertain*	*care*	*check*	*consider*	*decide*	*determine*
	disclose	*discover*	*establish*	*estimate*	*forget*	*guess*
	indicate	*inform*	*judge*	*know*	*learn*	*mind*
	notice	*observe*	*predict*	*prove*	*realise*	*recall*
	remember	*say*	*see*	*show*	*tell*	*think*
ii	*ask*	$concern_2$	*inquire*	*investigate*	*ponder*	*wonder*

$Concern_2$ means "be about": *The debate concerned how best to contain inflation.* The verbs in [i] license declaratives as well as interrogatives, while those in [ii] do not: compare *We'll establish that the contract is valid* and **We investigated that the contract is valid.* The verbs that exclude declaratives include the verbs of asking (interpreted broadly enough to include *wonder*), but they are not limited to these.[11]

There are also various verbal idioms that belong with the verbs of [i]:

[25] *find out, work out, have any/no idea/clue/notion, give a damn, make certain/sure, make up one's mind*

(e) Complement of a preposition

[26] i *They were divided in their beliefs* [*as to whether the diet was effective*].
ii *The result will be the same regardless* [*of whether you involve yourself or not*].
iii *He is preoccupied* [*with whether people find his behaviour socially acceptable*].
iv [*As for/to what should be done next,*] *I think your own proposal is best.*

[27] *about* *as for* *as to* *concerning* *into* *of* *on* *over* *with*

There are two complicating factors to note regarding this construction:

Relevance of higher construction

To a significant extent it is not the preposition itself that licenses the interrogative but the preposition in combination with the head item that governs the preposition. In [iii], for example, the interrogative is licensed by *preoccupied* + *with* – in contrast, say, to *equipped* + *with*. Similarly we find interrogatives after *depend on* but not *rely on*, after *the issue of* but not *the photograph of*, and so on. This applies equally when the

[11] *Ask* and *wonder* license declaratives when used with a different sense: *I must ask that you take more care* ("request"), *I wonder* (*that*) *he wasn't sacked* ("am surprised").

governing item is itself a preposition: for example, *regardless/irrespective* + *of*, but not *ahead* + *of*.

Nevertheless, the preposition itself can be the decisive factor – this is so with *about*, *as for*, *as to*, *concerning*, *on*, *over* – the ones having the "concerning" meaning that we included in the set of licensing classes in [17]. This is particularly clear in [26iv], but compare also *belief as to* in [26i] with *belief in* or *belief* on its own, neither of which allows an interrogative.

The preposition is sometimes optional

[28] i *They can't agree* [(*about* / *as to* / *on*) *who is the best person for the job*].
ii *I'm not certain* [(*about* / *as to* / *of*) *what she's asking for*].
iii *He ignores the question* [(*as to* / *of*) *whether the commissioner was impartial*].

There are many places, however, where the preposition can't be omitted:

[29] i *They were wrangling over who should be secretary.*
ii *He is anxious about whether he should accept their offer or not.*
iii *I overheard their discussion on how to combat tax-avoidance.*

In some cases, moreover, there is an appreciable difference in meaning between the constructions:

[30] i *She asked what changes they were planning to introduce.*
ii *She asked about what changes they were planning to introduce.*

Here [i] reports the content of the question she asked, whereas [ii] just gives the topic of her question (or questions). It is clear, therefore, that there can be no general rule allowing the omission of a preposition before an interrogative clause. Instead we take the optionality of the prepositions in [28] to be a matter of the head elements licensing either interrogative clauses or PPs as complement.[12] Following our earlier usage we will say that the interrogative clause is a core complement of the verb, adjective, or noun when it is immediately in construction with it, and an oblique complement when it is related via a preposition.

(f) Complement of an adjective

[31] i	*I'm not* [*sure why you are complaining*].			[core complement]
ii	*He's* [*only interested in how he can make a quick profit*			[oblique complement]
[32] i	*aware* (*of*)	*careful*	*certain* (*of*)	*clear*
	concerned	*fussy*	*sure* (*of*)	*worried*
ii	*dependent on*	*indicative of*	*interested in*	*relevant to*

There are no adjectives that take interrogatives as core complements but not as obliques. All of those listed in [32i] allow *about* or *as to*, while the ones so marked also allow *of*. With most, the prepositional construction is more frequent; the major exception is *sure*, which usually takes the interrogative as core complement. The adjectives in [32ii] are illustrative of those that license only oblique interrogatives.

[12] The verb *depend* licenses an interrogative as complement only when the subject is *it* (or perhaps *that*): the preposition is omissible in *It depends* (*on*) *how much you want it* but not in *My decision will depend on how you perform in the test.*

(g) Complement of a noun

Again we have a distinction between core and oblique complements:

[33] i *The minister has been reluctant to 'come clean' on [the question whether or not he intends to build any new towns].*

ii *This brings us to [the question of how much the proposals would cost].*

The core complement construction is mainly found with the noun *question*, but occasional examples with other nouns are found:

[34] i *[A decision whether to hold a public inquiry] in London will be taken after they report.*

ii *[The test whether damped fires are really alight] is to see whether they can burn up when poked.*

iii *They could be sent to US ports for [rulings whether cargo should be confiscated].*

A sample of nouns found with interrogatives as oblique complement is given in [35]; other prepositions from the "concerning" set [27] could also be used, and clearly the preposition plays a major part in the licensing of the interrogative.

[35]				
	apprehension as to	*argument over*	*belief as to*	*controversy over*
	debate as to	*discussion of*	*dispute about*	*indication as to*
	judgement on	*knowledge of*	*opinion on*	*wrangle over*

Postposing

Interrogative content clauses, like declaratives and other post-head dependents, may be postposed:

[36] *The question may be raised whether or not we are dealing with a common factor in anxiety and compulsivity.*

(h) Supplements

Interrogatives quite often function as supplements, with an NP as anchor. As they involve citation of the question, they can appear either as content clauses (subordinate) or as main clauses:

[37] i *Ch. 19 discusses the converse question, whether aboriginal customary laws should themselves be imported into the general legal system in some way.*

ii *We now turn to our final question: What place should brief, crisis-oriented preventive case-work occupy in our total spectrum of services?*

When the supplement is not adjacent to the NP anchor, main clause form is preferred:

[38] i *The question might be asked: Isn't the management aware of these facts?*

ii *Once again the question arises: When should the change be made?*

As noted in §4.5, supplements are required to be semantically compatible with their anchor NP, but are not syntactically licensed by the head of that NP:

[39] i *I had earnestly sought for some definition of the ultimate object of the whole great enterprise: whether, for example, Germany was to be destroyed, dismembered, or reorganised.*

ii *Their quarrels were always about the same thing – whether she should give up her job and get married.*

iii *Newton maintained that his conclusion could be reached without reference to any hypothetical commitments as to the nature of light – for example, whether it was corpuscular or wave-like in nature.*

The nouns *definition, thing,* and *nature* do not license interrogatives as integrated complements, and the occurrence of the interrogatives in these examples depends crucially on the interpretation of the underlined NPs. In [i] a definition of the object of the enterprise must provide the answer to various questions about it. In [ii] the context of quarrelling allows *the same thing* to be interpreted more specifically as "the same question/issue". And in [iii] the *as to* triggers the interpretation of *the nature of light* as a concealed question, i.e. as meaning "what is the nature of light?".

5.3.2 Question-orientation vs answer-orientation

Depending on the context in which they are embedded, subordinate interrogatives can be classified as having an orientation towards the question or towards the answer:

[40]	QUESTION-ORIENTATION	ANSWER-ORIENTATION
i	a. *She asked where he lived.*	b. *She told me where he lived.*
ii	a. *She wanted to know / didn't know where he lived.*	b. *She knew where he lived.*

Example [ia] reports an illocutionary act of asking a question, whereas [ib] reports an act of stating, giving the answer to a question that may or may not have been asked. These, being reports of illocutionary acts, represent the distinction at its clearest, but we can generalise to cases where no actual illocutionary act is necessarily being reported, as in [ii]. In [iia] she may or may not have asked the question, but her mental state was conducive to doing so, and in [iib] it is conducive to answering the question.

This distinction correlates with restrictions relating to the use of emotive modifiers, closed interrogatives, and subject–auxiliary inversion. For the last two of these we will need to work with a finer classification, distinguishing between strong and weak orientation to question or answer.

Emotive modifiers restricted to contexts with question-orientation

[41]	QUESTION-ORIENTATION	ANSWER-ORIENTATION
i	a. *Tell me how on earth you saved her.*	b. **I recall how on earth you saved her.*
ii	a. *I wonder who ever would do that.*	b. **I see who ever would do that.*

The emotive modifiers *on earth, the hell, ever,* etc., are used in main clause interrogatives like *How on earth did you save her?* or *Who ever would do that?* to indicate surprise that you did in fact save her, that someone would do that. They are admissible in corresponding subordinates only in contexts of question-orientation.

Restrictions on closed interrogatives

In the default case, contexts which accept open interrogatives also accept the closed type too, and vice versa. There are, however, contexts where the open type is admissible but where closed interrogatives are either: (a) of questionable acceptability; or (b) completely excluded. We will refer to these as involving respectively weak and strong answer-orientation.

(a) Marginal status of closed interrogatives in contexts of weak answer-orientation

[42]		QUESTION-ORIENTATION	WEAK ANSWER-ORIENTATION
	i	a. *Did she say if the door was locked?* *She didn't say if the door was locked.*	b. ?*She said if the door was locked.*
	ii	a. *Does he know whether it is ready?* *He doesn't know whether it is ready.*	b. ?*He knows whether it is ready.*

The [b] examples here are significantly less natural and acceptable than the [a] ones. If I know that [ib] is true, then I will typically also know either that she said the door was locked or that she said it wasn't locked – and in that case the expectation would be that I would use a declarative complement. *She said that the door was locked* and *She said that the door was not locked* are clearly more informative than [ib], and hence if I'm in a position to say one or other of these I would normally do so. Analogously for [iib]. The [a] examples involve non-affirmative contexts (interrogatives, negatives, etc.), and a number of the verbs governing interrogative complements occur most readily in such contexts. But it must be emphasised that this is a matter of pragmatically motivated preference, not of a syntactic rule. Compare, for example, [42iib] with *He must know whether it is ready*: this is still an affirmative context, but it is more acceptable than [42iib] because the *must* makes it more likely that the speaker doesn't know whether it is ready and hence is not in a position to use a declarative instead of the interrogative. Compare, similarly, *He knows whether it is ready but he won't tell me.*

The distinction between non-affirmative and affirmative contexts is of much less significance for open interrogatives. Affirmatives like *She said what she plans to do* or *He knows why she resigned*, for example, do not have the questionable status of the closed interrogatives in [42].

(b) Exclusion of closed interrogatives in contexts of strong answer-orientation

Some governing expressions license open but not closed interrogatives:

[43]		CLOSED INTERROGATIVE	OPEN INTERROGATIVE
	i	a. **It's amazing whether he wrote it.*	b. *It's amazing what he wrote.*
	ii	a. **He realised if she meant you.*	b. *He realised who she meant.*

The [a] examples here are not improved by making the matrix clause non-affirmative: **Is it amazing whether he wrote it?*; **He didn't realise if she meant you.* The governors generally take declarative complements with a factive interpretation: *It's amazing that he wrote it* and *He realised she meant you* presuppose respectively that he wrote it and that she meant you (cf. §7.4).[13] Note also that [ib] conveys that I know what he wrote – similarly with *It's surprising, I'm amazed*, etc. Another item which belongs here is the preposition *considering*: while the verb *consider* licenses a closed interrogative (*We were considering whether we should accept the proposal*), the converted preposition allows

[13] An exception is the complex governing expression *you wouldn't believe*, as in *You wouldn't believe who she's going to marry. You wouldn't believe that she is going to marry Fred* does not involve the same exclamatory use of *you wouldn't believe* and is not factive.

only a declarative or an open interrogative (*Considering what the conditions were like, it was a creditable performance*, but not **Considering whether it was her first attempt, . . .*). Similarly with *given*, except that here the verb from which it is converted does not take content clause complements at all.

Non-factive *careful*, *take care* behave in the same way: *Be careful what you say* but not **Be careful whether they see you.* Instead of the latter we need a declarative: *Be careful they see / don't see you.*

Subject–auxiliary inversion

Some varieties of English (quite widespread in the USA) allow subordinate interrogatives with subject–auxiliary inversion in contexts of strong question-orientation:

[44]	INVERTED ORDER	UNINVERTED ORDER
i	a. %*She asked what had she done wrong.*	b. *She asked what she had done wrong.*
ii	a. %*He wanted to know was she ill.*	b. *He wanted to know if she was ill.*
iii	a. **He didn't know was she ill.*	b. *He didn't know if she was ill.*

In [i] we have the open interrogative construction, with the two versions differing just in respect of subject–auxiliary inversion; [ii] has closed interrogatives, marked by inversion alone in [a], but by *whether* or *if* in the uninverted version. The inverted construction is limited to a subset of the question-oriented contexts – to contexts of what we are calling strong question-orientation. This is seen in the contrast between [iia] and [iiia]: both *want to know* and *not know* allow emotive modifiers like *on earth* (*He wanted to know / didn't know why on earth she put up with it*), but only the former allows inversion. The inverted construction is more characteristic of non-standard speech, but examples are certainly found in Standard English.

The inverted construction represents a blurring of the distinction between subordinate and main clauses. It is not to be equated with the main clause construction illustrated in [21ii], for this time the question is not cited: [44ia], for example, involves indirect reported speech, not direct (such as we have in *She asked, 'What have I done wrong?'*). We treat it therefore as a subordinate clause, recognising that in this variety inversion does not always distinguish main from subordinate clause interrogatives.

5.3.3 Dubitatives

A handful of items – the verbs *doubt* and *question* and the derived adjectives *doubtful* and *questionable* – allow closed interrogatives but not the open type:[14]

[45]	CLOSED INTERROGATIVE	OPEN INTERROGATIVE
	a. *I doubt whether he wrote it.*	b. **I doubt who wrote it.*

Moreover, the closed interrogative cannot contain an *or*-coordination marking an alternative question: **I doubt whether he wrote it or not*; **I doubt whether they'll appoint a man or a woman* (in the sense "uncertain which it will be"). From a semantic point of view, indeed, it is arguable that the interrogative clause in [45a] does not express a question at all but simply a proposition: it is equivalent to a declarative.

[14] The verb *question* takes open interrogatives as oblique complements (e.g. *He questioned them about where they had been*): we are concerned with core complements, as in *He questioned whether such drastic measures were really necessary*. An exceptional use of an open interrogative here is seen in *It might be questioned what he does learn at school*, but this is interpreted as "whether he does learn anything", with the suggestion that the answer is negative.

Compare in this connection the following pairs:

[46] DECLARATIVE / CLOSED INTERROGATIVE

i a. *She didn't say that he wrote it.* b. *She didn't say whether he wrote it.*
ii a. *She's not certain that he wrote it.* b. *She's not certain whether he wrote it.*
iii a. *I doubt that he wrote it.* b. *I doubt whether he wrote it.*

In [i] we have the typical case where there is a very obvious difference in meaning between declarative and interrogative. Example [ia] is quite consistent with her having said that he didn't write it, whereas [ib] is not. Strictly speaking the same applies in [ii]: it would be possible to say *She's not certain that he wrote it – on the contrary, she's certain that he didn't write it.* But when, as here in [ii], the matrix clause expresses uncertainty, the semantic distinction tends to be blurred pragmatically. The most likely context for [iia] is one where she isn't certain either way, hence one where [ib] would also be true. With the verb *doubt*, however, it seems that the semantic distinction is not just blurred but lost altogether, that [iiib] is equivalent to [iiia]. This would explain why we can add *or not* in [iib] but not [iiib]. *Doubt* expresses not uncertainty but an inclination to believe that the embedded proposition is not true.[15] This is why we can say [47i] but not [47ii]:

[47] i *I'm not certain that he wrote it but I'm not certain that he didn't write it either.*
ii #*I doubt that he wrote it but I doubt that he didn't write it too.*

On this account [46iiib] involves a mismatch between syntax and semantics: syntactically the complement is interrogative, whereas semantically it does not express a question.

A further point about *doubt* + *whether* is that it is normally restricted to affirmative contexts. This applies with both verb and noun *doubt*:

[48] i a. *I don't doubt that he wrote it.* b. ?*I don't doubt whether he wrote it.*
ii a. *There's no doubt he wrote it.* b. ?*There's no doubt whether he wrote it.*

The [b] examples would be possible only in some special context such as one of denial, as when you say *They think you doubt whether he wrote it* and I reply *I don't doubt whether he wrote it – only whether he intended it for publication.*

5.3.4 On the construction *He made I don't know how many mistakes*

A distinction needs to be drawn between the following constructions:

[49] i *He made some mistakes, though I don't know how many.*
ii *He made I don't know how many mistakes.*

In [i] *how many* is a reduced interrogative clause functioning as complement to *know*. This differs from the constructions we have been discussing only in the reduction of the interrogative clause; it is interpreted anaphorically as "how many mistakes he made". In [ii], however, there is no ellipsis, and *how many mistakes* is not an interrogative clause. It means very much the same as *I don't know how many mistakes he made*, and its form seems in some way derivative from the latter. But clearly *made* is the verb of the matrix clause and the proposition that he made some mistakes is the main assertion, not backgrounded information; and there is an implicature that he made a large number

[15] This is very evident in the attested example *He watched her go, a little pensive because he doubted whether he would ever have an excuse to meet her, perhaps not even to see her again. Not even* normally requires a preceding negative (cf. Ch. 9, §1.1) and its use here indicates that the *whether* clause is interpreted like a negative declarative.

of mistakes. Syntactically, *I don't know how many mistakes* must be an object NP with *mistakes* as head; *I don't know* functions as an irregular type of modifier to *how*.

A variant of *I don't know* is *God knows*. These modifiers occur with most of the interrogative words (though not *why*) – compare *They're inviting God knows who to the reception.*

5.3.5 Infinitival interrogatives

Subordinate interrogatives commonly have infinitival form, expressing what we have called direction questions:

[50] i *I was considering whether to get my jacket from the car.* [closed]
ii *Frequently readers request advice on how to establish a good lawn.* [open]

The answers have the force of directives and would characteristically be expressed as imperatives (*Get* / *Don't get your jacket from the car*, etc.).

We cover these in the present chapter because most expressions that govern interrogatives allow both finite and infinitival constructions. In terms of the classification suggested in [17] above, infinitivals are most often found with governors in the fields of knowing, asking, telling, deciding, and concerning. There are some cases where only the finite construction is permitted:

[51]	FINITE	INFINITIVAL
i	a. *I doubt whether I should accept.*	b. **I doubt whether to accept.*
ii	a. *It was amazing what they offered.*	b. **It was amazing what to offer.*
iii	a. *It depends on how much I must pay.*	b. **It depends on how much to pay.*
iv	a. *I don't care whether I go or not.*	b. **I don't care whether to go or not.*

Infinitivals do not occur with expressions of disbelief, surprise, dependence, or (for the most part) significance.

5.3.6 Interrogatives as adjunct: the ungoverned exhaustive conditional construction

There is just one construction where subordinate interrogatives function as adjunct: the ungoverned version of the exhaustive conditional construction. The meaning of the adjunct is the same as in the corresponding governed construction – compare:

[52] i *You got paid [whether business was good or bad].* [ungoverned]
ii *You got paid [regardless of whether business was good or bad].* [governed]

The underlining indicates the interrogative clause, the brackets the adjunct. In [ii] the adjunct has the form of a PP in which the interrogative clause is embedded, whereas in [i] it simply has the form of the interrogative clause itself. In [ii] the subordinate clause is governed by *of*, and is hence a complement; in [i] the subordinate clause is ungoverned, and hence an adjunct. In the governed version of the construction the adjunct is headed by *irrespective, regardless, independently* (which all take *of* + interrogative) or by *no matter* (which takes the interrogative as immediate complement: *You got paid [no matter whether business was good or bad]*).

The interrogative clause (like its non-embedded counterpart *Was business good or bad?*) expresses a question with two possible answers: "Business was good" and "Business was bad". Each answer defines a condition or 'case'. The meaning of [52] is that you got paid in either of these cases; they are equivalent to an *and*-coordination of *if* phrases (or of conditional clauses):

[53] i *Business was sometimes good, sometimes bad; you got paid in either case.*
ii *You got paid if business was good and (you got paid) if business was bad.*

The case where business was good and that where business was bad are assumed to constitute an exhaustive set of possibilities, so it follows from [52] that you got paid. Hence our term **exhaustive conditional** (see Ch. 8, §14.6).

The adjuncts in [52] differ from the prototypical adjunct of condition, as expressed in an *if* phrase, in that they are non-restrictive. *If* phrases are characteristically interpreted pragmatically as restrictive, i.e. as implicating "only if". But they do not have to be: restrictiveness is not an essential feature of conditionals. Consider the following range of *if* constructions:

[54] i *I'll do it if I have time.*
ii *You will fail your exam if you watch TV every evening.*
iii *We got paid even if business was bad.*

The restrictive use is illustrated in [i]: I'll do it only if I have time, for if I haven't time then I can't, hence won't, do it. Similarly, *You got paid if business was good* will normally be interpreted as giving a necessary condition for getting paid. *If* itself, however, does not mean the same as *only if*: without the *only* the restrictive meaning is implicated, not explicitly expressed. This is evident from [ii], which certainly does not say that the only condition under which you will fail your exam is if you watch TV every evening – I'm not guaranteeing that you will pass your exam if you don't watch TV every evening. And in [iii] the *even* explicitly rules out a restrictive interpretation: you got paid if business was bad but (it is implicated) you also got paid if business was good. Conditionals can therefore be non-restrictive, and the exhaustive conditional is a special case of a non-restrictive conditional.

Construction [52] is indeed quite similar in meaning to the *even if* example [54iii]. Both constructions convey that you got paid if business was good and also if it wasn't. The *even if* construction differs from the exhaustive conditional in that it mentions only one case: there is no explicit mention of the case where business was good, but there is an implicature that in this case too you got paid.

The use of interrogatives expressing embedded questions in conditionals is related to their use as complements to items whose meaning involves dependence and significance (cf. [17vi–vii]) – compare *Your getting paid didn't depend on whether business was good or bad* or *As far as getting paid was concerned, it didn't matter / wasn't relevant whether business was good or bad.* What distinguishes [52i] from these and from [52ii] is that in [52i] there is nothing external to the interrogative construction itself expressing the idea that the answer to the embedded question has no bearing on the issue.

Like interrogative clauses in general, those in exhaustive conditional function fall into two subclasses, open and closed:

[55] i *I'm going with them, whatever the consequences may be.* [open]
ii *I'm going with them, whether you like it or not.* [closed]

We consider them in turn before returning to certain special properties that they have in common. Both differ in various respects from interrogative clauses in complement function; indeed their analysis as interrogative clauses is by no means uncontroversial.

The open interrogative construction

Open interrogatives in the ungoverned construction differ from those in the governed one in that they require interrogative words in ·*ever*. Compare:

[56] UNGOVERNED / GOVERNED

		UNGOVERNED	GOVERNED
[56]	i	a. **Who we recommend, they will appoint Jones.*	b. [*Regardless of who we recommend,*] *they will appoint Jones.*
	ii	a. *Whoever we recommend, they will appoint Jones.*	b. *[*Regardless of whoever we recommend,*] *they will appoint Jones.*

Open interrogatives express variable questions whose answers supply values for the variable. In the present example, the question contains the open proposition "we will recommend *x*", and the answers consist of "We will recommend Smith", "We will recommend Baker", and so on. The meaning of [56] is that they will appoint Jones given any value of *x* – i.e. in any of the cases defined by possible answers to the question. In the governed construction [ib], the meaning that the actual value of *x* doesn't matter is expressed outside the interrogative, by *regardless*; in the ungoverned [iia], it is expressed inside the clause by ·*ever*. This has the free choice meaning found in one sense of *any*: "Take the case defined by any value of the variable – they will still recommend Jones in that case". This free choice sense of ·*ever* is likewise found in fused relatives: *They can appoint whoever they like*, "They can appoint anyone they want to appoint". The requirement that the [a] construction contain ·*ever* can be seen as motivated by the need to express the free choice meaning within the interrogative clause itself, given that there is no governing item such as *regardless* to express it outside the clause.

Open interrogatives compared with fused relatives

We have just noted that ·*ever* forms are elsewhere found in fused relative constructions, which means that as far as their internal form is concerned, open interrogatives in the ungoverned construction bear a close resemblance to fused relatives. Compare:

[57]	i	*They will appoint Jones, whoever we recommend.*	[open interrogative]
	ii	*They will appoint whoever we recommend.*	[fused relative]

The underlined sequence is in [i] an interrogative clause in adjunct function and in [ii] a fused relative construction functioning as object of *appoint*.[16] The free choice ·*ever* compounds do not occur elsewhere in interrogative clauses – the *ever* in examples like *What ever could have come over her?* has a different sense, and is usually written as a separate word (see Ch. 10, §7.13).

A further similarity between the ungoverned exhaustive conditional and the fused relative is that neither construction permits **whyever*: compare *[*Whyever she was late,*] *they won't forgive her* (interrogative) and **He complained* [*whyever she did*] ("for whatever reason she complained"). Fused relatives do not in fact allow *why* either (*[*Why he did it*] *was invalid*, "the reason why . . . "), whereas they are allowed in interrogatives, including the governed exhaustive conditional: *No matter* [*why she was late,*] *they won't forgive her.*

[16] *Whomever* is possible as a formal alternant of *whoever*, especially in [57ii].

Note also that, as in relatives, there can be no more than one ·*ever* compound:

[58] i **Whoever said whatever to whomever, we've got to put the incident behind us and work together as a team.* [interrogative]

ii **Whoever said whatever to whoever will be severely dealt with.* [relative]

Again the governed construction allows multiple interrogative words: [*No matter who said what to whom,*] *we've got to put the incident behind us and work together as a team.*

There are nevertheless compelling reasons for distinguishing between the constructions in [57] as respectively interrogative and relative.

(a) Meaning

The first point to note is that in [57ii] *whoever we recommend* denotes a person – they will appoint some person, and this construction indicates who it will be (namely the person we recommend). But the same expression in [57i] clearly does not denote a person: expressions denoting persons or concrete objects cannot function as adjunct in clause structure.

(b) Clausal status

Whoever we recommend is a clause in [57i] but not in [57ii]: in the latter it is an NP. This correlates with the point just made about meaning: it is NPs, not clauses, that denote persons. Syntactic evidence for distinguishing the constructions as clausal vs non-clausal is provided by facts concerning the placement of prepositions:

[59] i *He always antagonised whoever he worked with.*

ii **He always antagonised with whomever he worked.*

iii *Now, in whatever way government may be theoretically conceived, it is in practice a matter of the adjustment of a multiplicity of private interests.*

In [i] we have a fused relative with a stranded preposition; as shown in [ii] the preposition cannot be placed in front of *whoever*. In ordinary interrogatives, both orders are possible: *I can't recollect who he worked with* / *with whom he worked*. But [ii] is ungrammatical because the preposition has been placed at the beginning of an NP rather than a clause. The difference between [i] and [ii] is thus comparable to that seen between *He always antagonised those who he worked with* and **He always antagonised with those whom he worked.* The ungoverned exhaustive conditional, however, is a clause and thus allows a preposition to be placed in front position along with its complement, as illustrated in the attested example [iii]. This may be compared with the governed counterpart *no matter in what way government may be theoretically conceived.*

(c) Place in the system of exhaustive conditionals

Exhaustive conditionals are classified, as we have noted, on two cross-cutting dimensions, governed vs ungoverned and closed vs open:

[60]

	GOVERNED	UNGOVERNED
CLOSED	a. *They will appoint Jones* [*regardless of whether he's the best candidate or not*].	b. *They will appoint Jones whether he's the best candidate or not.*
OPEN	c. *They will appoint Jones* [*regardless of who we recommend*].	d. *They will appoint Jones whoever we recommend.*

On one dimension, the relation of [a] to [b] is the same as that of [c] to [d]; and on another the relation of [a] to [c] is the same as that of [b] to [d]. These relationships are most simply described if in other respects the constructions are all alike – i.e. all involve interrogative clauses.

(d) *Whatever the hell...*

Ordinary interrogatives allow emotive modifiers like *the hell* or *on earth* to follow the interrogative word: *What the hell do you want?* or *Who on earth said that?* This pattern is found also in the exhaustive conditional, as in the following attested example:

[61] *We* [sc. *women*] *must be attractive – whatever the hell that means – because, without that, we will find no place in this society.*

Fused relatives do not admit these expressions: **Whoever the hell said that was wrong.*

(e) The exclusion of multiple ·*ever* words

We noted above that it is not possible to have more than one word with free choice ·*ever*: see [58]. This appears to make the ungoverned exhaustive conditional more like a relative than like a governed interrogative since the latter allows more than one interrogative word. But the constraint is best seen as excluding multiple ·*ever* words, not multiple interrogative words as such. Note that if we replace the second and third ·*ever* words in [58i] by ordinary interrogative counterparts, the stark ungrammaticality is lost:

[62] ?*Whoever said what to whom, we've got to put this incident behind us and work together as a team.*

This seems to be more or less acceptable: certainly, it is strikingly better than the corresponding fused relative **Whoever said what to whom is going to be severely dealt with.*[17]

The conclusion must be that the ungoverned conditional is semantically and syntactically distinct from the fused relative. To some extent it is a blend between the relative and interrogative constructions, inasmuch as the ·*ever* forms can be regarded as primarily relative: only those forms which are used in fused relatives are established in the conditional, even though the counterparts without ·*ever* are regularly found in the governed construction and other interrogatives. But the interrogative features significantly outweigh the relative ones, and the construction is best analysed as a non-prototypical type of interrogative clause.

The closed interrogative construction

There are also differences between closed interrogatives in the ungoverned conditional construction and those which occur elsewhere, though this time it is a matter of an important restriction that applies. Closed interrogatives in general express either polar questions (*Is he the best candidate?*) or alternative questions (*Is the meeting in Paris or in Bonn?* or *Is he the best candidate or not?*) – see Ch. 10, §§4.3–4. Those expressing alternative questions contain an *or*-coordination, with each coordinate corresponding to one of the answers ("The meeting is in Paris" and "The meeting is in Bonn" or "He is the best candidate" and "He is not the best candidate"). In the ungoverned exhaustive

[17] A further point concerns the idiomatic interrogative construction with *what* + *be doing*: *What were they doing reading her mail?*, "Why were they reading her mail?" This is admissible in the exhaustive conditional (*I'm still going to complain about invasion of privacy, whatever they were doing reading my mail*), but is completely excluded from the fused relative (**She didn't complain about whatever they were doing reading her mail*).

conditional only the alternative kind of question is permitted, i.e. an *or*-coordination is obligatory:

[63] i *They will attend the meeting* [*whether it is in Paris or in Bonn.*) } [alternative]
ii *They will appoint Jones* [*whether he is the best candidate or not.*) }
iii **They will appoint Jones* [*whether he is the best candidate*]. [polar]

The interrogative clause in [iii] is perfectly admissible in the governed construction: *They will appoint Jones regardless of whether he is the best candidate.*

As with the case of the ·*ever* forms in the open construction, this special property of closed interrogatives in adjunct function can be related to the fact that there is nothing outside the clause itself to indicate that the choice between the various cases defined by answers to the question doesn't matter. In polar questions, one of the answers is left implicit: the obligatory presence of *or not* in [63ii] ensures that both answers are explicitly represented.

The status of *whether*

In traditional grammar the subordinate clauses in [63] are analysed as adverbial clauses, not subordinate interrogatives ('indirect questions'). Adapting to our descriptive framework, this would be to say that *whether* here is a preposition, not an interrogative subordinator. *Whether* would then be like *if*, belonging to both preposition and subordinator categories. While this distinction is certainly necessary in the case of *if*, however, we do not believe that it is in the case of *whether*. There is a clear semantic difference between the *if* of *I'll do it if I've time* and that of *I don't know if I've time*, but there is no such difference in the case of *whether* between, say, [60b] and [60a]: as we have said, the systematic relations between the four constructions in [60] are most simply described if all the subordinate clauses are analysed as interrogative. Note, moreover, that the two constructions are syntactically alike in that the ungoverned conditional, like all subordinate closed interrogatives, allows *or not* to follow *whether*:

[64] i *You'll have to stop now* (*regardless of*) *whether you have finished or not.*
ii *You'll have to stop now* (*regardless of*) *whether or not you have finished.*

On both semantic and syntactic grounds, therefore, we recognise just one item *whether*, an interrogative subordinator.

Reduction to participial or verbless construction

Conditional interrogatives commonly appear in reduced form:

[65] i *Whether hunting or being hunted, the fox is renowned for its cunning.*
ii *Whether taken neat or with water, the mixture can be quite lethal.*
iii *Whether historically a fact or not, the legend has a certain symbolic value.*
iv *The United Nations may not interfere in the political affairs of any nation, whether to unify it, federalise it, or balkanise it.*
v *Whatever their faults, they are not hypocrites.*
vi *However well-meaning, the very act of helping old people may reduce their ability to look after themselves.*

With closed interrogatives introduced by *whether* we have omission of subject + verb. In [i] the result is a gerund-participial, in [ii] a past-participial construction, and in [iii] a verbless construction with *a fact* as predicative complement. The interrogative clause in [iv] is verbless, not an infinitival: the infinitival is embedded within the interrogative clause as an adjunct of purpose. We could expand here as *whether it is to . . .* or *whether it does so to . . .* Examples [v–vi] illustrate the type of reduction found with open interrogatives. The conditional clause in [v] consists of the interrogative phrase followed by the subject, with the verb *be* understood: "whatever their faults are / may be". And in [vi] it consists just of the interrogative phrase, as predicative complement, with subject + *be* understood: "however well-meaning it is / may be".

6 Exclamative content clauses

Subordinate exclamatives, like main clause exclamatives, are marked by one or other of the exclamative words *what* and *how*:

[1] i *He soon realised what a terrible mistake he had made.*
ii *She told me how very aggressive he had been.*

In general, such clauses are identical in form with main clauses: subordination is not marked in the internal structure of the exclamative clause.

One difference between subordinate and main exclamatives is that subject–auxiliary inversion is restricted to the latter, but since it applies there very rarely this is a minor difference – quite unlike that holding between subordinate and main clause open interrogatives. As in main clauses, the subject may occur in postposed position: *They emphasised how imperative had been the need to take immediate action.*[18]

6.1 Exclamatives in relation to open interrogatives

How and *what* can be either exclamative or interrogative; the differences between the two uses are the same in content clauses as in main clauses, and have been described in Ch. 10, §8.1. The examples in [1] were chosen as ones that are unambiguously exclamative: interrogative *how* cannot modify *very*, and interrogative *what* cannot combine with the indefinite article. In many cases, however, no such features distinguish them: phrases like *how old* or *what games* occur in both types of clause. In main clauses, exclamatives are often distinguished from open interrogatives by the order of elements, but since subject–auxiliary inversion generally doesn't apply with subordinate interrogatives there is a much greater degree of overlap between the clause types in content clauses than in main clauses. Compare, for example:

		a.	b.
[2]	i	a. *How old were they?*	b. *What games do they play?*
	ii	a. *How old they were!*	b. *What games they play!*
	iii	a. *She forgot how old they were.*	b. *I know what games they play.*

The order difference marks [i] as interrogative and [ii] as exclamative, but the content clauses in [iii] can be either. The ambiguity of the content clauses is very evident here, precisely because they can be construed as the subordinate version of either [i] or [ii]. Thus [iiia] means either "She forgot what their ages were" (the interrogative reading) or

[18] Main clause exclamatives are commonly reduced to verbless constructions, and such reduction is also occasionally found in subordinate exclamatives: *She laughed to herself thinking what a stupid way to put it.*

"She forgot that they were remarkably old" (the exclamative reading), and similarly for [iiib] we have "I know what the games are that they play" and "I know that they play remarkable games (remarkable for either good or bad qualities)".

Where both interrogative and exclamative readings are possible, the exclamative will often be considerably more salient where *how* is used in its degree sense:

[3] i *This just shows how immature he was.* *I remembered how frail he was.*
ii *It's amazing/extraordinary/remarkable how old they were.*

We will normally interpret [i] as conveying that he was immature or frail to a remarkable degree, hence as exclamative. The exclamative reading is effectively more specific, more informative than the interrogative one, rather than being in conflict with it. If I remembered that he was remarkably frail, then I remembered the answer to the question "How frail was he?" – it's just that the answer involves a high degree of frailty. In [ii] the expression governing the content clause incorporates within its meaning something very akin to the "remarkable" feature that is associated with the exclamative construction, and this favours the exclamative interpretation so strongly that one would generally not use this form to express the interrogative meaning (where what is amazing is simply the answer, whatever it might be, to the question "How old were they?"). The context in [ii] is one of strong answer-orientation: I know how old they were. I will then normally be understood as conveying how old they were (namely, remarkably old) rather than as leaving the question unresolved. It must be emphasised, however, that the governing expressions in [ii] do take interrogative complements as well as exclamative ones (they belong to the class given in [17ix] of §5 under the label 'surprise'). This is evident from the fact that the complement is not limited to *how* and *what* but allows the full range of open interrogative words: *It's amazing who they appointed / which ones they preferred / where they took him.* There is an exclamatory component of meaning in such examples, but it derives from the matrix adjective *amazing*, not from the content clause.

6.2 Distribution of exclamative content clauses

Subordinate exclamatives occur in a subset of the environments where interrogatives are found; they always function as complement of some governing expression, and there are no expressions that license exclamatives but not interrogatives.

The functions that may be realised by exclamative clauses are illustrated in:

[4]	i	*What a blunder it was didn't emerge till later.*	[subject]
	ii	*It's incredible what a difference a little paint can make.*	[extraposed subject]
	iii	*I found it quite amazing what a fuss he was making.*	[extraposed object]
	iv	*She kept thinking what a fool she'd been to trust them.*	[internal comp of verb]
	v	*He expressed his dismay at what a raw deal she'd had.*	[comp of preposition]
	vi	*They were surprised what a good price we were offering.*	[comp of adjective]

Exclamatives in subject function are rare: they generally do not satisfy the pragmatic constraints described in Ch. 16, §7.1. Compare [ii] with #*What a difference a little paint can make is incredible!* Exclamatives are as impossible as declaratives as (non-preposed) object in the complex-transitive construction: **I found what a fuss he was making quite amazing*. And while a number of nouns allow interrogatives as core complements, none allow exclamatives: they occur in NP structure only as obliques. *At*, for example, is not omissible in [v], or in *I remember her amazement at how immaturely her husband had behaved*, and so on.

The governing expressions belong mainly in the semantic classes shown in [5], where the roman numerals match those in [17] of §5:

[5] ii	KNOWING	*We know what a disappointment it is for you.*
iii	GUESSING	*I couldn't have predicted what a disaster it would be.*
iv	TELLING	*She told them what bores they were.*
viii	CONCERNING	*He was holding forth about what a hard life he'd had.*
ix	SURPRISE	*It is surprising how little variation there was in these results.*

In general such governors license not only interrogatives and exclamatives but also declaratives: compare *We know that it is a great disappointment for you.* The only exception is that declaratives do not occur as complement of such prepositions as *at* and *about*, so that we cannot replace the exclamative by a declarative in examples like [4v] and [5 viii].

7 Mood, tense, and factivity

In this section we outline certain uses of mood (including the modal auxiliaries) and tense that are not in general found in main clauses but are characteristic of content clauses.

7.1 The subjunctive construction and specialised uses of modal auxiliaries

The term 'subjunctive' is generally applied to an inflectional category of the verb but, as explained in Ch. 3, §1.8.2, we are here reinterpreting it as the name of a syntactic construction – a clause that is finite but tenseless, containing the plain form of the verb. Leaving aside various fixed phrases like *So be it*, *Long live . . . !*, etc., the subjunctive is restricted to various kinds of content clause.

Three uses of the subjunctive in content clauses

The three main subordinate constructions where the subjunctive is found are illustrated in:

[1] i *We insist that she be kept informed.*

ii *Nothing in English has been ridiculed as much as the ambiguous use of words, unless it be the ambiguous use of sentences.*

iii *Our thanks are due to all our staff, whether they be in the offices, the warehouses, or the branches, for their help during this difficult time.*

The content clause in [i] belongs to the subjunctive **mandative** construction; in [ii] it is complement to one of a small set of prepositions (*if*, *unless*, *lest*, etc.) that can take subjunctive complements; and [iii] is an exhaustive conditional interrogative.

Alternatives to the subjunctive construction

In none of the above three cases is the subjunctive construction obligatory. Two other possibilities have to be considered, as in the [b/c] examples in:

[2] i a. *It is essential [that everyone attend the meeting].*
b. *It is essential [that everyone attends the meeting].*
c. *It is essential [that everyone should attend the meeting].*
ii a. *They must co-operate in order [that the system operate effectively.]*
b. *They must co-operate in order [that the system operates effectively.]*
c. *They must co-operate in order [that the system may operate effectively.]*

The [b] examples are ordinary declaratives, while [ic/iic] belong to what we call **the specialised-modal construction**. This involves a use of a modal auxiliary that cannot be identified with one of the uses characteristic of main clauses. The *should* of [ic], for example, is not the same as that seen in the main clause *Everyone should attend the meeting*: the latter does not accurately express the content of our demand since the *should* here is weaker than in [ic], allowing that not everyone will necessarily attend. Similarly the *may* of [iic] is not interpreted like that of the main clause *The system may operate effectively*, where it conveys epistemic possibility. The ordinary declarative contains a present tense or preterite non-modal verb or else a modal auxiliary with a sense that it can also have in a main clause: compare, for example, subjunctive *It is essential that everyone be able to see the screen* with ordinary declarative *It is essential that everyone is able to / can see the screen.*

Distinguishing the subjunctive from an ordinary declarative

The subjunctive construction contains the plain form of the verb, which is overtly distinct from a present tense only with the verb *be* or a 3rd person singular subject:

[3]			
	i *be* as verb	*It's vital that they be kept informed.*	[subjunctive]
		It's vital that they are kept informed.	[non-subjunctive]
	ii 3rd sg subject	*It's vital that he keep them informed.*	[subjunctive]
		It's vital that he keeps them informed.	[non-subjunctive]
	iii other	*It's vital that we keep them informed.*	[indeterminate]

In [i] *be* and *are* contrast overtly as plain form vs present tense and hence mark the clauses as respectively subjunctive and non-subjunctive (ordinary declarative). In [ii] the absence of agreement in *he keep* shows the *keep* to be a plain form and hence the clause to be subjunctive, while *keeps* can only be a 3rd person singular present tense form, so that the clause is distinctively non-subjunctive. But in [iii] *keep* could be either the plain form or the plain present tense form, and the clause could therefore be either subjunctive or non-subjunctive. This is not a matter of ambiguity, however, since there is no semantic difference between the subjunctive and non-subjunctive examples in [i–ii].

Two places where the morphological indeterminacy can be resolved in favour of the subjunctive are illustrated in:

[4] i *The nuns insisted [that their young ladies wear stockings].*
ii *It is vital [that they not accept the offer without first taking legal advice].*

Wear in [i] must be the plain form because if the subordinate verb were tensed backshifting would be required: *The nuns insisted that they* <u>*wore*</u> *stockings*, so the *wear* must be the plain form.[19] The mandative clause in [ii] is negative, and the tensed version would therefore require *do*: *that they do not accept the offer*. Negative subjunctives with verbs other than *be* are, however, quite rare and formal.

7.1.1 The mandative construction

Mandative clauses characteristically occur in construction with various verbs, nouns, and adjectives, such as *demand* and *mandatory* (to cite the two that contain the element *mand* on which the term 'mandative' is based).

[5] i *They* <u>*demanded*</u> [*that access to the park* <u>*remain*</u> *free*].
 ii *It is* <u>*mandatory*</u> [*that all pools* <u>*be*</u> *properly fenced*].

We will apply the term mandative not only to the subordinate clauses but also to the verb, noun, or adjective which licenses or governs them – for example, we will say that as used in [5] *demand* is a mandative verb and *mandatory* a mandative adjective.

Three types of mandative clause

On the basis of their internal structure we distinguish three types of mandative clause:

[6]	i	*They demand(ed)* [*that the park* <u>*remain*</u> *open*].	[subjunctive mandative]
	ii	*They demand(ed)* [*that the park* <u>*should remain*</u> *open*].	[*should*-mandative]
	iii	*They demand* [*that the park* <u>*remains*</u> *open*].	[covert mandative]
	iv	*They demanded* [*that the park* <u>*remained*</u> *open*].	

Those with the form of a subjunctive construction we refer to as **subjunctive mandatives**, those containing the specialised use of *should* as ***should*-mandatives**, and those with the form of an ordinary declarative content clause as **covert mandatives**. There is nothing in the internal structure of the bracketed clauses in [iii–iv] to distinguish them from the non-mandative content clauses in *I know* [*that the park* <u>*remains*</u> *open*] or *He said* [*that the park* <u>*remained*</u> *open*] – the mandative meaning derives entirely from the governing verb *demand*. Covert mandatives contain a present tense verb, or else a backshifted preterite, as in [iv]: we can't have an ordinary, past-time preterite (**They demand that the park remained open*).

Clear cases of the covert construction are fairly rare, and indeed in AmE are of somewhat marginal acceptability. In AmE the subjunctive is strongly favoured over the *should* construction, while BrE shows the opposite preference.

Semantic contrast between mandative and non-mandative clauses

A content clause in construction with *demand* or *mandatory* – or *require, stipulate, essential, necessary*, etc. – is always mandative, but others items such as *insist, suggest,*

[19] Strictly speaking, [i] is ambiguous. We are concerned with the mandative interpretation, where the nuns imposed a rule about wearing stockings, but there is also a non-mandative interpretation with *wear* a present tense verb: "The nuns emphatically asserted it to be the case that their young ladies wear stockings" (compare the contrast between [7ia/iia] below).

important can select either a mandative or a non-mandative clause as complement:

[7] i a. *She insisted [that he tell her the whole story].* [mandative]
b. *I suggest [you go and see a doctor].*
c. *It's important [that he should take us into his confidence].*
ii a. *She insisted [that he had been lying].* [non-mandative]
b. *I suggest [she doesn't like us very much].*
c. *It's not important [that the gift won't be a surprise].*

The difference in meaning is comparable to that between imperative and declarative clauses.[20] With mandatives it is a matter of bringing about the situation expressed in the content clause. As with imperatives, we can invoke the concept of 'compliance': in [ia] she insisted on compliance, in [ib] I'm advocating compliance in a relatively tentative way, and in [ic] compliance is said to be important. With the non-mandatives, by contrast, it is a matter of the truth of the proposition expressed in the content clause. In [iia] she insisted on the truth of the proposition, in [iib] I put the proposition forward as something that may well be true, and in [iic] the truth of the proposition is taken for granted, presupposed: it is treated as a fact, a fact that is said to be not important.

Ambiguity between mandative and non-mandative clauses

With the items that allow both mandative and non-mandative complements there may be ambiguity between them. Compare:

[8] i *She insists [that he take the eight o'clock train].* [mandative]
ii *She insists [that he took the eight o'clock train].* [non-mandative]
iii *She insists [that he takes / they take the eight o'clock train].* [ambiguous]

Example [i] is distinctively subjunctive. By contrast, [ii] is non-subjunctive and cannot be taken as a covert mandative because *took* is an ordinary past-time preterite, not a backshifted one: the time of his taking the train is earlier than that of her insisting. Both versions of [iii] are ambiguous. With *he takes* it can be a covert mandative equivalent to subjunctive [i]: the meaning is that she insists on his taking this train, either on some particular future occasion or habitually. But the more likely interpretation is non-mandative, that she emphatically asserts it to be the case that he takes this train – most probably a matter of his habitually doing so, but it could be a single future occurrence with a futurate interpretation ("She emphatically maintains that he is scheduled to take the eight o'clock train"). The version with *they take* has the same ambiguity, but on the mandative reading it is also syntactically indeterminate between the subjunctive and covert constructions.

Mandatives and modality

The mandative construction falls within the broad area of meaning that is known as modality. In our discussion of modality as expressed by the modal auxiliaries (Ch. 3, §9), we distinguished various dimensions of modal meaning, including 'kind' and 'strength'. Two of the main kinds of modality are deontic and epistemic: deontic modality is concerned with obligation and permission (as in *You must leave at once* or *You may leave as soon as you've finished*), while epistemic modality is primarily concerned with one's level of assurance about the truth of the proposition expressed (as in *He must/may have missed the train*).

[20] It has indeed been suggested that mandatives should be analysed syntactically as subordinate imperatives; we have argued against that view in Ch. 10, §9.8.

On the dimension of strength, *must* is strong and *may* weak, while *ought* is somewhere in between, of medium strength. Within this framework, mandatives clearly involve deontic modality: *It is necessary that you leave at once* is comparable to the above *You must leave at once*, with the deontic use of *must*.[21] As for the dimension of strength, mandatives show variation here, with *demand, insist, necessary*, for example, stronger than *advise, recommend, desirable*. In general, however, they occupy an area on the scale of deontic strength higher than that represented by permission: mandatives are rare with *allow* (*He won't allow that she attend the meeting*), questionable with *permit*, and quite impossible with *let* – verbs of permission generally take infinitival complements (*He won't allow/permit her to attend the meeting*).

Blurring of semantic contrast between mandative and non-mandative

Verbs expressing deontic modality (whether auxiliaries or lexical verbs) may of course appear in content clauses, and this may lead to a loss of the sharp distinction between mandative and non-mandative illustrated in [7i] vs [7ii]. Consider:

[9] i *She insisted [that he must / had to wear a hat when he went out]*.
ii *I suggested [that we might invite the Smiths at the same time]*.

There are grounds for saying that the bracketed clauses here are non-mandative. The modals *must* and *might* do not have plain forms and hence cannot occur in subjunctive or *should* mandatives; ***have*** is not morphologically restricted in this way, but *had* could not here be replaced by *have* (or *should have*), so we cannot plausibly argue that these clauses are covert mandatives. Note, moreover, that we could replace *insisted* and *suggested* by, for example, *said* and *added*, verbs that do not take mandative complements. Nevertheless, the meanings are very similar to the mandative *She insisted that he wear a hat when he went out* and *I suggested that we invite the Smiths at the same time*. This phenomenon is similar to that found with main clauses. *You must / have to wear a hat when you go out* and *We might invite the Smiths at the same time* are declarative clauses, not imperatives, and yet they are most likely to be interpreted in context as directives, as having much the same force as the imperatives *Wear a hat when you go out* and *Let's invite the Smiths at the same time* (cf. the discussion of declarative directives in Ch. 10, §9.6.2). This strengthens the analogy we have drawn between mandatives and imperatives on the one hand, non-mandatives and declaratives on the other. Mandatives and imperatives are inherently deontic; non-mandatives and declaratives are not, but when they incidentally contain deontic modal expressions their interpretation may come to merge with that of mandatives and imperatives respectively.

Modal harmony between mandative governor and its complement

One consequence of the resemblance between a modalised non-mandative and a mandative is that such items as *stipulate, essential, requirement*, which (unlike *insist* and *suggest*) normally allow only mandative complements, may nevertheless appear with a non-mandative that contains an appropriate deontic modal:

[10] i *The agreement stipulates [that an election must be held next year]*.
ii *These criteria must be satisfied within the overriding requirement [that work assessed must show literary merit]*.
iii *It is essential [that the radiochemical procedure for the assay of lead-210 shall provide for a high degree of decontamination from major fission products]*.

[21] Note that the adjective *necessary*, unlike the verb *must* or the adverb *necessarily*, is restricted to the deontic kind of modality, so that it takes mandative but not non-mandative clauses: we can say *He wasn't necessarily referring to you*, but not, equivalently, **It isn't necessary that he was referring to you*.

We will say that a non-mandative is allowed with such items if it is modally harmonic with them: the strong deontic modals *must* and *shall* here match the modality expressed by *stipulate*, *requirement*, and *essential*. (For further discussion of modal harmony, see Ch. 3, §9.2.3.)

Should-mandatives

In main clauses *should* expresses medium strength modality (like *ought*): *You should inform the police* countenances that you may not do so – I could add *but I don't suppose you will*, which would not be possible with strong *must*. Consider now its use in:

[11] i *They demanded [that he should be freed].* [*should*-mandative]
ii *She insists [that I should have told her].* [non-mandative]
iii *They insisted [that all murderers should be hanged].* [ambiguous]
iv *They suggested/recommended [that we should engage a consultant].*

Example [i] is clearly not a case of modal harmony, for *demand* is stronger than *should* is in its main clause uses: cf. the discussion of [2ic] above. It is for this reason that we recognise a specialised use of *should* as a grammatical marker of a distinct *should*-mandative construction, equivalent in meaning to the subjunctive. *Insist* in [11ii] is also strong, but here *should* is the ordinary medium-strength one that we have in the main clause *I should have told her*. Moreover, *insist* cannot here be being used mandatively, for the past time expressed by *have* rules out a mandative interpretation. The example is like [7iia], meaning approximately "She maintains that I should have told her". Example [11iii] can be interpreted in either way. As a *should*-mandative it is equivalent to subjunctive *They insisted that all murderers be hanged*, "They insisted on having all murderers hanged" (which implicates that they were in a position of power); in the non-mandative reading they forcefully expressed their view as to the right punishment for murderers (and hence may have been ordinary citizens).

More problematic is [11iv]: *suggest* and *recommend* are of medium strength and hence potentially harmonic with the ordinary *should*. This time, therefore, *We should engage a consultant* does accurately express the content of their suggestion/recommendation. We probably need to accept that the distinction between a *should*-mandative and a modally harmonic non-mandative is here neutralised; such examples are much more frequent than the clear cases of modal harmony like [10], but they are also considerably more frequent, especially in AmE and AusE, than strong *should*-mandatives like [11i].

Distribution of mandative clauses

In the most straightforward cases the mandative clause functions as (internal) complement to the governing mandative word or else, with nouns and certain adjectives, as subject or (much more likely) extraposed subject in the clause in which the governing item heads the predicative complement:

[12] i *the requirement that it be signed by a director* [complement]
ii *That it be signed by a director is no longer a requirement.* [subject]
iii *It is no longer a requirement that it be signed by a director.* [extraposed subject]

The syntactic relation between the mandative clause and the governing word may, however, be less direct:

[13] i *The main recommendation was that an outside consultant be engaged.*
ii *It seemed the most important thing in my life at this moment that she should know the real truth about me.*
iii *One of the qualities demanded of a politician by other politicians is that he or she always keep a confidence.*

In [i] *recommendation* is head of the subject while the mandative clause is complement of *be*: this is the specifying use of *be*, where properties of the variable (here the subject) carry over to the value (here the predicative complement). In [ii] the mandative property of *important* percolates up, as it were, so that it applies to the NP in which *important* is modifier. And [iii] combines these two extensions of the relationship: the main clause contains specifying *be* and the subject is mandative by virtue of *demand*, which heads the non-finite clause modifying *qualities*.

A sample of mandative verbs, adjectives, and nouns

We give here examples of items from these three categories that license mandative clauses. The annotation '†' signifies that the item readily takes ordinary, non-mandative, content clauses too (as illustrated for *insist, suggest,* and *important* in [7i–ii]).

[14]				
	advise/advice †	*agree/ ·ment* †	*allow* †	*arrange/ ·ment*
	ask	*beg*	*command /–*	*decide/decision* †
	decree/–	*demand/–*	*desire/–*	*determine/·ation* †
	enjoin	*entreat /·y*	*insist/·ence* †	*instruct/·ion*
	intend/intention	*move/motion*	*ordain*	*order/–*
	pledge/–	*prefer/·ence*	*propose/·al* †	*recommend/·ation*
	request/–	*require/·ment*	*resolve/–* †	*rule/·ing* †
	stipulate/·ation	*suggest/·ion* †	*urge/·ing* †	*vote/–*

[15]					
i	*advisable*	*appropriate* †	*compulsory*	*crucial* †	*desirable*
	essential	*fitting* †	*imperative*	*important*†	*necessary*
	obligatory	*preferable*	*proper*	*urgent*	*vital*
ii	*anxious*	*eager*	*insistent* †	*keen*	*willing*

List [14] gives verbs together, where applicable, with the corresponding nouns; the notation '–' indicates that the noun has the same lexical base as the verb.[22] The items in [15] are adjectives: with those in [15i] the mandative characteristically appears as subject or extraposed subject (*It's vital that she be kept informed*), while with those in [ii] it is normally complement within the AdjP (*I'm anxious that it should be settled quickly*). A few of these provide the base for de-adjectival nouns: *importance, necessity, eagerness,* etc. It should be emphasised, however, that there can be no question of giving a definitive list of mandative items: in spite of suggestions that have been frequently made that the subjunctive is dying out in English, this construction is very much alive, with attested

[22] The final *e* of the verb base is deleted before a suffix beginning with a vowel, as in *determination*, etc. (see Ch. 19 §5.15). With *wish*, mandatives are commonly found with the noun (*It is her wish that the matter be resolved quickly*), but are hardly possible with the verb, which takes, rather, a modal preterite (*He wishes he had told them*). Similarly mandatives are licensed by the noun *regulation* but not normally by the verb *regulate*. Besides *ruling*, there is a noun *rule* which takes only a mandative complement: *the rule that ties be worn.*

examples like *I would stress that people just be aware of the danger* suggesting that its distribution is increasing.

7.1.2 Content clauses governed by prepositions

Prepositions and prepositional idioms governing subjunctive or specialised-modal content clauses include the following (where '-T' indicates that the content clause cannot be expanded by the subordinator *that*):

[16]	i ADVERSATIVE	*for fear*	*lest* –T		
	ii CONDITIONAL	*if* –T	*in case* –T	*on condition*	*provided*
		providing	*though* –T	*unless* –T	
	iii PURPOSIVE	*in order*	*so*		

Adversatives

[17] i *He was bathed in perspiration, trembling [lest his authorship become known].*
ii *Both were tense with worry [lest things should somehow go wrong].*

Lest, which belongs to formal style, is the only preposition where the subjunctive is the preferred construction, though specialised *should*, as in [ii], is also readily used. Ordinary declaratives are possible, but comparatively rare.

Conditionals

[18] i *He struggles in vain against the proposition that [if the mind be immaterial,] its functions ought to be unaffected by the condition of the body.*
ii *He handed over the pretty sloop to Abel for keeps, [on condition that he never fail to let his brother accompany him whenever the younger boy wished].*
iii *[If you should need any help,] don't hesitate to call me.*
iv *They want flexibility [in case the market should fail].*
v *[If some thief should open her case,] he wouldn't easily find her jewellery.*

The subjunctive is fairly rare here, especially with verb-forms other than *be*; it belongs to formal style and verges on the archaic. Specialised *should* is regularly found, but much the most usual construction is with an ordinary declarative. *Should* can appear in either open or remote conditionals, as in [iii/iv] and [v] respectively. In the open construction *should* has a narrower range of use than an ordinary declarative: only the latter is found in cases where the condition is accepted as satisfied, where there is no element of doubt, as in *If it's as good as she says, let's go and see it.*

The noun *condition* takes mandative complements (*They wanted to impose a condition that full payment be made in advance*), so that there is an evident connection between the conditional and mandative constructions.

Purposives

[19] i *Extraordinary precautions were taken [so that no stranger be allowed in the city].*
ii *He issued white gloves [so that his customers should not soil their hands].*
iii *A true friend would change subjects [so that they could do projects together].*
iv *They say I am urging him to abdicate [in order that I may step into his shoes].*

Subjunctives and specialised *should* are found with both *so* and *in order*, but they are not common. *So* usually takes an ordinary declarative, very often containing the ***can*** of ability, as in [iii]. The combination of purpose and ability ***can*** might perhaps be regarded as a case of modal harmony: there is a close connection between purpose and enabling. *In order* is more formal than *so*, and this is reflected in the fact that the most frequent pattern with *in order* has *may* (or *might*), as in [iv]. This use of ***may*** is somewhat different from its use in main clauses, and hence counts as a specialised-modal construction. The main clause *I may step into his shoes* would most likely be interpreted epistemically ("I will perhaps ..."), and a deontic reading is also available ("I'm allowed to . . ."), but a dynamic, ability, reading is hardly possible.[23]

7.1.3 Content clauses functioning as exhaustive conditional adjunct

The subjunctive is found in the exhaustive conditional construction discussed in §5.3.6:

[20] i *It meets with continuing hostility from those who see themselves as fostering and guarding serious art,* [*whether it be in the theatre, in fiction, or on television*].

ii *Achieving the optimum blast design for a particular rock mass type,* [*be it in mining or quarrying,*] *can be an expensive and time-consuming procedure.*

iii *They realise that East–West friction,* [*wherever it take place around the globe*], *is in essence the general conflict between two entirely different societies.*

In [i] we have a closed interrogative expressing an alternative question: the meaning is approximately "irrespective of the answer to the question 'Is it in the theatre, in fiction, or on television?'". The subjunctive here is relatively formal and more or less confined to the verb *be*, so that we find *whether he likes it or not* but hardly ?*whether he like it or not.* Example [ii] is an alternant of the construction with *whether*, again belonging to formal style. Here the restriction to the verb *be* is absolute, and the following subject is usually a personal pronoun. The structural relation between *whether it be* and *be it* bears some resemblance to that between *whether it is* and *is it* (as found in main clause interrogatives), but the subjunctive *be* + subject order is not a case of normal subject–auxiliary inversion, which applies only with primary verb-forms. Example [iii] is an open interrogative, with the subjunctive much less common than a tensed construction (*wherever it takes place* . . .).[24]

Specialised *should* is hardly possible as an alternant of the subjunctive in such conditionals, but one commonly finds *may* in the open interrogative type, in what can be regarded as a case of modal harmony:

[21] [*Whatever one may choose to call it,*] *natural law is a functioning generality with a certain objective existence.*

This is equivalent to *whatever one chooses to call it*: *may* doesn't add a new modal meaning, but reinforces that inherent in the *whatever.*

7.1.4 Other specialised-modal constructions

Attitudinal *should*

Should is found, as an alternant of an ordinary declarative, in clauses governed by (or otherwise related to) items expressing various kinds of subjective attitude or

[23] This is not to say that *may* cannot have the ability sense in main clauses, but the main clause use is considerably more restricted than that found in purposive constructions. A second example, involving backshifted *might*, is seen in *A press conference was held in order that the consulting specialists might clarify the president's condition for the nation.*

[24] Two fixed phrases with postposed subjects, *come what may* ("irrespective of what may come/happen") and *be that as it may* ("however that may be"), also belong here. So too does the rare subjectless construction with verb + fused relative as complement: *She wandered up and down, trying turn after turn, but always came back to the house, do what she would* ("whatever she did").

evaluation:

[22] i *We felt incensed [that he should have been treated so leniently].*
ii *It is wrong [that a judge should sit while his conduct is under investigation].*
iii *What held his interest was the fact [that these two should have been there at all].*

In [i] the content clause is complement to the adjective *incensed*, in [ii] it is extraposed subject in a matrix with *wrong* as predicative, and in [iii] it is in a much less direct relation to *interest* (compare *It was interesting that . . .*). A sample of licensing expressions is given in:

[23]					
	a good idea	*a pity*	*appropriate*	*astonishing*	*can't bear*
	can't imagine	*distressed*	*expedient*	*extraordinary*	*fortunate*
	honoured	*impossible*	*improper*	*inevitable*	*intelligible*
	ironic	*lamentable*	*natural*	*perturbed*	*puzzling*
	remarkable	*right*	*sad*	*suitable*	*surprising*

This construction differs from the mandative in that the *should* clause is not replaceable by a subjunctive (cf. **We felt incensed that he have been treated so leniently*) – though there may be variation with certain items (such as *appropriate* and *proper*) as to whether they belong here or with the mandatives.

The attitudinal use of *should* is virtually but not quite restricted to content clauses: it is also found in main clause interrogatives like *Who should I see but Bill?*

May

May and *might* occur in the complements of governors such as *hope, pray, fear, dread,* and the like:

[24] i *We hope that he may make a complete recovery.*
ii *She had dreaded still more that he might return to England.*

These are equivalent to ordinary declaratives with *will*: *that he will make a complete recovery*; *that he would return to England.* The hope, that is, is not so much for the possibility of a recovery as for its actualisation, and analogously for the dread. With some items, such as *lest* and *for fear*, there is a choice between *may*, specialised *should*, and the subjunctive, but these last two constructions are not possible with *hope* or *fear* as a verb. Again there is variation over particular items: some speakers will have *pray* as a mandative and for others *dread* allows attitudinal *should*.

7.2 Modal preterites and irrealis mood

We use the term **modal preterite** for a preterite that expresses modal rather than temporal meaning, i.e. modal remoteness rather than past time (or backshift). By extension, the term applies to a clause with a preterite verb-form of this kind:

[25] i *Suppose [they were in London last week].* [ordinary preterite]
ii *Suppose [they were in London now / next week].* [modal preterite]

In [i] we see the primary use of the preterite to locate the situation in past time; in [ii], by contrast, the time is present or future and the preterite serves to imply that their being in London at the time in question is a relatively remote possibility. Example [ii] contrasts with *Suppose they are in London next week*, where the same situation is presented as an open possibility. The modal auxiliaries *could, might, should,* and *would* are found as modal preterites in main as well as subordinate clauses (*It could be over before next Tuesday*; *You might have been killed*), but with other verbs modal preterites are restricted to content clauses.

A clause with **irrealis mood** has *were* as verb in construction with a 1st or 3rd person singular subject. In general, modal preterite *was* has irrealis *were* as a somewhat more formal alternant:

[26] i *Suppose* [*she was in London now / next week*]. [modal preterite]
ii *Suppose* [*she were in London now / next week*]. [irrealis mood]

Modal preterite and irrealis content clauses are found in the following constructions (see also Ch. 3, §1.7, for uses of irrealis *were* by some speakers in contexts where it is not an alternant of a modal preterite).

(a) Remote conditionals

[27] i *If* [*he was / were still in Paris*] *she would call on him this evening.* [present time]
ii *If* [*he had been in Paris last week*] *she would have called on him.* [past time]

These constructions are described in detail in Ch. 8, §14.

(b) Complement to *wish*

[28] i *I wish* [*she was / were here*]. [present time]
ii *I wish* [*he hadn't told them*]. [past time]

These have counterfactual interpretations: [i] indicates that she isn't here and [ii] that he did tell them. They contrast therefore with *I hope she is here* and *I hope he didn't tell them*, which leave open the issue of whether she is here and whether he told them. There is, however, no such straightforward contrast between *wish* and *hope* with future situations. For *wish* we find the following distribution:

[29] i *I wish* [*she had come tomorrow*]. [doubly remote]
ii *I wish* [*semester ended next week*]. [futurate]
iii *I wish* [*you would come with us tomorrow*]. [volition]
iv #*I wish* [*you passed your driving-test tomorrow*].

Example [i] indicates that something has already happened to exclude her coming tomorrow (perhaps she has come today): it has two markers of modal remoteness, preterite and perfect (Ch. 3, §6.1). Example [ii] is a futurate, concerned with the present schedule: it indicates that semester doesn't end next week. In [iii] *would* is interpreted as indicating present-time volition: we understand that you won't come with us tomorrow, i.e. that you are not (now) willing to. But *wish* cannot be used with a 'pure' future, one where there is no present time involved: cases like this are still within the realm of hoping, so that instead of [iv] we would say *I hope you pass your driving-test tomorrow.*[25]

(c) *Would rather / sooner / as soon*

[30] i *I'd rather* [*I didn't have to go*]. [present time]
ii *I'd rather* [*you hadn't told her*]. [past time]
iii *I'd rather* [*she came tomorrow*]. [future time]

[25] A modal preterite is at best very marginal with *wish* as a noun: ?*He told nobody of his wish that he had married Angela.* A clausal complement to the noun *wish* is normally mandative (*He expressed a wish that the director drop dead*).

Again, [i] and [ii] are counterfactual: I do have to go and you did tell her. But the most usual case is with a future time situation, as in [iii], and this is certainly not counterfactual: it doesn't say that she won't come tomorrow. It is a tentative way of expressing a preference, allowing that she may not do so. *Prefer* is marginally possible with a modal preterite when in construction with *would/should* or some similar context (*I'd prefer she came tomorrow*), but it is much more usual to have *it* + remote conditional: *I'd prefer it if she came tomorrow.*

(d) *It **be** time*

[31] i *It is time [you were in bed].* [present state]
ii *It is time [we repainted the house].* [immediate future occurrence]

Here, [i] is straightforwardly counterfactual: "You aren't in bed but you should be". Example [ii] entails that the situation is not yet in progress: "We aren't repainting the house, but should do so". A perfect, as in *It is time you had finished it*, is interpreted as a modally remote version of the present perfect: "You haven't finished but should have done". This construction differs from the others in that it hardly allows an irrealis: *It is time he was/?were in bed.*[26]

7.3 Present tense with future time interpretation

In main clauses a simple present tense can be used with a future time interpretation only in what we are calling the futurate, e.g. with a future event that has already been scheduled, as in *She leaves for London next week.* This restriction does not apply in various types of subordinate clause, including relatives, comparatives, and content clauses (Ch. 3, §4.2.5). Content clauses allowing such pragmatically unrestricted futures are illustrated in:

[32] i *Let's go home before [it starts raining].* [comp of temporal preposition]
ii *We'll visit Jill if [there is time].* [comp of conditional preposition]
iii *We insist [that he answers all the questions].* [covert mandative]
iv *It doesn't matter [whether you do it this week or next].* [interrogative]
v *I hope [the weather clears up soon].* [comp of *hope*-type governors]

These constructions are discussed in Ch. 3, §4.2.5; [v] differs from the others in that *will* can be added without changing the meaning: *I hope the weather will clear up soon.*

7.4 Factivity

The lexical properties of the governing item determine whether or not a declarative content clause is entailed, and whether or not, in the default case, it is presupposed. Entailment is a semantic relation, while presupposition is a pragmatic one: this is why we need the default case proviso for presuppositions but not entailments.

[26] A rare attested example (from a British newspaper) is *It's high time the true cost of the monarchy were pointed out.* Examples are also occasionally found of mandative *should* or a present tense instead of the modal preterite: *%Perhaps it is time that the very principle of a public subsidy should be given a thorough examination*; *%It is about time we acknowledge the unconscionable fact that international trade benefits no one except the multi-nationals and international financiers.*

Definitions of entailment and presupposition

These concepts were introduced in Ch. 1, §5, and defined as follows:

[33] i *X* entails *Y* ≡ If *X* is true, then it follows necessarily that *Y* is true too.
ii *X* normally presupposes *Y* ≡ in saying *X* the speaker, in the absence of indications to the contrary, takes the truth of *Y* for granted, i.e. presents it as something that is not at issue.

We are concerned in this section with the special case where *Y* is a declarative content clause. Entailment may then be illustrated with the following examples:

[34] i *It happened [that Kim had left the country].* [entails [iii]]
ii *It seemed [that Kim had left the country].* [does not entail [iii]]
iii *Kim had left the country.*

If [i] is true, then [iii] must also be true, whereas in asserting [ii] I do not commit myself to the truth of [iii]: [ii] leaves open the possibility that Kim had not left the country. The difference is of course due to the properties of the governing verbs: with *happen* the complement clause is entailed, with *seem* it is not.

Presupposition is illustrated in the following:

[35] i *The insurance company knows [that Jill had lent Ed her key].* [presupposes [iii]]
ii *It is true that Jill had lent Ed her key.* [does not presuppose [iii]]
iii *Jill had lent Ed her key.*

Example [i] conveys two pieces of information: (a) that Jill had lent Ed her key (i.e. [iii]); (b) that the insurance company has knowledge of [iii]. In normal circumstances these two pieces of information will differ in their pragmatic status, with (a) backgrounded, taken for granted, while (b) is foregrounded, presented as the proposition whose truth is at issue. We say then that (a) is presupposed, while (b) is asserted. If you respond with *No, that's not so,* you will normally be taken to be challenging (b), not (a). With [ii], by contrast, that Jill had lent Ed her key is part of the assertion, and there is clearly no way of challenging [ii] as a whole which doesn't simultaneously challenge [iii]. Again the difference is attributable to properties of the governing items in the matrix clause: *know* triggers the presupposition that the complement clause is true, while *true* does not.

Differences between presupposition and entailment

It will be evident from the above account that presupposition and entailment are very different kinds of concept. One especially important difference emerges when we change the matrix clause by making it negative, interrogative, or complement of conditional *if*:

[36] i a. *The insurance company knows [that Jill had lent Ed her key].* (=[35i])
b. *The insurance company doesn't know [that Jill had lent Ed her key].*
c. *Does the insurance company know [that Jill had lent Ed her key]?*
d. *If the insurance company knows [that Jill had lent Ed her key], they may refuse to pay her.*
ii a. *It is true [that Jill had lent Ed her key].* (=[35ii])
b. *It isn't true [that Jill had lent Ed her key].*
c. *Is it true [that Jill had lent Ed her key]?*
d. *If it is true [that Jill had lent Ed her key], her claim will be refused.*

In [i] the presupposition that Jill had lent Ed her key holds for all of [a–d] in the absence of indications to the contrary. In the salient use of [ib], I know that Jill had lent Ed her key and assert that the insurance company doesn't know this. Similarly in [ic] I take it for granted that Jill had lent Ed her key and ask whether the insurance company knows this. And in the most likely context for [id] I know she had done so and entertain the possibility that the insurance company knows it too. In [ii], however, the entailment that Jill had lent Ed her key holds only in [a]. In [iib] of course we have the opposite entailment – that she had not lent Ed her key. Example [iic] is a question, and therefore does not have a truth value: questions themselves are neither true nor false. For this reason the issue of entailments does not arise: if the *X* in definition [33] has no truth value, the condition for *Y* being an entailment cannot be satisfied. And in [36iid] the whole sentence is not inconsistent with Jill's not having lent Ed her key: it excludes only the situation in which Jill had lent Ed the key but her claim will not be refused.

The conditional construction involves embedding the presupposing or entailing clause in a larger construction; other cases where the presupposing or entailing clause is embedded are illustrated in:

[37] i a. *I <u>hope</u> [the insurance company knows that Jill had lent Ed her key].*
b. *He <u>realised</u> [that the insurance company knows that Jill had lent Ed her key].*
ii a. *I <u>hope</u> [it is true that Jill had lent Ed her key].*
b. *He <u>realised</u> [that it is true that Jill had lent Ed her key].*

Both [ia] and [ib] convey that Jill had lent Ed her key: the presupposition of [36ia] is retained under embedding. In [37ii], however, only example [b] conveys that Jill had lent Ed her key: the entailment of [36iia] is lost when the entailing clause is embedded as complement to *hope*, but retained when it is embedded as complement to *realise*. The difference is due to the fact that [37iib], but not [37iia], entails [36iia]. Entailment is what is known as a logically transitive relation: if *W* entails *X* and *X* entails *Y*, then *W* entails *Y*.[27]

The difference with respect to preservation of presuppositions and entailments can therefore be stated as follows:

[38] i In the default case, presuppositions are preserved when the presupposing clause is negated, interrogated, or embedded.
ii Entailments are lost when the entailing clause is negated or interrogated, and also when it is embedded, unless it is itself entailed by the clause in which it is embedded.

Presuppositions that are also entailments of the positive declarative matrix clause

In the case of [36i] the positive declarative [a] (*The insurance company knows that Jill had lent Ed her key*) both entails and presupposes that Jill had lent Ed her key. The presuppositional status of the content clause *Jill had lent Ed her key* is retained under the operations of negation, interrogation, and embedding illustrated in [b–d], but its entailment status is lost, just as it is in [iib–d]. In [ib–id], the proposition that Jill had lent Ed her key is an implicature, not an entailment, and as such it can be cancelled. This

[27] The sense of 'transitive' in logic is quite different from the sense it has in syntax ("having an object"). Etymologically, the term has to do with the concept of 'going across'. How this applies in logic is transparent from the definition just given; in syntax it is based on the idea that the most prototypical transitive clause describes an action that 'goes across' from an agent to a patient.

could happen, for example, in a context where the insurance company is suggesting or claiming that Jill had lent Ed her key but where I, the speaker, question whether they have sufficient evidence to establish that. In this case *know* would bear contrastive stress to focus on the issue of whether it is indeed a matter of knowledge (as opposed, for example, to surmise). In [ib] I'm saying they don't have such knowledge, in [ic] I'm asking whether they do, and in [id] I'm presenting it as only a possibility that they do.[28]

It is also important to note that while the complement clause always has the status of an entailment in [36ia], its status as a presupposition can be cancelled. This could happen in a context similar to the one just discussed. It may be, for example, that you have doubts as to whether Jill had lent Ed her key and have questioned whether the insurance company have evidence to establish that she did: I can then say [36ia] with stress on *know* to indicate that they are indeed in the position of knowing it to be true. In this case I still convey that Jill had lent Ed her key, because this is an entailment, but the presuppositional status of the content clause is lost, just as in the contextualisations of [36ib–d] discussed in the last paragraph. That is, the information expressed in the content clause is not here taken for granted: the issue of whether Jill had lent Ed her key is foregrounded, not backgrounded.

Presuppositions that are not entailments of the positive declarative

Most cases where a content clause is presupposed are like the *know* example in having the content clause as an entailment of the unembedded positive declarative. But there are some places where no such entailment obtains:

[39] i *Ed went out before [his parents came home].*
ii *Ed regretted [that he had offended his parents].*
iii *Ed confessed [that he murdered her husband].*

Example [i] presupposes that his parents came home, but does not entail it. It is a truth condition for [i] that when Ed went out his parents had not come home, but not that they did in fact come home later. It may be, for example, that they were involved in a fatal traffic accident and never came home. That this is consistent with the meaning of *before* is evident from such examples as *Ed died before [he finished his thesis]*, which obviously does not entail that he finished his thesis after he died. The presupposition triggered by *before* – that the event expressed in its complement subsequently took place – thus has only the status of an implicature even in the positive declarative, and as such it can be cancelled.

The same applies with [39ii]: this presupposes, but does not entail, that he had offended his parents. Ed must have believed that he had offended his parents, but it is possible for him to have been mistaken. The implicature can therefore be cancelled, as in:

[40] *Ed believed that he had offended his parents and very much regretted that he had done so, but it turned out that he had been mistaken: they hadn't been in the least offended.*

Similarly with [39iii]. The default assumption is that confessions are true, so that what is foregrounded is the act of confession, not the issue of whether the content is

[28] One very common case where the presuppositional implicature associated with *know* is cancelled is in the present tense with a 1st person singular subject: *I don't know that she approves of our plan.* Again *know* may have contrastive stress, indicating that this issue is whether it's a matter of knowledge or mere belief, but it can also appear without such stress, in which case I'm casting doubt on the truth of the content clause.

true. But it is perfectly possible to make a false confession, so it cannot be an entailment of [39iii] that he murdered her husband.

Varying degrees of backgrounding

We have said that a presupposed proposition is backgrounded, so that its truth is not at issue. The examples examined show, however, that there can be varying degrees of backgrounding. It is appreciably greater with *regret*, for example, than it is with *know* (even though the complement of *know* is entailed in the positive declarative, while that of *regret* is not). This can perhaps be most easily seen by comparing interrogative forms like:

[41] i *Does he know that his plan has been modified?*
ii *Does he regret that his plan has been modified?*

In both cases, I am likely to be taking it for granted that his plan has been modified and asking whether he knows or regrets this. In [i], however, it is not difficult, as we saw for the earlier *know* example, to imagine a context where I don't know whether his plan has been modified: one aim of my question could be to determine whether it is a fact or merely supposition that his plan has been modified. But one would have to be very devious to ask [ii] with similar intent. Just as one cannot regret some proposition *P* unless one believes that *P* is true, so one would not normally ask whether someone else regrets that *P* unless one believes that *P* is true.

Factive and entailing governors

Verbs, adjectives, etc., whose content clause complement is normally presupposed are called **factive**. *Know*, *regret*, *confess*, for example, are factive verbs, while *before* is a factive preposition, and so on. There is no well-established name for items whose complement is entailed in the positive declarative: we will call them simply **entailing** verbs, adjectives, etc. A sample of governing items classified in terms of entailment and presupposition is given in [42]; in each case the items are given in the order verbs (or verbal idioms), adjectives, nouns, prepositions:

[42] i ENTAILING AND FACTIVE

a. *find out*	*forget*	*know*	*point out*	*realise*	*remember*
aware	*fact*	*after*	*although*	*because*	*since*
b. *amuse*	*bother*	*matter*	*offend*	*suffice*	*worry*
exciting	*important*	*odd*	*relevant*	*surprising*	*tragic*

ii ENTAILING AND NON-FACTIVE

a. *happen*	*prove*	*show*	*turn out*
b. *evident*	*inevitable*	*obvious*	*true*

iii NON-ENTAILING AND FACTIVE

a. *admit*	*confess*	*regret*	*resent*	*angry*	*sad*
sorry	*before*				

iv NON-ENTAILING AND NON-FACTIVE

a. *announce*	*appear*	*assume*	*believe*	*conclude*	*conjecture*
hope	*inform*	*insist*	*say*	*seem*	*tell*
certain	*confident*	*hopeful*	*sure*	*danger*	*evidence*
idea	*impression*	*if*	*lest*	*provided*	
b. *likely*	*possible*	*probable*			

Items in the sets labelled [a] take the content clause as post-head complement, as in *He found out* [*that she had left*] or *It happened* [*that there were a few seats still available*]. Those in [b] take it as subject, [*That I was taken in by their story*] *amused them*, or extraposed subject, *It amused* [*them that I was taken in by their story*].

Negative entailments and presuppositions

A small number of items entail or presuppose the negative of their content clause complement:

[43] i [*That we intended to defraud you*] *is simply false.*
ii *Ed wished* [*that her parents were still alive*].
iii *Jill pretended* [*that she was seriously ill*].

Example [i] entails that we didn't intend to defraud you. *False*, however, unlike *true*, is very rarely used with a content clause as subject (or extraposed subject): examples like this are unlikely to be encountered outside philosophical discourse. It would be much more natural to have either an NP (e.g. *the claim that we intended to defraud you*) or an infinitival clause (*It's simply false to say that we intended to defraud you*) – or else to have *not true*. Examples [ii–iii] convey that her parents weren't still alive and that she wasn't seriously ill. It is arguable, however, that these are presuppositions but not entailments – only strong implicatures. Thus [ii] entails that Ed believed her parents were not still alive, but it does not entail that this belief was correct. It could be that he had been misinformed, that unknown to him they were in fact still alive: this would not itself make [ii] false. Similarly for [iii]: this can be true if Jill believed she wasn't seriously ill, even if she was in fact seriously ill without being aware that she was.

Wish differs from *pretend* in two respects. Firstly, the negative presupposition is marked syntactically by the modal preterite form. And secondly, the degree of backgrounding is significantly greater. With *pretend* it is not unusual for the presupposition to be cancelled in the negative: *Jill wasn't* PRETENDING *that she was ill – she really was very sick indeed.* Cancellation is not impossible with *wish*, but much less likely.

Correlation with other properties

The distinctions between entailed and non-entailed, factive and non-factive, are not marked as such in the form of the content clause itself, but there are a number of places where we find some correlation between these and other categories.

(a) Subjunctive and mandative clauses are non-entailed and non-factive

[44] i *It is important* [*that the matter be / is / should be resolved without delay*].
ii *They avoided the subject, lest* [*it be too painful for her to talk about*].

Subjunctive clauses (whether mandative or not) and mandative clauses (whether subjunctive or not) are invariably non-entailed and non-factive, as in these examples. Note that some of the items that license the mandative construction are, elsewhere, entailing and factive. Compare [i], for example, with [*That no records were kept of these transactions*] *is very important.*

(b) Modal preterite and irrealis clauses are non-entailed and non-factive

[45] *If* [*she was/were still alive*] *she would be horrified.*

A modal preterite / irrealis clause is never entailed or presupposed; on the contrary, there is often an implicature of counterfactuality.

(c) Simple present tense with future time interpretation normally non-entailed, non-factive

[46] i *I'll certainly go* *if* [*they invite me*].
ii *I hope* [*you manage to get home in time*].

This does not apply to the futurate construction: *I realise* [*the match starts tomorrow*] entails and presupposes that the match starts tomorrow. But we have argued (Ch. 3, §4.2.4) that there is in fact a present time component involved here (a present arrangement), so this is not a pure future. One case where we do have entailment and/or presupposition is in the complement of temporal prepositions: *I'm leaving after/before* [*the meeting ends*].

(d) Attitudinal *should* occurs only with factive governors

[47] *It is extraordinary* [*that she should have taken it all so calmly*].

This may be contrasted with **It is possible* [*that she should have taken it all so calmly*]. Note, however, that this use of *should* is not licensed by all factive governors: most obviously, it does not occur with verbs of knowledge or coming to know such as *know* or *find out*.

(e) The *fact* normally insertable only with factive verbs/adjectives

		a.	b.
[48]	i	[*That she had to walk*] *didn't bother him at all.*	*The fact* [*that she had to walk*] *didn't bother him at all.*
	ii	[*That we've made a mistake*] *is quite likely.*	#*The fact* [*that we've made a mistake*] *is quite likely.*

Factive verbs and adjectives often allow both constructions shown here: in [ia] *bother* has the content clause itself as complement, whereas in [ib] the complement of *bother* is an NP with *fact* as head and the content clause as complement of *fact*. This is not normally possible with non-factive governors, as illustrated in [ii]. Items like *regret, resent, angry, sorry,* which we have classified as factive but non-entailing allow insertion of *the fact* in this way: *He resented* (*the fact*) *that they had given him false information.* But the version including *the fact* does entail that the content clause is true – by virtue of the properties of *fact* itself. Notice, however, that not all factive verbs allow *the fact* as complement. We cannot, for example, insert it with *know*: *I know I made a mistake*, but not #*I know the fact that I made a mistake.*

(f) Prohibition of gaps generally found only with factive verbs and adjectives

		a.	b.
[49]	i	*the errors which I think* [*I saw* __]	**the errors which I regret* [*I saw* __]
	ii	*Who is it likely* [*she'll invite* __]?	**Who is it strange* [*that she'll invite* __]?

In [i] the object of *saw* is realised by a gap linked to the relative pronoun *which*; the result is grammatical in [ia], where the content clause is complement of non-factive *think*, but not in [ib], where it is complement of factive *regret*. Similarly in [ii]: the gap linked to interrogative *who* is permitted in [iia], where the content clause is an extraposed subject licensed by non-factive *likely*, but not in [iib], where *strange* is factive. Such gaps are prohibited by the subset of factives that allow insertion of *the fact*, as discussed in (e) above.

Content clauses containing a bound variable

We should note, finally, that the content clause complement of a normally entailing or factive governor cannot properly be said to be entailed or presupposed in examples like:

[50] i *Every boy knew/resented that he was being watched.*
ii *Every boy was aware of the fact that he was being watched.*

We are concerned with the interpretation where the pronoun *he* has *every boy* as its antecedent. In this case *he* is not referring to any particular person, but is acting as a variable bound by the quantified NP *every boy*. The meaning of [i] can be represented along the lines of "For every boy *x*, *x* knew/resented that *x* was being watched". In this case the content clause expresses an open proposition and does not have a truth value – it doesn't make sense to ask whether "*x* was being watched" is true. For the same reason the content clause in [ii] does not express a fact, even though it functions syntactically as complement to the noun *fact*. For these reasons the content clauses here cannot satisfy the definitions of entailment and presupposition given in [33].

Examples of this kind serve as a useful reminder that content clauses are syntactically subordinate, differing in various features of form and meaning from main clauses. In particular, the subject pronoun of a main clause cannot express a bound variable like the *he* in [50]. In *Every boy was being watched and he very much resented it*, for example, *he* cannot have *every boy* as its antecedent: it must refer to some specific male person.

8 Some issues of syntactic analysis

The analysis of content clauses presented in this chapter differs in significant ways from that found in traditional grammar: in this section, therefore, we explain some of the changes we have felt it necessary to make.

8.1 Subordinators and the traditional category of 'subordinating conjunctions'

The three subordinators that we have recognised in content clauses, declarative *that* and closed interrogative *whether* and *if*, are traditionally regarded as belonging to a class of a dozen or so 'subordinating conjunctions': they are assigned to the same class as *although*, *unless*, *while*, *after*, *before*, *since*, etc. In terms of the present framework, this is to say that all these items are markers of clause subordination, that none of them are heads: traditional grammar does indeed say that expressions like *although the paper is poorly written* are subordinate clauses, just like *that the paper is poorly written*. The view we have taken in the present grammar, by contrast, is that these other words are grammatically very different from *that* and *whether* and should be analysed as heads of the construction they introduce, more specifically as prepositions heading PPs with a content clause as complement.

For purposes of exposition, we will divide the traditional 'subordinating conjunctions' into two classes, S (corresponding to our subordinators) and P (a subset of our prepositions):

[1] i S-class 'subordinating conjunctions': *that*, *whether*, if_1 ("whether")
ii P-class 'subordinating conjunctions': *after*, if_2 (conditional), *since*, *though*, etc.

Some of the P-class 'subordinating conjunctions' are homonymous with prepositions: *after*, for example, is traditionally analysed as a subordinating conjunction in *She left* [*after she had signed the documents*] and as a preposition in *She left* [*after the ceremony*].

Why P-class 'subordinating conjunctions' are heads

Unlike the S-class items, those in the P-class are not mere markers of subordination: they have evident semantic content, and this content is clearly the major factor in determining the function and distribution of the construction they introduce. Compare, for example:

[2] i *Please bring the washing in* [*before/if it rains*].
ii *His behaviour* [*after you left*] *was atrocious.*

Before it rains and *if it rains* in [i] are adjuncts of time and condition respectively, and are obviously construed in this way by virtue of the meanings of *before* and *if.* In [ii] the meaning of *after* makes the bracketed sequence a time expression, and this in turn allows it to function as modifier of *behaviour* (but not, say, of *boy*).

Why P-class 'subordinating conjunctions' belong in the preposition class

The traditional distinction between 'subordinating conjunctions' and prepositions is that the former introduce clauses while the latter introduce phrases – in our terms traditional prepositions normally enter into construction with noun phrases. Words like *unless* are just 'subordinating conjunctions', those like *on* just prepositions, and those like *until* belong to both categories, being analysed as subordinating conjunctions when they introduce clauses and as prepositions when they introduce phrases:

[3]	INTRODUCING CLAUSE	INTRODUCING PHRASE
i	a. *I won't do it* [*unless you pay me*].	b. **I won't go* [*unless payment*].
ii	a.**I'm banking* [*on you pay me more*].	b. *I'm banking* [*on an increase in pay*].
iii	a. *I left* [*before the meeting ended*].	b. *I left* [*before the end of the meeting*].

We reject this analysis for the following reasons.

(a) Difference in complementation doesn't justify a primary part-of-speech distinction

We have argued that the P-class 'subordinating conjunctions' are heads, and the same point applies to traditional prepositions. The differences illustrated in [3] are thus differences in the complementation of the underlined words. This difference in complementation, however, does not provide adequate justification for saying that *unless* and *on* belong to different parts of speech. It is normal to find differences in complementation between members of the same primary category, and the above difference between *unless* and *on* is matched within the class of verbs by that between, for example, *complain* and *prevent*:

[4]	CLAUSE AS COMPLEMENT	NP AS COMPLEMENT
i	a. *We* [*complained that they didn't consult with the staff*].	b. **We* [*complained the lack of consultation with the staff*].
ii	a. **He* [*prevented that they consulted with the staff*].	b. *He* [*prevented any consultation with the staff*].

The point is, then, that the difference in complementation provides no more reason for a part-of-speech distinction between *unless* and *on* than it does between *complain* and *prevent.* And just as we have seen that some items, such as *before* in [3], take either clauses or NPs, so there are verbs like *announce* whose complements can be of either kind (*He* [*announced that he was resigning*] vs *He* [*announced his resignation*]).

It should be noted, moreover, that the difference is not in fact between clause and NP as complement. Traditional grammar accepts that prepositions can take finite interrogative clauses (*It depends [on whether there is adeqate consultation with the staff]*) or gerund-participials (*We're banking [on there being adequate consultation with the staff]*),[29] so the crucial property of subordinating conjunctions is not that they introduce clauses as opposed to NPs, but that they introduce a particular kind of clause, finite declaratives. This makes the contrast between the [a] and [b] structures in [3] even less appropriate as a basis for a distinction between primary part-of-speech categories.

(b) Pre-head dependents

A further argument against making a part-of-speech distinction on the basis of the complements, the post-head dependents, is that items like *before* which occur with both kinds of complement take the same range of pre-head modifiers in the two cases:

[5] i a. *an hour before the meeting ended* b. *an hour before the end of the meeting*
ii a. *just/shortly before it ended* b. *just/shortly before the end*

What we find, therefore, is that *before* is head of a phrase that can have an NP or a content clause as complement, and in either case it takes modifiers like *an hour, just, shortly*. To say that the phrase belonged to different classes in the two cases would lead to a quite pointless complication of the grammar. Overall, then, there is overwhelming evidence that the *before* that combines with a declarative content clause is, from both a syntactic and semantic point of view, very much more like the *before* that combines with an NP than it is like the subordinator *that*. And of course the same applies to the other words that fall into both preposition and 'subordinating conjunction' classes: *after, since, until*, etc.

Analysis of the sequences *provided that, in order that*, etc.

One point that is sometimes made in support of grouping the P-class 'subordinating conjunctions' with *that* is that they are mutually exclusive with it: we can have *before the meeting ended* and *that the meeting ended*, but not **before that the meeting ended*. This argument is undermined, however, by the fact that some of the items we have to consider do combine with *that*, i.e. take expandable rather than non-expandable clauses as complement. A few of these are illustrated in:

[6] i *I'll do it [provided that you pay me].*
ii *They went hungry [in order that their baby would have food].*
iii *It looks like any other typewriter [except that it has phonetic symbols].*
iv *He intends to exercise his constitutional right to sit on the court, [notwithstanding that the commission of inquiry has not yet made its report].*

The traditional account of such constructions is that the *that* belongs with the preceding item – so that *provided that, in order that, except that, notwithstanding that*, and so on, are complex 'subordinating conjunctions'. This preserves a relation of mutual exclusiveness between what we are calling S-class and P-class 'subordinating conjunctions'. But there is compelling evidence that the *that* in fact belongs in the content clause, i.e. that the immediate constituents are as shown in [7b], not [7a]:

[7] a. *COMPLEX HEAD ANALYSIS b. SIMPLE HEAD ANALYSIS
provided that + you pay me *provided + that you pay me*

The most important point is that *that* can be repeated in coordination: *provided [that you pay me and that I'm allowed to do it my way]*. The first *that* must belong in the coordination,

[29] Traditional grammar also allows for gerund-participials to occur after certain 'subordinating conjunctions'. This creates further problems for the distinction between 'subordinating conjunctions' and 'prepositions', with *although living in London* having an initial 'subordinating conjunction', *despite living in London* an initial 'preposition'.

not with *provided*: the coordination here is between two expanded declaratives, two clauses introduced by *that*.

A second point is that the *that* is usually omissible: we can equally have *I'll do it provided you pay me*. Under analysis [7b] this is covered by the general rules for the omission of the subordinator *that* as described in §3.1; under analysis [7a] it has to be treated as a separate phenomenon.

Thirdly, *in order* allows an infinitival complement, with or without a subject:

[8] i [*in order*] [*that their baby have food*]
ii [*in order*] [*for their baby to have food*]
iii [*in order*] [*to save food for their baby*]

Traditional grammars commonly recognise two complex units here, *in order that* and *in order to*. But this doesn't cater for [ii]. The relation between [ii] and [iii] is just like that between *It is essential* [*for their baby to have food*] and *It is essential* [*to save food for their baby*]. If an infinitival clause contains a subject it takes *for* as subordinator, and *for* is permitted only when there is a subject. It is clear, then, that the structural division in [ii–iii] is between *in order* and the infinitival clause, as shown by the bracketing. And similarly in [i] the structural division comes before *that*, not after it; *that* as a marker of a finite declarative contrasts with *for* as the marker of an infinitival one with subject–predicate form. Similarly, items such as *notwithstanding, except, granted* take either a content clause or an NP as complement:

[9] i *notwithstanding* [*that the commission has not yet made its report*]
ii *notwithstanding* [*the delay in the publication of the commission's report*]

We don't want to say there are two items *notwithstanding that* and *notwithstanding*: there is just one item, the preposition *notwithstanding*, and *that* appears when the complement is a declarative clause but not, of course, when it is an NP.

Once it is established that the *that* belongs in the content clause, it is quite clear that *provided, in order, notwithstanding*, and the like are syntactically quite different from *that*. They are not markers of clause subordination contrasting with *that*, but prepositions functioning as heads of phrases that may contain declarative content clauses as complement.

8.2 Content clauses in relation to the traditional classification of subordinate clauses

In §1 we introduced a classification of finite subordinate clauses into three major categories: relative clauses, comparative clauses, and content clauses. Traditional grammar recognises the categories of relative clause and comparative clause,[30] but the major classification of subordinate clauses is into nominal, adjectival, and adverbial clauses (or noun, adjective, and adverb clauses):

[10] i *<u>That he must be guilty</u> is obvious to everyone.* ['nominal']
ii *They have all the equipment <u>they need</u>.* ['adjectival']
iii *The weather was so bad <u>that they cancelled the expedition</u>.* ['adverbial']

[30] In the case of comparative clauses, however, *than* and *as* are treated as subordinating conjunctions within the subordinate clause rather than prepositions governing the comparative clause, as in our analysis; this relates to the issue we have been discussing in §8.1.

This classification is based on functional analogies between the subordinate clauses and the three word categories. The above may be compared with, for example:

[11] i *His guilt is obvious to everyone.* [noun phrase]
ii *They have all the necessary equipment.* [adjective (phrase)]
iii *The weather was unprecedentedly bad.* [adverb (phrase)]

We have not retained this traditional classification in the present grammar, but will work with the one distinguishing relative, comparative, and content clauses on the basis of overt or covert differences in the structure of the clause. We find the classification as nominal, adjectival, or adverbial unsatisfactory for the following reasons.

(a) The traditional classification does not take proper account of the form of clauses

The classification is based on the function of the subordinate clause rather than its structure. The functions have to be stated in any case, however, and there is no point in attempting to repeat the functional analysis in the classification. In [10], for example, we have to say that *that he must be guilty* is subject in [i] and that *that they cancelled the expedition* is complement in AdjP structure in [iii], and nothing is gained by using that functional distinction to assign the clauses to different classes. There is no relevant syntactic difference in the form of the two clauses, so that each could occur in the function of the other:

[12] i *That they cancelled the expedition is highly regrettable.*
ii *His defence was so implausible that he must be guilty.*

Both are content clauses, and content clauses can fill either of these two functions. The case is comparable to that of a phrase like *last week*. Consider, for example, its use in:

[13] i *Last week was the wettest for several years.* [subject]
ii *I saw them last week.* [adjunct]

The **function** of *last week* is subject in [i], adjunct in [ii], but in both cases it belongs to the **category** NP – because it has a noun as head. There is no more justification for assigning *that he is guilty* to different classes of subordinate clause in [10i] and [12ii] than there is for assigning *last week* to different classes of phrase in [13i–ii].

Consider also the following set of examples:

[14] i *Things aren't always [as they seem to be].*
ii *Max was late for his appointment, [as he so often is].*
iii *Max was late for his appointment, [as he had been unable to start his car].*

The traditional analysis takes *as* as part of the subordinate clause, and in this framework the functional criterion will group [ii] and [iii] together as adverbial (the subordinate clauses here function as adjuncts) in contrast to [i] (where it is functioning as predicative complement, a position characteristically filled by adjectives or nouns, not adverbs). But this classification obscures the fact that in terms of their internal form [i] and [ii] belong together in contrast to [iii]. *They seem to be* and *he so often is* are alike in that there is a missing predicative complement (they could occur as main clauses only as elliptical constructions with a predicative retrievable from the context); *he had been unable to start his car*, by contrast, is structurally complete. On our analysis *he had been unable to start his car* is a content clause, while *they seem to be* and *he so often is* are comparative clauses – cf. the more transparently comparative constructions *They aren't as bad as they seem to be* and *Kim wasn't as late as Max so often is.*

(b) Problems with the traditional class of subordinating conjunctions

A high proportion of so-called 'adverbial clauses' are introduced by traditional grammar's 'subordinating conjunctions' (more particularly by what we referred to as P-class ones):

[15] i *They cancelled the match* [*because the ground was too wet*].
ii *I'll take on the job* [*if I can get secretarial assistance*].
iii *She left* [*before the meeting ended*].

We have argued in §8.1, however, that these items should be analysed as prepositions – prepositions that take clauses as complement. On this account the bracketed constituents in [15] are not clauses at all, but PPs. The subordinate clauses are *the ground was too wet*, *I can get secretarial assistance*, *the meeting ended*, and these are certainly not like adverbs: they are content clauses. The revised treatment of 'subordinating conjunctions', therefore, has the effect that a large proportion of traditional grammar's 'adverbial clauses' have to be discarded from the class. Since *before* can take an NP complement the subordinate clause in [iii] could be assigned to the noun clause category, but those in [i–ii] hardly bear a close functional resemblance to nouns.

(c) Functional differences between content clauses and nouns (or NPs)

There are many places where content clauses are not in contrast with NPs and where it is therefore misleading to call them noun clauses. This is so even if we confine our attention to those that traditional grammar does in fact analyse as noun clauses, i.e. if we leave aside those like *that they cancelled the expedition* in [10iii], traditionally analysed as an adverbial clause, or *the ground was too wet* in [15i], which on the traditional analysis is merely part of an adverbial clause introduced by *because*. Compare, for example:

[16] i *He* [*feared that he might lose his job*]. [complement of verb]
ii *He told me of his* [*fear that he might lose his job*]. [complement of noun]
iii *He was* [*afraid that he might lose his job*]. [complement of adjective]

The subordinate clause is complement of the verb *fear*, the noun *fear*, and the adjective *afraid* respectively, and on our analysis it is a content clause in all three cases. In [i] it could be replaced by an NP (*He feared the prospect of unemployment*), but in [ii–iii] it could not: a major difference between verbs on the one hand, nouns and adjectives on the other, is that the former can take NP complements, while the latter (with minor exceptions) cannot. The analysis of the underlined clause as a noun clause in all three is thus not in fact consistent with the principle of classifying subordinate clauses on the basis of functional similarity to various categories of word.

The traditional treatment of content clause complements of nouns as appositives

In cases like [16ii] traditional grammar justifies the classification of the subordinate clause as a noun clause by saying that it is in apposition to the noun *fear*: on this account it is noun-like since the function of appositive to a noun is characteristically filled by a noun (NP in our scheme), as in *Kim Jones, the bank manager*. This, however, does not provide a satisfactory account of why the subordinate clauses in [16] are assigned to the same class. In the first place, it loses the parallelism between them: in particular, the subordinate clause is treated as an appositive in [ii] and as an object in [i], two quite different functions. In fact, however, the function of the subordinate clause is the same in all three cases in [16]: it is a complement, licensed by the head of the VP, NP, or AdjP in which it occurs. Note, then, that replacing these head words by others may result in the subordinate clause becoming inadmissible: *He *used that he might lose his job*; **He told me of his injury that he might lose his job*; **He was fond that he might lose his job*. The verb *use*, the noun *injury*, the adjective *fond*, unlike those in [16], do not license content clause complements.

A second objection to traditional grammar's analysis of [16ii] is that the relation between the clause and the preceding noun is very different from standard cases of apposition. It is true that in [16ii] noun and clause could be identified one with the other in a specifying *be* construction (*His fear was that he might lose his job*), but there are numerous cases where this is not possible:

[17] i a. *Their insistence that the meetings should be held at lunch-time angered the staff.*
b. **Their insistence was that the meetings should be held at lunch-time.*
ii a. *His ruthless determination that his rival's reputation should be destroyed was distressing to witness.*
b. **His ruthless determination was that his rival's reputation should be destroyed.*

But even where the specifying *be* construction is acceptable it is very often not possible to omit the noun (together with the pre-head dependents) as it should be if this were a genuine case of apposition. Compare:

[18] i a. *Kim Jones, the bank manager, is to be congratulated on this initiative.*
b. *The bank manager is be congratulated on this initiative.*
ii a. *His fear that he might lose his job was increasing.*
b. **That he might lose his job was increasing.*
iii a. *They ridiculed his suggestion that he was being stalked.*
b. **They ridiculed that he was being stalked.*

We believe, then, that the classification of subordinate clauses as nominal, adjectival, or adverbial is a feature of traditional grammar that should be discarded. What we need is a classification based on the form of subordinate clauses themselves, not on supposed analogies with the parts of speech. As far as finite clauses are concerned, we claim that the first division is between relative clauses, comparative clauses, and the default category of content clauses.[31]

8.3 Content clauses and the function 'object'

Our argument in §8.2 that content clauses are distributionally very different from NPs and hence cannot be satisfactorily analysed as 'noun clauses' focused on content clauses functioning as complement to nouns, adjectives, and prepositions or as adjunct in clause structure. In the present subsection we turn our attention to content clauses functioning as internal complement to a verb, as in *He feared that he might lose his job* ([16i]). Traditional grammar not only analyses the subordinate clause here as a noun clause, but

[31] The term 'content clause' is due to Jespersen. In formal grammar the most usual term is 'complement clause', but this too we regard as unsatisfactory. In the first place, content clauses are not restricted to complement function: they also occur (though much less frequently) as adjunct, as in [52] of §4.7 (*What has happened, that you are looking so worried?*, etc.), and in the interrogative examples of §5.3.5 (*You got paid whether business was good or bad*, etc.). Secondly, it is not only content clauses that function as complement: comparative clauses do too – of the prepositions *than*, *as*, or *like*. Note, in particular, that *than* and *as* can take both comparative clauses and content clauses as complement: *More people came* [*than we'd expected*]; *It's not as good* [*as it was last year*] (comparative); *I'd rather you went overseas* [*than that you should risk being arrested*]; *He fell* [*as he was getting in the bath*] (content). Similarly with *like* in informal style: *It was just me and Eileen getting drunk together* [*like we used to in the old days*] (comparative); *It seems* [*like we're going to get into a speck of trouble*] (content).

assigns it the same function as that of the NP in *He feared the prospect of unemployment*, namely that of object of the verb. Again, however, we believe that the subordinate clause is not sufficiently like an NP to justify that analysis. With external complements there are good grounds for recognising a single function, subject, applicable to content clauses as well as NPs: the subject is distinguished from other functions in clause structure by a whole cluster of syntactic properties, and a significant number of these apply to content clauses as well as to subjects, as we noted in §4.1. The case with internal complements, however, is very different. Not all internal complements are objects, and the object has far fewer distinctive properties than the subject. The grammatical differences between content clauses and NPs make it inappropriate in general to include both within the functional category of object.

Differences between content clause complements and NP objects

(a) Linear position

One distinctive property of NP objects is that they generally come immediately after the verb. Certain kinds of complement can intervene between the verb and its object (namely indirect objects, as in *She gave Kim the key*, and particles, as in *He brought in the clothes*), objects can be preposed (*Most of them we rejected*) and heavy objects can be postposed (*I reject emphatically the suggestion that I was in any way responsible for the delay*). Apart from these special cases, however, the object occurs just after the verb. Content clauses, on the other hand, are not constrained to follow the verb in this way. Compare, then:

[19] i a. *He opened slowly the door. b. *He denied categorically that he had spoken to her.*
ii a. *He returned to me the key. b. *He mentioned to me that he was leaving.*

As far as position is concerned, therefore, we cannot say that content clauses behave like objects. Note again the contrast between this case and that of the subject: the default position for NP subjects is before the verb, and the fact that content clauses can occur here does provide evidence for saying that they can function as subject.

(b) Differences in the governing verbs

One important difference between an external complement (subject) and an internal complement is that all verbs which license a clause as subject also allow an NP, whereas this is not so with internal complements. There are verbs which take a content clause but not an NP:

[20] i *I often [marvel that intelligent people can at times be so petty].*
ii *She will [vouch that I didn't leave the house until six o'clock].*

The content clauses here are internal complements of the verbs, but beyond that they have no significant property in common with NP objects. Nothing is gained by diluting the concept of object in such a way that it applies to constructions of this kind.

Note that one can't avoid this problem by using the passivisation test. We saw in Ch. 4 that passivisation provides neither a necessary nor a sufficient test for objecthood: *She has lots of friends* can't be passivised even though *lots of friends* is object, while *Someone has drunk out of this glass* can be passivised even though *this glass* is not object. And as far as content clauses are concerned, passivisation is not restricted to verbs where the clause could be replaced by an NP object:

[21] i *Can it be wondered that they feel aggrieved?*
ii *It has been charged that Labour's failure to press for nationalisation of insurance was due to its financial links with the co-operatives.*

(c) Contrast between NP objects and NP obliques doesn't apply to content clauses

The main reason for the existence of verbs which take content clause complements that are not replaceable by NP objects has to do with the difference between NPs and content clauses with respect to prepositions. Unlike NPs, declarative content clauses cannot occur (in relevant constructions) as obliques, i.e. as the complement of the preposition governed by a prepositional verb:

[22] i *He rejoiced* [*at her decisive victory*]. [prep + NP]
ii **He rejoiced* [*at that she had won so decisively*]. [prep + content clause]

Instead of [ii] we find the content clause related directly to the verb: *He rejoiced that she had won so decisively*. It follows that the distinction that applies with NPs between an object of the verb and an oblique does not apply with declarative content clauses. Compare, for example:

[23]	NP AS COMPLEMENT	CONTENT CLAUSE AS COMPLEMENT
i	a. *He said some cruel things.*	b. *He said that Kim is an alcoholic.*
ii	a. *He insisted on an adjournment.*	b. *He insisted that we adjourn.*

In [ia] *some cruel things* is object of *say*, whereas in [iia] *an adjournment* is an oblique, a complement of the preposition *on* rather than of the verb *insist*. The absence of a preposition before the NP is a distinctive property of objects. But with content clauses the contrast between structures with and without a preposition is lost: there is no preposition in either of the [b] examples. The absence of a preposition in [ib], therefore, does not provide any evidence for saying that the content clause is an object. Content clauses behave differently from NPs with respect to prepositions, and the loss of the distinction between constructions with and without a preposition provides a strong argument for assigning the content clauses to the more general functional category of complement rather than to the more specific one of object.

An oblique/object distinction cannot be justified by invoking latent prepositions

It is sometimes argued that the distinction between an object and an oblique can be carried over to content clauses if we postulate a latent ('covert' or 'underlying') preposition in examples like [23iib]. On this account, the verb *insist* would take as complement a PP with *on* as head: if the complement of *on* is an NP the preposition is retained, but if it is a declarative content clause the preposition is omitted or deleted. With *say*, however, there is no preposition involved. The content clause complement of *say* can therefore qualify as an object, while that of *insist* is (covertly) an oblique. Similarly, the complements of *marvel* and *vouch* in [20] and of *wonder* and *charge* in [21] will be obliques, governed respectively by *at*, *for*, *at*, *with*. As a result, we would no longer have verbs taking objects with the form of content clauses that do not also take NP objects.

The main argument used to support this account involves constructions where prepositions are stranded, as in:

[24] i a. *Complete restitution was insisted on by the principal.*
b. *The drug's safety we can vouch for on the basis of long experience.*
ii a. *That they should all wear hats and blazers was insisted on by the principal.*
b. *That the drug is harmless we can vouch for on the basis of long experience.*

The structurally more basic alternants are as follows:

[25] i a. *The principal insisted on complete restitution.*
b. *We can vouch for the drug's safety on the basis of long experience.*
ii a. *The principal insisted that they should all wear hats and blazers.*
b. *We can vouch that the drug is harmless on the basis of long experience.*

In [25i] the prepositions appear in their default position before their NP complement. The suggestion is that the relation between [24ii] and [25ii] is the same as that between [24i] and [25i], and that this provides evidence for a latent preposition before the content clause complements in [25ii]: its actual absence is attributed to a rule that deletes prepositions when they immediately precede a declarative content clause complement.

There are, however, serious problems with this analysis, and we do not believe that it provides a satisfactory basis for generalising the distinction between objects and obliques from NPs to content clauses.

Marginal status of the examples and irrelevance of pseudo-clefts

The first point is that examples like [24ii] are of very questionable acceptability. They are made-up examples: genuine examples of this construction are very hard to come by. More acceptable are ones involving pseudo-cleft clauses:

[26] *What you must insist on is that they all wear their hats.*

Examples like this tend to be included with those in [24ii] as data supporting a latent preposition analysis of *insist* + content clause, and its greater acceptability appears to strengthen the argument. Syntactically, however, the content clause in [26] is complement of *be* (in its specifying sense): it is *what*, not the content clause, that is in construction with *on*. Pseudo-cleft clauses cannot be systematically derived from simpler non-clefts, as argued in Ch. 16, §9.3. Consider first the following examples without stranded prepositions:

[27] i *What I like about your watch is that it's so compact.*
ii *What they want apparently is that we should meet only twice a year.*

Here the non-cleft counterparts are ungrammatical: **I like about it that it's so compact*; **They want that we should meet only twice a year.* The admissibility of the content clause *that it's so compact* in [i] is due to the semantic fact that it describes a property of your watch and hence denotes something that one can like: there is no syntactic requirement that it satisfy the complementation requirement of the verb *like* in the fused relative. Similarly in [ii] *that we should meet only twice a year* denotes a state of affairs that one can want, but doesn't need to be admissible as a complement of *want.* Compare, then, the following examples with stranded prepositions:

[28] i *What I'm getting at is that he may have been trying to mislead you.*
ii *What we're counting on is that they won't all turn up.*

The non-cleft counterparts are ungrammatical, whether we retain the preposition or omit it: **I'm getting (at) that he may have been trying to mislead you*; **We're counting (on) that they won't all turn up.* Again, the admissibility of [28i–ii] reflects the fact that the content clauses satisfy the semantic requirement that they denote possible values for the variables defined in the fused relative: they do not have to be syntactically admissible complements of ***get*** + *at* and ***count*** + *on.* The pseudo-cleft [26] cannot, therefore, be used as evidence for a latent preposition in the non-cleft *You must insist that they all wear hats.* But fully acceptable examples like [26] may make those in [24ii] seem more acceptable than they otherwise would be. Those in [24ii] are like [26] in that the content clause is not directly in construction with the preposition, but differ in that there is an indirect relation with the preposition, mediated by passivisation or complement preposing.

The stranded preposition construction is quite impossible with many prepositional verbs

A second point is that [24ii] is not illustrative of a regular pattern: there are numerous prepositional verbs where examples of these kinds are completely unacceptable. Compare, for example:

[29] i **That the report represents a serious indictment of the banks they concur in.*
ii **That a peaceful resolution can be found we must all hope/pray for.*
iii **That everyone would soon forget this undertaking was gambled on by the Dean.*
iv **It was decided on eventually that he should be reinstated.*
v **It has been charged with that the documents were leaked by the treasurer.*

There is therefore no evidence from the stranded preposition construction to support an analysis of *They concur that the report represents a serious indictment of the banks*, etc., in which the content clause is complement of an abstract preposition. A few marginal examples like those in [24ii] cannot support a systematic distinction between objects and obliques among content clauses that parallels that found with NPs.

Note also that there are content clauses licensed not by a verb alone but by a verbal idiom:

[30] a. *It is time you were in bed.* b. *I had no idea what would happen.*

Although they follow a noun the content clauses here are not complements of that noun (as evident from the impossibility of **The time you were in bed has arrived*, **No idea what would happen occurred to me*, and the like). PPs are possible in such contexts (*It's time for bed*; *I had no idea of the possible consequences*), but again there is no possibility of stranded prepositions occurring with clausal complements: **That you were in bed it is time for*; **What would happen I had no idea of.*

Meaning differences

There are, moreover, places where the clausal complement does not have the same meaning as preposition + NP. Consider, for example:

[31] i a. *He objected that the meeting was being held on Sunday.* b. *He objected to the fact that the meeting was being held on Sunday.*
ii a. *They complained that there was no hot water.* b. *They complained about the water.*
iii a. *We decided that the proposal would be impossible to implement.* b. *We decided on a trip to the zoo.*

Examples [ia] and [ib] are understood quite differently. In [ia] the proposition that the meeting was being held on Sunday was put forward in objection to something else (e.g. to refute someone's contention that work commitments might prevent people attending the meeting), whereas in [ib] the timing of the meeting is itself what was objected to. Nor is [iia] strictly comparable to [iib]. In [iia] the subordinate clause gives the content of their complaint; it could be that they simply said *There is no hot water*, with the reporter interpreting this as a complaint. In [iib], however, the NP doesn't give the content of the complaint, but its topic: the *about* is therefore semantically motivated in this case, but not in the clausal complement construction shown in [ii]. Similarly in [iii]. The construction with *on* + NP expresses a choice concerning what to do, while the construction with a clausal complement may involve coming to the conclusion that a certain proposition is true. Note, then, that [iiia] could not be paraphrased as #*We decided on the impossibility of implementing the proposal.* The fact that *object*, *complain*, and *decide* can take complements with the form of a preposition + NP is therefore irrelevant to the analysis of the constructions with content clause complements: there is no justification for analysing these as containing obliques.

It is equally important to note that similar differences in meaning are to be found with non-prepositional verbs, verbs that take either a content clause or an NP as complement:

[32] i a. *She explained that the planets are in motion.* b. *She explained the motion of the planets.*
ii a. *I understand he was furious.* b. *I understand his fury.*

The difference in [32i] is similar to that in [31i]: in [a] she said that the planets are in motion in order to explain something else, whereas in [b] it is the motion itself that was explained. And in [32iia] *understand* means approximately "believe", not "comprehend", as in [iib].

Conclusion: content clause complements must be analysed independently of NPs

The traditional view of content clauses as 'noun clauses' suggests that they are equivalent to, or substitutes for, NPs, but it is not in fact satisfactory to handle them derivatively in this way. There are a considerable number of verbs taking content clause complements that cannot be replaced by either NPs or PPs without a change in the meaning of the verb – verbs such as *understand, explain, object*, mentioned above, or *conclude, contend, observe, reason, reflect, reply*, and so on. The dictionary entries for verbs must specify directly whether (and with what senses) they take content clauses as complement: it is not satisfactory just to say whether they take an NP or preposition + NP, allowing that in general abstract NPs may be replaced by content clauses, with consequent loss of any governing preposition.

The complex-transitive construction

One exceptional case where we do recognise a content clause in object function involves preposing in a complex-transitive clause. Consider the complex-intransitive and complex-transitive constructions together, as illustrated in:

[33]	COMPLEX-INTRANSITIVE	COMPLEX-TRANSITIVE
i	a. *His behaviour is odd.*	b. *I find his behaviour odd.*
ii	a. *That he lost his temper is odd.*	b. **I find that he lost his temper odd.*
iii	a. *It is odd that he lost his temper.*	b. *I find it odd that he lost his temper.*
iv	a. **Isn't that he lost his temper odd?*	b. *That he lost his temper I find odd.*

The ungrammaticality of [iib] is due to the fact that the content clause is non-initial. The ungrammaticality can be removed by preposing the content clause, as in [ivb], and conversely [iia] becomes ungrammatical if the subject is placed in non-initial position, as in the interrogative [iva]. Compare also *That he still has no job is a source of great worry to them* (content clause subject in initial position) and **I can understand why that he still has no job should be a source of great worry to them* (non-initial). There is therefore good reason to analyse the constructions in comparable ways: in the [a] construction the predicand is subject or extraposed subject, while in [b] it is object or extraposed object.

One reason why we have not analysed the content clause as an object in examples like *I noticed that she lost her temper* is that there are numerous verbs occurring in this construction which do not take NP objects. But this argument doesn't apply in the present case: all verbs which license complex-transitive complementation with a content clause as the predicand (as in [33iiib/ivb]) also license it with an NP as predicand ([33ib]).

9 Reported speech

What, following the grammatical tradition, we call **reported speech** covers the reporting of spoken and written text but also that of unspoken thoughts.

Direct vs indirect reported speech

There are two main types of reported speech, illustrated in:

[1] i *The premier replied: 'I have no intention of resigning.'* [direct]
ii *The premier replied that he had no intention of resigning.* [indirect]

Direct reported speech purports to give the actual wording of the original, whereas **indirect reported speech** gives only its content.[32] The conditions under which one is in a position to use direct reported speech are of course considerably more restricted than for the indirect variety – perhaps one has access to a written or recorded version of the original, perhaps the original was short enough for one to have been able to memorise it, or perhaps one is composing fiction, where the author can decide what the characters say.

We will use the term **original speaker** for the person who said (or thought) the text being reported (i.e. the premier in [1]) and **reporter** for the one reporting (i.e. in [1] the person who utters the whole sentence). And we will refer to *the premier replied* as the **reporting frame**, while the term 'reported speech' itself applies to the rest, the underlined sequence.

Major difference between direct and indirect speech: deixis

The main reflection of the distinction between reporting wording (or form) and reporting content (or meaning) is to be found in the use of **deictic** expressions such as personal pronouns, demonstratives, and tense. Deictic expressions are interpreted in relation to certain features of the utterance-act – the place, time, and participants (see Ch. 17, §1.1). In direct speech these expressions are interpreted in relation to the original utterance, whereas in indirect speech they are interpreted wholly or predominantly in relation to the act of reporting. In [1], for example, the original speaker is referred to in the direct version by means of the 1st person singular pronoun *I*, but in the indirect version by means of the 3rd person pronoun *he*, interpreted through its anaphoric relation to its antecedent, *the premier*. The indirect report *The premier replied that I had no intention of resigning* would thus mean something quite different from [1], with *I* now referring to the reporter. Note also the difference in tense, with present tense *have* in [1i] and the backshifted preterite in [1ii].

[32] If the text to be reported is in a foreign language a direct report may retain that language or provide a translation of the text. Some writers omit the 'reported' and talk simply of 'direct speech' and 'indirect speech', while others restrict the term 'reported speech' to the indirect type; we believe, however, that it is useful to have a term covering both. Further alternative terms for direct and indirect reported speech are 'oratio recta' and 'oratio obliqua' respectively.

9.1 Indirect reported speech

Embedded vs non-embedded reported speech

The two main syntactic constructions used for indirect reported speech are illustrated in:

[2]	EMBEDDED	NON-EMBEDDED
i	a. *She said that she lived alone.*	b. *She lived alone, she said.*
ii	a. *Did she say if I'll be invited?*	b. *Will I be invited, did she say?*

In [ia/iia] the reported speech is syntactically subordinate. It has the form of a content clause functioning as complement of the reporting verb *say*: the reported speech is thus embedded within a matrix clause. This is a straightforward case of complementation: the content clause is obligatory in that *she said* cannot stand alone as a sentence (except in certain cases of ellipsis), and the content clause, declarative in [ia], closed interrogative in [iia], is licensed by *say*. The reporting frame does not form a syntactic constituent. In [ia], for example, *she* is subject while *said* is head of the VP *said that she lived alone*.

In [2ib/iib], by contrast, the reported speech has the form of a main clause. It does not function syntactically as complement of *say*, and is not embedded. The reporting frame (*she said* and *did she say*) does not belong in a matrix clause, but has the status of a **parenthetical**, a kind of supplement. Note that it would not be valid to analyse the reported speech as a preposed complement. In the first place, there is a difference in the internal form of the reported clause: in [ia/iia] it has subordinate form, while in [ib/iib] it has main clause form, as just observed. And secondly, in cases like [ii], where the reporting frame is interrogative, the two versions have different meanings. Version [iia], with embedding, asks whether she gave the answer to the question of whether I'll be invited, but does not itself explicitly ask this latter question; version [iib], however, does ask this question, with the issue of whether she provided the answer being backgrounded. A response of *No* means "No, she didn't say" in the case of [iia] and "No, you won't be invited" in the case of [iib]. (For further discussion of the illocutionary force of the parenthetical construction, see Ch. 10, §5.3.)

The parentheticals in [ib/iib] follow the reported speech, but it is also possible for them to be inserted medially within it; in addition, the subject of a declarative parenthetical may be postposed to follow the verb if it is not a personal pronoun. Compare:

[3] i *When we got home, I told her, we would have to have the locks changed.*
ii *Is it likely, did she say, that the proposal will be accepted?*
iii *The person most likely to benefit, thought Jill, was herself.*

These structures, however, are less common than with direct reported speech, and we will look at them further in §9.2.

The syntactic constructions are not specific to indirect reported speech

The constructions illustrated in [2] are not syntactically distinct from ones used for other purposes than to report speech and thought:

[4] i *This proves that he was lying.*
ii *These tests will determine whether he needs to be hospitalised.*
iii *The minister, it seems clear, has already made up her mind.*

The verbs that take content clauses as internal complement are by no means limited to those that serve to report speech and thought, as evident from [4i–ii], where *prove* selects a declarative and *determine* a closed interrogative (see the sample lists in §§4.2, 5.3.1). Similarly, the parenthetical in [4iii] is not a reporting frame, but expresses the same kind of meaning as a modal adjunct such as *seemingly* or *apparently*. Moreover, the original speech is often reported not by a content clause but by an infinitival – as when *Get a doctor*, say, is reported as *She told me to get a doctor*. But again the infinitival catenative construction is obviously not restricted to the function of reporting speech – cf. *This entitles you to seek admission to the advanced course.*

Deixis

The major difference between direct and indirect reported speech, we have said, is that in the direct type deictic expressions are interpreted relative to the original text, whereas in the indirect type they are, at least for the most part, interpreted relative to the report. The contrast was illustrated in [1]; here we will consider a little further the indirect case.

Person

The most straightforward case involves the deictic category of person, which is invariably interpreted relative to the report. Compare:

[5]	i	ORIGINAL:	*I love you.*
	ii	REPORT:	*I said I loved you. You said you loved me. She / Sue / The doctor said she loved me. I told him / Max / Jill's brother that I loved him.*

Suppose that [i] was said to Max (Jill's brother) by Sue (Max's doctor): it might be reported indirectly by means of any of the versions in [ii], and many others too, depending on who is reporting it to whom. The first version is appropriate if Sue is reporting it to Max, the second if Max is reporting it to Sue, the third if Max is reporting it to someone else, and so on. The essential point is that in an indirect report we refer to the persons and other entities concerned in just the same way as we do in utterances that do not contain reported speech. Compare, for example, *It is obvious that Sue loves you, It is fortunate that she loves Max*, and so on.[33]

Tense

Indirect reports commonly have a preterite tense where the original has a present: compare the *loved* of [5ii] with the *love* of [5i]. This case is somewhat different from that of the personal pronouns. We have seen that there is nothing special about the use or meaning of the pronouns in [5ii]: it is the same as in non-reporting utterances. The *loved* of [5ii], however, does represent a special use of the preterite, what we call a backshifted preterite. An ordinary preterite, as in *She loved him for several years*, normally locates the situation of her loving him at a time prior to the time of speaking, but that is not what a backshifted preterite does. This is evident from examples like *I wish he realised she loved him*, where in the intended interpretation the situation of her loving him still obtains at the time of utterance. The phenomenon of tense backshift is discussed in detail in Ch. 3, §6.2.

[33] One qualification is that in a non-embedded report the parenthetical will not normally contain a pronoun with an antecedent located within the report. *The doctor, she said, loved Max even though he didn't love her*, for example, does not allow an interpretation where *she* has *the doctor* as its antecedent.

Other deictic forms

In general other deictic forms, such as demonstratives and various temporal and spatial expressions, follow the pattern described for person. Consider, for example:

[6] i ORIGINAL: *The lease expired yesterday.*
ii REPORT: *She said the lease had expired yesterday / the day before / last Friday / two weeks ago / on 17 June.*

Suppose the original was said on 18 June, so that *yesterday* refers to 17 June. Then, depending on when the report is uttered, any of the temporal expressions in [ii] could be used to refer to the day in question. Note in particular that the first version, with *yesterday*, will only be appropriate if the report is said on the same day as the original: i.e. *yesterday* is interpreted as the day before the day of the report, not the day before the day of the original. It is possible in certain circumstances, however, for this to be overridden, for *yesterday* (and other such deictic expressions) to be interpreted relative to the time of the original: *She realised the lease must have expired yesterday.* This could be used in a narrative context with *yesterday* referring to the day before that of the realisation rather than of the present time of the narration. This kind of deictic shift generally occurs, however, in free indirect speech rather than with an explicit verb of reporting, such as *realised* in this example: we postpone further comment, therefore, until §9.3.

9.2 Direct reported speech

Embedded vs non-embedded reported speech

This distinction applies to the direct mode as well as to the indirect, though this time it is not so clearly marked syntactically:

[7]	EMBEDDED	NON-EMBEDDED
i	a. *She replied, 'I live alone.'*	b. *'I live alone,' she replied.*
ii	a. *He asked, 'Where do you live?'*	b. *'Where do you live?' he asked.*

Direct speech purports to be identical to the original, and hence the embedded and non-embedded constructions do not differ with respect to the form of the reported speech itself.[34] There is thus nothing comparable to the distinction in [2], where the reported speech has the form of a subordinate content clause in the embedded version and of a main clause in the non-embedded one. Nevertheless, the contrast between the two constructions can be maintained on the basis of the reporting frames: in the [b] examples the reporting frame has the status of a parenthetical, while in the [a] examples the reporting verb is syntactically superordinate to the reported speech. This is reflected in the fact that the [a] construction as a whole can itself be subordinated, whereas the [b] type cannot:

[8] a. *I was taken aback when she replied, 'I live alone.'* b. **I was taken aback when 'I live alone,' she replied.*

Similarly, we can have *He hadn't expected her to reply, 'I live alone'*, but there is no corresponding construction with a parenthetical.

In the embedded construction we therefore take the reported speech to function as complement of the reporting verb. However, this complement – *I live alone* in [7ia] and

[34] We ignore here the punctuational difference between [a] and [b] in [7i]: the punctuation of direct reported speech is described in Ch. 20, §6.

[8a] – is not a content clause. It is not a subordinate clause of any kind. What is embedded in these examples happens to have the form of a clause, but it can be longer than that:

[9] *She replied, 'I live alone. My son lives alone too. We both prefer it that way.'*

The construction thus involves the embedding of a **text**, not of clauses as such.

Form of the parenthetical

The subject of a parenthetical reporting frame is often postposed. Compare:

[10] a. *'Your father's arrived,' Sue said.* b. *'Your father's arrived,' said Sue.*

Subject postposing is not permitted if the verb has an object (*Sue told them*, but not **told Sue them* or **told them Sue*); postposing of personal pronoun subjects (*said he*) is archaic.[35] As observed earlier, postposing is more usual with direct than with indirect reported speech, but in the direct case the parenthetical is predominantly declarative. There is no analogue here, for example, of the construction illustrated in [2iib]. Compare indirect *Will I be invited, did she say?* (as spoken, let us say, by Kim) with direct #*'Will Kim be invited?' did she say?*

Position of the parenthetical

The parentheticals in [7] and [10] occur after the reported speech; they are also often found medially within it:

[11] i *'Jennifer,' he called, 'have you seen my glasses?'*
ii *'In those days,' Sue admitted, 'we were heavily in debt.'*
iii *'One of the delegates,' Max added, 'had volunteered to move a vote of thanks.'*
iv *'I now realise,' Kim replied quietly, 'that I was probably in the wrong.'*
v *'The train leaves in two hours,' he screamed, 'and we haven't started to pack.'*

In [i–iii] the parenthetical follows the first element of the reported speech – a vocative, an adjunct, and the subject respectively. In [iv] it occurs between the verb and its clausal complement; it can also occur before an object provided it is relatively heavy: *'I have bought,' he insisted, 'only the things that were absolutely essential.'* In [v] it follows the first coordinate in a clause-coordination. It will be noted that these are all positions where we could insert an adjunct.

Reporting verbs

A sample of the large number of verbs that can be used to report direct speech is given in:

[12]

add	*admit*	*advise*	*agree* P	*answer*	*argue* P
ask	*beg*	*begin* P –C	*boast* P	*call*	*comment*
declare	*demand* P	*explain*	%*go* –C	*grin* P –C	*inquire*
maintain P	*mumble*	*observe*	*order*	*promise* P	*reason* P
remark	*reply*	*say*	*smile* P –C	*state*	*suggest*
tell P	*think*	*warn*	*wonder* P	*write*	*yell*

The embedding construction tends to prefer the more general verbs such as *say*, *ask*, *reply*, etc.; those in the list marked 'P' occur predominantly in the parenthetical

[35] It is also found in the non-standard or jocular !*says I*. Subject postposing is occasionally found in the embedded construction too, but it is largely restricted to journalistic writing: *Said manager Fred Kessels: 'This has been a very successful year, with profits up by 45% on 1998.'*

construction. Compare, then: *'It was a good try,' she smiled* and #*She smiled, 'It was a good try.'*

Most verbs that report direct speech can take content clauses; those with the annotation '–c' are exceptions, and hence do not occur with indirect reported speech in the embedded construction. Compare: *He goes, 'I don't know what you mean'* and **He went that he didn't know what I meant.*[36] Note also that with some of the verbs that take either direct speech or a content clause as complement there are significant differences in use:

[13] i	a. *She said, 'What did they want?'*	b. *She said what they wanted.*
ii	a. *'Why did you leave?' she demanded.*	b. **She demanded why we left.*

In [ia] *say* reports the asking of a question, but in [ib] it reports the answering of one – an indirect report of the asking would need a reporting verb (such as *ask* itself). In [ib] but not [ia] we could substitute *tell* + object: *She told me what they wanted*, but not #*She told me, 'What did they want?'* Content clauses, as we have seen earlier in this chapter, are subclassified according to clause type, i.e. as declarative, closed or open interrogative, and so on. The governing verbs are specified as to which type of content clause they can take as complement. Example [iib] is thus excluded because *demand* does not select an interrogative clause – it takes a declarative mandative, as in *She demanded that I tell her why we left* (it can also take an infinitival complement: *She demanded to know why we left*). There is no comparable grammatical restriction on the verbs taking direct speech, where it is semantic compatibility that determines acceptability. For *ask* with the approximate sense "inquire", for example, the syntactic restriction on a content clause complement is that it be interrogative, while the semantic restriction on its use with direct speech is that the latter have the force of a question. And the question need not have the form of an interrogative: *'You're leaving already?' she asked* (cf. Ch. 10, §4.7.2).

Other syntactic contexts for direct speech and citation

The cases of embedded direct speech considered so far have all been complements of reporting verbs. Other contexts where it is found are illustrated in:

[14] i *What he said was 'I'll see what I can do.'*
ii *Her response was 'That's all I have done.'*
iii *Kim's first question, 'Who called the police?', was never answered.*

In [i–ii] the direct speech is complement of ***be*** in its specifying sense, while in [iii] it is a supplement sanctioned by the anchor *Kim's first question*. Very similar to direct speech is citation, as in:

[15] i *The school motto is 'Dare to be wise!'*
ii *Next week's seminar will be on the topic 'Does God exist?'*

These are not reporting a particular speech act, but the form of the citation is of the kind that might serve as such a report.

[36] We mark *go* with the % symbol as it is mainly restricted to younger speakers in casual style; it is found predominantly in the historic present use of the present tense, as in this example. Another form found in casual speech for reporting direct speech consists of *be* + *like*: %*And he's like, 'I don't know what you mean.'*

Blurring of the distinction between direct and indirect reports

[16] i *The Chief Minister said that the territory's justice system was so biased towards offenders that it was 'totally corrupt'.*
ii *Mr Crabb stated that, 'during this first half, there was an appreciable strengthening in most non-ferrous metal prices, . . .'*

The distinction between direct and indirect reporting is not always sharply maintained. Direct quotation may be inserted into what is primarily an indirect report, as in [i]. The subordinator *that* and the backshifted tense in the two instances of *was* mark this as an indirect report, but the quotation marks around *totally corrupt* indicate that this phrase was used by the original speaker.[37] Example [ii] (from a company circular) represents a much less usual type of blend between the constructions: the reporting verb is followed by *that*, normally a marker of indirect reporting, but what follows *that* itself is wholly quoted. It would seem to be motivated by the fact that *state* does not readily take direct reported speech as complement, though it is commonly found in parentheticals.

9.3 Free indirect and direct speech

We have been concerned so far with **reported** speech, constructions where there is a reporting frame superordinate to the reported speech or parenthetical to it. It is possible, however, for the reporting frame to be left implicit, and in this case we have **free** indirect or direct speech. This phenomenon is normally restricted to certain types of written or indeed oral narrative.

Free indirect speech is illustrated in the underlined sequence in:

[17] *Max was feeling remorseful. <u>He shouldn't have spoken to them so harshly. He would have to apologise to them next time he saw them.</u>*

In the intended interpretation the last two sentences represent the thoughts of Max, not judgements by the narrator. We understand something along the lines of "He felt/told himself that he shouldn't have spoken to them so harshly", but the reporting frame is left implicit, recoverable from the first sentence. The form of the free indirect speech is the same as that of explicitly reported indirect speech. For further discussion and examples, see Ch. 17, §§3.1.4, 10.2.

Examples of free direct speech are seen in:

[18] i *The reason I'm interested in language is because I'm interested in mind. That is an unfashionable position. Most psychologists these days will tell you that minds can't be studied scientifically. <u>You can't measure them; all you can see is behaviour. So why not forget about minds and just study behaviour instead?</u>*
ii *She ate with her friends like an actor on stage, miming enjoyment of cotton-wool cakes and a glass of cold tea; leaned back and laughed as they sharpened their tastes on their host's choice of food, furniture, bathroom fittings, and friends. <u>See I eat, I laugh, I listen. I belong.</u>*

[37] In speech this might be marked prosodically, by setting *totally corrupt* off from the rest. Alternatively it might be marked by a parenthetical (. . . *was – and I quote – totally corrupt*). There is also a convention of using the expression *quote*, alone or followed by *unquote*: *the system of justice was, quote, totally corrupt* (*unquote*).

In [i] the underlined sequence represents the views of psychologists, not of the writer (the referent of *I* in the first sentence). We thus understand this sequence as though it were explictly reported direct speech: "You can't measure them", they say, "all you can see is behaviour . . . " Similarly in [ii], where *I* in the underlined sequence is co-referential with *she* in the first sentence.

12

Relative constructions and unbounded dependencies

Rodney Huddleston
Geoffrey K. Pullum
Peter Peterson

1 Terminological preliminaries

This chapter deals with what are traditionally called **relative clauses**. We use the more general term **relative constructions** because although it is reasonable enough to call the underlined construction in [1i] a relative clause, the term is misleading for the type of construction seen in [1ii]:

[1] i *I agree with most of the things that your father was saying.* [clause]
ii *I agree with most of what your father was saying.* [NP]

These two sentences are equivalent. But the phrase *what your father was saying* in [ii] is an NP: it corresponds not to the relative clause *that your father was saying* in [i], but to the larger NP containing it, *the things that your father was saying.* And we will see that there are syntactic as well as semantic reasons for treating *what your father was saying* in [ii] as an NP.

We therefore use the term 'relative constructions' to cover both the underlined sequences in [1], with 'relative clause' available as a more specific term applying to cases like [i]. Often, however, we will talk simply of 'relatives', leaving 'construction' or 'clause' understood.

2 Types of relative construction

This section presents an overview of the different types of relative construction that will be discussed in detail in subsequent sections. The two major dimensions of contrast yield what we will call **formal types** and **relational types**.

The formal types are distinguished according to whether they contain one of the special relative words *who, which,* etc., or the subordinator *that,* or simply a 'gap', a missing constituent.

The relational types are distinguished on the basis of their external syntax, their relation to the larger construction containing them. The traditional distinction between restrictive and non-restrictive relative clauses fits in here, but we shall use different terms and contrast them with two further categories, cleft and fused relatives.

In addition to these major contrasts, we need to invoke the more general distinction of finiteness: while most relative constructions are finite, infinitivals (and certain minor types) are also possible under certain conditions.

2.1 Formal types: *wh*, *that*, and bare relatives

Relative clauses are so called because they are related by their form to an antecedent. They contain within their structure an anaphoric element whose interpretation is determined by the antecedent. This anaphoric element may be overt or covert. In the overt case the relative clause is marked by the presence of one of the relative words *who*, *whom*, *whose*, *which*, etc., as or within the initial constituent: clauses of this type we call ***wh* relatives**. In **non-*wh* relatives** the anaphoric element is covert, a gap; this class is then subdivided into ***that* relatives** and **bare relatives** depending on the presence or absence of *that*:[1]

[1]			
i	*He'll be glad to take the toys*	*which you don't want.*	[*wh* relative]
ii		*that you don't want.*	[non-*wh*: *that* relative]
iii		*you don't want.*	[non-*wh*: bare relative]

In [i] *toys* is antecedent for the pronoun *which*, whereas in [ii–iii] there is no such pronoun, merely the absence of the understood object of *want*. We take *that* in [ii] to be a clause subordinator, not a relative pronoun as in traditional grammar. It is the same marker of clause subordination as we find in content clauses, and the distinction between *that* and bare relatives is analogous to that between expanded and bare declarative content clauses, as in *You said that you don't want the toys* and *You said you don't want the toys*. We present arguments in support of this treatment of *that* in §3.5.6.

2.2 The relational types: integrated, supplementary, cleft, and fused

Four types are distinguished according to the relation of the relative construction to the larger structure containing it:

[2]		
i	*The boys who defaced the statue were expelled.*	[integrated relative]
ii	*My father, who retired last year, now lives in Florida.*	[supplementary relative]
iii	*It was Kim who wanted Pat as treasurer.*	[cleft relative]
iv	*What you say is quite right.*	[fused relative]

The underlined sequence in [i–iii] is a clause, while that in [iv] is an NP; we will see, however, that fused relatives can also be PPs.

The integrated relative clause

The most central and most frequent type of relative construction is the **integrated** relative. It usually functions as a modifier within a nominal constituent: in [2i], for example, *who defaced the statue* modifies *boys*, which is the antecedent for the pronoun *who*. Integrated relative clauses are occasionally found as modifier to other kinds of head: a superlative adjective, as in *He's now the fattest he's ever been*, or an interrogative preposition, as in *Where can we eat that isn't too expensive?* (In this last example the relative clause is postposed instead of being in the default position immediately following the antecedent.)

Integrated relatives are so called because they are integrated into the construction containing them, both prosodically and in terms of their informational content. The prototypical integrated relative serves to restrict the denotation of the head nominal it

[1] Bare relatives are sometimes called 'contact clauses'.

modifies, and is often referred to by the term 'restrictive relative'. The set of boys who defaced the statue, for example, is smaller than the set of boys; here the information expressed in the relative clause is an integral part of that expressed by the matrix clause in that it delimits the set of boys under discussion.

The supplementary relative clause

A **supplementary** relative clause adds extra information about the antecedent, information not fully integrated into the structure of the containing clause and not needed to delimit the set denoted by the antecedent. In [2ii] the antecedent of *who* is not the nominal *father*, but the NP *my father*, which refers to a unique person: the clause *who retired last year* thus plays no role in identifying the referent, but adds some extra information about him. The information expressed in this type of relative is presented as supplementary, separate from that expressed in the rest of the sentence, and this is reflected in the fact that the relative clause is characteristically marked off prosodically or by punctuation from the rest.

The supplementary relative is also distinguished from the integrated relative in that it permits a much wider range of antecedents, as is evident from such examples as:

[3]	i	*Pat is afraid of snakes, which I'm sure Kim is too.*	[AdjP]
	ii	*Pat is afraid of snakes, which doesn't surprise me at all*	[clause]

The antecedents for *which* here are an AdjP in [i] and a whole clause in [ii], the relative clauses being interpreted as "I'm sure Kim is afraid of snakes too" and "That Pat is afraid of snakes doesn't surprise me at all". The antecedent can indeed be a piece of text syntactically unconnected to the relative, as when a lecturer finishes one topic and then moves on to the next with the supplementary relative *Which brings me to my next point.*

The cleft relative clause

The clause that occurs after the foregrounded element in an *it*-cleft construction is called a **cleft** relative clause. Consider the following set of examples:

[4]	i	*Kim wanted Pat as treasurer.*	[non-cleft]
	ii	*It was Kim who wanted Pat as treasurer.* (=[2iii])	[cleft]
	iii	*It was Pat that Kim wanted as treasurer.*	[cleft]

Example [i] is an ordinary, non-cleft, clause, while [ii] and [iii] are cleft counterparts of it, and the underlined clauses are the cleft relatives, differing in function and, in certain respects, their internal structure from integrated relatives. The cleft construction is so called because it divides the more elementary construction into two parts, one of which is foregrounded and the other backgrounded. In [ii] *Kim* is foregrounded and *wanted Pat as treasurer* backgrounded, whereas in [iii] the foregrounded element is *Pat*, with *Kim wanted as treasurer* backgrounded. The cleft construction is dealt with in Ch. 16, §9, and in the present chapter will be mentioned only incidentally.

The fused relative construction

Finally we consider the **fused** relatives, which are always of the *wh* type:

[5]	i	*What he did was quite outrageous.*
	ii	*Whoever devised this plan must be very naive.*
	iii	*You can buy whichever car appeals to you most.*

From a syntactic point of view this is the most complex of the four relative constructions. With the others we can separate a relative clause from its antecedent, but this is not possible with the fused construction. Compare, for example:

[6] i *It would mean abandoning that which we hold most dear.* [antecedent + clause]
ii *It would mean abandoning what we hold most dear.* [fused relative]

These are semantically equivalent (though [i] belongs to very formal style). Syntactically, *that* in [i] is antecedent, with *which we hold most dear* an integrated relative clause modifying it, but in [ii] *what* corresponds to *that* and *which* combined, so that it is not possible to separately identify antecedent and relative clause – hence the term 'fused'.

While the fused relatives in [5] are NPs, those based on *where* and *when* are PPs:

[7] i *Put it back where you found it.*
ii *He still calls his parents whenever he is in trouble.*[2]

Because the fused relative construction is so different from the integrated, supplementary, and cleft relative clause constructions, we will treat it separately, deferring further consideration of it until §6.

2.3 Finiteness

The great majority of relative constructions are finite, but with integrated relatives we find infinitivals of the *wh* type and corresponding ones without a relative word. The underlined parts of [8] are infinitival relative clauses:

[8] i *She found a good place from which to watch the procession.*
ii *She found a good place to watch the procession from.*

There are various other non-finite constructions which bear some resemblance to relatives, such as gerund–participials and past-participials that modify nouns (*anyone knowing his whereabouts, those killed in the accident*): these constructions are discussed in Ch. 14, §9.

3 The form of relative clauses

A relative clause, we have said, contains within its structure an overt or covert element that relates it anaphorically to an antecedent. Other kinds of clause may also contain anaphoric elements, of course. In *I lent Jill my bicycle last week [and she hasn't returned it yet]*, for example, *she* and *it* in the second clause are anaphorically related to *Jill* and *my bicycle* in the first. Here, however, the anaphoric relation is incidental: there is no anaphora in *I lent Jill my bicycle last week [and now there's a bus strike]*, but we still have the same syntactic construction, a coordination of main clauses. In relative clauses, by contrast, the anaphoric relation is an essential feature of the construction. What distinguishes relatives from other clauses is the specific nature of the anaphoric relation

[2] Other terms found in the literature corresponding to our 'fused relative (construction)' are 'free relative', 'headless relative clause', and 'nominal relative clause'. Terms incorporating 'clause' are unsatisfactory for the reasons we have given. In addition, 'nominal' is insufficiently general in that it doesn't cater for prepositional examples like those with *where* or *when*. And 'headless' is misleading in our view since the head of the containing phrase is not missing but fused with part of the modifying clause.

involved. In the central case of the integrated relative, the antecedent is the head that the clause modifies, and in all cases the anaphoric element itself has distinct properties. In *wh* relatives the overt forms *who*, *which*, etc., are distinct from the anaphoric forms that are used in main clauses; they are homonymous with interrogative words, but the latter are not anaphoric. In non-*wh* relatives the anaphoric element is a gap, but this too is distinct from other kinds of anaphoric gap with respect to the positions in which it can occur and the way it is interpreted.

3.1 Relativisation

The essential anaphoric element in a relative clause we call the **relativised element**. It is primarily in respect of this element that the relative differs in form from a comparable main clause. Consider first the case where the relativised element is subject:

[1]	i	*A letter drew our attention to the problem.*	[main clause]
	ii	*This is the letter$_i$ [which$_i$ drew our attention to the problem].*	[*wh* relative]
	iii	*This is the letter$_i$ [that __$_i$ drew our attention to the problem].*	[*that* relative]

The main clause in [i] has the ordinary NP *a letter* as subject. In the *wh* relative the subject is *which*, a relative pronoun anaphorically linked to the antecedent *letter*, as indicated in [ii] by the identical subscripted indices. In [iii], where *that* marks the clause as subordinate, the subject position is empty, but there is still an anaphoric link to the antecedent *letter*, which we indicate by attaching the same index to the symbol marking the gap. The meaning in both [i] and [ii], ignoring the definite article, can be given roughly as "This is letter *x*; *x* drew our attention to the problem". This kind of meaning, with two occurrences of a single variable, is an essential and distinctive feature of all relative constructions.

We take the antecedent of *which* and the gap to be *letter*, not *the letter*, since *the* enters into construction with the whole nominal *letter which/that drew our attention to the problem*: it is this, not *letter* by itself, that is presented as an identifying description that sanctions the definite article (see Ch. 5, §6.1).

In [1iii], as in almost all cases of subject relativisation in non-*wh* relatives, *that* is non-omissible: there is no bare relative counterpart **This is the letter drew our attention to the problem*. But where it is the object that is relativised *that* is optional, so we have all three types:

[2]	i	*My neighbour gave me some advice.*	[main clause]
	ii	*I accepted the advice$_i$ [which$_i$ my neighbour gave me].*	[*wh* relative]
	iii	*I accepted the advice$_i$ [that my neighbour gave me __$_i$].*	[*that* relative]
	iv	*I accepted the advice$_i$ [my neighbour gave me __$_i$].*	[bare relative]

As in [1], the main clause in [2i] has an ordinary NP as direct object, whereas the relative clauses do not. The *wh* relative [ii] again has *which* as relative pronoun, while the non-*wh* versions simply have a gap in object position. And as before the meaning involves two occurrences of a variable: "I accepted advice *x*; my neighbour gave me *x*".

Fronting to prenuclear position

In [2ii] *which* occurs in what we call **prenuclear** position, before the subject + predicate construction that constitutes the nucleus of the clause (cf. Ch. 2, §2). Formally, there is a gap after *gave me* in this construction as well as in the non-*wh* relatives. The difference is that while in [2iii–iv] the gap is related directly to the antecedent *advice*, in [2ii] it is related indirectly, via *which*. Example [2ii] can thus be represented as in [3], with the relative clause having the structure shown in [4]:

[3] *I accepted the advice$_i$ [which$_i$ my neighbour gave me _$_i$].*

[4]

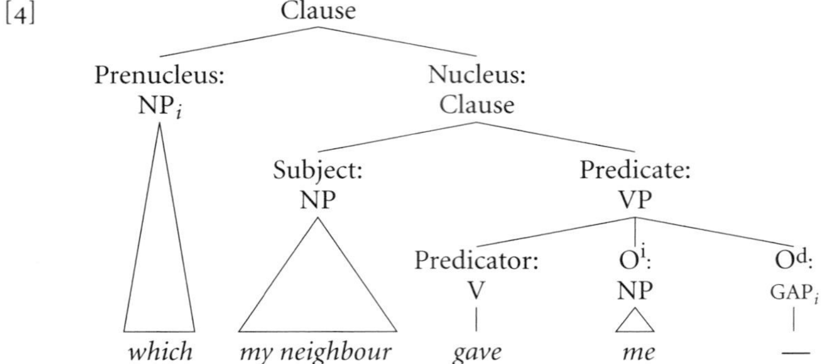

In the first instance it is the gap that is in object function, as indicated in the diagram. However, prenuclear elements that are linked to a gap are interpreted as having the function of that gap, and we can thus say in a secondary, derivative, sense that they have that function. On this account, therefore, *which* is object of the relative clause, just as it is in traditional grammar.

Relative clauses vs content clauses

Examples [1–2] show how the relativisation feature distinguishes relative clauses from main clauses. The obligatory presence of an (overt or covert) relativised element likewise distinguishes relative clauses from content clauses, the default kind of subordinate clause:

[5]	i	a. *They ignored the suggestion$_i$ [that Kim made _$_i$].*	[relative clause]
		b. *They ignored the suggestion [that Kim cheated].*	[content clause]
	ii	a. *Focus on the question$_i$ [which$_i$ your brother raised _$_i$].*	[relative clause]
		b. *Focus on the question [which of them stood to gain by it].*	[content clause]

The non-*wh* relative in [ia] has a gap in object position anaphorically linked to the antecedent *suggestion*: we understand that Kim made some suggestion. Thus, again ignoring the determiner, the meaning can be given as "They ignored suggestion *x*; Kim made *x*", with two occurrences of the same variable. But there is no gap in the content clause in [ib], where we understand the subordinate clause as simply expressing the proposition "Kim cheated". Similarly in [ii], except that this time the relative is of the *wh* type and the content clause is an open interrogative rather than a declarative.[3] We understand from [iia] that your brother raised some question: "Focus on question *x*; your brother raised *x*". But the content clause in [iib] is understood simply as "Which of them stood to gain by it?" In [iia] *which* is anaphoric, relative, while in [iib] it is non-anaphoric, interrogative.

If the verb in the subordinate clause is one that can be used both transitively and intransitively there may be ambiguity between the two constructions:

[3] In the interrogative case a preposition (*of* or *as to*) would often appear after the head noun.

[6] *They rejected the idea [that we had advanced].* [relative or content clause]

In the relative interpretation there is a relativised object, a gap, with *idea* as antecedent. We had advanced some idea: "They rejected idea *x*; we had advanced *x*". In the content clause interpretation, on the other hand, *that* introduces an ordinary clause (a complement to the noun *idea*): the meaning is that they rejected the proposition "We had advanced".

There are other factors that distinguish relative clauses from content clauses. In NP structure relatives function as modifiers, whereas content clauses are complements, compatible only with a fairly small subclass of noun. Our examples contain *suggestion, question, idea*: others are *fact, news, belief, concern, proposal,* etc., but innumerable nouns like *cat, boy, health, energy* allow relatives but not content clauses. Secondly, content clauses do not allow the alternation between the *wh* and *that* constructions found with relatives: for example, if we replace *that* by *which* in [6] it becomes unambiguously relative. In content clauses, *that* marks declarative clause type, while *which, who,* etc., occur only in open interrogatives, licensed by such nouns as *question.*

3.2 Relative words, relative phrases, and upward percolation

We refer to the initial phrase in *wh* relatives as the **relative phrase**; it occupies either subject or prenuclear position. A **simple** relative phrase consists of a relative word on its own: *who, whom, which, where,* etc. A **complex** relative phrase consists of a relative word together with other material. Compare:

[7] i *I can't find the book [which he recommended __].* [simple]
ii *We've never met the people [whose house we are renting __].* [complex]
iii *We admired the skill [with which she handled the situation __].* [complex]

In [ii–iii], as in almost all the complex cases, the relative phrase contains more than just the relativised element. In [ii], for example, the relative phrase in prenuclear position is the NP *whose house,* but it is just the genitive determiner within this NP, i.e. *whose,* that constitutes the relativised element: it is *whose* that derives its interpretation from the antecedent *people.* The gap in object position in the nucleus is thus not co-indexed with the antecedent, as it is in [i]. Rather, we have two co-indexed pairs of different extents, with *whose* linked to *people,* and the gap linked to *whose house,* for it is *whose house* that is understood as object of *renting.* Similarly in [iii], except that the gap is anaphorically linked to a PP rather than an NP. The anaphoric links can thus be shown as in [8], where the outer brackets in [ii–iii] enclose the relative clause, and the inner ones the complex relative phrase:

[8] i *I can't find the book$_i$ [which$_i$ he recommended __$_i$].*
ii *We've never met the people$_i$ [[whose$_i$ house]$_j$ we are renting __$_j$].*
iii *We admired the skill$_i$ [[with which$_i$]$_j$ she handled the situation __$_j$].*

Non-*wh* relatives do not contain a relative phrase, and consequently there can be no non-*wh* relatives matching *wh* relatives like [7ii–iii]:

[9] i *I can't find the book [that he recommended].*
ii **We've never met the people [that's house we are renting].*
iii **We admired the skill [with that she handled the situation].*

In describing the range of permitted complex relative phrases we will invoke the metaphor of 'upward percolation'. In [7ii], for example, the relative feature percolates upwards from the genitive determiner *whose* to the matrix NP *whose house* and in [7iii] it percolates upwards from the NP *which* to the PP *with which*. We invoked the same metaphor in Ch. 10, §7.9, in describing the structure of complex interrogative phrases, but the phenomenon is considerably more extensive in the case of relatives. Seven types of upward percolation may be distinguished in relative clauses, five involving percolation from the element on the right, two from the one on the left:

[10]	TYPE	PERCOLATION FROM	TO	EXAMPLE
	I	comp of preposition	PP	*behind which*
	II	PP	NP	*the result of which*
	III	PP	AdjP	*prominent among which*
	IV	NP	infinitival	*to refute which*
	V	NP	gerund-participial	*passing which*
	VI	genitive *whose*	NP	*whose essay*
	VII	determinative *which*	NP	*which suggestion*

We will examine each of these in turn. Where appropriate, we will contrast the examples with main clause constructions to show the basic, non-relative, form of the phrase.

3.2.1 Type I: from complement of preposition to PP (*behind which*)

In general, this type of upward percolation is optional:

[11] i *Kim was hiding behind the curtain.* [main clause]

ii *the curtain* [*behind which Kim was hiding*] [Type I applied]

iii *the curtain* [*which Kim was hiding behind*] [Type I not applied]

In [ii] the relative phrase is the PP *behind which*, with percolation of the relative feature from the NP *which* to the PP in which it is complement; the result is that the preposition is fronted along with its complement. In [iii] the relative phrase is just *which*, and fronting this time affects only the complement of the preposition, the latter being left **stranded**. The factors favouring, or in some cases requiring, one or other of these structures are discussed in detail in Ch. 7, §4.1.

3.2.2 Type II: from PP complement of noun to NP (*the result of which*)

Type II always combines with Type I in the PP, so that we have percolation from a relative NP to a PP and thence to a larger NP:

[12] i *She's just sat her final exam,* [*the result of which we expect next week*].

ii *She investigated all the complaints,* [*most of which were well founded*].

iii *They are members of an association* [*the first and most precious principle of which is mutual trust*].

iv *Police are looking for a Ford Escort* [*the licence number of which ends in 7*].

Much the most frequent preposition is *of*, and the construction is found more often in supplementary relatives ([i–ii]) than in integrated ones ([iii–iv]). Example [ii] illustrates the quite common case where *of which* is a partitive complement.

Like Type I, Type II upward percolation is in general optional. There is potentially alternation, therefore, between three different versions of the relative clause:

[13] i *He already knows the answers to the problems.* [main clause]
ii *problems* [*the answers to which he already knows*] [Types I and II]
iii *problems* [*to which he already knows the answers*] [Type I only]
iv *problems* [*which he already knows the answers to*] [Type I not applied]

In [ii] we have percolation from *which* into the PP *to which* (Type I), and from there into the NP *the answers to which* (Type II). In version [iii] only Type I applies so that we have fronting of just the PP complement of the NP object. Version [iv] has a simple relative phrase: there is no upward percolation at all.

Some factors relevant to choice between alternants

Examples like [13ii], with two steps of upward percolation, are characteristic of relatively formal style. Other factors include the following.

Preposition stranding not normally permitted at the end of the subject

[14] i a. *He came up with a strange plan,* [*the purpose of which escapes me*].
b. *He came up with a strange plan,* [*of which the purpose escapes me*].
c. *He came up with a strange plan,* *[*which the purpose of escapes me*].
ii a. *He came up with a strange plan,* [*the purpose of which I don't understand*].
b. *He came up with a strange plan,* [*of which I don't understand the purpose*].
c. *He came up with a strange plan,* ?[*which I don't understand the purpose of*].

In the last example in each set, fronting applies to *which* from the larger NP, leaving *of* stranded; in [ic], where the NP is subject, the result is quite ungrammatical, while [iic], where the NP is object, is much more acceptable – stylistically inelegant rather than ungrammatical.

Partitive *of* resists stranding

Constructions with a partitive *of* phrase normally have at least one step of upward percolation:

[15] i *She hadn't kept copies of her letters,* [*only five of which he'd answered*].
ii *She hadn't kept copies of her letters,* [*of which he'd answered only five*].
iii *She hadn't kept copies of her letters,* *[*which he'd answered only five of*].

Informational status

The main factor concerns what we are calling information packaging, the informational status of various parts of the message. Compare, for example:

[16] i *I sympathise with such complaints,* [*of which we receive many*].
ii *I sympathise with such complaints,* [*many of which I investigate myself*].

In the most likely interpretation of [i], the main information being conveyed is that the complaints are numerous: *many* occupies the basic object position and will carry the main stress, marking it as the focus of new information. *Many of which we receive* would suggest (if the focal stress is on *receive*) that some of the complaints are not received, i.e. are lost, or (if the stress is on *we*) that some of them are received by others. In [ii], where *many* is fronted along with its complement, the main information is that I investigate them myself.

In general, then, material will not be fronted if fronting it would leave the nucleus following the relative phrase with too little significant content:

[17] i a. *They are striving to explain phenomena [of which we have little or no direct knowledge].*

b. #*They are striving to explain phenomena [little or no direct knowledge of which we have].*

ii a. *Her first loyalty is to the programme [of which she is director].*

b. **Her first loyalty is to the programme [director of which she is].*

The [b] examples are unacceptable because of the radical imbalance between the content of the relative phrase in prenuclear position and that of the following nucleus. In [iib] *director* is head of the predicative complement, and it is doubtful if upward percolation of Type II could ever apply into an NP in predicative complement function, certainly where the verb is *be*: we have accordingly marked it as ungrammatical, not merely infelicitous.

Recursive application of percolation Types I and II

Since an NP containing a PP as complement can itself be the complement of a preposition, there can be a further application of Type I after Type II, and then a further application of Type II: the construction is recursive. Compare:

[18] i *He was wearing a tall black sheepskin hat [from the top of which dangled a little red bag ornamented by a chain of worsted lace and tassels].* [I + II + I]

ii *They will be involved in several other projects, [one of the most important of which will be to find ways to use the new superconductor in chips that can provide the brains of a new generation of supercomputers].* [I + II + I + II]

In [i] the upward percolation goes from *which* to the PP *of which*, then to the NP *the top of which* and finally to the underlined PP. In [ii] there are four steps: from NP to PP, PP to NP, NP to PP, and PP to NP.

3.2.3 Type III: from PP to AdjP (*prominent among which*)

[19] i *The many varieties of mammalian skin secretions perform a wide range of functions, [prominent among which is sexual attraction].*

ii *Several MPs were interviewed, [chief among whom was the Chancellor of the Exchequer, Douglas Durack].*

This type is rare and highly restricted: in general, the head of an AdjP containing a relative PP is not fronted with it but remains in the basic predicative complement position, as in *He had received a savage sentence for a crime of which he might quite possibly have been innocent* or *It concerns a part of the business for which I am no longer responsible.* This relates to the point about information packaging made in §3.2.2: fronting the adjective here would result in an imbalance between the informational content of the relative phrase and that of the following head clause. It is significant that the examples in [19] (which are semantically very similar) both have postposing of the subject, which is the locus of the main information in the relative clause.

Type III percolation is confined to supplementary relatives; it is obligatory in [19ii], while [19i] has the less favoured alternant *among which sexual attraction is prominent.*

3.2.4 Types IV and V: from NP to non-finite (*to refute which, passing which*)

Type IV: infinitivals – supplementary relatives only

[20] i *I felt the need of a better knowledge of Hebrew and archaeology to refute a higher criticism of the Bible.* [main clause]

ii *I became disturbed by a 'higher criticism' of the Bible, [to refute which I felt the need of a better knowledge of Hebrew and archaeology].* [Type IV]

This type is rare and very largely confined to purpose adjuncts and catenative complements that are semantically somewhat similar – e.g. *to please whom he had striven so hard*, but not **to please whom he had wanted so desperately* (only *whom/who he had so desperately wanted to please*).

Type IV combines (obligatorily) with Type I when the infinitival is complement of the preposition *in order*:

[21] *Here is Dr Van Buren, [in order to interview whom Phelps says he was prepared to fly to Copenhagen].*

Type V: gerund-participials – supplementary relatives only

[22] *They take a rigorous examination, [passing which confers on the student a virtual guarantee of a place at the university].*

This is again very rare and also highly formal in style – except in the expressions *speaking/talking of which/whom*, used to indicate the topic of what follows.

3.2.5 Type VI: from genitive *whose* to NP (*whose essay*)

Relative *whose* functions as subject-determiner in NP structure and obligatorily triggers upward percolation:

[23] i *He plagiarised the student's essay.* [main clause]

ii *the student* { *[whose essay he plagiarised]* [Type VI]

iii *the student* { **[whose he plagiarised essay]* [Type VI not applied]

Type VI percolation can combine with I, and hence also with II:

[24] i *I hadn't yet met the people [in whose house I would be staying].*

ii *She was lecturing on Tom Roberts, [an exhibition of whose work can currently be seen at the National Art Gallery].*

iii *You sometimes find yourself unable to describe the physical appearance of someone [with the very texture of whose thought you are familiar].*

The steps involved here are, respectively: VI + I; VI + I + II; VI + I + II + I.

3.2.6 Type VII: from determinative *which* to NP (*which suggestion*)

When *which* is a determinative rather than a pronoun, upward percolation to the containing NP is obligatory:

[25] i *They all enthusiastically endorsed this suggestion.* [main clause]

ii *I said that it might be more efficient to hold the meeting on Saturday morning, [which suggestion they all enthusiastically endorsed].* [Type VII]

iii *. . . *[which they all enthusiastically endorsed suggestion].* [Type VII not applied]

Determinative *which* is not itself a phrase, and cannot be separated from the head on which it is dependent, as evident from [iii]. We take the relativised element in [ii] to be the whole object NP, *which suggestion*: this is the phrase whose interpretation is given by the antecedent (*it might be more efficient to hold the meeting on Saturday morning*), though the presentation of it as a suggestion is of course contributed by the relative clause rather than being inherent in the antecedent itself. The double-variable gloss will thus be: "I said *x* (=it might be more efficient to hold the meeting on Saturday morning); they all enthusiastically endorsed suggestion *x*". This is the only type of upward percolation which does not yield a relative phrase that is larger than the relativised element.

Type vii percolation is found only in supplementary relatives. Further examples are seen in:

[26] i *They refuse to support the UN's expenses of maintaining the UN Emergency Force in the Middle East as a buffer between Egypt and Israel, and the UN troops in the Congo, [which expenses are not covered by the regular budget].*
ii *I may be late, [in which case I suggest you start without me].*
iii *I will return at 3 pm, [by which time I expect this room to be tidy].*
iv *Both horses, broken and trained by different trainers, were blundering jumpers until they were seven, [at which age they began to outgrow their carelessness].*
v *She has to comment on him standing there, and later, when the soldiers march away, has to tell him not to move yet – [neither of which remarks should be so obtrusive that the soldiers might notice them, but both of which should be clearly heard by the audience].*

Examples like [i], where the NP concerned is itself an element of clause structure, are quite rare and formal, verging on the archaic. It is much more usual for the NP to be complement of a preposition which is also fronted, and the head noun is then predominantly one of very general meaning such as *case* or *time*, as in [ii–iii]. In the last example the upward percolation involves three steps: vii (*which remarks*), i (partitive *of which remarks*), and ii (the whole NP).

3.3 What can be relativised

In this section we survey briefly the various elements in the relative clause that can be relativised, without at this stage distinguishing between *wh*, *that*, and bare relatives.

(a) Subject

[27] i *A man came to dinner.*
ii *The man$_i$ [who$_i$ came to dinner] turned out to be from my home town.*

(b) Object

[28] i a. *She received a letter from the Governor.* [direct object]
b. *This is the letter$_i$ [that she received __$_i$ from the Governor].*
ii a. *He showed a student the exam paper.* [indirect object]
b. **The student$_i$ [whom$_i$ he showed __$_i$ the exam paper] informed the police.*

Relativisation applies to direct objects but not normally to indirect ones.

(c) Predicative complement

[29] i a. *She is a scholar.*
b. *Her book displays the fine sceptical intelligence of the scholar$_i$ [she is __$_i$].*
ii a. *They consider it a good investment.*
b. ?*I don't think it is the good investment$_i$ [they consider it __$_i$].*

Relativisation of predicatives is comparatively rare, and almost entirely limited to the subjective type, i.e. those with the subject as predicand, as in [ib]. Example [iib], with the object as predicand, is of doubtful acceptability – it would be much more usual to have *they consider it to be __*.

With integrated relatives it is also very rare for the antecedent to be in other than a definite NP: we find the NP *the scholar she is* in [29], but it is hard to contextualise #*a scholar she is* as an NP. But in the right context indefinites are possible; for example, there is no syntactic ill-formedness to *Harry is basically a fat man searching for a thin man that he once used to be.*

(d) Complement of preposition

[30] i *He was trying to cut it with a penknife.*
ii *The penknife$_i$ [that he was trying to cut it with __$_i$] was blunt.*

In *wh* relatives the preposition may be fronted along with its complement: *the penknife with which he was trying to cut it.* This involves upward percolation, as described in §3.2 above, with the relativised element (still complement of a preposition) contained within the complex relative phrase.

(e) Adjuncts and associated complements

[31] i *We met Kim at the races one day.*
ii *Do you remember the day$_i$ [we met Kim at the races __$_i$]?*

The gap in [ii] is functioning as adjunct in its clause, like *one day* in [i]. A selection of the major types of adjunct or complement we are concerned with here is supplied in [32]:

[32] i	*It was a time in my life$_i$ [when$_i$ everything seemed to be going right __$_i$].*	[time]
ii	*I've finally found somewhere$_i$ [where$_i$ I can work undisturbed __$_i$].*	[location]
iii	*They want to go to the place$_i$ [where$_i$ they went last year __$_i$].*	[goal]
iv	*I shall go back the way$_i$ [I came __$_i$].*	[path]
v	*Look at the way$_i$ [he tackled the job __$_i$].*	[manner]
vi	*That's not really the reason$_i$ [she left him __$_i$].*	[reason]

This sort of case is to be distinguished from (d) above: here it is the whole adjunct or complement that is relativised, whereas in (d) what is relativised is just the NP functioning as complement within a PP. In [30ii], for example, what is relativised is not the instrumental adjunct itself, but just the complement of *with*. Case (d) is in fact broader than (e) since it can apply with virtually the full range of prepositions. For most of the categories in [32] there is an alternant of type (d): for example, [v] alternates with *the way in which he tackled the job*. We look further at such alternations in §3.5.4.

Two extensions of this kind of construction should be noted.

Extension I: special *wh* words

A number of additional adjunct categories can be relativised by means of the somewhat formal or archaic relative words *whence, whither, whereby, wherein*, etc.

[33] i *They returned to the place$_i$ [whence$_i$ they had come __$_i$].* [source]
ii *It is a scheme$_i$ [whereby$_i$ payment can be deferred for six weeks __$_i$].* [means]

Extension II: cleft relatives

Cleft relatives differ from ordinary ones in various ways, and one of them is that they allow for the relativisation of a very much wider range of complements and adjuncts, e.g. the beneficiary and purpose adjuncts in [34]:

[34] i *It wasn't for me$_i$ [that he made the sacrifice __$_i$].* [beneficiary]
ii *It's to avoid such a conflict of interest$_i$ [that I'm resigning __$_i$].* [purpose]

(f) Genitive subject-determiner

[35] i *Some client's measurements remain unknown.*
ii *One cannot tailor a suit for a client [whose measurements remain unknown].*

(g) Complement of auxiliary verb, and related constructions – supplementary relatives only

[36] i a. *I simply can't design it myself.*
b. *He told me to design it myself$_i$, [which$_i$ I simply can't __$_i$].*
ii a. *I called the police immediately.*
b. *They advised me to call the police$_i$, [which$_i$ I did __$_i$ immediately].*
iii a. *I'd very much like to go with him.*
b. *He's asked me to go with him$_i$, [which$_i$ I'd very much like to __$_i$].*

In [ib] the relativised element is complement of the auxiliary *can*. Auxiliary *have* and *be*, and of course the other modals, behave in the same way: *She said he had cheated$_i$ [which$_i$ indeed he had __$_i$]*, etc. Where the main clause counterpart does not contain an auxiliary, the relative construction requires *do*, as in [iib]. In this case, what is relativised is in effect the predicate, for it is *do* + *which* that derives its interpretation from the antecedent. In [iiib] it is the head of a *to*-infinitival VP that is relativised. This is possible only when the infinitival is complement of a catenative verb – compare, for example:

[37] i *It is certainly important to consult your lawyer.*
ii **He says you should consult your lawyer$_i$, [which$_i$ it is certainly important to __$_i$].*

Here the infinitival is in extraposed subject function. For further discussion of the constructions illustrated in [36], see Ch. 17, §§7.1–3.

3.4 Relativisation of an element within an embedded clause

The gap that is linked to the antecedent in non-*wh* relatives and to the fronted relative phrase in the *wh* type need not be located directly in the relative clause itself: it can be within a smaller clause embedded within the relative. Compare:

[38] i a. *She recommended a book.*
b. *This is the book$_i$ [that she recommended __$_i$].*

ii a. *I think she recommended a book.*
b. *This is the book*$_i$ [*that I think* [*she recommended* __$_i$]].

In [ib] the gap is object of the relative clause itself, whereas in [iib] it is object of the content clause functioning as complement of *think* – the outer pair of brackets enclose the relative clause, while the inner pair enclose the content clause embedded within it. It is by virtue of this possibility that relative clauses belong to the class of unbounded dependency constructions which we shall be examining in §7.

Relativisation is characteristically unaffected by embedding

Leaving aside various general constraints on unbounded dependency constructions, it for the most part makes no difference, as far as relativisation is concerned, whether the gap is directly in the relative clause itself or in a smaller clause embedded within it. In [38], for example, we have relativisation of a direct object, and in both [ib] and [iib] *that* can either be replaced by *which*, giving a *wh* relative, or else be omitted, giving a bare relative. Compare, similarly, the following cases of indirect object relativisation:

[39] i a. *I lent a boy my key.*
b. **They found the boy*$_i$ [*that I lent* __$_i$ *my key*].
ii a. *He said I lent a boy my key.*
b. **They found the boy*$_i$ [*that he said* [*I lent* __$_i$ *my key*]].

This time both relative clauses are ungrammatical: the indirect object can't be relativised. But again it makes no difference whether it is the indirect object of the relative clause itself, as in [ib], or of a clause embedded within the relative clause, as in [iib].

Subject vs embedded subject

There is just one exception to this pattern, one place where embedding does make a difference: when we have relativisation of the subject. Compare:

[40] i a. *This car is safe.*
b. *I want a car*$_i$ [*that* __$_i$ *is safe*].
ii a. *I know* [*this car is safe*].
b. *I want a car*$_i$ [*that I know* [__$_i$ *is safe*]].

The difference is that *that* is obligatory in [ib] but omissible in [iib]. We can thus have a bare relative in case [ii], but not in case [i]:

[41] i **I want a car*$_i$ [__$_i$ *is safe*]. [gap as subject of relative clause]
ii *I want a car*$_i$ [*I know* [__$_i$ *is safe*]]. [gap as subject of embedded clause]

We need therefore to distinguish between relativisation of the relative clause subject and relativisation of an embedded clause subject. The distinction is also relevant in *wh* relatives, where it has a bearing on the case of the pronoun ***who***, with some speakers allowing an accusative for an embedded subject (%*the man whom they say was responsible*) but not a relative clause subject (**the man whom was responsible*): see Ch. 5, §16.2.3.

3.5 The formal types: *wh*, *that*, and bare relatives

In this section we examine the various *wh* relative words, the omissibility and syntactic status of *that*, and factors relevant to the choice between *wh* and non-*wh* relatives.

3.5.1 *Who* and *which*

Which belongs to both pronoun and determinative categories. As a determinative, it occurs only in supplementary relatives, as illustrated in [25–26] above; as a pronoun it contrasts in gender with ***who***, as **non-personal** vs **personal**. The choice depends on the nature of the antecedent:

[42] PERSONAL ANTECEDENT | NON-PERSONAL ANTECEDENT

i a. *the people who were outside* b. *the things which matter most*

ii a. *a dog who was licking my face* b. *a dog which is always barking*

The distinction between ***who*** and *which* is very similar, but not identical, to the one between ***he/she*** on the one hand and ***it*** on the other. The two contrasts are compared in our discussion of gender (Ch. 5, §17.3),[4] and here we will merely add a few points of detail.

Who with antecedents denoting animals

Who occurs predominantly with human antecedents, but with antecedents denoting animals, both pronouns are possible, as shown in [42ii]: *which* is the default choice, but ***who*** is by no means uncommon. ***Who*** conveys a greater degree of empathy or personal interest and involvement. The most obvious cases where ***who*** is used are in references to pets, but it is also found with other creatures (or even collections of creatures), as in these attested examples:

[43] i *For eighty years, grizzly bears have been feeding at the rubbish dumps, often in great roaming bands who came down from the remote pine forests.*

ii *The more vigorous dance for a dilute source of nectar in turn recruits other bees, who then visit that dilute source instead of concentrated ones.*

Two special cases of *which* used with human antecedents

Ascriptive predicative complement of *be*

Which occurs with antecedents denoting human beings when the relativised element is complement of auxiliary *be* in a supplementary relative. Compare:

[44] i *They accused him of being a traitor$_i$, [which$_i$ he undoubtedly was _$_i$].*

ii *It turned out that he wasn't the person$_i$ [who$_i$ I'd thought he was _$_i$].*

Example [i] belongs to the construction illustrated in [36ib], with relativisation of the complement of an auxiliary verb. The complement in this case is a predicative, but we cannot relativise the predicative complement of a lexical verb such as *seem* in this way: **She thinks he's a fool, which indeed he seems.* The relativised predicative in the *which* construction will generally be of the ascriptive type, as in this example: the clause is concerned with the person's properties, what kind of a person he was, not his identity. *Who* would be impossible here, but is used in the integrated relative clause of [ii], with *be* used in its specifying sense: the issue is the identity of the person (I thought he was person *x*, but he turned out not to be). Note that in both [i] and [ii] the antecedent is in predicative complement function as well as the pronoun.

[4] Ch. 5 (§16.2.3) also deals with the choice between nominative *who* and accusative *whom*.

Complement of *have (got)*

[45] i *They've got a chief executive who can provide strong leadership, which we certainly haven't got at the moment.*
ii *Remember that they have a house-keeper, which we don't have.*

Again there is no issue of identity involved here: it is not that we have not got the same chief executive or house-keeper, but the same kind of chief executive, or just the same kind of thing (a house-keeper). This construction is found only with supplementary relatives, but it differs from [44i] in that *which* is not complement of an auxiliary verb.

Coordination of personal and non-personal antecedent nouns

[46] i *She spoke of the people and books which had brought her the greatest pleasure.*
ii *She spoke of the books and people who had brought her the greatest pleasure.*

Here the antecedent is a coordination of nouns differing with respect to the personal vs non-personal contrast. The conflict is typically resolved by means of the principle of proximity, with the gender of the pronoun determined by the last noun in the coordination. The conflict can of course be avoided by using a non-*wh* relative, in this example a *that* relative.

3.5.2 *Whose*

Used with both personal and non-personal antecedents

The contrast between personal **who** and non-personal *which* is neutralised in the genitive, where *whose* is the only form. It occurs with both personal and non-personal antecedents:

[47] i *She started a home for women [whose husbands were in prison].* [personal]
ii *The report contains statements [whose factual truth is doubtful].* [non-personal]

Alternation with *of* construction

We have seen (Ch. 5, §16.5.2) that with non-relatives, a genitive determiner characteristically alternates with a construction containing *the* + post-head *of* phrase:

[48] i a. *The child's parents were constantly quarrelling.*
b. *The parents of the child were constantly quarrelling.*
ii a. *The house's roof had been damaged in the storm.*
b. *The roof of the house had been damaged in the storm.*

The same alternation is found with *whose*, except that here we have two versions of the *of* construction, one with the *of* PP in post-head position, one where it is separated from the head:

[49] i a. *a child [whose parents were constantly quarrelling]* [genitive]
b. *a child [the parents of whom were constantly quarrelling]* [post-head *of* PP]
c. *a child [of whom the parents were constantly quarrelling]* [separated *of* PP]
ii a. *a house [whose roof had been damaged in the storm]* [genitive]
b. *a house [the roof of which had been damaged in the storm]* [post-head *of* PP]
c. *a house [of which the roof had been damaged in the storm]* [separated *of* PP]

In the post-head *of* PP construction the relative phrase is the whole NP, so that there is upward percolation of Type II, from PP to NP. In the separated *of* PP version the relative phrase is just that *of* PP, with Type II percolation not applying.

With non-relatives the genitive alternant is more likely with personal nouns than with non-personals, and this general tendency applies with relatives too, where it may well be strengthened by the morphological resemblance between *whose* and *who*: the great majority of instances of *whose* have personal antecedents. In [49i], therefore, the genitive alternant [a] is much the most likely of the three. With non-personal antecedents one or other of the *of* constructions will often be preferred, but it must be emphasised that genitives like [49iia] are completely grammatical and by no means exceptional.[5] One genre where they occur very readily is scientific writing: examples like *a triangle whose sides are of equal length* are commonplace.

Distributional restrictions on relative *whose*

Relative *whose* does not occur in the full range of genitive constructions (see Ch. 5, §16.3). It is permitted in the oblique genitive (*a friend of whose*), but otherwise occurs only as determiner in NP structure. Compare, for example:

[50]	SUBJECT-DETERMINER GENITIVE	PREDICATIVE GENITIVE
i	a. *It was the doctor's car.*	b. *The car was the doctor's.*
ii	a. *the doctor [whose car it was]*	b. **the doctor [whose the car was]*

Note that there is no *of* alternant available in [ib/iib] (**The car was of the doctor, *the doctor of whom the car was*), so the meaning has to be expressed by quite different means (e.g. *the doctor who owned the car / to whom the car belonged*).

3.5.3 Other relative words

Other words belonging to the relative class are *where, when, while, why, whence*, and various compounds consisting of *where* + preposition.[6]

Where

[51] i *She wanted to see the house$_i$ [where$_i$ she had grown up].*

ii *They met in the journalists' club$_i$, [where$_i$ he went every Sunday afternoon].*

iii *She often climbed the knoll behind the mission$_i$, [from where$_i$ she could look down on roofs and people].*

Where takes locative expressions as antecedent; within the relative clause it functions as adjunct of spatial location, goal complement, or complement of a locative preposition. A 'double-variable' representation of [i] is "She wanted to see house *x*; she had grown up in *x*": the "in" component is contributed by *where* together with its spatial location function, with the antecedent determining the value of the variable *x*. In [ii] we understand "to *x*", with the "to" component derivable from the goal function. And in [iii] we have "from *x*", with the "from" component overtly expressed. Analogously for the examples below.

[5] It is interesting to note that a number of usage manuals feel it necessary to point out that relative *whose* can have a non-personal antecedent: there are apparently some speakers who are inclined to think that it is restricted to personal antecedents.

[6] In traditional grammar, all these are classified as adverbs; in the present grammar, we take *why* as an adverb and the others as prepositions: see Ch. 7, §2.4.

When

[52] i *It happened at a time$_i$ [when$_i$ I was living alone].*
ii *In those days$_i$, [when$_i$ he was still a student,] he used to babysit for us.*
iii *He left college in 1982$_i$, [since when$_i$ I've only seen him twice].*

When takes a temporal expression as antecedent; it generally functions as an adjunct of temporal location within the relative clause, but it can also appear as complement to a temporal preposition such as *since.*

While

[53] i *From 1981 to 1987$_i$, [while$_i$ his uncle lived with them,] she had a full-time job.*
ii %*He wrote most of his poetry during the years$_i$ [while$_i$ he was in Paris].*

Relative *while* is mostly found in the fused construction, but it can occur in supplementary relative clauses and, for some speakers, in integrated ones. The antecedent denotes a period of time, and *while* can be replaced by *when* or *during/in which* (*time*).

Why

Relative *why* is used in a very narrow range of constructions – integrated relatives with *reason* as antecedent:

[54] i *That's the main reason$_i$ [why$_i$ they won't help us].*
ii *There was no reason$_i$ [why$_i$ he should stay at the dance any longer].*
iii *I can't see any reason$_i$ [why$_i$ you shouldn't have a little fun].*

The majority of examples are of the types shown in [i–ii]: either the specifying *be* construction, where it is a matter of identifying reasons, or the existential construction, where we're concerned with the existence of reasons. *Why* alternates with *for which*, as in the attested example *The Physical Training and Recreation Act of 1937 deals with the acquisition of playing fields, which may not be absolutely the reason for which an authority would wish to acquire property. For which*, however, is comparatively rare and formal: it could not idiomatically replace *why* in ordinary examples like [54].

Whence

[55] i *He sent his son with the papers to another congressman's house$_i$, [whence$_i$ they were spirited to a governor].*
ii *But this means that the Taniyama-Shimura conjecture is true$_i$, [whence$_i$ it follows that Fermat's Last Theorem is true].*

Whence belongs to formal style, serving in its primary sense to express spatial source, as in [i]. The "from" meaning can be incorporated in *whence* or expressed separately by the preposition *from*, which is obligatorily fronted. This use is in general somewhat archaic, though it is still found in journalistic writing. *Whence* is also used for logical source, normally in supplementary relatives, as in [ii]; this is the relative counterpart of the most common use of *hence.*

Compounds of *where* + preposition

There are a number of prepositions formed from *where* and a preposition: *whereat, whereby, wherefrom, wherein, whereof, whereon, whereto, whereupon*, and others. They have non-relative counterparts based on *here* and *there* (*thereat, hereby*, etc.). Most are archaic and rare, though *whereby* and to a lesser extent *wherein* and *whereupon* are still regularly used:

[56] i *His Lordship might make an order$_i$ [whereby$_i$ each side would bear its own costs].*
ii *Size segregation occurs when a powder is poured into a heap$_i$, [whereby$_i$ the larger particles run more easily down the slope of the heap].*
iii *Try to imagine a market$_i$ [wherein$_i$ the majority consistently wins what the minority loses].*
iv *She told him his essay was incoherent$_i$, [whereupon$_i$ he tore it up and stormed out of the room].*

In integrated relatives *whereby* is equivalent to *by which*, with *by* having approximately the "means" sense: typical antecedent nouns are *agreement, arrangement, mechanism, method, plan, proposal, scheme, service, suggestion*, etc. In supplementary relatives it can also occur with a clause as antecedent, as in [ii]. *Wherein* is equivalent to *in which. Whereupon* means approximately "immediately after which"; it is found only in supplementary relatives whose antecedent is a clause (or larger).

3.5.4 The choice between the *wh* and non-*wh* constructions

In this section we examine the choice between the *wh* and non-*wh* types in non-fused relatives – fused relatives invariably contain a *wh* phrase.

(a) *Wh* type required or strongly favoured in supplementary relatives

Supplementary relatives whose antecedent is an AdjP, VP, or clause, not an NP, always have a relative phrase:

[57] i *She said he was arrogant, [which I don't think he is].* [AdjP]
ii *He set out to redeem himself, [which he eventually did].* [VP]
iii *He wouldn't let us defend ourselves, [which was completely unfair].* [clause]

Where the antecedent is an NP the *wh* construction is also normally used, but some speakers do allow supplementary *that* relatives, as in the following attested examples:

[58] i *The patas monkey, [that spends almost all of its time in open grassland,] adopts just such tactics.*
ii *His heart, [that had lifted at the sight of Joanna,] had become suddenly heavy at the sight of Ramdez thumping after her.*
iii *February, [that in other years held intimations of spring,] this year prolonged the bitter weather.*
iv *She had long been accustomed to the solitary nature of her son's instincts, [that I had tried – and failed – to stifle].*

The remainder of this section will be concerned with integrated relatives.

(b) Upward percolation applies only in *wh* type

We have noted (§3.2) that upward percolation requires the presence of a relative word, and hence applies only in the *wh* type. With the few exceptions dealt with in (c) below, there are therefore no non-*wh* counterparts to clauses with complex relative phrases, such as:

[59] i *They won't register companies [whose directors are undischarged bankrupts].*
ii *It's a burden [of which they will never be free].*

Where upward percolation is optional, as in [ii], there will be an alternant with a simple relative phrase (*It's a burden [which they will never be free of]*) and if relevant conditions are satisfied this will have a non-*wh* counterpart (*It's a burden [they will never be free of]*).

(c) Time, reason, place, path, and means

Relatives introduced by *when* or *why* have non-*wh* counterparts, with or without *that*:

[60] i *I haven't seen them since the day [when/(that) Kim was born].*
ii *That's the reason [why/(that) she resigned].*

The notation '*when/(that)*' indicates a choice between *when* and optional *that*, so we have *the day when Kim was born*, *the day that Kim was born*, or *the day Kim was born*. Relatives introduced by *where*, by contrast, do not in general alternate with the non-*wh* type except where the antecedent is a very general noun such as *place*:

[61] i *This is much better than the hotel [where we stayed last year].*
ii *This is much better than the place [where/(?that) we stayed last year].*

The '?' annotation in [ii] applies to the version with *that* (?*the place that we stayed last year*); the bare relative (*the place we stayed last year*) is more acceptable.[7]

When the antecedent is *way*, in either the path or the means sense, we have non-*wh* relatives or *wh* relatives introduced by preposition + *which*:

[62] i *Go back the way [(that)/by which you came].*
ii *I admired the way [(that)/in which she handled the situation].*

How does not belong to the class of relative words (except very marginally in the fused construction, §6.4), so we cannot have **the way how she handled the situation*.[8] Note that if *way* is replaced by *manner* the non-*wh* construction is no longer possible: **the manner (that) she handled the situation.*

(d) *That which* and *all who*: obligatory *wh*

[63] i *That [which we so carefully created] he has wantonly destroyed.*
ii *All [who heard her speak] were deeply impressed by her sincerity.*

The very formal *that which* ("what") cannot be replaced by either *that that* or *that*, and when pronominal *all* applies to people **who** is required (cf. **all that heard her speak*).

(e) *Anything, all,* etc.: non-*wh* preferred

[64] i *Anything [(that) you say] may be used in evidence against you.*
ii *All [(that) I ask for] is a little peace and quiet.*

[7] The restriction to *wh* relatives does not apply when *where* is complement to stranded *at*: *the hotel where/(that) we stayed at last year. Where . . . at* seems to be a blend between *where* and *which . . . at*; note that with *in* we can have *which* but not *where*: *the hotel which/*where we stayed in last year.*

[8] Some non-standard dialects differ; hence the line *It ain't what you do, it's the way how you do it* in a rock 'n' roll song.

This case covers the compound determinatives (*anything, everything, nothing, something*) and non-personal fused determiner-heads *all, much, most, few, little, some, any*, etc. There is a preference for the non-*wh* type here, but of varying strength, with *everything which*, for example, significantly better than ?*all which*.

(f) Nominals with superlative modifiers: non-*wh* preferred

[65] i *She gave me the best meal* [(*that*) *I'd had for many years*].
ii *You should take the first appointment* [*that is available*].
iii *That fish is the biggest* [(*that*) *I've ever seen*].

There's a very strong preference for the non-*wh* type here, especially in fused-head NPs like [iii]. The non-*wh* type is also preferred, though not so strongly, after *only, next,* and *last*.

(g) Relativised element is ascriptive predicative complement: normally non-*wh*

[66] i *He's no longer the trustworthy friend* [(*that*) *he was in those days*].
ii *The interview turned out not to be the ordeal* [(*that*) *I had thought it would be*].

Which is virtually impossible here; we saw, however, in [44ii] (*It turned out that he wasn't the person who I'd thought he was*) that the *wh* type is permitted when the complement is specifying rather than ascriptive.

(h) Personal antecedent

With personal antecedents, there is a preference for *who* when the relativised element is subject, as in *the boy who threw the dart*, and for the non-*wh* type elsewhere, e.g. *the boy* (*that*) *they had found hiding in the cupboard*. The non-*wh* here avoids the choice between formal *whom* and informal *who*. It must be emphasised, however, that we are concerned here only with preferences: a phrase like *the boy that threw the dart* is certainly fully grammatical.

(i) Complexity

Increasing the distance between the relative clause and the head noun, notably by adding other post-head modifiers, favours the *wh* type (just as, within the non-*wh* type, it favours *that* over a bare relative). Thus *a material of great tensile strength and very remarkable electroconductive properties which has been widely used in the aviation industry* is preferred over the version with *that* in place of *which*.

3.5.5 Non-*wh* relatives: presence or absence of *that*

That relatives and bare relatives differ with respect to the presence or absence of the subordinator *that*. In its relative use, as with its use to mark declarative content clauses, *that* can very often be omitted, and in these cases we have alternation between the two types of non-*wh* relative.

Restrictions on omission of *that*

With the rather marginal exception of examples like [61ii] above, there are no constructions where *that* has to be absent: it is normally possible to add *that* to any bare relative to obtain a grammatical *that* relative. However, the converse does not hold: under certain very limited conditions, the subordinator cannot be omitted from a *that* relative without loss of grammaticality.

The relativised element is subject

That cannot normally be omitted if the relativised element is subject of the relative clause:

[67]	NON-SUBJECT	SUBJECT
i	a. *The car [that I took __] was Ed's.*	b. *The car [that __ hit us] was Ed's.*
ii	a. *The car [I took __] was Ed's.*	b. **The car [__ hit us] was Ed's.*

The [a] cases represent the default: *that* can be omitted from [ia] to produce the grammatical [iia]. In this example the relativised element is object, but any other non-subject would similarly allow omission of *that*: *He's not the man (that) he was a few years ago* (predicative complement); *I can't find the book (that) you asked for* (complement of preposition); *He's the one (that) they think was responsible for the first attack* (embedded subject), and so on. In all these cases *that* precedes the subject, but when the subject itself is the relativised element, and hence missing, *that* must be retained, as in [b].

The prohibition on dropping the *that* with relativised subjects is associated with the need to distinguish the subordinate relative clause from the matrix predicate. Since *hit us* in [ib] immediately follows *the car*, there is nothing to stop the listener construing *hit us* as the main clause predicate, with *the car* as its subject: *that* prevents such a misconstrual by explicitly signalling the start of a subordinate clause. This is not to suggest that there would always be a danger of misconstrual if *that* were omitted from clauses with a relativised subject. In **We didn't take the number of the car __ hit us*, for example, *the car* is complement of *of* and hence not a possible subject for a predicate *hit us*. The grammatical restriction preventing subject relativisation with bare relatives covers a wider range of cases, but the point is that it includes those where *that* serves a role in aiding perception of the structure.

Some varieties of English do allow *that* to be omitted from clauses with relativised subjects under certain conditions:

[68]			
	i	?*It was my father [__ did most of the talking].*	[*it*-cleft]
	ii	?*There's someone at the door [__ wants to talk to you].*	[existential]
	iii	!*Anyone wants this can have it.*	

Most such cases are clearly non-standard, like [iii]. The status of [i–ii], where the relative clause functions within an *it*-cleft and existential construction respectively, is less certain: they fall at the boundary between very informal and non-standard. Note that the position of the relative clause in [i–ii] is such that it could not be misconstrued as predicate of the matrix clause.

That not omissible when not adjacent to the subject

A second, less important, exception to the optionality of *that* is seen in examples like:

[69] *I found I needed a file [that only the day before I had sent to be shredded].*

That is needed here to mark the beginning of the subordinate clause: without it there would be the potential for the following adjunct to be misconstrued as belonging in the matrix clause. Bare relatives always have the subject in initial position.

That not omissible in supplementary relatives

We have noted that although supplementary relatives are normally of the *wh* type, examples with *that* are also found, as in [58] above. But it is quite impossible to omit the *that* in such cases (cf. **She had long been accustomed to the solitary nature of her son's instincts, I had tried – and failed – to stifle*).

Factors favouring or disfavouring the omission of *that*

In contexts other than the above, *that* is grammatically optional. It is somewhat more likely to be omitted in informal than formal style, and when the antecedent and the relative clause, or at least its subject, are both short.

In the following, where the antecedent is indicated by underlining, [i–ii] involve a slightly special case where a bare relative is preferred, while the others illustrate the kind of structure where dropping *that* is very strongly disfavoured:

[70] i *I'll go back the <u>way</u> [I came].*
ii *I haven't seen her since the <u>day</u> [Kim was born].*
iii *It was <u>with considerable misgivings</u> [that her parents agreed to this proposal].*
iv *It was <u>in order to avoid this kind of misunderstanding</u> [that I circulated a draft version of the report].*
v *<u>Something</u> has cropped up [that I hadn't expected].*

In [i–ii] the relativised element is respectively a path and time adjunct, and the antecedent is both short and prototypical for that kind of adjunct. Examples [iii–iv] belong to the cleft construction: the relativised element is an adjunct of a type that cannot be relativised in integrated or supplementary relatives and the antecedent, especially in [iv], is a relatively complex expression. In [v] the relative clause is postposed, so that it is not adjacent to its antecedent: *that* is here very strongly favoured, though a bare relative cannot be completely excluded.

3.5.6 *That* as a subordinator (not a relative pronoun)

Traditional grammar analyses the *that* which introduces relative clauses as a relative pronoun, comparable to *which* and **who**, but we believe that there is a good case for identifying it with the subordinator *that* which introduces declarative content clauses.

(a) Wide range of antecedent types and relativised elements

If *that* were a pronoun, or pro-form, its use would be much wider than that of the uncontroversial relative pronouns, or indeed of any pro-form at all in the language. Compare:

[71] i	*They gave the prize to the <u>girl</u> [that spoke first].*	[*who*]
ii	*Have you seen the <u>book</u> [that she was reading]?*	[*which*]
iii	*He was due to leave the <u>day</u> [that she arrived].*	[*when*]
iv	*He followed her to every <u>town</u> [that she went].*	[*where*]
v	*That's not the <u>reason</u> [that she resigned].*	[*why*]
vi	*I was impressed by the <u>way</u> [that she controlled the crowd].*	[**how*]
vii	*It wasn't <u>to you</u> [that I was referring].*	[no *wh* form]
viii	*She seems to be the <u>happiest</u> [that she has ever been].*	[no *wh* form]

It would not only cover the ground of all the simple '*wh*' words put together, as shown in [i–v]: it would also appear in a variety of constructions where no '*wh*' word could replace it, as in [vi–viii]. Particularly important here is the cleft construction shown in [vii], and in [70iii–iv] above. Note that, leaving aside the disputed case of the relative construction, there is no pro-form in English that takes as antecedent such complements and adjuncts as *to you* (in the sense it has in [71vii]), *with considerable misgivings, in order to avoid this kind of misunderstanding*, and the like. Instead of postulating a pro-form with such an exceptional range of use, we are saying that *that* relatives do not contain any overt pro-form linked to the antecedent: they simply have an anaphoric gap, like bare relatives.

(b) Lack of upward percolation

There are no *that* relatives matching *wh* relatives with a complex relative phrase:

		a.	b.
[72]	i	a. *the woman [whose turn it was]*	b. **the woman [that's turn it was]*
	ii	a. *the knife [with which he cut it]*	b. **the knife [with that he cut it]*

If *that* were a pronoun we would have to stipulate that it has no genitive form, and that it never occurs as complement of a preposition – or rather that when it is complement of a preposition the latter must be stranded, for *the knife that he cut it with* is quite grammatical. The severe restrictions here stand in sharp contrast to the remarkable versatility of the putative pronoun *that* illustrated in (a). In the analysis where *that* is a subordinator the ungrammaticality of [72ib/iib] is predictable. Subordinators do not inflect and must occupy initial position; there is no relative word and hence no possibility of the relative feature percolating upwards into a larger constituent.[9]

(c) Finiteness

That relatives are always finite, as are the declarative content clauses introduced by *that*. Note, then, that we cannot insert *that* into non-*wh* relative infinitivals like *a knife to cut it with* – cf. **a knife that to cut it with*. If *that* were a pronoun this would be a special fact needing explanation, but under the subordinator analysis it is exactly what we would expect, given that *that* is a finite clause subordinator.[10]

(d) Omissibility

As we have noted, *that* can be regarded as very largely omissible in relative clauses in the same way as in declarative content clauses. The conditions under which omission is prohibited are not the same in the two cases (those for content clauses are given in Ch. 11, §3.1), but in both they have it in common that they are related to the need to mark explicitly the beginning of a subordinate clause under certain structural conditions. And in both cases, moreover, *that* is more readily omitted in simple structures than in complex ones. There is no pro-form in English that is systematically omissible under remotely similar conditions.

[9] There are non-standard regional dialects of English in which *that's* does occur, as in *the man that's leg was broken*. We do not believe that such examples necessitate a pronoun analysis for the dialects concerned, and certainly they do not establish this analysis as valid for all dialects.

[10] The force of this argument is diminished by the fact that *which* can't occur here either: we have *a knife with which to cut it*, not **a knife which to cut it with*. The absence of **a knife with that to cut it* is then already covered under point (b). Nevertheless, the analysis of *that* as a finite clause subordinator does provide a very general account of why the only type of bare relative that can't be expanded by means of *that* should be the infinitival one.

4 The distinction between integrated and supplementary relative clauses

These two types of relative clause are illustrated in:

[1] i a. *They interviewed every student <u>who had lent money to the victim</u>.* [integrated]
b. *They interviewed Jill, <u>who had lent money to the victim</u>.* [supplementary]
ii a. *The necklace <u>which her mother gave to her</u> is in the safe.* [integrated]
b. *The necklace, <u>which her mother gave to her</u>, is in the safe.* [supplementary]

The terms **integrated** and **supplementary** indicate the key difference between them: an integrated relative is tightly integrated into the matrix construction in terms of prosody, syntax, and meaning, whereas a supplementary relative clause is related only loosely to the surrounding structure.

(a) Prosody and punctuation

A supplementary relative is marked off prosodically from the rest of the sentence by having a separate intonation contour; there is typically a slight pause separating it from what precedes and, if it is non-final in the sentence, from what follows. The pitch contour tends to match that of the one preceding it and containing the antecedent. An integrated relative, on the other hand, is prosodically bound to its antecedent, falling within the same intonation contour.

This prosodic difference is largely reflected in writing by a difference in punctuation. A supplementary relative is characteristically preceded and (if non-final) followed by a comma, or, less often, by a dash, or the clause may be enclosed within parentheses. Conversely, an integrated relative is not separated from its antecedent by a comma or other punctuation mark. In this chapter we consistently mark the distinction in this way, but it must be emphasised that punctuation is elsewhere not a wholly reliable guide: it is by no means uncommon to find clauses that are not marked off punctuationally even though the syntax and/or meaning requires that they be interpreted as supplementary.

(b) Syntax

An integrated relative clause usually functions as modifier within the structure of an NP. Those in [1ia/iia], for example, are constituents of the NPs *every student who had lent money to the victim* and *the necklace which her mother gave to her*. Note that *every student* and *the necklace* do not themselves constitute NPs in these examples.

The syntactic structure of sentences containing supplementary relatives is less clear: the relative clauses are only loosely incorporated into the sentence. In [1ib/iib] *Jill* and *the necklace* constitute NPs by themselves, but the supplementary relatives do not combine with them to form larger NPs. We suggest in Ch. 15, §5.1, that the antecedent + relative clause here is a special case of a **supplementation** construction, which is distinct from a head + dependent construction. The supplement is in construction with an **anchor** (in this case the antecedent), but does not combine with it to form a syntactic constituent.

(c) Meaning

The content of an integrated relative is presented as an integral part of the meaning of the clause containing it, whereas the content of a supplementary relative is presented as a separate unit of information, parenthetical or additional. We will see that there can be a range of reasons why the content of a relative should be presented as integral to the larger message, but our initial examples illustrate two very obvious cases. In [1ia] dropping the relative would drastically change the meaning: I would be saying that they wanted to interview every student, not just those who had lent money to the victim. And [1iia] implicates that there was more than one necklace, so if the relative were dropped it would be unclear which one I was referring to. The supplementary relatives here, by contrast, can be omitted without affecting the meaning of the remainder. Example [1ib] says that they interviewed Jill, and it would still say that if we dropped the relative. Example [1iib] says that the necklace was still in the safe, where I assume the necklace I'm referring to is identifiable in the context, and again the same would hold if the relative were dropped.

4.1 Major syntactic differences

(a) Differences with respect to the formal types

[2]	INTEGRATED	SUPPLEMENTARY
i *Wh* relatives	Yes	Yes
ii *That* relatives	Yes	Marginal
iii Bare relatives	Yes	No

All three types occur as integrated relatives, whereas only the *wh* type occurs freely in the supplementary construction. Supplementary relatives with *that* are found, as illustrated in [58] of §3, but they are comparatively rare and of questionable acceptability for many speakers.

(b) Differences with respect to relative words and phrases

[3]	INTEGRATED	SUPPLEMENTARY
i *Which* as determiner	No	Yes
ii Upward percolation, Types III–V	No	Yes
iii *Whereupon*	No	Yes
iv *Why*	Yes	No

Supplementary relatives allow a wider range of complex relative phrases than integrated ones. Complex relative phrases are those containing more than just the relative word itself: we have described these in terms of the concept of upward percolation (§3.2). Most importantly, phrases containing *which* + head noun (upward percolation Type VII) are found only in supplementary relatives:

[4] *He spent all breaks either riding racehorses – he won three steeplechases – or skiing, [in which sport he won a European under-18 downhill race].*

Rarer constructions involving upward percolation into an AdjP (*prominent among which*), an infinitival VP (*to refute which*), or a gerund–participial (*passing which*) are likewise limited to supplementary relatives. The same applies to such partitive expressions as *none/most/all/both of which*, etc.: *The new bedrooms, each of which will have its own private bath or shower, are all on the first floor.* Among the simple relative phrases, *whereupon* occurs only in supplementary relatives, *why* only in integrated ones, with ***reason*** as antecedent (cf. [56iv] and [54] of §3).

(c) Differences with respect to antecedents

The above differences concern the internal structure of the relative clause; in addition there are differences in their distribution, in the range of antecedents they can have. The most important of these are as follows:

Clauses

Only supplementary relatives can have a clause as antecedent:

[5] *He said he'd drafted the report, which I knew to be untrue.* [supplementary]

The antecedent of *which* is the clause *he'd drafted the report*; the relative clause in such cases can only be of the supplementary type, with a separate intonation contour.

Proper names

These occur readily as antecedent of a supplementary relative; they cannot normally take an integrated relative unless preceded by a determiner:

[6] i *You should speak to Sue Jones, who was here the whole time.* [supplementary]
ii *She is obviously not the Sue Jones they are looking for.* [integrated]

Sue Jones forms a full NP in [i], but not in [ii], where it is only a nominal. Example [i] represents the primary use of a proper name – to refer to the bearer of the name; [ii] involves a secondary use, which may be glossed in this example as "person called Sue Jones".

Quantification with *no, any, every*

Expressions consisting of *no, any,* or *every* morphologically compounded with ·*one*, ·*body*, or ·*thing*, or syntactically combined with a head noun, have non-referential interpretations and cannot serve as antecedent of a supplementary relative, but they can be followed by integrated relatives:

[7] i **No candidate, who scored 40% or more, was ever failed.* [supplementary]
ii *No candidate who scored 40% or more was ever failed.* [integrated]

Superlatives and interrogative prepositions

Integrated relative clauses almost always have nominals as antecedent, but there are other possibilities:

[8] i *He's now the fattest that he's ever been.*
ii *She ran the fastest that she's ever run.*
iii *When that wouldn't be too inconvenient for you could we hold the meeting?*
iv *Where can we go for lunch that isn't too expensive?*

That relatives of a very restricted type are also found in superlative AdjPs or AdvPs, as in [i–ii]. And the interrogative prepositions *when* and *where* – like nominal *time* and *place* – can serve as antecedents for integrated *that* relatives, which occur most readily in postposed position, as in [iv].

(d) Stacking possible only with integrated relatives

[9] i *I like those ties you wear that your sister knits for you.*
ii **They've given the job to Max, who has no qualifications, who starts next month.*

The integrated relative construction is recursive: an integrated relative can combine with its antecedent to form a larger unit which is antecedent for a second integrated relative. In [i], for example, *you wear* combines with its antecedent *ties* to give *ties you wear* and this is then the antecedent for the second relative, *that your sister knits for you.* This kind of recursion is known as **stacking**. It is limited to the integrated construction: antecedent + supplementary relative cannot serve as antecedent for a second supplementary relative, as illustrated in [ii].

(e) Non-declaratives and question tags found only with supplementary relatives

[10] i *He said he'd show a few slides towards the end of his talk, <u>at which point please remember to dim the lights</u>.*

ii *It may clear up, <u>in which case would you mind hanging the washing out</u>?*

iii *She may have her parents with her, <u>in which case where am I going to sleep</u>?*

iv *I didn't get much response from Ed, <u>who seemed rather out of sorts, didn't he</u>?*

Relative clauses mostly belong to the default declarative clause type, but with supplementary relatives other clause types are possible. Those in [i–iii], for example, are respectively imperative, closed interrogative, and open interrogative. And declaratives can have question tags attached, as in [iv]. These constructions are quite impossible with integrated relatives.

Analysis

The antecedents of integrated relatives are sub-phrasal, parts of a phrase. In the great majority of cases, the antecedent of an integrated relative is a nominal, and the relative clause combines with it to form a larger nominal, as in the following structure that we propose for [7ii]:

[11]

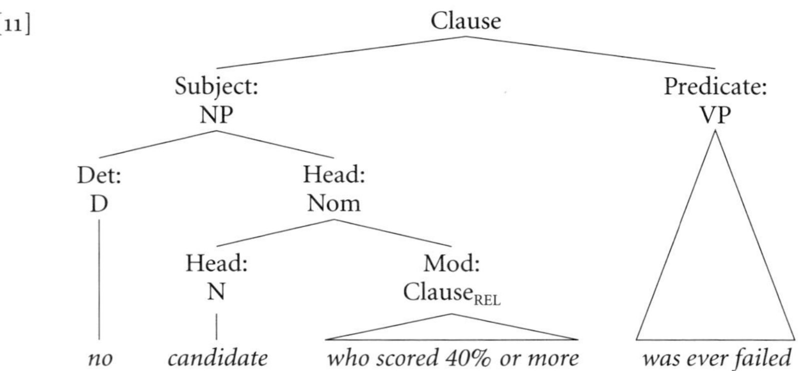

With supplementary relatives, on the other hand, the antecedents are full phrases, such as NPs, or larger constituents, such as clauses, and the relative clause does not function as a dependent of the antecedent. The structure we propose for [1ib] is as follows (and for [1iib] see Ch. 15: [52ii] of §5):

[12]

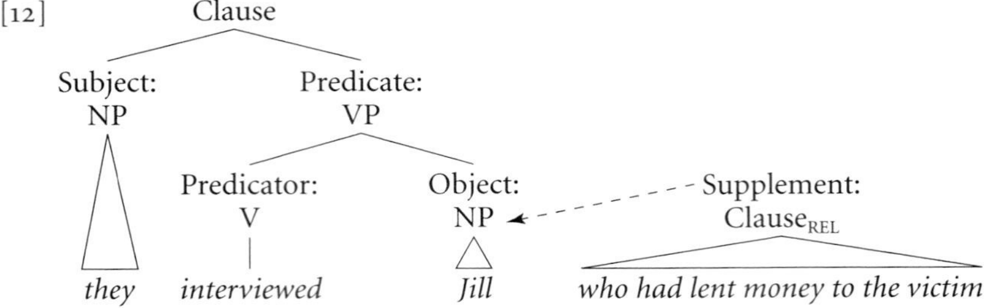

Consider these structures in the light of some of the syntactic differences noted above.

Non-declaratives

The non-declarative clauses in [10] provide evidence for the view that supplementary relatives are not dependents of a head. Except for the relativisation, the structures are like those found in main clauses, not clauses in dependent function – compare *At that point please remember to dim the lights*; *In that case would you mind hanging the washing out?*; and so on.

Stacking

The structure proposed for integrated relatives predicts the possibility of stacking. In [9i] *ties* is a nominal which combines with *you wear* to form a larger nominal *ties you wear*, and this in turn combines with *that your sister knits for you* to form the further nominal *ties you wear that your sister knits for you*, which enters into construction with the determiner *those*. In [9ii], however, the supplementary relative *who has no qualifications* does not form a unit with its antecedent, so *Max, who has no qualifications* is not a possible antecedent for the second *who*.

Quantification with *no, any, every*

The structure for [7ii] is given as [11]; the antecedent for the integrated relative is *candidate*, not *no candidate* – this is why the relative clause is not interpreted as "No candidate scored 40% or more".[11] In [7i], with a supplementary relative, the antecedent is *no candidate*, yet this NP has no reference – so there is no referent for the relative pronoun *who*. NPs of this kind can no more serve as antecedent for a relative pronoun than they can for a personal pronoun – compare the incoherence of #*I have no money; it's on the desk*, if *no money* is taken as antecedent of *it*.

Proper names

In [6i] the *who* of the supplementary relative has as antecedent the NP *Sue Jones*. This refers to the person of that name, and *who* refers to her too: it is coreferential with its antecedent. In [ii] *Sue Jones* is a nominal, not an NP, and as such does not refer; the integrated relative combines with it to form a larger nominal which is not a proper name and hence (given that it is count singular) it requires a determiner.

Definite descriptions

Consider, finally, the *necklace* examples in [1ii]. In the supplementary case [iib] (*The necklace, which her mother gave to her, is in the safe*) the antecedent is *the necklace*: this is marked as definite, indicating that the description *necklace* is assumed to be sufficient in the context to identify the referent. In the integrated case [iia], the antecedent is *necklace*; the relative clause combines with this to form the nominal *necklace which her mother gave to her*, and

[11] A more complex case is seen in *Nobody who scored 40% or more was ever failed.* Here there is grammatical fusion of the determiner and the head (see Ch. 5, §9.6), but semantically the negative is again not part of the antecedent.

the indicates that this nominal provides an identifying description of the referent. The relative clause thus forms part of the identifying description in the integrated case but not in the supplementary: hence the implicature in the former but not the latter that there is some other necklace from which the one being referred to needs to be distinguished.

4.2 Meaning and use

Supplementary relatives express true or false propositions, integrated ones do not

In describing the semantics of relative clauses, it is useful to consider again our initial examples:

[13] i *They interviewed every student <u>who had lent money to the victim</u>.* (=[1ia])
ii *They interviewed Jill, <u>who had lent money to the victim</u>.* (=[1ib])

In an ordinary use of [13ii] the supplementary relative expresses the proposition that Jill had lent money to the victim, and depending on the circumstances this will be true or false. But the integrated relative clause in [i] does not express a proposition that can be evaluated as true or false – in particular it does not express the proposition that every student had lent money to the victim. We represent the propositional content as "*x* had lent money to the victim", where '*x*' is a variable, and precisely because it is a variable "*x* had lent money to the victim" is an open proposition, one that is not itself either true or false. An integrated relative is comparable to an ascriptive modifier. Compare, for example, *every <u>generous</u> student* and *every student <u>who had lent money to the victim</u>*: it makes no more sense to ask whether the relative clause is true or false than it does to ask whether *generous* is true or false. This difference between the two types of relative clause correlates with the difference in syntactic structure we have proposed. The antecedent for *who* in [ii] is the full NP *Jill*, a referring expression, whereas the antecedent for *who* in [i] is a nominal, and nominals themselves do not refer.

Supplementary relatives normally have illocutionary force

We have noted that supplementary relatives select for clause type: they then characteristically have the same illocutionary force as other non-dependent clauses of the same type (cf. Ch. 10). The relative in [13ii], for example, would be used to make a statement, while those in [10i–iii] would be used as directive, indirect directive, and question respectively.

Supplementary relatives replaceable by clauses with non-relative anaphoric expressions

Supplementary relatives can be replaced by other kinds of supplements containing non-relative anaphoric expression, notably personal pronouns or demonstratives. Compare the following with the supplementary relatives given above:

[14] i *They interviewed Jill – <u>she</u> had lent money to the victim.* (cf. [1ib])
ii *The necklace – her mother gave <u>it</u> to her – is in the safe.* (cf. [1iib])
iii *He spent all breaks either riding racehorses – he won three steeplechases – or skiing (<u>in this sport</u> he won a European under-18 downhill race).* (cf. [4])
iv *He said he'd drafted the report; I knew <u>this</u> to be untrue.* (cf. [5])

Note similarly that the deviance of [7i] is matched by that of **No candidate – he or she scored 40% or more – was ever failed.*

The continuative use of supplementary relatives

[15] i *I gave it to John, who passed it on to Mary, and she gave it back to me.*
ii *They come to a cliff, where the deer suddenly stops and throws off the little boy, and boy and dog then fall into a pond.*

These examples illustrate a use of juxtaposed supplementary relatives in narrative contexts that is traditionally referred to as **continuative**: they serve to continue, to develop, the narrative. The effect is like that of *and* + non-relative anaphoric expression: *I gave it to John and he passed it on to Mary, . . .* Whereas elsewhere the information conveyed in a supplementary relative is somewhat backgrounded relative to that conveyed in the clause containing the anchor, the continuative relative has equality of informational status, presenting a further event in a narrative chain.

Content of integrated relative an essential component of matrix message

Integrated relatives have it in common that their content is presented as an integral part of the meaning of the clauses containing them. The prototypical integrated relative expresses a distinguishing property, as in:

[16] i *They only take in overseas students who they think have lots of money.*
ii *She was offended by the letter that accused her of racism.*

In [i] the relative clause distinguishes a subset of overseas students: the people referred to by *they* do not take in all overseas students, but only those from the subset they believe to have lots of money. In [ii] the relative distinguishes the letter she was offended by from other letters: it serves to identify which letter she was offended by. In cases like these, we find a very sharp contrast between the integrated and supplementary constructions. The supplementary counterparts of the above are:

[17] i *They only take in overseas students, who they think have lots of money.*
ii *She was offended by the letter, which accused her of racism.*

This time the relative clause in [i] does not pick out a subset of overseas students, but makes an assertion about overseas students in general. Similarly the supplementary relative in [ii] does not serve to distinguish the letter from other letters, but provides additional information about a letter assumed to be identifiable simply by the description *letter.*

Contrasts like these provide the basis for the traditional classification of relative clauses as 'restrictive' ([16]) and 'non-restrictive' ([17]). We prefer to distinguish the two classes as integrated vs supplementary because there are many places where the contrast is not a matter of whether or not the relative clause expresses a distinguishing property.[12]

Consider first the following attested example (from a novel) involving a definite NP:

[18] *The father who had planned my life to the point of my unsought arrival in Brighton took it for granted that in the last three weeks of his legal guardianship I would still act as he directed.*

[12] A term quite widely used instead of 'non-restrictive' is 'appositive'. We find the latter term unsatisfactory because the integrated vs supplementary contrast applies to apposition as well as to relative clauses. Compare, for example, *my brother the heart surgeon* (integrated) and *my brother, the heart surgeon* (supplementary).

The narrator is three weeks short of eighteen and is saying that his father took it for granted that during those three weeks he would continue to do as his father directed. The relative clause here belongs to our integrated class: it cannot be omitted or spoken on a separate intonation contour and allows *that* as an alternant of *who* (albeit somewhat less favoured). Yet it does not serve to distinguish this father from other fathers of the narrator: he has only one father. The reason for presenting the content of the relative clause as an integral part of the message is not, therefore, that it expresses a distinguishing property but that it explains why the father took it for granted that the son would do as he was told.

Compare similarly:

[19] i *He sounded like the clergyman he was.*
ii *She had two sons she could rely on for help, and hence was not unduly worried.*

Both underlined clauses are bare relatives and hence necessarily integrated. But we do not understand *he was* in [i] as distinguishing one clergyman from another: it conveys that he was a clergyman, and an obvious reason for presenting this as an integral part of the message is that sounding like a clergyman when you are one is significantly different from sounding like a clergyman when you are not. In [ii] it could be that she had more than two sons (in which case the relative would be serving a distinguishing role), but an at least equally likely context is one where she had only two sons. In this context the property expressed in the relative clause does not distinguish these sons from other sons she has, but is an essential part of the reason for her not being unduly worried.

The relative clause in [19ii] is embedded within an indefinite NP, and here it is very often the case that the crucial factor differentiating the integrated and supplementary constructions has to do with what we are calling information packaging rather than with whether the relative restricts the denotation of the antecedent. Consider:

[20] i *She had two sons(,) who were studying law at university(,) and a daughter(,) who was still at high school.*
ii A: *Have you been to Paris?* B: *Yes, often: I have a brother who lives there.*
iii *I've been talking to one of the porters, who says the train may be an hour late.*

Example [i] could be spoken/punctuated equally readily with integrated or supplementary relatives in a context where she has just two sons and one daughter. On the supplementary reading the primary information being imparted is that she had two sons and a daughter: the information given in the relative clauses is supplementary, secondary. On the integrated reading, by contrast, the content of the relatives is part of the main information. In [ii] a supplementary reading would be incoherent even if B has only one brother. It would involve presenting "I have a brother" as the primary message, whereas it has in fact no relevance by itself in the context of A's question: the crucial point is that the brother lives in Paris, since this explains B's having frequently been there. Example [iii] has a supplementary relative, dividing the message into two separate pieces of information. But if we replace *one of the porters* by, say, *a guy* it would be much more natural to have the relative integrated. This is because "I've been talking to a guy" is less likely to be considered worth presenting as a self-contained piece of information: the crucial information will be that concerning the train's delay.

4.3 Linear position

The normal position for a relative clause is immediately after the antecedent. Since integrated relatives have sub-phrasal antecedents whereas supplementary ones have phrasal antecedents, we find the sequence integrated + supplementary, but not the reverse:

[21] i *The contestant who won first prize, who is the judge's brother, sang dreadfully.*
ii **The contestant, who is the judge's brother, who won first prize sang dreadfully.*

The antecedent for the *who* of the integrated *who won first prize* is a nominal (*contestant*), while that for the *who* of the supplementary *who is the judge's brother* is an NP (*the contestant who won first prize*).

Postposing of relative clause

It is also possible, however, for the relative clause to occur in postposed position, at the end of the clause containing its antecedent.

[22] i *A stranger came into the room who looked just like Uncle Oswald.*
ii *Kim lent a book to Ed which contained all the information he needed.*
iii *I met a man the other day who says he knows you.*
iv *There was a fight reported in Monday's paper that put three people in hospital.*

This construction is most likely when the informational content of the relative clause is greater than that of the material that would follow it in the matrix clause if it occupied the default position following the antecedent.[13] It will generally be avoided if it would result in possible confusion as to what was the intended antecedent. Compare [i], for example, with *A man was talking to one of the check-out operators who looked just like Uncle Oswald,* where *one of the check-out operators* provides a more salient antecedent than *man.* And *She put a hat on her head that had corks hanging from it* too strongly evokes the picture of the head having corks hanging from it to be used with *hat* as intended antecedent.

Postposed relative clauses are predominantly of the integrated type. For example, [22i] becomes quite unacceptable if we replace *a stranger* by a proper name, which would require the relative to be supplementary: **John came into the room, who looked just like Uncle Oswald.* Nevertheless, postposed supplementary relatives do sometimes occur:

[23] i *Only the flower is used, which is not poisonous and is attached to the plant with a very fine stem.*
ii *She could hear her father in the next room, who was angrily complaining about the horrific telephone bill.*

Preposing

A supplementary relative with a coordinated clause as antecedent can precede it, following the coordinator:

[24] *The Net will open up opportunities to exploit tax differences and – which makes it even more of a headache than globalisation – it will make it possible to dodge taxes altogether.*

[13] There is one case where only the postposed position is possible – the case where we have 'split antecedents' (Ch. 17, §1.3): *There's a boy in Group B and a girl in Group E who have asked to be on the same team.*

5 Infinitival relative clauses

Integrated relatives may have infinitival form, with or without a relative phrase.

Wh type infinitivals

The most obvious kind of infinitival relative clause is illustrated in:

[1] i *I'm looking for an essay question with which to challenge the brighter students.*
ii *She is the ideal person in whom to confide.*
iii *The best place from which to set out on the journey is Aberdeen.*

This construction is limited to somewhat formal style. It is found only with integrated relatives, and is subject to the following severe structural restrictions:

[2] i The relative phrase must consist of preposition + NP.
ii There can be no expressed subject.

The first restriction excludes examples like **She's the ideal person whom to invite* and **I'm looking for an essay question which to challenge the brighter students with* (where the preposition is stranded rather than being part of the relative phrase). Condition [ii] rules out **She's the ideal person in whom for you to confide*, and the like. There is no evident explanation for the first restriction, but the second is predictable from the properties of *wh* relative clauses and infinitivals taken together: infinitivals allow subjects only when introduced by the subordinator *for*, but this cannot occur in *wh* relatives since both it and the relative phrase require to be in initial position.

Non-*wh* infinitivals

Infinitival relatives without a relative phrase allow a considerably wider range of structures:

[3] i *She's the ideal person [(for you) to confide in __].*
ii *I've found something interesting [(for us) to read __].*
iii *A systems analyst wouldn't be such a bad thing [(for her) to be __].*
iv *That is not a very good way [(for him) to begin __].*
v *You're not the first person [__ to notice the mistake].*

The relativised elements here are respectively complement of a stranded preposition, direct object, predicative complement, manner adjunct, and subject. Except in the latter case a subject can be optionally included, preceded by the subordinator *for*.

Where the relative clause is within an NP functioning as object or complement of a preposition, there is overlap with an infinitival adjunct of purpose. Compare:

[4] i *He found a video [for the kids to watch].* [relative]
ii *He got it [for the kids to watch].* [purpose adjunct]
iii *He got a video [for the kids to watch].* [ambiguous]

In [i] the infinitival is a relative with a meaning close to that of the finite relative *that the kids could watch.* A relative interpretation of this kind is excluded in [ii] because *it* does not permit modification by a relative clause (cf. **He got it that the kids could watch*); [ii] has, rather, a purposive interpretation: "He got it in order that the kids could watch it". This interpretation is not possible in [i] because finding is non-agentive and therefore does not allow purpose adjuncts. In [iii] the conditions for both constructions are met;

it can be construed in either way, though there is little effective difference in meaning between them.

Modal meaning

Infinitival relatives characteristically have a modal meaning comparable to that expressed in finites by ***can*** or ***should***. *Here's something interesting for you to read*, for example, is comparable to *Here's something interesting that you can/should read*. This modal meaning is indeed what makes relatives like those in [4] semantically so close to purpose infinitivals. Where the matrix NP is definite there is very often some explicit or implicit evaluative modification, such as *ideal* in [1ii] or *best* in [1iii].

Infinitivals where the relativised element is subject have a somewhat wider range of interpretations than others, allowing non-modal as well as modal meanings:

[5]	i	*She's obviously the person to finish the job.*	[modal]
	ii	*She was the first person to finish the job.*	[non-modal]

Example [i] is like the non-subject examples considered above: we understand "best, most appropriate" and "should" ("the person who should finish the job"). But [ii] has no such modal meaning, being equivalent simply to *the first person who finished the job*. Nominals containing relatives with this kind of interpretation usually contain a modifier such as *only*, *next*, *last*, or one of the ordinals *first*, *second*, etc.

6 The fused relative construction

Classification

An initial illustration of the range of constructions belonging to the fused relative category is given in [1]:

[1]		SIMPLE SERIES	·*EVER* SERIES	
	i	a. *I spent <u>what he gave me</u>.*	b. *I spent <u>whatever he gave me</u>.*	[NP]
	ii	a. *I gave him <u>what money I had</u>.*	b. *I gave him <u>whatever money I had</u>.*	[NP]
	iii	a. *I'll go <u>where you go</u>.*	b. *I'll go <u>wherever you go</u>.*	[PP]

On one dimension we have a contrast between the simple series and the ·*ever* series, the latter being marked by a relative word ending in ·*ever*. Cutting across this is the major category contrast: the fused relatives are NPs in [i–ii], PPs in [iii]. And within the NP category we have a further distinction according as the relative word is a pronoun, as in [i], or a determinative, as in [ii].

6.1 Fused relatives as phrases, not clauses

Traditionally, fused relatives are analysed as clauses, but the view taken here is that they are NPs or PPs. Let us focus on the NP case, examining the evidence for treating examples like the fused relatives in [1i–ii] as NPs. The starting-point is the equivalence between pairs like the one given as [6] of §2:

[2]	i	*It would mean abandoning <u>that</u> <u>which we hold most dear</u>.*	[antecedent + clause]
	ii	*It would mean abandoning <u>what we hold most dear</u>.*	[fused relative]

The fused relative is equivalent not to the relative clause *which we hold most dear* but to the NP containing it, *that which we hold most dear*. Compare similarly:

[3] i *The dog quickly ate the scraps that I'd left on my plate.*
ii *The dog quickly ate what I had left on my plate.*

These are not of course fully equivalent since [i] contains the lexical item *scraps*, but in [ii], no less than in [i], the object of *ate* denotes something concrete, a physical entity. Clauses, by contrast, denote abstract entities: propositions, events, and so on. These points demonstrate the semantic likeness between the fused relatives and NPs, but there is also strong syntactic evidence for analysing these constructions as NPs.

(a) Subject–verb agreement

[4] a. *What money she has is in the bank.* b. *What books she has are in the attic.*

The verbs here agree with the fused relatives in subject position. The crucial point is that the *are* in [b] shows that *what books she has* is plural, like the uncontroversial NP *all the books she has*. Clauses functioning as subject, by contrast, always belong to the default 3rd person singular category: *That she has so few books is rather surprising.*

(b) Subject–auxiliary inversion

[5] a. *What she suggests is unreasonable.* b. Is *what she suggests unreasonable?*

Fused relatives can occur in interrogative and other constructions with subject–auxiliary inversion. Again this differentiates them from clauses: compare *That she proposes to go alone* is unreasonable and **Is that she proposes to go alone unreasonable?*

(c) No extraposition

[6] a. *What she suggests is unreasonable.* b. **It is unreasonable what she suggests.*

Like ordinary NPs, fused relatives do not occur in the extraposition construction. Here too they differ from clauses: compare *That we should have to do it ourselves is unreasonable* and *It is unreasonable that we should have to do it ourselves.*

(d) No fronting of preposition

[7]	FUSED RELATIVE	INTEGRATED RELATIVE
i	a. *What she referred to was Riga.*	b. *The city which she referred to was Riga.*
ii	a. **To what she referred was Riga.*	b. *The city to which she referred was Riga.*

When the relativised element is complement of a preposition the fused construction requires that the preposition be stranded, as in [ia]: it cannot be fronted along with its complement, as it can in the integrated relative construction [iib]. The difference in grammaticality here reflects the fact that *which she referred to* is a clause while *what she referred to* is an NP. Fronting the preposition in the integrated construction places it at the beginning of the clause, while fronting it in the fused construction places it before the NP. The deviance of [iia] is thus comparable to that of **To the city which she referred was Riga.* In the integrated case the antecedent *city* and the relative pronoun *which* are distinct and the preposition can come between them, but in the fused case the antecedent and relative pronoun are not distinct and hence there is no place for a fronted preposition to occupy.

(e) Functional range of NPs

Fused relatives occur with the functions that ordinary NPs take:

[8] i *What he said was outrageous.* [subject]
ii *They criticise whatever I do.* [direct object]
iii *We'll give whoever needs it a second chance.* [indirect object]
iv *Things aren't always what they seem to be.* [subjective predicative comp]
v *She made him what he is.* [objective predicative comp]
vi *I was ashamed of what I had done.* [comp of prep]

And, most distinctively, they cannot occur as complement of a noun or adjective (except with exceptional adjectives such as *worth* that take NP complements: see Ch. 7, §2.2). Compare, for example:

[9] i *I'm sorry that you were inconvenienced.* [clause]
ii **I'm sorry the inconvenience / what I did.* [NP]

Sorry can take a clause as complement, but not an NP: an NP can occur only as an oblique complement, related by a preposition, as in *I'm sorry for the inconvenience / for what I did.*

(f) Occurrence with integrated relative

[10] i *Whatever they gave him that he didn't need he passed on to me.* [integrated]
ii *He told me he had done it himself, which was quite untrue.* [supplementary]

That he didn't need is an integrated relative with the nominal *whatever they gave him* as antecedent: it is part of the NP functioning as object of *passed.* As we have already noted, clauses can only be antecedent for supplementary relatives. This is seen in [ii], where the antecedent for *which* is *he had done it himself,* and where the relative clause has to be supplementary. The crucial point, then, is that a fused relative, like ordinary nominal expressions but unlike a clause, can take an integrated relative as modifier.

6.2 Fused relatives contrasted with open interrogatives

There is a considerable degree of overlap between fused relatives and subordinate open interrogative clauses. Compare, for example:

[11] i *I really liked what she wrote.* [fused relative]
ii *I can't help wondering what she wrote.* [open interrogative]
iii *What she wrote is completely unclear.* [ambiguous]

In [i] the complement of *liked* is an NP approximately equivalent to one with an antecedent nominal + integrated relative clause, such as *the material which she wrote.* In [ii] *what she wrote* expresses an embedded question: it is the subordinate counterpart of *What did she write?* An approximate paraphrase is "I can't help asking myself the question 'What did she write?'". But [iii] can be interpreted in either way. With a fused relative as subject, the meaning is "The material she wrote is completely unclear" (she failed to write clearly); with a subordinate interrogative as subject, [iii] means "The answer to the question 'What did she write?' is completely unclear" (e.g. it is unclear which parts of some book, article, or whatever were written by her). There is no ambiguity in [i] because *like* cannot take an interrogative clause as complement, while [ii] is unambiguous because *wonder* cannot (with irrelevant exceptions) take an NP as complement.

Open interrogatives, whether main clauses (e.g. *What did she write?*) or subordinate (*what she wrote*) normally express what we have called variable questions (Ch. 10, §4.5). The propositional content of such questions contains a variable ("She wrote *x*"), and the answers specify values of the variable (*She wrote the preface*; *She wrote a textbook on phonetics*, etc.). We have also analysed integrated relatives as containing variables, but here the variable is anaphorically bound to an antecedent. In the earlier *no candidate who scored 40% or more*, for example, we have an analysis along the lines of "no candidate *x* [*x* scored 40% or more]", i.e. "no candidate *x* such that *x* scored 40% or more". In the case of fused relatives the antecedent and pronoun are not syntactically discrete, but we still have linked occurrences of the variable in the interpretation, e.g. for [11i] "I liked the *x* such that she wrote *x*". Both relative and interrogative thus contain the "she wrote *x*" component: in the relative case, the variable is bound to an antecedent, whereas in the interrogative case the value of the variable is to be given in the answer to the question.

Consider the following further examples in the light of this account:

[12] i	*The dogs wouldn't eat <u>what she gave them</u>.*	[fused relative]
ii	*I told him <u>what she gave them</u>.*	[open interrogative]
iii	*I told him <u>what she suggested I tell him</u>.*	[ambiguous]

Again, the fused relative is roughly equivalent to an NP containing antecedent + integrated relative, e.g. *the food which she gave them*, so we might analyse [i] as "The dogs wouldn't eat the *x* such that she gave them *x*". There is again no ambiguity here because *eat* cannot take clausal complements. Example [ii] can be glossed as "I told him the answer to the question 'What did she give them?'" – i.e. "I told him the value of the variable in 'She gave them *x*'".

Tell can take NP complements, as in *I told him the news*, but the things you can tell are distinct from the things you can give, so there is no fused relative interpretation "#I told him the *x* such that she gave them *x*". However, if we change the example to remove this incompatibility, we can get an ambiguity with *tell*, as in [12iii]. The interrogative interpretation matches that for [ii]: "I told him the answer to the question 'What did she suggest I tell him?'" – i.e. "I told him the value of the variable in 'She suggested I tell him *x*'". And the fused relative interpretation is "I told him the *x* such that she suggested I tell him *x*".

The difference can be brought out by imagining the case where she suggested I tell him that his offer would have to be raised. In this scenario the interrogative interpretation of [12iii] is equivalent to *I told him that she suggested I tell him that his offer would have to be raised* (and I thereby implicitly distance myself from this evaluation of his offer), while the fused relative interpretation is equivalent to *I told him that his offer would have to be raised* (i.e. the value of *x* in "I told him the *x* such that she suggested I tell him *x*" is "his offer would have to be raised").

We have focused above on the semantic difference between the constructions. We now turn to the syntactic differences.

(a) NP vs clause

We have shown that fused relatives (other than the prepositional ones introduced by *where*, *when*, etc.) are NPs; interrogatives, however, are not: they are clauses. The points made in §6.1 above concerning agreement, subject–auxiliary inversion and extraposition, preposition fronting, and adjective complementation can therefore be applied to the distinction between fused relatives and interrogatives:

[13] i a. *What ideas he has to offer are likely to be half-baked.* [fused relative]
b. *What ideas he has to offer remains to be seen.* [interrogative]
ii a. *Is what she wrote unclear?* [fused relative]
b. *It is unclear what she wrote.* [interrogative]
iii a. *What he's referring to / *To what he's referring is Riga.* [fused relative]
b. *I can't imagine what he's referring to / to what he's referring.* [interrogative]
iv *He's not sure what he should say.* [interrogative]

The subject of [ia] is plural and must therefore be an NP: the corresponding clause in [ib] belongs to the default 3rd person singular category. In [ii] we have subject–auxiliary inversion in [a], so *what she wrote* must be an NP, and in [b] we have extraposition, so here *what she wrote* must be a clause. Note that both examples lack the ambiguity of *What she wrote is completely unclear* ([11iii]). In [13iii] the possibility of fronting the preposition in [b] shows that the complement of *imagine* is a clause, not an NP.[14] And the complement of the adjective *sure* in [13iv] can only be interrogative, matching the interpretation "He is not sure about the answer to the question 'What should he say?' ".

(b) Differences in unbounded dependency words

Who, whom, whose, which, why, and *how* are found in fused relatives only under very restrictive conditions (described below), but they occur freely in interrogatives. The contrast between fused relatives and interrogatives is quite clear:

[14] i a. *I agree with what she wrote.* b. **I agree with who spoke last.* } [relative]
ii a. *I accepted what he offered.* b. **I accepted which he offered.*
iii a. *I wonder what she wrote.* b. *I wonder who spoke last.* } [interrogative]
iv a. *I know what he offered.* b. *I know which he offered.*

Conversely the ·*ever* series of forms occur freely in fused relatives, but they are generally not permitted in interrogatives:[15]

[15] i a. *He accepted what/whatever she offered.* } [relative]
b. *He planted roses where/wherever there was enough space.*
ii a. *He didn't tell me what/*whatever she offered.* } [interrogative]
b. *He went to see where/*wherever there was enough space.*

(c) Elliptical reduction

Open interrogatives (whether main or subordinate) can be reduced to an interrogative phrase if the rest of the clause is recoverable anaphorically, but such reduction is quite impossible with fused relatives, just as it is with non-fused ones. Compare:

[14] This last point is of only limited value as a distinguishing test because the stranded preposition construction is often strongly preferred or else the only option even in the subordinate interrogative construction (cf. Ch. 7, §4.1), as in *I can't imagine what he's getting at / *at what he's getting.*

[15] We ignore here cases where *ever* (often written as a separate word) has a quite different sense, like that of *on earth*: *I can't imagine what ever he was thinking about.* There is, however, one type of interrogative where the ·*ever* forms are found, namely interrogatives functioning as exhaustive conditional adjuncts, as in *He won't be satisfied, whatever you give him.* This construction is discussed (and contrasted with the fused relative) in Ch. 11, §5.3.6.

[16] i a. A: *Jill gave him something last night.* B: *What?* } [interrogative]
b. *Jill gave him something last night, but I don't know what.*
ii a. **Jill gave him something last night, but he lost what.* [fused relative]
b. **Jill gave him a book last night, but he lost the book which.* [integrated relative]

In [ia] *what* is equivalent to interrogative *What did she give him?*, while [iia] shows that relative *what she gave him* cannot similarly be reduced to *what*. Analogously in [ib/iib].

(d) Infinitivals restricted to the interrogative construction

A further difference between open interrogatives and fused relatives is that only the former can be infinitival in form: *I wonder what to buy*, but not, say, **I can't afford what to buy* ("I can't afford that which I should buy").

6.3 Syntactic analysis

The analysis of NP structure given in Ch. 5 allows for the head to fuse with an adjacent dependent, i.e. for the two functions to be realised jointly. In *Many would agree with you*, for example, the determinative *many* jointly realises the determiner and head functions. As implied by the term, we invoke the same concept of functional fusion in our analysis of fused relatives. This time the head of an NP fuses with the relativised element in a relative clause.

As an example, take *what she wrote* as in [11i] above, *I really liked what she wrote.* We have demonstrated that the fused relative is an NP, and we take *what* to realise simultaneously the head of that NP and the prenuclear element in the relative clause:

[17]

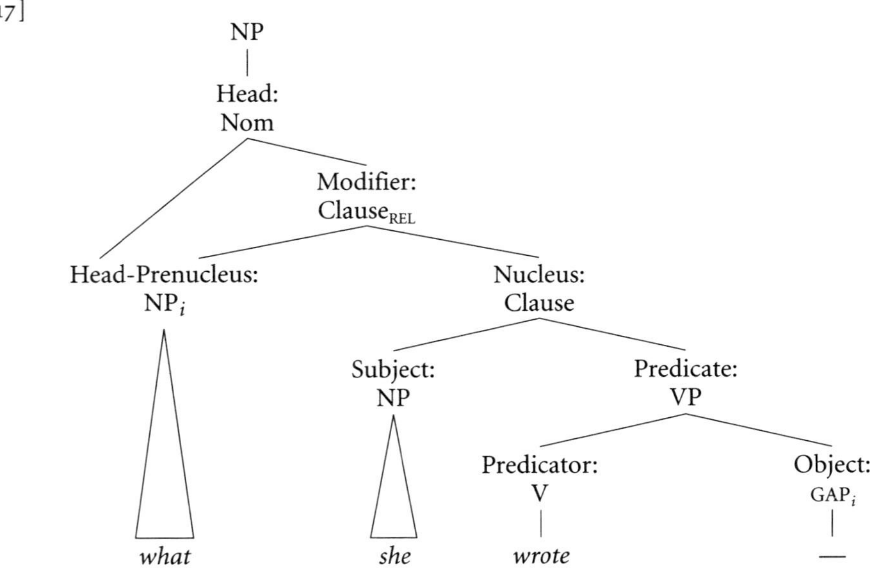

Case

The pronoun *what* in [17] is simultaneously head of the whole NP and object (in prenuclear position) in the relative clause. In constructions with personal ***who*** and ***whoever***, the pronoun has to satisfy the case requirements of both the relative clause and the matrix clause in which the whole NP is functioning. Compare:

[18] i *[Whoever is responsible for the damage] must pay for it.*
ii *He will criticise [whomever she brings home].*
iii ?*[Whomever he marries] will have to be very tolerant.*
iv ?*She lunches with [whomever is going her way after morning classes].*

In [i] both the whole NP (bracketed) and the relativised element (underlined) are subject of their respective clauses: the nominative form matches both requirements. In [ii] both the whole NP and the relativised element are objects, and accusative is fully acceptable though somewhat formal in style. In [iii–iv], however, there is a clash between the function of the whole NP and that of the relativised element – respectively subject and object in [iii], object of a preposition and subject in [iv] – and the result is at best very questionable. *Whoever* would be preferable in both, but many would regard it as less than fully acceptable in formal style.

6.4 Relative words in the fused construction

The relative words used in the fused construction are as follows:[16]

[19]								
i	SIMPLE	***who***	*what*	*which*	*where*	*when*	*how*	*while*
ii	COMPLEX	***whoever***	*whatever*	*whichever*	*wherever*	*whenever*	*however*	

Who and ***whoever*** have distinct nominative and accusative forms, illustrated for ***whoever*** in [18i–ii]; for the genitive of ***whoever*** see footnote 17.

The properties that distinguish ***who***, *what*, and *which* in fused relatives are the same as in interrogatives, so that the system is significantly different from that found in non-fused relatives:

[20]	FUSED RELATIVES or OPEN INTERROGATIVES	NON-FUSED RELATIVES
i PRONOUNS		
who	personal	personal
what	non-personal	—
which	—	non-personal
ii DETERMINATIVES		
what	non-selective	—
which	selective	(non-selective)

The gender contrast of personal vs non-personal is thus realised by ***who*** vs *what*, not ***who*** vs *which*, as in non-fused relatives. And *which* in fused relatives, as in interrogatives, is a determinative, contrasting with *what* as selective vs non-selective. In non-fused relatives determinative *which* is non-contrastively non-selective (and found only in the supplementary type). The same properties apply to the ·*ever* forms, as illustrated in:

[21] i *[Whoever finishes first] will win a prize.* [personal]
ii *[Whatever you can let us have] will be very much appreciated.* [non-personal]
iii *I'll use [whichever edition I can get hold of].* [selective]
iv *He appears to have lost [whatever interest he ever had in it].* [non-selective]

[16] There are also archaic variants of the ·*ever* series with ·*so*: *whosoever*, *whatsoever*, etc.

In [iii] it is a matter of selecting one edition from an identifiable set of editions, whereas there is no such feature in [iv]. Fused *which(ever)*, although a determinative, not a pronoun, can function as fused determiner-head, as in:

[22] [*Whichever of these two finished ahead of the other*] *would be the undisputed financial leader of the tour.*

Three of the simple items, ***who***, *which*, *how*, are virtually restricted to the particular use of the fused relative that we call the **free choice** construction; we will look at this first, and then turn to other uses, taking the ·*ever* and simple forms separately.

The free choice construction (*You can do whatever/what you want*)

[23] i *Invite* [*whoever/whomever/who/whom you like*].
ii *Liz can go* [*wherever/where she wants*].

In fused relatives like these the referent of the (overt or understood) subject of the matrix clause is given the freedom to choose: in [i] it is for you to decide who you invite, and in [ii] it is for Liz to choose where she goes. We have used 'free choice' to label one sense of *any*, and constructions with *any* + integrated relative are very close in meaning to the above: compare *Invite anyone you like* and *Liz can go anywhere she wants* (but see Ch. 5, §7.14, n. 32, for a slight difference).

There is no detectable difference in meaning between the ·*ever* and simple forms in this construction, and since ***who***, *which*, and *how* can hardly occur in other kinds of fused relative, it is plausible to see the ·*ever* as here omissible by virtue of being redundant: the "any whatever" meaning is entailed by the free choice and does not have to be explicitly expressed in the relative word. The verb in this construction belongs to a small class consisting primarily of *choose*, *like*, *please*, *want*, *wish*, and is interpreted as if it had a clausal complement – e.g. for [ii] "She can go wherever she wants to go". Note, then, that *Sack who you like* does not mean "Sack the persons that you like", but "Sack whoever you care to sack". However, the distinctive syntactic property of the construction – that of allowing certain simple forms which do not normally occur in fused relatives – is generally restricted to the case where the clausal complement is merely implicit, so that we have *Invite who you want*, but hardly ?*Invite who you want to invite*. Moreover, *please* does not in fact license clausal complements: *Go where you please*, but not, in Present-day English, **He pleased to go to Paris*. And with *like* the meaning differs aspectually from that of a construction with an infinitival complement. *I like to take the biggest portion*, for example, implies repeated taking (cf. Ch. 14, §5.6.1), whereas *Take which you like* does not. There are also constraints on the matrix clause. For example, the fused relative must follow the matrix verb: *I'll invite who you like* but not **Who you like I'll invite*.[17]

[17] The genitive forms *whosever* and (informal) *whoever's* are possible but rare in the free choice construction. Thus *Take whosever/whoever's you like* could serve as a response to the question *Whose bicycle shall I take?* The genitives are not admissible outside the free choice construction – cf. **They want to question whosever/whoever's dog was barking throughout the night* or **Whosever/Whoever's car is blocking my driveway must move it immediately*. The close grammatical association between the genitive determiner and the following head noun seems to suggest the anomalous meanings where it is the dog they want to question and the car that must move itself.

Further uses of the ·*ever* forms

[24] i *[Whoever told you that] can't have read the report carefully.*
ii *I'll accept [whatever price you suggest].*
iii *I'll go [wherever they tell me to go].*
iv *[Whenever I see her,] she's reading.*

The ·*ever* marks a phrase as non-referential: there is no reference to any particular person, price, place, or time in these examples. Such forms are found in several of the different kinds of non-referential phrases discussed in Ch. 5, §8.3. The bracketed phrase in [i] is a descriptive NP: we understand "the person *x* satisfying the description '*x* told you that'", with the implicature that I don't know who it was. The interpretations in [ii–iii] are non-specific: we are concerned with future acts of suggesting a price and telling me where to go. And in [iv] we have a multiple-situation-bound interpretation: it is a matter of a series of situations such that I see her at time *x* and she is reading at time *x*. The free choice construction shown in [23] is a special case of non-specificity, and the close paraphrase with *any* extends to the non-specifics in [24ii–iii]: cf. *any price you suggest; anywhere they tell me to go.* Often (as also with *any*) there is an implicature of "every, all": *I'll do whatever I can to help you.* This "every" interpretation is more clearly associated with the multiple-situation-bound case: [24iv] can be glossed as "Every time I see her, she's reading".

Use in coordination and supplementation

The ·*ever* series of fused relatives appear in the expected range of functions of NPs and temporal or locative PPs: subject in [24i], object in [24ii], and so on. Two common uses worth drawing attention to are as the final element in a coordination, or in a supplement:

[25] i *The central computer will simulate rape scenes or high-speed motor chases or [whatever stimulates their proletarian fancies].*
ii *There's always something different to do or eat or [whatever it happens to be].*
iii *They put on old coats or ducking jackets, [whichever they carried behind their saddle cantles].*

Reduction

The construction may be reduced to the relative phrase + an adjectival predicative complement (e.g. *possible, necessary, feasible*) or past participle:[18]

[26] i *They want to assist the impending assault in [whatever way possible].*
ii *She came to Atlanta, in the fall of 1888, to help [wherever needed].*

Further uses of the simple forms

As noted above, ***who***, *which*, and *how* hardly occur in fused relatives other than as alternants of the ·*ever* forms in the free choice construction. *Who* is found in archaisms preserved by quotation in the contemporary language, like *Who steals my purse steals trash* (from Shakespeare's *Othello*), but we cannot say, for example, **Who wrote this letter must have been mad*, or (with *which* as the relative word) **He always ordered which (one) was cheaper.* Examples with *how* are found but they are rare and quite marginal:

[18] In the coordination case we often find the ·*ever* word on its own: *Disturbed by this telephone call or whatever, she walked out into the night.* We take this to be a simple NP, though it might alternatively be regarded as a fused relative with something like "it was" understood.

%*We will not change how we use future contracts during the term of this Prospectus*; %*I don't like how it looks.*

What

The most frequent type of fused relative NP has *what* as fused head. It is found in non-referential NPs, like *whatever*, but it also readily occurs in referential NPs:

[27] i *I'll do* [*what I can*] *to help you.* [non-referential (non-specific)]
ii *They seem pleased with* [*what I gave them*]. [referential]

Determinative *what* (leaving aside the free choice construction) is restricted to non-count or plural NPs and has a paucal meaning that can be reinforced by *little* or *few* and is inconsistent with *much* or *many*:

[28] i *This will further erode* [*what* (*little*) *economic credibility the government has left*].
ii [*What* (*few*) *mistakes she had made*] *were all of a minor nature.*

The specifying *be* construction

Simple forms of the unbounded dependency words are commonly found within a matrix clause containing *be* in its specifying sense, and here it is by no means a straightforward matter to distinguish between the fused relative and subordinate interrogative constructions. Compare, for example:

[29] i *What caused the trouble was a faulty switch.* } [fused relative]
ii *A faulty switch was what caused the trouble.* }
iii *That's who I meant.* *That's not how to do it.* } [interrogative]
iv *He's not who she thinks he is.* }

Example [i] belongs to the pseudo-cleft construction (Ch. 16, §9.3), which is normally reversible, yielding in this case [ii]. There is no doubt that these involve fused relatives. Note, for example, that we can have subject–auxiliary inversion (*Was what caused the trouble a faulty switch?*) and that preposition fronting is completely impossible (*What I'm referring to is his intransigence*, but not **To what I'm referring is his intransigence*).

The examples in [iii–iv] are not reversible (cf. **How to do it is not that*, etc.), and there are grounds for saying that the underlined expressions are interrogative clauses even though they can be paraphrased by such NPs as *the person I meant*, *the way to do it*, *the person that she thinks he is.* Note first that *who* is found here, but not elsewhere in fused relatives, other than in the free choice construction. In particular, it cannot occur in the pseudo-cleft: **Who caused the trouble was your brother.*[19] Similarly, the infinitival of *how to do it* is not possible in fused relatives. Conversely, the one item that appears in relatives but not interrogatives, *while*, is not found here. *That was while we were in Paris*, for example, is quite different from [29iii]: it does not serve to identify the period during which we were in Paris but locates 'that' within this period.

A further difference between [29iii–iv] and the pseudo-cleft is that only the latter can incorporate an integrated relative (cf. the discussion of [10i]). Compare *What she left me that I treasure most is this little music-box* with **That's who she recommended who has the best qualifications* ("the person she recommended who has the best qualifications").

[19] *Why* (which has no counterpart in ·*ever*) appears freely in the interrogative construction, as in *This is why I'm leaving*, but is marginally possible in the pseudo-cleft: *Why I'm leaving is that/because there's no opportunity to use any initiative.* It does not occur elsewhere in fused relatives.

Finally, and most decisively, the specifying *be* construction of [29iii] allows preposition fronting: *That is precisely for what it was designed*; *That is exactly against what we should be fighting now.* This distinguishes them clearly from the pseudo-cleft construction and indicates that they must be interrogatives.

The likeness in meaning between the relative and interrogative constructions of [29] is consistent with the different syntactic analyses we have proposed. For [i] we have "The *x* such that *x* caused the trouble was a faulty switch": *a faulty switch* gives the value of the variable defined in the fused relative. And in *That's who I meant* the subject *that* gives the value of the variable in "He meant person *x*", the propositional content of the embedded question – i.e. it gives the answer to the question "Who did he mean?"[20]

The prepositions *when, where, while*

[30] i [<u>*When*</u> *it rains*] *they play in the garage.*
ii *We must put it* [<u>*where*</u> *no one will be able to see it*].
iii *They insisted on talking* [<u>*while*</u> *I was trying to get on with my work*].

These have paraphrases containing noun + integrated relative: *On occasions when it rains, they play in the garage*; *We must put it in a place where no one will be able to see it*; %*They insisted on talking during the time while I was trying to get on with my work.*

While differs from the other fused relative words in having no ·*ever* counterpart and in having no interrogative use.

Fused relatives or preposition + content clause?

An alternative analysis of examples like those in [30] is to treat *when, where,* and *while* as prepositions that take content clauses as complements – like *before, whereas, although,* etc. There are certainly some cases where the latter is the preferable analysis:

[31] i [<u>*When*</u> *they weren't home at six o'clock*] *I began to get worried.*
ii *Let me know* [*if and* <u>*when*</u> *you need any help*].
iii [<u>*Where*</u> *the British Empire was established with musket and gunboat,*] *America's empire has been achieved with the friendly persuasion of comedian and crooner.*
iv [<u>*While*</u> *I don't agree with what she says,*] *I accept her right to say it.*

In [i] we cannot gloss *when* as "at the time at which" since the temporal adjunct function within the subordinate clause is pre-empted by *at six o'clock*. In [ii] *when* is co-ordinated with *if*, which quite clearly takes a content clause as complement. Example [iii] illustrates a use of *where* that has been bleached of the basic locative meaning: it indicates contrast, like *whereas*. Moreover, it would conflict with the meaning to posit a location adjunct within the subordinate clause: the sentence does not say that America's empire was established in the same place as the British Empire. Example [iv] is similar: *while* here is used for contrast and its meaning does not involve temporal duration.

On the other hand, we find places where a fused relative analysis is required. The clearest cases are with *where* and *while* in such examples as:

[32] i *I put the key* [<u>*where*</u> *I always put it*], *in the top drawer.*
ii *It was fun* [<u>*while*</u> *it lasted*].

[20] Another case where an interrogative has an interpretation similar to that of a relative construction is illustrated in *There's an article in the weekend magazine on* <u>*how to grow orchids*</u>. We might instead say *on* <u>*the way to grow orchids*</u>, with an NP containing a relative clause. But *how to grow orchids* must be an interrogative, by virtue of the *how* and the infinitival. And again the meaning in fact fits the interrogative analysis: the magazine article is concerned with answering the question "How to grow orchids?"

Here the subordinate clauses must contain complements of goal and duration respectively because of the complementation requirements of the verbs *put* and *last*. Thus *I always put it* and *it lasted* are not themselves structurally complete, and could not occur as complement of a preposition. They must have a gap in final position that is linked to *where* and *while*: *where*$_i$ *I always put it* __$_i$ and *while*$_i$ *it lasted* __$_i$. In the light of examples [31–32], we conclude that both the fused relative and the preposition + content clause analyses are needed; some examples require just one, whereas others are consistent with either.

7 Unbounded dependency constructions

Relative clauses belong to a larger class of constructions known as **unbounded dependency constructions**. In this final section of the chapter we examine the properties of this more general category of constructions.

7.1 Definition and taxonomy

What is meant by an unbounded dependency construction can be seen by considering a set of examples such as those in [1]:

[1] i *This is the book*$_i$ [*which*$_i$ [*she recommended* __$_i$]].
ii *This is the book*$_i$ [*which*$_i$ [*I think she recommended* __$_i$]].
iii *This is the book*$_i$ [*which*$_i$ [*I think you said she recommended* __$_i$]].

The outer brackets enclose the relative clause, while the inner ones enclose the nucleus. The nucleus contains a gap in the position of object of the verb *recommended*, and this gap is linked to the relative phrase *which* in prenuclear position. The relation between the gap and *which* is comparable to that between an anaphoric pronoun and its antecedent – between, for example, *which* and its antecedent *book*. *Which* derives its interpretation from *book*, and the gap derives its interpretation from *which*: a component of the meaning of all three examples is "she recommended *x*", where *x* is some book. We will say, therefore, that the gap is anaphorically linked to *which*, i.e. that *which* is antecedent for the gap.

This relation between the gap and *which* is a **dependency** relation. Semantically, the gap derives its interpretation from *which*, as we have just seen. And syntactically *which* requires an associated gap: the object of *recommended* cannot be realised by an ordinary NP – compare **This is the book which she recommended 'War and Peace'*.[21] The dependency relation between the gap and its antecedent is **unbounded** in the sense that there is no upper bound, or limit, on how deeply embedded within the relative clause the gap may be. In [1i] the gap is object of the topmost verb in the relative clause. In [1ii] it is object of the verb that heads a clause embedded as complement to the topmost verb (*think*). In [1iii] there are two layers of clause embedding: the *recommend* clause is complement in the *say* clause, and the latter is complement in the *think* clause. And there is no grammatical limit on how many such layers of embedding there can be. Adding a third might give, for example, *the book which I think you said Kim persuaded her to*

[21] The dependency relation between a gap and its antecedent is not to be equated with that of a dependent to a head. Dependent and head are functions within a syntactic construction, and the gap is not a dependent of *which* in this sense. The gap and *which* are related anaphorically, not as functions within a construction.

recommend. And further layers still can be added without loss of grammaticality even though they may result in stylistically undesirable complexity.

A second unbounded dependency construction is the open interrogative, illustrated in:

[2] i *What*$_i$ [*does he want* __$_i$]?
ii *What*$_i$ [*do you think he wants* __$_i$]?
iii *What*$_i$ [*do you think she said he wants* __$_i$]?

The gap represents the object of *want* and is anaphorically linked to the interrogative phrase *what* in prenuclear position. This relationship indicates that the question concerns the object of *want*: the meaning contains the component "he wants *x*", and answers to the question supply a value for the variable *x*. Again, the dependency relation between the gap and the interrogative phrase is unbounded: the examples show the *want* clause progressively more deeply embedded, and again there is no grammatical limit as to how many layers of embedding are permitted.

In the light of these examples we may define an unbounded dependency construction as follows:

[3] An unbounded dependency construction is one which sanctions within it an anaphoric gap, with no upper bound on how deeply embedded the gap may be.

Constructions with and without unbounded dependency words

The two constructions considered so far, *wh* relatives and open interrogatives, have it in common that they are marked by the presence of a distinctive type of word functioning as or within the prenuclear element. *Which* in [1] is a relative word and *what* in [2] is an interrogative word. As we have seen, there is a large degree of overlap between relative and interrogative words, and we refer to them jointly as **unbounded dependency words**, i.e. words that are markers of an unbounded dependency construction.[22] Exclamative *what* and *how* also belong in this category, for exclamatives are also an unbounded dependency construction, as is evident from such examples as:

[4] i <u>*What a disaster*</u>$_i$ [*it was* __$_i$]!
ii <u>*What a disaster*</u>$_i$ [*it turned out to be* __$_i$]!
iii <u>*What a disaster*</u>$_i$ [*it seems to have turned out to be* __$_i$]!

Not all unbounded dependency constructions are of this kind, however. In preposing, the prenuclear position is filled by a phrase or clause that can also occur in a canonical clause construction. Compare:

[5] i <u>*The other chapters*</u>$_i$ [*she wrote* __$_i$ *herself*].
ii <u>*The other chapters*</u>$_i$ [*I think she wrote* __$_i$ *herself*].
iii <u>*The other chapters*</u>$_i$ [*I think she said she wrote* __$_i$ *herself*].

The other chapters is an ordinary NP, functioning as object in the canonical *She wrote the other chapters herself*, but in [5] it is in an unbounded dependency relation with a gap.

These examples illustrate the main preposing construction, with the preposed element in prenuclear position within a clause. It is also possible for the preposed element to

[22] These words are often referred to as '*wh* words'; the category, however, is obviously not unique to English, and we prefer to use a more general term.

occupy prenuclear position within a PP (see Ch. 7, §4.4):

[6] i [*Stupid*$_i$ [*though he is* _$_i$],] *he saw through their little game.*
ii [*Stupid*$_i$ [*though you no doubt think he is* _$_i$]], *he saw through their little game.*
iii [*Stupid*$_i$ [*though I expect you think he is* _$_i$]], *he saw through their little game.*

The outer brackets enclose the PP, and the inner ones its nucleus, containing a gap anaphorically linked to the preposed AdjP *stupid.*

Constructions with prenuclear and external antecedents

We have now introduced five unbounded dependency constructions: *wh* relatives, open interrogatives, exclamatives, preposing in clause structure, and preposing in PP structure. In all of these, the antecedent for the gap is located in prenuclear position. There are also unbounded dependency constructions where the antecedent is located outside the clause altogether. One clear case is that of non-*wh* relatives:

[7] i *This is the book*$_i$ [*she recommended* _$_i$].
ii *This is the book*$_i$ [*I think she recommended* _$_i$].
iii *This is the book*$_i$ [*I think you said she recommended* _$_i$].

These are just like the *wh* relatives in [1] above, except that they contain no relative phrase in prenuclear position. The gap is thus related directly to the nominal *book*, rather than indirectly, via the relative pronoun *which.* This construction still satisfies the definition given in [3]: the relative clause can contain an anaphoric gap that is embedded indefinitely deeply within it.

Another construction of this type is the comparative clause:

[8] i *Kim made more mistakes*$_i$ *than* [*Pat made* _$_i$].
ii *Kim made more mistakes*$_i$ *than* [*I think Pat made* _$_i$].
iii *Kim made more mistakes*$_i$ *than* [*I think you said Pat made* _$_i$].

Comparative clauses function as complement to a preposition (*than, as,* or *like*); the gap is within the comparative clause while the antecedent is outside. Comparative clauses, however, differ in significant ways from other unbounded dependency constructions with respect to the kind of gap allowed and the way it is interpreted: we examine them in detail in Ch. 13, §2, and will pay no further attention to them here.

Major and minor unbounded dependency constructions

The final distinction to be made contrasts the major constructions listed above with minor ones, such as hollow clauses:

[9] i *<u>The machine</u>*$_i$ *was too big* [*to take* _$_i$ *home*].
ii *<u>The machine</u>*$_i$ *was too big* [*to ever want to take* _$_i$ *home*].
iii *<u>The machine</u>*$_i$ *was too big* [*to imagine ever wanting to take* _$_i$ *home*].

The gap here is object of *take*, and has an external antecedent, *the machine.* As before, the gap can be embedded indefinitely deeply within the hollow clause. However, examples like [ii–iii] with respectively one and two levels of clause embedding are quite rare. Although there is in principle no limit to the depth of embedding this construction in practice allows deeply embedded gaps much less readily than those discussed above and for this reason can be regarded as a relatively minor member of the set of unbounded dependency constructions. Moreover, when the gap is located within a clause that is embedded within the hollow clause, the embedded clause must be non-finite, like the hollow clause itself. Compare:

[10] a. *The problem$_i$ is too difficult* [*to expect a ten-year-old to be able to solve* _$_i$].
b. **The problem$_i$ is too difficult* [*to expect* [*that a ten-year-old could solve* _$_i$]].

While [i] is fully acceptable, [ii] is ungrammatical. This is because the hollow clause (enclosed within the outer pair of brackets) contains a finite clause within it (enclosed within the inner brackets), and the gap is inside this finite clause. The same constraint applies to infinitival relatives and infinitival open interrogatives, and we accordingly include these too in the set of minor unbounded dependency constructions.

Summary taxonomy

Unbounded dependency constructions may be classified in terms of the above distinctions as follows:

[11]		
I	MAJOR CONSTRUCTIONS	
IA	**Prenuclear antecedent**	
IAi	Contain unbounded dependency word	*wh* relatives (finite), open interrogatives (finite), exclamatives
IAii	No such word	preposing in clause, preposing in concessive PP
IB	**External antecedent**	non-*wh* relatives (finite), comparatives
II	MINOR CONSTRUCTIONS	
IIA	**Prenuclear antecedent**	infinitival *wh* relatives and open interrogatives
IIB	**External antecedent**	hollow clauses, infinitival non-*wh* relatives

7.2 Gaps and antecedents

The syntactic functions of gaps

Gaps occur in certain functional positions. In most of the examples used in §7.1 the gap represents the object of a verb. This is not of course the only possibility, but there are severe constraints on what functions can be realised by a gap. One general constraint is stated summarily in [12]:

[12] A gap in an unbounded dependency construction can function only as either:
(a) a post-head dependent; or
(b) subject in clause structure (immediate or embedded).

Compare, for example, the following open interrogatives:

[13]		
i	*What$_i$* [*did you buy* _$_i$]?	[complement of verb]
ii	*What$_i$* [*are you referring* [*to* _$_i$]]?	[complement of preposition]
iii	*Where$_i$* [*did you see them* _$_i$]?	[adjunct of verb]
iv	*Who$_i$* [*do you think* [_$_i$ *was responsible*]]?	[subject of clause]
v	**Whose$_i$* [*did you borrow* [_$_i$ *car*]]?	[subject-determiner in NP]
vi	**How many$_i$* [*did they receive* [_$_i$ *applications*]]?	[determiner]
vii	**How serious$_i$* [*will it be* [_$_i$ *a problem*]]?	[pre-head modifier in NP]
viii	**Who$_i$* [*have they shortlisted* [_$_i$ *and Kim*]]?	[coordinate]

The inner brackets in [ii] and [iv–viii] enclose the constituent within which the gap is located: a PP in [ii], content clause in [iv], an NP in [v–vii], and an NP-coordination in [viii]. Examples [v–viii] are ungrammatical because the gap does not have one of the functions permitted by rule [12]. They can be corrected by making the gap conform to [12]:

[14] i *Whose car$_i$ did you borrow __$_i$?*
ii *How many applications$_i$ did they receive __$_i$?*
iii *How serious a problem$_i$ will it be __$_i$?*
iv *Who$_i$ have they shortlisted __$_i$ in addition to Kim?*
[complement of verb]

In addition to rule [12], certain more specific conditions apply:

Gaps not normally allowed in indirect object function

As we observed in Ch. 4, §4.3, one of the main syntactic differences between indirect and direct objects is that gaps are more or less excluded from the former function. The qualification 'more or less' is needed because there is some variation with respect to acceptability judgements on clauses with indirect object gaps, but for the most part there is a clear difference between the acceptability of direct and indirect object gaps. Compare:

[15] i a. *This is the CD$_i$ [she got me __$_i$ last Christmas].*
b. **He's the one$_i$ [she got __$_i$ that CD last Christmas].*
ii a. *The copies [he sold me __$_i$] were defective.*
b. **The person$_i$ [he sold __$_i$ them] seemed satisfied.*
iii a. *How much$_i$ do you owe them __$_i$?*
b. *?How many people$_i$ do you owe __$_i$ more than $50?*

In each pair the gap is direct object in [a], indirect object in [b]. Most verbs that take indirect objects also occur in an alternative construction with direct object + PP complement, and this construction can be used to express the meanings of the [b] examples: *He's the one$_i$ she got that CD for __$_i$ last Christmas*, and so on. (The prepositional construction will also often be preferred over a ditransitive one with indirect object + gap in direct object function – e.g. *the story$_i$ that he was reading __$_i$ to his children*, over *the story$_i$ that he was reading his children __$_i$*.)

Gaps in subject function

As we saw in §3.4, it is necessary to distinguish between an **immediate subject** (i.e. the subject of the topmost verb in the construction) and an **embedded subject** (the subject of a clause embedded within the unbounded dependency construction).

Embedded subject gaps are permitted only in bare content clauses, i.e. declaratives without the subordinator *that* (cf. Ch. 11, §3.1). Compare:

[16] i *He's the man$_i$ [they think [__$_i$ attacked her]].* [bare declarative]
ii **He's the man$_i$ [they think [that __$_i$ attacked her]].* [expanded declarative]
iii **He's the man$_i$ [they wonder [whether __$_i$ attacked her]].* [closed interrogative]

With immediate subjects we can have a gap in Type IB constructions (with external antecedent), but not in Type IA (with prenuclear antecedent). Compare:

[17] i *This is the copy*$_i$ [*that* [__$_i$ *is defective*]]. [immediate subject gap]
ii *This is the copy*$_i$ [*which*$_i$ *is defective*].
iii *Who signed the letter?* } [no gap]

In [i] *that* is the subordinator in prenuclear position, and the subject in the nucleus is realised by a gap anaphorically linked to the antecedent *copy*: this is a Type IB construction, with the antecedent of the gap external to the relative clause. (As we noted in §3.5.5, the subordinator *that* is generally not omissible when the gap is in immediate subject function.) In [ii–iii], by contrast, the subjects are realised not by a gap but by relative *which* and interrogative *who*: in the absence of convincing evidence to the contrary, we take the structure to be the same as that of the canonical clauses *This copy is defective* and *Kim signed the letter.* Note, moreover, that the preposing construction does not allow preposing of an immediate subject. Compare:

[18] i *The other chapters*$_i$ [*she wrote* __$_i$ *herself*]. [preposing of object]
ii *She wrote the other chapters herself.* [no preposing]

In [i] we have a gap in object position, but there is no gap, no preposing in [ii], where *she* is in its canonical position.

Hollow clauses

In the hollow clause construction the gap can only be complement of a verb or preposition: see Ch. 14, §6.

Function of the antecedent

In constructions with an external antecedent, the function of the antecedent is independent of that of the gap. Compare:

[19] i a. *Have you seen the book*$_i$ [*I got* __$_i$ *from the library*]?
b. *Where's the book*$_i$ [*I got* __$_i$ *from the library*]?
ii a. *Their proposal*$_i$ *was hard* [*to accept* __$_i$].
b. *We found their proposal*$_i$ *hard* [*to accept* __$_i$].

In [i] the bracketed clauses are non-*wh* relatives with the gap in object function. The antecedent is the nominal *book*, which is head of an NP, and this NP can occur in any NP function: it is, for example, object in [ia], subject in [ib]. In [ii] we have hollow clauses with the gap in object function. The antecedent is the NP *their proposal*, and again the function of this NP does not need to match that of the gap: in [iia] it is subject, while in [iib] it is object.

Prenuclear antecedents inherit function of the gap

The situation with antecedents in prenuclear position is quite different. These elements are located within the unbounded dependency construction itself, and thus do not have a function outside it. Because they fall outside the nucleus the only function that can be assigned directly to them is that of prenuclear dependent. This is shown in the following tree diagram for the preposing construction *The others I know are genuine*, corresponding to canonical *I know the others are genuine.*

[20]

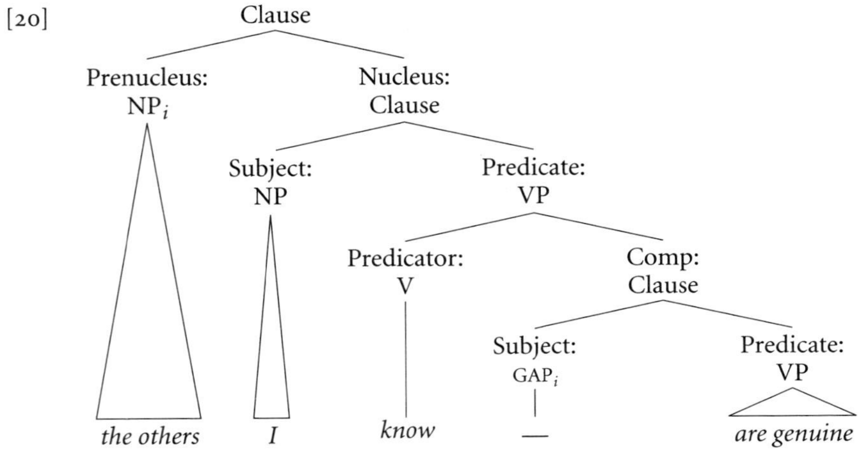

We could not label *the others* as subject, for it clearly does not stand in the subject relation to the clause of which it is an immediate constituent. Nevertheless, it is understood as subject of *are genuine*, just as it is in the canonical counterpart *I know the others are genuine.* Notice, moreover, that the verb form *are* agrees with *the others* – again, just as it does in *I know the others are genuine.* We will regard these prenuclear antecedents, therefore, as taking on the function of the associated gap. In a secondary, or derivative, sense, that is to say, *the others* is subject of the content clause whose head (predicate) is *are genuine.* This information is retrievable from the tree diagram as it stands: the secondary function of *the others* is that of the co-indexed gap. Similarly in *The others$_i$ I haven't yet read __$_i$* we will say that *the others* is, in this derivative sense, object of *read.*

The same applies with constructions where the prenuclear element consists of or contains an unbounded dependency word, as in:

[21] i *the letters$_i$ [which$_i$ [he says she wrote __$_i$]]*
ii *Who$_i$ [do you think __$_i$ wrote the letter]?*

We will say that *which* in [i] is object of *wrote* and *who* in [ii] is subject of *wrote.* This is of course what is said in traditional grammar too: our concern here has been to show how that kind of statement can be reconciled with the tree diagrams that are used to represent syntactic structure in this book. *Which* and *who* are not labelled object and subject directly, but are treated as inheriting this function from the gap with which they are co-indexed.

Match between antecedent and potential realisations of the gap function

The anaphoric relation between the gap and the antecedent means that well-formedness is subject to the following condition:

[22] The syntactic and semantic properties of the antecedent must normally match those of expressions which in other constructions can occur as overt realisations of the gap function.

In the simplest cases, the antecedent expression itself can elsewhere realise the function of the gap. Illustrations of this situation are provided by preposing and hollow clauses:

[23] i a. *To Kim$_i$ [they gave a bicycle __$_i$].* [preposing]
b. *They gave a bicycle to Kim.*
ii a. *Kim$_i$ is very hard [to please __$_i$].* [hollow]
b. *It is very hard to please Kim.*

In [ia] the PP *to Kim* is antecedent for the complement gap in the nucleus, and this PP can itself realise the same complement function, as shown in [ib]. Similarly in [ii]: the gap in [a] is object of *please* and the antecedent for this gap, the NP *Kim*, can elsewhere fill that function, as in [b]. These examples may be contrasted with the following:

[24] i **To Kim$_i$ [they bought a bicycle __$_i$].*
ii **That he comes home so late$_i$ is very hard [to enjoy __$_i$].*

In [i] the preposed complement contains the wrong preposition: we need *for Kim*, to match *They bought a bicycle for Kim.* In [ii] the antecedent is a content clause but *enjoy* does not license a complement of that kind: we need an NP, such as *his novels*, to match *I enjoy his novels.*

Compare, again, the following examples of the *it*-cleft construction:

[25] i *It was that jar$_i$ [that she says she put the key in __$_i$].* [NP ~ NP]
ii *It was in that jar$_i$ [that she says she put the key __$_i$].* [PP ~ PP]
iii **It was that jar$_i$ [that she says she put the key __$_i$].* [NP ~ PP]
iv **It was in that jar$_i$ [that she says she put the key in __$_i$].* [PP ~ NP]

In [i] the antecedent is an NP, and this is the category needed to realise the gap function, object of the preposition *in*. In [ii] the antecedent is a PP, which can realise the function of goal complement in the *put* clause, as in *She put the key in that jar.* The other examples are ungrammatical because the antecedent fails to meet the requirements of the gap function: compare **She put the key that jar* and **She put the key in in that jar.*

Condition [22] is formulated in terms of matching rather than identity: there is no requirement that the antecedent expression itself should be able to realise the gap function. Three very general cases where it can't are illustrated in:

[26] i *Every book$_i$ [we have consulted __$_i$] ignores this problem.* [non-*wh relative*]
ii *That's not the reason [why$_i$ [he did it __$_i$]].* [*wh* relative]
iii *__$_i$ Don't be so hard [to please __$_i$].* [hollow clause]

The bracketed clause in [i] is a non-*wh* relative of the integrated type. As explained in §4.1, the antecedent is the nominal *book*, not the sequence *every book*: the sentence doesn't say that we have consulted every book. A nominal as such cannot realise the gap function, which requires a full NP: **We have consulted book.* The antecedent can nevertheless be said to satisfy the matching requirement in that it can realise the gap function if an appropriate determiner is added to make it into a full NP: *We have read a book.*

The outer brackets in [26ii] enclose a *wh* relative clause, and here the relative phrase is required to occupy initial position, so relative *why* could not occur within the nucleus as a realisation of the gap function. The matching requirement is satisfied, however, in that *why* is a reason expression and non-relative expressions of that kind can realise the gap function, as in *He did it for that reason*. The same applies, of course, to other relative expressions.

In [26iii] the antecedent for the gap in the hollow clause is not overtly expressed. But it is understood, by virtue of being subject of an imperative, as *you*, and this can realise the gap function: *It is hard to please you*. In *Pat*$_i$ *wants* __$_i$ *to be hard* [*to please* __$_i$], the antecedent (the subject of the *be* clause) is likewise missing, but this time it is recoverable from the superordinate *want* clause.

Mismatches

There are a number of constructions where the matching requirement [22] is not strictly observed. They are illustrated in [27], but as all are dealt with elsewhere in the book only a summary commentary is needed at this point.

[27] i *Who*$_i$ [*did you give it to* __$_i$]?
ii %*He always chose those* [*whom*$_i$ [*he thought* __$_i$ *were most vulnerable*]].
iii [*What*$_i$ [*I'm hoping* __$_i$]] *is that nobody will notice my absence.*
iv *What on earth*$_i$ [*do you want* __$_i$]?
v *That no one realised such action might be illegal*$_i$ [*I find* __$_i$ *surprising*].
vi *That they'll give him a second chance*$_i$ [*I wouldn't gamble on* __$_i$].
vii [*Brilliant advocate*$_i$ [*though she is* __$_i$],] *she's unlikely to win this case.*

Examples [27i–ii] show that the inflectional case of prenuclear interrogative and relative ***who*** does not always match that of pronouns in the position of the gap. Compare the nominative *who* of [i], with accusative *them* in *You gave it to them*, and the accusative *whom* of [ii] with the nominative required in *He thought they were most vulnerable* (see §3.4 above, and Ch. 5, §16.2.3).[23]

Fused relative *what* in [27iii] is an NP, but *hope* does not license an NP complement: compare **I was hoping some respite*. *Hope* takes declarative content clause complements, and the presence of such a content clause following the fused relative is apparently necessary for *what* to be admissible: compare **What I was hoping was a little peace and quiet*. The fused relative in [iii] is subject within a pseudo-cleft clause (see Ch. 16, §9.3), and the same extended use of *what* is found with a few other verbs in pseudo-clefts. Compare, for example, *What we decided was to interview all the candidates*. Although *decide* does license NP complements, they don't stand in the same semantic relation to it as *what* does here – compare *The weather will decide the outcome*, but not #*We decided an interview*.

Example [27iv] is an open interrogative. Unlike relative phrases, interrogative phrases are not in general required to occupy initial position – compare *And so you want what, exactly?* (cf. Ch. 10, §4.5). Interrogative phrases containing emotive modifiers such as *on earth*, *the hell*, *ever*, etc., however, can only occur initially, hence not in the position of the gap in [iv]: **And so you want what on earth?*

The remaining examples in [27] are preposings. In [v] the function of the gap is that of object in a complex-transitive clause. The preposed content clause could not

[23] In constructions with an external antecedent the case of the antecedent will be determined by its function within its own clause, which is independent of the function of the gap. Compare *He*$_i$ *is hard to get on with* __$_i$ (where ***he*** is subject and hence nominative) and *I find him*$_i$ *hard to get on with* __$_i$ (where ***he*** is object and hence accusative). In [27i–ii], however, ***who*** is in prenuclear position, so its case does depend on the function of the associated gap.

occur in post-verbal position: instead of **I find that no one realised such action might be illegal surprising* we need the version with extraposition *I find it surprising that no one realised such action might be illegal.* In [vi] the preposed content clause could not replace the gap because the latter is complement of the preposition *on*, which does not license complements of this category: it requires an NP (see Ch. 11, §8.3, for further discussion of this very marginal type). Finally, [vii] has preposing of a predicative complement NP from within a concessive PP. Here there is a more systematic departure from the form found in non-preposed position, with the latter requiring an indefinite article: *Although she is a brilliant advocate, she's unlikely to win this case.*

Combinations of unbounded dependency constructions

It is possible for certain unbounded dependency constructions to combine in such a way that the gap in one is the antecedent in the other. In the following, for example, an open interrogative is combined with a cleft relative:

[28] i *Which jar*$_i$ *was it* __$_i$ [*that she says she put the key in* __$_i$]?
ii *In which jar*$_i$ *was it* __$_i$ [*that she says she put the key* __$_i$]?

These are the open interrogative counterparts of the declarative clefts given in [25i–ii] above. The first gap has the interrogative phrase as its antecedent, and itself serves as antecedent for the second gap. In both examples the matching requirement is satisfied. In [i] the gap in the *put* clause is object of *in*, and hence requires an NP antecedent: this requirement is met because the gap in the *be* clause has the overt NP *which jar* as its antecedent. Similarly in [ii] the gap in the *put* clause requires a PP antecedent, and this requirement is satisfied because the gap in the *be* clause has an overt PP as its antecedent. Interrogative counterparts of the ungrammatical [25iii–iv] will thus be ungrammatical too:

[29] i **Which jar*$_i$ *was it* __$_i$ [*that she says she put the key* __$_i$]?
ii **In which jar*$_i$ *was it* __$_i$ [*that she says she put the key in* __$_i$]?

But there is an additional constraint, illustrated in:

[30] **Which jar*$_i$ *was it* [*in* __$_i$]$_j$ [*that she says she put the key* __$_j$]?

The antecedent for the gap in the *put* clause is the PP headed by *in*: we have enclosed it in square brackets and co-indexed it with the gap in the relative clause. This PP contains a gap with the interrogative phrase as antecedent. What makes the sentence ungrammatical is that the antecedent for one gap contains another gap within it, so we have two gaps with different interpretations – "which jar" and "in which jar". Thus while the antecedent for a gap may itself be a gap, as in [28], it cannot merely contain a gap.

7.3 Location of gaps

We have said that there is no upper bound on how deeply a gap may be embedded within an unbounded dependency construction. This does not mean, however, that there are no constraints on whereabouts in the construction the gap may occur. Compare, for example:

[31] i *I told her* [*what*$_i$ [*you insisted that we need* __$_i$]].
ii **I told her* [*what*$_i$ [*that we need* __$_i$ *is agreed*]].

While [i] is acceptable, [ii] is completely unacceptable. And the cause of the unacceptability is clearly grammatical, not semantic. The meaning of [i] can be given as "I told her the value of *x* in the proposition 'You insisted that we need *x*'", and the intended meaning of [ii] is similarly "I told her the value of *x* in the proposition 'That we need *x* is agreed'". This meaning can in fact be expressed by means of the extraposition construction: *I told her what it is agreed that we need.*

The structure for the interrogative clause in [31i] is as follows:

[32]

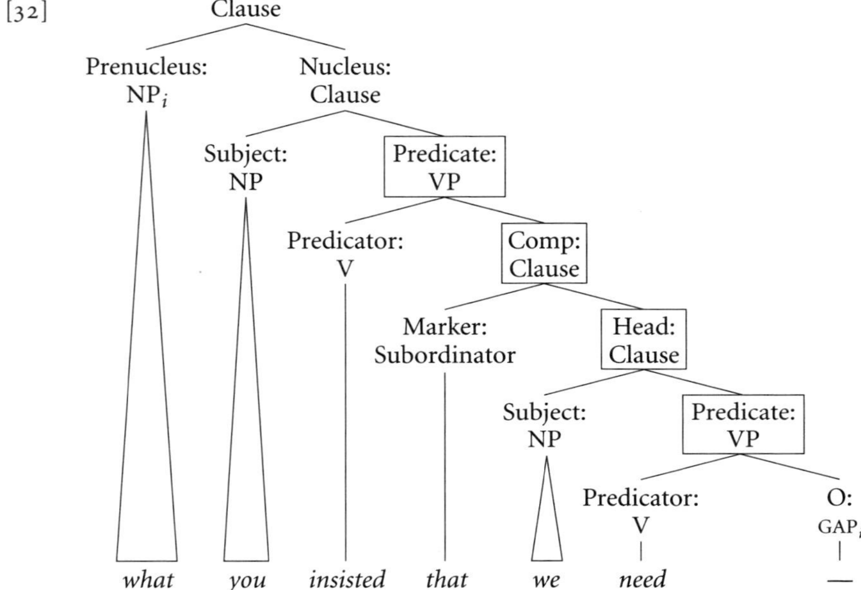

The boxes enclose points in the tree that lie on the path from the top down to the gap, and grammaticality depends on the function and category labels that occur on this path. The deviance of [31ii] is due to the fact that the path to the gap passes through a constituent with the form of a clause and the function of subject: *that we need* __ is subject of *is agreed.* Note that we are concerned here with the path to the gap, not with the gap itself. We noted in §7.2 that (under restricted conditions) the gap can be subject, as in *Who*$_i$ [*do you think* __$_i$ *wrote the letter*]?: what is not admissible is for the gap to be part of a larger clause that is functioning as subject.[24]

In this section we will review a range of constituent types, examining whether or not they may occur on the path leading to the gap. Before we start, however, two general points should be made. In the first place, while the status of [31i–ii] as respectively well-formed and deviant is quite clear, there are many intermediate cases where the status is uncertain. Secondly, while we can confidently say that [31ii] violates a rule of grammar, the acceptability of examples may also be affected by semantic considerations. Compare:

[33] i *That's a subject*$_i$ [*that Steven Jay Gould wrote a book about* __$_i$].
ii #*That's a subject*$_i$ [*that Steven Jay Gould despises a book about* __$_i$].

[24]Constituent types that do not allow gaps within them are often called 'islands'.

These have the same grammatical structure, differing only lexically, with [i] having *write* and [ii] *despise* as the verb of the relative clause. But they differ significantly in acceptability: [i] is clearly acceptable, while [ii] is very unnatural. This difference has a semantic explanation. The relative clause combines with the antecedent *subject* to form a nominal that denotes a class of subjects. In the case of [i], this class has some coherence: to say of some subject that Steven Jay Gould wrote a book about it points to a selection of significant topics in areas like evolutionary biology, geology, palaeontology, etc. The class denoted by the nominal in [ii] has no such coherence. What would have to be true of a subject in order for it to be an *x* such that Steven Jay Gould despises a book about *x*? Someone, at some time in history, has to have written a book about *x* that Gould despises for some reason (it is badly written, or was plagiarised, or has annoyingly pretentious page design, or is full of mistakes, or whatever reason there might be). The subject in question could be shoes, ships, sealing wax, cabbages, or kings. In other words, there is no sensible characterisation of a class of subjects in [ii] at all, and as a result the example seems anomalous.

Let us turn now to the review of constituent types. In the examples, we use one pair of square brackets to delimit the constituent in question, and another to delimit the unbounded dependency construction if it is less than the whole sentence. Antecedents are underlined if they contain more than the one word that carries the subscript index.

(a) VP in predicate function

[34] i *Most of the criticisms$_i$ he [accepted __$_i$ with good grace].*
ii *I don't know [where$_i$ he [found it __$_i$]].*
iii *It was to her cousin$_i$ [that she [sold the business __$_i$]].*

VP predicates readily allow gaps within them. In [i] we have a preposing with a direct object gap, in [ii] an open interrogative with an adjunct gap, and in [iii] a cleft relative with a complement gap linked to a PP antecedent.

(b) AdjPs in predicative complement function

[35] i *Whether it's ethical$_i$ I'm not [so certain __$_i$].*
ii *That's the only crime [of which$_i$ they could find him [guilty __$_i$]].*

Example [i] has preposing of a clausal complement of *certain*. In [ii] the relative PP *of which* is antecedent to the gap functioning as complement of *guilty*.

(c) Declarative content clause in post-head complement function

[36] i *It was here$_i$ [she said [she found the knife __$_i$]].*
ii *I don't know [who$_i$ he thinks [he is __$_i$]].*
iii *Here's a book$_i$ [I think [__$_i$ might help us]].*
iv *He's the only one$_i$ [that I'm [sure she told __$_i$]].*

Gaps are readily allowed here: an adjunct in [i], predicative complement in [ii], subject in [iii], object in [iv]. The adjunct case has the potential for ambiguity. In the interpretation indicated by the inner brackets in [i], the gap belongs in the *find* clause: it is a matter of where she found the knife. The gap could also be in the *say* clause: *It was here$_i$ [she said [she found the knife] __$_i$].* In this interpretation it is a matter of where her utterance took place.

(See Ch. 10, §7.12, for discussion of such ambiguities in open interrogatives.) In [iv] the content clause is complement of an adjective rather than a verb.

(d) Closed interrogative clause in complement function

[37] i *There are several books$_i$ here [that I'm not sure [if you've read __$_i$]].*
ii *The actor had to be careful with the amount of venom poured into a character [who$_i$ in the end we don't know [whether to hate or pity __$_i$]].*
iii $^?$*The woman boarding in front of me was carrying a huge sports bag$_i$ [that the cabin crew wondered [whether there was going to be enough room for __$_i$]].*

Interrogative content clauses accept gaps much less readily than declaratives. Examples are rarely found in published material, though [ii] is an attested example from a weekly magazine. Acceptability seems to diminish quite rapidly with increasing complexity, with [iii], for example, quite questionable in comparison with [i–ii].

(e) Open interrogative clauses in complement function

[38] i *These are the only dishes$_i$ [that they taught me [how$_j$ to cook __$_i$ __$_j$]].*
ii *The man in the dock was a hardened criminal$_i$ [that the judge later admitted he didn't know [why$_j$ he had ever released __$_i$ __$_j$ in the first place]].*
iii $^?$*Here's another photograph$_i$ [that I can't remember [where$_j$ we took __$_i$ __$_j$]].*
iv **It's Max$_i$ [that I'd like to know [who introduced __$_i$ to your sister]].*

Gaps are permitted in open interrogatives only under quite restrictive conditions. Example [i], with *how* as the questioned element (and with a very short interrogative clause), seems completely acceptable. Example [ii], with *why*, is more or less acceptable in speech but this type would not normally occur in published material. Example [iii], with *where*, is more questionable, whereas [iv] can be regarded as ungrammatical, and the same will apply to other examples where the interrogative phrase is in complement function. It will be noted that in [i–iii] there are two gaps, one associated with the open interrogative construction (and having the index *j*), the other with the relative clause in which the interrogative is embedded: compare the canonical construction *I cook spaghetti bolognese this way.*[25]

(f) Non-finite clause in post-head complement function

[39] i *It's you$_i$ [I want [to marry __$_i$]].*
ii *What$_i$ did you [tell the police __$_i$]]?*
iii *I wonder [what$_i$ they intend [doing __$_i$ about it]].*
iv *They are the ones [to whom$_i$ he had the weapons [sent __$_i$]].*

These illustrate all four types of non-finite clause: respectively *to*-infinitival, bare infinitival, gerund-participial, and past-participial. This category includes the non-finite complements of auxiliary verbs, as in [ii] or *What$_i$ are you [reading __$_i$]?*, etc.

[25] In **There are words or terms$_i$ in this Guide [that you may not be sure [what$_j$ they$_i$ really mean __$_j$]]* (taken with minor and irrelevant modification from an Australian government publication) the personal pronoun *they* is used instead of a gap linked to the antecedent *words or terms*. Pronouns used in place of a gap in relative clauses are known as 'resumptive pronouns'. In some languages they represent a regular feature of relative clause formation, but in English they are ungrammatical, as evident from their inadmissibility in simpler constructions like **words or terms [which$_i$ you may not understand them$_i$]*.

(g) PP

[40] i Some of us$_i$ he wouldn't even speak [to _$_i$].
ii This is the knife$_i$ [you should cut the tomatoes [with _$_i$]].
iii ?What day$_i$ will you not be able to return the book [until _$_i$]?
iv *Here is a list of the objections$_i$ [that they went ahead [despite _$_i$]].
v *You pay me$_i$, I'll do it [if _$_i$].
vi *It was this proposal$_i$ [that they sacked me [because I criticised _$_i$]].

In [i–iv] the gap is complement of a preposition and has an NP as antecedent. This results in what is called a stranded preposition – a transitive preposition with the complement missing but understood. It is a very common construction except in formal style: see Ch. 7, §4.1. Stranding is most generally permitted when the PP is in complement function, as in [i]. With PPs functioning as adjunct, acceptability depends on the semantic type of the adjunct and the particular preposition; for example, instrumental *with* strands easily, whereas *until* is fairly resistant to stranding, and with *despite* it is excluded.

PPs do not permit gaps linked to a finite clause antecedent, as illustrated in [40v]. The preposing here must apply to the whole PP, not just the complement: *If you pay me$_i$, I'll do it _$_i$*. Nor do they permit a gap **within** a finite clause that is complement of the preposition, as we see from [vi]. Again it can be corrected by having the gap in place of the whole reason PP: *It was because I criticised this proposal$_i$ that they sacked me _$_i$*.

(h) NP

NPs accept gaps considerably less readily than VPs. Gaps cannot occur as or within modifiers in NP structure (see subsection (i), Modifiers, below). Complements are normally either PPs or clauses, and we will consider these two cases in turn.

PP complements

[41] i Of which institute$_i$ did you say they are going to make him [director _$_i$]?
ii To which safe$_i$ is this [the key _$_i$]?
iii He knows little about any of the companies [in which$_i$ he owns [shares _$_i$]].
iv I can't remember [which country$_i$ she served as [prime minister of _$_i$]].
v What kinds of birds$_i$ have you been collecting [pictures of _$_i$]?
vi It's a topic$_i$ [that I'd quite like to write [a book about _$_i$]].
vii *It's a topic$_i$ [you should read [my philosophy tutor's book on _$_i$]].

In [i–iii] the gap itself functions as complement and has a PP as antecedent. In [iv–vi] the gap is complement of the preposition, yielding a further case of preposition stranding. The NP in [iv–vi] is indefinite, and this construction is clearly acceptable except in formal style. Where the NP is definite, however, and especially where it has a genitive determiner, acceptability is generally very much reduced, as in [vii].

Clausal complements

[42] i *That it was my fault$_i$ I emphatically reject [the insinuation _$_i$].
ii *How the accident happened$_i$ they haven't begun to address [the question _$_i$].
iii *How much$_i$ did the secretary file [a report that it would cost _$_i$]?
iv *He's someone$_i$ [I accept your contention that we should not have appointed _$_i$].
v How many staff$_i$ did he give you [an assurance that he would retain _$_i$]?

Examples [i–ii] have the gap itself in complement function, but this time – in contrast to [41] – the result is very clearly ungrammatical. Preposing must apply to the whole NP: *The insinuation that it was my fault$_i$ I emphatically reject __$_i$* and *The question how the accident happened$_i$ they haven't begun to address __$_i$*.[26] In [iii–v] the gap is within the declarative content clause functioning as complement in NP structure. In general, this construction is of low acceptability. There is, for instance, a very sharp difference between [iii–iv] and comparable examples where the clause is complement of a verb: *How much$_i$ did the secretary report that it would cost __$_i$?* and *He's someone$_i$ [that I agree we should not have appointed __$_i$]*. However, the construction is by no means wholly excluded. It is most acceptable in examples containing collocations of light verb + noun such as *give an assurance, make the claim, hold the belief*, etc., which have essentially the same meaning as the verbs *assure, claim*, and *believe* respectively (cf. Ch. 4, §7). Thus [v] does not differ appreciably in acceptability from *How many staff$_i$ did he assure you that he would retain __$_i$?*

The examples in [42] involve content clauses; with infinitival complements gaps are more generally admissible:

[43] i *What$_i$ had Dr Harris secretly devised [a plan to steal __$_i$]?*
ii *It is not clear [which felony$_i$ he is being charged with [intent to commit __$_i$]].*

(i) Modifiers

[44] i *That's the car$_i$ [that I'm saving up [to buy __$_i$]].*
ii *Which month$_i$ are you taking your holidays [in __$_i$] this year?*
iii **It's this river$_i$ [that I want to buy a house [by __$_i$]].*
iv **List the commodities$_i$ [that you have visited countries [which produce __$_i$]].*

Gaps occur very much less readily in modifiers than in complements. One type of modifier where they are unquestionably allowed, however, is an infinitival clause of purpose in VP structure, as in [i]. Example [ii] shows a gap inside a PP functioning as modifier of temporal location, but we noted in (g) above that the stranded preposition construction has a quite strong preference for PPs in complement function. Modifiers in NP structure very strongly resist internal gaps, as illustrated in [iii–iv]. In [iii] the gap is in a PP modifying *house*, while that in [iv] is in a relative clause modifying *countries*.

(j) Subjects

[45] i *They have eight children [of whom$_i$ [five __$_i$] are still living at home].*
ii **They have eight children [who$_i$ [five of __$_i$] are still living at home].*
iii **What$_i$ would [to look at __$_i$ too closely] create political problems?*

Gaps are almost wholly excluded from occurring within a subject. The main exception is the construction shown in [i], where the gap is complement within the subject NP and has a PP as antecedent. Examples like [ii–iii] are completely ungrammatical; in [ii] the gap is within a PP dependent in the subject NP, while in [iii] it is within a clause functioning as subject. The clause in this example is infinitival, but the same prohibition

[26] Examples like *Why he did it$_i$ I have no idea __$_i$* are acceptable, but here we take the interrogative clause to be a complement in the structure of the VP, not the NP: see Ch. 4, §6.

applies to finite clauses, as seen in the example used in the introduction to this section, [31ii].[27]

(k) Coordinates

We saw in §7.2 that a gap cannot itself function as a coordinate (cf. [13viii]), but there are also constraints on the occurrence of gaps within coordinates. Compare:

[46] i *Who was the guy$_i$ [that [Jill divorced __$_i$][and Sue subsequently married __$_i$]]?*
ii **Who was the guy$_i$ [that [Jill divorced Max] [and Sue subsequently married __$_i$]]?*

In general, a gap can occur within a coordinate element only if a gap with the same antecedent occurs in all other coordinates in the coordination construction. In [i], for example, each of the two coordinates (enclosed by the inner sets of brackets) contains a gap in object function with *guy* as its antecedent. The sentence presupposes that there was some guy *x* such that Jill divorced *x* and Sue subsequently married *x*. Example [ii] is ungrammatical because the gap figures in one coordinate but not the other.

There are certain conditions, however, under which this constraint is relaxed:

[47] i *There are some letters$_i$ [that I must just [go downstairs] [and check __$_i$ over]].*
ii *What is the maximum amount$_i$ [I can [contribute __$_i$] [and still receive a tax deduction]]?*
iii *He has built up a high level of expectations, [which$_i$ he must [either live up to __$_i$] [or suffer a backlash]].*

These are cases of asymmetric coordination, i.e. cases where the coordinates are not of equal status from a semantic point of view (see Ch. 15, §§2.2.3–4). This is reflected in the fact that such coordinations have approximate paraphrases where one coordinate is replaced by an adjunct. Compare *I'll go downstairs and check them over* with *I'll go downstairs <u>to check them over</u>*; *I contributed $1,000 and still received a tax deduction* with *<u>Although I contributed $1,000,</u> I still received a tax deduction*; *He must either live up to these expectations or suffer a backlash* with *<u>If he doesn't live up to these expectations,</u> he will suffer a backlash.* Note that in each case the gap appears in the coordinate corresponding to the adjunct in the paraphrase. We pointed out at the beginning of this section that the acceptability of gaps in various locations is not determined by purely grammatical factors, and the contrast between [46] and [47] is a clear instance where a grammatical constraint is overridden by semantic factors.

7.4 Nested dependencies

It is possible for a sequence containing a hollow clause gap and its antecedent to be nested between the gap of a major construction and its antecedent. This kind of construction is illustrated in examples like *Which of the two instruments will this piece be easier to play on?*

[27] The following is a rare attested example of a gap within an infinitival subject, showing that the constraint is not absolute: *The eight dancers and their caller, Laurie Schmidt, make up the Farmall Promenade of nearby Nemaha, a town$_i$ [that [to describe __$_i$ as tiny] would be to overstate its size].*

The analysis of this example is as follows:

[48]

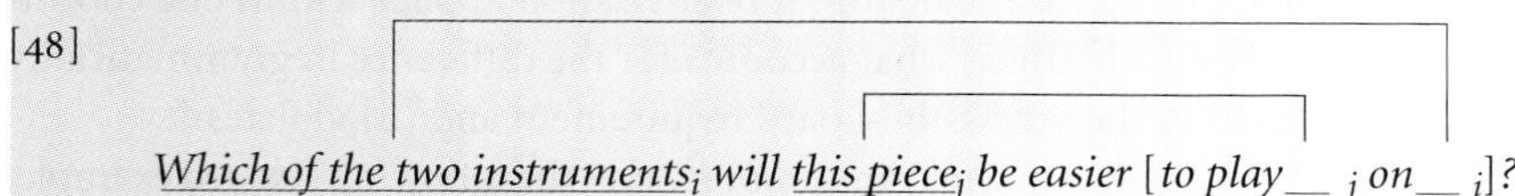

Which of the two instruments$_i$ *will this piece*$_j$ *be easier* [*to play*___$_j$ *on*___$_i$]?

The brackets enclose the hollow clause, and the underlining marks the antecedents of the two gaps, one functioning as object of the verb *play*, the other as object of the preposition *on*. One plays pieces of music on instruments, as reflected in a main clause such as *Kim will play the sonata on this piano.* The NP containing the noun *piece* will thus be the antecedent for the gap which is object of *play*, and the NP containing the noun *instruments* will be antecedent for the gap which is object of *on*.

It will be noted from the diagram that the first antecedent is linked to the second gap, and the second antecedent to the first gap: the pair with the *j* index is said to be nested between the pair with the *i* index. The dependency relations are required to be nested one within the other in this way. It is not possible for them to cross each other, as in:

[49]

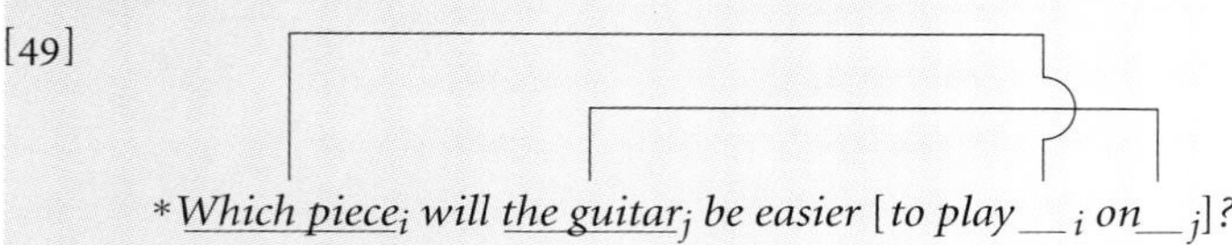

**Which piece*$_i$ *will the guitar*$_j$ *be easier* [*to play*___$_i$ *on*___$_j$]?

It is plausible to see this constraint as serving to facilitate understanding: if only [48] is an admissible structure, the hearer will know that the first gap encountered will be linked to the most recently perceived antecedent.

7.5 Parasitic gaps

Omission of personal pronoun with gap as antecedent

Under certain conditions it is possible to omit a non-reflexive, non-genitive personal pronoun whose antecedent is a gap in an unbounded dependency construction:

[50] i *They do an annual report*$_i$ [*that I always throw* ___$_i$ *away without reading it*$_i$].
ii *They do an annual report*$_i$ [*that I always throw* ___$_i$ *away without reading* ___$_i$].

The second gap in [ii] is called a **parasitic gap**. It is 'parasitic' in the sense that a gap is permitted in this position only if the antecedent is also a gap. Thus in *I always throw their annual report*$_i$ *away without reading it*$_i$ the antecedent of the pronoun *it* is an overt NP, and omission of the pronoun in this case leads to ungrammaticality: **I always throw their annual report away without reading* ___$_i$.

The most clearly acceptable cases of parasitic gaps occur, like that in [50ii], in non-finite clauses located within adjuncts functioning in clause structure.

Parasitic gaps distinct from across-the-board gaps

The construction with an ordinary gap + parasitic gap is to be distinguished from that where two ordinary gaps appear in coordinated constituents:

[51] *It was a proposal*$_i$ [*that* [*Kim supported* ___$_i$] [*but everyone else opposed* ___$_i$]].

Here the second gap cannot be replaced by a personal pronoun. There is thus nothing parasitic about the second gap here: it is required by the rules for coordination. As explained in Ch. 15, §2.1, a distinctive property of coordination is that such processes as relativisation must apply 'across the board': if relativisation applies within one coordinate it must apply within all. This is what accounts for the difference in grammaticality in [46], where [i] satisfies the across-the-board requirement and [ii] violates it.

Parasitic and across-the-board gaps can combine, as in the following attested example, where the parasitic gap is marked by an initial subscript 'p':

[52] *Fairbanks reached for a towel, a clean one and not the scarcely crumpled one*$_i$ [*that Comore himself had* [*used* $\_\__i$] [*and left* $\_\__i$ *thriftily on the ledge below the mirror rather than consign* $_{p}\_\__i$ *to the linen basket*]].

The outer brackets enclose a relative clause within which there is a coordination functioning as complement of the perfect auxiliary *have*. The two coordinates, enclosed by the inner pairs of brackets, each have an ordinary gap as object (of *used* and *left* respectively), but in addition the second coordinate has a parasitic gap in the adjunct headed by *rather*. Again, the parasitic gap could be replaced by the personal pronoun *it*, but the ordinary gaps could not.

13

Comparative constructions

Rodney Huddleston

1 Preliminaries

English has a rich system of specialised syntax and morphology for the expression of comparisons of various types. The two inflectionally marked terms in the system of **grade**, exemplified in such forms as *bigger* and *biggest*, have the expression of comparison as virtually their only use, and one of the three major kinds of finite subordinate clause – the type of clause underlined in *She is much bigger than she was then* or *She went to the same school as I went to* – is reserved for the expression of comparison.

We use the traditional terms **comparative form** and **superlative form** for the inflectional categories *bigger* and *biggest*, and **comparative clause** for subordinate clauses like *she was then* and *I went to*.[1] This chapter is concerned with constructions containing these categories and others bearing significant syntactic resemblances to them. In this preliminary section we introduce the main subtypes of comparative construction and a number of syntactic categories needed for their description.

1.1 Two cross-cutting distinctions: scalar vs non-scalar, equality vs inequality

Two intersecting dimensions of contrast yield the four types of comparative construction shown in [1]:

[1]	EQUALITY	INEQUALITY
SCALAR	*Kim is as old as Pat.*	*Kim is older than Pat.*
NON-SCALAR	*I took the same bus as last time.*	*I took a different bus from last time.*

Scalar vs non-scalar

Scalar comparisons are concerned with relative position on some scale, such as that denoted by ***old*** in [1]; ***old*** is a gradable adjective and scalar comparison is one type of grading, potentially more complex than grading by means of such degree adverbs as *very*, *quite*, *rather*, etc., but of the same general kind.

Non-scalar comparisons, by contrast, are concerned not with grading but with such issues as identity and likeness. *Bus*, for example, is not gradable, and the non-scalar

[1] Recall that on our analysis (see Ch. 11, §8.1) *than* is a preposition taking the comparative clause as its complement, not part of the subordinate clause as in traditional grammar.

comparisons in [1] compare the two buses (the one I took and the one I had taken last time) for identity.

Scalar comparison can be regarded as the more central type: inflectionally marked comparatives are scalar and, within the inequality category, comparative clauses are rare in the non-scalar constructions.

Equality vs inequality

These terms apply reasonably transparently to scalar comparison. If Kim is as old as Pat, then Kim's age is (at least) **equal** to Pat's, and if Kim is older than Pat, their ages are **not equal**.

We do not so readily invoke these terms in describing the meaning of non-scalar comparisons (for example, *I took the same bus as last time* does not mean "The bus I took equals the bus I took last time"). Non-scalar comparison is concerned with identity vs non-identity or likeness vs unlikeness. Grammatically, however, there are grounds for recognising a single contrast applying to scalar and non-scalar comparisons alike: *as* is the main marker of equality comparison, whether scalar (*as old <u>as</u> Pat*) or non-scalar (*the same bus <u>as</u> last time*), while *than* marks both scalar inequality (*older <u>than</u> Pat*) and certain types of non-scalar inequality (*other <u>than</u> Pat* or, in some varieties of English, %*different <u>than</u> last time*).

Subtypes of inequality: superiority and inferiority

Within certain kinds of scalar comparison we need to distinguish two different kinds of inequality, giving in all a contrast between three categories, not just two:

[2]	EQUALITY		*as heavy as*	*as careful as*
	INEQUALITY	**superiority**	*heavier than*	*more careful than*
		inferiority	*less heavy than*	*less careful than*

Superiority may be marked inflectionally (*heavier*) or analytically, by *more*, while the other categories are marked just analytically: **inferiority** is marked by *less*, and **equality** by *as*. What is standardly called the comparative inflection, therefore, is the marker of just one type of comparative relation, scalar superiority.[2]

Scalar orientation

Superiority and inferiority are to be interpreted relative to the particular scale at issue: *younger than* is just as much a comparison of superiority as *older than*. Scales have an **orientation**, or direction, which depends on the lexical meaning of the compared item. ***Old*** and ***young*** both denote scales concerned with age but have opposite orientations: the older something is, the further it is from age zero, whereas the younger it is the closer it is to that zero point. Superiority and inferiority are grammatical categories, marked as indicated above, whereas orientation is a matter of lexical meaning.

Scalar comparison of equality indicates "at least equal"

In the absence of indications to the contrary, a scalar comparison of equality is interpreted as "at least equal", not "exactly equal":

[2] The term 'equative' is often used in contrast to 'comparative' for what we are calling scalar comparison of equality. The view taken here is that *X is as heavy as Y* involves comparison just as much as *X is heavier than Y*, and syntactically they are alike in that the *Y* element can in both cases be realised by a comparative clause.

[3] i *Jill is as clever as Liz.* [Jill may be cleverer]
ii *Jill isn't as clever as Liz.* [Jill must be less clever]

Example [i] is consistent with Jill being cleverer than Liz: we can say *Jill's as clever as Liz, somewhat more so in fact.*[3] Scalar equality therefore normally excludes only the relation of inferiority: it gives a lower bound. And the negative in [ii] accordingly entails inferiority, ruling out both the case where Jill and Liz are equally clever and that where Jill is cleverer.[4] This is just as well for the practical use of the language, for while some scales (such as those involving physical size) allow precise measurement, most do not. It would normally be nonsensical to ask whether Jill is exactly as clever as Liz, for example.

The extent to which a comparison of equality is compatible with superiority will vary with the content and context: *He made as many as eighteen mistakes* carries a much stronger suggestion that perhaps exact equality holds, for example, than *He made as many mistakes as I did.*

Sanctioning of non-affirmative items

Non-affirmative items such as *any*, *ever*, etc., are permitted in three of the four subtypes of comparison given in [1]:

[4] i *She ran faster than <u>anyone</u> had expected.* [scalar inequality]
ii *She ran as fast as she had <u>ever</u> run before.* [scalar equality]
iii *It was different from <u>anything</u> I'd <u>ever</u> seen before.* [non-scalar inequality]
iv **It was the same as <u>anything</u> I'd ever seen before.* [non-scalar equality]

There is an evident connection in [i–iii] with negation (the prototypical context for such items). These sentences entail, respectively, that no one had expected her to run as fast as she did, that she had never run faster before, that it was not the same as, or not like, anything I'd ever seen before.

1.2 Term and set comparison

A further distinction within comparative constructions is between **term comparison** and **set comparison**:

[5] i a. *Ed is more tolerant than he used to be.*
b. *Kim's version is much superior to Pat's.* } [term comparison]
ii a. *Ed made the most mistakes of them all.*
b. *It sold for the highest price ever paid for a Cézanne.* } [set comparison]

The examples in [i] express comparison between a **primary term** and a **secondary term**, labels which reflect the fact that the secondary term is syntactically subordinate relative to the primary one. In [ia] the comparison is between how tolerant Ed is now, the primary term, and how tolerant he used to be, the secondary term: the primary term is expressed in the matrix clause, the secondary term in a subordinate clause (*he used to be*). In [ib]

[3] This can indeed apply also to ***equal*** itself, as in *Kim is the equal of Pat when it comes to solving crossword puzzles* (which is consistent with Kim being better) or *We hope to equal last year's profit* (consistent with bettering it).

[4] This applies to ordinary negation. With metalinguistic negation (Ch. 9, §1.2) it is possible to say *Jill isn't as clever as Pat, she's a good deal cleverer*: this rejects *Jill is as clever as Pat* not because it is false, but because it doesn't say enough.

the comparison is between Kim's version (primary) and Pat's version (secondary); in this case there is no immediate syntactic relation between the NPs expressing the two terms, but *Pat's* is lower in the constituent structure, and in that sense can be regarded as subordinate relative to the primary term.

The examples in [5ii] express comparison between the members of some set: in the type of set comparison illustrated here, one member of the set is picked out as being at the top of the scale. In [iia] the set is identified by the NP *them all*: the comparison is between the members of this set with respect to how many mistakes they each made, with Ed ranked at the top of the scale. It is possible to omit the PP *of them all*, in which case the set being compared is identified contextually. In [iib] the comparison is between the prices paid for paintings by Cézanne, and again one is picked out as being at the top of the scale.

Omission of secondary term in term comparison

The secondary term is commonly left implicit when it is recoverable from the context:

[6] i *Ed was pretty difficult in those days, but now he's <u>more tolerant</u>.*
ii *Pat's version is rather pedestrian: Kim's is <u>far superior</u>.*
iii *They have moved house four times in <u>as many years</u>.*

We understand "more tolerant than he was in those days", "far superior to Pat's version", "as many as four years",[5] with the missing material recovered from the preceding text. Alternatively, the secondary term may be simply recovered from the situation – as, for example, when you open the window in a stuffy room and I say *That's better!*

Equivalence between set and term comparisons

In general, set comparisons can be reformulated as equivalent term comparisons. For example, [5iia–b] are equivalent to:

[7] i *Ed made more mistakes than all the others.*
ii *It sold for a higher price than had ever been paid for a Cézanne before.*

In [5iia] *them all* identifies a set that includes Ed, whereas in [7i] *all the others* excludes Ed and expresses the secondary term in the comparison. Similarly, in [5iib] one price is ranked at the top of the scale for the set of all prices ever paid, while in [7ii] one price is compared with all the others as primary term vs secondary term.

The scalar vs non-scalar and equality vs inequality contrasts apply to both types

The two dimensions of contrast introduced in §1.1 apply to set comparisons as well as to term comparisons, as illustrated in [8–9]:

[8] SET COMPARISON

	Equality	**Inequality**
Scalar	*Sue and Ed are equally good.*	*Sue is the best of the three.*
Non-scalar	*Sue and Ed are in the same class.*	*Sue and Ed go to different schools.*

[5] This is one place where scalar equality is interpreted as exact equality rather than as giving a lower bound: we understand "in four years". Compare, similarly, *This is their sixth victory in as many matches* ("in six matches").

[9] TERM COMPARISON

	Equality	Inequality
Scalar	*Sue is as good as Ed.*	*Sue is better than the other two.*
Non-scalar	*Sue is in the same class as Ed.*	*Sue goes to a different school from Ed.*

Syntactic differences

The two most important syntactic differences between term and set comparisons are the following:

[10] i Comparative clauses occur only in term comparisons, where they are associated with the secondary term.

ii Superlative and comparative grades are used in comparisons of inequality; the superlative is restricted to set comparisons, while comparative grade is used predominantly in term comparison, but occurs also in set comparisons where the set has just two members.

The two uses of comparative grade are illustrated in:

[11] i *Jill is taller than her twin sister.* [term comparison]

ii *Jill is the taller of the twins.* [set comparison]

In this chapter we devote §2 to the description of comparative clauses, and §3 is concerned with a special type of comparison known as metalinguistic comparison (as in *I was more worried than angry*). We then deal in §§4–6 respectively with scalar term comparison, non-scalar comparison, and scalar set comparison.

1.3 Comparative complements, comparative governors, and comparative phrases

The secondary term in a term comparison may be expressed by a comparative clause or some other form of expression, typically a phrase:

[12] i *We performed better than <u>we did last year</u>.* [comparative clause]

ii *This year's performance was superior to <u>last year's</u>.* [other form (NP)]

While the comparative clause is a syntactically distinct construction appearing only in term comparisons, other forms of secondary term are not specialised to comparative constructions but occur readily elsewhere (cf. *It is too early to judge this year's performance, but <u>last year's</u> was excellent*).

Comparative complement – bare and expanded

Whether a comparative clause or not, the form expressing the secondary term has the syntactic function of complement. In the most central cases, as illustrated in [12], it is complement of a preposition which is itself governed, or selected, by some other item, as *than* in [12i] is governed by the comparative form *better* and *to* in [12ii] is governed by *superior*.[6] We will generalise to this construction the distinction between 'bare' and 'expanded', with **bare comparative complement** excluding the preposition

[6] In a few cases the secondary term is expressed in a genitive subject-determiner in NP structure, as in <u>*my*</u> *betters*, "those who are better than me".

and **expanded comparative complement** including it. As applied to the examples in [12], this gives:

[13]			
i	BARE COMPARATIVE COMPLEMENT	*we did last year*	*last year's*
ii	EXPANDED COMPARATIVE COMPLEMENT	*than we did last year*	*to last year's*

The main prepositions that occur in the expanded complement vary to some extent according to the type of comparison:

[14]	EQUALITY	INEQUALITY
SCALAR	*as*	*than, to*
NON-SCALAR	*as, to, with*	*than, to, from*

Comparative governors

The items which license comparative complements we call **comparative governors**. The following table shows the main governors (underlined) together with the prepositions they take in expanded complements; the governors are classified according to the four types of comparison, with the pluses indicating scalar and equality, the minuses non-scalar and inequality:

[15]	SCALAR	EQUALITY	
i	+	+	*<u>as</u> . . . as, <u>so</u> . . . as, <u>such</u> . . . as*
ii	–	+	*<u>same</u> as, <u>such</u> as, <u>similar</u> to, <u>equal</u> to/with, <u>identical</u> to/with*
iii	+	–	*·<u>er</u> than, <u>more</u> than, <u>less</u> than, <u>rather</u> than, <u>prefer</u> . . . to/than, <u>superior</u> to, <u>inferior</u> to*
iv	–	–	*<u>other</u> than, <u>else</u> than, <u>differ</u> from, <u>different</u> from/to/than, <u>dissimilar</u> to/from*

The ·*er* in [iii] represents the comparative inflection (whether realised as the suffix ·*er* or irregularly, as in *worse*, etc.). We include *such* in both scalar and non-scalar categories: scalar *such* expresses likeness of degree (*It isn't such a good idea as he would have us believe*), while non-scalar *such* expresses likeness of kind or identity (*I did such things as only one woman can do for another*). In addition we will see that comparison with *same* may have affinities with the scalar type when *same* modifies a gradable noun.

Governors taking bare complements

There are also items which take the secondary term as complement without any mediating preposition. These include *like* and *unlike* (which belong to both adjective and preposition categories), *as* and certain other prepositions such as *before* and *after*, a few verbs such as *equal, exceed, resemble* (it is the adjective *equal* that is listed in [15ii]), and so on. Thus we have *Ed is like his father*, not **Ed is like to his father*, etc. For *as* we need to distinguish the three occurrences shown in:

[16] i *It wasn't <u>as</u> expensive <u>as</u> she had expected.*
ii *It was reasonably cheap, <u>as</u> she had expected.*

The first *as* in [i], an adverb, is the governor, and it licenses a complement expanded by the second *as*, a preposition. In [ii] we have just one *as*, a preposition, which is the governor and takes a bare complement (just as *like* does). In both cases the comparative clause *she had expected* is complement of the preposition *as*, but in [i] this *as* is selected by the adverb *as* which introduces the comparison. In [ii] it is the preposition *as* itself that introduces the comparison.

Comparative phrase

We apply the term **comparative phrase** to a phrase containing a comparative governor. In [12], for example, the comparative phrases are *more satisfactorily than we did last year* and *superior to last year's*. In other cases it may be a larger phrase:

[17] *This may be a more serious problem than you think.*

Although *more* modifies *serious*, it is the phrase headed by *problem* that is the comparative phrase. This is another place where we can invoke the metaphor of upward percolation: the comparative feature percolates up from *more* to *more serious* and thence to the whole NP. We take up in §2.4 below the issue of how far such upward percolation can go, i.e. how much is encompassed by a comparative phrase.

Position of the comparative complement

The complement is found in a variety of positions relative to the head of the comparative phrase. They are illustrated in [18], where the comparative phrase is enclosed in square brackets, double underlining marks its head, and single underlining marks the expanded comparative complement.

[18]	i	*He took out [a bigger loan than was necessary].*	[post-head]
	ii	*She's [more experienced in these matters than I am].*	[postposed in phrase]
	iii	*[More people] attended the meeting than ever before.*	[postposed in clause]
	iv	*He chose Kim, than whom no one could be [more suitable].*	[preposed]
	v	*They've achieved [a better than expected result].*	[pre-head]
	vi	*[More people] oppose than support the proposed office reorganisation.*	[before delayed right constituent]

In more detail, the possibilities shown in [18] are as follows:

i The complement immediately follows the head, the noun *loan.*

ii The *than* phrase is separated from the head but is still within the comparative phrase. *In these matters* is also a dependent (another complement) of *experienced.*

iii The complement *than ever before* is separated from the head by the predicator and its object, and hence is not part of the same phrase as its governor *more* – not part of the comparative phrase.

iv The comparative complement occupies initial position in the clause, because *whom* is a relative pronoun and hence occupies prenuclear position (along with the preposition *than*) in the relative clause. This is a relatively rare construction, found only in formal style.[7]

v Here the comparative complement occurs in pre-head position within the comparative phrase. This pattern is largely restricted to inflectional comparatives with *than* followed by one of a handful of short expressions such as *anticipated, expected, hoped for, necessary, usual.*

[7] It is marginally possible also in open interrogatives (*Than whom is he less tolerant?*) and with complement preposing (*Than such a slogan, nothing could be more negative*). It is not found with comparisons of equality: **Kim, as whom no-one could be as suitable.*

vi This illustrates the delayed right constituent construction, which is more often found with coordination than with subordination (and hence is described in Ch. 15, §4.4). A typical coordinate example would be *Three-quarters of them oppose and only 15 % actually support the proposed office reorganisation.* The final NP, *the proposed office reorganisation,* is understood as object of both *oppose* and *support.* If the comparative complement were in final position, it would need a separately realised object: *More people oppose the proposed office reorganisation than support it.*

The most usual position for the comparative complement is at the end of the clause containing the comparative phrase, as in [18i–iii]. This means that if the clause contains material (other than the comparative complement itself) following the head, the complement will characteristically be postposed, very often to a position outside the comparative phrase. In [18ii–iii] postposing is optional: we can also have *She's more experienced than I am in these matters*; *More people than ever before attended the meeting.* The longer, or heavier, the complement is, relative to the other material, the more likely it is to be postposed. There are also cases where postposing is grammatically obligatory:

[19]	i	*He knew more about Paris than any of his friends.*	[postposing preferred]
	ii	*It is better to tell her now than to wait till after the exam.*	[postposing required]

Example [i] is more natural than the version without postposing because the *than* phrase is significantly heavier than *about Paris.* In [ii] postposing is obligatory because the main contrast is between *to tell her now* and *to wait till after the exam,* and as the former belongs to the primary term it must precede the latter, which belongs to the secondary term.

It will be clear, then, that expanded comparative complements are very often indirect complements, in the sense explained in Ch. 2, §5: in these cases they are licensed not by the head of the construction in which they occur, but by some dependent of the head. In [18i], for example, *than was necessary* is complement of the bracketed NP, but it is not licensed by the head of that NP, *loan.*

2 Comparative clauses

Comparative clauses form a subcategory of subordinate clauses, contrasting with relative and content clauses. They are found in the four types of term comparison, though the non-scalar inequality type is subject to dialect restrictions described in §5.4:

[1]	i	*It was better than I had expected.*	[scalar inequality]
	ii	*It wasn't as good as I had expected.*	[scalar equality]
	iii	*It was excellent, as/%like I had expected.*	[non-scalar equality]
	iv	*%It wasn't much different than I had expected.*	[non-scalar inequality]

In all cases, the comparative clause (*I had expected*) is complement of one of the prepositions *than, as,* and *like.*

Note that it is not the matrix clause expressing the whole comparison that is traditionally called a comparative clause, but the subordinate clause that expresses the secondary term. The major distinctive feature of comparative clauses is that they are structurally reduced relative to full main clauses: in varying degrees, material is left understood that would be overtly present in comparable full main clauses. *I had expected,* for example, is not grammatical as a sentence in its own right.

Variables vs constants

The comparison in [1ii] is between how good it was and how good I had expected it to be – but the sentence doesn't say how good it actually was or how good I had expected it to be. To describe the meaning we therefore need to invoke variables: we will informally represent the primary term as "It was x good" and the secondary one as "I had expected it to be y good". The governor, the comparative inflection, then indicates that x exceeds y: "$x > y$". This kind of comparison is thus to be distinguished from that where one or both of the terms is a constant. Compare, for example:

[2] i *It was better [than I had expected].* [variable–variable comparison]
ii *I stayed longer [than six weeks].* [variable–constant comparison]
iii *Sue is just like her mother.* [constant–constant comparison]

In [ii] the primary term again contains a variable "I stayed x long", but the secondary term this time is simply "six weeks". *Six weeks* here is an NP, not a clause: comparative clauses always express secondary terms involving a variable. Example [iii] illustrates the case where both terms are constants: this is simply a comparison between Sue and her mother.

Inversion

While a particular kind of structural reduction is the chief syntactic factor distinguishing comparative clauses from other clauses, there is also a difference with respect to the position of the subject, which can occur after the verb under conditions illustrated in:

[3] i *Spain's financial problems were less acute than were those of Portugal.*
ii **The water seems significantly colder today than was it yesterday.*
iii *It is no more expensive than would be the system you are proposing.*
iv **It is no more expensive than would the system you are proposing be.*
v **He works harder than works his father.*

The effect of the inversion is almost invariably to place a contrastive subject in end position: in [i], for example, *those of Portugal* contrasts with *Spain's financial problems.* In [ii], then, where the contrast is between the non-subjects *today* and *yesterday* the inversion is out of place: we need *than it was yesterday.* Note, moreover, that in [iii] the subject follows the sequence *would be*: it cannot invert with *would* alone, as we see from [iv]. The construction therefore has strong affinities with postposing (cf. Ch. 16, §4) – yet it also resembles subject–auxiliary inversion in that the verb normally has to be an auxiliary: we can have *He works harder than his father works* but not [v]. The construction therefore has something of the character of a blend between subject postposing and subject–auxiliary inversion, and this mix of properties is found only in comparative clauses.

2.1 Reduction of comparative clauses

We confine our attention in this section to the central case where the comparative clause occurs in an expanded complement headed by *than* or *as.* We look first at two cases of obligatory reduction, (a)–(b), and then move on to optional reduction, (c)–(g).

(a) Obligatory absence of counterpart to the comparative governor

The minimum reduction is seen in such examples as:

[4] i *The swimming-pool is as deep as [it is __ wide].*
ii **The swimming pool is as deep as [it is very / quite / two metres wide].*

The comparative governor, the underlined *as*, is a degree modifier of *deep* in the matrix clause, and the corresponding position in the bracketed comparative clause must be empty. This requirement is satisfied in [i], where the position of degree modifier (modifying *wide*) is empty, while [ii] is ungrammatical by virtue of this position being filled. The inflectional suffix ·*er* counts as equivalent to the analytic marker *more*, so that the position indicated by '__', which we will refer to as the **gap**, must likewise remain empty in *The swimming-pool is deeper than [it is __ wide].*

Although this position of the gap must remain syntactically empty, it is not semantically empty. The notation '__' is intended to suggest that some element is understood. What is understood is the value for the variable that we have already suggested is involved in the meaning of comparisons whose secondary term is expressed by a comparative clause.

Because of the missing but understood material, the comparative clause in [4i] does not have the same meaning as the main clause *It is wide.* The latter says that the pool is wide (relative to the norms for pools), but [4i] doesn't say this. Rather, we understand something like "The pool is x units deep; the pool is y units wide; and x is (at least) equal to y". In other words, there is an implicit degree modifier, and since this consists of a variable (y) whose value is unspecified, [4i] is consistent with the pool being wide, narrow, or in-between, depending on what the value turns out to be.

This implicit variable degree modifier explains the impossibility of filling the gap position with an explicit degree modifier, as in [4ii]: it can't be implicitly and explicitly filled at the same time. In the matrix clause the x variable is also implicit rather than actually expressed, but syntactically its position is taken by the comparative governor, expressing the relation between x and y.

(b) Counterpart of comparative phrase normally omitted unless distinct

Consider next:

[5] i *She is older than [I am __].*
ii *She went to the same school as [I went to __].*

The comparative phrases are *older than I am* and *the same school as I went to*, and counterparts to these, corresponding phrases minus the comparative governor and complement, i.e. *old* and *the school*, are understood but unexpressed in the comparative clause. We understand "I am y old", "I went to y school", but *old* and *school* must be left implicit as well as the y variables. The syntax thus excludes:

[6] i **She is older than [I am old].*
ii **She went to the same school as [I went to the school].*

The comparative clause can contain a counterpart to the comparative phrase when there is a contrast between them. This was the case in [4i], which has a contrast between the *deep* of the matrix clause and the *wide* of the comparative clause. Further examples are:

[7] i *She wrote more plays than [her husband wrote __ novels].*
ii *You couldn't be a worse polo-player than [you are a __ singer].*
iii *He is more afraid of her than [she is __ of him].*
iv *There is no more reason to invite him than [there was __ to invite her].*

In [i] *novels* contrasts with *plays* and hence we have an overt counterpart to the comparative phrase: both the comparative phrase and its counterpart are NPs functioning as object of their clause, the former headed by *plays*, the latter by *novels*. Example [ii] is similar, except that the comparative governor is here within an attributive adjective (*worse*) rather than a determinative (*more*). In [iii–iv] the contrast lies not in the heads of the comparative phrases (*afraid* and *reason*) but in the post-head dependents: '__ *of him*' is therefore an AdjP with a missing head (and missing degree modifier), and analogously for '__ *to invite her*'. It is possible to repeat the head in such circumstances; thus [iii] can be expressed as *He is more afraid of her than [she is __ afraid of him]*.[8]

(c) Stranding and *do*

The comparative clause is commonly further reduced by elliptical stranding of auxiliary verbs or infinitival *to*:

[8] i *She is right more often than [the others are __].*
ii *I didn't enjoy the concert as much as [Kim had __].*
iii *I don't hear from my brother as often as [I used to __].*
iv *She can get through more work in an hour than [I can __ in a day].*

Again the bracketing here identifies the comparative clause, while the underlining indicates matrix material that is ellipted. The ellipsis here is optional: the gaps could be filled out as *right*, *enjoyed it*, *hear from him*, *get through*, i.e. repetitions or variants of the matrix material. The elliptical versions are more frequent than those with repeated material. The gap comes at the end of the clause, as in [i–iii], or else is followed by contrastive material, as in [iv], where *in a day* contrasts with *in an hour* in the primary term. The resultant structures are like those found with stranding in non-comparative constructions (Ch. 17, §7) – compare [i] and [iv], for example, with the coordinations:

[9] i *She is right and the others are __ too.*
ii *I can't get through that much work in an hour, but I can __ in a day.*

What distinguishes the comparative construction is that any filling in of the gaps is subject to the restrictions covered in (a) and (b) above, so while we could expand the coordinative [9ii] to *I can get through that much work in a day* the maximum expansion of the comparative clause in [8iv] is *than I can get through __ in a day.*

The expressions that can be stranded are the same as in non-comparatives. Thus a lexical verb such as ***enjoy*** cannot be stranded in comparatives any more than in

[8] An exceptional case where a head is retained even though it is neither distinct nor accompanied by a distinct dependent is that where the head is contrastively stressed in a correction of what has just been said, as in A: *She writes as many books as you write articles.* B: *No, that's an exaggeration; but she writes as many books as I write* BOOKS.

non-comparatives:

[10] i *I didn't enjoy the concert as much as [Kim had enjoyed __].

ii *Kim enjoyed the concert and I enjoyed __ too.

The reduced VP is commonly headed by the verb **do**, which in some varieties of English is best considered as an auxiliary verb that can be stranded like those in [8] and in other varieties as a pro-form (see Ch. 17, §7.2):

[11] i *I get it wrong more often than [she does].*

ii *We treat our apprentices better than [they do their career employees].*

Here too the reduced comparative clauses are formally identical to non-comparative clauses found in other anaphoric constructions: *I often get it wrong and she does (too)*; *We treat our apprentices well and they do their employees.* And again the possible replacements for the **do** forms are subject to the restrictions given in (a)–(b), so while we can have *I often get it wrong and she often gets it wrong too*, we can't have **I get it wrong more often than [she often gets it wrong]*.

In varieties (especially BrE) where **do** is a pro-form, it can occur after auxiliaries or infinitival *to*, and this yields the possibility of a choice between the stranding and pro-form constructions. Compare, for example, [8ii] on the one hand and *%I didn't enjoy the concert as much as [Kim had done]* on the other.

Examples are occasionally found where the *do* clause is passivised in such a way that no simple replacement for the pro-form is possible. Compare:

[12] i *%We must attend to it more closely than [people have usually done].*

ii *%We must attend to it more closely than [has usually been done].*

We can expand [i] to *people have usually attended to it*. However, if we replace *do* in [ii] by a version of its antecedent the *it* will appear as subject, and *attended to* in place of *done*: *it has usually been attended to.* The subjectless passive that we have in [ii] bears some resemblance to the construction with an understood embedded clause, to which we now turn.

(d) Omission of embedded clauses

Another common type of reduction is seen in:

[13] i *The matter was more serious than [we had expected __].*

ii *More faults had been detected than [he was willing to admit __].*

iii *They finished the job earlier than [__ (had been) expected].*

iv *The difficulties are even greater than [__ appears at first sight].*

Here an entire subordinate clause is understood. We could make the meaning of [i] explicit by replacing the gap by *than we had expected that it would be*, or *than we had expected it to be.* It is much more usual, though, to omit the subordinate clause, as in the examples given.

In [13iii–iv] the missing clause is understood as subject. Expansion to make the meaning explicit would require extraposition (*They finished the job earlier than it had been expected that they would finish it*) – but note that extraposition *it* cannot be inserted if the clause is not added: **They finished the job earlier than it had been expected.*

In the passive construction, as in [13iii], some verbs, such as *expect*, allow the omission of auxiliaries (as indicated by the parentheses in [iii]), reducing the comparative clause to just a past participle (*than* expected). In [14] we give a sample of verbs figuring in this construction, with the annotation '–AUX' indicating the possibility of omitting the auxiliaries.

[14]	*acknowledge*	*admit* –AUX	*allow*	*anticipate* –AUX	*appear*
	assume –AUX	*believe*	*dream*	*expect* –AUX	*hope*
	imagine	*imply*	*indicate* –AUX	*intend* –AUX	*justify*
	like	*plan* –AUX	*predict* –AUX	*realise* –AUX	*recognise*
	remember	*require* –AUX	*schedule* –AUX	*show* –AUX	*suggest*
	suppose	*suspect*	*think* –AUX	*warrant*	*wish*

Dream takes the preposition *of*: *The Ariadne was going to be much hotter than our space people had ever dreamt of.*

The verbs in [14] are predominantly non-factive (in the sense explained in Ch. 11, §7.4), but it is worth noting that the class does include factive *realise.* Consider, then:

[15] i *The draft had more mistakes in it than I had realised.*
ii *I had realised that the draft had five mistakes in it.*
iii "The draft had five mistakes in it"

Example [ii] entails [iii]: if [ii] is true, [iii] must be true too. This property of *realise* might at first seem problematic for [i]. The secondary term in the comparison is "I had realised the draft had *x* many mistakes in it", which entails "the draft had *x* many mistakes in it" – yet the sentence says it had more than *x* mistakes in it. There is, however, no contradiction here: [ii] does not say that there were **exactly** five mistakes, only that there were **at least** five. If the draft contained seven mistakes it follows that it contained five, though one generally wouldn't **say** that it contained five if one knew that it contained seven (cf. Ch. 5, §5.2). This is why [i] makes perfect sense. It says that there were more mistakes in the draft than I had been aware of: contrast #*The draft didn't have as many mistakes in it as I had realised.*

In addition to the verbs listed in [14], we also find adjectives and other predicative expressions in these missing-clause comparatives:

[16] i *Don't spend any longer on it than* [__ *(is) necessary*].
ii *The score is higher than* [__ *would have been the case if no one had cheated*].
iii *The danger may be greater than* [*any of us is aware (of)* __].

The understood missing parts are something like "spending that long on it" in [i], "the score being that high" in [ii], and "the danger being that great" in [iii]. The lexical items allowing this sort of construction include:

[17]	*acceptable*	*aware*	*justifiable*	*necessary* –V	*normal* –V
	polite	*possible* –V	*usual* –V	*the case*	*one's habit*

With *necessary* and others marked ' –V', the verb *be* can be omitted, so that the clause may consist simply of the adjective: *than* [__ *necessary*].

(e) Verbless clauses: reduction to two (or more) elements

We turn now to constructions where the verb is omitted (beyond the special case mentioned in (d) above), beginning with those where at least two elements remain:

[18] i *Max didn't love Jill as much as* [*she* __ *him*].
ii *He didn't send as many postcards to his friends as* [__ *letters to his mother*].

In [i] just the verb is optionally omitted (we could insert *loved* or *did*), whereas in [ii] the subject is omitted as well as the verb (we could supply *he sent* or *he did*).

The resultant structures are again like ones found in various types of coordination:

[19] i *Max loved Jill and she __ him.*
ii *He sent postcards to his friends and __ letters to his mother.*

As before, the permitted expansions are different: in [19], for example, we could expand to *and she loved him even more* or *and he sent many letters to his mother*, but the *even more* and *many* cannot be added in [18] by virtue of conditions (a)–(b). There are also differences with respect to negation. In [18] the comparative clause is interpreted as positive ("as she loved him", "as he sent letters to his mother"), even though the matrix clause is negative – and changing the matrix to positive has no effect on the polarity of the comparative clause (cf. *Max loved Jill as much as she __ him* and *Max sent as many postcards to his friends as letters to his mother*). But to get a positive interpretation of the second coordinates in [19] we had to make the first coordinate positive too: *Max didn't love Jill and she __ him*, for example, doesn't allow the interpretation "and she loved him".

(f) Verbless clauses: reduction to a single element

The extreme case of reduction is where only a single element remains:

[20]	i	*We spend more time in France than [__ in Germany].*	[PP]
	ii	*He seems to play better drunk than [__ sober].*	[AdjP]
	iii	*More believed that it was genuine than [__ that it was a hoax].*	[content clause]
	iv	*It is better to try and fail than [__ not to try at all].*	[infinitival clause]
	v	*Sue phoned Angela more often than [(__) Liz (__)].*	[NP]
	vi	*He has more enemies than [__ friends].*	[nominal]

In all of these it would be possible to add material in the position of the gap: for [i] we could have *We spend more time in France than [we spend __ in Germany]*, and so on. Reduction to an AdjP, as in [ii], is restricted to cases where the AdjP is adjunct: we cannot omit the *it is* in [4i] (*The swimming-pool is as deep as it is __ wide*) where the AdjP is predicative complement.[9]

In [20iii], *that it was a hoax* is a content clause in terms of its internal structure: as a comparative clause it is reduced to just a complement with the form of a content clause, but permits expansion by the addition of *believed*, giving *than [__ believed that it was a hoax]*. Analogously for [iv].

The most common type of single-element construction has an NP standing on its own, as in [20v]. This example illustrates an obvious type of ambiguity resulting from reduction: it can be filled out as either *than [she phoned Liz __]* or as *than [Liz phoned her __]* (and such fuller versions are likely to be preferred where the context doesn't make clear which meaning is intended).

In [20vi] the complement of *than* is an NP, but the part following the gap is a nominal and cannot be replaced by a full NP such as *these friends*.

Pronoun case

Where the single element is a personal pronoun, the choice between nominative and accusative follows the general rules given in Ch. 5, §16.2. Compare:

[9] Examples like *He was more shy than rude* involve metalinguistic comparison (§3).

[21] SUBJECT NON-SUBJECT

i a. *She is older than* [*I* __]. b. **The decision affected Kim more than* [__ *I*].

ii a. *She is older than* [*me* __]. b. *The decision affected Kim more than* [__ *me*].

If the pronoun is understood as object or complement of a preposition it is accusative, as in unreduced clauses: *The decision affected Kim more than it affected me/*I.* If it is subject, the choice of case depends on the style. In formal style it appears as nominative, again as in unreduced clauses: *She is older than I am*; but informal style has accusative, as in [iia], where the missing verb cannot be inserted. Some speakers find *I* obtrusively formal and *me* obtrusively informal, and therefore avoid both constructions by retaining the verb: *She is older than I am.*

(g) Restrictions on omission of subject

In clauses where the verb is retained, the subject can be omitted only when it is the counterpart to the comparative phrase or is understood as an embedded clause, as in (d) above:

[22] i *More people came than* [__ *were invited*]. [counterpart to comparative phrase]

ii *He spent longer on it than* [__ *seemed necessary*]. [embedded clause]

iii **Liz works harder than* [__ *worked/did last year*].

To remedy [iii] we must either insert a subject (*she*) or else omit the verb too, giving *than last year.*

2.2 *Than/as* + single element (*Bob is as generous as Liz*)

The most frequent type of scalar comparison has a single element as complement to *than* or *as*, but the analysis of this element is problematic:

[23] *Bob is as generous as Liz.* [reduced clause or immediate complement?]

We have been assuming that in examples like this the complement to *than/as* is a clause reduced to a single element – that in this particular case *Liz* is subject, so that the structure is like that of *Bob is as generous as Liz is*, except that the reduction has been taken one step further. An alternative analysis is to say that *Liz* is here not a clause but simply an NP, that it functions directly, immediately, as complement of *as*. The two possible structures are as follows:

[24]

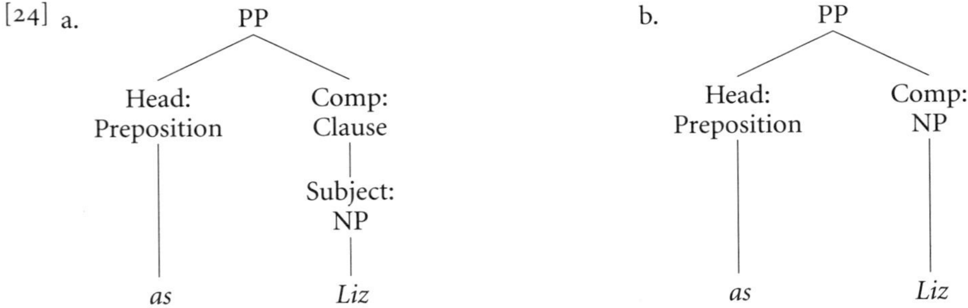

We refer to [a] as the **reduced clause** analysis and to [b] as the **immediate complement** analysis. On this immediate complement analysis, *Bob is as generous as Liz* will be syntactically like *Bob is similar to Liz*, where there is no question of *Liz* being a clause.

One initial point to make is that there are unquestionably some constructions where a single element following *than/as* is an immediate complement, not a reduced clause:

[25] *I saw him as recently as Monday. It is longer than a foot. He's inviting more people than just us. He's poorer than poor. Sue deals with matters such as sales. I saw no one other than Bob.*

The underlined expressions here can't be reduced clauses, because they can't be expanded into clauses: cf. **I saw him as recently as I saw him Monday*; **I saw him as recently as Monday is*; and so on.

The question then is whether all single element constructions should be treated alike or whether a distinction should be drawn such that some, like [25], are immediate complements while others, including [23], are reduced clauses. We review below a number of factors relevant to the choice between these analyses. They do not provide conclusive evidence in favour of one over the other. We have to allow, therefore, for co-existing alternative analyses.

Evidence for a reduced clause analysis

The immediate complement analysis is obviously the simpler of the two and hence initially the more viable. We therefore begin by dealing with three arguments that must be acknowledged as favouring a reduced clause analysis. We will point out, however, that each of the arguments is weakened by certain countervailing considerations.

(a) Potential for nominative case

The first is that in formal style the complement of *as/than* can be a nominative pronoun: *Bob is as generous as she.* A reduced clause analysis obviously accounts for this very simply: the pronoun is subject of the reduced clause and hence takes the same case as it would if the verb were included (*as she is*). The comparative clause construction will then differ structurally from the one with *after* or *before*: *Bob left after Liz.* Unlike [23], this does not allow a nominative: *Bob left after her/*she.* The nominative is impossible here because the pronoun is not subject of a clause but the immediate complement of a preposition.

The fact that less formal style allows an accusative in the comparative construction (*Bob is as generous as her*) is irrelevant because it is consistent with the pronoun being either an immediate complement or a reduced clause. This is because informal style has nominatives only when a primary form of the verb is present, allowing accusative subjects when the verb is omitted (*Kim will be giving the first lecture, me the second*), or is in a secondary form (*What, me wear a kilt?*).

The possibility of a nominative certainly supports a clausal analysis, but we do not regard it as conclusive, because nominatives are found (again in formal style) in certain constructions that we would not want to regard as clausal: *Everyone other than she had signed the petition.* This is like the examples in [25] in not allowing expansion by the addition of a verb; it differs in that *other than* falls within the subject, and it is this association with the subject that motivates the nominative case.

(b) Range of phrase types

A second factor favouring a clausal analysis is that the range of expression types following *than* and *as* in this construction is much wider than is normally found as complement to a preposition. Compare, for example:

[26] i a. *I'm more confident that Kim will support us than that Pat will.*
b. **I'd prefer that Kim supported us to that Pat did.*
ii a. *It is more important to do it well than to do it quickly.*
b. **To do it well is different from to do it quickly.*

Than is followed by a declarative content clause in [ia] and an infinitival clause in [iia], but these cannot function as complement to such prepositions as *to* and *from*. It's not just a matter of *than/as* allowing a large range of expression types, however: the important point is that the content clause in [ia] is not licensed by *than* but by *confident*, and similarly the infinitival clause in [iia] is licensed by *important*. On a reduced clause analysis *than* in [i] doesn't have a content clause but a comparative clause as its immediate complement: *that Pat will*, considered as a content clause, is complement of the understood *confident*, the item which licenses it.

The range of expression types that can occur with *than/as* is similar to that found with the coordinators: cf. *I'm confident that Kim will support us and [that Pat will]*; *It is important to do it well and [to do it quickly]*. There are indeed significant similarities between coordination and comparison. Coordinated elements are normally required to be syntactically alike (Ch. 15, §3), and this likeness is seen too in the comparative construction we are concerned with here – between *that Pat will* and *that Kim will support us*, between *to do it quickly* and *to do it well*, and so on.[10]

Nevertheless, *than* is a preposition here, not a coordinator: the comparative is a subordinative construction, not a coordinative one. The crucial difference between *than* and *and* is that *than* is dependent for its occurrence on a comparative governor, here *more*. Within the AdjP *more confident that Kim will support us than that Pat will*, the complements *that Kim will support us* and *than that Pat will* are not coordinate, not of equal syntactic status, because the former is licensed by *confident*, the latter by *more confident*.

The force of this argument is reduced, however, by the fact that there is a small set of prepositions which do take a similarly wide range of complement types. These are the prepositions of inclusion and exclusion/exception: *including*, *excluding*, *except*, *save* (see Ch. 7, §5.1). Compare, for example: *I'm not confident of anything except that Pat will support us.* There is no plausible analysis of this in which *that Pat will support us* is an elliptically reduced version of a larger clause, but the licensing of it still involves *confident*.

Nevertheless, even these prepositions do not behave entirely like *than/as*:

[27] i *He has more enemies than __ friends.* (=[20vi])
ii *He'll have no one voting for him except friends.*

We have seen that it is impossible to add a determiner to *friends* in [i], but in [ii] we could have, for example, *except his friends*. On a reduced clause analysis the restriction applying to [i] follows from the general rule given in §2.1 above that the counterpart to the comparative governor must be omitted, but on the immediate complement analysis we need an extra restriction, unique to the comparative construction.

[10] The connection between comparison and coordination is reflected in the fact that certain comparative expressions have uses in which they have been reanalysed as marginal coordinators (Ch. 15, §2.8), e.g. *as well as* in *We have a cat as well as a dog.*

(c) Potential for expansion

A third factor is already implicit from the discussion above. Examples like [23] (*Bob is as generous as Liz*) can be expanded into obvious clausal structures:

[28] i a. *Bob is as generous as Liz.* b. *Bob is as generous as Liz is.*
ii a. *I enjoyed it more than the film.* b. *I enjoyed it more than I enjoyed the film.*

It is not just that such expansion is possible; it is an important advantage of the reduced clause analysis that it brings out the difference between such examples and those like [25], where no expansion is possible. At the same time, it ties in with the semantics. *Bob is as generous as Liz* is interpreted as a variable comparison ("Bob is *x* generous, Liz is *y* generous, and *x* is (at least) equal to *y*"), whereas this kind of interpretation does not apply in [25] (recall the contrast between variable–variable and variable–constant comparisons illustrated in [2] of §2). Moreover, the reduced clause analysis offers a straightforward account of the ambiguity of examples like [20v] (*Sue phoned Angela more often than Liz*), with *Liz* subject of the reduced clause in one interpretation, object in the other. And given that a clause can be reduced to a sequence of two elements, as in [18], there would seem to be no principled reason for saying that it can't be reduced to a single element.

A problem emerges, however. It is not in fact a straightforward matter to determine whether or not a verb can be added. Consider such examples as the following:

[29] i *In a country as rich as Australia there should be no poverty.*
ii *He won't waste his hard-earned dollars on something as frivolous as exercise.*
iii *Criticism is as old as literary art.*
iv *Your guess is as good as mine.*
v *The field was as flat as a pancake.*
vi *He looks as fit as a fiddle.*

The relevant verb in all cases is *be*. It can be added readily enough in [i] (*as Australia is*), but for [ii–iv] it would be very unusual, for [v] it would be almost impossible, and for [vi] it is unthinkable.

The reason we can't add *is* in [29vi] is that *as fit as a fiddle* is an idiom meaning "very fit". It would be nonsensical to ask how fit a fiddle is (violins do not have states of health), and hence it is impossible to insert *is*. In the case of [v] it would not be nonsensical to insert *is* because pancakes are in fact flat; it is just highly unidiomatic, because *as flat as a pancake* is a familar established phrase. In this phrase it is possible to omit the first *as* (*was flat as a pancake*), and insertion of the *is* then becomes syntactically impossible. Example [iv] is also a familiar expression, one that this time includes the subject, not just the predicative AdjP. And this familiarity of the expression disfavours the addition of *is*, though not so strongly as in [v–vi].

In general, the more familiar the expression, the less readily will it accommodate the addition of a verb. But this does not provide a dichotomy between cases where the verb can be added and those where it can't. Moreover, it is not a matter of syntax as such. It is not clear, therefore, that we have grounds for making any structural distinction among the comparative complements in [29], or between them and [28].

We have been tacitly assuming here that potential expansion is a sufficient condition for a reduced clause analysis: that if you can expand to make a clause, the clausal analysis is the right one. But there is one context in which this would yield the wrong results, namely in the complement of the prepositions *before* and *after*. Compare:

[30] i *Sue phoned Angela before Liz.*
ii *Sue phoned Angela more often than Liz.* (=[20v])

Here [i] exhibits the same ambiguity as [ii], being expandable to either (a) *before Liz phoned her*, or (b) *before she phoned Liz.* But it would be wrong to say that *Liz* is a reduced clause in [i], because (as noted above) a pronoun in this position cannot appear in nominative case: **Sue phoned Angela before she* is ungrammatical. It would therefore be wrong to treat expandability as sufficient to establish that a reduced clause analysis is valid.

Evidence for an immediate complement analysis

We now present two arguments against treating every phrasal complement to *as* or *than* as some kind of reduced clause. Again, though, we note that there are complicating and weakening considerations; the arguments are not conclusive.

(a) Fronting and preposition stranding

Consider, first, the following constructions:

[31] i *It was decided by Judge Darwin, than whom no one could be more impartial.*
ii ?*How many of them do you regard yourself as better than?*

Example [31i] is a further example of the construction illustrated in [18iv] of §1. *Than* has a relative pronoun as complement, so that *than* + NP occupies prenuclear position in the relative clause, rather than the final position seen in the main clause *no one could be more impartial than Judge Darwin.* It would be quite impossible to have a clause as complement to *than* here, e.g. **than* [*who is* __] *no one could be more impartial.*

Whereas [31i] belongs to formal style, [ii] is informal, and indeed perhaps of only marginal acceptability. Structurally, it differs from [i] in that only the complement *how many of them* is fronted, with the preposition *than* left stranded in its basic position. And again the fronted element can only be a phrase, not a clause: **How many of them are do you regard yourself as better than?*

In these two constructions, then, *whom* and *how many of them* do behave syntactically as immediate complements of *than* rather than as clauses.

The force of this argument is limited, however, by the fact that these are very rare constructions: they don't provide a secure foundation for building an analysis of the much more central type seen in our *Bob is as generous as Liz* example.

(b) Reflexives

A second point concerns the optional occurrence of reflexive pronouns, as in:

[32] *He married a woman fifteen years younger than him/himself.*

It is not possible to add a verb here (**than himself was*), which suggests that the pronoun is an immediate complement.

Once again, the evidence is far from conclusive, because the reflexive form could be attributable to the omission of the verb, as in *I suggest that you give the first three lectures and myself the remaining two.*

Fused relative as complement: *than what* ...

Where the complement of *than/as* is a single element with the form of a fused relative introduced by *what*, a distinction is to be made between the following constructions:

[33] i *She apparently liked it more than what we gave her.*
ii %*She apparently liked it more than what we did.*

There is nothing special about [i]: *what we gave her* is not significantly different from any other NP, such as *the book we gave her*, for example. Note, in particular, that [i] could be expanded to *She apparently liked it more than she liked what we gave her*. The meaning of [ii] (at least in the salient and intended interpretation) is "She apparently liked it more than we liked it". Here *what we did* can't be expanded: on the contrary, *what* can be dropped to give *She apparently liked it more than we did*. It is therefore using a fused relative NP instead of a comparative clause. This second construction is commonly encountered in speech, but it is not normally found in published writing: it is very doubtful whether it can be regarded as belonging to the standard variety of English.

2.3 Likeness and contrast between comparative clause and matrix

Maximum and minimum likeness

The terms in a variable comparison are partly alike and partly different. The extremes on the scale of likeness are illustrated in these two examples, where underlining indicates material shared between the comparative clause and the matrix:

[34] i *She's as fit as [she is __] because she does so much swimming.*
("she is *x* fit", "she is *y* fit")

ii *More people came to the show than [we could find seats for __].*
("*x* many people came to the show", "we could find seats for *y* many people")

In [i] the terms differ only in the implicit variables (which are asserted to be equal). Syntactically, the comparative clause differs from the matrix only in the absence of a counterpart to the comparative phrase.[11] The minimum likeness required is that the comparative clause include, semantically, a counterpart to the comparative phrase. This is the case with [ii], where the likeness to the matrix is confined to the understood "many people".

Most variable comparisons fall between these extremes, having some overt contrast but also varying amounts of shared material, repeated (typically by pro-forms) or left understood:

[35] i *There were more boys in the class than [(there were) girls].*

ii *Jill spends more time in London than [(she does) at home].*

Multiple contrasts

Each of the examples in [35] involves a single contrast (apart from that between the implicit variables), but one commonly finds more, e.g. two in [36i] and four in [36ii]:

[36] i *There were more boys in IB than [(there were) girls in IC].*

ii *Kim lost more at the races in one day than [I earned at my job in a year].*

Implicit point of contrast in the matrix

There may be a contrast between an overt element in the comparative clause and one which is merely understood in the matrix:

[11] In this type of comparison there is generally an implicature that the value of the variables is relatively high – she's quite high on the scale of fitness. Similarly: *With the weather being as hot as it is, the weeds should dry out quickly enough.*

[37] i *The trains arrive on time more often than [they do in England].*
ii *It tastes better than [it does with sugar in].*

The implicit elements are recoverable deictically (i.e. from the time, place, or other circumstances of the speech act) or anaphorically (from previous mention). In [i] the contrast is between England and the country we are in or have been talking about; in [ii] we understand "like this/that, i.e. without sugar in".

Temporal contrasts

The main contrast may be a matter of time, expressed by tense:

[38] i *It is better than [it was].*
ii *It wasn't as good as [it is now].*

Note, however, that where contrastive present time is associated with the comparative clause the present tense normally needs reinforcing with a temporal modifier: it would be unusual to drop *now* from [ii].

Contrasts involving embedding

When the comparative phrase is contained within a content clause, the scope of the comparison may or may not extend upwards into the superordinate clause. Compare:

[39] i *Jill thinks Max is better off than [she is].* [narrow scope]
ii *Jill thinks Max is better off than [he is].* [wide scope]

The salient interpretation of [i] attributes to Jill the thought "Max is better off than I am", where the terms in the comparison are "Max is *x* well off" and "I (Jill) am *y* well off": here *Jill thinks* is outside the scope of the comparison. But the salient interpretation of [ii] does not attribute to Jill the nonsensical thought "Max is better off than he (Max) is". Rather, *Jill thinks* is within the scope of the comparison, whose terms are "Jill thinks Max is *x* well off" and "He (Max) is *y* well off". As will be evident from these examples, this distinction is not encoded grammatically, and strictly speaking both examples are ambiguous as to the scope of the comparison.[12]

2.4 The comparative phrase

We have so far been talking of the comparative phrase quite loosely as the one 'containing' the comparative governor: we need now to consider the concept rather more carefully.

Predicative vs attributive AdjP

Note first the following data:

[40] i *His motor-bike was more powerful than my car had been __.*
ii **He had a more powerful motor-bike than my car had been __.*
iii *He had a more powerful motor-bike than I had had __ / than mine had been __.*

[12] One respect in which there is a grammatical difference is that the comparative clause in examples like [39ii] can't be reduced to a pronoun in the 'sensible' reading, but allows a reflexive in the nonsensical one: *#Jill thinks Max is better off than himself.*

In [i] the comparative phrase is *more powerful* (*than my car had been*):[13] we understand the secondary term as "my car had been *y* powerful". In [ii], however, the comparative phrase is not *more powerful* but the larger sequence *a more powerful motor-bike*: this is why the example is anomalous, for we have to interpret the secondary term as "my car had been a *y* powerful motor-bike". Instead of this we need examples like [iii], where the secondary terms "I had had a *y* powerful motor-bike" and "mine had been a *y* powerful motor-bike" make sense. As suggested in §1.3, we can think of the comparative feature as 'percolating' upwards from the AdjP to the NP in which it functions as attributive modifier.

AdvP

Compare similarly:

[41] i *She spoke more persuasively than her father had __.*
ii *He was more conspicuously shy than Max was __.*
iii **He was more conspicuously shy than Max leered __ at Jill.*
iv *This is a more carefully researched article than I have read __ this semester.*
v **This is a more carefully researched article than his book was __.*

In [i] the comparative phrase is the AdvP *more persuasively.* In [ii–iii] it is the AdjP *more conspicuously shy*: [iii] is unacceptable because there is no place in the comparative clause for an understood "shy". And in [iv–v] the comparative phrase is *a more carefully researched article,* with [v] being anomalous because it requires the interpretation "his book was a *y* carefully researched article". Again, then, we have upward percolation of the comparative feature from the AdvP to the AdjP in [ii–iii], and to the NP in [iv–v].

Postpositive AdjP

Where an AdjP modifier is postpositive (after the noun) rather than attributive (before the noun) there is normally no such upward percolation:

[42] i **He had a more powerful motor-bike than my car had been __.* [attributive]
ii *He had a motor-bike more powerful than my car had been __.* [postpositive]

In [i] (discussed above as [40ii]) the comparative phrase is *a more powerful motor-bike,* whereas in [ii] it is just *more powerful*: the difference in acceptability reflects the fact that while a car can be powerful, a car cannot be a powerful motor-bike. The postpositive AdjP here behaves in the same way as a relative clause: *He had a motor-bike which was more powerful than my car had been.* It also behaves like a clause in that the comparative complement cannot be postposed out of it: *Anyone less thick-skinned than Kim would have resigned long ago,* but not **Anyone less thick-skinned would have resigned long ago than Kim.*

PP

In general upward percolation does not extend from an NP to a PP containing it, but there are nevertheless some constructions where it does:

[43] i *He lectured on more topics than __ were included in the syllabus.*
ii *He lectured on more topics than I had lectured on __ / *than I had lectured __.*
iii *He returned to us in a far less buoyant frame of mind than he had left us __.*

[13] Henceforth in this section we simplify by omitting the *than* or *as* phrase (the comparative complement) when citing comparative phrases.

In [i–ii] the comparative phrase is the NP *more topics*, not the PP *on more topics*: in [i] the missing subject is understood as "*y* many topics", not prepositional "on *y* many topics", and in [ii] *on* cannot be omitted from the comparative clause, as would be possible (and indeed required) if it were part of the counterpart to the comparative phrase.[14] In [iii], however, the comparative phrase is the PP *in a far less buoyant frame of mind*: we interpret the comparative clause as "he had left us in a *y* buoyant frame of mind" and it is not possible to add *in* after *us*.

Unexpected cases of upwards percolation

One finds occasional examples where the upwards percolation goes beyond what is allowed for on the above account. In the following it applies with postpositive AdjPs:

[44] i *They would have us face risks greater than President Kennedy's most influential advisers seem disposed to face* __.
ii *He made tables of veins, nerves, and arteries five times more exact than* __ *are described by any contemporary author.*

The gaps here require understood NPs, not AdjPs, since their functions are respectively object and subject: the comparative phrases must include *risks* and *tables of veins, nerves, and arteries*. Consider also the following, where the AdjP in the matrix is predicative rather than postpositive:

[45] i *This result is better than* __ *would probably be achieved by a vaccination policy.*
ii *The price was higher than he wished to pay* __ .
iii *When children start school they tend to get books that aren't as rewarding as they've had* __.
iv *The eastward movement of the Atlantic thermal ridge was forecast to be a little less than* __ *actually occurred.*

Again, the missing element from the comparative clause must be understood as an NP, not an AdjP: they are equivalent to '*. . . than the result that would probably be achieved . . .*', '*. . . than the price that he wished to pay*', '*. . . as the books they've had*', '*. . . than the movement that actually occurred*'. It is questionable whether such examples are frequent and systematic enough to qualify as grammatical; certainly the construction illustrated here is not generally permissible, as is evident from the clear ungrammaticality of **This candidate was much better qualified than they appointed* ("than the one whom"), and the like.

3 Metalinguistic comparison (*more apparent than real*)

Examples like *The problem was more apparent than real* differ both syntactically and semantically from the ordinary comparisons discussed so far. These differences are seen in:

[1] i *Ed is older than his brother.* } [ordinary comparison]
ii *Ed is older than middle-aged.* }
iii *Ed is more old than middle-aged.* [metalinguistic comparison]

In [i] we have a variable comparison between the degree to which Ed is old and the

[14] *On* can be omitted if *lectured* is too (*than I had* __), but that results in the stranding construction where more than the counterpart to the comparative element is omitted.

degree to which his brother is old. In [ii] we have a variable–constant comparison (like *Kim is taller than six foot*): *middle-aged* denotes a segment on the scale expressed by ***old*** and [ii] puts his age beyond that part of the scale. What [iii] says, however, is that Ed is more properly described as old than as middle-aged: we call this **metalinguistic comparison** because it is concerned not with segments on the age scale but with the relative applicability of the linguistic expressions *old* and *middle-aged.*

Syntactically, metalinguistic comparison differs from ordinary comparison in that it allows only analytic comparative forms: *older* in [ii], for example, excludes this metalinguistic interpretation. The construction here also excludes a comparative clause as complement to *than*/*as*: **Ed is more old than he is middle-aged.*

Other examples of metalinguistic comparison are:

[2] i *The office of Lord High Commissioner is now more ornamental than functional.*
ii *The buds were more red than pink.*
iii *He was more dead than alive.*
iv *It was more an error of judgement than a case of negligence.*
v *She had spoken more in sorrow than in anger.*

The commonly used expression illustrated in [iii] brings out the point that this kind of comparison can be used with non-gradable adjectives (contrast the ordinary comparison *#He was more dead than we'd expected*). The most obvious examples of metalinguistic comparison involve adjectives, where – at least with shorter ones – we can contrast the permitted analytic form (*more red*) with the excluded inflectional one (*redder*). But the category certainly applies more generally, as evident from [iv] (NPs) and [v] (PPs).

Note, however, that this construction does not apply to verbs: **We more expect than require you to make a contribution.*

Semantically similar to the above core cases of metalinguistic comparison are:

[3] i *He's old rather than middle-aged.*
ii *He's not so much stupid as lazy.*

These may be contrasted with the ordinary comparisons *I intend to do it my way rather than yours* or *I haven't got so much patience as you.*

4 Scalar term comparison

4.1 The major governors in comparisons of inequality

Scalar comparison of inequality is for the most part governed by the comparative inflection or the degree adverbs *more* and *less.* As well as being degree adverbs, however, *more* and *less* can themselves be inflectional forms of determinatives, so we need to begin by clarifying the two uses of these words.

4.1.1 *More* and *less*: analytic markers vs inflectional forms

More as an analytic marker corresponding to the comparative inflection

The inflectional system of grade applies to a large set of adjectives and a few adverbs, determinatives, and prepositions (see Ch. 6, §2.2). We illustrate here with adjectives and adverbs:

[1]

	PLAIN	COMPARATIVE	SUPERLATIVE
i ADJECTIVE	*tall*	*taller*	*tallest*
ii ADVERB	*soon*	*sooner*	*soonest*

Grade differs from other inflectional systems in English in that only a subset of adjectives and adverbs inflect: with others the comparative and superlative categories are marked analytically (i.e. by means of a separate word), rather than inflectionally (i.e. by morphological modification). For the comparative category, analytic marking is by means of the adverb *more*, which we will represent as *more*$_a$ (with subscript 'a' mnemonic for 'analytic'). Consider, then:

[2]

	INFLECTIONAL COMPARATIVE	ANALYTIC COMPARATIVE
i	a. *This is shorter than that.*	b. **This is more*$_a$ *short than that.*
ii	a. **This is porouser than that.*	b. *This is more*$_a$ *porous than that.*
iii	a. *This is commoner than that.*	b. *This is more*$_a$ *common than that.*

Some lexemes, like *short*, inflect and exclude *more*$_a$ (except in metalinguistic comparison); others, like *porous*, allow only the analytic form; and some, like *common*, allow both patterns – see Ch. 18, §3.2. *More*$_a$ thus provides an alternative means of expressing the meaning elsewhere expressed by the comparative inflection.

More as an inflectional form

In addition, *more* can be itself an inflectional comparative form of the determinatives ***much*** and ***many***. This *more*, which we represent as *more*$_i$, contrasts with the plain forms, as illustrated in:

[3]

	PLAIN FORM	INFLECTIONAL COMPARATIVE
i	a. *Did it cause much trouble?*	b. *Did it cause more*$_i$ *trouble than last time?*
ii	a. *Many people complained.*	b. *More*$_i$ *people complained than last time.*

We use interrogative examples in [i] because the plain form *much* is polarity-sensitive, occurring most readily in non-affirmative contexts (see Ch. 9, §4.1.2). *More*$_i$ is of course an irregular form, standing in, as it were, for regular **mucher* and **manier*. Note that *more*$_a$ does not enter into any such contrast with *much*: we can say *This is more porous than that*, but not **Is this much porous?*

The corresponding superlative form is *most*, so the set of forms matching those given in [1] above is:

[4]

	PLAIN	COMPARATIVE	SUPERLATIVE
DETERMINATIVE	*much/many*	*more*$_i$	*most*$_i$

The distinction applied to *less*: *less*$_a$ vs *less*$_i$

The case with *less* is similar, though with some differences of detail, and we again make a distinction between *less*$_a$ and *less*$_i$. We noted in §1.1 that there are two different kinds of comparison of inequality, superiority and inferiority; the former is marked inflectionally or analytically, by *more*$_a$, while inferiority is always marked analytically – by *less*$_a$:

[5]

	SUPERIORITY	INFERIORITY
i	a. *This is taller than that.*	b. *This is less*$_a$ *tall than that.*
ii	a. *This is more*$_a$ *porous than that.*	b. *This is less*$_a$ *porous than that.*

Less$_i$, by contrast, is an inflectional form – in the central cases, the comparative form of

little. As such, it contrasts with the plain form:

[6]	PLAIN FORM	INFLECTIONAL COMPARATIVE
	a. *We have little money.*	b. *We have $less_i$ money than we need.*

Again, the *$less_a$* that modifies the adjectives in [5] does not contrast with the plain form *little*: **This is little porous.* The *little* in [6a] belongs to the determinative category and is sharply distinct, in terms of both syntax and meaning, from the adjective *little* of *a little house*, etc.[15]

Difference in relations of *$more_a$* to *$less_a$* and of *$more_i$* to *$less_i$*

$More_a$ and *$less_a$* are markers of comparison of superiority and inferiority, respectively. If we include the comparison of equality, we have the three terms shown in [7] (with *strong* taking an inflectional comparative, *tactful* an analytic one):

[7]			
	i EQUALITY	*I'm as strong as Ed.*	*I'm as tactful as Ed.*
	ii SUPERIORITY	*I'm stronger than Ed.*	*I'm $more_a$ tactful than Ed.*
	iii INFERIORITY	*I'm $less_a$ strong than Ed.*	*I'm $less_a$ tactful than Ed.*

Like ***old*** and ***young***, as discussed in §1.1, the determinatives ***much*** and ***little*** are opposite in orientation: the more money you have, the further removed from zero is the amount of money you have, but the less money you have, the closer to zero it is. We will say that ***much*** and ***little*** have respectively **positive** and **negative** orientation, since *Much has been achieved* and *Little has been achieved*, say, are syntactically positive and negative respectively (see Ch. 9, §3.3). As inflectional comparatives, *$more_i$* and *$less_i$* (like *older* and *younger*) both express superiority, but there are no inferiority counterparts marked by *$less_a$* – cf. **I've $less_a$ much tea than Ed*; **I've $less_a$ little tea than Ed.* Thus instead of a one-dimensional contrast between three forms, as illustrated in [7], we have a two-dimensional pattern with four admissible forms:

[8]		POSITIVE ORIENTATION	NEGATIVE ORIENTATION
	i EQUALITY	*I've as much tea as Ed.*	*I've as little tea as Ed.*
	ii SUPERIORITY	*I've $more_i$ tea than Ed.*	*I've $less_i$ tea than Ed.*

Equivalences and entailments

Much and *little*

These determinatives denote scales that are effectively the same except for the positive or negative orientation. In comparisons the relations are as illustrated in:

[9]			
i	a. *Kim has $more_i$ money than Pat.*	b. *Pat has $less_i$ money than Kim.*	[a = b]
ii	a. *Kim has as much money as Pat.*	b. *Pat has as little money as Kim.*	[a ≠ b]

In [i], a comparison of superiority, [a] and [b] are equivalent: each entails the other. Neither of them says whether Kim or Pat has much or little money, the issue being merely their relative positions on the scales. The comparisons of equality, [ii], are not equivalent, however; [iib] indicates that both Pat and Kim have little money, whereas [iia] (like both examples in [i]) is neutral as to whether they have much or little money. The difference correlates with the fact that *much* is the more general member of the pair: it can be used more widely, and in particular without any implicature that an unmodified plain form

[15] The adjective ***little*** has *littler* as its comparative form, but this and superlative *littlest* are rarely used, the corresponding forms of ***small*** generally being preferred; see also the discussion of adjectival *less(er)* below.

would be applicable. *How much money do you have?*, for example, doesn't presuppose that you have much money, whereas *How little money do you have?* would generally be used only in a context where it has been established that you have little money.

Adjectives

Some pairs of adjectives show the same behaviour as *much* and *little*, whereas for others the relations are different. Consider the following comparisons of superiority:

[10] i	a. *Kim is older than Pat.*	b. *Pat is younger than Kim.*
ii	a. *Yours is better than mine.*	b. *Mine is worse than yours.*
iii	a. *Monday was hotter than Tuesday.*	b. *Tuesday was colder than Monday.*

In [i] we again have equivalence between [a] and [b]. In [ii] there is entailment in only one direction: [b] entails [a], but [a] does not entail [b]. This is because [iia] is neutral as to whether yours and mine are good or bad, whereas [iib] conveys that both are bad. And in [iii] there is no entailment in either direction: [iiia] conveys that both days were relatively hot, while [iiib] conveys that they were both relatively cold. Thus while *old* and *young*, *good* and *bad*, *hot* and *cold* are opposites, they are opposites of somewhat different kinds, and this of course is a matter of their lexical meaning.

Superiority and inferiority

Consider next the relation between the [a] examples in [10] and corresponding comparisons of inferiority:

[11] i	a. *Kim is older than Pat.*	b. *Pat is less old than Kim.*
ii	a. *Yours is better than mine.*	b. *Mine is less good than yours.*
iii	a. *Monday was hotter than Tuesday.*	b. *Tuesday was less hot than Monday.*

This time it is in [iii] that [a] and [b] are equivalent. In [i–ii] the [b] version entails the [a], but [a] does not entail [b]. In [ia] Kim and Pat could both be young, whereas [ib] conveys that both are relatively old, and similarly in [ii].

Relative infrequency of comparisons of inferiority

Of the three types of comparison, superiority, equality, and inferiority, the last is much the least frequent. We have seen that it is grammatically excluded with the determinatives *much* and *little*, and with adjectives it has to compete with various rival forms. Consider, then:

[12] i *The first problem was less difficult than the second.*
ii *The first problem was not as difficult as the second.*
iii *The first problem was easier than the second.* } [entailed by [i]]
iv *The second problem was more difficult than the first.* }

We noted in §1.1 that scalar equality is normally interpreted as "at least equal", i.e. equal or superior, and hence the negation of this is equivalent to inferiority: [i] and [ii] each entail the other. The superiority comparisons [iii–iv] are entailed by [i], but do not entail it because they don't entail that the first problem was difficult.

Less occurs readily with adjectives of two or more syllables (*less articulate*, *less interesting*, *less likely*, etc.) but not so commonly with short ones, especially where there is an adjective of opposite meaning available: *older* is likely to be strongly preferred over *less young*, *smaller* over *less big*, *worse* over *less good*, and so on.

Adjectival *less*$_i$

The *less*$_i$ that we have considered above is the comparative form of the determinative *little*, but *less*$_i$ can also belong to the adjective category:

[13] i *Is Soviet influence throughout the world greater or less than it was ten years ago?*
ii *They can employ apprentices provided they pay rates which are not less than those of the other workers.*
iii *They too had felt the influence of Christianity to a greater or less extent.*

Here *less*$_i$ contrasts with adjectival *greater* rather than with determinative *more*$_i$. A non-comparative construction corresponding to *less* in [i] might be *Soviet influence is now quite small*, just as a positive orientation version would be along the lines of *Soviet influence is now very great/considerable* (not *much*). Similarly, in [ii] a non-comparative would have an adjective such as *low* rather than determinative *little*: *These pay rates are low/*little.* Adjectival *less* is clearly a comparative form, but it cannot be identified as the comparative counterpart of any particular plain form. It is normally restricted to predicative function, as in [i–ii]; its occurrence in attributive function is virtually restricted to the particular phrase *a greater or less extent.* Note that in this example *less* is in construction with a count singular noun, which is not possible for the determinative *little.*

The double comparative *lesser*

[14] i *They too had felt the influence of Christianity to a greater or lesser extent.*
ii *We think this is a lesser risk than taking no action at all.*
iii *a lesser man/journal*

Lesser is found only in attributive function – in [i] as an alternant of *less.* The meaning is "smaller" ([i–ii]) or "less worthy/significant" ([iii]). From a morphological point of view *lesser* is a 'double comparative': it is formed by the addition of the regular comparative suffix to what is itself an irregular comparative form, *less.* Other double comparative forms, such as *worser*, are no longer current in Standard English.

4.1.2 Comparative forms of the degree determinatives

The count vs non-count distinction

The examples in [8] above have ***much*** and ***little*** as determiner to a non-count noun. With a plural count noun as head we have the following pattern:

[15]	POSITIVE ORIENTATION	NEGATIVE ORIENTATION
i EQUALITY	*I've as many shirts as Ed.*	*I've as few shirts as Ed.*
ii SUPERIORITY	*I've more*$_i$ *shirts than Ed.*	*I've fewer/less*$_i$ *shirts than Ed.*

Many and *few* are the count plain forms corresponding to non-count *much* and *little*, but in the comparison of superiority *more* is used with count as well as non-count nouns, while with negative orientation non-count nouns take *less*, and count nouns either *fewer* or *less.* The pattern is thus as shown in:

[16]	POSITIVE ORIENTATION		NEGATIVE ORIENTATION	
	Non-count sg	**Count pl**	**Non-count sg**	**Count pl**
EQUALITY	*as much*	*as many*	*as little*	*as few*
SUPERIORITY	*more*		*less*	*fewer/less*

The relation between *less* and *fewer* is fairly complex. In non-count singulars only *less* is possible: *Kim has less/*fewer money than Pat.* In plural NPs we have:

[17] i *She left less than ten minutes ago.*
ii *Less/Fewer than thirty of the students had voted.*
iii *He made no less/fewer than fifteen mistakes.*
iv *You pass if you make ten mistakes or less/?fewer.*
v *He took less/*fewer pains to convince us than I'd expected.*
vi *He made fewer/less mistakes than the others.*

Both [i] and [ii] have *than* + numeral. In [i] *ten minutes* expresses an amount of time rather than a number of individuated units, and in such cases *fewer* is virtually impossible – just as *few* would be in a comparison of equality: *She left as little/*few as ten minutes ago.* Similarly with *We paid less than thirty dollars for it*; *She's less than forty years old*; *We were going at less than ten miles an hour.* In [ii] we are concerned with countable individuals and *little* cannot be used in a comparison of equality (**as little as thirty of the students*); nevertheless, for inequality *less* is more common than *fewer* in this construction. The same applies with percentages: *Less/Fewer than 30% of the students had voted.* Construction [iii] has the comparative form following *no*: though the interpretation is count plural, *less* is here again more common than *fewer.* Construction [iv] has *or* after a numeral: *less* is the usual form here, with *fewer* quite marginal; this construction is widely seen in supermarkets, with the fast checkout labelled *eight items or less*, or the like. In [v] *pains* is plural but non-count rather than count (we can't ask how many pains he took), and here only *less* is possible. Finally in [vi] (as also in [15ii]) the comparative occurs directly with a count plural noun: both forms are found, but *less* is subject to quite strong prescriptive disapproval, so that *fewer* is widely preferred in formal style, and by many speakers in informal style too.[16]

Grading of count singular nouns

[18] i *Jill's more of a scholar than Tom is.*
ii *The delay turned out to be less of a problem than we'd expected.*

The comparative forms *more* and *less* are used in grading count singular heads in predicative NPs: it is a matter of the degree to which Jill is a scholar, and to which the delay was a problem. For the syntactic structure of these NPs, see Ch. 5, §9.2.

Degree adjunct in clause structure

[19] i *She trusts you [more than her own solicitor].*
ii *It hurt [less than I'd thought it would].*

The bracketed phrases are degree adjuncts modifying the verb. The plain forms *much* and *little* occur in comparisons of equality (e.g. *It hurt as much/little this time as on the previous two occasions*); unmodified *much* could occur only in non-affirmative

[16] Usage manuals are divided on the issue of *less* vs *fewer.* Some uncompromisingly brand such forms as *less mistakes* as incorrect, while others note that though commonly condemned they are often used by speakers of Standard English. Before the Early Modern English period (beginning around 1500) *more* was restricted to non-count NPs with *moe* used as the comparative of *many.* At that time *less* was used along with *fewer* for count NPs, but came to be stigmatised and quite rare in this use: it is only within the last generation or so that it has become frequent. The current revival seems inexorable, given the strong pressure of analogy with *more.*

contexts (*She doesn't trust you much*), while unmodified *little* does not occur in this position.

4.2 Less central governors in scalar inequality (*rather*, *prefer*, *superior*)

Rather

This contains the comparative suffix ·*er* but the original base *rath* (meaning "soon") has been lost, so that *rather* is no longer analysable as an inflectional comparative. It nevertheless retains clear semantic and syntactic affinities with ordinary comparative constructions. We consider four uses where it appears in construction with *than*.

(a) The idiom *would rather* ("would prefer")

[20] i *She would rather live in danger than die of loneliness and boredom.*
ii *I'd far rather give it to charity than to the government.*
iii *I'd rather you left the position vacant than that you appointed your son.*
iv *I'd rather he came on Tuesday than on Wednesday.*

These are term comparisons, with the terms marked by underlining. *Would rather* takes either a bare infinitival complement ([i–ii]), or a finite one ([iii–iv]). In either case the primary term can be either the whole complement, as in [i/iii], or part of it, as in [ii/iv] (which can be expanded to make them like [i/iii]: *than give it to the government, than that he came on Wednesday*). *Sooner* is an alternant of *rather*, and we can also have the comparison of equality *would as soon* (+ *as*).

(b) With bare infinitival and "in preference" meaning

[21] i *Many of them went to jail rather than pay the fine.*
ii *Rather than talk about it, let's do it.*

The meaning is related to that in (a), but syntactically the *than* complement is obligatory and must immediately follow *rather* – note, for example, the impossibility of putting *rather* before *went* in [i], or of omitting *than pay the fine* (without a change in the meaning of *rather*).

(c) Contrastive link, meaning "not, instead of":

[22] i *Care rather than skill is all you need.*
ii *Things like that would increase rather than be done away with.*

The meaning of "preference" has here been lost, and *rather than* belongs with the coordinators: see Ch. 15, §2.8. Note that in [ii] *rather than* is followed by a bare infinitival, but it differs syntactically as well as semantically from the construction of [21]. In use (c) a bare infinitival has to be paired with another one preceding *rather* (here *increase*) – compare **Things like that increased rather than be done away with* with [21i].

(d) Pleonastic use, with *rather than* equivalent to *than* alone:

[23] i *Wouldn't it be better to travel with friends, rather than total strangers?*
ii *These people are more likely to be referred to courts rather than to aid panels.*

Rather has no independent meaning here, repeating or emphasising the superiority feature expressed earlier in *better* and *more*. Usually, of course, we have *than* on its own, and *rather* is allowed only when *than* is fairly far removed from the main comparative governor – *than* can't be replaced by *rather than* in simple structures like *Kim is more patient than Pat.* Nor can it occur in combination with determinative *more*: **Kim has more patience in situations of this kind, rather than Pat.*

Prefer

The meaning is the same as that of *like better*, which is overtly comparative; *prefer* itself, however, is at the periphery of syntactically comparative expressions. It occurs in the following constructions:

[24] i *They prefer kangaroo meat to beef.*
ii *She prefers to read rather than watch television.*
iii ?*He'd prefer to put David over the cliff than let him have the land for building.*
iv *They preferred to sell their produce for gold rather than the local currency.*
v *He prefers plucking the guitar string to the bow-string.*

The most usual pattern is seen in [i], a term comparison with the primary term expressed by the object NP, the secondary one by the complement of the preposition *to*. *To* cannot take an infinitival complement, however, and hence can't be used when the primary term has this form: instead we generally find *rather than*, as in [ii]. This use of *rather than* can be related to use (d) above, except that with *prefer* omitting the *rather* is not fully acceptable: the construction with *than* alone, as in [iii], is rare (and generally condemned by prescriptivists, in spite of the clear analogy with *would rather*). *Rather than* is also used when the terms are contained within an infinitival clause, as in [iv], which allows expansion to *rather than sell it for the local currency.* Example [v] shows that *to* can also be used when the terms are contained within a clause, but this is normally restricted to gerund-participials: *to* cannot substitute for *rather than* in [iv]. *Prefer* can also take a declarative content clause; an overt secondary term is rare here, but the structure would follow the pattern of infinitivals (*I'd prefer that the meeting was postponed than that it should take place without you*).[17]

Superior, inferior

These adjectives come from Latin comparative forms, but their syntactic resemblance to English comparative forms is very limited. Most notably, they don't take *than*, but *to*:

[25] i *They believe their culture is superior to any in the world.*
ii *It is absurd to speak of philosophy as a superior enterprise to sociology.*

The meaning of *superior* here is "better" – and note that the attributive use in [ii] resembles the attributive use of a comparative form (as in *Students find philosophy a more difficult enterprise than sociology*) in that the head noun applies semantically to *sociology* as well as to *philosophy*, i.e. sociology is presupposed to be an enterprise (cf. [40] of §2.3).

The modifiers these items take can be like those of comparative forms (see §4.4): we could, for example, add *much* or *far* to *superior* in [25]. But they also accept the modifiers used with plain forms, such as *very*: *This is a very inferior design.* In such cases the comparative meaning is usually lost too, with *very inferior* interpreted simply as "very

[17] Other prepositions than those shown in [24] are occasionally found – e.g. *over*. This is more usual, however, with the noun *preference*: *their preference for the country over the city.*

poor quality"; the comparative meaning, "much poorer quality", is nevertheless also possible. Note finally that while an inflectional comparative cannot itself be compared, such recursive comparison is much more acceptable with these forms:

[26] i **Our forces are more worse than theirs than you acknowledge.*
ii *Our forces are more inferior to theirs than you acknowledge.*

Other adjectives deriving from Latin comparative forms are *anterior, posterior, prior, senior, junior, major,* and *minor.* Except for the last two these can occur in the predicative construction with a *to* complement, and *senior/junior* can take *far* and *much* as modifiers (cf. *He's far senior to me in experience*), but otherwise their syntactic resemblance to English comparative forms is negligible.[18]

4.3 Scalar comparisons of equality: *as, so, such*

The default degree adverb marking scalar equality is *as*: *Kim is as old as Pat. So* is also possible under restricted conditions:

[27] i *It's not so simple as that.*
ii *The floor and furniture didn't gleam nearly so much as yours do.*
iii *Is putting a rocket in orbit half so significant as the good news that God put his son, Jesus Christ, on earth to live and die to save our hell-bound souls?*

In this use, *so* occurs only in non-affirmative contexts – most are negatives, as in [i–ii], but other types are found too, such as interrogative [iii]. *As* can replace *so* in these contexts, where it is indeed somewhat more frequent. *So* is also used in some of the comparative idioms discussed in §4.5 below: *so/as far as I know*; *No one else in the family had so/%as much as heard of it.*

In addition, *such* occurs in scalar comparisons of equality (as well as non-scalar ones dealt with in §5.3):

[28] i *This country has never faced such great dangers as __ threaten us today.*
ii *Few industries were growing at such a rate as catering.*
iii *His second film wasn't such a success as his first.*
iv *Never again would the society assume such a high profile as in the late twenties.*

Like *so, such* in this use is normally restricted to non-affirmative contexts. This restriction does not apply to non-scalar *such,* nor to the use of degree *such* without an *as* phrase, a use where the comparative meaning is effectively lost and *such* serves simply as an intensifier: *It seemed such a good idea at the time!*; *They are such pedants!*

Omission of first *as*

Where the comparative complement consists of *as* + NP, the first *as* is sometimes omitted. This is primarily found with familiar similes like *good as gold, quick as lightning, safe as*

[18] *Senior* and *junior* allow the secondary term to be expressed as a genitive (cf. note 6 above), as in *She is* [*two years my senior*]. The syntactic analysis of the bracketed phrase is problematic. The genitive dependent suggests that it is an NP, but it cannot occur in core NP positions such as subject and object (cf. *[*Two years my senior*] *supported me*). It cannot, moreover, be pluralised (*They are two years my senior/*seniors*), and it alternates with the clearly adjectival *She is* [*two years senior to me*].

houses, etc.; cf. also the informal (*as*) *like as not*, "probably" (*He'd like as not prefer to eat his meals there*).

4.4 Modification

4.4.1 Degree modification

The governors of scalar comparison may be modified by such expressions as:

[29] i	INEQUALITY:	*much, far, immensely, a great deal, a lot, somewhat, rather, slightly, a bit, (a) little, no, any*
ii	EQUALITY:	*at least, about, approximately, roughly, every bit, easily, half, twice, nearly, nothing like, nowhere near*
iii	EITHER TYPE:	*hardly, scarcely, a third, three times*

The modifiers used in comparisons of inequality are the same with inflectional comparatives as with analytic ones: *far bigger, far more careful. Very* does not serve this function – we need *much* instead (*much bigger*, not **very bigger*, and so on). *Much* itself can as usual be modified by *very*: *very much bigger*. Except for *no*, the expressions in [29i] are found with the more peripheral comparative governors *superior, inferior, preferable.*

Note that while the multipliers *half* and *twice* are restricted to the equality type, *a third* and *three times*, etc., occur with both – with the semantic relations illustrated in:

[30] i	a. *I earn four times as much as Ed.*	b. *I earn four times more than Ed.*	[a = b]
ii	a. *I earn a third as much as Ed.*	b. *I earn a third more than Ed.*	[a ≠ b]
iii	*I earn a third as much again as Ed.*		[= iib]

In [i], the [a] and [b] versions are equivalent: if Ed earns $15,000 a year, I earn $60,000. The more usual version is [ia], and this is semantically straightforward: $15,000 is as much as Ed earns, and $60,000 is four times that. The less usual [ib] might be seen as a blend between *I earn more than Ed* and *I earn four times what Ed earns.* In [ii] there is no such equivalence between the two constructions. In [iia] I earn $5,000, one third of the sum Ed earns; in [iib] I earn $20,000, which is $5,000 more than Ed's $15,000, hence more by one third. This latter meaning can be expressed by a comparison of equality with *again*, as in [iii] – here I earn Ed's $15,000 plus a further third of that.

4.4.2 Modification by *the*

The main function of *the* is as determiner in NP structure, but it also occurs as modifier in various comparative constructions. Some of these involve set comparison (e.g. *It's Jill who wins the more/most often*) and are accordingly dealt with in §6.3.4 below. In term comparison one special case is the correlative comparative construction (as in *The more you practise, the easier it becomes*) described in §4.6; other cases are illustrated in:

[31] i *This didn't make her achievement [<u>any the less</u> significant].*

ii *In the Swedish context, notable for its tradition of peace and non-violence, the senseless futility of this act stands out [<u>the more</u> starkly].*

iii *The plight of the four British employees greatly perturbed Urquhart, [<u>the more</u>] because a request to the Governor for a contingent of Cossacks to escort them to safety had been turned down.*

iv *The result is [all the more disappointing] because she had put in so much effort.*
v *That's [all the more reason to avoid precipitous action].*
vi *He went prone on his stomach, [the better] to pursue his examination.*

The here modifies the following comparative (*more, less, better*), forming a phrase which in turn is modifier to an adjective ([i/iv]), an adverb ([ii]), a verb ([iii/vi]) or determiner to a nominal ([v]).[19] In [i–ii] *the* is freely omissible. In [iii] the underlined occurrence of *the* would be omissible if it introduced a modifier rather than a supplement (which would mean dropping the comma), but not as it stands. In [iv], *all the* might be glossed as "even", or *all the* + comparative as "especially"; *the* can only be omitted if *all* is omitted too. Example [v] is similar, except that *all the more* is here a DP functioning as determiner in NP structure. In [vi] *the better* is a fronted modifier in the infinitival clause of purpose; *the* is obligatory in this position but optional in the basic position – compare *in order to pursue his examination (the) better.*

The is completely excluded if the secondary term is expressed: **The result was the better than I had expected.* Nor is *the* permitted when the secondary term is recoverable anaphorically, from what has gone before. We cannot, for example, insert *the* in *It was cloudy and cold for the first two days but on the third day the weather was better*, where we understand "better than on the first two days".[20]

4.5 Comparative idioms and reanalysis

This section presents a sample of the numerous expressions containing comparative governors which in the course of time have become idiomatised or syntactically reanalysed.

(a) *More than*, *less than*, etc., as modifiers

In *Kim earns more/less than Pat (does)* the comparative forms *more* and *less* are heads (more precisely, fused determiner-heads), with the *than* phrases functioning as complements to them. But in some cases *than* merges syntactically with *more* or *less* to form a modifier of the item following *than.* A corresponding reanalysis is found with *as.* One clear case (not applying with *less than*) is where *than/as* is followed by a verb that can be a tensed form:

[32] i *This more than compensated for the delay.*
ii *She expects to more than double her capital in three years.*
iii *She never so much as turned her eyes on any other bloke.*
iv *He as good as admitted he'd leaked the information himself.*

More than compensated for the delay is a VP, and the head must be *compensated*, not *more* – note, for example, that we can drop *more than* but not *than compensated for the delay. More than* is therefore a modifier of the verb. Similarly in [ii]. Although *double* is a plain form of the verb, not a tensed form like *compensated* in [i], this is due to the ***expect*** + *to* construction and has nothing to do with *more than.* The crucial point is that

[19] Historically this *the* is not the usual definite article but the fossilised remnant of an Old English instrumental case-form meaning roughly "by so/that much". It came to fall together phonologically with the definite article, but its syntactic distribution still reflects its different origin.

[20] In such an example as *Kim was good but Pat was better* we can insert *the* but doing so changes the term comparison into a set comparison, for we understand not "better than Kim" but "the better of the two".

we can equally have a tensed form here: *She more than doubled her capital.* Example [iii] shows the same reanalysis with a comparison of equality; these tend to occur in non-affirmative contexts and to have the form *so much as*, as here; *as good as*, however, can also be used, as in [iv], meaning much the same as *virtually*.

She more than doubled her capital may be contrasted with *She did more than double her capital*, where *double* is required to be in the plain form: here there is no reanalysis, *more* being head, and *than double her capital* its complement. The construction with *do* allows *less* instead of *more* but the special construction of [32ii] does not. The two constructions differ semantically as well as syntactically. Suppose, for example, that her capital was initially $10,000. *She more than doubled her capital* means that she increased it to over $20,000. But that is not the meaning of *She did more than double her capital.* This says that she doubled her capital and more: the 'more' may involve a further increase in the capital or else something different, such as achieving promotion in her job.

The reanalysis also applies to *more than* and *less than* followed by an adjective or adverb, as in *He'd given a [more than satisfactory] explanation for his behaviour*, where *satisfactory* is head of the bracketed AdjP, and *more than* an optional modifier. (We do not postulate reanalysis, however, in examples like *more than fifty people*: see Ch. 5, §11).

(b) *No/any more than* + comparative clause

[33] i *The horses were no more on parade than was their driver.*
ii *Kim wouldn't do anything prematurely or in bad taste any more than Pat would.*

More in this construction is in modifier function, but the usual degree meaning has effectively been lost. We don't interpret [i] as a comparison between the degree/extent to which the horses were on parade and that to which their driver was: it can be glossed without a degree modifier as "The horses weren't on parade, just as their driver wasn't". The difference between this and an ordinary comparison may be fairly slight: *This prospect did not please Mrs King any more than did the possibility that her daughter might marry a Bohemian.* The literal interpretation compares degrees of pleasing (without saying what they were), whereas the idiomatic one says that neither the prospect nor the marriage possibility pleased Mrs King (at all). Where the subordinate clause expresses an obviously false proposition the rhetorical effect is to emphasise the negative: *Social invention did not have to await social theory any more than the use of the warmth of a fire had to await Lavoisier.*

(c) Idioms containing ***soon***

Sooner and *as soon* can be used as alternants of *rather* in the idiom with *would*: *I'd rather / sooner / as soon stay at home.* The inequality versions mean "I'd prefer", and the equality *as soon* "I'd like as much". In addition, both *as soon as* and *no sooner* have idiomatic meanings as well as their ordinary comparative ones:

[34] i	a. *The car may not be ready as soon as I said it would.*	[ordinary comparison]
	b. *I'll phone you as soon as the meeting is over.*	[idiom]
ii	a. *We got home no sooner than if we'd taken the bus.*	[ordinary comparison]
	b. *We'd no sooner got home than the police arrived.*	[idiom]
	c. *No sooner had we got home than the police arrived.*	[idiom]

Example [ia] is a variable comparison comparing how soon the car will (possibly) be ready and how soon I said it would be ready (cf. also the variable–constant comparison *It may be ready as soon as tomorrow*). But such a comparative meaning is lost in [ib], where *as soon as* is an idiom meaning "immediately" (and best regarded as a compound preposition).

Similarly *no sooner* has its literal comparative meaning in [34iia], but is an idiom in [iib–c], where the meaning is "The police arrived immediately after we got home". The version with fronting and subject–auxiliary inversion, [iic], is much the more frequent. The meaning is essentially the same as the construction with *hardly/barely/scarcely* + *when*: *We had hardly got home / Hardly had we got home when the police arrived.* And as a result of this equivalence blends between the constructions are found, with *when* appearing instead of *than* with *no sooner* and vice versa with *hardly*, etc.:

[35] i *<u>No sooner</u> had we got home <u>when</u> the police arrived.*
  ii *<u>Hardly</u> had we got home <u>than</u> the police arrived.*

Such blends are accepted as established usage by the liberal manuals, but still condemned by the more authoritarian ones.

(d) Idioms containing ***long*** and ***far***

[36] i *I'll look after them <u>as/so long as</u> you pay me.*
  ii *<u>As/So far as</u> I know, he's still in Paris.*
  iii *<u>As/So far as</u> the weather was concerned, we were very lucky.*
  iv *He went <u>so/as far as</u> to compare the proposal to a tax on sunshine.*
  v *<u>Insofar as</u> it's any business of mine, I'd say they should give up.*

With *as long as*, [i] is ambiguous between an ordinary variable comparison (comparing how long I'll look after them and how long you'll pay me) and one where *as long as* has lost its comparative meaning and been reanalysed as a compound preposition meaning "provided" ("I'll look after them provided you pay me"). In affirmative contexts like this, *so* is possible only in the idiomatic meaning. Similarly *so* alternates with *as* in the idiomatic preposition *as/so far as*. *As far as I know* means approximately "to the best of my knowledge"; *I know* is here a content clause, not a comparative clause. *As far as X is concerned* means "Regarding X"; *the weather was concerned* is again not comparative, and some speakers drop ***be*** *concerned*, making *as/so far as* a preposition taking an NP complement: %*As far as the weather, we were very lucky.* The idiom in [iv] is *go so/as far as* + infinitival VP; here I assert that he compared the proposal to a tax on sunshine, and indicate that this is a relatively surprising or extreme thing to do. *Insofar as* in [v] means "to the extent that".

(e) *Well, better, best*

As well (*as*) has the literal comparative meaning in *I doubt if I'll ever play as/so well again* or *She did as well as could be expected*; but it also has a range of idiomatic uses:

[37] i a. *They invited Kim <u>as well as</u> Pat.* b. *It was raining, <u>as well</u>.*
  ii a. *We might <u>as well</u> have stayed at home.* b. *You may <u>as well</u> leave it at that.*
  iii *It's just <u>as well</u> we called the doctor.*

In [ia] *as well as* means "in addition to", and like *rather than* in its "not, instead of" sense, is best regarded as having been reanalysed as a coordinator: see Ch. 15, §2.8. In

[ib] *as well* on its own means "in addition" and functions as a connective adjunct. The *as well* of [ii] normally combines with one of the possibility modals *may, might, could*; it is possible to have a comparative complement consisting of *as* + bare infinitival (*We might as well have stayed at home as come here*), but the version with the secondary term unexpressed is more common. This use of *as well* is idiomatic in that there is no corresponding non-comparative use of *well*: #*We stayed at home well.* In [iia] it serves to indicate dissatisfaction with what we have done: we're no better off than if we had taken the simpler course of staying at home. In [iib] it indicates an unenthusiastic, somewhat grudging suggestion: "There's no reason why you shouldn't leave it at that". In [iii] (*just*) *as well* means approximately "fortunate".

Idiomatic uses of *better* and *best* are seen in:

[38] i *I knew <u>better than</u> to question his decision.*
ii *We'll manage <u>as best</u> we can.*

Know better than to means "know one shouldn't". Example [i] has a negative implicature ("I didn't question his decision"), but *You know better than to talk with food in your mouth!* has a positive one ("You have been talking with food in your mouth"). In [ii] we have a curious use of the superlative form instead of the regular *as well as*: *as best* occurs only with ***can***. For the modal idiom *had better/best*, see Ch. 3, §2.5.6.

4.6 The correlative comparative construction

What we refer to as the **correlative comparative construction** has two versions, illustrated in [39i–ii] respectively:

[39] i a. *<u>The more</u> sanctions bite, <u>the worse</u> the violence becomes.*
b. *<u>The more conditions</u> I impose, <u>the less likely</u> is he to agree.* [fronted version]
c. *<u>The older</u> he gets, <u>the more cynical</u> he becomes.*
ii a. *The violence becomes <u>worse</u> <u>the more</u> sanctions bite.*
b. *He is <u>less likely to agree</u> <u>the more conditions</u> I impose.* [basic version]
c. *He becomes <u>more cynical</u> <u>the older</u> he gets.*

Both versions have paired – 'correlative' – comparative phrases (indicated by underlining). Very much the more common version is the one shown in [i], but it is the other that is syntactically the more basic. *The more sanctions bite* is a subordinate clause functioning as adjunct, and likewise *the more conditions I impose* and *the older he gets*; in [ii] they occupy the default position at the end of the matrix clause, whereas in [i] they occupy front position. The subordinate clause has the comparative phrase in front position in both versions, whereas the head clause has it fronted only when the whole subordinate clause is fronted. The comparative phrase begins with *the* when it is fronted; this is the modifier *the* discussed in §4.4.2 above. In the basic version it is possible but rare to have *the* in the non-fronted comparative phrase: *The violence becomes <u>the</u> worse, the more sanctions bite.*

The construction indicates parallel or proportional increase (or decrease, in the case of *less*) along the two scales expressed in the head and subordinate clauses.[21] It can be

[21] The basic version marginally allows a verb such as *increase* instead of a syntactic comparative: *The violence increases the more sanctions bite.*

approximately paraphrased by a construction in which the subordinate clause functions as complement to *as*:

[40] i *As sanctions bite more, so the violence becomes worse.*
ii *The violence becomes worse as sanctions bite more.*

Because of this parallel movement along the two scales it is often possible to reverse the direction of dependency:

[41] i *The more we pay them, the harder they work.*
ii *The harder they work, the more we pay them.*

In [i] the *work* clause is superordinate: the effort they put into their work increases as we pay them more. In [ii] it is the *pay* clause that is superordinate: the amount we pay them increases as they work harder. The two versions are not equivalent, however: for example, if they work harder each time we pay them more, but sometimes work harder for other reasons and without getting more pay, then [i] is true but [ii] is false.

Syntactic evidence that the first clause in [39i] (the fronted version) and the second clause in [39ii] (the basic version) is subordinate to the other is provided by examples like:

[42] i *Won't the violence become worse, the more the sanctions bite?*
ii *He is clearly the sort of person [who would be less likely to agree, the more conditions I impose].*

Example [i] is a closed interrogative, and it is marked as such by subject–auxiliary inversion in the main clause. The bracketed part of [ii] is a relative clause, and again it is the superordinate clause whose structure is affected by relativisation. Note that such operations as those forming interrogatives and relatives can be performed on the basic version, not on the fronted version. The fronted version can be subordinated, but only in ways that simply involve adding the subordinators *that* or a relative phrase modifier such as *in which case*:

[43] i *He realised [that the longer he delayed the more difficult the task would be].*
ii *She may call an election, in which case the sooner we resolve these differences, the better our chances will be.*

Structural reduction

Where the comparative phrase is a predicative AdjP, the verb *be* may be omitted, and in the fronted version it is possible to reduce either the head clause alone or both clauses to just the comparative phrase:

[44] i *[The harder the task,] the more she relished it.*
ii *The more directly the sun strikes walls and roof, [the greater its heat impact].*
iii *The sooner you leave the firm, [the better].*
iv *[The sooner,] [the better].*

Classification of subordinate clause

The subordinate clause in both versions of the correlative comparative construction belongs to the class of content clauses. In terms of its internal structure the only special feature it has is the fronting of the comparative phrase, but that same feature also applies to the head clause in the fronted version of the construction, and hence is not a marker of subordination. We noted in Ch. 11 that content clauses do not always differ structurally from main clauses, and the present construction is one of the cases where there is no internal marking of subordination.[22]

5 Non-scalar comparison

The differences between term and set comparison are less extensive in non-scalar comparison than in scalar comparison, and in this section we will therefore deal with them together. Two general points concerning the relation between the two types should be made before we review the various comparative governors in turn.

Potential ambiguity between set comparison and term comparison

[1] i *They offered the <u>same</u> deal to Kim and Pat.*
ii *Our views are <u>similar</u>.*

There may be ambiguity between a set comparison and a term comparison in which the secondary term is left unexpressed. For example, [i] may express a set comparison where the set consists of Kim and Pat: this is equivalent to the term comparison *They offered the same deal to Kim as to Pat.* But [i] can also be equivalent to *They offered the same deal as this to Kim and Pat*, with *this* referring to some deal just mentioned. In this latter case it is purely incidental that *Kim and Pat* refers to a plurality, whereas in the former case it is essential: *They offered the same deal to Kim* can only be a term comparison with an understood secondary term. Likewise [ii] can be a set comparison between the views of those referred to by the pronoun ***we*** or a term comparison between our views and some view or views identified earlier.

Set comparison and reciprocals

[2] i *These questions are very <u>different</u> (from each other).*
ii *The <u>same</u> question occurred to both of them: why had no one called the police?*

Set comparisons are often equivalent to term comparisons in which the secondary term is expressed by a reciprocal pronoun. The version of [i] without the parenthesised phrase is a comparison between a set of questions, whereas the version with the *from* phrase is a term comparison with the primary term expressed by *these questions*, the secondary one by *each other*. The set comparison construction is much more common than the reciprocal, which will often sound unnecessarily complex: compare *Kim and Pat have the same colour hair* and the less likely *Kim and Pat have the same colour hair as each other.* In cases like [ii] there is no equivalent reciprocal construction at all: **The same question occurred to both of them as to each other.* Leaving aside cases of preposing, the reciprocal is excluded in constructions where the comparative governor precedes the expression denoting the set, as *same* in [ii] precedes *both of them.*

[22] Some speakers, however, have *that* after the comparative phrase: %*The more that sanctions bite, the worse the violence becomes.* Another variant has a relative clause, as in the attested example *The more centralised information became and <u>the more uses to which the Australia Card was put</u>, the more unease the Law Council would have.* This, however, cannot be regarded as grammatical; it may have been used to enable the writer to avoid the stranding of the preposition in *the more uses the Australia Card was put to.*

5.1 *Same*

Inherent definiteness

In attributive function *same* is restricted to definite NPs, and in predicative function it occurs with *the*. Contrast, then, the distribution of *same* with that of *identical*:

[3]	i a. *The same mistake was made by Ed.*	b. *The identical mistake was made by Ed.*
	ii a. **A same mistake was made by Ed.*	b. *An identical mistake was made by Ed.*
	iii a. *The two copies are the same.*	b. *The two copies are identical.*
	iv a. *She treats them all the same.*	b. *She treats them all identically.*

In NPs *same* usually occurs with *the*, as in [ia], but demonstrative determiners are also found: *this same version*. In [iiia] *the same* is an AdjP rather than an NP, with *the* a dependent of an adjective, as in the comparisons of inequality discussed in §4.4.2. Similarly, in [iva] *same* is head of an AdvP with *the* as dependent.[23]

Term comparison with comparative clause

Same commonly occurs with *as* + comparative clause:

[4] i *He goes to the same school as his father went to __ / did.*
ii *She'll be using the same method as __ proved so successful last time.*
iii *They behaved in the same way as you had predicted __.*
iv *We achieved the same result as __ (was) obtained in the first experiment.*

The range of possibilities is broadly like that found in scalar comparison. One restriction is that it is not possible to have a contrast involving the head noun of the comparative phrase:

[5] i *He has the same phonetics tutor as he had __ last year.*
ii **He has the same phonetics tutor as he has __ syntax lecturer.*

Example [5ii] may be contrasted with the well-formed scalar comparative *He wrote as many symphonies as he wrote __ piano concertos*. Example [4iii] illustrates the construction discussed in (d) of §2.1, where an embedded clause is left understood ("you had predicted that he would behave in *y* way"), but it is considerably less frequent than with scalar comparisons. In [4iv] the missing counterpart to the comparative phrase is subject of a passive clause, and here the auxiliary verb *be* can be omitted.

With relative clause

Instead of *as* + comparative clause we often find an equivalent relative clause:

[6]	i *We're going to the same hotel as we stayed at __ last year.*	[comparative clause]
	ii *We're going to the same hotel that we stayed at __ last year.*	[relative clause]

The equivalence follows straightforwardly from the semantics of the constructions. With the comparative we have "We're going to hotel *x*; we stayed at hotel *y* last year; $x = y$". With the relative we have "We're going to hotel *x*; we stayed at *x* last year" (cf. Ch. 12, §3.1). In [i] the identity of the variables *x* and *y* is expressed by *same*; in [ii] the relative construction itself builds in the identity between the variables (as reflected in our use of the

[23] In casual speech *the* is omissible in a few expressions: *We stayed at home, same as usual/always. The* is also sometimes omitted in the anaphoric use of *same* seen in examples like *Thank you for the application form; I enclose (the) same herewith, duly completed.*

same symbol *x* in our representation of the meaning). *Same* is omissible in [ii],[24] but its presence serves to reinforce, to emphasise, the identity. Structurally the two constructions are very similar – in [6], for example, both subordinate clauses have the complement of *at* left understood. The main difference is that comparative clauses allow for a greater amount of reduction than relatives. There is, for example, no relative corresponding to *the same hotel as __ usual*, for the relative can't be reduced to a verbless structure like this. Note also that relatives do not allow the inversion that is characteristic of comparatives: *Sheep and goats turned up on Timor at the same time as/*that did the dingo.*[25]

Same as with NP complement

It is very common for the comparative complement to consist of *as* + NP. In some cases it is possible to add a verb, in others it is not:

[7]	i	a. *I am in the same class as Pat (is).*	b. *I left at the same time as Pat (did/ left).*
	ii	a. *Kim's views are the same as Pat's.*	b. *This version looks the same as that one.*

The examples in [i] are similar to scalar comparisons – e.g. *I am in a higher class than Pat (is); I left earlier than Pat (did/left).* Those in [ii] differ from scalar comparisons (such as *Kim's views are better informed than Pat's; This version looks more authentic than that one*) precisely by not allowing the addition of *be*; *the same as* here is similar to *identical to* or *equivalent to*, and the examples are best regarded as simply comparisons between constants – between Kim's views and Pat's, this version and that one. Gerund-participials can also appear in this construction: *Promising to do something is not the same as doing it.*

Blurring of distinction between scalar and non-scalar equality

When *same* occurs with nouns denoting measurable properties such as *age, size, height, length,* and indeed more generally with gradable nouns, the interpretation will often be similar to that of a scalar comparative:

[8]	i	a. *He'll soon be the same height as me.*	b. *He'll soon be as tall as me.*
	ii	a. *I don't earn the same salary as you.*	b. *I don't earn as much as you.*
	iii	a. *It's not the same quality as the earlier model.*	b. *It's not as good as the earlier model.*

The [a] examples, with *same*, will typically convey much the same as the [b] examples, which are central cases of scalar comparisons of equality. We take the view, however, that this is a matter of implicature: the [a] and [b] examples do not have the same truth conditions. The scalar equality expressed by *as* (. . . *as*) means "at least equal", but that is not the meaning of *same.* Consider the questions *Is he the same age as you?* and *Is he as old as you?* It is perfectly natural to answer the first with *No, he's two years older*, but this is not a natural answer to the second (where we would have *Yes, two years older, in fact* or the like). Similarly, [iia] can naturally be continued with *I earn $1,000 more*, but this would be possible as a continuation of [iib] only if the latter were interpreted as having metalinguistic negation. Or compare *If I*

[24] This leads some of the more authoritarian usage manuals to condemn the relative construction – on the grounds that *same* is here redundant. There is no empirical basis for proscribing it, however: it is very common and thoroughly acceptable.

[25] For these reasons we do not follow the common traditional practice of analysing *as* as a relative pronoun here: the examples in [6] belong to syntactically distinct constructions even though they are semantically equivalent.

earn more than you, then necessarily I earn as much as you and *#If I earn more than you, then necessarily I earn the same as you.*[26]

The same as as equivalent to (*just*) *as* or *like*

[9] i *They stay here the same as you do.* [=(*just*) *as*]
ii *You deserve a break the same as everyone else.* [=*like*]

This construction belongs to informal style. The interpretation of the subordinate clause in [i] would seem to be simply "you stay here": there is no counterpart of the comparative phrase. In this respect it is a marginal member of the class of comparative clauses. The connection with central members, however, is seen in the fact that it can be reduced to such forms as *as usual*: *We're going to the movies on Friday, the same as usual.*[27]

Anaphoric use of *the same* in term comparison

The comparative complement, and hence the secondary term in the comparison, is commonly left understood:

[10] i *He arrived on Tuesday morning and left for Sydney the same day.*
ii *Kim certainly tried, and the same can be said for Jill.*
iii *They rejected my application and the same thing happened to Kim.*

In [i] *the same day* is interpreted anaphorically as "on Tuesday"; in [ii] what can be said for Jill is that she certainly tried; and in [iii] they rejected Kim's application too. This represents one of the major anaphoric devices in English, not least in construction with *do* (as object) or *happen* (as subject) – see Ch. 17, §8.

The same in set comparison

[11] a. *Kim and Pat are the same age.* b. *We asked them all the same question.*

Example [a], where the set is expressed by a coordination, is equivalent to the term comparison *Kim is the same age as Pat.* The difference between the two versions is a matter of information packaging: in the term comparison Kim and Pat are differentiated as primary and secondary terms, whereas in [11a] they are of equal status as members of the set being compared.

Modification

In NPs *same* can be modified by *very*: *the very same mistake as you made last time.* Semantically this serves to reinforce the *same* rather than to indicate degree: it is comparable to that of *That's the very point I was making* rather than that of *That's very good.* The compound *selfsame* achieves the same emphasis. *Same* can also be modified by such items as *much, almost, roughly, exactly* preceding *the*: *much the same*, etc.; apart from *much*, these are the main items that modify scalar comparisons of equality (cf. [29] of §4).

[26] The implicatures commonly conveyed by the [a] examples in [8] are also found with NPs that have no overt comparison: *I don't earn your salary* will tend to implicate that I earn less. The similarity between such pairs as those in [8] provides the basis for the blend between non-scalar and scalar comparisons found in the attested example *He used a rod that was exactly the same length as the model tower was high.*

[27] There is a somewhat similar type of construction in more formal style: *In exactly the same way as we best see something faint (Halley's Comet, say) by not looking directly at it, so the thinking part of our brain tends to work better when we're not conscious of thinking.* Here too *in exactly the same way as* could be replaced by *just as*, and the comparative clause is not understood as having an implicit modifier matching *in exactly the same way.*

5.2 *Similar*

We here examine *similar* as representative of a set of comparative governors that occur with *to*, *from*, or *with*, but not the prototypical comparative prepositions *as* and *than*,[28] and hence not with comparative clauses.

Similar with a comparative complement

Similar selects *to* and is found in the following range of constructions:

[12] i *This festival is rather similar to Munich's Oktoberfest.* [predicative]
ii *The tribunal has powers similar to those of the courts.* [postpositive]
iii *She was using a similar argument to that outlined above.* [attributive:I]
iv *This problem is of similar complexity to the last one.* [attributive:II]

The secondary term in the comparison is in all cases expressed by the complement of *to*. Where *similar* is used predicatively the primary term is expressed by its predicand – the subject *this festival* in [i], the object in *They have made this festival rather similar to Munich's Oktoberfest.* In the postpositive use it is given by the part of the nominal preceding *similar*, here *powers* – the comparison is between the powers the tribunal has and the powers of the courts. In the attributive use of *similar* (much less frequent than the other two) there are two possibilities. In [iii] (Type I), the primary term is given by the comparative phrase – *a . . . argument.* In [iv] (Type II), it is given by some other NP – the subject *this problem.* Type I is the more usual construction; in the following pair, for example, [i] is much more likely than [ii]:

[13] i *She was using a similar argument to yours.* [attributive:I]
ii *She was using a similar argument to you.* [attributive:II]

Nevertheless, Type II examples are readily found:

[14] i *We should set up a local Labour Party along similar lines to the London one.*
ii *Errors on this new task take a very similar form to those which are made on the conservation or class inclusion task.*
iii *A semi-synthetic molecule available in Europe and Japan, artepon, has a similar mechanism of action to the drugs currently under study.*

The comparative complement is omissible if recoverable anaphorically, except in the postpositive case. If we drop *to those of the courts* from [12ii], for example, the general rules for the placement of adjectives will require that *similar* occupy pre-head position: *The tribunal has similar powers.*

Similar in set comparison

Set comparisons are found corresponding to two of the term comparisons illustrated in [12], namely the predicative and the Type II attributive:

[15] i *This festival and Munich's Oktoberfest are rather similar.*
ii *This problem and the last one are of similar complexity.*

[28] Examples with *as* are attested: *The average Australian retiring in twenty years will need up to $2 million in assets to live at a similar standard as today.* They are not, however, frequent or systematic enough to be regarded as grammatical; they appear to be restricted to relatively complex examples facilitating the analogical influence of *same*: we do not find examples like **My views are similar as yours* or **I have similar views as you.*

Modification

Similar is a gradable adjective, and hence can be modified by such adverbs as *very, quite, rather, extremely*, etc., and can itself be subject to scalar comparison (*The Opposition's policy is more similar to the government's than they care to admit*). In general the degree of likeness conveyed by *similar* falls short of complete identity, but it is sometimes used for the latter, allowing such modifiers as *exactly* and *almost.*

Lexical derivatives

The corresponding noun and adverb are seen in:

[16] i *The shooting had remarkable similarities with/ to a terrorist execution.*
ii *Purchase of state vehicles is handled similarly to all state purchases.*

The adjective *dissimilar* usually takes *to*, but *from* is found too.

5.3 ***Such***

We focus here on *such* as it appears in non-scalar comparisons with a comparative complement; for scalar *such*, see §4.3 above, and for the use of *such* with a resultative complement, see Ch. 11, §4.6. *Such* does not occur in set comparisons.

Such as with comparative clause

Such may precede or follow the noun head, as in [17i–ii] respectively:[29]

[17] i a. *Would you yourself follow such advice as you give me __?*
b. *We have been requested to discuss with you such matters as __ appear to us to be relevant.*
c. *Applications shall be made in accordance with such regulations as the Secretary to the Treasury may prescribe __.*
d. *Such roads as __ existed were pretty much open roads.*
e. *We were in the worst possible shape to deal with the immediate task of trying to co-operate with the Russians, who suffered from no such disadvantages as did we.*
ii a. *There were no homes for old people such as there are __ today.*
b. *A new payroll tax, such as the Minister proposes __, would be highly unpopular.*
c. *He questioned the value of certification, such as __ provided by these courses.*

The comparative phrase is the NP containing *such* and the counterpart to this is always missing in the comparative clause. Other features of the comparative construction are seen in the inverted order of [id] and the omission of the passive auxiliary *be* in [iic].

The central meaning of *such* concerns likeness of kind. For example, [17ia] might be glossed as "advice like that which you give me", [iib] as "a new payroll tax of the kind the Minister proposes". In [ic] – a type quite common in legal language – the sense of *such . . . as* is close to that of *whatever.* Example [id] is also comparable to a fused relative construction, but without the ·*ever*: *what roads existed.* It conveys that there were

[29] The *such* phrase can also be postposed: *No depression occurs such as is seen clinically or may be produced in normal persons by drugs.*

relatively few roads.[30] But in spite of the semantic similarity with relatives, *such*, unlike *same*, does not normally take a relative clause instead of the comparative complement. Examples like *Such overseas interests that Australian companies do have are summarised in Appendix 5* are attested, but rare, and of questionable acceptability.

Such + *as* is also found occasionally without a following head noun:

[18] i *The concern they felt for me was such as I shall never forget* __ .
ii *We are to admit no more causes of natural things than such as* __ *are both true and sufficient to explain their appearances.*

Note that the missing object in [i] cannot be recovered from the *such* phrase itself: we need to go to the subject NP (*the concern they felt for me*). In this respect the example differs from normal comparative constructions (but compare [45] of §2 above); it may represent a blend between the comparative and the resultative content clause construction *The concern they felt for me was such that I shall never forget it.* In [ii] *such* is fused modifier-head.

Such as with phrase

The most common use of *such* (. . .) *as* is with a single element after *as*, usually an NP:

[19] i *What is one to make of such statements as this?*
ii *The choice depends on such factors as costs and projected life expectancy.*
iii *Traditional sports such as tennis, cricket, and football led in popularity.*
iv *It is no interference with sovereignty to point out defects where they exist, such as that a plan calls for factories without power to run them.*

In the majority of cases (unlike those cited for scalar *such* in [28] of §4.3) it is not possible to add a verb, and the NP following *as* is best regarded as an immediate complement, not a reduced clause (§2.2). Especially when *such* follows the head noun, the element of likeness may be attenuated, with *such as* just introducing examples, as in [iii].[31]

5.4 *Different, other, else*

Term comparison: *different* + *from*

The comparative complement usually has *from* as head; the range of constructions matches that discussed above for *similar* + *to*:

[20] i *My brushes are different from those used by most watercolourists.* [predicative]
ii *They have an examination system not very different from ours.* [postpositive]
iii *You're answering a different question from the one I asked.* [attributive:I]
iv *Do Catholics have different attitudes from Anglicans?* [attributive:II]

In Type I attributives the primary term is expressed in the comparative phrase (*a . . . question . . .*), while in Type II it is expressed elsewhere, here in the subject.

[30] Such a deprecatory interpretation is also found in the idiomatic frame *such as they are*, etc.: *My opinions, such as they are, are my own* suggests that the opinions are of limited value or significance.

[31] In existential constructions with *thing* the comparison involves identity rather than likeness: *There's no such thing as a free lunch*, "There are no (genuinely) free lunches".

Construction [iv] is simpler than the equivalent Type I construction formed by replacing *Anglicans* by *those of Anglicans.*[32]

Different + *to* and *than*

While the verb *differ* selects only *from*, *different* also takes *to* or *than*:

[21] i *This version is very different to the one we shall hear in the simulcast.*
ii %*Records provide a different sort of experience than live music.*
iii %*The focus of interpersonal relationships is different in marriage than in a pre-marital situation.*
iv %*There was no evidence that anything was different than it had been.*

They are, however, very much less frequent than *from. Than* is subject to regional variation: it is hardly used at all in BrE, but is well established in AmE, though even there it is unlikely in the simplest predicative and postpositive constructions (?*My needs are different than yours*; ?*We expected a result rather different than this*). As elsewhere, *than* can be followed by a single element (NP in [ii], PP in [iii]) or a clearly clausal construction ([iv]). *From* and *to* are normally restricted to NP complements, so that replacement of *than* by *from* or *to* in cases like [iii–iv] requires a more complex formulation involving nominalisation, for example by means of a fused relative: *different in marriage from what it is in a pre-marital situation, different from what it had been.*[33]

Differently

The adverb is found with the same range of prepositions as the adjective:

[22] i *We need to remember that Israel treated sheep differently <u>from</u> us.*
ii %*People often behave differently in a crowd <u>than</u> they would individually.*

Note that in [i] the primary term is expressed by the subject *Israel*, but in [ii] it is given in the comparative phrase *differently*, understood as "in a different way". The comparison is between the way people behave in a crowd and the way they behave individually.

Set comparison

[23] i *The two versions of the incident are very different.*
ii *They proposed three different ways of solving the problem.*
iii *Different people hold different views on this matter.*
iv *The various candidates had reacted quite differently.*

Different, like *similar* above, is used in set comparisons in predicatives ([i]) or Type I attributives ([ii]). In the latter case *different* may occur in more than one NP, as in [iii]; the effect of the repetition is to pair people and views, excluding the case where a single

[32] A comparable simplification is seen in the predicative *Public attitudes to historical material were very different then from now.* The primary term here is expressed by *then*, not the subject, as it would be with *from what they are now.*

[33] The choice of preposition with *different* is much discussed in usage manuals. The most authoritarian insist that only *from* is correct, but the majority recognise that this rule is in clear conflict with accepted usage. American manuals accept *than*, especially with clausal complements, while British ones vary in their attitude to it: some defend it as permitting a simpler construction in cases like [21iii–iv] (and on the grounds that *different* takes modifiers like *no* and *much*, which makes it like a comparative form), but most do not allow it as standard in BrE.

person holds different views. Example [iv] illustrates the use of the adverb *differently* in set comparison.

Modification

Different (like *similar*) is a gradable adjective, allowing the usual range of modifiers for this class, such as *very* and a scalar comparative (*His views were more different from mine than I'd expected*). At the same time, however, it takes those found with scalar comparison of inequality (cf. [29] of §4): *no, any, much* (generally in non-affirmative contexts: *It isn't much different from the previous version*), *far, a great deal*, and so on.

Other + than

Other occurs only in term comparison. The comparative complement has *than* as preposition.[34] As an adjective, *other* occurs predicatively, postpositively, and in the Type I attributive construction:

[24]	i	*It turns out that the US policy is in fact other than he stated.*	[predicative]
	ii	*He has no income other than his pension.*	[postpositive]
	iii	*We must find some other means of restricting imports than tariffs.*	[attributive:I]

The predicative use is comparatively rare, and *other* here requires a complement. We cannot therefore say, for example, **Our policy is <u>other</u>*; instead we need *Our policy is <u>different</u>*. The construction with *other* used predicatively is the only one where the *than* can take a comparative clause, as in [i] – compare **He has no income other than the government provides* and *He has no income other than that which the government provides*, with an NP as immediate complement of *than*.

The attributive use is much less frequent than the postpositive, but syntactically more straightforward in that the *than* phrase is omissible and clearly a separate dependent in the structure of the NP. *Other* can be coordinated with a scalar comparative form, showing that we are here not far removed from the central type of comparative construction: *My mother had the faculty of gazing beyond people into space inhabited by other and more exciting ones than those who were actually in the room.* Also straightforward is the construction where ***other*** is a nominal pro-form: *These wrongs are public in the sense that they involve others than the agent*, with *others* head ("other people") and *than the agent* comparative complement.

In the postpositive construction *than* cannot be omitted: **He has no income other.* This is conducive to a reanalysis whereby *other than* is construed as a compound preposition with a meaning like "besides, except, apart from". Such a reanalysis certainly seems to have applied in the construction where *other than* is not in construction with a head noun, but introduces an adjunct:

[25]	i	[*<u>Other than</u> this very significant result,*] *most of the information now available about the radio emission of the planets is restricted to the intensity of radiation.*
	ii	*Little has changed* [*<u>other than</u> that it is now a silent and deserted place*].
	iii	*For a long time we didn't talk* [*<u>other than</u> to confirm our common destination*].

[34] *Other* is occasionally found in combination with *but* instead: *I wouldn't want any other pet but a dog* – a blend between *any pet but* and *any other pet than*. This is different from the combination with *except*, as in *He has no other friends except you*, which doesn't say that you are his only friend: the interpretation here is "He has no other friends than these except you" – i.e. there is an understood secondary term for comparative *other*.

Further constructions where *other than* appears to function as a constituent are illustrated in:

[26] i *Did he consider the possibility of recording other than popular music in this way?*
ii *No one suggests these deals are other than legitimate commercial operations.*
iii *He is at pains to define his key terms other than anecdotally.*

Again, *other* could not occur on its own in these positions, and it is doubtful if it can properly be regarded as head. The underlined sequences are NPs in [i–ii] and an AdvP in [iii], and it is plausible to take *music, operations,* and *anecdotally* as syntactic head with *other than* a modifier, comparable to the reanalysed uses of *more than* and *less than* discussed in §4.5.

Else

This is semantically equivalent to *other,* but it takes a complement headed by either *than* or *but* that is always optional: *anyone else (than/but you), nowhere else (than/but in France).* Like non-predicative *other,* it cannot take *than* + comparative clause: *anything else than what she gave you,* not **anything else than she gave you. Else* is restricted to occurrence with interrogatives (*who/what/how else,* etc.), the compound determinatives (*everyone, anything,* etc.), and *much, little,* and *all* in fused determiner-head function.

5.5 *As*

In this section we are concerned with term comparisons of equality where the preposition *as* appears on its own, without a superordinate comparative governor such as *same, such, so,* or a preceding *as*:

[27] i	*As you know, we face a difficult year.*	[adjunct of comparison]
ii	*I did it as I was told to do it.*	[manner]
iii	*The universe today looks just as it did millions of years ago.*	[predicative]
iv	*The plan as currently conceived is seriously flawed.*	[dependent of nominal]

This *as* is itself the comparative governor, and takes a bare comparative complement (cf. §1.3). It does not occur in set comparison: it always introduces the secondary term in term comparison.

We focus primarily on constructions where *as* takes a clausal complement, considering in turn the four categories illustrated in [27]. The causal *as* of *As it was raining they cancelled the match* and the temporal one of *She fell as she was going downstairs* are excluded as falling outside the domain of comparison: these simply take content clauses as complement, whereas the complements of *as* in [27] are comparative clauses.

Adjunct of comparison

The underlined adjunct or complement in [27ii–iv] is only incidentally comparative: the *as* phrase could be replaced without change of function by, for example, *carefully, remarkable, in its present state,* and so on. The adjunct in [27i], however, is inherently comparative, not replaceable by an expression with the same function that is not comparative: it is for this reason that we call it an adjunct of comparison, a semantic type of adjunct on a par with those described in Ch. 8. Further examples are given in:

[28] i *[As I have already observed __,] no reason has yet been offered for this change.*
ii *The event was sponsored, [as __ is the fashion these days,] by a brewery.*
iii *He didn't report the matter to the police [as you'd predicted __].*

The comparative clauses functioning as complement to *as* are structurally incomplete in that the clausal complements which their verbs would have in main clauses are missing. They are recoverable from the matrix: in [28i], for example, what I have already observed is that no reason has yet been offered for this change. Similarly in [ii]: what is the fashion these days is for comparable events to be sponsored by a brewery. Example [iii] is ambiguous: what you'd predicted may be that he would report the matter to the police or that he wouldn't.

Adjuncts of this kind cannot be foregrounded in the *it*-cleft construction (**It's as you know that we face a difficult year*). Nor can they fall within the scope of a negative – note, for example, that in neither interpretation of [28iii] does the negative have the subordinate clause within its scope: it cannot be used to convey that you had not predicted that he would/wouldn't report the matter to the police. They are generally prosodically detached, having the status of supplements. As for the interpretation, the truth of the subordinate clause is not at issue: it is taken for granted or presupposed.[35]

Other verbs often found in the comparative clause in this construction include:

[29]	*acknowledge*	*argue*	*claim*	*demonstrate*	*discover*
	expect	*find*	*hear*	*insist*	*note*
	promise	*remark*	*say*	*show*	*suggest*

These are verbs that take content clauses as internal complement; such adjectives as *aware* follow the same pattern (*as you will be aware*). The missing complement may likewise be understood as subject of these verbs in the passive (*as is widely known*), or of other expressions taking clausal subjects (*as happens frequently*), or verb + predicative (*as will be obvious*). The structure is like that found in central comparative constructions: compare [28iii] with *Not as many people came [as you'd predicted __]*. One difference, however, is that in the present construction the *as* phrase can occupy a range of positions, like many other adjuncts: front, end, or central (*We face, as you know, a difficult year*). This difference is attributable to the fact that the *as* here is itself the comparative governor, rather than being selected by some superordinate governor that it must follow.

Relationship with relative construction

The construction containing an adjunct of comparison bears a significant resemblance to one with a supplementary relative clause:

[30] i a. *He phoned home every day, [as he'd promised to do].* [comparative]
b. *He phoned home every day, which he'd promised to do.* [relative]

[35] *As I recall* (or *as I remember*) has a somewhat different interpretation from the examples in [28]. The truth of the subordinate clause is not here taken for granted; rather, the *as* phrase serves as a 'hedge', a modal qualification, indicating that the information in the matrix clause is based on recollection. The meaning is similar to that of *as far as I recall.* Note, by contrast, that *as I well recall* follows the usual pattern. Compare *As I recall, no one had raised any objections to the proposal,* and *The Society to which I myself belonged in my own college at Oxford was, as I well recall, of this latter sort.*

ii a. *She has recovered quickly,* [*as her doctor will confirm*]. [comparative]
b. *She has recovered quickly, which confirms that it wasn't serious.* [relative]

The underlining marks the subordinate clauses, comparative or relative, while the brackets in the [a] examples mark the adjunct of comparison. In [ia] we have a comparison of equality between two variables: "*x* (he phoned home every day); he promised to do *y*; x = y". In the relative construction [ib] we have two occurrences of the same variable: "*x* (he phoned home every day); he'd promised to do *x*". The end result is the same in the two constructions, just as we saw that *same* + *as* can be equivalent to *same* + relative (§5.1). Nevertheless, there are pragmatic and syntactic differences between the two constructions.

The informational content of the comparative clause is backgrounded, whereas the relative presents the information it expresses as separate from that of the main clause. In [30iia] *as* is much more likely than *which*, whereas in [iib] *as* would be impossible: the relative here takes the matrix as the starting-point or basis for new information of equal importance.

Syntactically, the comparative displays distinctive properties of the central comparative construction, as illustrated in:

[31] i *He was a devout Catholic,* [*as were _ both his brothers*].
ii *They claimed it as a deductible expense,* [*as _ permitted under US tax law*].
iii *Kim won convincingly,* [*as _ usual*].
iv *I've also felt at times like leaving my wife,* [*as she has _ me*].

In [i] we have postposing of the subject, which would not be possible in a relative: *which both his brothers were too*, but not **which were both his brothers too.* In [ii] the passive auxiliary *be* is omitted, and again this is not permitted in a relative: cf. *which is permitted*, but not **which permitted.* In [iii] the comparative clause is reduced to an adjective: *which* would require a finite construction, *which is usual.* And in [iv] *has* is stranded, but with an object following the missing verb: relative **which she has me* would again be quite impossible.

Reduction not always obligatory

One respect in which this *as* construction differs from more central types is that the subordinate clause is not necessarily structurally incomplete. Instead of [31iv], for example, we could have *as she has felt at times like leaving me*, with no material missing but understood. The minimum reduction required in central comparatives is that the counterpart to the comparative governor be missing (cf. §2.1), but in this construction the governor, *as*, is head of an adjunct which has no counterpart in the subordinate clause.

This is not to say, however, that reduction is always optional: it is most clearly obligatory in cases like [27i], [28], or [31ii–iii], where it would be impossible to add a pronoun in place of the missing complement (**as you know it*, **as I have already observed it*, etc.). In these cases the *y* variable is understood as embedded as complement of a verb or verb + predicative, rather than as constituting the whole complement of *as*.

No requirement for new or contrasting material

The comparative clause usually contains material distinct from that in the matrix: in [27i] *you know* appears only in the subordinate clause, in [31iv] we have contrasting subjects (*she* vs *I*) and contrasting objects (*me* vs *my wife*), and so on. But as with scalar comparisons of equality (*She's as fit as she is because* ...) the subordinate clause need not contain new or contrastive lexical material:

[32] i *If the aim is to create disunity, [as it is __,] we should reject his proposal.*
ii *She suggested he hadn't been honest with her, [as indeed he hadn't __].*
iii *The deadlock is a disappointment coming [as it does] after such a promising start.*

What makes these possible is that the matrix does not **state** that the proposition is true, whereas the comparative clause does. The latter does therefore introduce a new feature, but it is not a matter of the lexical content. In [i] *the aim is to create disunity* is complement to *if* and hence merely entertained conditionally, rather than stated, in the matrix. Similarly in [ii] the *x* variable is expressed by the complement of *suggested*, and hence is not entailed. And [iii] has non-finite *coming*, which is not itself a construction used for stating: note that we could not here replace *coming* by *because it comes*.

Reduction to a single element

The comparative clause can be reduced to a single element:

[33] i *In sport, [as in everything else], attitude is all important.*
ii *We took the precaution, [as always], of having the paintings authenticated.*
iii *These qualities are necessary today [as never before] if we are to march together to greater security, prosperity, and peace.*

We understand "as it is in everything else", "as we always do/did", "as they have never been before". Again the construction resembles central comparatives – cf. *Attitude is as all important in sport as in everything else*; *These qualities are more necessary today than ever before.* There is, however, one major difference: in the present construction a clause cannot normally be reduced to an NP understood as subject or object. For example, we can't omit the verb from [31ii]: **He was a devout Catholic, as both his brothers.* Instead we need *like*: *He was a devout Catholic, like both his brothers.*

Manner

Here the *as* phrase functions as manner element in the matrix and the comparative clause has an implicit manner element that is compared with it:

[34] i *He uses statistics [as a drunk uses a lamppost __], for support rather than illumination.*
ii *The louvres are constructed [as __ shown in the diagram].*
iii *These people don't know how to go about complaining [as Europeans do].*

Example [i] may therefore be analysed along the lines proposed for central comparatives: "He uses statistics in way *x*; a drunk uses a lamppost in way *y*; *x* = *y*". And again there is an equivalent with a relative clause: *He uses statistics in the way a drunk uses a lamppost.* Example [ii] gives another illustration of the past-participial construction, with the passive auxiliary *be* omitted; the missing subject can be interpreted as "how louvres are constructed".

There may be ambiguity between the manner and adjunct of comparison types, as in [34iii]. The manner interpretation is concerned with the way Europeans go about complaining – these people don't know how to go about doing it in this way. In the adjunct of comparison interpretation the equality is simply between what they don't know and what Europeans do know. Only the adjunct of comparison interpretation is possible if the *as* phrase is placed before *how*: *They don't know, as Europeans do, how to go about complaining.*

Predicative

Here there is a comparison between two kinds or states:

[35] i *His behaviour was [as we'd expected it to be __].*
ii *Make sure you leave everything [as you find it __].*
iii *The design of the building is [as __ shown __ in Figure 12].*

These fit the familiar analysis: "His behaviour was *x*, we'd expected it to be *y*; *x* = *y*", with the variables representing predicative complements. Example [ii] is equivalent to a relative construction with the noun *state* as head: *leave everything in the state in which you find it.* And [iii] is a further past-participial passive. The *as* phrase functions as predicative complement: subjective in [i/iii], objective in [ii]. The comparative clause has a missing predicative complement in [i–ii]; [iii] has a missing subject, interpreted as "the design of the building", and it is arguable that there is also a missing predicative complement here too: it's a matter of **how** Figure 12 shows the design.

In construction with a nominal or NP

[36] i *This is a photograph of the church [as it was __ in 1900].*
ii *Computer technology may make the car, [as we know it __,] a Smithsonian antique.*
iii *No one thought that Margot, [as she was then known __,] would last the distance.*

The *as* phrase in [i] is a modifier in the structure of the nominal headed by *church*, while those in [ii–iii] are supplements to the anchor NPs *the car* and *Margot.* This construction differs semantically somewhat from the others we have been considering, and doesn't lend itself to an analysis of the familiar kind involving variables *x* and *y*. Rather, the *as* phrase specifies some property or aspect of what is denoted by the head noun or the anchor NP: in [i] we are concerned with how the church was in 1900, in [ii] with how we know (conceive of) the car, in [iii] with how (by what name) the person concerned was known at the time in question.

Syntactically the complement of *as* is still a comparative clause, still structurally incomplete relative to a main clause. This is most obvious in [36i], which may be compared with main clause *The church was <u>in such-and-such a state</u> in 1900.* The comparative clauses in [ii–iii] may similarly be contrasted with *We know it <u>in such-and-such a form</u>* and *She was then known <u>as such-and-such</u>.*

Idiomatic uses

Examples such as the following are of limited productivity:

[37] a. *<u>As it happens</u>, I met her only yesterday.* b. *Do <u>as I say</u> / <u>as you like</u>.*

It happens is structurally incomplete in that it couldn't stand alone, but it is not clear what missing element is understood: *as it happens* is a fixed phrase. Compare also *as things stand, as it is.* Both versions of [b] have exceptional syntax in that *do* normally takes an NP object (cf. *Do this*; *Do what I say*); the pattern does not occur with other transitive verbs (e.g. **Take as you like*). A relatively recent such idiom is *as is*: *All items are sold as is* ("in their present state").

As if and *as though*

These introduce phrases with the same range of functions as those discussed above for *as* alone, except that they do not function as dependents to a noun:

[38] i *He had scurried up the hatch as if we were abandoning ship.*
ii *They were treated as if they were Commonwealth citizens.*
iii *There was a ragged edge to her voice now, as if she'd been crying.*
iv *The effect is as if he had materialised out of nowhere.*

The *as if* phrase is a manner adjunct in [i], a manner complement in [ii], an adjunct of comparison in [iii], and a predicative complement in [iv].

As if and *as though* as compound prepositions

In the examples of [38] it is possible to fill out the construction, inserting material between *as* and *if*:

[39] i *He had scurried up the hatch as he would if we were abandoning ship.*
ii *They were treated as they would be if they were Commonwealth citizens.*
iii *There was a ragged edge to her voice, as there would have been if she'd been crying.*
iv *The effect is as it would have been if he had materialised out of nowhere.*

This might suggest that there is nothing special about [38] – that the underlined phrases simply consist of *as* as head with the *if* phrase as complement. Thus [38iii], for example, would be comparable to *There was a ragged edge to her voice, as when she'd been crying.* There is strong syntactic and semantic evidence, however, for saying that *as* and *if* have merged into a single compound preposition taking a content clause as complement, that the examples of [38] cannot be analysed as reduced versions of [39].

The first argument for the compound analysis is that *as if* in [38] can be replaced without change of meaning by *as though*, whereas *if* in [39] cannot be replaced by *though.*

The second argument is that it is not possible to repeat *if* in coordination: **They were treated as if they were Commonwealth citizens or if they had resided here for ten years or more.*

The third argument is that expansion of the kind shown in [39] is very often not possible:

[40] i *Don't attack a mouth as if you're dipping a mop into a slop-bucket!*
ii *It was highly imprudent of him to drink as if he were a youngster like ourselves.*
iii *She acts as if she hates me.*
iv *It seems/looks as if we've offended them.*
v *Max seems/looks as if he's in difficulties.*
vi *As if this news wasn't bad enough, I found that the printer wasn't working either.*

In [i] we have a comparison of equality (interpreted as resemblance) not between two ways of attacking a mouth but between a way of attacking a mouth and the way of dipping a mop into a slop-bucket. In [ii] the comparison is not between the way he drank and the way he would drink if he were a youngster but between the way he drank and the way it would be acceptable, appropriate, or reasonable to drink if he were a youngster. Example [iii] could be expanded if it had modal preterite *hated* (*She acts as she would act if she hated me*), but it can't be expanded as it stands, with present tense *hates.*

Whereas in [40i–ii] the idea of comparison associated with *as* remains very evident, it is much attentuated in [iii]: it is more a matter of the way she acts suggesting that she hates me. This shift from comparison to the issue of whether the content clause is true is carried a step further in [40iv]. In the version with *seem, as if* could be replaced by *that* with virtually no change in meaning. In this construction the *as if* reinforces or harmonises with the modal meaning expressed in the verb (essentially medium strength epistemic modality, in the sense of Ch. 3, §9) – thus, roughly, "Judging from appearances, it is likely that we have offended them".

Other verbs of similar meaning likewise take a complement of this form: *appear, feel, sound, taste,* and also *be*.[36] In addition to the impersonal construction of [40iv] we find ordinary subjects, as in [v].

Finally, [40vi] involves a special use of *as if / though*, where the matrix clause presents some situation as a further instance of something, normally something bad – in this example, of further bad news. In this use, the *as if* always has a negative complement, and again it is less a matter of comparison than of the status of the content clause. This time the construction indicates that the content clause is true (not merely likely): this news wasn't bad enough (i.e. bad enough to satisfy a malevolent fate, as it were, bad enough to make it unnecessary to inflict further bad things on me).

The *as if/though* phrase standing on its own

The *as if / though* phrase may form an exclamatory clause by itself:

[41] i *As if I didn't have enough on my plate as it was!*
ii *As if I would try to cheat you!*

The first of these is a structurally incomplete version of the construction shown in [40vi]: the indication of what else I had on my plate is left unexpressed, being recoverable from the context. Example [41ii] presents the content clause as false: it is an indignant rejection of the suggestion that I would try to cheat you.

Irrealis *were* and the preterite

The *as if / though* construction is one of those that allow irrealis *were* or a modal preterite. Where the matrix clause has present tense, we have the expected contrast in the content clause between *were* or modal preterite and present tense:

[42] *He moves about on camera, angular, emaciated, graceful, as if his body <u>were</u> / <u>is</u> weightless.*

The version with irrealis *were* is motivated by the fact that his body is not actually weightless, i.e. by the counterfactuality of the content clause. The version with *is*, by contrast, presents his body's being weightless as an open possibility, thereby suggesting that he gives the appearance of being weightless. Compare also *She acts as if she hated me* and *She acts as if she hates me* (=[40iii]). The latter conveys that the way she acts suggests that she does hate me or may well do so, whereas the modal preterite *hated* presents her hating me as a more remote possibility (though it is certainly not presented as counterfactual).

Less straightforward is the case where the matrix clause is in the preterite:

[43] i *He was treated as if he were a Commonwealth citizen.*
ii *As the trooper left the room, the gambler turned to the army girl with an odd expression, as though he were remembering painful things.*

[36] With *be* in the negative we actually have an entailment that the content clause is false: *It's not as if he wasn't trying* entails that he was trying. This construction is used to deny a proposition that might otherwise have been deduced (perhaps he didn't perform as well as expected).

The natural interpretation of [i] is that he was treated like a Commonwealth citizen although he wasn't one. Example [ii], however, doesn't imply that he wasn't remembering painful things: on the contrary, it suggests that he was or appeared to be. In [i] we could have *as if he had been a Commonwealth citizen*, with the perfect marking backshift (or past time) and the preterite marking modal remoteness; it is, however, much more usual in such contexts to have an irrealis or simple preterite after *as if/though* than a preterite perfect.

The irrealis in [43ii] does not appear to be semantically motivated: certainly if we had a simple preterite in this context we would have no reason to regard it as a modal preterite. This *were* is therefore probably best regarded as belonging with the 'extended' uses of the irrealis discussed in Ch. 3, §1.7. Like them, it has the flavour of a hypercorrection: *was* is a less formal variant of *were* in modal remoteness constructions like [i], so that some speakers feel *were* to be stylistically preferable to *was* in similar constructions where *was* was not traditionally stigmatised.[37]

As if/though with infinitival and verbless complement

A further difference between *as if/though* and *if* is that the former can take a subjectless infinitival or verbless clause as complement:

[44] i *He examined the notes thoroughly, as if to see if they were real.*
ii *She combed her hair back with her fingers as if to see better.*
iii *Unruly hair goes straight up from his forehead, standing so high that the top falls gently over, as if to show that it really is hair and not bristle.*
iv *He rose up as if weightless.*

The infinitival is interpreted as involving purpose or intention. The subject of the matrix clause is normally a human agent: exceptional examples like [iii] are interpreted as involving personification, with the hair conceived of as acting purposefully. The force of the *as if/though* is much like that in [40iii]: his examining the notes thoroughly (or the way he did so) suggested that his intention was to see if they were real. Example [44iv] illustrates the case where subject + *be* is omitted to yield a verbless complement.

As if/though in scalar comparison

We have been concerned so far with non-scalar comparison (diluted in some cases in such a way that there is little sense of comparison at all). Consider, finally, examples of scalar comparison like the following:

[45] i *Our aim is to be <u>as</u> competitive <u>as</u> <u>if</u> we had rivals breathing down our necks.*
ii *The part of her that was in control was <u>as</u> calm <u>as</u> <u>though</u> she were just shedding an outer garment during a photo session.*

In [i] the second *as* is head of the comparative phrase and has the *if* phrase as its complement: *as if* is not here a compound preposition. Nevertheless one finds occasional examples with *though* instead of *if*, as in [ii]; they are, however, of questionable acceptability, and probably best treated as blends between the construction where *as* and *if/though* form a compound preposition, as in the non-scalar examples, and

[37] This extended use of irrealis *were* is occasionally found in constructions where the matrix has present tense: *It sounds from the guide book as if Verona were worth a visit.* The flavour of hypercorrectness is stronger here: the example falls under the use of *as if* seen in [40iv], which indicates that the content clause is relatively likely to be true, making the irrealis semantically inappropriate.

the one where *if* is head of the complement of the *as* marking scalar comparison of equality.

5.6 Like

Like occurs with a comparative sense in a wide range of constructions. We look first at those where it has an NP as complement, then in §5.6.2 at the use of *like* with finite clause complements, and then review summarily a variety of other constructions in §5.6.3. For the distinction between *like* as an adjective and as a preposition, see Ch. 7, §2.2.

5.6.1 *Like* + NP complement

With an NP as complement, *like* rather than *as* is used in non-scalar term comparisons of equality:

[46] i a. *Jill is like her mother.* b. **Jill is as her mother.*
ii a. *Like you, I welcome this decision.* b. **As you, I welcome this decision.*
iii a. *Jill was talking like a lawyer.* b. *Jill was talking as a lawyer.*

Here [ib] and [iib] are ungrammatical, while [iiib] is not a comparative construction, differing sharply in meaning from the comparative [iiia]. The latter expresses a comparison of equality (resemblance) between Jill and a lawyer with respect to the way she was talking; [iiib] says that Jill was talking in her capacity of lawyer. *As* here takes a predicative complement, so we infer that Jill was a lawyer – whereas in [iiia] she may or may not have been.

Like phrases with an NP as complement function in clause structure as predicative, manner complement, or adjunct, and they also function as dependent of a noun or as a supplement anchored to an NP.

(a) *Like* phrases as predicative

[47] i *Max is just like his father. It seemed like a good idea at the time. It feels like silk. The wine tasted like vinegar.*
ii *It is just like Max to be late.*
iii *The effect was to make him even more like his father.*
iv *I don't want Sally to see me like this. It would be better like this.*

Like phrases commonly occur as complement to *be* and other complex-intransitive verbs, especially the appearance verbs *seem* and *appear*, and the sense verbs *feel*, *look*, *sound*, and *taste*.[38] *Max is like his father* is a straightforward comparison of equality between Max as primary term and his father as secondary term, with equality interpreted as resemblance. The sphere of resemblance can be specified in a modifier such as *in his attitude to work*.

Example [47ii] illustrates a special use of *like* with the sense "characteristic of". In [iii] the *like* phrase is objective predicative complement. This is not a common construction: relatively few complex-transitive verbs readily allow a *like* phrase as predicative (cf. ?*I*

[38] *I feel like an intruder* belongs to this construction, but *I feel like a drink* does not: *feel like* is here an idiom meaning approximately "want", with *feel* a prepositional verb and *like a drink* a non-predicative complement. In *That looks like Kim over there* the meaning is not comparative "resemble" but modal "is probably / seems to be".

thought him like his father, **This got him like a raving lunatic*, and so on). In [iv] *like this* is a predicative adjunct.

(b) Manner complement

[48] i *Liz is behaving like a prima donna.*
ii *Jill treated Max like the others.*
iii *You shouldn't treat her like that.*

The few verbs that take a manner phrase as complement readily allow it to have the form of a *like* phrase. Thus [i] expresses resemblance between Liz and a prima donna with respect to the way or manner in which Liz is behaving. Example [ii] is ambiguous, in that the primary term in the comparison can be either Jill or Max: "Jill treated Max in the same way as the others treated him" or "Jill treated Max in the same way as she treated the others". This ambiguity is like that found in scalar comparisons such as *Sue phoned Angela more often than Liz* (=[20v] of §2), though there can be no question of analysing the complement of *like* as a reduced clause here. Finally, [iii] is an instance of what we have called a variable–constant comparison (cf. *I stayed longer than six weeks* discussed in §1.3). The meaning can be given as "You shouldn't treat her in manner *x*; *x* = that", so that it is equivalent to the non-comparative construction *You shouldn't treat her that way.*

(c) Non-predicative adjunct

Like phrases are very common in this function, where they have a rather wide range of interpretation. We consider three cases, though the distinction between the second and third is by no means sharp:

[49] i *Like his brother, Max is a keen gardener.* [likeness of predication]
ii *Max talks like his brother.* [likeness of manner]
iii *Like a fool, Max believed everything they told him.* [other likeness]

Likeness of predication

The likeness between Max and his brother in [49i] is that both are keen gardeners: in this type, something is said about the primary term that also applies to the secondary term. The primary term is almost always expressed by the subject of the clause, and hence we call this 'likeness of predication' in that the same predicate applies to both terms. The distinction we are drawing between the primary and secondary terms in a comparison is reflected here in the status of the two propositions conveyed: "Max is a keen gardener" is asserted as the main information, while "His brother is a keen gardener" is backgrounded, presupposed information, something that is taken for granted.

This type differs from the others with respect to negation, in that *like* can take the negative prefix *un·*. Compare, for example:

[50] i *Unlike his brother, Max is a keen gardener.*
ii **Max talks unlike his brother.*

Example [ii] is inadmissible in the meaning "Max talks in a way which is unlike that in which his brother talks" – it would be acceptable with a comma after *talks*, but in that case it would be the counterpart not of [49ii] but of *Max talks, like his brother*, which involves likeness of predication, not likeness of manner. Example [50i] has subclausal negation, *unlike* serving to negate the secondary proposition, so that the meaning is:

"Max is a keen gardener, but his brother is not". With clausal negation we have (changing the content of the propositions for greater naturalness):

[51] i *Like his brother, Max had not received a distribution from the family trust.*
ii *Max had not, like his brother, received a distribution from the family trust.*
iii *Max had not been to university like his brother.*

In [i] the *like* is outside the scope of negation: Max and his brother are alike in that they had both not received a distribution from the family trust. Example [ii] is ambiguous: *like* can be outside the scope of negation, giving the same meaning as for [i]; or it can be inside the scope of negation, so that Max and his brother are not alike – Max's brother had received a distribution, but Max himself had not. In abstraction from prosody, the same ambiguity applies in [iii]. If the sentence is read as a single intonation phrase, the *like* phrase is inside the scope of negation ("His brother had been to university, but Max hadn't"), but if *like his brother* is read as a separate intonation phrase it will normally be outside the scope of negation ("Both of them hadn't been").

Where the complement of *like* is a personal pronoun it normally takes accusative case; this is the only possibility when the *like* phrase precedes the subject or follows the VP, but when it comes between subject and verb nominative forms are occasionally attested:

[52] i *Like us/*we, Max is a keen gardener.*
ii *The Russians, like us/ %we, have an obvious interest in avoiding war.*

The nominative suggests that the pronoun is construed as a subject, but it is not coordinate with *the Russians* and could not in this position be expanded into a finite clause; it is probably best regarded, therefore, as a hypercorrection (cf. Ch. 5, §16.2).

In the great majority of cases, the primary term in the comparison is expressed by the subject of the clause – by *Max* in [52i], *the Russians* in [52ii], and so on. Departures from this pattern are illustrated in:

[53] i *Like any stray, his response to these comforts was instantaneous.*
ii *Like Moscow, the main streets in Leningrad are wide and tree-lined.*
iii *Like certain expensive restaurants, just sitting there gave you the illusion of being wealthy yourself.*
iv *Like so many great successes, the ideas are surprisingly simple.*

In [i] the primary term is expressed by the pronoun *his*, determiner within the subject NP, not subject of the clause itself. In [ii] it is expressed by the complement of *in* within the subject NP. In [iii] it is expressed by the locative adjunct *there* within the clause functioning as subject. And in [iv] it is not expressed at all, but is understood as the work or whatever whose ideas are surprisingly simple. Such examples are widely condemned in style manuals, and would generally be avoided in careful writing. This can be done by reformulating the clause so that the primary term is expressed by the subject (*he responded ...*), or by using a construction with *as* + PP (*as with so many great successes, ...*).

Likeness of manner

[54] i *These birds walk like human beings.*
ii *These birds don't walk like human beings.*

We interpret [i] as "These birds walk in the same way/manner as human beings" – hence the label 'likeness of manner'. In [ii] the *like* phrase falls within the scope of negation:

"These birds don't walk in the same way/manner as human beings"; the implicature is that the birds do walk, but in a different way from humans. As with manner complements, the NP following *like* can itself refer to a manner: *You should do it like this.* The comparison here is between the way you should do it and 'this'.

Again, the primary term in the comparison is not invariably expressed by the subject:

[55] i *He loved her like a sister.*
ii *Bergs will simply rip through sea ice like tissue-paper if the overall current is at variance to the top few metres of the watermass.*

Less specific likeness

[56] i *The girls shrieked their applause like a mob of cockatoos.*
ii *The afternoon sun shone through her chestnut hair like a fiery halo.*
iii *He just slid his hand slowly out again like a snake.*
iv *I followed his instructions, like a coward.*

The examples in [i–iii] bear some similarity to [54i], but the comparison is not with the manner in which a mob of cockatoos might shriek their applause, in which a fiery halo might shine through her hair, or in which he might slide a snake slowly out. It is simply that the girls resembled a mob of cockatoos as they shrieked out their applause, the afternoon sun resembled a fiery halo as it shone through her hair, his hand resembled a snake as he slid it slowly out again. *Like a coward* in [iv] is somewhat different. It is not a matter of any visual resemblance: rather, I was like a coward simply by virtue of following his instructions.

(d) Modifier of a nominal or supplement to an NP

[57] i *She gave an account of their meeting very like the one published in the press.*
ii *I don't think there'll ever be another rider like him.*
iii *Tossing around terms like 'new right' benefits no one but the left.*
iv *I hope that wearing a dress like this will give me confidence.*
v *There were others who ingested strange objects, like live fish.*
vi *?She had an accent like a Dutch kid I used to know.*

The *like* phrase in [i] can be expanded into a relative clause, *which was very like the one published in the press*: it is straightforwardly a matter of resemblance. A similar expansion is possible in [ii], but less natural: the interpretation is similar to that of a scalar comparison, *as good as him. Like* in [iii] is equivalent to *such as*: *new right* is an example of the terms in question. Some of the more authoritarian style manuals condemn this usage, but there is no empirical basis for doing so: it is very common and in no way restricted to informal style. *Like* expresses what we are calling a comparison of equality, and there is no requirement that the resemblance stop short of inclusion or identity. In [iv], for example, it is likely that 'this' is precisely the dress that will be worn: in this context the difference between *this dress* and *a dress like this* is that the latter is concerned with the **kind** of dress involved. In all of [i–iv] the *like* phrase is integrated into the structure of the NP as a modifier. In [v], by contrast, it is a supplement. Finally, [vi] is attested but of doubtful acceptability. The comparison is not between a Dutch kid I used to know and an accent, but between the Dutch kid and the referent of *she* – compare *She had an accent like that of a Dutch kid I used to know.* As it stands, [vi] is stylistically comparable to the examples in [53].

5.6.2 *Like* + finite clause

Like may take either a comparative clause or a content clause as complement:

[58] WITH COMPARATIVE CLAUSE
- i *He wanted to see if she was really like [she always seemed to be__ in his dreams].*
- ii *You talk like [my mother talks__].*
- iii *You didn't look both ways before crossing the road like [you promised__].*
- iv *She was pushing a pram, a high-riding one with large wheels like [you see __ in English movies].*

[59] WITH CONTENT CLAUSE
- i *It looked like [the scheme would founder before it was properly started].*
- ii *You look like [you need a drink].*
- iii *She clasped it in her hand like [it was a precious stone].*
- iv *It was like [I had lost something valuable in a vault full of my own money].*

In [58] *like* is in competition with *as* (or *such as* in the case of [iv]), and the bracketed clause is structurally incomplete in the way discussed above for the complement of *as* in §5.5. The missing element is predicative complement in [i], manner adjunct in [ii], complement in [iii], object in [iv] – compare *You see high-riding prams with large wheels in English movies*, and so on. In [59] *like* is in competition with *as if/though*, and its complement is structurally complete.

There is a quite strong tradition of prescriptive opposition to these constructions: it is alleged that *like* requires an NP complement and cannot take a finite clause (or, to put it in terms of the traditional analysis, that *like* is a 'preposition', not a 'conjunction'). Undoubtedly some speakers follow this rule, avoiding *like* in such examples as [58–59] in favour of the competing forms. Such speakers are, however, very much in the minority: both constructions are commonly used, though somewhat more widely in AmE than in BrE. In BrE they are mainly restricted to informal style; in AmE they are also associated with informal style, but less exclusively, as evident from such examples as:

[60] *There is nothing to suggest that the brain can alter past impressions to fit into an original, realistic and unbroken continuity like [we experience __ in dreams].*

5.6.3 Other constructions

(a) With PP complement

[61] *The shops stay open all night, just like [in the States].*

Here again, *like* is in competition with *as*, which would generally be preferred in formal style (and required by the more authoritarian prescriptivists). The construction is comparable to that where *than* or *as* is followed by a PP (*They aren't as good as in the States*): it may be that the complement of *like* should be analysed as a reduced clause (see §2.2). We should also include here examples like *They're going to Bournemouth like last year*; although *last year* is an NP, it is one of those that can function as adjunct, so that the example is comparable in acceptability to *They are going to Bournemouth like they did last year.*

(b) NP + PP

Like is often followed by the sequence (det) + nominal + PP, and it may be unclear whether the PP is a post-head modifier of the nominal (with the whole sequence therefore forming a single NP), or a separate element (with the sequence forming a verbless clause). Compare the bracketed word sequences in these examples:

[62] i *He looks like [a guy in my tutorial].* [single NP]
ii *She took to it like [a duck to water].* [NP + PP]
iii *At every problem he goes running to the sergeant like [a child to its mother].*
iv *Hate rose in him like [mercury in a thermometer].*
v *There were countless boats bobbing up and down like [corks in a bathtub].*

The two possible structures are illustrated in the first two examples respectively. In [i], *in my tutorial* is a modifier of *guy*, but *to water* in [ii] cannot be a dependent of *duck*, as evident from the ungrammaticality of **She saw a duck to water*, and suchlike. *Like a duck to water* is a familiar expression, but the same structure must apply in [iii]: *child* does not belong to the restricted set of nouns that can take a *to* phrase as dependent. Examples [ii] and [iii] are quite grammatical, and not subject to prescriptive condemnation; it would be unusual, of perhaps questionable acceptability, to replace *like* by *as* here. Examples [iv–v], and numerous similar ones, can be construed either like [i] or like [ii–iii]. There is nothing to stop the *in* phrase being modifier to *mercury* and *corks*, but nor is there anything to block the other structure, with the interpretations "as mercury rises in a thermometer", "as corks bob up and down in a bathtub". Note that the *in* phrase is relevant to the comparison, whereas in [i] it simply gives information limiting the denotation of the nominal. In [v] we could drop the PP because the boats were in the sea and corks would bob up and down in the sea as well as in a bathtub. But it would be pragmatically odd to drop the PP in [iv], for it is not a general characteristic of mercury to rise.

(c) Gerund-participials

The distribution of gerund-participials is very similar to that of NPs, so that in most of the constructions discussed in §5.6.1 above the NP complement of *like* could be replaced by a gerund-participial. Instead of *Max is just like his father*, for example, we can have *Talking to Max is just like taking an oral examination*. In addition, we should note the following uses of the gerund-participial:

[63] i *He shook the barman once more, like a bull-terrier shaking a rat.*
ii *The project looks like continuing another few years.*

Example [i] raises the same issues as were discussed in (b) above: it is unclear whether the complement of *like* is an NP (with *shaking a rat* a modifier to *bull-terrier*) or a non-finite clause (with *a bull-terrier* as subject and *shaking a rat* as predicate). Example [ii] illustrates a special use of *look* + *like*, with the gerund-participial an oblique catenative complement; the meaning is the same as for *look as if* (cf. *The project looks as if it will last another few years*).

(d) Reanalysis

[64] i *We have [nothing like finished].*
ii *His results aren't [anything like as good as they were last year].*

We noted in §4.5 a number of places where sequences containing scalar *than* or *as* have been reanalysed as modifying expressions: [64] illustrates a similar reanalysis with non-scalar *like*. Example [i] cannot be analysed in the same way as, for example, *We have nothing like this specimen*, where *nothing* is head of the object NP and *like this specimen* is modifier. Rather, the bracketed sequence is complement of perfect *have*, so its head must be *finished*, with *nothing like* a modifier; the example may be compared with *We haven't* [*even nearly finished*]. Similarly, in [ii] *anything like* is a modifier of *as*, and in *We found something like thirty major errors* the sequence *something like* is a modifier of *thirty*.

(e) *Like* as a noun and attributive adjective

[65] i *I'd never seen the like of it.*
ii *We want to protect our privacy from ID cards and the like.*
iii *She had no mind to condemn the Queen's weakness knowing herself guilty of the like.*
iv *A quarter of a million pounds was provided for preserving historic properties and a like amount for purchasing.*

In [i–iii], *like* is the head noun in the underlined NP, while in [iv] it is an attributive adjective modifying *amount*. The secondary term in the comparison is expressed by the complement of *of* in [i] and is recovered anaphorically in the other examples: the NPs are understood as "things like that", "a weakness like (or identical to) the Queen's", "a similar amount to that for purchasing". Pattern [i] allows a plural in informal style: *the likes of us*, "people like us".

(f) Set comparison: *like* and *alike*

[66] i *We are of like mind on this question.*
ii *They seem to be growing more and more alike.*
iii *She insisted on treating us all alike.*
iv *Revenues have been a great disappointment to planners and investors alike.*
v *The prospect of mediocrity and the dread of oblivion were alike past bearing.*

Like can be used for set comparison as an attributive adjective, as in [i], but elsewhere set comparison requires *alike*. It is a predicative adjective in [ii], a manner adverb in [iii], while [iv–v] illustrate its most frequent use, as an adverb associated with coordination. In [iv] it is adjunct in an expanded coordination (Ch. 15, §4.1), and in [v] distributive adjunct in clause structure: the coordination identifies the set being compared. Coordination inherently implies likeness between the coordinates, and *alike* simply makes this explicit.

5.6.4 *Unlike*

The negative form occurs in a subset of the constructions available with *like*:

[67] i *Like poles repel, unlike poles attract.*
ii *Jill is quite unlike her mother.*
iii *It's unlike Max to be late.*
iv *She came up with a proposal quite unlike any we had considered so far.*
v *Ice-bergs, unlike sea ice, are not greatly affected by winds.*

vi *<u>Unlike other fruits</u>, one cannot eat the skin of an avocado.*
vii *<u>Unlike in Europe</u>, very few popular books about the natural world were printed in in Australia.*

In [i–iv] it is an adjective (attributive, predicative, or postpositive), in [v–vii] a preposition. Example [iii] matches [47ii] above, with *unlike* interpreted as "uncharacteristic of". The modifier use in [67v–vii] matches the 'likeness of predication' use of *like*, with [v] illustrating the most usual pattern. Example [vi] departs from this pattern in that the primary term in the comparison is not expressed by the subject but by the complement of a preposition (*an avocado*) within the object NP – compare [53] for *like.*

Unlike does not take a finite clause as complement, but it is sometimes found with a PP, as in [67vii]. The acceptability status of this matches that of the corresponding *like* construction seen in [61]; note, however, that while *as* would be preferred in formal style to *like*, *as* has no negative counterpart that could be substituted for *unlike.*

6 Scalar set comparison

6.1 Plain, comparative, and superlative grade

We approach the description of superlatives by returning to the contrast between plain, comparative, and superlative forms, as illustrated in:

[1]	i *Sam is <u>good</u>.*	[plain]
	ii *Pat is <u>better</u> than Sam.*	[comparative]
	iii *Kim is the <u>best</u> of the three.*	[superlative]

A trio of examples like this can be joined together to form a coherent sentence (*Sam is good, but Pat is better and Kim is the best of the three*) and this might suggest that the three categories express progressively higher degrees of the property denoted by the lexical base. But it would be a mistake to interpret them in that way. In the first place, recall that *Pat is better than Sam* does not entail that Pat is good – Pat could be bad, but simply not as bad as Sam. *Older women*, moreover, is generally construed as denoting a subset of women whose average age is less than that of those denoted by the phrase *old women*: see below. Secondly, *Kim is the best of the three* is equivalent to *Kim is better than the other two* : there is no difference in degree.

The system of grade, therefore, is not a matter of different degrees ordered on a scale. The plain form differs from the others in that it does not express comparison. The main difference between the comparative and the superlative is that for the most part they express different kinds of comparison: the comparative is used predominantly for term comparison while the superlative is used exclusively for set comparison.

Thus [1i] does not explicitly compare Sam with anybody else. This is not to say, however, that there is no implicit comparison. Suppose Sam, Pat, and Kim are students and are being evaluated as to how good they are as students. Not all students are good students, so that saying Sam is good, or a good student, involves some comparison with the standards of students in general. Such relativity is particularly evident in examples like *Jumbo is a small elephant.* This does not say that Jumbo is small in any absolute sense: we interpret it as saying that Jumbo is small relative to the standards applicable to elephants. Note, moreover, that it is possible to express comparison in accompanying phrases: *Sam is a good student compared with the others in the class.* The point remains, however, that the plain grade does not itself express comparison.[39]

Example [1ii] is an instance of what we are calling term comparison; the terms in the comparison are either Pat and Sam (if we take the complement of *than* to be simply an NP) or the degree *x* to which Pat is good and the degree *y* to which Sam is good (if we take the complement of *than* to be a reduced clause). Example [iii] is a set comparison: the comparison is between the members of the set of three, with Kim ranked at the top of the scale of 'goodness' for that set.

Non-scalar set comparison has been dealt with in §5, and scalar set comparison of equality (as in *Kim and Pat are equally guilty*) needs no further discussion: our concern in this final section of the chapter is therefore with scalar set comparison of inequality. This is primarily marked by superlative grade, but we will look first at constructions containing comparative grade.

6.2 **Comparative grade in set comparison**

The central case: *the better of the two*

Comparative forms are found in set comparison when the set contains just two members:

[2]		COMPARATIVE	SUPERLATIVE
	i	a. *Pat is the more reliable of the two.*	b. *Pat is the most reliable of the three.*
	ii	a. *Which of the two is the better value?*	b. *Which of the three is the best value?*

Comparative *more* and *better* cannot substitute for superlative *most* and *best* in [b]: a superlative is required if the set contains three or more. In [a], however, the superlative is found as an alternant to the comparative, though it is generally restricted to informal style. The superlative is used more readily in those cases where the dual nature of the set is less immediately or explicitly indicated than it is in [ia/iia] themselves – as in the following example from a linguistics textbook:

[3] *For lexical units with identical grammatical properties, two alternative criteria for for membership of the same lexeme will be proposed. The first is the most important.*

Comparatives of the type *older women*

[4] i *The programme is designed for older women.*
ii *Taller students are asked to use the top shelves.*
iii *This was not one of his better suggestions.*

The comparatives here are better regarded as set comparisons than as term comparisons: it is not possible to add a *than* phrase (without a fundamental change of meaning), and such comparatives readily take definite determiners, as in *This programme is designed for the younger listener*, or *The obvious solution is for the taller students to use the top shelves* – or the genitive of [iii]. *Older women* implies a comparison within the set of women: it

[39] The traditional term for plain grade is 'positive grade', but we have preferred to restrict 'positive' to the sense where it contrasts with 'negative'. Another term found in the literature is 'absolute', but we regard this as semantically inappropriate for reasons given in the text; 'absolute comparative', moreover, is a traditional term for a comparative in which the secondary term is left unexpressed, as in *This is cheaper.*

denotes a subset who are above the mean age. In general, *older* covers a larger range of the scale of age than the plain form *old*: women of fifty, for example, might well be regarded as older women, but not as old.

The lexical comparatives *upper, inner,* and *outer*

These forms transparently contain the comparative suffix ·*er*, but it is here better regarded as a derivational suffix than as an inflectional one. *Upper*, *inner*, and *outer* are adjectives restricted to attributive position, whereas *up*, *in*, and *out* are prepositions, not adjectives. These comparatives do not license a *than* phrase (cf. **I'd rather live in an outer suburb than this*), and do not express term comparison.

However, in some uses at least, they express a type of set comparison over two-member sets. In such comparisons, *upper* is contrasted with *lower* (an inflectional comparative form)[40] and *inner* with *outer*:

[5]	i	a. *her upper lip*	b. *her lower lip*
	ii	a. *the outer suburbs*	b. *the inner suburbs*

Note also that ·*er* here does not contrast with ·*est*. Rather, ·*most* can be added after the ·*er* to form what might similarly be regarded as derivational superlatives, *uppermost*, *innermost*, *outermost*. (There are also forms in ·*most* without counterparts in ·*er*: *topmost*, *rightmost*, *northernmost*, etc.)

Former and *latter*

Here too we take the ·*er* to be a derivational rather than an inflectional suffix. Both forms enter into a further lexical word-formation process, namely suffixation of ·*ly* (*formerly*, *latterly*). Again they do not license a *than* phrase. They have both non-anaphoric and anaphoric uses, illustrated in [6i–ii] respectively:

[6] i a. *She has had to take out an injunction against her former husband.*
b. *The poem was written in the latter part of the twelfth century.*
ii a. *The wine may be chilled in a bucket of ice and water or the freezing compartment of a refrigerator, the former being far preferable.*
b. *If asked to choose between a terrible probability and a more terrible possibility, most people will choose the latter.*

The non-anaphoric use of *former* belongs in fact in the term comparison category: it involves reference to a time earlier than now (or than the time under consideration). The other cases, however, are set comparisons. Non-anaphoric *latter* picks out one of a set of two members (here subdivisions of the twelfth century); it is broadly equivalent to the inflectional comparative *later*. In the anaphoric use (described more fully in Ch. 17, §9.4), members of the set being compared are specified in the preceding text, with *former* picking out the first and *latter* the last, thus a bucket of ice and water in [iia] and a more terrible possibility in [iib]. In this use *former* and *latter* are commonly paired:

[7] *It is not easy to make an economic comparison between clay pots and the various substitutes; the former may last indefinitely with luck, while the latter are often expendable and used only once.*

Former is normally restricted to two-member sets, but it is not uncommon for *latter*

[40] There is also the archaic *nether*, found in the expressions *nether regions/garments*, and various place names.

to be used for the last-named of a larger set – a manifestation of the weak degree of grammaticalisation of the dual category in English. An alternative to *latter* in such cases is *last*, and the ordinal numerals can also be used in a similar way.

6.3 Superlatives

6.3.1 Inflectional and analytic superlatives

The formation of superlatives is very similar to that of comparatives. They can be marked inflectionally, with the suffix ·*est* corresponding to comparative ·*er*, or analytically, with the adverbs *most* and *least* corresponding to comparative *more* and *less*. Again we add subscript 'a' to indicate the analytic marker use:

[8]

	COMPARATIVE		SUPERLATIVE	
i SUPERIORITY	*easier*	*more*$_a$ *difficult*	*easiest*	*most*$_a$ *difficult*
ii INFERIORITY	*less*$_a$ *easy*	*less*$_a$ *difficult*	*least*$_a$ *easy*	*least*$_a$ *difficult*

Superlatives of superiority and inferiority are illustrated in:

[9] i *This is the most*$_a$ *difficult problem of them all.* [superlative of superiority]
ii *This is the least*$_a$ *difficult problem of them all.* [superlative of inferiority]

We have here a comparison on a scale of difficulty between the members of a set of problems: [i] picks out the problem at the top of the scale, [ii] the one at the bottom.

Like comparative *more* and *less*, superlative *most* and *least* can also be inflectional forms of the degree determinatives, and as before we add subscript 'i' to represent this inflectional use. The various forms are given in [10], with the superlatives illustrated in [11]:

[10]

	POSITIVE ORIENTATION		NEGATIVE ORIENTATION	
	non-count sg	**count pl**	**non-count sg**	**count pl**
PLAIN	*much*	*many*	*little*	*few*
COMPARATIVE	*more*$_i$		*less*$_i$	*fewer*/*less*$_i$
SUPERLATIVE	*most*$_i$		*least*$_i$	*fewest*/*least*$_i$

[11] i *Kim shows (the) most*$_i$ *promise.* [non-count } positive orientation]
ii *Kim has (the) most*$_i$ *friends.* [count
iii *Kim has (the) least*$_i$ *patience.* [non-count } negative orientation]
iv *Kim made (the) fewest/least*$_i$ *errors.* [count

The variation between *least*$_i$ and *fewest* is broadly similar to that between *less*$_i$ and *fewer*, but superlative *fewest* and *least*$_i$ are very much less frequent than *fewer* and *less*$_i$, and do not enter into the wide range of construction types that we noted for the latter pair.

There is a traditional prescriptive rule requiring *fewest* with count plurals. This is more often followed when the determinative is in construction with a plural noun than when it is functioning as fused determiner-head, as in *No one made many errors, but Kim made the fewest/least*$_i$.

Most$_i$ and *least*$_i$ also function as adjunct of degree in clause structure, but unlike comparative *more*$_i$ and *less*$_i$ they are not used in the grading of count singular nominals:

[12] i *Kim enjoyed it the most*$_i$/*least*$_i$.

ii **Of all my teachers Kim was the most*$_i$/*least*$_i$ *of a scholar.*

Adjectival *least*

Least$_i$ is not only a determinative but also an adjective:

[13] i *Its attractiveness as an investment is least during periods of high inflation.*

ii *[Even the least alteration to the plan] could prove fatal.*

iii *That's [the least of my worries].*

iv *She didn't seem [the least bit] interested in what they were saying.*

Least here is the opposite of *greatest*, and means "smallest/slightest". Example [i] illustrates the predicative use, where it is the superlative counterpart of adjectival *less*. In [ii–iv] *least* is used attributively: it functions as modifier in NP structure (fused with the head in [iii]). To a limited extent it here corresponds to adjectival *lesser* – [iii] is comparable with *That's the lesser of my worries*, and *to the least degree* with *to a lesser degree.*

6.3.2 Non-superlative uses of *most*

Most has a number of uses besides those where it is a superlative form or marker.

Intensifier *most*

[14] i	*Kim is a [most enthusiastic] supporter.*	[intensifying]
ii	*This one is [most useful].*	[superlative or intensifying]
iii	*This one is [cheapest].*	[superlative only]
iv	*You are [most kind].*	[intensifying as salient reading]

The *most* of [i], which belongs to relatively formal style, is an intensifier, a degree adverb meaning approximately "highly, very, extremely". It does not express comparison any more than other intensifiers such as *very.*

There is a clear semantic difference between *most enthusiastic* here and in the superlative *Kim is the most enthusiastic supporter I've come across*, where we do have a comparison within the set of supporters I've come across. In this case, the two uses of *most* are distinguished by the article, with *a* requiring the intensifying interpretation, *the* the superlative one. Example [14ii] is ambiguous between a superlative reading equivalent to "This one is more useful than all the others", and an intensifying one, "This one is extremely useful"; adding *the* before *most* forces the superlative reading.

In general, forms marked with the inflectional suffix ·*est* are not used in the intensifying sense: we cannot, for example, replace *most enthusiastic* in [14i] with such a form: **Kim is a keenest supporter. Cheapest* in [iii] is thus unambiguously superlative, and allows the insertion of *the* without change of meaning.

Example [14iv] has in principle the same ambiguity as [ii], but since *kind* allows inflectional marking of grade, we would expect *You are kindest* as the superlative. As a result, [iv] itself would generally be construed as intensifying.[41]

[41] One exceptional case where an inflected form expresses intensification rather than set comparison is with terms of endearment, as in *my dearest Anna* ("my very dear Anna"). Precisely because it is so exceptional, we retain the term superlative for the inflectional form and treat *my dearest Anna* as an intensifying use of the superlative form rather than saying, as we do of *a most enthusiastic supporter*, that it doesn't belong to the

There is no corresponding use of *least*. *This one is least useful*, for example, is unambiguous, meaning "This is the least useful one among them", not "This one is not very useful".

Proportional quantifier

[15] i *Most people think he's guilty.* } [proportional quantifier]
ii *I agree with most of your points.* }
iii *Kim had interviewed most candidates.* [superlative or proportional]
iv *Kim had interviewed the most candidates.* } [superlative only]
v *Kim had interviewed (the) least candidates.* }

Most in [i–ii] means "more than half, the majority": it expresses a kind of proportional quantification (Ch. 5, §7.11). *Many* and *much*, by contrast, are non-proportional: *I agree with many of your points*, for example, doesn't indicate whether or not the number of your points that I agree with exceeds the number that I don't agree with, and analogously for *I agree with much of what you say*.

The difference between this proportional sense and the superlative one can be brought out by considering ambiguous examples like [15iii]. In the superlative reading Kim had interviewed more candidates than anybody else: we have a comparison between the set of interviewers with respect to how many candidates each had interviewed, with Kim placed at the top of the scale. In this reading there is no indication as to what proportion of the candidates Kim had interviewed. In the proportional reading of [iii], Kim had interviewed more than half the candidates; this time there is no comparison between Kim and anybody else, no indication that anybody else was interviewing candidates.

The two readings are grammatically distinguished in that only the superlative one allows the insertion of *the*: [iv] is unambiguously superlative. Similarly *most* can be replaced by *least* or *fewest* only in the superlative reading, so that [v] is likewise unambiguously superlative: *least* expresses set comparison, not proportion.

Reduction of *almost*

Most can also be a reduced form of *almost*, as in %*I think most everybody would agree.* This use of *most* is found primarily in AmE and is characteristic of relatively informal style. It functions as modifier to *all*, *any*, and *every*, and compounds containing them, such as *anything*, *everybody* – and *always*.

6.3.3 Absolute and relative superlatives

NPs containing superlatives may have either **absolute** or **relative** interpretations:

[16] i *Kim lives in the smallest house in England.* [absolute]
ii *Of all members of the team, Kim had the most difficult job.* [relative]

In [i] the comparison is between the set of houses in England: the underlined NP refers to the member of this set which is at the top of the scale of smallness. The comparison here doesn't involve anything outside the NP containing the superlative form. In [ii], by contrast, the comparison crucially involves Kim: it is a matter of how difficult a job Kim had in comparison with how difficult a job other members of the team had. The

superlative category at all. One additional special use of intensifying *most* is in titles for people holding certain high offices in the judiciary or the church: *Most Honourable*, *Most Reverend*.

job here, then, is not the most difficult in an absolute sense, but only relative to the jobs assigned to members of the team. The difference can be brought out by comparing these set comparisons with equivalent term comparisons:

[17] i *Kim lives in a smaller house than any other house in England.*
ii *Kim had a more difficult job than any other member of the team.*

In [ii] *any other member of the team* means "any other member than Kim": Kim is involved in the comparison in [ii] but not in [i].

Most in [16ii] is the analytic marker; the determinative *most* $_i$, by contrast, is virtually always relative:

[18] *Kim scored the most points.* [relative]

An absolute use of this *most* might be *Kim scored the most possible points*, but this is quite marginal: we would generally express the intended meaning as *Kim scored the highest possible number of points* or the like.

Absolute superlatives are often concerned with possible maximum or minimum degrees:

[19] i *We want to ensure that the fullest discussion takes place.*
ii *I have the strangest feeling of having lived through this very same event before.*
iii *The ground was so soft that the lightest step made a deep imprint.*
iv *She hasn't the slightest/least recollection of what happened.*

In such contexts *the slightest/smallest/least* and the like are equivalent to *any at all*: *She hasn't any recollection at all of what happened.* Special cases of this use are seen in the phrases *at least, at most, in the least.* Note finally the contrast in meaning and structure in such a pair as the following:

[20] i *Kim was not the least concerned about what people might think.* [absolute]
ii *Kim was the least concerned about these developments.* [relative]

In [i] *the least* is a constituent modifying *concerned*: *the* is obligatory and the modifying phrase could be replaced by *the least bit, in the least, at all.* In [ii] *the* is optional and does not form a constituent with *least*, and the superlative implies a comparison between Kim and some set of which Kim is a member.

6.3.4 The structure of superlative phrases

In describing the structure of superlative phrases we need to distinguish between two cases, which we call **incorporated** and **free** superlatives. They are illustrated in [21i–ii] respectively, where the underlined sequence is the superlative phrase:

[21] i a. *They rejected [the two best novels she has written].* [incorporated]
b. *Kim has [the most valuable collection of all].*
c. *This is [her most perfectly constructed novel].*
d. *Pat made [the most mistakes].*
e. *He offered me [the least valuable of the paintings].*
f. *[The most we can hope for] is a 2% rise.*
ii a. *She's [the candidate most likely to be elected].* [free]
b. *These were the ones that the grown-ups laughed at loudest.*
c. *He's the least able to look after himself.*
d. *It was Jill who presented her case the most effectively.*

The superlative phrases in [i] are incorporated into the structure of an NP, marked by the bracketing – more precisely they occur before the head ([a–d]) or fuse with it ([e–f]). Those in [ii] are either not contained within an NP at all ([b–d]) or are in post-head position ([a]).

In [21ia–c] the superlative phrase constitutes all or part of a modifier of the head of the NP. The *the* in [ia–b] does not form part of the superlative phrase but is determiner in NP structure: it can be separated from the superlative by another modifier, as in [ia], and can be replaced by other definite determiners, such as the genitive in [ic] or a demonstrative (*this most recent edition*).

The *most* of [21id], however, is the inflectional superlative of *many*, and here *the most* forms a DP functioning as determiner in the NP; this *the* is optional and cannot be replaced by a genitive or demonstrative.

The same distinction applies in [21ie–f], where the superlative phrase is fused with the head of the NP. In [ie] *the* is determiner and *least valuable* fused modifier-head. Note again the possibility of inserting a modifier such as *two* between them. In [if] *the most* is fused determiner-head; *the* is obligatory this time, but again not replaceable by a genitive or demonstrative.

The free superlatives in [21ii] are more straightforward. The initial *the* in [iic–d] is not determiner in a matrix NP, but part of the superlative phrase; it cannot be separated from the superlative phrase and is not in contrast with definite determiners like genitives. We will see below that there are also differences between the free and incorporated constructions with respect to post-head elements.

Presence or absence of *the*

In free superlative phrases *the* is usually permitted but optional. It can, for example, be dropped from [21iic–d], and it can be inserted in [iia–b], though it is much more usual for it to be omitted in the construction shown in [iia], where the superlative phrase is an AdjP used postpositively, i.e. as post-head modifier in NP structure. One construction where it is not possible to have *the* is in supplements like those in [22].

[22] i <u>*Most important of all*</u>*, the weather at the time was dry: there was no rain to bring down the radioactive materials.*

ii <u>*Most surprisingly of all*</u>*, they continued to believe in his innocence.*

Incorporated superlatives generally confer definiteness on the NP containing them and are therefore incompatible with indefinite determiners: **a brightest girl in the class.*[42] *The* (or some other determiner) is always permitted in definite NPs, normally quite strongly preferred, and often obligatory. Consider the following, where the bracketing marks NPs:

[23] i *The prize was won by* [*the* <u>*youngest*</u> *competitor*].

ii *These are* [*the two* <u>*tallest*</u> *buildings in the city*].

iii *The programme gives* [(*the*) <u>*best*</u> *results*] *if you begin before the age of thirty.*

iv *The rebates should be given to those in* [(*the*) <u>*greatest*</u> *need*].

v *It was Kim who attracted* [<u>(*the*) *most*</u> *attention*].

[42] Occasional exceptions are found where the NP is indefinite: *Several of the competitors achieved personal best times.* Such examples tend to involve highly lexicalised collocations.

The is obligatory in [i–ii], optional in the others. In [i] *competitor* is a count singular noun and hence requires a determiner by the general rules of NP structure: the only effect of the superlative *youngest* is to add the requirement that the determiner be definite. In [ii] the impossibility of dropping *the* is not attributable to the head noun, but to the fact that omission of *the* would make *two* the determiner: this would mark the NP as indefinite, which is incompatible with the inherent definiteness conferred by the superlative.

No such factors apply in [23iii–v], and here *the* can be omitted. Note, however, that its omission does not result in a change of meaning – in particular, there is no change from definite to indefinite. In [v] *the* is part of the DP, as in [21id] above.

Relative clauses

One distinctive property of superlatives is that they can take integrated relative clauses as dependents even when not incorporated into NP structure:

[24] i *The price of gold is <u>the lowest it has been for ten years</u>.*
ii *The system seems to be working <u>the most efficiently that it has ever worked</u>.*

Lowest in [i] is an adjective, *efficiently* in [ii] an adverb, and there is no plausible reason to propose that the underlined phrases they head are NPs. Note, for example, that *wh* relatives are not permitted (**the lowest which it has been for years*) and that the equivalent term comparisons are simply *lower than it has been for ten years, more efficiently than it has ever worked before. The* is obligatory in this construction.

Other post-head dependents

Besides relative clauses, superlatives take such dependents as *ever, imaginable, possible, practicable*, and *of* phrases indicating the set whose members are compared:

[25] i a. *We'll aim for the <u>best</u> <u>possible</u> result.* b. *We'll aim for the <u>best</u> result <u>possible</u>.*
ii a. *Kim's essay was the <u>best</u> <u>of all</u>.* b. *Kim wrote the <u>best</u> essay <u>of them all</u>.*

With incorporated superlatives, the single word dependents are optionally delayed so as to become indirect dependents in the structure of the NP, as illustrated in [ib/iib]. Such delay is obligatory for *of* phrases (compare [iib] with **the best of them all essay*). Note also that *them* in [iib] can refer either to the set of essays, in which case we have an absolute superlative, or to the set of essay writers, in which case we have a relative superlative.

Pre-head dependents

These fall into two groups, as follows:

[26] i *very*; *next* and ordinal numerals other than *first*
ii *absolutely, almost, altogether, barely, by far, easily, entirely, fully, hardly, more or less, much, nearly, practically, quite, scarcely, virtually, ...*

Those in [i] follow *the*, while those in [ii] precede it:

[27] i *It was the <u>very</u> <u>best</u> performance I can recall.*
ii *Kim's the <u>second</u> <u>youngest</u> in the class.*
iii *This one works <u>easily</u> the <u>most efficiently</u>.*
iv *I made <u>by far</u> the <u>most</u> errors.*

Very here means "absolutely"; it occurs with inflectional but not analytic superlatives. The ordinal numerals indicate position in a rank ordering, counting from the top (or from the bottom in the case of comparisons of inferiority, as in *the third least expensive model*). In [27ii], for example, there is just one person younger than Kim. The fact that the items in [26ii] precede *the* means that with incorporated superlatives such as that in [27iv] they function as peripheral modifier in the structure of the NP rather than in the structure of the superlative phrase itself (see Ch. 5, §13).

14

Non-finite and verbless clauses

Rodney Huddleston

1 Preliminaries

1.1 Matters of form and function

Non-finite vs finite

Non-finite clauses are distinguished from finites largely but not wholly by the inflectional form of the verb. Clauses whose verb is a gerund-participle or past participle are always non-finite, and those whose verb is a preterite or present tense form (or irrealis *were*) are always finite: only the plain form appears in both classes of clause (Ch. 3, §1.8). Of the three main syntactic constructions having a plain-form verb, two are finite and one non-finite:

[1] i	IMPERATIVE	*Be patient.*	[finite]
ii	SUBJUNCTIVE	*It's essential that he be more careful.*	[finite]
iii	INFINITIVAL	*It's important for him to be more careful.*	[non-finite]

Infinitivals are distinguished from the two finite constructions by the following properties:

[2] i Most infinitivals, apart from the complements of modal auxiliaries and supportive *do*, contain the VP subordinator *to*: this is a clear marker of the infinitival.

ii Unlike imperatives, they do not take auxiliary *do* in negatives, etc.: compare *Don't be late* and *It's important not to be late.*

iii Unlike imperatives, they are almost invariably subordinate.

iv Unlike subjunctives, they usually have no subject, and where there is a subject it appears in accusative (or plain) form, not nominative (compare *him* in [1iii] with *he* in [1ii]).

v Whereas the most common type of subjunctive construction, the mandative, takes the finite-clause subordinator *that*, the infinitival subordinator (used only when a subject is present) is *for*.

Form-types

On the basis of the inflectional form of the verb we distinguish three main kinds of non-finite clause: **infinitival**, **gerund-participial**, and **past-participial**. We refer to these as **form-types**. They are illustrated by the bracketed clauses of [3] (all of which are complements of the preceding verb):

[3] i *Max wanted [to change his name].* [infinitival]
ii *I remember [locking the door].* [gerund-participial]
iii *His father got [charged with manslaughter].* [past-participial]

Precisely because it is only the plain form that can occur in both finite and non-finite clauses, it is only for [i] that we need a label that is not simply derived from the name of the inflectional form of the verb. For [ii–iii] we use gerund-participle and past participle for the verb-forms, gerund-participial and past-participial for the clauses.

Subtypes of infinitival: *to*-infinitivals and bare infinitivals

Infinitivals are subdivided into *to*-infinitivals and bare infinitivals according to the presence or absence of the subordinator *to*:

[4]	*TO*-INFINITIVAL	BARE INFINITIVAL
i	a. *They forced me to sign the petition.*	b. *They helped me move the furniture.*
ii	a. *You ought to sell it.*	b. *You should sell it.*
iii	a. *All I did was to ask a question.*	b. *All I did was ask a question.*

The *to*-infinitival occurs in a very wide range of constructions, whereas the bare infinitival is very restricted. It occurs primarily as complement to a small number of verbs, but these include the modal auxiliaries and supportive *do*, which makes it a very common construction.

Form-types, auxiliaries, and voice

The modal auxiliaries and supportive *do* are excluded from all non-finite clauses. Infinitivals admit the remaining three auxiliaries:

[5] i *I expect [to have finished soon].* [perfect *have*]
ii *I expect [to be working all week-end].* [progressive *be*]
iii *I expect [to be interviewed by the police].* [passive *be*]

Gerund-participials accept *have* and passive *be*, but not progressive *be*:[1]

[6] i *I regret [having told them].* [perfect *have*]
ii *I resent [being given so little notice].* [passive *be*]
iii **I remember [being working when they arrived].* [progressive *be*]

The past participle form of the verb has two uses, perfect and passive. Clauses with a perfect past participle as head occur as complement to auxiliary *have*, and accept progressive and passive *be*, while those with a passive past participle as head accept no auxiliaries:

[7] i *Ed has [seen her].* *Ed has [been seeing her].* *Ed has [been seen].* [perfect]
ii *He had it [checked by the manager].* [passive]

[1] Examples with progressive *be* are occasionally encountered in casual speech: *I've missed endless buses through [not being standing at the bus stop when they arrived].* This cannot, however, be regarded as an established construction in Present-day English.

Subjectless non-finites

The great majority of non-finite clauses have no subject, as in:

[8] i *Kim was glad* [_ *to reach home*].
ii *It has been a pleasure* [_ *meeting you*].
iii *Anyone* [_ *living nearby*] *will be evacuated.*
iv *The sum* [_ *spent on gambling*] *was extraordinary.*

Whereas the subject is an obligatory element in canonical clauses, there are no non-finite constructions in which a subject is required.[2] There are, moreover, many constructions where it is impossible to add a subject, as in [iii–iv], or the examples of [4] above.

It will be evident from this formulation that we take the subject to be an optional element in non-finite clauses, not an element whose presence is necessary for an expression to qualify as a clause. That is, the bracketed expressions in [8] are analysed as clauses that consist of just a VP rather than simply as subclausal expressions with the form of a VP. We take the VP to be the head of the clause and the presence of a VP is normally sufficient to establish clausal status. The main exception is with attributive VPs in NP structure:

[9] i *our rapidly approaching deadline*
ii *a poorly drafted report* } [VPs, not clauses]

Expansion of the verbs in this construction is virtually limited to adverbial modifiers preceding the verb: the range of structural possibilities here is quite different from that found in clauses.

Hollow clauses

In a relatively small number of constructions, almost exclusively *to*-infinitivals, some non-subject element is missing:

[10] i *The letter isn't legible enough* [*for you to read* _].
ii *The letter isn't legible enough* [*to read* _].
iii *I don't think they are worth* [*spending much time on* _].

The bracketed clauses here we call **hollow clauses.** The missing non-subject is normally recoverable from the matrix clause. In [i–ii] the object of *read* is recoverable from *the letter*, while in [iii] the object of *on* is recoverable from *they*. Missing subjects, by contrast, are not always recoverable from the matrix, as evident from [8ii] and [10ii].

Interrogative and relative *to*-infinitivals

Interrogative and relative clauses may have the form of *to*-infinitivals:

[11] i a. *I can't decide whether to go with them.* [closed interrogative]
b. *He doesn't know how to placate her.* [open interrogative]
ii a. *They have funds with which to conduct a survey.* [*wh* relative]
b. *Another option for you to consider is renting a caravan.* [non-*wh* relative]

These will receive little attention in the present chapter, as they are covered along with other subordinate interrogatives (Ch. 11, §5.3.5) and relatives (Ch. 12, §5).

[2] The subordinator *for* cannot occur without a subject, but we do not find constructions where *for* + subject is required.

Distribution of non-finite clauses

Non-finite clauses occur as dependent or supplement in a wide range of constructions.[3] The major distinction we draw is between non-finites in complement function, and those in non-complement function (modifiers or supplements); these are illustrated for infinitivals in [12i–ii] respectively:

[12]	i	a. *His aim was* <u>*to intimidate us*</u>.	[comp in clause structure]
		b. *She is [keen* <u>*to regain control*</u>*]*.	[comp in AdjP structure]
		c. *I've missed [the opportunity* <u>*to have my say*</u>*]*.	[comp in NP structure]
		d. *She left at six [in order* <u>*to catch the early train*</u>*]*.	[comp in PP structure]
	ii	a. *She left at six* <u>*to catch the early train*</u>.	[modifier in clause structure]
		b. *He's a charlatan,* <u>*to put it bluntly*</u>.	[supplement to a clause]
		c. *I've found [a box* <u>*to keep the tapes in*</u>*]*.	[modifier in NP structure]

The complement functions are similar to those of content clauses, but the non-complement uses are more varied and frequent than those of content clauses.

1.2 The catenative construction

The functions of complement non-finites in clause structure include the following:

[13]	i	<u>*To underestimate her*</u> *would be foolish*.	[subject]
	ii	*I found* <u>*talking to her*</u> *quite helpful*.	[object]
	iii	*I call that* <u>*taking liberties*</u>.	[predicative comp]
	iv	*It was natural* <u>*to be worried*</u>.	[extraposed subject]
	v	*I found it distressing* <u>*to see her so ill*</u>.	[extraposed object]
	vi	a. *She wants* <u>*to leave the country*</u>.	[catenative comp]
		b. *She seems* <u>*to like them*</u>.	[catenative comp]
		c. *She hopes* <u>*to hear from them soon*</u>.	[catenative comp]

In the case of [i–v] the non-finite clause has the same function as expressions of other kinds, e.g. NPs in [i–iii], finite clauses in [iv–v]. Compare:

[14]	i	<u>*Such behaviour*</u> *would be foolish*.	[subject]
	ii	*I found* <u>*the discussion*</u> *quite helpful*.	[object]
	iii	*I call that* <u>*an outrage*</u>.	[predicative comp]
	iv	*It was natural* <u>*that they should be worried*</u>.	[extraposed subject]
	v	*I found it distressing* <u>*that she was so ill*</u>.	[extraposed object]

In the case of [13vi], on the other hand, we take the view that the non-finite clause cannot be satisfactorily subsumed under a complement type filled by other classes of expression. The governing verbs *want*, *seem*, and *hope* appear elsewhere with such complements as we see in:

[15]	i	*She wants* <u>*a holiday*</u>.	[object]
	ii	*She seems* <u>*fond of them*</u>.	[predicative comp]
	iii	*She hopes* <u>*for an early reply*</u>.	[comp of prepositional verb]

[3] They also occur in some minor main clause constructions, such as polar echoes and certain kinds of directive: see Ch. 10, §§4.8.3, 9.6.3.

We will argue in §4.1, however, that the differences between these do not carry over to [13via–c], so that the latter cannot satisfactorily be regarded as containing respectively an object, a predicative complement, and the complement of a prepositional verb. Instead, we analyse the underlined clauses in [13vi] as examples of a distinct type of complement realised exclusively by non-finite clauses; we refer to them as **catenative complements**.

The term 'catenative' applies to a large class of constructions where a verb has a non-finite internal complement. The name reflects the fact that the construction can be repeated recursively, yielding a concatenation ('chain') of verbs:

[16] i *I wanted to arrange for Kim to do it.*
ii *She intends to try to persuade him to help her redecorate her flat.*

In [i] we have a chain of three verbs, with *for Kim to do it* complement of *arrange* and *to arrange for Kim to do it* complement of *want.* We apply the term 'catenative' both to the non-finite complement and to the verb in the matrix clause that licenses it, so that *want* and *arrange* here belong to the class of catenative verbs. The last verb in the chain, *do*, is not a catenative verb as it does not have a non-finite complement. Similarly, the underlined verbs in [ii] are catenative verbs with the non-finite complements shown in:

[17]	CATENATIVE VERB	CATENATIVE COMPLEMENT
i	*intend*	*to try to persuade him to help her redecorate her flat*
ii	*try*	*to persuade him to help her redecorate her flat*
iii	*persuade*	*to help her redecorate her flat*
iv	*help*	*redecorate her flat*

Note that *persuade* and *help* take an NP complement (an object) in addition to the catenative complement, namely *him* and *her* respectively.

Auxiliary verbs

Auxiliary verbs in their core use as markers of mood, tense, aspect, and voice also belong in the class of catenative verbs. On this account, *She may like it*, for example, will be analysed with *like it* a non-finite complement of *may* just as *to like it* is a complement of *seems* in *She seems to like it*; we take up this point in §4.2.

Simple vs complex catenative constructions

Catenative constructions may be classified on one dimension according to form-type, and on another as **simple** or **complex**, according as they lack or contain an **intervening NP**, i.e. an NP positioned between matrix and subordinate verbs and functioning as complement of one or other of them.

[18]	SIMPLE	COMPLEX	
i	a. *I hope to finish soon.*	b. *I advise you to sell it.*	[*to*-infinitival]
ii	a. *I helped wash up.*	b. *I made them apologise.*	[bare infinitival]
iii	a. *I stopped worrying about it.*	b. *I saw them fighting.*	[gerund-participial]
iv	a. *I got arrested.*	b. *I had my car stolen.*	[past-participial]

More precisely, the simple construction has no intervening NP in the active: passives like *You are advised to sell it* are subsumed under the complex construction.

Four subtypes of the (active) complex construction can then be distinguished:

[19] i *I arranged for them to go by bus.* [*for*-complex]
ii *I rely on them to look after themselves.* [oblique-complex]
iii *I resented their being given such favourable treatment.* [genitive-complex]
iv *I want them to be happy.* [plain-complex]
v *I resented them being given such favourable treatment.*

In the *for*-complex construction the intervening NP is preceded by the subordinator *for*; it is subject of the non-finite but in accusative (or plain) case. The oblique-complex is found with certain prepositional verbs: the intervening NP is an oblique complement of the matrix verb, i.e. complement of the preposition that the verb selects. In the genitive-complex the intervening NP is in the genitive case and functions as subject of the non-finite clause. Finally, in the plain-complex the intervening NP is in plain or accusative case, and (depending on factors discussed in §3) either object of the matrix, as in [iv], or subject of the subordinate, as in [v].[4]

1.3 *To*-infinitivals with and without a subject

To-infinitivals with overt subject require the subordinator *for*

To-infinitivals containing a subject are always introduced by the subordinator *for*:

[20] i *[For them to withdraw now] would be a mistake.* [subject]
ii *It's not necessary [for them to wait any longer].* [extraposed subject]
iii *The best plan would be [for them to go alone].* [predicative comp]
iv *I can think of no solution except [for them to sack him].* [comp of preposition]

If we drop the *for* we must also drop the subject, and conversely, *for* cannot appear without a following subject. Compare [20ii], for example, with:

[21] i *It is not necessary [to wait any longer].*
ii **It is not necessary [them to wait any longer].*
iii **It is not necessary [for to wait any longer].*[5]

Notice, moreover, that the interrogative *to*-infinitivals shown in [11i] and the *wh* relative [11iia] cannot contain a subject:

[22] i a. *I can't decide [whether to go with them].* (=[11ia])
b. **I can't decide [whether (for) us to go with them].*
ii a. *He doesn't know [how to placate her].* (=[11ib])
b. **He doesn't know [how (for) us to placate her].*
iii a. *They have funds [with which to conduct a survey].* (=[11iia])
b. **They have funds [with which (for) us to conduct a survey].*

The well-formed examples here all exclude *for* because the prenuclear position is occupied – by the interrogative subordinator *whether*, the interrogative phrase *how*, or the relative phrase *with which*. And because an infinitival cannot contain a subject

[4] The infinitival version of the plain-complex is often referred to as the 'accusative + infinitive construction'.
[5] There are, however, non-standard varieties where certain catenative verbs may take *for* without a subject: !*He wanted for to see you.*

unless introduced by *for* the asterisked examples here are as bad in the version without *for* as in the one where *for* illicitly appears.

The catenative construction not an exception

At first glance examples like the following might appear to cast doubt on the rule that *to*-infinitivals with a subject require *for*:

[23] i *They arranged for the performance to begin at six.* [*for* required]
ii *They expected the performance to begin at six.* [*for* excluded]
iii *They intended (for) the performance to begin at six.* [*for* optional]

For is required after *arrange*, excluded after *expect*, and optional after *intend*. The structural difference between [i] and [ii], however, is not just a matter of the presence or absence of the subordinator *for*: in [i] *the performance* is subject of the infinitival clause, but in [ii] it is object of the matrix clause. This means that [ii] is not an exception: there is no *for* here because the infinitival clause has no subject. And in [iii] the version with *for* has the same structure as [i], while the version without *for* has *the performance* as matrix object, like [ii].

Semantically, of course, *the performance* does belong with *begin* in [23ii], just as it does in [i], for the meaning is "They expected that the performance would begin at six". Nevertheless, there are several pieces of evidence showing that syntactically it belongs in the matrix clause, that *the performance* and *to begin at six* in [ii] do not combine to form a single constituent (a clause) but are separate complements of *expect*: object and catenative complement respectively.

(a) Passivisation

Examples [23i] and [ii] behave quite differently under passivisation:

[24] i *It was arranged for the performance to begin at six.*
ii **It was expected the performance to begin at six.*
iii *The performance was expected to begin at six.*

In the construction with *for*, passivisation is accompanied by extraposition, so that *for the performance to begin at six* becomes extraposed subject. But where *for* is absent the sequence *the performance to begin at six* does not become extraposed subject: rather it is just the NP *the performance* that is promoted to subject. This is strong evidence that *the performance* is a separate complement of *expect* in [23ii] – its object. Note that with *intend*, where *for* is optional, we have two passive versions: *It was intended for the performance to begin at six* (matching [24i]), and *The performance was intended to begin at six* (matching [24iii]). Thus *for* marks the beginning of the infinitival clause, with the following NP therefore subject of the subordinate clause, but where *for* is absent the NP behaves syntactically as object of the matrix clause.

It is true that not all catenatives taking an NP without *for* allow passives like [24iii]:

[25] i *They wanted the performance to begin at six.*
ii **The performance was wanted to begin at six.*

However, there is no other relevant difference between *want* and *expect*, and given that passivisation doesn't provide a necessary condition for objects, we shall not wish to assign different structures to the *want* and *expect* examples. Note, moreover, that *want* takes *for* when there is a preceding adjunct, but does not allow passivisation in the *for* construction either:

[26] i *They had wanted all along for the performance to begin at six.*
ii **It had been wanted all along for the performance to begin at six.*

This suggests that the deviance of [25ii] is due to a property of the verb *want*, not to the structure of the active clause [25i].

The important point, then, is that while there are verbs which exclude passives like [24iii], there are none that accept those like [24ii]: the latter is grammatically impossible because the sequence NP + *to*-infinitival does not form a constituent and thus cannot function as extraposed subject any more than it can function as an ordinary subject.

(b) Position of adjuncts

In general, adjuncts cannot occur between a verb and an NP object, but they are permitted between a verb and a clausal complement:

[27] i **We expected all along an improvement.*
ii *We expected all along that things would improve.*

In the catenative construction such an adjunct can follow the matrix verb in the construction with *for*, but not in the one without:

[28] i a. *He arranged at once for the performance to be postponed.*
b. **He expected all along the performance to be postponed.*
ii a. *I'd prefer if at all possible for you to do it tomorrow.*
b. **I'd prefer if at all possible you to do it tomorrow.*

As in the passive case, therefore, *the performance* behaves as an NP object of *expect*, rather than as part of a larger clausal complement. The contrast is particularly striking with verbs like *prefer* which occur with or without *for*: if we drop *if at all possible* from [ii] both versions are well formed.

(c) Pseudo-cleft

While a *for*-infinitival can occur as complement in pseudo-cleft and related constructions the sequence NP + infinitival VP cannot:

[29] i a. **What they expected was the performance to begin at six.*
b. *What they arranged was for the performance to begin at six.*
ii a. **All I want is you to be happy.*
b. *All I want is for you to be happy.*

Note again the particularly clear contrast with verbs like *want* in [ii] that occur in catenative constructions with and without *for*.[6]

(d) With some verbs the intervening NP is obligatory

There is a class of verbs including *believe*, *assume*, etc., where the intervening NP cannot be omitted even when it is coreferential with the subject of the matrix clause:

[30] i *Max believed Kim/himself to be in the right.*
ii **Max believed to be in the right.*

[6] In the catenative construction *want* takes *for* only when the catenative complement is preceded by an adjunct, as in [26i], but this is sufficient to sanction the *for*-infinitival in [29iib].

This indicates that there is a direct syntactic relation between the matrix verb and the NP: the NP is an obligatory complement of the verb. Note by contrast that in the *for* construction, where the NP is not a complement of the matrix verb, it can normally be readily omitted (along with *for*):[7]

[31] i *Max arranged for Kim to see a solicitor.*
ii *Max arranged to see a solicitor.*

(e) The intervening NP may belong semantically in the matrix clause

With some verbs appearing in the plain-complex structure the NP is semantically related to the matrix verb:

[32] *They persuaded the students to cancel the performance.*

Here there is no reason at all to suggest that *the students to cancel the performance* is a single complement, for the meaning is that persuasion was applied to the students in order that they should agree to cancel the performance. The only plausible structure is one with the NP and the infinitival as separate complements, and this structure is then available to accommodate examples like [23ii] above. We will examine the semantic difference in detail in §3.1.1, but what is relevant at this point is that [32] is like [23ii] with respect to all the properties discussed in (a)–(c) above:

[33] i a. *The students were persuaded to cancel the performance.* } [passivisation]
b. **It was persuaded the students to cancel the performance.* }
ii **They persuaded easily the students to cancel the performance.* [adjunct]
iii **What they persuaded was the students to cancel the performance.* [pseudo-cleft]

In passivisation the intervening NP is promoted to subject, adjuncts cannot come between the verb and the intervening NP, and the intervening NP + infinitival VP cannot form the complement of a pseudo-cleft.

The conclusion must be that there is no construction where the sequence NP + *to*-infinitival, with no preceding *for*, behaves as a subordinate clause, a single constituent.

1.4 The structure of infinitivals

Two special features of the *to*-infinitival construction are, firstly, the *for* that introduces the clause if it contains a subject and, secondly, the *to* itself that marks the VP. We consider them here in turn, and then take up briefly the bare infinitival construction.

1.4.1 The clause subordinator *for*

Historically, the *for* which introduces *to*-infinitivals containing a subject derives from the preposition *for*. This prepositional source is reflected in a number of current properties, but there are nevertheless good reasons for saying that it has come to be reanalysed as a subordinator.

[7] An exception is *call*: *He called for her to be released*, but not **He called to be released.* Note, however, that a reflexive is also normally excluded: **He called for himself to be released.*

Syntactic reflection of the prepositional source of *for*

(a) Case

Accusative rather than nominative forms of personal pronouns are used for the subject:

[34] *He arranged for her/*she to be interviewed first.*

(b) Subject must immediately follow *for*

No clause element can come between *for* and the subject NP:

[35] i *It's important for you to read the first one immediately.*
ii **It's important for the first one you to read immediately.*

Note the contrast here between *for* and the finite subordinator *that*: *It's important that the first one you read immediately.*

(c) Distribution

There is a very large overlap between the positions where we find *for* clauses and those where *for* PPs appear:

[36]		a.	b.
	i	a. *the need for peace*	b. *the need for us to cooperate*
	ii	a. *too cold for a swim*	b. *too cold for us to go out*
	iii	a. *ready for departure*	b. *ready for us to start*
	iv	a. *We arranged for a postponement.*	b. *We arranged for it to be postponed.*

Similarly, a *for* clause is like a *for* PP in that it can't generally occur as complement of a preposition:

[37] a. **I'm thinking of for a holiday.* b. **I'm thinking of for us to leave.*

Reanalysis of *for* as subordinator

The item *for* that appears with *to*-infinitivals differs in important ways from the one that takes NP complements. Although traditional grammars and dictionaries classify it as a preposition, there are strong grounds for analysing it as a subordinator, with the following NP functioning as subject of the infinitival VP. The subordinator *for* does for infinitival clauses with subjects what the subordinator *that* does for finite content clauses.

(a) Occurrence of *to*-infinitivals in non-PP positions

In spite of the similarities illustrated in [36], *for* clauses commonly appear in places that do not allow *for* PPs:

[38] i *For you to give up now would be tragic.* [subject]
ii *It's rare for the bus to be so late.* [extraposed subject]
iii *This made it necessary for the meeting to be postponed.* [extraposed object]
iv *I can't afford for them to see me like this.* [complement of *afford*]

Most importantly, they occur as subject or as extraposed subject/object, as in [i–iii]: PPs do not appear in extraposed position and appear as subject only under highly restrictive conditions. In addition, [iv] shows that the class of verbs taking *for* clause complements is not limited to those allowing *for* PPs: while [iv] is grammatical, **I can't afford for an investigation* is not (cf. also *agree* and *say*).

(b) Range of subject NPs

Except for the matter of accusative case, the NPs following *for* are the same as those which occur as subject of finite main clauses. Note in particular that dummy *there* occurs freely here though it can't occur as complement in a *for* PP, and the same applies to numerous NPs that form parts of idioms:

[39] i *It's essential for there to be no misunderstanding on this point.*
ii *He called for close tabs to be kept on the new recruits.*

(c) Constituent structure

It is clear that *for* + NP + VP forms a constituent – the subject of [38i], for example, is uncontroversially *for you to give up now*, and similarly for the other examples cited.[8] Within this sequence there is no reason to say that the NP combines directly with *for*; rather the NP and VP combine to form a clause nucleus showing the same range of contrasts as a main clause – or as a clause nucleus following the subordinator *that*:

[40] i *It's necessary* [*for both your parents to sign the form*].
ii *It's necessary* [*for the form to be signed by both your parents*].
iii *It's necessary* [*for your parents both to sign the form*].

The underlined clauses in [i] and [ii] contrast as active vs passive, while that in [iii] contrasts with [i] with respect to the position of *both*: the NP following *for* behaves like an ordinary clause subject.

(d) Absolute initial position and contrast with *that*

For must occupy initial position in the subordinate clause. We have noted that it can't occur in the interrogative and *wh* relative constructions [22]: this is because the initial position is there pre-empted by the interrogative subordinator *whether* and the interrogative and relative phrases. Its syntactic role is therefore closely parallel to that of the finite clause subordinator *that*, which is likewise excluded from interrogative and *wh* relative constructions. Like *that*, *for* has no identifiable meaning of its own, but serves as a syntactic marker of a particular syntactic construction. The functional similarity to *that* is particularly clear in such pairs as the following, where we find a direct contrast between finite and infinitival clauses:

[41] i a. *It is important that detailed records be kept.*
b. *It is important for detailed records to be kept.*
ii a. *That's the best course that you can take.*
b. *That's the best course for you to take.*
iii a. *In order that the bill may be passed major amendments were made.*
b. *In order for the bill to be passed major amendments were made.*

1.4.2 The infinitival subordinator *to*

Constituent structure

It is important that *to* enters into construction with a VP, not just a verb. This is shown by such data as:

[42] i *She wants me to lend him the money, so lend him the money I have to.*
ii *She wants me to lend him the money, but I don't have to* __.
iii *I have to lend him the money and find a solicitor for him.*

[8] Examples like *It would be good for us to have a period on our own* are ambiguous according as *for us* is a PP dependent of *good* (cf. *To have a period on our own would be good for us*) or part of the *to*-infinitival (cf. *For us to have a period on our own would be good*).

Lend him the money acts as a constituent in [i]. It is separated from *to* and occupies prenuclear position. In [ii] *lend him the money* as a whole is ellipted. And in [iii] it is coordinated with another constituent of the same category, *find a solicitor for him.*[9]

Traditional grammar treats *to lend* as a form of the lexeme ***lend***, as if *to* were an inflectional prefix, comparable to the inflectional suffix that marks the infinitive in such languages as Latin and French. This is quite inappropriate for English. The evidence from [42] shows that *to* is not syntactically in construction with the verb base, let alone morphologically bound to it.

Syntactic reflection of the prepositional source of *to*

Like *for*, *to* derives historically from the homophonous preposition. This source is again reflected in the present properties of the construction – though to a much lesser extent than in the case of *for*.

(a) Distributional restrictions

To-infinitivals, like PPs consisting of *to* + NP, do not in general occur as complement to a preposition:

[43] a. * *We're thinking of <u>to London</u>.* b. **We're thinking of <u>to travel by bus</u>.*

This is an extension of the point made above in connection with *for*: the restriction applies to *to*-infinitivals whether or not they contain *for*.

(b) Contrast with prepositions *from* and *against*

The prepositional history of *to* is reflected in the contrast we find between *to*-infinitival and *from* + gerund-participial complements with certain pairs of verbs of opposite meaning such as *encourage* vs *discourage*, *persuade* vs *dissuade*. Compare:

[44]	i	a. *I persuaded her <u>to</u> buy it.*	b. *I dissuaded her <u>from</u> buying it.*
	ii	a. *I assented <u>to</u> her proposal.*	b. *I dissented <u>from</u> her proposal.*

The non-finite complement is comparable to a goal in [ia] (metaphorically, persuasion moves someone towards an action, and assent to a proposal is likewise seen as movement towards it) and source in [ib] (dissuasion and dissent involve pulling back or moving away).

We find a somewhat similar contrast between a *to*-infinitival and *against* + gerund-participial with verbs like *warn*, though this time *to* is not used with NP complements:

[45] a. *I warned her <u>to</u> stay indoors.* b. *I warned her <u>against</u> staying indoors.*

Here [b] is equivalent to *I warned her not to stay indoors*, as [44ib] is equivalent to *I persuaded her not to buy it.*

However, points (a) and (b) are not nearly sufficient to justify treating infinitival *to* as a preposition in Present-day English. It cannot coordinate with any preposition (**I don't want you warning her to or against*); its complement cannot coordinate with

[9]The validity of coordination data as evidence for constituent structure is discussed in some detail in Ch. 15, §4.6. There are some types of 'non-basic' coordination where the coordinates are not constituents in corresponding non-coordinate constructions: in *the American proposal*, for example, *the American* is not a constituent but it occurs as a coordinate in *the American and the Russian proposals.* The fact then that we can say *I have <u>to chlorinate</u> and <u>to vacuum</u> the pool* does not demonstrate that *to chlorinate* is a constituent in *I have to chlorinate the pool*: it too involves non-basic coordination, in contrast to the basic, and much more likely, *I have to vacuum and chlorinate the pool.*

the complement of prepositional *to* (although *I agreed* [*to it*] and *I agreed* [*to go*] are both grammatical, **I agreed* [*to it and go*] is not); and the phrases it introduces cannot be systematically substituted for PPs or vice versa. It is quite clear that the distribution of *to*-infinitivals has to be described independently of that of PPs.

Reanalysis of *to* as a VP subordinator

To introduces phrases that function as predicate in clause structure, and all the evidence is compatible with these phrases being of the same category as phrases functioning as predicate in canonical clauses. That is, *to lend him the money* can be assumed to be a VP. And as already noted, *to* combines with a VP to make this larger VP. We can therefore assume the partial structure in [46].

[46]

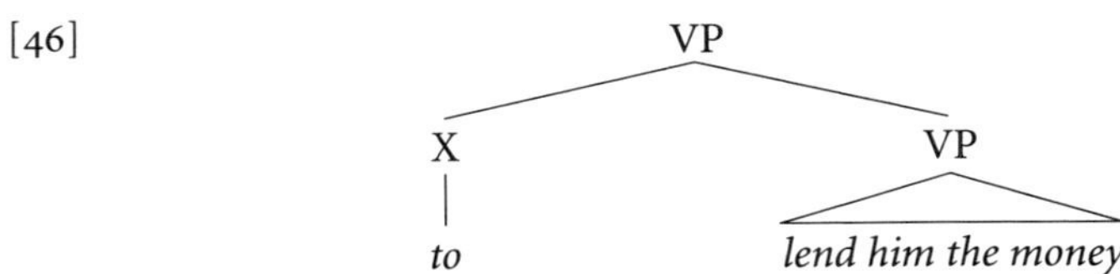

To fill out the details we must decide which constituent (*to* or *lend him the money*) is the head of the upper VP. If the constituent labelled X is the head, then it follows from general principles that it belongs to the verb category, and we would have the structure in [47a] below. The alternative is that *lend him the money* is the head. In that case *to* will have a function in the VP comparable to that of *that, whether,* and *for* in the structure of the clause, namely as a marker of the subordination, and we will have the structure in [47b].

[47] a. b.

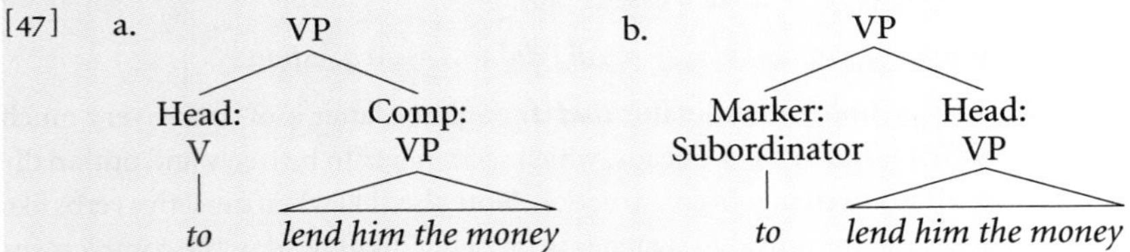

It is difficult to find compelling evidence to choose between these alternative analyses. It would not be impossible to maintain [a], if *to* were assumed to be an auxiliary verb, albeit a rather problematic defective one with no forms other than the plain form. Some linguists have defended that view. But the case for *to* being a VP subordinator is stronger. *To* has no meaning independently of the semantic properties of the infinitival complement construction as a whole. It functions with respect to the VP *lend him the money* in much the same way as *whether* functions in *whether she ever lent him the money*, or *that* in *that she lent him the money*. It would seem both syntactically and semantically appropriate to place *to* in the same category as *whether* and *that*, the category of subordinators.

It must be acknowledged that it differs from the clause subordinators in two significant respects, but those differences are not sufficient to motivate choosing structure [a].

The first difference is that in elliptical constructions, *to* can stand alone without the lower VP – i.e. it can be 'stranded', as in [42ii] (*I don't have to* __). Indeed, in this respect it is like the auxiliary verbs, for these can be stranded too (cf. *but I won't* __). The similarity is strengthened when we note the strong tendency not to stress secondary forms of auxiliaries stranded by ellipsis: *He* MAY *have* __ is preferred over ?*He may* HAVE __; *They* COULD *be* __ is preferred over

?*They could* BE __; and parallelling these, *You* HAVE *to* __ is strongly preferred over ?*You have* TO __. In this respect, *to* and the secondary forms of auxiliaries appear to function alike.

In response to this argument, however, note that there are special conditions on the stranding of *to* that do not apply to clear cases of auxiliaries (see Ch. 17, §7.3, on contrasts like *Not to would be a mistake* vs **To would be a mistake*). Some special mention of *to* is necessary either way: either it is the only subordinator that can be stranded under ellipsis of the constituent it introduces, or it is the only auxiliary verb subject to these special conditions on stranding. And the stress facts are expressible in a different way: we can say that it is strongly preferred for a stranded item that is stressed to bear tense.

The second acknowledged difference between *to* and clause subordinators is that *to* does not always occupy absolute initial position in the constituent it marks:

[48] i *She taught her children always to tell the truth.*
ii *I'll try not to underestimate the opposition next time.*

Always and *not* here belong in the subordinate clause, not the matrix, but they precede the subordinator *to*. With clause subordinators this is not the case (*He thought always that there would be some way to work it out* has *always* unambiguously interpreted in the matrix clause, and *He thought that always there would be some way to work it out* has it unambiguously in the subordinate clause – but see [13] in Ch. 11, §3). It is of course unlike the other subordinators anyway, in that it is a marker of VPs rather than clauses, so what we have to say is that the VP subordinator allows for various adjuncts in its VP to precede it.

Again, this does make *to* an unusual subordinator. But there are two further arguments that militate against its being treated as an auxiliary verb, one that suggests it is unlike heads in general, and one that weighs specifically against its being a verb. The argument that it is not a head is that under certain conditions it is omissible without any change in meaning or grammatical construction type. One such case is [49].

[49] a. *All I did was to ask a question.* b. *All I did was ask a question.*

In this respect *to* is like the finite subordinator *that* (though the latter is of course very much more freely omissible). It is not at all like heads, which seem never to be freely and optionally omissible in this way without a change of construction. Note also that when causative verbs like ***make*** and ***let*** are passivised, infinitival *to* switches from being disallowed in the complement to being required:

[50] i *They made the general public pay for it* / **to pay for it*.
ii *The general public was made* **pay for it* / *to pay for it*.

For a verb to select a different subordinator for its complement depending on whether it is active or passive seems less strange than for the head verb of the complement to be required to change.

Finally, the general argument against *to* being a verb is that there are no counterexamples in English to this very broad generalisation: **all verbs can occur as head of a main clause**. Even the highly anomalous verb *beware*, which has no inflected forms at all, occurs in main clauses like *Beware the jabberwock.* If admitted as a meaningless and defective auxiliary verb, the item *to* would be the unique exception to a principle that holds for all of English and, as far as we know, for all languages, because it can only appear in non-elliptical sentences when some other verb is superordinate to it. Being limited to subordinate clauses is precisely the property that we do expect in subordinators, and is a property that we expect never to find in verbs.

We conclude that *to* is a VP subordinator. Our analysis for a *to*-infinitival clause containing a subject can now be displayed in more detail:

[51]

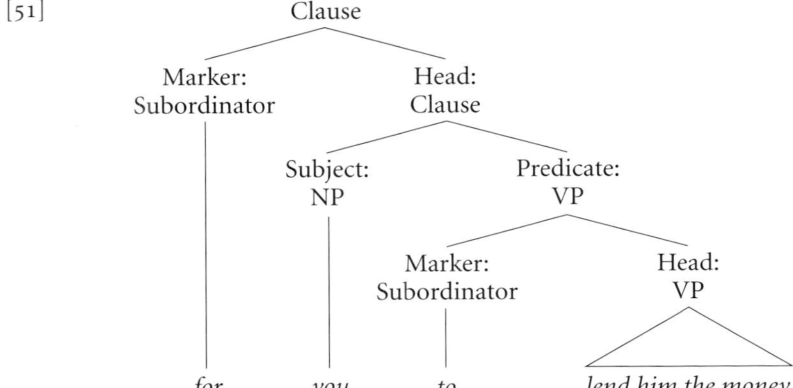

1.4.3 Bare infinitivals

These lack both the VP subordinator *to* and the clause subordinator *for*. They are almost always subjectless, in which case they consist simply of a VP headed by a verb in the plain form. There are two constructions, however, where a subject is present:

[52] i *Kim tell a lie! Surely not.*
ii *Rather than Kim give the introductory lecture, why don't you do it yourself?*

Example [i] belongs to the main clause polar echo construction discussed in Ch. 10, §4.8.3, while subordinate construction [ii] is found only as complement to *rather than*. The first is characteristic of informal style, and a personal pronoun would therefore generally appear in accusative case (*Me tell a lie!*), though a nominative cannot be entirely excluded. In [ii] we illustrate a rather rare construction where a nominative pronoun would be very unlikely – the choice of case for the subject is easily avoided by using a subjectless construction as in *Rather than have Kim give the introductory lecture, why don't you do it yourself?*

1.5 The structure of gerund-participials

The verb in gerund-participials ends with the suffix ·*ing*, a suffix which also appears on nouns and adjectives, so that it is necessary to distinguish (by the criteria given in Ch. 3, §1.4) between a gerundial noun, a gerund-participle form of a verb, and a present-participial adjective:

[53] i *She had witnessed the breaking of the seal.* [gerundial noun]
ii a. *There's no point in breaking the seal.* } [gerund-participle form of verb]
b. *They were entertaining the troops.*
iii *an entertaining show* [present-participial adjective]

Traditional grammar, we have noted, distinguishes between *breaking* in [iia], a gerund, and *entertaining* in [iib], a present participle – but since no verb lexeme has distinct forms in these constructions there is no basis for saying that they involve different inflectional forms: our gerund-participle thus covers both gerund and present participle of traditional grammar insofar as these terms are applied to verbs rather than nouns or adjectives.

Complement and non-complement uses of gerund-participials

We also take the view that even from a purely syntactic point of view the traditional distinction between gerundial and participial uses of the verb-form ending in ·*ing* is not well motivated: see §4.3. Instead, we distinguish primarily between gerund-participials with complement function and those in non-complement function (modifiers or supplements):

[54] i a. *Telling her father was a big mistake.* } [complement]
b. *He stopped seeing her.*
ii a. *Being a foreigner himself, he understood their resentment.* } [non-complement]
b. *Anyone knowing his whereabouts should contact the police.*

In terms of the traditional analysis, the non-complement uses all involve participles, while the complement uses contain primarily gerunds but also some participles.

Nominal source of the traditional gerund

Historically, the ·*ing* suffix derives from two distinct sources, corresponding respectively to traditional grammar's present participle and gerund. The gerund suffix formed nouns from verbs – as it still does in what we are calling gerundial nouns, such as *the breaking of the seal* ([53i]). In the course of time, however, the syntactic use of this form was greatly extended, so that it came to combine not just with dependents of the kind associated with nouns, as in that example, but also with those associated with verbs, as in *breaking the seal* in [53iia]. It was this extension that led to the split between nominal and verbal 'gerunds', though the traditional definition of the gerund as a 'verbal noun' fails to recognise the reanalysis of the form as a verb in the latter type.

The nominal source of the ·*ing* verb that is found in most gerund-participial complements is reflected in certain properties that still hold in the present-day language.

(a) Distributional similarity to NP

The distribution of gerund-participial complements is much closer to that of an NP than is that of any of the other non-finite form-types, or indeed of finite subordinate declaratives. In particular, they freely occur as complement to a preposition and can follow the verb in subject–auxiliary inversion constructions. Compare the gerund-participials with the *to*-infinitivals in:

[55] i a. *It's a matter of breaking the seal.* b. **It's a matter of to break the seal.*
ii a. *Is breaking the seal wise?* b. **Is to break the seal wise?*

With regard to extraposition, gerund-participials fall somewhere between NPs and *to*-infinitivals (cf. Ch. 16, §7):

[56] i a. **It was silly the breaking of the seal.* b. **It amused him the breaking of the seal.*
ii a. *It was silly breaking the seal.* b. #*It amused him breaking the seal.*
iii a. *It was silly to break the seal.* b. *It amused him to break the seal.*

Extraposition is normal with *to*-infinitivals, as in [iii], but not generally possible with NPs, as illustrated in [i]; with gerund-participials speaker judgements vary, but in general it tends to be possible over a short VP like the intransitive *was silly* but not over longer ones like transitive *amused him.*

(b) Hybrid constructions

Examples occasionally arise where the dependents are of mixed types:

[57] i a. *This constant telling tales has got to stop.*
b. *Let's have no more of this bringing food into the computer room.*
ii a. *There was no telling what he might do next.*
b. *There'll be no stopping her.*

The relevant heads are double-underlined. The pre-head dependents are characteristic of NP structure, the post-head ones characteristic of VP structure (except that *into the computer room* occurs readily in either).

The examples in [57i] are of somewhat marginal acceptability. Those in [ii] are fully acceptable in the present-day language, but this use of *no* with a gerund-participial is virtually restricted to the existential construction with *there*; we don't get, for example, **No telling what he might do next was possible.*

The examples in [57] illustrate the kind of hybrid construction that can arise when a historical change has not been fully carried through to completion. Such examples resist elegant description.

(c) Genitive case

The NP preceding the ·*ing* word can be in genitive case in the verbal construction just as in the nominal one:

[58] i *I resented [his constant questioning of my motives].* [noun]
ii *I resented [his constantly questioning my motives].* [verb]

That *questioning* is a noun in [i] and a verb in [ii] is evident from the contrast between *constant* (adjective) and *constantly* (adverb), and between *of my motives* (PP) and *my motives* (NP – object), but in both we have genitive *his.* And the characteristic use of genitive case is of course to mark the dependent of a noun, not of a verb.

Analysis of the genitive NP as subject of the gerund-participial

It might be argued that *his constantly questioning my motives* in [58ii] should be described in terms of some kind of nominal–verbal hybrid construction such as we evidently need for [57], but we believe it is better, for several reasons, to regard the genitive as having been reanalysed as a clause subject.

(a) Marginal status of the determiner + VP construction

The examples like [57] certainly involve a determiner in construction with a VP as head, but they are very peripheral to the present language-system by virtue of the questionable acceptability of [i] and the semi-formulaic nature of [ii]: this construction should not be allowed to determine our analysis of the much more central and productive construction with a genitive.

(b) Relation with accusative/plain case

The genitive can be replaced in informal style by an accusative (or plain) case: [*I resented*] *him constantly questioning my motives* (see §1.6 below). In this non-genitive construction the historical process of changing from noun to verb has been taken a step further: there is nothing noun-like about the structure here, and its analysis as a clause is unproblematic. It is then simpler to treat the stylistic alternation between genitive and non-genitive as a matter of the case of the subject NP than as a major difference between two quite separate constructions: the preference for the non-genitive in informal style can be seen as regularising the clausal construction.

(c) Optionality of the genitive NP

The genitive NP can normally be omitted:

[59] i a. *I regretted [his leaving the firm].* b. *[Your being a shareholder] is important.*
ii a. *I regretted [leaving the firm].* b. *[Being a shareholder] is important.*

The significant point here is that the presence or absence of the genitive NP is not like that of a genitive determiner in NP structure. In *I regretted his decision*, for example, we cannot drop *his*: **I regretted decision*. This is ungrammatical because *decision* is a singular count noun and requires the presence of some determiner. In the gerund-participial construction, however, the presence or absence of the genitive is like the presence or absence of the subject in a *to*-infinitival:

[60] i a. *I arranged [for him to leave the firm].* b. *[For you to be a shareholder] is essential.*
ii a. *I arranged [to leave the firm].* b. *[To be a shareholder] is essential.*

We interpret [59iia] as "I regret my leaving the firm" and [60iia] is interpreted as "I arranged for me to leave the firm"; and similarly [59iib] and [60iib] may be glossed roughly as "One's being a shareholder is important", "For one to be a shareholder is essential". Moreover, we have noted that the genitive can be replaced by a non-genitive: if *I regretted [his leaving the firm]* and *I regretted [him leaving the firm]* are analysed as quite different constructions, with only the second of them a clause, then which of the constructions would *I regretted [leaving the firm]* belong to? This problem would be particularly difficult to resolve with those gerund-participials where it is not possible to include an NP before the verb, as in *He didn't bother [giving me a copy]*. We avoid these problems by treating the optionality of the initial NP as simply a matter of the optionality of subjects in non-finite clauses.

The structure of the gerund-participial in [58ii] will therefore be as follows:

[61]

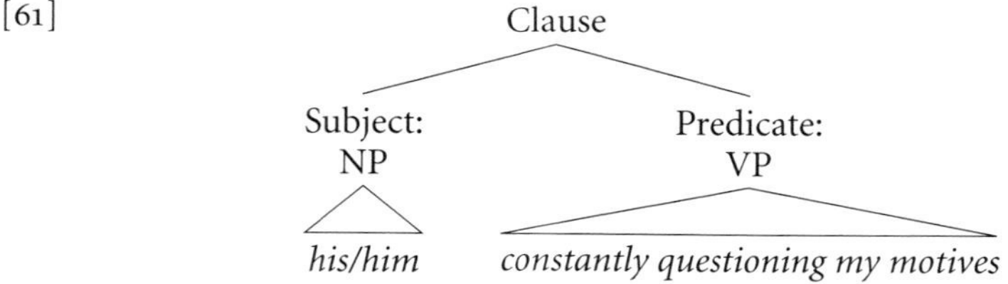

Subject must be in absolute initial position

Whether genitive or not, the subject always occupies initial position in a gerund-participial clause. It is therefore not possible to prepose elements or to postpose the subject:

[62] i *I resented [them/their going without me].*
ii **I resented [without me them/their going].*
iii *I remember [a troop of boy scouts suddenly appearing over the hill].*
iv **I remember [suddenly appearing over the hill a troop of boy scouts].*

Comparison between genitive marking and the subordinator *for*

Genitive marking in gerund-participials bears some resemblance to the marking of *to*-infinitivals by the subordinator *for*.[10] *For* marks the clause boundary, so that the following NP must belong in the subordinate clause; the genitive case relates the NP to the following VP and hence as again belonging in the subordinate clause. In *to*-infinitivals the subject must immediately follow *for* and in gerund-participials the subject must be the first element: neither construction allows for elements to be fronted to pre-subject position or for the subject to be postposed.

Nevertheless, the analogy is not a close one, for there are several important differences.

(a) Status and position

For is a separate word belonging to the category of subordinators; it occupies initial position in what we are calling the marker function. The genitive, by contrast, is an inflectional case. Compare, then, structure [61] with [51] above.

(b) Restrictions on NP

Genitive case is incompatible with certain types of NP: for example, we can't say **I resented this's being made public* – only non-genitive *this* is possible. No such restrictions apply to *for*.

(c) Omissibility

For cannot in general be omitted unless the following subject is omitted too, and in those constructions where it is omissible – after such catenatives as *intend*, *prefer*, etc. – its presence or absence correlates with a major difference in structure, the NP belonging in the subordinate clause when *for* is present but in the matrix clause when it is absent (cf. §1.4). The genitive inflection, by contrast, is systematically omissible (subject to considerations of style), and there is no reason to suppose that its omission has any further effect on the structure. Most importantly, genitive case is not necessary in gerund-participials for the sequence of NP + VP to form a constituent. This is evident from such examples as [63], where the status of the bracketed sequences as constituents is unproblematic in both genitive and non-genitive versions:

[63]	i	*I have no objection to [<u>their</u>/<u>them</u> taking notes].*	[comp of preposition]
	ii	*What he doesn't like is [<u>Kim</u>/<u>Kim's</u> taking all the credit].*	[predicative comp]
	iii	*[<u>His son's</u> / <u>His son</u> being a friend of the judge] hadn't helped at all.*	[subject]

1.6 Case of the subject NP in gerund-participials

Nominative or plain case in non-complement gerund-participials

Gerund-participials functioning as supplement to a clause may contain a subject; pronouns with a nominative–accusative contrast usually appear in the nominative, with accusative a somewhat marginal alternant in informal style, while other NPs take plain case:

[64]	i	*They appointed Max, [<u>he</u>/<u>him</u> being the only one who spoke Greek].*
	ii	*[<u>His mother</u> being ill,] Max had to withdraw from the expedition.*

This construction is the only one where we find a nominative subject in a non-finite clause; it belongs to fairly formal style, and hence the informal accusative form in [i] is

[10] Modern works that adopt a parallel treatment usually represent the elements as '*for–to*' and 'POSS–*ing*'.

unlikely: the alternation here is not like that between *It's I/me*, where the accusative is much more common.

Genitive vs non-genitive subjects in gerund-participial complements

When the clause is functioning as complement, we find both genitive and accusative/plain case, and our main concern in this section is to investigate the factors favouring one or other of them. A preliminary point to emphasise is that potential alternation between these cases arises only when the NP is subject of a gerund-participial clause – compare:

[65] i [*I enjoyed*] *his/*him reading of the poem.* [determiner in NP: genitive required]
ii [*I caught*] *him/*his reading my mail.* [object of matrix: genitive excluded]
iii [*I remember*] *his/him reading my mail.* [subject: genitive or accusative allowed]

In [i] *reading* is a noun: the preceding NP is therefore determiner and has to be in the genitive. Note then that while *Kim didn't like his singing* is ambiguous according as *singing* is a noun or a verb, *Kim didn't like him singing* is unambiguous, with *singing* necessarily a verb.[11] In [65ii] *him* is the object of *caught*, with *reading my mail* a second complement: *him* is not subject of the gerund-participial clause and therefore cannot be genitive. Only in [iii], where the pronoun is subject of the subordinate clause, do we have alternation between the cases. (For the structural distinction between [ii] and [iii], see §3.2.1.)

In constructions of this third kind, where the NP is subject of a gerund-participial complement,[12] the choice between genitive and accusative/plain depends on the following factors:

(a) Style

Genitives are more likely to occur in formal than in informal style.[13]

(b) Type of NP

Some NPs cannot take genitive marking, however formal the style: dummy pronouns (particularly *there*); fused-head NPs like *this, that, all, some*; pronoun-final partitive NPs like *both of them, some of us*; and so on. Such NPs cannot occur as determiner in NP structure but readily appear in non-genitive form as subject of a gerund-participial:

[66] i *He resented* [*there/*there's having been so much publicity*].
ii *I won't accept* [*this/*this's being made public*].

There are others which, while they do not exclude genitive marking in general, disfavour it in the subject of a gerund-participial:

[67] i *He objected to* [*the girls / ?the girls' being given preferential treatment*].
ii *It involved* [*the Minister of Transport / ?the Minister of Transport's losing face*].

[11] In the noun interpretation we are concerned with the **manner** of his singing (cf. *Kim didn't like his singing of this difficult aria*), whereas in the verbal interpretation it is a matter of the **activity** or **fact** of his singing (cf. *Kim didn't like him singing obscene songs*).

[12] We should also add the condition that the subject immediately precede the verb. If it is followed by a supplement, a non-genitive subject is required: *He resented Kim, after only two years, being promoted manager.* And the same applies if the verb is omitted in the gapping construction: *He objected to Kim having three tries and Pat __ only two.* Contrastive stress on the subject also strongly favours a non-genitive: *I've no objection to* KIM *doing it.*

[13] Modern usage manuals generally do not condemn non-genitives altogether (as Fowler did in early work), though they vary in their tolerance of them, the more conservative ones advocating a genitive except where it sounds awkward, stilted, or pedantic – by virtue of the type of NP involved (our factor (b)).

The regular plural *girls* in [i] is identical to its corresponding genitive in speech, but in writing they are distinguished by the apostrophe, and in this construction the form without the apostrophe is much the more likely. In [ii] the NP contains a post-head dependent PP *of Transport*, and while such NPs can take genitive marking when determiner to a noun (*the Minister of Transport's performance*), such marking is very unlikely in a gerund-participial.

More generally, the genitive in a gerund-participial is awkward with NPs of any significant length or complexity, especially those with post-head dependents. It is most likely with personal pronouns, and after that singular NPs that refer to people and have no more than one or two words as pre-head dependents.

(c) Matrix construction

A gerund-participial in subject function is somewhat more likely to select a genitive than one in other complement functions. There are also differences within the class of catenative verbs: verbs like *appreciate*, *countenance*, *mind*, etc. (class 2Ci of §5.3) take a genitive more readily than *like* and *hate* (class 2Bi), while with *stop* a genitive is not likely to occur at all (we find *She stopped them using it*, not **She stopped their using it*).

1.7 Understood subjects

Most non-finite clauses have no subject, but the interpretation requires that we find an 'understood subject': characteristically, the VP represents a semantic predicate and we need to find the argument that it is predicated of.

We distinguish three main ways in which the interpretation of a subjectless clause is completed:

[68]	i	*Pat persuaded <u>Kim</u> [to travel by bus].*	[controlled interpretation]
	ii	*Pat intended <u>Kim</u> [to travel by bus].*	[raised interpretation]
	iii	*It was necessary [to travel by bus].*	[non-syntactic interpretation]

In [i] and [ii] we understand it to be Kim who was to travel by bus, but there is a difference between them. In [i] *Kim* is associated with two semantic roles, patient of *persuade* (Pat applied pressure to Kim) and agent of *travel*, but in [ii] *Kim* has only the latter role: *intend* expresses a relation between Pat and the situation where Kim travels by bus. Nevertheless, *Kim* is syntactic object of the matrix clause in both.

These two cases involve **controlled** and **raised** interpretations of the missing subject. In [68i] the interpretation of the missing subject is controlled by an antecedent in the matrix clause – in this example by the matrix object, in *Kim wanted to travel by bus* by the matrix subject. In [ii] the missing subject is retrievable from the raised complement in the matrix clause. But [iii] is sharply different in that there is nothing in the sentence itself to identify the traveller: the understood subject here has to be identified from the context. It could be the speaker, someone else, or a group including or excluding the speaker. We say here that the interpretation is determined **non-syntactically**, i.e. the missing subject is not linked to an antecedent in some syntactically specified position.

The distinction between constructions with controlled and raised interpretations is discussed in detail in §§2–3, and we return at the end of the chapter to that between controlled and non-syntactic interpretations.

2 The simple catenative construction

Our primary concern in this section will be with the semantic status of the subject: in some cases it represents an argument of the catenative verb, whereas in others it does not, having a semantic role only with respect to the non-finite, so that it has the status of a raised complement. We will examine this distinction first in *to*-infinitivals and then in gerund-participials.

2.1 *To*-infinitivals (*I hoped to convince them* vs *I seemed to convince them*)

The semantic difference between the two kinds of subject can be illustrated with the verbs *hope* and *seem*:

[1] i *Liz hoped to convince them.* [ordinary subject]
ii *Liz seemed to convince them.* [raised subject]

In [i] *Liz* is an ordinary subject in that it is an argument of the verb: *hope* denotes a psychological attitude on the part of someone to some situation (here Liz's attitude to the later, potential, situation where she convinces them). But in [ii] *Liz* is not an argument of *seem*. The meaning is something like "Seemingly, Liz convinced them"; *seem* has a modal meaning, serving to make [ii] weaker than the unmodalised *Liz convinced them*. Syntactically *Liz* is subject of *seem*, but semantically it relates only to the subordinate *convince* clause, not to *seem*. *Liz* in [ii] is then a raised subject: the verb that *Liz* relates to syntactically is higher in the constituent structure than the one it relates to semantically.

In [1i], *Liz* has two semantic roles, as experiencer of *hope* and as agent of *convince*; but in [ii], *Liz* has only one semantic role, as agent of *convince*. The difference is like that between [68i] and [68ii] of §1.7 (*Pat persuaded Kim to travel by bus* and *Pat intended Kim to travel by bus*), and we will again say that the missing subject of the non-finite clause has a controlled interpretation in [1i] and a raised interpretation in [1ii]. Verbs like *seem* which take a raised complement are called **raising verbs.**

Evidence for the distinction between an ordinary subject and a raised subject

(a) Relation with finite complement construction

With verbs which take either infinitival or finite complements the semantic relations are more transparent in the construction with a finite complement. Compare:

[2] i *Liz$_i$ hoped that she$_i$ would convince them.* [two arguments]
ii *It seemed that Liz convinced them.* [one argument]

In [i] *hope* clearly has two arguments, represented by the subject and the content clause. The identical indices on *Liz* and *she* indicate that we are concerned with [i] in the interpretation where *she* has *Liz* as its antecedent: the double reference to Liz thus makes transparent that *Liz* has two semantic roles, as experiencer of *hope* and agent of *convince*. In [ii], by contrast, there is only one reference to Liz, in the subordinate clause: again, then, the construction shows transparently that *Liz* has just one semantic role, agent of *convince*. There is no syntactic relation between *Liz* and *seem*, and this reflects the absence of any semantic relation between them. The subject *it* is a dummy element: it satisfies the syntactic requirement for a subject but is not an argument of the verb. Thus while *hope* has two semantic arguments, *seem* has only one. The semantic difference is the same as in [1], but this time it is reflected syntactically because raised subjects are found only with non-finite complements.

(b) Relation with passive infinitivals

Compare now the following superficially similar pairs:

[3]	i	a. *Liz hoped to convince them.* b. *They hoped to be convinced by Liz.*	[voice-sensitive: a ≠ b]
	ii	a. *Liz seemed to convince them.* b. *They seemed to be convinced by Liz.*	[voice-neutral: a = b]

Such pairs bring out very clearly the difference between *hope* and *seem*, for with *hope* [a] and [b] differ sharply in meaning, whereas with *seem* they are equivalent. In [i] the content of the hope remains constant (namely, that Liz convince them or, equivalently, that they be convinced by Liz), but the experiencer is different: *Liz* in [ia], *they* in [ib]. The subject of *hope* has the experiencer role, and changing the subject therefore changes the meaning. In [ii], however, the subject is not an argument of *seem* and this is why it is possible to change the subject without affecting the overall propositional meaning: the equivalence of [iia] and [iib] matches that found in the main clause pair *Liz convinced them* and *They were convinced by Liz*, or in *It seemed that Liz convinced them* and *It seemed that they were convinced by Liz*. Here, then, the subject has a semantic role relative to *convince*, but not to *seem*. We speak of *hope*-type verbs as **voice-sensitive** and of *seem*-type verbs as **voice-neutral** – sensitive or neutral, that is, to a change of voice in the sequence consisting of their subject and the non-finite VP.

(c) Selection restrictions

Hope imposes selection restrictions on its subject: it must denote some entity capable of filling the experiencer role, and hence be animate and typically human. But *seem* does not restrict its subject: any NP is permitted provided only that it satisfies any selection restrictions imposed by the subordinate clause verb. Compare, then, the anomaly of [i] with the acceptability of [ii] in:

[4]	i	#*This news hoped to convince them.*	[violation of restriction]
	ii	*This news seemed to convince them.*	[no violation]

This property of *hope* demonstrates conclusively that there is a direct semantic relation between it and its subject. And the absence of restrictions with *seem* is predicted by the raised subject analysis: if there is no direct relation between the two elements there could be no comparable restrictions.

(d) Dummy subjects – subjects with no independent meaning.

With raising verbs, the dummy subject NPs *there* and *it* are possible:

[5]	i	*There seemed/*hoped to be enough food available.*	[dummy *there*]
	ii	*It seemed/*hoped to be unwise to dissent.*	[dummy *it*]

The subjects here have no identifiable meaning of their own, so the unacceptability of the *hope* versions can be seen as following from point (c) above: such NPs could not satisfy the requirement that the subject denote an animate being capable of filling the experiencer role.

(e) Choice between simple and complex constructions.

[6]

	SIMPLE	COMPLEX
i	a. *Ed expected to die.*	b. *Ed expected Pat to die.*
ii	a. *Ed arranged to go.*	b. *Ed arranged for Pat to go.*
iii	a. *Ed tried to help us.*	b. **Ed tried (for) Pat to help us.*
iv	a. *Ed seemed to faint.*	b. **Ed seemed (for) Pat to faint.*

Verbs entering into the simple catenative construction vary according to whether they can also appear in the complex construction – either the plain subtype, as in [i], or the one with *for*, as in [ii]. All raising verbs are like *seem* in being restricted to the simple construction. This restriction follows directly from the fact that they take raised subjects. In [iva] *Ed* represents an argument of *faint* but not of *seem*: *Ed* simply refers to the one who seemingly fainted; if we then add another NP as the subject-argument of *faint* there is no semantic role left for *Ed*, so [ivb] is uninterpretable. This problem doesn't arise with the non-raising verbs, many of which allow a choice between the simple and complex constructions. In [ia] *Ed* is the experiencer of *expect* and the theme of *die*: when we add *Pat* in [ib] it takes over the latter role but leaves the former to *Ed*. Similarly in [ii]: whether or not we have the subordinator *for* before the inserted NP is irrelevant to the issue of the semantic roles. There are nevertheless some non-raising verbs, like *try* in [iii], which are incompatible with either version of [b]. In such cases there is often a semantic explanation for the restriction. Thus trying involves internal effort that is necessarily directed towards one's own actions: Ed could try to persuade Pat to help us or try to make Pat help us, but it is not possible for the trying itself to apply directly to Pat.[14]

(f) Matrix passivisation

A few non-raising catenatives allow passivisation, with the infinitival appearing as extraposed subject, but this is quite impossible with raising verbs:

[7]

i	a. *We hope to return to this issue.*	b. *It is hoped to return to this issue.*
ii	a. *We seem to be in danger.*	b. **It is seemed to be in danger.*

Hope takes two arguments, and the passive allows the active subject to be left unexpressed, with the infinitival appearing as extraposed subject; *seem* takes only one argument, so passivisation is quite impossible.

Summary of differences between *hope*-type verbs and *seem*-type verbs

The six differences between non-raising verbs like *hope* and raising verbs like *seem*, described in (a)–(f) above, are summarised in [8]:

[8]

PROPERTY	NON-RAISING VERBS	RAISING VERBS
(a) Finite complement	Two arguments (or N/A)	One argument (or N/A)
(b) Infinitival voice	Voice-sensitive[15]	Voice-neutral
(c) Restrictions on subject	Yes	No
(d) Dummy subject	No	Yes
(e) Simple/complex choice	Yes for many verbs	No
(f) Matrix passivisation	Yes for a few verbs	No

For footnotes 14–15, see next page.

'N/A' in (a) means "not applicable": this is the case when the verb doesn't allow a finite complement; (e) and (f) provide a distinguishing criterion only in the case of a 'yes' answer, which indicates a non-raising verb, 'no' being consistent with either type.

The problem of agentivity

With so many factors involved, the distinction between ordinary and raised subjects is generally clear, but it is not always so. The main problem involves agentivity, and it arises primarily with aspectual verbs like *begin*. These verbs don't take finite complements, so point (a) is not applicable. Consider, then, the following examples:

[9] i *There began to be some doubt in our minds as to whether he was trustworthy.*
ii a. *His behaviour began to alienate his colleagues.*
b. *His colleagues began to be alienated by his behaviour.*
iii a. *Jill began to unwrap the parcel.*
b. ?*The parcel began to be unwrapped by Jill.*

In [i–ii] *begin* behaves like a raising verb. We see from [i] that it allows a semantically empty subject (property (d)), and hence does not impose selection restrictions (property (c)). In [ii] we have a clear example of voice-neutrality (property (b)). But [iiib] is not an acceptable alternant to [iiia]. The difference between [ii] and [iii] is that the situation described in the infinitival is non-agentive in the former, agentive in the latter: compare the corresponding main clauses *His behaviour alienated his colleagues* and *Jill unwrapped the parcel*, where *his behaviour* has a non-agentive role, *Jill* an agentive one. And if the whole situation of Jill's unwrapping the parcel is agentive, isn't the initial phase of it, the beginning, likewise agentive? If so, *Jill* in [iiia] will be an ordinary subject, not a raised one – which will account for the apparent difference in the relation of [a] to [b] in [ii] and [iii]. This reasoning has thus led to a position where *begin* can take either an ordinary or a raised subject according to whether the subordinate situation is agentive or not.

There are good grounds, however, for rejecting this solution to the problem posed by [9iiib]. The important point to note is that while [iiib] is of low acceptability it does not describe a different situation from [iiia]: there is no difference in truth conditions such as we have in [3i] (*Liz hoped to convince them* vs *They hoped to be convinced by Liz*). Indeed, we can find examples involving *begin* with an agentive infinitival where the two members of the pair are not only equivalent but also both fully acceptable: *Max began to court Jill* and *Jill began to be courted by Max* (or compare *They began to sell the shares at a discount* and *The shares began to be sold at a discount*). Voice neutrality does not require that the two alternants be equally likely and acceptable (for this condition does not hold for many simple active–passive pairs: compare *I opened my eyes* and ?*My eyes were opened by me*), only that they be truth-conditionally equivalent. The data in [9iii] are thus quite consistent with a unitary treatment of *begin* as a raising verb in all of

[14] Our model verb *hope* takes *for* (*She was hoping for Kim to return safely*), but a finite construction (*She was hoping that Kim would return safely*) is much more likely than the complex infinitival, and hence we have used other examples in [6].

[15] Examples are occasionally attested where non-raising verbs are treated as though they were voice-neutral: *The exam papers are trying to be marked by next week* ("We are trying to mark them"). There can be no doubt, however, that they are rare and unsystematic enough for us to be able to dismiss them as mistakes.

[9i–iii], which is much preferable to putting it in both classes, with a great deal of resulting indeterminacy over the analysis of particular examples.

The issue of agentivity also arises, but with a larger set of verbs, in cases like:

[10] i *It's time you began to relax.*
ii *It's essential that you at least* APPEAR *to be enjoying yourself.*

Here *begin* and *appear* occur in subordinate clauses where the matrix confers an agentive interpretation on their subjects: it is a matter of your volitionally bringing about the situations where you begin to relax and appear to be enjoying yourself. Although agentive subjects characteristically represent arguments of their verbs, it is reasonable to maintain that they don't necessarily do so, for in cases like [10] it is not the verbs *begin* and *appear* themselves that confer agentivity on the subject, but the larger context. These examples are comparable to the passive given in note 16 of Ch. 4, *They advised the twins not to be photographed together*, where *advise* confers agentivity on the understood subject of the infinitival, although the role assigned by *photograph* itself is clearly not agent. The fact that the agentivity in [10] is not attributable to the verbs *begin* and *appear* is quite consistent with *you* being a raised subject, i.e. as representing an argument of *relax* and *enjoy* rather than *begin* and *appear*.

2.2 Gerund-participials (*We enjoyed sailing* vs *We kept sailing*)

The distinction between ordinary and raised subjects applies to gerund-participials too:

[11] i *Kim enjoyed heckling him.* [ordinary subject]
ii *Kim kept heckling him.* [raised subject]

In [i] *Kim* is an argument of *enjoy*, with the semantic role of experiencer. In [ii], however, there is no direct semantic relation between *Kim* and *keep*: [ii] simply says that the situation in which Kim heckled him recurred over and over again. The parallel with the infinitival construction is made clearer by the fact that there are both raising and non-raising catenatives that take either infinitival or gerund-participial complements, e.g. raising *begin* and *continue*, non-raising *like* and *hate*.

Three of the six distinguishing properties discussed above apply here quite straightforwardly: we therefore first review these summarily together, and then take up the other three.

Passive infinitivals, selection restrictions, dummy subjects

[12] i a. *He enjoyed being heckled by Kim.* [≠[11i]: *enjoy* is voice-sensitive]
b. *He kept being heckled by Kim.* [=[11ii]: *keep* is voice-neutral]
ii a. *#My papers enjoyed blowing away.* [violates selection restrictions on subject]
b. *My papers kept blowing away.* [no selection restrictions on subject]
iii a. **There enjoyed being problems with the radio.* [dummy subjects excluded]
b. *There kept being problems with the radio.* [dummy subjects allowed]

These show respectively that the raising catenative *keep*, like *seem* and in contrast to non-raising *enjoy* and *hope*, is neutral as to the voice of the non-finite (property (b)), imposes no selection restrictions on its subject (property (c)), and hence allows dummy subjects such as *there* (property (d)).

Relation with finite complement construction

Property (a) is less useful as a diagnostic this time because fewer verbs taking a gerund-participial also allow a finite complement. None of the raising verbs do, but some non-raising ones do and exhibit the predicted behaviour:

[13] i *I regret giving him my address.*
ii *I regret that I gave him my address.* [two arguments]

It is transparent in [ii] that *regret* has two semantic arguments, represented by the subject and the content clause. *I* here has two semantic roles, experiencer of *regret* and agent of *give*.

Choice between simple and complex constructions

With respect to property (e), the gerund-participial construction differs from the infinitival in that there are raising as well as non-raising verbs that occur either with or without an intervening NP:

[14] i a. *Ed likes reading aloud.* b. *Ed likes me reading aloud.*
ii a. *Ed kept sitting on the stool.* b. *Ed kept me sitting on the stool.*

However, the semantic relation between the two constructions is not the same in the two cases. With *like*, which takes an ordinary subject, the difference is the same as in the infinitival case: the meaning of the verb remains constant and *Ed* remains experiencer, so that the difference is simply a matter of who is doing the reading – Ed in [a], me in [b]. But in [ii] the meaning of *keep* does not remain constant: in [b] it has a causative sense ("Ed made me stay sitting on the stool") and in [a] there is an element of interruption and repetition (Ed repeatedly got on and off the stool) that is missing in [b]. Given this difference in meaning, [iib] is not inconsistent with a raising analysis of [iia]: *Ed* is an argument (agent) of *keep* in [iib] but not in [iia].

Matrix passivisation

Gerund-participials differ from infinitivals in that they do not readily allow extraposition, so we focus here on the construction without extraposition. Matrix passivisation of this kind is predictably quite impossible with raising verbs; with non-raising verbs it tends to be somewhat marginal, but acceptability can be increased by adding motivating context:[16]

[15] i **Heckling people was kept by Kim.*
ii *?Heckling people was enjoyed by Kim.*
iii *Watching TV is enjoyed by far more people than reading novels.*

2.3 Concealed passives (*The house needs painting*)

With a small number of catenative verbs, notably *need*, *require*, *deserve*, and *want*, a gerund-participial may be passive while lacking the usual marking of the passive – we

[16] A fully acceptable type of passive is illustrated in *Swimming after a heavy meal is not recommended. Recommend* is clearly a non-raising verb, but it differs from *enjoy* in that the matrix subject is not the understood subject of the gerund-participial: in *Doctors don't recommend swimming after a heavy meal* it's a matter of people in general, not doctors, swimming after a meal.

refer to this as the **concealed passive construction**. Compare:

[16] i a. *The house needs to be painted.* } [ordinary passive]
b. *These books want to be taken back to the library.*
ii a. *The house needs painting.* } [concealed passive]
b. *These books want taking back to the library.*

The catenative complements in [i] are overtly marked as passives by the auxiliary *be* and the past participle forms *painted* and *taken*, while those in [ii] lack such marking although they are interpreted in the same way.[17]

In the absence of distinctive kinds of dependent there will often be syntactic ambiguity between a concealed passive gerund-participial and a gerundial noun, but commonly with negligible difference in meaning:

[17] i *The children need coaxing.*
ii *It's an attractive feature of avocados that they do not require processing.*

In [i] *coaxing* can be a verb, "to be coaxed", or a noun, as in *They need a little coaxing*, but we understand that the coaxing should apply to the children, so the meaning is effectively the same as with the verbal reading. Likewise in [ii]: *processing* can be a verb, "to be processed", or a noun, as in *processing of any kind*, and in either case it is a matter of processing the avocados. Similar examples can be formed with *training*, *teaching*, and numerous others.

The concealed passive is to be distinguished from a hollow clause, an active with a missing non-subject element, object of the verb or of a preposition:

[18] i *The article needs checking.* [concealed passive]
ii *The article is worth reading __.* [hollow: active]

Note that the first construction is possible only where there is a corresponding ordinary passive, but this is not so with the second. Compare, then:

[19] i **The article was had a careful look at.* [ordinary passive]
ii **The article needs having a careful look at.* [concealed passive]
iii *The article is worth having a careful look at __.* [hollow: active]

The deviance of [ii] here reflects that of the main clause [i], whereas the acceptability of [iii] matches that of an active main clause like *We will have a careful look at the article.*

A second point is that the concealed passive can contain the *by* phrase that appears in ordinary passives as an internalised complement:

[20] i *The article needs checking by the editor.* [concealed passive]
ii **The article is worth reading __ by the editor.* [hollow: active]

The concealed passive is found only with gerund-participials and in the catenative construction; the hollow active is more often found with non-catenative *to*-infinitivals, as in *an easy problem to solve* (§6).

3 The complex catenative construction

In the complex construction the matrix and subordinate verbs are separated by an intervening NP which functions as complement in one or other of the clauses. As with the simple construction, we look first at *to*-infinitivals and then at gerund-participials.

[17] *Want* with the sense "need" is more characteristic of BrE/AusE than AmE, and is more likely with a concealed passive gerund-participial than with a *to*-infinitival (where there is more danger of confusion with the primary sense of "desire").

3.1 *To*-infinitivals

3.1.1 The plain-complex construction (*I persuaded Liz to go* vs *I intended Liz to go*)

In this construction the intervening NP always belongs syntactically in the matrix: it functions as matrix object, as argued in §1.3 above. Semantically, however, we find a contrast according as the object represents an argument of the matrix (an ordinary object) or only of the subordinate clause (a raised object):

[1] i *Pat persuaded Liz to interview both candidates.* [ordinary object]
ii *Pat intended Liz to interview both candidates.* [raised object]

In [i] the syntactic structure matches the semantics quite straightforwardly. *Persuade* has three complements (*Pat*, *Liz*, and the infinitival) and each represents an argument: the matrix situation involves one who applies the persuasion (Pat), one to whom it is applied (Liz), and the situation aimed for (that Liz interview both candidates). *Liz* is thus an ordinary complement, an argument of the verb which governs it. But in [ii] there is no such simple relation between syntax and semantics. In particular, *Liz* is not an argument of *intend*: the situation simply involves one who has the intention (Pat) and the content of the intention (that Liz interview both candidates). With *intend*, therefore, we have three complements but only two arguments: *Liz* is a raised object.

The distinction is parallel to that discussed in §2 for the simple catenative construction: there we were concerned with the semantic status of the subject, here with that of the object (the intervening NP). We will therefore extend the term 'raising verb' to cover *intend* as well as *seem* – where necessary we can distinguish them as 'raised object verb' and 'raised subject verb' respectively. The first five factors discussed in §2 for the contrast between ordinary and raised subjects apply again here with suitable adjustments.[18]

(a) Relation with finite complement construction

Compare [1i–ii] first with corresponding finite constructions:

[2] i *Pat persuaded Liz_i that she_i should interview both candidates.* [three arguments]
ii *Pat intended that Liz should interview both candidates.* [two arguments]

Even more clearly than with the *hope* vs *seem* contrast the switch to a finite complement brings out the semantic difference between *persuade* and *intend*. In [2] *persuade* has three syntactic complements, and three semantic arguments, while *intend* has two of each – this time there is no dummy *it* to complicate the picture. In [i] the dual semantic role of Liz, as patient of *persuade* and agent of *interview*, is now transparent, with *Liz* appearing as matrix object and co-referential *she* as subordinate subject.[19] With *intend* the fact that there is no direct semantic relation between *intend* and *Liz* is likewise transparent in the finite construction, where *Liz* is not a complement of *intend*.[20]

[18] The sixth factor, matrix passivisation, does not apply here because in the complex catenative construction it is the intervening NP, not the infinitival, that is promoted to subject, and this kind of passivisation applies with ordinary and raised objects alike (though in either case there are some verbs which block it: see §5).

[19] There is a slight difference in meaning between the infinitival and finite constructions with *persuade*. Whereas [1i] entails that Liz agreed or undertook to interview the candidates, [2i] is a little weaker: she accepted that there was an obligation on her to do so. But this doesn't affect the semantic status of *Liz*: in both cases Pat applied persuasion directly to Liz, producing a change in her psychological state.

[20] We have noted that the subordinator *for* is like *that* in marking clause boundaries very clearly, so that the *for*-complex construction provides the same kind of evidence for a raising analysis with the few verbs that enter into both plain- and *for*-complex constructions. Compare, then, *I'd prefer Liz to do it herself* and *I'd prefer*

(b) Relation with passive infinitivals

Compare next the following superficially similar pairs:

[3]	i a.	*Pat persuaded Liz to interview both candidates.*	[voice-sensitive
	b.	*Pat persuaded both candidates to be interviewed by Liz.*	a≠ b]
	ii a.	*Pat intended Liz to interview both candidates.*	[voice-neutral
	b.	*Pat intended both candidates to be interviewed by Liz.*	a = b]

In [i] there is an obvious difference in meaning: in [ia] Pat applied persuasion to Liz, but in [ib] to the candidates. This shows that the object is an argument of *persuade*. In [ii], by contrast, [a] and [b] are equivalent, just as they are in the main clause pair *Liz interviewed both candidates* and *Both candidates were interviewed by Liz.* The fact that we can change the object in this way without affecting the propositional meaning shows that there can't be any direct semantic relation between it and the matrix verb.

(c) Selection restrictions

Persuade imposes selection restrictions on its object: except when used in an extended, metaphorical sense it requires that its object denote a sentient being capable of making decisions. But *intend* does not restrict its object: any NP is permitted that is compatible with the infinitival. Compare the anomaly of [i] with the acceptability of [ii] in:

[4]	i	#*Liz persuaded the spotlight to intimidate Pat.*	[violation of restriction]
	ii	*Liz intended the spotlight to intimidate Pat.*	[no violation]

(d) Dummy objects – objects with no independent meaning

Dummy objects are found with *intend*, but not *persuade*, and again the unacceptable versions with *persuade* can be regarded as special cases, more grammaticalised, of a violation of selection restrictions:

[5]	i	*Pat intended/*persuaded there to be one student on the board.*	[dummy *there*]
	ii	*Pat intended/*persuaded it to be easy to obtain a pass grade.*	[dummy *it*]

(e) Choice between complex and simple constructions

[6]	COMPLEX	SIMPLE
i	a. *Liz persuaded Pat to leave.*	b. **Liz persuaded to leave.*
ii	a. *Liz intended Pat to read it.*	b. *Liz intended to read it.*
iii	a. *Liz believed Pat to be ill.*	b. **Liz believed to be ill.*

We have noted that catenative verbs differ according to whether they enter into both simple and complex constructions or only one. In §2.1 the contrast was between simple only (*seem*) vs both (*expect*), whereas here it is between complex only (*persuade*) and both (*intend*). In [i] *Pat* is an argument in the matrix and is obligatory: even if the understood subject of the infinitival is referentially identical with the subject of *persuade* we need the intervening NP, which will be a reflexive, *Liz persuaded herself to try again.* In [ii] *Pat* has no role relative to *intend*, but is simply agent of *read*; if we make the agent of *read* identical with the experiencer of *intend* then it can be left understood, as in [iib]. As in §2.1 we find here an imperfect correlation with the ordinary vs raised distinction.

for Liz to do it herself: there is no perceptible difference in meaning and the lack of a direct semantic relation between *prefer* and *Liz* is transparent in the *for* construction.

The main complicating factor (one which has no evident semantic explanation) is that there is a rather large class of verbs of cognition and saying, like *believe*, which require an intervening NP even when there is referential identity with the matrix subject: instead of [iiib] we have *Liz believed herself to be ill.*

Summary of differences between *persuade* and *intend*

The distinctions between non-raising verbs like *persuade* and raised object verbs like *intend* are summarised in [7]:

[7]	PROPERTY	NON-RAISING VERBS	RAISING VERBS
	(a) Finite complement	Three arguments (or N/A)	Two arguments (or N/A)
	(b) Infinitival voice	Voice-sensitive	Voice-neutral
	(c) Restrictions on object	Yes	No
	(d) Dummy object	No	Yes
	(e) Simple/complex choice	Normally no[21]	Yes for many verbs

Property (e) provides a distinguishing criterion only when the answer is 'yes', indicating a raising verb, since a 'no' answer is consistent with either type.

3.1.2 The *for*-complex construction (*I arranged for her to go by bus*)

This construction is fairly straightforward: *for* is a subordinator marking the start of the non-finite clause and is obligatorily followed by the subject NP, in accusative or plain case. There are no catenative verbs that appear only in this construction. All but a few are found also in the simple construction with the meaning contrast illustrated in:

[8] i *I arranged for her to go by bus.* [*for*-complex]
ii *I arranged to go by bus.* [simple; control by subject]

In [i] the infinitival has an overt subject, in [ii] a covert one, controlled by the matrix subject – it's a matter of **my** going by bus.

The verbs which don't follow this pattern appear in contrasting complex constructions:

[9] i a. *He pressed for Ed to be admitted.* b. *He pressed Ed to join the club.*
ii a. *He called for Ed to be sacked.* b. *He called on Ed to resign.*

In [ia] *Ed* belongs straightforwardly to the subordinate clause, whereas in [ib] *Ed* is an ordinary object of *press* and controller of the understood subject of *join. Ed* has one semantic role in [ia], the 'admittee', but two in [b], patient of *press* and agent of *join.* The semantic difference is like that between *He intended Ed to be admitted* and *He persuaded Ed to be admitted* but with *press* the semantics is reflected directly by the syntax. Other verbs that follow the pattern of *press* are *push* (informal style) and *signal*; *ask* combines the contrasts shown by *arrange* and *press* (*He asked for Kim to chair the meeting*; *He asked to chair the meeting*; *He asked Ed to chair the meeting* – but see, further, §5.3). *Call* in [9ii] is similar to *press* except that in [b] *Ed* is an oblique, not an object: [9iib] belongs to the oblique-complex construction.

[21] There are one or two cases of non-raising verbs where the intervening NP is omissible, but the semantic effect is not the same as with raising verbs. For example, the difference between *I'll help you wash up* and *I'll help wash up* does not match that between [6iia] and [6iib], for in *I'll help wash up* it is a matter of helping some unspecified person(s).

3.1.3 The oblique-complex construction (*I signalled to her to move off the road*)

A few prepositional verbs take a subjectless infinitival complement as well as the prepositional one:

[10] i *I signalled to her to move off the road.*
ii *She relies on him to look after the shop while she's out.*

The oblique NP serves as controller for the missing subject of the infinitival. It cannot be a dummy pronoun, and hence not a raised complement: **I signalled to there to be a pause*; **She relies on there to be a daily delivery of fresh bread.*

3.2 Gerund-participials

Here too we need to distinguish according as the intervening NP is or is not an argument of the matrix verb – but syntactically the plain-complex gerund-participial construction is not wholly parallel to the infinitival one. We need to recognise three matrix verb types, not just two.

3.2.1 *Catch* vs *resent* (*I caught him doing it* vs *I resented him doing it*)

Semantic difference between *catch* and *resent*

From a semantic point of view, these verbs are comparable to *persuade* and *intend* respectively, in that the intervening NP is a matrix argument with *catch* but not with *resent*:

[11] i	*I caught Kim mistreating my cat.*	[matrix argument]
ii	*I resented Kim mistreating my cat.*	[not matrix argument]

Example [i] might be glossed as "I caught Kim in the act of mistreating my cat": *Kim* is the patient-argument of *catch*. In [ii], however, it wasn't Kim the person that I resented but the whole situation in which Kim mistreated my cat. This semantic distinction is borne out by the familiar kind of evidence:

[12] i	a. ?*I caught my cat being mistreated by Kim.*	[voice-sensitive: ≠ [11i]]
	b. *I resented my cat being mistreated by Kim.*	[voice-neutral: = [11ii]]
ii	a. **I caught there being several non-members present.*	[dummy excluded]
	b. *I resented there being several non-members present.*	[dummy allowed]
iii	*I resented that Kim mistreated my cat.*	[two arguments]

Catch doesn't take a finite complement, so only one example is given in [iii], but it still shows that *resent* behaves in the predictable way, with the NP appearing in the subordinate clause and hence transparently an argument of *mistreat*, not of *resent*.

Syntactic difference between *catch* and *resent*

When we turn to matters of syntax, however, we find that the relation between the two verbs is not the same as with *persuade* and *intend*. A crucial difference between gerund-participials and *to*-infinitivals is that a non-genitive NP can function as subject of the former but not of the latter unless *for* is present (cf. §§1.4–5):

[13] i *What I resented was Kim mistreating my cat.*
ii **What I intended was Kim to interview both candidates.*
iii *What I intended was for Kim to interview both candidates.*

We have no reason, therefore, to analyse the NP following *resent* as a raised object – instead we take it as subordinate subject, so that the syntactic structure matches the semantics:

[14] i *I caught Kim mistreating my cat.* [matrix argument; matrix object]
ii *I resented Kim mistreating my cat.* [not matrix argument; subordinate subject]

Evidence for a syntactic difference of this kind is as follows:

(a) Possibility of genitive marking

This can be added only when the NP is subject of the gerund-participial:

[15] i *I caught Kim/*Kim's mistreating my cat.* [matrix object: genitive excluded]
ii *I resented Kim/Kim's mistreating my cat.* [subordinate subject: genitive allowed]

(b) Matrix passivisation

The intervening NP can be promoted to subject only if it is matrix object:

[16] i *Kim was caught mistreating my cat.*
ii **Kim was resented mistreating my cat.*

With *resent* it is even marginally possible for the NP together with the gerund-participial VP to be promoted, especially with genitive marking: *?Kim('s) being given such an unfair advantage was deeply resented by everyone.*

(c) Choice between simple and complex constructions

[17]	COMPLEX	SIMPLE
i	a. *I caught myself apologising.*	b. **I caught apologising.*
ii	a. *I resent them being exploited.*	b. *I resent being exploited.*

Resent enters into both constructions: if the subordinate subject-argument is identical with that of the matrix it is left unexpressed. With *catch* the intervening NP is obligatory, part of the complementation of the verb: a reflexive is therefore required in comparable cases of identity, as in [ia].

3.2.2 *See* (*I saw him doing it*)

See falls in between the sharply distinct patterns found with *catch* and *resent*: it is like *resent* in that the intervening NP is not a matrix argument, but like *catch* in that it is syntactic object of the matrix clause:

[18]		MATRIX ARGUMENT	MATRIX OBJECT
i	*I caught Kim mistreating my cat.*	Yes	Yes
ii	*I saw Kim mistreating my cat.*	No	Yes
iii	*I resented Kim mistreating my cat.*	No	No

Semantically, *see* involves an experiencer and a stimulus: in [ii] the stimulus is the event wherein Kim mistreats my cat.[22] Generally, when one sees an event one also sees the participants in the event, so that it will normally be inferred from [ii] that I saw Kim – but this should not mislead us into thinking that *Kim* is an argument of *see*. For note first that I presumably also saw my cat, but there can be no question of *my cat* being an argument of *see* in [ii]. And, secondly, the intervening NP need not refer to something

[22] We ignore at this point the aspectuality: in *I saw Kim mistreating my cat* the subordinate clause is progressive in contrast to the non-progressive of *I saw Kim mistreat my cat* (see §5.4).

visible: *I saw the stress of these last few months taking its toll of her.*[23] Because the intervening NP is not a matrix argument, *see* behaves like *resent* with respect to voice-neutrality and the occurrence of dummy elements:

[19] i *I saw my cat being mistreated by Kim* [voice-neutral: = [18ii]]
ii *We had seen there developing between them a highly destructive antagonism.* [dummy allowed]

In the syntactic structure, however, the intervening NP belongs in the matrix clause, as object of *see*. *See* is therefore like our model verb *intend* in taking a raised object.[24] The evidence for this analysis is given in:

[20] i *I saw Kim/*Kim's mistreating my cat.* [genitive excluded]
ii *Kim was seen mistreating my cat.* [matrix passivisation]
iii **I saw opening the safe.* [simple construction excluded]

These examples show that *see* behaves syntactically like *catch*, not *resent* – compare [20i–iii] with [15–17] respectively.

3.2.3 Concealed passives with intervening NP (*He needs his hair cutting*)

Concealed passives are found in the complex as well as the simple construction:

[21] i *Your hair needs cutting by a professional.* [simple]
ii *You need your hair cutting by a professional.* [complex]

Semantically *your hair* is not a matrix argument in either case – we can gloss as "There is a need for your hair to be cut by a professional" and "You have a need for your hair to be cut by a professional". We take it to be a raised subject in [i], a raised object in [ii]. The syntactic structure is less clear than with *see* since there is here no possibility of matrix passivisation. The main reason for taking *your hair* as matrix object in [ii] is that genitive marking is completely unacceptable.

4 The catenative complement as a distinct type of complement

4.1 Non-finites in relation to NP and AdjP complements

The traditional classification of subordinate clauses as nominal, adjectival, and adverbial implies that they can be identified functionally with phrases headed by nouns, adjectives, and adverbs respectively. Certainly there are places where such identifications can validly be made. The clearest case is that of the subject, the type of complement that is syntactically most clearly distinguished from others:

[1] i a. *The first answer was wrong.* b. *Pretending you were ill was wrong.*

Another is the complement of *be* in its specifying use, where subject and predicative complement can be switched:

[23] This point is even more evident with *feel*: *I felt him running the feather down my back* clearly doesn't entail that I felt him.

[24] The catenative use of *see* is to be distinguished from that where the gerund-participial is an adjunct, as in *I saw Kim at the back of the class talking to her neighbour*; the two kinds of gerund-participial can combine: *I saw them walking across the courtyard, arguing vociferously.*

[2] i a. *His goal is total victory.* b. *His goal is to win at all costs.*
ii a. *Total victory is his goal.* b. *To win at all costs is his goal.*

The view taken in this grammar, however, is that it is not always possible to identify the function of subordinate clauses with that of non-clausal constituents such as NPs, AdjPs, and AdvPs. We argued this case for finite clauses in Ch. 11, §8.2; here we focus on catenative complements, arguing that they cannot be systematically analysed as objects or predicative complements.

Irrelevance to *to*-infinitivals of the distinction between object and oblique

With NPs we have a clear distinction between an object (related directly to the verb) and an oblique (related via a preposition), but this distinction does not apply to *to*-infinitivals, for they cannot occur as complement to a preposition (or at least not to a preposition of the relevant kind). Compare, for example:

[3] i a. *Kim started the riot.* b. *Kim started to riot.*
ii a. *Kim remembered the cat.* b. *Kim remembered to feed the cat.*
iii a. *They came to an agreement.* b. *They came to agree on the main points.*
iv a. *He proceeded to the next task.* b. *He proceeded to shred the documents.*

The underlined complements in the [a] examples are objects in [i–ii] but PP complements in [iii–iv] (where the NPs *an agreement* and *the next task* are related only obliquely to the verb), but the [b] examples show no such difference. There is then no reason to draw a functional distinction between the non-finite clauses of [ib/iib] and those of [iiib/ivb], and no reason to identify their functions with those of the object or oblique NPs in the [a] examples. The fact that the NP complements of *start* and *remember* in [ia/iia] are objects is not reason enough for saying that the non-finite complements are objects too, because there are significant syntactic differences between the two types of complement. For example, NPs can be promoted to subject through passivisation but *to*-infinitivals cannot: *The riot was started by Kim* but not **To riot was started by Kim.* Note, moreover, that as far as the non-finite complements are concerned the significant distinction is not between the constructions of [ib/iib] and those of [iiib/ivb] but between those with a raised subject, the *start* and *come* examples, and those with an ordinary subject, the *remember* and *proceed* examples.

Irrelevance to non-finites of the distinction between objects and predicatives

With NP complements we have a clear distinction between objects and predicative complements, but again this distinction is in general irrelevant to non-finite complements:

[4] i a. *Kim offered financial advice.* b. *Kim offered to help.*
ii a. *Pat needs a large loan.* b. *Pat needs to consult a solicitor.*
iii a. *Ed seems a nice guy.* b. *Ed seems to like him.*

Financial advice and *a large loan* are objects, while *a nice guy* is predicative complement. The main grammatical differences between objects and predicative complements concern passivisation and realisation by an AdjP, but these differences do not carry over to the examples with non-finite complements. Examples [ia] and [iia] can be passivised, though [iiia] cannot (*Financial advice was offered by Kim*; *A large loan is needed by Pat*; **A nice guy is seemed by Ed*); but none of the [b] examples can undergo passivisation. And with the NP complements *seem* again differs from *offer* and *need* in systematically allowing a replacement of the NP *a* *nice guy* by the AdjP *nice*, but here too there is no equivalent difference with the non-finites. It is true, of course, that we can replace *to like him* in [iiib] by *nice*, but this simply reflects the fact that *seem* can take a predicative complement as well as an infinitival one: it doesn't show that the latter is a predicative, for the relationship is not the same as with the replacement of *a nice guy* by *nice* in [iiia] (note, for example, that we couldn't replace the infinitival by an AdjP in *There seems to be a serious misunderstanding here*). It follows that there is no valid basis for generalising to the non-finites the analysis that applies to the NP complements. Again, the examples have been chosen to bring out the point that the syntactic grouping of verbs in the [a] examples is different from the semantic grouping in the [b] examples: with infinitival complements *need* belongs with *seem*, not *offer*, for *need* and *seem* take a raised subject while *offer* takes an ordinary one (cf. *There seems/needs/*offers to be ample justification for such a course of action*).

Application of the argument to the plain-complex catenative construction

The same points apply to constructions with two internal complements. Consider first:

[5] i a. *She taught <u>him</u> <u>Greek</u>.* b. *She taught <u>him</u> <u>to drive</u>.*
ii a. *She invited <u>him</u> <u>to her party</u>.* b. *She invited <u>him</u> <u>to chair the meeting</u>.*

In the [a] examples, *teach* takes two objects, *invite* an object and a PP complement, but this distinction is irrelevant to the [b] examples: there's no evidence for a comparable difference in structure here.

Similarly with the contrast between objects and predicatives:

[6] i a. *I told <u>him</u> <u>the new duties</u>.* b. *I told <u>him</u> <u>to sweep the floor</u>.*
ii a. *I consider <u>him</u> <u>a failure</u>.* b. *I consider <u>him</u> <u>to have failed</u>.*

The new duties in [ia] is direct object, *a failure* in [iia] a predicative complement (with *him* as predicand); and at the same time the function of *him* is different, indirect object in [ia], direct object in [iia]. But again the syntactic properties distinguishing [ia] from [iia] do not apply to the catenatives. For example, an indirect object is resistant to fronting in relativisation, etc. (cf. *[*the one*] *whom I told the new duties*), but such restrictions do not apply to plain-complex structures like [6ib] ([*the one*] *whom I told to sweep the floor*): the intervening NP here behaves like a direct object rather than an indirect one. There are semantic differences between [ib] and [iib], with *him* a matrix argument in [ib] but not [iib], and the time of the subordinate situation being later than that of the matrix one in [ib] but not [iib]; but these do not provide any basis for saying that they differ in syntactic structure in the way that [ia] differs from [iia].

Varying degrees of likeness to objects

Catenative verbs vary in the extent to which their non-finite complements resemble objects, but overall the similarities are fairly slight. Relevant factors are as follows:

(a) Passivisation

The catenative complements that are most like objects are those which can be promoted to subject by passivisation. All are gerund-participials, as in:

[7] i *<u>Kim's leaving early</u> wasn't mentioned.*
ii *<u>Going out alone at night</u> isn't recommended.*

All the verbs concerned also take NP objects, and passivise much more readily with an NP object than with a gerund-participial: the above construction is quite rare and felt to be rather awkward and marginal.

With a few verbs an infinitival complement can be promoted to extraposed subject:

[8] i *It is planned to complete the work in three stages.*
ii *It is hoped to return to this issue.*

This can hardly be regarded, however, as indicative of a significant resemblance to an object, for clauses with NP objects do not undergo this kind of passivisation, and while *plan* allows an NP object *hope* does not.

(b) Pronouns and clefts

It is not normally found with non-finite complements as antecedent: *Yes, I want it*, for example, is not an appropriate response to *Do you want to see them?*, nor *Yes, I avoided it* to *Did you avoid implicating your father?* Questioning with *what* is possible with some verbs: the questions *What do you want?*, *What have you decided?*, *What do you recommend?* might be answered respectively *I want to see the manager*, *I've decided to accept the offer*, *I recommend leaving things as they are.* But this is very restricted, especially with infinitivals: *I'd like to go to Spain*, for example, is not an answer to *What would you like?*, nor *You should stop drinking coffee* to *What should I stop?* Relativisation in a pseudo-cleft is possible with more verbs (*What I'd like is to go to Spain for a few days*; *All I ask is to be allowed to get on with my work in peace*) – but again with severe limitations (**What they began first was to arrange/arranging the cards in order*).[25] *It*-clefts are marginally possible with some gerund-participials (*It's having to do the job under such appalling conditions that I resent*) but quite impossible with infinitivals (compare *It's encouragement that she needs* and **It's to consult a solicitor that she needs*).

In general, gerund-participials tend to be more like objects than *to*-infinitivals, reflecting the nominal source of the traditional gerund. But there are considerable differences among them, and (except for the cases defined in §7) it is better to treat gerund-participials along with other non-finites in the catenative construction than to separate some of them out and handle them with NP complements as object.

4.2 The analysis of auxiliary verbs

The syntactic class of auxiliary verbs is defined in English by the NICE properties – occurrence with Negation, Inversion, Code, and Emphasis (see Ch. 3, §2.1). We have distinguished between **core** and **non-core** uses of the auxiliaries: in the core uses they appear with a following verb in one of its secondary forms (plain form, gerund-participle, or past participle), whereas in the non-core uses they take an NP, a finite clause, or some other kind of complement:

[9]	CORE USES	NON-CORE USES
i	a. *He <u>isn't</u> <u>working</u>.*	b. *He <u>isn't</u> <u>a liar</u>.*
ii	a. *I <u>haven't</u> <u>seen</u> it.*	b. %*I <u>haven't</u> <u>time</u>.*
iii	a. *<u>Would</u> you <u>regret</u> it?*	b. *<u>Would</u> you rather <u>I did it</u>?*

[25] In some cases a *to*-infinitival can occur instead of an NP as complement of a pseudo-cleft whose subject contains a prepositional verb: *What she agreed to was <u>his proposal for a cooling-off period</u> / <u>to accept a cooling-off period</u>* or *What he longed for was <u>her forgiveness</u> / <u>to know he was forgiven</u>.* But relatively few verbs behave in this way: compare, for example, *What he applied for was <u>two months' deferment</u> / *<u>to defer his enrolment</u>* or *What she decided on was <u>a partial sale of the business</u> / *<u>to sell part of the business</u>*, and so on.

All auxiliaries have core uses, whereas non-core uses are found only with *be*, stative *have* (in some varieties), and *would* in the idioms *would rather / sooner / as soon.*

There are two competing analyses of the core auxiliaries: on the **dependent-auxiliary analysis,** they are dependents of a following **main verb**, whereas in the **catenative-auxiliary analysis** they belong to the larger class of catenative verbs which take non-finite complements. Now that we have examined the catenative construction in some detail, we will present our arguments for adopting the catenative-auxiliary analysis; we first set out the case for the dependent-auxiliary analysis and then show why the catenative analysis is to be preferred.

4.2.1 The dependent-auxiliary analysis

Since the NICE properties are found with a few verbs which clearly take complements, as in the non-core uses illustrated in [9], these properties cannot provide the justification for taking the core auxiliaries as dependents rather than heads: the special treatment of core auxiliaries must be based on other factors.

General motivation for the dependent-auxiliary analysis

These other factors can be brought out by comparing the following constructions:

[10]	i	*Ed had a busy morning: he read the report.*	[sequence of main clauses]
	ii	*Ed says that he read the report.*	[finite subordination]
	iii	*Ed asked to read the report.*	[non-finite subordination]
	iv	*Ed had read the report.*	[auxiliary construction]

(a) Sequence of main clauses

In [10i] there are two main clauses; they are of equal syntactic status, neither being subordinate to the other. This relational independence is reflected in the internal independence of the two clauses. That is, each selects independently of the other for tense, polarity, clause type, subject, and so on. This is illustrated for polarity in:

[11]	i	*Ed <u>had</u> a busy morning: he <u>read</u> the report.* (=[10i])	[positive + positive]
	ii	*Ed <u>had</u> a busy morning: he <u>didn't read</u> the report.*	[positive + negative]
	iii	*Ed <u>didn't have</u> a busy morning: he <u>read</u> the report.*	[negative + positive]
	iv	*Ed <u>didn't have</u> a busy morning: he <u>didn't read</u> the report.*	[negative + negative]

Similarly for subject selection: as it stands, the subject of the second clause is related anaphorically to that of the first, but the two subjects could be quite unrelated, as in *Ed had a busy morning: the phone rang continuously.* And so on: there are no grammatical limitations on either clause imposed by the other.

(b) Finite subordination

As we move down to [10ii], we find that this internal independence of the two clauses has diminished, though to a relatively modest extent. Here, *that he read the report* is a subordinate clause serving as complement to *say:* there is therefore a clear structural interdependence in that one clause is functioning within the structure of the other. By virtue of its subordination, the *read* clause loses its potential illocutionary force. That is, in uttering [ii] I do not assert that he read the report (as I normally do if I utter the simple sentence *He read the report*): I don't make two separate assertions, as in [i], but a single composite assertion. Related to this is the fact that the choice of clause type in the complement clause is restricted. It would not be possible to have an imperative clause here. And a closed interrogative is just about excluded too (*[?]Ed says whether he read the report*) though it would become completely normal if we made the main clause negative or interrogative (*Ed doesn't say* / *Does Ed say whether he read the report?*), an indication of the interdependence between the two clauses. In other respects, however, the *read* clause has the same range of options available as in a main clause: the options for tense, polarity, subject, for example, are unaffected by the subordination (cf. *Ed says that the boss doesn't read the reports*, which differs in all three of these respects).

(c) Non-finite subordination

Moving from [10ii] to [iii] takes us from a finite to a non-finite subordinate clause, and non-finites have a reduced range of clausal options open to them. Non-finite clauses tend to be significantly less explicit than finite clauses: components of meaning that in finites are directly expressed are in non-finites often left to be derived from the context in which the clause appears. The non-finite has no inflectional tense – and no possibility therefore of including a modal auxiliary (the possible contrast in [10ii] between *that he may/must/can/will read the report* is not available in [iii]). Instead, the superordinate verb contributes a great deal to the interpretation of the lower clause: in [iii], for example, the reading is merely potential and in a time sphere subsequent to the time of asking, whereas in *Ed remembered to read the report* it is actual and not temporally separable from the remembering. Like most non-finites, the *read* clause of [iii] has no overt subject – but the understood subject is retrievable from the superordinate subject *Ed*.

(d) The auxiliary construction

Finally, when we come to [10iv], the range of structural options available is further reduced, so much so (the argument goes) that it is no longer justifiable to talk in terms of two clauses, one embedded within the other. Historically it is a two-clause construction, comparable to [iii], but the two clauses have lost their separate identities, merging together into a single clause. This evolution has been accompanied by a reinterpretation of the direction of grammatical dependence, with *have* now dependent on *read*, rather than the other way round.

The reduced independence of *have* and *read* in [10iv] relative to that of *ask* and *read* in [10iii] is reflected in a number of ways, most notably [12i–iii], which we examine in turn:

[12] i *Ask* takes an argument subject, whereas *have* takes a non-argument subject.
ii With *ask* there is a very clear distinction between negating *ask* itself and negating the complement, but *have* does not follow the same pattern.
iii *Ask* and its complement show a greater degree of temporal independence than we find with *have* and the following verb.

The distinction between argument and non-argument subjects

Both [10iii], *Ed asked to read the report*, and [10iv], *Ed had read the report*, have only a single subject, but there is nevertheless a major difference between them. In the semantic interpretation of [iii] we understand *Ed* to be an argument of both the verbs – to have two semantic roles. Ed is the 'asker' and also the (potential) 'reader'. But we cannot similarly attribute two distinct roles to Ed in [iv]. Ed is here the reader, but not the 'haver'. Semantically, *have* relates to Ed's reading the report as a whole, not just to Ed. This is the distinction we have discussed in contrasting *hope* and *seem* in §2.1, where we talked of ordinary subject vs raised subject; the way in which we defined 'raised subject', however, assumed a two-clause structure and hence the term is not appropriate in discussing the dependent-auxiliary analysis: we will simply say here that *ask* takes an argument subject, whereas *have* takes a non-argument subject. The distinction between the two kinds of subject is reflected in ways that will be familiar from the earlier discussion.

(a) *Ask* is voice-sensitive, *have* voice-neutral

[13] i	a. *Kim asked to interview the PM.*	}	[voice-sensitive: a ≠ b]
	b. *The PM asked to be interviewed by Kim.*		
ii	a. *Kim had interviewed the PM.*	}	[voice-neutral: a = b]
	b. *The PM had been interviewed by Kim.*		

In [i] there is a clear contrast in meaning, with Kim doing the asking in [a], the PM in [b]: *ask* is sensitive to the voice of the following infinitival. But in [ii] the propositional meaning is the same in [a] and [b]: *have* is voice-neutral. The relation between [iia] and [iib] is just the same as in the simple active–passive pair *Kim interviewed the PM* and *The PM was interviewed by Kim.* That is what we would expect if *have* were simply an optional dependent of *interview.*

(b) *Ask* imposes selection restrictions on the subject, *have* does not

[14] i	#*The knife asked to touch the baby.*	[selection restrictions apply]
ii	*The knife had touched the baby.*	[no selection restrictions]

Example [i] is anomalous because catenative *ask* imposes selection restrictions on its subject: normally it is only people who ask to do something. This indicates a direct semantic relation between *ask* and the subject: verbs generally impose selection restrictions on their arguments. Perfect *have*, by contrast, imposes no such restrictions. In [ii] *the knife* satisfies the restrictions imposed by *touch* (compare #*Infinity had touched the baby*). This indicates a direct relation between the subject and *touch* but not *have*: again this is what we would expect if *touch* were the head element, and *have* a dependent.

(c) *Have* allows subjects with no independent meaning, *ask* does not

[15] i	**There asked to be a mistake in the proof.*	[dummy *there* excluded]
ii	*There had been a mistake in the proof.*	[dummy *there* permitted]

Example [i] is unacceptable because *there* has no meaning of its own and hence cannot satisfy the selection restrictions imposed by *ask.* But [ii] is acceptable because *There was a mistake in the proof* is: adding *have* to this doesn't affect acceptability, and this too is what one would expect if it were a dependent of *be.*

Negation

With *ask* we find a sharp semantic and syntactic distinction between negating *ask* and negating its complement. Negation of the complement occurs most naturally with passives, so we may contrast [16ia–b], whereas with *have* we have the single negation [ii]:

[16] i a.	*She didn't ask to be included in the survey.*	[negation of *ask* clause]
b.	*She asked not to be included in the survey.*	[negation of complement]
ii	*She had not been included in the survey.*	

The dependent-auxiliary analysis treats *She had been included in the survey* as a single clause and hence predicts that there will be just one negation of it, as in [ii].

With the modals, moreover, we find that the clear semantic contrast between [16ia] and [16ib] may be syntactically neutralised. Compare:

[17] i	*You may not start yet.*	[external negation]
ii	*You must not start yet.*	[internal negation]

As explained in Ch. 3, §9.2.1, we use the term 'external negation' for the interpretation where the negation has scope over the modal, and 'internal negation' for that where the negation is within the scope of the modal. Thus [17i] is comparable semantically to [16ia] in that *may* (here indicating permission) falls within the scope of the negative, so that we have negation of the modality: it says that you do not have permission to start yet. It differs syntactically from [16ia] because *may* is an auxiliary and can hence be negated directly, without *do*-support. However, [17ii] is comparable semantically to [16ib] in that *must* (here indicating requirement or obligation) is outside the scope of the negative. The meaning is "You are required not to start yet" rather than "You aren't required to start yet"; what is negative, therefore, is not the modality but the propositional content that the modality applies to. This is why [17i–ii] effectively mean the same even though *may* and *must* themselves are of course very different in meaning. In spite of the difference in the semantic scope of the negative, however, they are syntactically alike, not just superficially in terms of the position of *not*, but more fundamentally in terms of their behaviour with respect to the tests for clausal negation set out in Ch. 9, §1.1; compare, for example:

[18] i a. *She didn't ask to be included in the survey and nor/*so did your brother.*
b. *She asked not to be included in the survey and so/*nor did your brother.*
ii a. *You may not start yet and nor/*so may your brother.*
b. *You must not start yet and nor/*so must your brother.*

In [ia] *ask* is negated and hence we have matching *nor* following, whereas in [ib] *ask* is positive and hence selects positive *so* following. But the parallel semantic difference between [iia] and [iib] is not reflected in this way: [17ii] no less than [17i] is treated as syntactically negative. This suggests that from a syntactic point of view *You must start* is a single clause, so that it has only one negative counterpart.

Temporal specification

Consider the following contrast:

[19] i *She asked to read the report on Saturday.*
ii *She had read the report on Saturday.*

Example [i] is ambiguous in that *on Saturday* can specify the time of the asking or the time of the (potential) reading. The ambiguity can be resolved in favour of the former meaning by moving the adjunct: *She asked on Saturday to read the report.* And it can be resolved in favour of the second meaning by changing *on* to *next*, giving *She asked to read the report next Saturday*, since the future meaning of the adjunct is incompatible with the past time meaning of *asked*. The point is that the asking and the reading are temporally quite distinct, and we can therefore add temporal specification relating to either. Or, indeed, to both: *She asked yesterday to read the report on Saturday*. But it would not be possible to say **She had yesterday read the report on Saturday*. Again, the data suggest that *have* and *read* have significantly less independence than do *ask* and *read*, and this can be captured by assigning them to a single clause.

The verb group

Under the dependent-auxiliary analysis, sequences like *had read, must start, was interviewed, had been interviewed*, etc., constitute single syntactic units, resulting from the historical reanalysis of earlier catenative constructions. We will call them **verb groups** ('VGps').[26] Within the structure of the VGp, the main verb functions as head and the auxiliaries as dependents.

[26] The term 'verb group' is an ad hoc one: if the main verb is head and the auxiliaries dependents, it would more properly be called a 'verb phrase'. The ad hoc term reflects our view that the category is not theoretically justified but may have some practical descriptive value. We prefer, therefore, to reserve the term 'verb phrase' for the unit which includes the complements and modifiers of the verb, in accordance with widespread usage in modern grammars. Traditional grammar generally uses the term 'verb' itself for the VGp as well as for the individual words within it, but it is undesirable to lose the distinction between the word and the larger unit.

The auxiliaries are optional elements, but their order is rigidly fixed. A simplified structure of the VGp (ignoring *do*, *use*, and the *have* of *I have to go*) is shown in [20], where parentheses indicate optionality:

[20]	(Modal)	(Perfect)	(Progressive)	(Passive)	Main Verb
	will	*have*	*be*	*be*	*take*
	can				*write*
	etc.				etc.

Such a structure accounts neatly for the possible combinations of auxiliary verbs and their relative order. Note, for example, that we have *She has been reading* (perfect + progressive), not **She is having read* (progressive + perfect). The fixed order of the modals and perfect ***have*** similarly handles such data as the following:

[21] i *I may have mentioned it yesterday.* [internal perfect]
ii *I should have mentioned it yesterday.* [external perfect]
iii *Kim needn't have written it.* [ambiguous]

In [i] the past time expressed by *have* is associated not with the modality, but with the proposition that the modality applies to, thus "It is possible that I mentioned it yesterday" (cf. Ch. 3. §9.9). In [ii], by contrast, the modality – which here involves the concept of the 'right' thing to do – falls within the semantic scope of *have*, for it is a matter of what was right in the past: "the right thing to do was (or would have been) to mention it yesterday". Example [iii] is ambiguous, for it can be interpreted in either way. The more salient reading follows the pattern of [ii]: "There was no need for Kim to write it yesterday" (with *need* inside the semantic scope of *have*); but it has a second interpretation along the lines of [i]: "It isn't necessarily the case that Kim wrote it" (with *need* now outside the scope of *have*). The phenomenon is similar to that involving negative scope illustrated in [17] – where *You must not start yet* is interpreted differently from *You may not start yet*. The development of a VGp unit with a rigidly ordered syntactic structure results in certain semantic scope distinctions being left implicit. The VGp selects as a whole for negative polarity and perfect tense, and the markers of these categories occupy a fixed syntactic position within the structure irrespective of their semantic scope.[27]

4.2.2 The catenative-auxiliary analysis

Although the category of VGp is in many ways descriptively very useful, the position taken here is that there are nevertheless compelling grounds for preferring an analysis of the modal, tense, aspectual and voice auxiliaries as catenative verbs taking non-finite complementation. On this account, [10iii–iv], *Ed asked to read the report* and *Ed had read the report*, have essentially the same structure. We will argue that there is no principled basis for drawing a structural distinction between catenative + complement and dependent-auxiliary + main-verb constructions.

[27] A further case of mismatch between syntactic and semantic scope is to be found in the position of adverbs. Although the order illustrated in *He must always/never have filed the letters* represents the usual one, it is also possible to have the adverb before the auxiliary, as in *He never/always must have filed the letters*. *Must* here has its epistemic sense, roughly "I am forced to conclude". And it is clear that the frequency adverbs relate semantically to the filing, not to the epistemic judgement: the meaning is "I am forced to conclude that he always/never filed the letters", not "I am always/never forced to conclude that he filed the letters". Semantically, then, it is comparable to *He promised always to do his best*, although the order matches that of *He always promised to do his best*: the semantic contrast between the two *promise* examples is lost with *must*.

The argument has both a negative and a positive side to it. The negative side involves reconsidering the differences between *ask* and *have* presented in the last section as supporting a dependent-auxiliary analysis, and showing that on closer examination they do not in fact do so. The positive side involves introducing other phenomena which can be handled more satisfactorily under the catenative analysis.

(a) The distinction between argument and non-argument subjects

The first point we made was that while *ask* takes an argument subject, *have* does not. But as we in fact noted when discussing this difference, it isn't only auxiliary verbs that take non-argument subjects: verbs such as *seem, appear, begin, tend* do so too. The following examples with *seem* thus match the above ones with perfect *have* in [13–15]:[28]

[22] i	a. *Kim seemed to intimidate the PM.* b. *The PM seemed to be intimidated by Kim.*	[voice-neutral: a = b]
ii	a. *The knife seemed to touch the baby.*	[no selection restrictions]
	b. *There seemed to be a mistake in the proof.*	[*there* permitted]

It is also important to note that the concept of catenative can be applied to adjectives as well as to verbs. Adjectives like *certain, likely, eager, keen* take non-finite complements, and can be chained together recursively in the same way as catenative verbs: cf. *She is likely to be keen to accept* or (with a mixture of verbs and adjectives in a chain of four catenatives) *She is likely to at least appear to be keen to try to win.* And catenative adjectives show the same split between those that take argument subjects and those that take non-argument subjects. Compare:

[23] i	a. *Kim was keen to interview the PM.* b. *The PM was keen to be interviewed by Kim.*	[voice-sensitive: a ≠ b]
ii	a. *Kim was likely to intimidate the PM.* b. *The PM was likely to be intimidated by Kim.*	[voice-neutral: a = b]

Furthermore, this split is to be found in the class of auxiliaries too: it is not quite true that all auxiliaries take non-argument subjects, for *dare* and the *would* of *would rather* take argument subjects:

[24] i	a. *Neither dare interview the PM.* b. *The PM daren't be interviewed by either.*	[voice-sensitive: a ≠ b]
ii	**The piano-lid daren't be open.*	[selection restrictions apply]
iii	**There daren't be any dust on the piano.*	[dummy *there* excluded]

What we find, then, is the cross-classification shown in:

[25]	ARGUMENT SUBJECT	NON-ARGUMENT SUBJECT	
i	*dare, would (rather)*	*be, can, have, may, need*	[auxiliaries]
ii	*expect, hope, try, want*	*appear, begin, seem, tend*	[lexical verbs]
iii	*anxious, determined, keen*	*apt, certain, liable, likely*	[adjectives]

The contrast in the semantic relation to the subject thus provides no basis for treating auxiliaries differently from lexical verbs. Moreover, the behaviour of *dare* and *would (rather)* is inconsistent with the dependent-auxiliary analysis: they are clearly heads, not dependents.

(b) Negation

Although the core auxiliary construction normally has just one negation, the possibility does in fact exist for contrasts in syntactic as well as semantic scope and for negating more than

[28] We have changed the non-finite complement of [13] because both *Kim seemed to interview the PM* and *The PM seemed to be interviewed by Kim* sound somewhat unnatural. They are equivalent, nevertheless.

one verb at a time. Compare:

[26] i *She can't always answer his questions, can she?* [negation of *can*]
ii *She can always not answer his questions, can't she?* [negation of *answer*]
iii *She can't always not answer his questions, can she?* [negation of both verbs]

There is an equivalence between [i] and *It isn't always possible for her to answer his questions, is it?*: the negation clearly includes the *can/possible* within its scope semantically, and the interrogative tag shows that it does so syntactically too – the standard type of tag reverses the polarity of the clause to which it attaches (cf. Ch. 9, §1.1).

By contrast, [26ii] is equivalent to *It is always possible for her not to answer his questions, isn't it?* ("to refrain from answering"), where the *can/possible* is now outside the scope of the negative, hence positive, as reflected in the negative tag. And [iii] is equivalent to *It is not possible for her to always not answer his questions, is it?* The two negatives here do not of course cancel each other out because they are negating different verbs; the tag is the same as in [i], because it is determined by the polarity of the *can* clause.

The *always* in these examples makes it easy to see the scope of the negatives. If we omit it, there is no longer anything in the linear sequence of elements alone to determine the scope: *She + can + not + answer his questions* could in principle have either the first or second interpretation. The second requires a special prosodic reading in which there is a break after *can* and the *not* is closely linked to *answer*; in writing *cannot* would force the first interpretation, whereas *can not* would tend to be used for the second. An inflectional negative always indicates that the negative has syntactic scope over that verb: *She can't answer his questions* unambiguously has the first interpretation.

The same range of possibilities is even available with perfect *have*:

[27] i *He has not always accepted bribes, has he?* [negation of *have*]
ii *He has always not accepted bribes, hasn't he?* [negation of *accept*]
iii *He has not always not accepted bribes, has he?* [negation of both verbs]

Have is negated in [i] and [iii], where *has not* is replaceable by inflectional *hasn't*, but in [ii] the *have* clause is positive (as evident from the tag), and the *not* belongs syntactically as well as semantically with *accept*: "It has always been his practice to not accept (i.e. to refuse) bribes".

Examples like [26ii/27ii] are just like the earlier [16iib] (*She asked not to be included in the survey*), and the catenative analysis enables them to be handled in just the same way, as non-finite complement negation, secondary negation in the sense of Ch. 9, §2.3. This is not possible in the dependent-auxiliary analysis, where they have to be treated as exceptions. The above contrasts show that the proposed VGp does not in fact form a unit with a single syntactic negation. It is true that examples like [i] represent the normal pattern, but the catenative analysis caters more satisfactorily for the range of options that the verbal system makes available.[29] (It should also be borne in mind that in the ordinary catenative construction negation of the matrix is much more frequent than negation of the complement.) Other

[29] Attested examples of the construction shown in [iii] are rare, but the following is a slightly more complex version of it: *Not since 1992 had Sampras not taken at least one among the Australian Open, French Open, Wimbledon and the US Open.* The initial negative phrase negates the *have* clause, while the second *not* negates the *take* clause.

examples of secondary negation after auxiliaries are given in:

[28] i *He will sometimes not answer the phone.*
ii *You should just occasionally not give everyone the benefit of the doubt.*
iii *They are always not accepting new orders.*

Temporal specification

The same kind of argument applies here. Initially we can distinguish two types of catenative: Type I are not temporally distinct from their complement, but Type II are. Some examples are given in:

[29] i *forget/remember (to); begin, continue, stop; manage, try* [Type I: non-distinct]
ii *ask, expect, intend, promise, want* [Type II: distinct]

With Type I it is not possible to give separate time specifications (of the same kind) or to give a time specification that conflicts with the time sphere required by the inflectional tense of the catenative, whereas with Type II it is:

[30] i **This morning it began to rain this evening.*
ii *This morning he promised to return this evening.*

On this dimension, Type II verbs clearly involve a higher degree of internal independence between the clauses than do Type I. Of the auxiliaries, however, only passive *be* and supportive *do* belong clearly to Type I – compare:

[31] i *At that time he was still arriving tomorrow.*
ii *He may have seen her yesterday.*
iii *We can now set out tomorrow.*
iv *When I arrived she had already left just a few minutes earlier.*
v *He had left when Kim arrived.*

Progressive *be* belongs to Type I when expressing progressive aspectuality but not with the futurate meaning seen here in [i]. The modals in general belong to Type II. In [ii], the *yesterday* gives the time of the seeing: it does not relate to the modality expressed by *may*, as evident from the fact that the modal is in the present tense. And in [iii] there are separate time specifications: *now* relates to *can*, *tomorrow* to *set out*. Perfect *have* also belongs basically to Type II. In [iv] *just a few minutes earlier* gives the time of her leaving, whereas *when I arrived* is associated with the *have*: it gives the time of orientation to which the leaving is anterior. Example [v] is ambiguous, in a way which parallels the earlier [19i] (*She asked to read the report on Saturday*). In one interpretation *when Kim arrived* gives the time of his leaving. In another it is like *when I arrived* in [31iv], and associated with *have* rather than *leave*: it specifies a time prior to which he had left. (Adding *already* after *had* makes this second reading more salient.) And in both the *have* and *ask* cases, moving the adjunct to the front just about forces its association with the first verb:

[32] i *On Saturday she asked to read the report.* [specifies time of asking]
ii *When Kim arrived he had left.* [specifies time of orientation]

The Type II behaviour of the auxiliaries provides strong support for the catenative analysis, where the time adjuncts can be assigned to the superordinate or complement clause as appropriate, just as they are when the catenative is a lexical verb.

Constituency

The dependent-auxiliary and catenative-auxiliary analyses assign different constituent structures. For *He was writing a letter*, say, we have (omitting functional labels):

[33]

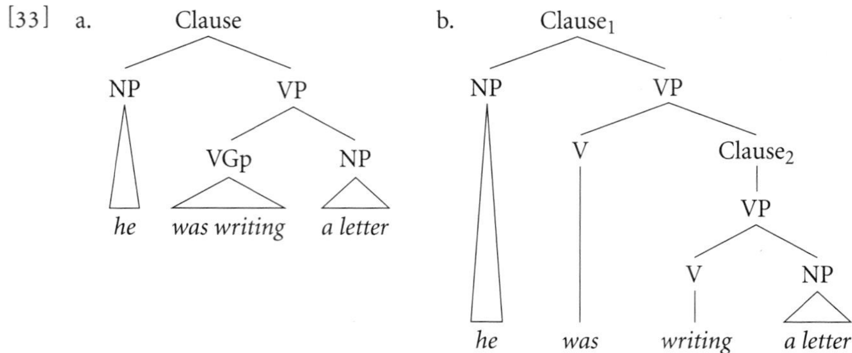

The major difference is that in [a], the dependent-auxiliary analysis, *writing* first enters into construction with the auxiliary *was* to form the VGp *was writing*, whereas in [ii], the catenative analysis, it first enters into construction with its complement *a letter* to form the VP *writing a letter*. Evidence supporting this second constituent structure is as follows:

(a) Preposing

The VP can occupy prenuclear position in the clause:

[34] *She said he'd be writing a letter, and* [*writing a letter he was*].

Here *writing a letter* has been preposed, and it is characteristic of fronting that it applies to whole constituents.

(b) Coordination

Coordination provides particularly strong evidence for the catenative analysis when it occurs in combination with negation:[30]

[35] i *You can't* [*join a debating society and not speak*].
ii *He surely hasn't* [*read the letter and failed to see its implications*].
iii *I'm quite sure he didn't* [*write the letter and not post it*].

Can't join and *can't join a debating society* are clearly not constituents in [i] (as they are predicted to be under the dependent-auxiliary analysis): it doesn't say that you can't join a debating society, but rather that you can't 'join-a-debating-society-and-not-speak'. Thus *join a debating society* must form a unit, which coordinates with (*and*)*not speak*, with the resulting coordination as a whole serving as complement to *can't*. The same applies to [ii], where we find coordination within the complement of *have*. And similarly in [iii], where the coordination is complement of supportive *do*. Such coordination would not be possible without *do* (**He wrote the letter and not post it*), but introduction of *do* detaches the tense inflection from *write*, making the way for coordination of two plain form VPs.

(c) Position of adjuncts

Adjuncts frequently occur between an auxiliary and the lexical verb: *He was slowly writing a letter*. It is difficult to see how this can be accounted for under the dependent-auxiliary analysis without invoking the concept of discontinuous constituents, whereas the catenative

[30] Coordination without negation is not so straightforwardly conclusive, for we can have either *He was writing a letter and listening to the radio* (favouring analysis [33b]) or *He has written or is writing his letter of resignation* (which might appear to favour [33a], but is best treated as a case of delayed right constituent coordination: see Ch. 15, §4.4).

analysis allows the construction to be handled with a simpler model of constituency. The ease with which we can insert elements between auxiliary and 'main verb' casts serious doubt on the idea that they form a syntactic constituent comparable with, say, NP, AdjP, PP, and the like.

Ordering constraints

Under the dependent-auxiliary analysis the fixed ordering of the auxiliaries is catered for by stipulating that the VGp has the structure shown in [20]. Under the catenative analysis the order results from certain independently needed constraints.[31]

(a) Initial position of the modals

This is attributable to their defective morphology: they have no secondary forms and so can't appear in the non-finite complement of another verb.[32]

(b) Final position of passive *be*

This is due to the fact that it is the following verb that is passivised: the preceding auxiliaries – the modals, *have*, and progressive *be* – don't have objects and are outside the scope of the voice contrast. Compare now:

[36] i *The king appears to be hated by his subjects.*
ii *The king may be hated by his subjects.*

Be occupies second position among the verbs in [ii] for the same reason as in [i]: *may*, like *appear*, is outside the scope of the passive.

(c) Fixed order of perfect and progressive

Be can't precede *have* because of a more general constraint excluding perfect *have* from the complements of aspectual verbs:

[37] i **He was having read the book.*
ii **He began having read the book.*
iii **He stopped having read the book.*

Conclusion

The dependent-auxiliary analysis has certain attractions for textual analysis, in that it very much reduces the amount of embedding that has to be recognised. *It may have been raining*, for example, will be a simple clause instead of a complex one with three layers of embedding. Given the high frequency of auxiliary verbs, this will result in a very considerable 'saving' in the analysis of most texts. It is also simpler in that we don't have to decide which clause temporal and similar dependents should be assigned to – e.g. whether *at noon* belongs with *be* or with *sleep* in *They were still sleeping at noon*. And the cases where we have shown it to give clearly unacceptable results are textually quite rare. Nevertheless, we believe we have shown that from a more theoretical perspective the catenative analysis is very much sounder.

It follows that in [10] above we distinguish just three categories, sequence of main clauses, finite subordination, and non-finite subordination. Within this last category, catenative

[31] In languages where mood, tense, and aspect are marked inflectionally there is some tendency for an aspect marker to be closer to the lexical base than a tense marker, and for the latter to be closer than a mood marker; the English syntactic order matches that morphological order.

[32] The *have* of *We have to stop* and the like is not a member of the syntactic category of modal auxiliaries, and in particular is not defective. It is therefore not catered for by structure [20] – e.g. it can precede or follow the perfect (*You have to have completed three years of undergraduate study*; *I have had to put it aside*). Nevertheless, in some varieties it can be used as a core auxiliary (Ch. 3, §2.5.6), and there is no evident reason why it should then be treated differently from other core auxiliaries.

complementation, we find a considerable range of differences in the degree of internal independence between the two clauses, but there is no principled basis for drawing a distinction between two quite different constructions. The dependent-auxiliary analysis implies that the auxiliaries have come, over time, to be reanalysed so as to lose their status as verbs taking non-finite complements: what we have seen, however, is that they have retained too much syntactic independence for this thesis to be sustainable. We believe, moreover, that the proposed analysis is much more viable in a descriptive framework that recognises the catenative complement as a distinct kind of complement – there is no question of suggesting that the non-finite complements of the core auxiliaries are objects or predicative complements.

4.3 The traditional distinction between 'gerunds' and 'present participles'

The verb-forms we are calling gerund-participles are traditionally divided into gerunds and present participles, as illustrated in:

[38] i a. *[Inviting the twins] was a bad mistake.* [gerund]
b. *We're thinking of [giving them one more chance].*
c. *I remember [seeing them together].*
d. *She found [talking to Pat] surprisingly stressful.*
ii a. *Those [living alone] are most at risk.* [present participle]
b. *[Not having read his book,] I can't comment.*
c. *She is [mowing the lawn].*
d. *We saw him [leaving the post office].*
e. *I caught them [reading my mail].*

We argued in Ch. 3, §1.4, that there is no justification for making any inflectional distinction: all the underlined forms belong to a single inflectional category. We call this form gerund-participle to reflect the fact that it covers the ground of both gerunds and present participles in other languages. At the level of words, what is important is to distinguish gerund-participle forms of verbs from nouns (*the reading of the poem*) and adjectives (*a very inviting prospect*). Our aim in this section is to show that even from a purely syntactic point of view no viable distinction can be drawn between the bracketed clauses in [i] and those in [ii]: we refer to them all as gerund-participial clauses.

In terms of their function we distinguish between complement and non-complement gerund-participials. Non-complement ones, we have noted, are traditionally present participles, while the complement ones include both traditional categories.

A difference in internal form: case of the subject NP

There is one respect in which 'gerund' and 'present participle' clauses differ in their internal form: with 'gerunds' the subject may take genitive case, with plain or accusative case a less formal alternant, but with 'present participles' the genitive is impossible and pronouns with a nominative–accusative contrast appear in nominative case, with accusative an alternant restricted to informal style.[33] Compare, then:

[39] i *She resented his/him/*he being invited to open the debate.*
ii *We appointed Max, he/him/*his being much the best qualified of the candidates.*

[33] We simplify here by ignoring constructions involving coordinate pronouns: see Ch. 5, §16.2.2.

This difference, however, is obviously relevant only to those constructions where the non-finite clause can contain a subject: it cannot be used to justify a distinction between 'gerund' and 'present participle' in the numerous constructions where no subject is permitted. In terms of our analysis, the contrast in the case of the subject is handled by our distinction between complement and non-complement gerund-participials: genitive case is restricted to the former, nominative to the latter. If the traditional distinction of 'gerund' vs 'present participle' is to be maintained, it must be based primarily on properties of the subjectless construction. But here there is no difference at all in the internal form of the constructions.

No viable distinction in function

The traditional distinction is based on the idea that 'gerunds' are like nouns while 'present participles' are like adjectives. In this respect, then, it is a reflection of the more general practice in traditional grammar of describing subordinate clause constructions in terms of functional analogies with the parts of speech. We have argued at length against this practice in the context of the classification of finite clauses (Ch. 11, §8.2) and of infinitivals (this chapter, §4.1); here we will consider the issue briefly with respect to catenative complements.

Some of our catenative complements are included in the 'gerund' class (e.g. [38ic]), while others belong with the 'present participles' (e.g. [38iid–e]); to make this distinction effectively requires that we analyse the former as objects and the latter as predicative complements, on the basis of analogies with NPs and AdjPs respectively. But the contrast between objects and predicative complements is no more applicable to gerund-participial catenative complements than to infinitival ones. Note first that there are a significant number of verbs that take adjectival predicatives but do not allow gerund-participials:

		a.	b.
[40]	i	a. *They seemed resentful.*	b. **They seemed resenting it.*
	ii	a. *He became remorseful.*	b. **He became feeling remorse.*
	iii	a. *This made them hostile.*	b. **This made them wanting to harm us.*

Constructions headed by 'present participle' verbs (as distinct from participial adjectives, as in *They seemed very interesting*, etc.) are not systematically substitutable for predicative AdjPs: their distribution is not predictable from that of AdjPs but has to be stated directly. Similarly, the possibility or otherwise of replacing a gerund-participial by an AdjP does not provide a plausible criterion for distinguishing between predicative complements and objects:

		a.	b.
[41]	i	a. *He kept staring at them.*	b. *He kept calm.*
	ii	a. *He went on staring at them.*	b. **He went on calm.*
	iii	a. *He stopped staring at them.*	b. **He stopped calm.*

The [a] examples belong together, all having an aspectual verb (or verbal idiom in the case of *go on*) in the matrix clause. The fact that *keep* licenses an adjectival predicative complement while the others do not is irrelevant, as is the fact that *keep* and *stop* license an NP object while *go on* does not (*He kept his cool*; *He stopped this annoying behaviour*).

The catenative construction is not syntactically close enough to constructions with NP and AdjP complements for us to be able to extend the distinction between object and predicative complements to the non-finites in a principled way.

Note also that there is an unsatisfactory asymmetry in the traditional treatment of catenative complements. The object vs predicative complement distinction is applied to both gerund-participials and infinitivals, but in the former case it provides the basis for a distinction between 'gerunds' and 'present participles' whereas no such distinction is drawn among the infinitivals. In neither case is there any difference in internal form in the subjectless construction, and the motivation for drawing a distinction within the gerund-participials but not in the infinitivals is primarily historical: 'gerund' and 'present participle' have different historical sources, whereas there is only one source for infinitivals. In a grammar aimed at describing the present state of the language, a syntactic distinction based on historical factors in this way cannot be justified.

No systematic difference in aspectuality

The traditional 'present participle' covers not only forms in modifier or supplement function but also the form of the verb that occurs with the progressive auxiliary *be*. It is evident, however, that 'present participles' do not always have progressive meaning, that there is no systematic difference in aspectual meaning between 'present participles' and 'gerunds'. Compare:

[42] i a. *On hearing his cry, she dashed into the garden.*
b. *Hearing his cry, she dashed into the garden.*
ii a. *Despite having no TV himself, he was able to see the programme.*
b. *Although having no TV himself, he was able to see the programme.*

In each pair, the verb in the underlined clause is traditionally analysed as a 'gerund' in [a] and a 'present participle' in [b], but in neither case is there any difference in aspectuality. In [ia/b] the aspectuality is perfective, while in [iia/b] it is imperfective but not progressive. Note, for example, that if we substitute a finite clause for the non-finite one in [iib], the appropriate form is the non-progressive *he had no TV himself.*

We conclude that there is no difference of form, function, or interpretation that correlates systematically with the traditional distinction between 'gerund' and 'present participle'. The distinction introduces an unmotivated complication into the grammar: it is one of the features of traditional grammar that should be discarded.

4.4 Catenative complements, adjuncts, and coordinates

In a number of cases, catenative complements bear some resemblance to various kinds of adjunct or to elements in a coordination.

Adjunct of purpose

In general, infinitival clauses functioning as adjunct of purpose are sharply distinct from catenative complements. Syntactically, they can be preceded by *in order* and characteristically can be moved to front position:

[43] i *He walked* [(*in order*) *to save money*].
ii [(*In order*) *to save money*,] *he walked.* } [purpose adjunct]

Semantically, they of course express the purpose of some agentive act, and we accordingly have a very clear ambiguity in:

[44] *He swore to impress his mates.* [catenative complement or purpose adjunct]

The catenative interpretation is "He swore that he would impress his mates (in some unspecified way)", whereas with an adjunct the meaning is "He swore in order to impress his mates (by swearing)". In the adjunct reading, *swore* receives greater phonological prominence and in writing is likely to be followed by a comma.

With a few verbs, such as *wait* and *hurry*, the semantic distinction is at times somewhat blurred – compare:

[45] i a. *She was waiting for his letter to arrive.* [catenative complement]
b. *She waited a while to make sure he wasn't coming back.* [purpose adjunct]
c. *She was waiting to use the photocopier.*
ii a. *He hurried to reassure her.* [catenative complement]
b. *He hurried, to prove he wasn't as slow as she claimed.* [purpose adjunct]
c. *He hurried to catch the train.*

With *wait* the contrast is clear in [ia–ib]: the catenative complement identifies the event she was waiting for and the adjunct gives the purpose of her waiting; [ic] can be construed as a catenative construction, but at the same time there is an element of purpose. Presumably she couldn't use the photocopier immediately (someone else was using it or it needed attention), so it was necessary for her to wait. In [ii] *hurry* is equivalent to *hasten* in [iia], where the meaning is that he quickly reassured her, or tried to do so; [iib] is straightforwardly purposive and readily allows *in order* and fronting; such fronting is very unlikely in [iii], but it is probably best treated as also purposive, for we could not here substitute *hasten*.

Go is a borderline member of the catenative category:

[46] i *She went to the Old Vic to see 'Hamlet'.* [purpose adjunct]
ii *She went to see 'Hamlet'.* [?catenative complement]

It is quite clear that in [i] the phrase *to the Old Vic* is a complement with the role of goal and the infinitival is an adjunct of purpose. In [ii] (spoken without any prosodic break after *went*) the concept of a spatial goal is very much backgrounded and it is not implausible to regard the infinitival as having been reanalysed as a complement: we certainly cannot insert *in order* and do not interpret it as answering the question *Why did she go?*

There is a use of *be* that is restricted to the perfect and has a similar sense to *go* as in *Jill has been to Moscow* (see Ch. 8, §4.3). This *be* too occurs with an infinitival, as in *She has been to see 'Hamlet'*. The infinitival here is in contrast with a goal such as *to Moscow*, and must qualify as a complement. Similar is *move*, as in *The government has moved to allay fears of a rise in interest-rates.* The sense of physical movement is lost, with *move* here meaning "take action"; the infinitival is virtually obligatory, and has the character of a complement rather than an adjunct.

Adjunct of result

To-infinitivals may be used as adjuncts to express a resultant or subsequent situation, but with some verbs it is not easy to distinguish sharply between this construction and the catenative one:

[47] i *I ran all the way to the station only to find the train had just left.* [adjunct]
ii *She opened the curtains to see that the ground was covered in snow.* [adjunct]
iii *She lived to be ninety / to regret her decision.* [complement]

The first two are clearly adjuncts: they are fully optional and there is here no question of licensing by the verb. In [iii], by contrast, the infinitival can hardly be said to be optional, for although *She lived* is acceptable, the interpretation is different than in [iii] (we would understand it as "She survived", i.e. "She didn't die"). Note that while [i–ii] can be roughly paraphrased with a coordinative construction (. . . *but found the train* . . . ; . . . *and saw that the ground* . . .), there is no comparable relation between [iii] and *She lived and was ninety* or *She lived and regretted her decision.*

We take *live* therefore to be a catenative. Likewise *go on*, as in *She went on to become Prime Minister.* Less clear are *wake* and *grow up*, as in *She woke to find he'd gone, He grew up to be a complete introvert*: they commonly occur in this construction, but the infinitival can be omitted without apparent effect on the meaning of what remains, and there is again a close relation with a coordinative construction, so that they are best treated with [47i–ii]. Note then that *grow up* differs from *grow*, which is undoubtedly a catenative in *He grew to like it.*

Adjunct of cause

A number of verbs appear in the following range of constructions:

[48] i *They rejoiced because they had won the war.* [adjunct]
ii *They rejoiced at their victory.*
iii *They rejoiced to hear they had won the war.*
iv *They rejoiced that they had won the war.* [complement]

The *because* phrase in [i] is clearly an adjunct and the finite content clause in [iv] a complement, while [ii–iii] fall towards the boundary between adjuncts and complements. Other verbs of this kind are: *blush, delight, grieve, grin, laugh, marvel, shudder, smile, tremble* (though only *grieve* and *marvel* of these readily enter into construction [iv]).

Depictive adjunct

Compare next:

[49] i *He came in / went out looking rather pleased with himself.* [adjunct]
ii *It came / went hurtling through the window.* [?complement]
iii *She sat/lay/stood reading the newspaper.* [adjunct]

The gerund-participial clause is undoubtedly an adjunct in [i], but it is somewhat closer to a complement in [ii]: it can be freely omitted in [i], but this is not possible in [ii] without a significant change of interpretation. In [iii] we illustrate a common construction for the positional verbs; the non-finite is not easily omissible here – but it is if we add a locative phrase like *on the patio*, and is probably better regarded as an adjunct than as a catenative complement.

Coordination

A link between catenative complementation and coordination is seen with *try* and *go*:

[50] i a. *I always try and please him.* b. *Try and not be so impatient.*
ii *Go get yourself something to eat.*

In [i] *and* is both semantically and syntactically more like a subordinator than a coordinator. As explained in Ch. 15, §2.2.3, *and* + VP here is best treated as a non-finite complement, a further form-type beyond those given in §1.1. *Go* occurs with *and* in coordination, as in *Go and get yourself something to eat*, *I went and got myself something to eat*, but under restrictive conditions it appears without *and*, as in [50ii]. Both verbs must be in the plain form and as the construction is specific to *go* it is best treated as a special case of bare infinitival complementation.

5 Classification of catenative verbs

In this section we present a classification of catenative verbs (together with some catenative idioms) based on the analysis given in §§2–4 above.

5.1 Framework of classification

Dimensions of classification

The primary dimension derives from the distinction we have drawn between the simple and complex catenative constructions. Class 1 verbs appear only in the simple construction, Class 2 in simple or complex, and Class 3 only in the complex construction. Within each major class, the first subdivision then concerns the form-types: *to*-infinitivals, bare infinitivals, gerund-participials, and past-participials.

Multiple entries

Where a verb has different senses in different constructions, we give it multiple listings, with subscripts distinguishing the uses. Compare, for example:

[1] i a. *He <u>intends</u> to leave at six.* b. *He <u>intends</u> leaving at six.*
ii a. *He should <u>try</u>$_1$ to eat less.* b. *He should <u>try</u>$_2$ eating less.*

Intend has the same meaning in [a] as in [b]: we therefore list it once, in the class of verbs taking either a *to*-infinitival or a gerund-participial. With *try*, on the other hand, we have a difference of meaning: in [a] it means "endeavour", in [b] "test the effectiveness of". We therefore list *try*$_1$ and *try*$_2$ separately, the former in the class taking a *to*-infinitival, the latter in the class taking a gerund-participial.

Passivisation

In considering whether the matrix clause can be passivised we distinguish three kinds of passive construction, and the symbols shown on the right in [2] will be used as annotations for verbs taking them:

[2] i a. *They advised me to enrol.* b. *I was advised to enrol.* [P]
ii a. *We intended (for it) to resume.* b. *It was intended (for it) to resume.* [P_X]
iii a. *We don't recommend getting involved in options trading.* b. *Getting involved in options trading isn't recommended.* [P_G]

In [i], with *advise* as the catenative verb, the intervening NP is promoted to subject; this is the usual case, and where 'passivisation' is used without qualification it is to be understood in this sense. In [ii] an infinitival complement (of *intend*) is promoted to extraposed subject, whereas in [iii] a gerund-participial complement (of *recommend*) is promoted to subject proper. With some verbs passivisation (of type [P]) is obligatory, and with others it is blocked, and these are marked as in:

[3] i a. **They said him to be ill.* b. *He was said to be ill.* [+P]
ii a. *They wanted him to see it.* b. **He was wanted to see it.* [−P]

Alternation with finite complements

In many cases the non-finite complement has a finite alternant or near-alternant:

[4] i a. *I believe him to be ill.* b. *I believe that he is ill.* [T_U]
ii a. *I'd prefer you to do it yourself.* b. *I'd prefer that you did it yourself.* [T_P]
iii a. *He decided to resign.* b. *He decided that he would resign.* [T_W]
iv a. *They demanded to be heard.* b. *They demanded that they be heard.* [T_M]
v a. *She persuaded me to go.* b. *She persuaded me that I should go.* [T_S]

The 'T' annotation is mnemonic for the *that* which occurs (usually optionally) in finite declarative complements. We distinguish five types, as marked by the subscripts. In [i] the finite is unmodalised (T_U), in [ii] a modal preterite (T_P), in [iii] it contains modal ***will*** (T_W), in [iv] it is mandative (T_M), in [v] it contains modal *should* (T_S). As noted earlier (§3.1.1), the constructions are not strictly alternants in [v].

Further annotations

To reduce the number of classes we add annotations to members of a class instead of dividing it into two or more smaller classes. The annotations used are as follows:

[5] B Takes bare infinitival (*I helped her mend the fuse*)
F Takes *to*-infinitival with *for* (*She asked for it to be postponed*)
N Occurs predominantly in non-affirmatives (*I don't mind waiting a little*)
NS Non-syntactic interpretation of understood subject (*She said to meet at six*)
P Matrix passivisation, with further specification as in [2–3]
PP Takes past-participial (*He reported them killed*)
T Also takes finite declaratives (with comparable sense); subtypes as shown in [4]

In addition, '?' indicates that the verb's membership of the class is questionable.

Omissions

We avoid setting up one-member or very small classes for verbs which have already been dealt with in the discussion – e.g. for *call*, the only verb appearing in *for*-complex but not simple constructions.

5.2 Class 1: catenative verbs appearing only in the simple construction

Here we need only two dimensions of subclassification, one based on the form-type of the non-finite, one on the semantic status of the matrix subject, whether raised or ordinary.

Class 1A: bare infinitival complement (*She may know the answer*)

[6]	*can*	*dare*$_1$	*do*	*had better*	*may*
	must	*need*$_1$ N	*shall*	*will*$_1$	*would rather*

This class consists of supportive *do*, the modal auxiliaries, and the modal idioms.[34] All take raised subjects, except for *dare* and *would rather*.

Class 1B: *to*-infinitival complement

1Bi: ordinary subject (*Kim decided to leave*)

[7]	*affect*	*aspire*	*choose*$_1$	*condescend*	*consent*
	$^{?}$*contrive*	*dare*$_2$ (B)	*decide* T$_W$ P$_X$	*decline*	*deign*
	demand T$_M$	*determine* T$_W$	*disdain*	*elect*$_1$	*endeavour*
	forget$_1$	$^{?}$*get*$_1$	$^{?}$*go on*$_1$	$^{?}$*grow*	*hasten*
	hate$_1$	*hesitate*	*know*$_1$	*learn*	*live*
	look$_1$	*manage*	*move*$_1$	*offer*	*omit*
	plot	$^{?}$*prepare*$_1$	*presume*$_1$	*pretend* T$_U$	*proceed*
	refuse	*regret*$_1$	*remember*$_1$	*resolve* T$_W$	*seek*
	serve	*stand*	*strain*	*strive*	*struggle*
	survive	*swear* T$_W$	*think*$_1$ N	*threaten*$_1$ T$_W$	*trouble*$_1$
	try$_1$	*undertake* T$_W$	*venture*	*volunteer*	*vow* T$_W$

In some cases it is not quite clear whether a *for*-complex is possible in addition to the usual simple infinitival; thus *contrive* and *prepare*$_1$ are marked questionable because of the marginal possibility of examples like $^{?}$*He had contrived for his son to be admitted to the course*; $^{?}$*I hadn't prepared for them to question me on that issue. Dare*$_2$ is a lexical verb, while *dare*$_1$ is an auxiliary: see Ch. 3, §2.5.5.

1Bii: raised subject (*She seemed to like it*)

[8]	*appear* T$_U$	*be*$_1$	*chance*$_1$ T$_U$	*come*$_1$	*fail*
	happen T$_U$	*have*$_1$	*have got*	*look*$_2$	*ought* (B)
	promise$_1$	*prove*$_1$	*seem* T$_U$	*tend*	*threaten*$_2$
	turn out T$_U$	*use*			

[34] Also in this class are (for the varieties of English that have them) the compounds *wanna, gonna, hafta, gotta,* etc., which incorporate *to* into the lexical base; see Ch. 18, §6.3. In the negative ***can*** occurs with an idiomatic use of *but* meaning "not": *It cannot but improve,* "cannot not improve – i.e. must improve". (This is to be distinguished from the *but* in conditionals: *if I could but explain how I feel,* "if only I could explain how I feel".)

For *ought* with bare infinitival and for *use* (*He used to like it*), see Ch. 3, §§2.5.4/9 *Be*$_1$ (quasi-modal *be*) is used only in primary forms (*There is to be another inquiry*). Verbs marked T$_U$ in 1Bii take a finite clause in the impersonal construction (*It appears I'm wrong*). In general the distinction between raised and ordinary subjects is clear, though *get* (*It had got to be quite late*), *go on*$_1$ (*She went on to become President of the Union*), and *grow* (*He had grown to love her*) are somewhat problematic: their meanings would lead us to expect them to be raising verbs (e.g. *grow* here means essentially the same as *come*), but they do not readily exhibit raising verb behaviour ($^?$*There had grown to be unanimity between them*). *Promise* and *threaten* illustrate the 'bleaching' (partial loss of primary meaning) that is sometimes associated with raising verbs. In *He promised*$_2$*/threatened*$_1$ *to tell the police* we clearly have ordinary subjects, but in *The weather promised*$_1$*/threatened*$_2$ *to change* the meaning of making a (characteristically verbal) promise or threat has been lost and the meaning is reduced to approximately "look likely", together with a favourable or unfavourable view of the likely event.[35]

Class 1C: *to*-infinitival or gerund-participial complement

1Ci: ordinary subject (*I propose to tell / telling her*)

[9]	*attempt*	*bother* N	$^?$*fear*$_1$	*neglect*	*propose* P$_X$
	scorn				

1Cii: raised subject (*He began to shout / shouting*)

[10]	*begin*	*cease*	*commence*	*continue*	*start*$_1$

Class 1D: gerund-participial only

1Di: ordinary subject (*We avoided being seen*)

[11]	*avoid*	*come*$_2$	*complete*	*consider*$_1$	*discontinue*
	escape	*evade*	*finish*	*get*$_2$	*go*
	postpone	*practise*	*quit*	*repent*	*resist*
	resume	*try*$_2$			

1Dii: raised subject (*Kim was writing the introduction*)

[12]	*be*$_2$	*end up*	*go on*$_2$	*keep*$_1$	*keep on*$_1$	*stop*$_1$

Most aspectual verbs have raised subjects, relating to the situation as a whole rather than specifically to the subject-argument, and hence belong in Class 1Dii, 1Cii, or 1Bii; there are, however, a few that have ordinary subjects, normally with an agentive interpretation: *discontinue, finish, quit, resume* (Class 1Di). Compare, for example, *It continued raining* and **It discontinued raining.*

Class 1E: past-participial only (*He got taken by a shark*)

[13]	*be*$_3$	*have*$_2$	*get*$_3$

The three verbs in this class all have raised construal. *Have* is the marker of perfect tense, auxiliary *be* and lexical *get* of passive voice.

[35] In its primary meaning *promise* allows an intervening NP and hence belongs in Class 2Ai, not 1Bi, like *threaten.*

5.3 Class 2: catenative verbs appearing in both simple and complex constructions

We include in this class only those verbs where the intervening NP can be omitted without a change in the meaning of the verb.[36]

Class 2A: *to*-infinitival but not gerund-participial

The simple construction has an ordinary subject, which controls the understood subject of the non-finite, except for *help* and *say*, marked 'NS' for non-syntactic interpretation.

2Ai: plain-complex, with ordinary object (*She asked to see him*; *She asked me to see him*)

[14]	*ask* T_M (F)	*beg* T_M (F)	*help* (B) N_S	*pay* (F)	*petition* (F)
	pledge T_W	*pray* T_W (F)	*promise*$_2$ T_W	*request* T_M	*train*

Most verbs that take an ordinary object in the complex construction do not enter into the simple construction (cf. *They persuaded him to leave*, but not **They persuaded to leave*), and so belong in Class 3 below. The few that do enter into both simple and complex constructions, the present Class 2Ai, exhibit three different relations between them:

[15]		a.	b.
	i	a. *Liz asked to leave.*	b. *Liz asked Pat to leave.*
	ii	a. *Liz promised to phone at six.*	b. *Liz promised me to phone at six.*
	iii	a. *Liz helped to clear up the mess.*	b. *Liz helped me to clear up the mess.*

In [i] the simple version [a] has control by subject, while the complex [b] has control by object: it's a matter of Liz leaving in [a] and of Pat leaving in [b]. In [ii] both versions have control by subject, with Liz the one to phone. Finally, with *help* [b] has control by object (I cleared up the mess, with Liz's help), whereas [a] has a non-syntactic interpretation – though it might also be said to have implicit control by object: we understand Liz to have helped someone, and this someone cleared up the mess.[37]

[36] It is for this reason that the following verbs are listed separately in Classes 1 and 3:

Choose:	*They chose*$_1$ *not to answer.* (1Bi)	*They chose*$_2$ *Kim to lead the party.* (3Ai)
Consider:	*He considered*$_1$ *resigning.* (1Di)	*He considered*$_2$ *it to be a fraud.* (3Aii)
Dare:	*He wouldn't dare*$_2$ *(to) go alone.* (1Bi)	*I dare*$_3$ *you to repeat that.* (3Ai)
Elect:	*He elected*$_1$ *to take early retirement.* (1Bi)	*They elected*$_2$ *Kim to lead the party.* (3Ai)
Fear:	*He fears*$_1$ *to go out alone.* (1Ci)	*She is feared*$_2$ *to have drowned.* (3Aii)
Get:	*I never got*$_1$ *to speak to her.* (1Bi)	*We got*$_4$ *them to move / moving.* (causative, 3Bi)
Have:	*I have*$_1$ *to leave now.* (1Bii)	*He had*$_3$ *them paint it black.* (3Bi)
Keep:	*He keeps*$_1$ *interrupting.* (1Dii)	*They kept*$_2$ *him waiting.* (3Cii)
Know:	*You know*$_1$ *not to cut it that way.* (1Bi)	*He knew*$_2$ *it to be impossible.* (3Aii)
Move:	*They moved*$_1$ *to allay her fears.* (1Bi)	*What moved*$_2$ *him to behave so aggressively?* (3Ai)
Prepare:	*He prepared*$_1$ *to attack.* (1Bi)	*We're preparing*$_2$ *her to take over as head.* (3Ai)
Prove:	*It proved*$_1$ *to be impossible.* (1Bii)	*She proved*$_2$ *it to be impossible.* (3Aii)
Stop:	*It has stopped*$_1$ *raining.* (1Dii)	*They stopped*$_2$ *me taking part.* (3Ci)
Think:	*I didn't think*$_1$ *to check his credentials.* (1Bi)	*He was thought*$_2$ *to be trustworthy.* (3Aii)
Trouble:	*He didn't trouble*$_1$ *to close the door.* (1Bi)	*May I trouble*$_2$ *you to close the door?* (3Ai)
Will:	*It will*$_1$ *be over soon.* (1A)	*You can't will*$_2$ *her to do it.* (3Ai)

[37] This kind of interpretation does not hold for all instances of *help*. The problem is that the helper and helpee may be involved in the subordinate situation in a range of different ways. In [15iiib], Liz and I cleared up together, and in [a] Liz and some unspecified person(s) did so. In *The commotion helped me to escape unnoticed*, on the other hand, it was only me who escaped, the commotion having merely a supportive role. And at the other extreme, consider *The eyebrows help to keep sweat out of the eyes.* The eyebrows have the primary role in keeping the sweat out, so much so that in this case we don't really reconstruct an understood helpee at all.

No other verbs follow the patterns of *help* and *promise*, and indeed [iib] is rather marginal: many speakers find this unacceptable and it would be much more usual to use a finite complement here (*Liz promised me that she would phone at six*). The case with *ask* is complicated by the fact that, under very restrictive conditions, control by subject applies (again somewhat marginally) in the complex construction. Compare:

[16] i *Liz asked Pat to be allowed to leave.* [control by matrix subject]
ii *Liz asked Pat to be photographed with the children.* [control by matrix object]

In [i] we understand that Liz asked for permission to leave, but it is only complements like *to be allowed* and synonyms that permit matrix subject control in this way. In [ii], for example, we have a passive infinitival, but it still takes control by object, like the active [15ib]. *Beg*, *pray*, *petition*, and perhaps *request* exhibit the same behaviour as *ask* (*begged Pat to be allowed to leave* has matrix subject control, *begged Pat to be photographed* does not). *Pay* is similar but takes control by subject in the complex construction under somewhat different conditions – compare:

[17] i *They paid her \$100 to dance naked.* [control by object]
ii *They paid her \$100 to see her dance naked.* [control by subject]

Example [ii] is one of those where the non-finite clause falls at the boundary between catenative complement and purpose adjunct (see §4.3). The complement expressing the price paid is of course irrelevant to the issue of control: *They paid (\$100) to see it. Pledge* and *train* follow the pattern of [15i] with no possibility of control by subject in the complex construction:[38]

[18] a. *They have pledged to end the fighting.* b. *She pledged herself to support us.*

Ask and the others marked '(F)' also allow *for* – compare:

[19] a. *He asked Pat to be interviewed.* b. *He asked for Pat to be interviewed.*

In [a] *Pat* represents the goal of *ask* as well as the patient of *interview*, but in [b] only the latter. Note here the contrast between *ask* and a raising verb like *intend*: *He intended Jill to be interviewed* and *He intended for Jill to be interviewed* are equivalent, whereas [19a–b] differ sharply in meaning.

2Aii: plain-complex with raised object (*I expect to finish soon*; *I expect you to finish soon*)

[20] *claim* T_U *desire* T_M (F) *expect* T_W *mean*$_1$ T_M (F) *profess* T_U
reckon *wish* –P (F)

2Aiii: *for*-complex (*He longed to return home*; *He longed for her to return home*)

[21] *ache* *agree* P_X ?*aim* P_X *apply* *arrange* P_X T_W
be dying *burn* *burst* *can afford* N *care*
clamour *hope* P_X T_W *itch* *long* *opt*
pine *say*$_1$ T_S NS *wait* *yearn*

Most of these also take complements of the form *for* + NP: compare *She longed for him to be dismissed* and *She longed for his dismissal*. The exceptions are *agree* (*They agreed for it to be postponed* ~ *They agreed to/on/*for a postponement*), *can afford* (*I can't afford for*

[38] With *pledge* the complex commonly has a reflexive object, but not invariably: *The treaty pledges the Sultan to co-operate with a democratically elected government.*

it to be postponed ~ *I can't afford a postponement* / **for a postponement*), and informal *say* (*She said for you to come at six* – no comparable construction with NP).

2Aiv: oblique-complex (*He signalled to stand up*; *He signalled to us to stand up*)

[22] *motion* *signal*

These allow the prepositional complement to be omitted but recoverable from the context, with the understood oblique controlling the missing subject of the infinitival. In *He signalled to stand up* we understand that he signalled to some person or persons that they should stand up. The simple catenative construction is to be distinguished from the non-catenative construction with a purpose adjunct, as in *He signalled to show us he was wounded.*

Class 2B: *to*-infinitival or gerund-participial

Except where otherwise indicated, the simple construction has an ordinary subject and the plain-complex has a raised object.

2Bi: both form-types can be simple or complex; genitive allowed (*I'd hate to see it*; *I'd hate you to see it*; *I hate wasting time*; *I hate his / him wasting time*)

[23] *can bear* N *can stand* N *hate*$_2$ *like* PP *loathe*
love *prefer* T

The genitive version of the complex gerund-participial (*He didn't like my interrupting him*) is generally restricted to formal style, and even there many would use only the non-genitive. None of these verbs allows passivisation: **He'd be hated to see it.* Most verbs of liking and not liking belong in this class, but *detest* and for the most part *dislike* are restricted to the gerund-participial, and hence belong in Class 2C. For the past-participial with *like*, see §5.6.2.

2Bii: both form-types can be simple or complex; no genitive (*I need to read it*; *I need you to read it*; *My hair needs cutting*; *I need my hair cutting*)

[24] *deserve* F? *need*$_2$ *require* *want*$_1$

The gerund-participials here are concealed passives. There can be no passivisation of the matrix, except with *require* in the *to*-infinitival: *The form is required to be returned by 1 May.* The complex *to*-infinitival with *deserve* is somewhat marginal: ?*He didn't deserve for his request to be turned down.*

2Biii: *to*-infinitival simple or complex, gerund-participial restricted to one or the other (*I intend to tell / telling her*; *I intended him to hear me*)

[25] *intend* P_X T_M (F) *plan* P_X T_W (F) *want*$_2$ –P PP

With the first two the gerund-participial is permitted only in the simple construction, whereas with *want*$_2$ it is found only in the complex (for *It wants washing* is a concealed passive with *want*$_1$ "need"):

[26] i a. *I intended to read / reading it.* [simple]
b. *I intended you to read / *reading it.* [complex]
ii a. *I want them standing when the Minister enters.*
b. *I don't want you bringing your dog with you.*

The gerund-participial with *want*$_2$ generally has a progressive interpretation, but in non-affirmative contexts it can be non-progressive. Example [iia] is equivalent to *I want them to be standing when the Minister enters*, contrasting with non-progressive *I want them to stand when the Minister enters.* But in [iib] the meaning is "to bring", not "to be bringing".

In the complex *to*-infinitival *intend* takes a raised object, *plan* an ordinary one:

[27] i *I intended there to be more time for discussion.*
ii *We planned the seminar to coincide with her visit.*

2Biv: *to*-infinitival plain-complex, gerund-participial simple (*He admits it to have been a mistake*; *He admits breaking it*)

[28] *ackowledge* T_U *admit* T_U *confess* T_U *deny* T_U

The simple construction has an ordinary subject, the complex one a raised object. These verbs belong semantically with the verbs of cognition/saying in Class 3Aii, but differ syntactically in allowing a simple construction with a gerund-participial.

2Bv : *to*-infinitival plain-complex, gerund-participial simple or complex (*I remember him to be irascible*; *I remember telling you*; *I remember his/him telling you*)

[29]	*advise* NS T_M	*encourage* NS	*forget*$_2$ T_U –P	*recollect* T_U –P
	recommend NS T_M	*remember*$_2$ T_U	*report* T_U PP	

Both genitive and non-genitive forms are permitted in the complex gerund-participial, with the genitive as usual more formal. In the simple construction, *advise*, *encourage*, and *recommend* have a non-syntactic interpretation of the missing subject, while the others have subject control. Compare :

[30] i *I wouldn't recommend buying it.* [potential buyer unspecified]
ii *I remember buying it.* [buyer = speaker]

2C: gerund-participial only

All verbs in this class allow a genitive subject in the gerund-participial. The non-finite complements here are relatively close to objects: except where marked '–P_G' they can marginally be promoted to subject through passivisation (whereas the intervening NP never can). There are two subclasses to distinguish.

2Ci: simple construction has control by subject (*You risk being arrested*; *I won't risk them/their seeing us together*)

[31]	*abhor*	*anticipate*	*appreciate*	*begrudge*	*can help* N[39]
	celebrate	*chance*$_2$	*contemplate*	*countenance*	*defer*
	delay	*describe*	*detest*	*discuss*	?*dislike*
	?*dread*	*endure*	*enjoy*	*envisage*	*fancy*$_1$
	foresee	*imagine*$_1$	*mention*	*mind* N –P_G	*miss*
	put off	*recall*	*regret*$_2$	*relish*	*resent*
	risk	*tolerate*	*welcome*		

[39] Non-affirmative *can help* also occurs with *but* + bare infinitival: compare *I couldn't help overhearing* / *couldn't help but overhear what you were saying to Jill.*

2Cii: simple construction has non-syntactic interpretation of the missing subject (*It will* <u>*mean*</u> *getting up earlier*; *It will* <u>*mean*</u> *you/your getting up earlier*)

[32]					
	advocate	*deplore* P_G	*deprecate* P_G	*discourage* P_G	*facilitate*
	fancy$_2$ N	*include*	*involve* $-P_G$	*justify*	*mean*$_2$ $-P_G$
	necessitate	*oppose*	*save* $-P_G$	*suggest*	*support*
	understand$_1$				

5.4 Class 3: catenative verbs appearing only in the complex construction

Class 3A: infinitival but not gerund-participial

3Ai: plain-complex with ordinary object (*She* <u>*urged*</u> *me to go*)

[33]					
	accustom	*aid*	*appoint*	*assist*	*authorise*
	back	*badger*	*beckon*	*beseech*	*blackmail*
	bribe	*bring*	*bring up*	*caution*	*challenge*
	choose$_2$	*coax*	*command*	*commission*	*compel*
	condemn	*constrain*	*dare*$_3$	*defy*	*design*
	direct	*discipline*	*drive*	*elect*$_2$	*empower*
	entice	*entitle*	*entreat*	*equip*	*exhort*
	fit	*forbid*	*force*	*implore*	*incite*
	induce	*inspire*	*instruct*	*invite*	*lead*
	leave$_1$	*make out*	*move*$_2$	*nag*	*nominate*
	oblige	*persuade* T_S	*pester*	*prepare*$_2$	*press* (F)
	pressure	*program(me)*	*prod*	*prompt*	*provoke*
	push (F)	*remind*	*school*	*second*	*select*
	sentence	*spur on*	*stimulate*	*stir*	*summon*
	teach	*tell* T_S	*tempt*	*thank*	*trouble*$_2$–P
	trust	*urge*	*warn* T_S	*will*$_2$	

This class includes certain verbs of causation such as *compel* and *force* which we discuss with some semantically related verbs under Class 3B.

3Aii: plain-complex with raised object (*I* <u>*assumed*</u> *there to be a mistake in the instructions*)

[34]					
i	*accept*	*affirm*	*allege*	*announce*	*argue*
	ascertain	*assert*	*assume*	*attest*	*believe*
	certify	*concede*	*conceive*	*conclude*	*conjecture*
	consider$_2$	*declare*	*deduce*	*deem*	*demonstrate*
	discern	*disclose*	*discover*$_1$	*establish*	*estimate*
	fear$_2$ PP	*find*$_1$	*gather*	*grant*	*guarantee*
	guess	*hold*	*imagine*$_2$	*intuit*	*judge*
	know$_2$ (B) T_U	*note*	*presume*$_2$	*presuppose*	*proclaim*
	pronounce	*prove*$_2$	*recognise*	*represent*	*repute* +P
	reveal	*rule*	*rumour* +P	*say*$_2$ +P	*show*$_1$
	state	*stipulate*	*suppose*	*surmise*	*suspect*
	take	*think*$_2$	*tip*	*understand*$_2$	*verify*
ii	*allow*	*cause*	*enable*	*let* –P B	?*make* B
	?*order* T_M PP	*permit*			

The 'B' annotation for *make* applies only in the active: in the passive it takes a *to*-infinitival:

[35] i *They made us feel guilty.* [active + bare infinitival]
ii *We were made to feel guilty.* [passive + *to*-infinitival]

This class contains a rather large number of verbs of cognition or saying, illustrated in [34i], and a handful of verbs of permission, ordering, and causation, listed in [34ii]. The verbs in [34i], except for informal *tip*, also occur with an unmodalised finite complement: *I assumed that there was a mistake in the instructions.*[40] All allow perfect infinitivals (*I assumed there to have been a mistake*) and, in the absence of perfect marking, the time of the subordinate situation is the same as that of the matrix. This means that we cannot have, say, **I believe her to win tomorrow's semi-final* corresponding to finite *I believe that she will win tomorrow's semi-final.* In the non-perfect the infinitival normally has a stative interpretation: *be* is especially common. Matrix passives are always possible and tend to be more frequent than actives; with *say* and others marked '+P' passivisation is obligatory: *He is said to be dying* (not **They say him to be dying*).

Consider now the verbs of permission and ordering in [34ii] (we take up the causatives in the discussion of Class 3Bi). *Allow* appears in examples like:

[36] i *Will you allow me to audit your course?*
ii *We mustn't allow there to be any repetition of this behaviour.*
iii *The weather didn't allow us to finish the game.*

Example [i] illustrates a conventional way of requesting permission, which might suggest an interpretation where *me* is an argument of *allow*, with the role of recipient of permission. In [ii], however, *allow* is clearly behaving like our model raising verb *intend*: there is certainly no question here of giving someone permission to do something. This is even clearer in [iii], where we have an inanimate subject. *Allow* has a much more general meaning than "give permission", the core being something like "not prevent, make possible, enable", and it would be difficult to maintain that the construction was ambiguous in such a way that in *He allowed Kim to take all the credit for this achievement*, say, the object is raised (it's fair to assume that Kim didn't seek permission to take the credit) while in *He allowed Kim to audit my course* we have an ordinary object (with Kim seeking and receiving permission). For even where giving permission is apparently involved we still find equivalence between active and passive infinitival constructions:

[37] i *He allowed the postgraduates to audit the course.*
ii *He allowed the course to be audited by the postgraduates.* } [voice-neutral]

The recipient of permission can be encoded with *give permission*, but even here it need not be, so that we have a contrast between *He gave them permission to audit the course* (recipient encoded) and *He gave permission for them to audit the course* (recipient not encoded). This contrast is not available with *allow*, which is best treated as a raising verb in all cases; it does not encode the giving of permission to anyone, though it

[40] It has been suggested that the finite and non-finite constructions are not entirely equivalent, that *I believe him to be telling the truth*, for example, is more acceptable than *I believe him to be lying* (by reason of being compatible with *I believe him*), but we are sceptical about the validity of a distinction along these lines.

may, in favourable circumstances, trigger an implicature that permission is given to the object-referent. *Permit* and *let* behave in essentially the same way. So indeed do the modals *can* and *may* in their deontic sense, except that here only one argument is encoded: the raised complement is thus subject, not object. *You can come in now* may be interpreted in context as "I give you permission to come in now", but the giver and receiver of permission are not encoded as arguments of *can*.

Order has a meaning comparable in specificity to *give permission* rather than *allow*: it involves issuing some (normally verbal) order. But the object clearly doesn't encode the recipient of the order in examples like *He ordered the documents to be destroyed*: this has a raised object and is equivalent to the finite construction *He ordered that the documents be destroyed.* Nevertheless, *order* differs from *allow* in that the cases where the object clearly does not represent the recipient of the order predominantly have passive infinitivals.[41] Thus whereas we can say *He ordered that the data be freely available to all interested parties*, the infinitival *#He ordered the data to be available to all interested parties* is anomalous (since it requires us to take the data as recipient of the order).

With a human object and active infinitival there is a strong implicature that the object represents the recipient, so that *He ordered Kim to unlock the safe*, say, is not equivalent to *He ordered that Kim unlock the safe. Command* is more straightforward in that it does not normally allow a raised object with a passive: *#He commanded the documents to be destroyed.*

3Aiii: oblique-complex (*Kim appealed to them to release the hostages*)

[38] *appeal* [*to*] *bank* [*on*] *count* [*on*] *depend* [*on*] *keep* on_2 [*at*] *rely* [*on*]

These take a catenative complement only in combination with a prepositional complement; in addition *call* uniquely occurs either in this construction or in the *for*-complex: cf. [9iia–b] of §3 (*He called for Ed to be sacked*; *He called on Ed to resign*).

Class 3B: infinitival, gerund-participial, or past-participial

Verbs in this class all take non-genitives in the gerund-participial. We distinguish two subclasses on the basis of matrix passivisation.

3Bi: no matrix passivisation (*I got them to talk / talking*; *I got my car repaired*)

[39] get_4 $have_3$ B

These belong semantically with the verbs of causation, but occur in a wider range of constructions than the others, which are found in classes 3Ai and 3Aii: we consider them all together here. The distinction between ordinary and raised complements is seen in:

[40] i *They forced/compelled Kim to unlock the safe.* [ordinary object]
ii *This caused both of us to overlook the inconsistency.* [raised object]

Force and *compel* (3Ai) impose selectional restrictions on the object and assign an agentive role to the covert subject of the infinitival: in [i] force/compulsion is applied directly

[41] Not exclusively, however: cf. *France has ordered nuclear testing to resume.* Occasional examples of this kind are also found with *instruct*: *I instructed prison routine to continue as normal.*

to Kim and the verbs clearly belong with our model verb *persuade. Cause* and *enable*, on the other hand, belong equally clearly with the raising verbs (3Aii): note, for example, the equivalence between [ii] and *This caused the inconsistency to be overlooked by both of us*; the second argument in [ii] is thus the whole event of our overlooking the inconsistency, and there is no direct relation between the matrix verb and its object. *Make, get,* and *have* are less clear-cut. *Make* could substitute with little effect on the meaning both for *force/compel* in [i] and for *cause* in [ii]. It does not readily take a passive infinitival, but [?]*Pat made both candidates be interviewed by Kim* seems to differ in propositional meaning as well as acceptability from *Pat made Kim interview both candidates*, suggesting that it takes an ordinary object, like *force/compel.* On the other hand, it can take a dummy object, certainly extrapositional *it*, as in *He made it appear that he had been acting under duress*, where it is difficult to see any direct relation between verb and object. *Make* thus seems to allow either control by object or raised construal, with a good deal of indeterminacy between the two. *Get* allows a wider range of objects than *force/compel* (cf. *He finally got the car to start*, where the car's role is non-agentive), but it cannot take dummy *there* as object (cf. **He finally got there to be a reconciliation*). As for voice, we have:

[41] i *He got a specialist to examine his son.*
ii *He got his son to be examined by a specialist.*
iii *He got his son examined by a specialist.*

Examples [i] and [ii] are not equivalent and *get* here clearly takes an ordinary object (as also with a gerund-participial). But [iii] is not an alternant of [ii]: *get* takes a raised object in the past-participial construction (which has no active counterpart). With *have* the analogue of [ii] is not acceptable (**He had his son be examined by a specialist*), and we have equivalence between *He had a specialist examine his son* and *He had his son examined by a specialist*; this indicates a raised object, which ties in with the fact that *have* is also used with a non-causative "undergo" sense: *He had the police call round in the middle of the night to question him about his secretary's disappearance*, where the visit was something that happened to him rather than something he arranged – and where there would seem to be no direct semantic relation between verb and object.

3Bii: matrix passive allowed (*I heard them arrive/arriving*; *I heard the window broken*)

[42]	*feel* T_U (B)	*hear* T_U (B)	*notice* T_U B	*observe* T_U (B)	*overhear* (B)
	see$_1$ T_U (B)	*watch* B			

These verbs, together with *smell* from Class 3Cii below, are the verbs of sensory perception. All take bare infinitivals, while those where the 'B' is parenthesised take a *to*-infinitival as well. For *see* we have the following possibilities:

[43]		a.	b.
	i	a. *We saw Kim leave the bank.*	b. **Kim was seen leave the bank.*
	ii	a. *We saw Kim leaving the bank.*	b. *Kim was seen leaving the bank.*
	iii	a. *We saw Spurs beaten by United.*	b. [?]*Spurs were seen beaten by United.*
	iv	a. *We saw him to be an impostor.*	b. *He was seen to be an impostor.*

We put the *to*-infinitival last because this does not represent the primary sense: it is not a matter of sensory perception but of mental inference. In this construction, *see* behaves like the verbs of cognition/saying (Class 3Aii), following their pattern of favouring a matrix passive and the verb *be* in the subordinate clause, of allowing the perfect (*He was seen to have altered the figures*), and of alternating with the finite construction (*We saw that he was an imposter*).

The primary sense, illustrated in [43i–iii], involves two arguments, an experiencer and a stimulus (the situation perceived): *Kim* in [i–ii] thus does not represent an argument of *see*. We demonstrated this for the gerund-participial construction in §3.2.2, but it holds for the other form-types too; this is why there is equivalence between [iiia] and *We saw United beat Spurs.*

The gerund-participial in [43ii] has progressive meaning: in [i] we saw the whole event of Kim's leaving the bank, in [ii] a segment of it – the contrast is the same as that between *Kim left the bank* and *Kim was leaving the bank.* The progressive auxiliary *be* cannot be used (**We saw Kim be leaving the bank*), and passive *be* is likewise omitted to give [iiia] instead of **We saw Spurs be beaten by United.*[42]

The bare infinitival does not allow matrix passivisation, as is evident from [43ib]. The *to*-infinitival, however, has a wider range of use in the passive than in the active:

[44] a. **We saw Kim to leave the bank.* b. *Kim was seen to leave the bank.*

It is therefore tempting to see [44b] as filling the gap created by the ungrammaticality of [43ib] (parallel to the case with *make*: *We made Kim leave the bank*; **Kim was made leave the bank*; *Kim was made to leave the bank*). Yet it is doubtful if the sense is quite the same: [44b] has at least a trace of the cognitive component of meaning noted above for [43iv]. Compare, for example:

[45] i *They had seen him drive, so everyone decided to go by bus.*
ii *He had been seen to drive, so everyone decided to go by bus.*

Notice that [i] is perfectly coherent, but [ii] is not. In [i] they had perceived the event, and hence the manner of his driving, and we infer that it was the latter that made them decide to go by bus. But in [ii] it is the fact of his driving that had been registered, and this doesn't provide an obvious reason for them to go by bus.

None of the other sense verbs shows quite the same range as *see*. The closest is *feel* but construction [43iii] is here virtually restricted to reflexives or body parts (*I felt myself/my leg grabbed from behind*). With *hear* and *overhear* [iv] is virtually excluded in the active (**We'd heard him to be an impostor*) and in the passive we have again the problem of distinguishing between the senses of [i] and [iv]: we do not have **He was heard to be an impostor* (where *see* would be quite normal), but only examples like *He was heard to lock the door*, which is very close to *They heard him lock the door.*[43] *Watch* wholly excludes the *to*-infinitival, whether active or passive. *Notice* and *observe* are hardly possible in [iii], and *notice* is also marginal in [iv]. *Smell* is generally restricted to [ii], and hence is listed in Class 3Cii below; it combines predominantly with *burn* (*I can smell something burning*).

[42] *Get*, however, is perfectly possible: *We saw Spurs get annihilated by United.*

[43] With a finite complement *hear* characteristically involves hearing something said; it also occurs in the fixed expressions *hear say/tell*, a simple catenative construction with contextual construal.

Class 3C: gerund-participial only

3Ci: genitive possible (*They prevented us/our speaking to her*)

[46]	*excuse* –P	*forgive* –P	*pardon* –P	*preclude* –P	*prevent*
	prohibit –P	?*stop*$_2$			

These verbs have alternants containing prepositions: *for* in the case of *excuse, forgive, pardon,* and *from* with *preclude, prevent, prohibit, stop*:

[47] i a. *Forgive me/my saying so, but . . .* b. *Forgive me for saying so, but . . .*
ii a. *He prevented us/our seeing her.* b. *He prevented us from seeing her.*

Passivisation is restricted to the prepositional construction (*He was never forgiven for abandoning his children*), except very marginally with *prevent* and *stop* (?*She was prevented/stopped writing to us*). *Stop* is a questionable member of this class because it does not generally allow a genitive in the [a] construction (**He stopped our seeing her*); moreover it has a wider range of meaning in [a] than in [b]. In the [a] construction we find the two meanings illustrated in:

[48] i *We must stop him coming back tomorrow.* ["not allow, prevent"]
ii *They stopped us playing before we had finished the first set.* ["made us stop"]

Construction [47iib], with *from*, generally yields the "prevent" meaning; *from* can thus be inserted in [48i] but not in [48ii]. In the second sense *stop* belongs with *keep*$_2$ and *start*$_2$ below (3Cii) as a causative of an aspectual verb.

In [47i] it is a matter of forgiving the offence in [a], the offender in [b], but the difference is negligible. In [47ii] the [a] version involves preventing an event, while [b] is more problematic. The [b] structure suggests that *us* is an argument of *prevent*, but some speakers allow dummy *there* here, %*We must prevent there from being any repetition of this error*. The semantically empty *there* cannot be an argument and hence must be a raised object, but the construction is unique in that the raised object precedes a PP rather than a non-finite VP; it is probably to be accounted for in terms of a blend between the [a] and [b] constructions.

3Cii: no genitive (*I caught them/*their smoking*)

[49]	*catch*	*discover*$_2$	*depict*	*envy* –P	*find*$_2$
	keep$_2$	*leave*$_2$	*picture*	*portray*	*see*$_2$ –P
	set	*show*$_2$	*smell*	*start*$_2$ –P	

There are several subgroups here. *Catch, discover,* and *find* clearly take ordinary objects, as do *depict, picture, portray,* and *show*; with all of these the gerund-participial has a progressive interpretation. *Leave* is more problematic: *I left them quarrelling among themselves* entails that I left them, suggesting an ordinary object; but *The quarrel left me feeling insecure* does not entail that the quarrel left me: the meaning here is approximately "result in", suggesting a raised object. *Keep, set,* and *start* have causative meanings; they allow a quite limited range of non-finites, especially the last two: they do not accept passives (**He kept them being washed*; **We started them being vaccinated*), and generally require dynamic situations (*It started them talking / *liking her*). *See*$_2$ (which usually occurs with *can*) is voice-neutral (*I can't see Kim beating Pat* = *I can't see Pat being beaten by Kim*), but differs from *see*$_1$ in not allowing passivisation: it is like *imagine*$_1$ (2Ci) and *fancy*$_2$ (2Cii) except that it is restricted to complex constructions.

5.5 Index to the classification

The following index includes all the verbs and verbal idioms mentioned in §§5.2–5.4, showing the class to which they belong.

abhor 2Ci	*accept* 3Aii	*accustom* 3Ai	*ache* 2Aiii	*acknowledge* 2Biv
admit 2Biv	*advise* 2Bv	*advocate* 2Cii	*affect* 1Bi	*affirm* 3Aii
agree 2Aiii	*aid* 3Ai	*aim* 2Aiii	*allege* 3Aii	*allow* 3Aii
announce 3Aii	*anticipate* 2Ci	*appeal* 3Aiii	*appear* 1Bii	*apply* 2Aiii
appoint 3Ai	*appreciate* 2Ci	*argue* 3Aii	*arrange* 2Aiii	*ascertain* 3Aii
ask 2Ai	*aspire* 1Bi	*assert* 3Aii	*assist* 3Ai	*assume* 3Aii
attempt 1Ci	*attest* 3Aii	*authorise* 3Ai	*avoid* 1Di	*back* 3Ai
badger 3Ai	*bank* 3Aiii	*be*$_1$ 1Bii	*be*$_2$ 1Dii	*be*$_3$ 1E
be dying 2Aiii	*bear* 2Bi	*beckon* 3Ai	*beg* 2Ai	*begin* 1Cii
begrudge 2Ci	*believe* 3Aii	*beseech* 3Ai	*blackmail* 3Ai	*bother* 1Ci
bribe 3Ai	*bring* 3Ai	*bring up* 3Ai	*burn* 2Aiii	*burst* 2Aiii
can 1A	*can afford* 2Aiii	*can bear* 2Bi	*can help* 2Ci	*can stand* 2Bi
care 2Aiii	*catch* 3Cii	*cause* 3Aii	*caution* 3Ai	*cease* 1Cii
celebrate 2Ci	*certify* 3Aii	*challenge* 3Ai	*chance*$_1$ 1Bii	*chance*$_2$ 2Ci
choose$_1$ 1Bi	*choose*$_2$ 3Ai	*claim* 2Aii	*clamour* 2Aiii	*coax* 3Ai
come$_1$ 1Bii	*come*$_2$ 1Di	*command* 3Ai	*commence* 1Cii	*commission* 3Ai
compel 3Ai	*complete* 1Di	*concede* 3Aii	*conceive* 3Aii	*conclude* 3Aii
condemn 3Ai	*condescend* 1Bi	*confess* 2Biv	*conjecture* 3Aii	*consent* 1Bi
consider$_1$ 1Di	*consider*$_2$ 3Aii	*constrain* 3Ai	*contemplate* 2Ci	*continue* 1Cii
contrive 1Bi	*count* 3Aiii	*countenance* 2Ci	*dare*$_1$ 1A	*dare*$_2$ 1Bi
dare$_3$ 3Ai	*decide* 1Bi	*declare* 3Aii	*decline* 1Bi	*deduce* 3Aii
deem 3Aii	*defer* 2Ci	*defy* 3Ai	*deign* 1Bi	*delay* 2Ci
demand 1Bi	*demonstrate* 3Aii	*deny* 2Biv	*depend* 3Aiii	*depict* 3Cii
deplore 2Cii	*deprecate* 2Cii	*describe* 2Ci	*deserve* 2Bii	*design* 3Ai
desire 2Aii	*determine* 1Bi	*detest* 2Ci	*direct* 3Ai	*discern* 3Aii
discipline 3Ai	*disclose* 3Aii	*discontinue* 1Di	*discourage* 2Cii	*discover*$_1$ 3Aii
discover$_2$ 3Cii	*discuss* 2Ci	*disdain* 1Bi	*dislike* 2Ci	*do* 1A
dread 2Ci	*drive* 3Ai	*elect*$_1$ 1Bi	*elect*$_2$ 3Ai	*empower* 3Ai
enable 3Aii	*encourage* 2Bv	*end up* 1Dii	*endeavour* 1Bi	*endure* 2Ci
enjoy 2Ci	*entice* 3Ai	*entitle* 3Ai	*entreat* 3Ai	*envisage* 2Ci
envy 3Cii	*equip* 3Ai	*escape* 1Di	*establish* 3Aii	*estimate* 3Aii
evade 1Di	*excuse* 3Ci	*exhort* 3Ai	*expect* 2Aii	*facilitate* 2Cii
fail 1Bii	*fancy*$_1$ 2Ci	*fancy*$_2$ 2Cii	*fear*$_1$ 1Ci	*fear*$_2$ 3Aii
feel 3Bii	*find*$_1$ 3Aii	*find*$_2$ 3Cii	*finish* 1Di	*fit* 3Ai
forbid 3Ai	*force* 3Ai	*foresee* 2Ci	*forget*$_1$ 1Bi	*forget*$_2$ 2Bv
forgive 3Ci	*gather* 3Aii	*get*$_1$ 1Bi	*get*$_2$ 1Di	*get*$_3$ 1E
get$_4$ 3Bi	*go* 1Di	*go on*$_1$ 1Bi	*go on*$_2$ 1Dii	*grant* 3Aii
grow 1Bi	*guarantee* 3Aii	*guess* 3Aii	*had better* 1A	*happen* 1Bii
hasten 1Bi	*hate*$_1$ 1Bi	*hate*$_2$ 2Bi	*have*$_1$ 1Bii	*have*$_2$ 1E
have$_3$ 3Bi	*have got* 1Bii	*hear* 3Bii	*help* 2Ai	*hesitate* 1Bi
hold 3Aii	*hope* 2Aiii	*imagine*$_1$ 2Ci	*imagine*$_2$ 3Aii	*implore* 3Ai
incite 3Ai	*include* 2Cii	*induce* 3Ai	*inspire* 3Ai	*instruct* 3Ai
intend 2Biii	*intuit* 3Aii	*invite* 3Ai	*involve* 2Cii	*itch* 2Aiii

judge 3Aii	*justify* 2Cii	*keep*$_1$ 1Dii	*keep*$_2$ 3Cii	*keep on*$_1$ 1Dii
keep on$_2$ 3Aiii	*know*$_1$ 1Bi	*know*$_2$ 3Aii	*lead* 3Ai	*learn* 1Bi
leave$_1$ 3Ai	*leave*$_2$ 3Cii	*let* 3Aii	*like* 2Bi	*live* 1Bi
loathe 2Bi	*long* 2Aiii	*look*$_1$ 1Bi	*look*$_2$ 1Bii	*love* 2Bi
make 3Aii	*make out* 3Ai	*manage* 1Bi	*may* 1A	*mean*$_1$ 2Aii
mean$_2$ 2Cii	*mention* 2Ci	*mind* 2Ci	*miss* 2Ci	*motion* 2Aiv
move$_1$ 1Bi	*move*$_2$ 3Ai	*must* 1A	*nag* 3Ai	*necessitate* 2Cii
need$_1$ 1A	*need*$_2$ 2Bii	*neglect* 1Ci	*nominate* 3Ai	*note* 3Aii
notice 3Bii	*oblige* 3Ai	*observe* 3Bii	*offer* 1Bi	*omit* 1Bi
oppose 2Cii	*opt* 2Aiii	*order* 3Aii	*ought* 1Bii	*overhear* 3Bii
pardon 3Ci	*pay* 2Ai	*permit* 3Aii	*persuade* 3Ai	*pester* 3Ai
petition 2Ai	*picture* 3Cii	*pine* 2Aiii	*plan* 2Biii	*pledge* 2Ai
plot 1Bi	*portray* 3Cii	*postpone* 1Di	*practise* 1Di	*pray* 2Ai
preclude 3Ci	*prefer* 2Bi	*prepare*$_1$ 1Bi	*prepare*$_2$ 3Ai	*press* 3Ai
pressure 3Ai	*presume*$_1$ 1Bi	*presume*$_2$ 3Aii	*presuppose* 3Aii	*pretend* 1Bi
prevent 3Ci	*proceed* 1Bi	*proclaim* 3Aii	*prod* 3Ai	*profess* 2Aii
programme 3Ai	*prohibit* 3Ci	*promise*$_1$ 1Bii	*promise*$_2$ 2Ai	*prompt* 3Ai
pronounce 3Aii	*propose* 1Ci	*prove*$_1$ 1Bii	*prove*$_2$ 3Aii	*provoke* 3Ai
push 3Ai	*put off* 2Ci	*quit* 1Di	*recall* 2Ci	*reckon* 2Aii
recognise 3Aii	*recollect* 2Bv	*recommend* 2Bv	*refuse* 1Bi	*regret*$_1$ 1Bi
regret$_2$ 2Ci	*relish* 2Ci	*rely* 3Aiii	*remember*$_1$ 1Bi	*remember*$_2$ 2Bv
remind 3Ai	*repent* 1Di	*report* 2Bv	*represent* 3Aii	*repute* 3Aii
request 2Ai	*require* 2Bii	*resent* 2Ci	*resist* 1Di	*resolve* 1Bi
resume 1Di	*reveal* 3Aii	*risk* 2Ci	*rule* 3Aii	*rumour* 3Aii
save 2Cii	*say*$_1$ 2Aiii	*say*$_2$ 3Aii	*school* 3Ai	*scorn* 1Ci
second 3Ai	*see*$_1$ 3Bii	*see*$_2$ 3Cii	*seek* 1Bi	*seem* 1Bii
select 3Ai	*sentence* 3Ai	*serve* 1Bi	*set* 3Cii	*shall* 1A
show$_1$ 3Aii	*show*$_2$ 3Cii	*signal* 2Aiv	*smell* 3Cii	*spur on* 3Ai
stand 1Bi	*start*$_1$ 1Cii	*start*$_2$ 3Cii	*state* 3Aii	*stimulate* 3Ai
stipulate 3Aii	*stir* 3Ai	*stop*$_1$ 1Dii	*stop*$_2$ 3Ci	*strain* 1Bi
strive 1Bi	*struggle* 1Bi	*suggest* 2Cii	*summon* 3Ai	*support* 2Cii
suppose 3Aii	*surmise* 3Aii	*survive* 1Bi	*suspect* 3Aii	*swear* 1Bi
take 3Aii	*teach* 3Ai	*tell* 3Ai	*tempt* 3Ai	*tend* 1Bii
thank 3Ai	*think*$_1$ 1Bi	*think*$_2$ 3Aii	*threaten*$_1$ 1Bi	*threaten*$_2$ 1Bii
tip 3Aii	*tolerate* 2Ci	*train* 2Ai	*trouble*$_1$ 1Bi	*trouble*$_2$ 3Ai
trust 3Ai	*try*$_1$ 1Bi	*try*$_2$ 1Di	*turn out* 1Bii	*understand*$_1$ 2Cii
understand$_2$ 3Aii	*undertake* 1Bi	*urge* 3Ai	*use* 1Bii	*venture* 1Bi
verify 3Aii	*volunteer* 1Bi	*vow* 1Bi	*wait* 2Aiii	*want*$_1$ 2Bii
want$_2$ 2Biii	*warn* 3Ai	*watch* 3Bii	*welcome* 2Ci	*will*$_1$ 1A
will$_2$ 3Ai	*wish* 2Aii	*would rather* 1A	*yearn* 2Aiii	

5.6 Further remarks on the form-types

5.6.1 *To*-infinitival vs gerund-participial

Which form-type(s) a particular catenative selects must be specified lexically for that verb: we cannot assign distinct meanings to the form-types and treat the selection as semantically determined. On the other hand, the selection is not random: verbs with similar meanings tend to select the same form-types, and where a verb allows both major form-types we very often find a difference in meaning that is at least partly motivated by their general characteristics.

We have noted (§1.4) that infinitival *to* derives historically from the preposition *to* and that while it has quite clearly undergone a syntactic change such that in this use it is no longer a preposition, certain aspects of its infinitival subordinator use reflect its origin. Prepositional *to* is characteristically associated with a goal, and a metaphorical association between *to*-infinitivals and goals is to be found in the fact that they commonly involve temporal projection into the future, as with the complements of *ask, choose, consent, hesitate, order, persuade, promise, resolve, strive, tell, threaten,* and countless other catenatives. Linked with this is the modal feature of potentiality. The gerund-participial, by contrast, is commonly associated with what is current and actual, as in *They enjoy walking, She finished working, He practised speaking with an American accent,* and it is plausible to see this as connected with the nominal source of most gerund-participial complements. But it must be emphasised that we are talking here of historically motivated tendencies and associations, not constant elements of meaning.

Catenative verbs that license both form-types

From the point of view of Present-day English the main interest is in those cases where the same verb allows both form-types. In some cases there is no discernible difference between the constructions, while elsewhere we find a variety of differences bearing some relation to the above broad outline.

(a) No discernible difference

This applies with *bother, intend, plan, propose*:

		a.		b.
[50]	i	a.	*He didn't bother to tell us.*	b. *He didn't bother telling us.*
	ii	a.	*He intends to leave tomorrow.*	b. *He intends leaving tomorrow.*

Note that [50iib] shows that futurity is not incompatible with a gerund-participial. *Attempt* also belongs in this group (contrast *try* in [56] below), though the gerund-participial is rather rare: *She attempted to walk / walking without the stick.*

(b) Aspectual verbs

With the subset of aspectual verbs given in Class 1cii, there is again often no perceptible difference in meaning: *He continued to see / seeing her every Sunday.* But, especially with *begin* and *start*, the constructions are not always wholly equivalent or interchangeable:

		a.		b.
[51]	i	a.	*I began to understand how she felt.*	b. ?*I began understanding how she felt.*
	ii	a.	?*Don't start to tell me how to run my life.*	b. *Don't start telling me how to run my life.*

The gerund-participial tends to suggest ongoing activity. In [i] the understand situation is too static for the gerund-participial: compare *She began explaining how she felt.* This is why the gerund-participial is not possible in the existential construction: **There began being some grounds for hope of an improvement.* The salient context for [ii] is one where you have already said something which I interpret as telling me how to run my life and in this case the infinitival is not appropriate: compare *If it starts to rain / raining, bring the washing in*, where either form-type is appropriate.[44]

(c) Verbs of liking (and not liking)

[52] i a. *I like to stay home at weekends.* b. *I like staying home at weekends.*
ii a. *I'd like to be a politician.* b. *I'd like being a politician.*

With [i] there are many contexts where [a] and [b] would be equally appropriate, but there are also some favouring one or the other. Suppose you ask me to go bushwalking next week-end but I wish to decline: [a] would here be more appropriate than [b]. Conversely if I am currently enjoying a week-end at home [b] is more appropriate than [a].

The infinitival is more associated with change, the gerund-participial with actuality. Thus someone who has recently turned forty or got married might say *I like being forty* or *I like being married.* An infinitival would be strange here, suggesting repeated changes from not being forty or married to being forty or married. In this case the meaning is close to that of *enjoy*, which only allows gerund-participials.[45] *Would like*, by contrast, projects into the future and resembles a verb of wanting, with a strong preference for the infinitival, as in [iia]; [iib] is possible, but the interpretation is roughly "I'd like/enjoy the life of a politician". If we change the example to *I'd like to start the meeting a little earlier this week* the gerund-participial becomes quite implausible: *I'd like starting the meeting a little earlier* suggests that the starting is itself something to be enjoyed, which is an odd idea.

Hate with a *to*-infinitival has an idiomatic use seen in

[53] *I hate$_1$ to tell you this, but your battery is flat.*

This can be thought of as involving projection into the immediate future: "I'm going to tell you, though I hate having to do so". What is special about this use (virtually confined to the 1st person) is the combination of simple present tense in the matrix and single dynamic event in the complement – contrast [52ia], where we have repetition of staying home; other verbs of liking and not liking do not allow this pattern, though it is found with adjectives: *I am happy / *like to tell you that you've passed your test* (cf. also *regret* in [56] below).

(d) Memory verbs

[54] a. *I remembered$_1$ to lock up.* b. *I remembered$_2$ locking up.*

In [a] the locking up is simultaneous with the remembering – but I remembered some kind of prior obligation to lock up and hence there is projection into the future with respect to that implicit earlier time. In [iib], however, I simply remembered some actual past event. *Forget* behaves in the same way, but *recollect* takes only the second form and meaning.

[44] It is sometimes said that the infinitival is preferred in examples like *I had just begun to sign / signing the cheque when he snatched it away*, where there is hardly time for ongoing activity, but many speakers find the two types equally acceptable here.

[45] *Detest* and for the most part *dislike* likewise are restricted to the gerund-participial.

(e) Gerund-participial expressing progressive meaning

[55] a. *I've finally got the program to work.* b. *I've finally got the program working.*

Here [a] entails that the program now works, [b] that it is now working: the difference of meaning here is therefore aspectual, with the infinitival non-progressive and the gerund-participial progressive. Compare also *want* in [26ii] – though *want* differs from *get* in that we can also have a progressive infinitival: *I want them to be standing when the Minister enters*, but not **I've finally got the program to be working.* This semantic contrast is more often found between the gerund-participial and a bare infinitival, as with the sense verbs of Class 3Bii and *have*$_3$ of 3Bi. The gerund-participial also has a progressive interpretation after certain verbs that don't take infinitivals: *catch*, *discover*$_2$, *find*$_2$, *smell* (from Class 3Cii).

(f) Some individual cases

[56] i	a. *She tried*$_1$ *to open the window.*	b. *She tried*$_2$ *opening the window.*
ii	a. *They fear*$_1$ *to go out at night.*	b. *They fear*$_1$ *going out at night.*
iii	a. *He scorns to compromise.*	b. *He scorns compromising.*
iv	a. *I regret*$_1$ *to inform you that . . .*	b. *I regret*$_2$ *telling her that . . .*
v	a. *They reported him to have left the safe unlocked.*	b. *They reported his leaving the safe unlocked.*

Try$_1$ ("endeavour") involves effort towards a goal: the opening is only potential; *try*$_2$ ("test the effectiveness of") indicates actual activity: she opened the window to see whether this would achieve the desired result. With *fear* infinitival [a] involves an element of volition/intentionality: [a] implicates that they don't/won't go out, while the gerund-participial [b] lacks this meaning and is comparable to an NP object (*They fear an attack*). Similarly [iiia] conveys that he doesn't/won't compromise, while in [b] the complement is more nominalised (cf. *He scorns compromise*) and arguably the missing subject is interpreted non-syntactically, i.e. it is a matter of compromising in general rather than specifically on his part. *Regret* usually takes a gerund-participial, describing some actual present state or past situation, as in [b]; with the *to*-infinitival, characteristically found with 1st person simple present followed by a verb of informing (cf. *hate* in [53] above), the subordinate situation follows (albeit immediately) the expression of regret. *Report* in [v] is one of the few verbs of cognition/saying that allows a contrast between the two main form-types; the difference is that [b] presents the report as true while [a] is non-committal – a difference that relates to that between actual and potential, and which also reflects the greater similarity of the gerund-participial to an NP, for *They reported his failure to lock the safe* likewise presupposes that he failed to lock it.

The doubl-*ing* constraint

Some verbs that license gerund-participial complements cannot themselves occur in the gerund-participle form when they have such a complement. Compare:

[57] i	a. *They started quarrelling.*	b. **They are starting quarrelling.*
ii	a. *The lawn needs mowing.*	b. **The lawn is always needing mowing.*
iii	a. *We considered buying one.*	b. *We are considering buying one.*

The succession of gerund-participles in [ib/iib] is excluded by what is known as the 'doubl-*ing* constraint'. As evident from [iiib], it applies to only a subset of catenative verbs – a small subset, in fact. The clearest cases are aspectual verbs such as *begin, cease, continue, start, stop*, and verbs taking concealed passives, like *need* in [ii]. We should probably also include others, such as *intend*, but there is a good deal of variation between speakers as to their acceptance of the [b] construction. We noted in §1.1 that gerund-participials cannot have the progressive auxiliary *be* as head (**They accused him of being running away when the alarm sounded*), and this can be seen as a special case of the constraint.

5.6.2 The minor form-types: bare infinitivals and past-participials

Bare infinitivals

Only a relatively small number of catenatives take bare infinitivals: the auxiliaries in Class 1A (the modals and supportive *do*), the sensory perception verbs (3Bii), and *have, let*, and *make* among the causatives. In addition a few are found either with or without *to*: *ought*, *dare*$_2$, *know*, and *help*.

Know takes a bare infinitival only in the perfect and with a special sense:

[58] i *I'd never known him (to) lose his temper before.*
ii *I know him to be thoroughly reliable.*

In [i] it's a matter of knowledge based on more or less direct experience of his losing his temper. The bare infinitival here is characteristic of BrE: AmE requires *to* in [i] as well as [ii].[46]

With *help* some speakers restrict the bare infinitival to cases of relatively direct assistance – compare:

[59] i *He helped me (to) finish on time by doing the bibliography for me.*
ii *He helped me to finish on time by taking the children away for the week-end.*

In [i] he actually did some of the work, whereas in [ii] he enabled me to do it myself. But it is questionable how widely shared such judgements are: many speakers would allow a bare infinitival in [ii] no less than [i], and there is certainly no clear-cut distinction between direct and indirect help.

The bare infinitival is virtually restricted to constructions where the matrix is active. *Have* and *let* do not passivise with infinitival complements, while the other transitive catenatives always take *to* in the passive: *He had never been known to lose his temper before.* With *make*, *to* is restricted to the passive: *They made her regret it* ~ *She was made to regret it*; for the relation between *They saw him pocket the key* and *He was seen to pocket the key*, see the discussion of Class 3Bii.

Past-participials

In the simple construction these occur with just three verbs (Class 1E): the perfect marker *have* and the passive markers *be* and *get*. In the complex construction they are found, as

[46] Some speakers of BrE also allow a bare infinitival with *find* with a sense like "see" or "notice": *Outside you will find Wren create new green dimensions with sensitive landscaping that creates a community and not just a row of houses.*

passives, with a fairly small subset of verbs taking infinitivals:

[60] i Most of the sense verbs (3Bii) – *I heard the window broken.*
ii *Get*$_4$ and *have*$_3$ (3Bi): *She got/had the house painted; I had my wallet stolen.*
iii *Like* from 2Bi, *want*$_2$ from 2Biii, *report* from 2Bv, *fear*$_2$ and *order* from 3Aii; here the past-participial is an alternant of a passive *to*-infinitival: *He'd like / wants them (to be) killed humanely; The captain was reported (to have been) killed; They are feared (to have been) abducted; He ordered it (to be) destroyed.*
iv *Need*$_2$ and *want*$_1$ from 2Bii as an alternant of the concealed passive: *He needs/ wants his hair %cut/ cutting*, but the past-participials are restricted to certain regional dialects such as Scottish.

Except with *report*, *fear*, and *order*, past-participials are wholly or virtually restricted to occurrence with an active matrix: **They were wanted killed; ?The door was heard slammed.* Past-participial complements are to be distinguished from adjectival passives (Ch. 16, §10.1.3), which are found with most verbs taking adjectival predicative complements: *He remained mistrusted by his colleagues; She considered it superseded*, etc.

6 Hollow non-finite clauses

6.1 General properties

Hollow non-finite clauses are clauses other than relatives or open interrogatives where some non-subject NP is missing but recoverable from an antecedent NP or nominal. The missing NP is normally object of the verb or object of a preposition. In the following examples, the hollow clause is enclosed in brackets, with the site of the missing NP, the gap, shown as usual by '__', and the antecedent that determines its interpretation is underlined:

[1] i *<u>The problem</u> took her only a few minutes [to solve __].* [object of verb]
ii *I found her father a very easy <u>person</u> [to get on with __].* [object of prep]

Examples that further illustrate the range of possibilities are as follows:

[2] i *<u>That he would do such a thing</u> is hard [to believe __].* [clausal internal comp]
ii *<u>Pat</u> is easy [to be intimidated by __].* [comp of passive *by*]
iii *?<u>An ideal husband</u> is not easy [to be __].* [predicative comp]
iv **You won't find <u>these kids</u> easy [to teach __ Greek].* [indirect object]

The gap can be object of the preposition *by* in the passive, though examples of this kind are very rare. Examples with the gap in predicative complement function, as in [iii], are at best very marginal. And indirect object function is excluded, as seen in [iv]: this is comparable to the resistance of the indirect object to being realised as a gap in open interrogatives, relatives, or preposing (cf. Ch. 4, §4.3). Since the missing element can be object of either the verb or a preposition, it is possible to find paired examples that are alike save with respect to which function in the infinitival clause is missing:

[3] i *<u>Serious music</u> is hard [to play __ on an instrument like this].* [object of verb]
ii *<u>An instrument like this</u> is hard [to play serious music on __].* [object of prep]

Construction [ii], however, with the missing element object of a preposition in a transitive clause, is relatively uncommon. It is most likely when the object is part of an idiom: *They are hard to make sense of __ / get the better of __ / do justice to __ / take advantage of __.*

Hollow non-finite clauses belong to the minor type of unbounded dependency constructions: see Ch. 12, §7.1. They usually have *to*-infinitival form-type; we examine these in §6.3 but look first at constructions involving hollow gerund-participials.

6.2 Gerund-participials

These are licensed as complement to the adjectives *worth* and *worthwhile*, and to the preposition *for* with a purpose sense:

[4] i *Your idea is certainly worth [giving some further thought to __].*
ii *The plan is so unpopular that it wouldn't be worthwhile [our pursuing __].*
iii *This knife isn't very good for [cutting meat with __].*

Recall (from §3.2.3) that the superficially similar construction governed by such verbs as *need* is a concealed passive not a hollow active, as evident from the possibility of having a *by* phrase: *The proposal needs [__ evaluating by a specialist]*. The missing element here, therefore, is subject, not object.[47]

6.3 Hollow *to*-infinitivals

There are six constructions where hollow *to*-infinitivals are required or permitted.

(a) As complement to predicative adjectives and nouns

[5] i *Max is impossible to live with __.*
ii *The assignment was an absolute pain to do __.*

A sample of adjectives and nouns (or nominals) licensing this construction is given in:

[6]	i a.	*awkward*	*bad*	*boring*	*convenient*	*cumbersome*
		dangerous	*depressing*	*desirable*	*difficult*	*dreadful*
		easy	*embarrassing*	*essential*	*exciting*	*expensive*
		fashionable	*fine*	*good*	*hard*	*ideal*
		impossible	*instructive*	*interesting*	*nice*	*odd*
		painful	*pleasant*	*safe*	*simple*	*tedious*
		ticklish	*tough*	*tricky*	*useful*	*wonderful*
	b.	*bastard*	*bitch*	*breeze*	*cinch*	*delight*
		devil	*doddle*	*dream*	*embarrassment*	*joy*
		nightmare	*pain*	*piece of cake*	*pig*	*pleasure*
	ii	*available*	*beautiful*	*fit*	*free*	*frosty*
		homely	*pretty*	*ready*	*soft*	*suitable*

The adjectives and nouns in [6i] have to do mainly with the ease or difficulty of the situation described in the infinitival clause or with one's emotional attitude to it. Note that *impossible* belongs in the class but *possible* does not: *That claim is impossible/*possible*

[47] *Bear* occurs with a very limited range of gerund-participials, as in the familiar phrase *It doesn't bear thinking about*; the complement here is probably a hollow clause rather than a concealed passive.

to substantiate. PPs with similar meanings are also occasionally found: *The temptation was beyond his capacity to resist.* A number of nouns used in this construction (including, for example, the first four cited in [ib]) belong to colloquial style. The adjectives in [ii] are semantically and syntactically less homogeneous. Some are collocationally quite restricted: *The air was frosty to breathe*; *They were pretty to look at*; *It was soft to touch.*

The main difference between [6i] and [6ii], however, is that the former also license ordinary *to*-infinitivals as subject or extraposed subject:

[7] i a. *His speech was embarrassing / an embarrassment [to listen to __].*
b. *It was embarrassing / an embarrassment [to listen to his speech].*
ii a. *The document is now ready [for you to sign __].*
b. **It is now ready [for you to sign the document].*

The semantic equivalence between [7ia] and [ib] bears some resemblance to that between constructions with infinitival and finite clauses as complement to verbs like *seem*, discussed in §2.1. Compare, for example:

[8] i a. *Her criticism was hard [for Ed to accept __].*
b. *It was hard [for Ed to accept her criticism].*
ii a. *Ed seemed [to accept her criticism].* [raised subject + non-finite comp]
b. *It seemed [that Ed accepted her criticism].* [dummy subject + finite comp]

We have said that with an infinitival complement *seem* takes a raised subject – that the *Ed* of [8iia], like that of [iib], is not a semantic argument of *seem* but only of *convince.* It has been suggested that a corresponding treatment is appropriate for [ia]. This would be to say that *her criticism* is likewise a raised subject, that it doesn't represent an argument of *hard* but only of *accept,* as is transparently the case in [ib]. On this account *her criticism* in [ia] and *Ed* in [iia] would both be raised subjects of the matrix clause, with *her criticism* and *Ed* interpreted respectively as an object-argument and a subject-argument of the subordinate clause.[48]

There is, however, an important difference between the two pairs that leads us to reject a raised subject analysis for [8ia]. The subject of *seem* in [8iia] can be a dummy element, but the subject of *be hard* in [8ia] cannot. Compare [9i–ii] with [9iii–iv]:

[9] i a. *It seems to have been Kim who leaked the news.*
b. *It seems that it was Kim who leaked the news.*
ii a. *There seems to have been a conspiracy between them.*
b. *It seems that there was a conspiracy between them.*
iii a. **It'll be hard for us to prove __ to have been Kim who leaked the news.*
b. *It'll be hard for us to prove it to have been Kim who leaked the news.*
iv a. **There will be hard for us to prove __ to have been a conspiracy between them.*
b. *It will be hard for us to prove there to have been a conspiracy between them.*

We are saying that with an infinitival complement *seem* has a raised subject: this means that *seem* itself imposes no constraints on what can occur in subject function but accepts any element that is licensed as subject by the infinitival clause predicate. In [ia] *it* is accepted as

[48] In the classical transformational-generative analysis *her criticism* appears in 'underlying structure' in the subordinate clause and is moved (raised) into the matrix subject position. The rule concerned is commonly called 'Tough movement', *tough* being one of the adjectives that allows this upward movement of a non-subject NP.

subject of the *seem* clause because the infinitival clause belongs to the *it*-cleft construction, which in finite clauses takes *it* as subject, as in [ib]. *Hard*, however, does not behave in this way. The infinitival clause *for us to prove it to have been Kim who leaked the news* is syntactically and semantically impeccable, but this does not suffice to sanction [iiia]. Similarly with dummy *there*. This is allowed as subject of *seem* in [iia] because it is licensed by the infinitival complement, which belongs to the existential construction. But again it is not acceptable as subject in [iva] in spite of the well-formedness of *for us to prove there to have been a conspiracy between them*. The conclusion must be that the external complement of *hard* + infinitival is not raised, not licensed purely within the infinitival clause. It must represent a semantic argument of *hard*.

In [8ia], therefore, *hard* + infinitival denotes a property that is predicated of her criticism: the subject must represent an entity of a kind that such a property can be ascribed to it. Cleft *it* and dummy *there* do not satisfy this requirement. The equivalence between [8ia] and [8ib] is quite consistent with this account. Her criticism has the property that for Ed to accept it is hard, but the fact that there is such a property is sufficient to establish that it is hard for Ed to accept her criticism. And if [8ib] is true it must follow that her criticism had the property that it was hard for Ed to accept it. Similarly, in the matching pair [3], [i] assigns a property to serious music, while [ii] assigns a property to the instrument, but each is deducible from the other. Note also the contrast in such a pair as:

[10] i *It has been a pleasure to listen to <u>someone with so much enthusiasm</u>.*
ii ?*<u>Someone with so much enthusiasm</u> has been a pleasure to listen to* ___.

The underlined NP is completely acceptable as the complement of the preposition in [i], but it is quite marginal as the subject of [ii]: if we were dealing with a raised subject construction there should be no such difference.

Potential ambiguity between hollow and ordinary constructions

For many of the items in [6] an infinitival internal complement must always be of the hollow type. Some of them, however, license ordinary as well as hollow complements, and there is then the potential for ambiguity:

[11] i *They are ready to use* ___. [hollow]
ii *They are ready to depart.* [ordinary]
iii *They are ready to eat* (___). [ambiguous]

In [i] *use* is transitive: the missing object is recovered from the antecedent *they*, while the user is not explicitly indicated. In [ii] *depart* is intransitive, with *they* antecedent for the missing subject – note, then, that an overt subject can be supplied for [i], but not [ii] (*They are ready for you to use* ___, but not **They are ready for you to depart*). *Eat* in [iii] is a dual-transitivity verb, so that *they* can be antecedent for either a missing object (cf. *The jam tarts are ready to eat* ___) or the missing subject (cf. *The guests are ready to eat*). *Ready* may be contrasted with, for example, *easy*, where we have hollow *This knife is easy to cut with* ___, but not ordinary **This knife is easy to cut*. Other adjectives that behave like *ready* include:

[12] *available* *bad* *fit* *free* *good* *nice*

(b) Licensed by an attributive adjective

[13] i *London is an <u>easy</u> place to get lost in* ___.
ii *The price was a <u>difficult</u> one to better* ___.

These initial examples bear a clear resemblance to the construction just discussed: they are comparable to *London is easy to get lost in* and *The price was difficult to better.* The applicability of the adjective is contingent on it being construed with the infinitival: [i] doesn't say that London is an easy place, but that London is a place which it is easy to get lost in. Likewise in [ii] it is not a matter of a difficult price, but of a price that it would be difficult to better. It makes sense, therefore, to treat the infinitivals here as indirect complements in the structure of the NP: they are licensed not by the head of the construction, the noun, but by a dependent of it, the attributive adjective.

Very often, however, the adjective is applicable derivatively to the noun:

[14] i *It's a difficult book to understand.*
ii *That wasn't a very sensible remark to make.*
iii *This was a surprising decision for them to take.*
iv *It is an extremely stressful and emotional decision for any woman to make.*

If a book is difficult to understand, that makes it a difficult book. In [ii] the remark itself as well as the act of making it will be construed as not very sensible. And likewise in [iii–iv] both taking or making the decision and the decision itself were surprising or extremely stressful and emotional. This is a very common type: compare similarly *a difficult person to get on with, an impossible price to pay, an easy problem to solve, a good book to buy.* Note that [iii], for example, is appreciably more likely than, say, *This was a surprising decision for them to criticise,* though the latter is certainly grammatical.

The range of adjectives used in the attributive construction is somewhat wider than that found in predicative function. Compare, for example:

[15] i *That's a stupid book to set as a text for Year 1.*
ii **The book was stupid to set as a text for Year 1.*

There is likewise no corresponding predicative use of *sensible* and *surprising* in [14ii–iii]; semantically similar adjectives such as *clever, unusual, exciting* show the same pattern. Note, however, that the attributive adjective construction usually has the adjective within an NP that is itself in predicative function, as in all the examples in [13–15i]. We would not say, for example, **The catalogue contained several stupid books to set as a text for Year 1*, **They are charging us a difficult price to better.* This restriction is less applicable to those cases like [14] where the adjective can be interpreted as applying to the head noun as well as to the subordinate clause: *She is married to a rather difficult guy to get on with.*

This construction is not sharply distinct from that containing a noun postmodified by a non-*wh* relative clause. Compare:

[16] i *The premier's health is another significant issue to bear in mind.* [relative]
ii *That would be an interesting issue to explore.* [structurally ambiguous]

In [i] the infinitival is quite independent of the attributive adjective *significant*, which could be dropped without affecting acceptability. An approximate gloss is "an issue that we should bear in mind which is significant". And [ii] can be interpreted in the same way: "an issue that we should/might explore which is interesting". But it can also be interpreted with the infinitival an indirect complement licensed by *interesting*: "an issue which it would be interesting to explore". Though there are two different syntactic structures, the meanings they yield are effectively the same. Cases where the present construction yields a clearly different meaning from the relative are illustrated in [15i] and [14iii]. The relative interpretation of the former would be the implausible "That's a book that we could/should set as a text for Year 1 which is stupid". And what differentiates [14iii] from a relative is that it conveys that the decision was in fact taken: the infinitival relative generally has a modal meaning, involving what could or should be done.

(c) As complement to verbs

There are five verbs that take hollow *to*-infinitivals as internal complement: *be* and the transitive *cost, need, require, take.*

[17] i *The decision is for you to make __.*
ii *The car cost over $1,000 to repair __.*
iii *The dispute needed/required a great deal of tact to resolve __.*
iv *The letter took me all morning to write __.*

With *be* the hollow clause usually has *for* + subject, but we also find exceptional cases of subjectless ones: *The house is to let __* and *You are to blame __*. These are restricted to *let* (perhaps also *rent*) and *blame*: compare **The house is to sell* or **You are to criticise.* The construction with the transitive matrix verbs shows the same alternation as we illustrated in [8] for the adjective *hard*;[49] compare [17ii–iv] with:

[18] i *It cost over $1,000 to repair the car.*
ii *It needed/required a great deal of tact to resolve the dispute.*
iii *It took me all morning to write the letter.*

(d) With dummy *there, have (got), with/without,* and predicative genitive

[19] i *There is/remains Kim [to consider __].*
ii *Jill has (got) her elderly parents [to look after __].*
iii *With her elderly parents [to look after __], Jill is finding life somewhat stressful.*
iv *The money wasn't yours [to spend __].*

The infinitival here has a modal interpretation. In [i–iii] it is a matter of deontic necessity: Kim needs to be considered, Jill's elderly parents need to be looked after. In [iv] it is deontic possibility, and since the matrix clause is negated we understand "You weren't entitled to spend the money".

In the deontic necessity case we again find a close relationship with the relative clause construction. Compare:

[20] *There are several assignments to mark / that I have to mark.*

The examples in [19] were chosen as ones where the object NP would not accommodate an integrated relative clause, with *Kim* a proper noun (in its proper name use) and *her elderly parents* containing a genitive determiner and being referentially fully determinate. The finite relative clause in [20] differs from an ordinary integrated relative, however, and it is uncertain whether the infinitival should here be included in the relative category or not.

[49] There is also an alternant for [17i] with *it*: *It is for you to make the decision.* But this does not belong to the same construction as [18]. In particular, *for you* is a PP functioning in the matrix clause, not subordinator + subject in the infinitival, as is evident from the fact that *for* is replaceable by *up to.*

(e) Complements licensed by *too, enough, sufficient(ly)*

[21] i *My coffee was too hot to drink ___.*
ii *I haven't enough money left to spare ___ for luxuries like that.*
iii *The proposal isn't sufficiently developed for us to accept ___ in its present form.*

These items also license ordinary infinitivals (*He's too young to go to school*): we discuss both types together briefly in §8.4.

(f) Purpose infinitivals

[22] i *I bought them to give ___ to the children.*
ii *I need it for the children to do their homework on ___.*

Again the purpose clause is not required to have a non-subject gap, and we therefore postpone further discussion of the construction to §9.

7 Non-catenative complements in clause structure

We have argued in §4.1 that non-finite complements of verbs cannot in general be assigned the same function as NPs or AdjPs, but are best analysed as constituting a distinct type of complement, the catenative complement. The cases not covered by the latter are illustrated in:

[1] i *For you to accept liability would be a serious mistake.* [subject]
ii *It is important to ascertain the cause of the malfunction.* [extraposed subject]
iii *He considers taking advice beneath his dignity.* [object]
iv *I thought it better to wait.* [extraposed object]
v *His aim is to gain control of the company.* [subjective predicative comp]
vi *I'd call that taking unfair advantage of a beginner.* [objective predicative comp]

The subject is an external complement sharply distinguished in English from other types of complement: there is therefore no problem in distinguishing the infinitival in [i] from our catenative complements and identifying it functionally with other forms of subject. The infinitival in [ii] is distinguished from catenatives by virtue of its relationship with the dummy element *it* in subject position.

In [1iii] the subordinate clause serves as predicand for the predicative complement *beneath his dignity*. The relationship between the gerund-participial and the PP matches that between NP object and PP in *He considers such action beneath his dignity* and is sufficient to distinguish the gerund-participial from a catenative complement and to enable us to subsume [iii] under the complex-transitive construction. In [iv] we have another extrapositional construction, and the relationship with *it* is again sufficient to distinguish the infinitival from a catenative complement.

Example [1v] is an instance of the specifying *be* construction, with the infinitival complement distinguishable from a catenative by its ability to switch function with the subject (*To gain control of the company is his aim*), a property it shares with other forms, such as the PP in *The best place is in the garden* ~ *In the garden is the best place* (Ch. 4, §5.5.2). We also include various other non-finite complements to *be* under the predicative complement function. The catenative uses of *be* are the progressive (*She is working*), the passive (*She was nominated for the position of treasurer*), and the quasi-modal (*Everyone is to remain seated*).

Finally, [1vi] is a further case of the complex-transitive construction, but this time the gerund-participial is in predicative function. The relationship between it and the object clearly matches that between adjectival predicative and object in *I'd call that unfair.* The distinction between catenative and non-catenative is not so sharp here. We take the gerund-participial in *He kept them waiting*, for example, to be a catenative complement, not a predicative, because the relationship between it and *them* is not the same as that between predicative and object in *He kept them warm.* Compare here the following sets:

[2]	i	a. *I call that unfair.*	b. *That is unfair.*
	ii	a. *I call that taking advantage of him.*	b. *That is taking advantage of him.*
	iii	a. *He kept them warm.*	b. *They were warm.*
	iv	a. *He kept them waiting.*	b. *They were waiting.*

The sets do not match because while the *be* of [ib/iib] is the same (the copula), this is not so for [iiib/ivb], where the former is the copula and the latter the progressive marker: *warm* is a predicative complement but *waiting* is not.[50]

7.1 Subject and extraposed subject

(a) *To*-infinitivals

[3]	i	a. *For you to take the children could seriously endanger our mission.*
		b. *To refuse her request would be unthinkable.*
	ii	a. *It embarrassed her to see him so drunk.*
		b. *It would be a good idea for you to consult a solicitor.*

Subjects of the infinitival are freely admissible, as in [ia] and [iib], though the subjectless form is much more frequent.

A sample of items that license infinitival subjects is given in:

[4]	i	*amuse*	*cause*	*cost*	*delight*	*disturb*
		embarrass	*occur* [*to*]	*pay*	*please*	*take*
	ii	*easy*	*essential*	*foolish*	*good*	*hard*
		impossible	*necessary*	*possible*	*ridiculous*	*usual*
	iii	*mistake*	*offence*	*pleasure*	*task*	*way*

Verbs, adjectives, and nouns are listed in [i–iii] respectively. With the verbs, the licensing often involves internal complements as well as the verb head: *It took courage to tell them*, but not **It took Kim by surprise to tell them*; *It didn't occur to me to invite him*, but not **It didn't occur last Tuesday to invite him.* The adjectives and nouns head phrases in predicative complement function, as in [3ib/iib]; this pattern is much more frequent than the one with verb as licensor ([3ia/iia]). PPs with meanings comparable to adjectives are also found: *out of the question*, *of considerable interest*, and so on.

There is a large overlap between the items that license infinitivals and those that license declarative finites (content clauses). The latter can be either mandative or non-mandative (Ch. 11, §7.1.1), and for those that take mandatives there is in general little difference in

[50] There is of course an interpretation of [2iib] where *be* is the progressive auxiliary, but that doesn't stand in any significant relation to [2iia], and hence is irrelevant to the argument.

meaning between the infinitival and finite constructions. Compare, for example:

[5] i a. *It is important for you to lock up carefully.*
b. *It is important that you lock up carefully.*
ii a. *It was necessary for him to walk to school.*
b. *It was necessary that he walk to school.*

Where the finite is non-mandative, it tends to be concerned with facts or propositions while the infinitival is concerned with situations (actions, events, states, etc.), though in some cases the difference is again very slight. Compare:

[6] i a. *It was good to be back at school.*
b. *It was good that they were back at school.*
ii a. *It pleased her to be honoured in this way.*
b. *It pleased her that she was honoured in this way.*

In [ia] the situation of being back at school was good (for whoever it was who was back at school), while in [ib] the fact of their being back at school was good (for whoever it was who judged it good – in the default case, the speaker). But there is no perceptible difference in [6ii].

The distinction is particularly clear with *possible* as the licensing adjective:

[7] i *It was possible for him to walk to school.*
ii *It was possible that he walked to school.*

With an infinitival complement, *possible* expresses dynamic or deontic modality, whereas with a finite complement it is epistemic. A rough paraphrase for [ii] would be *Maybe he walked to school*: concerning whether the proposition that he walked to school is true, [ii] says maybe it is. But in [i] the issue is not the truth of a proposition, but his abilities. Note, however, that the modal adjective *necessary* does not exhibit the same difference: the modality is deontic in both constructions in [5ii].

The tendency for non-mandative finites to be associated with facts/propositions and infinitivals with situations ties in with the two main cases of items restricted to one or other form of complement. These restrictions are stated in [8], and exemplified in [9].

[8] i Adjectives concerned with truth or likelihood take declaratives, not infinitivals.
ii Adjectives concerned with the ease or difficulty of doing something take infinitivals, not declaratives.

[9] i a. **It was obvious for him to be lying.*
b. *It was obvious that he was lying.*
ii a. *It was easy for me to sympathise with her.*
b. **It was easy that I sympathised with her.*

Obvious in [ib] can be glossed as "obviously true"; other adjectives likewise restricted to finites are *likely, probably, certain, clear, evident, apparent* – and *true* and *false.*[51] Conversely, facts or propositions can't be easy, hence the difference in [ii]. *Hard* can take a finite complement, but its sense is then quite different from the sense it has with an

[51] These last two can take an infinitival if its verb is *say* (or a near-synonym): *It's true that he cheated, It's true to say that he cheated* (with the content clause an internal complement of *say*, not an extraposed subject of *be true*), but not **It's true for him to have cheated.*

infinitival:

[10] i *It's hard for them to work twelve hours a day.*
ii *It's hard on them that they have to work twelve hours a day.*

The situation described in the infinitival is often merely potential rather than actualised, and this is reflected in the frequent occurrence of the infinitival in construction with *would be*, where the corresponding non-mandative finite has *if*, not *that*:

[11] i a. *It was good to invite them both.* b. *It would be good to invite them both.*
ii a. *It was good [that you invited them both].* b. *It would be good [if/*that you invited them both].*

In [iia] *good* is factive: it is taken for granted that you invited them both. This factivity is inconsistent with the conditional implication of *would be*, and hence we need a conditional adjunct in [iib] instead of a factive complement.

(b) Bare infinitivals

These are occasionally found, in informal style, as subject in the reversed version of the specifying *be* construction; the internal complement contains the verb *do*:

[12] i *Plead mitigating circumstances is all you can do.*
ii *Seek professional advice is what we should do.*

(c) Gerund-participials

[13] i a. *Their reporting him to the manager led to his dismissal.*
b. *Inviting your uncle was a bad mistake.*
ii a. *It's no use his/him asking for special consideration.*
b. *It has been nice meeting you.*

The subject of the gerund-participial is much more often left understood, as in [ib/iib], than overtly expressed. The overt subject is particularly unlikely in the extraposed construction.

The gerund-participial is considerably less frequent in these functions than the infinitival, and there is also a major difference with respect to the extraposed and non-extraposed constructions: infinitivals are usually extraposed, gerund-participials comparatively rarely. To a significant extent, then, the difference between infinitival and gerund-participial is a matter of information packaging: end position tends to favour the infinitival while basic subject position tends to favour the gerund-participial.

For the most part, items that license a gerund-participial also license an infinitival, and vice versa. An infinitival could, for example, be substituted for the gerund-participial in [13ib] and [ii]. But such substitution would not be possible in [ia]: **For them to report him to the manager led to his dismissal.* Compare, similarly:

[14] i *Paying off the mortgage last year has put us in a strong position.*
ii **It has put us in a strong position to pay off the mortgage last year.*

The gerund-participial here and in [13ia] denotes a specific, actualised situation, and although the infinitival is not wholly excluded in such cases (cf. *It was a mistake to invite your uncle*), its use is considerably constrained. Note, then, that if we change from actual to hypothetical, the infinitival becomes acceptable:

[15] i *(For them) to have reported him to the manager would have led to his dismissal.*
ii *To have paid off the mortgage last year would have put us in a strong position.*

The gerund-participial is certainly not restricted to actualised situations (cf. *Changing the arrangements would be very difficult at this stage*), but for non-actualised situations the infinitival will often be required or at least quite strongly preferred, especially where the non-finite contains a subject:

[16] i a. *It would be better for the lecture to be rescheduled.*
b. **The lecture's being rescheduled would be better.*
ii a. *To doubt her word would never have occurred to me.*
b. ?*Doubting her word would never have occurred to me.*

7.2 Object and extraposed object

As explained at the beginning of §7, we take non-finite clauses to be objects, rather than catenative complements, only when they occur in some distinctively object relation with some element other than the head verb. The main case is the complex-transitive construction:

[17] i *This made obtaining a loan virtually impossible.*
ii *I regard solving this problem as my first priority.*

Infinitivals cannot occur in this position between verb and predicative complement; normally, then, they occur in extraposed object position, though it is marginally possible for them to be preposed in prenuclear position, without extrapositional *it*:

[18] i *I thought it wise to adopt a low profile.*
ii *For them to sack him we would regard as a gross miscarriage of justice.*

A gerund-participial, generally short and simple in structure, can also function as indirect object in the ditransitive construction, though it is likely to be considered stylistically somewhat awkward:

[19] *We've been giving moving to Sydney a good deal of thought recently.*

7.3 Predicative complement

The construction most clearly distinct from the catenative is the reversible specifying construction, where the internal complement can be a *to*-infinitival, a bare infinitival, or a gerund-participial:

[20] i *His intention was (for the meeting) to begin at six* [*to*-infinitival]
ii *All I did was print out the table of contents.* [bare infinitival]
iii *The funniest thing was (Kim) trying to hide in the coal-box.* [gerund-participial]

The bare infinitival is restricted to cases where the subject NP contains *do* in a relative clause; as we have noted, *to* can be added here (*All I did was to print out ...*). Since a subjectless gerund-participial can also be catenative complement to progressive *be*, some examples are ambiguous between the specifying and progressive constructions. This potential ambiguity is exploited in the advertising slogan *Our business is working for you*: as a specifying construction this identifies what our business is; with *be* a marker of progressive aspect, it says what our business is doing.

In addition a *to*-infinitival can occur as purpose complement, replaceable by a purpose PP such as *for the purpose of . . .* :

[21] *The grid is to prevent the cattle from wandering off.*

One other construction that belongs here is the idiomatic one illustrated in:

[22] i *To discuss melodrama, then, is to raise questions about 'culture' itself and the categories and oppositions by which we conceptualise it.*
ii *For any German director to attempt to make a film about Josef Mengele, the notorious Auschwitz concentration camp doctor, is to court controversy.*

This construction has a *to*-infinitival as both subject and internal complement of *be*. It differs from the specifying construction in that it cannot be reversed – *To raise questions about culture itself . . . is to discuss melodrama* is not equivalent to [i]. The construction indicates what the situation described in the subject entails or necessarily involves: "The discussion of melodrama necessarily raises questions about culture itself . . . ". In general, it can be paraphrased by means of *if* or *when*: *If/When a German director attempts to make a film about Josef Mengele, they necessarily court controversy.*

Finally, we have noted that a gerund-participial can function as objective predicative complement under very restricted conditions, mainly with *call* as matrix verb, as in [2iia].

8 Further complement uses of non-finite clauses

8.1 Non-finite complements of adjectives

These are predominantly *to*-infinitivals. We review these first, and then turn very briefly to gerund-participials; adjectives do not license past-participial complements.

To-infinitivals

The construction where an adjective is followed by a direct complement – i.e. one licensed by the adjective lexeme itself – is to be distinguished from a number of superficially similar ones. Compare:

[1] i *You are [free to leave when you want].* [direct comp of adj]
ii *She's [too young to go to school].* [indirect comp]
iii *She's [young] to be going to school.* } [adjunct in clause structure]
iv *I was [mad] to volunteer.*
v *It would be [foolish] to ignore them.* [extraposed subject]

In [ii] the infinitival is a constituent of the AdjP, but is licensed by *too* rather than by the adjective *young*. It is therefore an indirect complement; complements of this kind are dealt with in §8.4. In [iii–iv] the infinitival is an adjunct, not a complement. It is not lexically licensed, and though it could not be preposed there is some evidence that it does not form part of the AdjP. Note in particular that the adjective + infinitival could not function as postmodifier in NP structure: compare **She is one of those young to be going to school* and **Anyone mad to volunteer can't expect much sympathy.* While [ii] says that she is young to a degree higher than that at which she can or should go to school, [iii] says that she is young relative to those who go to school: it is unexpected or noteworthy that someone as young as she is should be going to school. The meaning of [iv] is that I was mad in that I volunteered: vounteering was a mad thing to do on my part. Finally, the infinitival in [v] is extraposed subject (compare the version without extraposition, *To ignore them would be foolish*), and as such is not part of the AdjP; see §7.1 for this construction.

Hollow vs ordinary infinitivals

[2] i *Their argument was [impossible [to follow __]].* [hollow]
ii *Kim was [anxious [to follow the argument]].* [ordinary]

The first division within the infinitival complements licensed by the head adjective is between the hollow and ordinary types. Hollow clauses, like *to follow* in [i], have a gap in some non-subject function, normally object of a verb or preposition; they have been discussed in §6, and henceforth in this section we will confine our attention to ordinary infinitivals, those without such a gap, like *to follow the argument* in [ii].

Raising and non-raising adjectives

The distinction between catenative verbs like *hope* and *seem*, which take respectively an ordinary and a raised subject, applies also to adjectives functioning as predicative complement and taking an infinitival complement. Compare:

[3]

ORDINARY SUBJECT	RAISED SUBJECT
a. *<u>Liz</u> was determined to convince them.*	b. *<u>Liz</u> was likely to convince them.*

In [i] the subject *Liz* represents an argument of *determined to convince them*: the property denoted by the AdjP is ascribed to Liz. But in [ii] the likelihood applies not to Liz but to the situation of Liz's convincing them. The grammatical and semantic differences noted in our discussion of *hope* and *seem* in §3.1 apply in essentially the same way to the adjectival construction. Compare:

[4] i a. *<u>Liz</u>$_i$ was determined that <u>she</u>$_i$ would convince them.* [double reference to Liz]
b. *It was likely that <u>Liz</u> would convince them.* [single reference to Liz]
ii a. *They were determined to be convinced by Liz.* [≠ 3a]
b. *They were likely to be convinced by Liz.* [= 3b]
iii a. *#This news was determined to convince them.* [violates selection restriction]
b. *This news was likely to convince them.* [no violation]
iv a. **There is determined to be enough food left.* [dummy subject inadmissible]
b. *There is likely to be enough food left.* [dummy subject admissible]
v a. *Liz was determined for them to have a good time.* [infinitival admits subject]
b. **Liz was likely for them to have a good time.* [infinitival excludes subject]

Because the parallel with the verbal constructions is so close, only a brief commentary is needed. In [i] the infinitivals are replaced by finite clauses. In [ia] *Liz* remains subject, and is the antecedent for a personal pronoun in the *convince* clause, which is still complement of *determined.* In [ib], by contrast, the subject is now *it* and the *convince* clause is extraposed subject – compare the non-extraposed *That Liz would convince them was likely*, where it is even more transparent that *likely* has a single argument. The data in [ii] show that *determined* is voice-sensitive, while *likely* is not: [iia] differs in meaning from [3a] because the determination is ascribed to 'them' rather than Liz, while the synonymy between [4iib] and [3b] shows that the likelihood does not apply to Liz or 'them', but to the situation of Liz convincing them and their being convinced by Liz. In [4iii] the [a] example is anomalous because *determined* takes an animate subject, while [b] is acceptable because there is no direct semantic relation between *likely* and the subject. This is why *determined* does not permit a dummy pronoun like *there* as subject, while *likely* does, as shown in [4iv]. Finally, the examples in [4v] show that with *determined* but not *likely* the infinitival can take a different subject from the matrix clause: the raised subject in the *likely* clause belongs semantically in the infinitival clause, and there is therefore no possibility of adding another subject to the latter.

The adjectives taking a raised subject, besides *likely*, are as follows:

[5]	*about*	*apt*	*bound*	*certain*	*due*
	fated	*liable*	*set*	*sure*	*wont*

The complement is obligatory: omitting it leads either to ungrammaticality (*He is wont to be late* but not **He is wont*) or to a change in the meaning of the adjective (compare *She is sure to win*, "It is certain that she will win", and *She is sure*, "She is not in any doubt").

Adjectives taking ordinary subjects are much more numerous. A sample is given in:

[6]	*able*	*accustomed*	*afraid*	*annoyed*	*anxious*
	ashamed	*astonished*	*careful*	*concerned*	*content*
	curious	*delighted*	*depressed*	*disgusted*	*disposed*
	eager F	*eligible*	*embarrassed*	*fascinated*	*fit*
	free	*frightened*	*furious*	*glad*	*happy*
	hesitant	*impatient*	*impotent*	*inclined*	*indignant*
	interested	*jubilant*	*keen* F	*loath*	*perturbed*
	poised	*powerless*	*prepared*	*prompt*	*prone*
	puzzled	*qualified*	*quick*	*ready* F	*relieved*
	reluctant F	*satisfied*	*slow*	*sufficient* F	*surprised*
	thankful	*welcome*	*willing* F	*worried*	*worthy*

Many of these do not allow a subject in the infinitival clause, or do so only marginally: those that most readily accept *for* + subject are annotated with 'F'. Compare *They are willing <u>for the proposal</u> to be resubmitted* and **You are welcome <u>for your children</u> to come with you.*

Able is a somewhat peripheral member of this class. It differs from clear members in that pairs such as the following do not differ in truth conditions:

[7] i *Primary schoolchildren are able to solve these problems.*
 ii *These problems are able to be solved by primary schoolchildren.*

Are able to could here be replaced by *can*, which is a raising verb. Yet *able* differs from *can* in that it does not allow dummy pronouns as subject. Compare:

[8] i *There can't be any progress without goodwill on both sides.*
 ii **There isn't able to be any progress without goodwill on both sides.*

The clear inadmissibility of [ii] indicates that *able* cannot take a raised subject. The equivalence of [7i–ii] must then be handled along the lines suggested for the pair given in [8i] of §6. Example [7i] ascribes a property to primary schoolchildren, not to the situation of their solving these problems, and [7ii] ascribes a property to the problems. But if the children have the property that they are able to solve the problems, the problems must necessarily have the property that they are able to be solved by the children. The truth conditions of [7i–ii] must therefore be the same even though they do not belong to the raised subject construction.

Gerund-participial complements

The adjectives *busy* and *worth/worthwhile* license complements of this form:

[9] i *She was busy* [*preparing her report*]. [ordinary]
ii *These objections$_i$ aren't worth* [*bothering about* __ $_i$]. [hollow]
iii *It isn't worth* [*taking the matter any further*]. [ordinary; impersonal]

Numerous adjectives take gerund-participials as oblique complements, i.e. with a governing preposition (*engaged in preparing her report, keen on playing games*, etc.), but *busy* takes the gerund-participial directly, as in [i]. *Worth* and *worthwhile* take hollow gerund-participials, as in [ii], where the gap functioning as complement of *about* is anaphorically linked to the predicand *these objections*. They also license ordinary gerund-participials, as in [iii], where there is no non-subject gap in the bracketed clause. This type is restricted to the construction with impersonal *it* as subject; it is comparable to extraposition, but does not allow the subordinate clause to appear in subject position: **Taking the matter further isn't worth.*

8.2 Non-finite complements of nouns

Many nouns license non-finite complements, all *to*-infinitivals:

[10] i	*advice*	*aim*	*application* F	*appointment*	*arrangement* F
	attempt	*authorisation* F	*claim*	*command*	*compulsion*
	consent F	*decision*	*desire* F	*determination*	*exhortation*
	failure	*hope* F	*incitement*	*inducement*	*inspiration*
	instruction F	*intention*	*invitation*	*longing* F	*move* F
	need F	*obligation*	*offer*	*order* F	*permission* F
	plan F	*pledge*	*plot*	*pressure*	*promise*
	proposal F	*provocation*	*recommendation*	*refusal*	*reminder*
	request	*resolution*	*selection*	*struggle* F	*tendency* F
	threat	*undertaking* F	*vow*	*warning*	*will*
	wish F	*yearning* F			
ii	*ability*	*eagerness* F	*eligibility*	*fitness*	*freedom* F
	impatience	*keenness* F	*readiness* F	*reluctance* F	*willingness* F
iii	*chance* F	*concern*	*opportunity* F	*power*	*strength*

The great majority of the head nouns are morphologically derived from (or homonymous with) verbs of matching senses that take the same complementation, as with those in [i]. Those in [ii] are similarly derived from adjectives, while with those in [iii] the complementation is not predictable in this way. Compare then:

[11] i a *Kim decided to go to Bonn.* b. *Kim's decision to go to Bonn*
ii a. *Pat was eager to help us.* b. *Pat's eagerness to help us*
iii a. [no relevant counterpart] b. *the opportunity to make a quick profit*

We include *strength* in [iii], not [ii], because the adjective *strong* does not take an infinitival complement. Note, then, that the following do not have matching structures or interpretations:

[12] i *She was strong to withstand this pressure.*
ii *She had the strength to withstand this pressure.*

In [i] the infinitival is an adjunct in the clause; the meaning is that she withstood the pressure, this indicating that she was strong. In [ii] the infinitival is a complement, and the meaning is "She had the strength necessary to withstand the pressure".

All the nouns in [10] take subjectless infinitivals, and those with the annotation 'F' also allow the construction with subordinator *for* + subject:

[13] i *This provided an opportunity [for them to plan the next step].*
ii *Permission [for the ceremony to be held in the church itself] was finally granted.*

A number of other nouns in our list could probably also occur with *for* + subject in the infinitival, but it is in general a relatively infrequent construction, and judgements as to whether a given noun could appear here are not always clear-cut.

In the subjectless construction, the antecedent for the missing subject may be found within the NP (as genitive determiner or within a PP complement), as in [14i], or outside the NP, as in [ii], and in cases like [iii] there is no antecedent in the sentence at all:

[14] i a. *your/Kim's promise to help me with my tax return*
b. *a proposal by the government to introduce a goods-and-services tax*
c. *the willingness of the other members to agree to the proposal*
d. *an instruction to the secretary to call an extraordinary meeting*
ii a. *They gave me instructions [to evacuate the building].*
b. *I received instructions [to evacuate the building].*
c. *What I hadn't expected to receive was an instruction [to evacuate the building].*
iii *They were discussing a proposal [to introduce a summer semester].*

In general, the recovery of the understood subject is determined by semantic principles, not rules of syntax. But in some cases the matter is more grammaticalised; with *selection*, for example, the antecedent is normally required to appear as complement to *of*:

[15] i *The selection of Judge Carter to head the inquiry is to be welcomed.*
ii *The selection to head the inquiry hasn't yet been announced.*
iii *Judge Carter is their selection to head the inquiry.*

Nouns do not take raised complements

In general, clauses with raised complements, licensed by raising verbs or adjectives, do not have counterparts with the form of NPs:

[16] i	a. *Kim seemed to be distressed.*	b. **the seeming of Kim to be distressed*
ii	a. *I believe them to be genuine.*	b. **my belief in/of them to be genuine*
iii	a. *They are certain to resent it.*	b. **their certainty to resent it*

One exception involves the verb *tend*, which has the noun counterpart *tendency*. Corresponding to clausal *The tabloids tend to support Labour* and the equivalent *Labour tends to be supported by the tabloids* we have:

[17] i a. *the tendency for the tabloids to support Labour*
b. *the tendency for Labour to be supported by the tabloids*
ii a. *the tendency of the tabloids to support Labour*
b. *Labour's tendency / the tendency of Labour to be supported by the tabloids*

In [ia/ib] *the tabloids* and *Labour* are subjects of the infinitival clauses, and the equivalence between the whole NPs simply reflects the equivalence holding between the active and passive subordinate clauses they contain. In [ii], however, *the tabloids* and *Labour* are oblique or genitive complements of *tendency*: here, therefore, they appear to bear some resemblance to raised complements. There is, however, a major difference between the NP and clause constructions. Dummy elements can occur as raised complements in clause structure, but they cannot occur as oblique or genitive complement of *tendency* – or of any other noun. *There* does not have a genitive form and cannot normally occur as complement of a preposition, but these general restrictions do not apply to *it*, and yet this too cannot be used in the relevant positions when it is a dummy element:

[18] i a. *It tends to be the wife who provides this support.*
b. **its tendency to be the wife who provides this support*
ii a. *It tends to be more efficient to pay by credit card than by cheque.*
b. **its tendency to be more efficient to pay by credit card than by cheque*

Such data argue that nouns, unlike verbs and adjectives, do not take raised complements. We take *the tabloids* and *Labour*, therefore, to represent arguments of *tendency* in [17iia–b] respectively, though not of course in [17i]. The relation between [17ia] and [17iia] is thus the same as that between [8ib] and [8ia] of §6.3 (*It was hard for Ed to accept her criticism* and *Her criticism was hard for Ed to accept*).

The same applies to *failure*, derived from the raising verb *fail*. The verb allows dummy subjects, but the noun does not:

[19] i *It had failed to become apparent, even after a day, what their intentions were.*
ii **its failure to become apparent, even after a day, what their intentions were*

Consider finally the case of *order:*

[20] i a. *They ordered the building to be evacuated.*
b. #*the order to the building to be evacuated*
c. *the order for the building to be evacuated*
ii a. *They ordered the doctor to examine the victims.*
b. *the order to the doctor to examine the victims*
c. *the order for the doctor to examine the victims*

The verb takes a raised object: *the building* is not an argument of the verb in [ia]. But with the noun the complement of *to* is an argument, with the role of recipient of the order. Hence the anomaly of [ib]: one doesn't give orders to buildings. The nominal structure thus differs from the verbal one in allowing for this role to be explicitly encoded. It does not have to be, however, for we can also have [ic/iic]: these match the verbal (clausal) construction in not encoding who received the order. Here *the building* and *the doctor* function as subject of the infinitival, not as oblique complement of the noun. Again, then, oblique complements of the noun are not raised: they have to be interpretable as arguments of the noun.

8.3 Non-finite complements in the structure of PPs

Gerund-participials

These occur very freely as complement of a preposition:

[21] i *I'm looking forward [to (you/your) returning home].*
ii *[On hearing the news] she immediately telephoned her father.*
iii *She was reported [as saying that she would appeal against the ruling].*
iv *[Although claiming to have a Ph.D.,] he didn't in fact have any degree at all.*

Although more often occurs with a finite complement (as in *although he claimed to have a Ph.D.*). Such clauses can be reduced to gerund-participials, past-participials, or verbless clauses: see [3] of §10 for a list of prepositions of this kind.

To-infinitivals

In contrast to gerund-participials, *to*-infinitivals occur in this function only under very restrictive conditions. The only prepositional expressions that take *to*-infinitivals other than interrogatives as direct complement are purposive *in order*, and *as if/though*:

[22] i *We got up at five [in order to catch the early train].*
ii *He raised his hand [as if to defend himself].*
iii *She glanced out of the window at the phaeton [as though to say that he was not the only man to have a new carriage that morning].*

The *as if / though* construction is related to purpose in that it can be glossed as "as if/though with the purpose/intention of". *In order* allows *for* + subject, but *as if/though* does not.

Past-participials

These occur in the complement of prepositions like *although, until*, etc., that allow reduction of a finite complement, and also in comparative clauses (see Ch. 13, §2.1):

[23] i *Please remain seated [until requested to board your flight].*
ii *He had more debts [than previously acknowledged].*
iii *The problem turned out to be more serious [than expected].*

8.4 Indirect and matrix-licensed non-finite complements

Infinitivals indirectly licensed by *too, enough, sufficient, sufficiently*

[24] i a. *It is too late [for you to go out now].*
b. *Enough people turned up [to form a quorum].*
c. *The instructions weren't sufficiently clear [for us to be able to assemble it].*
ii a. *Too good [to miss __] is how I'd describe it.*
b. *The problem isn't important enough [to worry about __].*
c. *Have you had sufficient [to eat __]?*

The underlined degree expressions license ordinary infinitivals, as in [i], or hollow ones, as in [ii]. The complements are indirect in that in constituent structure they are not dependents of the licensor, but of a head item that is modified by the latter. In [ia], for example, the infinitival is a dependent of *late*, not directly of *too*. The infinitival strongly favours end position in the matrix clause: [ib], for example, is strongly preferred over *Enough people to form a quorum turned up*. The latter is not ungrammatical, however, and in the specifying *be* construction [iia], the infinitival cannot be moved to the end.

The licensors indicate degree relative to some need, purpose, desire, etc. *Too* expresses a degree that exceeds the maximum or upper bound consistent with fulfilling the need, purpose, or desire. In [ia] it is late to a degree higher than the maximum at which you can or should go out: it follows that you can't or shouldn't go out now. Note that *excessively* is not substitutable for *too*: compare *My coffee is too/*excessively hot to drink. Enough* and *sufficient(ly)* express a degree that is at least as high as the minimum or lower bound. In [ib], for example, the number of people who turned up was at least as high as that needed to form a quorum.

Hollow infinitivals indirectly licensed by an attributive adjective

[25] *That was a silly thing [to do __].*

The infinitival is licensed by *silly* but in constituent structure is a complement in the NP headed by *thing*; for this construction, see §6.3.

Matrix-licensed complements

A number of prepositions take non-finite complements if the larger construction licenses them (see Ch. 7, §5.1). There are three main cases.

(a) With prepositions of inclusion or exception *including, but, except, save*

[26] i *He does nothing but/save/except waste people's time.*
ii *I couldn't help but notice her embarrassment.*
iii *You have no choice but to accept her offer.*
iv *There's nothing he wants save to pursue his studies in peace.*
v *This would achieve nothing except to antagonise some of our supporters.*

In [i] the bare infinitival is licensed by *do nothing* + the preposition of exception: compare **He likes nothing but waste people's time* (in this context we need gerund-participial *wasting*) or **He does wonderful things but waste people's time*. In [ii] the licensor is the non-affirmative idiom ***can** help but*. The other examples have *to*-infinitivals, but the licensing is again a property of the matrix construction, with *choice, want, achieve* the decisive elements. *Want* straightforwardly takes a *to*-infinitival itself: *He wants to pursue his studies. Achieve* does not, but nevertheless to antagonise some of our supporters is to achieve something, and hence the infinitival is admissible: contrast **He found nothing except to antagonise our supporters.*

(b) With the prepositions of comparison *as* and *than*

[27] i *I'd rather stay at home than go out in this weather.*
ii *That wouldn't be as bad as for you to lose your job.*
iii *They visit the area for such recreational purposes as to attend hockey matches.*

In [i] the infinitival is permitted after *than* because the matrix *would rather* licenses a complement of the same form (*stay at home*). In [ii] the predicate *be bad* licenses infinitival subjects (*For you to lose your job would be bad*). And in [iii] the infinitival denotes a purpose.

(c) With *as* in purposive and resultative complements

[28] i *They were asked to stand back so as not to hamper the efforts of the firefighters.*
ii *Blood for transfusion cannot be chosen so as to exclude every possibility of sensitisation.*
iii *On this matter their views are so close as to be indistinguishable.*
iv *His art is such as to render the familiar original and mysterious.*
v *Will you be so good as to order your men not to molest my maid.*

The *as* here is itself licensed by *so* or *such.* In most cases, *as* + infinitival alternates with a finite clause optionally or obligatorily introduced by the subordinator *that*: *so (that) they would not hamper the efforts of the firefighters*; *so (that) it will exclude every possiblity of sensitisation*; *so close (that) they were indistinguishable*; *such that it renders the familiar original and mysterious.* No such replacement is possible in [v], where *be so good as to* is an idiom meaning "kindly". None of these constructions allows *for* + subject in the infinitival.

The *so* phrase in [28i] is a purpose adjunct, while that in [ii] is a manner adjunct; in the latter construction *so* can be separated from the *as* complement: *cannot be so chosen as to* ... Unlike *so* + finite clause, *so* + *as* + infinitival does not serve by itself as a resultative adjunct: there is no *as* + infinitival counterpart of examples like *He didn't wake up until ten, so that he wasn't able to see his mother before she went to work.*

8.5 Interrogative infinitival clauses

While the distribution of non-interrogative infinitival clauses is very different from that of content clauses, this is not so with interrogatives. Interrogative infinitival complements are found in a large subset of the environments where interrogative content clauses are licensed. Compare, for example:

	a.	b.
[29] i	*I don't know whether I should go.*	*I don't know whether to go.*
ii	*She decided what she would do.*	*She decided what to do.*
iii	*It doesn't matter what you say.*	**It doesn't matter what to do.*

The interrogative phrase cannot have subject function (**I don't know who to go first*), and no other subject is permitted either (**She didn't say what for me to do*). For further discussion, see Ch. 11, §5.3.5.

9 Non-finite clauses as modifiers and supplements

We turn now, very much more briefly, to non-finite clauses in non-complement function.

Post-head modifier in NP structure

[1] i	a. *This provides [a solid foundation on which to build].*	[*wh* relative]
	b. *This provides [a solid foundation to build on].*	[non-*wh* relative]
ii	a. *[People living near the site] will have to be evacuated.*	[gerund-participial]
	b. *I came across [a letter written by my great-grandfather].*	[past-participial]

Clauses in this function cannot contain an overt subject. Infinitivals, as in [i], belong to the class of integrated relative clauses; they are discussed in Ch. 12, §5.

Gerund-participials and past-participials are semantically similar to relative clauses: compare *people who live near the site* and *a letter that was written by my great-grandfather*. We do not analyse them as relative clauses since there is no possibility of them containing a relative phrase (cf. **people who living near the site*, etc.).

Past-participial modifiers are bare passives (Ch. 16, §10.1.1), as evident from the admissibility of a *by* phrase in internalised complement function. Gerund-participials can be active or passive. Passive gerund-participials contrast with the past-participials in aspectuality as progressive vs non-progressive, but with actives the progressive vs non-progressive distinction is lost:

[2]		VOICE	ASPECTUALITY	FORM-TYPE
i	*people earning this amount*	active	neutralised	gerund-participial
ii	*the amount being earned by Kim*	passive	progressive	gerund-participial
iii	*the amount earned by Kim*	passive	non-progressive	past-participial

The active neutralises the distinction between *people who are earning this amount* and *people who earn this amount*. Features of form or context in particular cases may favour or require one or other kind of interpretation – compare *anyone knowing his whereabouts* ("who knows") and *Who's the guy making all that noise?* ("who is making"). The construction itself, however, is quite neutral between the two interpretations. In the passive, on the other hand, [ii–iii] contrast like *the amount which is being earned by Kim* and *the amount which is earned by Kim*. Note, though, that we are concerned here with the semantic category of aspectuality, not the syntactic category of aspect (see Ch. 3, §3, for this distinction). It must be emphasised that *being* in [ii] is the passive auxiliary: as pointed out in §1.1, gerund-participials do not accept the progressive auxiliary.

Modifiers in clause structure

[3] i *They are saving up to buy a washing-machine.*
ii *They arrived home to find the house had been burgled.*
iii *He was a fool to say he'd go.*
iv *Liz was lying by the pool reading a novel.*

The infinitival in [i] is an adjunct of purpose, while that in [ii] indicates a resultant or subsequent situation. In [iii] it indicates the respect in which he was a fool, a reason or explanation for the judgement. The gerund-participial in [iv] is a depictive adjunct, giving descriptive information about Liz; note that it is interpreted with progressive aspectuality: "she was reading a novel".

Adjuncts that are integrated into clause structure as modifiers tend not to be sharply distinct from complements: see §§4.4, 8.1.

Supplements

[4] i a. *His hands gripping the door, he let out a volley of curses.*
b. *This done, she walked off without another word.*
ii a. *Realising he no longer had the premier's support, Ed submitted his resignation.*
b. *Born in Aberdeen, Sue had never been further south than Edinburgh.*
iii *Whether working or relaxing, he always has a scowl on his face.*

The underlined non-finites are supplements with the main clause as anchor. Those in [i] contain a subject, and belong to what is known as the **absolute** construction, one which is subordinate in form but with no syntactic link to the main clause. Those in [ii] have no subject, and are syntactically related to the main clause in that the missing subject is controlled by the subject of the main clause: it was Ed who realised he no longer had the premier's support, and Sue who was born in Aberdeen. In neither [i] nor [ii] is there any explicit indication of the semantic relation between the supplement and the anchor. This has to be inferred from the content of the clauses and/or the context. The natural interpretation of the supplement in [ib], for example, is temporal ("when this was done"), and of that in [iia] causal ("because he realised ... "). Both constructions allow gerund-participials or past-participials – and also verbless forms, as exemplified in §10. Example [iii] belongs to the exhaustive conditional construction discussed in Ch. 11, §5.3.5.

While the missing subject in [4ii] is controlled by the subject of the anchor clause, we also find supplements where it has to be interpreted non-syntactically:

[5] i *To put it bluntly, they're utterly incompetent.*
ii *But, judging from their reaction, the decision was a complete surprise to them.*
iii *Based on the latest inflation data, there'll be another rate-rise soon.*

Such supplements belong to the category of speech act-related adjuncts (Ch. 8, §18): they are concerned with the manner in which the main assertion is expressed, or the evidence for it. In [i–ii], the missing subject is understood by reference to the speaker, while with the past-participial in [iii] it is the prediction of another rate-rise that is based on the inflation data. The past-participial (which is less clearly established as grammatical than the others) is more or less restricted to *based on*; for the relation between the gerund-participials and deverbal prepositions, see Ch. 7, §2.3.

Non-finites can also serve as supplements to NP anchors:

[6] i *Kim and Pat, both of them suffering from hypothermia, were winched into the helicopter.*
ii a. *Kate's proposal – to dismiss the manager – was greeted with dismay.*
b. *Jim's hobby – collecting beermats – is taking up all his time.*
c. *There was only one thing to do: call in the police.*

The supplement [i] is of the ascriptive type, comparable to a relative clause (compare *who were both of them suffering from hypothermia*). Those in [ii], by contrast, are of the content-specifying type: see Ch. 15, §5, for this distinction. Note that while *proposal* licenses infinitival complements, *hobby* does not license gerund-participials. The supplements here are thus sanctioned semantically (collecting beermats is a possible hobby), rather than being lexically licensed.

10 Verbless clauses

We confine our attention here to verbless clauses in dependent or supplement functions comparable to those realised by non-finite clauses, as described in the main part of the chapter.

(a) Complement to *with* and *without*

[1] i *They were standing against the wall* [*with their hands above their heads*].
ii *They were wandering around* [*without any clothes on*].
iii [*With the children so sick,*] *we weren't able to get much work done.*
iv *Who is that guy* [*with his hands in his pockets*]?

The underlined clauses have subject + predicate structure, but with no verb in the predicate. *With* and *without* do not license finite complements, but non-finites are found in addition to the verbless forms (see §8.3 above). The bracketed PPs function as adjunct to a clause ([i–iii]) or post-modifier in NP structure ([iv]). *With* is semantically similar to *have*, and *without* to *not have*: [i–ii], for example, entail *They had their hands above their heads,They didn't have any clothes on.*[52]

(b) Complement to prepositions that license reducible clauses

We have observed that a number of prepositions like *although* usually take finite clause complements, but allow the complement to be reduced – either to a non-finite clause, as illustrated in §8.3, or else a verbless one, as in:

[2] i *Although no longer a minister, she continued to exercise great power.*
ii *Once away from home, she quickly learned to fend for herself.*
iii *He spoke in an injured voice, as though resentful of the fact that she had not given him proper warning.*
iv *He can be very dangerous when drunk.*
v *While in Paris, I visited Uncle Leonard.*

A finite clause can be reconstructed by adding a subject and a form of the verb *be*: *although she was no longer a minister*, and so on.

We noted in Ch. 12, §6.4, that *when* and *whenever, while* and *whilst* fall at the boundary between relative words and prepositions taking content clause complements; the fact that they enter into the present construction is a feature they share with the prepositions taking content clause complements. Including them, the governing items are:

[3]	*although*	*as if*	*as though*	*if*	*once*
	though	*when*	*whenever*	*while*	*whilst*

In addition to the construction illustrated in [2], *if, when(ever), where(ver)*, and marginally *unless* take *necessary* and *possible* as complements, as in:

[4] i *Don't hesitate to call me at home* [*if necessary.*]
ii *He was anxious to learn and helped me* [*wherever possible.*]

The interpretation of the missing subject derives from a proposition expressed in the matrix: we can expand as *if it is necessary to call me* and *wherever it was possible to help me.* Note that the locative meaning has been bleached out of *where* in this example: it could be replaced by *whenever.*

[52]This use of *on* applied to clothing is one where the construction with *be* is somewhat unidiomatic: ?*Their clothes weren't on.*

(c) Supplements

[5] i *His face pale with anger, he stormed out of the room.*
ii *The contestants, some of them primary school children, were kept waiting for two hours.*
iii *The Chinese, whether drunk or sober, never kiss in public.*

These are verbless analogues of the non-finite supplements given in [4i] and [6i] of §9.

Condensed structures and reanalysis

Verbless clauses may appear 'condensed', with the subject consisting of a single word even when it is a count singular noun:

[6] i *Dinner over, they resumed their game of chess.*
ii *He stood glowering at us, face red with anger.*
iii *They threw him head first into the pond.*

Note that *head first* in [iii] is integrated into clause structure, having the status of modifier rather than supplement.

A small number of expressions of this kind can function as predicative complement as well as adjunct. Compare:

[7]		a.	b.
	i	*They walked away arm in arm.*	*They were arm in arm.*
	ii	*He stood at the door, hat in hand.*	**He was hat in hand.*

Predicative complement is not a function that normally accepts verbless clauses, and it is plausible to suggest that *arm in arm* has been reanalysed, losing its status as a clause and coming to be construed as a PP. The head will be *in*, with the second *arm* an internal complement, and the first an external complement: see Ch. 7, §4.3.[53] It is also possible for such PPs to consist of an external complement NP + intransitive preposition, as in *face down* (compare *She was face down*, but not **She was palms up*). Further examples are: *side by side*, *back to back*, *inside out*, *upside down*.[54]

11 Further remarks on the interpretation of subjectless non-finites

The subject is an obligatory element in canonical clauses, and the interpretation of clauses which lack a subject requires that the omission be somehow made good. For non-finite clauses we have distinguished three cases, involving raised, controlled, and non-syntactic interpretations.

In the raised case, the missing subject is retrievable from the subject or object of the matrix clause. Raised complements are licensed only by verbs and adjectives; they have been discussed at length in earlier sections of the chapter and need not be considered

[53] The structure proposed bears a significant resemblance to that of the verbless clause. Thus *in* is also the ultimate head of *hat in hand* in [7iia], with *hand* an internal complement (*in hand* constituting the predicate) and *hat* an external complement (more specifically, the subject).

[54] *Upside down*, a reworking of earlier *up-so-down*, differs etymologically from the others in that *upside* postdates – and is probably derived by back-formation from – the whole phrase. PPs of the type discussed in Ch. 7, §4.2, with *ago* and *apart* as head (e.g. *a week ago* or *this apart*) also derive historically from absolute clauses. *Ago* derives from *agone*, related to the past participle of **go**, while *this apart* is comparable to the *dinner over* of [6i].

further here. The relation between the other two types of interpretation, however, does merit additional discussion.

The distinction between controlled and non-syntactic interpretations

The relation between a missing or covert subject and the controller is a special case of anaphora. It is thus analogous to the relation between a personal pronoun and its antecedent: compare *Jill expected to finish on time* and *Jill expected that she would finish on time* (in the interpretation where *she* is co-referential with *Jill*). We can thus use the familiar notational device of co-indexing: *Jill*$_i$ *expected* [__$_i$ *to finish on time*]. It is not only in the case of control, however, that a missing subject may be co-indexed with an antecedent located elsewhere in the sentence. Compare:

[1] i a. <u>*I*</u>$_i$ *hope* [__$_i$ *to see her next week*]. } [controlled interpretation]
b. *Jill asked* <u>*Pat*</u>$_i$ [__$_i$ *to help her*].
ii a. *This would involve* [__ *moving to Sydney*]. } [non-syntactic interpretation]
b. *All Sue*$_i$ *has had so far is a request* [__$_i$ *to accept nomination*].

In [i] the underlined NPs are the antecedents, and more specifically the controllers, of the missing subjects. In [iia] there is no antecedent at all, while in [iib] *Sue* is the antecedent, but not the controller. It is understood that Sue is the potential accepter of the nomination, but this interpretation is not determined by the syntactic relation between *Sue* and the missing subject. It is arrived at, rather, by semantic inference along the following lines:

[2] i The matrix clause (with specifying *be*) entails that Sue has had a request.
ii Sue therefore fills the semantic role of recipient of the request.
iii The understood subject of a non-finite complement to the noun *request* represents either the maker of the request (*his request to see the files*) or the recipient (*I received a request to make a donation to the Scholarship Fund*).
iv Only the recipient is expressed in [1iib], and the content of the request makes it more likely that the understood subject will represent the recipient of the request.

Similar factors are at work in:

[3] i *Jill*$_i$ *found it difficult* [__$_i$ *to understand what he was getting at*].
ii *Max*$_i$ *admitted it had been a mistake* [__$_i$ *to leave so little time for revision*].

In [i] the infinitival is extraposed object in a complex-transitive construction: this makes it the predicand of the adjective *difficult*. The missing subject in an infinitival predicand of *difficult* is co-indexed with the NP with the semantic role of experiencer, and this role is associated with the subject of *find*, i.e. *Jill*. Contrast this example with *This made it difficult to understand what he was getting at*: *make* assigns the role of causer, not experiencer, to its subject, so that this time we do not have co-indexing between matrix and subordinate subjects. In [ii] the infinitival is extraposed subject and predicand of *a mistake*: the missing subject represents the one who made the mistake, and *admit* in the next higher clause suggests that it was Max who made the mistake. Note, however, that it doesn't have to have been Max who left so little time for revision. This is a likely interpretation but not the only possible one: admitting something doesn't entail that one is responsible for it.

Control is the case where the identification of the missing subject can be described by reference to syntactic functions rather than in terms of semantic roles. One of the clearest cases is the catenative construction:

[4] i *Kim$_i$ wants [__$_i$ to enter the competition].* [control by matrix subject]
ii *Kim wants me$_i$ [__$_i$ to enter the competition.]* [control by matrix object]

Here, as in almost all non-raising cases, the simple construction has control by the subject of the matrix clause, while the plain-complex construction has control by the object.

To say that control is defined syntactically is not to suggest that it is semantically arbitrary. On the contrary, it is strongly motivated by the semantics. Compare, for example:

[5] i *Sue told Tim$_i$ [__$_i$ to arrange the interviews].* [control by matrix object]
ii *Sue$_i$ promised Tim [__$_i$ to arrange the interviews].* [control by matrix subject]

The infinitival subject is co-indexed with the object of *tell* and the subject of *promise*, but this reflects semantic differences between *tell* and *promise*. *Tell* belongs with the set of verbs of 'influence': it denotes an attempt to influence someone's behaviour, and the one (potentially) influenced corresponds to the missing subject of the infinitival complement. *Promise*, by contrast, belongs with the verbs of 'commitment', and the missing subject with such verbs corresponds to the one making the commitment. Control, then, is semantically motivated, but these examples differ from those like [1iib] and [3] in that the missing subject is anaphorically linked to an antecedent in a specified syntactic function. Notice, moreover, that the use of *promise* shown in [5] is quite rare: it is much more usual to have a simple catenative construction (*Sue$_i$ promised _$_i$ to arrange the interviews*) or to have a finite complement (*Sue$_i$ promised Tim that she$_i$ would arrange the interviews*). In the overwhelming majority of cases, then, the controller for the plain-complex construction is the matrix object.

A related difference between *tell* and *promise* concerns passivisation:

[6] i *Tim$_i$ was told by Sue [__$_i$ to arrange the interviews].*
ii **Tim was promised by Sue$_i$ [__$_i$ to arrange the interviews].*

Tell passivises readily, and it is now the subject that controls the missing subject of the infinitival. But *promise* does not passivise: the antecedent for the missing subject in [ii] is complement of the preposition *by*, and that is not a syntactically permitted function for a controller.

Non-finite clauses functioning in NP structure

The interpretation of non-finite clauses functioning in the structure of NPs is determined very differently. We observed in §8.2 that raised complements do not occur in NP structure, and the data in [7] show that we do not have syntactic control either:

[7] i *Tim was satisfied with [Sue's$_i$ promise [__$_i$ to pay the rent]].*
ii *Tim was satisfied with [the promise by Sue$_i$ [__$_i$ to pay the rent]].*
iii *Tim extracted from Sue$_i$ [a promise [__$_i$ to pay the rent]].*
iv *Tim will not be satisfied with [a mere promise [__ to pay the rent]].*

The missing subject of the complement of the noun *promise* is anaphorically linked to the NP denoting the one making the promise, irrespective of the syntactic function of that NP. And indeed, as we see from [iv], there does not have to be any such NP in the sentence: it can be left to the context to determine the interpretation.

As a second example, compare the verb *request* with the corresponding noun:

[8] i a. *Kim requested us*$_i$ [__$_i$ *to enter the competition*].
b. *We*$_i$ *requested* [__$_i$ *to enter the competition*].
ii a. [*Sue's*$_i$ *request* [__$_i$ *to enter the competition*]] *has not yet been considered.*
b. *We*$_i$ *received a request from Sue*$_j$ [__$_{i/j}$ *to enter the competition*].
c. *We still haven't received any requests* [__ *to enter the competition*].

The plain-complex catenative construction [i] has control by the object, with the object representing the recipient of the request, while the simple catenative [ii] has control by the subject, with the subject representing the maker of the request. But with the NP construction there is no control, no anaphoric link between the missing subject and an antecedent in some specified syntactic function. The antecedent may be in the NP headed by *request*, or it may be in the matrix clause, or there may be no antecedent at all, as in [iic]. Note, moreover, that [iib] is ambiguous, interpretable with either *we* or *Sue* as antecedent: Sue may have been requesting us to enter, or requesting to enter herself.

The verb *request* is a marginal member of a small class of verbs that allow the normal syntactic rule of control to be overridden under highly restrictive conditions. In *We*$_i$ *requested them* __$_i$ *to be allowed to enter the competition*, the antecedent is the subject, not the object, as in [8ia]. This, however, is a very exceptional departure from the normal pattern of object control, not possible beyond a very narrow range of cases like *to be allowed* (see the discussion of Class 2Ai in §5.3): it is not comparable with the situation found with non-finites embedded in NPs.

The anaphoric relation between the antecedent and the missing subject

In examples where the antecedent is a simple NP such as a proper name, the missing subject can be recovered quite straightforwardly: in *Kim*$_i$ *remembered* __$_i$ *to lock the door*, for example, it was Kim who locked the door. Where negation or quantification is involved, however, matters are more complex:

[9] a. *<u>No one</u>*$_i$ *intends* [__$_i$ *to harm you*]. b. *<u>Both of them</u>*$_i$ *hope* [__$_i$ *to speak first*].

Example [a] does not mean "No one intends that no one should harm you", and [b] does not mean "Both candidates hope that both candidates will speak first". We understand, rather, "No one intends that he or she should harm you" and "Each of the two of them hopes that he or she will speak first". What is understood is something more abstract than a repetition of the antecedent: we need to invoke the concept of variables, as in the informal representations "No one *x* intends [*x* to harm you]" and "Both of them *x* want [*x* to speak first]". This, however, is not a special feature of subjectless non-finites, but rather a quite general feature of anaphora, and for this reason further discussion can be left to Ch. 17.

It is also a general feature of anaphora that we can have a sequence of links between a missing element or pro-form and its antecedent, forming an 'anaphoric chain', as in:

[10] *Jill*$_i$ *intends* [_$_i$ *to try* [_$_i$ *to mediate between them*]].

The missing subject of *mediate* is controlled by the subject of *try*, but that itself is missing, controlled by the subject of the next higher clause, with *intend* as predicator. *Jill* is thus associated with the role of experiencer relative to *intend*, and agent relative to *try* and *mediate*.

15

Coordination and supplementation

Rodney Huddleston
John Payne
Peter Peterson

The preceding chapters have been concerned with constructions which consist of a head element, alone or accompanied by one or more dependents. In this chapter we turn to two types of **non-headed** construction, namely **coordination** and **supplementation**. Compare:

[1] i *I left the room and Pat followed me.* [coordination]
ii *The tourists – most of them exhausted – got into the bus.* [supplementation]

Construction [i] is non-headed because the two underlined constituents are of equal syntactic status: we cannot say that one is head and the other dependent. Construction [ii] is not so clearly distinct from a headed construction: the difference is that the underlined constituent is not tightly integrated into the syntactic structure. We treat it therefore as a supplement rather than as a dependent (such as we have in *The exhausted tourists got into the bus*). We look in detail at coordination in §§1–4, and then turn more briefly to supplementation in §5.

1 The structure of coordinate constructions

1.1 Coordinations, coordinates, and coordinators

Coordination is a relation between two or more elements of syntactically equal status, the **coordinates**; they are usually linked by means of a **coordinator** such as *and* or *or*:

[2] i *[Kim and Pat] speak excellent French.* [NP-coordination]
ii *He can see you [this afternoon or on Tuesday].* [NP/PP-coordination]

The equality of the coordinates is reflected in the fact that usually **either** of them could stand alone in place of the whole coordination (with adjustment of agreement features where necessary): *Kim speaks excellent French*; *Pat speaks excellent French.*[1] A second indication of the equality of the coordinates is that in the most straightforward cases we can reverse their order without significant effect on structure or meaning: *Pat and Kim speak excellent French*; *He can see you on Tuesday or this afternoon.*

Coordination as a non-headed construction

Coordination contrasts with subordination, where the elements are of unequal status. In subordination one element is head, the other(s) dependent, but precisely because

[1] In cases like *Kim and Pat [are a happy couple]*, such replacement is not possible, but the coordinates are again of equal status in that **neither** can replace the whole: see §1.3.2.

coordinates are of equal status the functions of head and dependent are not applicable to coordination. We therefore refer to *Kim and Pat* as an NP-coordination, not an NP: it is functionally like an NP but does not have the structure of one. Examples like [2ii] show, moreover, that the coordinates do not have to be of the same syntactic category, *this afternoon* being an NP, *on Tuesday* a PP. The whole cannot belong to either one of these categories, and we analyse it therefore as an NP/PP-coordination, i.e. a coordination of an NP and a PP.

Contrasting structures

The examples in [3] contain two coordinates and one coordinator, but there are other possibilities. We have three contrasts of structure to note.

(a) Binary vs multiple coordination

There can be more than two coordinates – in which case we speak of **multiple coordination** in contrast to **binary coordination**, with just two:

[3] i *Kim wrote a letter and Ed watched TV.* [binary coordination]
ii *She wants to live [in Sydney, in London, or in Paris].* [multiple coordination]

(b) Syndetic vs asyndetic coordination

Although the construction is usually marked by a coordinator, it does not have to be; the coordination is said to be **syndetic** when it is overtly marked in this way, and **asyndetic** when it is not:

[4] i *He invited [all his colleagues and all his students].* [syndetic]
ii *He invited [all his colleagues, all his students].* [asyndetic]

With multiple coordination we have two subtypes of syndetic coordination:

[5] i *He can see you [on Monday, Tuesday, or Friday].* [simple-syndetic]
ii *He can see you [on Monday or Tuesday or Friday].* [polysyndetic]

Example [i] has *or* marking just the final coordinate, whereas in [ii] it marks all except the first. These are the only possibilities even when we have more than three coordinates: all **medial** coordinates (those which are neither initial nor final) must be treated alike, either all unmarked (*on Monday, Tuesday, Thursday, or Friday*) or else all marked (*on Monday or Tuesday or Thursday or Friday*) – not, for example, **on Monday or Tuesday, Thursday or Friday.*

(c) Correlative vs non-correlative coordination

All syndetic coordination has a marker before the final coordinate; the initial coordinate may also be marked, by a determinative that is **correlative** (paired) with the one marking the final coordinate. *Both* correlates with *and*, *either* with *or*, and so on (see §2.3).

[6] i a. *He invited [both his father and his uncle].* [correlative]
b. *He invited [his father and his uncle].* [non-correlative]
ii a. *He can see you [either on Monday or on Tuesday].* [correlative]
b. *He can see you [on Monday or on Tuesday].* [non-correlative]

Either can appear in multiple coordination, and we then find again the contrast between simple-syndetic *either on Monday, on Tuesday, or on Friday* and polysyndetic *either on Monday or on Tuesday or on Friday.*

The most usual pattern has a single coordinator located before the final coordinate; the extra elements in correlative and polysyndetic structures emphasise the coordinative relation (but see also §2.3), while the absence of a marker in asyndetic coordination makes this not always clearly distinguishable from non-coordinative constructions.

Place of coordinators in the constituent structure

From a semantic point of view a coordinator expresses the relation between the coordinates, but syntactically it belongs with the coordinate that follows it (i.e. they form a constituent together), so that the structure for *Kim and Pat* will be as in [7]:

[7]

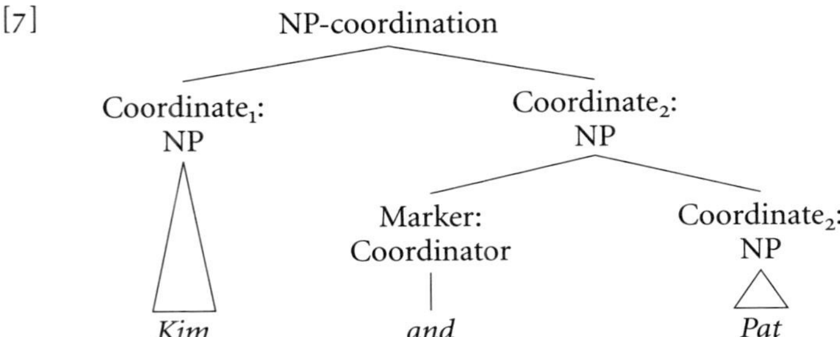

The numerical subscripts indicate the sequential order of the coordinates: as we have said, they are of equal syntactic status, and this is reflected in the fact that they are not differentiated in terms of syntactic function, but only in terms of their linear position.

There are three reasons for saying that the coordinator forms a syntactic constituent with the coordinate that follows:

(a) Variable position of second coordinate

Under certain conditions it is possible to vary the position of the second coordinate in a binary coordination (cf. §4.5). Compare:

[8] i a. *They allowed <u>the others</u> <u>but not me</u> a second chance.*
b. *They allowed <u>the others</u> a second chance <u>but not me</u>.*
ii a. *Did <u>the boss</u> <u>or her secretary</u> tell you that?*
b. *Did <u>the boss</u> tell you that <u>or her secretary</u>?*

In both versions the coordinator is located next to its coordinate: what varies is the position of *but not me* and *or her secretary*, which indicates that each of these forms a unit.

(b) Sentence-initial *and*, *or*, *but*

Such coordinators as *and*, *or*, and *but* can occur in sentence-initial position. For example, speaker A might say, *She thoroughly enjoyed it*, and B then add, *And so did her mother*. It is clear that *and* here forms a unit with *so did her mother*.

(c) Prosody and punctuation

The natural intonation break is before the coordinator, not after. This is particularly clear in polysyndetic and correlative coordination. A natural reading of *He invited his brother and his sister and his mother*, for example, will have a prosodic break before each *and*: He *invited his brother* | *and his sister* | *and his mother*. Similarly with writing: if punctuation is used between the coordinates, it occurs in these same places.

Bare and expanded coordinates

In [7] we have generalised the functional term 'coordinate' so as to have it apply not only to *Pat* but also to the larger element *and Pat*; where it is necessary to make clear which is intended, we use **bare coordinate** for *Pat* itself and **expanded coordinate** for *and Pat*. We also allow for an expanded coordinate to contain various modifiers in addition to (or instead of) a coordinator – modifiers like *too, as well, else*, and so on. The structure for the coordination in *He offended the guests and indeed his family too* will therefore be as in [9].

[9]

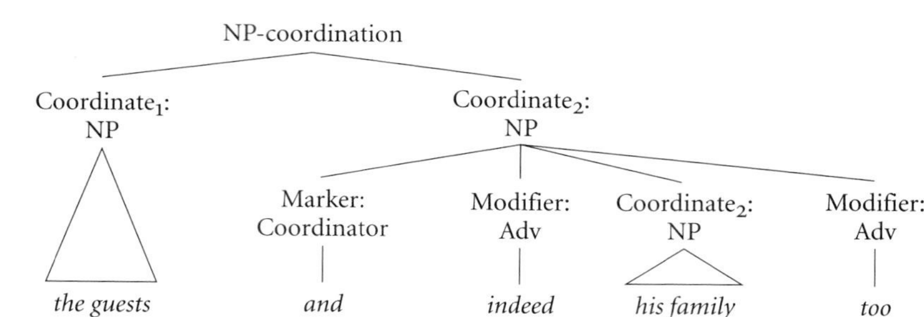

The bare coordinates are *the guests* and *his family* (just as they are in *He invited the guests and his family*), but *his family* is expanded by the modifiers *indeed* and *too*, as well as by the marker *and*. (See §4.1 for fuller discussion of this kind of expansion.)[2]

1.2 Layered coordination (*Kim and either Pat or Alex*)

A coordination can function as a coordinate within a larger one, resulting in what we call a **layered coordination**:

[10] i *We should invite [Kim and <u>either Pat or Alex</u>].*
ii *<u>I tried to persuade him and so did Kim</u>, but he was quite inflexible.*

The underlining marks the lower coordination. In [i] the NP-coordination *either Pat or Alex* is coordinated with *Kim* to form the larger NP-coordination enclosed in brackets, whose structure is as follows:

[11]

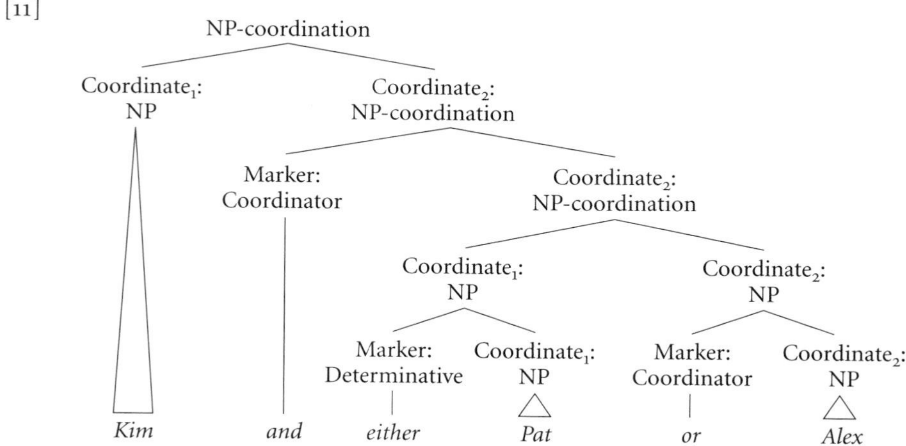

[2] Formal grammar often uses 'conjunction' in place of 'coordination', but we see no reason to change the traditional term, which contrasts transparently with 'subordination'. 'Conjunction' is in any case an unfortunate

Similarly in [10ii]: the underlined sequence is a clause-coordination which realises the first coordinate in a larger clause-coordination that forms the whole sentence. *But* is the coordinator at the upper layer, *and* at the lower.

The possibility of layering means that with three bare coordinates we can in principle have three contrasting structures, as shown in the following simplified representations:

[12]

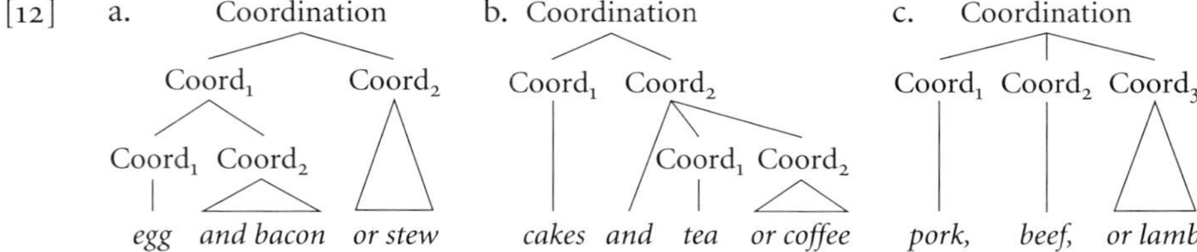

The word sequences in [a] and [b] are ambiguous, but the interpretations represented in the diagrams are the natural ones. In [a] the choice (*or*) is between egg and bacon on the one hand, stew on the other, whereas in [b] the choice is between tea and coffee. The second layer of coordination is on the left in [a], and on the right in [b], whereas in [c] there is only a single layer.

In [10] and [12a–b] it is immediately clear that there is layering because of the contrasting coordinators: *and* vs *but* or *and* vs *or*. Within any single coordination the coordinators must match: all non-initial ones must be identical and any initial markers must correlate with the non-initial ones, *both* with *and*, *either* with *or*, etc. Moreover, as we noted above in introducing polysyndetic coordination, if any **medial** coordinate is marked by a coordinator, all must be – which means that while [13i] may be a single coordination [13ii] cannot be:

[13] i *He invited [Kim <u>and</u> Tom <u>and</u> Pat <u>and</u> your parents].*
ii *He invited [Kim, Tom <u>and</u> Pat, <u>and</u> your parents].*

In [ii] we have four bare coordinates but only two coordinators, so that there must be layering. There are two possible structures: the first layer has either two coordinates ([*Kim, Tom <u>and</u> Pat*] + [*your parents*]) or three ([*Kim*] + [*Tom <u>and</u> Pat*] + [*your parents*]). Example [i] has no grammatical marking of layering, but it does not exclude a layered interpretation and indeed allows numerous different ones ([*Kim <u>and</u> Tom*] + [*Pat*] + [*your parents*]; [*Kim*] + [*Tom <u>and</u> Pat*] + [*your parents*]; and so on) – the layering in this case would have to be signalled purely by prosody or punctuation.

Scope

In [12a] (*egg and bacon or stew*) we say that *or* **has scope over** *and*, in that the *and*-relation holds within one of the coordinates linked by *or*. Scope is a semantic concept, but in simple examples like this it is reflected straightforwardly in the syntactic structure: *or* is a marker at the upper layer of coordination, *and* at the lower layer. An alternative type of formulation we shall use is to say that *or* has **wide scope** relative to *and* – or that *and*

choice because this term is used in logic for a relation corresponding closely to just one type of coordination, that marked by *and* as opposed to *or* (*or*-coordination corresponding in turn to logical disjunction) – see §2.2.1 below. In traditional grammar, moreover, 'conjunction' is used for a class of words used in both coordinative and subordinative constructions. 'Coordinate' is not widely used in traditional grammar, and for this concept formal grammar almost invariably uses 'conjunct'.

has **narrow scope** relative to *or*. In [12b] (*cakes and tea or coffee*), of course, the scope relations are reversed: here *and* has scope over *or*.

1.3 Syntactic constituency and semantic scope

1.3.1 Clausal and subclausal coordination

In **clausal coordination** the bare coordinates are full main clauses; other cases we refer to as **subclausal coordination.**

Semantic equivalence

In the absence of special factors, a subclausal coordination is semantically equivalent to the corresponding clausal coordination:

[14] i a. *There is a copy* [*on the desk and in the top drawer*]. [subclausal]
b. *They arrived* [*on Tuesday or Wednesday*].
c. *He told me* [*who she was but not what she wanted*].
ii a. *There is a copy on the desk and there is a copy in the top drawer.* [clausal]
b. *They arrived on Tuesday or they arrived on Wednesday.*
c. *He told me who she was but he didn't tell me what she wanted.*

Example [ia] is equivalent to [iia], and similarly for the other pairs. Note that coordination of subordinate clauses, as in [ic], is subsumed under subclausal coordination: the coordinates, although themselves clauses, are nevertheless constituents of the main clause just as much as the coordinates of [ia–b], and in that sense are subclausal.

Given this equivalence, we will say that the semantic scope of the coordinator is the same in both cases. So although the coordination is syntactically subclausal in [14i] the semantic scope of the coordinator extends over the whole clause, just as it does in [ii]. It can also be convenient to speak of [i] as a **reduction** of [ii], or of [ii] as an **expansion** of [i], with the understanding that this does not imply that [i] is syntactically derived by ellipsis from [ii].

Non-equivalence

There are also numerous cases where corresponding subclausal and clausal coordinations are not semantically equivalent. A typical example is found in:

[15] i *One candidate was* [*very young and very energetic*]. [subclausal]
ii *One candidate was very young and one candidate was very energetic.* [clausal]

In [i] there is a single candidate with two properties, whereas [ii] implicates that the one who was very young and the one who was very energetic were different candidates. Again we will talk in terms of semantic scope: in [ii] *and* has scope over the determiner *one*, so that a referent for *one candidate* is selected independently in the two coordinates. But in [i] *one* has scope over *and*, so that the two properties are predicated of the same candidate. Where the coordination does not have scope over the whole clause we say that it has **narrow scope**, and it is precisely when subclausal coordination has narrow scope that it is not equivalent to clausal coordination.

Further examples of narrow scope coordination are given in:

[16] i *No one [treats me like that and gets away with it].*
ii *Nothing is wrong with [the amplifier or the tuner].*
iii *Who [lives in college and has a car]?*
iv *Did she [go to the meeting and make her report]?*
v *The [first and most impressive] speaker was from Wales.*
vi *She'd like [a cricket bat or a tennis racquet] for her birthday.*

Example [i] doesn't say that no one treats me like that – but that no one gets away with it if they do. And [ii] is quite different from *Nothing is wrong with the amplifier or nothing is wrong with the tuner*, for the meaning is "Nothing is wrong with the amplifier **and** nothing is wrong with the tuner". These two illustrate one of the most frequent cases where scope factors prevent expansion: the case where the coordinator is within the scope of a negative (to be discussed in §2.2.2). In [iii] interrogative *who* similarly has scope over *and*: it is a single question asking about a set of people combining two properties, whereas the clausal coordination *Who lives in college and who has a car?* is two questions, asking about two sets of people. Example [iv] likewise expresses a single question as to whether she both went to the meeting and made a report, whereas *Did she go to the meeting and did she make her report?* is two questions about two separate events. In [v] *and* falls within the scope of the definite article *the*, so that there is a single speaker with the twin properties of being first and being the most impressive. Finally, the salient interpretation of [vi] has *or* falling within the scope of *would like*: she is as it were offering a choice, she would be happy with either a cricket bat or a tennis racquet.[3]

1.3.2 Joint coordination (*Kim and Pat are a happy couple*)

A special case of narrow scope coordination is **joint coordination**, which contrasts with the default **distributive coordination**:

[17] i *Kim and Pat know Greek.* [distributive]
ii *Kim and Pat are a happy couple.* [joint]

Example [i] is equivalent to *Kim knows Greek and Pat knows Greek*, but if we attempt to expand [ii] in the same way the result is incoherent: **Kim is a happy couple and Pat is a happy couple.* The difference is that knowing Greek applies to Kim and Pat **distributively**, i.e. individually or separately, but being a happy couple does not – it is Kim and Pat together, jointly, who are a happy couple (cf. Ch. 5, §5.1).

Further examples of joint coordination like [ii] are:

[18] i *Kim and Pat are two of his best friends.*
ii *Kim and Pat disliked each other.*
iii *Kim and Pat went to Bonn and Paris respectively.*

Example [i] is like [17ii] in that the coordination is within the scope of the predicative complement: we must first form a set consisting of Kim and Pat before we can assign the properties "a happy couple" and "two of his best friends". In [18ii] the coordination is within the scope of *each other* (*dislike each other* can only apply to a plural set) and

[3] Example [16vi] also has a less likely interpretation where *or* has scope over *would like*, and in this case it is equivalent to the clausal coordination *She'd like a cricket bat for her birthday or she'd like a tennis racquet for her birthday* (i.e. I'm not saying which she would like, with the implicature that I don't know).

in [iii] both coordinations are within the scope of *respectively* (hence the incoherence of **Kim and Pat went to Bonn respectively* and **Kim went to Bonn and Paris respectively*).

Ambiguity between distributive and joint coordination

Examples like the following allow both kinds of interpretation:

[19] i *Kim and Pat are in love.*
ii *Kim and Pat are studying law and economics.*
iii *Kim and Pat told me they were going to New York.*

The distributive interpretation of [i] is equivalent to the clausal coordination *Kim is in love and Pat is in love*, while the joint interpretation is equivalent to *Kim and Pat are in love with each other*: the reciprocal relation can be implicit. And the same applies to the respectively relation, so that [ii] has not only the distributive reading "Kim is studying law and economics, and Pat is studying law and economics", but also the joint one "Kim and Pat are studying law and economics respectively". In the distributive interpretation of [iii] there were two acts of telling, one performed by Kim, the other by Pat, whereas in the joint reading there was a single act of telling. This might have been in a letter from the two of them, but it could also be that in fact just one of them actually said this to me: if they were both engaged in the conversation it would be perfectly reasonable to attribute the information to the two of them jointly.

Distinctive grammatical features of joint coordination

Joint coordination differs from other kinds of coordination in the following respects:

(a) Restriction to *and*

Joint coordination virtually requires *and* as coordinator:[4]

[20] i	*Kim <u>or</u> Pat will be going to Bonn.*	[distributive]
ii	**Kim <u>or</u> Pat will be going to Bonn and Paris respectively.*	[joint]

(b) Exclusion of correlative *both*

For most speakers at least, *both* is not permitted in joint coordination:

[21] i	*<u>Both</u> Kim and Pat are friends of his.*	[distributive]
ii	**<u>Both</u> Kim and Pat are two of his best friends.*	[joint]

(c) No expansion by modifier

And cannot be accompanied by any modifiers to the coordination, such as *too, as well, especially, probably*, etc.:

[22] i	*Kim and <u>probably</u> Pat <u>too</u> resented your intervention.*	[distributive]
ii	**Kim and <u>probably</u> Pat <u>too</u> disliked each other.*	[joint]

The ambiguity of [19i–ii] is resolved in favour of a distributive interpretation if they are amended in any of these respects: *Kim <u>or</u> Pat had been in love*; *<u>Both</u> Kim and Pat had been in love*; *Kim and <u>probably</u> Pat <u>too</u> had been in love.* But the restrictions do not apply to the narrow scope coordinations cited in §1.3.1: [15i], for example, can be manipulated to give *One of the candidates was very young and <u>probably</u> very energetic <u>too</u>*; *One of the candidates was <u>both</u> very young and very energetic*; *One of the candidates was very young <u>but</u> very energetic.* Note also the contrast between reflexive and reciprocal pronouns, at

[4]The qualification 'virtually' is needed because *or* is marginally possible in a narrow range of cases when the predicate contains some such word as *choice*: *Hamburgers or sausages is a miserable choice to have to make.*

least with respect to correlative *both*:

[23] i *Both Kim and Pat had hurt themselves.* [reflexive: distributive]
ii **Both Kim and Pat had hurt each other.* [reciprocal: joint]

Example [i] is not strictly expandable (we can have *Kim had hurt herself and Pat had hurt himself* or the like, but this involves changing the pronoun and incorporating information about their sex that is not encoded in [i]). It is for such reasons that we prefer to contrast 'joint' with 'distributive' rather than 'separable': [i] doesn't belong to the joint construction, but it is not separable in the sense of involving wide scope coordination.

Verb agreement

In addition to the above, there is a fourth grammatical property, singular agreement, that holds distinctively for certain special cases of joint coordination:

[24] i *Two ham rolls and a glass of milk <u>were</u> hidden behind the lamp.* [distributive]
ii *Two ham rolls and a glass of milk <u>was</u> more than she wanted.* [joint]

The 3rd person singular verb-form *was* indicates that the subject is understood collectively as denoting a quantity – e.g. a quantity of food/drink to be consumed for lunch.

Other cases of joint coordination

Our examples so far have involved NP-coordinations in subject function, but joint coordination is found more widely than this.

In the first place, joint NP-coordinations occur in other functions besides subject:

[25] i *I introduced <u>Kim and Pat</u> to each other.* [object]
ii *I sat between <u>Kim and Pat</u>.* [comp of preposition]

Secondly, the coordinates may belong to other categories:

[26] i *He was <u>eating</u> and <u>reading</u> at the same time.* [verbs]
ii *The latter two were <u>French</u> and <u>German</u> respectively.* } [adjectives]
iii *He was wearing a <u>black</u> and <u>white</u> silk tie.* }
iv *<u>Telling him you were busy</u> and <u>then going out dancing</u> was a mistake.* [VPs]

Example [26i] is implicitly reciprocal in that the eating and reading were taking place at the same time as each other (this is the salient interpretation: it is just possible to take the coordination as distributive, with the events taking place at the same time as something specified in the preceding context). The joint interpretation of the coordination in [26ii] is due to the *respectively*, whereas that in [iii] reflects a "partly–partly" sense: we understand the tie in [iii] to be partly black and partly white. It is therefore quite different from the pragmatically unlikely *He was wearing a black tie and a white tie*, which has him wearing two ties. In [iv] what was a mistake was the combination of the two actions, not each of them individually; it is not equivalent to the clausal coordination *Telling me you were busy was a mistake and then going out dancing was a mistake* precisely because the latter says that the two actions were separately mistaken.

1.3.3 NPs with discrete set interpretations (*new and second-hand books*)

NPs containing a dependent with the form of a coordination may be interpreted as denoting discrete sets, each associated with a different coordinate. Compare:

[27] i *They sell [<u>new</u> and <u>second-hand</u> books].* [discrete]
ii *They offer [<u>new</u> and <u>highly sophisticated</u> programs].* [not discrete]

In [i] we have two discrete sets of books, a set of new books and a set of second-hand books; in [ii], by contrast, we have a single set of programs, all of them being new and highly sophisticated. The difference reflects the fact that while *new* and *second-hand* denote mutually exclusive properties, *new* and *highly sophisticated* do not.

These examples involve count plural NPs, but the distinction is found also with non-count NPs: *They sell new and second-hand furniture* (discrete types of furniture) vs *They offer new and highly sophisticated software* (not discrete: the software is simultaneously new and highly sophisticated). A discrete interpretation is inconsistent with a count singular NP, though it is possible for the head of a count plural NP to be singular when the coordination includes determiners (§4.4) – compare *a new and a second-hand copy* (discrete: two copies, one new, one second-hand) and *a new and highly sophisticated program* (not discrete, a singular NP: one program, simultaneously new and highly sophisticated).

Discrete set interpretations can also be found when the dependent does not itself have the form of a coordination but contains a coordination within it:

[28] i *It will be opposed by [the premiers of Queensland and Tasmania].* } [discrete]
ii *I need the names of [the hotels he stayed at in Rome and Paris].* }

These have discrete interpretations like [27i], but in the first the coordination is within the complement of *of* and in the second it is within the relative clause modifying *hotels.* The discrete interpretations here derive from the knowledge that Queensland and Tasmania are separate states and hence have separate premiers, that Rome and Paris are distinct cities and hence have different hotels (compare *the books he read in Rome and Paris,* where there is nothing to force a discrete interpretation).

Discrete vs not discrete can't be identified with distributive vs joint

The distinction illustrated in [27] bears some resemblance to that between distributive and joint coordination, but there are several reasons for not identifying it with the latter:

(a) Lack of grammaticalisation

The distinction in [27] is not reflected grammatically in the same way as that between distributive and joint coordination – indeed it can hardly be said to be grammaticalised at all. Thus both cases allow modifiers and coordinators other than *and: They sell new but also second-hand books*; *They offer new but nevertheless thoroughly tested programs.* And while correlative *both* strongly favours a discrete interpretation (it could readily be inserted before *new* in [i] but hardly in [ii]), it nevertheless does not require a discrete interpretation in cases of post-modification:

[29] i *Comments both favourable and critical had poured in.* [discrete]
ii *Comments both brief and to the point will be very welcome.* [not discrete]

(b) Relation with clausal coordination

Secondly, we do not find the same sharp difference as with distributive vs joint coordination when we compare with clausal coordination:

[30] i *They sell new books and they sell second-hand books.*
ii *They offer new programs and they offer highly sophisticated programs.*

Example [30i] is equivalent to [27i], but [30ii] does not contrast with [27ii] in the way that *Kim is in love and Pat is in love* contrasts with the joint (reciprocal) interpretation of *Kim and*

Pat are in love ([19i]), for it quite readily allows an interpretation where two properties are assigned to a single set of programs.

(c) Indeterminacy

Consider also the range of contexts for such an example as

[31] *I have seen the films showing on Saturday and Sunday.*

If there is a single film showing each night, [31] will be interpreted discretely, as involving two separate films (otherwise singular *film* would be used). Suppose, however, there is more than one film each night: the Saturday and Sunday films may then be completely different (programs change on Sunday – a discrete interpretation) or completely the same (perhaps programs change on Thursday). But it is also possible that some change and others don't – there is partial overlap. And we also have the case where only one film is showing on Saturday but more than one on Sunday, or vice versa, again with or without a change. There is no reason to say that these numerous different scenarios yield different **meanings** for the NP: it simply gives no indication concerning the distribution of the films over the two days (the same applies to *the films showing at the week-end*, where there is no coordination). It is for this reason that [27ii] is labelled 'not discrete' rather than 'non-discrete': it doesn't say that the sets are discrete, but nor does it actually **say** that they are non-discrete.

1.3.4 Constituent structure and scope ambiguities (*long poems and essays*)

In sequences of the form 'Dependent–X_1–C–X_2' or 'X_1–C–X_2–Dependent', where C is a coordinator and X_1 and X_2 are elements of the same kind able to function as head to the dependent, there may be ambiguity according as the dependent applies to just the X element adjacent to it or to the coordination 'X_1–C–X_2'.

The NP *long poems and essays*, for example, can have either of the following (simplified) structures:

[32]

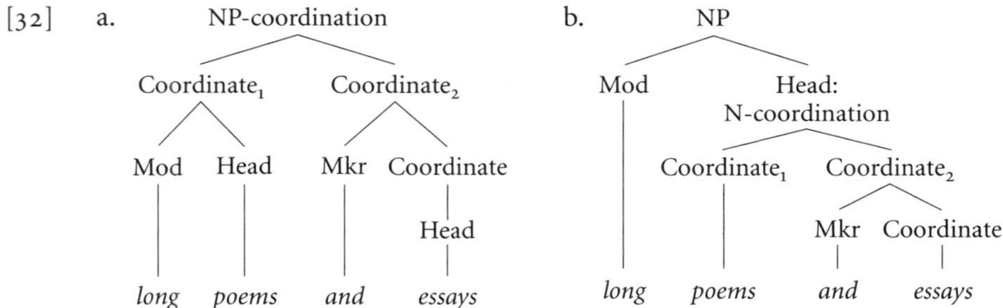

In [a] the dependent *long* belongs in the first coordinate and modifies just *poems*: this corresponds to the interpretation where the poems are long while the length of the essays is not specified. In [b] *long* modifies the coordination *poems and essays*, which matches the interpretation where both poems and essays are long: in this case the NP is equivalent to the NP-coordination *long poems and long essays.*

The example just given involves an adjective modifying a nominal head, but the structural contrast shown in [32] is found over a very wide range of dependent–head constructions, as indicated in the formulation given at the beginning of this section.

The range of the phenomenon is illustrated in the paired examples given below. In each pair, [a] has a salient interpretation where the dependent applies to just the adjacent 'X' element, and [b] one where it applies to the 'X' coordination: the constituent structures will thus be similar to [32i] and [32ii] respectively (or to their mirror images in cases where the dependent follows the head). Single underlining marks the dependent, double underlining the associated head: thus in [33ia] *extremely* modifies the adjective *rare* in [a] and the adjective-coordination *tired and irritable* in [b].

[33]	i	a. *It was [extremely rare or unique].* b. *He was [extremely tired and irritable].*	[Mod–Adj]
	ii	a. *He did it [very hurriedly but satisfactorily].* b. *She spoke [very quickly and fluently].*	[Mod–Adv]
	iii	a. *He [often goes to bed before nine and likes plenty of exercise].* b. *He [often gets up at six and has a swim before breakfast].*	[Mod–VP]
	iv	a. *Yesterday Ed was taken ill and the lecture's been cancelled.* b. *Yesterday Ed was taken ill and the lecture was cancelled].*	[Mod–Clause]
	v	a. *women and children under sixteen* b. *men and women over fifty*	[N–Mod]
	vi	a. *He [left and phoned his wife].* b. *He [hugged and kissed his wife].*	[V–O]
	vii	a. *I [went to bed and read the paper for a while].* b. *I [called the police and complained as soon as the party began].*	[VP–Mod]

Other things being equal, structure [b] – with the dependent applying to the coordination – is in general more likely. 'Other things being equal' requires that the dependent could apply equally readily to either 'X' element.[5] This condition is not met in four of the examples. In [33ia] the adjective *unique* is hardly gradable in this context: the choice must be between being extremely rare and being actually unique. In [iiia] going to bed before nine is a serial state but liking plenty of exercise is a non-serial state, and hence resists modification by *often* (cf. Ch. 3, §3.2). In [iva] the first clause is in the preterite (*was*), while the second is present perfect (*has been*), and as such excludes the modifier *yesterday* (cf. Ch. 3, §5.3.1). And in [va] women are all adults and hence not under sixteen.

In [33iia] a type [b] reading is excluded by the contrary-to-expectation combination of *hurriedly* and *satisfactorily* marked by the coordinator *but*. Example [via] allows in principle a type [b] structure, but it is very unlikely because leaving one's wife and phoning her are not normally comparable, the former being a major and drastic occurrence, the latter an everyday one. Finally in [viia] a type [b] interpretation is possible but unlikely because it is much more usual to go to bed, read for a while, and then go to sleep for the night than to go to bed, read for a while, and then get up.

[5] The 'other things being equal' proviso also implies the absence of special prosody: a sharp prosodic break after the first coordinate can signal a type [a] reading. Often, of course, this kind of interpretation can also be unambiguously conveyed by reversing the order: in *He was irritable and extremely tired*, for example, the dependent *extremely* clearly applies to *tired* alone.

1.4 Order of coordinates

Reversible and irreversible coordination

In the simplest cases, the order of bare coordinates is free, so that we can change the order without discernible effect on interpretation or acceptability:

[34] i *She [was very bright and had a warm personality].*
ii *She [had a warm personality and was very bright].* [reversible: i = ii]

We say here, then, that the coordination is **reversible.** In many other cases, however, the coordination is **irreversible**, so that changing the order of the bare coordinates leads to a different interpretation or to loss of acceptability, as in:

[35] i a. *She [fell ill and went back to her mother's].*
b. *She [went back to her mother's and fell ill].* [irreversible: ia ≠ ib]
ii a. *She had [far and away] the best outline.*
b. **She had [away and far] the best outline.* [irreversible: only iia is acceptable]

We interpret [ia] with the falling ill preceding the return to her mother's and [ib] with the opposite order of events, and in [ii] only [a] is acceptable since *far and away* is a fixed expression.

In this section we will consider certain general factors which cause the different orders to be less than fully interchangeable; certain more specific ones (such as that involved in [35i]) will be taken up in the discussion of the individual coordinators in §2.

Anaphora

Often, reversal is blocked for the simple reason that the second coordinate contains (or has as a supplement) an item explicitly or implicitly anaphoric to the first or to an element within it:

[36] i *Her father had once lied to her and because of this she never really trusted him.*
ii *Jill was rich and Pat, moreover, was even richer.*

In [i] *this* has the first coordinate as antecedent and *him* has *her father*: since an anaphoric item and its antecedent cannot in general be located in successive coordinates, the order can only be as in [i] itself. The same applies with [ii], where there is implicit anaphora: the supplement *moreover* means roughly "besides this", and *richer* is here understood as "richer than her". Quite similar are cases like *I'll tell the truth and nothing but the truth* or *You and you alone will be held responsible*, where there is repetition rather than anaphoric reduction. The second coordinate must follow because it presupposes the first: *I'll tell nothing but the truth* presupposes that I'll tell the truth, and so on.

Lexicalised coordinations

A large number of coordinations – mainly pairs of words joined by *and* or *or* – are partially or fully lexicalised. The **fully lexicalised** ones constitute composite lexical items with the order completely fixed and with meanings generally not fully predictable from those of the coordinates and the coordinator:

[37]

aid and abet	*betwixt and between*	*by and large*	*common or garden*
first and foremost	*hem and haw*	*high and dry*	*hither and yon*
let or hindrance	*part and parcel*	*rhyme or reason*	*rough and ready*
rough and tumble	*spick and span*	*to and fro*	*well and truly*

Some of these contain words that no longer occur in contemporary English other than in the coordination: *fro, hem, spick,* etc.

Partially lexicalised coordinations are combinations where the items regularly go together in a particular order; reversal is not impossible but represents a quite sharp departure from the expected order:

[38]	*buy and sell*	*come and go*	*cup and saucer*	*cuts and bruises*
	fish and chips	*for and against*	*friend and foe*	*head and shoulders*[6]
	hope and pray	*husband and wife*	*life and death*	*loud and clear*
	meek and mild	*tried and tested*		

In both [37] and [38] the coordinates are often either near-synonyms (*tried/tested, meek/mild, first/foremost*) or opposites of one kind or another (*come/go, husband/wife, buy/sell*).[7]

Ordering tendencies

In many cases, the fixed or preferred order of coordinates in fully or partially lexicalised coordinations reflects certain tendencies that favour one order over another in ordinary, non-lexicalised coordinations too.[8]

(a) Temporal order

Coordinates denoting periods or points of time tend to be ordered so as to match the temporal order: *past, present, and future*; *yesterday, today, and tomorrow*; *the morning, afternoon, and evening*; *sooner or later*; *on Tuesday, Wednesday, and Friday.* Similarly with states ordered in time, as in *life and death*, or parts of a whole, as *beginning and end.*

(b) Spatial hierarchy

With items arranged on the vertical dimension, there is a tendency to put the higher before the lower: *up and down*, *upstairs and downstairs*, *upper and lower, above and below*, *head and shoulders*, *top and bottom.* It may be that this order reflects the greater salience of the higher in important cases like *above and below ground, above and below the horizon*, and arguably a similar salience hierarchy is reflected on the horizontal dimension in the ordering of *front and back, fore and aft*, etc.

(c) Deixis

The order in *here and there, hither and thither, now and then, this and that* reflects a deictic hierarchy, with the reference of the first coordinate being closer to the deictic centre, the time and place of the speech act. With the category of person, however, the hierarchy is overridden by a convention of politeness, which has 1st person in final position. Compare *you and your sister* (which accords with the hierarchy: 2nd person before 3rd) and *my sister and I* (reversing the hierarchy, with 3rd person before 1st).[9]

[6] This is fully lexicalised in its metaphorical sense: *This model is head and shoulders above the rest.*

[7] Comparable to lexicalisation is institutionalisation in the form of proper names – of books, public houses, organisations, etc. Many such names consist of or include coordinations, and the order of the coordinates is of course fixed as part of the name: *Pride and Prejudice*; *the Hare and Hounds*; *the Department of Employment, Education and Training.*

[8] Lexicalisation may also have been facilitated in expressions following certain phonologically favoured patterns, such as shorter before longer (in terms of number of syllables, *stuff and nonsense, out and about,* or length of vowel, *stress and strain, brush and comb*), high vowels before low in monosyllables (*dribs and drabs, fits and starts*), more sonorant before less sonorant initial consonant (*high and dry, hope and pray*).

[9] Non-standard !*Me and my sister were alone* simply follows the deictic hierarchy. With time and space factors (a) and (b) may outweigh (c): *yesterday, today, and tomorrow*; *up there and down here.*

(d) Polarity and evaluation

Positive terms tend to precede negatives: *yes and no*, *admit or deny*, *accept or refuse*, *with or without*. The concepts of positive and negative are extended to many scales of evaluation, and it is again the positive (more highly valued) term that tends to come first: *good and bad*, *for [better or worse]*, *friend or foe*, *right or wrong*. The concepts are also relevant to pairs like *come and go* and *arrive and depart*, where the positive–negative contrast is a matter of being at a certain place and not being there.

(e) Social hierarchy

Another tendency is for the order to reflect social status: *employers and employees*; *officers and men*; *peers and commoners*. Two special cases of this hierarchy rank adults above children and males above females: *father and son*; *Mr and Mrs*; *the Duke and Duchess of Penzance*; *husband and wife*; *brothers and sisters*; *he or she*; *men, women, and children*. The male–female order is reversed, however, in *Ladies and Gentlemen*; *bride and groom*; *mums and dads*.[10] Precisely because the usual male–female order can be seen as reflecting the social hierarchy, it can be regarded as a case of 'sexism' in language – and it may then be consciously reversed for that reason; it has, however, received very much less attention and criticism than more obvious cases of sexist language such as the use of masculine terms like ***he*** to subsume females (Ch. 5, §17.2.4).

2 Coordinators and related linking items

Coordination, we have said, is a relation between elements of equal syntactic status, and as such contrasts with subordination, a relation between elements of unequal status, dependent and head. As so often, however, we find that while the central or prototypical cases of coordination and subordination are sharply distinct, there is no clear boundary between the peripheries of the constructions and therefore some uncertainty concerning the precise membership of the category of coordinators. In this section we will first outline the distinctive grammatical properties of prototypical coordination and its markers, and then consider in turn a range of linking items including those that are clear members of the coordinator category, others that lie at the periphery, and some with insufficient similarity to justify inclusion in the coordinator category.

2.1 Properties of prototypical coordinators

(a) Unlimited number of coordinates

Arguably the most important distinctive property of coordination is that there is no grammatical limit to the number of coordinates that can be joined in a single layer of coordination.

[10] The order in *Ladies and Gentlemen* is widely felt to be a matter of conventional politeness, though historically it may be related to the origin of *lady* as the female counterpart of *lord* and hence higher in the social hierarchy than *gentleman*. There is also a historical explanation for *bride and groom*: the second term derives from *bride's groom*, which followed *bride* because it is defined in terms of its relation to the latter. With names, the male–female hierarchy is likely to take second place to the pragmatic principle of ordering according to primary interest: in a context where Kim and Pat are married, for example, Kim's parents are likely to refer to them as *Kim and Pat*, Pat's as *Pat and Kim*, and so on.

[1] i *He invited Kim and Ed and Max and Pat and Tom and Bob and Sue and Di.*
ii *He invited Kim, Ed, Max, Pat, Tom, Bob, Sue, and Di.*

These have eight coordinates, but clearly we could add as many more as we wished: the limits are set by style, comprehensibility, etc., not by grammar.

Coordinators are in this respect clearly distinct from prepositions and subordinators: repetition of these necessarily involves further layers of subordination. Compare, for example, coordinator *and* with preposition *of*. There are three possible structures for a sequence '*X and Y and Z*', two with layering, one without (cf. §1.2), but for '*X of Y of Z*' there are only two, both with layering:

[2]

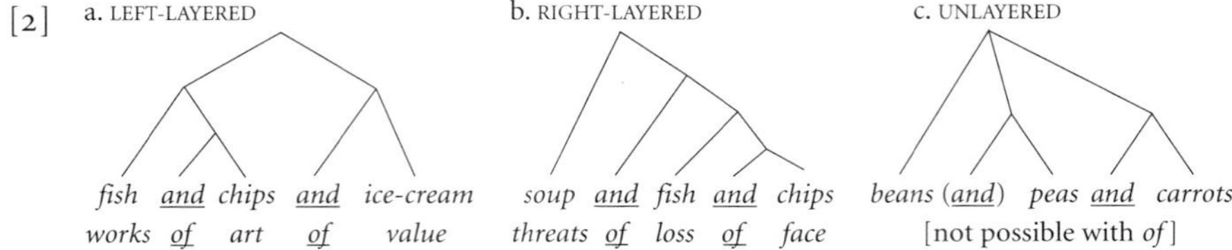

In [a] *fish and chips* and *works of art* form a unit on the left, and in [b] *fish and chips* and *loss of face* form a unit on the right; but in [c] (where the first *and* is omissible) there is no such intermediate grouping – and *of* cannot occur in this kind of structure. Similarly with *if* + clause: *Stay indoors if it's wet, if you want* has a left-layered structure comparable to [a], and *Don't appoint him if he'd panic if there was a crisis* has a right-layered one comparable to [b], but there is no possibility of an unlayered sequence '*X* (*if*) *Y if Z*'. The clause subordinator *that* allows unlimited iteration in structures like *Kim said that Pat thought that you had recommended that we accept the offer*, but again this clearly involves layering (on the right). There is therefore no subordinative analogue of the unlayered multiple coordination [c].

(b) Coordinates must be syntactically alike

Since coordination is a relation between elements of equal status, they must be syntactically alike. Just what this means is a question we take up in §3.1, but it is sufficient for present purposes to note that the coordinates are usually of the same syntactic category. Coordinators can thus be seen to contrast sharply with clause subordinators and prepositions, both of which relate a subordinate element to a superordinate one that can be syntactically quite unlike it:

[3] i a. *The [fact that he's a politician] makes it worse.*
b. *He was [unsure whether to accept her offer].* } [clause subordinators]
ii a. *His anger contrasted with his [mood before he'd seen them].*
b. *He [collapsed on hearing the news].* } [prepositions]

In [i] the clause subordinator *that* relates the finite clause *he's a politician* to the noun *fact*, while *whether* relates the infinitival clause *to accept her offer* to the adjective *unsure*. In [ii] the preposition *before* likewise relates a finite clause to a noun, *he'd seen them* to *mood*, while *on* relates non-finite *hearing the news* to finite *collapsed*. Substitution of coordinator *and* leads to complete unacceptability in all such cases – it requires structures like *She's a doctor and he's a politician*, *I plan [to resign and to accept her offer]*, etc., where like is coordinated with like.

(c) Wide range of categories that can be coordinated

Almost any syntactic category can be coordinated. The categories that can be related by a coordinator are thus considerably more numerous and diverse than those that can be related by a preposition.

Coordination of finite VPs

One category that occurs freely with coordinators but not with prepositions is that of finite VP:

[4] i *She finished the report and went home.* [coordination]
ii *She finished the report before going home.* [subordination]

Finite *went home* is impossible in [ii],[11] while gerund-participial *going home* is excluded from [i] by the requirement that the coordinates be alike (both finite or both gerund-participial).

Coordination of nominals

A second category of elements that can occur readily with coordinators but not generally with prepositions is that of nominals, elements smaller than full NPs:

[5] i *They found [her son and younger daughter].* [coordination]
ii **They found [her son with younger daughter].* [subordination]

In [i] the coordinates *son* and *younger daughter* are nominals, not NPs, for the determiner *her* is outside the coordination. The ungrammaticality of [ii] shows that the preposition *with* cannot similarly combine with a nominal, but requires a full NP: *They found her son with her younger daughter.*

(d) Impossibility of fronting an expanded coordinate

A coordinator and its coordinate cannot be moved to front position. Note here the contrast between the coordinator *but* and the preposition *although*:

[6] i a. *He joined the club but he had little spare time.*
b. **But he had little spare time he joined the club.* [coordination]
ii a. *He joined the club although he had little spare time.*
b. *Although he had little spare time he joined the club.* [subordination]

This restriction reflects the fact that the coordinates are of equal status. The structure we have assigned to a binary coordination is $\text{Coordinate}_1 + \text{Coordinate}_2$: the numerical subscripts indicate only the linear position, not a functional difference. There can therefore be no alternation between '$\text{Coordinate}_1 + \text{Coordinate}_2$' and '$\text{Coordinate}_2 + \text{Coordinate}_1$', for the latter is incoherent, given this interpretation of the subscripts.[12]

(e) Across the board application of syntactic processes

A special consequence of the requirement that coordinates be syntactically alike is that certain syntactic processes must apply **across the board**, i.e. to each one of the

[11] We can have *She finished the report before she went home*, but the complement of the preposition is here a clause, not a finite VP.

[12] We can of course have *He had little spare time but he joined the club*, but this has exactly the same structure as [6i] ($\text{Coordinate}_1 + \text{Coordinate}_2$); property (d) is concerned with expanded coordinates, not bare ones.

coordinates. Compare from this point of view the coordinative and subordinative constructions in:

[7] i *They attended the dinner but they are not members.* [coordinator]
ii *They attended the dinner although they are not members.* [preposition]

If we relativise these and embed them as modifier within NP structure, we must relativise both clauses in [i], i.e. across the board, but only the superordinate clause in [ii]:

[8] i *Those [who attended the dinner but who are not members] owe $20.*
ii *Those [who attended the dinner although they are not members] owe $20.*

The contrast here is very sharp: coordinates are treated alike, but a subordinate clause is unaffected by processes applying to its superordinate.

Compare now:

[9] i a. *You recommended the book and she enjoyed it so much.*
b. *It was a cold, wet evening and she enjoyed the book so much.* [coordination]
c. *He said that she enjoyed the book so much.* [subordination]
ii a. *the book [which you recommended and she enjoyed so much]*
b. **the book [which it was a cold, wet evening and she enjoyed so much]*
c. *the book [which he said that she enjoyed so much]*

This time, instead of a coordination of relative clauses, as in [8i], we have a coordination within a single relative construction, but the across the board requirement still holds. What it means here is that the relative pronoun *which* must relate to both coordinates: in [9iia] it is understood as object of both *recommended* and *enjoyed.* This is why [iib] is ungrammatical: the first coordinate is *it was a cold wet evening*, which is a complete clause, with no gap understood as linked to *which* ("the book"). The relative construction in [iic] also involves two clauses, but since they are related by subordination *which* does not have to have a role in each: it is understood simply as object of *enjoyed.*

For the same reason *which* cannot itself coordinate with a non-relative NP – compare *Kim and Pat invited them* and **I blame Kim, who and Pat invited them.* Similarly with other unbound dependency constructions such as open interrogatives: **Who and Pat invited them?*[13]

(f) Only one coordinator per coordinate

The coordinators are mutually exclusive, with a single coordinate containing at most one of them. This property distinguishes coordinators not from prepositions but from connective adverbs such as *yet, moreover*, etc.:

[10] i **She was extremely bright and but very humble.* [coordinator + coordinator]
ii *She was extremely bright and yet very humble.* [coordinator + adverb]

There is a very sharp contrast here between the adverb *yet*, which can combine with *and* (as a modifier within the expanded coordinate) and *but*, which can't – we need *She was extremely bright but very humble.*

[13] An interesting exception to this constraint is seen in the attested example *Even Barbara, [between whom and Juliet there should by rights have existed a great awkwardness,] was in some ways easier to grasp than Frances.* Such exceptions would seem to be restricted to relative clauses containing a coordination functioning as complement to *between.*

(g) Coordinators must occupy initial position

In expanded coordinates, the coordinator always comes first. Compare:

[11] i *It had rained all week and we were short of food.* [coordinator]
ii *It had rained all week; moreover, we were short of food.*
iii *It had rained all week; we were, moreover, short of food.* } [adverb]

Again, this property distinguishes coordinators from connective adverbs. The only position available to *and* in the second clause is the initial one shown in [i], but the adverb *moreover* can occur in a variety of positions, as illustrated in [ii–iii] (it could also occur after *we* or at the end of the clause).

The two most central coordinators are *and* and *or*: these have all the above properties. The next most important coordinator is *but*, which lacks property (a), however. *Nor* is also a clear member of the category. In addition, there are a few items, such as *as well as*, *plus*, etc., which in some uses have arguably been reanalysed to become marginal members of the coordinator category.

2.2 *And* and *or*

The relation between *and* and *or* is comparable to that between *all* and *some* – or universal and existential quantification (Ch. 5, §5.1). Compare:

[12] a. *We'll invite [Kim, Pat, and Alex].* b. *We'll invite [Kim, Pat, or Alex].*

Example [a] entails that we will invite **all** members of the set expressed by the coordination, while [b] says that we'll invite **some** member of that set. With *and* we are concerned with a set in its totality, whereas with *or* the members of the set are regarded as alternatives.

2.2.1 Logical conjunction and disjunction

We will focus first on clausal coordination of declaratives and subclausal coordination that is equivalent to it.

[13] i a. *He came to work by bus today and he has gone home early.*
b. *He came to work by bus today or he has gone home early.* } [clausal]
ii a. *There is a copy [on the desk and in the top drawer].*
b. *There is a copy [on the desk or in the top drawer].* } [subclausal]

In [i] the bare coordinates express the simple propositions "He came to work by bus today" and "He has gone home early", while the whole coordination expresses a composite proposition containing the two simple ones. In [ia], where the coordinates are joined by *and*, the composite proposition is true if and only if **both** simple propositions are true; in [ib], where they are joined by *or*, the composite proposition is true if and only if **either** simple proposition is true. Because the subclausal coordination in [ii] is equivalent to clausal coordination we can handle these examples in the same way: [iia] is true if and only if both simple propositions ("There is a copy on the desk" and "There is a copy in the top drawer") are true, while [iib] is true if and only if either of them is true.[14]

[14] When we talk of a clause or clause-coordination being true, this is a shorthand way of saying that the proposition that in some context it is or can be used to assert is true.

Or is most characteristically used when the speaker believes that only one of the component propositions is true. A plausible context for [13ib], for example, is one where his car is not in the place it would be expected to be if he had come to work by car and had not yet gone home: I am offering alternative explanations for the absence of the car, not envisaging the possibility that both might apply. And with [iib] it may well be that I have in mind a single copy that is in one or other location – in this case the component propositions are mutually exclusive, just as they are in *Kim is in the study or in the rumpus-room.*

But *or* doesn't **mean** that only one of the alternatives is true. Example [13ib] doesn't explicitly exclude the possibility that both explanations apply. And if we modify our contextualisation of [iib] so that there could be more than one copy, then the possibility arises of there being a copy in both locations. *There's a copy in the office or in the library*, for example, is perfectly consistent with both component propositions being true – and indeed I might say it knowing that both are true, using *or* rather than *and* because I'm thinking of a choice as to which copy to consult.

We will take up this point below, arguing that the 'only one' feature commonly associated with *or* has the status of an implicature. And where we have this implicature that only one of the component propositions is true, there will generally be a further implicature that the speaker doesn't know which it is. If I utter [13iib] in a context where there is only one copy, for example, you will normally assume that I don't know precisely where it is, whether on the desk or in the top drawer – because if I did know I would surely tell. But, very clearly, this is again not part of the meaning of *or* but a matter of pragmatics. There is, for example, nothing anomalous about *The question in Part 2 is on Molière or Racine, but I'm not telling you any more than that.* The second clause implicates that I do know which of the alternatives is the true one, and yet it is quite consistent with the *or* in the first clause – the *but* clause here cancels or blocks the "I don't know which" implicature commonly found with *or*.

The collective and alternative relations expressed by *and* and *or* in such examples as [13] correspond closely to the relations known to logicians as **conjunction** and **disjunction**. These are operations on propositions that are entirely defined by their effects on truth; the truth value of a proposition formed by conjunction or disjunction is fully determined by the truth values of the component propositions.

Conjunction

Suppose "P" and "Q" are two propositions. The logical conjunction of "P" and "Q" is often symbolised as "P & Q". By the definition of conjunction, "P & Q" is true if and only if both "P" and "Q" are true. In all other circumstances, "P & Q" is false. This matches what we said above about the coordinations with *and*. In [13ia] "P" = "He came to work by bus today" and "Q" = "He has gone home early", and the whole coordination is true if and only if both of these propositions are true, and likewise in [iia], with "P" now having the value "There is a copy on the desk", and "Q" the value "There is a copy in the top drawer".

Inclusive and exclusive disjunction

Logicians distinguish two kinds of disjunction: **inclusive** and **exclusive** disjunction. The inclusive disjunction of "P" and "Q" is often written "P $\vee$ Q". It is true if and only if at least one of the propositions "P" and "Q" is true. The exclusive disjunction of "P" and "Q" will be written here as "P $\underline{\vee}$ Q". It is true if and only if exactly one of "P" and "Q" is true.

Truth tables for conjunction and disjunction

Because these definitions are given entirely in terms of conditions under which propositions are true, we can express them in the form of truth tables. We assume that "P" and "Q" can be true or false independently of each other. We list the four possible combinations of truth values for them at the left of the table, and then show the truth values that "P & Q", "P ∨ Q", and "P ⊻ Q" would have for each of the four combinations:

[14]	Truth values		Conjunction	Inclusive disjunction	Exclusive disjunction
	P	Q	P & Q	P ∨ Q	P ⊻ Q
i	true	true	true	true	false
ii	true	false	false	true	true
iii	false	true	false	true	true
iv	false	false	false	false	false

For example, row [i] of the table corresponds to a situation in which "P" and "Q" are both true. In such a situation, "P & Q" makes a true claim, as shown in the column labelled 'Conjunction'; so does "P ∨ Q", as shown in the 'Inclusive disjunction' column; but "P ⊻ Q" is false, as the final column indicates. Row [ii] covers the case where "P" is true but "Q" is false, and so on.

And in [13ia/iia], we have said, expresses conjunction: the whole coordination is true in situations corresponding to [14i] and false in situations corresponding to [14ii–iv]. *Or* in [13ib/iib] expresses **inclusive** disjunction: the coordinations are true in situations corresponding to [14i–iii] and false only in a situation like [iv] – i.e. for [13ib], in a context where he didn't come to work by bus today and he hasn't gone home early, or for [13iib], where there is no copy on the desk and no copy in the top drawer.

Exclusiveness as an implicature of *or*

Of the three contexts where these *or*-coordinations are true, the ones I am most likely to intend in uttering [13ib/iib] are those corresponding to [14ii–iii], where just one of the alternatives is true. Indeed, the alternatives joined by *or* are often mutually exclusive, or are intended by the speaker to be seen as mutually exclusive:

[15] i *He was born on Christmas Day 1950 or 1951.*
ii *I shall walk or catch the bus.*
iii *You can have a pork chop or an omelette.*

In [i] we know that he can't have been born on two different Christmas Days; in [ii] it will normally be a matter of going the whole distance on foot or taking the bus; and [iii] will generally be used to offer or report a choice between two alternatives. It does not follow, however, that *or* here expresses exclusive disjunction. We shall say, rather, that *or* expresses inclusive disjunction but that a statement with the form '*P or Q*' is typically interpreted as carrying the implicature "P and Q are not both true".

Some *or*-coordinations are clearly not inconsistent with situation [14i]:

[16] i *There's a copy in the office or in the library.*
ii *Either the mailman hasn't got here yet or there's no mail for us today.*

As noted above, [i] does not exclude the possibility that there's a copy in the office and in the library – and we could indeed add *perhaps both*, explicitly allowing for it. Similarly[15]

[15] Compare also *They had contacted some or all of the witnesses*: in cases like this, if "Q" ("They had contacted all of the witnesses") is true then "P" ("They had contacted some of them") must be too (cf. Ch. 5, §5.2), so the choice is between contexts [14i] and [ii].

[ii] certainly does not rule out the case where the mailman is still on his way but has no mail for us. The *or* in [16] must be inclusive, which means that if we were to say that *or* expresses exclusive disjunction in [15] we would be saying that *or* is **ambiguous** between inclusive and exclusive meanings. There are, however, several reasons why it would not be satisfactory to handle the relation between [15] and [16] in terms of a difference between two meanings of *or*.

(a) Disambiguation

Assigning two meanings to *or* does not itself account for the exclusive interpretation of [15]: we would still have to show how *or* is disambiguated here, how we select one meaning, the exclusive one, rather than the other. In [15i], for example, the inclusive reading is ruled out by our knowledge that one cannot be born on successive Christmas Days. But instead of this knowledge selecting one meaning of *or* over another it can be seen as simply narrowing down the range of possible contexts for the whole coordination: *or* itself rules out only context [14iv] and our knowledge about the world (that you can't be born twice) further excludes context [14i].

(b) Not a matter of false vs true

If we analyse [15i] as having the logical form "P $\veebar$ Q" and [16i], say, as "P $\vee$ Q", we are saying that in context [14i] the former is false and the latter true, but this is not in fact how they differ. It is not that [15i] is **false** in this context, but that this context is not a practical possibility for [15i], so that the question of whether it is true in that context doesn't arise, or has no intuitively clear answer.

(c) Negation

Thirdly, and most importantly, a logically negated *or*-coordination is true only in context [14iv]:

[17] i *There isn't a copy on the desk or in the top drawer.*
ii *I shan't walk or go by bus.*

These entail that both alternatives are false, i.e. "There isn't a copy on the desk and there isn't a copy in the top drawer", "I shan't walk and I shan't go by bus". Logical negation reverses the truth value, and the truth values for these examples are the reverse of those for inclusive disjunction, namely false, false, false, true for contexts [14i–iv] respectively. Thus [17ii], for example, is true only when "I shall walk" and "I shall go by bus" are both false, i.e. in context [14iv]. If the *or* of [15ii] expressed exclusive disjunction, [17ii] should have the values true, false, false, true, "Maybe I'll both walk and go by bus, maybe I'll do neither", but that is clearly not what it means. It means I'll do neither. The force of this argument becomes even greater when we consider multiple *or*-coordination:

[18] i *They will appoint <u>Kim, Pat, or Alex</u> to oversee the election.*
ii *They won't appoint <u>Kim, Pat, or Alex</u> to oversee the election.*

Although [i] will normally **convey** that they will appoint just one of Kim, Pat, and Alex, this is not what it **means**, for [ii] is not the negation of the proposition that they will appoint just one of them. If it were, it would mean that they will appoint all three of them, or any two, or none at all: in fact, of course, [ii] means simply that they will appoint none of them.

The "not and" implicature associated with *or* belongs to the family of scalar implicatures – it is, for example, closely comparable to the "not all" implicature of *some* (cf. Ch. 5, §5.2).

A scalar implicature arises when two items are arranged on a scale where one is 'stronger' than the other: use of the weaker one implicates the negation of the stronger. *And* is stronger than *or*: '*P and Q*' entails '*P or Q*' (since whenever '*P and Q*' is true, i.e. in context [14i], '*P or Q*' is true too) but '*P or Q*' does not entail '*P and Q*' (since '*P or Q*' can be true while '*P and Q*' is false, namely in contexts [14ii–iii]). In general we don't use the weaker of two terms if we could use the stronger – e.g. we don't generally say '*P or Q*' if we know '*P and Q*' to be true. If I know they appointed Kim and Pat to oversee the election, it will normally be inappropriate to say *They appointed Kim or Pat to oversee the election*, for this is likely to suggest that they appointed just one but that I don't know which of the two it was. Similarly, if I intend to invite Kim and Pat to dinner, it is normally misleading to say *I'll invite Kim or Pat to dinner.* The most likely reason for saying '*P or Q*' rather than '*P and Q*', therefore, is that the latter would be false, which leads to the "not and" implicature. But that isn't the only reason for saying '*P or Q*': it may be that I know that one or other of"P" and "Q" is true, but don't know whether both are, as is likely to be the case in [16ii].

As usual, the implicature can be made explicit in a *but*-coordinate: *He'll invite Kim or Pat, but not both* (comparable to *He'll invite some of them, but not all*).[16] And it can be cancelled in similar ways: *He'll invite Kim or Pat, perhaps both* (comparable to *He'll invite some of them, perhaps all*).

When *or* implicates "and"

In certain cases '*P or Q*' has the opposite implicature, namely "P and Q":

[19] i *Houses are cheaper in Perth than in Sydney or Melbourne.*
ii *They are obtainable at Coles or Woolworths.*

In their salient interpretations, these are pragmatically equivalent to sentences with *and* instead of *or*.[17] The crucial feature is that although they present a choice it doesn't matter to the speaker which alternative is chosen. In [i] there is a choice (hence *or*) between comparing Perth with Sydney and comparing it with Melbourne, but it makes sense to state that Perth is cheaper than whichever alternative you might pick only in one circumstance: that Perth is cheaper than both. Similarly in [ii] you have a choice between obtaining them at Coles and obtaining them at Woolworths, but this choice presupposes that both stores stock them; hence the implicature that they are obtainable at Coles **and** at Woolworths. This phenomenon occurs in the same contexts as those where *any* is pragmatically equivalent to *all* (Ch. 5, §7.5). Such contexts most commonly involve comparison, as in [i], or – with varying degrees of explicitness – the modality of possibility, as in [ii] (cf. also *She can speak French, German, or Russian*, and so on).

[16] This provides further evidence against saying that *or* expresses exclusive disjunction: if '*P or Q*' has "not both P and Q" as part of its **meaning**, *but* should be inappropriate in '*P or Q but not both*', for it implies contrast (§2.5). The implicature can also be cancelled by metalinguistic negation (as opposed to logical negation: Ch. 9, §1.2), as in *They didn't appoint Kim* OR *Pat, they appointed* BOTH; metalinguistic negation of inclusive disjunction differs from logical negation of exclusive disjunction in that it doesn't allow situations corresponding to [14iv].

[17] In a less likely interpretation the "not both" implicature applies, accompanied by an implication of ignorance – e.g., for [ii], "They are obtainable at one or other of Coles and Woolworths, but I don't know (can't remember) which".

Or in questions

One special case where *or*-coordination is interpreted exclusively is the alternative question (Ch. 10, §4.4). In this type of question (which has an intonational rise on the initial coordinate, and fall on the final one) *or* is essential, whereas when it appears in other types of question it is merely incidental:

[20]	WITHOUT *OR*	WITH *OR*	
i	a. [not possible: *or* essential]	b. *Would you like tea↗ or coffee↘?*	[alternative]
ii	a. *Would you like a drink↗?*	b. *Would you like tea or coffee↗?*	[polar]
iii	a. *Who would like a drink?*	b. *Who would like tea or coffee?*	[variable]

In [ib] *or* does not appear in the answers, which are simply "I would like tea" and "I would like coffee" – they are presented as alternative answers, such that one and only one of them is true. "Both" is not a possible **answer** in that it rejects this presupposition of mutual exclusiveness. In [iib] and [iiib], *or* is retained in the answers: e.g. "Yes, I would like tea or coffee" and "No, I would not like tea or coffee" for [iib].[18]

2.2.2 *And* and *or* in combination with negation

When a subclausal *or*-coordination falls within the scope of a negative, it is equivalent to an *and*-coordination of negative clauses:

[21] i *I didn't like his mother or his father.*
ii *I didn't like his mother and I didn't like his father.*
["not A-or-B" = "not-A and not-B"]

Similarly *He can't read or write* means "He can't read and he can't write", *No one had seen Kim or Pat* means "No one had seen Kim and no one had seen Pat", and so on.

Conversely, when a subclausal *and*-coordination falls within the scope of a negative it is equivalent to an *or*-coordination of negative clauses:

[22] i *He isn't both treasurer and secretary.*
ii *He isn't treasurer or he isn't secretary.*
["not A-and-B" = "not-A or not-B"]

Note that both of [22i–ii] implicate that he is either treasurer or secretary. In the case of [ii] *or* triggers the usual "not and" implicature – that "He isn't treasurer" and "He isn't secretary" are not both true. It then follows from this that "He is treasurer" and "He is secretary" are not both false, i.e. that he is either treasurer or secretary. In the case of [i] the implicature that he is either treasurer or secretary derives from the familiar type of scalar implicature: [i] is weaker than *He isn't either treasurer or secretary* and hence implicates that the latter is not true.

Matters are complicated, however, by the fact that a negative does not always have scope over a following subclausal coordination. Whereas *and* falls within the scope of the negative in [22i], it is more often the other way round, with *and* having scope over the negative:

[23] i *I didn't like his mother and father.*
ii *I'm not free on Saturday and Sunday.*

[18] It is nevertheless likely to be dropped from a **response** in the interests of greater informativeness: *Yes, thank you, I'd love some coffee.* For the contrast between answer and response, see Ch. 10, §4.1.

Natural interpretations are "I didn't like his mother and I didn't like his father" and "I'm not free on Saturday and I'm not free on Sunday (i.e. I'm not free this week-end)". There is also a less salient reading in which the scopes are reversed, e.g. for [ii]: "I'm not free on **both** days" (with an implicature that I'm only free on one); this kind of interpretation characteristically has *and* stressed.

Or generally falls within the scope of a preceding negative, as in [21i], but wide scope readings are often possible as less likely interpretations:

[24] *He wasn't at work on Monday or Tuesday.*

The salient interpretation is "He wasn't at work on Monday and he wasn't at work on Tuesday", but it can also be read as "On Monday or Tuesday (I can't remember precisely which day it was) he wasn't at work".[19]

Not cannot have scope over a coordination of full main clauses. In *He didn't like it or he was in a hurry*, for example, the negative applies just to the first clause. To express negation of *or* and *and* we thus generally need coordination within a single main clause, either of phrases, as in [21i], or of subordinate clauses, as in *It's not the case that he was being investigated by the fraud squad or that he had offered to resign* (equivalent to *He wasn't being investigated by the police and he hadn't offered to resign*).[20] Analogously for *and*.

Equivalences in conditionals

The equivalence between narrow scope *or* and wide scope *and* seen in [21] in the context of negation is found also in the context of explicit or implicit conditionals:

[25] i a. *You'll see more if you walk or cycle.*
b. *You'll see more if you walk and if you cycle.*
ii a. *Those who are late or (who) are improperly dressed will be punished.*
b. *Those who are late and those who are improperly dressed will be punished.*

In [ia] *or* is within the scope of *if*, while in [iia] it is within a relative clause, but the whole construction is implicitly conditional, conveying "If anyone is late or improperly dressed they will be punished", where *or* is again within the scope of *if*.

2.2.3 Asymmetric constructions, I: *and* (*He got up and had breakfast*, etc.)

Example [13iia], *There is a copy on the desk and in the top drawer*, is **symmetric** in that it is equivalent to *There is a copy in the top drawer and on the desk*, where the coordinates appear in the reverse order. Similarly for the corresponding example with *or* and indeed the other examples considered in §§2.2.1–2. We have noted, however, that the order of coordinates is not always reversible in this way, and where the different orders convey different meanings we will speak of the coordination as **asymmetric**. The fact that the orders are not interchangeable indicates that the linked

[19] If the coordination is moved to the front, as in this gloss, it will be unambiguously outside the scope of the negative. Expanding the second coordinate by a modifier can also give the coordination wide scope, as in *He wasn't at work on Monday or perhaps Tuesday.*

[20] The qualification 'generally' is needed because there is another possibility, involving gapping (§4.2), as in *Kim hadn't been at home on Monday or Pat on Tuesday.* Here *or* is within the scope of the negative in the first clause, so that the meaning is "Kim hadn't been at home on Monday and Pat hadn't been at home on Tuesday".

terms are not, strictly speaking, of equal status, and hence the constructions concerned are not cases of prototypical coordination. We will see that they exhibit varying degrees of affinity with subordination: in particular, they do not always conform to the 'across the board' requirement that applies to symmetric coordination (cf. property (e) of §2.1).

We look first at asymmetric uses of *and* and then turn to *or* in §2.2.4.

Temporal sequence: '*X and Y*' implicates "X and then Y"

Where the coordinates denote occurrences rather than states, the linear order generally reflects the temporal sequence of the events:

[26] i *He got up and had breakfast.*
ii *I went over to Jill's and we checked the proofs.*

We interpret [i] as "He got up and then had breakfast", [ii] as "I went over to Jill's and then we checked the proofs (there)". Reversing the coordinates would reverse the sequence of events – *He had breakfast and got up*, for example, conveys that he had breakfast before getting up (i.e. he had breakfast in bed).

We analyse this "then" interpretation as an implicature, not part of a distinct meaning of *and*. There are three reasons for treating it in this way.

(a) Not dependent on *and*
The same implicature can be found across sentences with no coordinative link between them – e.g. if we substitute a full stop for *and* in [26ii].

(b) Variation in strength
The implicature varies in strength according to the context: for example, it is stronger in *In the afternoon I mowed the lawn and had a game of tennis* (narrating past events) than in *In the afternoon I will mow the lawn and have a game of tennis* (intended future events).

(c) Possibility of cancellation
Thirdly and most importantly, the implicature can be cancelled: *Before leaving town he handed in his resignation and phoned his wife, though I don't know which he did first.*

Nevertheless, the temporal sequence can be treated as part of the propositional content of the utterance, as when I ask: *Did he get up and have breakfast, or have breakfast and get up?* Moreover, this is one of the places where we find some relaxation of the usual 'across the board' requirement – notably in coordinations of VPs where the first expresses motion: *I've mislaid the proofs which I had gone over to Jill's and checked so carefully with her.*

Consequence: '*X and Y*' implicates "X and therefore Y"

Another common implicature is that the event expressed in the second coordinate is not only later than that expressed in the first but also a consequence of it:

[27] i *The principal came in and everybody immediately stopped talking.*
ii *I fell off the ladder and broke my leg.*

Here you will infer that the principal's entrance caused everybody to stop talking, that I broke my leg as a result of falling off the ladder.

Condition: '*X and Y*' implicates "if X then Y"

Closely related to consequence is condition, as in:

[28] i *I express the slightest reservation and he accuses me of disloyalty.*
ii *Come over here and you'll be able to see better.*
iii *Do that again and you'll be fired.*

Example [i] is interpreted as "If I express the slightest reservation, he accuses me of disloyalty". In the form given, it belongs to informal style, but a somewhat less restricted version is found with modal necessity added to the first coordinate: *I only have to express the slightest reservation and he accuses me of disloyalty.* Examples [ii–iii] illustrate the special case of the conditional implicature where the whole coordination has directive force (Ch. 10, §9.5). The implicature of [ii] is "If you come over here you'll be able to see better", which provides a reason for complying with the directive "Come over here". Similarly, [iii] implicates "If you do that again you'll be fired" but – assuming being fired is something you will want to avoid – this provides a reason for **not** complying with the apparent directive, so the end result is "Don't do that again". These examples have the form imperative + declarative; we also find two imperatives, as in *Join the Navy and see the world* (the fact that you'll see the world if you join the Navy is an incentive for joining), or the first coordinate can be of another form used with directive force, as in *I suggest you come over here and then you'll be able to see better.*

The logical link between conjunction and condition that facilitates the implicature is that both "P & Q" and "if P then Q" exclude the case where "P" is true and "Q" false, e.g. (for [28i]) where I express some slight reservation and he doesn't accuse me of disloyalty.

Concession: '*X and Y*' implicates "despite X, Y"

Here we have a "nevertheless/despite" relation between a second coordinate VP and the first:

[29] i *You can eat as much of this as you like and not put on weight.*
ii *They expect us to get up at 3 a.m. and look bright and cheerful.*

This is the opposite of consequence: your not putting on weight will be in spite of your eating as much as you like, not the result of your doing so. Again the inequality of status is reflected syntactically by relaxation of the 'across the board' condition. This time, however, we find unmatched extractions from the first rather than second coordinate: *How much of this can one eat and not put on weight?*

Temporal inclusion: '*X and Y*' implicates "X while Y"

In informal style *and* may be interpreted as "while":

[30] i *He came in and I was still asleep.*
ii *Did he come in and I was still asleep?*

The inequality of status is especially apparent in [ii], where the first clause is interrogative and the second declarative, and yet the whole is a single question: the question component has scope over the second clause just as it would if it were subordinate, as in *Did he come in while I was still asleep?*

Formulaic frames

Under this heading we include constructions of the form '*X and Y*' where X is fixed (or nearly so), but Y is not, and the whole is partially idiomatic.

(a) *Nice/good and* Adj/Adv

[31] i *The coffee is nice and hot.*
ii *He hit it good and hard.*

Example [i] is not understood in the same way as the ordinary coordination *The coffee is sweet and hot*: in the latter each coordinate expresses a property of the coffee, but in [i] *nice* applies rather to the heat ("It was nice by virtue of being hot, nicely hot, hot to a nice extent"), so that the interpretation is more like that of a subordinative construction than of a coordination. Compare also *It was nice and not too expensive* (ordinary) and *It was nice and cheap* (idiomatic – unless the *nice* and the *and* are each given prosodic prominence to mark the coordinates as of equal status). Only the ordinary case allows correlative *both*: *It was both nice and not too expensive.* Where the *Y* element is an adverb, as in [ii] (or *Take it nice and slowly*), the difference in status is reflected by a difference in syntactic category (adjective + adverb) – and thus only an idiomatic interpretation is available.[21]

(b) *Try / be sure and* V

[32]	PLAIN FORM + PLAIN FORM	PLAIN PRESENT + PLAIN FORM	
i	a. *Try and not be so touchy.*	b. *We always try and do our best.*	[*try*]
ii	a. *Be sure and lock up.*	b. [not possible]	[*be sure*]

This is very different, semantically and syntactically, from the ordinary use of *and*. Note first that, unlike the clausal coordination *We always try and we do our best*, [ib] does not entail that we do our best. Secondly, this idiomatic construction is syntactically restricted so that *and* must immediately follow the lexical base *try*; this means that there can be no inflectional suffix and no adjuncts: *She always tries and does her best* and *We try hard and do our best* can only be ordinary coordinations. There are two forms that consist simply of the lexical base: the plain form, as in [ia], and the plain present tense, as in [ib]. But the verb following *and* is always a plain form, as is evident when we test with ***be***: *We always try and be/*are helpful.* In spite of the *and*, therefore, this construction is subordinative, not coordinative: *and* introduces a non-finite complement of *try*. *And* can be replaced by the infinitival marker *to*, *and* being slightly more informal than *to*. *Be sure* works in the same way as *try*, except that the lexical base of ***be*** is only the plain form, so this time there is no plain present tense matching [ib]: *We are always sure and do our best* is not possible as an example of this construction (and unlikely as an ordinary coordination). Because the construction is subordinative, the across the board restriction does not apply: *This is something* [*that you must try / be sure and remedy*].

[21] The term 'hendiadys' is used for coordinations like [31], where the first coordinate is understood as modifying the second. In attributive position the *and* is omitted but we can still discern a difference between the idiomatic meaning of *I'd like a nice hot coffee* ("nicely hot, nice by virtue of being hot") and the ordinary meaning of *I'd like a large hot coffee* ("a hot coffee that is large, i.e. a large serving of hot coffee"). With *good* the range of second coordinates is very small and adverbs are restricted to words which also belong to the adjective category, like *hard* in [31ii]. In the predicative adjective case *nice* can be replaced by such related items as *lovely* and *beautiful*: *It was lovely/beautiful and hot.*

(c) *Go and* V

[33] i *The TV has gone and broken down.*
ii *He went and told the teacher.*

In this colloquial use of *go* the verb has lost its motional meaning and has a purely emotive role. The propositional content of [i] is simply "The TV has broken down", with *go and* adding an overlay of disapproval, annoyance, surprise, or the like. *He went and told the teacher* can be interpreted in the same way, or else literally, with *go* retaining its sense of movement. In the idiomatic sense *go* must immediately precede *and*: *He went to the office and told the teacher*, for example, can only have the literal movement interpretation. Any inflectional form of *go* is possible, and the following verb must match: both past participles in [i], preterites in [ii]. In this respect it is closer to coordination than the *try and* construction, but again there is no across the board restriction: *What a mess he's gone and made!* Even more colloquial is the multiple coordination *been and gone and* + past participle (*He's been and gone and told the teacher*), which has only the emotive idiomatic meaning.

(d) *Sit* (etc.) *and* V

[34] i *They sat and talked about the wedding.*
ii *Don't just stand there and watch.*

The first verb here is a verb of posture/stance, most often *sit, stand*, or *lie*. These verbs also take gerund-participials: *They sat talking about the wedding.* The latter is equivalent to [i], but the more informal coordinative construction arguably gives greater prominence to the talking; the sitting is backgrounded, and the impossibility of reversing the coordinates (without a change of meaning) reflects the difference in prominence assigned to them.

(e) *Be an angel* (etc.) *and* V

[35] i *Be an angel and make me some coffee.*
ii *Would you be an angel and make me some coffee?*

The two clauses here are of quite different pragmatic status: the second is the important one, the first having a role comparable to an adjunct like *kindly* or *please*. The first term allows for a range of alternatives to *an angel*: *a dear, a good boy/girl*, and so on. The coordinates can be imperative clauses, as in [i], or VPs within a clause used with indirect request force (Ch. 10, §9.6.1), as in [ii] – or in the reporting of a request: *She asked me to be an angel and make her some coffee.*

2.2.4 Asymmetric constructions, II: *or* (*Hurry up or we'll be late*, etc.)

Condition: '*X or Y*' implicates "if not X, then Y"

Or, like *and*, occurs in constructions with a conditional interpretation:

[36] i *I'm leaving before the end or I'll miss my train.*
ii *I left early or I would have missed my train.*
iii *Hurry up or we'll be late.*
iv *Don't do that again or you'll be fired.*

With *or* the implicated condition is obtained by negating the first coordinate: "If I don't leave before the end, I'll miss my train".[22] In [ii] the implied conditional is of the remote category, as indicated by the *would have*: "If I hadn't left early I would have missed my train", implicating that I did leave early and didn't miss my train. Again, modal necessity will often figure in the first coordinate: *I must leave before the end or I'll miss my train*; *I had to leave early or I would have missed my train.* In [iii–iv] the conditional interpretation provides a reason for complying with the directive given in the imperative: "Hurry up, because if you don't we'll be late"; "Don't do that again, because if you don't not do that again (i.e. if you don't refrain from doing that again) you'll be fired". Note that [iv] arrives via a different route at the same result as [28iii]. With *or* the second coordinate is always presented as the less desirable alternative, and may be left unexpressed: *Do as I say, or else!*

The pragmatic inequality between the clauses is again reflected syntactically in the relaxation of the normal across the board requirement. In *She hadn't spoken to John,* [*who had had to leave early or he would have missed his train*], for example, the first clause is relative but the second is not, and doesn't allow the replacement of *he* by *who.*

The logical link between coordination and condition is more direct with *or* than with *and*: "P or Q" says that one or other of the propositions is true, so if "P" isn't, then "Q" must be – "P or Q" entails "If not P, then Q".

Numerical approximations: *two or three*

Or-coordinations like *two or three, four or five,* etc., are commonly used as approximations rather than sets of alternatives. *I have three or four letters to write* can be interpreted literally as "I have either three or four letters to write (I'm not quite sure which)" but it is more likely to be taken as an approximation, "I have a few letters to write, something like three".

When *three* and *four* are taken as alternatives, they can be reversed, but the approximation interpretation is possible only where the smaller number comes first. With NPs we have a contrast between, say, *a glass or two,* an approximation, and *one glass or two,* a set of alternatives. *Three or so/thereabouts,* "about three", and the like can only be irreversible approximations.[23]

2.2.5 Coordinator-marked reduplication (*louder and louder, dozens and dozens*)

An idiomatic use of *and* is found in intensifying reduplication:

[37]	i	*The noise grew louder and louder.*	*She felt more and more confident.*
	ii	*I laughed and laughed and laughed.*	*I've told you about it again and again.*
	iii	*I made dozens and dozens of mistakes.*	*It rained for days and days.*

In [i] *and* joins inflectional comparatives (*louder*) or the marker *more* in analytic comparatives – and similarly *less* (*He was showing less and less interest in his family*). The meaning here is "progressively more/less". In [ii] we have verbs and adverbs, with the reduplication conveying a high degree of continuity or repetition. Prepositions can work

[22] Note that in deriving the conditional implicature of [i] we have changed *I'm not leaving* to *I don't leave*: this change reflects the different ways of referring to future time in conditionals and main clauses.

[23] For the use of *or* to present a revision, see the discussion of supplements in §5.2 below.

in the same way: *It went up and up and up.* In [iii] the reduplication is of nouns – measure nouns – and serves to indicate a large number or amount.

Like coordination proper, this construction allows an indefinite number of elements – but all except the first must be marked by *and* (thus not **I laughed, laughed, and laughed*). Usually the reduplicated items are words, so we do not have **She felt more confident and more confident* or **It rained for many days and many days.* An exception is seen in *She hit him and hit him and hit him,* but *him* is little more than a clitic here, and a lexical NP would not be possible: **She hit her attacker and hit her attacker and hit her attacker.*[24]

2.3 *Both* and *either*

The determinatives *both* and *either* function in the structure of NPs or of coordinations:

		a.	b.
[38]	i	a. *both players*	b. *both Kim and Pat*
	ii	a. *either player*	b. *either Kim or Pat*

In the NPs [ia/iia] they function as determiner, as described in Ch. 5, §§7.2, 7.7. In the coordinations [iia/iib] they function as marker of the first coordinate in correlative coordination: *both* is paired with *and,* while *either* is paired with *or.*[25]

Binary and multiple coordination

In NP structure *both* and *either* are restricted to sets of just two members: compare *both/either of her parents* and **both/*either of her three children.* In coordination, *both* is similarly restricted, occurring in constructions with just two coordinates, but *either* is used in multiple as well as binary coordination. Compare:

[39] i a. *The allegation was [both untrue and offensive].*
b. *Everything he suggested was [either unobtainable or too dear].* } [binary]
ii a. **I [both locked the doors and set the alarm and informed the police.*
b. *I'll either call out or bang on the door or blow my whistle.* } [multiple]

The fact that the duality restriction is maintained with *both* but not with *either* can plausibly be related to the fact that in NPs the duality feature is more explicit with *both* than with *either.* Thus *both players* itself denotes a set of two players, whereas *either player* does not: it is singular, but involves **selection** from a set of two.

[24]There are certain other cases where special interpretations are found with coordinator-marked reduplication. One is the existential construction *There are musicians and musicians*: this implies that there are **different kinds** of musicians, e.g. good musicians and bad musicians. Another involves *or,* as in *Is it hot or is it hot?,* where the identity of the coordinates makes the choice a spurious one, so that the question is rhetorical, conveying emphatically that it is hot. Similarly *You can have pork or pork or pork* draws attention, usually with humorous intent, to the absence of any alternative to pork. A comparable effect can be achieved with *and*: *The three most important things in real estate are location, location, and location.* These differ from the intensifying reduplication of [37] in that they are a matter of word play, involving implicatures deriving from the ordinary meaning of *and* and *or.*

[25]*Both* is occasionally found with other linking items than *and,* such as *as well as* (§2.8), *along with* (§2.9), *yet* (§2.10). *Either* also belongs to the category of adverbs, and as such serves as a connective adjunct, as in *Kim didn't go and Pat didn't, either.*

Distributional restrictions on correlative coordination

Correlative coordination is considerably more restricted in its distribution than the default non-correlative coordination.

(a) Largely excluded from position following a pre-head dependent

[40] i **It had been approved by [the both federal and state governments].*
ii **Your speech must be [very either witty or brief].*

The inadmissible correlative coordinations (underlined) are here located after the dependent *the* in NP structure and after the dependent *very* in AdjP structure. The ungrammaticality can be removed by dropping either *the* or *both* from [i], *very* or *either* from [ii].[26]

(b) *Both* (unlike *either*) can't be used before first coordinate in main clause coordination

[41] i **Both he overslept and his bus was late.*
ii *Either he overslept or his bus was late.*

(c) *Both* excluded from joint coordination

[42] i *Both Kim and Pat are happy.* [distributive]
ii **Both Kim and Pat are a happy couple.* [joint]

Both is also excluded from examples like *I want to see Kim and no-one else* / *Kim and only Kim*, where the second coordinate serves to exclude everyone other than Kim.

(d) *Either* excluded from alternative questions

[43] i *Are they coming on either Monday or Tuesday?*
ii **Are you either coming or not?*

Example [i] can only be a polar question, one with *Yes* and *No* as answers, while [ii] is simply inadmissible.

(e) Generally excluded from coordinations with asymmetric *and* and *or*

Both and *either* tend to emphasise the equality of the coordinates and hence do not in general combine with the asymmetric uses of *and* and *or* described in §§2.2.3–4 above. As we noted, *The coffee is both nice and hot* is not possible except as an ordinary coordination, assigning two separate properties to the coffee, and *He has both gone and told the teacher* likewise has only a literal interpretation. In *He both got up and had breakfast* and *I both fell off the ladder and broke my leg* the *both* is unexpected, and calls into question the temporal sequence and consequence implicatures of the versions without *both*. Similarly *either two or three* can't be used as an approximation like *two or three*, but presents two alternatives. There is, however, one asymmetric use of *or* that permits *either* in certain cases – the one where it has a conditional and directive interpretation, as in *Either you tidy your room or you lose your pocket money*. The *either* here reinforces the implicature ("Tidy your room!") by emphasising that there is no third alternative.

[26] Under certain conditions correlative coordination is possible in this position: *A similar [both very negative and very positive] appraisal of the theoretical importance of such research may be found in Jones (1982); It was clearly an [either misinformed or else simply malicious] suggestion.*

Either and the exclusiveness implicature

Either emphasises that one of the coordinates must obtain, and tends to strengthen the exclusive implicature that only one of them does. *I'll be seeing her on either Friday or Saturday* conveys somewhat more strongly than the version without *either* that I'll be seeing her on just one of these days. Exclusiveness nevertheless is still only an implicature: *They are obtainable at either Coles or Woolworths* emphasises the choice but, like the version without *either*, could readily be used in a context where they are obtainable at both stores.[27]

Linear position of *both* and *either*

The usual position for *both* and *either* is at the beginning of the first coordinate, as in all the above examples. They can, however, occur to the left of the basic position, as in [44i], or to the right, as in [44ii]:

[44] i a. *This was made clear both to [the men] [and their employers].*
b. *He was quite taken by either my [cheek] [or cheerfulness].*
c. *They will either have to [reduce expenditure] [or increase their income].*
ii a. *[He both overslept] [and his bus was late].*
b. *Usually he [is either too busy to come with us] [or else has no money].*
c. *We must prevent rapid changes [in either the mixed liquor] [or in the effluent].*

The coordinates are enclosed in brackets, and the markers underlined. With placement to the left, the coordinator is separated from the first coordinate; with placement to the right (which is less common, especially with *both*) it occurs non-initially within it. The most frequent cases involve constructions containing a preposition, as in [44ia/iic], or a determiner, as in [44ib].

Placement in these non-basic positions is quite common, particularly with *either*, though usage manuals tend to regard it as stylistically undesirable. In some cases, it is the only possibility other than omission or reformulation. This is so in [44iia]: the version with *both* at the beginning of the first coordinate is the ungrammatical [41i] above. Similarly in [44ib] placement of *either* before *cheek* gives **my either cheek or cheerfulness*, which violates constraint (a) above. Placement in non-basic position here can be avoided by repeating the determiner: *either my cheek or my cheerfulness*.[28]

By virtue of their ability to occur elsewhere than before the coordinate, *both* and *either* are clearly distinct from the coordinators. Given the relationship with the NP constructions shown in [38], we analyse them as determinatives which can realise the same function as coordinators. In some cases the position of the determinatives matches that of modifiers in clause structure: compare *It [will both solve the present problem] [and may also prevent future conflict]*, where *both* follows the auxiliary verb, like the modifier in *It will probably solve the present problem.*

[27] An explicitly inclusive *either* is found in this attested (but surely ungrammatical) example with *and/or*: **The majority of the manufacturing firms were engaged in importing, either of materials and components for use in production and/or final goods to complement their product range.*

[28] In *I always find myself next to some oaf who either overflows onto my seat or who talks endlessly about his hideous life* the non-basic position can be avoided only by omitting the second *who*, for a further restriction on correlative coordination is that the initial marker cannot precede a relative clause.

The tree structure we propose for *both to the men and their employers* in [44ia] is:

[45]

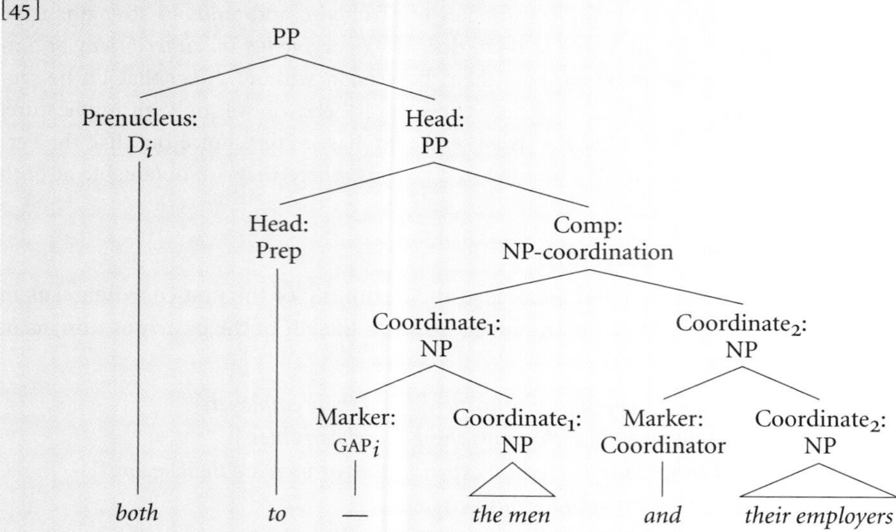

The marker for the first coordinate is realised by a gap that is co-indexed with the determinative *both* that occupies prenuclear position in the PP – compare the structure given for a relative clause in Ch. 12, §3.1. In [44iia] *both* occurs in prenuclear position in the VP *both overslept*, and is co-indexed with the marker element to the left of *he*.

2.4 *Neither* and *nor*

Neither as determinative and adverb

The determinative *neither*, like *both* and *either*, functions as a determiner in NP structure or as a marker in correlative coordination:

[46] a. *neither player* b. *neither Kim nor Pat*

In addition, it is an adverb functioning as connective adjunct in clause structure, like *either*:

[47] i *She wasn't impressed, (and) I wasn't either.*
ii *She wasn't impressed, (and) neither was I.* [*either*/*neither* as adverbs]

Example [ii] is related to [i] by the incorporation of the negative into the connective adverb; like other pre-subject negatives *neither* here triggers subject–auxiliary inversion. *Neither* differs from *either* in occurring in front rather than end position, but this construction is still clearly distinct from that of [46b] because of the possibility of having the coordinator *and* or *but* before it. That this *neither* is not a marker of coordination is also evident from the fact it can connect a main clause to a subordinate one: *If you don't complain, then neither will I.*

Neither as marker of coordination

As a marker of coordination, *neither* is usually paired correlatively with *nor*.[29] It can occur (like *either*) in multiple as well as the more usual binary coordination, and (like

[29] Examples are also found where *neither* is paired with *or*, as in *She was restrained by neither fashion or conformity* or *The Supreme Court's most recent affirmative-action decision is neither startling or new.* Usage manuals generally recommend *nor*, but there is no doubt that *or* is an established alternant.

both) it cannot occur initially in a coordination of main clauses:

[48] i *She found it [neither surprising nor alarming].* [binary]
ii *He was [neither kind, handsome, nor rich].* [multiple]
iii **Neither did he oversleep nor was his bus late.* [main clause coordination]

Position of *neither*

Like *both* and *either*, *neither* can occur to the left or right of its basic position:

[49] i *This serves the interests neither of [producers] [nor consumers].*
ii *[We are neither trying to keep out immigrants,] [nor are we favouring the well-to-do].*

Example [i] is again less favoured than *of neither producers nor consumers* (or *neither of producers nor of consumers*). The position of *neither* in [ii], however, is obligatory in view ofthe ungrammaticality of **Neither are we trying to keep out immigrants, nor are we favouring the well-to-do* (cf. [48iii]), but such structures are usually avoided in favour of subclausal coordination (*We are [neither trying to keep out immigrants] [nor favouring the well-to-do]*).

Nor as coordinator

Nor appears as a coordinator paired correlatively with *neither* ([50i]), or non-correlatively as a variant of *or* in negative contexts ([50ii]):

[50] i a. *[Neither Jill nor her husband] could help us.*
b. *A good conversationalist talks [neither too much nor too little].*
ii a. *The change won't be [as abrupt as in 1958 nor as severe as in 1959].*
b. *No state shall have a share [less than 50% nor more than 70%].*
c. *Serious art is not [for the lazy, nor for the untrained].*

In [ii] *nor* could be replaced by *or*, which is much more common: the version with *nor* perhaps gives added emphasis to the negation. There is no possibility of adding *and* or *but* before *nor* here, and hence every reason to treat *nor* as a coordinator in [ii] as well as in [i]. The difference is that in [i] all the coordinates are marked as negative, whereas in the non-correlative [ii] the first coordinate (*as abrupt as in 1958*, etc.) is not marked as negative within the coordination itself, but falls within the scope of a preceding negative.

Nor with subject–auxiliary inversion

The following non-correlative use of *nor* differs from that in [50ii] in that *nor* is not here replaceable by *or*:

[51] i *The Germans haven't yet replied; nor have the French.*
ii *He didn't attend the meeting, nor was he informed of its decisions.*
iii *He was one of those people who can't relax. Nor did he have many friends.*
iv *The hotel had good views and a private beach; nor were these its only attractions.*

In this use *nor* introduces a clause (normally a main clause) and triggers subject–auxiliary inversion. Some speakers allow a preceding *and* or *but* (cf. *%The Germans haven't yet replied and nor have the French*), so that for them *nor* here is a connective adverb, like the *neither* that could replace it (*... and neither have the French*). For many, however, this *nor* cannot combine with *and* and *but*,[30] and hence is again best regarded as a coordinator, though it very often occurs in sentence-initial position, as in [51iii].

This use also differs from that in [50ii] with respect to polarity. In [50ii] the first coordinate is within the scope of a negative; in [51] the first clause is usually negative, as in [i–ii], but in relatively formal style it need not be. In [iii] the first clause contains a negative but it is within the subordinate clause: the main clause itself is syntactically positive, though it has an obvious negative entailment, "He couldn't relax". In [iv], however, the first clause is completely positive.

Analysis of *neither* and *nor*

All three of the following are logically equivalent:

[52] i *She found it neither surprising nor alarming.* (=[48i])
ii *She didn't find it either surprising or alarming.*
iii *She found it both not surprising and not alarming.*

(The subclausal coordination in [iii] is in turn equivalent to clausal *She didn't find it surprising and she didn't find it alarming.*) It is tempting to analyse [i] as related to [ii] by the incorporation of the negative into *either... or*, reflecting the transparent morphological structure of *neither* as *n* + *either* and *nor* as *n* + *or*. This matches the analysis suggested for the adverb *neither* in [47]. The only difference is that while there is only one negative in [52ii], in [52i] the negative appears in both coordinates – but this could be regarded as a kind of negative agreement.

However, while the semantic analysis of *nor* as "not-or" is perfectly consistent with [50], it does not cater for all the cases of *nor* seen in [51]. It would be possible to regard [51i–ii] as negated disjunctions ("It isn't the case either that the Germans have replied or that the French have"), but a paraphrase like this is not possible in [51iii–iv], because the first clauses here are positive, as we have seen. It appears then that under the influence of the equivalence between negated disjunction and conjunction of negatives, *nor* has been reanalysed as "and-not", or "also-not".

2.5 *But*

But belongs to several categories: it is a coordinator in *He tried but failed*, a preposition in *I couldn't have done it but for your help*, an adverb in *He is but a child*, a noun in *Let's have no more buts.* We focus here of course on *but* as a coordinator, but we will see at the end of the section that the distinction between coordinator and preposition uses is not sharply drawn.

Adversative coordination

As a coordinator *but* characteristically has an adversative meaning, indicating a contrast between the coordinates:

[53] i *Kim left at six but Pat stayed on till noon.*
ii *My parents enjoyed the show but I didn't like it at all.*
iii *He wasn't [at all arrogant but on the contrary quite unassuming].*
iv *He has [many acquaintances but few friends].*
v *She likes [not only opera but also chamber music].*

[30] This is particularly so in AmE, but in other varieties too we find coordinator + *neither* much more often than coordinator + *nor*.

Here we have a direct contrast between Kim's departure time and Pat's, between my parents' reaction to the show and mine, and so on. Note that the coordinates differ in two respects: [i] Kim vs Pat, six vs noon; [ii] my parents vs me, enjoy vs not like; [iii] arrogant vs unassuming, positive vs negative; [iv] many vs few, acquaintances vs friends; [v] opera vs chamber music, negative vs positive.

A single difference is sufficient if it is located in a predicative or modifying element, but hardly otherwise:

[54] i *She loved her husband but betrayed him.* [predicator]
ii *He was [rich but very mean].* [predicative comp]
iii *He had a [demanding but low-paid] job in the public service.* [modifier]
iv **She likes opera but (she likes) chamber music.* [object]

In the above examples the contrast is derivable very directly from the content of the coordinates: from the grammatical opposition of positive vs negative, or lexical oppositions like *rich* vs *mean*, *opera* vs *chamber music*, and so on. More often it is derived indirectly, via various assumptions and inferences:

[55] i *He called round at Jill's, but she was out.*
ii *She was in considerable pain but insisted on chairing the meeting.*
iii *She likes opera but (she likes) chamber music too.*

In [i] we will assume that he called at Jill's with the aim of seeing her: her being out made this impossible, so we have a contrast between intention and actuality. Example [ii] illustrates a broad category of cases where the second coordinate contrasts with what one would or might expect on the basis of the first: if she was in considerable pain one might have expected her not to chair the meeting. In [iii] we have an explicit opposition between opera and chamber music, but we have noted that this is not sufficient (cf. [54iv]). The *too* introduces another implicit difference: *She likes opera* on its own might be pragmatically interpreted as "That's all (the only type of music) she likes", and *too* serves to deny that possibility, so that [55iii] entails [53v].

In general, *but* conveys "and" together with some further, non-propositional, meaning – commonly an adversative meaning such as we find in the connective adverbs *nevertheless, however, yet.* Thus [55ii], for example, might be paraphrased: *She was in considerable pain and yet insisted on chairing the meeting.* Such cases also allow paraphrases with subordinative *although*: *Although she was in considerable pain she insisted on chairing the meeting.* In some cases, such as [55iii], the implicit relation is "moreover": compare *She likes opera and moreover she likes chamber music too* (similarly with the coordinate negatives, *Kim hadn't read it, but Pat hadn't either*). Neither a "nevertheless" nor a "moreover" relation applies in cases like [53iii], where the second proposition entails the first (when negated, as here) and adds relatively little to it – compare similarly *He didn't go to work yesterday but stayed at home all day* – the relation here might be expressed by *instead.* Where, as in these two examples, the contrast is so sharp, it is barely possible to replace *but* by *and* + connective adverb.

Other cases which resist substitution of *and* + adverb are illustrated in:

[56] i *I would have gone, but I was too busy.*
ii *You may not believe this/it, but I usually keep the house quite tidy.*
iii *I'm sorry but you'll have to do it again.*
iv *He said it was your fault, but then he would say that, wouldn't he?*

Example [i] illustrates the preventative use of *but*: the situation expressed in the second coordinate prevents the realisation of the one hypothetically entertained in the first – my being too busy prevented my going (compare the remote conditional construction *I would have gone if I had not been too busy*). In [ii], the first coordinate contains a pronoun anaphoric to the second: *this*/ *it* is interpreted as "that I usually keep the house quite tidy". We call this anticipatory anaphora: the pronoun precedes its antecedent. This kind of anaphora is sanctioned by *but*, but not *and* (Ch. 17, §2.4). Example [iii] is similar except that the anaphoric relation is implicit: we understand "sorry to say this" or the like. *But then* in [iv] is idiomatic: it is used to indicate that what precedes is not surprising.

Restriction to binary structures

Unlike *and*, *but* is restricted to binary coordination:

[57] i *Kim is Irish but Pat is Welsh.*
ii **Kim is Irish but Pat is Welsh but Jo is Scottish.*

Dropping the first *but* in [ii] would make the example marginally acceptable, but it would be interpreted as a layered structure: the first two clauses would form an asyndetic coordination, so that Jo's being Scottish would be contrasted with the other two being Irish or Welsh.

Emphatic reaffirmation

But is occasionally used for emphatic effect with a repeated phrase:

[58] *Nothing, but nothing, will make me change my mind.*

The meaning is "absolutely nothing". The repeated expresssion is generally a negative, though we also find adjectives, particularly if they denote extreme values on a scale: *It was perfect, but perfect.*

But with the sense "except": preposition vs coordinator

[59]		a.	b.
	i	*Everyone but Jill was told.*	**But Jill, everyone was told.*
	ii	*Everyone but %I/ %me was told.*	*Everyone was told but me.*

But here has the same meaning as the preposition *except*, suggesting that it too is a preposition. It differs syntactically from *except*, in that it can't occur initially, as shown in [ib]: in this respect it is like a coordinator – cf. property (d) of §2.1. In [iia] both nominative and accusative forms of the pronoun are found, and this suggests that *but* can be construed as either a coordinator or a preposition. Following a coordinator, the pronoun will take nominative case because it is part of the subject (cf. *Neither Jill nor I was told*); following a preposition it will take accusative case (cf. *Everyone except / with the exception of me was told*). In *They told everyone but me* the accusative is obligatory, but provides no evidence as to the structure since a coordinate pronoun in this position would also be accusative (*They told neither Jill nor me*). Accusative is much the more usual case in [iia], with nominative very formal in style, and very much a minority variant: for most speakers *but* in this sense is a preposition. Notice, moreover, that in [iib], where *but* + pronoun is postposed, a nominative is virtually excluded even for speakers who have one in [iia]: it seems that in this position *but* is construed as a preposition by just about all speakers.

2.6 *Not*

'*X but not Y*' and '*not X but Y*'

Coordinates joined by *but* very often contrast as positive vs negative, or negative vs positive:

[60] i a. *Jill had been invited but her husband hadn't.* [clausal coordination]
b. *Jill hadn't been invited but her husband had.*
ii a. *They had invited [Jill but not her husband].* [subclausal coordination]
b. *They had not invited [Jill but her husband].*
c. *They had invited [not Jill but her husband].*

In clausal coordination the negation is expressed within one of the bare coordinates, the clause *her husband hadn't* in [ia], *Jill hadn't been invited* in [ib]. With subclausal coordination matters are more complex. In [iia] *her husband* is the bare coordinate, *but* the marker, and *not* a modifier (*not her husband* does not constitute an NP: we can't have **Not her husband accompanied her*, etc.). In [iib] the coordination is *Jill but her husband*, so the negation is not expressed within the coordination itself. However, the scope of the negative includes the first coordinate, but not the second: the meaning is, therefore, "They hadn't invited Jill but they had invited her husband". This is also the meaning of [iic], but here the *not* has been attracted into the coordination. We take *not* to be part of the coordination because it could not appear in this position in a non-coordinative construction (**They had invited not Jill*). The object here is therefore *not Jill but her husband*, with *not* a modifier expanding the first coordinate. Similar examples are:

[61] i *This is surely evidence [not of his guilt but of his innocence].*
ii *He married her [not because he loved her but because he was desperately lonely].*
iii *What she needs may be [not criticism, not advice, but simply encouragement].*

When *not* appears in an initial coordinate in this way, it is paired with *but* in the second: *not ... but* is thus comparable to *both ... and*, *either ... or*, *neither ... nor*. This might suggest that *not* should be treated as a marker of correlative coordination, like *both*, *either*, *neither*. The reason we don't analyse it that way, but take it rather as a modifier, is that the parallel with *both*, *either*, *neither* is only partial. This can be seen from [61iii], where *not* is repeated. The coordination here is layered. The first layer has *not criticism, not advice* as the first coordinate, and *but simply encouragement* as the second. The second layer then consists of a further, asyndetic, coordination with *not criticism* and *not advice* as coordinates. The fact that *not* can appear in a second coordinate and that *and* could be inserted before it (*not criticism, and not advice*) shows that – unlike *both*, *either*, *neither* – *not* has not taken on the function of a marker of the initial coordinate in a correlative construction.

'*X, not Y*'

It is possible to have '*X, not Y*' without a *but*:

[62] i *They had invited Jill, not her husband.*
ii *He died in 1984, not 1983.*

The meaning is not quite the same as that of '*X but not Y*'. With [60iia] (*They had invited Jill but not her husband*) we understand that they might in principle have invited both Jill and her husband, but in fact did not do so. In [62i], however, the issue is which of Jill and her husband it was that they invited. This is why it would be anomalous to add *but* to [ii]: it is not in principle possible for him to have died in both years.

2.7 ***Not only***

'*Not only X but Y*'

A special case of negative + positive coordinations with *but* involves *not only*; *but* is often accompanied by *also*, *as well*, or *too*:

[63] i *Our correspondents cover [not only this country but the whole world].*
ii *He [not only never went to school, but never even learned to read].*
iii *Not only was he incompetent, but he was also corrupt.*

Position of *not only*

Not only is often found to the left or right of its basic position, like *both*, *either*, and *neither*:

[64] i a. *He not only knew [soldiering] [but history and literature as well].*
b. *They had given copies not only to [the staff] [but the students too].*
c. *It is not only a question [of honour] [but of life and death].*
ii a. *[Complete power not only corrupts] [but it also attracts the mad].*
b. *He [had not only photocopied it] [but had even read it].*
c. *Religion offers the best rewards to those [who not only abide by its norms] [but who engage in good works].*

Like *not* on its own, however, *not only* can be repeated in layered coordination:

[65] *Practice among authorities varies [not only on the question of the parental means scale, not only in the way they assess parental incomes, but in the amounts which they give].*

It thus functions as a modifier, not a marker of correlative coordination. The location of *not only* then simply reflects the range of positions available to focusing adverbs like *only*.

'*Not only X, Y*'

Where *but* introduces a main clause, it is omissible:

[66] i *Not only was he incompetent, he was also corrupt.* (cf. [63iii])
ii *Complete power not only corrupts, it also attracts the mad.* (cf. [64iia])
iii *She said that he was not only ill, he was also penniless.*

It is questionable whether this construction is a case of asyndetic coordination or simply one of juxtaposition. It differs from clear cases of coordination in that it cannot be subordinated: **Since not only was he incompetent, he was also corrupt, they regarded him as a total liability.* The second clause thus has to be a main clause, although the clause containing *not only* may be a subordinate one, as in [66iii]. From a syntactic point of view it is unclear whether *he was penniless* here enters into construction with *that he was not only ill* (as suggested by the *not only . . . also* pairing) or with *she said that he was not only ill* (as suggested by the fact that this is the only other main clause).

Three emphatic variants of '*X and Y*':

[67] i *He was both incompetent and corrupt.* ['*both X and Y*']
ii *He was incompetent but also corrupt.* ['*X but also Y*']
iii *He was not only incompetent but also corrupt.* ['*not only X but also Y*']

All of these entail *He was incompetent and corrupt.* All emphasise the separateness of the coordinates: none of the three constructions can be used with the joint coordination of §1.3.2 (**Both Kim and Pat are a happy couple*; **Kim and also Pat are a happy couple*; **Not only Kim but also Pat is/are a happy couple*). In addition, [i] emphasises the equality of the coordinates; [ii] contrasts the coordinates and may suggest that there is something unexpected about the second; [iii] highlights the second coordinate at the expense of the first, which tends to be backgrounded. Note, then, that [iii] is the most likely of the three in a context where his incompetence is old information.

Alternative forms

Simply, solely, merely can substitute for *only* in all the above. *Just* is also possible, except that *not just* does not occur in clause-initial position (**Not just was he incompetent, . . .*), or pre-verbally (**He not just knew soldiering, . . .*).

Alternation with verbal negation

Where *not only/simply/solely/merely* precedes a tensed lexical (i.e. non-auxiliary) verb, we have alternation with the *do*-support construction. Corresponding to [64ia/iia], for example, we have:

[68] i *He did not only know soldiering but history and literature as well.*
ii *Complete power doesn't only corrupt, but it also attracts the mad.*

Here the negation is associated syntactically with *do* rather than with *only*. In [63–64], by contrast, we take *not* and *only* to form a single syntactic element.[31] This is particularly clear in cases like [63iii], where neither *not* nor *only* could appear without the other: compare **Not was he incompetent* and **Only was he incompetent.*

2.8 Expressions based on comparison (*as well as*, *rather than*, etc.)

Comparative constructions bear a significant resemblance to coordination in that they may relate syntactically like terms from a wide range of categories:

[69] i *He was [more sad than angry].* [predicative Adjs]
ii *He presented [not so much rational as emotional] arguments.* [attributive Adjs]
iii *His success was due [less to his own efforts than to his father's].* [PPs]
iv *I'd [rather resign than accept such humiliation].* [infinitival VPs]

[31] Examples where the *not* immediately follows an auxiliary verb, as in [64ic/iib], are structurally indeterminate as to whether *not* belongs with *only* or with the verb (as it does in the inflectional negatives *It isn't only a question of honour but of life and death* and *He hadn't only photocopied it but had even read it*). Another place where *not* and *only* do not combine into a single element is where *only* appears at the end of its coordinate: *Racial discrimination is not about racist discrimination only but also about the oppression of one racial group by another.*

In these examples the comparative meaning is clearly in evidence, and we analyse them in terms of the grammar of comparison described in Ch. 13, with *than* and *as* prepositions that function as head of comparative complements. There are some cases, however, where the literal comparative meaning is bleached away, yielding expressions that resemble coordinators.[32]

As well as

The literal use of *as well as* is seen in comparisons of equality like *He played as well as he'd ever done.* Here *well* is an adverb heading the underlined phrase, an adjunct of manner. There is also an idiomatic use meaning approximately "and, in addition to", illustrated in:

[70] i a. *She* [*means what she says*] [as well as *says what she means*].
b. [*Abstraction*] [as well as *impressionism*] *were Russian inventions.*
c. [Both *increasing ewe liveweight,*] [as well as *liveweight at mating,*] *influence ovulation rate and lambing performance.*
ii a. [*Beauty*] [as well as *love*] *is redemptive.*
b. *He will have,* [as well as *the TV stations,*] [*a book publishing empire*].
c. *I met her father,* [*whom*] *she had invited along* [as well as *her college friends*].
d. *She* [*has experience in management*], [as well as *being an actor of talent*].

In [i] *as well as* behaves like the coordinator *and.* In [ia] it links two finite VPs, a property characteristic of coordinators: cf. property (c) of §2.1. Note in this connection that while *She plays the piano as well as the violin* (with paired NPs) is ambiguous between a literal meaning ("as proficiently") and the idiomatic one ("and"), *She plays the piano as well as sings lieder* (with paired finite VPs) has only the idiomatic meaning. In [ib] the form *were* indicates that the subject NP is plural, just like *abstraction and impressionism.* And in [ic] we have not only such plural agreement, but also a correlative pairing of *both* with *as well as* instead of the usual *and.*

In [70ii], by contrast, *as well as* behaves markedly differently from a coordinator. In [iia] the 3rd person singular verb-form *is* indicates that this time the subject is singular: *is* agrees with *beauty,* so that *as well as love* is treated syntactically as an adjunct, not a coordinate. In [iib] *as well as the TV stations* precedes *a book publishing empire,* making it clearly an adjunct. *And* could not appear in the position *as well as* has here: cf. property (d) of §2.1. In [iic] relativisation has applied to just one of the bracketed constituents, contrary to coordinator property (e). And in [iid] the bracketed constituents are syntactically unlike, the first being a finite VP, the second a gerund-participial, contrary to coordinator property (b). Note that order reversal is possible in [iid] (*As well as being an actor of talent, she has experience of management*), but not in [ia] (**As well as says what she means, she means what she says*).

We must conclude that idiomatic *as well as* can be construed syntactically in two ways, introducing an element that is either coordinate (as in [70i]) or subordinate

[32] A similar pairing of a range of syntactically like terms is found with *if* and *though* (especially in combination with *not*): *He has read most if not all of her novels; This would minimise if not eliminate the problem; Several highly confidential, though not top secret, messages were intercepted.* Here, however, reversal is quite generally possible, making the construction more clearly subordinative: *He has read, if not all then certainly most, of her novels.*

(as in [ii]). In the former case, we take it to have been reanalysed as a compound coordinator. In the latter case there has been no such syntactic reanalysis, and here *as well as* does not form a constituent. This is evident from the fact that *as well* can occur on its own: compare *Beauty is redemptive and love is as well.* In [iia], then, the second *as* is a preposition taking the NP *love* as its complement, and the whole PP *as love* is an indirect complement in the AdvP *as well as love.* Similarly for the other examples in [ii].

As a coordinator, *as well as* is restricted to subclausal coordination: *She plays the piano as well as she sings lieder*, for example, has only the literal comparative interpretation. Even as a coordination, '*X as well as Y*' differs from '*X and Y*' in that the second term is backgrounded: *Y* often expresses information that is discourse-old, i.e. familiar from the prior discourse.

Rather than

The primary sense of *rather* is seen in [69iv] above, *I'd rather resign than accept such humiliation.* Here it is an adverb with a comparative meaning: approximately "more readily, in preference to". There are also uses where this meaning is largely or wholly lost – a change facilitated by the fact that the morphological base *rath·* no longer occurs without the *·er* suffix. Like *as well as*, *rather than* may introduce a constituent that is syntactically coordinate or subordinate. Compare:

[71] i a. *In the end he* [*survives*] [*rather than conquers*].
b. *The dilemma has* [*deepened*] [*rather than been resolved*].
c. *Wisdom and folly are* [*moral*] [*rather than intellectual*] *categories.*
ii [*Rather than individual security*] *it is* [*the security of an ideological group*] *that is basic.*

In [i] *rather than* links finite VPs, past-participials, and attributive adjectives, and it is plausible to suggest that it, like *as well as*, has been reanalysed as a coordinator. The meaning of coordinative '*X rather than Y*' is "*X*, not *Y*". In [ii], however, *rather than* cannot be a coordinator because of its position: there is no reason to postulate reanalysis here, and we take the first bracketed phrase to be an adjunct, with the adverb *rather* as its head. Note that such fronting of '*rather than Y*' is not possible in [i]. Compare [ia] in this respect with the clearly non-coordinative *They obeyed the order rather than suffer torture or death.* Here the underlined constituents are not syntactically alike (the first being finite, the second non-finite), and fronting is permitted: *Rather than suffer torture or death they obeyed the order.* In this case, unlike [71], *rather* has its comparative "in preference to" meaning.[33]

'*Not so much X but Y*'

The similarity between comparison and coordination is reflected in the not infrequent blending of comparative '*not so much X as Y*' and coordinative '*not X but Y*':

[72] *Insofar as science generates any fear, it stems* [*not so much from scientific prowess and gadgets*] [*but from the fact that new unanswered questions arise*].

[33] A less frequent variation of '*X rather than Y*' is '*rather X than Y*': *I rather sensed them than saw them.*

Much less, still less

These are found in non-affirmative contexts within a final coordinate. They occasionally combine with *and* and hence (by virtue of coordination property (f), §2.1) are not themselves coordinators, but function as modifiers:

[73] i *She was prettier than he had any right to [hope for,] [much less expect].*
ii *The conference decisions did not reflect the opinions of [the majority of party members] [and still less the party's supporters in the country].*

2.9 Expressions of addition, inclusion, etc. (*including*, *instead of*, *plus*, etc.)

In addition to, including, instead of, along with

Such expressions bear some resemblance to coordinators in that they can link phrases in a considerable range of functions ([74i]) and of syntactic categories ([74ii]):

[74] i a. *[Friends from Limpsfield,] [in addition to the villagers,] came to the party.*
b. *They got [free milk and free meat] [in addition to their wages].*
c. *I was subjected to [crippling fines,] [in addition to usurious interest on unpaid debts].*
ii a. *There is a need to provide [special,] [including institutional,] treatment as well.*
b. *She might have turned it [full] on [instead of faintly].*
c. *She would make him [stand face-to-wall in a corner] [instead of stay in after school].*

The first term is subject in [ia], object in [ib], complement of a preposition in [ic]. These constructions are nevertheless clearly not coordinative in that the PP can be moved to front position, or to the position before the term to which it is linked (*They got, in addition to their wages, free milk and free meat*). The similarity with coordination is greater in [ii], where the order cannot be changed in this way. Such examples provide some evidence for suggesting that *including* and *instead of* – like *as well as* and *rather than* – have a use where they are reanalysed as marginal members of the coordinator category.[34]

Plus

This is another item that straddles the boundary between prepositions and coordinators:

[75] i *Each boy's parents pay [$2,000 a term in fees,] [plus extras].*
ii *[The cost-billing system] [plus other control refinements] has reduced the deficit.*
iii *[His stamina] [plus his experience] make him unbeatable.*
iv *The committee consists of [two staff] [plus four students] [plus the secretary].*
v *[He spoke with a funny accent] [plus he wore socks with his sandals].*

Plus is predominantly followed by an NP, making it more like a preposition than a coordinator.[35] Examples like [v], where it introduces a main clause, are restricted to

[34] Compare also this example where *along with* is paired with *both* in a correlative coordination: *They emphasise the keeping of both the old covenant with its food laws, cultural traditions, circumcision and sabbath keeping, along with the new covenant.* This can hardly be regarded as an established construction, but it does illustrate the way in which the category of coordinators can extend beyond the clear-cut members.

[35] It can also occur in phrase-final position: *They were both forty plus*; there is of course no question of a coordination here.

informal style – a style where it has undoubtedly been assimilated to the coordinator category.[36] It differs from prototypical prepositions in that it does not permit fronting (**Plus other control refinements the cost-billing system has reduced the deficit*) and only very rarely occurs as head of a predicative complement (*The electrical charge is plus, of course, the initial pulse of current*). '*X plus Y*' tends to count as singular for agreement purposes, as in [ii], but it is sometimes taken as plural, as in [iii] – in the singular case it is being treated as a preposition, in the plural case as a coordinator. Example [iv] shows that it occurs in multiple as well as binary structures, which also puts it with the coordinators.[37] As a coordinator, however, it is largely if not wholly restricted to joining main clauses or NPs.

Let alone, not to say

The wide range of categories they can link suggests that these idioms might be regarded as marginal coordinators:[38]

[76] i *Few people [have seen the document,] [let alone know what's in it].* [finite VPs]
ii *His behaviour was in [questionable,] [not to say downright bad] taste.* [AdjPs]

2.10 Connective adverbs (*so, yet, however*, etc.)

So, in the sense "therefore, as a result", and *yet*, "nevertheless", appear in constructions where they are very clearly distinct from coordinators, but they also have uses where the resemblances are such that they may be regarded as marginal members of the coordinator category.

Differences from coordinators

(a) Links between non-coordinate elements

[77] i *The mill could be sold off, so providing much-needed capital.*
ii *He was gone, leaving her caught up to a pitch of excitement and ecstasy that was yet perilously close to tears.*
iii *Certain this menace was only imaginary, he yet stared in fascinated horror.*

Here *so* and *yet* are adverbs linking elements that are clearly not coordinate. In [i–ii] the adverb links a subordinate clause to the matrix, while in [iii] it links the main predication to the initial adjunct – compare also *Though he was certain this menace was only imaginary, he yet stared in fascinated horror*, where *yet* is correlative with *though*.

(b) Combination with coordinator

[78] i *This may make the task seem easier and so increase self-confidence.*
ii *You can look as fit as a fiddle and yet feel quite listless.*

[36] This is particularly evident when it links imperative clauses, as in the advertiser's *Save $300.00 plus choose $300.00 worth of free gifts.*

[37] This reflects its basic use in mathematics; in that register other operators such as *minus* and *times* behave in the same way, and are perhaps also marginal members of the coordinator category.

[38] *Not to mention*, though similar in meaning, can link unlikes (*He is a four-star general, not to mention also being president of the tiny country of Concordia*) and can introduce an adjunct in front position (*Not to mention other things, every day I am under the pressure of my concern for all the churches*).

Here it is *and* that marks the coordination relation: *so* and *yet* are thus modifiers within the second coordinate (cf. property (f) of §2.1). *So* combines just with *and*, while *yet* is also found with *but* and *nor* (*He was created not exactly immortal, nor yet exactly mortal*).

Similarities with coordinators

(a) Initial position

So and *yet* normally occupy initial position (save for the coordinator itself in examples like [78]); in this respect they are closer to coordinators than to such adverbs of similar meaning as *therefore, consequently, nevertheless, however*, etc., which readily occur in central or end position. Compare: *He therefore/*so had to resign* or *The two speeches were, however/?yet, very similar in content.*[39]

(b) Occurrence as sole linking item in coordinative construction

Although *so* and *yet* can combine with a coordinator, as in [78], they much more often occur without one:

[79] i [*There was a bus strike on,*][*so we had to go by taxi*].
ii [*The book was written ten years ago,*][*yet conditions are still the same*].

In cases like these, *so* and *yet* are just about indispensable elements of the construction. If we omit them the result is a mere juxtaposition of clauses rather than a coordination: it would therefore be misleading to treat the constructions here as asyndetic coordination. It is more plausible to analyse *so* and *yet* here as markers of coordination.

(c) Range of coordinates

Both *so* and *yet* can link finite VPs:

[80] i *He* [*wanted to avoid the rush-hour*][*so took the early train*].
ii *He* [*worked for peace all his life,*][*yet sadly died by a gun*].

In this respect they are like coordinators. But this use of *so* is quite infrequent: whereas *so* on its own is much commoner than *and so* as a link between main clauses,[40] the reverse is the case with subclausal coordination. *So* can also link adjectives (*It was an untried, so rather risky, undertaking*), but not NPs, subordinate clauses, non-finite VPs, etc. (note, for example, that *and* is not omissible from [78i]). *Yet*, on the other hand, is similar in meaning to the coordinator *but*, and occurs in a similar range of coordinative constructions – for example:

[81] i *A person* [*who has a master's degree,*][*yet who has not taken education courses,*] *is not permitted to teach in the public schools.*
ii *The speech was delivered in* [*simple*][*yet eloquent*] *words.*
iii *It was a proposal which* [*sickened*][*yet fascinated*] *me.*

[39] *Yet* occurs centrally in subordinative constructions such as [77ii–iii]. A rare example of central *so* is seen in: *It is found in the works of those who held the first chairs and lectureships when the monopoly on legitimate educational theory shifted to universities about a century ago, and who so set the tone for modern contemporary studies* – *so* could not precede relative *who* here. *Hence* can occur centrally (*They involve long computations and are not, hence, very useful in practice*), but is much less frequent in this position than *therefore*, etc.

[40] Note that *so* can link main clauses of unlike type, as in *It'll be quite cold, so take plenty of warm clothing*: it would hardly be possible to add *and* here, and the clauses are clearly not of equal status pragmatically – the first gives a reason for issuing or complying with the directive expressed in the second (compare the subordinative construction *Take plenty of warm clothing because it will be quite cold*).

Yet can link relative clauses, as in [i]; adjectives, as in [ii]; verbs, as in [iii], and so on. It is thus syntactically somewhat closer to the coordinators than is *so*.[41]

2.11 *For, only,* and resultative *so* + *that*

As used in [82], these items fall at the boundary between coordinators and prepositions (prepositions that take clausal complements, thus subordinating conjunctions in a traditional analysis). They lack the more positive features of each, so that their classification remains problematic.

[82] i [*He went to bed,*][*<u>for</u> he was exhausted*].
ii [*I would have gone,*][*<u>only</u> I was too busy*].
iii [*The dust clogged their throats,*][*<u>so that</u> the women were always making ice water*].

For is semantically quite close to the clearly subordinative *because*, but differs from it syntactically. *Only* is replaceable by the coordinator *but*, or the preposition *except* (which may take a content clause with the subordinator *that*: *except that I was too busy*). In [82ii] *only* has a preventative interpretation: "being too busy prevented me from going" (cf. [56i]), but it is also found with a limiting, excepting sense, as in *He's very like his father, only he has blue eyes.* Example [iii] has a resultative interpretation and is to be distinguished from the purposive *He left early* [*<u>so that</u> he would miss the rush-hour traffic*], which is clearly subordinative.

(a) Differences from coordinators

For, only, and resultative *so* + *that* lack most of the properties distinguishing prototypical coordinators from prepositions with clausal complements.

No requirement of syntactic likeness

The clause following them cannot contain any internal marker of subordination whereas the first clause can, which means that the two clauses may be syntactically unlike. Compare, for example:

[83] i *They've postponed the meeting till tomorrow,* [*which is a great nuisance*] [*<u>for</u> it means that several members will be unable to attend*].
ii *He said* [*that he would have gone,*][*<u>only</u> he had been too busy*].

In [i] relativisation does not apply across the board: we have *which* in the first clause but *it* in the clause following *for*, with *for* therefore relating syntactically unlike clauses. Similarly for *only* in [ii]: one clause is marked by the subordinator *that*, but we cannot insert *that* after *only*. Contrast here the behaviour of the coordinator *but* in *He said* [*that he would have gone,*] [*but <u>that</u> he had been too busy*].

[41] *However*, whose meaning is similar to that *of yet* and *but*, also has uses where it behaves like a coordinator for speakers who accept such examples as: %*Other services have been expanded to meet the need, however the situation is still critical* and *Please note that the costs are correct, however are subject to change prior to final payment.* A further item similar in meaning to *but* is (*al*)*though*; in general this differs syntactically quite sharply from *but* (cf. properties (d) and (e) of §2.1) and belongs to the category of prepositions taking a finite clause as complement. It too, however, is sometimes found linking finite VPs, as in *They both remembered Jane, though rarely spoke of her.* There is no possibility of fronting here (**They both, though rarely spoke of Jane, remembered her*), and this too might be regarded as a marginal coordinative construction.

Restriction to binary constructions

They cannot appear in multiple coordinations like '*X* (*and*) *Y and Z*'. Compare:

[84] *He went to bed, for he was exhausted, for he had been gardening all day.*

This kind of example would generally be avoided on stylistic grounds, but it can only be interpreted as a right-layered construction (cf. diagram [2b] of §2). The gardening explains the exhaustion not, directly, the going to bed, so the scope of the first *for* is *he was exhausted, for he had been gardening all day.* Unlike a coordinator in multiple coordination, the first *for* cannot be omitted.

Restriction to finite clauses

Coordinators can link a wide range of categories but the present items can be followed only by a finite clause. Note, for example, that while *only* can replace *but* in [56i], it differs from *but* in not allowing a following VP: *I would have gone, but/*only was too busy.* In the case of *so that* in [82iii] the *that* is the subordinator that introduces declarative content clauses.

(b) Differences from prototypical prepositions with clausal complements

They also differ significantly from prepositions such as *if, because,* purposive *so* (+*that*).

Inability to occur in initial position

The order of the bracketed elements in [82] is irreversible. Contrast here *for* and *because*: *Because/*For he was exhausted, he went to bed.* Similarly, resultative **So that the women were always making ice water, the dust clogged their throats* may be contrasted with purposive *So that he would miss the rush-hour traffic he left early.*

Inability to coordinate

The constituent formed by these items and the following clause cannot function as a coordinate:

[85] i **He went to bed, [<u>for</u> he was exhausted] [and <u>for</u> he had to get up early next day].*

ii **I would have gone [<u>only</u> I was too busy] [and <u>only</u> I was short of money].*

iii **The dust clogged their throats, [<u>so that</u> they quickly felt parched] [and <u>so that</u> the women were always making ice water].*

Again, this restriction does not apply to the clearly subordinative constructions with *because* and purposive *so.*

The (a) properties make these items like prepositions, the (b) properties make them like coordinators. On balance, we would favour putting them with the prepositions: in the absence of positive coordinator properties the ability to link unlike elements, as in [83], can hardly be reconciled with a coordinator analysis.[42]

[42] In terms of their meaning, they are very different from prototypical cases of coordination since they express relations that are clearly asymmetric. Nevertheless, *for* is traditionally classified as a coordinator – an analysis that may reflect the fact that its translation equivalent in Latin belongs syntactically with the coordinators. On a prepositional analysis, there is no need to treat *so* + *that* as a unit: *that* is simply the subordinator that introduces the content clause complement of *so*. The *that* is, however, obligatory in this construction: in the absence of *that*, so is the connective adverb discussed in §2.10.

3 The range of coordination: what can be coordinated with what

3.1 Conditions on the distribution and form of coordinations

Coordinations can occur at almost any place in the structure of a sentence. As a first approximation, we may put it as follows:

[1] If (and only if) in a given syntactic construction a constituent *X* can be replaced without change of function by a constituent *Y*, then it can also be replaced by a coordination of *X* and *Y*.

This may be illustrated by reference to sentence [2]:

[2] *Kim wanted to take them.*

Here *to* is a unique marker of the infinitival construction: it cannot be replaced by any other word and hence not by a coordination. But all the other constituents in [2] allow both simple and coordinative replacement. This is illustrated in [3] for the four words other than *to*:

[3]	A	B	C
i	*Kim*	*Pat*	*Kim and Pat wanted to take them.*
ii	*wanted*	*intended*	*Kim wanted and intended to take them.*
iii	*take*	*keep*	*Kim wanted to take and keep them.*
iv	*them*	*the others*	*Kim wanted to take them and the others.*

Column A gives the original word, B a simple replacement, and C the clause resulting from substituting a coordination of A and B for the original word in [2]. Similarly for the non-minimal constituents: *take them* can be replaced by *give them to Pat* and hence by a coordination of this and the original – *Kim wanted to take them and give them to Pat.*

The possibility of layered coordination (§1.2) can now be seen to follow directly from [1]. We can apply rule [1] to the coordination *Kim and Pat* in the C column of [3i]: *Kim and Pat* can be replaced by *Jill and Max* and hence by a coordination of the two coordinations, yielding the layered structure in *Both Kim and Pat and Jill and Max wanted to take them.*

Rule [1] says that there must be no change in function when we make the replacement. This condition excludes examples like:

[4] i **He left this morning and the room.*
ii **She became and admired the best teacher in the university.*

Example [i] is inadmissible because *He left this morning* has *this morning* as adjunct whereas *He left the room* has *the room* as object. Similarly [ii] is excluded because *the best teacher in the university* is predicative complement in *She became the best teacher in the university*, but object in *She admired the best teacher in the university.*

Rule [1] does not require, however, that *X* and *Y* belong to the same category, and hence allows for cases like *He left this morning or just after lunch*, where the first coordinate is an NP, the second a PP. The major condition on coordination, then, is that coordinates must be **alike in function**, they must stand in the same syntactic relation to any surrounding material.

It is to be understood that when *X* is replaced by *Y* the meaning of other expressions in the sentence remains unaffected. Take, for example, *This excited her interest*: if we replace *her interest* by *the children* the meaning of *excite* is changed (from, roughly, "arouse" to "stir up"), and hence such replacement doesn't sanction the coordination #*This excited her interest and the children*. Likeness of syntactic function must thus be accompanied by likeness of semantic relation.[43]

The requirement that the coordinates must be alike in function is not quite as straightforward as it might seem. Consider, for example:

[5] i a. *Kim and Pat saw it.* b. *Kim saw it and Pat saw it.*
ii a. *Kim saw it.* b. *Pat saw it.*

We cannot say that in [ia] *Kim* and *Pat* are functionally alike in that each is subject: it is the whole coordination *Kim and Pat* that has the function of subject, not the separate coordinates. The requirement must therefore be interpreted derivatively, by reference to the clausal coordination [ib] or the related clauses shown in [ii]: here *Kim* and *Pat* are both subjects. But it must be emphasised that we are not suggesting that [ia] is syntactically derived from [ib]. Such an analysis is out of the question because, as we have noted, subclausal coordination is not always equivalent to clausal coordination: *No buses were running or no trains were running* does not have the same meaning as *No buses or trains were running*. The relevance to [ia] of [ib] is the same as that of [ii]: the subclausal coordination in [ia] is **sanctioned** by the fact that [ib] and [ii] are well formed and have *Kim* and *Pat* in the same syntactic and semantic relation to *saw it*.

As it stands, rule [1] is considerably oversimplified. We will list summarily here various qualifications that must be made, and look in more detail at certain of them in subsequent sections.

(a) Agreement

If in *Kim underestimates herself* we replace *Kim* by *Kim and Pat* we must adjust the items which agree with *Kim*, giving *Kim and Pat underestimate themselves*. The subject *Kim and Pat* is plural and the agreement must be clearly with it as a whole, not with one or other of the bare coordinates. The interaction between coordination and agreement is discussed in Ch. 5, §18.3.

(b) Likeness of category

Rule [1] requires that X and Y be alike in function, as noted above, but in some cases there is a stricter requirement that they be alike in category. The clearest example is that of infinitival and gerund-participial clauses, which cannot coordinate. The gerund-participial subject in *Cycling there would be dangerous* can be replaced by the infinitival *to go on foot*, but these cannot be joined in a coordination:

[6] *[*Cycling there or to go on foot*] *would be dangerous.*

Instead we need either *To cycle there or to go on foot would be dangerous* or else *Cycling there or going on foot would be dangerous*, where the coordinates belong to the same category. Cases where a difference of category is permitted are outlined in §3.2.

[43] The requirement that the coordinates have the same syntactic and semantic relation to the context is sometimes flouted for humorous effect, as in *He lost his way and his temper* or *She was in the army and a difficult position.* This rhetorical device is known as syllepsis (or zeugma).

(c) Expanded coordinates

These cannot coordinate. In *Kim or Pat should give the course* we can replace *or Pat* by *and Max*, but not by a coordination of these:

[7] *Kim or Pat or and Max should give the course.

To express this meaning we need to repeat *Kim*, giving *Kim or Pat or Kim and Max.*

(d) *For, only,* and resultative *so*

As noted in §2.11, we cannot coordinate phrases headed by these items, in the senses discussed. This is the main property making them partially like coordinators, as the deviance of [85] of §2.2 (**He went to bed, for he was exhausted and for he had to get up early next day*, etc.) is comparable to that of [7] above.

(e) Grammaticised words

Words that are grammatically distinctive, e.g. by virtue of belonging to closed categories, tend to coordinate less freely than open category ones. For example, we do not say **my and this book* (but rather *my book and this book/one*).We take up this issue in §3.3.

(f) Departures from strict functional likeness

We occasionally find minor and semantically motivated violations of the requirement that coordinates be functionally alike, as in:

[8]	i	*all and only the corrected copies*	[predeterminer + focusing modifier]
	ii	*our and future generations*	[determiner + attributive modifier]

(g) Coordination of word-parts

In general, coordinates are whole words or larger expressions, hence the reference to syntactic construction in [1]. But to a limited extent it is possible to coordinate parts of words:[44]

[9]	i	*pro- and anti-marketeers*	*pre- and post-war living conditions*
	ii	*the [four- and five-year-old] boys*	*red- or auburn-haired*

Coordination of prefixes is found with a few pairs of opposite meaning, such as those in [i], or *inter·* and *intra·*. Coordination of bases is well established with numerals and in denominal adjectives formed by suffixation of ·*ed* (see Ch. 19, §5.8), as in [ii]; it is also commonly found in compounds formed from past participles: *Sydney- or Melbourne-based companies.*

(h) Joint coordination

Rule [1] does not allow for cases of joint coordination where one of the coordinates cannot replace the whole coordination:

[10] i *Kim and Pat are a happy couple.* (=[17ii] of §1)
ii *Kim and Pat are respectively scrupulously honest and an inveterate liar.*

Example [ii] can be seen as following from the acceptability of *Kim is scrupulously honest* and *Pat is an inveterate liar*, but this kind of solution is not available for [i]. Here we

[44] Very occasionally one finds coordination between a word and a prefix: *Please list all publications of which you were the sole or co-author.*

need to accept that an *and*-coordination of NPs can be used directly to enumerate the members of a set.

(i) Lexicalised coordinations

We must also go beyond [1] to allow for fixed phrases like *spick and span, to and fro*, etc. (§1.4).

(j) Special syntactic treatment of coordinates

Compare next:

[11] i a. %*They invited Kim and I.* b. **They invited I.*
ii a. *I need pen and paper.* b. **I need pen.*

In [ia] we have a nominative case pronoun where the corresponding non-coordinative construction would require accusative *me*; not all speakers accept examples like [ia], but for the many who do the rules for case selection in coordinations are clearly not the same as those applying elsewhere (cf. Ch. 5, §16.2.2). Similarly, [ii] shows that the normal rules concerning the requirement of a determiner with count singulars are sometimes relaxed in coordinations.[45]

(k) Avoidance of adjacency constraints

In such an example as *They disagreed as to whether it should be allowed* we could replace *whether* by *how often* but not by *to what extent*, and yet a coordination of *whether* and *to what extent* is perfectly possible:

[12] i **They disagreed as to to what extent it should be allowed.*
ii *They disagreed as to whether and to what extent it should be allowed.*

Open interrogatives beginning with a preposition are hardly permissible as complements to a preposition, especially when the prepositions are identical, as in [i]. But in [ii] the prepositions are not adjacent, and hence there is nothing to rule out the *to what extent* PP.[46]

3.2 Coordination of unlike categories

In the great majority of cases, coordinates belong to the same syntactic category, but a difference of category is generally tolerated where there is likeness of function. This section surveys the main functions allowing coordinations of this kind.

(a) Predicative complement

One of the most straightforward cases is the coordination of AdjPs, NPs, and PPs in predicative complement function:

[13] i *It was [extremely expensive and in bad taste].* [AdjP + PP]
ii *He became [very forgetful and an embarrassment to his family].* [AdjP + NP]

[45] Two other cases where a form is found in coordination that would not be permitted in a non-coordinate construction are illustrated in *Teachers have been uncertain how or if to incorporate grammar into the approach*, and *It was a hilarious scene as fat and thin alike swooped, swayed, tripped, and fell.* The interrogative subordinator *if* which appears in the first of these cannot normally occur with an infinitival complement: **They have been uncertain if to incorporate grammar into the approach.* In the second the adjectives *fat* and *thin* are functioning as fused modifier-head NPs, which would not be possible without the coordination.

[46] This example also belongs under (f), since *to what extent* has adjunct function, but *whether* does not: it is purely a marker of subordination and closed interrogative clause type.

It is also possible to coordinate an AdjP, NP, or PP with a non-finite clause:

[14] i *He's [in love and behaving quite irrationally].* [PP + gerund-participial]
ii *He is [known to have a gun and likely to use it].* [past-participial + AdjP]
iii *This process [is perfectly natural and to be welcomed].* [AdjP + infinitival]

Example [i] can be expanded to *He's in love and he's behaving quite irrationally*, where the *be* of the second clause marks progressive aspect. Similarly [ii] can be expanded to *He is known to have a gun and he is likely to use it*, where the first clause is passive. And expansion of [iii] gives *This process is perfectly natural and it is to be welcomed*, where the second coordinate contains quasi-modal ***be***.[47] The progressive and passive constructions can themselves combine: *He was living in the Latin Quarter and thought to have AIDS*. Mixed coordinations involving non-finites are much less usual than those in [13]: certainly in the case of passives, the version where *be* is repeated will often be preferred or required, as in *He was invited but was unable to accept* or *He was insolent and was dismissed.*

Coordinations like those in [14] are found only with *be. Get* can take an adjectival predicative complement (*He got insolent*) and any of the three non-finites (*He got going / sacked / to see it*) but these are all interpreted as different constructions, so that mixed coordinations like **He got insolent and sacked* are not acceptable. Similarly *He kept awake* and *He kept listening for her* involve different uses of *keep*, so that we cannot have **He kept awake and listening for her.*

(b) Other complements, including subject

Where a head element can take different categories as complement (without a change in sense), unlike coordinations are generally possible.

[15] i a. *[The stamp purchases and how the cash float was administered] were the subject of prolonged questioning yesterday.*
b. *It lists [the value of assets and which partner owned them before the marriage].*
c. *He was sure [of himself and where he was going].*
ii a. *I remembered [reading about you in the papers and that you lived here in Wigan].*
b. *We were told [to wait in the terminal and that we would be informed when we could reboard].*
iii a. *They reported [a deep division of opinion between the government and the people and that the African population was almost solid in its opposition to federation].*
b. *After [their rubber plantation failed, and her husband's death on the Upper Rewa in 1885], she maintained her three young children with a tiny store.*
c. *I was planning [a four-month trip across Africa and to then return to England].*
d. *They believe [in the fall of man and original sin and that all mankind is descended from a single couple].*
e. *The University provides a great opportunity [for adventures of the mind and to make friendships that will last a lifetime].*
f. *They want to know [his financial arrangements in Italy and about the people he met there].*

[47] Where ***be*** has a more centrally deontic interpretation, such coordination is not possible: we could not, for example, omit the second *you are* from *You are on duty and you are to remain in the guard-room until relieved.*

The head is an adjective (*sure*) in [ic],[48] a preposition (*after*) in [iiib], a noun (*opportunity*) in [iiie], and a verb in the others – with the complement external (i.e. subject) in [ia]. The examples in [i] illustrate what is probably the most common case, coordination of a finite interrogative with an NP; the latter will then often express a 'concealed question' (Ch. 11, §5.3), as in [ib] (*the value of assets* = "what the value of assets was"). The coordinations in [ii] are of non-finite and finite clauses; this order is obligatory with gerund-participials and almost so with infinitivals. A sample of other combinations are given in [iii]: NP + declarative clause (with and without *that*), NP + infinitival, PP + declarative clause, PP + infinitival, NP + PP.

(c) Adjunct

No difficulty arises in coordinating different categories within the adjunct function, including PPs with different kinds of complement (as in [iii] below, where the first PP consists of *because* + clause, the second of *for* + NP):

[16]	i	*She did it [slowly and with great care].*	[adverb + PP]
	ii	*I'll do it [tonight or in the morning].*	[NP + PP]
	iii	*He'll reject it [because it's too long or for some other reason].*	[PP + PP]
	iv	*He signed on [to please his wife but with no hope of success].*	[clause + PP]

(d) Modifier in NP structure

The most usual case involves post-head modifiers: PPs, AdjPs, participial clauses, and finite clauses, as in [17i]. Mixed coordinations in pre-head (attributive) modifier position, however, are not common. As illustrated in [17ii], they tend to involve adjectives and nominals belonging within a single semantic set.

[17] i a. *They still won't recommend grants for people [over the age of 65 or who have retired].*
b. *She won in a match [interrupted by showers but which lasted under an hour].*
c. *A man [in singlet and shorts and wearing a green baize apron] finally appeared.*
d. *It would be an opportunity to do something [quite new for me and in which I believed much more strongly than in our government's economic policy].*
ii a. *the civic, school, and religious life of the community*
b. *the state and federal laws*
c. *the Australian and New Zealand flags*
d. *in [daily or evening newspapers]*

The nominals *school, state, New Zealand, evening* are used here because there is no corresponding adjective.

A final possibility is the coordination of pre- and post-head modifiers:

[18] *The demise of the liberals has been [a long and complicated process but which now looks as though it is fairly decisive].*

This construction is comparatively rare: it would be more usual to drop the *but*, expressing the adversative relation between the adjuncts by a connective adjunct such as *however* within the relative clause.

[48] Strictly speaking there is indeterminacy as to whether the coordination is complement of ***sure*** (with the form PP + clause) or of *of* (with the form NP + clause), for the non-coordinative version could be either *he was sure where he was going* or *He was sure of where he was going.*

(e) Sentential coordinations

Finally there are coordinations which have no function within a larger construction but constitute a sentence. Mixed coordinations here consist of a fragment and a clause:

[19] i *Now I can only write, and that only when I get out of pain.*
ii *One more remark like that and I'm leaving.*

In [i] *that* is a pro-clause, interpreted anaphorically as "I can write"; [ii] exemplifies the implicit conditional construction discussed in §2.2.3.

3.3 Coordination of grammaticised words

We have noted that grammaticised words tend to coordinate less readily than others: in this section we survey the coordination possibilities for the main kinds of grammaticised word.

(a) Coordinators

The idiom *and/or* is an asyndetic coordination meaning "and or or":

[20] a. *They're inviting [Kim and/or Pat].* b. *They're inviting [Kim or Pat].*

We have seen (§2.2.1) that *or* on its own is characteristically associated with an implicature of exclusiveness, so that [b] suggests they're only inviting one of them: *and/or* then serves to block this implicature, explicitly allowing for the situation where they invite both Kim and Pat as well as that where they invite only one.

(b) Subordinators

The clause subordinators do not normally coordinate: *for* takes a different construction from *that* and *whether*, and the latter two are simply markers of different clause types. *Whether*, however, does coordinate with *not* or with an interrogative phrase in adjunct function:

[21] i *I don't know [whether or not he saw her].*
ii *They must consider [whether and in what circumstances it should be allowed].*

Example [i] is equivalent to *I don't know whether he saw her or not* (where *or* coordinates a clause with a clause fragment), but *whether or not* is probably best handled as a fixed phrase, a subordinator complex. *Whether or no* is sometimes found as a variant. In [ii] we understand "and if so . . . " (*if so* can be added as an adjunct to the second coordinate, but is commonly omitted) – the order is therefore fixed. The likeness here is that both elements are interrogative markers: only the first has a subordinating role.[49] *If* cannot substitute for *whether* in [i], and would be at best unidiomatic in [ii].

(c) Prepositions

These cover a considerable range on the scale of grammaticisation. At one extreme we have uses where the preposition is fully determined by the head element and hence – in accordance with [1] – cannot coordinate: *I'll give it to Kim*; *the search for gold*; *He's intent on revenge.* At the other extreme, numerous alternatives are available and coordination

[49] Because the marking of closed interrogatives is so different in subordinate and main clauses, there is no analogue in main clauses of this kind of coordination: we would have to say *Should it be allowed, and if so in what circumstances?*

is commonplace. This applies particularly in the areas of time and space, as in *before and after*, *above and below*, *at or near*, etc.; it is much more difficult to find plausible coordinations for such items as *although* or *because*, which take clausal complements. Some coordinations have the character of fixed phrases: *if and only if*, *if and when*.[50]

(d) Determinatives

Coordination of quantifiers, especially with *or*, occurs freely: *one or two mistakes*, *three or more witnesses*, *little or no money*, *some or all applicants*. The emphatic *each and every* is a fixed phrase.[51] But for the rest, determinative coordinations are comparatively rare, there being a preference for coordinating at NP level: *this copy and those*, for example, is more likely than *this and those copies*.

(e) Auxiliaries

Certain coordinations of modals occur very readily: *I can and will finish it*; *He must and will be punished*. Perfect *have* and progressive *be* are unique markers of these constructions and don't coordinate with any other lexemes. Nor can passive *be*, even though *get* is an alternative (non-auxiliary) marker of passive – there is no clear semantic distinction between them to motivate a coordination (**He was or got arrested*).

3.4 Coordination and genitives

We look first at constructions containing NPs other than personal pronouns, then at coordinations of personal pronouns, and finally at mixed coordinations, i.e. those involving a personal pronoun and an ordinary NP.

(a) NPs other than personal pronouns

There are three main types of coordination to distinguish:

[22]	i	*[Kim and Pat's] children*	[Type I: single genitive]
	ii	*[Kim's and Pat's] children*	[Type II: direct multiple genitive]
	iii	*Kim's children and Pat's*	[Type III: indirect multiple genitive]

In [i] we have Type I, the 'single genitive': there is a single marking of genitive case, applying to the NP-coordination *Kim and Pat* as a whole. In the others, there is multiple marking of genitive case. In [ii] the coordination is between the two genitive NPs themselves, i.e. *Kim's* and *Pat's*: this is Type II, which we will call the 'direct multiple genitive'. In [iii] the coordination is between two NPs that are not themselves genitive but contain genitive determiners, i.e. *Kim's children* and *Pat's* (equivalent to *Pat's children*): this is Type III, the 'indirect multiple genitive'.

Types I and II are not semantically contrastive. Both allow either a joint or a distributive interpretation of the genitive relation. In the joint interpretation of [22i–ii] the matrix NP denotes the set of children who have Kim and Pat as their parents, while in the

[50] This has some affinity with the coordination in [21ii]: in both cases the first coordinate cancels the presupposition normally associated with the second. *I'll do it when he pays me* presupposes that he'll pay me, but *I'll do it if and when he pays me* does not. Similarly, *They must consider in what circumstances it should be allowed* presupposes that there are circumstances where it should be allowed, but [21iii], with *whether*, does not.

[51] Another fixed phrase is *one or other*, a coordination of a determinative and an adjective; it functions as a determiner meaning "either/any".

distributive interpretation it denotes the set consisting of Kim's children and Pat's children. Note, then, that in a context where Kim is married to Pat we can appropriately use either Type I, *Kim and Pat's marriage*, or Type II, *Kim's and Pat's marriage*. Conversely, if Tom is married to Jill and Max is married to Sue, we can refer to the husbands as either *Jill and Sue's husbands* (Type I) or *Jill's and Sue's husbands* (Type II). The Type III construction, however, has only a distributive interpretation: [iii] denotes the set comprising Kim's children and Pat's children.

Two factors affect the choice between Types I and II. First, some speakers generally opt for Type II rather than Type I, at least in the relatively careful use of language, because they take it to be grammatically more 'correct' for an inflectional suffix to attach to single words than to coordinations. Secondly, Type I will often be preferred over Type II when the genitive relation is interpreted jointly, when there is a strong (and relevant) association between the referents of the coordinated NPs. Thus we say *Gilbert and Sullivan's popularity* rather than *Gilbert's and Sullivan's popularity* because we are concerned with them as a team rather than as individuals. This is why the contextualisation of [22] with Kim and Pat as parents of the same children is more salient for [i] than for [ii]. In the Gilbert and Sullivan case this second factor will strongly outweigh the first, whereas in [22] the factors are more evenly balanced, allowing for variation according to formality and speaker. The second factor also explains why a preference for Type I over Type II is more likely with *and* than with *or*: the kind of association relevant here is found only with *and*.[52]

In [22] the coordination is between NPs, but Types I and II are also found with coordination of nominals:

[23]	i	*her [mother and father's] letters*	[Type I: single genitive]
	ii	*her [mother's and father's] letters*	[Type II: direct multiple genitive]

(b) Genitive pronouns

The pattern with personal pronouns differs in two respects. In the first place, Type I, with a single genitive, is not admissible in the standard language. Secondly, there are two series of genitive pronouns, dependent (*my*, *your*, etc.) and independent (*mine*, *yours*, etc.). This gives two variants of Type II. Compare, then:

[24]	i	*[*you and my*] *letters*	[Type I: single genitive]
	ii	[*your and her*] *letters*	[Type IIA: direct multiple genitive – dependent]
	iii	*yours and hers*	[Type IIB: direct multiple genitive – independent]
	iv	*your letters and hers*	[Type III: indirect multiple genitive]

With pronouns, the Type II construction hardly allows a joint interpretation. *His and her children*, for example, strongly conveys that the children don't all have the same parents. Similarly *his and her quarrel* could hardly be used to denote a quarrel between him and her.

One common use of Type IIA is in examples like *Everyone must face his or her partner*, where the antecedent is a non-referential NP that is neutral as to sex (see Ch. 5, §17.2.4). Otherwise this construction is felt to be somewhat awkward, and tends to be disfavoured relative to Type III or to a non-coordinative plural genitive: *our/your/their letters*.

[52] Another case where the second factor outweighs the first is that involving measure expressions, as in *a week and a day's delay* ("eight days' delay"): *a week's and a day's delay* denotes two delays, one of a week, the other of a day.

(c) Mixed coordinations

The possibilities here are as follows:

[25]	PRONOUN FIRST	PRONOUN LAST	
i	a. ?[*you <u>and</u> Kim's*] *letters*	b. *[*Kim <u>and</u> your*] *letters*	[Type I]
ii	a. [*your <u>and</u> Kim's*] *letters*	b. [*Kim's <u>and</u> your*] *letters*	[Type IIA]
iii	a. *yours <u>and</u> Kim's*	b. *Kim's <u>and</u> yours*	[Type IIB]
iv	a. *your letters <u>and</u> Kim's*	b. *Kim's letters <u>and</u> yours*	[Type III]
v	a. *yours <u>and</u> Kim's letters*	b. [pre-empted by iib]	[Type III]

Type I is at best very marginal. The version with a genitive pronoun, [ib], is of the same status as [24i], though the construction with an independent pronoun may be slightly better (?*These are Kim and yours*). The version with a non-genitive pronoun, [ia], is most acceptable when the second coordinate contains a dependent genitive: *you and your partner's letters.* With pronouns that have distinct nominative and accusative forms, the accusative is clearly non-standard: !*me and Kim's letters.* The nominative is inadmissible with a 1st person pronoun, **I and my partner's letters*, but perhaps marginally acceptable for some speakers with a 3rd person, ?*they and their partners' letters.*

Type II is grammatical but again disfavoured relative to Type III or a non-coordinative construction. For Type III there is a variant in which the head noun (*letters*) appears in the second coordinate, as in [va]. An attested example (from an address by a managing director) is *It is mine and the board's responsibility to maximise profits.* The effect is to use an independent form of the pronoun in place of the dependent one that would normally be expected when the head noun comes at the end of the matrix NP, i.e. in place of *my* in *my and the board's responsibility.* There is no counterpart to [va] with the pronoun in final position, since it is only with pronouns that the distinction between independent and dependent genitives applies: *Kim's and your letters* will thus be construed as having the structure indicated in [iib] rather than [*Kim's*] [*and your letters*].

3.5 Coordination of clause types

Coordination of unlike types

Coordinated clauses are usually of the same type, but do not have to be: this is one reason why we take declarative, imperative, etc., to be categories of the clause rather than the sentence. Coordination of unlike types is seen in [26i] (main clauses) and [26ii] (subordinate clauses):

[26]			
i	a.	[*It'll be very hot,*] [*so take plenty of drink*].	[declar + impve]
	b.	[*They've finished the job,*] [*<u>but</u> why did they take so long?*]	[declar + interrog]
	c.	[*Did you make your own contributions to a complying superannuation fund*] [*<u>and</u> your assessable income is less than $31,000?*]	[interrog + declar]
	d.	[*You give the first three lectures*] [*<u>and</u> then I'll take over*].	[impve + declar]
	e.	[*Come around six,*] [*<u>or</u> is that too early?*]	[impve + interrog]
	f.	[*What a disaster it was*] [*<u>and</u> yet no-one seemed to mind*].	[exclam + declar]
ii	a.	*I knew* [*that he would come*] [*<u>and</u> what he would say*].	[declar + interrog]
	b.	*I remember* [*who was there*] [*<u>and</u> what a success it was*].	[interrog + exclam]

With main clauses such mixed coordinations characteristically involve a sequence of separate speech acts (statements, questions, directives, etc.), so that the coordinator will have wider scope than the illocutionary components. A normal utterance of [ia], for example, consists of a statement (or prediction) followed by a directive. Similarly, in [ib] we have a statement followed by a question, in [if] an exclamatory statement followed by an ordinary statement.

But this is not so in all cases. Most obviously, [26ic] (taken from an income tax form) expresses a single question, not question + statement: this is a rather unusual case where in a coordination of full main clauses a feature of the first coordinate (here the closed interrogative clause type) has semantic scope over the whole coordination.[53] A different case again is seen in [ie]. It is not a matter of a choice between a directive and a question: the question has priority, and only if the answer is negative does the directive stand ("Come around six if that is not too early").

Coordinations of like type

An unmixed coordination of main declaratives (*Kim is in Bonn and Pat is too*) can generally be taken as a single statement of a composite proposition, though (at least with *and*) it would make no effective difference if we regarded it as a combination of statements, each of a simple proposition. Analogously for imperatives.

The situation with interrogatives is more complex. *And*, as in *Who is it and what do they want?*, can be taken to join questions, though again this hardly differs from an interpretation as a single composite question (with answers like "It's Jill and she wants to borrow the saw"). *But* does not normally coordinate main interrogatives (we would not say *Who is it but what do they want?*).[54] With *or* we have several distinct possibilities:

[27] i	*Is it genuine or is it a hoax?*	[alternative Q]
ii	*Have you moved or are you about to move?*	[alternative or polar Q]
iii	*Either can you eat it or have I got one?*	[two polar questions]

Example [i] is a single question, with *or* marking it as of the alternative kind: the answers are "It is genuine" and "It is a hoax". Example [ii], discussed in Ch. 10, §4.4, could also be an alternative question, asking whether your move has already taken place or is imminent. But it can also be a single polar question, asked for example in order to find out whether the writer's record of your address needs changing: here the answers are "Yes, I have moved or am about to move" and "No, I have not moved nor am I about to move". This is comparable to [26ic], for in both of them the whole coordination expresses a single polar question, but whereas with *and* the second clause is declarative, with *or* it has to be interrogative. Example [27iii] is a coordination of questions: much less usual, but possible in a context where, for example, I am trying to solve a puzzle and say, *Give me a clue by answering one of the following questions: Either can . . .* The *either* in [iii] makes explicit that the coordination has wide scope, i.e that it is a coordination of questions. It could not appear at the beginning of [i–ii], where the coordination has narrow scope (coordination within a question). This scope factor accounts for the

[53] The same applies in informal speech in examples like *Did he come in and I was still asleep?* (=[30ii] of §2), or *How could you have been so spiteful, and her your best friend?* (where the second clause is verbless, and is interpreted as "given that she was your best friend"). A further case where an element in the first coordinate may have scope over the second is seen in *It might be up there and I can't see it*: here *might* has wide scope, the meaning being "it might be that it is up there and I can't see it".

[54] Exceptions arise when one of the interrogatives is used as an indirect statement: *Isn't it a bargain, but where could we put it?*

fact noted earlier (§2.3) that *either* can never correlate with the *or* of an alternative question.[55]

3.6 Level of coordination

Equivalence at different levels

It is an important property of coordination, we have noted, that it can occur at almost any place in constituent structure. As a result, we have equivalences such as those shown in:

[28] i	*They shot her father and they shot her mother.*	[clauses]
ii	*They shot her father and shot her mother.*	[VPs]
iii	*They shot her father and her mother.*	[NPs]
iv	*They shot her father and mother.*	[nouns]

(Coordinations at different levels may differ in meaning in ways described in §1.3: we will not be concerned with those differences in the present section.) The lower the level, the less repetition there is; but the most economical version, the one with the coordination at the lowest level, is not always the preferred one.

In general, lower-level coordination tends to suggest a closer association between the coordinates than higher-level coordination. Given that there is a very close association between one's father and one's mother, the word-level coordination in *They shot her father and mother* is perfectly natural; in the absence of special contextual factors, however, there is no similarly close association between one's father and one's solicitor, and hence one would be more likely to say *She was accompanied by her father and her solicitor*, with the coordination at phrase level, than ··· *by her father and solicitor*. Compare, similarly, *I need a shirt and tie* (strong association: coordination of nouns) and *I need a diary and a calculator* (weaker association: coordination of phrases). Or again: *my friend and colleague* (a single person) and *my boss and my secretary* (different people).

We have also noted that determinatives tend not to coordinate readily, with a higher-level coordination preferred in cases like *this copy and those*. Similarly, while *be* allows mixed coordinations as complement, a version where *be* is repeated will often be preferred or required when non-finites are involved, as in *He was insolent and was dismissed.*

Number constraints on coordination of nouns

In NP structure certain determiners are sensitive to the number of the head, as described in Ch. 5, §3.4. The demonstratives ***this*** and ***that*** agree with the head, and determiners such as *a, one, each* select singular heads, while *many, several, two*, etc., select plurals. Coordinations of nouns (or nominals) in head function are subject to various constraints illustrated in:

[29] i	a. **these elephant and giraffe*	b. **two elephant and giraffe*
ii	a. *this cup and saucer*	b. *a/one cup and saucer*
iii	a. #*this elephant and giraffe*	b. #*an/one elephant and giraffe*

The examples in [i] demonstrate that a coordination of singulars does not count syntactically as plural, and hence cannot combine with a plural demonstrative or a determiner

[55] In the case of [27ii] it is marginally possible to have *either* to the right of its basic position before the first coordinate, as in *Have you either moved or are you about to move?*

that selects a plural head. Such a coordination can combine with a singular demonstrative or a determiner selecting a singular head if there is a close association between the coordinates, as in [ii]. Thus a cup and a saucer can be conceptualised as a unit, but this would not normally be possible with an elephant and a giraffe. Instead of [iii], therefore, we would normally have coordination at the NP level, with separate determiners: *this elephant and this giraffe*, and so on. Note, moreover, that whatever the determiner, a singular cannot coordinate with a plural at the word level: *the women and the man*, not **the women and man.*[56]

The dissociating effect of higher-level coordination

When the close association factor could be expected to sanction a lower-level coordination, use of a higher-level one may serve to separate, to partially dissociate the coordinates. Compare:

[30] i *He had dinner and watched TV.* [VP-coordination]
ii *He had dinner and he watched TV.* [clause-coordination]

In [i] we have a common sequence of events, whereas in [ii] we might be listing more sharply distinguished events, and it does not convey as strongly as [i] that the events took place in the order in which they are expressed.

Coordination at unlike levels

We also find examples where the coordinates are at different levels in the hierarchy:

[31] i *If you are homeless, an orphan, a refugee in State care or your parents can't provide you with a home, care or support, you can get Austudy from the minimum school leaving age.*
ii *He was middle-aged, of sallow complexion and had penetrating blue eyes.*
iii *He reads widely, has a questioning mind and he's very mature for his years.*
iv *He had read the report, discussed it with colleagues and was now drafting a reply.*

In [i] the first three coordinates are phrases, each of which could occur as predicative complement to *be*, while the final coordinate is a clause. In [ii] the first two coordinates are phrases within a VP while the third is a full VP. In [iii] the first two are VPs, the third a clause. And in [iv] the first two are past-participials dependent on perfect *have*, while the third is a finite VP. The status of such examples is somewhat uncertain. They are more likely to be found in casual speech than in more carefully monitored speech or writing – but they do occur in the latter, as evident from [i], taken from an Australian Government document on its tertiary education allowance.

The examples in [31] cannot be described directly in terms of the structures outlined in §1, for the underlined expressions do not combine into a constituent with a definable function. If they are to be regarded as grammatical and given an analysis, we will need to treat the coordination as being at the level of the final coordinate, with ellipsis of elements at the beginning of the medial coordinates. Thus [ii], for example, would be a case of VP-coordination, with the second coordinate, *of sallow complexion*, having ellipsis

[56] Where a numeral higher than *three* combines with a noun-coordination the generally preferred interpretation is that where it applies to the coordinates jointly. Thus *ten elephants and giraffes* is most likely to be interpreted as denoting a set of ten animals in all. But a distributive interpretation ("ten elephants and ten giraffes") cannot be excluded.

of the verb *was*. This would put them in the category of non-basic coordination, to be discussed in the next section, but given their marginal status we will not consider them any further.

4 Non-basic coordination

So far we have focused on what we will now call **basic coordination**, in contrast to various more complex constructions, **non-basic coordination**, to which we now turn.

Basic coordination is illustrated in [1], and has the three properties summarised in [2]:

[1] [*Sue and her brother*] *live in Paris.*

[2] i Bare coordinates are normal constituents. That is, they can appear as constituents in corresponding non-coordinative constructions: *Sue lives in Paris*; *Her brother lives in Paris.*[57]

ii Coordinates appear in succession. In [1], for example, the second coordinate, including its marker *and*, immediately follows the first.

iii Bare coordinates appear alone or in combination with a marker. In [1] *Sue* stands on its own, while *her brother* is marked by *and.*

Non-basic coordination lacks one or more of these properties. We have already noted in connection with [2iii] that a coordinate can be expanded by a modifier as well as (or instead of) a coordinator, as in *Jill and her brother too live in Paris*: we look at this kind of expansion first, and then turn to various constructions differing from basic coordination in respect of properties [i] or [ii].

4.1 Expansion of coordinates by modifiers (*the guests and indeed his family too*)

In this construction an expanded coordinate contains one or more modifiers in addition to the bare coordinate and the marker (coordinator) if present:

[3]	i *He offended* [*the guests and indeed his family too*].	[expansion by modifier]
	ii *He offended* [*the guests and his family*].	[basic NP-coordination]

The second coordinate in [i] consists of *his family* as bare coordinate, *and* as marker, and *indeed* and *too* as modifiers – see [9] of §1 for a tree diagram.

Distinct constructions only with lower-level coordinates

Expansion by a modifier does not yield a special coordination construction with main clause coordinates (or their VPs). For here comparable modifiers have a place in the structure that is quite independent of coordination:

[4] i *He offended the guests and indeed he offended his family too.*

ii *He offended the guests. Indeed he offended his family too.*

[57] We have noted that in a joint coordination like *Sue and her husband are a happy couple* there are no non-coordinative counterparts, but the coordinates here can still be regarded as normal constituents in that their status as constituents elsewhere (e.g. in *Her husband is happy*) is quite unproblematic.

There is no coordination in [ii], but the modifiers *indeed* and *too* have the same function here as in [i]. For this reason we treat them as belonging within the bare coordinate in [i], so that [i] will be simply an instance of basic coordination of clauses.[58] Note that with a subordinate clause, by contrast, the modifier can be clearly outside the bare coordinate: *I can't recall any task which at first seemed so simple and yet which subsequently proved so troublesome.*

Types of modifier

The central type of modifier in this construction is one which reinforces the relation expressed by the coordinator, including as a special case negative *not* as modifier to the first term in a *but*-coordination:

[5] i *She had read the report and taken notes too.*
ii *It must have been a rat or else a very large mouse.*
iii *I want it not next week but now.*

These include additive focusing adverbs, as discussed in Ch. 6, §7.3. Others of this kind include *also, as well, in addition* (with *and* or *but*), *alternatively* (with *or*), *rather* (with *but*). Also common are various connective modifiers such as *consequently, by contrast, of course, on the one hand,* and modifiers expressing epistemic modality such as *perhaps, probably, certainly, obviously, no doubt* (cf. *They're inviting Jill and probably her husband as well*).

Similar to this construction is one where a coordinate is anchor to a supplement (cf. §5 below), as in *It had been affected by both the inflation rate and, more recently, devaluation.*

4.2 Gapped coordination (*Kim is an engineer and Pat a barrister*)

Gapped coordinates are structurally incomplete clauses: the predicator is omitted, so that there is a gap in the middle of the clause. Compare:

[6] i *Kim is an engineer and Pat is a barrister.* [basic coordination]
ii *Kim is an engineer and Pat __ a barrister.* [gapped coordination]

The gap, marked in [ii] by '__', is interpreted anaphorically from the underlined antecedent in the first clause. Usually a gapped coordination is semantically equivalent to a basic coordination in which there is repetition rather than a gap,[59] as [ii] here is equivalent to [i]. Gapping is possible only when the coordinates have parallel structures: the gap is flanked by elements which match elements of like function flanking the antecedent. In [ii], for example, *Pat* matches the subject *Kim* and *a barrister* matches the predicative complement *an engineer*. In multiple coordination all the coordinates after the first can be gapped: *Kim is an engineer, Pat __ a barrister, and Alex __ a doctor.*[60]

[58] An exception is *else*: even with clauses this does not normally occur except with *or* and hence should be treated as expanding the coordinate.

[59] The repetition need not be exact, since agreement features are irrelevant: the basic counterpart of *Kim is an engineer and the two boys __ doctors* will have *are*, not *is*.

[60] The term 'gapping' is taken from formal grammar; there is no established term in traditional grammar for this construction. It should be emphasised, however, that there are numerous constructions that we analyse in terms of a gap, and the term 'gapping' or 'gapped coordination' applies only to the one discussed in this section.

In the simplest case the gap has just the predicator of the first clause as antecedent, and is flanked on the left by the subject and on the right by a single element (complement or adjunct). In [6ii] the right element is a predicative complement, while in [7i–ii] it is object and adjunct respectively:

[7] i *Their daughter studied law, their son __ medicine.* [subject __ object]
ii *The PM arrived at six and the Queen __ an hour later.* [subject __ adjunct]

The gap in combination with the structural parallelism serves to tie the clauses together, so that *and* is more readily omitted than in basic coordination – compare [7i] with *Their daughter studied law, their son studied medicine*, where in speech it would be more difficult to decide whether we have asyndetic coordination or simply a sequence of two sentences.

More complex cases of gapping

Consider now the possible extensions of this elementary type of gapping.

(a) The antecedent may be a sequence of elements

[8] i *Jill came to Fiji in 1967 and her parents __ the following year.*
ii *Their daughter was studying law, their son __ medicine.*
iii *Kim expects to get a credit, Pat __ only a pass.*
iv *His father wanted him to marry Sue, but his mother __ Louise.*

This is particularly common in the catenative construction: the antecedent contains a verb – either an auxiliary (e.g. progressive *be* in [ii]) or a lexical verb (e.g. *expect* and *want* in [iii–iv]) – that takes a non-finite complement. It is possible for the whole of the non-finite complement to be included within the antecedent (*Ed wanted to join the firm because of the pay, Bill __ because his girlfriend worked there*), but more often only part of it is, as in the above examples, and this then means that the antecedent does not form a constituent: in [iv], for example, *wanted him to marry* is clearly not a constituent, for in constituent structure *to marry* combines first with *Sue*.[61]

One limitation is that the antecedent cannot end with a preposition or infinitival *to*, so that the underlined items cannot be omitted in [9] even though they appear in the first clause too:

[9] i *I went by car and Bill __ by bus.*
ii *Kim was hoping to go to university and Pat __ to join the family business.*

(b) A gapped coordinate need not contain a subject

We distinguish two cases of gapped clauses with no subject:

[10] i *On Monday she'd been in Paris and on Tuesday __ in Bonn.*
ii *Always do it with your left hand, never __ with your right.*

In [i] the subject (*she*) is part of the antecedent; this is possible only when the subject is preceded by another clause element. In this example the element preceding the subject is an adjunct, but it could also be a complement: *Some of them she cut with an ordinary knife, the others __ with a razor-blade.* In [ii] there is no subject in the gapped clause because the coordination is of subjectless clauses, imperatives. But we again have a

[61] It is possible, though considerably less usual, for the catenative verb alone to be the antecedent, and again this applies whether it is an auxiliary or a lexical verb: *Kim will lead the party and Pat bring up the rear*; *One was reading, the other __ watching television*; *Two of them intended to go to university, and one __ to join the army.*

pre-verbal element (here the modifier *never*) so that the gap is still medial, flanked on both sides by contrasting elements.

(c) The antecedent may be non-verbal

This very rare case is found with a verbless complement of *with*:

[11] *With [Jill intent on resigning and Pat __ on following her example], we look like losing our two best designers.*

(d) The gap may be followed by two elements

It is possible, but rare, to have more than one element after the gap – e.g. object + adjunct:

[12] *Ed had given me earrings for Christmas and Bob __ a necklace for my birthday.*

(e) There may be two gaps rather than one

[13] i *One had treated his whole family appallingly, the other __ only his wife __.*
ii *I wanted the Indian to win, my wife __ the Italian __.*
iii *Too few fathers had been rostered for Saturday and __ mothers __ for Sunday.*
iv *His criticisms of Kim were inaccurate and __ of Pat __ irrelevant.*
v *Max hadn't finished his assignment, nor __ Jill __ hers.*

In [i] we interpret the gapped coordinate as "the other had treated only his wife appallingly"; this sense of *treat* requires a manner dependent, so the antecedent must be the discontinuous sequence *had treated . . . appallingly.* In [ii] we understand "my wife wanted the Italian to win": we reconstruct both the main predicator and the infinitival complement following the object. In [iii] the determiner element in the subject, *too few*, is carried over as well as the verbal sequence *had been rostered*; note that the omission of the determiner (creating a secondary gap) is possible only in combination with the primary gapping of the predicator – we can't say **Too few fathers had been rostered for Saturday and __ mothers had volunteered for Sunday.* Secondary gapping of this kind is extremely restricted: it would hardly be possible, for example, if we replaced *too few* by *all the* or *five.* In [iv] the first part of the subject is likewise missing, this time determiner + head. Finally [v] could be expanded as *nor had Jill finished hers*, where *nor* triggers subject–auxiliary inversion, separating the auxiliary *had* from the past participle *finished.*

(f) Exceptionally, the gap may be in final position

[14] *In most households the adults make these decisions, but in ours the kids __.*

This possibility reflects the fact that the basic position for the adjuncts *in most households, in ours* is after the object: in the version without fronting of the adjuncts the gap will be in its normal medial position (*The adults make these decisions in most households, but the kids __ in ours*).

Case

The case of a subject pronoun in a gapped clause may be either nominative or accusative: *Kim took the upper route, I/me __ the lower one.* This is in accordance with the general rules for case assignment, which in a finite clause require a nominative when there is an overt verb but allow either case elsewhere, with the nominative representing the more formal alternant (see Ch. 5, §16.2.1). However, when a gapped clause consists of a subject pronoun followed by an object pronoun, an accusative subject is appreciably less acceptable: *Max loathed the Smiths and they/?them _ him*; informal style would tend to avoid the gapped construction here.

Possible non-equivalence with basic coordination

In all the examples so far the gapped coordination has been semantically equivalent to the corresponding basic coordination, as noted for [6]. But such an equivalence does not always hold:

[15] i	a.	*Kim can't have a new bicycle and Pat _ just a t-shirt.*	[a≠b]
	b.	*Kim can't have a new bicycle and Pat can't have just a t-shirt.*	
ii	a.	*Kim wasn't at work on Monday or Pat _ on Tuesday.*	[a≠b]
	b.	*Kim wasn't at work on Monday or Pat wasn't at work on Tuesday.*	

A context for [i] might be a discussion between parents concerning possible presents for their children. We interpret [ia] as something like "We can't allow/accept a situation where Kim has a new bicycle and Pat has just a t-shirt"; semantically there is just one "can't" but it applies to the composite situation in which Kim and Pat are treated so differently, Kim receiving a new bicycle, Pat just a t-shirt. Here, then, *can't* has scope over the coordination. In [ib], however, it does not, for this time "can't" appears twice, applying separately and independently to the two simple situations. A plausible response to [ia] might be *OK, let's give them both a new bicycle*, but this would be incoherent as a response to [ib], because [ib] rules out giving a new bicycle to Kim. The difference in [ii] is likewise a matter of scope. The meaning of [iia] is "It is not the case that Kim was at work on Monday or that Pat was at work on Tuesday". Semantically we again have just one negative here, with scope over the whole coordination. We have noted that "not A-or-B" is equivalent to "not-A and not-B" (*I didn't like his father or mother* = *I didn't like his father and I didn't like his mother*), and the same applies here, so that [iia] is equivalent not to [iib] but to *Kim wasn't at work on Monday and Pat wasn't at work on Tuesday*. Example [iia] says there were two absences, while [iib] implicates that there was just one.

Analysis

On the basis of the simple examples with which we began it is tempting to analyse gapped coordination in terms of the deletion of repeated material, but [15] shows that a syntactic analysis of this kind is not satisfactory. We must accept that the syntactic structure of the gapped coordinate is simply fragmentary (e.g. subject + predicative complement for [6ii]); the context enables us to derive a semantic interpretation, but this may be a more complex matter than just filling in missing words.

It was with such examples as [15ia/iia] in mind that we defined clausal coordination in §1.3.1 as coordination of **full** main clauses. This puts gapped coordination with subclausal coordination: it belongs here because, as in more central cases, the coordinator may fall within the scope of a preceding element.

Gapping in non-coordinative constructions

In general, gapping is not found with subordination: **I <u>will help</u> you if you _ me*; **Jill <u>danced</u> with Max because Liz _ with his brother.* There are, however, some exceptions, notably comparatives (which in other respects too have a good deal in common with coordinative constructions): *Max <u>loved</u> Jill more than she _ him*, or *I <u>wanted</u> the Indian <u>to win</u> as much as my wife _ the Italian _* (cf. [13ii]). The comparative and coordination cases are not entirely parallel, however, for they behave differently with respect to negation. In *Max didn't love Jill as much as she __ him*, for example, we interpret the gap as "loved", not "didn't love", but we could not similarly leave out *loved* in *Max didn't love Jill but she loved him.*

4.3 Right nonce-constituent coordination (*I gave $10 to Kim and $5 to Pat*)

This is coordination of sequences that do not form syntactic constituents elsewhere, e.g. in corresponding basic coordination:

[16] i *I gave $10 to Kim and I gave $5 to Pat.* [basic coordination]
ii *I gave $10 to Kim and $5 to Pat.* [nonce-constituent coordination]

In [i] *$10* and *to Kim* do not go together to form a constituent as they are separate complements of ***give***, and likewise for *$5* and *to Pat*; yet in [ii] these sequences *$10 to Kim* and *$5 to Pat* form the bare coordinates, and by virtue of that they are constituents. The term 'nonce-constituent' is intended to convey, therefore, that constituent status is conferred on the sequence simply by the coordination relation – they are constituents for the nonce, as it were, just by virtue of the coordination.[62] And we call it 'right' nonce-constituent coordination because the coordinates follow the head element on which the components are dependent, in this case *give.*

The structural parallelism requirement

The coordinated sequences are required to be parallel in structure. In [16ii], for example, each consists of a direct object followed by a *to* phrase complement. Further examples meeting this requirement are given in [17i], including one that has three elements within each coordinate, and [17ii] illustrates the deviance that results when the coordinates are not parallel:

[17] i a. *We persuaded one of them to cycle and the others to catch a bus.*
b. *It was criticised by some for being too short, by others for being too long.*
c. *Ted considered Kim too young and Pat too earnest.*
d. *Jill bought Kim a t-shirt and Pat some shorts.*
e. *I sent Ed a letter on Monday and Sue a postcard on Friday.*
ii a. **In the afternoon I wrote a report and my wife a letter.*
b. **He blamed his wife for the debts and the untidy state of the house on the boys.*

Examples [ic–e] are in fact ambiguous between this construction and gapping (where the meaning would be "... and Pat considered Kim too earnest", etc., but the right nonce-constituent reading is generally much more likely in such cases.[63] Similarly [iia] is grammatical as an instance of gapping (" ... and my wife wrote a letter"): the asterisk indicates that it can't be a case of right nonce-constituent coordination. This is because the two coordinates are not structurally alike or parallel: the first contains just a single element (direct object) while the second contains two (indirect object + direct object). In

[62] Precisely because these sequences are constituents of the coordination construction we prefer 'nonce-constituent' to the more usual term in formal grammar, 'non-constituent coordination'.

[63] This is where the NPs are all of the same type: in *Some of them considered me too young and others too old*, where *others* contrasts more naturally with *some of them* than with *me*, it is the gapped coordination reading that is more salient.

[iib] both coordinates contain two elements, but they reflect different complementation patterns for *blame*: '*blame X for Y*' and '*blame Y on X*'.[64]

Right nonce-constituent coordination in NP structure

Unlike gapping, the present construction is not restricted to clause structure, but is found also in NPs:

[18] *She's read* [*the lectures on Goethe by Dr Smith and on Schiller by Dr Jones*].

Possible non-equivalence with basic coordination

As with gapping, this construction is usually equivalent to corresponding basic coordination (as [16ii] is equivalent to [16i]), but it is not invariably so. The following examples of non-equivalence are of the same kind as those given in [15]:

[19] i a. *I can't give a new bicycle to Kim and just a t-shirt to Pat.*
b. *I can't give a new bicycle to Kim and I can't give just a t-shirt to Pat.* [a≠b]
ii a. *He said nothing to Kim about Pat or to Pat about Kim.*
b. *He said nothing to Kim about Pat or he said nothing to Pat about Kim.* [a≠b]

In [ia] a single composite situation is excluded, the one where I give a new bicycle to Kim and just a t-shirt to Pat, whereas [ib] excludes the two simple situations separately. In [ia] *and* has narrow scope relative to *can't*, whereas in [ib] *and* has wide scope. Similarly in [iia] the negative *nothing* has scope over *or*, and hence (by the equivalence of "not A-or-B" to "not-A and not-B") the sentence can be paraphrased not as [iib], but as *He said nothing to Kim about Pat and he said nothing to Pat about Kim.*

Analysis

In view of the non-equivalence shown in [19], it would not be satisfactory to derive the right nonce-constituent construction from basic coordination by deletion of repeated material. Instead we propose an analysis along the lines shown in [20], a simplified representation of the structure of the VP in [16ii].

[20]

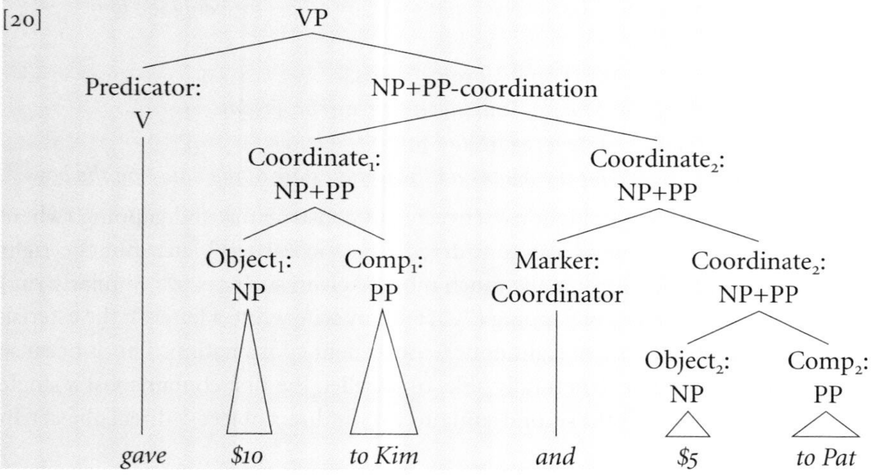

[64] Some speakers find acceptable such examples as ?*He left his daughter $20,000 and half that amount to each of his grandchildren*; it is certainly better than [17iib] and also than the opposite breach of parallelism seen in **He left $20,000 to his daughter and each of his grandchildren half that amount.*

The notation 'NP + PP' means a sequence of NP followed by PP. The sequence *$10 to Kim and $5 to Pat* is a coordination of such sequences, but no function is assigned to it: it is only the smaller elements *$10*, *$5*, *to Kim*, and *to Pat* that can be assigned clause-level functions, direct object for the first two, prepositional complement for the others.

Further evidence for saying that the first coordinate is the sequence *$10 to Kim* (rather than *I gave $10 to Kim* or *gave $10 to Kim*) is that it can be marked by correlative *both*: *I gave both $10 to Kim and $5 to Pat.*[65]

4.4 Delayed right constituent coordination (*knew of but never mentioned my work*)

In this construction the constituent which in basic coordination would appear as the rightmost element of the first coordinate is held back until after the final coordinate:

[21] i *She knew of my other work but never mentioned it.* [basic coordination]
ii *She knew of but never mentioned my other work.* [delayed right constituent]

In general, the effect is to heighten the contrast between the coordinates by removing from them material that would be the same in each. But the construction is appreciably more difficult to process than basic coordination, both for the addressee, who has to hold the first coordinate in mind until the sense is completed at the end, and for the speaker, who has to plan ahead to ensure that each coordinate ends in a way that syntactically allows completion by the delayed element – as *knew of* and *never mentioned* both allow completion by an NP complement.[66] Characteristically, there is a prosodic break after the final coordinate, signalling that the element that follows relates to the whole coordination, not just to the final coordinate.

Range of uses

We illustrate here a sample of the main types of coordination where a right constituent is delayed in this way.[67]

(a) Heads taking different complementation

Probably the most common case is where the heads of the coordinates differ in the syntactic complements they take. Example [21ii] is of this kind: *know* (in the sense intended) takes an *of* PP, while *mention* takes an NP object. Other examples are seen in:

[22] i *I'm interested in but rather apprehensive about their new proposal.*
ii *He ought to, but probably won't, make a public apology.*

[65] One type of example that does not readily fit into the structure shown in [20] is *We'll be in Paris for a week and Bonn for three days.* The complication here is that *for a week* is a clause-level function (adjunct of duration), but *Paris* is not – it is the complement of the preposition *in*. The best solution is probably to treat *in* as part of the coordination; we will then have a PP+PP-coordination, with ellipsis of *in* in the second coordinate.

[66] Examples are found where this condition is not satisfied. One case is illustrated in *?I always have and always will value her advice*, where the plain form *value* is an admissible continuation of *will* but not of *have*: compare basic *I have always valued her advice and always will value it.* Another involves coordination of comparisons of equality and inequality: *?It's as good or better than the official version*, where *as good* takes a complement headed by *as* not *than*. Such examples are not fully grammatical and would generally be avoided in monitored speech and writing; the second can be corrected to *It's as good as or better than the official version.*

[67] We focus on cases where the delayed element is a single constituent; occasional examples are found where what follows the coordination is not a single constituent but a sequence: *It had to be ascertained whether the managers had suitable people to put forward for possible appointment from persons* [*registered with, or applying to, them for employment*].

In [i] the heads *interested* and *apprehensive* take different prepositions, *in* and *about*. In [ii] *ought* and *will* take different kinds of infinitival complement, with *to* appearing only with *ought*.

(b) Contrasts of time or modality

A second pattern has the same verb in each coordinate but with differences expressing such concepts as time or modality:

[23] i *She was then, is now, and always will be, devoted to the cause of peace.*
ii *They regarded him, or appeared to regard him, as a complete liability.*

(c) Pairing of lexically simple and lexically complex coordinates

[24] i *He had either telephoned or written a letter to his son's boss.*
ii *You should welcome, not take offence at, the suggestions they make.*
iii *He was accused but found not guilty of stalking a woman for seven years.*

The first coordinates here are simple verbs, while the final ones are complex expressions: [ii] illustrates the fairly common case where one or more of the coordinates in this construction is a verbal idiom of the kind considered in Ch. 4, §6.4.

(d) Contrasting sequences of pre-head dependents in NP structure

[25] i *They have [five new and two second-hand copies of his novel].*
ii *[Neither the American nor the Russian people] want war.*

In [i] both dependents in the coordinated sequences contrast, whereas in [ii] only the second does. The repetition of *the* in [ii] is motivated by *neither* which could not occur between *the* and *American*, but such repetition is not restricted to cases where it is syntactically or semantically required: *He was comparing the American and the Russian versions.*

(e) Contrasting pairs of subject and verb

[26] *Kim may accept, but Pat will certainly reject, the management's new proposal.*

Construction not confined to coordination

Delayed right constituents occur predominantly in coordination, but they are found in some subordinative constructions too:

[27] i *I enjoyed, although everyone else seemed to find fault with, her new novel.*
ii *Those who voted against far outnumbered those who voted for my father's motion.*

These most closely resemble case (e) above in that the contrasting sequences (shown by underlining) that could combine with the delayed right constituent contain a subject: *I* vs *everyone else* in [i], and *who* in [ii].

Analysis

In some cases the present construction looks like the mirror image of right nonce-constituent coordination: compare *five new and two second-hand copies* with *gave $10 to Kim and $5 to Pat*, and so on. But there are two important differences. One is the point just noted, that a delayed right constituent can occur in subordination. The other is that the present construction does not require the parallelism that is found with right nonce-constituent coordination. In [24i], for example, the coordinates are *telephoned* and *written a letter to*, which are quite different in their internal structure.

One possible analysis is to take the right constituent as being related to the coordinates, in a way analogous to that in which a relative pronoun is related to a relative clause (and similarly in other unbounded dependency constructions: cf. Ch. 12, §7): [24i] might then be compared to *his son's boss* <u>*whom he had either telephoned or written a letter to*</u>. Applying this idea to [24i] gives a structure along the lines of [28]:

[28]

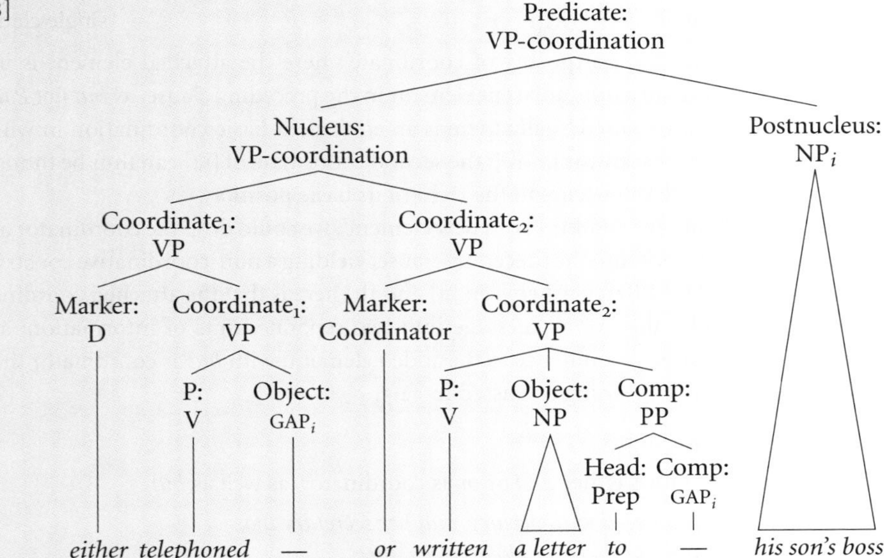

Both coordinates contain a gap co-indexed with the NP in postnuclear position, just as in the relative construction they will be co-indexed with the relative pronoun. The difference is that in the relative construction there may be, and most often is, only one gap (cf. *everyone whom he had telephoned*): the delayed right constituent, by contrast, is found only with gaps in two or more matching sequences, usually coordinate.

No functional label other than 'postnucleus' is assigned directly in [28] to the delayed right constituent. However (like the relative pronoun) it is understood as inheriting the functions in the coordinates of the gaps with which it is co-indexed. This caters for the case, illustrated in this example, where the delayed element is understood as having different functions in the coordinates: *his son's boss* is here understood as object of *telephoned* and complement of the preposition *to*. We leave open the question of whether this kind of structure is appropriate to all cases of delayed right constituents – in particular, those where there is no prosodic break before the final element, and where it can be an unstressed personal pronoun, as in *He's as old as or older than me*.

4.5 End-attachment coordination (*They had found Kim guilty, but not Pat*)

A subclausal coordinate may be attached at the end of a construction, following a clause; it may, but need not, have the informational status of an afterthought, in which case it has the status of a supplement. Two subtypes can be distinguished, as illustrated in [29ia/iia]:

[29] i a. *They had found Kim guilty of perjury but not Pat.* [postposing of coordinate]
b. *They had found Kim but not Pat guilty of perjury.* [basic coordination]
ii a. *I spoke to her, but only briefly.* [addition of new element]
b. *I spoke to her only briefly.* [single clause]

One subtype we call 'postposing of coordinate': here the attached element is in a coordinative relation to a non-adjacent element in the preceding clause, as *but not Pat* in [ia] is coordinate with *Kim*. Usually there is an equivalent basic coordination in which the coordinates are adjacent, as in [ib]; the second coordinate of [ia] can thus be thought of as 'postposed' in that it occurs to the right of its basic position.

In the second subtype, 'addition of a new element', we could drop the coordinator and integrate what follows it into the preceding clause, yielding a non-coordinative construction, as in [29ii]. The difference between [a] and [b] here is that the attached coordinate construction divides the overall message into two separate units of information, and thereby gives increased prominence to the added element; with *but* as coordinator there is also the adversative meaning discussed in §2.5.

Postposing of coordinate

This construction allows either *and* or *or* as coordinator, as well as *but*:

[30] i *Jill has been charged with perjury, and her secretary too.*
ii *Jill must have told them, or else her secretary.*

Note that where the basic position is within the subject, postposing has an effect on subject–verb agreement: in [i], for example, *has* agrees with *Jill* (compare *Jill and her secretary too have been charged* . . .). A special case of *or* is in questions, where we note that *Did Jill tell you that, or her secretary?* exhibits the same ambiguity as the basic coordination *Did Jill or her secretary tell you that?* It can be either an alternative question ("Which of them told you?") or a polar one ("Did one or other of them tell you?"), again with a clear intonational difference between the readings (Ch. 10, §4.4); note here that in the alternative interpretation the appended element wouldn't normally be an afterthought.

As with several of the other constructions considered in this section, factors such as negation may result in a difference of meaning between basic and non-basic coordination:

[31] i *Jill or her secretary hadn't complied with the regulations.*
ii *Jill hadn't complied with the regulations – or her secretary.*

Example [i] says that one or other of them hadn't complied with the regulations; this is a possible meaning of [ii] (with unstressed *or*), but in a more likely interpretation (with stressed *or*) it says that neither had. *Or* is outside the scope of the negation in [i], where *or* comes before *hadn't*, but potentially inside the scope of the negative in [ii], where their order is reversed.

Analysis

A major difference between this postposing of coordinate construction and basic coordination is that the coordinates do not combine into a syntactic constituent: in [29ib] the NP-coordination *Kim but not Pat* forms a constituent functioning as object, but in [ia] there is no such constituent. In the postposing construction the coordinative relationship is simply marked **linearly** by *but*: as far as the hierarchical constituent structure is concerned *but not Pat* is attached as an NP at the end of the clause and can be assigned the function 'coordinate object'. Note that it would not do to claim that the coordination was in fact of clauses: the full clause *They had found Kim guilty of perjury* and the clause fragment *but not Pat*. The appeal of such an analysis is that it brings the construction into line with normal coordination in that the coordinates would together form a constituent (co-extensive with the whole sentence), but whereas it might work for the majority of examples it doesn't cover cases like [31ii] above, or similarly:

[32] i *They hadn't issued sheets to the new recruits – or towels.*
ii *How many had they issued sheets to, but not pillow-slips?*

These exhibit the now familiar phenomenon of narrow scope coordination, so that they are not equivalent to the coordination of full clauses. Thus [i], for example, is not equivalent to *They hadn't issued sheets to the new recruits or they hadn't issued towels to them*: the latter says that either sheets or towels hadn't been issued, whereas [i] says that neither sheets nor towels had been. The difference is that in [i], but not in the clause-coordination, *or* is within the scope of the preceding negative. In [ii] there is no corresponding clause-coordination that is well formed (cf. **How many had they issued sheets to but how many had they not issued pillow-slips to?*), but even if there were (as would be the case if we substituted *and* for *but*) it would not be equivalent to [ii] since it would be questioning the number of two sets (those issued with sheets and those not issued with pillow-slips) instead of one (those issued with just sheets). In [ii], therefore, the coordinator is within the scope of the interrogative phrase *how many*. An analysis in terms of clause-level coordination fails to bring out that the second coordinate relates not to the whole of what precedes but to a particular constituent within it.

Addition of a new element

Further examples of this construction are given in:

[33] i *The match was won by Kim, and very convincingly too.*
ii *He was reading, but nothing very serious.*
iii *I'll drive you there, but only if you pay for the petrol.*

But is the most common coordinator in this construction; *and* is also possible, but *or* is not. The added element is very often interpreted as an adjunct, but it can also be a complement provided the verb is one that can occur with or without a complement of the type in question. In [ii], for example, *nothing very serious* is interpreted as object of *read*, this being a verb that occurs in both transitive and intransitive clauses. Example [iii] represents a rather special use of this construction. Normally *A but B* (like *A and B*) entails both A and B. This applies to basic coordination: *Kim left at six but Pat stayed on till noon*, for example, entails both that Kim left at six and that Pat stayed on till noon. It also applies to most cases of the present construction: [33i] entails that the match was won by Kim and that it was won very convincingly. However, [iii] does not entail that I'll drive you there – it has only the weaker, conditional entailment that I'll drive you there if you pay for the petrol. *But* here thus introduces a qualification that weakens what precedes it; note that *only* is not omissible, though *not* could take its place (*I'll drive you there, but not if you criticise my driving*).

The distinction between this construction and basic coordination is not completely straightforward; compare:

[34] i *He comes not from Alabama but from Georgia.*
ii *He's from Alabama, but from the city of Birmingham, not rural Alabama.*

Example [i] is a very clear case of basic coordination, the coordinates being *not from Alabama* and *but from Georgia.* We take [ii], however, as adding a new element: the two *from* PPs are not coordinates. An important difference in meaning is that while Georgia is distinct from Alabama, Birmingham is not – it is included within it. Example [ii] is like the earlier examples of the addition of a new element construction in that we can drop the *but* to yield a non-coordinative construction: *He's from Alabama, from the city of Birmingham, not rural Alabama.* We noted in §2.5 that *but* generally indicates a contrast between the coordinates, a contrast that is, however, very often derived indirectly via various assumptions and inferences; this is what is going on in [ii], where the *but* reflects an assumption that people's image of Alabama might be formed mainly by reference to rural stereotypes.

Analysis

In this construction *but* or *and* coordinates the added element to the whole preceding clause. Here, then, in contrast to the postposing of coordinate construction, the clause does have the form of a coordination between a clause and a clause fragment.

4.6 Coordination as evidence for constituent structure

It is a common practice in linguistic analysis, one we have followed a number of times in this grammar, to use the potential for coordination as evidence that a given sequence of words forms a syntactic constituent. The principle can be stated as follows:

[35] In general, if a sequence *X* can be coordinated with a sequence *Y* to form a coordination *X and Y*, then *X* and *Y* are constituents.

The qualification 'in general' is needed because, as we have noted above, exceptions are to be found in various kinds of non-basic coordination. In this final section, therefore, we examine the criterion in the light of the distinction between basic and non-basic coordination.

Coordination as evidence for a VP constituent

The example we will take is that of the VP: how does coordination support the analysis of a clause like *Sue found the key* into two immediate constituents, as in [36i], rather than three, as in [ii]?

[36] i *Sue | found the key.* [NP + VP: the VP analysis]
ii *Sue | found | the key.* [NP + V + NP: the 'no VP' analysis]

Principle [35] supports the VP analysis

The sequence *found the key* can be readily coordinated:

[37] *Sue <u>found the key</u> and <u>unlocked the door</u>.*

Only analysis [36i] is therefore consistent with principle [35]; other things being equal, it is to be preferred over [36ii] because it allows us to subsume [37] under basic coordination, so that it requires no special treatment. Principle [35], however, is qualified, not absolute, so we need to consider the matter further.

VP-coordination vs clause-coordination with ellipsis of the subject

An alternative treatment of the coordination here, one that is consistent with [36ii], is to say that the coordinates are clauses, the second having ellipsis of the subject. The first coordinate will then be not *found the key* but *Sue found the key*, and the second will be '__ *unlocked the door*. This accounts for the equivalence between [37] and *Sue found the key and she unlocked the door*. But we saw in §1.3.1 that there are many cases where no such equivalence obtains, as in:

[38] i *No one treats me like that and gets away with it.* [VP-coordination]
ii *No one treats me like that and no one gets away with it.* [clause-coordination]

An elliptical clause analysis doesn't provide a satisfactory account of coordination like [38i].

Basic vs right nonce-constituent coordination

Another alternative consistent with [36ii] would be to say that the underlined sequences in [37] are merely nonce-constituents, constituents in the coordination but not elsewhere. This is to treat [37] like our earlier example:

[39] *I gave* <u>*$10 to Kim*</u> *and* <u>*$5 to Pat*</u>. (=[16ii])

There are, however, two important differences between [37] and [39]. In the first place, the nonce-constituents in [39] have to be parallel in structure (as noted in §4.3), whereas those in [37] do not – compare, for example, *Sue found the key and departed*. Secondly, the reason why *$10 to Kim* is not a normal constituent is that there is no direct syntactic relation between the parts, *$10* and *to Kim*: they are, rather, separately dependents (complements) of *give*. *Found the key* in [37] is quite different: here there is a syntactic relation between the parts, *found* being head and *the key* dependent. The nonce-constituent analysis is a more complex type of construction than basic coordination, applying under restricted conditions (the requirement of parallelism) and justified by strong independent arguments against recognising the coordinates as normal constituents: in the case of [37] we have no reason to prefer the more complex analysis to the one that follows the general principle given in [35].

Basic vs delayed right constituent coordination

The relevance of [37] to constituent structure might be challenged on the grounds that it is also possible for coordination to group *found* with *Sue*:

[40] <u>*Max lost*</u> *but* <u>*Sue found*</u> *the key.*

If coordination can group *found* with either *the key* or *Sue*, the argument would go, then it can't provide evidence for a constituent grouping of *found* with just one of them, *the key*. But such an argument fails to recognise that there is a major difference between the coordination of [37] and that of [40]. The latter represents a much less usual type of coordination than [37], and this instance of it is indeed of somewhat marginal acceptability because of the low weight of *the key*; acceptability is increased by expanding to *the key to the safe* but greatly diminished by reducing to *it*. Example [40] would characteristically have special prosody, with a clear break before *the key*. But [37], by contrast, has no such limitations or special prosody,[68] and can be taken to represent the most elementary type of coordination: as such, it does provide valid evidence in support of the VP analysis.

[68] These properties do not hold for all cases of delayed right constituent coordination, but even when they do not there will be independent evidence for treating the coordination as non-basic. Take, for example, [24iii], *He was accused but found not guilty of stalking a woman for seven years*: it is evident that in the non-coordinative *He was found not guilty of stalking a woman for seven years* the *of* phrase is a complement of *guilty*, not *find not guilty*, because it regularly occurs with *guilty* quite independently of the presence of *find*, as in *He was/seemed guilty of treason*.

Conclusion: coordination provides a criterion, other things being equal

Coordination clearly does not provide a simple and absolute criterion for constituent structure: the qualification 'in general' in [35] is indispensable. It nevertheless remains a useful criterion: if a sequence *X* can be coordinated, then the simplest account will be one where it is a constituent entering into basic coordination, and we will adopt some other, more complex, analysis only if there are independent reasons for doing so.

5 Supplementation

We turn now to supplementation constructions, illustrated in such examples as:

[1] i *Pat – <u>the life and soul of the party</u> – had invited all the neighbours.*
ii *The best solution, <u>it seems to me</u>, would be to readvertise the position.*
iii *Jill sold her internet shares in January – <u>a very astute move</u>.*

The underlined expressions are **supplements**, elements which occupy a position in linear sequence without being integrated into the syntactic structure of the sentence.

5.1 General properties of supplementation

In the clear and central cases, supplements have the character of **interpolations** or **appendages**. An interpolation, as in [1i–ii], is located at a position between the beginning and end of a main clause: it represents an interruption to the flow of the clause. An appendage is attached loosely at the beginning or end of a clause. In speech, supplements are marked as such by the prosody: they are intonationally separate from the rest of the sentence. In writing, they are normally set off from the rest of the sentence by punctuation marks – commas, or stronger marks such as dashes, parentheses, or (in the cases of appendages in end position) a colon. Punctuation allows for different degrees of separation, as described in Ch. 20, §§4–5.

Supplementation in relation to dependency constructions and coordination

It is the lack of integration into the syntactic structure that distinguishes supplementation from dependency constructions and coordination. But supplementation is like coordination in being non-headed: since the supplement is not integrated into the structure it cannot function as a dependent to any head. The three types of construction are thus distinguished as shown in:

[2]

		INTEGRATED?	HEADED?
i	DEPENDENCY CONSTRUCTION	Yes	Yes
ii	COORDINATION	Yes	No
iii	SUPPLEMENTATION	No	No

It should be noted, however, that expressions introduced by a coordinator can have the status of supplements rather than coordinates in an (integrated) coordination construction:

[3] *Jill – <u>and I don't blame her</u> – left before the meeting had ended.* [supplement]

In spite of the *and*, the underlined clause is an interpolation, and is clearly not of equal syntactic status with the clause *Jill left before the meeting had ended.* We thus treat [3] as an instance of supplementation, not coordination, such as we have in *Jill left before the end of the meeting and I was sorely tempted to follow her.*

Supplements and anchors

Although supplements are not syntactically dependent on a head, they are semantically related to what we will call their **anchor**.[69] In [1i] the anchor is the NP *Pat*, while in [1ii–iii] and [3] it is a clause – the clause which the supplement interrupts or follows. Other possibilities are shown in [4], where double underlining marks the anchor, single underlining the supplement:

[4] i *When the patient closed his eyes, he had absolutely no spatial (that is, third-dimensional) awareness whatsoever.*

ii *The goal is to produce individuals who not only possess 'two skills in one skull', that is, are bicultural, but can also act as human links between their two cultures.*

In [i] the anchor is the adjective *spatial* (which functions as attributive modifier to the noun *awareness*); in [ii] it is the VP *possess 'two skills in one skull'* (first coordinate in a VP-coordination).

A supplement must be semantically compatible with its anchor. Compare, for example:

[5] i *This stipulation – that the amount of damages not be divulged – was ignored.*

ii #*This stipulation – whether the press could be informed – was ignored.*

The supplement in [i] is a declarative clause and as such can appropriately combine with the anchor *this stipulation.* The anomaly of [ii] stems from the fact that the supplement is an interrogative clause and hence is not semantically compatible with this anchor.

Supplements vs dependents

Semantic compatibility vs syntactic licensing of complements

The restriction illustrated in [5] is comparable to that which holds between a complement and the head nominal in NP structure:

[6] i *The stipulation that the amount of damages not be divulged was ignored.*

ii **The stipulation whether the press could be informed was ignored.*

This time, single underlining indicates the complement, double underlining the head. The noun *stipulation* licenses a declarative content clause as complement, but not an interrogative, so [ii] is inadmissible.

There is a significant difference between [5] and [6], however. The integrated construction shown in [6] requires that the complement be syntactically licensed, whereas in supplementation it is, as we said above, a matter of semantic compatibility. Compare:

[7] i a. *The stipulation that Harry could not touch the money until he was eighteen annoyed him enormously.*

b. **The codicil that Harry could not touch the money until he was eighteen annoyed him enormously.*

[69] Some writers use the term 'host', but we have avoided this because we use it elsewhere in its primary sense, where it applies to the word to which a clitic is attached (see Ch. 18, §6.2).

ii a. *This stipulation – that Harry could not touch the money until he was eighteen – annoyed him enormously.*
b. *The codicil in the will – that Harry could not touch the money until he was eighteen – annoyed him enormously.*

The examples in [i] belong to the integrated head + complement construction. *Stipulation* licenses a declarative complement, but *codicil* does not: hence the ungrammaticality of [ib]. In [ii] the content clause is a supplement, interpreted as specifying the content of its anchor NP. And this time the *codicil* example is acceptable: the NP it heads denotes an addition to a will and hence has propositional content which can be specified by a declarative content clause.

As a second illustration of the difference between the integrated and non-integrated constructions, consider:

[8] i a. *The question (of) where the funding would come from wasn't discussed.*
b. **The thing (of) where the funding would come from was rather more important.*
ii a. *The second question – where the funding would come from – wasn't discussed.*
b. *The thing they didn't discuss – where the funding would come from – was rather more important.*

Here the content clause is interrogative. In [ia] it is a dependent within the NP headed by the noun *question*: it may appear as an immediate complement or it may be related to the head noun by the preposition *of*. Again, the complement needs to be licensed by the head noun: *question* takes interrogative complements, but *thing* does not, so [ib] is ungrammatical. In [ii] the interrogative clause is a supplement and is subject to the weaker constraint that it be semantically compatible with its anchor. Example [iib] is therefore admissible because the anchor NP as a whole denotes a potential topic of discussion, so that the content of this topic can be specified by means of an interrogative clause supplement.

Form and interpretation of supplements realised by clauses

A further important difference between supplements and dependents is that the former may be realised by main clauses with their own illocutionary force:

[9] *Sue felt – can you blame her? – that she was being exploited.*

The supplement here has the form and interpretation of a main clause: there is no change in form or loss of independent illocutionary force such as is found with clauses realising a dependent function.

Supplements and non-restrictiveness

By virtue of not being integrated into the syntactic structure, supplements are necessarily semantically non-restrictive. Compare, for example, [8ia–iia]. In the former, the integrated construction, the content clause is semantically restrictive, distinguishing the question being referred to from other questions. It provides the identifying information that makes it appropriate to use the definite article *the*. By contrast, in [iia], the supplementation construction, *the second question* by itself constitutes a definite referring NP. The supplement doesn't serve to distinguish one second question from other second questions: it doesn't restrict the denotation of the head nominal.

The same contrast between dependency and supplementation constructions is commonly found with relative clauses and appositives:

[10] i a. *The necklace which her mother gave to her was in the safe.* [modifier]
b. *The necklace, which her mother gave to her, was in the safe.* [supplement]
ii a. *They are working on a new production of the opera 'Carmen'.* [modifier]
b. *Bizet's most popular opera, 'Carmen', was first produced in 1875.* [supplement]

In [ia] the relative clause is a modifier of the head noun *necklace* and serves semantically to identify which necklace is being referred to, but in [ib] it is a supplement to the anchor NP *the necklace*, which is assumed to be identifiable independently of the information given in the relative clause. Similarly, in [iia] the appositive *Carmen* is a modifier of *opera*, identifying which opera is being referred to, while in [iib] it is a supplement to the anchor NP *Bizet's most popular opera*, and since there can be only one entity satisfying that description the supplement is again non-restrictive.

However, we have noted in our description of relative clauses and appositives that the integrated construction is not necessarily semantically restrictive – see Ch. 12, §4.2, and Ch. 5, §14.3, respectively. Compare, then:

[11] i *The father who had planned my life to the point of my unsought arrival in Brighton took it for granted that in the last three weeks of his legal guardianship I would still act as he directed.*
ii *This is my husband George.*

In [i] the relative clause doesn't distinguish one father from another: the narrator has only one father, so the modifier provides non-restrictive information about him. And [ii] does not convey that the speaker has more than one husband.

It is for this reason that we have departed from the traditional account of relative clauses, in which the two main constructions are distinguished as 'restrictive' and 'non-restrictive'. A distinction in terms of integrated versus supplementary reflects the semantic difference more accurately and also matches the prosodic difference that distinguishes them in speech. It enables us, moreover, to capture the similarity between the unintegrated relatives and other elements that are semantically, prosodically, and syntactically unintegrated with the rest of the sentence: these can all be subsumed under the concept of supplement.

Syntactic representation of supplementation

A supplement, as we have seen, requires a semantically appropriate anchor: it cannot occur, as a supplement, without the anchor. Thus if we drop the anchor from [10ib], for example, the result is ungrammatical: **Which her mother gave to her, was in the safe.* And if we drop it from [10iib] '*Carmen*' takes on the status of an integrated dependent, the subject: '*Carmen*' *was first produced in 1875*. For this reason, we take the anchor and its supplement to form a construction – a supplementation construction. But the lack of integration of the supplement into the syntactic structure means that there is no good reason to treat the supplementation as a syntactic **constituent**. We propose, therefore, that in the syntactic representation supplements should be kept separate from the tree structure, related to their anchors by some different notational device, as in [12]:

[12]

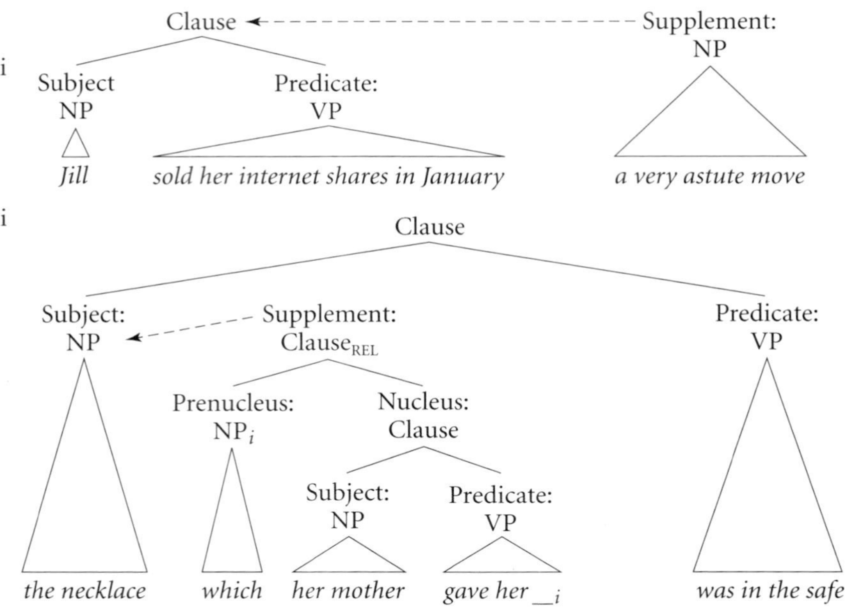

In [12i], representing the structure of example [1iii], the supplement *a very astute move* has the clause *Jill sold her internet shares in January* as its anchor: this is shown by the broken line leading from the functional label 'Supplement' to the category label 'Clause'. Similarly in [12ii] the broken line shows that the relative clause is a supplement to the NP *the necklace.*

Indicators

Supplements may contain **indicators** which serve to clarify the nature of their semantic relation to the anchor. In the following examples, the supplement is enclosed in square brackets and the indicator is marked with single underlining (with the anchor marked with double underlining, as above):

[13] i *No wonder that Pozzatti and I had at times difficulty in remembering the real purpose of our presence,* [*namely, Cultural Exchange*].

ii *Mature connective tissues are avascular,* [*that is, they do not have their own blood supply*].

iii *Much to everybody's amazement, I got along splendidly with Max;* [*that is, until I became an editor and hence a potential rival*].

iv *The poem asserts emotion without evoking it* – [*that is to say, it is sentimental*].

v *Other pairs of phonological subsystems also interact or overlap in this way;* [*for example, duration sometimes figures in both the vowel system and the intonation*].

vi *She was highly critical of both proposals,* [*especially the second one*].

Namely (like formal *viz* and *to wit*) indicates that the supplement has a specifying function: the real purpose of our presence **was** Cultural Exchange. *That is* and *that is to* *say* can be used in the same way, but they can introduce a wider range of supplement types, including finite VPs or main clauses, with the supplement typically providing an explanation of the anchor. It is also possible, however, for the supplement to serve as a qualification to the anchor, as in [iii], where we understand: "or rather I got along splendidly with him until I became an editor . . . ".

Indicators are to some extent analogous to coordinators in that they link together the elements in a construction. We will therefore generalise the contrast between syndetic and asyndetic to the supplementation construction. The supplementations in [13] are thus syndetic, while the corresponding constructions without the indicator are asyndetic. Compare syndetic [13iv], for example, with asyndetic *The poem asserts emotion without evoking it: [it is sentimental]*.

One difference between indicators and coordinators, however, is that some at least of the indicators can occupy non-initial position in the supplement:

[14] i *It is these other differences between North and South – [other, that is, than those which concern discrimination and social welfare] – which I chiefly discuss in this paper.*
ii *The therapist's level tone is bland and neutral – [he has, for example, avoided stressing 'you'].*

Linear position

When the anchor is a main clause, the supplement may interrupt it as an **interpolation**, or be loosely attached as an **appendage** at the beginning or end:

[15] i *He claimed – and everyone believed him – that it was all my fault.*
ii *Having reviewed all the evidence, they decided he had no case to answer.*
iii *He sent her some flowers – the least he could do in the circumstances.*

When the anchor is subclausal, there are two aspects of the position of the supplement to consider: its position relative to the anchor, and its position relative to the main clause that contains the anchor. Compare:

[16] i *It is almost mandatory for anyone in the financial business to have ready – that is, virtually real-time – access to sources of information about overseas markets.*
ii *Exeter clearly enjoyed full employment – as full, that is, as was attainable in the conditions of the time.*
iii *When political art (that is, art which challenges the status quo in some way) succeeds it is most often by reinventing the real.*
iv *One question still needs to be considered: who's going to pay for it all?*
v *Eric Hoffer once said that America was a paradise – the only one in the history of the world – for workingmen and small children.*

In [i] the supplement is adjacent to its anchor, the attributive adjective *ready*, but it is still an interpolation with respect to the main clause that forms the sentence as a whole. In [ii], by contrast, the supplement is an appendage to the main clause, but is separated from its anchor. Examples [iii–iv] are like [i–ii] respectively, but have an NP as anchor. But in [v] the supplement is not only an interpolation with respect to the main clause: it is also located internally within its NP anchor.

Multiple supplementation

Because they are syntactically only loosely related to the rest of the sentence, supplements naturally receive far less attention in grammars than do integrated constructions. It should be emphasised, however, that in many kinds of speech and writing they are extremely frequent. Moreover, sentences commonly contain more than one supplement:

[17] i *A recent newspaper report said there were five Negroes in the 1960 graduating class of nearly one thousand at Yale; that is, about one-half of one per cent, which looks pretty 'tokenish' to me, especially in an institution which professes to be 'national'.*

ii *Professionally a lawyer, that is to say associated with dignity, reserve, discipline, with much that is essentially middle-class, he is compelled by an impossible love to exhibit himself dressed up, disguised – that is, paradoxically, revealed – as a child, and, worse, as a whore masquerading as a child.*

In [i] there are three supplements. The first (*that is, about one-half of one percent*) has as its anchor the preceding content clause, the complement of *said.* The second (the relative clause *which looks pretty 'tokenish' to me*) is a supplement to the first, and then the third (*especially in an institution which professes to be 'national'*) is a supplement to the second. Example [ii] is more complex. It begins with the supplement *professionally a lawyer,* which is anchor to another supplement, *that is to say associated with dignity, reserve, discipline, with much that is essentially middle-class* (which, we may observe, contains two instances of asyndetic coordination, one between the two *with* PPs, one between the three NPs *dignity, reserve, discipline*). The participial adjective *disguised* is anchor for the supplement *that is, revealed,* which has another supplement, *paradoxically,* interpolated within it. Finally, *worse* is a supplement preceding its anchor, *as a whore masquerading as a child.*

5.2 The form of supplements

Supplements can be realised by a very wide range of categories. The indicator *that is,* in particular, can link supplements of most categories to anchors of the same category. In [4i–ii] above, for example, it links an adjective to an adjective, and a finite VP to a finite VP, a versatility comparable to that of a coordinator. The following review of types of supplement thus does not aim for exhaustive coverage.

(a) Relative clauses

[18] i *We called in to see Sue's parents, which made us rather late.*

ii *They'd given me two diskettes, both of which turned out to be defective.*

Supplementary relative clauses can have a clause or various kinds of phrase as anchor. In form they are a type of subordinate clause, but differ from integrated relative clauses in ways described in detail in Ch. 12, §4.

(b) NPs

Specifying and ascriptive supplements to NP anchors

In supplementations with one NP as anchor and another as supplement, the relation between the two is comparable to that between subject and predicative complement in a *be* clause. In particular, the distinction between specifying and ascriptive complements applies also to supplements. Compare [19i–ii], for example, where double underlining marks the subject of the clausal construction and the anchor in supplementation, single underlining the predicative complement and the supplement:

[19] i a. *The first contestant was Lulu.* [specifying]
b. *Kim Jones was a quite outstanding student.* [ascriptive]
ii a. *The first contestant, Lulu, was ushered on stage.* [specifying]
b. *Kim Jones, a quite outstanding student, won a scholarship to MIT.* [ascriptive]

In the [a] examples *Lulu* is interpreted as specifying who the first contestant was, while in [b] *a quite outstanding student* expresses a property that is ascribed to Kim Jones. One formal difference in the case of supplementation is that specifying NPs accept the indicators *namely, that is, i.e.,* etc.: *The first contestant, namely Lulu, was ushered on stage.*

Apposition

The construction with a specifying NP as supplement is known as **apposition**. More particularly, this is the supplementary type of apposition, corresponding to the integrated apposition of *the opera 'Carmen'* or *my husband George* (in [10iia/11ii] above). Thus the appositive NP can be substituted for the whole supplementation yielding an entailment of the original: [19iia] entails *Lulu was ushered on stage.*

Further examples of supplementary apposition are given in:

[20] i *The murderer, the man with the scar, will be arrested soon.*
ii *A university lecturer, Dr Brown, was arrested for the crime.*
iii *A surprise present, a bouquet of roses, was delivered to my door.*
iv *An entire genre, the comedy thriller, has been made obsolete by the invention of the mobile phone.*
v *A Seyfert galaxy – a galaxy with a brilliant nucleus – usually has a massive red-shift.*

Example [20i] is just like [19iia] except that the appositive is not a proper name but an NP with a common noun as head. Example [20ii] shows that the relation between supplementation and predication in a *be* clause is not always as straightforward as in the pair [19ia/iia]. Indefinite NPs are certainly not excluded from functioning as subject in a specifying *be* clause (cf. *One problem is the cost*), but they occur there much less readily than in appositive supplementation. Thus the predicational counterpart of the supplementation in [20ii] is anomalous: #*A university lecturer was Dr Brown.* The appositive is nevertheless clearly of the specifying type, and can be matched up with the predicational *The university lecturer arrested for the crime was Dr Brown.* In [20iii] both NPs are indefinite, and again may be compared with predicational *The surprise present delivered to my door was a bouquet of roses.*

The anchor NP in supplementary apposition is non-referential, in the sense of Ch. 5, §8.3. In [20i–iii] the appositive NP is referential, but examples [20iv–v] show that it too can be non-referential: in [iv] it is generic, and in [v] definitional.

In all the above examples the appositive is adjacent to the anchor, but where the anchor is non-final in its clause the appositive may be separated from it. In such cases the anchor is generally but not invariably indefinite:

[21] i *I met a friend of yours at the party last night – Emma Carlisle.*
ii *The two dominical sacraments stand out from all the rest – namely baptism and Holy Communion.*

Ascriptive NP supplements

Further examples of NP supplements with an ascriptive interpretation are given in:

[22] i *Her father, a die-hard conservative, refused to even consider the proposal.*
ii *Wilson, Secretary to the Cabinet, had informed the Prime Minister immediately.*
iii *Robert, no genius, is applying for a scholarship to Harvard.*

This construction does not qualify as apposition because the supplement cannot always be substituted for the whole construction in such a way as to yield an entailment of the original. In [ii], for example, the supplement is a bare role NP unable to take over the subject function: **Secretary to the Cabinet had informed the Prime Minister immediately.* And *No genius is applying for a scholarship to Harvard* is clearly not an entailment of [iii].

Ascriptive NPs are also found in such constructions as the following:

[23] i *United will be playing at home, a not inconsiderable advantage.*
ii *A die-hard conservative, her father refused to even consider the proposal.*

In [i] the anchor is not an NP, but a clause, or perhaps a VP: we understand that it is an advantage to play at home. In [ii] the supplement precedes the anchor. Although the subject NP *her father* is the predicand for the ascriptive NP (it is her father who was a die-hard conservative), it is arguable that the anchor for the supplement is the whole clause rather than just the subject NP, for we understand it as providing some explanation for her father's refusal to consider the proposal.

(c) Content clauses

Content clause supplements generally have an NP or another content clause as anchor:

[24] i *The excuse he gave – that the train had been late – seemed to satisfy the boss.*
ii *I don't know what its status is, that is, whether or not it is confidential.*

In [24i] we again have a parallel with a specifying *be* clause: compare *The excuse he gave was that the train had been late.* This construction, however, is distinct from apposition, for the systematic entailment relation that is an essential feature of apposition does not apply. Example [i] itself demonstrates this. It does not entail *That the train had been late seemed to satisfy the boss*: what seemed to satisfy the boss was the excuse, not the fact that the train had been late. As we noted in Ch. 5, §14.3, the same point applies to integrated constructions where a content clause is a dependent of a noun, as in *The suggestion that they cheated is quite outrageous*: the content clause here is a complement, not an appositive modifier.

We thus need to distinguish two kinds of specifying supplement with an NP as anchor. A specifying NP supplement is apposition, while the supplement in [24i] may be called **content-specifying**. This type of specifying supplement can also be realised by other categories than content clauses: see [25i] and [30i] below.

(d) Main clauses

Anchors for supplements with the form of main clauses again include NPs and clauses:

[25] i *I raised a more serious objection : it's against the law.*
ii *The universe is expanding, that is, the galaxies are receding from each other at immense speeds.*
iii *If he says he can't afford it – he usually does – tell him I'll pay for us both.*

In [i], with an NP anchor, the supplement clause is again of the content-specifying type. It cannot substitute for the whole supplementation (**I raised it's against the law*), and hence cannot satisfy the condition for apposition.

Supplement main clauses in final position (especially those without any indicator) are not clearly syntactically distinguishable from separate sentences. In speech, one can use intonation to link a clause to what precedes as supplement to anchor, and in writing punctuation serves to mark more explicitly whether a main clause is being presented as a supplement to what precedes or as a separate orthographic sentence.

Parentheticals and tags

[26] i *There are, I think, some grounds for optimism.*
ii *Such behaviour runs the risk, wouldn't you agree, of alienating our customers.*
iii *You're not proposing to go out in those trousers, are you?*

The underlined expressions here have the form of main rather than subordinate clauses, but they are syntactically distinct from canonical main clauses by virtue of being structurally incomplete. Those in [i–ii] are known as 'parentheticals', while *are you?* in [iii] is an interrogative 'tag'. The form and interpretation of these constructions is discussed in Ch. 10, §5.

(e) AdjPs

[27] i *The editor, angry at the delay, resigned from the project.*
ii *Too afraid to venture out, Kim stayed barricaded in the house all week.*
iii *The editor has been sacked and, worse, they're imposing strict censorship.*

These constructions are similar to those with an ascriptive, as opposed to specifying, NP supplement. Construction [iii] is exceptional in that *worse* has as its predicand not an NP, but a clause (*they're imposing strict censorship*); it is more usual to have a relative construction – *what/which is worse.*

(f) Verbless clause

[28] i *The tourists, most of them foreigners, had been hoarded onto a cattle truck.*
ii *The defendants sat in the dock, their heads in their hands.*
iii *The only household chore men excelled at was – drumroll please – taking out the rubbish.*

In [i] the supplement is comparable in function to a relative clause: compare *who were most of them foreigners* (or *most of whom were foreigners*). If the supplement consisted of *foreigners* on its own, it would be an ascriptive NP, like those in [22]; *most of them*, however, does not function as a modifier in NP structure, so *most of them foreigners* must be analysed as a reduced clause – one which could not stand alone as a sentence. The supplement in [28ii] could likewise not stand alone, but differs in its internal structure in that *their heads* is subject. An equivalent integrated construction would have a modifier with the form of *with* + verbless clause: *with their heads in their hands.*

The supplement in [28iii], by contrast, could stand alone as a sentence. It is simply a fragmentary main clause (with the illocutionary force of a directive) used as an interpolation.

(g) Non-finite clauses

[29] i *All things considered, the result was reasonably satisfactory.*
ii *Having read the report, Max was sure he had nothing to worry about.*
iii *Not to put too fine a point on it, he's an absolute layabout.*

Example [i] illustrates the construction where the non-finite clause contains a subject. Usually, however, the subject is understood; in most cases it is recoverable from the anchor, as in [ii] (where it is Max who read the report), but it may also be recoverable contextually, as in [iii], where it is the speaker who is putting it bluntly. For further discussion of these constructions, see Ch. 14, §9.

(h) PPs and AdvPs

[30] i *This final portrayal – of Stalin – does no credit to the author.*
ii *In my opinion, the idea isn't worth pursuing.*
iii *The Dean, as you know, is totally opposed to the proposal.*
iv *Frankly, I think we could do better ourselves.*
v *They go – probably – by bus.*

PPs can occur as supplement to an NP anchor, and here again the specifying–ascriptive distinction applies. Example [i] is of the specifying type – more particularly, the content-specifying type. It contrasts in the familiar way with the integrated construction *this final portrayal of Stalin.*

The other supplements in [30] have a clause as anchor, and their function is very much like that of a modifier. In cases like [v] there is a contrast with an integrated construction, *They probably go by bus*: the latter has the adverb in its default position, and it is only when set off intonationally as an interpolation that it can occur in the position it occupies in [v]. For the rest, there is little difference between supplements with a clause as anchor and modifiers, and in this book we generally treat them together, using **adjunct** as a general term covering both.

The supplements differ from the most central modifiers in that they do not fall within the scope of negatives in the anchor and cannot be made the complement of *be* in the *it*-cleft construction. In [ii], for example, *in my opinion* is outside the scope of the negative *isn't*: the meaning can be glossed as "My opinion is that the idea isn't worth pursuing", not "That the idea is worth pursuing isn't my opinion". Their inability to be foregrounded in the *it*-cleft construction is seen in the ungrammaticality of examples like **It is as you know that the Dean is totally opposed to the proposal.*

(i) Interjections

[31] i *Ah, so you were there after all!*
ii *Damn, we've missed the bus again!*

The general definition of interjection is that it is a category of words that do not combine with other words in integrated syntactic constructions, and have expressive rather than propositional meaning. Central members of the interjection category in English are such words as *ah, hey, oh, oops, ouch, sh, ugh, wow* (or the now dated *alas*), which in their sole or primary meaning are used as expressive exclamations, on their own, or as supplements with clausal anchors, as in [31i]. There are also a number of words such as *blast, bugger, damn, fuck* which are primarily verbs, but which in supplements like that in [ii] have lost their verbal meaning, and are best regarded as having been reanalysed as interjections.[70]

(j) Clauses and phrases introduced by a coordinator

As we have noted, expressions introduced by the coordinators can be set apart from the rest of the sentence like supplements instead of functioning as coordinates in integrated constructions:

[32] i *If he checks my story – <u>and he probably will</u> – I'll be sacked.*
ii *It's clear – <u>and let's not mince words</u> – that he's been embezzling the funds.*
iii *He told the manager – <u>and her secretary</u> – that the report was defamatory.*

The status of the expression as a supplement rather than a coordinate is clearest in examples like [i–ii], where it could not enter into a coordination relation with what precedes. In [i] it could not coordinate with *he checks my story* because the latter is a subordinate clause functioning as complement of *if*, whereas *he probably will* is a main clause outside the scope of *if*. The structure is thus quite different from that of *If <u>I tell that story and he checks it</u>, I'll be sacked*, where the underlined sequence is a coordination of clauses which together form the complement of *if*. It would be possible to have a coordination reading if the underlined expression were placed at the end: *If he checks my story I'll be sacked, and he probably will.* In [ii] the underlined sequence could not even be placed felicitously at the end: *#It's clear that he has been embezzling the funds and let's not mince words.* The clauses are not sufficiently alike in terms of their meaning to permit felicitous coordination.

Example [32iii] is closely related to the obviously coordinative construction *He told <u>the manager and her secretary</u> that the report was defamatory.* The difference is that in [32iii] *and her secretary* is set apart by dashes, and in the corresponding spoken version it is set apart by intonation. It is this punctuational or prosodic separation that gives *and her secretary* the status of a supplement in [32iii]: it is presented as secondary information rather than being on a par with *the manager*. Nevertheless, it is a marginal and exceptional kind of supplementation. Normally, supplements can be omitted without loss of well-formedness, but this is not always so in the present case:

[33] *The manager – <u>and her secretary</u> – have been charged with defamation.*

If the supplement were omitted, the verb-form *have* would have to be replaced by *has*: the supplement is relevant to determining the form of the verb, just as it is in the integrated

[70] The verbal origin is more relevant in expressions like *Damn these mosquitoes!* or *Fuck you!*, where they have an NP complement. Historically, the *blast* and *damn* constructions were understood with *God* as subject, but that doesn't match their normal interpretation now: there is no more reason to postulate an understood subject in *Blast you!* than in *Fuck you!* It may be best to regard such words as exceptional interjections that combine with an NP complement to form an interjection phrase.

structure *the manager and her secretary*. Note that in cases like this the dashes cannot be replaced by parentheses: see Ch. 20, §5.

Supplements introduced by *or* are used to express reformulations or corrections:

[34] i *I'm convinced it was masterminded by Tom – <u>or Ginger</u>, as everyone calls him.*
ii *They'll be finishing on Tuesday – <u>or at least that's what they said</u>.*

16

Information packaging

Gregory Ward
Betty Birner
Rodney Huddleston

1 Syntactic overview

Information-packaging constructions

Our concern in this chapter is with a number of clause constructions which we refer to collectively as **information-packaging constructions**, and which differ syntactically from the most basic, or canonical, constructions in the language. These information-packaging constructions characteristically have a syntactically more basic counterpart differing not in truth conditions or illocutionary meaning but in the way the informational content is presented. Compare, for example:

[1]		CANONICAL VERSION	NON-CANONICAL VERSION
	i	a. *Kim wrote the letter.*	b. *The letter was written by Kim.*
	ii	a. *Two doctors were on the plane.*	b. *There were two doctors on the plane.*
	iii	a. *We rejected six of the applications.*	b. *Six of the applications we rejected.*

In each pair [b] is an instance of one of the information-packaging constructions, while [a] is the syntactically more basic counterpart. In each pair the truth conditions are the same, so that [a] entails [b] and [b] entails [a]; and there is no illocutionary difference between them: all six examples are declaratives and would normally be used as statements. The syntax makes available different ways of 'saying the same thing', with the various versions differing in the way the content is organised informationally.

We have said that information-packaging constructions **characteristically** enter into relationships of the kind illustrated in [1]. The qualification is needed for two reasons. In the first place, for most of the constructions there are conditions under which the syntactically more basic counterpart is in fact unacceptable for syntactic or pragmatic reasons:

[2]			
	i	a. **The nanny said Kim to have been devoted to the children.*	b. *Kim was said by the nanny to have been devoted to the children.*
	ii	a. #*An accident was at the factory.*	b. *There was an accident at the factory.*
	iii	a. **I find that he got away with it for so long quite incredible.*	b. *That he got away with it for so long I find quite incredible.*

Secondly, the canonical and non-canonical versions do not invariably have the same truth conditions:

[3]			
	i	a. *Kim didn't sign many of them.*	b. *Many of them weren't signed by Kim.*
	ii	a. *Many MPs weren't in the House.*	b. *There weren't many MPs in the House.*
	iii	a. *I haven't met many of her friends.*	b. *Many of her friends I haven't met.*

In each pair the relative order of the quantifier *many* and the negative is different in [b] than in [a], and this affects the relative semantic scope. The difference is sharpest in [ii], where the issue has to do with how many Members of Parliament were in the House (the British House of Commons, let us assume). In [iia] *many* has scope over the negative: the meaning is that a large number of MPs were absent from the House. In [iib] the negative has scope over *many*: the number of MPs present in the House was not large. Thus in a context where we have 600 MPs, of whom 300 are present in the House and 300 absent, version [a] would rate as true, whereas [b] would not. These issues of relative scope are dealt with elsewhere (see Ch. 5, §5, & Ch. 9, §1.3.2), and need not be taken further in this chapter.

Overview of main information-packaging constructions

The main constructions to be considered are illustrated in [4], with the default counterpart given in the right-hand column; the underlining draws attention to the syntactic differences between the two versions.

[4] i	PREPOSING	*This one she accepted.*	*She accepted this one.*
ii	POSTPOSING	*I made without delay all the changes you wanted.*	*I made all the changes you wanted without delay.*
iii	INVERSION	*On board were two nurses.*	*Two nurses were on board.*
iv	EXISTENTIAL	*There is a frog in the pool.*	*A frog is in the pool.*
v	EXTRAPOSITION	*It is clear that he's guilty.*	*That he's guilty is clear.*
vi	LEFT DISLOCATION	*That money I gave her, it must have disappeared.*	*That money I gave her must have disappeared.*
vii	RIGHT DISLOCATION	*They're still here, the people from next door.*	*The people from next door are still here.*
viii	CLEFT	*It was you who broke it.*	*You broke it.*
ix	PASSIVE	*The car was taken by Kim*	*Kim took the car.*

For some of the information-packaging constructions we will be distinguishing various subtypes, and we shall also be introducing certain extensions and additional, relatively minor, constructions.

In the case of [4ix] there is an independent term, **active**, for the default version on the right (*Kim took the car*), but for the rest there are no established terms for the constructions that lack the distinctive properties of the non-canonical information-packaging constructions. For the latter we have largely retained established terms. Some of them can apply equally to clauses and constructions: *The car was taken by Kim*, for example, is a passive clause and is an instance of the passive construction. Similarly for 'existential' and 'cleft'. The others apply, in the form cited, to the construction rather than the clause. Thus *It is clear that he is guilty* in [v] illustrates the extraposition construction, but we do not refer to it as an 'extraposition clause' – it is a clause with an extraposed subject. Similarly, *This one she accepted* in [i] is not a 'preposing clause', but a clause with a preposed object. The inversion in [iii] of the subject (*two nurses*) and an internal complement of the verb (*on board*) is to be distinguished from the inversion of subject and auxiliary verb (as in *Were two nurses on board?*): we speak, therefore, of subject–dependent inversion and subject–auxiliary inversion. However, since subject–auxiliary inversion is of relatively little relevance to the concerns of this chapter we will often use 'inversion' on its own, as in [iii], as an abbreviation for 'subject–dependent inversion'.

Several of the terms in [4] are based on processes, and it is worth repeating at the beginning of this chapter that process terms are to be interpreted simply as a convenient metaphorical means of describing how one construction differs from a syntactically more basic one (cf. Ch. 2, §2). When we say that *this one* is preposed in *This one she accepted*, we mean only that in this construction it is in front position although the default or basic position for it is after the verb.

Reordering and realignment

The differences between information-packaging constructions and their more basic counterparts are in some cases simply a matter of the linear order of the syntactic elements, and in others a matter of how semantic elements are aligned with syntactic functions. Using process terminology with the interpretation just explained, we can say, then, that constructions [4i–iii] involve reordering, while the others all effect a realignment of semantic and syntactic elements.

In [4i–iii] the non-canonical version can be regarded as less basic than its default counterpart in that the order is not only less frequent but subject to pragmatic constraints that do not apply to the default version. In [iv–ix] the non-canonical version is syntactically less basic by virtue of its greater syntactic complexity: the realignment is accompanied by the addition of one or more elements, such as *there* in [iv], *it* in [v], the auxiliary ***be*** and the preposition *by* in [ix] and so on.

Combinations

Certain of the information-packaging constructions are mutually exclusive because the processes concerned apply under distinct conditions. For example, extraposition cannot apply in [4iv] because *A frog was in the pool* does not contain a subordinate clause, and conversely existential formation cannot apply in [v] because *That he is guilty is clear* has a subordinate clause as subject: no one clause can be an instance of both the existential and extraposition constructions. In the absence of such restrictions, however, the constructions can combine, as illustrated in [5]:

[5]	i	a. *My mother found some of them offensive.*	
		b. *Some of them she found offensive, my mother.*	[preposing, right dislocation]
	ii	a. *That she was joking became clear at that point.*	
		b. *It was at that point that it became clear she was joking.*	[cleft, extraposition]
	iii	a. *Everyone assumed that Jill would win.*	
		b. *It was assumed by everyone that Jill would win.*	[passive, extraposition]
	iv	a. *The police had interviewed Kim.*	
		b. *Kim it was who had been interviewed by the police.*	[passive, cleft, preposing]

2 Information packaging: concepts and general principles

The information-packaging constructions, we have said, characteristically differ from their default counterparts with respect to the way the information they convey is presented. In this section we introduce the major concepts we need to describe these differences, and outline certain general principles governing the way information is presented in the clause. We take information to cover entities and properties as well as propositions. Thus in an example like *My father was angry* we can talk about the informational status of the proposition "My father was angry", but also about that of the person referred to by *my father* and the property "angry". We will also apply the concepts to the linguistic expressions that represent the entities, properties, and propositions.

Familiarity status: old and new information

Familiar or **old** information is information that the speaker takes to be shared by speaker and addressee, contrasting with **unfamiliar** or **new** information. More specifically, we must distinguish between information that is old or new with respect to the discourse, and information that is old or new with respect to the addressee.

Discourse-familiarity status: discourse-old vs discourse-new information

Here we are concerned with the status of the information within the current discourse – or, for very long discourses (such as a book) within the currently salient stretch of discourse. Consider the following examples of discourse-old information:

[1] i *Two letters have arrived for Jill; she'll be calling round to pick them up.*
ii *I haven't heard from Jill for a long time – have you?*
iii *As a child, I used to pretend a unicorn lived in my backyard. I called him Joe.*
iv A: *What did Max tell Jill?* B: *He told her I'd been delayed at the office.*

In [i] the first clause introduces two letters into the discourse: we say then that the letters are **discourse-new**, and by extension that the linguistic expression *two letters* is discourse-new. In the second clause, however, the letters are **discourse-old** because they have already been mentioned (in the preceding clause); and again we will say that the corresponding linguistic expression, *them*, is discourse-old. This represents one of the most obvious cases of a discourse-old constituent, a pro-form with a preceding antecedent. Similarly, in a context where there has been no prior mention of Jill, the NP *Jill* has the status of new information, while the coreferential pronoun *she* represents old information. In [ii] the pronouns *I* and *you* can be regarded as discourse-old because they refer to participants in the discourse. Example [iii] (ignoring now the 1st person pronoun) is like case [i] in that *him* is discourse-old by virtue of its anaphoric link with *a unicorn* in the preceding sentence: we give a second example of this type to make the point that the status of an entity as discourse-old does not depend on its actually existing in the real world, or even on the interlocutors' belief that it exists. In [iv] it is not just the NPs *he* and *her* that are discourse-old, but the whole sequence *He told her*, or the corresponding open proposition "He told her *x*".

Discourse-old status applies not only to elements that have themselves been explicitly evoked in the prior discourse, but also to those that stand in some salient and relevant relationship to elements that have been evoked:

[2] i *I don't in general care for puzzles, but crossword puzzles are fun.*
ii *I tried to get into the library after hours, but the door was locked.*
iii *That book is awful; the author doesn't have any writing ability at all.*

In [i] *crossword puzzles* is discourse-old information because there has been prior mention of the more general class of puzzles: crossword puzzles are a kind of puzzle. In [ii] we have a part–whole relationship between the door and the library, so we can infer that *the door* refers to the door of the library; it has the status of discourse-old information as the latter has been mentioned. Similarly, books characteristically have authors, and hence we understand *the author* to refer to the author of the book just mentioned. It is of course possible for a book not to have an author (it could be an edited collection of papers), but that is irrelevant: there is a close relationship between books and authors, and this is sufficient to make *the author* discourse-old information in the context of the preceding NP *that book.*

The relationship in question must be a salient and relevant one if I am to be able to assume that you can make the necessary inference – from crossword puzzles to puzzles, from doors to libraries, from authors to books. Compare, for example:

[3] i *I walked into the kitchen.* [*On a stool was a large book.*]
ii *I walked into the kitchen.* [*#On an overcoat was a large book.*]

There is a salient relationship between stools and kitchens: kitchens commonly have stools in them. But there is no comparable relationship between overcoats and kitchens. Mention of the kitchen thus serves to give the underlined NP the status of discourse-old information in [i] but not in [ii]; and the bracketed clause of [ii] is then infelicitous, i.e. unacceptable in this context, because (as we shall demonstrate in §5.2) inversion requires the preposed constituent to represent a link to the prior discourse. The discourse-old information in [i] serves as such a link – that is, it acts as a point of connection between the information in the current utterance and what has already been evoked in the discourse; it is then the absence of any such link in [ii] that makes the discourse infelicitous.

In the same way, propositions can be discourse-old even if they have not been directly expressed in the prior discourse, provided they stand in some salient relationship to ones that have, and/or to features of the situation of utterance. Consider, for example:

[4] A: *Are those cupcakes for sale?* B: *No, they're a special order. But the bagels you can have.*

One component of the meaning of the underlined clause is the open proposition "You can have *x*". This hasn't been expressed in what precedes, but has the status of discourse-old information because it is inferrable from A's question, which conveys that A wants to buy (hence have) something.

Addressee-familiarity status: addressee-old vs addressee-new information

Information that is familiar from the discourse, by virtue of prior mention or a salient and relevant relationship to what has been previously mentioned, is necessarily familiar to the addressee. Discourse-old information is also **addressee-old information**. But the addressee can also be assumed to be familiar with things that have not been mentioned in the discourse or that cannot be inferred from what has been mentioned. Consider, for example, an utterance in the United States of the sentence:

[5] *The President is giving the State of the Union address later tonight.*

Here I can assume on the basis of common knowledge shared by citizens of the United States that you know who *the President* refers to, and this NP accordingly has the status of addressee-old information even though it is discourse-new.

Focus and focus-frame

The **focus** of a clause (or portion of a clause) is the constituent bearing the strongest, or 'nuclear', stress, as indicated by the small capitals notation:

[6] *Mary bought* RICE *yesterday.*

Here *rice* is the focus. The residue we refer to as the **focus-frame**. This can be given in the form of an open proposition containing a variable in place of the element represented by the focus: "Mary bought *x*". The phonological prominence given to the focus accords it prominence in the message: it is presented as the most informative element in the clause, with the focus-frame backgrounded. The focus typically represents **addressee-new information,** and the focus-frame addressee-old information.[1]

Foci come in a variety of sizes. Consider, for example:

[7] *She bought a bag of* RICE.

If I say this in response to the question *What did Mary buy a bag of?*, the focus is *rice* and the focus-frame "She bought a bag of *x*". If I say it in response to *What did Mary buy?*, the focus is *a bag of rice* and the focus-frame "She bought *x*". If I say it in response to *What did Mary do?*, the focus is *bought a bag of rice* and the focus-frame "She did *x*". The focus is a constituent containing the nuclear stress, but it can contain varying amounts of material in addition to the stressed syllable: for further discussion, see Ch. 9, §1.3.3.[2]

It is possible for a clause to have more than one focus:

[8] A: *What did they* BUY? B: MARY *bought a bag of* RICE, . . .

In B's response both *Mary* and *a bag of rice* are foci, with the focus-frame being "*x* bought *y*".

Focus and familiarity

We have said that the focus typically represents new information, but the sense in which it is new may be different from that considered in our discussion of examples like [1i–iii]. Consider:

[9] A: *Did they give the job to you or to Mary?* B: *They gave it to* HER.

Here *her* refers to Mary and is old information by virtue of prior mention. At the same time *her* is focus and as such is new. This apparent paradox can be resolved by distinguishing between the familiarity status of Mary considered as an entity, a person (from this point of view Mary is old information), and Mary considered as the value assigned to the variable in the focus frame "They gave it to *x*" (from this point of view Mary is new information). I assume you know who the referent of *her* is, but I don't assume you know that Mary was the one to whom they gave the job: that is precisely the new information that I'm imparting to you.

[1] Throughout this chapter 'focus' is to be understood as 'informational focus', as opposed to 'scopal focus': see Ch. 6, §7.3, for this distinction.

[2] The focus-frame is often called a 'presupposition', but this represents a different sense of the term presupposition from that adopted in this book (see Ch. 1, §5.4, and Ch. 11, §7.4). The two concepts overlap, but are not synonymous. Note, in particular, that the presupposition can contain the focus, as in *It's unfortunate that he gave the key to* KIM. Here the underlined content clause is presupposed by virtue of *unfortunate* being a factive adjective, but it contains the focus *Kim*, and hence is not a focus-frame – the focus-frame here is "It's unfortunate that he gave the key to *x*".

Weight: heavy constituents

The weight of a constituent is a matter of its length and syntactic and morphological complexity. The weight of a constituent is one factor that may affect its position in the clause. Compare, for example:

[10] i a. *Sue picked up the dog.* b. *Sue picked the dog up.*
ii a. *Sue picked up a couple of boxes containing old computer manuals.* b. ?*Sue picked a couple of boxes containing old computer manuals up.*

In [i] the particle *up* may precede or follow the object NP, but in [ii], where the NP is heavy, there is a strong preference for the particle to come first: version [iib] is at best of marginal acceptability. It will be evident from this example that weight is a scalar concept: *a couple of boxes* is heavier than *the dog*, but not as heavy as *a couple of boxes containing old computer manuals*. We will talk of 'heavy constituents', meaning ones that have considerable weight, but without any implication of a dichotomy between constituents that are heavy and those that are not.

There is a correlation between weight and familiarity status: heavy constituents are more likely to be new than old. Entities that have already been introduced into the discourse and hence are old can typically be referred to by relatively short and simple expressions – often, of course, by pronouns. Nevertheless weight and familiarity are distinct concepts, and there is no necessity for heavy constituents to be new, or vice versa:

[11] i *One of his daughters was running a computer store, while the other was still at university, reading law. The one running the computer store earned nearly as much as he did.*
ii *There's a toad in the pool.*

The underlined NP in [i] is heavy but discourse-old, while *a toad* in [ii] is new but not heavy.

Topic

The topic of a clause is what the clause is about. This is an intuitive concept, but it is notoriously difficult to provide criteria that enable one to identify clause-topics in English in a rigorous and convincing way, and we shall make relatively little use of the concept in this chapter.[3]

There are certain devices which serve to explicitly mark that a constituent denotes the topic:

[12] [*As for external funding,*] *Smith has a grant application pending.*

As for indicates that its complement, here *external funding*, expresses the topic of the clause; more specifically, it indicates a change of topic, typically to something that has been mentioned earlier. Other expressions that mark the topic include *regarding*, *speaking of*, *talking of*; in such cases, as in [12], the constituent containing the topic-expression functions syntactically as an adjunct. For the most part, however, English does not provide any explicit syntactic marking of the topic of a clause.

[3] Clause-topic (or sentence-topic in the terminology of those who use 'sentence' for what in this grammar is called a clause) is to be distinguished from discourse-topic, which is what a whole discourse, or a section of discourse, is about – the topic of a book or a chapter, a lecture, discussion, or the like. Another term often used instead of 'topic' is 'theme' (a sense of 'theme' quite different from the one it has in this book).

Some general tendencies regarding information structure

A few general tendencies are stated summarily in [13]:

[13] i Heavy constituents tend to occur at or towards the end of the clause.
ii The focus typically appears at or towards the end of the clause.
iii Subjects are the dependents that are the most likely to be addressee-old.
iv Information that is familiar tends to be placed before that which is new.
v Information-packaging constructions tend to be restricted with respect to the range of contexts in which they can felicitously occur.

In view of point [v], discussion of information-packaging issues in the following sections will be largely concerned with the constraints applying to the non-canonical constructions. It must be emphasised, however, that there are conditions under which the default version is inadmissible (due to ungrammaticality or infelicity; cf. [2] of §1), and there are others where it may sound awkward, less natural than the non-canonical construction. It should also be borne in mind that the choice of one of the non-canonical constructions may be motivated by stylistic considerations, by the need for variety: a discourse consisting of clauses all of which follow the default pattern would likely be perceived as tiresome and repetitive.

3 Complement preposing

Complement preposing is a construction in which a complement whose basic position is internal to the VP occurs in front position, preceding the nucleus of the clause:

[1] i *Most of it she had written __ herself.*
ii *Anything you don't eat put __ back in the fridge.*
iii *It appears [that from one of them he had borrowed several hundred dollars __].*

The underlined complements in these examples are in prenuclear position, rather than in their basic position, indicated here by '__'. Preposing occurs most readily in declarative main clauses, as in [i], and our discussion of the pragmatic constraints on complement preposing will concentrate on examples of this kind. The construction is certainly not restricted to such clauses, however, as is evident from [ii] (imperative) and [iii] (subordinate).[4]

Pragmatic constraints on complement preposing

Adjuncts may also be located in prenuclear position, but when complements occur there the construction is subject to pragmatic constraints on familiarity status that do not apply with initial adjuncts. Compare, for example:

[2] i *In New York there is always something to do.*
ii *#In a basket I put your clothes.*

While [i] could perfectly well occur as the opening sentence in a discourse, [ii] could not: it requires a context that motivates the preposing.

For complement preposing to be felicitous, the complement must be discourse-old, acting as a link to other entities evoked in the prior discourse. Compare, for example,

[4] Preposing is an unbounded dependency construction, as described in Ch. 12, §7.

the following, where speaker A is a customer and B the server:

[3] i a. A: *Can I have a bagel?* B: *Sorry, we're out of bagels.* A: *How about a bran muffin?* B: [*A bran muffin I can give you.*]

b. A: *Do you have any muffins?* B: [*A bran muffin I can give you.*]

c. A: *Can I have a bagel?* B: *Sorry, we're out of bagels.* [*A bran muffin I can give you.*]

ii A: *Where can I buy a pen like that?* B: *At the bookstore.* [*Six dollars it costs.*]

Example [ia] illustrates the simplest case: here the preposed constituent is identical with a preceding one. In [ib] *bran muffin* is related to *muffins* in that it denotes a subset of muffins. And in [ic] it is related to *bagels* in that both denote members of some contextually relevant set, the set of breakfast foods. In [ii] the relationship is less direct, but nevertheless still apparent: buying a pen evokes the concept of a price, and *six dollars* then denotes one of the set of potential prices.

Such examples may be contrasted with the infelicitous

[4] *I was in the library last night and* [#*an interesting guy I met*].

Here there is no relevant relationship between *an interesting guy* and anything in the preceding discourse to justify the preposing: mention of a library does not readily call to mind the set of people one might meet there. In this context, then, only the default version of the second clause would be acceptable: *I met an interesting guy.*

The requirement of an appropriate relationship to some preceding constituent applies in all cases of complement preposing. Most cases also satisfy a second condition, that the clause as a whole be related to what precedes via an open proposition that represents discourse-old information.

In [3i] this open proposition is "I can give you *x*", whose status as old rather than new information derives from the fact that A has been asking for something. In [3ii] the open proposition is "It costs amount *x*", and this is again evoked by the talk of buying a pen, and hence counts as discourse-old.

As two further examples, consider:

[5] i *Colonel Bykov had delivered to Chambers in Washington six Bokhara rugs which he directed Chambers to present as gifts from him and the Soviet Government to the members of the ring who had been most co-operative.* [*One of these rugs Chambers delivered to Harry Dexter White.*]

ii A: *Did you buy a whole new wardrobe for school?* B: *No, I have lots of clothes.* [*Most of my stuff my mom gets at Alexander's.*]

The requirement that the preposed complement itself relate to the preceding discourse is clearly satisfied: in [i] *one of these rugs* relates back to *six Bokhara rugs*, and in [ii] *most of my stuff* relates to *a whole new wardrobe* in that both are concerned with B's clothes. In addition, we have the open propositions "Chambers delivered the rugs to *x*" and "My mom gets my stuff at *x*", and these are both discourse-old in that they are inferrable from what has gone before. In [i] delivering rugs to various people is what Chambers had been directed to do. In [ii], speaker B is a student, so it is a reasonable inference that her mother buys her clothes for her, and this she must do at various stores.

Focus and non-focus complement preposing

The first division we make within the category of complement preposing constructions is between those where the preposed complement is, or contains, the focus and those where the focus follows. The examples in [3] are of the focus preposing type. In [i] the natural placement for the main stress is on *bran*, with the NP *a bran muffin* the focus in [ia/c], and just *bran* itself the focus in [ib] (bran muffins are contrasted with other kinds of muffins); in [ii] the stress will be on *dollars*, with the whole NP *six dollars* the focus (picking out this amount from the set of potential prices). In [5], by contrast, the natural place for the main stress is at the end, on *White* and *Alexander's*, the foci being *Harry Dexter White* and *Alexander's* respectively. The preposed complements here will certainly be stressed, for preposing does accord them a significant amount of intonational prominence, but the degree of stress will be less than on the final words. These then are examples of non-focus preposing.

We noted in §2 that a constituent may be discourse-old when considered as an entity and discourse-new when considered as specifying the value in an open proposition. This dual status will always apply in the case of focus preposing. The general constraint on complement preposing requires that the link be discourse-old in the first sense, but in focus preposing it is necessarily discourse-new in the second sense by virtue of being focus. As we observed for [3ii], for example, *six dollars* represents a price for a pen and as such is discourse-old in the context since there has been talk of buying a pen, but at the same time it specifies the value of the variable in "It costs *x*", and as such is discourse-new.

We will look first at non-focus preposing, in §3.1 and §3.2 (the latter dealing with one particular subtype, called 'proposition assessment'); then in §3.3 we return to focus preposing.[5]

3.1 Non-focus complement preposing

The preposed complement may belong to any of the major categories that function as a complement. The following examples have a preposed NP, PP, AdjP, and VP respectively:

[6] i *I work on the 6th floor of a building. I know some of the elevator riders well. [<u>Others</u> I have only that nodding acquaintance with] and some are total strangers.*

ii *Consume they did – not only 15 kegs of beer, which they guzzled like soda pop, but also the free Coors posters which they seized as works of art to adorn their dorm walls. [<u>For their heads,</u> they were given free Coors hats] and for their cars free Coors bumper stickers.*

iii A: *This is not another vulgar disgusting sexploitation film.* B: *[<u>Vulgar</u> it's not. <u>Dumb</u> it is.] Did we see the same movie?*

iv *As members of a Gray Panthers committee, we went to Canada to learn, and [<u>learn</u> we did].*

The NP case, also seen in [5] above, is the most common variety and needs no further commentary here. The VP case is found in the proposition assessment construction

[5] Complement preposing in general or, for some scholars, non-focus preposing in particular, is commonly called 'topicalisation'. We do not adopt that term here because we do not accept the implication that the (characteristic) function of the construction is to accord topic status to the preposed complement.

discussed in §3.2. In this section we will look further at preposing of AdjPs and PPs, the latter of which are characteristically locative.

Preposing of AdjPs

Preposing of AdjPs is less common than that of the other categories and subject to a different constraint. It is restricted to cases where we have an explicit contrast between one property and another, as between "vulgar" and "dumb" in [6iii]. Note, for example, that [6iii] would be infelicitous if we dropped the *Vulgar it isn't* clause, so that *dumb* was no longer contrasting with any other property expression.

Typically, as in this example, we have a pair of clauses with preposing, involving a salient set of two properties, one of which is affirmed and the other denied: the clauses are used in tandem to evaluate some salient discourse entity. This pattern is further illustrated in [7]:

[7] i *The Philadelphia Fish & Co. is grilling fresh seafood so good the competition is broiling mad.* [*Casual and affordable they are. Expensive they are not.*]

ii *The ratings no doubt will show that some small number of Americans failed to escape and ended up watching the two-hour NBC 'World Premiere Movie'.* [*A premiere it may be, but new it's not.*]

iii [*Pretty they aren't. But a sweet golden grapefruit taste they have.*]

In [i] the preposed complement is an AdjP (or AdjP-coordination) in both clauses, while in [ii] the first clause has a preposed predicative NP and in [iii] the second has a preposed object NP, property assignment here being expressed by means of *have* rather than *be*. As with complement preposing in general, the preposed complement is related to the preceding discourse. In [6iii] the property "vulgar" has been mentioned before and "dumb" belongs with it in a set of potential properties of sexploitation films. In [7i] the AdjPs denote members of a set of properties typically associated with restaurants and hence potentially applicable to the one under discussion.

The following examples illustrate relatively minor variations on the above pattern:

[8] i *'In the early days, our productions were cheap and cheerful', says producer John Weaver of London-based Keefco. 'We'd go into a seven-light studio, shoot the band in one afternoon and edit as we went along. The client would walk out with a tape that day.'* [*Today's tapes may still be cheerful, but cheap they are not.*]

ii A: *All my friends think she's wonderful and generous. Well, she's certainly generous . . .*
B: [*Wonderful you're not so sure about?*]

iii A: *I can't stand him. He's stupid, arrogant, and totally off-the-wall.* B: [*Stupid I wouldn't really say he is.*]

In [i] only the second of the paired clauses has the AdjP preposed, the first having the default order. In [ii] A affirms the property "generous" (with default order), while B queries A's evaluation of the person under discussion with respect to the property "wonderful". In [iii] A affirms a set of properties and B denies one of them. These examples have in common with [6iii]/[7] that there is a contrast between two or more properties that are explicitly evoked either in the prior discourse or in the speaker's own utterance.

Preposed locative complements

Semantically locative preposings differ from other types of complement preposing in that while the complement is still required to be related to some constituent in the prior discourse, there is with locatives no requirement of a discourse-old open proposition. Compare, for example:

[9] i *There are two issues we'll have to deal with.* [*One we can discuss tomorrow.*]
ii A: *Do you think you'd be more nervous in a job talk or a job interview?*
B: [*A job talk I think you'd have somewhat more control over.*]
iii *In the VIP section of the commissary at 20th Century Fox, the studio's elite gather for lunch and gossip. The prized table is reserved for Mel Brooks, and* [*from it he dispenses advice, jokes, and invitations to passers-by*].

In non-locative [i] the preposed *one* is straightforwardly related to the prior *two issues* and at the same time we have an open proposition, "We can discuss the issues at times *x*", which is inferrable from what precedes: if we have to deal with the issues there will be various times at which we can discuss them. Similarly in [ii]: the preposed complement denotes something already mentioned, and in addition A's talk of nervousness evokes the concept of having control over a situation, so the open proposition "You'd have *x* amount of control over the situation" counts as discourse-old. In the locative [iii], however, there is no such open proposition recoverable from the prior discourse. The NP *it* within the preposed PP relates of course to *the prized table*, but the proposition "He dispenses *x* from some location" is not inferrable from the context.

The relaxation of the usual requirement for a discourse-old open proposition applies only with static as opposed to dynamic situations. Compare:

[10] i *My neighbours have a huge back yard.* [*Through it they've run a string of beautiful Japanese lanterns.*]
ii *My neighbours have a huge back yard.* [*#Through it my kids like to run.*]

Here we have different interpretations of *run through*. In [i] it has a static interpretation: the clause is simply describing the location of the string of lanterns. In [ii], by contrast, it is interpreted dynamically, as denoting movement across a path. Example [ii] is then infelicitous because it fails to satisfy the general requirement of a discourse-old open proposition: "people like to do *x* through it" is not inferrable from the preceding sentence.

3.2 Proposition assessment

One special case of non-focus complement preposing has the focus on the polarity of the clause, positive or negative, and serves as a means of assessing the truth of the proposition expressed. The main stress typically falls on the auxiliary verb or the negative marker *not*:

[11] i *I've promised to help them* [*and help them I* WILL].
ii *It's odd that Diane should have said that, if* [*say it she* DID].
iii *The NBA's new collective-bargaining agreement sounds as though it was written by the IRS.* [*Simple it is* NOT.]

In all but a small range of exceptions that we will return to at the end of the section, the clause has emphatic polarity and hence requires the verb to be an auxiliary (see

Ch. 3, §2.1.3). The supportive auxiliary *do* is then required to carry the focal stress if there is no semantically contentful auxiliary in the corresponding unemphatic default order clause – compare *say it she did* in [ii] with *She said it.* Because the preposed element is a complement of an auxiliary it is very often a non-finite VP, like *help them* and *say it* in [i–ii], but other categories of complement are found with auxiliary *be* and (for some speakers) *have*, as seen in the preposed AdjP of [iii].[6]

Examples [11i–iii] illustrate respectively the three main types of proposition assessment: **proposition affirmation**, **proposition suspension**, and **proposition denial**. The first two are distinguished from other types of complement preposing in that the preposed complement has to be identical with a constituent in the prior discourse, save for minor differences such as the use of pro-forms or morphological changes like those in [12]:

[12] i *The developers either couldn't count or they didn't count on the city enforcing the law. [But enforce the law we did, all the way to the United States Supreme Court.]*

ii *Inside the truck was beer for the students' consumption. [Consume they did – not only 15 kegs of beer, but also the free posters which they seized to adorn their dorm walls.]*

In [i] the verbs differ in their inflectional form, whereas in [ii] we have a difference in lexical morphology, with *consumption* a noun, *consume* a verb. Note, however, that it would not be admissible to have *Drink they did* in this context: although consuming beer implies drinking, the present construction requires a close formal relation between the preposed complement and the prior discourse.

(a) Proposition affirmation

In the most common type of proposition assessment the speaker affirms a belief in or a commitment to a proposition explicitly evoked in the preceding discourse. This is what we have in [11i]: the preceding clause says that I've promised to help them, and the clause with complement preposing affirms that I will indeed do so.

Logically independent and dependent proposition affirmation

On one dimension we can distinguish two uses of proposition affirmation according to whether or not the proposition has already been presented as true. Compare:

[13] i *Asked what he thought about during today's race on a sultry day, Tour de France winner Greg LeMond said: 'I didn't think. I just rode.' [Ride he did.] LeMond won the time trial easily.*

ii *At the end of the term I took my first exams; it was necessary to pass if I was to stay at Oxford, and [pass I did].*

In [i] the prior evocation of the proposition that LeMond rode is in the form *I just rode*, which of course presents it as true, as factual. In [ii], by contrast, the prior discourse merely talks of the necessity of my passing if I was to be able to stay on at Oxford, and this itself does not entail that I passed. We will say that in [i] the affirmation is **logically dependent** on the prior discourse, while in [ii] it is **logically independent**. The logically dependent case involves affirmation of a previously asserted proposition, and for this

[6] The construction is often called 'VP preposing', but because auxiliary verbs are not wholly restricted to non-finite complements we find this an inappropriate term.

reason is distributionally more constrained than the independent case: one needs some justification or motivation for affirming what has already been affirmed.[7]

Concessive, scalar, and simple affirmation

On another dimension we distinguish between concessive, scalar, and simple affirmation. The first two can be either logically dependent or logically independent in the sense just explained, while the simple (or neutral) type is restricted to logically independent affirmation.

In **concessive affirmation** the proposition is affirmed in the context of some countervailing consideration that is conceded in the prior discourse.

[14] i *It was ironic that he eventually learned more of his mother's story from her papers and tapes than he had from her. [But learn her story he did.]*

ii *Waiting in long lines can be infuriating. Waiting in long lines to pay someone else money seems unconscionable. Waiting in long lines to pay someone else more money than they seem to be entitled to is lunacy. [But wait in line they did Monday in Chicago and the Cook County suburbs.]*

In [i] the suggestion is that one wouldn't have expected him to have to learn his mother's story primarily from indirect sources rather than directly from her, but nevertheless he did learn it. In [ii] waiting in line in the relevant circumstances is said to be lunacy, but in spite of this they did it. The examples are logically dependent and independent respectively. In [i] the prior discourse conveys that he did in fact learn her story, the issue being where he learned it. In [ii] the proposition that they waited in line is evoked but not entailed in the prior context. Another example of this type is [12i]: it is concessive in that we enforced the law in spite of their not counting on us to do so, and logically independent in that their not counting on us to enforce the law clearly doesn't entail that we did so. In all cases of concessive affirmation the clause is introduced by the concessive coordinator *but* or a concessive adjunct such as *yet* or *nevertheless*: replacing *but* by *and* in [14] would make the examples infelicitous.

Scalar affirmation affirms a proposition whose predicate can be construed as a scale on which the referent of the subject NP is assigned a high value:

[15] i *'This is one of the things that symbolises the best Evanston has to offer,' David Bradford, chairman of the Evanston Human Relations Commission, said at a public hearing Saturday. 'People will come out and talk about things.' [And talk they did.] For five hours more than 150 residents, police officers and officials, community leaders and politicians filled to capacity the City Council chambers in a public hearing.*

ii *Kenny Rogers had asked his fans to bring cans to his concerts to feed the hungry in the area. [And bring cans they did.]*

What is conveyed by the proposition affirmation in [i] is not simply that people talked but that they talked to a remarkable extent – and this is reinforced by the following sentence, which indicates that the talking lasted for five hours. The bracketed clause in [ii] likewise invites an interpretation in which the fans brought a remarkable number of

[7] In [13i] *I just rode* appears as direct reported speech, so the discourse preceding the bracketed clause does not strictly entail its truth. In this context, however, there is no question that what LeMond said was true: the proposition is treated as having been already asserted. Similarly in [15i] below.

cans. Example [13i] above is also of this kind: we understand not simply that LeMond rode but that he rode remarkably well and remarkably fast. Unlike [14], both examples in [15] are logically independent. In [15i], the fact that people will come out to talk does not entail that in this case they did so, and in [ii] Kenny Rogers had merely asked his fans to bring cans, from which it doesn't follow that they did.

Simple affirmation is then the residual category, where neither of the special factors found in the concessive and scalar types applies – and here only logically independent affirmations are felicitous:

[16] i *Andy bet me $10 he would get 100 on his exam, [and get 100 he did]. No one else got more than 80.*
ii *I'm so proud of Andy for getting 100 on his exam, [#and get 100 he did]. No one else got more than 80.*

Here there is no countervailing consideration to suggest that it was unlikely that he would get 100, and getting 100 doesn't lend itself to a scalar interpretation: it is difficult to imagine how one could be assigned a high value on a scale representing 'getting 100' (as opposed, say, to getting a good mark). Thus while [i] is perfectly natural, [ii] – where the preceding clause presupposes that Andy got 100 – is not: there is nothing further to affirm.

Affirmation with *it + be*

One highly specialised and idiomatic proposition-affirming construction has preposing of the complement of a clause with *it* as subject and *be* as verb:

[17] i A: *What would you like for breakfast?* B: *French toast.* A: [*French toast it is.*]
ii A: *At First Bank* YOU *choose the length of your certificates.* B: *What if I want a certificate for only fourteen days?* A: [*Then fourteen days it is.*]

Here A affirms or accepts B's choice from some previously evoked set – the set of breakfasts or certificate lengths. The affirmation signals an intention to accommodate the addressee's choice: A is committed to providing the French toast, or a certificate for fourteen days. The preposing is an essential feature of the idiom. *It is French toast*, for example, does not have a comparable meaning and cannot be regarded as a default order counterpart of *French toast it is*, as used in [i].

Affirmation with preposed *that*

Another specialised case of affirmation has anaphoric *that* as the preposed complement:

[18] i A: *It must have surprised you to hear we're home again.* B: *Yes,* [*that it did*].
ii A: *George Carlin is a great comedian.* B: [*That he is.*]
iii A: *Are you thinking about leaving?* B: [*That I am.*]

This construction is used to express emphatic agreement, as in [i–ii], or to give a positive answer to a polar question, as in [iii]. In the agreement case, it is more likely to be used in response to a subjective or evaluative statement than to a factual one. The response in [ii], for example, is more natural than if A had said *George Carlin is Emma's brother-in-law.*

(b) Proposition suspension

[19] *Mark submitted his report late, if [submit it he did].*

This type of proposition assessment functions syntactically as a complement of the conditional preposition *if*; the *if* phrase is used to suspend the speaker's commitment to a proposition that would otherwise be entailed. *Mark submitted his report* is an entailment of *Mark submitted his report late*, but not of [19] as a whole. The superordinate clause must contain information beyond that expressed in the subordinate one. If, for example, we drop *late* from [19] the result is anomalous: #*Mark submitted his report if submit it he did* is unacceptably tautological and uninformative.

(c) Proposition denial

The third type of proposition assessment is used to deny a proposition for ironic effect. It is restricted to clauses where the preposed element is a complement of copulative *be*:

[20] i *The NBA's new collective-bargaining agreement sounds as though it was written by the IRS.* [*Simple it is not.*]

ii *I will long cherish Mickey Rooney's appearance to receive a special Oscar in recognition of his 60 years as a performer.* [*Humble he wasn't,*] *but why should he be? As he told us rather curtly, he'd been the world's biggest box office star at 19.*

Commonly, as in these examples, proposition denial involves **meiosis**, or understatement, resulting in an ironic and colourful interpretation that would not necessarily be induced by the corresponding default-order construction. We understand from [i], for example, that the agreement was not merely not simple, but extremely complicated, and from [ii] that Mickey Rooney was the opposite of humble.

Proposition denial serves to express the speaker's evaluation of some salient person or other entity with respect to some salient or inferrable property. In [20i] (repeated from [11iii above]), "simple" belongs to the set of properties applicable to such documents as agreements and Internal Revenue forms; in [20ii], "humble" represents one of the inferrable properties associated with the ideal Oscar recipient. If the property in question is neither evoked nor inferrable, the construction is infelicitous:

[21] i *The TV repairman keeps looking in the mirror.* [*A sex symbol he's not.*]

ii *I don't think the TV repairman knows what he's doing.* [#*A sex symbol he's not.*]

In [i] the preceding sentence raises the issue of the man's physical appearance, and hence *a sex symbol* constitutes an acceptable link to the prior discourse, but in [ii] there is no evident connection between his appearance and his ability to repair television sets.

Epitomisation

One particular case of proposition denial is called 'epitomisation'. Here the preposed complement is a definite NP, typically a proper name, whose referent can be seen as the epitome of the relevant property:

[22] i [*Mount Everest it wasn't,*] *but Engineering School sophomore Benno Matschinsky prepares to rappel from the South St. Bridge yesterday afternoon, and then falls graciously with a safety rope toward the ground.*

ii *The triumphant mood is broken when an usher from the movie theatre next door strolls over. 'You're blocking our marquee,' he bellows in my ear, making it clear that I should move on – hastily.*

[*Carnegie Hall it isn't,*] *but for an amateur musician, a bustling sidewalk can be as good a place as any to begin.*

In [i] the relevant property is the height of entities to be climbed, and Mount Everest represents the highest value on the scale defined by this property. In [ii] the epitomised property is success as a musician, with the highest value on this scale represented by performance at Carnegie Hall.

Proposition assessment with lexical verbs

We noted at the beginning of this section that the preposed element in proposition assessment is normally the complement of an auxiliary verb. Compare, for example:

[23] i *He suggested I phone Emma,* [*#so Emma I phoned*].
ii *He suggested I phone Emma,* [*so phone her I did*].

In [i] we have the preposing of the complement of the lexical verb *phone*, and in this context, as an instance of proposition affirmation, the preposing is infelicitous. Instead we would have [ii], with preposing of the non-finite complement of auxiliary *do*.

There are, however, some exceptions – cases where the complement of a lexical verb can be preposed in proposition affirmation:

[24] *I've put Jones in the Green Room* [*and in the Green Room he stays*].

The first clause entails that Jones is in the Green Room, and the second affirms that that situation will continue to obtain. Note that in this context we could not have #*and stay in the Green Room he will*, because there has been no prior evocation of the proposition "He will stay in the Green Room". This extension of the normal pattern is highly constrained, hardly possible except with verbs that are semantically comparable to the auxiliary verbs – in this case, *stay* expresses the aspectual concept of continuity.

Inflection with perfect *have*

A special issue arises when the preposed element is a complement of perfect *have*. Compare:

[25] i *He said he wouldn't tell them,* [*but tell/told them he has*].
ii *He denies he has told them,* [*but tell/told them he has*].

Although *have* normally takes a past participle, it is the plain form of the verb that is preferred in [i]. The past participle is preferred in [ii], where it has been used in the preceding clause, but even here the plain form *tell* is acceptable.

3.3 Focus complement preposing

We turn now to cases where the preposed complement is focused:

[26] i *I made a lot of sweetbreads.* [*A couple of* POUNDS *I think I made for her.*]
ii *I had two really good friends.* [DAMON *and* JIMMY *their names were.*]
iii *I promised my father* – [*on Christmas* EVE *it was*] – *to write home at my first opportunity.*
iv A: *Did you want tea?* B: [COFFEE *I ordered.*]

In focus complement preposing the preposed constituent serves both as a link with the prior discourse and as the value of the variable in the discourse-old open proposition expressed by the rest of the clause. In [i] the open proposition is "I think I made *x* amount of sweetbreads for her", and *a couple of pounds* gives the value of *x*. Whenever a discourse involves mention of a relevant yet unspecified quantity (of time, space, objects, people, etc.), the focus in a clause with focus preposing may provide a specification of the quantity in question. The open proposition in [ii] is "Their names were *x*", where *x* stands for members of the set of names. The link *Damon and Jimmy* together with the preceding mention of two really good friends evokes this set. Examples of focus preposing with the verbs *name* or *call* are extremely common; apparently the mere mention of a new object or entity renders salient the proposition that the entity is called something. The open proposition in [iii], roughly "It happened at *x* time", is salient given the fact that events occur at particular times. Finally, [iv] illustrates the case where the link contrasts with a constituent in the prior discourse: tea and coffee are members of the set of drinks on the menu; "I ordered *x*" is inferrable from A's question, and the focus provides a correction to the specification of the value of *x*.

Echoing

Echoing is a special type of focus preposing in which the link is being called into question:

[27] i A: *Cheeseburger, large fries, and a large Coke.* B: [*Large* FRIES *you wanted?*]
ii A: *I wish Newt Gingrich were running.* B: [*Newt* GINGRICH *you'd vote for?*]
iii A: *Diane gets along with all her colleagues.* B: [DAVID *she gets along with?*]

As in focus complement preposing generally, the preposed constituent represents the value of the variable in a discourse-old open proposition: "You wanted *x*", "You'd vote for *x*", "Diane gets along with *x*". An echoing questions whether this link represents the correct value of the variable, reflecting uncertainty or disbelief on the part of the speaker. Examples [i–ii] illustrate the usual case of echoing, where the link repeats a phrase occurring in the preceding utterance. Example [iii] illustrates a less common case: David has not been explicitly mentioned, but he is one of her colleagues, so it follows from what A says that Diane gets along with David, and this is what B calls into question.

4 Postposing

An element is said to be postposed when it appears to the right of its basic position, at the end of the clause (save perhaps for one or more adjuncts):

[1] i *Spain's financial problems were less acute than* [*had been those of Portugal*].
ii *He seemed at that time very much more sympathetic to the idea than he is now.*
iii *There was in her manner a certain aloofness that I found quite disconcerting.*
iv *Chris put on the table a large blue bucket full of ice-cubes.*

The postposed elements here are respectively subject, predicative complement, displaced subject (in the existential construction), and direct object. For the subject the default position is before the predicator, and for the other three functions it is immediately after the predicator.

Weight and relative weight

One major factor that motivates postposing is weight: there is a tendency or preference for heavy constituents to appear late in the clause. The examples in [1] may thus be contrasted with the structurally similar ones in the right-hand column of [2]; here the postposed constituent is short, and the version with postposing is much less natural or acceptable than the one with default order shown on the left:

[2]		DEFAULT ORDER VERSION	VERSION WITH POSTPOSING
	i	a. *You weren't as ill as [I had been].*	b. #*You weren't as ill as [had been I].*
	ii	a. *She seemed sad at that time.*	b. ?*She seemed at that time sad.*
	iii	a. *There is some milk in the fridge.*	b. ?*There is in the fridge some milk.*
	iv	a. *Chris put his elbows on the table.*	b. #*Chris put on the table his elbows.*

The felicity of a postposing depends not simply on the weight of the postposed constituent, but on the relative weights of it and the constituent over which it is moved:

[3]			
	i	a. *You'll find the company's latest financial statement on your desk.*	b. *You'll find on your desk the company's latest financial statement.*
	ii	a. *You'll find the company's latest financial statement in the top drawer of the tall black filing cabinet alongside the window.*	b. ?*You'll find in the top drawer of the tall black filing cabinet alongside the window the company's latest financial statement.*
	iii	a. ?*You'll find the report that the company has prepared in response to the secretary's latest allegations on your desk.*	b. *You'll find on your desk the report that the company has prepared in response to the secretary's latest allegations.*

In [i] the object NP is considerably heavier than the locative PP and postposing is acceptable, though not obligatory. In [ii] we have the same object NP, but this time it is a good deal less heavy than the PP, with the result that postposing is barely acceptable. Conversely, in [iii] we have the same PP as in [i], but a much heavier object NP, and in this case postposing is more or less obligatory.

One place where it is particularly clear that **relative** weight is the crucial factor is in the object + particle construction (see Ch. 4, §6.2). Almost any NP is heavier than a particle, and postposing is normally permitted with any object other than an unstressed personal pronoun:

[4]			
	i	a. *I brought the chairs in.*	b. *I brought in the chairs.*
	ii	a. *I brought them in.*	b. **I brought in them.*

Postposing of NPs representing discourse-new information

Leaving aside the object + particle construction, where object postposing applies very freely, postposed NPs tend to be both heavy and discourse-new. Heavy NPs are likely to be discourse-new since entities that have already been referred to can generally be evoked a second time with few words, but as we noted in §2 there is only an imperfect correlation between weight and discourse-familiarity status. And in the present context we need to note that discourse-new status may be sufficient to motivate postposing when the NP concerned is not heavy:

[5] *Jenkins walked back into the office and glanced out of the window. Turning around, he saw on the desk a gun.*

A gun is not heavy (and in relative terms the locative PP *on the desk* is slightly heavier than the object), but in terms of information status *a gun* is discourse-new while *a desk* is discourse-old (by virtue of the prior mention of the office and the salient relation between desks and offices). It is this difference in information status that motivates the postposing. Postposing of this kind is less frequent than that motivated by weight. Whereas the default order version *he saw a gun on the desk* is quite neutral, the version with a postposed object emphasises the unexpectedness of the gun.

Subject postposing

Postposing of the subject is usually accompanied by preposing of another complement or an adjunct, giving the subject–dependent inversion construction seen in *More important are the moral objections*, etc.: this we deal with in §5 below. For the rest, postposing of the subject is found in two constructions. One is the comparative construction illustrated in [1ii]; here the postposing is motivated by weight, as we have seen. The other is with verbs of reporting:

[6] i *The best solution, suggested Pat, would be to install a security alarm system.*
ii *Said Manager Kim Kessels: 'This is our best result in 20 years!'*

Here subject postposing occurs predominantly in parentheticals, as in [i], but in journalistic style it is also found with the verb in initial position, as in [ii]. This is a different kind of postposing from the others considered in this section, since it is apparently not motivated by weight.

Object postposing

In the examples given so far, the object is postposed over a PP. Other possibilities are illustrated in [7]:

[7] i *I have read very carefully / several times all the articles she has written.*
ii *I found rather more promising the proposals that his sister had made.*

In [i] the object is postposed over an AdvP or NP in adjunct function, while in [ii] it is moved over a predicative AdjP. Where a complex-transitive clause has an NP rather than an AdjP as the predicative complement, postposing is less readily acceptable:

[8] ?*He considers an idiot just about anyone who disagrees with him.*

It is not possible to postpose an indirect object over a direct one. Most ditransitive clauses have an alternant with one object + a PP complement (see Ch. 4, §8.2.1), and the latter construction is used instead of indirect object postposing:

[9] i	*They gave anyone who scored over 90% a special prize.*	$[O^i + O^d]$
ii	**They gave a special prize anyone who scored over 90%.*	$[O^d + O^i]$
iii	*They gave a special prize [to anyone who scored over 90%].*	$[O^d + \text{PP comp}]$

One further syntactic restriction is that object postposing is hardly permitted in the complex catenative construction (see Ch. 14, §3):

[10] i *I believe one of the systems analysts we brought in from Ohio to be responsible.*
ii ?*I believe to be responsible one of the systems analysts we brought in from Ohio.*

5 Subject–dependent inversion

5.1 Syntactic issues

In subject–dependent inversion the subject occurs in postposed position while some other dependent of the verb is preposed. A considerable range of elements may invert with the subject in this way, as illustrated in [1]:

[1] i *George, can you do me a favour?* [*Up in my room, on the nightstand, is a pinkish-reddish envelope that has to go out immediately.*]

ii [*Immediately recognisable here is the basic, profoundly false tenet of Movie Philosophy 101, as it has been handed down from "Auntie Mame" and "Harold and Maude":*]*Nonconformism, the more radical the better, is the only sure route to human happiness and self-fulfilment.*

iii *She's a nice woman, isn't she?* [*Also a nice woman is our next guest*] ...

iv *Arrested were Nathan Johnson, 23, of New York, and his brother, Victor Johnson, 32, a 15-year Army veteran.*

v *This jacket and cap will keep you warm throughout the chilly autumn days. The jacket is made of a particularly heavy brushed denim, with rivets at the pockets and a brown suede collar.* [*Complementing the jacket is the cap, crafted of the same denim and featuring a brown suede visor.*]

vi *On Saturday they received an astonishing fourteen credit offers in the mail.* [*Three days later came another eight offers.*]

In the great majority of cases the preposed element is a complement, usually of the verb *be*; [vi] shows, however, that with other verbs it can be an adjunct. It is for this reason that we speak of subject–dependent inversion – inversion of the subject and another dependent of the verb.

The complements in these examples are a PP in [1i], an AdjP in [ii], an NP in [iii], and subjectless non-finite clauses, or VPs, in [iv–v]. The inversion of the subject with an NP in predicative function, as in [iii], is relatively rare: it results in a structure of the form 'NP + *be* + NP', which looks like that of a canonical construction with the first NP as subject and the second as predicative complement. We take *also a nice woman* as the predicative complement rather than the subject here for two reasons. In the first place, this matches the meaning: the propositional meaning is the same as that of *Our next guest is also a nice woman*, i.e. it ascribes the property of being a nice woman to our next guest. Secondly, this analysis is supported by the fact that the first NP lacks the important syntactic property of subjects of being able to invert with an auxiliary verb to form an interrogative: **Isn't also a nice woman our next guest?*[8]

Example [1v] merits further comment because the inverted clause does not correspond semantically to *The cap is complementing the jacket* but rather to the non-progressive *The cap complements the jacket.* Subject–dependent inversion cannot apply to the latter because *complements the jacket* is the entire VP, not a dependent thereof. The progressive form in [1v] thus does not have a non-progressive counterpart: **Complements the jacket the*

[8] Subject–dependent inversion is possible with *be* only in its ascriptive use. If one interchanges the NPs in a specifying *be* clause like *Kim was the chief culprit* to give *The chief culprit was Kim* the syntactic structure remains the same, with the first NP the subject and the second the predicative complement.

cap is ungrammatical. It is only in cases like this, i.e. when there is no competition with a corresponding non-progressive, that a preposed progressive VP lacks the expected progressive interpretation. Compare:

[2] i *Being driven out of office was Senator Johnson.* [progressive]
ii *Driven out of office was Senator Johnson.* [non-progressive]

Here [i] does have an inverted non-progressive counterpart, namely [ii], and in this case it has the same interpretation as the uninverted form *Senator Johnson was being driven out of office.*[9]

Subject–dependent inversion involves the postposing of the subject and the preposing of another dependent, but there are grounds for regarding it as a distinct construction rather than the mere combination of two separate and more general constructions, complement preposing and postposing. In the first place, it would very often be inadmissible to have one without the other. This is so with all of [1i–v] – compare, for example, [iv] with #*Arrested Nathan Johnson, 23, of New York, and his brother, Victor Johnson, 32, a 15-year Army veteran, were* (preposing only) and **Were arrested Nathan Johnson, 23, of New York, and his brother, Victor Johnson, 32, a 15-year Army veteran* (postposing only).[10] Secondly, as we shall see in §5.2 the pragmatic constraints on the construction are not simply a combination of those applying to complement preposing and postposing.

5.2 Pragmatic constraints on inversion

For inversion to be felicitous, the following conditions must obtain:

[3] i The preposed phrase must not represent information that is less familiar in the discourse than that represented by the postposed NP.
ii Unless the preposed dependent is semantically locative, the inversion requires an appropriate open proposition that is discourse-old.
iii The verb must not represent information that is new to the discourse.

Relative discourse familiarity of the preposed and postposed constituents

We have seen that with ordinary preposing the preposed element must be discourse-old; in inversion, however, the constraint is a relative one in that the preposed constituent must not be less familiar than the postposed one. Compare:

[4] i *They have a great big tank in the kitchen,* [*and in the tank are sitting a whole bunch of pots*].
ii *They have a whole bunch of pots in the kitchen,* [#*and in a great big tank are sitting all of the pots*].

In the felicitous example in [i], the preposed element is discourse-old while the postposed element is discourse-new, but in [ii] the former is new and the latter old, and the result is infelicitous.

[9]The same point arises with participial modifers in NP structure. *Those being investigated by the police* contrasts with *those investigated by the police* and therefore has a progressive interpretation, but with *those owning their own home* there is no such contrast and the gerund-participial does not have a progressive interpretation (see Ch. 14, §9)

[10]The example with preposing only is marked as infelicitous rather than ungrammatical because the construction is elsewhere quite acceptable: *I said they would be arrested and arrested they were!*

A large majority of inversions are of the type shown in [4i], with the preposed element discourse-old and the postposed subject discourse-new. Two other patterns are possible, but uncommon. In the following, both elements are discourse-new:

[5] *I had lunch at Ritzy's yesterday, and you wouldn't believe who was there.* [*Behind a cluster of microphones* *was* *Hillary Clinton,*] *holding another press conference.*

This shows that the problem with [4ii] is not that the preposed constituent is new: it is the combination of new followed by old that makes it infelicitous. Note that it is discourse-familiarity rather than addressee-familiarity that is relevant. In [5] the addressee is likely to be familiar with Hillary Clinton, the wife of the former President, but this has no bearing on the relative status of the inverted constituents: this is not a new + old inversion, like [4ii].

The combination of old + old is illustrated in [1v], and again in [6]:

[6] *Lieberman and Clinton go way back. When Lieberman made his run for the Connecticut Senate seat in 1970,* [*helping him* *as a young volunteer was* *Clinton,*] *a young Yale law student.*

Both the preposed pronoun *him* and the postposed subject *Clinton* are discourse-old by virtue of referring to people mentioned in the preceding discourse. Notice, however, that both here and in [1v] it is the more recently evoked information that appears in preposed position. In [6] *him* refers to Lieberman, who has been mentioned more recently than Clinton, and is thus arguably the more salient of the two at the point of the inversion. Similarly, in [1v] although both the jacket and the cap have been previously mentioned, the jacket has been mentioned more recently and is therefore the more salient of the two at the point of the inversion. With the NPs in the opposite order, the inversion is infelicitous in this context: #*Complementing the cap is the jacket, which also features zippered side pockets.*

Although the inverted constituents in [1v] and [6] are both old, there is a sense, therefore, in which the preposed one represents more familiar information. Condition [3i] says that the information expressed in the preposed element cannot be less familiar than that expressed in the postposed one, but it will now be evident that in almost all cases it is in fact more familiar.

Inversion in narrative contexts

An inversion commonly performs a scene-setting function at the outset of a narrative:

[7] *In a little wooden house in the middle of a deep forest lived a solitary woman who spent her days reading and gardening.*

Such an inversion provides a minimally informative setting relative to which the postposed NP can be interpreted. For this reason, the discourse is far more coherent when the topic of the following clause or clauses is the entity represented by the postposed NP rather than that represented by the NP within the preposed phrase. Thus [8i] would make a natural continuation, but [8ii] would not.

[8] i *She had recently won the lottery, and had hidden the money under her mattress.*
ii *It was badly in need of repairs, and everyone who saw it wondered whether it could hold up another year with its broken shutters and fractured foundation.*

Either of these, however, could felicitously follow the default order counterpart of [7],

A solitary woman who spent her days reading and gardening lived in a little wooden house in the middle of a deep forest.

Inversions like [7] have a strongly literary flavour. In the context of storytelling the preposed locative can be regarded as discourse-old: the narrative context evokes the notion of a setting, triggering the inference to a set of possible settings, and the preposed PP provides one of these. Outside of a storytelling context, clauses of this form are much less acceptable:

[9] *Hey, did you hear the weird report on the evening news?* [#<u>*In the basement of a department store*</u> *are living* <u>*a bunch of alligators*</u>.]

In the colloquial context the preposed PP represents discourse-new information, and though the new + new combination is not wholly excluded (as illustrated in [5]), it is out of place in the context of [9].

The discourse-old open proposition requirement

A second condition on the felicity of inversion is that, except with preposed locatives, an appropriate open proposition must be derivable from the prior discourse, with the value of the variable being given by the postposed subject. Compare:

[10] i *Two young men were hurt yesterday during a bungled convenience-store robbery, according to police. Two suspects were arrested at the scene and are now in custody.* [*Wounded were* <u>*Paul Randolph and Steve Seymour*</u>.]

ii *The Air & Water Show did not go as planned yesterday.* [#*Wounded were* <u>*Paul Randolph and Steve Seymour*</u>.]

iii *They had every kind of cake imaginable, all lined up in a row.* [*Adorning the first one was* <u>*a monstrous rose sculpted from white chocolate*</u>.]

In [i] the open proposition "*x* were wounded" is inferrable straightforwardly from the prior statement that two young men were hurt. In [ii], however, the mere fact that the show didn't go as planned is not sufficient to justify treating "*x* were wounded" as discourse-old information, and the inversion is infelicitous in this context; note that the default order version, *Paul Randolph and Steve Seymour were wounded* would be admissible here. In [iii] the open proposition "*x* adorned the first cake" is not so directly related to the prior discourse as the corresponding one in [i], but nevertheless it is easily inferrable from the fact that they had every kind of cake imaginable that one of them should have something adorning it.

Locatives

As with ordinary preposing, the requirement of an open proposition does not apply when the preposed element is locative and the situation is static. Compare static [11i–ii] with dynamic [11iii]:

[11] i *The low-income high-rises are universally considered to be among the ugliest complexes in the city.* [<u>*To the west of the group of ten buildings*</u> *flows the Grayson River, one of the most polluted in the country.*]

ii *My neighbours have a huge back yard.* [<u>*Through it*</u> *runs a string of beautiful Japanese lanterns.*]

iii *My neighbours have a huge back yard.* [#<u>*Through it*</u> *run my kids almost every afternoon.*]

Requirement that the verb not represent new information

The great majority of inversions have *be* as the verb; this is the ascriptive rather than specifying *be*, and accordingly has little if any semantic content. Verbs other than *be* are required to represent information that is evoked or inferrable in the context of the preceding discourse or of the inversion itself – compare [1vi] above and the following:

[12] i *He opened the door and took a folded canvas bucket from behind the seat.* [*Coiled on the floor* <u>*lay*</u> *a fifty-foot length of braided nylon climbing rope.*]
ii *Beneath the chin lap of the helmet* <u>*sprouted*</u> *black whiskers.*
iii *On the manager's desk* <u>*sat*</u> *a large manila envelope.*
iv [*At odds with the mayor* <u>*remain*</u> *the residents of the condos,*] *who are willing to fight a long battle over the additional taxes.*

In [1vi] the idea of offers coming has been evoked in the previous sentence, so *come* is salient in the context. In [12i] *lay* is inferrable from the preposed *coiled on the floor*, since an object that is coiled on the floor is known to be lying there; therefore, *lay* contributes no new information. In [12ii] *sprout* is inferrable from the mention of whiskers; that is, *sprout* itself adds no information, and could be replaced by *be* with no loss of information – and the same applies to *sat* in [12iii]. Finally, *at odds* in [iv] is an inherently predicative expression, so a complex-intransitive verb is inferrable, and *remain* merely adds the aspectual concept of continuation.

Verbs other than *be* tend to allow a more restricted range of preposed elements than are found with *be*. A high proportion are locatives, and the most common constituent category is PP. Temporals are not uncommon (cf. the *three days later* of [11vi]), but predicatives, especially with AdjP or NP form, are much less readily accommodated than with *be*.

5.3 Clauses with the form '*Here/There* + verb + NP'

Here and *there* can occur as preposed locative complements in ordinary subject–dependent inversions:

[13] i *. . . one of the major focal points of our concern is the South-Asian region.* [<u>*Here*</u>*, in two nations alone, are almost 500 million people, all working, and working hard, to raise their standards.*]
ii *At the distant edge of the river, I caught a glimpse of roofs and chimneys, and the quick glitter of glass that marked the hot-houses in the old walled garden that had belonged to the Hall.* [<u>*There*</u>*, too, lay the stables, and the house called West Lodge.*]

In addition, however, there are certain specialised clause constructions of the form '*here*/*there* + verb + NP' that differ syntactically and/or pragmatically from the inversion construction described above.

Here/there + be

[14] i a. <u>*Here was I*</u>*, an African woman on the grants committee of a British aid agency, suggesting that we scrap a paragraph that dealt with 'gender implications'.*
b. *And* <u>*there was I*</u> *imagining that underneath that hostile exterior there was a girl who really held me in high esteem.*

ii [viewing a photograph] *Here's/There's me, when I was six.*
iii a. *Here's/There's the money I owe you.*
b. *Here are your instructions. First, drive down to the bank, ...*

The examples in [i] differ from the inversion construction exemplified in [13] in that the postposed subject is a personal pronoun. At the same time, *here* and *there* are largely bleached of their locative meaning: the construction does not serve to indicate my spatial location, but is a stylistic device for presenting a personal narrative in a vivid way. It is possible for the subject to occupy its basic, pre-verbal position, and examples occur in which the two orders are used in successive clauses, as in *Then there was I, fighting for control, and there you were wanting to come close again.*

In [14ii] the personal pronoun is in the accusative case, indicating that in this construction *here* and *there* have been reanalysed as subjects, with the pronoun a predicative complement. *Here* and *there* are comparable to the demonstratives *this* and *that*, and like the latter would typically be accompanied by pointing, or some other indexing act.

The examples in [14iii] are inversions. Those in [iiia] can be interpreted as ordinary inversions, giving the location of the money I owe you and alternating with the uninverted construction *The money I owe you is here/there.* However, they also have a use in which they accompany the act of presenting the money to you, whereas the canonical versions could not be felicitously used in this way. In the case of [iiib] this is the only possible use if we assume that the instructions are not written down. In this presentation-accompaniment use *here* and *there* could again be replaced by demonstratives, but in [iiia/b] it is still the post-verbal NP that is the subject, as evidenced by the fact that the verb agrees with this NP. When the NP is a personal pronoun, it precedes the verb, in the nominative case: *Here they are.*

Here/there + come/go

[15] a. *Here comes the bus.* b. *There goes my last dollar!*

These too are syntactically inversions, but they are not replaceable in context by canonical *The bus comes here* and *My last dollar goes there.* They are comparable to running commentaries, describing a situation that takes place or is taking place as they are uttered. This accounts for the use of the simple present tense for a single present-time event (cf. Ch. 3, §4.2.1); compare the alternative way of announcing the arrival of a bus, with progressive aspect: *Look, the bus is coming.* A personal pronoun subject precedes the verb, as in *Here I come* and *There she goes.*

6 **Existential and presentational clauses**

We are concerned in this section with constructions containing the dummy pronoun *there*: **existentials**, which have *be* as the verb, as in *There's plenty of food in the fridge*, and **presentationals**, which have some verb other than *be*, as in *There remain many problems.*

6.1 Syntactic preliminaries

Dummy *there* vs locative *there*

Historically, dummy *there* derives from the locative *there* of, for example, *Don't leave your shoes there.* Locative *there* is an intransitive preposition contrasting with *here*: it has deictic and anaphoric uses, as described in Ch. 17, §9.1. In the constructions we are concerned with in the present chapter, *there* has been bleached of its locative meaning and reanalysed as a pronoun. The clear split between locative *there* ($there_{loc}$) and dummy pronoun *there* ($there_{pro}$) is reflected in the fact that they readily combine in the same clause, even in adjacent positions:

[1] a. *<u>There</u>*$_{pro}$ *is nothing <u>there</u>*$_{loc}$. b. *What is <u>there</u>*$_{pro}$ *<u>there</u>*$_{loc}$*?*

There$_{pro}$ is generally easy to recognise, being distinguished from *there*$_{loc}$ by the following properties:

[2] i *There*$_{pro}$ has no locative or other independent meaning.
ii *There*$_{pro}$ is always unstressed and has a weak form: /ðə^{r}/.
iii *There*$_{pro}$ functions only as subject or raised object, and can fill the subject position in interrogative tags: *There is something wrong, isn't there?*

As we have said, the original locative meaning has been lost, and *there*$_{pro}$ combines as readily with *here* as with *there*$_{loc}$: compare [1a] with *There*$_{pro}$ *is nothing here.* Hence our term 'dummy *there*'. It is simply the marker of a grammatical construction, serving to fill the subject position while the element that would be subject in the basic version is displaced to post-verbal position. The phonological property noted in [2ii] reflects this lack of semantic content, and *there*$_{pro}$ can never be focus. *There*$_{loc}$, by contrast, always retains its full vowel /eə^{r}/ and can occur as focus (*Don't leave it* HERE*: it belongs over* THERE$_{loc}$). It is property [2iii] that leads us to analyse dummy *there* as a pronoun (see Ch. 5, §10.1.1). It is comparable to certain uses of the pronoun *it*, which can also serve as a dummy subject (e.g. in the extraposition construction *It's a pity we missed them*); there are, indeed, certain cases where we have a paradigmatic contrast between *there*$_{pro}$ and *it*, as in *Who was there/it that was playing in the garden?* In the remainder of this section, *there* unless otherwise noted is to be understood as the dummy pronoun *there*$_{pro}$.

Subject and displaced subject

Many clauses with *there* as subject have syntactically simpler counterparts without *there*, and our analysis of the former is derivative from that of the latter. Compare:

[3] a. *Several windows were open.* b. *There were several windows open.*

In [a] *several windows* is the subject, whereas in [b] the subject function is filled by *there*, as argued in Ch. 4, §3.2.2. We accordingly analyse *several windows* as a **displaced subject**: it is an internal complement of the verb that is not syntactically a subject but corresponds semantically to the subject of the counterpart in [a]. Note in this connection that *several windows* is in both examples the predicand to which the predicative complement *open* applies. We then generalise the concept of displaced subject to clauses that have no simpler counterpart. Thus *There was an accident* has *an accident* as displaced subject even though there is no corresponding clause in which it is subject proper (**An accident was*).

There as a raised complement

There commonly occurs as the raised subject or object of a catenative verb, as described in Ch. 14, §§2–3:

[4] i *There seems to have been a mistake.*
ii *We hadn't expected there to be over a hundred people at the meeting.*

In [i] *there* is the raised subject of *seem*, but *a mistake* is the displaced subject of *be*, just as in the simpler construction *There was a mistake.* Similarly, in [ii] *there* is the raised object of *expect*, but *over a hundred people* is the displaced subject of *be*, just as in *There were over a hundred people at the meeting.* In both cases, then, we take the embedded *be* clause to be an existential even though *there* does not appear as subject of that clause but is located higher in the constituent structure of the sentence.

Position of the displaced subject

The default position of the displaced subject is immediately after the verb, as in [3b–4]. As an internal complement of the verb, however, it can undergo the processes of postposing and preposing, and in relativisation it need not be overtly present at all:

[5] i *There were in his in-tray no fewer than thirty unpaid bills.*
ii *How much is there in the other account?*
iii *Two further points there are that I must make before we leave this topic.*
iv *You can have everything* [*there is on the table*] *for $30.*

In [i] the displaced subject is postposed over the locative PP *in his in-tray.* Example [ii] is an open interrogative, with the displaced subject itself as the interrogative element, appearing in initial position. In [iii] we have complement preposing, but with the relative clause that modifies *points* postposed; the default order for the existential would be *There are two further points that I must make before we leave this topic.* Finally, in [iv] we have relativisation of the displaced subject so that it does not appear overtly in the existential clause: instead we have a gap anaphorically linked to the antecedent (*every*)*thing.*

6.2 The existential construction

Most clauses with *there* as subject have *be* as the verb, and these are called existential clauses. The general term 'existential' derives from the fact that one use of this construction is to express propositions concerning existence: *There aren't any unicorns*; *They were arguing about whether there is a God*; *How many different kinds of jelly-fish are there?* It should be borne in mind, however, that the category of existential clause is defined syntactically in terms of the combination of *there* and *be*: existential propositions can be expressed by other syntactic means (cf. *They were arguing about whether God exists*), existential clauses do not always express existential propositions (cf. *There is also me to consider*, which doesn't serve to assert my existence), and in pairs like [3a–b], where only [b] is an existential clause, the difference is a matter of information packaging rather than of propositional content.

6.2.1 Survey of structures

The distinction between bare and extended existentials

We draw a distinction between **bare** and **extended** existentials, as illustrated in [6]:

[6]		BARE EXISTENTIAL	EXTENDED EXISTENTIAL
	i	a. *There's no milk (again).*	b. *There's one copy on the table.*
	ii	a. *(Then) there was silence.*	b. *There's Sue to consider.*
	iii	a. *There was a short delay (because he'd mislaid his notes).*	b. *There were two sirens blaring.*

Bare existentials contain *there*, the verb *be*, and the displaced subject, alone or accompanied by adjuncts like those enclosed in parentheses in the [a] examples. These adjuncts are of no syntactic significance for the existential construction since they are admissible here under the same conditions as apply in other constructions: compare *She smiled (again)*; *(Then) they departed*; *He was embarrassed (because he'd mislaid his notes)*. Extended existentials contain, in addition to *there*, *be*, and the displaced subject, an **extension**, such as the underlined constituents in the [b] examples. These elements are of relevance to the existential construction, being either complements or adjuncts that are more constrained than those in the [a] examples in that they occur less freely in other types of clause. The locative *on the table* is a complement of *be*: note that it cannot be omitted from the non-existential counterpart *One copy is on the table*. In [iib] the infinitival complement *to consider* is licensed only by *be* and a few other verbs: compare **I saw Sue to consider*. In [iiib] *blaring* is not a modifier of *sirens* (as evident from the inadmissibility of examples like **Two sirens blaring were expected*): it is a separate element in clause structure licensed by the existential construction.

We look first at bare existentials, and then at the various kinds of extension.

(a) Bare existentials

[7] i *There are good teachers and bad teachers.*
ii *There is plenty of ice-cream.*
iii *There is bound to be an official inquiry.*
iv *Is there a bus to the library?*
v *There's no doubt we're in a lot of trouble.*
vi *There can be no turning back now.*

The verb *be* can hardly occur without an internal complement,[11] and there are accordingly no non-existential counterparts of examples like these: compare **Good teachers and bad teachers are*, and so on. Example [i] illustrates the case where the construction expresses an existential proposition – it would be used to assert the existence of good and bad teachers. Example [ii] illustrates the common case where there is an implicit locative: we would generally understand "here", "in the fridge", or the like. Many nouns denoting events are found in bare existentials, as with *inquiry* in [iii]: *be* in such cases expresses occurrence. Example [iv] asks not about the existence of buses but whether they run to the library – or about the existence of a bus-service to the library. *Doubt* in [v] is one of a set of nouns expressing modality that are commonly found in bare existentials: the clause

[11] Exceptions are largely limited to philosophical discourse (cf. *I think, [therefore I am]*) or fixed frames (*Time was when . . .*).

can be glossed as "Undoubtedly we're in for a lot of trouble". Example [vi] contains what we call a hybrid NP as displaced subject: an NP with a VP (*turning back*) as head – see Ch. 14, §1.6. This irregular type of NP is found predominantly in existentials.

(b) Locative and temporal extensions

[8]		NON-EXISTENTIAL	EXISTENTIAL
	i	a. *A friend of yours is at the door.*	b. *There's a friend of yours at the door.*
	ii	a. *One concert is on Sunday.*	b. *There's one concert on Sunday.*

One very common type of extended existential has a locative or temporal complement. In the examples given here both existential and non-existential versions are acceptable; often, however, pragmatic factors make one or the other infelicitous. This issue applies quite generally to extended existentials, and is dealt with in §6.2.2.

(c) Predicative extensions

[9]			
	i	a. *Two delegates were absent.*	b. *There were two delegates absent.*
	ii	a. *Two delegates were deaf.*	b. #*There were two delegates deaf.*
	iii	a. *Two delegates were employees of the sponsor.*	b. #*There were two delegates employees of the sponsor.*
	iv	a. *Is anything the matter?*	b. *Is there anything the matter?*

Existentials with predicative extensions systematically have acceptable non-existential counterparts. But there are quite severe constraints on the type of predicative permitted in the existential construction. In the first place, the predicative must denote a temporary state as opposed to a (relatively) permanent property, as illustrated in the contrast between [i] and [ii]. A sample of adjectives found in such existentials is given in [10]:

[10]						
	afoot	*alarming*	*asleep*	*available*	*awake*	*better*
	certain	*different*	*empty*	*missing*	*pleasing*	*present*
	right	*sick*	*surprising*	*vacant*	*worth*	*wrong*

Illustrative examples are *There's a scheme afoot to dump the premier*; *There are two plates missing*; *There are several points worth considering further.*

A second restriction is that predicatives with the form of NPs are normally excluded, as shown in [9iiib]. One exception involves the idiomatic expression *the matter* ("wrong"), as in [ivb].

(d) Infinitival extensions

[11]			
	i	a. *A few replies are still to come.*	b. *There are still a few replies to come.*
	ii	a. *One letter is (for you) to sign.*	b. *There's one letter (for you) to sign.*

In [i] *a few replies* is understood as subject of the infinitival, while in [ii] *one letter* is understood as object of the infinitival – see Ch. 14, §6.3.

(e) Participial extensions

Existential clauses in which *be* is followed by a noun that is in turn followed by a participial clause may be construed syntactically in two ways. Firstly, the subordinate clause may be a modifier of the noun and hence part of the displaced subject NP:

[12] i *There were [specimens measuring over twelve inches in length].*
ii *There were [some letters written by her grandmother] in the safe.*

Example [i] is a bare existential, while [ii] has a locative extension. Secondly, the subordinate clause may be an extension, not part of the displaced subject NP:

[13] i *There were [some boys] playing cricket.*
ii *There were [several people] killed.*

The non-existential counterparts of these are *Some boys were playing cricket* and *Several people were killed*, whereas the counterpart of [12ii] is *Some letters written by her grandmother were in the safe.* Example [12i], being a bare existential, has no non-existential counterpart, but we understand it as asserting the existence of specimens that measured over twelve inches in length.

There is ample evidence for the structure shown in [12]. First, nouns regularly take gerund-participial and past-participial clauses as modifiers. Second, the bracketed sequences in [12] occur elsewhere as NPs: *We had found [specimens measuring over twelve inches in length] / [some letters written by her grandmother]*. Thus, it follows that such NPs should also be able to occur as displaced subjects in existential clauses. Syntactic evidence for recognising a distinct construction of the kind shown in [13] is provided by examples like the following:

[14] i *There are [some people] going to be disadvantaged by the new tax system.*
ii *There were killed [some 650 infantry from the 2nd Battalion].*
iii *We postulate a system of particles [on which there are [some forces] acting].*

The *going* of [i] does not occur in clauses functioning as a modifier of a noun: compare **Those people going to be disadvantaged by the new tax system will have to be compensated in some way.* Example [ii] is comparable to [5i] above, with postposing of a heavy NP over the extension: this would not be possible if *killed* were a modifier of *infantry from the 2nd Battalion.* In [iii] the existential is a relative clause, which is enclosed by the outer pair of brackets, while the inner pair enclose the displaced subject. The corresponding main clause is *There are some forces acting on a system of particles.* Relativisation applies to an element within the *acting* clause, and again this would not be possible if this clause were a modifier of *forces.* There are thus good grounds for treating these examples as the existential counterparts of [15]:[12]

[15] i *Some people are going to be disadvantaged by the new tax system.*
ii *Some 650 infantry from the 2nd Battalion were killed.*
iii *We postulate a system of particles [on which some forces are acting].*

Note that the *be* in these examples is not the copula but the progressive or passive auxiliary.[13]

The position of the displaced subject after the verb *killed* in [14ii] makes this clause look like a presentational construction – compare *Then there had appeared some 650 infantry from the 2nd Battalion.* The resemblance, however, is only superficial: [14ii] differs crucially from

[12] An exceptional gerund-participial construction that doesn't belong with either [12i] or [13i] is found with *there* **be** *no use/point*, as in *There's no use/point complaining*, "Nothing is to be gained by complaining". There is also a past-participial construction that differs from those of [12ii] and [14ii]: %*There's a man been shot.* Here *been* is a perfect past participle, *'s* being a cliticised form of the auxiliary *has* (cf. *A man has been shot*) – but one which cannot be replaced by the full form.

[13] It is primarily because of examples with passive extensions, such as [13ii] and [15ii], that we prefer 'displaced subject' to the more usual 'logical subject' as the term for the NP corresponding to the subject of the non-existential counterpart. *Several people* and *some 650 infantry from the 2nd Battalion* are associated with the semantic role of patient, not agent, and hence are not logical subjects as that term is traditionally understood.

the latter in that the displaced subject follows *killed* as a result of postposing. If the NP were less heavy it could precede *killed*, as in [13ii], *There were several people killed.* This would not be possible if it were a presentational clause: compare **Then there had several people appeared.*

(f) Relative clause extensions

It may be that a distinction matching the one we have drawn between [12] and [13] applies also to existentials containing relative clauses. Compare:

[16]	i	*There are* [*people* <u>*that have an IQ far greater than that*</u>].	[modifier within NP]
	ii	*There was* [*one man*] <u>*that kept interrupting.*</u>	[relative clause extension]

In [i] the relative clause is naturally taken as a modifier of *people*: the sentence asserts the existence of people with an IQ far greater than 'that'. Example [ii], however, might be construed as the existential counterpart of *One man kept interrupting.* Note that the latter is a paraphrase of [ii], whereas [i] cannot be paraphrased as *People have an IQ far greater than that.*

The case for making a structural distinction along the lines indicated is much weaker with relative clauses than with the gerund-participials and past-participials discussed in (e) above, and it remains an open question whether the analysis suggested for [16ii] is valid. One piece of supporting evidence that can be adduced is the possibility of having a relative clause after a proper name. Thus in answer to the question *Who might be able to help?* one might reply: *Well, there's John you could try.* This cannot have an analysis like [i], for *John you could try* is not a possible NP.

6.2.2 Pragmatic constraints

The existential construction is characteristically used to introduce addressee-new entities into the discourse, and for this reason the displaced subject NP is usually indefinite. In many cases, the presence of an indefinite NP makes the existential pragmatically obligatory in that the corresponding non-existential is infelicitous:

[17] i *There is* <u>*a serious flaw*</u> *in your own argument.*
ii #<u>*A serious flaw*</u> *is in your own argument.*

Conversely, replacing an indefinite NP in an existential with a corresponding definite often results in infelicity:

[18] i *There is* <u>*a more serious flaw*</u>*, however, in your own argument.*[14]
ii #*There is* <u>*the more serious flaw*</u>*, however, in your own argument.*

We will examine these two constraints in turn, and then consider very briefly a constraint on the occurrence as displaced subject of NPs containing certain quantifiers.

Indefinites: preference for the existential over the non-existential

Bare existentials, as we have observed, normally have no non-existential counterpart: compare *There was a power failure* to the ungrammatical **A power failure was.* A choice between the constructions thus arises only in the case of extended existentials. With indefinite NPs, there is in general a preference for the existential.

[14]We have added the adjunct *however* in [18] to ensure that *in your argument* is construed as a complement of *be*, not a modifier of *flaw*.

In many cases the non-existential is infelicitous. Compare [19] and [20], where the non-existentials are felicitous in the former but not the latter:

[19] i a. *<u>A furniture van</u> was in the drive.* b. *There was <u>a furniture van</u> in the drive.*
ii a. *<u>Two copies of Sue's thesis</u> are on my desk.* b. *There are <u>two copies of Sue's thesis</u> on my desk.*

[20] i a. *#<u>Plenty of room</u> is on the top shelf.* b. *There's <u>plenty of room</u> on the top shelf.*
ii a. *#<u>A hole</u> is in my jacket.* b. *There's <u>a hole</u> in my jacket.*
iii a. *#<u>Sincerity</u> was in her voice.* b. *There was <u>sincerity</u> in her voice.*
iv a. *#<u>Peace</u> was in the region.* b. *There was <u>peace</u> in the region.*
v a. *#<u>An accident</u> was in the studio.* b. *There was <u>an accident</u> in the studio.*

When the indefinite NP denotes a physical entity, as in [19], both constructions are felicitous, but when it denotes an abstract entity, as in [20], the existential is generally required. Compare [20iva], then, with *A peace delegation was in the region.* A further relevant feature in [19iia] is that the indefinite NP contains a definite NP within it. *Sue's thesis* is likely to represent addressee-old information, and thus the subject introduces a new token of a previously known type, rendering it felicitous in subject position.

The above examples contain spatial locative complements. Similar contrasts are to be found with other extensions. Compare, for example, [21], where the PP is a temporal complement:

[21] i a. *<u>One performance</u> is at noon.* b. *There's <u>one performance</u> at noon.*
ii a. *#<u>A fireworks display</u> is tonight.* b. *There's <u>a fireworks display</u> tonight.*

Although indefinite (and abstract), *one performance* requires a context that establishes what it is a performance of – the ballet *Swan Lake*, for example. It will thus be related to the prior discourse and it is this relationship that makes it acceptable in subject position in [ia]. There is nothing in [iia], however, to indicate any such connection to prior discourse: the likely context is one where I'm informing you that a fireworks display will be taking place (e.g. with a view to suggesting we go and see it), and in such a context only the existential version is felicitous.

Displaced definite NPs

There is a strong tendency, we have noted, for the displaced NP to be indefinite. Compare such pairs as:

[22] i a. *I had a terrible fright in the kitchen today. I just turned on the light,* [*and sitting in the corner, looking at me, there was <u>a mouse</u>*].
b. *I saw a mouse in the kitchen today. I just turned on the light,* [#*and sitting in the corner, looking at me, there was <u>the mouse</u>*].
ii a. *President Clinton appeared at the podium accompanied by three senators and Margaret Thatcher.* [*Behind him there was <u>a bodyguard</u>.*]
b. *President Clinton appeared at the podium accompanied by three senators and Margaret Thatcher.* [#*Behind him there was <u>the Vice President</u>.*]

It must be emphasised, however, that definite NPs are certainly not excluded from the existential construction: they are admissible provided they represent addressee-new information.

The underlined definite NPs in [22ib/iib] clearly do not satisfy this condition. In [ib] the mouse is discourse-old (by virtue of having been introduced in the preceding sentence), and hence also addressee-old. In [iib] the Vice President is discourse-new but nevertheless addressee-old: you can be assumed to know of the Vice President's existence. It will be evident from our discussion of definiteness in Ch. 5, §6.1, however, that definite NPs do not always represent addressee-old information. We will review in turn five distinct cases where a definite NP satisfies the addressee-new requirement and hence can function as the displaced subject in a felicitous existential.

(a) Addressee-old entities treated as addressee-new

[23] i *The voters are in a resentful mood, and the governor is adept at exploiting that resentment. His opponent is plagued by other problems as well; he has been accused of dalliances with his underlings, and his support for the funding of controversial art has gained him no friends among conservatives. His waffling on budgetary matters has been noted by several major newspapers.* [*And then there is that resentment.*]

ii A: *I can't imagine what I'm going to make for dinner tonight.* B: [*Well, there's that leftover meatloaf.*]

Here the underlined NPs are addressee-old: the resentment in [i] was mentioned a few sentences before, while B in [ii] assumes prior familiarity with the leftover meatloaf on A's part, whether it has been mentioned in the preceding discourse or not. Nevertheless, the resentment and the meatloaf are treated as new, in the belief that the addressee may have temporarily forgotten them. Such cases have the flavour of reminders. The use of an indefinite in such contexts would incorrectly introduce into the discourse a brand-new entity, as though this resentment or meatloaf were not already familiar to the addressee.

We can also include under the present heading the use which echoes a reminder that has been offered by someone else:

[24] A: *I know you want to go to the party, but you've got a lot of homework to do first. And wait – didn't you promise your sister that you would spend this evening helping her practise for the school play?* B: *Well, yes –* [*there is that*].

Here, the existential echoes A's reminder of a forgotten promise, treating the promise on the one hand as new information but on the other as nonetheless previously known and therefore identifiable.

(b) Addressee-new tokens of addressee-old types

[25] i *Physics majors are required to take three courses in a foreign language,* [*and there is the same requirement placed on students in the other sciences*].

ii *The congressman's sex scandal has captured the entire country's attention.* [*There are the usual sleazy reasons for that, of course.*]

iii *The problem is* [*that there aren't the necessary funds to complete the project*].

A definite NP is admissible when it represents a new instance of a type that is addressee-old. The underlined NPs here have dual reference: they are being used to refer simultaneously to a type and a token. The definite article is justified because the type is known or inferrable: in [i] the requirement has been mentioned in the preceding clause; in [ii] I assume you are familiar with the sleazy reasons why sex scandals involving public figures capture the country's attention; and in [iii] you can infer, given a project, that some amount of funds will be required to ensure its completion. The occurrence of these NPs as displaced subjects is justified because the current instance of the type is addressee-new: in [i] we are concerned with the foreign-language requirement as it applies to students in sciences other than physics, in [ii] with the reasons for the interest in this particular sex scandal, and in [iii] with the funds needed for the particular project under discussion.

Because of the dual reference, either the type or the token may be available for subsequent pronominal reference:

[26] i *There was <u>the usual crowd</u> at the beach today. <u>They</u> were there yesterday, too.*

ii *There was <u>the usual crowd</u> at the beach today, but this time <u>they</u> were dispersed by the police for being a public nuisance.*

iii *There was <u>the usual crowd</u> at the beach today. <u>They</u> were there yesterday, too, but this time <u>they</u> were dispersed by the police for being a public nuisance.*

In [i], the anaphoric pronoun *they* is used to refer to the type, since the statement may be true even if some members of today's group differ from yesterday's.[15] In [ii], on the other hand, *they* refers to the current instantiation – the particular group of people who were dispersed on this occasion. Example [iii] shows that it is not a matter of *the usual crowd* being ambiguous, since both type and token readings apply at the same time.

The definite NP very often contains an adjective indicating that it refers to a type that is known (e.g. *same, usual, regular, traditional, obligatory, expected*) or inferrable (e.g. *ideal, correct, perfect, necessary, required*). All the examples cited are of this kind, but a demonstrative determiner can serve the same function:

[27] *Jones' stand on abortion angered Republicans for being too liberal and Democrats for being too conservative,* [*and there was <u>this problem</u> with many of his other views as well*].

(c) Addressee-old entities newly instantiating a variable

[28] i *I must be getting sensitive to garlic; it's upset my stomach twice this week. The first time was on Sunday, when I had way too much garlic bread.* [*Then there was <u>the spicy pasta that you and I shared at lunch yesterday</u>.*]

ii A: *What can I get Mary for her birthday?* B: [*There's <u>the new book on birdwatching we were talking about yesterday</u>.*]

The definite article in these examples is felicitous because the NP is addressee-old: I assume you know which pasta or which book I am referring to. But at the same time the NP serves to instantiate, i.e. to specify the value of, the variable in an open proposition that represents discourse-old information. In [i] the open proposition "*x* upset my stomach" is introduced in the prior discourse, and the displaced NP in the existential provides a new value for this variable. In [ii] the open proposition is "A can get Mary *x* for her birthday", which is a presupposition of A's question, and again the underlined NP provides a new value for *x*. If the definite NP (or coordination of definite NPs) doesn't

[15] There is an ambiguity here associated with the word *usual*: [26i] can mean either that the same general crowd was at the beach again today, or else it can mean that there was a crowd at the beach today, as usual. It is the first reading that we are interested in.

provide a new value for a variable in this way, the existential will be infelicitous. Compare, for example:

[29] i A: *Who was at the party last night?* B: [*There was Mary, Sue, Fred, Matt, and Sam.*]
ii *I had a really great time last night.* [#*There was Mary, Sue, Fred, Matt, and Sam at this party I went to.*]

In [ii], the relevant open proposition is not salient in the context, and the utterance is correspondingly infelicitous.

This variable-instantiating use of the existential often involves a list, as in [29i]: we are given a list of values for the variable in the open proposition "*x* was at the party last night". Where only a single value is provided, there is often an implicature of non-exhaustiveness. For example, in [28ii] B implicates that there are also other possibilities worth considering. The implicature can be denied, but infelicity will arise if there is no such denial and yet exhaustiveness is intended:

[30] i A: *What's in that drawer?* B: [*There's the stapler, but nothing else.*]
ii A: *What's in that drawer?* B: [#*There's the stapler.*]

In [i] *but nothing else* cancels the implicature that the stapler is one of a set of things in the drawer; in [ii] B seems to be giving an exhaustive answer without any such cancellation and the result is infelicitous – compare *Well, there's the stapler, for a start*, where the final adjunct reinforces the non-exhaustiveness implicature. Note similarly that B's existential in [28ii] would not be appropriate if A's question had been *What did you get Mary for her birthday?*, which invites an exhaustive answer.

(d) Addressee-new entities with identifying descriptions

[31] i *In addition to interest-rate risk, there is the added risk that when interest rates fall, mortgages will be prepaid, thereby reducing the Portfolio's future income stream.*
ii *In Johnson's latest article, there is the claim that earthquakes are affected by the tides.*
iii *There was the world's tallest man at the circus.*
iv *If you look at the map, you can see the intersection,* [*and then a couple of miles north of that, there is this road here that runs from the northwest to the southeast.*]
v *There was the sound of a sharp slap, and then a loud cry.*

Here the displaced subjects are not addressee-old in any sense, but a definite NP is in order because the content of the NP is sufficient to fully identify the referent, to pre-empt a *which* question. In [i], for example, the content clause functioning as a complement to *risk* fully defines the risk I'm referring to. Similarly in [ii], the proposition that earthquakes are affected by the tides constitutes a unique and fully identifiable claim. This may be compared with #*In Johnson's latest article there is the claim about earthquakes and tides*: the PP *about earthquakes and tides*, unlike the content clause in [ii], is not sufficient to identify the claim, and as a result the example is infelicitous. In [iii] the superlative makes *the world's tallest man* uniquely identifiable: there can only be one person satisfying this description. In [iv] the identification is achieved deictically, by means of *this* and *here*, which would normally be accompanied in such a case by a gesture (an indexing act, in the sense of Ch. 17, §1.1). In [v] *a sharp slap* is indefinite, but associated with any slap is its own individual sound: the identifiability of the sound justifies the definite article, but the NP is clearly new.

(e) False definite ***this***

There is one use of demonstrative ***this*** – described more fully in Ch. 17, §5.4 – that is pragmatically equivalent to *a* or *some*, and hence readily found in the displaced subjects of existentials:

[32] i %*Last week there was this strange dog wandering around the neighbourhood.*
ii %*Early in the 70s, there was this rock guitarist that I liked so much that I bought all of his albums.*

This strange dog here is replaceable by *a strange dog* but not by *the strange dog*. Hence the name 'false definite': the NP is definite in form, but indefinite in meaning. This use is characteristic of informal style and, as indicated by the '%' annotation, is not found in the speech of all speakers. In its ordinary ('true definite') use, ***this*** is excluded from displaced subjects unless the NP falls into one of the categories discussed above (as in [31iv]). Compare [32] with, for example, the anaphoric *this* of *Kim has just written another song about death* [#*and there is this song on the radio every day*]. Here *this song* refers to the one mentioned in the first clause: it thus represents addressee-old information and is inadmissible in the existential construction.

Quantified NPs

The felicity of existential clauses is also sensitive to quantification. NPs determined by the proportional quantifiers *most* and *all* or the universal distributive quantifiers *each* and *every* are subject to pragmatic restrictions on their occurrence as displaced subjects. In the following, for example, *most* and *all* are felicitous only in the non-existential version, whereas other quantifiers, such as *some, many, one, a* are admissible in both versions:

[33] i a. *Some/Many/Most/All small firms are experiencing difficulties.* b. *There are some/many/#most/#all small firms experiencing difficulties.*
ii a. *A/One/Each/Every student from my class was at the party.* b. *There was a/one/#each/#every student from my class at the party.*

As with definite NPs, however, there is no categorical ban on displaced subject NPs determined by *most, all, each,* and *every*. Under conditions that are not yet well understood, such NPs can also appear in existential clauses, as in [34]:

[34] i *Among our dresses there were most kinds of shabby and greasy wear and much fustion and corduroy that was neither sound nor fragrant.*
ii *There are all kinds of insurance policies that can meet your needs.*[16]
iii *There's still each student in Group C to be interviewed.*
iv *I think that's probably still a NASA job because of the number of contractors involved. [In firing room two, there's every contractor we've got, just about, over there.]*

[16] Note that *all kinds of insurance policies* is not interpreted literally as "every kind of policy", but rather something like "a lot of different kinds of policy". It is, as it were, 'false universal quantification', comparable to the false definite use of *this* in [32]. Similarly with *every* (but not *each*). In a sentence like *There's every reason to believe this winter will be especially mild*, the NP *every reason* means something like "good reason".

6.3 The presentational construction

Issues of form

Presentational clauses have dummy *there* as subject and some verb other than *be* as predicator:[17]

[35] i *After they had travelled for many weeks, there came a moonlit night when the air was still and cool.*
ii *Between the two candidates there exists a great deal of antipathy, the result of months of negative campaigning.*
iii *There remain only two further issues to discuss.*
iv *There seems little doubt that the fire was started deliberately.*

A sample of other verbs (or verbal idioms) found in this construction is given in [36]:

[36]					
appear	*arise*	*arrive*	*develop*	*emerge*	*enter*
escape	*follow*	*grow*	*lie*	*live*	*loom*
occur	*persist*	*sit*	*spring up*	*sprout*	*stand*

A high proportion have to do with being in a position or coming into view; note then the contrast between *At the edge of the cave there appeared a terrifying grizzly bear* and #*At the edge of the cave there disappeared a terrifying grizzly bear.*

Most presentational clauses are of the bare type or have a locative extension. *Remain,* however, allows an infinitival extension, as in [35iii], and also licenses a predicative (*There remained only two officers alive*).

Pragmatic constraints

The presentational construction differs from the existential with respect to the felicity conditions that apply to the occurrence of definite NPs as displaced subject. Compare [37iia–c], considered in a context where they are continuations of [37i]:

[37] i *President Clinton appeared at the podium accompanied by three senators and Margaret Thatcher.*
ii a. *Behind him there stood/was a bodyguard.*
b. #*Behind him there stood/were the senators.*
c. *Behind him there stood/*#*was the Vice President.*

We see from [iia–b] that both the presentational with *stand* and the existential with *be* accept indefinite *a bodyguard* and exclude definite *the senators,* which is discourse-old. The difference is exemplified in [iic]. *The Vice President* is discourse-new but addressee-old: such NPs are excluded by the existential (cf. [22iib] above), but admitted by the presentational. Thus while the existential requires that a definite displaced subject be addressee-new, the presentational makes the lesser requirement that it be discourse-new.

It follows that definite NPs occur more readily as displaced subjects in presentationals than in existentials: addressee-old NPs like *the Vice President* are permitted if

[17] Presentational clauses are generally intransitive, but transitives cannot be wholly excluded, as illustrated in the attested example *There seized him a fear that perhaps after all it was all true.*

discourse-new. At the same time, the presentational allows definites of the five categories discussed for existentials in §6.2.2:

[38] i *But remember, there still exists that first problem I mentioned.*
ii *Through the discussion there ran the usual thread of veiled hostility.*
iii *At first they could see nothing but the road and the trees. [But then, as they rounded the bend in the road, there came into view the grocery store, the barbershop, and the little ramshackle ice cream parlour.]*
iv *It's clear that the school needs a significant amount of work on its electrical and plumbing systems, as well as new textbooks and computers. [There remains the sticky issue of how this will all be financed in a district peopled with struggling taxpayers.]*
v %*I opened the door, [and in front of me there stood this enormous chest of drawers].*

These illustrate respectively an addressee-old entity treated as new (a reminder), a new token of an old type, an old entity newly instantiating a variable (in the open proposition "*x* came into view"), a new entity with the definite article rendered felicitous by the identifying description, and false definite *this*.

7 Extraposition

7.1 The central case: extraposition from subject of content and infinitival clauses

The most common and straightforward case of extraposition is illustrated in the [b] examples of [1]:

[1]		BASIC VERSION	VERSION WITH EXTRAPOSITION
	i	a. *That he hasn't phoned worries me.*	b. *It worries me that he hasn't phoned.*
	ii	a. *Why she told him is unclear.*	b. *It is unclear why she told him.*
	iii	a. *To resist would be pointless.*	b. *It would be pointless to resist.*

In the basic version the subject position is filled by a subordinate clause: a declarative content clause in [i], an interrogative content clause in [ii], and an infinitival clause in [iii]. In the version with extraposition, the subject position is filled by the pronoun *it* and the subordinate clause appears at the end of the matrix clause, in what we are calling extraposed subject position. An extraposed subject, like a displaced subject, is not a kind of subject, but an element that is related to a dummy subject. Semantically, the subordinate clause stands in the same relation to the verb (or verb + predicative complement) in [b] as in [a], but syntactically the switch from [a] to [b] transfers the subject properties from the subordinate clause to *it*, as demonstrated in Ch. 4, §3.2.2. The effect of extraposition is to place a heavy constituent at the end of the clause, in conformity with the general tendency noted in [13i] of §2 for heavy constituents to occur in this position.[18]

[18] Extraposed subjects can be followed by adjuncts provided they too are relatively heavy: *It worries me that he hasn't phoned, because he knows that we have to settle things before we leave for Cyprus tomorrow.*

Pragmatic constraints on the basic version

We regard the [a] examples in [1] as the basic version because they are syntactically simpler than their counterparts in [b] and because their clause structure is normally the only one of the two that is available when the subject is an NP: *His silence worries me* but not **It worries me his silence.*[19] Nevertheless, with examples like those in [1], where the element concerned is a content clause or an infinitival clause, the version with extraposition is much more frequent than the basic one, and it is to the basic version, not the one with the extraposed subject, that pragmatic constraints relating to familiarity status apply.

Non-extraposed content clause treated as background knowledge

Consider first the following examples:

[2] i a. A: *Jeffrey didn't turn in his term paper until a week after the deadline.*
B: *It's a miracle <u>that he did it at all</u>.*
b. A: *Jeffrey didn't turn in his term paper until a week after the deadline.*
B: *<u>That he did it at all</u> is a miracle.*
ii a. *It is amazing <u>that the real problems surrounding NATO's planned bombing raid on Serbia were never addressed during the marathon peace talks now underway in France</u>.*
b. #*<u>That the real problems surrounding NATO's planned bombing raid on Serbia were never addressed during the marathon peace talks now underway in France</u> is amazing.*

In [i] the underlined content clause represents old information: Jeffrey's completion of a term paper has been explicitly evoked in the prior discourse. Here, both the extraposed version [ia] and the basic version [ib] are acceptable. Example [iia] is taken from the beginning of a newspaper article. In that context the information represented by the content clause is new and only the extraposed version [iia] is acceptable: the basic version [iib] would be quite inappropriate as the first sentence of a newspaper article.

In [2i] the content clause information is discourse-old by virtue of prior mention. But felicity of the non-extraposed version is not limited to cases where the information in the content clause is discourse-old: all that is necessary is that the speaker be able to treat the information as familiar to the addressee – that is, as something that doesn't have to be presented as new because it can be assumed to be part of the shared set of background assumptions. Consider the following examples:

[3] i *<u>That the skin survives these daily torments</u> is a remarkable tribute to its toughness.*
ii [*<u>That Pierce Brosnan is the best 007 since Connery</u> is beyond doubt,*] *and for all its anachronisms this witty, occasionally thrilling 1995 effort (efficiently directed by Martin Campbell) served to reinvigorate what had long seemed to be an exhausted franchise.*
iii *His act takes on lunatic proportions as he challenges female audience members to wrestling matches, falling in love with one while grappling it out on the canvas.* [*<u>How he and feminist Lynne Marguiles (Courtney Love) became life partners</u> is anyone's guess.*]

[19] *It worries me, his silence* is perfectly acceptable but is a right dislocation; for the distinction between the two constructions, see §8.2.

Example [i] follows a paragraph describing the 'daily abuses' to which people subject their skin – stretching, scraping, gouging, exposure to excessive and injurious doses of sunlight and wind, and so on. The prior text doesn't assert that the skin survives these torments, but it is obvious common knowledge that it does. Example [ii] occurs in a newspaper column commenting on the movies that are to be shown on television during the following week: it is the first sentence in the piece on the James Bond (007) movie 'Goldeneye'. The information represented by the content clause is obviously discourse-new in this context, but the writer is presenting it as a proposition readers can be expected to be familiar with. Example [iii] is from a newspaper review of a movie about the American comedian Andy Kaufman, the referent of the pronoun ***he***. The information in the underlined clause is discourse-new; however, it is not being asserted, but rather is being treated as background knowledge.

Non-extraposed content clauses representing presupposed information

Very often a non-extraposed content clause represents presupposed information, information whose truth is not at issue. This is the case in the declarative examples [2ib] and [3i], and also in [3iii], where the interrogative clause presupposes that Kaufman and Marguiles became life partners. But the condition on the felicity of the non-extraposed version is not a matter of whether or not the content clause is presupposed. Note in the first place that the underlined clause in [2ii] is presupposed by virtue of the semantic properties of the factive adjective *amazing* (see Ch. 11, §7.4), but in context extraposition is obligatory. Secondly, a non-extraposed content clause need not be presupposed: the one in [3ii], for example, is not – it is asserted to be true. And it is no less possible for the matrix clause to deny the truth of the content clause: *That he was motivated by pure altruism is a complete myth.*

Extraposition and weight

Extraposition places the subordinate clause at or towards the end of the matrix clause, which is in general the preferred position for heavy constituents. In cases where both orderings are permissible, the weight factor may well result in the extraposed version being preferred. But acceptability of the basic version certainly does not require that the content clause be fairly short. This is evident from the following example, where the subject clause is very long and the matrix VP quite short:

[4] *But, we must never forget, most of the appropriate heroes and their legends were created overnight, to answer immediate needs. . . . Most of the legends that are created to fan the fires of patriotism are essentially propagandistic and are not folk legends at all . . . Naturally, such scholarly facts are of little concern to the man trying to make money or fan patriotism by means of folklore.* [*That much of what he calls folklore is the result of beliefs carefully sown among the people with the conscious aim of producing a desired mass emotional reaction to a particular situation or set of situations is irrelevant.*]

Here, the content clause serves as a summary of a long stretch of prior discourse and, as such, it represents familiar information and is thus felicitous in non-extraposed position despite being extremely heavy.

Processing factors

Extraposition places the subordinate clause in a position where it is easier to process than when it is in subject position. In particular, extraposition makes it possible to have multiple embedding of a type that is not permitted in the basic construction:

[5] a. #*That that he was angry was so obvious embarrassed her.* b. *It embarrassed her that it was so obvious that he was angry.*

The sequence of two identical subordinators in [a] makes this basic version unacceptably difficult to process, whereas the version in [b] is impeccable. Here extraposition applies to both the *embarrass* clause and the *be* + *obvious* clause.

Syntactic constraints on the basic version

There are also syntactic conditions under which the basic version is inadmissible. Most importantly, subjects with the form of declarative content clauses and infinitivals cannot undergo subject–auxiliary inversion, and where such inversion is required only the version with extraposition will therefore be allowed:

[6] i a. *<u>To pay now</u> would be better.* b. *It would be better <u>to pay now</u>.*
ii a. **Would <u>to pay now</u> be better?* b. *Would it be better <u>to pay now</u>?*

Exclamative content clauses are generally unacceptable in the basic version:

[7] a. #*<u>What a fuss some people make</u> is incredible.* b. *It is incredible <u>what a fuss some people make</u>.*

This constraint, however, is not absolute – compare *What a blunder it was didn't emerge till later* (cf. Ch. 11, §6.2); the unacceptability of [7a] and the like is therefore better handled in terms of the above pragmatic constraint than by a rule of syntax.

Syntactic constraints on extraposition

There are also syntactic conditions under which extraposition is not permitted:

[8] i a. *<u>How she escaped</u> is the question we ought to be addressing.* b. **It's the question we ought to be addressing <u>how she escaped</u>.*
ii a. *<u>That she survived at all</u> shows that she must have been very fit.* b. **It shows that she must have been very fit <u>that she survived at all</u>.*

In [i] the matrix clause verb is *be* in its specifying sense, and in such cases the basic version is required. In [ii] the matrix VP has a content clause as an internal complement, and the subject cannot be extraposed over this. The precise nature of this constraint remains unclear. Extraposition is also impossible in *Why they were allowed to get away with it is something I shall never understand*, where *I shall never understand* is a relative clause functioning as modifier in an NP structure: this suggests a more general constraint on extraposition over a finite clause. But cases where an extraposed clause immediately follows a finite clause are certainly attested, as in *It's going to depend on when Mum gets home whether we can go shopping this afternoon.*

Lexical constraints on the basic version

A number of verbs or verbal idioms occur with dummy *it* as the subject and a declarative content clause or infinitival in post-verbal position without an equivalent version where the subordinate clause appears as subject:

[9] i a. **<u>That he was dying</u> turned out.* b. *It turned out <u>that he was dying</u>.*
ii a. **<u>To notify her family</u> fell to me.* b. *It fell to me <u>to notify her family</u>.*
iii a. **<u>To short-list three of the candidates</u> was decided.* b. *It was decided <u>to short-list three of the candidates</u>.*

The main items concerned are given in [10]:

[10]	i	*appear*	*be*	*chance*	*come about*	*fall out*
		happen	*seem*	*strike*	*transpire*	*turn out*
	ii	*decide* P	*fall*	*hope* P	*intend* P	*remain*

Those in [i] take declarative content clauses, with *strike* transitive, the others intransitive.[20] Those in [ii] take infinitivals; with the ones marked 'P', the relevant construction is passive, as in [9iii]. It is debatable whether the function of the subordinate clause is in all cases to be subsumed under that of extraposed subject: this issue is discussed in Ch. 11, §4.3.1.

7.2 Further cases of extraposition

(a) Extraposition of gerund-participial subjects

Extraposition can apply with gerund-participials as well as content clauses and infinitivals:

[11] i a. *Complaining would be no use.* b. *It would be no use complaining.*
ii a. *Getting Ed to agree to our proposal will be no problem whatsoever.* b. *It will be no problem whatsoever getting Ed to agree to our proposal.*

We did not include this under the central case of extraposition because gerund-participials extrapose less readily and generally than content clauses and infinitivals. Compare, for example:

[12] i *It was stupid to tell my parents / ?telling my parents.*
ii *It would make things worse to call in the police / ?calling in the police.*

Here the extraposed infinitivals are impeccable, but the gerund-participials are at best very marginal, though the basic versions are quite unproblematic (*Telling my parents was stupid*; *Calling in the police would make things worse*). Gerund-participials with an overt subject, especially a non-pronominal one, are particularly resistant to extraposition: *Kim and Pat getting married had taken us all by surprise*, but not **It had taken us all by surprise Kim and Pat getting married.* Note that gerund-participials differ from infinitivals in that they can undergo subject–auxiliary inversion (cf. *Will getting Ed to agree to our proposal be a problem?*), so extraposition is not obligatory in this context.[21] Gerund-participials in complement function are the most NP-like of subordinate clauses, and the fact that they are less amenable to extraposition than the other subordinate clause categories is a further manifestation of this.

(b) Extraposition of NPs

NPs generally cannot be extraposed, but there is a very limited range of types that can:

[13] i *It's extraordinary the amount of beer he puts away.*
ii *It impressed me the way she disarmed him.*
iii *It's incredible the things they get up to.*

[20] *Appear*, *seem*, and *strike* allow the content clause to function as subject when they have a predicative complement: *That Kim is ill seems obvious / strikes me as obvious.*

[21] There is, however, one item that takes a gerund-participial – namely, *worth* – that enters into the pattern shown in [10]. We have, for example, *In discussing the future it is also worth considering the impact on Antarctica of human activities elsewhere on the globe*, but not **Considering the impact on Antarctica of human activities elsewhere on the globe is worth.*

The NPs concerned all have the form '*the* ... N + relative clause'. They are a special case of what we have called 'concealed questions' (see Ch. 11, §5.3): they are more or less equivalent to the interrogative clauses *how much beer he puts away*, *how she disarmed him*, *what they get up to*. At the same time, the matrix VP gives an exclamatory meaning: [i] conveys that he puts away an extraordinarily large amount of beer, and so on. Extraposition is optional: we can also have the basic versions *The amount of beer he puts away is extraordinary*, and so on.

(c) Extraposition of non-subjects

The dummy *it* of extraposition may function as object rather than subject, but here we do not find a contrast between a basic version and a version with extraposition comparable to that illustrated in [1]:

[14] a. **I find that he got away with it for so long quite incredible.* b. *I find it quite incredible that he got away with it for so long.*

The deviance of [a] is like that of [6iia]: in both, the subordinate clause is positioned between the verb and its complement. Note that if the subordinate clause in [14a] is preposed the result is well formed: *That he got away with it for so long I find quite incredible* (=[2iiib] of §1). For further discussion of clauses like [14b], see Ch. 11, §4.3.2.

8 **Dislocation**

A dislocated clause has a constituent, usually an NP, located to the left or right of the nucleus of the clause, with an anaphorically linked pronoun or comparable form within the nucleus itself. Compare, for example, the non-dislocated [1i] with the two dislocated versions given in [1ii–iii]:

[1] i *Her parents seem pretty uncaring.* [non-dislocated version]
ii *Her parents, they seem pretty uncaring.* [left dislocation]
iii *They seem pretty uncaring, her parents.* [right dislocation]

In [i] *her parents* is functioning in the nucleus of the clause (in this case as subject), with no element external to the nucleus. In [ii–iii], by contrast, *her parents* stands outside the nucleus, to the left and right respectively, and the coreferential pronoun *they* occupies the place filled by *her parents* in the non-dislocated version.

In §§8.1–2 we will examine the left and right dislocation constructions in turn, considering only the case where the coreferential form in the nucleus is a personal pronoun. Dislocation of this kind is often found in oral personal narratives and informal writing. In §8.3 we look at further possibilities and contrast dislocation with a number of superficially similar constructions.

8.1 **Left dislocation**

Range of functions of the pronoun

In [1ii] the pronoun that is anaphorically linked to the detached element functions as subject of the nucleus of the clause, but other functions are equally possible:

[2] i *But his mother – I really admire her.*
ii *This guy in my cognitive science class, I gave him my notes to copy.*

iii *My sister, someone threw a rock at her at the beach.*
iv *The people next door, the police have just arrested their son on a drugs charge.*
v *The other one, they don't think she'll survive.*

Her in [i] is the direct object, *him* in [ii] the indirect object, *her* in [iii] the object of a preposition, *their* in [iv] the subject-determiner within the object NP, and *she* in [v] the subject of a content clause embedded as a complement within the clause nucleus following the dislocated NP.

It is also possible for dislocation to apply to a clause-coordination. Compare:

[3] i a. *I eat garlic and pretty soon my stomach's upset.*
b. *I gave this guy in my class my notes to copy and he never returned them.*
ii a. *Garlic, I eat it and pretty soon my stomach's upset.*
b. *This guy in my class, I gave him my notes to copy and he never returned them.*

In [iia] there is just one personal pronoun anaphorically linked to the dislocated element, while in [iib] there are two, one in each of the coordinated clauses.

Left dislocation vs complement preposing

Left dislocation of a complement is to be distinguished from complement preposing. Compare:

[4] i *Her parents, I don't like them at all.* [left dislocation]
ii *Her parents I don't like __ at all.* [complement preposing]

In left dislocation there is an anaphoric link between the initial element and some overt pronoun in the nucleus, whereas in complement preposing there is a gap in the relevant place in the nucleus. The dislocation construction is syntactically less constrained than preposing: for the latter there are constraints on the function of the gap that do not apply to the overt pro-form. In the first place, preposing places an element before the subject, so we can't have preposing of the subject itself: there is no preposing counterpart of [1ii], for example. Secondly, preposing of indirect objects is generally quite restricted (see Ch. 4, §4.3): ?*This guy in my class I gave my notes to copy.* Thirdly, there is no preposing counterpart to examples like [2iv], for a genitive subject-determiner cannot be preposed: **The people next door's, the police have just arrested son on a drugs charge.*

Left dislocation differs from preposing not only in syntactic form, but also in pragmatic function. In preposing the prenuclear constituent must represent a discourse-old link to the prior context, but in left-dislocation it may introduce discourse-new information:

[5] *Some guys, they just show up without even calling first.*

Left dislocation vs marked topic

Left dislocation is also to be distinguished from the *as for* construction in which the initial element is explicitly marked as a topic (see §2 above):

[6] i *Her father, he didn't want to know about it.* [left dislocation]
ii *As for her father, he didn't want to know about it.* [marked topic]

As for assigns topic status to its complement, but in left dislocation the prenuclear element is not marked as topic: in this construction, as in clauses with no prenuclear element, there is no grammatical indication of what (if anything) is the topic of the clause. Consider, for example:

[7] A: *What kind of tips do you get dancing?* B: *Well, this one guy, he gave me a diamond ring that I still wear on my right hand and tell people is from my grandmother.*

The dislocated element here is *this one guy*, but it is much more plausible to interpret B's reply as being about the diamond ring than about the guy who gave it to her. A further difference between the constructions is that in the case of a marked topic there need be no anaphoric link with a pronoun in the nucleus of the clause:

[8] *As for the concert-hall, the architect excelled herself.*

The initial phrase indicates that the concert-hall is the topic, but there is no reference to this in the nucleus. The nucleus is nevertheless interpreted as saying something about the concert-hall – that is, that the architect of the concert-hall excelled herself in her design of it.

Pragmatic functions of left dislocation

(a) Simplification of processing (production or perception)

One common case where left dislocation has a simplifying function is illustrated in [2iv], where it serves to avoid having an awkward and complex genitive construction: ?*the people next door's son.* Left dislocation also avoids having a discourse-new element in subject position, which favours discourse-old elements:

[9] *My sister and her husband were having a terrible fight, and she started to scream.* [*The landlady, she went up,*] *and she told them she was going to call the police.*

Here the landlady is new to the discourse (and presumably to the addressee as well). The dislocated NP creates a new information unit and thus eases processing, because the entity is rendered discourse-old before its appearance in subject position in the clause, where it is represented here by the pronoun *she.*[22]

(b) Relationship to the previous discourse

We have observed that left dislocation differs from preposing in that the prenuclear constituent is not required to serve as a link to the prior discourse (cf. [5] above), but nevertheless it frequently does represent discourse-old information:

[10] i *I hate writing term papers.* [*An exam, you take it and you're done.*] *But papers seem to drag on forever.*

ii *Jane has an interesting idea for a science project. She's going to use three groups of mice.* [*One group, she'll feed them mouse food. Another, she'll feed them veggies.*]

As with preposing, the entity represented by the dislocated phrase in this type of left dislocation stands in a contextually relevant relation to some previously evoked entity or entities: in [i] exams belong with term papers in a set of assessment exercises; in [ii] one group and another group are included within the set of three groups mentioned in the preceding clause. Left dislocation differs from preposing, however, in that there

[22] The same effect can of course be achieved by numerous different means. For example, the new entity may be introduced in a separate clause with very little other content: *You know those letters we did this morning? They have to go off in today's mail.*

is no requirement for a discourse-old open proposition, as there is with complement preposing (see §3 above). In [ii], for example, the clause nucleus following the dislocated *one group* is *she'll feed them mouse food*, but we might equally have *she'll keep them in the bathroom* or *she'll ignore them*, or *a friend will take care of them*, and so on. Thus, there is no need for the clause to provide the value for a variable in an open proposition that is familiar from the prior discourse.

8.2 **Right dislocation**

Range of functions of the pronoun

The pronoun in right dislocation can have a wide range of functions within the nucleus, as we saw for left dislocation. Our original example [1iii] (*They seem pretty uncaring, her parents*) had dislocation of the subject; other functions are illustrated in [11]:

[11] i *I really like him, your dad.*
ii *I gave him a dollar, that man back there.*
iii *I've never spoken to her before, the Vice Chancellor.*
iv *What's his name, your son?*
v *There's no doubt they're unusually bright, your kids.*

Again we have a direct object in [i], an indirect object in [ii], an object of a preposition in [iii], a subject-determiner in [iv], and a subject in an embedded clause in [v].

Pragmatic functions of right dislocation

(a) Utterance processing function: clarification of reference

[12] i *My dad was telling my uncle about how you had said you'd solve the financial problems of your business. It took a while to explain it, because [he didn't really understand what you planned to do, my uncle].*
ii *I get back strain from carrying this heavy backpack, especially when I have to take home my huge science book and all of my lit folders. [It's ridiculously heavy, my science book,] and it's really not good for me to be hauling it back and forth all the time.*

Here, I utter a pronoun and then realise it may not be clear what the pronoun is being used to refer to. I then add this information in clause-final position, as a sort of 'afterthought'. In [i], for example, the referent of *he* may be unclear, in view of the presence of two potential antecedents (*my dad* and *my uncle*); the right-dislocated *my uncle* clarifies which is intended. In [ii] there is a similar potential for confusion between two possible antecedents for *it* – that is, *my huge science book* and *this heavy backpack*; again, the right-dislocated *my science book* provides the necessary clarification.

(b) Other cases of discourse-old information

[13] i *Frank has absolutely no social skills, and the way he dresses is an embarrassment. [He's a mess, that guy.]*
ii *Have you read this biography of Lincoln? I just started reading it this morning, and already I'm up to chapter 5. [It's fascinating, this book.] I never knew half of this stuff before.*

In examples like these there is no question of the dislocated phrase being needed to clarify what the pronoun refers to: in these contexts there is only one appropriate referent for the pronoun, Frank in [i], the biography of Lincoln in [ii]. Note, moreover, that the dislocated phrases *that guy* and *this book* provide very little identifying information about the referent.

Nevertheless, here, no less than in the disambiguating case, the dislocated phrase must represent discourse-old information. Compare:

[14] i *I had to take my car in for service again.* [*It's really in bad shape, that car.*]
ii *I just saw 'Titanic' for the eighth time.* [*He's so cute, that Leonardo DiCaprio!*]
iii *Dad took your old desk out to the curb to be taken away with the trash, but forgot that I had been keeping all my important papers in there. Luckily Diana checked the drawers and thought that the papers looked important, so she took them out.* [*#He looked them over, our attorney.*]

In [i] the right-dislocated *that car* has been explicitly evoked in the prior discourse, while in [ii] *that Leonardo DiCaprio* is related to the previously evoked movie 'Titanic' by virtue of being one of the major actors in it. In [iii], however, *our attorney* refers to someone who is new to the discourse and as a result the dislocation is infelicitous.[23]

Right dislocation and topicality

We have seen that *He looked them over, our attorney* is infelicitous in the context given in [14iii] because *our attorney* is not discourse-old. But it is not sufficient that the right-dislocated constituent be discourse-old: it must also represent topical information. Thus the bracketed clause of [14iii] could be replaced by [15i], but not by [15ii]:

[15] i *She showed a lot of foresight, that Diana.*
ii *#She had the foresight to call your lawyer, who came to get them immediately, that Diana.*

Example [i], but not [ii], is naturally interpreted as being primarily about Diana.

8.3 Extensions and contrasting constructions

(a) Left dislocated NPs with forms other than personal pronouns in the nucleus

[16] i *That brother of yours, the guy's a crook.*
ii *The guy next door, the lucky bastard's just won a million in the lottery.*

In [i] *the guy* effectively has no more content than the personal pronoun *he*, and it seems reasonable to regard this as an extension of left dislocation. Similarly with [ii], where *the lucky bastard* is an 'epithet' (cf. Ch. 5, §7.5).

[23] Because of this restriction to discourse-old information, the case where the pronoun is genitive, as in [11iv], is quite rare. Here it is necessary that both the genitive pronoun (*his*) and the NP containing it (*his name*) are discourse-old: your son will have been mentioned and his name is discourse-old by virtue of the standard association between people and their names. Note, then, the contrast in acceptability between *There's John.* [*#His whole family is obnoxious, that guy*], where *his whole family* is discourse-new, and *There's John's goofy sister.* [*His whole family is obnoxious, that guy*], where the prior mention of John's sister makes his family discourse-old.

(b) Left dislocation and contrast

[17] i *The people who earn millions and pay next to no tax, those are our targets.*
ii *Bill, Paul, Harry – managers like them should get the boot.*

In [i] the demonstrative *those*, although representing discourse-old information, is stressed, in order to contrast the people concerned with others who are not our targets. And in [ii] – where again *them* needs to be contrastively stressed – the relation between the prenuclear constituent and the subject of the nucleus is no longer one of coreference: Bill, Paul, and Harry form a subset of the managers.[24]

(c) The supplementary epithet construction

Dislocation is to be distinguished from the construction with a non-referential epithet in prenuclear position:

[18] i *That bastard next door, he's just won a million in the lottery.* [left dislocation]
ii *The bastard, he's taken my chair again.* } [supplementary epithet]
iii *He's taken my chair again, the bastard.* }

In [i] the NP *that bastard next door* is used referentially, and the fact that it is headed by the noun *bastard* is quite incidental: many other (non-pronominal) expressions referring to the person in question would do as well. In [ii–iii], however, *the bastard* is a supplement (cf. Ch. 15, §5); it is not referential but is used to express the speaker's attitude towards the person referred to by *he*. Any referential NP could be used in place of *he* in the nucleus (cf. *The bastard! Max has taken my chair again*). The epithet can occur within the nucleus, as *Max, the bastard, has taken my chair again* (which is again distinguished from apposition by the non-referential use of the epithet). And when it precedes the clause nucleus, the epithet is prosodically distinct from a left-dislocated NP in that it forms a separate intonational unit (and in writing an exclamation mark or dash will often be preferred to a comma).[25]

(d) Right dislocation vs extraposition

Right dislocation is to be distinguished from the superficially similar extraposition construction discussed in §7. Compare:

[19] i *It annoyed us both, having to do the calculations by hand.* [right dislocation]
ii *It annoyed us both that we had to do the calculations by hand.* [extraposition]

The *it* of [i] is a referential pronoun and functions like other personal pronouns (cf. *They annoy me, these calculations*); in this example, the pronoun refers to the situation expressed in the gerund-participial. The *it* of [ii] is invariant, on the other hand, and is best treated as a dummy, non-referential pronoun.

[24] Examples are occasionally attested where there is no explicit anaphoric link at all between the prenuclear NP and an NP in the nucleus: *The typical family today, the husband and the wife both work; Tulips, you have to plant the bulbs every year?* Such examples bear some resemblance to the marked topic construction illustrated in [8], differing in that they contain no explicit marking of the topic. The absence of any anaphoric link renders them distinct from left dislocation.

[25] Left dislocation is also to be distinguished from the use of resumptive pronouns in unbounded dependency constructions, as in *My boyfriend, [who I never know what he's going to say,] sometimes embarrasses me when I have friends over* – see Ch. 12, §7.3. This differs from left dislocation in that the placement of *who* in prenuclear position is obligatory, required by the relative clause construction.

In speech the two constructions are strikingly distinct prosodically. Unlike the extraposed constituent, the dislocated constituent almost invariably constitutes a distinct intonational phrase and is separated from the nucleus of the clause by an intonational boundary. In writing there will generally be a corresponding difference in punctuation, with the dislocated constituent, but not the extraposed one, set apart by a comma (or dash).

The prosodic difference correlates with a difference in the information status of the right-dislocated and extraposed constituents. As we have noted, the right-dislocated phrase is required to be discourse-old, whereas the extraposed constituent may be discourse-new. Compare the following as discourse-initial utterances:

[20] i #*It's really interesting, a book I'm reading.*
ii *It now seems likely that there'll be another price increase in the next few weeks.*

The dislocated [i] is infelicitous in this context: instead we would have *A book I'm reading is really interesting* or, more naturally, the existential *There's a book I'm reading that's really interesting.* Conversely, the extraposition [ii] is completely natural, while the version without extraposition, *That there will be another price increase in the next few weeks now seems likely* would be infelicitous in discourse-initial position.

Syntactically, extraposition is found predominantly with content clauses and infinitivals; these are rarely right-dislocated, though not wholly excluded from the construction (cf. *It's an interesting question, why the animals react in this way*). With very few exceptions, NPs can be dislocated but not extraposed. The main overlap between the constructions is thus found with gerund-participials: compare *It was interesting, listening to the debate* (right dislocation) vs *It was interesting listening to the debate* (extraposition).

9 Clefts

9.1 General properties of clefts

There are two main types of cleft clause, ***it*-clefts** and **pseudo-clefts,**[26] with the latter category having **basic** and **reversed** versions. These constructions are illustrated in [1] alongside the corresponding non-cleft clause:

[1]	i	*I bought a red wool sweater.*	[non-cleft]
	ii	*It was a red wool sweater that I bought.*	[*it*-cleft]
	iii	*What I bought was a red wool sweater.*	[basic pseudo-cleft]
	iv	*A red wool sweater was what I bought.*	[reversed pseudo-cleft]

'Cleft' is a process term: the idea behind it is that a cleft clause is formed by dividing a more elementary clause into two parts. In [1], for example, [ii–iv] can be thought of as being formed from [i] by dividing it into the two parts *a red wool sweater* and *I bought.* One of the two parts, here *a red wool sweater,* is **foregrounded**, and the other, *I bought,* **backgrounded.** Syntactically, the foregrounded element is made a complement of the verb *be* in its specifying sense – an internal complement in the *it*-cleft and basic

[26]The term 'cleft' is often used instead of *it*-cleft, i.e. in opposition to pseudo-cleft, rather than as a more general term covering both types. Pseudo-clefts are also called *wh*-clefts.

pseudo-cleft, a subject in the reversed pseudo-cleft.[27] The backgrounded component, by contrast, is subordinated by being placed in a relative construction.

We will say that [1ii–iv] have a foregrounded direct object, whereas [2ii–iv] have a foregrounded subject (and, as we will see, other constituents may also be foregrounded):

[2] i *The wording of the question confused me.* [non-cleft]
ii *It was the wording of the question that confused me.* [*it*-cleft]
iii *What confused me was the wording of the question.* [basic pseudo-cleft]
iv *The wording of the question was what confused me.* [reversed pseudo-cleft]

This way of speaking reflects the fact that *a red wool sweater* in [1ii–iv] corresponds to the direct object of the non-cleft [1i], while *the wording of the question* in [2ii–iv] corresponds to the subject of the non-cleft [2i]. Alternatively (and indeed preferably) we can explain the concept of foregrounded object and subject by reference to the relative construction: in [1ii–iv] the foregrounded *a red wool sweater* is the antecedent for the object of the relative, while in [2ii–iv] *the wording of the question* is the antecedent for the subject of the relative.

Backgrounding interpreted in terms of presupposition

In terms of information packaging, the effect of backgrounding is to mark the backgrounded information as presupposed. Examples [1ii–iv] presuppose that I bought something and assert that this something was a red wool sweater, and similarly [2ii–iv] presuppose that something confused me and assert that this something was the wording of the question. A presupposition, it will be recalled, is a proposition whose truth is taken for granted or not at issue.

Presuppositions are characteristically preserved under negation, and this is the source of an important difference between a cleft and the corresponding non-cleft. Compare:

[3] i a. *It was Tom that Sue married.* b. *It wasn't Tom that Sue married.*
ii a. *Sue married Tom.* b. *Sue didn't marry Tom.*

Both the positive cleft in [ia] and the negative cleft in [ib] convey that Sue married someone, but this is clearly not so in the corresponding negative non-cleft: [iib] can be used as readily in a context where Sue didn't marry anyone as in a context where she married someone other than Tom.[28]

The difference between non-clefts and clefts with respect to the effect of negation will not always be as sharp as this. Consider the following set:

[4] i a. *It was Sue who wrote the foreword.* b. *It wasn't Sue who wrote the foreword.*
ii a. *Sue wrote the foreword.* b. *Sue didn't write the foreword.*

Here both the negative clauses convey that someone wrote the foreword, but in the case of the non-cleft [iib] this feature of the interpretation is attributable to the use of the definite NP *the foreword*. This refers to some actual foreword, and one will therefore infer that someone wrote it. The point is, then, that in the cleft the presupposition is attributable to the cleft construction itself, whereas in the non-cleft if it is present at all it is not attributable to the general synactic structure but to independent factors.

[27] For the distinction between the specifying and ascriptive senses of *be*, see Ch. 4, §5.5.
[28] The presupposition that Sue married someone has the status of an entailment in [ia] and of a conversational implicature in [ib]: see Ch. 1, §5.4, for a fuller explanation of the concept of presupposition.

Foregrounded element as the expression of the value of a variable

The presupposition of a cleft clause can be given in the form of an open proposition containing a variable. For [1ii–iv] it is "I bought *x*", for [2ii–iv] it is "*x* confused me", and so on. The foregrounded element then expresses a value that is assigned to the variable by means of the *be* predication.

Exhaustiveness and exclusiveness

A further property of a positive cleft is that it implicates that the value assigned to the variable is exhaustive and exclusive. Thus [1ii–iv] implicate that a red wool sweater constituted the sum total of my purchase – that I didn't (on the occasion in question) buy anything else. This is not implicated by the non-cleft [1i], which is perfectly consistent with my having bought other things as well as the sweater. Compare, similarly:

[5] a. *I love you.* b. *It's you I love.*

This exhaustiveness implicature can be reinforced by adding *only*, or cancelled by negation of *only*:

[6] i *It is only on Tuesdays that they come to Baltimore.*
ii *It is not only you who will benefit from this decision.*

In the next two sections we will examine the syntax of *it*-clefts and pseudo-clefts in turn, and then in §9.4 we turn to pragmatic issues.

9.2 The form of *it*-clefts

It-cleft clauses have *it* as the subject of the matrix *be* clause, with the relative clause appearing in extranuclear position at the end. The *it* in subject function can be thought of as a place-holder for the variable, which is defined in a relative clause that is not syntactically part of the subject.

The *it*-cleft distinguished from other constructions containing an integrated relative clause

An *it*-cleft is superficially similar to a clause in which *it* is an ordinary referential pronoun and the relative clause is a modifier within the structure of the NP containing the antecedent, as in *It's something I've been wanting for a long time.* There may indeed be ambiguity between an *it*-cleft and a clause of this latter type. Compare:

[7] i A: *I hear they sacked the secretary.* B: *No, <u>it's the director who was sacked</u>.*
ii A: *Who's that talking to the police?* B: *<u>It's the director who was sacked.</u>*

In [i] the underlined clause is interpreted as an *it*-cleft: "the one they sacked is the director"; the non-cleft counterpart is *The director was sacked.* In [ii], by contrast, *it* refers to the person talking to the police and the relative clause *who was sacked* is part of the NP *the director who was sacked*, which functions as complement of *be*. In [i] the focal stress will fall on *director*, whereas in [ii] the default place for it is on *sacked.* A major distinguishing feature of the *it*-cleft construction is thus that the relative clause does not form a constituent with its antecedent. This correlates with the fact that the range of antecedents in an *it*-cleft is considerably greater than in the construction of [ii]. Note, for example, that *It's Kim who was sacked* could be substituted for B's response in [i] but not in [ii]: it is admissible as an *it*-cleft version of *Kim was sacked*, but *Kim who was sacked*, with an integrated relative clause, could not occur as the complement of *be* in [ii].

There is another, minor, construction that resembles the *it*-cleft more closely but is semantically quite distinct from it. It is found in proverbs like [8i], but also in new creations like [8ii]:

[8] i *It is a long lane that has no turning.*
ii *It is a foolhardy man, surely, who believes that the contrast had nothing to do with the expression of the tradition through, not only the Monarchy as an institution, but also the personal characters and examples set by George V and George VI.*

Example [i] is not an *it*-cleft version of *A long lane has no turning*; the meaning is, rather, "A lane that has no turning is a long one". Similarly for [ii] – not "A foolhardy man believes so-and-so", but "A man who believes so-and-so is foolhardy". The *be* here is ascriptive, not specifying.

Truncated *it*-clefts: omission of relative clause

The relative clause of an *it*-cleft construction can be omitted if it is recoverable from the prior discourse:

[9] A: *Who finished off the biscuits?* B: *I don't know; it certainly wasn't me.*

The underlined clause here can be analysed as a **truncated *it*-cleft**, equivalent to *It certainly wasn't me who finished off the biscuits.*

The cleft as an unbounded dependency construction

Relative clauses are unbounded dependency constructions, as described in Ch. 12, §7, and since the cleft contains a relative clause it too belongs in this family of constructions. Compare, then:

[10]	NON-CLEFT VERSION	CLEFT VERSION
i	a. *She wants a VW.*	b. *It's a VW she wants.*
ii	a. *She said she wants a VW.*	b. *It's a VW she said she wants.*
iii	a. *He thinks she said she wants a VW.*	b. *It's a VW he thinks she said she wants.*

The clefts here have foregrounding of the object of *want*: in [ib] *want* is the predicator of the relative clause itself, in [iib] it is the predicator of the clause functioning as a complement of *say* within the relative clause, and in [iiib] it is the predicator of the clause functioning as a complement of the *say* clause, which itself is a complement within the relative clause headed by *think*. And there is clearly no syntactic limit to how much further embedding of this kind we could add.

Range of elements that can be foregrounded

The foregrounded element in an *it*-cleft serves as the antecedent for a gap or pro-form in the relative clause, but this relative clause represents a distinct type, differing in certain respects from ordinary relative clauses, whether integrated or supplementary. Most importantly, it allows a somewhat broader range of elements to be relativised. In reviewing the elements that can be foregrounded, we need therefore to consider both the range of categories that can occur as complements of *be* in the matrix clause, and the range of associated functions in the relative clause.

(a) NPs

The most common type of *it*-cleft has an NP as the foregrounded element. We have already illustrated cases where a foregrounded NP is the antecedent for a subject or direct object in the relative clause; other functional possibilities are illustrated in [11], where the bracketing marks off the relative clauses:

[11] i *It's the president* [*I'm referring to* __]. [comp of preposition]
ii *It was only last year* [*that he got his tenure* __]. [adjunct]
iii *They made me secretary, but it wasn't secretary* [*I'd wanted to be* __]. [PC]
iv *It's you* [*whose head will roll*]. [subject-determiner in NP]

A more formal alternant of [i] is *It's the president* [*to whom I'm referring*]: see Ch. 7, §4.1, for the relation between these two variants. Relativisation of a predicative complement, as in [iii], is quite rare. A more common variant of [iv] has relativisation of the matrix NP rather than just the subject-determiner: *It's your head* [*that* __ *will roll*]. As with other relative constructions, relativisation of an indirect object is at best very marginal: ?*It was Sue* [*I gave* __ *the key*].[29]

(b) PPs

[12] i *It was with considerable misgivings that she accepted the position.*
ii *It's because you stood up for yourself that you were sacked.*
iii *It's downstairs they want to play.*

The next most common category is that of PP. In these examples we have *with* + NP complement in [i], *because* + clause complement in [ii], and a preposition with no complement, *downstairs*, in [iii]. Where the function is that of the adjunct rather than complement, it depends very much on the semantic category of the adjunct whether foregrounding is possible. Compare, for example, *It was because it was wet that they cancelled the trip* (reason) with #*It was although it was sunny that they cancelled the trip* (concession). The potential for foregrounding in the *it*-cleft construction is one of the parameters considered in the description of adjuncts in Ch. 8.

(c) Content clauses

Content clauses cannot generally be foregrounded:

[13] i #*It's that he did it deliberately that I'm inclined to think.*
ii #*It's why no one told us that I'm wondering.*

However, this restriction is not absolute:

[14] i *It's that he's so self-satisfied that I find offputting.*
ii *It's not whether you win or lose that matters, but how you play the game.*

In general, content clauses are foregrounded much more readily in pseudo-clefts than in *it*-clefts. Compare [13], for example, with *What I'm inclined to think is that he did it deliberately* and *What I'm wondering is why no one told us.*

(d) Non-finite clauses

[15] i *It's certainly not to make life easier for us that they are changing the rules.*
ii *It was listening to Sue's story that made me realise how lucky we have been.*

[29] For the choice between nominative and accusative case in foregrounded personal pronouns (*It is I/me who told them*), see Ch. 5, §16.2.

An infinitival purpose adjunct can readily be foregrounded, as in [i], but other infinitivals are hardly possible. In many cases the pseudo-cleft is again strongly preferred: compare *What I want is to be able to spend more time on research* with #*It's to be able to spend more time on research that I want.* Gerund-participials, as in [ii], are permitted, albeit uncommon. Compare, for example, the non-cleft *They began playing golf* with the *it*-cleft **It was playing golf that they began.* The inadmissibility of the latter correlates with the fact that the complement of catenative *begin* cannot be questioned with *what* (*They began playing golf* cannot be used to answer the question *What did they begin?*), and in such cases there is no pseudo-cleft either (**What they began was playing golf*).

(e) AdvPs

[16] i *It was only gradually that I came to realise how much I was being exploited.*
ii *She learns sex is something sordid,* [*and when she experiences it for the first time herself it is incoherently, clumsily, but half shyly and half inquisitively*].
iii *It isn't often they're as late as this.*

Example [ii] here is truncated, with omission of the relative clause *that she experiences it.*

(f) AdjPs

[17] i *It's not lonely he made me feel – it's angry.*
ii *It wasn't green I told you to paint it.*

Here we have foregrounding of an adjectival predicative complement, but (except in Irish English where examples like %*It's selfish you are* are quite normal in informal style) *it*-clefts of this type are very rare.

It as raised complement

The *it* of the *it*-cleft construction commonly occurs in a higher clause than the one with *be*: it can function as a raised subject or object. But, unlike the *it* of extraposition, it cannot occur as the object in a complex-transitive clause – we need a construction with *be*:

[18] i *It seems to be the switch that is defective.* [raised subject]
ii *I believe it to be her father who was primarily responsible.* [raised object]
iii **I consider it you who are to blame.* [object of complex-transitive]

Negation

An *it*-cleft clause is a complex structure having a matrix clause with *be* as head and a subordinate clause with the form of a relative. Either clause (or indeed both) can be negated:

[19] a. *It was Kim who didn't complain.* b. *It wasn't Kim who complained.*

The difference in meaning is very clear: if the negation is in the relative clause it is part of the presupposition, but if it is in the matrix clause it isn't. Thus the presupposition of [a] is "Someone didn't complain", while that of [b] is "Someone complained".[30]

Tense

In the default case the tense of the matrix matches that of the relative clause:

[20] a. *It is you she likes.* b. *It was you she liked.*

[30] In the case of [19a] there will generally be an implicature that there are one or more others who did complain.

But there is certainly no grammatical requirement that the tenses match in this way: instead of [b] we could equally well have *It is you she liked*, with present tense in the matrix clause and preterite in the relative clause. The felicity of such a mixed tense *it*-cleft will depend on the content of the clause. In *It was my great-grandfather who founded the company in 1892*, for example, it would be inappropriate to have *is* in the matrix clause.

Preposing of the foregrounded element

As an internal complement in the *be* clause, the foregrounded element can be preposed:

[21] A: *Was it Sue who polished off the cookies?* B: *No, [Pat it was who ate them].*

Extensions of the main pattern

(a) Non-finite clause in place of the relative clause

The element expressing the presupposition sometimes has the form of a gerund-participial or (for some speakers) infinitival rather than a relative clause:

[22] a. *Is it Kim making all that noise?* b. %*It is you to serve.*

These are equivalent to relatives containing the verb *be*: *who is making all that noise*; *who are to serve.*

(b) Demonstratives in place of *it*

A demonstrative, interpreted deictically, can be used instead of *it* in subject function:

[23] i *Those are my biscuits you're eating.*
ii *This is a serious problem we have here.*
iii *This is Jill speaking.*

Example [iii] is most likely to be uttered by Jill herself, to identify who is speaking – e.g. on the telephone.

It-clefts and this minor variant with a demonstrative as subject make up the class of clefts proper,[31] as opposed to pseudo-clefts, to which we now turn.

9.3 The form of pseudo-clefts

The pseudo-cleft has a fused relative construction defining a variable whose value is specified by the foregrounded element. As we have noted, the usual alignment is for the element defining the variable to occur as subject and the one giving the value as internal complement, but the reverse order is also possible:

[24] i *What I need is a long cool drink.* [basic pseudo-cleft]
ii *A long cool drink is what I need.* [reversed pseudo-cleft]

The relation between the syntax and the semantics of pseudo-clefts is more transparent than with *it*-clefts. In [24], the fused relative construction (discussed in detail in Ch. 12, §6) corresponds to "the *x* [I need *x*]" (or "the *x* such that I need *x*"), the foregrounded

[31] One other variant has *seem* instead of *be* as the verb: *It seems (like) only yesterday that we were worrying about which school to send her to*, "It seems as if it were only yesterday that . . . ". This pattern is very restricted: it's doubtful if anything other than a past time expression could be foregrounded – cf. **It seems (like) Kim who broke it.* It is exceptional in that *seem* does not normally take a specifying complement: #*The time I saw her last seems yesterday.*

element represents "a long cool drink", and *be* expresses identity, hence that "a long cool drink" is the value of the variable *x*.

Contrasting constructions

The pseudo-cleft needs to be distinguished from a number of other constructions that bear some superficial resemblance to it:

[25] i *What's going to happen next is a mystery.*
ii *What we can do to stop them is the question we ought to be addressing.*
iii *What they did was a disgrace.*
iv *Her performance was what I'd call extremely competent.*
v *The easiest such object to analyse is what we shall call a 'rigid body'.*

In the first place, we must distinguish between fused relatives and open interrogative clauses, as compared in Ch. 12, §6.2. While the underlined constituent is a fused relative NP in [iii–v], it is an interrogative clause in [i–ii], and this immediately excludes [i–ii] from the category of pseudo-clefts.

Secondly, we must distinguish between specifying and ascriptive uses of the verb *be*: it is the specifying *be* that occurs in pseudo-clefts. This excludes [25iii–iv], which have ascriptive *be*. Thus in [iii] the predicate *was a disgrace* expresses a judgement about what they did: it does not identify what they did. Similarly, [iv] (where the fused relative is an internal complement rather than a subject) does not identify the variable *x* in the open proposition "I'd call *x* extremely competent": rather, it expresses an evaluation of her performance, and is semantically similar to *Her performance was extremely competent.*

Finally, when we have a clause containing specifying *be* and a fused relative we have to distinguish between cases where the fused relative expresses the variable and those where it expresses the value: only in the former case do we have a pseudo-cleft. This is why [25v] (taken from a science textbook) is excluded. This clause does not serve to identify what we shall call a 'rigid body' (it is not a pseudo-cleft version of *We shall call the easiest such object to analyse a 'rigid body'*): rather, it serves to identify the easiest such object to analyse. Putting it slightly differently, the question that it implicitly answers is not "What shall we call a 'rigid body'?", but "What is the easiest such object to analyse?".

Range of elements that can function as the foregrounded element

(a) NPs

The foregrounded element is often an NP, as in [24]. This category itself includes fused relatives, so we may have two fused relatives in the one clause: *What I wanted was what you've just given Sue.* The NP category represents the main source of overlap between the *it*-cleft and the pseudo-cleft, as in [1] above (*It was a red wool sweater that I bought* and *What I bought was a red wool sweater*).

(b) Declarative and interrogative content clauses

[26] i *What I meant was that you don't have to come if you don't want to.*
ii *What puzzles me is why they didn't accept the offer in the first place.*

We noted above that content clauses are rare in the *it*-cleft construction; in the basic pseudo-cleft, by contrast, they represent the most common category.

(c) Non-finite clauses

[27] i *What would be better would be to try and find a compromise solution.*
ii *What you must do is (to) apply for special leave.*
iii *What annoys me is having to fill in all these forms.*
iv *What he's doing is simply repeating what his wife said.*

Again, non-finites occur predominantly with pseudo-clefts rather than *it*-clefts. In particular, they very commonly occur with *do* as the verb of the fused relative, as in [ii/iv], and here the *it*-cleft is normally inadmissible: **It is (to) apply for special leave that you must do*; **It is simply repeating what his wife said that he's doing*. Infinitival *to* is obligatory in [i] (as also in the corresponding non-cleft *To try and find a compromise solution would be better*), but optional in the construction with *do*.[32]

(d) AdjPs

[28] i *What her father is, if you want my view, is arrogant, dogmatic, and pig-headed.*
ii *Insensitive is how I'd be inclined to describe him.*

AdjPs are rare, but generally more acceptable than in *it*-clefts.

(e) PPs

[29] i *Up in the mountains is where I'd like to live.*
ii *In the morning is when I do my best work.*

PPs are found predominantly in *it*-clefts, but locative and temporal PPs are possible in pseudo-clefts like [29].

Range of relative lexemes

Not all relative lexemes are permitted in fused relatives, and hence in pseudo-clefts. Most importantly, ***who*** is excluded:

[30] **Who achieved the best result was Angela.*

Instead we need an *it*-cleft (*It was Angela who achieved the best result*) or some other specifying clause (such as *The one who achieved the best result was Angela*).

Pseudo-clefts with no non-cleft counterpart

Pseudo-clefts do not always correspond straightforwardly to non-cleft counterparts:

[31] i *What is unique about milk is its richness in minerals and vitamins.*
ii *What I like about it is that it is so compact.*
iii *What went wrong was that the timer malfunctioned.*
iv *What I object to is that they won't allow a secret ballot.*
v *What they want apparently is that we should meet only twice a year.*

For these the non-cleft counterparts are ungrammatical: **Its richness in minerals and vitamins is unique about milk*; **I like about it that it is so compact*; **That the timer malfunctioned went wrong*; **I object to that they won't allow a secret ballot*; **They want that we should meet only twice a year*.[33] Compare similarly [28ii] with **I'd be inclined to describe him insensitive.*

[32] In the *do* construction it is possible, in relatively informal style, for the value phrase to be a declarative content clause: *What they did was they threw us out and locked the door.*

[33] There are some AmE dialects in which this last is allowed, but for most speakers *want* does not take finite complements.

Related structures

Very similar in meaning to pseudo-clefts are the [b] examples in [32]:

[32] i a. *What impressed me was her wit.* b. *The thing that impressed me was her wit.*
ii a. *What I need is a little peace.* b. *All I need is a little peace.*
iii a. **Who deserves the credit is Jill.* b. *The one who deserves the credit is Jill.*

As noted above, [iiib] provides one way of filling the gap created by the inadmissibility of ***who*** in fused relatives. Like pseudo-clefts, the [b] examples contain *be* in its specifying sense, and the internal complement specifies the value of the variable defined in the subject. The subject, however, is not a fused relative, but an NP with a general noun as head (or fused determiner-head), and an integrated relative clause as modifier. This structure allows for expansion of the same kind as is found with NPs occurring in other kinds of clause – compare [ib], for example, with *The two things that impressed me were her wit and her modesty*; *The other thing that impressed me was her wit*; *One of the things that impressed me was her wit*; and so on.

On the term 'pseudo-cleft'

The points illustrated in [31–32] help explain why the construction is called 'pseudo-cleft'. The *it*-cleft can almost invariably be matched with an equivalent non-cleft,[34] and it clearly represents a distinct construction by virtue of the special use of *it* and the special type of relative clause. The pseudo-cleft, by contrast, can very often not be matched with an equivalent non-cleft, and rather than constituting a distinct construction it simply represents the particular case of the specifying *be* construction where the element defining the variable is realised by a fused relative. The difference between the [a] and [b] examples in [32] has to do with the form of the subject NP and has no real significance at the level of the clause.

Examples like [31] show that it would be unsatisfactory to attempt to describe the pseudo-cleft derivatively, in terms of a cleaving operation applied to a more elementary construction. Take [31ii], for example. There is no source for this because **I like about it that it is so compact* is ungrammatical. One reason for this is that *like* cannot normally take a content clause as a complement. But this grammatical property of *like* is irrelevant to [31ii] itself: the content clause is admissible here because it satisfies the semantic requirement that it describe a situation that one can like.

This grammar, of course, is not adopting a derivational mode of description, and process terms are serving simply as convenient metaphors. From this point of view, what examples like [31] show is that there is a considerably less systematic relation between pseudo-clefts and non-clefts than there is between *it*-clefts and non-clefts. But from an information-packaging point of view what pseudo-clefts have in common with *it*-clefts is that they divide the message into two parts, one presented as a presupposition, the other a specification of the value of the variable in the presupposition. This is so whether or not there is a corresponding non-cleft.

[34] The qualification is needed to accommodate examples like [14i] above, where the non-cleft counterpart is **I find that he's so self-satisfied offputting.* But the unacceptability here can be remedied simply by applying extraposition: *I find it offputting that he is so self-satisfied.*

9.4 Issues of information packaging: discourse status of the presupposition

9.4.1 Two types of *it*-cleft: old presupposition vs new presupposition

It-clefts fall into two types according to whether the information represented by the presupposition is discourse-old or discourse-new.

(a) Discourse-old presupposition

[33] i A: *Did you turn the air-conditioning off?* B: *No, it was Kim.*
ii *Inexperienced dancers often have difficulty in ending the Natural Turn in the correct alignment . . . It is usually the man who is at fault.*
iii *John only did the illustrations for the book. It was Mary who wrote the story.*

The context for [i] is one in which it is known that someone turned the air-conditioning off; B's response takes the form of a truncated *it*-cleft, a construction that permits the omission of discourse-old information. In [ii] the presupposition that someone is at fault follows from what has just been said. In [iii] the existence of the book suggests that someone wrote the story.

(b) Discourse-new presupposition

[34] i *It was fifty years ago that the first real computer was built in Philadelphia.*
ii *It is with great pleasure that I now declare this Exhibition open.*
iii *The Indians were helpful in many ways. It was they who taught the settlers how to plant and harvest crops successfully in the New World.*

In examples of this kind the bulk of the new information is conveyed by the relative clause. As in the first type, however, the information in the relative clause is presented as a presupposition, i.e. as shared or uncontroversial. The concept of presupposition is thus distinct from that of familiar information: information does not have to be familiar to be presupposed.

The foregrounded element in this second type of *it*-cleft may be an adjunct, as in [34i–ii], or a complement (typically a subject), as in [iii]. In the latter case, it will tend to represent old information.[35]

Foregrounding and focus

The kind of prominence given to an element by foregrounding it in an *it*-cleft bears a considerable resemblance to that which is given by marking an element prosodically as focus. Thus in the context of [33iii] *MARY wrote the story* may convey much the same information as *It was Mary who wrote the story.* Very often, moreover, the two kinds of marking are combined, with the foregrounded element being the prosodically marked focus: *It was MARY who wrote the story.* It is important to emphasise, however, that the foregrounded element does not have to be focus: the concepts of foregrounded element and presupposition cannot be identified with those of focus and focus-frame.[36]

First, the type of *it*-cleft that has a discourse-new presupposition generally has the focus within the relative clause, as it is the relative clause that expresses the new and most important information. Secondly, in the type with a discourse-old presupposition

[35] Example [34ii] shows that this construction is one place where the verb of a subordinate clause can be used performatively (see Ch. 10, §3.1).
[36] Many works, however, use the term 'focus' for what we are calling the foregrounded element.

there may be factors that override the default selection of the foregrounded element as focus:

[35] i *It* CAN'T *have been Jill who leaked the news to the press.*
ii *It was Jill who designed* THIS *house too.*

Example [i] has *can't* as focus: it is an instance of the emphatic polarity construction, used to deny a salient proposition. In [ii] the focus is located within the relative clause for reasons of contrast between one house and another.

Three other cases worth noting are illustrated in [36]:

[36] i A: *You cheated me.* B: *On the contrary, it was* YOU *who cheated* ME.
ii *It's* JILL'S *husband they've charged.*
iii *It was a very* TROUBLED *wife that greeted Harry on his return that night.*

In [36i] we have a discourse-old open proposition "*x* cheated *y*", and the new information is that the value of *x* is "you (i.e. A)" and the value of *y* is "me (i.e. B)". The formal structure of the *it*-cleft, however, allows only one variable to be specified by the foregrounded element. This must be a single constituent, and relative clauses (unlike open interrogatives) allow only one relative pro-form or gap, so we can't have **It was you me who cheated who.* Instead, one variable (corresponding to the subject) is specified by the foregrounded element, and the other by the focused element in the relative clause.

In [36ii] the focus is just part of the foregrounded element. The *it*-cleft construction assigns presuppositional status to "They've charged *x*", but the selection of *Jill's* as focus treats "husband" as old information too; the old information is thus "They've charged *x*'s husband", and the new information is that "Jill" is the value of *x*. In this example focus and foregrounded element can be made to match: *It is Jill whose husband they've charged.* Often, however, they can't: *It's Jill's* FORMER *husband they've charged, not her* PRESENT *one.* A modifier within an NP can't be foregrounded, so instead of *former* and *present* we must foreground a whole NP, with the focus picking out *former* and *present* as new.

Example [36iii] is an unusual type of *it*-cleft because, in spite of its form, it does not serve to identify who greeted Harry. Note, for example, that *a very troubled wife* would not constitute a felicitous response to the question *Who greeted Harry on his return that night?* Thus rather than specifying the value of the variable in the open proposition "*x* greeted Harry on his return that night", [36iii] in fact treats the value of *x* as old information, and the new information imparted concerns the state of the person concerned.

9.4.2 Pseudo-clefts in comparison with *it*-clefts

With pseudo-clefts, there is no analogue of the *it*-cleft construction with a discourse-new presupposition: in a felicitous pseudo-cleft the presupposed information expressed in the fused relative must always be discourse-old. Consider the following examples:

[37] i A: *You said you'd be home early.* B: *No, what I said was that I'd come home as soon as I could.*
ii *Why you would want to refinance is perfectly clear. What I can't understand is how you were able to refinance with such a lousy credit rating.*
iii *What I want to do in this lecture is to place Racine's work in a historical context.*

In [i] the presupposition represents information ("I said *x*") that has been explicitly evoked in the preceding discourse. It is more usual, however, for the relation between the presupposition and what has gone before to be somewhat less direct than this. In [ii] the relation is one of contrast – between being perfectly clear and being hard or impossible to understand; mention of something being clear makes salient the question of level of comprehensibility. Example [iii] might be the initial sentence of a discourse, specifically a lecture, and serves to show that the discourse-old status of the presupposition may derive from the context of situation rather than from prior mention. The context is one where I am beginning a lecture, and here it can be taken for granted that I have intentions about what I will discuss in the lecture.

The examples in [37] all have a clause as the foregrounded element, and we have noted that in such cases the pseudo-cleft is generally preferred over the *it*-cleft. Where the foregrounded element is an NP, the two constructions will often be equally felicitous:

[38] i a. *Sue is planning to buy a Camry, but it's a Lexus that I want.*
b. *Sue is planning to buy a Camry, but what I want is a Lexus.*
ii a. A: *You're a history teacher, aren't you?* B. *No, it's economics that I teach.*
b. A: *You're a history teacher, aren't you?* B. *No, what I teach is economics.*

The *it*-cleft is characteristically used when the foregrounded element is contrastive. In [38] the contrast is explicit: *a Lexus* vs *a Camry* and *economics* vs *history*. It may also be implicit, as when in answer to the question *Who broke the vase?* I reply, *It was Kim* or *It wasn't me*, with an implicit contrast between Kim or me and other potential culprits.

The pseudo-cleft can also be used in contexts of contrast – though there is no truncated version, and no form with ***who***, and hence no pseudo-cleft counterpart to *It was Kim* and *It wasn't me* in this question–answer context. The pseudo-cleft also readily occurs in the absence of contrast when the relevant presupposition is salient. Compare the following, where [ii–iii] are to be contextualised as the opening sentence of a lecture:

[39] i a. *That was hard work. What I need now is a long cool drink.*
b. *That was hard work. #It's a long cool drink that I need now.*
ii a. *What I want to discuss in this lecture is the historical context of Racine's work.*
b. *#It is the historical context of Racine's work that I want to discuss in this lecture.*
iii a. *#What my name is, ladies and gentlemen, is Kim Aldermaston.*
b. *#It is Kim Aldermaston, ladies and gentlemen, that my name is.*

The end of a piece of hard work makes the needs of the worker salient, though there is no contrast between a long cool drink and anything else. In this context, the pseudo-cleft [ia] is felicitous, but the *it*-cleft [ib] is not. The examples in [ii] can be similarly accounted for. In the context of beginning a lecture, as noted for [37iii], it can be taken for granted that I have plans as to what I am going to discuss. The open proposition "I want to discuss *x* in this lecture" will therefore be salient, and the pseudo-cleft [iia], unlike the *it*-cleft [iib], is accordingly felicitous. This context, however, does not make salient the proposition that I have a name, and hence in [iii] even the pseudo-cleft version is infelicitous.

There are also conditions under which the *it*-cleft is preferred:

[40] i *What is it you teach?*
ii *It is usual for a mare who has produced one winning jumper to produce others, even if not of the same standard, and generally in steeple-chasers it is the influence of the mare that predominates.*

In [i] the foregrounded element is questioned; in general this is not possible in pseudo-clefts: #*What is what you teach?* Even in polar questions the *it*-cleft is often more natural: compare *Is it history you teach?* and #*Is what you teach history?* In [ii] the foregrounded element contains a constituent (*the mare*) that is discourse-old even though it is focal (and hence new as an instantiation of the variable in "the influence of *x* predominates"). The pseudo-cleft *what predominates is the influence of the mare* has *the mare* in final position, which would be more natural if it were not discourse-old.

10 Passive voice

Passive contrasts with active in a system of voice, as illustrated in [1]:

[1] i *Oswald assassinated Kennedy.* [active]
ii *Kennedy was assassinated by Oswald.* [passive]

The general term **voice** applies to a system where the contrasting forms differ in the way semantic roles are aligned with syntactic functions, normally with some concomitant marking on the verb. The terms **active** and **passive** are applied on the basis of the alignment of roles with functions in clauses that express an action, like those in [1]. Example [i] is called active because here the subject, *Oswald*, is aligned with an active role, with the role of agent: Oswald performed the action. Example [ii] is called passive because the subject, *Kennedy*, is associated with a passive role, the role of patient: Kennedy was the one on whom the action was performed.

Many clauses of course do not express actions:

[2] i *Most members of the cabinet hated the premier.* [active]
ii *The premier was hated by most members of the cabinet.* [passive]

Most members of the cabinet is aligned with the role of experiencer rather than agent, and *the premier* is aligned with the role of stimulus rather than patient, but syntactically [2i] belongs with [1i], and [2ii] with [1ii], and for this reason they are classified as active and passive respectively. As usual, the names of the categories are based on semantic properties that do not apply to all members, but the issue of which clauses in English are active and which are passive is to be determined by their syntactic properties. We begin therefore by looking at the syntactic properties that distinguish passives from actives, and then in §10.2 consider some of the factors that favour or require the selection of an active over a passive or vice versa.

10.1 Syntax of the passive

10.1.1 Structural differences between active and passive clauses

From a syntactic point of view we find large-scale structural differences between an active clause and its passive counterpart. A representative pair of examples like those given in [3] differ in the four ways stated summarily in [4]:

[3] i *Pat stole my surfboard.* [active]
ii *My surfboard was stolen by Pat.* [passive]

[4] i The subject of the active (*Pat*) appears in the passive as the complement of the preposition *by*.
ii The object of the active (*my surfboard*) appears as the subject of the passive.
iii The verb of the active appears in the passive in the past participle form (*stolen*).
iv The passive contains an extra verb, the auxiliary *be*.

We will comment briefly in turn on these four points.

The internalised complement and the distinction between long and short passives

The PP *by Pat* in [3ii] we refer to as the **internalised complement**: in the active *Pat* is the subject and hence external to the VP, but in the passive it is internal to the VP.[37]

With a small number of exceptions, the internalised complement is omissible, and we accordingly distinguish between **long passives**, in which it is present, and **short passives**, which contain no internalised complement:[38]

[5]	LONG PASSIVES	SHORT PASSIVES
i	a. *My surfboard was stolen by Pat.*	b. *My surfboard was stolen.*
ii	a. *His plan was rejected by the board.*	b. *His plan was rejected.*

Short passives have no exact active counterpart. Example [ib] conveys much the same information as *Someone stole my surfboard*, but this is the active counterpart of the long passive *My surfboard was stolen by someone*. The difference between this and [ib] may be negligible, but often there will be a more significant difference between passives with and without an internalised complement. For example, [iib] is not pragmatically equivalent to *His plan was rejected by someone* (the passive counterpart of *Someone rejected his plan*): we will generally understand from [iib] that the plan was rejected by the person or body to whom it was submitted. On the other hand, an active clause will encode some information about the subject that is not explicitly encoded in a short passive even if part or all of it is implied or suggested. We return to this issue in §10.2; in the meantime, where we pair actives with short passives in the examples below, it is to be understood that we are not presenting them as fully equivalent.

The preposition *by* has numerous uses other than that of marking the internalised complement. *This result was achieved by dubious means* is thus a short passive, with the *by* phrase functioning as a means adjunct, just as it does in the active *They achieved this result by dubious means*.

Externalisation of the object from the VP of the passive

Just as the external complement of the active, the subject, appears internal to the VP in the passive, so the internal complement of the active, the direct object, is external to the VP in the passive, i.e. it appears as subject. Note that *by Pat* in [3ii] is a PP, not an NP,

[37] The internalised complement is very often referred to as the 'agent'; we avoid the latter term because it is also used (as in this book) as the name of a semantic role. As illustrated in [2ii], this element is not always associated with the agent role, and it is therefore important to maintain a clear distinction between syntactic functions and semantic roles.

[38] Exceptional cases where the internalised complement is not omissible include those with *precede* or *follow* used in a temporal sense: *Dinner was preceded/followed by several speeches.* Also *actuate* as used in *His behaviour was actuated by blind self-interest.* The fact that the *by* phrase is generally omissible leads many grammarians to treat it as an adjunct: see the discussion of this issue in Ch. 4, §1.2. In keeping with the terminology mentioned in footnote 37, short passives are often referred to as 'agentless passives'.

and hence not an object; the effect of switching from the active to the passive in [3] is thus to switch from a transitive clause to an intransitive one.

It is an invariant feature of the passive that the VP lacks a complement that is present in the corresponding active. The element that is externalised, however, is not invariably the direct object. Compare, for example:

[6]		ACTIVE	PASSIVE
	i	a. *My aunt gave Ed a pair of shoes.*	b. *Ed was given a pair of shoes by my aunt.*
	ii	a. *Everyone refers to her paper.*	b. *Her paper is referred to by everyone.*

In [i] it is the indirect object that is externalised, i.e. *Ed* is the indirect object of the active and the subject, or external complement, of the passive. In [ii] *her paper* is the object of a preposition in the active, and the subject in the passive. We review the various kinds of complements that can be externalised in §10.1.2.

Past participle inflection of the verb

The passive represents one of the two uses of the past participle form of the verb, the other being the perfect. The perfect use is normally found in the complement of auxiliary *have*, as in *Pat has stolen my surfboard*, and in such cases it is clearly distinguishable from the passive use. There are certain places, however, where passive and perfect uses are in immediate contrast:

[7] i [*Considered by many overqualified for the post,*] *she withdrew her application.*
ii [*Now fallen on hard times,*] *he looked a good deal older.*

The underlined form in [i] is a passive use of the past participle, while that in [ii] is a perfect use. The passive can be recognised by the internalised complement *by many*, and by the fact that the VP lacks the object that we have in active *Many considered her overqualified for the post*. In [ii], however, the VP is interpreted in just the same way as in *He had fallen on hard times*, which is explicitly marked as perfect by the auxiliary *have*.

The past participle form of the verb is almost, but not quite, an invariant feature of the passive. There is one construction in which the verb appears in the gerund-participle form, as in [8]:

[8] *This draft needs checking carefully by the editor.*

This sentence can be paraphrased as *This article needs to be checked carefully by the editor*. Like the latter, it contains a *by* phrase in internalised complement function, and this is sufficient to establish it as passive in spite of the exceptional morphology. We refer to this construction as a 'concealed passive', because it does not have the usual past participle form; for further discussion, see Ch. 14, §2.3.

Be-passives, *get*-passives, and bare passives

Consider finally the fourth difference between the active and passive clauses in [3], the presence of auxiliary ***be*** in the passive. We have noted that the verb of the active appears in the passive in the past participle form: auxiliary ***be*** then carries the preterite inflection that in the active appears on ***steal***. More generally, the auxiliary takes on the inflection of the active verb except for any person–number feature, which is determined by agreement with the subject. Compare, for example:

[9]			
	i	a. *Pat was examining the contract.*	b. *The contract was being examined by Pat.*
	ii	a. *Jill writes the reports.*	b. *The reports are written by Jill.*

The gerund-participle inflection carried in the active [ia] by ***examine*** appears in the passive on ***be***, with ***examine*** taking on the past participle inflection; the first ***be*** in [ib] (*was*) is the progressive auxiliary, matching that of [ia]. In [ii] the present tense inflection carried by active *writes* appears on ***be***, but the agreement is with the subject *the reports*.

Not all passive clauses contain ***be***; some have ***get*** instead, while there are also passives that contain neither of these verbs. These latter we call **bare passives**. Compare:

[10] i *Kim was mauled by our neighbour's dog.* [*be*-passive]
ii *Kim got mauled by our neighbour's dog.* [*get*-passive]
iii *He saw Kim mauled by our neighbour's dog.* } [bare passive]
iv *The guy mauled by our neighbour's dog is in intensive care.* }

Bare passive clauses usually have no overt subject, as here (*Kim* in [iii] being syntactically an object in the *see* clause: see Ch. 14, §5.6.2). Examples where a bare passive does have an overt subject are seen in [11]:

[11] i *All things considered, we're lucky not to have been sued for a lot more.* } [short]
ii *People really are inconsiderate – present company excepted.* }
iii *My house wrecked by a tornado is something I don't ever want to see.* } [long]
iv *Their vehicle immobilised by the mud, they had to escape on foot.* }

Because the verb is in the past participle form, such clauses are always non-finite and hence restricted to subordinate position: passive main clauses always contain either *be* or *get*, as in [10i–ii].

Expanded passives

Be and *get* are catenative verbs, verbs taking non-finite complements. The complement they have in [10i–ii] is the same as the second complement of *see* in [iii] and the modifier of *guy* in [iv] – i.e. a bare passive. We therefore take *be*- and *get*-passives to be **expanded passives**: they contain a bare passive augmented by means of a catenative verb that can carry the full range of verb inflections. This enables the passive clause to occur in any syntactic context instead of being restricted to dependent positions, like the passives of [10iii–iv] and [11]. As is clear from the examples given in [5] and [11], the distinction between expanded and bare (depending on the presence or absence of *be* or *get*) is independent of that between long and short (depending on the presence or absence of a *by* phrase as an internalised complement). The distinction between *be* and *get* as markers of expanded passives is discussed in §10.1.4; in the meantime, we will focus on the construction with *be*, which is the more frequent of the two.

Passives without an overt subject

Because the subject is crucially involved in the relationship between active and passive clauses we cannot have a straightforward voice contrast in a context where it is missing – that is, when the subject is understood. Compare, for example:

[12] i a. *The best solution is [for Dr Jones to examine your son].* b. *The best solution is [for your son to be examined by Dr Jones].*
ii a. *The best solution is [___ to examine your son].* b. *The best solution is [___ to be examined by Dr Jones].*

In [i] the bracketed subordinate clauses have overt subjects and stand in the normal active–passive relationship. In [ii], however, the subjects are left unexpressed and we no longer have equivalence: there is nothing in the context to lead us to interpret the missing subject of the active as identical to the NP of the internalised complement of the passive (*Dr Jones*) and the missing subject of the passive as identical to the object of the active (*your son*).

There are constructions, however, where the missing subject is recoverable from a higher clause so that changing an NP in that higher clause can result in the missing subject's being interpreted in such a way as to establish equivalence:

[13]	i	a. *Kim seems to intimidate Pat.*	b. *Pat seems to be intimidated by Kim.*
	ii	a. *Jill may chair the meeting.*	b. *The meeting may be chaired by Jill.*

Here the subject of the subordinate infinitival clause is recovered from the subject of the matrix clause. In [i] we thus interpret the subject of *intimidate* as *Kim* in the active, and as *Pat* in the passive, and analogously in [ii]. From a semantic point of view, [a] and [b] are equivalent in each pair, just as active *Kim intimidated Pat* and *Jill chaired the meeting* are equivalent to their passive counterparts *Pat was intimidated by Kim* and *The meeting was chaired by Jill.* But from a syntactic point of view, [b] is not the passive of [a] in [13i–ii]: it is not the matrix clauses headed by *seem* and *may* that are passive, but the subordinate clauses embedded within them. In the rest of this section, however, we will make use of examples like those in [13] from time to time, with the understanding that they illustrate the active–passive relationship indirectly rather than directly.

Verbal passives and adjectival passives

The verb *be* serves, of course, not only as a passive marker but also as a copula, taking a predicative complement in the complex-intransitive construction. And there can be ambiguity between the two constructions:

[14] *The vase was broken.* [*be*-passive or complex-intransitive]

As a passive (of the short variety) this describes an event, as does the active clause *Someone broke the vase.* As a complex-intransitive clause it describes a state – the state resulting from someone or something breaking the vase. In the first interpretation *broken* is a bare passive clause consisting of just the head, the verb *broken*; in the second *broken* is an adjective. We will follow the widespread practice of describing *broken* in the second sense as an **adjectival passive**, but it is to be emphasised that this represents an extended and derivative sense of the term 'passive'. We will look at the relation between adjectival passives and **verbal passives**, i.e. passives proper, in §10.1.3.

10.1.2 Complements externalised from the passive VP

The invariant feature of the passive, we have seen, is that the VP lacks a complement that is present in the corresponding active – a complement that appears as subject of the passive clause (or, if the clause has no overt subject, one that represents the understood subject). In this section we review the kinds of complement that can be externalised in this way, identifying them by their function in the active counterpart.

(a) Direct object of monotransitive clause

[15] a. *The hail damaged <u>the car</u>.* b. *<u>The car</u> was damaged by the hail.*

This represents the simplest and most common case. Most verbs taking just one object permit passivisation, but there are some which – either generally or in certain senses – do not, being restricted to active voice:

[16] i a. *A strange adventure befell him.* b. **He was befallen by a strange adventure.*
ii a. *He failed her.* b. **She was failed by him.*

The restriction applies to *befall* quite generally but to *fail* only in the sense of "let down": [iib] is perfectly acceptable when it means "not pass", as in some kind of test. In [17] we provide some further examples of actives containing verbs that, in the sense illustrated, do not occur in passive clauses:

[17] *Do you think [this behaviour becomes you]? This resort boasts the best beaches on the east coast. This bottle contains the milk you need for your breakfast. A packet of cigarettes costs around seven dollars. Three squared equals nine. These shoes fit me perfectly. Jill has the best qualifications. This auditorium holds about a hundred people. Most people lack the energy that she has. I don't think [they mind your criticism]. The enemy numbered over 5,000. They're talking politics again. This suitcase weighs exactly that amount.*

Because the objects here cannot be externalised by passivisation they differ sharply from prototypical objects. The view taken here, however, is that the resistance of the verbs in [17] to passivisation does not provide convincing grounds for saying that the post-verbal NPs are not objects: passivisation does not provide either a necessary or a sufficient condition for object status (see Ch. 4, §4.1).

It should also be noted that with some verbs, the direct object cannot be externalised when it combines with some other complement – a catenative or predicative complement:

[18] i a. *They want Paul to resign.* b. **Paul is wanted to resign.*
ii a. *People here like beer lukewarm.* b. **Beer is liked lukewarm.*

The [b] examples may be contrasted with the well-formed *That isn't [what is wanted]*, where *want* has no catenative complement, and *He isn't much liked by his colleagues*, where *like* has no predicative complement.[39]

(b) Indirect and direct object in ditransitive clauses

[19] i a. *My father gave me this watch.* b. *I was given this watch by my father.*
ii a. *My father gave me this watch.* b. *%This watch was given me by my father.*

In principle, ditransitive actives have two passive counterparts depending on whether it is the indirect or the direct object that is externalised, as in [ib] and [iib] respectively. The version with the indirect object externalised is called the **first passive**, while the one with the direct object externalised is the **second passive** – terms based on the linear position of the relevant object in the active construction. The first passive is much more common; the second is hardly possible in AmE, and even in BrE is acceptable in only a limited range of cases: for further discussion, see Ch. 4, §4.3.

[39] A further point about voice in the catenative construction is that most verbs taking object + bare infinitival in the active require a *to*-infinitival in the passive: compare *They made me do the cooking* and *I was made to do the cooking* (see Ch. 14, §5.6.2).

(c) Object of a preposition – prepositional passives

[20] i a. *My mother approved of the plan.* b. *The plan was approved of by my mother.*
ii a. *The committee didn't face up to these problems.* b. *These problems weren't faced up to by the committee.*
iii a. *The organisers seem to have lost sight of the main goal.* b. *The main goal seems to have been lost sight of.*
iv a. *Someone has slept in this bed.* b. *This bed has been slept in.*

Here the underlined NP in the active examples is an object not of the verb but of a preposition. In the passive this NP functions as a subject, with the result that a preposition which is transitive in the active is intransitive in the passive – hence the term **prepositional passive**. The preposition in the [b] examples is 'stranded', and as with other cases of preposition stranding (as, for example, the open interrogative *Which bed did you sleep in?*) the construction is often avoided in formal, written prose: see Ch. 7, §4.1.

Prepositional passives fall into two main types. In one, illustrated in [20i–iii], a particular preposition is specified by the verb or verbal idiom; in the other, the preposition is less constrained: compare [20iva], for example, with *Someone has slept on/under/near the bed.*

Type 1: preposition is specified by the verb or verbal idiom

The preposition may be specified by a prepositional verb (such as *approve*), or as part of a verbal idiom with the form 'verb + preposition + preposition' (*look up to*) or 'verb + NP + preposition' (*lose sight of*). We have argued that sequences like *approve of, look up to*, and *lose sight of* do not form syntactic constituents – that they cannot be analysed as 'complex verbs' (see Ch. 4, §6). Nevertheless, the occurrence of a preposition as the final component of a verbal idiom is one factor that may facilitate its stranding in a prepositional passive.

Note in the first place that it is only with idioms that we find prepositional passives where the preposition follows an object NP, as in [20iiib]. For example, prepositional passives are not permitted with transitive prepositional verbs: compare the active *They accused Kim of the murder* or *She explained the problem to me* with the passive **The murder was accused Kim of* or **I was explained the problem to.*

Secondly, there are cases where the same sequence of words beginning with a verb and ending with a preposition can occur in a prepositional passive when it has an idiomatic interpretation but not in the literal interpretation. Compare:

[21] i a. *A First World War uniform was easily come by.*
b. *She was a fine manager, one [who was looked up to by them all].*
ii a. *#We need to ask the march organisers [whether our shop is going to be come by].*
b. *#The top of the mountain was looked up to as the volcano erupted.*

The passives are acceptable in [i], where *come by* and *look up to* have the idiomatic meanings "obtain" and "respect", but infelicitous in [ii], where the same sequences have their literal meanings, and the stranded prepositions *by* and *to* are not specified by *come* and *look + up.*

The fact that a preposition is specified by a verb or verbal idiom is no guarantee, however, that it can be stranded in a prepositional passive. For each of the three cases shown in [20i–iii], there are other examples that are ungrammatical:

[22] i *He was taken after by his son. [verb + preposition]
ii *Justice is being cried out for. [verb + preposition + preposition]
iii *She had been curried favour with. [verb + NP + preposition]

Whether a specified preposition can be stranded in a prepositional passive is not something that can be predicted by a general rule: it has to be recorded in the dictionary as a particular property of the verb or idiom concerned.

Type II: locative preposition not specified by verb

Prepositions that are not specified by the verb (or verbal idiom) have a locative meaning: compare *My hat has been sat on* and *The bridge has already been flown under twice* with **Sundays were never worked on* and **The fog was set out despite* (cf. *We never worked on Sundays* and *They set out despite the fog*). The locative case is subject to pragmatic constraints that exclude such examples as *#The tree had been died near*; we take up this issue in §10.2.

(d) Subordinate clause complements

Complements with the form of a subordinate clause rather than an NP can also be externalised. The following examples contain a declarative, an interrogative, and a gerund-participial respectively:

[23] i a. *Her son suggested that we should call the police.* b. *That we should call the police was suggested by her son.*
ii a. *They haven't yet determined whether this is feasible.* b. *Whether this is feasible hasn't yet been determined.*
iii a. *You can't avoid paying taxes.* b. *Paying taxes can't be avoided.*

Where an active contains an object as well as a subordinate clause complement, it is the NP object rather than the subordinate clause that is externalised in the passive:

[24] i *My solicitor assured me that we would win the case.*
ii *I was assured by my solicitor that we would win the case.*
iii **That we would win the case was assured me by my solicitor.*

The passives in [23ib/iib] have content clause subjects, and as such have alternants in which the content clause is extraposed:

[25] i *It was suggested by her son that we should call the police.*
ii *It hasn't yet been determined whether this is feasible.*

As we noted in §7.2, extraposition of gerund-participials is severely restricted, and it cannot apply to [23iiib]: *#It can't be avoided paying taxes.*

We take an extraposed subject to be structurally outside the VP, and on this account there is a difference in the structure of the VP in the active and in the corresponding passive extraposition construction. For example, the active VP of [23iia] (at the level of the complement of perfect *have*) is *determined whether this is feasible*, while the passive VP of [25ii] is just *determined*.

Declarative content clauses

For the most part, subordinate clauses of this kind can be externalised. Nevertheless, there are a fair number of verbs that do not permit this; for example, there are no passive counterparts, with or without extraposition, to the actives in [26]:

[26] i *We complained that there was no hot water.*
ii *They rejoiced that the war was finally over.*
iii *He snarled that he would never agree to such terms.*

There are others that permit the passive only with extraposition:

[27] i *It was charged that they had used the funds for private purposes.*
ii *It was objected that the costs would be excessive.*

Interrogative content clauses

Verbs taking interrogative complements usually allow passivisation, but there are a few that do not, as illustrated in [28]:

[28] i *Nobody cares/minds what happens to us.*
ii *They are wondering whether they made the right decision.*
iii *No one had thought what the consequences would be.*

Gerund-participials

Passives with gerund-participial subjects are uncommon; a fair number of catenative verbs that take complements of this form do not allow passivisation. Compare:

[29] i *Taking out a mortgage wasn't considered/recommended/suggested.*
ii **Painting the house was begun/kept/hated/intended/remembered by Sam.*

Note that there is a difference in the interpretation of the corresponding actives. In *Sam remembered painting the house* the understood subject of *paint* is recovered from the matrix clause: it was Sam who painted the house. In *Sam recommended taking out a mortgage*, however, the subject of *take* is not specified syntactically but has to be contextually recovered. It is this type of gerund-participial construction that most readily allows passivisation.

Infinitivals

Infinitival clauses can occur as subject or extraposed subject in passive clauses in which they are related to a predicative complement; in other types of clause, infinitivals are restricted to just a few catenative verbs (e.g. *decide, desire, hope, prefer*), and then only in extraposed position:

	a.	b.
[30] i	*Not to go would be considered rude.*	*It would be considered rude not to go.*
ii	**To accept the offer was decided.*	*It was decided to accept the offer.*
iii	**To receive more help was expected.*	**It was expected to receive more help.*

Verbs restricted to the passive

A handful of verbs occur only in the passive, either generally or with a particular type of complementation. *Be*-passives containing such verbs are given in [31]:

[31] i *Pat is reputed to be very rich.*
ii *It is rumoured that there will be an election before the end of the year.*
iii *Kim is said to be a manic depressive.*

The verbs *repute* and *rumour* are wholly restricted to the passive – and are thus morphologically defective, having only a past participle form. *Repute* takes an infinitival complement, *rumour* either an infinitival or a declarative content clause (usually extraposed, as in [ii]). *Say* cannot occur in the active with an object + infinitival complement: **They say Kim to be a manic depressive*; in other constructions, of course, it occurs freely in the active.[40]

10.1.3 Adjectival passives

There is a large-scale overlap between adjectives and the past participle forms of verbs, and since the verb *be* can take complements headed by either of these categories we find a significant resemblance, and often an ambiguity, between a verbal passive and a complex-intransitive clause containing an adjectival passive as predicative complement. Compare:

[32]	i	*The kitchen window was broken by the thieves.*	[verbal: *be*-passive]
	ii	*They were very worried.*	[adjectival: complex-intransitive]
	iii	*They were married.*	[ambiguous]

Broken in [i] is a verb, *worried* in [ii] is an adjective, while *married* in [iii] can be either. The ambiguity of [iii] is very clear: in the verbal interpretation it is dynamic, describing an event, while in the adjectival interpretation it is static, describing the state resulting from some prior event. Compare *They were married last week in London* (verbal) and *Hardly anyone knew that they were married – that they had been for over ten years* (adjectival). We will see, however, that this sharp semantic distinction does not apply in all cases.

Adjectival passives are passive only in a derivative sense, and we will not say that [32ii–iii] in their statal interpretations are passive clauses: they belong to the complex-intransitive construction. The term adjectival passive applies only to the predicative complement, that is, to the AdjPs *very worried* and *married*. Thus the clause *They were very worried* is not itself an adjectival passive – it merely contains one. Passives in the strict sense are always verbal;[41] more specifically, we restrict the term *be*-passive to clauses like [i] or [iii] in its dynamic interpretation, i.e. to clauses in which *be* is a catenative verb taking a bare verbal passive as complement.

Grammatical tests for adjectival status

(a) Modification by *very*: a sufficient condition

Adjectives differ from verbs in that (if gradable) they can be modified by *very* and *too* (in the sense "excessively"), whereas verbs cannot (Ch. 6, §2.2). Compare:

		ADJECTIVE	VERB
[33]	i	a. *It was [very enjoyable].*	b. **We [very enjoyed it].*
	ii	a. *They are [too quarrelsome].*	b. **They [quarrel too].*

(The [b] examples can be corrected by inserting *much*: *We enjoyed it very much*; *They quarrel too much.*)

The presence of *very* in [32ii] thus makes this unambiguously adjectival. Similarly *He was too embarrassed by their behaviour to acknowledge that he was their son* can only be adjectival. This example shows that adjectival passives allow *by* complements (though

[40] For some speakers *take ill* is also restricted to the passive, as in *They were taken ill* ("became ill"); others allow an active intransitive with the same meaning, *%They took ill.* In BrE the past participle form spelt *born* is also restricted to the passive: compare *I was born in Boston* and *She had borne three children.* This use of *born* is found only in short passives (cf. **He was born by a Greek peasant*).

[41] Adjectival passives are sometimes called 'pseudo-passives', though this term is more widely used for prepositional passives.

there are restrictions we will return to below): the *too* is sufficient to establish that it is adjectival, for it is not permitted in the active verbal construction **Their behaviour embarrassed him too for him to acknowledge that he was their son.*

Not all adjectives are gradable, however, and the potential for modification by *very* thus provides a sufficient but not a necessary test for adjectival status. In *The new recruits were assembled outside the officers' mess*, for example, *assembled* cannot be modified by *very*, but this doesn't mean that the example cannot be adjectival – it is in fact ambiguous, like [32iii].

(b) Occurrence with other verbs taking predicative complements

Adjectival predicative complements are not restricted to occurrence with *be* but are found also with such verbs as *seem*, *look*, and *remain*. All of these can substitute for *be* in [32ii], but not in [i]: *They seemed very worried*, but not **The kitchen window seemed broken by the thieves.* Leaving aside *meant* and *supposed*, which involve semantic specialisation illustrated in [45] below, there are no adjectival passives that are restricted to occurrence with *be*, so this test virtually provides a necessary condition for adjectival status: if *be* can't be replaced by other such verbs, the passive in question is normally verbal. *It is believed to be a forgery* and *Someone was heard moving around in the attic*, for example, exclude such verbs and are unambiguously verbal. Note, then, that while *assembled* cannot be modified by *very* it can occur as a complement to *remain*: *The new recruits remained assembled outside the officers' mess for over an hour.* Replacement of *be* by *remain* also serves to remove the ambiguity of [iii] in favour of an adjectival reading: *They didn't live together <u>but they remained married</u>.* This test confirms, moreover, that adjectival passives may contain a *by* phrase: *He remained too embarrassed by their behaviour to acknowledge that he was their son.*

(c) The negative prefix *un·*

Many adjectives form opposites by prefixation of *un·*, but verbs do not take *un·* with the same sense:

[34]		ADJECTIVE	VERB
	i	a. *They were <u>unrepentant</u>.*	b. **They <u>unrepented</u>.*
	ii	a. *It was <u>unmemorable</u>.*	b. **We <u>unremembered</u> it.*

Where *un·* occurs with verbs, as in *untie*, *unhorse*, etc., it has a clearly different sense (cf. Ch. 19, §5.5). The presence of *un·* in the following thus marks them clearly as adjectival, for there are no verbs *unanswer* and *unnotice*:

[35] i *The letter was still <u>unanswered</u>.*
ii *The cat was <u>unnoticed</u> by the guests for several minutes.*

The adjectives here are ungradable, and hence can't be modified by *very* or *too*, but they pass test (b): *The letter remained unanswered*; *The cat remained unnoticed.* Notice again the *by* phrase in the indisputably adjectival example [ii].

Dynamic vs stative

Adjectival passives always have a stative interpretation. The clearest contrasts are between verbal and adjectival passives that differ as to whether they are interpreted dynamically or statively:

[36] i *They were <u>injured</u> when the platform they were standing on collapsed.* [verbal]
ii *She is <u>injured</u> and will have to miss the next two matches.* [adjectival]

Similarly, the obvious ambiguities are those that allow either a dynamic or a stative interpretation, such as *They were injured* on its own, *They were married* (=[32iii]), *The window was broken*, and so on.

It must be emphasised, however, that adjectival and verbal passives cannot be distinguished simply by asking whether the interpretation is stative or dynamic – it is for this reason that we have not included this among the tests for adjectival status. There are two points to be made.

(a) Verbal passives may have a stative meaning

The meaning of a verbal passive matches that of the corresponding active. Compare:

[37]		DYNAMIC	STATIVE
	i	a. *Everyone criticised her.*	b. *Everyone loves her.*
	ii	a. *She was criticised by everyone.*	b. *She is loved by everyone.*

Criticise has a dynamic meaning, while *love* has a stative meaning, and in both cases the active and passive have the same interpretation. The grammatical relation between [ii] and [i] is the same in both pairs, so we must allow [iib] to be a verbal passive – i.e. a passive proper – as well as [iia]. It follows that we must accept that verbal passives can be stative.

In such cases the difference in meaning between the verbal and adjectival constructions is neutralised. Consider:

[38] i *Kim was worried by the prospect of redundancy.*
ii *The village was surrounded by troops from the First Battalion.*

Example [i] can be construed as differing syntactically from the active *The prospect of redundancy worried Kim* in the same way as [37iia/b] differ from [37ia/b] respectively. We have to allow, therefore, that it can be an ordinary, i.e. a verbal, passive counterpart of the active clause. But at the same time it passes the tests for an adjectival passive, for *worried* can be modified by *very* and *be* can be replaced by such verbs as *seem* and *become*: compare the unequivocally adjectival *Kim seemed very worried by the prospect of redundancy*. Syntactically, [38i] can thus be either a verbal or an adjectival passive, but semantically, there is no real perceptible difference in meaning.

Example [38ii] is more complicated, because the verbal passive, like its active counterpart *Troops from the First Battalion surrounded the village*, is ambiguous between a dynamic and a stative interpretation: either the troops moved into position around the village or else they were already in that position. Note that adding the aspectual adjunct *still* to either the passive or the active version forces the stative reading. In addition, we have the adjectival construal, whose meaning is effectively the same as that of the stative reading of the verbal passive. We can show that there must be an adjectival analysis of the clause because although *surrounded* can't be modified by *very*, it can combine with other verbs than *be*: *The village remained surrounded.*

(b) Adjectival passives may function as the predicative complement of a dynamic verb

Compare next the following pair:

[39] i *It was magnetised.* [verbal or adjectival]
ii *It became magnetised.* [adjectival]

Example [i] displays the familiar ambiguity found in *They were injured*, *They were married*, and so on. It can have a dynamic interpretation, like the active *They magnetised it*, which describes an event: in this case it is a verbal passive. It can also have a stative interpretation, with *magnetised* denoting the state resulting from a prior event of magnetisation: in this case it is an adjectival passive. In [ii] *magnetised* is adjectival because it is a complement to *become*. The verb *become* denotes a change of state and thus has a dynamic meaning, so [ii] as a whole describes an event. But this is not in conflict with our statement that adjectival passives have a stative meaning: the dynamic component in the meaning of [ii] is attributable to *become*, while the adjectival passive *magnetised* still denotes the state resulting from magnetisation.[42]

Complementation

Verbs and adjectives differ to some extent in their complementation, so that some expressions are admissible as VPs of verbal passives but not as AdjPs in adjectival passives, or vice versa. One very general difference is that verbs but not adjectives can take predicative complements. In other cases there are restrictions applying to specific lexemes. Compare:

[40] i *Kim was regarded as / considered a liability.* [predicative complement]
ii *Max was known to be an alcoholic.* [infinitival complement]

These are unambiguously verbal passives, [i] because it contains a predicative complement, [ii] because the adjective *known* can't take an infinitival complement: compare *He became known as a champion of lost causes* and **He became known to be an alcoholic.*

By phrase complements

We have noted that *by* phrase complements are found in adjectival as well as verbal passives, but their occurrence in the adjectival construction is much more restricted than in the verbal one. Compare:

[41] i *The window was broken.* [ambiguous: verbal or adjectival]
ii *The window was broken by vandals.* [unambiguously verbal]

Example [i] displays the familiar ambiguity between a verbal passive clause describing an event ("Someone or something broke the window") and a complex-intransitive with an adjectival passive complement describing a state ("The window was in the state resulting from prior breaking"). The *by* phrase in [ii], however, is incompatible with the adjectival construction, so [ii] has only the verbal reading ("Vandals broke the window"). That *broken* but not *broken by vandals* can be adjectival is confirmed by the second of our tests for adjectival status, occurrence with complex-intransitive verbs other than *be.* Thus we can have *The window remained broken*, but not **The window remained broken by vandals.*

By phrases are permitted in adjectival passives when the meaning of the corresponding verb is stative but not when it is dynamic. Adjectival *worried by the prospect of redundancy* in [38i] is admissible because the corresponding verb, *worry*, has a stative meaning, but – as we have just seen – *broken by vandals* cannot be adjectival because the verb *break* is dynamic. The verb *surround* can have either a dynamic or a stative meaning, so [ii] construed as a verbal passive is ambiguous, but as we noted above it is unambiguously stative when construed as a complex-intransitive with an adjectival passive as a complement.[43]

There are also cases where the complement in an adjectival passive contains some other preposition instead of *by*:

[42] i a. *She was pleased at these results.* b. *She was pleased by these results.*
ii a. *He is known to the police.* b. *The answer was known by everyone.*

[42] Because the *become* construction presents the event as a change of state, the meaning is not quite the same as that of a verbal *be*-passive. In many cases the latter will be strongly preferred: *The house was painted*, rather than *#The house became painted*, and so on.

[43] For adjectival passives with the *un·* prefix there are no corresponding verbs, as we have noted. This construction allows *by* phrase complements more freely, as evident from *unnoticed by the guests* in [35ii].

The [a] examples are adjectival, while the [b] ones can be verbal or adjectival.

Adjectival passives with the negative prefix *un·*

We have noted that such examples as the following are unambiguously adjectival because there are no corresponding verbs *unrepair, unaccount, unsee*:

[43] i *The vehicle had to go unrepaired for several months.*
ii *Nearly half the money was unaccounted for.*
iii *He had remained unseen throughout the meeting.*

There are three further points to make about this construction.[44] In the first place, only AdjPs like those in [43] can occur as complements to the verb *go* in the sense "remain", as in [i]. Thus, although *It went black* is acceptable, *go* here means "become, turn", not "remain". Secondly, the adjective may incorporate a preposition, as in [ii]. Although we have argued that in *We accounted for more than half the money* the sequence *accounted for* is not a verb, and not a syntactic constituent, the *unaccounted for* of [ii] is a compound adjective. The difference in status is reflected in the fact that the verb can be separated from the preposition whereas in the adjectival construction the parts are inseparable. Compare *We have accounted already for the money* and **The money was unaccounted still for.*

Thirdly, the morphological process of forming such negative adjectives is highly productive, and in many cases the form without the prefix occurs in verbal but not adjectival passives. For example, *unseen* is an adjective, but *seen* is not: compare [43iii] with **He had remained seen throughout the meeting.* A sample of forms in *un·* found in adjectival passives is given in [44]:

[44]					
unaffected	*unaided*	*unattended*	*unbalanced*	*unchanged*	*undaunted*
undetected	*undeterred*	*unfettered*	*unharmed*	*unheeded*	*unhindered*
unimpeded	*unintended*	*unmoved*	*unopposed*	*unprotected*	*unseen*
unspoiled	*unsupported*	*unswayed*	*untouched*	*untroubled*	*unwanted*

Adjectival passives with specialised senses

There are a few adjectives that are morphologically related to the past participles of verbs but whose meanings have changed, so that they are no longer comparable to verbal passives with the same forms, and their connection with passives proper is purely historical:

[45] *She's bound to win.* *We're engaged (to be married).* *Aren't you meant to be working on your assignment?* *His days are numbered.* *Are you related?* *I'm supposed to pay for it.* *He isn't used to hard work.*

10.1.4 *Get*-passives

Get in passive and complex-intransitive clauses

Like *be*, the verb *get* functions not only as the catenative verb in an expanded passive but also as head of a complex-intransitive clause, as in *They got angry.* Since the predicative complement in the latter construction can have the form of an adjectival passive, we

[44] Adjectival passives of this kind are often called '*un*-passives'.

again have to distinguish between verbal and adjectival passives, with the potential for ambiguity between them:

[46] i *They got killed by the hijackers.* [verbal: *get*-passive]
ii *They got very frightened.* [adjectival: complex-intransitive]
iii *They got frightened.* [ambiguous]

Example [i] is synonymous with the *be*-passive *They were killed by the hijackers* and with the active *The hijackers killed them*, while the *very* in [ii] makes this example clearly adjectival, "They became very afraid". Example [iii] can be interpreted like [ii] without the degree modification: "They became afraid". But it can also be interpreted as a short passive, comparable to the long passive *They got frightened out of their wits by their teenage children, who turned off the power supply and pretended to be ghosts.*

Ambiguities between verbal and adjectival passives, however, arise much less often with *get* than with *be*. Compare, for example:

[47] i *The window was broken.* [ambiguous: verbal or adjectival]
ii *The window got broken.* [unambiguous: verbal only]

As we have seen, [i] is ambiguous, interpretable either as a verbal passive ("Someone or something broke the window") or as a complex-intransitive with an adjectival passive complement ("The window was in the state resulting from prior breaking"). Example [ii], however, has only the verbal passive reading: it describes the event of someone or something breaking the window, not the transition into the broken state. Thus *get* accepts adjectival passives as complements less readily than *be*.

The clearest cases of adjectival passives with *get* involve gradable adjectives like the *frightened* of [46]: *alarmed, carried away, depressed, distressed, interested, worried*, etc. A clear non-gradable is *lost*, as in *The children got lost in the woods* ("became lost"). Compare also adjectival *My coat got caught in the door* ("became caught") vs verbal *Tom got caught in the girls' dormitory* ("was apprehended"). With *married, dressed, changed,* and *shaved* there is a semantic contrast that can plausibly be attributed to the adjective vs verb distinction:

[48] i *They are getting married at the week-end.* [adjectival]
ii *They are hoping to get married by the bishop.* [verbal]

In [i] *married* is comparable to *engaged*, which we have already noted is (in the relevant sense) always adjectival – though *married*, unlike *engaged*, does not readily combine with *become*: *We became engaged/#married.* The *by* phrase in [ii] makes this clearly verbal – compare *They are hoping that the bishop will marry them.* Two other forms commonly found as adjectives with *get* (though again not with *become*) are *started* and *finished*, as in *Let's get started/finished* – compare verbal *The job got finished by their son.* The difference in these last examples is that with the verbal passives there is some explicit or implicit agent (expressed in [48ii] by *the bishop*) distinct from the subject-referent, whereas in the adjectival cases there is not. For example, [48i] means much the same as *They are marrying (each other)*, and *Let's get started* much the same as *Let's start.*

Differences between *get*-passives and *be*-passives

Be is much more commonly used in expanded passives than *get*, especially the long variety, i.e. those with an internalised complement. The main differences between the two types of expanded passive are summarised in [49]:

[49] i *Get*-passives tend to be avoided in formal style.
ii *Get*-passives are found only with dynamic verbs.
iii *Get*-passives are more conducive to an agentive interpretation of the subject.
iv *Get*-passives are characteristically used in clauses involving adversity or benefit.

Nothing further need be said about [i], but the other points merit brief discussion.

The restriction to dynamic verbs

Point [49ii] reflects the fact that other uses of *get* are all dynamic – compare *I got a t-shirt for my birthday*, *We had to get some more milk*, etc. It follows that *be* is not replaceable by *get* in such examples as:

[50] i *It was/#got believed that the letter was a forgery.*
ii *Obviously, the manager is/#gets feared by most of the staff.*

Note similarly that the dynamic–stative ambiguity of the *be*-passive [38ii], *The village was surrounded by troops from the First Battalion*, is lost when we substitute *get*: *The village got surrounded by troops from the First Battalion* describes the event wherein they took up position around the village.

Agentivity

Other things being equal, *get* tends to be preferred over *be* when the subject-referent is seen as having an agentive role in the situation, or at least as having some responsibility for it. Take for example the pair *Jill was/got arrested.* Either could be used to report an event where Jill simply had a patient role, but if I believe she set out to provoke the police into arresting her or was careless in letting it happen I will be more likely to use the *get* version. *Get* is thus the natural choice in *Jill deliberately got arrested*, and such constructions as:

[51] i *She managed to get transferred to the finance department.*
ii *Go and get checked out at the medical centre.*
iii *Getting elected president of the student union took a lot of time and effort.*
iv *He did a silly thing: he got caught downloading pornography on their computer.*

Adversity and benefit

Get occurs predominantly in passives representing situations that have an adverse or a beneficial effect on the subject-referent, or on someone associated with it, rather than in passives representing purely neutral situations. Typical examples are shown in [52]:

[52] i a. *Kim got sacked.* b. *Kim got promoted.*
ii a. *My watch got stolen.* b. *My letter got published.*

The situations described in [i] are normally thought of as respectively bad and good for Kim, those in [ii] as bad and good for me, the owner of the watch and writer of the letter. Such examples are much more natural than, say, *The milk got bought at the store down the road* or *The door got opened by a shabbily dressed old man*, where *be* is preferred.

There are some instances where *be* and *get* are not interchangeable:

[53] i *Kim was/*got seen to leave the laboratory with Dr Smith.*
ii *He saw Kim get/*be mauled by my brother's dog.*

Both of these involve sense verbs with non-finite complements. In [i] it is *see* itself that is passivised, and here *be* is required. In [ii] it is the complement of *see* that is passivised, and this time *be* is excluded – but an alternative to the *get* construction is a bare passive: *He saw Kim mauled by my brother's dog.*

Get in the complex catenative construction

The *get*-passive is a simple catenative construction, one with no intervening NP between *get* and the non-finite complement. *Get* is also found (unlike *be*) in the complex construction where there is an intervening NP:

[54] a. *I get my hair cut once a month.* b. *I got myself exempted from guard duties.*

Where the intervening NP is a reflexive, as in [b], the construction is explicitly agentive, with the subject-referent taking the initiative or being responsible (cf. *Watch out! You're going to get yourself run over*). This construction thus provides an alternative to *get*-passives with agentive subject interpretations. Compare, for example, [51i] with *She managed to get herself transferred to the finance department.*

Status of the catenative verb in *be*- and *get*-passives

In the light of the above examination of *get*, consider again the analysis of such clauses as:

[55] i	*The hospital board reprimanded both doctors.*	[active]
ii	*Both doctors were reprimanded by the hospital board.*	[*be*-passive]
iii	*Both doctors got reprimanded by the hospital board.*	[*get*-passive]

All three have the same propositional meaning, and on this basis we are treating [ii] and [iii] as alternative passive counterparts to active [i]. *Be* and *get* are catenative verbs taking a bare passive clause as complement: the *be* and *get* clauses are expanded passives in the sense that they include *be* and *get* in addition to the bare passive. The implication is that *be* and *get* are dummy verbs with no identifiable meaning of their own – comparable in this respect to the *do* of *do*-support constructions. That is, they have a purely syntactic role: they serve to mark the passive voice and to carry the preterite tense inflection that appears on *reprimand* in the active, as explained in §10.1.1.

As far as *be*-passives are concerned, this treatment seems amply justified, but *get*-passives are more problematic. It is clear that in the complex catenative construction illustrated in [54] *get* is not a dummy verb, nor a passive marker: the *get* clauses here are not themselves passive, but merely contain passive clauses as complements. The *get*-passive analysis of clauses like [55iii] thus treats this *get* in a radically different way from that of the complex construction [54] in spite of the semantic affinity between such pairs as *She managed to get transferred* and *She managed to get herself transferred.* An alternative treatment of [55iii] would be to say that here, as in [54], it is only the embedded complement that is passive, with the matrix *get* clause being active. However, the *get*-passive analysis is to be preferred on the grounds that the unembedded forms *She got transferred* and *She got herself transferred* do clearly differ, with the agentive feature being merely a possible implicature in the former.

10.2 Pragmatic factors favouring actives or passives

This section deals with issues of information packaging: when both active and passive versions are formally permitted, what factors favour the choice of one over the other? The long and short passive constructions will be considered separately because the former is sensitive to the relative discourse familiarity of the subject and the internalised NP.

Long passives

Major constraint: subject must not be less familiar in the discourse than the internalised NP

The felicity of a long passive requires that the subject not represent information that is newer in the discourse than the NP governed by the word *by* in the internalised complement. Compare:

[56] i *The mayor's term of office expires next month. [She will be succeeded by George Hendricks.]*
ii *George Hendricks will take office next month. [#The current mayor, Angela Cooke, will be succeeded by him.]*

In [i] the subject *she*, referring to the mayor, is discourse-old, while the internalised NP *George Hendricks* is discourse-new. But in [ii] the subject is discourse-new and the internalised NP old, with resulting infelicity. Instead we would have the active version *He will succeed the current mayor, Angela Cooke.*

As indicated in the formulation of the constraint, what matters is discourse familiarity, not addressee familiarity. Note, then, the contrast between:

[57] i *A press conference will be held by the President at 3 p.m. today.*
ii *#A press conference will be held by me at 3 p.m. today.*

Assuming there has been no mention of the president in the prior discourse, [i] is perfectly natural: *the President*, although addressee-old, is discourse-new, and hence the subject is not less familiar in the discourse than the internalised NP. But, as we observed in §2, the speaker and addressee count as discourse-old simply by virtue of their participation in the discourse, and [ii] therefore violates the constraint, with the subject being discourse-new and the internalised complement discourse-old.

The constraint is a matter of the relative discourse familiarity of the two NPs. It excludes new + old ([56ii], [57ii]), allowing not only old + new ([56i]), but also old + old and new + new, as in [58i–ii] respectively:

[58] i *Paul and Mary have agreed to help with the salads. We'll serve a pasta salad and a traditional bowl of tossed greens. [The pasta salad will be made by Paul,] and Mary will bring the greens.*
ii *Before the parade, a flag ceremony will be led by a troop of Girl Scouts.*

Comparison with subject–dependent inversion

The constraint on long passives given above applies also to subject–dependent inversion, as discussed in §5.2. This reflects the fact that the two constructions differ from their more basic counterparts in similar ways:

[59] i a. *Her doctor will be with her.* b. *With her will be her doctor.*
ii a. *Her doctor prescribed the pills.* b. *The pills were prescribed by her doctor.*

In both pairs the order of the underlined constituents is reversed, and this reversal is subject to the constraint that the one that comes to occupy first position must not be less familiar in the discourse than the one that comes to occupy a later position.

There are nevertheless significant differences between passivisation and inversion. In the first place, we have seen that (leaving aside the case of locatives) inversion requires a discourse-old open proposition, but passivisation does not:

[60] *An important new bill was introduced by Senator Jill Johansen at the State Capitol yesterday.*

This does not require a context in which the open proposition "*x* was introduced by somebody" has been evoked or is inferrable. Secondly, in terms of the distinction drawn in §1, passivisation involves realignment of syntactic functions with semantic roles, while inversion merely reorders. In [59i] *her doctor* is the subject in [b] as well as in [a], whereas in [ii] the active has *her doctor* as subject and *the pills* as object while the passive has *the pills* as subject and *her doctor* as object within the internalised complement. Because of this difference, passivisation but not inversion can interact with other syntactic constructions (whether in the information-packaging domain or not) which effect a different linear ordering of the elements than that shown in [59iib]:

[61] i *Which doctor were her pills prescribed by?* [open interrogative]
ii *By none of them was the question answered satisfactorily.* [preposing]

In [i] *which doctor* occurs in front position by virtue of being the interrogative phrase. Note that the final element in [59ib] cannot be fronted in this way, since *with her* is not the subject: **Which doctor will with her be?* An open interrogative can only be formed from the [a] version, giving *Which doctor will be with her?* In [61ii] *by none of them* is preposed (and since the NP within it is negative we have subject–auxiliary inversion). As it belongs to two of the information-packaging constructions, this example has to satisfy two constraints. The constraint on passivisation will be satisfied because the subject *the question* will not be less familiar in the discourse than *none of them* – the definite article in *the question* will reflect prior mention. The constraint on preposing requires firstly that *none of them* provide a link to the prior discourse (which it does through the anaphoric pronoun *them*) and secondly that the open proposition "The question was answered satisfactorily by *x*-number of them" be discourse-old, i.e. previously evoked or inferrable.

Short passives

As in long passives, the subject of the short variety may be discourse-old or discourse-new, but this time there can of course be no requirement that it not be less familiar than the internalised complement NP, because there is no such NP present:

[62] i *I was going to show you my new car [but yesterday <u>it</u> was stolen].* [old]
ii *Did you hear the news? [<u>A shop-keeper downtown</u> was shot last night].* [new]

The crucial difference between a short passive and an active clause is that the information expressed in the subject of the active is omitted in the passive. There may be a variety of reasons why a speaker might wish to omit such information, as illustrated in [63]:

[63] i *The house was built in 1924.*
ii *Very little is known about the cause of the disease.*
iii *Application forms can be obtained from the Departmental Secretary.*
iv *Mom! The vase got broken!*

v *The delay in attending to this matter is regretted.*
vi *The solution was drained under a hydrogen atmosphere, the deposits were washed with water and methanol and dried. A film of formvar was then cast on the deposit . . .*

A likely reason for the use of a short passive in [i] is that the speaker doesn't know who built the house – similarly in [62]. The most natural interpretation of [63ii] is that it is concerned with human knowledge in general. Example [iii] is comparable to *You/One can obtain . . .*: the short passive provides an alternative means of expressing general propositions of this kind. The short passive can also be used to avoid identifying the person responsible for some situation, as is quite likely to be the case in [iv]. Example [v] is from a letter from the Taxation Office illustrating the common use of short passives in material from government and similar institutions. The letter was ostensibly from the Deputy Commissioner but no doubt written by some relatively junior member of staff; the active *I regret . . .* would imply too direct and personal an involvement on the part of the signatory. Finally, [vi] is from a report of a scientific experiment. It is a well-known feature of scientific writing that it has a higher proportion of passives than most registers; many of the short passives, like those in this example, serve to avoid making explicit reference to the writer, and this is widely believed to give the writing a more objective flavour than is found in texts with 1st person references.

A somewhat different type of case is illustrated in [64]:

[64] i *Our solar system was formed billions of years ago.*
ii *The boat capsized and over twenty passengers were drowned.*
iii *In view of these losses Smithson is reluctantly closing his Fifth Avenue shop. He admits he feels as if his dream has been shattered.*

Here the cause of the event is too general and diffuse to name, and neither a long passive nor a transitive active would seem appropriate. Note that [i–ii], and for some speakers [iii], could be replaced by **intransitive** actives with hardly any change in meaning: *Our solar system formed billions of years ago*; *Over twenty passengers drowned*; %*His dream has shattered.*

Prepositional passives

Consider finally the pragmatic constraints applying to passives like [20ivb] above, *This bed has been slept in*, where there is stranding of a locative preposition that is not specified by the verb. Passives of this kind are felicitous only if the VP indicates either a significant property or a change in a significant property of the subject-referent. Compare:

[65] i a. *This bed was slept in by George Washington.*
b. *The valley could be marched through in less than two hours.*
c. *My new hat has been sat on.*
ii a. #*The river was slept beside.*
b. #*The village hall could be met in.*
c. #*The roof has been sat on all day.*

The fact that George Washington slept in the bed gives it some historical interest, so [ia] satisfies the constraint. Similarly in [ib]: if the valley could be marched through in less than two hours, this tells us something significant about its length and the terrain.

As for [ic], if someone has sat on my new hat it will presumably have been squashed or otherwise affected, so there will have been a change in a significant property of the hat. Our original example, *This bed has been slept in*, is of this latter kind: sleeping in a bed results in an important change, for it becomes rumpled and the sheets are likely to be treated as no longer clean enough for someone else to use them. No such factors motivate the use of the passive in [ii], though the corresponding actives are of course acceptable: *We slept beside the river*; *We could meet in the village hall*; *The protesters have sat on the roof all day*. Sleeping beside a river doesn't affect it or distinguish it in any significant way from other rivers. Village halls are quite generally used for meetings, so to say that we could meet in one doesn't say anything noteworthy about it. And merely sitting on a roof doesn't normally have any effect on it.

17

Deixis and anaphora

Lesley Stirling
Rodney Huddleston

1 Preliminaries

1.1 The concept of deixis

The reference of certain kinds of expression is determined in relation to features of the utterance-act: the time, the place, and the participants, i.e. those with the role of speaker or addressee. This phenomenon is known as **deixis** and the expressions concerned are called **deictic**. Examples of such expressions are given in:

[1] i *I bought a new stereo system yesterday.*
ii *Do you feel any pain here now?*
iii *Could you pick this up and put it with those boxes, please?*

Yesterday in [1i] and *now* in [ii] are interpreted in relation to the time of the utterance: *now* refers to a time including that of the utterance, while *yesterday* refers to the day before that on which the utterance takes place. This is a matter of **temporal deixis**.

Here in [1ii] refers to a location close to the speaker, and in [iii] *this* refers to something located close to the speaker and *those boxes* to boxes that are further away. This is **locative deixis**.

Finally, *I* in [1i] refers to the speaker, and *you* in [ii–iii] to the addressee. This is called **person deixis**.

It will be recalled that we are using such terms as 'utterance-act' and 'speaker' to cover written as well as spoken language. Example [1i] could be used with the same interpretation as readily in writing as in speech; the others are unlikely to be used in writing because the reference of *here*, *this*, and *those boxes* is determined by very local features of the utterance-act, whereas it is characteristic of writing that writer and addressee are in different places. But of course they don't have to be: if I had lost my voice, for example, I might communicate [ii–iii] to you in writing in your presence.

Varying reference

It follows from what we have said that the reference of deictic expressions potentially varies from one utterance to another. This of course applies to referring expressions generally: different utterances of *Where's Kim?* potentially involve reference to different people called Kim. What is significant for deixis is that the shifting reference is systematically tied to features of the utterance-act itself. The meaning of deictic expressions explicitly relates them to features of the utterance-act; for example, the difference in meaning between deictic ***this*** and ***that*** is primarily a matter of relative closeness to the speaker. Variation in the reference of *Kim*, by contrast, is simply due to the fact that many different people bear that name.

Deictic vs non-deictic location in space and time

Location in space and time may be indicated by deictic or non-deictic means:

[2]		DEICTIC	NON-DEICTIC
	i	a. *She lives here.*	b. *She lives in Paris.*
	ii	a. *He went to Spain last week.*	b. *He went to Spain the day after the exam.*

In [ia] the place where she lives is identified deictically in relation to the utterance-act: it might be the house where I'm speaking, the town, perhaps the country, but some area conceived of as including the place of utterance. In [ib] *in Paris* is non-deictic, and could in principle be used to refer to the same place wherever I am talking. Similarly *last week* in [iia] is deictic in that it identifies the time in relation to the time of speaking: it is the week preceding that in which the utterance-act takes place. In [2iib], by contrast, *the day after the exam* is non-deictic: it identifies the day in relation to the time of the exam, not to the time of speaking.

We noted above that referring expressions in general have varying reference, and this applies to *Paris* and *the exam* in these examples (in addition to the Paris in France there are several places named *Paris* in the USA), but there is nothing in the meaning of these expressions that relates them to the place or time of the utterance-act as there is in the meaning of *here* and *last week*.

Deictic expression and deictic marker

In [1iii] it is the whole NP *those boxes* whose referent is determined in relation to the location of the speaker. It is *those boxes*, therefore, that counts as the **deictic expression**. Nevertheless, it is just the demonstrative determiner *those* that incorporates the meaning "relatively distant from the speaker". We will call *those* the **deictic marker**. Deictic marker and deictic expression often coincide. What distinguishes *those boxes* in [1iii] from the other cases in [1] is that the marker does not constitute the whole referring expression. Similarly, in [2iia] the deictic expression is *last week*, while *last* is the deictic marker.

Indexing acts

Deictic expressions are frequently accompanied by **indexing acts** performed by the speaker in order to clarify their reference: gestures towards the intended referent by pointing with the fingers, head, or other body parts, touching or brandishing the referent, or merely eye-movements.[1] In some cases the indexing act is required for the deictic expression to be fully interpretable:

[3] *She's about so tall.* *He shook his head thus.* *Just put it down there.*

Similarly, some such indication would be needed to make clear just which area is intended by *here* in [1ii]. A less obvious but nevertheless important use of indexing acts is to pick out the addressee when there are other people present – for example, by eye contact. The necessity for an indexing act depends on the characteristics of the referent to some extent: if an object is large and in your field of vision, there will be less perceived need for me to point to it.

[1] The etymology of *deixis*, from a Greek word meaning "pointing/showing", reflects the close relation between deictic expressions and indexing acts. And an alternative term for 'deictic expression' is 'indexical (expression)', commonly used in the philosophy of language, with 'indexical' etymologically related to the Latin word meaning "pointing finger".

Pointing, eye-movements, and the like are prone to be somewhat vague in themselves, and we commonly find that an indexing act and a deictic expression work together in such a way that each clarifies the other. Suppose, for example, that I am in a room where there are a number of books, including several red ones, scattered around, and I say *Could you pass me that red book* with an accompanying gesture. The indexing act picks out which of the red books I'm referring to, while the nominal *red book* distinguishes the object I'm referring to from various other objects in the area I'm pointing at.

As noted above, in the case of writing the addressee usually does not witness the utterance-act, and hence there is much less scope for indexing. Nevertheless diagrammatic devices such as arrows can be used for indexing: *Our hotel room here* ↗; *This way up*⇑.

Deictic centre

Deixis is for the most part centred on the speaker. Consider, for example:

[4] i *This bowl holds twice as much as that one.*
ii *I started this letter two hours ago but I keep getting interrupted.*
iii A: *I'm going to sit here.* B: *I'd rather sit here.*

In [i] the two bowls are distinguished in terms of their location, and it is a matter of relative proximity to me, the speaker. In [ii], *two hours ago* measures the temporal distance between the time the letter was begun and now, and this 'now' is my time, the time at which I am writing. Your time – the time at which you read the letter – is irrelevant. Example [iii] illustrates the way in which the **deictic centre** switches from one speaker to another in conversation. The first *I* refers to speaker A and the second to B; and the first *here* is oriented with respect to A, the second with respect to B.

There are, however, conditions under which the deictic centre for some deictic expressions shifts from speaker to addressee or to some other person:

[5] i *Now wash your hands.*
ii *She realised Ed must have left at least a week ago.*

Example [i] appears as a notice in a public toilet; in this case *now* refers not to the time of writing the notice but to the time of reading it – and hence is constantly shifting with the passage of time. In [ii] *at least a week ago* could be interpreted at face value as "at least a week before the time of the utterance", but it is also possible for it to have the interpretation "at least a week before the time of her realisation". In this case I adopt the perspective of the person whose thoughts and experiences I am reporting (see §10.2).

1.2 Anaphora: anaphors and antecedents

Prototypical examples of anaphora are given in:

[6] i *Max claims he wasn't told about it.*
ii *The idea was preposterous, but no one dared say so.*

Anaphora is the relation between an **anaphor** and an **antecedent**, where the interpretation of the anaphor is determined via that of the antecedent. In the reading of [i] that we are concerned with, *he* is the anaphor and *Max* the antecedent, and *he* is understood to refer to the same person as *Max* by virtue of this relationship. Similarly, in [ii] we have an anaphoric link between *so* and the first clause, with *so* being thereby interpreted as "that the idea was preposterous".

In [6i] it happens that both anaphor and antecedent are subject of their respective clauses, but that is a fortuitous feature of the example: the same anaphoric relation is found in *Max claims that they didn't tell him about it* (antecedent *Max* as subject, anaphor *him* as object), or in *I told Max that he was wrong* (antecedent as object, anaphor as subject), and so on. Indeed, in most (but not all) kinds of anaphora it is possible for the antecedent to be in a separate sentence from the anaphor. For these reasons there will often be more than one potential antecedent for a given anaphor, leading to ambiguity:

[7] *I've just been talking to Max. I understand that Ed has told Frank that the Commission's report has exonerated him completely.*

As far as the grammar is concerned, any of *Max*, *Ed*, and *Frank* could serve as antecedent for *him* here. A thoughtful writer would tend to avoid such examples, at least in careful style, unless it was clear from the context which was the intended antecedent.

In the examples used in this chapter, and elsewhere in the book, we will commonly indicate the intended antecedent by underlining (*Max claims he wasn't told*) and/or by co-indexing (*Max$_i$ claims he$_i$ wasn't told*); this will make it unnecessary to keep qualifying our remarks by saying that they apply only in a particular interpretation.

Anaphoric marker and anaphor

In our introductory discussion of deixis we drew a distinction between deictic marker and deictic expression, so that in *Put it with those boxes*, the determiner *those* is the deictic marker and the whole referring NP *those boxes* is the deictic expression. A corresponding distinction for anaphora is needed to handle examples like:

[8] *We'd been listening to Paul: that guy certainly knows how to stir things up.*

It is the whole NP *that guy* that derives its interpretation from the antecedent *Paul*; *that guy* therefore counts as the anaphor, while *that* (as used here) serves as an **anaphoric marker** indicating that the interpretation of the NP is to be obtained from an antecedent. In the more frequent case illustrated by *he* and *so* in [6], the anaphoric marker constitutes the whole anaphor.

Our terminology is not quite parallel for deixis and anaphora: we use 'anaphor' in preference to 'anaphoric expression'. We make such frequent use of the concept of anaphor in this chapter that it is convenient to have a single-word term.

The close relation between anaphora and deixis

Anaphora and deixis are treated together in this chapter because they have a great deal in common. The nature of the relation between them will be clarified as we proceed, but two initial points can be made here.

(a) Forms may be simultaneously deictic and anaphoric

[9] i *Sue is coming over later; we are having lunch together.*
ii *I was born in London and have lived here all my life.*
iii *I was born in London and have lived there all my life.*

In the salient interpretation of [i] *we* refers to the set consisting of Sue and me: the speaker component of this is determined deictically by virtue of *we* being a 1st person pronoun, while the inclusion of Sue in the set is determined anaphorically by virtue of the previous mention of her. In [ii] *here* is anaphoric in that it obtains the interpretation "in London" from the preceding PP, but at the same time it is deictic in that it refers to a place which includes that where the utterance-act takes place. Similarly with [iii], except that this time the deictic component of *there* indicates that the place is relatively distant from where I am speaking. Because they have the same antecedent, the *here* of [ii] and the *there* of [iii] refer to the same place, but the different deictic meanings indicate that the utterance of [ii] takes place in London while that of [iii] does not.

(b) Some items can serve either as deictic markers or as anaphoric markers

[10]		DEICTIC	ANAPHORIC
	i	a. *What's <u>that</u> he's got in his hand?*	b. *He wants $30, but <u>that</u>'s too much.*
	ii	a. *She lives <u>only half a mile away</u>.*	b. *I didn't see her very often when I was at College: she lived <u>too far away</u>.*
	iii	a. *They'll be here <u>soon</u>.*	b. *She was stunned, but <u>soon</u> recovered.*

In [ia] *that* will be interpreted deictically as referring to some object present in the situation of utterance and relatively distant from me, whereas in [ib] it obtains its interpretation anaphorically, from the antecedent *$30*. The two uses of ***that*** are clearly related, and it is plausible to regard the anaphoric use as derivative from the deictic and in fact it retains some residual deictic meaning.

Spatial *away* in [10ii] is understood relationally, i.e. as away from some place, the source. In the salient or default reading of [iia] this is the location of the speaker at the time the utterance takes place: "only half a mile away from <u>here</u>", so *away* is implicitly deictic. In [iib] we understand "too far away from <u>College</u>": here the implied source is recovered anaphorically. Similarly, *soon* is interpreted in [iiia] as "in a short time from now", and in [iiib] as "in a short time after being stunned". In the deictic cases, therefore, the place or time referred to is identified relative to the place or time of the utterance-act, whereas in the anaphoric ones it is identified relative to a place or time given in the preceding text.

Retrospective and anticipatory anaphora

The examples of anaphora considered so far have it in common that the anaphor follows the antecedent. It is also possible, however, for the anaphor to come first. Compare:

[11]			
	i	*When <u>the headmaster</u> saw the damage, <u>he</u> called in the police.*	[retrospective]
	ii	*When <u>he</u> saw the damage, <u>the headmaster</u> called in the police.*	[anticipatory]

We refer to the two cases as **retrospective** and **anticipatory** anaphora respectively.[2] In [i] the anaphor *he* looks back, as it were, to find the antecedent that provides its interpretation, whereas in [ii] it looks forward into what follows.[3] Retrospective anaphora

[2] Etymologically, the term 'anaphora' is based on the retrospective case, and some writers restrict it to this, using 'cataphora' for the anticipatory case. 'Endophora' is sometimes used as a more general term applying to both. 'Antecedent' also has an etymology associated with retrospective anaphora, but its generalisation to the anticipatory case is quite standardly accepted.

[3] The term 'backwards anaphora' is commonly used for anticipatory anaphora. This seemingly perverse usage stems from early transformational analyses under which an example like [11ii] was assigned an 'underlying structure' like '*When <u>the headmaster</u>$_i$ saw the damage, <u>the headmaster</u>$_i$ called in the police*'. A transformational operation ('pronominalisation'), sensitive to identity of form and reference and certain other conditions, replaced the first occurrence of *the headmaster* by a pronoun, thus looking backwards from the unchanged occurrence to the 'pronominalised' one. Such analyses have long been abandoned, but the terminology has survived.

is much the more common and can be regarded as the default case, with anticipatory anaphora permitted only under quite restricted conditions (see §2.4).

Types of anticipatory anaphora: integrated vs non-integrated antecedent

We distinguish two cases where the anaphor precedes the antecedent, as illustrated in:

[12] i *None of those who actually saw it said the film should be banned.* [integrated]
ii *It's official: Bill Gates is now the richest man in the world.* [non-integrated]

In [i] the antecedent *the film* is integrated into a larger construction: it is subject of the clause *the film should be banned.* But in [ii] the antecedent is *Bill Gates is now the richest man in the world*, which is a supplement rather than a constituent of some larger syntactic construction. The order of antecedent and anaphor cannot be reversed in the latter type – compare:

[13] i *None of those who actually saw the film thought it should be banned.*
ii **That Bill Gates is now the richest man in the world is official: it.*

But the two types cannot be distinguished simply by reversibility, for we shall see that under certain conditions the integrated antecedent type is non-reversible. What distinguishes the non-integrated type of anticipatory anaphora is that it is non-reversible for a particular reason: when we replace the anaphor by the antecedent there ceases to be any work for the anaphor to do. This is why [13ii] is incoherent: the *it* appears to be referring to something, but I'm neither saying nor implying anything further about what is stated in the antecedent clause. In [12ii] the *it* acts as a provisional subject and the clause *Bill Gates is now the richest man in the world* then serves to provide an interpretation for it. So if we replace the anaphor by the antecedent we no longer need the anaphor.

Ellipsis

The concept of anaphor can be readily extended to cover various kinds of ellipsis. Compare:

[14] i *If you want me to invite Kim as well, I will __.* [retrospective ellipsis]
ii *If you want me to __, I will invite Kim as well.* [anticipatory ellipsis]

In [i] the infinitival complement of *will* is ellipted,[4] being recoverable from that of *want* in the conditional adjunct, whereas in [ii] the ellipsis is within the complement of *want*, with that of *will* providing the interpretation. *Invite Kim as well* can therefore be analysed as the antecedent, and the elliptical 'gap' as the anaphor. The retrospective vs anticipatory contrast seen here is the same as that in [11], so that [14i] illustrates the default case where the anaphoric gap follows the antecedent from which it derives its interpretation, while in [14ii] we have the less usual case – subject, we will see, to the same quite stringent grammatical conditions as generally apply with overt anaphors – where the gap precedes the antecedent. As with most kinds of overt anaphors, the antecedent for an elliptical gap may be in a preceding sentence:

[15] A: *Why don't you invite Kim as well?* B: *I don't want to __.*

[4] We use 'ellipt' as the verb corresponding to the noun 'ellipsis'; it is not found in traditional grammar, but has become reasonably well established in modern grammatical studies.

Anaphoric chains

In the examples so far we have had a single anaphoric link between an anaphor and its antecedent, but very often we find a sequence of such links forming what we will call an **anaphoric chain**:

[16] i *My daughter$_i$ tells me that her$_i$ car has been giving her$_i$ a lot of trouble recently. She$_i$ thinks she$_i$ may have to start cycling to work.*
ii *If he$_i$ hurts himself$_i$, Max$_i$ will undoubtedly blame you.*
iii *Ann$_i$ regretted _$_i$ committing herself$_i$ to the project.*

In [i] *my daughter* is antecedent to the first *her* (a genitive pronoun), and this in turn is antecedent to the second *her* (an accusative pronoun), and so on. In this example, each anaphor refers to the same person as its antecedent, so all the underlined NPs have the same reference. Similarly, in [ii] *Max* is antecedent for *he* (this being a case of anticipatory anaphora), and *he* is antecedent for *himself.* Elliptical gaps can also figure in anaphoric chains; for simplicity they were not marked in [i], but an elementary example is given in [iii]. Here the anaphor *herself* is linked to the covert subject of the *commit* clause, and this in turn is linked to *Ann.*

We talk in terms of a chain of anaphoric relations between anaphor and antecedent rather than say that in such an example as [16i] all the pronouns are related directly to *my daughter* as antecedent. There are a number of factors that support the chain treatment.

(a) Restrictions on permitted type of anaphor

The most important concerns various restrictions on the location of the antecedents of certain types of anaphor, most notably reflexive pronouns. In [16ii], for example, *himself* has *he* as antecedent, and *he* has *Max* as antecedent: *himself* cannot be directly related to *Max.* This is evident from the ungrammaticality of, say, **If they hurt himself$_i$, Max$_i$ will undoubtedly blame you.* Similarly, *herself* in [iii] could not be directly linked to the subject of the matrix clause: compare **Ann$_i$ regretted my committing herself$_i$ to the project.*

(b) Progressive changes in the nature of the entity referred to

A second point is that the nature of the referent being talked about may change during a sequence of events described:

[17] *Wash a bunch of fresh spinach well and then shred it finely. Sauté it in a little butter until it is wilted, drain __, then put a little into each ramekin.*

A little here is interpreted not as referring to a little of the bunch of fresh spinach, but rather to a little of the spinach that results after the shredding, sautéing, wilting, and draining.

(c) Potential distance between antecedent and anaphor

There can be a very large distance between the first antecedent in a chain and the final anaphor, greater than would typically be permitted for a direct link: it is the intermediate links that keep the referent salient in the context of discourse so that reference to it can be made by means of a personal pronoun or other anaphor with little intrinsic content.

1.3 The relationship between an anaphor and its antecedent

Traditionally an anaphor is said to refer to its antecedent, but that is a very different sense of 'refer' from that in which we say that an NP refers to a person or other entity in the outside world. We will not use 'reference' for the relation between anaphor and antecedent. 'Anaphora' itself is the term that names this relation. We will describe an anaphoric pronoun as **anaphoric to,** or **anaphorically linked to,** an antecedent. Our concern in the present section is therefore to give a brief account of the nature of this relationship.

(a) Coreference between NPs

The simplest and prototypical relation between anaphorically linked NPs is that of coreference:

[18] *The drummer was late because he had overslept again.*

In the intended interpretation, *he* is anaphoric to *the drummer* and by virtue of that relation refers to the same person as the latter phrase: we say then that antecedent and anaphor are **coreferential.** This underscores the point just made concerning the term 'refer': *he* in [i] refers to a person in the outside world, not the linguistic expression *the drummer.*

(b) Anaphorically linked NPs that are not coreferential: the bound variable interpretation

Two NPs can be coreferential only if both of them are referring expressions, but very often an anaphor and/or its antecedent do not satisfy this condition:

[19] i *No one put their hand up.*
ii *Every car had its windscreen smashed.*

Neither *no one* nor *their* has reference in [i]; the anaphoric relation here can best be described in terms of a bound variable, with the meaning represented roughly as "There is no person *x* such that *x* put *x*'s hand up" (see §2.3.2 below). Similarly for [ii]: "for every car *x*, *x* had *x*'s windscreen broken".

(c) NP anaphors with antecedents that are not NPs

Another important case where the relation between an anaphoric NP and its antecedent cannot properly be described as coreference is that where the antecedent is a clause, VP, or some similar expression:

[20] i *His digestion was upset, and this led him to the discovery of yoghurt.*
ii *He smiled and stuck a large finger with white hairs sprouting on it into his ear as though that might help.*
iii *If you don't go while you have a chance, you'll regret it.*
iv *They may bring the dog with them, which would make things difficult for us.*

Again, there cannot be coreference here because the antecedent is not a referring expression. The NP anaphors refer to various kinds of abstract entity such as states of affairs, actions, facts, propositions, etc. It is very often not possible to identify a constituent or sequence of the preceding text that can be said to express precisely the content of the anaphor. In [iv], for example, it is not the possibility of their bringing the dog but their actually bringing it, that would make things difficult. In [ii] the smiling is presumably irrelevant, but the fact that the finger had white hairs sprouting on it could well be irrelevant too, the issue being simply whether sticking a finger in his ear might help.

The relation between anaphor and antecedent in such cases is characteristically of a somewhat looser kind than we have in cases (a)–(b) above. The task of interpreting such anaphors cannot be reduced to that of identifying an antecedent. Nothing would be gained, for example, by saying that the antecedent for *which* in [iv] is *they... bring their dog with them*, rather than the continuous sequence underlined above.

(d) Anaphors that are not NPs

In many cases the anaphor is not an NP. A few examples of this kind are given in:

[21] i *I asked for a green shirt, but he gave me a white one.* [noun]
ii *If you want me to stay on I will do so.* [VP]
iii *Liz will complain, or at least I think she will __.* [VP gap]

In [i] the anaphoric relation is not between the NPs *a green shirt* and *a white one*, but between the nouns *shirt* and *one*. These are not referring expressions: we understand the antecedent and anaphor here to have the same denotation, not the same reference. Nor, of course, is there a relation of coreference between the NPs that have the anaphorically linked expressions as their heads, namely *a green shirt* and *a white one*. The relation in [ii–iii] is similarly one of like denotation: we understand "I will stay on" and "she will complain". In both of these the antecedent is a VP; in [ii] the anaphor is a VP too, while [iii] is one of a wide range of types of elliptical anaphora.

Although the relation between anaphor and antecedent in [21] is not itself one of coreference, there may be coreference between an NP **contained** within the antecedent and one implied by the anaphor:

[22] i *There's only one photograph of the children here: where's the other one?*
ii *If you want me to invite Kim I will do so.*
iii *Liz will win the prize, or at least I think she will __.*

In [i] we could replace the anaphor *one* by *photograph of the children*, with the understanding that it is the same children as are referred to in the first clause. Similarly, in [ii–iii] we can replace the anaphors by *invite Kim* and *win the prize*, and again it is the same Kim, the same prize as is referred to within the antecedent. But it is not always so:

[23] i *He's got lots of photographs of lions: why does he need to take another one?*
ii *I've never lodged a complaint before, but I'm going to __ now.*
iii *Ed always gets his kids to help in the kitchen: why don't you __?*

Lions in [i] does not refer to any particular lions, and so it is not a question of whether he needs to take another photograph of the same lions. Note, moreover, that neither antecedent nor anaphor indicates explicitly whether individual photographs are of one or more than one lion. In [ii], *a complaint* is non-referential (there is no prior complaint to refer to), so again there is no coreference.

Example [23iii] is different, since here we have an ambiguity between the following interpretations:

[24] i "Why don't you get his kids to help in the kitchen?" [implicit coreference]
ii "Why don't you get your kids to help in the kitchen?" [implicit bound variable]

In the first interpretation the VP gap implicitly refers to Ed's kids, so that there is implicit coreference with the NP *his kids* contained within the antecedent. In the second interpretation (pragmatically more likely) it is a matter of getting your own kids to help in the kitchen. To account for this reading we again need the concept of bound variable. It follows from the first clause that "x gets x's kids to help in the kitchen" holds where $x =$ Ed, and my question is about why it does not also hold where $x =$ you.

With a reflexive pronoun as the contained NP, only the implicit bound variable reading is available. *Max had hurt himself and Ed had __ too* does not have a reading in which Ed had hurt Max: the meaning is that *x* had hurt *x* holds for Ed as well as for Max. Gender makes no difference: we can say *Max had hurt himself and Julie had __ too*, meaning that Julie had hurt herself.[5]

(e) Split and 'missing' antecedents

[25] i *Kim$_i$ is better than Pat$_j$ but neither of them$_{i+j}$ is really suitable for the position.*

ii *I hadn't taken an umbrella with me$_i$, but Liz had __$_i$, and she was good enough to let me borrow it$_j$.*

The antecedent for an anaphor may be split into two or more separate parts. This is illustrated in [i], where the antecedent for *them* consists of *Kim* and *Pat* together. The first clause introduces Kim and Pat into the context of discourse (or maintains their salience if they have been introduced earlier), and this makes it possible to refer to the set comprising them both by means of the pronoun ***they***: whether or not they were introduced by means of a single constituent is irrelevant. Example [ii] shows that the antecedent for an anaphor may be merely implied by another anaphor. The clause *Liz had* contains an elliptical gap which is anaphoric to the underlined complement in the first clause: we interpret it therefore as "Liz had taken an umbrella with her". This introduces an umbrella into the context of discourse which can subsequently be referred to by the pronoun *it*. The term **missing antecedent** is commonly applied to constructions like [ii]: there is nothing that can, strictly speaking, be identified as the antecedent of *it*.

Discourse deixis

One case that needs to be distinguished from anaphora is discourse deixis:

[26] i *Take the bus to Murwillumbah. Shall I spell that for you?*

ii A: *It was a great lurk.* B: *Is that another Australianism?*

iii A: *Is this a dagger that I see before me?* B: *That was too loud.*

That in [i] refers to *Murwillumbah* the word, not Murwillumbah the town. *Murwillumbah* is not the antecedent but the referent. This, then, is not anaphora but deixis. It is comparable to the central deictic use of *What's that you're holding?*, differing, however, in that the referent is not physically present in the situation of utterance but is located in the discourse itself.[6] *That* in [ii] is very similar, referring to the word *lurk*; *lurk*, however, is

[5] Reading [24ii] is commonly labelled as involving 'sloppy identity' between anaphor and antecedent. The idea is that for the VP to be understood as "gets his kids to help in the kitchen" involves an exact match with the antecedent *gets his kids to help in the kitchen*, but for it to be understood as "get your kids to help in the kitchen" involves only an inexact or sloppy match ("your" does not match *his*). Likewise the match between "hurt herself" and *hurt himself*. We avoid this term because it runs the risk of being misconstrued as making a stylistic judgement. There is nothing stylistically sloppy about this kind of anaphora, even for the most authoritarian of prescriptivists.

[6] An alternative term for discourse deixis is textual deixis. With both terms it is to be understood that the discourse or text in question is the one that is currently ongoing. It is of course also possible to refer to entities in some other text that happens to be present in the context of utterance, normally in writing. Thus I might say, indicating a word in my son's school assignment, *This word is incorrectly spelt.* But there is nothing special about this phenomenon, which is more obviously distinct from anaphora than the examples in [26].

a common noun, and hence is not itself a referring expression in A's utterance. Again, then, *lurk* and *that* are not coreferential: rather *that* refers deictically to a word in the discourse. In [iii] *that* refers not to a word, or sentence, but to A's utterance (in a rehearsal of 'Macbeth', let us assume, with A the actor and B the director).

Discourse deixis is most clearly distinct from anaphora when the reference is to a word or phrase, as in [26i–ii]. Less obvious are cases like the following:

[27] i A: *Kim has been falsifying the accounts.* B: *That's terrible.* [anaphoric]
ii A: *Kim has been falsifying the accounts.* B: *That's a lie.* [discourse-deictic]

In [i] A's utterance is the antecedent for B's *that*, which refers to the situation that A has described. This belongs to the type illustrated in [20] above, where an NP anaphor has a clause as its antecedent. But in [ii] *that* refers to A's speech act, to a linguistic entity in the prior discourse.

The form *hereby* has the special property that it is used only in discourse deixis, as in *I hereby pronounce you husband and wife* or *You are hereby invited to forward any amendments to the secretary.* The meaning is essentially "by virtue of this speech act". The reference therefore is to the utterance that contains the deictic expression. Self-reference of this kind is also found in examples like *I should warn you that this conversation is being recorded.* But of course *this conversation* is not restricted to the discourse-deictic use.

1.4 **Pro-forms**

Pro-forms and pronouns

The traditional term 'pronoun' is based on the idea that words of this class 'stand for' nouns. Traditional grammar does not work with a constituent structure model like that assumed in this book, and hence does not draw the distinction we do between nouns and NPs. When adapted to the present framework, therefore, the traditional idea is that pronouns are words that 'stand for' NPs.

The most obvious kind of 'stand for' relation is anaphoric, with the pronoun used instead of repeating the antecedent, as in elementary examples like:

[28] i *Liz thinks she may be able to help.*
ii *The woman next door thinks she may be able to help.*

Example [ii] brings out the point that *she* stands for (is anaphoric to) an NP, not a noun: [i] illustrates the special case where the antecedent NP happens to consist of just a noun.

In the present grammar we retain the traditional category of pronoun, but introduce a further category based on the idea of 'standing for' – the category of **pro-form**. A pro-form is an anaphor with little inherent semantic content of its own: the interpretation derives from the antecedent, so that the anaphor need contain little descriptive information itself. Pro-forms are single words (or in a few cases idioms, such as *do so*): they constitute a subclass of anaphors. Thus *she* is a pro-form in [28], but in [8] above (*We'd been listening to Paul: that guy certainly knows how to stir things up*) the anaphor *that guy* is not a pro-form: it is a phrase with lexical content of its own.

The sets of pronouns and pro-forms overlap, but neither set is wholly contained within the other.

(a) Not all pronouns are pro-forms

Clear cases of pronouns that are not anaphors are interrogative ***who*** and *what*. To the extent that they can be said to stand for an NP, it is in the sense that they take the place in a question that would generally be filled by an NP in the answer. This falls outside the scope of anaphora: the interpretation of these pronouns is not mediated by an antecedent expression, and hence the interrogative pronouns do not qualify as anaphors. In addition, the 1st and 2nd person pronouns, especially singular ***I*** and ***you***, are predominantly used deictically rather than anaphorically.

From a syntactic point of view, ***who***, *what*, ***I***, and ***you*** belong with ***she***, ***he***, etc., in that they function as head in NP structure, differing from other words in this function in that they exclude determiners. This is what makes them all pronouns. Note, however, that while pronouns are traditionally regarded as a distinct part of speech, we are treating them as a subclass of nouns: they belong in the noun class by virtue of occurring as head in NP structure.

(b) Not all pro-forms are pronouns

Probably the most obvious pro-form that doesn't qualify as a pronoun is *so*, while another clear (but not so obvious) example is ***one***, as used in [29ii]:

[29] i *Kim may be too ill to attend; if so I'll have to ask you to chair the meeting.*
ii *This copy of the notice is blurred, but the other ones appear to be satisfactory.*

So is clearly a pro-form here, being interpreted anaphorically as "Kim is too ill to attend". But it could not be replaced by an NP, and there is no basis for saying that it constitutes an NP, hence none for saying that it is a pronoun. *Ones* in [ii] is anaphoric to the nominal *copy of the notice*, and like the latter functions as head in NP structure. It nevertheless fails to qualify as a member of the syntactic class of pronouns because it occurs readily with determiners: it is a common noun. Note, moreover, that like most common nouns, but unlike pronouns, it inflects for number.

Other pro-forms that are not pronouns include spatial *there* and temporal *then*:

[30] i *I put your letter in the top-drawer; I hope it is still there.*
ii *They are coming at around five o'clock; will you still be here then?*

We take these to be (intransitive) prepositions: they could be replaced by transitive PPs and typically have PPs as antecedents.[7]

Kinds of pro-form

Instead of talking simply of 'pro-forms', we will often use more specific terms such as '**pro-NP**' for an anaphor with an NP antecedent, '**pro-clause**' with a clausal antecedent, '**pro-nominal**' where the antecedent is of the nominal category,[8] etc.:

[7] *Then* and *there* are traditionally described as pronominal adverbs. 'Pronominal' is to be interpreted in this context as "resembling a pronoun": they are like (some central) pronouns in that they are used anaphorically (or deictically too).

[8] Notice that our hyphenated term 'pro-nominal' is distinct from the unhyphenated word 'pronominal,' often used as an adjective related to the noun 'pronoun'.

[31] i *The car is being serviced at the moment but it should be ready soon.* [pro-NP]
ii *If he was disappointed by her response he did not show it.* [pro-clause]
iii *This photo of Ann is much better than the other one.* [pro-nominal]
iv *I think she'll be there – I certainly hope so.* [pro-clause]
v *I met her last time I was in Paris but she doesn't live there now.* [pro-PP]

In [i] *it* has an NP as antecedent, and if it were replaced by an equivalent expression that was not a pro-form, this too would be an NP (*the car should be ready soon*). Similarly in [ii] the antecedent is a clause, and we could replace *it* by a clause (*he did not show that he was disappointed by her response*).

We will use this 'pro-X' formulation only when both the antecedent and the potential replacement belong to the same category X. This is the usual case, but there are some places where it does not apply:

[32] i *She had expected to find the church empty, but three women were there.*
ii *The Opposition vehemently objected to any increase in the powers of local government, so much so that the new system which was inaugurated in April 1934 was thrown out in August of the same year.*

The antecedent in [i] is an NP, but the anaphor *there* is a PP, and its replacement would require a preposition: *three women were in the church*. Example [ii] represents a more restricted case: when modified by *so much* in this way the pro-form *so* cannot be replaced by any matching form, whether a clause like the antecedent or not.

2 The personal pronouns

The full set of personal pronouns is given in Ch. 5, §10.1.1; the ones we will be concerned with here are as follows:

[1]

	SINGULAR	PLURAL
1ST PERSON	***I***	***we***
2ND PERSON	***you***	***you***
3RD PERSON	***he, she, it***	***they***

In this section we are generally concerned with the pronouns as lexemes, with ***I*** subsuming the forms *I*, *me*, *my*, *mine*, and *myself*, and so on. The distinction between reflexive *myself* and the non-reflexive forms is closely bound up with anaphora and will be taken up in §3 below, but that between nominative *I*, accusative *me*, dependent genitive *my*, and independent genitive *mine* is a matter of case, and not of concern in the present chapter.

Personal pronouns are so called because they are the ones to which the grammatical system of **person** applies. This is the system whose terms are differentiated by reference to the utterance-act roles of speaker and addressee:

[2] i 1ST PERSON Characteristically used for the speaker or a group including at least one speaker.
ii 2ND PERSON Characteristically used for the addressee or a group including at least one addressee but no speaker.
iii 3RD PERSON The residual category – not 1st or 2nd.

2.1 3rd person as the default category

Any NP that is not explicitly marked as 1st person by ***I*** or ***we*** or as 2nd person by ***you*** is 3rd person. ***He***, ***she***, ***it***, and ***they*** are given in [1] as personal pronouns because they belong in the same syntactic class as 1st and 2nd person ***I***, ***we***, ***you***, but pronouns of other categories such as interrogative *what* and **who**, and NPs that are not pronouns (*Kim, the doctor, those boxes*) are 3rd person too.

At the language-particular level 3rd person is defined by the absence of the 1st and 2nd person markers ***I***, ***we***, and ***you***. It should be emphasised, however, that 3rd person NPs do not explicitly exclude reference to the speaker or addressee: unlike 1st and 2nd person, 3rd person is not a deictic category. Thus it is perfectly possible to refer to oneself or to the addressee in the 3rd person:

[3] 3RD PERSON REFERENCE TO THE SPEAKER/WRITER
- i A: *Ann is going to volunteer.* B (Ann): *She/Ann is going to do no such thing.*
- ii *The writer has to admit that he cannot see the logic of this argument.*
- iii *Your reviewer is unable to find any merit in this film.*

[4] 3RD PERSON REFERENCE TO THE ADDRESSEE
- i *And how is young Francis this morning?*
- ii *Does Madam / His Lordship require anything further?*
- iii *The reader no doubt recalls that this issue also arose in Ch. 2.*

In [3i] the speaker refers to herself as *she* or *Ann*, following A's reference to her as *Ann*. One plausible context for this usage is where A was unaware that Ann was present or able to hear: Ann uses the form that would be appropriate if A's assumption were correct, but the fact that it is she herself who is using it draws attention to A's mistake. It could equally be that Ann is known to be present: her use of the 3rd person here matches A's 3rd person *Ann* and draws attention to A's failure to use a 2nd person form, A's failure to consult her. In either case, *she* acquires its referential interpretation anaphorically, not by person-deixis. In [3ii–iii] the underlined NPs can likewise be used to refer to the speaker/writer: they permit self-reference without the use of 1st person ***I***. And in the intended interpretations of the examples in [4] the underlined NPs are used to refer to the addressee. Note also that a 3rd person NP can be used to refer to one member of a group of addressees. In a seminar discussion, for example, I might say *Emily's suggestion sounds promising: would you like to elaborate?*, with the first clause addressed to the group as a whole, the second to Emily in particular.

That the underlined NPs in [3–4] are all 3rd person, not 1st or 2nd, is evident from the form of the verb, which agrees in person and number with the subject: in [3i] we have *is* not *am*, in [ii] *has*, not *have*, and so on. As so often, therefore, it is necessary to distinguish carefully between meaning or reference and grammatical form: the reference here is to speaker/writer or addressee, but the form is 3rd person. Thus 3rd person does not mean that the reference is to an entity other than speaker or addressee: it means only that the reference is not derivable from the person feature, as it is with 1st and 2nd person.

The same applies where there is reference to a set rather than an individual:

[5]
- i *All members of the cabinet support this proposal.*
- ii *Do all members of the cabinet support this proposal?*
- iii *The McCarthys have owned this estate for five generations.*
- iv *Everyone in the team is going to have to improve their performance.*

It is perfectly possible for [i] to be said by a member of the cabinet and for [ii] to be addressed to one. Analogously for [iii–iv]. There is nothing in the form or meaning of these NPs to indicate whether the speaker or addressee is included in the set referred to. They contrast in this respect with NPs like *all of us/you in the cabinet, we McCarthys.* Note also that it may be possible to explicitly indicate inclusion of speaker or addressee by means of an anaphoric 1st or 2nd person pronoun: *Everyone in the team is going to have to improve our/your performance.*

2.2 1st and 2nd person

2.2.1 Primary uses

We look first at what we will call the primary uses of ***I***, ***we***, and ***you*** – the uses which match the general definitions given in [2]. Here the interpretation is determined deictically.

Singular *I* and *you*

[6] a. *I have just finished my assignment.* b. *Have you hurt yourself?*

I refers straightforwardly to the speaker, ***you*** to the addressee: no further commentary is needed.

Plural *we*

(a) Single speaker vs plurality of speakers

We refers to a set of two or more that includes a speaker.

[7] i *Hurry up! We are going to be late.*
ii *Why are we waiting?*
iii *We accept your offer subject to the conditions stated below.*

Usually the set consists of a single speaker together with one or more others, as in the likely interpretation of [i]. The relation between ***we*** and ***I*** is thus very different from that between *books* and *book*, and we take them to be distinct lexemes, not plural and singular forms of a single lexeme. It is, however, perfectly possible for the group to contain a plurality of speakers, as in plausible interpretations of [ii–iii]. In the case of speech this use involves speaking in unison, as in singing, praying, chanting, and the like: [ii], for example, is commonly chanted by a crowd of spectators when the start of the event they have come to watch has been delayed. In the case of writing, it may be a matter of joint signatories, of a letter, contract, petition, etc., as in [iii] (note the formula *we, the undersigned, . . .*), or joint authorship, as of a book, for example.

(b) Inclusive and exclusive

A second issue is whether or not the set includes one or more addressees in addition to the speaker:

[8] i *Why don't we go together instead of taking two cars?* [inclusive]
ii *We could lend you a couple of hundred dollars if that would help.* [exclusive]

In the natural interpretation of [i] it is a matter of you and me (and possibly others too) going together, whereas in [ii] it is unlikely that you are a member of the set that would lend you the money. The terms **inclusive** and **exclusive** are standardly used to distinguish these cases: inclusive or exclusive of the addressee, that is. We noted in §1.1 that deixis is generally centred on the speaker, and the priority accorded to the speaker over the addressee (which leads us to call them respectively 1st and 2nd person) is reflected in the fact that a set containing both speaker and addressee is referred to by 1st person ***we***, not 2nd person ***you***.

Many languages have distinct pronouns for inclusive and exclusive 1st person plural reference, but as far as English is concerned there is just one place where the distinction is grammaticalised. The 1st person plural imperative, marked by a special use of *let*, is always interpreted inclusively, and here *us* can be, and almost always is, reduced to the clitic form *'s*. Compare:

[9] i *Let's finish this off tomorrow.* [1st person imperative]
ii *Please let us have our ball back.* [2nd person imperative]

In [i] the *'s* necessarily includes the addressee(s) as well as the speaker. In [ii], *let* has its ordinary meaning of "allow" and *us* cannot be reduced to *'s*.

(c) Variation in the size and specificity of the set referred to

We stipulates that the set referred to contains someone with the role of speaker, but this leaves great scope for variation with respect to who else is included. Compare, for example:

[10] i *I went out to dinner with my uncle and aunt on Monday: it cost us nearly $300.*
ii *When we were trying to sell our home we had it valued independently.*
iii *We have lived here for three generations.*
iv *When I was at school we had to share the oval.*
v *How did you get on during that storm we had at the week-end?*
vi *We are seriously overtaxed as it is.*
vii *We have many more back problems than other primates.*

In [i] the remaining membership is determined anaphorically, via the antecedent *my uncle and aunt*. In [ii] the group probably consists of me and my partner, while in [iii] *we* may apply to a family – with the predication applying jointly to the set as a whole, not to the members individually. In [iv] I'm talking about the school population, and in [v] about those present in the area affected by the storm. As we move to [vi] the set grows: I'm here probably talking about the population of a country. And in [vii] *we* refers to humankind in general.

Plural *you*

The 2nd person plural is distinct from the singular only in the reflexive form *yourselves*.[9] It applies to a set consisting of an addressee and one or more other non-speakers. The size and specificity of the group can vary in the same way as was illustrated above for ***we***. Compare:

[11] i *I saw Jill the other day – have you two had a fight?*
ii *Did you have your house valued independently before you sold it?*
iii *I'm told you have lived here for three generations.*
iv *Did you get any rain over in Whittlesea?*
v *You seem to be even more heavily taxed in this country than we are back home.*

[9] There are dialectal forms that distinguish a plural non-reflexive: *youse* (found in North America, Australia, Scotland, Ireland) and *you-all*, or *y'all* (primarily US Southerners).

2.2.2 Secondary uses

(a) Authorial *we*

Written works authored by a single person often use ***we*** as a means of involving the reader and/or avoiding the 1st person singular pronoun ***I***. Many people feel that ***I*** should be used very sparingly, if at all, in certain types of writing, particularly scientific papers or books: the idea is that reference to the speaker as an individual may make the text appear inappropriately personal and subjective.

[12] i *We have seen in Ch. 3 that this methodology has a number of drawbacks.*
ii *In the next chapter we will describe the methodology used.*

It can be argued that in examples like [i] *we* has plural reference to the author + readers and hence is an instance of the primary use of ***we***. Such an explanation is harder to justify in [ii], for it will in fact be the author alone who will describe the methodology. No sharp boundary can be drawn between the two cases, however, and even in [ii] there remains some suggestion that the reader is being invited to engage in a joint enterprise.

(b) *We* for single speaker

[13] *Give us a lick of your icecream.*

This can be interpreted with *us* referring to the speaker alone; as such it is a very colloquial form characteristic of the speech of children or intimates. It applies only with accusative and perhaps genitive forms. At the opposite end of the stylistic spectrum is the honorific singular *we* of Queen Victoria's *We are not amused*, but this usage is no longer current.

(c) *We* for addressee or third party

[14] i *How are we feeling this morning? Have we taken our medicine?*
ii *Oh dear, we are a bit cranky this morning, aren't we?*

Example [i] might be used to ask about the addressee: "How are you feeling this morning? Have you taken your medicine?" This usage is generally found in contexts of illness (doctor, nurse, etc., to patient) or tuition (teacher to pupil: *We need to practise our scales*); it runs the risk of being construed as patronising.[10] Examples like [ii] convey mockery; they might be used in talking to or about the person concerned. The latter is likely to be someone I have a regular association with: my boss or teacher, perhaps, or a child I have in my care.

(d) Non-referential *you*

[15] i *You can get fined for parking on the footpath.*
ii *I think Smith's a really great speaker, whether you agree with him or not.*
iii *You have to avoid that sort of thing when you're eight months pregnant.*
iv *You couldn't hear yourself talk, it was so noisy.*

Singular ***you*** is commonly used as a less formal variant of ***one***: compare *One can get fined for parking on the pavement*, and so on. Unlike singular ***you*** in its primary use, this ***you*** does not refer to a specific person, the addressee, but is used to talk about people in

[10] In the attested example *Let's just hop up on the couch and have a look at you, eh?* we have an unusual switch in interpretation between the coordinates: it is the patient who is to hop onto the couch but the doctor who is to have a look (note the ordinary 2nd person *you* here).

general. There can be a fairly clear ambiguity according as ***you*** is interpreted referentially or not. Take [ii], for example. With referential ***you*** this could be used (though of course does not have to be) in a context where you have expressed disagreement with Smith: in this case I convey that in spite of your disagreeing with him I myself think he's a great speaker. With non-referential ***you***, by contrast, what I convey is that one doesn't have to agree with him to recognise that he is a great speaker. The non-referential ***you*** in [iv] is used in talking about some particular event in the past, and is understood as applying to those present at the time (most likely including the speaker).

The connection between the two uses of ***you*** is that what holds for people in general will characteristically hold for you personally. If one can be fined for parking on the footpath, then you personally may be fined if you park there. However, a general statement involving non-referential ***you*** need not apply in fact to the addressee: [15iii], for example, could be addressed to a man. Note also the apposition in the following attested example, spoken by an actor: *Playing these slightly unsavoury characters that I do, I think it tends to leave an aroma on you, the actor.*

(e) Play-acting

[16] *I commit suicide before they discover it was you who murdered the duke.*

In a highly restricted set of contexts the 1st and 2nd person pronouns can be used to refer not to the actual speaker and addressee themselves but to characters in a play or the like.

2.3 3rd person

2.3.1 Anaphoric and non-anaphoric uses

While the 1st and 2nd person pronouns are generally used deictically, the characteristic use of the 3rd person personal pronouns ***he***, ***she***, ***it***, and ***they*** is anaphoric:

[17] i *If you see Paul, please tell him that the lawn needs mowing.*
ii *I've just been talking to your sister. She seems rather depressed.*
iii *What's that you've got there? Give it to me.*
iv *I'd made several mistakes, but fortunately they weren't very serious.*

The pronouns here are definite referring expressions, and in this subsection we will confine our attention to such uses. The use of a definite referring expression implies that the speaker takes the referent to be identifiable without further description, and in these cases it is identifiable by virtue of having been introduced into the context of discourse by the antecedent.

Agreement between pronoun and antecedent

The 3rd person pronouns can be classified in terms of number and gender as follows:

[18]

MASCULINE SINGULAR	FEMININE SINGULAR	NEUTER SINGULAR	PLURAL
he	***she***	***it***	***they***

The number and gender provide descriptive information about the referent, and at the same time narrow down the range of possible antecedents:

[19] *Liz*$_i$ *had bought the tickets*$_j$ *for Tom*$_k$ *but he*$_k$ *hadn't yet paid her*$_i$ *for them*$_j$.

The masculine singular feature links *he* to *Tom*, the feminine singular links *her* to *Liz* and the plural feature links *them* to *the tickets*. We follow the traditional account and say that the pronoun agrees with its antecedent in person, number, and gender, but as pointed out in the more detailed description given in Ch. 5, §17.2, it is a somewhat loose sense of agreement because the information encoded in the pronoun need not be encoded in the antecedent too:

[20] i *Did you know <u>the Vice-Chancellor</u> was getting married on Saturday? <u>Her</u> former husband died only a few months ago.*
ii *We've just appointed <u>a new chief executive</u>, but <u>she</u> won't be starting until June.*

The nouns *vice-chancellor* and *executive* are neutral as to sex, but the pronouns indicate that the referents are female. The extra information conveyed by the pronoun may be already known to the addressee, as is likely to be the case in [i], where you probably know who the Vice-Chancellor is, or it may be new, as is likely in [ii]. What is required, then, is not that the antecedent encode all the meaning of the pronoun, but that it be consistent with it. *The Vice-Chancellor*, for example, is consistent with either ***he*** or ***she*** – but not with ***it***. Note, however, that as far as the category of person is concerned we have agreement in the strict sense: a 1st or 2nd person pronoun cannot be the antecedent for a 3rd person one.

Because of the minimal descriptive information contained in the pronoun, there will often be more than one NP to which the pronoun could be anaphorically linked. Typically, however, the content of the clause containing the pronoun will strongly favour one of the potential antecedents:

[21] *Liz told Jill that <u>she</u> was going to Paris at the week-end.*

Though it is certainly possible for *Jill* to be the antecedent, *Liz* is a far stronger candidate: it is commonplace for me to tell you what I will be doing, whereas it is only under restricted conditions that I tell you what you will be doing. Where there are no comparable factors favouring one NP as the antecedent, ambiguity is occasionally avoided by repeating the intended antecedent NP in apposition to the pronoun.

[22] *Ed told me that he had been informed by Max that <u>he</u>, Max, had been nominated for an excellence in teaching award.*

Non-anaphoric uses

Although the 3rd person pronouns are usually interpreted via an antecedent, they certainly do not have to be. We group these non-anaphoric uses under four headings.

(a) Reference to contextually salient entity

[23] i *Isn't <u>she</u> lovely!*
ii *<u>She</u> looks as if <u>she</u>'s going to fall.*
iii *Why's the meal so late? Isn't <u>he</u> home yet?*
iv [Pointing at a painting] *<u>He</u> certainly knew how to paint.*

The intended context for [i] is where I'm admiring a baby, say, that I have just encountered. There is no need for any prior mention: *she* can be interpreted directly by virtue of the presence of the referent in the situation of utterance. A possible context where [ii] might be used in this kind of way is one where we are watching a tightrope walker at a circus. The prominence of the person on the high wire together with the content of the predication makes it obvious who I'm referring to without the need for an antecedent or a more contentful referring expression. Note that the *she* that is applied to ships or other inanimates can be used in this way: *Here she comes.*

Contextual salience does not require that the referent be actually present in the situation of utterance. Thus [23iii], for example, might be used in a family context with *he* referring to the father. If the regular family routine is for the meal to be served when the father returns from work, the delay suggests that he may not have returned yet, and in this context the content of *he* ("male one") is sufficient to make clear who I'm talking about.[11] In [iv] I point at a painting and use *he* to refer to the painter. This case has been called 'indirect ostension': ostension is showing or indicating, as by pointing, and it is indirect in that what I am pointing at is not the painter but something closely associated with him. By drawing attention to the painting I create a context in which the painter is salient and hence can be referred to by a mere pronoun.

Some works subsume the use of pronouns illustrated in [23] under the concept of deixis, on the grounds that the referent is identified by virtue of features of the context of utterance. There is, however, a crucial difference between these pronouns and genuine deictic expressions such as *I, you, this, those boxes*, etc. In their deictic use these expressions encode the relation between the referent and features of the situation of utterance: *I* refers to the speaker of the utterance, *this* to something relatively close to the speaker, and so on. But there is no such meaning expressed in the 3rd person personal pronouns. They are merely **definite** and this is not a deictic category. The referential use of a definite NP indicates that the speaker takes the referent to be identifiable by the addressee, and in the case of the pronouns in [23] the identifiability results from the contextual salience of the referent, not from anything in the meaning of the pronouns that relates the referent to features of the situation.

This use of 3rd person pronouns is comparable to that of the underlined NPs in:

[24] i *Please close <u>the door</u>.*
ii *<u>The Prime Minister</u> is being interviewed on TV tonight.*
iii [Host at dinner party] *Would you like to sit next to <u>Angela</u>.*

In [i] the intended referent will normally be the door of the room in or outside which the utterance takes place, and in the salient non-anaphoric interpretation of [ii] reference will be to the prime minister of the country in which the utterance takes place. Similarly with the proper name *Angela* in [iii]: there are innumerable people with this name, and in the context given the intended referent is identifiable by virtue of her presence at the dinner table. As in [23], there is nothing in the meaning of these expressions that relates them to the situation of utterance. We believe, therefore, that it would represent an unnecessary and undesirable dilution of the sense of deixis to extend it to cover cases like [23–24].

(b) Quasi-anaphoric uses

[25] i *I went to the corner shop but <u>he</u> wouldn't sell me any stamps.*
ii *Tom's getting married at the week-end. <u>She</u>'s already three months pregnant.*
iii *I heard from Sue yesterday. Did you know <u>they</u> had moved again?*
iv A: *How's baby?* B: *Oh, she's crying now.* A: *Yes, <u>they</u> do tend to cry.*

[11] It can seem rude to someone to assume that they are so salient that they need no name or title. Children who refer to their mother as *she* with no other identification are sometimes rebuked for it (*Who's 'she' – the cat's mother?*).

He in [i] refers to the person serving at the corner-shop, *she* in [ii] to the person Tom is going to marry, *they* in [iii] to Sue's family, and *they* in [iv] is interpreted generically as "babies". *The corner shop* in [i] is not the antecedent for *he*, but it serves the same kind of role as an antecedent: once I have introduced the corner shop into the universe of discourse I can refer to entities associated with it without needing to use a descriptive NP that includes a reference to the shop. We will say therefore that this use of *he* is **quasi-anaphoric**.

The case is closely parallel to the indirect ostension in [23iv]: there pointing at the painting makes the painter conceptually accessible enough to be referred to with a pronoun, while here mention of the corner shop achieves the same result with respect to the person serving there. Similarly *marry* cannot be regarded as the antecedent for *she* but it creates a context of discourse involving a marriage partner, and this person can then be referred to by a pronoun. In [25iii] there is again an association between Sue and the referent of *they: Sue* is a member of the set referred to (a couple, perhaps), making the set salient. And in [iv], *baby* is straightforwardly an antecedent for *she*, but talk of one baby makes it an easy conceptual move to talk of babies in general.

Examples like those in [25] belong to informal or relatively casual style: in more carefully monitored speech or writing one would be more likely to use more explicit expressions.

The boundary between anaphora proper and quasi-anaphora is not entirely clear-cut. One borderline case is illustrated in:

[26] *We've just joined the local squash club, but <u>they</u> won't let schoolkids play on Saturday and Sunday afternoons.*

They refers to the people who run the local squash club, so that we have an association between the referent of the pronoun and the entity introduced into the context of discourse by the NP *the local squash club*: from this point of view this case is like the quasi-anaphoric ones in [25]. But it would also be possible to replace *they* by *the local squash club*, which makes the latter very much like an antecedent. This is especially so for speakers (more in BrE than in AmE) who treat it as a collective allowing a plural verb: *The local squash club don't let schoolkids play on Saturday and Sunday afternoons.*

(c) *He who . . .*

[27] *He who committed this infraction of taste would promptly discover how little mercy liberals were disposed to allow to libertarians who appeared to them libertines.*

This use is now rare (though familiar from proverbs and the Bible). It is mostly found with non-referential uses of what we have called the purportedly sex-neutral ***he***; but ***he*** is in principle possible with its primary "male" sense, and likewise ***she*** with the "female" sense. Neuter ***it*** and plural ***they***, however, are not used in this way: instead we have demonstrative ***that*** (cf. §5.4).

(d) Institutional and non-referential ***they***

[28] i *<u>They</u>'ve closed the bridge for repairs following last week's floods.*
ii *<u>They</u>'ve increased the cost of a passport from $50 to $100.*
iii *I think this is what <u>they</u> call a 'fait accompli'.*
iv *I don't know what <u>they</u> use alfalfa for.*

They is commonly used to refer vaguely to some unspecified institution or authority: the department of transport or the local council perhaps in [i], the government in [ii]. The bridge has been repaired and the cost of a passport increased by the people who have the authority to do this. This use may merge with those described in (a) and (b) above in examples like *They won't let you in without a tie*, said in the context of a proposed visit to a yacht club. The referent of *they* here will be the people with the authority to refuse you entry and these people are associated with an establishment in the context of discourse by virtue of our being on our way there and/or by virtue of having been mentioned in the preceding text.

In [28iii–iv] ***they*** conveys very much the same as non-referential ***you***. The 3rd person version may have a slight distancing effect. Example [iii] may suggest (as the version with *you* would not) that *fait accompli* is not an expression that I myself regularly use. Syntactically ***they*** is much less versatile than ***you***, being for the most part restricted to the nominative form. Note, for example, that *you* could not be replaced by *them* in such examples as *This wine gives you a terrible hangover, doesn't it?*

Clauses with institutional or non-referential *they* as subject are generally pragmatically equivalent to short passives (i.e. those without a *by* phrase): *The bridge has been closed for repairs following last week's floods*; *I think this is what is called a 'fait accompli'*; etc.

2.3.2 Semantic relations between pronoun and its antecedent

(a) Coreference with a definite antecedent

[29] i *<u>My father</u> says <u>he</u> can lend us the money.*
ii *The police wanted to speak to <u>the manager</u>, but <u>she</u> was out.*
iii *We tried <u>the door</u>, but <u>it</u> was locked.*
iv *I can't find <u>my shoes</u>. Have you seen <u>them</u>?*

This represents the most elementary case: antecedent and anaphor are definite referring expressions with the same referent.

(b) Coreference with an indefinite antecedent

[30] i *<u>One of your friends</u> phoned while you were out, but <u>she</u> didn't give her name.*
ii *I bought <u>some little cakes</u>, but nobody liked <u>them</u>.*
iii *I've written <u>a letter to Kim's solicitor</u>. Would you mind reading <u>it</u> over?*

Another common case is where the antecedent is indefinite. The antecedent introduces some entity into the context of discourse, and the pronoun refers to that entity.

(c) Reference to a hypothetical entity introduced by the antecedent

[31] i *If she caught <u>a fish</u>, she will no doubt have given <u>it</u> to her father.*
ii *I want to buy <u>a filing-cabinet</u>. We could keep all these papers in <u>it</u>.*
iii *Dig <u>a large hole</u> and hide these bones in <u>it</u>.*

The antecedents here do not have reference: existence of actual fish, filing-cabinets, or holes is not entailed. But in each case I envisage a hypothetical situation in which an entity of the kind described does exist, and this makes it possible to refer to this hypothetical entity.

(d) Anaphor falls within the quantificational or interrogative scope of its antecedent

Singular antecedents

[32] i *Every woman in the group said she supported the proposal.*
ii *Each boy was asked to talk about his favourite game.*
iii *Nobody thought they had been unfairly treated.*
iv *Has anyone got their copy of 'Macbeth' here?*
v *Who thinks they can solve the problem?*

In [i] *she* has *every woman in the group* as its antecedent, but could not be replaced by a repetition of the antecedent: the meaning is quite different from that of *Every woman in the group said that every woman in the group supported the proposal.* The difference can most easily be brought out by considering the direct speech counterparts. According to this latter example, every woman said: *Every woman in the group supports the proposal,* but what every woman said in [i] was: *I support the proposal.* This is the kind of reading for which we invoke the concept of a variable: "*x* said that *x* supported the proposal" holds for every woman in the group. One way of representing this is to attach the first instance of the variable to the antecedent NP: "Every woman in the group *x* said that *x* supported the proposal". Syntactically, therefore, the quantifier belongs in the NP functioning as subject of the matrix clause, but semantically it has scope over the pronoun *she.* Because the variable expressed by *she* is within the scope of a quantifier, it is said to be **bound** by that quantifier: the pronoun here therefore expresses a **bound variable.** There is of course a reading of *Every woman in the group said she supported the proposal* in which *she* has an antecedent in a preceding sentence, and is not in the scope of *every.* In this case, what every woman said was: *She supports the proposal.*

Each behaves in just the same way as *every,* so that the meaning of [32ii] can be given as "Each boy *x* was asked to talk about *x*'s favourite game". These first two examples were chosen as ones where the head of the antecedent NP is feminine or masculine, so that the pronoun required is simply ***she*** and ***he*** respectively. *Nobody* and *anyone* in [iii–iv] are neutral as to sex and require a pronoun which likewise has a sex-neutral interpretation. The various possibilities (***they***, ***he*** *or* ***she***, ***he***, ***she***, etc.) are discussed in Ch. 5, §17.2.4; here we have opted for ***they***, which is now much the most common choice. Again, then, we represent the meaning of [iii–iv] as "Nobody *x* thought *x* had been unfairly treated" and "Has anyone *x* got *x*'s copy of 'Macbeth' here?" Interrogative phrases in variable questions work in the same way, so that for [v] we have "Who *x* thinks *x* can solve the problem?"

Plural antecedents

[33] i *All the suspects had their fingerprints taken.*
ii *Many of them acknowledged that they had not given the matter enough thought.*
iii *The visitors had taken their coats off.*

The anaphors here likewise have bound variable interpretations. In [i], for example, "*x* had *x*'s fingerprints taken" holds for all the suspects. In [iii] the quantification that binds the variable is just plural number: "*x* had taken *x*'s coat off" holds for members of the set of visitors. We understand that it holds for all members of this set, or at least more or less all. Note that although they (presumably) had only one coat each the plural form *coats* is required since together they removed a plurality of coats.

It is also possible in principle for a pronoun anaphorically linked to a plural NP like these to have a coreferential interpretation. The examples given in [33] were chosen as ones that (perhaps with the exception of [iii]) pragmatically force or favour the bound variable interpretation, but there are others where a coreferential reading is required or more likely. Compare [ii] with *Both candidates said they should be interviewed simultaneously*: what they said here was not *I should be interviewed simultaneously*, but *We should be interviewed simultaneously*. Or compare [iv] with *The visitors said they would have to leave at six*. Notice that the latter does not convey that each visitor spoke: it is quite likely that just one person spoke on behalf of them all.

(e) Variable interpretations with other kinds of quantification

[34] i *Anyone who thinks they could be of help is requested to contact the secretary.*
ii *If he sees a dog that isn't on a lead he is terrified that it is going to attack him.*
iii *Every time we had gone overseas we had brought back a souvenir, but it had always languished unused in the cupboard afterwards.*
iv *Everyone who has a cat should ensure that it is kept indoors at night.*

These are similar to the examples given under (d) in that they involve quantification, but here the quantification is not expressed in the antecedent NP. In [i] the anaphoric link falls within a relative clause functioning as modifier within a quantified NP. The antecedent of *they* is the relative pronoun *who*, and this itself expresses a bound variable within the scope of *any*. The meaning can be given as "Any person *x* such that *x* thinks *x* could be of help is requested to contact the secretary".

Example [34ii] is a conditional construction, like [31i], but whereas the latter involves a singulary situation, [34ii] expresses a multiple situation. *If* here means more or less the same as *whenever*: we are concerned with repetition of the subsituation in which he sees a dog that isn't on a lead and is terrified that it, the dog, is going to attack him. Neither antecedent nor anaphor refers to any one dog, so again it is a matter of linked variables, not coreference between constants. We also have a multiple situation in [iii], this time with the quantification explicitly expressed by *every time*. For each instantiation of the multiple situation there is some particular souvenir that we brought back and that languishes unused in the cupboard. Example [iv], like [i], has a relative clause integrated into the structure of a quantified NP, but this time only the antecedent (*a cat*), not the anaphor (*it*), falls within the relative clause. Again we have a multiplicity of cats, and the meaning is that, for each cat *x*, *x*'s owner should keep *x* indoors.[12]

(f) Variable is associated with an NP contained within the antecedent

[35] *The brother who left his estate to charity will be remembered longer than the one who left it to his children.*

Here we have two brothers and two estates, so that *it* is not coreferential with its antecedent *his estate*. This example is like [23iii] of §1 (*Ed always gets his kids to help in the kitchen: why don't you __?*) except that the anaphor is a personal pronoun, not an elliptical gap. The common

[12] Examples like [34iv] are sometimes referred to as 'donkey sentences', after an example commonly used in discussing them: *Every farmer who owns a donkey beats it.* They have received considerable attention in the logical and formal semantic literature because the meaning cannot be represented by means of the standard predicate calculus.

factor is that we have two layers of anaphora: at the upper level *his estate* is antecedent and *it* anaphor, but *his estate* contains the anaphor *his* with the first *who* as antecedent. *It* is interpreted as "his estate", but with the genitive pronoun now having the second *who* as antecedent. A rough way of indicating the meaning would be: "The brother *x* such that *x* left *x*'s estate to charity will be remembered longer than the brother *y* such that *y* left *y*'s estate to his children".[13]

This use of the personal pronouns is rare and subject to severe constraints. It remains unclear, however, what the constraints are, and we merely give two examples here where this kind of interpretation is not permitted:

[36] i *Jill adores her son, but Liz doesn't like him at all.*
ii *Jill gets on very well with the people she works with, and Liz gets on with them quite well too.*

Him in [i] is understood as referring to Jill's son, not Liz's. And in [ii] the people Liz gets on with quite well must be the same as those Jill gets on very well with.

(g) Antecedent is a clause (or sequence of clauses)

[37] i *Tom's just phoned to say we've won the case. I can hardly believe it.*
ii *Bruce has finally been sacked. I can't understand why it took them so long.*
iii *If you don't go while you have a chance, you'll regret it.* (=[20iii] of §1)
iv *I'd like to come with you, but it would cost too much.*

The antecedents here are not referring expressions, and hence can't be coreferential with the pronoun. The *it* serves a nominalising role, making it possible to refer to propositions, facts, events, actions, and the like that have been introduced into the context of discourse by means of clauses.

2.4 Order of anaphor and antecedent

Retrospective anaphora as the default type

Most of our examples so far have involved retrospective anaphora, where the pronoun follows its antecedent. This is the default order: it is almost always permitted, and in many cases it is the only possible order. The following constructions, for example, do not normally allow anticipatory anaphora:

[38]	RETROSPECTIVE	ANTICIPATORY
i	a. *Ann wrapped a towel around her.*	b. **She wrapped a towel around Ann.*
ii	a. *Ann applied for a grant and they gave her $50,000.*	b. **She applied for a grant and they gave Ann $50,000.*
iii	a. *Ann realised she couldn't win.*	b. **She realised Ann couldn't win.*

The asterisk in the [b] examples indicates that they do not admit an interpretation where *she* is anaphorically linked to *Ann*. Example [i] illustrates the case where antecedent and anaphor are in the same clause, related to the verb directly or via a preposition. In [ii] they are in separate coordinate clauses. In [iii] the second element is in a clause that is subordinate to the one containing the first element.

[13] The term 'pronoun of laziness' is often applied in the theoretical literature to pronouns like *it* as used here: *it* is simply a shorter way of saying *his estate*. The classic example, on which ours is closely modelled, is *The man who gave his paycheck to his wife was wiser than the man who gave it to his mistress.* As with the 'donkey' type mentioned in footnote 12 above, the anaphoric links cannot be formalised in the predicate calculus.

Our focus in this section will therefore be on cases where anticipatory anaphora is permitted or obligatory. We confine our attention here to the non-reflexive forms of the personal pronouns. Reflexives are dealt with separately in §3, and non-pronoun cases follow the general principles outlined here and will be dealt with briefly, where appropriate, in the relevant sections.

First-mention vs repeat-mention anticipatory anaphora

We have anticipatory anaphora when a pronoun is anaphorically linked to a full NP (or other constituent type) that follows. In some cases, as in [39i], the pronoun will represent the first mention of the entity concerned, but often it will also have been mentioned earlier in the discourse, as in [39ii]:

[39] i *Susie Connor says that from the moment she began working for him, her boss sexually harrassed her.*

ii *A go-ahead was recently given for a documentary to be made about Peter Bland, the first Australian to reach both the South and North Magnetic Poles. The documentary should screen on the ABC in January and will have the potential to be seen in about 75 million homes worldwide.*

It is remarkable that Bland reached the North Magnetic Pole only 12 months after major heart surgery. This was in February 1998 when he and four British men pulled sledges across the frozen Arctic Sea for 650 kilometres.

Two years before, he and others had sailed to the South Magnetic Pole in an 18 metre sloop. During this trip he risked his life by diving overboard into the icy waters to cut a line free from the yacht's propeller.

On his return, Bland began to plan a visit to the North Magnetic Pole.

Example [i] is a newspaper synopsis of a film scheduled to be broadcast on television: the sentence constitutes the whole of the synopsis, so that the first mention of Susie Connor's boss is by means of the pronoun *him*. In [ii] the person under discussion is first referred to as *Peter Bland* and then *Bland*; there follow three instances of retrospective *he*; then in the final sentence quoted we have *his* in the initial PP and *Bland* in subject position. The *his* is anaphorically linked to *Bland*, so that this is a case of anticipatory anaphora, but it is a special case of it because of the previous mentions, by proper name or pronoun.

We will distinguish these two cases as **first-mention** and **repeat-mention** anticipatory anaphora. The repeat-mention type is acceptable in a somewhat broader range of contexts than the more constrained first-mention type, as illustrated in this further attested example (where B's *was* is understood as "was completely feral"):

[40] A: *I was talking to Michael's dad and he said: 'He's completely feral.'*
B: *What, his dad said Michael was?*

Here anaphoric *his* is determiner within the subject NP. This would be unacceptable if there had been no previous mention of Michael. Similarly, examples like the following (which follow the general pattern of the inadmissible [38iiib]) are widely judged to be acceptable only if there has been a previous mention of the person concerned:

[41] i *He would have been like a son to both of us, if my wife and I could have kept Paul away from the influence of his family.*

ii *He'll do it, because Paul always does what I tell him to do.*

In what follows it is to be assumed that the construction under consideration permits both types of anticipatory anaphora unless otherwise stated.

Anaphoric chains

We have noted that a link between anaphor and antecedent is often part of a chain of such relations, and it is important to bear this in mind when distinguishing between retrospective and anticipatory anaphora. Compare, for example:

[42] i __ *Realising she couldn't win, Ann withdrew from the competition.*
ii *__ *Realising Ann couldn't win, she withdrew from the competition.*

In [i] the missing subject of *realising* has *Ann* as its antecedent: this is a common case of anticipatory anaphora. At the same time, the missing subject is antecedent for the pronoun *she*; the anaphora here is retrospective, just as it is in *Ann realised she couldn't win.* There is no direct anaphoric link between *she* and *Ann*, so this *she* is not an instance of an anticipatorily anaphoric pronoun. The fact that [ii] is inadmissible does not therefore mean that we have here a case of a pronoun obligatorily preceding its antecedent. The inadmissibility of [ii] follows from that of **She realised Ann couldn't win* ([38iiib]): it has nothing to do with the fact that *Ann* precedes the *she* of the *withdrew* clause.[14]

2.4.1 Central cases of anticipatory anaphora

Three major constructions

Most of the central cases of anticipatory anaphora belong to the following constructions:

(a) Anaphor is located within a subordinate clause

[43] i *If [she has any sense], your mother will hang on to the shares.*
ii *The news [he had received that morning] depressed my father more than I would have expected.*
iii *As [he moves through life], each man seeks the same kind of reward.*
iv *When [she was 5 years old], a child of my acquaintance announced a theory that she was inhabited by rabbits.*
v *[Her parents being overseas,] Ann has to deal with these problems herself.*
vi *The news [that his application had been rejected] sent Ed into a paroxysm of rage.*

Here the anaphor is inside a clause (marked off by the square brackets) that is subordinate, directly or indirectly, to the one containing the antecedent. It is also possible for the antecedent to be located within another subordinate clause, as in:

[44] i *Although [it is over 400 pages long], everyone agrees [that the Commission's report contains very little that is new].*
ii *Even though [it is not absolutely certain], there are very good grounds for [believing that Ann was responsible for the change of policy].*

As the examples show, the subordinate clause containing the pronoun can have a range of functions: complement of a preposition ([43i]), modifier of a noun ([ii]), non-finite adjunct in the matrix ([v]), and so on. Cases where the subordinate clause is subject, as in *[That he wasn't invited] didn't bother Tom at all*, are hardly possible except with repeat-mention anticipatory anaphora.

[14] The same applies to nominalisations like **The realisation that Ann couldn't win led her to withdraw from the competition*: the noun *realisation* still implies an experiencer argument, just as in the construction with an overt subject–determiner, **her realisation that Ann couldn't win.*

Most examples of anticipatory anaphora have definite antecedents, but indefinites are also found, as in [43iii–iv]; [44ii] illustrates the case where the antecedent is a clause rather than an NP. The examples also show that genitive forms of pronouns are admissible in this construction as well as non-genitives – see [43v–vi].

(b) Pronoun occupies a subordinate position within a larger NP

[45] i *[The repeated attacks on him] had made Max quite paranoid.*
ii *[These rumours about him] made us wonder whether Ed would have to resign.*
iii *[His demotion] had left my brother completely demoralised.*
iv *Most of [her colleagues] thought that Sue was quite outstanding.*
v *We told [his wife] that Frank would be travelling on the later flight.*
vi *In [his first report to a meeting of 120 union members yesterday], Mr Combet proposed setting up five internal departments in the ACTU.*

These are similar to those in [43–44] in that the anaphor is in a subordinate position, but this time it is located within an NP rather than a subordinate clause. Often, indeed, the NP concerned can be replaced by one of very similar meaning containing a subordinate clause – e.g. *the fact that people were repeatedly attacking him* and *the rumours that were circulating about him* for [45i–ii]. Example [vi] illustrates a particularly common case of this type of anticipatory anaphora: the pronoun is genitive determiner in the NP complement of a preposed PP (cf. also [39ii]).[15]

(c) Anaphor within a preposed PP: anticipatory anaphora may be obligatory

		a.	b.
[46]	i	*[Around her] Ann wrapped a towel.*	**[Around Ann] she wrapped a towel.*
	ii	*[Only a few inches away from her] Ann noticed a red-back spider.*	**[Only a few inches away from Ann] she noticed a red-back spider.*
	iii	*[Not far from her house] Ann had found an injured koala.*	**[Not far from Ann's house] she had found an injured koala.*
	iv	*[Without the support of her mother,] Ann would not have survived.*	**[Without the support of Ann's mother,] she would not have survived.*

Here the order anaphor + antecedent is not only permitted but required: the [b] versions are inadmissible with *Ann* as antecedent for *she*. The PP is here in non-canonical position, and the versions with canonical order (*Ann wrapped a towel around her*, etc.) likewise have the pronoun in the locative phrase; note further that the non-genitive type [ia/iia] is also exceptional in that in constructions where, as here, antecedent and anaphor are related to the same verb, directly or via a preposition, the anaphor is usually reflexive (see §3).

The examples in [46] all have the second element in subject function; elsewhere retrospective anaphora is generally permitted: *Without the support of Ann's mother, I wouldn't have been able to persuade her to seek medical help.* Even with subjects the retrospective type may be acceptable, as in *In view of Paul's special circumstances, he was given extra time.* The clearest cases where it is excluded are those with locative PPs, as in [i–iii].

[15] Instead of being inside a larger NP, the pronoun is occasionally simply subordinated within an AdvP ([*Unfortunately for them,*] *the bandits' plans had been leaked to the police*) or PP ([*According to her,*] *Sue had been warned not to ask any awkward questions*).

Qualifications and extensions

The account presented above represents something of an oversimplification, for the possibility or necessity of anticipatory anaphora is not determined by purely syntactic properties, and it should also be borne in mind that judgements of the acceptability of many examples show considerable variation among different speakers.

Restrictions on anticipatory anaphora

Anticipatory anaphora is not acceptable in all cases having the structures described in (a)–(b) above. Compare, for example:

[47] i *[*One of them*] *suggested that the boys should complain.*
ii *[*Her problem*] *is that your mother is rather set in her ways.*
iii **If* [*there's a problem with her*], *it's that your mother is rather set in her ways.*

In [i–ii] the pronoun occupies a subordinate position within a larger NP like the acceptable cases in [45]. *One of them* belongs to the partitive construction, and this systematically excludes anticipatory anaphora. It is less clear why [47ii] should differ in acceptability from [45]. It may be related to the fact that in [47ii] there is less semantic independence between the NP containing the pronoun and the antecedent than there is in [45]: the problem necessarily involves your mother. In [47iii] the pronoun is located within a subordinate clause, like those in [43], and again it is not clear why it should differ in acceptability from the latter. It may be due to the fact that [47iii] implicates [ii], with the inadmissibility of the latter carrying over to it.

The effect of distance and complexity

Increasing the distance between pronoun and antecedent, and thus the complexity of the construction, can make anticipatory anaphora more acceptable:

[48] i ?*Her husband had supported Ann throughout the ordeal.*
ii *All her friends and relatives had supported Ann throughout the ordeal.*

The type shown in [i], with the pronoun determiner in a simple subject NP, is hardly admissible ([40] is a rare example, but requires stress on the antecedent); increasing the length and complexity of the subject NP, as in [48ii], makes it significantly better, certainly for the repeat-mention case. Note also that a similar increase in complexity can make retrospective anaphora more acceptable in the construction with a preposed locative PP illustrated in [46]. The unacceptable [b] versions of [46] may be compared with, for example, the appreciably better *Just behind the shed that Ann had been repairing she noticed a red-back spider.*

Coordination that is pragmatically comparable to subordination

We noted at the outset that anticipatory anaphora is not normally permitted when the linked NPs are in separate coordinate clauses – see [38ii]. Exceptions to this syntactic constraint are found, however, in examples like the following:

[49] i [*She was only in office for ten months,*] *but* [*Sue achieved a remarkable amount in that time*].
ii [*They may still call Australia home*] *but* [*for 300,000 Australians 'home' is really an address overseas*].
iii [*Make even the slightest criticism of him*] *and* [*Max will lose his temper*].

What makes the anticipatory anaphora admissible here is that the coordinates are not of equal status from a pragmatic point of view. In [49i–ii] the first clause is interpreted as concessive and in [iii] it has a conditional role. Although formally coordinate, therefore, the constructions behave for the purposes of anaphora like the subordinative constructions to which they are pragmatically equivalent, namely:

[50] i *Although [she was only in office for ten months], [Sue achieved a remarkable amount in that time].*
ii *Although [they still call Australia home], [for 300,000 Australians 'home' is really an address overseas.*
iii *If [you make even the slightest criticism of him], Max will lose his temper.*

2.4.2 Further cases of anticipatory anaphora

In this section we introduce three special cases of anticipatory anaphora beyond the more general ones considered so far.

(a) Anticipatory anaphora for rhetorical effect

It is a quite common feature of journalism and novels to use anticipatory anaphora as a device to catch the listener's or reader's attention: pronouns are used to tempt the curious reader or listener into continuing to pay attention – so that they can find out who or what the pronoun refers to. In these cases reference by pronoun may continue across a number of sentences before a full NP provides the required identification. Two newspaper examples are as follows:

[51] i *Peter Costello calls her a Labor Party hireling, but she could be the academic that ultimately saves the Government's bacon on the goods and services tax. Ann Harding will today become one of only two witnesses in the five-month Senate ordeal on the GST that all sides want to hear from.*
ii *They started a penchant for expensive cars and real estate and their respective business enterprises – the Rebels and the Bandidos – turned a healthy profit. Both lived in the fast lane, but police records show that, unlike most executives, they preferred the black market to the stock exchange.*
But despite their similarities, there was not much love lost between millionaire Rebels boss Alex Vella and Bandidos president Michael Kulakowski.

(b) Anticipatory anaphora with a following main clause as antecedent

[52] i *It's ridiculous! They've given the job to Pat.*
ii *It's a complete mystery to me: Why did he turn down such a marvellous offer?*
iii *It's a tremendous nuisance! How could he have cancelled the meeting at such short notice?*
iv *I think it disgraceful. He's given the job to his son.*
v *There's no doubt about it: you've done us proud.*

This is the type of anticipatory anaphora, mentioned in our initial survey in §1.2, where the antecedent is not integrated into a larger construction but is a main clause standing on its own. Examples [i–ii] represent the central and most straightforward case. *It* is in subject position, and the predicate expresses a judgement or evaluation about the state of affairs or whatever that it refers to. The interpretation of *it* is given by the second clause (declarative in [i], interrogative in [ii]): what is ridiculous is that they've given the job to Pat, what is a complete mystery to me is why he turned down such a marvellous offer.

The second clause has no structural relation to the first and, being syntactically a main clause, cannot be substituted for the anaphor without modification. However, in this example all we need to do is to add the subordinator *that* in [i] and drop the inversion in [ii]: we get *That they've given the job to Pat is ridiculous* from [i], and *Why he turned down such a marvellous offer is a complete mystery to me* from [ii]. When we do this the anaphor is simply dropped: it does not take the place of the antecedent (cf. **That they've given the job to Pat is ridiculous. It.*). This is what distinguishes this construction from the central cases of anticipatory anaphora discussed in §2.4.1.

In [52iii] the interpretation of *it* is not the content of the second clause itself, but rather its presupposition – namely, that he cancelled the meeting at such short notice. In [iv] *it* is in direct object position, while in [v] it is object of a preposition: replacement of *it* by the antecedent would here require greater modification, and in the case of [iv] at least would most likely involve a change in the construction of the first clause – e.g. *I think his giving the job to his son was disgraceful.*

The clause containing the *it* normally has to be asserted by the speaker. It would be quite impossible for *it* to be anaphorically linked to a following independent clause in constructions like **Kim insists that it is a disgrace: he's given the job to his son.*

(c) Right dislocation

[53] i *They've really taken a dislike to me, your parents.*
ii *What did you think of it, that suggestion of Paul's?*

Here too we have an anaphoric link between a 3rd person pronoun and a following expression, this time normally an NP. The latter could replace the pronoun, and the pronoun would then again be simply dropped, giving the canonical versions *Your parents have really taken a dislike to me, What did you think of that suggestion of Paul's?*

This construction is discussed in Ch. 16, §8.2; here it is sufficient to note summarily that it differs from (b) in the following respects:

[54] i The antecedent is attached to the clause in postnuclear position, rather than being structurally independent.
ii All 3rd person personal pronouns are found, and the antecedent is normally a coreferential NP.
iii The antecedent represents discourse-old information, not new information.

2.5 Special uses of *it*

In this section we review briefly those uses of *it* that are not anaphoric (or at least not clearly so), and do not refer directly to contextually salient entities. We are concerned here, therefore, with constructions where *it* cannot be replaced by other 3rd person personal pronouns.

(a) Extrapositional and impersonal *it*

[55] i *It's ridiculous that they've given the job to Pat.*
ii *I think it disgraceful for him to have given the job to his son.*
iii *It seemed that / as if things would never get any better.*

The extraposition construction of [i–ii] is discussed and compared with right dislocation in Ch. 16, §§7–8; for the impersonal construction illustrated in [iii], see Ch. 11, §4.3.1.

We take *it* as a dummy, semantically empty pronoun, an obligatory and non-contrastive feature of the constructions, though there is clearly some resemblance here to the use of *it* in anticipatory anaphora illustrated in [52] and [53ii].

(b) The *it*-cleft construction

[56] i A: *It was your father who was driving.* B: *No it wasn't, it was me.*
ii *It was precisely for that reason that the rules were changed.*

No independent meaning can be assigned to *it* here, and no part of the construction can be regarded as its antecedent: we again regard it as a dummy subject. It is an invariable part of a distinct grammatical construction, which we describe in Ch. 16, §9.

(c) Weather, time, place, condition

[57] i *It is raining. It became very humid.*
ii *What time/date/day is it? It is five o'clock / 1 July / Monday.*
iii *It is only two weeks since she left / until we go on holiday.*
iv *It is very noisy in this room.*
v *It is more than five miles to the nearest post office.*
vi *It would be wonderful if you could spend the week-end with us.*
vii *It is a crime when families are starving because a man cannot get a job.*
viii *I don't like it when you behave like this.*

It is used as a dummy subject with verbs and predicative adjectives denoting weather conditions, as in [i]. It does not represent a semantic argument and cannot be replaced by any other NP: it has the purely syntactic function of filling the obligatory subject position.[16] *It* is also used with various expressions of time as predicative complement, as in [ii]; compare also *I don't even know what month/year it is.* For clock-time and date *it* is replaceable by *the time/date*: *The time is five o'clock*; *The date is 1 July.* But we do not say, with a corresponding meaning, **The day is Monday*; **The month is July* (though we can say *Today is Monday*). In [iii] *it* is an invariable subject with a predicative of temporal extent together with an adjunct expressing the starting-point or endpoint; the two are found together in *It is only three weeks from now until Christmas.* In [iv] the predicative describes the condition applying in a certain place – cf. also *It can be very cold in Edinburgh.* Example [v] is the spatial counterpart of [iii].

The last three examples in [57] bear some resemblance to extraposition inasmuch as what would be wonderful would be your being able to spend the week-end with us, what is a crime (understood here as, roughly, "a scandal") is the fact that families are starving because a man (the father) can't get a job, and what I don't like is your behaving like this. But they differ from extraposition in that the final elements are not content clauses, not potential replacements for *it*, and it is for that reason that we include them under the present heading.

[16] There are some rather marginal constructions in casual style where *it* behaves more like a semantically contentful pronoun. *It is trying to rain* involves a kind of personification with *it* assigned an agent role by virtue of being subject of *try*; in %*It rained and flooded the basement*, the *it* is subject of a VP-coordination that includes a non-weather verb.

(d) *It* as subject with other predicative NPs

[58] i a. *It was a perfect day.* b. *The day was perfect.*
ii a. *It's a wonderful view.* b. *The view is wonderful.*

Example [ia] here might be grouped with the weather clauses discussed above, but has [ib] as an alternant. The latter, however, is very unidiomatic in the sense of [ia]; the contrast is even sharper with such a pair as *It's a beautiful day, isn't it?* and *The day is beautiful, isn't it?*: the latter is grammatical, but it is not idiomatic, not the kind of clause we use in commenting about the weather. There is, however, a greater degree of referentiality about the *it* in [ia] than in the earlier weather examples. It is possible to replace *it* by demonstrative *this* without significant change of meaning or any sharp loss of idiomaticity. And in [iia] *this* would be a perfectly natural replacement for *it*.

(e) *It* in idioms

Finally, *it* appears with no identifiable independent meaning in a large number of generally colloquial idioms. A sample is given in:

[59] i *What's it to you? How's it going?*
ii *Beat it, kid. He was camping it up, as usual. You'll catch it if you're wrong. Don't come it with me. Just cool it, OK? We'll have to go it alone. I can't hack it. They don't exactly hit it off. Hold it! We finally made it. Make it snappy. We'll play it safe. I'm going to have to wing it.*
iii *Let's get on with it. He made a go of it. He had a hard time of it. Now you're in for it! She made the best of it. Don't go just for the sake of it.*

It is subject in [i], object of the verb in [ii], and object of a preposition in [iii]. Some of the verbs in [ii] do not otherwise allow objects (e.g. *come* and *go*). These idioms allow little syntactic manipulation; in particular, those in [ii] do not allow passivisation and require *it* to immediately follow the verb.

3 Reflexive pronouns

Reflexive pronouns are inflectional forms of the personal pronouns, formed morphologically by the compounding of ***self*** with another form: the dependent genitive (*myself*), the accusative (*himself*), or the plain form (*oneself*).

Complement vs emphatic uses of reflexive pronouns

Reflexive pronouns have two uses: in one they function as complement, in the other they have an emphatic effect. Compare:

[1] COMPLEMENT USE
i *Rhiana feeds herself now.* [complement of verb]
ii *Liz talks to herself.* [complement of preposition]

[2] EMPHATIC USE
i *Rhiana wrote the report herself.* [adjunct in clause structure]
ii [*Liz herself*] *presented the prize.* [modifier in NP structure]

In the complement case, the reflexive may be complement of a verb or of a preposition, while an emphatic reflexive may function in the structure of a clause or of an NP.

An important difference between complement and adjunct reflexives is that only the former are in competition, as it were, with non-reflexive forms: non-reflexive personal pronouns do not have a comparable emphatic use. In complement function we can have either reflexive or non-reflexive forms, and we need to investigate the factors influencing the choice between them. This is the issue that we will be concerned with in §3.1, and we will then return to emphatic reflexives in §3.2.

3.1 Reflexive pronouns in complement function

While the choice between the different cases of the personal pronouns – nominative, accusative, and genitive – depends on the function of the pronoun in the construction containing it, the choice between reflexive and non-reflexive forms depends primarily on the structural relationship between the pronoun and its antecedent. Compare, for example:

[3] i *Ann$_i$ blames herself$_i$ for the accident.* [reflexive form]
ii *Ann$_i$ realises that they blame her$_i$ for the accident.* [non-reflexive form]

In [i] the pronoun is a complement of the same verb as the antecedent, whereas in [ii] it is a complement of a different verb. Broadly speaking, reflexives are used when there is a close structural relation between pronoun and antecedent. From a communicative point of view, the reflexive provides a more specific indication as to the location of the antecedent. In [i], for example, *Ann* is the only possible antecedent for the pronoun, and conversely the absence of a reflexive in *Ann blames her for the accident* excludes *Ann* as a possible antecedent for the pronoun. In [ii] we have attached indices to show the intended interpretation, but it would also be possible for *her* to have its antecedent in a preceding sentence, or indeed for its intended reference to be determined non-anaphorically, e.g. by pointing.

Status of the reflexive: mandatory, optional, and inadmissible

With respect to the choice between reflexive and non-reflexive forms we have the three possibilities illustrated in [4], where the labels give the status of the reflexive:

[4] i *Ann$_i$ blames herself$_i$/*her$_i$ for the accident.* [mandatory]
ii *Ann$_i$ tied a rope around herself$_i$/her$_i$.* [optional]
iii *Ann$_i$ realises that they blame *herself$_i$/her$_i$ for the accident.* [inadmissible]

A reflexive form is **mandatory** if it cannot normally be replaced by a non-reflexive form with the same antecedent. The reflexive *herself* in [i] is thus mandatory since, as we have observed, *Ann blames her for the accident* cannot be interpreted with *Ann* as antecedent for the pronoun. A reflexive is **optional** if it is replaceable by a non-reflexive form with the same antecedent, as in [ii]. And a reflexive is **inadmissible** in contexts like [iii] where only the non-reflexive form is permitted.

Overrides

The mandatory and optional reflexives in [4i–ii] we take to be **basic** reflexives, as opposed to the **override** reflexives in:

[5] i *The draft had been prepared by Ann and myself.*
ii *Ann claimed that junior lecturers like herself were being exploited.*

The idea behind the term is that the default form of a pronoun in these contexts is non-reflexive, and the reflexive can therefore be regarded as overriding the default or normal form; mandatory reflexives are thus always basic, while optional ones may be either basic or override. Override reflexives do not require the close structural link between pronoun and antecedent that characterises basic reflexives. Indeed, they can occur without any antecedent at all in the 1st and 2nd person, as in [5i], where the pronoun is interpreted in a purely deictic way.[17] We take this to be the major criterial feature distinguishing override from basic reflexives. A further factor supporting the distinction, however, concerns the distribution of the reciprocal pronouns *each other* and *one another*. As we will see in §4, these are like reflexives in that they require a close structural relation with their antecedent – and we find that they occur in the environments that permit basic reflexives but not in those limited to override reflexives.

Override can also work in the opposite direction, with a non-reflexive form appearing instead of the normal reflexive:

[6] *Why don't you buy something for* <u>YOU</u> *for a change, instead of spending all your money on your kids?*

The normal form here would be reflexive *yourself*: non-reflexive *you* is used to emphasise the contrast between you and your kids, though reflexive forms can also be used contrastively. It was to allow for such overrides that we defined mandatory reflexives as those which cannot **normally** be replaced by the non-reflexive counterpart: we take the reflexive in *You bought it for yourself* to be mandatory, clearly different in status from the optional reflexive of [4ii]. Override non-reflexives like [6] are largely restricted to informal style, and much less common than override reflexives: we need not consider them further.

The domain of a reflexive pronoun

We have said that basic reflexives require a close structural link between pronoun and antecedent, and we must turn now to the task of clarifying what is meant by that.

Verb domain reflexives

In a large and central class of cases, the reflexive and its antecedent are related to the same verb, directly or by means of a preposition. This is illustrated in [7], where single underlining marks the pronoun and its antecedent, double underlining the head verb:

[7] i *<u>Sue</u> <u>defended</u> <u>herself</u>.*
ii *The fact [that <u>Sue</u> <u>bought</u> <u>herself</u> a new car] is irrelevant.*
iii *<u>Sue</u> <u>lives</u> by <u>herself</u>.*

In [i] the pronoun and its antecedent are complements of the verb *defended*, and similarly in [ii] both are complements of *bought*. In [iii] the antecedent is a complement of *lives*, while the reflexive is complement of the preposition *by*, with the whole PP being a dependent of *lives*. We refer to the pronouns here as **verb domain** reflexives: pronoun and antecedent are linked via their relationship to a verb. It doesn't make any difference

[17] In examples like *<u>I</u> hurt <u>myself</u>* we take the reflexive to be simultaneously deictic and anaphoric. The deictic feature links it to the speaker while the anaphoric feature links it to the antecedent *I*. It stands in the same structural relation to *I* as *herself* does to *Ann* in *Ann hurt herself*; this relation, unlike that in *They asked <u>me</u> if <u>I</u> needed help* and *They asked <u>Ann</u> if <u>she</u> needed help*, is one which makes the reflexive obligatory. The crucial property of [5i] is thus that there is no such anaphoric link to a 1st person pronoun antecedent.

whether the verb is head of a main clause, as in [i/iii], or of a subordinate clause, as in [ii].

Noun domain reflexives

We also find reflexives that are linked to their antecedent via their relationship to a noun, and we speak here of **noun domain** reflexives:

[8] *They rejected [Ed's representation of himself as a victim].*

Here the antecedent, the genitive NP *Ed's*, is subject-determiner of the noun *representation* to which the reflexive is related via the preposition *of*.

Dual-head domain reflexives

Consider next such an example as:

[9] *Max found a photograph of himself in Jill's wallet.*

Here the relationship between pronoun and antecedent is not as close as in [7–8]. The antecedent *Max* is a complement of the verb *found*, while the pronoun is related via the preposition *of* not to the verb but to the noun *photograph* which is head of the object of *found*. Pronoun and antecedent are thus not related to a single head element, and we therefore speak here of the reflexive as occurring in a **dual-head domain**. This particular example has a verb–noun domain, but other types will be introduced below.

Summary classification of complement reflexives

By contrast with [9], the earlier examples [7] and [8] can be grouped together as having a **single-head** domain. This then gives the following classification of complement reflexives, where the annotation on the right gives the number of the example used above to illustrate the type in question:

[10]

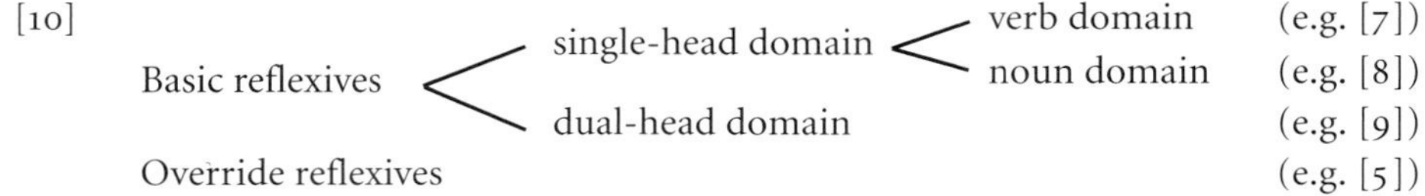

These four types will be examined further in §§3.1.1–4 respectively.

Verb and noun are the only two categories that figure in single-head domains. Only they have a sufficiently rich array of dependents to cover both antecedent and pronoun; more particularly, only they take external complements – subjects.

Ellipted antecedents and anaphoric chains

Reflexives often occur in subjectless clauses with the same relation to the understood subject as they have to an overt subject in other clauses:

[11]	OVERT SUBJECT	COVERT SUBJECT
i	a. *Sue defended herself$_i$/*her$_i$.*	b. *Sue$_i$ tried __$_i$ to defend herself$_i$/*her$_i$.*
ii	a. *She tied a rope around herself$_i$/her$_i$.*	b. *__$_i$ Tie a rope around yourself$_i$/you$_i$.*

Example [ib] contains an anaphoric chain in the sense of §1.2: *Sue* is antecedent for the missing subject of *defend*, and this missing subject is the antecedent for the pronoun. Such examples are thus verb-domain reflexives. Note that the reflexive is here mandatory, just as it is in [ia]. We likewise have a verb domain reflexive in [iib], the antecedent being the covert subject, recoverable non-anaphorically as *you* by virtue of the imperative construction. The reflexive here is optional, just as it is in [iia]. In the discussion which follows we will include such examples as [ib/iib] under verb domain reflexives without special comment – and without marking the gap.

3.1.1 Basic reflexives in verb domains

Where antecedent and pronoun are related to the same verb, a reflexive form is almost always admissible; when they are both related to it directly, rather than via a preposition, the reflexive is (with one minor exception) mandatory.

In clauses with canonical constituent order, a reflexive must follow its antecedent. For this reason, the antecedent is usually the subject of the clause – and the subject cannot itself be reflexive:

[12]	i	*Sue defended herself.*	[subject as antecedent]
	ii	**Herself defended Sue.*	[subject as reflexive anaphor]

We will review in turn the various functions where verb domain reflexives occur in the simplest constructions, and then turn briefly to clauses with non-canonical order.

(a) Reflexive pronoun in direct object function

Here the antecedent is subject and the reflexive mandatory:[18]

[13] i *The protesters chained themselves to the Embassy railings.*
ii *Tim considered himself a victim of the system.*
iii *Liz believes herself to be suitable for the job.*
iv *Everyone committed themselves to continuing the fight.*
v *Sue was the only one [who defended herself].*

These examples illustrate reflexive objects in a range of transitive constructions. Example [i] represents the elementary case where antecedent and pronoun represent arguments of the same verb. In [ii] we have a complex-transitive clause with the object *himself* predicand for the following predicative complement. In [iii] *herself* is a raised object (Ch. 14, §3.1.1). These first three examples have the pronoun coreferential with the antecedent, while [iv] illustrates again the case where a pronoun expresses a bound variable, as discussed for non-reflexive forms in §2.3.2. In [v] anaphor and antecedent are located within a subordinate (relative) clause.[19]

Verbs that select mandatory reflexives

A number of verbs select objects that are required to be anaphorically linked with the subject, and these must then be reflexive in form:

[14]	i	a. *He cried himself to sleep that night.*	b. *Ed prides himself on his tolerance.*
	ii	a. *Ann acquitted herself extremely well.*	b. *You express yourself very clearly.*

Example [ia] illustrates the special case where a reflexive object occurs with a basically intransitive verb: the object is not an argument of the verb, but enables it to take a

[18] In the ditransitive construction it is in principle possible for the direct object to have the indirect object as antecedent, but in practice pragmatic factors normally exclude an anaphoric relation between the two objects, so that examples like #*They sold the slave himself* ("They sold the slave to himself") are at best highly contrived. With some verbs a reflexive object can be omitted without loss of meaning: *Ed shaved*, for example, is generally interpreted as equivalent to *Ed shaved himself*: see Ch. 4, §8.1.3.

[19] The feminine gender of the pronoun in [13v] matches that of *Sue* although there is no anaphoric link (not even an anaphoric chain) between *Sue* and *herself*: the matrix clause specifies identity between Sue and the referent of the second NP, so that the feature "female" is assigned to *one* and hence to the relative pronoun *who*, the antecedent of the reflexive.

resultative goal or predicative (see Ch. 4, §5.3). *Pride*, used as in [ib], doesn't allow a non-reflexive object at all. *Acquit* does allow non-reflexive objects, but only in a different sense (*They acquitted her*), and *express* with a human-denoting object also belongs in this class (we don't find #*You express me perfectly*). Other verbs of this kind are given in [15]; some take PP complements as indicated in addition to the object, as *pride* in [ib] takes an *on* phrase. Those marked † are like *pride* in having a reflexive as the only (or virtually the only) type of object permitted:

[15]	*absent* (*from*) †	*apply* (*to*)	*avail* (*of*) †	*behave* †	*busy* †
	comport †	*compose*	*conduct*	*content*	*demean*
	enjoy	*excel*	*exert*	*ingratiate* †	*perjure* †

(b) Indirect object

[16] a. *Liz didn't leave herself enough time.* b. *I bought myself a new car.*

Again, the antecedent is subject, and the reflexive mandatory – except that in some dialects, mainly US, an accusative is found in informal style as a variant of the reflexive. This usage occurs predominantly with a 1st person pronoun: %*I bought me a new car*; %*Let's get us a hamburger.*[20]

(c) Predicative complement

[17] a. *I'm not feeling myself today.* b. *You should just try to be yourself.*

Once more, the antecedent is subject and the reflexive mandatory. It is, however, relatively rare for the predicative complement to be anaphorically linked to the subject, and both [i] and [ii] here are idiomatic. Example [i], with the verb *feel*, means roughly "I'm not feeling completely well" or "I'm not feeling in good spirits", while [ii], with *be*, means "You should just try to act naturally". There is one case where the non-reflexive is strongly favoured, namely where the proposition is concerned with identity: *If you weren't you, who would you like to be?*

(d) Object of preposition

We turn now to constructions where the pronoun is related to the verb not directly but via a preposition. The structural relation between pronoun and antecedent is thus not so close as in (a)–(c), and here a reflexive may have any of the three statuses we have defined: mandatory, optional, or inadmissible. These are illustrated in [18i–iii] respectively:

[18]	REFLEXIVE FORM	NON-REFLEXIVE FORM
i	a. *He was beside himself with anger.*	b. **He was beside him with anger.*
ii	a. *Liz wrapped the rug around herself.*	b. *Liz wrapped the rug around her.*
iii	a. **I haven't any money on myself.*	b. *I haven't any money on me.*

Mandatory reflexives

This represents much the most common pattern and can be regarded as the default case. Further examples are given in [19], where the pronoun cannot be replaced by a non-reflexive form with the same antecedent.

[20]The meaning, however, is not always quite the same. While *I caught myself some fish* implies that the fish were specifically for me, %*I caught me some fish* does not. There is also a non-standard use of *me* where the standard dialect would not have an indirect object at all: !*I seen me a mermaid once*; !*I want me a house by the beach.*

[19] i a. *He doesn't look after himself.* b. *She believes in herself.*
ii a. *He thinks of himself as overworked.* b. *Can't you do anything for yourself?*
iii a. *I never get any time to myself.* b. *Max had done it by himself.*

This case includes PPs functioning as complement of prepositional verbs (Ch. 4, §6.1) – for example, *after* in [ia] is selected by *look*, *in* in [ib] by *believe*, and so on. Also in this category are constructions where the object of the preposition is predicand for a predicative complement, as in [iia]. In [iiia–b], and also [18ia], the complement is required to be anaphorically linked to the subject: the reflexive is selected by the preposition, or the idiom containing it. Thus **I never get any time to him* is impossible, while *Max had done it by me* and *He was beside her* have only the literal locative senses of *by* and *beside.*

The antecedent in all these examples is the subject; it is also possible, though very much less usual, for the antecedent to be the object of the verb or even of a preposition:

[20] i *I had to save Mary from herself.*
ii *[Tim praises Mary to herself] but criticises her to everyone else.*
iii *He told Mary about herself as a young girl.*
iv *Liz talked to Tim about himself.*

These are still in accordance with the general rule that the antecedent precedes the reflexive anaphor. In the double PP construction [iv], the *to* phrase normally precedes the *about* phrase (*?Liz talked about Tim to himself*), but the reverse order is possible in a context of contrast (*Liz talked about Tim to himself very differently from the way she talked about him to her friends*).

Optional reflexives

[21] i *Rhiana saw a spider near her/herself.*
ii *Phil kept the radio next to him/himself the whole trip.*
iii *Mary made sure [she directed the stream of champagne away from her/herself].*

The governing prepositions indicate spatial location, with the PPs being either adjuncts, as in [i], or complements, as in [ii–iii]; the antecedent is in all cases subject. There is variation across speakers and also particular examples, but for many the non-reflexive form is preferred except in contexts of contrast (e.g. *Tim wanted the radio but Phil insisted on keeping it next to himself the whole trip*).

Inadmissible reflexives

[22] i *She looked about/around her/*herself.*
ii *He liked having children around him/*himself.*
iii *They took their cousin with them/*themselves.*
iv *You have your whole adult life before you/*yourself.*

The prepositions again involve spatial location (though with a metaphorical interpretation in [iv]). The complements of the preposition are required to be anaphorically linked to the subject, so that we can't say, with the same interpretation of verb and preposition, **She looked about him*, **He liked having children around me*, and so on. In this respect they are like [18ia] and [19iiia–b], but this time it is the non-reflexive form that is required.

Non-canonical constituent order

The basic rule, we have noted, is that a reflexive pronoun must follow its antecedent. It can precede the antecedent, however, in cases of preposing:

[23] i *To herself, the coordinator allocated the first watch.*
ii *Himself, he excused from these onerous duties.*

These correspond to the canonical structures:

[24] i *The coordinator allocated the first watch to herself.*
ii *He excused himself from these onerous duties.*

In [24] the order is determined by the basic rule, and in [23] the choice as to which of the linked NPs is treated as anaphor and which as antecedent is the same as in the corresponding canonical structure. Again, then, we cannot have a reflexive as subject of a main clause: **To the coordinator*$_i$, *herself*$_i$ *had allocated the first watch.*

Where the antecedent is object rather than subject (as in [20i], *I had to save Mary from herself*) such a reversal of the order of a reflexive and its antecedent is in principle possible in clauses with heavy-object postposing, but in practice examples of this kind are of questionable acceptability:

[25] ?*Tim was not able to save from herself even the ordinary middle-class girl he had met in the drug rehabilitation clinic.*

Coreference with and without an anaphoric link

Consider now the contrast between reflexive and non-reflexive forms in:

[26] i *Paul voted for himself.*
ii A: *Who voted for Paul?* B: *Well, Paul himself voted for him, but I doubt whether many others did.*

Example [i] is a straightforward case of a mandatory reflexive of the kind we have been considering. It might appear from [ii] that the reflexive of [i] is optional, since here we have non-reflexive *him* in the same environment. The reason why we have *him*, however, is that the antecedent is not the subject *Paul himself* but the previous occurrence of *Paul* in A's question. The fact that *him* and the subject are coreferential is incidental, not a consequence of any anaphoric link between them. This is evident from the fact that *Paul* can appear as object without reduction to a pro-form at all; compare, for example:

[27] i *Only Paul voted for himself.* [anaphoric coreference]
ii *Only Paul voted for Paul.* [non-anaphoric coreference]

Because of the quantification expressed by *only*, there is a sharp difference of meaning between these: [i] says that nobody else voted for themselves, [ii] that nobody else voted for Paul. We can give the meaning roughly as "x voted for x is true only for $x =$ Paul" and "x voted for Paul is true only for $x =$ Paul". The repetition of x in "x voted for x" in the first indicates an anaphoric relation between the corresponding NPs *Paul* and *himself*: hence the reflexive form. And conversely the absence of such repetition in "x voted for Paul" in the second indicates that there is no anaphoric link and we therefore have a full NP in both positions.

3.1.2 Basic reflexives in noun domains

Examples of constructions where a reflexive is related to the same noun as its antecedent are the bracketed NPs in:

[28] i [*Sue's nomination of herself for the headship*] *took us by surprise.*
ii [*Tim's confidence in himself*] *had dropped dramatically.*
iii [*Ed's portrayal of himself as a helpless victim of fate*] *was very hard to accept.*
iv *We finally came across* [*Mary's letters to Max about himself*].

We suggested in Ch. 5, §16.5.1, that genitives like those in [i–iii] combine the function of determiner with that of subject of the NP, and one of the factors that motivates the extension of the concept of subject to NPs is that these genitive phrases, like subjects in clause structure, are prototypical antecedents for a reflexive in the phrase. Nouns, however, do not take objects, so all the reflexives are objects of a preposition rather than of the head noun itself. Most of the nouns found in this construction are morphologically related to verbs, and in such cases there is a particularly close relationship with the clausal construction: compare [i], for example, with *Sue nominated herself for the headship.* Example [iv] differs from the usual pattern in that both antecedent and pronoun are governed by prepositions: it is comparable to the clause construction *Mary wrote to Max about himself.* Reflexives in this construction are mandatory.

In NPs generally there is often alternation between a construction with a genitive subject-determiner and one with *the* and a following *by* phrase: *Jill's purchase of the shares* ~ *the purchase of the shares by Jill.* This latter pattern is sometimes found with reflexives, resulting in a structure in which the reflexive precedes its antecedent:

[29] [*The annual nomination of himself by this loathsome creature*] *caused a great deal of resentment.*

Nouns with reflexive obliques vs compound nouns in *self-*

An alternative to the syntactic construction where a noun has a complement consisting of preposition + reflexive pronoun is a morphological one with *self* incorporated into the head noun. In some cases both patterns are available, while elsewhere only one or other is acceptable:

	a.	b.
[30] i	*Jill's confidence in herself*	*Jill's self-confidence*
ii	*Rembrandt's portrait of himself*	*Rembrandt's self-portrait*
iii	**Mary's abnegation of herself*	*Mary's self-abnegation*
iv	*Ed's portrayal of himself as a victim*	**Ed's self-portrayal as a victim*

The compound in *self-* does not require there to be an NP standing in a relation to it matching that of antecedent to anaphor in the syntactic construction: *an exhibition of self-portraits*; *Self-confidence is essential in this situation.*

3.1.3 Basic reflexives in dual-head domains

We turn now to a range of constructions where pronoun and antecedent are related to different heads, so that the structural link between them is more indirect.

(a) Verb or noun + predicative adjective

[31] i *I was thoroughly ashamed of myself.*
ii *She found him rather too preoccupied with himself.*
iii *I don't accept [your description of Bill as completely preoccupied with himself].*

The reflexive is mandatory and the antecedent is predicand – subject in complex-intransitive clauses like [i], object in complex-transitives like [ii], complement of a preposition in the nominalisation [iii]. Semantically, the predicand is an argument of the adjective, and hence there is a close semantic link between pronoun and antecedent. Syntactically, however, the predicand is not a dependent of the adjective, but of a verb or noun which takes the adjective as complement (immediate or oblique).

(b) Verb + noun

[32] i *Sir Harry presented [a bust of himself] to the Library.*
ii *For a moment he had [a vision of himself at primary school].*
iii *I've had [a horrible revelation about myself].*
iv *[The photograph of himself] he has on his web page makes Ed look like a crook.*

Here the antecedent is complement of the verb (subject in [i–iii], object in [iv]), while the reflexive is an oblique dependent of a noun heading another complement of that verb (object in [i–iii], subject in [iv]). Unlike the examples in [28], these latter NPs do not have a subject-determiner, the favoured function for the antecedent in the noun domain case.

The reflexives in [32] are mandatory, but there are other cases of the same general form where they are optional:

[33] i *Sue found a picture of herself/her taped to the notice-board.*
ii *Ed was angered by the rumours about himself/him published in the local press.*
iii *He turned the worst things about himself/him to cheery self-mocking dazzle for the delectation of people at parties.*
iv *A voice within herself/her was urging her to press on in spite of these setbacks.*

It remains unclear what factors determine whether the reflexive is mandatory or merely optional, and judgements may differ as to which type we have in particular examples. As illustrated in [32iv] and [33iv], it is possible in both cases for the reflexive to precede the antecedent. The nouns heading the NPs containing the reflexive commonly denote representations of various kinds, such as pictures, photographs, etc., and for this reason these reflexives are often referred to as 'picture noun reflexives'.

(c) Verb + verb

The final case to consider is that where pronoun and antecedent are dependents of different verbs, and are hence located in different clauses:

Reflexive is subject of non-finite clause

[34] i *Harry arranged for himself to be arrested.*
ii *Sue hadn't called for herself to be nominated.*
iii *Paul disapproved of himself being pilloried in the press.*

The pronouns in this construction are not in the same clause as their antecedents, for they are subjects of their own clause. Nevertheless we have mandatory reflexives here: it is as though the pronoun were being treated like a phrase within the matrix clause rather than as part of a subordinate clause. This construction is, however, quite rare and generally requires that the pronoun be contrastive. Without such contrast we would normally have ellipsis of the subject, as in *Harry$_i$ arranged $\_\__i$ to be arrested*; *call* is exceptional in not allowing a subjectless complement, but it is still rare for the subject of the infinitival to be anaphorically linked to the subject of *call*.

Clefts and related constructions: antecedent in subordinate clause

[35] i *It wasn't for himself that Ed had bought the shares.*
  ii *I tend to favour the opinion that when young men do well it is because of their parents, and [when they do badly it is because of themselves].*
  iii *The only one Ed embarrassed was himself/HIM.*

Here the reflexive is, or falls within, the complement of *be* in its specifying use, while the antecedent is in a subordinate clause.[21] Examples [i–ii] belong to the *it*-cleft construction, and here the reflexive is mandatory; in [iii] the antecedent is in a relative clause within the subject NP, and the reflexive is optional, a non-reflexive being permitted if stressed.

With respect to the structural relation between pronoun and antecedent this construction is highly exceptional, in that the antecedent is in a subordinate position relative to the pronoun. It is plausible to see the reflexive here as derivative from that found in the more elementary structures that are entailed:

[36] i *Ed didn't buy the shares for himself.*
  ii *They do badly because of themselves.*
  iii *Ed embarrassed himself.*

Basic reflexives: summary

If we set aside this last construction, which we have suggested is best accounted for as derivative from more elementary constructions, the following generalisations can be made about the structural relation between a reflexive and its antecedent:

[37] i The antecedent is related to a verb or noun as head; the reflexive is related (directly or via a preposition) to that same head or to a dependent thereof.
  ii Generally, the antecedent is superordinate to, and precedes, the reflexive.

Point [i] caters for the distinction between the single-head and dual-head domains. As for [ii], the antecedent is generally superordinate in the sense that it occupies a higher position in the constituent structure. The prototypical antecedent is subject, in the structure of a clause or NP, and as such it is higher than other dependents of the head verb or noun. Antecedent and pronoun can be at the same structural level when they are both related to the head verb or noun via a preposition, but this is relatively rare. The only case where the reflexive is structurally higher than the antecedent is when it is preposed in clause structure (as in [23ii], *Himself, he excused from these onerous duties*), and we suggested that this too should be regarded as derivative from a more elementary structure. Note, then, that in a dual-head construction where the heads are verb and noun, it is the antecedent that is related to the verb, not the reflexive. Examples like the following are thus quite inadmissible:

[38] *[*The bride's father*] / *[*The father of the bride*] *put herself first.*

[21] In [35ii] the relative clause of the cleft is omitted: we understand *It is because of themselves that they do badly.*

A reflexive in the position of *herself* must take the whole subject NP as antecedent, not a subordinate element within it – compare the single-head construction *The bride's father / The father of the bride put himself first.*

3.1.4 Override reflexives

Override reflexives are those that occur in place of a more usual non-reflexive in a restricted range of contexts where there is not the close structural relation between reflexive and antecedent that we find with basic reflexives. Crucially, the constructions concerned admit a 1st or 2nd person reflexive with no antecedent at all, and this represents the most frequent and central case of the override. The use of override reflexives, especially 1st person singular *myself*, has been the target of a good deal of prescriptive criticism; there can be no doubt, however, that it is well established, though there is a good deal of variation among speakers as to how commonly and in how wide a range of syntactic contexts it occurs.

Types of override constructions

(a) Coordination

[39] i *Both the local authority and myself have gone to the minister.*
ii *Ann suggested that the reporter pay both the victim and herself for their time.*
iii *They had invited Tim as well as myself.*

There is of course no override in coordinations like *He trusts only himself and his wife*, for here the reflexive is mandatory and is identical with the form that would appear in the corresponding non-coordinate construction, *He trusts only himself.* But in [39] the reflexive is optional and in [i–ii] it would be inadmissible without the coordination: **Myself have gone to the minister*; **Ann suggested that the reporter pay herself for her time.*

(b) Comparatives

[40] i *They were all much better qualified than myself.*
ii *A doctor such as yourself would be welcome in any rural town.*
iii *She told him he should marry a woman like herself.*
iv *Now Abel turned his head to look at his brother. Mark held the wheel loosely, . . . Mark looked easily older than himself, settled, his world comfortably categorised.*

(c) Inclusion, exclusion; *as for* and *what/how about?*

[41] i *Everybody, including yourself, will benefit from these changes.*
ii *Liz couldn't understand why nobody except herself had complained.*
iii *As for myself, it doesn't worry me which one they choose.*
iv A: *What did you think of the play?* B: *I enjoyed it – how about yourself?*

(d) Complement of specifying *be* or of a preposition in predicative complement function

[42] i *The only one they didn't invite was myself.*
ii *I confess [that the novel is really about myself].*
iii *All Ann's novels are really about herself.*

Note that in [iii] the antecedent is just part of the subject NP: as illustrated in [38] this is not possible with basic reflexives. Compare, similarly, *An individual's genes are unique to itself.*

(e) With 'picture nouns'

[43] i *The photo of myself that he'd chosen for the brochure was hardly flattering.*
ii *Tim knew that the letters about himself were libellous.*
iii *The Lord Mayor sighed. The portrait of himself newly presented to the gallery had been hung in an obscure alcove.*

These differ from examples like [32–33] in that the pronoun has an extraclausal antecedent or no antecedent at all. In [32–33], moreover, the reflexive is either mandatory or at least as highly favoured as the non-reflexive form, whereas in the present case the non-reflexive can reasonably be regarded as the default form.

(f) Some exceptional extensions of the override

Normally, override reflexives do not occur as object of the verb or object of those prepositions that in verb domain anaphora take mandatory reflexives:

[44] i **They will try to persuade yourself to go with them.*
ii **Liz didn't realise that I was talking to herself.*

Nevertheless, there are examples where an override in these positions is at least marginally acceptable:[22]

[45] i *The fact [that Paul had nominated myself for the position] didn't please Frank.*
ii *Liz couldn't hide her elation. The fact that Paul had nominated herself for the position was a huge vote of confidence.*
iii *It was Kennett's flamboyant self-indulgence that allowed himself to become an election issue at the expense of his own achievements.*

Factors favouring or disfavouring reflexive override

(a) 1st person

Much the most common override is 1st person *myself*. The reflexive avoids the choice between nominative *I* and accusative *me*, and this may well favour its use in coordinate and comparative constructions, where there is divided usage and hence potential uncertainty for some speakers as to which is the 'approved' case (see Ch. 5, §16.2).

(b) Perspective

Overrides with 3rd person reflexives characteristically occur in contexts where the antecedent refers to the person whose perspective is being taken in the discourse. Typical are such free indirect style examples as [40iv] and [43iii], which can be seen as an extension of the central 1st person case. Compare, then:

[46] i *Paul was determined to be promoted ahead of Sue. That profile of himself in the company newsletter would certainly help.*
ii *Sue was surprised at how many people had heard Paul's name. That photograph of him/*himself in the company newsletter must have reached a wide audience.*

In [i] it is Paul's perspective on events that is being taken, whereas in [ii] it is Sue's. As a result, a reflexive linked to *Paul* is acceptable in [i] but not in [ii].

[22] We have even found an example in subject function: *Each side proceeds on the assumption that itself possesses infinite courage, but that the other side consists of poltroons who can be frightened by bluster.* This is highly exceptional in that a deictic 1st or 2nd person reflexive could not occur in subject function.

(c) Intervening NP

Override reflexives may be disfavoured or excluded if an NP is located between the antecedent and the pronoun, especially one with the same gender and/or number features:

[47] i *Sue knew that there was a photograph of herself on the noticeboard.*
ii **Sue knew that Mary had put a photograph of herself on the noticeboard.*
iii ?*Sue knew that Paul had put a photograph of herself on the noticeboard.*
iv *Sue knew that the BBC had put to air an interview with herself which she had done in Nairobi in 1988.*

The override is fully acceptable in [i], where only the dummy *there* intervenes between *Sue* and the picture NP, but it is inadmissible in [ii], because *Mary* pre-empts the role of antecedent. More acceptable is [iii], because of the gender incompatibility between *Paul* and *herself*, while [iv] is again more or less fully acceptable, given that *the BBC* refers to an organisation, and hence is manifestly not a potential antecedent for the reflexive.

(d) Contrast

Acceptability of the override reflexive is increased if it is contrastive. For example, [45ii] requires stress on the reflexive to contrast Liz with other possible nominees; in [iii] we have a contrast between Kennett (Kennett's personality) and his achievements. Similarly, in the example of footnote 22 there is contrast between one side and another. Consider finally the result of combining stress with foregrounding by means of the cleft construction:

[48] i ?*She had wanted him to marry herself.*
ii *It was herself she had wanted him to marry.*

Here [ii] is fully acceptable even though the canonical counterpart [i] is questionable.

3.2 The emphatic use of reflexive pronouns

Four positions

Emphatic reflexives occur in one of the four positions illustrated in:

[49] i *I myself do not regard it as important.* [modifier in NP structure]
ii *I do not myself regard it as important.* [central]
iii *I do not regard it as important myself.* [end position]
iv *Myself, I do not regard it as important.* [front position]

In [i] *myself* functions as modifier within the structure of the larger NP *I myself*, while in [ii–iv] it is an adjunct in clause structure (see Ch. 8, §20.1, for explanation of the three positions). Reflexives in front position are predominantly 1st person, and the reflexive on its own here is hardly distinguishable from the PP *as for myself*. In clauses with no auxiliary and a 2nd/3rd person subject, there are generally just two possibilities:

[50] i *The manager herself detected the error.* [modifier in NP structure]
ii *The manager detected the error herself.* [end position]

Clause adjuncts

Emphatic reflexives functioning in clause structure always have the subject as antecedent:

[51] i $\_\_{}_i$ *Having read the report herself*$_i$, *Liz*$_i$ *was able to confirm what I said.*
ii **They gave Max the key himself.*

The subject antecedent is overt in [49ii–iv], missing but understood in [51i]. Example [51ii], with *himself* anaphoric to the indirect object, is inadmissible.

Modifiers in NP structure

NPs containing a reflexive as modifier can occur in most NP functions:

[52] i *[The President himself] had made the decision.* [subject]
ii *We saw [the President himself].* [object of verb]
iii *She had addressed the letter to [the President himself].* [object of preposition]

The predicative complement function, however, is very restricted. In *Liz is an engineer herself*, for example, the reflexive is a clause adjunct with *Liz* as antecedent, not a modifier in the NP headed by *engineer*. Nevertheless, predicative complement function is possible in examples like *You will be the President himself* (where 3rd person *himself* cannot have *you* as antecedent). One absolute restriction is that neither the antecedent nor the whole NP can be genitive. Compare:

[53] **I met Mary's herself son / Mary herself's son / Mary's herself's son.*

To express the intended meaning we need an *of* phrase rather than a genitive: *I met the son of Mary herself.* Note, then, that the subject of a gerund-participial cannot be genitive if it contains a reflexive modifier:

[54] i *They objected to Tom/Tom's doing it himself.*
ii *They objected to Tom/*Tom's himself doing it.*

Emphasis and contrast

The emphatic effect of the reflexive may be comparable to that of *none other than* or *no less than*; these items could be added with little change to the meaning in, for example, [52]. Very often there is explicit or implicit contrast:

[55] i *Funds should be provided for the maintenance of both the dwellings themselves and the spaces between them.*
ii *The rules of conduct which must be enforced on the inferior masses do not apply to the rulers themselves.*
iii *Then, in chronological order, Mr White covers the primary campaigns, the conventions, and the presidential campaign itself.*
iv *When his father told stories about the war a curious happiness came over him which the stories themselves did not explain.*

The contrasting terms may be alike or different with respect to the predication. In [i], for example, the funds are for the dwellings and the spaces between them, while in [ii] the rules apply to the inferior masses but not to the rulers. In cases of explicit contrast such as [i–iii], the reflexive will tend to attach to the term that is in some sense more important, either inherently or in terms of the context of discourse. In [iii] for example, the primaries and conventions are preliminaries, while the presidential campaign is the major stage in the election of the president.

Special use: direct involvement

In addition to what we will call the 'ordinary use' illustrated above, the emphatic reflexive may be used to indicate the direct involvement of the subject referent. Compare:

[56]	ORDINARY USE	DIRECT INVOLVEMENT USE
i	a. *Liz had a swim herself.*	b. *Liz had solved the problem herself.*
ii	a. *Did you like it yourself?*	b. *Did you make these cakes yourself?*

The salient interpretation of [ib] is that Liz solved the problem without help, that this was her own accomplishment. Similarly in [iib] the implied contrast will most likely be between your making the cakes and simply buying them ready-made (or getting someone else to make them). This kind of meaning can be expressed more explicitly by means of such PPs as *by oneself* or *on one's own*: *Liz had solved the problem by herself / on her own.* Compare also *I want to see the evidence myself* and *I want to see the evidence for myself.*

The direct involvement sense strongly favours end position: [56ib], for example, is considerably more likely for the sense described than *Liz herself had solved the problem* or *Liz had herself solved the problem.* In negative clauses an ordinary emphatic reflexive falls outside the scope of negation, whereas one with the direct involvement sense falls inside the scope. Compare:

[57] i *I don't feel hungry myself.* [reflexive outside scope of negation]
ii *I didn't write the report myself: Jo wrote it.* [reflexive inside scope of negation]

Example [i], with an ordinary emphatic reflexive, can be glossed as "Personally, I don't feel hungry": the negative applies to the feeling hungry but not to *myself.* In [ii], however, what is negated is my direct involvement in writing the report. Where a direct involvement reflexive is inside the scope of negation, there will generally be an implicature that the action or whatever was, is, or will be performed by someone else. In [ii] this implicature is explicitly confirmed in the following clause (included in the example precisely to force the direct involvement reading), but it is also conveyed by the relevant reading of *Liz hadn't solved the problem herself,* and the like: other things being equal you will infer that the problem was solved, with someone helping Liz or doing it for her.

A further difference between the two uses is illustrated in the following pair:

[58] i **Any mother herself will understand what I mean.* [ordinary use]
ii *Any mother should be able to do this herself.* [direct involvement use]

In the ordinary use the antecedent is usually definite and normally has to be referential: hence the anomaly of [i]. But no such restriction applies with the direct involvement use.

Emphatic reflexives in ascriptive supplements

[59] i a. *John, [<u>himself</u> a religious man,] defended the exhibition.*
b. *John, [a religious man <u>himself</u>,] defended the exhibition.*
ii a. *[<u>Himself</u> a bachelor,] Ed knew well how to entertain his bachelor friends.*
b. *[A bachelor <u>himself</u>,] Ed knew well how to entertain his bachelor friends.*

Ordinary emphatic reflexives commonly occur in ascriptive supplements (cf. Ch. 15, §5.2). They may precede the predicative element, as in [ia/iia], or follow, as in [ib/iib].

In either case, the supplement can follow or precede the antecedent, as in [i] and [ii] respectively.[23]

4 Reciprocals

4.1 Form and meaning

Compound vs split constructions

Reciprocal meaning is expressed by *each* or *one* in combination with *other*. The two components may form a compound reciprocal pronoun (*each other* or *one another*) or remain separate, with *each* and *one* determinatives, ***other*** a common noun: we will speak of **compound** and **split** constructions. Compare, then:

[1]	i	*They are required to consult with each other / one another.*	[compound]
	ii	*They are each required to consult with the other.*	[split]
	iii	*They are required to consult one with the other.*	[split]

The pronouns *each other* and *one another* are semantically equivalent, with *each other* the more frequent of the two.[24] In the split construction, however, *each* and *one* differ both syntactically and semantically, and we will therefore compare them separately with the compound construction.

The split construction with *each* compared with the compound construction

[2]	i	a. *Each girl trusted the others.*	[split]
		b. *Each of the girls trusted the others.*	[split]
		c. *The girls each trusted the others.*	[split]
		d. **The girls trusted each the others.*	[split]
	ii	*The girls trusted each other / one another.*	[compound]

Each can occur within the subject NP itself (as pure determiner in [ia], fused determiner-head in [ib]) or as an adjunct following the subject, as in [ic]. *Each* can follow an auxiliary verb (*The girls had each trusted the others*), but it cannot immediately precede the NP containing *others*: instead of [id] we have the compound construction [ii], with *each other* or *one another* a pronoun functioning as head of the object NP. The distributive determinative *each* behaves in just the same way as in non-reciprocal constructions: compare *Each girl* / *Each of the girls* / *The girls each won a prize*. Similarly *the others* is quite independent of *each*: compare *I trusted the others* or *Only a few of the girls trusted the others.*

The same patterns are found where *the others* is object of a preposition:

[3]	i	a. *Each girl / Each of the girls / The girls each shook hands with the others.*
		b. **The girls shook hands each with the others.*
	ii	*The girls shook hands with each other / one another.*

[23] Alternatively, we might say that the construction has an ellipted subject, and in this case the reflexive would not be directly linked to the following *Ed* but to the preceding covert subject.

[24] There has been a prescriptive tradition of saying that *each other* is appropriate for sets of two, *one another* for sets of three or more: *Kim and Pat like each other* but *Kim, Pat, and Alex like one another*. The empirical evidence, however, does not support this rule and there is not even any historical basis for it; most modern usage manuals recognise that the pronouns cannot be distinguished along these lines.

Suppose there are three girls, Sue, Jill, and Pam. It then follows from [2ia–c] that Sue trusted Jill and Pam, Jill trusted Sue and Pam, and Pam trusted Sue and Jill. And the compound version [2ii] conveys the same. Notice, however, that the split version allows for a more precise expression of the relationships where larger sets are involved:

[4] i *Each of the girls trusted a few / some / most of the others.*
ii *Each of the girls trusted each of the others.*

The compound version [2ii] is obviously not equivalent to [4i], but it is not equivalent to [4ii] either: the latter specifies that the relationship holds between every pair of girls, but given a reasonably large set of girls the truth conditions for [2] would be somewhat less stringent. That is, each girl trusted the rest of the set as a whole, but not necessarily every individual one of them. We should also observe that the split construction differs from the compound one in that it distinguishes between sets of two and sets of three or more. For a set of two we would have singular *other*: *Each of the girls trusted the other.*

The split construction with *one* compared with the compound construction

[5] i *They were placed one on top of the other.* [split]
ii *They were placed on top of each other / one another.* [compound]

The split construction with *one* usually has *one* as adjunct preceding a PP containing *other*, as in [i]. It will be noted that the syntactic position of *one* in the split construction is different from that of *each*: see [1ii–iii]. *One* occurs after rather than before the verb: compare [5i] with **They were one placed on top of the other.* A further difference is that the *one* construction doesn't allow *one* as adjunct to combine with *the other* as object – compare **They followed one the other through the tunnel* with the *each* counterpart in [2ic] (*The girls each trusted the others*).

Kinds of reciprocity

In the split construction *one* is used for a broader range of reciprocal relations than *each*. Compare the following:

[6] i *They were placed one on top of the other.* (=[5i]) [linear: asymmetric]
ii *They were sitting one beside the other in the back row.* [linear: symmetric]
iii *They are required to consult one with the other.* (=[1iii]) [non-linear]

Suppose *they* refers to a set of four: A, B, C, and D (they might be mattresses in [i], people in [ii–iii]). The relation in [i–ii] is **linear** in that A–D are ordered: in [i] A is on top of B, B is on top of C, C is on top of D, and in [ii] A is beside B, B is beside C, and C is beside D. A is thus not (immediately) on top of or beside C, and B is not (immediately) on top of or beside D. The relation in [iii], by contrast, is **non-linear**. Here there is no ordering, and A consults directly or immediately with all of B, C, and D, B consults with all of A, C, and D, and so on. Within the linear type we then have a distinction between **asymmetric** and **symmetric**. *On top of* expresses an asymmetric relation in that *A is on top of B* entails *B is not on top of A*; and *beside* expresses a symmetric relation because *A is beside B* entails *B is beside A*. The compound reciprocal pronouns, like the split construction with *one*, can be used for all three kinds of relation, but the split construction with *each* is restricted to the non-linear type, the most central case of reciprocity.

In our contextualisation of the asymmetric [6i]/[5], the intermediate mattresses B and C are both on top of some mattress and have a mattress on top of them: this is what makes the situation like more central cases of reciprocity. But the outer mattresses A and

D do not have this property of entering into the relation in both directions: A doesn't have any mattress on top of it and D is not on top of any mattress. If the set in question contains only two members, there won't be any member that enters into the relation in both directions, and the situation will not then qualify as reciprocal. In this case the compound construction is inappropriate:[25]

[7] i *The two jars had been placed one inside the other.* [split]
ii #*The two jars had been placed inside each other / one another.* [compound]

Even with sets of more than two, the compound construction is less readily used for asymmetric linear reciprocity than for the other kinds. Compare, for the meaning "They were slaughtered in turn":

[8] i *They were slaughtered one after another / the other.* [split]
ii #*They were slaughtered after each other / one another.* [compound]

One within the subject NP

The examples of the split *one* construction considered so far have had *one* as a post-verbal adjunct. It is also possible for *one* to occur within the subject:

[9] i *One crisis followed another at frequent intervals.*
ii *Crises followed each other / one another at frequent intervals.*

In [i] the NP *one crisis* is interpreted non-referentially: it doesn't refer to any one crisis. Examples where an NP of this form is used referentially, as in *One girl criticised the others*, have non-reciprocal interpretations.

Antecedent of reciprocal pronouns must denote a set of two or more

A reciprocal relation necessarily involves at least two entities, and the antecedent for the reciprocal pronouns must therefore denote a set of two or more. Usually it is a plural NP (as in the examples given so far) or an *and*-coordination of NPs (*Kim and Pat mistrust each other*). In a few cases, however, it can be syntactically singular:

[10] i *Everyone knew each other.*
ii *One couple clearly hated each other's guts.*

Singular *everyone* implies some contextually given set of people, and the reciprocal relation of knowing each other holds over this set. Notice, however, that NPs with *every* as determiner do not behave in the same way. We cannot have, for example, **Every girl knew each other*: a plural such as *all the girls* would be used instead. In [10ii] *couple* is a singular collective noun denoting a set of two people, and the relation of hating each other's guts holds for this set. The acceptability of such examples varies somewhat according to the particular collective noun involved; [10ii] seems better, for instance, than *The cabinet/government didn't like each other very much*, where many speakers would prefer an explicit plural such as *members of the cabinet/government.*

[25] Examples are occasionally found, but they are generally regarded as mistakes – cf. this letter to the editor of a London newspaper: *We read the instructions on 'How to condense milk by magic' in last week's Colour Magazine, but we can't find two jam jars which will fit loosely inside each other. We have found two jam jars one of which will fit loosely inside the other. Will the magic still work?* The lack of reciprocal meaning is not restricted to cases where the set has just two members. Consider *The jars had been stored one inside another.* It could be that there are ten jars, five of one size and five slightly larger, with each of the smaller ones stored inside one of the larger ones. No one jar would then be both inside a second jar and have a third jar inside it, and again, then, there would be no reciprocity.

4.2 The distribution of reciprocal pronouns

Reciprocals and reflexives

Our concern in the remainder of this section will be with the compound construction. Reciprocal pronouns have it in common with reflexives that there has to be a close structural relation between pronoun and antecedent. Thus both types of pronoun are inadmissible in contexts like:

[11] i *Kim and Pat claim that I misled themselves.
ii *Kim and Pat claim that I favoured each other.

Just as the meaning "Kim and Pat claimed that I misled Kim and Pat" cannot be expressed by [i], so the meaning "Kim claimed that I favoured Pat and Pat claimed that I favoured Kim" cannot be expressed by [ii].

At the same time, reciprocals differ from reflexives in several ways, the most important of which are as follows:

[12] i Reciprocals always function as complement: there is no emphatic use.
ii Unlike reflexives, reciprocals have genitive forms, *each other's, one another's.*
iii Reflexive is an inflectional property, but reciprocal is not.

Point [i] is illustrated by the ungrammaticality (and semantic incoherence) of examples like **We each other enjoyed the show* or **The girls solved the problem each other.* Point [ii] is illustrated by the contrast between *They blamed each other's parents* and **They blamed themselves' parents.*

Point [12iii] concerns the different status of reflexives and reciprocals in the system of pronouns: the reflexives are inflectional forms of the personal pronouns, while the reciprocals are independent pronouns. This difference has a number of consequences. Note in the first place that we can correct [11i] by replacing the reflexive form of ***they*** by the accusative form: *Kim and Pat claim that I misled them.* But we cannot correct [11ii] by adjusting the inflectional form of the pronoun: we need a more radical change that eliminates the pronoun altogether, as in the split construction *Kim and Pat each claimed that I favoured the other.* A second consequence is that the mandatory vs optional distinction that we need for reflexives is inapplicable to reciprocals. Compare:

		a.	b.
[13]	i	*They hurt themselves/*them.*	*They hurt each other.*
	ii	*They tied the ropes around themselves/ them.*	*They tied the ropes around each other.*
	iii	*They say I misled *themselves/ them.*	**They say I favoured each other.*

With reflexives, the issue is which form of the pronoun we get in a given context, reflexive or non-reflexive. There are three possible answers: in [ia] only the reflexive is permitted, so it is mandatory; in [iia] both forms are permitted, so the reflexive is optional; in [iiia] only the non-reflexive is permitted, so the reflexive is inadmissible. With reciprocals, the issue is simply whether the pronoun is admissible ([ib/iib]) or inadmissible ([iiib]).

Syntactic contexts admitting reciprocal pronouns

Reciprocal pronouns occur in essentially the same range of contexts as those where we find basic reflexives. These have been described in §§3.1.1–3, and hence need only a summary treatment here. We illustrate with *each other,* with the understanding that *one another* would also be possible.

(a) Verb-domain reciprocal pronouns

[14] i *Kim and Pat love each other.* [subject; direct object]

ii *They never gave each other presents.* [subject; indirect object]

iii *We sat opposite each other.* [subject; comp of prep]

iv *We must protect them from each other.* [object; comp of prep]

v *I talked to Kim and Pat about each other.* [comp of prep (both)]

The annotations on the right give the functions of the antecedent and pronoun respectively; in [v] both have the function of complement of a preposition.[26] As with reflexives, the pronoun cannot have subject function: **Each other love Kim and Pat.*

(b) Noun-domain reciprocals

[15] i *We were alarmed at* [*their growing hostility to each other*].

ii *She wrote a poem about* [*the love of Karl and Sophie for each other*].

iii *The story is about* [*the love for each other of two teenage students who had both been rejected by their parents*].

Here antecedent and anaphor are related to the same noun, the pronoun by means of a preposition, the antecedent by genitive case or a preposition. Example [iii] shows that in this construction the pronoun can precede the antecedent.

Extensions

The same types of extension are found with reciprocals as with reflexives, except that reciprocals are hardly possible as complement in the *it*-cleft construction: ?*It was each other that they criticised most harshly.*

(a) Predicative adjective domain

[16] i *They seem very fond of each other.*

ii *The competition had made them somewhat antagonistic towards each other.*

The pronoun is oblique complement of a predicative adjective, and the antecedent is the predicand – subject in [i], object in [ii].

(b) Subject of non-finite complement of verb

[17] *They arranged for each other to be nominated by one of the directors.*

(c) Mixed verb–noun domain

[18] i *They had had* [*nightmares about each other*].

ii *Lady Mary and Sir Harry had presented* [*portraits of each other*] *to the Gallery.*

iii *Kim and Pat sued* [*each other's parents*].

Examples [i–ii] are comparable to the reflexive examples [32–33]. In [18iii] the reciprocal is genitive subject-determiner to the noun *parents*, while the antecedent is subject of the verb *sue*; this pattern is much more common than that of [i–ii] but, as we have observed, has no reflexive counterpart because reflexives do not have genitive forms. Note that in the mixed verb–noun domain it is not possible for the antecedent to be a genitive (**The girls' assignments had been typed by each other*); genitive antecedents are found only in noun-domain anaphora, as in [15i].

[26] As with reflexives, the preferred order in [14v] has the *to* phrase before the *about* phrase: ?*I talked about Kim and Pat to each other.*

Ellipted antecedents

[19] i *Now __ hug each other.*
ii *__ Keeping a wary eye on each other, they woo Concordia.*

As with reflexives, the antecedent (typically the subject) may be ellipted. In the imperative [i] we understand *you* as antecedent, while in [ii] the covert subject of the subordinate clause is itself anaphorically linked to the following *they* in the matrix clause.

Coordination

Reciprocal pronouns can be coordinated with a reflexive or some other NP:

[20] i *They no longer respected themselves or each other.*
ii *You must help not only each other but also your families.*

5 Demonstratives

5.1 Preliminaries

Forms

There are two demonstratives, proximal ***this*** and distal ***that***. Both inflect for number:

[1]		SINGULAR	PLURAL
i	PROXIMAL	*this*	*these*
ii	DISTAL	*that*	*those*

Dependent and independent uses

The demonstratives have both **dependent** and **independent** uses, as illustrated in:

[2] i DEPENDENT: *[This milk] is sour. Where's [that boy of yours]? [These two] are mine. Please pass [those knives]. He's not often [this late]. It didn't cost [that much].*
ii INDEPENDENT: *[All this] is mine. [That]'s not true. Can I have a few of [those]? His manner was like [that of a schoolmaster]. [Those who broke the law] could expect no leniency.*

In the dependent use they function as pre-head determiner or degree modifier; in the independent use they function as fused determiner-head in NP structure (see Ch. 5, §§7.1, 9.2).

Singular independent demonstratives mostly restricted to inanimates

Independent *this* and *that* cannot in general be used of humans or animals:

[3] i *Those who obtain a score of 90% will win a prize.*
ii **That who obtains the highest score will win a prize.*
iii *He/That saved my life.*
iv *The population of Victoria far exceeds that of Queensland.*
v **The premier of Victoria will be meeting with that of Queensland.*

Those in [i] is understood as denoting a set of people, but the corresponding singular *that* in [ii] is inadmissible. In [iii] *he* and *that* contrast in animacy, *he* referring to a person or animal, *that* to an inanimate. And in the anaphoric cases in [iv–v] *that* is acceptable with the interpretation "the population" but not "the premier". No such restriction applies to dependent *this* and *that*: *This guy* / *That guy saved my life.*

This and *that* can have animate reference, however, when they function as subject of the verb *be*:

[4] i *This is my husband, Peter.*
ii *Look over there. Isn't that your biology tutor?*

Such examples normally involve the specifying use of ***be***: we can't have **This isn't very well today* or **That is President.*[27] Note also that the singular forms are used even when more than one person is involved: *This is Alice and Robert Penfold*; *That's your parents over there.*

5.2 The central deictic use

The primary use of the demonstratives is in NPs referring to objects present in the situation of utterance, with ***this*** applying to objects relatively close to the speaker (proximal), and ***that*** to objects relatively distant from the speaker (distal):

[5] i *This apple looks riper than that one.*
ii *Is this yours?*
iii *What's that you're eating?*

If the demonstrative NP contains a postmodifier that itself participates in the proximal vs distal distinction, demonstrative and postmodifier must agree: *this book here*, *those flowers over there*, but not **this book there.*

What counts as proximal and what as distal is not determined by purely objective features of spatial location: there may be a subjective element involved. For example, I might be holding something in my hand and still have a choice between saying *What is this?* and *What is that?* In this context *this* would be the default choice, but *that* could be used to indicate some negative attitude such as disapproval. Or suppose we are in a department store looking for a jacket: I might refer to one quite close to me, saying *How about this one?* or *How about that one?* One possible factor in the choice could be whether I am the one wanting to buy (favouring *this*) or whether you are (favouring *that*).

Demonstratives can be used deictically not only to pick out physical objects in the situation of utterance, but also in reference to properties of such objects or to actions taking place or other abstract features of the situation of utterance:

[6] i *I hadn't expected there to be this much damage.* *I've never seen a computer this small before.* *I'm not comfortable like this.* *Hold your head up like this.* *This is what he was doing.* *When we first travelled with Matthew he was younger than this.*
ii *Stop that.* *I'm looking for something about that size.* *Don't look at me like that / that way.* *That is not how to do it.*

As observed in §1, deictic demonstratives are often accompanied by indexing acts such as pointing – as in the last example of [i], where the speaker points at the child whose

[27] The ascriptive *be* construction is permitted under certain circumstances with an NP as predicative complement: *That is an extraordinarily tall man over there*; *This is a beautiful baby.*

age is compared with Matthew's. For the use of *this* in temporal deixis (as in *this week*, etc.), see §10.1.2 below.

Demonstratives are also commonly found in discourse deixis (see [26] of §1):

[7] i A: *You look about fifteen.* B: *Is that meant to be a compliment?*
ii *I hope this conversation isn't being recorded.*
iii *Taking the Waltz first, a group of figures that really must be included are Natural Turn, Closed Change, and Reverse Turn, danced in that order.*

In [i] *that* refers to A's statement; in [ii] *this conversation* refers to the one in which the utterance of *this conversation* takes place; and in [iii] *that order* refers to the order in which the three figures have just been mentioned.

5.3 **Anaphoric uses**

(a) With NP as antecedent

[8] i *There was a glass pane in the front door, and through this he could see into a hallway where a plump woman with red hair was arranging flowers.*
ii *I raised some money by hocking the good clothes I had left, but when that was gone I didn't have a cent.*
iii *It appears Tom did most of the damage. That boy's becoming quite a problem.*
iv *I bought another copy, but that one was defective too.*
v *The 1978 Report recommended that a State Plan be adopted to develop 99 public libraries throughout South Australia over an eight-year period. The development programme to achieve this State Plan has been highly successful.*

A demonstrative NP and its antecedent NP are characteristically coreferential, as in [i–iv]; in [v] *a State Plan* is non-referential, but we understand that the recommendation was adopted, so that there does exist an actual plan for the anaphoric NP to refer to. The demonstratives in [i–ii] are independent, the others dependent. In these dependent cases, the demonstrative determines a nominal which in [iii] (*boy*) represents new information; in [iv] (*one*) is itself an anaphor with the nominal *copy* as antecedent; and in [v] (*State Plan*) is repeated from the antecedent NP. Note that in [iv] we have one anaphoric link at the level of nominals between *one* and *copy*, and another at the level of NPs between *that one* and *another copy*.

As evident from the examples cited, both ***this*** and ***that*** can be used anaphorically – and in general one could be replaced by the other with very little effect on the meaning. Note that ***this*** and ***that*** cannot be used contrastively in the anaphoric use as they can in the deictic use: #*I went Christmas shopping and bought a t-shirt*$_i$ *and a CD*$_j$; *that*$_i$ *is for Kim, and this*$_j$ *is for Pat.* It would be possible to replace the demonstrative NPs in [8] by personal pronouns, and indeed personal pronouns are very much more commonly used as anaphors to coreferential NPs than are demonstratives.

The anaphoric and deictic uses of demonstratives are not mutually exclusive:

[9] A: *Look at the necklace she's wearing.* B: *That's the one I gave her.*

That is here anaphoric to *the necklace she's wearing*, but as the necklace is present in the situation *that* also has distal deictic force.

(b) Antecedents with the form of clauses

[10] i *Harold would be absent in Salonika for some days; this made the arrangement for her own timetable much simpler.*
ii *He discovered that she had slept with several other boyfriends before him. That shocked him a good deal, and they had a quarrel about it.*
iii *A fire had just been lighted and things had been set out for drinks, and his response to these comforts was instantaneous.*
iv *At first he took no notice of their taunts, but he was soon forced to abandon that approach.*
v *He chopped part of Pa's door down before he stopped. He might not have gone that far if Pa hadn't been locked in laughing fit to shake the house.*

Except in [v], where *that* is a degree modifier, the anaphor is an NP, and hence has a nominalising role. We noted that where the antecedent is an NP, as in [8], independent demonstratives are less common than personal pronouns, but the reverse is the case here. While *it* would be possible in [10i–ii], demonstratives are more likely. Note that [10ii] contains an anaphoric chain, with *that* anaphoric to the preceding clause but antecedent to the following *it*.

(c) Antecedents with the form of AdjPs or AdvPs

[11] i *She was incredibly depressed. In this mood she couldn't do anything.*
ii *They had a blue rug, but that isn't the colour I wanted.*
iii *They were running very slowly. At that speed they didn't have a hope of catching the train.*
iv *Her skin is brown and so clear. No one in Europe ever had skin that clear.*

The anaphor is again an NP except in [iv], and hence has the same kind of nominalising role as in [10].

(d) Independent demonstratives with nominals as antecedent

While the antecedent of an independent demonstrative can be a full NP, as in [8i–ii] and [9] above, it can also be just a nominal. There are two subcases to be distinguished, one involving deictic ***this*** and ***that***, the other non-deictic ***that***.

Deictic ***this*** and ***that*** with nominal antecedents

[12] i *[This copy] is clearer than [that].*
ii *[The wine we had yesterday] was too sweet for my taste but [this] is perfect.*

That in [i] and *this* in [ii] are clearly deictic, referring to entities in the situation of utterance, and with distal and proximal senses respectively. At the same time, however, they are anaphoric, for we understand "that copy" and "this wine". We analyse independent ***this*** and ***that*** as realising a fusion of determiner and head functions (as explained in Ch. 5, §9.5), and it is here just the head component that is interpreted anaphorically, as having the same denotation as the underlined antecedent. These examples thus differ clearly from independent *that* in [9], which is also simultaneously deictic and anaphoric. In [9] the anaphoric relation is between *that* and the NP *the necklace she's wearing*, with the relation interpreted as coreference; in [12], however, the anaphoric relation is between *that* or *this* (or the head function component of them) and the nominals, or nouns, *copy* and *wine*: there is no anaphoric relation and no coreference between the bracketed NPs.

Non-deictic ***that*** with nominal antecedent

[13] i *Their names weren't on [the list of the dead], nor on [that of the missing].*
ii *[The shops in the suburban shopping centres] resemble [those of an English village].*
iii *[The speech she actually made] was quite different from [that which had been released to the media].*

Again, the antecedent is a nominal rather than a full NP, but this time ***that*** lacks the deictic meaning that it has in [12]. Non-reduced versions of the NPs here would contain *the* rather than ***that***: *the list of the missing, the shops of an English village, the speech which had been released to the media.* This correlates with the fact that there is no distal–proximal contrast in the present construction, for ***this*** is inadmissible: cf. **Their names weren't on the list of the dead, nor on this of the missing.* In this use, ***that*** has been bleached of its primary distal demonstrative meaning and as far as its determiner function is concerned it serves as a pure marker of definiteness, like *the. The* itself is one of the few determinatives that cannot function as a fused determiner-head (we cannot have **Their names weren't on the list of the dead, nor on the of the missing,* with *the* interpreted as "the list"): ***that*** in this bleached, non-deictic sense can therefore be regarded as filling this gap in the system.

In each of the examples in [13] the bracketed NPs are referentially distinct: *the list of the dead* and *that of the missing* refer to distinct lists, and so on. The relation between the NP containing the antecedent and the one containing ***that*** is not always of this kind, however:

[14] i *[His image of her] was [that of a woman in her early thirties].*
ii *Penalties, too, have a more severe impact on [Aboriginal people]. An appreciable number of [those convicted and fined] go to jail rather than pay the fine.*

In [i] there is just one image: the second NP, in predicative complement function, provides further descriptive information about the referent of the first. In [ii] we have a subset relation: the second bracketed NP, interpreted as "the Aboriginal people (who are) convicted and fined", refers to a subset of Aboriginal people in general.[28]

Independent demonstratives and the pro-form ***one***

Independent ***this*** and ***that*** are often equivalent to NPs with the pro-form ***one*** as head. An alternant of [12i], for example, is *This copy is clearer than that one,* and similarly [13iii] is equivalent to *The speech she actually made was quite different from the one which had been released to the media.* The general relationship between the fused determiner-head construction and NPs with pro-form ***one*** as head is discussed in §6.1 below, but we will comment briefly here on the special case where the fused determiner-head is ***that***. The main differences between the present use of ***that*** and ***one*** are as follows:

[15] i ***That*** incorporates a definite determiner.
ii Non-deictic ***that*** requires a post-head dependent.
iii ***That*** allows a singular non-count antecedent.

Point [i] reiterates our analysis of independent ***that*** as representing a fusion of determiner and head functions; ***one*** by contrast functions simply as head and as such combines with

[28] Like most fused determiner-heads (see §6.1 below) non-deictic ***that*** can take an explicit or implicit partitive: *[The houses on the agent's list] – or at least [those (of them) that were within our price range] – weren't big enough for our needs.* Here the full NP *the houses on the agent's list* is antecedent, but it is antecedent for the explicit or implicit partitive.

separate determiner elements (obligatorily so in the singular). Thus *that* in [12i] and [13iii] corresponds not to *one* alone but to *that* + *one* and *the* + *one*. As for point [ii], both ***one*** and ***that***, in the uses we are concerned with here, require the presence of a dependent, but while ***one*** allows both pre-head and post-head dependents (e.g. *the earlier one, the one from Sydney*), with ***that*** it can only be in post-head position.[29] Point [iii] is illustrated in:

[16] *The crockery reminds me of [that which we used to have in College].*

The demonstrative NP here could not be replaced by *the one that we used to have in College*, which requires a count antecedent.

Anticipatory anaphora

This occurs in anticipatory anaphora with a separate, non-integrated antecedent:

[17] i *There are still these candidates to interview: Lugton, Barnes, Airey, and Foster.*
ii *This is what I want you to do: Pick up Sue from the airport (she's arriving on Qantas flight 122) and take her to the Astoria Hotel in Brunswick Street . . .*

If we replace the anaphor by the antecedent in [i] the anaphor is simply dropped (instead of switching places with the antecedent), giving *There are still Lugton, Barnes, Airey, and Foster to interview*. The length of the antecedent in [ii] makes it an unsuitable replacement for *this*, but a shorter expression (such as *Pick up Sue at the airport*) could occur as subject, with consequent dropping of *this*.

Instead of *these candidates* in [17i] we could have non-anaphoric *four candidates*. In both cases the following names serve to identify the candidates, but there is a significant difference between the two constructions. The indefinite *four candidates* does not require any further specification: the names could be omitted without affecting the coherence of the utterance. But *these candidates* is definite and its use implies that the referent is identifiable: the following names provide that identification, and for this reason can be regarded as having the status of antecedent.

We distinguish between an antecedent and mere elaboration or clarification, although the boundary is not clear-cut. Compare [17] with, for example:

[18] i *The next day he was caned for six for wagging school, but he never told. That was the good thing about Herbie: no matter what happened to him, he never told.*
ii *This/That is strange: the door is unlocked.*

In [i] *no matter what happened to him, he never told* clarifies how *that* is to be interpreted, but *that* is nevertheless anaphoric to what precedes and the clarification is not obligatory: we therefore treat cases like this as ordinary retrospective anaphora. In [ii] the second clause again clarifies the reference of the demonstrative, but what is strange is something in the situation of utterance, and hence the demonstrative is deictic; again the clarificatory clause might be omitted. Note that instead of the second clause we could have *I'm sure I locked the door when I went out*: this doesn't itself say what is strange (and hence couldn't plausibly be analysed as an antecedent), but it likewise serves to clarify what is strange about the current situation. It would seem that there are no cases of distal ***that*** that can properly be regarded as involving anticipatory anaphora.

[29] It will be apparent from some of our examples that ***that*** permits a somewhat wider range of post-head dependents than ***one***. Note, for example, that we could not substitute *the* + ***one*** in [13ii] or [14i].

5.4 Other uses of the demonstratives

(a) Recognitional uses

[19] i *You never wore that scarf I bought you.*
ii *He'd look at you with those big, brown scowling eyes, and he'd look right into you.*
iii *It's time something was done about these blackouts we've been having.*
iv *What's all this I hear about you and Alex getting into trouble at school?*

In the intended contextualisations of these examples, the demonstrative NP refers to an entity that is not present in the situation of utterance and has not been mentioned in the preceding discourse, but I assume you can identify it on the basis of specific past shared experience or knowledge. Such recognitional uses mostly involve dependent ***that***, as in [i–ii], with the distal element of meaning motivated by the fact that the shared experience occurred at some time in the past. However, ***this*** is also possible, as in [iii–iv], when the shared grounds for identification are current. The demonstrative cannot stand alone in this use: some elaboration is needed, normally in the form of a head nominal, as in [i–iii], or a postmodifier, as in [iv].

(b) False definite dependent *this*

[20] i %*He's been married and got this half-grown kid.*
ii %*I was in Penang and I met this man, and he gave me your address and a present for you.*
iii %*She was wearing these enormous earrings that she'd bought at the duty free.*

The demonstrative NPs here are **false definites** in that they have the form of a definite NP but do not satisfy the conditions for the felicitous use of one. They introduce new entities into the discourse and do not have sufficient descriptive content to identify the referent for the addressee. This usage is characteristic of very informal conversation; although extremely common in that style, there are many speakers who would use indefinite *a* or *some* rather than ***this*** in such contexts: hence the '%' annotation.

(c) *That* with post-head dependents

[21] i *Amy intended to reap* [*that share of life's experiences that was her due*].
ii *She was certainly not one of* [*those people you could talk with easily*].
iii *We always prefer* [*that which is familiar*] *to* [*that which is not*].
iv *The council will show no leniency towards* [*those who break its laws*].

The demonstrative NPs here are again neither deictic nor anaphoric: the dependents themselves contain sufficient information to identify the referent, so that these are genuine definites. ***That*** is dependent in [i–ii], independent in [iii–iv], with the singular in [iii] inanimate, and plural *those* in [iv] human. *That which* is relatively formal, the fused relative construction being much more usual: compare *What he said was nonsense* with the very unlikely *That which he said was nonsense.* This use, like the anaphoric one with obligatory dependent illustrated in [13], is restricted to ***that***, which here has little of its central distal meaning.

(d) *That* as non-deictic, non-anaphoric degree modifier

[22] i *I'm not feeling (all) that well today.*
ii %*The movie was that boring I fell asleep.*

As degree modifiers of adjectives or adverbs the demonstratives are usually either deictic (as in *I hadn't expected it to be that big,* said as I point at the object in question) or anaphoric (*Kim is 6 foot and Pat is nearly that tall too*), but those in [22] do not belong to either of these types. In [i] the meaning of *that* (or *all that*) is roughly "particularly", while in [ii] (with a following resultative clause) *that* is a variant of *so*; both cases belong to informal style, and [ii] is predominantly BrE.

6 Other types of reduced NP: pro-nominals, fused heads, and ellipsis

Our main concern in this section will be with NPs headed by the pro-forms ***one*** and ***other***, and with NPs where the head is fused with the determiner or a modifier:

[1]	i	*I asked for a key but he gave me [the wrong one].*	[pro-nominal head]
	ii	*There are only four cups here: where are [the others]?*	[pro-nominal head]
	iii	*She wanted some bread but we didn't have [any].*	[fused determiner-head]
	iv	*This bus is full: we'll have to wait for [the next].*	[fused modifier-head]

Any in [iii] and *the next* in [iv] could be replaced by *any bread* and *the next bus,* and hence appear to be elliptical; we argued in Ch. 5, §9.5, however, that an analysis in terms of ellipsis does not provide a satisfactory general account of this construction, and we are accordingly saying that *any* combines the functions of determiner and head, and similarly that *next* is here functioning simultaneously as modifier and head.

The pro-nominal and fused-head constructions have it in common that they do not have a separate head filled by an ordinary noun with inherent lexical content. The interpretation thus generally requires that the content of the head be filled out from the context. In the examples given in [1] the interpretation is determined anaphorically – as "the wrong key", "the other cups", "any bread", "the next bus". We thus refer to the bracketed phrases as **reduced** NPs. They differ from those considered in §§2–4 in that the head is not a pronoun (recall the distinction between pronoun and pro-form drawn in §1.4), but we have encountered one case of the fused determiner-head construction in §5, with the independent demonstratives as fused head. The fused-head and pro-nominal ***one*** constructions are very similar in their uses and are often interchangeable. For this reason we will consider them together in §6.1, and then return to pro-nominal ***other*** in §6.2.

Ellipsis plays a relatively minor role in NP reduction and does not require extended discussion. It is limited to the omission of post-head dependents, as in

[2] i *The plays she directed were more successful than [the musicals __].*
ii *There were lots of books in the attic, but [the majority __] were trashy novels.*

In the salient interpretation of [i] there is ellipsis of the relative clause *she directed.* Example [ii] illustrates one of the most common types of ellipsis, that of a partitive complement (*of them*).

6.1 Pro-nominal *one* and the fused-head construction

These two constructions, we have observed, are often interchangeable. Examples of this kind were noted in our discussion of demonstratives – compare *This copy is clearer than* [*that one*] and *This copy is clearer than* [*that*]. Other cases where one can be replaced by the other without any change in meaning are seen in:

[3] i a. *These seats are still available:* [*Which one(s)*] *do you want?* [***one*** as head]
b. *These seats are still available:* [*Which*] *do you want?* [fused head]
ii a. *What seats have you got? I want* [*the cheapest one(s) available*]. [***one*** as head]
b. *What seats have you got? I want* [*the cheapest available*]. [fused head]

In each pair, example [a] has pro-nominal ***one*** as head, while [b] has the head fused with a dependent, the determiner *which* in [ib], and the modifier *cheapest* in [iib]. And in each pair both examples are interpreted anaphorically with *seats* as antecedent, giving "which seat(s)" and "the cheapest seat(s) available". Instead of repeating *seats* we either substitute the pro-form ***one*** or simply omit it, letting the dependent (determiner or modifier) incorporate the head function. The contrast between singular and plural is marked inflectionally on ***one*** but is not expressed in the fused-head NP.

Limitations on interchangeability

The overlap between the constructions is only partial, primarily because of limitations on the elements that, like *which* and *cheapest* in [3], can occur in both, i.e. immediately preceding pro-nominal ***one*** and as a fused head.

Modifiers

As described in Ch. 5, §9.3, there are severe limitations on the modifiers that can occur in the fused-head construction. They include ordinal numerals, comparative and superlative adjectives or AdjPs, and certain adjectives describing physical properties; they are more acceptable following the definite article or cardinal numerals as determiner than after the indefinite article and other determinatives. For example, ***one*** cannot be omitted in:

[4] i *It was, frankly, a hypothesis – albeit* [*an excellent one*].
ii *The present company is a combination of* [*several smaller ones*].

Determiners

Some determiners permit both constructions, others only one or the other:

[5] i *These are excellent biscuits. Can I have* [*another*] / [*another one*]*?*
ii *We have two keys but we need* [*three*] / *[*three ones*].
iii *He asked for some paper clips, but we had* [*none*] / *[*no ones*].
iv *We've ten glasses left, but* *[*every*] / [*every one*] *is cracked.*

Another admits both constructions, *three* and ***no*** only the fused head,[30] *every* only pro-nominal *one*. The restrictions on ***one*** here apply only where the determiner immediately precedes: *three extra ones, no fresh ones*, and so on, are completely well-formed. Determinatives can then be classified as to which construction they occur in:

[6] i BOTH: ***this***, ***that***, *which, another, each, any, either, neither*
ii FUSED ONLY: cardinal numerals, *all, both, many, some, several, a few, few,* ***no***
iii *ONE* ONLY: *every, the, a*

[30] ***No*** appears in the independent form *none* in the fused-head construction; most of the genitive personal pronouns likewise have an inflectional contrast between independent forms (*mine, yours*, etc.) and dependent ones (*my, your*, etc.): see Ch. 5, §16.4.

The status of genitive NP determiners is somewhat problematic. They are occasionally found with ***one***, but such examples are of rather questionable acceptability: [?]*She's finished her assignment, but I've only done half of* [*my one*]. Instead of *my one* we would normally have *mine*.

The cannot normally occur with pro-nominal ***one*** unless the latter is accompanied by a dependent, except in predicative complement function:

[7] i *This fish isn't as big as* [*the one I caught*].
ii A: *I can't find that letter from the tax office.* B: *Is this* [*the one*]?
iii **I can't find that letter from the tax office. I'm sure I left* [*the one*] *on my desk.*

Instead of *the one* in [iii] we need the personal pronoun *it* (which could also be used in [ii]).[31]

A one is generally restricted to non-affirmative contexts in informal style:

[8] i *We turn them on at 6 in the morning and off at 5.30 every night, six days a week, and not a one of them has ever gone down on us.*
ii *I have never met another woman like her, you see, and I do not suppose I shall ever meet such a one again.*

In [i] a form with an attributive adjective would usually be preferred: *not a single one*.[32]

Pro-nominal $\textbf{\textit{one}}_{ct}$ vs determinative $\textit{one}_{d}$

The singular form of pro-nominal ***one*** is homonymous with the determinative *one*, and since the latter (like cardinal numerals in general) can occur as a fused head, it is sometimes difficult to distinguish between the homonyms. Pro-nominal ***one*** belongs to the category of common nouns – more specifically, of count nouns – and we will represent it, for convenience, as $\textbf{\textit{one}}_{ct}$, with the determinative represented as $\textit{one}_{d}$.[33]

The main syntactic differences between $\textbf{\textit{one}}_{ct}$ and $\textit{one}_{d}$ are as follows:

[9] i $\textbf{\textit{One}}_{ct}$ functions only as (non-fused) head in NP structure; $\textit{one}_{d}$ functions as determiner or modifier, either with a following head or in fusion with the head.
ii $\textbf{\textit{One}}_{ct}$ inflects for number (with *ones* as plural form); $\textit{one}_{d}$ does not.
iii Singular $\textit{one}_{ct}$, like other count singular nouns, requires a preceding determiner.
iv $\textit{One}_{d}$ cannot normally follow a modifier in NP structure.

It is because of [ii] that we are representing $\textbf{\textit{one}}_{ct}$ in boldface, to highlight the distinction between it and $\textit{one}_{d}$. The following instances of *one* and *ones* can be assigned unequivocally to one or other category by virtue of these four properties respectively:

[10] i *She had taken* [*only* $\textit{one}_{d}$ *book*]. [not in head function]
ii *These cakes are better than* [*the* $\textit{ones}_{ct}$ *I made*]. [plural form]
iii *This brush won't do: I want* [$\textit{one}_{d}$ *with a handle*]. [no preceding determiner]
iv *This knife is blunt: have you got* [*a sharper* $\textit{one}_{ct}$]? [follows modifier]

[31] A less general exception to the rule that *the one* requires a dependent is seen in *I know the one*; like the predicative complement case, this is concerned with identification. We understand: "I know the/which one you are referring to".

[32] There is also a non-anaphoric use of *a one* which belongs with the 'special' interpretation case of *one* illustrated in [20iv] below: *I'm not much of a one for exercise*, and the colloquial *You're a one!* (an idiomatic use where I pretend to be slightly shocked by your behaviour, but convey amused approval).

[33] There is also homonymy with the plain form of the personal pronoun $\textbf{\textit{one}}_{p}$, as in *One can't be too careful, can one?* However, the meaning and syntax of the latter (described in Ch. 5, §10.1.1) make it easy to distinguish it from $\textbf{\textit{one}}_{ct}$ and $\textit{one}_{d}$, and we can confine our attention here to these two.

The bracketed NP in [i] has *book* as head and hence is not reduced. Of the three reduced NPs, [ii] and [iv] belong to the pro-nominal head construction, while [iii] has a fused determiner-head. The major difference is that if we expand to a non-reduced NP we simply replace ***one***$_{ct}$ by a new, non-reduced head (*the cakes I made, a sharper knife*), whereas *one*$_{d}$ is replaced by a sequence of determiner + head (*a brush with a handle*). This of course matches the difference in syntactic analysis that we have proposed. ***One***$_{ct}$ is a count noun occupying head position, and expansion of the reduced NP simply involves replacing it with a head that has more intrinsic content. *One*$_{d}$ is a determinative combining here the functions of determiner and head, and expansion results in a structure with separate determiner and head.

The result of expanding fused determiner-head *one*$_{d}$ may have either *one*$_{d}$ itself as the determiner or else the indefinite article *a*. Compare:

[11] i *We need three keys, but at the moment we've [only one*$_{d}$*].*
ii *I've foolishly come without a pen: can you lend me [one*$_{d}$*]?*

In [i] *only one* is equivalent to *only one key*: here *one*$_{d}$ contrasts with larger cardinal numerals. In [ii], on the other hand, fused *one* is equivalent to *a pen*: here *one*$_{d}$ is not in contrast with cardinal numerals, but behaves like a stressed form of the indefinite article. As we have noted, the indefinite article cannot itself function as fused determiner-head, and this gap in the system is filled by *one*$_{d}$ in a way which is analogous to that in which ***that*** fills the gap resulting from the inability of the definite article *the* to function as fused determiner-head.[34]

One$_{d}$ as fused modifier-head

In [10iii] and [11] *one*$_{d}$ functions as fused determiner-head, and such cases are easy to distinguish from the pro-nominal ***one***$_{ct}$ construction by virtue of property [9iii]: singular *one*$_{ct}$ cannot occur without a preceding determiner. More difficult to distinguish from the pro-nominal construction is that where *one*$_{d}$ is fused modifier-head, i.e. a fused head following a determiner. Cardinal numerals can occur in this position, as is evident from examples like *any two, those three*, etc., and *one*$_{d}$ follows this general pattern. A *one* in head position following a determiner, therefore, could in principle be either *one*$_{d}$ or *one*$_{ct}$: the properties given in [9] do not suffice to resolve the issue of which *one* we have in this context. Compare, then:

[12] i *Six issues declined for [every one*$_{d}$ *that advanced] on the Paris Stock Exchange.*
ii *It's a small victory, but the industry needs [every one*$_{ct}$ *it can get].*

We can expand [i] to *every one issue that advanced*, but we cannot similarly expand [ii] to *#every one victory it can get*: we would have, rather, *every victory it can get.* On this basis, therefore, we take *one* to be the determinative in [i] and the pro-nominal in [ii]. We noted in our commentary on [11] that in fused determiner-head function *one*$_{d}$ may correspond to either *one*$_{d}$ or the indefinite article *a* in the expanded counterpart, but in fused modifier-head function the expanded counterpart will always have *one*$_{d}$, for the indefinite article does not occur in modifier function. This means that in fused modifier-head function *one*$_{d}$ is always in contrast with larger cardinal numerals (and as such is always stressed). This is what distinguishes the examples in [12]: there is no such contrast in [ii], whereas in [i] there is – cf. *Six issues declined for every five that advanced.*

[34] In Ch. 5, §7.6, we distinguished the two uses of *one*$_{d}$ illustrated in [11] as respectively numerical and singulative; as noted in that earlier discussion, the distinction applies also to dependent uses of *one*$_{d}$, i.e. those where there is a following head.

Compare similarly the following attested examples with *any*:

[13] i *Notice 88-38 now says that after figuring the withdrawal amount for each account, you may take the total minimum from [any one*$_{d}$ *or more of them].*

ii *They could have sent their child to [any one*$_{ct}$ *of the many integrated private or public schools in their neighbourhood].*

The coordination *one or more* in [i] requires that *one* be taken as cardinal numeral. In [ii], however, there is no numerical contrast, and the closest non-partitive counterpart would be *any integrated private or public school* . . . rather than *any one private or public school* . . . ; we accordingly take the *one* here to be *one*$_{ct}$. An instance of *one* in head position immediately following a determiner is most likely to be *one*$_{ct}$, but we will analyse it as *one*$_{d}$ in those cases where it is replaceable by a higher cardinal numeral.

Restrictions on the distribution of *one*$_{ct}$

(a) Antecedent must be a count noun or nominal

One$_{ct}$ is a count noun, and hence cannot take non-count nouns or nominals as antecedent:

[14] i * *The advice you gave was more useful than [the one I received from the Dean].*

ii * *The arrival of the king was followed by [the one of the queen].*

These can be corrected by using *that* (*that which I received from the Dean, that of the queen*), though this is quite formal, and other reformulations would generally be preferred (e.g. *Your advice was more useful than the Dean's*).

(b) ***One***$_{ct}$ requires elaboration: it cannot occur without one or more dependents

One$_{ct}$ cannot constitute an NP by itself, even in the plural, where there is no requirement for a determiner:

[15] i **I'm looking for travel guides: do you sell ones?*

ii **Kim has doubts about the proposal, and Pat may have ones too.*

It would be possible to repeat the underlined phrases here (*do you sell travel guides?*; *Pat may have doubts about the proposal too*), but it is not possible to reduce them to *ones*. (The most likely anaphor in [i] would be *them* and in [ii] the fused determiner-head *some*, or else we would have ellipsis of the complement of *have*: *Pat may have __ too.*) ***One***$_{ct}$ must be accompanied by some dependent – and, as noted above, this must normally have more content than simply *the* and *a*, pure markers of definiteness and indefiniteness.

(c) Restrictions on complementation with relational noun antecedents

Although ***one***$_{ct}$ requires one or more dependents, there are restrictions on what kinds are permitted. Compare:

[16] i a. A: *Which movie did you like best?* B: *The one about dinosaurs.*

b. A: *Which house did they choose?* B: *The one you recommended.*

ii a. A: *Which king did you see?* B: **The one of Belgium.*

b. A: *Which sleeve did you mend?* B: **The one of the dress.*

c. A: *Whose mother is she?* B: **The one of Kim.*

d. A: *Which proposal do you prefer?* B: **The one that we hold a referendum.*

The examples in [i] illustrate the default case: the expanded versions are *the movie about dinosaurs* and *the house you recommended*, and the reduced versions simply have ***one***$_{ct}$ in head position and the same dependents. But [ii] departs from this pattern: *the King of Belgium, the sleeve of the dress, the mother of Kim, the proposal that we hold a referendum* are all perfectly good NPs, but this time we cannot replace the head by ***one***$_{ct}$. The post-head dependent in

[iid] is a content clause complement, and dependents of this kind are quite generally excluded from occurring with ***one***$_{ct}$. The inadmissible dependents in [iia–c] are complements with the form of PPs, and the acceptability of complements of this kind depends on the nature of the antecedent noun, for such complements are permitted in examples like:

[17] i [*This proof of Taylor's theorem*] *is better than* [*the one of Parzival's inequality*].
ii [*The production of Madame Butterfly*] *was better than* [*the one of Tosca*].

The cases where complementation is inadmissible, as in [16ii], include antecedent nouns of the following kinds:

[18] i Role nouns: *boss, friend, dean, king*
ii Nouns denoting a part–whole relationship: *cover, leg, sleeve*
iii Kinship nouns: *mother, father, sister*
iv Agent nominalisations: *designer, student, supporter*

Uses of the fused-head and pro-nominal *one* constructions

In Ch. 5, §9.1, we distinguished three main uses of the fused-head construction, simple, partitive, and special, with the partitive subdivided into implicit and explicit cases. The same classification applies to the pro-nominal *one* construction. Compare, then:

[19] THE FUSED-HEAD CONSTRUCTION

i	*How many glasses do we need? Will* [*ten*] *be enough?*	[simple]
ii	*We have twenty glasses, but* [*several*] *are cracked.*	[implicitly partitive]
iii	[*Most of these glasses*] *are cracked.*	[explicitly partitive]
iv	*He's considered a prophet, by* [*some*].	[special]

[20] THE PRO-NOMINAL *ONE* CONSTRUCTION

i	*That glass is OK, but* [*this one*$_{ct}$] *is cracked.*	[simple]
ii	*There were five apples left, and Ed took* [*the biggest one*$_{ct}$].	[implicitly partitive]
iii	[*Every single one*$_{ct}$ *of the glasses*] *was cracked.*	[explicitly partitive]
iv	*Kim's not* [*the one*$_{ct}$ *responsible for the delay*].	[special]

It is the simple and implicitly partitive uses that are of relevance to the primary concerns of this chapter, and little need be said about the others. ***One***$_{ct}$ does not commonly occur in explicit partitives, and in particular the plural form *ones* is of questionable acceptability. *Which of the apples*, for example, is strongly preferred over ?*which ones of the apples*.

The special interpretation of ***one***$_{ct}$ is "person": [20iv] can be glossed as "Kim's not the person responsible for the delay". This is comparable to the interpretation of *some* in [19iv] as "some people", though the fused-head construction has a range of special interpretations, depending on the determinative concerned.

Anaphoric interpretations

In the simple and implicitly partitive uses the interpretation is usually determined anaphorically, from an antecedent. In the simple use, the antecedent is the head element in an NP, a nominal – *glasses* in [19i] (*ten* is understood as "ten glasses"), *glass* in [20i] (*this one* = "this glass"). The implicitly partitive case is not so straightforward. Here we take the antecedent to be a full NP, but it provides the interpretation of the missing partitive oblique. *Several* in [19ii] is equivalent to *several of them*, where the antecedent for *them* is the NP *twenty glasses*. Similarly, *the biggest one* in [20ii] is equivalent to *the biggest one of them*, with *them* having *five apples* as its antecedent. In the implicitly partitive case the reduced NP denotes a subset of the set denoted by the antecedent, whereas there is no such relation in the simple case.

Non-anaphoric interpretation: contextually salient denotation

It is also possible for such examples to be interpreted non-anaphorically, with the denotation derivable from something present in the context of utterance but not actually mentioned. Suppose, for example, there is a plate of little cakes on the table and I have just had one. I might then say *Can I have another?*, with the "cake" meaning coming from the context rather than from an antecedent. I might similarly pick up a glass and say *This one is cracked*, or I might see Ed take the biggest apple on the plate and say *He's taken the biggest one, as usual.* The distinction between the simple and implicitly partitive constructions tends to be neutralised in such cases, for expansion could involve adding either a noun (*Can I have another cake?*) or a partitive PP (*Can I have another of these cakes?*).

Extent of the antecedent in anaphoric interpretations of the simple constructions

Since one nominal can occur inside another there may be more than one possible antecedent in the simple use of the fused-head and pro-nominal ***one*** constructions. Compare:

[21] i [*Jill's first semantics book*] *was clearer than* [*her second* (*one*)].
ii [*Sue's first semantics book*] *was clearer than* [*Jill's*].
iii [*Sue's first book on semantics from CUP*] *was clearer than* [*Jill's*].

The salient interpretation of [i] has *semantics book* as the antecedent, with the comparison being between Jill's first and second semantics books. *First* cannot be part of the antecedent because it contrasts with *second* in the reduced NP. There is no such contrasting element in the reduced NPs in [ii–iii], and here the most salient interpretations include *first* in the antecedent: "Jill's first semantics book" and "Jill's first book on semantics from CUP". In general, the preferred interpretation is the one where the antecedent is the largest nominal that does not contain contrastive material (like the *first* in [i]).

Other interpretations are possible, especially with appropriate placement of the main stress. Compare, for example, *Sue's* FIRST *semantics book was clearer than Jill's, but her* SECOND *certainly wasn't*, where we understand "Jill's semantics book" (or perhaps even "Jill's book"). It is not possible, however, for the antecedent to be discontinuous. Thus *Jill's* cannot be interpreted in [21ii] as "Jill's first book", because in the preceding NP *first* and *book* are separated by *semantics*, and hence do not constitute a nominal. Similarly, *Jill's* in [iii] cannot be interpreted as "Jill's book from CUP", and so on.

6.2 **Pro-nominal *other***

Pro-nominal ***other*** occurs in all four of the constructions discussed above for the fused-head and pro-nominal ***one*** constructions:

[22]	i	*These* <u>*boxes*</u> *are more suitable than* [*the* <u>*others*</u>].	[simple]
	ii	*One of* <u>*the plates*</u> *was broken and* [*the* <u>*other*</u>] *was chipped.*	[implicitly partitive]
	iii	*He focussed on international monetary policy while* [<u>*others*</u> *of his colleagues*] *embraced protectionism.*	[explicitly partitive]
	iv	*Kim doesn't show much consideration for* [<u>*others*</u>].	[special]

In [i] *others* is interpreted anaphorically as "other boxes": here it takes the nominal *boxes* as antecedent. The simple construction also allows a non-anaphoric interpretation, with the denotation retrievable from the situation of utterance: you offer me a biscuit, and I say *No thanks, I prefer the others.* In [ii] the full NP *the plates* provides the interpretation of the understood partitive: "the other (one) of the plates". In [iii] we have an overt partitive complement, which is quite rare with ***other***. And in [iv] *others* has the special interpretation "other people".[35] In [i] ***other*** is subject to the same restrictions on complementation that we have noted for ***one***$_{ct}$. Thus *all the others of this opera* is permissible with an antecedent such as *production*, but we can't have **all the others of England* interpreted with *king* as antecedent.

Relationship with the pro-nominal *one* and fused-head constructions

The construction with ***other*** as head is in some respects like the pro-nominal ***one*** construction and in others like the fused modifier-head construction. ***Other*** is like ***one***$_{ct}$ in that it inflects for number, with *others* as the plural form. This establishes quite clearly that it is a noun: we will represent it as ***other***$_{ct}$ to distinguish it from *other*$_{a}$, the adjective from which it is derived by conversion. Like ***one***$_{ct}$, ***other***$_{ct}$ occurs only in head function; the structure of *the others* in [22i], for example, is simply determiner + head – there is no syntactic fusion of two functions.

At the same time, the ***other***$_{ct}$ construction resembles the fused-head one semantically in that when we expand to a non-reduced form we retain *other*: *the other boxes.* What is retained, however, is not the noun ***other*** but the lexical base, which is now syntactically an adjective. Note also that although the plural inflection shows that ***other***$_{ct}$ has been converted into a noun, it retains some distributional properties of the adjective *other*$_{a}$, as illustrated in:

[23] a. **the red other boxes* b. **the red others*

Attributive *other*$_{a}$ cannot follow an adjective, and the same applies to the head ***other***$_{ct}$. Instead of [a] we have *the other red boxes*, and hence the only pro-form available is ***one***$_{ct}$: *the other red ones.*

Other$_{ct}$ vs *other*$_{a}$ + *one*$_{ct}$

Pro-nominal ***other***$_{ct}$ is in competition with *other*$_{a}$ + pro-nominal ***one***$_{ct}$: we can have either *the other(s)* or *the other one(s)*, either *one other* or *one other one*, and so on. As far as the singular is concerned, both constructions are common following the determiners *the* and *one*$_{d}$, with the *one*$_{ct}$ construction generally preferred elsewhere, often quite strongly: *your other one* is preferred over ?*your other, that other one* over ?*that other*, and so on.[36] In the plural, both constructions are generally available, except that *other ones* cannot replace *others* in the special "other people" interpretation illustrated in [22iv].

[35] It would be a mistake to argue that the "people" meaning is determined anaphorically from *Kim*, the name of a person. We cannot say *I prefer London to others* with the interpretation "I prefer London to other cities" unless there is an antecedent ***city*** in the text: the mere fact that London is a city is not sufficient. It is thus a special fact about *others*$_{ct}$ that it can mean "other people": this is why we have treated [22iv] as belonging to the 'special' construction.

[36] Neither construction is available after the indefinite article (**an other*, **an other one*): instead, we have the compound determinative *another*, which can function by itself as a fused head or else as determiner to *one*$_{ct}$.

7 Reduced VPs and clauses, and related constructions

The last four sections have been concerned almost exclusively with NPs, and we turn now to reduced constituents of other categories. We will be concerned primarily with constituents headed by verbs, i.e. VPs and clauses, but there is also a limited amount of reduction of AdjPs, AdvPs, and DPs to be considered. As with NPs, reduction may be a matter of ellipsis or the use of pro-forms, though there are places where the distinction between those two devices is somewhat unclear, namely with certain uses of ***do*** and *so*.[37]

7.1 Stranding of auxiliary verbs

We say that an auxiliary verb is **stranded** when it occurs before a structural gap – in the simplest case, an ellipsis site. In the following examples, the stranded auxiliary is marked by double underlining, while single underlining indicates the antecedents which provide the interpretation of the ellipsis:

[1] i *I couldn't hear what he was saying, but fortunately Kim could __.*
ii *Sue will help me, won't she __?*
iii A: *They may have mended it by now.* B: *I certainly hope they have __.*
iv *Everyone expects her to perform well, and I'm sure she will __.*
v *Kim is on the committee, I think, but Pat is not __.*
vi *He thinks there is a mistake in the program; is there __?*
vii A: *It is important to keep them informed.* B: *Yes, it is __.*
viii *She says she'd rather stay at home, and indeed I would __ too.*

The auxiliary occupies the position immediately before the gap or else is separated from it by a narrow range of dependents, primarily the subject ([ii/vi]) or the negative marker *not* ([v]). Very often the antecedent is complement of the same auxiliary verb as is stranded, e.g. ***can*** in [i], ***will*** in [ii], and so on. This is not a condition for stranding, however, as is evident from [iv]: here the antecedent, together with the infinitival marker *to*, is complement of ***expect***, but what is ellipted is the complement of ***will***.[38]

In [1i–iv] we have ellipsis of the non-finite complement of an auxiliary verb. In [v–vii] the stranded verb is ***be***, which enters into a wider range of constructions than other auxiliaries. In [v] there is ellipsis of a locative complement, and in [vi–vii] of sequences of two complements: displaced subject + locative, and predicative + extraposed subject. In [viii] what is ellipted is *rather* (which is part of the idiom *would rather*) and the infinitival complement. The last three examples show that what is ellipted need not be a syntactic constituent.[39] Where the auxiliary immediately precedes the ellipsis site, the VP consists just of the auxiliary as head; where the auxiliary is followed by the subject, the structure involves subject–auxiliary inversion, so that the VP is completely empty: the head position is empty because the auxiliary is in prenuclear position, while the dependent positions are empty because of the ellipsis.

[37] Because we will be quite often concerned with inflection we use the boldface representation of lexemes throughout this section, except when displaying lists of lexemes.

[38] In Ch. 3, §2.1.4 we distinguished between 'old-verb stranding', for cases where the auxiliary is repeated, and 'new-verb stranding' for cases like [1iv] where it is not – and we noted that the range of items that can be stranded is slightly more restricted in the latter type.

[39] Auxiliary-stranding ellipsis is often called 'VP deletion' or 'VP ellipsis', but it is clear from these examples that what is ellipted need not be a VP.

Inclusion of dependents in the reduced VP

The usual pattern is for all dependents in the VP to be ellipted, as in [1]. It is also possible, however, for some to be retained:

[2] i A: *You had better stay at home.* B: *Yes, I'[d better __].*
ii A: *Could you wash the car?* B: *OK, I [will __ after lunch].*
iii A: *Can you come on Monday?* B: *Yes, I [can __ on Monday], but I'll be away from Tuesday to Saturday.*
iv A: *Could you mow the lawn this afternoon?* B: *No, but I [will __ tomorrow].*
v A: *Have you invited Max?* B: *No, but I [have __ his brother].*

In [i], *better* is part of the idiom *had better*, and is retained even though it is present in A's utterance too: it could also be ellipted, giving *Yes, I had __*. Retention is of course obligatory if *better* could not be recovered anaphorically: *I haven't read the report, but I suppose I'[d better __]*. In [ii] there is ellipsis of *wash the car* and *after lunch* is added as an adjunct. In [iii] *on Monday* is present in A's utterance and could be ellipted along with the verb *come*; it is repeated for reasons of contrast: speaker B can come on Monday but not on subsequent days. In [iv–v] the adjunct *tomorrow* and the object *his brother* contrast with *this afternoon* and *Max* respectively in the VP containing the antecedent for the gap. Note that in [ii–v] the dependent in the reduced VP is not a dependent of the stranded auxiliary that is head of the VP, but of the verb that is understood as filling the elliptical gap.

There are quite severe restrictions on the construction illustrated in [2iv–v], where the dependent in the reduced VP contrasts with one of the same kind in the VP containing the antecedent. This is especially so where the element concerned is a complement rather than an adjunct. Compare:

[3] i **Kim had seemed fairly confident even though Pat [had __ extremely pessimistic].*
ii **I haven't put the TV in the bedroom: I [have __ in the lounge].*

Ellipsis is inadmissible in [i] because *extremely pessimistic* is a predicative complement. And in [ii] *in the lounge* is a PP complement; PPs are generally admissible in this construction only if they are adjuncts, as in *You can't cut that with scissors though you probably [could __ with a razor blade].*

Sequences of auxiliaries

If the unreduced form of a VP would have a sequence of two or more auxiliaries it is in principle possible for any one of them to be stranded:

[4] i a. A: *They must have made a mistake.* B: *Yes, they must __.*
b. A: *They must have made a mistake.* B: *Yes, they must have __.*
ii a. A: *It should have been checked by the dean.* B: *Yes, it should __.*
b. A: *It should have been checked by the dean.* B: *Yes, it should have __.*
c. A: *It should have been checked by the dean.* B: *Yes, it should have been __.*

Minor differences between antecedent and expanded version of the reduced VP

In all the examples considered so far the gap could be replaced by an exact copy of the antecedent. In [2], for example, we could have *I'd better stay at home, I will wash the car after lunch, I can come on Monday, I will mow the lawn tomorrow, I have invited his brother*.[40] This is not an absolute requirement of the auxiliary stranding construction, however: certain kinds of difference between antecedent and potential replacement are found. We consider first two minor cases that have little or no effect on acceptability, and then take up the issue of major differences.

(a) Inflection

The inflectional form of the verb that would fill the gap is determined by the stranded auxiliary: modals select a plain form, perfect ***have*** a past participle, and so on. The form of the verb in the antecedent depends on the construction containing it, which, as we have noted, need not be the same as that containing the gap. Inflectional differences are illustrated in [5], where the form required to fill the verb position in the gap is given on the right:

[5] i a. *He says he likes it, but I'm sure he doesn't* __. [*like*]
b. *She hasn't written it yet, but I'm sure she soon will* __. [*write*]
c. A: *Are you going by car?* B: *Don't I always* __*?* [*go*]
ii a. ?*Kim may be questioning our motives, but Pat hasn't* __. [*questioned*]
b. *I'm sure Bob will tell her soon, but he hasn't* __ *yet.* [*told*]
iii a. ?*Kim won't enter the competition, but Pat is* __. [*entering*]
b. ?*They may all move south, and in fact some of them already are* __. [*moving*]

In [i] the verbs required in the context of the gap are all plain forms, while the antecedent verbs are respectively 3rd person singular present tense, past participle, and gerund-participle; differences of this kind do not in general affect the acceptability of the reduced VP.[41] In [ii] the gap context requires a past participle, while the antecedents are a gerund-participle and a plain form. Here there is some loss of acceptability. Thus [iia] is quite marginal: one would generally prefer a form such as *Pat hasn't done so*, where the perfect is marked more explicitly. However, [iib] is appreciably better: it is acceptable in informal contexts though some speakers would avoid it in more formal ones. It is more acceptable than [iia] because there is a simple contrast concerning the time of Bob's telling her, whereas in [iia] there is also a difference in aspect, progressive vs non-progressive. In [iii] there is necessarily a difference in progressive aspect, and the examples are of somewhat marginal status, though the adjunct *already* in [iiib] improves it slightly; fuller marking of the progressive (e.g. *is/are doing so*) would generally be preferred.

Be and perfect ***have*** tend to resist ellipsis when there are inflectional differences of any of the above kinds. In the following examples they follow another auxiliary verb, but omitting them to leave this other verb stranded would lead to unacceptable (or at best very marginal) results:

[6] i *Ed was being interrogated when I left and soon Max will be* __.
ii *He has been sick several times, and doubtless will be* __ *again.*
iii *Kim was interrogated yesterday and is being* __ *again today.*
iv *It will be demolished soon, if it hasn't been* __ *already.*
v A: *Have they made a mistake?* B: *They must have* __.

[40] There are some constructions where the gap cannot be filled, where the ellipsis is obligatory. This is so, for example, in the interrogative tag of [1iii]. But this doesn't affect the general point being made here, for we can make a small change to the construction, replacing the interrogative tag by an ordinary interrogative clause, and then it would be possible to replace the gap with an exact copy of the antecedent: *Won't she help me?*

[41] Also fully acceptable are cases where there is an implicit difference in the number of an NP in predicative complement function: *Kim and Pat are already members, and I will be* __ *soon* (where we understand singular "a member").

(b) Polarity-sensitive items

[7] i *You said there wasn't any milk in the fridge, but there was __.*
ii *You may not be able to see anything wrong with it, but I can __.*
iii *He says they haven't finished the report yet, but I rather think they have __.*
iv *Jill won't resign until she's found another job, but I think Sue will __.*
v ?*Kim won't be working in this section any longer, though of course Pat will __.*

The gap in [i] cannot be filled by *any milk in the fridge*: instead we need *some milk in the fridge*, with the positively-oriented *some* instead of the negatively-oriented *any* (see Ch. 9, §4, for the concept of polarity-sensitive items). This switch is quite automatic, and does not affect acceptability. Similarly, expansion of [ii] gives *I can see something wrong with it*, with *something* instead of the antecedent *anything*. In [iii] the full form would be *they have already / (by) now finished the report*. In [iv] we would have *Sue will resign before she's found another job* – and in formal style *before* might well be preferred to *until* in the antecedent. Example [v] is slightly different from the others since there is no positively-oriented item closely corresponding to negatively-oriented *any longer*. As a result the example is not so clearly acceptable: at least in formal style, a more explicit form such as *Pat will be carrying on* is likely to be preferred.

Major differences between antecedent and expanded version of the reduced VP

Examples are occasionally found where the antecedent and the expanded version of the reduced VP differ more radically, for example in voice:

[8] i ?*A cyclone of that degree of ferocity was expected to damage property, but not to the extent that the council houses were __.*
ii ?*We have implemented it on a Mac, but it doesn't have to be __.*

The interpretations of the reduced VPs are passive ("were damaged" and "to be implemented on a Mac"), although the antecedents are active. We have marked these with a question mark even though they are attested examples, because we do not believe they can be considered fully grammatical. Speakers vary in their judgements about such examples, and there is no doubt that such changes of voice are not systematically permitted, as is evident from the clear ungrammaticality of examples like:

[9] i A: *Have the police been informed?* B: **I don't know; I certainly haven't __.*
ii A: *You ought to notify the police.* B: **Why? They don't need to be __.*

The reason is that voice is a property of the clause as a whole, whereas auxiliary stranding concerns the form and interpretation of VPs. In [i] the intended interpretation is "I haven't informed the police", but there is no VP in A's utterance to provide the necessary antecedent, for *the police* is in subject function. In [ii] the VP in A's utterance is *notify the police*, and again this is not a suitable antecedent for a gap interpreted as passive "notified".

Restrictions on stranding of gerund-participle forms of auxiliaries

[10] i %*They have all volunteered, but I think some of them regret having __.*
ii %*Kim is being investigated by the police, and I think Pat is being __ too.*
iii A: *When is the building going to be demolished?* B: %*It already is being __.*
iv %*I've been Rex's mistress for some time now, and I shall go on being __, married or not.*

The only auxiliaries with gerund-participle forms are ***be*** and ***have***, and the stranding of these forms is subject to dialect variation. Very few speakers accept the stranding of *having*, as in [i]. Stranded *being* is inadmissible in AmE, but accepted in some varieties of BrE. In [ii] *being* can itself be ellipted, since it heads the complement of another instance of auxiliary ***be*** and is recoverable from the preceding clause. It could not be ellipted in [iii] (since *It already is* __ would be interpreted as "It is already demolished") or in [iv] (where it does not follow an auxiliary verb).

Anticipatory anaphora and non-anaphoric use

The antecedent for the elliptical VP can follow the gap under the conditions for anticipatory anaphora described in §2.4:

[11] i *If I can* __, *I'll speak to him.*
ii *I shouldn't* __, *but I'll let you have the key if you want to pay your last respects.*

It is also found occasionally with the interpretation of the gap provided by the non-linguistic context rather than by an antecedent expression, but this use is very unusual. It is basically limited to a few phrases with special conventionalised senses. Thus *Shall we?* is conventionally used to ask someone if they wish to dance, *May I?* can be used to request permission to take something (the salt and pepper, another cake, a spare chair), *Don't!* can be used to warn people away from something they are about to do, and so on with a few other cases. But in general, VP ellipsis demands that a suitable VP meaning should be found in the immediate linguistic context.

Stranding of auxiliaries in supplementary relatives

The examples of stranding considered so far have contained an elliptical gap, but there is also a type of supplementary relative construction which strands auxiliary verbs. Compare:

[12]	ELLIPSIS	SUPPLEMENTARY RELATIVES
i	a. *He says she'll win, and she will* __.	b. *He says she'll win, which she will* __.
ii	a. *He says there's plenty of milk in the fridge, and there is* __.	b. *He says there's plenty of milk in the fridge, which there is* __.
iii	a. **She says he's ill, and he seems* __.	b. **She says he's ill, which he seems* __.

In [ia/iia] the auxiliary occurs before a gap created by ellipsis, while in [ib/iib] the gap results from relativisation, so that instead of post-verbal complements we have *which* in the prenuclear position. The verbs that can be stranded in the two constructions are the same: ***seem***, for example, is not an auxiliary verb and, as shown in [iii], cannot be stranded in either construction.

7.2 *Do*: supportive auxiliary or lexical pro-form

The auxiliary stranded by the ellipsis described in §7.1 may be the ***do*** that is required in the three main ***do***-support constructions when there is no semantically contentful auxiliary present (see Ch. 3, §2.1):

[13] i *I liked it, but Kim didn't* __. [primary verb negation]
ii *I liked it; did* YOU __ ? [subject–auxiliary inversion]
iii *He says she doesn't like him, but she* DOES __. [emphatic polarity]

The unreduced versions of the final VPs here would contain ***do*** (*Kim didn't like it*; *did* YOU *like it?*; *she* DOES *like him*); it is clear, therefore, that such examples have ellipsis of the complement of the supportive auxiliary ***do***. Our concern in the present section will be with reduced VPs headed by a ***do*** that would not be present in the non-reduced version:

[14] *I liked it, and Kim did too.*

Here the non-reduced version would be simply *Kim liked it too*: the ***do*** in [14] is thus specifically attributable to the use of a reduced form.

In this construction we find important dialect differences, with some dialects admitting only the primary inflectional forms of ***do***, others admitting the secondary forms as well:

[15] PRIMARY FORMS OF DO (All dialects)
- i *Jill complained, or at least I think she did.*
- ii *I like it and I think Kim does too.*
- iii A: *Did you like them?* B: *I did most of them.*
- iv *If Kim does, will you accept nomination too?*

[16] SECONDARY FORMS OF DO (BrE, but not AmE)
- i %*I didn't tell you at the time; I wish now that I had done.* [past participle]
- ii %*I wasn't enjoying the course then, but I am doing now.* [gerund-participle]
- iii %*I haven't written the letter yet, but I will do soon.* } [plain form]
- iv %*I like it now, but I didn't do then.* }

In both cases, the antecedent cannot have an auxiliary verb as its head:

[17]
- i **Jill will be here soon, or at least I think she does.*
- ii **I hadn't been very well at the time, and Jill hadn't done either.*

Thus *does* cannot be interpreted as "will be here soon", nor *done* as "been very well at the time".

We suggested in Ch. 3, §2.1.4, that in the dialect which allows only primary forms this ***do*** is best regarded as a special case of the supportive auxiliary ***do***. In this dialect, the auxiliary-stranding construction, like primary verb negation, subject–auxiliary inversion, and emphatic polarity, requires the presence of an auxiliary verb; if the non-reduced version of the VP does not contain an auxiliary then ***do*** must be added to allow elliptical reduction, leaving ***do*** as the stranded auxiliary. For example, the rules governing ellipsis do not permit the omission of the underlined sequence in *I liked it and Kim liked it too*: instead we introduce supportive ***do*** to occupy the position before the elliptical gap and to carry the verbal inflection, as in [14].

In dialects which accept secondary as well as primary forms, this ***do*** is a pro-form, substituting for a verb alone (e.g. *complained* in [15i]) or a verb together with internal dependents (e.g. *likes it* in [15ii] or *told you at the time* in [16i]). Pro-form ***do*** is a lexical verb, and combines with supportive auxilary ***do*** in constructions like the negative [16iv]. As a pro-form functioning as head in VP structure, ***do*** is comparable to the pro-form ***one*** which functions as head in NP structure, and substitutes for a noun alone or together with internal dependents.

Reduced VPs with primary forms of *do*

Reduced VPs headed by primary forms of ***do*** allow the same range of possibilities as we have surveyed in §7.1. This is illustrated by the examples in [15]. In [iii] ***do*** has a dependent that is understood as a complement of the unexpressed verb retrieved from the antecedent: "I liked most of them". Example [15iv] has anticipatory anaphora.

Reduced VPs with secondary forms of *do*

Content clause and main clause examples of this construction are given in [16]; it is also commonly found in comparative clauses:

[18] i %*He was working harder than he had ever done before.* [past participle]
ii %*She was making faster progress than her son was doing.* [gerund-participle]
iii %*I'd like to travel more than I've been able to do in the past.* [plain form]

The dialect that does not permit reduced VPs with secondary forms of ***do*** can generally avoid them by simply dropping ***do***, giving an equivalent construction with ellipsis; for [16i–iii], but not [16iv] or [18], there is also an alternant with ***do*** *so*. Compare, then, [16i] and [18i] with:

[19] i *I didn't tell you at the time; I wish now that I had __ / had done so.*
ii *He was working harder than he ever had __ before.*

Of the three secondary forms, the most widely acceptable is the past participle. It is normally restricted to perfect uses: compare the passive **Most of them were rejected but a few of them weren't done.* The gerund-participle form *doing* is found only in a subset of the dialects that have *done* – those that allow stranding of the gerund-participle of auxiliary verbs. The plain form *do* occurs after modal auxiliaries, as in [16iii], or infinitival *to*: %*She doesn't play much golf now, though she certainly used to do.*[42]

Minor and major differences between antecedent and non-reduced counterpart of the *do* VP

In many cases the ***do*** VP could be replaced by a full form identical with the antecedent – e.g. *complained* in [15i], *enjoying the course* in [16ii]. Elsewhere, we find minor differences in inflection (e.g. *liked* rather than *like* in [15iii]) or polarity-sensitive items (e.g. *Kim didn't make any mistakes, but Pat did*, where we would have *Pat made some mistakes*). And again we find examples of major differences between the antecedent and the understood VP:

[20] i ?*This problem was to have been looked into, but obviously nobody did.*
ii ?*This complaint deserves a response, but before you do, check with our legal department.*

In [i] the antecedent is passive, while the reduced VP is equivalent to active *looked into it.* And in [ii] the antecedent is an NP, while the non-reduced version of *do* is a VP, *respond* or *make a response.* Such examples are of the same status as those in [8]: they are

[42] In the *to*-infinitival case there is some evidence that acceptability varies to some extent according to the verb governing the infinitival complement: *used to do* or *wanted to do*, for example, seem to be more widely acceptable than *is going to do* or *happened to do.*

certainly found in unmonitored speech (and occasionally in writing), but they represent extensions of the normal patterns, not constructions that are systematically admissible.

7.3 Reduction of VPs with infinitival *to*

Stranding of *to*

Like auxiliary verbs, infinitival *to* can be stranded before a structural gap:

[21] i *I haven't submitted a formal complaint yet, but I still intend to __.*
ii *If you'd like to __, we could have a stopover in Singapore.*
iii *She wants to finish her thesis this year, but it's not clear she'll be able to __.*
iv *She invited me to go with them, which I'd quite like to __.*

In [i–iii] the gap arises from the ellipsis of a VP, while in [iv] the VP is relativised (cf. [12]). Unlike auxiliary verbs, *to* must immediately precede the ellipsis site: compare *They suggested I call the police but I decided not to __ / *to not __.*

Be **and** ***have***

Where the non-reduced form of the infinitival would begin with ***be*** or perfect ***have***, the verb will normally be retained, giving stranding of the auxiliary rather than of *to*:

[22] i A: *Will Jill be there?* B: *She's quite likely to be __.*
ii A: *Had they forged his signature?* B: *They aren't likely to have __.*

Restrictions on *to* stranding

To-stranding ellipsis is subject to fairly severe constraints, though again there is considerable variation in judgements. The infinitival clause is generally internal complement of a verb or adjective, such as *intend*, *like*, and *able* in [21]. Compare:

[23] i **She wants to sell it, but I'm sure that to __ at this stage would be a mistake.*
ii **If you complete the course, you'll be the first teenager to __.*
iii A: *How does she do it?* B: **I don't know: her ability to __ amazes me.*

In [i] the infinitival clause is subject (thus external rather than internal complement of the verb), in [ii–iii] it is a dependent of a noun (modifier and complement respectively), rather than of a verb or adjective. Ellipsis is not possible here: instead we would have the complex pro-form ***do*** *so*: *to do so at this stage would be a mistake*, and so on.

Negating the infinitival clause or adding a subject, however, often makes the ellipsis acceptable. Compare, [23i], for example, with:

[24] i *You'll have to sell your shares; not to __ could lead to a conflict of interest.*
ii *You'd better do it yourself; for anyone else to __ would be too hazardous.*

Stranding of auxiliaries and the pro-form *do* after *to*

The constraints illustrated in [23–24] apply not only to the construction where *to* is stranded, but also to those where *to* is followed by a stranded auxiliary or by the pro-form ***do***. Compare:

[25] i **He hadn't resigned; to have __ would have been to admit liability.*
ii **He hadn't resigned; to have done would have been to admit liability.*
iii *He had resigned; not to have __ would have been dishonourable.*
iv *%He had resigned; not to have done would have been dishonourable.*

7.4 Ellipsis of complement of lexical verbs and adjectives

Various lexical verbs and adjectives that take complements can occur with the complement left unexpressed when retrievable anaphorically:[43]

[26] i *I asked Max to tidy up his room, but he refused* __.
ii *She said she didn't touch it, but I saw her* __.
iii A: *Have you finished your assignment yet?* B: *I haven't even started* __.
iv *The meeting was a waste of time. I blame Kim* __.
v A: *I can't come with you.* B: *But you promised* __.
vi A: *Have they appointed a new director yet?* B: *I don't know* __.

The second clauses here are equivalent to the following expanded forms:

[27] i *He refused to tidy up his room.*
ii *I saw her touch it.*
iii *I haven't even started my assignment.*
iv *I blame Kim for the fact that the meeting was a waste of time.*
v *You promised to come with me / that you would come with me.*
vi *I don't know whether they have appointed a new director yet.*

Although a wide range of complement types can be left understood in this way, only a relatively small number of head items permit it. This is especially so in the case of direct objects, as in [26iii]; the verbs that allow anaphoric ellipsis of the object hardly extend beyond such aspectuals as *begin*, *start*, *finish*, where an NP object is pragmatically equivalent to an infinitival clause: *I've started my assignment* is understood as "I've started doing / working on my assignment", and so on. We will confine our attention in this section to the ellipsis of non-finite and content clause complements.

Ellipsis of non-finite complements

[28] i *I don't know whether I'll be able to do it by the week-end, but I'll try* __.
ii *I hadn't wanted to lead the procession, but they made me* __.
iii *They wanted Jill to introduce the guest speaker, but she wasn't willing* __.

Where the missing complement is a *to*-infinitival, there is alternation with the much more widely available type of reduction with stranded *to*: *I'll try to*; *she wasn't willing to.*

Try enters into the simple catenative construction: *I'll try to do it by the week-end*; *make* enters into the complex one (with an object as well as the non-finite complement): *They made me lead the procession.* Other verbs which behave like *try* and *make* respectively are given in [29i–ii]:

[29] i	*agree*	*begin*	*continue*	*refuse*	*stop*	*volunteer*
ii	*beg*	*force*	*hear*	*let*	*see*	*stop*

While verbs with like meaning often have like syntactic properties, we find a sharp contrast in the present construction between *try*, which allows ellipsis, and *attempt*, which does not: **I don't know whether I'll be able to do it by the week-end but I'll attempt.*

[43] The term 'null complement anaphora' has been used for this construction in some of the linguistics literature.

Differences from auxiliary-stranding ellipsis

The following examples are similar in that they both have an ellipsis site following a verb which licenses the ellipsis:

[30] AUXILIARY-STRANDING ELLIPSIS
a. *They've asked me to mend the fuse, but I can't __.*

LEXICAL VERB COMPLEMENT ELLIPSIS
b. *They've asked him to mend the fuse, but he won't even try __.*

There are, however, a number of differences which lead us to recognise distinct constructions.

(a) No relative counterpart to lexical verb complement ellipsis

[31] a. *They've asked me to mend the fuse, which I can't.*
b. **They've asked him to mend the fuse, which he won't even try.*

We saw in §7.1 that we can form supplementary relative clauses corresponding to the auxiliary-stranding ellipsis construction, but this is not possible with lexical verb complement ellipsis.

(b) Lexical verb complement ellipsis requires ellipsis of full complement

[32] a. *I can't attend the first session, but I can __ the others.*
b. **I won't try to attend the first session, but I will try __ the others.*

Here [a] is interpreted as "I can attend the others": what is ellipted is just the verb, not the full VP, and *the others* is understood as the object of the missing verb. The asterisk in [b] applies to the corresponding interpretation of this example: "I will try to attend the others".

(c) Lexical verb complement ellipsis allows change of voice

[33] a. **The program needs to be corrected: why won't Jill __ ?*
b. *The program needs to be corrected: why won't Jill try __?*

We cannot interpret [a] as "why won't Jill correct the program?", whereas the corresponding interpretation of [b], "why won't Jill try to correct the program?" is available. We noted in §7.1 there there are some marginal cases where auxiliary stranding does occur with a change of voice, but in general this is not possible; lexical verb complement ellipsis allows it much more readily.[44]

Ellipsis of finite complements

[34] i *I suggested the price was too high, and she agreed __.* [declarative]
ii *I don't know if she's going to buy it: she didn't say __.* [closed interrogative]
iii A: *How long will it last?* B: *You can't tell __.* [open interrogative]

We interpret [i] as "she agreed that the price was too high", with a declarative complement; [ii] as "she didn't say whether she's going to buy", with a closed interrogative complement; and [iii] as "You can't tell how long it will last", with an open interrogative complement.

[44] A further point is that with lexical verbs a missing complement can in general be more readily retrieved non-anaphorically, from the situation of utterance. For instance if I see you struggling to open a window I might say simply: *Let me try.*

Verbs and adjectives that take this kind of ellipsis include the following, where the annotations 'D' and 'I' indicate whether the ellipted complement clause is understood as declarative or interrogative.[45]

[35]	*agree* D	*ask* I	*convince* D	*explain* I	*forget* D/I	*hear* D/I
	inquire I	*know* D/I	*mind* D/I	*persuade* D	*recall* D/I	*remember* D/I
	say I	*see* I	*suppose* D	*tell* D/I	*certain* D/I	*sure* D/I

In [34] the type of clause understood to be ellipted is derivable directly from the antecedent (the underlined clause). In other cases, the clause type and other features of the interpretation are less straightforwardly retrievable. Compare:

[36] i *He may have committed suicide. We'll never know* __.
ii *You could take it home and return it in the morning. No one would know* __.
iii *I did everything I could: ask Kim* __.

In [i] modal *may* is sufficient to trigger an interrogative interpretation, "whether he committed suicide or not". In [ii] we again have the modality of possibility, but this time the interpretation is that if you took it home and returned it in the morning no one would know that you had done so. *Ask* in [iii] doesn't allow a declarative complement, so we interpret the ellipted complement as the closed interrogative counterpart of the declarative antecedent: "ask Kim whether I did", the implicature being that Kim's answer will confirm what I have said.

Some special cases

There are a number of places where we find ellipsis following verbs that do not normally permit it. One common case is in the complement of conditional *if*: *Take a taxi if you want* __; *We could make it Tuesday if you prefer* __; similarly *if they like, if you choose*. Compare the non-conditional **I didn't go because I didn't want* __, and so on. We also find various fixed phrases, such as *Allow me*, expressing a polite offer to help – to open a door, carry something heavy, or the like.

7.5 *Do so*

In addition to functioning on its own as a pro-form in certain dialects, ***do*** functions as head of complex pro-forms. We look first at ***do*** *so*, and then turn to those where ***do*** combines with NPs such as *it* and *that*.

The complex pro-form ***do*** *so* serves as an anaphoric VP which in many cases is a slightly more formal alternant to the types of reduced VPs considered in §§7.1–3. Compare, for example, the following responses to such a question as *Has he informed the police?*:

[37]	ELLIPSIS OR PRO-FORM *DO*	PRO-FORM *DO SO*
i	a. *No, but he will* __ *tomorrow.*	b. *No, but he will do so tomorrow.*
ii	a. *No, but he still intends to* __.	b. *No, but he still intends to do so.*
iii	a. *He may have* __.	b. *He may have done so.*
iv	a. %*He may have done.*	

[45] There are some dialect differences here. *Suppose* allows ellipsis in AmE and AusE, whereas BrE has the pro-form *so* (*I suppose so*); *know* allows declarative ellipsis in BrE and AusE, whereas AmE would have a pro-form such as *it*.

Like the ***do*** of the earlier constructions, ***do*** *so* is inadmissible if the head of the antecedent is an auxiliary:

[38] a. **I told him to be tactful and he did.* b. **I told him to be tactful and he did so.*

Nevertheless, the constructions are by no means always interchangeable. There are contexts where, relative to ellipsis or pro-form ***do***, the ***do*** *so* construction is excluded or disfavoured, and some where it is required or preferred.

Contexts where *do so* is excluded or disfavoured relative to ellipsis (or pro-form *do*)

(a) ***Do*** *so* does not admit contrastive complements

[39] *I didn't invite Kim, but I did Pat / *but I did so Pat.*

The *did* of *I did Pat* does not correspond to a full VP, but only to the verb, and *Pat* is object of an understood *invite*, contrasting with *Kim* in the preceding clause; ***do*** *so*, however, must substitute for a VP consisting at least of the verb and its complements.

(b) ***Do*** *so* is inadmissible in comparative constructions

[40] i *She earns more than I do / *than I do so.*
ii *He thought it was good, as I did / *as I did so.*

(c) ***Do*** *so* cannot in general be anaphoric to a stative VP

[41] *He liked it; at least he said he did / *did so.*

Like denotes a state, and as such cannot head the antecedent of ***do*** *so*, which must be dynamic.

(d) ***Do*** *so* excluded or disfavoured in various tags and responses, and in non-anaphoric use

[42] i *Jill had written it, hadn't she? / *hadn't she done so?*
ii A: *Jill had written it.* B: *Had she? / *Had she done so?*
iii A: *Jill had written it.* B: *No she hadn't. / *No she hadn't done so.*
iv A: *Had Jill written it?* B: *Yes, she had. / *Yes, she had done so.*
v [No antecedent] *Don't! / *Don't do so!*

Ellipsis (or primary forms of pro-form ***do***) must be used in preference to ***do*** *so* in interrogative tags ([i]), and in responses such as those illustrated in [ii–iv]. In [ii] B responds to A's statement with the corresponding polar question, either to acknowledge that the information is new and somewhat surprising or to challenge the truth of A's statement. In [iii] B contradicts A's statement, and in [iv] answers A's polar question. In all of [i–iv], then, the issue is simply yes or no, and in such contexts the version with the greater reduction of the VP is required. Similarly in the non-anaphoric use of reduction illustrated in [v], where the interpretation derives from salience in the context of utterance rather than from a linguistic antecedent: it may be, for example, that you are about to hit your young brother and I'm telling you not to. We have noted that this use of ellipsis is rare, but ***do*** *so* does not permit it at all.

(e) ***Do*** *so* is disfavoured in chaining and with crossed anaphoric links

[43] i A: *Are you going to help them? I think you should __.* B: *I may __; I'd certainly like to __, but I'm not sure I can __.*

ii A: *You should phone her$_i$ and ask if she has finished$_j$.* B: *I will __$_i$, but I'm pretty sure she hasn't __$_j$.*

Ellipsis lends itself to repetition much more readily than ***do*** *so*, which would be unnatural though not ungrammatical in examples like these. In [i] we have an anaphoric chain, while in [ii] the anaphoric links cut across each other: the missing complement of *will* is linked to *phone her* and that of *hasn't* to *finished.*

Contexts where *do so* is required or preferred relative to ellipsis (or pro-form *do*)

(a) Reduced VP contains a non-contrastive adjunct

[44] i *She agreed to help, but she did so / *did reluctantly.*

ii *Those who take part do so / *do at their own peril.*

In [i] the adjunct *reluctantly* adds a specification of manner but does not contrast with anything in the previous clause. Similarly in [ii] the adjunct *at their own peril* does not contrast with anything in the relative clause which contains the antecedent.

(b) Various kinds of non-finite clause

[45] i *We didn't complain: there was no point in doing so / %doing.*

ii *We didn't complain: we knew that to do so / *to do would be pointless.*

In [i] we have a gerund-participial clause and, as we have noted, pro-form ***do*** on its own would be inadmissible for all but a minority of speakers. In [ii] the clause headed by ***do*** is infinitival; in such clauses pro-form ***do*** by itself or the stranding of *to* is subject to constraints dealt with in §7.3 above. See also the discussion of [5ii–iii] above.

Minor and major differences between antecedent and the non-reduced counterpart of *do so*

Differences between the antecedent and the full VP that could replace the reduced form are tolerated somewhat more readily by ***do*** *so* than by the auxiliary-stranding and pro-form ***do*** constructions. Example [45i] illustrates the case where we have a minor difference in inflection (*complain* vs *complaining*): such cases are completely acceptable because the required inflection – here the gerund-participle inflection – is overtly carried by ***do*** rather than being lost with the ellipted verb, as in [5ii] above. Major differences are seen in:

[46] i *The intention behind the legislation was to ensure that the money should be used for reinstatement where it was possible and economic to do so.*

ii *The financially secure can contemplate travel alone when it was unseemly for a woman who was not a suspect adventuress to do so in previous generations.*

In [i] the antecedent is passive, while the non-reduced form would be active, *use the money for reinstatement.* And in [ii] the antecedent *travel alone* is an NP while the full form would be a VP (though homonymous with the NP). Such examples would be widely regarded as stylistically infelicitous, but they are certainly attested, and are more acceptable than comparable forms in ellipsis – compare [8] and [20].

Function and position of *so*

So functions syntactically as complement but it is not an object, and hence there is no passive with *so* as subject (**The papers had to be filed and so was done by Kim*). *So* is usually positioned immediately after ***do***, but it can also precede the verb in gerund-participials and (rarely) *to*-infinitivals, a highly exceptional position for a complement:

[47] i *We don't want to initiate an inquiry but we are in the process of so doing.*
ii *The lease may be terminated by Council after having given not less than 12 months' notice in writing of its intention so to do.*

7.6 *Do it, do that, etc.*

Do enters into a number of complex pro-forms in which it takes an NP as object, mainly the 3rd person personal pronoun *it* and the demonstratives *that* and *this*:

[48] i *If we are going to live together, we may as well do it properly.*
ii *There are times when I'd just like to go down to the library and get some books, but often you can't do that on the spur of the moment.*
iii *We need to make absolutely clear what the goals of the various courses are: only if we do this will people be able to make an informed choice between them.*

Restriction to agentive situations

One difference between these combinations and ***do*** *so* is that they require an agentive interpretation whereas ***do*** *so* can denote a non-agentive dynamic situation. Compare, then:

[49] *When the tree fell, it did so / #did it with a loud crash.*

The tree's falling is dynamic rather than stative, and hence ***do*** *so* is permitted; but the tree does not have the role of agent, and this excludes ***do*** *it*, ***do*** *that*, and the like. Note, however, that like other uses of ***do***, this one does not allow an antecedent headed by ***be*** even when the latter has an agentive interpretation: **You must be more tactful – if you don't do that, you won't get anywhere.*

The non-idiomatic nature of these combinations

Do *so* is an idiom: its meaning and syntactic properties cannot be derived by combining those of ***do*** and *so*. ***Do*** *it* and ***do*** *that/this*, however, are not idioms: their meaning and properties can be predicted from those of ***do*** and the NP as used in other combinations. The anaphoric nature of the VPs headed by ***do*** in [48] is attributable to *it* and the demonstratives, for ***do*** occurs with the same meaning in non-anaphoric VPs, as in *I've just done something very stupid* or *They can't do anything about it*. We have seen that the demonstratives are often used deictically, and this carries over to their use in combination with ***do***, as in *Don't do that* (with ***do*** *that* understood as denoting the action you are currently performing) or *He was doing this* (said as I demonstrate the action in question). And because the NPs are objects, there can be corresponding passives in which they function as subject: *They climbed all four peaks in one day – it/this had never been done before.*

The ***do*** we have here is thus a verb of very general meaning that can be used of a great range of actions that could be expressed by verbs with more specific meanings; we will call it the general agentive verb ***do***, and represent it as ***do***$_{ga}$. English has no verb that is itself interrogative or relative, but ***do***$_{ga}$ can be used in combination with interrogative or relative pronouns to permit questioning or relativisation of a VP:[46]

[50] i *What will they do?* [open interrogative]

ii *[What they did] was clearly wrong.* [fused relative]

iii *There are several things [we ought to do].* [integrated relative]

iv *They climbed all four peaks in one day, [which had never been done before].* [supplementary relative]

Similarly there is no general deictic verb and no anaphoric verb (except for the dialect-restricted pro-form ***do***), and ***do***$_{ga}$ combines with appropriate NPs to form deictic and anaphoric VPs. It also combines with various comparative expressions such as *the same (thing)*, *likewise*, or *otherwise*, and these retain the semantic and syntactic properties that they exhibit elsewhere.

To obliques with patient role

Do$_{ga}$ can take other complements in combination with those mentioned above. Most importantly it can take a *to* PP with the oblique NP associated with the semantic role of patient:

[51] *They questioned Jill for over an hour before letting her go: I hope they don't do that to me.*

The interpretation here is "I hope they don't question me for over an hour before letting me go"; the oblique *me* contrasts with the object *Jill* in the VP containing the antecedent. Such *to* PP complements are found with the full range of ***do***$_{ga}$ constructions: compare deictic *Don't do that to me* or interrogative *What did they do to you?*, etc.

Happen as a general dynamic verb

Very similar to the general agentive verb ***do*** is the general dynamic verb ***happen***:

[52] i *I was hoping that they wouldn't speak English so I would have been forced to use Chinese but unfortunately it didn't happen.*

ii *If you do too much last minute cramming you can end up too tired to do the exam. That happened to me last week because I studied pretty late for it.*

iii *I can't believe this is happening to me.*

iv *What's happening?*

v *We came back early because it started to snow, which happens sometimes even in May.*

vi *What happened was we didn't have a quorum, so the meeting was adjourned.*

While ***do***$_{ga}$ combines with such NPs as *it* and the demonstratives as object to form VPs, ***happen*** combines with them as subject to form clauses. In [i–ii] the ***happen*** clause is anaphoric, interpreted as "They didn't not speak English so that I was forced to use Chinese" (i.e. they spoke English, so I was not forced to use Chinese) and "I ended up too tired to do the exam", whereas in [iii] the clause is interpreted deictically. Similarly,

[46] Relativisation with the general agentive verb ***do*** is to be distinguished from that discussed in §7.4; the latter occurs with auxiliary verbs and pro-form ***do***, needn't be agentive (*He said it would rain, which indeed it did*), and cannot be passivised.

while ***do***$_{\text{ga}}$ combines with *what* or *which* to permit questioning or relativisation of the VP, ***happen*** combines with them to permit questioning or relativisation of the clause, as in interrogative [iv], supplementary relative [v], and fused relative [vi]. ***Happen*** indicates that the situation was dynamic rather than stative, but unlike ***do***$_{\text{ga}}$ it does not imply agentivity.

Comparison between *do so*, *do it*, and *do that*

Two differences between ***do** so* and the ***do***$_{\text{ga}}$ constructions have emerged from the above discussion: ***do** so* need not be agentive whereas ***do***$_{\text{ga}}$ always is, and ***do** so* is always anaphoric, whereas ***do***$_{\text{ga}}$ has a much wider range of uses. Within the anaphoric use, a further difference relates to the fact that *it* and *that* are definite NPs. Anaphoric ***do** it* and ***do** that* characteristically denote specific events, either the same event as that denoted by the antecedent VP or at least the same action involving the same participants as those expressed by the internal complements of the antecedent VP. In contrast, ***do** so* VPs often denote merely the same **kind** of event as the antecedent. Compare, for example:

[53] i a. *Jill nearly caught a fish yesterday.* b. *Tomorrow she's sure she will do so.*
ii a. *Jill nearly caught that fish yesterday.* b. *Tomorrow she's sure she will do it.*

In the salient interpretation of [ia] there is no particular fish that I have in mind as one Jill nearly caught, and [ib] is then a more likely continuation than [iib]. ***Do** so* is here interpreted as "catch a fish", with no requirement that it be the same fish as the one she nearly caught yesterday. In [iia] I am referring to a particular fish that I take to be identifiable to you (probably by virtue of previous mention), and here the more likely continuation is [iib]; *do it* is interpreted as "catch that fish", where it must be the same fish as she nearly caught yesterday. The issue in the sequence [iia] + [iib] is Jill's ongoing battle with a certain fish, where in the sequence [ia] + [ib] it is the more general situation of catching a fish.

The *it* of ***do** it* (like the *so* of ***do** so*) is unstressed, while the *that* of ***do** that* readily takes stress, giving contrastive focus on the action concerned. Compare, for example:

[54] i A: *I've sent in my resignation.* B: *Why did you do it?*
ii A: *I've sent in my resignation.* B: *Why did you do that?*

The exchange in [i] is likely to occur in a context where the possibility of A's resigning is already in the air. B's question, with stress on *do*, then asks why A went through with it. The exchange in [ii], by contrast, is likely in a context where the issue of A's resigning is new.

Summary of different uses of *do*

We conclude this section by listing summarily the different uses of ***do*** that we have distinguished in this grammar:

[55] i *She doesn't regret it.* [auxiliary]
ii %*I like it more than I used to do.* [pro-form]
iii *I enrolled for the course but soon regretted doing so.* [head of pro-form ***do** so*]
iv *You shouldn't do that. What is he doing?* [general agentive verb]
v *She did a somersault. She does a lot of writing.* [light verb]
vi *She did well. That'll do. They are doing 'Macbeth'.* [ordinary lexical verb]

The auxiliary is used only in the four ***do***-support constructions; it has only tensed forms, except that plain *do*/*don't* occur in emphatic or negative imperatives. ***Do*** in [ii–vi] is a lexical verb, and combines with auxiliary **do** in the **do**-support constructions: %*I like it now, but I didn't do then*; *He didn't do so*; and so on. The pro-form **do** is found in BrE but not normally in AmE; it is restricted to anaphoric use. ***Do*** *so* is an idiom, likewise used anaphorically. The ***do*** of [iv] associates an agent role with its subject; it generally combines with an NP object, permitting the formation of anaphoric and deictic VPs, the questioning and relativisation of VPs, and so on. The ***do*** of [v] is a light verb, like the ***make*** of *They made an offer*, the ***take*** of *She took a decision*, the ***give*** of *He gave a grunt*, and so on: see Ch. 4, §7. There is nothing grammatically special about the ***do*** of [vi], an ordinary lexical verb with a range of senses; the examples given illustrate intransitive and monotransitive constructions, and it can also be ditransitive, as in *They did me a favour.*

7.7 *So*

So has a very wide range of uses, only some of which are deictic or anaphoric. Given the concerns of this chapter, it is these we will focus on here, in §§7.7.1–2 respectively, but we will then summarily review other uses in §7.7.3.

7.7.1 Deictic *so*

Adverbial *so* can be used deictically, indicating degree (generally modifying an adjective) or manner (as an adjunct to a clause):

[56] i *She was about so tall.*
ii *You then fold the paper in two, so.*

In the degree sense, *so* must be accompanied by an appropriate indexing act; in saying [i], for example, I will indicate, typically by hand, how tall she was. In the manner sense *so* is accompanied by the performance of the action in the manner concerned. Degree *so* is equivalent to demonstrative *this* or *that*, and manner *so* to the relatively formal *thus*. An alternant of the manner adverb *so* is the PP *like so* (cf. *like this*).[47]

The use of *so* as predicative complement of such verbs as *name* and *call* is a case of discourse deixis (§1.4):

[57] *The ark module is so named in keeping with the distributors' talmudic interests.*

So here stands not for the denotation of *ark module*, but for that linguistic expression: "The ark module is named *ark module* . . . ".

7.7.2 Anaphoric *so*

So combines with **do** in the complex pro-form ***do*** *so* discussed in §7.5 above. Other anaphoric uses are as follows.

[47] The idiom *so far* can be used either deictically or anaphorically. The deictic use is seen in *I have so far marked about half of them* ("up to now"); the anaphoric use in *I had so far marked about half of them* ("up to then").

(a) Pro-clause complement with finite antecedent: *I think so*

[58] i A: *Are they putting the price up?* B: *I think so. / I'm afraid so. / It seems so.*
ii *She thought he was wrong but was too polite to say so.*
iii *She was totally opposed to the idea and told the premier so.*
iv *Will she accept the recommendations, and if so how will they affect us?*

So here stands for a clause in complement function: we understand "I think they are putting the price up", and so on. The understood clause is always declarative, though the antecedent can be interrogative, as in [i/iv]. This construction is found with the conditional preposition *if*, the adjective *afraid*, and a fair number of verbs, a sample of which are given in:

[59]	*appear*	*assume*	*believe*	*fear*	*gather*	*guess*
	hope	*imagine*	*presume*	*reckon*	*regret*	*say*
	seem	*suppose*	*suspect*	*tell*	*think*	*trust*

Appear and *seem* take impersonal *it* as subject: *it seems so*. Many of the others allow passivisation, with *so* then in extraposed subject position: *It is believed so*, etc. Verbs which, by contrast, do not allow *so* to substitute for a clausal complement include *confirm, doubt, realise, resent.*[48]

A number of the verbs in [59] also allow *it* or *that* as a pro-clause anaphor. In most cases there is a fairly clear difference in meaning between *so* and these NPs. It is particularly clear in 1st person singular present tense examples like *I believe so* vs *I believe it/that.* With *I believe so* the main issue is the truth of the antecedent proposition: I might well use this in response to a polar question to give a modally qualified positive answer. With *I believe it/that* the main issue is whether I believe the proposition concerned (and this time the antecedent could hardly be interrogative). The difference emerges very sharply if we add *yes.* In *Yes, I believe so,* the *yes* relates to the proposition expressed by *so*; in *Yes, I believe it/that* the *yes* relates to the matrix proposition: "Yes I do believe". Or take the verb *regret. I regret so* is understood as "Yes, regrettably", while in *I regret it/that* the truth of the proposition expressed by the complement is taken for granted, and what is asserted is that my attitude to it is one of regret.

Polarity: *so* and *not*

So normally expresses a positive proposition, with *not* being used as the corresponding negative pro-form. In response to *Will Kim be there?*, for example, *I hope so* is understood as "I hope Kim will be there" and *I hope not* as "I hope Kim will not be there".[49] There is likewise a straightforward contrast with *if* between positive *so* and negative *not.* With *say* and *tell,* however, *so* readily substitutes for a negative clause and *not* is quite rare and often inadmissible outside responses to questions:

[60] i *She didn't approve of the idea and told them so/*not.*
ii A: *Will they be accepting the proposal?* B: *She says not.*

[48] In general *know* belongs with these, but there is an established somewhat jocular use of *know so* when an explicit contrast is being made between knowing and merely thinking – e.g. A: *Do you think so?* B: *I* KNOW SO.

[49] A number of the verbs in [59] occur in the negative with what we have called increased specificity of the negation (Ch. 9, §5), so that *I don't think so* is typically interpreted as equivalent to the less frequent *I think not.*

Preposed *so*

[61] i *They seem diametrically opposed, or so I thought until I investigated further.*
ii *The optical and mechanical first principles could be inferred directly from experiments – or so Newton would have his readers believe.*
iii *Five of us, so I believe, have had fiction published in magazines or anthologies.*
iv A: *The clock has stopped.* B: *So I see.*
v *So wrote a ten-year-old student in a letter to his parents from St Aidan's.*
vi *Nor, so did I believe, had anyone yet effectively caught the gaping contrast between the heedless flow of time and the fleeting evanescence of existence.*

Most of the verbs in [59] (but not the preposition *if* or the adjective *afraid*) allow *so* to be fronted, and indeed there are a few verbs, such as *see* and *write* in [61iv–v], that occur with *so* in front but not end position (cf. **I see so*). Examples [i–iv] have the default subject + predicator order, and [i–ii] illustrate one of the most common uses of this construction – in an *or*-coordinate that serves to qualify the speaker's commitment to the proposition expressed in the first coordinate. It is also possible for preposing of *so* to be accompanied by subject postposing, as in [v], or (rarely) subject–auxiliary inversion, as in [vi]. Preposed *so* does not contrast with *not*, and can have a negative antecedent.

(b) *So* in lieu of non-finite complement of lexical verb

[62] *You can, if you so wish/choose, join for a trial period of three months.*

The interpretation here is "if you wish/choose to join for a trial period of three months". This construction characteristically occurs in the complement of *if* and with *so* in preverbal position; it is found with only a small number of verbs, the most common being *wish, choose, desire*. We also find past-participial passives: *if so ordered*, etc.

(c) Pro-predicative

[63] i *They were very happy at that time, or at least they seemed so.*
ii *The bible was already a symbol of class struggle, and remained so for a long time.*

So here functions as predicative complement; the antecedent is most often an AdjP, but other categories are possible, as in the NP of [ii]. With the verb *be* comparable reduction usually takes the form of ellipsis (*Kim was enthusiastic and Pat was __ too*), but *so* is not altogether excluded: *In the general sense of 'political' – having to do with the distribution and exercise of political power – jury trials and the legal system are very clearly so.* Note also its use with a dependent modifier in *or*-coordinations: *Because nets cannot be projected any great distance, they are generally stationary, or nearly so, when in use.*

(d) *So* as head of clause with dependent modifiers or complements

[64] i *Step-parents have to break through a layer of resistance,* [*more so than other people trying to join any close-knit community*].
ii *The Coo-ee cordial factory prospered almost at once,* [*so much so that my father bought a new house at Coorparoo*].
iii *He was respected in international political forums,* [*and properly so*].
iv A: *Did they get permission from the Dean?* B: [*Probably so*].
v *Jo was hard-working and well regarded by her colleagues;* [*not so her brother*].

The bracketed sequences here are reduced main clauses, with *so* as head, accompanied by one or more dependents. One common type has a degree modifier, with a following comparative or resultative complement, as in [i–ii]. In [iv] *so* is accompanied by a modal adjunct; this construction is like that covered under (a) in that we have a polarity contrast between positive *Probably so* and negative *Probably not.* Other modal adjuncts found in this pattern include *perhaps, maybe, necessarily, allegedly,* while *certainly* allows *not* but not *so*. Compare, similarly, *Why so?* and *Why not?* In [v] *her brother* contrasts with *Jo* in the first clause, and hence is understood as subject: "Her brother was not hard-working and well regarded by his colleagues".[50]

(e) *So* as anaphoric manner adjunct

[65] *Employment in services of one kind or another may be expected to increase as the towns approach maturity; indeed, in the country generally the proportion of people so employed is growing steadily.*

Anaphoric *so* can function as a manner adjunct, characteristically in combination with a past participle in its passive use, and equivalent to *thus* or *in this way*; it is interpreted in this example as "in services of one kind or another".

(f) *So* as complement of auxiliary verb: exclamatory confirmation

[66] A: *Jill has misspelt our name.* B: *So she has!*

B's response here serves to confirm A's statement and to express some emotive meaning – that the fact is surprising or remarkable. Syntactically *so she has* is a special case of the emphatic polarity construction, and hence requires supportive ***do*** in the absence of any auxiliary in the preceding clause: the response to *Jill misspelt our name* would be *So she did.* It is not possible to repeat the full VP: *So she has misspelt it!* belongs to a quite different construction, with *so* meaning "therefore" (as in [71] below). For this reason we take the *so* of [66] as complement of *has*, interpreted anaphorically as "misspelt our name". The antecedent will most often be a non-finite clause, but with *be* and *have* can be non-clausal (A: *Jill is in the attic.* B: *So she is!*).[51]

Category status of anaphoric *so*

The *so* discussed in this section does not fit readily into our system of word categories, except for the manner adjunct use seen in [65], which can be classified as an adverb. The pro-predicative use of [63] can substitute for predicatives of a range of categories, AdjP, NP, PP, and there seems to be no good reason to treat it as the head of any one of these categories. The *so* that substitutes for a clausal complement, as in [58], is classified in dictionaries as a pronoun, but that reflects the traditional analysis of content clauses as 'noun clauses', which we have argued against in Ch. 11, §8.2. Certainly, the distribution of this *so* is very different from that of anaphoric NPs such as *it* or *that* – for example, it cannot occur in subject function. In [64] *so* is the head of a clause; clauses normally have a verb as head, but *so* lacks the important inflectional properties of verbs. Overall, then, we prefer to classify anaphoric *so* simply as a pro-form; its properties are unquestionably unique, and we do not believe that anything is gained by forcing it into one or more of our general part-of-speech categories.

[50] Two idioms contain *so* as head in a use which bears some resemblance to the one considered here: *quite so*, said as an expression of agreement, and *even so*, "nevertheless".

[51] Some varieties allow *so* to follow the auxiliary verb, the effect this time being to deny a negative statement, as when A says *Jill didn't sign the petition* and B responds %*She did so!* ("That's not true: she HAS signed it"). This differs prosodically from the idiomatic ***do*** *so* construction of §7.5 in that the *so* is strongly stressed; moreover, this *so* occurs with other verbs than ***do***, so that to A's *Jill hasn't signed the petition* B could respond %*She has so!* As a complement of auxiliary verbs *so* is comparable to *that* in some regional dialects: %*That it is* or %*It is that*, said in response to *It's an absolute swindle.*

7.7.3 Other uses of *so*

(a) Initial *so* in correlation with *as*

[67] i *Just as Renaissance scholars had to reconcile Platonism with Christianity, so the Victorian Platonist dons had their particular reconciliation to do too.*
ii *As infections increased in women, so did infections in their babies.*

As and *so* indicate likeness between the situations expressed in the subordinate clause (the complement of *as*) and the main clause (introduced by the adjunct *so*). Subject–auxiliary inversion is optional: for [i] we could have *so did the Victorian Platonist dons have . . .*, and for [ii] *so infections increased in their babies.* The *so* is optional (with inversion permitted of course only when it is present): it serves to reiterate the likeness expressed by *as*. *So* is here at most only marginally anaphoric, indicating likeness with what has gone before: "in the same way / at the same time as that".

(b) Other cases of initial *so* with subject–auxiliary inversion

[68] i *Jill will certainly notice the mistake, and so will Max.*
ii A: *Tom is very nervous.* B: *So would you be in his position.*

In these examples there is a very clear anaphoric relation between the second clause and the first: we understand "Max will certainly notice the mistake" and "You would be very nervous in his position". It is probably best, however, to attribute this to ellipsis, with *so* then being a connective adjunct indicating likeness between the two clauses.

So is restricted to positive clauses: **Jill won't notice the mistake and so won't Max.* The corresponding negative construction has *neither* or *nor*: *Jill won't notice the mistake, and neither will Max.* There are, however, significant differences between *so* and *neither*/*nor*. In the first place, *so* can combine with *too* (itself a connective adjunct with positive orientation), as in *and so too can Pat*: there is no comparable combination for the negatives. Secondly, the clause introduced by *so* must contrast with the preceding one with respect to its subject, whereas *neither*/*nor* appear in a wider range of contexts:

[69] i a. **He can play the piano, and so can he sing.* b. *He can't play the piano, and neither can he sing.*
ii a. **She has invited Max, and so does she intend to invite Paul.* b. *She hasn't invited Max, and neither does she intend to invite Paul.*

The VP following *so* is almost invariably reduced. It would be at best highly unidiomatic, for example, to add *notice it* at the end of [68i]. It is possible under certain circumstances, however, to have a full VP:

[70] *This forecast is admittedly way above the estimate of most analysts in several recent surveys. But so is reality generally far off from the consensus.*

It is for this reason that we analyse this construction differently from that in [66], taking *so* as an adjunct rather than an anaphoric complement.

(c) Connective adjunct of reason, consequence

[71] i *There had been a power failure, so all classes had had to be cancelled.*
ii *I've no more to say, so I suggest we move on.*

Here too *so* functions as a connective adjunct, this time marking reason or consequence. As with many other connective adjuncts, there is a slight anaphoric component in the meaning: "for this reason, as a result of this".

(d) Manner, purpose, result, licensing a content clause complement

[72] i *The timetable had been so arranged that Fridays were kept free of lectures.*
ii *We usually cut up her spaghetti so (that) she can eat it with a spoon.*
iii *There had been a power failure, so that all classes had had to be cancelled.*

In [i] *so* is an adverb functioning as manner adjunct in clause structure in pre-verbal position and licensing the *that* clause following the verb (cf. Ch. 11, §4.6); without such a following clause, manner *so* is deictic or anaphoric, as in [56i] and [65] above. In [72ii–iii] *so* is a preposition functioning as head of a purpose and result adjunct respectively; here the content clauses are complement of *so*. With purpose adjuncts the complement can have the form of *as* + infinitival: *so as to enable her to eat it with a spoon* (see Ch. 8, §12.2, for discussion of these constructions).

In [72ii] the subordinator *that* is optional, as indicated. If we drop the *that* from [iii], however, we no longer have clause subordination, as evident from the fact that the coordinator *and* can be added before *so*. This is why quite different structures are assigned to [72iii] and [71i]: in the latter *so* does not have a complement but functions as adjunct in a main clause (see Ch. 15, §§2.11).

(e) *So* in idiomatic coordinates: *or so, and so on*

Or so is often combined with expressions of measure or quantification, as in *a week or so, fifteen or so candidates / fifteen candidates or so*, to give the meaning "approximately": "approximately a week", "about fifteen candidates". There is an evident connection to the productive anaphoric uses, in that we can gloss it as "or something like that". Similarly for other coordinative idioms *and so on/forth*, "and more / other things of this kind".

7.8 Further cases of ellipsis

7.8.1 Ellipsis of grammaticised words at the beginning of a main clause

A range of grammaticised items, such as personal pronouns and auxiliaries, can be omitted from the beginning of a main clause in casual style. In general, this type of ellipsis is not dependent on the presence of an antecedent.

(a) Ellipsis of personal pronoun subject

[73] i *Hope you're right. Can't think what I was doing.* [*I*]
ii *Doesn't matter. Serves you right. Must be time for bed, isn't it?* [*It*]
iii *Should be a screwdriver on the bench.* [*There*]

This occurs mainly with 1st person *I* and the dummy pronouns *it* and *there*, as in these examples. Ellipsis of other pronouns is also possible, however: *Looks a bit put out, doesn't he?* There may also be a preceding antecedent, as when you ask *What's the new guy like?*, and I reply, *Can't play at all*, with ellipsis of *he*.

A number of the reduced forms, such as *Serves you right*, have something of the character of fixed phrases. *Thank you* allows *I* as subject in some contexts, but hardly when it follows *yes* or *no*, for example. The omission of *you* from imperatives is different from the subject ellipsis illustrated in [73], in that it is not a feature of casual style but is the default form.

(b) Ellipsis of subject pronoun + auxiliary

[74] i *Glad you think so. Never seen anything like it!* [*I + am/have*]
ii *Strange how the ants come in when it's about to rain.* [*It + is*]

The omitted material is shown on the right. The most likely pronoun is 1st person *I* or dummy *it*, while the most likely auxiliary is ***be***. Perfect ***have*** is retrievable in [i] by virtue of the past participle *seen*. *Sorry* is particularly common here: *Sorry to have kept you waiting*. Without a complement and used as an apology, *sorry* is hardly to be regarded as elliptical: its status is comparable to that of *thank you*.

(c) Ellipsis in closed interrogatives of auxiliary or auxiliary + subject pronoun

[75] i *Anyone seen my glasses? Anyone at home? That you, Liz?*
ii *Want any more beer? Ever driven a Porsche? Feeling any better?*

These are reduced versions of questions with closed interrogative form: the initial auxiliary is missing, and in [ii] the subject is too. The auxiliary is retrievable from the form of the verb when there is one: ***do*** with a plain form (*want*), ***have*** with a past participle (*seen, driven*), ***be*** with a gerund-participle (*feeling*); when the predicate is verbless (*at home, you*) the understood auxiliary is ***be***. The pronoun ellipted in subject position will normally be understood as *you*, and if understood as 3rd person virtually requires an indexical act.

(d) Determiner in NP structure

[76] i *Trouble is, we have to be there by six. Friend of mine's been there.* [*The*; *A*]
ii *Pity you can't stay. Car still in hock?* [*It's a*; *Is your*]

In [i] the subject NP has lost its determiner, *the* and *a* respectively. The examples in [ii] show that this kind of ellipsis can combine with types (b) and (c) above.

7.8.2 Radical ellipsis in open interrogatives

Open interrogative clauses can be reduced to the interrogative phrase – or this phrase + a stranded preposition:

[77] i A: *I've decided to withdraw.* B: *Why/When?*
ii A: *I sold my bicycle this morning.* B: *Who to?*
iii A: *We've included 'Macbeth' in the syllabus.* B: *And what else?*
iv A: *That woman is a saint.* B: *What woman?*

In [i] the interrogative clause is reduced to an adjunct: B is asking for information about the reason or time. The rest of the clause is recoverable anaphorically: "Why/When have you decided to withdraw?" Example [ii] illustrates the case where a preposition is stranded: the non-reduced version would be *Who did you sell your bicycle to?* The fronted counterpart, *To whom?*, would be markedly formal, but stranding is somewhat more restricted in the reduced construction than elsewhere: it is not possible when the interrogative word is determiner in NP structure. Thus while *Which car will you be travelling in?* is fully acceptable, **Which car in?* is inadmissible as a response to, say, *We'll be following later* – we need the non-stranded version *In which car?* In [iii] the interrogative phrase contains the modifier *else*: "What else besides 'Macbeth' have you included in the syllabus?" Emotive modifiers such as *on earth, the hell, ever* are not permitted unless followed by a stranded preposition, *else*, or (in the case of *why*) *not*: *Who ever to?, And what on earth else?, Why ever not?*, but not **Why ever?*

Example [77iv] is somewhat different from the others. While it is possible to expand the interrogative phrase in the same way as in [i–iii], i.e. *What woman is a saint?*, a more natural expansion would be *What woman do you mean / are you referring to?* A's use of the definite NP *that woman* implies an assumption that B will be able to identify the referent, and B's response indicates that this assumption was false.

Subordinate clauses

This type of anaphoric reduction is also common in subordinate interrogatives:[52]

[78] i A: *They got in without a key.* B: *I wonder how.*
ii *There's going to be a special meeting, but when I don't know.*
iii *The police had been tipped off, but she didn't say who by.*

7.8.3 Radical ellipsis in declarative responses

Responses to questions are very often reduced to a single element of clause structure:

[79] i a. A: *When did she get home?* B: *Yesterday morning.*
b. A: *Why did they sack him?* B: *Because he's incompetent.*
c. A: *What did she give you?* B: *A t-shirt.*
d. A: *What were they doing?* B: *Playing cards.*
ii a. A: *Did you read them all?* B: *No, only the first three.*
b. A: *Were they fighting?* B: *No, just shouting at each other.*

In [i], B's response gives an answer to A's question. In [ia–c] it has the form of a phrase with the same function as the interrogative phrase in the question, so that [ia] is an elliptical version of *She got home yesterday morning*, and so on. The question in [id] concerns the complement of progressive ***be*** and the response serves as a replacement for ***do*** + *what* (cf. §7.6): *They were playing cards.* In [ii] B gives a negative answer to A's polar question, and then asserts a contrasting positive proposition. B's responses are thus equivalent to *I didn't read them all: <u>I read</u> only the first three* and *They weren't fighting: <u>they were</u> just shouting at each other.*

Radical reduction is also found with contrastive negation, as in:

[80] i A: *They've invited Jill.* B: *Yes, but not her husband.*
ii A: *They were shouting at each other.* B: *But not fighting.*

Her husband is contrasted with *Jill*, so that we understand "They have not invited her husband". And similarly for [ii]: "They were not fighting".

7.8.4 Gapping

'Gapping' is the name given to the construction where the medial segment of a clause is ellipted when anaphorically retrievable:

[81] i *Kim <u>lives</u> in Perth, Pat __ in Melbourne.*
ii *Tom <u>will</u> play the guitar and Mary __ sing.*
iii A: *I <u>will now show you how to make</u> clafouti.* B: *And I __ custard.*

[52] There are also a few fixed phrases where the missing material is not recoverable anaphorically: *Say when* ("when to stop pouring" – typically used as I pour you a drink); *I'll tell you what* (roughly "what we should do" – used to announce a suggestion); *Guess what* ("what has happened", or the like – invites the response *What?*, enabling me to go on to impart some new information). The subordinate interrogative construction illustrated in [78] is sometimes referred to in formal grammar as 'sluicing'.

In the simplest cases, the ellipted segment is just the verb, as in [i–ii], equivalent to *Pat lives in Melbourne* and *Mary will sing*. Often, however, what is ellipted consists of the verb together with following material, as in [iii]: *I will now show you how to make custard.* Note that in this case the ellipted material, shown by the underlining, does not form a syntactic constituent. In some cases the ellipted material is not a continuous sequence:

[82] *I had expected the Indians to win, Peter __ the Sri Lankans __.*

A distinctive property of this construction is that the gap (the first gap in cases like [82]) is flanked on either side by contrastive material: *Pat* and *in Melbourne* contrast with *Kim* and *in Perth*, while *Mary* and *sing* contrast with *Tom* and *play the guitar*. Note, then, that we cannot have **Tom will play the guitar and he __ sing too*, for there is no contrast between *Tom* and the coreferential *he*. In [81iii] the subject has the same form *I* in both clauses, but it has a different reference (to speaker A and speaker B respectively), and this is what matters for the contrast requirement.

The gapping construction is almost entirely restricted to coordinative constructions, and for that reason our main discussion of it is presented in Ch. 15, §4.2.

8 Comparatives

Anaphora contributes to the interpretation of comparative expressions in three main ways:

[1] i *The result wasn't as good as [I'd thought it would be __].*
ii *There were three apples on the plate; Ed took [the biggest].*
iii *I'd rather talk to Jill than Max: she is [more approachable].*

In [i] the bracketed sequence is a comparative clause, and such clauses are generally structurally incomplete relative to main clauses. In this case there is a missing predicative complement, which we interpret anaphorically as an AdjP headed by *good*. In [ii] the bracketed sequence is an NP with a superlative adjective as fused modifier-head; it is implicitly partitive, and we interpret it anaphorically as "the biggest of the three apples". In [iii] the bracketed sequence is a comparative phrase without a *than* complement expressing the secondary term in the comparison: this, however, can be recovered anaphorically as "than Max (is)". We will look very briefly at the first two cases, and then take up the issue of the recovery of an implicit secondary term.

Comparative clauses

Comparative clauses form a distinct subclass of subordinate clauses by virtue of the special kind of reduction they exhibit:

[2] i *Jill can run faster than [Ed can __].*
ii *She certainly went to more countries than [I went to __] / [I did].*
iii *The debate lasted longer than [__ was necessary].*

Ed can might appear to be an instance of the elliptical auxiliary stranding construction discussed in §7.1 above, where it could be used, say, as a response to the question *Who can run fast?* There is, however, an important difference in interpretation. In this latter context it is a reduced version of *Ed can run fast*, but that is not how it is interpreted in [i]. The comparative clause contains an implicit degree modification of *fast*, the comparison being between how fast Jill can run and how fast Ed can run, and there is no entailment that Ed can run fast. Analogously with *I did* in [ii], where ***do*** can be either the supportive auxiliary or the pro-form, as discussed in §7.2 above. The interpretation of *I did* when used as a response to *Did you go to many countries?* is "I went to many countries", but again that is not how it is interpreted in [ii], where the comparison is between how many countries she went to and how many I went to. Moreover, *I went to* in [ii] (with missing complement of the preposition) and *was necessary* in [iii] (with missing subject) could not occur as elliptical main clauses at all. For these reasons, the form and interpretation of comparative clauses has to be described separately from the constructions of §7: it is dealt with in Ch. 13, §2.

Fused-head NPs and related constructions

Comparative and superlative adjectival expressions can function as fused modifier-head, as described in §6.1 above. They normally have a partitive interpretation, with the partitive phrase either expressed overtly (*the younger <u>of the boys</u>*; *the most useful <u>of their suggestions</u>*) or merely implicit. In the latter case, the understood partitive is generally recovered from an antecedent, as in [1ii]. It can also be recovered non-anaphorically when the set concerned is salient in the situation of utterance, as when Ed takes an apple from a bowl on the table and I say *Look: he's taken the biggest again.* Closely related to the fused-head construction, as we have seen, is that with pro-form ***other*** as head: *Two of the apples are rotten, but you can have the others*, "the other apples (in that set)".

Recovery of an implicit secondary term in the comparison

When the secondary term in a comparison is overtly expressed, it takes the form of a PP headed by *than, as, to, from*, etc. Very often, however, the secondary term is not expressed in the comparative phrase, but is inferred from the context. Thus in [1iii] *more approachable* is interpreted as involving a comparison with Max. In this example, it would be possible to insert an overt *than* phrase (*she is more approachable <u>than him</u>*), and we can therefore legitimately talk of ellipsis of the comparative complement. But there are other cases where a secondary term is understood but could not be expressed within a comparative complement. In *Max and her other friends*, for example, the second NP refers to friends of hers other than Max, but this construction doesn't admit a *than* phrase: **Max and her other friends than him.* We won't analyse such cases in terms of ellipsis, therefore, but we can still say that *her other friends* is interpreted anaphorically – in the sense that it involves comparison with a secondary term which is recovered from an antecedent expression.

We will review here the way the comparison is interpreted when the secondary term is merely implicit, whether or not it could be expressed overtly within a comparative complement.

(a) Scalar comparison

[3] i *John works very hard, but Jill works <u>even harder</u>.*
ii *It's two metres long, maybe <u>a little longer</u>.*
iii *He has had three accidents in <u>as many months</u>.*
iv *I played a lot of tennis when I was <u>younger</u>.*
v *Can't you go <u>any faster</u>?*

In [i–iii] the secondary term is recovered anaphorically. Example [i] illustrates the elementary case of what we have called variable comparison. Here we could supply a comparative clause as complement of *than*: *even harder than John works*. In [ii] we have an implicit variable–constant comparison, with *a little longer* understood as "a little longer than two metres". The secondary term is also a constant in [iii], but here it would be at best highly unidiomatic to express the secondary term overtly: #*He has had three accidents in as many months as three/that.*

The implicit secondary term in [3iv–v] is recovered not anaphorically but from some aspect of the current situation. The comparison is with how young I am now and with how fast you are going now.

(b) *Same*

[4] i *She flew over to Paris at daybreak and returned to London later* <u>*the same day*</u>.
ii *While one arm of the US government was secretly selling arms to Iran, another arm was endeavouring to trap 17 individuals doing* <u>*the same thing*</u>.
iii *Suppose that instead of Irene leaving Soames for Bosiney, Soames had left Irene on account of* <u>*that same young architect*</u>.
iv *You find businesses going down the gurgle one week and almost immediately* <u>*the same people*</u> *bob up under a new name without any repercussions.*
v *Current sales and earnings are well up on the results achieved during* <u>*the same period last year*</u>.

Examples [i–iii] are straightforwardly anaphoric. In [i] we understand "the same day as (the day) she flew over to Paris at daybreak". In [ii] the interpretation is "the same thing as the first arm was doing"; *the same thing* is object of the general agentive verb ***do***, and the VP *doing the same thing* is interpreted as "secretly selling arms to Iran". In [iii] the underlined NP is coreferential with its antecedent *Bosiney*; where, as here, the NP has a demonstrative as determiner rather than the definite article it cannot be expanded to include an overt *as* phrase. Example [iv] illustrates what we have called the quasi-anaphoric use of expressions: there has been no prior mention of people as such, but the first clause does mention businesses, and *the same people* is understood as the people associated with those businesses – or, more specifically, the people running them. In [v] the secondary term is recovered from the situation of utterance: "the same period last year as we are now in".

In [4] *same* functions as modifier to a following head noun, but it is also commonly found as fused modifier-head or as head of an AdjP:

[5] i *Managers in commerce and industry must increase efficiency to help get us out of the economic slump, and* <u>*the same*</u> *applies to public-service managers.*
ii *If we give Kim a second chance, we'll have to do* <u>*the same*</u> *for Pat.*
iii A: *Jill's more interested in schoolwork than in boys.* B: *Sue is* <u>*just the same*</u>.

In the fused-head construction of [i–ii] *same* has a special interpretation, essentially "the same thing", in an abstract sense. The secondary term is in all three examples derivable anaphorically – "as applies to managers in commerce and industry", "as we do for Kim", "as Jill is".[53]

[53] There are some idiomatic uses where the comparative sense is largely bleached away – e.g. *I'm going* <u>*all the same*</u>, "nevertheless".

(c) *Such*

[6] i *His first film was a major hit, but this one has not been [such a success].*
ii *I've never had to wait [such a long time] before.*
iii *Cricket, football, and [such games] are played with the aim of instilling team spirit in the children.*
iv *Duvern wrote scripts for the Crawford police dramas and it was on [one such script] that he met Lynn Bayonas.*
v *Sure, it was tough financially to go on the road with the Socceroos but [such sacrifices] came with the job.*

Here *such* is an adjective functioning as modifier in NP structure. It may be concerned with either degree or kind.[54] The degree sense is seen in [i–ii] – compare *so great a success, so long a time.* In [i] the secondary term is retrieved anaphorically: "such a success as his first film". In [ii] (or at least the intended contextualisation of it) the secondary term is retrieved from the situation of utterance: "such a long time as this, i.e. as the time I'm currently having to wait".[55]

Examples [6iii–v] illustrate the 'kind' sense of *such*: we understand "games of this kind", and so on. All three are interpreted anaphorically; the antecedent is here in the same sentence, but very often it is in the preceding one. In [iii–iv] the antecedent is an NP; by virtue of the coordination in [iii] we understand *such games* as other games like cricket and football, whereas in [iv] *one such script* refers to a member of the set denoted by the antecedent, so that it is equivalent to *one of these scripts.* In [v] the antecedent is a clause, with the head noun *sacrifices* serving to categorise the act of going on the road with the Socceroos in a way which matches the predicative AdjP *tough financially.*

It is also possible, though less common, for *such* to occur without a head noun:

[7] i *Stories of Renamo 'slave camps' compete with those of Frelimo 'work camps'. Refugees fear both armies. But [such] is the nature of war in Africa.*
ii *Christ, Mahomet, [such] are the names that shepherds here have long invoked.*

Compare also the fixed expression *Such is life!* This use of *such* is found only with the verb ***be*** followed by an NP: the latter is subject and *such* is an adjectival predicative meaning approximately "like that, of that kind". But the non-canonical inverted order is obligatory: we can't have **But the nature of war in Africa is such.*

A special case of *such* forming a phrase on its own is as complement of *as*:

[8] i *This substance is poisonous and should be labelled as such.*
ii *It offers valid clues, even if they are only seen as such in retrospect.*
iii *He says that her stories are 'first-rate melodrama', though he thinks as such they're 'period pieces', as if melodrama had no twentieth-century cultural history.*
iv *We don't have a secretary as such.*

In this construction *such* is bleached of its usual comparative meaning. In [i–iii] it behaves like a non-comparative anaphor: we understand "labelled as poisonous", "seen as valid

[54] In legal register *such* may be concerned simply with identity: *This agreement shall be for an initial term of two years from the commencement date and may be terminated at the expiration of [such term] by either party giving to the other at least six months written notice in advance of its intention to do so. Such* here means much the same as ***this***: there can hardly be said to be any comparison.

[55] In the degree sense there need be no implied comparison at all: *It's such a pity Jill can't be with us,* "It's a great pity . . . "; the same applies with the degree adverb *so,* as in *It's so hot today.*

clues", "as (first-rate) melodrama". In [iv] *as such* has an idiomatic and metalinguistic sense: "We don't have a secretary in the strict sense of that term".

(d) *Different, differently*

[9] i *Older than Ed by two years, Tim was [very* <u>*different*</u> *in looks and temperament].*
ii *It is also important that the standards developed overseas will be suited to [the* <u>*different*</u> *conditions experienced by vehicles in Australia].*
iii *I've described massage with the recipient lying down, but this time we'll do it [*<u>*differently*</u>*] – sitting up.*
iv *Last time I came here I got [a very* <u>*different*</u> *reception].*
v *Things would have been [very* <u>*different*</u>*] if only they'd appointed Jo as manager.*
vi *You always like to be [*<u>*different*</u>*], don't you?*

Examples [i–iii] have *different* as a predicative or attributive adjective and *differently* as a manner adverb; in all three the secondary term in the comparison is recoverable anaphorically: "different from Ed", "different conditions from those obtaining overseas", "differently than with the recipient lying down". The salient interpretation of [iv] has the secondary term derived from the situation of utterance: "a very different reception from the one I'm getting now". Example [v] might occur in a context where its interpretation is anaphoric: it may be that I have just described how things actually were, so that *very different* would be understood as "very different from this, from what I've just described". But there need not have been any such description, the interpretation being simply "very different from what they are/were". Finally, [vi] has a special interpretation: we understand "different from other people".

(e) *Other* and related forms

[10] i *We were heading to Thursday Island and [the various* <u>*other*</u> *islands thereabouts].*
ii *When the film was shown to American troops fighting* <u>*the Second World War,*</u> *Conway's self-doubts were snipped, as were [*<u>*other*</u> *overtly anti-war scenes].*
iii *In Bombay itself this reformer ferreted out extortionists, embezzlers, and those guilty of [*<u>*other*</u> *corruption].*
iv *Haven't you got [any* <u>*other*</u> *shoes] you could wear?*

Other is here an adjective functioning as modifier in NP structure. In [i–iii] the secondary term is again recovered anaphorically – e.g. "other islands than Thursday Island". The head noun denotes a property common to both terms in the comparison, and hence serves to categorise the secondary term as well as the primary one: [ii], for example, conveys that the scene of Conway's self-doubts was an overtly anti-war scene. In [iii] the secondary term is not given directly by the nouns *extortionists* and *embezzlers* but by the abstract nouns morphologically related to them: we understand "other corruption than extortion and embezzlement". A natural contextualisation of [iv] illustrates the case where the secondary term is derived from the situation of utterance: "any other shoes than those you are wearing".

The following examples have the count noun ***other*** as head in NP structure:

[11] i *I was feeding the cat with one hand and pulling on my tights with [the* <u>*other*</u>*].*
ii *Each of the countless levels of the multi-storey car-hell is just like [the* <u>*others*</u>*].*
iii *No thanks, I prefer [the* <u>*others*</u>*].*

Example [i] is doubly anaphoric. In the first place, the secondary term is retrieved from the antecedent NP *one hand*: I was pulling my tights on with the other hand than the one I was feeding the cat with. Secondly, ***other*** is a pro-form interpreted from the antecedent nominal *hand* as "other hand". Similarly in [ii], though here the interpretation is complicated by the quantification expressed by *each*: we need to invoke the concept of bound variable, giving (in simplified form) "Each level *x* was just like the levels other than *x*". In the intended contextualisation of [iii] both the implicit secondary term and the denotation of pro-nominal ***other*** are derived from the situation of utterance – as, for example, "the other cakes, as distinct from these".

The compound *another* is a determinative; it can occur with a following head or else fuse with the head, but the interpretation follows the same principles as apply with the above adjective and noun forms:

[12] i *Whether she or [<u>another</u> terrorist] fired the fatal shot is unclear.*
ii *He has two children and his wife is expecting [<u>another</u>].*

These illustrate the alternative and additive senses of *another*: see Ch. 5, §7.9.

Otherwise rarely occurs with a *than* complement, and in many cases does not allow one. It has a range of uses, as illustrated in:

[13] i *You must certify that you will not sell or <u>otherwise</u> dispose of the property.*
ii *You'd better leave now; <u>otherwise</u> you'll get caught up in the rush-hour traffic.*
iii *It may have been an accident, but the evidence suggests <u>otherwise</u>.*
iv *I'll assume you'll be joining us unless you let me know <u>otherwise</u>.*
v *A person is presumed innocent until proved <u>otherwise</u>.*
vi *I wouldn't have wished it <u>otherwise</u>.*
vii *We are not yet able to determine the correctness or <u>otherwise</u> of this hypothesis.*

In [i] *otherwise* is a manner adjunct and can be glossed straightforwardly as "in any other way than by selling". In [ii] it is a conditional adjunct, equivalent to *if* + negative: "if you don't leave now". In [iii–iv] it serves as a pro-clause anaphor, with some resemblance to *so* and *not* as discussed in §7.7 above (though we noted that *know* does not admit the latter): "that it wasn't an accident", "that you won't be joining us". There is also a similarity with *so* in [v–vi], where *otherwise* is a pro-predicative: "proved not innocent (i.e. guilty)", "wished it (to be) other than it was". Finally, in [vii] *otherwise* appears as the second term in an *or*-coordination, indicating the opposite or negation of the first term, here "incorrectness". The part-of-speech classification of *otherwise* raises problems similar to those discussed for *so* at the end of §7.7.2.

(f) *Else*

[14] i *They don't realise that tastes differ just as much in sex as in [anything <u>else</u>].*
ii *Like [everything <u>else</u> in Rome, ruins and monuments alike], this house is lived in.*

As a comparative marker, *else* is semantically like *other*, but syntactically it occurs only as post-head dependent to certain fused determiner-heads and pronouns (*all, much, someone, nobody, what,* etc.).[56] The examples cited are interpreted anaphorically: "anything else than sex", "everything else besides this house".

[56] *Else* is also used to reinforce the disjunctive coordination expressed by *or*: see Ch. 15, §4.1.

9 Spatial location and change of location

Adjuncts and complements expressing location and change of location in space have been discussed in some detail in Ch. 8, §4; here we return to them with a view to examining the role that deixis and anaphora play in this area, beyond that covered in our discussion of the demonstratives.

9.1 *Here* and *there*

The intransitive prepositions *here* and *there* are distinguished as proximal and distal, like the demonstratives ***this*** and ***that*** respectively.

Deictic use

[1] i *Shall we put it <u>here</u>, or would you rather leave it over <u>there</u>?*
ii *Could you put it <u>here/there</u>, on the coffee table.*
iii *I've got a terrible pain just <u>here/there</u>.*
iv *You can't grow strawberries <u>here/there</u>.*
v *You come <u>here</u> to learn the piano, not to meet boys.*
vi *We'll have to stop <u>here/there</u> and continue next week.*

Here and *there* are commonly used deictically. *Here* refers to a location close to the speaker, *there* to one that is further away: [i] is an elementary example of this contrast. Both *here* and *there* can be followed by another locative expression that specifies the place more precisely, as in [ii], and likewise both are often accompanied by indexing gestures achieving the same effect, as would typically be the case in [iii]. As with the demonstratives, the proximal vs distal distinction is not a matter of purely objective physical location: there is a subjective element involved. In [ii–iii], for example, either could be used in reference to the same place, with different conceptualisations of it as close or not. One difference between *here* and *there* is illustrated in [iv]. These could both be used with quite local reference to a garden bed, for example, again relatively near with *here* or further away from me with *there*. But *here* could also be interpreted in a broader sense as "in this region, in this part of the world", whereas a corresponding interpretation for *there* ("in that region, in that part of the world") would generally be achieved anaphorically, by previous mention of the area, rather than deictically.

Expressions denoting spatial location often refer not primarily or exclusively to some physical place but rather to the institution, event, or activity associated with the place. This is seen for deictic *here* in [1v], where the reference might be to a piano class, say. In [vi] we have a temporal use of spatial *here* and *there*, interpreted as "at this/that point (in the progression of our activity)". Compare also *Christmas is here again*. Discourse deixis is illustrated in the interpretation of *You have a point there* where *there* refers to what you have just said. For the construction with initial *here* and *there*, as in *Here's/There's your money*, see Ch. 16, §5.3.

Anaphoric uses

[2] i *I put the keys <u>in the top drawer</u>; they should still be <u>there</u>.*
ii *The dog chased the boy <u>up a gum tree</u> and kept him <u>there</u> for an hour before going away.*

iii *Many Australians do not yet understand how much China has changed and what great trade opportunities exist there for Australia.*
iv *At the age of twenty-five he had walked into the mission as if he belonged here and had become a Christian.*
v *The main stadium was almost finished. Here, on the opening day of the games, participants from every country would parade.*

Anaphoric uses mainly involve *there*, *here* being primarily deictic. *There* in [i–iii], though primarily anaphoric, retains a distal deictic component of meaning, for it still indicates a place relatively removed from where I am now. In [iv] *here* is likewise simultaneously deictic and anaphoric: the utterance takes place in the mission, so that *here* has its primary deictic sense, but the antecedent provides a more specific referential interpretation. In the intended contextualisation of [v] the utterance takes place elsewhere than in the stadium: *here* is in this case non-deictic, purely anaphoric. It is debatable whether spatial expressions following *here* and *there* such as *here/there on the coffee table* in [1ii] should likewise be regarded as antecedents: if so, this will involve anticipatory anaphora as well as deixis.

Here and *there* can occur as complement to a preposition: *in here*, *from/to there*, and so on. When there is no governing preposition, they may be interpreted with the same reference as a prepositional antecedent. In [2ii], for example, *there* is interpreted as "up the gum-tree". But they may also be understood as incorporating some relatively neutral locative preposition such as *at*, *in*, *to* that is not present in the antecedent. Thus in [2iii/v] the antecedents are simply the NPs *China* and *the main stadium*, but we understand "in China", "in the main stadium". Similarly, in *Kim is in Paris and wants us to go there too*, we understand "to Paris", with "to" predictable from the goal role.

In casual style the antecedent is sometimes not even an NP but a modifier within an NP:

[3] i *This Canadian lady, she couldn't believe how cold it was and of course you know they get minus thirty or something over there.*
ii *Many a motel owner – when we've stopped there again – has remembered us and has said he preferred our dogs to most children.*

There is understood as "in Canada" in [i] and "at the motel" in [ii]; note that in this latter example the antecedent occurs within a quantified NP, and hence *there* is understood as expressing a bound variable, just like the personal pronoun *he* that follows.

Other uses

In addition to the deictic and anaphoric uses of *here* and *there* we find some specialised and more or less idiomatic uses. *Here and there* means "in various places" – compare *now and then* in §10.1.1 below. *Here's to the happy couple / the bride and groom / ...* is used for toasts. In *I want to climb the mountain simply because it is there* we understand "because it exists (as a challenge)".

9.2 *Come* and *go*

Deixis plays a major part in accounting for the relation between the verbs *come* and *go*, and certain similar pairs, such as *bring* and *take*. *Come* and *go* are verbs of motion and as such involve implicitly or explicitly a source and a goal (see Ch. 8, §4.3):

[4] i *Jill came to Melbourne from Sydney by bus.*
ii *Jill went from Sydney to Melbourne by bus.*

Here Sydney is the source, Melbourne the goal. The source is the place where the journey begins and is characteristically marked by *from*, while the goal is the place where it finishes and is characteristically marked by *to*.

Goal vs source orientation

One important difference between *come* and *go* is reflected in the specification of time:

[5] a. *Jill came home at four o'clock.* b. *Jill went to school at eight o'clock.*

In [a] *at four o'clock* gives the time of reaching the goal, whereas in [b] *at eight o'clock* gives the time of leaving the source (even though the source is not overtly expressed while the goal is). We will say, then, that *come* is **goal-oriented**, while *go* is **source-oriented**.

Initial contrast in terms of speaker's location at time of utterance

The simplest case of the contrast between *come* and *go* is seen in pairs like:

[6] i a. *Come in.* b. *Go away.*
ii a. *Come to the window.* b. *Go to the window.*

In [i] the complements of *in* and *away* are left unexpressed, but the implicit complements are understood deictically, i.e. in relation to features of the utterance-act. With goal-oriented *come* my location gives the implicit goal, while with source-oriented *go* it gives the implicit source. Thus we interpret *Come in* as "Come into the room where I am (or some other type of location than a room – a vehicle, tent, or whatever)", and *Go away* as "Go away from here". In [ii] the goal is explicitly expressed – but there is still an implicit deictic component in the interpretation. *Come to the window* implies that I am at the window, so just as before I am asking you to come to the place where I am located. *Go to the window* implies that I am not at the window, and again I am asking you to go to a place that is distal rather than proximal to where I am.

Come

The goal for *come* and source for *go* are not always identifiable in terms of the speaker's location at the time of utterance. We will survey the range of possibilities in the first instance for *come*. One variable factor is the time of the speaker's location at the goal. In [6] it is a matter of where I am now, at the time of utterance, but it does not have to be:

[7] i *Carla came to Tahiti to do a commercial while we were holidaying there.*
ii *Jill came round last night but I missed her as I was working late at the office.*

What motivates the *come* in [i] is that I was in Tahiti at the time of Carla's visit. In [ii] I was not at the goal location at the time of Jill's visit; it could be that I am there now, but it could just as well be that I am currently elsewhere – at the office again, perhaps. In the latter case, then, my association with the goal is just that this is where I typically am (on occasions of the relevant kind – i.e. in the evenings), that it is, as it were, my 'base'. The three possibilities are not mutually exclusive. If I'm at home, for example, and say *Jill's coming round to see me this evening*, the implicit goal is where I am now, where I will be at the time she comes, and also my base. The point is, however, that any one of them is sufficient to make *come* appropriate.

A second variable factor concerns what we have called the deictic centre. So far we have considered only the default case where the deictic centre is the speaker, where the goal is identifiable with my location now, then (at the time of the event), or typically. But the deictic centre can instead be the addressee. Here I present the matter from your perspective:

[8] i *OK, I'm coming.*
ii *I'm told Carla came to Tahiti to do a commercial while you were holidaying there.*
iii *Jill says you were out when she came round to see you last night.*

Thus [i] is a typical response to a summons: the goal is where you currently are. In [ii] the goal is where you were at the time of the event. And in [iii] you weren't there then and needn't be there now: in this case the goal is your base. Your perspective and mine may of course coincide: in *Jill's coming round to see us tonight*, it may be a matter of where you and I are now, and will be then, and/or where we have our base.

It is also possible for the deictic centre to shift to someone else who is prominent in the discourse:

[9] i *Ed wants me to come over immediately and check the proofs with him.*
ii *Ed says Carla came to Tahiti to do a commercial while he was holidaying there.*
iii *Ed says Jill came round to see him last night while he was out.*

In these examples I take Ed's perspective rather than my own. In [i] it is a matter of coming to where Ed is now; in [ii] Carla came to where Ed was then; and in [iii] (uttered, let us assume, at the workplace I share with Ed) Jill came to Ed's base.

The range of possibilities is summarised in [10], where the deictic centre is the person whose perspective is being taken, the person whose location at the goal satisfies the conditions for the use of *come*:

[10] i The deictic centre may be the speaker, the addressee, or someone else in the context of discourse.
ii The person who constitutes the deictic centre may be located at the goal at utterance-time, event time, or typically.

Go

The same possibilities are available for *go*, this time applying to the source rather than the goal, but again not mutually exclusive:

[11] i a. *Will you please go and get my slippers.*
b. *We went to the movies last night.*
c. *The children will be going to school by bus while we are in Scotland.*
ii a. *Could you go and check whether I turned the oven on.* (said on the telephone)
b. *Did you go to the movies last night?*
c. *Will the children be going to school by bus while you are in Scotland?*
iii a. *If that's Ed on the phone, ask him to go and see if I left my hat in his car.*
b. *Ed went to the movies last night.*
c. *Will Ed's children be going to school by bus while he is in Scotland?*

The deictic centre is the speaker in [i], the addressee in [ii], and Ed in [iii]. And in each set the implicit source is the place where the person constituting the deictic centre is now in [a], was at the time of the event in [b], and has their base in [c].

In a great many cases the same event can be expressed with *come* or *go*, depending on the perspective taken. Consider, for example:

[12] i *Phil came to the office yesterday morning.*
ii *Phil went to the office yesterday morning.*

Among the numerous scenarios allowed for in the above account is one where I work at the office concerned but am at some other place at the time of utterance. *Come* then reflects my perspective: I was at the office at the time he came and/or have the office as my base (i.e. the place where I typically am during working hours). *Go*, by contrast, reflects Phil's perspective: the place he set out from was (necessarily) where he was at the time of departure and (possibly) where he had his base (his home). There are, however, circumstances in which one of the verbs is required or at least strongly preferred. The examples in [6] are of this kind: here the time of the event is the immediate future and one of the terminal points in the journey is where I am now. *Come* is required if that place is goal, *go* if it is source. Similarly for the past time event in [12]: if I am at the office at the time of utterance, *come* is virtually obligatory, but if I am not there, and don't work there, *go* will be preferred, especially if I am now or was then at Phil's home base.

Combination with *here* and *there*

In general, *come* selects proximal *here* from the *here/there* pair as goal, while *go* selects distal *there*:

[13] i a. *Come here.* b. *Go over there.*
ii a. *She's coming here next week.* b. *She's going there next week.*

Come, however, can certainly combine with *there* as goal:

[14] i *If you don't be quiet, I'll come over <u>there</u> and sort you out.*
ii *I met Ed in Cairns. He had come <u>there</u> after graduation in 1988 and was working for a firm of stockbrokers.*

In [i] *there* is deictic and the distal meaning reflects my perspective, whereas *come* takes your perspective, the goal being where you are now. In [ii] *there* is anaphoric, while *come* is motivated by the fact that at the time which is salient in the discourse (the time of my meeting Ed) both he and I were at the place referred to by *there*. On the other hand *go* is not normally compatible with *here* as goal: #*They went here last year too.*[57]

9.3 Further cases of deictic and anaphoric interpretations of spatial expressions

(a) Implicit location

We have noted in our discussion of *come* and *go* that source and goal elements can be left unexpressed while nevertheless being understood. This is in fact a very pervasive phenomenon, extending far beyond these two verbs. Other cases are discussed in Ch. 7, §2.4, and Ch. 8, §4.3; here we will confine ourselves to the prepositions *away* and *back*,

[57] One special case where *go* can take *here* as goal is when *here* is accompanied by an indexing act, pointing for example to a place on a map.

with a view to illustrating how the interpretation derives from the deictic and anaphoric concepts introduced above. First, *away*:

[15] i *Don't wander away.*
ii *The bird perched on the balcony rail and then flew away again.*
iii *Next week-end is a public holiday, so a lot of people will be away.*
iv *Liz regretted that her parents lived so far away.*

Away is understood as "away from source *x*", with this unspecified source recoverable from the context. In [i] it is implicitly deictic, with the speaker as deictic centre: "away from here, i.e. where I am now". In [ii] the interpretation is derived anaphorically: "flew away from the balcony rail". Example [iii] has the 'base' interpretation: "away from home"; there is an anaphoric component too inasmuch as it's a matter of being away from **their** base. Example [iv] illustrates the close relation between deixis and anaphora. We can think of the interpretation as deriving anaphorically, as "away from Liz", but we can also handle it in terms of deictic shift, with Liz the deictic centre, giving "away from the place where the person constituting the deictic centre, Liz, has their home base".

Back in the following is understood with an implicit goal or location:

[16] i *Off you go, then, but hurry back.*
ii *She travelled from Sydney to Melbourne by train and flew back two days later.*
iii *Max felt more secure now that his parents were back.*

In [i] we have an implicit deictic goal: "back here, to where I am". The salient interpretation of [ii] is anaphoric: "back to Sydney". Example [iii] has the 'base' interpretation: "back home", but it can be Max's home, not just the parents'.

(b) Orientation

Certain prepositions or prepositional idioms, such as *behind* and *in front*, sometimes involve orientation with respect to an assumed observer. Compare:

[17] i *He has parked his car behind the town-hall.*
ii *There's a snake behind that rock.*

A town-hall has an inherent front and back, and *behind* / *in front of the town-hall* may be interpreted with respect to that inherent orientation. The *behind* phrase in [i] can therefore be understood as, approximately, "at the back of the town-hall". But that is not the only possibility, and for [ii] there is no interpretation of this kind because a rock, unlike a town-hall, has no inherent front and back. The natural interpretation of [ii], then, is "There's a snake on the other side of the rock, i.e. on the side opposite that closest to me, the observer", and the corresponding reading is available for [i]. In this case the implicit observer is the speaker, constituting the deictic centre, but again the perspective can be that of some other person involved in the situation, as in *Liz found a snake behind the rock.*

Behind and *in front* also allow for an understood complement to be left unexpressed. Compare, then:

[18] *There's a huge furniture van behind.*

In the absence of further context inducing an anaphoric reading, this is likely to be interpreted along the lines discussed above for [16i/17ii], with the complement implicitly deictic, giving "behind us". A plausible scenario is that we are travelling in a car or other vehicle, and vehicles, like town-halls, have an inherent front and back. The back of the vehicle then provides the orientation for the interpretation of *behind*, the back being the end closer to the furniture van.

9.4 Location of antecedents and referents in the discourse

One special case of location is location in the discourse:

[19] i [*The above-mentioned processes*] *will be discussed more fully in Ch. 3.*
ii *There are no data to confirm* [*the above formulas*].

In [i] *above-mentioned* indicates that the processes have been mentioned earlier in the discourse, and hence that there is an anaphoric link to a preceding antecedent. In [ii] *the above formulas* refers to formulas that themselves appear earlier in the discourse: this, then, is a case of what we have called discourse deixis. Location in the discourse can be conceptualised in either spatial or temporal terms: compare *mentioned above* and *mentioned earlier.* Spatial terms are generally restricted to written texts (or reading from a prepared written text), while the temporal terms are neutral as to the medium; we will cover both types in this subsection, which thus provides a transition between the present major section on spatial location and the next one on temporal deixis and anaphora.

Antecedents are, by definition, part of the discourse, but for the most part anaphors do not directly indicate where in the discourse the antecedent is to be found. Note in this connection that the demonstratives ***this*** and ***that*** express respectively proximal and distal meaning when used deictically,[58] but are not in their anaphoric use distinguished in terms of the relative distance between antecedent and anaphor. Our concern with anaphora here, then, is limited to those cases where the anaphor does express information about the spatial or temporal location of the antecedent.

Many spatial and temporal expressions can be used indifferently for location in discourse or for location elsewhere. We can use *the last paragraph* to refer to the preceding paragraph in the current written discourse, but we can equally have *the last president.* Similarly with terms such as *preceding* or *following, earlier* and *later, first, second, next,* and so on. But there are a few items that are specialised to the location in discourse use, and it is these we will focus on here.

Above and related expressions

Above is primarily a preposition (transitive or intransitive), but also belongs (by conversion) to the adjective category, where it is used either attributively or as fused modifier-head:

[20] i	*the discussion above*	[preposition: post-head modifier]
ii	*the above discussion*	[adjective: pre-head modifier]
iii	*Her conclusion is the same as* [*the above*].	[adjective: fused modifier-head]

The preposition use is not restricted to location in the discourse, but the adjective *above* is. Thus we have *the room above* meaning "the room above a certain room, the one I'm in or one previously mentioned", but *the above room* cannot be interpreted in this way. Unlike *above, below* has no special discourse-location use: it belongs only to the preposition

[58] In discourse deixis they differ in that only ***this*** can be used in reference to what follows.

category, so we have either *the discussion below* (location within this discourse) or *the room below* (ordinary spatial location), but not **the below discussion.* We do, however, have *under-mentioned* matching *above-mentioned*, both of them belonging to formal style.

Adjectival *above* is predominantly used in discourse deixis, with *above-mentioned* (or legal register *aforementioned*) used for anaphora, as in [19], but *above* is also used in the "above-mentioned" sense, as in *the above scholars*, etc.

Former and *latter*

[21] i *They moved from [the old Treasury Buildings]$_i$ to Government House ballroom across the road; American military authorities were in [the former place]$_i$.*
ii *Other recent papers include Voegelin & Voegelin 1977 and [Hill 1980]$_i$; [the latter paper]$_i$ contains an extensive bibliography on the subject.*
iii *Many people are inclined to speak of all 'public relations' as ballyhoo or [propaganda], perhaps overlooking the early meaning of [the latter word].*
iv *Max never did learn what [Lee]$_i$ wanted, for [the latter]$_i$ shook hands and moved towards the door.*
v *It is not easy to make an economic comparison between [clay pots]$_i$ and [the various substitutes]$_j$; [the former]$_i$ may last indefinitely with luck, while the [latter]$_j$ are often expendable, used only once.*

The adjectives *former* and *latter*, containing the comparative suffix ·*er*, are used attributively, as in [i–iii], or as fused modifier-head, as in [iv–v]. Example [iii] is another case of discourse deixis: *propaganda* is the referent, not the antecedent, of *the latter word*; in all the other examples there is an anaphoric link between the NP containing *former* or *latter* and the bracketed co-indexed element. In the attributive use *former* and *latter* have other senses not concerned with location in the discourse (*her former husbands*; *the latter half of the nineteenth century*), but the fused-head uses are always anaphoric.

In their anaphoric or discourse deictic uses, *former* and *latter* imply a set of potential antecedents or discourse referents: *former* then picks out the first in the set (e.g. *clay pots* in [v]), while *latter* picks out the last in the set (thus *the various substitutes* in [v]). Precisely because there is a set of potential antecedents or discourse referents, the locational feature expressed by *former* and *latter* makes them more appropriate than, say, the personal pronouns: *it* in [ii], for example, would be quite incomprehensible. The set concerned usually has just two members, but it is not uncommon (at least with *latter*) for it to contain more than two. Ordinal numerals such as *first*, *second*, etc., can be used in a comparable way, but these are clearly not specialised for location in discourse in the way that *former* and *latter* are.[59]

[59] Another pair of terms occasionally used with the same effect as *former* and *latter* are *one* and *other*: *[The sublime]$_i$ and [the beautiful]$_j$ are indeed ideas of a very different nature, [one]$_i$ being founded on pain, [the other]$_j$ on pleasure.* These, however, do not express any ordering meaning, so that the pairing of antecedent and anaphor is not determined semantically, as it would be with *former* and *latter*. Compare, for example, *Kim and Pat had both done brilliantly, one having scored 99%, the other 95%*, which does not force an interpretation where it was Kim who scored 99%.

A related phenomenon: *respective* and *respectively*

The order in which expressions occur in the discourse may also be relevant to the interpretation of clauses containing the adjective *respective* and the adverb *respectively*:

[22] i *Hercule Poirot and Lord Peter Wimsey (the respective creations of Agatha Christie and Dorothy Sayers) have retained Holmes' egotism but not his zest for life and eccentric habits.*

ii *The letters D, E, and X in the column following each field of study indicate that this programme is offered as a major study by day, evening, and external courses, respectively.*

Respective in [i] serves to pair *Hercule Poirot* with *Agatha Christie*, and *Lord Peter Wimsey* with *Dorothy Sayers*; similarly, *respectively* in [ii] pairs *D* with *day*, *E* with *evening*, and *X* with *external*. This time, however, the relation between the paired items is not that of antecedent to anaphor, nor referent to deictic referring expression. Rather, the plural in *creations* and the coordination *day, evening, and external* are interpreted distributively, and the pairing indicates how the distribution is to be understood. Thus Hercule Poirot is Agatha Christie's creation while Lord Peter Wimsey is Dorothy Sayers' creation; and similarly D indicates that the programme so annotated is offered as a major study by day course, that the one annotated with E is offered by evening course, and that the one with X is offered by external course.

Such pairing is not invariably found – indeed it occurs with only a small proportion of the uses of *respective*. Compare, then:

[23] i *Liszt played this version through to Berlioz and Wagner on their respective visits to Weimar.*

ii *Two of the children were later the celebrated eighteenth-century beauties the Gunning sisters, who became respectively Countess of Coventry and Duchess of Hamilton.*

iii *For the two subsequent years the Government has set indicative planning levels of 110,000 and 125,000, respectively.*

In [i] *respective* merely indicates that Berlioz and Wagner visited Weimar separately rather than together. In [ii], one of the sisters became Countess of Coventry and the other the Duchess of Hamilton, but the sisters are not separately referred to. In [iii] 111,000 is the indicative planning level for one year and 125,000 for the other; again there is no separate reference to the two years, but we understand that 111,000 is the level for the first of them, 125,000 for the second. (Indeed, a likely but not necessary interpretation of [ii] is that it was the elder sister who became Countess of Coventry.)

Syntactically, *respective* functions attributively within a plural NP, while *respectively* is always associated with a coordination. In [23ii] *respectively* precedes the first coordinate and in [23iii] it follows the last coordinate, but it can also be located higher in the constituent structure than the coordination itself, as in [22ii], where it follows an NP containing the coordination as pre-head modifier.

10 Temporal deixis and anaphora

Deixis and anaphora play a major role in the domain of time as well as in that of space. One very important case of deixis is that of primary tense, the inflectional contrast between preterite and present tense:

[1]	PRETERITE	PRESENT TENSE
i	a. *I promised to do it this week.*	b. *I promise to do it this week.*
ii	a. *She lived in Melbourne.*	b. *She lives in Melbourne.*

In elementary examples of this kind, preterite indicates past time and present tense indicates present time, where past and present time are deictic concepts. In the intended interpretation of [i] we are concerned with a single act of promising; in [ia] this act is located at a time earlier than the time of utterance, whereas in [ib] the time of the act is identified as the time of utterance. The examples in [ii] are imperfective, her living in Melbourne being a state; I am not concerned with the state in its entirety but am referring to a time at which it obtained or obtains. *She lived in Melbourne*, for example, does not entail that she doesn't live in Melbourne now (cf. *She already lived in Melbourne at that time*). But again the time actually referred to in [ia] is past, prior to the time of utterance, while in [ib] it is present.

There is, of course, a great deal more to inflectional tense than this: the question is dealt with in detail in Ch. 3, §4. Our concern in this section is with other ways of locating a situation in time, with temporal expressions having the form of PPs, NPs, or AdvPs.

10.1 Basic uses

We look first at what we will call 'basic uses' of temporal expressions, as opposed to those where there is a shift in the deictic centre, which we take up in §10.2.

10.1.1 *Now* and *then*

Proximal *now* and distal *then* are the temporal counterparts of spatial *here* and *there* respectively. *Now* is predominantly deictic while *then*, in its temporal sense, is usually anaphoric.

Deictic *now*

[2] i *He is now twenty-eight.*
ii *He estimates there'll be only half as many Europeans in 100 years as there are now.*
iii *Now you know why I'm so afraid of the ID card they want to introduce.*
iv *She was here just now.*
v *I want you to do it now, as soon as you've finished lunch.*

In its primary use, *now* refers to an interval of time that includes the moment of utterance, as in [i–iii]. The use of *now* often involves a contrast between the present and the past or future. Such a contrast is explicit in [ii], implicit in [iii]: we understand in the latter that recent events (typically something that has been said in the discourse) have brought about a changed situation where you know something you didn't know before. *Now* can take a content clause complement specifying what distinguishes the present time from the pre-now period: *Now that the exams are over, we can start enjoying ourselves again.*

The proximal meaning of *now* does not require that its reference actually include the moment of utterance. In [2iv] it refers to a time just before the moment of speech; this is hardly possible without the modifier *just*. In [v] *now* is used for the very near future. Such cases are comparable to the use of *here* for a place that does not include that where the speaker is located but is close by; this use is much commoner with *here* than with *now*, however, no doubt because the nearby location can be identified indexically, whereas that is not possible for time.

Deictic *then*

[3] A: *Did you hear a scream?* B: *When?* A: *Just then.*

Distal *then* is mostly used anaphorically, but it can refer deictically to a time in the very recent past, as here. A different case is where I am watching a film or video, or looking at a photograph depicting past events, and say, for example, *We were happier then.*

Anaphoric *then*

[4] i *They were married in 1982; he was then just short of twenty-one.*
ii *He first stood for Parliament in the 1968 election, for the Mount Hagen constituency where he was then working.*
iii *In the lower forms, you will remember, I was a good student and already then I felt myself specially ear-marked for fame.*
iv *They were fighting as usual about money, and it was then I realised I had to get away.*
v *She did some gardening and then had a rest.*
vi *The review had been ordered by the then Premier, Mr Dunstan.*

Example [i] illustrates the simplest case, with the antecedent a temporal PP. In [ii] the antecedent PP refers to an event, with *then* interpreted as "at the time of the 1968 election". In [iii] *in the lower forms* is not itself a temporal expression, but we understand "when I was in the lower forms", and that is the time *then* refers to. In [iv] we have the common case where the antecedent is a clause; *then* is coreferential with the preterite tense of this clause. Very often *then* refers not to the same time as that of its antecedent but to a time closely following, as in [v]: we understand "after that". As well as functioning as adjunct in clause structure, *then* can modify a noun, as in [vi] – or an attributive adjective: *It travelled at the then incredible speed of 420 mph.* The reference here is to the time of the situation expressed in the clause containing *then.*

Other uses

Now and then is an idiom meaning "sometimes, but not very often". *Then* is commonly used as a conditional connective, as when you say *Kim will be at the party* and I reply *Then you can count me out* ("in that case"). Both forms are also used as pure discourse connectives: *Now, where were we up to?*; *Now then, what's all the trouble?*

10.1.2 Other temporal expressions

The ternary system pre-proximal vs proximal vs post-proximal

While *now* and *then* contrast in a binary system of proximal vs distal, there is in addition a quite elaborate system of temporal deictic expressions based on a ternary contrast of

pre-proximal vs **proximal** vs **post-proximal**. It is illustrated initially in the pronouns:

[5]	PRE-PROXIMAL	PROXIMAL	POST-PROXIMAL
	yesterday	*today*	*tomorrow*

Today refers to the day on which the utterance takes place, *yesterday* and *tomorrow* to the days immediately before and after that day. The three terms also have secondary senses in which *today* refers more generally to the present, *yesterday* and *tomorrow* to the past and future: *Today the inflation rate is less than 3%*; *We're not interested in yesterday's designs – only the current ones will do.*

Syntactically complex expressions contain temporal nouns denoting culturally determined time-units, which fall into two classes, **non-positional** and **positional**, as in [6i–ii] respectively:

[6] i *day, week, month, year, century, millennium*
ii a. *morning, afternoon, evening, night*
b. *Sunday, Monday, Tuesday, Wednesday, Thursday, Friday, Saturday*
c. *January, February, March, April, May, June, July, August, September, October, November, December*
d. *spring, summer, autumn, winter*

The non-positional nouns denote time intervals that follow each other immediately, while the positional ones denote intervals that form part of a cycle: a day is followed by another day, but a morning is followed by an afternoon. 'Positional' indicates that the interval has a fixed position within the cycle.[60]

The regular realisation of the ternary system is by means of *last*, *this*, and *next*:

[7]	PRE-PROXIMAL	PROXIMAL	POST-PROXIMAL	
i	*last week*	*this week*	*next week*	[non-positional]
ii	*last Thursday*	*this Thursday*	*next Thursday*	[positional]

There are irregular forms for *day*, which have already been given in [5],[61] and for the positional nouns in [6iia], which are as follows:

[8]			
i	*yesterday morning*	*this morning*	*tomorrow morning*
ii	*yesterday afternoon*	*this afternoon*	*tomorrow afternoon*
iii	*yesterday / last evening*	*this evening*	*tomorrow evening*
iv	*last night*	*tonight*	*tomorrow night*

Non-positional terms for shorter intervals than a day do not enter into this system, though the proximal forms *this second/minute* are readily used deictically (*You must do it this minute*). *Fortnight* (BrE) and *decade* belong semantically in the non-positional set, but hardly enter into the ternary system, though again the proximal form is possible (*I've not received my pay this fortnight*; *The problem is unlikely to be solved this decade*).

[60] Positional *night* also forms a cycle with *day* in a positional sense, distinct from non-positional *day*, which denotes a period of 24 hours. Similarly, positional *weekend* contrasts with *week* in a positional sense distinct from the non-positional *week*, which denotes a period of seven days – cf. *at the weekend or during the week.* (There is also a term *weekday*, but it does not form a cycle with *weekend*, and does not form deictic expressions of the kind we are concerned with here.)

[61] *This day* can be used instead of *today* in complement function (*This day has been one of the happiest I can remember*), and very occasionally as an adjunct (e.g. in real estate agents' notices: *Auction this day*).

Interpretation with non-positional terms

Here the proximal form refers to the time-unit containing the moment of utterance:

[9] i *I only learnt about it this week.*
ii *I promise I'll finish the job this week.*

These locate the learning and finishing situations within the week containing the day on which I utter the sentence, with other factors indicating earlier and later respectively. *Last week* and *next week* then refer to the weeks immediately preceding and following this week. There is, however, some ambiguity or indeterminacy over the boundaries between one week and another. *Week* may be interpreted calendrically, as a period beginning on a fixed day (with the added complication that while the first day is usually taken as Sunday, there are some speakers, mainly BrE, for whom it begins on Monday), or non-calendrically, as a seven-day period beginning today.

Interpretation with positional terms

Matters are here more complex, and there are differences among speakers with respect to the use of some forms. There are also differences with respect to the sets given in [6ii].

With the four parts of the day, the forms are given in [8], whose interpretation is quite clear. *This morning* refers to the morning of today, whether I am speaking during the morning or later in the day. *Yesterday morning* refers to the morning of yesterday and *tomorrow morning* to that of tomorrow. Similarly for the other forms.

With the months of the year, a proximal form such as *this July* can be used unproblematically to refer to the month containing the day on which I am speaking. It can also be used when it is not now July to refer to a month that is relatively close to the current one (before or after) – in keeping with the ordinary proximal meaning of demonstrative *this*. It will typically fall within the current year, but it does not have to: *this February*, said in December, is more likely to refer to the February of the following year than to that of the current one. We saw in discussing the spatial demonstratives that there is no absolute, objective difference between proximal and distal, so that I might refer to an object reasonably close to me as either *this* or *that*, and the same applies with temporal deixis. If we are now in July I might refer to the April of this year as *this April* or *last April*, and to the October of this year as *this October* or *next October*. *This* will normally be used to the exclusion of *last* and *next* for a month adjacent to the current one, and will be preferred for a month one and perhaps also two steps further away, especially in the future. In such cases *last* and *next* can be used to refer to a month one year further away, i.e. to the specified month on an earlier or later cycle. A further possibility is to use the preposition *in* with the month-name by itself: *She was married / is getting married in April.* This form is not normally used for the current month, but can apply deictically to the nearest April in the past or future.

Essentially the same principles apply with the seasons and the positional term *weekend*: *They moved to Paris last autumn*; *We're getting married next weekend.* The prepositional construction, however, is not often used deictically with the seasons, and with *weekend* has *at* (BrE) or *on* (AmE, AusE) rather than *in*: *What did you do at/on the weekend?*

The days of the week work in a similar way except that such forms as *this/last/next Tuesday* are not normally used for today, yesterday, or tomorrow; and some speakers restrict *this* to future time. Many speakers would also avoid *this/last/next Tuesday*, etc., in reference to the days standardly referred to as *the day before yesterday* and *the day after tomorrow*. The preposition this time is *on*: *They left last/this/on Tuesday* could all be said on Friday in reference to the preceding Tuesday. It is also possible, especially in AmE, to omit the preposition: %*They left / are leaving Tuesday for Chicago.*

Complex forms involving two temporal nouns

There are also numerous expressions that are syntactically more complex, involving the embedding of one phrase within another:

[10] i *the day before yesterday, the day after tomorrow, a week from today, the Sunday before last, the Sunday after next*
ii *today week, a week today, a week on Tuesday, a week last/next Saturday*

The interpretation of expressions like those in [i] is straightforwardly predictable from the form (with *last* and *next* elliptical for "last/next Sunday"). Those in [ii], however, do not fit into ordinary NP constructions. *Today week* and *a week today* both mean the same as *a week from today*, so if today is Monday they refer to next Monday. The *today week* frame allows *tomorrow* or a day-name such as *Tuesday* as replacements for *today* and (mainly in BrE) *fortnight* as a replacement for *week*. The *a week today* pattern allows quantification of the first phrase (*two weeks today*), replacement of *week* by *fortnight, month, year*, and replacement of *today* by *tomorrow*. Some speakers have the pattern %*a week Tuesday* in the sense "a week next Tuesday".

Other deictic expressions

A sample of other temporal expressions that are or can be interpreted deictically is given in [11] (and see also the discussion of the aspectual adjuncts *already, still, yet, any longer* in Ch. 8, §8):

[11] i PAST *in the past, formerly, hitherto, recently, previously, two weeks ago, in days gone by, in former/previous times, up till now*
ii PRESENT *at present, at this time, these days, nowadays, currently*
iii FUTURE *in future, later, immediately, straightaway, soon, in two weeks, in the coming weeks, in the weeks ahead, henceforth*

Two weeks ago and *in two weeks* are illustrative of general patterns, with other time-measures able to replace *two weeks*; *ago* measures backwards from now, while *in* measures forwards. It will be noted that the motion verbs *come* and *go* figure in some expressions, so that we have *gone* for past and *coming* for future. *Coming* also combines with proximal *this*, making explicit that reference is to the future: compare *this Tuesday* (past or future) and *this coming Tuesday* (future only). The metaphor here is of time moving past the world from the future into the past, with now the goal for *come* and the source for *go*. Compare similarly *Summer has come and gone already, The days are going past so quickly*, and so on. A different metaphor has time as a spatial line along which the world is moving from the past into the future: hence expressions like *the weeks ahead* – and formulations like *the tasks that lie before us* or *These problems are now behind us.*

Anaphoric uses and counterparts

Some of the expressions mentioned above can be used anaphorically as well as deictically, while for others there are distinct anaphoric counterparts. Compare:

[12] DEICTIC / ANAPHORIC

i a. *We will soon be home.* b. *He ran off and was soon out of sight.*

ii a. *She's going to Bath next week.* b. *She arrived in London on 3 June and planned to go to Bath the following week.*

Soon refers to a time shortly after some time of orientation, which can be the time of utterance, as in [ia] ("soon after now"), or a time defined in the context of discourse, as in [ib] ("soon after then – i.e. after the time when he ran off"). In [ii] *next week* refers to the week after the one containing today, but for the week after the one containing 3 June we need *the following week* (or *the next week*).

Other expressions which follow the pattern of *soon* are given in [13], while contrasting deictic and anaphoric forms are shown in [14]:

[13] *at this time, afterwards, before, previously, later, recently, in April*

[14] i *yesterday, last week* — *the previous day/week, the day/week before*

ii *today, this week* — *that day/week*

iii *tomorrow, next week* — *the next/following day/week, the day/week after*

iv *a week ago* — *a week before/earlier/previously*

In + month-name is predominantly deictic, but is included in [13] because anaphoric examples like *They went to Washington in January 1978 but came home again in April* (i.e. "April 1978") are also possible. Very often, however, a distinctively anaphoric expression would be preferred, such as *in the April of that year* or *the following April.* With days of the week, only this latter type of expression is possible: *They arrived on Monday 10 January and left on the (following) Friday. On Friday* here would have only a deictic interpretation ("last Friday").

Expressions with demonstrative *that* are virtually restricted to anaphoric use;[62] the predominantly deictic *this* can also be used anaphorically, but not normally in NPs like *this week* in adjunct function (as indicated in [14ii]):

[15] i *1934 was a bad year. That summer the gambling houses were closed, . . .*

ii *She lost her job soon after her father died. She was still in her fifties at this time, much too young for retirement.*

10.2 Shift of deictic centre

So far we have been concerned with cases where deictic expressions are interpreted in relation to the speaker's 'now', the time of utterance. But it is also possible for the deictic centre to be shifted away from the speaker. One rather minor instance of such a shift is where *now* is interpreted in relation to the time of decoding rather than encoding. This has been illustrated with examples of written notices such as *You are now leaving West Berlin* or *Now wash your hands.*

More important is the deictic shift that occurs in free indirect style:

[62] The qualification 'virtually' is to allow for cases like *There were a lot of jacarandas out that November, weren't there?*, said while watching a video of a November wedding (cf. the similar example given for *then* in §10.1.1 above).

[16] *Cheryl . . . had turned into such boring company; the suggestion that she come back to Robertson with Emma for a couple of days she treated as if she was being asked to take a canoe down the Limpopo. And to think that* <u>*only four years ago*</u> *her friend had been the epitome of sixth form rebellion.*

This passage from a work of fiction is reporting the thoughts of the main character, Emma, and the time referred to by *only four years ago* is four years before the time at which she was having these thoughts – not four years before the time of writing. Emma's perspective is also reflected in the use of *come* (cf. §9.2) – but the shift doesn't affect the category of person, so that we have *Emma*, not *me*, and *her friend* (i.e. Emma's friend Cheryl), not *my friend*. It is precisely the use of a deictic rather than anaphoric expression (*only four years before*) that indicates that the passage is in free indirect style, taking the perspective of the person involved rather than of the narrator. *Now* can be used in the same way:

[17] *They had stripped him of his musket and equipment and* <u>*now*</u> *they were pulling his boots and jacket off.*

18

Inflectional morphology and related matters

Frank Palmer
Rodney Huddleston
Geoffrey K. Pullum

1 Preliminaries

This chapter and the next are concerned with morphology, that part of a grammar that deals with the form of words. As explained in Ch. 1, §4.3, morphology is divided into two subcomponents: we look first at inflectional morphology and then in Ch. 19 turn to lexical word-formation.

Inflectional morphology vs lexical word-formation

The distinction between these two subcomponents of morphology may be illustrated with reference to a set of words such as the following:

[1]	i	*simple*	*simpler*	*simplest*	
	ii	*simpleton*	*simpletons*	*simpleton's*	*simpletons'*
	iii	*simplify*	*simplifies*	*simplified*	*simplifying*

The three words in [i] are forms of the same lexeme, which we represent in bold face as ***simple***. *Simpleton* and *simplify*, however, are not forms of this lexeme: they are forms, together with the other words in [ii–iii] respectively, of the lexemes ***simpleton*** and ***simplify***.

As is implied by saying that they are forms of the same lexeme, *simple*, *simpler*, and *simplest* represent the same lexical item, the same vocabulary item. They are forms of this item that are required or permitted in different syntactic constructions. In the frame '*This is __ than that*', for example, only the comparative form *simpler* is permitted, and similarly the frame '*This is the __ of them all*' requires the superlative form *simplest*. And if we replace the lexeme ***simple*** by another adjective, we will still need a comparative and superlative form in these constructions: *This is cheaper than that* and *This is the cheapest of them all*, and so on.

Simpleton and *simplify*, by contrast, represent different vocabulary items, different lexemes. From a syntactic point of view, the fact that *simpleton* is formed by adding an affix to *simple* is irrelevant: its syntactic distribution is no different from that of nouns that are not derived from an adjective. *Simpleton* and *fool*, for example, are syntactically alike: the grammatical difference between them is purely morphological. Similarly, the morphological structure of *simplify* is of no syntactic significance: the grammatical difference between *I'll simplify the problem* and, say, *I'll solve the problem* is again purely morphological.

The various forms of a lexeme are, more specifically, its **inflectional forms**, and it is with the morphological description of these that the bulk of this chapter is concerned. However, we also include in the final section of the chapter a description of various non-inflectional variations in form that involve different pronunciations for certain grammaticised words – variation such as that between strong and weak forms of certain auxiliaries, personal pronouns, prepositions, etc. There is, for example, a clear difference between the pronunciations of *at* in *What are you looking at?* (the strong form, /æt/) and *Look at this!* (the weak form, /ət/). This is not a difference in inflection, but the phenomenon has it in common with inflection that it is concerned with a difference in form that depends in part at least on the grammatical context.

1.1 Lexical base, morphological operations, and alternation

Lexical base

The starting-point for the description of the inflectional forms of a lexeme is the **lexical base**. A lexical base may be **simple**, as with *dog*, or **complex**, as with *worker*, which is divisible into smaller morphological units, *work* and ·*er*.[1] The difference between simple and complex lexical bases is, however, of hardly any relevance to inflectional morphology, and that is why we can leave the description of complex lexical bases to the next chapter. Note, for example, that the plurals *dogs* and *workers* are formed from the lexical base in the same way.

In English it is almost always the case that one of the forms of a variable lexeme is identical with the lexical base. In [1], for example, the first word in each of [i–iii] is identical to the lexical base. Exceptions are to be found among certain **defective** lexemes, i.e. lexemes which do not have the full set of inflectional forms found with other lexemes of the same syntactic category. For example, the plural noun-form *dregs* has no singular counterpart, but it nevertheless has *dreg*· as its lexical base. Moreover, there are lexemes where more than one inflectional form is identical with the lexical base. An obvious example is ***sheep***, where the (plain, or non-genitive) plural form as well as the singular is identical with the lexical base. Lexical base is thus a distinct concept: it cannot be subsumed under that of inflectional form.

Morphological operations

The plural forms *dogs*, *workers*, and *dregs* are formed by adding ·*s* to the lexical bases. We refer to this as a **morphological operation** – specifically, the operation here is that of **suffixation**. This is in fact the major type of operation involved in English inflectional morphology. However, it is not the only one. The plural *teeth*, for example, is formed by changing the vowel of the base *tooth*, and the same applies to the preterite form *rang*, formed from the base *ring*. In the case of *knives*, suffixation is accompanied by modification of the base (with voicing of the final consonant in speech and corresponding replacement of *f* by *v* in writing). Other, relatively minor, operations will be introduced as they are needed.

Present-day English has a very simple system of inflection – much simpler than Latin, for example, or indeed than earlier stages of English such as Old English. There are few inflectional categories and relatively few types and combinations of operation are involved in their formation. Most inflectional forms are either identical with the lexical

[1] We use the notation '·' when citing suffixes (like ·*er*) or prefixes (like *un*·) and, where relevant, for marking morphological divisions within words (*dog*·*s*).

base or formed directly from it, as in the above examples. There are some, however, where two steps are involved. One obvious example is the genitive plural, with *children's*, say, formed by suffixation from the plural *children*, not from the base *child*. A second example is provided by a small subset of past participles like *trodden*: this is formed not from the base *tread*, but from the preterite form *trod*, by suffixation of ·*en* (with doubling of the final *d* in the spelling).

Alternations

We speak of **alternation** when a morphological unit has different realisations depending on the context in which it appears. For example, the plural ending is realised in writing as *s* in *cats* but as *es* in *boxes*: there is alternation between the suffixes ·*s* and ·*es* in the formation of plural nouns. A good deal of this chapter will be devoted to the description of such alternations.

Regular and irregular forms

An inflectional form is **regular** if it is formed in accordance with a general rule applying without reference to particular lexemes. *Cats* and *boxes*, for example, are regular plurals (and the alternation they exhibit between ·*s* and ·*es* is likewise said to be regular), and similarly the verb-form *talked* is a regular preterite and past participle. *Children* and *bought*, however, are **irregular**: the dictionary entries for ***child*** and ***buy*** must contain specific information about the plural and preterite forms respectively. *Thieves* too is irregular, for although the suffixation of ·*s* follows the general rule, the voicing of the base-final consonant, together with addition of *e* in the spelling, is not general throughout the language; we have *thief* ~ *thieves* but not *chief* ~ **chieves*, *hoof* ~ *hooves* but not *proof* ~ **prooves*, etc. For lexemes like ***thief*** and ***hoof*** the dictionary must record that the plural suffix is added to a special alternant of the base. Note, by contrast, that the preterite and past participle *knitted* is fully regular, for the modification of the written base by doubling the final *t* does follow a general rule.

Syncretism

When two or more inflectional forms of a lexeme are pronounced or spelled alike, we say that there is **syncretism** between them, or that they are **syncretised**. To return to the example used above, ***sheep*** has syncretism between the singular and plural forms.

1.2 Overview of inflectional categories

(a) Nouns

Prototypical nouns inflect for number and case:

[2]

	SINGULAR	PLURAL
PLAIN (NON-GENITIVE)	*dog*	*dogs*
GENITIVE	*dog's*	*dogs'*

The non-genitive singular is identical with the base, and the plural is formed from it as described in §4.1; the genitives are formed from the corresponding non-genitives (§4.2). The two demonstrative determinatives ***this*** and ***that*** also inflect (irregularly) for number. The forms are *this* ~ *these* and *that* ~ *those*; they do not require further discussion here.

Pronouns

Most of the personal pronouns have nominative and accusative case forms, separate dependent and independent genitive forms, and reflexive forms in which number functions as an inflectional category in all three persons. The nominative–accusative contrast is also found with relative/interrogative ***who***. The forms have been listed in Ch. 5, §10.1.1. The reflexive forms are morphologically compounds, formed with *self* (singular) or *selves* (plural) combining with the dependent genitive in the 1st and 2nd persons, and with the accusative in the 3rd person. There are no other significant morphological generalisations to be made about pronouns, so they are not dealt with further in this chapter.

(b) Grade

The system of grade applies to many adjectives and a few other lexemes:

[3]	PLAIN	COMPARATIVE	SUPERLATIVE	
	weak	*weaker*	*weakest*	[adjective]
	soon	*sooner*	*soonest*	[adverb]

The plain form is identical with the lexical base, and the inflectional comparative and superlative are formed, for the bases that permit inflection, by simple rules of suffixation, with very few irregularities in either speech or writing. Our discussion, in §3, also deals with the distinction between, on the one hand, inflectional comparatives and superlatives, such as those in [3], used with a large but restricted class of bases, and, on the other, analytic ones, such as *more careful*, *most careful*, used with all other bases.

(c) Verbs

For the great majority of verbs six inflectional forms must be distinguished, as argued in Ch. 3, §1, and illustrated here for ***take***:

[4]

PLAIN PRESENT	3RD SG PRESENT	PRETERITE	PLAIN FORM	GERUND-PARTICIPLE	PAST PARTICIPLE
take	*takes*	*took*	*take*	*taking*	*taken*

The plain present tense and the plain form are identical with the lexical base: ***be*** is the only verb without syncretism between the base and a present tense form. In addition to the categories in [4], auxiliary verbs have negative forms.

1.3 **Speech and writing**

Syntactic description of English can quite often ignore not only interdialectal differences but also the distinction between spoken and written English. Morphological analysis cannot. To a small but not negligible extent we find different morphology in the spoken and written forms of the language. Spoken forms will be represented here in terms of the transcription system presented in Ch. 1, §3.1.2; when citing individual words we normally indicate stress only if the lexical base contains more than one syllable.

Different alternations in speech and writing

The most obvious point that must be made regarding the differences in inflectional morphology between written and spoken English is that in numerous cases the alternations found in writing are different from those found in speech. Consider, for example, these preterite verb-forms:

[5]								
i	*sighed*	*kissed*	*waited*		/saɪd/	/kɪst/	/weɪtɪd/	
ii	*sighed*	*rubbed*	*tried*	*loved*	/saɪd/	/rʌbd/	/traɪd/	/lʌvd/

In [i] the three forms are all alike in writing in that they involve the addition of ·*ed* to the lexical base, but the three spoken forms are all different, with three suffixes added: /d/, /t/, and /ɪd/. In [ii] it is the other way round; the spoken forms have the same suffix /d/, while the written forms are different. All again involve the addition of ·*ed*, but in those other than *sighed* the lexical base is modified: in *rubb·ed* the final consonant of the base *rub* is doubled, in *tri·ed* the final *y* is replaced by *i*, and in *lov·ed* the final *e* of the base is dropped before the suffix (as it also is in *lov·ing*).

Primacy of speech

In some cases the spoken rules are clearly primary, the written ones derivative. One very obvious example concerns the alternation between ·*es* and ·*s* in forming the plurals of words ending in a consonant:

[6]						
i	*gases*	*boxes*	*buzzes*	*bushes*	*churches*	*stomachs*
ii	/gæsɪz/	/bɒksɪz/	/bʌzɪz/	/bʊʃɪz/	/tʃɜːʳtʃɪz/	/ˈstʌməks/

Bases ending in *s*, *x*, *z*, *sh*, and (usually) *ch* take ·*es* rather than ·*s*, but this reflects the fact that the spoken forms have /ɪz/. In speech the presence of the vowel /ɪ/ in the suffix depends on the phonological properties of the base. If the immediately preceding sound is one of the subclass of consonants called sibilants, comprising /s/, /z/, /ʃ/, /ʒ/, /tʃ/ and /dʒ/, then the vowel /ɪ/ is required in the suffix. The presence of *e* in the written suffix, on the other hand, depends on how the suffix is pronounced in speech. Note, for example, that while most bases ending in *ch* take ·*es*, as in the above *churches*, there are a few that take ·*s*, as in *stomachs*, *epochs*, *eunuchs*. The choice depends not on the spelling but on the pronunciation: in the former case *ch* corresponds to sibilant /tʃ/, so that the suffix in speech is /ɪz/, whereas in the latter case it corresponds to non-sibilant /k/, which takes /s/ as the suffix in speech. There is nothing about the letters *ch* (or indeed *s*, *x*, etc.) that calls for ·*es*: it is simply a matter of matching the pronunciation.

Inflectional classes in speech and writing

For the most part, we will be able to deal with matching written and spoken forms together in the same sections, because there is close correspondence between the membership of the inflectional classes of the written and spoken language. The nouns and verbs that have regular morphology in the written language generally have regular morphology in the spoken, and vice versa. But there are some exceptions:

[7]				
i	*say* ~ *says*	*pay* ~ *paid*	*house* ~ *houses*	*money* ~ *moneys, monies*
ii	/seɪ/ ~ /sez/	/peɪ/ ~ /peɪd/	/haʊs/ /haʊzɪz/	/ˈmʌni/ ~ /ˈmʌniz/

The 3rd person singular (henceforth '3rd sg') present tense form of ***say*** is regular in writing but irregular in speech, where there is a change in the vowel of the base. Conversely, the preterite (and past participle) of ***pay*** is regular in speech, but irregular in writing, where *y* is changed to *i* and the suffix is ·*d*, not regular ·*ed* (contrast the regular *play* ~ *played*). Again, the plural of ***house*** is regular in the written form, but irregular in the spoken, since the final consonant of the base is voiced in the plural, changing from /s/ to /z/. And while ***money*** is regular in speech, in writing there is variation between regular *moneys* and irregular *monies* (irregular because replacement of *y* by *i* normally applies only if *y* is preceded by a letter representing a consonant).

In ordering the material in this chapter we have given priority to the spoken forms: the sections on regular plurals and verb-forms deal with those that are regular in speech, and cover the corresponding written forms whether regular or not.

Forms that are irregular in both writing and speech can usually be assigned to the same subclasses. The verb ***read*** is an exception, however, as we see from these preterites and past participles:

[8]	i	*meet* ~ *met*	*hit* ~ *hit*	*read* ~ *read*
	ii	/miːt/ ~ /met/	/hɪt/ ~ /hɪt/	/riːd/ ~ /red/

Meet belongs to a subclass where there is a change in the base from /iː/ to /e/ in speech and *ee* to *e* in writing, while ***hit*** belongs to a subclass where the preterite and past participle are identical with the base in both speech and writing. With ***read***, however, we see that it belongs with ***meet*** in speech but with ***hit*** in writing. Again, it proves easier and more illuminating to base the classification on the spoken form. The divergent case of ***read*** will therefore be handled primarily in the appropriate spoken class, i.e. with ***meet***, but it will also be given a secondary mention in the discussion of the class to which it belongs in writing, i.e. with ***hit***.

Symbols and letters, vowels and consonants

As explained in Ch. 1, §3.2, we use the term **symbol** for the minimal unit of writing that corresponds to a unit of speech. Symbols may be **simple**, consisting of a single letter, or **composite**, consisting of two or more letters. *Through*, for example, contains three symbols: composite *th* + simple *r* + composite *ough* (corresponding to /θ/, /r/, and /uː/ respectively). The categories **vowel** and **consonant** apply primarily to speech and only derivatively to writing. Except where there could be no possible confusion we will not use these terms on their own when referring to writing: instead we will talk of **vowel symbol** and **consonant symbol** – or **vowel letter** and **consonant letter**, for the case where the symbols are simple. Note, then, that *y* is a vowel letter in *fully* (representing /i/), a consonant letter in *yes* (/j/), and just part of a composite vowel symbol in *boy* (/ɔɪ/). Similarly, *u* is a vowel letter in *fun* (/ʌ/), a consonant letter in *quick* (/w/), and part of a composite symbol in *mouth* (/aʊ/).

2 General phonological and spelling alternations

Before looking in turn at the various lexeme categories mentioned in §1.2, we introduce a number of phonological and spelling alternations which apply independently of particular categories.

2.1 Phonological alternations

In this section we look at the main phonological rules relating generally to alternation in inflectional suffixes or in the bases to which they are attached.

2.1.1 The sibilant suffixes: /ɪz/ ~ /s/ ~ /z/

There are three places in the inflection of nouns and verbs where we have a suffix containing an alveolar fricative, indicated in the spelling by *s*: the plural of regular nouns, the genitive, and the 3rd sg present tense of verbs. There are three alternants, with the alternation conditioned by the phonological features of the final consonant of the base.

[1] i /ɪz/ after sibilants (/s/, /z/, /ʃ/, /ʒ/, /tʃ/, and /dʒ/)
ii /s/ after all other voiceless consonants (/p/, /t/, /k/, /f/, /θ/)
iii /z/ after all other sounds

Thus the vowel /ɪ/ is present only where it separates two sibilants; and in its absence elsewhere the remaining consonant is subject to **voicing assimilation**, that is, it assumes the same voicing as the immediately preceding sound.

We illustrate the alternation in [2], where most of the examples can belong to any of the three categories of plural, genitive, and 3rd sg present:

[2]		PLURAL	GENITIVE	3RD SG PRES
i	/mɪs·ɪz/	*misses*	*miss's*	*misses*
	/geɪz·ɪz/	*gazes*	*gaze's*	*gazes*
	/wɪʃ·ɪz/	*wishes*	*wish's*	*wishes*
	/ruːʒ·ɪz/	*rouges*	*rouge's*	*rouges*
	/mætʃ·ɪz/	*matches*	*match's*	*matches*
	/dʒʌdʒ·ɪz/	*judges*	*judge's*	*judges*
ii	/kʌp·s/	*cups*	*cup's*	*cups*
	/reɪt·s/	*rates*	*rate's*	*rates*
	/reɪk·s/	*rakes*	*rake's*	*rakes*
	/naɪf·s/		*knife's*	*knifes*
	/deθ·s/	*deaths*	*death's*	
iii	/klʌb·z/	*clubs*	*club's*	*clubs*
	/men·z/		*men's*	
	/sjuː·z/			*sues*

2.1.2 The alveolar plosive suffix of the preterite and past participle: /ɪd/ ~ /t/ ~ /d/

This suffix, written *ed*, attaches to regular verb bases, and has the three alternants shown in [3], with examples in [4]:

[3] i /ɪd/ after alveolar plosives (/t/ and /d/)
ii /t/ after all other voiceless consonants (/p/, /k/, /f/, /s/, /ʃ/, /tʃ/)
iii /d/ after all other sounds

[4]				
i	/heɪt·ɪd/	*hated*	/lænd·ɪd/	*landed*
ii	/lɑːf·t/	*laughed*	/hɪs·t/	*hissed*
iii	/lʌv·d/	*loved*	/steɪ·d/	*stayed*

Again /ɪ/ is present just where it prevents the juxtaposition of two similar sounds (this time two alveolar plosives) and where it is absent there is voicing assimilation between the consonant of the suffix and the final sound of the base. The alternation thus matches that for the sibilant suffixes, and hence has been included in this section even though the suffix attaches only to verbs.

2.1.3 Bases ending in syllabic /l/ (/ˈhʌmbl̩/ ~ /ˈhʌmblɪŋ/)

For many speakers words like *humble*, *couple*, *rattle* are pronounced with a syllabic /l/ following the plosive – i.e. the /l/ (represented below as /l̩/) forms a syllable by itself. When a suffix beginning with a vowel is added to the base, however, the /l/ loses its syllabicity, becoming simply the initial consonant of the syllable containing the suffix. This is found with the comparative suffix /əʳ/, superlative /ɪst/, or gerund-participle /ɪŋ/,[2] but not with suffixes beginning with a consonant such as preterite or past participle /d/ and plural or 3rd sg present /z/. Compare, then, the forms in [5i], with non-syllabic /l/, and those in [5ii], where syllabic /l/ is retained:

[5]	i /ˈhʌmblə/	/ˈhʌmblɪst/	/ˈhʌmblɪŋ/	(*humbler*	*humblest* *humbling*)
	ii /ˈhʌmbl̩/	/ˈhʌmbl̩d/	/ˈhʌmbl̩z/	(*humble*	*humbled* *humbles*)

Other speakers have /əl/ instead of syllabic /l/ (/ˈhʌmbəl/ ~ /ˈhʌmbəld/ ~ /ˈhʌmbəlz/), but the /ə/ drops before the vowel-initial suffixes, so that the forms are again as in [i].

Bases such as *cudgel*, *funnel*, *quarrel*, *pummel*, and *squirrel*, where a vowel letter preceding the *l* appears in the spelling and the preceding consonant is an affricate or sonorant rather than a plosive, tend (though there is interspeaker variation) to have /əl/ throughout the paradigm: ?/ˈkʌdʒlɪŋ/ for *cudgeling* would be unusual compared to /ˈkʌdʒəlɪŋ/.

2.1.4 Bases ending in post-vocalic /r/: alternation in non-rhotic accents (/reəʳ/ ~ /reərə/)

As discussed in Ch. 1, §3.1.1, non-rhotic accents such as BrE have the sound /r/ only in pre-vocalic position: in these accents the forms we are representing with superscript /ʳ/ are pronounced without any base-final /r/ sound. Thus *rare* and *mar*, for example, which we represent as /reəʳ/ and /mɑːʳ/ are actually pronounced /reə/ and /mɑː/. When a suffix beginning with a vowel is added to a base of this kind, the /r/ becomes pre-vocalic, and hence is not lost. Lexical bases like *rare* and *mar* thus have two alternants in non-rhotic accents, one with final /r/ occurring before a vowel, and one without /r/ occurring in other positions.

[6]	i ***rare***	/reə/	/reərə/	/reərɪst/	*rare*	*rarer*	*rarest*	[adjective]
	ii ***mar***	/mɑː/	/mɑːd/	/mɑːrɪŋ/	*mar*	*marred*	*marring*	[verb]

With adjectives, the alternant with /r/ appears in both the comparative and superlative forms. With a verb, it appears in the gerund-participle – but not in the preterite and past participle, where the suffix is /d/.[3]

[2] See §3.1 for some exceptions. Compare also the past participle suffix ·*en*, which is pronounced as syllabic /n/ after certain consonants: see §5.3.3.

[3] The /r/ that appears before the vowel-initial suffix is a special case of linking /r/. Some speakers also have an intrusive /r/ in forms like *drawing*, *sawing*, and *thawing*: again, see Ch. 1, §3.1.1.

2.2 Spelling alternations

There are likewise spelling alternations – or spelling rules – that apply across different lexeme classes; for most of them, however, there are exceptions, which we will deal with in the appropriate sections. Three rules affect the final letter of the base, while one involves alternation in the form of the inflectional suffix itself:

[7] i	CONSONANT DOUBLING	*hop* ~ *hopp·ing*	[alternations in base]
ii	*e*-DELETION	*hope* ~ *hop·ing*	
iii	*y*-REPLACEMENT	*pity* ~ *piti·ed*	
iv	·*s* ~ ·*es* ALTERNATION	*cat·s* ~ *fox·es*	[alternation in suffix]

The three rules affecting the base apply in both lexical and inflectional morphology: we focus here on inflection and take up these rules again, more briefly, in the context of lexical word-formation (Ch. 19, §5.1.5).

2.2.1 Consonant doubling (*bat* ~ *batt·ing*)

The general case of this rule applies to bases ending in a single consonant represented by a single consonant letter; the letter is doubled before suffixes beginning with a vowel under the following conditions:

[8] i The final syllable of the base must have a single-letter vowel symbol.
ii The base must be stressed on its final syllable.

Monosyllabic bases necessarily have the stress on the final syllable and hence always satisfy [8ii]. The examples in [9i] illustrate doubling of the base-final consonant letter, while those in [9ii] have no doubling because one or other of the conditions in [8] is not satisfied:[4]

[9] i	a. *bat*	*batt·ed*	*batt·ing*	[monosyllabic base]
	b. *trod*	*trodd·en*		
	c. *fat*	*fatt·er*	*fatt·est*	
	d. *prefer*	*preferr·ed*	*preferr·ing*	[disyllabic base with final stress]
	e. *forgot*	*forgott·en*		
	f. *unfit*	*unfitt·er*	*unfitt·est*	
ii	a. *bleat*	*bleat·ed*	*bleat·ing*	[condition [8i] not satisfied]
	b. *beat*	*beat·en*		
	c. *neat*	*neat·er*	*neat·est*	
	d. *offer*	*offer·ed*	*offer·ing*	[condition [8ii] not satisfied]

Bases like *equip* satisfy condition [8i] because *u* is here a consonant symbol representing /w/, so the doubling rule applies to give *equipp·ed* and *equipp·ing*.

The inflectional suffixes that trigger the doubling in [9i] are the preterite or past participle ·*ed*, the irregular past participle ·*en*, the gerund-participle ·*ing*, the comparative ·*er*, and superlative ·*est*. For historical reasons, as noted in Ch. 1, §3.2, ·*ed* counts as a vowel-initial suffix even when it corresponds to phonological /t/ or /d/, and base-final *r* counts as a consonant letter even in non-rhotic accents, where post-vocalic /r/ has been lost in speech.

[4] The verb ***combat*** may be stressed on either syllable and the suffixed forms are accordingly spelled with or without doubling: *combated*/*combatted*; *combating*/*combatting*.

In addition the plural or 3rd sg present suffix begins with a vowel when the base ends in a sibilant (§2.1.1), and hence we have the following patterns of doubling:

[10] i	*quiz*	*quizzes*	*quizzed*	*quizzing*	[verb]
ii	*fez*	*fezzes*			[noun]

The letters *h*, *w*, *y*, and *x* are not doubled

It follows from the account of the rule given above that base-final *h*, *w*, *y*, and *x* will not be doubled: they do not represent single consonants. Compare, then:

[11]		VERBS		ADJECTIVES		
i	*hurrah*	*hurrahed*	*hurrahing*	[no adjectives ending in *h*]		
ii	*saw*	*sawed*	*sawing*	*raw*	*rawer*	*rawest*
iii	*stay*	*stayed*	*staying*	*coy*	*coyer*	*coyest*
iv	*box*	*boxed*	*boxing*	*lax*	*laxer*	*laxest*

On the traditional classification of all letters other than *a*, *e*, *i*, *o*, *u* as consonants, examples like these have to be treated as exceptions. But they are not exceptions on the account given here. The letters *h*, *w*, and *y* are never consonant symbols when they occur at the end of a base with final stress: they are always parts of composite symbols (*ah* /ɑː/, *aw* /ɔː/, *ay* /eɪ/, *oy* /ɔɪ/ in the examples of [11]). As for *x*, in base-final position this too is not a consonant symbol; it is a single-letter symbol representing the two-consonant sequence /ks/, and hence it does not fall within the scope of the rule either.

Exceptions to the consonant doubling rule

There are two exceptions to be stated for the doubling rule.

(a) Doubling in bases with non-final stress

[12] i	*travel*	*travelled*	*travelling*	*cruel*	*crueller*	*cruellest*	[BrE]
ii	*travel*	*traveled*	*traveling*	*cruel*	*crueler*	*cruelest*	[AmE]

For certain kinds of base, condition [8ii] is waived. The most general case is with bases ending in *l*, where doubling applies in BrE, but not AmE. Condition [8i] on the type of vowel still holds, so that there is no doubling with *travail* (which can take stress on either syllable), just as there isn't with *prevail* (which has final stress), because the vowel symbol is the composite *ai*. For further cases of doubling with non-final stress, see §5.1.

(b) Bases ending in *s*

With these (unlike those in *z*, as illustrated in [10]) doubling is not always found before ·*es* in bases satisfying conditions [8i–ii]. There are, however, significant differences between nouns and verbs, with doubling much less usual in nouns. ***Gas*** as a noun has *gases* as its plural form, while as a verb it has *gasses* as its 3rd sg present. The noun ***bus*** has the plural form *buses*, while with the verb both *busses* and *buses* occur. We will thus take up this matter in the separate sections on the noun and the verb.

2.2.2 *E*-deletion (*like* ~ *lik·ing*, *subdue* ~ *subdu·ing*)

A base-final *e* is generally dropped before suffixes beginning with a vowel. *Like*, for example, loses its final *e* in *lik·ing* but retains it in *like·s*.

We distinguish three cases of base-final *e*:

[13]						
i	SIMPLE VOWEL SYMBOL	*acme*	*acne*	*be*	*cafe*	*the*
ii	COMPOSITE VOWEL SYMBOL	*blue*	*dye*	*eye*	*free*	*sortie*
iii	MUTE *e*	*edge*	*hope*	*love*	*plane*	*simple*

The *e* in [i] constitutes a vowel symbol by itself, corresponding to /i/, /iː/, /eɪ/, or /ə/. In [ii] the *e* is part of a composite two- or three-letter vowel symbol at the end of the base: *ue, ye, eye*, etc. **Mute** *e* in [iii] is the residual case, including any base-final *e* not covered in [i–ii].

The *e*-deletion rule does not apply to case [i]; there are few words of this kind and very few places where such bases occur before a vowel-initial suffix, but note the retention of the *e* of *be* in *be·ing* and *be·en*. The main place where *e*-deletion occurs is thus case [iii], where there are few exceptions, at least in inflectional morphology. We take this case first, and then turn to case [ii]; nothing further needs to be said about [i].

(a) Mute *e*

Application of *e*-deletion is illustrated in:

[14]						
i	*edge*	*edg·ing*	*edg·ed*			
ii	*hope*	*hop·ing*	*hop·ed*			
iii	*take*	*tak·ing*		*tak·en*		
iv	*simple*				*simpl·er*	*simpl·est*
v	*square*	*squar·ing*	*squar·ed*		*squar·er*	*squar·est*

As with consonant doubling, ·*ed* counts as beginning with a vowel even when it represents /d/ or /t/, as in *edged* and *hoped*, and post-vocalic *r* counts as a consonant in non-rhotic as well as rhotic accents, so that bases like *square* end in mute *e* and undergo the rule.[5]

E-deletion applies before the same suffixes as consonant doubling. The result is that with such verb-base pairs as *hope* and *hop* or *plane* and *plan*, distinguished by the presence or absence of mute *e*, the forms with vowel-initial suffixes are distinguished instead by absence or presence of doubling: *hope* ~ *hoping* ~ *hoped* vs *hop* ~ *hopping* ~ *hopped*, or *plane* ~ *planing* ~ *planed* vs *plan* ~ *planning* ~ *planned*.[6]

With the suffixes other than ·*ing* we have assumed that the morphological division is before the *e*, e.g. that *hoped* is analysed as *hop·ed*, not *hope·d*. On this account the alternation is in the base, not the suffix. There are two arguments in favour of this analysis.

First, the omission of *e* before ·*ing* shows that there is unquestionably alternation in the base: the proposed analysis is simply a generalisation of the rule of *e*-deletion needed for the gerund-participle form. Note here that *e* also drops before non-inflectional suffixes beginning with *i*: compare *pure* ~ *pur·ity*, *simple* ~ *simpl·ify*, etc.

Second, with ·*er*, ·*est*, and ·*en* the proposed division matches the pronunciation: *nic·er*, *nic·est*, *tak·en*, for example, match /naɪs·əʳ/, /naɪs·ɪst/, /teɪk·ən/, and the same holds for ·*ed* for bases ending in an alveolar plosive, as in *hat·ed* /heɪt·ɪd/ and *sid·ed* /saɪd·ɪd/. The only troublesome case is ·*ed* corresponding to /t/ or /d/, but we have already noted that this behaves like a vowel-initial suffix with respect to consonant doubling, so the present analysis again involves a generalisation of rules motivated elsewhere.

[5] BrE has mute *e* in bases like *centre*, whereas AmE has the spelling *center*, with non-final *e*; the *e* therefore drops in the inflected forms of BrE (*centr·ing* ~ *centr·ed*), but not in AmE (*center·ing* ~ *center·ed*).

[6] Note, however, that in the much rarer type of pair seen in *bathe* vs *bath* the distinction is lost in the inflected forms *bathing* and *bathed*: *e*-deletion applies to *bathe* but consonant doubling cannot apply to *bath* because it doesn't end in a single consonant letter.

(b) The *e* is part of a final composite vowel symbol

Bases ending in *ue*

[15] i	*subdue*	*subduing*	*subdued*		
ii	*blue*	*bluing/blueing*	*blued*	*bluer*	*bluest*

Most such bases undergo *e*-deletion, with no *e* appearing in the gerund-participle form: compare *arguing, ensuing, imbuing, pursuing, rescuing, ruing.* There are, however, a few monosyllabic bases where the rule is optional, as with *blue*: others of this kind are *clue, cue, glue.*[7]

Bases ending in *ee, oe, ye*

[16] i	*free*	*freeing*	*freed*	*freer*	*freest*
ii	*hoe*	*hoeing*	*hoed*		
iii	*dye*	*dyeing*	*dyed*		

Deletion does not apply here, except that with *eye* (where final *e* is part of a three-letter vowel symbol) it is optional: *eying/eyeing.*

Bases in *ie*

[17] i	*sortie*	*sortieing*	*sortied*
ii	*lie*	*lying*	*lied*

In [i] *ie* represents /ɪ/, and the *e* is retained, as with *ee, oe, ye*; other examples are *birdieing* and *stymieing.* In [ii] *ie* represents /aɪ/; what we have here is not *e*-deletion, but alternation between *ie* and *y*: we return to this case in §2.2.3 below.

Problems of segmentation

We have not indicated the morphological boundaries in the above forms because in a number of cases the morphological analysis is problematic. The problem arises with those verbs such as ***free*** which retain *e* before ·*ing*: where does the boundary fall in the other forms? Take *freed,* for example. *Fre·ed* is implausible precisely because we do not have **fre·ing.* But *free·d* has the disadvantage of requiring alternation in the suffix, which otherwise is invariably ·*ed* in regular verbs. A possible explanation, perhaps, is in terms neither of *fre·ed* nor of *free·d*, but rather that one *e* has to be omitted because the sequences *eee, oee, yee,* and *iee* are not permissible in English (**freeed,* **hoeed,* **dyeed,* **sortieed*), so that the situation is quite different from that of ·*ing* – and it is then immaterial which *e* it is that is said to be omitted. Similar arguments hold for the adjectives *freer* and *freest,* and also with forms like *died* in [20ii].[8]

2.2.3 *Y*-replacement (*silly* ~ *silli·er, try* ~ *trie·s*)

Bases ending in a *y* as a single-letter vowel symbol show the following alternation:

[18] i	before a suffix beginning with *i*	*y* is retained	*try* ~ *try·ing*
ii	before plural or 3rd sg present ·*s*	*y* is replaced by *ie*	*try* ~ *trie·s*
iii	elsewhere	*y* is replaced by *i*	*silly* ~ *silli·er, silli·est*

The inflectional suffixes that trigger replacement of *y* by *i* all begin with *e*, but other types work the same way in lexical word-formation (*deny* ~ *deni·al, embody* ~ *embodi·ment,*

[7] The loss of *e* in *catalogue* ~ *catalogu·ing* falls under the mute *e* case, with *gue* a composite consonant symbol, while the retention of *e* in *segue* ~ *segueing* is due to its being a single letter vowel symbol, representing /eɪ/.

8 Notice that spelling facts from lexical word-formation reinforce this: while *freelance* and *freewheeling* are spelled as unhyphenated words, in *free-enterprise system* a hyphen is called for to prevent the impossible ∗*freeenterprise.*

etc.). Note that *y*-replacement does not apply where *y* is part of a composite vowel symbol. Compare, then, the verbs in [19i], the adjectives in [ii], and the nouns in [iii]:[9]

[19]	SINGLE VOWEL SYMBOL			COMPOSITE VOWEL SYMBOL		
i	a. *try*	*tries*	*tried*	b. *stay*	*stays*	*stayed*
ii	a. *silly*	*sillier*	*silliest*	b. *coy*	*coyer*	*coyest*
iii	a. *city*	*cities*		b. *guy*	*guys*	

Again it must be emphasised that the rule cannot be stated simply in terms of letters: we need to consider what sounds they represent. Both *guy* and *soliloquy*, for example, end in *uy*, but whereas *y*-replacement does not apply to the former because *uy* is a composite vowel symbol (representing /aɪ/) it does apply to *soliloquy* since *u* is here a consonant symbol (representing /w/) and *y* a simple vowel symbol: the plural form is therefore *soliloquie·s*.

A handful of verbs have final *ie* rather than *y* in the base: ***die***, ***lie***, ***tie***, ***vie***. The other forms, however, are the same as for ***try***:

[20]	i	*try*	*trying*	*tried*	*tries*
	ii	*die*	*dying*	*died*	*dies*

For ***die*** the *ie* is the default spelling, so that the replacement works in the opposite direction: *ie* is replaced by *y* before the ·*ing* suffix.

Analysis of the plural and 3rd sg present forms

It will be noticed that in [18ii] we have analysed the form *tries* as *trie·s* rather than *tri·es*, even though this necessitates special mention of the plural or 3rd sg present suffix: if we had *tri·es* it could be subsumed under the general case of replacement of *y* by *i*. There are two reasons why we have opted for *trie·s*. In the first place, we have just seen that such verbs as ***die*** clearly have an alternation between *ie* and *y* – and note that these spellings also alternate as variants of the diminutive suffix, as in *aunty* ~ *auntie*. Secondly, ·*s* is the default alternant of the plural and 3rd sg present suffix (as will be demonstrated in the next section), and there is no reason why the ·*es* alternant should appear in such words as *tries* and *cities*: note that it doesn't normally occur in words with a base ending in *i*, as we see from *alibis* and *taxis*.

2.2.4 Alternation between ·*s* and ·*es* in the plural and 3rd sg present tense

This alternation can be most economically described by stating the conditions under which ·*es* is used, and then saying that ·*s* appears everywhere else: it is in this sense that ·*s* can be regarded as the default alternant. This suffix is very different from the default preterite and past participle suffix ·*ed*. The difference is particularly clear in pairs like *sip·s* and *sipp·ed*, where ·*ed* triggers doubling of the base-final consonant letter *p*.

(a) Bases which in speech end in a sibilant

Bases with a final sibilant take ·*es*, matching the /ɪz/ of speech. There is no difference between the noun plural suffix and the verb 3rd sg present.

Bases spelled with final *s*, *x*, *z*, or *sh*

These are the most straightforward cases, always taking ·*es*:

[21]	*gas·es*	*box·es*	*buzz·es*	*wish·es*
	miss·es	*fix·es*	*fizz·es*	*lash·es*

[9] For some exceptions among the verbs, see §5.1.

The bases here end in /s/, /z/, or /ʃ/ (*x* represents /ks/, the second component of which is sibilant /s/). We have seen that a single *z* doubles and a single *s* may do so, but the suffix is still ·*es*: *fezz·es*, *gas(s)·es*.

Bases spelled with final *ch*

These take ·*es* when the base ends in sibilant /tʃ/ but ·*s* in the less common case where *ch* represents non-sibilant /k/:[10]

[22]	i	*bench·es*	*branch·es*	*catch·es*	*coach·es*	*lunch·es*	[(*t*)*ch* = /tʃ/]
	ii	*epoch·s*	*eunuch·s*	*monarch·s*	*stomach·s*	*triptych·s*	[*ch* = /k/]

Bases ending in mute *e*

Bases ending in the sibilant /dʒ/ have mute *e* in the spelling: *edge, judge, age, change.*[11] The same applies to the relatively small number ending in /ʒ/ (*mirage, barrage, rouge*), and to some of those in /s/ (*dose, niece*), or /z/ (*gaze, nose*), and a small number in /ʃ/ (*douche, niche*). This *e* drops before a suffix beginning with a vowel by the *e*-deletion rule (§2.2.2), giving *edg·es, mirag·es, dos·es*, etc.

An alternative analysis is *edge·s*, which does not involve loss of the base-final *e*. We adopt the analysis *edg·es*, however, since this both matches the pronunciation (/edʒ·ɪz/) and allows a more general statement of the alternation, namely that ·*es* occurs with all bases ending in a sibilant. Note, moreover, that these bases do lose the *e* when they are followed by the ·*ing* suffix: *edg·ing, chang·ing, gaz·ing*, etc. (see §5.1 for a few exceptions).

(b) Bases ending in *o*

Bases with final *o* take the ·*es* alternant if the *o* is preceded by a symbol representing a consonant sound; otherwise they take the default ·*s*:

[23]	i	*echo·es*	*go·es*	*hero·es*	*potato·es*	*veto·es*	[*o* follows consonant]
	ii	*boo·s*	*embryo·s*	*radio·s*	*studio·s*	*zoo·s*	[no preceding consonant]

The default [ii] covers cases where *o* follows a vowel symbol (*i* or *y*) and those where it is part of a composite vowel symbol (*oo*). There are some exceptions to this rule, with ·*s* used after consonant + *o*; almost all involve plural nouns where there is no homophonous verb, such as ***dynamo***: see §§4.1.1, 5.1.

3 Grade

The inflectional system of grade applies primarily to adjectives, but also to a few adverbs that do not end in the ·*ly* suffix and a handful of determinatives and prepositions (see Ch. 6, §2.2). We look first at the inflectional forms, and then at the distinction between inflectional comparatives and superlatives (e.g. *taller*, *tallest*) and analytic ones (*more distinct, most distinct*).

[10] Bases ending in *nch* can be pronounced with /nʃ/ instead of /ntʃ/ (except that in *nudibranch* and *elasmobranch* – types of mollusc and fish – it represents /ŋk/, so these take ·*s*). The base *loch* may be pronounced with a velar fricative rather than /k/, but in either case the base does not end in a sibilant and hence takes ·*s*.

[11] Foreign words like *hadj* and *raj* are exceptions, but the plurals of these words rarely occur and have somewhat questionable status.

3.1 Inflectional comparative and superlative forms

The inflectional suffixes marking comparative and superlative are /əʳ/ and /ɪst/ in speech, ·*er* and ·*est* in writing. The spelling alternations illustrated in [1] have been described in §2.2 and need not be repeated in this section:

[1] i	*big*	*bigg·er*	*bigg·est*	[consonant doubling]
ii	*nice*	*nic·er*	*nic·est*	[*e*-deletion]
iii	*pretty*	*pretti·er*	*pretti·est*	[*y*-replacement]

Monosyllabic *dry* and *shy* are optionally exceptions to the *y*-replacement rule, allowing either *y* or *i* before the suffix: *dry* ~ *dryer*/*drier* ~ *dryest*/*driest* and *shy* ~ *shyer*/*shier* ~ *shyest*/*shiest*.

Phonological changes in the base

Addition of the suffixes affects the base as follows:

(a) Syllabic /l/

We noted in §2.1 that a base-final syllabic /l/ loses its syllabicity before the suffixes, as they begin with a vowel. The adjectives ***little*** and ***brittle***, however, are exceptions in that the /l/ may optionally remain syllabic – compare:

[2] i	/ˈsɪmpl̩/	/ˈsɪmplə/	/ˈsɪmplɪst/	(*simple*	*simpler*	*simplest*)
ii	/ˈlɪtl̩/	/ˈlɪtl̩ə/, /ˈlɪtlə/	/ˈlɪtl̩ɪst/, /ˈlɪtlɪst/	(*little*	*littler*	*littlest*)

(b) Irregular adjectives in /ŋ/

There are only three adjectives with bases ending in /ŋ/ that normally inflect for grade, and all three are irregular in speech (though not in writing), adding /g/ before the comparative and superlative suffixes:

[3] i	/lɒŋ/	/lɒŋg·əʳ/	/lɒŋg·ɪst/	(*long*	*longer*	*longest*)
ii	/strɒŋ/	/strɒŋg·əʳ/	/strɒŋg·ɪst/	(*strong*	*stronger*	*strongest*)
iii	/jʌŋ/	/jʌŋg·əʳ/	/jʌŋg·ɪst/	(*young*	*younger*	*youngest*)

These forms are described as irregular, rather than as following a regular rule of /g/ addition between /ŋ/ and a suffix. This is because there is no evidence of any such rule in standard dialects.[12] Verb bases ending in /ŋ/ take vowel-initial affixes such as /ɪŋ/, as in /sɪŋ·ɪŋ/ (*singing*) and never add /g/, even when they are phonologically identical with the bases in [3] (e.g. /lɒŋ·ɪŋ/, *longing*). Non-inflectional suffixes beginning with a vowel never induce addition of /g/ after /ŋ/, even when they are phonologically identical with the comparative suffix (e.g. /ˈsɪŋ·ə/, *singer*). Regular adjective bases ending in /ŋ/ that are semantically eligible to inflect for grade happen to be almost entirely absent. *Wrong* does not occur in the inflectional comparative or superlative (it may be best treated as a lexical exception), but native speakers read the spelling *wronger* as /rɒŋəʳ/ (and the noun *wronger* /rɒŋəʳ/ "one who wrongs someone", which is attested, is so pronounced). *Cunning* is likewise seldom if ever found inflected, but the pronunciation /ˈkʌnɪŋɪst/ seems reasonably plausible in comparison with */ˈkʌnɪŋgɪst/.

[12] In the dialects of the north of England, there is no irregularity, because /ŋg/ is found instead of final /ŋ/: *long* is pronounced /lɒŋg/, and the comparative and superlative /lɒŋgə/ and /lɒŋgɪst/ are regular. What has happened in all other dialects is that word-final /g/ has been lost after /ŋ/ but retained in the inflected forms of ***long***, ***strong***, and ***young***, creating a mismatch with the base.

Irregular inflection

The following have irregular forms:

[4] i	*good, well*	*better*	*best*
ii	*bad, badly*	*worse*	*worst*
iii	*much, many*	*more*	*most*
iv	*little*	*less*	*least*
v	*far*	*farther/further*	*farthest/furthest*

As indicated in [i–iii], the distinction between *good* and *well, bad* and *badly, much* and *many* is lost in the comparative forms. *Well* and *badly*, moreover, can be adjectives or adverbs. Compare, for example:

[5] i	a. *This one is good.*	b. *That one is better.*	[adjective]
ii	a. *I'm feeling well.*	b. *I'm feeling better.*	[adjective]
iii	a. *They played well.*	b. *They played better than ever.*	[adverb]

Better in [iib], moreover, is ambiguous between the ordinary comparative sense "better than before", and the sense "recovered, well again".

In addition, ***old*** has the regular forms *older* and *oldest*, but also irregular *elder* and *eldest*, as used in:

[6] i	*my elder brother*	*her eldest daughter*
ii	*the elder (of the two)*	*the eldest (of them)*

These forms are highly restricted both semantically and syntactically. Semantically, they indicate relative order of birth within a family – contrast **the elder of the two editions*. Syntactically, they modify a following noun, as in [i], or appear in fused modifier-head function, as in [ii]. *Elder* can't be used predicatively (**Which one is elder?*) or with *than* (**an elder brother than Max*). The regular forms can be used as variants of the irregular ones in [6]. *Elder* is also used in the idioms *elder statesman/stateswoman* and is the source for the converted noun ***elder***.

3.2 Inflectional vs analytic comparatives and superlatives

Adjectives

Many adjectives allow both types, many others only the analytic type, and a few only the inflectional:

[7]		INFLECTIONAL		ANALYTIC	
i	***lively***	*livelier*	*liveliest*	*more lively*	*most lively*
ii	*public*	**publicer*	**publicest*	*more public*	*most public*
iii	***good***	*better*	*best*	**more good*	**most good*[13]

There is no simple set of rules to indicate which adjectives take which type: in many cases it is a matter of more or less likely rather than possible or impossible.

[13] The asterisks here apply to the use of these expressions as ordinary comparatives/superlatives. *More good* is possible in metalinguistic comparison, where inflectional comparatives are excluded: *I'd say it was more good than excellent* ("more properly classified as good than as excellent"). *Most good* has *most* as an intensifier, not a strict superlative marker: *It was most good of you to invite us.*

There are some generalisations that can be made, however. One is that participial adjectives, as illustrated in [8], take only analytic forms:

[8]							
i	*amazing*	*amusing*	*boring*	*frightening*	*pleasing*	*wearing*	*worrying*
ii	*amazed*	*amused*	*bored*	*frightened*	*pleased*	*worn*	*worried*

(A marginal exception is ***tired***, though *more tired* is much more usual than *tireder*.)

The remaining generalisations are best dealt with by separating adjectives out into sets according to the syllabic composition of the base.

(a) Monosyllables

Adjectives with monosyllabic bases almost always have inflected forms, but there are some that do not. First, the generalisation mentioned just above overrides monosyllabicity: participial adjectives do not have inflected forms even when they are monosyllabic. Second, there are also a few morphologically simple exceptions:

[9] *cross, fake, ill, like, loath, prime, real, right, worth, wrong*

These do not inflect – or at least, their inflected forms are in practice virtually never encountered. This is not because these adjectives do not express gradable properties: there can certainly be degrees to which one can be cross with someone, loath to do something, or in error; yet **crosser, *loather*, and **wronger* appear never to occur.

Most monosyllables allow analytic forms, either as an alternative to inflection or as the only way to express comparative or superlative degree, but the irregular inflectional forms *better, worse, further* pre-empt use of **more good, *more bad, *more far*, and the inflectional forms are very much more usual with such common adjectives as ***big***, ***large***, ***small***, ***high***, ***low***, ***fat***, ***thick***, ***thin***, ***long***, ***tall***, ***short***, ***fast***, ***slow***, ***hot***, ***cold***, ***cool***, ***old***, ***young***, ***clean***, ***great***, ***wide***.

(b) Disyllables

With disyllables the analytic forms are always possible, while the inflectional ones are sometimes possible and sometimes not. Many of the conditions making inflection impossible relate to the ending of the lexical base. With initially stressed bases, the endings in [10i] (only the first two of which have the status of suffixes) generally permit inflection, while those in [10ii] reliably exclude it:

[10]			
	i	*·y*	*angry, dirty, early, easy, funny, happy, hungry, noisy, pretty, silly*
		·ly	*beastly, costly, deadly, friendly, ghastly, ghostly, likely, lovely, manly*
		le	*able, ample, feeble, gentle, humble, little, noble, purple, simple, subtle*
		ow	*hollow, mellow, narrow, sallow, shallow, yellow*
	ii	*·ful*	*bashful, careful, cheerful, faithful, graceful, harmful, skilful, useful*
		·ish	*boorish, boyish, brutish, fiendish, foolish, priggish, sheepish, ticklish*
		·al	*focal, global, legal, lethal, local, moral, primal, rural, venal, vital, vocal*
		·ic	*caustic, chronic, comic, cyclic, epic, magic, manic, public, septic, tragic*
		·ous	*anxious, bumptious, callous, cautious, conscious, famous, jealous, porous*

There can be no doubt, however, that the matter is very much lexically determined, and certainly not a matter of phonology; note, for example, the following contrasts between pairs of disyllabic initially stressed bases with phonologically identical endings:

[11] i *stupid handsome common clever wicked pleasant* [inflection allowed]
ii *placid awesome wanton eager rugged mordant* [no inflection]

The above examples all have the stress on the first syllable, but we find the same differences among bases with stress on the final syllable. Thus *demure, mature, obscure, polite* can inflect but *secure, superb, effete,* and *replete* do not. It should also be borne in mind that there is no hard and fast boundary between those that can inflect and those that can't: speaker judgements are by no means wholly uniform.[14]

(c) Bases with more than two syllables

These normally allow only the analytic forms.[15] One systematic exception is where the prefix *un·* is added to a disyllabic adjective that inflects: *unhappy* ~ *unhappier* ~ *unhappiest.* There are one or two other exceptions, such as *shadowy* and *slippery*, but the forms *shadowier, slipperier*, etc., are rare and perhaps only marginally acceptable.

Adverbs

Most gradable adverbs take analytic forms: *softly* ~ *more softly* ~ *most softly.* Only a handful of adverbs have regular comparative and superlative inflection:

[12] ***early fast hard late long often soon***

The majority of gradable adverbs have bases formed with *·ly*, and the inflectional endings are never attached to bases of this kind: *early* of course is not an exception, since it is not formed from an adjective base **ear.*

All the adverbs in [12] except ***often*** and ***soon*** are homonymous with adjectives. ***Often*** is a somewhat marginal member of this class: the analytic forms are much more frequent and for some speakers are the only possibility. With the others, however, only the inflectional forms are normally possible: *The meeting lasted longer / *more long than usual.*

Earlier and *later* have a wider range of meaning than the corresponding plain forms. In such examples as *Earlier he had adopted a rather aggressive position* and *I later realised he had been joking*, where a *than* complement could not be added, the meanings are approximately "previously" and "subsequently"; the plain forms have no corresponding use.

Adverb pairs of the type *loud* ~ *loudly*

There are a number of pairs of adverbs where one is formed from the adjective by *·ly* suffixation and the other by conversion: *loud* ~ *loudly, easy* ~ *easily, slow* ~ *slowly, quick* ~ *quickly.* The ones with simple bases have regular inflection (*loud, louder, loudest*), while those with the *·ly* suffix take analytic *more/most* (*loudly, more loudly, most loudly*). The former are of more limited distribution than the latter, and are commonly subject to

[14] Historically, there has been a trend to move increasingly towards the analytic, though with fluctuations in the treatment of disyllabic adjectives during the twentieth century. Early Modern English used the inflectional type more freely (*apter, privatest*) and sometimes allowed both types to be combined (*the most unkindest cut of all*) – a doubling damned out of existence by prescriptivists – and even in the nineteenth century there were occasional examples like *properer, playfullest, scornfullest, sociablest.*

[15] Lewis Carroll's **curiouser and curiouser*, involving a trisyllabic base in *·ous*, is ungrammatical, and was intended jocularly, or as indicating that his young heroine Alice had not quite grasped the limitations of the inflectional system yet.

prescriptive criticism. The inflected forms, however, tend to be somewhat less restricted and more acceptable than the plain form without ·*ly*:

[13] i a. *They complained loudly/*loud about the service*
b. *They complained louder than anyone else*
ii a. *He was walking quite slowly/?slow because of his injury*
b. *He was walking slower than usual*

4 Nouns

Prototypical nouns inflect for number and case. The singular non-genitive is identical with the lexical base, and genitive marking is added after the plural marking: we will therefore look first at plural formation and then at genitives.

4.1 Plural formation

There are a number of types of plurals: regular ·*s* plurals, ·*s* plurals accompanied by modification of the base (as in *wives*), base plurals (identical in form to the singular, and hence to the base, such as *species*), plurals with vowel change (such as *geese*, from base *goose*), a small set with the suffix ·*en* (*oxen*, etc.), and foreign plurals of various kinds.

4.1.1 Regular ·*s* plurals (*cats, dogs, horses*)

We begin with nouns whose plural is regular in speech, presenting first the phonological alternation, and then the spelling ones.

Plurals in speech: the alternation between /ɪz/, /s/, and /z/

This alternation (already described in §2.1) is entirely predictable in terms of the final consonant of the base:

[1] i /ɪz/ after the sibilants /s/, /z/, /ʃ/, /ʒ/, /tʃ/, and /dʒ/
ii /s/ after other voiceless consonants
iii /z/ after other voiced sounds (including all vowels)

[2] i	/hɔːʳs·ɪz/	/bʊʃ·ɪz/	/mɪrɑːʒ·ɪz/	/tʃɜːʳtʃ·ɪz/	(*horses*	*bushes*	*mirages*	*churches*)
ii	/kʌp·s/	/kæt·s/	/wɪk·s/	/klɪf·s/	(*cups*	*cats*	*wicks*	*cliffs*)
iii	/kʌb·z/	/rɒd·z/	/hɪəroʊ·z/	/zuː·z/	(*cubs*	*rods*	*heroes*	*zoos*)

Plurals in writing: spelling alternations

Nouns ending in *y*

As we noted in [19] of §2.2.3, *y* remains intact when it forms part of a composite vowel symbol; otherwise (when it represents a vowel sound on its own) the *y* drops and the plural has *ies*:

[3] i	*guy* ~ *guys*	*quay* ~ *quays*	*donkey* ~ *donkeys*	*honey* ~ *honeys*
ii	*lady* ~ *ladies*	*baby* ~ *babies*	*city* ~ *cities*	*soliloquy* ~ *soliloquies*

Two optional exceptions are *money* and *trolley*: the plurals can be spelled *monies, trollies* as well as *moneys, trolleys*. And the replacement rule does not apply to compounds in ·*by* (*laybys, standbys*); to the informal *poly*, a clipping formed from *polytechnic* (*polys*); or to proper nouns (see §4.1.8).

The alternation between ·*s* and ·*es*

(a) Bases ending in a sibilant take ·*es*, matching spoken /ɪz/, as described in §2.2.4; where the base ends in *e* it is deleted before the vowel of the suffix:

[4] *bench·es* *box·es* *bush·es* *buzz·es* *judg·es* *kiss·es* *ros·es*

(b) With bases ending in *o*, where *o* does not follow a consonant symbol (i.e. where it is preceded by a vowel or is part of the composite vowel symbol *oo*), the plural takes ·*s*:

[5] *bamboos, cameos, embryos, folios, kangaroos, patios, radios, studios, zoos*

(c) Where *o* does follow a consonant, the plural has to be specified for the lexeme concerned. There are three classes:

[6] i ·*es* only: *echo* ~ *echoes*. Also ***domino***, ***embargo***, ***hero***, ***mango***, ***negro***, ***potato***, ***tomato***, ***torpedo***, ***veto***

ii ·*s* or ·*es*: *motto* ~ *mottos/mottoes*. Also ***archipelago***, ***banjo***, ***buffalo***, ***cargo***, ***dado***, ***dodo***, ***grotto***, ***halo***, ***innuendo***, ***manifesto***, ***mulatto***, ***proviso***, ***tornado***, ***volcano***

iii ·*s* only: *bistro* ~ *bistros*. Also ***calypso***, ***do***, ***dynamo***, ***beano***; clippings such as ***demo***, ***kilo***, ***memo***, ***photo***; nouns of Italian origin: ***cello***, ***concerto***, ***contralto***, ***libretto***, ***maestro***, ***piano***, ***quarto***, ***solo***, ***soprano***, ***virtuoso*** (but see also §4.1.6); and names of ethnic groups: ***Chicano***, ***Eskimo***, ***Filipino***, ***Texano*** (see also §4.1.3).

Cargo and ***volcano*** are marginal members of class [ii]: they usually take ·*es*, but the forms *cargos* and *volcanos* are sometimes found.[16]

(d) Other bases take the default alternant ·*s*. This includes bases ending in a vowel other than *o*: *arenas, cafés, alibis, tutus*. A marginal exception is that *taxies* is very occasionally found instead of the more normal *taxis*.

Doubling of final consonant of the base

The general rule of final consonant doubling (§2.2.1) is of very limited relevance to plural formation, since the default suffix ·*s* does not begin with a vowel. Doubling is found only before ·*es*; after base-final *z* it is obligatory, while after *s* it is sometimes available as a less favoured alternant, but most often excluded:

[7] *quiz* ~ *quizzes* *plus* ~ *pluses/plusses* *bus* ~ *buses*

In accordance with the general rule, doubling is not normally permitted in bases like *atlas* or *surplus* that have non-final stress; *biasses* and *focusses* are very occasionally found, but these spellings are very largely restricted to the 3rd sg present verb-forms.

Plurals with *'s*

An apostrophe may be used to separate the plural suffix from the base with letters, numbers (notably dates), symbols, abbreviations, and words used metalinguistically:

[8] i *p's and q's, 1960's, &'s, Ph.D.'s, if's and but's*

ii *She got four A's and two B's.*

[16] For ***do*** in the colloquial sense of "social event", which is converted from the verb and pronounced /duː/, the plural is sometimes spelled *do's*, with the apostrophe separating the suffix from the base, so that it is not misconstrued as affecting the pronunciation of *o* (cf. also [8]).

This practice is less common than it used to be; with dates and abbreviations ending with an upper case letter, the form without the apostrophe is now more usual: *in the 1960s, two candidates with Ph.D.s.*

4.1.2 Irregular ·*s* plurals: modification of the base (*wives, mouths, houses*)

We turn now to nouns where the plural is irregular in speech in that it involves an unpredictable change from a voiceless to a voiced final consonant. The consonants concerned are /f/, /θ/, and (one example only) /s/; only with /f/ is the change reflected in the spelling, with *f* being replaced by *v* or *ve.*

(a) Bases with final /f/

There are three classes of noun here: those where voicing is obligatory, those where it is optional, and those where it is excluded.

[9]	i	***knife***	/naɪf/		/naɪvz/	*knife*		*knives*	[/v/ only]
	ii	***wharf***	/wɔː^{r}f/	/wɔː^{r}fs/	/wɔː^{r}vz/	*wharf*	*wharfs*	*wharves*	[/f/ or /v/]
	iii	***chief***	/tʃiːf/	/tʃiːfs/		*chief*	*chiefs*		[/f/ only]

While native-English bases with final /f/ can have *f* or *fe* in the spelling, those with final /v/ always have *ve.* When modification applies, therefore, final *f* is replaced by *ve*, as in *wharve·s.* Membership of the three classes is illustrated in:

[10]	i	/v/ only	***calf, elf, knife, leaf, life, loaf, self, sheaf, shelf, thief, wife, wolf***
	ii	/f/ or /v/	***dwarf, half, handkerchief, hoof, roof, scarf, wharf***
	iii	/f/ only	***belief, chief, cliff, muff, oaf, photograph, proof, safe, tough, waif***

Nouns with compound bases such as ***cloverleaf*** and ***housewife*** generally belong in the same class as the final base, i.e. class [i] for these examples. However, ***cloverleaf*** in the sense of a complicated road junction would normally belong in [iii], with the regular plural *cloverleafs*, as would the expression ***still life***. ***Dwarf*** is a rather marginal member of [ii]: the voiced variant is comparatively rare. With ***half***, by contrast, voicing (shown in the spelling *halves*) is normal in the sense "half-portions", with the plural in /fs/ restricted to various other senses, such as "half-backs" in soccer or rugby. ***Handkerchief*** and ***roof*** belong in [ii] only with respect to speech: in writing they belong in [iii]. Nouns spelled with anything other than a single final *f* or *fe* are all regular, belonging in [iii].

(b) Bases with final /θ/

Voicing may be obligatory, optional, or excluded, with no change in the spelling:

[11]	i	***mouth***	/maʊθ/	/maʊðz/	*mouth*	*mouths*	[/ð/ only]
	ii	***oath***	/oʊθ/	/oʊθs/, /oʊðz/	*oath*	*oaths*	[/θ/ or /ð/]
	iii	***death***	/deθ/	/deθs/	*death*	*deaths*	[/θ/ only]

[12]	i	/ð/ only	***mouth***
	ii	/θ/ or /ð/	***lath, oath, sheath, truth, wreath, youth***
	iii	/θ/ only	***berth, birth, breath, death, length, moth, strength***

Path belongs to [i] in BrE but to [ii] in AmE, and ***hearth*** belongs to [ii] in BrE but to [iii] in AmE. For ***youth*** in the sense "boy, young man" the plural is normally /juːðz/, with /juːθs/ confined to the sense "period of age" (e.g. *in our youths*).

(c) Bases with final /s/

There is just one noun, ***house***, that has obligatory voicing, but no change in the spelling; all other such nouns are regular:[17]

[13]	i	***house***	/haʊs/		/haʊzɪz/	*house*	*houses*
	ii	***dose***	/doʊs/	/doʊsɪz/		*dose*	*doses*

4.1.3 Base plurals (*cod, bison, series, Chinese, craft*)

With some nouns, the plural has the same form as the singular and is thus identical with the base: we speak here of **base plurals**. Compare, for example: *A sheep has escaped* (singular), *Two sheep have escaped* (plural). This case is to be distinguished from that where a noun has no plural form: ***sheep*** has syncretism between singular and plural, ***equipment*** has only a singular form. We also exclude items like ***cattle*** and ***police*** which are invariably plural. Finally, we take examples like *She's six foot tall* to involve a special use of the singular form rather than a base plural: the difference between this and *How many feet are there in a mile?* is a matter of syntax rather than of inflectional morphology. These exclusions leave the following cases of base plurals.

(a) Nouns denoting edible and game fish

[14] ***carp***, ***cod***, ***haddock***, ***hake***, ***mackerel***, ***perch***, ***roach***, ***salmon***, ***trout***, ***turbot***

These (and others of the same semantic class) almost always have base plurals: *We caught three salmon*. However, with some, if not all, the regular ·*s* plural might be used when referring to fish being purchased for food, especially when there is reference to individuals, as in *three herrings* – as well as with reference to "kinds of", as with count uses of basically non-count nouns (Ch. 5, §3.1). The noun ***fish*** itself, with base plural *fish* and regular *fishes*, is also of this type, and similarly such compounds as ***goldfish*** and ***swordfish***.

(b) Nouns denoting game animals and birds

This is an area where there is a good deal of variation in usage, but we can broadly distinguish the following classes:

[15]	i	***bison***, ***deer***, ***grouse***, ***moose***, ***swine***	[base plural only]
	ii	***elk***, ***quail***, ***reindeer***	[base or regular plural]
	iii	***elephant***, ***giraffe***, ***lion***, ***partridge***, ***pheasant***	[base plural restricted]

The nouns in [i] do not have a regular ·*s* plural, only the base plural. Those in [ii] allow both types: *We saw three elk/elks*.[18] Those in [iii] normally have a regular plural as the only possibility, as in *The three elephants/*elephant were the main attraction*; base plurals, however, are found in the context of hunting and shooting (*They were hunting elephant*) or when referring to collections of them (*a herd of elephant*). It is arguable, however, that the latter construction involves not a base plural, but a special use of the singular in certain syntactic contexts (comparable to the *six foot tall* construction mentioned above).

[17] Including ***spouse***, since here there is alternation between /s/ and /z/ in both singular and plural.
[18] ***Swine*** belongs in [ii] when used as a term of abuse, usually applied to humans.

(c) Nouns with bases ending in /s/ or /z/

Regular nouns of this kind take the /ɪz/ suffix (e.g. *loss* ~ *losses*), but there are various kinds which have the same form as the singular:

[16] i ***barracks, crossroads, dice, gallows, headquarters, innings, kennels, links, means, mews, oats, series, species, works***
ii ***Chinese, Japanese, Lebanese, Maltese, Portuguese, Vietnamese; Swiss***

Many of those in [i] look like ordinary plural forms, but in fact can be used as either singular or plural: *There is one more crossroads* ~ *There are two more crossroads; She played a good innings* ~ *two good innings; It is the biggest meatworks in the state* ~ *There are few meatworks still operating.* The ·*s* element in such cases is therefore to be interpreted as part of the lexical base (see Ch. 5, §3.2.3). *Dice* is etymologically the plural of *die*, but the latter is virtually no longer in use (outside the fixed phrase *The die is cast*), with *dice* reanalysed as the lexical base: *another dice* ~ *a pair of dice.*

The items in [ii] are nationality terms in ·*ese*, together with *Swiss*. In some varieties of English, these behave as singular nouns with base plurals: *a Chinese/Swiss* ~ *two Chinese/Swiss.* However, this usage is lessening in frequency, and count noun usages like *a Chinese* sound old-fashioned or even slightly offensive to some speakers, for whom plurals like *the Chinese* and *the Swiss* are acceptable but have the structure of generic plural constructions with nationality adjectives, like *the French* or *the English* (cf. **a French*, **two English*); see Ch. 19, §5.6.2.

(d) Tribal and ethnic names

Such names as the following have both base and regular plurals (*The Kikuyu/Kikuyus do not share these beliefs*):

[17] ***Apache, Bantu, Bedouin, Hopi, Inuit, Kikuyu, Navaho, Sotho, Xhosa***, . . .

Sioux has only a base plural in writing, but in speech the singular is /suː/ and the plural /suː/ or /suːz/.

(e) Other cases

Craft and ***offspring*** have only base plurals: *One craft was damaged* ~ *Two craft were damaged.* The usual plural of ***ski*** is the regular *skis*, but *ski* is also found. Compounds in ·*man* also belong here in speech, with *policeman* and *policemen* both pronounced with /mən/, and conversely such French borrowings as ***chassis*** and ***corps*** have base plurals in writing but not in speeech (§4.1.6).

4.1.4 The vowel change plurals (*teeth, mice, men*)

There are seven nouns where the plural is formed by changing the vowel of the base:

[18]									
i	a. /tuːθ/	/tiːθ/	*tooth*	*teeth*	b. /mæn/	/men/	*man*	*men*
ii	a. /guːs/	/giːs/	*goose*	*geese*	b. /ˈwʊmən/	/ˈwɪmɪn/	*woman*	*women*
iii	a. /fʊt/	/fiːt/	*foot*	*feet*				
iv	a. /laʊs/	/laɪs/	*louse*	*lice*				
v	a. /maʊs/	/maɪs/	*mouse*	*mice*				

The only generalisation that can be made about these is that the [a] examples involve alternations between a back vowel in the singular and a front vowel in the plural – in [ia–iiia] /uː/ or /ʊ/ alternating with /iː/, and in [iva–va] /aʊ/ alternating with /aɪ/ (where it is just the second component of the diphthong that alternates). For the [b] items ***man*** and ***woman***, the changes in the written form are alike (*a* to *e*), but they are quite different in the spoken form (/men/ and /wɪmɪn/). In complex bases in ·*man* the vowel difference between /æ/ and /e/ is normally lost, with both reduced to /ə/: the result is that these therefore have base plurals in the spoken language, as noted above.[19]

4.1.5 The ·*en* plurals (*oxen, children, brethren*)

Three nouns show fossilised remnants of an Old English weak ending ·*en*:

[19] i	/ɒks/	/ɒksən/	*ox*	*oxen*
ii	/tʃaɪld/	/tʃɪldrən/	*child*	*children*
iii	/ˈbrʌðəʳ/	/ˈbreðrən/, /ˈbreðrɪn/	*brother*	*brethren*

Only the first has a simple addition of ·*en* to the base. With *children* there is also the addition of *r* and a vowel change in speech, while *brethren* has vowel change in both speech and writing. ***Brother*** also has a regular plural, *brothers*: the form *brethren* is restricted in its application to members of an organisation or religious group.

4.1.6 Foreign plurals (*formulae, curricula, phenomena, crises*)

Many words borrowed from other languages have been completely anglicised and have only regular plurals. Others have the plurals of the languages from which they are taken, either as the only possibility or as a variant of a regular plural. Many of the foreign plurals are restricted to scientific or technical genres or to formal style. In informal speech the regular plural forms tend to be preferred where they exist; except in specialised contexts, use of the more exotic foreign plurals is often regarded as pedantic or affected.

One problem is that there is no way of identifying foreign words from the form of the base. Although some endings are found with one type of foreign word, others are found with words of quite varied origin – for example, final *a* is characteristic of one class of nouns in Latin, but is also found in such words as *algebra* (from Arabic) and *phobia* (from Greek). Furthermore, an ending may be indicative of a particular foreign language origin, but not restricted to the class of nouns having a certain type of plural. While *us*, for example, is found with a fair number of nouns from Latin that have *i* in the plural (e.g. *alumnus* ~ *alumni*), ***corpus*** (plural *corpora*) does not belong to this class; nor do ***foetus*** and ***prospectus***. Similarly, ***polygon*** does not belong to the same class as ***phenomenon*** in Greek.

Some words that are etymologically foreign plurals have been reanalysed as singulars in English: this has happened where the original singular form is relatively uncommon or no longer in use at all (see Ch. 5, §3.2.4). The reanalysis may be complete, as with *agenda*, which is no longer used as a plural (and is in fact the base for a regular plural *agendas*), or incomplete, with singular and plural uses co-existing, as with *data*. See the comments below on *algae, data, insignia, candelabra, bacteria, strata, media, criteria, confetti, macaroni.*

[19] Pluralisation by vowel change is now effectively dead, and new uses and adaptations of the above words are beginning to show regular plurals. Thus when ***louse*** is used to mean "despicable person" it has the plural *louses*, and *mouses* is becoming increasingly common as the plural of ***mouse*** in the sense of a computer cursor-movement peripheral.

Latin plurals

From Latin there are four common patterns:

[20]		LATIN PLURAL	REGULAR PLURAL
i	*formul<u>a</u>*	*formul<u>ae</u>*	*formul<u>as</u>*
ii	*radi<u>us</u>*	*radi<u>i</u>*	*radi<u>uses</u>*
iii	*curricul<u>um</u>*	*curricul<u>a</u>*	*curricul<u>ums</u>*
iv	*ind<u>ex</u>*	*ind<u>ices</u>*	*ind<u>exes</u>*

The Latin plural involves changing the ending of the base, while the regular plural adds the plural suffix to the base. For patterns [i–iii] there are some words which allow only the Latin plural, some that allow either, and others that allow only the regular plural. Thus for [i] *larva* takes only the Latin plural, replacing *a* by *ae* (*larvae*/**larvas*); *formula* takes both (*formulae*/*formulas*); and *arena* takes only the regular English plural (*arenas*/**arenae*). For pattern [iv] we have only the second and third of these possibilities.

(a) Bases ending in *a*

Bases of the three types just distinguished are shown in [21], those in [i] taking only the Latin plural, those in [ii] allowing either, and those in [iii] taking only the regular English plural:

[21]			
	i	*ae* only	***alga***, ***alumna***, ***larva***
	ii	*ae* or *s*	***amoeba***, ***antenna***, ***fibula***, ***formula***, ***lacuna***, ***nebula***, ***persona***, ***retina***, ***tibia***, ***vertebra***
	iii	*s* only	***algebra***, ***area***, ***arena***, ***dilemma***, ***encyclopedia***, ***guerrilla***, ***phobia***, ***quota***, ***replica***, ***rumba***

The nouns in [iii] have a variety of origins – Arabic (***algebra***), Greek (***phobia***), Spanish (***rumba***): only ***area*** and ***arena*** belong etymologically with those in [i–ii]. The normal pronunciation of *ae* is /iː/, but /aɪ/ is found as a variant in *algae*, *formulae*, *lacunae*, and /eɪ/ in *vertebrae*. Singular *alga* is uncommon and *algae* is often reanalysed as non-count singular.

(b) Bases ending in *us*

The Latin plural of bases ending in *us* replaces this ending by *i*; the default pronunciation of this is /aɪ/, but the nouns marked † in [22] have a variant pronunciation with /iː/.

[22]			
	i	*i* only	***alumnus***, ***bacillus***†, ***homunculus***, ***locus***, ***rectus***, ***stimulus***†
	ii	*i* or *es*	***abacus***, ***cactus***†, ***focus***†, ***fungus***†, ***hippopotamus***, ***narcissus***, ***nucleus***†, ***radius***, ***stylus***, ***syllabus***, ***terminus***, ***thesaurus***, ***uterus***
	iii	*es* only	***apparatus***, ***census***, ***excursus***, ***foetus***, ***hiatus***, ***impetus***, ***prospectus***, ***status***, ***virus***

Foci with the /aɪ/ suffix usually has /s/ rather than /k/ in the base. None of the nouns in [iii], apart from ***virus***, belongs etymologically with those of [i–ii]. Similarly, ***corpus***, ***genus***, and ***opus*** do not belong in this group etymologically; they have either the Latin plurals *corpora*, *genera*, *opera*, or the regular ones in *es*. ***Octopus*** does not belong here etymologically either (it derives, indirectly, from Greek); it behaves like the nouns in [ii], though *octopuses* is more common than *octopi* (which is often criticised by prescriptivists).

(c) Bases ending in *um*

The Latin plural here replaces *um* by *a*, normally pronounced /ə/. Again we have three classes:

[23] i	*a* only	***addendum, bacterium, corrigendum, datum, desideratum, erratum, labium, ovum, pinetum, quantum***
ii	*a* or *s*	***aquarium, candelabrum, curriculum, honorarium, maximum, memorandum, millennium, moratorium, plectrum, podium, referendum, spectrum, stadium, stratum, symposium, ultimatum***
iii	*s* only	***album, asylum, chrysanthemum, conundrum, forum, geranium, harmonium, mausoleum, museum, pendulum, premium***

Agenda and *insignia* belong here etymologically but the forms in *um* are no longer used: *agenda* is now a count singular with a regular plural and *insignia* is treated as either plural or non-count singular. *Candelabrum* is also rare: for many people it is no longer in use, with *candelabra* now a singular like *agenda*. Similarly, singular *bacterium* is rare outside scientific contexts and *bacteria* is elsewhere often used as either singular or plural. *Strata* can also be found reanalysed as a singular with the meaning "level in society" and with *stratas* as plural, but this usage is widely regarded as non-standard. ***Medium*** in the sense "spiritualist" belongs in [iii], with *mediums* as plural; *media* is used in a range of senses, most commonly as a cover term for television, radio, and the press: here it is either plural (but with singular *medium* extremely rare) or non-count singular.

(d) Bases ending in *ex* or *ix*

The Latin plural replaces these endings by *ices*. This time we distinguish just two classes; the nouns in [24i] allow either the Latin or the regular plural, and those in [ii], which do not belong to the same etymological class, have only regular plurals:

[24] i	*ices* or *es*	***apex, appendix, cervix, codex, cortex, helix, ibex, index, latex, matrix, tortix, vortex***
ii	*es* only	***annex, crucifix, reflex, spinifex***

Dictionaries give only *codices* for **codex**, but the term is an uncommon and technical one and without reference to a dictionary one might well use *codexes* (and similarly for ***tortix***). There are no examples comparable to ***larva*** in [21], ***stimulus*** in [22], ***desideratum*** in [23], where regular plurals are quite clearly out of the question. With ***index*** the two plurals usually correspond to different senses, *indexes* applying to alphabetical reference lists in publications, *indices* to raised numerals in mathematics. With ***appendix*** the Latin plural is commonly used for additions included at the end of a publication and the regular plural for parts of the body, but the correlation is a good deal weaker than with ***index***.

There are also a few nouns in *x* that have *ges* in the plural: *larynx* ~ *larynges*; similarly ***pharynx*** and ***coccyx***. These are also found with regular plurals.

Greek plurals

There are two types to be considered.

[25] i	*basis*	*bases*	/ˈbeɪsɪs/	/ˈbeɪsiːz/
ii	*phenomenon*	*phenomena*	/fəˈnɒmɪnən/	/fəˈnɒmɪnə/

For the spoken versions of type [ii] the plural simply drops the final /n/ of the base.

Bases ending in *is*

Most nouns ending in *is* are from Greek and follow the pattern of ***basis***, with *es* replacing *is*; there are a few with a regular plural, *es* being added instead of replacing *is*, but there are none with alternation between the two types:

[26] i change *is* to *es*: ***analysis, antithesis, arsis, axis, crisis, diagnosis, ellipsis, emphasis, genesis, hypothesis, metamorphosis, neurosis, oasis, paralysis, parenthesis, psychosis, synopsis, synthesis, testis, thesis, thrombosis***

ii add *es* after *is*: ***iris, metropolis, pelvis, penis***

The last two of the nouns in [ii] derive from Latin rather than Greek (as indeed does ***testis*** in [i]). Note that while the plural of ***basis***, *bases*, is the same in writing as the regular plural of ***base***, the two plurals are pronounced quite differently, /ˈbeɪsiːsz/ vs /ˈbeɪsɪz/; the same applies to *axes* (from ***axis*** or ***axe***) and *ellipses* (from ***ellipsis*** or ***ellipse***).

Bases ending in *on*

The foreign plural replaces *on* by *a*. Again there are three classes:

[27] i *a* only ***criterion, phenomenon, prolegomenon***

ii *a* or *s* ***automaton, ganglion***

iii *s* only ***electron, neutron, positron, prion, proton, skeleton***

Horizon, pentagon, polygon, etc., do not belong to the same etymological class as the above, but are like [iii] in having only regular plurals. With ***criterion***, examples of the regular plural *criterions* are in fact attested, but they are very rare; much more common is the reanalysis of *criteria* as a count singular (?*No criteria exists*), but it is not widely regarded as acceptable. Nor is the (less common) use of *phenomena* as a singular.

French plurals

French words ending in *s* have base plurals in writing, whereas in speech the singular has no final consonant and the plural a regular /z/ ending. There are others, ending in *eau* or *ieu*, that are again regular in speech but in writing have a French plural in *x* as well as a regular one in *s*:

[28] i	/ˈʃæsi/	/ˈʃæsiz/	*chassis*	*chassis*
ii	/ˈplætoʊ/	/ˈplætoʊz/	*plateau*	*plateaux/plateaus*

Other lexemes following these patterns are:

[29] i Like ***chassis***: ***chamois, corps, faux pas, patois, rendezvous***

ii Like ***plateau***: ***adieu, bureau, chateau, milieu, tableau***

Other foreign plurals

Two further patterns, from Hebrew and Italian, are the following:

[30] i	*kibbutz*	*kibbutzim*	[Hebrew]
ii	*paparazzo*	*paparazzi*	[Italian]

The Hebrew plural in *im* is found in religious language with ***cherub*** and ***seraph***, and in borrowings via Yiddish like ***goy***. It coexists, however, with regular English forms: plurals like *cherubs*, *goys*, and *kibbutzes* will be found and are quite acceptable.

The contrast between Italian singular *o* and *i* plural seen in [30ii] is extremely marginal in English. Words such as *paparazzi* and *graffiti* were borrowed into English as plurals; the singulars followed later and are not well established. Thus *one of the paparazzi* is more usual than *a paparazzo*. Pasta terms like *cannelloni, capellini, macaroni, ravioli, spaghetti, tagliatelli*, and *tortellini*, and some similar words such as *confetti*, are likewise plurals in Italian. In English, however, they are non-count singulars; and *paparazzi* and *graffiti* already show signs of following them in this.[20]

In contrast, a number of Italian borrowings in the sphere of classical music are known primarily through their singulars: ***concerto***, ***contralto***, ***libretto***, ***soprano***, ***tempo***, ***virtuoso***, etc. For these, however, the regular plurals are much more common than the foreign ones in *i*, which are generally restricted to very specialised contexts such as concert programme notes and likely to be perceived as affected elsewhere. There are thus almost no signs of the *o* ~ *i* pattern being active in English.

Dictionaries sometimes contain various other plurals from certain other languages (e.g. *erg* ~ *arag* "sand dunes" from Arabic; *as* ~ *aesir* "gods" from Norwegian), but none of them are in common use.

4.1.7 Compound nouns (*grown-ups, commanders-in-chief*)

Plural marked on second element

Most compounds form their plurals with the regular ·*s* suffix added to the second element: *grown-ups, overcoats, shopkeepers*, etc. Where the second element is a noun with an irregular plural, the compound normally exhibits the same irregularity: *grandchildren, policewomen, werewolves*. There are a few exceptions, however. ***Reindeer***, we have seen, has a regular plural as well as a base one, whereas ***deer*** has only the latter. In speech ***handkerchief*** has an irregular plural in /vz/ as well as the regular one in /fs/, while the rarer ***kerchief*** has only the regular one. Compounds in *man*, such as ***policeman***, normally have no stress on the *man* syllable, so it is pronounced /mən/ in both singular and plural; hence, in effect, these forms have base plurals in speech despite the vowel change plural of ***man*** itself (§4.1.3).

Plural marked on first element

With some compounds, usually ones where the second element is an adjective or a PP, the first element may carry the plural marking. In some cases this is the only possibility, but in others there is alternation with a plural marked on the second element:

[31]	i	1st only	sg: *man-of-war*	pl: *men-of-war*
	ii	1st or 2nd	sg: *attorney general*	pl: *attorneys general, attorney generals*
[32]	i	1st only	***commander-in-chief, passer-by***	
	ii	1st or 2nd	***court martial***; ***sister-in-law***, ***son-in-law***, . . . ; ***spoonful***, ***mouthful***, . . .	

Where both plurals exist, the one with marking on the first noun is generally the more favoured one in formal style. The exception is the set of nouns in ·*ful*, ***spoonful***, ***bucketful***, ***mouthful***, and the like: these differ from the others in being written without space or hyphen, and the form with final ·*s* is more frequent and recommended by manuals.

[20] While not as widely accepted in non-count singular use as *data* or *media*, these words are beginning to be thus attested; note, for example, the occurrence of *its* in this 1997 example: *With his mother gone, there is an expectation the paparazzi will turn its lenses on Prince William.*

Plural marked on both elements

This is found when the first base is *man* or *woman* and it stands in an ascriptive type of relation to the second: *menservants. Menservants* should be contrasted with *man-eaters*, where the relationship is not ascriptive: menservants are men, but man-eaters are (generally) not.

4.1.8 Proper nouns (*Joneses, Marys*)

Proper nouns may be used in the plural in constructions like *The Hudsons have invited us over*; *We must keep up with the Joneses*; *There are five Davids in the class* (Ch. 5, §20.4). In such cases the base always remains unchanged in both speech and writing, and takes the regular suffixes: the Wolf family are referred to as *the Wolfs* (not as **the Wolves*), people called *Mary* can be referred to collectively as *Marys* (not **Maries*).

This principle extends to common nouns used as proper names. For instance, three copies of the publication 'Woman' would be referred to as *three Womans.*

4.2 The genitive

In this chapter we are concerned solely with head genitives, those that are marked on the head noun of the genitive NP, as in [*the <u>duke's</u>*] *children*; phrasal genitives like [*the Duke of <u>York's</u>*] *children* are discussed in Ch. 5, §16.6.

From the point of view of inflectional morphology there are two types of genitives, which we call **'s genitives** (as in *dog<u>'s</u>*) and **bare genitives** (as in *dogs<u>'</u>*).

The *'s* genitive

This is the default alternant: it occurs except in the special circumstances described below where the non-genitive ends in /s/ or /z/. In speech the ·*'s* suffix has the same three alternants as we have in regular plurals and 3rd person sg present tense verbs – /ɪz/ after sibilants, /s/ after voiceless non-sibilants, and /z/ after voiced non-sibilants:

[33] /hɔːʳs·ɪz/ *horse's* /kæt·s/ *cat's* /dɒg·z/ *dog's*

In writing it is invariantly *'s.* The apostrophe separates the suffix from the base, which does not undergo any of the regular or irregular modifications that apply in plural formation:

[34] i	*wife's*	*lady's*	*potato's*	*quiz's*	[genitive singulars]
ii	*wives*	*ladies*	*potatoes*	*quizzes*	[non-genitive plurals]

The bare genitive

In writing this has the form of an apostrophe at the end of the word: *dogs'*. In speech it has no realisation at all, such genitives being identical with the non-genitive: /dɒgz/. Notice then that, as spoken, /dɒgz/ is ambiguous between genitive singular *dog's*, non-genitive plural *dogs*, and genitive plural *dogs'*.

The bare genitive is normally restricted to nouns ending in *s*. It is either obligatory or else optional, with the *'s* genitive as a variant:

[35] i	*cats'*	*dogs'*	*horses'*	*wives'*	*indices'*	*theses'*	*species'*	[obligatory]
ii	*Socrates'*	*Xerxes'*	*Moses'*	*Jesus'*	*Burns'*	*Jones'*	*James'*	[optional]
iii	*Socrates's*	*Xerxes's*	*Moses's*	*Jesus's*	*Burns's*	*Jones's*	*James's*	

The bare genitive is obligatory with plural nouns ending in *s*, regular or irregular, including foreign plurals like *indices*. Nouns like *species* which have identical singular and plural forms with final *s* take a bare genitive in the singular as well as the plural, and in writing this will apply to nouns like ***chassis*** too (§4.1.6). The bare genitive is likewise the only possibility in more or less fixed phrases with *sake*: *for goodness'/convenience' sake* (the latter having spoken /s/ but not written *s*).

An optional bare genitive is found in certain types of proper names, where it is more likely in writing than in speech, in formal style than in informal. There is a good deal of variation here and it is not possible to give hard and fast rules. The bare genitive is most widely used with classical, religious, and literary names like the first five in [35ii]. Elsewhere it is normally restricted to names pronounced with voiced /z/ rather than voiceless /s/ (as in all the names in [35ii] except ***Jesus***). Examples like *Ross'* are sometimes attested but they are of questionable acceptability: *Ross's* is the normal form, and in speech the /ɪz/ is required. Even with final /z/, a bare genitive is hardly possible if /z/ is preceded by a vowel, as in ***Les*** or ***Ros***.

5 Verbs

All non-defective verbs other than ***be*** have syncretism between the plain form and the plain present tense, both identical with the lexical base. Many verbs, including all regular ones, also have syncretism between the past participle and the preterite. And a few have syncretism between these last two and the plain form. Lexical verbs thus have five, four, or three overtly distinct forms:

[1]

PLAIN FORM	PLAIN PRESENT	PRETERITE	PAST PARTICIPLE	3RD SG PRESENT	GERUND-PARTICIPLE
take		*took*	*taken*	*takes*	*taking*
love		*loved*		*loves*	*loving*
cut				*cuts*	*cutting*

The gerund-participle is regular in speech for all verbs, and the 3rd sg present for all but four: our major focus will therefore be on the preterite and the past participle.

We begin in §5.1 with the forms of regular verbs, and then deal briefly in §5.2 with the irregular present tense forms, before turning to the preterite and past participle forms in §5.3. In these first three sections we consider only verbs with simple bases, but the analysis extends very straightforwardly to verbs with complex bases, as shown in §5.4. Finally, in §5.5 we examine the formation of negative auxiliary verbs.

5.1 Regular forms

In this section we consider those inflectional forms that are regular in speech: with some of them there are spelling alternations that make them irregular in writing.

The gerund-participle

This is regular in speech for all verbs, even ***be***; it is formed by means of the suffix ·*ing*, phonologically /ɪŋ/:[21]

[2] /laɪk·ɪŋ/ *lik·ing* /pleɪ·ɪŋ/ *play·ing* /biː·ɪŋ/ *be·ing*

The 3rd sg present tense

The suffix here is identical with that of regular plural nouns and has been discussed in §2.1. It is written as *s* or *es* and in speech has the alternants /ɪz/, /s/, and /z/, depending on the phonological features of the base:

[3] /wɪʃ·ɪz/ /sɪp·s/ /rɒb·z/ *wish·es* *sip·s* *rob·s*

The preterite and past participle

Regular forms of these are always the same, and have the suffix written as *ed* and pronounced /ɪd/, /t/, or /d/, depending again on the phonological features of the base:

[4] /heɪt·ɪd/ /laɪk·t/ /pleɪ·d/ *hat·ed* *lik·ed* *play·ed*

Spelling alternations

Four sets of spelling alternations were discussed in §2.2, but there is a little more to be said about each of them.

Doubling of base-final consonant letter before suffixes beginning with a vowel

The general rules given in §2.2.1 account for such forms as those in [5], where doubling applies to the final consonant letter of a base preceded by a vowel symbol consisting of a single letter and stressed on the final syllable.

[5] i	*bat*	*batted*	*batting*	
ii	*occur*	*occurred*	*occurring*	
iii	*gas*	*gassed*	*gassing*	*gasses*

Doubling extends to some bases meeting the above conditions except that they have non-final stress:

[6] i	*level*	*levelled/leveled*	*levelling/leveling*	
ii	*focus*	*focussed/focused*	*focussing/focusing*	*focusses/focuses*
iii	*worship*	*worshipped/worshiped*	*worshipping/worshiping*	
iv	*handicap*	*handicapped*	*handicapping*	

We noted in §2.2.1 that bases of this kind ending in *l*, as in [i], take doubling in BrE but not AmE. This applies quite systematically, except that BrE doubling is optional with ***parallel*** (no doubt because the base already contains one instance of double *ll*). The base in [ii] ends in *s*: ***bias*** is the one other verb of this kind.

Worship and ***handicap*** are representative of a number of other verbs taking optional or obligatory doubling respectively; further examples are as follows:

[7] i Optional: ***bayonet***, ***benefit***, ***diagram***, ***kidnap***, ***program***
ii Obligatory: ***format***, ***hobnob***, ***humbug***, ***leapfrog***, ***sandbag***, ***waterlog***

[21] In non-standard dialects in both the BrE and AmE families, and also in some now largely extinct upper-class dialects in Britain, the ·*ing* suffix is pronounced /ɪn/ in the gerund-participle use (but much less so where it is part of the lexical base, as in *belongings*, *planking*, *railings*, etc.).

Where both forms are used, the one with doubling tends to be characteristic of BrE, the other of AmE.[22] For the most part these verbs have, or look as though they have, complex bases – and the doubling can then be seen as following the pattern of complex bases with a verb as final element, such as ***wiretap***. In the latter, the inflection matches that of the simple verb, irrespective of the stress, so that we have obligatory doubling, as with ***tap***: *wiretap* ~ *wiretapped* ~ *wiretapping* (see §5.4). Note the contrast with such items as the following (likewise with non-final stress) where doubling does not occur: ***develop***, ***dollop***, ***gallop***, ***gossip***, ***hiccup***, ***scallop***.

Comparable to consonant doubling is the (obligatory) addition of *k* after final *c*, as in:

[8]	*picnic*	*picnicked*	*picnicking*

Other verbs of this kind include: ***bivouac***, ***frolic***, ***magic*** (*away/up*), ***panic***, ***tarmac***, ***traffic***.[23]

Presence or absence of base-final *e*

The earlier rules (§2.2.2) deal with such cases as:

[9]	i	*hope*	*hoped*	*hoping*
	ii	*hoe*	*hoed*	*hoeing*

With verbs ending in *inge*, mute *e* is retained before ·*ing* in some, optional in others, and omitted (in accordance with the general rule) in others:

[10]	i	*singe*	*singeing*	Also: ***swinge***	[*e* retained]
	ii	*tinge*	*tinging*/ *tingeing*	Also: ***binge***, ***hinge***, ***whinge***	[*e* optional]
	iii	*cringe*	*cringing*	Also: ***fringe***, ***impinge***, ***syringe***	[*e* dropped]

The *ge* of the base indicates that the final consonant is /dʒ/, and so marks the distinction in the gerund-participle between *singeing* (/sɪndʒɪŋ/) and *singing* (/sɪŋɪŋ/), *swingeing* (/swɪndʒɪŋ/) and *swinging* (/swɪŋɪŋ/). Another example of the retention of *e* before ·*ing* is BrE *routeing* /ruːtɪŋ/: the *e* serves to distinguish *routeing*, a form of ***route***, from *routing*, a form of ***rout***. (AmE has the pronunciation /raʊtɪŋ/ and the spelling *routing* for the former.) With ***age***, both *ageing* and *aging* are found, with the former more usual in BrE (contrast the regular ***wage***, where *e* is obligatorily dropped).

Alternation between *y* and *i*(*e*)

We have noted that, following a consonant symbol, *y* is changed to *i* before ·*ed*, but not before ·*ing*, and that *ie* is changed to *y* before ·*ing*:

[11]	i	*deny*	*denied*	*denying*
	ii	*lie*	*lied*	*lying*

However, there is a mixed situation with two verbs that end in *i*: ***taxi*** and ***ski*** (both formed by conversion from nouns):

[12]	i	*taxi*	*taxied*	*taxiing*/ *taxying*
	ii	*ski*	*skied*/ *ski'd*	*skiing*

[22] In BrE the base *program* is used only in the sense relating to computers; for other senses the base is *programme*, which itself contains double *mm*.

[23] ***Arc***, where the *c* follows *r*, optionally takes *k*: *arced*/*arcked*, *arcing*/*arcking*.

Taxying is clearly formed by analogy with *lying*, while the use of the apostrophe with *ski'd*, to establish that the base is *ski*, may be motivated by a recognition that *skied* might be taken to be the preterite or past participle of the verb ***sky***.[24]

Where *y* forms part of a composite vowel symbol, it normally remains unchanged, but there are three verbs in *ay* which have *aid* in the preterite and past participle – compare:

[13] i	REGULAR	*pray*	*prayed*	*praying*	Also: other regular verbs
ii	IRREGULAR	*pay*	*paid*	*paying*	Also: ***lay***, ***say***

Say does not strictly belong here, for it is an irregular verb in speech by virtue of a vowel change not matched in the spelling (/seɪ/ ~ /sed/): see [54].

Alternation between ·*s* and ·*es* with bases ending in *o*

We have seen (§4.1.1) that there are a considerable number of nouns ending in *o*, some of them forming their plurals in ·*s*, others in ·*es*, others again in either. There are only a few verbs in *o*, and all are homonymous with nouns. Apart from ***radio*** (which takes ·*s* because the *o* is preceded by a vowel symbol) almost all the verbs take the ·*es* suffix, like the corresponding nouns:

[14] *echoes* *embargoes* *goes* *torpedoes* *vetoes*

(*Does*, from the verb ***do***, also has ·*es*, though the verb is irregular and its 3rd sg present is pronounced differently from the plural of the noun ***do***.) One exception is *photos* with ·*s* in both verb and noun – but the verb ***photo*** is quite rare: for the verb we usually use the non-clipped ***photograph***.

5.2 Irregular present tense forms

Irregular 3rd sg present

Just four verbs have irregular forms in the 3rd sg present:

[15] i	***be***	/biː/	/ɪz/	*be*	*is*
ii	***have***	/hæv/	/hæz/	*have*	*has*
iii	***do***	/duː/	/dʌz/	*do*	*does*
iv	***say***	/seɪ/	/sez/	*say*	*says*

The first two are irregular in both speech and writing; the 3rd sg present of ***be*** is suppletive (phonologically unrelated to the base), while that of ***have*** drops the base-final /v/, as do the preterite and past participle. The 3rd sg present forms of ***do*** and ***say*** are irregular only in speech, where they have a different vowel from the base.

Non-3rd sg present forms of *be*

Be differs from all other verbs in having a distinct form for the 1st sg, *am* /æm/. The default present tense form, used for all person–number combinations other than 1st/3rd sg, is also suppletive: *are* /ɑːʳ/.

Modal auxiliaries

The modals are highly irregular in that they show no person–number distinctions at all, and may be treated as having neither the plain present nor the 3rd sg present, but

[24] An apostrophe is also optionally found in *mascara'd*, where the motivation seems to be merely to avoid the unusual sequence *aed*.

just a single undifferentiated present tense form. *Must* and *ought* derive historically from preterite forms.

5.3 Irregular preterite and past participle forms

We have seen that with all regular verbs the preterite and the past participle are identical; the same holds for many irregular verbs too, and we therefore treat the two forms together in this section (and where they are identical we will normally give the form only once in the examples below). Some verbs have regular forms as variants of the irregular ones: these are indicated by the notation 'R' in the lists that follow.

The classification is based on the spoken forms, as explained in §1.3. We have four broad classes, each with several subclasses. An index to the classification is given in §5.3.5.

5.3.1 Class 1 verbs: secondary ·*ed* formation (*burn, keep, hit, lose*)

A number of common verbs are clearly somewhat irregular, but can nevertheless be treated in terms of the ·*ed* formation, supplemented by four other operations: devoicing of the suffix, vowel shortening, consonant reduction, and devoicing in the base. Seven subclasses of these verbs may be recognised, each involving one or more of these operations. In all cases the preterites and past participles are the same.

Class 1A: devoicing of the suffix

With eight verbs ending in /l/ or /n/ there is both a regular form with /d/ and one in which the suffix is /t/, despite the voicing of the final consonant of the base. The variation is normally reflected in the spelling, with *t* instead of *ed* (and *ll* reduced to *l*).

[16]	***smell***	/smel/	/smeld/, /smelt/	*smell*	*smelled, smelt*
	burn	/bɜːʳn/	/bɜːʳnd/, /bɜːʳnt/	*burn*	*burned, burnt*
[17]	Also: ***dwell, earn, learn, spell, spill, spoil***				

Earn is an exception orthographically: it has only the regular form *earned.*

Class 1B: vowel shortening

With several monosyllabic verbs there is a change in the vowel from /iː/ to /e/; this is matched in the spelling by the change from *ee* to *e*, though *ea* remains unchanged:

[18]	***keep***	/kiːp/	/kept/	*keep*	*kept*
	leap	/liːp/	/lept/	*leap*	*leapt*
[19]	Also: ***creep, sleep, sweep, weep***				

This can be treated in terms of 'vowel shortening': /iː/ is a member of the class of long vowels and /e/ a member of the class of short vowels, and the long vowel is replaced by a short one when followed by two consonants. In addition to the vowel shortening there is a change in the vowel quality (/iː/ is close and /e/ is half open), but the spelling (generally using the same vowel letters) indicates that there has been a historical change. This change is reflected elsewhere in the language, as in /sə'riːn/ (*serene*) vs /sə'renɪti/ (*serenity*). All the verbs in this class end in /p/ and therefore have the /t/ alternant of the suffix.

Class 1c: consonant reduction

With some verbs the preterite and past participle form is identical with the base:

[20]	***hit***	/hɪt/	/hɪt/	*hit*	*hit*
	spread	/spred/	/spred/	*spread*	*spread*

[21] Also: ***bet*** R, ***bid***$_1$, ***burst***, ***bust*** R, ***cast***, ***cost***$_1$, ***cut***, ***fit*** R, ***hurt***, ***let***, ***put***, ***quit*** R, ***rid*** R, ***set***, ***shed***, ***shut***, ***slit***, ***split***, ***thrust***, ***wed*** R, ***wet*** R

As indicated above, the notation 'R' means that the verb has regular forms as variants: *He had wet/wetted it.* BrE has only regular forms for ***fit***; otherwise, there is generally a preference for the irregular forms, especially in BrE. The regular forms of the colloquial ***bust*** are found primarily in AmE or when it has the sense "arrest". Irregular *rid* is required in adjectival passives like *At last we were rid of them.* The taboo verb ***shit*** (again with regular alternants) also belongs here, but it has an additional preterite variant with vowel change, *shat.*

There are phonologically similar verbs such as ***knit***, ***shred***, ***sweat*** that have only the regular forms. Similarly, although ***cost***$_1$ "be priced" is in class 1c, ***cost***$_2$ "estimate the cost of" is always regular. ***Bid***$_1$ "make an offer" has different forms from the ***bid***$_2$ of ***bid*** farewell, ***bid*** *someone do something*, which belongs in Class 3e. In writing ***read*** belongs here too, but in speech it is like ***bleed*** and is therefore listed in Class 1f.

The identity of the preterite and past participle with the base might seem to suggest that there is no suffix and that these verbs are like the base plural nouns of §4.1.3, but it may be argued that it is significant that all of these verbs end in an alveolar plosive /t/ or /d/. An alternative analysis, therefore, is that these verbs are irregular by virtue of having the suffixes /t/ and /d/ rather than regular /ɪd/ – just like verbs with bases ending in consonants other than /t/ and /d/. Addition of /t/ and /d/ to the bases here would give */hɪtt/ and */spredd/, but English phonology does not permit doubled consonants at the end of a word, so these forms would be reduced to /hɪt/ and /spred/. This is plausible in itself, and it also receives support from the discussion of Class 1f below.

Class 1d: vowel shortening with devoicing of the suffix

Six verbs have both devoicing of the suffix and reduction of /iː/ to /e/, reflected in the spelling change from *ee* to *e*, with *ea* again remaining unchanged. The bases end with alveolar /l/ or /n/, except for one instance of /m/:

[22]	***feel***	/fiːl/	/felt/	*feel*	*felt*
	mean	/miːn/	/ment/	*mean*	*meant*

[23] Also: ***deal***, ***dream*** R, ***kneel***, ***lean*** R

Class 1e: consonant reduction with devoicing of the suffix

Six verbs combine these two operations:

[24]	***bend***	/bend/	/bent/	*bend*	*bent*
	build	/bɪld/	/bɪlt/	*build*	*built*

[25] Also: ***lend***, ***rend***, ***send***, ***spend***

The verbs in this class all end in an alveolar sonorant plus voiced plosive (/n/ or /l/ followed by /d/) in the base, but in a sonorant plus voiceless /t/ in the preterite and past participle. This can be accounted for by the combination of consonant reduction (*/bendd/ and */bɪldd/ giving */bend/ and */bɪld/) and devoicing of the suffix (giving /bent/ and /bɪlt/). The archaic ***gird*** (with *girt* /gɜːʳt/ as its preterite and past participle) is similar but would need to be explained in terms of another sonorant, /r/; this would be correct for rhotic accents but, as we have noted, the /r/ has been lost in modern BrE and is reflected by vowel quality alone.

Class 1F: vowel shortening with consonant reduction

These operations combine in:

[26]	***bleed***	/bliːd/	/bled/	*bleed*	*bled*
	lead	/liːd/	/led/	*lead*	*led*

[27] Also: ***breed***, ***feed***, ***meet***, ***read***, ***speed***

These verbs have vowel shortening from /iː/ to /e/, like those in Classes 1B and 1D above. The bases also end in an alveolar plosive, /d/ or /t/, which appears to be unchanged in the preterite and past participle, but can again be accounted for in terms of consonant reduction, with */bledd/ becoming /bled/, and so on. Indeed these verbs provide further evidence for consonant reduction. The vowel shortening in Classes 1B and 1D applies before two consonants (thus not, for example, with bases ending in a vowel, such as ***free***), so that vowel shortening in the present class is explained if we postulate forms with two consonants like */bledd/, with reduction to /bled/ following from the prohibition on double consonants.

In writing *ee* again changes to *e*; this time *ea* also becomes *e* in ***lead***. In ***read***, on the other hand, the spelling remains unchanged in the preterite and past participle, as in the verbs of Classes 1B and 1D. Thus in writing ***read*** shows no change at all, and belongs in Class 1C.

There are three other verbs that can be handled in terms of vowel shortening and consonant reduction, but the vowels are different from the above:

[28]	***slide***	/slaɪd/	/slɪd/	*slide*	*slid*
	light	/laɪt/	/lɪt/	*light*	*lit*
	shoot	/ʃuːt/	/ʃɒt/	*shoot*	*shot*

The vowel changes in the first two from /aɪ/ to /ɪ/, and in the third from /uː/ to /ɒ/. Both can be seen as vowel shortening, since diphthongs such as /aɪ/ are phonologically long vowels – and this particular change is found elsewhere in English, e.g. in /dɪ'vaɪn/ (*divine*) vs /dɪ'vɪnɪti/ (*divinity*). The same vowel changes are found with ***bite*** (3D) and ***shoe*** (4A). All three verbs in [28] end in an alveolar plosive and so fit in with the account in terms of consonant reduction. ***Light*** is often regular in AmE, or in the idiom ***light*** *upon*.

Class 1G: devoicing in the base with vowel shortening

These operations apply in:

[29]	***leave***	/liːv/	/left/	*leave*	*left*
	lose	/luːz/	/lɒst/	*lose*	*lost*

Leave and ***lose*** are the only clear examples of this pattern. ***Bereave*** and ***cleave*** are usually regular (*bereaved*, *cleaved*); the irregular forms /bɪ'reft/ and /kleft/, *bereft* and *cleft*, also occur, but they are more often found as participial adjectives than as verbs (and see 3F for *cloven*).

5.3.2 Class 2 verbs: vowel alternations (*drink, dig, find, come*)

With many of the irregular verbs there is a change in the stressed vowel of the base to form the preterite and/or the past participle. Usually there is a front vowel in the base but a back vowel in the preterite or past participle, a pattern we will speak of as the **back vowel formation**. Most again have syncretism between the preterite and the past participle, but the forms are distinct in Classes 2A and 2E.

Class 2A: /ɪ/ ~ /æ/ ~ /ʌ/

Nine verbs have the vowels /ɪ/, /æ/, and /ʌ/ (spelled *i*, *a*, and *u*) for base, preterite, and past participle respectively:

[30]	***drink***	/drɪŋk/	/dræŋk/	/drʌŋk/	*drink*	*drank*	*drunk*
	ring	/rɪŋ/	/ræŋ/	/rʌŋ/	*ring*	*rang*	*rung*
	begin	/bɪˈgɪn/	/bɪˈgæn/	/bɪˈgʌn/	*begin*	*began*	*begun*

[31] Also: ***shrink***, ***sing***, ***sink***, ***spring***, ***stink***, ***swim***

In the written form, the vowels suggest the basic vowel triangle *i a u*, a familiar pattern in languages that have only three vowels. But this is not reflected in the spoken form in all dialects; most have /ʌ/ instead of /ʊ/ corresponding to *u* (those of northern England being exceptional in preserving the earlier system).

Class 2B: /ɪ ~ /ʌ/ ~ /ʌ/

The verbs in this class are similar to those in 2A except that there is syncretism between the preterite and past participle. In general, the /ʌ/ corresponds to *u* in writing; ***win*** is exceptional in spelling it with *o*.

[32]	***dig***	/dɪg/	/dʌg/	*dig*	*dug*
	win	/wɪn/	/wʌn/	*win*	*won*

[33] Also: ***cling***, ***fling***, ***sling***, ***slink***, ***spin***, ***stick***, ***sting***, ***string***, ***swing***, ***wring***

All except ***dig*** and ***stick*** (which were formerly regular) end in a nasal. There is some overlap between this class and the last. All the verbs in Class 2A are also occasionally found with the /ʌ/ vowel in the preterite, e.g., /rɪŋ/ ~ /rʌŋ/ ~ /rʌŋ/, *ring* ~ *rung* ~ *rung*; these preterites, however, are considered non-standard, in varying degrees. Conversely, ***swing*** from [33] may occasionally be found in speech with the preterite /swæŋ/), and there is an archaic preterite of ***spin***, *span*.

Class 2C: /aɪ/ ~ /aʊ/ ~ /aʊ/

This class has a change from front to back in the last element of a diphthong in speech, but from *i* to *ou* in writing:

[34]	***find***	/faɪnd/	/faʊnd/	*find*	*found*

[35] Also: ***bind***, ***grind***, ***wind***$_1$

(***Wind***$_2$, converted from the noun ***wind*** and pronounced /wɪnd/, is regular.)

Class 2D: miscellaneous vowel alternations

Several other miscellaneous alternations, most of them between front and back vowels, are seen in the following dozen verbs:

[36]						
abide R	/ə'baɪd/	/ə'boʊd/	*abide*	*abode*	Also: ***dive*** AmE
fight	/faɪt/	/fɔːt/	*fight*	*fought*	
get BrE	/get/	/gɒt/	*get*	*got*	
hang	/hæŋ/	/hʌŋ/	*hang*	*hung*	
heave	/hiːv/	/hoʊv/	*heave*	*hove*	
hold	/hoʊld/	/held/	*hold*	*held*	
shine	/ʃaɪn/	/ʃɒn/	*shine*	*shone*	
sit	/sɪt/	/sæt/	*sit*	*sat*	Also: ***spit***
sneak AmE	/sniːk/	/snʌk/	*sneak*	*snuck*	
strike	/straɪk/	/strʌk/	*strike*	*struck*	

Heave belongs here only in its nautical sense: elsewhere it is regular. ***Dive*** and ***sneak*** are regular in BrE, though *snuck* is used jocularly. In AmE ***strike*** has *stricken* as a variant of the past participle; in BrE this is used only in the passive (or as a participial adjective), with the sense "afflicted", as in *He was stricken with arthritis/fear.* ***Sit***, ***spit***, and ***hang*** each have two of the vowels involved in Class 2A. ***Hang*** tends to be regular in the execution/suicide sense; *hung* is certainly found in this sense (e.g. *hung in effigy*), but is condemned in some usage manuals. For AmE ***get***, see Class 3F.

Class 2E: vowel change in preterite, past participle identical with base

Just two verbs show this pattern:

[37]						
come	/kʌm/	/keɪm/	/kʌm/	*come*	*came*	*come*
run	/rʌn/	/ræn/	/rʌn/	*run*	*ran*	*run*

5.3.3 Class 3 verbs: past participles formed with the ·*en* suffix (*see, ride, take*)

There are verbs in which the past participle has the suffix we refer to as ·*en*. This suffix is never used for the preterite in standard English, though there are some forms, notably *done* and *seen*, that are used as preterites as well as past participles in certain non-standard dialects.

The suffix is most often added to the base, as in *eat·en*, sometimes with modification of the base, as in *swoll·en*, but there are also verbs where it is added to the preterite form, as in *brok·en*.

In speech it is pronounced /ən/, /n̩/ (syllabic /n/), or /n/, normally under the following conditions:

[38]						
i /ən/	after /l/ or /k/	/fɔːlən/	/teɪkən/	*fallen*	*taken*
ii /n̩/	after /t/, /d/, /v/, /z/	/biːtn̩/	/tʃoʊzn̩/	*beaten*	*chosen*
iii /n/	after vowels	/siːn/	/groʊn/	*seen*	*grown*

There is variation between /ən/ and /n̩/ after consonants other than /l/, so that /n̩/ can occur instead of /ən/ in *taken*, etc., and vice versa in *beaten*, *chosen*, etc.

The spelling alternations for bases taking ·*en* are the same as with other vowel-initial suffixes with respect to deletion of final *e*, as in *tak·en* (formed from *take*), and doubling of final consonant, as in *trodd·en* (formed from *trod*). We also have consonant doubling in such forms as *ridden* and *written*: the bases *ride* and *write* end in an *e* that forms part of a discontinuous symbol representing the diphthong /aɪ/, but the change to the short vowel /ɪ/ leads to the dropping of the *e*, so that the *d* and *t* are now in final position and hence subject to doubling.

In addition ·*en* is reduced to ·*n* after a composite vowel symbol, and *i* replaces *y* at the end of such a symbol; with bases ending in *re*, both the *e* of the base and that of the suffix are dropped, with /r/ therefore remaining post-vocalic and pronounced only in rhotic accents:

[39] i	after composite vowel symbol	*see*	*seen*	*sew*	*sewn*
ii	after composite vowel in *y*	*slay*	*slain*	*lay*	*lain*
iii	after *re*	*tore*	*torn*	*wore*	*worn*

The *e* of ·*en* is retained after the single-letter vowel symbol of *be* to give *been*. With the three verbs ***do***, ***go***, ***bear*** the suffix has the exceptional spelling *ne*: *done*, *gone*, *borne*.

Some of the verbs have similar vowel changes to those that have already been considered in §§5.3.1–2. We distinguish eight subclasses.

Class 3A: regular preterite, ·*en* added to base

There are eight verbs here, all with regular alternants:

[40]	***show*** R	/ʃoʊ/	/ʃoʊd/	/ʃoʊn/	*show*	*showed*	*shown*

[41] Also: ***hew*** R, ***mow*** R, ***prove*** R, ***saw*** R, ***sew*** R, ***sow*** R, ***strew*** R

Apart from ***prove***, all have bases ending in a vowel; in writing they have a composite vowel symbol in *w*, and hence the suffix ·*n*. With some, notably ***show***, ***sow***, ***strew***, the irregular past participle is preferred, but ***prove*** is again the odd one out: in BrE *proved* is much more common than *proven* as a verb (as distinct from the participial adjective of *a proven friend*, etc.).[25] *Proven* can be pronounced with /uː/ or with /oʊ/ — in the latter case the verb belongs in Class 3B.

Class 3B: regular preterite, vowel change in past participle

Two verbs:

[42]	***shear*** R	/ʃɪəʳ/	/ʃɪəʳd/	/ʃɔːʳn/	*shear*	*sheared*	*shorn*
	swell R	/swel/	/sweld/	/swoʊlən/	*swell*	*swelled*	*swollen*

Class 3C: /aɪ/ ~ /oʊ/ ~ /ɪ/

These verbs have a different vowel in each form.

[43]	***ride***	/raɪd/	/roʊd/	/rɪdn̩/	*ride*	*rode*	*ridden*

[44] Also: ***drive***, ***rise***, ***shrive*** R, ***smite***, ?***stride***, ***strive***, ***thrive***, ***write***

The change from base /aɪ/ to past participle /ɪ/ might be regarded as vowel shortening, but without the two consonants that normally condition it – compare ***slide*** in [28]. ***Stride*** is marked '?' because the past participle form *stridden* is very dubious and may not occur. For ***strike*** and the form *stricken*, see Class 2D.

[25] *Shaven* is used only as a participial adjective and hence is not included in our list.

Class 3D: vowel shortening in preterite and past participle

Three verbs can be treated in terms of the secondary ·*ed* formation, with the preterite having consonant reduction and vowel shortening from /aɪ/ to /ɪ/:

[45]	***bite***	/baɪt/	/bɪt/	/bɪtn̩/	*bite*	*bit*	*bitten*
[46]	Also: ***chide*** R, ***hide***						

The past participle might appear to be formed from the preterite, but it is simpler to treat it as formed from the base, as with most verbs: it is just that the past participle also involves vowel shortening of /aɪ/ to /ɪ/, as it does in the verbs of Class 3C (where there is no question of the past participle being formed from the preterite).

One other verb that may be considered here is ***beat***:

[47]	***beat***	/biːt/	/biːt/	/biːtn̩/	*beat*	*beat*	*beaten*

This too can be seen in terms of consonant reduction in the preterite, but it is unusual in that there is no vowel shortening as there is with all similar verbs: if there were vowel shortening as in ***meet*** or ***lead*** (and compare ***bite***) the forms would be */bet/ and */betn̩/.

Class 3E: vowel change in preterite, ·*en* added to base

There are some other verbs that have past participles formed by the addition of ·*en* to the lexical base, with various vowel changes in the preterite:

[48]	***bid***$_2$	/bɪd/	/bæd/	/bɪdn̩/	*bid*	*bade*	*bidden*
	blow	/bloʊ/	/bluː/	/bloʊn/	*blow*	*blew*	*blown*
	draw	/drɔː/	/druː/	/drɔːn/	*draw*	*drew*	*drawn*
	eat	/iːt/	/et/	/iːtn̩/	*eat*	*ate*	*eaten*
	fall	/fɔːl/	/fel/	/fɔːlən/	*fall*	*fell*	*fallen*
	give	/gɪv/	/geɪv/	/gɪvn̩/	*give*	*gave*	*given*
	see	/siː/	/sɔː/	/siːn/	*see*	*saw*	*seen*
	slay	/sleɪ/	/sluː/	/sleɪn/	*slay*	*slew*	*slain*
	take	/teɪk/	/tʊk/	/teɪkən/	*take*	*took*	*taken*
[49]	Also: (like ***blow***) ***grow***, ***know***, ***throw***; (like ***take***) ***forsake***, ***shake***						

Alternative pronunciations of the preterites of ***bid*** and ***eat*** are /beɪd/ and (especially in AmE) /eɪt/. ***Bid***$_2$ has the sense "give a greeting/order", and is somewhat archaic; for ***bid***$_1$, see 1C. In BrE ***know*** is not quite like ***blow*** in that the preterite has /j/: /njuː/.

Class 3F: vowel change in preterite, ·*en* added to preterite

There is another set of verbs that have past participles formed by the addition of ·*en* to the preterite, rather than the lexical base, with various vowel changes:

[50]	***break***	/breɪk/	/broʊk/	/broʊkən/	*break*	*broke*	*broken*
	choose	/tʃuːz/	/tʃoʊz/	/tʃoʊzn̩/	*choose*	*chose*	*chosen*
	lie$_1$	/laɪ/	/leɪ/	/leɪn/	*lie*	*lay*	*lain*
	speak	/spiːk/	/spoʊk/	/spoʊkən/	*speak*	*spoke*	*spoken*
	tear	/teəʳ/	/tɔːʳ/	/tɔːʳn/	*tear*	*tore*	*torn*
	tread	/tred/	/trɒd/	/trɒdn̩/	*tread*	*trod*	*trodden*
	wake	/weɪk/	/woʊk/	/woʊkən/	*wake*	*woke*	*woken*
[51]	Also: (like ***speak***) ***cleave*** R, ***freeze***, ***steal***, ***weave***; (like ***tear***) ***bear***, ***swear***, ***wear***						

AmE ***get*** belongs here, with the forms /get/ ~ /gɒt/ ~ /gɒtn̩/, *get* ~ *got* ~ *gotten* (the same vowel pattern as ***tread***), except that there is a variant of the past participle that is identical to the preterite, as it always is in BrE. ***Lie***$_1$ has the meaning of position: ***lie***$_2$ "tell a lie" is regular. The preterite of intransitive ***lie***$_1$ is homophonous with the base of transitive ***lay*** (listed in [13ii]): compare *It lay on the floor* (***lie***$_1$) and *He asked me to lay it on the floor* (***lay***). ***Lay***, however, is often confused with ***lie***$_1$ and used intransitively, but this usage is regarded as non-standard: !*He asked me to lay on the floor.* In BrE, the past participle of ***bear*** is spelled *born* only in the passive, in the childbirth sense (*He was born in 1900*) or metaphorical extensions thereof (*His anti-social behaviour was born of frustration at being constantly ignored*); elsewhere it is *borne* (*It has borne fruit*). ***Cleave*** has *cleft* as a variant for the preterite and past participle (Class 1G).

Class 3G: vowel change in both preterite and past participle

There are two verbs that have an ·*en* suffix but different vowels (other than shortened vowels) in all three forms:

[52]	***do***	/duː/	/dɪd/	/dʌn/	*do*	*did*	*done*
	fly	/flaɪ/	/fluː/	/floʊn/	*fly*	*flew*	*flown*

Class 3H: suppletive preterites

Two verbs have suppletive preterites, and both have past participles with a version of the ·*en* suffix:

[53]	***be***	/biː/	/wɒz/–/wɜːʳ/	/biːn/	*be*	*was–were*	*been*
	go	/goʊ/	/went/	/gɒn/	*go*	*went*	*gone*

Be is idiosyncratic in that it has two preterite forms, *was* for 1st/3rd sg and *were* elsewhere; its ·*en* suffix is phonologically /n/, as normal after a vowel. (*Were* with a 1st/3rd sg subject is an irrealis mood form: see Ch. 3, §1.7.) The past participle of ***go*** is irregular in both speech and writing, having an idiosyncratic vowel change in speech and *ne* as the spelling of the suffix.

5.3.4 Class 4 verbs: other formations (*flee, hear, stand, buy, can*)

There are some verbs that have features that are not covered in the previous discussion. Most of them appear to have an ·*ed* type suffix, but with vowel changes that are not typical of the secondary ·*ed* formation.

Class 4A: vowel shortening and ·*d* suffix

There are three verbs with bases ending in a vowel that have a /d/ suffix together with a vowel change in the preterite and past participle:

[54]	***flee***	/fliː/	/fled/	*flee*	*fled*
	say	/seɪ/	/sed/	*say*	*said*
	shoe	/ʃuː/	/ʃɒd/	*shoe*	*shod*

Flee has the same vowel change as ***keep*** (1B), while ***shoe*** has the same change as ***shoot*** (1F). ***Say*** has a completely idiosyncratic vowel change – the same, however, as in the 3rd sg present form /sez/. The vowel change in all three verbs might be regarded as vowel shortening, but again we do not here have the two final consonants that condition vowel shortening in the central cases, such as ***keep***.

Class 4B: vowel change and ·*d* suffix

Very similar, but with vowel changes that clearly do not involve shortening, are:

[55]	**hear**	/hɪəʳ/	/hɜːʳd/	*hear*	*heard*	
	sell	/sel/	/soʊld/	*sell*	*sold*	Also: **tell**

Class 4C: loss of consonant

There are three verbs of this type:

[56]	**have**	/hæv/	/hæd/	*have*	*had*
	make	/meɪk/	/meɪd/	*make*	*made*
	stand	/stænd/	/stʊd/	*stand*	*stood*

Have and ***make*** would be regular except for the loss of /v/ and /k/. ***Stand*** has both vowel change and loss of /n/; the final /d/ can be taken to be either the final consonant of the base or the suffix /d/ with consonant reduction.

Class 4D: forms with *ought* and *aught*

There are seven verbs, with various types of base, that have preterite and past participle forms ending in /ɔːt/ (*ought* or *aught*):

[57]	**beseech**	/bɪˈsiːtʃ/	/bɪˈsɔːt/	*beseech*	*besought*
	bring	/brɪŋ/	/brɔːt/	*bring*	*brought*
	buy	/baɪ/	/bɔːt/	*buy*	*bought*
	catch	/kætʃ/	/kɔːt/	*catch*	*caught*
	seek	/siːk/	/sɔːt/	*seek*	*sought*
	teach	/tiːtʃ/	/tɔːt/	*teach*	*taught*
	think	/θɪŋk/	/θɔːt/	*think*	*thought*

Fight has been listed in Class 2D as its base ends in /t/, but it could also be included here.

Class 4E: preterites of the modals

Four of the modal auxiliaries have preterite forms, though not past participles; all are highly irregular, three of them ending in /ʊd/ (*ould*), with an *l* that does not correspond to a phonological /l/ in any extant dialect.

[58]	**can**	/kæn/	/kʊd/	*can*	*could*
	may	/meɪ/	/maɪt/	*may*	*might*
	shall	/ʃæl/	/ʃʊd/	*shall*	*should*
	will	/wɪl/	/wʊd/	*will*	*would*

5.3.5 Index to the classification

abide 2D	***be*** 3H	***bear*** 3F	***beat*** 3D	***begin*** 2A	***bend*** 1E	***bereave*** 1G
beseech 4D	***bet*** 1C	***bid***$_1$ 1C	***bid***$_2$ 3E	***bind*** 2C	***bite*** 3D	***bleed*** 1F
blow 3E	***break*** 3F	***breed*** 1F	***bring*** 4D	***build*** 1E	***burn*** 1A	***burst*** 1C
bust 1C	***buy*** 4D	***can*** 4E	***cast*** 1C	***catch*** 4D	***chide*** 3D	***choose*** 3F
cleave 1G	***cling*** 2B	***come*** 2E	***cost*** 1C	***creep*** 1B	***cut*** 1C	***deal*** 1D
dig 2B	***dive*** 2D	***do*** 3G	***draw*** 3E	***dream*** 1D	***drink*** 2A	***drive*** 3C
dwell 1A	***earn*** 1A	***eat*** 3E	***fall*** 3E	***feed*** 1F	***feel*** 1D	***fight*** 2D

find 2C	***fit*** 1C	***flee*** 4A	***fling*** 2B	***fly*** 3G	***forsake*** 3E	***freeze*** 3F
get 2D,3F	***gird*** 1E	***give*** 3E	***go*** 3H	***grind*** 2C	***grow*** 3E	***hang*** 2D
have 4C	***hear*** 4B	***heave*** 2D	***hew*** 3A	***hide*** 3D	***hit*** 1C	***hold*** 2D
hurt 1C	***keep*** 1B	***kneel*** 1D	***know*** 3E	***lead*** 1F	***lean*** 1D	***leap*** 1B
learn 1A	***leave*** 1G	***lend*** 1E	***let*** 1C	***lie*** 3F	***light*** 1F	***lose*** 1G
make 4C	***may*** 4E	***mean*** 1D	***meet*** 1F	***mow*** 3A	***put*** 1C	***quit*** 1C
read 1F	***rend*** 1E	***rid*** 1C	***ride*** 3C	***ring*** 2A	***rise*** 3C	***run*** 2E
saw 3A	***say*** 4A	***see*** 3E	***seek*** 4D	***sell*** 4B	***send*** 1E	***set*** 1C
sew 3A	***shake*** 3E	***shall*** 4E	***shear*** 3B	***shed*** 1C	***shine*** 2D	***shoe*** 4A
shoot 1F	***show*** 3A	***shrink*** 2A	***shrive*** 3C	***shut*** 1C	***sing*** 2A	***sink*** 2A
sit 2D	***slay*** 3E	***sleep*** 1B	***slide*** 1F	***sling*** 2B	***slink*** 2B	***slit*** 1C
smell 1A	***smite*** 3C	***sneak*** 2D	***sow*** 3A	***speak*** 3F	***speed*** 1F	***spell*** 1A
spend 1E	***spill*** 1A	***spin*** 2B	***spit*** 2D	***split*** 1C	***spoil*** 1A	***spread*** 1C
spring 2A	***stand*** 4C	***steal*** 3F	***stick*** 2B	***sting*** 2B	***stink*** 2A	***strew*** 3A
stride 3C	***strike*** 2D	***string*** 2B	***strive*** 3C	***swear*** 3F	***sweep*** 1B	***swell*** 3B
swim 2A	***swing*** 2B	***take*** 3E	***teach*** 4D	***tear*** 3F	***tell*** 4B	***think*** 4D
thrive 3C	***throw*** 3E	***thrust*** 1C	***tread*** 3F	***wake*** 3F	***wear*** 3F	***weave*** 3F
wed 1C	***weep*** 1B	***wet*** 1C	***will*** 4E	***win*** 2B	***wind*** 2C	***wring*** 2B
write 3C						

5.4 Verbs with complex bases (*underpin*, *become*)

Regular verbs

Where a verb with a complex base is formed from a regular verb, it too is regular. Moreover, if there are spelling alternations, they match those of the verb from which it is formed. This is seen in the doubling of the final consonant in:

[59] i	*underpin*	*underpinned*	*underpinning*
ii	*wiretap*	*wiretapped*	*wiretapping*

The stress pattern of the complex base verb cannot account for the doubling in [ii], because the last syllable is not stressed; there is doubling because there is (predictable) doubling in the simple form.[26] As suggested in §5.1, this probably also accounts for such verbs as ***hobnob***, ***humbug***, ***worship***, ***handicap***, ***kidnap***, etc., which likewise have doubled consonants before ·*ed* and ·*ing*, even though the last syllable is not stressed. Whatever their actual status, these are apparently treated as if formed from ***nob***, ***bug***, ***ship***, ***cap***, and ***nap*** (and with ***kidnap*** this analysis would appear to be etymologically correct).

Irregular verbs

The same applies here: the complex verb has irregular forms matching those of the simple verb in final position. For example, ***arise*** has the forms *arise* ~ *arose* ~ *arisen*, matching those for ***rise***, the preterite and past participle of ***retell*** is *retold*, and so on. This pattern

[26] Compare the two verbs ***relay***. In the sense "lay again" it is a derivative of ***lay*** and shares its irregular preterite and past participle: *relaid*. In the sense "send by relay" it has no morphological connection with ***lay***, and is regular: *relayed*.

applies even where the meaning of the complex verb is relatively opaque. For example, ***mistake*** is like ***take*** and ***understand*** like ***stand***, in spite of the fact that there is no evident semantic relation between the simple and complex verbs:

[60]	i *take*	*took*	*taken*	*mistake*	*mistook*	*mistaken*
	ii *stand*	*stood*	*stood*	*understand*	*understood*	*understood*

The inflectional-morphological relationship is thus maintained long after the semantic connection has been lost. A sample of complex verbs of this kind is given in:

[61]	***become***	***befall***	***behold***	***beset***	***betake***	***forbear***
	forbid	***forecast***	***forgive***	***forgo***	***forswear***	***hamstring***
	overbear	***overcome***	***oversee***	***overtake***	***partake***	***undergo***
	undertake	***uphold***	***upset***	***withdraw***	***withhold***	***withstand***

Forbid derives from ***bid***$_2$ "order" of Class 3E: *forbid* ~ *forbade* ~ *forbidden*. ***Forget*** has the forms *forget* ~ *forgot* ~ *forgotten*, following the model of ***get*** in AmE, except that the past participle has only the form with ·*en*. ***Beget*** normally follows the same model (*beget* ~ *begot* ~ *begotten*), but it also has a distinct archaic preterite *begat*.

Exceptions

There are a very small number of exceptions, where a complex verb has regular forms even though the simple one is irregular. One example is ***gainsay***, which differs from irregular ***say*** in that it retains the vowel /eɪ/ of the base in the 3rd sg present tense (/geɪnseɪz/ vs /sez/) and optionally does so in the preterite and past participle too (/geɪnsed/ or /geɪnseɪd/ vs /sed/ only); in writing ***gainsay*** follows the pattern of ***say*** (with irregular change of *y* to *i*).

A second exception is ***broadcast***, which in addition to the irregular preterite and past participle *broadcast*, matching that of ***cast***, has the regular form *broadcasted*; likewise the more recent ***telecast***. Similar is ***deepfreeze***, but here the irregular *deepfroze* and *deepfrozen* are the normal forms and the regular form *deepfreezed* is of only marginal acceptability.

5.5 Negative forms of auxiliaries

A distinctive property of the English auxiliary verbs is that they have negative forms, marked by the suffix /nt/, spelled *n't*. The verbs concerned are ***be***, ***have***, ***do***, the modals, and (for some speakers) aspectual ***use***. The negative suffix appears only in finite clauses: on preterite and present tense forms (and the irrealis form of ***be***), and in the auxiliary ***do*** used in imperatives.

Regular forms

Most of the negative auxiliary forms are regular, with the suffix simply added to the preterite or present tense form. This applies with the following:

[62]	*aren't*	/ɑːʳnt/	*couldn't*	/kʊdn̩t/	*daren't*	/deəʳnt/	*didn't*	/dɪdn̩t/
	doesn't	/dʌzn̩t/	*hadn't*	/hædn̩t/	*hasn't*	/hæzn̩t/	*haven't*	/hævn̩t/
	isn't	/ɪzn̩t/	*mightn't*	/maɪtn̩t/	*needn't*	/niːdn̩t/	*oughtn't*	/ɔːtn̩t/
	shouldn't	/ʃʊdn̩t/	*wasn't*	/wɒzn̩t/	*weren't*	/wɜːʳnt/	*wouldn't*	/wʊdn̩t/

We omit ?*mayn't* (/meɪnt/, /meɪənt/); though current in the earlier part of the twentieth century, it has now virtually disappeared from the language.

Irregular forms

Half a dozen negative auxiliary forms are irregular, either in speech alone or in both speech and writing.

Forms that are regular in writing but irregular in speech

[63] i *do* — *don't* — /duː/ — /dəʊnt/
ii *must* — *mustn't* — /mʌst/ — /mʌsn̩t/
iii *used* — %*usedn't* — /juːst/ — %/juːsn̩t/

In [i] there is a change of vowel, and in [ii–iii] the final /t/ is lost before the negative suffix. *Usedn't* is the only form where the suffix is added to a preterite with the ·*ed* suffix, and it has a variant irregular spelling *usen't* in which the final consonant is dropped in writing too (see Ch. 3, §2.5.9).

Forms that are irregular in both speech and writing

[64] i *can* — *can't* — /kæn/ — /kɑːnt/ (BrE), /kæːnt/ (AmE)
ii *shall* — *shan't* — /ʃæl/ — /ʃɑːnt/ (BrE), /ʃæːnt/ (AmE)
iii *will* — *won't* — /wɪl/ — /woʊnt/

All the negative forms in this group lose the base-final consonant, and with ***will*** there is also a change of vowel, in both speech and writing. In BrE, *can't* and *shan't* have a change of vowel in speech.

The form *cannot*

Can has an additional variant form *cannot*, unique in that *not* (the etymological source of the /nt/ suffix), complete with its vowel, is attached to the lexical base. This form is more common in the written language than in speech, though the distinction in writing between the single word *cannot* and the word sequence *can not* is matched in speech by that between /ˈkænɒt/ (one /n/ and stress on the first syllable) and /kən ˈnɒt/ (two /n/'s and stress on the second syllable). In *cannot*, as in *can't*, the negative is invariably external, having scope over the modality, whereas this is not so with the analytic negative *can not*: see Ch. 3, §9.10.

Cannot is more formal in style than *can't*. It is hardly possible in pre-subject position: *Can't* / ?*Cannot we stay a little longer?*; *Not only can't* / **cannot he find the key, he's not even sure the papers are in the office anyway!*

The form *ain't*

This form, pronounced /eɪnt/, serves as the negative of any of the present tense forms of ***be*** and ***have***: *am, are, is, have, has.* There is a long tradition of prescriptive condemnation of it. In BrE it is reasonably called non-standard,[27] occurring (for example) in working-class speech but not (except jocularly) in academics' discourse; but in AmE it is more widely used and accepted in informal style. Educated American speakers use it not only in ordinary informal speech but also at times in writing.

[27] Until the nineteenth century or even later, however, *ain't* was common in colloquial upper-class BrE speech. Its effective proscription has been one of the greatest successes of prescriptivists.

The negative of *am*

The regular negative form %*amn't* is restricted to certain dialects, notably of Scotland and Ireland. In interrogatives with subject–auxiliary inversion /ɑːʳnt/ is widely used: *Aren't I going to be invited?*; *I'm right, aren't I?* The earlier spellings *a'n't* and *an't* have given way to *aren't*, reflecting its homophony with the negative of *are*. *Aren't I* is fully established in BrE or AmE, though in informal AmE *ain't I?* would often be substituted.

However, in uninverted constructions **I aren't* is not admissible even in informal style. Those who have *ain't*, use that here, while others use analytic negation: *I am not* or *I'm not.*

6 Phonological reduction and liaison

Inflectional morphology is concerned with the form of grammatically distinct words that belong to a single lexeme, but we turn now to certain cases of phonological variation in the form of a single grammatical word. Compare, for example:

[1] a. *I think Pat <u>has</u> seen it.* /əz/ b. *I haven't seen it, but Pat <u>has</u>.* /hæz/

We are dealing here with the same word *has* (the 3rd sg present tense form of ***have***), but a natural pronunciation in the context of [a] is /əz/, whereas in [b] it is pronounced /hæz/. These are called **weak** and **strong** forms respectively.

The weak form can be regarded as phonologically reduced relative to the strong form, but this kind of reduction is found on a much larger scale in rapid casual speech. Compare, for example, the three pronunciations of *What do you want?* shown in:

[2] i /ˈwɒt duː juː ˈwɒnt/
ii /ˈwɒt dʊ jʊ ˈwɒnt/
iii /ˈwɒdʒə ˈwɒ̃ʔ/

Version [i] contains strong forms of *do* and *you*, and represents a somewhat unnatural pronunciation, involving unusually careful or emphatic enunciation. Version [ii] contains weak forms of *do* and *you*, and represents a natural pronunciation in ordinary connected speech. Version [iii] involves a much greater degree of reduction (with /ɒ̃/ indicating a nasalised vowel in place of vowel + nasal sequence, and /ʔ/ indicating a glottal stop in place of /t/) and is restricted to casual style.

There are of course more than three possible pronunciations of the sentence, showing varying degrees of phonological reduction. The study of pronunciation in rapid casual style belongs to the field of phonology, and is outside the scope of this book. Weak forms do merit some consideration, however, for two reasons. In the first place, they are used, as we have said, in ordinary connected speech and in many cases represent the default or stylistically neutral pronunciation. The natural pronunciation of *Look at the cat*, for example, is /lʊk ət ðə kæt/; the version with strong forms of *at* and *the*, namely /lʊk æt ðiː kæt/, would generally be unnatural to the point of unacceptability, sounding like a sequence of disconnected words. Secondly, the use of weak forms interacts with the grammar in that it is subject to grammatical restrictions: it is not possible, for example, to have a weak form of *has* in [1b].

We will also consider in §6.2 **clitic** forms, which represent a somewhat greater degree of reduction. A clitic is a form which merges phonologically with an adjacent word, as when the first two words of *Pat has seen it* are pronounced /pæts/ (the written language indicates this with the spelling *Pat's seen it*).

6.1 Weak forms

There are around fifty words that have one or more weak forms as well as a strong form, as shown in the following table:[28]

[3]

ITEM	STRONG	WEAK	ITEM	STRONG	WEAK
a	/eɪ/	/ə/	*me*	/miː/	/mi/
am	/æm/	/əm/	*must*	/mʌst/	/məst/, /məs/
and	/ænd/	/ənd/, /ən/	*my*	/maɪ/	/mɪ/
are	/ɑːʳ/	/əʳ/	*of*	/ɒv/	/əv/
as	/æz/	/əz/	*shall*	/ʃæl/	/ʃəl/
at	/æt/	/ət/	*she*	/ʃiː/	/ʃi/
be	/biː/	/bi/	*should*	/ʃʊd/	/ʃəd/
been	/biːn/	/bɪn/	*sir*	/sɜːʳ/	/səʳ/
but	/bʌt/	/bət/	*some*	/sʌm/	/səm/
can	/kæn/	/kən/	*than*	/ðæn/	/ðən/
could	/kʊd/	/kəd/	*that*	/ðæt/	/ðət/
do	/duː/	/dʊ/, /də/	*the*	/ðiː/	/ði/ ~ /ðə/
does	/dʌz/	/dəz/	*them*	/ðem/	/ðəm/
for	/fɔːʳ/	/fəʳ/	*there*	/ðeəʳ/	/ðəʳ/
from	/frɒm/	/frəm/	*to*	/tuː/	/tʊ/, /tə/
had	/hæd/	/həd/, /əd/	*us*	/ʌs/	/əs/
has	/hæz/	/həz/, /əz/	*was*	/wɒz/	/wəz/
have	/hæv/	/həv/, /əv/	*we*	/wiː/	/wi/
he	/hiː/	/hi/, /i/	*were*	/wɜːʳ/	/wəʳ/
her	/hɜːʳ/	/həʳ/, /ɜːʳ/, /əʳ/	*who*	/huː/	/hʊ/, /ʊ/
him	/hɪm/	/ɪm/	*will*	/wɪl/	/wəl/, /əl/
his	/hɪz/	/ɪz/	*would*	/wʊd/	/wəd/, /əd/
is	/iz/	/ɪz/	*you*	/juː/	/jʊ/, /jə/

Except for *sir*, these words belong to one (or more) of the grammatical categories auxiliary verb, pronoun, determinative, preposition, coordinator, and subordinator. The weak form /ðət/ applies to *that* as a subordinator, not a determinative; /ðəʳ/ applies to *there* as a dummy pronoun, not a locative preposition; /hʊ/ and /ʊ/ apply to *who* as a relative rather than interrogative pronoun.

With the definite article *the*, the weak form /ðə/ is generally used before consonants and /ði/ before vowels: /ðə ˈpeəʳ/ (*the pear*) and /ði ˈæpl/ (*the apple*). There is, however, a certain amount of variation: some speakers use /ðə/ throughout – and there are also those who have this as a strong form.

[28] Forms containing /ə/ followed by /l, m, n/ have an alternate possible pronunciation with no vowel and syllabic /l̩, /m̩, /n̩; these phonologically predictable alternants are not shown in the table.

Distribution of strong and weak forms

Strong forms are used when the word is stressed, weak forms when it is unstressed.

One completely general factor that leads to a word being stressed is emphasis or contrast, as with the articles in [4i] or the verb *was* in [ii]:

[4] i *I didn't say I'd found* THE *missing key: I said I'd found* A *key.*
ii *I never said I* WAS *a member.*

As far as the articles are concerned, the strong forms are found only under conditions of this kind (see Ch. 5, §6), where they are not only stressed but also the informational focus.

For the rest, there are certain grammatical contexts that require strong forms:

[5] i a. *Who did you give it [to _]?*
b. *We'll help you if we [can _].* [stranding]
c. *They want me to resign, but I don't intend [to _].*
ii *How long will it be before she comes [to]?* [intransitive use]
iii *I haven't any money: can you lend me some?* [fused-head]
iv *Thank you, sir.* [not the appellation use]

In [i] we have stranding of a preposition, auxiliary verb, or infinitival *to*; in [ia] *to* is followed by a gap linked to interrogative *who*, while [ib–c] are elliptical. In [ii] the preposition has no complement at all; this use of *to* is highly restricted, and there are no comparable uses of the other prepositions in [3]. The generalisation covering cases [i–ii] is that prepositions, auxiliaries, and infinitival *to* are stressed when they are the sole or final element in a phrase-level constituent, a PP or VP.[29]

Examples [5iii–iv] illustrate more specific conditions. Determinative *some* is always stressed when in fused-head function; for its pre-head use, see Ch. 5, §7.5. The weak form of *sir* is used only in pre-head position in a proper name, as in *Sir James*; the same applies to *saint*, whose weak form /sənt/ is found only in names like *Saint/St Joan.*

6.2 Clitic versions of auxiliary verbs

Certain tensed forms of auxiliary verbs have, in addition to their weak forms, **clitic** versions, which merge phonologically with an adjacent word, their **host**. Thus *we've* is pronounced like *weave*, and *he'll* like *heel*, while *I'm* rhymes with *time*, and so on. For the most part, as in these examples, the clitics attach to a preceding word: they are then called, more specifically, **enclitics**. There is, however, one **proclitic**, attaching to a following host: this is the clitic version of *do*, which merges with *you* in examples like *D'you like it?*

Clitic forms are more restricted in their syntactic distribution than weak forms – but in varying degrees. The most restricted is the proclitic form of *do*, which attaches only to the pronoun *you* in clauses with subject–auxiliary inversion: *D'you want it?*; *What d'you want?* The enclitics we will consider under three headings.

[29] This statement may need to be qualified to cater for constructions where the gap is preceded by a sequence of two (or more) auxiliaries or prepositions, as in *I didn't tell her, though I realise I probably should have _* or *What did she make it out of _?* While strong forms are required for the first element (*should* and *out*), both strong and weak forms are found for the second (*have* and *of*). The strong version is the more usual, however, and it may be that the weak forms are confined to the rapid casual style that falls beyond the scope of this book.

(a) Most restricted: clitic forms of *am, are, have,* and *will*

These attach only to a preceding subject pronoun, as in:

[6] /aɪm/ *I'm* /wɪəʳ/ *we're* /ðeɪv/ *they've* /hiːl/ *he'll*

The clitic forms of *am, have,* and *will* consist of a single consonant: /m, v, l/. In the case of *are* it is not possible to give a satisfactory representation for the clitic itself, as the host + clitic combination may not be phonologically divisible into two corresponding parts. For example, *they're* in BrE is usually homophonous with locative *there.* Matters are complicated by the rhotic vs non-rhotic contrast and by the fact that the host + clitic combination may itself have strong and weak forms. Thus *you're* has a number of strong forms, including /jɔːʳ/ (rhyming with *sore*) and /jʊəʳ/ (rhyming with *pure*), but also a weak form /jə/.

The distributional restrictions on these clitics can be seen by comparing the examples in [6] with those in [7], where cliticisation is not normally possible:

[7] i *Jo and you are in for a shock.*
ii *Both of you have been pretty inconsiderate.*
iii *The Smiths will be there, and so will I.*

In [i–ii] *you* is not itself the subject, only part of the subject; and in [iii] *so* is a connective adjunct. We are concerned here with the phonology: *so will,* for example, can't be reduced to /soʊl/ (homophonous with *soul*). In writing, the use of contraction marked by an apostrophe is somewhat more extensive, at least for *'ll* and *'ve.* In *Pat'll do it,* for example, *'ll* corresponds to the weak form /əl/, and in *You could've been hurt* the *'ve* corresponds to weak /əv/.

The contrast between [6] and [7] is very clear. The difference between clitics and weak forms can, however, be quite slight, and there would seem to be some variation among speakers concerning the use of these clitics. Some, for example, accept non-subject interrogative words as host, as in *Where have you put the keys?* (%/weəʳv/).

(b) Least restricted: the clitic forms of *is* and *has*

The clitic form of both these verbs is /z/ (or /s/, after a voiceless consonant). Thus in *Jean's here* and *Jean's taken it* we have /dʒiːnz/, homophonous with the plural form *jeans.* The loss of the distinction between the two auxiliaries can lead to ambiguities: *It's finished,* for example, can mean either "It is finished" or "It has finished".[30]

These clitics place fewer requirements on what may serve as their host, allowing hosts that are not subject pronouns; but they are still interestingly restricted. Compare:

[8]	i	*Which dog's been on the sofa?*	[NP subject]
	ii	*That they're wet's obvious enough.*	[clausal subject]
	iii	*Get the one that's up in the bedroom.*	[subordinator *that* in relative]
	iv	*What do you think's going to happen?*	[matrix clause + subject gap]
	v	*Ed, I think, is going, and so's Sue.*	[connective *so* (or *neither/nor*)]
	vi	*Here's what you need.* *There's the bus.*	[locative *here/there*]
	vii	*Why's this happening?*	[monosyllabic interrogative word]
	viii	*What the hell's she doing?*	[interrogative + emotive modifier]

[30] In examples like *What's it matter?* the /s/ is a clitic version of *does,* but this use belongs to a more casual style of speech than we are concerned with here.

ix %*<u>What salad</u>'s that man over there eating?* [multi-word interrogative]
x %*Don't use more force <u>than</u>'s absolutely necessary.* [comparative *than*]
xi **She <u>often</u>'s right about things.* [central adjunct]
xii **<u>Never</u>'s it going to be easier.* [other preposed constituent]

The clitic may attach to the last word of the subject, which does not have to be an NP. In [iii–iv] it attaches to the word preceding a subject gap: the subordinator *that* in relative clauses, or the last word of the matrix in content clause complements (in [iv] '*__'s going to happen*' is complement of *think*: compare *I think something absolutely terrible's going to happen*, where the subject is present in the content clause). The elliptical construction shown in [v] may have *neither* or *nor* instead of *so*: *Ed isn't going and <u>neither</u>'s/<u>nor</u>'s Sue.* With prenuclear non-subject interrogative phrases, the clear cases are those consisting of a monosyllabic interrogative word, alone or followed by one of the emotive modifiers *the hell*, *on earth*, *ever*, etc. Some speakers allow other interrogative phrases, as in [ix]. There is also variation with respect to comparative *than* in [x]. But [xi–xii] illustrate constructions where cliticisation is excluded: following an adjunct in central position (between the subject and the verb), and preposed constituents other than interrogatives and the connectives of [v].

(c) Intermediate: the clitic forms of *had* and *would*

These auxiliaries have /d/ as their clitic form: in *He'd gone* and *He'd go* we have /hiːd/, homophonous with *heed*. Again, then, ambiguities can arise: *I'd put it away* can mean either "I had put it away" or "I would put it away". Such ambiguities, however, are much rarer than with *is* and *has* because there is less overlap in the distribution of *had* and *would*.

The clitic /d/ occurs only after vowels: in *Jan had seen it*, for example, the auxiliary can't be cliticised to yield a form rhyming with *sand*. Syntactically, it is less restricted than the clitic forms of *am*, *are*, *have*, and *will*: it may, for example, attach to *to* in *The person you were talking to'd been in prison.* But it seems somewhat more restricted than /z/: for example, it can hardly attach to connective *so* in *and so had/would I*. For many speakers *had* cliticises somewhat more readily than *would*, so that reduction to /d/ would be more likely in *Who <u>had</u> she been seeing?*, say, than in *Who <u>would</u> you vote for?*

6.3 Incorporation of the infinitival marker *to*

In some varieties, especially in AmE, the initial *to* of an infinitival catenative complement may, in informal speech, be morphologically incorporated into the preceding head word. This is found with the seven items listed in [9]; it is often shown in very informal styles of writing (typically the written representation of casual speech) by non-standard spellings:

[9] i	*going* + *to*	/ˈgənə/	*She's <u>gonna</u> fall.*
ii	*got* + *to*	/ˈgɒtə/	*You've <u>gotta</u> help me.*
iii	*have* + *to*	/ˈhæftə/	*We'll <u>hafta</u> give it away.*
iv	*ought* + *to*	/ˈɔːtə/	*You <u>oughta</u> tell them the truth.*
v	*supposed* + *to*	/səˈpoʊstə/	*He's <u>supposta</u> be at work.*
vi	*used* + *to*	/ˈjuːstə/	*I <u>usta</u> like her.*
vii	*want* + *to*	/ˈwɒnə/	*They <u>wanna</u> get a new car.*

This phenomenon is to be distinguished from the regular phonological reduction of *to* (infinitival marker or preposition) to the weak form /tə/, as in:

[10] a. *I hope to see her.* /hoʊp tə/ b. *They drove to Paris.* /droʊv tə/

The most significant difference is that the forms in [9] can be stranded, whereas the reduction to a weak form illustrated in [10] does not take place in this kind of context (cf. [5i] above). Compare, then:

[11] i a. %*He doesn't want me to tell her but I'm gonna* __.
b. %*I asked them to help but they don't wanna* __.
ii a. *I'm not sure I'll see her, but I hope to* __. [/hoʊp tuː/, /not */hoʊp tə/]
b. *That's not the place they drove to* __. [/droʊv tuː/, not */droʊv tə/]

In this respect the case is similar to that of negative forms like *can't* or *isn't* (§5.5), and we again regard it therefore as a matter of morphology, not mere phonological reduction. But it is much less systematic than the negative case, applying to just seven words which do not in other respects belong together as a class; it thus falls within the sphere of lexical morphology, not inflection.

This is to say that the forms in [9] are morphological compounds. And because the infinitival marker has been incorporated into the compound the catenative complement is a bare infinitival, not a *to*-infinitival. For the same reason they can only enter into the simple catenative construction, not the complex one. The ordinary verb *want* can enter into either: *They want to get a new car* (simple) or *They want me to get a new car* (complex). There is naturally no compounded counterpart of the latter example because *want* and *to* are not adjacent. But even when the object NP is fronted so that the *to* does immediately follow *want*, the compound is still excluded. Compare, then:

[12] i a. %*Who do you want to invite* __? b. %*Who do you wanna invite* __?
ii a. *Who do you want* __ *to win?* b. **Who do you wanna* __ *win?*

In [ia] *who* is object of *invite*, whereas in [iia] it is object of *want*. Example [ia] thus belongs to the simple catenative construction (like *I want to invite Kim*) and hence allows incorporation of *to*, as in [ib]; [iia] belongs to the complex construction (like *I want Kim to win*) and hence has no counterpart with *wanna*, for the compound verb licenses only a single complement, a subjectless bare infinitival.[31]

Two of the seven compounds display the inflectional contrast shown in:

[13]

		3RD SG PRESENT	PLAIN PRESENT OR PLAIN FORM
i	***hafta***	/hæstə/	/hæftə/
ii	***wanna***	/wɒnstə/	/wɒnə/

The inflectional marking of the 3rd sg present form is on the head element, the verb base, just as in plural compounds like *passers-by* it is on the noun base. In contexts requiring some other inflectional form, only the ordinary, non-compounded construction is available: *They had to leave*; *We're having to sell it.* Note that in ellipsis these behave like [11ii], not [11i], so that in *We asked them not to leave but they had to*, for example, we have /hæd tuː/, not */hædə/. In addition, /juːstə/ can be either a preterite form (*I usta like it*) or a plain form (*I didn't*

[31] A minority of speakers appear to allow the pronunciation /wɒnə/ in [12iib], but we would regard that not as a case of morphological compounding but a matter of phonological reduction. The complex catenative construction provides no evidence for a morphological explanation of the kind illustrated in [11].

usta like it), the syncretism here reflecting the homonymy in the non-compounded *I used to like it* and *I didn't use to like it*. The /gɒtə/ of [9ii] is a past participle form governed by perfect ***have***; the latter is often omitted, however, leading to the reanalysis of /gɒtə/ as an invariant present tense form. The /ɔːtə/ of [iv] is an invariant present tense form or a non-standard plain form used in the negative with supportive ***do*** (*!He didn't oughta*). Also invariant are /gənə/ and /səpoʊstə/, the former being part of an idiom headed by progressive ***be***, the latter a participial adjective likewise found only after ***be*** (cf. Ch. 16, §10.1.3).

6.4 Liaison

There are two instances in English phonology and morphology of transitional consonants that are inserted between words, or parts of words, to avoid a hiatus between two vowels. This phenomenon is widely known as **liaison**, a term taken over from the grammar of French.

One case is that of linking and intrusive /r/ found exclusively in non-rhotic accents. This is of morphological relevance in the formation of gerund-participles, as discussed in §2.1.4. For the rest, it is a quite general phonological phenomenon, and it is not necessary to add here to the account given in Ch. 1, §3.1.1. It is never reflected in the orthography.

The indefinite article

The other case is specific to one grammaticised word, the indefinite article, which has *an* as a liaison form before vowels:

[14] i	a. *a fool*		b. *an idiot*
ii	a. *a by no means ugly man*		b. *an in some ways handsome man*

Historically, the indefinite article derives from an unstressed form of the cardinal numeral *one*: the /n/ of the latter has been lost in *a* but retained in *an*. As far as Present-day English is concerned, the result is that the indefinite article is unique in having a distinct liaison form. It has /ən/ as its weak form, /æn/ as its strong form.

An is used when the next word begins with a vowel. The choice between *a* and *an* depends purely on the phonological context. The liaison form occurs before a vowel sound, not before particular letters. Thus *uncle* and *epic* are pronounced with an initial vowel, so we have *an uncle* and *an epic*, but *unit* and *eunuch* are pronounced with an initial consonant (/j/), giving *a unit* and *a eunuch*. Or compare *an onion* and *a once-in-a-lifetime opportunity* (where *once* begins with /w/).

The only complication concerns words spelled with initial *h*. We need to distinguish three sets of words beginning with *h*:

[15] i	*heir*	*honest*	*honorarium*	*honour*	*hour*
ii a.	*ˈhabitat*	*ˈhero*	*ˈhistory*	*ˈhostel*	*ˈhysterectomy*
b.	*haˈbitual*	*heˈroic*	*hisˈtorical*	*hoˈtel*	*hysˈterical*

The words in [i] do not have an /h/ in their pronunciation, and hence require the liaison form: *an heir*, *an honest man*, etc. There are relatively few such words: those listed, together with derivatives and compounds (*heirloom*, *hourly*) – and, in AmE but not BrE, *herb*.

The words in [15iia–b] all have initial /h/ when spoken in isolation. The difference is that with those in [iia] the syllable beginning with /h/ is stressed, while with those in [iib] it is unstressed. The [iia] words never take the liaison form: we have *a hero*, not **an hero*, in accordance with the general rule. The initial /h/ of an unstressed syllable, however, may optionally be dropped in connected speech, as in *Did you see him?*, *this habitual criminal*, *its historical development*, and so on. Loss of the /h/ results in a word beginning with a vowel, thus providing the context for the liaison form, again in accordance with the rule: /ənə'bɪtʃʊəl 'krɪmɪnəl/.

This is unproblematic as far as speech is concerned, but in writing the status of expressions like *an habitual criminal*, *an heroic trek*, *an historical novel*, *an hysterical outburst* is less clear. Usage manuals generally agree that *an* is permissible, but not obligatory, in such cases – which reflects the fact that /h/ is optionally, but not obligatorily, omitted in speech. The manuals suggest, however, that the present trend is towards always using *a* before words of type [15iib]: *a habitual criminal*, *a heroic trek*, *a historical novel*, *a hysterical outburst*. *A hotel* is often mentioned as a special case, with the suggestion that *an hotel* is now old-fashioned and to be avoided.

19

Lexical word-formation

Laurie Bauer
Rodney Huddleston

This is the second of two chapters dealing with the form of words. The main topic of Ch. 18 was the formation of inflected words from their lexical base, while the present chapter is concerned with the form of lexical bases, i.e. with the lexical side of word-formation.

1 Preliminaries

1.1 Established words and potential words

To a very large extent speakers know words as individual items of vocabulary. We know, for example, that the word for the area over which a bishop has charge is *bishopric*, not **bishopdom* – and conversely that the word denoting the area over which a king rules is *kingdom*, not **kingric*; that there are words *unfaithfulness* and *infidelity*, but not **infaithfulity* or **unfidelness*; and so on. Words like *bishopric, kingdom, unfaithfulness, infidelity* we will refer to as **established** words: they are recognised as part of the vocabulary of the language.

Established words are individually familiar to speakers of the language and can be found in standard dictionaries. The inventory of items included in such dictionaries is not, however, identical to the set of words. A dictionary includes many multi-word expressions that have idiomatic meanings or are otherwise known as individual items (*give in*, *take advantage of*, *the more the merrier*, and so on). Conversely, and more importantly for the purposes of this chapter, not all words are established words. In speaking or writing we do not always restrict ourselves to established words: we can create new words or use words we have heard before but which have not yet become established.

Creating new words is in general subject to rules or constraints. For example, the rules of Present-day English word-formation allow *policeability* as a word, but not **priestric* or **pick-basket*. People vary in their subjective reaction to new words, and some will find *policeability* inelegant or otherwise open to criticism, but it nevertheless differs very clearly in its linguistic status from **priestric* and **pick-basket*. *Policeability* is formed from the established verb *police* by adding the adjective-forming suffix ·*able*, and then adding a further suffix, with modification of ·*able*, to yield a noun that might be used in such a sentence as *The Commissioner questioned the policeability of the new regulations.* But **priestric* and **pick-basket* do not conform to the present-day rules; **priestric* is analogous to *bishopric* but ·*ric* is no longer available as an element for forming new words, and the pattern seen in *pickpocket* (plain form of the verb + noun in a direct object relation) is likewise no longer available for forming new words so **pick-basket* is not admissible.[1]

Words which conform to the rules of word-formation we will call **grammatical**, extending this term from syntax to morphology. Similarly, words that do not conform to these rules and which are not established we call **ungrammatical** and mark with the familiar asterisk notation. Grammatical words like *policeability* which are not established will be referred to as **potential words**: they have the potential to become established.[2] Words which have been used but have not become established are commonly called 'nonce-words'; as we have defined 'potential' word as a grammatical word that is not established the category will cover nonce-words as well as words that have not in fact been used.

An ordinary dictionary deals with the established words more or less item by item, whereas a grammar describes the structural patterns and interrelationships within the full set of established and potential words, and the principles and rules governing the formation of new words: this is our concern in the present chapter.

1.2 Morphological structure

Complex and simple words

A **complex word** is one that is analysable into a sequence of smaller units, while a word that is not so analysable is **simple**:

[1]	i	*trap*	*child*	*father*	*elephant*	[simple words]
	ii	*mouse·trap*	*child·care*	*father-figure*	*elephant-tusk*	[complex words]
	iii	*en·trap*	*child·ish*	*father·ly*	*elephant·ine*	

Bases and affixes

The two main morphological categories that figure in the structure of words are **bases** and **affixes**. In English bases are characteristically **free** while affixes are normally **bound**, where an element is free if it can stand alone as a word and bound if it can't. Among the minimal units in [1] the bases are *trap, child, father, elephant,* and *mouse, care, figure, tusk.* Note that although the bases *mouse, trap,* etc., do not form words by themselves in [ii] and [iii] they have the potential to do so, and hence satisfy the definition we have given for 'free'. The affixes in [1] are *en·*, *·ish*, *·ly*, and *·ine*. These cannot normally stand alone as words but attach to a base;[3] affixes which precede the

[1] We continue to use the '·' notation introduced in the last chapter to mark suffixes (like *·able*) or prefixes (like *pre·*) and, where appropriate, for marking morphological divisions within words except when there is a hyphen in the orthography.

[2] Established words like *bishopric* and *pickpocket* which do not conform to the present-day rules of word-formation could be called 'agrammatical'; we return to them below in discussing the concept of lexicalisation. In the morphological literature the term 'grammatical word' is commonly used in other senses (generally contrasting with lexical word, lexeme, orthographic word, and so on), but these senses are so different from that adopted here that there can be no danger of confusion.

[3] The qualification 'normally' is added to cater for cases like that where one responds to the question *Was it small?* by simply saying *Ish*. This represents a jocular ellipsis of *small* and doesn't affect the status of *·ish* as an affix rather than a base. More problematic is the case of items such as *mega·*, *mini·*, *anti·*, *pro·*, which are historically affixes but have developed uses where they can stand alone as words: *She was wearing a mini* or *I'm very anti that sort of behaviour*, etc. Since these uses come from the bound form and are probably still felt as related to it, there seems little point in reanalysing *mini·dress* and the like as consisting of two bases.

base, like *en·* in *en·trap*, are **prefixes**, and those which follow, like the other three, are **suffixes.**

Bound bases

We have said that English bases are characteristically free, but we also find bound bases, bases which cannot stand alone as a word. Compare:

[2]	i	*perish·able*	*starv·ation*	*abus·ive*	*pre·judge*	*dis·aggregate*	[free base]
	ii	*dur·able*	*dur·ation*	*aggress·ive*	*pre-empt*	*dis·perse*	[bound base]

The underlined elements in [2i] are straightforward bases of the kind illustrated in [1]: they have the potential to stand alone as words. (*Starve* and *abuse* lose their final *e* when followed by a vowel-initial suffix, but that is simply a matter of spelling alternation.) But there are no words *dure, aggress, empt*, and *perse* in English, so the underlined elements in [2ii] are bound. We nevertheless classify them as bases, not affixes, because they fill the same role in the structure of the word as the central type of base seen in [i] – the examples are chosen to show the same affixes attaching now to a free base, now to a bound one. All words contain at least one base, and since *·able, ·ation, ·ive, pre·*, and *dis·* are clearly affixes, there is no problem in identifying the underlined elements in [i] as the base of these words.

Dur·, *aggress·*, *·empt*, and *·perse* are quite unlike affixes in that they do not attach to free bases to form words. The reason the [2ii] words have bound bases is historical: they were not created by the word-formation processes of English itself. *Durable*, for example, was borrowed into English from Old French, and the Old French word in turn came from Latin; the *·able* part, however, is easily identifiable with that of *perishable* and this enables us to analyse the whole into base + suffix. Precisely because *dur·* is bound, however, *durable* does not conform to the rules of Present-day English word-formation, and the same applies to the other words in [ii].

Combining forms

The underlined elements in [3] are known as **combining forms**:

[3]	i	*anglo·phobe*	*aster·oid*	*auto·gamy*	*electro·lyte*	*pseudo·carp*
	ii	*Anglo-Soviet*	*meteor·oid*	*auto·hypnosis*	*electro·magnet*	*pseudo·science*

Combining forms generally have their origin in one of the classical languages, usually Greek. Protypically, one such form combines with another to form a word, as in [i] (and many of them must combine in this way), but some can also combine with a free base, as in [ii]. We will take combining forms to be a special case of bound bases, though they are less clearly distinct from affixes than other bases; they are discussed more fully in §4.5.

Constituent structure

Words containing three or more elements have a hierarchical constituent structure comparable to that of larger grammatical units. The **immediate constituents** (ICs) of *un·gentle·man·ly*, for example, are *un* + *gentlemanly*: it is formed by adding the negative prefix *un·* to the adjective *gentlemanly*, not by adding the adjective-forming suffix *·ly* to a non-existent noun **ungentleman*. At the next layer of structure, the ICs of *gentlemanly* are *gentleman* + *·ly* (not *gentle* + *manly*). And finally *gentleman* is divisible into *gentle* + *man*. The constituent structure can be represented in the familiar type of tree-diagram, as in [4], where we also give an analysis of *disinterestedness*:

[4] a. b.

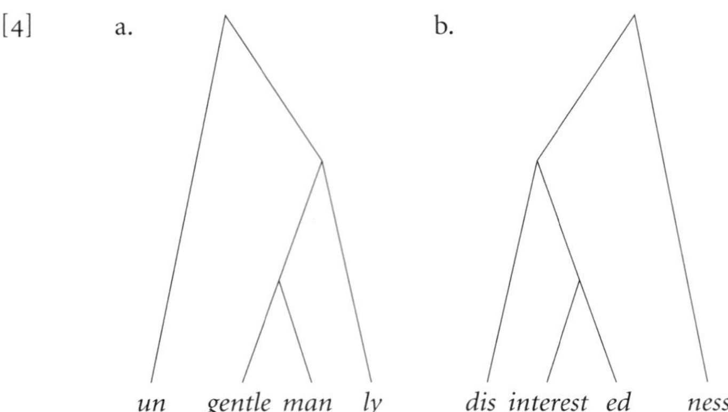

In complex words one base occurs as a constituent of another. *Boy·ish*, for example, is a base that contains the base *boy* within it. In [4] the bases in [a] are *gentle*, *man*, *gentleman*, *gentlemanly* and *ungentlemanly*, and in [b] *interest*, *interested*, *disinterested* and *disinterestedness*. Note that while a base may be contained within a larger base, we do not speak of a word being contained within a larger word. *Gentle* and *man*, for example, are bases but not words when they occur in the word *gentleman*. The sentence *He behaves like a gentleman*, for example, contains just five words: *gentleman* is here both a base and a word, while *gentle* and *man* are just bases. In *He is a very gentle man*, by contrast, *gentle* and *man* are simultaneously bases and words.

We can now define various kinds of base as follows:[4]

[5] i **Compound base**: one whose ICs are themselves bases
ii **Derivative base**: one with an affix as an IC
iii **Simple base**: one not divisible into smaller morphological constituents
iv **Lexical base**: one that is not part of a larger base formed by a process of lexical word-formation

Gentleman is therefore a compound base, but *gentlemanly* and *ungentlemanly* are derivative bases; *gentle* and *man* are simple bases. Compound and derivative bases are defined by their internal structure, and simple bases by their lack of any such structure. A base of any of these three types may or may not be a lexical base, depending on the larger morphological structure, if any, in which it is contained. *Gentleman*, for example, is a lexical base in *He behaves like a gentleman*, but not in *He behaves in a gentlemanly way*.

Morphophonological alternation

Bases and affixes often exhibit variation in phonological form depending on the structure of the base in which they occur: this phenomenon is known as **morphophonological alternation**. In [4i], for example, *man* has a reduced vowel /ə/ instead of the full vowel /æ/ that it has when it is not part of a compound. The final consonant of *electric* is normally /k/, but in *electricity* we have /s/ instead. Commonly, as in these examples, the morphophonological alternation is not reflected in the spelling, but there are also

[4] An alternative term for 'base' is 'stem' (though the latter is also used in other senses); and 'root' is commonly used for a simple base. We allow the term 'base' to apply to words as well as to parts of words in order to achieve greater generality. For example, as far as the internal structure of 'gentlemanly' is concerned, it doesn't make any difference whether it is standing alone as a word or is merely part of the larger word 'ungentlemanly': in either case it is a derivative base.

cases where it is, as with the negative prefix seen in *inattentive*, *impossible*, *illegal*, *irrelevant*. Morphophonological alternation is particularly frequent in derivative bases, and is discussed in that context in §5.1.2.

Morphological analysability vs etymology

Words are most clearly analysable into constituent parts when the latter occur with the same or similar meaning elsewhere, as with *bed·room*, *un·kind*, *soft·ness*, etc. But this is by no means a necessary condition for analysability. There is no difficulty in recognising *straw·berry* and *draw·ing-room* as compounds even though the meaning of the whole is not predictable from the meanings of the component bases: it is enough that the second base is formally and semantically identifiable with the *berry* and *room* that occur as separate words or in semantically more transparent compounds like *black·berry* and *bed·room*. Similarly with derivative bases like *dur·able* and the others listed in [2ii], even though affixes characteristically have less specific meanings than bases.

There are even cases where neither component contributes a clearly separable component of meaning to the whole. The meaning of *black·mail*, for example, is not predictable from the meanings of *black* and *mail* as independent words, but *black* remains easily recognisable as a separate morphological unit because it occurs in a considerable number of compounds and phrases where it likewise does not have its literal meaning: *blackleg*, *blacklist*, *blacksmith*, *black magic*, *black mark*, *black market*, *black spot*, and so on.

The case of *blackmail* is to be distinguished from that of *blackguard*. *Blackmail* is morphologically analysable but semantically opaque as a result of historical change. (The original meaning of the *mail* component was "coin, rent" and with *black* having the meaning "illicit" still seen in *black market*: the compound was interpretable as "illicit money".) But with *blackguard* historical change has resulted in the loss of /k/ from *black*, and /blægɑːʳd/ is now a simple base, not a compound: the first syllable is neither phonologically nor semantically identifiable with /blæk/.[5] The original base *black* is retained in the spelling, but this can be seen as a reflection of the historical source rather than as a justification for treating *blackguard* as a compound. Compare, similarly, /kʌbəd/ *cupboard*, /brekfəst/ *breakfast*, and so on. With *husband* even the orthography gives no indication of the original compounding of *house* and *bōnda* "householder", a word which has now vanished from the language. Any analysis of such words as *blackguard*, *cupboard*, *breakfast*, *husband*, and the like belongs therefore to the field of **etymology**, the study of the historical source of words, not to the field of **morphology**, the study of the grammatical structure of words. There is nothing in the present-day language system to motivate an analysis of such words into smaller morphological units.

Historical change may likewise yield simple bases from what were originally derivatives. *Mongrel*, for example, is not morphologically analysable even though historically it was formed by suffixation. The original suffix was also used in the formation of such words as *mackerel*, *doggerel*, *scoundrel*, but these words are too few in number and too opaque semantically to justify a base + suffix analysis in Present-day English. Again, then, we take the view that any analysis of *mongrel* is a matter of etymology, not morphology.

It is not always so easy, however, to decide whether one is doing morphology or etymology. Take again the case of *durable*. Evidence for recognising *dur* as a base is

[5] Some speakers pronounce *blackguard* as /blægəʳd/: here the second syllable is likewise neither phonologically nor semantically identifiable with /gɑːʳd/.

provided by the semantic relation between *durable*, *duration*, and *endure*, and evidence for taking ·*able* as a suffix comes from the relation with such words as *perishable* and also from the adjective–noun relationship between *durable* and *durability* (compare *repeatable* ~ *repeatability*, *readable* ~ *readability*, and countless others). That adds up to quite a strong case for a morphological analysis. But consider now the words *stable*, *soluble*, *voluble*. These enter into the same adjective–noun relationship (compare *stability*, *solubility*, *volubility*), so we can't say there is no evidence for morphological analysis here. It is, however, very slight, even when we add in the relation between *soluble* and *solution*. In the case of *stable* a division between *st* and *able* gives a base without a vowel and the wrong vowel quality for the suffix (/eɪ/ rather than /ə/), while a division between *sta* and *ble* (which is in fact etymologically correct) doesn't have the suffix that is found in words whose morphological analysability is clear (i.e. words like *repeat·able*).

Or take the adjective *pregnant*. Etymologically it is divisible into the three components *pre*· "before in time" (cf. *prejudge*, *premature*), *gn* "having to do with begetting" (cf. *cognate* or, with an intervening vowel, *gonad*, *genus*), and the adjective-forming suffix ·*ant* (cf. *expectant*, *malignant*). The division between *pre* and *gn* can safely be regarded as purely etymological: *gn* is not a phonologically possible base, and the semantic connection with *prejudge*, *cognate*, etc. is not transparent enough to sustain a morphological analysis. Evidence for a division between *pregn* and *ant* is provided by the adjective–noun relationship seen in *pregnant* ~ *pregnancy* (cf. *flippant* ~ *flippancy*, *militant* ~ *militancy*, etc.), but this is not as widespread as the *durable* ~ *durability* pattern and not accompanied by the other evidence favouring a morphological analysis of *durable*.

As a final example consider such words as *commit*, *demit*, *emit*, *compel*, etc. Evidence for a morphological analysis *com·mit*, *de·mit*, *e·mit*, *com·pel*, etc., is provided by the set of relationships between the verbs in [6i] and between these verbs and the corresponding nouns shown in [6ii]:

[6]	i	*commit*	*demit*	*emit*	*permit*		*remit*
		compel		*expel*		*propel*	*repel*
		compose	*depose*	*expose*		*propose*	*repose*
		conceive	*deceive*		*perceive*		*receive*
	ii	*commission*	*demission*	*emission*	*permission*		*remission*
		compulsion		*expulsion*		*propulsion*	*repulsion*
		composition	*deposition*	*exposition*		*proposition*	
		conception	*deception*		*perception*		*reception*

However, the number of words entering into these relationships is quite small – not remotely comparable to the number entering into the ·*able* ~ ·*ability* relationship (or indeed the ·*ant* ~ ·*ancy* one if we include the ·*ent* ~ ·*ency* variant seen in *consistent* ~ *consistency*, etc.). Moreover, the putative prefixes *com·*/*con·*, *de·*, *ex·*/*e·*, *per·*, *pro·*, *re·* and bases *mit*, *pel*, *pose*, *ceive* cannot be given constant independent meanings from which the meanings of the whole words could be predicted.

The view taken here is that no sharp boundary can be drawn between morphological analysis and pure etymology – and we will leave open the question as to whether forms like those in [6i] are to be taken as morphologically analysable in Present-day English. Our primary focus in this chapter will be on cases whose morphological analysability is transparent or very nearly so, but a restriction of this kind is motivated by limitations of space and is not inconsistent with a broader interpretation of the field of morphology.

1.3 Productivity and lexicalisation

Productivity of a process as availability for use in the creation of new words

We say that a particular kind of morphological process, or a particular affix, is **still productive** if it is still available for the creation of new words. For example, the process of combining two nouns into a compound noun that was used in the Old English period to form the source of *husband* is still productive, enabling us to create new words such as *housemate* (cf. the established *flatmate*). Similarly, we can form new words like *policeability*, as mentioned above, so that the process of forming an adjective by adding the suffix ·*able* to a verb and the process of forming a noun by adding the suffix ·*ity* to an adjectival base ending in ·*able* are still productive.

These examples contrast with processes that have been used in the formation of words in the past, but are no longer productive. The ungrammatical words **pick-basket* and **priestric* discussed in §1.1 provide examples. **Pick-basket* is ungrammatical because the type of verb + noun compounding process that gave us *pickpocket* with the meaning "person who picks pockets" is not now productive. And **priestric* is not a potential word because the suffix ·*ric* found in *bishop·ric* and *arch·bishop·ric* is no longer productive.

Lexicalisation

The converse of productivity is **lexicalisation**: words that are or were earlier morphologically analysable but which could not be formed with their present meaning by the current rules of word-formation are said to be lexicalised.[6] The implication of the term is that properties of these words have to be specified individually in the dictionary rather than being consistent with the grammatical rules of word-formation.

Numerous examples of lexicalisation are provided by words already discussed. *Bishopric* and *pickpocket* are lexicalised in that the processes by which they were formed are no longer productive. *Blackmail* is lexicalised even though the process of forming a compound by combining an adjective and noun is still productive, because the meaning of the whole is not predictable from the current meanings of *black* and *mail*. Derivatives with bound bases like *durable* and the others in [2ii] are likewise lexicalised in that the still productive use of the affixes concerned attaches them to free bases, not bound ones. The words of [6] (*commit*, *demit*, etc.) are lexicalised since, whether or not they are morphologically analysable at all, they certainly could not be formed by the current rules – hence the impossibility of filling the gaps in the table. The extreme case of lexicalisation is seen in words like *husband* and *mongrel* which are no longer morphologically complex.

Lexicalised words tend to have rather more specialised meanings than non-lexicalised ones. Compare, for example, *blackmail* with a potential compound such as *dog-radio*. Out of context it is not clear how the latter is to be interpreted. It could mean "a radio which resembles a dog", "a radio which is attached to a dog", "a radio for calling dogs on", "a radio with a picture of a dog on it", or various other things. But a lexicalised compound like *blackmail* does not have this wide range of possible meanings. It cannot mean "a type of coat of mail which is typically black", nor "illicit post", and so on: its central meaning is "extorting money from someone by threatening to reveal damaging information".

Such specialisation of meaning is typical of words that are lexicalised. But it is not restricted to them: it tends to be characteristic of the larger class of established words.

[6] Alternative terms that can be found in the literature include 'frozen', 'fossilised', 'petrified'; these focus on the fact that lexicalised words are fixed in meaning and not open to the range of meaning available for a newly coined word.

Take, for example, the compound *wheelchair*. In principle, it could be used for any type of chair that has some strong association with wheels – by virtue of having wheels, being made from wheels, being in the shape of a wheel, and so on. In practice, however, it is restricted to the type of chair used by invalids. A pushchair has wheels, but that does not make it a wheelchair. You can push a wheelchair, but that does not make it a pushchair. *Wheelchair* thus has a specialised meaning, but while it is an established word, it is not lexicalised: it is formed by a perfectly productive process of compounding from two nouns that are readily identifiable with the independent words *wheel* and *chair*, and its meaning is quite consistent with its having been formed by compounding *wheel* as modifier with *chair* as head.

Degree of productivity

If a word-formation process is still productive, we need also to consider its **degree of productivity**. This is a matter of how readily words can be formed by means of the process. To a large extent this is determined by the size of the class of bases available to the process.

We can illustrate this concept by comparing the suffixes ·*ness* and ·*ity*. Both can be added to adjectives to form nouns. Some bases allow either: *porousness* and *porosity*, for example, are both established words. Other bases allow or strongly prefer just one: *bearded* can only take ·*ness* (*beardedness*, not **beardedity*), while *linear* strongly prefers ·*ity* (*linearity*, but hardly ?*linearness*). But overall ·*ness* is used more widely than ·*ity*, and there is evidence that speakers today forming new words strongly prefer those in ·*ness*: we say then that ·*ness* has a higher degree of productivity than ·*ity*.

Words produced by the most freely productive processes rarely become established. It would be inappropriate, for example, for a dictionary to attempt to list all words formed on the pattern of *brown-eyed, smooth-skinned, chocolate-coated, red-covered, two-bedroomed* (though some of them, such as *tight-fisted* or *small-minded* do have to be recorded because of their specialised meanings). Such highly productive processes are comparable to the rules for forming syntactic phrases: we don't need to list *brown-eyed* in the dictionary any more than we need to list *with brown eyes*. Similarly, there is no more reason for a dictionary to list the thousands of grammatical compounds in ·*like* (*axe-like, cheese-like, dog-like, orange-like, dream-like, . . .*) than there is for it to list the corresponding phrases (*like an axe, like cheese, . . .*).

We will not try here to quantify degrees of productivity, but will work rather with broad categories such as 'highly productive', 'of low productivity', and the like, or with relative productivity, saying (as in the ·*ness*/·*ity* example) that one process is more productive than another.

1.4 Introduction to the description

Processes and morphological structure

We have pointed out that a chapter dealing with the grammar of words must deal with the ways in which new words can be created as well as with the properties of existing words. At times, therefore, the focus will be on **processes**, on **word-formation**, while at others it will be on **morphological structure**, on the **form of words**. To a large extent, a description in terms of processes and one in terms of morphological structure are equivalent. Compounding, for example, is the process whereby two bases are put together to form a third, but the result is a compound, defined in structural terms as a base whose ICs are themselves bases. Similarly, derivation is the process of attaching an affix to a base, and this yields a base with the structure of a derivative, i.e. one consisting of a base and an affix, so again a description in terms of formation process and one in terms of morphological structure are equivalent. But the relation between formation process and resultant structure is not always so straightforward: not all word-formation processes yield words of a distinct morphological structure. An obvious example is back-formation, the process by which *edit*, for example, was formed from *editor* by dropping the suffix. Here the resultant form is just a simple base and in terms of morphological structure the relation between *edit* and *editor* is the same as that between *write* and *writer*: whether the derivative is older or (as in the usual case) newer than the simple base is a purely historical question.

Organisation of the chapter

We deal first, in §§2–3, with those processes which (like back-formation) do not result in words of a distinct morphological structure. Next, §§4–5 are mainly devoted to compounding and derivation respectively. We have, however, departed from an organisation based purely on the type of process or resultant form in order to give greater weight to meaning. Thus §4 is almost completely limited to compounding involving noun, adjective, and verb bases, while compound verbs beginning with such preposition bases as *out*, *over*, *under*, etc., are dealt with in §5, along with the derivatives, and in this latter section we group together affixes that have the same kind of meaning (such as those deriving diminutives, reversatives, and so on) or have the same syntactic effect (such as deriving adjectives from nouns or verbs). It is hoped that the heterogeneity of the classification, in reflecting the heterogeneity of the material, will allow some patterns to emerge more clearly than they would with a classification based entirely on processes or one based entirely on meaning.

We will not be concerned with the borrowing of new words from other languages (as with *blitzkrieg*, from German, for example): although this enlarges the vocabulary, it does not involve **forming** a new word. Nor will we be concerned with the development of new meanings for existing words. Most attention will be given to processes that are still productive.

Data

All the examples given here are attested words. Established words have been taken from dictionaries, including various dictionaries of new words and neologisms. Words from these sources show the continued productivity of the processes they illustrate. The few nonce-words used have the same function.

Notational convention: the symbol '~'

The meaning of a derivative usually involves in some way the meaning of the base to which the affix is attached. In giving glosses for the meanings of such derivatives, we will make use of the swung dash symbol '~' to represent the meaning of the base. For instance, one meaning of the suffix ·*ise* can be glossed as "make ~", so that *vulgarise* means "make vulgar", *immortalise* means "make immortal".[7]

[7] The '~' symbol is commonly used in dictionaries to stand for the base itself, but as we use it within double quotes it will be evident that we are concerned with meaning.

2 Minor word-formation processes

This section deals with various word-formation processes that are marginal in some way. They do not yield words of a distinct morphological structure or result in new combinations of independently meaningful components. Those in §2.2, moreover, are based on spelling rather than on pronunciation, and hence irrelevant to languages without an established writing-system.

2.1 Manufacture

Word manufacture is an extremely rare process creating a new word simply on the basis of the phonological resources of the language:

[7] *nylon*, *quark*, *boff* ("have sex with") AmE slang, *scag* ("heroin")

From a structural point of view these are simple bases: they are not made up of smaller morphological units. The relation between form and meaning is quite arbitrary – deliberately so in a high proportion of cases. One use of this process is for tradenames, as in *Kodak* and (originally) *nylon*.

2.2 Initialism

This type of word-formation process has its basis in the written language: in the central cases a base is formed by combining the initial letters of a sequence of words (or of the parts of a complex word). There are two main types, **abbreviations** and **acronyms**.

Abbreviations

[8]	i	*CIA*	*Central Intelligence Agency*
		EEC	*European Economic Community*
		FBI	*Federal Bureau of Investigation*
		LA	*Los Angeles*
		MIT	*the Massachusetts Institute of Technology*
		UN	*United Nations*
	ii	*DJ*	*disc jockey*
		DNA	*deoxyribonucleic acid*
		EFL	*English as a foreign language*
		ESP	*extrasensory perception*
		HQ	*headquarters*
		MC	*Master of Ceremonies*
		MP	*Member of Parliament*
		TV	*television*
		VIP	*very important person*
	iii	*pc*	*postcard, personal computer*
		ps	*postscript*

Abbreviations are pronounced as sequences of letters: /siːaɪeɪ/, /iːiːsiː/, etc. They are normally written as here, or else with full stops (periods) after each letter (*C.I.A.*, etc.). Occasionally, however, they are spelled out as ordinary words, as in *deejay*, an alternative spelling of *DJ*. The full form is virtually always available as an alternant in the language system (though individual speakers will not always be aware of it, as for example in the case of *DNA*).[8]

The examples in [8i] are proper names – of institutions or places. Some require the definite article when functioning as head in NP structure, while others appear without it: compare *She works at the UN* and *She works at MIT*. The use of initialisms for institutions is extremely common, but many of them are very localised or ephemeral.

Most words formed by abbreviation are written with upper-case letters, but some have lower case, as in [8iii] (where *PC* and *PS* are alternants). Abbreviations of Latin phrases such as *e.g.* (*exempli gratia* "for example"), *i.e.* (*id est* "that is"), *n.b.* (*nota bene* "note") are written in lower case, but there is no reason to say that these abbreviations are single words. The examples in [8], however, are words: they belong to the category of noun, and behave grammatically like ordinary nouns. *MC, MP, VIP*, for example, are count nouns and inflect for plural in the regular way. Note particularly the contrast between *MCs* or *MPs* and *Masters of Ceremonies* or *Members of Parliament*; similarly *HQ* has a distinct plural *HQs* whereas the plural of *headquarters* is identical to the singular. Abbreviations, like other bases, can in principle enter into other word-formation processes, as with *ZPG-er* ("supporter of the zero population growth movement").

In addition to the above types, we also find compounds where the first base is abbreviated, while the second is retained in full, as in *email* (← *electronic mail*) or *g-suit* (← *gravity suit*). (Here and below, we use an arrow to indicate the source of the cited word.)

Acronyms

[9]	i	*NATO*	*the North Atlantic Treaty Organisation*
		UNESCO	*the United Nations Educational, Scientific and Cultural Organisation*
	ii	*AIDS*	*acquired immune deficiency syndrome*
		TEFL	*teaching English as a foreign language*
		TESOL	*teaching English to speakers of other languages*
		TESSA	*tax-exempt special savings account* BrE
		WASP	*white Anglo-Saxon protestant* AmE
	iii	*dinky*	*double income, no kids yet* BrE
		laser	*lightwave amplification by stimulated emission of radiation*
		radar	*radio detecting and ranging*
		scuba	*self-contained underwater breathing apparatus*

Acronyms differ from abbreviations in that they are pronounced like ordinary words, with the letters having their characteristic phonological value: /neɪtoʊ/, /juːneskoʊ/, /eɪdz/, /tefəl/, etc. This imposes constraints on the letter sequence that don't apply with abbreviations: *FBI*, for example, can only be an abbreviation because it is not a possible spelling of an ordinary word – though the initialism *SCSI* (*small computer system interface*) is unexpectedly pronounced as an acronym, /skʌzɪ/. Some abbreviations could of course be pronounced as ordinary words, and it is then a matter of convention which initials give rise to abbreviations and which to acronyms – contrast here the abbreviation *EFL* and the acronym *TEFL*.[9]

[8] One example where the full form is not used is *OK*, historically an abbreviation of *ol korrect* (with non-standard spelling). Especially with the spelling *okay*, this is a very marginal example of initialism.

[9] One occasionally finds words that are part acronym, part abbreviation, as in *CD-ROM* (/siːdiːˈrɒm/, "compact disk with read-only memory").

Acronyms are commonly formed from proper names, as in [9i] – and not infrequently an organisation chooses a name for itself that will yield an effective acronym. Like the initialism *MIT*, proper name acronyms stand as full NPs without the definite article: *She works for NATO/ UNESCO*, not **the NATO / *the UNESCO*.

Like abbreviations, some acronyms are written with upper-case letters, others with lower case – and again some can be written in either way (e.g. *UNESCO* or *Unesco*, with initial capital because it is a proper name). Full stops are not used with the lower-case letters and are less likely than with abbreviations with upper-case letters. The upper-case type are recognisable as acronyms by their written form, and again their connection with the unreduced forms is maintained by the use of the latter as alternants: in both speech and writing we can have either *NATO* or *the North Atlantic Treaty Organisation*, either *AIDS* or *acquired immune deficiency syndrome*, and so on. Lower-case acronyms are strikingly different. These are formally indistinguishable from ordinary words in both speech and writing, and in general the unreduced forms are not used as alternants. Notice in this connection that with the recent coinage *dinky* the meaning ("married couple with [double income but no kids yet]") incorporates that of the full form rather than being identical to it: the full form could not therefore be an alternant. For these reasons, the acronym status of such words as [9iii] is largely a matter of etymology, and speakers may well be unaware of it (especially with those that have been in the language a considerable time, such as *laser*, *radar*, *scuba*).

Departures from strict initialisms

In some cases letters are used which are not the initial of a word or smaller morphological unit. In *TB* /tiːbiː/, from *tuberculosis*, the *B* is not an initial letter, and likewise the *D* of *ID* /aɪdiː/, from *identification* (meaning "identification document" or, as a verb, "verify someone's identity by means of such a document"). In the recent coinage *NIREX* /naɪreks/, from *nuclear industry radioactive waste executive*, the *w* of *waste* is omitted while the non-initial *x* of *executive* is included: this kind of departure from the central pattern is used to make the form fit the phonological system. As a final example, consider the form *yuppie*. This is not itself an acronym, but it is formed by adding the suffix ·*ie* to the bound base *yup* (with regular doubling of the consonant letter);[10] this *yup* is an acronym standing for *young urban professional* or *young upwardly-mobile professional*, and in the latter interpretation the *m* of *mobile* is likewise omitted.

2.3 Clipping

The operation of **clipping** involves cutting off part of an existing word or phrase to leave a phonologically shorter sequence: *ad* from *advertisement*, *chute* from *parachute*, etc. We call the word that is the source of the clipping the **original**; the phonological material that is cut away will be called the **surplus**, and the remaining material that forms the new base the **residue**. Thus the original *advertisement* has the surplus material spelled *vertisement* cut away to form the residue *ad*, which is then a new base of the type known as a clipping.

The historical fact that a base was formed via the clipping operation is not a grammatically relevant fact about the present-day language. But since the clipping process is

[10] Compare the addition of ·*ie* to various clippings, discussed in §2.3.2 below.

still productive – in some dialects extensively so – a description of the process involved is a relevant part of the grammar of Present-day English.

Clippings often have restricted uses in that they are deployed only in informal style or even constitute slang when they are first coined. Thereafter, however, they may wholly or largely displace the original, as with *mob* (from *mobile*, itself a shortening of the Latin *mobile vulgus*) or *pram* and *movie* (where the originals *perambulator* and *moving picture* are now rarely used). They can also develop special meanings that differentiate them from the original: compare *curio* and *curiosity*, *fan* ("devotee of sport, famous person, etc.)" and *fanatic*, *pants* and *pantaloons*. Clipping has been a part of English word-formation for a long time, but it is more widely used in some dialects than in others; Australian English (AusE) is particularly rich in clippings.

We divide the words formed by the clipping operation into two types, **plain clippings**, which consist of just the residue from clipping, and **embellished clippings**, in which other operations apply to the residue to produce a longer word. In the above examples, *movie* is embellished, the others plain. We will ignore the fairly extensive numbers of nicknames for places (e.g. *Brum* from *Birmingham*) and, especially, nicknames for people (e.g. *Joe* from *Joseph*, *Gussie* from *Augustus*); personal nicknames in particular often introduce extraneous complications stemming from baby-talk simplifications.

2.3.1 Plain clippings

We can distinguish three kinds of plain clipping, naming them by reference to the location in the original of the surplus (not the residue).

(a) Back-clippings: surplus removed from the back, i.e. word-final, part of the original

[10]	*coke* (← *cocaine*)	*deb* (← *debutante*)	*deli* (← *delicatessen*)
	doc (← *doctor*)	*lab* (← *laboratory*)	*mike* (← *microphone*)
	pen (← *penitentiary*)	*prom* (← *promenade*)	*quad* (← *quadruplet/quadrangle*)

(b) Foreclippings: surplus removed from the front

[11]	*bus* (← *omnibus*)	*cello* (← *violoncello*)	*chute* (← *parachute*)
	coon (← *raccoon*)	*phone* (← *telephone*)	*pike* (← *turnpike*; AmE)

(c) Ambiclippings: surplus removed from both beginning and end

[12]	*flu* (← *influenza*)	*fridge* (← *refrigerator*; BrE)	*tec* (← *detective*; BrE)

General remarks on plain clippings

(a) Much the most common type is the back-clipping, and there are very few cases of ambiclippings (indeed *tec* is hardly in current use any more). Some back-clippings are based on the first word of a phrase rather than on a single word: *prefab* (← *prefabricated building*); *pub* (← *public house*, BrE); *ute* (← *utility vehicle* "pickup truck", AusE/NZE); *zoo* (← *zoological garden*, with adjustment of the vowel for those who pronounce the full form /zoʊlɒdʒɪkəl/). There are also cases where both words of a phrase are back-clipped to form a **clipping compound**: *elint* (← *electronic intelligence*), *kidvid* (← *kid's video*).

(b) In some cases there may be sporadic modification of a consonant or vowel in the clipping; thus *bike* comes from *bicycle* with pronunciation of the *c* as /k/ instead of /s/, and *pram* loses the first vowel of *perambulator*.

(c) Plain clippings are almost always monosyllabic, but there are a few clear exceptions to this, such as *deli* and *cello*, cited above, *exam* (← *examination*), *medic* (← *medical student/practitioner*), *photo* (← *photograph*), *polio* (← *poliomyelitis*).

(d) Clipping normally yields nouns. Note, for example, that *ad*/*advert* and *exam* are clipped from *advertisement* and *examination*, not *advertise* and *examine*. *Photograph* can be either a noun or a verb, whereas *photo* is quite marginal as a verb.

2.3.2 Embellished clippings

Some words consist of a clipping followed by a suffix. *Turps* (← *turpentine*) has ·*s*, *soccer* (← *association football*)[11] and *rugger* (← *rugby football*) have ·*er*, while *preggers* (← *pregnant*), *shampers* (← *champagne*), *Honkers* (← *Hong Kong*) and *starkers* (← *stark naked*) have ·*er* + ·*s*. The words in ·*ers* are semi-jocular and distinctively BrE or AusE.

Embellished clippings in AusE

Words of this kind are particularly common in AusE. Though informal or colloquial, they often appear in print in newspapers and magazines, and thus most have orthographic forms. In addition to the above ·*er*, seen (together with the plural suffix) in *bathers* (← *bathing shorts*), *swimmers* (← *swimming shorts*), the main suffixes are ·*ie* (or ·*y*) /i/ and ·*o* /oʊ/:

[13]	i	*barbie* (← *barbecue*)	*blowie* (← *blowfly*)	*frenchie* (← *French letter*)
		pollie (← *politician*)	*rellies* (← *relatives*)	*sunnies* (← *sunglasses*)
	ii	*garbo* (← *garbage-collector*)	*journo* (← *journalist*)	*rego* (← *(car) registration*)

The ·*ie*/*y* can be identified with the diminutive suffix (see §5.2.1), but overall the suffixes have mainly rhythmic or decorative function, hence the term 'embellished'.[12] A significant phonological point about the embellished clippings in AusE is that the fricatives /s/ and occasionally /f/ are often voiced when suffixation puts a residue-final fricative between two vowels: *this arvo* /ˈɑːvoʊ/ (← *afternoon*); *Aussie* /ˈɒzi/ (← *Australian*); *cossie* /ˈkɒzi/ (← *(swimming) costume*); *mozzie* /ˈmɒzi/ (← *mosquito*); *possie* /pɒzi/ (← *position*).

2.4 Blending

Blending is the formation of a word from a sequence of two bases with reduction of one or both at the boundary between them, as in *brunch* from *breakfast* + *lunch* or *gues(s)timate* from *guess* + *estimate*.

From a formal point of view we can distinguish the following types:

[14]	i	*paratroops* (*parachute* + *troops*)	*telebanking* (*telephone* + *banking*)
	ii	*breathalyser* (*breath* + *analyser*)	*newscast* (*news* + *broadcast*)
	iii	*heliport* (*helicopter* + *airport*)	*stagflation* (*stagnation* + *inflation*)
	iv	*motel* (*motor* + *hotel*)	*sexploitation* (*sex* + *exploitation*)

In [i] the blend consists of the first part of the first base + the whole of the second base. In [ii] it consists of the whole first base + the final part of the second. In [iii] it consists of the first part of the first base and the final part of the second. And in [iv] the central part is common to the two bases: there is overlap between them. In some cases there

[11] *Soccer*, however, has the vowel /ɒ/, not /oʊ/; /sɒkə/ represents a spelling pronunciation, one based on the way the form is spelled.

[12] A further suffix occasionally found is ·*a* /ə/, as in *Maccas* (← *MacDonalds*).

may be overlap in writing but not in speech (*smog*, /smɒg/, from *smoke* + *fog*, /smoʊk + fɒg), or in speech but not in writing (*ballute*, /bəluːt/, from *balloon* + *parachute*, /bəluːn + pærəʃuːt/. The blends in [i–ii] can be regarded as compounds, whereas the morphological status of the bases in [iii–iv] is somewhat indeterminate. There is some evident resemblance between clippings and blends, but what distinguishes a blend from a clipping is that it always begins with the first part of the first source base and ends with the final part of the second.[13]

Usually the blend is no longer than the longer of the two bases from which it is formed, but exceptions can be found among blends of type [iv], such as *musicassette* (*music* + *cassette*) or the nonce-word *glasnostalgia* (*glasnost* + *nostalgia*). The bases involved are normally free, but occasional examples are found with a bound base, a combining form, as in *electrocute* (*electro* + *execute*).

Some blends provide models for the formation of new words of the same kind. The jocular *chocaholic*, for example, is formed on the model of *workaholic* (← *work* + *alcoholic*). Similarly, *Reaganomics* (← *Reagan economics*) has been the model for numerous nonce-words, with the name of a politican as first component, such as *Thatchernomics.* Such blends effectively give rise to new morphological elements, ·*aholic*, ·*nomics*, falling at the boundary between affix and base.[14]

2.5 Back-formation

Back-formation is the coining of a new word by taking an existing word and forming from it a morphologically more elementary word. It is usually a matter of deleting an affix. In the following, for example, the words with affixes had already been in the language for some time when the ones without affixes were coined:

[15]	SOURCE	BACK-FORMATION	SOURCE	BACK-FORMATION
	baby-sitt·<u>er</u>	*baby-sit*	*edit·<u>or</u>*	*edit*
	headhunt·<u>er</u>	*headhunt*	*jogg·<u>er</u>/jogg·<u>ing</u>*	*jog*
	lip-read·<u>ing</u>	*lip-read*	*recycl·<u>ing</u>*	*recycle*
	televis·<u>ion</u>	*televise*	*underachiev·<u>er</u>*	*underachieve*
	<u>un</u>·couth	*couth*	*<u>dis</u>·abled*	*abled*

As far as morphological structure is concerned, back-formation does not yield a distinct type of base. *Edit* and *jog*, for example, are simple bases, just like *write* and *run*; *recycle* is a derivative base (analysable into prefix + base), just like *rebuild*; *underachieve* is a compound base like *underact*; and so on. That *television* was established in the language before *televise* is a fact of history, not something that is relevant to the structure of the language today, where the morphological relation between *televise* and *television* is the same as that between *revise* and *revision.*

Nevertheless it is clear that back-formation is one of the processes by which new words are created, and that this process is still productive today: the examples in [15] range from nineteenth-century ones like *edit* to quite recent ones like *headhunt.* Back-formation by deletion of ·*ing* or ·*er* is indeed one of the main avenues for the creation of verb compounds

[13] There are nevertheless places where the distinction is blurred. *Cheeseburger*, for example, might be regarded as a blend from *cheese* + *hamburger*, but since *burger* exists as an independent word, a clipping from *hamburger*, *cheeseburger* can also be analysed as a compound formed from two free bases.

[14] Such elements are sometimes called 'splinters'.

with the structure noun base + verb base: besides *baby-sit*, *headhunt*, and *lip-read* from the list above we have *brainwash*, *day-dream*, *house-hunt*, *house-keep*, *sleep-walk*, *spring-clean*, etc., and more recently *break-dance*, *plea-bargain*, *skateboard*, *windsurf*. One respect in which the origin of these compound verbs as back-formations is of relevance to a descriptive, non-historical study, is that irregular preterite and past participle forms are sometimes unacceptable. Compare, for example, *He had been <u>day-dreaming</u> all morning* (regular gerund-participle) and **He had <u>day-dreamt</u> all morning* (irregular past participle).

Back-formation may result in a base that is close in meaning to one that is already established. *Self-destruct*, for example, was formed from *self-destruction* by reversing the suffixation process seen in the derivation of words like *abduction* and *construction* from *abduct* and *construct*, and it yields a base *destruct* alongside the long-established *destroy*, but with a more restricted meaning and correspondingly limited distribution. As remarked above, back-formation usually deletes an affix from a derivative base,[15] but other types of reversal are occasionally found. The compound verb *spoon-feed*, for example, was formed from *spoon-fed* by reversing the process that applies in forming the simple past participle *fed* from the lexical base *feed*.

Like other productive processes, back-formation can be used in a jocular way, as with *couth* from *uncouth*.

2.6 Phonological modification

We consider here certain phonological changes that accompany the shift of a word from one syntactic category to another.

(a) Stress shift

There are numerous pairs of disyllabic verbs and nouns that are spelled alike but pronounced differently, with the verb being stressed on the second syllable, the noun on the first, as in the following illustrative examples:

[16]		VERB	NOUN		VERB	NOUN
i	*digest*	/daɪ'dʒest/	/'daɪdʒest/	*incline*	/ɪn'klaɪn/	/'ɪnklaɪn/
	insert	/ɪn'sɜː^{r}t/	/'ɪnsɜː^{r}t/	*insult*	/ɪn'sʌlt/	/'ɪnsʌlt/
	torment	/tɔː^{r}'ment/	/'tɔː^{r}ment/	*transfer*	/træn'sfɜː^{r}/	/'trænsfɜː^{r}/
ii	*accent*	/æk'sent/	/'æksənt/	*conduct*	/kən'dʌkt/	/'kɒndʌkt/
	conflict	/kən'flɪkt/	/'kɒnflɪkt/	*contest*	/kən'test/	/'kɒntest/
	convert	/kən'vɜː^{r}t/	/'kɒnvɜː^{r}t/	*convict*	/kən'vɪkt/	/'kɒnvɪkt/
	decrease	/dɪ'kriːs/	/'diːkriːs/	*escort*	/ɪ'skɔː^{r}t/	/'eskɔː^{r}t/
	export	/ɪk'spɔː^{r}t/	/'ekspɔː^{r}t/	*fragment*	/fræg'ment/	/frægmənt/
	permit	/pə^{r}'mɪt/	/'pɜː^{r}mɪt/	*present*	/prɪ'zent/	/'prezənt/
	rebel	/rɪ'bel/	/'rebəl/	*record*	/rɪ'kɔː^{r}d/	/'rekɔː^{r}d/
	reject	/rɪ'dʒekt/	/'riːdʒekt/	*suspect*	/sə'spekt/	/'sʌspekt/

In [ii] the stress difference is accompanied by a difference in vowel quality, with unstressed /ə/ corresponding to a variety of stressed vowels, and unstressed /ɪ/ to stressed /iː/ or /e/.

[15] In some cases a back-formation reflects an etymologically incorrect analysis of the source word. The verb *burgle* for example, was formed from *burglar*, indicating that the latter was analysed as *burgl·ar* although the *ar* was not originally a suffix.

In many of the above pairs the verb is older than the noun, the latter having been formed from the verb by a process that is like conversion except for the shift in the position of the stress (and, frequently, consequential change in vowel quality) – a shift reflecting the fact that nouns typically have the stress earlier in the word than verbs.

There are also verb–noun pairs where the noun has stress on the first syllable, while the verb can have either initial or final stress. In cases like *protest* and *refund* there is no difference in meaning, whereas in others the initially stressed verb has a more specialised meaning that matches that of the noun (or one sense of the noun). For example, the verb *abstract* in the sense "remove" is pronounced /æb'strækt/, but with the meaning "make an abstract or summary" it is /'æbstrækt/, like the noun. There are also regional differences, with AmE having, for example, /'segment/ and BrE /seg'ment/ for the verb. With *research* both noun and verb are found with either initial or final stress; the former is the usual AmE pronunciation, but has been the subject of a certain amount of prescriptive criticism in BrE.[16]

(b) Vowel change

Some pairs of words that are spelled alike but belong to different syntactic categories are differentiated phonologically not by stress but just by vowel quality:

[17]						
i	V or N	*compliment*	*document*	*implement*	*ornament*	
ii	V or N	*certificate*	*estimate*	*graduate*	*isolate*	
iii	V or Adj	*deliberate*	*desolate*	*intimate*	*legitimate*	*separate*

In [i] *ment* is pronounced /ment/ in the verb, /mənt/ in the noun. In [ii–iii] ·*ate* is pronounced /eɪt/ in the verb and /ət/ in the noun or adjective. In all these cases the final vowel of the noun or adjective is reduced to /ə/ while the verb has an unreduced vowel or diphthong: as with the stress differences in [16], therefore, the end part of the verb is phonologically stronger than that of nouns or adjectives.

The vowel contrasts illustrated here are found in very few items: they are remnants of differences in other languages, and have never involved productive word-formation processes in English.[17] Note in this connection that the words in [17i] can hardly be analysed into base + suffix, and even in [ii–iii] subtracting ·*ate* as a suffix leaves predominantly bound bases.

(c) Base-final voicing contrasts

There is a small set of noun–verb pairs where the noun ends in a voiceless fricative, and the verb in the voiced counterpart:

[18]						
i	N: /f, θ, s/	*belief*	*sheath*	*wreath*	*mouth*	*house*
ii	V: /v, ð, z/	*believe*	*sheathe*	*wreathe*	*mouth*	*house*

For the first three the difference is reflected in the spelling. We have seen that this modification is found also in inflectional morphology: there is obligatory voicing in the plurals *mouths* and *houses*, optional voicing in *sheaths* and *wreaths*. The pattern is no longer productive in lexical word-formation, and there are very few such pairs. An even

[16] There are also a few verb–adjective pairs differentiated by the position of the stress: *abstract* /æb'strækt/ vs /'æbstrækt/, *frequent* /frɪ'kwent/ vs /'friːkwənt/, *present* /prɪ'zent/ vs /'prezənt/.

[17] The same applies to the vowel contrasts (reflected this time in the spelling) between the pairs of intransitive and transitive verbs *fall* ~ *fell*, *lie* ~ *lay*, *rise* ~ *raise*. The rarity of this relationship contrasts with the frequency of the case where the same verb appears in intransitive and transitive constructions (cf. Ch. 4, §8.1.4).

smaller set have a voicing contrast between the alveolar plosives /d/ and /t/: *ascend* ~ *ascent*; *descend* ~ *descent*; *extend* ~ *extent*. This reflects a French pattern and has never been productive in English.

3 Conversion

3.1 The domain of conversion

Conversion normally involves changing a word's syntactic category without any concomitant change of form, as in the creation of the verb *humble* from the adjective *humble* or of the noun *attempt* from the verb *attempt*. It also covers the creation of a word from an affix, as in the conversion of the suffix ·*ism* into a noun or the conversion of the prefix *anti*· into a preposition: this resembles the usual case of conversion in that a word is formed from a pre-existing morphological unit by simply giving it new grammatical properties.

We include conversion within the set of lexical word-formation processes because we see it as creating new words. The noun *attempt*, for example, is a different word from the verb *attempt*: it has different inflectional properties and enters into different inflectional paradigms. By generalisation, we regard any difference in primary category as sufficient to establish a difference between one word and another, and hence we take conversion to cover such cases as the creation of the preposition *contrary* (as in *Contrary to your predictions, the meeting was a great success*) from the homonymous adjective (*Such a decision would be contrary to common sense*), even though neither of these words has any inflectional property. We do not, however, take a change of secondary class as a matter of conversion. Consider the verb *frighten*, for example: this is primarily a transitive verb (*I don't want to frighten you*), but it can also appear in intransitive constructions (*I don't frighten easily*). There is nevertheless no reason to say that intransitive *frighten* is a different word from transitive *frighten*, and hence no reason to say that this extension in the use of *frighten* is a matter of lexical word-formation, more specifically of conversion. Similarly we exclude cases where common nouns arise through the establishment of new meanings for what are primarily proper nouns, as with *newton*, *pascal*, *wellington*, etc.

Also excluded from the domain of conversion, though not from that of word-formation, is the case where a word is formed by fusing a sequence of words into one, as in *his <u>couldn't-care-less</u> attitude*. The word *couldn't-care-less* consists of a combination of bases and hence is a compound: it is formed by the process we refer to as 'dephrasal compounding' (§4.1).

The normal effect of conversion is to create a pair of corresponding words belonging to different parts of speech, or primary categories. This same effect is very often produced by affixation, especially suffixation. Compare:

[19]	CONVERSION			AFFIXATION		
i	*spy*$_{\text{V}}$	→	*spy*$_{\text{N}}$	*kill*$_{\text{V}}$ + ·*er*	→	*killer*$_{\text{N}}$
ii	*arrest*$_{\text{N}}$	→	*arrest*$_{\text{N}}$	*manage*$_{\text{V}}$ + ·*ment*	→	*management*$_{\text{N}}$
iii	*humble*$_{\text{ADJ}}$	→	*humble*$_{\text{V}}$	*marginal*$_{\text{ADJ}}$ + ·*ise*	→	*marginalise*$_{\text{V}}$

The effect is the same but the means are different: affixation introduces a new morphological element whereas conversion does not. A base formed by affixation is always a derivative, whereas one formed by conversion is of the same type as the source: the noun *spy* is a simple base, the verb *blacklist* is a compound (like the corresponding noun), and the verb *package* is a derivative (again like the noun from which it is formed). Conversion, therefore, has no effect on the morphological structure.

Because the effect of conversion is like that commonly brought about by affixation, many works treat it as a special case of affixation, 'zero-affixation' (or 'zero-derivation'). This is to say that the noun *spy*, for example, is derived from the verb by the addition of an affix that happens to have no phonological realisation – a zero affix. We find this an unsatisfactory way of looking at it: we want to say that there is no affix at all, not that there is an abstract or covert affix. A major problem for the zero-affixation approach is that with ordinary affixation we have a range of different affixes, some of them producing different effects (e.g. *manager* and *management* are different kinds of nominalisation of the verb *manage*), some of them varying simply according to the base to which they are attached (e.g. *arriv·al*, *clos·ure*, *distribut·ion*, etc.). This raises the question of how many 'zero-affixes' are involved in conversion. If we say there is just one, then we do not in fact have a close resemblance between conversion and (ordinary) affixation. If we say there is more than one we have the problem of determining how many there are and of how to distinguish between them when they are phonologically null. A further weakness of a zero-affix analysis is that it implies a difference in morphological structure between input and output. As noted above, we want to say that the verbs *spy*, *blacklist*, and *package* have respectively a simple, compound, and derivative base, but under a zero affix analysis all would be derivatives. This is to introduce an unwarranted complication into the morphological structure: it attempts in effect to reflect the historical origin of a word in its present-day structure.

Most cases of conversion involve the three major part-of-speech categories noun, verb, and adjective. The following subsections deal with the three pairs within this set, while other cases of conversion are dealt with in the chapters on words belonging to the output category (e.g. Ch. 7 for the conversion of adjectives, nouns, and verbs into prepositions).

3.2 Conversion between nouns and verbs

It is a notable property of English that it has a great deal of homonymy between nouns and verbs. In a considerable number of cases it is unclear which is the earlier of the two, but there are also many examples where one is clearly semantically more basic than the other. The noun *bottle* is more basic than the verb since the verb means "put into a bottle" rather than the noun meaning "container into which something is put when it is bottled". Conversely *arrest* is primarily a verb, with the noun denoting the event wherein someone is arrested. Examples are given in:

[20] i VERB TO NOUN CONVERSIONS

arrest	*attempt*	*bore*	*cheat*	*coach*	*control*
cough	*desire*	*flirt*	*go*	*hoist*	*laugh*
read	*smile*	*sneak*	*spy*	*whisper*	*whistle*

ii NOUN TO VERB CONVERSIONS

butcher	*butter*	*can*	*cash*	*duel*	*enamel*
eye	*finger*	*fish*	*foal*	*gesture*	*knife*
knot	*lamb*	*motion*	*panic*	*parody*	*parrot*
queue	*shepherd*	*ski*	*skin*	*trumpet*	*water*

Quite a number of semantic classes are involved. One involves instrumental nouns, with the more basic member of the pair usually the noun (*knife, hammer, mop*), but sometimes the verb (*hoist, whistle*). Closely related are pairs where the noun denotes a body-part and is always basic: *eye, elbow, finger, head, knee*, etc. In some pairs the noun denotes a person, defined by profession, relationship, behaviour, or character: the noun is basic in *butcher, doctor, shepherd, usher*, the verb in *bore, cheat, flirt, spy*. Another class, with the noun basic, has the verb meaning "apply ~ to" or "remove ~ from" ("apply" in the case of *enamel, grease, sugar, water*; "remove" with *hull, shell, skin, weed*). The verbs involved in noun–verb conversion (in either direction) are usually dynamic rather than stative – though there are some, such as *smell* and *taste*, which can be either.

As for formal properties, a high proportion of the paired nouns and verbs have simple bases. Derivatives tend to resist conversion, though some examples can be found: *action, package, stretcher*, etc., are primarily nouns, while *dislike* is a rare case of one that is primarily a verb. Compound nouns convert quite often to verbs: *blacklist, keyboard, network*; this is one of the main sources of compound verbs. Both directions of conversion are still productive, with noun-to-verb conversion being considerably more common.[18]

3.3 Conversion between adjectives and nouns

(a) From adjective to noun

A considerable number of nouns are formed by conversion of adjectives. Examples include:

[21]						
	comic	*dear*	*drunk*	*empty*	*female*	*heavy*
	human	*intellectual*	*local*	*medical*	*natural*	*original*
	positive	*potential*	*primary*	*private*	*professional*	*regular*
	right	*royal*	*short*	*social*	*special*	*sweet*

In most cases the resulting noun is equivalent to a nominal consisting of the adjective + an understood noun, and often there will be two or more senses differing with respect to what noun is understood, as in *comic* ("person/periodical"), *empty* ("bottle/box"), *positive* ("photograph/feature/quantity"), *regular* ("soldier/customer"), and so on. A number belong to informal style (at least in one of their senses): (*old*) *dear, heavy* ("minder"), *local* ("pub", BrE), *natural, regular* ("customer"), *royal* ("member of royal family"). In many cases the resultant noun denotes a type of person. Another group is that of colour terms: compare *His tie is brown* (adj) and *His tie is a dark shade of brown* (noun); some of these also have other specialised meanings, as with *white* ("white part of egg", "white part of eye", or "person with white skin"). Time-period adjectives like *daily, weekly, monthly* convert to nouns denoting periodicals, though some have other meanings too (e.g. "cleaner who comes daily"). Some of the nouns appear normally or exclusively with the plural inflection: *basics, greens* ("green vegetables"), *marrieds, smalls* ("underwear"), *woollies*.

Conversion of an adjective into a noun is to be distinguished from the use of an adjective as a fused modifier-head, as in *Is it the new version or the <u>old</u>?* or *The tax will disadvantage the <u>poor</u>*: see Ch. 5, §9.3.

[18] Changes from verb to noun are often accompanied by a change in the placement of the stress, as in *recall*, and hence involve stress shift rather than conversion (§3.1). Note also that nouns like *hang-out, pay-back, take-away* involve compounding, not conversion: in *I'll take away the food*, for example, *take away* is a two-word sequence, not a compound verb.

(b) From noun to adjective

Conversion in this direction is, by contrast, very rare. Historically, we find examples of noun-to-adjective conversion in such words as *rose* and *orange*, where the senses of the nouns (denoting flower and fruit respectively) are clearly distinct from the colour senses of the adjectives. But there are few modern examples. School grammars tend to say that in expressions like *the Clinton policy* the word *Clinton* is (or 'is used as') an adjective but, as we have argued in Ch. 6, §2.4.1, this is to confuse the word-category adjective with the function modifier of a noun. Any noun (other than a pronoun) can occur in this function, given a suitable head noun, so the appropriate way to handle such data is in terms of syntax (the distribution of nouns), not in terms of word-formation (the creation of new words).

To establish that a noun has been converted into an adjective we need to show that it has acquired distinctively adjectival properties. Since the ability to modify a noun is not restricted to adjectives this will normally mean showing that it has become gradable and takes the distinctive degree modifiers that are found with adjectives but not nouns, notably *very* and *too*. One often-cited example is *fun* (and the fact that this example is cited so often reflects the paucity of clear examples): many speakers, especially younger ones, accept expressions like *a very fun person*, indicating that *fun* has been assimilated into the adjective category. Another example is *Oxbridge*: *He has a very Oxbridge accent* or *His accent is very Oxbridge*. It is arguable that we should also include certain adjectives in ·*ist* and ·*ite*: these suffixes primarily serve to form nouns, but such derivatives as *sexist* and *Thatcherite* satisfy the conditions for adjective status: *That remark was very sexist/Thatcherite*. But noun-to-adjective conversion is a very minor type of word-formation process.

3.4 Conversion between adjectives and verbs

(a) From adjective to verb

[22]	*bare*	*blind*	*blunt*	*brave*	*calm*	*clear*
	dim	*dry*	*empty*	*free*	*humble*	*muddy*
	narrow	*slow*	*smooth*	*tame*	*tense*	*weary*

This pattern has been fairly productive for several hundred years, though there are far fewer verbs converted from adjectives than from nouns. The most common meanings of the resultant verbs are "become ~" (intransitive) and "make ~" (transitive), with some verbs, such as *clear*, *cool*, *empty*, having both these meanings. In a third type, illustrated by *brave*, *brazen*, *gentle*, *savage*, etc., the adjectival meaning applies to the manner in which something is done: to savage someone is to attack them in a savage way, to brave the storm is to endure it bravely, and so on. The bases are generally simple, but there are some derivatives in ·*y* (*dirty*, *muddy*, etc.), some compounds in ·*proof* (*soundproof*, *waterproof*) and – exceptionally in the field of conversion or indeed word-formation generally – cases of inflected forms (*better*, *best*).[19]

[19] *Lower* is even more exceptional in that inflected bases that undergo word-formation processes, whether conversion or affixation, are generally irregular ones.

(b) Verb to adjective

A process which differs significantly from central cases of conversion is the formation of an adjective homonymous with the gerund-participle or past participle form of a verb, as in:

[23]	i	*amusing*	*boring*	*entertaining*	*stunning*	*tiring*	*worrying*
	ii	*amused*	*bored*	*spoilt*	*stunned*	*tired*	*worried*

For many verbs, this applies with both forms, for others only one – for example, there are no adjectives *entertained* and *spoiling*. One important difference between this and the central cases is that here it is not the lexical base of the verb that is converted but an inflected form. A second difference is that it is very much more productive than the conversion processes involving lexical bases. Nevertheless, this process has it in common with uncontroversial cases of conversion that we have homonymous pairs of words of different primary categories. For discussion of the contrast between the verb-forms and the participial adjectives, see Ch. 3, §§1.3–4.

4 Compounds

4.1 Preliminaries

Morphological compound vs syntactic construction

A compound base, we have said, is one composed of two (or occasionally more) smaller bases. A major problem that arises in the description of compounds, however, is how to distinguish cases where two bases combine to form a single word, a compound, from those where they constitute separate words in a syntactic construction:

[1]	i	*greenhouse*	*sweetheart*	*cotton-plant*	*newspaper*	[morphological compound]
	ii	*green house*	*sweet taste*	*cotton shirt*	*quality paper*	[syntactic construction]

In general the problem arises where the final component is a noun rather than an adjective or verb. With adjectives, for example, we take *tax-exempt* as a compound adjective and there is no contrasting syntactic construction where an adjective has a noun (or NP) as modifier. With verbs the distinction between, say, a compound such as *baby-sit*, and a syntactic construction *babies cry* is unproblematic. It is for this reason that our discussion of this problem is included in the chapter on the noun phrase. The contrast between the examples of [i] and [ii] is relatively sharp because a number of criteria give convergent results. Those in [i] are written as single words, while those in [ii] are written as word sequences; those in [i] are pronounced with the main stress on the first component while those in [ii] have it on the second; those in [i] exclude modification of the first component while those in [ii] allow a very wide range of modification such as is found elsewhere with phrases headed by adjectives or nouns – compare *an unusually bright green house, a very much sweeter taste, an Egyptian cotton shirt, a better-quality paper than I'd expected.* The examples in [1] were chosen as ones where the criteria converge, but there are places where the boundary between morphological compound and syntactic construction is unclear; this problem is discussed in Ch. 5, §14.4, and in the present chapter we confine our attention, except where otherwise stated, to uncontroversial cases of compounds.

Hyponymy

A high proportion of compounds, especially compound nouns, are **hyponymic**: the compound as a whole is a **hyponym** of the base that functions as head. Hyponymy is a semantic relation that can in the first instance be most easily explained by reference to nouns. We say that noun *X* is a **hyponym** of noun *Y* when *X* denotes a subset of what is denoted by *Y*. This relation may hold between morphologically unrelated words. For example, *tulip*, *daffodil*, and *rose* are hyponyms of *flower*, while *alsatian*, *poodle*, and *cocker-spaniel* are hyponyms of *dog*: a tulip is a kind of flower, an alsatian is a kind of dog, and so on. With compounds, the relation of hyponymy is reflected in the morphological structure: *wall-flower* consists of *wall* as dependent and *flower* as head, and denotes (in its literal sense) a kind of flower; *bulldog* has *bull* as dependent, *dog* as head, and denotes a kind of dog. We can generalise from nouns to compounds of all categories by talking in terms of entailment rather than subsets. *This is a wall-flower* entails *This is a flower*, but *This is a flower* does not entail *This is a wall-flower*. Similarly for such an adjective as *paper-thin*: *This is paper-thin* entails *This is thin*, but not conversely. And for a verb like *hand-wash*: *They hand-washed it* entails *They washed it* but again the reverse entailment does not hold.

For a compound to be hyponymic can be regarded as the default case: it is when the compound is not a hyponym of the head that we need to consider why this is so. There may be a variety of reasons why a compound fails the entailment test for hyponymy. Consider:

[2] *hotshot, glow-worm, cholesterol-free, sunset, breath-taking, redskin*

The informal term *hotshot* does not denote a kind of shot, but a person who is skilled or successful in some field: this illustrates the common case where the non-hyponymic property of a compound is simply a matter of lexicalisation, an idiosyncratic feature of the particular compound in question. *Glow-worm*, which denotes a kind of beetle, is also lexicalised, but in this case there has also been a historical change in the meaning of *worm*, which earlier had a broader denotation than is now current, being applicable to any animal that crawled, such as snakes, legless lizards, caterpillars, and long-bodied insects like glow-worms. *Cholesterol-free* is not lexicalised but it is non-hyponymic because *free* in the sense it has here cannot stand alone as a phrase but requires a complement. The sense of *free* in *It is free of/from cholesterol* is not the same as in *It is free. Sunset* involves a particular sense of *set* which occurs only as a verb (the corresponding noun being the derivative *setting*), so again *It was a beautiful sunset* doesn't entail *It was a beautiful set.* Similarly with the adjective *breath-taking*: there is no adjective *taking* (except with the specialised sense of "captivating"), and hence *His arrogance was breath-taking* does not entail *His arrogance was taking. Redskin* "Red Indian" is another example of lexicalisation, but it illustrates a pattern of compounding which necessarily results in a non-hyponymic form. It belongs to the pattern (discussed in §4.2.1 below) where the literal meaning gives a property of the entity the compound denotes: a redskin is not a kind of skin but a kind of person, the kind that has (or is perceived as having) red skin.[20]

[20] Compounds formed by patterns that invariably result in non-hyponymic compounds are commonly called 'exocentric', with others being, by contrast, 'endocentric'. Considerable problems arise, however, in giving rigorous definitions for these categories, and we shall not make use of this taxonomy in the present discussion.

Subordinative and coordinative compounds

The great majority of compounds are **subordinative**, in that one base can be regarded as head, the other as dependent. The head is normally the second element. Note, for example, the contrast between *birdcage* and *cage-bird*. *Birdcage* has *cage* as head and denotes a kind of cage; *cage-bird* has *bird* as head and denotes a kind of bird (one that is kept in a cage or of the sort that is customarily kept in one). In both, then, there is a clear difference in status between the component bases, the first being a dependent of the second.

There are also compounds where the component bases are of equal status: these we call **coordinative**. In, for example, the noun *secretary-treasurer*, the adjective *bitter-sweet*, or the verb *cook-chill*, neither component is dependent on, subordinate to, the other. Coordinative compounds can normally be glossed with 'and': a secretary-treasurer is someone who is both secretary and treasurer, not (or not just) a kind of treasurer.

Dephrasal compounds

We apply the term **dephrasal compound** to the underlined elements in:

		a.	b.	
[3]	i	a. *He's a <u>has-been</u>.*	b. *the usual <u>rent-a-crowd</u>*	[noun]
	ii	a. *<u>hard-core</u> pornography*	b. *his <u>holier-than-thou</u> attitude*	[adjective]
	iii	a. *Don't <u>cold-shoulder</u> us.*	b. *He might <u>short-change</u> you*	[verb]
	iv	a. *<u>old-maid</u>ish*	b. *a <u>fly-by-night</u>er*	[nominal base of derivative]

Such elements, usually written with hyphens, as here, consist of a sequence of free bases and hence satisfy the definition of compounds. They arise, however, not by the normal morphological process of compounding but rather through the fusion of words within a syntactic structure into a single lexical base. The distinction is particularly clear in [ia] and [iib] since normal morphological compounding would not allow the internal inflections that are present in these words.

In the next three subsections we review in turn the patterns to be found in compound nouns, compound adjectives, and compound verbs, dealing with contrasts between hyponymic and non-hyponymic and between subordinative and coordinative as we go. The last two subsections then deal with types of compound that in part at least cut across this primary dimension of classification into noun, adjective, verb: §4.5 discusses neo-classical compounds such as *geography, sociology, ambidextrous, audiovisual*, while §4.6 reviews the minor category of compounds that are motivated by the phonological form, involving reduplication, rhyme, or vowel change, as in *goody-goody, razzle-dazzle, zigzag.*

4.2 Compound nouns

The largest number and the largest variety of compounds are to be found in the category of nouns. We discuss them here under two main headings, **noun-centred** and **verb-centred**:

[4]	i	*blackbird, egghead, footpath, girlfriend, tearoom*	[noun-centred]
	ii	*busdriver, city-dweller, fox-hunting, life-guard, take-away*	[verb-centred]

The compounds in [ii] are verb-centred in that the head element is the lexical base of a verb or else formed from one by suffixation or conversion. *Driv·er, dwell·er*, and *hunt·ing* are formed from verbs by suffixation, *guard* is formed by conversion, while with *take-away* (which has the first element as head) there is no reason to say that *take* itself is anything other than a verb. The meanings of such compounds depend centrally on the meanings of the verbs: a busdriver is someone who drives buses, a life-guard is concerned with guarding (protecting) lives, a take-away is a restaurant that sells cooked food that one takes away to eat elsewhere (or, in a second sense, the food itself). With the noun-centred compounds in [i], by contrast, the head element is purely or at least primarily a noun. With *girlfriend*, for example, *friend* can only be a noun, and with *egghead*, the meaning is based on that of the noun *head*, not the verb (which was formed by conversion from the noun).

4.2.1 Noun-centred compound nouns

These compounds have a noun as the final base. In almost all cases the first element is a dependent, the final one the head, but there are some small-scale coordinative patterns to be noted.

We will look in turn at noun-centred compounds where the first base is a noun, adjective, verb, or some other category, but will leave until the end a special kind of non-hyponymic compound known as **bahuvrihi** compounds, where the first base can be either a noun, as in *egghead*, or an adjective, as in the *redskin* example of [2].

Noun + noun compounds

[5]					
	ashtray	*bedtime*	*beehive*	*birdcage*	*breadcrumb*
	broomstick	*bulldog*	*cowshed*	*goldfish*	*handbag*
	honey-bee	*horsehair*	*liferaft*	*motorcycle*	*palm-tree*
	pillow-case	*placename*	*shirt-sleeve*	*steamboat*	*tearoom*

This is by far the most productive kind of compounding in English, and indeed the most productive kind of word-formation. There is an immense variety of semantic relationships between the component bases, as will be evident from the following few examples:

[6]	i	*eye-rhyme*	"thing which appears to the eye to be a rhyme"
	ii	*footpath*	"path designed for people who are on foot"
	iii	*liferaft*	"raft designed to be used for saving life"
	iv	*timberline*	"apparent line formed by the highest extent of timber growth"

It does not seem likely that we could devise an exhaustive classification of such compounds into a reasonably small set of types according to the semantic relationships between the bases. Rather than assume that the meaning of the compound is systematically predictable from the meanings of the component bases, we see such compounds as lexical structures designed to act as mnemonics. In hyponymic compounds, the modifying element provides a rough reminder of how the subset denoted by the compound is distinguished from the larger set denoted by the head. This kind of explanation accounts for the fact, noted in §1.3, that *wheelchair* denotes a different subset of chair from *pushchair* (a verb + noun compound) even though a wheelchair is not uniquely identified by having wheels nor a pushchair by the fact that it can be pushed. It also accounts for the fact that a new compound such as *rain-snake* may be ambiguous out of context – does it mean "a snake which comes out in the rain", "a snake made of rain", "a snake which causes rain", or something else entirely?

There are many lexicalised compounds of the form noun + noun that are non-hyponymic: a shoe-tree is not a kind of tree, nor a ladybird a kind of bird. Similarly for *network*, *oilfield*, or (perhaps less obviously) *ash-tray*, *boathouse*, and so on.

Coordinative compounds: dvandvas and others

[7]	i	*Alsace-Lorraine*	*Austria-Hungary*	*Bosnia-Herzegovina*	*Schleswig-Holstein*
	ii	*Fletcher-Challenge*	*Hewlett-Packard*	*Metro-Goldwyn-Mayer*	*Rank-Xerox*
	iii	*comedy-thriller*	*murder-suicide*	*secretary-treasurer*	*singer-songwriter*

These are coordinative in that the bases are of equal status instead of being in a relation of subordination. One feature of this type which makes it comparable to coordination as a syntactic construction is that there can be more than two bases, as in *Metro-Goldwyn-Mayer* (where the first component is clipped) or *secretary-treasurer-editor*, denoting a person filling all three offices.

The examples in [7i–ii] illustrate a special type of morphological construction known as **dvandva compounds**, a term taken from Sanskrit grammar. As far as English is concerned, this is a very minor category. Dvandva compound nouns in English are mainly proper nouns referring to the combination or union of the referents of the component parts – territories in [i], businesses in [ii]. *Alsace-Lorraine* refers to the area composed of Alsace and Lorraine together, while the business names normally result from merging two smaller businesses into a larger one.

The coordinative compounds in [7iii] differ from the dvandvas in that the components apply individually as well as jointly. *She is secretary-treasurer of the society* entails *She is secretary of the society and she is treasurer of the society*, but *She was born in Alsace-Lorraine* does not entail *She was born in Alsace and she was born in Lorraine* – on the contrary, she can't have been born in each of them separately. Similarly with the business names: *I bought it from Hewlett-Packard* does not entail *I bought it from Hewlett and I bought it from Packard*. A company merger typically involves the original companies losing their separate identities, so that the question of whether I bought it from Hewlett or from Packard would not arise. Most dvandvas are proper names, but one technical term much used in the present grammar provides an example of a dvandva compound belonging to the class of common nouns: *gerund-participle*. We coined this term precisely for the union of what is denoted by the traditional terms *gerund* and *present participle* because we do not believe the traditional distinction between them is sound: in saying that such and such a form is a gerund-participle, therefore, we are not saying that it is simultaneously a gerund and a participle, but that it belongs to a single category covering both traditional ones.[21]

Ascriptive compounds

[8]	*apeman*	*foodstuff*	*fuel-oil*	*girlfriend*	*handlebar*
	houseboat	*maidservant*	*manservant*	*pathway*	*washerwoman*

We call these **ascriptive compounds** because the relation between the first noun and the second is comparable to that between an ascriptive modifier and the head noun in NP structure, as in *handsome man*, *male servant*, etc. (cf. Ch. 6, §4.1). They are similar to coordinative compounds, more specifically to the non-dvandva ones in [7iii], since a

[21] Some works use the term 'dvandva' to apply to all coordinative compounds.

manservant is both a man and a servant just as a secretary-treasurer is both a secretary and a treasurer.[22] We treat them as subordinative rather than coordinative on the grounds that the components are of unlike types such that the first can be thought of as defining a subset of the set denoted by the second.[23] *Manservant*, for example, is comparable to the syntactic construction *male servant*, where *male* is dependent and *servant* head. Similarly, a houseboat is more a kind of boat (one fitted up for living in) than a kind of house (one that floats on water). But the distinction is not a sharp one, and not everyone will share our judgements about all the examples.

Manservant differs from the others in that the plural is marked on both components, not just the head – note the contrast between *menservants* and *maidservants*. This special feature of ***man*** is parallelled by that of ***woman*** or ***gentleman*** in syntactic constructions of the type *woman doctor* ~ *women doctors*, *gentleman farmer* ~ *gentlemen farmers*.

Compound with an ·*s* at end of the first element

[9]	i	*beeswax*	*bullseye*	*hogshead*	*lambswool*
	ii	*almshouse*	*clothes-peg* BrE	*clothes-pin* AmE	
	iii	*batsman*	*headsman*	*huntsman*	*swordsman*

The ·*s* in the examples in [i] derives from a genitive: the genitive apostrophe is dropped unless the word is written with a hyphen (e.g. *bull's-eye*). The orthographic convention of writing these elements together reflects the stress pattern, which in turn reflects lexicalisation: in examples like *hogshead* (denoting a type of cask or a unit of liquid measure) this is seen in the unpredictable meaning of the word, in *lambswool* it is merely related to frequent usage. Nevertheless, there is no apparent reason behind writing *bullseye* as a single word but *mare's nest* ("illusory discovery") as two. Nor is there any apparent reason why *hare's-foot* (denoting a type of clover) should have the *s*, while *harelip* does not.

The first base in the compounds in [9ii] is a plural-only noun (cf. Ch. 5, §3.2.1), but the forms are irregular in that the ·*s* is usually missing in compounds – compare *trouser-press*, *pyjama-top*. The ·*s* in [iii] is also a plural in origin, though it no longer carries any plural meaning. There is again no obvious reason why the ·*s* should be present in these ·*man* compounds but lacking in *boatman*, *doorman*, *rifleman*, etc. The two versions are found with the same meaning in *lineman* and *linesman*. Both are apparently productive, with *bagman* and *locksman* being recent formations.

Adjective + noun compounds

[10]	*blackbird*	*blacksmith*	*blueprint*	*busybody*	*commonwealth*
	Englishman	*grandmother*	*grandstand*	*greenhouse*	*greyhound*
	handyman	*hotbed*	*hotline*	*madman*	*mainland*
	shortbread	*sick-bed*	*smalltalk*	*tightrope*	*wetnurse*

There are many compound nouns of this form in the vocabulary, and the type is still productive, as is evident from such relatively recent formations as *freeway*, *hotline*, *software*, *wetsuit*, etc. The degree of productivity is nevertheless fairly low: this pattern is

[22] *Girlfriend* and *boyfriend* are somewhat marginal members of the class from this point of view since they tend to be applied to a wider age-range than the nouns *girl* and *boy* used as separate words.

[23] An alternate term for this type is 'appositional compound'.

not widely used for the creation of new words. We include *smalltalk* and *grandstand* in the noun-centred rather than verb-centred category because the verbs *talk* and *stand* do not enter into construction with comparable adjectives.

The great majority of adjective + noun compounds involve a quite high degree of semantic specialisation and lexicalisation: the compound differs significantly, therefore, from a syntactic construction consisting of an attributive adjective + head noun. *Blackbird*, for example, is quite different in meaning from *black bird*: it denotes a species of bird, not a bird of a certain colour, so that *white blackbird* is not contradictory. In many cases the compound is not even hyponymic: a busybody is not a kind of body, nor a commonwealth a kind of wealth, and analogously for *greenhouse*, *hotbed*, *shortbread*. In a good number of cases the property denoted by the adjective does not apply to the denotation of the noun base but to something else that is understood: with *sick-bed*, for example, it is not the bed that is sick, but the person in it. Similarly a blacksmith works with black things, a greenhouse is a building containing green plants, and so on. Adjective + noun compounds are almost always distinguishable from syntactic constructions by their phonological as well as semantic properties. They normally have the main stress on the adjective component, so that morphological *'blackbird* contrasts with syntactic *'black 'bird*. Exceptions (like *black'currant* for the majority of speakers) are quite rare.

The adjectives that appear as first element in compound nouns are of one or two syllables, and usually of Germanic rather than Romance origin. They are almost invariably simple bases: examples like *<u>earthen</u>·ware*, with a derivative adjective, are exceptional. Take *Chinese restaurant*, for example. Its meaning is comparable to that of some of the compounds discussed above since it provides a classification of the restaurant, so that *German Chinese restaurant*, like *white blackbird*, is not contradictory. Nevertheless, *Chinese* is a complex base, not a simple one, and *Chinese restaurant* is not a compound.

Grand is used in a specialised sense in kin terms like *grandmother* or *grandson* to indicate a further degree of lineal distance beyond that expressed in the head. Such forms can themselves be modified by *great* (with the same meaning) in a morphological construction that is recursive: there is no linguistic limit on how many *great*'s are permitted in compounds like *great-great-great-grandmother*.

Verb + noun compounds

[11]	i	*copycat*	*crybaby*	*driftwood*	*glow-worm*	*hangman*
		hovercraft	*playboy*	*screechowl*	*search-party*	*workman*
	ii	*borehole*	*call-girl*	*mincemeat*	*punch-ball*	*push-button*
	iii	*bakehouse*	*blowtorch*	*dance-hall*	*driveway*	*fry-pan*
		grindstone	*payday*	*plaything*	*searchlight*	*springboard*
		swearword	*swimsuit*	*washday*	*washroom*	*workbench*

These differ from the verb-centred compounds in having the verbal element in dependent position, but they are similar in that the semantic relation between the two components is comparable to that found in a clausal construction between the verb and an NP. In [i] the noun matches up with a clausal subject: compare *The baby cries*; *The man hangs* (*people sentenced to death*). In [ii] the match is with a clausal object: a punchbag is a bag that one punches, and so on. In [iii] the clausal relation would be mediated by a preposition: compare *wash (clothes) <u>on</u> this day* / *<u>in</u> this room*, *work <u>at</u> this bench*, etc. The relations involved here include instrument (*grindstone, swearword*), location (*bakehouse, driveway*), time (*payday, washday*).

Compounds of this form are mostly hyponymic, but again there is in many cases a high degree of semantic specialisation – cf. *call-girl, plaything, searchlight, springboard,* and others. Non-hyponymic examples include *glow-worm* (cited in [2]) and *copycat,* which denotes a kind of person, not a cat.

A great many lexical bases in English can be either verbs or nouns, and as a result there may be uncertainty or indeterminacy as to whether a component of a compound is one or the other. For example, *payday* might be glossed as "day on which people are paid" (taking *pay* as a verb) or "day on which people receive their pay" (with *pay* as a noun). *Dance-hall* might similarly be glossed as "hall where one dances" or "hall for dances". Our purpose here, however, is simply to illustrate the range of patterns to be found within the set of compound words, not to establish a system of classification that will yield a unique analysis for every compound; our account is therefore consistent with the fact that some words could be construed as fitting more than one pattern.

Verbal element has the ·*ing* suffix

[12]	*chewing-gum*	*drinking-water*	*eating-apple*	*frying-pan*	*hiding-place*
	living-room	*talking-point*	*turning-point*	*walking-stick*	*whipping-boy*

These characteristically have a purposive meaning: "gum for chewing", "pan for frying in". Again such compounds are mainly hyponymic, but there are a few lexicalised exceptions, such as *whipping-boy*, "scapegoat". In some cases there is alternation between a compound where the verbal element is morphologically simple, as in [11] above, and one where it has the gerund-participle form, as here: *frying-pan/fry-pan, swimming-costume/swim-suit*; BrE tends to prefer the suffixed verb, AmE the unsuffixed one.

Other categories of first base

[13]	i	*after-effect*	*backwater*	*downside*	*in-joke*	*inroad*
		off-chance	*outbuilding*	*outpatient*	*overcoat*	*underdog*
	ii	*six-pack*	*he-man*	*she-wolf*		

The main other type of noun-centred compound has a preposition as first element, as in [i]; there are also a few beginning with a numeral or a gender-specific personal pronoun.

Bahuvrihi compounds

[14]	i	*lazybones*	*loudmouth*	*paleface*	*redhead*	*redskin*
	ii	*birdbrain*	*butterfingers*	*egghead*	*skinhead*	*suedehead*

Compounds of this type denote the entity characterised by having the property indicated: a redhead is a person who has red hair (and hence a red head); a birdbrain is a person who has (or rather who is presented as having) a brain the size of a bird's, i.e. someone very stupid; an egghead is someone presented as having a head resembling an egg, i.e. a high forehead, hence an intellectual. Note that *lazybones* and *butterfingers* contain the plural suffix on the head element but they usually apply to a single person and are then syntactically singular: *He's a lazybones/butterfingers.*

The label **bahuvrihi** again comes from Sanskrit grammar, with the meaning "having much rice", which thus illustrates the kind of construction it denotes. The first base is an adjective in [14i], a noun in [ii]. English has only a relatively small number of compounds of this kind but, as is evident from the last two examples in [ii], this type of formation is still productive.

Bahuvrihi compounds in English mostly denote kinds of people, and are generally derogatory. Some are readily used as vocatives: *Hey, birdbrain!* There are also compounds of this type that denote animals (*redbreast*), plants (*longleaf, whitethorn*), and inanimates (*greenback*, a type of banknote; *blackhead*, a kind of pimple; *hatchback*, a type of car).

4.2.2 Verb-centred compound nouns

Verb-centred compound nouns are those where the central element is 'verbal', its form being identical with that of the lexical base of a verb (*hand·<u>shake</u>*) or derived from it by suffixation (*theatre·<u>goer</u>*).[24] One initial point to make is that the relation between the parts is characteristically comparable to that between a verb and NPs in clause structure, which is typically a relation of complementation rather than modification. For this reason, glosses in terms of 'a kind of' tend to be less applicable or less plausible than with noun-centred compounds. We shall hardly want to say, for example, that a handshake is a kind of shake or a theatre-goer a kind of goer. This is because *shake* and *goer* are unlikely to be used on their own with the relevant sense, so that *a kind of shake* and *a kind of goer* are pragmatically unnatural expressions.

We look first at compounds where the verbal element combines with a noun, and then at those where it combines with a preposition.

The non-verbal element is a noun

Here the noun usually occupies first position, but we begin with a minor type with the reverse order.

(a) Verb + noun: *pickpocket* type

[15]	*breakwater*	*cut-throat*	*dreadnought*	*lickspittle*	*lockjaw*
	makeweight	*pickpocket*	*scarecrow*	*spoilsport*	*turnkey*

There are only a few established words formed on this pattern, which is no longer productive. The noun corresponds to the object of a clausal construction, and the compound as a whole denotes the person or thing that carries out the action: a pickpocket is a person who picks ("steals from") pockets, a scarecrow is something that scares crows away. The meaning is therefore like that found in the productive pattern *letter-writer*, but the form is exceptional in that the verbal element comes first; compare also *breakwater* and *windbreak*. The V + N form is comparable to that seen in [14] above, but the meaning of the latter is very different: a call-girl, for example, is not someone who calls girls (for sex), but a girl whom people call, and this is why we have taken *call-girl* to be noun centred.[25]

[24] Compounds where one base is derived from a verb by suffixation are often called 'synthetic compounds'. We avoid this potentially confusing term because in its primary sense 'synthetic' contrasts with 'analytic' and applies to marking by modification of the form of a word rather than by means of a separate word (e.g. *taller* is a synthetic comparative while *more intelligent* is an analytic one). In this general sense all compounds are synthetic. The motivation for calling words like *life-saver* and *fox-hunting* synthetic compounds is that the semantic relation between *save* and *life* or *hunt* and *fox* is here expressed within a single word rather than a clausal construction such as *They save lives / hunt foxes.*

[25] The *pickpocket* type is often classed together with bahuvrihi compounds like *paleface*: calling someone a pickpocket because they pick pockets is comparable to calling someone a paleface because they have a pale face.

(b) Noun + verbal element without suffix: *bee-sting, bloodshed, gunfight*

[16]						
	i	*bee-sting*	*bus-stop*	*cloudburst*	*daybreak*	*dogfight*
		earthquake	*fleabite*	*footstep*	*frostbite*	*headache*
		heartbeat	*landslide*	*nightfall*	*nosebleed*	*plane-crash*
		rainfall	*snowdrift*	*sunset*	*sunshine*	*waterfall*
	ii	*birth-control*	*bloodshed*	*car-park*	*chimney-sweep*	*dress-design*
		haircut	*handshake*	*life-guard*	*self-control*	*windbreak*
	iii	*boat-ride*	*daydream*	*field-work*	*gunfight*	*handstand*
		homework	*moon-walk*	*pub-crawl*	*table-talk*	

In [i] the initial noun corresponds to the subject of a clausal construction (compare *bee-sting* with *The bee stings*), in [ii] to the object (compare *bloodshed* and *They shed blood*), and in [iii] to the object of a preposition (compare *gunfight* and *They fight with guns*). There are a few cases such as *sunset* and *bloodshed* where the second base (with the sense it has in the compound) is purely verbal, but for the most part the second base can occur alone as either a verb or a noun. It may then not always be clear which is primary, and hence whether the compound belongs to the verb-centred or noun-centred pattern. Indeed it may be that the answer in a particular case will vary according to the meaning, as with 'dress-design', for example: compare *a new dress-design* (where the compound is a hyponym of the noun *design*) and *I'm in dress-design* (where *design* is verbal, and could be replaced by *designing* with no change of meaning).

(c) Noun + deverbal noun in ·*er*: *stage-manager, lawn-mower, city-dweller*

[17]					
	i	*gamekeeper*	*life-saver*	*matchmaker*	*radio-operator*
		rat-catcher	*shoemaker*	*songwriter*	*stage-manager*
		stakeholder	*whistleblower*	*window-cleaner*	*wrong-doer*
	ii	*clothes-drier*	*dishwasher*	*honey-eater*	*lawn-mower*
		nutcracker	*oyster-catcher*	*pen-holder*	*place-holder*
		record-player	*screwdriver*	*shock-absorber*	*tongue-twister*
	iii	*city-dweller*	*factory-worker*	*freedom-fighter*	*gate-crasher*
		grasshopper	*house-breaker*	*theatre-goer*	*town-crier*

By virtue of the ·*er* suffix the whole compound denotes the person or thing corresponding to the subject in a clausal construction, so this time there are no cases like [16i] where the first noun has the subject-like role. In [i] and [ii] the first noun corresponds to the object of a clause, those in [i] denoting humans (a rat-catcher is someone who catches rats), those in [ii] non-humans (a lawn-mower is a machine for mowing lawns). In [iii] the noun corresponds to the object of a preposition: a city-dweller dwells/lives <u>in</u> a city, a freedom-fighter fights <u>for</u> freedom, a theatre-goer goes <u>to</u> the theatre, and so on. The unexpressed preposition can be regarded as the default one for the particular verb–noun pair.

In general, this type of compound has a relatively narrow range of meanings. The fact that the semantic relation between the bases matches that found in clause structure means that *stage-manager*, for example, can only mean "one who manages the stage": it cannot be interpreted as "phoney manager" (compare *stage whisper*), "manager who operates over particular sectors" (compare *stage-coach*), "manager intended to be seen on stage" (compare *stage-play*), and so on. Most of the established words on this pattern are limited in their denotation to persons, animals, or machines that characteristically perform the action expressed in the verbal element.

Compounds of this kind are among those where the constituent structure is not entirely straightforward. We have assumed that the ·*er* is part of the second base, so that the ICs of *shoemaker*, for example, are *shoe* and *maker*, not *shoemake* and ·*er*. This reflects the fact that there is a word *maker* (which might occur in the phrase *a maker of shoes*), but not a word *shoemake*. With some of them the corresponding compound verb is established (e.g. *stage-manage*, *gate-crash*), but these are normally back-formations: the major point is that this pattern does not presuppose the existence of such a verb, and that the natural gloss is of the form "one who manages the stage / saves lives", not "one who stage-manages/life-saves", and so on. The IC structure of these words is therefore different from that of *first-nighter*, *flat-earther*, *left-hander*, etc., which are not compounds but derivatives formed by suffixing ·*er* to the nominal expressions *first-night*, *flat-earth*, *left-hand*.

(d) Noun + deverbal noun in ·*ing*: *letter-writing*, *churchgoing*

[18]						
	i	*book-keeping*	*brainwashing*	*dressmaking*	*fox-hunting*	*housekeeping*
		letter-writing	*peace-offering*	*shadow-boxing*	*sightseeing*	*town-planning*
	ii	*churchgoing*	*handwriting*	*night-flying*	*shop-lifting*	*sky-writing*
		sleepwalking	*spring-cleaning*	*star-gazing*	*sun-bathing*	*window-shopping*

Again the first noun corresponds in [i] to an object in clause structure, and in [ii] to the object of a preposition. *Cockfighting* might seem to be a case where it corresponds to a subject, but the term applies not to the activity where cocks fight each other but to that where people set them fighting. The compound generally denotes an activity, but other meanings are seen in *peace-offering* (which differs from the others in being a count noun) and *handwriting*.

(e) Noun + other deverbal noun: *book-production*

[19] *book-production* *car-maintenance* *heart-failure* *self-denial* *word-formation*

These are similar to the compounds in ·*ing*, but involve other forms of nominalisation of the verb. In *heart-failure* the first noun corresponds to a subject, in the others to the object.

The non-verbal element is a preposition

(a) Unsuffixed verb + preposition

[20]					
	breakthrough	*drop-out*	*hang-up*	*lean-to*	*look-out*
	phone-in	*pullover*	*runabout*	*runaway*	*run-up*
	show-off	*sit-in*	*stand-off*	*take-away*	*take-off*

These compounds contain the lexical base of a verb followed by a preposition: this is still a productive process. In most cases (but not, for example, in *hang-up* and *lean-to*) the verb and preposition occur adjacently in related clausal constructions: *He's going to drop out of the race*; *I will run up to the wicket*; *We must phone in our results*. In such cases the process of forming the noun bears some resemblance to conversion – it differs from it, however, because the verb and preposition in the clausal construction are separate words, so that the effect of combining them into a noun is to form a compound. Note also that the stress pattern is different. While the syntactic construction has the main stress on the preposition, the compound has it on *phone*: the difference between the noun *phone-in* and the verb + preposition sequence *phone in* matches that between noun *import* and verb *import* discussed in §2.6. These compounds have meanings ranging over persons (*drop-out, runaway, show-off*), concrete objects (*lean-to, pull-over*), events (*breakthrough, stand-off*). *Sit-in* belongs to a group widely used in the 1960s: *love-in, kneel-in, read-in, swim-in*, etc.

(b) Preposition + unsuffixed verb

[21]	*downturn*	*intake*	*offshoot*	*offspring*	*onset*
	outlook	*overflow*	*overkill*	*underlay*	*upkeep*

Here the preposition occupies initial position. A few compounds of this type match up semantically with verb + preposition constructions (e.g. *intake* with *take in*), a few are formed by conversion of compound verbs (e.g. *overflow*), but overall the relation to verbal constructions is not very systematic. *Outlook* contrasts with *look-out* in [20]: compare also *off-spin* and *spin-off, outbreak* and *break-out, out-fall* and *fall-out.* It is clear, therefore, that the choice between the verb + preposition and preposition + verb orders is determined neither by the preposition nor by the verb.

(c) Verbal element carries the ·*er* suffix: *passer-by, bystander*

[22] i	*diner-out*	*hanger-on*	*looker-on*	*passer-by*	*runner-up*
ii	*bystander*	*onlooker*	*outrider*		

The nominalising ·*er* suffix is added to the verbal base, usually giving an agentive interpretation. The preposition follows the verbal element in [i], precedes it in [ii], but carries the main stress in both cases. We exclude from [ii] examples like *underwriter*, which is a derivative from the verb *underwrite.* There are only a few compounds of the types shown in [22]; some match up closely with clausal constructions (cf. *They look on / pass by*), while others do not (verbal *run up* does not have a meaning comparable to *runner-up* "winner of second place in a competition"). Plurals are formed by adding ·*s* to the noun in ·*er*: for [i] this means that the plural suffix precedes the preposition: *hangers-on, runners-up.* This is a clear indication that the preposition is a dependent element: the plural suffix is added to the head noun, as in [ii] and in nouns generally.

The pattern in [22ii] is no longer productive, yet it appears to have left a trace behind, since non-standard nonce-words are sometimes heard with two ·*er* suffixes (e.g. [!]*blower-upper*, "a shell which should be blown up"). In nouns of this second type the plural is marked at the end of the word, in line with the most general inflectional pattern.

(d) Verbal element carries the ·*ing* suffix: *summing-up, upbringing*

[23] i	*dressing-down*	*going-over*	*summing-up*	*talking-to*	*washing-up*
ii	*infighting*	*outpouring*	*upbringing*	*uprising*	

As in [22], the preposition carries the primary stress whether it occurs in final or initial position. Again there are few examples of these types; we exclude from [23ii] examples like *undertaking* (a derivative from *undertake*), and from [i] we exclude the underlined sequences in *the bringing in of the furniture, the taking away of the rubble, the closing down of the store*, which we take as head + complement sequences in the structure of NPs. This syntactic construction allows a very wide range of complements, including an AdjP in *the burning alive of the missionaries* and a transitive PP in *the bringing to a close of these proceedings*, and so on. Most of the compounds in [23] match up with clausal constructions, but not all (cf. *infighting*). Unlike the nouns in [22i], those in [23i] do not readily occur in the plural: neither ?*dressings-down* nor ?*dressing-downs* sounds acceptable.

The non-verbal element is an adjective

[24] i	*best-seller*	*free-thinker*	*high-flier*	*loud-speaker*	*new-comer*
ii	*sharp-shooter*	*shortcoming*	*shortfall*	*well-being*	

There are few established compounds in this pattern: most have the ·*er* suffix attached to the verb. In most cases the relation between adjective and noun is comparable to that between adverb and verb (cf. *sell best, think freely*), but there is a high degree of lexicalisation, so that few can be paraphrased with the corresponding clausal construction.

4.3 Compound adjectives

Our initial classification here is again based on the category of the central element. We distinguish three categories: adjective-centred (*cholesterol-free, red-hot*), verb-centred (*fun-loving, MIT-trained, germ-resistant*), and a residual category centred on nouns (*highbrow*) or having the form of preposition + noun (*upmarket*).

4.3.1 Adjective-centred compound adjectives

Noun + adjective compounds

The majority of compounds with an adjective as second component have a noun as the first. In general, there is no contrast here between a compound and a syntactic construction since adjectives take only a highly restricted type of NP as pre-head dependent (cf. Ch. 6, §3.2): the syntactic dependents of adjectives are generally pre-head adverbs or post-head PPs and clauses. Many noun + adjective compounds involve a high degree of lexicalisation, as in:

[25]	*colour-fast*	*foot-loose*	*headstrong*	*threadbare*	*top-heavy*

Although there is a more or less obvious connection between the meaning of the whole and that of the adjective head, none of these satisfy the test for hyponymy. *He is headstrong*, for example, does not entail *He is strong*, and something can be top-heavy even though it is as a whole relatively light. We will not attempt a comprehensive review of the patterns to be found, but will illustrate a selection of the more productive ones.

Comparative/intensifying

[26] i	*bone-dry*	*crystal-clear*	*dirt-cheap*	*dog-tired*	*feather-light*
	ice-cold	*paper-thin*	*razor-sharp*	*rock-hard*	*stone-deaf*
ii	*bottle-green*	*brick-red*	*jet-black*	*snow-white*	*steel-blue*

Here the noun indicates a standard of comparison: "dry as a bone", "clear as crystal", etc. Very often, as in [i], the effect is to intensify: *bone-dry* means "extremely/completely dry", and so on. A special case of the comparative type is that of colour adjectives, as in [ii]; *jet-black* and *snow-white* are intensifying, but the others simply specify a particular shade of the colour. Compounds of this type are clearly hyponymic: if you are dog-tired, then necessarily you are tired, and so on.

Measure terms

[27] *ankle-deep* *shoulder-high* *skin-deep* *state-wide* *week-long*

This is a productive pattern, with the noun indicating extent. *Wide* here has to do with area rather than the one-dimensional measure denoted by *wide* on its own, and *skin-deep* "superficial" is a further example of lexicalisation. Compounds formed on this pattern are non-hyponymic: *The water was ankle-deep*, for example, does not entail *The water was deep*. We noted earlier that there may be a variety of reasons why a compound might fail the hyponymy test: in the present case it is due to the fact that the adjectives are gradable ones that can apply either to the scale generally (*How deep is the water?*) or to an area of the scale greater than some relevant norm (*The water is deep*). The compound involves the first use, whereas the adjectives are generally interpreted in the second way when standing alone.

Incorporated complement/modifier

[28] *accident-prone* *burglar-proof* *camera-shy* *carsick* *cholesterol-free*
class-conscious *girl-crazy* *oil-rich* *power-mad* *praiseworthy*
snow-blind *tax-free* *travel-weary* *user-friendly* *watertight*

These are comparable to syntactic constructions where the adjective has a following PP as dependent, complement, or modifier – compare *prone to accidents*, *proof against burglars*, *crazy about girls*, *rich in oil*, etc. *Free* (both in the sense "not having to pay", as in *tax-free*, and in the sense "not containing", as in *cholesterol-free*) is particularly productive. Some adjectives, such as *crazy*, *free*, *mad*, *rich*, *weary*, *worthy*, occur readily both in compounds and in syntactic constructions, while others, such as *proof* and *tight*, prefer or require the compound form.[26] Others again take syntactic complements but hardly form compounds: *fond of animals*, *keen on sport*, *eager for revenge* (compare **animal-fond*, **sport-keen/*sports-keen*, **revenge-eager*). Where the noun corresponds to a syntactic complement, the compounds are generally not hyponymic: tax-free goods aren't (necessarily) free, nor is a user-friendly computer manual a friendly one. With *prone* and *proof* the issue does not in fact arise since they cannot stand alone without complements – and indeed the same applies to *free* and *conscious* in the senses they have in *cholesterol-free* and *class-conscious*.

Self· compounds

[29] *self-confident* *self-concious* *self-evident* *self-important* *self-righteous*

There are a great many adjectives with *self·* as the first component; many belong in the verb-centred category (*self-denying*, *self-declared*), but there are a considerable number which are adjective-centred, like those in [29]. A high proportion apply to humans (but cf. *self-evident*, *self-contradictory*). A few are hyponymic (*self-confident*, *self-contradictory*), while others are clearly not (*self-important*, *self-righteous*).

Adjective + adjective

There are far fewer established compounds of this form. We distinguish two cases.

[26] *Fail-safe* and *tamper-proof* are exceptional in that the first base is a verb rather than noun.

Coordinative

[30] *bitter-sweet* *deaf-mute* *shabby-genteel* *Swedish-Irish* *syntactic-semantic*

The components here are of equal status. The last two illustrate highly productive patterns, both of which are predominantly used in attributive function: *Swedish-Irish trade*, *a syntactic-semantic investigation*. In general these can be glossed with coordinative *and*: "bitter and sweet", "deaf and mute", etc. In some, however, there is an understood "between" relation: "trade between Sweden and Ireland".

Subordinative

[31] *dark-blue* *icy-cold* *pale-green* *red-hot* *white-hot*

As with nouns, it is not always easy to distinguish between coordinative and subordinative types, and some analysts include these with the coordinative type. We regard them as subordinative because we take the first element to be semantically modifying the second: *icy*, *red*, and *white*, for example, have an intensifying role. *Bright*, *dark*, *light*, *pale* occur productively with colour terms. Compounds combining two colour terms, such as *blue-grey* or *orange-red* probably belong here too, with the first identifying a particular shade of the colour denoted by the second.

4.3.2 Verb-centred compound adjectives

Gerund-participle as head

Noun as first component

[32]	i	*awe-inspiring*	*breath-taking*	*heart-breaking*	*thought-provoking*
	ii	*animal-loving*	*cost-cutting*	*degree-conferring*	*fact-finding*
	iii	*law-abiding*	*ocean-going*	*theatre-going*	*winter-flowering*

This is a very productive type of compound, covering a number of patterns. Usually, the noun corresponds to the object in a syntactic construction, as in [i–ii]. *Awe-inspiring* corresponds to the VP *inspire awe*, *degree-conferring* to *confer degrees*, and so on. But it is also possible for the noun to correspond to the complement of a preposition, as in [iii], where the verbs are intransitive: *abide <u>by</u> the law*, *go <u>on</u> the ocean* / *<u>to</u> the theatre*, *flower <u>in</u> winter*. In all cases the understood subject of the verb derives from the head of the NP when the adjective is used attributively and from its predicand when it is used predicatively: in *a thought-provoking lecture* and *The lecture was extremely thought-provoking* or *They found the lecture thought-provoking* it is the lecture that provokes thought.[27] Many adjectives of this kind, such as those in [i], are gradable and occur in both attributive and predicative function, while there are others, illustrated in [ii], that are normally ungradable and restricted to attributive function (with the syntactic construction being preferred to the predicative use of the compound: *This institution confers degrees* rather than ?*This institution is degree-conferring*). *Self-* is a common first component: *self-respecting* (attributive only), *self-financing*, *self-pitying*.

Adjective/adverb as first component

[33] *easy-going* *far-seeing* *hard-working* *long-suffering* *strange-looking*

[27] *Mouth-watering* is exceptional in that it is one's mouth that waters: the head or predicand is understood to have a causative role, making one's mouth water.

Verbs like *look*, *smell*, *taste*, *seem*, etc., which take adjectival predicative complements, occur in compounds matching the clausal construction: *a strange-looking object* matches *an object that looks strange*, *a desperate-seeming suggestion* matches *a suggestion that seems desperate*, and so on. But *good-looking* and *high-sounding* are lexicalised – we can say, for example, *Your prospects look good*, but not #*Your prospects are good-looking*. With other kinds of verb there is also a good deal of lexicalisation, as in *easy-going*, *far-seeing*, *long-suffering*. *Hard-working* corresponds to *work hard*, with adverbial *hard*, but we need to distinguish between compound adjectives of this form and adverb + verb syntactic sequences like *rapidly diminishing* (*returns*). One difference is that we can say *They seem hard-working*, but not **They seem rapidly diminishing*.

Past participle as head

Based on passive use of past participle

[34] i	*drug-related*	*home-made*	*MIT-trained*	*moth-eaten*
	safety-tested	*sex-linked*	*taxpayer-funded*	*weather-beaten*
ii	*clean-shaven*	*French-based*	*high-set*	*new-born*

Those in [i] have a noun as first component, a highly productive pattern. These compounds generally correspond to syntactic passives with a PP: *related to drugs*, *made at home*, *tested for safety*, *funded by taxpayers*, etc. A relatively small proportion are gradable: *very moth-eaten/weather-beaten*. *Self-* is again often found as first component, often with a high degree of lexicalisation: *self-taught*, *self-appointed*, *self-made*, *self-confessed*, *self-possessed*. Those in [ii] have an adjective or adverb as first element. For these there is generally no closely corresponding syntactic construction with adjective/adverb (?*shaven clean*, **based French* – compare similarly *foreign-built* but not **built foreign*). This type is of low productivity except for the subtype illustrated by *French-based*: with proper names of countries and to some extent other locations the adjective is used in past-participial compounds when one is readily available – compare *French-based* (*French* an adjective) and *Guernsey-based* (*Guernsey* a noun), *Paris/Parisian-based* and *London-based*.

Based on active use of past participle

[35]	*plain-spoken*	*short-lived*	*well-behaved*	*well-travelled*

These are semantically related to clauses involving the active rather than the passive use of the verb: *plain-spoken* applies to a person who speaks plainly, not to words or whatever that are spoken plainly. Similarly, a well-travelled person is someone who has travelled well, or widely. There are few compounds of this form, all lexicalised.

Deverbal adjective as head

Finally we find compounds of the form noun + deverbal adjective:

[36]	*drug-dependent*	*germ-resistant*	*self-reliant*	*tax-deductible*

These match syntactic constructions involving verb + NP object (*resist germs*) or verb + PP (*depend on drugs*). They are therefore closely comparable to the compounds in [32], where we also saw that the syntactic distinction between an NP that is object of the verb, and one that is related to the verb by a preposition is lost in the morphological compound. But they are also similar to the compounds in [28–29], since there are also paraphrases with AdjPs (*dependent on drugs, resistant to germs*): the initial noun of a compound adjective can represent a semantic argument whether the head is verbal or adjectival.

4.3.3 Other forms

We saw in Ch. 5, §14.2, that the attributive modifier function in NP structure can be realised by a very wide range of expressions. They include ordinary AdjPs (*an extraordinarily good movie*), DPs (*the almost eighty students present*), nominals (*a gold watch*), VPs (*the retreating troops*). In addition there are expressions that do not fit into the regular structures for these categories:

[37]	*an all-time high*	*a hands-on approach*	*a high-rise building*
	inflight entertainment	*the London–Glasgow express*	*a no-win situation*

Such expressions are typically nonce-forms, restricted to attributive modifier function. This is an area where it is difficult to draw a clear line between syntax and morphology, but it may be best to treat them as compound adjectives.

One productive type that merits mention involves measure expressions with a singular noun base: *a three-inch nail, a five-mile walk, a two-year moratorium.* These do not qualify as nominals, which have plural forms of the noun: *The nail is three inches long*; *We walked five miles*; and so on. These compound adjectives can combine with adjectives to form larger compounds (belonging with the subordinative adjective + adjective compounds of §4.3.1): *a three-metre-wide pool, a two-year-old child.* Those with *old* as head readily convert to nouns: cf. *two three-year-olds.*

4.4 Compound verbs

There are far fewer compound verbs than there are compound nouns or compound adjectives. A high proportion of them, moreover, are formed by other processes than compounding, namely back-formation and conversion. Back-formation is most commonly from nouns in ·*er* (*ghostwriter* → *ghostwrite*) or ·*ing* (*job-sharing* → *jobshare*), or adjectives in ·*ed* (*hen-pecked* → *hen-peck*); for some, more than one source may be available (*chain-smoker/chain-smoking* → *chain-smoke*; *freeze-dried/freeze-drying* → *freeze-dry*). Conversion is generally from compound nouns (*blacklist*$_N$ → *blacklist*$_V$). Most compound verbs that arise directly from compounding have a preposition as the first base, as in *over-react, outlast, underestimate.* Direct formation of compounds with a noun as first base is very rare, and it is not easy to establish that the verb preceded the corresponding noun in ·*ing.* Verbs of this kind that do appear to have been formed directly include *speed-read, hand-wash,* and perhaps *gift-wrap.* There are also verbs like *cold-shoulder* that are formed by what we have called dephrasal compounding: see §4.1 above.

The following types of compound verb may be distinguished according to the component bases involved. In the lists of examples we add annotations in the case of those verbs formed by some process other than ordinary compounding: 'B' for back-formation, 'CV' for conversion, and 'DP' for dephrasal compounding.

[38] i NOUN + VERB

baby-sit B	*brainwash* B	*chain-smoke* B	*daydream* CV	*ghostwrite* B
hand-wash	*henpeck* B	*hood-wink* B	*job-share* B	*mass-produce* B
nosedive CV	*proofread* B	*sky-dive* B	*sleepwalk* B	*spoonfeed* B
springclean B	*stage-manage* B	*tape-record* B	*whitewash* CV	*window-shop* B

ii NOUN + NOUN

bar-code CV	*handcuff* CV	*honeymoon* CV	*snowball* CV	*stone-wall* DP

iii ADJECTIVE + NOUN

blacklist CV	*fast-track* DP	*shortchange* DP	*soft-soap* DP	*wisecrack* CV

iv PREPOSITION + NOUN/VERB

backdate	*background* CV	*bypass* CV	*downgrade*	*downsize*
input CV	*offset*	*onsell*	*outclass*	*outgrow*
outsource	*overcharge*	*overdose* CV	*overflow*	*underachieve* B
undercharge	*underlie*	*undersell*	*uphold*	*upstage* CV

v VERB + VERB COORDINATIVE COMPOUNDS

blow-dry	*cook-chill*	*freeze-dry*

One marginal type of compound verb formed by conversion from a noun is seen in:

[39] *They went* <u>*deer-hunting*</u>. *They spent their holiday* <u>*trout-fishing*</u>.

These are defective in that there are no verb-forms other than the gerund-participle: cf. **They deer-hunted*. Nevertheless, the forms in [39] would seem to be verbs, not nouns. *Go* in the relevant use is restricted to this kind of expression, but *spend* accepts uncontroversial gerund-participials, while not admitting NPs: *They spend their holiday* <u>*touring Europe*</u>.

4.5 Neo-classical compounds

A neo-classical compound is a compound where at least one of the component bases is a combining form. Combining forms are usually of Greek or Latin origin, but they appear in great numbers of compound nouns and adjectives which are not themselves of classical origin. Words like *holograph* and *hydrology*, for example, are made up of classical components but are modern coinages. Combining forms are thus used productively in English word-formation: this is why we speak of **neo**-classical compounds. Such compounds figure extremely prominently in scientific terminology and learned vocabulary generally.

The central type of neo-classical compound consists of two combining forms: *astronaut*, *autocrat*, *carnivore*, *fratricide*, *pseudonym*, *psychology*, and so on. Forms occurring in initial position we refer to as **initial combining forms** (ICFs), those in final position as **final combining forms** (FCFs). A few examples are given in [40i–ii] respectively:

[40]

i	*aer(o)*	*andr(o)*	*anthrop(o)*	*audio*	*aut(o)*	*bio*
	electro	*geo*	*heter(o)*	*hom(o)*	*hydr(o)*	*neur(o)*
	palae(o)	*pseud(o)*	*psych(o)*	*quadr(i)*	*socio*	*tele*
ii	*cephaly*	*ectomy*	*emia*	*gamy*	*geny*	*icide*
	ivore	*(o)crat*	*(o)graph*	*oid*	*(o)logy*	*onym*
	ophile	*(o)phobe*	*pathy*	*phone*	*saurus*	*scope*

Many of the items in [ii] are found only in combination with ICFs, and such combinations form the prototypical examples of neo-classical compounds. The morphological status of the bracketed vowels is problematic: we take up this issue below; we also set aside at this stage the issue of analysing such forms as *pathy* as *path·y*. Combining forms are generally bound, but there are also some that can stand alone as words, such as *mania, phobia, ology* ("a science or theory"), and a number that have arisen as informal clippings: *homo* ("homosexual"), *pseud, psycho, phone, physio*, etc.

There are also neo-classical compounds where one of the components is an ordinary free base rather than a combining form:

[41] i *aero<u>space</u>* *Anglo-<u>Irish</u>* *auto-<u>suggestion</u>* *bio<u>degradable</u>* *electro<u>magnet</u>*
hyper<u>market</u> *micro<u>chip</u>* *neuro<u>surgeon</u>* *pseudo-<u>science</u>* *socio-<u>economic</u>*
ii *<u>addresso</u>graph* *<u>insect</u>icide* *<u>jazz</u>ophile* *<u>merit</u>ocrat* *<u>speed</u>ometer*

The ordinary free base is compounded with an ICF in [i], with an FCF in [ii]; the former type is much the more common of the two. The word *neo-classical* itself is of this kind, *ne(o)* being an ICF that combines with FCFs in such words as *neology, neontology, neonate*.

The medial vowel

An important feature of neo-classical compounds is that they normally have a vowel at the boundary between the bases. Where the ICF ends in a vowel and the FCF begins with one, there is very often a loss of one vowel. We find the following patterns (though some of the example words are very rare):

[42] i a. $o + o \rightarrow o$ *anthropology, biology, geode, phonograph, pseudonym, theocrat*
b. $i + i \rightarrow i$ *omnivore*
ii a. $o/i + \mathrm{V} \rightarrow \mathrm{V}$ *aer·iferous, anthrop·oid, aut·archy, heter·acanth, hom·axonic, hydr·emia, neur·ectomy, pseud·aesthesia, psych·agogue, quadr·ennium, tyrann·icide*
b. $\mathrm{V} + o \rightarrow \mathrm{V}$ *agara·phobe, arche·logy, Dixie·crat, genea·logy, tele·graph*

'V' in [ii] represents a vowel symbol other than *o* – we include *·oid* here as the vowel symbol is *oi*, not *o*.[28] The above examples contain two combining forms, but there are also cases where the final vowel of an ICF is omitted when it attaches to a free base: *hom·organic, micr·acoustic, palae·ontology, quadr·angle* (compare also *meg·ohm*, where the omitted vowel is *a*). These, however, are relatively old words – in more recent formations the practice is to retain the vowel of the ICF:[29]

[43] *aero-engine, autoerotic, hydro-electric, microanalysis, neo-impressionism, pseudo-intellectual, psychoanalysis*

With the words in [42ii] the boundary between the bases is clear, but for those in [42i] it is more problematic: we might argue for *ge·ode, pseud·onym*, but in other cases the boundary may be indeterminable. In the representations in [40], therefore, we have enclosed the boundary vowel in parentheses only where it may be dropped by the processes shown in [42ii].

[28] In the case of [42iia], *h* behaves like a vowel, with the *o*/*i* of the ICF being omitted, as in *pseud·haemal, ant·helion*.
[29] There are also cases where we find alternants with and without the vowel: *ne(o)arctic*; *palae(o)ichthyology*.

Many elements have alternants without the boundary vowel which appear in other morphological constructions. Compare, for example:

[44]	a. *anthropopathy* ~ *philanthropy*	b. *Anglo-Irish* ~ *Anglicist*
	carpophagous ~ *pseudocarp*	*ethnography* ~ *ethnic*
	morphology ~ *ectomorph*	*socio-economic* ~ *society*
	pathology ~ *osteopath*	*theology* ~ *theism*

The pairs in [a] have an element appearing as ICF in the first member and as FCF in the second: in the former case it has a vowel at the end, in the latter at the beginning. The pairs in [b] have an element which in the left member is an ICF with *o* at the boundary, and in the right member appears with an affix attached but without the *o*. (*Society* was borrowed from French rather than formed in English and is not easily analysable into base + suffix; nevertheless the first part is clearly related to the ICF *socio*.)

Instead of treating *anthropo·* and *Anglo·* as ICF alternants of *anthrop·* and *Angl·*, we could say that the *o* does not belong to the combining form itself but is simply a linking element introduced by the neo-classical compounding process. This analysis has a good deal to commend it; in particular, it provides a natural account of why the *o* follows *carp* in *carpophagous*, but precedes it in *pseudocarp*, and so on. Instead of the processes of vowel sequence reduction given in [42], we would have constraints on the insertion of a linking vowel. In general, the insertion of the linking vowel would serve to break up a sequence of consonants at the medial boundary (thus *pseud·o·carp* instead of the inadmissible **pseud·carp*), though there are also places where *o* follows a vowel rather than a consonant and hence has no such phonological motivation – cf. *archaeology*, *ichthyomancy*, *palaeolith*, etc.

We have preferred to analyse the vowel as belonging to one or both of the ICFs mainly because in Present-day English combining forms are commonly added to existing words (i.e. free bases), and in such cases the medial vowel generally appears irrespective of the phonological form of the free base. This was illustrated above in [43]: there seems little doubt that in Present-day English *aero·*, *auto·*, *hydro·*, *micro·*, *neo·*, *pseudo·*, *psycho·*, etc., are single units available for use in the formation of new words. Or take the case of *·ology*. Etymologically, the *log* here is the same as that in *logical*, but the fact that *·ology* attaches very readily to proper nouns to form nonce-words such as *Kremlinology*, *Buffetology*, etc., suggests that it too behaves as a word-forming unit – and the fact that *ology* exists as a word by itself (comparable to *ism*) provides strong support for this analysis. Similarly, the productivity of the process involved in such words as *fungicide*, *germicide*, *herbicide*, *insecticide*, *pesticide*, *spermicide* provides evidence that Present-day English has an element *icide* used to form words with the meaning "chemical for killing ~". The etymological source is ultimately Latin *caedere* (or *·cidere*) "kill", with no initial *i*, but if we took the FCF to be *cide* with the *i* a linking vowel we would need to stipulate that compounds in *cide* take *i* rather than the default *o* as the linking vowel: it is simpler just to say that the *i* is part of the FCF. Such examples may be contrasted with *quadricycle*, *quadrisyllable*, *quadrivalve*, where the *i* is clearly part of the ICF.[30] A further point is that there are a few cases where we do not in fact have a medial vowel at all – for example, there is a vowel before *·pathy* in *allopathy*, *antipathy*, *telepathy* but not in *sympathy*. The linking vowel analysis would add *o* in *allopathy* (and *osteopathy*, etc.); the insertion of *o* in *antipathy* and *telepathy* would be blocked by the vowel at the end of *anti*

[30] Some ICFs have alternants with different marginal vowels, with *quadri·* one of the clearest examples. The default alternant has *i*, but *a* is found in a few words such as *quadragenarian*, *quadraphonic* and *u* in *quadrumanus*, *quadruped*, etc.

and *tele*, but its absence in *sympathy* would require special provision. We prefer to say simply that the ICFs here are *allo·*, *anti·*, *tele·*, and *syn·* (the latter appearing in the variant *sym* before bilabial /p/). Compare, similarly, *holo·gamy*, *micro·gamy*, and *syn·gamy*.

In the default case we take a single marginal vowel to belong to the ICF: *anthropo·morphism*, *geo·mancy*, *micro·lith*, *neo·nate*, *philo·sophy*, *quadri·plegia*. For it to be assigned exclusively or jointly to the FCF we need specific evidence. There is no need to include an *o* in *geny*, for example: it doesn't occur in *eugeny* and in words like *biogeny* or *ontogeny* the *o* can be assigned to the ICF. The two main kinds of evidence that the vowel belongs (exclusively or jointly) to the FCF were mentioned in the last paragraph. One is that the vowel appears when the element combines with a free base, as in *address·ograph*, *insect·icide*, *Kremlin·ology*. Note, however, that the argument for *·ology* applies where the meaning is "science, knowledge, study related to ~": as far as English is concerned, this element can be distinguished from the FCF *·logy*, which is found, with various senses, in such words as *eulogy*, *trilogy/tetralogy*, *syllogy*. (The last of these has no medial vowel, since the ICF is an alternant of *syn·* – compare the same alternation with the prefix *in·*: *inactive*, *impossible*, *illogical*). The second case is where the FCF selects *i* as the boundary vowel, as in *insect·icide*, *herb·ivore*, *frug·iferous*.[31] A third, much more specific, kind of evidence is provided by the ICF *syn·*, which differs from normal ICFs in that it does not end in a vowel. Compare, then, the above *anti·pathy* and *sym·pathy* with *antonym* and *synonym*. The *o* in the latter pair must belong to the FCF, not the ICF: if the FCF were *·nym* rather than *·onym*, combination with *anti·* and *syn·* would yield forms matching the combinations with *·pathy*, namely **antinym* and **synnym*.[32]

Combining forms contrasted with affixes

Combining forms are generally bound, and in that respect are like affixes rather than bases, which are characteristically free. Nevertheless, there are good grounds for including them in the category of bases, not affixes.

In the first place, the prototypical neo-classical compound consists of two bound combining forms, as in many of the examples above: *astronaut*, *bibliophile*, *osteopath*, etc. Such words could not have the structure 'affix + affix' (since an affix is always attached to a base) and as there are no grounds for treating one component as base and the other as affix we take both as bases.

Secondly, although only relatively few combining forms are free, a considerable number can serve as the base to which affixes are attached: *an·<u>anthrop</u>·ism*, *an·<u>emia</u>*, *<u>aqua</u>·tic*, *<u>hydr</u>·ic*, *<u>phon</u>·al*, *<u>phot</u>·ism*, and so on (cf. also the examples in [44b]). From a semantic point of view, there is a variable relationship between the elements in a neo-classical compound just as there is in a native one, and the meanings of combining forms are generally more specific than is typical of affixes. Nevertheless, we find a number of cases where a combining form and an affix have similar meanings – compare the ICF *micro·* and the prefix *mini·*, or ICF *hyper·* and prefix *super·*.

Combining forms are most like affixes when they combine readily with ordinary free bases. Examples include *micro·* (cf. *microcard*, *microchip*, *microcircuit*, *microclimate*, *microdot*,

[31] It may well be that we need to make a distinction between *·icide* and *·cide* parallel to that between *·ology* and *·logy*. The meaning of words such as *fratricide*, *regicide*, *suicide* is distinguishable from that of *insecticide*, etc., and they could be analysed as *fratri* + *cide*; this would accommodate the fact that there is a sense of *autocide* which is equivalent to *suicide*.

[32] The analysis *syn·onym* reflects the etymology, with *·onym* coming from the Greek *onum* "name"; compare also *an·onymous* "with no name (known or acknowledged)".

microfiche, microfilm, microgroove, micro-organism, micro-processor, microstructure, microwave, etc.) and *bio·* (cf. *bio-contamination, biodegradable, biodestructible, bioengineer, bioethics, bioexperiment, biohazard, biomedicine, biorhythm, biosatellite, bioscience,* etc.). What makes these elements nevertheless combining forms rather than affixes is that they also combine with bound combining forms, and retain the potential to enter into new combinations of this kind: *microcosm, microphone, microscope, biogen, biognosy, biolysis,* and so on. Note also that compounds consisting of combining forms normally have a vowel at the boundary; for the most part, then, prefixes which end in a consonant or suffixes which begin with one are phonologically distinguishable from combining forms. Thus *arch·* (/ɑːʳtʃ/), for example, as in *archdeacon* or *arch-enemy,* is a prefix, although the etymologically related *archi·* (/ɑːʳkɪ/), as in *archidiaconal, archilithic, archimage* ("chief magician"), *archinephron,* etc., is a combining form. This does not provide a necessary condition for combining form status, however, for we have noted that the ICF *syn·* does not end in a vowel: in analysing this as a combining form we have given priority to the fact that it can combine with FCFs, as in the above *sympathy, syngamy, syllogy.*

Neo-classical compounds, clippings, and blends

Neo-classical compounds, like other words, can undergo clipping and blending. *Photo,* we noted, is a clipping from *photograph,* so *photo-album* ("photograph-album") is a compound with a clipped first base, not a neo-classical compound like *photometer* ("instrument for measuring light"). *Telephone* is neo-classical, but *telegenic* is a blend of *television* + *photogenic,* and *telebanking* is a blend of *telephone* + *banking. Autocide* with the meaning "automobile suicide" is a blend, but we have noted that it can also be a neo-classical compound meaning "suicide".

Attachment of suffixes to or within neo-classical compound bases

A high proportion of words containing FCFs end in suffixes. Typically, we find a family of words differing only in the suffixes:

[45] i *theology, theologise, theologism, theologist, theologian, theologaster, theological*
ii *microcephaly, microcephalous, microcephalic*
iii *xenophobe, xenophobia, xenophobic*

The analysis of such sets poses considerable problems. Consider first set [i]. From a semantic point of view it would seem that *theology* has special status within the set, in that the meanings of the others are dependent on that of *theology*: *theologian,* for example, denotes a person skilled in theology. Instead of saying that all the forms are derived from a bound base by attachment of various affixes, we prefer to say, therefore, that the other forms are derived from *theology* by replacement of the affix *·y* by other affixes (for discussion and further illustration of this kind of affixation, see §5.1.4 below). *Theology* itself will then be a compound with *theo* as ICF and *(o)logy* as FCF, the latter being further analysable as base + the suffix *·y*. The set of affixes found in the established words is, however, specific to *theology* – for *biology* we have *biologist* and *biological,* for *psychology* we find *psychologist, psychological, psychologism,* and so on. For this reason we take the ICs of *theologian,* say, to be *theolog·* and *·ian,* which makes it a derivative, with a compound internal base. Similarly in [ii] we take the noun *microcephaly* to be a compound and the two adjectives to be derivatives from it. In [iii] it would be possible to take *xenophobia* as a derivative from *xenophobe,* but we prefer to take it too as a compound, since it corresponds to the nouns of the other sets and because *phobia* is a free base, so that *xenophobia* can be construed as a kind of phobia, a phobia of foreigners. *Xenophobic*, however, we again take to be a derivative (from one or other of the compounds). There are other ways of handling morphologically related sets of words like those in [45] (e.g. by saying that all, other than *xenophobe*, are derivatives with bound compound bases, or that all are compounds, with the affix belonging within the second base). We do not have knock-down arguments in support of our proposed analysis, and recognise that there is a certain amount of indeterminacy as to the IC structure of such words. Certainly, the identification of FCFs is less straightforward than that of ICFs.

4.6 Phonologically motivated compounds

There are a few items which, although they are treated orthographically as if they were compounds, and in some cases meet all the requirements for being ascriptive compounds, nevertheless are formed according to stipulations which are normally irrelevant in compound formation:

[46] i *clap-trap*, *cop-shop* (BrE slang "police station"), *gang-bang*, *walkie-talkie*
ii *boogie-woogie*, *fuzzy-wuzzy*, *super-duper*, *teeny-weeny*
iii *fuddy-duddy*, *helter-skelter*, *hodge-podge*, *hoity-toity*, *hurdy-gurdy*, *mumbo-jumbo*, *namby-pamby*
iv a. *chitchat*, *shillyshally*, *tittletattle* b. *knickknack*, *zigzag*
v a. *clipclop*, *crisscross*, *singsong* b. *dingdong*, *pingpong*

The examples in [i] are normal compounds formed from two independently existing words, and it just so happens that the two words rhyme. Compounds of this kind often have the effect of trivialising what they denote: compare, for example, *gang-bang* with *gang·rape*. In the examples in [ii], this rhyming feature is maintained, but the second base has no independent meaning, and serves purely to provide a rhyme. The particular consonant that is used at the start of the second base is not generally predictable, though labial consonants (including /w/) seem to be preferred. Note that if these were normal compounds, the right-hand base would be the head, but here the only meaningful element is the left-hand one. In the examples in [iii] neither base has any independent meaning (at least in Present-day English): the rhyme is the fundamental principle involved in the creation of these words. The examples in [iv] and [v] show words motivated not by rhyme but by vowel contrast. In [iv] there is change from /ɪ/ to /æ/, in [v] from /ɪ/ to /ɒ/, either with the right-hand base being the original meaningful element, as in the [a] examples, or with neither base being independently meaningful, as in [b]. There are also a few examples like *ticktock* where the lefthand base is the meaningful element. The /ɪ/ ~ /æ/ alternation is also found in the syntactic phrases *dribs and drabs* and *tit for tat*.

5 The core of English lexical word-formation: mainly derivation

The focus in this section is on derivation, though we shall make further reference to some of the processes already surveyed when they serve to achieve the same effect as is achieved by certain affixes.

5.1 Affixation and derivation: formal issues

Affixation is the process of forming a new base by the addition of an affix. Affixation is widely used in both inflectional and lexical morphology: **derivation** is then the more specific term for the formation by affixation of lexical bases, or **derivatives.** In the central type of derivation an affix is simply added to a base: *un·* + *happy* → *unhappy*; *read* + *·able* → *readable.* There are also places, however, where it is more helpful to see derivation as involving the replacement of one affix by another – to see *baptism*, for example, as deriving from *baptise* by replacement of *·ise* by *·ism*, rather than as simply involving the addition of *·ism* to the bound base *bapt·*.

5.1.1 Kinds and combinations of affixes

The syntactic effect of affixation

Affixes differ with respect to whether and, if so, to what extent they affect the syntactic distribution of the base to which they attach. We distinguish three main types:

(a) Affixes which change the primary category

One very important role of affixes, especially suffixes, is to create nouns, verbs, adjectives, etc., from bases of another category. Adding *·ness* to an adjective, for example, changes it into a noun: we refer to it as a **de-adjectival noun** and the process is a special case of **nominalisation.** Similarly, adding *·able* to a verb creates an adjective, adding *·ise* to a noun changes it into a verb, and so on:

[1]		RESULTANT BASE	PROCESS
	i *wet*$_{ADJ}$ + *·ness* → *wetness*$_{N}$	de-adjectival noun	nominalisation
	ii *read*$_{V}$ + *·able* → *readable*$_{ADJ}$	deverbal adjective	adjectivalisation
	iii *terror*$_{N}$ + *·ise* → *terrorise*$_{V}$	denominal verb	verbalisation

Affixes can also serve to nominalise or adjectivalise phrasal sequences, as in the <u>*old-maid*</u>*ish* and <u>*fly-by-night*</u>*er* examples of §4.1; particularly common here is the use of *·ed* to form dephrasal adjectives like *red-nosed, two-faced*, etc. Lexical word-formation processes of nominalisation, adjectivalisation, and verbalisation (whether by affixation or by other means) are described in §§5.7–9 respectively.

(b) Affixes which change the subclass

Less often, the primary category is preserved, but there is a change in the subclass:

[2]		a.	b.
	i	*He <u>moaned</u> about the lack of funds.*	*He <u>bemoaned</u> the lack of funds.*
	ii	*She hadn't yet become a <u>star</u>.*	*Her rise to <u>stardom</u> was meteoric.*

Moan, as in [ia], is an intransitive verb (here taking a PP complement): prefixing *be·* makes it transitive, as in [ib]. In [ii] *star* is a concrete count noun, whereas *stardom* is abstract and normally non-count.

(c) Affixes which have no effect on the syntactic distribution

There are also affixes, predominantly prefixes, which leave even the subclass unchanged:

[3]					
	i	*happy/<u>un</u>happy*	*fiend/<u>arch</u>fiend*	*judge/<u>mis</u>judge*	*read/<u>re</u>-read*
	ii	*tiger/tigr<u>ess</u>*	*kitchen/kitchen<u>ette</u>*	*green/green<u>ish</u>*	*good/good<u>ly</u>*

It should be borne in mind, however, that affixes do not always behave in a uniform way across all the bases to which they attach. *Be·*, for example, changes the subclass in the above example of *bemoan*, but it changes the primary category in *befriend* (a denominal verb) and *becalm* (de-adjectival). *Pre·* generally has no syntactic effect, as in the verb *pre-heat* or the adjective *pre-human*, but in words like *pre-war* it derives an adjective from a noun.

Restrictions on the category of base to which the affix is attached

For the most part affixes attach to free bases belonging to one or other of the three major syntactic categories, noun, verb, and adjective. Some affixes are found with bases of all three categories – cf. *counter-example* (N), *counter-act* (V), *counter-productive* (Adj). But these are very much in the minority: most affixes attach to bases of just one or two of the three categories (at least in their currently productive uses). For example, *·ity* and *·ness* attach to adjectives (*public·ity*, *wet·ness*), as does the verb-forming suffix *·en* (*light·en* – *strength·en* and *length·en* are lexicalised exceptions). Similarly, *fore·* and *re·* are normally found with verbs or (verb-related) nouns (*fore·warn*, *fore·taste*, *re·consider*, *re·birth*).

Such restrictions can provide useful evidence about constituent structure in cases where the structure is not obvious from the meaning. Consider, for example, words like *un·fair·ness*, consisting of an adjectival base together with a nominalising suffix and the negative prefix *un·*: are the ICs *unfair* + *·ness* or *un·* + *fairness*? The semantics doesn't provide a clear answer because there is no decisive contrast between "the state/condition of being unfair" and "the opposite of fairness". There is, however, a strong formal argument in support of an analysis as *unfair* + *·ness*: this IC structure enables us to make the general statement that this *un·* (as opposed to the one with the "reversal" sense of *un·tie*, etc.) normally attaches to adjectives. There are a great many adjectives consisting of *un·* + simple base: *uncertain*, *unclear*, *uncommon*, *uneven*, *unfair*, *unhappy*, *unready*, *untidy*, and so on. Here *un·* obviously attaches to an adjective, and we can simply generalise this analysis to words like *unfairness* if we take the ICs as *unfair* + *·ness*. We find, by contrast, only a handful of nouns containing this *un·* as prefix but no nominalising suffix: *unconcern*, *unease*, *unrest*, and the like; these must be regarded as lexicalised exceptions to the general pattern.[33]

Restrictions on occurrence of affixes with bound bases

Affixes generally attach to free bases – nouns, verbs, adjectives (and occasionally, in colloquial and often mildly jocular formations, to prepositions, as in *downer*, *iffy*, *uppity*). There are also words containing an affix attached to a bound base; but only a subset of affixes are found in words of this kind. Examples are given in [4i], while a sample of affixes restricted to free bases is given in [4ii]:

[4]	i	ALLOW BOUND BASES:	*dis·gruntled*,	*en·quire*,	*pre·empt*,	*re·vise*,
			dur·able,	*feas·ible*,	*bapt·ism*,	*evangel·ist*,
			atroc·ity,	*aggress·ive*,	*auth·or*,	*visc·ous*
	ii	REQUIRE FREE BASES:	*fore·warn*,	*un·happy*,	*un·do*,	*under·felt*,
			care·ful,	*boy·hood*,	*fair·ish*,	*red·ness*,
			friend·ly,	*wild·ly*,	*cream·y*	

Words with bound bases are characteristically loans rather than the result of English word-formation processes, and in many cases (e.g. in words like *compel*, *precede*, *resume*,

[33] The prefix *in·* attaches more readily to nouns than does *un·*, so that we have contrasts such as *unjust* vs *injustice*, *unequal* vs *inequality*. Note that the different IC structures of *unfairness* (*unfair* + *·ness*) and *injustice* (*in·* + *justice*) reflects the lack of any sharp semantic contrast between the nominalisation of a negative adjective and the negation of a de-adjectival noun.

etc.) it is questionable whether a word that is etymologically divisible into base + affix can properly be assigned a morphological analysis of that kind in Present-day English – see the discussion of this issue in §1.2.

Ordering of affixes

There are some affixes which appear only as first or last derivational affix. For example, the ·*ly* which forms denominal adjectives like *friendly* never occurs following another suffix, although it can itself be followed by another suffix, as in *friend·li·ness*. Thus from the noun *business* we can form *businesslike*, but not **businessly*. Conversely, ·*hood* can follow other suffixes, as in *magic·ian·hood*, but can never be followed by another derivational affix, so that forms like **child·hood·ic* are ungrammatical.

In addition there are constraints on the relative ordering of affixes, particularly suffixes. In general those with a Germanic source occupy more peripheral positions than those coming from Latin and Romance. For example, we have words like *nerv·ous·ness* and *hope·ful·ness*, where native ·*ness* follows Romance ·*ous* or native ·*ful*, but not **care·ful·ity* or **king·dom·ous* with Romance ·*ity* and ·*ous* following native ·*ful* and ·*dom*.

5.1.2 Morphophonological alternation

Affixes can affect the phonological form of the base to which they are attached: if we add the suffix ·*ion* to *persuade*, for example, the base takes the form /pəʳˈsweɪʒ/ instead of the default /pəʳˈsweɪd/. The different forms an element takes in different morphological environments (e.g. /pəʳˈsweɪd/ and /pəʳˈsweɪʒ/) we refer to as **morphophonological alternants**. Such alternants may differ in stress, in their vowels, or in their consonants: we accordingly speak of stress alternations, vowel alternations, and consonant alternations.

Affixes and stress

Affixes, particularly suffixes, may affect the position of the stress. We can distinguish the following four types of suffix, though it has to be borne in mind that suffixes do not always behave in a completely regular way, so that there are some exceptions to the patterns described below.

(a) Derivative follows stress rules for simple words

Consider first the simple bases *Aˈmerica* and *veˈrandah*. In *Aˈmerica* the stress falls on the third syllable from the end, the **antepenult**, whereas in *veˈrandah* it falls on the second syllable from the end, the **penult**. The difference in the location of the stress is due to a difference in the phonological structure of the words: although in both cases the last three syllables all have short vowels, the vowel of the penult is followed by a single consonant (/k/) in *America*, but by a two-consonant cluster (/nd/) in *verandah*. Now consider the following words in ·*al*:

[5]		STRESS REMAINS CONSTANT	STRESS SHIFTS
	i	a. *conˈjecture* ~ *conˈjectural*	b. *ˈmedicine* ~ *meˈdicinal*
	ii	a. *ˈfraction* ~ *ˈfractional*	b. *ˈparent* ~ *paˈrental*

The position of the stress is unaffected in the [a] examples: *conjecture*, for example, has a phonological structure like that of *verandah* and hence has the stress on the penult, while *conjectural* is comparable to *America*, with the stress therefore on the antepenult. In [b], however, the addition of the affix leads to a shift in the location of the stress. In [ib] it yields a word with a phonological structure like that of *America*, so the stress shifts to what is now the antepenult. And in [iib] the derivative has a structure parallel to that of *verandah*, and hence takes the stress on what is now the penult. Other suffixes that behave in this way include ·*ive* and ·*ous*:

[6] i a. *'secret* ~ *'secretive* b. *'product* ~ *pro'ductive*
ii a. *'murder* ~ *'murderous* b. *'portent* ~ *por'tentous*

(b) Stress falls on the syllable preceding the suffix

[7] i a. *a'naemia* ~ *a'naemic* b. *'photograph* ~ *photo'graphic*
ii a. *bron'chitis* ~ *bron'chitic* b. *as'tronomy* ~ *astro'nomic*

Adjectival derivatives in ·*ic* have the stress on the penult, the syllable just before the suffix. In most cases, this involves a shift in the placement of the stress, as seen in the [b] examples. Note that in [iib] the phonological structure of *astronomic* is in relevant respects like that of *astronomy*: the difference in the placement of the stress must therefore be attributed specifically to the effect of the ·*ic*.[34] The examples in [a] illustrate the case where there is no shift in the location of the stress – because ·*ic* replaces *ia* and *is*.

Such suffixes as ·*ify* and ·*ity* similarly take the stress on the preceding syllable, though they could also be placed in group (a) since their phonological form makes that position predictable:

[8] i a. *'beauty* ~ *'beautify* b. *'person* ~ *per'sonify*
ii a. *in'firm* ~ *in'firmity* b. *'tranquil* ~ *tran'quillity*

(c) Stress falls on the suffix itself

[9] i *Victori'·ana, salu't·ation, absen't·ee, electio'n·eer, Japa'n·ese*
ii *pictu'r·esque, kitche'n·ette*

In [i] the affixes ·*ana*, ·*ation*, ·*ee*, ·*eer*, and ·*ese* contain long vowels of the kind that characteristically attract stress if they fall within the final three syllables of a word. This can be illustrated for words with simple bases in such contrasts as we find in *gui'tar* vs *'gutter* or *I'raq* vs *'Arab* (stressed /ɑː/ vs unstressed /ə/), *do'main* vs *'curtain* or *ex'plain* vs *'extra* (stressed /eɪ/ vs unstressed /ə/), *ba'leen* vs *'barren* or *ca'reen* vs *'Karen* (stressed /iː/ vs unstressed /ə/). The suffixes ·*esque* and ·*ette* in [ii] have short vowels, and there is no phonological motivation for their special behaviour with respect to stress placement.

(d) Stress-neutral suffixes

Finally, there are suffixes which have no effect on the stress: the stress falls on the same syllable as in the base:

[10] a. *mi'raculous* ~ *mi'raculousness* b. *pe'dantic* ~ *pe'danticness*

Other stress-neutral suffixes besides ·*ness* include ·*dom*, ·*er*,[35] ·*hood*, ·*ise*,[36] ·*ish*, ·*ly*, and adjectivalising ·*y*. For the most part ·*ess* belongs here too, but there are some words such as *stewardess*, *hostess* where speakers vary as to whether they treat it as belonging to the present group (*'stewardess*) or to group (c) above, attracting the stress onto itself (*stewar'dess*).

[34] There are a number of exceptions, such as *'Arabic*, *'catholic*, *'lunatic*. Note also that we are concerned only with the ·*ic* that forms adjectives: compare *arith'metic* (adj) and *a'rithmetic* (noun).

[35] *Pho'tographer* is best handled in terms of ·*er* replacing the ·*y* of *pho'tography*, rather than the addition of ·*er* to *'photograph*.

[36] Exceptions where the stress shifts are seen in *ca'nal* ~ *'canalise*, *im'mune* ~ *'immunise*.

Vowel alternations

There is an immense amount of vowel alternation in English, some of which has been described in the last chapter – cf. especially the discussion of the contrast between strong and weak forms. For present purposes, there are two main cases to note.

Alternations resulting from the Great Vowel Shift

One group of alternations very common in established vocabulary were brought about by changes in the vowel system known as the Great Vowel Shift, which took place between the fifteenth and seventeenth centuries, approximately:

[11]			
i	/aɪ/ ~ /ɪ/	*crime* ~ *criminal*	*malign* ~ *malignant*
ii	/iː/ ~ /e/	*gene* ~ *genotype*	*obscene* ~ *obscenity*
iii	/eɪ/ ~ /æ/	*profane* ~ *profanity*	*voracious* ~ *voracity*
iv	/aʊ/ ~ /ʌ/	*abound* ~ *abundance*	*profound* ~ *profundity*

Oversimplifying somewhat, we can say that alternations that were once simply a matter of vowel length came to be a matter of vowel quality as a result of changes in the pronunciation of the long vowels (and to some extent the short vowels). The spelling reflects the earlier pronunciation and hence the morphological relationship between the paired words is more evident in writing than in speech.

Vowel reduction

One extremely common type of alternation is between a stressed full vowel and the unstressed reduced vowel /ə/. Alternation between full vowel and /ə/ (or sometimes /ɪ/) is therefore regularly associated with shifts in the location of the stress of the type discussed above. Compare, for example:

[12]	/ˈpeərənt/ ~ /pəˈrentəl/	/dʒəˈpæn/ ~ /dʒæpəˈniːz/	/ˈpedənt/ ~ /pɪˈdæntɪk/
	(*parent* ~ *parental*	*Japan* ~ *Japanese*	*pedant* ~ *pedantic*)

There are also cases, less widespread and systematic, where vowel reduction involves the complete loss of the vowel:

[13]	/ˈæktəʳ/ ~ /ˈæktrəs/	/ˈhʌŋgəʳ/ ~ /ˈhʌŋgri/	/məˈdɪsənəl/ ~ /ˈmedsən/
	(*actor* ~ *actress*	*hunger* ~ *hungry*	*medicinal* ~ *medicine*)

Consonant alternations

A number of affixes either trigger consonantal alternation in the base or themselves undergo such alternation. Among the most important of these alternations are the following:

[14] i NASAL ASSIMILATION/OMISSION: /n/ ~ /m/ ~ ∅
inaudible ~ *impossible* ~ *illegal*/*irrelevant*
conurbation ~ *commixture* ~ *collateral*/*correlation*

ii VELAR SOFTENING: /k/ ~ /s/; /g/ ~ /dʒ/
electric ~ *electricity*, *analogous* ~ *analogise*

iii ALVEOLAR PLOSIVE VERSUS FRICATIVE: /t/ ~ /ʃ/ or /s/; /d/ ~ /ʒ/ or /z/
transmit ~ *transmission*, *hesitate* ~ *hesitation*; *diplomat* ~ *diplomacy*
invade ~ *invasion*; *divide* ~ *divisible*

iv ABSENCE VERSUS PRESENCE OF PLOSIVE WITH NASAL: ∅ ~ /g/ or /b/
paradigm ~ *paradigmatic*, *sign* ~ *signify*; *iamb* ~ *iambic*

In [i] we have certain prefixes ending in a nasal; the default alternant has alveolar /n/, but this assimilates to /m/ before a bilabial, and drops before /l/ and /r/ (with the spelling having *ll* and *rr*): /ɪ'liːgəl/, /ɪ'reləvənt/). The negative prefix *in·* shown in [i] is clearly recognisable from its meaning, the prefix *con·* "with" very much less so. 'Velar softening', [ii], is the term standardly used for the replacement of the velar plosives /k/ and /g/ by fricative /s/ and affricate /dʒ/ respectively. This alternation applies to a base-final velar before /ɪ/ or /aɪ/; note that the spelling remains unchanged. The alternation in [iii] is between an alveolar plosive and a sibilant fricative; the sibilant generally matches the plosive in voicing, but there may also be devoicing, as (optionally) in *divide* ~ *divisive*. Two cases of [iv] may be distinguished. In the first it applies with bases spelled with final *g* + *m/n*: the spoken form has /g/ only when the base is followed by a vowel. In the second case the base is spelled with *mb*: the spoken form again has /b/ only when there is a following suffix such as *·ic*.

These modifications of the base or of the affix itself apply with some affixes, but not with others. Nasal assimilation/omission, for example, does not apply to *un·*: compare *unauthorised, unpardonable, unlikely/unreasonable* with the examples in [i]. Velar softening occurs before *·ic, ·ise, ·ism, ·ist, ·ity*, noun-forming *·y* (*analogy*), but not before *·ish*, diminutive *·ie/y*, or adjective-forming *·y* (cf. *snakish, roguish, cookie, doggy, creaky, plaguy*). Similarly, the alternation in [iii] applies with *·ion, ·ible*, noun-forming *·y*, but not with *·able* or *·ing* (cf. *understandable, transmitting*). And with [iv] we have /g/ in *signal, signatory* but not in *signer* or *signing*, and likewise /b/ in *bombard* but not in *bomber*.[37]

5.1.3 Class I and Class II affixes

The last two subsections have introduced a number of logically independent parameters with respect to which affixes can be classified, but there is in fact a very significant correlation between them. We can therefore distinguish two broad classes of affix, I and II, with the following properties:

[15]		Class I	Class II
i	Can occur with bound base	Yes	No
ii	Affect stress placement	Yes	No: stress-neutral
iii	Occupy central or peripheral position	Central	Peripheral
iv	Trigger/undergo morphophonological alternation	Yes	No

There is a tendency for Class I affixes to have their etymological source in Latin and the Romance languages and for Class II affixes to have theirs in the Germanic languages. The labels I and II are based on the ordering dimension: from the perspective of building up a complex word in stages from its minimal elements, the Class I affixes are attached first, and hence occupy more central positions than the Class II affixes. The ungrammaticality of the above **carefulity* and **kingdomous*, then, is attributable to the attachment of a Class I suffix to a base ending in a Class II affix.

It must be emphasised that the correlation between the properties is by no means complete. The division of affixes into Class I and Class II is therefore best thought of

[37] Exceptionally, the inflectional suffixes *·er* and *·est* trigger the appearance of /g/ in the irregular forms *longer/longest, stronger/strongest, younger/youngest* (see Ch. 18, §3.1); note that such forms as *dumber/dumbest* follow the regular pattern in having no /b/.

as providing an account of the correlation which holds in the default case. Where the various properties match in the way shown in [15] nothing further needs to be said, but cases which diverge from this pattern need to be noted. Stress-neutral ·*ise*, for example, occurs before ·*ation* in words like *privatisation*, although ·*ation* is not stress-neutral. Similarly, stress-neutral ·*er* precedes the non-stress-neutral ·*ial* in *managerial* – and so on. Some morphophonological alternation differs from the cases presented in [14] in not being associated with Class I affixes. For example, the voicing of the fricatives /v/, /s/, and /θ/ which applies in some irregular inflectional forms, is also found in a few cases of lexical word-formation, as in *thief* ~ *thievish*, *glass* ~ *glazier*, *smith* ~ *smithy*, with triggering by Class II affixes. There are also places where, for historical reasons, a Class II affix is attached to a bound base. For example, we have *gormless* "stupid" but no free base *gorm*: *gormless* was originally *gaumless*, derived by ordinary attachment of ·*less* to a dialectal word *gaum* "understanding".

A second general point to make is that the classification has greater relevance to suffixes than to prefixes. Prefixes that are still productive normally behave like Class II affixes. Prefixes combine less readily than suffixes, so the question of the order in which they occur is of less importance, and since they attach at the beginning of a word they do not affect the position of syllables in the base as final, penult, or antepenult, and hence they have much less effect on the location of the stress. Forms that one might wish to regard as Class I prefixes tend to be of questionable analysability in English, such as *de*, *ex*, *re*, as in such words as *deduce*, *expel*, *refute* – and matters are complicated by the fact that the same orthographic forms are also found as productive Class II prefixes in such words as *debug*, *ex-president*, *repaint*. One reasonably clear contrast is found within the negative prefixes, with *in*· belonging to Class I, *un*· to Class II. We have noted that the nasal assimilation/omission alternation [14i] applies to *in*·, but not *un*·. And *in*·, unlike *un*·, cannot precede a productive (Class II) use of such prefixes as *re*·, etc.: compare *irrefutable* (with *re* unanalysable or Class I) and **irrepaintable*.

5.1.4 Paradigmatic relations and affix-replacement

So far in this section we have focused on **syntagmatic** relations within derivatives – on the formation of bases by combining two elements, base and affix. But it is also important to consider **paradigmatic** relations – relations of contrast or choice between sets of affixes (or sets of derivatives differing only in their affixes).

Affix-replacement

One place where paradigmatic relations are of particular relevance has already been mentioned – the case where a set of affixes are in construction with a bound base, as in:

[16]				
	i	*bapt·ise*	*hypnot·ise*	*plagiar·ise*
	ii	*bapt·ism*	*hypnot·ism*	*plagiar·ism*
	iii	*bapt·ist*	*hypnot·ist*	*plagiar·ist*

Such forms do not arise independently through the syntagmatic attachment of an affix to a bound base: rather those in [ii] and [iii] are different kinds of nominalisation of the verb in [i]. Compare also *terror·ise*, *terror·ism*, *terror·ist*, where the internal base is free, but where the nouns are semantically related more closely to the verb in ·*ise* than to the nominal base *terror*. The implication is that affixation may involve the replacement of one affix by another rather than simply the independent addition of an affix to a base.

There are in fact a great many places where this kind of derivation seems appropriate. Further examples are given in [17], those in [i] being neo-classical compounds:

[17] i	a. *bigamy*	*biology*	*biography*	*philosophy*	*kleptomania*
	b. *bigamist*	*biologist*	*biographer*	*philosopher*	*kleptomaniac*
ii	a. *aggressive*	*analogous*	*archaic*	*compulsory*	*diary*
	b. *aggression*	*analogy*	*archaism*	*compulsion*	*diarist*
iii	a. *glory*	*hilarious*	*relevant*	*treacherous*	*vacant*
	b. *glorify*	*hilarity*	*relevance*	*treachery*	*vacancy*

In each of the pairs of nouns in [i] the one denoting a person, [b], is plausibly viewed as deriving by affix-replacement from its counterpart in [ia]: *bigamist*, for example, means "someone who commits bigamy", *biologist* means "scientist working in the field of biology", and so on.

The problem of boundaries

Very often the paradigmatic relations between words are clearer than the syntagmatic divisions within them. Take a pair such as *hesitate* and *hesitation. Hesitation* is obviously the abstract noun derived from the verb *hesitate*, but its division into base + affix(es) is less obvious. The ICs might be taken as *hesitate* + *ion*, but we might also say that the nominalising suffix is ·*ation*, since this is certainly a noun-forming suffix in words like *causation*, *flirtation*, etc.; on this second analysis ·*ation* would replace ·*ate*, and there are a number of places where ·*ate* is quite clearly replaced (cf. *tolerate* ~ *tolerant*, *abominate* ~ *abominable*). Again, the paradigmatic relation between *accurate* and *accuracy* is more salient than the syntagmatic division of the latter into base + affix. A plausible analysis would be *accurate* + *y*, with /t/ modified to /s/ in accordance with the alternation given in [14iii]; but there are a considerable number of nouns ending in *acy* and since this ending clearly has the status of a suffix in *supremacy* it might also be analysed as such in *accuracy*, *obstinacy*, *intimacy*, etc. Precisely because the morphological boundaries may be unclear or indeterminate we will at times refer to the last part of a word as an **ending**, a preliminary term which leaves open the question of whether or not it has the status of a suffix. Endings will be cited without the '·' notation that signals a morphological boundary.

Paradigmatic dependency relations between affixes

There are also cases where the existence of one type of derivative presupposes the existence of one or more others. Compare, for example:

[18] i	*atheism*	*egotism*	*naturalism*	*plagiarism*	*spiritualism*
ii	*atheist*	*egotist*	*naturalist*	*plagiarist*	*spiritualist*
iii	*atheistic*	*egotistic*	*naturalistic*	*plagiaristic*	*spiritualistic*

There is a tendency for adjectives in ·*istic* to occur in sets like those in [18], where there is not only a noun in ·*ist* but also one in ·*ism*. Exceptions can be found (e.g. *cannibalistic*, *stylistic*), but the tendency is strong enough to confirm that there is a significant paradigmatic relation between these affixes.

5.1.5 Spelling alternations

In our description of inflection we presented three rules which affect the final consonant of a base when various kinds of suffix are added: consonant doubling, *e*-deletion, and *y*-replacement (Ch. 18, §2.2). The same rules apply in lexical word-formation, though with somewhat more exceptions.

Consonant doubling

A base ending in a simple vowel symbol followed by a simple consonant symbol has the last letter doubled before a vowel provided the base is stressed on the final syllable. The derivatives in [19i] have doubling in accordance with this rule, while the other bases do not satisfy the conditions for application of the rule, those in [iia] having a complex vowel symbol, and those in [iib] having stress on a non-final syllable:

[19]	i		*bagg·age*	*bedd·ing*	*committ·al*	*deterr·ence*	*dogg·ie*	*fatt·y*
			gladd·en	*nunn·ery*	*pigg·ish*	*pott·er*	*propell·ant*	*two-legg·ed*
	ii	a.	*balloon·ist*	*broad·en*	*steam·er*	*wood·en*		
		b.	*human·ist*	*item·ise*	*London·er*	*utter·ance*		

As with inflection, the final stress condition is relaxed in BrE for *l*, so that BrE *tranquill·ity* and *travell·er* are distinct from AmE *tranquil·ity* and *travel·er*. We do not have doubling in such words as *a'tom·ic* and *E'ton·ian*, even though the stress falls just before the suffix: it is the position of the stress in the free bases *'atom* and *'Eton* that is decisive.

Exceptions to the consonant doubling rule are relatively few in number. *Johnn·y* and BrE *wooll·en* and *wooll·y* have doubling even though the preceding vowel symbol is complex. Bases with unstressed *·gram* have doubling in such derivatives as *diagrammatical* and *epigrammatic* (as also in BrE inflectional *diagrammed*) – contrast regular *problematic*. With some bases in stressed *·fer* we have variant spellings with and without doubling: *inferable/inferrable*, *transferable/transferrable*. *Preferable* has no variant with doubling, though it can be stressed on either the first or second syllable. The recent nonce-word *fattism* has an irregular variant without doubling, *fatism*. And the BrE extension of *l* doubling to unstressed syllables mentioned above does not apply in such words as *equal·ity* or *verbal·ise*.

E-deletion

Mute *e* is generally deleted before a vowel-initial suffix. The application of this rule with a range of different suffixes is illustrated in:

[20]	*abus·ive*	*believ·able*	*bibl·ical*	*captiv·ity*	*cliqu·ish*	*compos·ure*
	coupl·ing	*creat·ion*	*driv·er*	*fam·ous*	*forc·ible*	*Gladston·ian*
	hast·en	*lodg·ing*	*pop·ery*	*refus·al*	*restor·ation*	*Rom·an*
	satir·ise	*serv·ant*	*statut·ory*	*stor·age*	*tru·ism*	*typ·ist*

Mute *e* is a base-final *e* that is neither a vowel symbol itself (as it is in *be*) nor part of a composite vowel symbol like that in *canoe*. With such composite vowel symbols, *e* is generally deleted from *ue*, just as in inflection: *argu·able*, *constru·able*, *continu·ation*, *devalu·ation*, etc. *Blue* and *glue* retain the *e*, however, in *blue·y* and *glue·y*; this avoids the *uy* sequence which characteristically corresponds to /aɪ/ – compare *blu·ish*, where there is no comparable motivation for retaining the *e*. Other composite vowel symbols are rarely found before derivational suffixes, but we may note the different treatments of *oe* in *obo·ist* and *canoe·ist*.

Deletion of *e* before a consonant

A few words have mute *e* exceptionally deleted before a consonant-initial suffix. Such deletion is obligatory in *du·ly*, *tru·ly*, *whol·ly*, and *aw·ful*, optional in *abridg·ment*, *acknowledg·ment*, *judg·ment*, and *fledg·ling*. Note that with *awful*, and to a lesser extent *duly*, the semantic connection with the base is tenuous, while the base *fledge* is rarely used on its own.

Retention of *e* before a vowel

Derivatives where mute *e* is optionally or obligatorily retained before a vowel are more numerous. Examples of various types are given in:

[21] i *enforceable, peaceable; changeable, manageable, marriageable; courageous*
ii *hireable, likeable, moveable, nameable, rateable, saleable, sizeable, timeable*
iii *cagey, gamey, grapey, holey, horsey, matey, phoney, pricey*
iv *acreage, mileage; ageism*

In [i] *e* follows *c* or *g* and is obligatorily retained before *a* and *o*. The bases concerned are pronounced with final sibilants /s/ and /dʒ/, and the motivation for keeping the *e* is that dropping it would give the sequences *ca/co* and *ga/go*, where *c* and *g* characteristically correspond to the plosives /k/ and /g/. Most derivatives to which this rule applies have the ·*able* suffix, but there are other ·*able* derivatives where *e* is optionally retained in BrE, as in [ii]. Most of these words have monosyllabic bases with long vowels or diphthongs, as with all those cited in [ii]; a few departing from this pattern are also found, such as *liveable* and *mistakeable*. The other suffix where a fair number of bases retain *e* is ·*y*, as used in forming denominal adjectives, as in [iii]; again the bases are monosyllables with long vowels or diphthongs. All have variant spellings without *e*, except for *holey* ("with holes in"), which *e* distinguishes from the homophonous *holy* ("sacred"). In [iv] we give a miscellaneous set of other exceptions; for the last two the regular spellings *milage* and *agism* are also found, and are the usual forms in AmE.

Deletion of *e* in compounds

The three spelling alternations normally apply in derivatives but not in compounds. *E*-deletion, however, is seen in *wherever* and the rare *whosever* – compare *whereabouts*, *wherein*, *whereof*, *whereupon*, etc., with a vowel letter other than *e* in the second base.

Y-replacement

A base-final *y* that itself constitutes a simple vowel symbol is normally replaced by *i* before suffixes that do not begin with *i*:

[22]			
	apply ~ *appli·cant*	*carry* ~ *carri·age*	*comply* ~ *compli·ance*
	deny ~ *deni·al*	*duty* ~ *duti·able*	*embody* ~ *embodi·ment*
	glory ~ *glori·ous*	*kindly* ~ *kindli·ness*	*likely* ~ *likeli·hood*
	mercy ~ *merci·less*	*plenty* ~ *plenti·ful*	*pretty* ~ *pretti·ly*

The *y* is retained in derivatives like *betray·al*, *pay·able*, *joy·ful*, where it is part of a complex vowel symbol, and in *busybody·ism*, *fairy·ism*, *Tory·ism*, etc., where the suffix begins with *i*, so that retention of *y* avoids the rare sequence *ii*. In addition *y* is exceptionally retained in a handful of words where the normal conditions for replacement are satisfied:

[23] *baby·hood; busy·ness; fairy·dom, gipsy·dom, puppy·dom; lobby·ward*

Babyhood contrasts with regular *likelihood*, but there are no established examples where ·*dom* and ·*ward* trigger *y*-replacement. The *y* is retained in *busyness* to distinguish this nominalisation of *busy* from the highly lexicalised *business*.

In addition to derivatives like those in [22] where a spelling rule replaces the letter *y* by *i*, there are a considerable number where we have morphological replacement of base-final *y* by a suffix beginning with *i*, as in *pretty* ~ *prettify*, *military* ~ *militar·ist*, *scrutiny* ~ *scrutin·ise*, etc.

5.2 Evaluative morphology

5.2.1 Diminutives

The term **diminutive** applies to affixes which indicate small size and also, by extension, ones which (additionally or instead) mark the off-spring of animals, affection or informality, resemblance or imitation.

·*ette*

This suffix marks small size in such words as *kitchenette*, *statuette*, *novelette* (often derogatory), *cigarette* (with specialisation of meaning). It can also indicate imitation, as in *flannelette*, *leatherette*, or female sex, as in *usherette* and *suffragette*.

·*ie/y*

This is the most productive of the diminutive markers in Present-day English, especially in Scottish, Australian, and New Zealand varieties. It is found in numerous hypocoristics (pet names): *Billy*, *Betty*, *Jimmy*, *Susie*, etc. Secondly, it is commonly used in language spoken to or by children: *granny*, *daddy*, *doggie*, *piggy*, *sweetie*, etc. In both these cases the role of the suffix is to mark emotional attachment rather than small size.[38] In some words it serves to form a noun from an adjective (*brownie*, *goodie*, *softy*) or from a verb (*cookie*). This suffix is also found in many embellished clippings: *brolly*, *hanky*, *nightie*, *tummy*, *undies*; in such cases, as also in the recent coinages *druggie*, *greenie*, *groupie*, it contributes to marking the informal style, often adding derogatory connotations.

·*ish*

[24] i *baldish, bluish, coldish, largish, narrowish, sickish, stupidish, youngish*
ii *bookish, boyish, brutish, fiendish, foolish, modish, prudish, sheepish, waspish*

In [i] ·*ish* attaches to an adjective to form another adjective with the meaning "approximately/somewhat ~". The same meaning applies when it is added to numbers: *tennish*, "about ten" (especially for times and ages: "about ten o'clock, about ten years old"). In [ii] ·*ish* forms denominal adjectives with the meaning "resembling ~ in some way". Uses [i] and [ii] are both still productive. For the non-diminutive ·*ish* of *Danish*, etc., see §5.6.1.

·*let* and ·*ling*

These noun-forming suffixes are now only marginally productive, if at all. The first indicates small size in *booklet*, *flatlet*, *ringlet*, *tartlet*; it is used with a few animal names to denote offspring (*piglet*, *eaglet*) or a small variety (*auklet*). This suffix is occasionally

[38] Small size may be concomitantly involved in *piggy*. *Pinkie* (mainly AmE and ScotE) means "little finger, i.e. the smallest in the hand", but the base *pink* itself means "small" (not "finger").

found with other meanings (e.g. in *eyelet* it is probably best glossed as "resembling ~", though an eyelet is also small), but the ·*let* of *anklet, wristlet*, etc., is probably a different (and non-diminutive) suffix.

The suffix ·*ling* is used to indicate small or young animals: *codling, duckling, gosling* (with phonological modification of *goose*), *spiderling*; compare also *nurseling, suckling*, and, for plants, *sapling, seedling*. Applying to adult persons it indicates contempt: *princeling, squireling, hireling* (with a verb rather than noun as base), *weakling* (adjective as base).

micro· and *mini·*

These are both productive elements, used only to indicate small size:

[25] i *mini-budget, minibus, minicab, minigolf, minipill, mini-series, miniskirt*
ii *microchip, microcosm, micrometer, microorganism, microscope, microwave*

Mini· is a relatively new prefix, formed by clipping from *miniature*. *Micro·* is a combining form, as evident from its ability to form compounds with such final combining forms as *cosm, meter, scope, phone*. But it combines readily with ordinary free bases like *cassette, film, processor* and hence is one of the combining forms that are very much like prefixes. *Micro·* indicates a significantly greater degree of smallness than *mini·*, as evident from one of the few cases where they appear with the same base: *microcomputer* and *minicomputer*.

·*o*, ·*a*, ·*er*, ·*s*, and irregular diminutives

We take these together as they occur in what we have called embellished clippings (§2.3.2 – cf. also ·*ie* above). The first is particularly common in AusE: *arvo* (← *afternoon*), *compo* (← (*worker's*) *compensation*); but it is also found more generally: *aggro* (← *aggravation*), *ammo* (←*ammunition*). As we noted, the use of this suffix has as much to do with rhythm and decoration as with the expression of emotional attitude. The minor variant ·*a* is virtually restricted to proper names: *Gazza* (← *Gascoigne*). The ·*er* is seen in *rugger* and *soccer*, but more often occurs in combination with ·*s*: *preggers* (← *pregnant*), *Twickers* (←*Twickenham*).

The suffix ·*s* also occurs after diminutive ·*ie* in such playground words as *onesies, twosies, widesies*: it is doubtful whether it is here marking plural number. In addition it is found in various terms of address, such as *ducks* or *Pops*. Finally, there are some totally irregular diminutives characteristic largely of baby-talk such as *drinky-poo, teeny* (as a variant of *tiny*), and the rhyme-motivated *teeny-weeny*.

·*een*, ·*en*, ·(*e*)*rel*, ·*et*, ·(*i*)*kin*

These suffixes have been used with diminutive force during the history of English, but many of the resultant words are no longer morphologically analysable: *colleen, kitten, doggerel, scoundrel, bullet, bumpkin*. The ·*een* suffix is recognisable with the "imitation" meaning in a few words like *velveteen* and *sateen* (with modification of the base *satin*), while ·*en*, ·*erel*, ·*et*, ·(*i*)*kin* are separable in *maiden, cockerel, baronet, lambkin, manikin*.

5.2.2 Augmentatives

Augmentatives typically indicate large size or high – often excessive – degree. In all the types presented below, the augmentative marker occupies initial position, whether as prefix or first component of a compound.

arch· and *archi·*

The prefix *arch·* (/ɑːʳtʃ/) attaches primarily to nouns denoting humans. It can mean "chief, highest-ranking", as in *archbishop, archdeacon, archduke.* It is also used as an intensifier, "extreme", where it normally has very negative connotations: *arch-criminal, arch-hypocrite, arch-villain.* In this sense it is still productive, witness such recent formations as *archmonetarist. Arch(i)* (/ɑːʳkɪ/) is the corresponding combining form: *archidiaconal, archiepiscopacy,* and (with omission of the *i*) *archangel.*

macro·

This is a combining form with the meaning "large" or "on a large scale": *macrocephalic, macrocosm, macroscopic* ("large enough to be seen by the naked eye"), *macro-economics.* There are not many established words with this combining form, but it is currently productive, being found in such recent coinages as *macrochange, macrocontract, macroscale.*

maxi·

This prefix, contrasting with *mini·*, flourished in the 1970s as the fashion for the minidress waned. It is used primarily of clothes, as in *maxicoat, maxidress,* but also came to mean "large" as in *maxi-series, maxi-taxi, maxi-yacht.*

mega·

This combining form means "of a very large size or number", as in *megalith, megacephalic* (an alternant of *macrocephalic*), or in scientific usage "a million", as in *megabyte, megaton(ne), megahertz.* In recent years it has become very productive in colloquial style: cf. *megaschool, megabucks,* or, with the meaning of an intensifier ("extremely"), *megaswish.* For some speakers it has been converted into an adjective of approbation, able to be used predicatively: %*It's really mega!*

out·

One use of *out·* is to produce compound transitive verbs incorporating a comparative meaning of "exceed, surpass". It generally combines with nouns ([26i]) or verbs ([26ii]):

[26] i *outclass, outdistance, outgun, outnumber, outpace, outrank, outwit*
ii *outdo, outfight, outlast, outlive, outperform, outrun, outshine, outweigh*

In general, those formed from nouns mean "have higher/better/more ~ than", and those formed from verbs mean "~ better/more/longer than", but there is a good deal of lexicalisation and specialisation of meaning. For example, *outshine* means "surpass in excellence", *outweigh* "have greater importance/influence than", *outdistance X* "get far ahead of X", and so on. *Outsmart* is exceptional in having an adjective as the second base, and *outsize* in being itself an adjective.

super·

In its augmentative sense this prefix is currently very productive. It combines with adjectives [27i] or nouns [27ii], the usual meaning being approximately "very large/great (in size or power)" or "greater than ~":

[27] i *superfast, superhuman, supernatural, super-rich, supersensitive, supersonic*
ii *supercomputer, superglue, superhero, superhighway, superman, supermarket, superphosphate, superpower, superset, superstar, superstate, supertanker*

■ *hyper·*

Etymologically speaking, *hyper·* is the Greek cognate of Latin *super·*, but while *super·* is a prefix, *hyper·* is a combining form, as can be seen from such technical words as *hyperaemia, hyperon, hyperosmia, hypertrophy.* Compounds in *hyper·* commonly have the meaning "excessive(ly) ~", as in the adjectives *hyperactive, hypercritical, hypersensitive,* and the noun *hypertension.*[39] It can also mean "very large", and can then be in competition with *super·*, as in *hypermarket*, which denotes something bigger than a supermarket. In recent computing jargon *hypertext* is used to indicate complex organisation of data in a database.

■ *ultra·*

One sense of *ultra·*, matching its Latin origin, is "beyond"; this is found primarily in scientific terms such as *ultrasound, ultraviolet* (but cf. also *ultramarathon* "footrace beyond the distance of a marathon"). In general usage, however, it has come to mean "extreme, excessive"; in this sense it has quite a high degree of productivity, attaching mainly but not exclusively to adjectives: *ultraconfident, ultraconservative, ultrafashionable, ultramilitant, ultramodern, ultrarational, ultraroyalist, ultraviolent.*

5.3 Gender-marking morphology

Gender is morphologically marked in nouns denoting females, human or animal, much more than in nouns denoting males. For this reason gender-marking is widely perceived as one of the areas where the language displays a sexist bias, and campaigns for linguistic reform from around the 1970s have certainly brought about a change in attitudes and usage, so that – especially with nouns denoting human occupations – many speakers now to a large extent avoid the use of gender-marked human nouns in favour of ones that are gender-neutral.

■ *·ess*

For most of the history of English this suffix has been the preferred marker of feminine gender in human nouns. *Lioness* and *tigress* are common terms for female animals, but apart from these the suffix is rarely used for non-humans.

We can distinguish two classes of human *·ess* words according as the unmarked counterpart applies to males alone or to both males and females (though there are differences within this second class as to how readily or acceptably the unmarked form can be used of females):

[28] i *abbess, countess, duchess, empress, princess*
ii a. *actress, authoress, manageress, poetess, sculptress, stewardess, waitress*
b. *adulteress, heiress, hostess, jewess, murderess, negress, villainess*

The forms in [i] derive from *abbott, count, duke, emperor, prince,* which are restricted to males: an abbess is not an abbot, nor a countess a count, and so on. These *·ess* forms are generally considered unobjectionable. The unmarked counterparts of the derivatives in [ii] can be used of women as well as men: an authoress, for example, is an author, and a manageress is a manager. The forms in [iia] denote professions/occupations, an

[39] Note the semantic specialisation in the linguistic term *hypercorrect*, which involves excessive striving for correctness that leads in fact to incorrectness.

area where the case for avoiding discriminatory terms is particularly compelling: the marked term suggests some difference in status, and may imply lower standards or achievement. This is particularly clear in the case of *authoress, poetess, sculptress*, and the like; these indeed have long been recognised as disparaging terms and are rarely used. The same kind of objection can be levelled against such words as *manageress, stewardess*, or *ambassadress. Waitress* is a marginal member of class [ii] in that the unmarked *waiter* is predominantly used for males: for this reason the marked *waitress* is not easily avoidable and hence remains quite common. Gender-differentiation in the *actor* ~ *actress* pair is motivated by the fact that males and females normally play different roles; note also that while *actor* is readily applied to women when used predicatively (*She is an excellent actor*) or with a proper name appositive (*the actor Penelope Harcourt*), the singular form is not so often used referentially of a woman (*An actor who had just joined the company expressed her support for the beleaguered director*).

Among the forms in [28iib], *jewess* and *negress* risk being perceived as involving both sexual and racial bias, and hence now tend to be avoided in most contexts. One salient use of *heiress* is in the context of marriage, as in *He was hoping his brother would marry a good Irish heiress*: in such contexts the gender feature is obviously highly relevant, and substitution of the unmarked *heir* would scarcely be possible, though it would be quite normal in examples like *She was now (sole) heir to her father's vast fortune*. We should note, finally, that there are one or two derivatives like *governess* where semantic specialisation has applied to the ·*ess* form but not to the unmarked counterpart: *governor* is a dual gender noun, but a governess is not a governor.

As far as the morphology is concerned, a good number of the bases to which ·*ess* is attached have the ·*er* suffix. The /ə/ of this suffix is often dropped (*actress, ambassadress, conductress, tigress, waitress*), but in some cases it is retained (*manageress*). With bases ending in *er·er*, the ·*ess* replaces the final ·*er*: *adulteress, murderess, sorceress*.

·*ette*, ·*ine*, and *trix*

We deal with these together as minor members of the set of feminine markers. The ·*ette* suffix is relatively recent, the earliest attested use of it for gender-marking apparently being in *suffragette* at the beginning of the twentieth century (with ·*ette* replacing the gender-neutral suffix ·*ist*). Apart from this, the only place where it may still be used as an emotively neutral feminine suffix is *usherette* – and perhaps (*drum-*)*majorette* in AmE. Such words as *undergraduette* are now obsolete. However, ·*ette* has retained some degree of productivity in the formation of such pejorative nonce-words as *editorette, reporterette, jockette* (from *jockey*), where the disparaging tone is connected with the primary use of ·*ette* as a diminutive marker (§5.2.1) – compare *bimbette*, where in current usage the clearly derogatory base *bimbo* is itself virtually restricted to females.

The suffix ·*ine* is found in a number of feminine proper names such as *Bernadine, Clementine, Pauline*. In common nouns it is clearly analysable as a gender marker in *heroine*; this has provided the basis for such relatively recent coinages as *chorine* ("chorus-girl"), but they have generally been short-lived. The ending *trix* occurs only in a handful of loanwords, especially legal terms – *administratrix, aviatrix, executrix*; all have gender-neutral counterparts ending in *tor*: *administrator*, etc. Though we have cited the form as *trix*, it is probably best analysed as a suffix ·*ix* added to the ending *tor*, with dropping of the /ə/.

he·/she· compounds

These pronouns are used as gender-markers in such animal terms as *he-goat* and *she-ass*. This type of compounding is still productive, but the resultant forms rarely become established. The pronouns are also found in a few lexicalised human nouns: *he-man*, *she-devil* (where we may note that the former generally involves positive evaluation, the latter obviously negative).

·man/·woman compounds

Compounds in *·man* mostly fall into one of the three types illustrated in:

[29] i *Englishman, Frenchman, Scotsman; businessman, policeman*
ii *doorman, fireman, infantryman, milkman, workman*
iii *chairman, ombudsman, spokesman*

In [i] the *man* element clearly introduces two components of meaning "person" and "male": a female can't be an Englishman or a businessman, etc. These words all have established feminine counterparts in *·woman*: *Englishwoman, businesswoman*, etc. The compounds in [ii] are likewise restricted to males but differ from those in [i] in that they do not have established feminine counterparts. They are occupational terms and the absence of feminine counterparts reflects the fact that in the past the jobs concerned were normally performed exclusively by males. The linguistic form of these compounds makes them discriminatory terms, and recognition of this fact has led to a reduction in their use, especially in the field of labour relations and recruitment. In the *Dictionary of Occupational Titles* published by the US Department of Labor in 1977, for example, all such terms were dropped in favour of gender-neutral terms: *firefighter* instead of *fireman*, and also *police officer* instead of the paired forms *policeman* and *policewoman*.

The compounds in [29iii] are commonly defined in dictionaries in terms that make no reference to gender: "the presiding officer of a meeting, committee, board, etc.", "someone who works for a government or large organisation and deals with the complaints made against it", "a person who is asked to speak as the representative of other people". Such definitions reflect the usage where these terms, unlike those in [i–ii], are applied to women as well as to men: %*They've asked her to stay on as chairman*; %*The chairman used her casting vote to defeat the motion*; %*Madam Chairman*. The apparent loss of the "male" meaning here may have been facilitated by the phonological reduction of /mæn/ to /mən/, but it is nevertheless evident that these words are not genuinely gender-neutral terms.[40] Their connection with the independent word *man* is transparent in writing, reflected in the irregular plural form in *·men* and reinforced by the fact that the great majority of compounds in *·man* do have "male" as part of their meaning (as seen in [i–ii]). This incontestably gives them a strong bias towards males: they are likely to be interpreted, consciously or unconsciously, as conveying that in the absence of indications to the contrary, the holder of the office is male. These terms, particularly *chairman*, have been one of the main foci in the campaign against sexual discrimination in language, and many organisations and individuals now avoid them, while manuals of usage commonly recommend against *·man* forms other than in specific reference to males.

[40] It is sometimes suggested that as a result of the phonological reduction *·man* has effectively come to have the status of an affix rather than being a base in a compound – compare the relation between the suffix *·ful* and the word *full* (§5.8). However, the fact that in many words *·man* contrasts with *·woman* is compelling evidence against its classification as an affix. One word in which the vowel remains unreduced is *caveman*.

Chairman and *spokesman* have established counterparts in ·*woman*, but since there is often no reference to any particular person, the need is for a genuinely gender-neutral term. Compounds in ·*person* have been coined for this purpose, with *chair* an alternative preferred by many in the particular case of the first item. The pseudo-neutral sense of ·*man* compounds seems to be more widely maintained in words formed by suffixation from the compound bases – words such as *chairmanship, gamesmanship, marksmanship, sportsmanlike,*[41] *workmanlike.* And there is one ordinary compound, *freshman*, that continues to be usually interpreted as applicable to females as well as males (though BrE tends to prefer *fresher*): *They decided to get married at the end of their freshman year.*

Man also occurs as the first component of compounds. In a few cases like *manservant* it has the "male" meaning, but more often it has the pseudo-neutral sense, so that such words as *manhole, mankind, manpower, manslaughter* again raise the issue of sexual bias in language. *Mankind*, in particular, is now commonly avoided in favour of *humankind*, though the high degree of lexicalisation in *manslaughter* makes this more resistant to change. *Woman* as first element is less clearly integrated into word structure. It may be written as a separate word or with hyphenation: *woman doctor* or *woman-doctor.* The same applies to *lady*, though the connotations of this term make it more restricted in its collocational range. For example, *lady-doctor* is often used (though found objectionable by some), but we do not find *lady-priest.*

5.4 Location in space and time

We have seen (Ch. 8, §7.1) that prepositions can often be used to indicate position in both space and time: *at the gate* or *at noon, in the lake* or *in the afternoon, on the roof* or *on the next day*, and so on. Prefixes, too, commonly have both a spatial and a temporal use, though there are some (as is again the case with prepositions) that are restricted to one or the other sphere. This section reviews these spatial and temporal uses of prefixes and initial combining forms, together with various extended uses where the locations are interpreted metaphorically. As with so much of English word-formation, we find elements with different etymologies (English, Latin, Greek) being used in rather different ways.

In front and before: *ante·*, *fore·*, *pre·*

Ante·, Latin in origin and not very common, is used with spatial meaning mainly in architectural terms like *antechamber* or *anteroom*, while its temporal meaning is found mainly with adjectives such as *antediluvian, antenatal, antenuptial, antepenultimate.*

Fore· is of English origin and is never attached to Latin bases, and rarely to French ones; it is probably no longer productive. The spatial meaning is found with noun bases, as in *forecourt* or *foreground* – especially ones denoting parts of the body or of a ship: *forearm, forefinger, forehand* (with semantic lexicalisation), *forehead, forelock, foreskin*; *foredeck, foremast.* The temporal meaning is found with verbs, as in *forebode, foresay, foretell, forewarn*, and with nouns, mainly but not exclusively deverbal ones: *forefather, foresight, forethought.*

[41] *Sportsman* itself has two senses. With the sense "man who engages in sport" it belongs in group [29i], with *sportswoman* as its feminine counterpart. With the sense "one who exhibits qualities highly regarded in the world of sport" it belongs in group [iii], and here there is as yet no well established genuinely neutral term.

Pre· is of Latin origin and words like *precede* and *predict* are of questionable analysability. But *pre·* occurs with many free bases and is much more widely used than *ante·* or *fore·*. In some words the pronunciation /pri/ is replaced by /pre/ or /prɪ/, as in *premature* and *prescribe*, but these are not productive patterns. The most common use, clearly still productive, is temporal, where we have verbs (*pre-cook*, *prejudge*, *pre-ordain*, *pre-record*), adjectives (formed from adjectives, as in *pre-marital*, *pre-Raphaelite*, *pre-scientific*, or from nouns, as in *pre-AIDS*, *pre-war*), and nouns (*preconception*, *pre-condition*, *pre-school* "school for children below the age at which compulsory education starts"). The spatial "in front of" sense appears particularly in technical terms like *premolar* and *prescrutum*. *Pre·* can also mean "before" in the transferred sense of "ahead of, better than others": *pre-eminent*, *prepotent*.

Behind and after: *after·* and *post·*

The preposition *after* combines almost exclusively with nouns, forming compounds like *after-care*, *after-life*, *afterthought*. These examples are all hyponymic: aftercare is a type of care – care given after something else. *Afternoon* is non-hyponymic: *noon* is interpreted like the complement of the preposition, so that the whole denotes the period following noon. In all of these the meaning is temporal, as also in the intransitive preposition *afterwards* and the adjective *aftermost*. The spatial sense is found in a few anatomical and nautical terms: *afterbrain*, *afterdeck*.

The prefix *post·* is the opposite of *pre·*, and like the latter is most commonly used with a temporal sense. It forms verbs (*post-date*, *postsynchronise*), adjectives (again formed either from adjectives, as in *post-classical*, *post-nuptial*, or from nouns, as in *post-war*), and nouns (*post-communion*, *postgraduate*). The relatively rare and technical spatial use is seen in *post-ocular*. This prefix is clearly still productive, witness its occurrence in the names of various modern intellectual movements: *post-feminism*, *post-modernism*, etc.

Around: *circum·* and *peri·*

The prefix *circum·* is used only with words of Latin origin and has only a spatial sense, attaching mainly to adjectives (*circumpolar*) and verbs (*circumnavigate*). A high proportion of words with this prefix, however, have bound bases and are semantically somewhat opaque, so that they are not obviously analysable in English: *circumcise*, *circumscribe*, *circumspect*, *circumstance*, *circumvent*, etc.

Peri· is a combining form which likewise has only the spatial sense. It is used only in scientific and learned words, combining with classical bases. A few of these coincide with English words, as in *pericranium* or *perinatal*, but more often they are bound: *pericarp*, *perigee*, *perihelion*, *perimeter*.

Above and over: *over·*, *super·*/*supra·*, *sur·*

The prepositional base *over·* occurs with a range of spatial meanings comparable to those it has as a separate word: *overarch* ("form arch over/above"), *overcoat* ("coat worn over / on top of another"), *overturn* ("cause to fall over / to an inverted position"), and so on. Much the most common meaning in compounds, however, is "to excess". In this sense it attaches mainly to adjectives (*over-eager*, *over-zealous*) and verbs (*over-charge*, *over-eat*).

The prefixes *super·* and *supra·* are variants in Latin. *Super·* has spatial meaning ("above, on top of") mainly in scientific words: nouns (*superaltar*, *superstratum*, *superstructure*) or adjectives (*superglacial, superjacent, supermarine*). More often it expresses high degree/size/power (*super-rich, supercomputer*) or powers that go beyond those associated with the base (*superhuman*): this use has been covered in our discussion of augmentatives. The "excessively" meaning noted for *over·* is sometimes found, but it is much less prevalent. Compare, for example, *overheat* with the technical term *superheat* ("heat (a liquid) above its boiling-point without vaporisation"); in *super-sensitive* it can mean either "extremely" or "excessively", whereas *over-sensitive* has only the latter meaning. *Supra·* is much less common, and generally attaches to adjectival bases; the spatial sense is seen in technical terms such as *supraorbital, suprarenal*, while the "beyond, transcending" sense applies in *supranational.* The Greek equivalent, *hyper·*, discussed in §5.2.2 above with the augmentatives, is not used with a spatial sense; in some cases, as we saw, it has the "excessively" meaning: *hyper-sensitive*, for example, is equivalent to *over-sensitive.*

The prefix *sur·* is found in very few words, mostly borrowed directly from French. In some cases it has a spatial meaning, as in *surtitle* and one sense of *surmount*, but more often it indicates "going beyond, exceeding" in a non-spatial sense (*surpass, surreal*) or "additional" (*surcharge, surtax*).

Below, underneath: *hypo·, infra·. sub·, under·*

The combining form *hypo·* is the Greek opposite of *hyper·*, but is not used in English formations outside the scientific sphere, where it is mainly used in a spatial sense, as in *hypodermic* "introduced beneath the skin". The common terms *hypocrisy* and *hypochondria* are loans where the connection with the spatial sense is purely etymological.

Infra· is an uncommon prefix of Latin origin. It is used with a spatial sense contrasting with *supra·* in such words as *infraorbital, infrarenal.* It occasionally contrasts with *ultra·*, as in *infrasonic.* The two most common words are the lexicalised *infra-red* and *infrastructure.*

The spatial meaning of the much more widely used prefix *sub·* is seen in *subjacent, suborbital* (= *infraorbital*), *subterranean, subway.* There are a considerable range of extended senses, such as "less than" (*subhuman, subnormal*), "lower in rank/importance" (*subdean, sublieutenant, sub-editor*), "lower in a hierarchy of classes" (*subbranch, subclass, subdivision, subheading*).

Under· is a prepositional base contrasting with *over·* and forming compounds with a range of senses overlapping those of *sub·*. There is a tendency for *sub·* to prefer Latinate bases and *under·* other bases. The spatial sense of *under·* is seen with nominal and verbal bases in *underclothes, underground, undergrowth, underlie.* Matching the "lower rank" sense of *sub-treasurer* we find *under-clerk, under-secretary*, and the like. But, unlike *sub·*, *under·* is commonly found with the sense "inadequately/insufficiently", attaching to verbs, as in *undercharge, underestimate, underexpose, undervalue.*

Inside, internal: *endo·, in·, intra·, mid·*

Endo· is a combining form of Greek origin having the spatial sense "internal"; it occurs in technical terms such as *endogamy, endoplasm, endoskeleton.*

Prepositional *in·* is sometimes used as a compound element, nearly always with monosyllabic bases (*income, indoor(s), inflow, inroad, insight*) or with gerund-participle and past participle forms of monosyllabic verbal bases (*inbreeding, incoming, infighting, ingrowing, indebted*). This pattern is still productive (*in-car, in-country, in-patient*), but recent formations are often based on the use of *in* to mean "fashionable, chic", as in *Motorcycle jackets are in this year* – cf. *in-crowd.*

Intra·, a prefix of Latin origin, has only a spatial meaning, and is used exclusively in the formation of adjectives. It often contrasts with *supra·*, *infra·*, and *extra·*, mainly in technical terms: *intracranial, intramural, intravenous.* While this use is still productive (cf. *intracloud*), recent formations tend to contrast with forms in *inter·* – cf. *intragovernmental, intrastate.*

The prefix *mid·* has a more specific meaning: "in the middle of". It attaches mainly to nouns, but is also found with adjectives, as in *mid-Victorian.* The spatial sense is seen in *midbrain, midship, midstream,* the temporal one in *mid-career, mid-morning, mid-September,* and in the semantically specialised *midday, midnight, midsummer.*

Outside, external: *ex·/exo·, extra·, out·*

Exo· is a combining form of Greek origin contrasting with *endo·* and having the spatial sense "external". Like *endo·*, it is restricted to technical terms: *exogamy, exoplasm, exoskeleton.*

Ex· is the corresponding prefix of Latin origin. The spatial sense is found in only a few words, such as *exterritorial* (less common than *extraterritorial*), *exurb* (cf. *suburb*), and perhaps *ex-directory.* With the temporal meaning "former", however, *ex·* is very productive: *ex-husband, ex-president,* etc.; it is the source for the informal converted noun *ex,* "former spouse/partner".

The prefix *extra·* contrasts with *intra·* and forms comparable technical terms: *extracranial, extramural, extravehicular,* or, with a somewhat extended sense, *extramarital, extrasensory.*

Prepositional *out·* occurs with the meaning "outside" or "outward" in such compounds as *outcast, outdoor, outhouse, outlaw, out-patient, out-tray.* But its most frequent and productive use is with the sense "exceeding/excelling", as in *outclass, outlast, outnumber, outstare,* etc., as discussed in §5.2.2.

Between: *inter·*

The spatial sense of this prefix is found in such words as *intergalactic, interstellar,* and scientific terms like *interdigital, intermolecular.* Besides simple location, there may be movement from one to another of the places specified in the base, as in *inter-city (express), interplanetary (travel).* The temporal sense is illustrated by *interglacial, inter-war.* In addition, *inter·* often indicates reciprocal action or mutual involvement: *interact, intercommunicate, interdependency.* It contrasts with *intra·*, and the two are often coordinated, as in *inter- and intra-departmental (projects).*

Beyond, through: *meta·, trans·*

The "beyond" meaning is associated with a number of forms already discussed: *over·*, *super·*, *out·*, and also *ultra·* (covered under the augmentatives, but cf. also *ultra-violet*).

Meta· is a combining form (as is evident from such compounds as *metaphor* or *metazoa*) with a number of different meanings. In anatomical and zoological terms it commonly indicates "at the back, behind, beyond": *metathorax, metacarpal.* It may indicate change (of condition, etc.), as in *metamorphosis.* One clearly productive use is in the names of sciences such as *metabiology, metachemistry, metapsychology*: the subject matter here goes beyond, transcends, that covered in the basic science.[42] A compound of particular relevance to this book is *metalanguage*, "a second-order language, a language used to talk about (a) language".

The prefix *trans·* carries the spatial meaning "beyond" or "across" in *transatlantic, transalpine, translunary, transcontinental.* In a few cases the meaning is "through", as in *transpierce.* Like Greek *meta·*, it may indicate change: compare Latin-based *transformation* with the above *metamorphosis.*

On this side of: *cis·*

The rare prefix *cis·* is the opposite of *trans·*: compare *cisatlantic, cisalpine, cislunar.* Unlike *trans,* however, it has a temporal as well as spatial sense, as in *cis-Elizabethan,* though normally *post·* would be preferred (and there are no established examples where the point of reference is in the future, making it equivalent to *pre·* rather than *post·*).

5.5 Negatives and reversatives

In this section we survey a number of prefixes expressing various kinds of oppositeness and related concepts, as in *un·reasonable* (negation), *un·fasten* (reversal), *un·horse* (removal), and *anti·British* (opposition).

5.5.1 Negation

There are five prefixes that express negation, illustrated in [30] with adjectives:

[30]	i	*a·*	*amoral, apolitical, asexual, asymmetric, atonal, atypical*
	ii	*dis·*	*discourteous, dishonest, disingenuous, disloyal, dispassionate, dissimilar*
	iii	*in·*	*inanimate, indiscreet, inflexible, inhuman, insecure, intangible, intolerable*
	iv	*non·*	*non-committal, non-essential, non-existent, non-standard, non-violent*
	v	*un·*	*unclear, uncommon, unedifying, unhelpful, unintelligible, unjust, unwise*

Phonological and spelling alternation

In· is a Class I prefix subject to the morphophonological process of assimilation/omission mentioned in §5.1.2. It thus has alternant forms determined by the first consonant of the base to which it attaches:

[31]	BEFORE	ALTERNANT	EXAMPLES			
i	/p, b/	/ɪm/ *im*	*im·pure*	*im·balance*		
ii	/m, n, r, l/	/ɪ/ *im, in, ir, il*	*im·mobile*	*in·numerable*	*ir·regular*	*il·legal*

In [i] the nasal of the prefix is assimilated to the bilabial position of the following consonant; in [ii] it is lost in speech, while the spelling has doubling of the initial letter of the base.[43] We also find alternation with *a·*, which has the form *an·*, as in *an·alphabetic, an·iconic*; there are few words, however, where the initial *an* is still clearly analysable as an alternant of *a·*.

[42] The original model for these terms appears to have been *metaphysics*, although etymologically the *meta* of *metaphysics* simply meant "after" ("the works of Aristotle after the Physics"); note, moreover, that the relation of metaphysics to physics is certainly not the same as that of metabiology to biology, etc.

[43] These alternations apply in all styles for all speakers. In speech there may be further optional assimilation yielding variant pronunciations such as /ɪnkəm'pliːt/ and /ɪŋkəm'pliːt/ (*incomplete*), and so on. This kind of optional assimilation is also found with the Class II prefix *un·*: compare /ʌn'kɒmən/ and /ʌŋ'kɒmən/ (*uncommon*), /ʌn'pɒpjʊləʳ/ and /ʌm'pɒpjʊləʳ/ (*unpopular*), and so on.

Productivity and choice between the prefixes

Negative *in·* is no longer productive, while *a·* and *dis·* are now rarely used to create new words. *Non·* has a fairly high degree of productivity, but *un·* is much the most productive of them all. Note, however, that there are some common bases that resist prefixation by any of the negative prefixes – especially those like *good, bad, big, small, strong, weak, deep, shallow,* that have morphologically unrelated opposites.[44] Similarly, negatives of adjectives with the suffix *·ful* tend to have negative counterparts in *·less* rather than with a prefix (*useful* ~ *useless*, not **unuseful*), though there are certainly a fair number with *un·* (*unfaithful, unhelpful,* etc.).

With many bases only one of the prefixes is established and acceptable. *A·* is from Greek and is used largely with classical bases. In addition to the clearly analysable words in [30i], where the vowel is /eɪ/, it is found with the pronunciation /æ/ or /ə/ in a number of scientific terms (*abranchiate, anaesthesia, anorexia, aphasia*) and in such words as *anarchy, amorphous, anomalous,* though it is very questionable whether these can be regarded as analysable in Present-day English. Historically, *in·* tended to be attached to Latinate bases, while English bases (and even French ones) took *un·*. This gives distinctions like *inedible* vs *uneatable, inadmissible* vs *unpresentable,* and so on. But there is a great deal of untidiness in the established vocabulary, as reflected in such pairs as *unable* ~ *inability, uncivil* ~ *incivility, unequal* ~ *inequality, unjust* ~ *injustice* (with the adjective taking *un·*, the noun *in·*). In recent formations, one place where *non·* is consistently used to the exclusion of *un·* is in forming adjectives (normally attributive) from nouns or verbs: *non-skid, non-standard, non-stick, non-stop.*

Alternation and semantic contrast

There are a number of bases which accept both *in·* and *un·* without any difference in meaning, and with varying preferences for one or the other: *advisable, consolable, controllable, distinguishable, elastic, escapable, practical, supportable.* We also find alternation between *a·* and *un·* in *atypical/untypical,* and between *non·* and *in·* or *un·* in *non-eligible/ineligible, non-aligned/unaligned,* and so on.

In some cases, different prefixes attached to the same base yield different meanings. *Non-human,* for example, means simply "not human", whereas *inhuman* means "cruel, brutal". *Amoral* means "without moral principles, unconcerned with morals", while *immoral* means "morally wrong". *Unsatisfied* means "not satisfied, unfulfilled" and characteristically applies to abstract entities (*Their need for guidance remained unsatisfied*); *dissatisfied* generally applies to humans, with the meaning "discontented" (*He remained thoroughly dissatisfied with his job*). The relation between *uninterested* and *disinterested* is less straightforward. *Uninterested* means "not interested, indifferent", whereas *disinterested* (which is much more common) can mean either that or "impartial, not influenced by considerations of personal advantage", as in *We can rely on her to give a completely disinterested ruling.*[45]

While most of the distinctions given above are lexicalised, and in principle unpredictable, distinctions between *un·* and *non·* are semantically predictable. We have such

[44] The opposite situation is found with such words as *inept, non-commital, ungainly*: here there is no word consisting of the base without the prefix (cf. **ept*, etc.).

[45] The use of *disinterested* in the sense "not interested" (as in *He seems quite disinterested in maintaining contact with us*) is subject to a great deal of prescriptive criticism, but is nevertheless very common.

contrasts as *non-repeatable* ("cannot be repeated") vs *unrepeatable* (which can also mean "too foul to repeat"), *non-productive* ("not productive") vs *unproductive* (also "fruitless"), *non-professional* ("not professional") vs *unprofessional* (also "unbecoming for a member of the profession"). The forms with *non·* are emotively neutral and non-gradable, while those with *un·* have a wider range of meaning, so that they may convey criticism and gradability (allowing them to take such degree modifiers as *very*, *extremely*, etc.). Compare, similarly, neutral *non-American* vs *un-American*, as in *non-American behaviour* ("unlike characteristically American"), vs *un-American activities* ("hostile to America").

Nouns and verbs

In· and *un·* (in its negative, as opposed to reversal, sense) attach primarily to adjectives – and are then found also in many nouns derived from those adjectives (*illegality*, *unfairness*). Only relatively rarely do they attach directly to nouns. An example for *in·* (in the bilabial alternant) is *imbalance*; for *un·* we find *unease*, *unemployment*, *unperson*, *unrest*; cf. also, for *dis·* the recent term *disinformation*. Much the most productive negative prefix for nouns is *non·*. It is especially used with nouns denoting persons (*non-member*, *non-resident*, *non-student*, *non-subscriber*) and with nouns derived from verbs (*non-adherence*, *non-payment*, *non-performance*, *non-recognition*). There is specialisation of meaning in *non-event* ("something which turned out to be insignificant, uninteresting, in spite of expectation to the contrary") and *non-person* ("someone whose existence is denied, deleted from official registers").

Very few verbs take negative prefixes. The one prefix that is found is *dis·*, as in *disagree*, *disallow*, *discontinue*, *dislike*, *disobey*, *distrust*.

5.5.2 Reversal

Although the prefixes with simply negative meaning rarely attach to verbs, two of those listed above, *dis·* and *un·*, also have a reversative sense where they readily combine with verbs, while *de·* occurs with the reversative but not the negative sense:

[32] i *unbutton*, *unclamp*, *undress*, *unfasten*, *unfreeze*, *unfurl*, *unlock*, *unstick*, *untie*
ii *disaffiliate*, *disconnect*, *disengage*, *disentangle*, *disentwine*, *disestablish*, *disunite*
iii *decentralise*, *declassify*, *de-emphasise*, *de-militarise*, *desegregate*, *desensitise*

All these verbs occur in transitive constructions, some in intransitive ones too: *She unlocked the gate* or *The gate wouldn't unlock*. In general, the effect of adding the reversative prefix is to indicate that the affected entity returns to the state obtaining before the process expressed in the base verb took place: to unlock a gate, for example, is to return it to the state it was in before it was locked. But as so often there are numerous instances of semantic specialisation, where this simple account does not apply – cf. *disinfect*, *disqualify*, *disinherit*, etc. *De·* is used productively with verbal bases ending in *·ate*, *·ify*, and especially *·ise*, while *dis·* is generally selected before *·en*, but *un·* is again much the most productive.

5.5.3 Removal

Closely related to reversal is removal, where the same three prefixes are found. In the central cases they attach to noun bases:

[33] i *unfrock, unharness, unhook, unhorse, unhouse, unmask*
ii *deforest, defrock, defrost, degrease, delouse, dethrone*
iii *disambiguate, disarm, disillusion, dismast, disrobe*

There is a clear connection between this sense and the last: for example, unharnessing a horse can be thought of as removing the harness from it or as reversing the process of harnessing it. All the above have transitive uses, but the object can refer either to the entity from which something is removed (*unharness X, defrost X* = "remove ~ from X") or to what is removed (*unhorse X, dethrone X, dismast X* = "remove X from ~"). There are a considerable number of lexicalised words with specialised meanings related to the concept of removal: *unbalance, unnerve, devalue, disbar, disgrace, dishonour, dismember, displace*, etc.[46]

5.5.4 Opposition

There are three prefixes to be considered under this heading.

anti·

This is a very productive prefix used predominantly in the formation of adjectives ([34i]) and nouns ([34ii]):

[34] i *anti-British, anticatholic, anti-semitic; anti-abortion, anti-missile, anti-tank*
ii *anti-depressant, anti-freeze, anti-hero, anti-oxidant, anti-perspirant*

A common pattern among the adjectives has *anti·* prefixed to a noun to yield an adjective that is used wholly or predominantly in attributive function (*an anti-abortion rally*). The main meaning is "against", in the sense of "opposed/hostile to those who are ~" (*anti-British*), or "acting against, acting to prevent (damage by)" (*anti-missile, anti-coagulant*). In the first sense *anti·* contrasts with *pro·* (*pro-British, pro-abortion*). *Anti-freeze* in [ii] is exceptional in that *anti·* attaches directly to a verb base. A further sense is "the opposite of", as in *anti-hero* ("central character in a play, etc., who lacks traditional heroic properties"); in BrE this sense is also found in the adverb *anticlockwise*, corresponding to AmE *counterclockwise*. There are numerous cases of semantic specialisation: *anti-body, anti-climax, anti-nuclear, anti-social*, and the recent *anti-choice* ("opposed to allowing the choice of abortion").

counter·

This prefix, borrowed from French, has its most productive use in nouns like *counter-attack, counter-claim, counter-culture, counter-demonstration, counter-offer, counter-espionage, counter-propaganda*, where the meaning is "~ made in reaction/opposition to (an)other ~". The main stress is usually on the prefix, but the last two examples have it on the base. Some of the above are verbs as well as nouns, but otherwise *counter·* is found in relatively few verbs; one is *countersign*, where there is no meaning of opposition. With adjectives we have *counterfactual, counter-intuitive, counter-productive.*

contra·

This comes from the Latin word meaning "against". It is found in only a small number of words (some with bound bases, such as *contradict, contraception*, if indeed these are

[46] *Dis·* also has an intensifying meaning, "completely, utterly", in combination with a few bases which themselves involve reversal, removal, etc.: *disembowel, disannul.*

morphologically analysable in English), but has nevertheless been used instead of the more frequent *counter* in a few recent formations: *contraflow* ("a temporary traffic flow system where traffic is diverted into lanes that normally carry traffic in the opposite direction"), *contra-indication, contra-suggestible.*

5.6 Words based on proper names

5.6.1 Adjective and noun derivatives

(a) ·*an*, ·*ian*

These suffixes are found with a great many names of persons and places. Examples where they are clearly separable from the base are:

[35] i *Chicagoan, Elizabethan, Lutheran, Tibetan, Uruguayan*
ii *Christian, Churchillian, Freudian, Iranian, Jordanian, Wagnerian*

The ·*ian* variant is still very productive, and is much more widely used than ·*an*, certainly with personal names: *Elizabethan* and *Lutheran* are lexicalised exceptions. Very often, especially with geographical names, the base ends in *a*, *ia*, or *e*:

[36] i *African, American, Jamaican, Kenyan, Nicaraguan, Oklahoman*
ii *Australian, Columbian, Hawaiian, Indian, Russian, Victorian*
iii *Chilean, European, Gricean, Korean, Zairean, Zimbabwean*

In [i] we have the not uncommon problem of an indeterminate boundary between base and suffix: *Kenyan* derives from *Kenya* + ·*an*, with reduction of *a* + *a* to a single *a*, which cannot be assigned uniquely to base or affix. Similarly in [ii], where we also have a neutralisation of the distinction between ·*an* and ·*ian*, since *Australian* could be derived by reduction of *ia* + *ian* or *ia* + *an*. Likewise in *Haitian* (← *Haiti*), *Italian* (← *Italy*), etc.

A small number of bases in *a* have ·*ian* in the derivative: *Canada* ~ *Canadian, North Carolina* ~ *North Carolinian*. In [36 iii] the *e* may or may not represent a vowel sound in the base when it stands alone (it does in *Chile*, but not in *Europe*), but in speech they all have the same ending as those in [ii]. An *e* is also found in various derivatives from Classical names, such as *Epicurean, Herculean, Promethean*. These include *Caesarean* (← *Caesar*, with no *e* in the base), though there is also a more regular spelling with ·*ian*. There is occasionally variation between ·*an* and ·*ian*, as in *Alabaman, Alabamian*. Bases in *o* generally drop the *o* before ·*an*: *Mexican, Moroccan, San Franciscan* (but note the exceptional *Chicagoan*).

The ·*ian* suffix occurs in a good number of names in *on* (*Baconian, Bostonian, Etonian*), and this has given rise to an ending *onian* that occurs in *Aberdonian, Buffalonian, Torontonian* (← *Aberdeen, Buffalo, Toronto*). Compare also the linking *n* in *Panamanian* (← *Panama*). Other forms involving irregular changes to the base include:

[37] *Belgian* (← *Belgium*) *Norwegian* (← *Norway*) *Glaswegian* (← *Glasgow*)
Laotian (← *Laos*) *Mauritian* (← *Mauritius*) *Peruvian* (← *Peru*)

Derivatives formed with these suffixes have a range of meanings, and may be adjectives or nouns. The basic meaning is "associated with ~". With place names, it may be a matter of where someone or something comes from: *a Scandinavian playwright, a Roman urn*; or it may be applied to properties or features of the place or events that take place there: *the Parisian climate, the Russian Revolution*. With personal nouns, the adjective may have such interpretations as "by ~" (*a Shakespearean tragedy*), "typical of or like things produced by ~" (*a Johnsonian remark*), "from the time of ~" (*an Elizabethan manuscript*). Nouns denote inhabitants or languages (see §5.6.2 below). They may also be used for supporters, devotees, or followers of the person (*a Kantian/Wagnerian*) – cf. ·*ist* and ·*ite* below.

Although they attach predominantly to proper nouns, ·*an* and ·*ian* are also to be found on some common nouns: *publican, republican, equestrian, pedestrian.* The two main semantic categories involved are specialists or practioners in various fields, especially in combination with ·*ic* (*beautician, phonetician, theoretician, veterinarian*) and in zoological classification (*crustacean, mammalian, reptilian*).

(b) ·*er*

One of the numerous uses of this suffix is to form nouns denoting inhabitants of the place named in the base:

[38] *Dubliner, Icelander, Londoner, New Yorker, New Zealander, Queenslander*

This suffix attaches fairly readily to place-names ending in ·*land* or *Island* (*Prince Edward Islander*), and it occurs with a fair number of American names, but otherwise ·*er* is quite rare in this use.

(c) ·*ese*

The main use of this suffix is to derive adjectives from place-names:

[39] i *Genoese, Maltese, Milanese, Portuguese, Tyrolese, Viennese*
ii *Burmese, Chinese, Japanese, Javanese, Nepalese, Vietnamese*

Those in [i] involve European, especially Italian, places, while those in [ii], to which a good few others could be added, relate to places in the Far East. A final *a* in the base drops when ·*ese* is added, while *Portuguese* (a loan) drops *al.* The ·*ese* derivatives are also nouns, denoting inhabitants and, where relevant, languages. This latter use is extended to apply, with negative connotations, to idiosyncratic styles of speaking/writing. The base here can be a place-name (*Brooklynese*), a personal name (*Carlylese*) or, more often and still productively, a common noun: *bureaucratese, computerese, journalese, officialese.*

(d) ·*esque*

The main productive use of this suffix is to derive adjectives meaning "in the style of ~" from personal names: *Disneyesque, Pinteresque.* The older pattern with common nouns which gave *picturesque* (actually adapted from French *pittoresque*), *statuesque*, etc., is found in the occasional recent formation (*robotesque*), but has never been widely used.

(e) ·*i*

This suffix is found in borrowed words attached to names of regions in or near the Middle East. It forms adjectives or nouns, the latter denoting inhabitants or (where relevant) languages:

[40] *Bangladeshi, Iraqi, Israeli, Kashmiri, Kuwaiti, Pakistani, Yemeni*

(f) ·*iana*

This suffix is usually attached to a personal name, following the form of the adjective in ·*ian*, and derives a noun meaning "the collected sayings, wisdom, or artefacts connected with ~": *Shakespeariana, Burnsiana*, etc. The most common ·*iana* derivative is *Victoriana*, which now means "objects, especially ornaments and bric-à-brac, made in the Victorian period"; it may have a somewhat dismissive flavour, and this carries over to such modern coinages with common noun bases as *railroadiana*.

(g) ·*ic*

This suffix is found extensively with common nouns but with only a relatively small number of proper nouns, chiefly names of countries and peoples: *Arabic, Celtic, Gallic, Greenlandic, Icelandic, Teutonic.* Nouns in ·*ic* are used for languages, usually obscure ones or scientific names for language families – compare, for example, *Turkish* with *Turkic*, "a branch of the Altaic family, including Turkish, Azerbajani, . . .". The ·*ic* suffix is found with only a few personal names: *Byronic, Miltonic* (a variant of *Miltonian*), *Socratic.*

(h) ·*ish*

One major use of this suffix is to form adjectives relating to countries or ethnic groups:

[41] i *Danish, Finnish, Jewish, Polish, Scottish, Swedish, Turkish*
ii *British, English, Irish, Spanish*

In [i] the suffix is added to a noun denoting a person from the country or group; in [ii] it attaches to a bound base relatable to the country name. *French* and *Welsh* belong here etymologically, and they are also like *English* and *Irish* in forming compounds in ·*man. Flemish* ("pertaining to Flanders") directly copies the Flemish word. Where applicable, the ·*ish* words, as nouns, are used for the languages spoken in the countries concerned.

(i) ·*ite*

This suffix attaches primarily to names of places and persons:

[42] i *Brooklynite, Canaanite, Israelite, Muscovite, New Jerseyite, Wisconsinite*
ii *Darwinite, Jacobite, McCarthyite, Paisleyite, Thatcherite*

Derivatives from place-names are mainly nouns denoting inhabitants. Numerous such forms are found among biblical names (and note that *Israelite* applies only to biblical Israel, the corresponding form for modern Israel being *Israeli*); there are also several with the names of American states as base. *Muscovite*, "inhabitant of Moscow", is based on *Muscovy*, a now archaic name borrowed from French. Derivatives from personal names, as in [ii], primarily denote followers or supporters of the person concerned. Especially in the case of political personages, the ·*ite* word is often coined by opponents, and hence tends to have a derogatory tone which is not found with comparable suffixes such as ·*ist* and ·*er*; this certainly does not apply in all cases, however (cf. *Jacobite*). *Pre-Raphaelite* departs semantically from the usual pattern, applying to a group of artists/writers aiming to produce work in the spirit of that done before the time of Raphael.

A few words in ·*ite* have bases other than proper names: *socialite, suburbanite.*

(j) Compounding with ·*man*/·*woman*

This type of compound, discussed in §5.3 above, forms a handful of inhabitant terms with adjectives as the first base:[47]

[43] *Dutchman, Englishman, Frenchman, Irishman, Scotsman, Welshman*

[47] *Chinaman*, with a noun as first base, is no longer used other than as a non-standard offensive term.

5.6.2 Derivatives from the names of countries, continents, etc.

In this section we examine the formation of adjectives and of nouns denoting inhabitants from the names of countries and similar entities. Almost all the word-formation processes involved have been covered in the last section: our purpose here is to present the general patterns to be found in the sets of four terms – place-name, related adjective, individual inhabitant noun, generic. By 'generic', we mean the form used in definite plural generic NPs, as in *The Chinese/French/Greeks do it this way.*

With a small number of exceptions, the four-term sets fall into two major classes, each with two subclasses:

[44]

	COUNTRY	ADJECTIVE	INHABITANT(S)	GENERIC
1A	*China*	*Chinese*	*Chinese*	*the Chinese*
1B	*Australia*	*Australian*	*Australian(s)*	*the Australians*
2A	*England*	*English*	*Englishman/men*	*the English*
2B	*Sweden*	*Swedish*	*Swede(s)*	*the Swedes*

In Class 1, which represents the default case, the inhabitant noun is homonymous with the adjective – and can be regarded as formed from it by conversion. In Class 2, by contrast, the inhabitant noun is distinct from the adjective. The difference between 1A and 1B is simply inflectional: in 1A the inhabitant noun has the same form in the plural as in the singular, whereas in 1B it has different singular and plural forms. The subclasses of Class 2 are distinguished by the form used for the generic: with 2A it is the adjective, whereas with 2B it is the inhabitant noun, though the adjective can generally also be used as a less favoured variant: *The Swedes/Swedish do it this way.*

Class 1A

This class contains those sets where the adjective is formed with ·*ese*, and also the set for *Switzerland*, where the adjective is the irregularly formed *Swiss*. Some speakers feel uncomfortable with the singular use of the inhabitant noun, especially in the case of *Swiss*, and avoid sentences like *They've appointed a Swiss as the new manager.*

Class 1B

This is the largest set. It contains those where the adjective is formed with ·*an*/·*ean*/·*ian* or with ·*i*. Also belonging here are a few sets where the adjective has no suffix: *Germany* ~ *German*; *Greece* ~ *Greek*; *Thailand* ~ *Thai.*

Class 2A

This is a small class mainly comprising those where the inhabitant noun is a compound in ·*man*/·*woman*: compounds of this kind are never used in the definite generic construction. Also belonging here is *Britain* ~ *British* ~ *Briton* ~ *the British.* The fact that for modern Britain the adjective form is used for the generic is related to the fact that generic *the Britons* refers to the inhabitants of South Britain before the Roman conquest; *Briton* (which is homophonous with *Britain*) can also be used in a similar way and is not widely applied to inhabitants of modern Britain.[48] The adjective members of Class 2A sets have the ·*ish* form, except for the irregular *Dutch*, *French*, and *Welsh.*

[48] The clipping *Brit* is a colloquial term for the modern inhabitants, which – like other colloquial nationality terms – is often pejorative.

Class 2B

This class contains all others where the adjective has the ·*ish* suffix. With one exception, the inhabitant noun in these cases is the base to which ·*ish* is attached: *Denmark* ~ *Danish* ~ *Dane* ~ *the Danes*. The exception is *Spain*, with *Spaniard* as the inhabitant noun. Also included in this class are those where the adjective is formed with ·*ic*.

Sample lists of Class 1 and Class 2 sets

For Class 1 sets we give just the place-name and the adjective, underlining the latter for Class 1A items. We omit place-names ending in *ia* (of which there are many), as they are entirely predictable, having adjectives in *ian*.

[45] CLASS 1

Afghanistan ~ *Afghan/Afghani*
Africa ~ *African*
America ~ *American*
Argentina ~ *Argentinian*[49]
Bangladesh ~ *Bangladeshi*
Belgium ~ *Belgian*
Brazil ~ *Brazilian*
Canada ~ *Canadian*
China ~ *Chinese*
Costa Rica ~ *Costa Rican*
Cuba ~ *Cuban*
Ecuador ~ *Ecuadoran*
Egypt ~ *Egyptian*
Europe ~ *European*
Germany ~ *German*
Ghana ~ *Ghanaian*
Greece ~ *Greek*[50]
Guatemala ~ *Guatemalan*
Guyana ~ *Guyanese*
Haiti ~ *Haitian*
Hungary ~ *Hungarian*
Iran ~ *Iranian*
Iraq ~ *Iraqi*
Israel ~ *Israeli*
Italy ~ *Italian*
Jamaica ~ *Jamaican*
Japan ~ *Japanese*
Jordan ~ *Jordanian*
Kashmir ~ *Kashmiri*
Kenya ~ *Kenyan*
Korea ~ *Korean*
Kuwait ~ *Kuwaiti*
Lebanon ~ *Lebanese*
Libya ~ *Libyan*
Mexico ~ *Mexican*
Nepal ~ *Nepalese*
Nicaragua ~ *Nicaraguan*
Norway ~ *Norwegian*
Oman ~ *Omani*
Pakistan ~ *Pakistani*
Paraguay ~ *Paraguayan*
Portugal ~ *Portuguese*
Senegal ~ *Senegalese*
Siam ~ *Siamese*
Sri Lanka ~ *Sri Lankan*
Surinam ~ *Surinamese*
Switzerland ~ *Swiss*
Taiwan ~ *Taiwanese*
Tibet ~ *Tibetan*
Uganda ~ *Ugandan*
Uruguay ~ *Uruguayan*
Venezuela ~ *Venezuelan*
Vietnam ~ *Vietnamese*
Yemen ~ *Yemeni*
Zaire ~ *Zairian*
Zanzibar ~ *Zanzibari*
Zimbabwe ~ *Zimbabwean*

For *Saudi Arabia* we have the regular *Saudi Arabian*, but *Arabian* is commonly omitted, *Saudi* on its own being then the adjective and inhabitant noun (with plural form *Saudis*). *Arabia* refers to the peninsula between the Red Sea and the Persian Gulf, with *Arabian* as the adjective, applying for example to flora and fauna of this area. It is also the inhabitant noun, but this is very uncommon in comparison with *Arab*, which has a much wider application, covering Semitic people from the Middle East generally. *Arab* is commonly used attributively (*Arab policies/philosophy*) but hardly as a predicative adjective (*They are Arabs*, but not **They are Arab* – compare *They are Greeks/Greek*). *Arabic* as a noun denotes the language and as an adjective relates primarily to the language, script, and literature (e.g. *Arabic lettering/numerals*), but is sometimes used also of people (*She learnt the dance from Arabic friends in Paris*).

[49] Also spelled *Argentinean*. The country is also known as *the Argentine Republic* or, less formally, *the Argentine*: corresponding to this term we have *Argentine* as adjective and inhabitant noun.

[50] There is also an adjective *Grecian* whose application is largely restricted to Ancient Greece (especially art and architecture, etc.).

For Class 2 we give place-name, adjective, and inhabitant noun, with the adjective underlined for Class 2A, and the inhabitant noun for Class 2B.

[46] CLASS 2

Britain ~ *British* ~ *Briton*	*Iceland* ~ *Icelandic* ~ *Icelander*
Denmark ~ *Danish* ~ *Dane*	*Ireland* ~ *Irish* ~ *Irishman*
England ~ *English* ~ *Englishman*	*Poland* ~ *Polish* ~ *Pole*
Finland ~ *Finnish* ~ *Finn*	*Spain* ~ *Spanish* ~ *Spaniard*
France ~ *French* ~ *Frenchman*	*Sweden* ~ *Swedish* ~ *Swede*
Greenland ~ *Greenlandic* ~ *Greenlander*	*Turkey* ~ *Turkish* ~ *Turk*
Holland ~ *Dutch* ~ *Dutchman*	*Wales* ~ *Welsh* ~ *Welshman*

An alternative to the place-name *Holland* is *the Netherlands. New Zealand* has *New Zealander* for the inhabitant, but no derivative adjective: the nominal itself is used attributively (*the New Zealand economy*), but its inability to function predicatively shows that it has not been converted to an adjective: **Her parents are New Zealand* (we need *New Zealanders*, or *from New Zealand*). For *the United States* there is no established derivative adjective or inhabitant noun. With *Scotland* there is threefold variation in each of the other terms: *Scotland* ~ *Scots/Scottish/Scotch* ~ *Scot/Scotsman/Scotchman* ~ *the Scots/Scottish/Scotch. Scotch* (etymologically a contraction of *Scottish*) is not now normally used by the Scots themselves except in a number of collocations (*Scotch broth/eggs/mist/terrier/tweed/whisky*, etc.), but it is still used outside Scotland, especially outside the UK. For the adjective, *Scottish* is much more widely used than *Scots*, though the latter appears in the names of regiments such as *the Scots Guards*; as a noun *Scots* is the name of the language of the lowlands of Scotland (derived from English but not comprehensible to ordinary English speakers). For the generic, *the Scots* is much preferred over the other terms.

Combining forms

For a number of areas there are established initial combining forms which are used in neo-classical compound adjectives (*Anglo-American*) or nouns (*Anglophobia*). A sample of these, paired with the ordinary adjective, are given in:

[47]

Americo[51] ~ *American*	*Anglo* ~ *English*	*Austro* ~ *Austrian*
Franco ~ *French*	*Germano* ~ *German*	*Graeco* ~ *Greek*
Italo ~ *Italian*	*Russo* ~ *Russian*	*Sino* ~ *Chinese*

5.7 Nominalisations

As a word-formation process, nominalisation prototypically involves the formation of a noun from bases of other classes, by affixation, conversion, or phonological modification. We also include comparable cases where one type of noun is formed from another, such as abstract *friendship* from *friend* or personal *mountaineer* from *mountain*. Certain cases of compounding may also be regarded as a matter of nominalisation – most clearly, the formation of compound nouns from verb + preposition, as in *take-off, phone-in*, etc. The main focus in this section will be on affixation, but reference will be made to

[51] *Amerindian* is not a neo-classical compound but a blend of *American* and *Indian*.

other kinds of nominalisation as appropriate. We divide the material into two sections, the first dealing with processes which serve primarily to form nouns denoting persons or instruments, the second with those whose output consists primarily of nouns denoting actions, states, and processes. We omit from this section a number of elements covered elsewhere – e.g. suffixes deriving nouns for persons from certain geographic areas (covered in §5.6.2), the ·*ie*/·*y* suffix which is primarily diminutive (§5.2.1), the ·*man* of compounds like *policeman*, which generally marks gender as well as serving as a nominaliser (§5.3).

5.7.1 Person/instrument nominalisations

We take person and instrument nominalisations together as there are some processes that are used for both. Suffixation by ·*er* is a clear example: compare *bottle-washer* (person) and *dish-washer* (instrument). There are a fair number of suffixes used only for persons, but none used only for instruments.

(a) ·*ant* and ·*ent*

These suffixes, of which ·*ant* is much the more frequent, attach to verbs:

[48]	i	a. *assistant, complainant, informant*	b. *disinfectant, relaxant*
	ii	a. *correspondent, president, resident*	b. *absorbent*

Neither suffix appears to be productive. The basic meaning is "person who ~s" (in the [a] examples) or "instrument for ~ing" (in [b]). *Débutant*, apparently with a noun base, is a loan from French. The suffix ·*ate* is dropped from the verb base in *accelerant*, *irritant*, etc.

(b) ·*ard*

This is no longer productive and is still recognisable in only a handful of words, such as *drunkard, dullard, sluggard.* Forms in ·*ard* generally have a deprecatory meaning.

(c) ·*arian*

This suffix, never very widely used but still productive, attaches to abstract nouns to form nouns denoting persons: *disciplinarian, sectarian.* It frequently replaces a final ·*y* or other ending: *Trinitarian, humanitarian, vegetarian.* The resultant nouns usually denote holders of a particular doctrine, but in some cases this meaning has been lost through lexicalisation, as in *parliamentarian.*

(d) ·*ee*

This comes from a French past participle ending, and hence is generally attached to verb bases. Usually it relates to the passive use of a past participle, giving the meaning "one who is ~ed": *appointee, employee, divorcee, payee, nominee* (again with deletion of ·*ate*), *laughee* (corresponding to a prepositional passive: "laughed at"). There are also words relating to the perfect (active) use of a past participle: *escapee, retiree.* In rare cases like *patentee* and *absentee* the bases are respectively noun and adjective. Usually there is a contrasting noun in ·*or*/·*er* (*examiner* ~ *examinee*; *interviewer* ~ *interviewee*); this facilitates the formation of *biographee*, with ·*y* dropped from the noun base. The ·*ee* suffix is still productive, especially in AmE, though relatively few words in ·*ee* become established.

(e) *·eer*

This suffix is usually attached to nouns, deriving nouns meaning "person concerned with ~": *auctioneer, engineer, mountaineer.* Very often they are derogatory: *profiteer, racketeer, sonneteer. Gazetteer,* "geographical index", is exceptional (as a result of historical change) in not denoting a person, while *privateer* is exceptional both in meaning (it denotes a type of military ship associated with private persons) and in having an adjective base. The suffix is still productive – cf. such nonce-words as *conventioneer* and *weaponeer.* One or two earlier words belong here semantically but have the spelling *·ier* (e.g. *bombardier*).

(f) *·er, ·or,* and *·ar*

These are probably best regarded as variants of the same suffix. The *·ar* variant is found in very few words, such as *beggar, bursar,* and *liar.* In general, *·or* occurs in words of Latin origin (*instructor*), following the suffix *·ate* (*activator*), in technical, especially legal, words (*adjustor, mortgagor*), or with bound bases (*author, doctor, tailor, traitor*), while the much more frequent *·er* is found in most other places, and can be taken as the default variant. The *·er* variant behaves in general like a Class II affix. One respect in which it departs from the Class II behaviour described in §5.1.3 is that it occurs with bound bases in such words as *biographer, philosopher,* etc.; these, however, are neo-classical, and we have suggested that they are best handled in terms of the replacement of *·y* by *·er,* rather than by simple attachment to a bound base. The *·or* variant is closer to a Class I affix: it attaches more widely to bound bases, and note also the shift of stress in the salient (legal) sense of *executor* (*'execute ~ ex'ecutor*). With some bases both spellings of the suffix are found: *adapt, advise, convene, execute,* etc.; overall, *·or* is losing ground to *·er.* A few words have the variant *·ier* (*clothier, grazier*) or *·yer* (*lawyer, sawyer*), while *·erer* occurs uniquely in *fruiterer* (for in such words as *upholsterer* the first *er* belongs to the base).

The highly productive *·er* variant attaches to a considerable range of bases besides verbs:

[49] i *executioner, golfer, freighter, petitioner; Londoner, New Yorker*
ii *fiver, oncer, southerner; dogooder, fast-tracker, nine-to-fiver*

The bases in [i] are nouns, or proper names, while in [ii] we have a numeral, an adverb, an adjective, and a sample of dephrasal compound bases. Deverbal *·er* nouns figure very productively in compounds such as *hairdresser, stage-manager,* etc. (see §4.2.2).

Nouns in *·er* exhibit a wide range of meanings. The central case is that of a deverbal noun denoting a person filling the agent role with respect to the verb: *baker, commander, singer*; many such words can be used for professions. A non-agentive reading is found in words like *admirer, loser.* Lexicalised animal names are seen in *pointer, warbler,* instruments in *boiler, eraser, silencer,* other kinds of causer in *reminder, eye-opener.* Some *·er* words (at least in some lexicalised senses) correspond not to the subject of the verb but to the complement of a preposition: *diner, sleeper* ("railway carriages to dine/sleep <u>in</u>"), *kneeler* ("stool to kneel <u>on</u>"), *slipper* ("shoe to slip your feet <u>into</u>"). In AusE and NZE a processual meaning is found in forms like *killer* and *bottler* ("something to be killed/bottled)".

Deverbal nouns in *·er/·or* often take complements corresponding to the object of the verb in a syntactic phrase: *the writer <u>of the editorial</u>, <u>Kim's</u> attacker, the governor <u>of Maryland</u>.*

(g) *·ist*

This is an extremely productive suffix, and we can illustrate here only a few of its uses:

[50] i *atheist, baptist, evangelist, exorcist, fascist, hedonist*
ii *extremist, idealist, isolationist, Marxist, nationalist, socialist, transcendentalist*
iii *agist, classist, racist, sexist, speciesist*
iv *bigamist, monogamist; agronomist, economist, geologist, psychologist*
v *anglicist, classicist, physicist, psychiatrist, semanticist*
vi *cellist, cymbalist, harpist, pianist, trombonist, violinist*

As noted in §5.1.4, there is a strong paradigmatic relation between *·ist* and *·ism*: this is illustrated by the words in [i–iii], which all have counterparts in *·ism*. Those in [i] have bound bases and, we have suggested, are best regarded as deriving by affix-replacement from the *·ism* words. Words in *·ism* commonly denote various philosophies or systems of belief: the *·ist* derivative then denotes a person holding these beliefs, as in [ii] and several of those in [i]. With [iii], the words in *·ism* have the meaning "prejudice based on ~", while the *·ist* words denote persons having such prejudice; these are relatively new creations and form a model for numerous nonce-words. There is a significant paradigmatic link between *·ist* and other suffixes besides *·ism*; this is illustrated in the words in [iv], which all have counterparts in *·y* – compare also *colonist, diarist, militarist, therapist*, etc. Several of the words in [v] show a similar relation with words in *·ics*. Many *·ist* words denote persons professionally or otherwise pursuing some field of scholarship, as in [v] and the last four words of [iv]. The *·ist* suffix is also the main way of forming nouns denoting persons playing particular musical instruments, as in [vi] (with the *o* dropped from *cello* and *piano*): *drummer* and *trumpeter* are exceptions to the usual pattern.

As evident from the above examples, *·ist* normally forms nouns from nouns. Etymologically that holds for *typist* too, but its present meaning relates more directly to *type* as a verb; note, however, that unlike *writer*, for example, it cannot take an *of* phrase corresponding to the object of the verb: *the writer/*typist of this letter.*

(h) *·nik*

This suffix, originally from Russian via Yiddish, started to gain popularity in English in the 1950s, but it had only a short period of high productivity. The meaning is broadly "person associated with ~", as in the original *beatnik*, "member of the beat generation". It is found in more or less jocular words, particularly for groups seen as anti-establishment (*peacenik, refusenik*) or fans of a certain kind of music (*folknik, jazznik*).

(i) *·ster*

In old words such as *songster, spinster* (originally gender-neutral), *webster*, this suffix again means "person connected with ~". Later forms are often derogatory (*rhymster, punster*), with a significant group having connotations of shadiness or illegal dealings (*gangster, mobster, gamester*). The bases are generally nouns (but cf. *youngster* and *oldster*). The suffix is still productive, especially in AmE, and doesn't necessarily have negative connotations (cf. *funkster*, "practitioner of funk music").

(j) Conversion

Conversion from verbs may yield nouns denoting persons (*bore, spy*) or instruments (*clip, rattle*), but neither process is very widely used. However, there are a fair number of nouns denoting persons that are converted from adjectives (*drunk*, *intellectual*, *professional*).

5.7.2 Action/state/process nominalisations

This section covers actions, states, and processes together: the view taken here is that any distinction between them is more a matter of the context in which the nouns are used than of any inherent quality of the affixes or processes involved. Several of the suffixes have additional uses besides that of forming action/state/process nominalisations.

(a) *·age*

This suffix, originally French, occurs in a large number of nouns but is no longer productive. It attaches predominantly to nouns and verbs, but is also found with the occasional adjective (*shortage*). It has a wide range of meanings, some of which are illustrated in:

[51]	i	*baggage, coinage, fruitage, leafage, wordage*	[collectivity]
	ii	*bondage, parentage, peerage, pupilage, shortage*	[state, condition, rank]
	iii	*breakage, marriage, stoppage, wastage, wreckage*	[result]
	iv	*anchorage, hermitage, orphanage, parsonage, vicarage*	[place]
	v	*acreage, dosage, mileage, tonnage, voltage*	[amount or rate]
	vi	*anchorage, cartage, corkage, haulage, postage*	[charge]

Many words have more than one such meaning, as shown here for *anchorage*.

(b) *·al*

This suffix attaches to disyllabic verbs with stress on the final syllable: *a'rrival*, *de'nial*, *re'fusal*, *re'moval*, *'trial*. *'Burial*, which does not conform to this constraint, has a different etymological source. Few *·al* nouns have been created since the nineteenth century (*referral* appears to be one), and it is questionable whether the suffix is still productive.

(c) *·ance* and *·ence*

These suffixes, of which *·ance* is much the more common, are based on Latin models; some English formations are found (*riddance*, *utterance*), but the suffixes are no longer productive. They form nouns from verb or adjective bases:

[52]		VERB BASES	ADJECTIVE BASES
	i	a. *acceptance, disturbance, performance*	b. *arrogance, fragrance, relevance*
	ii	a. *emergence, interference, resurgence*	b. *prudence, sentience, violence*

With verbs the suffixes simply attach to the base, except that verbs in *·ate* lose this suffix: *dominate* ~ *dominance*. With adjective bases, the nominal suffixes replace the adjectival ones, so that *arrogance* is the nominalisation of *arrogant*, *prudence* of *prudent*, and so on. Some verbs form both nouns and adjectives: *dominate* ~ *dominance* ~ *dominant*, *differ* ~ *different* ~ *difference*, and similarly for *observe*, *persist*, etc. The verb bases include some prepositional verbs, and here the same prepositions occur in complements to the noun (*adhere/adherence to*, *comply/compliance with*, etc.).

No fully general rules can be given for the choice between the *a* and *e* spellings, but in many cases the spelling matches that of paradigmatically related suffixes where the vowel is not reduced to /ə/ – compare *tolerance* and *tolerate* (/eɪ/), *influence* and *influential* (/e/). In addition, *e* is predictable after *qu* (*sequence*), *sc* (*luminescence*), *c* representing

/s/ (*munificence*), or *g* representing /dʒ/ (*emergence* – contrast *extravagance*, where *g* represents /g/). For nouns in ·*ancy* and ·*ency*, see (n) below.

(d) ·*ation*, ·*ion*, ·*ition*, ·*sion*, ·*tion*, ·*ution*

These suffixes occur with verb or bound bases. The only one which is English is ·*ation*: all the others are virtually restricted to loan words from Latin or French (often not clearly analysable in English), as in *confus·ion*, *perd·ition*, *compul·sion*, *absorp·tion*, *sol·ution*. Examples like *demot·ion*, created from English *demote* by analogy with *promot·ion*, are very rare. Some contrasting pairs are to be found, such as *affection* and *affectation*, but both of these go back to Latin models (and at earlier periods of English, though hardly today, they could be synonyms). There are very few such contrasts, however, and on the whole we can say that these suffixes are variants of a single form, with ·*ation* the only one productive in Present-day English. Established words include some where the verb base bears no suffix (*experimentation*, *flirtation*, *starvation*), but in uses where it is still productive it attaches to verbs with the following suffixes:

[53] i ·*ise* *atomisation*, *civilisation*, *fertilisation*, *legalisation*, *privatisation*
ii ·*ate* *alternation*, *education*, *intimidation*, *metrication*, *moderation*
iii ·*ify* *glorification*, *justification*, *purification*, *ratification*, *yuppification*

In [ii] the ·*ate* again drops, and in [iii] *c* is added before the suffix (as it also is with a few verbs in ·*ply*: *imply* ~ *implication*). No other suffix (apart from the special case of ·*ing*) is now used for nominalising verbs of these three kinds.

(e) ·*dom*

Originally a noun (etymologically related to present-day *doom*), this suffix yields nouns with a number of meanings. The most general or neutral is "state/condition of being ~", as in *boredom*, *martyrdom*, *stardom*. In such words as *dukedom* and *earldom* it means "territory under the jurisdiction of / associated with ~". Words like *fairydom* fit in here but differ in being non-count. The suffix has also developed the sense "collectivity of ~", as in *gangsterdom*, *officialdom* (where it has a deprecatory tone), and in jocular words like *puppydom*. The base is almost invariably a noun; the few exceptions include *freedom* and *wisdom* (derived from *wise* but with the vowel change making the relation less transparent). Many ·*dom* words have been created, but relatively few of the older ones have survived and relatively few of the more recent ones have become established. It is clearly still productive, especially in AmE (cf. *couch potatodom*, *yuppiedom*).

(f) ·*hood*

Like ·*dom*, this suffix comes from what was originally an independent noun; the ·*head* of *godhead* and *maidenhead* (not etymologically related to the present word *head*) is a variant. It is also like ·*dom* in sense, yielding nouns meaning "condition of being ~", as in *bachelorhood*, *sainthood*, *widowhood*, or "collectivity of ~", as in *brotherhood*, *priesthood*; *neighbourhood* can have the latter interpretation, but its usual meaning is locative. The base is normally a noun, with de-adjectival *falsehood* and *likelihood* the main exceptions still in common use; *livelihood*, "means of living", is not semantically based on *lively* nor etymologically formed by suffixation of ·*hood*. Though much less frequently used than ·*dom*, it is still available for use in new words – witness nonce-words like *bumhood*.

(g) *·ing*

We are concerned here with the lexical *·ing* that forms gerundial nouns from verbs, as in *the/his accidental killing of the birds*, as distinct from the inflectional *·ing* that forms the gerund-participle form of verbs, as in *I'd heard about him/his accidentally killing the birds*: see Ch. 3, §1.4, for this distinction.

With a good number of verbs, suffixation with *·ing* is the only way of forming a deverbal noun: *coming, feeling, forgetting, opening, painting, rendering, understanding, undertaking, writing.* In other cases, we find a difference in meaning or in the range of permitted complements between the *·ing* noun and a noun formed from the same base by another suffix or by conversion: compare such pairs as *breakage* ~ *breaking, laughter* ~ *laughing* (*his constant laughing/*laughter at me*), *knock* ~ *knocking, work* ~ *working.* In other cases, an *·ing* noun can substitute for some other deverbal noun without a change of meaning: *classification/classifying, completion/completing, postponement/postponing, removal/removing.* In such cases the *·ing* formation often tends to sound (in varying degrees) less idiomatic, less natural than the other, but not to the extent of being ungrammatical.

As well as being used in the formation of abstract nouns, as above, *·ing* commonly appears in nouns denoting the concrete result of some process (*building, clearing, drawing, savings*). It also attaches to noun bases in examples like *bedding, fencing, flooring, railing.* In a few cases it attaches to prepositions: *inning, outing.*

(h) *·ism*

Most *·ism* words fall into one of the three semantic groupings illustrated in:

[54] i *Buddhism, capitalism, Darwinism, expressionism, fanaticism, federalism*
ii *Americanism, archaism, colloquialism, Gallicism, spoonerism, vulgarism*
iii *alcoholism, autism, embolism*

The nouns in [i] represent a broad range denoting doctrines, systems of philosophical, religious, or political beliefs, intellectual or artistic movements. Related senses include modes of life (*monasticism*), attitudes or conduct (*absenteeism, defeatism, favouritism*), prejudice (*racism, sexism*), and so on. The bases are nouns (including numerous proper nouns), together with some adjectives, bound bases, and dephrasal compounds (*go-it-aloneism*). As we have noted, there is a strong paradigmatic link with nouns in *·ist*, and as with *·ist*, there may be a derogatory tone. This use continues to be very productive. The words in [ii] illustrate a smaller group denoting some special linguistic usage or peculiarity of speech. The bases are mainly adjectives or proper nouns, though there are also a few bound bases, as in *euphemism, solecism*; the latter, like *mannerism*, extends from language to other forms of behaviour. A third group are used for abnormal medical conditions, as in [iii]. In addition we find a small number of words where *·ism* simply forms a de-adjectival noun with the meaning "state/condition of being ~", as in *bilingualism* or *magnetism* (with loss of *·ic*, as also in the above *archaism*).

(i) *·ity*/*·ety* and *·ness*

These are the most common suffixes used in de-adjectival nouns with the general meaning "quality/state of being ~". They contrast strikingly in their behaviour, providing prototypical examples respectively of Class I and Class II affixes. Many words in *·ity* came into English as loans from French rather than being created by an English word-formation process, and this is reflected in the fact the base very often differs significantly in form from the free adjective. Words in ·*ity* have the stress on the syllable preceding the suffix, and this frequently leads to a shift of stress relative to the adjective base:

[55] *actu'ality, besti'ality, curi'osity, eccen'tricity, no'bility*

The stress shift affects the vowel quality – and vowel change without stress shift is seen in *chastity, sincerity*, etc. Velar softening (§5.1.2) applies with bases in ·*ic*: *electricity, rusticity*, etc. The adjectival ending ·(*i*)*ous* is lost in such words as *assiduity, atrocity, hilarity, superfluity*, while *fidelity* and *humility* have no corresponding English adjectives (and *duplicitous* and *felicitous* are formed from the nouns *duplicity* and *felicity* rather than providing the base for them). It does not attach to adjectives containing a Class II suffix such as ·*ed*, ·*ful*, ·*ish*, ·*less*, ·*ly*. The variant ·*ety* is found in only a small number of words: *gaiety, nicety, dubiety, notoriety* (the last two with loss of ·*ous*), and so on. A great many ·*ity* words have adjective bases in ·*able*/·*ible*: *amiability, compatibility*, etc. In general, ·*ity* is the preferred nominalising suffix for adjectives of this form; this is especially so where the adjective has the meaning "able to be ~ ed"; with some other ·*able* adjectives we find ·*ness*: *charitableness, peaceableness, reasonableness*. It is most clearly with ·*able* bases that ·*ity* is still productive (cf. recent forms such as *deniability, sustainability*); elsewhere, ·*ness* tends to be preferred for new formations, though ·*ity* may appear in technical terms such as *connectivity*.

Unlike ·*ity*, ·*ness* does not affect the stress or induce other changes: compare *clearness* and *clarity, gentleness* and *gentility, nobleness* and *nobility*, etc. It also differs from ·*ity* in its ability to attach to bases of other word classes than adjective (*nothingness, oneness, whyness*), to compound adjectives (*straightforwardness, user-friendliness, watertightness*), to dephrasal compounds (*matter-of-factness, more-than-one-ness*). The meaning is almost entirely regular, with *business, Highness* (indicating status), *wilderness*, and *witness* lexicalised exceptions. In general, ·*ness* can be regarded as the default suffix for forming new de-adjectival nouns; it is sometimes used instead of other suffixes when the established form is temporarily forgotten (e.g. *saneness* for *sanity*), or to give a new meaning (e.g. *impossibleness* instead of *impossibility* for the noun corresponding to the colloquial sense of *impossible*, as applied to persons).

(j) ·*ment*

This suffix has been very widely used in the past, but is now only marginally productive, if indeed productive at all. The suffix is of French origin, but became naturalised as English very early on, and yields nouns from French and English verb bases. It is particularly common with verbs containing the prefixes *en*·/*em*· and *be*·: *ennoblement, embodiment, bewilderment*. Besides abstract nouns like *astonishment, betterment, development*, etc., we find nouns in ·*ment* with concrete meanings (in addition to or instead of the abstract): *advertisement, embankment, reinforcement*. There are a small number denoting location: *encampment, settlement*. In the past ·*ment* was occasionally added to adjectives; *oddment* is the only survivor of this type, though *merriment*, formed from an obsolete verb *merry*, now looks to be de-adjectival.

(k) ·*ship*

This suffix attaches primarily to nouns denoting persons, again yielding nouns with the general meaning "state or condition of / associated with ~": *apprenticeship, companionship, friendship, kinship*. *Hardship* is an exceptional example with an adjective base.

A more specific sense found in a considerable number of words is that of office, rank, position, or of emoluments associated with such positions: *governorship, headmastership, scholarship, tutorship* (*lectureship* is unusual in having *lecture* rather than *lecturer* as base). *Dictatorship* can belong with these, but more often denotes a type of government. The ·*ship* suffix can also carry connotations of skill or craft; this is especially common with compound bases in ·*man*: *craftsmanship, marksmanship, statesmanship*. Except with such senses as are lexicalised in *township, Ladyship*, and the like, the suffix is still productive (cf. *chairpersonship*, for example), though it is not widely used.

(l) ·*th*

This suffix, no longer productive, is found mainly in de-adjectival nouns such as *warmth*, but also in one or two deverbal ones (e.g. *growth*). In most cases the phonological relation between base and derivative is irregular (*long* ~ *length, die* ~ *death, bear* ~ *birth*), and in several cases the semantic relationship has been lost, so that there is no longer any morphological relationship between such pairs as *dear* and *dearth, foul* and *filth*.

(m) ·*ure*

Most nouns in ·*ure* are loans; there have been a fairly small number of formations in English, such as *composure, departure, enclosure*, but the suffix is probably no longer productive. It is found with bound bases (*capture, leisure, treasure*), verbs (*composure, failure, mixture, pressure*), and the occasional adjective (*rapture*) and noun (*candidature*).

(n) suffixes ending in *y*

A great number of nouns, mainly abstract, end in *y*. In some cases, such as *fury, glory, luxury*, there is no semantic evidence for analysing the word into base + suffix, while in others, such as *privacy*, the boundary between base and suffix is problematic (*priv·acy* or *privac·y*): there are many places where it is difficult to distinguish between morphological and etymological analysis. We begin with nouns unproblematically containing ·*y* itself as a suffix, and then turn to various larger suffixes ending with *y* or endings where the division between base and suffix is uncertain; ·*ity* (together with its variant ·*ety*), however, has been dealt with already and need not be further considered here.

·*y*

This is most straightforwardly recognisable as a suffix forming abstract nouns when it attaches to free bases: adjectives, as in *difficulty, honesty, jealousy, modesty*; verbs, as in *delivery, entreaty, injury, perjury*; nouns, as in *beggary, victory*. With bound bases its status as a suffix may be established by its paradigmatic contrast with other suffixes. One large class of cases of this kind involve neo-classical compounds: compare *biography* ~ *biographer, euphony* ~ *euphonic, philology* ~ *philologist, philosophy* ~ *philosophise*. Others are seen in *history* ~ *historic, memory* ~ *memorable, treachery* ~ *treacherous, usury* ~ *usurer*.

acy, cy, sy

The ending *acy* is found in many nouns that are paradigmatically related to words ending in /t/, or /t/ + suffix. Particularly numerous are contrasts between nouns in *acy* and nouns or adjectives in *ate*: *privacy* ~ *private*, and similarly for *accuracy, advocacy, intimacy, obstinacy*, etc. Another group have the ending *cracy* contrasting with *crat*: *aristocracy* ~ *aristocrat*, and likewise *bureaucracy, democracy*, etc. Other examples include *diplomacy* ~ *diplomat, lunacy* ~ *lunatic*. The same kind of contrast is seen for *cy* in *idiocy* ~ *idiotic*, and for *sy* in *ecstasy* ~ *ecstatic*, *heresy* ~ *heretic*, *hypocrisy* ~ *hypocrite*, *idiosyncrasy* ~ *idiosyncratic*, and so on.

The most plausible analysis of these cases is to say that the suffix ·*y* is attached to a base in *t*, with /ti/ becoming /si/ by morphophonological alternation, reflected in spelling as *cy* or *sy* (see §5.1.2). On this account *privacy* will be divided as *privac·y*. Nevertheless, there are so many words ending in *acy* that it has something of the character of a suffix, and indeed it must have that status in *supremacy* where it attaches to a free base. (And in *conspiracy* we have a contrast both with *conspire* and with *conspiratorial*.)

We must also recognise a suffix ·*cy*; it attaches to a larger group of free bases, mainly nouns denoting ranks or offices (*baronetcy*, *captaincy*, *chaplaincy*, etc.), but also the occasional adjective (*bankruptcy* and *normalcy*). The ·*sy* of *minstrelsy* seems to be a spelling variant.

·*ty*

This suffix forms a small number of de-adjectival nouns such as *certainty*, *cruelty*, *loyalty*, *safety*, *subtlety*. *Admiralty* is exceptional in having a noun base.

·*ery* and ·*ry*

These can be regarded as variants of the same suffix, with ·*ery* the more common of the two. They occur in a good number of nouns, expressing such meanings as condition (*slavery*), behaviour (*debauchery*), collectivity (*machinery*, *citizenry*), location (*piggery*, *printery*). The bases may be nouns (*creamery*, *bigotry*, *dentistry*, *gimmickry*), adjectives (*bravery*, *gallantry*), verbs (*bakery*), or, in a few cases, bound (*chivalry*, *sorcery*, *surgery*).

A fair number of nouns in ·*ery* are in paradigmatic relation with agentive nouns in ·*er*: compare *baker* ~ *bakery*, *brewer* ~ *brewery*, etc. In some cases, the ·*er* is attached to a bound base, as in *butcher*, *grocer*, *haberdasher*, *milliner*: the forms in *y*, *butchery*, *grocery*, etc., might here be analysed as having ·*ery* replacing agentive ·*er* or as having ·*y* added after it. The latter proposal is probably preferable since it is the only one of the two that will generalise to cases like *embroidery* and *upholstery*. In these words *er* is part of the verb base, and the agentive nouns have ·*er* added after it: *embroiderer*, *upholsterer*. It seems clear, then, that we must analyse the former pair as *embroider·y* and *upholster·y*, allowing that one use of the ·*y* suffix is as a variant of ·*ery* attaching to a base ending in *er*. This then raises the possibility that forms like *bakery* should be analysed as deriving from *baker* by affixation of the ·*y* variant, rather than from *bake* by affixation of ·*ery*.

·*ancy* and ·*ency*

These are restricted to nouns in paradigmatic relation to a word in ·*ant* and ·*ent*, usually an adjective, as in such pairs as *blatant* ~ *blatancy*, *vacant* ~ *vacancy*, *decent* ~ *decency*, *lenient* ~ *leniency*, but occasionally a noun, as in *infant* ~ *infancy*, *vagrant* ~ *vagrancy*. We have noted that the same paradigmatic relationship holds for one use of ·*ance* and ·*ence*, and there is no apparent principled basis for the choice of one nominalisation over the other. In some cases both are found: *competence*/*competency*, *complacence*/*complacency*, *relevance*/*relevancy*; the version with *y* tends to be countable (e.g. *competencies*), and in one or two cases has a more specific meaning as in *dependency*, "territory controlled by another", or *Excellency*, a status term.

There are two possible analyses for ·*ancy* and ·*ency*: one is to treat them simply as variants of the ·*ance* and ·*ence* suffixes, the other is to say that the suffix ·*y* is added to the form in ·*ant*/·*ent*, with /t/ modified to /s/, as suggested for *privacy*, etc.

(o) Minor suffixes

There are a few further suffixes that can be recognised as such in a small number of deverbal nouns but are no longer productive: *laugh·ter, merg·er, hat·red, complain·t.*

(p) Phonological modification, conversion, and compounding

A number of the word-formation processes covered in earlier sections include deverbal nouns within their output. Final consonant devoicing is seen in *belief, ascent, extent* (§2.6). A considerable number of nouns are formed from verbs by shifting the stress to the first syllable, sometimes with an associated change in vowel quality: *'digest, 'rethink, 'decrease.* Many others involve no phonological change at all, arising simply by conversion: *arrest, push, swallow, whimper,* etc. Nominalisations with the form of compounds commonly arise from lexicalised verb + preposition combinations: the preposition may be placed first and stressed, as in *'downfall, 'intake, 'upkeep,* or, more often, remain in second position with the stress shifted from it to the verb base, as in *'blow-out, 'make-up, 'stopover.*

5.8 **Adjectivalisation**

Adjectivalisation is primarily a matter of forming adjectives from words of other categories, nouns and verbs, usually by suffixation. It also covers the formation of one adjective from another when the process is the same as or similar to that applying to other bases: for example, suffixation of *·y* generally forms adjectives from nouns (*thirst·y*) or verbs (*weep·y*), but also occasionally from adjectives (*lank·y*), and we include the latter as well as the former in the category of adjectivalisation. The formation of adjectives from proper nouns and numerals is dealt with in §§5.6, 5.10, and need not be further considered here.

(a) *a·*

The *a·* prefix we are concerned with here has its source in the preposition *on*; a high proportion of the derivatives it forms are themselves prepositions, but there are also adjectives (including some very common ones such as *afraid, asleep, awake*), and a few adverbs (*aloud*). The bases for adjectival derivatives may be nouns (*afoot*), adjectives (*askew*), or verbs (*atremble*). The formation of adjectives in *a·* is still productive, but probably only with verbal bases, in a small number of (often poetic) coinages, such as *aclutter* or *awhir.*

(b) *·able* and *·ible*

The *·ible* member of this pair is mainly restricted to loans from Latin or forms created in English with Latin bases – compare, for example, Latin-based *edible* and *legible* with English-based *eatable* and *readable.* A very minor third variant, *·uble,* is seen in the loans *soluble* and *voluble*: compare the variation between *·ation, ·ition,* and *·ution* in §5.7 above. With a relatively small number of bases both *·able* and *·ible* derivatives are found. In general, the meaning is the same (cf. *deductable/deductible, extractable/extractible*), but there are a few cases where the *·able* form has a different or more restricted sense (cf. *contractable* "liable to be contracted (e.g. of a disease)" vs *contractible* "liable to contract / be caused to contract"; *accessable* "able to be accessed (e.g. of a computer file)" vs the much more general *accessible*).

The ·*ible* variant has the properties of a Class I affix. It precedes the Class I suffix ·*ity*; it occurs with bound bases (*audible, credible, feasible*, etc.); it triggers morphophonological alternation in the base (*divide* ~ *divisible, perceive* ~ *perceptible*); and there are one or two cases of stress shift (*neg'lect* ~ *'negligible*). Adjectives in ·*ible*, moreover, usually form negatives with the Class I prefix *in*· (*ineligible, indestructible, imperceptible*). The ·*able* variant, however, exhibits mixed behaviour. It too precedes ·*ity* and occurs with bound bases (*durable, vulnerable*), but it is also found with dephrasal compound bases (*get-at-able*). It often triggers omission of ·*ate*, but there are a good many cases where ·*ate* is optionally retained (*navigable/navigatable, separable/separatable*). Other alternations rarely occur with ·*able*, and we find pairs like *defensible/defendable*, with alternation triggered by ·*ible* but not by ·*able*. There are words where ·*able* triggers stress-shift but forms where the stress remains unchanged are found as alternants (*'comparable/com'parable, 'preferable/pre'ferable*). Some negatives are formed with Class I *in*· (*irreparable, intolerable, inviolable*), others with Class II *un*· (*undeniable, unremarkable*).

These affixes are the only ones in English whose primary meaning is modal. The central case, clearly still productive, has ·*able* attached to a transitive verb giving an adjective with the meaning "capable of being ~ ·ed". This corresponds, therefore, to a passive verbal construction. In a few cases, however, the adjective has an active interpretation, as in *perishable*, "liable to perish". *Adaptable* and *changeable* illustrate the case where both interpretations are possible, "able to adapt / to be adapted", etc. The modal meaning is generally like that of *can*. Sometimes, however, it is stronger, like that of *must* or *will*. Compare, for example, *It is payable at any post office* ("can be paid") with *It is payable by 15 June* ("must be paid") or *The question isn't answerable* ("can't be answered") with *The minister is answerable to Parliament* ("has to answer"). Note also *The deposit is refundable* ("will be refunded"). The modal meaning may also be a matter of fitness/worthiness, as in *laughable* or one sense of *comparable* (cf. *The style is comparable with Voltaire's*). In general, the modality is of the kind we have called dynamic (Ch. 3, §9), a matter of capability or ability, but there are some cases where it is deontic, a matter of permission. *Photocopiable*, for example, may indicate feasibility (dynamic) or legality (deontic). Semantic specialisation is found (co-existing with a regular meaning) in such forms as *appreciable* and *considerable* "fairly large", *tolerable* "fairly good", and so on.

The bases to which ·*able* attaches are generally verbs. These include a number of prepositional verbs, the usual pattern being for the preposition to be omitted: *dependable* ("on"), *dispensable* ("with"), *disposable* ("of"), *laughable* ("at"). In a few formations, however, the preposition is retained, and either precedes the suffix (*un-put-downable*) or follows (*liveable with*). The ·*able* variant also occurs with nouns: *knowledgeable, peaceable, reasonable, seasonable*. A few of these have a passive-type meaning matching that of the deverbal adjectives: *objectionable* ("that may be objected to"), *saleable* ("fit to be sold").

(c) ·*al*, ·*ar*, ·*ial*, ·*ual*

These suffixes come originally from Latin and are usually found attached to Latin, Greek, or French noun bases (even where these have also been borrowed into English): *accidental, baptismal, cultural, monophthongal, pastoral*, etc. Only rarely are they added to native English words, as in *tidal*. They generally form denominal adjectives with the general meaning "pertaining/related to ~", but there are numerous cases of semantic specialisation, as in *familiar, occasional, singular, usual*, etc. And there are also many with bound bases, as in *medieval, regal*, etc. Some of these correspond semantically to morphologically unrelated English-based nouns – compare *oral* ~ *mouth, manual* ~ *hand, dorsal* ~ *back, filial* ~ *son*, etc.

The different variants are illustrated in:

[56] i *additional, alkaloidal, central, conventional, natural, regimental*
ii *lunar, molecular, nuclear, oracular, polar, vulgar*
iii *bestial, confidential, editorial, ministerial, proverbial, substantial*
iv *eventual, gradual, habitual, intellectual, sensual, spiritual*

The ·*al* variant is particularly productive with bases ending in *tion*, ·*ment*, and ·*oid*. We find ·*ar* immediately after /l/, or with /l/ in the preceding syllable, but in the latter case there may be a contrast with ·*al* (*linear* vs *lineal, familiar* vs *familial*). Where the base ends in syllabic /l/, *u* is commonly added, as in *oracular* from *oracle*; note also the relation between adjectives in *ular* and verbs in *ulate* (*regular* ~ *regulate, popular* ~ *populate*). The ·*ial* variant seen in [iii] commonly occurs after ·*or* (but we also find others with just ·*al*: *doctoral, electoral*), and in paradigmatic contrast with nominal ·*ance*/·*ence* (*circumstance* ~ *circumstantial, existence* ~ *existential*). In a fair number of these latter cases there is also a semantically distinct adjective (*confidence* ~ *confident* ~ *confidential, difference* ~ *different* ~ *differential*). Note that in such words as *familial, secretarial, territorial*, the *i* belongs to the base, rather than to the suffix. The *u* in such words as those in [iv] is part of the suffix as far as English is concerned, but etymologically it belongs with the base in Latin and this is reflected in the fact that it is commonly found with other suffixes attaching to the same bases – compare *eventuate, graduate, habituate, sensuous, spirituous*. A few words such as *funereal* and *marmoreal* end in *eal*, but as the bases are bound the precise division into base and suffix remains uncertain. For adjectives in ·*ical* see (j) below.

(d) ·*ant* and ·*ent*

Adjectives with these suffixes mostly go back to present participles in Latin or (in the case of ·*ant*, but not ·*ent*) French. For this reason, the base may be bound: *elegant, evident, present, virulent*. But there are also a good number where the base is an independent English word: *defiant, observant, repentant, triumphant, absorbent, excellent*. Others are in paradigmatic contrast with verbs in ·*ate*: *arrogant, radiant, stagnant, tolerant*. With verbs in ·*ify* we again find *c* at the boundary: *magnificent, significant*. There are others where the base differs in vowel quality from the corresponding verb: *abundant* (*abound*), *apparent* (*appear*), *errant* (*err*). These suffixes are probably no longer productive.

(e) ·*ary*

Many adjectives with this suffix are direct loans from Latin; again, therefore, some have bound bases (*ordinary, voluntary*). In English, the suffix is added mostly to noun bases ending in ·*ion*, especially *tion* (*cautionary, discretionary, reactionary, visionary*), and *t*, especially ·*ment* (*complimentary, fragmentary, parliamentary, dietary*). The pattern may still be productive with such bases, but certainly not elsewhere.

(f) ·*ate*

This suffix has never been widely used in the creation of English adjectives. Such words as *celibate, fortunate, intricate* are loans, not English formations. There are numerous learned words using classical bases (*corporate, degenerate, geminate*), but the clear English formations are based on nouns ending in ·*ion*: *affectionate, extortionate, passionate.*

(g) ·*ed*

This suffix attaches to nouns (*bearded*) or, more often, nominals consisting of a dependent + a head noun (*one-eyed, red-faced*). Plural nominals lose the plural inflection: *three-bedroomed*, not **three-bedroomsed.* The construction is extremely productive; the basic meaning is simply "with ~", but there are many lexicalised examples with specialised meanings: *barefaced, blue-eyed, two-faced*, etc. The suffix is in general identical to that used in the formation of regular past participles – note in particular the alternation between /ɪd/ (*red-handed, hard-hearted*), /t/ (*humpbacked*), and /d/ (*one-armed*). The /ɪd/ variant, however, occurs exceptionally in a handful of lexicalised words (*crooked, dogged, ragged, wicked, wretched*) and in forms containing *legged* (e.g. *three-legged*, though /legd/ is an alternative pronunciation). For participial adjectives in ·*ed*, see (t) below. Where the base is a noun rather than a nominal, the formation of the adjective may involve the prefix *be*· as well as the suffix ·*ed*: *bejewelled, bespectacled.*

(h) ·*en*

A small number of nouns denoting materials form adjectives in ·*en*:

[57] a. *earthen, wooden, woollen* b. *golden, leaden, silken*

The meaning is either "made of ~" or "resembling ~", the latter often in a figurative sense. The adjectives in [a] are used in both ways, while those in [b] are now virtually restricted to the second. Much the most usual way of expressing the first meaning is by means of a noun, rather than a denominal adjective: *a stone wall, a copper kettle*; compare, then, *a gold watch* and *a golden age, a lead pipe* and *a leaden sky, a silk tie* and *long silken hair.* The second sense is found in both attributive and predicative function (*a wooden performance*; *His performance seemed rather wooden*), whereas the first sense is generally attributive (*a wooden box*).

(i) ·*ful*

This suffix attaches mainly to nouns, originally yielding adjectives that can be construed as meaning "full of ~", reflecting the etymological source of the suffix in the adjective *full*: *careful, sinful, sorrowful.* More generally, the meaning might be glossed as "having/displaying ~" or, in some cases, "causing/exciting ~": *delightful, fearful, shameful.* It also attaches to a number of verbs, giving the meaning "prone to ~": *forgetful, fretful, resentful.* In the usual use of the common word *awful* (/ɔːfəl/, "bad, unpleasant") the connection with *awe* is lost, but it can be reinstated with the pronunciation /ɔː fʊl/ (and sometimes the spelling *awe-ful*) to mean "awe-inspiring". Derivation with ·*ful* may be no longer productive (unlike compounding with *full*, which is certainly still used).

(j) ·*ic*, ·*atic*, ·*ific*, ·*ical*, ·*istic*

The suffix ·*ic* is one of the most widely generalised adjectivalising suffixes, especially on noun bases of Greek or Latin origin. Some of the main types of base with which it occurs are illustrated in:

[58] i *allergic, economic, geographic, harmonic, philosophic, telepathic*
ii *anaemic, bronchitic, democratic, genetic, parasitic*

A great many nouns form adjectives by replacement of final ·*y* by ·*ic*, as in [i]. Often the ·*y* is a noun-forming suffix in neo-classical compound bases – compounds in ·*graphy*, ·*logy*, ·*phily*, ·*phony*, ·*trophy*, etc. There is usually a paradigmatic relation with other suffixes too (*economy* ~ *economic* ~ *economist*, *harmony* ~ *harmonic* ~ *harmonise*). The words in [ii] exemplify patterns where ·*ic* adjectives are formed from nouns in ·*ia*, ·*itis*, ·*cracy*, ·*sis*, ·*ite*.

The variants ·*atic* and ·*ific* are seen in:

[59] i *cinematic, dogmatic, dramatic, paradigmatic, problematic*
ii *beatific, horrific, scientific, terrific*

The bases in [i] end in *m* or *ma*; in the latter case, we can take the affix to be ·*tic* or ·*atic* with omission of base *a*; *operatic* is a rare example where the base has no *m*. Except for *scientific*, the bases in [ii] are paradigmatically related to verbs in ·*ify*.

The ending ·*ical* looks like a combination of ·*ic* and ·*al*, but is best regarded as a single suffix, a variant of ·*ic*. For a great many nouns (though fewer than in the past), both formations are found: *analytic/analytical, fanatic/fanatical, ironic/ironical, philosophic/philosophical.* A number of such pairs exhibit differences of meaning and/or collocation, as illustrated in:

		a.	b.
[60]	i	a. *a classic example of pedantry*	b. *classical music*
	ii	a. *a comic opera*	b. *his comical appearance*
	iii	a. *economic theory*	b. *an economical use of time*
	iv	a. *an electric current*	b. *electrical appliances*
	v	a. *this historic occasion*	b. *a historical novel*
	vi	a. *lyric poetry*	b. *a lyrical description of their courtship*

The close relation between the two suffixes is reflected in the fact that the distinction is neutralised in the formation of adverbs: except for *publicly*, the adverbs corresponding to both ·*ic* and ·*ical* adjectives end in ·*ically*.

Consider finally the ending ·*istic*. As we have noted, it is usually in paradigmatic contrast with ·*ism* and ·*ist*: cf. *hedonism* ~ *hedonist* ~ *hedonistic*. It looks like a combination of ·*ist* and ·*ic*, but as with ·*ical* we prefer to analyse it as a single suffix rather than a sequence of two. In the first place, there are a few adjectives in ·*istic* that lack noun counterparts in ·*ist*: *autistic, cannibalistic, characteristic, euphemistic, logistic.* Secondly, where there is a noun in ·*ist* the meaning of the adjective tends to relate more directly to that of the noun base preceding ·*ist*, or to the one in ·*ism*, than to the ·*ist* noun. A stylistic analysis, for example, is an analysis of the style, and need have nothing to do with a stylist. Syllogistic logic has to do with syllogisms, rather than syllogists. Note, moreover, that nouns in ·*ist* that do not have counterparts in ·*ism* do not in general form adjectives in ·*istic*; *linguist* is one that does, but note again that *linguistic* means "pertaining to language", not "pertaining to linguists".

(k) ·*ine*

This derives (via French) from a Latin suffix, and usually occurs in words borrowed from Latin or built on a Latin model: *alpine, bovine, canine, equine, feline, crystalline* – or, with the pronunciation /ɪn/ rather than /aɪn/, *masculine* and *feminine.* It is probably no longer productive.

(l) *·ive, ·ative*

Most adjectives in *·ive* are derived from Latinate verbs in /d/, /t/, /s/. In the case of /d/ and very often /t/, the base appears in an alternant with /s/:

[61] *attract* ~ *attractive, permit* ~ *permissive, evade* ~ *evasive, coerce* ~ *coercive*

The basic meaning is "tending to ~". There is a very strong paradigmatic link with nouns in *·ion* (and its variants): compare *attraction, permission, evasion, coercion.* This link is also apparent in cases with bound bases, such as *aggressive* and *cognitive.* Some of the bases end in *·ate*, giving rise to derivative pairs like *appreciative* ~ *appreciation, decorative* ~ *decoration*, etc. – and just as *·ation* appears as a separate suffix independent of *·ate*, so too does *·ative*: compare *cause* ~ *causative* ~ *causation, exploit* ~ *exploitative* ~ *exploitation. Talkative* is exceptional in having no *·ation* counterpart. Each variant of the suffix is found with a few noun bases: *instinctive, sportive* (unusual also in having a native English base), *authoritative, qualitative.* We also find *·ive* with dephrasal compound bases, especially with subsequent nominalisation by *·ness*: *stick-to-it-iveness* (AmE).

(m) *·less*

This suffix attaches productively to nouns to derive adjectives with the meaning "without ~ / having no ~": *careless, fearless, meaningless.* It is the negative counterpart of *·ful*, and the examples just given are among the numerous cases where there is an opposite in *·ful*: *careful, harmful, meaningful.* But just as there are adjectives in *·ful* such as *beautiful, respectful, successful*, with no established *·less* counterpart, so there are many in *·less* without an opposite in *·ful*: *headless, matchless, penniless, priceless.* Note also that while adjectives in *·ful* often form opposites with *un·* (*unfaithful, unfruitful*), the negative affixes *un·* and *·less* do not normally combine. The *·less* suffix (like *·ful*) is found with a small number of verb bases: *countless, fathomless, relentless, tireless.* The first two of these have modal passive paraphrases: "that can't be counted/fathomed".

(n) *·like*

This combines with nouns to form adjectives with the meaning "resembling ~": *childlike, godlike, ladylike.* These examples are established words, but in general words formed in this way do not become established, though the process is available for coinages as needed: as noted in §1.3, such words can be formed as productively as the corresponding syntactic phrases (compare *cudgel-like* and *like a cudgel*, etc.). Since it occurs with the same form and meaning as a separate word, we take *like* to be a base, forming compounds, rather than a suffix, forming derivatives, but it merits inclusion in this section in that it serves an adjectivalising role in essentially the same way as an affix.

(o) *·ly*

This suffix is found mainly with noun bases: *cowardly, friendly, manly, rascally.* The basic meaning is "like / characteristic of / befitting ~", but there is a considerable amount of semantic specialisation (cf. *lovely, orderly, shapely*). One special use is with nouns denoting time-periods: *daily, weekly*, etc., with the meaning "recurring every ~". The suffix is also found with a number of adjective bases: *deadly, goodly, poorly.* It has not been productive since the beginning of the nineteenth century: its main semantic domain appears to have been taken over by *·like.*

(p) *·ory, ·atory*

These suffixes attach to Latinate bases, usually verbs; they are probably no longer productive. With a few exceptions such as *perfunctory* (which has a bound base) and *sensory*, adjectives in ·*ory* have noun counterparts in ·*ion*, and are probably best regarded as related to them by affix-replacement, especially where the base cannot stand alone as a verb: *compulsory* ~ *compulsion* (cf. also *illusory, satisfactory, transitory*). Similarly we have pairs with ·*atory* and ·*ation*: *accusatory* ~ *accusation* (also *condemnatory, explanatory, obligatory, respiratory*). The suffix ·*ory* bears some resemblance to ·*ary* (see (e) above), but differs in that it replaces ·*ion* rather than being added to it: compare *satisfact·ion* ~ *satisfact·ory* and *react·ion* ~ *react·ion·ary*.

(q) *·ous, ·eous, ·ious, ·atious*

Many words in ·*ous* are loans from French or Latin, though there are also numerous English coinages from the fourteenth through to the nineteenth centuries. In most cases ·*ous* attaches to noun bases: *advantageous, courageous, hazardous, poisonous, virtuous*. With nouns in *y*, the vowel may drop (*analogous, blasphemous, monotonous, treacherous*) or be retained, with the suffix then spelled either ·*ious* (*glorious, industrious, perfidious, prodigious*) or ·*eous* (*beauteous, bounteous, piteous*). Both these latter variants are also found elsewhere: *spacious, uproarious, righteous*. The ·*ious* variant is often in paradigmatic contrast with nominal ·*ion*, as in the pair *ambitious* ~ *ambition*, and similarly for *cautious, rebellious, religious*, etc. And we have the same contrast between ·*atious* and ·*ation*: *disputatious* ~ *disputation*, and similarly for *flirtatious* and *vexatious*. In the form ·*ious* (or ·*tious*) the suffix has since at least the early twentieth century been used in jocular coinages such as *bumptious, rumbustious, scrumptious*.

(r) *·some*

This suffix is found with bases of all three major categories: nouns (*awesome, gamesome*), verbs (*irksome, meddlesome*), adjectives (*fulsome, wholesome*); in cases like *fearsome* and *quarrelsome*, the base could be taken as noun or verb. There were numerous words of this kind at earlier stages of the language, but many have dropped out of use, and some of those that survive no longer have recognisable bases (*handsome, winsome*) or indeed a recognisable base + suffix form (*buxom, lissom*). The suffix was being used to form new words from verb bases into the nineteenth century, but may no longer be productive.

(s) *·y, ·ey*

A great many adjectives have been formed with this suffix. It is found mainly with noun bases, generally giving the meanings "full of ~, covered with ~, having the quality of ~": *bloody, cloudy, dirty, rainy, silky*. There are also a good number with verb bases with the meaning "inclined/apt to ~": *floppy, sleepy, squeaky, sticky*. A handful have adjective bases: *lanky, purply*. The bases are rarely more than two syllables long, and belong to everyday vocabulary; *angry* and *hungry* have obligatory dropping of /ə/ from the base. A fair number of ·*y* adjectives have an informal and rather disparaging tone (*catty, choosy, horsy, lanky, nosy, piggy*), but this is certainly not a necessary feature of the suffix. It is probably the most productive of the adjective-forming suffixes in current English; it is common in child language, in forms which do not become established, but it is also found in numerous neologisms: *glitzy, nerdy, trendy, yucky* – or *rootsy*, where ·*y* follows an inflectional suffix.

The minor variant ·*ey* is used when the base ends in a complex vowel symbol in *y*: *clay·ey*;[52] for retention of base-final *e* in the spelling of words like *cagey*, see §5.1.5.

(t) Conversion and phonological modification

We noted in §3.3 that there is relatively little conversion of nouns into adjectives, but that conversion of gerund-participle and past participle forms of verbs is extremely productive: *It seems very promising*; *He looked devastated*. Adjectives formed from the past participles *blessed* and *cursed* have the pronunciations /blesɪd/ and /kɜːʳsɪd/ as well as the unmodified /blest/ and /kɜːʳst/; the forms with /ɪd/ are generally used in attributive position, as in *a blessed/cursed nuisance*.[53]

5.9 **Verbalisation**

Verbalisation is primarily a matter of the formation of verbs from nouns and adjectives, but as before we include cases where the same processes yield verbs from verbs.

(a) ·*ate*

The vast majority of verbs in ·*ate*, if not direct loans from Latin, were based on Latin forms rather than on English ones. Although we may recognise the ·*ate* in such words as *alleviate*, *equate*, *locate*, etc., the bases are bound and can be found only in other words borrowed from Latin or founded firmly on Latin models. Even those words which appear to have English bases are frequently, from a historical perspective, either back-formations from nouns in ·*ation* (*orientate*, *vaccinate*) or based on Latin (*captivate*, *domesticate*). Nevertheless, there are some genuinely English formations mainly from noun bases, such as *hydrogenate*, *hyphenate*, *orchestrate*, or (with adjective base) *activate*. This suffix has also been used in the production of mock-learned words such as *absquatulate* and *discombobulate*. In addition, there are a very few verbs where ·*ate* occurs with a verb base, as in *fixate* or *prolongate*; again, however, such verbs probably did not arise by the affixation of ·*ate* to the bases *fix* and *prolong*, but by back-formation from the nouns *fixation* and *prolongation*.

(b) *be*·

This is a very marginal member of the class of verbalising affixes, for although a good number of verbs have been formed with this prefix, in the great majority of cases the base too has been a verb. Originally *be*· was simply an unstressed form of the preposition *by*, and it is found in prepositions as well as verbs (*because*, *behind*, *beneath*, *beyond*, etc.). In some verbs historical change has resulted in its losing its morphological status as a prefix: such forms as *behave* and *believe* are not now morphologically analysable. In others the only connection with the original base is in the shared irregular inflection (*become*, *befall*, *betake*). The most salient uses of *be*· as a verbal prefix are to intensify (*bespatter*) and to form transitive verbs from intransitives (*bemoan*, *besprinkle*). The only use of *be*· that is probably still productive is in the formation of adjectives like *bejewelled* (see (g) in §5.8). The verbalising role is seen in a few de-adjectival formations such as *becalm*, *befoul*, *belittle*, and such denominals as *befool*, *behead* – and also, from a present-day perspective,

[52] The rarely used derivative from *sky* can be spelled *skyey* or *skiey*.

[53] The same variation is found for *accursed* and *beloved*, though here the verbs *accurse* and *belove* which provide the historical source are no longer in use, so that the forms now have the analysis prefix + base + suffix.

befriend and *beguile*, though etymologically these were formed from now obsolete verbs.

(c) *·en*

This suffix is found in a good number of de-adjectival verbs: *brighten, dampen, deafen, harden, loosen, sicken, worsen*. Historically speaking, many such verbs were derived from verbs rather than adjectives, but that is no longer apparent, and not relevant to their morphological analysis. A few *·en* verbs have noun bases: *frighten, hearten, lengthen, strengthen, threaten*, but this pattern is no longer productive. Bases in the de-adjectival formation have been restricted to those ending in a plosive or a fricative, and in the last century or two the phonological restriction has been even more severe, with the only bases used ending in an alveolar plosive, /t/ or /d/. Most verbs formed by *·en* suffixation have both intransitive and transitive uses: *He weakened* ~ *This weakened his resolve.*

(d) *em·, en·, in·*

These prefixes have been used to form a considerable number of verbs, but many are now obsolete, and the pattern is probably no longer productive. Leaving aside loans with bound bases (e.g. *enamour*), the bases may be nouns, adjectives, or verbs:

[62] i *embody, empower, encage, encompass, endanger, enrapture, enslave*
ii *embitter, enable, endear, enlarge, ennoble, enrich, ensure*
iii *enhearten, enliven, entrust, entwine, enwrap*

The main meaning for the denominal verbs in [i] is "put in ~"; there is also a type, represented here by *enslave*, with the meaning "make ~", which is like that of the de-adjectival formations in [ii]. The verbal bases in [iii] include some containing the suffix *·en* covered in (c) above; compare also *embolden*, where the base *bolden* is no longer in use as a verb. The *em·* variant appears before bilabial /b/ and /p/. In the "put in ~" sense the prefix is semantically comparable to native *in·*, and a number of verbs have alternate spellings with *en·* and *in·*. For the most part the form with *e* is now preferred – but not, for example, in *inure* or *instate*. *Ensure* and *insure* co-exist with different meanings, and in BrE a distinction is often made between *enquire*, "ask" (e.g. about the times of trains), and *inquire*, "conduct an investigation", with AmE having *in·* for both.

(e) *·ify*

Like *·ate*, this suffix appears mainly with Latinate bases, even if the words were coined in English rather than Latin. With adjective bases it usually means "make ~", as in *humidify, purify, simplify*. Such verbs as *falsify* and *justify* have gained other meanings through lexicalisation. With noun bases, the meaning is generally "make into ~", especially with technical words, such as *mummify* and *personify*. Other meanings can, however, be found in this set – for example, in *beautify, classify, glorify*. In some words the suffix has a clearly derogatory flavour, as in *countrify, Frenchify, speechify, preachify*. The last of these, perhaps modelled directly on *speechify*, is very unusual in being formed from a verb base (but cf. also the relatively recent *scarify*, "make scared"). The *·ify* suffix has never been used to make many words, but is still productive: witness such neologisms as *yuppify*. A form *·fy* is recognisable in a number of loans, such as *liquefy, rarefy, satisfy, stupefy* (all of which form nouns in *·faction*), but the form used in English word-formation is always *·ify* (replacing *y* in cases like *beautify*).

(f) ·*ise*, ·*ize*

These are variant spellings of a single suffix; in BrE both are widely used, AmE has ·*ize*, while AusE and NZE increasingly prefer ·*ise*. The variation does not apply to words ending in an *ise* or *ize* that is not a suffix but part of the base; there are a considerable number of such words in *ise* (e.g. *advertise, advise, circumcise, comprise, despise, exercise, improvise, surprise, televise*, etc.), but very few in *ize* (*capsize, size*).

This is the most productive suffix for forming verbs in Present-day English; relatively recent examples include *colourise, computerise, walkmanise*. So productive is it, indeed, that prescriptive criticism is levelled against what some perceive as the unnecessary proliferation of ·*ise* verbs.

Most ·*ise* verbs are transitive, but we also find intransitives such as *deputise, philosophise, theorise*. With adjective bases the meaning is typically "make ~": *equalise, italicise, legalise, liquidise, urbanise*. Often, however, there are more specialised meanings, as in *penalise, rationalise, visualise*. With noun bases, there is no single generalised meaning: compare *anthologise, burglarise, computerise, hospitalise, idolise, itemise, pasteurise, scrutinise, standardise, terrorise*, etc. Noun bases drop final ·*y*, as in *apologise, colonise, economise*; there are also cases where ·*ise* attaches to a bound base (or a bound form of one) and can be seen as replacing ·*ic*: *dramatise, hypnotise, systematise*. The ·*ise* suffix is in competition with other verbalising processes, and with some bases we find different formations with the same meaning (*legitimise/legitimate, syllabise/syllabify*) or with contrasting meanings (*equalise, equal, equate*).

This suffix is one of those that does not behave consistently as a Class I or Class II suffix. It is like a Class I suffix in that it regularly comes before ·*ation* (as in *marginalisation*) and causes the base-final /n/ of *solemn* to be pronounced (contrast *solemnly*, with Class II ·*ly*). but it is like a Class II suffix in that it can follow ·*er* (as in *containerise*) and is normally stress-neutral (compare ˈ*masculinise* and *mascuˈlinity*, with Class I ·*ity*).

(g) Prefixes expressing removal: *de*·, *dis*·, *un*·

These prefixes were discussed in §5.5.3, but in one of their uses they have a verbalising role, creating verbs from nouns: *degrease, disarm, unhorse*. As we have observed, it is relatively unusual for prefixes to change the primary category of the base in this way.

(h) Back-formation, conversion, and dephrasal compounding

Several types of word-formation discussed in earlier sections may have a verbalising role. Back-formation yields verbs from nouns (e.g. compound *baby-sit*, neo-classical *televise*, simple *burgle*) and to a lesser extent from adjectives (compounds like *gobsmack* and occasionally simple bases like *laze* from *lazy*). Conversion gives verbs from nouns (recent examples being *bus, leverage, handbag*) and from adjectives (e.g. *humble* – convincing recent examples are hard to find). Dephrasal compounding is seen in such examples as *fast-track* and *soft-soap*.

5.10 Numerals

We use the term **numeral** for linguistic expressions and **number** for meanings. For example, *five* is a numeral expressing the number "5" – and *fifteen hundred* and *one thousand five hundred* are different numerals expressing the same number, "1,500".

Numerals cut across the division between syntax and morphology: cardinal numerals expressing numbers below 100 are single words, while those expressing higher numbers are syntactically composite. The syntactic structure of the latter is to a significant extent distinct from that of other phrases, and we accordingly treat them in this chapter together with the single-word forms. We also include in this section a brief account of fractions and dates, which are also syntactically composite but closely related to numerals.

5.10.1 Cardinal numerals

The single word numerals

Numerals expressing numbers below 100 are morphologically of four types: simple bases, derivatives in ·*teen*, derivatives in ·*ty*, and compounds:

[63]	SIMPLE	DERIVATIVE		COMPOUND
	1 *one*			21 *twenty-one*
	2 *two*		20 <u>*twenty*</u>	22 *twenty-two*
	3 *three*	13 <u>*thirteen*</u>	30 <u>*thirty*</u>	23 *twenty-three*
	4 *four*	14 *fourteen*	40 <u>*forty*</u>	24 *twenty-four*
	5 *five*	15 <u>*fifteen*</u>	50 <u>*fifty*</u>	25 *twenty-five*
	6 *six*	16 *sixteen*	60 *sixty*	26 *twenty-six*
	7 *seven*	17 *seventeen*	70 *seventy*	27 *twenty-seven*
	8 *eight*	18 <u>*eighteen*</u>	80 <u>*eighty*</u>	28 *twenty-eight*
	9 *nine*	19 *nineteen*	90 *ninety*	29 *twenty-nine*
	10 *ten*			
	11 *eleven*			
	12 *twelve*			

The suffix ·*teen* indicates the addition of ten to the number expressed in the base, while ·*ty* indicates its multiplication by ten.[54] The compound forms consist of a ·*ty* derivative followed by a simple base in the range 1–9, with the meaning of addition; those in [63] are representative of the eight sets of such forms.[55]

The underlined forms in [63] exhibit minor irregularities:

[64] i 13, 30: /θɜːʳ/, *thir*·, as a variant of /θriː/, *three*.
ii 15, 50: devoicing of /v/ to /f/, matched in the spelling; shortening of /aɪ/ to /ɪ/, reflected in the spelling by loss of base-final *e*.
iii 18, 80: reduction from double to single /t/, *t*.
iv 20: /twen/, *twen*·, as variant of /tuː/, *two*.
v 40: *forty* lacks the *u* of *four*.

Historically, *eleven* and *twelve* are complex forms too, but although this is reflected in the partial similarity between them and in the *tw* of *twelve* shared with *twenty* and (in writing) *two*, the present-day forms cannot usefully be analysed into base + suffix and

[54] Words in ·*teen* – like many other words used attributively – have variable stress: compare *He had* '*fourteen* '*books* / *four*'*teen clari*'*nets* and *We need four*'*teen.* The stress falls on the base if the next word in the phonological phrase is stressed near the beginning, otherwise generally on the suffix. The suffixes /tiː/ and /tiːn/ are phonetically quite similar, especially in attributive position, and it is not uncommon for speakers to take special measures (such as exaggerated enunciation of the /n/ of /tiːn/) to guard against misperception. The suffix ·*teen* has given rise, by conversion, to a noun *teen*, covering numbers in the range of 13 to 19; it applies primarily to ages, as in *a boy in his teens, a teenager* – but cf. also *temperatures in the teens.*

[55] The second base can also be *something*, as in *thirty-something*, for ages in the range 31–39. Such forms can convert to nouns: *thirty-somethings*, "people in their thirties".

are better treated as simple bases. As evident from [63], therefore, the words are not as regular and systematic as the representations in figures.

The syntactically composite numerals

The numerals expressing numbers above 99 have a syntactic structure consisting of a head obligatorily preceded by a **multiplier** and optionally followed by an **addition**:

[65]		MULTIPLIER	HEAD	ADDITION	
	i	*five*	*hundred*	*and three*	503
	ii	*five hundred*	*thousand*	*and ninety-seven*	500,097
	iii	*two hundred and three*	*thousand*	*six hundred and ten*	203,610
	iv	*four thousand five hundred*	*million*	*seven hundred thousand*	4,500,700,000

The meaning of the dependent functions is as indicated by the labels; [i] thus comes out as "$(5 \times 10^2) + 3$", [ii] as "$(500 \times 10^3) + 97$", and so on. The multiplier position is itself filled by a numeral, a single word, as in [i], or a syntactically composite one, as in [ii–iv]. The addition position is filled by what we will call an 'additional numeral': this consists of either *and* followed by a single-word numeral, as in [i–ii], or just another syntactically composite numeral, as in [ii–iii]. The fact that one numeral can occur within the structure of another means that the construction is recursive: just as there is no largest number, so there is no limit to how many layers of embedding there can be of one numeral within another.

The power-of-ten words

The head position is filled by a word with a meaning involving a power of 10:

[66] *hundred* ("10^2"), *thousand* ("10^3"), *million* ("10^6"), *billion* ("10^{12}" or "10^9"), *trillion* ("10^{18}" or "10^{12}"), *quadrillion* . . .

Outside the numeral system these words appear with the plural inflection, usually with a following *of* phrase: *hundreds of dollars, thousands of people* (see Ch. 5, §3.3). In numerals, however, they are always uninflected: *five hundred and three*, not **five hundreds and three*. The forms *billion, trillion*, etc., can be morphologically analysed into a prefix + the bound base ·*illion*. The meaning of ·*illion* can be given as "$1{,}000 \times 1{,}000$"; the prefix indicates a power, and the ambiguity is a matter of whether it applies to "$1{,}000 \times 1{,}000$" itself or just to one of the 1000's. *Billion*, with *b*· a variant of *bi*·, "two", can thus mean "$(1{,}000 \times 1{,}000)^2$", i.e. "a million million, 10^{12}", or "$1{,}000 \times 1{,}000^2$", i.e. "a thousand million, 10^9". In AmE it has the latter meaning, and in BrE this meaning is now the predominant one, with the older "million million" meaning somewhat outdated. Etymologically, ·*illion* is a base extracted from *million*, and this is reflected in the fact that *million* itself is best regarded as morphologically simple, the variant of ·*illion* that occurs when there is no prefix: an analysis as *m·illion* would leave us with a prefix that didn't occur elsewhere and was semantically unmotivated.

Restrictions on the embedded numerals

The embedding of one numeral within another is subject to the following restrictions:

[67] i The head word in a subordinate numeral must be lower than that in the matrix, except that, with high numbers, the head word in the multiplier may be the same as that in the matrix.

ii When the head word is *hundred* the multiplier cannot be *ten* or a ·*ty* derivative.

Restriction [i] excludes [a] in favour of [b] in the following examples, where the head word of the matrix numeral is underlined:

[68] i a. **two thousand hundred and ten* — b. *two hundred thousand and ten*
ii a. **six hundred hundred and one* — b. *sixty thousand and one*
iii a. **one hundred two thousand and six* — b. *two thousand one hundred and six*
iv a. **two hundred one hundred and one* — b. *three hundred and one*

The exception allowed for is illustrated in forms like *two billion billion* – in contrast to **two hundred hundred* or **two thousand thousand*.[56] Restriction [67ii] excludes forms like [69ia/iia], but otherwise the system allows for different ways of expressing the numbers in the range 1,000–9,999:

[69] i a. **ten hundred* — b. *one/a thousand*
ii a. **sixty hundred and fifteen* — b. *six thousand and fifteen*
iii a. *nineteen hundred and ten* — b. *one thousand nine hundred and ten*
iv a. *sixty-one hundred and forty* — b. *six thousand one hundred and forty*

A as variant of *one*, and omission of multiplier

The indefinite article *a* occurs as a variant of *one* when it is the first numeral word, but *a* is dropped if the matrix numeral is functioning as dependent in NP structure and is preceded by a determiner:

[70] i a. *one hundred and ten* — b. *a hundred and ten*
ii a. *two thousand one hundred and ten* — b. **two thousand a hundred and ten*
iii a. *the one hundred pounds I owe you* — b. *the hundred pounds I owe you*

5.10.2 **Ordinal numerals, fractions, and dates**

Ordinals are formed from cardinals. The form depends on the final base of the cardinal, so that *twenty-one*, *two hundred and one*, etc., form ordinals in the same way as *one*, giving *twenty-first*, *two hundred and first*, etc. Similarly, *forty-five*, *three thousand and sixty-five*, etc., form ordinals in the same way as *five*: *forty-fifth*, *three thousand and sixty-fifth*. The rules applying to the final base are as follows:

[71]

	BASE	CHANGE	EXAMPLES		
i	*one*	replace by *first*	*first*	*twenty-first*	*thirty-first*
ii	*two*	replace by *second*	*second*	*twenty-second*	*thirty-second*
iii	*three*	replace by *third*	*third*	*twenty-third*	*thirty-third*
iv	*five, twelve* } *eight, nine*	add /θ/, ·*th*, and modify base	{ *fifth* *eighth*	*twelfth* *ninth*	*twenty-fifth* *twenty-eighth*
v	. . . ·*ty*	add /əθ/, ·*eth* ($y \rightarrow i$)	{ *twentieth* *fiftieth*	*thirtieth* *sixtieth*	*fortieth* *seventieth*
vi	Others	add /θ/, ·*th*	*fourth*	*sixth*	*seventh*

The modification of base *five* in *fifth* is the same as in *fifteen* and *fifty*, while the devoicing of /v/ applies also to *twelve* (which doesn't enter into the other derivatives). With *eighth* and *ninth* the modification is purely a matter of spelling: double *t* is again reduced (whereas

[56] The form *a/one thousand thousand* might be used in a definition (*A million is a thousand thousand*), but hardly elsewhere (*She earns over a million* / **thousand thousand pounds a year*).

/t/ is retained in speech before /θ/), and there is irregular dropping of base-final *e* with *nine*. The replacement of *y* by *i* in the ·*ty* forms follows the general rule (§5.1.5).

Fractions

Fractions are expressed by NPs in which the numerator functions as determiner and the denominator as head:

[72]	$^1/_2$	*(a/one) half*	$^1/_3$	*a/one third*	$^2/_3$	*two thirds*
	$^3/_4$	*three quarters*	$^5/_8$	*five eighths*	$^3/_{200}$	*three two hundredths*

The head is a noun or nominal converted from an ordinal numeral: note the contrast between singular and plural forms. The determiner is realised by a cardinal numeral, except that the indefinite article can be used instead of *one*. With *half* as head the only possible numerator is "1", and the determiner is here omissible: *I ate half of it* (see Ch. 5, §12).

Dates

There are numerous ways of representing dates, as illustrated in:

[73]	i	*2 June 1980*	*2nd June 1980*	*June 2, 1980*	*June 2nd, 1980*
	ii	*2/6/80*	*2.6.80*	*2-6-80*	*2.vi.80*
	iii	*the second of June, nineteen eighty*		*June the second, nineteen eighty*	

In writing, the day and year are normally given in figures: written forms like those in [iii] are more or less restricted to legal documents. The month may be given as a word or figure, as in [i–ii] respectively. In recent times the versions of [i] with cardinal numerals have become increasingly favoured over those with ordinals. As shown in [i], the day may precede or follow the month, and the first three versions of [ii] are ambiguous between "2 June 1980" (BrE) and "February 6, 1980" (AmE). The fourth version is unambigous, with roman *vi* indicating the month – but this represents very much a minority usage in English.

The most usual way of giving dates in speech is as in [73iii], but shorter versions matching the written forms of [i–ii] are also found (e.g. /tuː dʒuːn naɪntiːn eɪti/). Forms such as *the second of June* clearly have an ordinary NP structure. *Second* functions here as fused modifier-head: compare *the second day of June*, found in legal texts.

The year, whether accompanied by day/month or not, is usually given in speech as in [73iii], but the version with a complex cardinal numeral – *nineteen hundred and eighty* – is found as a formal alternant. Note that for years in the range 1100–1999 we count in hundreds, not thousands – thus not **one thousand nine hundred and eighty* (cf. the alternation shown in [69iii] for other uses of numerals). For years in this range ending in '00', *hundred* cannot be omitted: "1900" is expressed as *nineteen hundred.* For years ending in '01'–'09', the version matching [73iii] gives the last two digits separately: /naɪntiːn oʊ wʌn/ for "1901", and so on. This pattern has not been preserved into the new millennium, however: at the time of writing, we have such forms as *two thousand and one* for "2001", but not */twenti oʊ wʌn/.

5.10.3 Words incorporating numerical elements

Many words have meanings which incorporate numbers: the numbers in such cases may be expressed by means of the ordinary English numeral bases or by elements originating from other languages, primarily but not exclusively Latin and Greek. The numerical components may be prefixes (such as *semi·* from Latin or *demi·* from French), combining forms (all the Greek elements, and such elements as *quadri·* from Latin), or other bases (free, as with all the English elements, or bound, as with Latin *sept·*, etc.). A sample of such words is given in [74], where the numerical element is underlined and classified according to its etymological source; we have also included a few incorporating quantifying rather than numerical elements.

[74]

NO.	ENGLISH	LATIN	GREEK
1	*one-sided*	*uni·lateral*	*mono·logue*
2	*two-faced*	*bi·focal, du·plex*	*di·graph, duo·poly*
3	*three-speed*	*tri·angle*	*tri·hedron*
4	*four-poster*	*quart·et, quadri·plegia, quadra·phonic, quadru·ped*	*tetra·hedron*
5	*five-star (hotel)*	*quint·et, quin·centenary, quinqu·ennium*	*penta·tonic*
6	*six-shooter*	*sext·et, sex·foil, sexi·syllabic*	*hexa·gram*
7	*seven-year (itch)*	*sept·uplet, septi·valent*	*hepta·meter*
8	*eight-hour (day)*	*octo·syllabic, oct·ennial*	*octo·pus*
9	*nine·pins*	*non·ary, nona·gon*	*ennea·hedron*
10	*ten-gallon (hat)*	*dec·ennium, decem·pedal*	*deca·pod*
20		*viges·imal*	
100	*hundred·weight*	*cent·ennial, centi·grade*	*hecto·litre, heca·tomb*
1,000		*mill·ennium*	*kilo·gram*
few		*pauc·ity*	
many	*many-sided*	*multi·faceted*	*poly·math*
all	*all-powerful*	*omni·potent*	*pan·sophy*

In the English column we have given only lexicalised words; some word-formation processes, however, are completely productive, so that other numerals can be incorporated in such nonce-words as *thirty-two-sided.* The Latin and Greek columns involve a good few variant forms; one reason for this is that the original source may be an ordinal numeral rather than a cardinal, while another concerns the presence or absence of medial vowels in neo-classical compounds (see §4.5 for discussion of this issue). The Greek and Latin numerals for 2, 3, 8, and 10 were similar, and this is reflected in the likeness or identity between the corresponding elements in [74].[57]

Words incorporating the numbers 50, 60, 70, 80, 90 are based on Latin: *quinquagen·arian, sexagen·arian, septuagen·arian, octogen·arian, nonagen·arian*, where the Latin elements are themselves derived from the numerals for 5, 6, etc. Units of measure involving numbers greater than 1,000 contain combining forms based on Greek:

[75] 10^6: *mega·byte* 10^9: *giga·watt* 10^{12}: *tera·bit* 10^{15}: *peta·joule* 10^{18}: *exa·hertz*

The Greek sources here, however, do not themselves denote large numbers: *mega·* is from *megas* "great", *giga·* from *gigas* "giant", *tera·* from *teras* "monster", while *peta·* and *exa·* are based on the above forms for 5 and 6, *penta·* and *hexa·*.[58]

[57] Derivatives with *bi·* attaching to a temporal expression such as *weekly, monthly, yearly* are ambiguous between the interpretations "every two ~" and "twice per ~". The meanings are, however, distinguished by the base in *biannual* "twice a year" and *biennial* "every two years".

[58] The opposite case is seen in such words as *millipede* and *quintessence*: the underlined elements have numerals as their etymological source, but the meanings of these words do not incorporate numbers.

Words incorporating fractions are illustrated in:

[76] i $\frac{1}{2}$: *half·time* *semi·circle* (Lat) *hemi·sphere* (Grk) *demi·god* (French)

ii $\frac{1}{10}$: *deci·bel* $\frac{1}{100}$: *centi·metre* $\frac{1}{1000}$: *milli·litre*

iii $\frac{1}{10^6}$: *micro·watt* $\frac{1}{10^9}$: *nano·gram* $\frac{1}{10^{12}}$: *pico·curie* $\frac{1}{10^{15}}$: *femto·ampere*

$\frac{1}{10^{18}}$: *atto·second*

For "$\frac{1}{2}$" we have four different elements, all distinct from the terms for integral numbers; the three non-native ones combine in the word *hemidemisemiquaver* (BrE). The elements in [ii] come from Latin; leaving aside the question of the medial vowels, the forms are the same as for the corresponding whole numbers in [74], but the standard international system for units of measure systematically uses Latin elements for units involving the fractions in [76], and Greek ones for those incorporating the corresponding non-fractions, 10, 100, and 1,000, as in [74]. In [76iii] *micro·* and *nano·* are from the Greek words meaning "small" and "dwarf" respectively – the opposites of *mega·* and *giga·* in [75]; *pico* is a Spanish word meaning "beak, little bit", while *femto* and *atto* are adapted from the Danish/Norwegian words for 15 and 18.

20

Punctuation

Geoffrey Nunberg
Ted Briscoe
Rodney Huddleston

1 Preliminaries

1.1 The domain of punctuation

The central concern of punctuation is with the use of the various **punctuation marks**, such as the full stop, comma, semicolon, colon, question mark, quotation marks, parentheses, and so on. These serve to give indications of the grammatical structure and/or meaning of stretches of written text. The punctuation marks are all **segmental** units of writing – i.e. they fully occupy a position in the linear sequence of written symbols. There are, however, various **non-segmental** features which can serve the same kind of purpose as the punctuation marks. For example, titles of literary or other works may be italicised as an alternative to being enclosed in quotation marks. And while the end of a sentence is indicated segmentally by a punctuation mark (a full stop, question mark, or exclamation mark), the beginning of a sentence is indicated non-segmentally by capitalisation of the first letter. We will therefore regard punctuation as covering the use not only of punctuation marks but also of such non-segmental features as italics, capital letters, bold face, and small capitals. Ordinary lower-case roman represents the default form, and these non-segmental features can be regarded as **modifications** of the default form.

One other important aspect of punctuation is the use of space, notably to separate one word from the next. Space between words is a segmental unit: like the punctuation marks, it occupies the whole of one position in linear sequence. For example, in this sentence a word space occupies the fourth position, the thirteenth position, and so on. We will use the term **punctuation indicator** as a general term covering punctuation marks and the other devices that fall within the domain of punctuation. The classification is thus as follows:

[1]

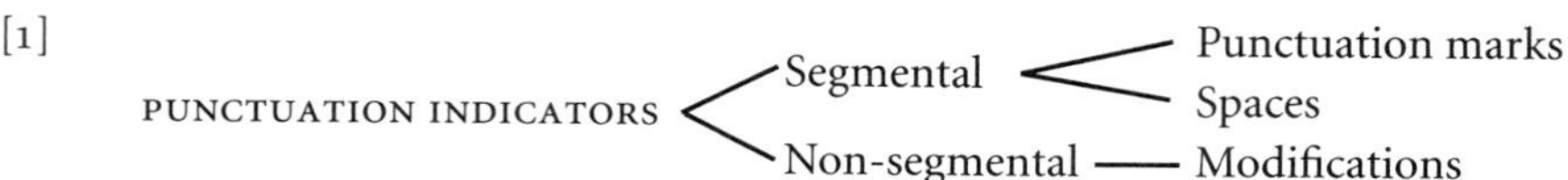

On another dimension, we need to clarify the domain of punctuation with respect to the size of the unit to which the punctuation applies. The punctuation marks mentioned above generally occur within a sentence (including its final boundary) but outside the individual words. There are two punctuation marks, however, that are normally word-internal: the apostrophe and the hyphen. Words may also contain various non-segmental marks, **diacritics**, but we do not regard these as falling within the domain of punctuation. For example, accents (which do not of course appear in native English words, but are nevertheless found in some words that are otherwise fully anglicised, such as *fiancé*)

are simply a matter of word-spelling.[1] There are also punctuation marks that can apply beyond the sentence: parentheses and quotation marks can enclose stretches of writing longer than a sentence. In addition, the division of a text into paragraphs (marked by a new line and, usually, indentation space) can also be regarded as a matter of punctuation. It is not usual, however, and nor would it be helpful, to extend the domain of punctuation to cover the lay-out of larger units (division into chapters or sections, use and format of headings, and so on). It follows that a non-segmental feature such as italics counts as a punctuation indicator when it serves to mark quotation, a title, or emphasis, but not when it is used for a heading of a certain hierarchical level in the organisational structure of a book or comparable document.

1.2 Indicators and characters

In virtually all written material the apostrophe is physically – or, as we shall say, graphically – identical with a single quotation mark. We need, therefore, to distinguish between two kinds of concept which we will call **indicators** and **characters**. The characters are the graphical shapes, or symbols, that **realise** the indicators. Apostrophe and single quotation mark are then distinct indicators that may be realised by the same character.

For reasons we will discuss in §6, we take single and double quotation marks as distinct indicators, but each of them can be realised by three different characters. Quotation marks normally occur in pairs, and there is one character that is used to open the quotation (‘ or “), another which is used to close it (’ or ”), and a third that is used in both positions in fonts (such as the standard typewriter keyboard) that do not have the separate opening and closing characters (' or "). We do not have opening and closing quotation marks as distinct indicators because the choice of character is predictable from the position: they are contextual variants of the same indicator. But the apostrophe has to be distinguished from the single quotation mark because it can never be realised by the character used to open a quotation – even when it is used at the beginning of a word, as in *rock ’n’ roll* (not **rock ‘n’ roll*).

The distinction between indicator and character is also important with respect to dashes and hyphens. We distinguish three indicators, illustrated in:

[2]	i DASH	*He’s late – he always is.*
	ii (ORDINARY) HYPHEN	*non-negotiable*
	iii LONG HYPHEN	*the doctor–patient relationship*

We also distinguish three characters: em-rule (—), en-rule (–), and hyphen-character (-). Depending in part on the resources available (the standard typewriter keyboard has only the hyphen-character), in part on the publisher’s house style, the dash indicator may be realised by any of the three characters or by a sequence of two hyphen-characters; the en-rule and the single hyphen-character are flanked by spaces, while the other two realisations may or may not be. The ordinary hyphen is realised by a hyphen-character without flanking spaces. The long hyphen is a relatively minor punctuation mark with a very restricted use; in some styles it is not used at all, the ordinary hyphen taking over

[1] The diaeresis (¨) is a borderline case. In morphologically simple words like *naïve* or *Brontë*, it is again simply a matter of spelling, but in AmE *coöperate* its function is comparable to that of the hyphen (cf. *co-operate*).

its functions (as in *the doctor-patient relationship*), but when it is recognised as a distinct indicator it is normally realised by the en-rule without flanking spaces.[2]

Consider finally the full stop and ellipsis points. The full stop is used to mark the end of a sentence or an abbreviation (as in *Col. Blimp*), but as these always have the same realisation we regard them as different uses of a single indicator. There is, however, a distinct indicator that is used to mark omission (as in *The President said, 'We will send as many troops as it takes . . . to restore order in the region'*); this indicator, which we call **ellipsis points**, is realised by a sequence of three dot characters or a single character consisting of a sequence of three dots.

In most other cases we have a simple one-to-one relation between indicator and character. The following table lists the punctuation marks we shall be concerned with, giving their realisation and commonly used alternative terms:

[3]	INDICATOR	REALISATION(S)	ALTERNATIVE TERMS
i	full stop	.	period (AmE)
ii	question mark	?	
iii	exclamation mark	!	exclamation point (AmE)
iv	comma	,	
v	semicolon	;	
vi	colon	:	
vii	dash	— – - --	
viii	parenthesis	( )	round bracket (BrE)
ix	square bracket	[ ]	bracket (AmE)[3]
x	ellipsis points	. . .	ellipsis
xi	double quotation mark	" " "	double/single quote (mark),
xii	single quotation mark	' ' '	inverted commas
xiii	apostrophe	' '	
xiv	slash	/	stroke, solidus, virgule
xv	long hyphen	–	en-dash
xvi	ordinary hyphen	-	-
xvii	asterisk	*	

1.3 The status of punctuation rules

A great deal of the written material that we read is put out by publishers (of books, newspapers, journals, etc.) with the text edited by people whose profession is precisely to prepare text for publication. To a significant extent this process involves the conscious application of codified rules, set out in manuals specific to a particular publishing house or accepted more widely as authoritative guides. Those outside the publishing trade are generally likely to be unfamiliar with at least some of the more technical rules, and in

[2] The em-rule and en-rule are so called because their length is (approximately) that of the letters *m* and *n* respectively. The em-rule and en-rule characters are often called em-dash and en-dash respectively, but from our perspective these are unfortunate terms, blurring the distinction between characters and indicators. 'Long hyphen' is not a well-established term, but since its function is manifestly much more like that of an ordinary hyphen than that of a dash we prefer this term to the more usual 'en-dash.'

[3] In BrE the term 'bracket' is commonly used as a cover term for both the indicators [3viii–ix], which are distinguished as respectively 'round' and 'square'.

the context of preparing text for potential publication many writers will defer to the advice of handbooks and the like. It is true, of course, that style guides commonly deal with points of grammatical usage too, but here they have a less influential role: a very high proportion of our use of language involves spontaneous speech, with no need or opportunity to consult such works. For this reason, we ourselves in writing this chapter on punctuation have given greater weight to the prescriptions of major style manuals than we have in the chapters on grammar. But we should also note that many of the rules of punctuation that have been mastered by competent writers are part of tacit linguistic knowledge no less than the rules of spoken language are, and as such are never mentioned in usage manuals or style guides.

Variation

In spite of the codification mentioned above, punctuation practice is by no means entirely uniform. On some matters, such as whether or not to mark abbreviations with a full stop, we find variation from one publishing house to another. More important, there is some significant regional variation, most notably with respect to the interaction between quotation marks and other punctuation marks.[4]

It is worth noting, however, that we do not find social variation between standard and non-standard such as we have in grammar: there is no punctuational counterpart of grammatically non-standard usage like *I ain't done nothing* or *Who done that?* – that is, a repertory of variants that are used in a consistent way by one social group but not by another. Moreover, the style contrast between formal and informal is of relatively limited relevance to punctuation. One might say that the multiple question marks and exclamation marks in [4] belong to informal style:

[4] i *They're coming for a week: what on earth are we going to do with them??*
ii *Thanks for inviting us – we had a wonderful time!!*

It is true that such uses of punctuation are rarely if ever found in the formal style of academic or legal writing. But we should bear in mind that there are many writers who would never use punctuation in this way: such usage is not comparable with the informal style grammar of, say, *I don't know who he's referring to*, which virtually all speakers would use in all but quite formal contexts in preference to *I don't know to whom he's referring*.

What we do find, however, is a distinction between **light** and **heavy** punctuation styles that is independent of regional and publishing house variation:[5]

[5] i *On Sundays they like to have a picnic lunch in the park if it's fine.* [light]
ii *On Sundays, they like to have a picnic lunch in the park, if it's fine.* [heavy]

This distinction has to do with optional punctuation, especially commas: a light style puts in relatively few commas (or other marks) in those places where they are optional rather than obligatory.

[4] There is also an appreciable amount of historical variation. One notable change is that capital letters are no longer used for common nouns as well as proper nouns. An example of a more specific change is that the semicolon is not now admissible in the construction illustrated in, say, Jane Austen's *His good looks and his rank had one fair claim on his attachment; since to them he must have owed a wife of very superior character to any thing deserved by his own.*

[5] Alternative terms are 'open' and 'closed' respectively.

1.4 Units of syntax and units of writing

The orthographic sentence

Syntax is traditionally defined as the study of the way words combine to form sentences, but from a syntactic point of view the delimitation of the sentence is quite problematic. A sentence may have the form of a clause or of a sequence of clauses, and while sentences with the form of a clause can generally be delimited straightforwardly, it is not so clear when successive clauses are syntactically combined into a larger unit. The central cases of sentences with the form of a sequence of clauses are those where the clauses are coordinated, with at least one of them being marked by a coordinator. The syntactic construction of coordination, however, does not have to be explicitly marked by means of a coordinator: coordination can be asyndetic (Ch. 15, §1.1). This is evident from the examples like <u>*Her family*</u>, <u>*her friends*</u>, <u>*her colleagues*</u> *had all rallied to her support*, where the underlined NPs combine to form an asyndetic NP-coordination that functions as subject of the clause. Note also that the gapping construction can occur with asyndetic coordination. Compare, then:

[6] i *Kim went to the concert, but Pat stayed at home.*
ii *Some went by bus, some by train.*
iii *Some went to the concert, some stayed at home.*

In [i] the coordination is marked by the coordinator *but*. In [ii] omission of the verb of the second clause, by gapping, serves to mark unequivocally that the clauses belong together in a larger syntactic unit. But in [iii] there is no overt marking of the coordinative relation between the clauses.

Coordination, moreover, is not the only syntactic relation that need not be marked by any formal device. The same applies with supplementation (Ch. 15, §5). Compare:

[7] i *There's another reason why we should hesitate – (namely,) the likelihood that interest rates will rise again in a few months.*
ii *There's another reason why we should hesitate – (namely,) it is likely that interest rates will rise again in a few months.*

In [i] the supplement is an NP, while in [ii] it is a main clause; in both cases *namely* is optional, so that in the version of [ii] without *namely* there is no structural marking of the relation between the two clauses.

For these reasons there will often be no syntactically marked distinction between a sentence with the form of a combination of two successive main clauses and a sequence of two sentences each of which has the form of a main clause. In writing, one function of punctuation is precisely to indicate whether successive clauses belong together or are to be treated as separate. In speech, prosody also serves to convey information about the relation between successive clauses, but it is important to emphasise that punctuation cannot be described as a means of representing the prosodic properties of utterances. When we are talking about the relation between successive main clauses, therefore, we cannot be neutral between the spoken and written medium. The term **orthographic sentence** is therefore applied to the unit that is defined by punctuation: leaving aside complications that we will take up below, an orthographic sentence is a unit of writing that begins with a capital letter and ends with a full stop, question mark, or exclamation mark. The term 'orthographic sentence' embodies no commitment as to whether or not the unit concerned is syntactically a sentence, a question which may have no determinate answer. Since this chapter is about punctuation, however, we will henceforth take it for granted that the term 'sentence' on its own is to be understood as "orthographic sentence" unless we explicitly indicate otherwise.

The orthographic word

Similar issues arise with the word. In the grammar we make a distinction between a morphologically complex word and a syntactic construction containing separate words:

[8] i *I left the watering-can in the greenhouse.* [complex word]
ii *Who lives in that green house opposite?* [syntactic construction]

In [i] *greenhouse* is a single complex word (more specifically, a compound) denoting a building made of glass used for growing plants that need warmth; in [ii] *green house* is a sequence of two words forming a nominal with the structure modifier + head and denoting a house that is green in colour. The basis for drawing this distinction is discussed in Ch. 5, §14.4, but again the criteria do not always yield clear-cut results, and even where they do the grammatical analysis will not always match up with the written form. We therefore need the concept of an **orthographic word** that is defined by punctuation: leaving aside again certain complications, an orthographic word is a minimal unit of writing that is flanked by spaces which are either immediately adjacent to it or are separated from it by punctuation marks. As with 'orthographic sentence', the term 'orthographic word' is neutral as to whether or not the unit is grammatically a single whole word, and again for the remainder of this chapter the term 'word' on its own is to be understood as "orthographic word" unless otherwise specified.

1.5 Functions and classification of punctuation indicators

Four main functions

The punctuation indicators serve a range of functions which can be grouped (leaving aside a few minor special purpose uses) into four main types.

(a) Indicating boundaries

[9] i *You will have to make a decision soon. It is not for me to try to influence you.*
ii *By all means take the book with you, but be sure to return it.*

In [i] we have a succession of two sentences, their boundaries being marked by the capital letter at the beginning and the full stop at the end. In addition, the spaces mark the boundaries between words. In [ii] the comma marks the boundary between two main clauses that are combined within a single sentence. Boundary marking can be regarded as the primary function of punctuation marks; it is not mutually exclusive with the other functions, and indeed is at least incidentally involved in virtually all uses.

(b) Indicating status

[10] i *What does Frank think about it?*
ii *The boys' behaviour was hardly likely to make her change her mind!*

The question mark in [i] serves to mark the sentence boundary, but at the same time it indicates that the sentence is a question; and the capital letter at the beginning of *Frank* indicates that this expression has the status of a proper name. In [ii] the apostrophe marks the noun as genitive, while the exclamation mark combines the functions of marking the sentence boundary and indicating that the sentence has the status of an exclamation.

(c) Indicating omission

[11] i *She goes on to say, 'But Johnson . . . was willing to accept a fee for the work.'*
ii *'F*** off!' he yelled, 'or I'll call the police.'*

The ellipsis points indicator in [i] marks the omission from the reported speech of one or more words that occupied this position in the original. In [ii] the asterisks mark the suppression of letters from the taboo word *fuck*, while the apostrophe signals the reduction and cliticisation of the word *will*.

(d) Indicating linkage

[12] i *The Management will continue to concentrate on completing the redevelopment/ acquisition programme outlined above.*
ii *I met her in the dining-car of the London–Glasgow express.*

The slash and the two types of hyphen serve to link, to relate the items on either side of them. In [i] we understand "the programme of redevelopment or acquisition"; in [ii] the ordinary hyphen joins the two noun bases into a compound noun, while the long hyphen joins the two place-names into a single modifier of the head *express* (with the interpretation "express going from London to Glasgow").

Prevention of misreading

We have noted that punctuation marks are often optional, with light and heavy styles differing with respect to how many of these optional marks are inserted. Even in what is overall a light style, however, such indicators will tend to be added if their omission might lead to an initial misreading of the sentence. Indeed, indicators may be inserted to prevent confusion of this kind even in places where they would not normally be permitted. Compare:

[13] i *Liz recognised the t-shirt he took from the bag and gasped.*
ii *Liz recognised the man who entered the room, and gasped.*
iii *Most of those who can, work at home.*

While [i] has no internal punctuation, [ii] – which has the same syntactic structure in relevant respects – has a comma which serves to make clear that it was Liz who gasped, not the man. In [iii] the comma marks the boundary between subject and verb, contrary to the general rule prohibiting punctuation in this position; what makes it justifiable here is that without it *work* is likely to be at first taken as head of the complement of *can* rather than of the matrix predicate.

Organisation of this chapter

It will be evident from the brief survey with which we began this section that a number of indicators have diverse functions. Most notably, perhaps, the full stop can mark the end of a sentence or indicate an abbreviation. As a consequence, it is not possible to draw up a satisfactory unidimensional classification of the punctuation indicators. The organisation of the rest of this chapter, therefore, represents a compromise between treating them in successive subsets and dealing with them function by function.

In §2 we describe what we call the **primary terminals**: the full stop as used to end a sentence, and the question and exclamation marks. With the latter two the function of marking status is more important than that of marking a terminal boundary, and they are not constrained to occur at the end of a sentence; nevertheless, they are mutually exclusive with the terminal full stop, and hence form a natural group with it.

A second group, dealt with in §3, consists of the comma, the semicolon, and the colon, which we refer to as **secondary boundary marks**. They are secondary in the sense that they mark boundaries within a sentence, not between sentences. Or rather, that is invariably the case with the comma and the semicolon, and predominantly the case with the colon.

We turn next, in §4, to parentheses. These occur in pairs (with distinct opening and closing characters), enclosing units which are usually smaller than a sentence, but do not have to be. In §5 we turn to the dash; in most of its uses this is a secondary boundary mark, but it has considerable affinities with the parenthesis, and hence is best dealt with at this point in the exposition.

The following section, §6, covers the related functions of quotation, citation, and naming. Quotation marks, single or double, are the main indicators for these functions, but italicisation is used too, and there are also places where there is no punctuational indication at all. Square brackets and ellipsis points occur primarily within quotations and are thus dealt with in this section. Related in some respects to quotation is capitalisation, the topic of §7.

Finally, §8 deals with those aspects of word-level punctuation not already covered. By **word-level punctuation** we mean the marking of word boundaries and the use of punctuation marks (mainly hyphens and apostrophes) within a word. Other punctuation we will refer to by contrast as **higher-level punctuation**. We treat the slash as a word-level punctuation indicator on the grounds that it is not (or at least not normally) flanked by spaces.

2 Primary terminals

For the most part, discursive written text consists of a sequence of sentences, each beginning with a capital letter and ending with a primary terminal – a full stop, a question mark, or an exclamation mark.

The full stop that marks the end of a sentence we refer to as the **terminal full stop**, as opposed to the **abbreviation full stop** (and various more specialised uses of this indicator). We suggested above that the primary function of the question and exclamation marks is to indicate status rather than boundaries, and this is reflected in the fact that they differ from the terminal full stop in being able to occur medially, internally within a sentence, and to be followed by other punctuation marks:

[1] i *She had finally decided – and who can blame her? – to go her own way.*
ii *Her son – what a scoundrel he is! – is threatening to sue her.*
iii **Southern liberals – There are a good many. – often exhibit blithe insouciance.*

Medial questions and exclamations do not normally begin with a capital letter except in the case of quotation (see §6): the expressions interpolated between the dashes in [i–ii] are thus grammatical clauses but not orthographic sentences.

Sentence terminals and clause type

In sentences with the form of a single clause, there is a significant correlation between terminals and clause type. The default relations are illustrated in:

[2]		CLAUSE TYPE	SENTENCE TERMINAL
i	*Kim has arrived.*	declarative	full stop
ii	*Let me know if you need any help.*	imperative	
iii	*Have you seen my glasses?*	interrogative	question mark
iv	*What nonsense they talk!*	exclamative	exclamation mark

The correlation, however, is very imperfect: the punctuation marks match the meaning and illocutionary force much more directly than do the syntactic clause type categories (see Ch. 10, §3, for the concept of illocutionary force and its relation to clause type).

Question mark

As the name implies, this indicates that the constituent it terminates has the status of a question.

Terminal of unembedded question

In the simplest case the question mark occurs at the end of an unembedded question, in contexts where it is in contrast with the full stop and (normally) the exclamation mark. It is the default punctuation mark following an interrogative main clause, whether closed or open. It is also used after other clause types with the punctuation itself signalling the question meaning, as rising intonation does in the corresponding spoken forms:

[3] i *Have you seen today's paper?* [closed interrogative]
ii *Why do fools fall in love?* [open interrogative]
iii *You saw him, then?* [declarative]
iv *Take it back on Saturday?* [imperative]

With imperatives (and likewise exclamatives) such cases are generally restricted to echo questions.

Examples where the sentence has the form of a sequence of main clauses are:

[4] i *It would be hard to criticise the measures, wouldn't it?*
ii *Where did you get it from and how much did it cost?*
iii *It certainly looks very good, but isn't it rather expensive?*

In [i] *wouldn't it?* is an interrogative tag; its effect is to make the whole sentence a question. Example [ii] is a coordination of two interrogatives but has just one question mark, at the end: it is punctuated as a compound question. In [iii] we have a coordination of declarative (statement) and interrogative (question): the semantic scope of the question mark is thus just the second clause, but it serves as terminal boundary mark for the whole sentence.

The question mark is often replaced by one of the other sentence terminals in questions that are used as indirect speech acts:

[5] i *Would you tell Jill that I'll be replying to her letter shortly.*
ii *Why don't you try to get this report to me by tomorrow.*
iii *Aren't they lucky to have got away with it!*
iv *Who cares what I think about it, anyway!*

Examples [i–ii], with the form of a closed and open interrogative respectively, are used as indirect directives, and may be punctuated according to the illocutionary force, not the grammatical form or literal meaning. There is a considerable range of interrogative constructions used with directive force, and some accept full stop punctuation more readily than others: see Ch. 10, §9.6.1. Examples [iii–iv] have the force of exclamatory statements and again are here punctuated accordingly; there is alternation with a question mark in the open type [iv] but not normally in the closed type [iii].

Embedded questions

When a question is embedded, the punctuation depends on the grammatical form: it normally takes a question mark if it has main clause form, but not if it has the form of a subordinate content clause. Compare:

[6]		MAIN CLAUSE SYNTAX	SUBORDINATE CLAUSE SYNTAX
	i	a. *She asked, 'Where is Kim going?'*	b. *She asked where Kim was going.*
	ii	a. *Again the question arises: why were we not consulted?*	b. *Again the question arises as to why we were not consulted.*
	iii	a. *Her son (you remember him, don't you?) has just been arrested.*	b. [no subordinate version]

Note that where the question has main clause syntax it may or may not begin with a capital letter. Example [ia] is a case of direct reported speech (Ch. 11, §9.2); here a capital is required if the question is enclosed in quotation marks, but otherwise lower case is permissible, especially with relatively short questions (*I'm afraid he always asks himself, what's in it for me?*). In [iia] the question is cited or identified, and here capitalisation is optional.[6] In [iiia] the question is parenthesised (and for this type there is no matching subordinate construction); here capitalisation, while not impossible, is relatively unlikely.

Parentheticals

Sentences containing interrogative parentheticals, or parentheticals in construction with an interrogative main clause, are illustrated in:

[7] i *There is nothing in the structure of English that prohibits us from referring to a woman as John Smith or, shall we say, George Eliot.*
ii *Will he tell them?, she asked.*
iii *Will he tell them, I wonder?*
iv *Will he tell them, do you think?*

Parentheticals like *shall we say, dare I say, would you believe* have interrogative main clause syntax but no inquiry force, and generally have no question mark, as in [i]. Examples [ii–iii] look alike syntactically, but they are understood, and hence punctuated, differently. In [ii] the whole sentence is a statement, reporting her asking a question. But *I wonder* in [iii] indicates that the sentence is posing a question, so the question mark

[6] In *And guess who they were sure inflicted them?* the question mark has scope over the matrix imperative clause, not the embedded interrogative clause, signalling that the whole sentence has the (indirect) force of a question, to which I'm asking you to guess the answer. An exclamation mark, however, is the more usual terminal for the *guess* + subordinate interrogative construction. Where the question consists simply of an interrogative phrase, the distinction between main and subordinate clause syntax is lost, and here a question mark may or may not be used: *She wondered why* or *She wondered, why?* (or *She wondered, Why?*).

goes at the end. In [iv] we have a sequence of two interrogatives, but they express a single question, and permit only a single question mark, at the end (see Ch. 10, §5.4).

Use of question mark to indicate doubt

[8] i *Michaelangelo Merisi (b. 1571?, Milan? – d. July 18, 1610, Port'Ercole, Tuscany)*
ii *He lives with an ophthalmologist (?) in Kensington.*

Example [i] illustrates the use of the question mark to indicate uncertainty about attributed dates and places; in some cases it is placed before the item in doubt (*b. ?1571*). In [ii] the question mark is enclosed in parentheses; this belongs to relatively informal style but again indicates uncertainty about the correctness of the item concerned (I may have doubts as to whether the person is in fact an ophthalmologist – or perhaps I'm unsure about the spelling).

Exclamation mark

Terminal of unembedded exclamation

[9] i *To hell with you!* *Up the Socceroos!* *Blast!* *Fire!* *Talk about arrogance!* *If only we had listened to her!* *That it should have come to this!* *Quick!*
ii *What a mess they made of it!* *How kind you are!*
iii *Look out!* *Get some water!*
iv *That's cheating!* *They had come without any money!*
v *Isn't it fantastic!* *What does it matter, anyway!*

Exclamation marks are often used with sentences whose form departs from the major main clause constructions: a variety of patterns of this kind are illustrated in [i]. Replacement of the exclamation mark by a full stop in such cases would be impossible or else would completely change the interpretation (several of them, for example, could occur with a full stop when standing as an elliptical answer to a question). The remaining examples have ordinary main clause form. Those in [ii] are syntactically exclamative, and here the exclamation mark is strongly preferred over a full stop. The examples in [iii] are imperative; as noted above, the full stop is the default terminal for imperatives, but the exclamation mark is also commonly used. It may serve to impart a sense of urgency, and/or to give the directive the force of a command or an entreaty, as opposed, say, to a request. With declaratives, as in [iv], the exclamation mark indicates that the content is regarded as remarkable or sensational, something that merits or requires special noting. Exclamation marks are also found with interrogatives, as in [v], when the illocutionary force is that of a statement: see the discussion of [5iii–iv] above.

Embedding

Like questions, exclamations can be embedded within a matrix sentence, and may also be subclausal:

[10] i *He replied, 'I've never been so insulted in my life!'*
ii *At first things went smoothly, but soon, alas!, the casualties began and we had to devise a new strategy.*

Exclamative clauses do not show the clear difference between main clause and subordinate clause internal syntax that we illustrated for interrogatives in [6]. Nevertheless, we still find that clauses identifiable as subordinate exclamatives do not take exclamation marks. Compare:

[11] i *She remembered what a struggle it had been in those days to make ends meet.*
ii *It's amazing what a difference a good night's sleep can make!*

In [i] the exclamative clause is complement of *remembered*, with the matrix clause a declarative terminated by a full stop. It [ii] the exclamative clause is embedded as extraposed subject; the matrix is declarative but takes an exclamation mark as terminal because of the exclamatory meaning associated with its predicate *is amazing*.

Multiple terminals

It is possible for question and exclamation marks to be iterated for emphatic effect, and for an exclamation mark to follow a question mark:

[12] i *Who, I wonder, is going to volunteer for the late shift??*
ii *Guess what – we've sold the house at last!!*
iii *Did you see his face when she mentioned the doctor?!*

This again reflects the fact that the main function of these two indicators is to indicate status: there is no comparable use of the terminal full stop, a pure boundary marker. In [iii] the question mark signals that the sentence is a question, while the exclamation mark conveys that there was something remarkable about the situation – presumably his face showed strong emotion of one kind or another. Examples like those in [12] tend to be disfavoured by the manuals; as observed in §1.3, they are restricted to informal style.

Punctuation of phrases and coordinate main clauses as separate sentences

[13] i *He had broken the vase. Deliberately.*
ii *The house needs painting. And there's still the roof to be fixed.*

The default punctuation here would be as a single sentence. In [i], where *deliberately* is interpreted as an adjunct relating to the verb *broken*, the division into two sentences has an information-packaging function: it presents the whole as a sequence of two messages, which serves to give extra importance to the contribution of the adjunct. In speech the same effect is achieved by setting the adjunct apart prosodically. The division of a clause-coordination, as in [ii], may be motivated by the same consideration, but it may also serve simply to keep the sentences shorter than they would otherwise be, and for this reason is particularly common in journalism.

3 The secondary boundary marks: comma, semicolon, and colon

While the terminal full stop marks the boundaries between successive sentences, the comma, semicolon, and colon normally mark boundaries within a sentence, and hence can be regarded as secondary boundary marks. They indicate a weaker boundary than the full stop, and we will see in §3.1 that there are grounds for regarding the comma as weaker than the colon or semicolon, so that these indicators may be arranged into a hierarchy of relative strength as follows:

[1] full stop > {colon / semicolon} > comma

In the present section we confine our attention to sentences containing neither parentheses nor dashes. The dash is also a secondary boundary mark in its main use, but we defer consideration of it until §5, after the discussion of parentheses.

Exception: colon marking a non-final sentence

One exception to the distributional distinction between the primary and secondary boundary marks is that the colon is sometimes followed by a capital letter:

[2] i *Libraries have not tried hard to compete in this domain: Their collections are still dominated by books.*
ii *A number of questions remain to be answered: Who will take responsibility for converting the records to digital form? How are the old records to be stored? Who will have access to the digital files?*

It seems best in such cases to take the colon as marking the boundary of a sentence, so that [i] will consist of a sequence of two sentences, and [ii] as a sequence of four. Clearly, however, a sentence with a colon as terminal could never be the last sentence in a text.

3.1 Some formal preliminaries

Asymmetry between marking of left and right boundaries

There is an important asymmetry in the marking of boundaries:

[3] i Constituents whose right boundary is marked very often have no marking of their left boundary.
ii Constituents whose left boundary is marked almost always have their right boundary marked – by a mark at least as strong as the one on the left.

Compare the following examples, where the relevant constituents are underlined:

[4] i a. *There'll be no problem because <u>anyone can take part</u>, provided they're over eighteen.*
b. *She suggested that <u>the most important factor had been overlooked</u>: the cost.*
c. *He has written books <u>on Babe Ruth</u>; on Tinker, the shortstop, Evans, the second baseman, and Chance; and on Hank Aaron.*
d. **Jill was <u>in fact</u>, keeping her options open.*
ii a. **Anyone can take part, <u>provided they're over eighteen</u> so there'll be no problem.*
b. **He told the press his reason: <u>he did not want have to renegotiate his contract</u>, but he did not give any explanation to the team owners.*
c. **He has written books on Babe Ruth; on Tinker, the shortstop, Evans, the second baseman, and Chance; <u>and on Hank Aaron</u>, and they've all sold well.*
d. *Kim, Pat, <u>and Alex</u> had done most of the organising.*

Examples [ia–c] have constituents with respectively a comma, colon, and semicolon at the right boundary, but no mark at the left – and they are completely well-formed. There are certainly some cases (discussed in §3.2.5) where a comma at the right boundary requires a mark at the left too, as evident from [id]; but they do not represent the general pattern. In [iia–c] we have constituents with a comma, colon, and semicolon on the left and no mark, or a weaker one, on the right, and they are strongly deviant. The only systematic exception involves the comma, and is virtually restricted to coordination, as in [iid].[7]

The strength hierarchy

It is constraint [3ii] that justifies the hierarchy of strength given in [1] above. In particular, it provides evidence that the comma is weaker than the colon and semicolon. A constituent with a colon or semicolon on the left cannot have a comma on the right, as illustrated in [4iib–c]. It is not possible to establish any categorical difference between colon and semicolon in this respect, and it is for this reason that we have placed them at the same position in [1]. Compare, for example:

[5] i *He told the press his reason: he did not want to have to renegotiate his contract; but he did not give any explanation to the team owners.*
ii *With a book as complex and anarchic as this, such reductionism is misleading. You could as easily say it was about the failure of Sixties' radicalism; the decline of the dollar; the hegemony of television culture: it is all these, and more.*

In [i] we have a colon on the left and a semicolon on the right. The structure of the whole sentence, at the top level, is '*X; but Y*': the semicolon marks the terminal boundary of all that precedes it, and hence can be said to have scope over the colon, which is included within the *X*. In [ii] we have the converse situation. The underlined NP has a semicolon on the left and a colon on the right. At the top level, the sentence has the form '*X: Y*', for the part following the colon provides an elaboration on the whole of what proceeds, not just the underlined NP. This time, then, the colon has scope over the semicolon, which is included within the *X*. It is much more usual for a semicolon to have scope over a preceding colon than vice versa, but neither relation is formally excluded, and we cannot therefore establish any strict hierarchical ordering between these two punctuation marks.

The single level constraint on the colon and semicolon

Two colons or semicolons may not occur at different levels within a single construction (leaving aside cases where one is located within a parenthesised element). Compare:

[6] i *I wouldn't recommend it, but he can certainly take part, provided he's eighteen.*
ii **A new policy has been instituted: the evaluation will be made by groups that will have only one responsibility: to prepare the year-end reports.*
iii **All students had to take a language; Sue took French; she already spoke it well.*

In [i] the first comma separates the two main clauses linked syntactically by *but*; the second comma then marks off an adjunct located in the second of the coordinated clauses. The second comma thus marks a boundary at a lower level than that marked by the first. This is not permitted with colons and semicolons, however, as illustrated by the unacceptability of [ii–iii]. In [ii] the second colon marks the boundary between *only one responsibility* and the supplement *to prepare the year-end reports*, which provides an elaboration of it. The first colon marks the boundary between two main clauses, and

[7] An unsystematic exception is seen in the second sentence of *It has been asked: what are the predominant characteristics of Scottish cookery? The answer: simplicity, good sense and an instinct for dietetic values, and what more could one ask?* Such examples are rare, and can be regarded as punctuationally ill-formed. This one can be remedied by replacing the comma after 'values' with a full stop.

since *only one responsibility* is a constituent of one of them, the second colon is at a lower level than the first. The same applies with the semicolons in [iii], though perhaps not so obviously. The second clause, *Sue took French*, provides an elaboration on the first: we infer that Sue is one of the students, and the sentence moves from a statement of a general requirement applying to all students to a particular statement concerning one student's satisfaction of the requirement. The third clause then provides an elaboration of the second: a natural interpretation is that Sue chose to take French because she already spoke it well. There is then no direct relation between the third clause and the first: the third is a supplement to the second, and the second is a supplement to the first. This means that the second semicolon is at a lower level than the first, as in [ii], and hence violates the single level constraint.[8]

Further constraints on the colon

The colon is subject to two further constraints. Firstly, unlike the comma and the semicolon, it is not used to separate elements in a coordinative relation, but is restricted to constructions containing just two terms. Compare:

[7] i *Many welcomed the proposal, some were indifferent, a few strongly opposed it.*
ii *Many welcomed the proposal; some were indifferent; a few strongly opposed it.*
iii **Many welcomed the proposal: some were indifferent: a few strongly opposed it.*

Combined with the constraint illustrated in [6], this means that whenever a sentence contains two colons they will belong in separate constituents, as in:

[8] *The press secretary gave them the rules: they were not allowed to speak to the committee directly; all other members were forbidden to discuss what the committee had decided: a hiring freeze would take place.*

Here the topmost constituent division is the one marked by the semicolon, and the colons thus occur in distinct constituents of the sentence. Neither has scope over the other.

Secondly, a constituent whose left boundary is marked by a colon cannot be followed by further material in the same clause:

[9] **Smith has written books on the Risorgimento, which was an exciting period; on the topic of this conference: <u>the Neapolitan Revolution of 1799</u>; and on the 'Italietta' period of the late nineteenth century.*

Here the colon marks a boundary within a non-final coordinate that is subclausal: only a comma (or a dash) would be admissible in this context.

3.2 Uses of the secondary boundary marks

We observed in §1 that the syntactic relations of coordination and supplementation need not be formally marked, so that with a sequence of main clauses there may be

[8] Examples are occasionally found which violate this constraint: *Several of the demonstrators and the bishops recognised one another; some had been seminary students together; others had worked together as priests.* The sense requires that we take the second and third clauses together in a coordinative relation, with the combination as a whole providing an elaboration of the first clause. Such examples are not common or systematic enough to invalidate the proposed constraint, and again, therefore, we would regard them as punctuationally ill-formed.

indeterminacy as to whether or not they are syntactically related in a coordination or supplementation construction. For this reason we will look first, in §§3.2.1–2, at these constructions in cases where they are formally marked (i.e. they are **syndetic** rather than **asyndetic**) and/or involve constituents lower in the hierarchy than main clauses (i.e. they are **subclausal**, with the understanding that this covers subordinate clauses). Then in §3.2.3 we consider asyndetic combinations of main clauses. The last two subsections, §§3.2.4–5, deal with remaining cases of subclausal boundaries, the first covering cases where there is no requirement that the left boundary be marked as well as the right, the second with what we call **delimiting** commas, where both boundaries must normally be marked.

3.2.1 Coordination, syndetic or subclausal

In coordination, punctuation is commonly used to separate one coordinate from the next. The comma is the default mark; under certain conditions, however, a semicolon (but not a colon) is used instead. We will look in turn at **bare** and **expanded** coordinates, i.e. those that respectively lack or contain a coordinator (see Ch. 15, §1.1).

Non-initial bare coordinates: left boundary mark obligatory

[10] i *The President will chair the first session, Dr Jones will chair the second, and I myself will look after the third.*
ii *The President, Dr Jones, and I myself will chair the first three sessions.*
iii *Do you call this government of the people, by the people, for the people?*
iv *They can, should, and indeed must make due restitution.*
v *It has a powerful, fuel-injected engine.*

The underlined coordinates are neither initial nor marked by a coordinator; in this context, the indicator at the left boundary is strictly obligatory. In the case of modification in the structure of nominals, as in [v], the punctuation distinguishes coordination from the stacking of modifiers (see Ch. 5, §14.2). In [v] itself, then, *engine* is modified by a coordination of adjectives, giving the meaning "engine that is both powerful and has fuel injection". In *a powerful fuel-injected engine*, by contrast, there are two layers of modification: *engine* is modified by *fuel-injected* to form the nominal *fuel-injected engine*, and this is in turn modified by *powerful*, allowing a somewhat different interpretation – "engine that is powerful by the standards applicable to fuel-injected ones".

Non-initial expanded coordinates

With coordinates introduced by a coordinator, we have no categorical rule comparable to the one given for bare coordinates. This is an area where we find variation between heavy and light punctuation, the former style including more commas in this position than the latter. The major factors that influence the choice between the presence and absence of a comma are illustrated in:

[11] i *Kim and Pat were planning a trip to France, Spain (,) and Portugal.*
ii *Their friendship for Augusta became rather hollow, and the news that Byron had left her practically all his money caused it to crumble to oblivion.*
iii *He packed up his papers and stormed out of the room.*
iv *I'll do my best, but I doubt whether I'll get very far.*

In the first place, a comma is more likely in multiple than in binary coordination. In [i], for example a comma is inadmissible before *and Pat*, but optional before *and Portugal*. The parenthesised comma here – one preceding the final coordinate in multiple coordination – is called a 'serial comma', and house styles commonly have a policy concerning the inclusion or exclusion of such commas. Secondly, punctuational marking is more likely before a long and complex coordinate than before a short and simple one. Thus, other things being equal, a comma is more likely before a clause than before a subclausal constituent: compare [ii] and [iii], and note again the inadmissibility of a comma in *Kim and Pat* in [i]. Thirdly, a comma is somewhat more likely with *but*, as in [iv], than with *and* and *or*. Punctuation may also be added to prevent misreadings, as illustrated in [13ii] of §1 (*Liz recognised the man who entered the room, and gasped*).

Use of the semi-colon in coordination

A semicolon can be used instead of a comma, typically in relatively formal style, under conditions illustrated in:

[12] i *In the 1890s Chicago had more Germans than any of Kaiser Wilhelm's cities except Berlin and Hamburg; more Swedes than any place in Sweden except for Stockholm and Göteborg; and more Norwegians than any Norwegian town outside of Christiana (now Oslo) and Bergen.*

ii *After the war, the United States produced half of the world's goods; our manufacturers had no peers; and our military, bolstered by the atomic bomb, had enemies but no equals.*

iii *His band members are Phil Palmer, guitar; Steve Ferrone, drums; Alan Clark and Greg Phillinganes, keyboards; Nathan East, bass; and Ray Cooper, percussion.*

iv *Professor Brownstein will chair the first session, and the second session will be postponed; or I will chair both sessions.*

v *He had forgotten the thing he needed most: a map; and he was soon utterly lost.*

In [i] the semicolon is motivated by the length and complexity of the coordinates. This is a rather untypical example, however, in that none of the coordinates contains a comma; usually one or more of them do, as in [ii–iv]. In such cases the punctuation helps in the perception of the hierarchical structure, with the semi-colon separating constituents higher in the tree structure than the commas. A special case is seen in [iv], where we have layering of coordination: *and* joins the first two clauses into a single unit which as a whole is coordinated to the third by means of *or*. It is *or*, then, that marks the upper layer of coordination, and which is consequently preceded by the stronger boundary indicator. In [v] the first coordinate contains not a comma but a colon. In this case a comma could not replace the semicolon (see the discussion of [4iib]), whereas it could occur as a less preferred option in [12i–iv].

3.2.2 Supplementation, syndetic and subclausal

Markers of supplementation

As noted in Ch. 15, §5, supplements may be marked by such expressions as *namely*, *that is*, *that is to say*, *viz*, *for example*, *in particular*, and so on. Supplements introduced by such items may be preceded by any of the secondary boundary markers. Examples [13i–ii] have subclausal and main clause supplements respectively:[9]

[13] i a. *The nineteenth century cases on which the Act was based were mainly sales between businessmen and organisations, that is, sales by manufacturers and suppliers.*

b. *This statement is still valid today, since 'resemblances' lead us to think in 'as if' terms; that is, in metaphorical terms.*

c. *Wittgenstein's treatment of the 'Other Minds' problem is an extended illustration of a point in philosophical logic: namely, that the meaningfulness of some of the things we say is dependent on contingent facts of nature.*

ii a. *Mature connective tissues are avascular, that is, they do not have their own blood supply.*

b. *One way of speaking about this is to say that images in a dream seem to appear simultaneously; that is, no part precedes or causes another part of the dream.*

c. *Pneumatic bearings also have a considerable application which has not been developed outside gyroscopes: for example, a patent has recently been taken out covering the use of a pneumatic bearing for a glass polishing head.*

Asyndetic subclausal supplementation

The left boundary of subclausal supplements may be marked by a comma or a colon, though the constraints outlined in §3.1 mean that the colon is admissible only if the supplement follows the clause containing the anchor:

[14] i *Bishop Terry Lloyd, the only Welshman in the college, had opposed the plan.*

ii *They went to Bill Clinton, the only man who could help them.*

iii *It was her face that frightened him most of all, the frosty smile, the brilliant unblinking eyes.*

iv *Either eat your breakfast or get dressed, one or the other.*

v *The ship steered between the buoy and the island: the only course that would avoid the rocky shoals.*

vi *Areas with a high concentration of immigrants tend also to be areas of ethnic conflict: Los Angeles, Miami, Adams-Morgan, Crown Heights.*

In [iii–v] either a comma or a colon could be used. But it is not always so: a colon would be out of order in [ii], for example. This is because the supplement provides descriptive, not identifying, information – compare *They went to the only man who could help them: Bill Clinton*, where the supplement does identify. In [vi], on the other hand, the colon could not be replaced by a comma.

3.2.3 Asyndetic combinations of main clauses

In combinations of main clauses with no coordinator or supplementation marker, there is no grammatical indication of the nature of the relation between the clauses. In some cases, notably where *and* or *but* could readily be inserted, they can be interpreted as coordinate; in others, the second provides an elaboration of the first – an explanation,

[9] The supplementation marker itself is usually followed by a delimiting comma, but examples are found with no punctuation mark on the right. It is also possible to have a comma before the marker and a colon after it, as in *Among the few arrests was one person charged with being in possession of stolen goods, to whit: 500 milk crates.*

an exemplification, a consequence, and so on. In general, the absence of any grammatical link strongly favours a stronger indicator than a comma to separate the clauses. Thus, although examples like the following occur, they would be widely regarded as infelicitous in varying degrees:

[15] i ?*The locals prefer wine to beer, the village pub resembles a city wine bar.*
ii **Your Cash Management Call Account does not incur any bank fees, however, government charges apply.*

Example [i] illustrates what prescriptivists call a 'spliced' or 'run-on' comma, with the implication that the sentence should be split into two. A special case of this is where the second clause begins with a connective adjunct such as *however, nevertheless, thus,* and the like; while [ii] is an attested example, it would generally be regarded as unacceptable.

Nevertheless, there are certainly conditions under which a comma is acceptable, and we will accordingly give in turn examples of these asyndetic main clause combinations marked by a comma, semicolon, and colon.

Comma

[16] i *It was raining heavily, so we decided to postpone the trip.*
ii *To keep a child of twelve or thirteen under the impression that nothing nasty ever happens is not merely dishonest, it is unwise.*
iii *Some players make good salaries, others play for the love of the game.*

Example [i] might be called 'quasi-syndetic': although *so* here does not belong to the syntactic category of coordinators, it serves a similar linking function, and a comma is strongly preferred over a semicolon or colon. *Yet* behaves in the same way: see Ch. 15, §2.10. Example [ii] is representative of constructions where a positive clause follows a negative, especially one where the negation combines with *only, simply, merely,* or *just.* In such cases the positive clause is often introduced by *but,* giving syndetic coordination; the asyndetic construction without *but* is also common, however, and readily allows a comma (as well as other marks: see below). In [iii] the comma is justified by the close parallelism between the clauses and their relative simplicity.[10] The comma-linked cases are thus broadly coordinative in interpretation.

Semicolon

[17] i *They came on the Mayflower; they came in groups brought over by colonial proprietors; they came as indentured servants.*
ii *The Latin, for example, was not only clear; it was even beautiful.*
iii *Some colonies started under the rule of private corporations that looked for the profits in fish, fur, and tobacco; some were begun by like-minded religious seekers.*
iv *All students had to take a language; Sue took French.*
v *The bill was withdrawn; the sponsors felt there was not sufficient support to pass it this session.*

The semicolon allows both coordinative and elaborative interpretations. Example [i] has three clauses at the same hierarchical level, putting it very clearly with the coordinative

[10] A special use of comma punctuation is seen in *Order your furniture on Monday, take it home on Tuesday.* Syntactically, this consists of a sequence of imperatives, but it is interpreted as a conditional statement, "If you order your furniture on Monday you can take it home on Tuesday" (see Ch. 10, §9.5); a semicolon would allow only the literal interpretation as a compound directive.

type. Examples [17ii–iii] are comparable to [16ii–iii], but have a semicolon instead of the comma. Again we note that here the first clause contains internal commas, so the semicolon serves to show that the boundary it marks is higher in the hierarchical structure of the sentence. These two examples can also be subsumed under the category of asyndetic coordination: the clauses could be linked by *but* and *and* respectively. In [iv–v], on the other hand, the relation is elaborative rather than coordinative, and here the semicolon could be replaced by a colon but not by a comma.

Colon

[18] i *Roosevelt was not a socialist: his solution was not to eliminate capital, but to tame and regulate it so that it could coexist harmoniously with labour.*
ii *He told us his preference: Jan would take Spanish; Betty would take French.*
iii *The rules were clear: they were not allowed to speak to the committee directly.*
iv *Brown pointed out the costs to the community on the radio last night, and McReady mentioned the political consequence in this morning's paper: the bill will cost the taxpayers more than $100,000 in the first year, and may be seen as giving the Republicans an unfair electoral advantage.*

The colon, we have seen, is not used in syndetic coordination, and in aysndetic combinations it indicates an elaborative rather than coordinative interpretation. What it elaborates on may be a whole clause, as in [i], or a smaller element, such as *his preference* in [ii] or the non-final NP *the rules* in [iii]; indeed, there may be more than one such item, as in [iv], where the clause following the colon elaborates on both *the costs* and *the political consequence.*

Like the comma and semicolon, the colon can separate a positive–negative sequence, where the first clause contains *not* + *only/simply/merely/just*:

[19] *The Romans built not only the Fort of Othona: they had a pharos, or lighthouse, on Mersea.*

This does not invalidate our statement that the colon cannot be used to separate clauses in a coordinative relation. It is, rather, that the elaboration relation makes perfect sense in this context: the second clause provides an explanation or demonstration of what is said in the first clause. Note, then, that it would be quite impossible to insert *but* after the colon.

3.2.4 Further cases of simple boundary marking at the subclausal level

Between verb and direct reported speech complement: obligatory comma or colon

[20] i *Kim asked plaintively, 'What am I going to do?'*
ii *He added: 'Some missiles missed their targets, resulting in collateral damage.'*

In this construction the reported speech is complement of the reporting verb – see §6 for the construction where the reporting verb is in a parenthetical. The direct reported speech complement (whether enclosed in quotation marks or not) is required to be preceded by a punctuation mark, usually a comma. A colon is also possible provided the reported speech is relatively long and complex. Note the contrast with indirect reported speech, where such punctuation is inadmissible: **He added, that some missiles had missed their target.*

- Before certain types of complement: optional colon

[21] i *The seminar will cover: superannuation; financial planning; personal insurance; home and investment loans.*
ii *The question to be considered next is: 'How long should artificial respiration be continued in the absence of signs of recovery?'*

The complement in [i] has the form of a list; this type is semantically comparable to appositive supplementation, with the list anchored to some such expression as *the following topics.* In [ii] the colon occurs before the complement of *be* in its specifying sense – a complement, moreover, which has the form of a main clause; this case has affinities with the reported speech construction. Constructions [20–21] are exceptional: in general, a verb may not be separated from its complement by punctuation.

- Between the main constituents of a gapped clause: optional comma

[22] i *The first film was released in October in just a few large cities and the second, in Christmas week in more than 400 theatres across the country.*
ii *Some of the immigrants went to small farms in the Midwest; others, to large Eastern cities.*

The second clauses here belong to the gapping construction (Ch. 15, §4.2), with the comma marking the place where material is missing: *was released* and *went* respectively. In short and simple cases, however, it is more usual not to mark the gap, especially if the gapped clause is itself preceded by a comma: *One of them was French, the other German.*

- Between subject and verb: comma under exceptional circumstances

[23] i **The right of the people to keep and bear arms, shall not be infringed.*
ii *What he thought it was, was not clear.*

In Present-day English there is normally a strong prohibition on punctuation separating subject and verb: examples like [i] are now completely inadmissible. The rule is relaxed, however, in certain cases. In [ii], for example, the comma prevents any confusion that might be caused by the juxtaposition of two tokens of the verb-form *was.* And in *Most of those who can, work at home* ([13iii] of §1) it prevents *work at home* being taken as complement of *can.*[11]

3.2.5 Delimiting commas

Simple examples of **delimiting commas** are seen in:

[24] i *Some, <u>however</u>, complained about the air-conditioning.*
ii *The plumber, <u>it seems</u>, had omitted to replace the washer.*
iii *Henry, <u>who hasn't even read the report</u>, insists that it was an accident.*
iv *I suggest, <u>Audrey</u>, that you drop the idea.*

[11] Some manuals nevertheless disapprove of exceptions like [23ii], suggesting that the problem should be solved by recasting the sentence. A similar issue arises with the boundary between VP and extraposed subject. Normally a comma is inadmissible (cf. **It was revealed, that our conversation had been taped*), but the rule is relaxed in examples like *It is clear to anyone who truly believes, that the power of faith is unabated even in this age,* where the comma prevents *that* from being misconstrued as introducing the complement of *believes.*

Here the commas mark both left and right boundaries of a subclausal constituent that is set apart from the main part of the sentence, usually indicating that it is in some sense less central to the message. If the left or right boundary coincides with that of a larger construction that is marked by a stronger indicator, then the comma is superseded by, absorbed into, the latter:

[25] i *Most of them liked it. However, some complained about the air-conditioning.*
ii *Things are quite difficult: unlike you, I don't get an allowance from my parents.*
iii *We've been making good progress; even so, we've still a long way to go.*
iv *The plumber had omitted to replace the washer, it seems.*
v *They want to question Henry, who hasn't even read the report: it's quite unfair.*
vi *I suggest you drop the idea, Audrey; it would be better to stay where you are.*

Examples [i–iii] show the left boundary superseded by a full stop, colon, and semicolon respectively, and [iv–vi] show the same for the right boundary.[12] In most cases, as in these examples, this arises when the delimited constituent is initial or final in the construction containing it. It is not of course possible for both boundaries to coincide with a higher one, so a delimited constituent will normally have a comma marking at least one of its boundaries.[13] Colons and semicolons do not serve this function of setting a constituent apart. They could thus not replace the right commas in [i–iii] or the left commas in [iv–vi].

Types of delimited element

The above examples illustrate the range of elements that are commonly delimited. In [25i–iii] we have an adjunct, in [iv] a parenthetical, in [v] a supplementary relative clause, in [vi] a vocative. With parentheticals and vocatives delimitating punctuation is required. Supplementary relative clauses, and similarly detached participials, are usually set off punctuationally, but (contrary to the rules given in the manuals) examples without punctuation are certainly attested.[14] Supplementary NPs interpolated within a clause also take delimiting punctuation, as seen earlier in [14i]. In addition, commas are obligatory with the peripheral elements in left and right dislocation structures (Ch. 16, §8): *My neighbour, she's just won the lottery* (left dislocation); *I don't think a lot of him, the new manager* (right).

[12] If the delimited constituent is the first element in a text, the left boundary is marked by the beginning of the text, not by a punctuation mark as such.

[13] In light punctuation style a left comma may be omitted when the boundary doesn't actually coincide with the clause boundary but is separated from it by a coordinator (*But if that's not convenient, you can drop them off tomorrow*) or short connective adjunct (*Thus although I have a lot of sympathy for them, there's really nothing I can do to help*). One also finds examples where the adjunct is separated from the beginning of the clause by a subordinator that is not itself preceded by punctuation (*It was clear that failing agreement, both parties would be locked in a legal battle for a considerable time*); this latter type of example, however, would be widely regarded as deviant and would tend to be corrected by professional copy editors.

[14] The distinction between integrated and supplementary relative clauses is not as straightforward as is often thought (see Ch. 12, §4), but published examples are attested where the relative clause is very clearly of the supplementary type and yet has no delimiting commas, as in *The temperatures in hydrogen clouds vary considerably but the mean value is about −175°C which represents the equilibrium temperature between the heat gained on collisions between clouds and the heat lost by radiation from the material of the clouds* or *I went to see Orinda who had finally returned from her weekend and answered the telephone.*

Constituents introduced by coordinators

We have seen that commas are often used to separate coordinates but, less commonly, they have a delimiting function:

[26] i *The students, and indeed the staff too, opposed all these changes.*
ii *She laughed, and laughed again.*
iii *He seemed to be both attracted to, and overawed by, the new lodger.*

The effect in [i] is to present the underlined NP as a parenthetical addition rather than an element on a par with the preceding element in terms of information packaging: we treat this too as a kind of supplementation rather than genuine coordination. In [ii] the second VP is clause-final, so it is not immediately obvious that the comma is delimiting; this becomes apparent, however, when we add a complement: *She laughed, and laughed again, at the antics of the little man.* Example [iii] belongs to the delayed right constituent construction (Ch. 15, §4.4); the commas, though optional, help show that *the new lodger* is understood as complement not only of *by* but also of *to*.

Adjuncts and complements

Because the function of delimitation is to set an element off from the central part of the message, it applies in clause structure predominantly with adjuncts rather than complements. Delimitation of a complement in its basic position is normally highly deviant: **He blamed, the accident, on his children.* With adjuncts, there is considerable variation as to when delimiting commas are used: this is the area where the contrast between the heavy and light styles of punctuation is most evident.

The main factors influencing the use of delimiting punctuation are:

[27] i length and complexity of the constituent
ii whether or not there are punctuation marks nearby
iii the linear position of the constituent
iv the semantic category of an adjunct
v the possibility of misparsing
vi prosody

Other things being equal, a short simple constituent is less likely to be marked off than a long complex one (e.g. one with the form of, or containing, a subordinate clause). The influence of nearby punctuation is seen in such a pair as:

[28] i *She was not sorry he sat by her, but in fact was flattered.*
ii *She was not sorry he sat by her but, in fact, was flattered.*

In [i] we have a comma before *but*, separating the coordinate main clauses, and the following adjunct *in fact* is not marked off. Conversely, in [ii] there is no comma before the coordinator and the adjunct is delimited. It would be possible to combine the comma of [i] with those of [ii], but to have three commas in such close proximity is likely to be perceived as noticeably heavy punctuation.

As for position, delimiting commas are most likely with adjuncts located internally within the clause. And they are more likely with elements in front position than at the end of the clause. This latter point applies, indeed, to complements too: in the relatively few cases where complements are delimited they are in front position. Compare, then:

[29] i a. *You'll have to train every day to have any chance of winning.*
b. *To have any chance of winning, you'll have to train every day.* [adjunct]
ii a. *He's not humble.*
b. *Humble, he's not.* [complement]

A delimiting comma before a final adjunct of a type that readily occurs without one may have the effect of presenting the content as a separate unit of information; it may also serve to mark the semantic scope of a negative. Compare:

[30] i *He had seen her at the supermarket, only two days earlier.*
ii *She didn't buy it, because her sister had one.*

In [i] the comma has an information-packaging function, dividing the whole message into two units of information. In [ii] the comma indicates that the negative does not have scope over the reason adjunct: we understand "Her sister having one was the reason for her not buying it" , not "Her sister having one was not the reason for her buying it".

Consider next the semantic category of the adjunct. We have noted that complements are not normally delimited and this reflects the fact that they are more tightly integrated into the main predication; similarly, within the very wide range of adjunct types, those that are related most directly to the verb and its complements are less likely to be marked off by commas than the semantically more peripheral ones. Within the (necessarily incomplete) list of categories given in [1] of Ch. 8, §1, the later ones thus tend to favour delimitation more than the earlier ones. Among the categories that most strongly favour commas are adjuncts of result, evaluative adjuncts (especially when non-initial), speech act-related adjuncts, and connectives:

[31] i *They increased the rent, so that it now took 40% of our income.*
ii *No one had noticed us leave, fortunately.*
iii *Frankly, it was an absolute disgrace.*
iv *It now looks likely, moreover, that there will be another rate increase this year.*

The use of delimiting punctuation to forestall possible misparsings is illustrated in:

[32] *Most of the clothes, my father had bought at Myers.*

The initial element here is a complement, and hence would not generally be marked off, but the comma serves to forestall an initial reading where *my father* is subject of a relative clause modifying *clothes*.

Consider finally the relevance of prosody. We have emphasised that punctuation cannot be regarded as a means of representing the prosodic properties of utterances, but there is no doubt that there is some significant degree of correlation between the use of delimiting commas and the likelihood that the constituent concerned would be set apart prosodically in speech. Compare, for example:

[33] i *That is probably true. However, we should consider some alternatives.*
ii *That is clearly unsatisfactory. Thus the original proposal still looks the best.*

In speech an initial *however* is characteristically prosodically detached from the rest, while *thus* is not, and this correlates with the fact that delimiting punctuation is very much more frequent with *however* than with *thus*.

4 Parentheses

In their primary use parentheses occur in pairs and enclose what we will call a **parenthesised element.**[15] Their function is to present that element as extraneous to a minimal interpretation of the text, as inessential material that can be omitted without affecting the well-formedness and without any serious loss of information.[16] They provide an elaboration, illustration, refinement of, or comment on, the content of the accompanying text.

Range of parenthesised elements

[1] i *Amazingly, only about 500,000 legal immigrants entered the US in the whole of the 1930s. (In those days there was little illegal immigration.)*
ii *Southern liberals (there are a good many) often exhibit blithe insouciance.*
iii *But listening to his early recordings (which have just been re-issued by Angel), one has the impression of an artist who has not yet found his voice.*
iv *If your doctor bulk bills (that is, sends the bill directly to the Government) you will not have to pay anything.*
v *It seems that (not surprisingly) she rejected his offer.*
vi *The discussion is lost in a tangle of digressions and (pseudo-) philosophical pronunciamentos.*
vii *Any file(s) checked out must be approved by the librarian.*
viii *One answer might be that only different (sequences of) pitch directions count as different tones with respect to the inventory.*

A very great range of expressions can be parenthesised. In [i] we have a sentence – and indeed it could be a sequence of sentences or a whole paragraph. In [ii] we have a main clause (it could not be punctuated as a sentence), and in [iii] a subordinate clause (a supplementary relative). The parenthesised element in [iv–v] is a phrase (VP and AdvP respectively), in [vi] a combining form, and in [vii] an inflectional suffix. Finally, [viii] shows that it need not be a grammatical constituent: *sequences* is head of the NP *sequences of pitch directions*, while *of* is the first word of the complement PP.

In all these examples except [ii], the parenthesised element is **integrable** in the sense that the parentheses could be omitted or (as in [iii–v]) replaced by commas (at the left or both left and right boundaries).[17] With the **non-integrable** type the status of the parenthesised element cannot be changed in this way. Where it is medial within the containing clause, the parentheses could only be replaced by dashes, which would make

[15] We use this term in preference to 'parenthetical' since the latter term is not tied specifically to written expressions marked off by parentheses; in this book we use it, more specifically, for expressions like *she said, it seems*, and so on, which are characteristically delimited by commas (see Ch. 10, §5.3). Besides the primary use that is our concern in this section, parentheses have a number of more specialised, secondary uses. One is to enclose numerals or letters used to order items in a list, as in *Our three chief weapons are: (a) fear; (b) surprise; and (c) ruthless efficiency.* In this use it is possible to omit the left parenthesis. A further use is to enclose dates in certain styles of bibliographic reference: *This point was first made by Jespersen (1924).*

[16] The only systematic exception to this generalisation is that when the indefinite article precedes a parenthesised element its form (as *a* or *an*) depends on the properties of the first word within the parentheses: *She made an (interminable) movie about a (supposedly endangered) owl.* The choice between *a* and *an* is made on a phonological basis (see Ch. 18, §6.4), and always on the basis of the sentence as it would sound if read aloud with the parenthesised element included.

[17] In the case of [1vi] the word-space before *philosphical* would drop with the parentheses.

hardly any change to its informational status; where it is final, a colon or semicolon could be used to separate it from what precedes. The non-integrable type characteristically has the form of a main clause; we also find sequences like that in:

[2] *The facts of her background include a beloved older brother who was institutionalised in his early twenties for 'dementia praecox' (schizophrenia, probably) and died there some ten years later.*

This consists of an NP followed by a modal adjunct, and if the order were reversed it would be integrable.

Linear position

Non-integrable parenthesised elements must follow the constituent they are associated with, their anchor. Compare [1ii], for example, with **The committee included a group of (there are still a few around) Southern liberals.* Integrable ones occupy the same position as they would if the parentheses were dropped, but there is a constraint prohibiting parenthesisation of an element at the absolute beginning of a clause. Thus we can parenthesise an element following a clause subordinator, as in [1iv], or following a coordinator – as in *but (not surprisingly) she rejected his offer* – but not right at the beginning: **(Not surprisingly) she rejected his offer.*

Combination with other punctuation marks

Punctuation within the parentheses depends mainly on the requirements of the parenthesised element itself. Thus terminal question and exclamation marks are used when it has the appropriate status. A full stop, and associated initial capital, however, is permitted only when the parenthesised element is not embedded within a sentence: compare [1i–ii]. The hyphen in *(pseudo-) philosophical* is required to be inside the parentheses because if *pseudo* were dropped the hyphen would drop too.

Punctuation outside the parentheses depends on the requirements of the containing sentence: it is the same as it would be if the parenthesised element were omitted. Any such punctuation normally follows, rather than precedes, the parentheses, as in [1iii].[18]

The single layer constraint

It is normally inadmissible to have one pair of parentheses included within another (leaving aside the secondary uses mentioned in footnote 15). Some manuals recommend that where the need for such embedding arises square brackets should be used at the lower level, but this is very much a minority usage. The usual way of solving the problem is to have parentheses at one level, dashes at the other, with no constraint on which of them occurs at the higher level:

[3] i *There was a time when the Fourth of July was an occasion for re-creating the days of the American Revolution. (I hope that it makes a comeback, despite the assaults of a misguided – and, it has to be said, self-defeating – 'multiculturalism'.)*

ii *Measures by Britain – land of la vache folle (mad cow disease) – to contain the problem have been ineffective.*

[18] Examples where the external punctuation precedes are sometimes encountered: *Talks, strongly backed by the US, (which has most to gain) have stalled again.* Such cases conflict with the rules given in the manuals and are widely regarded as unacceptable.

The insulating effect of parentheses

Parentheses set the enclosed material apart from the main text in such a way that the latter cannot depend on it for its well-formedness or interpretation. This is why such examples as the following are inadmissible:

[4] i **Kim (and Pat) have still not been informed.*
ii **She brought in a loaf of bread (and a jug of wine) and set them on the table.*
iii **Ed won at Indianapolis (and Sue came in second at Daytona) in the same car.*
iv **Languages like these (which linguists call 'agglutinating') are of great interest. Agglutinating languages are found in many parts of the world.*

In [i] the parenthesised element is included within the subject that determines the form of the verb. In [ii] it is included within the antecedent for the pronoun *them*. In [iii] it is included within the comparison expressed by *same*: Ed and Sue drove the same car. In [iv] it provides an explanation of the term 'agglutinating', which is used in the following sentence. In all these cases dropping the parenthesised element naturally maintains the anomaly, but dropping the parentheses (with commas substituted in [iv]) removes it.

5 The dash

Dashes occur either in pairs or singly, marking an ostensible break or pause in the production of the text. They are not used to separate coordinates, and hence, unlike the comma and the semicolon, they do not occur in open-ended series.

Paired dashes

[1] i *There's a difference over goals, but the end – namely freedom – is the same.*
ii *Exeter clearly enjoyed full employment – as full, that is, as was attainable in the conditions of the time – while Coventry languished in the grip of severe unemployment.*
iii *The book – and the movie – were strongly condemned by the Legion of Decency.*
iv *Immigrants do come predominantly from one sort of area – 85% of the 11.8 million legal immigrants arriving in the US between 1971 and 1990 were from the Third World; 20% of them were from Mexico – but services have not adapted to that reality.*
v *Many of Updike's descriptions of Hollywood – the place – are nicely observed.*
vi *In theory – no, no theory! – ideally, both description and dialogue should forward narrative.*

When they occur in pairs they serve to set off some constituent from the rest of the text, giving it the character of an interpolation. The interpolation typically provides an elaboration, explanation, or qualification of what precedes.

In this function dashes are in competition with delimiting commas and parentheses; either could replace them in [i–ii], while commas could in [iii]. They mark a clearly stronger break from the surrounding text than commas, and allow a larger range of constituent types to be delimited – including, for example, a main clause, or combination of main clauses, as in [iv]. The distinction between integrable and non-integrable parenthesised elements drawn in §4 thus applies to dash-interpolations too.

There are also significant differences between paired dashes and parentheses. Dashes cannot enclose part of a word or a separate whole sentence: they could not, for example, replace the parentheses in [1i/vi/vii] of §4. They would also be at best very questionable in [viii], where *sequences of* is a non-constituent that is not coordinated or otherwise paired with a comparable one. No less important is the functional difference. We noted that a parenthesised element is presented as inessential to and insulated from the accompanying text. This is often not so with dash-interpolations. In [1v] of this section, for example, *the place* is understood in a semantically restrictive sense, serving to distinguish Hollywood the place from Hollywood the industry: with parentheses it would give descriptive rather than identifying information, like a supplementary relative clause (as in *Hollywood, which is a place*). In [vi] the interpolation serves to justify the correction of *in theory* to *ideally*, and the dashes are neither omissible nor replaceable by parentheses. Example [iii] shows that dashes do not insulate the interpolation: the verb-form *were* agrees with *the book* together with the interpolation. Note, then, that all but one of the deviant examples in [4] can be corrected by replacing the parentheses with dashes. The exception is [iii], where comparison with *same* requires that the coordinates be of equal status; compare, similarly, **Kim – and Pat – are a happy couple.*

Single dashes

[2] i *We could invite one of the ladies from next door – Miss Savage, for example.*
ii *Initiative, self-reliance, maturity – these are the qualities we're looking for.*
iii *We've got to get her to change her mind; the question is – how?*
iv *You may be right – but that isn't what I came here to discuss.*
v *But we would like your permission to do – that is, to go further if need be.*
vi *'I think – ' 'I'm not interested in what you think,' he shouted.*

In many cases a single dash is like the first member of a pair of dashes with the second member being superseded by or absorbed into an indicator that marks a higher-level boundary. This is illustrated in [i], which may be compared with *One of the ladies from next door – Miss Savage, for example – could be invited.* There are other cases, however, where a single dash has a somewhat different function. Example [ii] is a special case of the left dislocation construction (Ch. 16, §8.1): the dash follows a coordination in initial position which provides the antecedent for an anaphor in the clause nucleus, typically a demonstrative, as here. A colon might be used in this construction, but a dash is the usual punctuation. In [iii] the dash matches a prosodic pause in speech, serving to highlight the final complement; this use is also found after supplementation indicators such as *namely, that is, for example,* etc. In [iv] the dash signals an abrupt change of topic, and in [v] a change in grammatical construction. Finally, in [vi] it signals simply a breaking off, an interruption with no resumption.

Relations with other indicators

A dash can follow a question or exclamation mark and a closing quotation mark or parenthesis, but otherwise it is normally mutually exclusive with other indicators – in particular, the comma:

[3] i **Some of them – Sue, for example, – wanted to lodge a formal complaint.*
ii **As he had no money – he'd spent it all at the races –, he had to walk home.*

These are both corrected by dropping the comma and retaining the dash:

[4] i *Some of them – Sue, for example – wanted to lodge a formal complaint.*
ii *As he had no money – he'd spent it all at the races – he had to walk home.*

The omission of the comma in [4i] is simply a further case of the absorption of the second of a pair of delimiting commas into an indicator that marks a higher constituent boundary: the comma-delimited constituent *for example* in [3i] is part of the larger dash-interpolation. But in [3ii] it is the comma that has wider scope, marking the top-level division between all that precedes and the main clause that follows. So in [4ii] we have the unusual phenomenon of an indicator that marks the boundary of one construction superseding the indicator that would be expected to mark the boundary of a larger construction. This relationship arises only between the dash and the comma; for another example, see [1ii]. It is, however, subject to severe constraints, as is evident from:

[5] i **Kim and Pat, who were easily the best qualified candidates – both had Ph.D.s – were the only ones shortlisted.*
ii **Only four people came to the meeting: Ed, Mr Lake – Ed's father – Sue and me.*

In [i] the second dash occurs at the end not only of the main clause interpolation but also of the relative clause supplement, and the need for a comma to mark the latter boundary is too great to permit its absorption by an indicator at a lower level. Example [ii] is even more sharply deviant. Here the second dash marks the boundary of the supplement *Ed's father* and also of the second coordinate, which in this context requires a following comma. Both examples could most easily be corrected by substituting parentheses for the dashes and adding the comma; in [ii] we could also use semicolons to separate the coordinates, with the second dash then being absorbed into the higher boundary mark: *Ed; Mr Lake – Ed's father; Sue; and me.*[19]

As far as the strength hierarchy shown in [1] of §3 is concerned, the dash can be placed on a level with the colon and the semicolon. Example [4i] shows that a dash can have scope over a comma, while the impossibility of having a comma in place of the second dash of [4ii] shows that a comma cannot have scope over a dash. Both scope relations hold between dash and colon or semicolon. In [1iv] the second dash has scope over the semicolon, while the semicolon has scope over the dash in *The results are somewhat disappointing – 20% down on last year; nevertheless, we are confident that the full year's results will match last year's.* Similar pairs can be found for dash and colon.

Like the colon, the semicolon, and parentheses, the dash cannot occur at two different hierarchical levels within a single constituent. The functional similarity between dashes and parentheses, however, means that where the need for such embedding might arise, the formal constraint can be avoided by alternating between the two different indicators, as in [3] of §4.

[19]The ban on combining a dash with a comma, illustrated in [3], is subject to some variation. The use of a comma in examples like [3ii] was in fact explicitly advocated in some earlier manuals. One exceptional case where the combination would still be widely accepted is seen in *'I would say –,' he began, but she didn't let him finish*: i.e. in reported speech, with a dash signalling interruption.

6 Quotation marks and related indicators

Functions of quotation marks

Quotation marks serve to assign a special status to the stretch of text they enclose, which may be anything from a word to a sequence of paragraphs.[20] Usually they indicate that the wording of the matter enclosed is taken from another source instead of being freely selected by the writer, as with ordinary text. The main categories of enclosed matter are as in [1], with corresponding examples given in [2]:

[1] i direct speech
ii quotation from written works
iii certain kinds of proper names, e.g. titles of articles, or radio/TV programmes
iv technical terms, or expressions used ironically or in some similar way
v expressions used metalinguistically

[2] i *'Let's not bother,' he replied.*
ii *Fowler suggested that many mistakes made in writing result 'from the attempt to avoid what are rightly or wrongly taken to be faults of grammar or style'.*
iii *'Neighbours' is Channel Nine's longest-running soap.*
iv *Their 'mansion' was in fact a very ordinary three-bedroom house in suburbia.*
v *He doesn't know how to spell 'supersede'.*

Single and double quotation marks

The above functions can all be indicated by means of either single or double quotation marks. AmE predominantly uses the double marks, while usage in BrE is divided, though British manuals tend to favour single marks. Strictly speaking, then, all examples containing quotation marks should have the % annotation, but we will simplify by omitting them, allowing this general statement to stand instead. (Our practice in this book is to differentiate between the two types, with single marks used for general purposes and double marks used for the special metalinguistic function of indicating meanings.)

When quotation marks are needed at different levels there is agreement that the two kinds of quotation marks should alternate:

[3] i *Wilson's claim that 'Shakespeare's "To be or not to be" is surely the most famous line of English literature, or any other' is disputed by French critics.*
ii *Wilson's claim that "Shakespeare's 'To be or not to be' is surely the most famous line of English literature, or any other" is disputed by French critics.*

In the rare cases where there are more than two levels the alternation continues: whichever type is used at level 1 is used again at level 3, while the other is used at level 2 and again at level 4, and so on. It is because of this pattern of alternation, and also the possibility of distinguishing them for special purposes, that we regard single and double quotes as distinct indicators, not merely different characters realising a single indicator (cf. §1.2 above).

The pairing of quotation marks

Quotation marks normally come in pairs, with one member marking the beginning, the other the end, of the quotation. One departure from this pattern is sometimes found in

[20] Very occasionally, indeed, they can enclose part of a word: *He couldn't be more un-'macho'.*

fictional writing. If a single character's speech extends over more than one paragraph, an opening quotation mark may be used at the beginning of each successive paragraph, with the closing one being reserved for the end of the final paragraph of the entire sequence. This is especially common in older (e.g. Victorian) novels, some of which have whole chapters told by a character in the 1st person, with opening quotation marks at the beginning of every paragraph. However, it is found in contemporary fiction as well.

Quotation marks in combination with other punctuation marks

When an expression is enclosed within quotation marks inside a larger matrix sentence we need to consider the distribution of punctuation marks within the quotation itself and in the matrix sentence. This is a matter on which there is a good deal of variation, firstly between AmE and BrE, and secondly, within BrE (and other non-American varieties), between different publishing houses.

Let us begin with an untypically simple example:

[4] *She replied, 'Why are you wasting my time?' and stormed out of the room.*

We will say that the question mark is **internal**, i.e. within the quotation marks, while the comma and full stop are **external**, outside the quotation marks. And what makes the example simple is that the formal location of the punctuation marks matches the meaning. The quotation is a question and hence needs a question mark; the matrix is a (non-exclamatory) statement and hence needs a full stop, while the comma separates the matrix verb from its direct speech complement. We take this to represent the default situation even though it is unusual: we need deal only with those cases which depart from this pattern. We will examine them under four headings.

(a) An internal terminal full stop cannot occur medially within the matrix

[5] i *'I don't know.' she said, and stormed out of the room.*
ii *She said, 'I don't know.' and stormed out of the room.*
iii *Nor would he consider trying to join Leslie and his men, rumoured to be close at hand and making for Scotland, 'which I thought to be absolutely impossible. I decided instead to make for France', where it was hoped that Louis would back the royalist cause.*

The inadmissibility of such examples is something on which all varieties are agreed. In [i] we need to replace the internal full stop with a comma – whose position is discussed in (d) below. Example [ii] can be corrected by simply dropping the internal full stop, while [iii] requires radical reconstruction. The rule does not exclude examples like:

[6] i *She replied, 'I don't know. Does it matter?'*
ii *Yet Craig remains confident that the pitching 'will come round sooner or later. We just have to hope everybody stays healthy.'*

As far as the orthography is concerned, each of these consists of a sequence of two sentences, separated by a full stop. The quotation marks thus enclose part of the first sentence and the whole of the second.

(b) Raising of semicolons and colons

[7] i *We ought to get going; the train leaves in half an hour.*
ii *'We ought to get going,' she said; 'the train leaves in half an hour.'*

When a sentence containing a semicolon is quoted, and divided at the boundary marked by the semicolon, the latter is positioned in the matrix after the reporting frame, with a comma taking its place in the quotation. The same applies with colons. A dash can be treated in the same way, but it is more usual to place it within the second set of quotation marks:

[8] *'We ought to get going,' she said '– the train leaves in half an hour.'*

(c) Quotations at end of matrix sentence: combinations of sentence terminals

With quotations in final position it is usual to suppress one of the sentence terminals:

[9]	i	*She added, 'It wasn't your fault.'*	[suppression of matrix full stop]
	ii	*So I asked, 'Whose fault was it?'*	
	iii	*Did he really say 'I couldn't care less'?*	[suppression of internal full stop]
	iv	%*Did he really ask, 'Whose fault was it?'?*	

If both terminals would be full stops, the matrix one is suppressed, as in [i]. If one is a full stop and the other a question mark, the full stop is suppressed, as in [ii–iii]. If both are question marks, there is variation: in [iv] both are retained, but it is probably more usual to drop one or other of them. Exclamation marks behave in the same way as question marks.

(d) Relative order of comma or full stop and closing quotation mark

AmE has a rule that when a comma or full stop is adjacent to a closing quotation mark the latter must follow, irrespective of the relative semantic scope. BrE tends to position the punctuation marks according to scope, i.e. the meaning, subject to the constraints covered in (a)–(c) above. Meaning, however, does not always provide an unequivocal criterion, so we find a certain amount of variation within BrE practice.

The following cases are straightforward and uncontroversial, with the versions given here representing uniform BrE practice:

[10] i *He'd apparently just been trying to 'help one of my patients'.*
ii *Instead of doing his homework he was watching 'Neighbours'.*
iii *I replied, 'It was all Angela's fault.'*

In [i–ii] the quotation is subclausal and does not license any internal punctuation; the full stop thus belongs semantically in the matrix and is hence located externally (contrary to AmE practice). In [iii], the quotation is a sentence and thus sanctions a full stop; from a semantic point of view the matrix also merits a terminal full stop, but this is suppressed in accordance with (c) above, so that this time BrE matches AmE practice.

Less straightforward are cases like the following:

[11] i %*'It was all Angela's fault,' I replied.*
ii %*She said, 'It was all Angela's fault', but no one believed her.*
iii %*'In that case,' she said, 'we'll do it ourselves.'*
iv %*'Some of them', she said, 'look very unsafe.'*

In [i] the quotation would have a full stop if it stood alone, but cannot have one here because of point (a): it is in medial position within the matrix. It can be argued, then, that the comma does duty for the inadmissible full stop, and hence belongs internally. In [ii] the quotation is the same, but this time it can be argued that the matrix has a stronger claim on the comma, as it were, since it is needed to separate the coordinate clauses of the matrix compound sentence. In [iii] the quotation would quite likely have a comma after the adjunct *in that case* if it stood alone, so an internal comma is justified. In [iv], we could not have a comma after the subject *some of them* if the quotation stood alone, so this time there is no scope justification for an internal comma. Some styles will thus punctuate the examples in the way shown here; others, however, will prefer a simpler rule that locates all the commas externally (and likewise those in [7ii] and [8]) on the grounds that they are separating the quotation from other elements in the structure of the matrix sentence – a rule that gives the opposite result to the AmE one.

Marking alterations to quotations: ellipsis points and square brackets

Two indicators are used to mark alterations made to quoted matter – ellipsis points indicate omissions and square brackets indicate substitutions or additions made by the quoting writer:

[12] i *He goes on to say, 'But Johnson . . . was willing to accept a fee for the work.'*
ii *She concluded: 'The first [model] fails the test of descriptive adequacy.'*
iii *According to Jones, '[N]o other language has such an elaborate tense system.'*
iv *It says that 'the first version has been superceded [sic] by a cheaper model.'*

In [i] some of the original text has been omitted after *Johnson.* In [ii] the writer adds *model* to clarify the denotation of what in the original was presumably an anaphorically reduced NP (*the first* or *the first one*). In [iii] the square brackets round *N* indicate a change from a small to a capital letter, a change made to satisfy the requirement that a quotation with the form of a main clause begin with a capital letter, except when it follows a subordinator, as in [iv]. Example [iv] illustrates the use of square brackets to enclose a comment by the writer: *sic* indicates that (contrary to appearances – in this case the misspelling) what precedes is faithful to the original text.

Alternatives to the use of quotation marks

Block quotes

In expository texts, quotations of a substantial length (more than five lines, according to some style manuals) are often presented as **block quotes**, indented and set off from the surrounding text (and often in smaller type). In this case, no quotation marks are used:

[13] *As J. P. Quincy wrote in 1876:*

> *To the free library we may hopefully look for the gradual deliverance of the people from the wiles of the rhetorician and stump orator. As the varied intelligence which books can supply shall be more and more widely assimilated, the essential elements of every political and social question may be confidently submitted to that instructed common sense upon which the founders of our government relied.*

The founders of the library movement envisioned the public library as an equal partner of the public school in achieving these goals.

Italics and other modifications

For the less central functions of quotation marks given in [1iii–v], italics are often used instead. With titles, it is common to make a distinction between various categories, with quotation marks used for articles in periodicals or chapters in books, for example, and italics for whole monographs or journals.[21] Bold face and small capitals provide alternative means of indicating technical terms, and works on language will typically employ a variety of indicators for different kinds of metalinguistic use, as we do in this book. Italics are also commonly used for foreign language expressions, or for emphasis:[22]

[14] i *I now realise that the baroque love of* trompe l'oeil *had a spiritual dimension.*
ii *Ed is a writer – a* writer! *– and Sue composes crossword puzzles for magazines.*

Absence of overt indication

Direct reported speech – in the broad sense of the term – is not always marked as such by punctuational means, especially when it is a matter of thought or interior monologue:

[15] i *Where can she be?, he wondered.*
ii *I bet she's missed the train, he thought.*

In texts consisting of dialogue, it is common practice just to give the speaker's name followed by a colon or dash.

7 Capitalisation

The use of capital letters has two main functions: to mark a left boundary and to assign special status to a unit. As a boundary marker, capitalisation normally applies to the first letter of the first word of a sentence, though in verse it occurs at the beginning of a new line. The use of capitals to mark sentence boundaries has already been dealt with, and in the present section we will confine our attention to capitalisation as a marker of status.

Kinds of special status

As status markers, capitals are prototypically used with institutionalised proper names and functionally comparable expressions. In addition, they can mark personal and relative pronouns anaphoric to the name of a deity (*God in His infinite mercy*), personification (*We can conceptualise this as a game played against Nature*), emphasis or loudness (*I said, Don't Do That!*; *He must be a Really Important Guy in your life*), or key terms in technical and legal texts (*the Tenant shall be responsible for all damage*). Capitals are also used in many initialisms – abbreviations (*TV, VIP*) or acronyms (*AIDS, TESOL*): see Ch. 19, §2.2. And there is the use of *I* for the nominative form of the 1st person singular pronoun.[23]

Grammatical categories marked by capitals

[1]	i NP	*Kim Smith, the Bishop of London, The Times*
	ii noun (or nominal)	*next <u>Monday</u>, a <u>Ford Cortina</u>, a <u>Beethoven</u> symphony*
	iii adjective	*French, Edwardian, Pinteresque, un-<u>American</u>*
	iv clause	*What's Up, Doc?; Alice Doesn't Live Here Anymore*

[21] Names may end in a question or exclamation mark (as for example in the film titles *What's up, Doc?* and *Oklahoma!*) and if such names occur in final position there will be obligatory suppression of a matrix full stop and optional suppression of a matrix question or exclamation mark – see [9]. If the name is set in italics rather than enclosed in quotation marks, a sequence of two punctuation marks is more likely to be avoided (by suppression or rephrasing).

[22] Since we are using italics for all our examples we here follow the convention of switching to roman font to mark an expression that would be in italics if the surrounding text were in roman.

[23] Historically this usage was introduced for typographical clarity rather than to mark special status.

The most common case is that of the NP – which may of course consist of just a noun, as in *Kim did it.* We also have nouns or nominals that are part of an NP that is not capitalised as a whole, as with the examples in [ii], the first two of which have head function, while *Beethoven* is here a modifier. Capitalised adjectives are derived from nouns that have capitals, as *French* from *France*, and so on. Both noun and adjective categories can apply to bases in complex words as well as to whole words: *mid-October, un-American.* Capitalised clauses are normally restricted to the titles of artistic works, which are functionally like NPs – cf. *They saw 'What's Up, Doc?' three times.*

The precise way in which capitalised expressions are marked is subject to some variation, but the above examples illustrate a very common practice. Each word in a capitalised NP or clause has a capital letter except for short transitive prepositions (such as *of, in, on*), coordinators, and, under certain conditions, the articles. The latter have a capital when part of the official title of a publication (such as *The Times*) or the official name of an institution (e.g. *The European Union*), but not in reference to holders of offices (*the Bishop of London, the Queen*) or when not part of the official title (*the New Scientist*). With an increasing number of compound proper nouns invented as product or business names, initial capitals appear in separate bases within the word even when there is no hyphenation: *PetsMart, WordPerfect.*

Semantic categories

Capitalised expressions are used to refer to or denote a great range of different kinds of entity: indeed there would seem in principle to be no limit to it. Many are personal names, where surnames, given names, and initials are capitalised (*Jane Austen, T. S. Eliot*). A personal name may be preceded by a capitalised appellation, abbreviated or not (*Dr Jones, Professor Chomsky, Ms Greer, General Noriega, Rabbi Lionel Blum*). Capitalisation is also used with the names of places (*London, Steeple Bumstead*), a geographical or topographical feature (*the Thames, the Black Forest, the Gulf Stream*), a monument or public building (*The White House, the Cenotaph*), an organisation (*the Home Office, Amnesty International, Shell, Dolland and Aitchison*), a political or economic alliance (*The European Union*), a country, nation, or region (*Great Britain, Scotland, Tyneside*), languages and peoples (*English, Chinese*), historical or cultural periods or events (*the Renaissance, the South Sea Bubble*), social or artistic movements (*Chartism, Decorated style*), days of the week, various special days, and months (*Tuesday, Christmas Day, September*), deities (*God*), honorifics (*Her Majesty*), trademarks (*Coca-Cola*), computer software (*Word, Emacs*), a kind whose name is taken from a proper name (*a Chevrolet, an Oscar, a Boeing 747*), and more. Capitalisation is commonly accompanied by italicisation or quotation marks in the titles of published and artistic works, as described in §6 above.

Common nouns denoting roles or institutions are often capitalised when used in combination with the definite article in reference to a particular individual or entity:

[2] i *Shortly afterwards, the Bishop ordered a pastoral letter to be read.*
ii *I hear the University has increased its student intake again.*

These may be contrasted with such examples as *In those dioceses, the bishop has considerable autonomy* or *I'm told the oldest university is Fez, in Morocco.* With such expressions as *the board of directors* or *the chief executive* the choice between capital and small letters tends to reflect perspective: they will be capitalised when used by members of the company, especially in official material, but commonly not when used by outsiders.

8 Word-level punctuation

8.1 Word boundaries

Word boundaries are marked by space, immediately adjacent to the word or separated from it by one or more punctuation marks. Opening quotation marks, parentheses, and square brackets are located between the space and the left boundary of the word, other punctuation marks between the right boundary of the word and the following space. The dash is exceptional among the higher-level punctuation marks in that it is immediately adjacent to both the word on its left and the one on its right or is separated by space from both (as in the style used in this book). These points are illustrated in sentence [1i], whose ten (orthographic) words are listed separately, in abstraction from the higher-level punctuation, in [1ii]:

[1] i *The vice-consul – Ed's 'companion' – hasn't (I'm told) seen* Oklahoma! *yet.*
ii *the vice-consul Ed's companion hasn't I'm told seen Oklahoma yet*

The quotation marks in [i] enclose a single word, but this is incidental and they are not part of the word itself. Similarly, the exclamation mark is part of the punctuation of a proper name which happens to contain just one word, but need not (for the distinction between proper names and proper nouns, see Ch. 5, §20.1).[24] The first word is listed in [ii] as *the* because the capital letter in [i] is a matter of sentence punctuation; the initial capitals in *Ed's, I'm,* and *Oklahoma,* however, are inherent features of these words.

8.2 Hyphens

8.2.1 Some initial distinctions

There are two hyphen indicators, an ordinary hyphen and a long hyphen, which is realised by an en-rule and of very limited distribution. As noted in §1.2, when the en-rule character is not available (as in handwriting or material written on a conventional typewriter), the functions of the long hyphen are taken over by the ordinary one.

At the first level we can distinguish three uses of the (ordinary) hyphen:

[2] i To join grammatical components in complex words: the **hard hyphen**
ii To mark a break within a word at the end of a line: the **soft hyphen**
iii To represent in direct speech either stuttering ('*When c-c-can I come?*') or exaggeratedly slow and careful pronunciation ('*Speak c-l-e-a-r-l-y!*')

The terms 'hard' and 'soft' are taken from word-processing: a hard hyphen is introduced into a document by a keystroke, while a soft one is inserted by the word-processing

[24] We noted in §4 that parentheses may enclose subparts of a word, as in *live(s)*: in such cases – where one of the parentheses has no space on either side – they do form part of the orthographic word. Likewise for the quotation marks in *un-'macho'*.

program. We will devote most of our attention to the hard hyphen. Nothing further need be said about use [iii], but a few comments should be made about [ii].

The soft hyphen

The purpose of this hyphen is to allow the amount of space between words on different lines to be relatively uniform. It occurs especially, but by no means exclusively, in typeset and right-justified text, and in these cases the division is made by the printer or the word-processing program. Normally, the division is made in a manner designed to facilitate reading, based on a mixture of morphological, phonological, and purely visual criteria. The precise rules used will depend on the publishing house style or the word processing system, but there is also significant regional variation, with AmE tending to favour breaks at syllable boundaries (e.g. *democ-racy*) and BrE those at morphological or etymological boundaries (*demo-cracy*). Regional differences are likely to diminish with the increasing internationalisation of publishing, and the increasing tendency to rely on automatic word separation provided by word processing systems, which are for the most part developed in the United States and not redesigned to take account of other countries' traditional hyphenation practices.

Divisions are not normally permitted within monosyllabic words, or within components that have (or could have) a hard hyphen at one of their boundaries (thus *school-master*, but not **schoolmas-ter*). They also tend to be disallowed if they would yield a unit spelt the same way as some unrelated word (**of-ten*, **the-rapist*, or **putt-ing*, as a form of the verb ***put***).

8.2.2 Hard and long hyphens

Among the hard hyphens we can distinguish (though not always sharply) between those that are **lexical** and those that are **syntactic**. The lexical hyphens are found in morphologically complex bases formed by processes of lexical word-formation, as described in Ch. 19. Syntactic hyphens join forms together when they occur in a specific syntactic construction, namely as attributive modifier in a nominal.

Lexical hyphens

The hyphen may join the bases of a compound (*bee-sting*) or the affix and base of a derivative (*ex-wife*).

Compounds

We have noted that the component bases of what from a morphological point of view is a compound may be written in three ways: **juxtaposed**, as in *blackboard*; **hyphenated**, as in *stage-manager*; or **separated**, as in *Nissan hut*. It is an area where we find a great deal of variation, with respect either to particular items (e.g. *startingpoint*, *starting-point*, or *starting point*) or to different compounds of the same morphological type (e.g. *dressmaking* vs *letter-writing*). There are two general tendencies to be noted. First, compounds which are long established are more likely to be written in juxtaposed format than more recent ones (compare *dishwasher* and *chip-maker*). Second, AmE tends to use hyphens somewhat less than BrE.

To a large extent, the choice between the three formats has to be specified individually in the dictionary. We illustrate in [3], however, a range of morphological types where hyphens are found in most or a high proportion of cases (the categories and concepts invoked here are explained in Ch. 19):

[3] i	compound adjective	*bone-dry, oil-rich, red-hot, snow-white*
ii	contains transitive prep	*free-for-all, sergeant-at-arms, sister-in-law*
iii	intransitive prep as 2nd base	*break-in, build-up, drop-out, phone-in, stand-off*
iv	coordinative compound	*Alsace-Lorraine, freeze-dry, murder-suicide*
v	nominal compound + ·*ed*	*one-eyed, red-faced, three-bedroomed*
vi	numerals and fractions	*twenty-one, ninety-nine, five-eighths*
vii	dephrasal compounds	*cold-shoulder* (V), *has-been* (N), *old-maidish*
viii	verb with noun as 1st base	*baby-sit, gift-wrap, hand-wash, tape-record*
ix	1st base is letter-name	*H-bomb, t-shirt, U-turn, V-sign*
x	rhyming-base compounds	*clap-trap, hoity-toity, teeny-weeny, walkie-talkie*

Type [iii], with the preposition at the end, may be contrasted with the type where it occupies first position and is generally juxtaposed: *downside, outbreak, uptake.* Words of type [v] are themselves derivatives (formed at the top level by suffixation of ·*ed*), but they contain a compound base whose components are joined by a hyphen, and the same applies with *old-maidish* in [vii]: the hyphen in such cases does not mark the top-level morphological division within the word. Hyphens are used in compound numerals expressing numbers between "21" and "99". With fractions there is variation between hyphenated forms (*two-thirds*) and separate words (*two thirds*); hyphens are not used if either the denominator or the numerator contains a hyphen (*thirteen twenty-eighths*), but otherwise hyphenation is more likely than separation when the denominator is greater than "4".

There are also particular bases which always or usually take a hyphen: *great,* as used in kinship terms, always does (*great-uncle*), while *self* and the combining form *pseudo*· usually do (*self-knowledge, pseudo-science*).

Derivatives

Suffixes are almost invariably juxtaposed, whereas there are a number of prefixes which in BrE are usually or commonly hyphenated: *non*·, *pre*·, *post*·, *pro*·, *anti*·, *ex*·, *co*·, *mid*· (but compare such semantically specialised forms as *nonentity, midnight,* etc.). It is also the usual practice, in both BrE and AmE, to insert a hyphen where there might otherwise be a danger of confusion caused by successive vowel letters or repeated sequences (*re-elect, de-emphasise, de-ice, re-release*), or to distinguish a word where the prefix is used in its productive sense from one where it is no longer analysable as a separate component (e.g. *re-form,* "form again", from *reform*; or *re-cover,* "cover again", from *recover*). Prefixes are generally hyphenated before a base beginning with a capital letter: *un-American.*

Conflicts of scope

In general a space marks a division at a higher level of constituent structure than a hyphen. The immediate constituents of *oil-rich kingdom,* for example, are *oil-rich* and *kingdom* not *oil* and *rich kingdom.* There are cases, however, that depart from this pattern:

[4] i *inter- and intrastate, pre- or post-industrial, Australian-born and -educated*
  ii *ex-army officer, non-mass market, pro-United States, mass market-style*

The coordination of prefixes, as in the first two examples of [i], is not uncommon; that of bases, as in the third, much less so – and one occasionally finds this latter type without the second hyphen. In non-coordinative examples like those in [ii] some writers resolve the conflict between punctuation and scope or constituent structure by inserting extra hyphens (e.g. *ex-army-officer*); note, however, that in *unselfconscious* (from the base *self-conscious*) the problem is solved by using juxtaposition instead of hyphenation.

Syntactic hyphens

Hyphens are also used to join into a single orthographic word sequences of two or more grammatical words functioning as attributive modifier in the structure of a nominal:

[5] i *a well-argued reply, a Bradford-based company, a hard-drinking man*
ii *a four-point plan, a fast-food outlet, the small-business sector*
iii *out-of-town shopping, the Hobart-to-Sydney classic, a creamier-than-average taste, a never-to-be-repeated offer, the what-was-it-all-for? factor*

The forms in [i] have a past participle or a gerund-participle as their final element, those in [ii] have a noun, and those in [iii] have forms which do not freely occur as attributive modifiers (see Ch. 5, §14.2). Hyphenation is not used with AdjPs (*a very old cat*) nor, generally, with past participles and gerund-participles modified by an adverb in ·*ly* (*a beautifully executed performance, rapidly diminishing returns*). With noun-headed modifiers, hyphens are used very commonly but by no means invariably – compare *an affirmative action policy, city council elections*; they are not used with proper names: *United States agents*. The hyphen explicitly indicates that the linked items form a constituent and hence may remove potential constituent structure ambiguities. Thus *small-business sector*, for example, means "sector comprising small business", while *small business sector* can mean either that or "business sector of small size".[25]

The syntactic hyphen is used with expressions in modifier function that either do not occur elsewhere in the same grammatical form (*The plan contains four points/*point*; *The company is based in Bradford/*Bradford-based*) or occur elsewhere without hyphens (*The reply was well argued*;[26] *We shop out of town*).

The long hyphen

This is used instead of an ordinary syntactic hyphen with modifiers consisting of nouns or proper names where the semantic relation is "between *X* and *Y*" or "from *X* to *Y*":

[6] *a parent–teacher meeting* *a French–English dictionary* *the 1914–18 war*

It can be used with more than two components, as in *the London–Paris–Bonn axis*. It is also found with adjectives derived from proper names: *French–German relations*. There is potentially a semantic contrast between the two hyphens – compare, for example, *the Llewelyn–Jones Company* (a partnership) and *the Llewelyn-Jones Company* (with a single compound proper name). This hyphen is also used in giving spans of page numbers, dates, or the like: *pages 23–64*; *Franz Schubert (1797–1828)*.

[25] In the last example of [5iii] the question could be enclosed in quotation marks, and in that case the hyphens could be dispensed with: *the 'what was it all for?' factor*.

[26] Prescriptive manuals attach considerable weight to this distinction as it applies to *well* + past participle; there are, however, some combinations where the hyphens are lexical, occurring in predicative as well as attributive function: *The steak was well-done*; *They look very well-heeled*.

8.3 The apostrophe

The apostrophe has three distinguishable uses:

[7]						
i	GENITIVE:	*Kim's*	*dog's*	*dogs'*	*Moses'*	**it's*
ii	REDUCTION:	*can't*	*there's*	*fo'c's'le*	*ma'am*	*o'clock*
iii	SEPARATION:	*A's*	*Ph.D.'s*	*if's*	*1960's*	

The apostrophe occurs as a case marker on the last word of genitive NPs, except those with one of the core personal pronouns as head (thus *its former shape*, not **it's former shape*; *This is yours*, not **This is your's*). There are two types of genitives: *'s* genitives (*Kim's*, *dog's*) and bare genitives, marked in writing by the apostrophe alone and homophonous in speech with the non-genitive counterpart (*dogs'*, *Moses'*); for the choice between the two types, see Ch. 18, §4.2.

The most common uses of the abbreviating apostrophe mark are for the negative inflectional forms of auxiliary verbs, as in *can't*, and the cliticisation of auxiliary verbs, as in *There's no time* (see Ch. 18, §§5.5, 6.2). *Fo'c's'le* is an alternative spelling of *forecastle*, one which matches the pronunciation. *Ma'am* is related to *madam*, but there are differences of use/meaning between the two forms. The apostrophe in *o'clock* reflects the etymology (*of the clock*), but there is no alternation with the full form in the current language. The abbreviating apostrophe does not normally appear at the left or right boundary of a word in established spellings: such forms as *'phone* or *'flu* are now clearly archaic. The form *'n'*, however, is an abbreviation of *and* used in a small number of fixed expressions, mainly *rock 'n' roll* and *fish 'n' chips*. Omission of initial *h* (*the 'ammer*) or the final *g* of the gerund-participle suffix (*huntin'*) is found in the representation of direct speech to indicate socially distinctive pronunciations.

A minor use of the apostrophe is to separate the plural suffix from the base, as in [7iii]; this occurs when the base consists of a letter (*She got three A's in philosophy*), certain kinds of abbreviation, a word used metalinguistically, or a numeral (see Ch. 18, §4.1.1).

8.4 The abbreviation full stop and minor reduction markers

The full stop as a marker of abbreviation

The full stop is commonly used to mark an abbreviation – in a broad sense of that term, covering certain kinds of contraction and acronyms. This use is subject to a great deal of variation. The omission of the abbreviation full stop is more common in BrE than in AmE, and more common in recent publications than in those of, say, the 1970s or earlier. While there are certain kinds of reduced form where a full stop is categorically excluded, it is doubtful if there are now any cases where a full stop is required in all varieties and house styles.

The alternation is illustrated in [8] for various categories of abbreviation:

[8]				
i	*Gen/Gen. Smith*	*Mr/Mr. Smith*	*fig/fig. 3*	*5 kg/kgs/kg./kgs.*
ii	*T S Eliot/T. S. Eliot*	*JFK/J. F. K.*		
iii	*eg/e.g.*	*cf/cf.*	*RSVP/R.S.V.P.*	
iv	*FBI/F.B.I.*	*pc/p.c.*		
v	*NATO/?N.A.T.O.*	*radar/*r.a.d.a.r.*		
vi	*demo/*demo.*			

The abbreviations in [i] occur in a limited range of contexts: the first two with following proper names, the last two with numerals. For example we don't (normally) write **Smith was a fine Gen(.)* or **We need one more kg(.) of sugar.* There has been a tradition in BrE of distinguishing 'abbreviations' from contractions: in the former the last part of the full word is missing, while in the latter at least the last letter of the full word is retained. One rule is then to have a full stop for the 'abbreviations' (*Gen.*) but not for the contractions (*Mr*); this rule, however, is much less widely followed than it used to be, and BrE tends to favour *Gen* as well as *Mr*, etc. With measure terms there is variation as to whether the plural is marked with ·*s*; in either case some styles specifically exclude a full stop with these terms. In [ii] we have initial letters of personal names. Where the surname follows, the version with stops (*T. S. Eliot*) is still much the more usual, whereas with full initials referring to a famous figure the stops are commonly omitted (*JFK*). Many abbreviations are based on phrases or words from foreign languages, especially Latin, as in [iii]; the version with stops is the more usual, though the other version is now by no means rare. The words in [iv–v] are formed by the process we have called 'initialism': see Ch. 19, §2.2; those in [iv] are pronounced as sequences of letters, while those in [v] are acronyms, with the letters having their usual phonological values. Full stops are becoming somewhat marginal in acronyms consisting of capital letters, and are excluded in those consisting of small letters. *Demo* in [vi] illustrates the category of back-clippings (Ch. 19, §2.3.1), and again the full stop is inadmissible.

Terminal full stop omitted after abbreviation full stop

The abbreviation full stop is part of an orthographic word and as such can be followed by higher-level punctuation marks. A terminal full stop, however, is suppressed after an abbreviation full stop to avoid a sequence of two full stops. Compare:

[9] a. *Why did she go to Washington, D.C.?* b. *She lives in Washington, D.C.*

Asterisk and dash

The asterisk or dash can be used to reduce taboo words (though such reductions are much less common than they used to be); the dash is also found in other types of reduction, for example of names:

[10] *F*** off!* *B– off!* *Count von O–*

8.5 The slash

We include the slash among the word-level indicators since it usually occurs without flanking spaces:

[11]	i	*director/secretary*	*flat/apartment*	*and/or*	*he/she*
	ii	*the June/July period*	*staff/student relations*		

In [i] it indicates an "or" relationship (an inclusive "or", in the sense of Ch. 15, §2.2.1), while in some styles it occurs as an alternant of the long hyphen, as in [ii]. A special case is *s/he*, "she or he", equivalent to the above *he/she*; the slash in effect indicates that the initial *s* is optional, and hence is here doing duty for a pair of parentheses, which are not permitted in initial position – **(s)he*. The slash is also used in a few abbreviations, such as *a/c* and *c/o*.

Further reading

It would not be feasible for us to attempt a comprehensive guide to the vast literature on English grammar; such a work would itself fill a large volume. Even giving an account of all the works we have consulted in the preparation of this grammar would go beyond reasonable size limits. But for a few of the cases we have been significantly influenced by particular works or have drawn analytical insights of major importance, and for those topics it is appropriate to explain where the reader can turn to begin further research. We stress, however, that neither these notes nor the bibliography that follows can be regarded as even a representative sample of the literature, and that we have consulted, and profited from, many more books and articles than can be mentioned here. We should also note that the inclusion of a work in this list does not imply that we adopted its position or think its claims are correct; in some cases the value of a work lies mainly in its defending an analysis with sufficient clarity to permit the reader to see how to improve on it. In those cases, just as in the cases where we have followed other authors closely, much credit for the virtues of this grammar is due to the scholars cited below (though of course we alone are responsible for the errors and failings of this book).

The English language

Amongst the thousands of books about English and its use around the world, Trudgill & Hannah (1985) presents a useful survey of differences between major regional varieties of English, and Crystal (1997) gives an account of how English has achieved the status of a global language.

Dictionaries

The most important of all reference works on the English language is the *Oxford English Dictionary* (*OED*) in its second edition – the finest and most complete dictionary ever compiled for any language. A dictionary of American English with particularly good attention to controversial matters of usage is the *American Heritage Dictionary* (4th edn, 2000). The standard dictionary of Australian English, which we have also used, is the *Macquarie Dictionary of Australian English.* At least two other dictionaries have been of considerable assistance because of their excellent collections of examples from actual corpora: the *Cambridge International Dictionary of English* edited by Paul Procter (1995) and the *Collins COBUILD English Language Dictionary* edited by John Sinclair (1987).

Terminology

Two very useful guides to the terminology of linguistics that we have made considerable use of are Peter Matthews' *Concise Oxford Dictionary of Linguistics* (Matthews 1997) and Larry Trask's *Dictionary of Grammatical Terms in Linguistics* (Trask 1993).

Grammars

One of the most complete grammars for English in the first half of the twentieth century was the seven-volume work by Otto Jespersen (1909–1949), which every serious English grammarian consults on a regular basis. A somewhat earlier work of a similar sort is Poutsma (1926–1929). The fullest and most influential grammar published in the second half of the twentieth century was that of Quirk et al. (1985), the culmination of a series of grammars published from the early 1970s onward, stemming from the research of the Survey of English Usage at University College London. The corpus-based grammar by Biber et al. (1999) employs essentially the same analytical scheme but devotes an unusual amount of space to quantitative details concerning frequency of occurrence for different constructions in different styles and registers of spoken and written English. We have found the *Collins COBUILD English Grammar* useful for its numerous lists of words sharing various grammatical properties, and we also profited from consulting Renaat Declerck's *A Comprehensive Descriptive Grammar of English* (1991a). Relatively few comprehensive studies of English syntax have been produced by transformational-generative grammarians; Stockwell, Schachter, & Partee (1973) was an early collaborative project of fairly wide scope, and McCawley (1998) is the best and most detailed transformational work published since then.

Usage manuals

As an example of a fairly authoritarian traditional usage book of the sort we discuss critically in Ch. 1, see Phythian (1979). An excellent example of modern non-authoritarian empirically-based writing on usage is *Merriam-Webster's Dictionary of Contemporary English Usage* (1994), which was an occasional source of useful examples for us. The usage notes in the *American Heritage Dictionary* (2000) are also very useful. Other usage manuals we have consulted include Burchfield (1996), which is a third edition of Fowler's classic *Modern English Usage*, and *The Right Word at the Right Time*, published by the Reader's Digest (1985).

History

We stress in Ch. 1 that we do not attempt a historical account of the English language here. Jespersen (1909–1949), on the other hand, was explicitly historical in approach, and is still of great value. The *OED* is also a vast compendium of material on the history of English grammar. For research on the history of English syntax, the four-volume survey by Visser (1963–1973) is extremely important. *The Cambridge History of the English Language* (in six volumes: Hogg (1992–2002)) provides a thorough survey of the history of the English language, probably the fullest available.

Pronunciation and spelling

We do not attempt to cover the phonetics and phonology of English in this book, except to provide the transcription scheme introduced in Ch. 1, which is needed for the material on inflection in Ch. 18. For those who wish to pursue the pronunciation of English further, Wells (1990) is now the definitive pronunciation dictionary for English, covering standard versions of both British and American English. For the reader without expertise in phonetics, Pullum & Ladusaw (1996) may be useful as a reference work on phonetic symbols and their uses. Mountford (1998) is an important recent book on English spelling, introducing the important concept of written symbol, which is invoked in Ch. 18.

Verbs

The verbal system of English has been much studied. Among the most important works influencing the treatment in Ch. 3 are Palmer (1987) and Leech (1987). Comrie (1985) provides a general survey on tense, and significant works on tense in English include Binnick (1991), Declerck (1991b), and McCoard (1978). See also the articles by Huddleston (1995a, 1995b), which argue for the analysis adopted here. On the topic of aspect, see Comrie (1976) and Tobin (1993). On modal verbs and modality generally, see Coates (1983), Palmer (1990, 2001), and Duffley's (1994) discussion of the properties of *need* and *dare*. Jacobsson (1975) is a relevant study of the English subjunctive.

Complements in clause structure

From the very large literature on complements in clause structure that influenced the development of Ch. 4, we would cite Halliday (1967–1968) as an early influential work; Matthews (1981) and Dixon (1991) as useful overviews; and for an extremely useful reference catalogue of the complementation system, Levin (1993). The topic of thematic roles is developed by a number of the papers in Wilkins (1988) and by Dowty (1991); see Palmer (1994) for a general survey of this topic. Seppänen, Granath, & Herriman (1995) is a useful source on subjects in non-canonical constructions, and likewise Seppänen & Herriman (1997) on the distinction between objects and predicative complements. Declerck (1988) is particularly valuable for its detailed account of copular clauses. Other works we have made particular use of include Wierzbicka (1982) on certain light verbs. The complex subject of the prepositional verb is one on which there has been considerable previous research; we profited especially from Bolinger (1971), Cattell (1984), and Cowie & Mackin (1993), among others.

Nouns

Works on number and countability in nouns include Reid (1991), Wickens (1992), and Allan (1980). A wide-ranging cross-linguistic study of the feature of gender is presented in Corbett (1991). Bauer (1998) presents an alternative view on the relation between compound nouns and modifier + head noun constructions.

Determinatives and determiners

This grammar presents an analysis under which determinatives function in noun phrase structure not as heads but as dependents of a particular kind, namely determiners. Payne (1993) is a discussion of some of the theoretical issues that relate to this controversial point. John Hawkins (1991) studies the use of the indefinite and definite determinatives. Roger Hawkins (1981) and Alexiadou & Wilder (1998) contain useful material on genitive ('possessive') determiners. The determinatives (like *all* and *some*) that are known as quantifiers represent an extremely important topic in semantics and logic; representative studies in the modern semantics literature (generally very difficult and technical works, it should be noted) include Barwise & Cooper (1981), Keenan & Stavi (1986), and Bach, Jelinek, Kratzer, & Partee (1995).

Noun phrases

For general studies of the structure of noun phrases (NPs) in transformational-generative terms see Jackendoff (1977) and Selkirk (1977). Partitive constructions are treated extensively in the contributions to Hoeksema (1996). Reuland & ter Meulen (1987) and Christopher Lyons (1999) are devoted to definiteness and indefiniteness of NPs. Those

NPs that function semantically as definite descriptions have been intensively studied by philosophers as well as linguists; Ostertag (1998) is an anthology devoted to the topic. Several papers on generic NPs are collected together in Carlson & Pelletier (1995). Nominalisations are the topic of Lees (1960) and Koptevskaya-Tamm (1993). Apposition is studied by Acuña-Fariña (1999).

Adjectives and adverbs

Ferris (1993) is a valuable source on the complex semantic correlates of prenominal attributive adjective position. Generative works with some information on the internal structure of adjective phrases and adverb phrases include Jackendoff (1977). The title essay in Dixon (1982) discusses the interesting question of why some languages have dramatically smaller numbers of adjectives than English does.

Prepositions and preposition phrases

Two transformational-generative works have been particularly influential and important in connection with our description of prepositions and the matter of distinguishing them from adverbs: Emonds (1972), and Jackendoff (1973). Burton-Roberts (1991) and Lee (1998) also provide discussion of the distinction between prepositions and adverbs. Hill (1968) is a useful pedagogical work listing the prepositions of English and distinguishing their many different senses and uses. Our account of word sequences like *in front of* has been much influenced by Seppänen, Bowen, & Trotta (1994). Herskovits (1986) is an interdisciplinary study of prepositional meanings.

Adjuncts

Our treatment of the highly diverse material in Ch. 8 benefits from study of many works, more than can be referenced here. Ch. 9 of Jackendoff (1991), Ch. 9 of Jackendoff (1995), and Ch. 11 of Baker (1995) are useful introductions in transformational-generative terms. More advanced theoretical works on the syntax of adjuncts include Bellert (1977), Cinque (1999), and (offering an alternative to the kind of account Cinque adopts) Ernst (2001). Among the works devoted to specific types of adjunct, we should mention Parsons (1990), especially Ch. 4 (on modifiers in general) and Ch. 11 (on temporal modifiers); Bolinger (1972) on degree modifiers; Lewis (1975) on frequency modifiers; and Traugott (1986) and Dudman (1994) on conditionals.

Negation

Klima (1964) is a classic transformational syntactic treatment of negation, and Stockwell, Schachter, & Partee (1973) is another early treatment with wide coverage. McCawley (1998, Ch. 17) is a more recent transformational analysis. The notion of direction of entailment, and much of the treatment of polarity items in Ch. 9, owes a lot to Ladusaw (1980). Horn (1989) gives a thorough account of many semantic aspects of negation that is a major source for our account of increased specificity in Ch. 9, §5.

Clause type and illocutionary force

The general issue of illocutionary force derives from the philosophy of language, specifically Austin (1962). Cole & Morgan (1975) contains a number of relevant papers, Searle's contribution on indirect speech acts being particularly important. There is a fairly rich literature on interrogatives, from which we would mention in particular the following: Bolinger (1978) on the distinction between polar ('yes/no') and alternative questions;

Hirschbühler (1985) for coverage of multi-variable questions; Duffley & Enns (1996) on infinitival interrogatives; Ohlander (1986) on subordinate interrogatives; Karttunen (1977) for the semantic classification of lexemes licensing interrogative complements; and Huddleston (1994) for a fuller treatment of the distinction between the syntactic category of interrogatives and the semantic category of questions. Useful works on imperatives include Bolinger (1977, Chs. 8–9) and Davies (1986); and for exclamatives, see Elliott (1974).

Relative constructions

McCawley (1981) provides a valuable general study of relative clauses within a transformational framework, while Sag (1997) is a recent non-transformational theoretical account. Bresnan & Grimshaw (1978) deals with fused relatives ('free relatives', in their terminology). Green (1992) discusses the relation between infinitival purpose clauses and infinitival relative clauses. Auwera (1985) considers the category status of relative *that*, and Jacobsson (1994) provides valuable data concerning the distinction between (in our terminology) integrated and supplementary relative clauses.

Unbounded dependencies

Ross (1986), which originates in a 1967 doctoral dissertation, is an important early transformational-generative source on constraints relating to unbounded dependency constructions. There is a vast transformationalist literature on unbounded dependencies that we do not attempt to review here. The description given in Ch. 12 has more in common with the non-transformational treatment introduced in Gazdar (1981) and developed in Gazdar et al. (1985).

Comparative constructions

Among the useful works we consulted in studying comparatives (Ch. 13) are Bresnan (1973), a major transformational-generative study, and Kuno (1981), which utilises some functionalist notions in its description. Allan (1986) and Mitchell (1990) provide a number of insights into the semantics.

Non-finite clauses

Mair (1990) and Duffley (1992) are valuable studies of infinitival constructions. Our approach to catenative constructions in Ch. 14 owes much to Palmer (1987, Ch. 9). Postal (1974) is a full-length study of what we call the complex catenative construction, while Akmajian (1977) looks specifically at the catenative complements of verbs of perception. Pullum & Zwicky (1998) describes the syntax of certain constraints on inflection applying to verbs and the head verbs of their complements. Sag & Pollard (1991) is a useful study of control, showing how semantic the phenomenon is.

Coordination and supplementation

Oirsouw (1987) is a useful study of coordination in general, while Payne (1985) is a comparative cross-linguistic survey. Gazdar et al. (1985, Ch. 8) presents a detailed (and fairly technical) description of coordination that may be compared with the one presented in Ch. 15 of this book. Ross (1986) is the source for some of the general properties that characterise coordination. Schachter (1977) deals with the issue of the kind of likeness normally required between coordinates, and Sag et al. (1985) discusses further the cases of coordination of syntactically unlike categories. Peterson (1998) deals with some of the issues concerning what we here call supplementation.

Information packaging

The pragmatic constraints on a number of the information-packaging constructions dealt with in Ch. 16 (complement preposing, postposing, subject–dependent inversion, right dislocation, existential and presentational clauses, and long passives) are discussed in more detail in Birner & Ward (1998), which provides the basis for the account given here. Prince (1992) is the source for the distinction between discourse-new and discourse-old information, and between addressee-new and addressee-old information ('hearer-new' and 'hearer-old' in Prince's terminology); and our account of the addressee-new condition on the displaced subject of existentials is a modified version of that presented in the same work. In addition, Erdmann (1976) and Lumsden (1988) are important early studies of existential sentences. Our discussion of proposition affirmation has benefited from Horn (1991). We are indebted to Prince (1997) for discussion of left dislocation. Tomlin (1986) is a useful source on the passive. Prince (1978) and Delin (1995) provided valuable insights into the functions of clefts, and Collins (1991) was a useful source of data on these constructions. Lambrecht (1994) is an excellent general source of information on topic and focus articulation in English.

Deixis and anaphora

John Lyons (1977, Ch. 11) provides a valuable theoretical discussion of deixis and anaphora. For more on deixis see Anderson & Keenan (1985), Jarvella & Klein (1982), and Fillmore (1997). McCawley (1998, Ch. 11) provides a useful account of anaphora within a transformational framework, and Hankamer & Sag (1976) is an important work dealing with the classification of anaphoric devices. Halliday & Hasan (1976) includes a valuable detailed and comprehensive description of anaphoric constructions in English, while Wales (1996) deals specifically with pronouns. The treatment of reflexive pronouns in Ch. 17 of this book owes much to the ideas of Pollard & Sag (1992), Reinhart & Reuland (1993), and Zribi-Hertz (1989). Edmondson & Plank (1978) gives a detailed survey of the range of uses of emphatic reflexives, and for reciprocal pronouns Kim & Peters (1998) is a valuable recent contribution. Our discussion of anticipatory anaphora has benefited particularly from Carden (1982) and Mittwoch (1983). Van Hoek (1997) has useful chapters on reflexives and on anticipatory anaphora.

Inflection

The discussion of inflection requires some attention to details of pronunciation, and for this we have relied in Ch. 18 mainly on Wells (1990). An introduction to morphological analysis of the sort undertaken in Ch. 18 is provided by Matthews (1991), and a more advanced theoretical discussion of morphological theory compatible with this approach may be found in Anderson (1992). The morphology (and other aspects) of the English verb are treated in detail in Palmer (1987). Inflection of adjectives for comparative and superlative grade is discussed in Rowicka (1987). Many details concerning the syntactic conditions on pronunciation of clitic auxiliaries can be found in theoretical work on the subject by Selkirk (1980, 1984) and Kaisse (1985).

Lexical word-formation

Barnhart et al. (1990) and Knowles (1997) are dictionaries that are particularly useful in connection with lexical word-formation (Ch. 19). Standard surveys include Jespersen

(1909–1949, part vi: Morphology, 1942), Marchand (1969), Adams (1973), Bauer (1983), and Szymanek (1989). Among the relevant transformational-generative studies are Lees (1960), Aronoff (1976), and Plag (1999). On compounds, see Ryder (1994), and for a useful corpus-based study of productivity see Baayen & Renouf (1996).

Punctuation

One of the most comprehensive guides to English punctuation (Ch. 20) may be found in Ch. 5 of the *Chicago Manual of Style*. A more popular account is provided by Partridge (1953). Other useful books devoted to punctuation include Sumney (1949) and Meyer (1987), the latter containing a considerable amount of statistical information about what patterns of punctuation occur. Nunberg (1990) presents a more theoretical discussion of the topic of punctuation marks and the rules that govern their distribution. For the history of the subject, see Parkes (1992).

References

This list of references contains only the works specifically mentioned in the notes above. Well-known dictionaries and other major reference works are listed under their names rather than the names of their general editors. City of publication is given only where it is not immediately obvious from the name of the publisher, and for works published in the USA and Australia we add the postal abbreviation for the state name if that is not obvious.

Acuña-Fariña, J. C. (1999), 'On apposition', *English Language and Linguistics* 3, 59–81.

Adams, Valerie (1973), *An Introduction to Modern English Word-Formation*, London: Longman.

Akmajian, Adrian (1977), 'The complement structure of perception verbs in an autonomous syntax framework', in Culicover, Wasow, & Akmajian, 427–460.

Alexiadou, Artemis, & Chris Wilder, eds. (1998), *Possessors, Predicates and Movement in the Determiner Phrase*, Linguistik Aktuell, 22, Amsterdam: John Benjamins.

Allan, Keith (1980), 'Nouns and countability', *Language* 56, 541–567.

Allan, Keith (1986), 'Interpreting English comparatives', *Journal of Semantics* 5, 1–50.

American Heritage Dictionary of the English Language (2000), 4th edn, Boston, MA: Houghton Mifflin.

Anderson, Stephen R. (1992), *A-Morphous Morphology*, Cambridge University Press.

Anderson, Stephen R., & Edward L. Keenan (1985), 'Deixis', in Timothy Shopen (ed.), *Language Typology and Syntactic Description*, Vol. iii, 259–309, Cambridge University Press.

Aronoff, Mark (1976), *Word Formation in Generative Grammar*, Cambridge, MA: MIT Press.

Austin, J. L. (1962), *How to Do Things with Words*, Oxford: Clarendon Press.

Auwera, Johan van der (1985), 'Relative *that* – a centennial dispute', *Journal of Linguistics* 21, 149–179.

Baayen, H., & A. Renouf (1996), 'Chronicling the *Times*: productive lexical innovations in an English newspaper', *Language* 72, 69–96.

Bach, Emmon, Eloise Jelinek, Angelika Kratzer, & Barbara Partee, eds. (1995), *Quantification in Natural Languages*, Dordrecht: Kluwer.

Baker, C. L. (1995), *English Syntax*, 2nd edn, Cambridge, MA: MIT Press.

Barnhart, R. K., C. Steinmetz, & C. L. Barnhart (1990), *Third Barnhart Dictionary of New English*, New York: H. W. Wilson.

Barwise, Jon, & Robin Cooper (1981), 'Generalized quantifiers and natural language', *Linguistics and Philosophy* 4, 159–219.

Bauer, Laurie (1983), *English Word-formation*, Cambridge University Press.

Bauer, Laurie (1998), 'When is a sequence of two nouns a compound in English?', *English Language and Linguistics* 2, 65–86.

Bellert, Irena (1977), 'On semantic and distributional properties of sentential adverbs', *Linguistic Inquiry* 8, 337–351.

Biber, Douglas, Stig Johansson, Geoffrey Leech, Susan Conrad, & Edward Finegan (1999), *Longman Grammar of Spoken and Written English*, Harlow: Longman.

Binnick, Robert I. (1991), *Time and the Verb*, Oxford University Press.

Birner, Betty, & Gregory Ward (1998), *Information Status and Noncanonical Word Order in English*, Amsterdam: John Benjamins.

Bolinger, Dwight (1971), *The Phrasal Verb in English*, Cambridge, MA: Harvard University Press.

Bolinger, Dwight (1972), *Degree Words*, The Hague: Mouton.

Bolinger, Dwight (1977), *Meaning and Form*, London: Longman.

Bolinger, Dwight (1978), 'Yes–no questions are not alternative questions', in Henry Hiż (ed.), *Questions*, 87–105, Dordrecht: Reidel.

Bresnan, Joan (1973), 'Syntax of the comparative clause construction in English', *Linguistic Inquiry* 4, 275–343.

Bresnan, Joan, & Jane Grimshaw (1978), 'The syntax of free relatives in English', *Linguistic Inquiry* 9, 331–391.

Burchfield, R.W. (1996), *The New Fowler's Modern English Usage*, 3rd edn, Oxford: Clarendon Press.

Burton-Roberts, Noel (1991), 'Prepositions, adverbs and adverbials', in Ingrid Tieken-Boon van Ostade, & J. Frankis (eds.), *Language Usage and Description*, 159–172, Amsterdam: Rodopi.

Cambridge International Dictionary of English (1995), ed.-in-chief Paul Procter, Cambridge University Press.

Carden, Guy (1982), 'Backwards anaphora in discourse context', *Journal of Linguistics* 18, 361–387.

Carlson, Gregory N., & Francis J. Pelletier, eds. (1995), *The Generic Book*, University of Chicago Press.

Cattell, Ray (1984), *Syntax and Semantics 17: Composite Predicates in English*, Orlando, FL: Academic Press.

Chicago Manual of Style (1993), 14th edn, University of Chicago Press.

Cinque, Guglielmo (1999), *Adverbs and Functional Heads*, Oxford: Basil Blackwell.

Coates, Jennifer (1983), *The Semantics of the Modal Auxiliaries*, London: Croom Helm.

Cole, Peter, & Jerry L. Morgan, eds. (1975), *Syntax and Semantics 3: Speech Acts*, New York: Academic Press.

Collins, Peter (1991), *Cleft and Pseudo-cleft Constructions in English*, London: Routledge.

Collins, Peter, & David Lee (1998), *The Clause in English: In Honour of Rodney Huddleston*, Amsterdam: John Benjamins.

Collins COBUILD English Grammar (1990), London: Collins.

Collins COBUILD English Language Dictionary (1995), ed. John Sinclair, New York: HarperCollins.

Comrie, Bernard (1976), *Aspect*, Cambridge University Press.

Comrie, Bernard (1985), *Tense*, Cambridge University Press.

Corbett, Greville G. (1991), *Gender*, Cambridge University Press.

Cowie, A. P., & R. Mackin (1993), *Oxford Dictionary of Phrasal Verbs*, Oxford University Press.

Crystal, David (1997), *English as a Global Language*, Cambridge University Press.

Culicover, Peter W., Thomas Wasow, & Adrian Akmajian, eds. (1977), *Formal Syntax*, Orlando, FL: Academic Press, 1977.

Davies, Eirlys E. (1986), *The English Imperative*, London: Croom Helm.

Declerck, Renaat (1988), *Studies on Copular Sentences, Clefts and Pseudo-clefts*, Louvain University Press.

Declerck, Renaat (1991a), *A Comprehensive Descriptive Grammar of English*, Tokyo: Kaitakusha.

Declerck, Renaat (1991b), *Tense in English: Its Structure and Use in Discourse*, London: Routledge.

Delin, Judy (1995), 'Presupposition and shared knowledge in *it*-clefts', *Language and Cognitive Processes* 10, 97–120.

Dixon, Robert M. W. (1982), *Where Have All the Adjectives Gone?: And Other Essays in Semantics and Syntax*, Berlin: Mouton de Gruyter.

Dixon, Robert M. W. (1991), *A New Approach to English Grammar, on Semantic Principles*, Oxford: Clarendon Press.

Dowty, David (1991), 'Thematic proto-roles and argument selection', *Language* 67, 547–619.

Dudman, V. H. (1994), 'On conditionals', *Journal of Philosophy* 3, 113–128.

Duffley, Patrick J. (1992), *The English Infinitive*, London: Longman.

Duffley, Patrick J. (1994), '*Need* and *dare*: the black sheep of the modal family', *Lingua* 94, 213–243.

Duffley, Patrick J., & Peter J. Enns (1996), '*Wh*-words and the infinitive in English', *Lingua* 98, 221–242.

Edmondson, Jerry, & Franz Plank (1978), 'Great expectations: an intensive self analysis', *Linguistics and Philosophy* 2, 373–413.

Elliott, Dale (1974), 'Toward a grammar of exclamations', *Foundations of Language* 11, 231–246.

Emonds, Joseph E. (1972) 'Evidence that indirect object movement is a structure-preserving rule', *Foundations of Language* 8, 546–561.

Erdmann, Peter (1976), *'There' Sentences in English*, Munich: Tudov.

Ernst, Thomas (2001), *The Syntax of Adjuncts*, Cambridge University Press.

Ferris, D. Connor (1993), *The Meaning of Syntax: A Study in the Adjectives of English*, Harlow: Longman.

Fillmore, Charles W. (1997), *Lectures on Deixis*, Stanford, CA: CSLI Publications.

Gazdar, Gerald (1981), 'Unbounded dependencies and coordinate structure', *Linguistic Inquiry* 12, 155–184.

Gazdar, Gerald, Ewan Klein, Geoffrey K. Pullum, & Ivan A. Sag (1985), *Generalized Phrase Structure Grammar*, Oxford: Basil Blackwell; and Cambridge, MA: Harvard University Press.

Green, Georgia M. (1992), 'Purpose infinitives and their relatives', in Diane Brentari, Gary N. Larson, & L. A. Mcleod (eds.), *The Joy of Grammar: A Festschrift in Honor of James D. McCawley*, 95–127, Amsterdam: John Benjamins.

Halliday, M. A. K. (1967–1968), 'Notes on transitivity and theme in English', *Journal of Linguistics* 3, 37–81 and 199–244, and 4, 179–215.

Halliday, M. A. K., & Ruqaiya Hasan (1976), *Cohesion in English*, London: Longman.

Hankamer, Jorge, & Ivan A. Sag (1976), 'Deep and surface anaphora', *Linguistic Inquiry* 7, 391–426.

Haspelmath, Martin (1999), 'Explaining article–possessor complementarity: economic motivation in noun phrase syntax', *Language* 75, 227–243.

Hawkins, John (1991), 'On (in)definite articles', *Journal of Linguistics* 27, 405–442.

Hawkins, Roger (1981), 'Towards an account of the possessive constructions: *NP's N* and *the N of NP*', *Journal of Linguistics* 17, 247–269.

Herskovits, Annette H. (1986), *Language and Spatial Cognition: An Interdisciplinary Study of the Prepositions in English*, Cambridge University Press.

Hill, L. A. (1968), *Prepositions and Adverbial Particles: An Interim Classification, Semantic, Structural and Graded*, Oxford University Press.

Hirschbühler, Paul (1985), *The Syntax and Semantics of Wh-constructions*, New York: Garland.

Hoeksema, Jacob, ed. (1996), *Partitives: Studies on the Syntax and Semantics of the Partitive and Related Constructions*, Berlin: Mouton de Gruyter.

Hogg, Richard M., gen. ed. (1992–2002), *The Cambridge History of the English Language* (6 vols.), Cambridge University Press.

Horn, Laurence R. (1989), *A Natural History of Negation*, University of Chicago Press.

Horn, Laurence R. (1991), 'Given as new: when redundant information isn't', *Journal of Pragmatics* 15, 305–328.

Huddleston, Rodney (1994), 'The contrast between interrogatives and questions', *Journal of Linguistics* 30, 411–439.

Huddleston, Rodney (1995a), 'The English perfect as a secondary tense', in Bas Aarts & C. F. Meyer (eds.), *The Verb in Contemporary English: Theory and Description*, 102–122, Cambridge University Press.

Huddleston, Rodney (1995b), 'The case against a future tense in English', *Studies in Language* 19, 399–446.

Jackendoff, Ray (1973), 'The base rules for prepositional phrases', in Stephen R. Anderson & Paul Kiparsky (eds.), *A Festschrift for Morris Halle*, New York: Holt, Rinehart and Winston.

Jackendoff, Ray (1977), *$\bar{X}$ Syntax: A Study of Phrase Structure*, Cambridge, MA: MIT Press.

Jackendoff, Ray (1991), *Semantics and Cognition*, Cambridge, MA: MIT Press.

Jackendoff, Ray (1995), *Semantic Structures*, Cambridge, MA: MIT Press.

Jacobsson, Bengt (1975), 'How dead is the English Subjunctive?', *Moderna Språk* 69, 218–231.

Jacobsson, Bengt (1994), 'Non-restrictive relative *that*-clauses revisited', *Studia Neophilologica* 62, 181–195.

Jarvella, Robert J., & Wolfgang Klein, eds. (1982), *Speech, Place and Action: Studies in Deixis and Related Topics*, Chichester: John Wiley.

Jespersen, Otto (1909–1949), *A Modern English Grammar on Historical Principles* (7 vols.), Copenhagen: Munksgaard. (Republished, Heidelberg: Carl Winter; London: George Allen and Unwin.)

Kaisse, Ellen (1985), *Connected Speech: The Interaction of Syntax and Phonology*, New York: Academic Press.

Karttunen, Lauri (1977), 'Syntax and semantics of questions', *Linguistics and Philosophy* 1, 3–44.

Keenan, Edward L., & Jonathan Stavi (1986), 'A semantic characterization of natural language determiners', *Linguistics and Philosophy* 9, 253–326.

Kim, Yookyung, & P. Stanley Peters (1998). 'Semantic and pragmatic context-dependence: the case of reciprocals', in Pila Barbosa, Danny Fox, Paul Hagstrom, Martha McGinnis, & David Pesetsky (eds.), *Is the Best Good Enough?*, 221–247, Cambridge, MA: MIT Press.

Klima, Edward S. (1964), 'Negation in English', in Jerry A. Fodor & Jerrold J. Katz (eds.), *The Structure of Language: Readings in the Philosophy of Language*, 246–323, Englewood Cliffs, NJ: Prentice-Hall.

Knowles, Elizabeth (1997), with Julia Elliot, *The Oxford Dictionary of New Words*, Oxford University Press.

Koptevskaya-Tamm, Maria (1993), *Nominalizations*, London: Routledge.

Kuno, Susumo (1981), 'The syntax of comparative clauses', in Roberta A. Hendrick, Carrie S. Masek, & Mary Frances Miller (eds.), *Papers from the 17th Regional Meeting, Chicago Linguistic Society*, 136–155, Chicago Linguistic Society.

Ladusaw, William A. (1980), *Polarity Sensitivity as Inherent Scope Relations*, New York: Garland.

Lambrecht, Knud (1994), *Information Structure and Language Form*, Cambridge University Press.

Lee, David (1998), 'Intransitive prepositions: are they viable?', in Collins & Lee, 133–147.

Leech, Geoffrey N. (1987), *Meaning and the English Verb*, London: Longman.

Lees, Robert B. (1960), *The Grammar of English Nominalizations*, The Hague: Mouton.

Levin, Beth (1993), *English Verb Classes and Alternations*, University of Chicago Press.

Lewis, David K. (1975), 'Adverbs of quantification', in Edward L. Keenan (ed.), *Formal Semantics of Natural Languages*, 3–15, Cambridge University Press.

Lumsden, Michael (1988), *Existential Sentences: Their Structure and Meaning*, London: Croom-Helm.

Lyons, Christopher (1999), *Definiteness*, Cambridge University Press.

Lyons, John (1977), *Semantics* (2 vols.), Cambridge University Press.

Macquarie Dictionary (1991), 2nd edn, ed. Arthur Delbridge et al., McMahon's Point, NSW, Australia: Macquarie Library.

Mair, Christian (1990), *Infinitival Complement Clauses in English: A Study of Syntax in Discourse*, Cambridge University Press.

Marchand, Hans (1969), *The Categories and Types of Present-Day English Word-Formation*, Munich: Beck.

Matthews, Peter H. (1981), *Syntax*, Cambridge University Press.

Matthews, Peter H. (1991), *Morphology*, 2nd edn, Cambridge University Press.

Matthews, Peter H. (1997), *The Concise Oxford Dictionary of Linguistics*, Oxford University Press.

McCawley, James D. (1981), 'The syntax and semantics of English relative clauses', *Lingua* 53, 99–149.

McCawley, James D. (1998), *The Syntactic Phenomena of English*, 2nd edn, University of Chicago Press.

McCoard, Robert W. (1978), *The English Perfect: Tense-choice and Pragmatic Inferences*, Amsterdam: North-Holland.

Merriam-Webster's Dictionary of Contemporary English Usage (1994), Springfield, MA: Merriam-Webster.

Meyer, Charles F. (1987), *A Linguistic Study of American Punctuation*, New York: Peter Lang.

Mitchell, Keith (1990), 'On comparisons in a notional grammar', *Applied Linguistics* 11, 52–72.

Mittwoch, Anita (1983), 'Backward anaphora and discourse structure', *Journal of Pragmatics* 7, 129–139.

Mountford, John D. (1998), *An Insight into English Spelling*, London: Hodder and Stoughton Educational.

Nunberg, Geoffrey (1990), *The Linguistics of Punctuation*, Stanford, CA: CSLI Publications.

Ohlander, S. (1986), 'Question-orientation versus answer-orientation in English interrogative clauses', in D. Kastovsky and A. Szwedek (eds.), *Linguistics across Historical and Geographical Boundaries*, Vol. II: *Descriptive, Contrastive and Applied Linguistics*, 963–982, Berlin: Mouton de Gruyter.

Oirsouw, Robert R. van (1987), *The Syntax of Coordination*, London: Croom Helm.

Ostertag, Gary, ed. (1998), *Definite Descriptions: A Reader*, Cambridge, MA: MIT Press.

Oxford English Dictionary (1989), 2nd edn (20 vols.), prepared by J. A. Simpson & E. S. C. Weiner, Oxford University Press.

Palmer, F. R. (1987), *The English Verb*, 2nd edn, London: Longman.

Palmer, F. R. (1990), *Modality and the English Modals*, London: Longman.

Palmer, F. R. (1994), *Grammatical Roles and Relations*, Cambridge University Press.

Palmer, F. R. (2001), *Mood and Modality*, 2nd edn, Cambridge University Press.

Parkes, Malcolm (1992), *Pause and Effect: An Introduction to the History of Punctuation in the West*, Aldershot: Scolar Press.

Parsons, Terence (1990), *Events in the Semantics of English*, Cambridge, MA: MIT Press.

Partridge, Eric (1953), *You Have a Point There*, London: Routledge and Kegan Paul.

Payne, John (1993), 'The headedness of noun phrases: slaying the nominal hydra', in Greville G. Corbett, Norman M. Fraser, & Scott McGlashan (eds.), *Heads in Grammatical Theory*, 114–139, Cambridge University Press.

Payne, John (1985), 'Complex phrases and complex sentences', in Timothy Shopen (ed.), *Language Typology and Syntactic Description*, Vol. II, 3–41, Cambridge University Press.

Peterson, Peter (1998), 'On the boundaries of syntax: non-syntagmatic relations', in Collins & Lee, 229–250.

Phythian, B. A. (1979), *A Concise Dictionary of Correct English*, London: Teach Yourself Books; Totowa, NJ: Littlefield, Adams.

Plag, I. (1999), *Morphological Productivity: Structural Constraints in English Derivation*, Berlin: Mouton de Gruyter.

Pollard, Carl, & Ivan A. Sag (1992), 'Anaphors in English and the scope of binding theory', *Linguistic Inquiry* 23, 261–303.

Postal, Paul M. (1974), *On Raising*, Cambridge, MA: MIT Press.

Poutsma, Hendrik (1926–1929), *A Grammar of Late Modern English*, Groningen: Noordhoof.

Prince, Ellen F. (1978), 'A comparison of *wh*-clefts and *it*-clefts in discourse', *Language* 54, 883–906.

Prince, Ellen F. (1992), 'The ZPG letter: Subjects, definites and information-status', in William C. Mann & Sandra A. Thompson (eds.), *Discourse Descriptions: Diverse Analyses of a Fundraising Text*, 295–325, Amsterdam: John Benjamins.

Prince, Ellen F. (1997), 'On the functions of left-dislocation in English discourse', in Akio Kamio (ed.), *Directions in Functional Linguistics*, 117–143, Amsterdam: John Benjamins.

Pullum, Geoffrey K., & William A. Ladusaw (1996), *Phonetic Symbol Guide*, 2nd edn, University of Chicago Press.

Pullum, Geoffrey K., & Arnold Zwicky (1998), 'Gerund participles and head-complement inflection conditions', in Collins & Lee, 251–271.

Quirk, Randolph, Sidney Greenbaum, Geoffrey Leech, & Jan Svartvik (1985), *A Comprehensive Grammar of the English Language*, London: Longman.

Reader's Digest (1985), *The Right Word at the Right Time: A Guide to the English Language and How to Use it*, London: Reader's Digest.

Reid, Wallis (1991), *Verb and Noun Number in English: A Functional Explanation*, London: Longman.

Reinhart, Tanya, & Eric Reuland (1993), 'Reflexivity', *Linguistic Inquiry* 24, 657–720.

Reuland, Eric, & Alice ter Meulen, eds. (1987), *The Representation of (In)definiteness*, Cambridge, MA: MIT Press.

Ross, John R. (1986), *Infinite Syntax!*, Hillsdale, NJ: Erlbaum.

Rowicka, G. (1987), 'Synthetical comparison of English adjectives', *Studia Anglica Posnaniensa* 20, 129–149.

Ryder, M. E. (1994), *Ordered Chaos: The Interpretation of English Noun-Noun Compounds*, Berkeley: University of California Press.

Sag, Ivan A. (1997), 'English relative clause constructions', *Journal of Linguistics* 33, 431–483.

Sag, Ivan A., Gerald Gazdar, Thomas Wasow, & Steven Weisler (1985), 'Coordination and how to distinguish categories', *Natural Language and Linguistic Theory* 3, 117–171.

Sag, Ivan A., & Carl Pollard (1991), 'An integrated theory of complement control', *Language* 67, 63–113.

Schachter, Paul (1977), 'Constraints on coordination', *Language* 53, 86–103.

Searle, John R. (1975), 'Indirect speech acts', in Cole & Morgan, 59–82.

Selkirk, Elisabeth O. (1977), 'Some remarks on noun phrase structure', in Culicover, Wasow, & Akmajian, 285–316.

Selkirk, Elisabeth O. (1980), *The Phrase Phonology of English and French*, New York: Garland.

Selkirk, Elisabeth O. (1984), *Phonology and Syntax: The Relation between Sound and Structure*, Cambridge, MA: MIT Press.

Seppänen, Aimo, Rhonwen Bowen, & Joe Trotta (1994), 'On the so-called complex prepositions', *Studia Anglica Posnaniensia* 29, 3–29.

Seppänen, Aimo, Solveig Granath, & Jennifer Herriman (1995), 'On so-called "formal" subjects/objects and "real" subjects/objects', *Studia Neophilologica* 67, 11–19.

Seppänen, Aimo, & J. Herriman, (1997) 'The object/predicative contrast and the analysis of "She made him a good wife"', *Neuphilologische Mitteilungen* 98, 135–146.

Stockwell, Robert P., Paul Schachter, & Barbara Hall Partee (1973), *The Major Syntactic Structures of English*, New York: Holt, Rinehart and Winston.

Sumney, G. (1949), *Modern Punctuation*, New York: Ronald Press.

Szymanek, B. (1989), *Introduction to Morphological Analysis*, Warsaw: Panstwowe Wydawnictwo Naukowe.

Tobin, Yishai (1993), *Aspect in the English Verb*, London: Longman.

Tomlin, Russell S. (1986), *Basic Word Order: Functional Principles*, London: Croom Helm.

Trask, R. L. (1993), *A Dictionary of Grammatical Terms in Linguistics*, London: Routledge.

Traugott, Elizabeth C., ed. (1986) *On Conditionals*, Cambridge University Press.

Trudgill, Peter, & Jean Hannah (1985), *International English: A Guide to Varieties of Standard English*, 2nd edn, London: Edward Arnold.

Van Hoek, Karen (1997), *Anaphora and Conceptual Structure*, University of Chicago Press.

Visser, F. T. (1963–1973), *An Historical Syntax of the English Language* (4 vols.), Leiden: E. J. Brill.

Wales, Katie (1996), *Personal Pronouns in Present-day English*, Cambridge University Press.

Wells, John C. (1990), *Longman Pronunciation Dictionary*, London: Longman.

Wickens, Mark A. (1992), *Grammatical Number in English Nouns: An Empirical and Theoretical Account*, Amsterdam: John Benjamins.

Wierzbicka, Anna (1982), 'Why can you *have a drink* when you can't **have an eat?*', *Language* 58, 753–799.

Wilkins, Wendy, ed. (1988), *Syntax and Semantics 21: Thematic Relations*, New York: Academic Press.

Zribi-Hertz, Anna (1989), 'Anaphor binding and narrative point of view: English reflexive pronouns in sentence and discourse', *Language* 65, 695–727.

Index

The index is divided into two parts, lexical and conceptual; in addition, there are two specialised indexes given in the main text of the book, one covering the classification of catenative verbs (Ch. 14, pp. 1239–40), one the inflection of verbs with simple bases (Ch. 18, pp. 1608–9).

In the lexical index we have in general cited lexemes (but in ordinary italics) rather than the separate inflectional forms, unless there are syntactic reasons for mentioning the latter. Thus there are no entries for *took* or *children*, which are covered under *take* and *child* respectively, in references to Ch. 18 (pp. 1567–1619). However, participial adjectives (such as *distressing* or *worried*) are listed. The number of lexical items mentioned in Ch. 19 is too large to permit them all to be included. For derivatives quoted in §5 of this chapter we have largely confined ourselves to listing the affixes; words ending in ·*able*, for example, will be found in the references for that heading. Similarly we have listed combining forms rather than the neo-classical compounds containing them. Other compounds cited only in the numbered displays in §4 (pp. 1644–66) are likewise not included in the index.

Idioms and comparable expressions, such as *cross swords with* and *at the behest of*, are located in the alphabetical listing on the basis of the head word (*cross*, *at*). As will be clear from the discussion in the text, the listing of expressions of this kind does not imply that they form syntactic constituents.

Cross-references are indicated by means of an arrow, interpreted as "see" or "see also". They are very largely confined to the conceptual index: there is, for example, no cross-reference from conceptual 'universal determinative' to lexical '*all*' and '*both*'. Since *all* and *both* are the two universal determinatives, such a cross-reference would be entirely predictable; in cases of this kind, however, there are likely to be significantly more references under the lexical heads than under the conceptual ones.

Major references (typically the topic of a chapter, section or subsection) are marked in bold face, and similarly major headings in the conceptual index are printed in bold face. The annotation 'n' indicates that the reference is to a footnote; it is not used if the topic is mentioned in the main text of the page concerned as well as in a footnote. References of the type '742–5' indicate that the item in question is dealt with on each page within the span, whether it is a matter of a single discussion or of independent mentions.

Lexical index

Conceptual index